Black Ship to Hell

Novels by Brigid Brophy

HACKENFELLER'S APE

THE KING OF A RAINY COUNTRY

BLACK SHIP
TO HELL

Brigid Brophy

———————

'. . . je comprenais ce que signifiaient la mort,
l'amour . . . Car si les noms avaient perdu pour
moi de leur individualité, les mots me découvraient
tout leur sens. La beauté des images est logée à
l'arrière des choses, celle des idées à l'avant. De
sorte que la première cesse de nous émerveiller
quand on les a atteintes, mais qu'on ne comprend
la seconde que quand on les a dépassées.'

(LE TEMPS RETROUVÉ)

HARCOURT, BRACE & WORLD, INC.,
NEW YORK

LIBRARY OF CONGRESS CATALOG CARD NUMBER: 62-8477

PRINTED IN THE UNITED STATES OF AMERICA

For
Sally Backhouse

Contents

CONTENTS

Note

In writing fiction, the great problem is from whose point of view to tell your story. When you have settled that, you have only to write it. With non-fiction, it is a question of whom to tell the story *to*.

Many of the things I recapitulate, especially in Chapter One, knowledgeable readers will know quite as well as I do. I beg their patience; and I have tried to alleviate their impatience by the method of the school arithmetic books—providing fresh examples. But other readers may not be conversant with all the matters I touch on; and it is in order to give them the utmost opportunity to check up on my assertions that I have adopted a policy of annotating everything, to the verge of absurdity.

Since, however, nothing is more irritating than to chase up a footnote and find that it leads only to a reference, I have taken the precaution, wherever a footnote supplies nothing except a reference, a date or a translation, of hedging-about its number in the text with discouraging brackets, as signals that the reader need not interrupt himself.

It is only fair, before inviting the reader into a book of this size, for which I have drawn my material from as wide an area as I could lay my hands on, to offer him a brief guide to its contents.

The theme of the book is man as a destructive and, more particularly, a self-destructive animal: a theme whose urgency is obvious at a time when he is threatening to commit suicide as a species.

Chapter One plunges straight into the self-destructive impulse subterraneanly at work in persons and groups whose conscious intention is only to destroy others. Taking its illustrations where it finds them—mythology, opera, a famous murder—it builds up to an analysis of the hidden but mortally effective suicidal tendency in societies and in civilisation itself.

Chapter Two is a first step towards framing a morality which shall take these disclosures into account. It is a step which goes by way of a vindication of Sigmund Freud, Bernard Shaw and the most neglected of great poets, Lucretius, and a reasoned demolition of the claims and influence of religion. Here and throughout the book I am addressing myself not only to moralists, sociologists, educationists and the like, but also to artists, in an attempt to understand both the morality and the biology of art; if we go on practising art without such an understanding, art will soon find itself cut off from its instinctual sources, and starving.

Chapters One and Two having been both a plea for and an exercise in reason, Chapter Three provides a history of the liveliest movement which has ever disturbed human thought, rationalism—together with an analysis of the psychological reasons for its failure (which is primarily a failure to understand and control the destructive impulse) in all the manifestations in which it has yet been tried.

The last chapter makes an attempt to track down the destructive impulse to its origins in our biological nature.

Invocation to the Reader

" 'But tell me, Circe, who is to guide me on the way? No one has ever sailed a black ship to Hell.'

" 'Odysseus,' the goddess answered me, 'don't think of lingering on shore for lack of a pilot. Set up your mast, spread the white sail and sit down in the ship . . .' "[1]

[1] E. V. Rieu's translation of *Odyssey*, x, 501-7:

"'Ὦ Κίρκη, τίς γὰρ ταύτην ὁδὸν ἡγεμονεύσει;
εἰς ῎Αϊδος δ' οὔ πώ τις ἀφίκετο νηῒ μελαίνῃ."
'Ὣς ἐφάμην, ἡ δ᾽ αὐτίκ᾽ ἀμείβετο δῖα θεάων·
"διογενὲς Λαερτιάδη, πολυμήχαν᾽ Ὀδυσσεῦ,
μή τί τοι ἡγεμόνος γε ποθὴ παρὰ νηῒ μελέσθω,
ἱστὸν δὲ στήσας ἀνά θ' ἱστία λευκὰ πετάσσας
ἧσθαι·"

I

BLACK SHIP . . .

1. *Hell—1*

I began work on this book under the impression that I was simply going to psycho-analyse the Greek myth of the Underworld. It turns out, however, that the subject is not only much vaster than a single, discarded myth but also a great deal more pressingly important. The reader, if he will go with me so far, can still find this essay in the interpretation of myths towards the end of the book. Hell is still our destination; but it is in a very urgent, present-day sense that I am inviting the reader to make the journey which Dante took in the company of Virgil and on which Homer dispatched Odysseus.

The Greek Underworld (which was not in every account *under* the world) was the home of all the dead, containing a bloodless elysium for the righteous as well as a torture-house for sinners. Christian mythology sharply separated Heaven and Hell (adding the halfway-house of Purgatory and the cul-de-sac Limbo) and resolved the pantheon into a single God, who was all goodness, and his opposite and enemy, the Devil. But no sooner did it insist that there was only one God, and that one omnipotent, than it found it had posed quite pointedly the problem which had already disturbed Aeschylus, namely how God could be benevolent or even just, when it was he who bore the ultimate responsibility for inflicting on the sinners in Hell a punishment much crueller than anything they could have inflicted on their victims on earth, since the tortures in Hell were never-ending. God had to be all-creating and omnipotent: it was on those grounds that we were invited to worship him exclusively: yet in that case, it must be he who had created death and pain, and who licensed Satan to tempt men to everlasting destruction. The rationalists began their antiChristian crusade by impugning the moral character of Jehovah-God the Father[1], exactly as Aeschylus, who had elsewhere gone so far towards building him into a supreme, almost a monotheistical, embodiment of justice, found himself, in the *Prometheus Vinctus*, painting Zeus as a tyrant.

All the myth-making in Christendom could not really separate Heaven and Hell; they kept creeping back to the proximity in which Odysseus found them, both comprised in the domain of Hades. All the theologising could not satisfactorily distinguish the persons of God and Satan. It was Sigmund Freud who uncovered the psychological stringency which had forced the myth into this paradox[2], by tracing both supernatural figments to our infantile and unconscious image of our natural father, towards whom we are constrained, by the Oedipal circumstances of our infancy, to feel a strong ambivalence of love-hatred. God and Satan are projections of our contradictory emotions towards a single personage; we have only to compare the trappings of their respective myths to remark that Satan 'is made to provide a mirror image of the Deity'[3].

In fact, the Greek myth had already told us as much, not once but twice over, in the unconsciously metaphorical language to which—before Freud—we lacked the key. Not only did it lump together the good and the bad dead, Zeus's friends as well as his enemies, under the jurisdiction of the awful, protosatanic death-god Hades; it also went

[1] Thomas Paine in 1795: 'There are matters in that book' (sc. the Bible) 'said to be done by *the express command* of God, that are as shocking to humanity, and to every idea we have of moral justice, as anything done by Robespierre, by Carrier, by Joseph le Bon, in France; by the English Government in the East Indies; or by any other assassin in modern times ... To believe therefore the Bible to be true, we must *unbelieve* all our belief in the moral justice of God ... And to read the Bible without horror, we must undo everything that is tender, sympathizing, and benevolent in the heart of man.' (*The Age of Reason*, II). Thomas Evans Bell in 1851: 'Is this bargaining, vacillating, bloodthirsty, and repenting Deity the same God whom we find described in our modern theological works as just, merciful, and all-wise?' (*The God Of The Bible*, IX). Bernard Shaw in 1921: 'The idol was, as Shelley had been expelled from Oxford for pointing out, an almighty fiend, with a petty character and unlimited power, spiteful, cruel, jealous, vindictive, and physically violent.' (*Preface* to *Back to Methuselah*)

[2] Cf. Freud: *Collected Papers*, Volume IV, XXIV ('A Neurosis of Demoniacal Possession In The Seventeenth Century')

[3] G. Rattray Taylor: *Sex In History*, VI

out of its way to insist that Hades and heavenly Zeus were aspects of a single person, by making Hades Zeus's brother. Indeed, Hades is, according to Homer, a 'subterranean Zeus'[1]. Geographically and genealogically, he is an extension of Zeus.

Our filial love and our filial hatred, neither of which can dispense with the other, constitute the tension which has produced religion. In mythology we can trace how they hoist up and dash down the figures whom a whole religious or national group has adopted as its communal parents—whom our imagination subjects to quite literal ups and downs in the form of apotheoses and damnations; in ritual and in the myth-making process itself, we can trace the ambivalence Freud discerned[2] in the primitive totem feast, whereby the very act of worship and love contrives, at the same time as exalting and magnifying the god, to diminish and aggress against him.

Yet these religious phenomena, fascinating though they are in themselves, and potent in historical influence, are still not the end of the subject. The idea of Hell is not a mere mistake, like the idea of phlogiston—a mistake that is automatically discarded when someone puts forward a hypothesis more satisfying to the intellect. Hell is an emotional hypothesis—in other words, a fantasy; and so emotionally satisfactory that men will cling to it at the cost of distorting their intellectual processes. If men conceived, believed and, by every kind of casuistic rationalising, persisted in the idea that there is a God who condemns sinners to everlasting torture, it was not by error but because they wanted it to be true. The myth of Hell is the classic repository of mankind's daydreams about torture. It leads us straight into the most pressing problem civilisation has to face, the problem of violence.

We do not avoid this problem by sloughing off the gods. Once we have recognized that the moral and social law emanates not from God but from society, which invents its various gods as mouthpieces for the law, we have simply substituted society for God and undertaken God's dilemma ourselves. If he, in punishing sinners, commits a crueller sin than they did, then society, in punishing its enemies and criminals, commits a crueller crime. The disciplinarian who wants to whip the thug because the thug has knocked an old

[1] Ζεύς καταχθόνιος (*Iliad*, IX, 457). Virgil copies this by calling Hades's wife an infernal Juno (*Aenid*, VI, 138)

[2] *Totem And Taboo*

lady on the head is giving expression to precisely the same emotion as the thug; the law of capital punishment makes society commit murder in its turn by assassinating the assassin; when we filch ten years from the life of the convicted jewel-thief, we are stealing from him something much more valuable and irreplaceable than all the jewelry in the world. And not one of these punishments will render the old lady unknocked on the head, restore the murdered victim to life or even restore the jewelry to its original owner.

Society might be rationally justified in its behaviour if it had shewn that punishing criminals was the most effective way of dissuading people from committing crimes. Such enquiries as have been made do not suggest that it *is* the most effective way; but in any case society itself, as it speaks through its legislators and law courts, does not rest its case on a rational enquiry of this kind at all (it does not even admit an obligation to make one) but on a principle of justice, according to which society has an absolute, though not in its own eyes an unlimited, right to exact retribution from people who have transgressed its laws. Thus it sets itself up, like God, as not to be reasoned with or about; and it promptly incurs the same reproach as God, namely that its justice is not even just but merely cruel, and that it punishes criminals not because it must, in order to safeguard the majority (a point which only reason could establish) but because it likes doing so. It is indulging the same destructive lust as the criminal was indulging in his crime; and it goes further in the indulgence than he does because, being stronger, it is able to. So long as it refuses to submit the matter to argument, and refuses to acknowledge the basic identity between its own aggressive acts and the criminal's, society is in no position to justify itself by claiming that it is making a carefully controlled use of its own destructive propensities for a constructive purpose, and it has no defence against the suspicion that it is in fact being carried along by its lust to destroy, which it intends to gratify whether reason shows the ultimate result to be constructive or not. Tacitly, therefore, society lends its approval in principle to the criminal's appeal to force, but punishes him for not having had sufficient strength to back it up. Like God, society rests its claim to our obedience on its superior power. It tells the criminal: 'When you assault, it is wrong; when we do, it is right; and the only difference between wrong and right is that we are many and you are one.'

2. *Crime Story*

The situation is, of course, decently clothed in fictions, the chief and hoariest of which is that society and its rules draw their sanction from God, a pretence which, to our secret satisfaction, turns God into a bully and muddlehead whom no moral person could respect, let alone worship. Our covert attempt to blacken God's reputation has freest play in a work of fiction, where God is not a character but appears indirectly through the manifestation of his wrath: Don Juan, for example, is punished at the hands of God's supernatural agent, the walking statue of the dead Commendatore (himself, of course, an outraged father). The legend of Don Juan has never required belief; but it is safe to assume that in its original form, whenever that may have taken shape[1], it was a parable of soundly orthodox tendency, warning profligates of the danger of failing to repent in time, and that its message, though not its narrative, was meant to be believed. In Don Juan, however, the moralisers had unwittingly created an antagonist to God capable of shewing God up; and it is probably thanks to this that the incredible old melodrama—'cette mauvaise Pièce espagnole' according to Carlo Goldoni[2]—was still enjoying in the eighteenth century, in both its French and its Italian version, a popularity which Goldoni could not account for. ('The Italian actors were amazed themselves', he wrote; 'some of them, either as a joke or through ignorance, said that the author . . . had entered into a contract with the devil to sustain him'.) Neither had it only a popular success. Goldoni makes it plain that his chief reason for producing his own rationalised version[3] was that 'Molière and Thomas Corneille occupied themselves with it'; it was treated in several operas; and Gluck made his ballet of it in 1761. Finally, in

[1] 'The prototypic Don Juan, invented early in the XVI century by a Spanish monk . . .' (Bernard Shaw: *Man and Superman*, Epistle Dedicatory); 'The legend of Don Juan . . ., the origins of which are unknown, was first made into a play by the Spanish poet Tirsó de Molina (1630)' (Introduction to the vocal score, Boosey and Hawkes)

[2] This and the other quotations are from a passage in Goldoni's memoirs cited in Alfred Einstein: *Mozart . . .* , 22

[3] 1736.

1787, Mozart and Lorenzo da Ponte used the methods of psychological music-drama to bring out the indictment of God which had always been inherent in the story. The supernatural machinery which Goldoni had rejected,[1] is retained together with the moral at the end, when the sextet of survivors tells the 'good people' in the audience 'We all repeat happily the very ancient refrain: such is the end of the man who does wrong'[2].

Yet they are retained as arguments against rather than for God, and perhaps even as reminders that Don Giovanni, though swallowed into Hell, has not died but is an immortal personage. The 'good people', whatever they are told by the libretto, are left by the dramatic music in not the smallest doubt which is the nobler figure: the deus ex machina who, in order to browbeat Don Giovanni into repentance, brings to bear the forces of supernatural terrorisation and of that superior, more than physical strength of his whereby the very grip of his hand thrills Don Giovanni with the unbearable chill of the grave; or the Don who, though he has broken society's rules and God's, seduced women and killed an outraged father in a duel, will not break his own rules, will not admit remorse, but withstands even the ultimate threat the statue can deploy and lets himself be carried off to unending torture. Mozart and da Ponte have done what Molière did before them and Bernard Shaw was to do after: they have inverted the morality of the old morality play and created what can be read as a vindication of the rebel and a tract against the oppressive God the Father. (Obviously we can never know for sure that Mozart intended the effect he undoubtedly made, but there is no reason why we should think him any less conscious of the religiously revolutionary message in *Don Giovanni* than of the politically revolutionary motifs in *Figaro* and *The Magic Flute*. Yet in all three operas

[1] explaining himself in language very like that wherein Racine justifies himself in ironing out the supernatural motifs in Greek stories. Goldoni objects not to the supernatural morality but only to the machinery. 'I did not see fit to suppress the thunderbolt which wipes out Don Jouan, because the man who sins must be punished: but I managed this event in such a way that it could be an immediate effect of the wrath of God, and that it could also issue from a combination of second causes, always directed by the laws of Providence.'

[2] E noi tutti, o buona gente,
ripetiam allegramente
l'antichissima canzon:
Questo è il fin di chi fa mal. (II, vi)

his is essentially a Homeric, a novelist's view of the conflict; tran-
scendently he is interested less in the moral issue than in the human
nature of moral issues, and morality is swallowed up in psychology.
Don Giovanni in Mozart's version has retained the popularity which
puzzled Goldoni about its earlier versions, and yet it has remained
intellectually a problem opera: the fact that it is concerned, though
at many melodramatic removes, with the Christian religion, and that
it deals with serious events—a man is killed, a daughter grieved—has
prevented us from seeing that it is to be taken at exactly the same
level as *Figaro*, namely as drama in the purest sense, a psychological
study of characters at loggerheads.)

One disadvantage of society's foisting this God on its children is that
not all the children who see through him are Molières or Shaws or
even Don Giovannis. The child who has exposed society's fraudulence
in fobbing him off with God as an administrative convenience may
simply argue that there is nothing to prevent him being as cynical as
society. Perceiving that society has put forward no better reason for
making the laws than that it wants to and has the power to, he may
claim that he needs no justification for breaking them except that
he wants to and has the power to get away with it. If he is clever,
but not inventive enough to be an artist, he may hit on that most
inartistic of ideas (because it negates the imagination), the idea of creating a work of art in real life. There may issue much more real harm
than the attempts—so often unsuccessful—to satisfy the sexual voracity
of the women of Spain, and the single manslaughter committed in
self-defence, which followed from Don Giovanni's treating seduction
as an art. If the young man is a more determined unconscious
masochist than Don Giovanni, and at the same time less imaginative,
the perfect work of art he plans to create in real life will be a crime.
His deepest ambition is to bring punishment on himself. He is one of
those aggressors whose acts of aggression are really designed to provoke
society into committing violence against him. Therefore the content
of the crime—or so he believes—is indifferent to him, providing its
enormity is sufficient. He plots an unmotivated, unprovoked crime,
so that there can be no question of mitigating circumstances. Indeed, he
will detach his act from circumstances; it will be pure crime, like
pure art. He has, in other words, conceived the acte gratuit, the
nucleus of Dostoievsky's hysterical masterpiece *Crime And Punishment*[1],

[1] Where the finding of the magistrates, after Raskolnikov's confession, was
that at the time of the crime 'the accused was suffering from a monomania of

an idea which lay about near the surface of that delicately festering lily-pond, the nineties, to be finally fished up in 1914 by André Gide and woven into his witty and unrelenting tour de force *Les Caves Du Vatican*. But the admirable cruelty of *Les Caves Du Vatican* is literary cruelty. Ten years afterwards, in Chicago, two more than averagely, but not transcendantly, clever young men acted out the acte gratuit: kidnapped a boy they had chosen at random, murdered him, and played with the police until their crime was discovered, whereupon they admitted the act but declined to feel remorse.

The famous, often fictionalised crime and trial of the young men, Nathan Leopold and Richard Loeb, form a locus classicus for our problem. Psychologically, the case is a rich demonstration of the versatility of sado-masochism. Ostensibly the two men were infatuated with their own cleverness. They had borrowed from Nietzsche the notion that their superiority to ordinary people raised them to the plane of supermen, where the only wrong they could commit was to make an intellectual mistake or to be found out in something that would have been a crime for ordinary people. But the habitual daydreams they described to the doctors who examined them after their confession were of the opposite kind: Leopold's 'imaginings about a slave who was intensely devoted to a king or master . . . our daydreamer himself, who was in the vast majority of his phantasies the slave, was bound to his king in later phantasies by a golden chain which he easily could have broken'; Loeb's 'picturization', in which 'he very strangely pictured himself frequently as being a prisoner in a jail yard. He would imagine himself stripped of clothing, shoved around and being whipped.'[1]

In effect, the two men did not want to be supermen: each wanted the other to be. The bullying was all of that subtle kind which the underdog exerts on the master, forcing him, whether by flattery, rebellion or provocation, to be more and more harshly masterful; one understands in what sense it was the slave who, in Leopold's fantasy, insisted on the chain. The crime itself was something that neither young man could have committed in isolation but the result of each of them manœuvring the other into the position of

murder and robbery for the sake of murder and robbery without any ulterior motive or any considerations of personal gain' (Epilogue, I, David Magarshack's translation)

[1] from the medical reports on the two men, published in Maureen McKernan: *The Amazing Crime And Trial Of Leopold And Loeb*, pp. 113, 119

aggressor. Their sole falling out after their confessions was on the question of who had performed the actual killing, of which each accused the other: but this was not really an accusation (there was no question of trying to shift the blame) but a compliment; they behaved like two over-polite people, each refusing to go through the door first, or two lovers each insisting the other is the more attractive.

And as a matter of fact there was in their case that homosexual element which so often underlies the acte gratuit, and which is to be discerned also in Don Giovanni, the Byronic contemner and destroyer of women. The content of the crime was not so immaterial as the criminals thought. Their unconscious motives are clear in the random choice of a boy, almost any boy (there was one other proviso) so long as it *is* a boy; in the kidnapping by car—allegory of seduction; in the mutilation of the body (an attempt to make identification harder by concealing its sex); in the criminals' care—the only other condition they imposed on the random choice—to pick a boy with a rich father, so that they might exact ransom which in fact they themselves were too rich to need. The boy and the murder itself take on the appearance of a mere pretext, a method of bringing the criminals into relation— into protracted commercial negotiation—with the father. They had eliminated the son in order to take his place themselves. As they planned the crime (a plan disrupted by the premature discovery of the body), their real duel was to be with the father—an elaborate warfare of wits, a flirtation even, designed to begin after the gratuitous act of violence was over.

So with Don Giovanni. Mozart and da Ponte have chosen a starting-point for their opera which thrusts it on the audience that Don Giovanni's real interest in seducing Donna Anna begins when the seduction is over or foiled. The whole attempt is his method of calling the person he is really concerned with, her father, on to the scene. The uproar of the bungled seduction does, indeed, call out the Commendatore—in both senses: he arrives and draws his sword on Don Giovanni: and one has only to pun a little further, saying that it rouses him or calls him up, to expose Don Giovanni's violence (which is in any case reluctant) as a mere mask. (After all, Don Giovanni is trying to conceal his face throughout the scene.) The story is playing on the common phallic significance of unsheathing a sword[1]: the

[1] Cf. the case analysed by Ernest Jones and quoted by Freud (*Psychopathology Of Everyday Life*, IX) wherein ' "The next memory was of a dream, plainly

provocation Don Giovanni offers the Commendatore—which includes taunting him that he is too old—is erotic.

In fact, Don Giovanni's famous seductions of women are so many actes gratuits. Their very number, together with the disgust with which he promptly discards his mistresses, confesses that the content of the act is nothing to him. Seduction no more affords him great sensual pleasure than murder did Leopold and Loeb[1]. The opera makes the point (as Bernard Shaw did by the alternative method of simply denying the legend, and making *his* Don Juan a sexual puritan, afraid of, and pursued by, women) by introducing Don Giovanni to us in the very act of amateurishly mismanaging a seduction. Of course it dutifully records the legend of the dashing, proficient seducer—but in reportage. What it actually shews us in the course of the action is the opening failure with Donna Anna, the ludicrous contretemps with Donna Elvira, and a further failure with Zerlina[2]: enough to make it plain that Don Giovanni not only lacks any strong wish to succeed in his seductions but has so positive a desire to be found out and foiled that his mismanagements can only be accounted for by taking them to be unconsciously intended.

Not that Don Giovanni is lying when he boasts that women are more necessary to him than the bread he eats and the air he breathes[(3)]. But what he really needs are the jealous fathers, fiancés and authorities who protect these women; the pleasure of matching his wits against these paternalistic figures; and the hope—which makes it necessary for him to bungle his seductions—of being caught and punished. He is really outraging not women but society—to the point where it must administer the punishment he craves; and he contrives to bring the final punishment on himself through the agency of a father. If

of a homosexual-masochistic nature; in it a man . . . attacked the subject with a 'sword' " '

[1] Thus, from one of the medical reports on Leopold : 'He got no pleasure from the crime. He got no sexual reaction from the crime.' (Maureen McKernan: *The Amazing Crime And Trial* . . . , pp. 100-1).

[2] Even Don Giovanni's serenade to Donna Elvira's maid (Act II, No. 17) comes to nothing (because of Masetto's appearance on the scene). Later Don Giovanni tells Leporello that, after disposing of Masetto, he has been involved in an adventure with another woman; but the woman somehow recognised him and screamed, and Don Giovanni had to run away. (Act II, iii, opening recitative:—'non so come mi riconosce, grida; sento gente; a fuggire mi metto.')

[(3)] Act II, recitative after No. 15

he has, by bravado and ingenuity, escaped from Don Ottavio and the police, it was to preserve himself for the avenger of his choice.[1]

Thus Don Giovanni—or the Nietzschian superman whom Bernard Shaw had the insight to equate with him[2]—tosses off his acte gratuit, his criminal beau geste, in order to engage society's attention. His crime is gratuitous in the sense of being superfluous. It is necessary merely to precipitate about his head the punishment he earned long before—by the undiscovered crime, which he committed not in fact but in unconscious wish, of his homosexual advances to the father. Of course, in seeking unconsciously to bring on his own punishment, he chooses a method which (by the common mechanism of neurotic compromise-formations) allows him to repeat the crime which originally incurred the guilt; and he exploits the masochistic quality in his erotic desires. Punishment is welcome to him because it is an act, an assault (again the play on the erotic and the violent senses of assault) committed on him by the paternal authorities or by society itself whose child he is. If he can oblige society to use him violently, for its own gratification, he will have corrupted and seduced the father, forcing the father to reciprocate his advances in kind. It is society which discountenances cruelty: the criminal who, by tossing off a cruel crime, makes society use him cruelly in turn, has stripped society naked and made it expose in itself the same lusts that it condemned in him.

If Don Giovanni had to bungle his crime in order to be caught, Leopold and Loeb had to bungle theirs, for they could neither seduce society nor realise their masochistic fantasies until they were found out. The would-be slave must first be captured; the prisoner will not get into the gaol yard until he has been detected. Leopold and Loeb's behaviour, both in committing the crime and afterwards (when they displayed the same compulsion as Dostoievsky's Raskolnikov to bring themselves to the notice of the police before they were suspected) is an exercise in psychic counterpoint, like the counterpoint between Don Giovanni's legend as a seducer and his actual performance: the unconscious pursues its course subterraneanly, meticulously undoing

[1] Cf. Shaw (*Man And Superman*, Epistle Dedicatory): 'No anxiety is caused on Don Juan's account by any minor antagonist: he easily eludes the police, temporal and spiritual; and when an indignant father seeks private redress . . . Don Juan kills him without an effort. Not until the slain father returns from heaven as the agent of God . . . does he prevail against his slayer and cast him into hell.'

[2] *Man And Superman*

everything the conscious has woven. The crime which was meant to establish their intellectual superiority and, being planned by superior minds, to be perfect and undetectable, was in point of fact traced to them, and promptly confessed by them, inside a fortnight. It was a crime which the prosecution (seeking to prove thereby that the criminals were perfectly sane and responsible) could call 'one of the most carefully planned murder cases . . . ever heard about', and the defence, with equal truth, could call so clumsy and obvious 'that no one, unless he had an afflicted mind . . . could possibly have done it'[1]. The clinching triumph for the criminals' unconscious desire to be caught was one of those acts which, as Freud discerned[2], express the wishes of the unconscious but pass unnoticed by the conscious— or, when brought to notice, are taken for accidental blunders. The murderers were found out because Nathan Leopold, with no idea he had done so, let fall his glasses near the victim's body: an act in which the State's Attorney, who prosecuted, more than once re- marked 'the hand of God'[3].

The psychological significances of the crime were lost on prosecu- tion and defence alike: the whole case is a demonstration of America's psychological ignorance in 1924. The medical reports—couched in neither English nor American nor the language of science—are a parade of amateurism. Yet the psychological ignorance is nothing compared with the moral confusion displayed by everyone—law, newspapers, public opinion—by a whole society, in fact, when it was confronted by the two young men who did not feel remorse. If one's humanitarianism is bound to applaud the judge's (comparatively) humane decision to pass a sentence of life imprisonment rather than the death sentence, one can only deplore that the result was achieved by a piece of pleading so specious (though from the rhetorician's point of view it is brilliantly ingenious) as Clarence Darrow's 'sum- mation'. What emerges from reading an account of the case is a failure—or, rather, a confusion—on the part of society, which, in all its dealings with Leopold and Loeb, in their education and in what amounted to their further education, their trial, never offered them any reason why they should not murder or why they should feel remorse.

What it did offer them was God, and they saw through him. 'He gave up the idea that there was a God,' states one of the medical

[1] Maureen McKernan: *The Amazing Crime And Trial* . . . , pp. 247, 175
[2] *Psychopathology Of Everyday Life*
[3] Maureen McKernan: *The Amazing Crime And Trial* . . . , p. 271

reports on Leopold, 'saying that if a God exists some pre-God must have created him. In this line of thinking he reasons by analogy . . .'[1] (The medical report includes this statement under the heading 'Phantasies'.) Having been taught that the moral law drew its sanction from God, the young men were simply being logical in concluding that to jettison God was to jettison the moral law as well. Indeed, this, in society's eyes, was their crime—or at least the crime of Leopold, the more intelligent of the two: he reasoned. And, having worked out his position by reason, he could not be induced to change it under emotional pressure from the threat of death[2]. As the medical report records, 'he stated that consistency has always been a sort of God to him'.[3]

Society could make nothing of Leopold except to classify him as abnormal, by which it meant he was a non-conformer—in his sexual tastes, his interests, his very imagination: 'the normal child', says the medical report categorically, 'identifies himself with the persons in his immediate environment, he daydreams of being a motorman, an engineer, a policeman, showing thereby in his desires a normal response to the influences which surround him'. Leopold had made a conscious effort to subordinate his emotions to his reason; and this 'separation of intellect and emotions with certainty indicates mental abnormality'. When his intellect led him to atheism, that was abnormal. 'He discussed atheism and the denial of immortality' with an older friend who was a doctor. 'The doctor's attitude seems to be quite a normal one, and the patient did not learn to correct his own mistakes by conversation with the doctor.' When, on the other hand, imagination led him to contemplate the scene which has moved so many saints to ecstasy, that, too, was 'peculiar'. 'One of the earliest of Leopold's waking dreams was related to his peculiar religious interests; he persistently visualized the Crucifixion . . .'

The 'abnormalities' which the defence employed as a shield for the

[1] Maureen McKernan: *The Amazing Crime And Trial* . . . , p. 90

[2] Thus, from the medical report: 'If he is going to have to die at the hands of the law, he . . . wants to write . . . his autobiography . . . He would include an apologia or interpretation which would, among other things, show that he played his part and went to his end consistently, that he did not change as many expected he would.' (Maureen McKernan: *The Amazing Crime And Trial* . . . , p. 110)

[3] This, and the quotations in the next six paragraphs are from Maureen McKernan: *The Amazing Crime And Trial* . . . , pp. 110, 113, 112, 88, 113, 269, 268, 245, 242-3, 242, 112, 111, 109, 86, 87, 86, 107-8

accused, the prosecution flung in their faces: 'these two perverts', 'these cowardly perverts'; 'this man, who does not believe in God'; 'these two perverts, these two atheists, these two murderers'. (All the same, the prosecution must be credited with recognising that Leopold's glasses did not fall by accident. 'He has proclaimed since he was eleven years of age that there is no God. "The fool in his heart hath said there is no God." I wonder now, Nathan, whether you think there is a God or not. I wonder whether you think it is pure accident that this disciple of Nietzschian philosophy dropped his glasses or whether it was an act of Divine Providence to visit upon your miserable carcasses the wrath of God in the enforcement of the laws of the State of Illinois'.) What gave the worst offence to the prosecution was a 'blasphemous and sacrilegious statement' emanating not from Leopold but from the medical reports on him:- a suggestion that his belief in his own intellectual superiority might be tending towards the delusion that he was God. 'Who said that this young pervert ever thought he was the Christ child?' demanded the prosecution, pointing out, quite correctly, that it was 'without a syllable of evidence any place'. Indeed, it seems to be no more than the doctors' hyperbole for the impressive sense of his own intelligence which they encountered in Leopold—plus, perhaps, an attempt on their part to bring his 'abnormality' closer to a recognised clinical disease.

Leopold's conviction that he was more intelligent than the rest of the community was, for the doctors, the heart of the case. The trouble is his 'pathologically developed ego', his 'delusional ego', his 'delusionally cherished ego'. Yet all their efforts to establish that Leopold had a delusion of superiority really constitute evidence that he *was* superior. The irony is that, while they were saving his life by establishing his deluded state, the very nature of the reports in which they sought to establish it shews how little it was a delusion.

The doctors speak for the confusion of a community which pays lip-service to reason, which pretends that it is educating its children in the use of reason, but it is in practice doing its best to anaesthetise their minds with athletics[1] and impose on them the arbitrary laws of a religion which is anti-rational. Such a society must in practice

[1] The doctors seem to consider it a significant part of Leopold's 'abnormality' that he 'never developed any great appetite for outdoor games and sports, and seldom participated. He used to be bored at watching a baseball game, although he now enjoys watching football and basket-ball games.' (Maureen McKernan: *The Amazing Crime And Trial* . . . , p. 87)

disparage intelligence, imagination and enquiry, in favour of the unreasoning conformity it names morality. But it dare not openly say that it disparages them, any more than it can confess that its morality will not withstand two seconds' reasoning about it. Leopold's crime was that he did what society said it wanted him to do, instead of what it really wanted him to do: he exercised his intelligence—and discovered that society's morality was based on nothing but terrorisation, disguised by sentimentality.

The medical reports make it plain that any intellectual enquiry, if pursued with enthusiam, is in the doctors' eyes an aberration in itself[1]. The first (chronologically) report, by two doctors, is gravely suspicious of Leopold's ornithological and linguistic studies and of his sheer cleverness. A stark paragraph relates: 'He writes in his memoranda with Sanskrit characters forming French words.' Scribbles in his notebooks are 'in various languages, some of which can be identified as French, German, Sanskrit, Russian, English' (one imagines the relief with which the doctors come on this last); and the doctors go on to conclude that the drawings and scribbles 'show that the man's subconscious mind had a much greater range than the average person's and turned to subjects quite foreign to the thinking of normal people.' But the clou of this report is its comment on Leopold's reading: 'He read extensively in non-academic books, along a great many different subjects, but rather especially along unusual lines. For example, Russian novels of vivid morbid psychology[2], ancient books, many of them bizarre.' It is the language of a Customs official.

The aberration of being intelligent was all the worse, in Leopold's case, for having begun when he was a child. In the second report, four doctors tell us: 'He was not only precocious in his mental interests, but these interests assumed a degree of intensity and showed themselves in special directions which were in themselves indications of abnormality'. But when we go on to the examples cited to support

[1] Thus: 'Another feature of Leopold's personality characteristics, which students of abnormal psychology all recognize as belonging to the same picture, namely, that of the paranoic personality, is concerned with the abnormal and intense energy which he has for many years displayed . . . There is much that bears upon this point. When interested in the study of birds he would remain up all night in preparation for his early morning observations.' (Maureen McKernan: *The Amazing Crime And Trial* . . . , p. 110)

[2] Perhaps this reference indicates that Leopold had read about Raskolnikov's acte gratuit.

this, they turn out to indicate nothing but the ordinary imaginative piety of childhood (though tinged already with masochism) co-existing with a capacity for ordered and enquiring thought which a society that really wanted to educate its children would have been delighted to see: 'when about five he showed an intense preoccupation with questions of religion, cataloguing churches, insisting upon visiting the different ones in his neighbourhood, learning the names and something of the lives of the minor Saints of the Catholic Church, dwelling upon the idea of the Crucifixion, which he now states had a peculiar fascination for him, and wondering greatly why there should be so many different ideas about God.' This was not the end of Leopold's childish abnormality. The report goes on: 'And at this time he exhibited other curious interests, such as in the specific meanings of words . . .' However, it is so curious to find the doctors regarding this as a 'curious' interest for a small boy that perhaps we ought to suppose they do not mean what they say. They are so nearly illiterate that they have difficulty ·in expressing what they do mean. Indeed, the next phrases of this same sentence (a reference to the beginnings of Leopold's interest in the comparative study of languages) catch them out in ignorance of the meaning of the very word *meaning*:— '. . . such as in the specific meanings of words, especially the meaning of "Yes" in different languages'.

3. *Crime as War*

If society was so confounded by Nathan Leopold, we cannot be surprised if it was still more confounded by that other Nietzschian, Adolf Hitler. This time the confusion, and its results, were on a world scale. If Leopold and Loeb's was a compact, for the purpose of crime, between two young men neither of whom could have committed the crime without the other, here was a compact between a man and a whole nation; and although we can be sure that the man could not have dispensed with the nation, we cannot be sure that, if Hitler had been confined in a lunatic asylum or had been talented enough to express his will through painting, the people would not merely have adopted another Hitler, which might have given the crimes a different content but would not have altered the final results or the motivation. Fundamentally, in accepting them, a people creates—

even invents—its leaders, just as it does its gods. We cannot blame the bloodthirsty visions of Hell entertained by the Fathers of the Church, or by the Jesuits who educated Stephen Dedalus[1], on the bloodthirstiness of God the Father: it is the bloodthirstiness of Christians which has created God the Father.

Already, the relation between society and the leader or god it invents for itself has led us deep into the thickets of sado-masochism. For the method by which the community shapes God the Father into an expression of its own will is not to bully and dominate him. On the contrary: the community prostrates itself before him. It proclaims first that God's will *is* absolute: everything which is is because he wills it. Then it goes on to the contradiction which is inherent in religious thought, and which really betrays the impotence of God in the hands of the people—it begs God to do his will.

Mankind bullies God by the unctuous and flattering humility of the prayers in which it persistently harangues him. Similarly with its leaders. The community which keeps its leader most tightly in its control, and which will have least to do with the democratic notion that a leader, even if he is an elected representative of the people, has a duty to act on his own conscience, is the one which flatters him with the grossest glamour and offers him the most abject obedience. Between Leopold and Loeb, it is the more craven masochist who does the bullying and exerts the stronger influence. Leopold builds Loeb into the superman and invites him to impose penalties on Leopold if Leopold should be disloyal—'at your discretion, to break friendship, inflict physical punishment, or anything else you like . . .'[2]. Yet Leopold knows that this superman is really his, the underdog's, creation. It is Leopold who undertakes to 'explain my system of the Nietzschian philosophy with regard to you'; and it is a system which does not confer its extraordinary privileges on the superman 'without also putting on him extraordinary responsibility'. The superman has risen above bourgeois morality only to be caught in the much finer-meshed, much more niggling, conventions imposed from below by his slave. He becomes liable to receive these long, nagging letters from Leopold, in which Leopold anatomises his conduct: 'the superman is held to have committed a crime every time he errs in judgment—a mistake excusable in others'; 'the other

[1] James Joyce: *Portrait Of The Artist As A Young Man*, p. 3

[2] This and the other quotations from Leopold's letters to Loeb are cited in Maureen McKernan: *The Amazing Crime And Trial . . .*, pp. 216-19

night you . . . insisted that Marcus Aurelius Antonius (sic)[1] was practically the founder of Stoicism. In doing so you committed a crime. But it was a slight crime, and I chose to forgive it.'

Just so might the community, if it was articulate, write to its leader. It is the community, the creator, which is the stronger of the two and which wields the ultimate threat; it can insist, as Leopold did to Loeb, that its superman satisfy 'first one and then the other requirement, upon which'—again it might be the people addressing the leader—'I agreed to refrain from attempting to kill you or refusing to continue our friendship'.

If the leader is ultimately the people's puppet, whom they manipulate into leading them in the direction they are in fact determined to take, we can usually distinguish the psychic quality in him which makes him serviceable. The chances are that it will be a paranoia which has taken for its subject-matter nationalistic or dynastic politics. He is a man who can repress his impulses of homosexual love towards other men only by the method of contradicting them and making the unconscious assertion that he hates other men; but, unable to acknowledge these impulses of hatred as his own, he projects them and sees them coming in towards him from the outside world[2]; with the result

---

[1] I do not know whether the mistake of writing Antonius for Antoninus crept into Maureen McKernan's book on the case or into Clarence Darrow's speech at the trial, where these letters from Leopold were quoted, or whether it originated with Leopold himself. It would be interesting if Leopold had unconsciously elected to make a slip on the same subject as his friend, for the letter which contains the slip records his determination to share equally in his friend's guilt in the minor law-breakings they committed together before the murder:—'I . . . want you . . . to feel that we are on an equal footing legally, and therefore, I purposely committed the same tort of which you were guilty . . . The enclosed document should secure you against changing my mind in admitting the facts, if the matter should come up, as it would prove to any court that they were true.'

[2] Thus Freud: 'what lies at the core of the conflict in cases of paranoia among males is a homosexual wish-phantasy of *loving a man* . . . it is a remarkable fact that the familiar principal forms of paranoia can all be represented as contradictions of the single proposition: "*I* (a man) *love him* (a man)" . . . The proposition . . . is contradicted by . . . "I do not *love* him—I *hate* him." This contradiction . . . cannot, however, become conscious to a paranoiac in this form. The mechanism of symptom-formation in paranoia requires that internal perceptions, or feelings, shall be replaced by external perceptions . . . "I hate him" becomes transformed by *projection* into . . . "*He hates* (persecutes) *me*,

that the powers and statesmen round him appear to him to be closing
in on him in a monstrous conspiracy to crush him. If it was the father
whom he originally loved in a forbidden way, we can see why it is
these paternalistic figures who now appear as his persecutors. (The
megalomania in his condition applies not to himself but to the father.
Even in the act of hating him, he pays the father the compliment of
letting none but the biggest and most powerful occupy the father's
persecuting rôle[1].) Once he can see himself as the victimised son—
denied, perhaps, his fair share of the inheritance—he is justified in
arming himself by whatever means he can and attacking the unjust
father. The modern world-conqueror may even force his father into
the injustice of disinheriting him: he casts off the very name he got
from his father and adopts one of his own choice. In the ancient world,
he could compliment his ideal of the father by promoting him to
divine status and at the same time eliminate his real father. The pane-
gyrists of Julius Caesar ignore his immediate ancestry in favour of
the legendary lineage which he traced, via Aeneas, back to Venus,
thus making him kin to Zeus in person; according to Ovid, it is
Venus who rescues the soul of her descendant after his murder and
establishes him, deified, as a star, all at the behest of the supreme
father—genitor—Zeus[2]. And rumour seems to have understood the
psychology of Alexander the Great when it suspected him of being implicated in the murder of his father Philip, and at the same time put it about
that he was really the son not of Philip at all but of Zeus Ammon[3].

It is not hard to pick out a standing force which is always ready to
take immediate advantage of the leader's paranoia: the unconscious
homosexual feelings which constitute the esprit de corps, the camer-
aderie, of a professional army[4] or a militaristic officer caste. Only
when it takes the field does the army put women and homes utterly

which will justify me in hating him." And thus the unconscious feeling, which
is in fact the motive force, makes its appearance as though it were the consequence of an external perception: "I do not *love* him—I *hate* him, because
HE PERSECUTES ME." ' (*Collected Papers*, Volume III, IV, III)

[1] Cf. Freud: 'When a paranoiac names a person of his acquaintance as his
"persecutor", he thereby elevates him to the paternal succession . . .' (*Totem
And Taboo*, II, 3 (b))

[2] *Metamorphoses*, XV, 807 foll.:—'talibus hanc genitor . . .'

[3] Plutarch's *Life* of Alexander the Great

[4] Edward Glover: *War, Sadism And Pacifism*, X; Freud: *Group Psychology
And The Analysis Of The Ego*

behind it, sweeping along with it civilian men as well, whom it has the triumph of seducing into its own enclosed world of sublimated, but often sentimental, masculine affection. Evidently this rejection of women occasions the soldiers some guilt, for they do not make it absolute until a war gives them the pretext. As a matter of fact, war, which facilitates the indulgence and therefore aggravates the guilt, by the same stroke furnishes an opportunity for expiating the guilt: the soldier expunges his debt to women and home by risking the sacrifice of his life in defence of them.

The leader and the army constitute the instrument of war, one that will always come to hand when the community wants it, being readily supplied from the world's stock of unconscious homosexuals and paranoiacs. The curious thing about this instrument is that half its destructive force is directed not outwards but against itself. The leader fantasises himself as a victim: the soldiers picture themselves perhaps as heroic self-sacrificers, perhaps as so many put-upon pawns, reduced to the anonymity of a number, and thrown away in handfuls by generals, by the leader, by the statesman and civilians at home—by the very women who are prepared to accept their sacrifice. Both led and leader, by their métier, are moved by an unconscious desire to expiate their guilt. Such an instrument of war might bring to mind the standard joke which called the recruit in the British army in the war of 1939-1945 'Hitler's secret weapon'—or its prototype, the comment on his troops usually attributed to the Duke of Wellington, 'I don't know if they frighten the enemy but, by God, they frighten me'.

Certainly, this is an ambiguous weapon—a boomerang—to be wielded in war by a nation which wants simply to overcome the enemy and secure its own advantage. But we have to ask whether its own advantage ever is a nation's only motive in starting—or in being provoked to—war. We say nowadays that there will be no new war because it is not to anybody's advantage, now, to fight one. But the comfort of this saying evaporates when we wonder whether it ever has been to anybody's advantage. To certain sections of the communities involved, yes; the opening phases of wars of conquest, yes: but expansionist powers do not stop when they have achieved their objective—they merely expand their objectives; and in every war the soldiers on both sides, and the people on both sides, always suffer more than they gain. Indeed, for the individual soldier no prospect of gain can outweigh the risk that he may be killed—or for the civilian the risk that he may be bereaved.

So long as we bind ourselves to supposing that aggression is motivated simply by self-advancement (a resolutely unpsychological attitude which is shared by capitalist and communist societies alike) we are at a loss to explain why so many shrewd rulers, let alone so many averagely intelligent soldiers and citizens, have miscalculated so badly. When the disadvantages begin to overtake the advantages, when the ground under dispute has lost its value by being so furiously contended, why do the people not use the power they always possess to refuse to continue their friendship with the leader? Admittedly, it is difficult and dangerous to overthrow any leadership; but nothing like so difficult and dangerous as prosecuting a war.

If we say the people are restrained by loyalty to the leader, we are approaching an answer. But not if we regard loyalty purely as love. How is it an expression of love for the leader to keep him on a course which may bring about his destruction as well as everyone else's, and make him guilty of thousands of deaths? We come closer if we add to the love a feeling of shame. The people have a sense of guilt, of being in debt to the leader and to their country; and this they seek to expiate by suffering for leader and country.

If we conclude that every nation in a war is unconsciously as much bent on suffering as it is consciously bent on making the enemy suffer this is only the same conclusion which is forced on us if we judge the motives of a war by its results, which are always devastating. When we judged Don Giovanni on his performance and not his legend, it became clear that he did not want to succeed as a seducer. When we judged Leopold and Loeb on performance instead of professions, it became clear that with Leopold's intelligence (and we may add Loeb's extensive reading of detective stories[1]) the young men could not have been in any doubt that their conduct would lead to their detection and punishment. But this knowledge of theirs was not conscious. Their conscious and rational processes were entirely subverted by their unacknowledged wish to be punished.

4. 'Why do the Nations . . .?'

Just such a subversion takes place in nations contemplating or prosecuting a war. Their conscious purposes and calculations of where their interest lies, their reasoning, their very morality are all made a mockery

[1] Maureen McKernan: *The Amazing Crime And Trial* . . . , p. 70

of—by the unconscious lust to bring destruction on themselves by way of punishment. Their morality becomes a tissue of pretexts, their reasoning a mere web of rationalisation, as impressive but as insubstantially grounded as the self-consistent delusionary systems of madmen. And the danger is that when we—that is to say, civilisation—set ourselves to diagnose the causes of war, with a view to putting an end to war, our intellects will be subverted in the same way. If we really want to stop war, why do we let Edward Glover plead with us in vain to spend money and intelligence on analysing war as a phenomenon? Or is the situation really that we are so addicted to this sport, which turns out to be the sport not of wicked kings but of civilised communities, that we have made up our unconscious minds never to let the truth about it be exposed, never to do anything, while professing to do everything, that might make war impossible?

How far we have let our intellect be subverted we can judge from the misconceptions we swallow about war. We have trained our minds and our language to consider war an 'outbreak'. We divide nations into the bad, aggressive ones, led by aggressive leaders; and the good, non-aggressive ones, by which we mean those who do not put their aggressive leaders in command, who do not want to injure their neighbours, who do not, in short, embark on exactly the same activities as the enemy, until the enemy has done it first. The act of aggression is, we maintain, a simple act of babyish greed, covetousness of another nation's territory, wealth or prestige, which bursts through the barriers of civilised restraint; resistance to aggression is a natural reaction to it. Yet when it takes days to mobilise and months to deploy an army, and when it may take the statesmen years to manœuvre into their starting positions, we have no excuse for thinking war a rash act. Still less is it a natural, instinctive, animal-spirited activity. It requires the utmost civilised constraint in armed men to use their arms only against the other side and spare their own even when their own officers threaten to shoot them if they run away from being shot by the enemy. War is notable for its organisation, its discipline and, above all—that most civilised and social of concepts —its legality, whereby a statesman's pen licenses or, rather, compels the soldier to perform assaults which in peacetime would be crimes. This is worlds away from the instinctual aggressions and reactions of animals.

As for the theory that the aggressor is motivated by simple covetousness, it is not adequate to explain the peccadillos of a kleptomaniac, let alone the organised conflict of two nations who are perfectly in a position to see that in the end even the winner will be impoverished. If they do not see, we must take it that they will not. We must know by now that we cannot trust the professions even of our self-declared villains, our Richard the Thirds and Iagos: there always are motives in them which they are unwilling to expose both to our view and to their own. We have no business, at this stage of civilisation's peril, to go on believing our kleptomaniacs when they assure us that they steal for the simple reason that they want something for nothing[1] or to go on believing Leopold and Loeb when they tell us there was no motive for their murder. And as a matter of fact even the burglar, ambiguous as *his* motives probably are, does not pretend that self-interest leads him to burgle the police station. Greed might explain empire or encroachments on weak nations, though even then we are left to explain greed itself and shew how the egoist's instinctual appetite, which is normally responsive to and regulated by his needs, can become so enlarged as to covet more than he can use. But the world conqueror is never satisfied by fraud and stealth. If he snaps up trifling prey, it is so that the snapping of his jaws may waken the larger powers. It is impossible to believe that he is such a poor judge of men that he cannot guess that the result of his conduct will be to unite the major powers against him. He is in fact conjuring up and creating the impromptu police force which he proceeds to attack.

However, it may happen that the world cannot, even by coalitions, put up any satisfactory power to oppose him, and then his self-destructive lust shews itself nakedly, as he sighs for new worlds to conquer—or for something capable of conquering him. Unable to

---

[1] In Raskolnikov's case, the court was struck by the fact that he had never used the monetary proceeds of his crime but had hidden the purse probably without even looking to see what was in it. It was this surprising fact which led the magistrates to the conclusion that he was a gratuitous murderer. (He made rather the same impression on the court as Leopold and Loeb: 'All this strongly pointed to the conclusion that Raskolnikov was not at all like any ordinary murderer, felon, and robber, but that they were dealing with something quite different here.') But to the 'intense disappointment' of 'those who had some smattering of psychology', Raskolnikov himself 'answered . . . with most offensive accuracy that the cause of it all was his wretched material position, his poverty and helplessness, and his desire to assure his financial position during the first period of his career . . .' (*Crime And Punishment*, Epilogue, I, David Magarshack's translation)

encounter resistance, he soldiers on into the spaces of the earth, until he becomes exhausted by over-extending his lines of communication and is defeated by geography. If he cannot persuade someone to kill him on a battlefield near home, he must succumb to a fever in Babylon.

Our modern Alexanders, however, have experienced very little difficulty in getting us to do the fever's work. Twice in this century the agents of retribution have been British and American, peace-loving peoples, not militaristic, and not given to heel-clicking and parading about in uniforms; yet it is notable that if you want to see military ceremonial efficiently performed with men reduced to the uniformity of automata, you will see it best in Britain; if you want to find an army lavishly equipped with weapons of destruction you will find it in the United States; and notable that these nations have twice proved more effective wagers of war than the Germans. Either we must believe that the stroke of the statesman's pen transforms our characters—or else confess that it is our characters which covertly work towards the declaration of war. Of course we are merely passive partners to the aggressor's crime: we wait to be provoked; we insist on being in the moral right; and by the time we have waited there is no doubt that we *are* in the moral right. Yet just this provides the pretext for *our* lust for self-sacrifice. It is our moment for expiating the egoism and slovenliness we indulged in during the peace, and we exclaim:

> Now, God be thanked Who has matched us with His Hour . . .
> Oh! we, who have known shame, we have found release there,
> Where there's no ill, no grief, but sleep has mending . . .
> Nothing to shake the laughing heart's long peace there
> But only agony, and that has ending;
> And the worst friend and enemy is but Death.[1]

Why, then, we must obstinately ask, did we behave so shamefully in the first place if it was not with a view to this ultimate expiation?

Since we are so prompt (having once waited for the enemy to begin it) to copy the enemy's example, to outdo him in military efficacy and even, as we did at Hiroshima, to outdo him in the uncontemplatable horror of our methods, it would be foolish not to ask whether our behaviour in the period of waiting really was calculated, as we

[1] Rupert Brooke: *1914*

believed, to restrain his excesses and make war less likely. Can we be so stupid that we had not observed that traditional diplomacy very seldom has prevented war, that the system of checks and balances has repeatedly given way? Or was it with unconscious knowledge of what we were doing that we trusted ourselves to instruments so often proved faulty? Are we so genuinely clumsy and unworldly-wise that our diplomatic blunders must be regarded as pure accidents and mistakes? Or ought we to conclude that, while our conscious minds designed them in all sincerity to preserve the peace, their ineptitude was shaped by our unconscious, which had no desire to do any such thing and perceived perfectly clearly that these were the tactics most likely to lead to war?

The test comes when we ask why, if we are genuinely concerned with peace, and if our insistence on our own legal position is not mere wool pulled over our own eyes, we have always drawn back from the one act which seems to hold any least promise of ending war and which is, at the same time, the only way to put the whole use of force on a legal footing. We refuse to forgo one tittle of our national sovereignty in order to pay it into the common pool of a supra-national authority; and we refuse in the name of each nation's right to order its own affairs. But consider what, for the sake of preserving this right, we risk in the way of likelihood of war. If we refuse to create any legal way whereby we can prevent Hitler from massacring the Jews in his own country, then we shall be forced, if we want to prevent him, to manœuvre him into attacking the Poles in order that we may have our chance to put a stop to his assaults on Poles and Jews alike. By the time we have achieved this, we have made nonsense of Germany's right to order her own affairs; we have abolished it, and have brought about instead a state of affairs whereby overnight, by the stroke of our pen, 'democracy' changes in Germany from a dirty to a good word— or, rather, it changes in part of Germany; for we have had to divide the country with the ally we could not dispense with, and *his* decree is that 'people's democracy' shall be the good word and 'western democracy' the bad.

The grounds on which we pass our decree are simply that we were stronger. Until we are prepared to proclaim on our side that, if we should begin to massacre Jews, foreign countries would have a moral duty to stop us, and that we should be morally wrong to oppose them, the virtue of our argument to Hitler amounts to no more than this: 'We can offer you no legal, let alone a moral, reason why you should not massacre Jews except that, if you do, we will inflict bigger massacres on you.' We cannot be surprised if Germans conclude that so long as Hitler was the stronger it was right to massacre Jews, and when we became stronger it became wrong.

Thus we put ourselves in a position not of reforming the criminal, nor of limiting the damage done, but of covertly provoking his fury to exceed all bounds. We are not even a primitive, legalistic police force which punishes the criminal as vindictively as the criminal commits his assaults. We are not a police force at all; we have refused all legal standing. By insisting on national sovereignty we declare our belief that there is one moral law in Britain and a different one in Germany and that both are right to the extent that they can get away with it. In short, we proclaim international anarchy; and all that our wars can prove is that we are the stronger bandit.

5. *The Double Entendre*

The unconscious homosexuality implicit in the soldier's calling has not exhausted itself when it has established the soldier's comradely feelings towards the men on his own side. There are also men on the opposite side. It seems that the soldier's conscious mind will tolerate love providing it is 'aim-inhibited'[1]—does not carry the instinctual impulse through to its bodily expression; or else it will tolerate a violent, physical act providing the loving nature of the impulse behind it is kept obscured. The unconscious eroticism of fighting can come to expression only by fusing itself to the acknowledged aggressive impulse.

It is not only on the battlefield but in all human activity that we encounter the erotic undertones in aggression and the aggressive ones in love. The soldier's loving impulse towards his enemy is only part of our universal ambivalence not only towards one another as objects of love or hatred but also towards sexuality and death themselves. Mankind's most persistent double entendre is the assonance between *l'amour* and *la mort*. 'The stroke of death is as a lover's pinch,' says Cleopatra, 'Which hurts, and is desir'd'; and the dramatic irony has already foreshadowed this passage in her real Liebestod by Enobarbus's satirical comment on the feigned deaths Cleopatra dies in the

[1] Freud: *Group Psychology And The Analysis Of The Ego*, VIII; XII

course of love, 'I do think there is mettle in death which commits some loving act upon her, she hath such a celerity in dying'[1]. This is not a question of a coincidence pressed into occasional service, a matter of the unconscious, when it seeks to express a forbidden phallic idea, making use of the convenient shape of guns, spears, swords, arrows—as it may, so dreams shew us, make use of almost any reasonably appropriate common object[2]. The fusion of loving and killing, being loved and being killed, is rooted in our biological nature, in our usefulness as vehicles for the continuity of the species. It is in achieving the loving act of union and the creative act of perhaps propagating a new life that we begin to die. At this moment we cross over from being the protected and favoured child, whom nature conspires to foster, into being, potentially, parents—and instantly we have marked ourselves down to be discarded by the species; we have begun to be not merely superfluous in function but in naked economic fact impediments to the development of the new generation of favoured children.

Thus the unconscious has an inevitable biological foundation (which is reinforced by the psychological material inevitably formed, during infancy, by the clash of instinct on reality) for the equation it is constantly making between sexual penetration and penetration with a weapon, between imposing or suffering an orgasm and imposing or suffering death.

The equation is not simply an important branch of the *language* of the unconscious but essential to the unconscious's thinking. Metaphor comments not on a similarity of appearances but on an ambivalence of feeling when it repeatedly compares the striving tangle of lovers' bodies to the combat of mortal enemies. Children who witness an act of intercourse reveal the ambivalent nature of their own puzzled but violent sexual impulses[3] when they regularly misconstrue what they see as an act of violence by the man against the woman[4]. We

[1] *Antony And Cleopatra*, V, ii; I, ii

[2] Cf. Freud's remark that in the description of the sexual organs 'the symbolism of dreams is as indefatigable as human wit'. (*The Interpretation Of Dreams*, VI, (E))

[3] Cf. Freud's description of the child's earliest (phallic) impulses of sexual love: 'obscure impulses are roused . . . to do something violent, to press in, to knock to pieces, to burst open a hole somewhere'. (*Collected Papers*, Volume II, VI)

[4] —so regularly that Freud listed '*the sadistic conception of coitus*' among the 'typical sexual theories' entertained by children in their attempts to solve the

scarcely need the psycho-analytic textbooks to remind us that orgasm, with its sweat, its agony, its breathlessness which simulates that giving up of the ghost in which the soul flies away, is sometimes called 'the little death'; we have Dryden's witty conceit on the subject of sexual simultaneity and of that 'celerity' which Cleopatra had in dying:

> Whil'st *Alexis* lay prest
> In her Arms he lov'd best . . .
> He found the fierce pleasure too hasty to stay,
> And his soul in the tempest just flying away.

> When *Cœlia* saw this,
> With a sigh, and a kiss,
> She cry'd, Oh my dear, I am robb'd of my bliss;
> 'Tis unkind to your Love, and unfaithfully done,
> To leave me behind you, and die all alone.

> The Youth, though in haste,
> And breathing his last,
> In pity dy'd slowly, while she dy'd more fast;
> Till at length she cry'd, Now my dear, now let us go,
> Now die, my *Alexis*, and I will die too.[1]

The phallic connotation of weapons is written deep into mythology. The snake itself, most ancient, revered and geographically distributed of phallic symbols, the one who insinuated sexuality to Eve, is a lethal weapon. (Snakes which coil and rear before striking provide a caricature of erection.) The sword is unsheathed—pulled out from its owner's clothing—and flourished, before being plunged into a body: our language points up the comparison by adopting, for the receptive

riddle of sex. 'Whatever detail it may be that comes under their observation, whether it is the position of the two people, or the sounds, or certain accessory circumstances, in all cases they arrive at the same conclusion . . . seeing in it something that the stronger person inflicts on the weaker by force, and comparing it, especially the boy, to a fight as they know it from their childish play, in which, by the way, an admixture of sexual excitation is also not wanting.' (*Collected Papers*, Volume II, VI)

[1] *Marriage-à-la-Mode*

sexual organ in a woman's body, the Latin name for 'sheath', *vagina*[1]. Weapons which are shot through the air describe schematically sexual ejaculation; and it is a weapon of this type which furnishes mythology and folk lore with their most famous and blatant phallic symbol, the arrow of the god of love. Again Dryden displays his insight by giving a specific sense to the pain this love-weapon imparts, in the song where Cupid, enlightening a puzzled virgin,

> Then show'd her his Arrow, and bid her not fear,
> For the pain was no more than a Maiden may bear.[2]

This symbolism the soldier transposes into his own homosexual world. He has chosen to spend his life in the places, barracks and battlefield, where there is the greatest profusion of weapons—and of young men; and where he may expend skill and expertise, and take pride, in devotedly bringing both to the apex of efficiency. Scrutinised, the image of Don Giovanni manœuvring the Commendatore into crossing swords with him proves to be an image of homosexual lovers; and so with the manœuvres of two bodies of men preparing to come into a contact which, even if they are separated by the range of artillery, always has the intimacy of producing a galvanic physical result by physical impact.

Don Giovanni, however, is rather in the situation of Dryden's Cœlia. He kills the Commendatore, swiftly enough, at the very outset, and then has to wait through the swelling tension of the entire opera for the Commendatore to come sufficiently back to life to return and kill *him*. The soldier has sacrificed much that Don Giovanni enjoyed; he submits to discipline, whereas Don Giovanni is a buccaneer fighting for himself alone: but the soldier gains the advantage of being more promiscuous. The object of his erotic hostility is not one body at a time but a whole body of men, with the result that if he kills one he can still be killed, almost in the same moment, by another. He has a much better chance than Don Giovanni of finishing the engagement with his breathless body lying on his lover's—that parody of mutual orgasm which was, after so much striving, achieved by

---

[1] Plautus converts the metaphor to a homosexual sense. One of his characters teases another (a military man): 'When the soldier went on guard duty at night and you went too, did his sword fit your scabbard?'—*conveniebatne in vaginam tuam machaera militis*? (*Pseudolus*, 1180-1)

[2] *Sylvae*

Tristan and Isolde. The battlefield is *Tristan Und Isolde* on orgiastic scale.

If soldiers seduce civilians on their own side into the inexplicit homosexuality of army life, they practise violent seductions on the other side. Or, rather, it is a case of reciprocal seduction. Dryden shewed us Cupid's weapon giving pleasure and pain in the act of defloration. Weapons of war do no less: they kill the flower of a nation's youth.

We can pursue this curious metaphor into *The Interpretation Of Dreams*, where Freud remarks the ancient and sanctified use of flower and plant metaphors in a sexual sense[1], and the phallic significance in dreams and myths of a branch bursting into blossom[2], and then goes on to note (in the course of analysing a young woman's dream which, like the ribald song, punned on *violet* and *violate*) that these formations symbolise 'the human sexual organs by flowers, the sexual organs of plants'[3]. We can see why its young soldiers are the flower of a nation. They are, quite precisely, the nation's sexual organs; and war cuts them off before they can leave the nation any progeny. Two nations at war are engaging in a reciprocal castration.

Why to offer himself for castration by the enemy should fulfil the soldier's homosexual desires is revealed by the infantile situation from which adult sexuality has evolved. Among children's sexual theories, the one which is most cogently enforced, by a hundred strands of Oedipal logic and necessity, and which most regularly persists into adult life (where it influences both men's and women's social attitude to women[4]) is the notion which explains girls as boys who have been castrated[5]. The little boy is afraid that the father will choose the logical punishment of castration to inflict on the boy in return for the boy's daring to rival him in the mother's affections—

---

[1] 'the "vineyard" of the Lord, the "seed" of Abraham, the "garden" of the maiden in the *Song Of Songs*' (*The Interpretation Of Dreams*, VI, (D)).

The same symbolism allowed the drawing-room balladist to bypass his audience's—and, no doubt, his own—prudery, and suggest to his beloved 'If I should plant a tiny seed of love/In the garden of your heart . . .'

[2] 'Just as the angel bears a lily-stem in the Annunciation' (*The Interpretation Of Dreams*, VI, (D) footnote)

[3] *The Interpretation Of Dreams*, VI, (E)

[4] e.g. Freud: *Collected Papers*, Volume V, XVII; XXIV

[5] See, cardinally, Freud: *Collected Papers*, Volume V, XVII; Volume II, VI

or daring to persist in sexual activity, even auto-erotic activity, at all. He fears that the part of his own body which it gives him so much pleasure to play with will be taken away from him, like other valuable and fragile objects he has gone on playing with after being forbidden to. Yet, with the optimistic versatility which is characteristic of instinctual life, the boy is capable of turning even this immense dread, which is the hinge of the whole Oedipus situation, to his own pleasure. The discovery that women have, as he thinks, really been castrated makes his dread worse: it proves the thing can happen. But he can also see that women have not made such a bad job of their deprived state; and, among women, this is especially true of his mother, who has the love of his father. If he cannot prize the parental couple apart by ousting the father, he will try to do it by ousting the mother and putting himself in her feminine place. If the father is going to castrate him or at least impose restrictions on his sexual life which are tantamount to castration, the boy can regard this mutilation as something which turns him into a woman[1]. He insists on receiving the father's oppression or assault on him as a rape; and because he always apprehends the assault as a castration, and regards women as castrated, it becomes his opportunity to offer himself to the father homosexually.

Just so does the soldier unconsciously regard his chances of being killed—that is, castrated—in battle: with dread of the ultimate punishment, and yet with the sense that he can turn even this into a gratification not only of his self-destructive impulses but also of his homosexual impulses. To be killed by the enemy is to be penetrated by a man; and if this castrates him, it confirms him in the woman's rôle. It is this delicately balanced instinctual compromise which makes war possible by making its risks tolerable to the soldiers. Without it, the fighting force would revolt and the nations would lack an instrument for their aggressive and self-destructive desires.

Love surprises us by its aggressive undertones—especially where there is a virgin to be deflowered; and sometimes a storyteller can

---

[1] Thus Catullus in the rhapsodic poem (LXIII) which describes the self-castration of Attis, heroic type of the castrated priests of Cybele, makes at the moment of Attis's self-mutilation a striking change from the masculine to the feminine gender in speaking of him. Attis, no longer he but she, calls on the eunuch priests of Cybele not as *Galli*, their usual name, but in the feminine form of *Gallae*; Lamb's translation sums up: 'Thus Atys, female now, to female comrades sung'. Similarly, the castrated priests of Cybele appear in *The Golden Ass* (VIII, 26) as girls, *puellae*.

wriggle past his own internal psychic censorship, and society's censorship at the same time, by shewing us an erotic act under the disguise of an aggressive one. A nineteenth-century operatic composer would never let us see a bride coming out of her bridal chamber with her nightdress stained with her own blood: but Donizetti can give his audience a perfectly respectable erotic frisson by bringing Lucia di Lammermoor forth stained with her husband's blood and letting us know that on her wedding night it is Lucia who has played the man and penetrated her husband. In war, the great field of men's rivalry and aggression, it is the other way about, and the frisson is one of homosexual tenderness. Again it is achieved by a psychic change of sex. Once he is seen as the victim whose blood is shed, the soldier joins the female sex, that vast class of persons who bleed when men deflower them and bleed again when they give men progeny. Only when he is in mortal danger can his fellow men lay aside their sexual rivalry with the soldier and admit a tenderness forbidden in peacetime; but the tenderness actually takes the form of creating the mortal danger; and it is expressed by an act, also forbidden in peacetime, which puts the soldier out of the way as a rival for ever. Women and enemies are both subjugated, removed from rivalry, by an act of penetration.

Fully to unravel the paradox whereby two nations' castrating one another is equal to the procreative act of sexual intercourse leads deep into the double entendre of sexuality. But we can see straight away that nations do not regard war as sterile. Its very locality has the name of a fertile place, a battle*field*. The implicit metaphor of war likens the spilling of the soldier's blood in the service of his country to the ejaculation of his semen in the service of the species: is not the blood of the martyrs the seed of the church? And when the young Adonis died—of a wound in the groin—his blood, sinking into the earth, made the earth fertile, and there came up the blood-red anemone[1].

Comparing our soldiers to flowers, we are drawing on the harvest metaphor[2] of the grass which is cut down in its flower so that its

[1] Ovid: *Metamorphoses*, X, 715 foll.

[2] Cf. the metaphor with which Aricie laments the death in war, without issue, of her brothers (Racine: *Phèdre*, II, i):

> Je suis seule échappée aux fureurs de la guerre:
> J'ai perdu dans la fleur de leur jeune saison
> Six frères . . . Quel espoir d'une illustre maison!
> Le fer moissona tout

seed may be scattered and come up next year; and at the same time we equate the soldier with the girl who will only be fertile if the flower of her maidenhead is reaped by man. Civilisation enshrines its pity for its soldiers, and its infatuation with their physical beauty, in the great metaphor which turns them into a bouquet, the nosegay we present to our lovers or the wreath we sacrifice to our dead[1]. The Flanders poppies of the 1914-1918 war have their precursor in Virgil's description of the death of the beautiful young soldier Euryalus:

> His snowy neck reclines upon his breast,
> Like a fair flow'r by the keen share oppress'd—
> Like a white poppy sinking on the plain,
> Whose heavy head is overcharg'd with rain[2];

and in the beautiful, appalling metaphor which the pity of war made to blossom in an unmetaphorical language:

$$\mathit{\dot{o}\rho\tilde{\omega}\mu\epsilon\nu\ \dot{a}\nu\theta o\tilde{v}\nu\ \pi\acute{\epsilon}\lambda a\gamma o s\ \mathrm{'}A\iota\gamma\tilde{a}\iota o\nu\ \nu\epsilon\kappa\rho\tilde{o}\iota s}^{3}$$

'we saw the Aegean sea flower with corpses'.

6. *Freud's Analysis of the Individual in Society*

If we want to carry the discussion of war beyond the army, which is only the instrument, and bring it home to the people, which supplies the thrust, we shall have to take into account Freud's analysis of social groups[4], for that is where we find an illumination of the loyalty

---

[1] Having remarked that we employ the sexual organs of plants to symbolise those of human beings, Freud adds that 'presents of flowers between lovers may perhaps have this unconscious significance' (*The Interpretation Of Dreams*, VI (E)). Surely this is likewise the significance of our giving flowers to the dead: it is a token self-castration on our part; we pay off our unconscious hostility towards the dead whom we regard as, essentially, dead parents, by sacrificing to them the very thing which was in dispute when the hostility was aroused.

[2] Dryden's translation (IX, 581-4) of *Aeneid*, IX, 435-7

[3] Aeschylus: *Agamemnon*, 659

[4] *Group Psychology And The Analysis Of The Ego* (1921); *Totem And Taboo* (1919)

which makes a people submit to prosecuting a war even though it is, or even after it has become, profitless. At this point I shall have to beg the indulgence of the reader who knows his Freud, and invite him to skim through the next two sections, merely keeping an eye on whether I have reported Freud fairly and giving a critical glance to my own embroideries round the border; and I must ask the non-Freudian to be indulgent, too, since I am only giving him a concentrated account of those of Freud's conclusions I am going to build on, and cannot begin to convey the cogency and elegance of Freud's own arguments.

Freud quickly establishes that a human group, whether mob or nation, is a collection of people whose feeling of solidarity with one another is enforced by something more pressing and more enduring than proximity or common conditions of work. Everyone had observed that a group behaves differently from how its members would individually behave in the same situation: it has abdicated the faculties of self-criticism and of rationally appreciating its situation which are to be found in most of its members taken one by one. But to affix to the influence under which this abdication is made, the academic psychologists could lay their hands on no more explanatory or meaningful label than group suggestion or herd instinct. Freud perceived that if the members of a group have given up these faculties it is because they hand them over to someone else—their leader. A leader is essential to the formation of a group. (Panic, so often regarded as a group phenomenon, Freud diagnosed as really the mark of a group's disintegration under the loss of its leader or of faith in him; panic is what the individual experiences when he resumes his own critical faculty and recognises the real dangers of his situation, which he failed to notice while his critical faculty had been usurped by the leader.) The leader is not always a person. Indeed, if a group is to keep its identity from generation to generation and outlive any particular constituents, the leader, too, must become immortal: he must be deified or replaced by something abstract, a leading idea.

For the unworkable and unwarrantable hypothesis of a herd instinct, Freud proposed to substitute an instinct which undoubtedly does exist, the sexual instinct, and to attribute the cohesion of social groups to the members' love for one another. But this social love was obviously a modification of the sexual instinct, since it did not seek a physical union between two people to the exclusion of the rest. Freud accordingly looked for its origin in the great school of aim-inhibition, the family, where the infant's sexual desire attaches itself to its first beloved, the mother, and encounters the father standing in its way: an intractable situation which forces the child into an evolutionary creative upheaval, from which it emerges with the prohibition against incest built-in to its own psychic apparatus instead of being imposed by the presence and rights of the father, and with its sexual ambitions towards its own kin tamed to the aim-inhibited character of family affection.

From this family feeling the group benefits. Freud's primary insight into the group's structure was to perceive that it is modelled on the family's structure. The leader's position is that of a communal adoptive father; and it is in their common submission to him, and their common renunciation of their own sexual rights in his favour, that the members become capable of the brotherly love which binds the group into a unit.

By going back to the family situation, and by considering the child as a being whose psyche is actually evolved under the pressures of that situation, Freud had discovered the bridge between individual and social psychology. The intellectual excitement of following his discovery consists in observing how perfectly the span which rises from the social and anthropological side meets and slots into the span which rises from the individual. The family is a society; and a society is a family. If mankind's social evolution has proceeded from family, via clan, to extended group, the capacity to form social relationships susceptible to these developments has been evolved in the individual during his experience of the primary social situation.

The key to Freud's social psychology was, therefore, his view of the individual infant's psychic evolution, a view in which the original psyche, the baby's mental equipment at birth, consists solely of the Id, that wholly unconscious and chaotic fund of pure instinctual impetus, which lunges blindly out in search of gratification and soon finds its impulses shattered and constrained by the hard walls of the real world. These encounters with the environment force the Id into the first stage of its evolution. It buds off from itself a new agency, the Ego, part of which it thrusts up into consciousness. The Ego's function is to mediate between the outside world and the vulnerable, permanently babyish Id, testing the reality of the images which are presented to the psyche by its own fantasies or by sense-stimuli, and directing the Id's impulses into channels that really will yield gratification.[1]

[1] Thus Freud (*The Question Of Lay Analysis*, II; III): 'So we represent the Ego as the outer layer of the psychical apparatus, the Id; a layer modified by

The actual mechanism of our social susceptibility is created, Freud was able to shew, during the evolution of the Ego. At the time when the Ego is setting in coherent shape, there is congealed into its very stuff, and thus into the very stuff of our individuality, a hook which, through the psychic act of identification, makes us apt to adhere to a society. This formation is influenced both by the successive modes of sexuality through which the infant progresses and by the different kinds of relationship he becomes capable of forming when he acquires an Ego.

Even before the development of the Ego, the baby has formed a relationship: with its mother; and its first gratification is that of eating her. How the baby experiences this relationship can be pieced together from the many survivals into later life of the babyish concept of relationships. To love the mother and to eat her are equivalent; and both are equivalent to being fused, identified, with her. In the baby's gratification at mealtimes there is nothing to choose between the idea that the baby, enclosed in the external womb formed by her arms, her bosom and her lap, has been reabsorbed into the mother's body, and the idea that the baby is sucking her substance into its own body.

This earliest, oral mode of gratification, and the relationship of love by identification whose vehicle it is, have left their deposit in magical, religious and childish systems of thought, which hold that to eat something is to become it—or vice versa.

> It's a very odd thing—
> As odd as can be—
> That whatever Miss T. eats
> Turns into Miss T.[1]

the influence of the outside world (reality) . . . The Ego lies between reality and the Id, which is the psyche proper'; 'everything which goes on in the Id is unconscious and remains so, and . . . the processes in the Ego (they alone) *may* become conscious. But they are not all conscious'; 'If it is the instinctual forces from the Id which provide the propulsion, yet it is the Ego which does the steering—without which, no goal can be reached. The instincts of the Id press for immediate satisfaction, regardless of all else, and in this way either fail of achievement or actually do damage. It is the Ego's task to avert these mishaps, to mediate between the pretensions of the Id and the preventions of the outer world . . . In taming the impulses of the Id in this way the Ego replaces the pleasure principle, which was earlier the sole regulating force, by the so-called *reality principle*, which indeed pursues the same ends but takes into account the conditions imposed by the outer world.'

[1] Walter de la Mare: *Peacock Pie*, Miss T

It is in this manner that the Catholic communicant seeks union with his God (and he incidentally revives the baby's circumstances, too: he does not use his hands to help himself to his food but has himself intimately waited-on by a parent, the priest whom he addresses as Father and to whom he is a spiritual son). But his is not the baby's original food, the mother; nor the food of the weaned child—Miss T.'s 'porridge and apples, mince, muffins and mutton'. (Miss T. already has so definite a notion of her own identity—so well formed an Ego—that she knows it is these bits of her environment which turn into her and not she into them, even though her nanny has probably instilled a touch of magical thinking into her mind by threatening that if she eats too much of the mutton she will turn into a sheep.) What the Catholic eats, and for a very good reason, is the father; and this to him is a sacramental act affirming his love of the person he eats; just as it is to the cannibal, who 'has a devouring affection for his enemies and only devours people of whom he is fond'[1].

The baby's union with its mother is subject to painful interruptions. As a matter of fact, the original union has already been decisively interrupted—by birth, when the baby, turned out into the cold world, has to set about getting its sustenance by new forms of muscular exertion, drawing air into its lungs and milk into its stomach. But while it is cuddled and fed, it must seem to the baby (or, rather, it would seem, if the baby had any objective perception of its standing vis-à-vis the mother) that this separation has been patched up[2]—until the mother puts it down away from her and it presently wakes up, hungry, and experiences a lapse of time before its hunger is satisfied. In the womb there was no lapse of time between a need and its gratification. These separations from the mother are so many small-scale repetitions

[1] Freud: *Group Psychology And The Analysis Of The Ego*, VII

[2] Thus Freud: 'just as the mother originally satisfied all the needs of the foetus through her own body, so now, after its birth, she continues to do so, though partly through other means. There is much more continuity between intra-uterine life and earliest infancy than the impressive caesura of the act of birth allows us to believe. What happens is that the child's biological situation as a foetus is replaced for it by a psychological object-relation to its mother. But we must not forget that during its intra-uterine life the mother was not an object for the foetus, and that at that time there were no objects at all as far as it was concerned. It is obvious that in this scheme of things there is no room for the abreaction of the birth-trauma.' (*Inhibitions, Symptoms And Anxiety*, VIII)

of birth. The effect of birth, which we from outside can see to be decisive for the baby's becoming a distinct psychic identity on its own, is impressed on the baby itself only by a whole course of similar experiences, culminating in the grand severance of weaning, which is really the completing phase of being born. Even the bottle-fed child has to be weaned; and this, like the original birth itself, entails a separation from the mother's close support and forces the baby to make new muscular efforts—and presently to use its hands—in order to get the difficult solid food into its body.

As Freud discerned, the separations and lapses of time in the baby's relationship with its mother force it into a recognition of its own distinctness first from the mother and then from the environment in general—force it, that is, to develop an Ego. 'It must make the strongest impression on' the baby 'that many sources of excitation, which later on he will recognize as his own bodily organs, can provide him at any time with sensations, whereas others become temporarily out of his reach—amongst these what he wants most of all, his mother's breast—and reappear only as a result of his cries for help. Thus an "object" first presents itself to the ego as something existing "outside", which is only induced to appear by a particular act.'[1]

No sooner has the Ego marked off the baby's psychic life into a continuous and delimited selfhood than it becomes capable of a new form of relationship: the self will treat various not-selves, which it has only lately differentiated, as objects. The ambitions of the Id, while that was the sole governing force, were towards *being* the thing at the other side of whatever relationship it established. When the Ego takes control of the Id's impulses, it directs them towards *having*. Eating no longer implies a fusion between the eater who experiences gratification and the food which provides it, but is a matter of objectively selecting bits of the environment and using them in such a way that they yield pleasure; there is no confusion now about which side of the border experiences the pleasure. Toys are no longer to be eaten; they are to be employed as objects, used for pleasure: and they can be possessed even though they are not converted into the self.

Just at the time when it becomes capable of apprehending its own bodily sensations *as* its own, the child begins to receive stimulations which are sexual not simply in that wider sense of the word whereby the oral impulses, with their lust for satisfaction, are sexual, but in

[1] Freud: *Civilization And Its Discontents*, I

the precise and local sense of genital; and it is not long before the child, equipped now with the Ego's intellectual apparatus and faculty of appreciating reality, begins to speculate how these promptings can be applied to objects in the real world in such a way as to yield pleasure.

It is possible that the child first listens to the new impulses because its instinct to love, to form relationships, has recently been balked of oral expression—by weaning. Freud noted: 'The old paediatrician Lindner [1879] once remarked that a child discovers the genital zones (the penis or the clitoris) as a source of pleasure while indulging in sensual sucking (thumb-sucking): I shall leave it an open question', Freud went on, 'whether it is really true that the child takes the newly found source of pleasure in exchange for the recent loss of the mother's nipple—a possibility to which later phantasies (fellatio) seem to point.'[1] That it *was* really true seems to have been the imaginative opinion of John Donne, who considered that the only conceivable predecessor to the lover's pleasure was the suckling's—or even (if we may interpret his metaphor) the unconscious pleasure of the unawakened embryo in the womb:

> I wonder by my troth, what thou, and I
> Did, till we lov'd? were we not wean'd till then?
> But suck'd on countrey pleasures, childishly?
> Or snorted we in the seaven sleepers den?[2]

Whether as a substitute or not, the genital mode of sexuality *is* accepted into the child's instinctual character, in which it eventually becomes dominant[3], and is at once applied in the new relationship with objects. And it seems likely that weaning is the decisive precipitator of this new type of relationship. It is then that, in its relationship with its food (which used to mean with its mother), the child is for the first time encouraged to use its hands—or is even able to, for this is the first time it is given food which *can* be picked up; and hands are

---

[1] *Collected Papers*, Volume V, XVII   [2] *The Good-Morrow*

[3] —a dominance perfectly described by Felix Krull: sexuality 'began very early to play a role in my life, to occupy my thoughts, to shape my fancies . . . Lacking any other means of description, I grouped all my emotions and fancies together under the heading of "The Best of All" or "The Great Joy." . . . As far back as I can remember, this "Great Joy" took up a commanding position in my inner life . . .' (Thomas Mann: *Felix Krull* . . . , I, 8, translation by Denver Lindley)

the great users and holders of objects: to have an object is, fundamentally, to hold it in the hand. When man adopted his upright stance, he set his hands free not only to use tools but to own them, and he developed that human sense of possession which is not quite shared by the animals who have to carry things in the mouth or whose hands are still needed for locomotion so that they find it hard to hold on to their goods at the same time as running away from a would-be thief.

At weaning, the child is repeating this piece of the species's evolution. If it is to take solid food, it may no longer lounge on its back in its mother's arms but must sit up and support itself; and presently it learns to stand and walk upright, too. Just like early man, the child thus sets his hands free to take possession first of his food and then of objects generally. The little boy's hand, exploiting its new potentiality and freedom, quickly discovers an object which is always with him: a part of himself, which can none the less be held; at once a tool, a toy, and a fiercely valued possession whose theft he dreads (and whose apparent theft from herself the little girl laments the moment she learns that boys still have it). It is the hand, now set free and mobile, which supplies the connecting link in the transition from oral to predominantly genital sexuality. The hand's first act, when the child is weaned, is to thrust its thumb into the child's mouth to take the place of the nipple which has been withheld. The child supplies himself with a gratification that was formerly supplied by someone else's body, thus converting sucking into an auto-erotic activity; and presently he learns that his hand can also supply gratification by genital masturbation. In adults' irrationally—and often violently—repressive reaction to thumb-sucking we are probably seeing the result of their unconscious recognition (that is, their own suppressed memory) of the fact that thumb-sucking is oral masturbation.

However, there is a great psychic distinction between the oral and the genital masturbation. Thumb-sucking takes the place of a gratification the infant really has experienced and later lost; but genital masturbation, which the adult may adopt as a substitute for experiences he has really had, is for the child an anticipation of experience. Not the least significant result of man's taking to the upright position is that it facilitated manual masturbation, an activity whose contribution to human culture we usually overlook. In the child's masturbation fantasies, we can discern the beginnings of both his imaginative and his rational life. Since he is anticipating experience he has to make deductions, and to invent and try out hypotheses, about the puzzle of sexual physiology. Masturbation must have been a comparable intellectual stimulus in the development of early man, by liberating the human sexual instinct from its dependence on immediate stimulation by something in the environment: the superiority of the human intellect lies in its power to summon images rather than simply react to those the world presents, and to concentrate its attention inwardly as well as passively having it caught by something external.

However, civilisation is built not only on the liberation of man's sexual instinct but on its renunciation; and here, too, masturbation must have played a decisive part in man's development, by piling on to him that load of guilt to expiate which he is prepared to renounce pleasures. If masturbation helped to make him more independent of the environment (and even, perhaps, of the species, for it may have been his developing imagination which freed him from seasonal sexuality) it also made him capable of defying the parents—who, as they do in every mammalian family, stand protectively between the child and the environment, controlling the aspects in which the environment may present itself to the child. Just because the child *is* a mammal, the father, no matter how jealous (or—our civilised derivative from jealousy—puritanical), cannot prevent the environment from presenting the child with the earliest source of sexual stimulation, the mother. As soon as the child is weaned, it can be snatched away from her seductive[1] influence and immured in a chaste and spartan world. But to no purpose: for, in being weaned, it has acquired the weapon of imagination, which no father can control, and has learnt that it always has about its person an instrument of self-gratification. Auto-erotic acts and the fantasies which accompany them become the expression of the son's rebellion against the father's pervasive government. It is not surprising that when the communicant expiates his guilt by humbly submitting himself to the father, part of his submission consists of renouncing the use of his hands.

The communicant also renounces something he acquired at the same

[1] Freud points out that the mother, by her care of the child's body, becomes the first seducer. Indeed, the mother's attention frequently awakens the child to masturbation, a fact which is reflected in 'the very common phantasy' of seduction by the mother or nurse; and 'I have . . . learned', Freud wrote, 'to unravel many a phantasy of seduction and found it to be an attempt at defence against the memory of sexual activities practised by the child himself'. (*Collected Papers*, Volume V, XXIV; Volume I, XIV)

time: the standing posture. To abase oneself by kneeling or prostration; even, perhaps, the token of lopping a few inches off his height by removing his hat which modern man pays to the presence of his god or his king (or the dead): these are a son's marks of his submission to paternal authority, wherein he disclaims rivalry to the father by going back on his childish ambition to be as tall as the father. Yet when we remember in what the son's original rivalry to the father consisted, and what discovery, in both the individual's and the species's history, accompanied learning to stand up, we can read these gestures as symbolic self-castrations, too—expiations and abdications of sexual activity in favour of the father. In symbol the son is paying the price he understands the father to require of him. His gesture of obeisance is a promise, an undertaking, which means 'I will not be erect, I will not raise myself up, I will not stand', in the precise sense of the metaphor Mercutio uses when he flaunts the power of purely imaginary images, independent of the object's presence, over human sexual activity:

> in his mistress' name
> I conjure only but to raise him up[1].

It is in the same sense that Donne's impatient *Elegie: Going to Bed* (adumbrating the bodily encounter between lover and mistress in terms of the encounter between armies) chides:

> The foe oft-times having the foe in sight,
> Is tir'd with standing though they never fight.

Equipped with an Ego and with new modes of sexuality, the child has acquired a capacity for forming a new type of relationship, but nothing has happened to make him change the direction in which he tries to form his most important relationship. It is still the mother towards whom his love flows[2]; but where he used to seek identification with her, he now seeks to make her the object of his love. And it is now that he finds the father in his way.

[1] *Romeo And Juliet*, II, i

[2] The genital instincts are not at first equipped to find satisfaction on their own but follow where the self-preserving instincts have already established a relationship. The mother has satisfied all the child's other bodily needs, so it looks to her for satisfaction of the new sexual need as well. (Cf. Freud: *Collected Papers*, Volume IV, III, II)

This situation the Ego treats by reverting to the older method of forming relationships, love by identification. If the father cannot be budged, he must be ingested into the child's own personality. It is by an external repetition—developed and modified by a long course of social evolution—of this psychic act that the Christian ingests his father at the communion. The child conceives an admiration for the father, an ambition to model himself on him: the Ego has taken the image of the father to itself and set it before itself as an ideal. (The little boy may also try out a homosexual solution to his problem, whereby it is the mother he identifies himself with and the father whom he makes the object of his love. Just this arrangement provides the girl with what is for her the heterosexual solution: the great psychic determinant which edges her more firmly than the boy towards this solution is that she is reacting to the fact that she has been castrated, whereas the boy reacts to the fear that he will be.[1])

The Ego-ideal formed in the father's image is, in fact, the hook by which the individual is caught into society; its creation completes the individual's evolution from asocial baby, through anti-social egoist, into potential citizen. The Ego-ideal, created by identification with an object which stood in the child's path, may in a sense be externalised again: it may be identified with a person in the outside world who now becomes suffused with the aura of the ideal. The ego-ideal is like a beam of light which the Ego projects in advance of itself; and a group is formed when a collection of Egos focus their beams on a single person, who becomes their common leader. The members of the group have identified their several Ego-ideals with the same leader, and as a result their several Egos become identified with one another.

The group hands over to the leader the functions which the Ego-ideal normally performs inside the individual psyche. The Ego-ideal is in the habit of criticising the Ego and chiding it for lagging so far behind its ideal. When the group sinks its Ego-ideal in the leader, it gives away its faculty of self-criticism; the leader is immune from criticism by the people, because he is the ideal; and the people have also handed over to him the function of choosing a purpose and a direction for their life's labours.

The people's love for the leader is, of course, aim-inhibited: a sexless infatuation. And Freud does compare the bond between group and leader with the bond between two people in love. The couple, unlike

[1] Freud: *Collected Papers*, Volume II, XXIII; Volume V, XVII; XXIV

the group, have sexual ambitions, but these are mixed with an aim-inhibited love which gives their union its power of enduring beyond the gratification of the sexual aims. Purely sensual love makes the beloved its object; being in love seeks identification with him as well. There are love affairs where the beloved is identified with the Ego-ideal and becomes immune to criticism, while the lover shrinks into a mere Ego disparaged in the comparison with his ideal; and love affairs where the pair achieve a fusion of their Egos, with the result that whatever is in the beloved's interest becomes the lover's self-interest, for his self-love encompasses the other person's as well as his own Ego. (Don Ottavio expresses the lover's state of mind with his

> Dalla sua pace
> la mia dipende;
> quel che a lei piace,
> vita mi rende,
> quel che le incresce,
> morte mi dà . . .
> e non ho bene
> s'ella non l'ha.[1]

Donna Anna, however, sings nothing of the sort about *him*. Rather, she fulfils the Ego-ideal's function of urging him to catch up with his duty; and in Don Ottavio's concern with her *peace*—'On her peace, mine depends'—we can hear the efforts of a man trying to satisfy and allay the Ego-ideal's demands on him.)

Still closer to the group bond is the relationship between the hypnotist and his subject: indeed, this was not, Freud said, properly comparable to the group formation but the very same thing. Hypnosis had in common with the loving couple that it was a relationship between two people (even in the demonstrations of mass hypnosis which have recently been popular, there is no relationship between the several hypnotised subjects, who remain oblivious of one another, but only between each and the hypnotist) but it resembled the group's bond with the leader in that the love paid to the hypnotist was purely aim-inhibited. The hypnotic relation was 'a group formation with two members', in which the subject makes an absolute concentration

[1] Act I, No. 11 (On her peace, mine depends; what pleases her renews my life, what causes her regret gives death to me . . . and I have no good if she has it not)

of his attention on the hypnotist, to the exclusion of every other object, and has even handed over to him the business of testing the reality of things. 'No wonder', Freud comments, 'that the ego takes a perception for real if its reality is vouched for by the mental faculty which ordinarily discharges the duty'[1].

7. *Freud's 'scientific myth'*

This approach to the group by way of the individual's early history and the individual's psychic evolution Freud was able to supplement by conclusions he had already reached from another direction, the study of the early history and biological evolution of mankind which he had made in *Totem And Taboo*, a commentary on Frazer which, though anthropology has since improved on the data on which it was based and challenged the universality of its application, remains our most penetrating and fertile insight into primitive psychology. It was, to be precise, in considering the consolidating phase of man's transition from an animal species, which has evolution, to homo sapiens, who has history, that Freud produced one of the most daring, dazzling and yet cogently persuasive acts of imagination in the whole course of scientific thinking: his reconstruction[2] ('associated with a hypothesis of Charles Darwin'[3]) of the earliest human social unit as a band or 'primal horde', an extension of the mammalian family, which is dominated by the strongest male.

This 'primal father' is the original superman. ('He, at the very beginning of the history of mankind, was the *Superman* whom Nietzsche only expected from the future'[4].) He takes for himself all the spoils and privileges of the group's existence, including the sexual use of all the females; and obliges the males, most of whom really are his sons, either to give up their sexual ambitions altogether or to direct them outside the group, a redirection which is the forerunner both of the

[1] *Group Psychology And The Analysis Of The Ego*, VIII

[2] —a 'scientific myth'; 'a "Just-So Story", as it was amusingly called by a not unkind critic' (Freud: *Group Psychology And The Analysis Of The Ego*, XII B; X)

[3] Freud: *Totem And Taboo*, IV

[4] Freud: *Group Psychology And The Analysis Of The Ego*, X

exogamy rules in force in primitive tribes and of society's prohibition against familial incest.

By abdicating sexual claims within the group, the sons put an end to sexual rivalry among themselves. Once this greatest cause of internecine hostility has been removed, brotherly love can grow up between them. This is made possible by the hypnotic dominance of the primal father. In their common submission to him, the members of the horde become bound to one another by social ties which are the prehistoric forerunners of the bourgeoisie's sense of civic responsibility. The superman, on the other hand, is recognised, as he always will be throughout his career, by his freedom from any social bond, his lack of compunction or obligation towards any one else, and his flouting of the group's sexual code.

The sons submit to sexual restrictions or sexual abstinence through terror of the father; and the very lack of direct gratification feeds their aim-inhibited group love. Presently love for the group begins to inhibit their wish to couple as individuals, for the couple, itself a more compact group, is a social disintegrator. 'Two people coming together for the purpose of sexual satisfaction, in so far as they seek for solitude are making a demonstration against the herd instinct, the group feeling.'[1] (In *Nineteen Eighty-Four* George Orwell depicts a society where the group feeling is so predominant that copulation is a political act of rebellion.) Conceivably, the sons in the primal horde were less inhibited in homosexual relations among themselves[2], but their relation to the primal father must have remained as non-sexual as that of subject to hypnotist. Even in sophisticated groups, where the original terrorisation of the sons has been idealised into the notion of a reciprocated love between them and the leader, the cohesion of the group depends on the members' believing that they all share equally in the love the leader bears them. The group will fall into internecine rivalries and be disrupted if any one member either takes arms against the father or seeks his special favour by offering himself to the father homosexually. 'A democratic character runs through the Church',

[1] Freud: *Group Psychology And The Analysis Of The Ego*, XII. D

[2] Freud points out that a group's cohesion has a better tolerance of homosexual than of heterosexual couples, and he even conjectures that the sons in the primal horde gathered the courage to cast off their inhibitions and rebel against the father by advancing 'from identification with one another to homosexual object love'. (*Group Psychology And The Analysis Of The Ego*, XII, D; X, footnote)

for example, 'for the very reason that before Christ everyone is equal, and that everyone has an equal share in his love'[1]. Even where the gap between leader and led is graded down through a hierarchy, we can still see the essential democratic character. (In the Catholic Church, the hierarchy is in any case transcended by the supremacy of Christ: everyone is equal before Christ, though everyone may not be before the Pope.) Not only is there an internal egalitarianism in each level of the hierarchy, but there is even a fellow-feeling, on the part of the underlings, towards the father who oppresses them from the grade above, for they know (a knowledge which holds armies together) that in the grade next above there is a super-father who oppresses *him*.

Although the sons are tyrannised, they are not necessarily tyrannised without genuine benefit to themselves, in the shape of an addition to the individual Ego's powers of self-protection. Each member now has the support of the group in conflicts with strangers and in winning a livelihood from the environment. This benefit of what is just beginning to be civilisation and civil peace is made available only through common submission to the tyrant. However hard his rule and gross his selfishness, he must be loved as well as hated because he is indispensable. Just so, in another state of emergent civilisation, the dreaded sternness of a paterfamilias or a headmaster may yet make him loved as a protector, because where his rule does not hold the child is subjected to the anarchy of the nursery, where each fears each and all[2].

Thus even the primal horde has the glimmerings of a constitution, the outline of an implicit social contract negotiated between the father and the sons. The relationship between the father and sons is what gives the group its existence; and the group's structure is defined by the bargain struck between them. The sons must always negotiate circumspectly for fear of disrupting the group and falling into panic and anarchy, states in which they can no longer rely on one another. It is only gradually that they can force the father to submit to the rule of law and deal justly with his subjects. In the first place

[1] Freud: *Group Psychology And The Analysis Of The Ego*, V. Certain Greek religious festivals (such as the Kronia) made a point of egalitarianism among the worshippers: 'all social distinctions were for the time being abolished, and master and man feasted together' (H. J. Rose: *A Handbook Of Greek Mythology . . .*, III)

[2] The paulopostprimal father is summed up in a remark (cited under Anonymous in the *Oxford Dictionary Of Quotations*) about a nineteenth-century headmaster: 'A beast, but a just beast'.

he obliged them to renounce their mothers and sisters: presently they insist that he, too, undertake half of this renunciation and submit to the law that no father may have sexual intercourse with his own daughters—though a trace of his original privilege remains in his right to give them in marriage, ceding to the man of his choice the prerogative that was once his own. The father may even have to re-inforce himself by turning himself into a limited company: he is no longer a single paternal personage but a whole patrician class, whose members are one another's peers. Now the sons are also solidified into a self-recognising class, and can negotiate quite explicitly with the paternal class about their rights to own the land and what it produces. But only the appearance of the argument, not its essence, has changed. What is in question is still the disposal of the sons' instinctual potential for forming relationships with objects—the original question of who is to have and use the mother.

The striking characteristic in the social relation of sons to father is its necessary ambivalence. The sons, no matter how much they fear him, must wish the father's government to continue; and to ensure its continuation they will even go to the length of immortalising him. At the same time they are for ever clipping away at his privileges; but they must do it carefully and covertly. Eventually—so Freud's momentous conjecture concludes—the sons in the primal horde devised a method of doing away with the father while keeping the group intact, thus breaking up the primal organisation and precipitating civilisation into its next social stage. The group rebelled as a whole. Everyone shared the guilt of striking at the father, and everyone took an equal share of the inheritance—thus loading on to society itself the guilt of that most original of sins, the Oedipal sin of parricide. This act is still discernible in rituals which descend from the primitive totem feast, wherein the whole tribe is responsible for murdering the totem animal who represents their common ancestor, and each citizen identifies himself with a bit of the father—but no one citizen more than any other—by the oral method of eating a piece of his body.

This solution was implicit in the formation of the primal horde from the start; the psychic act of identification, by which the paternal Ego-ideal is formed in the first place, 'is ambivalent from the very first'[1]. If you fuse your identity with something, are you destroying it or suffering it to destroy you? The wish for identification is

---

[1] Freud: *Group Psychology And The Analysis Of The Ego*, VII

two-edged even when the baby applies it to the mother. If it could, the baby would gobble up the mother and destroy her utterly, just like that lethal little worm which Cleopatra suckled in place of a child—

> Peace, peace!
> Dost thou not see my baby at my breast,
> That sucks the nurse asleep?[1]

Of course the baby, with its purely Id organisation and indifference to the laws inherent in reality, has no appreciation of the contradiction implicit in its relation to the mother. But it is significant that the moment when the mother weans it, and thus propels it into a more realistic relationship with the world, is dictated by its acquisition of teeth—and thereby of the power to put the hostile component in its desire into effective practice.

(Of course, in many societies children are suckled long past that date: the mother may not be allowed or may masochistically not wish to act on her instinct of self-preservation. It is interesting that society usually does lay down, either by rule or by fashion, some age by which time the child must be weaned or else be regarded as obscene. The Talmud, for example, records Rabbi Eliezer's opinion that 'A child should be nursed twenty-four months. From then on, it is as if it sucked a detestable thing'. Evidently the memory that oral pleasure is sexual pleasure is repressed not far below the level of society's consciousness. It can be surprised out of its hiding by a witticism: the juxtaposition of the idea of the baby's sucking the breast, which we like to think of as a sexless activity, with circumstances which are sexually stimulating to an adult constitutes the wit in the country visitor's comment on the decolleté dresses in Paris, that he had not seen such a sight since he was weaned[2]. Once the child becomes capable of conceiving of the mother's breast as an object, he is trespassing on the father's territory, and becomes liable to that primary disgust which society reserves for incest. A second opinion recorded by the Talmud even understands that weaning is what precipitates the child into relationships with objects: after that, there can be no going back to the infantile pleasures without committing a sort of incest. Rabbi Joshua's opinion is: 'The child may nurse even for four or five years, but if it stopped at twenty-four months and then started again,

[1] *Antony And Cleopatra*, V, ii
[2] G. Rattray Taylor: *Sex In History*, XI

then it should be regarded as if it were sucking a detestable thing.'[1])

The Ego, however, when it performs its identification with the father, *can* appreciate the contradiction between swallowing his image in order to get him out of the way and, on the other hand, modelling itself on his image, an act which makes sure that the son's narcissistic love will embrace the father as well as the son's self: and the psyche experiences the contradiction in the form of the conflict and tension, the peculiar nagging relationship, between Ego-ideal and Ego. The Ego must scramble after the ideal and yet take care to keep it at arm's length, out of reach of hostility: if the ideal were to be caught up, it would be robbed of its influence. Just so the Catholic *must* perform his oral unions with God—at least once a year by the modern regulations (and these regulations by which the Church lays down maxima and minima for the layman's communions and for the priest's celebrations of the Mass, remind one of the rules by which folklore and, sometimes, religious lore govern the frequency of married couples' sexual intercourse[2]): but the communicant must *not* conceive that, by means of this union by identification, he has become God. From this danger, which would carry all the penalties of parricide, of usurping the father[3], he is protected by the same device which protected the individual son in the primal horde. The Mass is a social rite, a sacrifice undertaken by the whole community of God's children. The intercourse it accomplishes is not a coupling but the cementation of a whole society; the whole society is united in an oral orgy to its communal father. The priest is forbidden to celebrate Mass in solitude[4]; and no single communicant can become

[1] Leo Auerbach's selected edition of the Babylonian Talmud, p. 86

[2] We are moré accustomed to the Christian church's attempt to restrict the frequency; but the Talmud, for instance, records: 'The *Torah* prescribed the marital duties as follows: Men who are unoccupied: every day; labourers, twice a week; ass-drivers, once a week; camel-drivers once in thirty days; sailors, once in three months. These are the words of Rabbi Eliezer.' (Leo Auerbach's selected edition of The Babylonian Talmud, p. 85)

[3] Before making his own communion, the celebrant prays against the danger of over-presumption: 'Let not the receiving of thy body, O Lord Jesus Christ, which I, though unworthy, presume to take, turn against me unto judgment and damnation . . .' (translation from an English Missal)

[4] 'In all private Masses the priest must, in the absence of an indult, have at least a server to represent the body of the faithful. Solitary Masses, once celebrated by indulgence or privilege in monasteries, are now strictly forbidden.' (*Catholic Dictionary*, 'Mass')

God when God is equally embodied in each of the millions of wafers the Church has put into the mouths of his sons. This world-wide distribution of God (symbolised by the actual fragmentation of a wafer during the ritual[1]) serves the same end as the tearing in pieces of the totem animal. Each son is prevented from disrupting the group through a too-close approach to the father and is obliged to extend his love sideways—to his fellows who become his brothers through their common participation (the communion of saints) in the meal.

The Id, in which 'there are no conflicts; contradictions and antitheses exist side by side'[2], simply dispatches its desire for identification into the world without considering the self-contradictoriness of the desire: it is reality, on which the desire strikes, that shivers it and reveals its two components. At first, of course, the mother interposes between the child and reality; the earliest prohibitions put in the child's way are not the experienced facts that fire burns and over-eating produces indigestion but the mother's interdiction on playing with fire and eating too much; and it is the mother who cuts short the child's oral desires by weaning it. Once this has happened, however, the child is in direct relationship with the real world; and it is its own Ego which must take over the mother's function of controlling its impulses before they strike disastrously against the real world. In discharging this function, the Ego cannot tolerate contradictions in its aim and therefore makes it its business to sort out the two wishes of love and of destruction, admitting one to consciousness and repressing the other. The result is that when the members of a group focus their Ego-ideals on a common leader, their conscious love for him is continually shadowed by unconscious destructiveness. The destructiveness is seldom allowed to become conscious; yet this does not mean it goes without expression in acts which do harm to the father, but only that the people's conscious is blinded to the real character and effect of what they do.

Primitive groups do not so much suppress their hatred of the father as cut the whole of their desire towards him, love and hatred alike, free from themselves and treat it as an independent force, whose origin in their own emotions they refuse to acknowledge. Freud's

[1] —where the priest (in the words of an English Missal) 'takes the host and breaks it in half over the chalice . . . He puts the portion that is in his right hand on to the paten; he then breaks off a small piece from the portion which is in his left hand . . . He puts the particle into the chalice . . .'

[2] Freud: *The Question Of Lay Analysis*, II

great achievement as an anthropologist was to decipher taboo, a force which 'still exists in our midst'[1], imposing on us irrational social compulsions and prohibitions, just as his personal neurosis imposes private ones on the neurotic. In many primitive societies, taboo provides the acknowledged legal and religious system that regulates existence. Taboo resides in figures whom Freud demonstrated to be representatives of the father: rulers, priests, gods, the dead (essentially, dead parents), the totem animal. Its force is passed like a contagion from them to whoever or whatever comes in contact with them; and the effects of taboo, when someone is infected with it, are both saving and searing, holy and polluting (an ambiguity which, Freud pointed out, was still inherent in the ancient world's concept of the sacred).

If the taboo force, which is the channel of the father's influence over his people, is two-edged, that is in reflection of their two-edged desire towards *him*. By setting their desire free of themselves and allowing it to govern life like a second natural law, the people escape the punitive consequences of their destructive wish. Admittedly, taboo governs—indeed, oppresses—them, just as his private taboo does the neurotic; but in both his case and theirs, what the taboo compels its slaves to do edges nearer and nearer to what they unconsciously wish to do. Taboo obliges the people to hedge the ruler about with ritual and protocol, protecting him from every profane contact; and gradually this too-insistent veneration eats so far into his freedom as to render his life hateful to him[2]. Letting the seemingly impersonal force of taboo do the work for them, the people have imprisoned their leader in the same nagging net as Nathan Leopold cast about *his* superman.

In *Totem And Taboo*, Freud illuminates society's history-long ambivalence towards its common fathers. The riddle of totemism, which had baffled the anthropologists, he was able to solve by juxtaposing the fact that the totem tribe often claims the totem animal as its ancestor with facts known to him from clinical experience: namely, that a small boy in the Oedipus phase, who has made a particular friend of a certain species of animal, will sometimes suddenly reverse his attitude and develop an intense phobia of the animal.

[1] Freud: *Totem And Taboo*, Preface

[2] Frazer collected instances and recognised the aggressive *effect* of primitive peoples' veneration towards the leader in 'The Burden of Royalty' (*Taboo And The Perils Of The Soul*, I). It was Freud who recognised the unconscious aggressive desire.

Analysis shewed that the loved-dreaded animal represented the father. In the throes of the Oedipus conflict, the boy had added, to his original love for the father, a strain of hostility against him, which, not daring to express itself directly, was diverted against the animal; and the boy, fearing that the object of this hostility would punish him (by castration) for his hatred, developed a phobia in which his only hope of safeguarding his dearest possession was to keep out of the way of the animal-father. From the anthropological data Freud shewed that the totem group had behaved like the boy and had incarnated the father in the totem species. As a rule it kept the totem species sacrosanct and treated it with reverence and affection. But on certain sacramental occasions, the group acting as a whole would dare to do what one member alone could not do except on pain of all the penalties exacted for parricide: it would turn on the father in his embodiment as the totem animal and cruelly kill it.[1]

Towards this proto-god, archaic ancestor of the many still partly animal gods of classical religion, the primitive tribe displays a simple unconscious hypocrisy: protects and fosters it; tears it to bits and eats it; laments and apologises to it[2]. But as society's Ego (the several Egos of the citizens, which have become identified with one another when they jointly identify their Ego-ideal with the leader) progresses further into self-consciousness and recognition of reality, it can no longer tolerate these open contradictions. In the animal sacrifice of Greek and Roman religion, Freud deciphered archaic vestiges which shewed that the murdered animal had originally been recognised as the god himself; but by classical times this knowledge has been suppressed, and theology had invented the more devious hypocrisy of sacrificing *to* the god an animal who was still unconsciously treated *as* the god. The Christian sacrament brought the original totemistic truth into the open again, boldly professing that in this sacrifice the victim (whom it identified with the sacrificial lamb of the Jews) was the same person as the God in whose honour the sacrifice was made; and, by means of the sacred myth which maintained that the victim had offered—sacrificed—himself[3], it justified the consummate

[1] Freud: *Totem And Taboo*, IV; *Collected Papers*, Volume III, II; *Inhibitions, Symptoms And Anxiety*, IV

[2] Frazer: *Spirits Of The Corn And Of The Wild*, XIII, 'Killing The Divine Animal'

[3] The Christians made their eucharist the successor to the Jewish animal sacrifice by identifying their God not only with the murdered animal (as the

hypocrisy whereby it was no longer the depersonalised compulsions of taboo, but the personal command of God himself, which obliged his sons to perform the hostile act of eating God.

The sacrament is a social rite, reaffirming the group's internal loyalty and ratifying its contract with the father; and towards the father it contrives to be an act of worship with the right hand, and of murder with the left. And if this act, at least in later times, is justified by reference to a myth, the very course of myth-inventing expresses the same two conflicting wishes towards the father. Mythologising exalts him to the skies, and at the same time gets rid of him from the earth. It makes his power supernatural and eventually omnipotent, and by the same stroke clips away his privileges. (As a matter of fact, this twofold process must have begun in the primal horde itself [where the glamour attributed to the father was the earliest manifestation of man's myth-making faculty]. While allotting all freedom and enjoyment to the father, the sons contrived to place one important restriction on his gratification of his instincts. They must have agreed among themselves not to approach him homosexually. While this was a sacrifice on their part, they undertook it not in deference to the father but for their own sakes, in order to preserve the group; and the result must have been to cut the father off from homosexual gratifications.) The deity is exalted above human frailty and mortality— and made incapable of precisely those gross pleasures which are in dispute between father and son, and which the primal father forced his sons to allot to him for his exclusive enjoyment. The gods of the pantheon are carnal only in myth; it is only in the believers' minds that they continue to exercise the license and freedom from social

Mass on Easter Sunday proclaims, in the words of *I Corinthians*, V, 7: 'Pascha nostrum immolatus est Christus', 'Christ our passover is sacrificed for us') but also with the priest who conducted the sacrifice. Eusebius exercises his ingenuity to trace Christ's spiritual descent from the Jewish priests 'after the order of Melchisedek', getting round the difficulty that the Gospels do not record Christ to have been anointed priest by the fact that Melchisedek was never anointed either, and arguing that Christ, having received his being directly from God before the world was put together, 'holds his priesthood, deathless and ageless, to limitless aeons' (*Ecclesiastical History*, I, iii, 16-18). The people's covert hostility to the father takes as its target both the heavenly father and the priest who represents him on earth; and this hostility achieves its ultimate triumph in the idea that the sacrifice which the people offer God consists of God's sacrifice of God and the priest's sacrifice of the priest.

restraints which characterised the original superman. The inventors of the Christian myth, while promoting God to an unrivalled and omnipotent exaltation, robbed him of even such pleasure as was left to the pantheon and created a heavenly father who, even in myth, must beget his son by an intercourse so bodiless as to leave his consort a virgin.

8. *The Group and the Revolutionary Poet*

This analysis of Freud's throws its illumination into every corner of our problem. It is no longer so surprising to find a collection of doctors solemnly setting down Nathan Leopold as abnormal on the grounds that from childhood he displayed precisely those characteristics of intelligence and logical consistency which in the first place distinguished the human species from all the other animals. Freud points out that from the start humanity has possessed two types of psychology: the individual psychology which in the primal horde belonged to the father alone; and the group psychology of the sons.[1]

The mark of the group psychology is that 'an individual's separate emotion and personal intellectual act are too weak to come to anything by themselves and are absolutely obliged to wait till they are reinforced through being repeated in a similar way in the other members of the group. We are reminded', Freud continues, 'of how many of these phenomena of dependence are part of the normal constitution of human society, of how little originality and personal courage are to be found in it . . .'[2]

The love between the members of the group, which has taken the place of their original rivalry, has not done so without letting them express a trace of their old hostility to one another. Theirs is a group feeling based on the equality of each member's renunciations—on the individual's sense that he can bear to forgo the freedom enjoyed by

[1] Freud adds that even in the primal horde a transition from group to individual psychology was possible, for it must have been regularly made whenever it was necessary to appoint a successor to the father. The successor was probably the youngest son, the one least in thrall as yet to the group bonds; and he was able to achieve individual psychology when he was afforded and took the chance of directly gratifying his sexual instincts. (*Group Psychology And The Analysis Of The Ego*, X)

[2] *Group Psychology And The Analysis Of The Ego*, IX

the father only if all his neighbours forgo it, too; and so it is the part of each member of the group to protest, with their nursery cry of 'It's not fair', against the elevation of any other member; each one makes it his business to hold his fellows down by holding them to their renunciations.[1]

We can see, therefore, how an intelligent and independent-minded member of the group appears to his fellows: as a criminal rebel who is trying to usurp the father's prerogative of individual psychology. (It is still the great cry of Catholics that people who reason independently about religious matters are being arrogant.) The rebel in fact tempts the others to act on their own repressed wish to rebel. Indeed, the reprehensible quality of the criminal consists in his power to tempt; his example acts as a summons by association to other people's unconscious wish to do the same.[2] If the criminal were to remain among the others, they would suffer anxiety or have to redouble their psychic precautions against their own impulses; and so their reaction is the reaction to all tempters, to bruise him underfoot[3]—that is to say, to get him out of sight; he must be expelled from the body politic, either outlawed, killed, or shut up in a prison (which serves to hide the criminals from the public as well as vice versa).

Yet we can see even from our own popular culture that the criminal, who really does what everyone else has to repress the wish to do, and especially the fictitious criminal, who acts out the reader's unconscious fantasies, is something of a hero as well; he dares to free his intelligence from social obligations and becomes a master-mind—acquires the mentality of a master. In primitive societies, the criminal may come, perhaps through his use as a scapegoat, to be a holy criminal; and this is precisely the part he plays in the imaginative world of Dostoievsky[4]. For Dostoievsky, the criminal is already well on his way towards identification with the Christian hero who, though guilty of no crime himself, suffers a criminal's death in expiation of the crimes of all mankind.

[1] Freud: *Group Psychology And The Analysis Of The Ego*, IX

[2] Freud: *Totem And Taboo*, II, 4

[3] 'And the woman said, The serpent beguiled me . . . And the Lord God said unto the serpent, Because thou hast done this, thou art cursed above all cattle . . . upon thy belly shalt thou go, and dust shalt thou eat . . . I will put enmity between thee and the woman, and between thy seed and her seed; it shall bruise thy head, and thou shalt bruise his heel.' (*Genesis*, III, 13- . . . 15)

[4] Freud: *Collected Papers*, Volume V, XXI, 'Dostoevsky And Parricide'

It is open to one of the egalitarian band of brothers to rise above the group and occupy the father's place: a process which is the mechanism both of those cultural revolutions whereby one religious system replaces another, and of political revolution. The prototype of revolution is to be found in the primal horde where, Freud conjectured, the sons eventually welded themselves into a fraternal conspiracy and murdered the primal father. The state which followed was a drab republicanism, in which all the brothers were equally oppressed by their equal share in the primal guilt of parricide—a state of fraternity and equality and, it is true, liberty from the primal father's oppressions, but in which each man had become his brother's oppressor and made it his business to see that no one brother enjoyed more liberty than any other. The group was freed from its guilt only when one brother singled himself out and claimed to have murdered the father single-handed, thereby incurring all the guilt himself and simultaneously all the glory. This Napoleonic figure—George Orwell gave him, in token of his psychic history, the name of 'Big Brother'—replaces the original father and becomes the new father to his lesser brothers. He has, in fact, achieved identification with the original father, either swallowing up the original father's identity in his own, or merging with him in that indissoluble one-ness which the Athanasian Creed postulates between Father and Son. (The group understands intellectual independence in the mythological sense. Reading its own unconscious wishes in other people's acts, it interprets intellectual independence as a bid to become the father; the doctors are unable to conceive the idea that Nathan Leopold disbelieves in God in any other sense than that Leopold has murdered God in order to become God himself.)

The son's method may be defiance: the mythological hero is the only person brave enough to slay the father (who often still wears his totemistic disguise and appears in the myth as an animal or animal-monster); and the people whom he has freed from the monstrous father's tyranny promptly elevate the hero in the tyrant's place, making him king and founding-father of their polity, and immortalising him by awarding him a cult. The alternative is the method of the scapegoat without blemish. The Christians' Big Brother is sinless. That is to say, his will does not in any least particular oppose his father's will; he has so completely identified his self-interest with the father's interest that he and the father become one. (The Christian method, whereby it is not the original father but, through his own self-sacrifice, the hero who is murdered, has a peculiar and stabilising psychic economy: the sons do not need to enter into a conspiracy all over again and rebel against the father's successor, because he has already been murdered; they can quite lawfully commemorate and re-enact his murder, and simultaneously give expression to their hostile feelings against the original father, who is one with the suffering victim.)

Whichever method the heroic brother adopts, he must possess himself utterly of the father's power. He must succeed—as Hitler did, and Leopold failed—in becoming the focal point of his brothers' Ego-ideals. Otherwise he will be only a half-made hero, and his heroic exploit will remain a crime, just as Jesus's daring in claiming to identify himself with the Father's godhead appeared to Jewish society as criminal blasphemy.

For the political hero, the gravest problem is his own mortality. Even if he does not sacrifice himself voluntarily or become, like Julius Caesar, a quasi-totemistic sacrifice, hacked to pieces by a band of brothers, he must die sooner or later. If he is to survive his death, he must enlist help from mythology, which will resurrect and deify him or else permit him to establish a ruling dynasty in which, the people superstitiously believe, some magical essence of divine right is reincarnated in the son at the moment of the father's death. In *Julius Caesar* Shakespeare dramatised an instant in history when the succession to a Big Brother stood in doubt. Julius Caesar is the hero who puts an end to the republican period which followed the over-throw of the primal kings; and now the hero is killed in his turn, by conspirators taking vengeance on behalf of the republic, led by the namesake and descendant of the Brutus who originally took the lead in expelling the kings. The conspirators, of course, fall into rivalry and dissension among themselves; and their crisis comes in that great scene between Brutus and Cassius when Brutus refuses to become guilty of having killed Caesar in order to replace him[1]. Brutus turns away from Cassius's offer to sacrifice himself for Brutus; he clings to

---

[1] IV, iii: Did not great Julius bleed for justice' sake?
    What villain touch'd his body, that did stab,
    And not for justice? What! shall one of us,
    That struck the foremost man of all this world
    But for supporting robbers, shall we now
    Contaminate our fingers with base bribes . .

And Antony's threnody (V, v) recognises Brutus's refusal to take Caesar's place:
    All the conspirators save only he
    Did that they did in envy of great Caesar . . .

the republican fraternalism despite Cassius's efforts to single him out from the conspirators and elevate him as the new father-substitute ('Good-night, my lord', says Cassius; 'Good-night, good brother', replies Brutus): and in the instant of Brutus's refusal the previous father-substitute is assured of his immortality. Brutus has barely bidden his colleagues good-night when the ghost of Caesar appears in his tent.

The ghost of Caesar is a dramatic condensation of the immortality which Caesar in historical fact secured through both the methods open to a dead father-replacement. Religion and poetry deified Caesar; and at the same time he was perpetuated in a dynasty of Caesars: and presently the two methods, and mankind's two great superstitious awes towards the father, came together and blended (restoring the primitive union of king-father with god-father) in a dynasty of deified emperors.

His reconstruction of the primal horde and its passing provided Freud with a skeleton timetable of mankind's religious myth-making. In the primal horde itself, the father has not yet been deified. There is no need for him to be, until the sons have murdered him and incurred a guilt they can expiate only by paying him this honour, which comforts them by assuring them that, though murdered, he is not really dead. Even so, when, after murdering him, they enter on their republican state, it is not the father they deify, but the mother, creating those maternal figures who are probably the oldest deities; for the only way the brothers can maintain their absolute equality among themselves is to fill all the leading positions, the figurehead positions, in the mythological order—and possibly in the real social order, too[1]— with women. It is not until the emergence of the hero, who lightens the brothers' parricidal guilt by taking it all on himself, that male gods appear. One of these is, of course, the hero; but he brings with him the resurrected memory of the primal father, to whom amends are now made by deifying him, and from whom the hero borrows paternal characteristics.[2]

Thus the primal father in his divine form is created, as it were, old: complete with an apparent past history (just as the last-ditch fundamentalist was driven to supposing the earth had been created

[1] But see IV, 10

[2] Freud: *Group Psychology And The Analysis Of The Ego*, XII, A; *Totem And Taboo*, IV

with a palaeontological record already contained in it[1].) Zeus, that quintessential father, epithetically the 'father of gods and men'[2], was really a jumped-up hero. In the chronology of religion, his worship replaces the mother religions of primitive Greece; but his myth records a different usurpation, because it comes into existence trailing behind it the memory of the murdered primal father. Implicit in the myth-figure of Zeus is the story of how the supremacy previously belonged to his father Kronos, whom Zeus heroically usurped; and behind Kronos is *his* father, Uranos, whom Kronos rebelled against, castrated and replaced[3]. This history, however, is all in the myth and is barely reflected in cult. Kronos had only a few festivals; and as for Uranos, 'it does not appear', says H. J. Rose's exhaustive and excellent *Handbook*, 'that the Greeks at any time or place worshipped him'[4].

The emergence of the hero Jesus Christ achieved very much the same effect through the transplantation of Christianity from its native

---

[1] Edmund Gosse: *Father And Son*, V

[2] Homer's πατὴρ ἀνδρῶν τε θεῶν τε

[3] The castration of Uranos by his son, as Freud was not slow to notice (*The Interpretation of Dreams*, V, (D) (b); VII (F)) is another of Greek mythology's contributions to our understanding of the Oedipal situation, second only to the myth of Oedipus himself. Here is the rivalry between father and son: Uranos oppresses his sons; their mother (we can read the wish-fulfilment of the child's desires) takes their side against him; Kronos, conspiring with his mother, dares to rebel. Kronos is not, however, jealous only of his father's political authority, which he finally usurps; that he is sexually jealous as well is made plain by the occasion he chooses for his assault on his father in Hesiod's (that is, the oldest extant) account of the story. 'Bringing night with him, great Uranos (Heaven) came and, being desirous of love, lay round Gaia (Earth) and entirely spread himself on her. The son from his ambush stretched out with his left hand, with his right took the monstrous, long, toothed sickle, and swiftly cut away the sexual organs of his dear father' (*Theogony*, 176-181). The word *dear* reads to us as one of the quaintest examples of the inflexibility of epic epithets in Greek verse. Yet as a matter of fact the refusal of these epithets to yield to any recognition of contradictions is just the kind of thinking which results from emotional ambivalence. For Hesiod to speak of Kronos's dear father at the moment when Kronos is mutilating him, or for Homer to apply the epithet 'noisy' to dogs which he says have not barked (*Odyssey*, XVI, 4-5)—these are marks of the primitive in being examples of a type of thought-process which has directly survived from a world governed by that most self-contradictory of concepts, taboo.

[4] *A Handbook Of Greek Mythology* . . . , II

land to Rome and the Roman Empire at large. Jehovah had, of course, been worshipped before his son appeared; but not at Rome; from a Roman point of view, the son arrived bringing his father with him.

Thus both the hero and the father God owe their emergence to a repressed memory which is resurrected through an act of imagination; imagination is humanity's great medium of rebellion. It was, Freud says, 'the first epic poet' who 'invented the heroic myth'; and the myth 'is the step by which the individual emerges from group psychology'. Whereas the primal father was really murdered by the whole group, the poet invents the story of the hero who performs the deed independently. (As Freud points out, the invented hero is really the poet himself. And indeed, poet and hero are blatantly combined in Orpheus.) The poet tells his story to his fellow members of the group, and it is by identifying themselves with the daring, individualist hero that the members advance into psychic independence.[1]

The theorists of crime as art are not so far wrong. Their mistake is to neglect imagination, but they have correctly perceived the nature of the artistic impulse and the fundamental content of the artist's fictions. The attempt to raise crime to the dignity of art will always remain, when it is practised in real life, a crime and, when it is practised in fiction, a tour de force which holds good only in a world of artificial-comedic convention. (Gide tried to create such a world elsewhere, but Les Caves Du Vatican was his single success.) The attempt must retreat into a world where morality is suspended, because (like another sealed-in system, religion) it ignores the real-life moral distinction between fact and imagination. Taken the other way about, however, the comparison works. There may be a masochistic motif in Thomas Mann's insistence that the artist is a sort of criminal, but his determination to view art through crime did produce a raking illumination of the nature of art—especially in his late, vital, baroque masterpiece Felix Krull, where the attractiveness, the independence and the opportunism of the confidence man stand as a metaphor for the seductive attractiveness, the temptation-value, of art and the artist's supermanly independence of social bonds.

Freud's reconstruction of his first appearance contains the outlines of the artist's subsequent career in society. He is in a sense a purveyor of dreams, of opium—and thus a 'confidence man'; his figments are fantasy fulfilments of his own and the audience's wishes. Yet since

[1] Freud: Group Psychology And The Analysis Of The Ego, XII, B

these are repressed wishes, which he summons into the light, he is at the same time a revolutionary, a rebel—above all, an emancipator, who liberates men from the group and impels them into individual psychology. Art, like copulation, is a demonstration against the group feeling.

Accordingly, the artist stands in the same divided light as the criminal who may become a hero. Sometimes he is forced, like Orpheus, to follow out in person the life-course of the suffering hero who is sacrificed; he will be pelted, like a scapegoat, with excremental language, and torn to pieces by frenzied reviewers; after which—it is usually after his death—he achieves immortality in his works, which society now accepts into its canon of perpetual remembrance, and may even be granted a personal semi-deification by bardolatry. In other cases, society's attempt to put the tempter out of its sight takes the form not of making him invisible by shredding him to atoms, nor of concealing him beneath filth so unlovely that no one will want to look at him, but of withdrawing its attention. The artist is isolated from society by neglect or by a peculiar belittlement. Society's Ego is in this case performing on him just the same repression by isolation whereby the obsessional neurotic's Ego defends itself against temptation. The obsessional neurotic begins by forbidding himself contacts in the sexual sense[1], and proceeds to sexualise and, in consequence, to forbid the whole idea of contact. He develops the 'délire de toucher' which Freud recognised as an idiosyncratic version of the primitive social rule which forbids the savage to come in contact with an object containing taboo, for fear of being infected.

(Here we can draw together three ideas. When the child advances from purely oral relationships to relationships with objects, he discovers the power of touching in a sexual sense. It is just this sexual sense which makes the neurotic inhibit touching and forbid himself contacts in general. The savage is forbidden contact with a taboo-ful object in every sense, including one which is a regression to the oral phase, for he must not eat the flesh of the sacred totem species which

---

[1] 'To "touch" a woman has become a euphemism for using her as a sexual object. Not to "touch" one's genitals is the phrase employed for forbidding auto-erotic gratification.' At the same time, Freud points out, contact is the 'first requisite of destructiveness, too'—that physical impact which is essential to the love-death struggle of the battlefield; and the prohibition against contact becomes the Ego's defence against its own aggressive, as well as its erotic, impulses. (Freud: *Inhibitions, Symptoms And Anxiety*, VI)

represents the father. [That this is in fact a regression, and that the impulse has made its way back *through* the more recent idea of tactile contact with objects, is borne out by the ancient Egyptian belief that to eat the flesh of pigs—originally a totem species—would bring on punishment in the particular form of a skin disease[1].])

The prohibition against touching is carried out by the obsessional neurotic in the mental sphere. He cannot totally forget the tempting idea, as the hysteric can, but he isolates it and will not let it into contact by association with his everyday ideas, for fear it should pollute them[2]. Similarly, society may resist the temptations art puts in its way either by refusing to pay any attention to the whole subject or by isolating art in a special category of entertainment, which is not allowed to come in contact with ordinary living. There is really nothing to choose between the philistine who denigrates the whole business, the ignoramus who ignores it and the Victorian gentleman who permitted himself to enjoy performances on the stage or platform but not to come into social contact with the entertainers. The Victorian's successor has dropped his social pretensions, or even inverted them and made the artist a social lion, but he still fences-in art to the category of entertainment. He tolerates—or, rather, he prefers—baddish art which can be said to be 'good theatre'; the emotions he is prepared to experience about art constitute a spectrum of their own which he keeps strictly separate from the emotions whereby he responds to real life.

To belittle art as something less than serious is quite consonant with paying the artist not a little adulation and a comparatively good wage. Society paid Shakespeare enough for him to set up as a bourgeois; Mozart it praised highly and allowed to scrape an inadequate living. But the instant circumstances permit, it will transform its isolation of the artist into the act of amnesia it could not quite manage before. It records for ever the histories of Queen Elizabeth and Frederick the Great; but—to the irritation of bardolators who want to canonise them in later centuries—they are no sooner dead than society forgets Shakespeare's biography and the very whereabouts of the pauper's grave in which it has buried Mozart.

Isolated in this way, often by the spotlight which picks him out as an entertainer, the artist becomes not so much a holy criminal as a

[1] Frazer: *Spirits Of The Corn And Of The Wild*, IX
[2] Freud: *Inhibitions, Symptoms And Anxiety*, VI; *Totem And Taboo*, II, 4

holy idiot, like Dostoievsky's hero Prince Muishkin. His imagination itself is turned against him to prettify and vaporise him: he is puffed away by the thought that it is all, after all, *only* imagination. Shakespeare, through Theseus's mouth, classes the poet and the lunatic together on the point of their imagination (and adds a third, the lover[1], that other great demonstrator against the group feeling, who breaks every social bond in favour of the one union which claims his whole attention). None the less, Shakespeare does not fail to point out the sense in which art *is* serious: it makes its figments real to our imaginations. Theseus's view is that the lovers' account of what happened in the wood near Athens is the product of their lunatic poetic imagination. Yet Hippolyta objects:

> But all the story of the night told over,
> And all their minds transfigur'd so together,
> More witnesseth than fancy's images,
> And grows to something of great constancy,
> But, howsoever, strange and admirable.

The dramatic irony at this moment is against Theseus, because we in the audience have seen, as he has not, what took place in the wood; *our* minds have been transfigured so together that we have seen it made real, brought to something of great constancy, by Shakespeare's poetry.

9. *Our Hostility to Culture*

The group, then, turns away from its criminals and poets or puts them out of view because they are incitements to the group's own repressed wish to rebel. But we do not properly understand the situation unless we remember that the group itself is at the same time

[1] Shakespeare has learnedly, though anachronistically, put into Theseus's mouth a genuinely Greek view. Theseus's 'The lunatic, the lover, and the poet Are of imagination all compact' (*A Midsummer Night's Dream*, V, i) is a condensation of Plato's four categories of divine madness (cf. E. R. Dodds: *The Greeks And The Irrational*, III). Plato's ritual and prophetic madnesses have been garbled together as simple lunacy: but the poetic and the erotic survive intact.

acting on this very wish: not by the criminal's method of a conscious act in real life, nor by the artist's method of a conscious act of imagination; but by an action in real life which is a symptom of society's unacknowledged ambivalence—one of those unconscious compromises which makes its act of worship or obedience at the same time an assault against the god or leader.

Here, in a stroke, is the reason why the education society gives its children can only *appear* to foster intelligence, imagination, logic. The group has an emotional vested interest in stupidity and philistinism. Not only does it lust to hand over its critical faculties to a leader; it makes use of that abnegation to deceive itself about the nature of its love for the leader. Logic in cold blood and the artist's imagination in hot blood are capable of exposing the contradiction in society's deepest allegiances. Society is against them because they may detect and interrupt it in its accustomed course of undermining the ideals it worships and obeys. Straightforward reason, straightforward rationalism even, are not the smallest use to us in this situation, because they are up against instinct—against what people *want* to do. Indeed, reason is quickly bent into a compromise with the unconscious instincts of the reasoner. We shall be nowhere until we turn the Freudian revolution to account by building ourselves a twentieth-century rationalism (based, as psycho-analysis is, in biology) which shall apply the instrument of reason to examining the instinctual sources of all our behaviour, including reasoning. Until then we are only piling logically consistent furniture into a structure which itself has no foundation in reality. Society has long known how to contain many of its best brains and even subvert them to its own purposes. The Jesuit may be as logical as he likes within the framework of Catholicism; the statesman may apply all the reasoning power in the world to securing peace providing he does it through the stultifying medium of international politics.

It is on this question of war or peace that our ambivalence reaches its crisis. It is a long time since anyone has consciously wanted war. Yet we have wars, arguing to ourselves that our conscious purposes have been overmastered by circumstances. But in fact there are in war no decisive circumstances except those of human psychology. The animals, though they prey on one another, are incapable of the organised activity which we mean by war. If mankind was removed from the planet, the mineral deposits in the earth, which are what we so often have in mind when we attribute war to circumstance, would not rise up and make wars on their own. What we are over-mastered by is our own unconscious wish for war.

This wish is created by a number of ambivalences, beginning with the group's ambivalence towards its leader, all of which find their discharge in a single situation which is punitive plus self-punitive, and destructive plus dangerous. War alone allows the people to pull the leader down on top of them into a more and more intimate and impassioned sado-masochistic embrace, which ends with the pair suffering—or even toppling—together. War affords the best chance of glorifying the leader (who must take a more supreme and uncontested position of power at home, as well as standing to gain in glory by defeating the enemy) and also the best hope of his destruction (for if the enemy defeats him, though it may not kill him, it certainly will kill the people's faith in him; revolution ferments fastest in defeated nations). War obliges the leader to maintain discipline by harsh and unconstitutional measures towards his people, and thereby to furnish them with justification for their murderous wishes against him: and in the same breath it provides the people with the chance of expiating those very murderous wishes by sacrificing their lives in obedience to the leader.

None the less, the modern war leader is not a genuine tyrant like the primal father, who really did terrorise his sons by force and paternal prestige. The leader may be cast in the primal father's rôle because the people are attracted by his supermanly qualities of remorse-lessness and freedom from obligation, but he has not won his position by the exercise of these qualities. If he has power and prestige, it is because the people have given them to him. (They are in the people's gift because the people took them from the primal father.) The people merely enjoy the fantasy that the leader has power over them.

The real successors to the primal father, and the real inheritors of his position as target for the people's ambivalence, are the forces which really do exert power over the people, imposing on them genuine renunciations of instinct, namely the leading ideas of the group. (The leader may owe some of his influence to seeming to personify an idea.) In the modern world, the most universally compelling leading idea has been the figure, half abstract, half personified, of one's country: the patria, the land of our fathers (those never-to-be-emulated fathers, whose legendary valour constitutes an historical Ego-ideal which the present-day Ego can never catch up with), the common ancestor which gives to all its sons the shared family name of Englishmen, Frenchmen or whatever they may be. Yet patriotism, that loyalty to the patria which makes the people fight in its interest, at the same time serves the people's destructive wishes against their country. Nothing can be sacrificed *for* a country except the country itself, the wealth and citizens it consists of, the very human beings in whose memories its tradition is deposited. The people's belief in the rightness of patriotism makes sure that their patria shall be depleted, by making sure that a force always exists which will rob it. If patriotism is right, and is nothing but loyalty to the self-interest of whichever land we happen to have been born in, then the enemy's soldiers and statesmen are just as much in the right as our own. We have, in effect, legalised wars of depredation; we have lent our own beliefs to sanction the self-interest of rival countries; and thus ultimately we are sanctioning the depredations and suffering they inflict on our own country.

Some perception of this ambivalence forces some peoples to shift their allegiance from the patria as such to a moralised patria and perhaps eventually to a principle of international legality or some moral ideal. These ideals do not, however, escape becoming the targets of our potent unconscious hostility. The war which we fight for our morality is the very thing which exposes it as no morality at all, but a naked assertion that might is right. The soldier knows that the ideals he is fighting for today will turn into tomorrow's diabolical misconceptions if the fortunes of war go against him; and in this moralistically vengeful world he will not even be protected, as the simple patriotic soldier was, by both sides' agreement that it was the duty of both sides to fight. The soldier begins the war an idealist and ends it a cynic. We would almost think that we fought our wars with no other purpose than to bring our morality down off its pedestal.

Our hostility to our own morals is, however, only one aspect of our fundamental hostility to civilisation and culture themselves. We may not share any particular social, moral or cultural organisation with the enemy, and we may fight him because he does not share our systems. What we do share with him is the fact of having *some* system, of being socially organised at all. It is human civilisation in its widest sense which has from the start imposed on us all renunciations of our sexual and aggressive instincts. The parents and the group-parent figures who impose renunciations on us are only passing on a pressure which is exerted by culture itself.

This ambivalence, whereby we hate the very thing our individual and social evolution is striving towards, the very thing for whose sake we have made our renunciations, is the price we have paid for becoming human—that is, psychological—beings as well as biological beings. An animal species which renounces life in the sea and takes to the land builds-in the renunciation to the instinctual pattern of the species. The individual land-dweller has not renounced his instinct for water-dwelling: the instinct he is endowed with from birth is a land-dwelling instinct. The worker bee has not abnegated sexuality: her species, through the instinctual pattern of behaviour it implanted in her fellows, has seen to it that she never received the diet which could turn her into a fertile female. The social organisation of bees, the contract whereby some classes renounce certain functions and undertake others exclusively, is decreed once and for all by their species. Two colonies of bees of the same species are organised on the same pattern, and the colonists are incapable of changing the pattern without transmuting themselves into a new species. Only our species produces individuals with so fluid an instinctual endowment that a single species can encompass the social and cultural organisations of ancient Babylon and modern London. The only social rule our species imposes on us is that we shall be social: we must, in response to our diverse historical and geographical environment, evolve some organisation. We are bound to no one pattern of civilisation, but since we are human and psychological we must be in some sort civilised.

When we employ war as a discharge for tensions in our own national group, as a means of expressing hatred against our leader and our social ideals, we are merely taking advantage of the enemy: we cast him in the almost passive rôle of a rock on to which we drive our ship in order to shatter the contract between captain and crew, simultaneously murdering the captain, and punishing the crew for mutiny, by drowning both. But when we take vengeance on civilisation itself, we are expressing the internal situation of humanity as a whole, and we draw the enemy, who is just as human as ourselves, into active collaboration with us. The conflict between his self-interest and ours, or between his ideals and ours, is only the pretext for a gigantic collusion between him and us. He and we are conspirators against the idealised but oppressive father of us all, human civilisation. Our wars prey on civilisation; they break down not one social system but the concept, the very influence, of sociability. In old-fashioned wars, the damage we inflicted was local and temporary. Now we see our way to razing civilisation altogether; we are even capable of wiping out what is genuinely the father, the ancestor of us all, the human species—the only species capable of species-suicide. If we are to act not on this largely unconscious wish but on our conscious intention of preserving the human race, then we must bend all the powers of our rational consciousness to isolating, and thus perhaps to controlling, our unconscious hatred of civilisation and our resentment of being human.

10. *The Pendulum*

The internal situation does not produce a steady stream of self-destructive impulses either in a national group or in the human race. War, which is a characteristically human activity, is an intermittent activity. Our conspiracy with our enemies has phases of quiescence, when we are at peace. We can go some way towards understanding this by considering another item in Freud's analysis of the relation between the Ego and the Ego-ideal in an individual. For some people, the ideal is never set far in advance of the Ego, while others take to themselves an exalted model which keeps up a tension between itself and the inevitably lagging Ego, which it browbeats with criticism. From this observation Freud goes on to the hypothesis that these two states may exist, successively, in a single person, and that the relationship between the Ego and its ideal can be invoked in order to give an account of the psychic condition where an individual, without any determining change in his outside circumstances, passes from melancholia, through a phase of happiness, into a state of manic exaltation, and then regularly plunges back into melancholia. The melancholia Freud reads as the reproaches directed against the unworthy Ego by a distant Ego-ideal. The Ego is presently stung into rebellion and moves closer to the ideal, producing a self-complacency in the individual; then the Ego triumphs utterly by swallowing up its tormentor, and exults in the feeling that there is no longer anything which can find fault with any of the Ego's actions; and finally the Ego succumbs to the guilt of this murder, resurrects the Ego-ideal and starts again to endure its criticisms.[1]

Something akin to, but not precisely the same as, this cycle seems to govern the internal relation of a group to its leader and to the abstract ideals which the leader may personify; and the psychic

[1] Freud: *Group Psychology And The Analysis Of The Ego*, XI

pendulum perhaps decrees the intervals between wars. When a nation goes to war, it looks back on the peace as a period of shame—Rupert Brooke's cry of 'Oh! we who have known shame, we have found release . . .'. But this is not so at the time. Peace is a period of self-complacency, of neglecting the group (from the point of view both of its internal solidarity and of its national glory in the world of foreign affairs) in favour of the individual's self-interest. Our phraseology couples peace with prosperity: we follow the Christmas wish of peace on earth with the wish for a prosperous new year. Evidently peace is a time when society's Ego-ideal is not uncomfortably far in advance of its Ego; and this situation society reflects in its choice of leaders. It rejects the politician who urges it to efforts or points to faults in its constitution, and adopts if possible a business man—certainly someone who will do the minimum of governing, impose the least discipline and ask for the smallest self-sacrifices.

In the individual manic-depressive, we should expect this self-complacency to end by rising into exultation by the Ego, in which every consideration of conscience and remorse is swept away. But this is not quite what happens to a group. When it moves out of the self-complacency of peace towards war, the group does experience exultation; the conscience which in peacetime forbids us to kill any of our fellow human beings *is* swept away—yet only in respect of half of our fellows. But at the same time the warlike mood has characteristics which in an individual would signal the depressive phase. There is an increase in criticism directed against the Ego, manifested in the revulsion from the selfish carelessness of the peace. So far from being caught up and controlled, the Ego-ideal is set far ahead and calls for the Ego to make self-sacrifices: the relaxing leader is dismissed in favour of one who promises blood and toil.

War, therefore, stands in contrast to the self-complacent phase and represents both extremes of the manic-depressive axis—which, of course, it is perfectly adapted to do by its nature. The great difference between the situation of a nation at war and the situation of an individual manic-depressive is that the nation has an enemy. Merely to fight is to exult and to triumph over conscience; but at the same time there is a risk that the Ego will be subjected to the ultimate criticism and sacrifice of being killed. Unlike the individual melancholiac, however, when his self-reproaches reach the pitch of suicide, the nation (and its soldiers as individuals) need not perform this office for itself. The collusion between a nation and its enemy consists in the two forming together one giant manic-depressive, gambling over the apportionment of the manic and the depressive phases: to the victor, the manic exultation, the position which cannot be criticised; to the defeated, the melancholia.

II. *The Beloved Enemy*

We have noticed that the soldier, when he commits an assault on his enemy which puts the enemy for ever out of his way as a rival, does so by an act which also makes the enemy the object of his sadistic love; and now we have detected two enemy nations making their rivalry the excuse for conspiring together against the safety of civilisation and forming a union in which each performs an indispensable office for the other. They exchange between them the rôles of aggressor and sufferer; each in turn discharges for the other some of the functions of the Ego-ideal.

Having noticed this, we can no longer put off recognising that the precept of the Sermon on the Mount, 'Love your enemies', which seems so difficult and impossibly ideal, is really one which we carry out only too well.

And as a matter of fact it is a very curious precept. Examined closely, it yields the clue to how the church which began by being horribly persecuted turned into the world's most effective and long-lasting persecutor. Indeed, this text is the kernel of the striking (though, of course, sentimentalised—that is, hypocrisised) sado-masochistic ambivalence which is Christianity's particular contribution to our culture. 'Love your enemies', it reads, 'bless them that curse you, do good to them that hate you, and pray for them which despitefully use you and persecute you; That ye may be the children of your Father which is in heaven'[1]. It does *not* read: 'Take care to have no enemies; educate your children in such a way that no one curses or hates anyone; so order the world that there are no acts of spiteful persecution'. Instead, it firmly implies that we cannot be the children of our heavenly father unless we lend our credence to supporting the existence of a diabolical father, too, keeping up by hook or by crook the world's supply of diabolical agents in order that they may persecute us. It is the old game of exalting an internal leader by raising up external enemies; and then

[1] *Matthew*, V, 44-5: ἀγαπᾶτε τοὺς ἐχθροὺς ὑμῶν . . .

exacerbating and propping up the strength of the enemies with our left hand, while our right searches for peace.

In our dealings with our enemies, we are not moved by pure hatred, which (so far as we, with our experience of inevitably mixed emotions, can conceive of it at all) would simply seek to annihilate the hated object by refusing to form any relationships with it, utterly withdrawing instinctual impulses from its direction, and which would avoid, above all, any physical contact with it. Instead we are moved by that particular blending of love and hatred which constitutes the wish to be identified with an object; we do not attempt to annihilate our enemies by any other method than achieving some sort of union with them. We do seek bodily contact with the enemy—or at least a reciprocal physical impact. The soldier is united and brought down to an equality with his enemy in the democratic embrace of death. The cannibal seeks a still more primitive and wholesale fusion with his enemy, to whom he pays the compliment of eating him, a compliment which in its literal form most men reserve for the first-loved person in their lives, the mother; but it is just this compliment which the Ego extends by a psychic act to the image of the father and which Christians and savages extend in the quasi-literal form of a sacrament to the super-father, the most adulated person in their world, the god.

Our very concept of enmity implies a compliment, an idealisation. Either the enemy is something we should like to be (though, if it is clearly he who attacks us, this may be nothing more than warlike: yet we unmistakably *should* like to be warlike, just as he is, or we should not resist him at all but capitulate); or else he has created something—a culture, perhaps—which we should like to have (we should like to have been its creator ourselves). What higher praise can the German offer the Frenchman, as he marches over the frontier, than his wish to turn all the French people into German citizens—and to become, himself, an inhabitant of Paris?

We are forced to the conclusion that its enemy, at least in some aspects, figures to a group as its father. This is really no more than we can guess from perceiving that the enemy, when he inflicts pain and loss on us, has become an agent of our own self-punishment and is helping to discharge one of the functions of our own internal Ego-ideal[1]. The unconscious, with its inability to recognise that there are

[1] —or than we can guess from the group's readiness to share in the leader's paranoia in relation to the enemy, since 'with the paranoiac it is precisely the

external events beyond the control of its own wishes[1], can no more conceive that the enemy could harm us gratuitously than it can conceive that an earthquake harms us by accident and not in punishment of some sin on our part. In the enemy, however, we are dealing with something responsive, which really will, unlike the earthquake, react to us—not, of course, to our mere wishes and sins in thought, but to our deeds; and the unconscious contrives so to shape our deeds that they really do, though covertly, manipulate the enemy into punishing us.

The diagnosis that the enemy is conceived as a father is instantly confirmed by the fact that primitive societies include enemies, along with gods and rulers, in the category of people who are full of taboo by virtue of standing in a paternal relation to the tribe. The savage warrior apologises to the enemy he has killed, and must undergo a ritual purgation of his guilt.[2] In other words, he uses the enemy and the totem animal with the same unconscious hypocrisy: both represent the father to him. Even when orthodox classical religion had suppressed the memory of the paternal nature of the animal victim, archaic vestiges in the rite preserved the fact that the sacrifice had once been a crime. As Freud and Robertson Smith pointed out, it was the guilt of the totemistic crime which was still expiated at Tenedos when 'the sacrificer of the booted-calf was stoned and driven into the sea'[3]. At the Athenian Bouphonia (a sacrifice whose name[4] means not simply the killing but the murder of an ox), the inanimate weapon which had done the crime was formally tried, found guilty and thrown into the sea[5]. That this is a relic of a primitive group's social sacrament is divinable from the fact that the god it honoured was Zeus Polieus—Zeus the keeper of the city (of Athens): the community shares the crime of assassinating its father-keeper in order to reaffirm the bonds of citizenship.

most loved person of his own sex that becomes his persecutor' (Freud: *Collected Papers*, Volume II, XIX)

[1] —that is, its belief in 'the omnipotence of thought' (Freud: *Totem And Taboo*, III, 3)

[2] Freud: *Totem And Taboo*, II, 3 (a). Cf. Frazer: *Taboo And The Perils Of The Soul*, IV, 4; 5, 'Warriors tabooed'; 'Manslayers tabooed'

[3] Smith's *Dictionary Of . . . Antiquities*, 'Sacrificium', C

[4] as Robertson Smith first pointed out, and Frazer emphasised (*Spirits Of The Corn And Of The Wild*, IX)

[5] Frazer: *Spirits Of The Corn And Of The Wild*, IX; Smith's *Dictionary Of . . . Antiquities*, 'Sacrificium'; Freud: *Totem And Taboo*, IV, 4

To this day the Catholic priest who re-offers the Lamb's self-sacrifice incurs a guilt which he must ritually purge. After he has himself communicated (and 'if there are any communicants, he should give them communion before purifying') the priest 'washes his fingers, wipes them and takes the ablution'[1].

In all these purifications we can detect the same motive which makes society push the criminal out of sight. Warrior and sacrificer tempt their fellows because they suggest the idea of killing the father. What they must really purge themselves of is their temptation-value for the rest of the community. Either they must symbolically wash away the blood the sight of which is an incitement; or else they must absent themselves from social intercourse long enough for the memory of the association between their persons and the forbidden deed they have committed to die down.

Tribal society[2], Victorian bourgeoisies and present-day royal families impose the same restriction on people who have been bereaved —who have lost, in the cardinal instance, a parent. The bereaved person must stay away from the group's social functions and may be put still further out of sight by being obliged to wear inconspicuously coloured clothes. Thus society lives up to the unconscious's rule that there are no accidents: whoever has wished for a death, albeit unconsciously, is guilty of that death; whoever has lost a parent has murdered a parent: and society tacitly admits that any reminder of this murder incites other people to copy the murderer's example[3]. A

[1] from an English Missal

[2] Frazer: *Taboo And The Perils Of The Soul*, IV, 2, 'Mourners tabooed'

[3] Cf (A) Freud: 'When a wife loses her husband, or a daughter her mother, it not infrequently happens that the survivor is afflicted with tormenting scruples ... which raise the question whether she herself has not been guilty, through carelessness or neglect, of the death of the beloved person ... Not that the mourner has really been guilty of the death ... but still there was something in her, a wish of which she herself was unaware, which was not displeased with the fact that death came .. Such hostility, hidden in the unconscious behind tender love, exists in almost all cases of intensive emotional allegiance to a particular person, indeed it represents the classic case, the prototype of the ambivalence of human emotions' (*Totem And Taboo*, II, 3 (c)) and (B) Bernard Shaw's scene in Hell between Don Juan and Doña Ana (who is still wearing mourning for her father—of whose death she really has been almost guilty by her carelessness):

DON JUAN. . . . You may remember that on earth—though of course we never confessed it—the death of anyone we knew, even those we liked

taboo is the mark of an ambivalence and, by the same token, of an unconscious temptation. A taboo rule is a reinforcement of society's defences against temptation; and the personage who is surrounded by the uncanny aura of taboo, whether god or devil, artist or criminal, has to be veiled in taboo because he is an incitement. Society will venerate him or put him away in order to keep its own unconscious wish in suppression: yet we can have no doubt of the existence of the wish or of its power, since the very act which is designed to suppress it tends more and more to be an expression of it. We suppress our own impulse to assassination by assassinating murderers; we control our impulse towards regicide by imposing a living death on our kings.

12. *Father Into Enemy*

In treating an enemy as a father, the unconscious is arguing by its favourite fallacy. It states its own feeling, 'My father is my enemy'; or, rather (to rearrange the singular proposition in its traditionally-logical form of universal proposition, which at the same time comes closer to the psychic content of the statement), it proposes:

All people who represent my father
to me are my enemies;

and from this it fallaciously draws the immediate inference:

Therefore all my enemies are people
who represent my father to me.

This fallacy, which consists in ignoring the distribution of a term (in this case ignoring that *enemies* in the original proposition does not cover the whole class of enemies, with the result that the whole class cannot properly appear in any inference drawn directly from the original proposition[1]) is in fact the foundation of the unconscious's thinking. Brought out into the open and given a speciously rational

best, was always mingled with a certain satisfaction at being finally done with them.
ANA. Monster! Never, never.
DON JUAN [*placidly*]. I see you recognize the feeling . . .

[1] the fallacy of converting an S a P proposition (which, because P is undistributed, can really yield only P̆ i S̆) into P̄ a S̆

form, it produces argument by analogy: in the actual processes of the unconscious, it produces those metaphorical formations which we recognise as symbols, or symptoms. To make a snake a phallic symbol is to argue 'Snakes are long, rounded, boneless, muscular things; phalloi are long, rounded, boneless, muscular things: therefore snakes are phalloi'. This is argument by the association of ideas without distinguishing whether the two ideas are associated as separate parts of a given class or whether they wholly coincide. In this same sense, the neurotic or hysteric attributes guilt by association to some neutral and everyday circumstance which he has associated with a sexual activity. Because to masturbate comes into the class of manual activities, he will inhibit the whole class and condemn his arm to paralysis; because to be alone is the prerequisite of—among other things— masturbation, he will defend himself from temptation by an agoraphobia in which he cannot bear to go out unaccompanied.

It is by a fallacy of this kind that the small boy—or the totem group—transmutes the father into an animal. 'The child', as Freud remarks, 'unhesitatingly attributes full equality to animals; he probably feels himself more closely related to the animal than to the undoubtedly mysterious adult, in the freedom with which he acknowledges his needs'[1]. But it is on just this question of freedom that the fraternity of child and animals is presently disrupted and the animal, like the singled-out heroic brother, is hoisted into paternal eminence. As the child grows, he finds himself subject to social restrictions, and notices that these are not imposed on the animal, whom nobody expects to control either its temper or its bodily functions. Eventually the child encounters the culminating social restriction, the ban on sexual relations with his mother; and what he notices now—indeed, it is the very crux of his jealousy—is that this ban is not imposed on his father. It does not matter that the father, though he may resemble the animal in uncertainty of temper, does not enjoy the animal's freedom of bodily function; and neither does it matter that the animal is not the mother's lover; the boy has perceived his analogy and proceeds to draw the fallacious syllogism:

My father is allowed to do many things I should like to do (especially make love to my mother);
The animal is allowed to do many things I should like to do (though not including making love to my mother):

[1] *Totem And Taboo*, IV, 3

Therefore:—
The animal is my father[1].

Once this is achieved, the boy has swept out of his path the objection that the animal did not enjoy sexual freedom in respect of the mother; he is well on his way to inventing the god who seduces the inaccessible maiden, or enters the mother's (the queen's) bed in the shape of an animal: Zeus is able to triumph over Europa's vow of perpetual celibacy by disguising himself as a bull in order to abduct her, and it is as a snake that he enters Queen Olympias's bed and there begets Alexander the Great.

Of course, the totemistic syllogism manages to degrade the father as well as adulate him. The child who has become subject to restrictions which never trouble the animal knows quite well that the animal remains free not because it is above but because it is beneath restrictions; and the totem tribe demonstrates that the unhappy animal is really not a powerful, divine personage when the animal shews itself unable to escape its cruel death. (The animal is real, but its sacredness is a myth; the primitive sacrament already conforms to definition[2] by being an outward and visible sign of an inward and spiritual grace. Already the progenitor is the creature of those who call themselves his descendants; and they have created him in order to misuse him). To equate the father with an animal is therefore an attempt to bring him into his sons' power and put him beneath them in rank; it is an insult to the father. The conclusion of the totemistic syllogism is readily converted into 'My father, who sleeps with my pure and chaste mother, is a beast'. The father becomes a disgusting monster, half animal, half man—like the satyr whom Alexander the Great, in one of his dreams, had so much trouble in subduing[3].

None the less it is by the marks of the superman (even though

---

[1] fallacious because the middle term is distributed in neither of the premises:

$$\bar{P} \; a \; \breve{M}$$
$$\bar{S} \; a \; \breve{M}$$

$$S \; a \; P$$

[2] '*Question.* What meanest thou by this word *Sacrament*? *Answer.* I mean an outward and visible sign of an inward and spiritual grace given unto us . . . *Question.* How many parts are there in a Sacrament? *Answer.* Two: the outward visible sign, and the inward spiritual grace.' (Church of England Catechism)

[3] Plutarch's *Life* . . .

these marks are really fictions, devised to serve the sons' unconscious hostility) that the animal is recognised as the father: by his sexual license and freedom from group obligations. The animal does not belong to our society; he is alien to us; he belongs to a different species. And it is just the same thought-process which makes the enemy identifiable as the father; for the enemy is, in the first place, the stranger. Our very word *hostility* embodies this origin, being derived from the Latin *hostis*, whose common meaning of 'enemy' has developed out of its primary meaning of 'stranger'[1].

This alien person presents himself to us as someone who is free from the rules of our group. This, in accordance with our old habit of xenophobia and our slightly more recent habit of ideological intolerance, we take to be a threat to our rules, though in fact the threat resides in our own resentment of our own rules. The emancipated foreigner, like the emancipated criminal, tempts us to break free ourselves; and sometimes we treat him as we do the criminal or regard him as no better than an animal—in the lowly sense of animal. We may even raid the foreigners in their enviable freedom, as we do the animals in their wildness, and, bringing them home, turn them into domesticated cattle, a sub-human species, our slaves.

Yet the stranger, like the criminal, is capable of rising to heroic status in our estimation; and he does it by reminding us so forcibly of the father that he begins to exert the same claims as the father on our (ambivalent) loyalty. Just as, with the divine animal, we ignore the fact that the animal is subject to restrictions imposed by his own species, which are really much more limiting than those our social group imposes on us, so we ignore the fact that the stranger is under an obligation to his own society. It is enough that he is free of *our* bonds and that we therefore, in envying, hate him. These two factors supply us with our analogy: the person who is free of our bonds and whom we hate is the father.

And indeed this primal enemy, the stranger, performs exactly the same function for the group, by terrorising it from outside, as the primal father does by terrorising his sons from within it. The enemy is the group's external father, the single point on which all the members focus their fears; and their shared relation to this terrifying object drives them into a closer identity with one another, a group solidity in which they all undertake equal sacrifices of their egoistic ambitions

[1] *hostis*: 'I. Prop., *a stranger, foreigner* (old or poet.) . . . II. Praegn., *an enemy, foe* . . . ' (Lewis)

in face of the common threat. This the word *hostis* reflects: the hostis, the stranger who becomes an enemy, is essentially a public enemy[1], the common foe of a group; and something of the enemy's paternal rôle is preserved in the English idiom which makes the enemy singular, while we, his estranged, hostile sons, are plural.

Like the primal father, the group's enemy exerts on the group the father's original taboo-ful influence, the influence of the hypnotist.[2] The stranger has caught our attention—because, being different from ourselves, he is conspicuous; and now, like the hypnotist, he holds our attention focussed on himself to the exclusion of everything else. Indeed, it is a hypnotic phenomenon that we ignore every aspect of him except the one in which he coincides with the father: it is the father in him that we are concentrating on. This total concentration on one object, to the exclusion of every other, is characteristic of the lover's infatuation, too. ('From being in love to hypnosis is evidently only a short step . . . There is the same humble subjection, the same compliance, the same absence of criticism . . . There is the same absorption of one's own initiative . . . It is only that everything is even clearer and more intense in hypnosis, so that it would be more to the point to explain being in love by means of hypnosis than the other way round.'[3]) When we go to war with our enemy, we have made enmity the excuse for bending on him the minute and exclusive concentration the lover devotes to the beloved. The lover employs every stratagem to find out what the other person is thinking: and so does the intelligence service. In war, as in a reciprocal love affair, both sides are the hypnotist and both the subject. Morale, which is so important, is a matter of which side exerts the greater influence and retains more of its own initiative.

13. *The Stranger*

Although the enemy becomes a father of a kind (we have still to explore what kind) he is no substitute for the primal father inside the group. Historically he is less primal. We cannot suppose that the group was formed in the first place under pressure from an external threat, but

[1] in distinction from *inimicus*, a private enemy (Lewis)
[2] Freud: *Group Psychology And The Analysis Of The Ego*, X
[3] Freud: *Group Psychology And The Analysis Of The Ego*, VIII

only that an external threat could force it, once formed, to become closer compacted. For if we ask why the group regards the enemy as terrifying, it is precisely because he threatens its existence as a group. The individual would often preserve himself better by capitulating to the enemy; but instead of doing so he risks his own utter destruction in order to preserve the group intact; and the only force which can bring him to this point of self-sacrifice is his loyal obligation to a group already formed.

The original threat which the stranger offers the group is that he may disrupt it by inciting the members, in emulation of his freedom, to burst their own bonds. But as soon as the stranger begins, by exerting his terrifying influence, to figure as the father (leaving aside for the moment the exact psychic content of this identification) he presents a threat in a new and paradoxical form. The danger is now that a member of the group will act on his impulse to put temptation out of sight and murder the stranger: in which case he will have murdered the father. This strange man who provokes him and whom he would like to kill is the same person as the strange man whom Oedipus (when both were travelling away from home) met at a triple cross-roads, disputed the right of way with, and killed.[1]

If the group is to avoid the penalties of parricide which overtook Oedipus, it must be protected from its murderous impulse against the stranger. Taboo protects the primitive from acting on his own criminal wishes against the father within the group, and does it in the guise of protecting the father; and now taboo extends its protection to the external father, the stranger, and thereby protects the members of the group from incurring the penalties of killing him.

This taboo rule survived intact into Greco-Roman civilisation in the form of the law of hospitality, the absolute obligation to receive and treat amicably the wanderer who appeared at one's gates. The idea of the stranger whom one would like to attack extends itself to create the idea of the stranger whom one attacks at one's peril: the word *hostis* extends itself to form the compound *hospes*[2]. *Hospes*, like its derivatives in modern romance languages[3], signifies either party in a relationship which is reciprocal: it means both 'host' and 'guest' (as well as preserving the original meaning of *hostis*, 'stranger')[4]: and in

---

[1] Sophocles: *Oedipus Rex*, 798 foll.

[2] hospes: 'hostis + R.POT—' (Lewis)   [3] Italian, *ospite*; French, *hôte*

[4] hospes: 'I. Lit., *an entertainer, host* . . . II. Meton. A. *A Sojourner, visitor, guest* . . . B. Praegn., *a friend, one bound by ties of hospitality* . . . C. *A stranger, foreigner*' (Lewis)

this reciprocal relationship between parties who are impulsively enemies, we scent the beginnings of the collusion between opponents in a war.

The law of hospitality is fundamentally pure, impersonal taboo, independent of theology. But when theology laid hands on it and began to rationalise it, it had no hesitation in pointing out that the reason why the stranger must be well treated is the risk of killing the father—a risk it mythologised into the risk that the stranger might be a god in disguise. The scriptural text which justified the law was the passage in *The Odyssey* where one of the suitors, speaking on behalf of the whole group of them, reproves another for striking the unknown stranger (who is in fact the hero, god-descended Odysseus, in disguise): 'you did wrong to strike the wretched vagabond. You're a doomed man if he turns out to be some god from heaven. And the gods do disguise themselves as strangers from abroad, and wander round our towns in every kind of shape to see whether people are behaving themselves or getting out of hand'[1].

It is this passage which Diodorus Siculus[2] cites to shew his Greek audience that there is nothing absurd in the Egyptians' belief that their sacred animals were manifestations of the gods. The strange man and the alien animal have both become divine on the point of their resemblance to the father.

As a matter of fact, myths have so accustomed us to the equation of stranger with father that we are no longer surprised when the unknown wanderer who appears in the city turns out to be a demigod (or even, like Oedipus himself, the real heir to the throne who has been estranged from his native land) or when the mysterious stranger, in sentimental dramas like Jerome K. Jerome's once popular play *The Passing Of The Third Floor Back*, proves to be a figure of Christ. Indeed, Christ begins his myth-career true to the heroic pattern by arriving as an impoverished traveller at the royal town of Bethlehem—as his religion was later to arrive at imperial Rome. His precepts enlarge the law of hospitality beyond strangers to include everyone in need[3], and he teaches quite explicitly that to behave lovingly to these people is to behave lovingly to God. Yet this spiritualised and idealised

[1] E. V. Rieu's translation of *Odyssey*, XVII, 483-7   [2] I, 12

[3] as, apparently, ancient Egyptian religion did. The dead Egyptian, at *his* judgment, had to be able to disclaim acts of oppression and, indeed, acts which could make his fellow men weep, and to assert that he had fed the hungry and clothed the naked. (Frazer: *Adonis Attis Osiris*, Volume II, I)

reason for loving the needy is not so far removed, indeed, it cannot be divorced, from Homer's cynical idea that the god may have put on a beggarly disguise in order to spy on his people. It is at the last judgment that the righteous will be rewarded for their good deeds offered to God through the persons of paupers and strangers[1]; and the last judgment shall come on the peoples of the world 'as a snare'[2].

Already in the myth where a god is disguised as a down-and-out, we can discern a little of the suppressed hostility to the father. Even as we tell ourselves that we must not treat the vagabond badly because he may be a god, we have managed to subject the god temporarily to the discomfort of *being* a vagabond. It is not such a big step from *hospes*, the stranger whom we must resist our impulse to kill, to the fully-fledged meaning of *hostis*, the stranger-enemy whom we may— or, rather, must—kill. Etymology will yield us one more piece to the puzzle, the completing piece, a figure who is divine and sacrosanct and yet whom we destroy, a father whom we love and yet must murder. The same verbal root[3] which gives us *hostis* gives us also *hostia*, one of the names[4] for the victim in the Roman animal sacrifice, and the name which Christianity borrowed to apply to the Host, the sacrificed god, in the Mass.

Christianity admitted that our victim, the hostia, was the god. But since this totemistic truth had been lost to the classical religion, Ovid was able to derive *hostia* directly from *hostis*, on the grounds that the *hostia* was an enemy subdued[5]; and he goes on to explain that the sow

[1] 'Then [sc. at the last judgment] shall the King say unto them on his right hand, Come, ye blessed of my Father . . . For I was an hungered, and ye gave me meat: I was thirsty, and ye gave me drink: I was a stranger, and ye took me in . . . Then shall the righteous answer him, saying, Lord . . . When saw we thee a stranger, and took thee in? . . . And the King shall answer and say unto them, Verily, I say unto you, Inasmuch as ye have done it unto one of least of these my brethren, ye have done it unto me.' (Matthew, XXV, 34- . . . 40)

[2] *Luke*, XXI, 35

[3] HAS-, *hurt*, whence also the English *host* in the sense of 'army' (Lewis)

[4] *hostia* was used of the smaller, *victima* of the larger animals (Smith's *Dictionary Of . . . Antiquities*, 'Sacrificium')

[5] Similarly he derives the alternative name for the sacrificed animal, *victima*, from *vincere*, to conquer, on the grounds that the victim falls to a victorious right hand (*Fasti*, I, 335-6):

> victima, quae dextra cecidit victrice, vocatur;
> hostibus a domitis hostia nomen habet.

was sacrificed to Ceres because it had made itself her enemy by rooting up her sacred crops, and the goat to Bacchus because it had nibbled his vines[1]. The animal who had originally been the god could now be called the god's enemy; and this had the advantage of disguising from us that it is really the god who is *our* enemy.[2]

And this disguise is really our whole motive in identifying the father with the stranger or the animal who is so alien to us. It is not the father but our hostile feelings towards him which we are estranging from ourselves; making the father unknown to us, we make our parricidal impulses unknown—unconscious—to us. If Oedipus kills the traveller and marries Queen Jocasta in ignorance of the fact that the traveller and Jocasta are his father and mother, his ignorance is how the myth represents the unconscious nature of his parricidal and incestuous wishes.

14. *The Lottery*

This myth-figure of the strange man appears again in a related context which has been analysed by Edward Glover[3]: the psycho-pathology (one might almost say the mythology) of prostitution. This time it is the girl's Oedipal problem which is in question: that second bout of the conflict, which is peculiar to her, in which she must accommodate herself to what she has discovered about the physiological status of her sex, abandon the wish to become her mother's lover and, identifying herself with her mother, take the father as the object of her love. The prostitute, who often remains more or less overtly homosexual, has not completely subdued her sexual love for her mother. The mother still figures to her as a desired person who was unfaithful to her: the mother went to bed with at least one of her

[1] *Fasti*, I, 349 foll.

[2] Compare the history of the pig which was sacrificed to Osiris. The pig, Frazer inferred, had originally been a manifestation of Osiris; but later it became identified with Osiris's enemy and murderer, Typhon. Frazer remarks: 'the examples of Dionysus and Demeter, if not of Attis and Adonis, have taught us that the animal which is sacrificed to a god on the ground that he is the god's enemy may have been, and probably was, originally the god himself.' (*Spirits Of The Corn And Of The Wild*, IX)

[3] in his lecture *The Psycho-Pathology Of Prostitution* (I.S.T.D.)

daughter's rivals, namely the daughter's father. It is with her mother as the pattern of the unfaithful woman that the prostitute identifies herself in the practice of her profession; and it is this debased image of the mother to which, for similar Oedipal reasons on their part, the prostitute's clients make love.

Identified thus with her mother, the prostitute sets about seeking out the one man whom she wishes to make the object of her emotions: the father, the man who certainly and quintessentially was her mother's lover. Her profession allows her to seek him high and low. In the long series of her lovers, she is really in quest of this one (as the ancient-world institution of sacred prostitution makes clear: for the sacred prostitute to offer herself to a chance passerby, or a series of them, is tantamount to offering herself to a god; her child, being the child of an unknown man, may even be regarded as the god's). At the same time her profession is the prostitute's defence against her incestuous desire for her father, enabling her to escape the penalties of finding and loving him. She has sought safety doubly: in numbers; and again in the idea of strangeness, in the fact that her clients are casual acquaintances who remain virtually anonymous to her (and she to them)[1].

In Oedipus's case, it is his murderous wish that is made strange to him when the myth makes his father a stranger; with the prostitute, it is her incestuous wish that is alienated from her by the strangeness of her lovers. Yet the prostitute remains something of a male, of an Oedipus, as well. The wish towards the father which she is disowning

[1] The father is someone whose name you know, and who knows yours, because his name *is* yours. (The totem tribe [Freud: *Totem And Taboo*, IV, i] takes its name from *its* father, the totem species.) The anonymity between client and prostitute is not only a practical but also a psychic safeguard, an assertion that they cannot be father and daughter. Our modern usage about names perfectly embodies the psychic facts of a child's identification with its parent. Son and daughter are alike synonymous in surname with the father; but whereas the son is an exact replica, Mr Smith just as his father is Mr Smith, the daughter is only Miss Smith (and, unlike her brother, she will not be addressed simply as 'Smith' at school)—a reminder to her that she must overcome her original identification with her father and make first him, and eventually a substitute for him, the object of her love. It is the mother she must identify herself with, to the extent of wishing to become Mrs, but she must cast about for a different surname from the one her mother has adopted; and when the substitute for her father has been found (the father himself will 'give her away' to him), she must betoken her utter renunciation of the father by giving up his name and assuming the substitute's.

is only partly the wish to make love to him, for this feminine desire has been superimposed on her still earlier infantile situation, in which she still reacted as though she were a boy, and saw her father as a hated rival. Towards the clients in whom she is seeking her father, the prostitute is by no means loving. 'Strange man' means 'enemy' to her, as it does to the primitive. If the primitive receives the stranger kindly, it is not on impulse but under compulsion from the taboo rules of hospitality, which bid him make a demonstration against what are really his murderous impulses—'Look, I am not attacking the father but entertaining him.' The prostitute not merely entertains but performs an act of love with her strange man. Yet this, too, is not spontaneous. It is done for money and in obedience to a compulsion of her own, which obliges her to repeatedly contradict her homosexual impulses towards her mother. The prostitute is demonstratively and compulsively heterosexual, as who should say, 'Look, I am not making love to my mother but to all these men.'

This demonstration does not save her from hating all these men on her mother's account. Any one of them—and this is the value to her of them all—might be the loathed rival with whom her mother betrayed her. By the casual way she meets and treats them, and by so multiplying their number that she cannot remember which is which, the prostitute makes her clients the object of her contempt and indifference. If she debases the female sex because her mother was seduced, she takes care to debase the male sex too because her father was the seducer. She murders her father by her coldness to her clients. The phenomena of sexual intercourse even permit her to—in a sense—inflict on the client the castration by which she would have liked to put a stop once and for all to the rivalry her father offered her in relation to her mother. The client's virility is extinguished in orgasm, but the prostitute makes no reciprocal surrender to him. Instead she diminishes him twice over, because she takes his money too.

When the myth dissociates Oedipus from his unconscious desires, it places him at the mercy of fate. Fate in tragic drama is an external, impersonal representation of what are really the tragic hero's wishes: fate impels him where he wants, but may not let himself know he wants, to go[1]. It was prophesied of the baby Oedipus that he would kill his father, and it was because of the prophecy that his father exposed him to die[2]. In this casting out of the accursed baby from his

[1] Freud: *The Interpretation Of Dreams*, V (b)
[2] Sophocles: *Oedipus Rex*, 711 foll.

family, we can see the incestuous and parricidal wishes being outlawed from society; and in the fact that the baby did not die but was rescued, we can read an admission that the repression of the wishes was unsuccessful. Once estranged from his own family, to be brought up elsewhere, Oedipus was condemned to ignorance of who his parents were—we read that he was condemned to ignorance of what his wishes towards his parents were, that his wishes had been condemned to the unconscious: and now it is up to fate to bring him to the fulfilment of his wishes. Fate must direct him to the accidental encounter at the crossroads, and then turn his steps towards Thebes and its widowed queen.

The prostitute, by disowning *her* wishes towards her father, has similarly placed herself at the mercy of fate. (This is the secret of her literary appeal. She is a person of no fixed address, a person who makes no attempt to impose her will on the environment by cultivating her garden, but lets fate carry her where it will—in which we, quite correctly, discern the hero's quality of being prepared for whatever adventures may come.) The prostitute's relations with the strange man who may be her father depend entirely on chance. Moreover, she tempts fate (as the tragic hero may do by his hubris). She takes refuge from her love for her mother by asserting that she is heterosexual, a lover of men; and she contradicts her incestuous desire for the one man who really engages her attention by embracing hundreds: but just this casting her net wide in the sea of the male sex gives her the highest possible chance of catching in it, there to be simultaneously loved and destroyed, the one man she is avoiding.

She has, in fact, improved on the tragic conception of fate by adding to it the numerical idea of chance. The male sex is a lottery, in which the prostitute has bought the highest possible number of tickets. Any one in her holding may be the winning number, the father she is seeking; but since no one knows which is he, it is the series as a whole which becomes the object of her sexual and aggressive desires. For the prostitute, every professional act of intercourse is an act of incest and, at the same time, an attack on her father. In exercising her profession, she gratifies her incestuous wish (and its murderous companion), yet the fact that it is a game of hazard allows her to plead not guilty to incest. Just so, if one member, no one knows which, of the firing squad has drawn a blank cartridge, all may feel innocent of the killing but the execution none the less gets done.

The same psychology is manifest in the very usage of modern European languages, where the plural *you*, *vous*, *sie* is a politer way of addressing one person than the singular *thou*, *tu*, *du*. The singular, which is used reciprocally between child and parent (the God whom the children pray to counting as a parent), preserves the ambivalence one would expect of such a relation: it may signify intimacy or insult. It is used to social inferiors, a habit which correctly interprets the class barrier as the incest barrier, and also to animals—it is the pure psychology of totemism which couples the animal with the father. The second person plural, on the other hand, is politer because it is incapable of the hostility which lurks in the singular. The chances of the speaker's hostility hitting the person addressed have been reduced by multiplying him into a plurality. He is made less of a target by being made less explicit. (Italian carries this inexplicitness further still when it makes its politest form of address not even *voi siete* but *Lei è*, *it* [*feminine*], sc. excellency, *is*. Similarly, the English servant used to reassure his master that he felt no hostility and his mistress that he had no [incestuous] sexual ambitions by renouncing *you* in favour of 'His Lordship is . . .', 'Madam is . . .'. He and the polite Italian have both abnegated even that primitive power over another person, conjuration, which is exercised by calling him up directly.)

The prostitute has her counterpart in Don Giovanni, another adventurer who carelessly lets fate carry him where it will (and eventually to the doom which in fact he has willed) and another compulsive heterosexualist—one who (in order, we may understand, to back up his constant disclaimer of homosexuality) actually keeps a catalogue[1] of his heterosexual clients. Chivalry cannot conceal that Don Giovanni's women *are* his clients and that he is a professional prostitute, indiscriminately available to satisfy their needs—though it is true that he has no mercenary interest in his profession, it being enough for him to relieve his clients of their good repute. Like the female prostitute, he has no real taste for heterosexual intercourse. Physiology does not allow him to use her expedient of remaining non-participant during the act; but his disinclination expresses itself by so often getting him prevented from performing the act at all that he has in effect done the next best thing and become a tease.

In Don Giovanni we can discern the outline of the genuine heterosexual romantic, who really does fall in love—copiously—with women

[1] Leporello (No. 4): 'Madamina, il catalogo è questo, delle belle che amò il padron mio . . .'

(though he may reject the idea of actual intercourse with them) and who is searching, in the multitude of women, for the one inaccessible woman who shall represent his mother. But Don Giovanni, though he has a touch of the troubadour, is not a romantic. He has overcome his desire for the mother, but only at the cost of fixing his ambitions for ever on the father. Unlike the romantic, he uses his women with contempt and matter of factness, as the prostitute does her clients; what he is really searching for in the lottery of women is the male personage who stands protectively behind the woman, the father. In other words, his quarry is the same as the female prostitute's. *Her* desires resolve themselves into a comparatively superficial incest wish, beneath which lies the older desire to harm the father. With Don Giovanni it is the other way about. His aggression against the father (the murder of the Commendatore) is only a provocation, designed to bring the father upon him in a homosexual assault. Even so, whereas the prostitute expresses both her desires through what is in form an act of love, albeit an unloving one, Don Giovanni has to perform both seductions and a murder; and when he prevails upon the Commendatore to return his homosexual affection, the affection has to be disguised as an act of violence which kills Don Giovanni.

Don Giovanni is a halfway house between the prostitute, who uses love to express violence, and the soldier, who uses violence to express love. We have noticed already that Don Giovanni's promiscuity is less successful in bringing him to a mutual Liebestod with his enemy-lover than the soldier's; and at once it becomes clear that the serial technique, the device of the lottery, which is employed alike by Don Giovanni and the female prostitute, is an insufficient protection against the unconscious desires. When the father manifests himself in a succession of strange men, who come one by one, he is still recognisable; the law of hospitality has to protect the single foreigner because he may be the god. It is only when the strange men come simultaneously, as an army, a host, that the group dares to recognise them explicitly as the enemy and put its hostility into practice.

The prostitute and Don Giovanni cannot adopt this method of declaring themselves, because the medium of expression to which they have confined themselves (even when what they express is in fact an aggression) is sexual intercourse, whose nature limits it to two participants at a time. Sexual love is capable of making two people one, binding them into the firmest possible identity, creating a society of two[1]; but it is unable to build upwards from the pair by adding a third, a fourth, a fifth partner[2]. The society of two is actually a disintegrating force in society at large. When the couple creates a third person, the child, he is not received as an equal partner, but has to set about inserting himself into the original pair by eliminating and taking the place of one or other parent; and it is from his rejection from a place in the society of two, and his acceptance of being rejected, that those bonds of social, aim-inhibited affection are formed which eventually bind him into his place in the wider society.

This is the advantage war has over sex and the reason why, although it is so uncivilised, civilisation has more ungrudgingly made room for it[3]. The sexual orgy does not work, because the presence of the other people is never a necessity[4]. A coupling of two people, though religions have employed it in a sacramental sense, does not exert enough obligation on the other people to serve as the symbol of a community's bonding together. It is only through acts of violence, at a shared meal or on the battlefield (where the presence of the other people *is*, most urgently, necessary), that an orgy can really take place and a group can orgiastically celebrate and reaffirm the union of each member with each and all of the others.

Don Giovanni may be tinged with the heroic and the woman prostitute tinged with the holy (like Sonia Marmeladov to whom Dostoievsky offers such veneration[5]; or she may first have, like the Magdalen, to repent and be sentimentalised): but in society's eyes they remain essentially criminal and outcast, never completely taking on the nimbus of the holy criminal. Society's good opinion is reserved for the soldier, who buys all his lottery tickets at once and takes his chance (of killing the father and being killed by him) in relation to a

---

[1] Donne actually considers the pair of lovers under the political metaphor in *The Anniversary*:

> Who is so safe as we, where none can do
> Treason to us, except one of us two?

[2] Freud: *Civilization And Its Discontents*, V

[3] Cf. a remark of V. S. Pritchett's (apropos Vladimir Nabokov's novel *Lolita*, in the English edition of which it is quoted): 'By what perversion of moral judgment does society regard murder as "clean" and sex as "dirty" as a subject?'

[4] Cf. Freud: 'a third person is at the best superfluous and in the extreme case is condemned to a state of painful expectancy'. (*Group Psychology And The Analysis Of The Ego*, X, footnote)

[5] *Crime And Punishment*

multitude of strange men at once. By his crime of aggression against
the estranged father, the soldier becomes a hero. The fortunes of war
are a massive lateral extension of the prostitute's lottery principle.
The soldier is another homeless adventurer, a prostitute of violence,
perhaps; for, unlike Don Giovanni, he is paid for his services.

However, if Don Giovanni were to attain to full heroic status, he
would at least keep all the glory for himself. Here the soldier contrasts
with him. Although the soldier's glory is so much more glorious and
socially respectable, he has to share it with his comrades. Don Giovanni,
on the other hand, is never one of a troupe. The nearest he comes to
comradeship is with his henchman, who is always shocked by Don
Giovanni's latest exploit and dissuasive about his next. Other men may
follow Don Giovanni's psychic pattern, but each is *a* Don Giovanni,
an entirely individual, new Don Giovanni: Don Giovanni will never
make them his allies. 'The soldier', on the other hand, means 'soldiers':
it is a type which is repeated throughout the army, a touch anonymous. The soldier is a number, a unit in a regiment, always the
unknown soldier.

Yet though we do not know *who*, we know *what* the soldier is:
he is one of the egalitarian band of brothers which, acting as a whole,
aggresses against the father. It is not one soldier but the army which is
the hero who usurps the father's possessions, rights and glory. In this
case, the father is the estranged father, the enemy; and his estranged
sons dare to attack him precisely because they are a fraternity, united
by equal sacrifices, with the result that no one man incurs more of the
guilt than his brothers. In an army this is ensured by the lottery principle of the fortunes of war: the chances of doing the crime and of
being punished for it by death are distributed, no one knows in
what proportions, throughout the ranks.

15. *The Sparagmos (with a non-psychological Note on Beans)*

Freud[1] has shewn us precisely this principle operating in another
scene of violence, the totem feast where the whole community tears
up and eats the animal father[2].

[1] *Totem And Taboo*, IV

[2] Cf. Frazer's multifarious examples from primitive practice of 'the homeopathic magic of a flesh diet' (*Spirits Of The Corn And Of The Wild*, XII). To
eat an animal is to possess oneself of its specific virtues of strength, courage,

The tearing in pieces, the sparagmos, is the group's and the individual's safeguard. Everyone gets and eats a piece; the divine essence is distributed among the sons, and so is the guilt of the crime: and thus it serves as the sacrament which ratifies the group's grouphood. Even when totemism has given place to animal sacrifice and the worshippers have forgotten that the animal was the god, the ancient taboo rule holds good: the whole of the animal's body must be consumed at the sacramental occasion, because it is full of the father's ambivalent taboo power. If an individual comes on some of this dangerous material that has been left over, he is tempted: he risks incurring personally the penalties of usurping the father's power, and the group is in danger from him because he will have taken into himself some of the father's glory without sharing it with his brothers. Therefore *Exodus* rules[1] that 'if ought of the flesh of the consecrations, or of the bread, remain unto the morning, then thou shalt burn the remainder with fire: it shall not be eaten, because it is holy'—which is at the same time a perfect example of the ambivalence of the primitive concept of holiness, and also of taboo's resemblance to an infection[2].

The primitive totem, originally always an animal, may by extension be also a plant[(3)]. Christianity in a sense revived the totem animal when it equated the sacramental food with the sacrificial lamb of the Jews, but the tangible forms of the food are the vegetable substances of bread and wine. It was Frazer who pointed out that this was a revival of the notion that to eat cereal was to eat Ceres herself, and to drink the wine sacred to him was to drink Bacchus's blood. The sacramental meaning of this idea had been so thoroughly lost that Cicero had remarked that to call corn Ceres and wine Bacchus was a mere figure of speech, which no one was insane enough to believe literally—on which Frazer commented that 'the Roman philosopher little foresaw that in Rome itself . . . the belief which he here

cunning or whatever; that is, to eat the animal, whose freedom from restraint reminds one of the father, is to acquire the father's freedom. The homeopathic magic of a divine diet is that to eat the god puts one in a (god-like) state of grace.

[1] XXIX, 34—on the subject of the ram sacrifice in the consecration of priests

[2] Freud: 'The magic power attributed to taboo goes back to its ability to lead man into temptation; it behaves like a contagion, because the example is contagious . . .' (*Totem And Taboo*, II, 2)

[(3)] Freud: *Totem And Taboo*, IV, i

stigmatises as insane was destined to persist for thousands of years'[1]

Having re-asserted the identity of the edible victim with the god, Christianity applied to its sacrament the essential rules of the totem feast for assuring the equal guilt of all the fraternity members. The god's body is parcelled out in wafers, and the god is symbolically subjected to a sparagmos when the priest breaks the Host. The rule that the whole taboo-ful meal must be eaten up at once holds good in the sense that consecrated Hosts may only be reserved by the Church, with proper precautions. For a communicant to refrain from eating the Host given him and carry it away is a dangerous crime likely to bring taboo penalties on the criminal—as we can see from Uccello's minatory chronicle-picture[2], which relates how a woman, who has kept back a Host in this way, lets it come into the hands of Jews, who attempt to destroy it: it proves indestructible and magic—it bleeds when maltreated: and, the crime being thus discovered, the Jewish family is burned, the woman executed and the Host ceremonially returned to the safekeeping of the Church.

Even in classical religion, the totemistic truth was not so utterly lost as the orthodox cults would imply. The Orphic sect (whatever, in precise, historical terms, that was) kept alive a more or less conscious identification between its mystic sacrificial animal and the god Dionysos (who, like all classical gods, was a father to mankind[3]). Worshippers of Dionysos practised[4] an impromptu sacrament (although there were days appointed for it, the victim was not kept for the purpose but was picked on wild during the wanderings of the worshippers) where an animal (perhaps on occasion a human) was set on by the frenzied group and subjected alive to sparagmos, the pieces of the body being eaten raw. The rite commemorated (or perhaps was later justified by the invention of) the myth that, during his infancy, the animal-god Dionysos-Zagreus was set on by the fraternity of the

---

[1] *Spirits Of The Corn And Of The Wild*, XII, citing *De Natura Deorum*, iii, 16. 41

[2] *The Profanation Of The Host*, Urbino

[3] e.g. Ovid: *Fasti*, III, 761; 789, where Dionysos is referred to, and addressed as, *pater*

[4] not only in Greece but also in Rome and Roman Italy, where there was a mass-hysterical outbreak of Dionysian orgies in 186 B.C., which the authorities had the utmost difficulty in suppressing (Mommsen: *History Of Rome*, III, XIII)

Titans, who tore him up, cooked and ate him—after which he was miraculously resurrected.[1]

The Orphic devotees preserved to the full the ambivalence of the primitive totem tribe, which, when it is not performing the violent tribal sacrament against the totem animal, abstains absolutely from harming the totem species or eating its flesh. This rule the Orphics extended from a single sacred species to the whole animal kingdom. At their sacrament, the victim might be any animal: conversely, their gentleness at other times was extended to all animals and they abstained from all animal flesh.

(It is a hitherto unexplained curiosity that the Orphic rule was to abstain from meat, fish—and beans[2]. As a matter of fact, this is only one instance of the ancient world's superstitious attitude to beans, which played a part in several religious and folk ceremonies[3]. Commenting on one of these[4], even Frazer confesses himself baffled. 'In antiquity beans were the subject of such a tangle of superstitions that it is seldom or never possible to single out the separate threads and follow them up to their starting-point in the muzzy brain of primitive man'[5]—a desperate resort for Frazer, who was usually primitive man's prime apologist and was, in fact, the first to demonstrate that primitive thought, though unrealistic, was by no means unmotivated.

(If I may allow my readers the luxury of a non-psychological explanation for once, I think the trouble was that Frazer never went into the kitchen. If you put fresh broad beans in water and boil them, they give out a light red liquid which gradually turns the boiling water the colour of blood. No doubt primitive man observed that when beans are maltreated by boiling them they bleed —rather like that other sacred vegetable substance, the Host in Uccello's picture. Primitive man concluded that in some magical, probably ghostly, way beans were really animals, and treated them as such in his totemistic religious ceremonies; and beans are

---

[1] Smith's *Dictionary Of . . . Antiquities*; E. R. Dodds: *The Greeks And The Irrational*, V

[2] Smith's *Dictionary Of . . . Antiquities*, 'Orphica'

[3] Smith's *Antiquities* suggests, for example, that the Orphic prohibition against beans may be accounted for by the use of beans at funerals—itself unexplained, of course.

[4] the burning of beanstalks, at the Parilia, as described by Ovid in *Fasti*, IV, 734

[5] Appendix (note on IV, 733) to Frazer's (Loeb) edition of Ovid's *Fasti*

really included under the heading of animals in the Orphic rule[1].)

The baby Zagreus is only one of several fathers and heroic father-replacers to be subjected in myths to sparagmos. (There is no contradiction in a baby being a father—witness the cult of the infant Christ. Zagreus's and Christ's divinity assures them of father-status in any case; and as a matter of fact the myth emphasises their infancy in order to shew them as aspiring supplanters of the father, at the very moment of the Oedipal crisis.) Sparagmos is, indeed, the distinguishing mark of the totemistic victim, who is so full of the father's mana that only the parcelling out of the guilt among his assassins makes his murder possible. But although the murder takes place, it still has to be compensated for, and this is done by maintaining that the father is not really dead at all but immortal or resurrected. Just as the totem animal is automatically resurrected in the person of the next animal of his species to fall into the tribe's hands (indeed, he is perpetually immortal in the perpetuity of the totem species), so, when myth sets to work on his anthropomorphic equivalent, it frequently records that his body is pieced together again after the sparagmos and that he is resurrected or deified—made immortal. Between the as yet untheologised idea of the totem animal's resurrection by virtue of its species and the full-grown myth of a murdered god's personal resurrection (though this, if the resurrection is commemorated annually, is still linked to the yearly renewal, the immortality, of plant species), there are intermediate stages. When the worshippers have eaten the flesh, the skin of a sacrificed animal may be stuffed and the animal set up again, resurrected.[2] A more sophisticated theology will devise a doctrine of reincarnation[3]. When the god has become personal and

---

[1] While this book was in the press I found my whole theory confirmed by Lucian's dialogue *Philosophies For Sale* (6), where Pythagoras is asked why he abstains from beans as well as meat. He replies that beans are holy, one of his reasons for thinking so being that 'if you boil them and put them out in the moonlight . . . you will make blood'.

[2] This happened to the ox murdered at the Bouphonia (Frazer: *Spirits Of The Corn And Of The Wild*, IX)

[3] By some versions of the myth, the soul of Osiris removed itself, after his death, into the sacred bull Apis, who then remained perpetually alive by a series of personal reincarnations. The idea that the Apis *was* Osiris, who had already suffered totemistically once and for all, probably accounts for the fact that the Apis, unlike so many holy animals, was allowed to live his life out. When he did die, of natural causes, he was deeply mourned, and the

anthropomorphic, he may be resurrected whole; or perpetually preserved or renewed in the pieces of his sparagmos; or both, like Christ, who is annually (yet also perpetually, and yet again only once, historically) resurrected, and also immortally renewed, since the fund of pieces of his body never fails—except on Good Fridays[1]. Orpheus, in name at least the inspiration of the mystery cult of Dionysos, the great father of the Dionysian church, was himself the victim of a Dionysian sacrifice: the saint imitates the pattern of the suffering original. After his sparagmos, his body was pieced together by the Muses, and he attained the sort of immortality which really is accessible to poets, in the currency of the hymns attributed to him—together with a fabulous apotheosis whereby his lyre was placed among the stars.

The motif of the worshippers comforting themselves that their victim is not really dead is carried a stage further when the victim actually offers himself for the sacrifice and commands his followers to renew and re-offer his sparagmos. Christ, of course, is the supreme example here, but as a matter of fact a presage of his self-sacrifice had already crept into the Greco-Roman animal sacrifice. The rule was that the animal must go willingly to its death (it was a bad omen otherwise)[2]. When we think about these sad animals, whose carnage was written-in to the classical religion, it is this terrible fancy of their willingness which most violently displays man's sanctimoniousness— that is to say the hypocrisy to which his ambivalence condemns him; and at the same time this sanctimonious rule confirms that the victim originally was the god and his killing a crime, because otherwise there would be no need for the rule to exist.

The whole totemistic nexus is most tellingly exemplified by the Egyptian myth of Osiris, who, being identified with the sun[3], is another annual—indeed, both a diurnal and an annual—resurrection- ist. Osiris, great benefactor and educator of his people (it is an interest- ing totemistic pointer that he was said to be the first person to induce

---

priests had the task of seeking out his reincarnation, another animal not merely of the same species but personally recognisable by the same distinguishing marks as his predecessor. (Diodorus Siculus, I, 85)

[1] when there is no Mass.

[2] Smith's *Dictionary Of . . . Antiquities*, 'Sacrificium'. The rule enabled Ovid, for example, to refer to heifers 'offering' their necks to the axe—colla . . . praebent ferienda iuvenci (*Fasti*, I, 83)

[3] Diodorus Siculus, I, II. Frazer (*Adonis Attis Osiris*, Volume II, VII) doubts whether Osiris was originally the sun

mankind to give up cannibalism[1]), was the victim of a conspiracy led by his brother, who wanted to usurp the throne: (a *Hamlet*-like displacement of what is, in the primal and family situation, the son's wish to usurp the father's place. We can perhaps guess that Osiris himself was once a member of a fraternity which usurped the original father, that he was singled out to become Big Brother and did not manage to avoid the jealousy of one of his subaltern brothers. And in genealogical fact, Osiris is the son of a pair of proto-deities, an earth god and a sky goddess, whom the Greeks identified with Kronos and Rhea, the parents of Zeus[2]. No doubt the Greeks were right in sensing that Osiris, like Zeus, was really a heroic supplanter of the father, and arrived bringing the memory of his forefathers with him. This probably accounts for another item in the myth, where there has again been a displacement from the primary to a secondary degree of kinship. Osiris, in raising himself from the son's to the father's position, has not dared quite to fulfil the son's primary incest wish, but contents himself with breaking one of the father's secondary prohibitions: he is married to his sister Isis.) After Osiris has been murdered, his body is chopped up into twenty-six[3] pieces, the chief conspirator giving one piece to each of his lieutenants.

Diodorus's account of the Egyptian myth states quite specifically the motive for this sparagmos, and it is the one Freud inferred in the case of the totem feast: 'he wanted them all to share the pollution, by which method he thought he would have them as firm coadjutors and guardians of his government'[4].

The widowed Isis, however, avenges the murder and collects the fragments of Osiris's body, which she treats as though they were so many Hosts. She enshrines each piece, as though in a monstrance, in a wax statue of Osiris, and distributes the twenty-six statues to twenty-six groups of priests, each of which buries its own statue and institutes a cultus at the burial-place of the god. At the same time, Isis gives a specific command that the father-quality of Osiris be transferred

[1] Diodorus Siculus, I, 14

[2] Frazer: *Adonis Attis Osiris*, Volume II, I

[3] according to Diodorus Siculus. The number varies in various accounts (Frazer: *Adonis Attis Osiris*, Volume II, I): it is the fact of sparagmos which matters.

[4] Diodorus Siculus, I, 21: . . . βουλόμενον πάντας μετασχεῖν τοῦ μύσους, καὶ διὰ τούτου νομίζοντα συναγωνιστὰς ἕξειν καὶ φύλακας τῆς βασιλείας βεβαίους.

into a quasi-totem animal: each group of priests is to choose an animal from those native to the particular district and consecrate it to Osiris; while the animal lives, it is to be honoured as though it were Osiris, and when it dies be given a funeral like his.

The fragments of Osiris's body are not, however, all of equal value. The twenty-six whose history has been traced are; and the twenty-six subordinate conspirators have equal shares in the guilt: but it is a subordinate part of the guilt which is apportioned between them. The very essence of Osiris's taboo, of his father-status, is contained in the part of his body by whose exercise he is capable of becoming a father. It is the sexual organs which the chief conspirator takes as his part of the body—which is why, we may surmise, he is confident of remaining the chief. When Isis pursues him, he throws them into the Nile, and they are never recovered; Isis has to have an effigy made and venerated[1]. When the chief murderer throws away his booty, he throws away his chance of ever replacing Osiris in the position of communal father and, like Brutus, dooms himself to die in expiation of his crime. There is nothing for it but for Osiris, like Julius Caesar, to rise again and reign immortal.

Thus the myth brings us back to the very crisis of the conflict between father and sons, the crisis of castrate or be castrated. As a matter of fact, we can add to the meaning of sparagmos. A sparagmos is always an expression of the sons' wish to castrate the father. What happens at the murder of Osiris, where there is a chief conspirator, is the very thing which does *not* happen when the group is acting as a perfectly egalitarian fraternity without a leader. In that case, the whole series of dismembered pieces of the body stands as a disguise for the one all-important member. The lottery principle is making sure that the phallos *will* be removed but that, once removed, it will be lost to sight in the raffle.

Indeed, the whole idea of killing the father presents itself to the infantile mind primarily as the surest method of castrating the father, which is itself the most absolute method of preventing him from castrating his son. When the father triumphs over death, he is really triumphing over castration. His resurrection is the renewal of his generative powers. The totem animal is immortal simply in the generative power of its species; and when mythology accords the

[1] which Diodorus, in his anxiety to prove that the Greek Dionysos was really the Egyptian Osiris, compares with the phallic worship in the Dionysian mysteries. (Diodorus Siculus, I, 22)

god a personal resurrection it does so in terms of metaphors no less recognisable, in which the central point of similarity, round which the metaphor is built, is that the dead lie down—they cannot move or raise themselves—just as the quiescent sexual organ lies down; and when the organ re-asserts its sexual power it does so by rising again.

The ox which was murdered at the Bouphonia was resurrected by being stuffed—that is to say, it was set up again[1] (and the Commendatore cannot return to the struggle and inflict on Don Giovanni what Don Giovanni has inflicted on him until he has been re-erected in the form of a statue). The same metaphor lends its shape to the career of the god or the hero who (as Christ did after his death and Orpheus did before his, foreshadowing his castration-by-sparagmos and resurrection) descends into Hell, the realm of death, and comes up again. The god's resurrection is easily linked with the springtime resurrection of the plants which phallically push up their shoots and rise again—also from beneath the earth. Indeed, Osiris's powers of resurrection caused him to be amalgamated both with the corn[2] itself and with the sun whose repeated resurrections makes the resurrection of the corn possible. Osiris's myth leaves us in no doubt that the god's triumph over death is the phallos's triumph over castration. One version of the story relates that Isis, hovering in the form of a hawk over her husband's dead body, conceived a child by him[3]. Her presence above the inert thing, the corpse and its powerless sexual organ, conjures the god—just as his mistress's name is meant to conjure Romeo—to rise again.[4]

[1] —'the stuffed animal was set on its feet and yoked to a plough as if it were ploughing' (Frazer: *Spirits Of The Corn And Of The Wild*, IX); that is, the animal was set up again at its task, which is no longer a sexual one from the animal's point of view, of making the earth fertile for agricultural man.

[2] Frazer: *Adonis Attis Osiris*, Volume II, V, 1, 'Osiris a Corn-God'

[3] Frazer: *Adonis Attis Osiris*, Volume II, I

[4] Frazer tells us that 'in the chambers dedicated to him at Philae the dead god is portrayed lying on his bier in an attitude which indicates in the plainest way that even in death his generative virtue was not extinct'. (No wonder that, as Diodorus records, the oath 'by Osiris who lies at Philae' was the strongest an Egyptian could swear.) The exact sexual meaning of resurrection as rising again was no doubt demonstrated by the 'obscene images' of Osiris, which Frazer reluctantly mentions—images which the women used to carry round the villages at the festival of Osiris and which 'they set in motion by means of strings'. (Frazer: *Adonis Attis Osiris*, Volume II, V, 3; Diodorus Siculus, I, 22)

16. *The Unheavenly Father*

If the group's fury against its communal god is primarily a rage to castrate the father, exactly the same is true of a group's fury against its public enemy. A group's ambition towards an enemy country is to cut off its young men before they beget children; and this is incidentally a gratification of the group's sexual instinct by turning the enemy's young men into girls.

The rage against the god is, however, set loose and legitimised only on the occasions of the group's sacrament. At all other times, and whenever a member of the group is acting individually, the god must be venerated—or his predecessor, the totem animal, must be spared and cherished. This, we can see as soon as we have recognised the enemy as an external father to the group, is a precise parallel to the paradox at the heart of human civilisation, the fact that whereas murder (and particularly, under the rules of hospitality, the murder of a stranger) is an abhorrent crime, war is legitimate. The actual killers in a war are only the hirelings of the nation at large, and none of them bears more or less of the guilt than any other of the citizens. The guilt of the double crime, aggression plus homosexual assault, is distributed among the members of the community, and only this distribution renders war legitimate. War is, in effect, the community's external sacrament.

This distribution we can achieve, in the case of war, without inflicting a sparagmos on the father we murder. We have no need to: the enemy, although we refer to him in the singular, is already broken up into innumerable pieces—all his soldiers, all his citizens. He has made this obliging provision for us because, from his point of view, it is we who are singular and he who is the band of brothers. He and we are in a reciprocal relation, in which each represents father to the other.

The numericalness of the enemy—even in the simple sense, whereby his numbers frighten us and hold us off—serves to keep the enemy at a distance from us (just as *her* lottery principle keeps the father distant from the prostitute). This distance, this strangeness, between a nation and its enemy is like the distance between an Ego and its Ego-ideal —which is also modelled on the father; and we have remarked that

the enemy performs some of the functions of the Ego-ideal. Not that
the enemy *is* the nation's Ego-ideal. On the contrary: he is its counter-
ideal. Whereas the ideal is everything we should like to be and fear
we shall never be good enough to become, the enemy is what we
should hate to be and dread becoming[1]. And, whereas the Ego feels
itself the unworthy object of criticisms directed against it by its ideal,
it is, by contrast, the nation which unceasingly criticises the enemy for
his shortcomings.

Now we are beginning to understand just in what sense the enemy
represents our father. He represents the deteriorated or debased image
of the father; he is the bad strange man, just as the prostitute, who
represents and has identified herself with the debased image of the
mother, is the bad strange woman. We are quite familiar with these
alternative images, exalted and debased, in mythology, where they
present themselves as god and devil; animal-cum-anthropomorphic
god, and miscegeneous monster; madonna, and witch or bitch. This
resolution of the father into a native Ego-ideal, probably embodied
in our own leader, and a foreign counter-ideal embodied in the
enemy is part of the Ego's attempt to sort out the ambivalent strains
of its emotion towards the father and create one father who can be
simply loved and one who can be purely hated.

The attempt for ever fails. We do not purely hate the enemy:
any more than we purely love the god against whom we aggress
so violently at our totem festivals and Masses. On the contrary: we
are so fascinated by the enemy that we never take our eyes off him;
and our love for him comes to direct expression in the homosexual
metaphor concealed in the act of killing him in war. Even our feeling
that we should hate to be like him plays us false. No sooner has war
started than retaliation gives us our excuse for imitating the enemy.
If he bombs civilians or uses poison gas, then we do too. By the
same token we withdraw some of our criticisms of him: bombing
civilians cannot be so bad after all if we are permitted by our Ego-ideal
to do it too. Striving to catch up our Ego-ideal, we find we have caught
and made ourselves resemble the counter-ideal. In effect, ideal and
counter-ideal are rapidly interchangeable; the execrated enemy merges
with the idealised internal leader. If we recognise that the sacrificed
animal, who is killed because he is said to be the enemy of the god,

[1] Not only do we dread becoming as bad (barbaric, decadent, undemo-
cratic) as the enemy; we dread quite literally that he will conquer us and transform our nationality into his own, making us him.

really *is* the god, what of the foe whom we kill because he is said to be the enemy of our ideal?

We have come full cycle—back to the fundamental identity between God and God's enemy, the devil. This identity, which genetically depends on the fact that both images are descended from the image of the father, depends economically on the fact that the devil is indispensable to God. 'The devil is, in fact, the best way out in acquittal of God,' Freud remarked[1]. If we are to keep our hatred of God under any sort of restraint, if we are to manage to love him at all, then we must keep the devil in existence too. Neither Job nor the Christian could afford to purely hate Satan; that is to say, they could not annihilate Satan, by removing their attention from him utterly, because to do so would be a crime against God: that portion of the aggressive impulses which has been diverted against Satan and found an economic outlet there would promptly be switched back to God and would murder God.

God's economic dependence on Satan is paralleled by a government's economic (in the sense of psychic economy) dependence on enemies abroad: government at home is only possible so long as there is a supply of enemies outside. Thus we can understand the actual psychic content, the moment-to-moment working, of the identification between enemy and father. It is no mere coincidence in our psychic history that the image of the enemy has grown out of the father: it is a naked fact of psychic economics that we cannot aggress against the enemy without becoming guilty of an aggression against the father. Any one enemy country we may of course attack, even destroy. What we cannot do is dry up the supply of enemies; we cannot destroy and annihilate the whole concept of national enemies without harming our internal leaders and ideals.

Mankind's political refusal to submit to supra-national authority resembles its persistent refusal to accept monotheism. Many civilisations held out for a long time against even a nominal monotheism. Greco-Roman polytheism, for example, was akin to our international anarchy of sovereign states. Each sovereign god retained the undivided ambivalence of the taboo-possessor and, like our nation-states, might be fiend or divinity according to whose side you were on and who was paying off scores against whom. The process of sorting out the exalted images from fusion with the debased, and of grouping the two kinds into two distinct camps, had only begun—

[1] *Civilization And Its Discontents*, VI

notably in the antithesis between heavenly Zeus and his infernal brother, Hades, and in the grouping together of all the heavenly deities under the chairmanship of Zeus—when polytheism yielded to Christianity. Even so, the new monotheism (itself a good deal less monotheistic, with its Trinity, than Judaism) *was* only nominal. No religion has ever been truly monotheistic, because no religion has annihilated that counter-god, the devil.

If we do not accept religion's own terminology but simply describe its mythology dispassionately, we have to describe the devil as a god (just as we have to describe the angels, with whom religion classes him, as lesser gods) because he is supernatural and immortal. Immortality is the loving gift we confer on our public father to make amends for our crime of murdering him, to expiate our guilt, to comfort ourselves that it was really not such a bad crime since it did not end him finally—and to make it possible for us to commit the crime against him all over again, to eternity. Just so with our public enemy. Nothing better demonstrates our secret love for him than that we never knock him down without setting him up—resurrecting—him again. We have made him immortal—by our refusal to eradicate war. Of course, his is not a personal immortality. He has to undertake many rapid transmigrations of soul—like the one whereby everything the Germans represented to us in 1944 was represented to us a decade later by the Russians. What we will not do without is *an* enemy.

By immortalising our enemies, we immortalise war, just as, once the god is immortal (or the totem animal in his species), the feast at which our hatred of him is legitimised becomes a recurrent festival. Moreover, we can now understand the part the enemy plays in the cycle which carries us successively through a self-complacent peace and into the combined crisis of melancholia and mania which is what a war is. Since we really do incur guilt for our incursions on the enemy, our remorse when we conquer him is the unbearable remorse of having conquered the father, a remorse which we can expiate only by setting the father up again and hazarding ourselves as sacrifices to him. The defeated have at least the satisfaction of having been punished. Probably it is the position of the victors which is the more intolerable psychologically, and it is in the guilt of the victors that we see the start of the next war—often in the falling out of former allies over the apportionment of their spoils. Here is the lottery of war extended into a new, grandiose field; we have become possessed by gambling fever. Our spoils (whether they are territorial and tangible or consist in prestige, the father's mana, the right to decree whether 'democracy' shall be a word of praise or execration) sit uneasily on us because we have incurred guilt in getting them. We feel, in fact, that they do not belong to us, but to the game; and we are not appeased until we have thrown them back into the game and, risking the unbearable victory of winning still more, risk also the absolute loss of everything we have.

Primitive communities, which insist on ritually purging the warrior's guilt (even though the community commissioned him to kill the enemy), have probably found a means of limiting the guilt of war. It is a fixed quantity of guilt which moves round a closed circuit from crime to expiation. We, however, have lifted the guilt from the soldier and placed it square on the community—only to deny, to repress, the fact that it *is* guilt. We represent our own and the enemy's aggressions as the virtue of self-interested patriotism; and as for the soldier's part in the matter, we have so euphemised him that we are barely capable of stating the plain facts of what his profession consists of. A member of the public can say (it is only an extra irony that the man she is speaking of is a murderer): 'I know he would never deliberately harm anybody. His whole ambition was to be a soldier like his dad'[1].

As soon as one community—the Romans, for example, among the Italian tribes—breaks out of the primitive equilibrium and stagnation, it embarks on a cumulative course of guilt. The advance into civilisation is accompanied by an advance in the methods of waging war—and a retrogression in our ability to wipe out our guilt from a war by any other means than hazarding ourselves in the next one. As Ovid said about one of the supreme examples of civilisation's gambling fever, if she had not taken arms against the whole world Rome would still be full of straw huts[2].

Civilised communities sometimes attempt to limit the guilt they incur during a war by limiting the crime committed. Codes of warfare confine the belligerents to chivalrous ways of harming people: beleaguered populations may be starved but not poisoned, women and children may not be maimed by any method other than widowing and orphaning them. But usually we set ourselves these limits only to overstep them—or else to break out in some still more barbaric

[1] reported in the *Daily Express*, 22 January 1960

[2] *Amores*, II, IX, 17-18: Roma nisi inmensum vires movisset in orbem,/ stramineis esset nunc quoque tecta casis

direction, which does not contravene the rules only because it is so horrible that when the rules were drawn up no one thought of ruling it out. Making rules for ourselves, we behave like the neurotic who, in his self-destructive pessimism, agrees with himself to take as a bad omen something he surely knows will happen. The net result of the existence of rules is simply to blacken our guilt when we break them. Thucydides certainly means us to suppose that the Athenians lost the Peloponnesian War because of the inexcusable and unprovoked atrocities they had committed during it. He speaks in theological imagery borrowed from the tragic dramatists, and implies that destiny punished the Athenians for hubris; but if we translate him into psychological terms we can perfectly well credit him and read that the Athenians' sense of guilt was determined to bring on their punishment. But unfortunately there is not a word of comfort in the lesson, which simply teaches us that conscience more easily makes defeatists of the more civilised side. For a nation to recognise its own wrongdoing may be a sign of grace in the theologian's eyes and of civilisation in the historian's; but from the practical point of view of the moralist, conscious remorse is as wasteful as unconscious guilt and hardly less dangerous. If the Athenians really felt sinful, they took the logical course of prolonging the war and their expiatory suffering until they underwent a total and bloody defeat which was ultimately fatal to the whole of antique civilisation.

The primitive still retains enough knowledge of his own guilt to expiate acts of war by ritual means; but the community which has achieved a more highly developed consciousness of itself as a community has banished guilt from its community consciousness. It has legitimised war by parcelling out the guilt among the fraternity; and this parcelling out serves once again as a repression; the guilt is lost to sight among the series. Even so, it might be possible to confine war to merely reproducing itself from generation to generation. Sometimes, when war is the sport of monarchs and the monarchs are locked in a carefully arranged balance of power, something of the sort does happen for a while. But by its very nature, which is that of a gamble, war cannot be guaranteed to equalise things out by always defeating the nation which was the victor last time. The very variation in the depth of unconscious guilt two communities will incur for the same amount of crime ensures that the equilibrium will be broken and sooner or later someone will emerge into the intolerable position of an unpunished victor. Among civilised nations, therefore, the unconscious need to be punished is cumulative; and consequently the wars in which we seek punishment grow progressively more violent. Apart from imperialistic frontier incidents and one or two anachronistic throwbacks to earlier fashions, we regularly expect each war to be worse than the one before; and we have rarely been disappointed, since the time when Thucydides began his history: 'Thucydides an Athenian chronicled the war of the Peloponnesians and Athenians as they waged it, having begun his task as soon as the war broke out in the expectation that the war would be great and worth discussing beyond its predecessors . . .'[1]

Our gambling fever compels us to pursue this progressive course until we can expunge for ever the possibility of anyone's being the victor. This is precisely what we have now arrived within sight of: a war from which no one will emerge the victor because no one will emerge. Now that we are within striking distance of our objective, there has been an interesting change in our methods of subterraneanly making war probable while consciously trying to avert it. In old-fashioned warmongering, we used to attribute all the evil intentions and the fatal moves to the villainous foreigner, even while we covertly did our utmost to provoke him. Now, under the shadow of the final war, we admit our collusion with the foreigner openly. Even the most ill-educated jingoist has seen the folly of blaming it all on the foreigners. He can recognise that, to the foreigners, he is a foreigner; and he admits the foreigner is much the same sort of person as himself. But by this he does not mean that he and the foreigner are alike possessed of a raging wish to kill, and a wish to be punished for that wish so insatiable that they will provoke or procure someone into killing them in return—a wish to attack civilisation and to be punished for it by the utter destruction of civilisation. No: he means that he and the foreigner are both decent civilised fellows who could never wish anything of the kind.

If we ask under what shield we perform this monstrous suppression of the facts about our human nature, the answer is science. Science has brought us to the pitch where our wars really can destroy civilisation; and science provides us with our excuse for unconsciously doing our best to do it. Primitive thought did not believe in the independence of external nature, but attributed every event of which the human mind took cognisance to a wish in some human mind. In various theological guises, this primitive animism survived the first—

[1] I, 1

the Greek—scientific revolution and became embodied in Christianity, which attributed omnipotence not to human but to divine wishes. It was not until the second scientific revolution of the sixteenth and seventeenth centuries that—at least for educated people—God's hold was broken, nature was given back its autonomy and we recognised that earthquake and tempest were not manifestations of God's wishes responding to impious wishes on our part, but simple extraneous accidents.

Now, however, having recognised that there is an autonomous natural system and having developed a dozen sciences for exploring its natural laws (laws, that is, which are not willed by anybody), we have equipped ourselves with a perfect screen on to which we may project those of our own wishes which we will not acknowledge. We shield ourselves from recognising them by calling them accidents and attributing them to natural law. Our collusion with the enemy takes the form of exculpating both him and ourselves, arguing that neither of us wants a war; if we are likely to get one, it is because we have both been overwhelmed by certain natural laws operating in human civilisation which are beyond our control—including a law, even, of 'human error', as though Freud had never shewn us that there are no non-significant human errors. In our feeble attempts to diagnose the causes of war, which are feeble precisely because we are determined not to let them succeed, we call in the help of economics, geography, sociology—any science, in fact, except those which are capable of displaying to us the instincts of living beings: biology and its top branch, psycho-analysis, the science of the human unconscious.

Like any tragic hero, we have projected our own unconscious wish on to the heavens and have only to wait here until the heavens let it fall on us; we call it not destiny but natural law. Telling both sides they are not to blame for war, we imply that they can do nothing to prevent it; this is our contribution to making it come. The primitive stood in the thunderstorm believing it had been conjured about his head by his own sin of breaking a taboo rule, or by the malicious desires of a witch or the vengeful desires of a god. We conjure war about our heads and persuade ourselves that there is no more con-nexion between this and our wishes than, so we have discovered, there really is between thunderstorms and our wishes; and this allows us to cry:

then, let fall
Your horrible pleasure; here I stand, your slave . . .

It is our modern inversion of the pathetic fallacy. The pleasure is really not heaven's but our own.

17. 'It IS Beethoven'

We are, therefore, utterly mistaken if we hope there will be no new war on the grounds that neither side can win it. That is more likely to allure both sides towards war. As Edward Glover has remarked, 'the actual and potential destructiveness of the atomic bomb plays straight into the hands of the Unconscious. The most cursory study of dreamlife and of the phantasies of the insane shows that ideas of world-destruction (more accurately destruction of what the world symbolizes) are latent in the unconscious mind . . . Nagasaki destroyed by the magic of science is the nearest man has yet approached to the realization of dreams that even during the safe immobility of sleep are accustomed to develop into nightmares of anxiety.'[1]

As a matter of fact, mankind has long set before itself the vision of a violent end to human civilisation, to the human race itself; and the idea of punishment, of a final settling and expiation of all guilts, has always been part of the vision. The confusion, terror and nakedness of mankind in that moment, and even the landscape of an atom-devastated world, were imagined four and a half centuries ago by Luca Signorelli and can be seen in his end-of-the-world frescoes in Orvieto cathedral. The Christian awaited the day of reckoning divided between joy and dread: it was still a lottery, like an old-fashioned war, and his own part might be the victor's; though, even so, nothing could outweigh for him, as for the individual soldier in a war, the chances that his own individual lot might be total destruction. De-Christianised, the vision of salvation for some and damnation for others yields to the vision of the complete and reciprocal destruction of everyone, and gives us *Götterdämmerung*. There is no longer even an unsuccessful attempt to divide the joy and the dread between the images of Heaven and Hell. They are fused. No one who has experienced *Götterdämmerung* can doubt its joy; and it is the joy of pure destruction.

Nothing is new in our present prospect except its scientific trappings.

[1] *War, Sadism And Pacifism*, XIV

Or, rather, we have merely exchanged the language of the old science of theology for the newer one of the natural sciences. In one respect Christian theology was more up to date than Wagner's. Whereas Wagner had to set his in a distant mythological past, Christianity could set its dies irae exactly where science fiction or political probability sets it now: just round the corner in the near future. When the belief that it would come before the expiry of Christ's generation[1], or at least St Paul's[2], had been belied by history, it was converted into the expectation of a millennium due six thousand years (to correspond to the six days of the Creation) after the founding of the world[(3)] or variously expected whenever the rounder numbers of the Christian era came in sight.

However, the world was never in genuine danger from the Christian god. It is we who, disappointed of God's or the Wagnerian gods' ability to put our fantasy into effect, have transferred our allegience to our new god, science. This, of course, is a god whom we can manipulate into giving real performances. If we want it to, this magic really works.

The beauty and joy of our destructive fantasies, and how essentially fantastic they are, is what is brought home to us by Bernard Shaw's masterpiece *Heartbreak House*. First the whole truth about our personal sadistic fantasies in an erotic context is summed up by Hesione Hushabye's dictum[(4)] 'Yes: cruelty would be delicious if one could only find some sort of cruelty that didnt really hurt'. (Compare this with Freud's observations on the common childish masturbation fantasy whose content is that a child is being beaten. 'It might . . . be expected', he says, 'that the sight of another child being beaten at school would also be a source of similar enjoyment. But as a matter of fact this was never so. The experience of real scenes . . . produced in the child who witnessed them a peculiarly excited feeling . . . in which repugnance had a large share. In a few cases the real experience . . . was felt to be intolerable. Moreover, it was always a condition

---

[1] '. . . there be some standing here, which shall not taste of death, till they see the Son of man coming in his kingdom' (*Matthew*, XVI, 28; and also *Mark*, IX, 1; *Luke*, IX, 27) '. . . this generation shall not pass, till all these things be fulfilled' (*Matthew*, XXIV, 34; and also *Mark*, XIII, 30)

[2] '. . . we which are alive and remain unto the coming of the Lord . . . Then we which are alive and remain shall be caught up together with them in the clouds, to meet the Lord in the air' (*I Thessalonians*, IV, 15- . . . 17)

[(3)] Gibbon: *The Decline And Fall* . . ., XV, II   [(4)] Act II

even of the elaborated phantasies of later years that the punishment should do the children no serious injury.'[1]) Then[2] the play moves on to mankind's group acts of destruction. Above the noise of the aeroplane and the bombs (those, to us, quaint, amateur, ineffectual, nineteen-sixteenish aeroplanes and bombs: Shaw, the perfect Wagnerite, knows that Wagner's day has not yet come) we hear Hesione's transcendent 'Did you hear the explosions? And the sound in the sky: it's splendid: it's like an orchestra: it's like Beethoven'—and Ellie's triumphant reply, 'By thunder, Hesione: it *is* Beethoven'.

If we succumb to the beauty of this vision, it will be because Beethoven, Wagner, Signorelli and Shaw were not enough for us—art being precisely what Mrs Hushabye was looking for, a method of being cruel which does not hurt. In his letter to Albert Einstein, Freud points out that the effect of the evolution of culture has been to internalise man's aggressive impulse, that cultured people rebel against war as part of their evolutionary progress, hating its ugliness almost as much as its cruelty, because it is 'in the crassest opposition' to culture. 'We are pacifists because we are obliged to be for organic reasons.'[3] If in spite of this we get our war, it will be because we have gone against the grain of our evolution—indeed, subverted it. Whereas man first distinguished himself by intellect and imagination, we, while professing to educate our children, offer them anti-culture. We force the group mind upon them, with its anti-thought and anti-imagination. The heroes we offer them are world conquerors (our lessons themselves, let alone our social behaviour, make it clear we do not rate twenty thinkers and artists the equal of one world conqueror) and the saints and martyrs who lust to submit themselves to God or country in a voluptuous surrender and exquisite self-sacrifice, and whose virtue consists in their belief that it would be sinful—taboo— to allow reason to come in contact with God or country. We cannot be surprised if the group pays its unreasoning loyalty to some version or other—perhaps a deified Science—of that original superman, the primal bully; and, this being so, we cannot be surprised if the group, ambivalent as always, bullies its superman into leading it where it wants to go, namely to the destruction of civilisation.

[1] *Collected Papers*, Volume II, XVII   [2] Act III
[3] 1932. *Collected Papers*, Volume V, XXV

II

MORALITY FOR TODAY

1. *Two Mainstays*

Well then: if we are to save civilisation, we must re-form our attitude towards it.

I cannot pretend the task is anything short of monumental, even in its intellectual aspect, let alone the practical (which authors, not being vested with statutory powers, always have to leave to chance). It consists of thinking out what society *should* have taught Nathan Leopold—that is to say, constructing a new rationalism and laying the foundations of a twentieth-century morality.

Fortunately, the twentieth century, as I have already more than hinted to my readers, provides us with two great mainstays: Bernard Shaw and Sigmund Freud, respectively metabiologist and hyper-biologist. Historians of manners will note that both belong to the bearded company of Victorian giants and possessed all the solid respectability of family physicians (in which they contrast with many of the revolutionary thinkers of the eighteenth century). The ironist may discern, in the—purely literary—relationship between Shaw and Freud, a clash between Dublin's notion of respectability and the softer Jewish-Viennese version. Anyone could have predicted that the puritan Shaw would be shocked by Freud's disclosures about sexuality and that Freud would be for him, 'an author . . . utterly void of delicacy'—though even so, Shaw admitted, 'instructive'[1] (Shaw rarely contradicts the findings of psycho-analysis, though he is at pains to ignore them): but it is more surprising to discover, in Freud's reference to 'Bernard Shaw's malicious aphorism to the effect that being in love means greatly exaggerating the difference between

[1] Shaw: *Sixteen Self-Sketches*, IX

one woman and another'[1], a miniscule hint that Freud—and on the very subject of sexuality—had been shocked by the Voltairean anti-romantic (or the sheer Dublin deflationist) in Shaw.[2]

Yet though they never co-operated, the two are for us complementary beacons. Both deal with us under our evolutionary aspect, illuminating our biological status as the political animal (Shaw took the *political* au pied de la lettre, as well)—the animal whose species compels him to partake in a civilisation of some sort, and to submit to culture of some sort, but resolutely abstains from dictating what sort.

Our preliminary task of reformation is to reform our attitude to these two bearded masters. We usually do, and frequently remark that we do, turn spiteful against our great men as soon as they are dead—a phenomenon which arises, once again, out of our ambivalence towards the father whose psychological position vis-à-vis ourselves the great man has occupied. Freud has shewn us[3] that our mourning for the dead, our prohibition (whether a primitive taboo rule or a question of good taste, the secular successor to taboo) against saying anything about them that is not complimentary, and the lavish rites of ancestor-worship or the funeral parlour, have their obverse in our dread of ghosts. If the dead person is so loved and so benevolent, why are we so scared of his returning that we take every possible magical precaution against it? For no other reason than that the dead person is unconsciously hated as well as loved; we are glad he has gone and we do not want him back. The malice of ghosts and demons, the dangers they seem to threaten to us, are projections of our malice towards the dead persons whose spirits they are.

It is just this situation which Shaw dramatised in the ghostly Epilogue to *Saint Joan*, where Joan's canonisation (the last word in eulogising the dead, which the Church specifically reserves to the dead) is accompanied by a resolution on the part of those left alive not to let her return to earth; her worshippers are the very people who, when she was on earth, dispatched her from it by burning her.

Our usual reaction against just-dead masters is deepened, in Shaw's case, by his peculiar gifts. We have let him be posthumously assassinated by his own genius for personal publicity. Whereas so many English

[1] *Group Psychology And The Analysis Of The Ego*, XII

[2] Ernest Jones (*Sigmund Freud . . .*, II, 13) relates how Freud quoted from *Man And Superman* but adds that Freud 'never came to like Shaw's writings, probably because of their widely differing conceptions of womanhood'.

[3] *Totem And Taboo*, II, 3 (c)

writers have turned aside the animosity of the mob by camouflaging themselves in the mob, posing in the attitudes of cricketers or rough-shooters, with a tankard of faux bonhomme ale in their hand (and ending, of course, by betraying their evolutionary mission and sinking into the mediocrity they began by imitating), Shaw never left the English public in a moment's doubt of his intellectual and moral superiority. Moreover, his vast intellectual range carried him everywhere; there was not a profession or a party which stood unrebuked by his exposure of our hypocrisies. Intellectually, he occupied the position, which is peculiarly the father's, of being omni-present and all-seeing—the very faculty which has in so many mythologies made the all-seeing sun into a god-the-father[1]; and the result was that we construed his virtues not as an example but as a reproach to us. We made him a conscience; and only after his death did we dare re-kill him by endorsing his death with obloquy and oblivion.

As a matter of fact, I am one of the people who are entirely sympathetic and acquiescent to Shaw's personality (and as a vegetarian I am immunised against the blood guilt his vegetarianism induced in his critics[2]); and there are five or six of his plays which I cannot pick up to re-read casually, or even to verify a reference, without their moving me—physically and irrepressibly—to tears, just as Shakespeare's tragedies do. Still, I should be quite willing to indulge the people who cannot stand Shaw at any price, and the world could well wait for them to blow themselves out, were it not that we have no time left for this childish making and smashing of father images, but need every second we can get to apply Shaw's lessons. In our present danger we would do best to make a sacrifice of our personal fantasies and attend to Shaw as a major philosopher; and in decency we might give him credit at the same time for his other achievements: the rescue of English prose from Art for Art's sake and Style for Style's (here Shaw followed in the much less flexible footsteps of

[1] It is apropos the sun-god Osiris that Diodorus cites Homer's tag 'the sun who sees all and hears all' (Diodorus Siculus, I, 11; Odyssey, e.g., XII, 323)

[2] 'My vegetarianism has a quaint effect on my critics. You read an article purporting to be a review of my latest book, and discover that what the critic is really doing is defending his private life against mine . . . the blood of the Deptford Victualling Yard chokes him, and the horrible carcass groves of Farringdon Market rise up before him . . . All my other fads are familiar to them, and often shared by them. But this is a matter of blood-guilt . . .' (Shaw, Sixteen Self-Sketches, IX)

Samuel Butler who wrote Latin, as it were, to Shaw's Greek), restoring prose to its eighteenth-century vigour and giving style a new lease of life by re-attaching it to meaning[1]; the resuscitation of one of the eighteenth-century's literary forms, the pamphlet, which Shaw re-issued under the designation of Prefaces; and the re-animation of the drama of ideas, which had lain more or less inert where it had been left by Euripides.

With Freud, on the other hand, there can be no question of a public reaction against his personality. He had no public face: only the psycho-analytic movement. If he had constructed a public personality for himself he would have been as false to his scientific purpose as Shaw, in the literary climate of the nineties, would have been to his artistic mission if he had not. The true personality of Freud, though in its bold outlines it can now be apprehended through the biography by Ernest Jones, distils its intimate essence only to those who piece it together from his own reticent work, and is the surprising personal reward of learning about psycho-analysis. For intellect, and for the combination in it of range and grasp, Freud has no equal in the history of the world except Aristotle, whom he resembles: only with Aristotle does he share the faculty of being both the pioneer whose imagination has dared the collossal break-through, and at the same time the consolidator who brings the material under systematic cultivation.

He shares, too, Aristotle's gift of naïveté. Freud's vision is a non-fiction equivalent to—not Fra Angelico's; there is nothing sweet and singing in Freud's work; but perhaps the naked and tragic vision of Masolino and Masaccio, pioneers with whom Freud may have felt an affinity, since he hung a reproduction of their Carmine frescoes in his study[2]. Freud's *is*, in a sense, a tragic personality—because, I think, of his courage, which permitted him to follow logic to the point of rejecting all comfort from illusions. It is to his courage that we should attribute his incomparable intellectual integrity. There has never been an original thinker so willing—indeed, resolved—at every stage to rethink the entire structure he was building. Freud was determinedly undazzled by his own brilliance. He did not allow a single easy solution, let alone a specious one, to get by; he never minimised a difficulty; he met every objection with the

[1] See Shaw's Epistle Dedicatory to *Man And Superman*

[2] as one can see in the photograph in Martin Freud's *Glory Reflected* (facing p. 25)

open-mindedness of a man who is seeking not to parry objections, make points or establish a case, but simply to discover the truth.

Though he was, of course, too knowledgeable to be surprised, Freud remained, in his naïveté, shocked to realise that his work was an intellectual revolution; but having realised it, he stuck to his position with logical, sweet-tempered integrity. It is his courage we see at every turn in his life-history, in the terrible journey he made out of the darkness of universal neglect, into the unkind light of almost universal disparagement—and then on into the still more comfortless landscape (it is the nonsensual, the postsensual world of such final masterpieces as *The Tempest* and *The Magic Flute*) of his ultimate position, which consisted of his having diagnosed mankind's ill with an accuracy so precise as to be almost painful, and of his knowing, as part of the diagnosis, with the perfection of disillusionment, that mankind would not believe him.

We cannot analyse Freud's courage further than to say that there was not a trace in him of hatred of life. Similarly—which cannot be said for all scientists, or even for many intellectual revolutionaries—there was not a trace of hatred of culture. He plaits his revolutionary discoveries into continuity with our cultural past; he is for ever tacitly reminding us that we need take nothing from him that we have not already gladly received in other forms from Shakespeare, Goethe and Sophocles. Gently rebellious on behalf of his discoveries, he surrenders to beauty, the final mystery in human psychology and one he repeatedly confessed. ('Unfortunately, psycho-analysis, too, has less to say about beauty than about most things'[1].) His own susceptibility was to mountainscape and to the arts of sculpture, painting and literature. He had no ear for music[2]. Even so, Mozart's[3] and da Ponte's *Marriage Of Figaro* had made its way to him, probably because it is a masterpiece of literature as well as music, and as trenchant in its psychology as in its drama—capable, indeed, of anticipating Freud by putting into pointed, dramatic practice a principle not enunciated formally until Freud wrote his *Psychopathology Of Everyday Life*[4]. Waiting for a train one day, Freud expressed his own impulses

[1] *Civilization And Its Discontents*, II   [2] Martin Freud: *Glory Reflected*
[3] Ernest Jones records that Freud could as a rule be tempted to the theatre only by a Shakespeare play or a Mozart opera (*Sigmund Freud . . .*, II, 15)
[4] Although the opera owes some of its shapeliness and bravura to Beaumarchais's dry little play, it is Mozart and da Ponte who gave depth to the dramatic climaxes by endowing the characters with psychology and thereby

of rebellion by singing[1] to himself Figaro's antipatrician aria *Se vuol ballare, signor Contino*; falling asleep on the train, he wove Figaro's ideas into one of his dreams—and later disentangled them for *The Interpretation Of Dreams.*

2. *AntiFreudianism: Simple . . .*

The reaction, then, has been not against Freud, whom the public does not know, but against Freudianism. Yet at once the question arises whether the public has any better a knowledge of Freudianism. We have quantities of lipservants to the belief that psycho-analysis has revolutionised life and thought; any literate person's list of influences on the twentieth century begins with psycho-analysis and Marxism. But is it true? Can we believe that psycho-analysis has exerted any general influence whatsoever when we encounter in every direction such a profound general ignorance of what psycho-analysis is?

Part of the trouble lies with the popularisers who practised in the twenties and thirties. Consciously at least, they intended nothing but good to Freud. But their work was in any case superfluous: Freud had already explained himself in everyday language; and with that immense intellectual control of his he was capable, no matter what point of complexity he had reached, of going back and explaining things from scractch for beginners or from first principles for the unconvinced. At the worst, the populariser did Freud the gross disservice of presenting his conclusions as if they were revealed doctrines and omitting the painstaking and honest process of argument by which Freud had arrived at them.

Often enough one can see the populariser's motive and sympathise with it: it is the excitement of his own cure from some neurotic condition. Freud's arguments, which he read long ago, seem dim and

making them moving (see Michael Levey: *Aspects Of Mozart's Heroines*, II [Journal of the Warburg and Courtauld Institutes, XXII, 1-2, 1959]); and it is they, not the more consciously shrewd Beaumarchais, who hit on the famous anticipation of Freud (Susanna's mistaken Si's and No's, in her Act III duet with the Count, which betray her unspoken intentions). There is not a hint of it in Beaumarchais's parallel scene (III, ix).

[1] 'Possibly another person would not have recognized the tune'. (Freud: *The Interpretation Of Dreams*, V, (B) IV, II)

unimportant to him compared with this living demonstration; so he sets down, unsupported, Freud's conclusions, which now seem to him self-evident, and he sincerely hopes, of course, to pass on the news of the cure to his fellow-sufferers. Meanwhile, the figure of Freud is in a position to say 'I told you so all along', like a father whose baby has tumbled and received a demonstration of facts the father has been urging on it by description and argument.

This was just what the popularisers achieved when they presented the public with a list of doctrines in place of Freud's clinical experience and scientific arguments, and with categorical descriptions of the Ego and the Id in place of Freud's subtle, psychological and clinically-tested working hypotheses[1]. The result was to elevate a wholly false image of Freud into a father figure. To this day one meets people who are in reaction against this chimaera (a reaction that would be admirable if the chimaera existed), and who conceive that the psycho-analytic movement is a sort of society of Jesuits[2], a closed circle in which Freud plays the authoritarian part of God, and which explains objections to it in its own terms as *resistance*, exactly as theology explains that lack of faith is caused by lack of faith—whereas in truth, as one cannot too often emphasise, Freud was first and last a reasoner[3], and psycho-analytic theory a body of reasoning. Indeed, the analogy is

---

[1] 'As to the material from which the psychical apparatus is constructed, I must ask you not to enquire of me. That is no concern of psychology, where the question is a matter of just as much indifference as would be in optics the question whether the sliding parts of a telescope were made of metal or cardboard . . . We do, in fact, suppose the unknown apparatus . . . to be actually like an instrument, made up of various parts—which we call agencies—each of which performs a special function; and there is a fixed spatial relationship between them. That is, the spatial aspect, "before" and "behind", "superficial" and "deep", only has the immediate meaning of something to represent the regular succession of functions . . . it is a hypothesis, and science makes use of many. The earliest always prove to have been somewhat crude, and should be labelled "open to revision".' (Freud: *The Question Of Lay Analysis*, II)

[2] Whereas what Freud actually compared it to was the Salvation Army. (This was not, however, the movement as it stood but as Freud hoped it might be, 'a corps to give battle to the neuroses springing from our civilisation.' To this his fictitious interlocutor [in *The Question of Lay Analysis*, VII] replies 'Aha, a new sort of Salvation Army', and Freud's answer is: 'Why not? Our phantasy always works on existing patterns.')

[3] Indeed, he was later to deplore not, of course, his lack of authoritarianism but his lack of authority, in the early period of psycho-analysis. As he wrote in

drawn precisely the wrong way round. It is impossible to have faith in psycho-analytic theory, just as it is impossible to have faith in the conclusions of a theorem or a syllogism. Faith must replace or defy reasoning, or it is not faith but common sense. The resistance of a person who agrees that psycho-analysis logically must be true but none the less refuses to believe it is a classic example of faith.

However, just as there are some people who insist on denying psycho-analysis in spite of reason, so there are some people who insist on embracing it without making use of reason, thereby turning themselves into worshippers of Freud. They have done Freud much harm in the world, and when we consider the ambivalent feelings worshippers usually entertain towards their god we can hardly doubt that harm is just what they unconsciously intended to do. Certainly, the person who deifies Freud must in his heart think very poorly of Freud, since he has to ignore Freud's own patiently rational example and precepts; and there is a certain malice in wanting to set up as infallible someone whose judgment was so patently fallible. Not only did Freud—another instance of his courage—go back and correct his early mistakes; there are also, on the periphery of his main work, mistakes or at least inadequacies which he never retrieved. His insight into wit, brilliant in passing through the surface, stopped there. His early gingerly analysis of poetic inspiration could have been told him straight off by a self-aware poet such as Keats. He never wholly corrected his romantic view of Moses.[1] In the end[2] he succumbed to the absurdity of thinking it probable that the works of Shakespeare were written by somebody else[3].

As a matter of fact, we can see in Freud's attitude to Shakespeare

1914, 'I myself did not venture to put forward a technique which was still incomplete, or a theory which was still in the making, with that authority which, if I had, would perhaps have spared the [other early psycho-analysts] many a pitfall' (Freud: *Collected Papers*, Volume I, 'On the Early History Of The Psycho-Analytic Movement')

[1] *Wit And Its Relation to The Unconscious;* 'The Relation Of The Poet To Day-Dreaming' (*Collected Papers*, Volume IV, IX); 'The Moses Of Michelangelo' (*Collected Papers*, Volume IV, XVI); *Moses And Monotheism*

[2] becoming convinced in 1926-8

[3] which became a point of collision between Freud and Ernest Jones, who, having worked out in full Freud's original brief analysis of *Hamlet* as an Oedipal story, stuck to his view that *Hamlet* was by Shakespeare after Freud had changed his mind. Jones (*Sigmund Freud . . .*, III, 16) connects this peculiarity of Freud's with a 'family romance' theme in Freud's fantasy-life, remarking that with

not only wrong-headedness but ironic tragedy: Freud had joined a movement for doing to Shakespeare exactly what his detractors did to Freud. 'I have always felt it as a gross injustice,' wrote Freud, 'that people always refused to treat psycho-analysis like any other science'.[1] The ultimate reason for this refusal is, of course, the actual material of psycho-analysis, which insists on disclosing facts we would much rather keep hidden from ourselves—and which we have been at pains to hide. People will leap at any opportunity for supposing that the findings of psycho-analysis, unlike those of other sciences, cannot be established by reason: and what gives them their opportunity is the very magnitude of Freud's scientific achievement. If you judge the scientificness of a statement not by test but by the outward appearance of the science it comes from, you are almost bound to commit this gross injustice to psycho-analysis. We have grown used to sciences whose history takes the form of X conceiving a hypothesis, Y correcting and improving it, and Z completing it. And this is precisely the form the history of psycho-analysis takes—except that, instead of the several X, Y and Z, there is one name, Freud's. The discovery of psycho-analysis is the achievement of one man—though corroborated, one should add, and in minor ways extended by hundreds of psycho-analysts. As the history of a science, this is unique, but it says nothing either for or against the scientific soundness of the discovery; it is a wholly specious pretext which it offers us for claiming, as we have been wanting to do all along, that psycho-analysis is not a science. With Shakespeare, our crisis is more personal, since it is a question of art. We are not out to demote the value of his achievement, but to demote him from his sole authorship and share out the virtue of the achievement a bit more generally among mankind. History does

each of the three great men who particularly interested Freud (Shakespeare, Leonardo and Moses) 'questions of identity arose in one form or another'. Freud's change of mind left its traces in his *Autobiographical Study* (VI), where he records that his original analysis adduced the fact that 'Shakespeare wrote *Hamlet* very soon after his father's death'. To this Freud adds the later footnote: 'I have particular reasons for no longer wishing to lay any emphasis on this point'. Yet if one turns to Freud's original account of *Hamlet* (*The Interpretation Of Dreams*, V (D) (b)), one finds him adducing another biographical point much harder to de-emphasise: 'It is known, too, that Shakespeare's son, who died in childhood, bore the name of Hamnet'. The anti-Shakespearean movement ought really to be in search of a candidate with the right dates *and* a son named something like Hamlet.

[1] *An Autobiographical Study*, V

not allow us, as it quite plausibly does in the case of Homer, to maintain that the work was really written by a committee or a tradition. The
best we can do is to elevate the writer, who we have to admit was
singular, from the grammar school at Stratford on Avon and transform him into at least a graduate and a courtier, and preferably an
aristocrat as well. But this compliment is accompanied by its destructive wish. We have not touched the value of the work, which still
stands unique and incomparable. But in elevating the author to high
places, we have made him subject to draughts—we have set him
among the intellectual eddies of the Italian renaissance. This colossal
achievement, we are saying, is to be attributed not only to its author
but to the influences which were playing on the English court and
universities at the time. We are half-way to claiming that it was the
Italian renaissance which wrote *Antony And Cleopatra* (despite that
renaissance's failure to achieve anything of half the stature in its
native tongue); and if we have made our Shakespeare an aristocrat
we are also giving some of the credit for his plays to the selective
breeding practised by his ancestors. With Shakespeare we argue:—
we cannot and do not deny that this is art; but because it is art, it
cannot be the product of a provincial petty bourgeois too close to the
ground to have felt the winds of the time. With Freud, we say:—
we know this is the work of one Moravian Jew; it cannot be
science.

Simple antiFreudians are for the most part throwing tomatoes at
the chimerical figure of an authoritarian Freud whom they have met
either in popularisations or in other people's reactions to popularisation.
They can be deflected by the simple question how much Freud they
have read. To ask this is to imply that people *should* read Freud himself
—and this not only because he is more reliable than his popularisers,
but because he is also more competent and more pleasing as a writer.
All his work has the charm of truth and reason: even the savagery
of Brill's translations cannot distort the proportion and fidelity of
Freud's reasoning: and the lateish, briefish, better translated mono-
graphs (such as *Group Psychology And The Analysis Of The Ego*, and
The Question Of Lay Analysis[1]) possess the same charm of form as

[1] *Group Psychology* . . . (1921) was described by Freud (in *An Autobiographical
Study*, V) as one of the works 'of my later years' where 'I have given free rein
to the inclination which I kept down for so long to speculation'. On the other
hand, . . . *Lay Analysis*, like the *Autobiographical Study* itself, is one of the works
for beginners, its sub-title being 'An Introduction To Psycho-Analysis'.

Plato's Socratic dialogues, on which in many cases Freud modelled their manner, though not their titles.

Indeed, Freud is the most accessible and least demanding of important authors. The reader need bring with him neither background reading nor knowledge of the jargon; he will not need to fight to ferret out Freud's arguments; he will not need to work himself up into a devotional mood. Yet it would be unfair to recommend Freud to the general public without a warning that he is, in another sense, the most difficult of authors. What his very simplicity amounts to is that he is asking the reader for that most difficult of self-disciplinary achievements, an open mind. All he asks us to do is discard (at least till we have examined them and seen objectively whether they are worth putting on again) the swaddling bands of those prejudices and assumptions which we call our culture—which, like Victorian clothes, we wrap round us neither for use nor for beauty but as a matter of purest taboo. To discard them is, of course, very difficult. Only the puritan can so defy plain experience as to go on pretending that it is easy (fatally easy, as he says) to undress in public. The puritan would feel safer, though not perhaps happier, if he could get it into his head that sexual licence is, for most people, simply too difficult. The same is true of the revolutionary ideas which the puritan so often associates with sexual licence (an association in which he is not wrong from a fundamental psychological point of view but often, of course, blunderingly wrong in practice: it is as though he treated an unconscious homosexual as a homosexual, without remembering that the unconscious homosexual is precisely the person who feels the strongest abhorrence for homosexuality). Because of the weakness of his own defences against pleasure, the puritan always underestimates other people's difficulty in accepting both sexual experience and revolutionary ideas; and so he always overestimates the—as he sees it—danger of both. When someone invites us to strip our minds of prejudices, we receive the proposal primarily as indecent and secondly as foolhardy: we are always afraid our minds might catch a chill if we exposed them to what we habitually call cold reason.

3. . . . and Complex

Simple antiFreudians, who will hear nothing of Freud, are less damaging to psycho-analysis than complex antiFreudians, whose cry is that they have already heard all about Freud. The subtlety of their argument is simply that they have not. These are the people who tell us what a tremendous influence psycho-analysis has had on the twentieth century. Freud has had his day, they maintain; all honour to him; the world has absorbed his lessons. But since they cannot give the barest coherent account of what his lessons were, and can be floored just as easily as the simple antiFreudians by the question how much Freud they have read, it is obvious that their claim to know already everything Freud told us is meant to excuse them from finding out what it was.

Nowhere is this voluntary ignorance more profound than in the medical profession. I recently met a doctor who practises exclusively in a mental hospital who told me in the same breath that Freud had been immensely influential, that Freud was now out of date and that he himself had never read a word of Freud's writings. And it must be confessed that in England at least the medical profession has swallowed psycho-analysis in order not to practise it. (It prefers latter-day versions of the 'electrotherapy' which had already, before the turn of the century and before psycho-analysis was discovered, disappointed Freud by its utter inability to relieve neurotic conditions[1].) The attitude of the medical profession to psycho-analysis is that of Nero to Britannicus: 'J'embrasse mon rival, mais c'est pour l'étouffer'[2]. The results of the stifling embrace are to be seen in, for example, the English edition of *The Question Of Lay Analysis*, where Freud argues that the world stands in such urgent need of quantities of trained psycho-analysts that it cannot afford to insist that each of them expend his time and money on being trained as a doctor first, acquiring knowledge of 'the anatomy of the metatarsal bones, of the properties of carbo-hydrates, of the courses of the cranial nerves', etc. etc., all of which, Freud points out, though valuable in itself, is not the smallest

[1] See Freud: 'On The History Of The Psycho-Analytic Movement', I (*Collected Papers*, Volume I)

[2] Racine: *Britannicus*, IV, iii

help in curing a neurosis and does not even 'sharpen the intellectual faculties on which his professional activity will make such demands'. This argument of Freud's is preceded in the English edition by a Foreword in which Ernest Jones, on behalf of the British psycho-analytical movement, confesses that 'the flooding of the profession with lay practitioners' (the very thing Freud was asking for) would 'alienate it from medical co-operation'; and a Translator's Note records that the British Institute of Psycho-Analysis requires, as one condition for admitting a candidate for training as a psycho-analyst, 'either the study of medicine or some other equivalent previous study or work'[1].

(British psycho-analysis has not, of course, remained unaffected by being swallowed. Not only is it restricted; it imposes restrictions on itself: it is in danger of coming to think of psycho-analytic theory as though it really were something as highly technical and as inaccessible to people without a medical training as the anatomy of the metatarsal bones. In the same monograph, Freud explains to his imaginary interlocutor: 'We take our stand on the ground of everyday experience, and recognise in man a psychical organisation which is interpolated between his sensory stimuli and perception of his bodily needs on the one hand, and his motor activity on the other . . . We call this organisation his "I" . . . we recognise another psychical sphere, vaster and more obscure, and we name it "the It". . . . You may feel dubious over our choice of simple pronouns . . . instead of high-sounding Greek names. But in psycho-analysis we like to remain in touch with popular ways of thinking. . . That is no merit to us—we must proceed in this way, since our teaching must be understood by our patients, who are often highly intelligent but are not always highly educated. The impersonal *it* comes quite naturally into the speech of normal people. "It upsets me" one says; "it was too much for me." *C'était plus fort que moi.*' But at this point British psycho-analysis intervenes once again to make nonsense of Freud, and the translator has to add a footnote: 'In accordance with the usage adopted by psycho-analysts in England, these terms "I" and "It" have been replaced by "Ego" and "Id" throughout the remainder of this translation'[2]—and everyone else has had to fall into the same line.)

Even so, complex antiFreudianism in Britain has not reached

[1] Freud: *The Question Of Lay Analysis* . . ., translated by Nancy Procter-Gregg, with foreword by Ernest Jones, M.D., Imago, 1947
[2] *The Question Of Lay Analysis*, II

anything like the subtlety and efficacy it has achieved in the United States
—where Freud had already noticed in 1925 that psycho-analysis was
both extremely popular and suffering from watering-down[1]. One
has only to look at American psycho-analytical writing to realise that
since then there have been great draughts of further dilution. Psycho-
analysis appears under the wing of the churches, an adjunct to pastoral
care or 'counseling', the clergy writing off Freud's own reasoned
views on religion with the same facile insolence with which my
old English teacher—acting, as she believed, for the good name of
English literature—emasculated Shelley and reduced all his high passion
to cosiness by telling her class that 'of course Shelley wasn't *really* an
atheist'. On the other hand, psycho-analysis is packaged into a technique for helping copywriters to sell more cars, and a correspondence-
course for helping consumers to 'adjust to' not being able to buy
more cars: so much for Freud's vision of a new Salvation Army.
And meanwhile a psycho-analyst propounds the theory, which is
meant to bring Freud up to date, that a psycho-analysis does not really
put the patient in possession of information which was previously
unavailable to his conscious mind but only gives him a fresh attitude
to what he already knew[2]. (It is interesting not merely formally but
as a clue to the methods the Ego adopts in defending itself against
reason that this is precisely the objection which—with far better justification—John Stuart Mill brought against the syllogism, when he
accused it of petitio principii on the grounds that in order to state its
premisses we had already to be acquainted with the conclusion[3].)

All these attacks are said to be favours done to Freud, correcting his
mistakes and carrying his influence into fresh fields. Resistance to
psycho-analysis has a counterpart in the world of art, where it goes
by the name of philistinism; and America's resistance takes a form
sadly familiar to artists: it consists of covering the pianist with so
much adulation that there is no time left to listen to his playing.
America is a patient which agrees so completely, so utterly without
objection or argument, with every word Freud is said to have said
that there is no getting home to it what he did say—a difficulty sometimes encountered by the Catholic Church whose peasant parishioners
are so anxious, in terror for their souls, to subscribe to the Church's
dogmata unheard that it becomes very hard for their priests to instruct

[1] *An Autobiographical Study*, V
[2] Karen Horney: *New Ways In Psychoanalysis*, I
[3] Cf. H. W. B. Joseph: *An Introduction To Logic*, XIV

them in what those dogmata are. America seems determined to turn Freud into a dogmatist and itself into a worshipper: it rushes to clasp Freud in its irrational embrace, thereby stifling its own opportunity of accepting him reasonably.

The theory that psycho-analysis has already made its effect has lately devised a new twist: not only do we not need to know what psycho-analysis is, but now we no longer need that immense influence it is said to have exerted without our knowing what it is; for it has, by its very influence, so changed human nature that human beings no longer need psycho-analysing. How sadly untrue the argument is can be seen from our misconceptions about war. In any case, if psycho-analysis really has had any influence, it is only on the middle classes; and one can promptly see how superficial its influence even on them has been by their startling ignorance of it. Psycho-analytic terminology is on every semi-educated lip; but an understanding of the concepts to which the words were originally attached is nowhere to be found. Bandying the words about, turning them into idioms, we have squeezed out their significance. In particular, we have drained the meaning from Freud's cardinal discovery, the fact that unconscious processes *are* unconscious. Indeed, idiomatically we prefer the non-Freudian word *subconscious*, which allows us to forget that towards our unconscious processes we really are unconscious, just as we are unconscious to the outside world when we are in a faint, and lets us suppose that the subconscious is just beneath the threshold and that we have only to pause and introspect for a second to recover ideas which were only hiding at (the older idiom employs a slightly different spatial metaphor) the back of our mind. Thus an American patient can note down: 'Felt no guilt at all this time and today haven't even been troubled by any subconscious guilt'[1].

If we allow ourselves to lose the concept of the unconsciousness of the unconscious, we shall be going back on a fundamental scientific discovery, retreating not only into a dark age for science but also, since the science concerned is man's knowledge of man, into a less advanced state of human awareness. Moreover, such is the peculiar content of this fact we are allowing ourselves to forget, that we cannot forget it without imperilling civilisation. And it is just on this point, the question of our violent impulses against civilisation, that we meet the crux of our need for further education in Freudianism.

[1] cited, but not as meaningless, in a case history in Frank S. Caprio's *Female Homosexuality*, XIII

4. Facts of Life and Facts of Death (with a Note on 'The Greek Myths')

The world received such a shock from Freud's disclosures about sexuality that it has evidently decided to take its revenge by remaining fixated at the point of its trauma and associating Freud's name with sexuality and nothing else for ever more. The truth is, however, that Freud's analysis of human instinct eventually isolated not one but two fundamental, irreducible instincts: the (in the widest sense) sexual instinct, which he named Eros 'exactly in the sense in which Plato uses the word "Eros" in his Symposium'[1]; and another which he called by the Greek name for death, Thanatos. The impetus of Eros is towards uniting, towards creating relationships, that of Thanatos towards dividing, and breaking them off.

If psycho-analysis really has made any effect on the world at large, it is solely in our attitude towards Eros.

Even here, the change may have been largely independent of psycho-analysis. Long before Freud, the world had had several periods in which people were comparatively free-spoken and liberal in behaviour about sex (as G. Rattray Taylor has shewn us[2]). It may well be that after 1918 we were due to swing into a liberal phase and simply attached the convenient name of Freud to a change we would have spontaneously made in any case. Often, of course, the change is only vocabulary-deep; it is characteristic of those who believe that Freud has had his influential day that they mistake the absence of a verbal censorship in many middle-class milieux for an absence of censorship on our emotions. The same mistake may, of course, be made by simple antiFreudians. Robert Graves in his Penguin volumes *The Greek Myths* argues:—'Oedipus's remorseful self-blinding has been interpreted by psychologists to mean castration; but though the blindness of . . . Phoenix . . . was said by Greek grammarians to be a euphemism for impotence, primitive myth is always downright, and the castration of Uranus and Attis continued to be recorded unblushingly in Classical text books'[3]. However, the internal censorship in dream- and myth-making is not concerned simply with

[1] Freud: *Collected Papers*, Volume V, XXV   [2] in *Sex In History*
[3] II, p. 14

sparing blushes or euphemising the facts of sex, but with disguising
our unconscious wishes about where we should like to apply those
facts. The myth has never admitted that Oedipus *wanted* to commit
the incestuous crime which it represents as an accident designed by
fate; if it disguises the true nature of his self-punishment, that is
because the logic of the punishment is too stark: self-castration, which
puts a stop to one's desires, gives away the fact that it was one's desires
which sinned in the first place.

(This is not the only misconception disseminated by *The Greek
Myths*, on the subject either of psycho-analysis or of Greek mythology. The reader must allow me a parenthesis to protest against the
unfairness of loosing this extraordinary work on the public, and
especially the Greekless, and therefore defenceless, public to whom it
is particularly directed[1], under the description of 'mythological
dictionary'[2] without a word of warning that much of the matter,
though not presented as such, is hypothesis, and that the manner is
that of Mr Graves's historical fiction. Each section, dealing with one
myth or group of myths, is divided into two parts: a narrative retelling the actual story of the myth; and a commentary. In one of
the narratives we read:—'In recent times, the Amazon queen . . .
set out from her Albanian court to meet Alexander the Great. . .'[3].
The explanation of how Alexander's times can be recent times is to
be found nowhere in the two volumes of *The Greek Myths*, but in

[1] 'written specially as a companion to the Penguin Classics' (front cover)
[2] I, p. 22. The blurb, in claiming that *The Greek Myths* is the first attempt
for over a century 'to provide for the English reader a complete "mythology"',
ignores the 1928 *Handbook* by H. J. Rose (a Professor of Greek at St.
Andrews who died in 1961), which is in some items more complete. (For
instance, the story of Side, who does not appear in the Graves index and is
not mentioned in any of the entries about her husband Orion, is related by
Rose [V] in the words of Apollodorus). My preference for Rose is not excited
by Mr Graves's antiFreudianism: Rose himself is utterly nonFreudian, indeed
nonpsychological. And of course neither compiler could give all the versions
of all the myths. Rose's selections, however, have the merit of at least referring
to items which to him are nonsignificant but in which other people may find
significance. His account of the castration of Uranos condenses Hesiod fairly
and indicates, though in rather veiled Victorianish language, that the occasion
on which the son castrated the father was the sexual intercourse of the parents.
Mr Graves (a further example of his incompleteness) relates that Kronos and
his brothers 'surprised Uranos as he slept' (I, p. 37)
[3] II, p. 127

one of Mr Graves's works of avowed fiction. Those who have been
fortunate enough to read his novel *The Golden Fleece* will remember
that in his introduction he explains:—'. . . a historical novelist should
always make it clear at what vantage-point he is standing. Here it
would have been unwise to tell the story as from the thirteenth century
B.C.. . . To tell it as from the present day would . . . have prevented
me from believing whole-heartedly in the story. . . I have therefore
allowed the phrases "to this day" and "today" to occur here and there
in the book. Historians will gather from the concluding page that
"today" means not later than the 146 B.C. when Lucius Mummius
sacked Corinth'[1]. But though the historical novelist feels an obligation
to state his vantage-point, the compiler of a work of reference evidently does not.

(As for the sections of commentary, the blurb claims that they
interpret the classical version of the stories 'in the light of today's
archaeological and anthropological knowledge'. When Mr Graves's
commentary on the Oedipus myth opens with the categorical statement that the story 'has been deduced from a set of sacred icons by a
deliberate perversion of their meaning'[2], the unlearned reader to
whom the work is addressed may be forgiven if he supposes that
today's archaeologists have dug up this set of icons and put them on
view in some museum[3]. The unlearned reader might also take seriously
both the use of the word *instinct* and the statement of historical fact
in Mr Graves's assertion: 'The Freudian theory that the "Oedipus
complex" is an instinct common to all men was suggested by this

[1] *The Golden Fleece*, p. 26   [2] *The Greek Myths*, II, p. 12

[3] Other misinterpreted icons occur passim. An icon on p. 277 of Volume II
has become so definite and unhypothetical as to be no longer *an* icon but *the*
icon: 'This tale is mistakenly deduced from the icon which showed Heracles
being given an apple-bough by the Hesperides'. The commentary on the
myth of Tereus tells us (I, p. 167): 'This extravagant romance seems to have been
invented to account for a series of Thraco-Pelasgian wall-paintings, found
by Phocian invaders in a temple at Daulis . . . , which illustrated different
methods of prophecy in local use.' I realise this hypothesis is covered by the
word *seems*: yet it may not be clear to readers that the *seems* applies not only to
theory of misinterpretation but to the very existence of the monuments which
are said to have been misinterpreted. I can, of course, be refuted instantly by
the production of these various icons and wall-paintings; but if they can be
produced why, in a book 'large enough in its scope for all normal requirements
of the student' as well as the 'general reader' (I, p. 22), does Mr Graves not
give details of where they are?

perverted anecdote'[1]. Freud's own account of how the movingness of the tragedy which Sophocles made out of the 'perverted anecdote' corroborated Freud's belief, based on clinical experience, that the situation occurred 'in the minds of the majority of children' is to be found in *The Interpretation Of Dreams*[2].)

Still, no matter how ignorant we remain, and whether or not the change has to any serious extent been influenced by psycho-analysis, there has been a change. Homes advised by Dr. Spock[3] are incomparably more hygienic psychically than the family home of the Gosses. In sexual questions we have begun to mend our manners. (We are slower to amend our laws.) We are no longer shocked by, we are no longer simply determined not to see, what used to be called the facts of life. It is the facts of death which still throw us into all the panic, the scientific obscurantism and the moral confusion people used to display at the thought of sex. Scarcely a mother in western Europe is disturbed or embarrassed to find her child fingering its sexual organs: our confusion and our hypocrisy begin when he fondles his toy gun. Indeed, as I mean presently to shew, it has been Thanatos even more than Eros which has been the stumbling-block —particularly for pre-Freudian and nonFreudian rationalists—all along.

Irrationalists, however, have no need to go so far before they stumble. Sexuality is quite enough to upset them, and their revulsion has produced a movement of

5. *CounterFreudianism*

Whereas antiFreudians have nothing against Freud except their ignorant belief that he was unreasonable, counterFreudians have nothing against him except their knowledge that he was reasonable. CounterFreudians cannot be wholly ignorant of Freud (though they usually choose to get their knowledge of him at secondhand, on the same principle whereby we are bound to get all our knowledge of early Christian heresies and early objections to Christianity from

[1] II, p. 13

[2] V, (D) (b). Cf. Freud's account of how 'the ubiquity of "the Oedipus complex" gradually dawned on me' (*An Autobiographical Study*, VI)

[3] 'Dr. Benjamin Spock's . . . Baby And Child Care'

polemics against them written by the orthodox—who eventually managed to suppress the documents they had earlier tried to contradict): the two effective counter-movements were both started by pupils of Freud who found the light too strong for them and groped back into the dark. Both attempts, C. G. Jung's and Alfred Adler's, seemed to Freud in 1925 to have 'blown over without doing any harm'[1]—a judgment still probably true of Adlerianism, which appears to be hardly more than a branch of boy-scouting. But Jung is having quite a hey-day.

In spite of Jung's remarkable learning, it is not by intellectual victories and convictions that Jungianism has remained alive. It is not a reasonable theory and has virtually abdicated any claim to be. Jung placed himself among the obscurantists. So much can be said fairly of a writer who discusses the psychology[2] of the Mass and, when he comes to the words of the Consecration, cites them in Latin and adds this footnote:—'According to the edict of the Church these words ought not, on account of their sacredness, to be translated into any profane tongue. Although there are missals that sin against this wise edict, I would prefer the Latin text to stand untranslated'[3].

From a reasonable point of view, Jung's psychology was succinctly demolished by Freud himself[4], and has since been irretrievably refuted, item by item, by Edward Glover in his book *Freud Or Jung*. Sometimes Jung teaches boldly as a prophet having authority in his own right; but every now and then he feels the need to reinforce himself by some other authority and, forgetting that he is not on the

[1] *An Autobiographical Study*, V

[2] though only 'from the phenomenological angle, for the realities of faith lie outside the realm of psychology'

[3] from Jung's contribution, 'Transformation Symbolism in the Mass', to a symposium, *The Mysteries* (English publication 1955), consisting of papers delivered at Eranos meetings. The best defence of Jung's obscurantism would be to claim that these papers were not intended to illuminate—so one might judge from the introductory *Note* (not by Jung) which says:—'. . . set in a garden on Lake Maggiore, all of the Eranos meetings have taken place. Against the background of ever-moving archetypal images, the actors (here speakers) move and play their parts. The scholarly form of their lectures becomes transparent, and the actual image or symbol of their respective themes seems to grip them. A scholar . . . gripped by such an image becomes the channel for its energy.'

[4] *Collected Papers*, Volume I, 'On The History Of The Psycho-Analytic Movement'

side of reason, claims to have reason on his side. In fact the only whiff of reason to be found in Jungianism comes from the Freudianism it has turned inside out. As Dr Glover makes clear, such systematic theory of the mind as Jung has uttered consists of negativing Freud on every point—regardless of the fact that to negative one consistent system does not produce another.

Even more preposterous than Jungianism's own claims is the idea that a true or even a workable psychology can be made by mixing Freud with Jung. It is Dr Glover's purpose to shew that, Jungianism being untrue to the facts and inconsistent with itself, nothing but a doubly meaningless mush can be expected from mixing it into a systematic body of theory of which it is a contradiction. Jungians, unconcerned with consistency, are often quite willing for the mixture to be made: their execration of Freud is mixed with a sort of condescending politeness to him, whereby they may take credit for being peacemakers at the same time as trying to reduce Freud to a mere forerunner. But the chief support for the idea of synthesising the two psychologies comes from baffled outsiders who, without investigating the matter for themselves, have been imposed on by the Jungians, and are under the misapprehension that here are two systems with equal claim to serious and scientific notice. The pity of this confusion is that the meaningless mixture, with its appearance of being unbiased, has a great appeal for public and academic authorities, who pay for it to be taught to social and educational workers under the impression that they are equipping them with a training in psychology. The effect is to blunt psycho-analysis in the very places where society needs it most urgently, and to discredit the whole idea of psychological science; the workers who are so anxious to help their fellow men are unknowingly equipped as mischief-makers.

Jung's general appeal is his anti-reasonableness, and he has been swept into the movement of revolt against what is felt to be the tyranny of reason. He has taken up and been taken up by the religionists, though his help to them is often rather teasing, since it is necessarily nonsectarian. Yet he remains useful to religion because what it asks from him is not simply unreason, which religion can supply for itself, but the specious appearance of reason: he appears to correct Freud into something acceptable to religion or at least so nebulous that religion need not reject it. As Freud pointed out, it is not the content that is the strength of either Adlerianism or Jungianism, but the fact that they seem to offer a way round the conclusions of psycho-analysis 'without the necessity of rejecting its actual material'[1].

Psycho-analysis is a hypothesis in the sense that the evolution of species is a hypothesis, and no more than evolution is to be point blank denied by reasonable people. Its discovery was just as shaking to religion as evolution was, and religion treated it in the same way, trying first to neglect or blast it out of existence and, when that failed, to convert its conclusions to the greater glory of religion. The instrument that came to the religionists' hand for this purpose was Jungianism, which had already begun its specious re-shaping of psycho-analysis.

What Jungianism shares with religion is a determination to make use of reason rather than to respect it. They both make play with reason so long as it argues on their side and will even help it along a little by employing fallacious arguments; but ultimately—or whenever you point out their fallacies—they throw up the whole business and proclaim that reason does not matter, it being inspiration, faith or decent feeling which counts. (John Locke had remarked this characteristic of religionists as long ago as 1690. 'I find every sect, as far as reason will help them, make use of it gladly: and where it fails them, they cry out, It is a matter of faith, and above reason'.[2])

Jungianism does not confine itself to reconciling religion to a false psychology. Devoted to eradicating Freud's footsteps, it has had to follow Freud into aesthetics, sociology and anthropology, where it has managed to turn soggy a good part of the intellectual life of the twentieth century. Today it is almost axiomatic that if you open a book of literary or social criticism and find in paragraph one a really gross blunder of argument or expression, paragraph three will betray, by an archetype here or a transformation symbol there, the influence of Jung. Christianity had long told the simple-minded that they had equal (or better) hopes of being saved with the intelligent; only Jung tells people that it is really much more intelligent of them to be stupid than to be intelligent.

What Jung is primarily concerned to obliterate is, as Freud perceived, the discovery which has provoked most of the cries of disgust uttered at psycho-analysis, the fact of infantile sexuality. As Freud pointed out[3], some nursemaids had always known that children had sexual feelings. Perhaps it was the desire to keep themselves in ignorance

[1] *An Autobiographical Study*, V
[2] *An Essay Concerning Human Understanding*, IV, XVIII, 2
[3] *The Question Of Lay Analysis*, IV

of children's sexuality which persuaded every married couple rich enough to aim at respectability to hand their children over to nursemaids, even though that cost the parents the pleasure of their children's company. What was known only to nursemaids was to all intents and purposes unknown, for the nursemaids were too inarticulate to publish it and were, moreover, female: general knowledge was the monopoly of men. Freud's pioneering began with his being the first father to enter the nursery unawed, with his scientific wits about him. It was by being as matter-of-fact about infancy as a nursemaid that he was able to establish, both from direct observation of children and by resurrecting childhood memories in adults, that a child experiences sexual pleasure not only genitally but in the regions where sexual pleasure is considered perverse, and directs its sexual attentions to the very people who presently become implacably forbidden by the incest ban. When psycho-analysis had published these facts (or when we had spontaneously become prepared to recognise them), the usefulness of the nursemaid ceased; and, the moment social changes put the smallest pressure on it, the office of nursemaid virtually vanished. (Of course middle-class mothers still get people to help them take care of their children; but they get people of their own social class and educational standing.) It was left to Jung to try to close the nursery up again, and his method, the facts being undeniable, was to reinterpret them into a spiritual allegory where sexuality no longer meant anything sexual; and in order to keep this interpretation plausible he had to turn his and his patients' attention away from the analysis of childhood[1].

To my taste Jung's version is very far from being prettier than Freud's, but in any case the prettiness of either has nothing to do with the correctness of either. Yet it is precisely on the grounds that it is unpretty, without a murmur about whether it is true or not, that Jung assails Freud's concept of sexuality. Freud's concept, Jung says, 'depreciates' sex. The 'obscenity and blindfold stupidity of the Freudian literature' make sex seem 'repulsive and disgusting'[2]. I do not find infantile sexuality disgusting, but that does not make it true; Jung does find it disgusting, but that does not make it untrue. One might as well deny the truth of what a medical text-book says about the

[1] See Freud: *Collected Papers*, Volume I, 'On The History Of The Psycho-Analytic Movement,' III

[2] C. G. Jung: *Contributions To Analytical Psychology*, 'Analytical Psychology And Education'

intestines on the grounds that it makes the intestines seem disgusting.

Jung's great mistake is to suppose that because he is a religionist and a prophet Freud must be, too[1], and that Freud, instead of discovering the facts, was advocating the practice, of sexuality. The popular impression is hardly different; since the twenties Freud's name has been good for a giggle in London theatres on the strength of the public's belief that he preached the discarding (as though they could be simply discarded) of sexual inhibitions. Since his death Freud has become a little more respectable, but the popular complaint is still that 'he exaggerates the importance of sex'—to which the reply must be 'Exaggerates it in comparison with what? With the part sex really does play in human life, or with the part someone thinks it ought to play?' Even when he made his famous description of infants as polymorphously perverse Freud was, as he explained later, 'only using a terminology that was then current: no moral judgement was implied by the phrase'[2]. Most people accept nowadays that he did not mean to condemn by the word *perverse*, but there are still people who suppose he meant to praise.

If an attack on Freud is to be valid, it must demolish his facts and not merely to impugn their tendency: for if the facts and arguments are correct the attacker is impugning not Freud but reality. Jung's accusations against Freud are all formed by comparing psychoanalysis with what Jung thinks reality should be like, not with any tenable thesis of what it is like.. Unable to prove that Freud reported reality incorrectly, Jung is reduced to saying that 'immense damage is done to the feelings through Freudian doctrine'; and he adds:— 'while it is just through decent feeling, and through this alone, that we can hope to advance towards the solution of the sex-problem'[3]. What Jung means by *the sex-problem* I do not know; but if it is to be solved by decent feeling alone it cannot be the intellectual problem of discovering and describing the true facts about sexuality. Much of Jung's writing as good as confesses that fact-finding is no concern of

[1] Cf. Freud's 'My courage fails me . . . at the thought of rising up as a prophet before my fellow-men, and I bow to their reproach that I have no consolation to offer them; for at bottom this is what they all demand—the frenzied revolutionary as passionately as the most pious believer'. (*Civilization And Its Discontents*, VIII)

[2] *An Autobiographical Study*, III

[3] *Contributions To Analytical Psychology*, 'Analytical Psychology And Education'

his, because it consists not of facts and arguments but of moral exhortation. However, it persists in claiming to deal with facts, and it supposes that they can be dealt with by moral exhortation—a supposition that is religious in the same sense as the belief that the way to move mountains is to have faith or the way to cure the sick is to pray for them.

6. *Psycho-analysis and Morals*

Moral exhortation cannot sensibly be addressed to the unconscious. Yet this is really what the Jungians are doing; they are saying that if the human unconscious really is full of crude sexual imagery, it shouldn't be, and we ought not to let our unconscious minds dwell on such obscenities—which shews, of course, that they have not understood that the unconscious *is* unconscious. They cannot try to obliterate infantile sexuality without trying to obliterate also its persistence in the unconscious of adults; and so they come back to the antiFreudian game of draining the unconsciousness out of the concept of the unconscious. And of course it is only by doing that that anyone can imagine Freud to have been so wasteful of breath as to encourage mankind to persist in unconscious sexuality.

Indeed, though sexuality has provoked most of the squeals, it is the unconscious which has given the deepest offence of all Freud's discoveries—as Freud himself recognised when he remarked[1] that the discovery of the unconscious was the latest of three historical affronts to mankind's self-esteem: we had to admit first that our planet is not the centre of the universe; then that our species is not a superior creation but the descendant and relative of the animals; and finally that we do not even know everything which goes on in our own minds and can gain a measure of control over the effects of our unconscious impulses only by constantly paying a price and not even knowing that we are paying it.

The affront wounds us in several respects but most gravely—if we may judge from our defensive reactions—in our moral sense. To begin with, psycho-analysis has described our moral codes, and the very apparatus through which they function, our conscience, as phenomena resulting from human evolution—just like our upright

[1] *Collected Papers*, Volume IV, XX

stance or the hairlessness of our faces. There is no guarantee that the promptings we receive from our conscience will be moral, or even that it is moral to *have* a conscience: all we can say is that it was necessary for mankind to get one if it was to evolve culturally. And as a matter of fact, it turns out that the conscience is part of the blackmail money we pay to our unconscious instincts, with the result that, so far from being a moral body in itself, the conscience has actually been shaped by those very instincts which are beyond our moral control.

Psycho-analysis seems, therefore, to carry us into a world where moral judgments are meaningless, where we can no longer blame the murderer, any more than we can praise the just judge for being just, but simply have to observe that the antecedents of each have made each what he is and prevented him from being otherwise.

The first thing to remark is that psycho-analysis is not the only science which seems to suggest this determinism. The puzzle is, in fact, as old as thought. *Something* must have caused the difference between the murderer and the judge, whether it is education, heredity, the accidents of glandular imbalance or the caprices of the grace of God. If the judge has opened his heart to the voice of God and the murderer has hardened his against it, something must have made the one receptive and the other not. Determinism is the immediate suggestion of all sciences which distinguish causes—including theology, determinism being only another version of the old puzzle of predestination.

Secondly, of course, we cannot impugn psycho-analysis because it seems to lead us into determinism. Unless we can prove that psycho-analysis has reported reality wrongly, it is not psycho-analysis but reality which is urging determinism on us. Moreover, if the universe really is one in which morality is nonsense, it will not change its nature according to whether we accept or refuse to accept psycho-analysis. No more than logical necessity was invented by Aristotle, and no more than species ceased to have been created according to *Genesis* at the moment when Lamarck or Darwin enunciated the theory of evolution, will the unconscious cease to exist if we, in wounded feeling, withdraw our recognition from it.

These things said, we can consider whether psycho-analysis does make morality meaningless.

The first person to analyse morality as a psychic phenomenon was Socrates, who conducted an enquiry (reported in the *Protagoras*) into the nature of virtue. To the moral question he did not find an answer;

but he did succeed in returning, to the purely psychological question of what people mean by 'the good', the purely factual answer that they mean what gives them pleasure. This turned out to be so irrefutable that the people who claimed that they had chosen evil in preference to good because they were over-ruled by pleasure could be routed on the grounds that to choose pleasure is nothing else than to choose good. This argument, which in Socrates's mouth was so bracing, has been capable ever since of being used by the self-indulgent against the self-sacrificial; the self-indulgent have only to point out that the self-sacrificer could not choose to sacrifice himself unless that were more pleasing to him than to save himself, that if he claims he does it to please God that is only to say it pleases him to please God, and that his only distinction from the self-indulger lies in the peculiarity of his tastes—in other words, in his masochism.

The undeniable fact that people do sometimes choose pain in preference to pleasure Socrates put down to their long or short-sightedness. If they choose to undergo surgery that is because they are long-sighted enough to recognise that a worse evil will come on them if they refuse; if on the other hand they succumb to the temptation to eat too much, that is because they cannot properly perceive the long-term pain waiting for them at the other side of the banquet. Virtue was, therefore, a matter of learning to see pleasure and pain in the perspective of time, and to evaluate them correctly despite the fact that the more distant looked the smaller; non-virtue was simply ignorance of this technique; and virtue could, therefore, be taught. Socrates ended by advocating education. (It was, incidentally, precisely this argument that was adopted and dramatised by the Christian religion, which set before mankind the prospect of a long-term pleasure, heaven, for whose sake men would be well advised to forgo short-term pleasures; and a long-term pain, Hell, for fear of which they should undergo short-term pains. Christianity, too, advocated education, though it was to be exclusively education in imagining the promise and the threat of heaven and Hell. In comparison with that, other education was vain. 'An old woman', according to Savonarola[1], 'knows more about the Faith than Plato. It would be good for religion if many books that seem useful were destroyed'. We may compare a more recent pronouncement [from the 1950 edition of the *Catholic Dictionary*[2]]: 'Few Catholics would hesitate

[1] according to Burckhardt (*The Civilization Of The Renaissance*, VI)
[2] article on Galileo

to say, even now, that it would have been to the unspeakable advantage of European society and individual souls if the bad book by Renan' [sc. his *Vie De Jésus*] '. . . had been summarily suppressed at its birth, and the writer imprisoned, at least "formally" '.)

Socrates's diagnosis was completed by Freud, who filled in the unconscious half of our motivations. The people who chose short-sightedly were not necessarily simply short-sighted with no more to be said; their judgment might have been subverted by unconscious motives. Simple conscious education might be powerless to give them longer sight; they might need education in the subject of the unconscious, to wit psycho-analysis. Moreover, subversion could not take place unless it were that the personality is not whole but is, unknown to itself, divided against itself; with the result that what is pleasant to one part is sometimes unpleasant to another, and it may even constitute pleasure for one part to have pain inflicted on it by another. The division of the personality is made when the infant's basic pleasure-seeking comes in contact with reality and is frustrated. Sooner than submit to frustration for ever, the impulse towards pleasure, in accordance with its nature, agrees to compromise. Part of it actually devotes itself to frustrating the rest, in order to save the rest from the still more devastating frustrations that would be imposed by reality; and an inner wall of restraint is built which the simple pleasure-seeking runs its head against before it ever reaches the outer wall of the real world.

The completed Socratic-Freudian account of our motivations binds us firmly to the pleasure-pain principle. All our moralities are limited by the fact that we cannot desire anything which we do not desire. Yet we have already distinguished it in several elements which may help us elucidate our problem: instinct, reality and a clash of the one on the other, which precipitates what is in effect an evolutionary development.

7. *Psycho-analysis and Evolution*

The mammals in general and par excellence the human species, which has made its babies particularly—that is, psychically—sensitive, have arranged to inflict on their babies a colossal disturbance of the environment and the climate. The comparatively stable era of womb-life is suddenly ended by the process of birth and its extension, weaning: and to the child this disturbance must feel like one of those tremendous upheavals of the environment ('great changes in the distribution of land and sea, and therefore of climate, dependent on great earth-movements'[1]) which, putting an end to a major geological era, precipitated animal species into a period of rapid and far-branching evolution.

Weaning initiates in the child just such a hectic course of evolution, which proceeds at top speed until the end of infancy (infancy being in Freudian terminology the first five years of life), whereupon the child is so exhausted that he enters the 'latency period' (in which he does not seek out new relationships but reacts to the experiences he has already had, repressing his memory of them into the unconscious) and does not undergo a renaissance till puberty.

This, too, tallies with the history of species, which, after the big upheavals, during which 'new families, orders and even classes tended to come into being', settled into 'a condition of faunal stability', where 'evolution has greatly slowed down'[2]. Although all the mammals use birth and weaning as a stimulus to their individuals' development, mankind is the only species which has arrived at the evolutionary position of slowing down before the next spurt. In effect, a human being is born and weaned twice, once as a baby and once as an adolescent. He achieves sexual maturity, which is what species mean by maturity, in two phases, suffering a 'double onset' of sexuality—a phenomenon which, Freud suspected, had 'much to do with the transition to humanity'. It seemed to him evidence of an imperfect join in the development of one species out of another, and he surmised that man 'is derived from a species of animal that was sexually mature at five years'. At the same time[3], Freud distinguished that this double onset is what gives man his unique predisposition to neurosis—and also, we may add, to civilisation. We are wholly weaned from our families, we have abandoned our ambition towards incest and have become capable of forming an Ego-ideal, by the end of infancy. Yet it is not till adolescence that the results of this weaning are passed on to society. Not till then do we become—perhaps by a solemn initiation which mimics birth and is, in effect, a re-birth—full members of the society which is our adoptive family. Again, it is not

[1] A. Morley Davies: *Evolution And Its Modern Critics*, II
[2] A. Morley Davies: *Evolution And Its Modern Critics*, II
[3] *Moses And Monotheism*, III, I, 3

until adolescence that the Ego takes its final step forward into self-consciousness, completes our view of ourselves as finite entities in time and seals us off for ever into our own individuality—thus separating us from the timeless conception of the world which children share with the animals. Post-adolescent man is the only animal afraid of wasting time.

The psyche's response to the environmental upheaval in infancy (the Id differentiating out of itself an Ego, which forms the nucleus of the conscious mind; the Ego differentiating out of itself an Ego-ideal, which forms the nucleus of a third agency, the Super-Ego) is in every sense an evolutionary response. The adaptable living being —the instinctual being—is accommodating itself to the environment and to the new aspects of the environment presented to it. And each new piece of evolution enables the human being to form a new type of relationship—that is, to negotiate his environment in a new mode. He moves from the Id's simple relationships by identification to the Ego's relationships with objects, and thence to the more sophisticated, social identifications we make through the medium of the Ego-ideal.

Obviously, this psychic evolution differs in method from the evolution of species, precisely because it is the evolution of an individuality. Although the species presides over the process (it is our species which has chosen the all-important determining factors that we shall be born of two parents, suckled by one of them and brought up in a mammalian family—of which society itself is only a cultural extension), the species has also decided to set each individual comparatively free, by endowing him with the instinctual capacity to make his own response to his own particular environment and create his own character by living through his own formative psychic history; and it is by this method that our species achieves its unique degree of individual variety.

Moreover, whereas the evolution of a species is accomplished, once and for all, as an historical fact, the psychic evolution which a human individual undergoes as a baby remains simultaneously present, and in use, in the adult. As Freud pointed out[1], whereas you do not find the baby's skeleton inside the adult's, and no more do you find the tiger's invertebrate ancestor inside the tiger, if you analyse an adult psyche, the still-living baby psyche is precisely what you do find. And it can never be dispensed with. The baby's instinctual endowment from its species is all we possess by way of instinctual endowment. It remains alive so long as the individual remains alive, and it is the reservoir on

[1] *Civilization And Its Discontents*, I

which he must draw for all the instinctual energy he disposes of in his negotiation of his environment. Thus Freud's account of psychic history is at the same time an account of psychic economics. The historical course from Id to Ego is also the path which must be taken by every instinctual impulse in its passage to expression in the relationships a human being forms with the outside world.

It is as though the human species had passed on to its individuals a particular version of the ability, which belongs to a species as a whole, to draw on its evolutionary past as it may need in order to adapt itself to present circumstances—the species's ability to adapt its embryos to a womb filled with liquid by making them recapitulate the ancestral history which began in the sea, or even to loose its embryos into direct dependence on a real watery environment, so that they pass the first act of their life-history as water-animals before turning into frogs or dragon-flies. But it is only a psyche which, by preserving images, can keep past experience alive; and thus it is only in the psychic species that the tadpole can remain alive—indeed, remain the dynamic force—in the frog. This evolution, which our psychic processes are perpetually recapitulating, is, however, the individual's own experience and property. We do not pass on by heredity what we personally have evolved by this method, but only the capacity to evolve on the same principle.

None the less, we need not resign ourselves to passing nothing on to our children. We do, as a matter of fact, distribute among them certain hereditary predispositions, whose influence on their psychic development no one has ever been able quite to determine; and it may well be that the psychic evolution of the human species is being carried forward by the hereditary method of biological evolution. But we have also managed, though doubtless not to supersede, certainly to supplement this method. This is what we are doing whenever we bring up our children to a particular language and in a particular cultural tradition. We can see the presages of a cultural tradition in the training a young bird or young mammal receives from its parents[1]; but the method could not receive its decisive acceleration, the cultural inheritance

[1] Not only is the animal's capacity for being trained limited (to substitute human parents for its own does not make a puppy able to evolve a human consciousness), with the result that what animal parents can pass on culturally to their children has only a limited individual variability, but the children's impressionability vis-à-vis the parents seems to be largely innate and passed on by heredity (though a Lamarckian evolutionist can argue that it must have

could not become so influential in the individual's life in comparison
with the innate one, and cultural traditions could not themselves
progress into a variety which almost matches our individual variety,
until the development of language.

When we educate our children, we are passing on to them Shakespeare's or Aristotle's individual experience of the environment. Here
is a method indeed of by-passing heredity. We are perpetuating not
only a species or a family but a cultural group (and we cannot perpetuate our species without perpetuating *some* sort of culture). If we
diagnose that the cultural group holds together by making Shakespeare
or Aristotle one of its communal father-figures, that is the mark of
how far our extra-biological version of evolution copies the biological
original. The mammalian family depends on physical kinship; a culture
is an adoptive family, which depends on the cultural transmission of
a common tradition.

We can see, moreover, that each of our separate cultural traditions
is doing its best to replace by social rules the rigid laws an animal
species imposes by heredity. We are always trying to make what
culture forbids—murder, for instance, or incest—as unthinkable as
it really is unthinkable for a tiger to take to wings or become a vegetarian; and sometimes—as in the case of incest—we deceive ourselves

come in the first place from their ancestors' individual experience). The
innate susceptibility of young birds to certain shapes suggesting enemy or
parent, independent of their personal experience, though naturalists have recently
re-discovered it (see Konrad Z. Lorenz: *King Solomon's Ring*), was known to
William James, who (*Text Book Of Psychology*, XXV) describes the experiments of a much less humane naturalist than Konrad Lorenz whereby he was
adopted as a mother-figure by newly-hatched chickens responding to the
first large moving figure they set eyes on. As a matter of fact, Freud concluded
that in the human Oedipus situation there was likewise a measure of innate
response. Marking himself a Lamarckian by his belief that the individual
psychic experiences of our ancestors could pass into the genetic inheritance of
our species (*Moses And Monotheism*, III, I, 5), he conjectured that humanity's
primeval, perhaps even, strictly speaking, pre-human, experience in relation
to the primal father had become part of our biological inheritance and
accounted, for instance, for our susceptibility to the paternal influence of the
hypnotist (cf. *Group Psychology And The Analysis Of The Ego*). But since hypnosis is an animal phenomenon as well as a human one, we could perhaps
proceed directly from the innate proto-Oedipus situation in animals to the
innate vestiges in our own, which have perhaps been superseded rather than
reinforced by human psychic development.

into supposing that our cultural abhorrence really is an innate, bio-logically-transmitted abhorrence.

Every civilisation is an attempt to lay down a regimen for the whole human species. It is, in effect, a proto-species, and it behaves as a true species must at the start of its career, by sealing itself into an isolation where it can breed true to its newly-acquired form. But once again we often forget that our breeding is accomplished not by heredity but by education. When we argue that there is an innate abhorrence to the mating of a Chinese with a European, or something as unnatural in the marriage of pink to black as there would be in the marriage of tiger with kangaroo, we deceive ourselves into misunderstanding the purely psychic nature of our cultural inheritance, and we under-estimate the catholicity of our unique species. It seems that none of the branches of the human species has yet succeeded in setting itself up as an independent species in the biological sense; so far as we can tell, the baby of pink parents who is adopted into Chinese culture behaves exactly as though he were Chinese—or at least with no more idiosyncrasies than one would expect from his reacting to the fact that he is not the same shade as his fellows or than heredity might have distributed to him through Chinese parentage.

The human race may be proceeding, by means of hereditary select-ion, towards a point where one section of it will make a particular adaptation to the environment and genetically cut itself off from the rest. But we can guess that this tendency is not going to receive any very decisive prod from the environment, as other evolutionary steps have done, because the method of evolutionary adaptation which the human race has already achieved is one which by-passes the necessity for transforming part of a species into a new species. When we are obliged to alter our relationship to the environment, we do not need to become a different sort of animal; we simply change our social, cultural—and perhaps our political—constitution.

8. *The Risk Life Has Taken*

Once we have recognised the psyche as the product of the human species's evolutionary response to the environment, we can see just in what sense Freud called consciousness the Ego's sense-organ[1];

[1] *The Question Of Lay Analysis*, III

and culture is the sense-organ evolved by the human species in groups—each of which is always taking it on itself to behave as though it were the whole species.

Evidently our species has made a distribution to its individuals of some of the elasticity, the adaptibility, the very evolutionary principle, which is normally reserved to the species as a whole. We cannot suppose that our species has made this distribution gratis. Like every other evolutionary change, it must serve the purpose of giving the species better security of tenure in the environment. But this particular change is an enormous and radical step, comparable in size only with the change from monocellular to multicellular life. It has altered the whole mode of the relationship between life and environment, and conceives of security of tenure in new terms. Every other species has achieved a measure of security in relation to one given environment; and if the environment changes, the species must transform itself or perish. But now it is as though life had grown tired of its long experimental history of adapting itself to the water only to find that the rivers dry up, and adapting itself to the land only to find that too successful an adaptation leads to the population outstripping the food supply, and had at last produced, in human beings, creatures capable of lifting their noses just an inch from the grindstone of negotiating the environment, and looking about them. Other creatures are adapted to air or water, and have a sort of recognition of air and water. But in us the sense-system has developed beyond this warning-system, which serves the needs of recognition, and has grown into a psyche, the conscious part of which is actually capable of asking what air and water *are*, and of forming not a recognition of one environment but a generalised concept of environment itself.

We are not, of course, anything like independent of our environment, which must still provide us with sustenance and can still overwhelm and destroy us at a moment's notice; but, unlike the animals, we are capable of altering the environment as scientists and imaginatively re-arranging it as artists; and these faculties are in turn derived from our much more flexible instinctual response to the environment. The other animals must wait for the environment to move before they —or their species—respond. But we are a jump ahead, because we are capable of imagining moves on the part of the environment and putting to ourselves the ideas of 'if' and 'as if'. The psychic system is an improvement on the sense-system because it can anticipate crises, and it owes its power to having undergone its own individual evolution and to keeping its evolutionary past alive inside itself. All our intellectual achievements depend on memory; and our conscious faculty of memory depends on the unquenchable vividness of the unconscious, which is continually serving up to us the fragments of past experience which are the images our reason and our imagination make use of in creating our relationship to the world. In negotiating the world, we are the most flexible of creatures, because we supplement our motor activity by a constant stream of psychic activity. A thought being only a thought, we can experiment without committing ourselves. By thought and communication, individuals annihilate time and space. Moreover, cultures evolve not only more rapidly but less dangerously than animal species, which have to go through the generations-long business of physically breeding improvements into their stock and then, if the improvement turns out to cost more than it is worth, breeding it out again. If we wish to be longer-sighted, we need not develop a new eye but have only to invent the telescope. We can instantly share our discovery with our contemporaries by publishing it, and transmit it by educating our children. And when it is bedtime and long sight turns out to be an impediment to the astronomer who merely wants to take his socks off, we have no need to de-evolve an eye but can simply put the telescope down.

None the less, our own particular improvement, even though it is not merely another useful organ but an actual advance in method of living, may yet turn out to be one of those improvements whose value is eventually outweighed by its disadvantages. Man's success on the earth, though run-away, has been comparatively short so far; and it may be that our psychic flexibility, like some animals' speed, is counter-balanced by its having left us unarmoured. The very individuality of the psyche is one danger. Potentially it is each individual who is a proto-species in himself; each of us has the possibility of setting up as the leader of a group modelling itself on his individuality; and our social problem is to balance the centrifugal anarchy of these millions of individuals against the deadweights they impose on progress when they do submit themselves to someone else's leadership—whereupon they at once forget that a thought is only a thought and treat it, in the fashion of taboo civilisations, as an act, and at the same time, forgetting that a culture is superior to a species because it is more flexible, try to make the laws whereby culture controls thoughts as rigid as those whereby a species controls actions.

Standing to gain so much in the way of a new kind of security of tenure, life also took an unprecedented risk when it created the human species. In being set free of the leading-reins, we have forfeited some of the guarantees which most animals have from their species. Our species gives us no innate dietary rules which should draw us towards wholesome food and save us from noxious—and this is supposing that we *want* to be saved: our species is unique in giving us no guarantee of that. Even our babies do not necessarily want to breathe but may prefer, if they cannot have womb-life for ever, not to have life at all; the midwife has to shake them into life; and the species, if it wants to keep up the supply of living babies, has to rely not on an innate prompting in mothers to shake their newly-delivered babies, but on the chancy cultural formations whereby society does, in the majority of cases, send a midwife to attend the birth and equips her with a folklore or a scientific training in how to treat the baby.

For if we have to do without safeguards from our species, no less has our species, in abdicating direct control over us, placed itself at our mercy. Our instincts are all passed through the medium of a psychic system, where they constitute the pleasure-pain axis. When men of science set up as sexologists and tell us that 'nature' is not concerned with morals or any other human system, but only with reproduction[1], they are not telling us anything which is true of human nature (or which is even certainly true of the human body, whose relation to the psyche is so mysterious to us). It makes better science to say that human nature is concerned not with reproduction but with pleasure; and in our peculiar condition of psychic freedom we have to think of our sexuality as an independent and original instinct of pleasure-seeking, which our individual psychic evolution eventually (and then not in every case) 'presses . . . into the service of reproduction'[2]. It would be possible for us, as for no other species, to deny the species its perpetuation by diverting the instinct which in the other animals has no raison d'être except reproduction. We might well all become exclusively homosexual or else practitioners of contraception to the

[1] e.g., 'Nature is not concerned with chastity. On the contrary she is only concerned with reproduction.' (Eustace Chesser, *New Statesman*, of 4 April, 1959)

[2] Freud: *Collected Papers*, Volume II, III. Similarly, 'the catastrophe of the Oedipus complex (the abandonment of incest and the institution of conscience and morality) may be regarded as a victory of the race over the individual' (*Collected Papers*, Volume V, XVII)

exclusion of parentage; and thus by employing two of the fruits of culture, neurosis and scientific ingenuity, we should defeat the purpose to promote which our species made us capable of culture.

In practice, however, our danger comes not from Eros but from Thanatos, which in the animal species is kept as rigidly under control as the sexual instinct. The species dispenses with the tiger when it has used him as a reproductive unit, and takes steps to ensure that he cannot *want* to dispense with himself prematurely. It has balanced what risks it can afford for him to take—what risks it must have him take if tigers are to retain their foothold on the earth; but it absolutely refuses to let him throw himself away by attacking a volcano, just as it will not let him refuse to want to mate providing the environment lets a mate come his way. The individual animal can succumb only to the will of his species or to an accident in the outside world. The species will have done its best to ensure that accidents do not overtake more than a certain proportion of its individuals; but of course the history of evolution is full of species which miscalculated their exact position in the tight-packed ecology of the earth and were outdone by rivals or else perished in an environmental upheaval that left them no time to reform themselves. Even so, these species perished through an actual failure: they could not wish to fail. The human species, in achieving its measure of insurance against actual failures has had to make us capable of anticipating the accidents of the environment in more than one sense. We can turn Thanatos against our own individual entities before the species is ready to write us off; and by the same token that we, alone of animals, can commit individual suicide, so we can force our species to commit suicide too.

9. *Evolution and Morals*

The unique achievement of our species is to have brought us into a relationship with reality which is at once more and less direct than any other animal's: more, because we have a grasp, however infirm, on reality itself, instead of merely recognising those bits of it which immediately concern us through our senses; less, because our relationship to it is mediated through a psychic system liable to distortion. When the amoeba responds with motor activity to the presence of an obstacle, it need have and can have no doubt that the obstacle is real; it lacks any system where it could store the memory of some previous encounter which could now hallucinate it. Hallucinations, like dreams, are the exclusive property of animals which have the elements of a psychic system and whose past thus remains alive, and in part recapturable.

Yet, whatever distortions our psyche may impose on us through being an organic instrument (that is, something evolved essentially out of instinct, wish, rather than perception of fact), it is capable of seeing the world squarely enough to deduce the existence of certain 'laws of reason', by which we really mean laws of reality, and to observe that these remain consistently true in all the behaviour of reality; there is no field where a thing can be both A and not-A. This perception becomes our touchstone, by which we can correct the distortions of our own perceptions: and if it was Aristotle's revolutionary achievement to apply it to our conscious arguments, it was Freud's to apply reason to the data gathered by our conscious perceptions in such a way as to expose the unconscious thought-processes which supply the motive power of all our conscious thoughts.

Here we begin to glimpse a little light in our moral problem. Psycho-analysis assumes, as all sciences do (and probably all arts), that there is such a thing as outside reality, and that the 'laws of reason' reflect its nature. (It is the privilege of philosophers to argue for ever how far the reality we see is the real reality, how far our reason is limited in perceiving it, and how far we can trust the evidence that other people's perception is consistent with our own.) Once we grant this assumption, we can see how psycho-analysis dares to correct distortions in people's minds. It is not on the statistics-collecting principle of a Kinsey report, and not on the majority-collecting principle of the doctors who found Nathan Leopold abnormal, a principle on which we should have to suppose that in 1100 A.D. it was insane to think the world spherical and insane today to think it flat: it is rather on the test of the reasonableness of our beliefs (and we must remember that anyone who thought in 1100 that the world was spherical without any reasonable grounds for doing so probably *was* insane).

Psycho-analysis can shew us patients to whom reality is so distasteful that they seek refuge in fantasy; it can shew us these same patients asserting that their real allegiance is, after all, to reality, since they are asking the analyst to relieve them of their belief in the fantasy. It can shew us obsessional neurotics in whom it is conscience that is the villain, the distorting agency; and it can shew us the analysts themselves, who are urged by nothing else than conscience to seek out the truth of the matter and make it available to the patient. And there is not a penny to choose between the fantasy and the realistic vision, or between the two consciences, except the reasonableness of the one and the irrationality of the other.

Yet before we go leaping to the conclusion that reason is morality, we have to consider that reason is only the instrument of our relationship to reality. Unless it is animated by instinct, it can no more function than an eye whose owner is dead or a camera whose owner has left it alone in the room. The laws of reason would remain true if every last human being had been wiped off the earth, but no reasoning can take place unless the instinct of a living creature has first created attention—has entered into relationship with the environment. Our reason waits to be animated by Eros, which attaches the mathematician and the novelist to their subjects just as it attaches the baby to its prey, the nipple.

What we can say, with some justification, is that to reason is moral; but all we can mean by that is that to reason (or to fantasise, as artists do, knowing that it is a fantasy), and thereby to come into a juster relation with reality, is ultimately more satisfying to us than to fantasise unconsciously—it is a more pleasurable fulfilment of our instinct towards pleasure. We cannot get away from the definition that the good is what pleases us. We can only note that, to judge from the particular equipment it has put it in our way to acquire by our individual evolutions, our species does seem to fulfil its evolutionary purpose if our instinct forms an ever juster and more precisely appreciative relationship to reality; and, since we are instinctual beings, to fulfil its purpose is our most satisfactory happiness and therefore our best morality. We have to bear in mind that our impulse to seek pleasure, though capable of negating our species's purpose, is the creature of the evolutionary urge in living beings; the Freudian conception of instinct, already anticipated by Schopenhauer's concept of Will[1], is coming very close to the Shavian Life Force (which had likewise been anticipated by Schopenhauer[2]).

Having remarked the limitation on our morality, on all our moralities, which prevents us from seeking anything but pleasure, we can go on to proclaim that psycho-analysis, so far from reducing morality

[1] Freud: *Collected Papers*, Volume IV, XX; *An Autobiographical Study*, V
[2] Shaw: *Back To Methuselah*, Preface, 'Discovery Anticipated By Divination'

to nonsense, is an urgent moral necessity. If we want to serve the evolutionary purpose of keeping the human species on the earth, psycho-analysis is the only practical and therefore the only moral, way of setting about it, for civilisation has put no other instrument in our hand capable of helping us even to see straight—let alone begin to control—our desperate crisis in relation to our own destructive impulses. Indeed, it is not until we achieve a realistic vision of the facts that we can begin to discuss morality at all.

The subject under post-hypnotic suggestion who has had artificially implanted in his unconscious the desire to leave the house at midnight and sing outside his front door invents plentiful rationalisations for his conduct, rationalisations his own intelligence would quickly see through if it had not been subverted from below. It is the business of psycho-analysis to free intelligence from spontaneous distortions of this kind and set the instinct towards pleasure, whose tortuous course has created them, back on the road towards reality; and until that is done there is no profit to be had from moral persuasion. The religious fanatic who believes that he is fulfilling the Christian moral precepts when he burns heretics is not making a moral mistake but an intellectual one. Moral argument will get nowhere with him, because he is convinced he is morally right; our only hope is to point out to him his unacknowledged destructive wish, which has blinded him to the logical necessity whereby loving one's neighbour is incompatible with burning him; and only when he has perceived this can we profitably begin to discuss with him the moral rights and wrongs of loving and burning.

If we can accuse the Jungians of nonsense in addressing moral exhortation to the unconscious, it is hardly too much to say that it is equally nonsense to address moral exhortation to the conscious, so long as the conscious remains at the mercy of unconscious subversion. The command to love one's neighbour was enjoined on the Jews by *Leviticus*[1] and passed on to the Gentiles by Christianity; the history of Judaism and Christendom is witness to our imperviousness to it. 'There does not appear to have been any lack of sublime moral precepts', wrote the Victorian rationalist Evans Bell, 'in every age and almost every nation. The value of moral precepts is in truth very small.'[2] That is at their best: at their worst, a precept quickly turns into a pretext, for it has only to set up as God-given and superior to reason, and it will connive at the subversion of reason.

[1] XIX, 18　　　　[2] *The God Of The Bible* (*The Task Of Today*), VII

Our concern today is with bigger bonfires than we burned the heretics in, but our fear is precisely the same: namely that in despite of our conscious wish to preserve life something will persuade us that destroying it is somehow compatible with saving it. Nuclear physics itself does not tell us that it is either right or wrong to drop nuclear bombs; it is simply a technique, and what it tells us is that if we want to destroy the world, here is the most effective way of doing it. Psycho-analysis, too, does not make a primary contribution to the moral problem—though it may help ultimately. Primarily, it, too, is a technique, but it is a technique for dealing with ourselves; and what it tells us is that if we really do not wish to destroy the world, and wish to make sure that we shall not do it in spite of ourselves, *here* is the most effective way of refraining.

10. *Psycho-analysis and Intelligence (with a Note on Tests)*

If, heeding this statement, our statesmen were to adopt psychoanalytic ways of thought, they would promptly be turned out of office—unless the habit of psycho-analysis had spread to the electorate. An attempt to apply psycho-analysis in communal life generally would run into the problem which has already impeded its application to such particular sections of the community as criminals: the problem whether the people concerned, criminals or the electorate (or, indeed, the politicians themselves) are, simply, intelligent enough. Psycho-analysis consists of the use of reason to restore the reason to control. There must be reason to use and to be restored.

This is, of course, the final problem of all government. Government by a minority was superseded when it became clear that none of the methods of selecting the minority came anywhere near being methods of selecting the most intelligent rulers, though a few minority rulers had clouded the issue by behaving intelligently enough in their own interest, the trouble being that their interest conflicted with the people's. For those who had heard only the ultima ratio regum, it was an understandable mistake to suppose that vox populi would be vox dei. The French Revolution made it plain that it was no such thing; but the conduct of minority rulers had made it no less plain that their voice, too, was far from being divinely right. When the franchise was extended in nineteenth-century England, it was thought to be a concomitant that the new voters should be educated into divine wisdom, and education was not merely thrown open to them but forced upon them. The horses were taken to the water and the trough was emptied over their heads: and it turned out that most of them would drink very little and some would not drink at all. The problem was no longer education but educability. The conclusion was forced on us that such a quality as intelligence existed, the potentiality for reasoning, and that most people had very little of it, an assessment confirmed when methods were devised of roughly measuring it.

By the beginning of the twentieth century it was obvious to Bernard Shaw that, since the majority of people were too stupid even to calculate correctly where their own interest lay, the only hope for government, as opposed to anarchy, was to produce a more intelligent race. We needed not one superman, who can govern the people only by oppressing them and provoking their animosity, but a whole breed of supermen, an evolutionary step forward. The obvious method was the same sort of selective breeding whereby we can produce racehorses and fancy dogs; but the trouble with human eugenics, from our present point of view, is that it would take much too long—as well as running into the same vicious circle as psycho-analysis, namely that the people whom we most need to win over to it are the least persuadable. (The idea of coercing them, like all coercions by minorities, has to be rejected if only because of the impossibility of selecting the minority.)

It seems, therefore, that we shall have to try our alternative method of evolution, education. Here we run into an enormous difficulty: at present, we are not intelligent enough to try to be more intelligent. We can see now the absolute viciousness of an educational system which pretends to develop reasoning power but is really doing its best to damp down reason, imagination and initiative. Yet as a matter of fact it is just in this viciousness that we can glimpse our only hope. If we really are damping down intelligence, then we really do possess potentially more intelligence than we at present allow to shew itself; and we can dare to hope that our present threat of extinction may work on us, as similar threats have worked throughout the history of species, to force us out of the childish stupidity of the masses, of the group mind, in which we are at present taking refuge, and oblige us to liberate our unused potentiality of intelligence.

With stupidity, as with other commodities, we simply do not know whether demand creates the supply or whether what is available dictates the market. Should we be thankful that civilisation requires a lot of dull jobs to be done, which can be gratefully done by dull people; or should we attribute the dullness of most people to the preponderance of dull jobs? Our very intelligence tests cannot distinguish, among the people who return dull answers, those who tried and failed from those who were not interested enough to pay attention. We do not know how many people our civilisation has discouraged from paying attention. Again, we cannot be sure that our educators are right in regarding intelligence as an innate endowment, which may grow naturally with age but is not much to be influenced by education. Have they not, perhaps, fallen victim to fatalism? And, since the same hands control both the tests and the education, they can repeatedly prove themselves right by employing the tests to weed out the dull children and then never giving those dull children the kind of education which might have made them more intelligent. Recently, psychologists have had to recognise that intelligence is probably not an innate and fixed quality at all but improves with education and cultural background—in which case the use educators make of the tests is topsy turvy: the children should be given tests at the end as well as at the start of their school careers and the difference be used to measure the efficacy of the teachers.

In fact, however, the tests often seem to be working towards the suppression of intelligence even in the children they pick out as intelligent. I cannot be accused of personal prejudice in this matter, because in my own schooldays I was very good at intelligence tests, which seldom made me out anything less than a genius. But nowadays when I read through the tests which are used in England to select children for grammar schools I wonder whether my 'intelligence' amounted to anything more than a facility in hypocrisy, and whether my 'genius' consisted in an ability to perceive anything more valuable about the real world than the answers the testers wanted—which is not always to credit them with great intelligence themselves. When I read the question where the child is asked to fill in the blank in 'Black as—', I have to admit that an intelligent child probably has noticed that the accepted cliché in this comparison is 'coal' or 'night', though I give a thought to the child whose family employs the not very stringent simile 'black as your hat'; but I also wonder what is the fate of the child who has observed and, in his simplicity, does not doubt that the examiner has also observed that night in cities is not black, and that coal usually presents glittering metallic faces which are no more black than the faces of a diamond—or the fate of the child who has read *A Midsummer Night's Dream* and fills in 'black as Acheron'.

(This conformism, this preference for the child who knows its clichés and, still worse, for the child who is prepared to accept the rules as they are taught in defiance of its own experience of the spoken language, is no less striking in the language tests, which ask the children not to comment on but categorically to correct such idiomatic English as 'Everyone went on their bicycles', and sentences where 'none' is followed by a plural verb. I have one examination question to put to the educationist who devised this last: Consider Andrew Marvell's sublime contribution to world literature

> The Grave's a fine and private place,
> But none I think do there embrace

and correct it in such a way that it still makes sense.)

11. *Psychology versus Mechanics*

How we assess our chances of responding to our dire need by acquiring more intelligence depends on which view we take of the methods of evolution. The question whether, in order to become more intelligent, we must first be more intelligent, or whether we can become more intelligent by wanting to, is a new limb to the old controversy whether the giraffe[1] got his long neck because he already had it or because he wanted it.

As Shaw never tired of pointing out, there are two versions of evolution. (He also pointed out that the British public never managed to grasp the distinction[2]; neither, one may add, have the biologists:

[1] Shaw: 'I do not remember how this animal imposed himself illustratively on the Evolution controversy; but there was no getting away from him then; and I am old-fashioned enough to be unable to get away from him now'. (*Back To Methuselah*, Preface, 'The Moment And The Man')

[2] 'I have pointed out elsewhere' (sc. in the Preface to *Androcles And The Lion*) 'that the British nation does not consist of atheists and Plymouth Brothers; and I am not now going to pretend that it ever consisted of Darwinians and Lamarckians. The average citizen is irreligious and unscientific . . .

if you keep an eye on their public pronouncements and their professional controversies, you can see quantities of them veering round towards Shaw's point of view without the least notion that it *is* Shaw's.) The neo-Darwinian point of view (Shaw exonerated Darwin in person from ever claiming that this was the only method employed by evolution) was that nothing could be passed on by heredity except what had been acquired by heredity: the variety of species was therefore the result of variations from the strict norm of a species's pattern, variations which are always distributed by the lottery of inheritance among a small part of the population of a species, but which in normal conditions counted, if anything, as disadvantages; yet if there was an environmental change, some of the odd animals out would find themselves better adapted, by virtue of their accidental quirks, than their normal fellows, would outdo their fellows and thus become the breeding-stock of the new species, to which they would pass on as normal the characteristics which had previously marked them as eccentrics.

To this mechanistic theory, which at the present time is still virtually the only one accepted as respectable in western biological cricles, Butler and Shaw opposed a neo-Lamarckian, essentially psychological[1] concept of evolution as the product of a wish, an instinct, inherent in life—an instinct which takes advantage of the environment where it can, and which, when the environment threatens to extinguish it, achieves miracles of adaptation rather than surrender life altogether. By this version the giraffe got his long neck in obedience to the pleasure-principle: his desire for the better leaves at the top was so great that he tried until he succeeded: and it followed, of course, that some of the adaptations an individual made on his own account could—if the life instinct was touched—be passed on by heredity.

To the adherents of the dynamic, psychological theory one must add Freud, who is so often ignorantly accused nowadays of being a nineteenth-century mechanist. Having noted 'the present attitude of biological science which rejects the idea of acquired qualities being

Nothing will knock into his head the fateful distinction between Evolution as promulgated by Erasmus Darwin, and Circumstantial (so-called Natural) Selection as revealed by his grandson.' (*Back To Methuselah*, Preface, 'Why Darwin Converted The Crowd')

[1] Consider Shaw's refutation as unpsychological of Weismann's neo-Darwinian experiments and conclusions (*Back To Methuselah*, Preface, 'Traumatic Selection')

transmitted to descendants', he went on: 'I admit, in all modesty, that in spite of this I cannot picture biological development proceeding without taking this factor into account'[1].

The proponents of the two views might argue as long as they liked about the method evolution has adopted, but they had to agree on the final (so far) result of the process, man. If the mechanical method of selection really was as ruthlessly efficient as the neo-Darwinians maintained, then it had finally vindicated its efficiency by producing a creature who was not mechanical but reasoning. The strict mechanists, however, would not admit this, but argued that logic and consciousness were not really logic and consciousness at all but strictly determined reflex actions, and that the reasoner could no more avoid going through certain mental paces than a tadpole could avoid turning into a frog.

As a construction set on reality, this point of view is irrefutable (though so is its contradiction); but as a justification (a concept which, strictly speaking, it makes meaningless) of certain courses of action, it is nonsense. Whether or not man really has a measure of freedom, one thing is quite certain: he has the impression (or maybe illusion) that he has. When the capitalist argued that the distress of the poor was inevitable, a side-result of inevitable competition, itself the inevitable biological result of the principle of the survival of the fittest; when Karl Marx argued that the triumph of the proletariat would be the inevitable result of unavoidable historical processes[2]; when the laboratory worker explains his inconceivably cruel assaults on animals by saying that he cannot help himself but is inevitably doing, as a member of the human species, what all species have done in the course of evolution—assault the weak in order to secure their own (in this case scientific) advancement: each of these arguments (besides making use of a logical and persuasive form which the arguer must believe is really neither logical nor persuasive) is denying the one cardinal and undeniable fact about man, that he believes he has choice.

The tiger cannot possibly avoid springing on its prey, and neither had its ancestors any choice open to them but to outdo the less efficient tigers: but what evolution has now produced is a laboratory worker who cannot help believing that he might one morning go to work

[1] *Moses And Monotheism*, III, I, 5

[2] It is Shaw who diagnosed Marxism as an extension of neo-Darwinism: to Marx 'civilization was an organism evolving irresistibly by circumstantial selection' (*Back To Methuselah*, Preface, 'Darwin And Karl Marx')

and liberate the animals he had intended to make his victims. If there is any inevitability our species binds on us, it is that we must believe we can choose and must, therefore, be moral beings in some sort, just as we must be cultural and social beings. Our inevitabilities, whatever they are, are mediated through a psychic system. We are psychological first and last. The man who confides himself for an instant to the direct support of biological or historical inevitability will end up, plump, on the floor; and he will instantly find himself consulting the pleasure-pain axis, quite as though within its limits he had free choice, about whether he should or should not get up again.

12. *Our Religious Revival*

The strict mechanist view, which by the end of the nineteenth century seemed so certain to prevail, nowadays has currency only in the communist part of the world, where it has suffered the paradoxical fate of being turned into an atheist religion—one which, with its puritanism, asceticism and belief in inevitability, resembles nothing so much as Calvinism. In the west, mechanism is confined to the laboratories (and is not to be found even in all of those), leaving the rest of us to rush headlong into a religious revival plus its concomitant, a revival of diabolism. Even the God of the Bible, whose cruelties were exposed by Evans Bell, the very God of *Genesis*, whose unfounded claims were disposed of by Darwin, has been revived in his original form; and the devil who has to accompany him in an attempt to mitigate his cruelty is identified with the anti-Christ of communism by quite large numbers of people, who would solemnly like us to destroy communism by force, at no matter what cost to our own lives, let alone our own morals, solely on the grounds that communism is atheistical.

For the most part, however, the religious revival does not care to be too specific about which god it is reviving. It has something to say for the oriental faiths, some of which manage to be faiths without *having* a god; but it is predominantly Christian, and yet nonsectarian or, if sectarian, oecumenical. There is a certain tolerance among religionists nowadays towards those who share at least their belief in religious belief, even if they cannot agree on a particular creed. But it would be a mistake to suppose that this tolerance is extended to rationalists who do not believe in the virtue of religious belief at all; indeed, it is their common intolerance of rationalism which has drawn the religionists together. Often it is the vaguest and most latitudinarian religionists who want to destroy the communists on the same principle that the Catholic Church destroyed heretics. The communists fortunately are protected against this intolerance by their own armed forces: in our present lack of international law and an international constitution, nothing else would protect them. Atheists at home are better off; they are protected from the fury of religionists by a constitutionalism that has been won step by step from the theocratic monarchies which formerly governed Europe. But if it were not for the British constitution I should, as a rationalist-atheist, go in fear for my life of the parson and priest who are personally so nice to me. As it is, if I lived in a Catholic country, I should go in fear of some discomfort; and in England I am quite aware of the religionists' doing all they can to edge the irreligious point of view out of every forum of public debate and instruction, in a way that the irreligionists, for their very principles, cannot even wish to edge out the religious point of view.

It is done, of course, without personal animus: just as the Church let heretics go to the fire without personal animus. The religionist of today, for all his tolerance of heterodox religionists, is the direct heir of the religionist who treated the believer in a different faith as no better than a total disbeliever. If the religionist is now a little misty on the subject of which god should be worshipped, that is because he feels the need to obscure God's responsibility for Satan. He may no longer insist that schools should inculcate exclusively the Presbyterian or the Anglican view of God; he may not even insist solely on a Christian view: but you will never find him proposing that our children should be allowed to consider the merits of reason, as well as those of faith, on religious questions. He cannot. He cannot fight for the rationalist's right to put his case, and the children's right to hear it, in the way that the rationalist must fight for the religionists' freedom; and this is not solely because he suspects he might lose in an open competition, but also because he believes it would be sin to give any larger currency to sin—that is, to the rationalists' point of view. Intolerance is written-in to his very code of faith.

The religious revival makes it its object to put the mystery back into the universe, the mystery having supposedly been plucked out by reason. This, Herbert Spencer pointed out, is an attitude curiously distrustful of the universe (and in fact the religious revolt against reason is nothing but a revolt against reality), as well as grossly flattering to reason. It was this eminent and now unjustly neglected Victorian reasoner who demonstrated by reason the inadequacy of reason in explaining the universe, which might be either self-existent, self-creating or created by an external agency; and all three possibilities Spencer shewed to be, strictly speaking, inconceivable[1]. The cause of the universe, according to Spencer, was a true mystery, and this he took to be the central, true mystery embodied in all religions. But religions, instead of simply recognising the unknowable, made, in their dogmata, statements about it; whereupon Spencer accused them of irreligion, because they were de-mysterising the central mystery. Moreover, when their dogmata were one by one refuted, the religionists even began to doubt the central mystery: 'Religion secretly fears that all things may some day be explained; and thus itself betrays a lurking doubt whether that Incomprehensible Cause of which it is conscious, is really incomprehensible'[2].

In accusing religionists of irreligion Herbert Spencer was taking a philosophic, not a psychological, view of them. It was, after all, he, not they, who selected consciousness of an incomprehensible cause of the universe as the nucleus of religion. Philosophy can always drive religionists back on this position, but historically and psychologically religions start from much more specific mysteries. Spencer, who was trying to find some general truth in religion which he could reconcile with some general truth in science, and who meant (so completely did science seem in 1862 to be winning the controversy) to be kind to religion, really dealt impertinently by it. The mystery he picked on differs in kind from a simple lack of knowledge by being a logical conundrum, an assertion that knowledge cannot know. But this mystery, being forced on us by the facts, requires no faith for its recognition and is different in kind again from what religion means by a mystery. The ground where Spencer reconciles religion and science is simply the no-man's-land that does not belong to either of them.

None the less, Spencer performed a correct and useful service, because in practice religionists will always claim the no-man's-land if no one disputes it with them. The moment you postulate that the cause of the universe is x, of which you can assert nothing except the

[1] *First Principles*, Part I, II   [2] *First Principles*, Part I, V, 28

impossibility of knowing what it really is, the religionist leaps in with 'Why not call the x God?', and at once begins behaving as though you had assented to the idea that the universe was caused by the God of whom the Athanasian Creed displays such detailed knowledge.

13. *The Absolute Immorality of Religion*

But though it was straining the words to accuse religion of irreligion, there would have been no strain if Spencer had accused it of immorality. Faith and morals, which the Roman church lumps together as the sphere of its own infallibility, are in reality, and of the very nature of reality, separate magnets which must pull contrary to one another.

Morality sets up a single objective, truth, and binds man to it by his moral obligation to explore it. Religion sets up this objective, too, but together with another, God. Not for a moment does religion admit that the two obligations may pull against one another; and it proves they cannot by equating the two and pronouncing that God is truth.

If it had stopped there, religion would have done no more than postulate Herbert Spencer's x, and no one would quarrel with it; but it would no longer be religion. Obviously, truth cannot be refuted. It is not possible that it is true to say that truth does not exist. Likewise a God who is simply truth cannot be refuted unless he himself intimates, on the authority of being God, that God does not exist.

However, truth, though it can be respected, cannot be worshipped. The religionist is bent on worshipping—and, what is more, on being wanted to worship. He has to turn God into a person and make statements about him which are liable to refutation. This liability the religionist denies by quickly turning God back into the abstract, truth, and extending the irrefutability of truth to cover the statements made about God the person; and every time you say to him that you doubt the existence of God the character who appears in *Genesis* or the Athanasian Creed, he replies that God's existence cannot be doubted because God is truth.

In fact, as practical experience quickly shews, it is impossible to argue with a religionist, because he cannot seriously conceive that the statements of religion are incorrect; and he cannot conceive it because he believes it would be sinful of him to conceive it. The most ingenious of the devices whereby religion perpetuates itself is to have made faith a virtue. And it is just this—which admits that religious belief, unlike reasonable belief, is a voluntary, wished, act—which exposes the psychology of religion and the absolute immorality which lies at its heart.

The theologians were able to maintain that faith was virtuous, whereas knowledge was not, by making the distinction that, while matters of faith and matters of knowledge were both certain, matters of faith were not evident. Thus, in the words of Franz Hettinger, 'an assent of faith is determined . . . not by evidence of the truth of the doctrines proposed, but solely by evidence of the truth of the teaching authority.' Knowledge is something we cannot help believing because of the evidence. But with faith, when we must trust in the authority, 'it is always possible to refuse to believe, and an act of faith must always be preceded by an act of obedience. . . It is this submission of the will which renders faith meritorious, while the contrary act . . . makes unbelief a sin. Its guilt consists in the deliberate denial of the truth of God's Word, and the deliberate preference of human reason as the more trustworthy authority.'

Hettinger's difficulty comes when one asks him on what evidence one is to trust God as a better authority than human reason, since the answer he has to give is:—human reason. The 'existence of God, as the one personal Creator and Rewarder, is made known to all men by the use of reason'[1].

A God who was simply truth would have been delighted when mankind was delivered from a long-standing error by the discovery that the world had not been created in six days. Christians, however, seemed to know very well that their God was not truth. So far from supposing him delighted, they conceived they would please him by finding some—or, rather, *any*—means of maintaining that it *was* made in six days, even though this duty involved them in the immorality of disingenuous argument. Only when science had utterly routed them and was on the point of ridiculing them out of their profession did they suddenly switch the debate from a factual plane to a metaphorical one. The controversy over the facts has become out of date and is dismissed by the now impolite adjective 'nineteenth-century'. Christians have taken to behaving as though the Christian tradition, to continue which is their only claim to authority, never *had* believed *Genesis* literally.

Apart from a few literalists left behind by their own churches,

[1] Franz Hettinger: *Revealed Religion*, I

Christians nowadays claim and are often granted licence to use words in a way no one else can use them and still be thought both sane and honest. Forced to admit that religious statements are not true, they fall back on claiming they are none the less valid, like artistic fictions. Yet the religionist cannot admit that his creed is a fiction or that it may properly be judged as a work of art: in that case religion would be a matter of taste, and there could be no question of sinning if one discarded or never found faith. The religionist claims for his creed the impossible best of both worlds, that it is more factual than art, and more valid than fact.

The controversies of the eighteenth and nineteenth centuries have left religion blatantly exposed in an untenable position, defying reality itself by the claim that, while every other kind of statement must be true or untrue, religious statements are excused from the dilemma and can be both—indeed, supertrue. Faith consists of maintaining a fantasy in the teeth of reality. It would be a very spiritless rationalist who did not admire the dazzling impudence whereby the religionists simply turn morality upside down and assure us that to defy reality is good, and to be in an untenable position virtuous. In western society, however, the religionists have gone beyond impudence into imposture. Anxious to avoid any further collisions with science, religion has proposed a non-aggression pact: let science stick to its sphere and religion will stick to *its*; a proposition which looks reasonable and magnanimous, for which religion gladly accepts the credit, until one notices that religion has no just claim to possess a sphere and is not a sovereign state at all, but an impostor, whose claims are grounded in no part of the real world.

Where it can no longer impose itself by force, religion still enjoys a success out of proportion to the amount of belief in it, because the unreligious let themselves be imposed on, allowing religion to drive a grossly unjust bargain. In English schools, instead of making religious instruction something available to those children whose parents ask for it, we let it pass for normal, leaving it to the unreligious parent to take steps to have his child exempted and risk the child growing up crassly ignorant (for no instruction in the history, influence and content of Christianity is available untainted by propaganda); and of course by making it appear strange not to go to scripture lessons the religionists impose their will on unreligious parents who are not prepared to force their children into eccentricity. Thus the religionists succeed in having religious statements taught to our children at school together with the statements of history and physics—but not on an equality with them: for while the child is taught that it is common sense to believe the physics text-book, he is told that it is virtuous to believe the scriptures; and while all the other lessons teach him to sift evidence and argue reasonably, the scripture lesson teaches him that belief is an act of will and that he must try not to disbelieve. When the religionist claims morning prayers in the schools, and evening homilies on the television, the authorities who arrange the timetable believe they are doing something conducive to the people's moral well-being by letting the religionist have his opportunity. But should the atheist claim an opportunity to refute religion, the timetable maker does not believe that to grant it him is conducive to anyone's moral well-being; the most he will give the atheist is one thousandth part of the opportunity given to religionists, and he will think himself tolerant and broad-minded for giving anything at all. If it comes to a dispute, the religionist need have no delicacy towards atheists' feelings and need be at no pains to point out his opponent's sincerity. Indeed, if he regards unbelief as a sinful act of disobedience, it is only with some difficulty and mental juggling that he *can* believe his opponents are sincere. But the atheist, if he wishes not merely to avoid condemnation for bad taste but to be allowed to speak publicly at all, must shew the utmost respect for religious susceptibilities, and whenever he mentions that he considers religion a mistake must quickly append that he believes it a sincere one.

Indeed, secular society makes a great point of the religionists' sincerity: it professes itself dazzled by it, and accords to the religionist a public respect it would not dream of paying to the lunatic who believes himself to be Napoleon. The lunatic's undoubted sincerity does not persuade us that his opinion about his identity is correct or, if not absolutely correct, socially valuable because of its sincerity. We do not hand our children over to him to be taught that they will be doing something dreadful if they ever cease to believe he is Napoleon. If we make this great distinction in the way we treat the lunatic's and the religionist's claim, it must be because one of them is useful to us. A society which is not prepared to put—or at least to try and put—its morality on a rational basis does not want rational questions asked about it; it is glad to call in help from the myth that morality is something delivered pat, and sanctioned, by God. So long as we cannot explain to our children why they should not hate one another, it is expedient to have them told that the answer is because

Jesus loves them. *We* may not believe it, but it is expedient that our neighbour should, because we want him to refrain from acts of murder. It is therefore important for us to believe in the religionists' sincerity, for it seems to shift the burden of hypocrisy from ourselves. *We* cannot sincerely indoctrinate our children with the Christian myth, but, so long as there are people who can, we will send our children to them to be indoctrinated, putting up with the slight moral discomfort we feel when the priests berate us for not accompanying our children to church ourselves.

In other words, because we think it to our advantage to do so, we accept the religionists' claim that to teach religion is the only way to teach morality. We do not trouble ourselves with questioning the morals of a morality which can only be taught together with an untruth, because we point out to ourselves that to the religionists it is not an untruth. We insist on believing them sincere. Yet as a matter of fact, we can no more believe them sincere than they can believe the atheist to be sincere, and for the same reason, namely that they profess faith and lack of faith to be voluntary acts. The religionist actually boasts that he believes not because he must but because he wants to.

This places the religionist in a much less harmless category than the lunatic. We know what has happened to the lunatic: his desire to believe in fantasy is so overwhelming, and his dread of the penalties of perceiving reality is so terrifying, that they have actually encroached on his faculty for judging reality. His is a genuine delusion, which he cannot help believing any more than the dreamer can help, while he is asleep, believing the vision he experiences as fact. But the religionist is a mere *day*dreamer. He insists that he is a *voluntary* hysteric, for he insists that he *can* help believing. (Even when he is a spontaneous hysteric as well, undergoing hysterical seizures and perceiving visions which are peculiar to himself, though their subject-matter is borrowed from the common mythology, he does not, in his waking moments, reiy on the absolute conviction these must impress on his senses [Indeed, he maintains they are untrustworthy and may emanate from the devil], but still places his emphasis on his voluntary act of faith.)

This he must do if he is to claim his religion as virtuous, for there can no more be virtue in crediting a delusion than in crediting a solid fact. Here lies the essential immorality of religion: it cannot be content with mere truth. The creed must be not simply something which *is* untrue, an honest mistake that could be abjured without the least sense of sin, but something which the religionist *knows* is untrue. If every clause of the Apostles' Creed were proved tomorrow to be historical and scientific truth, the religionists would have to disclaim the common-sense method of arriving at the knowledge or else cease to be religious.

Before he can assert his faith in any particular creed, the religionist must assert his faith in faith. This is why he is immoral—unlike the lunatic, who would not dream of wanting us to believe something that is untrue but invites us to agree that he is Napoleon solely on the grounds that he *is* Napoleon.

Naturally the scientific progress of the eighteenth and nineteenth centuries left religion unshaken. Since it did not include a psychological science, it had no understanding of the religionists' faith in faith. The scientists were merely pressing rational arguments about reality on someone who did not accept either reason or reality. All they could do was to force religion out of one fortuitously immoral position it had taken up, and oblige it to stop claiming that its creed was true on the common-sense level as well as the supernatural. Those who had accepted the religionists' conclusions on what were really grounds of probability, for want of a better hypothesis, were shaken off the religious tree, leaving the real religious stock stronger than ever for being clearly shewn in its necessarily unreasonable position. To the eighteenth-century rationalist, the problem about religionists was whether they were fools or hypocrites. Psychology sets the more delicate problem whether they are, like the lunatic, unconscious hypocrites or whether we should accept their own claim and read them as opting for self-delusion. We are back at the problem whether a man can wish not to see straight.

Whether by choice or necessity, religionists are daydreamers, and they are not yet so completely dominated by their fantasy as to set it free to return to them like an independent visitation, in the manner of a real dream or a hysterical vision. (And in fact if the village should suffer an outbreak of hysterical panic—a belief in ghosts or black magic—the sceptics and materialists will not find a doughtier rock to stand beside than the parson and the priest, the one acting in the name of common-sense and the other through dread of superstition, by which he means any belief in miracles not emanating from his Church. Their strength lies precisely in their hypocrisy: being intimate with the supernatural, inducing a miracle on the altar every Sunday and regularly preaching the resurrection of the dead, they know quite well that the supernatural does not really manifest itself, that its power is all in the mind and it does not really hurt.) The creed is a fantasy, a statement in the form of narrative of what is really a wish. When the religionist asserts the value and power of faith, he is asserting the value and power of the human imagination. Up to this point he preaches exactly the same doctrine as the artist—indeed, as any cultured person. But the powers of the mind are not enough for him. He *will* go further and insist that his myths are true in some literal as well as in a literary way, with the result that he finally alienates even the artist who, sharing his daydreamy temperament, is his natural ally.

To entrust our children's education to these literal-minded fantasists is an act of confusion—or at least it would be if we genuinely wanted to educate our children. The two things we profess to ask education to impart, knowledge and reasoning, religion is bound to deprecate even when it is not in panic dead against them. If it is comparatively rare for religion to contradict a demonstrable fact and find itself maintaining that the sun *does* go round the earth, it must all the time, and regardless of the content of any particular fact, belittle the importance of facts. No religion counts curiosity a virtue. Christianity's attitude to it was fixed by the fourth century and summed up by Eusebius's sarcasms[1] on those heretical Christians some of whom 'actually study Euclid's geometry and admire Aristotle and Theophrastus', an attitude presently enshrined in that unscupulous anti-curiosity parable the Faust legend. Religion has always held that learning, experiment and reason are not only superfluous to faith but actively dangerous, being attractive enough to distract man from salvation. The coming of science, which could not merely distract men's minds but factually contradict religion's statements, only forced religion to tighten a repression it had practised all along. From astronomy to anatomy there is hardly a branch of knowledge that Christianity has not tried to wither or lop off and burn. Savonarola's conviction of the superiority of faith to imagination and intelligence (still to be found—just as puritanical but a trifle secularised, faith having been transmuted into 'character'—in English schools) is the only consistent attitude for Christians to adopt. It is nothing short of burglary when Christians nowadays seek to persuade us that western culture is inseparable from Christianity, and try to place

[1] approvingly quoted from a still earlier Christian writer (Eusebius: *Ecclesiastical History*, V, XXVIII). Cf. Lecky's remarks (*History Of European Morals. . .* IV) on the 'positive disfavour' with which the early monks regarded learning.

Christianity in the centre of our defence of a cultural tradition in which they must take care to mention Botticelli more often than the Inquisition.

That Christianity so often and so fruitfully did play the patron to art and scholarship we owe either to the inconsistency or to the worldliness, as complained of by Savonarola, of Christians. The monasteries preserved, no doubt partly in ignorance but partly also superstitiously, the relics of a pagan civilisation which the preservers were professionally bound to consider worthless or dangerous. If this inconsistency made the renaissance possible, our own educational tradition has been able to pass down to us a touch of the renaissance's classical enthusiasm thanks to the illogicality—or sometimes perhaps the hypocrisy—which kept it alive in Christian universities and schools and, often with notably scholarly results, in the very vicarages and rectories themselves.

14. *Classical Education*

Although we seldom pause to remark its strangeness, it *is* psychologically very strange that the remains of antiquity were nursed, at first rather uncomprehendingly and then with idolatrous admiration, in the bosom of Christendom, the most intolerant social-religious system the world has ever experienced.

No doubt we owe this strangeness, like so many others, to human ambivalence towards God. The very severity with which God the Father insisted on being our exclusive god, and set his face against reason, forced us to keep alive a secret and subversive source of rebellion against him. The teeming Greek mythology implicitly mocked at the intellectualised but intellectually impossible three-in-oneness of the Christian God and the purely mental feat of his bodiless conception; and at the same time Greek literature preserved towards its own mythology, and thereby by implication towards the Christian mythology too, a tradition of arrantly rational scepticism.

If we decide now to do away with classical education we shall be shutting down an underground river which has been marvellously, if secretly, fertilising. Scientific and technical education cannot begin to match the unorthodoxy, the sheer anti-conformism, which unknown to ourselves we let the Greeks propagate from the very centres and seminaries of Christian orthodoxy. In English public schools, with their chaplains, their headmasters in holy orders or the grip of lay enthusiasm, and equally (as Roger Peyrefitte's novel, *Les Amitiés Particulières*, lets us know) in priestridden French schools, young men being respectably instructed in classical literature and antiquities have for generations pursued a tacit but systematic course not only in pagan mythology and categorical rationalism but also in republican politics and homosexuality.

This last has been a more potent influence towards social noncon-formism than we usually acknowledge. Any sexual unorthodoxy may be the first step towards social rebellion; but this particular un-orthodoxy has its step bent in that direction by particular causes. When the public schoolboy seeks out younger boys, he is defying the class-system, the class-divisions by age, of school, just as he will later defy the social class-system by seeking out young men in the prole-tariat. It is to homosexuals that we should give the credit of having implicitly understood the psychic structure of society and of discerning in modern civilisation the unerased outline of the primal horde. Unconsciously the homosexual recognises the social class barrier for what its equivalent really is at school, an age barrier—quintessentially, the barrier between generations, the ban on incest between the parental and the filial generation. He recognises that the patrician and the proletariat are father and sons. (And we can learn a good deal about the psycho-sexual nature of society from the fact that no such interpretation of social class is written-in to women's homo-sexuality.)

Fundamentally, we can argue, the homosexual must devote himself to keeping class barriers in existence because it thrills him to trans-gress them (and he must also want to preserve the public schools where he first exercised his homosexuality and first learned to think of himself as a member of a patrician class). But often he will represent to himself that his excursions across the barriers are the acts of an egalitarian; he will see himself, as Oscar Wilde did, as a socialist: and from this we have the benefits at least of his conscious liberalism and of some genuine knowledge of other classes which he will inevitably bring back with him. Similarly we enjoy the benefits of the intellectual curiosity of the classical scholar who may have been attracted to ancient Greece in the first place by its comparative tolerance of homosexuality and its recognised institutionalisation of certain homosexual feelings. No doubt Johann Joachim Winckelmann (failing of course to foresee the circumstances of his own violent death, that tremendous irony of the homosexual basis in so much classical scholarship) argued to himself, as John Addington Symonds was to do publicly, that no great harm could result from affections condoned by Plato. The soil of Athens is the classical meeting-place of homosexual feelings, reformist feelings and impulses of intellectual curiosity, whether they are all combined in one person or whether the man who first takes refuge there against the heterosexual tyranny imposed on our manners by Christianity comes away infatuated by the talkative, restless and egalitarian (so long as one forgets the slaves) image of Athenian democracy. What we preserved in preserving antiquity was a world half given over to rationalism and half devoted to irrational assumptions which were the very opposite of the irrational assumptions of Christianity. Our education had at its centre something which prompted us to question, either on rational grounds or on grounds of sheer comparison, every Christian prejudice from monotheism to the divine right of kings. We are in debt to our civilisation's conception, and often in its misconception, of antique civilisation for a good part of our political freedom as well as for the vast and still disturbing enrichment loosed into our imaginative life by the artists of the renaissance; for the renaissance love of Greece presently transformed itself into the Byronic love of Greek liberty.

If the schools and universities, whose business was to impose orthodoxy, actually taught Greek rebellion, it was probably the touch of homosexual propaganda in the classical tradition which prevailed on them to do so. This motive was of course unconscious, but, like all unconsciously homosexual institutions, these congregations of boys and men, kept in segregation from women, unconsciously sailed as near the wind as they could. They made homosexuality the worst of crimes, second only to heterosexuality. But heterosexuality, as a matter of fact, had been put right out of court, made impossible, by segregation; whereas homosexuality by the same token was made the most possible of crimes—and at the same time sanctioned by Plato. Yet the boy who misinterpreted the unconscious homosexuality of the institution as conscious, and took Plato literally, was caught out and severely punished.

In sailing near the wind, the schools—like the homosexuality of ancient Greece itself—were taking advantage of 'how easily erotic wishes develop out of emotional relations of a friendly character, based upon appreciation and admiration, . . . between a master and a pupil'. In other words, 'compare', as Freud adds in this connexion, 'Molière's "Embrassez-moi pour l'amour du grec" '[1].

15. *Religious Education*

Thus Christianity throws us, as readers of history, into a position where we must in retrospect be thankful to either the illogicality or the hypocrisy of Christians. It is a similar dilemma which religious education or influence presses on us as parents. When we hand over our children to the religionists (who exert their influence not only in schools, from which some countries exclude them, but also in the newspapers, on television and in the whole climate of publicly-approved respectability), we are having them brought up either so uneducated that they do not notice inconsistency or else so accomplished in hypocrisy that they do not care.

This is not to say that English rationalists should aim at turning the religionists out of the schools. The experience of Catholic France and religion-lorn America does not suggest that an enforced divorce between religion and public schooling produces reasonable people or indeed does anything more than exacerbate the religionists into using more and more unscupulous methods of influencing children outside school. Rather, the rationalist should insist, equitably enough, on *all* the religions being represented in the schools, together with the rationalist point of view. But he should also insist that the process of education itself does not fall into the hands of people whose religious profession marks them as anti-educationalists, by committing them to belittle both fact and logic. The divorce the rationalist should seek is of religion from its exclusive hold on respectability.

The dilemma which religious education imposes on parents is actually experienced, of course, by the child. 'Religious education' is a contradiction: religion and education will pull the child in opposite directions, religion telling him that it is sin to be disloyal to Jesus, education telling him that it is immoral—uneducated, stupid—to be false to his own perception of truth.

It is not simply that the moral obligation (which is an obligation to be educated, to be in relation to reality) *may*, on some issue of fact,

[1] *Group Psychology And The Analysis Of The Ego*, XII, B

pull contrary to the God in whose name we enjoin moral obligation: they must pull against one another of their nature. The Catholic Church has to admit that, in a conflict between religion and conscience, conscience must win; but every church presses on the unbeliever the conscienceless advice that he should pray to the God he does not believe in to grant him belief.

Very few children are so stupid that they do not notice that the headmaster (or the youth leader, the general or the politician) believes in the existence of God in a quite different manner from how he believes in the existence of chairs and tables; and as a matter of fact religion, with its emphasis on faith, is always bringing the difference to their attention. The creed, in being presented as a matter of faith, is presented as an act of imagination, a fantasy—something which the child understands perfectly well: and then suddenly the educator changes ground and demands that the child believe the fantasy as though it were really true.

Giving a child a religious education, we do nothing else than tie him down on a rack—the same rack on which the hero of *Nineteen Eighty-Four* was tortured until he submitted to doublethink. It was, of course, religious faith which originated doublethink, which is simply the religionist's ability to believe that a thing can be both A and not-A. The religious doublethinker maintains that by a mental act he can hold contradictions apart and prevent them from being contradictory. He withdraws his attention from the fact that A and not-A will always cancel one another out in the real world, regardless of who is looking at them, and proposes to the scientist and the moralist his pact of non-aggression, which consists of suggesting that if both sides agree not to look at the contradiction it will no longer *be* a contradition by its logical nature.

It was J. M. Barrie who devised the perfect allegory of religion and copied in the theatre the torture by sentimentality (that is, the torture between loyalty and false loyalty) which we inflict on our children in the schools and Sunday schools. We unfold the story, which the children can see we believe only in the theatrical and not the literal sense; and then, by one of those violent changes which constitute the essential technique of the torturer, we break the convention and demand from the audience a real act which shall affirm real belief in the drama. Tinker Bell 'says she thinks she could get well again if children believed in fairies'; whereupon the fictitious hero throws out his arms to the real children in the audience and invites them: 'Do you believe in fairies? Say quick that you believe! If you believe, clap your hands!'[1]

Most of our children cheat the rack by swooning and never properly regaining consciousness. There is for them no conflict between faith and morals. They have withdrawn attention by retreating into stupidity, and the inspirational words of society's leaders (together with the rebellious words of society's artists and thinkers) will for ever pass over them as unheeded as the chaplain's or the scoutmaster's homilies did at school. Education has reduced them to the non-attention, the non-mind, which we have suspected was society's unconscious aim all along, even while it consciously professed to do the opposite; and we may suspect that society, in choosing to submit them to what it pretended was the bracing influence of religion, unconsciously picked out this route as the shortest way there.

Among the small number of children who remain alert, the majority quickly copy the hypocrisy of their instructors and leaders; our intelligence tests are efficiently designed to select those with the aptitude. A few refuse to submit to hypocrisy (or doublethink) and remain fully perceptive of the contradictions inherent in society's morality. The first educational dose having failed on them, we name them juvenile delinquents and double the dose. That is to say, we let the terrorisation society practises on its citizens come more nakedly home to them, by submitting them to sadistic discipline in some sort of prison or quasi-military camp, and at the same time we double the dose of sanctimoniousness: it is notable that we seldom permit educators to increase their harshness against children without also increasing the number and the sentimentality of the religious influences we loose on them.

Some delinquents give in, of course, and become either stupid law-abiding citizens or stupid, repetitive criminals. But again there remain a few whom the treatment merely toughens. In these few we have raised a crop of that rarity, the perfect cynic. They are our potential Leopolds and Loebs. They genuinely disbelieve in everyone's sincerity, including their own; and when they meet an artist or a moralist, they truly believe that he is 'putting it on' and has no more real love for beauty or morals than the headmaster or prison governor has for God.

It is a nice point whether their acute cynicism is more deadly to culture than the unconscious cynicism of the bourgeois, who does not really believe either in God or in art and morals but who imagines he

[1] *Peter Pan*, IV

believes in all three. (Indeed, his approval of art and morals is ultimately, though vaguely, based on his approval of God.) He is just as bitterly against the artist and the moral reformer as any delinquent, but instead of dismissing them on the honest grounds that he thinks beauty and morality so much guff, he attacks them on the grounds that they, the artist and the reformer, are destroying beauty and morals.

16. *Keeping Tinker Bell Alive*

If religion is driven by logic into moral and intellectual doublethink, it is because it delights to be there: that is why it set up to challenge reality. Its illogic is the vehicle of religionists' unconscious hatred of God. If the religionist secretly knows that this father, whom he loves and flatters so piously, is really only a fantasy, then he has to hand a secret and perpetual means of attacking the father, deflating him, and reducing him to non-existence. He can murder God by stopping believing in him. This is why he dreads blasphemy, which could do no harm to a god who objectively existed. Blasphemy reveals the blasphemer's wish that God should cease to exist.

God is an enormous balloon floating above the world, which can be kept in existence only if the worshippers, by affirming their faith in it, pump pump pump the life into it. No wonder disbelief is a sin: it is the act of taking one's hand from the pump and thereby willing the death of God the Father. Of course the religionist knows his God is not real, or he would not have to pump: disbelief could not be thought a sin if God were thought real: but at the same time the religionist really has killed God by insisting he is only a fantasy which cannot be kept in existence except by communal wishing—that is, belief.

J. M. Barrie's metaphor is perfectly exact. The child who will not affirm his belief in Tinker Bell by clapping his hands is made responsible for the extinction of Tinker Bell. Just so, the religionists make unbelievers responsible for the extinction of God, thereby confessing their knowledge that God is not an objective fact at all, but an imaginary fact, which the volume of our applause—our prayers and piety—can make and unmake exactly as the electrician fades and resuscitates Tinker Bell.

Herein lies the secret of religion's intolerance. It is simply dramatic intolerance, which cannot afford to have a scoffer in the house but must sweep us all along in a communal act of imagination. Religion, however, has so enlarged the theatrical conventions that they encompass the whole of reality; it takes the universe for its auditorium. Knowing that his god is an illusion, the religionist knows that his god is diminished by anyone's unbelief. The religionist can never agree to tolerate your scepticism because by your failure to believe you have deprived *him* of a little of what he believes in. Religion's case against knowledge (and thereby against intelligence, curiosity and education) is that it kills a little of this God who, not being real, is vulnerable to, and resuscitable by, thoughts. The whole case is stated by Peter Pan, with his 'Children know such a lot now. Soon they don't believe in fairies, and every time a child says "I don't believe in fairies" there is a fairy somewhere that falls down dead'[1].

The simple reason why the religionist was not shaken when his creed and his Bible were discredited is that he never believed they were true in the first place: he believed they were desirable. So habituated is he to judging the reality of statements by their prettiness that discussion with him will get nowhere unless you can undermine this standard. What he really believes is that death *ought* not to be the end of us, that virtue *should* be rewarded and that it is too poignant to be bearable if the martyrs have died for an illusion. When you question survival after death, he does not really understand you to be questioning the fact, but takes you to mean that you do not want it to be true —for which he judges you immoral and heartless. An atheist to him is someone who *wants* God to die. He cannot get it into his head that the rational atheist is not expressing a wish about the matter at all, but only an opinion about whether God really does or does not exist; and the reason why he cannot get it into his head, and why he continues to shew a superstitious fear of the atheist's disbelief, which would be powerless to harm a god who *was* real, is that the religionist himself, by playing with his own sense of reality, is all the time indulging his own dreaded, unconscious wish to make the father, in the guise of God, not exist.

Discussion with the religionist is maimed by his two peculiarities: he is quite unaffected by your reasoned arguments; but the conclusion you have drawn from them, namely your unbelief, he treats as something personally wounding and grievous to himself. You will find no way to him through his fantasy-life unless you can isolate and make

[1] *Peter Pan*, I

him notice the faith in faith which underlies his fantasy—the belief that he makes God exist by praying to him: and even then you will have to address your appeal to a quality which may not exist, the will (or the life instinct) which can make us exercise our intelligence. But the religionist—or part of him—is of the opinion that his instinctive quest for pleasure draws him the other way. He is addicted to his fantasy like opium; he confesses what the priest at Brompton Oratory told Bernard Shaw, that he could not live without his religion[1]. This, in the mouths of incautious religionists, soon changes from a statement of what is supposed to be psychological fact into an argument—indeed a boast; for they are so accustomed to assuming the truth of what they set out to prove that they believe the strength of their faith will support the existence of God, and they say that the good God would not have made life without God intolerable unless there was a God.

17. *The Religion of Lucretius*

It is on moral grounds that irreligionists like myself are irreligious. Our loyalty to the one objective set up by morals, though it takes its direction from reason, is in intensity a passion.

It is not the least bit of good our trying to argue that reason itself draws us to truth, for reason does not draw one to anything; it is a mere technique for distinguishing the truth, not a force capable of fixing attention on the problem. What does draw us to the truth is our instinct towards continuing life. Reason then judges that the most efficient adaptation to living in the real world is made by recognising the facts of the real world. A rationalist pure and simple would have to confess he could see no rational justification for the instinct to live. To the prime proposition made implicitly by every living creature, 'Il faut que je vive', he would have to reply, 'Je n'en vois pas la nécessité'.

We might reverse Spencer's dictum and call ourselves religious irreligionists; and our temperament is certainly religious, though it has been re-directed. Some of us are unable to say with Freud[2] that

[1] *Back To Methuselah*, Preface, 'In Quest Of The First Cause'
[2] See, e.g., his *Collected Papers*, Volume V, XXII

we have never felt the need of religion; out of our own temperament we can readily understand worshippers, whether they worship God or Freud. We even admire the devotion that makes them insist the world is something it is not on the grounds that it would be more beautiful if it were: but we ourselves are so devoted to Keats's confusing religion in which truth is beauty that we unavoidably find the ugliest reality more beautiful than the most beautiful fantasy.

Our moral indignation with the religionists insists on having it both ways. On the one hand, we do not like to see so purely human a product as religion extolled as possessing superhuman authority. On the other, we do not like to see ·man's best achievements snatched away from him and attributed to God. It is easy for religion to shew that man is nothing in comparison to God if it attributes to God all men's best ideas, including the idea of God.

Irreligionists of this class have as their great exemplar the finest of Latin poets, Lucretius, who was an atheist on every point except the ultimate, technical one of the gods' existence. This he had to leave intact because he was unable to see how the idea of the gods could be a human idea, but he set about denying the gods' intervention in human existence—which as a matter of fact is as far as reason can go with any possibility of being certain. If religionists care to postulate a super-real, superhuman plane where the gods exist, no one can prove them wrong any more than they can prove themselves right. It is only when they build bridges from the superhuman to the human and postulate, in Tennyson's metaphor, that the whole world is bound with gold chains to the feet of God (the chains consisting of divine intervention in human affairs and human intervention—by means of prayer and fasting—in divine); it is only then that their bridges and chains, being made of mundane substance, can be refuted.

This refutation Lucretius performed to the best of his ability with the material available to him at the time; and in performing it he contributed a masterpiece to the world's religious literature. The poem which announces that it is at last religion's turn, after terrorising men so long, to be trampled under men's feet, and which proclaims that the gods are not affected by human activities[1], begins by inviting Venus to intervene in the poet's cause—thus implying not one but two contradictions; for if the gods *were* the kind of gods who respond to prayer, it would still be suicidal of Venus to give her help to Lucretius.

[1] I, 79-80; 44-9

Lucretius has apprehended that a man who lived by reason alone would not live at all; and he knows that if he is to appeal to us to be reasonable, he must address his appeal not to our reason but to a will, an instinct, in us. His conception of this instinct is thoroughly scientific: he knows that it is external reality, 'the nature of things', which has endowed us with an instinct attaching us to reality; and his teaching is that if we will only throw away our fantasies and devote our imaginations to reality we shall in fact be much better pleased. What he invokes is that tiny measure of free will which, we have to suppose, is the motive force of evolution by enabling a living thing to turn towards or away from life; and he gives us a biological panorama of the living world which, whether for passion or for intellectual penetration into the nature of reality, has no parallel in the whole range of ancient civilisation.

Lucretius's prayer to the Life Force under the name of Venus is cast in a form thoroughly liturgical. Indeed, since Horace and Ovid[1] use the same device (which turns up again, desubtilised but still effective, in the prose doggerel of the Christian paean *Gloria in excelsis*[2]), it was perhaps from the prayers he was brought up on that Lucretius borrowed the insistent, incantatory *te*:—

> te, dea, te fugiunt venti, te nubila caeli
> adventumque tuum, tibi suavis daedala tellus
> summittit flores, tibi rident aequora ponti . . .
> aeriae primum volucres te, diva, tuumque
> significant initum perculsae corda tua vi.[3]

The tradition, however, must go back to the most primitive methods of conjuration; and to this Lucretius, as poet, was co-heir with the religionists. The artist, too, has to invoke a power of whose origin his conscious mind knows nothing, and which he therefore images to himself as a visitor from outside. Lucretius's scientific imagination has led him to go on from biology to psychology; he possesses a shrewd insight into the nature of the poet's unconscious inspiration, and seeks

---

[1] Horace (apostrophising Jupiter): *Odes*, I, 12, 56-60; Ovid (in the birds' lament for Orpheus): *Metamorphoses*, XI, 44-6

[2] Laudamus te. Benedicimus te. Adoramus te. Glorificamus te. Gratias agimus tibi. . . Quoniam tu solus sanctus. Tu solus Dominus. Tu solus altissimus. . . . (Order of Mass)

[3] I, 6- . . . 13

poetic help from the force which perpetuates species[1], figured as the goddess of erotic love. Lucretius's personal cult of Venus was inherited, after the lapse of centuries, by Botticelli, who illustrated, in the shell-like ripples which lap *The Birth Of Venus*, what Lucretius meant when he addressed Venus with the words 'tibi rident aequora ponti', and, in the carpeted floor of the *Primavera*, what Lucretius meant by 'tibi suavis daedala tellus summittit flores', and whose *Mars And Venus* is rich with the lazy, summery atmosphere of making love instead of war—the very atmosphere of Lucretius's description of Mars the conqueror being himself conquered by 'the eternal wound of love'[2]. (Botticelli does not depict the same incident as Lucretius [whose Mars is lying back in Venus's lap, gazing up at her, his breath hanging on her lips] for the very good reason that his imagination has penetrated deeper into the essentials of the situation. Lucretius sees the eternal wound of love as the prick of desire, Botticelli as the wound which comes on the man, the warrior, when desire is satisfied, when he has used his weapons and is disarmed. Botticelli's Venus, inscrutable and ambiguous, is awake, while Mars, separated from her and from his arms, lies in exhausted sleep.) At the centre of the *Primavera*, watching Flora emerge from winter, and raising her hand to bless, at the other side, the Graces (one of whom, at the instigation of Venus's son with his arrow, has just fallen in love), stands the madonna-like figure of Venus, presiding, just as Lucretius invokes her to do, over the propagation of humans and plants, and, by implication, over the artist's imagination, too.

The poet, no less than the religionist, must work, work his imagination—that is, work himself into a state of faith in his fantasy: but where the magician supposes that his rhythmical spell-casting makes his fantasy come true, and the religionist hypnotises himself into believing that he believes, the poet pretends to nothing except the miracle wrought by evolution: our ability to summon into psychic being, and communicate to others, a purely mental image which can be contemplated without deluding or deceiving either audience or creator.

[1] He describes a rout of animals under the power of Venus, who brings it about that they all 'cupide generatim saecla propagent' (I, 20)

[2] aeterno devictus vulnere amoris (I, 34)

18. *Genesis and Exodus*

Lucretius had to leave the gods secure on their own plane because he could not see how men had ever formed the notion of them unless they existed. Obviously he did not believe in divine revelations and inspirations; but he knew that men sometimes dreamed of the gods (observation had led him, though uncomprehending, straight to the unconscious) and he had to believe that what men caught in their dreams were genuine, though accidental, glimpses of gods who really existed[1].

The argument that the idea of God could not have come into being unless there were something real to which it corresponded, though not a very good one (it applies equally to the idea of fairies), has always been used by religion. The religionists asked how men had ever framed the notion unless God existed and had himself (the easy next stage of the argument) implanted the notion in their minds. The simple sceptics replied that men's desire for a God was obviously the father of the intimations they had of him. Neither side could prove its point; and neither side put forward a convincing theory of the genesis of religion (though there were various possible ones) until Freud gave us the evolutionary view of both the individual psyche and human culture, laid bare the still-active baby, still emotionally dependent on his parents, who is buried alive in the foundations of every adult, and made it clear that the cardinal fact of our bio-psychological nature is that man is a weaned mammal.

'Instinct in general' Freud saw as 'a kind of elasticity of living things, an impulsion towards the restoration of a situation which once existed but was brought to an end by some external disturbance'[2]. When an external disturbance puts an end to a certain situation of animals in the environment, the species takes steps to prevent the individual's instinct from trying to restore it: a species that has once found its feet on dry land is overwhelmed if the sea gives it an opportunity to go back by flooding the land. But instinct in the human psyche retains its elasticity. When birth and weaning have disrupted the baby's union with the mother, the baby's instinct is prepared to snap back and restore it; and all the adaptations which reality forces it to undergo

[1] V, 1169-71   [2] *An Autobiographical Study*, V

succeed only in pegging the elastic in certain positions, not in making it abandon its intention and tendency to snap back.

When religion maintained that man's intimations of God were intimations of a parent; when it said that man had once lived in intimate union with this parent, but the union had been disrupted by sin on man's part; and when it said that man was constantly striving to restore the union—psycho-analysis quite agreed. Psycho-analysis, wrote Freud, 'confirms what the pious were wont to say, that we are all miserable sinners'[1] : but of course it confirmed religion in a way unacceptable to religion, because, instead of proving the myths true, it shewed how they had exerted so much power without being true. The psychic-evolutionary account of religion left the religionists in the same difficulty as the evolution of species. Here was all the evidence of a process having taken place which was quite adequate to account for everything that happened: either they must maintain that the process, though lying to hand, was not the method God used: or else they must push God back to the start of the evolutionary chain, which reduced him to Herbert Spencer's x, who bears not the smallest resemblance to the pictures of God delivered to mankind at the end of the chain.

The instinct of the weaned baby sets itself to restore the union with the mother, but its encounters with reality—and in particular with that glaringly intractable piece of reality, the father—force it to propose to itself wider and wider détours on its route. It is obliged in effect to progress forwards (as it does, for example, when it advances from a purely oral sexual character into a sexuality enriched by the anal and genital modes; but even these enrichments may in fact be détours, each new mode being acceptable to the child only as a partial substitute for the previous one, on whose track the child's instinct has been frustrated[2].) Yet it never loses sight of its ambition to work its way round, and back, to its starting-point.

These adaptations are reflected in the religious myth; indeed, in the whole religious *feeling*. Religion, too, is obliged to progress forwards. It has switched our instinctual goal from the beginning of life to the end; if it still records the tradition that mankind inhabited paradise at the start of its career, it also projects a mirrored image of that paradise to the end, and holds up to individuals the hope of regaining paradise in the form of entering heaven after their deaths. As for the father, religion has taken him into account to the extent of

[1] *Totem And Taboo*, II, 4   [2] Cf. I, 6

deifying him. Indeed, it has changed the parent we desire to be re-united with. Whereas the baby originally hungers and thirsts after the mother's breast, and presently figures to itself the desire to re-enter the kingdom of the mother's womb, religion represents the kingdom of heaven as ruled by a father, shews us a promised land flowing not with mother's milk but with some ethereal manna provided by the father (perhaps even the bread of angels which he provides from his own body) and insists that it is only by courtesy of the father, through a reconciliation with him, that we shall go through the gates of heaven. In this myth, it is possible to distinguish the stages of our infantile détours round reality, and even the successive deposits left by our misconceptions of reality and of what it demands of us.

At weaning, the child is finally and irrevocably frustrated of its desire to restore the union with its mother in oral terms; and presently society makes it plain that to return to the breast after having once been weaned is indecent, a trespass on the father's property, a kind of oral incest[1]. Already, however, the child has begun to conceive of new terms in which the union might be effected. It would like, as its physical promptings suggest, to enter the mother's body and use her as an object which yields pleasure.

As a matter of fact, if the child really did this, it would be on its way to restoring a union which is even older than the oral union; and the child gets an inkling of this fact when its physical promptings set it to speculate intellectually about the difference between the sexes, about how the mother *could* be penetrated, and thus eventually[2] about how she *was* penetrated by the father, and how the baby left her body.

It is at this point that the child encounters the father, both in its attempt to form a sexual relation with the mother, which is inter-rupted because the father claims that right for himself alone, and in its intellectual enquiries: the father intrudes himself into the

[1] Cf. the parenthesis on weaning in I, 7

[2] Freud's original opinion was that children's curiosity first tackled the question of where babies come from and was led from that to the distinction between the sexes. Observation shewed that it was usually the other way about. The distinction between the sexes is a pressing problem emotionally as well as intellectually, because it suggests to the girl that she has been deprived, and to the boy that he may be reduced to her level by being deprived, of the male sex's distinguishing mark. (*Collected Papers*, Volume II, VI; Volume V, XVII)

intellectual puzzle because the child has to ask in what sense a baby is his as well as the mother's.

The child's enquiries, Freud points out[1], are straitened by two pieces of inevitable ignorance, two blanks in its own experience. It does not know that the penis can emit another substance besides urine; and it does not know that there is a third channel in and out of the woman's body besides the two whose existence it can surmise from its own excretory functions. 'Inter urinas et faeces nascimur', as Freud was fond of quoting[2] from St. Augustine: and when the child puts together from its own experience an account of what copulation and birth must be like, it reconstructs them as something between urination and defecation. The only account of childbirth which seems tenable to children is their 'cloaca theory', according to which a baby is passed by the anus—a theory whose persistence, Freud observed, is capable of leading an insane woman to regard her faeces as a child; and he observed also that 'occasionally an "innocent" girl on her wedding night is still indignant because the man has "urinated into her"'— her innocence being the persistence of the child's enforced ignorance of the existence of semen.

The infantile confusion between semen and urine can be seen in the myth of Zeus impregnating Danaë by means of the golden rain, where the fluid has taken its colour from urine. This same unconscious association permits the prostitute to aggress against her client by taking from him first semen and then money (together, a golden rain) without giving anything of herself in return. (And in fact her refusal to be sensually or emotionally participant in the union reduces the client's part in it to a lonely one, just as though it really were, like urination, a matter of his merely easing his own discomfort. The prostitute is not far removed from the indignant innocent bride. Her implicit complaint is that the client makes a convenience of her. And having, by her professional coldness, made him play a selfish part, she feels justified in making him pay for the convenience.) The resemblance between prostitution and the myth was evidently not lost on the High Renaissance painters who shew Danaë spread on a bed in the pose of a courtesan (Titian[3] has her abetted by an avaricious old procuress); and the point was brought satirically home when Anne-Louis Girodet-Trioson painted an actress who

[1] *Collected Papers*, Volume II, VI; Volume III, II, II

[2] e.g. *Collected Papers*, Volume III, I, I   [3] In the *Danaë* at Leningrad

had married for money as a Danaë, thereby scandalising the Salon of 1799[1].

To such an extent does the child have to take the father into its scheme of things that mythology, besides representing our future heaven as man's reconciliation with his divine father, may even make out that the child's original union was with the father and that it was by a sin against the father that the child disrupted it. The Oedipus conflict has retrospectively coloured the past—a past which the child comes to know of only under stimulation from the Oedipus conflict: the child learns that it once *was* in the mother's body only as part of learning that the father forbids it to go back.

The story of man's original sin against the father, how Adam and the woman were punished for eating fruit from the one tree in the middle of the Garden, which the father had forbidden them[2], has been deciphered by Theodor Reik[3], and it turns out that this proto-typic dispute between father and children was a totemistic dispute. Reik's interpretation, so simple and convincing as to make anyone acquainted with the rules of totemism wonder how he failed to be as perceptive as Reik, is that the special tree in the middle was, his-torically, the totem species. The prohibition against eating it was the totemistic prohibition against eating the totem animal or plant. In other words, originally—in purely taboo times—the tree *was* the father (later anthropomorphised by mythology into God the Father, who now gives the command not to eat it): mankind's primal sin was to aggress against him by eating him. (It is not surprising that the human beings are *tempted* into this sin, taboo rules being a precaution against unconscious temptation.) The primitive myth does not achieve its complete development until Christianity, when the crime of eating the father which was so terrible a sin for the world's only two individuals in the Garden, becomes feasible, indeed dutiful, for their descendants performing a social rite as a group, and the whole of God's family partakes of his body in another vegetable manifestation.

Jewish religion as a whole was so exclusively concerned with the relation between Jehovah and his sons, and so anxious to wipe out the sons' guilt by imposing sacrifices on them in favour of the father, that it has almost completely erased any anthropomorphic references the myths may once have made to the mother of mankind, Jehovah's mate. Jehovah, in *Genesis*, behaves like a widower, doing for his

[1] e.g. J. Robiquet: *La Femme Dans La Peinture Française*
[2] *Genesis*, III   [3] *Myth And Guilt*

children what their mother would normally do: it is a singularly touching item of the myth, worthy of Homer's civilised, domestic genius, that, when the time for their expulsion came, 'Unto Adam also and to his wife did the Lord God make coats of skins, and clothed them'. None the less, the mother is present in *Genesis*: if Jehovah creates two children, he must have created them in a woman: it is simply that she has a territorial, not a personal, manifestation.

This, indeed, is her regular fate in the unconscious mythology of politics. When the nomadic primal horde settles down and learns agriculture, the body of the mother, to enjoy which is the father's prerogative, is transmuted into the body politic, figured as the native land itself. It is over this that the father and the sons must now bargain or contend, each striving to dispossess the other of the instrument which metaphor represents both as a weapon, which can castrate a sexual rival, and as an agricultural implement—a tool which can violate, deflower and fertilise. (Thus Agrippa tells us of the royal wench,

> She made great Caesar lay his sword to bed;
> He plough'd her, and she cropp'd.[1])

Hesiod's cosmology makes use of something between the bloodless personifications of politics and the personalities of myths; and here we find that the aboriginal mother, the very start of the divine family tree, is again territorial: Gaia is the name both of a person and of the earth. The land, in which men drive furrows, drill holes and plant seed, with a wealth of sexual metaphor, also feeds them all just as a mother feeds all her sons from her breasts.

'Broad-breasted Gaia'[2] has been put out of her sons' way, so that she may no longer tempt them to incest, not only by deification (the method by which the father is put out of reach of his sons' hostility) but also by being pushed back beyond the reach of cult, into a mytho-logical past. And probably her identification with the earth, though turned to conscious purpose in an attempt to answer intellectual speculations about the universe, is unconsciously another attempt to fend off the incest wish by desexualising her. Her husband Uranos is likewise put out of reach of mankind's jealousy of the father by being the sky, whose showers of rain fertilise the earth; but the parental pair

[1] *Antony And Cleopatra*, II, ii
[2] Γαῖ' εὐρύστερνος (Hesiod: *Theogony*, 117)

have not been so far desexualised that one of their sons cannot express his jealousy of their coition by preventing it by castrating his father.

The superannuation of Gaia did not, however, suppress the incest temptation from Greek mythology. It was quickly resurrected in the persons of more attractive divine mothers, often Gaia's lineal descendants, some of whom had to be protected from mankind's filial infatuation with the mother by undertaking perpetual virginity. Jewish religion, more anxious about the penalties of succumbing, was more vigorous in effacing the tempting image. Even so, *Genesis* has removed only the name and personality of Jehovah's wife: it has left her womb. We have no difficulty in recognising the Garden of Eden as a womb: a garden is a sheltered, enclosed place where fruits grow, just as a womb is a sheltered, enclosed place where babies grow. The Garden has, in fact, been planted by God the Father, and it is in this enclosed place that he puts the son he has created[1]; and he exercises the rights of a husband by 'walking in the garden in the cool of the day'.

The Jewish embargo on ascribing a mate to Jehovah was broken by Christianity, which restored her to a place in mythology, cult and (presently) heaven, though stopping short of deifying her. Mankind still needed to be protected from its incestuous aspirations towards the wife of its divine father, and to this end Christianity adopted the Greek device of making Mary 'always a virgin', even though the myth fully admitted that she was a mother who had borne several children to two different consorts[2]. Cult and theology, of course, went further and adopted her as the universal mother[3]. As mother of God, who is himself the father (or brother) of all mankind, she is bound to be the mother of all mankind. Moreover, as so many altarpieces insist when they place her high up, facing out towards the

[1] *Genesis*, II, 8

[2] Theology, however, quickly rescinded the second part of this admission. By the end of the fourth century it had become heretical to believe that Jesus's brothers, named in *Mark*, VI, 3, *were* his brothers. The Greek Church chose to interpret them into Joseph's sons by an earlier marriage; the Latin Church, with its tendency to hold that Joseph himself must have been a virgin, developed the view that the brothers were really cousins. (Gibbon: *The Decline And Fall . . .*, XVI; *Catholic Dictionary*, 'Brethren Of Our Lord'). As a matter of fact, St. Mark mentions not only Jesus's brothers but his sisters (αἱ ἀδελφαὶ αὐτοῦ), but these were dropped from the controversy.

[3] Patristic tradition made Mary a second Eve: she had achieved by privilege the purity which, until the Fall, belonged to Eve by nature. (*Catholic Dictionary*, 'Immaculate Conception')

congregation as she gives her breast to her baby son, she is also the universal nursing-mother, who offers her breast to everyone: we are all sucklings in the orbit of her comfort. It was a not uncommon theme of baroque painting to shew her nourishing the saints (especially St. Bernard in the 'lactatio Sancti Bernardi'), or even sinners in hell-fire, with her milk, the moral being that Christ succours with his wound, Mary with her breast[1]. But the Church can improve on this metaphor and feed us, more concretely, on another product of Mary's body: the little boy whom we see in the altarpieces, whose flesh is spread out as a universal meal on the altar table.

Christianity had, in fact, thoroughly taken the analogy between fruits growing in a garden and babies growing in a womb. The fruit of Mary's womb and the fruits of the earth which the Eucharist consecrates as his body are pointedly compared in the picture[2] where Botticelli shews us the Madonna holding her baby son with one hand and with the other fingering a bunch of grapes stuck with ears of corn. In the background, through an opening like a window, we catch a glimpse as it were of the past (by analogy with the primitive convention whereby paintings shew previous incidents in the background of present ones): a landscape in which a broad shallow river winds past two hills—a reminiscence or, rather, an infantile reconstruction of the passage whereby the fruit left the womb.

Elsewhere[3], Botticelli's madonnas have backgrounds of roses and trees; this is all that the renaissance and his own genius for close-ups have left of the hortus conclusus in which medieval iconography placed the Virgin. This pretty garden with its profusion of roses repeats the symbolism of the Garden of Eden and is perhaps a conscious emulation of it: it signifies both the most fertile place in the world, Mary's womb, and at the same time (witness its incorporation into pictures of the Madonna nursing her baby) the most comforting external approximation to it, the enclosed orbit of the mother's arms and bosom.

By such methods Christianity does, of course, permit men to express their longing to return to the mother—and most notably the longing

[1] 'Christus vulnere, Maria ubere'. See A. Pigler: *Barockthemen* . . ., Volume I, pp. 506-7

[2] *The Madonna Of The Eucharist*, Boston

[3] *The Virgin Of The Roses*, Uffizi; *The Virgin And Child With The Infant St. John*, Louvre

to return to her breast. For this desire the symbolism of the garden-womb and its fruit provides an apt vehicle. We feed on Mary's breast and on her son, who is her fruit: and we have only to think of the many madonna-and-child paintings which the artist has littered with fruits, usually apples or pears, to realise that iconography has pressed into service that simple resemblance between breasts and fruits which no one from childhood up has failed to remark[1]. The altarpieces are so many expressions of the weaned child's yearning—indeed, of his prayer. Each picture could be translated, like the dramatised series of pictures which constitutes a dream, into the statement of a wish.

Consider, for example, the dream of a four-year-old boy, recorded and interpreted by Freud[2]. He dreamed of 'two large Emperor-pears, of which he was given one to eat. The other lay on the window-sill of the living-room.' The child woke, Freud continues, 'with the conviction of the reality of what he had dreamt, and obstinately asked his mother to give him the second pear; it was, he said, still lying on the window-sill.'

Freud interprets: 'The two pears—*pommes ou poires*—are the breasts of the mother who nursed him; the window-sill is the projection of the bosom, analogous to the balconies in' dreams of houses. The dream 'is to be translated: Mother, give (show) me the breast again at which I once used to drink. The "once" is represented by the eating of the one pear, the "again" by the desire for the other.'

It is just this translation which we can give of madonna-and-child paintings in general. Moreover, if we turn to Bellini's Morelli Madonna[3], we find the mother and her baby sitting behind the para-pet which Bellini so often uses to frame his madonnas. The parapet is the window-sill or balcony of the dream; and on the parapet stands the one pear.

Yet though Christianity allowed men to express this wish towards the Madonna, it allowed them to do it only through the father. It is only through her nursling (with whose body our other holy mother, the Church, provides us), and only by putting ourselves in his place in the picture, that we can feed on Mary's breast. And as a matter of fact, Mary is our mother only by courtesy of, and by virtue of her relation with, the male God, who in his three persons is respectively her father (her creator), her son, and her husband (the Holy Ghost who impregnates her). The parental creative power, and its extension,

[1] See Further IV, 12   [2] *The Interpretation Of Dreams*, VI, (E) 9
[3] *Accademia Carrara*, Bergamo

the redemptive power, are entirely reserved to him, which is why Mary is not a goddess[1]. If we may hope to be reunited to her in heaven, it is he who will admit us; and as a matter of fact we shall only find her in heaven because he summoned her there and crowned her.

Of course Christianity is not alone in making use of the obvious similarity between fruit and breast. Painters sometimes visually compare the tempting apple in the Garden with Eve's naked breast[2]; and in fact the comparison is implicit in the Garden of Eden myth itself, which has not yielded up all its meaning when Reik has shewn us its totemistic nature. In the totemistic bargain between Jehovah and his sons, the other trees in the Garden, which Adam and the woman *may* eat from, are simply the neutral, non-taboo trees belonging to other species than the totem species. But clearly, in another layer of the myth, this idea of eating fruits in the comfortable, timeless, warm (Adam and the woman do not *need* clothes) Garden represents the idea of feeding from the mother's breasts. (Indeed, it is probably at the insistence of this idea that Jehovah adopts a fruit-tree as the totem species in which he embodies himself.) In this layer of the myth, the Garden is the external womb, the mother's embrace; and the expulsion from it is weaning. God allows the children to eat from the mother's breast up to a certain time, after which to encroach further —to eat of the tree in the centre—becomes a sin of aggression against him. We know exactly where this forbidden point comes. It is the time of the first genital promptings, when the child begins to desire the mother as an object, and thereby infringes the father's rights: the

[1] Comparing the powers of Mary and her son, the *Catholic Dictionary* ('Immaculate Conception') quotes Bossuet: 'Thou' (Christ) 'art innocent by nature, Mary only by grace; Thou by excellence, she only by privilege; Thou as Redeemer, she as the first of those whom Thy Precious Blood has purified'.

[2] Titian's picture of Adam and Eve, in the Prado, makes almost a visual pun —or rather it shews Adam having just not made a significant mistake. Eve is reaching up to touch the apple on the tree; and Adam counterpoints this with a similar gesture in the opposite direction—towards her: he is reaching out to restrain her, and his hand makes contact with her shoulder, just missing her breast, as though Titian were shewing us that when they *have* succumbed to the temptation of the apple, it really will be Eve's breast which tempts him and which he does touch. In Hans Baldung's painting of Ada mand Eve (in the Thyssen-Bornemisza collection) Adam's hand *is* touching Eve's breast— and Eve's hand holds the apple.

time when 'the eyes of them both', the father's son and his daughter, 'were opened, and they knew that they were naked'—and, we may add, different from one another.

The two layers of significance are, we must observe, perfectly fused psychologically. As soon as the child abandons identification with the mother and makes her his object, he is driven into identifying himself with the father instead. It is the father who does, of exclusive right, use the mother as an object. If the child tries to do the same, he is trying to replace the father by his own person. To eat the breast-fruit is permissible so long as it serves identification with the mother. But let it become an act of object-love towards her, and the child *is*, in effect, eating the father and the forbidden totem species—that is to say, the child is wishing to *be* the father. It is in order to defend him against his wish to become the father by eating him that the tribesman is forbidden to eat the totem; and so the serpent is quite correct in telling the woman that if she and Adam do eat the tree (which Reik makes clear is a god), they will become 'as gods'.

The expulsion from the Garden is thus an account of three distinct happenings: the birth of the children; their weaning; and their quarrel with the father over the subject of the mother. But the earlier two are seen from the point of view of the last, and this has made the father the principal agency in the whole affair. The children have reconstructed their own weaning and birth in the light of the father's prohibition on incest. As they imagine the story, it is as though the father had come to caress his property, the mother's breasts, and had found the children there; and as though, when he entered the mother's body sexually, he found the children *there*: and in his anger at finding them usurping his place, he expels them from both her bosom and her womb.

Turned out of the Garden, the children never go naked again. In this symbol the myth records something from each of the three events it describes: the children's discovery of sexual shame when they incur sexual guilt by their dispute with the father; that tremendous change of climate which is such a stimulus to evolution when the embryo experiences it at birth; and—by an inversion—the fact that after weaning the mother will never bare her breast to them again.

When we remember that children believe babies to be a sort of faeces, we can understand why God, in creating man, formed him 'of the dust of the ground'[1], and likewise why, in another account,

[1] *Genesis*, II, 7

Prometheus[1] creates man of earth and water—in which we can recognise both excretory products. Similarly the childish theory allows us to understand the disgust with which (in another account, Ovid's[2], of mankind's separation from its divine parents) the gods, who have hitherto shared the earth with men, remove themselves into more rarified places, offended by men's sin.

And perhaps these stories historically refer to the period, whose importance Freud pointed out[3], when man, having withdrawn from the earth to the extent of taking up his lofty, head-in-the-air stance, had to overcome his dependence on smell, detach his sexuality from it and thereby from any instinctual connexion with excretion, and train himself to regard excrement with disgust. 'The training of children', Freud goes on to point out, 'is very energetic in this particular'; and it has to be, since children originally regard their faeces with pleasure and pride—which alone allows them to think of themselves as born like faeces.

It is this childish pride, unconsciously persisting, which creates the curious symbolism wherein dreams and fairytales equate faeces, which adult man treats as his most waste, least regarded, product, with gold, his most precious possession[4]. And it is this symbolism which allows us to understand Hesiod's account of the genesis of mankind. If babies are a sort of faeces, and faeces are gold, then it is not surprising that 'the immortals . . . made first of all a golden race of mortal human beings'[5].

The Fall which followed this genesis is, according to Hesiod[6], a gradual decline. The golden generation gives way to a silver, and that to a brazen; and thus (after a temporary improvement, the heroic age) to the present iron generation. Here is an account of the restrictions which, stage by stage, tighten round the infant's pleasures— and particularly those anal pleasures[7] against which training crusades so vigorously. From the symbolism that gold equals faeces, Hesiod has wrung an account of the progressive devaluation of man's instinc-

---

[1] The same infantile misconception appears in the story of Orion's birth from an oxhide on which three gods had urinated. (Smith's *Classical Dictionary*, Prometheus; H. J. Rose's *Handbook*, V)

[2] *Fasti*, I, 247 foll.   [3] *Civilization And Its Discontents*, IV, footnote

[4] Freud: *Collected Papers*, Volume II, IV

[5] *Works And Days*, 109-110   [6] *Works And Days*, 109-201

[7] One might claim another classical acknowledgement of the sexual character of anal sensations and functions in 'Cloacina . . . a surname of Venus' (Lewis)

tual life. He has, moreover, marked several of the socially crucial stages on the way. The golden generation, for example, is evidently still breast-fed. Hesiod tells us that the earth ungrudgingly and 'automatically' provided the men of the golden age with fruit in plenty; and he emphasises that they were therefore happy and like the gods. Even the silver generation retains the infant's close and timeless dependence on the mother. A child in that epoch, Hesiod tells us, would spend a hundred years in his own home with his dear mother, remaining utterly uneducated. But when the silver men *did* grow up, they were disrespectful to the gods, and this prompted Zeus to destroy them. Thus already it is the father who is interrupting the childish idyll, and the children are already irked by his rule. The next generation is all aggression and strife, and has to be destroyed. (In these righteous destructions by the father we can read how each of our infantile epochs is, at the insistence of the father's influence, repressed into the unconscious, though it cannot be destroyed: and in fact Hesiod specifically tells us that each generation, after its destruction, though wiped off the face of the earth, *does* survive in spirit form, whether in the earth, in the realm of Hades or in the Islands of the Blessed.) Next comes the improvement, the heroes or demi-gods, a race like the gods—in which we can read that the child has formed his Ego-ideal on the father, and wishes to be like the father; and there is probably also a historical reference to the period when the heroic myths and religions emerged. But in Hesiod's view, this solution is only a truce in the Oedipal conflict. He is sure that Zeus will have to destroy also the iron race which has replaced the heroes, and he prophesies little for this generation except Oedipal strife: 'the father will not agree with his children nor the children with him, nor' (the juxtaposition shews Hesiod's unconscious understanding of the taboo rule of hospitality[1]) 'the guest with the host . . .'

No doubt the association of faeces with gold owes something to the colour of the other waste product; and that, too, has monetary associations. The person who 'spends money like water' has not yet conformed to the adult system of valuing things as possessions and according to their rarity, but retains some of the child's delight in the golden liquid his body produces, a delight not yet diminished by the fact that the liquid is common and, so adults insist, dirty (it is dirt common, dirt cheap): the child values it not as an object but for his pleasure in producing it. It is just this pleasure in emission which

[1] Cf. I, 13

212 BLACK SHIP TO HELL

allows the unconscious to persist in the infantile confusion between urine and semen. Now it is semen which is spent like money, as the Danaë myth demonstrated. The lover's impulse is to spend money on the person he has fallen in love with; when convention requires the intending bridegroom to buy his fiancée an engagement ring, it is asking for proof of his virility; and for some people the act of spending money in any context must be counted among the sexual pleasures and as an assertion of their sexual freedom.

Let us now go back to the *Genesis* myth for the last time and consider how unerringly, in depicting it, a Christian artist has followed its psychic contours: that is to say, he has re-created the story as what it psychically is, namely an account at the same time of birth and of weaning, both reconstructed from the point of view of the child in the Oedipus situation.

I have already remarked that when Botticelli makes a reference to weaning (which he does by expressing our desire to go back on it: the picture is like a dream which restores the weaned child to the breast by making the statement 'the child is being nursed by his mother'), he throws in what I take to be a reminiscence of the earlier separation which was enforced at birth. And I believe that in giving us this reminiscence he has unconsciously employed the convention which allowed primitive painters to shew successive incidents within the same picture. If we now look at Roger van der Weyden's beautiful *Expulsion From Paradise*, in the Prado, we find him consciously employing the convention in the ordinary way. Here in the foreground are a large-scale Adam and Eve coming out through the high, narrow, ecclesiastical gate of paradise; and if we look through the gate into the Garden they are leaving behind them, we are looking into the past, and see the incident which led to the foreground incident. There is the tree, with the serpent in it; and standing beside it are another Adam and Eve, much smaller because they are in the distance (but we can make out that these two are not wearing the leaves with which their later fallen selves in the foreground conceal their nakedness).

Thus the convention, by allowing van der Weyden to shew us two Adams and Eves, allows him to shew us two expulsions: from the breast and from the womb. Because of the myth's retrospective point of view, he has reversed Botticelli's order and shews us what is really the more recent expulsion as the more distant (it is happening to smaller people—as it were to younger children); but we need be in no doubt that this background incident does refer to feeding at the breast, because the tree's thick foliage is profusely dotted with little round orbs of fruit. (No doubt it was a nostalgia for Italy as the mother and nurse of civilisation which Goethe expressed when he asked

Kennst du das Land, wo die Zitronen blühn,
Im dunkeln Laub die Gold-Orangen glühn . . .?)

In the foreground van der Weyden shews us the children emerging from the womb, and shews it in terms of the infantile theory of child-birth. There are only two passages out of this Garden: one the way through the gate, which Adam and Eve are taking, and the other a stream of water running out parallei to it, at the spectator's left—a reference to the myth's own recognition that 'a river went out of Eden'[1]. (We can also see that Adam and Eve, in reaching the gate, have had to cross a river or a moat, and this no doubt represents the uterine waters; but I do not think it is a mistake to see the other stream as the channel through which urine flows, parallel to what children conceive to be the common channel of defecation and child-birth, because the water here is enclosed under an arch and sluiced down steps—which I take to be a reference to the control which children, after the last separation from the mother, are expected to exert over their own excretory functions.) In effect, van der Weyden has given us, in a literary disguise, something like a child's anatomical drawing: a glimpsed view, through the narrow entrance of the passage which leads to it, of the wide, fertile womb beyond.

As I keep saying, the whole story is told from the point of view of the child's Oedipus conflict with the father. The father is present in van der Weyden's picture only through the person of his emissary, the angel who sits above the gate, waiting for Adam and Eve to pass through, when he will become the guardian who forbids them ever to return. And as a matter of fact, this guardian, with the 'flaming sword which turned every way'[2] denotes not only God the Father's expulsion of the children from the Garden, but his purpose in being there himself and keeping it for his own use. As we might guess from his sword's prowess, the angel is a concentrated symbol of the father's phallic power. The winged angel with his weapon is a mythological formation of exactly the same significance as the winged god of love with *his* weapon (of whom more presently[3]: for the moment it is

---

[1] *Genesis*, II, 10   [2] *Genesis*, III, 24   [3] IV, 16

enough to remark that angels share with Cupid the tendency to grow younger as their iconographical tradition grows older).

We have come back to the fundamental dispute between father and son. If the father's sword is so phallicly raised in van der Weyden's picture, it is raised in the father's exercise of his own exclusive sexual rights against the son's claims. What the picture asserts is the tremendous and cardinal threat which the son apprehends from the father in the Oedipus dispute. If the son should try to get back to the womb he has been expelled from—and we know with which part of his body he will venture in at the gate—then the father's weapon is waiting to descend and cut him off.

19. *Art and Religion*

To say that Lucretius's passion was religious in nature is to say no more than that art and religion are divergent directions taken by the same mental activity, and that Lucretius was an artist—a truth about him missed by many of his commentators, who misread the lines[1] where he claimed to use poetry as a children's doctor used honey, to sweeten a bitter draught. To take this as a confession that Lucretius was less than an artist is to misread all art and misprize its passionateness. Every artist's first passion is to get his draught swallowed, and it is always a bitter draught; but quite often the artist himself has such an enthusiastic faith in its health-giving qualities that he spends years forcing it down people's throats before their constant rejection of it makes him notice that it is bitter to them. It is only then, and then only in consideration of the fact that a rejected draught cannot bring health to anyone, that the artist sets about making what he wants to communicate palatable. The artist who has no pill to sugar is merely sugary. Propagandist artists like Lucretius differ from 'pure' artists only in administering two pills in one. The poetry is no less bitter than the propaganda, and the artist who purveys poetry alone must sugar it just as much as the artist-propagandist, poetry being a disturbing,

[1] I, 936-50. Cyril Bailey takes care not to mistake his author. Although he holds that Lucretius 'is first and foremost a missionary', he goes on to say that '. . . perhaps most important, Lucretius is a poet, and his philosophy is the poet's philosophy' (Prolegomena, I, 10; 14)

moving and painful experience which no audience would undergo if the artist had not taken pains to seduce it.

Of course, the artist holds that art is more than health-*giving*; it is, rather, the purpose for which we want to be healthy, art being, in the human race, a function of the life instinct. This belief is the core of the artist's temperament, and the core of the artist's resemblance to the religionist. The religionist holds that the worship of God, the artist that the practice and appreciation of art, is a self-justifying activity. The artist's faith in the goodness of a good work of art is an evolutionary absolute.

(At this point, of course, there begins that immense problem of how a good work of art can be distinguished from a bad one, and how judgment of this kind can ever amount to more than two personal convictions at loggerheads. But without tackling the problem itself one can say that a large part—though admittedly the easiest part—of the problem would vanish if the world began to take art seriously and looked to it not for poppy seed but for the seeds of salvation. It is true that among the few people who do take art seriously aesthetic controversy is a bitter affair, and perhaps one can only ask for aesthetic quarrels to take the place of religious and ideological ones. Yet even this would be pure gain: aesthetic controversies do not lead to the fire or the executioner's block; time reconciles and sifts them more quickly than it does religious controversies; and the aesthetic faculty, if it is cultivated, is capable of evolving rapidly without the impediments loyalty places on the religious sense. The artist is not obliged to believe that his taste as a child was pure, but can confess and forswear his past mistakes without accusing himself of treachery.)

None the less, it is true that the impulse to art (in both the artist and the audience) begins by being a search for sweetness. Poems begin as daydreams or, rather, poetry develops out of daydreaming[1] (though some audiences never develop beyond expecting the artist to provide them with daydreams). This psychological origin art shares with religion. Both are fantasies, created in the first place as refuges against the inclemency of the real world outside.

Their social history, so far as it can be traced and conjectured, leads back to the same point. Art and religion, which in primitive cultures are still not wholly separable, have grown out of a single seed, magic. Ritual performances of primitive magic seem to be the origin of religious ceremonial on the one hand and, on the other, of the arts of

[1] Cf. Freud: *Collected Papers*, Volume IV, IX

dancing, music, mime and drama; and if Reinach was right in thinking that prehistoric painters intended not to decorate walls but to conjure magically the objects they depicted[1], then magic is likewise the origin of both idolatry and the visual arts. And magic is, ultimately, fantasy.

Magic, we are accustomed to say, is imitative: the rainmaker mimics a shower of rain, the witch makes a copy of her enemy's body and imitates on it the lacerations she wants him to suffer. But 'imitation' is shorthand for what really takes place. The rainmaker is imitating not rain but the content of his own wish for rain. Ultimately, of course, our wishes derive their imagery from something we have perceived in the real world, but we are at liberty to re-arrange and fuse the images; otherwise, our wishes would not be wishes at all but perceptions. Having seen rain and having seen blue, we can wish for blue rain; having seen her enemy whole and sound, and knowing that people can be hurt, the witch can put the two together and wish for her enemy to be hurt. The unconscious has already fused the two and presents a fait accompli, as though it were a perception. A dream does not state 'I wish I were in Italy', but shews the dreamer Italy as though he were in it. But once we leave the unconsciousness of sleep, this image of being in Italy, which my unconscious presents to me, has to contend with another image presented to me by my conscious perceptions, which insist that I am somewhere quite different; and now the unconscious statement 'I am in Italy' has to translate itself into a conscious wish, so that I state 'I am in London, but I wish I were in Italy'.

So long as I remain asleep, however, my unconscious wish has all the power of a real perception. I cannot help believing its assertion that I am in Italy just as seriously as, when I wake up, I will believe my conscious when it informs me I am in London. The magician's concern is to make this power, which is vested in the unconscious, available in waking life, and he does it by copying the content of his wish into something which is real in the external world, an artifact —a ritual dance, the witch's figurine. Here is embryonic art: a truthful external delineation of a wish. But here is also embryonic religious faith: the magician believes that the potency of his wish, whose complete control over the unconscious is asserted every time he dreams, has been transferred, by means of his magic ceremonial, into the outside world, and that by making a palpable representation of his

[1] an idea Freud considered in *Totem And Taboo*, III, 3

wish for rain he has empowered his wish to create rain in the outside world.

The belief (christened, by a patient of Freud's, belief in the omnipotence of thought[1]) that every wish issues directly in something we can perceive, and that everything we perceive is valid because it is the content of someone's wish, belongs in its absolute form to the unconscious. But the magician, in company with children, savages, neurotics, solipsists and Christian Scientists, clings to some of this inner world. He has given up some of it, or he would not be a conscious being at all; his belief in the omnipotence of thought is partial, operating in some cases and not in others—a compromise between the inner and outer worlds, whose claims to be real conflict. The rainmaker bows to the real world to the extent of admitting that it is *not* raining—yet. The concession is wide enough for consciousness to creep in, together with the beginnings of art, the ceremonial in which he embodies his wish for rain. But the magician has yielded as little as he can and insists that the sheer potency of wishes is such that the ceremonial in which he embodies his wish will oblige the outside world to copy it and produce rain.

When they both develop out of magic, it is on this point that religion and art diverge. Art is more completely a fantasy, for it seals itself off from the real world altogether. Yet precisely this brings it back into accord with reality. Unlike religion, it cannot directly conflict with reality because it never for a moment pretends to be real. Art, in Coleridge's classic apothegm, requires a 'willing suspension of disbelief for the moment'. Religion requires a permanent suspension that shall be at the same time willed and necessary.

Artist and religionist both encourage their fantasy, because both believe it to be good. The artist makes enormous claims for his, but these are all claims about its value and its relation to reality via the evolution of the human race; the religionist claims that his fantasy *is* reality. The psychological similarity between the artist and the religionist is that both perform acts of faith (as, indeed, Coleridge made clear[2]). An audience, no less than a congregation, must marshal, nurture and discipline its belief in what is taking place in its presence—in which the stallholder imaginatively participates no less than the communicant. The artistic creator, if he is to achieve his beatific

[1] Freud: *Collected Papers*, Volume III, III, II (b); *Totem And Taboo*, III

[2] '. . . that willing suspension of disbelief for the moment, which constitutes poetic faith' (*Biographia Literaria*, XIV)

vision and make his sacramental act efficacious, must perform an act of sustained belief in the product of his own imagination no less arduous and ardent than the dedication of the hierophant or saint— to which not only successful artists can testify but also failed ones, who, having begun a work of imagination, have experienced the tragedy of losing their faith.

Religion has preserved from its magical origin the magician's obstinacy. It insists that it is real and that, in a conflict between them, its psychic images prevail over outer reality: it is the outwardly real heaven and earth that shall pass away, the images that shall remain[1]. For magical formulae religion has substituted prayer, which introduces a complication that is not in magic; but the fundamental belief behind prayer is the same as behind magic. The magician believes that by wishing it graphically, the religionist that by wishing it prayerfully, he makes his wish come true. Religionists, as one can see by turning to the prayers for special occasions in a prayer book or missal, still believe they can make rain by ceremonially wishing it, and they still so far consider their prayers to be magic formulae which will operate automatically that they take care not to wish for too much rain[2].

Prayer is a wish expressed; and religion holds it to be efficacious if the wish is intense enough. It can be intensified by repetition, or by a number of people expressing it at the same time ('Almighty God, who . . . dost promise that when two or three are gathered together in thy Name thou wilt grant their requests. . .'[3]) or if it is prayed by one person who has generated sufficient intensity by his sanctity. The saints, being more sanctified than ordinary people, have more efficacy attached to their praying; and so the ordinary Catholic addresses his prayers to the saint, asking the saint to address his, more efficacious,

[1] 'Heaven and earth shall pass away, but my words shall not pass away' (*Matthew*, XXIV, 35)

[2] 'O God . . . who . . . hast promised to all them that seek thy kingdom . . . all things necessary to their bodily sustenance: Send us . . . such moderate rain and showers, that we may receive the fruits of the earth to our comfort, and to thy honour . . .' (Book of Common Prayer). 'Be appeased by the gifts which we offer up, O Lord . . . and grant us in season the blessing of sufficient rain . . .' (Missal). These prayers observe, though the other way about, the same caution as the jingle we teach our children to chant: 'Rain, rain go away And come again another day.'

[3] A Prayer of Saint Chrysostom (Book of Common Prayer)

prayers to God. (Some saints are more efficacious even than other saints. St. Rita of Cascia is 'the saint of impossibilities'[1]; and 'God has granted to St. Jude extraordinary powers in cases where others seem to have failed, and it is especially in difficult cases that his wonderful help is experienced'[(2)].) Indeed, the Catholic dispatches his prayers round the circuit in both directions. Not only does he pray to the saints to intercede for him with God, but he prays to God to grant him the intercessions of the saints[3].

20. *The Two Magics: the one which pretends, and the one which pretends and works*

In conceiving of prayer as a transmissible charge of energy, religion remains in the mental world of taboo and its more sophisticated successor, magic. In pure taboo, the potency of wishes is set free of any wisher and roams the world infecting people as impersonally as contagion. Magic re-asserts the person who does the wishing, at least to the extent of letting him attach his own wishes to the currents of magic power which are flowing about the world, rather as we can attach our ideas to radio waves: it provides a technique for harnessing the powers of magic to human will. When religion replaces magic, it completes the process of reuniting thoughts to persons; but it still believes in the dynamic potency of thought in its own right.

Intellectually and morally, religion is a tremendous advance; but not an unadulterated one. The savage had to keep watch over his actions with the minuteness of an obsessional neurotic because he could—so unjustly, as it seems to our concept of law—be punished for accidentally blundering into a taboo rule. But if he could be punished

---

[1] A prayer addresses her as 'Voi che tutti chiamano la Santa degl' *Impossibili*', who 'foste da Dio prescelta per avvocata dei casi più disperati'. (From an Italian 'holy picture', 'con approvazione ecclesiastica')

[(2)] from an English 'holy picture', *Perpetual Novena in honour of St. Jude*, Permissu Superiorum 20 July 1940; Carmelite Press, Kent.

[3] The Occasional Prayers in the English Missal include three 'to beg the intercession of the saints'—e.g., 'Grant, we beseech thee, almighty God, that the intercession of holy Mary, mother of God, of all the holy apostles, martyrs, confessors and virgins, and of all thy elect, may ever gladden us; that we who celebrate their merits may enjoy their patronage . . .'

for a deed with no intention behind it, at least he could not be punished for a wish that had not issued in a deed. Religion, with its emphasis on intentions, sets the religionist to watch his thoughts—an encouragement to the introspection and the psychological turn of mind which are the very basis of civilised culture and law. Yet this very advance was also a retreat towards restoring the omnipotence of thought, for it insists that something really happens in the world outside one's own mind—a sin is registered—when one entertains a sinful wish, whether or not it is expressed in a deed. 'Ye have heard that it was said by them of old time, Thou shalt not commit adultery: But I say unto you, That whosoever looketh on a woman to lust after her hath committed adultery with her already in his heart.'[1] But religion did not allow conscience to be something autonomous; it was to be scrupulous and active only in God's cause; it was not to question the prohibition on adultery, which emanated from God. The conscience could not even be trusted to relay God's commands efficiently, since individual consciences gave diverse accounts of them. An organisation which could persuade itself that God had made it his representative could therefore put itself in the place of all these inconsistent individual consciences and do its best, by whatever method it could devise, to reduce the amount of sin in the world by stopping certain thoughts from ever being thought and certain adulteries in the heart from ever being entertained. Inadvertently Jesus prepared the way, via the confessional, for the Thought Police.

Having removed thought from the public domain by recognising its personal and psychological nature, religion at once spoilt the effect by making everything depend on the personal psychology of God. The taboo system had mistaken certain pronouncements of the human unconscious for forces at work in the external world; the religionists were to attribute earthquakes to the will of God. Instead of merely externalising the unconscious prohibition on incest and parricide, and setting it free as an autonomous force in society, religion both externalised and projected it—shot it up to heaven, whence it came thundering back as the divine command that man must love and submit to the heavenly father. God's commands were no more to be reasoned about or moralised than the prohibitions ordained by taboo.

The disadvantage for the savage is that, having disclaimed responsibility for his thought and set it free, he cannot recall it and control

[1] *Matthew*, V, 27-8

it by a purely mental act. Even magic is still a machine which responds to deeds, not wishes, and responds quite automatically. The Sorcerer's Apprentice cannot by mere wishing reverse the effect of the wish—the spell—he cast. In the world of taboo there is no forgiveness. The transgression, once performed, is automatically punished because no one admits ownership of the punishing force.

Magic is credited so long as the people are too afraid to put it to the test—so long as transgressors die of fright and no one dare omit the rain-making ceremony for fear of drought. But should it, by some accident, be seen to fail, it must either resign or transform itself into religion, which can explain anything by the elastic will of God. Someone's mood, someone's anger—so the religionist explains to the disappointed magician—has interposed between spell and effect. The religionist has the advantage over the savage that he *can* be forgiven; but whether he *is* forgiven depends entirely on the caprice of God. The religionist still casts his wishes in the spell-like form of prayers and ceremonies, and seeks by them to influence God in the direction he wants; but while incorrect performance may mar, correct performance alone does not guarantee the efficacy of prayer. God must accept the worshipper's intention.

Magic takes in many respects a more scientific view of the world than religion does—or at least one which could more easily blossom into science. Being a sort of inferior science itself, it has none of religion's power to resist science; once scientific thinking has established itself, magic must retreat into half-ashamed, undefended, only half-serious superstition, while the church remains as intellectually and socially respectable as ever. Magic's experimental technique is wrong, and it does not know the rules of evidence; it may fake evidence in its favour; but at least it has not set itself to defy the validity of evidence. It draws strength from fear and—when no one dares to suspend the rain-making ceremony—by assuming what it thinks to demonstrate; but religion puts an end to the experimental frame of mind altogether when it forbids us to test God's existence on the grounds that God himself has ruled that we may not tempt the Lord our God. Magic rests on mistaken belief: religion devalues all demonstrable belief—in favour of faith; it killed experiment by making it virtuous to embrace a mystery.

Religion has, indeed, a distaste for the very material in which experiments have to be conducted and the very senses which conduct them. It lumps the world and the flesh in with the devil; painting all matter as either gross or disgusting or at best mere, uninteresting matter, it tries to condition man—by giving him shocks of disgust and guilt whenever he has looked out—to look solely inward at the world of his psychic images. If magic attributed too much to the outside world, religion has internalised—psychologised—everything. The sum of things exists because God thought of it. God is the solipsist: religion asserts the omnipotence of God's thought.

The tendency to psychologise everything has been taken further than ever by religion's latest ally, Jung—who comes near to giving the game away and admitting in so many words that it is the worshipper who is the real solipsist and who creates God by believing in him. In the introduction to his book, *Answer To Job* (an introduction addressed to the benevolent reader[1]; I do not think it was eavesdropping of me to read it) Jung writes:—' "Physical" is not the only criterion of truth: there are also *psychic* truths which can neither be explained nor proved nor contested in any physical way. If, for instance, a general belief existed that the river Rhine had at one time flowed backwards from its mouth to its source, then this belief would in itself be a fact even though such an assertion, physically understood, would sound utterly incredible. Beliefs of this kind are psychic facts which cannot be contested and need no proof. Religious statements' (he continues in a new paragraph) 'are of this type.'

This makes it obvious, for a start, why Jung's help to the religionists is necessarily nonsectarian. The immunity from test or proof which he extends to statements of this kind (it is interesting that Jung begins by admitting fairly that they *cannot* be proved, but a few lines later has it that they *need* not) covers pagan, savage and Mohammedan statements as well as Christian—and also, of course, such once widely believed statements as that the earth is flat and that geese grow out of barnacles. Of course it is true that belief in these things is a fact. It is true, also, that any picture which has ever flashed across the mind of man or beast is a psychic fact, whether or not it corresponds to anything in the external world—the point made by formal logic when it asserts that a term may have connotation but no denotation[2]. But in fact religious statements are not 'of this type' at all. The people who assert as an article of faith that the Red Sea parted or the Rhine flowed backwards are not asserting it as a psychic fact but as a concrete and externally true one: not as something additional to what happened

[1] Lectori Benevolo
[2] Cf. Susan Stebbing: *A Modern Introduction To Logic*, III, 4

on the given date, but *as* what happened. Religionists certainly do not mean to assert that God came into existence at the moment a general belief in him began, or that the miracle of the loaves and fishes became true when, some years after the date of the supposed event, belief in it became widespread. They are not telling us the history of religion, but its content, and the content must be either true or untrue. We may not be able to discover which, but that does not mean the answer does not exist.

Jung, however, is trying to divert us from the question about external truth by insisting that every belief is a psychic fact, which must be true because it has been thought. It is as though the power of thought can outweigh, outvalidate, the state of things in the external world: belief is a generating machine; it can *make* a thing true—if it is believed sufficiently. And here Jung bludgeons us with numbers. The curious word in the passage is *general*; the curious assertion is that the backward movement of the Rhine is a psychic fact if there is general belief in it. The truth is that it is neither more nor less of a psychic fact if many people believe it than if one solitary madman believes it. Jung has reverted to the primitive notion that thought is a generating machine: if enough people believe the same thing, that thing will be propelled into a kind of extra reality: not quite physical reality (neither Christians nor Jung can afford to assert that baldly) but a kind of special validity sufficient to blot out the additional question whether it is physically real or not. It is unfortunate for the religionists that psychic factuality belongs to all religious beliefs and not only to one church's; and it is still more unfortunate that it belongs equally to the delusion of the madman and the unique perception of the solitary genius. In none of these cases can we afford to judge that the psychic fact is so valid that we may neglect the question whether it tallies with external fact, because if we do not ask that question we have no means of distinguishing between true religion and false or between madman and genius.

Since to God 'all hearts be open, all desires known'[1], the ceremonial confession of an adultery committed in the heart might seem superfluous. Similarly, the natural conclusion for a lazy Christian to draw from the words 'Almighty God . . . who knowest our necessities before we ask, and our ignorance in asking'[2] is that human beings

[1] Communion Service collect, Book of Common Prayer

[2] Collect 'to be said after the Offertory, when there is no Communion', Book of Common Prayer

lack either occasion or ability to frame prayers. By introducing an omniscient God, religion runs the risk of relapsing into an omnipotence of thought more primitive than magic, in which it may even go back on the need for such external artifacts as prayers and ceremonies. Quite to disregard the outer world is to be unconscious; and the Christian mystic in ecstasy approaches unconsciousness. The real world fades from him and leaves him possessed by the fantasy which emanates from his unconscious. He is rapt into exclusive communion with his unconscious, or—as he might prefer to put it—he has made his conscious aware of nothing in the external world except the God who is everywhere in it. But, whereas some lunatics secure themselves in their fantasies and ignore the outside world for ever, the mystic emerges from his ecstasy. The world and his flesh reassert themselves in his awareness—for which the Church must be grateful; for the mystic, so long as his direct union with God lasts, has made redundant the Church and its ceremonies, both of which are intermediaries for uniting man to God. The mystic's ecstasy is no rival to the Church providing it is precarious, short-lived and difficult to attain; but the Church is none the less usually mistrustful of mystics during their lifetimes.

Whereas the mystic is solitary and has no security in his direct communion with God, the Church, which is social, offers certain guarantees of efficacy for its own, less direct, methods of communion; and this means that it retains for them some of the automatic efficacy of magic. Sacred objects, confession and prayers carry a partly automatic effect, the Catholic Church going so far as to state how much efficacy can be expected from reciting a given prayer or devotion. Even Jesus Christ, who so insisted on will by both sides of the transaction between man and God, acknowledged the contagiousness of taboo, and admitted that the woman who touched his clothes had drawn off some of his healing taboo power even though he himself did not will to transmit it[1]. For one ceremony the Catholic Church guarantees a completely automatic effect, the Mass. The mystic may or may not succeed in inducing the actual presence of his God, but that actual presence is invariably to be found in the consecrated Host. The words of the Consecration are a magical formula which works automatically, even though the priest personally be in mortal sin. (St. Teresa of Ávila, whose direct communions with God made her suspect, during her life, to the Church, but who always devotedly used and com-

[1] *Mark*, V, 25-34

mended the Church's method of Communion, had the truth of this doctrine demonstrated to her, at the very occasion of the Church's Communion, in one of the most direct of her visions[1].)

By retaining some magical value for its ceremonies Christianity retains the need for artifacts and so keeps a foot in the real world, saving itself from the danger, which some oriental religions apparently run into, that the devotee will make his aim the complete renunciation of reality and the complete return to unconsciousness. But if the introduction of God into the magical scheme brings liability to this danger, it also brings an advantage to religion which outweighs it. The magician's fantasy has defined limits, depends on certain misconceptions and no others, and affords the magician a refuge from reality only to a defined extent. Though he hide his head, reality will sooner or later find him out from the rear and unavoidably insist that the real world does not tally with the fantasy. But the religionist has spun himself an elastic fantasy; and the more reality insists, the deeper he can dive into it. The mystery of God and the mysteriousness of his ways will stretch to any extent and shape required.

Magic, which consists of a certain number of rigid keys, is always caught out when reality presents a lock of the wrong shape. Religion overcame this liability in just the spirit that a clever child, reading a fairytale where a man is offered fulfilment of three of his wishes by magic, cannot understand why the man does not break through the system by making his first wish the wish that all his wishes from then on should be fulfilled. This is the point of sophistication which religion has reached: and it invents a god to whom all desires are known. God is the supreme artifact of man's making, the key to all keys, and the formula of all formulae.

Nobody wants to believe something that is not true. When the religionist believes his fantasy because he wants to believe it, he is wanting something he does not want. Perceiving the impossibility of this, Socrates decided that men could not be immoral except through ignorance; and the rationalists of the eighteenth and nineteenth centuries similarly decided that men could not be religious except through ignorance. But ignorance is by no means the simple

[1] when she saw devils at the priest's throat while he administered the Communion. 'Then the Lord Himself told me . . . that he had allowed this in order that I might realize what power there was in the words of consecration, and that God never fails to be present however wicked the priest who pronounces them.' (Autobiography, 38, in J. M. Cohen's translation)

explanation it appears, since it does not explain why men, instead of acknowledging their ignorance and leaving a blank space on their maps, as Herbert Spencer invited them to do, filled the space with fabulous inventions, to believe which gave them so much pleasure that they called it virtuous. Moreover, in the event, the dispersal of ignorance does comparatively little to disperse either religion or immorality. Indeed, religion, if forced by analysis, turns out to be a species of immorality. Yet it also turns out to be a species of pleasure-seeking, and morality turns out to be nothing but pleasure-seeking. How, then, can religion and morality, be, as they necessarily are, enemies?

The psycho-analytic answer, like the Socratic, is 'by ignorance', but ignorance of a special kind—repressing the wish which is not to be known into the unconscious. Only one instinct is strong enough to defeat the instinct to pleasure, and that is the instinct to pleasure. The disparity between morals and religion is a case of the pleasure instinct turning on and subverting itself, and that it can get away with only by acting in the dark.

Antonio, the villain in *The Tempest*, called his conscience 'This deity in my bosom'[1]; and although as a matter of fact he was denying the existence of any such deity in his own bosom, he gave a perfectly correct account of what conscience is. (There is, by the way, a compact intellectual history to be read in the change of locale which had taken place by the eighteenth century, when Pope called conscience 'The God within the mind'[2].) Conscience has no more claim to be an absolute than the God in heaven has. We can give an account of both in terms of our psychic evolution: both are images of the father: both are targets for our ambivalence towards the father. The religionist lets fly with his secret hatred of God when he drives God off the earth and up to a heaven which he knows quite well is a fantasy; his unconscious feeling towards the father is expressed by a myth-making process which desexualises, etherealises and finally vapourises him. It is a similar end we often pursue by different means with conscience. Many of those most attached to it detest it; they may derive a fawningly affectionate pleasure from being bullied by it, but any gratitude they feel for this pleasure does not prevent them from blackening its character and ruining its good name. The puritan and the killjoy are secret rebels, hoping to tempt the oppressor into worse and worse acts of violence and so to make rebellion inevitable and justified.

[1] II, i　　　[2] *Essay On Man*, II, 204

In the obsessional neurotic, conscience has become such a bully that the Ego has to appeal over its head to another, more ultimate, standard and in the name of reason seek out the psycho-analyst who can relieve the patient of some of the imperatives his conscience presses on him.

That the appeal can be made is our sole justification for pronouncing conscience more capable of morality than religion is. It is an appeal, of course, to what is really another kind of conscience: an appeal, mediated via reason, to another irrational imperative, the instinct which insists absolutely 'Il faut que je vive'. But it *is* mediated through reason, and thus establishes us in a relation to reality; and this is its superiority to religion, which has set its face against reason and reality.

The appeal to the life instinct does not hand us over to moral anarchy. Dreadful as we know human nature to be, we need not be more afraid of what people might do if they were without a God or absolute taboo-like moral canons than we are afraid now. We must remember that people *now* do what they like. No god or moral superstition has prevented them from revealing to us the dreadfulness of human nature. All that taboos and religions achieve is to dress up our lust for cruelty in sanctimoniousness.

And in fact, when we consider humanity's record of cruelty, human sanctimoniousness is the worst horror—not simply in the psychological sense that it is the most repulsive to contemplate, but in the sense of actual harm as well: it is possible that if they had not been cloaked in sanctimoniousness many of the foulest atrocities would never have been done. Sanctimoniousness is called in wherever a strong party is going to victimise a weak one; it enables the stronger to pretend either that chastisement is for the victim's good or even that it is he, the stronger, who is really the victim.

As Dickens knew, sanctimoniousness was the cover under which we pursued our long social history of physical and mental cruelty to children; and it is still the cover for our relationship to another class of defenceless and inarticulate beings, the animals. The Greek or Roman religionist who draped garlands or ribbons on the animal he was leading to the sacrifice, and the tribesman who worships the animal he is going to murder, are not more hypocritical than the audience which is moved to admiration, and sexual excitement, by the 'courage' of the bullfighter, when it is in fact the bull who is doomed to die. At Easter we give our children dear little fluffy replicas of the chicken whose throat we will cut as soon as we have fed it up plump enough: the replica-giving is magic by imitation, a fertility rite for ensuring the meat supply for the coming year and the coming generation.

The definitive textbook of human sanctimoniousness was written towards the end of the fifteenth century: the *Malleus Maleficarum*—which is also a valuable source-book of psychological evidence. It reveals that the witches, with their hysterical fantasies of copulating with the diabolical father[1], were in the same case as the prostitute: incestuously desiring the father, and yet seeking to injure him by befouling his reputation. We can see (what we might have guessed from a stray remark of Burckhardt's, that during the renaissance 'a woman who, without youth and beauty, nevertheless exercised a powerful charm on men, naturally became suspected of witchcraft'[2]) that, just as her consort is a father to men (the father of lies, in fact), so the witch is a mother, whom men have debased in an attempt to

[1] *Malleus Maleficarum*, I, question 6; II, question 1, IV. The latter section records what may well (in spite of embellishments such as that on some rare occasions a black vapour was seen afterwards to arise from the witch) be factual observations of witches' hysterical seizures: 'the witches . . . have often been seen lying on their backs in the fields or the woods, naked up to the very navel, and it has been apparent from the disposition of those limbs and members which pertain to the venereal act and orgasm, as also from the agitation of their legs and thighs, that, all invisibly to the bystanders, they have been copulating with Incubus devils' (Montague Summers's translation, which I quote throughout). Compare Freud's 'General Remarks on Hysterical Attacks' (*Collected Papers*, Volume II, VIII) which begin: 'When one psycho-analyses a patient subject to hysterical attacks one soon gains the conviction that these attacks are nothing but phantasies projected and translated into motor activity and represented in pantomime.' Freud goes on to remark that a 'dream frequently takes the place of an attack'; and it is with dreams of flying, which Freud interpreted as representations of sexual intercourse, that G. Rattray Taylor connects the night rides through the air to which witches sometimes confessed. (G. Rattray Taylor: *Sex In History*, VI; Freud: *The Interpretation Of Dreams*, VI, (E); *Malleus Maleficarum*, I, question 1) I think it likely that in many cases the witch's confession was based on a dream of this sort, but one accompanied by a physical experience which persuaded her that it was more than a dream, namely a spontaneous orgasm during sleep. This phenomenon, which is comparatively rare in women, probably indicates a persistence in a fantasy of masculine-type sexuality of the clitoris (indeed, as Freud remarks, dreams of flying may be erection dreams); and so we may conjecture that the witch further resembled the prostitute by remaining unconsciously homosexual.

[2] *The Civilization Of The Renaissance*, VI

overcome their incestuous desires towards her. The witch, as G. Rattray Taylor[1] makes clear, is the obverse of the Virgin Mary, deteriorated image to exalted. The witch fills something of the social rôle later taken by the prostitute—who is already adumbrated in Christian mythology as the other (the obverse) Mary, the Magdalen[2].

Moreover, the celibates appointed[3] to enquire into and put down the mischief supposedly[4] worked by witches have not overcome their incestuous desires. The results they attribute to the witch's practices plainly reflect their own unconscious dread of the punishment for incest. The cardinal ill worked by witchcraft is castration—that is, a blight on the fertility of crops or cattle, and impotence in men[5]. Quite correctly, the authors of the *Malleus* pronounce that 'All

[1] *Sex In History*, VI

[2] Evidently the witch had become associated with an exalted virgin goddess of ancient mythology (now of course debased as pagan)—and also with a prostitute-figure from the New Testament: the *Malleus* (I, question 1) quotes an earlier ecclesiastical opinion on the subject of witches who claimed to have ridden 'with Diana or Herodias'. (*The Catholic Dictionary* quotes this Council [Trier, 1310] as referring to 'Diana or Herodiana'—by which 'was meant the daughter of Herodias'.) The particular form of this fantasy perhaps confirms that the witch's strongest unconscious attachment was to the mother.

[3] Henry Kramer and James Sprenger, 'Professors of Theology, of the Order of Friars Preachers' (i.e., Dominicans), appointed in 1484 by a Bull of Pope Innocent VIII

[4] The *Malleus* maintains not only that witchcraft itself, which involves renunciation of Catholic doctrines, is a heresy but also that it is a 'heresy, or rather infidelity' to maintain that witchcraft does not exist; it prescribes that suspects be made to formally abjure both heresies (I, question 2; III, question 24). By 1950 the *Catholic Dictionary* ('Witchcraft') had gone so far as to admit that it need not be believed that any of the supposed compacts between witches and evil spirits really did take place; but the opinion that 'any commerce between human beings and evil spirits is imaginary and impossible . . . cannot be held by Catholics'.

[5] The *Malleus* (II, question 1, VI) describes how witchcraft causes impotence in men and sterility in women and goes on (II, question 1, VII) to relate how a witch can cast a 'glamour' over the male sex organ, whose owner becomes unable to see or feel it. The predominance of mischief of this kind it explains by saying that God allows the devils 'more power over this act, by which the first sin was disseminated, than over other human actions' (II, question 1, VI). Indeed, (I, question 3) the devils' power over men is 'confined to the privy parts and the navel', since in men it is from the privy parts that semen falls, 'just as in women it falls from the navel'.

witchcraft comes from carnal lust'[1], but they have placed it all on the women (like the son who expresses his own Oedipal wish by a fantasy that the mother wants to seduce him), and rule that woman is more prone to witchcraft because 'she is more carnal than a man'[2].

It is when we come to the third part, which deals with the ecclesiastical and civil proceedings against witches, that the *Malleus* turns into the sanctimonious hypocrite's vade mecum. In dealing with the witch hysteric, it is the Catholic Church and the monopolistically Christian state which pose as the injured parties. 'And finally' (that is, after torture) 'let the Judge come in and promise that he will be merciful, with the mental reservation that he means he will be merciful to himself or the State; for whatever is done for the safety of the State is merciful'[3] (a doctrine recently adopted by secular states).

The Church itself, of course, only tortures witches, handing them over to the state to be killed, though it knows the state *will* kill them. The Church takes care not to be polluted by their death: the sentence handing them over to the secular court 'ought not to be pronounced on a Festival or Solemn Day, nor in a church. . . For it is a sentence which leads to death; and it is more decent that it should be delivered on an ordinary day and outside the church; for a Feast Day and the church are dedicated to God'[4]. None the less, 'witches should be questioned on the more Holy Days and during the solemnization of the Mass'[5]; and a woman gravely suspect of witchcraft 'is not to be altogether released, but must be sent to the squalor of prison for a year, and be tortured, and be examined very often, especially on the more Holy Days'[6].

All this bitter cruelty and sanctimoniousness was practised in the name of a god said to be love. So poorly did the priests imitate him in this respect, that we can only doubt the validity of their love for their god—as, indeed, we must in a religion whose chief spiritual exercise is to contemplate the torture of its god. Before torturing the witch in her second examination, the judge is advised by the *Malleus* to attach to his body certain holy objects and symbols—including a script of the words Christ uttered in *his* torture[7]. The section which begins 'The Judge should act as follows in the continuation of the torture', continues with the information that witches cannot weep true tears, and recommends that the judge or priest conjure the victim to tears 'by

[1] I, question 6   [2] I, question 6   [3] III, question 16
[4] III, question 28   [5] III, question 16   [6] III, question 25
[7] III, question 16

the bitter tears shed on the Cross by our Saviour . . . and by the burning tears poured in the evening hour over His wounds by the most glorious Virgin MARY, His Mother . . .'[1]

What we do *is* what we like. The myths of God and of moral idealism have only permitted us to do it in the name of duty. If we discard them, we shall at the very worst have gained a frank evil in place of a hypocritical one; and at best there is a hope that access to the sources of our behaviour will give us the means of controlling it.

For all their common origin, the god in the bosom and the god in heaven quickly become irreconcilable because, while conscience has at least the chance of moving towards reality, religion is driven by its own nature further and further from reality, into the fantasy of a super-reality, where the religionist maintains that man's highest virtue is to love God and his deepest pleasure to dwell on and promote the religious fantasy. Scientists, philosophers and artists are all driven by conscience to oppose this view. The first two find virtue in directly exploring reality: but the artist is just as imaginative a fantasist as the religious believer—with the crucial difference that he never puts his fantasy in the place of reality by pretending that it is the literal truth.

The result is that morality must be, at the lowest, permissive towards art. The least value art can claim is therapeutic: it affords a retreat from reality pour mieux sauter.

However, this low value, which is all the amateur artist puts on his own work, limiting its efficacy to himself, by no means satisfies the serious creator or the serious lover of the arts. The creator's own conscience certainly does more than permit him to practise art: it obliges him to. This obligation he tends to spread from himself to mankind in general, and most people who are in favour of culture are implicitly in agreement with him. Cultured people acknowledge a feeling that everyone has a duty to art: to create it if possible and, if not, to make himself into that kind of educated and impassioned spectator whose enjoyment of a work of art consists in re-creating for himself as nearly as possible the creative experience of the original artist.

When artists propagandise for this duty they are often behaving with mere professional patriotism and are concerned for their own self-importance, just as religious propaganda has sometimes been inspired more by the ambitions of priests than by the wish to save

[1] III, question 15

souls. Ever since the romantic movement of the early nineteenth century, some artists have aspired to be the priests of modern society: some want the superstitious reverence paid to the lean and crazed prophet; some want the pomp of the cardinal. But when the artist is serious enough to devote himself to the cause not of artists but of art, then he has a good case for impressing mankind with its obligation to art. He can make much of the permissive aspect: it is very probable that the only way that human beings can be kept out of the mischief of wars and oppressions is by the relief to their boredom which can be achieved by a passionate devotion to art. To this day, there are people who argue in favour of churches on the grounds that they keep young delinquents off the streets: art can claim to be more effective and also to have the advantage of being morally innocuous.

However, art, like religion, makes a positive claim to virtue as well as this negative one. The only objection to religion's claim to be the most important subject in the world is that its magic-making is simply not true. Art makes the same claim to importance without, in one sense, claiming to be true. But in another sense its magic-making genuinely works. There is a sense in which thought really is omnipotent. So long as it does not claim to do so palpably and literally, imagination is quite justified in claiming that it annihilates time and space. It conjures what is not there into a kind of existence. The magician makes the claim that he brings reality into accordance with human wishes by the techniques of magic. Science, we can see, has made this claim good by improving on magic's technique: science really can alter the environment and make it as we want it to be: and its technique for doing so is passed on and enlarged by our system of cultural inheritance. The artist does the same thing but all within the sphere of the mind. All he requires from reality, the only things he really alters in the environment, are paper and ink, canvas and paint. If we pass these, and the knack of reading them, to our descendants, we have passed on his mental magic-making.

Moreover, once it has abandoned the primitive's claim to affect external reality, art can insist that it does affect the mind. It alters the human beings who practise (or re-experience) it. The purpose which religion claims God intends for mankind does not exist, because God does not exist. But mankind is quite capable of giving itself a purpose: our evolutionary progress has set us free to do so.

The mind, which can leap in an instant to the state where our present difficulties, which look so likely to overwhelm us, have all been solved, instantly demands what is the purpose of solving them. And indeed, if the dynamic view of evolution is correct, without a purpose we shall never solve them. When we have arranged a world free from wars and oppressions, when all the people are educated, when science protects us from the environment in the form of germs and earth-quakes and has taken care of our material needs by inventing machines to do the dull work, and when we have gained the political wisdom to effect a re-distribution of labour and turn the machines into our working class—what is the point? Hence the connexion, vaguely grasped by a number of artists and socialists, though in practice often negated by both sides, between art and socialism. Art is a religion in which the worshippers acknowledge that they have created the deity—thereby freeing themselves of hatred towards him. Creating art, men create the destiny of mankind. Instead of creating the fantasy of gods and paying court to it as though it were real, they have made it real. They have made themselves, as creators, gods—or, in evo-lutionary terminology, super-men. If we want to make this advance without becoming supermen in Nietzsche's sense: without committing the immoralities of the primal father and the deified bullies, and without incurring the odium which attends them and keeps up the wearisome cycle whereby they are pulled down only to be resurrected; then we shall have to observe the prime distinction morality draws, that between real and imagined acts: and we shall have to make our advance in the cultural—that ·is, the imaginative—realm to which our evolution has adapted us.

III

THE EMANCIPATION OF REASON

1. 'On se mêle de raisonner' (Voltaire in 1735)[1]

Since 1804, when Beethoven angrily rescinded the dedication of his 'heroic' symphony to Bonaparte on learning that Bonaparte had transformed himself from a First Consul into an Emperor[2], everyone who advocates reason and champions the rights of man considered as a reasonable being has been put at a disadvantage by history: by the fact that modern Europe has already attained to an Age of Reason, in which reason was given its chance and failed.

To be just, the Age of Reason did no worse than most of the preceding ages of unreason. But that, as rationalists are bound to admit, was not the point. Reason must do much better than unreason; otherwise people are quite justified in exercising their preference, even though it is a purely capricious one, for oppression and bloodshed allied to unreason rather than oppression and bloodshed allied to reason. Since the climactic failure of reason at the end of the eighteenth century, rationalism has had to contend not only with reaction but with its own doubts.

The fanfare of the eighteenth century was sounded, a decade before the century opened, in John Locke's italicised pronouncement that *'Reason must be our last judge and guide in everything'*[3]. The question at issue was religious revelation and the authority based on it. Locke demonstrated (the point that was to trip up Franz Hettinger's argument in favour of religious authority[4]) that even if we accept the

[1] letter to M. de Cideville, 16 April
[2] See, e.g., the introduction to the Eulenburg (miniature) edition of the score
[3] 1690. *An Essay Concerning Human Understanding*, IV, XIX, 14
[4] Cf. II, 13

possibility of revelation we must still depend on reason to establish whether the prophet really did receive a message and, if so, whether it really came from God. This perception became one of the great common thoughts of the eighteenth century. Locke's argument was still being urged at the very end of the century by the impassioned deist and noblest of men Tom Paine, in his eponymous tract for the times *The Age of Reason.* 'No one will deny or dispute the power of the Almighty to make such a communication if he pleases. But admitting, for the sake of a case, that something has been revealed to a certain person . . . it is revelation to that person only . . . and *hearsay* to every other; and consequently they are not obliged to believe it'.[1]

The human race did not suddenly become more reasonable at the approach of the eighteenth century. Locke himself remarked that 'God has not been so sparing to men to make them barely two-legged creatures, and left it to Aristotle to make them rational'[2]; and still less did he suppose God had left it to John Locke. However, as Aristotle's Edwardian champion H. W. B. Joseph rejoined, 'Had God made men barely two-legged creatures, Aristotle would in vain have taught them to be rational, for they would not have understood his teaching'[3]. Aristotle's formulation of logic marks an advance not in man's rationality but in his self-consciousness. It is the point where culture became formally conscious of its own rationality. If logic is the syntax of reasonable thought, Aristotle drew our attention to the fact that we had been arguing in syntactical prose all along.

The eighteenth century's discovery of reason marks just such an advance in self-consciousness on the part of postclassical man. Obviously, the eighteenth century was not saying that men always reasoned correctly—or that sharpest of weapons, eighteenth-century satire, would have lacked material on which to do execution. On the other hand, neither was it simply affirming what Christian theology and mere common sense had already maintained, namely that man was capable of reason. Locke's argument was neither that reason may be nor that it *should* be our last judge and guide, but that it must be: if we are to have any judge and guide at all, we cannot help making it reason; to say that we will ignore reason and take some irrational

[1] 1794. *The Age of Reason,* I
[2] *An Essay Concerning Human Understanding,* IV, XVII, 14
[3] *An Introduction To Logic,* I (first edition 1906)

authority for our guide is not really to abandon reason at all but merely to reason badly.

Locke had in effect recognised man as an animal whose consciousness is his sense-organ—which is true as far as man's Ego is concerned; and in fact the Ego was as far as the concern of the rationalist movement went. Locke's denial of the existence of innate ideas in the human mind[1] acknowledges that our species (or, in his pre-biological terminology, our creator) has not imposed an instinctual pattern of behaviour on the human race; the human mind acquires its stock of notions from the imprint on it of its own experience, and has nothing on which it can rely to bind it into a consistent and instinct-gratifying relationship with the environment except the rational use of whatever stock it has collected.

It is this recognition of man as a particular kind of creature which defines the advance the eighteenth century made in human self-consciousness. The faculty of being human, man's distinction alike from divinities and from animals, now meant not merely to be capable of reason but to be necessarily dependent on reason: if man was to pursue the instinctual quest for happiness which could be observed in the animals and postulated as achieved in God (who was perfect—that is, satisfied and, like heaven, harmonious), then he must make use, well or badly, of his reason. The advance was nothing else than a consciousness of man in the generic sense. Never before had so many men anatomised, apostrophised, epigrammatised on man. The century is spanned and defined by its great books on the themes *man* and *human*: *An Essay Concerning Human Understanding; Essay On Man; The Rights Of Man*[2].

2. Men and Man

If the Age of Reason was a crucial step in modern civilisation's emergence into self-awareness, it was only the second spurt of a process which began with the renaissance. Moreover, the whole process (including a trial and failure of rationalism) had already been gone through in ancient Greece; and for both the renaissance and the eighteenth century the great mark of their own development of self-consciousness,

[1] *An Essay Concerning Human Understanding*, I, 'Of Innate Notions'
[2] 1690; 1733-4; 1791-2

and the great spur towards developing it further, was their re-awakening, reconstruction and, often, misconception of classical experience.

Like Aristotle's discovery of logic, the eighteenth-century discovery of reason was a step in *formal* consciousness; and as such it was in several respects antithetical to the renaissance. The renaissance had no need to rediscover either logic or Aristotle. Both were embodied—or, rather, embalmed—in the theology of St. Thomas Aquinas and in the formal logic taught by the universities; they belonged, in fact, to the medieval system of thought which the renaissance was engaged in picking holes in. Medieval thought was already only too formal: that is to say, it was highly logical and not in the least reasonable. There was no reasonable connexion between the intricate, gothic structure of theology's picture of the universe and the real universe it supposedly rested on. Probably it was its sense of not being based in reality which gave medieval thinking its characteristic anxiety—an anxiety whose symptoms we can recognise in its obsessive schematisation and in the great knots of conscious and arbitrary symbolism with which it decorates and impedes the flow of its arguments.

This characteristic turn of medieval thought persisted into the renaissance. It is medieval formalism which gives shape to the neo-Platonic allegories and obsessive symbolisation round which Botticelli built his mythology pictures, and to the elaborately worked-out conceits of renaissance poetry. Indeed, it is still there in the seventeenth century, giving even a shape on the printed page to some English metaphysical poems and filling them with geometric, cosmological and even alchemical metaphors; and it is still the medieval concept of thought as a formal exercise like jousting which gives Racine the pretext for indulging his positive delirium of antitheses. But the content which is framed in this way differs in kind from the content of medieval thought. Even though the renaissance was not so wholesale a break as nineteenth-century scholars supposed, and even though the dark and middle ages had contained proto-renaissances of their own, it is still true to say that those were sporadic and isolated breaks in the clouds, and that it was only the renaissance proper which achieved a steady climate of complete consciousness. The relation to reality, the psychological experience of reality, has been re-established. Botticelli has found a way out of medieval constrictions not through neo-Platonism, whose message is carefully wrapped so as to be indiscoverable to the uninstructed eye, but through art, which appeals directly to the world at large; the allegories and symbols, whatever they were, have been quite swallowed up and digested by the picture, which presents itself to us not as an intellectual and philosophical but as a sensuous and artistic experience. The metaphysical poets are using their rigid conventions, as Bach was to use his, only to intensify the personal and poignant states of emotion they convey to us; and Racine reveals to us through his formalities a free play of individuals' psychology in relation to one another, which, for flexibility and the modern tone of its psychological curiosity, was not to be equalled until the novels of the nineteenth century. The renaissance had forced its way through the medieval paving stones, cracking them apart and making use of bits of their rigidity where it liked; and it was only after it had re-established the contact between human consiousness and reality, and only after civilisation had taken in, and absorbed into the cultural tradition, a whole fresh store of experience, that there was any call for reason to set to work on the new material and formulate fresh rules about the nature of reality.

Whereas the eighteenth century at once began to define natural laws on the subject of man, of whom it had just become conscious, the renaissance made do, for rules, with fragments of the medieval system it had shattered and such bits of the classical system as it could bring to light, and devoted its consciousness to men. The renaissance view is epitomised in Hamlet's satirical 'What a piece of work is a man! How noble in reason'.'[1], the eighteenth century's in an unconscious 'improvement' on it which we still incline to make, taking the nobility perfectly seriously and misquoting Hamlet's *a man* as simply *man*. The renaissance was individualistic, centrifugal, anti-democratic. It was asserting individual and diverse men against the dominance of the medieval Church and God—who had, in a sense, forced men into a consciousness of themselves as man, and had imposed a sort of democracy on them: but their common humanity was summed up in the name of Adam, the punished sinner, and the democracy was the democracy of their all being, like Adam, dust; it is that frightful equality and fraternity asserted by medieval Triumphs of Death. The Church laid down catholic rules by observing which everyone equally might hope to circumvent the universal sway of death and end in heaven. The renaissance placed its emphasis on the qualities by which nature unfairly distinguished one man above another. Complaining with a bittersweet agony of the fact of death, it occupied itself with the means whereby an individual might

[1] II, ii

outlast mortality: by impressing his personal merits—his courage, beauty or artistic genius—on the cultural tradition.

> So long as men can breathe, or eyes can see,
> So long lives this, and this gives life to thee[1].

The poet's poem is his child—his posterity, his immortality; and it may be at the same time the child of the beloved person to whom he has, in a marriage of true minds, mated his genius:

> But were some child of yours alive that time,
> You should live twice,—in it and in my rime[2].

Unable to produce a single tenable generalisation about human nature, the artists of the renaissance created human beings—an ability which reached its historically highest peak with the creation of that most individualised of human beings, Hamlet. Any general conclusions we wish to draw from *Hamlet* must be extracted and shewn us by Freud and Ernest Jones. The author tells us nothing about nature. He has simply done what nature does, and created a man whole. His genius commented Keats[3], 'was an innate universality'.

The tendency of the renaissance was naturalistic, and artists were concerned with the idiosyncrasy of a personality, the distinction of a figure, the personal beauty or grotesquerie of a face. Often, however, and especially in visual arts, this tendency took on a more formalistic appearance by being disguised as a search for an ideal, an ideal of beauty or a heroic ideal; we find an almost medieval quest for types— though the ideal is now, of course, a classical one. If this happens particularly in painting and sculpture, it is no doubt through their connexion with the science of anatomy, which really does demonstrate an unvarying type beneath the skin. Yet the moment an artist succeeded, as, most notably, Michelangelo did, in creating figures who, for all the naturalism of their presentation, are recognisably ideal types of the generic man, the renaissance quickly found an outlet for its true tendency and turned the tables on the artist's intention. Foiled of idiosyncrasy in his paintings and statues, people picked on the idiosyncrasy of Michelangelo himself and adulated in him not generic man but individual genius.

[1] Sonnet XVIII   [2] Sonnet XVII   [3] Houghton: *Life And Letters* . . .

It was, in fact, the renaissance which invented, largely round Michelangelo and Leonardo, our concept of the genius, which it propounded as a secular rival to canonisation. It was part of its centrifugal quality to substitute this individual genius, whose baptism was a direct descent of inspirational fire, for that social and fraternal being, the anonymous craftsman, whose skill was automatically induced by formal and prolonged initiation.

Even where it did create societies—in the political sphere—the renaissance emphasised their differences from one another: that is, it began to create nationalism. To some extent it did so by breaking up Christendom. Although the political unity of Christendom had long before been split by its various monarchs, it was the renaissance which put a stop to its old catholic culture by abandoning Latin—a move forced on the renaissance by the preference its individual poet-geniuses shewed, following the route pioneered by Dante, for the less canonical and less impersonal vulgar tongues, each of which was a closed book to the others.

Whereas the renaissance had been humanist, the eighteenth century was humanitarian. Like all humanitarian movements, it can be accused of losing sight of men in the clarity of its vision of man; but we can equally accuse the renaissance of lacking any social sense whatsoever. It has to be admitted that the eighteenth century lost the benefit of some of its predecessors' finest individual imaginings, but we often blame it for blindnesses it did not really shew or which were not its own. It is true that it did not recover Botticelli from oblivion; but then it was not eighteenth-century but High Renaissance taste which had eclipsed him in the first place. We often think that the eighteenth century in England, with its academic or merely theatrical-catchpenny determination to 'improve' him, came within an ace of losing Shakespeare. But Pope and Johnson were his servitors; and if we can get over the bardolater's outraged feeling that Dryden committed a blasphemy when he wrote a play on a theme Shakespeare had already touched (it is true, divinely), our ear will have to recognise that Augustan poetry is saved from the mechanical and academic—remains, for all its wit, poetry—precisely because it was constantly irrigated by the metaphors and vocabulary of Shakespeare. It is to the Forest of Arden and the wood near Athens that we must trace the descent of English eighteenth-century pastoral, a genre incarnated for all time in *Acis And Galatea*. The libretto of that ravishing musical masterpiece, with its

Hush, ye pretty, pretty warbling choir

and its

As when the dove
Laments her love
All on the naked spray,

is saved from both the slackness and the mere efficiency of journalism
by the everlasting felicity of its conventions, in which is distilled and
preserved a sort of essence of Shakespeare.

It is no idle coincidence that the libretto of *Acis And Galatea*[1] comes
from Ovid[2], the source-book from which Shakespeare borrowed and
adapted his own pastoral and sylvan images (and filched the very
name of Titania[3]). The librettists[4] have transmuted Ovid into the
idiom Shakespeare created from the same material. Moreover, they
have picked out of Ovid a story which, like the resurrection of
Orpheus, is a metaphor of the immortality through art which preoccupied Shakespeare. Galatea, as a minor goddess, has—within
limitations[5]—the power to bring her dead lover back to life. She
metamorphoses him into a stream, which she conjures out of the
rock beneath which he lies crushed:

thus I exert my pow'r divine;
Be thou immortal, though thou art not mine.

In other words, she has given him to the cultural tradition. This
stream, whose constant flow Handel's music so prettily imitates[6],
is the immortal stream of music itself. 'Acis now a god appears', sing

[1] a subject used by various earlier eighteenth-century and just pre-eighteenth-
century works. (See the sleeve of the Oiseau-Lyre recording)

[2] *Metamorphoses*, XIII, 738 foll., which Part II of the libretto sticks to remarkably closely. Acis's dying words are a translation of the Latin; Polyphemus's speeches preserve his very similes from Ovid, and his famous 'I
rage—I melt—I burn' is represented by the more intellectualised and less
effective thought of line 867, 'uror enim, laesusque exaestuat acrius ignis'.
Ovid himself had borrowed the chain of similes from Polyphemus's speech
in Theocritus's *Idyll* XI.

[3] *Metamorphoses*, III, 173

[4] The libretto, according to the Oiseau-Lyre sleeve, was attributed to John
Gay and includes lines by John Hughes, Dryden and Pope.

[5] Ovid (but not the libretto) remarks on these limitations (line 885).

[6] No. 29

the chorus, hailing him as 'Shepherds' pleasure, Muses' theme'. At the same time, the stream's constancy is the lover's (a constancy his human weakness[1] prevented him from achieving in real life). As in the final couplets in Shakespeare's sonnets, the metamorphosis of life into art has immortalised the lover's love:

> Through the plains he joys to rove,
> Murmuring still his gentle love.

We can guess that Galatea's strangely limited pow'r divine is that power of making limited magic which belongs to artistic genius.

3. *The Benefits of Comparison*

Reason was liberated, and with such éclat, in the eighteenth century thanks to the preceding three centuries, which had provided it with fresh material to work on in the shape of mathematical and scientific discovery, the discovery of unguessed-at parts of the earth, and the rediscovery of a barely guessed-at antiquity.

Psychologically it was the last two which were particularly stimulating, because they forced comparisons on the attention. Eventually the same effect was made by the rift to which Christianity succumbed at the Reformation; and it is the Reformation, the new world and the ancient world which, in our psychological history, are the promoters of rationalism. The advance in self-consciousness followed on taking more of the external world into consciousness. Once reason's appetite was aroused, it gladly gobbled up material about the external world provided by the natural sciences, and often learned its discipline from them. Physics and mathematics are just as capable as formal logic of taking the intellect for its daily exercise. But such is their emptiness of human material that by themselves they would probably no more have promoted the sceptical turn of mind than formal logic did during the middle ages.

No amount of argumentation could have done half so much for

[1] This is not simply a question of his being unable to resist death. The serenata (the Novello score's word for it; Oiseau-Lyre call it a masque) begins as, but for Galatea's divine power, it would have ended, with Galatea lamenting Acis's absence. What has removed him is not explained.

scepticism as the simple demonstration that other moeurs existed (a demonstration exhaustively completed between 1890 and 1915, when *The Golden Bough* became the rationalists' handbook without containing a word of rationalist advocacy. Not that Frazer concealed his own opinions; but he was aware that the compilation of fact would speak for them, and he explicitly acknowledges the benefits of comparison. 'The old view that the principles of right and wrong are immutable and eternal is no longer tenable. . . Few things, perhaps, can better guard us from narrowness and illiberality in our moral judgments than a survey of the amazing diversities of ethical theory and practice which have been recorded among the various races of mankind in different ages; and accordingly the Comparative Method applied to the study of ethical phenomena may be expected to do for morality what the same method . . . is now doing for religion, by enlarging our mental horizon . . . throwing light on the origin of current beliefs and practices, and thereby directly assisting us to replace what is effete by what is vigorous, and what is false by what is true'[1].) Once you know that the Aztecs (or, if you are a Catholic, the Protestants) receive as self-evident truth a whole series of propositions quite different from your own self-evidently true system, and practise as though in obedience to innate laws a series of customs which contradict yours, you have the means of questioning both systems. It is, once again, the hypnotic power of the stranger, who fixes our attention by his conspicuous difference from ourselves. The stranger's system begins to exert a tug on our loyalties contrary to our own system, and we are led to question the basis of all loyalty. The Church had been wise in its generation in suppressing heresy: not that heresies like witchcraft or Calvinism were so immediately more attractive than the Catholic faith that the people, if left free to do so, would have flocked to them, but because the mere knowledge that two contradictory heartfelt faiths can exist ultimately urges people to have done with faith altogether.

The great perception of the eighteenth century was to realise that in the face of several contradictory systems of apparently revealed truth, our only possible criterion is reason. But before the perception could be made, the mélange of information had to be laid in front of the mind. Historically we owe eighteenth-century rationalism to the sort of travellers' tales Shakespeare made fun of[2], even while inventing a better, in *The Tempest* (and which had already inspired Elizabethan

[1] Preface to *Taboo And The Perils Of The Soul*   [2] III, iii

Gonzalos to imagine utopian commonwealths in implicit criticism of contemporary principalities), to terrestrial globes of the sort Holbein placed with his sitters[1], and to the popular redactions of the outlandish mythological beliefs entertained by the Greeks and Romans.

It was not intended that any of this should lead to scepticism; often the very opposite. The Protestants sought to restore Christianity to the unsullied faith of the archaic Christian movement, which had not yet allowed the Church and the Pope to intervene as monitors between it and its credulity; but the result of their labours was towards undermining faith and credulity altogether. The missionaries of every sect who went out to the newly opened territories in order to Christianise the natives contributed ultimately to the de-Christianising of Europe, by sending home reports of benighted pagan customs which in the end suggested to the recipients that Christian customs would, with just as good reason, look equally benighted to a pagan.

The eighteenth century, on the other hand, did intend that comparisons should point out our ultimate dependence on reason. The marvellously cold eye which eighteenth-century satire cast over the world is an attempt to induce such a stimulus artificially. The result was a lively but a pamphleteering rather than a psychologising literature. Candide was dispatched on his adventures so that the reader might through him see the world (not childhood) from knee-height (a device Swift used, in reverse, more literally)—through the naïf eyes of a child but without the child's limitation of depending on, and therefore wanting to be assimilated to, the status quo. Candide is quite independent: that is, he depends on his reason. The picaresque tradition was enlarged to take in the modish theme of exoticism (this genre, too, Voltaire tried his hand at), and a European traveller would be cast away on a sultry shore, or a dignified, exotic prince brought to Europe, there to ask disconcerting questions. It was all propaganda for reason as our only possible guide and judge. The unanchored vision and the anomalous point of view forced the reader to notice the arbitrariness of the established conventions; and the moral was that between those and the conventions of savagery there was not a penny to choose—unless reason was set to work.

The pamphleteers, and likewise the practitioners of the new, conversational skill of journalism, were addressing themselves to a new social phenomenon, a public. Renaissance artists had spoken to patrons as individualistic as themselves. The patron's interest in the

[1] 'The Ambassadors', National Gallery

matter was that he hoped to hop on the vehicle of artistic genius and thus be conveyed, in all his individuality, to posterity. By the eighteenth century, patronage had proliferated and lost much of its influence (Johnson's set-piece on the subject would have been unthinkable to Shakespeare) and the practice was merging into the modern one of literary back-scratching and reputation-fixing. Reputation was beginning to carry more kudos than nobility, and the sounding-board of reputation was the public. Even patrons were now attempting to secure influence with the public, rather than remembrance by posterity.

The new material released into culture by the renaissance pioneers had been assimilated by a whole class, a literate bourgeoisie. Naturally this class was more social in its aims than the individual patron. No one member could hope for a personal immortality by patronising the arts. Rather, as he sought to be educated and to be kept informed, as he read the magazines and miscellanies, the individual was performing a social duty; he was trying to keep up with the rest of his cultural class. The old individual ambition of leaving a great name behind, or achieving an apotheosis or a triumph such as seventeenth-century painters had accorded to noble patrons, had to be gradually replaced by an ideal that could be shared by a group; and this was, of course, the transcendent eighteenth-century ideal of Taste.

In pursuit of Taste, the eighteenth century made a discovery of its own. To the new world and the ancient world, it added the old world. Its eyes were opened to Europe. As well as succumbing to the glamour of the exotic, it succumbed to the glamour of the merely foreign. Laurence Sterne told his public that they ordered this matter (by which his public understood every matter) better in France[1], and the impression on the British bourgeoisie has never been effaced. (To ask someone what he thinks of the French remains the most stringent test of social class in modern England. If he replies that they are foul, frog-eating foreigners, he is a member of the working class.)

There had been travellers in other centuries; the eighteenth century invented tourists—and a tourist might turn into a travel-writer and thence, like Joseph Addison, into that other eighteenth-century invention, a journalist. The great flow was of northerners going south in order to cultivate taste; but many returned to exercise it by summoning Italian painters and decorators home to England. Painting still depended on individual patrons; but music began to catch up with writing (which had, of course, got a head start because it could

[1] *A Sentimental Journey* . . ., I

be disseminated in print). With the development of popular opera and, in England, popular oratorio, composers and executives began to address themselves less to the nobleman who paid by stipend and pension and more to the public who paid by subscription and the price of a box. This, too, bred international exchanges. Everyone depended on Germany and Austria for great composers, and the English public depended largely on Italy for singers.

These exchanges made possible a continual comparison between the Protestant and Catholic sections of Europe; and the result is instantly apparent in the stop which the eighteenth century promptly put to sectarian wrangles. By the middle of the century, an English Protestant no longer needed to travel to discover that the papists were human; the knowledge would come to him at his university at home—where it came to Edward Gibbon, who in the flush of discovery became one himself. It was to be divested of Catholicism that Gibbon was sent abroad, and there turned into a cosmopolitan whose first published work was in French; soon comparison made its usual effect and, having discovered that neither Protestants nor papists were more than human, Gibbon soared into his circumspect scepticism towards both sides.

4. *The Comparison with Antiquity*

What drew the tourists south was not Catholicism but classicism, the fount of Taste. In historical fact it was the study of antiquity which had opened the first fissures in the Christian monopoly, by providing Europe with its first standard of comparison since the death of Julian the Apostate. We know or can guess that the thought that the great writers and philosophers of antiquity had believed in pagan gods or no gods at all led several individual minds of the renaissance on tiptoe to an inexplicit, perhaps even an equivocal or a worldly, scepticism. But, true to the asocial quality of renaissance culture, most of the renaissance sceptics seem to have had no eagerness to proselytize. Indeed, the renaissance tradition about what to do with important intellectual knowledge was not to throw it open to as many people as possible, but to conceal it, as a dangerous and powerful mystery, in symbolical trappings whose meaning should be revealed only to initiates. And of course if a sceptic did, like the reckless Christopher

Marlowe[1], attempt to propagate his ideas, he found himself in danger from the government, whether that was Catholic or Protestant.

What the pagan myths meant to the renaissance painters who plunged into them we can only guess from their paintings. For Titian and Veronese, here, obviously, was a way round Christian puritanism and into sensuality. But this need imply no conscious rejection of the accepted Christian standards, still less an intellectual criticism of them; the importance of the classics as a fount of rebellion is that they were always accepted as perfectly respectable. Neither can we have the least doubt that Botticelli took his Christianity seriously and personally, though we may surmise that he was tortured between a Savonarolesque Christianity and the nonChristian moral import of the neoPlatonic lessons he dressed up in pagan clothes. But whatever his intellectual position, the emotion he conveys to us through his mythology pictures is a nostalgia for the mythological world itself, the imaginary world he knows never objectively existed.

Venetian mythology pictures, with their strapping, glorious, mature gods and goddesses, seem to be suggesting to us what an adulthood men and women might have enjoyed if (though the criticism is only implied) Christianity had not imposed its embargoes on sensuality. Veronese's marvellous *Venus And Adonis*, in the Prado, breathes the very high-summer air of *Antony And Cleopatra*: the nobleness of life, it asserts, is to do thus. But when we consider the Florentine mythological tradition (a tradition primarily of Botticelli's own creating, but with contributions from Piero di Cosimo and from Signorelli in his *Pan*[2], a Florentine commission), although we find there, too, a sensual world, it has, rather, the sensuality of childhood. Everything is, in a sense, sexualised, down to the very grass and the flowers in it, but sexuality itself has not yet been objectively and knowingly perceived in its social setting: however we may interpret Botticelli's Venus, she is innocent in a manner inconceivable to Veronese's—or to Shakespeare's—Cleopatra.

Some of the difference between these attitudes must be attributed to

[1] See the 'Note' (reprinted in the Havelock Ellis edition of Marlowe's plays) 'Contayninge The Opinion Of One Christofer Marlye, Concernynge His Damnable Opinions And Judgment Of Relygion And Scorne Of Gods Worde', which affirms that Marlowe not only held blasphemous opinions himself 'but almost in every company he commeth, perswadeth men to Atheisme willinge them not to be afrayed of bugbeares and hobgoblins . . .'

[2] at Berlin, now destroyed

history. The Florentine tradition, much more than the unlearned and late-awakened Venetian culture (or English culture), was aware of antiquity as something dug up in incomplete fragments, pieced together as far as scholarship could manage, but in its entirety poignantly irrecapturable. The archaeological metaphor struck the Florentine imagination (just as it proved irresistible to Freud, whose profession consisted of bringing to light and reconstructing the fragments of people's individual pasts; he invoked an archaeological simile in describing psycho-analysis[1], was himself a collector of archaeological finds[2], and recorded how disturbingly moved he was when he at last stood on the Acropolis[3].) Their own renaissance was to the Florentines an adolescence, a final bursting-through into complete individual self-consciousness, after which no return is possible: antiquity was, from this point of view, the irrecapturable childhood of the world.

We can understand why the painters interested themselves less in the factual history of the ancient world than in the imaginary histories recorded in its myths. What is lost to the Florentine renaissance—or, rather, what it would like to recapture but cannot—is not the objective nature of childhood but childhood as it is experienced by the child. The Venetian painters have made use of the myths by embodying in them a state which is irrecapturable only at one remove: flesh and sexuality really exist; it is simply that the real world has never allowed us to liberate them. But what the Florentines convey to us through the myth-world is much more subtly irrecapturable. It is the child's own experience of a timeless world, a world of eternal summer, and the child's own sense of being immortal—before complete self-consciousness has shewn him himself finite in the context of time; and this universe of childish experience, like the universe created by the myths, really never did exist objectively.

The Florentine painters, by sympathetically including in their mythological pictures animals and animal-men mixtures, like Pan or the Centaur whom Botticelli[4] shews us being tamed by Pallas Athena, give us a glimpse into childhood which includes even the equality which children feel between themselves and animals, and which is the common starting-point from which both the animal phobias and tribal totemism spring into an ambivalence towards

[1] *Civilization And Its Discontents*, I [2] Martin Freud: *Glory Reflected*
[3] *Collected Papers*, Volume V, XXVIII [4] *Minerva Taming A Centaur*, Uffizi

animals[1]. Piero di Cosimo[2] has poignantly depicted the very instant when the lucid cocoon of timelessness, in which this equality exists, is split by the recognition of death, just as the immortality of paradise is split, in *Back To Methuselah*, by the death of the fawn.

Ultimately, therefore, Botticelli is asserting the very same wish in his pagan mythologies as he is in his madonna and child pictures[3]: the wish to restore infancy. If we surmise that he felt an intellectual conflict between pagan and Christian, we may also surmise that what kept him from quite succumbing to its strain was this identity of unconscious content between the opposites. But from the conscious point of view, there remains the cardinal difference that the mythological picture admits that its case is hopeless, whereas the religious picture insists that paradise can be re-gained in real life—providing certain conditions are observed in real life.

Here lies the fundamental importance of pagan mythology to painting, indeed to culture, in general. It afforded Christendom its first respite from Christianity's insistence on impinging on people's imaginations with its supposed realities. Antiquity was beloved not, primarily, as antiChristian but as aChristian, a return to the time when the most exacting of babies combined with the most exacting of fathers had simply not yet been conceived and placed in his manger. It was a world suspended, to which the critical questions posed by Christianity, questions on which salvation turned, simply did not apply— like that Limbo, isolated from the Christian scheme of damnation and salvation, in which Dante placed the great pagans, who had never had to decide for or against Christ and who therefore lived out their eternal lives suspended[4] (one of whom, as though to map out the way the renaissance was to go, he takes with him as guide for his exploration of the Christian scheme).

For painting, the antique was all-important, because it was the step whereby the art secularised itself—became, in fact, an art instead of an adjunct to religious magic-making. (Dante had begun the secularisation of literature by preferring the vulgar tongue to the tongue of the Vulgate; although his point of view is eminently Christian, it is also most pointedly that of a layman.) The religious tradition in which painting grew up was always indulging in religion's habit[5]

---

(1) Freud: *Totem And Taboo*, IV
(2) Mythological subject ('The Death of Procris'), National Gallery
(3) Cf. II, 18
4 'che 'n quel limbo eran sospesi' (*Inferno*, IV, 45)   (5) Cf. II, 15

of breaking through the artistic conventions. The altarpiece propelled its demands through the dimensions of the picture and out into the congregation, insisting 'The madonna depicted here really exists outside this frame and can be addressed' or 'The figure you see here being tortured to death really is suffering at this moment because of your sins'. The antique myths, on the other hand, could make no demands on real belief, only on imaginative belief; and so they provided a cul-de-sac into which the art of painting could retreat and there develop an aesthetic—criteria by which a painting could be judged in its own conventions and without extraneous intervention.

Antiquity as a repository of the imagination survived into the eighteenth century, when Giambattista Tiepolo was still peopling it, in the tradition of Veronese, with magnificent imagined personages and sophisticated, impossible magic. But culture had meanwhile turned round in its cul-de-sac and was prepared to spring out of the picture-frame again, armed now with a developed aesthetic in the shape of the Rules of Taste—one of which was to stab Tiepolo in the back and prefer, to his transcendent creations, the work of Mengs. Taste was hardly better than religion at judging a picture within its own conventions. It let itself think that the mythology pictures were ridiculous because their subjects were impossible. The neo-classic movement to a large extent dropped ancient mythology in favour of ancient history with all the trappings pedantically reconstructed—that is, not imagined, in the sense that Tiepolo imagined the trappings of *his* pictures, at all. Tiepolo was the last of the renaissance geniuses, the final exponent of a cultural tradition passed from one individual imagination to another. When he fell into unpopularity, painting succumbed to the social age.

5. *The new catholicism*

Inspiration, whether of the religious or the artistic variety, visits its saints and geniuses capriciously. Reason, on the other hand, is a great leveller, its conclusions being the same for everyone and at all times. The Age of Reason was necessarily social. Even taste, which we incline to think of as partly a personal inspiration and not to be disputed about, was to the eighteenth century eminently to be disputed about, because by and large (there had, obviously, to be a natural endowment of sensibility) correct taste, like correct morals, could be established by reason. And therefore, of the great eighteenth-century trinity, Morals Taste and Reason, the greatest of these was Reason.

In every sphere, the eighteenth century substituted the appeal to reason for faith in authority: and the paradoxical result was to establish a new catholicism. Reason achieved what had eluded faith for centuries, the cultural unity of Europe. Reason had evolved a common syntax for all the vulgar tongues. Not since the gothic had there been so truly international a style. The eighteenth-century manner was of course far more susceptible to fashion than gothic had been, yet the whole century is united—not by one particular style, but by its common quest, from a common basis, for style itself. Cultural continuity from one nation to the next was barely interrupted even by wars; and the continuity of the age from one decade to the next is only emphasised by its great stylistic upheavals—the convulsive rejection of rococo, the debate between Roman and Grecian, the militancy of neo-classicism. These controversies could not disrupt a society which responded as a whole to their touch: it was merely as though fashion was blowing ripples through the entire, brilliant, integral expanse of silk which the cultivated classes were weaving across Europe and down the decades.

Baroque genius, whether of a Rubens or of a St. Teresa of Ávila, though it might be still admired, would have been as out of place here as in the middle ages. And in a sense eighteenth-century culture, a gothic world transmuted into classical terms, *was* a middle ages—reconstituted in the sun, the threatening shadow of God the Father having been rolled away from the sky. But his place had been taken by something equally unitive in its effects on humanity below, the abstract Ego-ideal of a self-aware bourgeoisie, which promulgated, in place of ten commandments, the canons of taste and morality.

Just as medieval Christendom was always seeking a blessing (that is, a fertility) from its own past, and invoking the remote fathers of the Church or its latest, just-dead, miracle-working saint, so the new catholicism sought guidance from antiquity and visited its shrines. Antiquity was, to the eighteenth century, an age of miracles inasmuch as it was endowed with miraculously good taste: where medievalism believed Christ had given the Church a guarantee that she could never fall into error in matters of faith, the eighteenth century believed that antiquity had been guaranteed against straying into vulgarity. Thus eighteenth-century Europe, too, had its regular, international pilgrim routes. But perhaps in this respect we should compare its unified culture not so much with Christendom as with its beloved model, the Greco-Roman world. It had revived the Hellenistic notion of travel as a university education; and its pilgrims flocked romantically, half self-mockingly and a touch vulgarly (having become self-conscious and aware of good taste, the age had become capable of vulgarity), to the places which spoke—as with the only half-credited voice of an oracle—of the ancient world and gods.

Reason recognised and insisted on a creative principle in the universe. The only revelation Tom Paine would recognise—but on this he poured out his adoration—was the universe itself and man's internal sense of morality: God's 'universal display of himself in the works of the creation, and . . . that repugnance we feel in ourselves to bad actions, and disposition to good ones'[1]—in other words, the very two things which, according to the much-quoted conclusion of his *Critique Of Practical Reason*[2], awed another eighteenth-century thinker, Immanual Kant. Reason had also to recognise, though often with a certain distaste, a lesser creative or inspirational principle, which had informed works of art and religious revelation. But it was no longer feasible to anthropomorphise the creative principle as a Jehovah and totemise it as a dove or, as Tom Paine called him, 'a flying pigeon' (Paine added in a footnote that the Gospel 'might as well have said a Goose—the creatures are equally harmless, and the one is as much a nonsensical lie as the other'[3]); and we know that the Maréchale de Luxembourg's comment on the Bible considered as the work of the Holy Ghost was that it was a pity the Holy Ghost had so little taste[4].

The new catholicism was thus Christendom reconstituted without Christ. It was a case of getting rid of the miracles and finding that the whole world had fallen at the feet not, as Rousseau had prophesied, of Christ but of a Supreme Being—an almighty principle figured, one can barely say personified, by the Freemasons as the great architect and by Tom Paine as 'the great mechanic of the creation'. Paine insists that we can have no idea of this creator's wisdom except through

[1] *The Age Of Reason*, II

[2] 'Two things fill the mind with ever-increasing wonder and awe . . .: the starry heavens above me and the moral law within me'

[3] *The Age Of Reason*, II

[4] Her remark (Quel effroyable ton! ah, Madame, quel domage que le Saint Esprit eût aussi peu de goût!) has been made famous by Lytton Strachey (*Books And Characters*, 'Madame du Deffand')

knowledge of the principles of science: 'the Creator of man is the Creator of science'; and the Almighty is 'the first philosopher and original teacher of all science'. The religious concept of the creator (in which Paine has rightly discerned the essential magician, a reflexion of the religionists' own magic-making) is not consonant with the awareness man has achieved in the Age of Reason: 'it is a puerile and pitiful idea to suppose the Almighty to say, Let there be light! It is the imperative manner of speaking that a conjurer uses when he says to his cups and balls, Presto! be gone'.[1]

If eighteenth-century culture informally healed the rift between Catholic and Protestant, it did so by transcending it. This was not a case merely of both sides agreeing, with so many international exchanges going on, to practise an expedient toleration on the grounds that displays of fanaticism could only be fruitless bad manners. Rather, both sides had come together in a fanatical hatred of bad manners, and in this respect the age was not tolerant at all. Society, using coercion by scorn, did its best to suppress every kind of religious enthusiasm, including that of the ardent atheist: Paine can think of no worse insult to Christianity than to analyse it as 'a species of Atheism'[2]. In this society of fanatical anti-fanaticism, the old-fashioned religious fanatics, judged now by morals instead of faith, have become social hobbledehoys:

> For modes of faith, let graceless zealots fight;
> His can't be wrong whose life is in the right[3].

The Catholics' faith in the authority of the Church and the Protestants' in the authority of the Bible have alike been translated into the new idiom. The Catholic Alexander Pope and the Protestant Joseph Addison adopt the same accents—having come together on the common ground of ancient Rome. ('Touch'd by thy hand', says Pope to Addison[4], 'again Rome's glories shine'.) Pope, following the fashion for 'improvement', translates into the new idiom the 'rugged and most unmusical' satires of the 'old poet'—and Anglican divine—John Donne, including Donne's off-hand strictures on Pope's fellow-papists[5]. It is into the same idiom that Pope charmingly translates the

[1] *The Age Of Reason*, II   [2] *The Age Of Reason*, I
[3] Pope: *Essay On Man*, III, 305-6   [4] Epistle to Mr. Addison
[5] Donne's (Satire II) 'yet their State/Is poor, disarm'd, like Papists, not worth hate' has become Pope's 'Yet like the Papist's is the poet's state/Poor and disarm'd, and hardly worth your hate!' (*The Satires of Dr. John Donne . . . Versified*, 1735)

mythological world of *The Iliad* and the magical world of *The Odyssey*, which he treats as though they were by his favourite model for imitation, Horace. Neither does he change his tone when he addresses God, who is no longer the god of either Church or Bible, but simply Herbert Spencer's depersonalised x, the unknowable creative principle, and the common grain of truth to which all religionists, including Pope's favourite primitives, have been aspiring:

> Father of all! in every age,
> In every clime adored,
> By saint, by savage and by sage,
> Jehovah, Jove, or Lord![1]

Moreover, both Pope and Addison have a vocabulary and a stock of concepts in common with the deist Tom Paine. Paine tells us that the 'only idea man can affix to the name of God is that of a *first cause*'[2]; and Pope's *Universal Prayer* has already addressed God as 'Thou great First Cause'. Addison's paraphrase of the nineteenth psalm is grist to Paine's deism[3], because Addison has transmuted the wild prose-poetry of the Authorised Version into the measured and reasonable verse of the Age of Reason. 'The heavens declare the glory of God', says the psalm, and Addison feels obliged to gloze its extravagant metaphor with

> What tho' no real voice, nor sound,
> Amidst their radiant orbs be found,
> In reason's ear they all rejoice . . .

6. *The Normative Age*

Logic, its textbooks insist, is a normative science; and it has to be admitted that the eighteenth century, at least in its attitude to the arts, was a dreadfully normative century. But it is stupid of us to—as we regularly do—let this mislead us into misconceiving the century's actual record in the arts.

One trouble is that we still see it through the romantic haze of the

[1] *The Universal Prayer* (1738)   [2] *The Age of Reason*, I
[3] Paine: *The Age Of Reason*, I

nineteenth century's reaction against it; another that we know too many of its own pronouncements, in which it was exceptionally articulate and which are exceptionally accessible to us, and have let them prejudice our view of its practice. Knowing that it demoted 'enthusiasm' into a derogatory word, had a distaste for the poetic inspiration which was to be adulated in the nineteenth century, and shewed a certain dis-esteem of genius, we permit ourselves to suppose that it produced no geniuses and no poetry. It is as though we went on quoting the standard anti-eighteenth-century joke, the epitaph which praises the clergyman for discharging his duties for so many years 'without enthusiasm', and paid no attention to Dean Swift and the melancholy poetry of *his* epitaph[1].

There have been fashions, for the most part superficial and mis-representing, for the 'charm' and 'decorativeness' of the eighteenth-century manner in general; but we still undervalue the highly individual (and, in all conscience, poetic) genius of Tiepolo, Piazzetta, Watteau and Gainsborough—four incomparable painters whom the eighteenth century *did* produce, even if it produced them against its grain. We have never praised Pope for the excellent poet he was, nor his precursor Dryden. Neither have we given adequate thanks to the eighteenth-century writers who, taking up what Dryden had begun, fashioned modern prose—that is, prose in the vulgar tongue—into a sharp and flexible instrument of literature. We speak of this civilised and highly-evolved ascent into prose as though it were a descent into the prosaic—as though we had never read the poetry purveyed in the medium of prose by Laurence Sterne and Choderlos de Laclos. The eighteenth-century prose idiom transcended even the native differences between English and French. The medium which Voltaire touched into the wit of genius made a plain and serviceable vehicle for the purity of Tom Paine's heart, and lent itself equally to the circuitous-ness of Gibbon's and the obliquity of Laclos's.

Meanwhile architecture and music, the arts which approximate most closely to the condition of logic, throve on the normative spirit of the age. In England and Ireland, English architecture achieved the world's golden age of building (which lasted, unabated, into the twenties or thirties of the next century). Again, it was in a sense a re-directed gothic civilisation, building secular cities instead of cath-

[1] *Ubi* saeva Indignatio Ulterius Cor lacerare nequit. *Abi* Viator Et imitare, si poteris, Strenuum pro virili Libertatis Vindicatorem (Memorial Tablet in St. Patrick's Cathedral, Dublin)

edrals and precincts; and it had the gothic characteristic that even provincial builders and anonymous ironworkers were touched by a felicity that could not fail. But their felicity came, in the eighteenth century, from the pattern books and the dissemination, in this most social of societies, of architectural ideas. In the intellectuality of its approach, in the currency of thoughts—and disputes—about the art, and in the interest taken by fashionable people and noblemen (at least one of whom was himself an excellent architect), the English eighteenth century is, rather, to architecture what the Italian renaissance was to painting.

This, however, no one would guess from the condescending tone native architectural commentators still take to the age or from the wanton destruction we still practise of its monuments. Where we do not destroy, we despoil, effacing perspectives and making nonsense of the period's social city-planning; sometimes we imitate eighteenth-century work or even criminally 'restore' eighteenth-century buildings in the inept and spiritless style we have offensively christened by the travestying name of 'Georgian'. Groups of private persons do their best to save buildings of the golden age; but of course its goldenness lies in its having created not only buildings but whole vistas, whole societies, of buildings; and the private groups (which in a fully civilised country would not need to exist—already we need no groups to campaign against scraping down the canvasses in the National Gallery or demolishing Gothic cathedrals) have no power against the great municipalities who, by act or permission, are responsible for the crimes. In the last five years no one prevented London from finally finishing off Nash's Regent Street by obliterating the effect Nash so nicely calculated for All Souls', Langham Place; no one prevented Dublin from tearing down Hardwicke Street[1] and thereby defouling the admirable approach to Francis Johnston's church.

In music the eighteenth century cannot be called a second renaissance, because neither the renaissance nor antiquity conceived anything like it. The eighteenth century virtually presented the world with a new art, complete—indeed, more than complete, since it threw in with the gift Mozart, the only artist the human race has produced to set beside Shakespeare.

Yet even here, as in the other arts, the age undervalued its artists.

[1] A photograph of the 'new corporation flats' appeared in *The Manchester Guardian* of 6 July, 1957; a photograph shewing a little of the beautiful terrace they replaced appears (41) in John Harvey's *Dublin* . . . (Batsford)

Its admiration for the sublime quartet of J. S. Bach, Handel, Haydn and Mozart had to be wrung from it and was shared on equal terms with inferior composers. Not a master in any of the arts could rely on fashion staying with him for five years at a time—and if it deserted him, he was edged into starvation, usually by a trumpery rival. Not that the inferior artists fared much better[1]. The intellectual movement of the eighteenth century, unlike that of the nineteenth, was not towards bad art but towards no art. It was art itself which was undervalued[2] (the absurdity of our present position being that we, who have begun to estimate art more justly, still have not rescued the eighteenth-century artists whose practice fought against the unjust estimation of art in their own times). Some of the aesthetic legislation which everyone who could put his tongue round a period poured out on the artists must be read as an unconscious attempt to stamp out art altogether. But we should also remember that some of the canon-making, especially in literature, was directed by the artists themselves to the public. Reputations had once existed in the esteem of patrons and artists (even Vasari, that influential reputation-maker, was an artist of sorts). Now, however, a writer's reputation began to depend on the public; but his access to the public lay through channels which were corrupt even by our standards of the twentieth century: prejudice and faction controlled the whole business of publication, publicity and criticism (or 'puffs'). The great cry that went up from eighteenth-century writers was that they should be judged on merit and merit alone. Some of the rule-making is simply the logical consequence of the cry, since if the new public was to judge on merit it must be equipped with standards by which to do so.

Here, in theory, even if it was not achieved, was the basis of a much freer and juster aesthetic world than that in which artists had depended on the arbitrary caprice of individual patrons. The tyranny of eighteenth-century taste made provision for its own repeated over-throw and reformation: if reason formulated the rules, then the rules

[1] Einstein (*Mozart . . .*, 24) quotes a journalist's complaint, written two years after Mozart's death, that the pursuit of the latest fashion in music and the 'inordinate fuss' about Mozart were unjustly obscuring the reputation of Johann Friedrich Reichardt.

[2] I shall always honour the exception of General Wolfe, even though I do not share his taste; he proves the rule inasmuch as it became a famous paradox for a successful general to have said he would rather have written a good poem.

could be argued with. Taste was aiming at an aesthetic counterpart of the great goal of the period's political theorists, constitutional government; Addison expressed it by coining the notion of 'the republic of letters'.

And in fact, this same normative spirit which laid such a questionable hand on the arts led, in political theorising, to an absolute libertarianism. The eighteenth century did not manage to set man free, though it made a beginning in England and America, which made a limited application of the principle one man, one vote (but neither there nor anywhere else did anyone act on the principle of one man, one income); if the eighteenth century began intellectually in 1690 with Locke's treatise on Reason, politically it began in 1688 with the English Revolution: but it did set thought free. Reason, having got to work on the authority of Christianity, quickly perceived that Christendom had rested on the gigantic hearsay (Paine's word) of the Gospels; whereupon thought swept away all the particularly revealed authorities and produced freethinkers, who acknowledged no authority except natural law, which could be directly perceived or reasonably deduced by everyone equally. Just so with the authority of princes and oligarchies. Thought perceived that natural law imposed no hereditary constitution on the human species, pre-electing a few to govern and the rest to be governed; it perceived, in other words, that 'man is born free'; and political theory at once swept away all the authorities which had imposed themselves by pretending to be naturally based on a hereditary principle. Reason could recognise no quality as sovereign, as fit to govern, except the capacity for reason; and this was the distinguishing mark not of certain classes, races or royal houses, but of man as a species. Reason rushed to what slow-witted and anti-logical people call extremes: that is, it recognised reality. Logic would support no authority except the equal authority of all human beings; government could find no justifiable stopping-place until it had so widened its basis as to take in the whole of humanity.

The reformers adopted antiquity as a talisman, although as a matter of fact they far outstripped it in logical stringency. Antiquity had always stopped arbitrarily short of recognising that slaves—or even, in some respects, women—were included in the human race. But the most reasonable minds of the eighteenth century, accepting that reason could not admit of any arbitrary limits on reason or justice of any expedient exceptions to justice, proposed to extend equal

sovereignty to all men and women, and to accord to children the
utmost liberty consistent with their safety—and to the animals, who
made the claims of instinctual if not reasonable beings, the right to
life and the pursuit of happiness un-cut-off by man's gourmandism.

What was particularly suggestive to progressive minds (the concept
of a progressive is another eighteenth-century innovation) was that
ancient Rome (and with it all that was left of Greece) had fallen into
decline from the moment it accepted a tyranny in place of the republican rule of law. This was the spectacle Addison put on the stage
in his tragedy *Cato*[1], to which Pope wrote a Prologue dismissing individual tragedies (by the morality of common sense and commonwealth: 'In pitying love, we but our weakness show, And wild
ambition well deserves its woe') in favour of social ones, which
excite humanitarian sympathy:

> Here tears shall flow from a more generous cause,
> Such tears as patriots shed for dying laws:
> He bids your breasts with ancient ardour rise,
> And calls forth Roman drops from British eyes.

Gibbon exploited a still more suggestive and equally social spectacle.
Instead of contemplating the brief noonday of Roman constitutional
virtue and the dramatic instant of its fall to Julius Caesar, he paraded
the long history of its subsequent prostitution. Here was a new way
of comparing the modern with the ancient world: not to point up the
contrast, but to draw out the similarity of their follies. The unreasonable
pretensions of all spiritual and temporal authorities are classically
incarnated in the absurdity of the Roman Empire, in the centuries
when Caesar and Augustus were no longer the personal names of
outstandingly able or unscrupulous men but the hereditary titles of
nonentities whom their subjects regularly and unexcitedly elevated
into gods and worshipped—a hereditary monarchy so little commanding that it never properly established itself as a monarchy at
all, and so inept that biology itself seemed to hold aloof and regularly
deny it the minimal blessing of an undisputed succession, with the
result that it was not properly hereditary either.

The comparison was all the more piquant because Christianity,

---

[1] 1713. Dr Johnson (Preface to his edition of Shakespeare, 1765) records
that '*Voltaire* expresses his wonder, that' Shakespeare's 'extravagances are endured
by a nation, which has seen the tragedy of *Cato*'.

which Gibbon approaches as though it were an indelicate subject, had during this era put forward its own candidate for deification. We may think poorly enough of the intellectual standing of the pagan Empire, with its superstitions, its desperate, try-anything religious panic, and its unwieldy fiction that the religious and the political fathers had coalesced in the persons of the deified emperors: but human reason took a still deeper and much icier plunge, which carried Europe (and Gibbon) deep into the ages of darkness, when a single non-tolerating religion won the monopoly of credulity, and the government of civilisation was divided between a Christian Church and Christian states. Enquiry, enlightenment and toleration were now outlawed formally and by decree: legislating for the Empire, Justinian began his code with the title 'Of the Most High Trinity and the Catholic Faith and that no one dare publicly to dispute it'[1]. Gibbon obliges his readers to observe that the impossible superstitions of paganism and the impossibility (as Tertullian deliberately hailed it —it was later to be quoted as the absurdity[2]) of the new faith were formed by the same historical forces, in which he discerns the self-interest of a few and the ignorance and folly of the majority. By merely chronicling the genesis of the primitive Church, he deals an impartial one in the eye to Catholicism, as the heir of the primitive Church, and to Protestantism, which aimed to restore it: meanwhile in his footnotes he keeps up a commentary of comparison with the absurdities of latterday theologians: with the result that his book is both a compendium of our knowledge about the Roman Empire and a source for our knowledge of the eighteenth century; not only a history but also, true to its age, the most extended pamphlet in literature.

[1] De Summa Trinitate et Fide Catholica et ut nemo de ea publice contendere audeat (quoted by P. N. Ure: *Justinian And His Age*, VIII)

[2] prorsus credibile est, quia ineptum est . . . certum est quia impossibile est (cited by the *Oxford Dictionary Of Quotations*, *De Carne Christi*, 5)

7. The Gigantic Repression

In Gibbon we can observe par excellence eighteenth-century literature's nonpsychologising trend. Perceptive as he is about the nature and results of Christianity, he has no insight into its motives. The ignorance of the age in which it was born is to him a sufficient explanation. He has little to say about why mankind preferred this fable to any of the others available at the time or why the new myth took this particular form: he might almost be grateful that circumspection, which obliges him to treat Christianity ironically as the one true light, has excused him from offering an explanation—were it not that as a matter of fact his curiosity has not been aroused by the problem at all.

Writing, at the age of fifty-one, about his own youthful conversion to Catholicism, Gibbon epitomises the eighteenth-century's psychological incomprehension. 'To my present feelings it seems incredible that I should ever believe that I believed in transubstantiation, but my conqueror oppressed me with the sacramental words "Hoc est corpus meum" . . . No sooner had I settled my new religion than I resolved to profess myself a catholic. Youth is sincere and impetuous; and a momentary glow of enthusiasm had raised me above all temporal considerations'[1]. What is remarkable is not the lack of insight, which any other period could match even in intelligent men, but the lack of desire for insight. Gibbon conducts no research into himself for the source of his enthusiasm; the literary trick of personification lets him out of the problem altogether, and he writes not 'I was conquered and oppressed' but 'my conqueror' (in whose power to do any such thing Gibbon does not concretely believe) 'oppressed me'. It has simply become incredible that he—or anyone else, we may add on the evidence of The Decline And Fall—ever believed he believed.

The eighteenth century was, in fact, engaged in a gigantic repression. The cultivated stratum, that amazingly unified European bourgeoisie, was performing for society the offices of an Ego. It worked, as an Ego always does[2], towards organisation and unity. It possessed the

[1] Memoirs Of My Life And Writings

[2] 'The Ego is an organisation, marked out by a very noteworthy tendency towards unity and synthesis; the Id has not this character—it is, so to speak, all in pieces, and its individual impulses pursue their ends independently and regardless of one another.' (Freud: The Question Of Lay Analysis, II)

Ego-characteristics of reasonableness, self-awareness and articulateness. And it engaged in the Ego's business of repressing the irrational impulses of the human unconscious—whose manifestations the eighteenth century inexplicitly but unerringly recognised by its own distaste for them, its sense of 'Quel effroyable ton!'

Up till the eighteenth century the world had taken an enormous interest in the unconscious, but without a scientific theory capable of recognising it as such. Christendom bent its attention on the ecstasies and the hallucinatory temptations of saints, and from time to time developed an obsessive interest in the psychopathological manifestations of witchcraft. Indeed, religion itself is nothing but a serious communal interest in a fantasy emanating from the unconscious. Theology, of course, ascribed the myth not to the unconscious but to God, in accordance with the quasi-scientific theory that ideas and emotions which enter the mind from a source unknown to the consciousness, which are not direct responses to perceptions or are quite disproportionate to the perception, come from an external, supernatural source which has temporarily taken possession of the mind. In the ancient world, dreams are said to emanate not from the dreamer but from the two gates[1], one of ivory and one of horn, whence they visit the sleeper; those from the ivory gate cheat him, those from the gate of horn are revelatory, usually of the future. Infatuate states of emotion are sent upon Homer's heroes by the gods[2]; and anyone, prophet, oracle-monger or lunatic, who utters ideas of which he himself can give no account, is touched with the supernatural and treated with the awe due to someone infected by taboo[3]. To this ancient theory Christendom more or less consistently adhered, after translating it into its own terms: there were now only two, and quite

[1] *Odyssey*, XIX, 560 foll.

[2] E. R. Dodds: *The Greeks And The Irrational*, I

[3] Even a dream, as a minor form of possession, was full of taboo. It was by origin divine, and yet by the taboo concept of divinity a man might have to purify himself of its polluting effect—an idea which has perhaps coalesced with pollution by sexual dreams. The ambivalence typical of taboo is perfectly expressed in a line of Aristophanes: 'Heat some water, so that I may wash off the divine dream' (*Frogs*, 1339-40, θέρμετε δ' ὕδωρ,/ὡς ἂν θεῖον ὄνειρον ἀποκλύσω: it is a baleful dream, which occurs in Aeschylus's parody of Euripides). Perhaps Pontius Pilate, himself a Roman, followed the Greco-Roman tradition and, in washing his hands of blood-guilt for Jesus's death, was also washing off the dream his wife had had about Jesus (*Matthew*, XXVII, 19;24)

distinct, supernatural agents that might possess the mind; and the generalised response to a person possessed as taboo-infected must now be sharply divided into reverence and abhorrence, according to whether the possession was divine or diabolical.

The theory of possession implies, of course, that the irrational be treated by irrational methods: from the saint you borrow a holy magic relic, and you arm yourself with holy magic talismans ('The Relics of the Saints . . . are of especial virtue'[1]) in your war against the witch's magic. The saint has not convinced you by argument but impressed you supernaturally; and you do not argue with the witch but impress her with instruments of torture. None the less, both the ancient world and Christendom were in daily traffic with the unconscious. They never translated the traffic into scientific terminology; yet they had to hand all the material from which a scientific psychology could be, and eventually was, extracted.

This advantage—indeed, this material—the eighteenth century threw away. Its distaste for enthusiasm was a distaste for what previous centuries had regarded as possession, 'enthusiasm' being simply the Greek for the theory of possession[2]. With the exception of the Quakers (who were nonconforming to the age and themselves non-normative) and the Swedenborgians, the intellectual movement of the age was towards severing the connexion with the unconscious. The language of the unconscious, as manifested in dreams, myths and symptoms, is everything a conscious Ego campaigns against: unorganised—that is, unbalanced; inconsistent; metaphorical and unargued—in that its symbols are created out of false analogies[3]. This to a large extent is also the language of art, which, though it is organised, is organised on different principles from rational arguments, and which falls on the mind like a revelation, with a mere inarticulate shout, making an impression rather than persuading; the eighteenth century was self-consistent when it extended a certain distaste to art and took certain repressive measures against it.

If music and architecture came through the repression least scathed, it is because their metaphors are abstract and carry with them in their passage from the unconscious no fragments of the actual human imagery of the unconscious's language. In Mozart we have to

[1] *Malleus Maleficarum*, III, question 16

[2] ἐνθουσιάζω, '*To be . . . inspired or possessed by the god . . .*' (Liddell and Scott)

[3] Cf. I, 12

recognise what we cannot call a superiority to the other supreme composers the century produced, but a sense in which he is more widely
human, just as Shakespeare is the most widely human of writers;
and this is precisely because Mozart stood most firmly out against the
tendency of the age. He reunites his abstract art to human imagery,
using music, as Shakespeare does poetry, in a manner essentially
psychological. It is not simply that his finest work is composed for
the human voice singing words that convey meaning—which is true
of Handel and Bach as well. Mozart is not content with oratorio and
the old static, masque-like opera, with their habit of periodically
alienating the audience from its absorption in the action and musically
inviting it to meditate for a minute; and neither is he to be confined
by his mid-eighteenth-century idiom, though he is a master in it.
He can hang his work from the most air-borne pinnacle of the courtly
or the ecclesiastical rococo, and yet the content of the work will be
profound emotion or (especially, of course, in *Figaro*) psychological
drama. (Only the Victorians were so offended by the sensuous delights
of Mozart's rococo manner that they could not see the content through
it.) Sometimes he even pours into the rococo moulds what is blatantly
romantic music (the Sinfonia Concertante or the C major quartet[1]);
in *Don Giovanni* he creates a psychological melodrama and fastens it
on a story which actually belongs to the outmoded Counter-Reformation world of demonology. (Perhaps it was because this world was
fundamentally much closer to nineteenth-century comprehension
than to eighteenth, and also no doubt thanks to the melodrama, that
Don Giovanni alone of Mozart's operas never needed reviving.) At
the end of his life he works contemporaneously on his *Requiem*, a
sombre and moving return to the baroque manner of Handel[2]
(which the next century could therefore accept as *really* religious,
unlike Mozart's rococo ecclesiastical music), and on *The Magic Flute*.
This latter is a thorough-going late-eighteenth-century opera, with
its Temples of Prudence, Work and Arts[3], and its freemasonic
allegorised religion, its revolutionary presages[4], and its strains of the
exotic and bizarre: yet at the same time, both in the flexible characterisation of Pamina and in its musical folk-tune plainness, this

[1] K.364; K.465
[2] several of whose vocal works, including the *Messiah* and *Acis and Galatea*
(K.572; K.566), Mozart had orchestrated
[3] Tamino's recitative, No. 8
[4] Alfred Einstein: *Mozart . . .*, 23

proletarian singspiel reaches out to anticipate and almost render superfluous the whole future course of romantic music.

By these explorations and, above all, by what he made of opera, Mozart bursts out of the unpsychological eighteenth century and bursts *into* the conventions of a work of art, just as secular painting retreated into the picture frame: he has created psychological music-drama. 'I have tried to express her feelings', he writes of one of Constanze's arias[1], and it is significant that he has had to alter its wording; from Mozart's complaint in this letter[2] that German librettists 'do not understand the theatre', it is only a brief step to Wagner's complete music-drama practice of composing both words and music. Mozart avowed that to write operas was his greatest desire[3]: only by fulfilling it, and giving a new meaning to opera, could he fulfil his psychological genius.

Society, however, accepted him not as a psychologist but as an entertainer—and paid him accordingly. 'People pay plenty of compliments', he wrote from Paris[4], '. . . but there it stops . . . I play and hear them exclaim: *"Oh, c'est un prodige, c'est inconcevable, ce'st étonnant!"*, and then it is—*Adieu.*'

If Christendom disparaged artistic revelation, it was in comparison with the religious kind. The eighteenth century persistently belittled both. Art had the advantage of its entertainment value; refreshment could be sucked from it before it was thrown aside by fashion, whereas religion was dull. On the other hand, religion, if allegorised and de-ecstasised, might exert a stabilising influence on society.

The eighteenth century had, in fact, discredited the theory of possession, without putting another in its place. It knew that religious myths did not come into currency through the inspiration of the Holy Ghost or the devil, and it knew that a work of art was not whispered to the artist by a Muse. What it would not do was turn its attention to the problem of where they did come from; and in this refusal we can perceive an enormous fear—the fear that to pay attention, however reasonably, to manifestations of the irrational would open the way for the irrational methods of treating them to return.

[1] *Seraglio*, No. 6, 'Ach, ich liebte'

[2] to his father, from Vienna, 26 September, 1781

[3] letter to his father, from Mannheim, 4 February, 1778. Mozart (witness his father's letter of 28 May, 1764) had operatic ambitions and projects at the age of eight.

[4] to his father, 1 May, 1778

The fear was not unjustifiable. Even in the twentieth century, Freud had no sooner undertaken a rational exploration of the irrational than Jungianism arose to advocate an irrational awe of irrational mental forces; and the eighteenth century was much more nearly terrified than we are of a return to the scientifically barbarous ages—to the intolerant monopoly of Christianity or, worse still, to the intolerant sectarian disputes of the seventeenth century.

Against this threat, the eighteenth century took merely emergency precautions. Left with the empty vocabulary of the possession theory on its hands, it filled this shell, the word 'enthusiasm', with an emotional (and enthusiastic) distaste of its own, which was no more rational than the awe primitives pay to psychopathological disturbances. For all their wit, Voltaire and Gibbon can really only make a frontal attack on Christianity just as Tom Paine does; they keep coming back to this obstinate phenomenon they cannot explain, with the irritation of a sore tongue seeking out a gumboil; but they will not attempt to explain it or even admit there is a problem. They could win over only the people who would never have been more than coerced and conforming Christians in any case; after this point, the frontal attack could only solidify the religionists. That, however, was the smallest danger in the eighteenth century's lack of psychology. The worst danger was to rationalism itself, which was being built on an emergency measure of repression, concealing a volcano: in withdrawing attention from the irrational, reason was beginning to behave as though the irrational did not exist.

Time and again the eighteenth century passed over the very opportunities Freud was eventually to take for directing reason to the subject of the unconscious. We can understand that Gibbon's historical circumstances prevented him not only from saying but from wanting to know anything about the unconscious sources of the Christian myth; but as a matter of fact his intellect is equally frigid to the question of how the pagans came to conceive of *their* myths. The more mythological bits of Homer affect Gibbon like a long and enthusiastic Christian sermon. During Odysseus's voyage to the Underworld (the reader must not blame Homer for the metaphorical sense I have given it in this book), Gibbon's attention wanders: 'The xith book of the Odyssey', he notes, 'gives a very dreary and incoherent account of the infernal shades'[1]. Mozart's family friend, Franz Anton Mesmer,

[1] Pindar and Virgil, 'though more correct than their great model, are guilty of very strange inconsistencies' (footnote, *The Decline And Fall* . . ., XV)

had, like Mozart, a succès d'estime in Paris and Europe generally, with his demonstrations of hypnotism; but again it was as an entertainer and not in any serious sense as a psychologist. Tom Paine hit on the very subject which was to afford Freud his decisive opportunity for deciphering the language of the unconscious. The third part of *The Age Of Reason* opens with an 'Essay on Dream', in which Paine takes a promisingly psychological tone, affirming that the only material which can go to create a dream is material available to the mind which has the dream (a view not unknown in the ancient world[1]) and making the accurate observation that 'it may rationally be said that every person is mad once in every twenty-four hours'. But the crucial question of what makes our nocturnal insanity take one particular form rather than another never occurs to Paine. Once he has perceived that the dreamer is a lunatic, his interest passes to other matters, notably the absurdity of taking Joseph's dream in the first chapter of *Matthew* as the foundation of a religion; he is interested in us only when we are awake and sane.

This nonpsychological trend hardened, during the nineteenth century, into the determined and prejudiced antipsychological stand taken by science. The eighteenth century did not want to explain the irrational: nineteenth-century materialism moved towards the wholly irrational, indeed religious, position of maintaining that what was not consonant with the explanations it had given did not exist. At the time when Freud reasonably asked how dreams were created, science had 'handed them over to superstition. . . It seemed quite inconceivable that anyone who had done serious scientific work could make his appearance as an "interpreter of dreams" '[2]. Here was the culmination of the eighteenth century's superstitious dread that to pay

---

[1] e.g. the lyric Petronius throws into the *Satyricon*, attributing its philosophy to Epicurus. (Somnia . . ./non delubra deum nec ab aethere numina mittunt/ sed sibi quisque facit; in Burnaby's translation:—When in a Dream presented to our view,/Those airy Forms appear so like the true;/Nor Heaven nor Hell the fancy'd Visions sends,/But every breast its own delusion lends.) (*Satyricon*, II). However, one should not conclude from seeing the lyric in isolation (it is conveniently included, for example, as an antique precursor of the medieval, in Helen Waddell's *Medieval Latin Lyrics*) that it represents Petronius's opinion. Rather, the story implies the opposite. In its context, the lyric is Eumolpus's attempt to persuade his adversaries to disbelieve dreams which have revealed to them something which is in fact perfectly true.

[2] Freud: *An Autobiographical Study*, IV

any attention at all to irrational phenomena was to invite the demons and spirits back. With rarer phenomena than dreams, the process could go further still. Nineteenth-century medicine, secure in having recognised that hysterical symptoms were not caused by possession by devils, let itself believe that they must be caused by shamming; and the very facts of hypnosis, which Mesmer had so fully demonstrated in the eighteenth, were by the nineteenth century 'looked upon as . . . a hoax'[1].

8. *The Eruption*

Even the eighteenth century could not pretend that reason alone could keep a man alive for two days together, though Pope admitted that, on the face of it, it looked as though it would have been better if it could[2]. One solution was to demote reason into a mechanical response and maintain that a man was in any case not really alive but was only a complex machine—a view which Sterne protested against[3] and which is perhaps reflected in the eighteenth century's curious fascination with automata, but which did not reach its culmination until the nineteenth century. The eighteenth century in general, so far from demoting reason, inclined towards deifying it, a process the French Revolution carried to the point of a sort of allegorical literalness. None the less, reason, which neither animals nor babies possess, although it may be sovereign, is plainly not self-sufficient. The eighteenth century had to admit another life-motivating force, instinct.

Here was a promising and psychological beginning. But in framing a concept of instinct the eighteenth century was hampered by its lack

[1] Freud: *Collected Papers*, Volume V, XIV

[2]
> Better for us, perhaps, it might appear . . .
> That never passion discomposed the mind.
> But all subsists by elemental strife;
> And passions are the elements of life.
> The general order, since the whole began,
> Is kept by Nature, and is kept in man.

(*Essay On Man*, I, 165-. . . 172)

[3] 'I felt every vessel in my frame dilate—the arteries beat all chearily together, and every power which sustained life, perform'd it with so little friction, that 'twould have confounded the most *physical precieuse* in France: with all her materialism, she could scarce have called me a machine—' (*A Sentimental Journey* . . ., I)

of a biological science. Accurate observations of living animals and even the habit of observing them nonanthropomorphically had not yet passed into accepted culture; and in any case there was no framework, in the shape of an accepted evolution theory, to receive them. In the course of the eighteenth century and its overspill into the first decades of the next, evolutionary and transformist ideas shaped themselves in several minds, many highly intelligent, some merely eccentric like Lord Monboddo's, and even became intellectually fashionable, but a concept of evolution never became part of the century's general consciousness. The 'vogue of Evolution, begun by Goethe and maintained by Darwin's grandfather, faded out in 1830'[1] —that is, with the last influences of the eighteenth century. When evolution returned, and did manage to enter the common culture, it did so in the mechanist version; and for the victory of this markedly anti-psychological version which was so far from being the earliest, we have to blame the psychological indifference of the eighteenth century.

Against the general acceptance of an evolutionary theory one of the eighteenth century's favourite concepts stood sentinel: the Supreme Being. All that was left to God of the many detailed characteristics ascribed to him by Christianity was the historical act of creating the universe including mankind and the flora and fauna. It was as creator that he had been left just sufficient personality for Pope to address him as Father. Lucretius's rationalism had had to leave the gods in existence because he supposed that visions and dreams of them must represent actual glimpses. The eighteenth century had got round that with the cursory explanation that dreams were nonsense in any case and that the other revelations were foisted on humanity by the priest-craft of the few and the ignorance of the many; but whereas Lucretius, after specifically rejecting the idea that the gods created the universe[2], was able to formulate a picture of universal evolution, from a raw material of atoms to the production of living creatures from the earth, the eighteenth century accepted the universe as a revelation of its creator, and took the consistency of the natural world, the fact that gravitation always works and that two and two always make four, as evidence of the consistency—that is, the reasonableness and wisdom—of the creator.

In the eyes of the eighteenth century, the universe argued up to God and creation had proceeded down from God. In the Chain of

[1] Shaw: Preface to *Back To Methuselah*, 'The Advent Of The Neo-Darwinians'
[2] V, 156-94

Being, the pyramid which built up from the lowest animals to God, growing more intellectual at every step, man was, according to Edward Young[1], a 'Distinguish'd link'; and the gap between man and God was filled, according to Henry Brooke[2], by 'the seraph's intellectual ray'. It is in just the same spirit that Tom Paine described God as the 'original teacher of all science', and that the century's great biological scientist, Linnaeus, classified living creatures on the principle that 'there are as many different species as the infinite Being originally created different forms'[3].

Since Nature was a revelation—indeed, the only acceptable revelation—of God (in 1776, the American Declaration of Independence referred to 'the laws of nature and of nature's God'), it followed that Nature must be semi-deified, along with Reason; and it was to Nature that Reason made its appeal. The classical and normative spirit appealed to the fact that the planets kept regular and mathematical timetables and that the animals' instinctual search for pleasure kept within the limits laid down by the creator of species[4]. Nature was incapable of extravagant or enthusiastic gestures: and thus Nature justified the classical orders of architecture and social good manners based on a recognition of what was fitting to the occasion. It was possible, however, to look at Nature and read a quite different lesson: a storm at sea was nothing if not extravagant; natural landscape followed no pattern and observed no balance, since every feature was singular and there were no ends—no borders—and no repetitions. Nature would thus justify freer and wilder landscape-gardening, Shakespeare[5], a taste for genre paintings in which terra-cotta-coloured

[1] *Night Thoughts*, I, 74

[2] quoted by M. M. Fitzgerald: *First Follow Nature*, II, I

[3] Species tot sunt diversae, quot diversas formas ab initio creavit infinitum Ens (quoted by A. Morley Davies: *Evolution And Its Modern Critics*, I)

[4]   God, in the nature of each being, founds
        Its proper bliss, and sets its proper bounds
(Pope: *Essay On Man*, III, 109-10)

[5] Dr Johnson, comparing Addison's *Cato* with the plays of Shakespeare: 'The work of a correct and regular writer is a garden accurately formed and diligently planted, varied with shades, and scented with flowers; the composition of *Shakespeare* is a forest, in which oaks extend their branches, and pines tower in the air, interspersed sometimes with weeds and brambles, and sometimes giving shelter to myrtles and to roses; filling the eye with awful pomp, and gratifying the mind with endless diversity.' (Preface to Johnson's edition of Shakespeare)

peasants search for fleas, for seascapes like Marco Ricci's, for architecture which, supposedly modelled on 'gothic' castles or cottages,
displayed neither order nor balance, for antique ruins (balanced
classical buildings eroded into imbalance by Nature), for nightmares
and nightmarish fictions, and eventually for grandeur and bizarrerie
sought out for their own sakes. This romanticising trend grew out of
the cult of Nature along with classicism; but the social quality of
eighteenth-century culture managed on the whole to tame it (and
where it could not tame it, as in William Blake, to ignore it), and it
did not burst into open flood until the nineteenth-century romantic
movement, by which time the informal but orderly social unity of
eighteenth-century culture had been destroyed.

The deification of Nature encompassed human nature; in its original
state, as it issued from the creator, human instinct must have been
supremely good. It was here that the eighteenth century missed its
opportunity of discerning a clash between natural instinct and reality,
the product of which clash, it might have concluded, was reason.
Instead, in its conviction that Nature was the harmonious revelation
of a harmonious Supreme Being, it saw reason and instinct as merely
re-inforcing one another. 'Reason or instinct', reads the *Argument* to
Pope's *Essay On Man*, 'operate alike to the good of each individual'[1].

Neither would Pope admit any necessary conflict between these
several individual goods and the common good:

> Thus God and Nature link'd the general frame,
> And bade self-love and social be the same[2].

This was essentially the position taken later in the century by Rousseau,
whose apparent romanticism was not opposed but complementary to
the classical spirit of the enlightenment. Instinct and reason, the whole
enlightenment agreed, worked towards the same benevolent end; it
was merely a question of whether one should employ reason to ferret
out what instinct intended (thus the Voltaireans) or (thus the Rous-
seauists) start from scratch with the child, refuse to educate him and
wait for instinct to declare its natural benevolence through him
naturally. Both sides agreed that in the natural, primitive state, un-
corrupted by human misreadings of nature, there was a natural consonance between instinct and reason, and between individual freedom
and a just social organisation. For Pope the link consisted of the Chain

[1] Epistle III   [2] *Essay on Man*, III, 317-18

of Being, which proceeded in an orderly fashion from the creator
down. What holds the several species and several individuals in their
places is natural instinct. This is, of course, an instinct of self-seeking;
but Pope has socialised and benevolised it, thereby benevolising life
itself, on the theory that instinctual necessity binds living creatures
into interdependence. The animate world of Nature is a harmonious
society designed by a god who

> as he framed a whole, the whole to bless,
> On mutual wants built mutual happiness:
> So from the first eternal Order ran,
> And creature link'd to creature, man to man[1].

In giving up the Christian quest for godliness, the world had come
back to Socrates's pursuit of the good—and it ended, like Socrates,
by discovering the morality of our instinct to seek out our own
pleasure. Socrates's argument that the glutton and the abstainer were
both motivated by the quest for pleasure was rediscovered by
Edward Young[2], who pointed out that for pleasure's sake 'the black
assassin draws his sword' and equally for pleasure's sake 'the saint
abstains'. Like Socrates, Young can account for the black and anti-
social desires only by attributing them to an intellectual error, a mis-
valuation of the pleasure to be had from the black course of action;
black desires result when the natural passions 'Mistake their objects, or
transgress their bounds'. In its natural context, pleasure is virtuous
('Pleasure is nought but virtue's gayer name') and not merely beneficial but essential to human life (for which reason alone cannot provide
the motive-power): without the quest for pleasure, exclaims Young,
'How would all stagnate!'

Thus, like Socrates, the eighteenth century was committed to the
original virtue of man, the moral necessity of some kind of education,
and, even more than Socrates had been, to a purely conscious psychology. The deluded and oppressed state of society was to be explained
at a purely conscious level: by the self-interest of priests and rulers. Yet
the eighteenth century had concluded, like Socrates but from different
premises, that self-interest was good. It must be, therefore, that the
frauds and oppressors had taken a distorted view of where their interest
lay; the trouble, like the original cause of Christianity, was ignorance;

[1] *Essay On Man*, III, 111-14
[2] *The Complaint, or Night Thoughts*, VIII (1742-4)

and the remedy for society's distress was, as Rousseau made clear, education.

The ideal education Rousseau prescribed for Émile was rather different from the education Socrates gave the young men who argued with him at Athens: it consisted very largely in avoiding books, cities and argumentation, and of being brought up in the country in intimate contact with Nature. If Rousseau is the great exponent of the wild and romantic cult of Nature, he has come to the same point as the most rigorously classicising intellects: a certain distaste for culture. By whichever direction the eighteenth century approached Nature, it seemed to approach the conclusion that the villain was civilisation itself, and that it was human learning which had produced human ignorance; and this was perhaps the inevitable conclusion to be drawn from the creationist view of instinct, which saw civilisation as a process which had spoilt human nature, human nature having been delivered pat from the hand of God, rather than seeing civilisation as the product of the unique freedom human nature had wrested from the evolutionary process.

The most civilised and artificial of centuries accordingly gave itself up to trying to reconstruct the untampered-with nature of primitive man. Out of two previous creationist myths, the Hesiodic Golden Age and the Biblical Eden[1], it compiled a quasi-scientific myth of its own, in which

> The state of Nature was the reign of God[2].

Primitive man, on this theory, was by no means an intellectual groper[3]; he could rely on not only an unclouded reason but also an instinct which had not yet been corrupted by civilisation. He has the benefits of society, but is free; he does no harm; he is happy; and, since no one is greedy, Nature produces enough for everyone. It is precisely the life *Acis And Galatea* ascribes to the prehistoric shepherds of Sicily:

> O the pleasure of the plains!
> Happy nymphs and happy swains!
> Harmless, merry, free, and gay,
> Dance and sport the hours away. . .

[1] Cf. M. M. Fitzgerald: *First Follow Nature*, I

[2] Pope: *Essay On Man*, III, 148

[3] M. M. Fitzgerald points out (*First Follow Nature*, I, 1) that, among the blessings believed to be lost by the Fall from Eden into civilisation, 'man's superior mental endowments seem to have impressed the poets most'.

> For us the winters rain,
> For us the summers shine,
> Spring swells for us the grain,
> And autumn bleeds the vine.

Quintessentially eighteenth-century in this picture, *Acis And Galatea* also tackled, in Polyphemus, the century's great problem of natural evil—whether it regards Polyphemus as an ugly, rejected jealous lover or as a personification of Mount Etna: and it may be said to have taken a more realistic view than the century's political philosophers, since it acknowledges that the volcano exists and erupts.

Not content with taunting civilised man with the social harmony and individual happiness achieved by primitive man, the eighteenth century took to taunting him with the virtues of the animals, to whom it attributed a courage and loyalty latterday man never attained, regardless of the fact that their instincts really leave the animals no choice but to be courageous or timid according to their kind. Similarly, ignoring the fact that we—in Freud's words[1]—'know by our own feelings that we should not think ourselves happy in any of these communities of the animal world' (that is, the 'state institutions' of bees, ants, termites), the eighteenth century was capable of envying the animals their instinctual happiness: 'proud Man!' says one writer[2], 'search Nature, and you'll see An insect's happier far than thee'. Similarly Pope has Nature bid man take instruction from 'The ants' republic, and the realm of bees'. Man is to learn from them how to hold wealth in common, and how to enjoy 'anarchy without confusion'[3].

When Pope reconstructs the age before man had become so proud (it is significant that his golden age lacks arts as well) he takes the opportunity to postulate a perfect amity between primitive man and the animals. Like its religious originals, Pope's myth of the golden age is a reconstruction of infancy, including the child's egalitarianism towards animals; and Pope has hit on—or, rather, revived from his classical studies[4]—the very notion which totemism makes

[1] *Civilization And Its Discontents*, VII

[2] cited (from the miscellany *The Honeysuckle*, 1734) by M. M. Fitzgerald: *First Follow Nature*, II, 3

[3] *Essay On Man*, III, 172-86

[4] A. O. Lovejoy and George Boas (*Documentary History Of Primitivism*, I, 34, cited by M. M. Fitzgerald) points out that Pope's description of the state of Nature is borrowed from Empedocles—'some of the couplets might serve for free translations of some of Empedocles's lines'.

such ferocious play with, namely that to kill an animal is murder.

> Pride then was not; nor arts, that pride to aid,
> Man walk'd with beast, joint tenant of the shade;
> The same his table, and the same his bed;
> No murder clothed him, and no murder fed[1].

The normative and classical approach has brought Pope intellectually to vegetarianism, which Shelley was to reach by a wild pantheistic sympathy: Pope adds:

> Ah! how unlike the man of times to come!
> Of half that live the butcher and the tomb;
> Who, foe to Nature, hears the general groan,
> Murders their species, and betrays his own[2].

Having drawn on a reconstruction of the past, the myth of the primitive drew also on the newly discovered outlandish parts of the world, and became fused with the exotic myth of the noble savage, manifestations of which dot the eighteenth century from the four Indian kings who visited London in 1710, there to be remarked by the Spectator, to the Bashaw in Mozart's *Seraglio*, who so pointedly proves himself so much more noble than his Christian opponents. The myth of primitive man was by origin, and in the hands of many of its proponents remained, Christian: it was still possible to argue that the primitive perfection which had been lost at the Fall could not be recovered by natural means, but only through grace. The myth of the noble savage, on the other hand, was a direct blow at the doctrine of original sin: the noble savage was primitive man still living, and capable of being emulated; his intellect and instinct had retained their natural state, out of reach of corrupting civilisation. 'To the Europeans who failed to observe them carefully and misunderstood what they saw', wrote Freud[3], 'these people seemed to lead simple, happy lives —wanting for nothing—such as the travellers who visited them, for all their superior culture, were unable to achieve'. Eventually the misconception was shattered by Frazer, with his monumental compilation of authenticated travellers' tales, and by Freud himself, who shattered also the false picture of infancy on which the myth was based, elucidating the obsessive tensions of primitive life by means of

[1] *Essay On Man*, III, 151-4   [2] *Essay On Man*, III, 161-4
[3] *Civilization And Its Discontents*, III

the tensions of infantile life. Against the eighteenth century's quasi-scientific creationist myth, Freud set his own evolutionary 'scientific myth' of the primal horde, with its very different concept of primitive social organisation and of primitive man's relation to the animals.

But long before Freud achieved this by a more rational application of reason, the eighteenth century's concept of the nature of man had been overwhelmed—by an eruption of the nature of man. To bene-volise instinct had been the most stupendous and the most doomed act of the repression the century consistently practised. Having laughed the devils out of existence and snubbed the Holy Ghost, it managed also to argue away original sin, the last of the innate ideas to be erased by the followers of Locke. The theory of primitive or savage perfection did, it is true, postulate that there had since been a Fall on the part of civilisation; but it was an error, a mistake in man's social technique, which had not altered man's nature, and there was nothing necessary about its consequences being passed on to all the generations of mankind[1]. Man's original endowment of benevolent instinct was still given to each member of the race at birth, and there was no need of an external visitation of supernatural grace to redeem the baby from mankind's historical mistakes: Nature was sufficient. Reason had only to uncover the route back to Nature, education had only to refrain from spoiling Nature, human society had only to be liberated from unjust and absurdly pretentious tyrannies, and mankind would be free to return to its natural benevolent state. The opportunity was created at the French Revolution—'And I presume you know', said Lady Bracknell a century afterwards[2], 'what that unfortunate movement led to?'

[1] Thus Tom Paine: 'man stands in the same relative condition with his Maker he ever did stand since man existed; and . . . it is his greatest consolation to think so. Let him believe this and he will live more confidently and morally than by any other system. It is by his being taught to contemplate himself as an outlaw, as an outcast, as a beggar, as a mumper, as one thrown, as it were, on a dunghill, at an immense distance from his Creater . . . that he conceives either a contemptuous disregard for everything under the name of religion . . . or turns what he calls devout. In the latter case he consumes his life in grief . . . His humility is ingratitude. . . He despises the choicest gift of God to man—the GIFT OF REASON. . .' (*The Age Of Reason*, I)
[2] Oscar Wilde: *The Importance Of Being Earnest*, I

9. *The Age of Eros*

Rationalism had met the same crisis, and in similar historical circumstances, two thousand years before; and here too a civilisation which had achieved a tremendous advance in consciousness was so terrified of a return to the old religious habit of worshipping the unconscious that it neglected its opportunity—and its danger if it failed—to frame a scientific psychology of the unconscious.

From its isolated beginnings among the pioneer philosophers and their separate groups of disciples, Greek rationalism emerged as a movement, and was put into currency[1] in a coherent, self-recognising intelligentsia, at Athens about the time of the Peloponnesian War. Here Socrates formulated the belief which was to govern the eighteenth century, that morality could be discovered by reason and propagated by education: and the eighteenth-century conviction that government could not reasonably rest on anything less than the rational faculty of all the citizens (that is, their power to convince and be convinced by one another in argument) had achieved an actual political embodiment in Athenian democracy—with the limitation that slaves were not citizens. The eighteenth century itself enjoyed this state of affairs only in England (where it was still subject to arbitrary limitations as well as corruption) and, presently, America (which, however, admitted the institution of slavery—against which Tom Paine began the crusade); with the results that continental freedom-lovers like Voltaire and Mozart[2] were anglophile, European freedom-lovers presently became americanophile, and the entire liberal movement was in love with Athenian democracy and its copy[3] at Rome. The political manifesto of the eighteenth century had been composed two millenia in advance by Thucydides[4] in the

[1] Cf. E. R. Dodds: *The Greeks And The Irrational*, VI

[2] Mozart to his father (from Vienna, 19 October, 1782): 'Indeed I have heard about England's victories and am greatly delighted too, for you know that I am an out-and-out Englishman'. Witness also, of course, Blonde (significantly a proletarian) with her 'Ich bin eine Engländerin, zur Freiheit geboren' (*Seraglio*, II)

[3] Probably a deliberate copy from the start, in the spirit of the Roman embassy sent in 454 B.C. to study the laws of Solon

[4] II, 35-47

shape of the definition of Athenian political practice which he puts in the mouth of Pericles to be pronounced at the public funeral of the first Athenian dead of the war.

Like its eighteenth-century counterpart, the Athenian enlightenment coalesced out of an intense comparison with other moeurs, a comparison which, as Pericles-Thucydides knew[1], had been brought home to Athens by Athenian sea power. (Like the eighteenth century, it had behind it, though not so far behind it, a renaissance, in the shape of the age of Themistocles and Aeschylus. This was quite literally a renaissance: Aeschylus gave a new lease of life to the heroes, the heroic dynasties and the vocabulary of the old epic poetry; Themistocles revived the glory, which had perhaps been exaggerated, of Athens under Theseus. In other words, behind the renaissance there lay a genuine antiquity: the Mycenean civilisation, itself a fruit of the sea, whose scriptural legacy was Homer.) Both enlightenments rose into self-consciousness as a result of the rise into self-consciousness and self-expression of a commercial bourgeoisie. Socrates's circle and the salons of the eighteenth century are alike borne up on the bourgeoisie's will to be educated. Indeed, illuminati who need to earn a living often do so literally by teaching. They become sophists at Athens; and in the eighteenth century, before they emerge as translators, journalists and pamphleteers, they frequently serve a term in the century's other great métier, that of tutor.

In both cases the bourgeois intelligentsia is sprigged with fashionable and aristocratic persons turned liberal constitutionalists. Pericles's ward and kinsman Alcibiades leaves an ineffaceable impression of his aristocratic insouciance on the heart of Socrates and his friends, just as in the last phases of eighteenth-century enlightenment Byron leaves an impression of his on the heart of all Europe, including Greece itself. In Alcibiades, as in some of the noblemen who sided with the French Revolution, there was a certain aristocratic unaccountability, a trace of the tradition of exercising power without being held accountable, which was capable of impressing a bourgeois philosopher both as something erotically desirable and as something which, belonging to a master and to the parent-class, was unattainable and forbidden. The philosopher's bond to a figure of this kind was truly romantic:

[1] The Funeral Oration points out (38-39) that the produce of the whole world came into Athens, there to be enjoyed by the Athenians as familiarly as their own native goods, and that the Athenians, in contrast to the xenophobic Spartans, held their city open to foreigners.

being incestuous, it must doom the lover by way of punishment: and more than once such a bond was one of the threads which, usually drawing him into political intrigue, netted a philosopher in destruction.

Both intelligentsias opened a new period of social history, indeed a more truly *social* period, by discovering the city (the new art-form created by eighteenth-century architecture), which ceased to be only a citadel and a market, and became a talking-shop. Socrates's attachment to Athens[1] prefigures Dr. Johnson's to London and almost every other eighteenth-century intellectual's to Paris. The intelligentsia is, of course, informally constituted. It has informally re-made the social system along lines not of class or commercial interest but of intellectual interests. In the enlightened society, any interesting person can meet any other interesting person. Protagoras has only to come from Abdera to Athens and he will meet Socrates; Madame de Staël has only to set foot in Germany and she will meet Goethe. The informal unity is maintained only by conversation (supplemented in the eighteenth century by print)—and by love affairs, which are sociably discussed in conversation.

Here the all-masculine Socratic circle had an advantage over the salons: it could meet at the palaestrae[2], to study, discuss and flirt with the boys who did their gym there, and rely on the advantage homosexual love has over heterosexual, that it is (in Freud's words[3]) 'far more compatible with group ties, even when it takes the shape of uninhibited sexual tendencies'. The intellectual élite of the eighteenth century, however, contained many notable and passionate women, some of whom, like Madame de Staël and Mary Wollstonecraft, were campaigning for a de jure recognition of women's position in society; and the results were that a good part of the century's intellectual effort was deliberately given over to trying to socialise the anti-social bond between one man and one woman, an attempt which even turned into an attempt to communalise marriage, while in practice salons and more intimate groupings often collected round individuals like Madame de Staël or (a less successful example) Shelley who, perhaps because they had themselves preserved a certain bisexuality intact from childhood, possessed the gift of accreting rather than exchanging lovers and of making their lovers friends instead of rivals—a gift they usually exercised at the expense of their own happiness.

[1] *Crito*, 52 B-E   [2] Vide *Lysis*
[3] *Group Psychology And The Analysis Of The Ego*, XII, D

Though they were dealing with different kinds of love and friendship, both enlightenments agreed in fusing love and friendship with the passion for instruction. Eighteenth-century social life is full of brilliant and attractive women instructing brilliant and attractive young men in political economy—or learning German or philosophy from them; the homosexual eroticism of the Socratic group has developed out of 'emotional relations of a friendly character . . . between a master and a pupil'[1]. And it is precisely here that we can find the means to penetrate into the whole nature of the enlightenment, and of the repression it practised, in both epochs.

Every society depends on the socialisation of love to bind it together, and every revolution or reaction re-makes the social bargain on which the social structure rests. The peculiarity of the enlightenment and the democratic revolution was that they attempted to make a community through love alone and to abolish the whole system of pitting one social section against another. What was emancipated at the emancipation was love, or, as the eighteenth century preferred to call it, benevolence. Christianity had insisted that Christians love one another and love Christ, but also that they hate sin and the devil; the new catholicism of the eighteenth century re-made Christendom without Christ (for whom it substituted man) and also without the devil. The essence of the enlightenment is incarnated in that informal social gathering, that symposium, where, mimicking parliamentary democracy, each of the diners is called on to speak in turn in praise of Eros.

In the primal horde, the sons are forced into their socialised and fraternal love for one another by the tyranny of the father. Later developments—short of democracy—only substitute the tyranny of a class for the tyranny of a man, and at the same time give the oppressed a better opportunity to make their hostility felt in the class above. In Sparta, for example, which Pericles's speech is all along tacitly contrasting with Athens, oppressors and oppressed have wedged one another into immobility: the state as a whole is so fixed in conservatism that it cannot pursue its own best advantage; and the oppressors, who must devote their lives to armed vigilance against insurrection, are hardly freer than their serfs and never enjoy the benefits of the tyranny they practise. But when the Athenians abolish class tyranny, one of the first fruits is enjoyment—as Pericles points out when he praises not only the Athenians' political freedom but their freedom

[1] Freud: *Group Psychology And The Analysis Of The Ego*, XII, C

from suspicion of one another; an Athenian is not angered by his neighbour's pursuit of happiness[1].

It is just this which the emancipation has achieved in the moral sphere: the liberation of the instinct to pursue happiness. In the democracy every disciplinary decision may be debated (a habit which, Pericles insists, actually renders the Athenians stronger than the Spartans, who maintain the traditional discipline which is passed down through a hierarchy): and meanwhile the intelligentsia sets itself to question all the arbitrary tyrannies which religion and moral taboos have imposed on human desire. Euripides, like Shelley and Byron, can even raise in his fiction the question of the absoluteness of the incest taboo, though of course he raises a scandal as well[2]; in the eighteenth century the Marquis de Sade even speaks up for the right to pursue happiness on behalf of those whose happiness lies in being tyrants. Yet, true to the social age, Sade puts himself forward as a social philosopher; his fantasies run to orgy[3]; he is trying to socialise sadism and debauchery just as other theorists and practitioners of the period try to socialise marriage.

The American Declaration of Independence expressly counted among the inalienable rights of man the right to pursue happiness, but as a matter of fact the unspoken assumption of all democracies goes beyond that and asserts that the citizen usually does pursue happiness, though of course the pursuit may be blocked by unjust tyrannies. It is just as necessary to Pericles's political philosophy as it is to Socrates's moral philosophy to hold that man is motivated primarily by self-love. There was no more difficulty at Athens than there was to be in the eighteenth century in reconciling individual self-loves with the social love of one's fellows and of the state: a truly passionate self-love will compel a man to use reason to determine where his best advantage lies, whereupon he will at once see that it lies in association, and that he will be well advised to sacrifice or risk some of his own short-term advantages in favour of the long-term advantage of the state; a democratic state pursuing its own interest by policy is pursuing the happiness of its citizens. The association of free citizens in the Athenian state, and of free states in the Athenian Empire, is voluntary inasmuch as each member is motivated by his own self-interest; but behind this lies the great involuntary

[1] ... οὐ δι' ὀργῆς τὸν πέλας, εἰ καθ' ἡδονήν τι δρᾷ, ἔχοντες (37)
[2] E. R. Dodds: *The Greeks And The Irrational*, VI
[3] Cf. Simone de Beauvoir: *Must We Burn De Sade?* pp. 44-5

compulsion Socrates assumed in human nature, that one cannot help pursuing one's own interest.

How far one's picture of one's own interest coincides with one's true interest in the real situation depends, according to the enlightenment, on one's knowledge and eyesight; decisions taken in democratic debate will not be to the real advantage of the state unless the debators have argued reasonably: and it is in improving knowledge and vision that education must play its all-important part. Pericles is as quick as Socrates to single out education: summing up, he defines that the rôle of Athens in the international community is to be 'the education of Hellas'[1]. As for the education of Athens itself, he nominates the governing idea of the eighteenth century, a rational élite: although Athens is a democracy and everyone is equal before the law, the democracy honours and esteems individuals according to their merit. It was to this idea that Socrates subscribed when he admitted that the oracle had, in a sense, spoken the truth when it named him as the wisest man in the world[2].

It is education, the pursuit of virtue conceived as knowledge, which makes Eros fluid and carries its binding power beyond the couple and out into the community. Socrates himself develops the process to its utmost with his dialectical manner of argument. If the method of the *Symposium* mimics a parliament, the dialectical method mimics a law court, by confining itself to the interpenetration of two points of view. We can read this interpenetration of wits either in the hostile or in the flirtatious sense: it is the situation of a pair of rivals, seeking to disarm and render one another impotent, each making it his object to impale the other on logic; or else it is the situation of a pair of lovers, where the defences to be penetrated are the virgin's, and the act of penetrating actually wins the assaulted on to the assaulter's side and skewers the two into unity. But whichever sense we take it in—or whichever of the innumerable compass-degrees through which the one sense shades into the opposite—the social result is the same: the impulse in its native form tends to isolate a pair from the community, but it has here been transmuted into a social act, an act of public instruction.

In these intimate duels between Socrates and his interlocutor, there is always a third party: the audience, present or implied. The audience

[1] Ξυνελών τε λέγω την τε πᾶσαν πόλιν τῆς Ἑλλάδος παίδευσιν εἶναι . . . (41)
[2] *Apology*, 20D-22E

is no mere eavesdropper, like a novelist; and though there is a chapter of a novel to be read *through* each of the Socratic dialogues (by translating Socrates's arguments back into the instincts of love and hostility), Plato does not conceive his readers' primary interest in them to be the novel-reader's interest in the confrontation of two individual psychologies, but the pamphlet-reader's in the confrontation of two conceptions of human psychology. The audience, which, like a jury, stands for the whole of the citizenship or the whole of mankind, has tacitly shaped the conversation; the arguments are addressed to the audience, and the two speakers are not content when they have persuaded or communicated with one another. But unlike a jury the audience is not called on simply to judge the case between the two duellists: it is more likely that it will be asked to judge the nature of justice itself or the validity not of the arguments but of argument itself. Socrates is examining the generalities on which human civilisation itself rests; he is re-writing the moral code of Athens—of the world—while we watch; and when he was actually put on trial he (or his reporter) managed to turn it into just such a discussion and to make his trial his last-but-one act of educating the public.

The enlightenment was, in fact, bound to generalise, abstract, intellectualise. Only by transmuting it into terms of thought, which can be communicated by language, could Eros be made fluid enough to perform the unitive task which it now had to undertake without the co-operation and collusion of tyranny. A word is an act of love vaporised, a holy ghost, a breath potent with meaning, which is capable of inseminating and disseminating. To communicate fulfils the nature of Eros: it unites the speaker and the listener; it creates a temporary identification between them by lodging the same image in their separate consciousnesses: and yet there is no limit to the number of people who may be inseminated by a single breath of the same speaker and who may thereby become identified with one another.

Both the enlightenments therefore concern themselves with what can be universally or at least widely communicated, and with abstracting certain general principles common to all men. Socrates directs his enquiries into general principles and habitually[1] conducts them in a nontechnical vocabulary with everyday examples, so that his conclusions may be both intelligible and applicable to the largest possible number of men. In trying to define the common skeleton

[1] *Symposium*, 221 E

beneath the multifariousness of individuals, the enlightenment has a scientific character—or, more precisely, a philosophical one, in the ancient sense of a philosophy which comprehends science. This philosophical enquiry is not, however, limited to what we should call nonfiction. Fiction in the form of tragic poetry (though as a rule[1] the tragedians did not invent their plots) is, according to Aristotle, more philosophical, and therefore more excellent, than history (the would-be tragic poets of the eighteenth century shared his opinion); and the reason Aristotle gives is precisely that tragedy is concerned with more general truths. 'In what manner, for example, any person of a certain character would speak or act, probably or necessarily— this is general; and this is the object of poetry. . . But what Alcibiades did, or what happened to him—this is particular truth'.[2]

However, this philosophical attempt is unable to discover—or to discover in time—enough common material for Eros to work on. A society will not hold together simply through each of its members possessing a rational faculty. Eros is obliged to bring the members closer together; reason insists they use their several reasons in such a way as to make them have more in common. The quest changes into a quest for law and principle in the secondary significance our language gives them; the scientific character of the enquiry changes into a legislative character.

Already in Pericles we can discern the eighteenth-century contrast between political libertarianism and a highly normative spirit towards manners and art. He has already set up the eighteenth-century idol of taste, with that insistence on keeping a mean which, if it is given a long run, condemns art to mediocrity or extinction. Indeed, taste, he tells us at the outset, has almost prevented him from giving us his own excellent piece of rhetorical artistry at all, it being so difficult to speak 'measuredly' on such an occasion; and at the end taste quite prevents him from addressing to the widows of the dead soldiers anything more than an injunction not to fall short of the standards set for their sex by Nature (here in her chilliest eighteenth-century manifestation), combined with the repressive epigram that the most glorious woman is the one with the least reputation, in either the good or the bad sense, among men. Between these two sacrifices to taste, he has counted as one of the glories of Athens the good taste with which the Athenians decorate their homes; but he has also counted

[1] Aristotle cites and approves of various exceptions and partial exceptions.
[2] *Poetics*, Thomas Twining's translation, II, VI

it as another that the Athenians do not push their intellectual bent to extremes or their artistic bent to the point of 'soppiness'[1].

It is at the junction where its enquiry into natural law turns into legislating that the enlightenment misses its opportunities in relation to both science and art. Already by concentrating on what *is* common to all men and on what *can be* communicated, it has put itself in a position where it may have to do violence to art; and the moment it turns its attention to what *should be* communicated, it begins to close in for the smothering. Aristotle is already in something of the eighteenth-century dilemma between idealisation and naturalism[2]. He believes that the poet (and the portrait-painter) should 'produce a likeness, and at the same time improve on the original'; but he is prepared to excuse a poet who depicts ill-mannered characters on the grounds of truth to fact; and he admits to his canon both Sophocles, who 'drew mankind such as they should be' and Euripides, who drew them 'such as they are'[3]. Aristotle's canon is, in fact, saved by his always referring back to the artistic effect as his criterion. His rules are the rules whereby a poet may make a tragic effect on the audience: they are drawn from and proved by the audience's response: the 'strongest proof' that the principles of tragedy distinguished by Aristotle are the correct ones is the fact that 'upon the stage, and in the dramatic contests' it is the works which exemplify these principles which 'have always the most tragic effect'[4]. In other words, he legislates only within the conventions of the art. His imperatives, whether they urge naturalism or idealisation, are sanctioned by what gives the audience pleasure; and he has seen that what gives it pleasure in the theatre, namely to be moved to pity and terror, is not identical with what gives it pleasure in life.

If the eighteenth century failed to produce such a penetrating literary aesthetic, it was partly because it lacked a free and vital theatre.

[1] φιλοσοφοῦμεν ἄμευ μαλακίας

[2] a dilemma perfectly expressed in Dr Johnson's comments (Notes to *King Lear*) on the death of Cordelia: 'A play in which the wicked prosper, and the virtuous miscarry, may doubtless be good, because it is a just representation of the common events of human life: but since all reasonable beings naturally love justice, I cannot easily be persuaded, that the observation of justice makes a play worse; or, that if other excellencies are equal, the audience will not always rise better pleased from the final triumph of persecuted virtue.'

[3] *Poetics*, Thomas Twining's translation, II, XV; IV, III

[4] *Poetics*, Thomas Twining's translation, II, XII

Politics (at least in France) imposed a formal censorship from one side, whereupon the enlightenment leapt in to impose an informal censorship from the other and insisted on idealisation not, as Aristotle had done, in order to heighten the tragic effect on the audience but in order to heighten the moral effect on mankind. (Some of the eighteenth century's curious judgments on Shakespeare must be the result of its so seldom taking Aristotle's advice and kitchen-testing him in the theatre; and, by scarcely allowing the public to see him —as opposed to reading him—unimproved, it was able to claim public approbation for the improved versions[1].) Unwilling to waste time legislating for the microcosmic society constituted by the audience in a theatre, the eighteenth century insisted on legislating for all mankind, one of its methods being through the medium of art, and thereby it shattered and made nonsense of the conventions of art. It failed to take Aristotle's point that an action on the stage which pleases the audience's moral sense may still not please their dramatic sense[2]. The business of art became not merely to please the moral sense but to serve its purpose. Fictions were to put forward a pattern for people to imitate, with the result that art would help to make people more like one another by making each of them more like the ideal. What passed unnoticed was that this destroys the morality of the actual practice of art.

Of all the arts, the eighteenth-century enlightenment sought first and most to annex literature, because of its peculiar powers of infecting people by imitation—powers which *The Sorrows Of Young Werther* demonstrated by provoking a spate of suicides in hysterical imitation. Goethe, however, helped by the isolation of the German language from the normative literary centres of Paris and London,

[1] Thus Dr Johnson records how Nahum Tate provided *King Lear* with an ending happy for Cordelia and (although the Spectator had the sense to see that thereby 'the tragedy lost half its beauty') concludes: 'In the present case the publick has decided. *Cordelia*, from the time of *Tate*, has always retired with victory and felicity'. (To this 'general suffrage', Johnson adds his own experience of being 'so shocked by *Cordelia's* death that I know not whether I ever endured to read again the last scenes of the play till I undertook to revise them as an editor'. (Notes to *King Lear*)

[2] 'Nor, again, should the fall of a very bad man from prosperous to adverse fortune be represented: because, though such a subject may be pleasing from its moral tendency, it will produce neither pity nor terror' (*Poetics*, Thomas Twining's translation, II, XI)

was one of the few writers who managed to contribute to the enlightenment while keeping its legislative grip off the artist's integrity;
and thus he managed at the same time (helped here, also, by the length
of his life) to hold a space open for the entrance of romanticism. (It
is significant that he did this, and that Schiller actually ushered in
romanticism, largely in the theatre, which supplies its own society;
and it was in the theatre that Mozart, too, found a refuge from the
normative spirit and a space in which to express his individuality in
his own version of romanticism.) Goethe was shocked by the French
enlightenment in the person of Madame de Staël (Christopher Herold's
biography makes it plain how precisely she *did* personify the enlightenment), because of its Socratic habit of philosophising 'in a social setting'.
Madame de Staël, Goethe remarked, habitually 'carried speech and
repartee to matters of thought and feeling which by right should
never be discussed except between the individual and his God'. Equally,
Madame de Staël was shocked by Goethe's unconcern over the
suicides his Werther had provoked. She herself, who believed that
literature had achieved a higher status in the eighteenth century by
ceasing to be 'a mere art' and becoming 'a weapon in the service of
the spirit of man', altered the suicidal ending of her own novel
Delphine in accordance with a change in her views on the morality
of suicide.[1]

Goethe foreshadows the desocialisation of art in the nineteenth
century, when the industrial revolution utterly divorced the cultivated stratum from the rest of society, and the bourgeoisie would
no longer support an élite but was more given to reviling it. Indeed
the élite, deprived of its social function, found itself no longer a
coherent social class but so many isolated individuals whose communication was often limited perforce to discussions between the
individual and his God.

The law-making of the enlightenment was of course based on
natural law: explicitly in the eighteenth century and implicitly at
Athens, where both Socrates and Pericles assume the predominance of
the instinct towards pleasure, and where Socrates's cult of naïveté,
simplicity and intellectual innocence is only another dress for the
eighteenth-century cult of the natural and primitive. When he justifies
the oracle in the sense that he is indeed the wisest man inasmuch as
he is the most aware of his own ignorance, Socrates approaches the

[1] J. Christopher Herold: *Mistress To An Age*, A Life of Madame De Staël,
13; 11; 12

eighteenth-century conclusion that it is culture and learning which befuddle civilised man's intelligence.

However, the concept of Nature on which the legislation was based was inadequate. Once the enlightenment had begun to weaken the authorities of class, taboo and religion on which the old social order stood, it found itself under the urgent necessity of raising a new authority by deliberately making laws. It felt obliged to foreclose the enquiry and hurry on to legislation. Moreover, since it was to the task of Eros, the task of binding society together, that the legislation was directed, it was Eros which drew attention to itself in Nature, to the neglect of the other instinct, 'which works in silence'[1].

It is the laws, the nomoi, which, Pericles tells us[2], impose social restraint on the Athenians; and he includes both the formal laws of the state and the unwritten laws, whose sanction is public opinion— in which we can see the presages of the eighteenth-century's informal laws of taste and their weapon, scorn. We know more about the nomoi from the great part they occupy in Socrates's conversation. He has rightly discerned that their authority is that of a parent: 'we begot you, we brought you up, we taught you', he imagines the laws saying to him[3]. The enlightened bourgeoisie has once again played the part of an Ego, and it has replaced an external father with an abstract Ego-ideal, whose commands are represented by the nomoi.

Naturally the nomoi are the educators, since education is the medium whereby parental authority is passed on to the children. In the old dispensation, education was a matter of submitting to one's immediate father until the time came for the son to take his place in the social order; and what that place should be was immutably decreed by the community's fathers—God, the ruling class or ancestral custom. Education in the ancien régime was a training for one particular function in the social order. The Spartans, as Pericles pointed out[4], are educated specifically and exclusively in the practice of arms; the Christian is educated primarily and often exclusively in the practice of prayer and faith, in preparation for his position as a servant of God; and in both cases the individual's supreme duty is to submit to the discipline appropriate to his place in the hierarchy. The Anglican catechism expressly recognises that man's social obligation is not to create a just social order but to preserve the social order as it stands: it defines 'my duty towards my Neighbour' as including 'To submit

[1] Freud: *An Autobiographical Study*, V   [2] Thucydides, II, 37
[3] *Crito*, 51 C   [4] Thucydides, II, 39

myself to all my governors, spiritual pastors and masters; To order myself lowly and reverently to all my betters ... and to do my duty in that state of life, unto which it shall please God to call me'. The enlightenment's concept of education does away with all this submission and substitutes a positive duty to question everything: the teacher joins in the enquiry as senior partner; his job is not to supply the answers but to provoke the questions, and if he is wiser than his pupil his wisdom consists in his greater knowledge of how ignorant he is. Thus the enlightenment performed the Ego's business of taking authority out of the hands of parent-representatives and placing the responsibility for education on the child's own relationship to reality, the duty to question everything being nothing less than the Ego's function of scrutinising all the images which present themselves to consciousness and testing their reality.

The enlightenment is, therefore, a movement towards liberalising the relation between parents and children (and when the reaction came it picked on Socrates in his essential character of educator; it perceived that the centre of the whole business was the relationship between generations, and its accusation was that the liberal education Socrates had been providing consisted of corrupting the younger generation). Where democracy casts down the barriers between the parent class and the child class in society, the educational revolution casts them down intellectually. It will have no numinous awe paid to the teacher, and will let him retain none of the magical prerogatives of a primal father. It will have nothing of the idea that knowledge, being invested with all the dangers of taboo power, should be kept arcane by some hieratic secret society within society. The new élite has abolished secret diplomacy. It is no priesthood but rests on the general suffrage; its enquiries are open to the public, and are for the public to judge; the wisdom wrung from them is meant for dissemination. The worry now is not that knowledge may leak out, but that the public may not want it when the tap is turned full on.

In this, however, as in the task of building a coherent social and cultural unit, the enlightenment trusts itself to Eros. It will trust the young to become attached to their educators, the masses to the élite, the democracy to the nomoi, through the power of love. The implicit argument is that self-love will bind a man so firmly to reality that he will be obliged to make use of his reason and read from reality back to the necessity of becoming educated in his own interest. The fallacy was to suppose that the laws and consistency of reality are directly binding on man, instead of through an evolutionary process of which reason is only the final result. It was again an evolutionary and psychological ignorance which prevented the enlightenment from discovering that it is not the whole man but only his Ego which pursues self-interest and must, therefore, pursue reality, and only the Ego which cares tuppence for unity and consistency. It would have been better for the enlightenment if the gods had really existed up to the moment when the enlightenment took the governance of man out of their hands.

The nomoi are recognised as the creation of the people they govern; a democracy knows it is self-governing in the same sense as an individual is governed by his own Ego. What the enlightenment failed to recognise is that the gods and taboos of the ancien régime have likewise been created (though this time unconsciously) by the people they govern; and that in fact all the self-contradictory forces which Socrates pointed out[1] in the nature of the gods had gone to create the nature of the nomoi, too. The relationship of the people to their Ego-ideal was as fraught with ambivalence as their relationship to the old authorities, for the reason that both relationships are extensions of the child's primary ambivalence towards the father. Evans Bell described Jehovah as a 'bargaining, vacillating, bloodthirsty, and repenting Deity'[2], but still without having taken the psychological point that Jehovah came into existence in reflexion of the wishes of the people. When the people created a deity which they admitted was of their own wishing—the sovereign people, whose voice was vox dei—it turned out to be a bargaining deity capable of the corrupt compromises entered into by the French Revolution, a vacillating and repenting one capable of resolving in parliamentary debate to massacre the prisoners who had surrendered at Lesbos and countermanding the order only just in time, and finally a deity so bloodthirsty that it destroyed not only the enemies of the Revolution and the enemies of the Athenian democracy but the Revolution and the democracy themselves.

These collapses put to the democrat his classical dilemma: what should he do when a democracy, whose justification can be established only by reason, behaves unreasonably; what should he do when it even turns against its own interest and democratically gives its voice against democracy and for tyranny? This was the net which caught Socrates, and the instrument of his destruction was his

[1] *Euthyphro*   [2] *The God Of The Bible*, IX

own ignorance of the psychological nature of the nomoi. He begins his suicide when he refuses to try to persuade the court by any method except reason and seals it with his refusal to escape after his condemnation. On his premiss that everyone is motivated by self-love, he has built a picture of the state as a pure Ego: the citizen must either obey the nomoi or persuade the state to change them[1]. To escape would be to weaken the authority of a concept of law to which he has himself subscribed—in which, so to speak, part of his own Ego is embodied; it is not for him, he argues, to seek to destroy the nomoi simply because the nomoi think it just to destroy him[2]. The true situation, however, is that although the nomoi have no existence and force except in the will of the people, they do not represent the whole of the will of the people. The people do not want to destroy Socrates because, as he supposes, they think it just[3], but simply because they *want* to; and in this want they disregard both justice and (which is to Socrates the same thing) their own advantage. It is not he who has failed to persuade them, but they who have set aside the whole basis of rational persuasion. Yet though we can perceive Socrates's ignorance of the people's psychology, we must add that he would probably have behaved in just the same way if he had known. His martyrdom for the values of the Ego is probably the only truly unavoidable and wholly justifiable martyrdom in history; although a scientific psychology is bound to re-arrange the pieces in the struggle, it can only come to the conclusion that there really was an irreconcilable conflict between Socrates and his assassins, the conflict between the two irreducible and irrational instincts of Eros and Thanatos. Greater knowledge could not have made the struggle non-existent; but, as Socrates would have leapt to perceive, it might have provided—and in the future may provide—Eros with more effective weapons. And indeed only if it does so will the whole of civilisation avoid dying on the same deathbed as Socrates.

As he announced in the *Symposium*[4], it was as an encomiast of Eros, and a practitioner and propagandist of 'erotics', that Socrates saw himself. He was aware of the irrational force of Eros, the 'great daimon'[5]; and he shewed himself an astute psychologist of love,

---

[1] *Crito*, 51C . . . πανταχοῦ ποιητέον, ἃ ἂν κελεύῃ ἡ πόλις καὶ ἡ πατρίς, ἢ πείθειν αὐτὴν ᾗ τὸ δίκαιον πέφυκε . . .

[2] *Crito*, 51A

[3] δίκαιον ἡγούμενοι εἶναι

[4] 212 B   [5] *Symposium*, 202 D. Δαίμων μέγας

who had recognised object-love as an extension of self-love, and
began to attack the problems of self-identification involved in loving
someone else[1]. We cannot go on repeating Aristotle's criticism[2]
that he underestimated the influence of the passions and ignored the
unreasoning part of the soul (a part which had to be re-instated by
Plato), when we have Socrates's remark that the greatest of the good
things in human life come to us through madness[3], and when he
was in the habit of attributing his own major decisions to the commands
of a daimon. But we can see in him the same neglect which is to be
seen in the enlightenment as a whole, the failure to make a scientific
approach to the irrational motivations. Like Bernard Shaw's nine-
teenth-century-rational St. Joan, he is at pains to vindicate the daimon
by shewing that what it commands is, in fact, the rational and moral
thing to do, thereby making it clear to us that the daimon's voice
really emanates from his own mind. But whether he has recognised
as much himself is not clear. We do not know for sure the answer
even to the more superficial question whether his daimon is his
metaphor for a moral imperative or a description of a genuinely
hallucinatory experience. Neither does he explain what he conceives
to be the relation of his daimon to the great daimon, Eros, or to the
external gods whom he took seriously enough to send them a sacrifice
from his deathbed, or to the oracle—whose voice he vindicates in the
same manner as his daimon's. When so explicative a person fails
to explain, we may take it that he is not interested in the problem.
For Socrates it is enough to establish the rationality and morality of
what his personal inspiration says, just as for the eighteenth-century
enlightenment it is enough to establish the irrationality and immorality
of what the Christian revelation says. Tom Paine judges the Bible
by the standard his century so regularly applied to art, namely its
social results (a standard which can be legitimately applied to the
Bible, since that *does* set up as a model for imitation); and he finds
that 'the obscene stories, the voluptuous debaucheries, the cruel and

[1] In *Lysis* he points out that Hippothales, in composing songs of praise to
the boy he loves, is really praising himself; and in *Euthyphro* he considers the
same problem of the relation of lover to loved in terms of whether holiness
is loved by the gods because it is holy or whether it is holy because it is loved
by the gods.

[2] Cf. the Introduction by A. D. Lindsay to the Everyman translation of
the Socratic discourses

[3] Cf. E. R. Dodds: *The Greeks And The Irrational*, III

torturous executions, the unrelenting vindictiveness with which more than half the Bible is filled' have 'served to corrupt and brutalise mankind'[1]. The problem of how the Bible's authors came to be imposed on by their revelation interests him no more than it did Gibbon: the person concerned 'may have been deceived, or may have dreamed it; or he may be an impostor, and may lie'[2].

Paine has, however, been led one step further than Socrates—by the fact that the Bible *is* immoral. He can see that the imposture, voluntary or involuntary as it may be, would still be an imposture even if the model it proposed for the world to imitate were virtuous and beneficial: even the morality of the supposed revelation, he points out[3], would not guarantee that it *was* revelation. (In remarking that the moral tendency of a play was no guarantee of its tragic effectiveness, Aristotle had made just the same point about the revelation a work of art constitutes to its audience; and indeed the immorality of the eighteenth-century artists who surrendered their integrity to the enlightenment is that a moral tale masquerading as a work of art is an imposture.) Socrates has not considered Paine's point because he has established that his revelation is moral and enquires no further into it. But even Paine, given the immorality of the Bible, never puts the crucial question why the fantasy which shoulders its way up in a dream, bursts in as a hallucination or comes idly to mind when the impostor sets out to concoct a falsehood should have taken the obscene, voluptuous, cruel and vindictive form it has, and what relation this content bears to mankind's willingness to swallow it.

The enlightenment looked at Nature, saw life and deduced the existence of Eros. It has to its credit a tremendous advance in our concept of Eros, in that it ceased to oppose self-love to the moral and social forms of love. Having recognised that moral and social love come from inside the individual and not from a supernatural visitation, it recognised that they were extensions and evolutionary adaptations of self-love, and that we can love our neighbour only by a psychic process which makes him identical with our self. Thus the eighteenth century built its social morality on private hedonism. 'We must begin', wrote Madame du Chatelet, 'by saying to ourselves that we have nothing else to do in this world but seek pleasant sensations and feelings'[4]. Socrates has gone into the question

[1] *The Age Of Reason*, I   [2] *The Age Of Reason*, II   [3] *The Age Of Reason*, II
[4] quoted in evidence of the re-instatement of self-love in the eighteenth century in Simone de Beauvoir: *Must We Burn De Sade?*, p. 61

more analytically: he recognises that both the sexual love of an object and the love of virtue in noble deeds are extensions of the love of self —extensions forced on the self by the certainty of its death; he puts forward the Shakespearean view that the self can be furthered and prolonged beyond the limit imposed by death only by begetting progeny, or by having one's virtue remembered, re-embodied, in the community[1]; Eros is the desire for immortality. Just so, Pericles holds that the soldiers who have died for Athens will really live longer than they would have done had they lived out their lives: they have given up their bodies, which are subject to decay and death, and taken in exchange praise which cannot grow old[2].

Yet though the enlightenment had fixed on death as what forces self-love to undertake its transformations, it did not manage to conceive scientifically the existence of a counter-Eros, capable of similar compounds and transformations, turning from the destruction of others to the destruction of self, working with a dis-unitive purpose, dissolving relationships between individuals, withdrawing recognition from logical relationships, breaking off the individual's negotiations with his environment, and finally dissolving those internal bonds which make the individual a self and hold him in the state where he is capable of functioning as an entity. The enlightenment failed to take account of death as part of Nature. The distinction we are looking for in the case of Socrates is not that he ignored what Plato distinguished as the irrational part of the soul, or that he wholly ignored (psycho-analysis having re-cast Plato's single distinction into two) the Id in favour of the Ego, or the unconscious in favour of the conscious: there has seldom been a man more aware of the irrational and unconscious force of libido: it is, rather, that he acknowledged Eros to the neglect of Thanatos and, though his insight did penetrate into the unconscious, his concept of the unconscious never went *beyond the pleasure principle.*

The great exception to the Greek enlightenment's exclusively Erotic and pleasurable view of human psychology is Euripides, the Mozart of the Greek theatre. To Aristotle, Euripides 'seems clearly to be the most tragic of all poets'[3]; and it is the study of the tragic effects made by Euripides and Sophocles which brings Aristotle to his own appreciation of the part Thanatos plays in creating dramatic pleasure. Contracting out of the normative rationalism of the age, but

[1] *Symposium,* 207D-209 E   [2] Thucydides, II, 43
[3] *Poetics,* Thomas Twining's translation, II, XII

equally refusing to conform to ancien-régime religion, Euripides became what Professor Dodds calls an irrationalist[1], concerned himself with psychological studies of crime which no one could with any certainty construe as moral tales, and, in a light comedy, actually named and personified on the stage the other instinctual daimon, Thanatos. The eighteenth century produced no such appreciation of Thanatos, though Choderlos de Laclos gave the world what is still the most brilliant account it possesses of the rapier-thrust implicit in the act of seduction, in a novel whose very title, *Les Liaisons Dangereuses*, qualifies the erotic noun with the thanatic adjective. A scientific appreciation of Thanatos was approached only by the Marquis de Sade. Sade's fictions, to judge from such examples as one is allowed to read, are artistic failures through being demoralising tales in the same sense that so many eighteenth-century fictions are moralising tales; their sensuous barrenness, the whiff of (Sade's own title) la philosophie dans la boudoir, deprives them of even pornographic effectiveness. But Sade's philosophy, as one can see from Simone de Beauvoir's monograph, is working towards a recognition of the destructive instinct: Sade has at least looked at Nature and perceived an anti-benevolence[2].

Even Sade, however, can bring Thanatos to light only in fusion with a strong dose of Eros, the very fusion we mean by sadism. He does not acknowledge the autonomy of the destructive instinct, but regards it as a perversion of love and, like any Rousseau-ist, attributes the destructive bent of his heroes to soçial causes[3]. It is sexuality which he sees as the prime motive of human life; he has even perceived its multifarious character[4]: and it is through this multifariousness, it is in its anal-sadistic form, and not nakedly per se, that Thanatos enters his picture of the world. Sade's destructiveness merges into his coprophilia and thence into his desire to be degraded and humiliated—a desire which, in life and fantasy, he expresses by masochistic and by passively homosexual behaviour; in the end he is asserting crime in the sense the true masochist asserts it, as the thing which makes the criminal deserve to be humiliated and punished[5].

Simone de Beauvoir points out that narration is for Sade more piquant and criminal than action, pornography than debauch; not

[1] *The Greeks And The Irrational*, VI
[2] Simone de Beauvoir: *Must We Burn De Sade?*, p. 63
[3] *Must We Burn De Sade?*, p. 19
[4] *Must We Burn Da Sade?*, pp. 55-6   [5] *Must We Burn De Sade?*, p. 35

only is narrative his own preferred method of expression, but his heroes echo it, and commit one crime by describing their crimes before they commit a second by acting them[1]. This predilection for narrative is, I think, a sign that Sade's fictional fantasies grew out of masturbation fantasies: and in those masturbation fantasies mentioned by Freud[2], which make it a condition of their sadistic images that the imaginary victim shall not be really damaged, we can discover the psychological vindication for another of Simone de Beauvoir's perceptions about Sade, namely that it is a mistake to think that his ultimate erotic objective was murder[3]. It is true that Sade's heroes sometimes have recourse to it, but, as Simone de Beauvoir points out, they do so because murder is the greatest of crimes. In other words, they arrive at it, like Leopold and Loeb, unsensually: and in their creator's letting them come to that point we can detect the weariness of the masturbator; their destructiveness is really Sade's self-destructiveness.

Sade cannot, in fact, play the torturer without admitting a measure of sympathy and self-identification with his victim; and his chosen medium of narrative allows him to inhabit both sides of the relationship. The unitive purpose of Eros is never wholly defeated, because in Sade's conception the torturer and victim tend towards what Simone de Beauvoir calls a genuine couple[4]. Sade is aware that the torturer's real crime will be not simply to inflict pain but to seduce and corrupt the victim into being his accomplice and wanting pain to be inflicted. The relationship comes close to being a game which the partners know is a game—it approaches the sharing of a masturbation fantasy.

Thus Sade was unable to prepare either himself or the eighteenth century for an eruption of Thanatos that was no game, in which, so far as the conscious could perceive, there was not the least hint of voluptuousness in the executioners or of complicity in the victims. Sade, himself a revolutionary, was shocked by the Revolution and imprisoned by it for being too moderate. We are still less humanitarian than he insofar as we can contemplate a more or less naked Thanatos without shock, and condemn it only when it is allied to so strong a force of Eros that we cannot avoid noticing its voluptuous character. Scenes where people are killed 'cleanly' though none the less agonisingly call forth no censorship; Sade's fictions we regard as obscene

[1] *Must We Burn De Sade?*, p. 47   [2] *Collected Papers*, Volume II, XVII
[3] *Must We Burn De Sade?*, p. 43   [4] *Must We Burn De Sade?*, p. 84

because his heroes insist on inflicting pleasure on their victim before
or actually as the concomitant of inflicting pain. We have driven the
prostitutes off the street and invited the soldiers to parade through it.

Although Thanatos appeared without any fusion to voluptuousness,
it was carried into expression in alliance with self-love. It shewed, as
it were, through the cracks between nation and nation and individual
and individual, and seemed at first merely to reveal self-love in what
appeared to be the truer light of a dissociative rather than unitive
force. In Hellas the question seemed to be whether the self-interest of
Athens could any longer pose as the education of minor states which
Athens had to keep down by force; the Spartans took on the paradoxical colour of the champions of freedom, just as the European powers,
having set out with the reactionary intention of punishing the French
Revolution for daring to liberate itself from a king, ended by defending
the civil liberties of the world against an emperor. The breakdown
of Athenian democracy and the dissolution of the Revolution in the
Terror seemed to prove the anarchical results of so many unchecked
self-loves contending with one another. The world took fright at
the enlightenment's bold admission that the nomoi which control
the individual are actually set up by himself in his own interest. Thus
Greek rationalism, as Professor Dodds says, while it did not 'enable
men to behave like beasts', did enable them 'to justify their brutality
to themselves'[1]. It was the same situation which horrified Sade:
'The Terror, which was being carried out with a clear conscience,
constituted the most radical negation of de Sade's demoniacal
world'[2].

The conscience of the Terror was, however, only as clear as the conscience of the Inquisition. The nomoi which admit to being man-
made are neither more nor less liable to subversion than the canons
which claim to come from God but are really invented by man; and
we stand not the smallest chance of arming them against their overthrow until we recognise Thanatos as well as Eros in the forces that
create them. The anarchy of conflicting self-loves in which the enlightenment ends is, in fact, a perfectly concerted social movement
towards self-destruction, which has merely taken advantage of the
desire to preserve oneself which is all that presents itself to consciousness. Athens is determined to lose not merely her civil liberties but
the war; the men who perpetrate the Terror are not such fools that

[1] *The Greeks And The Irrational*, VI
[2] Simone de Beauvoir: *Must We Burn De Sade?*, p. 26

they cannot see the dangers to their own lives and power. The Revolution was bent on creating the situation where Napoleon had to stop the Revolution and put himself in its place, where the will of the people had to re-incarnate the murdered king in a hero and set up a new supernatural revelation, the vulgar little Napoleonic version of the heroic myth, in place of the realistic Ego-values of the enlightenment. In this case the hero, unlike the king, did not even believe his own myth. Napoleon's view of human psychology was exactly that of the enlightenment, namely that everyone is motivated by self-love, and he set cynically out to manipulate other people's self-love in order to prosper his own. In the end, however, it was he who was manipulated, not by anyone's self-love but by everyone's self-destructiveness. He was forced to become a merchant of death on a larger scale than even his egoism would have spontaneously commanded, and on a much larger scale than his egoism *could* have commanded had it not been reinforced by the will of the people: his egoism became the tool of his subjects' determination to destroy themselves.

10. *From Reaction to Reaction*

The reaction began while the enlightenment was still in progress. The current flows both ways in Euripides: compared with Socrates, he takes a philosophically retrogressive step; but to Aristophanes, who had gone so much further into reaction, Euripides appeared in retrospect as an irresponsible sceptic teaching people to experience and question everything[1].

(Aristophanes, it is interesting to notice, is judging art on behalf of the reaction by precisely the same criterion as the enlightenment used: its social results. When he stages the posthumous contest between Aeschylus and Euripides in the Underworld, he has both poets agree that a poet is to be judged by whether his poetry performs a public service by producing better citizens[2], and he has each poet claim that his poetry did just that. Euripides, it is true, claims that he made people better citizens by teaching them to talk freely, to which Aeschylus [whose own claim rests on his having made the citizens eager to fight for their country] replies that it would have been better if he hadn't. Euripides, who is made to speak on behalf of the

[1] *Frogs*, 971 foll.   [2] *Frogs*, 1006 foll.

enlightenment, unwittingly exposes the practical weakness of the enlightenment's attitude to art: once it has agreed to justify art only by its social utility, the enlightenment has subscribed in principle to the censorship a Napoleon or a Catholic Church practises on precisely those grounds.)

In the event, the Greek enlightenment was not extinguished with the débâcle of democracy and the defeat of Athens, even though the reaction reached a howling climax at that time in the manifestations Professor Dodds[1] has summarised: prosecutions of enquiring minds, Socrates only one among several, on charges of atheism and religious subversion; outbreaks of superstitious panic in the community; the return to currency not only of extravagant religious cults and claims but also of magic and witchcraft themselves. Even when reaction had become the prevailing climate, there was still time for the religio-rationalist synthesis (or contradiction), the effort to capsulate the enlightenment within the folds of a state-priesthood's robes, which Professor Dodds calls 'Plato's attempt to stabilise the situation'. If Plato's was rearguard rationalism, rationalism already defeated, it is the more remarkable that it was later still, in the very embers of the enlightenment, that Plato's favourite pupil produced the firmest achievement of the whole enlightened movement and, by systematically observing and collecting the material and then classifying it, founded half a dozen studies and sciences, including the science of logical classification.

Political pressures deprived the enlightenment of its historical and social coherence, and it was fragmented by religious persecution (not always unallied to political persecution); Athens brought the now customary charge of impiety against Aristotle, too. If the spirit of enquiry and instruction survived so long, it was because the man of destiny does not always come prompt upon his hour. The persecution remained as sporadic as it had made the enlightenment. No one had yet systematised anti-logic and intellectual anarchy, and no one had yet disciplined the dis-sociative forces of Thanatos into a death machine. Athenian demagogues, Spartan admirals, Theban generals, Sicilian tyrants were all proposed or proposed themselves for the rôle of hero of Hellas, and failed. Plato himself, whose writings had endowed the reaction with a theoretical constitution, was posthumously pressed into personal service; a faction proposed that he was a son of Apollo and perhaps even accorded him the cult of a

[1] *The Greeks And The Irrational*, VI

god[1]; and his being sold—or at least his being believed to have been sold—as a slave is the germ of a saviour religion, the motif of the hero descending into abjection (dying a criminal's death, going down into the Underworld or, by actually committing a crime, descending into the social Underworld of the criminal classes) before rising again as a deified hero. Even so, Plato, like the other candidates, failed to consolidate the heroic status. It took sixty-eight years[2] to replace the nomoi by a revelation, and to offer Hellas a pattern of heroic valour in place of the liberal education once offered it by Athens. (The hero was another reputed son of a god, and came to Hellas, as Napoleon did to France, from the position of a semi-foreigner.) Aristotle was forty-one when, anticipating the fashion of the eighteenth-century intellectuals, he took up his appointment as tutor to a boy of thirteen and thus helped to make Alexander what Napoleon was, a child of the enlightenment who, as the hero always does, eclipsed his parent.

The agony Hellas underwent in procuring itself a master was matched by the convulsive experience of Rome. It would not be fair to contrast the eleven years in which France progressed from rejecting a monarch to re-incarnating him in an emperor with the centuries Rome took about the same transition, because the French enlightenment had spiritually emancipated itself from the king long before it could physically budge him, and the Romans did not expel the father-principle from their political life until long after they had expelled their kings. The Roman state, as Mommsen discerned[3], was an expansion of the patriarchal household, in which absolute power belonged to the paterfamilias. The effect of expelling the monarchy was only to make the state's paterfamilias many-headed, in the form of the patrician class. The political, juridical and ecclesiastical authority which had been attached to the office of king was split up among the magistracies of the republican constitution and its legislative assembly, the Senate; but the magistracies and the Senate were the expression exclusively of the patrician class, which practised a remarkable egalitarianism within its own rank[4] but excluded the proletariat from all

[1] E. R. Dodds: *The Greeks And The Irrational*, VIII, note 36; VII, note 9

[2] from the capitulation of Athens in 404 B.C. to Alexander's accession to the throne of Macedon in 336 B.C.

[3] *History Of Rome*, I, V

[4] Mommsen argues that the internal egalitarianism of the patricians was already established under the monarchy, and that the king was in effect only a president, in whom the patricians vested their power for reasons of efficiency,

political rights and powers whatsoever. The patrician class in effect became the absolute monarch of Rome; and its egalitarianism, combined with the system of annual magistracies, with, at the top, a double consulate wherein each consul could check his colleague, was designed to make its many heads speak with a single, patriarchal voice.

The primal father had thus been replaced by, and had become immortal in, the self-renewing powers not of a single royal line but of the whole patrician class, which was more truly self-renewing than a king can be, since it could—and did—marry only within itself. The sons of Rome were divided into a self-perpetuating elder brother, the patriciate, and a perpetually disinherited younger brother, the plebs. The patricians, as their name implied (and likewise the name of the Senate and the senators, and the senators' title *patres*), constituted an everlasting elder generation in the state, to which the perpetually younger generation could never succeed; and the incest barrier between the generations was formalised as the law forbidding intermarriage between the classes. The function of the plebs was merely to fill out[1] the state. The status of the plebs was proletarian;

but who remained no more than their equal in rank. In this case, we can surmise that the patricians themselves represented a group of brothers who had once overthrown a primal father. The king no doubt represents an attempt on the part of one brother to replace the primal father; but the others rejected him, as they had the right to do, and proceeded not so much to establish as to re-establish a republic. The ineradicable and politically important abhorrence the Romans always felt towards a monarchy was perhaps originally provoked by the primal father, whose person was later blotted out from their historical memory; the abhorrence of him, however, survived; but it became attached to the kings who had in fact failed to become tyrants and who therefore hardly seem to deserve the odium which pursued them. After the failure of the king, there were no more attempts from among the patrician class itself to single-out a Big Brother; and the reason for this was the growth of Rome, which had added a whole new population *below* the patricians; with the result that the patricians, while still maintaining fraternity among themselves, had en bloc replaced the primal father in relation to the rest of the community. The hero who singled himself out and emerged from their revolution was in fact the great instrument of their political power, the Senate.

[1] *plebs* from root PLE-, fill (Lewis): '. . . the "multitude" (*plebes*, from *pleo, plenus*), as they were termed negatively with reference to their want of political rights . . .' (Mommsen: *History Of Rome*, I, VI)

that is, it supplied the state with children[1]—children who could never, in the political sense, grow up. The patricians, on the other hand, based their title on their being the heirs to the father, the replacement of the paternal stock; they were the sons who *did* grow up, who took over the father's position; and they even withheld from the proletariat the right to a fully legal marriage, so that they might treat the whole proletariat as bastards disinherited in the state[2].

What the patricians arrogated to themselves were all the constitutional rights which are expansions and adaptations of the earliest constitutional right in history, the father's right to the mother and the whole female sex. This prerogative, the right to fertilise the female and dispose of the produce, is asserted by a landowning patriciate over the mother in her territorial manifestation—as the land which feeds all the citizens. The father's claim is that 'he plough'd her, and she cropp'd'; he alone is the husbandman; and presently he extends his claim to the political rights which develop out of the possession of land. Thus it comes to be the state itself, the public thing, the respublica, which represents the communal mother; and while this common parentage lays social and national obligations on all the children the patricians claim that they alone, representing the father, are legally married to the republic and thus own the right to govern it.

Even after the republic had been established in name, Rome was not a republic but a patriarchy, and the primal struggle between father and sons over the mother had still to be fought in the contest between patriciate and proletariat over constitutional rights. Perhaps it was the sharpness of the struggle at home, and an unconscious attempt to unite the two classes against common enemies, which forced the Roman community into military expansion; and as soon as the military nature of the state had been established, the proletarians could assert their indispensability as soldiers and use the proletarian weapon of the strike[3] to procure their first political rights. They had to work at first through a system of apartheid, aiming at recognition for their own separate assembly and separate magistracies; but once

[1] ' "children-producers", *proletarii*' (Mommsen: *History Of Rome*, I, VI); *proletarius* (from *proles*, progeny) 'affording the state only children' (Lewis)

[2] 'the Roman burgesses assumed the name of the "fathers' children" (*patricii*), inasmuch as they alone in the eyes of the law had a father' (Mommsen: *History Of Rome*, I, V)

[3] the secession of the plebs, 494 B.C., by which the plebs achieved the creation of the tribunate

they had achieved those, they used them to break down the legal barrier to intermarriage between patricians and plebians, and to win their entrance into the Senate and the magistracies of the whole community. Only when they had done this was the republic achieved in fact. A sort of democracy held all the sons together under the matriarchal tutelage of the republic, embodied in the city of Rome and personified in its warlike goddess Bellona.

The democracy was caught up first in Italian and then in the Punic Wars which constantly suggested to it, as the Peloponnesian War did to Athenian democracy, the need for an authoritarian military commander. From there it was inveigled into imperialist expansion, and the existence of the empire at once began to cry out for an emperor. No one planned the acquisition of the empire, and many Romans opposed it even while it was happening; it was undertaken perhaps as the only action which could conceal the still bitter class feud and, indeed, the only positive move permitted by the carefully-designed conservatism of the constitution. But each fresh acquisition increased the administrative difficulties of the politicians; and each fresh campaign created a new occasion of class struggle with the repeated demand of the veteran soldiers for land. The republic, who possessed a strong character but, unlike Athens, few intellectual principles, was longing for one of her sons to single himself out and marry and master her. Her first sketches for the hero, the brothers Gracchus (personally the sons of a matriarch full of republican virtue), made use of the new political power of the plebs; but after their failure, the republic turned regularly to the political power of the plebeians considered as soldiers and applied to any man who had an army behind him. For the rest of the republic's agonisingly drawn-out life, Roman politics played with the idea of a coup d'état consisting of a march on Rome by a general returning from extending or defending the empire; and the feeling that emperors were to be made by armies lasted into the imperial period. The state tried Marius, Sulla and Pompey in turn, all of whom failed it through awe or fear of the republic (in Sulla's case, an ancien-régime patrician republic). Only after throwing itself into a convulsive civil war did the republic prevail on Julius Caesar to master it, and then the defenders of the republic assassinated him, provoking another civil war before Augustus could be finally established, a century after the murder of his forerunner Caius Gracchus.

Augustus (and still less Alexander, who did not cope at all with the problem of making himself immortal in a dynasty, a problem which *was* overcome, though only clumsily, at Rome) did not put a stop to the malaise of the world. To do that required a more radical hero, capable of actually destroying a whole culture. In the longest view, the decline of the civilisation of the ancient world dates from the traumatic effect of rationalism's failure at Athens. The 'fear of freedom' and 'the return of the irrational', which Professor Dodds[1] describes as following on the collapse of rationalism, merges into the state of mind of the first century A.D., when, in Freud's[2] words, the consciousness of guilt 'was no longer restricted to the Jews; it had seized all Mediterranean peoples as a vague discomfort, a premonition of misfortune the reason for which no one knew'. There were of course arrests in the process of decline and even temporary ascents half way up the hill again, revivals imported often enough by the very conquerors, censors and authoritarians who are really the enemies of freedom; the world time and again put itself into a state where we must count as a progressive anyone capable of restoring order and public energy. But the whole picture is of civilisation imploring the coup de grâce which was finally administered by Christianity.

Both Freud and Professor Dodds remark that to account for the end of the ancient world in terms of the decadence or the ageing of its civilisation is merely to label the symptoms without explaining them. And in fact a civilisation is, precisely, a thing which is immune to ageing; the device of cultural heredity is Eros's greatest triumph over Thanatos. Our research for something which *made* ancient civilisation become decadent will never find its object, because it rests on the Socratic fallacy that a civilisation, like an individual, must want to remain alive and vigorous. This is to ignore guilt, the great hinge which admits Thanatos into our social relations. Civilisation is built on society's primary guilt for having deposed the primal father, which was the method whereby citizens first advanced into individual psychology. The hidden tendency of civilisation is towards making amends by setting up a new father and sacrificing to him the individuality which was won by deposing the old. This unconscious lust to sacrifice the self has all the reserves of Thanatos to draw on; the forces which seem to be fighting a local engagement for this person's self-advancement here and that person's there are really employed in a concerted bombardment against the self of civilisation. We fail to account for the decadence of the ancient world for the same reason that

[1] *The Greeks And The Irrational*, VIII   [2] *Moses And Monotheism*, III, II, 8

the ancient world itself failed to arrest it: it neglected to read its own symptoms, its premonitions of misfortune, as evidence of its own unconscious resolution to be misfortunate.

The lust to destroy the self develops as an attack on the values of the Ego. It lays low the nomoi by which the Ego governs itself; it fractures rationality, which is the Ego's instrument of self-defence, and, not satisfied with sporadic and tolerant irrationality, it creates and compulsorily imposes a system of irrationality. It was these new elements of absolute nontoleration and of systematic doublethink which Christianity introduced to the chaotic superstitiousness of the ancient world, proposing a faith whose glory was its illogicality. (By the fifth century[1], when the orthodox core of the Church had to meet the arguments not only of disbelievers but of heretics, it had become necessary to set out the contradictions of the Christian faith in the systematic logical form adopted by the Athanasian Creed.) Having proclaimed itself anti-rational, putting forward its illogicality as its greatest claim on man's allegiance, and announcing also its opposition to such other fruits of the enlightenment as sensuous enjoyment, self-love and unrestricted sexual pleasure, Christianity had only to wait for all the forces campaigning against civilisation to enlist under its labarum. The 'miracle' cited by Christians, whereby the faith of a tiny Jewish sect grew into the religion of the world, is really a miracle the other way about, the wonder being that Christianity took so long to establish itself and that the fragments of civilisation held out against it so stubbornly.

As Freud remarked[2], it was a Jew, St. Paul, who, by drawing on the peculiar relationship of Jewish culture to the image of the father, was able to give a theologico-mythical shape to the sense of guilt and the desire for self-destruction, by explaining to the Mediterranean world that its malaise had been caused by mankind's sin against God the Father, and persuading it to channel its self-destructiveness into the form of sacrificing the self to him. But if St. Paul provided the myth, it was Plato who had long before foreseen the social form the attack against culture must take. It was a blueprint for Catholic Christendom which he drew up with his programme of banning the arts, prosecuting free thought, and imposing a compulsory religion. The terrifying passage Professor Dodds[3] quotes from the *Laws*

[1] A. E. Burn (*An Introduction To The Creeds* . . ., VI, VI) dates the Athanasian Creed to 420-430

[2] *Moses And Monotheism*, III, II, 8

[3] 942, A-B (*The Greeks And The Irrational*, VII, note 44)

The principal thing is that none, man or woman, should ever be without an officer set over him, and that none should get the mental habit of taking any step, whether in earnest or in jest, on his individual responsibility . . . in a word, we must train the mind not even to consider acting as an individual or know how to do it

is a prevision of the spiritual surveillance that was to be practised by Christianity. The Ego renounces its own relation to reality, becomes as a little child and places its hand (via a hierarchy) in the hand of the parent. The Ego's expiatory regression from individual psychology back into group psychology is what we mark by the end of the ancient world and the start of the dark ages. The Ego really is doing its best to go back on its acquisition of consciousness; by destroying the common historical memories and the common artistic and scientific consciousness which are embodied in a culture, the dark ages really do impose restrictions on individual consciousness. The lesson of antiquity is that, if our psychological ignorance affords them cover, our impulses of self-destruction, our hatred of culture, our preference for sleep rather than consciousness, all working through guilt, really are capable of destroying a civilisation.

Guilt, however, is the trapdoor which admits Eros as well as Thanatos; if it is through guilt that we destroy civilisations, it is also through guilt that we direct our destructive impulses to holding down the impulses of the Id and thus raise ourselves into consciousness and society into culture. The uniqueness of man among the animals is that his instincts are not capable of being satisfied by a given pattern of gratification. The situation of a human being is never tolerable—which is why mankind is doomed to have a history.

With the invention of the Christian religion, a sizeable and more or less cut-off section of the human race seemed to have taken to itself an infallibly efficient mechanism for allaying the primal guilt of humanity by sacrificing a good part of its human consciousness. However, being irremediably psychic animals, Christians were incapable of achieving, under the Catholic hierarchy, the instinctual equilibrium achieved by ants and bees in the hierarchy imposed by their species. Christianity could not do what we are perhaps capable of doing today, namely put a stop to the human race itself (though in its first passion for chastity and its expectation of an immediate second coming, it almost threatened to); with the result that the necessary ambivalence of a psychic being towards the father to whom all these sacrifices had been made was bound to assert itself. The guilt-allaying mechanism turned out to be not so efficient. The people who were the worst oppressed by a sense of guilt and unworthiness were not the sinners but the pious and the saintly, the leaders of blameless lives, who had avoided all offence, who had most thoroughly sacrificed reason and sunk themselves deepest in the dream of faith. Neither were they wrong, psychologically considered, the Christian myth being actually wrought of the filial ambivalence whose guilt it allays. The saint could signal his devotion to God only by meditations which were in fact voluptuous daydreams of assassinating God; he could discharge his debt to God and at the same time take comfort from God only through a sacrament consisting of a cannibal assault on God: with the result that the more he expiated his original sin, the more he became aware of a guilt which he had incurred by his unrecognised secondary sin.

Once this oppressive character in Christianity made its weight felt, it was inevitable that the hostility to Christ which had always been concealed in the religion would eventually be forced into the open and would attack Christianity itself in an attempt to shift the oppression of guilt. The first revolts were acts of rebellion and acts of mental individuality, rather than assertions that rebellion and mental individuality were right. Consciousness re-asserted itself through works of art—often Christian, but tacitly claiming an artistic value quite independent of their religious import. These artistic values were gathered together, explicitly recognised and coherently arranged during the renaissance, which restored to society an aesthetic consciousness that had been dead since antiquity. The renaissance not only was artistic; it knew it was artistic. Art had in fact secularised itself even while much of its subject matter and the intentions of many artists remained Christian. Even so, the aesthetic consciousness was, strictly speaking, only paraChristian, though it at once challenged Christianity to a comparison. Philosophy did not achieve secularisation until the seventeenth century; and it was only in the eighteenth that culture, which had been committing acts of rebellion against the group mind ever since its rebirth, was able to propound an explicitly antiChristian philosophy of emancipation.

The emancipation was nothing less than culture's coherent consciousness of itself. It was this consciousness which was stunned by the French Revolution. Our history since then has been the history of our dizziness from the blow; it is not yet decided whether we will choose to give up consciousness wholly and finally.

11. *Disenlightenment*[1]

Rationalism's one certainty, the benevolent nature of man, having been refuted, the world leapt back in fright into an irrational faith first in a superman and, when he proved destructible, in God. English Protestants, who had nothing more irrational to retreat into than the mild contradictions of the Church of England (which in many cases had not made too great demands even on the faith of the enlightenment), had to build up the numinous defences of their Church by gothicising its decorations and Catholicising its theology and ceremonial. Even this did not afford sufficient protection, and by the time of the Oxford Movement dozens of them were leaping one after the other out of their own shallow trench into the deeper irrationalism offered by the Catholic Church. Even those already entrenched in Catholicism had felt the panic impulse to dig deeper still. The faith into which John Henry Newman was received in 1845 was already much more passionately irrational, and much more positively self-sacrificial towards authority, than the quiet Catholic piety, with its resignation to authority, for which many believers had bravely suffered during the Revolution; and it was not until 1870 that the Catholic Church reached the abyss of the anti-rational panic started by the Revolution, and explicitly declared the infallibility of the Pope. Similarly in politics: the Revolution frightened Europe first into reaction as a temporary expedient, like the dictatorship of Napoleon, and then into a reaction that had become habitual, a mere automatic gesture of repression against the mob whose nature had revealed itself in the Revolution. The bourgeoisie had decided to turn its ever-increasing power *against* the proletariat. Aesthetically it embraced philistinism, a no-aesthetic; its rebels expressed themselves through romanticism: rebels and philistines alike opposed themselves to the age of reason and taste.

Immediately after the débâcle there were still elements of the French enlightenment which refused to draw what seemed to most French people the obvious and immediate conclusion, Napoleon: but even they were fully aware of what had been lost. The sight of the mob which penetrated the Tuileries, wrote Madame de Staël, 'could for

[1] the romantic salvation preached by Zacharias Werner (J. Christopher Herold: *Mistress To An Age*, 16)

ever destroy the respect which the human race should inspire'. Her friend François de Pange described himself as refusing to admit that there was 'any necessary connection between abstract ideas and murder'.[1]

In other words, eighteenth-century rationalism was revealed for what it really had been all along, an act of faith, based on a gigantic psychic repression. Voltaire's and Gibbon's inability to explain the irrational was now complicated by the rationalists' inability to explain their own rationalism. The rationalist faith had previously been a positive assertion: now it became a mere obstinate refusal, and took up an embattled position. Moreover, it was embattled not simply through being outnumbered by irrationalism, which it probably always had been, but because progress had deserted it. The people who expanded the consciousness of Europe during the nineteenth century did so from within the reaction. They took paths which led away from society and which the main body of the reaction, the philistine bourgeoisie, condemned as perverse and wicked; but if they offended the new respectable régime, they would equally have offended the old eighteenth-century culture, by turning into individual byways inaccessible to the broad philosophical front of the enlightenment. Madame de Staël was already a little old-fashioned as soon as the Revolution had taken place—though as a matter of fact she was later able to retrieve her position: thanks to her liberal and old-fashioned obstination against Napoleon, she was able to skip the reaction's first tentative phase and pioneer the form in which it was to endure, romanticism. Towards the end of her life she and her friends were toying with the whole irrational gamut, to which she had introduced herself by way of German romanticism: Catholicism, occultism, the more openly erotic types of mysticism and what Socrates-Plato would have described as (Professor Dodds's translation) 'the blessings of madness'.

Madame de Staël herself did not wholly surrender to any of these— or perhaps it was already a case of could not. As the nineteenth century continued and the reaction dug itself more deeply in, the position of the rationalists was increasingly that of people who, to their own regret, could not be vanquished. The defensive tone of rationalism towards religion and a society built on religious conventions deepened into an (in the modern sense) apologetic tone. The enlightenment had treated loss of faith as cheerfully as the loss of a toothache and had

[1] J. Christopher Herold: Mistress To An Age, 7; 10

proselytized, passing on the cure, wherever it could. The Victorian age produced a crop of uneasy agnostics, major and minor Matthew Arnolds and Leslie Stephens, who treated their loss of faith as a tragedy which had left a vacuum behind. The effect of their bereavement was to make them abstain, like mourners, from society. They bound themselves to a paralysed ineffectuality by vowing that they would no more infect other people with their own painful disbelief than tamper with the innocence of children. It was this attitude which set the fashion, which society still follows for self-interested motives, for nonbelievers to expose children to the contamination of religion with a sense of thereby doing something moral.

Rationalism was, in psychic fact, in mourning: it was expiating the sins of the Terror. In atonement, the survivals of the enlightenment sacrificed the enlightenment's first fruit, the pursuit of happiness. To enjoy a day's happiness in the unreligious state would have seemed to them to re-murder all the victims of the guillotine. Whereas Madame de Staël (following what was only, after all, the aristocratic fashion of the ancien régime) had flouted conventions and flaunted her lovers, her Victorian successors embraced the discomfort of the notion that they were penitents on probation, their spiritual condition an acute purgatory. Their conduct was meant to avoid bringing worse disrepute on a faith the Revolution had already covered with opprobrium: it was a long demonstration that, if they dispensed with the Bible in taking their oath, they were none the less as scrupulous and truthful as the pious; if they dispensed with marriage, their unmarried couples could outdo the respectable in respectability. The people who really flouted the Victorian proprieties did so not in the name of free thought but in the service of a private God; the erotic mystics petted by Madame de Staël had more than one Victorian descendant.

A good part of Victorian rationalism was thus not a continuation of the enlightenment but a particular, neutralised version of the reaction against it. Guilt and self-punishment had here taken the form not of sacrificing reason but of binding it immobile. The rationalist's purgatory was the nightmare sensation of the body's being paralysed while the mind goes on working; and, like that sensation when it occurs in a dream[1], the rationalist's anxiety signified a conflict of will, in which the censored and inadmissible wish was his desire to be swept away by one of the currents of the reaction.

[1] Freud: *The Interpretation Of Dreams*, VI (D)

Those currents had developed in force out of what had been under-currents in the enlightenment. Napoleon himself was no more than a one-man élite, cut off from the rational consent of the governed but still supported on popular faith. His programme was merely to impose by the sword, the police and the Code Napoléon the cultural uniformity which the enlightenment had already informally spread over Europe by means of liberal education. In itself, even his personal absolutism might not have been displeasing to Voltaire, who, having noticed a tendency in democracies to put philosophers to death, had preferred to cast himself as Aristotle to an Alexander, and had put his faith in the benevolence of enlightened despots rather than of mankind at large. Voltaire would never have incurred the reproach which Dr Johnson brought against a far more radical progressive, Alexander Pope, that he 'nursed in his mind a foolish dis-esteem of Kings'[1]. (Dr Johnson himself represents one of the points where the enlighten-ment responds to the tug of a counter-enlightenment flowing out of sight below. If we can penetrate his immense Englishness, we come on the surprising discovery of a Plato in him; he has some of Plato's fraught but refined emotionalism; and something of Plato's attempt 'to stabilise the situation' is repeated in Dr Johnson's attempt to fix on a quality of common sense and mental soundness which he can oppose on the one hand to reason and on the other to the extremes which have not yet revealed themselves but which he senses irration-alism to be capable of.) But whereas the enlightenment had created a new catholicism, on the basis of the self-evident benevolence of a deified Nature, Napoleon had to fall back on the old supernatural Catholicism and even on the old aristocracies and monarchies. He would thereby have forfeited his claim in Voltaire's eyes to be en-lightened, though Voltaire might have approved the cynicism with which he manipulated the Pope and the royal houses. One again, however, what Napoleon proposed cynically other people accepted sincerely. The world not only swallowed the Napoleonic myth; it swallowed the Catholic myth with which he had bolstered his own: and long after Napoleon had vanished, the Church retained, and actually increased, its power over the mind.

Napoleon, in fact, like the deified Augustus, was too rational a deity to satisfy his worshippers' lust. His divinity was too evidently a human creation, since its continuance depended on his continuing to be able to work miracles on the field of battle; even his victoriousness

[1] Boswell, 1781

was supplied through the visible device of conscription: he never became powerful enough to safeguard his power by promulgating the law that the people were not to tempt the lord their god. The lust for unreason demanded an illusion in which the strings that supported the puppet could not be seen; and for this the enlightenment, even in its Napoleonic version, and the classical antiquity it reflected, were too bright.

The solution the world adopted was a plunge away from the antique and into the old: out of the Age of Reason and back into the ages of faith. The world ran out of the sunlight into the obscurity of the Gothic, an obscurity whose only illuminations were oblique, opaque and tinted by stained glass, creating an atmosphere where illusions shaped and suggested themselves to the mind without anyone having to produce them by theatrical mechanisms.

As a matter of fact, even while it looked as though Napoleon might still be the saviour instead of the èclipse of the Revolution, and even while the French constitution was reviving the names and forms of the Roman republic, fashion had already begun to set classical antiquity aside. The vogue Napoleon brought home from his Egyptian campaign was for a Romanised Egyptian, but the Roman dress was thin enough to shew the images of another type of antique culture—one which, so far from being reasonable and enlightened, was barbaric, cruel and authoritarian. This brief Egyptianising vogue, which vanished with Napoleon, constitutes, like Napoleon himself, the transition between the eighteenth and the nineteenth century.

Considered as a manifestation of the eighteenth century, this vogue was simply one finger of the long arm of the taste for the exotic, whose other fingers had already reached Pompeii, India and China. English architecture, which kept to the eighteenth-century course through and beyond the era of Napoleon, was still expressing the pure exoticism of the enlightenment when it assembled the motifs of chinoiserie beneath the minarets of a Turkish encampment: the splendid beauty which Nash and the Prince Regent achieved with their full-scale Pavilion at Brighton preserves an unbroken line of feeling from 1716, when Effner and the Elector Max Emanuel began to build their tiny pavilion, the Pagodenburg[1], the most exquisite monument of the exotic.

The taste for the exotic was itself a development of the picaresque spirit, which first of all simply had, and presently was intended to

[1] at Schloss Nymphenburg, Bavaria

have, the effect of making European institutions look less absolute and inevitable by shewing them juxtaposed with outlandish. The lesson was that civilised moeurs were no more reasonable than uncivilised ones. Even when the taste for the exotic had begun to *like* outlandish motifs for their own sakes, the point of the comparison was still being made: the exotic style created not only chinoiserie but singeries. But just as the eighteenth century came to envy the animals their freedom, so it came to envy men who had not been tamed by civilisation; and the cult of Nature intervened in the argument to suggest that uncivilised men, being more natural, were actually *more* reasonable than civilised men, and, in consequence, better.

The spectacle of the Revolution discredited Reason but not Nature. Wordsworth was preaching exactly the same doctrine of salvation through a return to Nature as Pope had preached before him. (Wordsworth, like Socrates, paid his homage to the natural by insisting on an everyday vocabulary.) What had been dropped from the argument was the belief that Nature was reasonable and orderly. Uncivilisation was still thought more natural, and consequently still thought better, than civilisation; but now it was thought better precisely because it was *less* reasonable. The creeping hostility which the eighteenth century had manifested towards culture was now brought into the open: it was from the arguments of the eighteenth century that the reaction drew fuel for its bid to sweep away culture, including the eighteenth century's consciousness of culture.

The moment Nature ceased to imply Reason as a necessary consequence, classical antiquity lost its exclusive and necessary function. It could no longer be argued that the return to Nature must go by way of Horace's country villa and Theocritus's idyllic shepherds; that is the precise difference between Wordsworth's pursuit of Nature and Pope's. The Napoleonic Egyptian vogue belongs to the nineteenth century inasmuch as it lets something unclassical shew through; but as soon as the nineteenth-century spirit developed in force it swept the Egyptian away, because its dress was still too classical. Egypt might have survived the taint of being associated with Napoleon (indeed, that association, when Napoleon had become a respectable, ancestral martyr, led to the anomalous revival of his sphinxes and eagles in a Victorian setting) but it could not live down the fact that it had been Romanised. The nineteenth century found nearer home a reservoir of the barbarian and the irrational which had the advantage that it had never been incorporated in the Roman Empire, with the result that its language remained unlatinised, and its syntax, thought and institutions unlegalised and unlogicalised.

When Napoleon exiled the French enlightenment from France, he virtually forced it—again in the person of Madame de Staël—to explore Germany. But as a matter of fact Voltaire had already, at the very height of the enlightenment in the seventeen-thirties, regarded the passion for geometry and physics which was sweeping Paris as a sort of Germanisation. 'Sentiment, imagination and the graces are banished', he wrote. 'If a man who had lived under Louis XIV were to come back to earth he would no longer recognise the French; he would think the Germans had conquered this country'[1]. To be conquered by the Germans, in one sense or the other, was in fact the future history of France. Madame de Staël's duel-flirtation with German culture in 1803-4, and her return home with a booty of German philosophy and German philosophers destined to conquer her, adumbrated the interpenetration between the two cultures which has constituted the history of Europe ever since. The duel was renewed in three Franco-German wars, in which it would be hard to say which side was more deeply enamoured of the other or which was imitating the glamorous militarism and nationalism of which. Napoleon found his most efficient imitator in Hitler, who conquered, though he did not suppress, France; and when Hitler's armies were at last expelled from France, it turned out that a large part of the French opposition to Hitler had in fact subscribed or succumbed to Hitler's glamour, since it at once set out to pursue military and imperialist glory on precisely the Napoleonic pattern which Hitler had been imitating, and even imitated directly from Hitler what had been his own contribution to the Napoleonic machine, the systematic use of torture.

Against this the intellectual section of the former Resistance firmly protested; but the intellectual climate out of which the protest came represented another victory in France for the glamour of German ideas. The philosophy which was carried into predominance by the French Resistance and the liberation had been borrowed by France, before the war[2], from Karl Jaspers and Martin Heidegger, who had themselves developed it from an original not merely extra-latin but

[1] Le sentiment, l'imagination et les grâces sont bannis. Un homme qui aurait vécu sous Louis XIV et qui reviendrait au monde ne reconnaîtrait plus les Français; il croirait que les Allemands ont conquis ce pays-ci. (Letter to M. de Cideville, from Paris, 16 April, 1735)

[2] Cf. Guido de Ruggiero: *Existentialism*

extra-German. Søren Kierkegaard was posthumously translated from an outpost to the centre of European culture: first to Germany, where he was unofficially canonised, and then on to France, where the French genius for parnassusisation, for turning authors into classics, has fixed him as the hero—the Oedipus-Hamlet[1]—of our age.

It was in Germany that the reaction first took on its Gothic character; it was German Catholicism to which Madame de Staël extended her sympathy, while continuing in her rationalist detestation of the French and French-Napoleonic versions. But once Germany had shewn it what to look for, the reaction noticed that all Europe had once been Catholic (and began in England to insist that the Church in England still was) and that all Northern Europe had once been Gothic. (Italy, where the Gothic buildings often did not look Gothic, was a more difficult case and had to wait for special interpretation by Ruskin.) The universal cry was raised to go back beyond the Age of Reason, perhaps even back to pre-Raphael (back, that is, to before Raphael sanctified the classical ideal)—back, in short, to Christendom.

12. *Gothick, Gothic and Vandal*

Here again the reaction had only to take up a strand which had run through the enlightenment. The eighteenth century had occasionally pastiched the architecture of medieval castles, expressing thereby a minor interest in the political irrationalities of feudalism; but the supernatural irrationalities of medieval Christianity (and its obverse, diabolism) excited it to a new genre, the Gothic novel of horrors, in which it revived subjects no one had thought about since John Webster,

[1] That he was Oedipus is clear from his relation to his father; that he was Hamlet from his relation (under the shadow of his filial relationship) to his Ophelia, Regine Olsen; that he was both from his Journals:—'I could perhaps reproduce the tragedy of my childhood, the terrifying, mysterious explanation of religion which a frightful foreboding played into my hands . . .—all in a novel called "the mysterious family". It would begin on a completely idyllic, patriarchal note so that no one suspected anything until suddenly the word sounded which translated everything into terror' (1843); 'It made a terrible impression on me the first time I heard that the *indulgences* contained the statement that they remit *all* sins: "*etiam si matrem virginem violasset*" ' (1837); 'If something is really to become depressing . . . it must lie in the family history. . . . That is why Hamlet is so tragic' (1837)

and to a pronounced ecclesiastico-Gothic strain in its architecture. That strain was manifested at Nymphenburg in a ruined hermitage[1] and was still being manifested a century later in the Monk's Cell which Sir John Soane added in 1824 to the idiosyncratic residence and monument he was compiling around himself in Lincoln's Inn Fields. In the last decade of the eighteenth century, *The Monk* had a success so great as to blot out the author's christian name[2] and get the novel read even by the anti-literate sporting public which Jane Austen satirised in John Thorpe[3]. Indeed, the entire enlightenment (and most idiosyncratically Alessandro Magnasco) was stiff with a delighted horror at the very idea—the very Gothic idea—of monks and nuns, whose morbid meditations on death and contemplations of deaths-heads were hardly more horrifying to it than their chastity. The frisson of terror imparted by the Gothic horror novel is only a very easily penetrated disguise for an erotic frisson (as Jane Austen implicitly recognises: she cures Catherine Morland's fit of the Gothic horrors by the same universal remedy she almost brutally prescribes for the emotional disorders which are subtly present in all her heroines, namely a man); and the ghostly celibates who stalk through the Gothic novels are really the same figures as the nuns whose profession Casanova accepted as a challenge to seduction.

Casanova, Sade and Don Giovanni (in his Mozart-da Ponte incarnation, on which Casanova himself wrote some improvements[4]), the three great destructive heroes of the eighteenth century (we should perhaps add Byron), are the precursors of romanticism. They are already caught, like true romantics, in the mother's tresses. Casanova is impelled to seduce nuns, Sade to combine blasphemy with his crimes of assault, by an infatuation with the woman whom paternal authority sets out of bounds—the same infatuation which makes the truly romantic Kierkegaard quicken his interest when he learns that the Church would absolve the guilt even of someone who had violated

[1] the Magdalenenklause which Effner built in 1725-8 (Nymphenburg, Official Guide)

[2] Matthew Gregory Lewis, called Monk Lewis

[3] *Northanger Abbey*, 7 (written in 1798-9)

[4] Alfred Einstein (*Mozart . . .*, 22): Casanova 'seems not to have been entirely satisfied with da Ponte, for among his papers there is preserved a new version for the text of the Sextet in the second act'.

the virgin mother[1]. The complete situation of the romantic, to find desirable only the one woman who is unattainable, was given expression when John Keats chose to treat the myth of Endymion's liaison with that inaccessible, virginal lady, 'the Queen-Moon'. But even before the romantic revolution, the sentimental revolution, led by Goethe and Laurence Sterne, had received intimations of an inaccessible eternal feminine (eternal, because she existed before her child, who is in love with her, was conceived; that is, she existed at a time inconceivable by him): and Sterne accidentally incorporated the essence of the romantic situation in a phrase struck off by the mere wandering association of his uncollected ideas, with surrealist irrelevance to his drift, 'I had an affair with the moon'[2].

Sterne, of course, tries to come down at once from the romantic heights by adding 'in which there was neither sin nor shame'. But in fact the idea of suffering is indispensable to the sentimental hero. Sterne is not yet prepared to admit that the hero suffers in punishment; still less to go the whole way with Keats and admit that the hero might be half in love with easeful death—or with the eternal easeful sleep which was Endymion's punishment: yet in the sentimentalists the enlightenment was already taking out its handkerchief and preparing to pay the price for having questioned and experienced everything by now being moved to tears by everything.

Not so Casanova-Sade-Don Giovanni. He remains an eighteenth-century hero, an assertion of the Ego and self-love. So far from falling in love with death and being prepared to kill off his Ego, he will not submit it even to the discomfort of a moment's remorse. It is true that his guerilla raids against society foreshadow the reaction's attack on the values of the Ego; but he is unwilling to loose his destructiveness directly on himself. All the same, his conduct is already working towards the romantic's end, self-destruction; but he does not know it is; and his self-destruction is brought about by his destruction of others, notably the women on whom he takes vengeance for the fact that they are not *the* woman (sometimes insulting them and making them superfluous by preferring boys or by taking the woman's part himself). His egoism and destructiveness are to this extent Napoleonic—or, rather, Napoleon is his utmost development. But he keeps one foot

[1] (Cf. the Journal for 1837 [the passage already quoted in a footnote to this chapter].) Luther also was shocked by this popular interpretation of the power of indulgences. (R. H. Fife: *The Revolt Of Martin Luther*, 14)

[2] *A Sentimental Journey* . . ., I

deeper in the eighteenth century than Napoleon, because he has not yet socialised his destructive wishes and created a machine for dealing death. This, of course, he cannot do, because he is an essentially singular adventurer, a lover: Thanatos in him is still in its eighteenth-century subservience to the purposes of Eros.

The horrors in eighteenth-century Gothic fiction tell the same story as the assaults in Sade's fiction: Thanatos has been admitted only as piquancy to the erotic quest for pleasure. Indeed, eighteenth-century Gothic as a whole is only the spikiest branch of eighteenth-century exoticism. Moreover, something of the eighteenth-century's cool attitude to the Gothic survived even in the unlikeliest places, the very ardours of the reaction. Scott himself, translator of Goethe, antiquarian collector of Scottish folklore, retained a touch of Goethe's own ability to face historically both ways. The influence of his rapturous improvisations on Scottish themes went out to convert all Europe to the Gothic; yet he was not quite cut off from the enlightenment, being the editor of Dryden and Swift. In Soane, the enlightenment survives intact right through the first wave of reaction. He keeps a Gibbonian detachment from the Middle Ages, which he is re-creating only to use them, not to surrender to them. He exercises the eclecticism of a curio-collector—the very opposite of the jealous and consuming passion of romantic love: an Egyptian sarcophagus thrills him equally with a monk's tomb; he juxtaposes his illuminated manuscripts to his collection of portraits of Napoleon[1].

This unserious Gothic was nothing to the reactionaries' purpose until they had altered its emotional content as radically as they altered the enlightenment's arguments about Nature. Some of the bad taste of the neo-Gothic movement comes from its having taken seriously what had been to the eighteenth century not exactly a joke but a highly sophisticated quirk. The reaction was determined to lose itself in a dream which the eighteenth century, with its immense self-consciousness, had always held at arm's length and recognised as a fantasy.

The enlightenment had felt no awe for the God of the Middle Ages and none for the style in which his cathedrals had been built. Indeed, it subjected the Gothic to the same utilitarian treatment as it did Shakespeare: Batty Langley's pioneering treatise[2] was not simply on Gothic architecture—it was *Gothick Architecture Improved*. Neither had the enlightenment any thought of sanctifying the residences into which it imported bits of ecclesiastical furnishing: the medieval God,

[1] *A Description Of The Residence . . .*, p. 98   [2] 1742

like the equally disbelieved-in gods of the ancient world, was simply decoration. The enlightenment's Abbeys, Fonthill[1] or the fictitious Northanger ('An Abbey! Yes, it was delightful to be really in an Abbey!'), carefully preserved the fruits of the Reformation by being not abbeys but houses[2], and were directed to the glorification not of God but of their owners.

The reaction, on the other hand, took both the God and his Gothic appurtenances seriously. Often it was the appurtenances which had pointed the way back to the God. Newman, for example, going through the exercise books he had kept from his schooldays, was amazed to discover that in one of them he had at the age of nine drawn a crucifix and a rosary; he was sure that his Anglican upbringing (at a time when Anglicanism was much less ritualistic than it was to become later under his influence) had suggested no such ideas, and surmised that he had got them from the Gothic novels[3]. Once the God was established and it was clear, moreover, that his authority rested not on reason but on tradition (that is, history), he in his turn hallowed the Gothic paraphernalia. The reaction became not merely pedantic but bardolatrous in its espousal of the Gothic style; and it proceeded to employ the style in diffusing the holiness that emanated from the God.

In medievalising and Gothicising as many as it could of the useful and decorative articles of its everyday life, the reaction *did* mean to sanctify its everyday life. It had abandoned the great eighteenth-century preoccupation with morality, and taken up a concern with morals in the vulgar sense the Victorians gave the word of sexual respectability. It made a serious ideal out of the medieval adulation of sexual purity, which to the eighteenth century had been a source only of titillation combined with a touch of pleasurable hypocrisy. At the end of the fifties Tennyson began to issue the *Idylls Of The King*, which combined feudalism with supernaturalism in an imprecisely dated medieval world: the phallic authority of the father appeared as a sword, whose naked assertion of force was decently clothed in white samite of a magic, indeed mystic, character; the most yearned-for objective in the world, the mother's womb, appeared in the appropriate shape of a cup, which, like a womb indeed, actually *contained* Christ in his

[1] finished 1807
[2] or schools, like the one Jane Austen attended at Reading.
[3] *Apologia* . . ., I: 'I suppose I got these ideas from some romance, Mrs. Radcliffe's or Miss Porter's'.

sacramental form; and the attainment of this holy Grail was expressly
reserved to the son who had made the utmost, self-castrating sacrifice
to the father's sexual tyranny by undertaking a complete sexual
purity. The ideals expressed in the medievalising saga were transported straight into the now medievalised outside world. Chivalry
and feudal loyalty to a leader (ultimately to an immortal principle
of royalty: King Arthur is the king who never dies, rex quondam
rexque futurus[1]) were practised in the Gothic quadrangles of the
public schools, and the sacrifice of sexuality exacted; and the ogival
windows, and the stained glass over the stairs or above the door,
deposits of the Victorian era still to be seen in English suburbs, really
were meant to let in to the home the devotional atmosphere and the
thoughts of purity engendered by the school chapel.

The most amusing of Jane Austen's heroes, Henry Tilney, is still a
man of the eighteenth century in which he was created but not published: a clergyman (indeed, a lesser Sydney Smith) whose ideal is
still the rational, he takes his Gothic in the form of *The Mysteries Of
Udolpho* which, he says, 'when I had once begun it, I could not lay
down again; I remember finishing it in two days, my hair standing on
end the whole time'[2]. But if we transpose him into the thirties of the
next century, we have to imagine that the Catholic and ritualistic
hints conveyed, as Newman witnesses, by Mrs. Radcliffe's fictions
have shaped themselves into doctrinal ideas, and that Henry Tilney
now takes his Gothic to heart, his hair standing on end with numinous
reverence—or, perhaps, with fear of the Catholic Church which seems
likely to reconquer everything. Rather than flirting with Catherine,
he will be agonising inwardly over the question whether his Anglican
orders, no matter what the lax Church of England says, do not bind
him to celibacy. Whichever way he decides, he will not have been
able to ignore the attempt to re-Catholicise the Anglican Church which
is being carried out by the Tractarian movement, whose opponents are
already saying that soon 'every man, and especially every clergyman, will be compelled to make his choice'[3]. By 1839 Newman had
not only taken part himself in restoring an unquestioning feudal
obedience to a Gothic God but had recognised that the movement
owed its success to 'a re-action from the dry and superficial character
of the religious teaching and the literature of the last generation or
century'; and as the influential figures in the reaction he names

[1] Malory: *Le Morte D'Arthur*, XXI, VII

[2] *Northanger Abbey*, 14   [3] quoted by Newman, *Apologia . . .*, II

Wordsworth and Southey, Coleridge (although 'he indulged a liberty of speculation, which no Christian can tolerate') and 'Walter Scott, who turned men's minds in the direction of the middle ages'[1].

The reaction's bad taste was, however, no temporary accident resulting from its adapting eighteenth-century modes to serious uses. The reaction was a concerted move against Taste, just as it was against Reason and the free thought and discussion through which the previous century had intended to arrive at Taste. Taste now appeared as one of the pretexts which had justified the eighteenth century in its frivolity and eroticism; the medievalising drive intended to bring art back to the position it had held in Christendom, where it should be controlled and licensed by religious sentiment. This time religious sentiment was exercised not only through a Church but through a philistine bourgeoisie; and while the intellectual reactionaries were covering Europe with Gothic churches, and public buildings indistinguishable from churches, in a determination that temples of Reason should never be raised again, the bourgeoisie extinguished art under a carbunculous teacosy of sheer quantity of material. The bourgeoisie had been bribed by comfort, by the goods put on display at the Great Exhibition; it behaved like a man who has resigned both artistic and directly sexual pleasure in exchange for being allowed to stuff himself with food. Thanatos worked on the bourgeoisie in the name of prosperity and material progress, on the intellectuals in the name of discipline and renewed vitality, but in fact it was performing its business of cutting off the negotiation of reality. The bourgeoisie became so insulated in its dream that it did not hear the industrial proletariat beneath it; Newman wasted the immense scrupulousness of his conscience in re-fighting the old Protestant-Catholic battle of the sixteenth and seventeenth centuries and debating, like any Athanasius, the niceties of the nature of a God who he (unlike Athanasius) could perfectly well have found out was imaginary.

It was on this point that the neo-Gothic did violence to the historical Gothic artists it imitated, whose belief had been unforced, who had no access to a civilisation which could have enlightened them and who were not trying to destroy a civilisation while pretending to advance it, the enlightenment of the ancient world having been so utterly destroyed, so long before, as to be quite beyond their reach. The bad taste of the neo-Gothic is the bad taste of a factitious belief

[1] quoted (*Apologia* . . ., II) by Newman from an article he published in 1839

which can only be kept up by destroying the evidence. The eighteenth century had thought of the true Gothic, wrongly, as destructive, indeed, what it liked in it was its supposed barbarism; and for that reason the enlightenment used it sparingly and with improvements, as the dash of Thanatos which threw pleasure into relief. The reaction, even though it acquired a much greater scholarly knowledge of it, did not understand the true Gothic much better than the enlightenment had done—as, in fact, its architectural imitations make plain. In its heart, it stuck to the eighteenth-century interpretation whereby the Gothic equalled the barbaric; and it was precisely this, its confidence that the Gothic was destructive of all the values of civilisation, which endeared the Gothic to its heart. The very name of the Gothic, which bears so little relation to either its history or its historical character, was an indication of where the neo-Gothic wishes tended: a Goth was next door to a Vandal.

13. *Spleen et Idéal*

Fortunately for civilisation, the reaction also possessed a black, a splenetic aspect.

The German Gothic which Madame de Staël encountered at the turn of the century was not only religious but erotic, and not only erotic but gloomy, bloody and putrescent[1]. It still bore more resemblance to Mrs. Radcliffe than to Pugin or William Morris except that, being taken philosophically, it was already taken seriously. Everything but its seriousness had to be refined out of it before it could be converted into the stained-glass twilight which formed the established religion of respectability in nineteenth-century Europe. (In England this presently paled into the Celtic twilight [dating perhaps from the eighteen-sixties, when the Celtic bee entered Matthew Arnold's bonnet] in which a factitious belief was induced not merely in God but in the fairies.)

The black romantics, on the other hand, preserved both the eroticism

[1] e.g. the doctrine that 'death . . . must be ecstatically embraced; putrefaction, which restores us to the infinite by uniting us with it, must be fervently desired', which J. Christopher Herold (*Mistress To An Age . . .*, 16) quotes from Zacharias Werner, who stayed with Madame de Staël at Coppet in 1808 and was converted to Catholicism in 1810.

and the destructiveness of the original reaction. They had turned against reason and enlightenment no less passionately than the philistines: but, by directly developing and not reversing the content of what had been the black strain in the enlightenment itself, they were able to react against the eighteenth century without breaking continuity with it. This gave them the invaluable literary advantage of preserving the eighteenth century's sense of style. Charles Baudelaire plunged into a Catholicism which would have horrified Newman—or, equally, Voltaire; a Catholicism in which God was necessary as a guarantor of Hell and Satan, and Satan was 'le plus savant et le plus beau des Anges, Dieu trahi. . . .'[1]: yet Baudelaire took with him into the depths a lifeline which had also supplied Voltaire, but which the author of *The Dream Of Gerontius* had lost most irrecoverably.

Whereas the eighteenth-century concepts of morality and goodness were not the smallest use to a generation in quest of godliness and the Holy Grail, eighteenth-century wickedness and irrationality, which had never been rationally understood in the first place, lent themselves to the black romantics' purpose. It was the old Gothic horror tale of the eighteenth century which crossed the Atlantic and had some genuine nastiness injected into it by Edgar Allan Poe: even so, it retained some of the absurdity of a joke which the provinces had taken seriously until Baudelaire re-translated it to Europe and style. Baudelaire, who modelled his appearance on the eighteenth-century figure of Laurence Sterne (emphasising the facial resemblance by borrowing the finger-to-forehead pose he had seen in the portrait prefixed to Sterne's works[2]), had in fact inherited his whole property cupboard from the eighteenth century: the horror tale, the destructive postures of Sade, the very concept of Spleen. But he brings to these properties precisely the psychological insight which the eighteenth century itself refused to give, and the lack of which makes Sade's fictions so dry; he added to Sade's consciousness of the destructive wish the full romantic recognition that it is the self which is to be destroyed. At the same time, he perserved the stylistic tradition in which the eighteenth-century hero had destroyed himself unknow-

[1] *Les Fleurs Du Mal*, Les Litanies De Satan

[2] Thus Théophile Gautier: '. . . il rasa sa moustache . . . Ainsi dégagée de tout duvet superflu, sa tête rappelait celle de Lawrence (sic) Sterne, resemblance qu' augmentait l'habitude qu'avait Baudelaire d'appuyer, en parlant, son index contre sa tempe; ce qui est, comme on sait, l'attitude du portrait de l'humoriste anglais, placé au commencement de ses oeuvres'.

ingly; and the line runs unbroken from the Hell Fire Club, though Byron, to 'ce dandysme sobre'[1] of Baudelaire. The rush to Hell was an exaggeration of the eighteenth-century habit of going to the dogs. It swept on, still without forfeiting its dandyism, carrying Rimbaud down to pass une saison en enfer in 1873, illuminating another Underworld in the brothel scenes of Toulouse-Lautrec, creating genuinely Baudelairean images in the stylish and perverse drawings of Aubrey Beardsley. By that time, however, the decadents were unintentionally giving back to the Hell tradition a little of Mrs. Radcliffe's absurdity, by treating of evil without a psychology to lend it insight. Oscar Wilde's *Salome* was merely silly until Beardsley and Richard Strauss, on their separate occasions, redeemed it for Hell again. All the decadents' hints about nameless vice boiled down to one predilection which, as its propagandists knew quite well, is not a vice and which is explicitly, if monotonously, nameable. Oscar Wilde and the Yellow Book authors, Henry Harland and Corvo, preserved little from their Baudelaire-Rimbaud lineage except an obsessive connexion between homosexuality and Roman Catholicism. Yet even within these limits, and well into the twentieth century, the Baudelairean line produced in Ronald Firbank one last, left-over, washed-out but authentic fleur du mal, a final—the guise in which he slipped himself into his own fiction[2]—orchid, 'a dingy lilac blossom of rarity untold'.

14. *The Renaissance of Psychology*

The Hell-bound romantics exploited their destructiveness and self-destructiveness (their *wish* to be decadent) to the utmost benefit for civilisation.

Obviously, their awareness of Thanatos gave them both an artistic and a moral advantage over the Holy Grailists, who had blindly adopted the vision of heaven in order to set themselves free to smash the civilisation on earth; and as a matter of fact it was also an advantage over the enlightenment itself. To say that the reaction took up and yet reversed tendencies concealed in the enlightenment is to say that the reaction let loose, without recognising them, the destructive tendencies the enlightenment had kept under lock and key also without

[1] Gautier (in 1868) on Baudelaire in 1849   [2] *Prancing Nigger*, XII

recognising them. Like all gaolers, the enlightenment was the prisoner of what it was repressing; and if the repression, the dictatorship of Taste, had ever absolutely hardened it would have achieved through mediocrity the devastation the philistine age actually did achieve through muddle.

Civilisation could in fact be saved only if there was a recognition of the destructive impulses inherent in it, to understand them being the only hope of controlling them. That the black romantics often had no intention of saving civilisation, but in some cases the opposite, made no difference to the result. Diving into the Pit, they came upon the instrument which, if cultivated, was capable of saving civilisation— an instrument which had not been much cultivated since Shakespeare. When Baudelaire plunged into the exploitation of Spleen (itself a concept left over from an early attempt at a scientific psychology) he took possession of a new realm of psychological understanding.

Using hindsight—knowing, that is, what was to come of 'free association'—we can see a beginning of psychology, or at a least a beginning from which a psychology could be made, in Laurence Sterne's great destructive exploit, which consisted of breaking up the eighteenth century's periodical sentence, and its logical principle for treating literary material, into those mere halves and thirds of senten-ces, those ideational streamers, whose flutterings on the page record the currents of Sterne's whimsicality. Sterne had a right to the Shakes-pearean persona of Yorick which he chose as the mask through which to speak his melancholy, because he was in effect bringing the English language back to the condition in which Shakespeare established it, the condition of a vulgar tongue: it has to be admitted that the tran-scendence achieved by the enlightenment, the uniformity it managed to impose on English and French, came largely from writing both languages as though they were Latin.

Certainly, when one goes from the enlightenment to the proto-black-romanticism of Benjamin Constant and the Shakespeare-enthusiast Stendhal, it is the new psychological tone which instantly engages the ear. Stendhal is not much *more* of a romantic than Don Giovanni; the difference lies in his knowledge and curiosity about his own state. We can pick out the constant romantic characteristics: the revolt against reason; the infatuation with the mother; the not quite easy self-identification with the rebellious and destructive hero (Satan or Napoleon). This time, however, the romantic's own atten-tion is caught by his states of mind, and it is in Stendhal's own obituary notice of himself that we find not only 'He adored Shakespeare and had an insurmountable repugnance for Voltaire and Mme. de Staël' and 'He respected one man alone: Napoleon' but also 'He liked none of his relatives. He was in love with his mother, whom he lost when he was seven'[1].

Benjamin Constant also felt, in another sense, an insurmountable repugnance towards Madame de Staël. He, too, was in love with an image of the mother; in his case the love took the form of being also in love with Madame de Staël.

Constant and Stendhal are writers belonging to our own literary epoch (the epoch of the novel), because in them the psychological order of ideas has—though with a struggle—taken precedence over the logical order. (A similar revolution did not come to painting until the Impressionists turned a picture into a lyric, something done at a sitting, expressing not the logical nature of the thing represented but an instant in the painter's psychological autobiography.) It is the same psychological tone which speaks—to *us*, it seems, directly—in the letters of Keats. In the ode *To A Nightingale*, that minute scrutiny of psychological experience, Keats employs (having first disciplined it) Sterne's method of mental association: stanza melts cinematically into stanza on a point of psychic or even verbal assonance. And of course it was in Keats par excellence that Shakespeare was revived. It makes no difference that Keats lingers in the Grecian (a romanticised Grecian) and at other times adopts the chivalry, the faery, the knights-at-arms of avant-garde medievalism, which he has got from studying Chaucer and Spenser. His very eclecticism is not entirely his own: if its foreground is the emotional opportunism of the romantic, we can read through it to the dramatic opportunism, the renaissance eclecticism, of Shakespeare. Granted also that eighteenth-century pastoral had preserved the fragrance of Shakespeare's manner. With Keats it is not a question of preserving. 'Cold Pastoral!' as he said in another context. He has stepped not into Shakespeare's vocabulary but into the very articulation of Shakespeare's thought. This is not a revival so much as an impersonation. Reading the marvellous poetry which came of Keats's baptism by total immersion into Shakespeare, one recognises the historical fact that Shakespeare had never been properly understood before.

Keats himself knew perfectly well that what he was introducing or re-introducing into poetry was psychology. He knew, moreover,

[1] Stendhal: *Memoirs Of An Egotist*, T. W. Earp's translation, pp. 136; 143

that the revolution consisted in discarding the ancient, religious theory of possession, which had contented Socrates, and which the enlightenment, though dissatisfied with it, had not troubled to replace, and applying to the mind itself for an account of behaviour which, seeming unaccountable, had once been attributed to an alien source. Keats not only puts to himself startlingly psychological questions but insists that they *are* psychological:

> Why did I laugh tonight? No voice will tell:
> No God, no Demon of severe response,
> Deigns to reply from Heaven or from Hell.
> Then to my human heart I turn at once.[1]

He finds himself writing an ode to the mind itself, in its personification as Psyche, who was to lend her name to the new science: Psyche has been personified too late in antiquity to receive the cult of a goddess; and therefore Keats himself ('I am more orthodox than to let a heathen goddess be so neglected'[2]) will accord her a cult that is not religious but psychological:

> Yes, I will be thy priest, and build a fane
> In some untrodden region of my mind,
> Where branched thoughts, new-grown with pleasant pain,
> Instead of pines shall murmur in the wind.

The lyric genius of Keats and Baudelaire, like the prose talent of Benjamin Constant (and a good part of that of Stendhal) is autobiographical. This was where the new psychological age shewed to its most obvious advantage over the enlightenment: one has only to think of Gibbon's positive *un*desire for autobiographical insight: the very title of Baudelaire's *Mon Cœur Mis À Nu* would have set him shivering. But the contrast is equally great between Baudelaire and Newman—though Newman actually shares Baudelaire's objective. So far from feeling distaste at the thought of laying his heart bare, Newman tears away at himself to get the covers off until he is lacerated and exhausted; but he might just as well have refused, like Gibbon, to try, because he has himself glued the covers on. He is wholly committed in advance to the antipsychological view inherent in the theory of possession: he will see no fundamental motive in

[1] Sonnet of 1819   [2] letter of 1819 (Houghton: *Life And Letters . . .*)

his conversion except the grace of God, coming from outside. The best his intellect can do is construct logical postures within the theological system, in which it is just as securely imprisoned as the medieval intellect had been. He carries his scrupulous introspection to the point of tracing his earliest intimations of Catholicism to Mrs. Radcliffe; but the connexion, which was obvious to Jane Austen, between the Gothic and the erotic is invisible to him. He is committed to not pursuing his analysis of his faith into an analysis of its emotional sources. (If he had been willing to make the attempt, he might have begun by asking himself why, in a letter written in the month after his conversion, he quoted in application to himself the epigram Pericles applied specifically to women[1].) Thus he tidies and logicalises the furniture of his medieval keep, but he will never let down the drawbridge to reality, being persuaded that to do so would be to commit the sin of Liberalism[2].

The black autobiographers and (Stendhal's word) egotists pursued psychology through introspection and took up, as it were, the lyrical and the descriptive-atmospherical aspects of Shakespeare's genius. Meanwhile his dramatic aspect belatedly found an heir in the novel, which had been trying to be born all through the eighteenth century. Even while keeping the novel within its epistolary confines, Choderlos de Laclos, by pushing his letter-writers' self-knowledge to a point of ruthlessness where the book is their, rather than his, tour

[1] in his letter to Cardinal Acton (which Newman quotes in *Apologia* . . ., IV): 'did your Eminence know me, you would see that I was one, about whom there has been far more talk for good and bad than he deserves'. Newman is in fact an example not of a man who is celibate because the Church demands it but of a celibate who has gone to the Church which justifies celibacy. Among the anticipations of Catholicism which lodged in his mind before he had any thoughts of Catholicism, he mentions, though 'with great reluctance', the conviction 'that it would be the will of God that I should lead a single life', an idea which 'took possession of' him when he was fifteen. (*Apologia* . . ., I)

[2] by which he meant 'false liberty of thought, or the exercise of thought upon matters, in which, from the constitution of the human mind, thought cannot be brought to any successful issue. . . Among such matters are first principles . . . and of these the most sacred and momentous are . . . the truths of Revelation. Liberalism then is the mistake of subjecting to human judgment those revealed doctrines which are in their nature . . . independent of it, and of claiming to determine on intrinsic grounds the truth and value of propositions which rest for their reception simply on the external authority of the Divine Word'. (*Apologia* . . ., Note A)

de force, had been able to produce at the very end of the century one incomparable but also inimitable masterpiece. The form had already become more elastic, and had been accepted as the most popular vehicle for entertainment, before Jane Austen provided it with psychological material to exercise its elasticity on.

Jane Austen's theme is the same as Laclos's or Richardson's, namely the eighteenth-century duel between the sexes. She treats it less outspokenly but not a bit less incisively: she is giving an account of the perils of women in a society where they are not emancipated and must steer, with the utmost realism of vision, between the danger of being left spinsters and the danger of being seduced. Seduction is the shipwreck which occurs off-scene in her novels but whose clamour and frightfulness provide the background of terror just as perceptibly as in the Gothic adventures, Laclos or even Sade.

To this theme Jane Austen applies the psychological curiosity and analysis of the new century; but her focus is still determined by the eighteenth. As a rule (but the exception to this rule is *Emma*, the incomparable novel, the novel of novels) her curiosity, like the eighteenth century's, is caught by society—that is, by relationships; almost to the neglect of the people between whom the relationships subsist. She is after the dramatic interpenetrations of character, the tennis-game between pride and prejudice, or sense and sensibility, rather than character itself: she is a Shakespeare without the introspective soliloquies, the lyrics, the descriptions of nature, the fantasy, the genre scenes of low life—in other words, a Racine.

The critics invariably point out how little attention Jane Austen gives to the political events of her time—barely an allusion to the military events, and none at all to the issues behind them. (It is symptomatic that she declined[1] an invitation to meet that transcendent European figure whose one concern was with issues, Madame de Staël.) But in fact this very closing up of interest is the mark of Jane Austen's swift response to the spirit of her time. Of course the narrowness of her subjects is occasioned by her being a woman, a provincial and a spinster; but it is really the spirit of the time whose character we are defining when we find it capable of being exemplified in a provincial spinster. Jane Austen has gone beyond the Johnsonian reaction against the enlightenment; we can see in her that distrust of abstract ideas to which François de Pange refused to yield after the

---

[1] cited, from the Biographical Notice to Bentley's edition of Jane Austen (1833) by R. W. Chapman: *Jane Austen . . .*, IX

Revolution. The enlightenment has pulled in its horns: the question of defining man in the generic, the problems of a just society, the negotiation of a reasonable social contract between the classes have all proved too puzzling and dangerous. To this impaired confidence, Jane Austen responds as Racine did to the inhibiting effect of absolute monarchy and absolute Catholicism—by eschewing all large abstract ideas whatever. She finds herself at the centre of civilisation through staying at home and treating of the old eighteenth-century preoccupations, morality and society, in terms of a few individuals' experience of loyalty and false friendship, and their judgments about vulgarity and gentlemanliness.

Of course this might have betokened only a reduction to the trivial; but in Jane Austen—and in the novel as a form—the reduction in scale is the occasion for a deeper searching of the elements. In coming down to the domestic, she has isolated the primal family. If she makes no comment on the social contract, she has picked out its psychological essence, the conflict between paternal authority and the younger generation's claim to a free choice of mate. Moreover, although, like any eighteenth-century propagandist, she is worried about the moral tendency of her work when it is loosed on society, her beautiful doubt prevents her from drawing a moral, and fixes her in the Shakespearean position of simply creating whole. 'I leave it to be settled by whomsoever it may concern', she concludes *Northanger Abbey*, 'whether the tendency of this work be altogether to recommend parental tyranny or reward filial disobedience'.

15. *Psychology Implicit*

Jane Austen already has—and, what is more, knows she has—the moral ambiguity which was to reach its most tremendous intensity in *The Golden Bowl* and which is the particular grace of the novel as a genre, the fluid in which its psychologising is carried. Again, she is already a Shakespeare, not in the scope or variety of her creativeness, but in the wholeness of what she does create: her moral ambiguity is simply nature's, reality's: and the great age of the novel which she initiates. is an age of artistic creation, a fruitfulness, a harvest, without precedent in the history of civilisation. The great and the nearly-great, Jane Austen, Dickens, Dostoievsky, George Eliot, Flaubert, Henry

James, George Meredith, Proust, Stendhal, Thackeray, Tolstoy, Turgeniev, thunder like apples from the tree, and every apple a world: it was whole cosmoi which the authors dropped into our cultural consciousness: it was not a renaissance but a new *Genesis*. Human beings have never crammed so much genius into one century and one artistic form.

It was the novel above everything else which brought psychology into our culture. It is to the habit of reading novels, a habit the ancient world had to do almost entirely without, that all of us at this moment owe our curiosity about one another's motives, our attempts to divine and define one another's susceptibilities—the whole psychologising cast of mind with which we conduct and civilise our social intercourse. Not only the great masters but the successor states, and even the commercial prostitutes if they are skilful enough, exercise us in the use of psychological imagination, the great task of postulating what it would be like to be someone else. There are still people who, like those who called down Jane Austen's famous wrath[1], deny the cultural importance of novels: but we should read their opinion as what they wish rather than what they think to be true. Their stand is against psychology: they are people who would deny that they ever had daydreams.

Psychology in novels is, of course, implicit, as science always must be in art. The novelist's psychologising is science in the sense that Keats's poetic practice is itself a critical commentary on Shakespeare and was, in fact, the world's first critical introduction to him, and that Tiepolo's paintings are our most illuminating commentary on Veronese's—the very sense in which Baudelaire affirmed his belief 'that the best critique is amusing and poetic, not cold and algebraic. . . The best account of a picture would be a sonnet or an elegy'[2].

Yet for all that their psychological knowledge is implicit, we cannot think of the nineteenth-century novelists as less aware of its implied existence than Baudelaire of the art-criticism that may be implied by

[1] in which she took care to point out the psychological perceptiveness of the novel, commenting, on the 'common cant' of the 'Oh! it is only a novel!' attitude:—'in short, only some work in which the greatest powers of the mind are displayed, in which the most thorough knowledge of human nature, the happiest delineation of its varieties, the liveliest effusions of wit and humour, are conveyed to the world in the best chosen language'. (*Northanger Abbey*, p. 5)

[2] Curiosités Esthétiques, Salon of 1846, I, cited by Frank P. Chalmers: *The History Of Taste . . .*, VI

a sonnet. The novelists were certainly not prehistoric builders or working elephants, applying the principles of leverage without a notion that there could be principles. Even in the ancient world, Aristotle distinguished tragedy as more philosophical than history— that is, more scientific. We cannot be sure that Sophocles himself when he wrote the *Oedipus Rex* was so far as we usually assume from enunciating the Oedipus complex as a psychological principle. Certainly Aristotle, in analysing the greatness of the play (although he distinguishes Euripides as the most tragic poet, it is the *Oedipus* which he obviously considers the Greek theatre's masterpiece; the *Oedipus* is so to speak the hero of the *Poetics*) stands on the threshold of recognising the universal validity of Oedipus's situation. 'Terror and pity', he says[1], 'may be raised by the decoration—the mere spectacle; but they may also arise from the circumstances of the action itself; which is far preferable and shows a superior poet. For the fable should be so constructed that, without the assistance of the sight, its incidents may excite horror and commiseration in those who hear them only: an effect which every one who hears the fable of the *Oedipus* must experience'. Aristotle's constant concern with the effect on the *audience* keeps bringing him back to psychological considerations: he has the germ—though he does not let it germinate—of the universal principle Freud was to isolate in Sophocles's play. 'The *Oedipus Rex*', wrote Freud[2], 'is a tragedy of fate; its tragic effect depends on the conflict between the all-powerful will of the gods and the vain efforts of human beings threatened with disaster. . . Modern authors have therefore sought to achieve a similar tragic effect by expressing the same conflict in stories of their own invention. But the playgoers have looked on unmoved at the unavailing efforts of guiltless men to avert the fulfilment of curse or oracle. . . If the *Oedipus Rex* is capable of moving a modern reader or playgoer no less powerfully than it moved the contemporary Greeks, the only possible explanation is that the effect . . . does not depend on the conflict between fate and human will, but upon the peculiar nature of the material by which the conflict is revealed. There must be a voice within us which is prepared to acknowledge the compelling power of fate in the *Oedipus*, while we are able to condemn the situations of *Die Ahnfrau* or other tragedies of fate as arbitrary inventions. And there actually is a motive in the story of King Oedipus which explains the verdict of this inner voice.

[1] *Poetics*, Thomas Twining's translation, II, XIII
[2] *The Interpretation Of Dreams*, V, D (b)

His fate moves us only because it might have been our own, because the oracle laid upon us before our birth the very curse which rested on him.'

To what extent, through the terminology of the thought of the ancient world, Sophocles apprehended this, we shall never know. But if we imagine his Oedipus put in full possession of the facts by Freud, and addressing himself explicitly, not merely through the moving effect of the play, to the audience, he would say to them: 'My curse is your curse; and if you do not recognise it explicitly as your own, but only implicitly, by being moved, that is because you have obscured your memory of your infancy by the process of unconscious hypocrisy Freud calls repression.' And by the nineteenth century we find that something of the sort *is* being explicitly said— by the autobiographical hero, the 'I' of Baudelaire's lyrics, who addresses[1] *his* audience as

Hypocrite lecteur,—mon semblable,—mon frère!

The reason why we must suppose the nineteenth century novelists to have been much more explicit and articulate psychologists than Sophocles, or at least than Sophocles *need* have been, is contained in Freud's remark that modern authors aim at the tragic effect of the *Oedipus* through stories *of their own invention*. Aristotle had pointed out to the writer in the ancient world that, though he might invent new subjects or devise novelties in his treatment of the old, he was 'not at liberty' to alter the essential outline of the 'received tragic subjects: Clytaemnestra must die by the hand of Orestes, and Eriphyle by that of Alcmaeon'[2]. If this restricted the writer's liberty, it also spared him a responsibility. He could select from a bunch of themes which had been already sifted in advance: not he but tradition would guarantee that the theme of his choice possessed that 'importance' which Aristotle named[3] as the first requirement in a tragic plot: and since the anonymous agency which had performed the sifting really was external to himself, he really was relying on something like divine possession or inspiration by a Muse. With the advent of the novel (whose English name, unlike the French and Italian, actually remarks that it is something new, originating with its author) the

[1] *Les Fleurs Du Mal*, Préface
[2] *Poetics*, Thomas Twining's translation, II, XIV
[3] *Poetics*, Thomas Twining's translation, II, I

author undertook the whole responsibility. He himself must sift the ideas which have lodged in his consciousness by the interplay of stimuli from his unconscious and stimuli from the observed world outside running to clasp one another. He alone must decide which of the external constellations his own unconscious fantasy can supply with sufficient motive-power to sustain the act of faith, the suspension of disbelief, which creates a book; and at the same time he is responsible for isolating in his own fantasy-life the elements which are significant—as Aristotle would say, important—for mankind as a whole: and thus he is required to be both more personally introspective and more generally scientific than Sophocles.

The theory of possession or, put more mildly, of divine providence, in terms of which Newman insisted on viewing his own life story, and which the unpsychological rationalism of the enlightenment had been powerless to replace, was really exploded by the novel. It was not only that the novelist had to admit that his own imperatives, however mysterious, came from within: he was also obliged to break the grip of fate because he was forced to impersonate fate in relation to his characters. No one told him by whose hand his victims and villainnesses must die: it was, rather, in *his* hand that the fates of all his characters reposed. So far as any external constraint was concerned, he was free to throw them all away in a railway accident or involve them in a brawl where they hacked one another to pieces. However, he quickly discovered that his own inner artistry did not leave him free to do any such thing. An author cannot dispose of a character in an accident without putting up in the background some sort of implicit philosophy of whether accidents are random and meaningless or whether they are providential retributions on human guilt. It is against the unspoken screen of his own picture of reality that the author must project his characters' apprehension of it. They may of course disagree with him, refusing a responsibility he believes, or shews, to be theirs, or punishing themselves for crimes he believes to be accidents of the environment. But if his book is to be coherent at all, he must hint an account of how the characters came to their beliefs in terms of reality itself as he sees it. Already, in recognising influences on their behaviour which they themselves do not recognise, the author is exercising a wider consciousness than his characters; and it may be that his picture of reality is so cogent as to suggest unconscious motives in the characters which actually contradict those they are conscious of. If, for example, he decides, instead of having his characters killed on the railway or in an earthquake, to have one of them killed by another, he may find himself exploring not only the unconscious wish to be punished in the murderer but—as Dickens does—the unconscious psychology whereby the victim elects and foredooms himself. The unconscious appears in the *Oedipus* in the shape of Fate, whose actions have been irrevocably dictated by myth; the novelist has to invent Fate.

It is in this sense that the novelist puts himself in the creative place of nature, and that a novel is a world. In creating characters, the author creates not only what they know about themselves but also what they do not know. (He can even by a tour de force reveal what a character does not know about himself through a first-person narrative confined to what he does know.) The characters' unconscious motivations are consistent not with their but with the author's picture of reality; the author has forbidden himself to break the continuity of *his* reality by intervening as a deus ex machina and whisking a character away: he can whisk characters away only if it is justified by his, though not necessarily their, apprehension of reality. In other words, the novelist is compelled to supply implicitly the essentials of an explicit scientific psychology: a self-consistent and scientific view of reality (not necessarily, of course, a true one); and an account of the characters' psychology which shall be realistic in terms of the author's view of reality.

16. *The World in Search of Psychology*

The novelists might break the hold of fate in literature, but they could not be of any immediate help in shattering the theory of possession in real life. Their business, which they more than adequately performed, was to nurture an art which had been half smothered by the enlightenment and then nearly dashed against a stone by the philistine reaction. They had no direct lesson to teach the world about how to comprehend its own destructive impulses: such a lesson could come only from an explicit science of psychology.

Indeed, the first effect of the novel-reading habit was to exacerbate the sufferings of a world which lacked a psychology—sufferings we can painfully observe in the journals of Kierkegaard (whose sensibilities have been enlarged by reading novels and who would seek therapy in writing them if he could[1]). Kierkegaard's personal agony brings home to us the perils of living in a world where one could not yet apply to psycho-analysis—like the perils of living in a world which had not yet discovered anaesthetics. But his philosophical agony is much more deeply symptomatic: he is the symbol of the fact that, from the moment of the romantic reaction, the world was looking for psychology. (Nothing better indicates the urgency of the nineteenth century's search—or the credulity which educated, scientific minds could shew towards Science—than the unquestioning seriousness with which even sceptical reasoners like George Eliot took up the elaborate and baseless 'science' which attempted to do the work of a psychology by exploring the shape of facial features and bumps on the head.)

Kierkegaard not only suffers his experience of guilt and anxiety; he must suffer also the guilt and anxiety of being unable to discover a scientific framework into which he can fit his experience. When he considers writing literature, he perceives clearly that his *literary* problem is a question of finding a psychology: 'I must take up my Antigone again. The problem will be to develop and motivate the foreboding of guilt psychologically'[2]. But he cannot quite take the analogous step in real life because, whereas psychological literature exists, scientific psychology as yet does not. Kierkegaard is afraid of his original impulse of destruction against his father and against God: yet he is also afraid of the lust for self-punishment which submission to religion would gratify. Not being a philistine, he can see, as Newman cannot, that the self-punishment implicit in submitting to authority is every bit as destructive as rebellion, whether it acts through puritanism of the kind which obliged Kierkegaard to break off his engagement or through the paralysing awareness of guilt, which became in Kierkegaard, who constantly manipulated fate into threatening him and crushing his will, an atmosphere as lowering as the doom in the *Oedipus Rex*. All that literature can do for Kierkegaard is

[1] He plans a novel about his family; he begins a story which 'could of course contain things which would astonish the world; for I have experienced more poetry in the last year and a half than all the novels put together'; he throws into his journal a story about a son and his father which allegorises the relation of man to God, under a sub-title which names the effects of Kierkegaard's ambivalence and at the same time the novelist's virtue of ambiguity, 'De omnibus dubitandum est'. (Journals, 1843; 1842)

[2] Journals, 1843

increase his pain by adding to the beauty which lies under threat of destruction. Until he is eased of his guilt, he is not free to enjoy art either as reader or writer. He approaches the very verge of naming the science that would release him, almost admits he is seeking a psychological account of sin, actually sketches the ambivalence of which he is a victim, and then has to skid back into the theory of possession. 'The nature of original sin has often been considered, and yet the principal category has been missing—it is *dread*, that is what really determines it; for dread is a desire for what one fears, a sympathetic antipathy; dread is an alien power which takes hold of the individual. . .'[1]

Kierkegaard had to return to the only two sciences he knew, philosophy and theology; and his effort to cram his experience into them nearly burst both apart—which, indeed, he was longing to do; but equally he could wish for no such success, since these two inadequate frames were the only coherent homes offered to his intellect in the world. Psychology was left to literature, where it remained implicit even when authors would have been capable of stating the psychological import of their books in unequivocal scientific prose. Henry James—he was, after all, a contributor to the Yellow Book—can have been in no doubt about the significance of *The Turn Of The Screw*, despite the strange idiom his imagination had adopted when it chose to revive the Gothic horror tale, a tradition which exerted its claims on him through its American branch, the stories of Nathaniel Hawthorne and Poe. By the time he had finished writing the story, he must have made it entirely clear to himself that the supernatural in his story was nothing but a symbol of what was still called at the time unnatural, and that in his idea of ghostly haunting there was no overplus of horror, nothing which was not accounted for by the conversion into imagery of the obsessive guilt which haunts a homosexual desire.

Literature could not come to the rescue of life because it had its own charge to look after: the novelist could not draw an open hostility on his books by stating explicitly what the public might let pass while it remained implicit—though behind this safety lay the risk of drawing the public's implicit hostility, its philistinism. One attempt, though it was both unconscious and wholly unsystematic, to give psychological knowledge the practical and transmissible form of a science was made in the unlikeliest literary quarter—though on a second look, the

[1] Journals, 1842

unlikeliness diminishes, Wilde's self-destructive indiscretion being almost as marked as James's self-preservative discretion. Wilde's vehicle, the epigram, is in fact an adaptation of the logical axiom and the scientific definition. The Irish—perhaps originally the theological —habit of paradox, which he loaded on to his vehicle and shot to heights no intellectual feu de joie has reached before or since, is (like the paradoxical mysteries of Christian theology itself) nothing else than an exposure of the ambivalence concealed in our morality; and it was to this end that Wilde constantly used it, revealing to society that it also loved what it was most aware of hating, and vice versa. Naturally Wilde did not succeed in his attempt to write the conclusions of a scientific psychology in a nutshell without first scientifically establishing the premisses from which they were drawn. It remained for Freud to elicit the evidence from which he built up, for example, the picture of the child's being forced by the Oedipal pressures to identify itself with one of its parents, acquiring a heterosexual orientation if the parent concerned is the one of its own sex, and an unhappy homosexuality if it fails to accept that parent as the model and lingers in the desire to accept the other; but the picture, once built up, could only corroborate the brilliance of the glimpse Wilde had revealed[1] in 1895 from the stage of the St. James's theatre:

JACK: . . . You don't think there is any chance of Gwendolen becoming like her mother in about a hundred and fifty years, do you, Algy?

ALGERNON: All women become like their mothers. That is their tragedy. No man does. That's his.

JACK: Is that clever?

ALGERNON: It is perfectly phrased! And quite as true as any observation in civilised life should be.

Henry James must have felt that *The Turn Of The Screw* was quite as true as any novel in what was not yet properly civilised life should be. We must suppose that so far from finding any difficulty in deciphering his own symbolism he was afraid that it would be only too clear to other people. The monumental hesitations of his later style are the gestures of a man pulling up the blankets to cover his form. Fortunately, however, the stronger his desire to cover up, the stronger his desire to communicate; his evasions at last carry him into sanctuary

[1] *The Importance Of Being Earnest*, I

so deep that he can tackle any subject he likes—even the implicitly incestuous subject of *The Golden Bowl;* and this subject itself is only incidental to his theme, because he has left scandal as far behind him as Gothic horror and is gazing into the moral horror, the naked instinct of Thanatos itself.

By the nineties, the novel had acquired a name for being what in fact it had been from the moment it became the acknowledged invention of one mind: psychological. 'What would those modern psychological novelists, of whom we hear so much, say to such a theory as that?' Sir Robert Chiltern[1] was asking in 1895. The science which had been so painfully needed had been named and recognised. All that was missing was its material and discoveries. What William James taught under the name of psychology was simply a mélange of medicine with philosophy. He was, of course, quite innocent of the fraud he was committing—and would have been amazed to know that by the middle of the next century a reference to the psychological genius of James would summon to mind his brother Henry.

17. *St. George Into Dragon*

If one asks why the enlightenment was not wholly overwhelmed in a new dark age, and likewise if one asks why the pained and grieving agnostics of Victorian belles lettres could not surrender to religion, the answer is the progress of science. Equally, it was the progress of science which made the agnostics *want* to surrender to religion. Again, the progress of science was what made the world leave the science of psychology to be discovered by Freud, who came on the scene so long after the need for it became obvious; and even then it was science again which militated against the acceptance of psychoanalysis.

To the enlightenment, science had appeared as a haloed St. George on the horizon, galloping steadily forward into the picture and destined to liberate the people from the chains of superstition. Voltaire grumbled for a moment that the fashion for science was obscuring literature, but hastened to point out that it was only the exclusiveness and tyranny of the fashion which he objected to; he stated his ideal as

[1] Oscar Wilde: *An Ideal Husband,* I

'to pass from an experiment in physics to an opera or a comedy'[1]. The ability to pass from science to art was continued in Shelley and Goethe, and was still to be found in Goethe's biographer, George Henry Lewes, who combined the two not only in his own practice but in the household he set up with George Eliot. Yet science had already lost its halo: George Eliot's friend Herbert Spencer felt the need to reconcile it to religion: science was already far advanced into the metamorphosis which was to change St. George into the dragon and make it the artist's and the liberal's nightmare.

None the less science was—and is—indispensable to the liberal (artists might try to do without it, but only at the risk of locking themselves into the infertile cul-de-sac of art for art's sake) because it is a fortress in which rationality *has* to be preserved. It is an area of life in which everyone—not merely the electrical engineer—must maintain his belief that two and two make four and that nature is a self-consistent continuum. Otherwise the electric light would fail—and we should really go back to the dark ages. The reaction might revive the belief that the hand of God intervenes through miraculous rents in the natural fabric, but science kept up a constant protest and contradiction by inducing tangible miracles which could not have worked unless nature were self-consistent; and the protest was reinforced, and its area extended, by the irresistible momentum of the industrial revolution.

Civilisation, of course, soon noticed the disparity between its medieval ideals and its industrial practice. As a matter of fact, science, which, so far from setting the people free, had chained them to the wheels of machinery, was failing to implement its own implied ethic of the enlightenment as well as opposing the ethic of medieval Christianity; and the early socialists, whose brave endeavour it was to combine the two ethics, made a still braver endeavour to unthink the industrial revolution. Presently the socialist argument was carried into the realm of aesthetics. There had been no crisis for taste when George IV had Brighton Pavilion supplied with gaslight[2], because

[1] Les belles-lettres périssent à vue d'oeil. Ce n'est pas que je sois fâché que la philosophie soit cultivée, mais je ne voudrais pas qu'elle devînt un tyran qui exclût tout le reste . . . aucun art, aucune science, ne doit être de mode. Il faut qu'ils se tiennent tous par la main . . . je veux passer d'une expérience de physique à un opéra ou à une comédie . . . (Letter to M. de Cideville, from Paris, 16 April, 1735)

[2] 1821 (J. G. Bishop: *The Brighton Pavilion . . .*)

the eclectic exoticism of the Pavilion had never attempted to contradict the laws of reality on the observation of which engineering is based. But there was a crisis when the reaction's neo-Gothic asked to be believed-in in the religious as well as the artistic manner. A terrible taint of moral hypocrisy, expressed through aesthetic bad taste, attached to a civilisation which wanted to use both modern plumbing and the religious concepts of Christendom, and tried to get over the difficulty by disguising the plumbing as a medieval moat. William Morris's solution, which consisted of throwing the factory-made into the moat and returning to the homespun, had at least the moral virtue of honesty. Unfortunately, this virtue, unless translated into the artistic conventions, is a vice in art, art being, from the literal-minded point of view, one enormous lie, illusion and counterfeit from start to finish. (Most of the arts have long since overcome the literal-minded argument: no one bothers to point out that it is a lie to hang a landscape painting on your drawing-room wall when your drawing-room window really looks out on a commercial garage: it is perfectly obvious that there is no reason to have pictures at all unless they tell lies. Architecture alone still lingers in the puritanical atmosphere of William Morrisland, because of course there *is* a functional reason for having buildings. This has become the pretext under which philistinism triumphs. We have forgotten that a building as a work of art is just as much a fiction as the most avowed fairy tale, and let ourselves be convinced not by artistic but by moral arguments, according to which a building that does not expose the function for which it was made is committing the sin of hypocrisy, and decoration is judged to be deceit—on exactly the principle whereby the early Christians turned against 'the practice of shaving the beard, which, according to the expression of Tertullian, is a lie against our own faces'[1].)

Towards the end of the nineteenth century, art in England was for the most part immured in a daydream; and it was largely science which had driven it there—by exercising the tyranny Voltaire had feared. Science seemed to have the monopoly of reason and thus of the approaches to reality, and at the same time it seemed militantly philistine: art was cut off from its resources and had to eat itself. The results are plain as a pikestaff in the works of Oscar Wilde. The art Wilde wrote for art's sake consists of pretty little fairy tales plus his ludicrous dives into the Baudelairean Pit, from which he emerged with what he labelled—indeed, over-labelled—evil but which was

[1] Gibbon: *The Decline And Fall* . . ., XV

unmistakably nonsense. He achieved a masterpiece only when, cutting out even the passages of high melodrama which had interspersed the wit of his earlier plays, he composed an outright farce for the commercial theatre: the tyranny of science had actually brought it about that bourgeois crudity was a healthier atmosphere for art than aestheticism.

Science became a monster precisely because it had preserved and extended the rationalism of the enlightenment. It was in nineteenth-century science that the anticultural and antipsychological tendencies of the enlightenment attained their utmost and iron-hardest manifestation. The eighteenth-century deification of Nature had grown into the nineteenth-century religion of Science—in which Nature had become satanised: it only needed Darwin's version of evolution and the coda added to it by Karl Marx to create a supposedly rationalist and realist picture of the human race in which human animals were quite unable to prevent themselves from engaging in a bloody competition to the death.

By taking care not to be equipped with a science of psychology, the priests of Science were able to remain quite unaware what fantasies of their own they were expressing by means of this picture. In order not to have a psychology, they had to neglect, or even deny the existence of, plain facts like the phenomena of dreams and hypnosis. Psychological ignorance once achieved, they were equipped to overlook the still more glaring fact that the product of evolution was a human animal who at least believed himself capable of ordering his own destiny. Science really had become a religion, not merely in occupying the place of religion in men's emotions, but in its actual psychic genesis: it was devoted to a deliberate, an induced repression of certain aspects of reality in order to set upon others a construction which amounted to a fantasy.

Moreover, the tendency of this fantasy was precisely what one would expect of a religious fantasy: it was towards the immolation of man, his punishment and castration in an effort to punish himself. Once Science had become caught up in the determinist puzzle, it had elevated a new form of fate to take the place of the will of God; and towards this new fate man now made continual obeisance by sacrificing all those rebellious aspirations towards will, towards culture, towards individual psychology, which constitute a son's sins against the father. Science took out its telescope and its microscope and discovered that there was no heaven above the clouds and no soul hidden in the heart, but that everything a man was could be described in terms of matter and physical energy: whereupon, instead of congratulating matter for being able, under the influence of evolution, to form a man capable of finding all this out, it set its own interpretation—that is, its own fantasy—on the facts it had discovered, and used the word 'matter' in a derogatory sense. Perhaps it had hoped to find a soul and a heaven: its disappointment at not finding them was the infant's on discovering that the faeces it produces from its own body is not a real, living baby.

'Matter' became a term with which to smear man, to humiliate and punish him for his aspiration to a soul. It gave the Marxist a savage pleasure to boil down the professions of the religionist and the idealist to economic self-interest, and the physiologist a savage pleasure to reduce the artist's inspiration to diseased eyesight: it did not occur to either that the analysis, if correct, had in no way changed the fact and the quality of the pleasure to be got from art and morality, or that his own pleasure in trying to deface it was itself susceptible of psychological analysis. The religion of Science was telling man precisely what *Genesis* and the doctrine of original sin had told him, that he had been thrown, as Tom Paine put it, on a dunghill and that he was in fact made of dust and dirt—that is to say, excrement. (The religion of Science even took away the small comfort offered by the original religion to the effect that this had been done by a conscious and thinking god, who held out hopes of redemption.) The Marxists enriched this diagnosis by the unconscious equation which maintains that faeces equals gold, and told man that he was made of—that his being was conditioned by—economics. The materialists meant this analysis to be taken as an insult, and the spiritualists and would-be spiritualists received it as such. (The unhappy agnostics suffered the expiation through dirt quite as bitterly as the materialists themselves, who had at least their savage joy.) To neither side did it occur that there is nothing inherently degraded about matter or even excrement, and that, if we take it for insulting, it is only thinking— that is, our psychology—which has made it so. The materialists had not only, as Bernard Shaw said of them[1], emptied the baby out with the bathwater: they believed the baby had dirtied water for ever.

Man was not the only victim of the scientists' disappointment. On the animals they visited not insults merely but unthinkable tortures. Half a glimpse of psychology could have made it plain that the

[1] *Back To Methuselah*, Postscript

fantasy of scientific necessity in whose name this was perpetrated rested on the discovery of evolution, which in a sense made the animals what the totemistic assassins of animals had long before claimed, our ancestors—that is, our father. The totemist had for that reason held the animal to be divine: the scientist's fury was all the worse because the animal had been instrumental in disappointing man of heaven, by shewing that his ancestry was *not* divine. The ecclesiastical system which the classical animal religions had developed out of primitive totemism was replaced by the ecclesiasticism of deified Science. In place of the temple, the laboratory became the centre of wholesale, ritualised slaughter and worse than slaughter. Science produced its own bigotry, superstition and magical incantations, and devoted itself to scanning the past and the present through the entrails of animals with the same religious blindness with which antiquity had divined the future. Of course science was on the right lines and has probably achieved more practical successes by applying rational principles than divination achieved by hazard while applying irrational ones; but the credulity and self-ignorance of scientific practitioners have often been hardly smaller than those of the priests; and in both cases the people have accepted what was said as unquestionable truth, and what was done as moral and necessary, not through any rational or even religious judgment at all, but through simple awe of the taboo-possessor, the magic-man.

When St. George really did come, it was in the dazzling intellectual armour of George Bernard Shaw, off which the epigrams glinted in a shower which was Irish but, unlike Oscar Wilde's, systematic. The first employment for Shaw's lance was to prick the hermetically sealed partition which had separated science from art. Humanism was let into science; the supposed moral justification of vivisection was demolished; evolution was displayed in quite another, and just as valid, light: and by the same token a great draught of realism, of subject matter and of genuine style—style evolved to grapple with subject matter—was let in to the suffocating compartment in which art had been eating for art's sake.

18. L'Apprenti Sorcier

All this Shaw achieved through what he called 'my own Irish eighteenth-centuryism', which 'made it impossible for me to believe anything until I could conceive it as a scientific hypothesis'[1]. He had single-handed brought back the enlightenment in its original form, with the additional advantage of placing in the centre of the picture the eighteenth- and early nineteenth-century concept of evolution, which the enlightenment itself had left to one side. Shaw fished up not only Lamarck but the theory of evolution considered as the everlasting transmutations of the Holy Ghost which Lorenz Oken had published in 1809, and pointed out that Oken had 'made a contribution of extraordinary biological importance' because he had '*thought* very hard to find out what was happening to the Holy Ghost'[2]. Thus, in the course of restoring intelligence to literature, Shaw also revived the enlightened notion of science as an activity of the intelligence.

It was just this notion which had become swamped when the determinists let themselves suppose that reasoning was not really reasoning at all but mechanical responses, an idea which naturally undermined the rational basis of science. By the end of the nineteenth century, science had lost itself in the sort of romantic magniloquence which had already been anticipated in painting by Benjamin Haydon. Since it did not really believe that there was any such thing as thought, it fell into the notion that it could give its activities significance only by doubling and tripling the amount of activity that went on, and that patterns would emerge—without being read—only from constant and large-scale experimentation on the part of people who themselves were behaving purely mechanically. What academic science will never forgive in Freud is that, although he maintained the utmost scientific objectivity in collecting his material, he collected as an observer and not a mere mechanical recorder and, having got his material, did not stop there, but sat down to examine it in the light of reason, arranging and re-arranging his motifs like a Cubist arranging and re-arranging his wine-bottle, newspaper and mandolin. The

[1] *Back To Methuselah*, Preface, 'My Own Part In The Matter'
[2] *Back To Methuselah*, Preface, 'Discovery Anticipated By Divination'

comparison is not idle: Freud's method did restore classicism to a science which had been lost in romanticism. What emerged from his procedure were *principles* of psychology, attainable only by thought. A romantic nineteenth-century scientist, having collected the dreams Freud worked on in *The Interpretation Of Dreams*, would have set out merely to reduplicate the material; with no thought of discovering the principle which produces dreams of flying, he would have set himself to discover the incidence of dreams of flying—a procedure which, by the way, is incapable of shocking anyone. And in fact to this day we still get served up to us in the name of science, even in the name of psychology, public opinion polls which, while offering no illumination of the psychic nature of incest or homosexuality, record how many people per thousand of the population are conscious of having succumbed to them.

Shaw restored the psychological version of the evolution of species: Freud added the psychic evolution of the human individual. It was precisely at the turn of the century (Freud corrected the proofs of *The Interpretation Of Dreams* in the winter of 1899, 'though its title-page was post-dated into the new century'[1]) that reason was emancipated from the last of its captors, the romantic fantasy of the religion of Science.

The world took not the smallest notice, any more than it took any real notice of Bernard Shaw, while making him the most famous and highly paid comedian in the world. The ecclesiastical machine of deified Science moved on, as it seemed, inexorably, and plunged mankind into the World War of 1914-18—which Shaw called the betrayal of western civilisation, pointing out that the obvious conclusion of the neo-Darwinian belief that the survival of the fittest could be ensured only by competition was the mutual extinction of the fittest at one another's throats.

It might have been thought that that war was indeed a conclusion and a culmination, and that the anticultural lust would be satisfied when it had destroyed so much of culture. The machine, which had already enslaved and ground down so many thousands in industrial darkness, must have seemed to have reached its final apotheosis when it took the name of the machine gun and mowed down its thousands openly. But that was to reckon without the later developments of the flying machine. The fantasy which the religion of Science is still nightmarishly acting out is the fantasy of the machine getting out of hand and marching on the machinist.

[1] Freud: *Collected Papers*, Volume V, XXVII

There is of course nothing new in this fable, which had often been related about the earlier sort of magic. It is all contained in the story of the Sorcerer's Apprentice, invented by Lucian, embodied in a ballade by Goethe, turned into a famous piece of programme music by Paul Dukas, and thence transmitted by Walt Disney to yet another generation in the film which he set to Dukas's music, identifying the apprentice with his own rebellious son-hero, Mickey Mouse. The crime of the sorcerer's apprentice is to rebel against the father, the venerable old sorcerer himself, by skipping the hierarchy. Instead of waiting to undergo the long and punitive initiation by apprenticeship which will eventually give him the right to share the sorcerer's arcane knowledge and exercise his magic powers, the rebellious apprentice usurps the knowledge and exercises the powers to his own pleasure, without having first paid the price in lack of pleasure. Just what the magic power is, the story leaves us in no doubt when it shews us the apprentice conjuring a broomstick into life and setting it to work for his purposes: it is that ancient power, the original of all magic and all conjuring, of galvanising an inert object—the broomstick which cannot stand but has to be propped—into what seems a defiance of the laws of nature[1], so that it becomes a tool apparently endowed with a life of its own. This power is, of course, quintessentially the father's: it was by exercising it that he *became* a father: and the story sees to it that the son, who by sexual rebellion is trying to put himself in the father's place and is really putting himself in the way of becoming a father himself, is punished by the magic power turning against him.

The same theme was treated by Mary Shelley in the story of the monster created by Frankenstein, a story which is the very point where the Gothic horror tale turns into modern science fiction. Again the crime is to conjure an inert substance, the 'lifeless thing'[2] Frankenstein has put together from dead or inanimate material. It is conjuration in the most primitive magical sense of conjuring up the dead;

[1] Cf. Freud's remark, apropos of dreams of flying (sorcery, it will be remembered, can also make broomsticks fly): 'Dr. Paul Federn (Vienna) has propounded the fascinating theory that a great many flying dreams are erection dreams, since the remarkable phenomenon of erection, which constantly occupies the human phantasy, cannot fail to be impressive as an apparent suspension of the laws of gravity (cf. the winged phalli of the ancients).' (*The Interpretation Of Dreams*, VI (E))

[2] *Frankenstein*, V

and at the same time it plays on the magic power of the phallos in the same sense that the resurrection religions do when they insist that their son-hero has proved himself identified with the father by his miraculous ability to rise again. What is new to *Frankenstein* is that it is modern science which is cast for the criminal rebel, from whom vengeance will be exacted. Already in 1818 it was clear to Mrs. Shelley's imagination that Science had usurped the religious position of the old sorcerer, the venerable Nobodaddy, and had taken to itself the paternal privilege of breathing life into inert dirt which Nobodaddy had exercised in *Genesis*. The ancient hero-criminal who rebelled against and usurped the unjust father has been replaced by the scientist Frankenstein— 'Or', as Mary Shelley called him in her sub-title, 'The Modern Prometheus'.

In fables of this kind, our sense of irony requires that the magic tool or machine which gets out of hand should not merely pursue an independent course unforeseen by the magician but turn pointedly against him and defeat him. It is this irony, like the tragic irony in myths, which reveals to us that the independent malice the machine seems to bring to bear against us is in fact a reflexion of the destructive wish we unconsciously embodied in creating the machine.

Both these points Mary Shelley knew. The monster which Frankenstein has liberated sets to work to murder the people nearest and dearest to Frankenstein; and Frankenstein even recognises this as a reflexion of himself. 'I considered the being whom I had cast among mankind', he says, '. . . nearly in the light of my own vampire, my own spirit let loose from the grave, and forced to destroy all that was dear to me'[1]. Mary Shelley takes as her eponymous hero the man who makes the monster; it is we whose vulgar error it is to apply the name Frankenstein to the monster itself, making it the hero and implying that it acts autonomously. Similarly it is we who are forgetting that deified Science, like the myth of any other god, is our creation. If the god, whether maliciously or with the unthinking inexorability of a machine, is carrying out the destruction of the people, that is because the people invented his myth in order to express their hostility to him.

In other words, the religion of Science is the supreme expression of our hostility to culture—which, of course, includes science. Science was the stronghold of rationality during the romantic reaction, and we contrived to transform it into a fantasy negation of reason more

[1] VII

romantic than romanticism itself. And now the question is whether we are going to use the machinery of science to obliterate science for ever. It is dangerous, of course, precisely because it *has* preserved rationality, with the result that its magic, unlike that of sorcery, really works. The reaction could not *go back* to the dark ages, because of our need to keep the electric light going: but that is not to say that we cannot *progress* into the dark ages. We have merely to use science to build bombs which will wipe out the power stations.

Because science, unlike God, works, we can no longer afford to rely on the simple unpsychological argument of eighteenth-century rationalism, still being advanced by the Marxists, that self-interest will keep us alive. So long as we continue to deify Science, we must by the rules of god-making keep the fact that we created the god unconscious to ourselves, by endowing him with a life of his own; and all the hostility which we so plainly see threatening us in him will never be claimed by us as a projection of our own hostility to the civilisation which schools us like a parent. We shall march blindly on to the fulfilment of our unconscious desire, bringing about the destruction of civilisation and, in the same blow, the destruction of ourselves in punishment therefor: and we shall march in the train of the progress of Science which, so long as it remains antipsychological, really does move with the blind inexorability of a machine. The machine *cannot* see, any more than the god *could* take pity on us.

IV

... TO HELL

———————————

1. *Ego Tyrannus*

The eighteenth century represents the triumph of the Ego; it is the conclusive and coherent assertion of the Ego's right to judge reality for itself, against the parental claims of authority to judge for it.

However, in the fierceness of the juridical struggle for its rights, the rationalists neglected to make a scientific enquiry into the Ego's constitution. Although they had discarded God, they remained frozen in the old belief that reason was God-given (a position they tried to logicalise by bringing back a Supreme Being); and they had, therefore, no call to look for the sources of reason at the other end of the scale, in man's biological nature.

The result was that the eighteenth century had emancipated itself from authority only to be tyrannised by a misinformed Ego. The rationalists' intention was to cede to nothing less cogent than reality itself, in whose case there can be no question of tyranny, reality always possessing both the upper hand and absolute rights by virtue of being real. But while the Ego remained blind to so relevant a section of reality as the sources of its own power to reason and to recognise reality, it was bound to exercise an unwitting tyranny, drawing lines and imposing inhibitions in the name of reality and nature in places where reality and nature did not in fact impose them at all; and the effects are to be seen in the cramping dictatorship by legislation which eighteenth-century theory was constantly proposing not merely for man's behaviour but for his feelings.

It was because the Ego was insecure in its command of man's feelings, including his feelings towards authority, that it was unable to over-come its ignorance of the sources of its command. Presented with a fantastic belief, the eighteenth century scrutinised only those aspects which it needed to establish that it *was* fantastic: the very act of judging was a triumph over authority which had denied the right to judge. Rationalism asked about the statements made by a myth or a dream the question which traditional logic asks about every proposition, Is it true or false? and those it found false it simply discarded, repressing them by the absolute and summary mechanism of withdrawing its attention. It behaved with all the propriety of a jury, whose business is simply to pronounce on the guilt or innocence of the prisoner at the bar: if it finds him innocent, it has no competence to go on to ask, 'Who, then, did commit the crime?' The juror is a logician: it is the detective, whose business it is to find an explanation of the facts, who is the scientist.

The eighteenth century was not equipped for psychological detection, because it had not developed a filter fine enough to admit the content of a fantastic belief to its attention as an object of study, without admitting the quality of believing. It was still afraid that to dwell on a myth was equivalent to believing a myth. Thus it was trapped in a vicious circle wherein its psychological ignorance led it to psychological ignorance. When the question arose of where myths came from, the rationalists could not really propound any alternative to the old theological theory that they came from God. This the rationalists could not admit (for the perfectly honourable reason that they could not believe it): so they put the question aside as one likely to lead to a false conclusion, namely God: and the result was that their attention was never focussed on the material from scrutinising which they could have learnt where myths do come from.

It was the lack of a fine filter which bedevilled the eighteenth century's relations with another sort of fantasy, art. Having no more idea of how and whence artistic fictions arise than it had in the case of religious fictions, rationalism began to confound even the moral distinction between fantasies which claim to be true and fantasies which glory in not being. It could not go so far as to accuse the artists of deliberately trying, like the religionists, to impose a false report of events on its belief; but since art was in fact just as false as myth, rationalism could and did accuse it of being a waste of time, and was a great deal less permissive towards it than even a quite unpsychological morality need be. Music and architecture escaped the most stringent type of theorising simply because, since they do not make statements, they could not be accused of falsehoods (though architecture had to carry the weight of being treated as propaganda for ancient Rome or ancient Greece). But they did not escape the belittling and artistically poisonous theory that their value was that they were useful for amusement and relaxation. Literature and painting found their ability to narrate stories and describe images enlisted to be more directly useful, and they were invited to lend their actual content to propping up morality and manners. Even so, just as Tom Paine could see that the best moral influence in the world emanating from a myth did not make the myth true, so the aesthetic theorists could not get over the fact that the most imposing grand manner in a painting, and the most elevating distribution of rewards and punishments at the end of a novel, did nothing to remove the work of art concerned from the realm of fiction.

Aesthetic theory nattered away at the problem, demanding from the arts a more and more literal truth to nature. The only genres with which it was quite at ease were portraiture from the painters and history from the writers. But ease did not breed respect; the aestheticians continued to accord more prestige to the genres of epic drama and history painting: yet they could never settle on a theory they regarded as adequate to control the artist's fantasy within those genres. The immediate effect of this uneasiness with fantasy was to push painting and decoration to the utmost limits of fantasticalness, where they produced the marvellous fabrications of the rococo. Miraculous themes from Christian or classical mythology, chosen perhaps *because* no one any longer believed them literally, were deliberately presented as though they were the contrived miracles of the operatic stage[1]; the painters and stuccoists performed conjuring tricks of trompe l'œil; and the whole performance incisively insisted, with the unrelenting self-consciousness characteristic of its century, that it *was* a performance and the fabrication *was* a fabrication. Then the rococo suddenly fell from fashion. But this, though it constituted a revolution in style and taste, proceeded from no revolution in psychic attitude but only from pushing the same distrust of fantasy a little further. The neo-classic movement, in excising fantasy from painting altogether, was only the culmination of the whole eighteenth century's tendency; and in the last year of the century Jacques-Louis

[1] See Michael Levey: *Painting In XVIII Century Venice*, I; *Tiepolo's Treatment Of Classical Story At Villa Valmarana* (Warburg Journal XX, 3-4, 1957)

David was propounding the new style with the inveterate eighteenth-century sentiment—'How . . . happy it would make me, if . . . I could help the arts towards their true destiny, which is to serve morality and elevate men's souls!'[1]

It was, in general, a century which had no use for fantasy. Not having recognised fantasy as part of the human life-activity, it would neither use it directly in creating and appreciating art—that is, in the actual process of living a human life—nor consider it as one of the symptoms of life which a biological science must study. As a corollary, it had small use for childhood. Eighteenth-century civilisation presents itself to us as the most grown-up of worlds. It dressed its children as miniature adults and prized them for their precocity. It would sometimes prettify childhood but never enquire what it was like to be a child. Its very passion for education was, until Rousseau, designed to hurry the child into adulthood as quickly as possible: and even Rousseau was so incurious about the actual facts of childhood as to consign what might have been his material to an orphanage. The enlightenment could no more conceive of an interest in childhood that was not itself childish than it could conceive of a nonreligious interest in religion. With a tremendous effort of intellectual self-control, it carried out an intellectual rebellion by means of liberating the rebelliousness of sons against fathers without bringing up to the surface with the movement of rebellion any actual data about sons.

The self-control, the realism and the reasonableness were all being devoted to what was, in effect, a fantasy—but the rationalists, unlike the rococo painters, did not know it was. If education was hurrying the child into adulthood, it was in order to set him up as an independent Ego: independent not only of the parents but of his immediate ancestry within his own personality, the child he had lately been. The eighteenth century was man's attempt to live not merely as an adult but as an adult who had never been a child. The tyranny of the Ego took the form of the Ego's proclaiming itself self-supporting and doing its best to isolate its factual judgments of reality from the irrational wishes promoted by the Id.

What the Ego had lost sight of was that the act of judgment is itself dependent on a wish: on the complex of instinctual forces which creates life—which is alone capable of paying attention. Moreover, even the most austerely factual and scientific estimate of reality is inflexible and quite unable to improve its acquaintance with reality

[1] *Artists On Art*, compiled by R. Goldwater and M. Treves

unless it is continually supplied with wishes—indeed, with fantasy, scientific hypotheses being nothing but fantastic fictions of a particular kind destined to be treated in a particular way by the conscious Ego. Accordingly the tyranny of the eighteenth-century Ego was operating, unknown to itself, to the intellectual detriment of science: and at the same time, from the point of view of its own psychic functioning, it was strangling the life-line on which its own tyranny depended.

In this respect the Ego was worse off than the irrational authority it had replaced. Irrational authority had at least been able to compromise surreptitiously with the irrational forces of the Id, and had allowed the Id's impulses some outlet, however oblique. The Ego, on the other hand, was prevented from arranging a compromise by the very logical stringency with which it perceived that it would be inconsistent of it to do so. Logically, it could take no course but to blanket the Id; and the more efficiently and consistently it did that, the more it made sure not only that there would eventually be an explosion of revolt against it but also that its own power to control the revolt would have been weakened by starvation.

The revolt which came in the nineteenth century was not, as the Ego's own revolt against authority had been, an intellectual revolution but an eruption of feeling, liberating anarchic impulses of destruction —some of which set about destroying civilisation itself with the cudgel of Victorian philistinism. The material which the eighteenth century had coldly suppressed was indeed brought to the surface; but in the violence of the upheaval which brought it, there was scarcely an Ego left sufficiently in command of itself to make disciplined use of the material for the purposes of either art or science. Baudelaire, by pursuing the fastidious intellectual dandyism of the eighteenth century, made great poetry out of dreams and perverse day-dreams; George Eliot, who, by the sheer steely exercise of her nonconformist will, managed to live the life of an eighteenth-century rationalist deep into the nineteenth century and actually to grow rich by doing so, reconstructed the feelings of childhood in one of the most adult novels ever written—and Proust followed her example: but the eighteenth-century fear that an interest in childhood would itself be childish was justified by a literary infantilism which, foreshadowed in Dickens, reached its peak in Rudyard Kipling and Mark Twain—and then went on to an absolute summit, which no one who did not live to see it would have believed possible, in J. M. Barrie.

Brought to the attention of adults, childhood provoked in them violently contradictory emotions—which resulted in such distortion that the facts of childhood were hardly more discernible in the Victorian age, when everyone was thinking about childhood, than they had been when the eighteenth century was refusing to consider the subject at all. Victorian sentimentality over children, accompanied as it was by the industrial exploitation of poor children and the sexual exploitation of upper-class boys as whipping fodder in the public schools, has the sanctimoniousness of the huntsman's love for animals. We can measure the sexual temptation children constituted to Victorian adults by the sexual purity the adults insisted on attributing to children—an attempt to overcome temptation by blanching the loved object, rather than the lover, of sexual feelings, comparable to the attempt to overcome the son's incestuous love towards the mother by turning her into a virgin goddess. We can conjecture, moreover, that the reason why children were tempting is that the sight of them threatened to summon into the Victorian adult's consciousness the memory he had rigorously suppressed of his own adventures in sexual sensation during his own childhood: so that the Victorian obsession with children's purity was an attempt to contradict an unconscious certainty, founded on personal experience, that they were *not* pure.

Thus the sight and thought of childhood summoned, by association, the sexual desires of the adult. But it also called forth, to counteract and control those desires, an unconscious desire on the part of the adult to punish his own infantile sexual feelings retrospectively— which could now only be done on the persons of those who were still children. Both contradictory desires were therefore tending towards some sort of action done to children; and the two together found a compromise release in sadistic assaults, physical or moral, by the adult on children. These were justified by the sanctimonious argument that they were for the children's own good, an argument which could be accepted in good conscience because, as always with sanctimoniousness, the love it implied was perfectly genuine: it was only its quality, and in what sense the assault was an act of love, which were concealed.

Literary fantasies took the same course, with the result that whole passages of Victorian literature, and of the essentially literary painting[1]

[1] Two prime examples belong to the Tate Gallery. In one, parents and bearded doctor watch by the sick child's melodramatically-lit bed; in the other, the more gruesome for its anecdotal irony, the distraught mother has taken

of the period, collectively deserve Gustav Mahler's title Kindertoten-
lieder. The depths of authors' and readers' desire to inflict death on the
pure little children can be divined from the orgasmic ecstasies of
regret they suffered at the bedside: and it was the sharpest of turns on
the screw of moral sadism which recommended these long-drawn
songs of the deaths of children as improving reading for children—
as though veal were recommended as an improving sight for calves.
Sometimes religion would give sadistic fantasy an excuse to pursue
the child beyond the deathbed, and then it produced such moral
monstrosities as the extracts Lecky protestingly quoted[1] from a
Catholic tract 'for children and young persons', which described in
babytalk the tortures inflicted on children in Hell: 'The little child is
in this red-hot oven. Hear how it screams to come out. . . It stamps its
little feet on the floor. . . God was very good to this child. Very likely
God saw it would get worse and worse, and would never repent, and
so it would have to be punished much more in hell. So God in His
mercy called it out of the world in its early childhood'.

The Victorians' sadistic idolatry of childhood—or, rather, in this
more specialised case, of masculine adolescence—also produced a
literary genre of its own, the school story. This contained plenty of
tortures, but few deathbeds. Yet the authors found a substitute for
them in dwelling on the fleetingness of adolescence. The schoolboy
hero dies when he has to leave school; and the author dwells with
agonised regret not only on his departure but on his imminent loss
of his boyishness.

The world the hero is eventually called out of is an all-masculine
family, sealed off by family loyalty against other public schools and
by class loyalty against the people who have not been to a public school
at all; while the internal structure of the school community is a translation into terms of social rank of the relations between father and
son. The crisis for the schoolboy hero is whether to resist or identify
himself with the power of the master who stands to him, as the master
often points out, in loco parentis. All three Oedipal possibilities for
their relationship—the subjugation of the boy; the boy's identification
with the master (which is achieved by the master's 'licking' the boy
into shape); the boy's offering himself to the master to be used

the small invalid into the sunshine in the garden, and neither of them sees a
man carrying a scythe pass by outside. (Luke Fildes: *The Doctor*, 1891; H. H. La
Thangue: *The Man With The Scythe*, 1896)

[1] W. E. H. Lecky: *History Of European Morals* . . ., IV, footnote

homosexually—are condensed into the cardinal symbolic act of the school story, wherein the master bids the boy offer his buttocks for a beating. The relationships in the school story turn on the absolute power one rank holds over another to inflict bodily sensations. Master may beat adolescent boy, and adolescent boy may beat fag: it is on the use, abuse or abnegation of these rights that the school story builds the imbroglio of its plot, explodes its jokes and creates its tone of masochistic loyalty.

Aptly enough, since the public schools not only constantly studied but also borrowed from the institutions of ancient Rome, the school story plays on this social situation exactly the same kind of sentimental comedy—implicitly homosexual, actively sadistic and obsessively flagellant—as Plautus and Terence played on the social situation of the Roman family. These authors, in whom the pupils might have seen their own world reflected, were not much read at the public schools, perhaps in the belief that they were too sophisticated—a misapprehension based on the fact that the characters usually include prostitutes, and fostered by the scholarly conceit which translates the bits of Greek which occur in the Latin text into French. But the truth is that the women characters, who are usually slaves as well as prostitutes, are reduced to the sexual nullity of mere chattels[1]—which Plautus emphasises by his habit of making them mutes with not a line to say; and though the plot may be set off by a young man's desire for one of them, this heterosexual love makes not the smallest emotional contribution to the play. The presence of the women characters in no way disturbs what is really the same sealed atmosphere as the school story's—a sealing which heightens the sexual titillation. The person of lower rank, the schoolboy or the slave (the disenfranchised proletarian, the permanent child), is sexually tempting because of his weakness: his inability, which is an inability of rights as well as of power, to resist whatever may be done to him. In the closed world, he is all the more tempting because utterly disenfranchised. There is no appeal against the institution of slavery, and no appeal to the wider world outside the public school. Kipling makes his school-story headmaster say while he administers a beating (a speech to which Kipling lends a pointedly sexual effect by the headmaster's 'stopping to talk between executions'): 'Among the—lower classes this would

[1] No wonder it is on the authority of Terence that the *Malleus Maleficarum* (Part I, question 6) adds to a long list of the shortcomings of women that women are, intellectually, children.

lay me open to a charge of—assault. You should be more grateful for your—privileges than you are.'[1]

The Latin plays are, of course, less hermetically closed than the school story. Confined within the comedic convention, the playwrights cannot raise the emotional pressure by pumping in religious and patriotic appeals; and the explicitness of theatrical presentation keeps them well below the proficiency in pornography which Kipling achieved in the torture chapter[2] of *Stalky & Co.* by a masterly inexplicitness and a narrative manner which employed to masturbatory effect rhythms and repetitiveness borrowed from the Authorised Version or from the Authorised-Version-like saga-style into which the public schools translated Homer. None the less, the Plautine-Terentian comedy is creating its emotionally milder world out of the same ingredients, which now take the form of a rich father's absolute right to withold money from his adolescent son, and free citizens' right to flog their slaves. The son has nothing to oppose to the father's severity except his adolescent charm and what practical help, in the way of subterfuges, he can get from the slave; and the slave in his turn has nothing to put between himself and a beating except his wits. The comedy which arises out of this is the comedy of threats: verbally one character belabours another with what he will do to him if——; and the comedy of situation consists of narrow escapes from that threatened *if*. The imbroglio depends on a rebellion on the part of the son and the slave; but it is only a cardboard rebellion, the son possessing no more genuine independence of spirit than his schoolboy counterpart—who possesses no more than he will need when he has become a subaltern in the Indian Army. The end in both genres is a sentimental reconciliation between master and rebels. The father succumbs to the freckled, tousled charm of the scapegrace son, and to the witty ingenuity with which the slave has gulled him: the son acquiesces in the father's authority (which, after all, he will presently inherit) and the slave responds with the masochistic devotion servants and horses are traditionally supposed to feel towards firm handling. (Terence, in the *Hauton Timorumenos*, is as contemptuous of indulgent fathers as the school stories are of weak schoolmasters.) The status quo is only the more solidly established after the seeming rebellion, which has merely tightened the erotic bonds between the classes. The charm which the rebels hold for the masters is cheekiness, which in itself implies that the rebel knows his place; it is the charm the

[1] *Stalky & Co.*, 'The Impressionists'   [2] 'The Moral Reformers'

proletarian holds for the upper-class homosexual. The master insists on his absolute right to be severe: if the rebel gets off, it is not of right but through the master's generosity; and if the master is to be generous, he insists on being won—seduced—into it by the rebel's charm. The master has, therefore, the masochistic delight of thinking of himself as twisted round his underling's little finger, even while he retains his full sadistic rights over the underling. He has exploited the underling emotionally and sexually: it is the mark of the underling in a homosexually closed world that he has to pay for whatever concessions he may win by continually being sexually attractive; he is a sexual court jester.

Thus Victorian literature re-instated childhood and adolescence in the public attention. But, as the quality of the attention makes clear, they were often carried into prominence on the crest of certain emotional impulses towards them. In the same way, the nineteenth century restored religion to intellectual currency but only in the course of a religious revival. It had reversed the direction of the process, but it stuck to the eighteenth century's misapprehension. Neither did it disentangle the eighteenth-century confusion about fantasy. Even more censoriously than the eighteenth century, it judged the content of artistic fantasies by criteria of morality and decency; and where the eighteenth century had asked for only a long-term moral tendency, the Victorians found it necessary to ban the very representation of objects and acts the mere sight of which might call up by association the desires they regarded as immoral and indecent. As far as religious art was concerned, the religion and the art were still felt to be inseparable: Protestants found it impossible to appreciate the baroque poems and canvasses of the Counter-Reformation; and people who wanted to enjoy medieval art tried to induce in themselves a sort of belief in the Christianity and the feudalism which had supplied its iconography and occasion. Eventually the confusion included secular art as well. The eighteenth century had been inclined to forgo all fictions because it did not want the religious ones. The nineteenth came to believe it must have religious fictions if it was to have fictions at all—a belief it was provoked into by the philistinism of science, which often behaved as though it had disproved the arts along with the book of *Genesis*: and the aesthete of the nineties wore his Roman Catholicism on his sleeve as a badge of his artistic sensibility.

2. Logic the Ego's Lieutenant

The enlightenment was fortified in its misapprehensions by logic. Logic was not, of course, responsible for them; it was psychic, not intellectual, forces which drove the eighteenth century into them: but once there, the enlightenment raised on its psychic situation an intellectual superstructure whose very weight helped to perpetuate its misapprehensions—even through the reaction against it.

The vicious circle whereby the eighteenth century's psychological ignorance deepened its psychological ignorance was in fact the vicious circle inherent in a deductive logic which refuses to call in the help of the imagination—or the inductive methods—of science. Deduced conclusions are only as good as the propositions from which they are drawn. If the premisses are false, all the deductive logic in the world can yield only a more and more searching acquaintance with what would have been true if the premisses had been true.

The enlightenment might have taken warning from the history of traditional logic, which had enjoyed its great period in the middle ages in the dearth of science. Aristotle's own discovery of logic was a manifestation of his elastic scientific curiosity. Yet by his discovery he unwittingly set up a shelter in which the intellect could take refuge from reality without forfeiting its intellectuality or its faculty of judgment: and the impulsion to use that shelter was applied by Christianity.

If it was not to give up nonfiction thought altogether, Christianity had to choose between the sciences, which might contradict it, and logic, which could formally demonstrate the contradictoriness of contradictions. Wisely from its own point of view, it chose logic. Having threatened all its children that it was sinful to take an interest in the tangible world and the palpable flesh, it was now able to seduce the cleverest of them by flattery, suggesting that it was a waste of time to enquire into particular aspects of reality when one could study its essence by learning logic. The danger to science lay not in the nature of logic, but in its prestige: the man who possessed himself of the scientia scientiarum, the knowledge of knowledge, could feel excused from acquiring any particular branch of knowledge. Logic was promoted to the vice-regency of Christendom, second only to theology itself, and was enlisted to prove the contentions of theology.

This, of course, logic was incapable of doing: all it could prove was the self-consistency of the theological system. The only statements which *must* be true in a logical process are the ones logic cannot prove but has to assume from the start, truths of the order of 'A thing cannot be both X and not-X'. These truths logic tosses into the logical process, where they behave as a catalyst, emerging unchanged after provoking a reaction among the other statements fed into the machine.

The logician derived part of his prestige from his daily familiarity with essential truths of this kind, even though he could not analyse them or encroach on them in any way. Another part of his prestige, however, came from what he was *not* familiar with—from what he did not handle at all; and it was here that superstitition began to build up a numinous reputation round logic, and presently round philosophy, to the detriment of science. Logic is, in fact, an exercise in seeing the propositions submitted to it solely in the light of these catalyst-truths. Confronted with a concept or a statement, logic distinguishes in it nothing but its possibilities for being formally related to another. The imagery and the import of a proposition are immaterial to logic, which is the knack of seizing on the assertion and not seeing its content. Of all studies, logic is the one with the least content; even mathematics, which symbolic logic presently came to resemble when it banned from logical practice even the possibility of perceiving an image by accident, deals in quantities. Logic makes the most dazzling display of concentration: it is in pointed contrast to the associative method whereby an artist exploits images for their sensuous and emotional content, and equally in contrast to the train of associations followed by the scientist's curiosity.

Logic never maintained, of course, that the human mind always functions in this concentrated way, but only that it must be made to do so for the purposes of logic. The danger to knowledge began only with the belief that those purposes were the noblest the human mind could entertain. Logic could claim a redoubled share of the intellectual superiority which really does belong to theory. An architectural theory which can account for how buildings stand up really is more deeply thoughtful than the mere practice of making them stand up; and it seemed that logic, as the theory of theory, must be equally much more thoughtful than any of the theories.

As a matter of fact, the analytical effort required is probably the same for all theories, including logic; and the others can actually claim an advantage over logic, because they make use of imagination into the bargain. But in any case, the prestige of logic was not really based on a belief in the superiority of thought, but on the unadmitted but inveterate belief that matter is equivalent to faeces, and that those who come in contact with it are childish. The artisan was consigned to the proletariat not because he did not understand the theory of what he was doing—no more did the feudal baron or the gentleman squire—but because he could not keep his hands clean. It was the taint of the manual which gave painting and sculpture such a hard struggle before they were accepted among the liberal arts[1]—the taint, that is, of a childish preoccupation with giving shape to lumps of matter or with smearing surfaces with moist, sticky, smelly material. By this criterion, logic truly was one remove more abstract than any of the arts or sciences. It had banished not merely material but the imagist value in concepts of material. It abstained from mental contact with matter; it was a complete intellectual structure raised on exercising the mind's power to repress ideas by isolating them. In its alliance with theology, logic held the intellect of Europe in isolation from physical matter; and the sciences did not advance until they had broken this grip and allowed themselves to consider matter, disclosing its properties by accepting the stimulus it offered to curiosity.

Here again the eighteenth century might have taken warning from the fact that the grip of theology was broken not by a more stringent application of logic but by a flood of information into Europe. But instead of taking the warning, it set about processing everything that came to its notice through the logical machine. The prestige of logic spread to its inseparable companion, metaphysics[2]; and the mechanical infallibility which logic really did possess in its limited sphere was attributed to the quite unlimited and amorphous study of metaphysics. The century abandoned itself to a riot, a positive folly of philosophy—which paternally subsumed even the physical sciences.

It was the prestige of the philosophers which provided the intellectual pretext for the fantasy-attempt the eighteenth century was making to live in and for the Ego alone. John Oulton Wisdom

[1] Vide, e.g., Anthony Blunt: *Artistic Theory In Italy* . . ., IV

[2] 'Logic . . . cannot be separated from metaphysics; indeed, it derives its chief importance from its connexion therewith'. (H. W. B. Joseph: *An Introduction To Logic*, VII)

has written a persuasive book[1] analysing one eighteenth-century philosophy, Berkeley's attempt to banish matter from reality, as an expression of Berkeley's ambivalence towards and unconscious hatred of faeces. But in fact what Berkeley attempts to do for the universe by the actual import of his philosophy is only what all philosophy does for its own field of study by its method. The intellectual tendency of the eighteenth century as a whole achieved exactly the same result as Berkeley without going to the imaginative effort of elaborating a fantasy in philosophical form, by illegitimately extending the philosophical method and sifting every approach to reality through philosophy. Logic had become the henchman of philosophy, whereas in the middle ages it had been the henchman of theology: it was serving the tyranny of the Ego, in place of the tyranny of authority; and logic plus philosophy began to perform just the same repression through isolation which had been the intellectual instrument of Christianity's tyranny.

The natural sciences had to emancipate themselves all over again; and they did not burst into their period of rapid growth until, in the nineteenth century, they had broken the hold of philosophy. Many of the scientists shared precisely the philosophers' estimation of matter and used their discoveries about it to smear philosophy, in the belief that they were discrediting philosophy not only in its illegitimate extension but altogether. Now, when science has invented the atom bomb and seems about to destroy us, the balance of superstition has bobbed up again in the philosopher's favour. Unconsciously holding that to probe matter is dirty and that to pursue scientific enquiry is to be curious about things the father has forbidden us to investigate, we conceive that science is recoiling on us in punishment. Our response to the scientific robot marching on us is not to press further into science and seek to understand the mind which controls the robot, but to propitiate the father by promising not to play with science any more. Those who cannot run all the way back to theology find philosophy ready to receive them, with its ability to consider facts without seeing their content and its refusal to dabble in matter. The philosopher has recovered much of his primitive prestige; he shines out as a holy simpleton, an uncontaminated innocent, whose great claim on our respect is that he does not wield any factual information whatsoever.

At the end of the nineteenth century, however, and the beginning

[1] *The Unconscious Origins Of Berkeley's Philosophy*

of the twentieth, science was still held in repute, if not always happily (which was thanks in great measure to the philistinism, cruelty and science-superstition of scientists), and logicians were anxious to claim the protection of scientific achievements. The great logical textbooks of the period do not, of course, pretend that formal logic had played any part in the development of science; in fact, they honourably point out that scientific thought—indeed, logical thought— is quite independent of the study of logic. But there remained, for logicians who had not gone symbolist, one sphere in which they could exercise a sort of disingenuousness: the selection of examples. The remarkable thing about the examples which illustrate the discourse in logical textbooks is that they are all true[1] and most of them scientific: the author has not only mustered his own mathematics and classical history but has evidently applied to colleagues at High Table. The content of an example is, of course, immaterial from the logical point of view; and this convenient blindness on the part of logic enabled the logicians to ignore, even while they deliberately created, the psychological effect made on the reader by logic books filled with true statements about the rays of the sun, the properties of carbon and the classification of ruminants or rodents—all of which conspired to suggest, without stating, that there was a necessary, instead of a merely possible, connexion between logic and science, and at the same time thoroughly masked the truth, which is not only historical but highly relevant to the nature of logic, that logic can and once did proceed just as logically within a pre-Galileo cosmology and a pre-Lamarck biology—or, indeed, within medieval theology.

(Once one begins to consider the actual content of logical examples —that is, to consider them psychologically instead of logically—one has to consider them as symptoms of the author as well as implicit messages to the reader. [Many examples are, of course, Aristotelian or traditional—though even here one may wonder why the scholastic tradition laid such repetitive emphasis on the mortality of Socrates.] H. W. B. Joseph's choice of examples reveals his concern with ecclesiastical and sectarian politics: and from this taken together with his

---

[1] H. W. B. Joseph points out (*An Introduction To Logic*, VII) that the very nature of a judgment is to assert its truth, and that a lie is not a judgment. But while Joseph's text consists of his own judgments, there is no reason why his illustrations should make assertions Joseph himself believed to be true; they would still be examples of judgments if he did not, providing somebody once had.

predilection for scientific examples one can almost read his great *Introduction To Logic* in a sense which never slipped into a line of his text: as an attempt to reconcile science to religion, within the cover of logic. Something more personal about Joseph is perhaps revealed by his rendering of an example [itself drawn from tradition, but this time not logical tradition] in his 'Appendix On Fallacies'[1]. He mentions the old trap of requiring someone to answer Yes or No to the question 'Have you stopped beating your wife?': but according to Joseph the question runs 'Have you left off beating your mother?')

Yet although the other sciences emancipated themselves during the nineteenth century, the science of psychology did not. The material was there, having been thrust up into notice by the romantic reaction, but it remained in the province of literature. The worst literature could do was to add to the psychopathological material which a science of psychology would eventually be able to elucidate. The best was, of course, the psychological novel—in which, however, the psychology remained implicit and unformulated and therefore inaccessible except through and for art. The science of psychology still did not appear, although it had been named and a place left vacant for it. Logical text-books expressly distinguished logic from psychology and indicated the area which psychology should occupy. But how little the logicians were prepared for what a psychology would say when it did arrive in scientific form is revealed by a remark Bernard Bosanquet made in his lectures on logic[2]: 'Several of those present have, I believe, attended a previous course of lectures on Psychology. They have learned, I presume, to think of the mind as the course of consciousness, a continuous connected presentation. . .'[3]

[1] The appendix is actually a chapter (XXVII) as well. The decision to have it both ways reflects Joseph's uncertainty whether to have it all: the appendix-chapter begins by doubting whether it is advisable to discuss fallacies at all in a work devoted to the principles of correct reasoning. This over-strict— that is, not wholly rational—conscience, which also forbids Joseph to employ logical examples for whose truth he is not prepared to vouch, probably had its prickly part to play in what I surmise to be Joseph's need to reconcile science and religion. It is interesting that he insists (bringing it up again in his discussion of whether to discuss fallacies) that logic is a science.

[2] *The Essentials Of Logic*, I (first published 1895)

[3] To be fair, Bosanquet does go on to say (my italics): 'This course of consciousness, *including certain latent elements, the existence of which it is necessary to assume*, is an invididual mind. . .' He had presumably recognised that without these latent elements the individuality and continuous identity of our minds

For all the logicians' courtesy in making a place for it, it was logic which was standing in the way of psychology, just as it had earlier stood in the way of the other sciences. Psychology had in this respect a disability the others did not: it dealt with the same material, mental judgments, as logic. Since there already existed a perfectly good science for analysing and classifying mental judgments, it was difficult to see in practice what was left for psychology to do, though the logicians attempted to point it out in principle. They themselves, however, were not entirely clear about the distinction between the reasonableness of logic and the reasonable faculty which allows a human being to apply it. The reasonableness of rational judgment is justified by the direct appeal logic makes to reality: but this appeal asks reality for no sort of account of how a living organism is capable of making it. Logic had provided a logical critique of itself, not a biological one—which, of course, it was its precise duty to do; but logic and philosophy allowed themselves to be so impressed by this achievement that they behaved as though, reason being reality-justified, it was also reality-given (or, via the hypothesis of a Supreme Creator of reality, God-given). The lingering kudos of logic and philosophy was tacitly suggesting that there was no need to ask *how* a human being judged reasonably since it was so obviously reasonable for him to do so.

3. *The Final Emancipation*

When the science of psychology at last emerged, at the turn of the century, the method it perfected was to scrutinise the very things which logical method systematically ignores.

Psycho-analytic technique, as opposed to logical technique, is the knack of seeing the content of a belief—through the eyes of the person who holds it. Obviously, psycho-analysis is also concerned with whether or not the belief is reasonable—given, that is, the information available to the believer; but in any belief, whether reasonable or unreasonable, true or false, it is concerned as well with the actual imagist content, since to discover the significance these images hold for the believer, by means of following up his associations with

would not survive a night's sleep; or perhaps he was only considering the smaller problem of memory.

them, is the only access we have to the instinctual sources of his act of judgment.

A completely fantastic belief, such as what the dreamer believes to be happening while he is in the course of dreaming, is evidently much closer to being wholly shaped by instinctual forces than a belief which is conscious, reasonable and true. Yet even the soberest, most factual, scientific belief in the world is not created as a mental act, though it may be justified as a logical act, by the external state of affairs it reports or is consistent with. There still remain to be described the instinctual forces which create the attention the believer's mind is paying to reality—attention being precisely what noninstinctual, inanimate activity cannot pay. Instinct has a great deal of latitude in determining what we shall *notice* in order to judge about it reasonably or realistically—as well as being able, of course, to interrupt our rational faculty or partially blind it, withdrawing instead of creating attention and, instead of supplying the faculty of rational and conscious judgment, starving it into closing down. Indeed, we cannot bear to remain conscious, let alone rational, for a day and a night together but become mad, as Tom Paine remarked, once in every twenty-four hours.

Psychology found itself, therefore, picking up a great deal of its material out of the wastepaper-baskets of the eighteenth century. It rediscovered childhood; it brought out and examined the contents of the myths, dreams and delusions the eighteenth-century philosophers had discarded the moment they found them untrue. What this amounted to was the re-instatement of fantasy—of wish: and it was expressions of wishes which Aristotle had specifically refused to regard as propositions, thereby excluding them from consideration by logic, because they did not make a factual assertion that was capable of being true or false. 'Not every sentence is a proposition, but only one which has it in it to be true or false. This capacity is not in all; for example, a prayer (εὐχή—prayer, vow, wish, curse) is a sentence but not true or false'.[1]

The eighteenth century, in its overestimation of logic's legitimate field, had concluded that, because logic had nothing to say about

---

[1] *Organon*, 17a. L. S. Stebbing (*A Modern Introduction To Logic*, IV) glozes Aristotle: 'It is clear that commands, requests, exclamatory sentences and expressive sighs are not propositions.' Joseph (*An Introduction To Logic*, VII) completes a similar list by adding interrogations. (This is not perhaps a complete account if one considers Latin questions: those in -ne are clearly not propositions, but one might argue that those beginning num or nonne are.)

wishes, reason had nothing to say about them. Once again the nineteenth century concurred in the mistake; for, although it brought
out much of the fantasy-material the eighteenth century had discarded, it treated the material fantastically, not rationally. In this
respect, psycho-analysis made a synthesis of the intellectual achievements of the two preceding centuries: it treated nineteenth-century
material in the light of eighteenth-century reason. It had, however,
extended the concept of reason beyond logic to science. If the eighteenth century established, once and for all, man's right to reason, it
was psycho-analysis which for the first time used the right at full stretch.

The eighteenth century had taken the logical point that all untrue
beliefs are equally untrue (and, the rationalists added, equally worthless morally). But it went on to make the scientific mistake of treating
them all as much of a muchness: in Tom Paine's view, the New
Testament might just as well have made the Holy Ghost a goose as a
dove. Psycho-analysis corrected him on the scientific (though not the
moral) issue by shewing that, when a belief has been established as
logically unjustifiable, it is not thereupon consigned to a chaotic
world, from which we can imagine the contents of the belief to have
been assembled by the most arbitrary chance. On the contrary, the
contents have been promoted by wishes, whose behaviour is just as
much to be explored by reason as the behaviour of planets or amoebae,
though wishes, planets and amoebae are not themselves able to reason.
Conversely, when a belief has been vindicated as reasonable by its
consistency with certain general conditions of reality, those conditions
do not promptly take over from wish (itself, of course, perfectly real)
the responsibility of having brought the belief into existence. Logic
questions whether a belief *is* reasonable, and enquires into the conditions in which it can be judged so: psychology questions what has
created the belief in its reasonable or unreasonable form, questioning
whether the wish for the belief to be true has predominated over the
wish to explore reality. Wrong arguments and untrue belief, which
held so little value for logic that H. W. B. Joseph hesitated to treat of
them at all, were of the utmost value to psycho-analysis, not as object
lessons (the use traditional logic found for them), but as symptoms
leading back to the wishes which create reasonable as well as unreasonable judgments.

The mark that a logical judgment is taking place is the timeless,
depersonalised 'is' which serves as the copula in a proposition, indicating that the proposition claims that one thing is or is not predicated

of another. Psycho-analysis was to trace the evolutionary connexion between an assertion—in the sense of an impulse—of instinct and the conscious, factual mental assertion of which this 'is' is the formal mark, a mark which bears the same relation to a psychic act as a geometric point to a place.

4. Man and Subman

The re-instatement of wish was a re-instatement of instinct; a biological point of view had been imported into thinking about mental processes. The mark of a living organism, which distinguishes it from a dead or inanimate one, is that it *wants*. We know it is alive because it is selfish: and it *is* a self in a sense that other entities and processes are not, namely that some of its organisation directly expresses a wish on the part of that organisation to keep its entity intact. We cannot imagine that a whirlwind is expressing any wish to go on being a whirlwind or takes any steps to prevent itself from being dispersed and fused with calmer processes of the air. But the activity we call life is invariably organised in such a way that by taking place at all it prepares for the perpetuation of life, whether in the same organism or its descendants: and, within the limits of the organism's mortality, it is also directed towards preserving the organism's self from being merged with the environment.

Here, at the very roots of life, discernible in even the most rudimentary life-activity, is a tremendous faculty of discrimination, whereby the self holds itself discrete from not-self. We must recognise, even in the amoeba's behaviour, the instinct of Eros, which compels the amoeba to create relationships with things which are not itself and to convert some of them by bringing them within the jurisdiction of its own organisation; and we must at the same time recognise the instinct of Thanatos, which asserts that between the self and certain other non-self things no relationship is to exist. A living body consists of nothing but certain portions of the environment caught up into the self's sphere and used for its purposes; but the self must also have constantly at its disposal the discriminatory power to preserve the identity of its selfhood, and to make sure that what it takes in becomes subservient to *it* and not vice versa. Life is the play of the two instincts. An organism is prolonged in time, and perhaps extended in space, by the voracious activity of Eros. But this would not prolong and extend the organism's life at all, though it might some other organism's, if the organism's self were not defined and delimited, sealed into its own continuous identity, by the discriminating power of Thanatos.

The most deeply searching of Freud's achievements was to discern that our unconscious psychic life is conducted on the same twofold instinctual principle as the metabolic life of a single cell. The psyche negotiates its environment by means of an act of instinctual judgment exerting the force of either Eros or Thanatos or both in a certain combination. This is an unconscious and subjective version of the judgment which logic later objectifies and intellectualises. The logical judgment is an affirmation of the *fact* that something is or is not predicated of a Subject Term. In the psychic judgment, the subject does its own judging, and the judgment is the self's own affirmation of its instinctual *wish* to be or not to be related to not-self. 'Expressed in the language of the oldest, that is, of the oral, instinctual impulses', wrote Freud[1], 'the alternative runs thus: "I should like to eat that, or I should like to spit it out"; or, carried a stage further: "I should like to take this into me and keep that out of me". That is to say: it is to be either *inside* me or *outside* me.'

As a matter of fact, this judgment, which we have to represent as 'I should like', does not appear in those terms to the unconscious psyche which makes it—any more than it does to the amoeba when it makes a similar judgment. In the amoeba, which is not subject to what Freud called[2] the 'procrastinating character of thought', an impulse to action and the action itself are one and the same. The amoeba makes no distinction between wishing to do and doing; and it is from its deeds that we infer the existence and quality of its instinctual impulses. Or, to be more precise, we infer them from its attempts; for it may, of course, be prevented from achieving its deed. If, however, some external interruption does frustrate it in this way, the amoeba experiences the frustration only in the form of the renewal of the impulse. It tries again; but, since it lacks any psychic system in which to store traces of its experiences and compare one with the other, it does not conceive that the renewed impulse *is* a repetition.

The baby, of course, is endowed with the psychic capacity the amoeba lacks. It *can* store traces of the sensations it has experienced and rearrange them into images. In one sense, however, the

[1] *Collected Papers*, Volume V, XVI
[2] *Collected Papers*, Volume V, XVI

unconscious psychic system continues to function like the amoeba. Just as the amoeba's instinctual impulse is translated directly into an attempt at bodily action, the baby's is translated directly into psychic action—that is, into images of the sensations of doing the action: in other words, into fantasy.

We have to represent the baby's instinctual impulses by a formula in which we imagine the baby to be saying 'I should like'. But this is because we are concerned with the question whether the baby really does take this into its mouth or spit that out. The unconscious, however, is not concerned with that question, which, indeed, it cannot raise; and it knows no 'should like'. We, as conscious beings, mean by a wish something which is necessarily not so; to wish for sunshine means that the sun is not shining in the outside world. To the unconscious, on the other hand, the wish cannot present itself in any other form than that of a perception that the sun is shining. The succession of events we experience during a dream *is* a wish: it is the only statement of wish the unconscious can entertain.

It is in this sense that unconscious desires are immortal and can be only repressed, not killed. Like the instinctual impulses of the amoeba, they can, of course, be frustrated from outside or—which does not apply to the amoeba—by another agency within the psyche. But the unconscious has no more appreciation than the amoeba of frustration or of the fact that a wish has failed. An unconscious impulse can mark the fact that it has not been discharged only by presenting itself again.

Once the baby has undergone enough sensational experience to create a stock of images, it has at its disposal a means of psychically satisfying its impulses merely by stating them. Fantasy is a self-contained system: frame a wish in the form of a fantasy and you experience its fulfilment—which, so long as you remain unconscious, you cannot distinguish from the experience of its fulfilment in real life. We all retire into this closed system every night. However, as the baby quickly discovers, a series of fantasy meals, though it satisfies something, does not satisfy the needs of the body; and the baby quickly receives sensory signals from its body which cause it a disquiet that is not allayed except by a real-life meal. This situation, into which the mammalian species deposit their babies, is the great prod to psychic development, obliging the unconscious Id to produce an Ego, and presently a conscious Ego, capable of sorting out which sensations come from the baby's body when it is isolated and which of its bodily sensations depend on the presence of the not-self who supplies its food. But the whole power of the Id to learn from frustration lies in its power to evolve the Ego; the Id itself remains unteachable.

The Ego wields the great power of judging reality, which it does in relation to the organism's instinctual selfishness: it mediates between the instinctual impulses and the outside world which is their prey. The Ego's is the power to compare the psychic images, in which the wish is embodied, with the state of affairs outside. It judges whether an image present in the psyche is *only* present in the psyche or whether it is corroborated by something corresponding to it in the outside world.

At the start of its career, the psyche has, as Freud pointed out, no need for such a power, for 'originally the mere existence of the image serves as a guarantee of the reality of what is imagined'[1]. The newly born baby is as undeludable as the amoeba. It is only when it has stored up enough images to begin to exercise its faculty of fantasy that necessity obliges it to evolve an Ego capable of distinguishing fantasy from fact.

In order to perform this new type of judgment, the psyche adapts the faculty of instinctual judgment it has possessed all along. The new judgment decides whether an object is present only in the imagination or whether it exists outside as well: 'once more', as Freud remarked, '. . . the question is one of *external* and *internal*'. In the earliest form of judgment, Eros asserted that there was to be an identity between the self and the object. In the intellectual judgment, Eros is no longer propounding the wish for identity: it is stating that there is a similarity between internal image and external object; but it is still fulfilling its erotic task of binding the two things together, though it is perceiving rather than creating an identity. Similarly, the negative intellectual judgment, when it denies that there is any identity between the internal image and the outside world, is employing the instinctual power of Thanatos to cut off the self from relationships with not-self; it is expelling or repelling not-self from self. In Freud's words, 'negation, the derivative of expulsion, belongs to the instinct of destruction.' (This power, if it ran riot unchecked by Eros, would lead to biological suicide by completely enclosing the psyche in its own world and breaking off the life-negotiation with reality; indeed, Freud traces 'the passion for universal negation, the

[1] This and the other quotations in the remainder of this section are from *Collected Papers*, Volume V, XVI

BLACK SHIP TO HELL

"negativism", displayed by many psychotics' to a withdrawal of the Eros component from impulses which as a rule consist of Eros and Thanatos in fusion.)

5. *A good word for Aristotle*

Anyone who reads Freud's condensed and suggestive paper on 'Negation', from which I have already quoted extensively, must respond by awarding full marks to Aristotle for the psychological perceptions he embodied in what he meant to be a logical analysis.

Aristotle's finding was that the proposition (the expression of a mental judgment) concerns two Terms; that it is either affirmatory or negative—either relates the two Terms or denies that they are related; and that the relationship it affirms or denies between them is that of predication: the proposition affirms or denies one thing of another[1]. The 'logical form' of a proposition was therefore Subject-copula-Predicate: S is (or is not) P: and into this form traditional logic undertook to squeeze even those statements whose idiomatic form was quite different.

It was not difficult for modern logicians to shew that this did violence not only to idiom but to analysis. As they ranged over the whole realm of the relationships which the human intellect can perceive and state, they discovered that there are several which cannot be adequately expressed as predications. The traditional practice of re-arranging such a proposition as 'Brutus killed Caesar' into 'Brutus is a man who killed Caesar' was, according to Susan Stebbing[2], 'as logically futile as it is practically absurd'. Moreover, once it was granted that a proposition might state a relationship by some other copula than 'is', it was clear that certain relationships necessarily subsist between more than two fixed points. A complete statement about, for example, a relationship of giving (a notion which includes owing and teaching) must tell us who gives what to whom[3]. (Gertrude Stein's most memorable remark was perhaps an attempt at expressing a three-pointed proposition in traditional logic form.)

[1] *Organon*, 24a: Πρότασις μὲν οὖν ἐστὶ λόγος καταφατικὸς ἢ ἀποφατικὸς τινὸς κατά τινος.

[2] *A Modern Introduction To Logic*, IV, 1

[3] Cf. L. S. Stebbing: *A Modern Introduction To Logic*, IV, 2

The traditional copula was also attacked as misleading even in its task of expressing predication. It could be said that the 'is' was a mere sign of predication, did not mean 'is' in the sense of 'exists' at all, and might as well be replaced by some out-and-out symbol. Against this Joseph put up a defence which was more psychological than logical: 'if there were no special appropriateness in the verb *to be*, as the sign of predication, it is strange that so many languages should have agreed to use it'[1].

Here—if one quite abandons logic and goes wholly over to psychology —is the germ of a vindication not merely for the use of 'is' to express predication but for the use of predication to express all the other relationships. What Aristotle was insisting on, though unknown to himself, was a 'special appropriateness' of the verb *to be* in forming relationships at all. Aristotle's insight had led him towards the emotional primacy of relationships of identification or exclusion; and in classifying propositions as affirmative or negative he picked on the principles of Eros and Thanatos. Naturally—from the point of view of psychology, though wrongly in logic—there are only two Terms in the proposition: they reflect the primal Terms in every relationship created by a living being, self and not-self. To dissociate one of these Terms from the self that is doing the judging; to perceive relationships between objects which are not connected with oneself by any impulse of Eros more primal than that one is paying attention to them: this belongs to a much later stage of psychic development— indeed, to the functions of the Ego. To do something *to* an object, whether kill it or love it; to have an object—still more to have it and give it: these relationships in themselves (and even more the perception of their existence between objects in the outside world) all have to be derived, by the Ego which employs them, from the original impulse in the self towards fusion with an object or exclusion of it.

As a matter of fact, Aristotle's analysis of propositions even goes on to hint at the manner whereby the Ego achieves its new power. Having divided propositions into affirmative and negative, he made a further division according to whether they affirm or deny the Predicate of the whole Subject Term or only part of it; so that to the two basic forms of proposition, All S is P and No S is P, he added two more, Some S is P and Some S is not P. If one translates the logical Subject Term back into the psychological subject, the self which does the judging, this new discovery is analogous to the

[1] *An Introduction To Logic*, VII

discovery which is forced on the baby by the repeated experience of mealtimes: the union the baby postulates between itself and the mother is not a fusion of beings at all, but a partial union; it is not eating the mother and becoming the mother, but eating the mother's milk, which becomes *it*, the baby.

In logic, the discovery leads on to the habit of thought, which some logicians deplore and others regard as the essence of logical method, of treating the Subject and Predicate Terms as classes: the proposition becomes a statement of how far their memberships overlap. The classes may, of course, wholly exclude one another, a case which the logic books represent diagrammatically by two entirely separate circles: two intersecting circles shew that part of S's membership coincides with part of P's: while if the whole of S is contained in P, the diagram consists of a large circle P, with a small circle S inside it[1].

The resemblance of these logical diagrams to the sketches and micro-photographs by which the biology textbooks illustrate the life-activity of the amoeba is more than formal and more than fortuitous. An amoeba engulfing its prey is making an instinctual assertion that one class is to be wholly subsumed within another: henceforth the prey is to *be* the amoeba; and an amoeba which has divided into two, and has just severed its last organic connexion with what was previously part of the first amoeba's substance and came under the domination and organisation of its self, is putting into action the principle which asserts intellectually that No S is P.

However, when a single cell divides but does not physically sever itself—though it does physically separate itself—from the new individuals which are produced, Eros and Thanatos are performing a much more complicated operation. Indeed, it is no longer proper to

[1] a situation which formal logic cannot differentiate from the case where S and P are co-extensive. 'All four-footed animals are quadrupeds' would be represented by an S and a P circle exactly on top of one another, whereas 'All pelicans are birds' is an S circle inside a P circle; but since there is nothing in the *form* of the proposition to distinguish the two cases (to make the distinction one has to know what pelicans are), logic for safety treats all propositions in this form as cases of S being contained in P, which must be true though it may also be true that in fact S and P are co-extensive. The diagrams also have difficulty in illustrating 'Some S is P' and 'Some S is not P', statements which insist only that some of S be shewn inside or outside some of P, and make no indication of how the diagram should dispose of the rest of S and the rest of P.

speak of the new cells as individuals but only as individual sub-units. The unit of individuality now resides in a higher class: the multi-cellular organism.

The relationship of the cells to one another in a complex animal or plant rests on a highly sophisticated development of the instinctual capacities. There is, so to speak, enough Thanatos exerted to keep the cells discrete, but enough Eros to bind each to its neighbour; and yet Eros must never insist on its original objective of complete fusion, by engulfing or being engulfed by its neighbour.

The cells have, in fact, undertaken a considerable renunciation of their own individuality, involving for most of them, in an organism of any complexity, such complete specialisation that they become incapable, in natural circumstances, of living independently. They have been prevailed on to make these sacrifices by the introduction of a higher unit, to belong to which offers them certain protections that independent life does not. In other words, the Eros which binds cell to cell has been induced to modify itself—persuaded to allow a certain Thanatic separateness to intervene between itself and the objective of fusion—through the influence of the common relationship which holds all the cells bound to the organism as a whole: the cells are bound to one another through the medium of being bound to the whole.

This situation has remarkable affinities with what happens in the psychic sphere when the baby discovers that it cannot be identical with its mother. The baby, of course, is not a new species of animal evolving a new way of life for the first time; it does not have to be induced to make certain sacrifices in the sense that cells must have been the first time they ever combined. The baby's psychic evolution consists largely of its recognising and accommodating itself to conditions which in fact its species has already imposed on it. Factually, it has no choice but to accept them; but psychically it still has to be induced to. Indeed, a whole section of its psyche never is prevailed upon to make any such surrender. The baby which is all Id is quite lively enough, from an instinctual point of view, to live, but quite unfitted to live the life its species has in fact imposed on it. The species has to impose on it also a parent, who will impose on it the sacrifices it cannot yet undertake for itself. The viable human unit is baby plus parent or, later, baby plus Ego (these being the constituents of a human adult).

Thus the baby never has really experienced the complete fusion of its own identity with another (unless we suppose it to preserve a trace of the experience of the sperm and the ovum in losing themselves in one another). The foetus's experience of an identity between itself and its mother when it is in her womb is subjective and rests on the foetus's having no standard of comparison. All the same, the baby has to be forced from one side and bribed from the other into giving up the goal of identification and accepting in its place the faculty of loving an object. Even so, the Oedipus situation has only to put obstacles in the way of the child's getting the object it wants, and the original desire for identification re-asserts itself. It does so, however in the modified form to which the Ego can reduce it. Instead of seeking a merger with the father, the child is content to take the image of the father into its own psychic constitution.

It is by virtue of this modification that the child becomes psychically (though once again history will have seen to it that he was objectively so from the start) a member of a social group. His relationships are now carried on, as logic unwittingly predicted they would, in terms of the overlapping or exclusion of classes. The psyche has traded some of its independence for membership of a group, which affords it parental-type protections in its relations with the environment. It has cut out some of the frequencies of its erotic impulse, with the result that its group ties are of an aim-inhibited kind; and the love which binds it to its fellow-members in the group operates only through the medium of the common bond between each member and the communal father.

This is not a complete parallel to the cells' sacrifice in the interest of the multicellular individual, since that individual would not exist at all but for the contributions made by the cells, whereas the father-leader stands outside the group, however much he imprints his own character on it and however much its subservience to him creates his character. (Indeed, by releasing him from the group mentality, it gives him the chance to *have* an individual character.) In one sense, however, the father really does exist only in the existence of his children, and that is if we take him as the representative and temporary embodiment of the continuity of the species. It is true to say that the children sacrifice some of their independence to the species—though again the psychic sacrifice is only a recognition of what has already been exacted from them biologically.

In the social insects, birds and mammals, the species itself arranges that the individual's sacrifice shall be to the advantage not only of the species but of a smaller unit within it, the social group—and in most cases the instrument of this arrangement seems to be to impose on the baby a period in which it is helpless and has to be cared for by the community or the parents. Man, who is not only bodily but psychically helpless as a baby, is the most flexible of animals in his development: he evolves by making his own response to his infantile circumstances, with the result that not only are human individuals more variously differentiated from one another than other animals but so are human social groups. Yet though the group is no longer imposed directly by the species, it is still making use of the form of the species and exists by virtue of the individuals' sacrifice to it. The group, like the species, can maintain its own continuous identity despite the death and replacement of the individuals in it. It has become a super-individual[1]: the historian can chronicle it as though it were an individual, writing 'France succeeded; the church failed', just as the natural historian can chronicle the species or, indeed, the family or Order, and tell us that the dinosaurs at first succeeded and then failed. Human groups have even become rivals to the species, so many attempts at breakaway movements, in which the father-leader sets up as founding father; but the method by which he hopes to imprint his own character on his descendants is psychic and cultural instead of hereditary. The species depends for its perpetuation on Eros in its sexual manifestation. This the group must make use of, too: it cannot outlast its individual members unless they have children: but it has cast its own interest on the vehicle provided by the species, and insists that the children, besides receiving through heredity the marks of the species, also receive through education the cultural marks of the group. And what is effective in achieving this is, of course, the aim-inhibited love which binds citizen to citizen through their common love for the leader who is culturally their father.

Thus the human group owes its existence to a modification of the sexual impulse which the species has placed in its individuals, just as the multicellular individual came into existence through a modification of the voracious Eros of the individual cell: 'we shall be reminded', Freud wrote in his analysis of the group's psychic structure[2], 'of a valuable remark of Trotter's, to the effect that the tendency towards

[1] Traditional logic, with its habit of treating the Subject Term as a class, had to treat individuals, when they occurred in propositions, as classes: the form of 'Socrates is a man' was analysed as All S is P.

[2] *Group Psychology And The Analysis Of The Ego*, III

the formation of groups is biologically a continuation of the multi-cellular character of all the higher organisms'.

6. 'Since By Man Came Death'

Speculation—if it is carried, as Shaw carried it in the last part of *Back To Methuselah*, 'as far as thought can reach'—would dearly like to know where Thanatos, the death instinct, came from. Of course, it would also like to know where Eros came from, which is equally a mystery. But that is at least a mystery we are familiar with. We are quite accustomed to understanding that we do not understand how certain chemical substances, undergoing certain chemical reactions, became possessed of this instinct which, although it is dependent on chemistry, is itself not a chemical reaction at all, and which is capable of wanting, so inexorably, to extend and continue life. 'The manifestations of Eros', wrote Freud, 'were distinct and audible enough'[1], whereas Thanatos 'works in silence'[2].

Theology had its own account of how death was introduced into the scheme of living things: it was in punishment for man's disobedience to the father who had created him. There was, as a matter of fact, a certain economic difficulty in the story, since the destructive principle must have been introduced before man could be disobedient. Disobedience to an authority is nothing short of an attempt to destroy the authority; and indeed we know from Theodor Reik that Adam's crime was to attempt to destroy the father in his totem manifestation. It was for wishing to kill God that Adam and Eve suffered the punishment of being made subject to death. The myth is quite aware of this economic difficulty and meets it by having the destructive idea, the notion of disobedience, suggested to the children by an outside agency, the serpent. However, the myth is not successful in concealing from us that the serpent is really the same person as the creative father. Indeed, with its phallic shape, the serpent represents the father in the very essence of his creativeness. (Homer emphasises that a god is always and quintessentially a father [and a goddess a mother] by having Poseidon tell a nymph he has just seduced that she will bear a child

[1] *Civilization And Its Discontents*, VI
[2] *An Autobiographical Study*, V

'since the embraces of gods are not infertile'[1].) What the serpent whispers is the very message that the thought of the father's phallos does convey to the son, namely 'You, too, could possess this creative power; you could replace the father; you, too, could be a god—that is, a father.'

Thus man did not really escape the responsibility. The original wish to do away with someone was already in man, who responded to temptation. And in fact theology, though it denied that man was responsible for the idea, which it attributed to Satan, did not deny that man's was the moral responsibility for making use of the idea, and accepted it as quite just that man should be killed for having wanted to kill God. This put into religion's hands the great hope it regularly holds out to mankind. If myth maintains that man is mortal because of a sin he once committed, it is open to myth to elaborate a story in which a man who is heroic enough can undo the effect of his predecessor's deed, either by reconciling man to God and winning God's forgiveness for the crime, or else by finishing off the crime his predecessor bungled and destroying the God who is inflicting this punishment of mortality on man. 'Since by man came death', Handel has the chorus announce in weighty sad notes—and then, after a pause, they burst out allegro 'by man came also the resurrection of the dead'[2].

The whole process is an illustration of the unconscious habit of taking the wish for the deed, and vice versa. Presented with the fact of man's mortality, the myth cannot interpret it except as an expression of a wish that he should be mortal, whether it is God who wishes it or man himself in the form of wishing to sin or, afterwards, wishing to be punished for sin. Conversely, the myth states its own wish as a fact: man's mortality is wished away by a narrative in which a hero overcomes death. Unfortunately, the immortality which the mystery religions, including Christianity, procured for their adherents remained

[1] (*Odyssey*, XI, 249-50.... ἐπεὶ οὐκ ἀποφώλιοι εὐναὶ ἀθανάτων.) Poseidon's claim is not always true of at least the manifest content of Greek myths. The marriage of his brother Hades to Persephone is without issue. But Persephone is so closely united in cult and personality to her mother Demeter that they are often regarded as aspects of a single personage (Frazer: *Spirits Of The Corn And Of The Wild*, II); perhaps, in the division of duties between them, Demeter has taken all the divine maternalness—which is, in fact, manifested in her passionately maternal love for Persephone.

[2] *Messiah*, No. 46 (*I Corinthians*, XV, 21)

in the realm of psychic images—in the afterlife or, like the resurrection of the body, in the future. The fact of mortality was still obstinately there in the real world, not only unsubdued but unexplained.

The myth does confirm one conclusion which psycho-analysis had already reached from experience and speculation, namely that there is a single instinct of destruction which may be directed either outward towards objects or inward against the self. But apart from this indirect value to the science of psychology, the myth appeared to have lost all scientific value—all its face-value, that is, as an account of the origin of death—when it turned out that organisms had not only lived but died for thousands of years before the appearance of man, who was supposed by his crime to have brought mortality on them.

Yet no sooner had biological science dismissed the myth than it discovered a fact which vindicated the myth—and vindicated it, moreover, not as a psychological document but as a straightforward account. The myth had erred in naming humanity as the level at which mortality was introduced. But mortality really had been introduced. 'Natural death' was not natural at all in the sense of being inherent in life: the amoeba was a form of life which was not subject to it. This observation, which was made by Weismann, suggested to Shaw the idea of bringing out the old Garden of Eden account of death and re-writing it in terms of evolutionary biology[1].

For the belief that by man came death, biology had substituted the idea that by multicellularity came death.

Freud's own brilliant speculation into the ultimate nature of Thanatos was that (consistently with the conservative nature of instinct in general—the tendency to snap back and restore a previous state of affairs that had been interrupted) it was an impulse to return living material to its original inanimate state. As a matter of fact, complex animals and plants are continually returning material to the common pool of inanimate material in the environment—not merely their waste products but actual cells which have been living and are now cast off dead. The selfhood of one of these organisms does not dominate one particular portion of matter throughout its life, but is maintained over a continual turnover of matter, like someone who stays in the same place by balancing on a turning wheel. What we call natural death is prepared for by a decline in the organism's power to draw on the environment in order to replace what is lost by this constant creeping death. The decline in the power of piecemeal self-renewal

[1] Back To Methuselah, Preface, 'Voluntary Longevity'; Postscript

(which is associated in the lifespan with the decline in the power of the individual as a whole to reproduce himself sexually) renders an organism vulnerable. A minor accident may be fatal to the senescent; and a minor accident in these circumstances is what we mean by natural death.

This is precisely what never happens to the amoeba, which is age-less: although we can measure its lifetime, it is never characterised by youth or senility. No inner susceptibility on its own part to acci-dents forces it to that final and wholesale act of excretion whereby complex organisms return their entire corpse to the compost heap. The speck of protoplasm over which the amoeba's self reigns ceases to live only if it is shattered by a major accident from outside. If Thanatos is an impulsion to return matter to the inanimate, we have to note that in the amoeba it does not succeed in its ambition.

Even so, this is not quite to assert what is often claimed for the amoeba, that it is, barring accidents, immortal. An amoeba *could* be kept in its immortal state, but only if it failed to encounter not only the unhappy accident which is capable of killing it but also the happy ones which present it with a mate and with enough to eat. The amoeba, having no age, has no mature period at which it is ripe to reproduce: it reproduces when it has grown big enough to split in two: and the moment this takes place, there is an end of the amoeba's immortality. Neither of these new amoebae is the original amoeba. From the point of view of the original, both these new ones are not-self. The original self, the first amoeba, no longer exists: it has died in giving birth to two descendants. We are deceived into thinking we see the original amoeba in its descendants; but in fact they are only making use of their parent's substance; what deceives us is that there is no substance left over, remaining the property of the parent or being returned to the inanimate. All that is really continuous and immortal in this process is the species—as it is in every act of reproduction. The difference is merely that in this case the species has managed the transaction without any waste of amoeba-substance; it has sacrificed nothing but the individuality by which the substance was previously governed. All the protoplasm concerned is still living, and still amoeba: but it is no longer *that* amoeba.

Much the same is true of the amoeba's curious act of copulation (which seems to have no necessary connexion with its act of repro-duction). The amoeba possesses two characteristics which romantic —that is, infantile—love would like to believe of human beings:

in itself it is ageless; and in its union with another it achieves a complete fusion—of substance and identity. Human sexual intercourse can give only an illusion of merging: the most consummate lovers cannot really share a single experience but can only depend on and make use of one another for the production of two separate experiences at the same time. This inadequacy is the perpetual complaint of the romantic lover against sexual intercourse. Lucretius expressed it in lines[1] which unite something of the intimacy of Donne's vision of sex with something of the bitterness of Shakespeare's: indeed, just as in attacking religion Lucretius wrote the best religious poetry in Latin, so he wrote some of the most passionate love-poetry in his disappointment with love. He has remarked that the earliest oral appetite, that for food, really does take the desired object into the body, with the result that the appetite can be satisfied; but when this method of loving is applied to a human being, the lover can assimilate from the body he desires nothing but frail images; Venus mocks lovers with images; although their gaze and hands roam, as Donne would say, 'behind, before, above, between, below', they cannot rub off anything of the limbs they uncertainly wander over. Even in their final embrace, when the man is on the point of (Lucretius employs the oldest of sexual metaphors) sowing the furrows of the woman, body clings greedily to

[1] IV, 1073-1120

> . . .
> nam cibus atque umor membris assumitur intus;
> quae quoniam certas possunt obsidere partis,
> hoc facile expletur laticum frugumque cupido.
> ex hominis vero facie pulchroque colore
> nil datur in corpus praeter simulacra fruendum
> tenvia; . . .
> . . . in amore Venus simulacris ludit amantis
> nec satiare queunt spectando corpora coram
> nec manibus quicquam teneris abradere membris
> possunt errantes incerti corpore toto.
> denique cum membris collatis flore fruuntur
> aetatis, iam cum praesagit gaudia corpus
> atque in eost Venus ut muliebra conserat arva,
> adfigunt avide corpus iunguntque salivas
> oris et inspirant pressantes dentibus ora,
> nequiquam, quoniam nil inde abradere possunt
> nec penetrare et abire in corpus corpore toto;
> nam facere interdum velle et certare videntur:
> . . .

body, salivas flow together, teeth press lips—in vain: the lovers cannot achieve what they are striving to do: they cannot tear off a piece, nor wholly penetrate or lose one body in another.

That, however, is precisely what the amoebae *can* do—yet only at the cost of demonstrating the ambiguousness inherent in the idea of love by identification. After their union, the two amoebae separate again—but in fact we are not entitled to say so much. Certainly, two amoebae separate, but which two? We cannot really identify these two individuals with the original two who went into this thorough embrace: rather, the two originals have lost their identities in becoming one, and that one then loses its identity in becoming two.

It is obvious why Eros in the amoeba has to have resort to reproduction, even though it uses it only sporadically and not as its regular vehicle. The aim of Eros is to bring as much inanimate material as possible under the cultivation of life. If Eros devoted itself solely to extending the amoeba's selfhood over a bigger and bigger area, it would fail of its purpose; giant amoebae might severally be less vulnerable to external accidents than normal-sized ones; but, on the other hand, the more amoeba-substance there was in one place and under one organisation, the more of it each accident would kill at a blow. Eros is obliged, therefore, to spread the risk by increasing the amoeba population whenever the food supply is sufficient to support it, and by making each increase capable of increasing further. In other words, Eros itself creates not only the individual but the species; every living individual must belong to some species and be subordinate to it. What the species exacts from the amoeba is that when it reaches a certain size it must abdicate in favour of two new amoebae: this criterion of size is the amoeba's equivalent to the comparative time-criterion of youth and senility by which other organisms are controlled.

To achieve this object, Eros has to enter into a new alliance with Thanatos. The amoeba has been held in being the whole time by impulses of Thanatos, which keep its self discrete from the environment; and now it looks almost as though the increase in the amoeba's size, with the increase in energy that places at the amoeba's disposal, had built up a greater force of Thanatos than the self can use in defending its borders. Perhaps the more substance a self has under its control, the more easily it can define its self, with the result that in the enlarged amoeba a surplus of Thanatos, no longer engaged in repelling not-self, begins to attack the self—to assert not-self of what was previously self; with the result that the organism divides in two.

Whatever the mechanism, it is clear that it is only simple growth by assimilation, as practised by the amoeba up to the point of its maximum size, which is a manifestation of Eros pure and simple. Once growth also takes the form of reproduction, there is an antithesis between the ambition of the species and that of the individual: the species is obliged to sacrifice the individual's continuity in favour of its own. Multicellularity was perhaps in the first place an attempt to overcome this antithesis: the cell contrived to keep its children with it and use their presence and contribution to make the multicellular individual less vulnerable. But again Eros was not content with a reduced vulnerability but insisted on multiplying the chances of survival by making the individual multiply himself.

Strictly speaking, a multicellular organism's method of growth is more like the amoeba's method of reproduction than the amoeba's method of growth. In other words, in a multicellular organism neither reproduction proper nor the process of growth and self-renewal is a manifestation solely of Eros, but the result of a complicated alliance between Eros and Thanatos. In this alliance, however, Eros has a superior loyalty, in that it is committed to extending the species in preference to the individual. Eros is only on loan to the individual's self; whereas Thanatos, whose very business is to define the self, remains with him. Consequently, when the individual has served his term as a potential parent, Eros withdraws from its attachment to his self or—in psychic beings—his Ego; the life pattern implanted by its species brings about in the individual a diminution at the same time in the power of reproduction proper and in the power of replacing material that has been cast off dead. The individual still has the Thanatic power to cast off old cells; what he lacks is the Erotic power to breed new ones; similarly he still disposes of the Thanatic capacity to separate a child from himself, but lacks the power to create one. The result is an overbalance of Thanatos, which has more ability to work than it has material to work on; and in the absence of any resistance by Eros—of any fresh material brought in for Thanatos to exercise its appetite on—Thanatos is free to turn on the individual's self and disintegrate the internal Erotic bonds on which the organisation of the self depends.

('The assumption of the existence of a death instinct or a destruction instinct', wrote Freud[1] in 1929, 'has roused opposition even in

[1] *Civilization And Its Discontents*, VI

analytical circles'. It continues to do so; Freud's argument has recently been powerfully criticised by Ronald Fletcher[1], himself a proFreudian, and no one who has read this criticism can doubt that—at the least—Freud's insight had, in this ultimate speculation, run ahead of his own powers of expression and perhaps even of his own understanding. None the less, I believe that it *was* insight and I adhere to Freud's conclusions—for Freud's own reason, namely that 'they provide us with that simplification, without either ignoring or doing violence to the facts, which is what we strive after in scientific work.' Probably Freud allowed himself to make too much of the antithesis between Eros and Thanatos, which he occasionally seems to understand in an almost directly moral sense, and too little of his notion of life itself being the interplay between them. For the remarkable thing about life is that it not only lives but dies: and not only dies but, during life, is limited to a self. We can take into account these extraordinary and mysterious phenomena of mortality and individuality only by postulating a divisive instinct within the organism, working towards and eventually achieving a state of no-relationship with the surroundings[2]. The silence in which Thanatos works, out of sight of our observation, is precisely the inevitability of that inevitable accident which constitutes mortality.)

7. *L'Amour and La Mort*

Even so incomplete and unsatisfactory a discussion as this of the instinctual status of the act of reproduction ought to help elucidate a little further the psychic construction which human beings place on that act—and, above all, humanity's persistent double entendre between l'amour and la mort.

The Erotic instinct which animates the Id is implanted by the species and serves the ambitions of the species—though without, as it were, knowing that it is doing so. Eros presses blindly forward towards its objective of fusion, without regard to the results. In practice, the results will serve the interest of the species and, which for a time co-incides with it, the interest of the individual. The blind Erotic impulse

[1] *Instinct In Man*, II, VI

[2] though here again Freud stressed the triumph of Thanatos in the individual, at the expense of the triumph of Eros in the stock.

to merge the self with not-self will attach the baby to the nipple and get the food inside it; and when the same impulse has been enriched by the sensations of genital sexuality, it will get the individual into genital contact with another body of a shape to receive him.

Sexual intercourse is not, however, capable of fusing the two entities, or even the two bodies, which meet in it. It might seem, therefore, that for the sexual impulse to present itself as an impulse towards fusion is an anachronism, an evolutionary survival from the time when life was conducted by independent single cells. And such no doubt it is. But when a species retains this sort of fluidity, when it reserves the right to call on earlier forms in its evolutionary past, it seems to do so with a view to adapting itself to its present circumstances. If the larva of a winged insect makes use of a wingless ancestral form, that increases the eggs' and grubs' chances of survival; if the human species puts its embryos through a short-course of evolutionary recapitulation, it is making use of the recapitulation in adapting the embryo to womb-life and perhaps in adapting the mother to serve as an eggshell. Similarly, if the species insists on holding back the infantile phase of psychic life—that is, permanently, the Id—at a level of development more appropriate to the life of a one-celled animal, that is probably for the very good reason that the species has chosen to start each of its individuals *as* a one-celled animal.

The impulse towards fusion which underlies the impulsion towards sexual intercourse *can* be, and in fact *is*, gratified—but not within the borders of the two personalities which experienced the sexual desire. It is the living sperm and ovum which fuse. Their fusion is a satisfaction for Eros in so far as Eros is serving the interest of the species; but it is just here, of course, that the interest of the species parts company with that of the individual.

We ought, in other words, to be wary about the sense in which we read the psycho-analytic grouping of the reproductive instinct together with the self-protective instinct in the concept of Eros[1]: we have to remember at the same time the distinction psycho-analysis draws between Eros as it manifests itself in the Id and those Erotic impulses which, coming from the Id, have attached themselves to the Ego and constitute the individual's narcissistic self-love. The Ego (like the original development of multi-cellularity) is attempting to place itself athwart the flow of the species's continuity and divert some of the potential immortality of the species to the individual: the Ego

[1] Freud: *An Autobiographical Study*, V

collects some of the Erotic impulses to itself in an attempt to make the Ego immortal[1]. The evolution of the Ego out of the Id is thus analogous to the evolution (which is repeated, in the behaviour of the fertilised egg-cell, at the conception of each individual) of a multicellular organism from the single cell.

Thus while reproduction is a triumph for Eros, it is not a triumph for narcissism. The species has been obliged to encourage the development of an Ego, because an individual capable of taking care of himself is, in the first instance, necessary to the species. But the ability to take care of himself, which depends on the Ego's appreciation of reality, could not be built up without diverting some of the actual wish for preservation from the species to the Ego. With its greater realism, the Ego is able to work out the consequences of acting on the impulse towards identification and perceive that it implies a loss of self. At the same time it recognises that the species, in impelling the individual towards reproduction, has betrayed the individual by employing his destructive impulses not merely to separate the self from not-self but actually to attack the integrity of the self and cut off a part of it.

The two acts which complete the process of reproduction are both acts of expulsion: the father must expel the sperm from his own body, and nine months later the mother must expel the baby from hers. In both cases the self is compelled to bring the divisive power of Thanatos to bear on something which was previously under the dominance of self. For all that these acts are—supremely—creative, the Ego apprehends them also as suicidal, diminutions of the self, just as it at first construes the expulsion of faeces, which children so regularly confuse with childbirth, as a loss to the self. Later, of course, the Ego becomes reconciled to this loss, on the grounds that what is expelled is an object noxious to the self. But to begin with, the Ego's own narcissism lends value to the faeces, which are prized as products of the self—as its projection into the outside world. Indeed, when the savage collects the nail-clippings or other bodily offscourings of his enemy, and believes that these put the enemy in his power, he is treating them as external and detached continuations of the enemy; and conversely, the child who dreads the loss of his nail-clippings, teeth or hair is dreading the loss of part of himself. But once the Ego has precisely defined the limits of its own selfhood, it recognises that what is done to the faeces, the nail-clippings or the hair is not experienced

[1] Cf. Freud: *Collected Papers*, Volume IV, III

by the self: and similarly it realises that whatever may be experienced by the detached sperm (in fact, the achievement of fusion) or by the detached baby (a new lease of life) is not experienced by the self which has projected it into its independent existence. None the less, the parent's Ego does in the end come back to esteeming the child as a projection of itself, but it does so by means of psychic identification. Parental love, as Freud points out[1], is nothing but the parent's lapping the child in the warm waves of overestimation with which, during his own infancy, he lapped himself—a narcissistic tide which reality forced to retreat; it is a version of the same compulsive infatuation and over-estimation with which lovers treat one another, when they have taken one another not only as objects of love but as subjects of self-identification.

The little boy's narcissism concentrates its love and esteem on one particular member, the penis; and everything he dreads the outside world may do to him is concentrated in his fear that it may deprive him of it[2]. Indeed, Freud concluded[3] that the Ego, which has never experienced anything like death but has experienced loss (of the nipple, of the faeces), apprehends death in terms of the dread of castration. Moreover, although the child himself has arrived at it solely through its value to him as a source of sensation, the little boy's high estimation of his penis is biologically perfectly correct[4]: so long as pleasure from this source remains at his disposal, that is a mark that Eros has not yet fulfilled its purpose of by-passing his Ego in favour of the next generation.

This particular member invites the suspicion that it will be taken away from its owner, because, while it is part of him, it is not, like a limb, self-moving (except on one, seemingly magical occasion) and is therefore also regarded as an object in his possession. It is an instrument—one which suggests it can serve an Erotic purpose by linking the self to someone else; and at the same time a channel, which offers itself for the creative purpose of projecting the self and extending its domination into the outside world. Yet this very channel is one which

[1] *Collected Papers*, Volume IV, III
[2] Cf. Freud: *Collected Papers*, Volume II, VI
[3] *Inhibitions, Symptoms And Anxiety*, VII
[4] Freud points out (*Collected Papers*, Volume II, VI) how often 'those components of the sexual instinct which are already active in the childish organism' lead the infantile sexual speculations to a flash of biological truth—concealed, of course, in immense elaborations of wish-fulfilment.

performs the Thanatic act of expelling substances from the body. And in fact the high value which the Ego sets on the penis is based not only on its potentialities as a tool in love, but on its potentialities as a weapon; not only on the sexual sensations it yields, but on the joy with which it can be used to destroy—a joy which in childhood is confined to its use for urination, which can attack and besmirch any object or enemy the boy turns it against. Conversely, the Ego's dread of castration is a dread both of losing sexual pleasures and of being disarmed.

Here is the crux of the opposition in instinctual character between the Id and the Ego. The Id has no weapons and no defences because it needs none; indeed, it apprehends no harm coming to it from the outside world: it is completely immersed in its own world of psychic reality, where each impulse achieves its gratification in fantasy, and failure or loss is impossible. Such Thanatic impulses as it directs outwards are probably used in excluding the Ego and rejecting what the Ego has to tell it about reality. When the species permits Thanatos to encroach and break down the organism itself, the Id raises no objections; it has no objections to dying. The Ego, on the other hand, is an organisation whose whole purpose is to object to dying, and it has not only marshalled Eros to serve its self-perpetuation but has, as Freud remarks, enlisted Thanatos to the same end: it directs Thanatos outward, in the form of aggression, and thus diverts some of its force from the process of internal destruction[1]. The Ego is able to experience a pure joy in aggression: it is loving itself and increasing its own chances of survival by destroying objects outside itself.

The situation is, therefore, that Eros and Thanatos are always and necessarily at work even at the level of the individual cell. The balance between them holds the individual in equilibrium until such time as Eros deserts him in favour of passing its impetus on to the next generation; and when this happens, there is nothing to counteract Thanatos in the activity it has been carrying on all the time of eroding the individual himself. The great developments in the individual's complexity are all attempts to corner Eros and save it for the individual: the single-celled organism becomes multicellular; the psychic being

[1] Thanatos 'would thus have been pressed into the service of Eros, in that the organism would be destroying something animate or inanimate outside itself instead of itself. Conversely, any cessation of this flow outwards must have the effect of intensifying the self-destruction which in any case would always be going on within'. (Freud: *Civilization And Its Discontents*, VI)

evolves, out of his single Id, the discrete mental agencies of the Ego and the Ego-ideal, one of which, the Ego, is capable of diverting Thanatos from the process of internal erosion by aggressively directing it outside; and the individual, by means of the Ego-ideal he has now acquired, becomes a unit in a social group. All these achievements depend on new compounds of Eros and Thanatos: and none of the new forms has managed to prevent Eros from by-passing the individual and thereby releasing a great force of Thanatos to intensify its constant erosion of the individual himself, dissolving the very bonds by which he is bound into his society, undoing the love between Id and Ego, diminishing the Ego's power to safeguard itself by externalising Thanatos, and eventually breaking off the organism's relationship with the world altogether.

8. *Expulsion*

With the waste products which are expelled from the body, it is comparatively easy for the Ego to progress from its earliest belief, which is that these are treasured extensions of the self and that to part with them is a loss, to the more highly developed phase in which it takes pleasure in the destructive act of expelling them. The child who begins by hoarding its faeces or urine inside itself and resisting the idea of giving them up discovers that retention has produced an additional bodily pleasure in the act of expulsion when it does take place. (For little girls, the retention of urine is probably a genital stimulant as well.) This pleasure reconciles the child to the idea of expulsion, and enables the Ego to make the final step in deducing that these substances are, after all, not part of the self. But there is still a way in which they can be turned to the greater glory of self. The child conceives the idea, which remains common enough among adults like Bishop Berkeley and readers of advertisements for constipation remedies (indeed Berkeley himself composed a panegyrical advertisement for a more-than-constipation remedy of his own[1]), that to retain the waste products is actually harmful to the self. The faeces have come to be regarded as poisonous, which is the natural conclusion for the child to draw from the adult teaching that they are

[1] John Oulton Wisdom: *The Unconscious Origin Of Berkeley's Philosophy*, VII

dirty. The Ego is anxious, therefore, to get them out of the self—and, what is more, on to someone else; for the Ego has learnt to safeguard itself from internal destruction by directing its inherent destructive instinct outward. Verbal aggression consists of figuratively pelting the victim with faeces; while the stream of urine can actually be used by the little boy as a missile and aimed at a target. To get these substances out of the child's own body, which they would poison if they remained there, and use them as aggressive weapons has become a complete analogue of the Ego's attempt to further itself by directing outwards the Thanatic forces which, if they remained within, would destroy it.

In its aggression in the cause of narcissism, the Ego's favoured weapon is the penis. But the discovery of the sexual functions of the penis entails certain discoveries which are disquieting to the Ego and disturb the balmy atmosphere of its self-love. In the first place, the sexual and the excretory functions of the penis are mutually exclusive; Freud pointed out some of the cultural results of this antithesis in his brilliant paper on 'The Acquisition of Power over Fire'[1]. For the Ego this means that on every occasion when it employs the penis as a tool in an Erotic sense, it forefeits the use of it as a weapon which channels destruction away from the Ego.

This in itself implies that sexual activity entails a release of Thanatos to work within the Ego. But the Ego has still another discovery to make, which is that if the excited penis follows its instinctual promptings to the point of emission, the result is an exhaustion which the Ego, as metaphor lets us know, construes as death—or, which is to the Ego the same thing, castration. The result of orgasm is, for the man, temporary impotence: the very situation to which Botticelli shews us the potent Mars reduced. (The Ego may reach this conclusion not only through experience but from observation, though in that case it rests on erroneous grounds: an analysis of Freud's records the case of a little boy who watched his parents' sexual intercourse and 'felt sympathy with his father' because 'during the coitus . . . he had observed the penis disappear'[2].) That the man suffers temporary castration in intercourse is, obviously, of the utmost importance in the psychic construction the woman sets on intercourse. The prostitute turns this to her peculiarly aggressive purpose[3]; but it is also true in general

[1] *Collected Papers*, Volume V, XXVI
[2] *Collected Papers*, Volume III, V   [3] Cf. I, 14

that, in G. Rattray Taylor's words[1], 'Uncomfortable as the idea may be to us, . . . sexual detumescence is a little death, and the woman is always, in some sense, the castrator of the male'.

This paradox, that the Ego apprehends the completion of sexual intercourse, so far as the man is concerned, as castration, is the very centre of the double entendre between sexuality and death. It is, moreover, another example of the psyche's arriving at a biological truth, since the exhaustion of the lover, which Petronius lamented[2], really is a physical token of the species's determination to have done with him as soon as it has sufficiently used him as a parent. It is recognised as a biological phenomenon in the Latin tag with which Mr. Duchemin distressed his guests at breakfast[3], 'Post coitum triste omne animal'. Here resides the precise uncomfortableness which the idea holds for the Ego. The Ego cannot, of course, afford to cut itself off economically from the Id; from nowhere else can it draw the supplies of Eros it needs to foster its self-love. On the other hand, once it admits the sexual impulses of the Id, it has admitted impulses which press onward towards the fulfilment of the species's purposes, without considering that in reality this entails an internal activation of Thanatos which works towards the dissolution of the self.

The Ego solves its problems as best it may. One method, Don Giovanni's, is to use the sexual tool as far as possible in an aggressive sense, hoping to save the self from destruction by wreaking destruction on the women who are used. Carried a step further, this method turns Don Giovanni into a homosexual, whose narcissism is so great that he can love only those people who reflect himself; his Ego has set such a narcissistically high value on the possession of a penis that it cannot contemplate associating itself with a person who lacks one. Both Don Giovanni and the out-and-out homosexual are fixated in the typical shock which the narcissism of small boys receives when they discover the castration which has apparently been inflicted on women[4].

An alternative, and perhaps even more highly romantic, method is Sir Galahad's. The boy's shock now bears the construction not that women are too disgusting (that is, frightening) to be made love to, but that they are too frail and pure. This chivalrous attitude to them,

[1] *Sex In History*, XII
[2] Foeda est in coitu et brevis voluptas,/et taedet Veneris statim peractae
[3] Ford Madox Ford: *Some Do Not*, V
[4] Freud: *Collected Papers*, Volume II, VI

which survived into civilised manners and was re-intensified by the Victorian revival of medieval chivalry, makes a point of course, of women's physical inferiority. Mary Wollstonecraft was quite shrewd enough to read it in that sense. 'I lament', she says[1], 'that women are systematically degraded by receiving the trivial attentions, which men think it manly to pay to the sex, when, in fact, they are insultingly supporting their own superiority. It is not condescension to bow to an inferior.'

At the peak of chivalry, Sir Galahad or his Victorian re-incarnation refrains from sexual activity altogether. Galahad is 'a clene virgin above all knights, as the flower of the lily'[2]. It is clear that his Ego conceives that by refraining from employing the sexual instrument, it obtains an enhanced use of the weapon. His strength is the strength of ten *because* his heart is pure. It is an ideational pun on potency. Sexual potency, semen itself, has become, on the analogy of urine and faeces, something which is to be hoarded within the body; and only in this way can it be converted into aggressive potency which is then directed to the outside world, to the benefit of the self and of the Ego's self-esteem. Sir Galahad's strength depends on his saintliness, and his saintliness on his awareness of not having polluted himself—not having expended any of his potency.

An Ego which adopts this method is, of course, under great pressure from the Id; and the Id's promptings may embody themselves in a superstition which is the obverse of Sir Galahad's about the source of his strength, namely that sexual abstinence is physically bad for the abstainer. If sexuality can harm others when it is converted into swordplay, then it can harm the self, too: semen—again on the analogy of urine and faeces—poisons its owner if it is retained. An Ego caught between these pressures is likely to succumb to psycho-sexual impotence, unless it can escape into homosexual relations with a lover of the same sex who, because he is not himself castrated, offers less threat of castration in intercourse. Sir Galahad's chaste frigidity is not so far removed from the promiscuous frigidity by which another knight errant, Don Giovanni, betrays his unconscious homo-sexuality. Don Giovanni is, moreover, threatened by psychic impotence—a threat which he can counter only by compulsively contradicting it. In both Sir Galahad and Don Giovanni, the Ego is

[1] *A Vindication Of The Rights Of Woman*, IV
[2] Thomas Malory: *Le Morte D'Arthur*, XVII, XVIII

attempting to hoard the Erotic impulses in order to devote them to self-love. Neither has yet found a partner whom he can sufficiently identify with himself to make it worth his while to expend his love on the partner as well as on himself; and we can surmise that each is being unconsciously urged towards a partner with whom it will be easier to identify himself because the partner is made in the same masculine image.

All these attempts to save up Eros are attempts on the Ego's part not to grow old. It is as though it believed that the species, which is resolved to cast off the individual when he is too old to procreate, could be cheated into holding its hand if he refrains from procreating. In reality, however, the species does no such thing but ages the virgin ascetic at the same rate as the roué. The Ego is obliged to yield to reality to the extent of transferring the immortal youth it hopes to enjoy to heaven, and the ascetic religions postulate a distinct relationship between chastity on earth and the believer's chances of immortality in heaven. The transfer is made by way of a social construct, a myth; and in order to enjoy the benefit of it the Ego has to sacrifice some of its narcissism and perform a sufficient self-identification with people outside itself to become a member of a social group. The path which the communal Ego of a religious group takes to immortality is the sacrament—whose efficacy in fact depends on the paradoxical assonance between sexual intercourse and castration.

9. 'Death And The Maiden'

Naturally, the situation reads very differently to the girl, who does not possess the organ by which the male Ego sets such store.

Not that the girl values it less highly. The first problem of her Ego is whether to succumb to the sense of deprivation, of lessened self-esteem, which must follow on recognising such a loss, or whether to withhold recognition from the loss.

The girl's Ego can, as a matter of fact, withhold recognition without wrapping itself in a complete fantasy: it needs only a comparative fantasy. Once again, infantile sexuality has been led by its own practical instinctual needs to a glimpse of biological truth, this time the fact that, anatomically, the clitoris is 'an organ homologous to the penis'[1]. The little girl does not have to imagine the importance of the penis to the little boy. She knows it from her own experience: during the early 'phallic' phase of her sexuality, she exploits her own stunted penis and makes it the centre of narcissism and auto-erotic activity just as the boy does its counterpart.

If the woman's sexuality is to remain fixated in this phase, she has only to shut out the comparison with men, who possess what is in effect the same equipment but in a more versatile and forceful version. In this case, the adult woman's behaviour will be dictated by an unconscious fantasy in which she *is* a man—a fantasy based on the anatomical half-truth. It will mean that she never exploits her own vaginal sexuality[2] and remains physically unresponding in sexual intercourse: it is as though, even in intercourse with a man, the woman does not allow the facts about men's bodies to come close enough to her for a comparison to be made between them and herself. The fantasy may of course be expressed in real life by an exclusive homosexuality; the woman may ape men in behaviour; and quite often her aim is not so much to love women as to exclude men, by building round herself a fantasy reconstruction of society into which the comparison which is so disturbing to her self-esteem never intrudes. But the same fantasy may, in different circumstances (and perhaps the simple accident of whether the woman is or is not beautiful is enough to determine its direction) produce a result which is outwardly so different as to pass for antithetical. The woman who is living in a fantasy of being a man is in this case the most 'feminine' of women—indeed, determinedly feminine. However, she suffers rather than enjoys

[1] Freud: *Collected Papers*, Volume II, VI

[2] However, the change from the sexuality of the clitoris to that of the vagina is not so great as most psycho-analytic writers imply. The change is primarily in psychic disposition: the woman becomes willing to be passively penetrated in order to obtain what is still an active-type pleasure. Physically, the vagina always has been the site of orgasm, and the clitoris remains the site of sexual sensations. (Paul Bousefield [*The Elements Of Practical Psycho-Analysis*, V] is one of the rare writers to emphasise this; he even argues that in the few cases where vaginal sensations occur they are in the nature of a regression to anal sexuality.) Frigidity in sexual intercourse is a mark less of unconscious homosexuality per se than of unconscious defences against it: the woman is refusing to recognise not the dissimilarity but the similarity of her sexuality to a man's: and it is thus that frigidity can be characteristic of the lesbian and the very feminine woman, both of whom are engaged in not entertaining the comparison between men and women.

the embraces of her lovers (she regards enjoyment as unfeminine), accepting from them not so much love as tributes to her beauty. A woman of this very frequent type is, as Freud remarks[1], completely self-contained in her own narcissism. This is, as a matter of fact, the narcissism of the infantile Ego, which she has preserved intact by never according mental recognition to the comparison with men which could damage it. It is notable that she lays it down, as the first requirement of femininity, that women should never compete with men. Her narcissism is like that of another closed system, Christendom; and that, too, was finally shattered by comparison[2].

If, on the other hand, the little girl concurs in the real state of affairs and takes a recognition of it into her Ego, the result is an irreparable wound to the Ego's narcissism. The future development of her Ego is built on the various substitutions the Ego can find—or, rather, by the usual conservative principle of sexual development, which it can be seduced into accepting—for the lost member. From the moment of discovery, the psychological divergence of the girl from the boy 'corresponds', in Freud's words[3], 'to the difference between a castration that has been carried out and one that has merely been threatened'. The boy must compromise with the father in order to keep safely what he still has; the girl finds herself turning towards the father with a view to making good her deficiency. Girl and boy agree, however, that she *is* deficient; and this inferiority which both sexes unhesitatingly attribute to the female body is, Freud points out[4], the grain of truth in Adler's theory of 'organ inferiority'.

As both boy and girl construe the female body, it has been actually and physically wounded. The girl once had a penis: so the boy argues because he has one still, and the girl because she still has, so to speak, the stump. The external appearance of the girl's genital region lends itself to this interpretation because it really does look like the lips of a wound; and when, at puberty, the girl's sexual emotions are reactivated, the old wound also acquires the uncanny property, round which so much superstition has accumulated, of painfully bleeding

[1] *Collected Papers*, Volume IV, III, where Freud notes that the most self-sufficiently narcissistic women are very often those who are most beautiful, but also refutes the Adlerian notion that psychic maladjustments can be traced to physical shortcomings.

[2] Cf. III, 3   [3] *Collected Papers*, Volume V, XVII

[4] *Collected Papers*, Volume I, 'On The History Of The Psycho-Analytic Movement'; Volume V, XVII

once a month—in ritual memory, it seems, of the original mutilation. These infantile observations and interpretations re-emerge later in myth and religious practice when the son is concerned to reconcile himself to the father by a token of self-castration. Besides the many tokens where something—hair, a tooth, a foreskin—is actually removed from the body, the worshipper may be slashed, ritually or in a frenzy in which he inflicts the wound on himself; and these scars emulate the original first-observed castrated state of the woman's body. The singled-out heroic brother, who reconciles all the sons to God by his own sacrifice, suffers a similar wound and has also borrowed from the girl the capacity to renew the bleeding ritually whenever the Mass is celebrated. Christian mythology lays great emphasis on the hero's (Christ's or the saint's) symbolic castration, and its miracles are much concerned with bleeding Hosts, wounds into which enquiring fingers may enter, liquefactions of old blood, and scars: the stigmata denote that the hero has, by self-submission to the father, incurred the same irreparable loss as the girl.

The conversation of any little girl of three or four years old who has been allowed freely to compare herself with boys and not forbidden to comment leaves no doubt that the girl's prime deficiency is in the way she urinates. Not only must the girl alone forfeit the dignity of standing, which at this age is still recently acquired; she is also unable to —our metaphors still preserve a trace of the infantile prowess—be a big noise or make a splash. That this is more grievous than any sexual deficiency which the little girl may be able to surmise is a point nicely taken in a story Colette recounts[1] about a woman named Loulou who, after hesitating between her husband and her lesbian lover, finally chose her husband. She tells her lesbian lover: ' "I have thought it all out and he can do something you can't do." "Of course", said Lucienne, furious. "No, it's not what you think at all", replied Loulou. "I am not so keen about that. . . But I'll tell you. When we go out together, in the country to a restaurant, when we travel together, everyone thinks you're a man, naturally. But it humiliates me to be out with a man who can't raise his leg like a dog against a wall." ' On this story, which is told her by a second lesbian, Colette reports herself as commenting: ' "it's childish, utterly childish" '; and her interlocutor replies: ' "Childish! But, my little darling, it was absolutely the most horrible thing, the most insulting remark Loulou could think of." '

[1] *These Pleasures*, III, 4 (anonymous translation)

What the woman is deficient in is the power to externalise Thanatos in the form of aggression. This is precisely what society has always thought of her—that she cannot wield arms because she cannot direct a stream of urine at a target. The psychological concomitant is a great increase of Thanatos working against the Ego internally. The psychology of women is distinguished by feelings of insufficiency and self-reproach which are inherent to the Ego and are not based on idealism—in contrast to the reproaches and commands which are addressed to the man's Ego by his Ego-ideal and Super-Ego[1].

Certainly the self-destructive bent of the woman's Ego is what makes women acquiesce in society's estimate of them, which has for so long placed them outside the pale of full citizenship. But society has given us very little chance to discover whether women also exclude themselves, spontaneously and necessarily, or whether the various substitutes the woman may psychically accept for her loss are capable of regularly (it is evident already that they can in some cases) building up in her again an Ego which is, so to speak, that of a man who happens also to be a woman.

It is a question whether women are capable of *two* psychologies. Insofar as she is specifically a woman, the woman's Ego must (unless it remains concentrated on the fantasy that her own clitoris *is* a penis) address itself to the father in a relationship which turns on the fact that he has and she has not a penis. But it may be that by means of this relationship the woman's Ego can restore itself to a sufficiently masculine condition for the woman to be able to take part in the great social debate between sons and father, a debate which turns on the fact that *both* parties have a penis, as though she were a man. In social relations she would count as a man and behave as a man: that is, she would achieve a social identification with her fellow citizens by means of identifying her Ego-ideal with the common father.

The first substitute for the lost penis is offered the girl at puberty when she develops breasts, a twin sexual organ with no equivalent on the man's body—for which reason the girl would often prefer, at first, to decline the gift, as an encumbrance which renders her not more but less like a man. Even so, in the sexual disgust which is often the means whereby the adolescent tries to counter the infantile sexual impulses which have re-emerged at puberty, the girl may accept

[1] Cf. Freud (*Collected Papers*, Volume V, XVII): 'Women's super-ego is never so inexorable, so impersonal, so independent of its emotional origins as we require it to be in men'.

her breasts, and the boy pay tribute to them, *because* they emphasise the difference between girl and boy. They are taken as a sign of the girl's superiority to the more 'animal' male. To the legend of women's greater sexual purity, a legend promulgated by men and women alike, nothing contributes more tellingly than the fact that a woman can have a sexual organ on the upper part of her body, quite removed from the contamination of the excretory functions.

In what sense the breast is a sexual organ it does not at first announce, having, unlike the penis, no spontaneous sexual activity. Its capacity to serve the girl as a substitute-penis and produce sensations of sexual pleasure (probably in association with the pleasures of the clitoris) has to be discovered through an accident or a caress. The breast thereupon becomes more acceptable to its owner, having revealed that its tip is composed of genuinely erectile material, capable of behaving in the same masculine way as the clitoris. 'We do not ask the breast what it thinks of the caress', wrote Colette[1], 'yet it immediately becomes stripped of all mystery, demanding and shamefully virile'.

Modern corsetry can compensate the girl further still by thrusting the whole breast up into an erect position and holding it rigid there; and girls in America are said[2] to be persuaded by advertisements that breasts treated in this way will bring their owner prestige and confidence, while breasts which are not so treated or are not amenable to treatment induce feelings of inferiority. The fashion is perhaps a genuine attempt by women to make themselves the equals of men: yet since it seems provoked chiefly by men's admiration, it should perhaps rather be read as men's attempt to reassure themselves after the shock of discovering women's castration and to prevent themselves responding to the shock by the homosexual solution of turning towards the sex which still possesses the real sexual organ. Certainly, it is a very superficial analysis which construes the fashion as evidence of 'matriarchy' in the United States and imagines it shews the yearning of American men, more than any other men in the world, to return to the mother's breast. The position into which the breasts are pushed is the one position in which they could be of not the smallest use to the suckling. Indeed, one corsetry advertisement claims to 'correct' all types of breast, including 'the natural'.

However, much as lesbians may wish it could[3], the breast is not

[1] *These Pleasures*, III, 5 (anonymous translation)
[2] Fredric Wertham: *Seduction Of The Innocent*, VIII
[3] See Simone de Beauvoir: *The Second Sex*, IV, IV

capable of becoming genuinely rigid or of penetrating. It is not a weapon even sexually; and when it does, fulfilling its biological purpose, emit a liquid, it is very far from answering the Ego's need for an instrument which can expel a death-working substance from the self by turning it to the disadvantage of someone else. Feeding the baby can be construed only as a diminution of the mother to the baby's advantage. The opportunity offered by her breasts can do no more than temporarily divert the girl in her perpetual search for a substitute for what she lost in infancy; and already in infancy she has conceived the idea of making good her own loss by turning to the sex which has not suffered the loss. This idea determined the approach which she made in infancy to her father, only to encounter the female extension of the Oedipus situation, which compels her eventually to renounce incest. When her sexual ambitions re-appear and direct themselves, now, outside the family, they are still animated by the desire to borrow from the man what she had been deprived of herself. The amputation supposedly practised on the girl, and her whole sexual intention in approaching men, is plainly expressed in the coarse and come-onish rhyme little girls chant to the boys in the North of England:

> Chase me, Charley, chase me, Charley—
> Lost the leg o' me drawers:
> Chase me, Charley, chase me, Charley—
> Have to lend me yours.

In fact, however, the woman can borrow from the man only a very temporary use of his possession. The beast with two backs is two people with one sexual organ; and when the man reaches orgasm and is deprived of the use of his possession for a while, the woman is deprived of the use of it, too. In one sense, she is actually *more* castrated by his castration in orgasm than he is. For him, desire is necessarily exhausted at the same time as capacity, and in his temporary impotence he can desire only to desire again: but the woman may still actively desire, either because she did not experience orgasm when he did or because her desires are more quickly revived afterwards than his.

The woman's initiation into sexual intercourse is a painful and often bloody repetition of the mutilation by which this region of her body was supposedly assaulted in infancy; and it is the penetration of virgins which language most pointedly likens to killing: yet even after her initiation sexual intercourse keeps, in the woman's eyes, some of the character of a castration—a cheat, a theft, which is unfairly practised against her more than against the man; and this endorses her original sense of being 'wronged'[1].

The woman may, however, be sustained in this situation by the hope of something which she can, by this means, acquire from the man, and which will be hers in a more nearly permanent sense: a baby. The quest for the organ which has been removed from her becomes fused with a quest for a baby 'by means—there is no other way of putting it—of the equation "penis = child" '; and, as Freud goes on to say[2], the girl's approach to the father in her Oedipus situation is made 'with this purpose in view'.

Economically, the idea of having a baby is the most satisfactory substitute the girl's Ego can adopt, thanks to the confusion of childbearing with the expulsion of the faeces. Here, at last, is a way in which the Ego can channel Thanatos out of itself, an aggressive weapon which, moreover, girls do and boys do not possess. It is probably by means of this economic device that the girl who has approached the father in love is also able to direct an active hostility against her rival, the mother. And in adult life to bear children, especially sons who may become soldiers, is how the woman makes her contribution to the aggressive resources of the group, a contribution she is disabled from making in her own person. Unconsciously, 'the conceptions *faeces* (money, gift), *child* and *penis* are seldom distinguished and are easily interchangeable'[3].

Yet although the idea of acquiring a child is added to the idea of getting back the lost organ—an addition which must be made if the girl is to exploit the aggressive potentialities of her sex—it seems impossible to agree with Freud that the girl actually 'gives up her wish for a penis and puts in place of it a wish for a child'[4]: for in that case we should have to suppose that the unconscious motivation which impels women to take part in sexual intercourse consisted of nothing but the wish for a child. And as a matter of fact, when the woman does become pregnant, it is the original and still unallayed wish for a penis which is offered a very plausible fulfilment. The woman

[1] Freud: *Collected Papers*, Volume IV, XVIII
[2] *Collected Papers*, Volume V, XVII
[3] Freud: *Collected Papers*, Volume II, XVI
[4] *Collected Papers*, Volume V, XVII

no longer feels castrated: the monthly bleeding which commemorated her original wounding is staunched. Moreover, what gradually takes place in her body resembles a slow-motion tumescence, as her abdomen—the substitute is situated this time in the correct half of the body—rises into rigidity; and presently this grotesque counterpart to an erection takes on, in the magical fashion of the erect penis, a life of its own and flutters with movements its owner cannot control. The pregnant woman, with her great access of self-confidence, is probably experiencing, for the first time in her life since infancy, the Ego-state of a man; her only anxieties concern the ending of her pregnant condition.

For, of course, she is doomed to expel the very thing which has restored her Ego to a sense of wholeness. If the fear of childbirth is, as it seems to be, the great promoter of the pain of childbirth, then we must trace both pain and fear to the woman's unconscious unwillingness to give up her child. The birthpangs are a physical analogue of maternal possessiveness. The unconscious Ego must look forward to the delivery of the child as the fulfilment of its archaic wish; it conceives that, at last, an attachment really is protruding between the woman's legs: but no sooner has it become visible that it is cut off from her. Neither can the Ego, in the end, take the destructive comfort it has promised itself from the expulsion, as it learns to do from expelling the faeces once it has recognised them as inanimate and not-self; the baby is animate and the mother has very closely identified herself with it, building her narcissism round it in the same way as the man builds his round the penis.

Childbirth constitutes to the mother, therefore, a recastration[1], a painful re-enactment of the infantile wound. Moreover, when she has completed her part in the reproductive act, the species signals its eventual intention of withdrawing its support from her Ego by a lassitude and exhaustion which are a large-scale counterpart to those which overcome the man after he has completed *his* part in the process. Thus for both sexes, the fulfilment of the species's creative

[1] No doubt it is men's unconscious apprehension of childbirth and menstrual bleeding as forms of castration undergone by the woman which promotes the pervasive primitive taboos (and their modern folklore equivalents) that surround women on these occasions, the taboo representing a defence against the unconsciously understood incitement to inflict such wounds. (Frazer: *Taboo And The Perils Of The Soul*, IV, 3 'Women tabooed at Menstruation and Childbirth')

demands signifies a death to the Ego, a death which takes the form of a loss to the self and which the self interprets as castration. In the days following childbirth, the woman seems to have suffered a shattering of her identity; her Ego is like a holed earth from which a moon has been torn out and made independent.

10. *Gynaecocracy and other myths*

For the woman, all sexual and reproductive experience—including sexual intercourse, in which she must be penetrated—has a certain resemblance to being killed or recastrated; and this is not always compensated—certainly not simultaneously—by the direct pleasure which may bribe the man into repeatedly undergoing his castration in orgasm. The economic result for the woman is an Ego perpetually suffering internal destruction; and while it is possible that a woman can build up a second Ego-psychology, in which she functions socially and intellectually as the equivalent of a man, it seems highly improbable that she could ever acquire a third psychology in which—in the so telling comparison with men—she actually believed herself and was believed by men to be the superior.

Psychological probability seems therefore to be against the theory that primitive society was matriarchal in the sense, which certain scholars insist on, that women dominated men. All that is psychologically probable is that during the republican period which followed the sons' communal rebellion against the primal father, the sons, in order to preserve their egalitarianism among themselves, awarded figurehead positions to women[1]. Indeed, the success and prosperity which have very often attended the reigns of women sovereigns, when the chances of heredity and the absence of Salic law have brought them to a throne in modern Europe, are probably owed to a lessening of hostility against the leader and of internecine rivalry among themselves on the part of the male subjects: if queens have seemed more successful rulers than kings, it may be because subjects are more easily ruled by someone they conceive to be inferior to them. Certainly, the accessions of Elizabeth I and Victoria did not initiate a change in the social order of England. There was no accession of women in general to power over men: perhaps it was even the reverse.

[1] Cf. I, 8

Psychological probability would, of course, have to give way before solid evidence; but as a matter of fact the evidence, which is drawn from myth and iconography, is equivocal. If an archaeologist of the future uncovers a Roman Catholic church intact, he will easily ascertain that Christendom was a society in which women dominated men. He will find that the greatest cult, in the way of candles and votive offerings, is paid to statues and paintings of the Goddess, who rules heaven in unique splendour (he will find her, depicted alone, trampling the moon beneath her feet) and who, on earth, is shewn enthroned, her small naked son supported on her knee—a reminder that all men are naked and helpless babies in the strong hands of the Mother. He will notice that the Goddess's consort, who presumably fathered her child, is so unimportant as a mere man that he is not pictorially represented at all. Indeed, the only depictions of an adult man to which much attention seems to be paid shew him, again naked, being agonisingly done to death and unable to save himself: and these depictions, which are usually small, wooden and uncoloured, are scattered about as penitential reminders of the frailty of man. If the archaeologist has the luck to uncover a vestry as well, he will notice from the long, embroidered robes hanging there, which resemble those worn by the Goddess herself, that the powerful and rich priesthood which served her was composed entirely of women.

Myths have, since the arrival of modern archaeology, received a tremendous historical vindication against the eighteenth-century belief that they were arbitrary nonsense (a belief which nineteenth-century historians scarcely improved on when they decided that myths might be charming literary fairytales, suitable, when expurgated, for recounting to children, but historically valueless). Modern scholarship has dug out of myths many grains of historical truth: legendary journeys correspond to tribal migrations which really did take place, divine and heroic family-trees to dynastic powers which really did flourish and fall—all recorded in myth in distorted shape. It is important to remember, however, that the myth record *is* a distortion of the historical truth. Archaeologists uncovered a labyrinthine palace at Knossos and evidence of a bull-cult or bull-sport; but we should not behave as though they have proved that a Cretan queen fell in love with a bull and bore it a child half bull and half human. Whereever there is distortion we must call in psychology to give an account of why, and also why the distortion took one form rather than another. To imagine, when we have found a grain of historical truth in a myth, that this accounts for the genesis of the myth, and for all the material in it, is to make the mistake of those who believe that when we can point to an external stimulus—a noise, for example—which has become incorporated in a dream, we have given an account of why the dream was dreamt and why it took the form it did. The classic instance of this mistake is 'Hildebrandt's "alarm-clock dreams" ', which Freud discussed in *The Interpretation Of Dreams*[1]. During the production of each of these dreams, an alarm clock really did go off, and its noise was incorporated into the dream-narrative. Once it was fitted into a Sunday scene, and appeared as church-bells; in a winter pastoral, it becomes sleigh-bells: in a domestic comedy it becomes crashing crockery. But it is, of course, nonsense to suppose that when we have learnt about the alarm-clock, we have explained the dreams or vindicated them as historical records of the ringing of the alarm bell, when this one event can appear so variously in them: 'we shall be compelled to ask', comments Freud, 'why the same causal stimulus evoked so many different results, and why just these results and no others'.

As a matter of fact, if a myth has picked on an historical event, it will have done so less in scholarly zeal to record history than in the hope of working over this particular historical event and transforming it into something more acceptable, just as the alarm-clock dreamer is likely to work over the noise of the alarm and convert it into something which need not wake him up. '*The dream*', in Freud's dictum[2], '*is the guardian of sleep, not its disturber*'. The myth is the guardian of another sort of sleep: the lazy, unrealistic and unindividualised thinking of the group mind. It was as a shatterer of myths that Freud recognised himself as one of those who had 'disturbed the sleep of the world'[3]. The dream may incorporate a contemporaneous noise or events which really took place on the previous day, but neither of these is ever the cause or explanation of the dream[4]. Indeed, when the dreamer is finally woken by the alarm clock, the dream has failed in the purpose for which it incorporated the noise; and perhaps the cases where a myth lets us see through to historical fact, cases we are tempted to greet as triumphs of the scientific spirit because they come so

[1] I (C)

[2] *The Interpretation Of Dreams*, V (C)

[3] *Collected Papers*, Volume I, 'On The History Of The Psycho-Analytic Movement'

[4] *The Interpretation Of Dreams*, VII (C)

gratefully to *our* scientific spirit, are really thanks to a failure in the myth-making process.

The myth-making spirit is what the scientific spirit develops from, but it is not itself scientific—or, indeed, it would have produced science instead of myths. It is very closely similar to the infantile sexual curiosity, from which scientific curiosity may presently develop; and myths are very closely similar to the infantile sexual theories. And in fact mythology in general has the same subject matter as the child's speculations. Myths about gods and goddesses, their matings and their progeny, are nothing but the child's attempt to spy on its parents in the bedroom. The divine pedigree, and likewise the story of the Creation (the two may, witness Hesiod, be interwoven), answer for the social group the question which excites the child's curiosity, 'Where did I come from?'

The question, however, having been stimulated in the first place by the child's own desires, is by no means disinterested; and neither is the answer supplied by myth or infantile theory. This is clear enough when the myth relates how Actaeon chances to see the goddess (the mother) naked. That the chance is no chance but the result of curiosity; and that the curiosity itself is not impartial and scientific but derived from an incestuous wish: this the myth makes clear by having Actaeon promptly punished by the loss of his life. Just as in the theological theories of the virgin birth and the immaculate conception of the Virgin, which contrive to answer the childish puzzle about the father's part in procreation at the same time as wishing it out of existence, Actaeon's curiosity is combined with an Oedipal wish. The glimpse is equivalent to a sexual assault; it is a visual violation of the mother.

Conversely, the child (or the myth) is quite capable of not seeing the facts when they are presented to its eyes, if they are disagreeable to its wishes. The little boy 'Hans', whose castration phobia Freud analysed in detail[1], was allowed to watch his baby sister in her bath but contrived not to see that she lacked a penis, because he could construe such a lack only as a threat that he might suffer the same amputation himself; he consoled himself that her penis was very small and would presently grow to the usual size. Commenting on this and other precisely similar instances, Freud remarks[2]: 'One might well feel horrified at such signs of the premature ruin of a child's intellect. Why did not these young enquirers state what they really

---

[1] *Collected Papers*, Volume III, II　　[2] *Collected Papers*, Volume III, II, I

saw . . .?' So far is the infantile sexual curiosity from disinterested scientific observation; and so far are myths.

The myth, whose genesis and content cannot be accounted for by an external event, depends, like a dream or an infantile theory, on a wish in its maker. We have a difficulty, of course, in the fact that we do not know who the myth-maker is, or even if he is one or many. But the difficulty is not so great as it seems, when we remember that a myth becomes the property of a group, and that the group is bound together by the Ego-identification of its members with one another. It does not greatly matter to us, though it would be interesting to know, *who* invents the myth, since the very thing which distinguishes the myth from a private fiction, hallucination or dream, is that it becomes common property. We can even guess that myths sometimes originate in a private person's dream, which, on being recounted, is accepted into the group; the group identifies its own unconscious wishes with those expressed in the dream: and we can be sure that what makes the myth—whatever its origin—acceptable to the group, as a vehicle for the group's wishes, is that it deals in some way with the great social bargain between sons and father on which the group's existence as a group depends.

With our dreams we are, as Freud points out[1], anxious to deny our own authorship and to maintain that the dream came to us from outside; and our pretext for doing so is that we were asleep at the time. With myths, the very anonymity of the story serves the same purpose. The authorship is lost in the crowd; the origin of the myth has become unconscious to any given member of the crowd; each can claim that the myths came to him from outside—though in fact it is his and his fellows' inner concurrence in the story which has made it a myth. The process is comparable to that whereby we banish from our own consciousness our hostile or incestuous impulses towards the father by losing the father in a multitude[2].

The analogy between myth-making and dream-making is recognised explicitly in Jane Harrison's dictum that myth is the dream-thinking of the people[3]; and we can insist on the precise psychological exactitude of her dictum in that the myth, like the dream[4], represents the fulfilment of a wish. This being so, we can go on to insist on the

[1] *The Interpretation Of Dreams*, I (E)
[2] Cf. I, 14
[3] cited by E. R. Dodds: *The Greeks And The Irrational*, IV
[4] Freud: *The Interpretation Of Dreams*, III

literal psychological truth, in exactly the same sense, of Frazer's remark[1] that the supposed primitive matriarchy (or, as he preferred to call it, with the spiny elegance of the Greek language, gynaecocracy) is 'a dream of visionaries and pedants'. The matriarchising scholars ignore the fact that the state of affairs in heaven and in myths generally is a reflexion not of the state of affairs on earth but of the wishes of the myth-inventors and myth-promulgators on earth. They are mistaking pyschological evidence for historical evidence. Items which can truly be picked out of the myths as evidence of matriarchising *wishes* in the society which entertained the myths are taken to be evidence of matriarchal facts in the society. This way of treating evidence is so visionary and unscientific that we are entitled to consider it as a private and latterday extension of the myth-making process itself. If the original myth worked on facts by wish to make them more accept-able, the scholar is working on the facts of mythology in the same way; he has picked out the evidence in myths of matriarchising wishes, and is treating it by means of his own matriarchising wishes.

There are two great wishes, widely expressed in myth because of their intimate connexion with the psychic structure of groups, which are likely to lead the interpreter—or to give him his pretext for going—astray. One is the ambivalent wish on the part of the son to be reconciled to the father and, by the same stroke, to acquire some of the father's authority for himself. The reconciliation is achieved by some sort of castration undergone by the son, in which he renounces some of those sexual ambitions which set him up in rivalry to the father: his accession at the same time to some of the father's power is achieved by making this sacrifice on the son's part the means and occasion of his initiation into a higher rank of the group's hierarchy. Thus the son, even though in token castrated, identifies himself more closely with the phallic authority and power of the father. What is liable to mislead the interpreter of the myths and sacraments which concern this bargain is the fact that, to the unconscious, a son who has been castrated is a daughter. An inner and powerful circle composed of these ceremonially castrated beings will have a confusing resem-blance to a ruling class composed of women. Indeed, it was just these circumstances which confused our imagined archaeologist of the future into thinking that the Catholic Church had an exclusively female clergy. The Catholic priest undergoes an effective self-castra-tion when he takes his vow of chastity; the monk adds to this the

[1] *Adonis Attis Osiris*, Volume II, XII, 2

castration symbol of the tonsure; and both assume the long-skirted dress of a woman: but in fact the priest has acquired over the layman a little of God the Father's power, and has become sufficiently identified with God the Father to represent God to the people; indeed, it is when he puts on the clothes of a woman that he acquires the title of 'Father'.

The second wish of which the interpreter must beware is more properly matriarchising, because it concerns the mother directly. It is, indeed, nothing short of an attempt to build the mother up again into wholeness and to overcome the infantile shock her son sustains when he discovers that she lacks the organ his own narcissism prizes so highly. The shock itself and the horror it causes are expressed by several mythological horror-symbols—one of them the severed (castrated) head of Medusa[1]. The simple course for fantasy to take in order to undo the shock is to restore the lost phallos. Ancient art devoted a whole genre to statues of hermaphrodites[2]; and more than one ancient goddess consists of the mother with a penis—the Egyptian goddess Mut, for example, who is implicated in Freud's elucidation of Leonardo da Vinci's 'vulture-fantasy'[3].

However, supposing that fantasy does manage to restore the image of the mother (in exactly the sense in which the restorer has to supply missing members to ancient statues), the son immediately encounters a second threat. At the original discovery, his feelings ran: 'My mother has been castrated, so I could be castrated, too'; and, under this threat, he withdraws from her in disgusted fear. But if his fantasy restores her to soundness, the way is opened again for his incestuous desires to flow towards her again, whereupon the Oedipal threat intervenes, which the boy interprets: 'If I make love to my mother, my father will castrate me'.

The little boy's dread balances between these two thoughts; and myths and folklore, like the infantile theories and phobias themselves, are uncertain whether the threat comes from the mother or the father. In pre-Freudian times, when it was not uncommon for the threat to be put baldly in words, it was often the mother who spoke them; it

[1] Freud: *Collected Papers*, Volume V, X
[2] Cf. Freud: *Collected Papers*, Volume II, VI
[3] (Freud: *Leonardo Da Vinci* . . ., III). Lemprière records that even Aphrodite 'was often represented with a beard, and the male parts of generation, with a sceptre in her hand, and the body and dress of a female'. (*Classical Dictionary*, Venus)

was usually she who found the child playing with his sexual organ. Even so, she might appeal to the re-inforcing authority of a father figure. 'Hans', for example, was threatened by his mother[1]: 'If you do that, I shall send for Dr. A. to cut off your widdler.'

Nowadays parents are more cautious. But the child scarcely needs a spoken threat, since he is perfectly familiar with having something taken away from him which he wants to play with, and has also had to submit to minor bodily amputations—of his hair or his nails, perhaps even his teeth. Through symbols derived from these experiences he expresses his own dread (witness the obsessive interest children shew in surgical operations, especially amputations); and through similar symbols he can read the implied threat in such informal myths as the story of the three blind mice. (They are three because of the threefold shape of the male sexual organs; they are doubly castrated—by having their tails cut off, and by the Sophoclean symbol of blinding; and although it is the mother who has cut their tails off, it is the father's jealousy which is ultimately responsible, since the mice have committed the cardinal Oedipus crime of running after the farmer's [the father's] wife.) As Freud pointed out[2], it is castration which children are dreading when they shew an irrational fear of having their hair or nails cut. Struwwelpeter's crime was to rebel and resist these operations—and in the same book another rhyme[3] gives an exact account of a parental threat that the child will be castrated in punishment for masturbation in its oral form, namely[4] thumb-sucking. Here again, it is the mother who tells her son that 'The great tall tailor always comes To little boys that suck their thumbs'. The mother goes out, leaving Conrad alone; loneliness figures, as in some phobias, as a temptation to masturbation, and Conrad puts his thumb into his mouth; whereupon the demon tailor, the father at one remove, arrives and subjects the child to a token castration by snipping off his thumbs[5].

Myths and religious rites refer to castration in the same symbolic language. As Freud goes on to say, it is by some such token as

[1] *Collected Papers*, Volume III, II, I
[2] *Totem And Taboo*, IV, 6
[3] Heinrich Hoffman: *Struwwelpeter*, 6 'The Story Of Little Suck-A-Thumb'
[4] Cf. I, 6
[5] In one version of his story (see H. J. Rose: *A Handbook . . .*, IV) to bite off his own thumb was the token self-castration whereby Orestes appeased the Erinyes and expiated his guilt.

tooth-pulling or hair-cutting, perhaps combined with the most blatant token of all, circumcision, that primitive tribes signify that sacrifice of the son's sexuality to the communal father by means of which the son is ritually adopted into the group-family. These tokens often remain the sacramental marks of initiation:- the monk's tonsure; the *depositio barbae* wherein the Roman youth signified his initiation into manhood by dedicating to a god the product of his first shave[1]; the shaving of the whole head, which was practised by the priests of Isis, along with the castration symbol[2] of slashing, which left the naked head covered with scars[3]. When the group turns on the father in his animal embodiment, it may signify *its* desire to castrate *him* in a similar token. The victim at the Greco-Roman animal sacrifice suffered, before its death, the ritual cutting off of a handful of hair from its forehead[4]. (The bullfighter possesses himself of the bull's sexual organ under the token of its ear, which he cuts off and may present to a woman. Vincent Van Gogh employed the same symbol for his melancholy castration of himself; and in sending his severed ear to a prostitute he displayed his unconscious knowledge of what prostitutes wish to do to their clients.) At the totemistic sacrament, the use of symbolism serves not only as a disguise of the group's wish but also as a safeguard of its grouphood, by preventing any one citizen from assimilating all the father's virility (even the bullfighter is kept at the rank of hero and may not turn into the god or monster he would become if he could really filch the bull's virility). The shift of emphasis from the really important detachable member of the body to one of neutral significance is parallel to the shift, at the sparagmos, from one to a whole lottery of pieces of the body. Yet even in its disguise the token member may be so full of mana that it must be, like the phallos of Osiris, lost—put beyond the citizen's reach: and this was achieved at the classical animal sacrifice by burning the clipped hair in the flame on the altar[5].

Totemism castrates the father in animal form; the animal phobias

[1] Jérôme Carcopino: *Daily Life In Ancient Rome*, VI, 3
[2] Cf. IV, 9
[3] Carlo Pietrangeli: *I Monumenti Dei Culti Orientali* (Capitoline catalogue), p. 55
[4] Smith's *Dictionary Of . . . Antiquities*, 'Sacrificium'
[5] unless there was a special reason to insist on the sharing of the totemistic guilt. If the sacrifice ceremonialised a treaty, for instance, the parties were bound together by dividing and sharing the hair.

expect castration from him, again in his animal form[1]. Some years ago, in a train in Italy, I picked up a paper someone had abandoned in the carriage, and found in it a drawing which is a pendant to the set of comic drawings about a maidservant and her small charge which Ferenczi found in a Hungarian comic paper at the turn of the century, and which Freud published in *The Interpretation Of Dreams*[2] as a graphic and unwitting illustration of the symbols and wishes involved in dream-making. The Italian drawing purports to illustrate a 'news item' (a hen pecks out a child's tooth, which it has mistaken for grain): in fact it vividly sets out the whole psychic content of the infantile animal phobias; the very attitude the boy sits in leaves no doubt of the meaning concealed in the tooth symbolism. Like the Hungarian drawing of so long before, the Italian one comes from that unchanging proletarian underworld which children share with servants and peasants (and share, in the comedy of Plautus and Terence, with slaves), where the content of infantile wishes and theories still lives a vigorous existence beneath the consciousness of the bourgeoisie—which plays the part of society's Ego. (Thus Freud[3] on the organisation of the psyche: 'Our mind . . . is no peacefully self-contained unity. It is rather to be compared with a modern State in which a mob, eager for enjoyment and destruction, has to be held down forcibly by a prudent superior class.')

Much of Greek mythology, with its multiplication of goddesses exalted and deteriorated, is an attempt to allay the infantile dread of castration. Like the dread itself, the myth hesitates on the question of which aspect to consider, that in which the mother horrifies because her castrated state threatens castration to the child, or that in which she no longer horrifies but attracts her children to the crime whose punishment is castration. Pallas Athena represents the mother cautiously restored, the restoration stopping short of the point where the temptation to incest would begin. She is not given the male organ, but she is given the character of a male warrior and, emblematically, his penetrative weapon; her birth uniquely from Zeus, without the intervention of a mother, suggests that she is an extension of his phallic prowess[4]: yet, in case this unhorrifying figure

---

[1] But in *Three Blind Mice* it is the child who has turned animal.

[2] VI (E)   [3] *Collected Papers*, Volume V, XXVII

[4] Athena seems to have exercised a phallic function through her connexion with an obscure trio of goddesses (the daughters of Kekrops) who represented the glistening dew—that is to say, the semen which fertilises the (mother)

should tempt men too far, her armour and weapon are used in repelling assailants and in defending the exalted and unapproachable character—which she maintains in spite of being sometimes addressed as 'mother'[1]—of a virgin.

The same compromise is also attempted by splitting the mother into the two, not quite separable personalities of Demeter and Persephone. The safely aged and sexually unattractive[2] mother is left on earth—visible, that is, to consciousness. There she mourns the loss of her daughter and searches for her, a mourning and search which movingly sum up for ever the woman's irreplaceable loss, culminating in the loss of the final substitute, her child. Meanwhile this child has been made invisible to consciousness by being repressed to the dark Underworld (at least for half[3] of each year. As a matter of fact, in dividing Persephone's time into a portion spent above and another spent below the earth, the myth is only reiterating what it has already done by dividing the mother into Demeter above and Persephone below. The new division was an elaboration which could usefully be made to explain the seasons, the exact fraction of year allotted to the Underworld being adapted to whatever calendar was in fashion; but the myth never insists on it in terms of personalities, and Persephone the queen of the Underworld is never missing from her ghostly kingdom.) Persephone, as the mother's child, represents the mother's penis; and it is the image of this which is repressed, because to leave it in unity with the mother makes the mother dangerously attractive. And, indeed, the young and charming personality of Persephone represents the infantile memory of the mother, a mother not yet made frightening to the child by the discovery of her mutilation.

Although repressed, this Persephone is still too dangerous to leave intact; having been stolen by Hades, she has to be mutilated by him,

---

earth. (H. J. Rose: *A Handbook* . . ., V). We can guess that this trio was a trio because the male sexual organs are tripartite. Since they are female, they seem to represent the mother's male organs. Their cult would naturally be absorbed by Athena in her character of male mother.

[1] H. J. Rose: *A Handbook* . . ., V

[2] Thus when the grieving Demeter disguises herself as a mortal (one of her most cult-commemorated manifestations) she appears 'in the likeness of a very old woman, cut off from childbearing and the gifts of Aphrodite' (Homeric Hymn *To Demeter*, 101-2).

[3] or, by some (perhaps the more orthodox) versions, a third of the year. (Homeric Hymn *To Demeter*, 399)

submitting to the defloration which re-iterates the woman's castration. (Persephone's association with flowers[1] and with vegetation in general is all a pun on defloration—turned to exegetic use, which helped also to disguise its sexual content.) This story the myth tells in appropriately infantile symbolism, picturing sexual union in terms of oral union[2]. When Demeter at last discovers what has become of Persephone, she applies to Zeus to have the lost child restored to her. Zeus promises to make Hades give the girl back, providing she has not eaten anything during her stay in the Underworld with him. Hades secretly gives her pomegranate seed to eat[(3)], and then dispatches her to the upper world to meet Demeter. In the beautiful, touching, sophisticated and amused account[(4)] which the Homeric Hymn gives of the interview between mother and daughter, Demeter runs headlong to meet her child, 'like a Maenad down a wooded mountain', and flings her arms round her: and then, like any mother recovering a daughter who has run away from finishing school and gone off with a man, she finds her heart misgiving her in the middle of the embrace, stops caressing Persephone and asks: 'My child, surely you didn't eat anything when you were in the Underworld? Speak out and hide nothing, so that we both may know'. Persephone has, of course, eaten the seed of the Underworld pomegranate—that is, she has received Hades's seed into her body. Zeus cannot, therefore, allow her to remain in the upper world: he cannot annul a marriage that has been consummated.

Persephone's marriage to Hades appears in the myth solely as the instrument of Persephone's mutilation. Mystery cult and doctrine, in the furtherance of their promise to initiates of overcoming death, elaborated a story in which Persephone mates with her own father, Zeus, and bears the resurrection-hero Zagreus: but in her orthodox

[1] Thus (in her own account of the circumstances of her kidnapping) Persephone and her maiden friends were 'playing and gathering lovely (ἐρόεντα—the word preserves the erotic connexion) flowers' when Hades erupted from beneath the earth. (*To Demeter*, 425 foll.)

[2] Freud points out (*Collected Papers*, Volume II, VI) that if the infantile theory that children are passed like faeces should persist, it becomes, later in childhood, augmented (and partly disguised) by an oral theory. 'It is like that in fairy-tales', he comments. 'One eats some particular thing and from this one gets a child'. In the fairy-tale about Persephone, this is how she marries; but she significantly does not get a child.

[(3)] Homeric Hymn *To Demeter*, 371-2   [(4)] 385 foll.

marriage with Hades, Persephone is never compensated for her mutilation by bearing a child (thus breaking Poseidon's rule that the matings of divinities are always fertile). Persephone is for ever the maiden raped and the mother discovered to be castrated. The myth has fused rape and discovery, as, indeed, the woman's own Ego does; and it is this act which transforms Persephone's pretty and desirable personality into that of the dreaded death-goddess. The sterility of her marriage, and the darkness and terror of the deathly kingdom she rules jointly with Hades, image the sterility and death threatened to the son by the existence of the mother who has been castrated.

A similar attempt to mend the mother but not too completely can be observed in the personality of Artemis (Diana). Moreover, here, too, the mother image has been split—this time into three; or perhaps several ancient mother deities have been welded into one image, and the image is the trinitarian one of Diana Triformis (or the triple Hecate), who has three manifestations, Selene (Luna), Artemis and Hecate, appropriate respectively to the spheres of above, on and beneath the earth. Since the first person of this trinity is hardly more than a theological-explanatory personification of the moon, it looks as though tripleness has been imposed on the moon-mother, who was originally split simply into an exalted virgin and a deteriorated image of a witch. The imposition is itself an attempt to restore to the mother the lost masculine sexual character, since tri-partness, with which the Christian father-god is also stamped, is the mark of the male sexual organs[1]; and the attempt to accomplish this by theological means has taken the form of modelling the mother's theological character on the great trinity of brothers—Zeus, Poseidon and Hades—in whom the phallic power of the father is shewn extending, respectively, above, on and beneath the earth[2].

The association of the moon with the mother probably comes about in the first place through the infantile conception of childbirth as

---

[1] Cf. (e.g.) the dream of 'a straw hat of peculiar shape, the middle piece of which is bent upwards, while the side pieces hang downwards' or the dream (dreamt by a policeman's wife) in which the penis appears as a policeman accompanied by two tramps, who go along with him 'quite peaceably'. (Freud: *The Interpretation Of Dreams*, VI (E)).

[2] This prolongation of Zeus's power is perhaps itself an indication of phallic prowess, like the 'endless prolongation' of a riding-whip, which, in a dream of Bismarck's analysed by Freud, 'can hardly signify anything else but an erection'. (*The Interpretation Of Dreams*, VI (E))

defecation and the resemblance of the moon to a profile view of the buttocks. Better acquaintance both with the facts of childbirth and with the influence of the moon would strengthen the association, by drawing a parallel between the uterine waters and the tides which are subject to the moon. A parturition dream of a woman patient of Freud's consists of the dreamer flinging herself 'into the dark water at the place where the pale moon is reflected in the water'. On this Freud comments: 'The place from which one is born may be recognized if one thinks of the humorous sense of the French *"la lune"*. The pale moon thus becomes the white "bottom", which the child soon guesses to be the place from which it came.'[1]

No sooner is the moon equated with the mother than a very good reason intrudes itself for equating it with the castrated mother: the moon's monthly cycle tallies with the monthly bleeding of the woman's wound. The moon becomes dangerous—dangerous enough to drive men mad; and one aspect of the moon-goddess becomes the horrid figure of Hecate[2], who is made invisible to consciousness by being relegated to the hours of darkness or to the Underworld itself (where she is associated, and sometimes confused or even amalgamated, with the death-goddess Persephone), and who presides over black magic worked with the help of unclean substances. On the other hand, Hecate's exalted counterpart, Artemis, retains enough of the character of the mother to be the goddess of childbirth, even though she has been put out of reach of mankind's incestuous desires by being made a virgin.

Artemis would not, however, stand in need of this protection if she had not first been built up again into something like the original attractive state of the mother. The restoration has been made by awarding her, as her emblem, that most phallic of weapons, the bow and arrow—the very emblem which emphasises Cupid's phallic character and which, in the hands of Artemis's brother Apollo, represents the fertilising rays of the sun (one of which, in Annunciation pictures like Crivelli's[3], symbolises the Holy Ghost's power to impregnate the Virgin Mary). With this weapon, Artemis, accompanied

---

[1] *The Interpretation Of Dreams*, VI (E)

[2] who seems to have been depressed into this deteriorated rôle after an earlier manifestation as a perfectly respectable—indeed highly honoured—goddess, whose special character was to be the guardian of the very young. (See Hesiod: *Theogony*, 411-52)

[3] National Gallery

by a group of virginal followers similarly armed, hunts wild animals; and we can understand this vendetta of hers if we take the wild animal in the totemistic sense it held for the followers of Diony-sos—as an embodiment of the father who, when hunted down, suffers castration at the hands of the group in the form of sparagmos. Artemis is the woman at her most hostile to men, trying to steal back from them what she herself has lost; and that her hostility to animals represents her hostility to men is confirmed by the story in which Actaeon accidentally catches sight of her naked as she bathes, whereupon she changes him into a stag and he is presently subjected to a sparagmos—that is, a castration—by his own hounds. (The punishment which is unconsciously expected for the crime of spying on a divine copulation was, so it was rumoured, inflicted—under one of the commonest and in this case the most appropriate of symbolic disguises—on Philip of Macedon: 'It is . . . said he lost one of his eyes, which was that he applied to the chink of the door, when he saw the god in his wife's embraces in the form of a serpent'[1].)

The story of Actaeon, perhaps originally and certainly in the hands of Ovid[2], makes an allusion to the mystery cults, with their promise to reveal to the initiate something occult about the true nature of a deity, and their threat that an uninitiated intruder or an initiate who lets the secret out will suffer a punishment which we can take as equal to castration. Shakespeare gives us a glimpse of pure mystery psychology (the tradition having been passed on, no doubt, through some renaissance secret society) in the compact between Viola and the sea captain in *Twelfth Night*[3]. We can take at its full value as a castration symbol the blindness which the sea captain calls down on himself if he should ever betray Viola's secret; and indeed, the secret itself shews us what Shakespeare's thoughts are playing on, for she is to present herself to Orsino in men's clothes—disguised, however, not as a man but as a eunuch. 'Be you his eunuch, and your mute I'll be', says the captain; and finishes the couplet with the mystery oath:

> When my tongue blabs, then let my eyes not see.

Psychologically, the mysteries are built on the infant's sexual curiosity. To reveal the true nature of a god or goddess is to shew the

[1] J. and W. Langhorne's translation of Plutarch's *Life* of Alexander the Great

[2] *Metamorphoses*, III, 173 foll.   [3] I, ii

father or mother naked—perhaps even to let the child spy on their mating; the initiates at Eleusis seem to have witnessed some theatrical and perhaps symbolical representation of a divine coitus. No doubt the theological mystery entrusted to initiates made an attempt to interpret the facts into something more acceptable to the infantile wishes— to explain, for example, that the mother in her secret true form had after all not been castrated and therefore held out no threat to her sons; the very goddess of death is explained as a comforting mother offering immortality to initiates.

When the unhappy Actaeon blunders (though we can interpret the accident, like Oedipus's ignorance, as the unconscious nature of what were really desires) into a glimpse of the mother naked, we can read his action as simultaneously sexual enquiry and incestuous wish. Similarly with the castration which comes on him as a result. If it is the obvious punishment for his wish, it is also the natural consequence of satisfying his curiosity. His is the classic shock of the boy who discovers that the mother has been castrated, a discovery which entails the horrifying deduction that he might be, too. It is partly Actaeon's own horror which the myth shews us in his horrifying death.

For the mystery cults it was easy to point the moral: this is what happens to the intruder who penetrates the mysteries (an intellectual version of penetrating the mother) without first undergoing the initiation which makes the knowledge innocuous by explaining it away. Initiation made knowledge innocuous by expiating, and thus making innocuous, the sexual wish behind the original desire for knowledge. Conversely, the mystery belief (which survived explicitly into the renaissance and still inexplicitly animates our thinking about science) that knowledge is dangerous and should be revealed only to initiates who have made some form of expiation is based on the child's original sexual concept of knowledge—indeed, his sexual interest in knowledge.

The mystery cults, the neo-Platonists of the renaissance, and the Freemasons of the eighteenth century were all in the habit (which is a sort of flirting with the perils of exposure) of publicly stating or alluding to the secret truth, but in an allegorical disguise impenetrable to the uninitiated eye. Conceivably, in 'The Birth of Venus'— really, of course, not her birth but her landfall—Botticelli painted an allegory of allegory itself. As the naked Venus is blown to land, a figure on the shore (whom, from her resemblance to the figure at the right of the *Primavera*, we can take to be Flora or Earth or some other personification of Nature) holds a cloak ready to wrap round the goddess. The allegory reads:- when the divine principle, the naked truth[1], comes among men, it must be cloaked in allegories made from material drawn from the natural world. The beauty of the picture does not, of course, depend on the allegory, but is drawn from the infantile situation behind the allegory; the sadness in Venus's face is a reflexion of the artist's sadness. Botticelli is again treating his constant theme, the irrecoverability of infancy: the moment when Venus steps ashore will be the very moment when the union between child and mother is split and the mother cloaks herself for ever against the child's enquiring and loving gaze.

Knowledge itself is, by the infantile and mystery concept, full of the ambiguous power of taboo. The taboo rules protect the savage from his own unconscious sexual wishes, and neo-Platonic allegory protects the layman from his own unconscious sexual curiosity—both of which, if indulged, would incur the penalties of an attack on the father. It is in order to safeguard themselves that some people, and especially those who do not belong to the fathers class in society, deliberately abstain from knowledge: knowledge is something which appertains to the mana of the father; to acquire it would be to be pretentious or 'stuck-up' (that is, hubritious) and would invite a disaster to punish it. Curiosity itself is still tainted with the infantile sexual curiosity, which in its turn cannot be divorced from the guilty wish to encroach on the father's rights.

Ovid, with his genuine and remarkable, though vulgar and unintellectual, psychological insight, and also with that delicate sensitivity to the scandalous which is second only to Colette's, does not hesitate to turn Artemis into a lesbian gym-mistress surrounded by a troupe of devoted tomboys. He understands perfectly that the blundering Actaeon has split open the fantasy in which Artemis, with her skirt hitched up[2], is maintaining that she is as good as a man; he makes great play with Artemis's disgust when she discovers that one of her maidens has been seduced by a male (in fact Zeus—who evidently understands the relationship between Artemis and her followers, since he is shrewd enough to disguise himself as Artemis before making his advances to the maiden)[3]; and perhaps Ovid is taking the

---

[1] On the subject of comparable personifications of the naked (philosophic) truth, see E. Panofsky: *Studies In Iconology* . . ., V

[2] *Metamorphoses*, I, 695. Smith includes a drawing of the Louvre statue of a short-skirted Artemis.

[3] *Metamorphoses*, II, 409 foll.

opportunity to hint at lesbianism in one of the Roman religious rites reserved to women.

Myth-historians often contrast the virgin goddess whom Ben Jonson called 'Queen and huntress, chaste and fair' with the far from fair and, by implication, far from virginal manifestation she had in her cult at Ephesus (where St. Paul came into conflict with a silversmith who made shrines for her[1]). The Ephesian Artemis is profusely maternal: hieratic swaddling bands mysteriously conceal all her body except her naked and innumerable breasts. Her promise seems to be of maternal succour to all mankind, insisting that she can suckle numbers of children at once, like a mother animal; and no doubt it is to a mother animal that the image-makers were comparing her when they covered her with tiny animals so that she resembles an orange stuck with cloves (a comparison whose mythological basis would be Artemis's reputation as a huntress or, more probably, the origin of that reputation, an earlier totemistic association between Artemis and animals). However, in making these breasts resemble an animal's dugs, the statuary has unwittingly betrayed the unconscious wish which is embodied in the cult figure. The narrow, pointed cylinders of flesh which protrude from Artemis bear little resemblance to a woman's breasts (the image-maker has even—so much for the promise of succour for mankind—suppressed the nipples) but a considerable resemblance to the male sexual organ. Artemis is both woman and man.

This bisexual character is emphasised by the figures worked in the goddess's robes. Up each side of her crawls a line of bees, the bees alternating with open flowers. It is the metaphor of the old-fashioned love song 'You are my honey, honeysuckle; I am the bee'. Artemis, however, has arrogated to herself both sexual characters. Alternately she is the flower, which waits immobile to be fertilised, spread receptively open and yet concealing the channel by which it can be penetrated until it yields to the bee, and she is the bee which actively crawls, aspires and penetrates, and whose body, with the abdomen protruding just below the flanking wings, the carver has turned into a diagram of the male sexual apparatus.

Thus the contrast between this maternal Ephesian Artemis and the virgin goddess vanishes: both are mothers in the sense that both are the result of childish curiosity and desire exercised on the image of the female body, which to the child is par excellence the mother's body; and both are mothers to whom the infantile fantasy has, for

[1] *Acts*, XIX

self-interested motives, restored some of the sexual character of a male. The Ephesian goddess's multiple breasts supply the same lack as the huntress's arrows; and if the huntress's chastity and weapons warn men against succumbing to her restored desirability, the Ephesian goddess holds them at a distance by her monstrous, half-animal nature.

11. *The Sacramental Journey*

If we arrange schematically what we can learn from Freud about the psychology of sexuality, it turns out that there are three occasions on which the Ego finds itself threatened with castration. The first is at the discovery that the mother has been castrated. The second is when the son has overcome the first fear sufficiently to address himself incestuously to the mother, in which case he fears that the father will castrate him. These two are inter-connected: we have just been exploring some of Greek mythology's hesitations about which of them to pacify at the expense of increasing the other. The third occasion is, so to speak, the real one—when the fear is justified and the species, satisfying its own purposes by fulfilling the Erotic impulses of the Id, really does inflict a temporary castration, a little death, on the Ego. (Although for women this experience does not come until after parturition, in another sense the whole of the woman's sexual life is an experience of a perfectly real castration; and out of this experience the woman is capable of supplying the psychic elements necessary for her to share the citizenship on a common basis with men.)

The life of the Ego represents an attempt to capture some of the species's immortality, which is only on loan to individuals and is really embodied in the continuity of the reproductive chain. The Ego's difficulty is that it cannot live in economic isolation, but has to bargain with the Id and, through the Id, with the species. The life of the group—that is to say, of a number of Egos identified with one another—is a further attempt in the same direction: the group is wringing its own immortality out of that of the species. The group, too, has its economic difficulties; it cannot afford to inhibit the sexual impulses wholly, and yet its cohesion as a group depends on their being partly inhibited.

The greatest danger to the group comes from its guilt towards the communal father. The sons' constant unconscious hostility towards him, together with their assertion of their sexual desires when he has claimed the exclusive right to sexuality, constitute a crime which brings the sons under the threat of being castrated by him in punishment. The group's Ego is threatened with strangulation—with being cut off from the instinctual source of life, the Id. This situation can be relieved only by an adjustment of the economic bargain, which is achieved at the group's sacrament. We can perfectly accept the Catechism's definition of a sacrament as 'an outward and visible sign of an inward and spiritual grace': it is a symbolic, symptomatic act whose inward result is economic—the release of a flood of energy, of 'grace', to the starved Ego.

This access of grace comes in the form most welcome to an Ego: the promise of immortality conveyed to the initiate in the mysteries or to the baptised (that is, initiated) Christian who makes regular use also of the eucharistic sacrament. The initiation sacrament foreshadows the initiate's entrance into immortal life by being explicitly a re-birth. Baptism is 'a new birth unto righteousness', the baby emerging, with obstetrical correctness, head first, breaking the waters with its skull.

However, baptism is also, the Catechism insists, 'a death unto sin'. It is, indeed, a token death by drowning, parallel to the ordeals by fire and water Tamino undergoes at *his* initiation in *The Magic Flute*. The initiation sacrament consists not only of the initiant's re-birth into immortality but of a sacrifice on his part which is tantamount to forgoing his hopes of immortality. That is to say, in one form or another he undergoes a castration: it may be in fact (as the priests of Cybele did) or by a direct token, like circumcision, or by a token death; it may be by a period of sexual abstinence or by a vow of sexual renunciation—which the baptised baby undertakes, only a little less rigorously than the Catholic priest, when he promises by proxy to give up the world, the flesh and the devil; it may be by means of the dangerous initiation course, itself a token death, through which he must labour, his heroic prototype in this case being Herakles.

The same is true of the eucharistic or totemistic sacrament. The worshippers are in fact assaulting their god; but, by the unconscious hypocrisy which is so striking in religious acts, they regard this as *their* sacrifice of praise and thanksgiving, though if they are Catholics they will be careful to say that they are merely re-offering a sacrifice originally made by the God's son. Moreover, they are not mistaken in seeing themselves as the sacrificed. The group sacrament really does re-affirm the group's subjection to its leader; and, by sharing the guilt of assaulting him, the members really do become bound both to one another and to the sacramental wheel, whereby their guilt can be expiated only by more and more sacrifices of the same kind.

The sacrament is thus a paradox: it fulfils the worshipper's Oedipal wishes (the communicant becomes the father by ingesting him; the initiate comes to see and know the mother in her naked truth; the ordained priest becomes a Father) and at the same time it is a sacrifice of the worshipper's own sexuality in favour of the father. I do not see any way fully to unravel the paradox except to recognise that the sacrament is actually playing on the biological situation, and is making use of the fact that sexual intercourse is tantamount to temporary castration. If the son is to be sacrificed and castrated in the rite, he takes care that the occasion of it shall be that of the phallos's castration-in-orgasm.

Psychically, the sacramental rite follows two patterns in one: it acts out both death and sexual intercourse. The shape of the experience which is undergone at the ceremony or at the course of initiation describes the sexual experience of the phallos, working up to a culmination in orgasm—an experience which can easily be converted into thanatic terms: that is, it may also represent either inflicting death on the god or the worshipper undergoing death himself. And in fact the fusion of castration and orgasm is contrived by means of the worshipper's identification with the father or the father's heroic son. The worshipper's own sacrifice of himself is amalgamated with the death he inflicts on the god; and, having made himself one with the god in this respect, he is able to make himself one with the god when the god, by the father's prerogative, enters the mother's body in a sexual sense. The sacramental rite is a journey both in this sexual sense, which culminates in the death in orgasm, and at the same time in the sense that the worshipper or initiant is journeying into death.

From the point of view of the sacrament, the two branches of Oedipal desire are inseparable; the one is included and understood in the other. The son cannot assault the father sadistically without incurring the concomitant of sexually assaulting the mother. He cannot wish to take the father's place without it being unconsciously understood that that place is in the mother's bed. (Neither can he fulfil his wish to make love to the mother without becoming guilty of parricide: the matriarchising religions whose heroes achieve sexual union with the mother goddess, and whose initiates enjoy, visually or symbolically, a sacramental copulation with some representative of the goddess, have included the aggressive act against the father in the sexual act with the mother.) Thus the communion wafer enables the son to munch and destroy the father: but at the same time this morsel of the father's flesh (a morsel which, by the lottery of the sparagmos, specifically enshrines sexual power) forms a connecting link between two bodies and thus sketches the union which is sacramentally taking place between the communicant and the mother, the Church. The sketch is acted out in oral terms, and the communicant, who is really the active person, takes the passive rôle: as he spiritually penetrates the body of the Church, the wafer penetrates his mouth, sketching on him what he is doing, just as the tongue may prefigure sexual intercourse in a kiss. (Proust, meditating on Albertine's kisses, compares her tongue to the eucharistic wafer which is slipped into the mouth of the dying: '. . . Albertine glissait dans ma bouche, en me faisant le don de sa langue, comme un don du Saint-Esprit, me remettait un viatique. . .'[1]. Naturally, the tongue may play a phallic part— and with the utmost precision—in castration-symbolism as well. Thus, in Gibbon's words[2]: 'Jerome, in his Legend of Paul the Hermit, tells a strange story of a young man, who was chained naked on a bed of flowers, and assaulted by a beautiful and wanton courtezan. He quelled the rising temptation by biting off his tongue.')

Similarly, the course of suffering which the worshippers inflict on the father or heroic son represents at the same time the phallic journey which the worshippers, in their identification with him, undertake into the body of the mother. The meditation on 'The Way Of The Cross' is not only one of the most lingeringly and deliberately cruel exercises the human imagination has ever devised, but it is also one of the world's most daring and effective masterpieces of pornography. It offers a complete sadistic parody of the phallos's progress to orgasm—in its dwelling account of how the hero, who has already been beaten, makes his labouring ascent up the hill of Calvary, repeatedly stumbling on the way, and is there stripped naked, suffers his flesh to be penetrated and is at last raised in his public elevation on the cross, where he expires with a final tremendous exhalation of breath; after which comes the swift and anticlimactic descent and burial—the little death, the relaxation into sleep. (It is the same progress which the Host

[1] *La Prisonnière*   [2] *The Decline And Fall . . .*, XVI, note

follows at the Mass, working up to the climax of its elevation.)

The initiation sacrament makes the same play on the occasions of castration. If we ask 'How can the priest be becoming a father if he is also divesting himself of sexuality?', the answer is that no one can become a father *without* suffering a castration in the act which makes him one. The sacrament is, precisely, an act in which the punitive castration, which the son has incurred by his guilt in respect of the father, is made to coincide with the castration which inevitably follows after the son's sexual intercourse—and which is not only inevitable but deserved if the son's intercourse is with the mother. The ceremonial progress of the initiant symbolises his sacrifice and castration of himself and at the same time his penetration into the mother's body. The initiated citizen is one who has acquired the right to use the body of the land which belongs to the state; the religious initiate has penetrated to secrets which are forbidden to outsiders—and this may even be physically demonstrated in the actual building of the church or temple with its three-dimensional resemblance to the body of the mother[1], by his being allowed to enter, first, the body of the church and then, at the next stage of initiation, the inner sanctuary which would be violated if a non-initiate set foot there.

In the Ego's attempt to make itself immortal, the group really has a hope of immortality which is not available to the individual Ego. Thus it comes about that the religious group offers its members the promise of immortal life through the sacrament which re-affirms the group's solidity and releases a new fund of psychic energy for the group's continuation. The miniature death and castration which the worshipper suffers at the sacrament has been fused with the occasion on which the species really does secure its immortality. At the sacrament the group really does direct this genuine immortality to the furtherance of the group; and the more sophisticated religions offer it back to the individual Ego in the form of a promised personal immortality after death, which is to be secured through use of the sacraments.

These religions have, in fact, equated the individual's death with the phallos's descent into temporary deadness, and the Ego's descent into unconsciousness, after orgasm; and they are pretending that the

[1] The human body is, according to St. Paul (*I Corinthians*, VI, 19), 'the temple of the Holy Ghost' (. . . τὸ σῶμα ὑμῶν ναὸς τοῦ ἐν ὑμῖν ἁγίου πνεύματός ἐστιν)—the temple, that is, of the agency which penetrated the maternal body of the Virgin Mary.

genuine chance of survival which this event gives to the species can be made an assurance of survival for the individual. Thus the sacramental hero in myth descends into Hell and rises again—a pattern which the initiant follows in ritual when he goes through the ordeal of token death and emerges re-born. This heroic journey traces out the same psychic pattern as the sacramental ceremony. It is not only a death inflicted by the hero on himself but also a death which he inflicts on the father—because it also represents the sexual intercourse of the hero with the mother. And at the same time it represents a raid by the Ego on the economic resources of the Id.

The climactic acts of Eros and Thanatos have thus coalesced in the metaphor of a journey (which may also be acted out in ritual): the journey of the dead soul to the other world, and at the same time, the sexual journey of the active phallos into the female body—a journey (or flight) which culminates in the soul flying away in the orgasmic exhalation. It is the prerogative of the sacrament, which makes us all heroes, to combine these two senses; and myth signifies the combination by allowing certain privileged heroes, certain sons of gods, to make *two* journeys to Hell, one in the normal way after death and one during their lifetime, from which they are permitted, by the hero's privilege of resurrection, to return. As the Sibyl tells Aeneas:

> The gates of hell are open night and day;
> Smooth the descent, and easy is the way:
> But to return, and view the cheerful skies—
> In this the task and mighty valour lies.
> To few great Jupiter imparts this grace,
> And those of shining worth, and heav'nly race.[1]

The economic efficacy of the sacrament is obviously a highly important factor in the history of religion. When the totemistic secret that the sacrificed animal was the father dropped out of the worshippers' consciousness, the animal-sacrifices of classical religion must have lost much of their efficiency. There was evidently an unconscious search for a sacrament which would really work in inducing a state of grace in the worshipper's Ego—a search reflected in the curious situation whereby the mystical and mystery cults, which in one form or another had preserved or re-instated the totemistic identification, were tolerated, more or less willingly, alongside the

[1] Dryden's translation (VI, 192-7) of Virgil: *Aeneid*, VI, 126-31

orthodox cults. It was a sort of confession that the orthodox cults were insufficient. Indeed, in the longest and most psychological view, the uneasiness, gathering towards panic, of the classical world as a whole, and its persistent feeling of guilt and decline, is probably the result of the Ego's panic fear of being starved to death, a fear induced progressively by the decay of the totem sacrament. The Ego did not re-assure itself until one of the unorthodox groups found the self-confidence to put itself and its sacrament forward to the exclusion of every other group and sacrament—thus becoming the new orthodoxy, and destroying the whole of ancient civilisation in the process.

If the mysteries owed their efficacy to partly re-instating the father-animal-victim identification of primitive totemism, it is no surprise that the eventual winner among mystery cults was Christianity, which was the most open in identifying its vegetable paschal lamb with the god. The totemism of its nearest rival, Mithraism, was less open[1]; it was left to Freud to recognise [2] Mithras as the singled-out hero who kills the tyrannical father in his totem manifestation as a bull.

Christianity and Mithraism had in common that they virtually suppressed the mother or reduced her to a nonpersonal representation. They are both cases where the sexual significance of the sacramental rite is included and understood in the aggressive significance, and the fulfilment of the incestuous Oedipal wish is included in the fulfilment of the violent wish against the father. The only overt meaning in the sacramental journey is now Mithras's heroic labour in overthrowing the tyrant or Christ's in sacrificing himself. The hero identifies himself with the father, and the worshipper with the hero; and only by becoming the father in this sense does the worshipper fulfil his ambition to become what the father is, the mother's lover.

With the matriarchising mysteries, it is almost the other way about. Here the great figure is the goddess, with whom the initiate attains a sexual union more or less disguised—disguised perhaps as an oral union (like the union he attained with Demeter in the eucharistic meal of the Eleusinian mysteries) or perhaps as a marriage of minds, of which Apuleius is probably giving an allegorised account when he tells the story of the marriage of Cupid and Psyche[3]. The relationship

[1] The stages of Mithraic initiation made use of the totem formula of man into animal, the lowest being a raven, the highest emerging openly as father.

[2] *Totem And Taboo*, IV, 6

[3] which Shakespeare, a devoted reader of *The Golden Ass*, was perhaps thinking about when he wrote (Sonnet CXVI) of 'the marriage of true

of goddess to initiant is summed up in her appearing to him in an illuminating—and no doubt theatrically illuminated—apparition during his initiation. Apuleius probably gives a disguised (rather than fictionalised) description of one of these apparitions, together with an account of the dreamy sensation priestly stagecraft induced in the initiant, in the dream Lucius has of Isis—who not merely identifies herself as a consummate mother figure (she claims to be the same person as the infernal Persephone, the Eleusinian Demeter, Dictynnian Artemis, the Phrygian 'mother of the gods', etc., etc.) but also hints, by calling herself 'the parent of natural things' and 'the uniform aspect of the gods and the goddesses'[1] that she is in fact the bisexual mother, the mother with a penis, of infantile fantasy.

(The mysteries made much play with lighting, probably in sudden contrast to darkness [in some cases, the darkness of Hell] or to the veiling of the initiant: Apuleius, for instance, tells us that during his initiation he saw the sun shining brightly at midnight[2]. One might compare the Council of Trent's statement[3] that Holy Mother Church has 'instituted certain rites, to wit that certain things be pronounced in the mass in a softened, and others in a raised tone. She has likewise made use of ceremonies, such as mystic benedictions, lights, fumigations of incense . . . whereby both the majesty of so great a sacrifice might be recommended, and the minds of the faithful be excited, by these visible signs of religion and piety, unto the contemplation of those most sublime things which lie hidden in this sacrifice.' And with both one might compare Freud's[4]: 'The hypnotist asserts that he is in possession of a mysterious power which robs the subject of his own will . . . This mysterious power . . . must be the same that is looked upon by primitive people as the source of taboo, the same that emanates from kings and chieftains and makes it dangerous to approach them (*mana*). The hypnotist, then, is supposed to be in possession of this

minds'. The pagan allegory of the marriage between the soul (Psyche) and the god of love seems to have been early acceptable to Christians, since the two figures, kissing, appear on a sarcophagus along with a figure of Christ (No. 48 in S. Aurigemma's catalogue *The Baths Of Diocletian*).

[1] *The Golden Ass*, XI, 4: rerum naturae parens; deorum dearumque facies uniformis

[2] *The Golden Ass*, XI, 23

[3] quoted, from Session XXII, by Wylie Sypher: *Four Stages Of Renaissance Style*, Mannerism, VI

[4] *Group Psychology And The Analysis Of The Ego*, X

power; and how does he manifest it? By telling the subject to look
him in the eyes; his most typical method of hypnotising is by his look[1].
But it is precisely the sight of the chieftain that is dangerous and unbearable for primitive people, just as later that of the Godhead is for
mortals. . . It is true that hypnosis can also be evoked in other ways,
for instance by fixing the eyes upon a bright object or by listening to
a monotonous sound. . . As a matter of fact these procedures merely
serve to divert conscious attention and to hold it riveted. . . The
hypnotist . . . makes the person upon whom he is experimenting
sink into an activity in which the world is bound to seem uninteresting
to him; but at the same time the subject is in reality unconsciously
concentrating his whole attention upon the hypnotist . . . in this withdrawal of interest from the outer world lies the psychological characteristic of sleep, and the kinship between sleep and the state of hypnosis
is based upon it.' So, one might add, is the resemblance between
religious faith and the deep slumber of the group mentality.)

At Eleusis the initiate's entering into the mother's body was further
symbolised by including in the initiation some form of holy charade
(with further opportunities for stagecraft) in which the initiant visited
the dark region of Hell—that is, we can construe, the womb, the
secret and forbidden underground bourne in the body of the mother
earth, ruled over by Demeter in her Persephone extension. Evidently
the Isiac initiation included something of the same kind (Isis, besides
claiming identity with Persephone, describes herself as queen of shades—
regina manium), since the brief description which is all Apuleius may
give of his initiation includes the statement: 'I went to the border of
death and set foot on the threshold of Persephone'[2]. 'D'où venons-
nous? Que sommes-nous? Où allons-nous?', asks Paul Gauguin's
painting[3], posing the three great questions of mankind; and the

---

[1] Cf. 'Pfungst has described how easy it is to elicit fear reactions in monkeys
by staring into their eyes, and even by showing them drawings which look
like eyes. . . A female mandril looks at a white sheet of paper without fear.
But if a pair of eyes is drawn upon it, the animal reaches for it anxiously and
averts its head' (David Katz: *Animals And Men*, 7, translated by H. Steinberg
and A. Summerfield)

[2] *The Golden Ass*, XI, 23: Accessi confinium mortis et calcato Proserpinae
limine. . .

[3] (at Boston). Gaugin himself gave a significant account of the unconscious
origin of the questions (*Artists On Art*, compiled by R. Goldwater and M.
Treves): the words appeared in his mind when he 'woke up' after painting, and

mysteries demonstrate how the first, which is the original enquiry made by the infantile sexual curiosity, is transformed into the intellectual and theological third—to which the mysteries returned an answer in terms of the original question, when they shewed the initiant his future life by leading him to a representation of the womb.

The matriarchising mysteries seem to have fulfilled this ambition for the initiate without expressly encountering the father who should forbid it and whose power drives it, in Christianity and Mithraism, to conceal itself. Apuleius's dedication is primarily to Isis; it is as an afterthought that he dedicates himself to her consort Osiris[1]—who seems, in this Greco-Roman extension of his cult, to have almost reverted to what he may have been by origin, namely not a father but a jumped-up hero who, in marrying his sister, was really marrying his mother[2]. Certainly, the best that several of the mysteries can produce in the way of a male god is a hero who attains to a liaison with the mother; and in the couples[3] formed by Astarte and Adonis, and by Cybele (the Magna Mater) and Attis[4], the young hero is still subservient to the goddess.

None the less, the father is present by implication. Attis and Adonis suffer the fate reserved for the son who commits incest with the mother (so, indeed, does Osiris): and it can only be the power of the unseen father which has inflicted it on them. In the end, however, it is the son who wins: slain though he is, and even explicitly castrated, he and his sexual power are resurrected. He has taken the father's place to the extent of banishing the father from the myth. Even so, he has not acceded to all the father's glory in cult, but remains subordinate. He belongs to the republican period of the group's history, when the

he inscribed them on the canvas as 'not a title, but a signature'—or, as one might say in Freud's words, 'a certificate of origin, as it were, like "Made in Germany" '. (The inscription also appears on Gauguin's preparatory drawing but must have been added after the painting was finished, when Gauguin turned the drawing into a souvenir. Cf. No. 180 in the catalogue of the exhibition *Les Sources Du XXe Siècle*, Paris, 1960–61.)

[1] 'I was only religious to the goddess Isis, but not yet sacred to the religion of great Osiris. . .' (Adlington's translation, *The Golden Ass*, XI, 27)

[2] Cf. I, 15

[3] See C. Pietrangeli: *I Monumenti Dei Culti Orientali* (Capitoline catalogue), pp. 8–9

[4] Perhaps at Eleusis Demeter and Triptolemos are a sketch for a couple of this kind, not yet completely emerged from the myth-making process.

mother is glorified, but it is the group as a group which is the real ruler; so it is not surprising that this hero, in whom the father is swallowed up, is himself swallowed up in the initiate. It is the initiate who, identifying himself with the hero, really takes the father's place in union with the mother. But the father's power is only suspended: it may still visit the punishment on the offending son—if the initiate breaks his oath of secrecy.

This punishment was inflicted on Actaeon, whom Ovid construes as something between an intruder into the mysteries and an initiate who betrays the secret—as we can tell from the words he puts into Artemis's mouth as she changes him into a stag: 'Now you may tell, if you can, how you saw me with my clothes off'[1]. Apuleius treats him as more of the unauthorised intruder, and at the same time is franker about the sexual curiosity implicit: in the very house where Lucius is warned against dabbling in witchcraft, there is a statue of Artemis, which he describes in detail, among the details being images of Actaeon looking at the goddess 'with curious gaze'[2], and beginning to be turned into a stag.

Apuleius's interpretation has already lost the taboo quality of the primitive story, where, by the rules of taboo, Actaeon is punished for an accidental mistake, and has substituted for it Actaeon's conscious and prying curiosity. Lucius himself is curious ('At ego curiosus'[3], he says); which is why he disregards the warning, attempts to get himself changed by sorcery into an owl and finds himself instead changed into an ass. It is after the long buffoonery of his ass-adventures that he is finally delivered by Isis, who has appeared to him in his dream, and is initiated into her mysteries—which has sometimes been read as a religious ending tacked-on to a bawdy fiction, but which is, I think, susceptible of quite a different explanation.

Both the myth of Actaeon and Apuleius's novel deal with metamorphoses (which is in fact the proper title of *The Golden Ass*) and thus with totemism, a metamorphosis being nothing but the psychic process which turns the human father into the animal or plant totem. In the metamorphotic myth the process is put on display and caught in the very act of symbol-formation. Moreover, we can associate the totemistic metamorphosis with the very spring of the mystery cults, since one of the most potent inspirations of the animal phobias, those idiosyncratic versions of totemism, is that the child's sexual

[1] *Metamorphoses*, III, 192-3   [2] curioso obtutu (*The Golden Ass*, II, 4)
[3] *The Golden Ass*, II, 6

curiosity, balked when he applies it to the parents and their mating, can be satisfied by observation of animals[1]. The child dreads that the father will castrate him, and makes the father an animal; the totem group makes the father an animal, and castrates him by sparagmos. It is just this sparagmos Actaeon suffers: he has seen what only the father may see and is therefore castrated as a guilty son—or should we say that by usurping his place he has become the father, and has thus incurred the hostility of the group?

As a matter of fact, Actaeon, who undergoes no resurrection, so that he cannot be cut down again annually in cult, remains more of the guilty son; his attempt to replace the father has not achieved a mythological success. But his experience points the way for the initiant to make his successful attempt. Towards the end of *The Golden Ass*, Lucius describes how, restored to human form, he entered on his initiation, and warns the 'studious reader' that he cannot tell, and the reader cannot hear, the inmost secrets of what happened during it without incurring the penalty for rash curiosity. He rehearses briefly his visit to Hell, and concludes: 'There, I have told you things which, although heard, you are none the less obliged to remain ignorant of; therefore only what can be told without sin to the understanding of the profane will I report'[(2)]. In other words, Apuleius admits that he has said, and will say, more than meets the uninitiated eye; he is telling the secret truth in the wrapped-up form in which it is permissible to give it to outsiders. If this is true of the paragraph he has just written about his visit to Hell, and if it will be true of the rest of the book that is still to come, why should it not be true of the book as a whole?

If it is, then Lucius's ass-adventures are not irrelevant to the end of the story, and neither are they merely, though they certainly are in part, a broad allegory of the uninitiated soul's asinine gropings. They are a precise account of the preliminary stage of the initiation, in which the initiant really did dress up as an animal, just as primitive worshippers dressed up as animals in order to honour and at the same time mock their animal-god. The initiant thus became the father first

---

[1] Freud: *Totem And Taboo*, IV, 3. See *Collected Papers*, Volume III, V, for a case where what a child remembered later as a parental coitus may originally have been a coitus he observed between dogs.

[(2)] Ecce tibi rettuli quae, quamvis audita, ignores tamen necesse est: ergo quod solum potest sine piaculo ad profanorum intellegentias enuntiari, referam (XI, 23)

in his totem form, whereupon he incurred the hostility of the rest of the group: to run this gauntlet constituted his ordeal. This part of the ceremony, which corresponds to mocking or 'humorous' episodes in other religious rites, was probably explained as an allegory of the initiant's blindness before he is illuminated by the celestial vision; the ass's head or mask is equivalent to the veil at Eleusis. From Lucius's adventures we can divine that the initiant was tricked—the fate of the blind man in blind man's buff and of the baited animal; Lucius believed he could enter the higher flights of initiation straight away and become an owl; it is by a mistake with a box of magic ointment that he becomes an ass, and, having done so, he is led to believe that he will be quickly restored. Instead, one vicissitude introduces the next. The ass gets beaten and overloaded, and narrowly escapes from death and castration, which he hears threatened for him. No doubt part of the joke against the initiant was to treat and speak of him as though he really was an animal, just as part of the Lucius joke is that people speak and behave in his presence as though he was an ass, although he has, as he points out, retained the sense and understanding of a human[1]—a joke which perpetuates the cruel totemistic doublethink of treating the animal as though it really did possess the powers and understanding of a god.

In the initiant, as in the totem animal, it is the father's sexuality which, by a softened version of castrating him, is mocked; and it is this which lends Apuleius's novel its curious sadistic-bawdy tone. The initiant's dressing-up evidently did not fail to insist on the sexual virility which is the point of the comparison the child makes between the animal and the father. Thus the three-year-old 'Hans', who presently developed a totemistic phobia of horses, first asked his father 'Papa, have you got a widdler too?' and then, watching his mother undress, commented to her, 'I thought you were so big you'd have a widdler like a horse'[2]; and 'neither could I see any comfort in my transformation', says Lucius as he describes undergoing it, 'save that the nature of my members was increasing'[3]. Lucius in his ass form even has a love affair with a rich and influential matron who has become infatuated with him and makes herself 'an asinarious Pasiphaë'[4]; and he only just escapes being put on public show copulating with a human. The strongly sexualised teasing of the initiant which we can read through all this (which no doubt really did

[1] III, 26   [2] Freud: *Collected Papers*, III, II, I
[3] Adlington's translation, III, 24   [4] X, 19

bring him, like Lucius, nearly to suicide[1]) was none the less the prelude to the union the initiant would achieve with the goddess when he put off his disguise and entered on the solemn final stage of the initiation. But it also served a genuinely sadistic purpose. The initiant as animal, a figure who disappears from the later stage of the rite, is the only representative in the initiation sacrament of the father. The initiant's sufferings do duty both for his own castration in the father's favour and for the castration the group inflicts on the father while professing to honour him; the next time the initiant takes part in such a ceremony he will be among the assaulters, enjoying the initiate's privilege of making the attack on the father which only the group as a whole can make with impunity. The wanderings and picaresque escapades of Lucius describe the sacramental journey in both its sexual and its thanatic sense.

(The Apuleian situation of a woman enamoured of a man-ass was—purged of its grossness—put on the English stage some three decades after the publication of William Adlington's translation of Apuleius. The woman is now not merely rich and influential but the fairy queen—that is, a disbelieved-in goddess; she retains the divine influence over crops and weather[2], and the nocturnal habits of the moon goddess; and Shakespeare has given her the name, Titania, which Ovid applies to the moon goddess Artemis in the passage where he describes Actaeon's metamorphosis, so much less amusing than Bottom's, into an animal. From Apuleius Shakespeare has borrowed not merely the situation but the spell which, in *A Midsummer Night's Dream*, brings it about. Apuleius places the spell in the Cupid and Psyche episode, which is set in train by Venus's jealousy of Psyche: to punish Psyche, Venus asks Cupid to shoot at Psyche and afflict her with love [a plan frustrated when Cupid, to Venus's further jealousy, falls in love with Psyche himself]. Venus begs that Psyche may [in Adlington's words[3]] 'fall in desperate love with the most miserable creature living, the most poor, the most crooked, the most vile. . .'. In other and more imaginative words,

> Be it ounce, or cat, or bear,
> Pard, or boar with bristled hair,
> In thy eye that shall appear
> When thou wak'st, it is thy dear.
> Wake when some vile thing is near.

[1] IV, 2; X, 29 [2] *A Midsummer Night's Dream*, II, i [3] IV, 31

Indeed, the juice of the flower which maidens call Love-in-idleness, and which owes its magic potency to having been accidentally struck by Cupid's arrow[1], is itself an extension and variant of Cupid's arrow. And the air-borne god whom Apuleius-Adlington had described as 'rash enough and hardy' and 'of his own proper nature sufficient prone to work mischief'[2], achieved one of his last and most beautifully imagined manifestations in 'that shrewd and knavish sprite' who can 'put a girdle round the earth in forty minutes' in order to fetch the poisonous weapon he so mischievously distributes.)

The mythological material by which I should like to elaborate this account of the paradoxical psychic content of sacraments flows to my pen in such quantity, and so interconnected, that all I can do with it is threaten my readers with another book. Here and now I can only invite them to plunge for a moment, in the steps of the heroes, into the Underworld, in order to assure themselves that this realm to which such heroes as Odysseus, Herakles, Orpheus and Theseus descend (heroes who psychologically are, and were perhaps consciously taken as, types of the mystery initiant) fulfils precisely what we should expect of it if the heroic journey into death is a sketch of the sacramental act.

12. *Hell—2*

From the economic point of view, the sacrament is a raid, initiated by the unconscious Ego, on the unconscious resources, which the Ego would like to divert from the species's to its own immortality; and it is remarkable that, in the Underworld which the sacramental hero visits and of which he brings back a description, the myth has given us a very fair representation of the unconscious—in terms very similar to the spatial metaphor adopted by psycho-analysis.

Moreover, the myth understands very well the value of these subterranean resources to the Ego. The decaying and infertile kingdom is also a source of wealth, and Hades himself is associated or amalgamated with Ploutos and Dis, whose very names indicate riches.

As a matter of fact, the Underworld is not always under the world. The canonical description of it, given in Homer's account[3] of Odysseus's visit, places it at the end of the earth, in the remote West,

[1] *A Midsummer Night's Dream*, II, i   [2] IV, 30
[3] in Books X and XI of the *Odyssey*

beyond the river Oceanus which surrounded the disk of the earth. The alternative account, by which the Underworld was beneath the earth (the entrance being through some fissure in the ground—like the famous one at Taenarum in the Peloponnese) eventually became the more accepted in spite of Homer's authority. Virgil models Aeneas's approach to Hell closely on Odysseus's, though with more melodramatic effects. Aeneas, however, does not journey to the end of the earth but finds the entrance near Cumae—where, obviously, Virgil did not conceive Hell was to be found above ground; so the Hell to which he sends Aeneas, despite his reverence for Homer and the slight ambiguity of the language he has respectfully modelled on Homer's, is evidently *under* the ground. (But in fact Homer himself seems not quite sure which version to adopt; in the very book where Odysseus prepares to make the journey to the West, a soul apparently goes *down* to Hades's realm[1].) By the time that the good dead had been segregated from the bad, both versions could be used without contradiction, the good dead going happily west to the Isles of the Blessed, while the wicked were sent beneath the earth—where Dante visited them (in a Hell which borrowed several physical features and inhabitants from the classical version) when it was his turn to write a Christian epic modelled on Virgil.

The two versions are, of course, only alternative representations of a single idea, which is the remoteness and inaccessibility of the realm in which the dead are confined. It is impossible for the dead souls to get back to the light of day; and it is both arduous and terrifying for the hero to visit them: in other words, it is impossible for repressed material to make its way back into consciousness, and it is extremely hard for the conscious, even if it can be persuaded to make the attempt, to recover what has been relegated to the unconscious. When psycho-analysis did develop a technique whereby the conscious Ego could undertake the hero's journey in an intellectual sense, patients spontaneously adopted in their dreams both the metaphors the myth uses. Freud records[2] that 'persons who are undergoing psychoanalytic treatment frequently dream of it... The image chosen for the treatment is as a rule that of a journey'; and he continues: 'If the "uncons-

---

[1] *Odyssey*, X, 560: ψυχὴ δ᾽ Ἀϊδόσδε κατῆλθεν. The force of the kat- might here be no stronger than it is in *katabasis* or the 'Down' trains; but when he called Hades a katachthonic Zeus Homer can only have meant to place him underground.

[2] *The Interpretation Of Dreams*, VI (F) 9

cious", as an element of waking thought, is to be represented in the dream, it is replaced, appropriately enough, by subterranean localities'.

Freud had, of course, noted in passing that psycho-analysis was a 'sojourn in the underworld'[1]; indeed he gave *The Interpretation Of Dreams* the epigraph 'Flectere si nequeo superos, Acheronta movebo'. Moreover, he called in the Underworld myth as a simile to help him describe the nature of repressed wishes—and, in doing so, incidentally interpreted the myth. The wishes represented in dreams, he says[2], are 'not always current wishes. They may also be bygone, discarded, buried and repressed wishes, which we must nevertheless credit with a sort of continued existence, merely on account of their reappearance in a dream. They are not dead, like persons who have died, in the sense that we know death, but are rather like the shades in the Odyssey which awaken to a certain degree of life so soon as they have drunk blood.'

The myth has, in describing the unconscious, perfectly described the wishes which are repressed there, as dead souls. They are dead but immortal; they can neither cease to exist nor come into the upper world and achieve expression—which it is their constant ambition to do: 'Put me on earth again', says the dead soul of Achilles, 'and I would rather be a serf in the house of some landless man, with little enough for himself to live on, than king of all these dead men that have done with life'[3]. But the whole geography of Hell, a fortress surrounded by impassable rivers, is designed to frustrate their escape to expression. In the monstrous watchdog Cerberus, who never sleeps (though a hero can drug him or, as Herakles did, drag him off by main force—but he had to be returned), the myth has even given us a sketch of the 'censor' which prevents our wishes from escaping in our dream unless they first disguise themselves[4]. (The myth knows, incidentally, that dreams come from the region where the dead souls are kept. Homer describes the passage to Hell from the upper world of the newly-dead souls of the suitors: 'they went past the streams of Oceanus and the white rock, past the gates of the sun, and the land of dreams'; and it is 'soon' after this that they come to 'the asphodel meadow where the souls live, the wraiths of men'[5].)

None the less, it is the energy of these dead souls, these repressed

[1] *Collected Papers*, Volume I, 'On the History Of The Psycho-Analytic Movement'
[2] *The Interpretation Of Dreams*, V (D) (b); see also VII (c), note
[3] E. V. Rieu's translation of *Odyssey*, XI, 489-91
[4] *The Interpretation Of Dreams*, IV   [5] *Odyssey*, XIV, 11-14

wishes, that the sacramental hero has come to tap—at a time when his own Ego is starved of energy to fulfil its own purposes, a time when his luck has run out. Thus when Odysseus asks the magical Circe for luck and begs her to send him home, which is his heart's desire, she replies: 'But first it is necessary for you to undertake another journey and visit the halls of Hades and dread Persephone, to consult the soul of Teiresias the Theban, the blind prophet'[1]. The hero's Ego must be reinforced by power—that is, knowledge—which is confined with the shades. He must undertake the journey which so terrifies him that the mere thought makes him weep: and when he arrives, the transfer of power from the dead souls to him is accomplished by his sacrifice—a token of that self-castration the hero undertakes in the sacrament, a reiteration of his quasi-suicide in going down to Hell at all. Odysseus makes his sacrifice of a young ram and a black ewe, and when the soul of Teiresias has drunk the blood it is able to express itself—not in the upper world, but to Odysseus; and by enlisting the force of the repressed wish, Odysseus learns—that is, acquires the power to govern—his future.

The authority which incarcerates these wishes in the unconscious is, originally, the father's, presently incorporated into the psyche itself in the form of the Super-Ego. This the myth makes quite plain to us, since the supreme governor and gaoler of the Underworld is Hades—the unconscious Super-Ego and the subterranean extension of Zeus, that quintessential 'father of gods and men', whose parental status is bodily built-in to the Latin version of his name[2]. But while the fundamental meaning of Zeus's name is 'bright', connecting him with heaven and the light of day[3], the very name of Hades indicates that he is unseen[4]; and he presently lends his name to the kingdom he rules, which is likewise essentially dark, a region where things are made invisible to consciousness. There in the dark Hades relentlessly defends the father's privileges: indeed, when he erupted on to the earth in the character of rapist, he was asserting the primal father's exclusive right to sexual enjoyment, carrying off Persephone in her adolescence

[1] *Odyssey*, X, 490-3

[2] Jupiter: *Jovis* plus *pater*. Similarly, maternal status is built-in to the second half of Demeter's Greek name.

[3] Both his Greek and his Latin name are from a root DIV- DIAV-, whence also *dies*, day (Lewis). Cf. H. J. Rose: *A Handbook* . . ., III

[4] According to H. J. Rose (*A Handbook* . . ., IV), the god originally had no proper name but was simply called Hades ("Άιδης from ΑϜίδης), 'the Unseen'.

before a mortal (that is, a son) could lay hands on her, and installing her as his Underworld consort, who has become the warning, deathly image of the mother.

By the paternal authority of the unconscious Super-Ego, all the dead are confined; and some are actively punished as well. Odysseus witnesses the punishments of Tityos, Tantalus and Sisyphus[1]; in later accounts of Hell, the list of sinners and punishments has been augmented, and the punishments are segregated in the dungeon, the pit, of Tartaros, the deepest section of the Underworld. Not surprisingly, these famous sinners have committed for the most part Oedipal crimes. Ixion committed adultery with Zeus's wife; Tityos raped Zeus's mistress; Theseus and Peirithoos, who were imprisoned for a period in Hell, had raided Hell in an attempt to carry off the deathly mother herself, Persephone. Tantalus killed his own son (a displacement, as it were, of his wish to kill the father); the Danaides all killed their husbands on their wedding night—evidently through an incestuous fixation on their father, who loaned them the knife. Salmoneus tried to usurp Zeus by driving about in a chariot and aping Zeus's effects of thunder and lightning; Phlegyas objected to Apollo's exercising the primal father's prerogative and burned down Apollo's temple after Apollo had raped his daughter; Sisyphus made a similar objection against Zeus as well as spying on the parental love-making— he saw Zeus carrying off a nymph and informed on him.

The punishments inflicted for these crimes are intensifications of the frustrations imposed on all the dead souls. They remind us of Freud's finding, that 'every punishment is ultimately castration'[2], since they are all calculated frustrations of appetites or endeavours; and since, in this psychic realm which the Underworld represents, a wish can never be done to death, the appetite or endeavour is immortally renewed to be be immortally frustrated. A banquet is offered which the sufferer is not allowed to eat; or, like Tantalus, who has lent his name to an English verb of teasing, he is perpetually thirsty, and the means of quenching his thirst is continually presented to him and withdrawn. Even the sinner's craving for punishment may be frustrated, as he lies beneath a stone which for ever threatens to fall and does not fall. Tityos is tortured by vultures (or a serpent) which continually eats away his liver—the seat of the passions[3]; the liver constantly renews itself,

---

[1] *Odyssey*, XI, 576-600   [2] *Collected Papers*, Volume V, XXI

[3] ἧπαρ—liver: 'often in Trag. as the seat of the passions . . answering therefore to our "heart" ' (Liddell and Scott)

446 BLACK SHIP TO HELL

so there is always more passion to be frustrated. Ixion, strapped to his wheel, can progress only in a circle; Sisyphus rolls his boulder uphill without ever reaching the top; the Danaides fill a cistern with leaky pitchers. Theseus and Peirithoos (until Herakles, in the course of *his* heroic raid to the Underworld, releases them) are punished by the dream-sensation of inhibited movement[1]—they are stuck fast in their chairs.

It is into this world of frustration that the sacramental hero plunges when he visits Hell. He is, as we know, undergoing the sacramental castration, which the myth betokens by his leaving the light behind him and descending into the dark. To enter Hell is to become blind (it corresponds, indeed, to the veiling of the Eleusinian initiant, whose course of initiation also included a symbolic or theatrical visit to Hell) and to become blind is to be, in token, castrated. Thus blinding himself was Oedipus's own symbol of his remorseful self-castration[2], an appropriate punishment for the infantile desire of the mother which is so often expressed visually—by, in Actaeon's fashion, seeing her naked.

However, the essence of the sacrament is that the son's castration implies its own compensation. Even folklore assures us that if we submit to one symbolic castration by having our ears pierced we shall be rewarded by achieving sharper eyesight. The mystery initiant is compensated for his temporary blindness by being allowed to see some revelation others have not seen; St. Paul achieved a personal initiation into Christianity on similar lines; Teiresias, the prophet who tells Oedipus the truth about his crime and whom Odysseus goes to Hell to consult, has acquired his prophetic vision in exchange for his bodily sight.

(As a matter of fact, myth has initiated—and castrated—Teiresias more than once[3]. As a boy, his sexual curiosity led him to come accidentally on the parental mating—that is to say he found two snakes copulating on a mountainside. [It is interesting that he still pictures the mother as well as the father in phallic shape.] The infant Teiresias intervenes sexually himself—that is, he strikes the snakes with his own stick: whereupon he is castrated—he is turned into a girl. In other words, Teiresias emerges from his infantile Oedipal conflict

[1] a sensation Homer evidently knew well, since he describes Achilles's pursuit of Hector round the walls of Troy as 'like a chase in a nightmare, when no one, pursuer or pursued, can move a limb' (E. V. Rieu's translation of *Iliad*, XXII, 199–200)

[2] Freud: *The Interpretation Of Dreams*, VI (E) note

[3] Ovid: *Metamorphoses*, III, 324 foll.

by adopting a homosexual orientation. But at puberty, when the sexual conflict is re-activated, he reverses this; or, as the myth puts it, seven years later he again finds two snakes mating, strikes them again and recovers his original sex. This first castration is already compensated by the acquisition of a special wisdom, inasmuch as Teiresias has now had the unusual experience of having belonged to both sexes; and so, when Zeus and Hera fall into dispute about whether men or women derive the greater pleasure from sexual intercourse, they have the witty idea of calling in Teiresias to adjudicate. He offends against that female canon whereby to enjoy sexual intercourse is unfeminine, by ruling that it is the woman who has the greater pleasure. Hera punishes him by blinding him; and Zeus makes it up to him by giving him the gift of prophecy.[1])

The myth of the hero's sacramental journey does not neglect to wring two senses out of the darkness of the realm he is visiting. If to be blinded is to be castrated, it is also true that blindness is the very condition of the phallos as it performs its sexual work. The phallos cannot see its way; it has to grope: and this is what determines the blindness of the phallic love-god Cupid. Hades, the god who is unseen, is also unseeing: his talisman, a magic helmet which makes him invisible when he puts it on[2], has also a phallic significance—as helmets in myths and dreams not infrequently have; like gnomes' caps, they symbolise the foreskin. The extension of the phallic power and pre-rogative of father Zeus, Hades, who stretched out to snatch Persephone from mankind, exercises his phallic rights by groping about in the darkness of his own kingdom. And if we ask what this kingdom is which Homer regularly calls the 'dank house' or the 'halls' of Hades[3], the answer is that it has the significance which houses or rooms so regularly have in dreams[(4)]: it is nothing but the body of the mother, Persephone herself. The 'halls of Hades' are also 'the halls of Hades and

[1] Another account of Teiresias's blindness is an Actaeon-like episode, still emphasising the infantile sexual curiosity and the castration significance of blindness, in which Teiresias is punished for seeing Athena bathing. (H. J. Rose: *A Handbook . . .*, VIII)

[2] The helmet was made by the Cyclops, and is the one Perseus used on his expedition against the Gorgons.

[3] e.g. . . . εἰς Ἀΐδεω ἰέναι δόμον εὐρώεντα (*Odyssey*, X, 512). The 'house' is sometimes singular, sometimes plural; εὐρώεις, 'mouldy, dank and dark' (Liddell and Scott)

[(4)] Cf. Freud: *The Interpretation Of Dreams*, VI (E)

dread Persephone'[1]: they are Persephone's body, and also Hades's to enjoy; and it is his exclusive right to them which makes her 'dread'—a danger to anyone else who should dare to penetrate there.

On this point the myth clinches its condensation of the two meanings of blindness and the two occasions of the hero's castration. His sacrifice coincides with his pleasure; plunging into the darkness, he is penetrating the mother. 'Many of the landscapes seen in dreams', says Freud[2], 'especially those that contain bridges or wooded mountains, may be readily recognised as descriptions of the genitals. Marcinowski collected a series of examples in which the dreamer explained his dream by means of drawings'. Whereas, 'naïvely regarded, they seemed to represent plans, maps, and so forth, closer investigation showed that they were representations of the human body, of the genitals, etc., and only after conceiving them thus could the dream be understood'. So with the myth: only after conceiving it thus can one understand the verbal map Circe gives Odysseus of his route to the kingdom of Hades (a map which is, saga-fashon, repeated line by line when Odysseus makes the journey). We can understand the watery approaches to the realm (that it is hot as well as moist is symbolised by the fiery river Pyriphlegethon) and we can take the allusion to the pubic hair. Odysseus's ship must cross Oceanus, and then, Circe tells him[3], 'you will come to a wild coast and to Persephone's Grove, where the tall poplars grow and the willows that so quickly shed their seeds. Beach your boat there . . . and march on into Hades's kingdom of Decay. There the River of Flaming Fire (Pyriphlegethon) and the River of Lamentation, which is a branch of the Waters of Styx, unite round a pinnacle of rock to pour their thundering streams into Acheron'.

A view up the channel which leads into this landscape is shewn us in Patinir's painting[4], of Charon's boat conveying a dead soul to its place. It is, as a matter of fact, a composition which Patinir painted more than once; in this picture he has tied it to the myth which exploits the same subject matter.

There remains to consider Persephone herself, the queen of this realm and the queen of death. The emblem which classical iconography

[1] . . . 'Ἀΐδαο δόμους καὶ ἐπαινῆς Περσεφονείης (Odyssey, X, 491)
[2] The Interpretation Of Dreams, VI, (E)
[3] E. V. Rieu's translation of Odyssey, X, 509-15
[4] in the Prado, Madrid

places in her hand is the pomegranate: mythologically, an allusion to the story of her marriage; psychologically, a comforting assurance that she is a mother to mankind, another play on that resemblance between the edible fruit and the edible breast which no one has ever failed to notice—certainly no Greek; it is, after all, the Greek language which charmingly calls a brassière an 'apple-holder'[1].

A later iconography associates the pomegranate, like other fruits, with another mother-figure, the Virgin Mary. The pomegranate, however, is particularly well placed among fruits to offer divine comfort to men, since when its rind splits the seeds are visible inside. Christianity took these as the seeds of immortality and made the pomegranate an emblem of eternal life[2]—St. Paul[3] and funerary art having perceived an assurance of the resurrection of the dead in the fact that the seed is buried before it sprouts. (The Ego is again resting its case for immortality on the immortality of species.) No doubt the Eleusinian initiate took the seeds of Persephone's pomegranate to his comfort in the same sense. But the message of the pomegranate is not only re-assuring. When the rind splits, it reveals the red flesh inside, creating the two red lips of a wound—and reminding the worshipper of the disquieting wound that has been inflicted on the mother. The Virgin Mary has been compensated for this, and the picture which associates her with the pomegranate associates her also with her small son, who is her substitute—for a while—for what she has lost; but in time everything the pomegranate's wound implies will have to be suffered by him (and in some pictures[4] his hand as well as hers plays with the fruit). Persephone, by contrast, has no child (indeed, it is she who *is* the child, rapt from her mother). The implications of the wounded fruit she holds are passed directly to the worshipper; and at the heart of the kingdom of death sits the menace of the mother who has been castrated.

(This reading of the split pomegranate is interestingly confirmed by another dehiscent fruit in a painting by Tintoretto—where its symbolic use, though not all the implications, must, I think, have been perfectly conscious to the painter. The subject is Vertumnus and

---

[1] μηλοῦχος

[2] Mrs Jameson: *Sacred And Legendary Art*, Introduction, IV

[3] 'But some man will say, How are the dead raised up? and with what body do they come? Thou fool, that which thou sowest is not quickened, except it die' (*I Corinthians*, XV, 35-6)

[4] e.g. in Botticelli's *Madonna of the Magnificat*, in the Uffizi

Pomona[1]. Vertumnus, 'a deity among the Romans, who presided over the spring and over orchards . . . endeavoured to gain the affections of the goddess Pomona': he approached her in various disguises 'but all to no purpose, till, under the form of an old woman, he prevailed upon his mistress and married her' [2]. The picture shews him in his old-woman disguise stealing upon the all but naked goddess, his gaze concentrated lasciviously on the genital region of her body. This, however, we cannot see, because the goddess's leg is in the way; and perhaps he cannot either, since she has some drapery thrown over her. But in the left foreground of the picture one of the many fruits which litter the scene (Pomona is goddess of gardens) has been specially chosen to shew us, as if by an arrangement of mirrors: a dehiscent melon reflects the message to us out of the picture, drawing our attention to the wounds in its flesh and the seeds inside.)

Once we have recognised Persephone as the mother, lure to the romantic, repugnant threat to the homosexual, we understand why the conduct of that romantic-homosexual, Don Giovanni, was unconsciously leading to no other end than his being swept off to Hell—where da Ponte, with surprising mythological accuracy, represents him as 'with Persephone and Hades', 'con Proserpina e Pluton'. Moreover, this rebel against society's taboos has achieved the first half of the privilege accorded to the successfully rebellious hero. He has gone to Hell without dying first; he leaves no corpse behind him, and the quintet who rush on to the scene of his last supper[3] are horrified to learn that he has simply vanished. Here, as with other undying

[1] I am grateful to Michael Levey for identifying the subject. The picture, which belongs to the Marquess of Bath, is listed by Berenson (*Italian Pictures Of The Renaissance*, Venetian Schools, 1957) as 'Allegorical couple in a garden' and was exhibited at Burlington House as 'Angelica And The Hermit(?)' (R.A. Exhibition, 1960, 'Italian Art And Britain')

[2] Lemprière

[3] Commentators on the opera seem to have missed the most blatant of Don Giovanni's claims to heroic status, namely that he apes Christ by holding a last supper (cena) before descending into Hell. It is possible that, at some stage in the story's transformations, this imitation was conscious on Don Giovanni's part and was intended blasphemously—a Black Last Supper, like a Black Mass. Even in the Mozart-da Ponte version, Don Giovanni is in a position at least to guess that the evening on which he holds his supper party will be his last: before he invites the statue to supper, the statue has rebuked his laughter by telling him 'You will be finished with laughter before dawn' (II, iii).

personages like Elijah and King Arthur, is a hint that he may return. If Don Giovanni were to complete the transformation from criminal-outcast to heroic Big Brother, he would no doubt complete the heroic journey, and come back from Hell within his lifetime. Orthodox society hopes, of course, that he will do no such thing. It wants him, together with the unconscious desires in society itself on which he acts as an incitement, to remain incarcerated, though admittedly unkillable, in the unconscious. Therefore the antichissima, indeed age-old, canzon at the end of the opera, which speaks for society, expresses the explicit wish 'Let him stay' where he is:

> Resti dunque quel birbon
> con Proserpina e Pluton!

I cannot emerge from this brief exploration of the Underworld without thanking the reader for coming so far. *Heureux qui, comme Ulysse, a fait un beau voyage.*

13. *The Perpetual Cinema-Show*

Freud's discovery that the unconscious was a region of wishes, and that unconscious wishes are incapable of representing themselves except as statements of fact, illuminated a whole sphere of behaviour which a psychology confined to the conscious could make nothing of. To the eighteenth-century philosopher it seemed inconceivable that the myths had been devised and put forward as serious statements of fact. Psycho-analysis was able to answer that they had not been: they were serious statements of wishes. Despite the astral myths and vegetation spirits which were so dear to nineteenth-century interpreters (perhaps because they were so 'innocent'), myths were not, in Freud's words[1], 'read off direct from the heavens'. It was more like the case[2] where the child dreams of the parents' copulation 'as an event taking place between heavenly bodies'. The mythological material is often shaped into offering a sort of explanation of natural phenomena, but it never loses touch with its genesis, namely the wishes which promote and direct the unconscious (that is, infantile)

[1] *Collected Papers*, Volume IV, XV
[2] Freud: *Collected Papers*, Volume III, V, note

sexual curiosity—to which stories like those of Actaeon and Teiresias actually refer. The mystery religions were not slow to improve on the sense in which all mythology and theology offer an opportunity to spy on the parents. They played a sophisticated, intellectual and theological variation on the runes and riddles which occur in more primitive sagas and myths, and in fairytales, and which are, as Freud said, an 'after-echo' of the infantile problem of where babies come from[1]. To this day, old men sometimes take a perhaps not wholly innocent pleasure in baffling children with the great mystery of how the baby got inside the mother, a mystery they present to the children in the form of a tangible riddle, the question being how the fully rigged ship got into the narrow-necked bottle. (The symbolism of the narrow entrance-exit channel of a bottle was seized on, far from innocently, by Pope for his Cave of Spleen, where 'maids turn'd bottles call aloud for corks'[2].)

Primitive and neurotic thought are created when the Ego clings to the psychic reality of the unconscious's world and fails to test whether the unconscious narrative is true in the external world as well. The primitive and the neurotic take the deed, when it is accomplished in the real world, for the wish—which is always represented in the psychic world as an accomplished deed. Taboo law punishes not the guilty intention of the criminal but the guilt—the uncleanness—of the deed; the wish is taken for granted, since the deed has really happened. As a civilisation's consciousness becomes more realistic, the law has, of course, to recognise the distinction between deliberate and accidental infractions of the taboo rules. Even so, the accidental blunderer does not escape punishment: indeed, he cannot escape the pollution which comes on him inevitably from contact with a tabooful object: but society may mitigate his punishment, though it takes care to remove the pollution from its midst. Thus Talmudic law distinguishes between the deliberate murderer, who is to suffer death, and the accidental manslaughterer who has, without meaning to, caused an unclean thing, a corpse, to come into existence. The manslaughterer may get off lightly by being allowed to escape into exile. Yet the Talmudic doctors cannot quite believe that the accident can be accident if the person who commits it has also a wish to commit it; and one of them[3] gives it as his opinion that, if the manslaughterer

[1] *Collected Papers*, Volume II, VI   [2] *The Rape Of The Lock*, IV, 54
[3] Rabbi Yosi ben Yehuda. (Leo Auerbach's selected edition of the Babylonian Talmud, pp. 139-40)

happens to be an enemy of the deceased, then he should suffer the same capital punishment as the deliberate murderer, because he is a 'potential deliberate murderer'.

This is precisely the neurotic psychology of Hamlet[1]. As soon as the death of the elder Hamlet is accomplished as a real fact, his son unconsciously recognises himself as a potential deliberate murderer. He has wished the death; and unconsciously he cannot interpret the real death as expressing anything but his own wish. Called on to avenge the death by punishing the murderer, Hamlet finds that he cannot punish Claudius, because Claudius has only stolen a march on him and got to the murder first; to his own way of thinking it is he, Hamlet, who is the murderer; and in the end he does contrive his own capital punishment. So with the saint[2]. The marks of the saint are an outwardly blameless life and an inner conviction of guilt and sin: his consciousness exonerates him of the accusation of sin, but in the unconscious, where a wish cannot fail to be put into effect, he cannot have failed to succumb to those temptations which often present themselves to his mind with the vividness of visions.

Just as Hades is not content with imprisoning the shades but has to inflict torment on the most dangerously—that is, Oedipally—rebellious of them as well, so the unconscious parts of the Ego and Super-Ego are not content with suppressing the Id's fantasy-narratives but generate punitive counter-narratives of their own. In this world where every wish counts as an act, the only way to undo wishes is by an act of aggressing against them. Probably no repression can take place without being embodied in some sort of fantasy; and in some sado-masochistic people the fantasy has grown to giant size and become a source of pleasure in itself. The life of the unconscious wishes is a perpetual cinema-show, in which the libidinous imaginings of the Id run side by side with the sadistic oppressions of the Ego and Super-Ego. A complete account of the Underworld would describe the tortures of the sinners going on at the same time as a repetition of their sins— and in fact, in accounts of Hell, the very mention of the sinner's name achieves virtually this effect, since it prompts the narrator to recount the crime which brought the sinner to Tartaros. Punishment itself is thus by origin a fantasy; and we can in fact see this in the behaviour of authoritarian fanatics who insist on retribution for its own sake, quite apart from the attempt to amend the criminal or prevent the

[1] Freud: *The Interpretation Of Dreams*, V (D) (b)
[2] Freud: *Civilization And Its Discontents*, VII

crime: they are living in that unrealistic world where crimes cannot be prevented or stopped and the only counter-action which can be taken is perpetual punishment.

The accusations which Hamlet and the saint unconsciously make against themselves become known to us in their neurotic—that is, otherwise inexplicable—feelings of guilt and in neurotic behaviour whereby they bring punishment on themselves. The paranoiac, on the other hand, may quite dissociate himself from the sensation of guilt, and the accusations made by his unconscious may come to him from outside, in the form of the voices he hears gossiping disparagingly about him. There is one interesting instance where the same result may be achieved by a less drastic method—by using the normal mechanism whereby our dreams seem to come to us from outside; and by this means a person may accuse himself of murder publicly and be, in a sense, believed, without being any the less well thought of by the community. This happens when someone apparently has a prophetic dream—'apparently', because the cases I am thinking of are those where, as in a case analysed in an early paper by Freud[1], no dream in fact takes place. In that instance, the patient said, in good faith, that she had dreamt of seeing a certain man outside a certain shop, and next day really saw him there: but when the case was analysed she came to the conclusion that the dream had in fact come to her, as a false memory of having dreamt, at the moment when she really did set eyes on the man concerned. This particular false dream is remarkable for its triviality. Dreams which are claimed as prophetic are rarely connected with shopping; they more often announce a death, and usually that of someone who is geographically very distant from the dreamer. Many of these dreams (where there is no record of the dream which dates from before the news which fulfils the dream) probably work by the same mechanism as 'Frau B's' trivial dream which Freud exploded: that is to say no dream is in fact dreamt but the conviction that it was arrives simultaneously with the real news of the death. It is not hard to reconstruct what happens. The news of the death is on the point of summoning a concurrence in it: the hearer's response is about to be 'Yes, I wished for that'. This wish (it is usually a near relation who is concerned) is, of course, inadmissible. But we are regularly in the habit of giving a sort of hearing to inadmissible wishes—in our dreams; and so it is, naturally enough, into a false dream that the wish is transposed. The supposed dreamer

[1] *Collected Papers*, Volume V, V (1899)

then tells the world that he had prior intelligence of the death. In what sense this is a self-accusation—indeed, a confession—is clear from the old detective-story trick where the murderer reveals himself by knowing too much: 'But how did you know X was murdered at three o'clock with a stiletto', says the detective, 'when the information has not yet been published? *You must be the murderer.*' However, the manufacturer of prophetic dreams has taken good care not to be suspected of a real murder. In the most typical examples, the death of which he is forewarned takes place a long way away; and this fits him out with a perfect 'alibi'. And it is just this which allows him to reap kudos from his self-accusation, since it lets him claim—which makes him an interesting person—that his dream *must have been* clairvoyant or telepathic. And this in its turn is the means whereby he effectively and publicly contradicts his original wish that the person concerned should die, for the supposed bond of telepathy suggests that he and the person who has died were en rapport—that they loved one another[1].

14. *Not*

When the conscious Ego puts the world of fantasy, of purely psychic reality, behind it, it develops the power of judging whether the psychic image does or does not correspond to the external state of affairs; and this power Freud shewed to be a derivative of the instinctual power of assimilating or excluding things from the self. To judge a thing true is to identify ourselves with it; to judge it untrue is to repel it.

The negative intellectual judgment is therefore, Freud points out, a manifestation of Thanatos, and he went on[2] to shew that by means of this device Thanatos makes our conscious intellectual processes possible. Originally, the excluding power of Thanatos is applied to untrue psychic images in order to repress them and exclude them from consciousness. However, when it has acquired the power of intellectually judging *not*, the Ego has possessed itself of a mechanism for

[1] As a matter of fact the suppressed wish out of which Frau B's dream was fabricated (in Freud's paper) was a wish for a lover's meeting.

[2] *Collected Papers*, Volume V, XVI

half-lifting the embargo. The content of the image that would otherwise have been repressed can now enter consciousness, where,
preceded by the *not*, it can be thought about. This device is the foundation of the human intellect's unique powers: by virtue of it, 'the
thinking process frees itself from the limitations imposed by repression
and enriches itself with the subject-matter without which it could not
work efficiently'[1].

Unconscious fantasy we share with all the animals that dream[2].
The dog knows as well as we do, when he wakes up, that the events
he perceived during his sleep are not true. But he can acknowledge
their unreality only by withdrawing his attention from them: his
consciousness cannot retain them as objects of thought while making
the condition that they are not real. The dog can learn to recognise
a great deal of human vocabulary, but the word *not* remains meaningless to him because there is no device in his intellect to which it corresponds. He may understand your 'No' as a prohibition on an action
he has already begun: but if you tell him he is *not* going for a walk,
he runs to fetch his lead exactly as though you had told him he *was*.

Similarly, although the dog has unconscious fantasies, he does not to
any great extent share our faculty—our artistic faculty—of consciously
creating fantasies[3] or enjoying those created by other people; neither
has he much of the faculty for prefacing his fantasies by 'if' or 'as if',
a faculty which is the mother of invention and science. The label
'fiction' and the label 'hypothesis' are large-scale, comprehensive
versions of *not*: each is the mark of a repression which none the less
admits the content of the image into the mind.

The philistine is a person who has not perfected this artistic device:
he does not understand the significance of the label 'fiction'. His
impulse towards the work of art is to repress it completely, to destroy
it, so that its content is no longer available to consciousness. (He may,
of course, pretend to be a lover of the arts, but he is always offering
them a protection, a traditionalism, which they do not need and
whose tendency is, in fact, to destroy them. The philistine art-lover is

[1] Freud: *Collected Papers*, Volume V, XVI

[2] Freud (*The Interpretation Of Dreams*, III): 'What animals dream of I do not
know. A proverb . . . professes to tell us, for it asks the question: "What
does the goose dream of?" and answers: "Of maize". The whole theory that
the dream is the fulfilment of a wish is contained in those two sentences.'

[3] though his own playing does include pure make-believe: he pretends to
be hunting or fighting.

the one who, with the utmost reverence and loving care, wishes the great painting to remain invisible under its layer of dirty varnish.) Because he has not understood the label 'fiction', the philistine treats the content of a work of art literally, as though it were real. When Picasso shews him a painting of a woman's head seen simultaneously in profile and front-face, the philistine would like to take an axe to it, just as he would to the 'monstrosity' of a chicken born with two heads. He may, however, spare the chicken—if he has got past the stage of thinking it a portent wished on him by the gods—because he knows the chicken cannot help it. But he knows that Picasso *can*. He recognises the painting, quite correctly, as the expression of a wish, and he would like to repress it. He is treating art as witchcraft: in the painted 'monstrosity', he sees a wish to plague him with monsters, perhaps even to make *him* a monster. If the mother can be castrated, thinks the small boy, so can I. If the woman can have two heads, thinks the philistine, so can I.

It is thanks to this label 'fiction' that we can enjoy tragedy; and thanks to it that the artist can create not only tragedy but comedy out out of infantile and inadmissible material. He summons up not only pictorial images and narratives, but, it may be, the actual images of sensation. Music is just as much fiction as paintings or novels are, and yet it recreates for us sensations almost completely devoid of concrete imagery. (This, which made music the least offensive of the arts to the literal mind of the eighteenth century, since it did not raise problems by counterfeiting events, is probably what makes it also the only human art which animals enjoy.) Some of this sensory subject-matter is undoubtedly erotic—as, indeed, the sensations induced by the rhythm of any work of art are; but music in particular has the very form of sexual sensation, since it consists of a basis of, as it were, bodily rhythm, on which is superimposed a line of melody which is by origin a vocal line, the 'tune' played by the breath. Notably, music is the blind art; and if this gives it its power to reproduce phallic sensations, it also enables it to take us further back in time and reconstruct round us another sort of union: we are lapped in music ('Lap me in soft Lydian airs', says L'Allegro) and transported by it, as though we really had recovered the actual kinaesthetic sensations of being supported and transported in what we did not at the time know was a womb.

The answer to civilisation's question 'What ought we to *do* with Thanatos?' is provided by the two labels 'fiction' and 'hypothesis', which are the marks respectively of our artistic and our scientific mental activity. Each of them is a larger construct arising out of the power of thought. Thought is made possible by the disposition of Thanatos which creates *not*; art and science by a wider and more particularised disposition of the power to say *not*. Instinctually considered, both—though in very distinct ways—are to a great extent destructive activities. (This is, of course, quite apart from any destructive or sadistic *content* they may have.) Indeed, they provide a counterpart and, which is civilisation's one hope, an alternative to the psychic efficacy of the Eros-Thanatos fusion achieved in the religious sacrament.

The scientist is engaged in what is, in a particular sense, the destruction of his own personality. His ambition is to disprove his hypotheses insofar as those are fantasies emanating from his own imagination. He is continually transferring the responsibility for their truth from his own inner world of psychic reality to the world of external reality, withdrawing credence from everything that has nothing to vouch for it except his personal world. The correct hypothesis, the one which has been proved true, is one from which he has withdrawn the stamp of his own personality.

Of course, scientific hypotheses are (though not much more, perhaps, than the fictions of naturalistic novelists) stimulated in the first place by observation of the facts which eventually justify them. But the difference between the uninspired scientist and the scientific genius is a matter of imagination. The uninspired scientist is precisely the one to whom the facts do *not* suggest a hypothesis. The genius has a particular wealth of fantasy (or has particularly easy access to it), which he can constantly call on to provide a fund of material to be moulded this way and that until it fits the framework of observed fact. It is in the end, not the sources, of his fantasy that the scientist is distinguished from the artist—or, indeed, from the magician and myth-maker. The theory of evolution no doubt arose (though already it was better bolstered by facts on its way up) from the same unconscious identification of animal with father as the theology of totemism (whose more sophisticated derivative, the transmigration of souls, Frazer pointed out[1] as an anticipation of Darwinism). In the alchemists' quest for the philosopher's stone or the pre-scientists' reduction of matter to a handful of basic elements, we can perceive a yearning towards a universal principle and a universal substance (the Ego's desire to rebuild a single parent image out of the fragmented

[1] *Spirits Of The Corn And Of The Wild*, XVI

images created by our ambivalence towards the parents), which elsewhere inspired, severally, religious syncretism and monotheism, the romantic ideal of monogamy (or even of a chastity in which the son is wedded to the god or goddess), and the scientific view of the chemical elements as so many variations on basic constituents or of various forms of physical energy as convertible into one another. Indeed, it is to some such emotional basis that we should attribute the whole scientific search for simple, economic, universal principles. The difference between the superstitious and the scientific theory is that the scientist, having reached his theory on a ladder of fantasy wishes, kicks down the ladder on which he arrived. His Ego has ventured its hopes of immortality on nothing but a perfectly correct reflexion of the external world.

Compared with this, the artist looks at first blush much more creative—more the agent of Eros—and much more of an Egoist. Instead of reflecting the external world, he is projecting into it some of his own inner world, giving it a solid existence in the existence of a work of art; and this work is validated solely by the validity of his internal world. Not only does he not look to the outside world for justification; he is, as Felix Krull exemplifies, entirely opportunist in his relations with the outside world, where he finds nothing so sacred that he will not use and convert it to his own ends, shewing the superman's disregard both of social bonds and of an Ego's obligation to reality. From the work of art, which he hopes to make comparatively immortal (so long, that is, as culture lasts and men can read), the stamp of its creator's personality can never be removed, art ceasing to be art the moment it is. But the personality which he projects and immortalises in his fictions is not a direct reflexion of the author's personality such as we can trace in the fantasy-creations of the hysteric, which have not been subjected to artistic discipline. The work of art is, rather, in a special sense—and not the conventional one—an idealised self-portrait of its author. The artist does not offer life and immortality to every image which comes bubbling up. On the contrary, he is the most ruthless of eugenists, continually killing off material in which his personality seeks to express itself and selecting only those ideas which are—artistically—fit to live. The joy of artistic creation, of projecting, is absolutely inseparable from the companion joy of pure destruction: it is the joy of precision, of pinning down—of giving to the inner fantasy the one form of expression which is the 'right' one, to the absolute exclusion and excision of every other possibility.

15. Psycho-analysis as naïveté

Having recognised the *not* as 'the hall-mark of repression, a certificate of origin'[1], the psycho-analyst proceeds to do with his patients' negative statements something which Freud described as taking a liberty: he ignores the *not*, and considers only the content of the idea which has come into the patient's mind.

The patient can admit the idea to his conscious only on condition that he repudiates it when it arrives there. He may do this by giving it the lie direct. In Freud's example, he says: ' "You ask who this person in the dream can have been. It was *not* my mother." ' Freud comments: 'We emend this: so it *was* his mother'. Alternatively, the patient may repudiate the idea by attributing it to the analyst: ' "Now you'll think I mean to say something insulting, but really I've no such intention" '. Often this unconscious disingenuousness plays a double game. The patient repudiates the idea only to reclaim it; or he attributes it to the analyst, insists it is wrong, and then throws in something which shews it is right.

One does not need to be a psycho-analyst to encounter this last situation. It is enough to be interested in psycho-analysis and to have friends who know. A friend of mine once described to me her particular fear of walking downstairs if there should be someone following behind her. I made no comment, but my friend immediately supplied me with thoughts in order to contradict them. 'Of course you, with your Freudianism—you'll at once think it has something to do with sex, or even the Oedipus Complex. But you're quite wrong', she went on; 'I should feel exactly the same if it was my own father walking down behind me.'

(As a matter of fact, it is to an incident of this kind that Freud owed the discovery of the symbolism round which my friend's phobia was constructed, a symbolism which also creates the sexual significance of staircases in dreams. It was Freud whose enquiries established that these dreams *do* have this significance, and he who understood the comparison which makes it possible for them to do so ['with rhythmical intervals and increasing breathlessness one reaches a height, and may

[1] This and the quotations in the next paragraph are from Freud: *Collected Papers*, Volume V, XVI

then come down again in a few rapid jumps']; but the original perception was made by someone whose object was to contradict Freud.
One might say that this contradictor had made the discovery but
chose to publish it only by denying it, by presenting it as something
not true. It is another instance of the contradictor giving a piece of
information which really confirms what he takes to be the analyst's
position—but in this case his own perception, though denied, has led
him to see what must be Freud's position before Freud had seen it
himself. Thus in Freud's account: 'I learned that a psychologist who
is unfamiliar with our work remarked to one of my friends that we
were surely over-estimating the secret sexual significance of dreams.
He stated that his most frequent dream was that of climbing a flight of
stairs, and that there was surely nothing sexual behind this. Our
attention having been called to this objection, we directed our investigations to the occurrence in dreams of flights of stairs . . . and we
soon ascertained that stairs . . . represent a definite symbol of coitus'[1].)

When it leaves patients behind it and moves out into the wider
world, psycho-analysis continues to take exactly the same liberty of
ignoring the *not*. Psycho-analysis interests itself in the content of ideas:
it restores the knack, which was wholly lost to the eighteenth century,
of looking at the content instead of looking solely at context or form,
whether the form in question is logical, linguistic or aesthetic.

By virtue of this knack, psycho-analysis is a sort of applied naïveté,
a gift of looking—though not as sentimentalists would mean it or
hope to see—through the eyes of a child (or the unconscious) and
thus laying bare the child in the adult psyche and the savage in the
civilised. It is the child or the psycho-analyst who asks 'Why do we
say a *flight* of stairs?' For the adult, the phrase is too deeply embedded
to be raised; when the child does raise it, it is a funny question and the
answer is 'We just do'.

The context and the form which psycho-analysis momentarily sets
aside are, in fact, the assumptions and distinctions on which civilised
life rests. Only a peasant can walk round a museum or an Italian
church and see nothing but the content of the works of art—and we
must suppose a peasant who has escaped a devotional upbringing. The
civilised mind sets to work immediately and automatically to perceive
the artistic form in the content and to set the whole in an historical,
aesthetic and iconographical context: the cultured person sees not only
a woman standing on a cloud supported by babies but, in the same

[1] *The Interpretation Of Dreams*, VI (E) note

physical object, a late Rubens, an example of the baroque manner and a manifestation of the Counter-Reformation. The psycho-analytic mind possesses this faculty to the best of its ability; but it *also* possesses the power to divest itself of all this and look through the eyes of the peasant; and as a result of looking in this way it discovers that half of Christian iconography is devoted to the idea of *mother*, while the other half gloats on precisely the imagery which is to be found in sadistic horror comics.

Promptly the psycho-analyst is jumped on by the Christians, crying that if he cannot distinguish between violence enjoyed for its own sake and violence enjoyed for the love of God, he is an idiot. On the whole, there is a smaller outcry from lovers of art, who have been re-assured in an entirely practical way, namely by the fact that no one's artistic sensibility ever has been damaged by psycho-analysis: but occasionally a lover of art will add that the psycho-analyst is an idiot if he cannot distinguish between cheap commercial drawing and the hand of an old master.

And, of course, if he could not, he would be. Fortunately, however, psycho-analytic naïveté, since it can be put on and off at will, is not an affliction of the faculties but an addition to them: so great an addition that the psycho-analytic revolution can claim to be the culminating vindication of man's unique intellectual prowess. Genetically (that is to say, in the history of civilisation, in the history of the individual's development from baby to adult, and in the course traced by every psychic impulse from origin to conscious expression) our instinctual judgment of assimilating or rejecting a certain image is earlier than the intellectual judgment which distinguishes its form and describes its context; and the intellectual judgment is an evolutionary derivative of the instinctual: and therefore unless we equip ourselves with the means of perceiving how instinctual judgment treats the content of images we do not possess a complete account of our faculty of intellectual judgment.

It is only when psycho-analysis exercises its knack and ignores the civilised distinction between murder and warfare that we can perceive that the instinctual content of the two acts is exactly the same, though intellectually considered they are as far apart as an old master Crucifixion and a horror comic. This perception is our clue to understanding the pre-civilised behaviour which does not properly distinguish between them but treats the warrior as polluted in the same sense as the murderer. Similarly, it is our clue to the neurotic behaviour which

of Christianity but actually to augment it—iconographically, at least —with a fuller understanding of its significance.

As a matter of fact, this revealing little god Eros, latinised as Cupid, was under the protection of fiction almost from the start. The god as we know him is scarcely related to the serious god who appears in Hesiod[1] and who, although he had a cult (but a rare one) was more of a first principle than a person. The mythological person, who is the naughty son of Aphrodite and a father variously given as Ares, Zeus and Hermes, appears first in the epigrammatic poets and Euripides and Sophocles[2], and received a more detailed characterisation from Apuleius's novel within a novel, which describes the god's love affair with Psyche. Thus he comes so late to mythology as to be taken over almost at once by poetic and allegorical fiction. That perhaps accounts for his vitality and his immunity to the decay of religious belief. Effortlessly absorbed from the learned into the popular tradition, where it is preserved in his mispronounced[3] statue at Piccadilly Circus, his image still has import on St. Valentine's day, with the result that his bow and arrows still make (phallic) sense to lovers who have never heard of Apollo's or Artemis's.

Cupid is, indeed, the only one of the classical gods to remain spontaneously alive into the modern world. More than that: he has actually grown younger. The reduction of Cupid from a young man to a baby began in the ancient world, where he was sometime shewn as a baby, perhaps playing with other babies[4], and was completed by the renaissance. Even Apuleius's story perhaps hints in this direction, by Venus's reluctance to recognise that her son is grown-up enough to have a love-affair; and by the same token it hints at the incestuous love between the mother and son—it is Venus's possessive jealousy, as bitter as a wife's, which pursues Psyche.

By reducing the love-god to babyhood, the myth was, of course, making its implicit affirmation that sexual life begins in infancy; and by multiplying Cupid into a decorative profusion of amoretti[5], it

[1] *Theogony*, 120   [2] Cf. Smith's *Classical Dictionary*, Eros
[3] though not *so* mispronounced as a hasty pedantry suggests. The *e*, it is true, *must* be short; but the *o*, which in classical Greek is long, was, according to Smith, short in the older poets.
[4] Smith's *Classical Dictionary*, Eros
[5] Apuleius, besides narrating the love-story of the individual and grown-up Cupid, can refer to Venus as 'waited upon by all the court of Cupids'—toto Cupidinum populo comitata (Adlington's translation, *The Golden Ass*, II, 9)

does not distinguish between my enemy's accidental death from measles and my unconscious wish that he should die. However, once we have understood this unconscious world of psychic reality, we are also in a position to come back and question the civilised assumptions on which we distinguish the inner from the outer reality. Uncivilised man mistook accidents for intentional acts: but civilised man, until Freud investigated his tiny and 'practically unimportant'[1] blunders under the eye of psycho-analytic naïveté, was in the habit of attributing his small unconsciously intended actions to accident or random chance. If it is the mark of the gentleman that he does not notice the speaker's belch, it is the mark of the intellectual that he does not notice the printer's error (or, if he does, only to mentally correct it) because it is not significant in the intellectual context. It is the child or Freud who puts that context momentarily out of mind and asks of what the error *is* significant. Only if it employs on a large scale the naïf technique Freud has given it will civilisation ever be able to question its major assumptions such as the justification of violence by love for God and the justification—or, rather, as we are now beginning to let ourselves think it is, the accidental nature—of war. Psychoanalysis, because it is the only scientific instrument for exploring the claims made by the unconscious world of psychic reality, is the ultimate instrument we possess for aligning our intellectual judgments with the external, instead of the internal, reality.

16. *Eros In Person*

It was by grace of the label 'fiction', with its power to remove the repression on the content of images, that an implicit psychology— that is, a psychology of content—was able to exist and accumulate material in the realm of art, long before Freud chiselled a science of psychology out of the same infantile material. But of course this implicit psychology, though entirely free within the goldfishbowl of art, was entirely confined within it. If the whole theory that the dream is the fulfilment of a wish is 'contained' in the proverb which tells us the goose dreams of maize[2], then the whole theory of infantile

[1] Freud: *Psychopathology Of Everyday Life*, I
[2] Freud: *The Interpretation Of Dreams*, III

sexuality is contained in Titian's painting[1] of 'The Venus Worship'. But it is, notably, *contained*. Freud had nothing to teach Titian about infantile sexuality—except how to liberate the import of his own picture.

The label 'fiction', which the renaissance painters could prefix to their pagan mythology pictures, was very much more of a liberator —within the artistic convention—than the label 'devotional' which had to be prefixed to Christian paintings. The devotional label, which insisted that the myth concerned was true, behaved as a disguise as well as a justification for the content of the painting. (Now that the veil of religious sentiment has been largely torn down, connoisseurs have had to devise intellectual veils of their own to disguise the brutal content of much Christian painting. Modern art history has a very remarkable tendency to pursue aesthetics or style criticism, both in themselves laudable enough ends, to the exclusion of the ability to see the subject matter at all. Pictures are criticised in terms solely of spirals and diagonals, and catalogued minutely as to where they fit in chrono-logically to the author's œuvre, while the subject is dismissed with the barest mention—a disproportion in which it is hard not to see the connoisseur in retreat from what Christian fantasy might reveal to him about human nature.) In his Christian pictures, the painter was restricted not only by the need to keep to what he or the Church regarded as historical fact but also by his own or, as Veronese dis-covered to his cost, the Church's notion of reverence. Pagan mytho-logy, on the other hand, provided him with properties which he could re-arrange more freely in expression of his own fantasy.

Accordingly, there grew up an unrecognised convention in which certain pagan themes were treated iconographically as the counter-part of certain Christian themes. God the Son not only balances but borrows some of the appearance of God the Sun—he has the Apollo-nian physique and manifests himself in the sky radiating light. The flaying of Marsyas becomes a rarer counterpart to the ubiquitous Crucifixion; Danaë's miraculous impregnation by golden rain counterbalances the Virgin's by a gold ray from heaven; amoretti play the same decorative part in pagan pictures as putti in Christian (in Poussin's convention, the two types of baby are quite interchange-able). Most notably, the Virgin has her secular counterpart in Venus. Venus is depicted alone; or with her baby son; or with her two sons— so that Venus with Eros and Anteros becomes analogous to the

[1] in the Prado, Madrid

women of the Holy Family shewn with the infant Christ and the infant John the Baptist, who play together like Eros and his brother: and by applying to another part of the myth the painters found, in the death of Adonis and Venus's mourning for him, a counterpart to the Pietà.

Since these resemblances were based on the painter's unconscious apprehension of the resemblance in material between the two myths, the freer pagan pictures provide us with an illumination of the fantasy content which in the Christian painting has had to be expressed in a more condensed and cryptic symbol. The Madonna and child picture can shew us only the infant son's oral desires towards the mother's breast. Bronzino can shew us, in his marvellously sensual pagan allegory in the National Gàllery, a nearly grown-up Cupid fondling his mother's naked breast; and she responds by parting her lips in a smile of pleasure and is on the point of letting him kiss her mouth.

In another mannerist painting, the *Venus And Cupid*[1] after a design of Michelangelo's, the naked Venus lies in the receptive pose of a Danaë—for, although she is pretending to be reluctant and is turning the upper part of her body away from the naked small boy, he has captured the lower part of her body, hooking his leg over hers and splaying her thighs apart, and his arm round her neck is turning her face towards receiving his kiss. Venus, her grave eyes half closing, is not looking at him: she is looking at nothing—or, perhaps quite idly, at the fingers of her outstretched arm: and in fact these long mannerist fingers reveal to us precisely what is in her mind; for, playing absently and caressingly with Cupid's arrows, they have half-pulled one of them out of the quiver in preparation. It is a shock to remember, after looking at this deliberately erotic picture of intending lovers, that the author and his contemporary audience were perfectly acquainted with the fact that the pair are mother and son.

Christian painting cannot, of course, shew anything half so explicit about the Christian mother and son. Yet their cult titles effortlessly make the same mythological point, proposing for mankind's supreme veneration Our Lord and Our Lady, a couple whom a stranger ignorant of their theology would naturally take for husband and wife.

When Christianity put an end to literal belief in the pagan myths, it did them the service of labelling them fiction; and the result was a vitality which, directly nourished by the imagination of artists, was able not merely to keep the pagan mythology alive during the reign

[1] at Naples

affirmed the universality of its finding. Yet Cupid is not always a baby. The two traditions about his age exist side by side, without much reference to stages in his history. (It is not a parallel case to pictures of the infant Dionysos or the infant Christ contrasted historically with their adult selves.) Late into the renaissance, he still keeps—witness Bronzino—his ability to appear on occasion almost full-grown. It seems, therefore, that the myth has taken the affirmation of infantile sexuality as the occasion of condensing into it yet another reference to the phallic quality of this thoroughly over-determined little symbol. His arrows denote his ability to penetrate[1]; and now the uncertainty about his size refers to the phallos's power of becoming erect and then, as it were, shrinking.

Not that this is the only allusion the myth makes to erection. Cupid's wings (which each of his arrows possesses, too) and his power of flight are nothing else. The down on Cupid's wings, says Apuleius, fluttered while he slept[2]. Perhaps he was dreaming of flying: for it is in the same erotic sense as dreams of hovering and flying that his wings must be interpreted. (It is these dreams, together with staircase dreams, which answer the question why we say a *flight* of stairs.) Cupid is, indeed, a personification of 'the winged phalli of the ancients' which Freud mentions in interpreting the dreams of flying; and Freud goes on to mention the 'fascinating theory' that these dreams, whose erotic significance is independently established, owe their symbolism to the fact that 'the remarkable phenomenon of erection, which constantly occupies human phantasy, cannot fail to be impressive as an apparent suspension of the laws of gravity'[3]. It was comparatively late in his career that Cupid acquired one further phallic attribute, which I have already mentioned, namely his blindness[4]: and it is in a play whose entirety is a dream that we are given this piece of iconographical interpretation:

[1] His phallic associations are emphasised in statues like the late Hellenistic one at Budapest which shews him, his wings outspread, leaning on an ithyphallic herm. (Bulletin du musée national hongrois des beaux-arts No. 13, 1958)

[2] *The Golden Ass*, V, 22: 'quamvis alis quiescentibus extimae plumulae tenellae ac delicatae tremule resultantes inquieta lasciviunt'.

[3] *The Interpretation Of Dreams*, VI (E)

[4] Professor Panofsky points out that Cupid is never blind in ancient art but became blind or blindfolded for the first time early in the thirteenth century. (*Studies In Iconology* . . ., IV)

Love looks not with the eyes, but with the mind,
And therefore is wing'd Cupid painted blind.[1]

(Perhaps Cupid acquired his blindness from a confusion of the motifs of the Cupid and Psyche story told by Apuleius. Psyche, at the start of their love affair, is visited by Cupid only in the dark and is forbidden to see him—an edict which effectively makes her blind or blindfold. This characteristic, which accords so well with his phallic nature, Cupid probably borrowed from his mistress. The story makes him a god who cannot [lawfully] be seen; medieval confusion, with sound unconscious reason, turned him into a god who cannot see.

(The original blindness, Psyche's, is a representation of unconsciousness. Not to know who her lover is remains Psyche's, and the pious reader's, last defence against recognising that her love affair is incestuous—within the metaphor whereby myths, like the sociological mythology of prostitution and homosexuality, represent the barrier between generations in the family as a class barrier. At the start of the story, Venus's jealousy is provoked because Psyche, a 'mortal girl', is receiving the homage properly owed to the goddess[2]. The love affair which follows between this mortal and the goddess's divine son is tinged with scandal—hence the interest the story holds for Apuleius; and here, as in Ovid's collection of divine-mortal love affairs, the scandal lies in the fundamentally incestuous content. Christendom discovered a counterpart to this ancient-world frisson in the particular scandalous flavour which in Catholic countries attaches to stories of love affairs between women and their spiritual fathers.)

In 'wing'd Cupid' we can see a pointed analogy with the adult angel or baby putto. (By the period of the rococo, sacred putti and profane amoretti were indistinguishably confused; and it is this period which produced the last major manifestation of Cupid in European art—under the sacred name of a cherub. Beaumarchais's Chérubin, the adolescent and mischievous page to Count Almaviva, was transformed into Mozart's and da Ponte's Cherubino, who gives us, in his fluttering aria 'Non so più'[3], what amounts to a soliloquy by the excited phallos: 'I no longer know what I am, what I'm doing; one moment I'm fire, the next ice; every woman makes me change colour; every woman sets me a-flutter.' He even confesses to—in default of better—auto-erotic activity. 'Parlo d'amor', he sings, 'to

[1] A Midsummer Night's Dream, I, i   [2] The Golden Ass, IV, 29
[3] Le Nozze Di Figaro, No. 6

the water, to the shade, to the mountains, to the flowers', etc. etc., 'and if I have no one to listen to me, parlo d'amor con me.') The angel is also winged and also uncertain in size; and he is a concrete representation of the father's phallic power, visiting mankind in a punitive, a protective or, at the Annunciation, a procreative sense.

However, we know on whose behalf the angel is representing this power and whom it belongs to. With Cupid, that is not so. If we would naturally assume his is the phallic power of his father, we at once meet the myth's uncertainty about who his father is. The myth seems to be saying that that is of no importance; or even that Cupid has no father. The stories seem to link him only with his mother. He is, so to speak, a detached phallos flying mischievously round the world—but never very far from his mother.

And this, as a matter of fact, is exactly the sense in which we should understand him. He is that organ which, infantile fantasy maintains, the mother's body once possessed. He is restored to her, when she has a child, only to be detached again. We have here the whole explanation of Cupid's late appearance in Greek mythology. Originally, there was no need for a separate Cupid: he was part of Venus[1]. (The bisexual Cyprian Venus actually shewed them as one.) Only when this fantasy had become superseded and untenable did the myth need to supply her with a son. (By the sixteenth century it was possible for a painter to conceive, in fanciful, probably literary and perhaps satirical terms, of the death of Cupid, and the workshop of Antoine Caron produced an amusing painting[2] of Cupid's funeral. The livid little corpse is strapped to the bier [the painter has had the insight to place the gauzy binding round Cupid's loins, taking the opportunity to pun on the drapery with which painters politely veil nudity] and it is followed by a procession of mourning humans: other humans run to see: and the cortège is led by winged babies, with black mourning hoods, holding aloft torches to which Cupid's emblems, including each of his wings, are severally attached. But the moral is less sad than it seems, since the mother and son have the same nature: humanity need not mourn

[1] Cupid's specific power of making people fall in love belonged originally to his mother (as, e.g., the Homeric Hymn *To Aphrodite* demonstrates). Later iconography even began to restore the union between mother and son: Professor Panofsky remarks on the 'strong tendency' of German art 'to personify Blind Cupid by a nude female figure' (*Studies in Iconology* . . ., IV).

[2] in the Louvre (no. 142 of the exhibition 700 *Tableaux* . . . *Tirés Des Réserves*, 1960–61)

the death of Love too deeply, because Love, in the person of Venus, is still present and presiding in her chariot in the sky above the scene.)

The identification of the child with the phallos appears, of course, in dreams, where children 'often signify the genitals, since men and women are in the habit of fondly referring to their genital organs as "little man", "little woman", "little thing" '[1]. (This German idiom occurs in a letter from Mozart to his wife describing how he has an erection. The translation[2] reads 'my little fellow', and the epithets that follow—like the fondness Freud refers to—are just the sort which literature applies to Cupid: 'rascal', 'rogue', 'knave'.) Pursuing the symbolism of dreams[3], Freud remarks: 'The "little brother" was correctly recognized by Stekel as the penis. To play with . . . a little child is often the dream's representation of masturbation.' Elsewhere, it is beating which represents masturbation; the fantasy, so common among girls, in which a child is being beaten, contained at its deepest level, Freud decided[4], 'a confession of masturbation', in which the child which was beaten was 'nothing more nor less than the clitoris itself'. The rhythmical action of beating has been assimilated to the rhythmical action of sexual caressing and stimulation. Taking Cupid at his full value as the little fellow, indeed as the mother's little fellow, we can see in just what pleasurably mischievous sense he is the naughty boy we meet in the poets—a little boy whose naughtiness invites us to give him a good beating[5].

When we consider the dream significance of playing with the little brother, it is scarcely surprising that the myth gives Cupid a little brother to play with. The name of this brother, Anteros, seems originally to have been construed not as opposition to love but as a counterpart to it: the prefix was taken in its second[6] sense and the name interpreted as love reciprocated. Yet ancient art was in no doubt that the

[1] Freud: *The Interpretation Of Dreams*, VI (E)

[2] by Emily Anderson. The letter is 565 in her edition (23 May, 1789, from Berlin).

[3] *The Interpretation Of Dreams*, VI (E)

[4] *Collected Papers*, Volume V, XVII

[5] Compare the painters' theme of Cupid beaten, bound, having his wings plucked or being otherwise punished (as, for example in Rubens's *Garden Of Love*, in the Prado).

[6] ἀντί—'I . . . *opposite, over against* . . . II . . . *instead, in the place of* . . .' (Liddell and Scott)

brothers were opposed to one another as rivals[1]; and psychologically we must read their antithesis as a representation of the antithesis between the two functions of the penis which are, as Freud says in his paper on 'The Acquisition Of Power Over Fire'[2], 'as incompatible as fire and water'. Eros, as god of passion, is god of fire, equipped with the emblem of the torch, whose flames are scarcely less pointed in significance than his arrows. Understood in this sense, the brothers are rivals: and out of this the myth has probably been able to fuse the purely erotic sense of Eros playing with his little brother to the slightly sadistically tinged sense of Eros beating his little brother. Certainly, later iconography exploited the fusion: Cartari's sixteenth-century collection of ancient myths includes an engraving which shews Eros and Anteros as naked small boys wrestling together[3]—to which one might append Freud's observation[4] that 'the first sexual sensations often have their origin in the scufflings and wrestlings of childhood'.

When, in this rivalry between them, Anteros is in the ascendant, the sexual power of Eros is in abeyance; and this state of affairs, which is generally represented in Cupid's iconographical tendency to grow big and small, is quite precisely set out—and in relation to Anteros—in a story about them which I found in a little nineteenth-century handbook[5] of classical myths and have been unable to trace in the classical sources or the reference books. I am, as a matter of fact, not without hope that the nineteenth-century compiler made it up: if so, he shewed a remarkable unconscious comprehension of the mythological material, fusing into one nexus, the incompatibility of the two functions and the notion that a stimulating playmate is indispensable to Eros in his sexual function. His story, which is nothing short of perfect, runs: 'In one of the myths about Eros, Aphrodite

[1] Professor Panofsky (*Studies In Iconology* . . ., IV, footnote 79a) cites ancient examples of their rivalry at wrestling, in a torch race, in a fishing contest, and remarks that this rivalry was often misinterpreted by the renaissance as a contest between virtue (Anteros) and sensual love.

[2] *Collected Papers*, Volume V, XXVI. Cf. *Civilization And Its Discontents*, III, note

[3] The engraving, which is from the illustrated edition (1571) of Cartari's *Le Immagini Colla Sposizione Degli Dei Antichi*, is reproduced in J. Seznec: *La Survivance Des Dieux Antiques*

[4] *The Interpretation Of Dreams*, V (D) (b) note

[5] *The Myths And Legends Of Ancient Greece And Rome*, Being A Popular Account . . ., by E. M. Berens. Fifth edition, Blackie, 1892

is described as complaining to Themis, that her son, though so beautiful, did not appear to increase in stature; whereupon Themis . . .
advised his mother to let him have a companion. Aphrodite accordingly gave him, as a play-fellow, his younger brother Anteros . . . and
soon had the gratification of seeing the little Eros begin to grow and
thrive; but, curious to relate, this desirable result only continued as
long as the brothers remained together, for the moment they were
separated, Eros shrank once more to his original size.'

This curious little mythological personage is, as it were, the seed
of that Eros whose name Freud uses 'exactly in the sense in which
Plato uses the word'[1] in the *Symposium*, and whose struggle with
Death Freud called 'this battle of the Titans'[2]. Civilisation's hope of
surviving the present bout of the struggle lies with the mighty Eros.
Yet just as we cannot deny and cannot afford to ignore, so we ought
not to despise this Eros's descent from the smaller god. There are
few ways in which ˙man can be more innocently employed than in
making love. In one form or another, it is to this tutelary deity that
we must commit and commend ourselves—and to his mother who,
as Lucretius pointed out, because she alone can conquer 'Mars potent
in arms', is 'alone able to bless mortals with tranquil peace'[3].

[1] *Collected Papers*, Volume V, XXV
[2] *Civilization And Its Discontents*, VI
[3]   nam tu sola potes tranquilla pace iuvare
             mortalis, quoniam belli fera moenera Mavors
             armipotens regit, in gremium qui saepe tuum se
             reicit aeterno devictus vulnere amoris, . . .
                                                    (I, 31-4)

Books Cited

Addis, see *Catholic Dictionary*.

Aeschylus: *Works*, Oxford text (Gilbert Murray, 1938), Clarendon Press, Oxford, 1947.

Anderson, ed., see Mozart.

Apuleius: *The Golden Ass* (*Metamorphoses*), Loeb ed. (with Adlington transl., 1566; rev. by S. Gaselee, 1915), Heinemann, London, 1958.

Aristophanes: *Works*, Loeb ed., Vol. II (B. B. Rogers, 1924), Heinemann, London, 1950.

Leo Auerbach, ed.: *The Babylonian Talmud*, selection ed. and transl., Skeffington, London, n.d.; Philosophical Library, New York, 1944.

S. Aurigemma: *The Baths of Diocletian and The Museo Nazionale Romano* (catalogue), transl. by J. Guthrie, rev. by A. W. Van Buren, Ente provinciale per il turismo, Rome, 1955.

Jane Austen: *Works*, Adelphi ed., Heffer, Cambridge, England; *Complete Novels*, Modern Library, New York, 1933.

Bailey, see Lucretius.

J. M. Barrie: *Peter Pan* (1928), Hodder and Stoughton, London, 1942; Scribner's, New York, 1940.

Charles Baudelaire: *Les Fleurs du Mal* (with an essay by Theophilé Gautier), N. Lévy Frères, Paris, 1869.

Pierre A. Caron de Beaumarchais, *Théatre de Beaumarchais* . . ., procédé d'observations littéraires, par N. Sainte-Beuve, Garnier Frères, Paris, 1866.

Simone de Beauvoir: *Must We Burn De Sade?* (*Faut-Il Brûler Sade?*, 1953), transl. by Annette Michelson, Peter Nevill, London, 1953; Associated Booksellers, Westport, Conn., 1953.

—— *The Second Sex* (*La Deuxième Sexe,* 1949), transl. and ed. by H. M. Parshley, Cape, London, 1953; Knopf, New York, 1953.

Ludwig van Beethoven: *Symphony in E♭ major* (*Eroica*). Introd. by W. Altmann, Eulenburg.

Evans Bell: *The God of the Bible, A Searching Study of the Christian Creed,* Watts, London, 1943 (abbreviated republication of *The Task of Today,* 1851).

E. M. Berens: *The Myths and Legends of Ancient Greece and Rome,* 5th ed., Blackie, Glasgow, 1892.

The Holy Bible, Authorized King James Version.

J. G. Bishop: *The Brighton Pavilion . . .,* by special authority of the Brighton Town Council, Brighton, 1892.

Anthony Blunt: *Artistic Theory in Italy 1450–1600,* Clarendon Press, Oxford, 1940.

Bolton, see Soane.

The Book of Common Prayer . . . according to the use of the Church of England.

Bernard Bosanquet: *The Essentials of Logic . . .* (1895), Macmillan, London, 1928.

James Boswell: *The Life of Samuel Johnson, LL.D.,* etc., ed. by P. Fitzgerald, reprint of 1888 ed., 3 vols., Allen and Unwin, London, 1924; T. Whittaker, New York, 1897.

P. Bousfield: *Elements of Practical Psycho-Analysis,* Kegan Paul, London, 1922.

Bowden, see Hettinger.

Rupert Brooke: *Poetical Works,* Faber, London, 1946; Dodd, Mead, New York, 1941.

Bulletin du musée national hongrois des beaux-arts, No. 13, Budapest, 1958.

Jacob Burckhardt: *The Civilization of the Renaissance* (1860), transl. by S. G. C. Middlemore, 2nd ed., Phaidon, London, 1945; Harper, New York, 1958.

A. E. Burn: *An Introduction to the Creeds,* etc., Methuen, London, 1899.

Burnaby, see Petronius.

Joseph Campbell, ed.: *The Mysteries, Papers from the Eranos Yearbooks*, transl. by R. Mannheim and R. F. C. Hull, Routledge and Kegan Paul, London, 1955; Pantheon, New York, 1954.

Frank S. Caprio: *Female Homosexuality*, Peter Owen, London, 1957; Citadel, New York, 1954.

Jérôme Carcopino: *Daily Life in Ancient Rome* (1941), ed. by H. T. Rowell, transl. by E. O. Lorimer, Penguin, Harmondsworth, 1956; Yale University Press, New Haven, 1955.

A Catholic Dictionary . . . by W. E. Addis and T. Arnold, rev. by T. B. Scannel and P. E. Hallett. Nihil Obstat and Imprimatur, 1950. 15th ed., Virtue, London, 1952; Herder, St. Louis, 1952.

Frank P. Chambers: *The History of Taste*, Columbia University Press, New York, 1932.

R. W. Chapman: *Jane Austen, Facts and Problems* (Clark Lectures), Oxford University Press, London, 1948.

Samuel Taylor Coleridge: *Biographia Literaria* . . ., ed. by W. G. T. Shedd, Harper, New York, 1884.

Colette: *These Pleasures*, anonymous transl. of *Ces Plaisirs*, White Owl Press, London, 1934.

Dante Alighieri: *Works*, Salani ed., Florence, 1929.

Walter De La Mare: *Peacock Pie* (1913), Constable, London, 1936; Holt, New York, 1936.

Diodorus Siculus, *Works*, Loeb ed., Vol. I (C. H. Oldfather, 1933), Heinemann, London, 1946; Putnam, New York, 1933–54.

E. R. Dodds: *The Greeks and the Irrational*, University of California Press, Berkeley, Calif., 1956.

John Donne, *Poems*, Everyman ed., Dent, London, 1931; Dutton, New York, 1931.

——*The Metaphysical Poets*, ed. by H. Gardner, Penguin, Harmondsworth, 1957.

Fyodor Dostoyevsky: *Crime and Punishment*, transl. by D. Magarshack, Penguin, Harmondsworth, 1951.

John Dryden: *The Works of Virgil*, transl. into English verse. Ed. of 1818; American Book Exchange, New York, 1881.

——*Poetry, Prose and Plays*, sel. by Douglas Grant, Hart-Davis, London, 1952; Harvard University Press, Cambridge, Mass., 1952.

Alfred Einstein: *Mozart, His Character, His Work* (1946), Cassell, London, 1956; Oxford University Press, New York, 1946.

Ellis, see Marlowe.

Eusebius: *Ecclesiastical History*, Loeb ed. (K. Lake, 1926), 2 vols., Heinemann, London, 1949.

R. H. Fife: *The Revolt of Martin Luther*, Columbia University Press, New York, 1957.

Ronald Firbank: *Prancing Nigger*, Brentano, New York, 1924.

Margaret M. Fitzgerald: *First Follow Nature, Primitivism in English Poetry, 1725–1750*, Columbia University Press, New York, 1947.

Ronald Fletcher: *Instinct in Man* . . ., Allen and Unwin, London, 1957; International Universities Press, New York, 1957.

Ford Madox Ford: *Some Do Not* (1924), Penguin, Harmondsworth, 1948; T. Seltzer, New York, 1924.

J. G. Frazer: *Adonis Attis Osiris* (1906), 2 vols., 3rd ed., Macmillan, London, 1919.

——*Spirits of the Corn and of the Wild*, 2 vols., Macmillan, London, 1912.

——*Taboo and the Perils of the Soul*, Macmillan, London, 1911. See also Ovid.

Martin Freud: *Glory Reflected, Sigmund Freud—Man and Father*, Angus and Robertson, London, 1957; Vanguard, New York, 1958.

Sigmund Freud: *An Autobiographical Study* (1925), transl. by J. Strachey, 1935; 2nd ed., Hogarth Press, London, 1946; W. W. Norton, New York, 1952.

——*Civilization and Its Discontents* (1929), transl. by J. Rivière, Hogarth Press, London, 1939; Doubleday, New York, 1958.

——*Collected Papers*, transl. supervised by J. Rivière, 1924, 1925, 1950; 5 vols., Hogarth Press, London, 1953; Anglobooks, New York, 1952.

——*Group Psychology and the Analysis of the Ego* (1921), transl. by J. Strachey, 1922, Hogarth Press, London, 1949.

——*Inhibitions, Symptoms and Anxiety* (1926), transl. by A. Strachey, 1936, Hogarth Press, London, 1948.

——*The Interpretation of Dreams* (1900), transl. by A. A. Brill, 1913, Allen and Unwin, London, 1945; ed. by J. Strachey, Basic Books, New York, 1955.

———*Leonardo Da Vinci, A Psychosexual Study of an Infantile Reminiscence*, transl. by A. A. Brill, 1922, Kegan Paul, Trench, Trubner, London, 1932; Dodd, Mead, New York, 1932.

———*Moses and Monotheism*, transl. by K. Jones, 1932, Hogarth Press, London, 1951; Knopf, New York, 1939.

———*Psychopathology of Everyday Life* (1914), transl. by A. A. Brill (?) 1938, Penguin, Harmondsworth, 1942; Macmillan, New York, 1915.

———*The Question of Lay Analysis* . . . (1926), transl. by N. Procter-Gregg, Imago, London, 1947; Norton, New York, 1950.

———*Totem and Taboo* . . ., transl. by A. A. Brill, 1919, Penguin, Harmondsworth, 1942; Random House, New York, 1960.

Gautier, see Baudelaire.

Edward Gibbon: *The History of the Decline and Fall of the Roman Empire* (1776–88), 7 vols., Oxford University Press, London, 1903–1906.

———*The Miscellaneous Works, with Memoir* . . . *by himself*, ed. by Lord Sheffield, Vol. I, 2nd ed., John Murray, London, 1814.

André Gide: *Les Caves du Vatican*, Gallimard, Paris, 1922.

Edward Glover: *Freud or Jung*, Allen and Unwin, London, 1950; Norton, New York, 1950.

———*The Psycho-Pathology of Prostitution*, lecture, 1943, Institute for the Study and Treatment of Delinquency, London, 1943.

———*War, Sadism and Pacifism* . . ., Allen and Unwin, London, 1946; Macmillan, New York, 1948.

R. Goldwater and M. Treves, compilers and editors: *Artists on Art*, Kegan Paul, London, 1947; Pantheon, New York, 1945.

Edmund Gosse: *Father and Son* (1907), Landsborough, 1959; Scribner's, New York, 1916.

Robert Graves: *The Greek Myths*, 2 vols., Penguin, Harmondsworth, 1955.

———*The Golden Fleece*, Cassell, London, 1944; British Book Service, New York, 1951.

Luisa Hager (revised by): *Nymphenburg, Official Guide*, Munich, 1955.

G. F. Handel: *Acis and Galatea*, vocal score, Novello, London; recording, Oiseau-Lyre OL 50179–80.

———*Messiah*, vocal score, Novello, London.

John Harvey: *Dublin* . . . , Batsford, London, 1949.

J. Christopher Herold: *Mistress to an Age, A Life of Madame de Staël*, Hamish Hamilton, London, 1959; Bobbs-Merrill, Indianapolis, 1958.

Hesiod: *Works, with the Homeric Hymns*, etc., Loeb ed. (H. G. Evelyn-White, 1914), Heinemann, London, 1954.

Franz Hettinger: *Revealed Religion*, ed. by H. S. Bowden. Nihil Obstat and Imprimatur, 1895. Burns Oates and Washbourne, London, 1905.

Dr. Heinrich Hoffman: *Struwwelpeter* (*The English Struwwelpeter or Pretty Stories and Funny Pictures*), recent ed., Routledge and Kegan Paul, London, n.d.

Homer: *Iliad*, Oxford text (D. B. Monro and T. W. Allen), Clarendon Press, Oxford, 1919.

———*The Iliad*, transl. by E. V. Rieu, Penguin, Harmondsworth, 1950.

———*Odyssey*, Oxford text (T. W. Allen, 1908), Clarendon Press, Oxford, 1954.

———*The Odyssey*, transl. by E. V. Rieu, Penguin, Harmondsworth, 1945.

Homeric Hymns, see Hesiod.

Karen Horney: *New Ways in Psychoanalysis* (1939), Kegan Paul, London, 1947; Norton, New York, 1939.

Houghton, see Keats.

Mrs. Jameson (Anna Jameson, née Murphy): *Sacred and Legendary Art* (1848), Longmans, London, 1891; Houghton Mifflin, Boston, 1881.

Samuel Johnson, *Prose and Poetry*, sel. by Mona Wilson, Hart-Davis, London, 1950; Harvard University Press, Cambridge, Mass., 1951. See also Boswell.

Ernest Jones: *Sigmund Freud, Life and Work*, Vols. II and III, Hogarth Press, London, 1955, 1957; Basic Books, New York, 1953, 1957.

H. W. B. Joseph: *An Introduction to Logic* (1906), 2nd ed., Clarendon Press, Oxford, 1946.

James Joyce: *Portrait of the Artist as a Young Man*, Cape, London, 1930; Modern Library, New York, 1944.

C. G. Jung: *Contributions to Analytical Psychology*, transl. by H. G. and C. F. Baynes (1928), Kegan Paul, London, 1945; Harcourt, Brace, New York, 1928.

———*Answer to Job* (1952), transl. by R. F. C. Hull, Routledge and Kegan Paul, London, 1954. See also Campbell.

David Katz: *Animals and Man*, transl. by H. Steinberg and A. Summerfield, Penguin, Harmondsworth, 1953.

John Keats: *Poems*, Everyman reprint, Dent, London, 1916; Dutton, New York.

——*Life and Letters of Keats*, ed. by R. Monckton Milnes, Lord Houghton (1848), Everyman reprint, Dent, London, 1938; Dutton, New York.

Søren Kierkegaard: *Journals* ..., sel., ed., and transl. by A. Dru (1938), Collins (Fontana), London, 1958; Harper, New York, 1959.

Rudyard Kipling: *Stalky & Co.,* Macmillan, London, reprint 1922; Doubleday, New York, 1922.

Henry Kramer and James Sprenger: *Malleus Maleficarum*, transl. by Montague Summers (1928), Pushkin Press, London, 1951.

Choderlos de Laclos: *Les Liaisons Dangereuses*, Charlot, Paris.

Langhorne, see Plutarch.

W. E. H. Lecky: *History of European Morals from Augustus to Charlemagne* (1869), Watts, London, 1946; Appleton, New York, 1913.

J. Lempriere: *A Classical Dictionary* . . ., Routledge, London, 1911; Lippincott, Philadelphia, 1866.

Michael Levey: "Aspects of Mozart's Heroines," *Journal of the Warburg and Courtauld Institutes*, XXII, 1–2, London, 1959.

——*Painting in XVIII Century Venice*, Phaidon, London, 1959.

——"Tiepolo's Treatment of Classical Story . . .," *Journal of the Warburg and Courtauld Institutes*, XX, 3–4, London, 1957.

Charlton T. Lewis: *A Latin Dictionary for Schools*, Clarendon Press, Oxford, 1889; Harper, New York, 1899.

H. G. Liddell and R. Scott: *A Greek-English Lexicon* (1843), Clarendon Press, Oxford, 1890; American Book Co., New York, 1897.

A. D. Lindsay, Introd. to *Socratic Discourses* (Plato and Xenophon), Everyman (1910), Dent, London, 1944; Dutton, New York.

John Locke: *An Essay Concerning Human Understanding* (1690), ed. and abridged by R. Wilburn, Everyman, Dent, London, 1947; Dutton, New York.

Lucretius, *Works*, ed. by Cyril Bailey, 3 vols., Clarendon Press, Oxford, 1947.

Malleus Maleficarum, see Kramer.

Sir Thomas Malory: *Le Morte D'Arthur*, 2 vols., Everyman (1906), Dent, London, 1910; Dutton, New York, 1906.

Thomas Mann: *Confessions of Felix Krull, Confidence Man* (1954), transl. by D. Lindley (1955), Penguin, Harmondsworth, 1958; Knopf, New York, 1955.

Christopher Marlowe: *Works*, ed. by Havelock Ellis, Ernest Benn, London, 1948; Scribner's, New York, 1903.

Maureen McKernan: *The Amazing Crime and Trial of Leopold and Loeb,* Signet Books, New York, 1957.

The Missal, compiled by lawful authority from the Missale Romanorum. . . . Nihil Obstat and Imprimatur, 1921.

Theodor Mommsen: *The History of Rome* (1854–56), transl. by W. P. Dickson, 1911, Everyman, 4 vols., Dent, London, 1931; Dutton, New York, 1911.

A. Morley Davies: *Evolution and Its Modern Critics,* Thomas Murby, London, 1937.

W. A. Mozart: *Don Giovanni*, vocal score, Boosey and Hawkes, London and New York, 1953.

———*The Magic Flute*, vocal score, Boosey and Hawkes, London and New York, 1956.

———*Le Nozze di Figaro*, vocal score, Novello, London.

———*Il Seraglio*, vocal score, Novello, London.

———*The Letters of Mozart and His Family*, transl. and ed. by Emily Anderson, 3 vols., Macmillan, London, 1938.

Musée National d'Art Moderne: *Les Sources du XXe Siècle* . . . (Catalogue of Exhibition, 1960–61), Paris, 1960.

Musée National du Louvre: *700 Tableaux . . . Tirés des Réserves* (Summary Catalogue of Exhibition), Paris, 1960.

Vladimir Nabokov: *Lolita* (1955), Weidenfeld and Nicolson, London, 1959; Putnam, New York, 1957.

John Henry Newman: *Apologia Pro Vita Sua* (1865), Longmans, London, 1890; Houghton Mifflin, Boston, 1956.

The New Testament in the Original Greek, ed. by B. F. Westcott and F. J. A. Hort (1885), Macmillan, London, 1904.

Nymphenburg, see Hager.

George Orwell: *Animal Farm*, Secker and Warburg, London, 1945; Harcourt, Brace, New York, 1954.

———*Nineteen Eighty-Four,* Secker and Warburg, London, 1949; Harcourt, Brace, New York, 1949.

Ovid: *Amores* (with *Heroides*), Loeb ed. (G. Showerman, 1921), Heinemann, London, 1947.

——*Fasti*, Loeb ed. (J. G. Frazer, 1931), 2 vols., Heinemann, London, 1951.

——*Metamorphoses*, Loeb ed. (F. J. Miller, 1915), 2 vols., Heinemann, London, 1951.

The Oxford Dictionary of Quotations, Oxford University Press, London, 1940.

Thomas Paine: *The Age of Reason* (1794–95), Watts, London, 1945; in *Complete Writings*, Citadel Press, New York, 1945.

—— *The Rights of Man* (1791–92), Everyman (1915), Dent, London, 1944; Dutton, New York.

Erwin Panofsky: *Studies in Iconology* . . . (Mary Flexner Lectures, Bryn Mawr, 1937), Oxford University Press, New York, 1939.

Petronius: *Satyricon*, transl. by William Burnaby (1694), Simpkin Marshall, London, n.d.; Modern Library, New York, 1929.

Carlo Pietrangeli: *I Monumenti dei Culti Orientali* (Cataloghi dei Musei Communali di Roma: Musei Capitolini), Rome, 1951.

A. Pigler: *Barockthemen* . . ., 2 vols., Budapest/Berlin, 1956.

Plato: *The Apology*, ed. by St. G. Stock, Clarendon Press, Oxford, 1899.

——*Crito*, ed. by J. Adam (1888), Cambridge University Press, Cambridge, England, 1940.

—— *The Symposium*, ed. by R. G. Bury, Heffer, Cambridge, England, 1932. See also Lindsay.

Plautus, *Works*, Oxford text, Vol. II (W. M. Lindsay, 1905), Clarendon Press, Oxford, 1940.

Plutarch: *Lives of Alexander* . . . *and Julius Caesar*, transl. by J. and W. Langhorne (1770), Cassell, London, 1886; Lovell, New York, 1889.

Alexander Pope: *Collected Poems*, Everyman, Dent, London, 1949; Dutton, New York, 1949.

Marcel Proust: *À la Recherche du Temps Perdu*, N.R.F., Paris, 1931.

Jean Racine, *Théatre Complet*, J. Gilbert, Paris.

Theodor Reik: *Myth and Guilt, The Crime and Punishment of Mankind*, Hutchinson, London, 1958; G. Braziller, New York, 1957.

E. V. Rieu, see Homer.

Arthur Rimbaud: *Une Saison en Enfer* (1873), Mercure de France, Paris, 1951–52.

J. Robiquet: *La Femme dans la Peinture Française*, Les Éditions Nationales, Paris, n.d.

H. J. Rose: *A Handbook of Greek Mythology Including Its Extension to Rome*, Methuen, London, 1928; Dutton, New York, 1928.

Guido de Ruggiero: *Existentialism*, transl. by E. M. Cocks, Secker and Warburg, London, 1946; Social Sciences Publishers, New York, 1948.

J. Seznec: *La Survivance des Dieux Antiques*, Warburg Institute, London, 1940.

William Shakespeare: *The Complete Works*, ed. by W. J. Craig (1905), Oxford University Press, London, 1952.

George Bernard Shaw: *Androcles and the Lion* (1916), Penguin, Harmondsworth, 1946.

———*Back to Methuselah* (1921), World's Classics, with Postscript, Oxford University Press, London, 1945.

———*Heartbreak House*, etc., Constable, London, 1919; Rialto Service Bureau, New York, 1920.

———*Man and Superman* (1903), Penguin, Harmondsworth, 1946.

———*Saint Joan* (1924), Penguin, Harmondsworth, 1946.

———*Sixteen Self Sketches*, Constable, London, 1949; Dodd, Mead, New York, 1949.

Mary W. Shelley: *Frankenstein or, The Modern Prometheus* (1818), Everyman (1921), Dent, London, 1951; Brentano, New York, 1925.

William Smith, ed. (with others): *A Dictionary of Greek and Roman Antiquities* (1842), 2 vols., John Murray, rev. ed., London, 1890–91.

———*A Classical Dictionary* . . ., ed. rev. by G. E. Marindin (1894), John Murray, London, 1904.

Sir John Soane: *A Description of the Residence of* . . . (1835), ed. by A. T. Bolton and issued as an official handbook, Oxford, 1930.

Sophocles, *Works*, ed. by R. C. Jebb, Cambridge University Press, Cambridge, England, 1897.

Herbert Spencer: *First Principles* (1862, 6th ed. 1900), Watts, London, 1946; Appleton, New York, 1910.

Benjamin Spock: *Baby and Child Care*, Pocket Books, New York, 1946.

L. S. Stebbing: *A Modern Introduction to Logic* (1930), Methuen, London, 1945.

Stendhal: *Memoirs of an Egotist,* transl. by T. W. Earp, Turnstile Press, London, 1949.

Laurence Sterne: *Works,* Routledge, London, n.d.; *Works and Life,* Clonmel Society, New York, 1904.

Lytton Strachey: *Books and Characters* (1922), Chatto and Windus, London, 1929; Harcourt, Brace, New York, 1922.

Summers, see Kramer.

Wylie Sypher: *Four Stages in Renaissance Style . . . 1400–1700,* Anchor Books, Doubleday, New York, 1955.

Talmud, see Auerbach.

G. Rattray Taylor: *Sex in History,* Thames and Hudson, London, 1953; Vanguard Press, New York, 1954.

Terence: *Hauton Timorumenos,* ed. by E. S. Shuckburgh (1877), Macmillan, London, 1924.

St. Teresa: *The Life of Saint Teresa of Avila by Herself,* transl. by J. M. Cohen, Penguin, Harmondsworth, 1957.

Thucydides, *Works,* Loeb ed. (C. F. Smith), 4 vols., Heinemann, London, 1919.

Percy N. Ure: *Justinian and His Age,* Penguin, Harmondsworth, 1951.

Virgil, *Works,* Oxford text (F. A. Hirtzell, 1900), Clarendon Press, Oxford, 1942. See also Dryden.

Voltaire: *Lettres Choisis,* Classiques Larousse, Paris.

Helen Waddell, ed.: *Medieval Latin Lyrics* (1933), Constable, London, 1947; Holt, New York, 1933.

Fredric Wertham: *Seduction of the Innocent,* Museum Press, London; Rinehart, New York, 1954.

Oscar Wilde, *Three Plays,* Pan, London, 1951.

John Oulton Wisdom: *The Unconscious Origin of Berkeley's Philosophy,* Hogarth Press, London, 1953.

Mary Wollstonecraft: *A Vindication of the Rights of Women,* Vol. I (1792), Humboldt, New York, 1891.

Edward Young, *Works,* Tegg, 1854; Sanborn and Carter, Portland, Me., 1848.

———*The Complaint, or Night Thoughts,* Tegg, 1812; Sanford and Carter, Portland, Me., 1848.

Index

RACE AND RACES
CASES AND RESOURCES FOR A DIVERSE AMERICA

By

Juan F. Perea
Cone, Wagner, Nugent, Hazouri & Roth and
University of Florida Research Foundation Professor of Law
University of Florida
Fredric G. Levin College of Law

Richard Delgado
Jean Lindsley Professor of Law,
University of Colorado-Boulder

Angela P. Harris
Professor of Law
University of California at Berkeley School of Law

Stephanie M. Wildman
Professor of Law, Emerita
University of San Francisco School of Law
Visiting Professor and Acting Director, Center for Social Justice
University of California at Berkeley School of Law

Jean Stefancic
Research Associate in Law, University of Colorado-Boulder
Project Editor

AMERICAN CASEBOOK SERIES®

**WEST
GROUP**

ST. PAUL, MINN., 2000

ISBN 0–314–22709–1

 TEXT IS PRINTED ON 10% POST CONSUMER RECYCLED PAPER

Acknowledgements

Juan Perea would like to thank Rick Matasar, Charles McClain, Michael Olivas, Chris Slobogin, Rennard Strickland, and Rob Williams, Jr. for their expertise and generous assistance. Special thanks to Kenneth Nunn for his expertise and collegial, constructive criticism that contributed significantly to Chapter 2. Thanks to Lisa Brooks, Sylvia Caballero, Dena Copulsky and Graham Penn for excellent research assistance. Marilyn Henderson, Kamil Díaz, Marla Wolfe and the members of the Faculty Support Services office, University of Florida, Fredric G. Levin College of Law, deserve special thanks for their assistance in preparing the manuscript.

My family, Jan Snyder Perea, Alexander Snyder Perea, and Daniel Snyder Perea, makes everything worthwhile.

Richard Delgado and Jean Stefancic would like to thank Ida Bostian, Adam Furst, and Kristen Kloven for first-rate research assistance. Linda Spiegler, Diana Stahl, Kay Wilkie, and Cindy Winn prepared the manuscript with intelligence and dispatch.

Angela Harris would like to thank John SW Park and Monika Batra for fabulous research assistance. Special thanks to Stephanie Wildman, to whom I owe debts both intellectual and inspirational, and to Lauren Andersen, whose organization, perseverance, and good cheer made all the logistics fall into place.

Stephanie M. Wildman would like to dedicate her efforts on this book to the memory of Trina Grillo, valued colleague, mentor, and friend.

Margalynne Armstrong deserves special recognition for teaching these materials in draft form. I appreciate the many colleagues who offered helpful advice about materials for this casebook, especially Marina Hsieh, Martha Mahoney, David Cruz, George Grossman, Joel Dobris, Adrienne D. Davis, and Catharine Wells. Thank you to the Markkula Center for Applied Ethics at Santa Clara University.

The book would never have been completed without the administrative support of Gloria González, Saralee Buck, Priscilla Battis, and librarian Ellen Platt. Librarian extraordinaire Lee Ryan was always ready to provide a needed document or other support.

Special thanks go to the student research assistants who helped on many phases of this project: Rex de Guia , Katy Filner, Tina Hunt, Ilana Kohn, and Jenn Sheetz.

Finally, I want to credit my family, Michael Tobriner, Becky Wildman-Tobriner, and Ben Wildman-Tobriner, with providing all the unseen support that an author needs.

*

Summary of Contents

Table of Contents

_____

Table of Cases

The principal cases are in bold type. Cases cited or discussed in the text are roman type. References are to pages. Cases cited in principal cases and within other quoted materials are not included.

*

Table of Authorities

patriation in the 1930s. Albuquerque: University of New Mexico Press, 1995, 320

Baldwin, James. The Fire Next Time. New York: Dial Press, 1963, 470

Baldwin, Margaret A., Public Women and the Feminist State, 20 Harv. Women's L.J. 47 (1997), 897

Barnes, Robin D., Black America and School Choice: Charting a New Course, 106 Yale L.J. 2375 (1997), 685, **724**

Barrett, James R. & David Roediger. How White People Became White. In Critical White Studies: Looking Behind the Mirror, edited by Richard Delgado & Jean Stefancic. Philadelphia: Temple University Press, 1997, **445**

Basso, Keith H. Portraits of "The Whiteman:" Linguistic Play and Cultural Symbols among the Western Apache. New York: Cambridge University Press, 1979, **1123**

Bell, Derrick A., Jr. And We Are Not Saved: The Elusive Quest for Racial Justice. New York: Basic Books, 1987, 105, 1002

Bell, Derrick A., Jr., Brown v. Board of Education and the Interest–Convergence Dilemma, 93 Harv. L. Rev. 518 (1980), 684, 1121

Bell, Derrick A., Jr. Faces at the Bottom of the Well: The Permanence of Racism. New York: Basic Books, 1992, 41

Bell, Derrick A., Jr. Race, Racism, and American Law. 3d ed. Boston: Little, Brown, 1992, 104, 105, 130, 131, 430, 583, 758

Bell, Derrick A., Jr., Racial Realism, 24 Conn. L. Rev. 363 (1992), 1092

Bell, Derrick A., Jr., Serving Two Masters: Integration Ideals and Client Interests in School Desegregation Litigation, 85 Yale L.J. 470 (1976), 722

Bell, Derrick A., Jr., White Superiority in America: Its Legacy, Its Economic Costs, 33 Vill. L. Rev. 767 (1988), 499

Bell, Lavinia (Interview, 1861, Canada). In Slave Testimony: Two Centuries of Letters, Speeches, Interviews, and Autobiographies, edited by John W. Blassingame. Baton Rouge: Louisiana State University Press, 1977, **112**

The Bell Curve Wars: Race, Intelligence, and the Future of America, edited by Steve Fraser. New York: Basic Books, 1995, 937

Benjamin, Stuart Minor, Equal Protection and the Special Relationship: The Case of Native Hawaiians, 106 Yale L.J. 537 (1996), 245

Bennett, Lerone. Before the Mayflower: A History of Black America. 5th ed. New York: Penguin Books, 1982, 131

Bennett, Lerone. The Challenge of Blackness. Chicago: Johnson Pub. Co., 1972, **1135**

Berger, Bethany Ruth, After Pocahontas: Indian Women and the Law, 1830 to 1934, 21 Am. Indian L. Rev. 1 (1997), **919**

Berkhofer, Robert F., Jr. The White Man's Indian: Images of the American Indian from Columbus to the Present. New York: Knopf, 1978, 862

Berkman, Eric Thomas, Responses to the International Child Sex Tourism Trade, 19 B.C. Int'l & Comp. L. Rev. 397 (1996), **898**

Berry, Mary F. Toward Freedom and Civil Rights for the Freedmen: Military Policy Origins of the Thirteenth Amendment and the Civil Rights Act of 1866. Washington, D.C.: Dept. of History, Howard University, 1975, 152

Biegel, Stuart, School Choice Policy and Title VI: Maximizing Equal Access for K–12 Students in a Substantially Deregulated Educational Environment, 46 Hastings L.J. 1533 (1995), 752

Blauner, Robert. Racial Oppression in America. New York: Harper & Row, 1972, **16**

Bosniak, Linda S., Exclusion and Membership: The Dual Identity of the Undocumented Worker under United States Law, 1988 Wis. L. Rev. 955, at **48**, **49**

Bosniak, Linda S., Opposing Prop. 187: Undocumented Immigrants and the National Imagination, 28 Conn. L. Rev. 555 (1996), 50

Bowen, William G. & Derek Bok. The Shape of the River: Long–Term Consequences of Considering Race in College and University Admissions. Princeton, N.J.: Princeton University Press, 1998, 746

Branch, Taylor. Parting the Waters: America in the King Years, 1954–63. New York: Simon and Schuster, 1988, **588**

Brand, Johanna. The Life and Death of Anna Mae Aquash. Toronto: J. Lorimer, 1978, 782

Brave Bird, Mary, with Richard Erdoes. Ohitika Woman. New York: Grove Press, 1993, 782

Brown, Dorothy A., The LSAT Sweepstakes, 2 J. Gender Race & Just. 59 (1998), 743

Brown, Kevin, Do African–Americans Need Immersion Schools?: The Paradoxes Created by Legal Conceptualization of Race and Public Education, 78 Iowa L. Rev. 813 (1993), 724

Brownmiller, Susan. Against Our Will: Men, Women, and Rape. New York: Simon and Schuster, 1975, 897

Broyles–González, Yolanda. El Teatro Campesino: Theater in the Chicano Movement. Austin: University of Texas Press, 1994, **976**

Bryant, Meredith Lee, Combating School Resegregation Through Housing: A Need for a Reconceptualization of American Democracy and the Rights it Protects, 13 Harv. BlackLetter L.J. 127 (1997), 709

Luna, Guadalupe T., An Infinite Distance?: Agricultural Exceptionalism and Agricultural Labor, 1 U. Pa. J. Labor & Emp. L. 487 (1998), 320

Lungren, Daniel E. & Mark L. Krotoski, The Racial Justice Act of 1994—Undermining Enforcement of the Death Penalty Without Promoting Racial Justice, 20 U. Dayton L. Rev. 655 (1995), 1087

Lynd, Staughton. Slavery and the Founding Fathers. In Black History; a Reappraisal, edited by M. Drimmer. Garden City, N.Y.: Doubleday, 1969, 104

MacDonald, Andrew (William Pierce). The Turner Diaries: A Novel. 2d ed. Hillsboro, W. Va.: National Vanguard, 1980, **489**

MacKinnon, Catharine A. Crimes of War, Crimes of Peace. In On Human Rights: The Oxford Amnesty Lectures 1993, edited by Stephen Shute & Susan Surley. New York: Basic Books, 1993, **895**, 897

MacKinnon, Catharine A. Feminism Unmodified: Discourses on Life and Law. Cambridge: Harvard University Press, 1987, 897

MacKinnon, Catharine A. Only Words. Cambridge: Harvard University Press, 1993, 835

Maclin, Tracey, Race and the Fourth Amendment, 51 Vand. L. Rev. 333 (1998), 1057

Magee, Robin K., The Myth of the Good Cop and the Inadequacy of Fourth Amendment Remedies for Black Men: Contrasting Presumptions of Innocence and Guilt, 23 Cap. U. L. Rev. 151 (1994), 1057

Mahoney, Martha R., Segregation, Whiteness, and Transformation, 143 U. Pa. L. Rev. 1659 (1995), **654**

Mankiller, Wilma P. Entering the Twenty-First Century—On Our Own Terms. In A Voice of Our Own: Leading American Women Celebrate the Right to Vote, edited by Nancy M. Neuman. San Francisco: Jossey–Bass Publishers, 1996, **1096**

Mann, Coramae Richey. Unequal Justice: A Question of Color. Bloomington: Indiana University Press, 1993, **1037**, 1038, 1039, **1042**

Margolick, David, A Mixed Marriage's 25th Anniversary of Legality, N.Y. Times, June 12, 1992, at B20, at 919

Marshall, Thurgood, Reflections on the Bicentennial of the United States Constitution, 101 Harv. L. Rev. (1987), **108**

Martin, Luther. Genuine Information. In U.S. Constitutional Convention. The Records of the Federal Convention of 1787, edited by Max Farrand. Rev. ed. Vol. 3. New Haven: Yale University Press, 1966, **105**

Martinez, George A., The Legal Construction of Race: Mexican–Americans and Whiteness, 2 Harv. Latino L. Rev. 321 (1997), **432**

Martinez, George A., Legal Indeterminacy, Judicial Discretion and the Mexican–American Litigation Experience, 1930–1980, 27 U.C. Davis L. Rev. 555 (1994), 310, 675

Martinez, John, Trivializing Diversity: The Problem of Overinclusion in Affirmative Action Programs, 12 Harv. BlackLetter L.J. 49 (1995), 746

Martini, Bill, Preserve Unity: Make English the Official Language, Star–Ledger, Oct. 16, 1996, **846**

Matsuda, Mari J., Beside My Sister, Facing the Enemy: Legal Theory Out of Coalition, 43 Stan. L. Rev. 1183 (1991), 894, **1114**

Matsuda, Mari J., Public Response to Racist Speech: Considering the Victim's Story, 87 Mich. L. Rev. 2320 (1989), 824

Matsuda, Mari J., Voices of America: Accent, Antidiscrimination Law, and a Jurisprudence For the Last Reconstruction, 100 Yale L.J. 1329 (1991), **551**, **561**

Matthiessen, Peter. In the Spirit of Crazy Horse. New York: Viking Press, 1983, 782

Matthiessen, Peter. Sal Si Puedes: César Chávez and the New American Revolution. New York: Random House, 1969, 325, 782

McBride, James. The Color of Water: A Black Man's Tribute to His White Mother. New York: Riverhead, 1996, 55

McClain, Charles J. In Search of Equality: The Chinese Struggle Against Discrimination in Nineteenth–Century America. Berkeley: University of California Press, 1994, 370, 373, 374, 375, 377, 378, 382, 384, 389, **395**

McClellan, Frank M., The Dark Side of Tort Reform: Searching for Racial Justice, 48 Rutgers L. Rev. 761 (1996), 1154

McGovney, Dudley O., The Anti–Japanese Land Laws of California and Ten Other States, 35 Cal. L. Rev. 7 (1947), 400

McIntosh, Peggy. White Privilege and Male Privilege: A Personal Account of Coming to See Correspondences through Work in Women's Studies. Wellesley, Mass.: Wellesley College Center for Research on Women, 1988, **459**

McLoughlin, William G. Cherokees and Missionaries, 1789–1839. Norman: University of Oklahoma Press, 1995, **192**, 207

McNeil, Genna Rae. Groundwork: Charles Hamilton Houston and the Struggle for Civil Rights. Philadelphia: University of Pennsylvania Press, 1983, 155, **156**

Means, Russell. Where White Men Fear to Tread: The Autobiography of Russell Means. New York: St. Martin's Press, 1995, 782

Meares, Tracey L., Social Organization and Drug Law Enforcement, 35 Am. Crim. L. Rev. 191 (1998), **1047**

Meier, Deborah. The Power of Their Ideas: Lessons for America From a Small

School in Harlem. Boston: Beacon Press, 1995, 696

Meierhoefer, Barbara S., The General Effect of Mandatory Minimum Prison Terms: A Longitudinal Study of Federal Sentences Imposed. Washington, D.C.: Federal Judicial Center, 1992, 1040

Meierhoefer, Barbara S., The Role of Offense and Offender Characteristics in Federal Sentencing, 66 S. Cal. L. Rev. 367 (1992), 1040

Menchaca, Martha, Chicano Indianism: A Historical Account of Racial Repression in the United States, 20 Am. Ethnologist 583 (1993), **265**, 266

Méndez, Miguel A., Hernandez: The Wrong Message at the Wrong Time, 4 Stan. L. & Pol'y Rev. 193 (1993), 579

Mexican Workers in the United States: Historical and Political Perspectives, edited by George C. Kiser & Martha Woody Kiser. Albuquerque: University of New Mexico Press, 1979, 320

Miles, Robert. Racism. New York: Routledge, 1989, 32

Miller, Jerome G. Search and Destroy: African–American Males in the Criminal Justice System. Cambridge; New York: Cambridge University Press, 1996, 1036

Milner, David. Children and Race: Ten Years On. London: Ward Lock Educational, 1983, 471

Monge, José Trias. Puerto Rico: The Trials of the Oldest Colony in the World. New Haven: Yale University Press, 1997, 326

Montejano, David. Anglos and Mexicans in the Making of Texas 1836–1986. Austin: University of Texas Press, 1987, **271**

Montoya, Margaret E., Máscaras, Trenzas, y Greñas: Un/masking the Self While Un/braiding Latina Stories and Legal Discourse, 17 Harv. Women's L.J. 185 (1994); 15 Chicano–Latino L. Rev. 1 (1994), **1145**

Montoya, Margaret E., Of "Subtle Prejudices," White Supremacy, and Affirmative Action: A Reply to Paul Butler, 68 U. Colo. L. Rev. 891 (1997), **1089**

Moran, Rachel F., Bilingual Education as a Status Conflict, 75 Calif. L. Rev. 321 (1987), 304

Moran, Rachel F. Interracial Intimacy (forthcoming 2000), 866, 908

Morgan, Edmund S. American Slavery, American Freedom: The Ordeal of Colonial Virginia. New York: Norton, 1975, **98**, 871

Morris, Aldon D. The Origins of the Civil Rights Movement: Black Communities Organizing for Change. New York: Free Press, 1984, 91, 161, **162**, 163

Morrison, Toni. The Bluest Eye. London: Chatto & Windus, 1979, c1970, **470**, 865, 996

Morrison, Toni. Playing in the Dark: Whiteness and the Literary Imagination. Cambridge: Harvard University Press, 1992, 470

Moynihan, Daniel Patrick. The Negro Family, the Case for National Action. Washington, D.C.: United States Department of Labor, 1965, **937**

Mueller, Mark, Hate Groups Spewing Venom on Net, Boston Herald, Sept. 15, 1996, at 1, at **485**

Mura, David, How America Unsexes the Asian Male, N.Y. Times, Aug. 22, 1996, at C9, at **908**

Murray, Yxta Maya, The Latino–American Crisis of Citizenship, 31 U.C. Davis L. Rev. 503 (1998), 325

Nabakov, Peter. Tijerina and the Courthouse Raid. 2d ed. Berkeley: Ramparts Press, 1970, 299

Nalty, Bernard C. Strength for the Fight: A History of Black Americans in the Military. New York: Free Press, 1986, 152, 153, 155

Nash, Gary B. Red, White, & Black: The Peoples of Early America. 3d ed. Englewood Cliffs, N.J.: Prentice–Hall, 1992, 173

Natapoff, Alexandra, Trouble in Paradise: Equal Protection and the Dilemma of Interminority Group Conflict, 47 Stan. L. Rev. 1059 (1995), 1087

National Criminal Justice Commission. The Real War on Crime, edited by Steven R. Donziger. New York: HarperPerennial, 1996, 1018, **1036, 1038, 1040**

Nelson, Vednita, Prostitution: Where Racism & Sexism Intersect, 1 Mich. J. Gender & L. 81 (1993), 900

Neuman, Gerald L. Strangers to the Constitution: Immigrants, Borders, and Fundamental Law. Princeton, N.J.: Princeton University Press, 1996, 264

Note, Racial Violence Against Asian Americans, 106 Harv. L. Rev. 1926 (1993), **1019**

Novick, Michael. White Lies, White Power: The Fight Against White Supremacy and Reactionary Violence. Monroe, Me.: Common Courage Press, 1995, 489

Nunn, Kenneth B., Rights Held Hostage: Race, Ideology and the Peremptory Challenge, 28 Harv. C.R.-C.L. L. Rev. 63 (1993), 140

Olivas, Michael A., "Breaking the Law" on Principle: An Essay on Lawyers' Dilemmas, Unpopular Causes, and Legal Regimes, 52 U. Pitt. L. Rev. 815 (1991), 1144

Olivas, Michael A., The Chronicles, My Grandfather's Stories, and Immigration Law: The Slave Traders Chronicle as Racial History, 34 St. Louis U. L.J. 425 (1990), **319**

Olivas, Michael A., The Education of Latino Lawyers: An Essay on Crop Cultivation, 14 Chicano–Latino L. Rev. 117 (1994), 743

Olivas, Michael A. The Law and Higher Education: Cases and Materials on Col-

RACE AND RACES

CASES AND RESOURCES FOR A
DIVERSE AMERICA

*

INTRODUCTION

At the beginning of the new millennium, the United States is, in important ways, a different country from the one the Framers envisioned. The principal racial issues confronting the Framers were the conquest of Indian nations and the perpetuation of black slavery. Our historical and cultural inheritance includes the unresolved legacy of those early racial dilemmas as well as additional, complex racial issues that we confront today as a result of our demographics. For example, are African Americans and Mexican Americans due reparations, as the government decided were due to Japanese American families imprisoned during World War II? Should members of these groups receive a formal apology for the treatment suffered by their ancestors, as Congress expressed in a recent joint resolution apologizing for the colonization of Native Hawaiians? Should African Americans and members of other racial minority groups receive affirmative action in hiring, government contracting, and admissions to higher education? What, if anything, should be done to improve the legislative representation of minority groups, who may otherwise be outvoted consistently? What happens when one group uses a constitutional right, such as free speech, to demean and hector another? How can tensions between racial groups be eased? In the end, how can we do more justice in our racially diverse society?

As of 1997, persons of color constituted nearly one-third of the U.S. population: African Americans (12.7%); Latinos/as (11%); Asian Americans (3.7%); and American Indians (.9%).[1] Because these groups are growing more rapidly than Whites, persons of color will likely outnumber Whites in the United States sometime near the middle of the next century. The demographics of our future will become ever more complex, more multiracial, as members of different racial groups intermarry, adding to the racial complexity already evident today.

Each of us has taught and written about race for most of our careers. We have all confronted the need for and the difficulty of assembling varied interdisciplinary and historical materials to cover race and racism comprehensively, in a manner that accounted for each of the principal racial groups in the United States—African Americans, Indians, Latinos/as, Asian Americans, and Whites.

This casebook is the first to present race and racism in a manner that corresponds to the racial complexity of United States society. Teachers and students committed to understanding our multiracial

1. Estimates, as of 1997. U.S. Bureau of the Census, *Statistical Abstract of the United States:* 1998 (118th ed.) Washington, D.C., 1998 (Table 13, Resident Population Characteristics—Percent Distribution and Median Age, 1850 to 1997, and Projections, 2000 to 2050).

1

society require ready access to historical, legal, and interdisciplinary materials that shed light on our continuing and changing problems of race. To ease and amplify understanding of the increasing complexity of American racial dynamics, we have written this book.

We explore the cutting edges of theory with respect to race, giving central attention both to the *continuity* across history of certain understandings of race and the *evolution* of those understandings, a process which continues today. Thus this book includes materials on the difficulties in defining and understanding the meanings of "race;" the nature of "racism," and "oppression;" Omi and Winant's theory of racial formation; the differing implications of colonization and immigration; the formation of stereotypes; unconscious racism; the gendered and sexualized nature of race; and the situation of biracial and multiracial persons.

This book also provides a rich historical introduction to the particular histories of four major racial groups in the United States, African Americans, Indians, Latinos/as, and Asian Americans, and their encounters with white Europeans and their descendants. Each of these minority groups has a long legal history documenting its presence and its attempts to use the courts and other means to fight racial discrimination in the United States. This legal history, much of which is often ignored in discussions of race, seems to us essential in understanding the situation faced by each of these groups today. This history also enables comparisons among the experiences of these different racialized groups.

Many discussions of race and racism in the United States focus solely on the experiences of racial minorities. It is just as important, in our view, to focus on the development of "Whiteness" and the white race. Demonstrating the evolution of racial categories, membership in the white race has changed over time for complex reasons. For example, Irish immigrants during the nineteenth century and European immigrants of the early twentieth century used to be considered nonwhite. Today, persons with such ancestry are considered White. How did this happen? Whiteness, the unstated norm of racial identity in the United States, requires close examination and study just as other racial identities do.

Readers will notice that much seemingly unrelated law fits together when race and racism are used as organizing principles. The law of slavery and the ceaseless African–American struggle for civil rights are essential to understanding the development of doctrines of equality under the Constitution and statutory law. A different process—conquest, and its legal ratification by Congress and justification by the Supreme Court—is essential to understanding the racialization of Indians, Mexican Americans, and Puerto Ricans. Immigration law also plays a crucial role in the law of race. Supreme Court decisions upholding Chinese exclusion and Alien Land Laws are central in producing the racialization of Asian Americans. And the Supreme Court's many determinations of who was "White" and who was not for purposes of naturalized citizenship were of crucial importance in defining the legal bounds of Whiteness.

This book also explores the themes of race and racism in a variety of doctrinal contexts. What is the meaning of racial equality? What understanding of racial equality finds expression in the crucial realms of education and voting rights? How do racial themes find expression in doctrines of freedom of speech? What are the popular images and stereotypes of people of color and Whites that pervade the media? How does race influence our understanding of sexuality and the family? And how does race intersect with crime?

This book makes it possible for readers to make these and other connections among race, history and legal doctrine. Yet the task is not easy—reading about race and races requires us to think critically about the powerful and ingrained modes of thinking about and expressing racial ideas. Here are some critical questions that should guide your study of race:

1. MAKE THE IMPLICIT EXPLICIT. Look for the assumptions underlying discussions about race and state them. Many implicit assumptions, when articulated to the world, demonstrate their own inadequacy. Is one racial group being privileged over another? What unstated assumptions about gender, sexual orientation, wealth, or physical ability are part of discussions about race?

2. LOOK FOR THE HIDDEN NORM. What perspective is being universalized as the perspective for all people? Is that view really representative and objective? Is "the way things are" being used to perpetuate oppression?

3. AVOID WE/THEY THINKING. In a country based on the ideal of democratic inclusion, consider whether race is being used to foster that inclusion. We/they thinking is usually designed to render some group outside the polis. Who is defining the included "we" and for what purpose?

4. REMEMBER CONTEXT. People do not live in the abstract; they live situated lives. Examining the context in which a problem arises may reveal levels of unsuspected complexity, but will also avoid facile solutions that fall into the traps listed above.

5. SEEK JUSTICE. Be skeptical of traditional lawyerly arguments to avoid change such as "the slippery slope," the intent of the framers (who excluded from voting representation Indians, women of all colors, and only counted African Americans as 3/5 persons), or reliance on discriminatory precedent. Ask the question, "What is a just result that fosters democratic inclusion?"

6. CONSIDER THE NATURE OF THE HARM. Is it minimal or serious? Whose characterization is being given credibility? Be sure to listen to the voices of those most harmed.

7. TRUST YOUR INTUITION. Trina Grillo wrote: "[W]e must believe what our bodies tell us. They teach us to check for the deep, internal discomfort we feel when something is being stated as gospel but does not match our truth. Then they teach us how to spin that feeling out, to analyze it, to accept that it is true but to be able to show why that is so. They also teach us to be brave." Trina Grillo, *Anti–Essentialism and Intersectionality: Tools to Dismantle the Master's House*, 10 Berkeley Women's L.J. 16, 22 (1995).

8. ASK, WHO BENEFITS? Practices, rules, and legal doctrines often benefit one group (usually the majority) at the expense of another. Ask

yourself, why was this rule adopted and who benefits from its observance? If a rule turns out to be unfair, what prevents us from changing it?

This book offers tools, histories, and analysis for the study of race. No single volume, however, can begin to capture the full richness and varied experiences of race in a large, multiracial society like ours. Readers may wish to pioneer new forms and subjects of critical analysis to examine further themes we explore or mention. For example, how does race intersect with territorial status? How do race and racism play out in the history of insular peoples? With gays and lesbians? What is the intersection of race with issues of class? Readers may want to examine issues of comparative and international law. How have other western, industrialized societies dealt with race and status questions, or with hate speech? What about non-European or non-industrialized societies? What do different world religions have to say about racial justice and social reform?

Much, then, remains to be done. In the hope that a comparative, historical, and politically engaged discussion of race can begin to illume what has been called—and what seems to remain—America's most intractable problem, we offer this book.

Juan F. Perea, Richard Delgado, Angela Harris, Stephanie M.Wildman

Note on Nomenclature:

Given the complexities in the meaning and understanding of the words "race" and "racism," we thought it useful to outline briefly our reasons for the use of certain terms in our discussions of racial groups. Each term refers to a group that is "pan-ethnic"–composed of more or less distinct subgroups that may vary by origin, history, language, and culture, among other factors that constitute a people. Thus each term in fact refers to an aggregation of peoples who are more or less alike and different, in their own perception and in the perceptions of others. Readers should not lose sight of this complexity.

In referring to the various racial groups, we have chosen the following terms: "African American" or "Black," "Indian," "Latino/a," "Asian American," and "White" because of their widespread usage and acceptance. We prefer "Latino/a" to "Hispanic" because it seems to us that the term "Hispanic" misleads by emphasizing the Spanish, European origins of the few conquerors who made their way to this continent, as opposed to the origins of a majority of persons who constitute the group to which the term refers, who are predominantly mixed, of indigenous and African ancestry. We have generally capitalized references to races by color, such as "Black" and "White," since these references typically function as proper names for their respective racial groups.

We have also, however, preserved as much as possible the original terms used in the excerpts quoted in this book out of fidelity to the original texts as well as to preserve the context, the sense of the time during which a piece was written, and the full meaning of the original sources.

Chapter 1

DEFINING RACISM AND RACE

Many people argue that racism flourishes in the contemporary United States. It is not always clear, however, what they mean by "racism." This chapter explores the relationship between the practices described as "racism" and the concept of "race."

It might be useful to begin by distinguishing "race" from the concept of "ethnicity." Ethnicity has been defined in many different ways, but for our purposes we may define an ethnic group as a group of people larger than an extended family whose boundaries are marked by a social practice or experience perceived as distinct: a history or a religion; customs or traditions; a language or alphabet; perhaps even a geography. (Consider the many ethnic groups in the Balkans, for example.) An ethnic group, in other words, is defined by the perception of a unique *culture*.

Ethnocentrism—seeing one's own ethnic group as "normal," or as superior in some way to other ethnic groups—has been ubiquitous throughout human history. Conflict and competition among ethnic groups, therefore, is universal in human societies. The practice of systematic ethnic subordination justified by a theory of *racial difference,* however, is a phenomenon that emerged in late eighteenth century Europe (some scholars place it earlier) and that reached full force in the nineteenth century.

Racism has a material component that is both collective and individual. The collective aspect of material racism includes the effort to structure social life and state policy along lines of racial difference, so that one "race" (throughout history, usually the "white" race) has greater access to economic, political, and social goods than the other(s). The individual aspect of material racism includes efforts to help or hurt particular individuals because of their perceived "race." Historically, these two aspects of the material component of racism have been expressed through many different social practices, including colonialism, slavery, segregation, immigration restrictions, discrimination, and genocide. In United States history, moreover, these practices often have been state policy, enforced by law. Examples of material racism sanctioned by law include: the rule indenturing African servants in perpetuity, whereas European servants would serve for a period of years; antimiscegenation statutes prohibiting persons of different races from marrying one another; "Jim Crow" segregation rules forbidding "white" and "nonwhite" persons from sharing public accommodations; restrictive covenants preventing real estate from being transferred to persons of a certain race; and the rule that individuals seeking to become naturalized U.S. citizens had to be "white".

In addition to its material component, racism also has an ideological component: a pool of beliefs, symbols, metaphors and images that justify and "naturalize" its practices. The belief that people are divided by biology into "races" that are similar to animal species; the assumption that each "race" has unique physical, mental, emotional, and/or moral characteristics; the association of black people with animals, particularly apes; phrases like "Indian giver" and taunts like "Chink Chink Chinaman;" caricatures of the Japanese as short people with slanted, near-sighted eyes and buck teeth; and the assumption that white people represent the American "norm" are all examples of the ideological component of racism.

Understanding racism is complicated by the way different people define it differently. In Section 1 of this chapter, we will explore various definitions of racism in search of a common vocabulary and understanding. As we do so, reflect on your own starting point. When you meet a new person do you make a mental note of his/her race? Do you think about his/her ethnicity? Does your answer to these questions depend upon whom you are meeting? What do *you* think racism is?

SECTION 1.   DEFINING RACISM

A.   HISTORICAL ORIGINS OF RACISM

BENJAMIN B. RINGER AND ELINOR R. LAWLESS

Race–Ethnicity and Society
21, 87, 88, 91, 93–94, 95–97, 99, 100–101, 103, 104–105 (1989).*

[S]ociety may define as a distinctive category * * * an aggregate of people who lack common culture, an internal structure, and a sense of folk, but who share certain distributive characteristics, and by forcing them into a common environment of arbitrary and discriminatory treatment, create[] a sense of shared fate and identity among them. This has been more or less the history of relations between peoples with different racial characteristics in which one racial group subordinates another. * * *

[T]he colonial expansion of the white European from the fifteenth century onward brought under his control vast areas and regions of the world that were comprised of racially different populations. * * *

In some of these conquered territories, such as in the Caribbean, the white European virtually exterminated the native population and brought in an enslaved labor supply for his plantations. In such areas he literally built a colonialist plural society from scratch. In other areas as in Africa and Southeast Asia, he subdued the native population, let most of them live, and superimposed a colonialist structure on the back of the traditional system. The form of colonial administration that he established to insure his control varied in part with the political style of the colonial power. For example, the British in Africa generally relied more heavily on the traditional system in the colony and on indirect rule than did the French who preferred their own direct rule. Perhaps of even greater importance in the colonialist's choice of administrative style was the state of political and social development of the conquered people. In Africa, for example, when the colonialists conquered a society with a developed set of governing institutions, they sought to coopt this structure of traditional authority and to harness it to their own purposes. * * * Contrastingly, when the European colonialists conquered "stateless" African societies, they resorted to direct rule. * * *

Despite efforts through church missions, schools, and public media to diffuse his values and beliefs throughout the colony, the colonialist in most colonies did not see himself constructing anything resembling a national community within the colony. He did not view the colony as a collective entity toward which he had civic responsibilities and with which he could identify. * * *

In the last several decades a number of colonialized people have ousted the colonialist from political power through revolutionary or other means and have established the colony as an independent state; however, it has not been easy for these societies to expunge the influence of their colonial past. For example, the status and elite models of colonial days continue to guide the life-style of much of the new elite. In fact, in some British Caribbean countries * * * color gradations persist as a major dimension of status: being black still means being on the bottom of the social scale, being white is still associated with being at the top. * * *

* * * In many respects the Western modes of administration have not only been retained but also expanded as governmental action and intervention has moved into an ever widening range of activities.

And finally the colonialist has bequeathed the new state an economic system that is still basically dependent on the metropolitan country. * * * Accordingly, much of the economic destiny for the foreseeable future rests in the hands of groups within the metropolitan country. The goal of modernization moves the population increasingly away from traditional economic activities and places them at the mercy of the marketplace and of the economic development programs of the new government. * * *

Colonial powers established the political boundaries that continue to define those of the new states. They did so on the basis of imperial design in the struggle with other colonial powers and paid little or no attention to the question of ethnic coherence. As a result, diverse ethnic groups were arbitrarily included within these boundaries. In addition, these boundaries all too frequently cut through ethnically homogenous territories. * * * In colonies where indirect rule in particular was practiced, the colonialist power would * * * strive to divide and to conquer the established tribes by pitting one against the other, by awakening dormant ethnic and tribal ties and antagonisms, and by favoring certain tribes over others in granting access to schooling and to minor government positions. * * *

Pervasive as was the effort of the white European to conquer nonwhite races and to impose upon them a system of exploitation, in a number of conquered territories he did something more. He also assumed the role of colonist and founded a permanent settlement in which he created a society whose institutions were molded in his racial, religious, and national image and with which he closely identified. In those settings he dominated the colonial plural structure and defined his status as a permanently established, not as a sojourner, elite. At the same time he viewed himself as the people of the colonist society. His rights and immunities in both structures stood in sharp contrast with those of the racial groups that comprised the subjugated strata of his colonialist plural society. * * * [Eds. Ringer and Lawless describe such societies as "dual" because they contain two different forms of political organization: an egalitarian community among the racial elite, and an inegalitarian relationship between the racial elite and the racially oppressed.]

The earliest and perhaps most widespread historical export of duality happened during the conquest and settlement of the New World, first by the Spanish, then by the English, and finally by other Europeans. They built their dual societies in South America, Central America, and North America. They eventually lost them as these societies became independent nations still bearing the marks of their dualistic heritage.

By the time the white European moved onto the continents of Asia and Africa, he had become, by and large, a colonialist who was interested in building an imperial system for his home country. * * * In some places, however, he settled permanently and evolved a colonist society too. As a result, duality resurfaced in such places as South Africa, Zimbabwe (Rhodesia), Australia, and New Zealand.

In Australia and New Zealand the white European overwhelmed an indigenous population that was pushed to the perimeters of the white society as a racial minority, much as the Indian was in the United States. In South Africa and Zimbabwe the situation was different. Whites built their own society as a small minority among a vast population of subjugated nonwhites. As might be expected, the dual structures built in these societies reflected the marked variations in population proportions of white and nonwhite as well as the different historical circumstances * * *

Within two decades after Columbus's discovery of the island of Hispaniola, the Spanish conquistador had not only wrested the land and its resources from the Indians, but had also imposed upon them a system of forced labor that was to remain in effect in the Spanish colonies for the next several centuries. Under this system of the *encomienda*, first elaborated and institutionalized by Governor Ovando, the successor to Columbus's successor as governor, Indians were parcelled out to Spaniards in numbers ranging from a few to several hundred. The number any Spaniard received depended on his status and his role in the conquest of Hispaniola. * * *

Most of the Indians were employed in the mining of gold and of other precious ores; others, in cultivating foodstuffs for the Spanish conquistador. They had to endure backbreaking manual labor for long hours under intolerable conditions. For them the encomienda was a brutal and coercive system of labor control not unlike slavery. Thus was set in place a colonial system of political control and economic exploitation divided along racial lines.

So harsh were the working conditions that by the end of Ovando's governorship in 1509, the mortality rate among Indians had risen catastrophically. Some scholars have insisted that the rapid rise was not entirely due to the working conditions. They also attribute it to the Indians' vulnerability to the diseases brought to the island by the conquistador. But whatever the reason, many died. Others did not wait to die; they escaped into the wilderness or fled to nearby islands. As a result, by 1520 the Indian population had declined so markedly that it no longer functioned as an adequate labor supply for the island. * * *

The demand for labor for sugar plantations * * * intensified pressures for a new source of labor that would fill the gap created by the dwindling supply of Indians. Thus was erected another colonial edifice of exploitation: this time on the backs of the enslaved blacks. * * *

In promulgating the Laws of Burgos [Eds. in 1512], the king gave the system of encomienda as designed for the New World a legal standing it lacked before. It was now incorporated into the laws of the Spanish empire and was no longer merely a practice sanctioned by king and local authorities. In addition, the system's axiom that Indians had inherently evil and slothful inclinations which had to be remedied was adopted as a cardinal principle of the legislation itself. In legitimizing the system, the king also surrounded it with normative constraints that were meant to protect the Indians from its more coercive features. Furthermore, the *encomendero* was to assume the paternal-like obligations of civilizing and Christianizing the Indians so that they would not only lose their evil and slothful ways but would also in time become "free vassals" of the king.

By casting the encomienda in this normative mold, the king hoped to impose an organically interlocked status hierarchy, similar to the estate structure in Spain, upon what was essentially a dehumanized colonial system of racial exploitation and forced labor. In doing this, he was prepared to include the Indian in his hierarchic domain of subjects, though initially as wards of the Crown, just as the Church was prepared to include them in its hierarchic domain of souls. * * *

Another link between the dual structures that the colonist forged almost from the moment that the first one set foot on the soil of Hispaniola was with the Indian woman. Primarily young and unattached, many of these men soon developed liaisons with the native women. According to [one writer], "in a way, the Spanish Conquest of the Americas was a conquest of women. The Spaniards obtained the

Indian girls both by force and by peaceful means." * * * [I]nterracial unions flourished but relatively few led to marriage. * * *

By the eighteenth century miscegenation in Spanish America had produced, according to various scholars, an elaborately refined, hierarchically arranged "Sociedad de Castas." In New Spain, for example, the nomenclatures of "castas" identified eighteen different categories; in Peru, fourteen. They were based on the interracial unions of Spaniards, Indians, blacks, and their mixed offspring of varying racial combinations. The major divisions were "invested with different legal status as well as the strong element of corporative privileges." * * *

[The] unifying external value framework [of the caste society] was provided by the Crown and Church. Its internal system of stratification was organized around a "color" axis into what a Chilean scholar has called a "pigmentocracy." * * *

Seeking to duplicate the colonial success of the Spanish in the New World, the English finally succeeded, almost a century after Columbus's first voyage and after several abortive attempts, in establishing a settlement in Jamestown under a royal charter given to the Virginia Company of London. However, unlike the Spanish conquistadors, the English settlers did not try to achieve their economic goals on the backs of the Indian as a captive labor force. Instead, they fought the Indian for his land and resources; and once they defeated him forced him to move beyond the perimeter of the settlement. They relied on their own labor at the beginning, and in the process they built a colonist society, first within the organizational framework of the Virginia Company and then as a distinctive territorial and political community under the Crown. * * *

[T]he company bequeathed two policies that structured the economy of the colonist society and gave it its distinctive character during the first half century. One was the headright provision that granted 50 acres of land to anyone who paid his own way and 50 additional acres for each person whose transportation he paid. From this developed an economy "filled with little farms a few hundred acres in extent, owned and worked by a sturdy class of English farmers," whose primary crop was tobacco. * * *

The second policy inherited from the company was the system of indentured servitude. It had its origins in the earliest days of the settlement when the company underwrote the transportation and other expenses of planters who were then obliged to work on company land for a certain number of years * * *

So widespread did this practice become that an estimated four out of five immigrants arrived in Virginia under terms of an indenture. From the very beginning, the servitude of the indentured white servant was defined as a contractual arrangement between two parties and of temporary duration. * * * Upon completion of his indenture, the white servant was accorded full membership in the colonist community of the people and a claim for "freedom dues" to facilitate his transition to this status. * * *

Even as the colonist society was being built under the yeoman planter, the foundations for a racially segmented colonialist plural society were also being laid. The arrival of a Dutch ship in 1619 marked the beginning of the involuntary flow of black slaves which grew only gradually during the next several decades. During this period their legal status was ambiguous; the nature of their servitude, unclear. Slowly through court decisions and finally through enactments of the Virginia legislature their servitude was defined as being in perpetuity and their legal status as being objects of ownership. [Eds. Some historians have argued that the divergence between the statuses of white indentured servants and black indentured servants was a deliberate policy to curtail growing political and economic alliances that threatened the elites.]

By the first decade of the eighteenth century black slaves had been * * * enmeshed in a web of legal and extralegal coercive constraints and oppressive controls that placed them completely at the mercy of their white masters. Their numbers had increased markedly by then. By mid-century the flow of black slaves reached flood proportions, just as the flow of white indentured servants had been reduced to a mere trickle. The result was the replacement of indentured white servants by black slaves as the major source of labor in Virginia. Their place of work, though, was not the small farm of the indentured servant but the large tobacco plantation of the white slave owner. And so a racially segmented colonial plural society reached maturity in Virginia that ended only with the Civil War.

TESSIE LIU

Teaching the Differences Among Women from a Historical Perspective:
Rethinking Race and Gender as Social Categories
14(4) Women's Studies International Forum 265, 272–74 (1991).*

In colonial societies as different as Dutch Indonesia, British Nigeria, and the American plantation South, we find bifurcated visions of womanhood. Women of European descent became the guardians of civilization. Thus, the Victorian cult of domesticity in the colonial world must be seen in the context of demarcations between groups. Because the structure of colonial race privileges focused particularly on limiting access to European status, the elevation of white women as civilization's guardians also confined them within narrow spheres. As the reproducers of the ruling elite, they established through their daily actions the boundaries of their group identity; hence their behavior came under group scrutiny.

By contrast, the images and treatment of colonized women resulted from more complex projections. On the one hand, colonized women were not viewed as women at all in the European sense; they were spared neither harsh labor nor harsh punishment. On the other hand, as the reproducers of the labor force, colonized women were valued as one might value a prize brood mare. Equally, men of European descent

eroticized colonized women as exotic, socially prohibited, but available and subjugated sexual objects. In this case, prohibition and availability are intimately connected to desire. Because such unions were socially invisible, the progeny from the union could be denied. Sex, under these conditions, became a personal rather than a community or racial matter. In other words, in sexual unions with women from a socially prohibited category, men could step outside the normal restrictions and obligations imposed on sexual activity by shirking responsibility for their progeny.
* * *

* * * In the latter half of the nineteenth century, the imperatives of competition for empire in a world already carved up by Europeans filtered back into European domestic politics in the form of anxiety over population decline and public health. In the eyes of the state, responsibility for the fitness of the nation rested on women's reproductive capacity, their place in the economy, and their role as mothers in protecting the welfare of children (the future soldiers for the empire). Debates over the Woman Question, in the form of feminist demands for greater equality within marriage and for political, economic, and reproductive rights, were debated in the context of colonial politics and concerns over the vitality of the master European races. Competition among European nations for colonial empire and their anxieties about themselves as colonizers set the terms for curtailing women's demands for greater freedom of action and autonomy. Anti-feminist projects such as economically restrictive protective legislation, bans on birth control, and pronatalist politics went hand in hand with the campaign against women's suffrage.

In the twentieth century, within the European heartland, German National Socialists took * * * shared assumptions about the relation between national fitness and women's activities to their terrifying extreme. * * * [O]bsession with race purity and population strength led to a policy of compulsory motherhood with the criminalization of abortion for Aryan women of the superior race and forced sterilization for the inferior races as part of their ultimate extermination. This study of the differential effects of racial policy on women's reproductive rights shocks us into recognizing that the division of women into breeders and nonbreeders is wholly consistent with the logic of racial thinking, whether we encounter such divisions in European dynastic politics or as part of the effort to establish boundaries between colonizers and the colonized. The most disturbing aspect of racial thinking is that it is *not* limited to the terrifying circumstances of genocide for some and compulsory motherhood for others. It is, in many respects, its very banality which should trouble us.

MICHAEL OMI & HOWARD WINANT

Racial Formation in the United States: From the 1960s to the 1990s
65–66, 67 (2d ed. 1994).*

For most of its existence both as European colony and as an independent nation, the U.S. was a *racial dictatorship*. From 1607 to

1865—258 years—most non-whites were firmly eliminated from the sphere of politics. After the Civil War there was the brief egalitarian experiment of Reconstruction which terminated ignominiously in 1877. In its wake followed almost a century of legally sanctioned segregation and denial of the vote, nearly absolute in the South and much of the Southwest, less effective in the North and far West, but formidable in any case. These barriers fell only in the mid–1960s, a mere quarter-century ago. Nor did the successes of the black movement and its allies mean that all obstacles to their political participation had now been abolished. Patterns of racial inequality have proven, unfortunately, to be quite stubborn and persistent.

* * * The centuries of racial dictatorship have had three very large consequences: first, they defined "American" identity as white, as the negation of racialized "otherness"—at first largely African and indigenous, later Latin American and Asian as well. This negation took shape in both law and custom, in public institutions and in forms of cultural representation. It became the archetype of hegemonic rule in the U.S. It was the successor to the conquest as the "master" racial project.

Second, racial dictatorship organized (albeit sometimes in an incoherent and contradictory fashion) the "color line" rendering it the fundamental division in U.S. society. The dictatorship elaborated, articulated, and drove racial divisions not only through institutions, but also through psyches, extending up to our own time the racial obsessions of the conquest and slavery periods.

Third, racial dictatorship consolidated the oppositional racial consciousness and organization originally framed by marronage and slave revolts, by indigenous resistance, and by nationalisms of various sorts. Just as the conquest created the "native" where once there had been Pequot, Iroquois, or Tutelo, so too it created the "black" where once there had been Asante or Ovimbundu, Yoruba or Bakongo. * * *

Racial rule can be understood as a slow and uneven process which has moved from dictatorship to democracy, from domination to hegemony. In this transition, hegemonic forms of racial rule—those based on consent—eventually came to supplant those based on coercion. * * *

Notes and Questions

1. The history of racial oppression in the Americas is examined more closely in Chapters 2–5.

2. Ringer and Lawless describe "the white European" as "he." Is this accurate? What information does Liu add to their account of colonizing societies?

3. Omi and Winant define "hegemony," a concept elaborated by the Italian Communist Antonio Gramsci, as "the incorporation by the ruling group of many of the key interests of subordinated groups, often to the explicit disadvantage of the rulers themselves. * * * [I]n order to consolidate their hegemony, ruling groups must elaborate and maintain a popular system of ideas and practices—through education, the media, religion, folk wisdom, etc.—which [Gramsci] called 'common sense.'" Omi & Winant,

Racial Formation in the United States at 67. How might hegemony disadvantage the rulers?

4. Omi and Winant suggest that "equality" as a core American value is quite new. For most of American history, racial hierarchy rather than racial equality has been the fundamental organizing principle. For a historical examination of the principle of "equality," arguing that African Americans were among its principal architects, see Celeste Michelle Condit & John Louis Lucaites, *Crafting Equality: America's Anglo–African Word* (1993).

B. RACISM(S) AND THEORIES OF OPPRESSION

IRIS MARION YOUNG

Justice and the Politics of Difference
40–42, 46–47, 48 (1990).*

* * * In its traditional usage, oppression means the exercise of tyranny by a ruling group. Thus many Americans would agree with radicals in applying the term oppression to the situation of Black South Africans under apartheid. Oppression also traditionally carries a strong connotation of conquest and colonial domination. * * *

New left social movements of the 1960s and 1970s, however, shifted the meaning of the concept of oppression. In its new usage, oppression designates the disadvantage and injustice some people suffer not because a tyrannical power coerces them, but because of the everyday practices of a well-intentioned liberal society. * * * In this extended structural sense oppression refers to the vast and deep injustices some groups suffer as a consequence of often unconscious assumptions and reactions of well-meaning people in ordinary interactions, media and cultural stereotypes, and structural features of bureaucratic hierarchies and market mechanisms—in short, the normal processes of everyday life. We cannot eliminate this structural oppression by getting rid of the rulers or making some new laws, because oppressions are systematically reproduced in major economic, political, and cultural institutions.

The systemic character of oppression implies that an oppressed group need not have a correlate oppressing group. While structural oppression involves relations among groups, these relations do not always fit the paradigm of conscious and intentional oppression of one group by another. * * * The conscious actions of many individuals daily contribute to maintaining and reproducing oppression, but those people are usually simply doing their jobs or living their lives, and do not understand themselves as agents of oppression.

I do not mean to suggest that within a system of oppression individual persons do not intentionally harm others in oppressed groups. The raped woman, the beaten Black youth, the locked-out worker, the gay man harassed on the street are victims of intentional actions by identifiable agents. I also do not mean to deny that specific groups are beneficiaries of the oppression of other groups, and thus have an interest in their continued oppression. Indeed for every oppressed group there is a group that is *privileged* in relation to that group. * * *

Assuming an aggregate model of groups, some people think that social groups are invidious fictions, essentializing arbitrary attributes. From this point of view problems of prejudice, stereotyping, discrimination, and exclusion exist because some people mistakenly believe that group identification makes a difference to the capacities, temperament, or virtues of group members. This individualist conception of persons and their relation to one another tends to identify oppression with group identification. Oppression, on this view, is something that happens to people when they are classified in groups. Because others identify them as a group, they are excluded and despised. Eliminating oppression thus requires eliminating groups. People should be treated as individuals, not as members of groups, and allowed to form their lives freely without stereotypes or group norms.

* * * While I agree that individuals should be free to pursue life plans in their own way, it is foolish to deny the reality of groups. * * * As both markets and social administration increase the web of social interdependency on a world scale, and as more people encounter one another as strangers in cities and states, people retain and renew ethnic, locale, age, sex, and occupational group identifications, and form new ones in the processes of encounter. Even when they belong to oppressed groups, people's group identifications are often important to them, and they often feel a special affinity for others in their group. I believe that group differentiation is both an inevitable and a desirable aspect of modern social processes. * * *

* * * In complex, highly differentiated societies like our own, all persons have multiple group identifications. The culture, perspective, and relations of privilege and oppression of these various groups, moreover, may not cohere. Thus individual persons, as constituted partly by their group affinities and relations, cannot be unified, themselves are heterogenous and not necessarily coherent.

Notes and Questions

1. Is it "foolish to deny the reality of groups," as Young suggests? Much contemporary liberal thinking places particular emphasis on the individual. Indeed, a tension between individual and community arguably permeates Western culture. Does acknowledging the reality of groups prevent us from treating the individual as paramount? Is that result desirable? For an argument that political liberalism must accept the reality of groups in order to treat individuals fairly, see Will Kymlicka, *Liberalism, Community, and Culture* (1989).

What are the implications for antidiscrimination law if we attempt to recognize the reality of groups? Young describes "discrimination" as "a methodologically individualist concept." Iris Marion Young, *Five Faces of Oppression* in *Rethinking Power* 174 (Thomas E. Wartenberg ed. 1992).

2. Young identifies five different "faces" of oppression: exploitation, marginalization, powerlessness, cultural imperialism, and violence.

By exploitation, she means "a steady process of the transfer of the results of the labor of one social group to benefit another. * * * Social rules about what work is, who does what for whom, how work is compensated, and the social process by which the results of work are appropriated operate to enact relations of power and inequality. These relations are produced and reproduced through a systematic process in which the energies of the have-nots are continuously expended to maintain and augment the power, status, and wealth of the haves." *Justice and the Politics of Difference* at 49–50.

By marginalization, Young means that "[a] whole category of people is expelled from useful participation in social life and thus potentially subjected to severe material deprivation and even extermination." *Id.* at 53.

Powerlessness describes the lack of "authority, status, and sense of self that professionals tend to have." *Id.* at 57. For Young, professionals enjoy a sense of "progressive development of capacities and avenues for recognition * * *, considerable day-to-day work autonomy," and the expectation and habit of being treated with "respect." *Id.*

Cultural imperialism, according to Young, means "the universalization of a dominant group's experience and culture, and its establishment as the norm." *Id.* at 59.

Finally, Young treats violence as a face of oppression, noting that "[m]embers of some groups live with the knowledge that they must fear random, unprovoked attacks on their persons or property, which have no motive but to damage, humiliate, or destroy the person." *Id.* at 61. Young also includes under violence "less severe incidents of harassment, intimidation, or ridicule simply for the purpose of degrading, humiliating, or stigmatizing group members." *Id.*

Young offers this framework as a way to analyze oppression in a more sophisticated way than simply asking "whether" or "how much" a group is oppressed. Consider this framework as you read the rest of this chapter.

3. Young's framework is meant to account for the many different ways in which groups can be oppressed. To what extent do racialized groups in the United States differ from one another in terms of their encounters with oppression? Is the major distinction between "white" and "nonwhite" groups, or are there significant differences within those broad categories? Consider the following excerpt.

ROBERT BLAUNER

Racial Oppression in America
51, 52, 53–56, 68–69, 71–72, 73–74 (1972).*

As the term *third world* has been increasingly applied to people of color in the United States, a question has disturbed many observers. Is the third world idea essentially a rhetorical expression of the aspirations and political ideology of the young militants in the black, brown, red, and yellow power movements, or does the concept reflect actual sociological realities? * * *

The fundamental issue is historical. People of color have never been an integral part of the Anglo–American political community and culture because they did not enter the dominant society in the same way as did the European ethnics. The third world notion points to *a basic distinction between immigration and colonization as the two major processes through which new population groups are incorporated into a nation.* Immigrant groups enter a new territory or society voluntarily, though they may be pushed out of their old country by dire economic or political oppression. Colonized groups become part of a new society through force or violence; they are conquered, enslaved, or pressured into movement. * * * The third world perspective returns us to the origins of the American experience, reminding us that this nation owes its very existence to colonialism, and that along with settlers and immigrants there have always been conquered Indians and black slaves, and later defeated Mexicans—that is, colonial subjects—on the national soil. * * *

Native Americans, Chicanos, and blacks are the third world groups whose entry was unequivocally forced and whose subsequent histories best fit the colonial model. Critics of the colonial interpretation usually focus on the black experience, emphasizing how it has differed from those of traditional colonialism. Rather than being conquered and controlled in their native land, African people were captured, transported, and enslaved in the Southern states and other regions of the Western hemisphere. Whether oppression takes place at home in the oppressed's native land or in the heart of the colonizer's mother country, colonization remains colonization. However, the term *internal colonialism* is useful for emphasizing the differences in setting and in the consequences that arise from it. The conquest and virtual elimination of the original Americans, a process that took three hundred years to complete, is an example of classical colonialism, no different in essential features from Europe's imperial control over Asia, Africa, and Latin America. The same is true of the conquest of the Mexican Southwest and the annexation of its Spanish-speaking population.

Other third world groups have undergone an experience that can be seen as part colonial and part immigrant. Puerto Rico has been a colony exploited by the mainland, while, at the same time, the islanders have had relative freedom to move back and forth and to work and settle in the States. Of the Asian–American groups, the situation of the Filipinos has been the most colonial. The islands were colonies of Spain and the United States, and the male population was recruited for agricultural serfdom both in Hawaii and in the States. In the more recent period, however, movement to the States has been largely voluntary.

In the case of the Chinese, we do not have sufficient historical evidence to be able to assess the balance between free and involuntary entry in the nineteenth century. The majority came to work in the mines and fields for an extended period of debt servitude; many individuals were "shanghaied" or pressed into service; many others evidently signed up voluntarily for serflike labor. A similar pattern held for the Japanese who came toward the end of the century, except that the voluntary element in the Japanese entry appears to have been considerably more significant. Thus, for the two largest Asian groups, we have an original entry into American society that might be termed semicolonial, followed in the twentieth century by immigration. Yet the exclusion of Asian immigrants and the restriction acts that followed were unique blows, which marked off the status of the Chinese and Japanese in America, limiting their numbers and potential power. For this reason it is misleading to equate the Asian experience with the European immigrant pattern. Despite the fact that some individuals and families have been able to immigrate freely, the status and size of these ethnic groups have been rigidly controlled.

There is a somewhat parallel ambiguity in the twentieth-century movement from Mexico, which has contributed a majority of the present Mexican–American group. Although the migration of individuals and families in search of work and better living conditions has been largely voluntary, classifying this process as immigration misses the point that the Southwest is historically and culturally a Mexican, Spanish-speaking region. Moreover, from the perspective of conquest that many Mexicans have retained, the movement has been to a land that is still seen as their own. Perhaps the entry of other Latin Americans approaches more nearly the immigrant model; however, in their case, too, there is a colonial element, arising from the Yankee neocolonial domination of much of South and Central America; for this reason, along with that of racism in the United States, many young Latinos are third world oriented. * * *

The essentially voluntary entry of the [European] immigrants was a function of their status in the labor market. The European groups were responding to the industrial needs of a free capitalist market. Economic development in other societies with labor shortages—for example, Australia, Brazil, and Argentina—meant that many people could at least envision alternative destinations for their emigration. Though the Irish were colonized at home, and poverty, potato famine, and other disasters made their exodus more of a flight than that of other Europeans, they still had some choice of where to flee. * * *

Because the Europeans moved on their own, they had a degree of autonomy that was denied those whose entry followed upon conquest, capture, or involuntary labor contracts. They expected to move freely within the society to the extent that they acquired the economic and cultural means. Though they faced great hardships and even prejudice and discrimination on a scale that must have been disillusioning, the Irish, Italians, Jews, and other groups had the advantage of European ancestry and white skins. * * *

Thus, the entrance of the European into the American order involved a degree of choice and self-direction that was for the most part denied people of color. Voluntary immigration made it more likely that individual Europeans and entire ethnic groups would identify with America and see the host culture as a positive opportunity rather than an alien and dominating value system.

* * *

The present-day inclination to equate racism against third-world groups with the ethnic prejudice and persecution that immigrant groups have experienced is mistaken. Compare, for example, intolerance and discrimination in the sphere of religion. European Jews who followed their orthodox religion were mocked and scorned, but they never lost the freedom to worship in their own way. Bigotry certainly contributed to the Americanization of contemporary Judaism, but the Jewish religious transformation has been a slow and predominantly voluntary adaptation to the group's social and economic mobility. In contrast, the U.S. policy against Native American religion in the nineteenth century was one of all-out attack; the goal was cultural genocide. Various tribal rituals and beliefs were legally proscribed and new religious movements were met by military force and physical extermination. The largest twentieth-century movement, the Native American Church, was outlawed for years because of its peyote ceremony. * * *

American capitalism has been partially successful in absorbing third world groups into its economic system and culture. Because of the colonial experience and the prevalence of racism, this integration has been much less complete than in the case of the ethnic groups. The white ethnics who entered the class system at its lowest point were exploited, but not colonized. Because their group realities were not systematically violated in the course of immigration, adaptation, and integration, the white newcomers could become Americans more or less at their own pace and on their own terms. They have moved up, though slowly in the case of some groups, into working-class and middle-class positions. Their cultural dynamic has moved from an initial stage of group consciousness and ethnic pluralism to a present strategy of individual mobility and assimilation. The immigrants have become part of the white majority, partaking of the racial privilege in a colonizing society; their assimilation into the dominant culture is now relatively complete, even though ethnic identity is by no means dead among them. In the postwar period it has asserted itself in a third-generation reaction to "overassimilation" and more recently as a response to third world movements. But the ethnic groups have basically accepted the overall culture's rules of "making it" within the system, including the norms of racial oppression that benefit them directly or indirectly. * * *

Because the colonized groups have been concentrated in different regions, geographical isolation has heretofore limited the possibilities of cooperation. When they have inhabited the same area, competition for jobs has fed ethnic antagonisms. Today, as relatively powerless groups, the racial minorities often find themselves fighting one another for the modicum of political power and material resources involved in antipoverty, model-cities, and educational reform projects. Differences in culture and political style exacerbate these conflicts.

The third world movement will have to deal with the situational differences that are obstacles to coalition and coordinated politics. One of these is the great variation in size between the populous black and Chicano groups and the much smaller Indian and Asian minorities. Numbers affect potential political power as well as an ethnic group's visibility and the possibilities of an assimilative strategy. Economic differentiation may be accelerating both between and within third world groups. The racial minorities are not all poor. The Japanese and, to a lesser extent, the Chinese have moved toward middle-class status. The black middle class is also growing. The ultimate barrier to effective third world alliance is the pervasive racism of the society, which affects people of color as well as whites, furthering division between all groups in America. Colonialism brings into its orbit a variety of groups, which it oppresses and exploits in differing degrees and fashions; the result is a complex structure of racial and ethnic division.

* * * By its very language the [third world] concept represents more than a negation of the immigration analogy. By its very language the concept assumes an essential connection between the colonized people within the United States and the peoples of Africa, Asia, and Latin America, with respect to whom the idea of *le tiers monde* originated. The communities of color in America share essential conditions with third world nations abroad: economic underdevelopment, a heritage of colonialism and neocolonialism, and a lack of real political autonomy and power.

This insistence on viewing American race relations from an international perspective is an important corrective in the parochial and ahistorical outlook of our national consciousness. The economic, social, and political subordination of third world groups in America is a microcosm of the position of all peoples of color in the world order of stratification. This is neither an accident nor the result of some essential racial genius. Racial domination in the United States is part of a world historical drama in which the culture, economic system, and political power of the white West has spread throughout virtually the entire globe. * * * The oppression of racial colonies within our national borders cannot be understood without considering worldwide patterns of white European hegemony. * * *

What is not clear is whether an international strategy can in itself be the principle of third world liberation within this country. Since the oppression, the struggle, and the survival of the colonized groups have taken place within our society, it is to be expected that their people will orient their daily lives and their political aspirations to the domestic scene. * * * Average levels of income, education, and health for the third world in the United States are far above their counterparts overseas; this gap will affect the possibility of internationalism. Besides which, group alliances that transcend national borders have been difficult to sustain in the modern era because of the power of nationalism.

Thus, the situation of the colonized minorities in the United States is by no means identical with that of Algerians, Kenyans, Indonesians, and other nations who suffered under white European rule. Though there are many parallels in cultural and political developments, the differences in land, economy, population composition, and power relations make it impossible to transport wholesale sociopolitical analyses or strategies of liberation from one context to another.

Notes and Questions

1. Classroom exercise: Consider the following scenarios. Both before and after reading the rest of this section, ask: Is "racism" involved? What factors indicate the presence or absence of racism?

A. On a college campus in a northern state, students frequently decorate their dorm rooms with posters and other images. One February—Black History Month—many African–American students display kente cloth and images of Malcolm X and Martin Luther King, Jr. A young white woman hangs a Confederate flag in her window. Several African–American students protest to their resident assistant, arguing that the display is racist. The woman who hung the flag denies this; she is a Southerner and sees the flag as a statement of pride in her identity, just as the image of Malcolm X is a statement of pride in black identity. She denies any racist intent; indeed, she is surprised and hurt that her actions have been understood as hostile. The African–American students disagree and urge that she be forced to take the flag down and be sanctioned under the campus "hate speech" code.

B. On another college campus, the mascot of the football team is a Native–American man in a long headdress, and the team is called the "Redskins." Indian students on campus protest that this is racist and that the name of the team should be changed and the mascot eliminated. Other students object that their mascot is a symbol of pride, not denigration, and that the mascot and the team name have a long and distinguished history. Indeed, they point out that the school consulted Indian leaders before adopting the mascot and were told they had no objections.

C. An African–American man is standing on the street one night, trying to flag down a taxi. He is wearing a well-tailored business suit and carrying a briefcase, and he is standing in the financial district of a large city. Seeing him, taxicab drivers slow down, then quickly speed up again without stopping. Finally, one cab driver, an immigrant from Pakistan, stops and gives the man a ride, and the passenger expresses his frustration. The cab driver explains that he seldom stops for black men, because they are more likely to rob him. Disclaiming any racial animus, he accurately cites statistics that, proportionally speaking, more black than white men are arrested, charged with violent crimes including armed robbery, and incarcerated for longer periods of time. He also points out that recently some thieves who prey on taxi drivers have taken to wearing suits and other "respectable" clothes.

D. A group of African–American high school students call one another "nigga" in a friendly, casual way. Hoping to be accepted by the group, a white student refers to one of the African–American students in the group as a "nigga."

E. A white, middle-class person disparagingly refers to working-class white people as "poor white trash." A black militant leader does the same in an angry speech.

F. A newspaper editorial praises Asian Americans as a "model" minority, and lauds "Asian values" such as education, hard work, obeying the law, and a commitment to family.

G. A student who was brought up to think of herself as "White" seeks to join a Latino/a student organization because her grandfather emigrated from Venezuela to the United States and she wishes to "explore her roots." The leaders of the organization refuse to allow her to attend meetings on the grounds that she cannot speak Spanish and that, having been raised as "White," she is not a "real" Latina. Two years later she reapplies, having learned to speak fluent Spanish by means of self-study and a semester in Spain.

H. "In 1983, a study by the United States General Accounting Office (GAO) found that three out of four landfills in the Southeastern region of the United States are located in predominantly poor and African American communities. The United Church of Christ (UCC) found similar disparities on a national level in its 1987 study. The UCC study measured the demographic patterns associated with commercial hazardous waste facilities and uncontrolled toxic waste sites. As for the demographic characteristics of communities with commercial hazardous waste facilities, the study found that race proved to be the most significant variable in determining the location of commercial hazardous waste facilities. Communities with the greatest number of commercial hazardous waste facilities had the highest percentage of nonwhite residents. Its study of uncontrolled waste sites produced similar findings: Three out of every five African American and Latino residents lived in communities with uncontrolled toxic waste sites. Furthermore, African Americans were heavily over-represented in the populations of metropolitan areas with the largest number of such sites." Sheila Foster, *Justice from the Ground Up: Distributive Inequities, Grassroots Resistance, and the Transformative Politics of the Environmental Justice Movement,* 86 Calif. L. Rev. 775, 788–89 (1998).

I. On entering a fancy hotel, you encounter a man of color standing by the front desk, which is almost deserted. You ask: "Excuse me, do you work for the hotel?" Later, you notice that nearly all the maids are either African Americans or Latinas, whereas the hotel managers are nearly all White. Similarly, the waiters in the restaurant are predominantly White, while the busboys and cooks seem to be Latino.

J. "On the major islands of Hawaii, Maui, Oahu, and Kauai * * * military airfields, training camps, weapons storage facilities, and exclusive housing and beach areas remind the Native Hawaiian of who owns Hawaii: the foreign, colonizing country called the United States of America.

But colonization has brought more than physical transformation to the lush and sacred islands of our ancestors. Visible in garish "Polynesian" revues, commercial ads using our dance and language to sell vacations and condominiums, and the trampling of sacred *heiau* (temples) and burial grounds as tourist recreation sites, a grotesque commercialization of everything Hawaiian has damaged Hawaiians psychologically, reducing our ability to control our lands and waters, our daily lives, and the expression and integrity of our culture. The cheapening of Hawaiian culture (*e.g.,* the traditional value of *aloha* as reciprocal love and generosity now used to sell everything from cars and plumbing to securities and air conditioning) is so complete that non-Hawaiians, at the urging of the tourist industry and the politicians, are transformed into "Hawaiians at heart," a phrase that speaks worlds about how grotesque the theft of things Hawaiian has become. Economically, the statistic of thirty tourists for every Native means that land and water, public policy, law and the general political attitude are shaped by the ebb and flow of tourist industry demands. For Hawaiians, the inundation of foreigners decrees marginalization in our own land. Haunani–Kay Trask, *From a Native Daughter: Colonialism and Sovereignty in Hawai'i* 3 (1993).

K. Citing the wishes of its customers (mostly white businessmen) an airline resolves to hire only attractive Asian women as flight attendants, and its advertising campaign stresses the importance of catering to the passengers' every whim. Coincidentally, a close friend of yours, a Caucasian male, is planning to marry an Asian–American woman whom he describes as "petite, pretty, and absolutely devoted to me."

2. There are no universally agreed-upon definitions of the term "racism." Indeed, in the United States debates about racism are often confused and angry because the parties have different understandings of what "racism" means. Moreover, it is sometimes asserted that racism is not one thing, but many. As you read the materials that follow, consider whether the following definitions of racism are too narrow or too broad, useful or not useful, and for what purposes.

Theories and definitions of racism can be grouped along several dimensions. First, different kinds of racism are sometimes described in terms of the perpetrator. For example, distinctions are commonly made among *individual racism, cultural racism,* and *institutional racism.* Second, different kinds of racism are sometimes described in terms of their relationship to individual or collective intent. Thus, for example, individual racism is sometimes divided into *conscious* racism and *unconscious* racism; writers also sometimes make distinctions between *ideological* racism, meaning beliefs about race that can be described as racist, and actual *practices* that can be described as racist without reference to any motivation (institutional racism has this connotation as well). As you read the materials that follow, see if these distinctions are helpful in sorting out what we mean by "racism" generally.

Finally, consider whether racism should also be distinguished in terms of its victims and its methods. As to victims, is racism against American Indians the same as racism against Asian Americans? Is there something unique about American anti-black racism? Should we speak of racism with a racial modifier to clarify this issue (for example, "anti-latino/a racism")?

As to methods, is racism through forced exclusion and racism through forced inclusion the same? Should we use a method modifier when describing racism?

JOEL KOVEL

White Racism: A Psychohistory
180, 54, 95–96 (1970).*

* * * We are all scarred by the same society, and most of us at least feel impulses in varying combinations and at varying times, toward some part of racist behavior. The varieties of racist experience are mixed in the real individual. No one behaves simply; he is the amalgamated product of a host of historical, cultural and personal influences.

Nonetheless, Ideal Types * * * can be discerned, and their consideration will prove fruitful * * *

1. The type who acts out bigoted beliefs. Whether a Night Rider in the South or a member of a mob protesting open housing in Chicago, he represents the open flame of race hatred. The true white bigot expresses

* Copyright © 1970 by Joel Kovel. Reprinted by permission. Kovel is a professor   at Bard College.

a definite ambition through all his activity: he openly seeks to keep the black man down, and he is willing to use force to further his ends; let us call him the *dominative racist*.

2. The type who believes in white race superiority and is more or less aware of it, but does nothing overt about it. An intrapsychic battle goes on between these sentiments and a conscience which seeks to repudiate them, or at least to prevent the person from acting wrongly upon them. This often means not to act at all, and such inaction serves as the only resolution of the inner conflict. Because of this, the person tends to behave in ways that avoid the issue: he tries to ignore the existence of black people, tries to avoid contact with them, and at most to be polite, correct and cold in whatever dealings are necessary between the races. We call this complex type the *aversive racist*, in accord with his most characteristic style of handling the race problem. Within this type we find at one extreme those individuals who, upon threat—such as when a black gets "too close"—lapse into dominative racism; and at the other, those who, impelled by a strong social conscience, consider themselves liberals and, despite their sense of aversion (which may not even be admitted inwardly), do their best within the given structure of society to ameliorate the conditions of the Negro. * * *

3. He who does not reveal racist tendencies at all—except as the unconscious persistence of what may be considered mass fantasies. * * *

[Kovel describes these fantasies as rooted in the historical association of blackness with badness and dirtiness, and in the further association of dirt with excrement, "the inside of the body turned out and threatening to return within."]

* * * [W]e insist that racism is not synonymous with race prejudice. The prejudice against race is a special psychological issue in which specific people may handle their specific problems by drawing on * * * racist fantasies. Racism includes this, but also the more fundamental phenomenon of the generation and sustaining of these fantasies. Prejudice is the surfacing of racism. Racism is the activity within history and culture through which races may be created, oppressed, and fantasied about without the aid of bigots. * * * The problem of racism is part of the problem of Western culture. And thus, its central aspect is not that blackness whose many meanings we touched upon in the previous chapter, but its cognate, whiteness. For the world is neither black nor white, but hued. A lightly-hued people—aided perhaps by fantasies derived from their skin color—came to dominate the entire world, and in the process defined themselves as white. The process that generated this white power also generated the fear and dread of black.

* * * [T]he general direction of American reform has been to paint over an older symptom with a newer one in order to protect the underlying disease. Thus did slavery yield to late-nineteenth-century racism. In terms of the ideal types we have been employing, dominative racism was succeeded by aversive racism as the principal mode employed by our culture to utilize and defend against the darkness within it. * * *

Racism, which began with the random oppression of another person, and moved from directly dominative, systematic control of his being, into abstracted averted use of his degradation, now passes beyond consciousness, holding only to its inner connections with the symbolic matrix. Metaracism is a distinct and very peculiar modern phenomenon. Racial degradation continues on a different plane, and through a different agency: those who participate in it are not racists—that is, they are not racially prejudiced—but metaracists, because they acquiesce in the larger cultural order which continues the work of racism. * * *

The paradigmatic example of metaracism is modern Army life. Here is a system, immensely powerful and capable of exercising its will upon individual personalities, which has elevated the lot of black men within its ranks to the highest general level that they have enjoyed in American history. * * * No wonder then that the Moynihan Report proclaimed the military as perhaps the best way to black manhood. Yet what kind of manhood is so fostered by military life? * * * Nowhere in our culture is there less freedom, less autonomy, less originality, joy and affirmation; nowhere is there more cold calculation, more mindless regimentation, more dullness, more banality—and more racial equality. And nowhere else is the integrated anal-sadistic wish of the Western matrix raised to such a pitch of perfection, nowhere else is the exteriorized destructivity of our culture so perfectly expressed.

Though we find it here in pure form, metaracism may be said to exist wherever the hand of the modern State reduces people to its own ends, and whenever it finds it expedient—not ethical, but useful—to eliminate race distinctions in the process. Metaracism exists wherever bureaucracies exist to reduce people to numbers—a white number and a black number are, after all, not so different; whenever "demonstration Negroes" are summoned up to improve a corporation's image; or when advertisers need them to sell more synthetic junk to keep the wheels of production turning. Note that no direct oppression occurs, and that certain real gains are made. A few black people are at long last afforded decent employment (though it is hard to conceive of significant numbers being admitted to high executive positions), and the crippling racist stereotypes are at long last dismantled. * * * Metaracism exists wherever the ends of the large-scale system of the modern Industrial State are considered more important than the human needs of men; it exists whenever production is rationalized, and "order" restored; and it exists wherever we are implored to heal our racial wounds so that, in effect, we can put on a good face to the world.

Anti-black racism has held a unique position in America. To be sure, racist thinking and belief has been applied in this country toward a whole host of non-Teutonic peoples. Even without blacks in our history we might still have been a significantly racist people. But it is to be greatly doubted whether we would have been *equally* racist. * * *

Notes and Questions

1.   Is anyone today racist in Kovel's sense? Is "metaracism" racism at all?

2.   Does Kovel's analysis apply to racism against non-black people? Do you agree that racism against black people is "unique"?

3. Is the military the best institutional example of "metaracism"? Consider the argument sometimes made that the military is the best example of a nonracist American institution. To what extent does the "don't ask, don't tell" policy of the U.S. military with respect to sexual orientation contribute to or undercut the argument that the military is metaracist?

ROBERT A. WILLIAMS, JR.

Documents of Barbarism: The Contemporary Legacy of European Racism and Colonialism in the Narrative Traditions of Federal Indian Law
31 Ariz. L. Rev. 237 (1989).*

The writings of Albert Memmi * * * deserve much closer scrutiny than they have previously received by theorists of Indian-white race relations in the United States. Memmi was a Tunisian Jew who wrote one of the most influential works to emerge out of the Third World decolonization movement, *The Colonizer and the Colonized.* * * * Memmi drew on his intensely personal experiences as a colonized Jew to construct a genealogy of European racist-imperial discourse * * * His * * * discussion * * * identified four related strategies by which European-derived cultures sanctioned and upheld their exercise of colonial power over non-European races. Memmi's essay first suggested the following definition of racism within the European-derived imperial context:

> Racism is the generalized and final assigning of values to real or imaginary differences, to the accuser's benefit and at his victim's expense, in order to justify the former's own privileges or aggression.

His "analysis of the racist attitude" revealed the following "essential" elements, or discursive strategies, of European-derived racist-imperial discourse.

1. Stressing *the real or imaginary differences* between the racist and his victim.

2. *Assigning values* to these differences, to the advantage of the racist and the detriment of his victim.

3. Trying to make them *absolutes* by *generalizing* from them and claiming that they are final.

4. *Justifying* any present or possible *aggression* or *privilege.* * * *

The strategy of stressing differences between European "civilization" and the New World savage in order to intensify the separation by which the Indian was placed outside white society recurs throughout the seventeenth and eighteenth century texts discussing tribalism's deficiency and unassimilability. [John] Locke's use of the American Indian as his primary philosophical strawman in illustrating his argument on possessive individualism and natural rights to private property is but the most famous use of the Indian's difference in the narrative tradition on tribalism's incompatibility with the norms and values of a superior civilization. And for the advocates of Removal who appropriated the tradition's principal themes of the Indian's inferior culture, habits and usages of land to sustain their arguments for exclusion of tribalism from the eastern United States, the savage's normative difference was repeatedly emphasized as evidence of the Indian's incompatibility with white values. * * *

The assigning of negative values to tribalism's difference with white society has been a persistently deployed strategy in the narrative tradition of tribalism's deficiency and unassimilability since the invasion of America by Englishmen. In the biblically infused discourse of the New England Puritans, and in the arguments made by the promoters of the Virginia Company's New World colonization venture, the Indian's divergent culture, norms and particularly land use practices were consistently devalued in relation to those of a civilized race of cultivators. * * *

Memmi's third postulated strategy of a racist discourse generalizes about the differences between the racist and his victim, and asserts those differences as final. "So the discriminatory process enters the stage of generalization, 'totalization.' One thing leads to another until *all of the victim's personality* is characterized by the difference, and *all of the members* of his social group are targets for the accusation." The narrative tradition of tribalism's deficiency and unassimilability illustrates the efficacy of this totalizing strategy. In the post-revolutionary war Indian policy discourses of John Knox and Abraham Lincoln, for example, all tribal Indians were assumed to suffer from the defects of tribalism, although there were many types of tribes, and all tribal Indians, because of their normative differences, were unassimilable and doomed to extinction in the face of white civilization.

In the case of the Removal era discourse of opposition to tribal sovereignty, the thematic device of totalization was a particularly potent discursive weapon. Removal was most strongly argued as necessary for the salvation of the Five Civilized Tribes, an oxymoron if there ever was one in European-derived racist discourse. As President John Quincy Adams' final message to Congress in 1828 admitted, the southern tribes had learned "the arts of civilization" and "the doctrines of Christianity." But to Adams, a "remedy" was still mandated that might "do justice to those unfortunate children of nature," while at the same time recognize the superior rights of white society to the lands they claimed. So long as the southern Indians remained as tribal communities, their difference could never be assimilated within white "civilization." * * *

According to Memmi, the final essential element of European-derived racist and imperial discourse relies on the mythology of the deficient, dehumanized victim to justify and explain the racist's own privileges and aggression. Memmi's pointed exposition of this strategy suggests the close relationship between white society's historical and continuing repression of tribalism's devalued difference and the thousand-year-old legacy of European racism and imperialism. He explains:

> Whatever is different or foreign can be felt as a disturbing factor, hence a source of scandal. The attempt to wipe it out follows naturally. This is a primitive, virtually animal reaction, but it certainly goes deeper than we care to admit.... However that may

be, the mechanism remains the same. By an accurate or falsified characterization of the victim, the accuser attempts to explain and to *justify* his attitude and his behavior toward him.

It was the tribal Indian's strange and disturbing difference that, according to the narrative tradition of tribalism's inferiority, justified the English colonists' privilege of dispossessing the Indian of the New World. It was this same devalued difference that justified early nineteenth century white society's removal of a race of people long-doomed as an obstacle on civilization's intended path.

Today, the white man's courts, his executive branch and his elected legislators increasingly rely on law and legal arguments in their public discourses on Indian policy to justify the imposition of constraints on contemporary tribalism. Disturbingly, as white society finds itself confronting a resurgent discourse of tribal sovereignty, and as its intercourse with once remote Indian Nations in the West grows more frequent, it increasingly draws upon themes of tribalism's supposed deficiency and unassimilability to sustain its privileges as "rightful judge" in the Indian's Country. These privileges, sustained by legal argument, are unashamedly declaimed in public discourses which assume white society's superior right to dictate the implied limitations on tribal sovereignty, the philosophy that ought to govern tribal economic development initiatives, and the procedural and substantive norms that ought to be enforced in tribal courts. These contemporary discourses of opposition to tribal self-determining autonomy, which draw so heavily on familiar themes of tribalism's deficiency and unassimilability, appear to be clearly situated within the same narrative tradition that once explained white society's privilege to colonize the Indian's America and to remove the Indian from the eastern United States.

Notes and Questions

1. How does Memmi's account of racism, summarized by Williams, differ from Kovel's? Are these writers explaining the same phenomena?

2. Public debates about racism often focus on discrimination against minority citizens. To what extent is racism also implicated in the question of who may become a citizen in the first place? Consider the following excerpt.

ROBERT S. CHANG & KEITH AOKI

Centering the Immigrant in the Inter/National Imagination
85 Calif. L. Rev. 1395, 1400–03, 1408, 1414 (1997); 10 La Raza L.J. 309 (1998).*

* * * Fear of immigration, often discussed in generalized terms, is colored so that only certain immigrant bodies excite fear. In the midst of cries to limit legal immigration, the Immigration Act of 1990 included legislation to encourage immigration from northwestern European countries such as Ireland. In the midst of cries to limit illegal immigration, the figure of the Mexican border-crosser or of the Chinese boat person makes the evening news, whereas the fact that Italians constitute the largest group of undocumented immigrants in New York is obscured.

(After the Italians, the most numerous groups of undocumented immigrants in New York come from Ecuador, Poland, Ireland, and Russia.) These examples show how the "problem" of legal and illegal immigration is colored in the national imagination: fear over immigration is not articulated solely around foreignness per se; it includes a strong racial dimension. * * *

Etienne Balibar, writing in the European context, describes the new racism, centered around the category of immigration, as:

> a racism of the era of "decolonization," of the reversal of population movements between the old colonies and the old metropolises, and the division of humanity within a single political space.... It is a racism whose dominant theme is not biological heredity but the insurmountability of cultural differences, a racism which, at first sight, does not postulate the superiority of certain groups or peoples in relation to others but "only" the harmfulness of abolishing frontiers, the incompatibility of life-styles and traditions * * *.[19]

In the United States, this differentialist racism might be termed nativistic racism. Nativistic racism * * * signifies that both nativism and racism are mutually constitutive of the other and operate in tandem to preserve a specific conception of the nation.

The nativist movements directed against immigrants from Southern and Eastern Europe, immigrants who were ostensibly White, reflect the constitutive relationship between nativism and racism. * * * [N]ativism against those groups did not gain real currency until scientific racism provided a language that allowed them to become targets of nativistic racism. Southern and Eastern European immigrants were represented as racially other to "White" Americans and could therefore be discriminated against. To combat this discrimination, these immigrants engaged in an identity politics in which they claimed a White identity. This eventually proved to be a successful strategy—by claiming a White identity, they could become "American" and escape the animus of nativistic racism.

Blacks, already present in the geographic space of the United States, posed a different problem. Ironically, the granting of freedom and formal national membership to Blacks provided the predicate for a new form of

---

19. Etienne Balibar, *Is There a "Neo-Racism"?*, in *Race, Nation, Class: Ambiguous Identities* 17, 21 (Etienne Balibar & Immanuel Wallerstein eds. & Chris Turner trans. 1991). This "differentialist racism" is precisely the basis of pluralism as articulated in the United States in the first quarter of this century. Compare Balibar's words with those of Lothrop Stoddard, who wrote in the early part of this century:

No theoretical questions of "superiority" or "inferiority" need be raised. * * * The really important point is that even though America (abstractly considered) may not be nearly as good as we think it is, nevertheless it is ours. * * * That is the meat of the matter, and when we

discuss immigration we had better stop theorizing about superiors and inferiors and get down to the bedrock of difference.

Lothrop Stoddard, *Re-Forging America: The Story of our Nationhood* 103 (1927), quoted in Walter Benn Michaels, *Our America: Nativism, Modernism, and Pluralism* 65 (1995). We see, then, the dark side of pluralism, which entails that "the commitment to difference itself represents a theoretical intensification rather than diminution of racism, an intensification that has nothing to do with feelings of tolerance or intolerance toward other races and everything to do with the conceptual apparatus of pluralist racism." Michaels, *supra*, at 65.

racial nationalism, the ideology underwriting "the identification of American with White (and the colonization or, failing that, segregation of Blacks)." The demise of the master/slave relationship and the formal ban against racial discrimination necessitated new technologies of racism to preserve White privilege. The Supreme Court provided a new technology in *Plessy v. Ferguson*, setting forth the "separate but equal" doctrine that marked

> a new development in racial thinking * * * [that] affirmed racial distinction as such; it affirmed, that is, racial distinction independent of any other legal consideration so that the relation between black and white was radically distinguished from the relation between master and slave. Slaves, in principle, could become free; blacks could never become white.

Racial nationalism, or "the identification of American with White," required that Blacks never become American. The doctrine of "separate but equal" enabled the economic disempowerment, political disfranchisement, and physical terrorization of Blacks, preserving the national community as White.

From these examples, we see that nativistic racism and racial nationalism helped to construct Black and White as racial and national formations. In a similar fashion, nativistic racism and racial nationalism have helped to construct Asian American and Latina/o as racial and national formations. * * *

The logic of the new world order requires that conquest be resisted. Our borders must be protected from the unlawful encroachment of certain foreigners and their cultures. This is to be accomplished through a renewed policing of national and institutional boundaries through immigration restrictions, affirmative action rollbacks, curriculum control, and welfare reform. Undocumented and legal immigrants, including naturalized citizens, have become the targets of recent political attacks. The new world order is accompanied by a new local order where membership in the national community is being constricted.

This creates a special problem for those of us who are perceived as foreign, because foreignness is used as a proxy for exclusion from the national community, such that our demands for justice and fair treatment may be ignored. We hear the response, "if you don't like it here, go back where you came from." But many of us do not have a place to which to return. For many, that place exists only as an "imaginary homeland."

This sense of in-between-ness, of being not quite part of the (imagined) national community and yet not having a homeland, is a strong component of Asian–American and Latina/o identities. * * *

Measures such as Proposition 187 target illegal immigrants, who are presented as the problem. They take jobs away from those who belong here. They use public services so that there is less for everyone else. Blaming illegal immigrants slides quickly into blaming all immigrants. The Federal Welfare Reform Act of 1996 allows states to cut off aid to even legal immigrants. Although these measures focus on immigration and citizenship status, problems arise, because that status is not evident from an individual's features. Foreign-ness then becomes a proxy for questionable immigration status. Foreign-ness triggers further scrutiny.

This presents a special problem for Asian Americans and Latina/os. Because of the construction of the national community as White and Black, Asian Americans and Latina/os are discursively produced as foreign. Foreign-ness is inscribed upon our bodies in such a way that Asian Americans and Latina/os carry a figurative border with us. This figurative border, in addition to confirming the belonging-ness of the "real" Americans, marks Asian Americans and Latina/os as targets of nativistic racism. It renders us suspect, subject to the violence of heightened scrutiny at the border, in the workplace, in hospitals, and elsewhere.

Notes and Questions

1. Asian Americans have been present in the United States since at least the 1850s, and Mexican Americans living in the southwestern states were granted federal citizenship by the 1848 Treaty of Guadalupe Hidalgo. Why are these groups still described as "foreigners"? See Natsu Taylor Saito, *Model Minority, Yellow Peril: Functions of "Foreignness" in the Construction of Asian American Legal Identity*, 4 Asian L.J. 71 (1997). Why aren't immigrants from England, Russia, and Ireland described in the same way? Are African Americans treated as foreigners?

2. Does "nativistic racism" operate in the fashion Joel Kovel describes? Does it operate in the fashion Albert Memmi describes? Are these writers describing the same or different phenomena?

3. Can you synthesize the preceding materials into a comprehensive definition of racism? Consider the definitions in these international documents:

> Article 2. Racism includes racist ideologies, prejudiced attitudes, discriminatory behaviour, structural arrangements and institutionalized practices resulting in racial inequality as well as the fallacious notion that discriminatory relations between groups are morally and scientifically justifiable; it is reflected in discriminatory provisions in legislation or regulations and discriminatory practices as well as in anti-social beliefs and acts; it hinders the development of its victims, perverts those who practise it, divides nations internally, impedes international co-operation and gives rise to political tensions between peoples; it is contrary to the fundamental principles of international law and, consequently, seriously disturbs international peace and security.

Declaration on Race and Racial Prejudice, UNESCO Doc. 20C/3/1.1/2 (Nov. 27, 1978).

> [Racial discrimination is] any distinction, exclusion, restriction or preference based on race, color, descent, or national or ethnic origin which has the purpose or effect of nullifying or impairing the recognition, enjoyment or exercise, on an equal footing, of human rights and fundamental freedoms in the political, economic, social, cultural or any other field of public life.

International Convention on the Elimination of All Forms of Racial Discrimination, opened for signature Mar. 7, 1966, 660 UNTS 195.

Are these definitions overbroad? Are they incomplete? Are they coherent without a definition of terms like "race," "color," "descent," or "national or ethnic origin"?

4.   The race theorist Robert Miles argues that the definition of racism has been wrongly "inflated" to include "all actions and processes (whatever their origin and motivation) which result in one group being placed or retained in a subordinate position by another." Robert Miles, *Racism* 52 (1989). The result is that racism is a charge easily made but difficult to substantiate. Do you agree?

5.   Can individuals or groups be "racist" if they lack the power to "nullify or impair the recognition, enjoyment or exercise * * * of human rights and fundamental freedoms"? If not, does this mean that people of color cannot be racist? Consider this argument:

> There is no black racism because there is no centuries-old system of racialized subordination and discrimination designed by African Americans to exclude white Americans from full participation in the rights, privileges, and benefits of this society. * * * While there are black Americans with antiwhite prejudices, and there are instances of blacks discriminating against whites, these examples are not central to the core operations of U.S. society and are not part of an entrenched structure of institutionalized racism that can be found in every nook and cranny of this country.

Joe R. Feagin & Hernán Vera, *White Racism* ix-x (1995).

Compare this statement:

> We have little patience with the argument that racism is solely a white problem, or even a "white disease." The idea that non-whites cannot act in a racist manner, since they do not possess "power," is another variant of this formulation.
>
> For many years now, racism has operated in a more complex fashion than this, sometimes taking such forms as self-hatred or self-aggrandizement at the expense of more vulnerable members of racially subordinate groups. Whites can at times be the victims of racism—by other whites or non-whites—as is the case with anti-Jewish and anti-Arab prejudice. Furthermore * * * it is difficult to contend that racially defined minorities have attained no power or influence, especially in recent years.

Michael Omi & Howard Winant, *Racial Formation in the United States* at 73.

Suppose a black personnel director excludes Latinos/as from managerial jobs, or vice versa. Should this conduct be described as "racism"?

6.   How does individual racism operate? Kovel's framework relies on Freudian psychology. More recently, theorists of racism have turned to the new "cognitive" psychology to understand how individuals incorporate and act upon racist beliefs and perceptions. Consider the following excerpt.

LINDA HAMILTON KRIEGER

The Content of Our Categories: A Cognitive Bias Approach
to Discrimination and Equal Employment Opportunity
47 Stan. L. Rev. 1161, 1168–1170, 1175–77, 1187–88, 1198, 1200–02 (1995).*

Section 703 of Title VII [of the Civil Rights Act of 1964] prohibits employers from failing or refusing to hire, or from discharging or otherwise discriminating against any individual because of his or her race, color, religion, sex, or national origin. It would be reasonable to interpret this language as simply requiring proof of causation without proof of intent. In other words, a Title VII claimant would need only establish that his or her protected status "made a difference" or "played a role" in a challenged employment decision.

This is not, however, how section 703 has been construed. Under existing law, the disparate treatment plaintiff, whether proceeding under Title VII or under 42 U.S.C.A. sections 1981 or 1983, must prove not only that she was treated differently, but that such treatment was caused by purposeful or intentional discrimination. Particularly in the context of race and national origin, discrimination is represented as resulting from the decisionmaker's discriminatory animus towards members of the plaintiff's racial or ethnic group. This stands in marked contrast to the law's construction of age discrimination. Consider the following language, which originated in the Seventh Circuit and was subsequently adopted by many other courts:

> Unlike race discrimination, age discrimination may simply arise from an unconscious application of stereotyped notions of ability rather than from a deliberate desire to remove older employees from the workforce: "Age discrimination is not the same as the insidious discrimination based on race or creed prejudices and bigotry. Those discriminations result in nonemployment because of feelings about a person entirely unrelated to his ability to do a job. This is hardly a problem for the older jobseeker. Discrimination arises for him because of assumptions that are made about the effects of age on performance."

It is hard to understand why a court would assume that race discrimination could not, as easily as age discrimination, result from the unconscious application of stereotyped notions of ability or other characteristics. It is also difficult to understand why a court would assume that race discrimination results exclusively from a deliberate desire to exclude members of a particular racial group from the workforce. Yet, in equating the causation requirement of section 703 with discriminatory intent, courts have constructed disparate treatment theory on these two dubious assumptions.

This is not to say that one cannot find language in disparate treatment cases acknowledging that race, sex, or national origin discrimination can be subtle or even unconscious. But one can literally count on one hand the number of published Title VII decisions in which, after acknowledging the existence of unconscious bias, the court rules for a race or national origin discrimination plaintiff or reverses a trial court ruling for the defendant. Many more courts, after acknowledging the existence in society generally of subtle or unconscious forms of bias, rule against the disparate treatment plaintiff on the grounds that she has failed to prove the existence of such bias in her case. * * *

During the late 1930s through the early 1950s, research and theoretical work on prejudice centered primarily around the question of intrapsychic etiology. The problem was straightforward: If prejudice were irrational and unjustifiable, as the academy had collectively come to believe, how could its geographical and temporal ubiquity be explained? Psychodynamic theory provided a ready explanation: Prejudice is a defense mechanism. It subconsciously diverts inner conflicts, needs, and externally induced frustrations onto less threatening external targets. The universality of these intrapsychic phenomena explained the temporal and geographical ubiquity of prejudice.

After World War II, the theoretical paradigm shifted somewhat. While prejudice was still seen as psychodynamically based, its origins were no longer sought in universal psychodynamic processes. Rather, prejudice was seen as stemming from a particular pathological personality structure. Thus the problem confronting students of intergroup relations became identifying the prejudice-prone personality—the bigot. Primary symptoms of this pathological personality structure included "stereotypy," the tendency toward "either-or," categorical thinking, and hostility towards racial or ethnic "outgroups."

By 1954, when Gordon Allport wrote his now classic work, *The Nature of Prejudice*, a mind-dazzling number of definitions of prejudice had been proposed. Among them all, there existed at least two points of agreement: first, that prejudice is a negative orientation, and second, that prejudice is an "attitude." * * *

* * * Seen in this way, prejudice, an attitude, causes discrimination, a behavior. Mediating between the two is conscious behavioral intention. Discrimination, in other words, is the intentional, behavioral manifestation of prejudice.

The parallels between these psychological models of discrimination and current disparate treatment jurisprudence are apparent. Discrimination—at least in race and national origin contexts—is construed as resulting from hostile animus towards and accompanying negative beliefs about an individual because of his or her membership in a particular group. Mediating between prejudice and discrimination is the "discriminatory motive," which is seen in both the psychology and race/national origin discrimination jurisprudence as a conscious behavioral intention to create social distance by denying outgroup members certain benefits and opportunities.

[Eds. In contrast to this view, Krieger introduces the "social cognition" approach, which relies on more recent psychological research.] * * * The social cognition approach to discrimination comprises three claims relevant to our present inquiry. The first is that stereotyping

* * * is nothing special. It is simply a form of categorization, similar in structure and function to the categorization of natural objects. According to this view, stereotypes, like other categorical structures, are cognitive mechanisms that all people, not just "prejudiced" ones, use to simplify the task of perceiving, processing, and retaining information about people in memory. They are central, and indeed essential to normal cognitive functioning.

The second claim posited in social cognition theory is that, once in place, stereotypes bias intergroup judgment and decisionmaking. According to this view, stereotypes operate as "person prototypes" or "social schemas." As such, they function as implicit theories, biasing in predictable ways the perception, interpretation, encoding, retention, and recall of information about other people. These biases are cognitive rather than motivational. They operate absent intent to favor or disfavor members of a particular social group. And, perhaps most significant for present purposes, they bias a decisionmaker's judgment long before the "moment of decision," as a decisionmaker attends to relevant data and interprets, encodes, stores, and retrieves it from memory. These biases "sneak up on" the decisionmaker, distorting bit by bit the data upon which his decision is eventually based.

The third claim follows from the second. Stereotypes, when they function as implicit prototypes or schemas, operate beyond the reach of decisionmaker self-awareness. Empirical evidence indicates that people's access to their own cognitive processes is in fact poor. Accordingly, cognitive bias may well be both unintentional and unconscious. * * *

Stereotypic expectancies may arise from one's own experiences with members of other social groups. Alternatively, * * * they may be absorbed in much the same way as folklore is learned, through the vicarious experiences of stories, television shows, movies, newspaper reports, and so forth. But wherever they come from, stereotypes can be expected to bias our subjective perception of the covariation between group membership and traits stereotypically associated with that group. We do not ignore evidence and choose to act instead on the stereotype. Rather, the stereotype, acting as an associative construct, biases the way we see the evidence. We recall, through the same cognitive processes that result in other forms of illusory correlation, stereotype-confirming instances as having occurred more frequently than they actually did. * * *

Consider the following scenario. A twenty-five-year-old, 5–foot, 6–inch woman with a 2–year degree in paralegal studies enters the police academy in a major urban area. One of her classmates is a twenty-five-year-old 6–foot male with a 2–year college degree in physical education. Their instructors, who must evaluate them and eventually decide whether they will become part of the police force, ask as they meet these two new cadets, "Is it a police officer?" and "How will it perform as a police officer?" To answer these initial questions using normative rules of inference would be an elaborate process indeed. But whatever those normative rules might prescribe, the training officers are not likely to follow them. Rather, they are likely to form an initial impression through the use of a cognitive shortcut which psychologists Daniel

Kahneman and Amos Tversky call the "representativeness heuristic." According to Kahneman and Tversky, a person attempting to estimate the likelihood that a person or an object falls into a particular category or class matches salient attributes of the stimulus object (in our case, the cadet) with equally salient attributes characterizing the viewer's schema or prototype of the category in question ("police officer"). If these two sets of salient attributes match, the person judges the object likely to be a member of the category or class. If these sets do not match, the person judges the object unlikely to be a member of the category or class.

Thus, the specific content of the training officer's schema "police officer" can powerfully influence whether the officer initially perceives each of our two cadets as a good candidate for the job. If the most salient features in the training officer's schema for "police officer" include attributes such as "dominating," "physically imposing," or "authoritarian," or if he pictures a male as the prototypical police officer, he may less readily categorize the female cadet as "police officer material." If, instead, the training officer's schema for a police officer includes attributes such as "calms people down in tense situations," "is skilled at interviewing witnesses and writing reports," or "can understand legal rules and apply them in novel situations," he may judge the female cadet, with her degree in paralegal studies and her less intimidating physical aspect, more favorably in this initial implicit assessment. In short, the initial categorization of a person or event is influenced by schematic expectancies. In forming our initial impressions, we judge other people by the content of our categories. * * *

* * * [P]eople categorize objects in their environment in a particular way because it proves useful in understanding their environment and predicting future events. It would be difficult to argue credibly that racial, ethnic, or gender distinctions have no utility in understanding American society or negotiating experience within it. The antidiscrimination laws themselves make gender, racial, and ethnic distinctions salient. The American history of slavery, race-based immigration restrictions, Jim Crow laws, and persistent segregation in housing, schools, and economic status all further serve to make race salient. Indeed, a fear that one might be racist or sexist, or a desire not to be perceived as such, will make race and gender salient, even highly charged. As a theoretical matter, the notion that racial, ethnic, or gender distinctions could be ignored in the priming of schematic expectancies is, at best, implausible. As an empirical matter, it is simply insupportable. Because gender, ethnic, and racial distinctions are often perceptually apparent, and because these categories are made salient by our social and cultural context, we can expect race, ethnic, and gender-based schemas to be implicated in the processing of information about other people. Once activated, the content of a schema will profoundly affect how we interpret a person's subsequent behavior, what about that behavior we remember, and how we use the behavior in judging the person later.

Notes and Questions

1. Social psychology research also suggests that members of groups that are subject to negative stereotypes perform less well in stressful

situations when they suspect they will be judged in terms of the stereotype. For example, Claude Steele of Stanford University and Joshua Aronson of the University of Texas have conducted several studies that reveal what they call "stereotype threat." Their experiments showed that African–American Stanford undergraduates taking a pencil and paper test, when made aware that the test diagnosed "intellectual ability," showed defensiveness about racial stereotypes, showed symptoms of anxiety, and actually performed less well on the test than in the absence of such "racial priming." See Claude M. Steele & Joshua Aronson, *Stereotype Threat and the Intellectual Test Performance of African–Americans*, 69 J. Pers. & Soc. Psych. 797 (1995). What are the implications of these findings for antidiscrimination law and policy?

2. If stereotyping operates unconsciously, is there any hope that racist attitudes and behavior can be altered? Some researchers believe that conscious efforts to override these cognitive processes can result in less stereotyping. See, *e.g.*, Jody David Armour, *Negrophobia and Reasonable Racism: The Hidden Costs of Being Black in America* (1997).

To control a bad habit, a person first must recall it consciously, and then intentionally inhibit it as he or she responds in ways consistent with his or her consciously endorsed beliefs and attitudes. Are there ways to legally enforce this practice? Should it be legally enforced? See Barbara Flagg, *Was Blind But Now I See: White Race Consciousness and the Law* (1998).

3. The Equal Protection Clause of the Fourteenth Amendment, like the disparate treatment theory of Title VII, has been interpreted by the courts as protecting individuals only against conscious, intentional racism. See *Personnel Administrator of Massachusetts et al. v. Feeney*, 442 U.S. 256 (1979) ("Discriminatory purpose," * * * implies more than intent as volition or intent as awareness of consequences. It implies that the decisionmaker * * * selected or reaffirmed a particular course of action at least in part "because of," not merely "in spite of," its adverse effects upon an identifiable group."). What is the justification for this rule? See Chapter 7.

4. Ample evidence suggests that racial stereotypes are used in courtroom advocacy. See, *e.g.*, Sheri Lynn Johnson, *Racial Imagery in Criminal Cases,* 67 Tul. L. Rev. 1739 (1993). Should attorneys have a duty to avoid triggering racial stereotypes? What if they are defense attorneys in a criminal case, who have a special duty of "zealous advocacy" to their clients? See Anthony V. Alfieri, *Defending Racial Violence,* 95 Colum. L. Rev. 1301 (1995); see also Anthony V. Alfieri, *Race Trials,* 76 Tex. L. Rev. 1293 (1998). For more readings on race in the criminal courtroom, see Chapter 13, § 2B.

If a lawyer encourages jury members to recall their prejudices but hold them in check, is the lawyer "playing the race card?" Is such behavior on the part of the lawyer permissible under the rules of professional responsibility? See Alfieri, *id*.

CHARLES R. LAWRENCE III
The Id, the Ego, and Equal Protection: Reckoning with Unconscious Racism
39 Stan. L. Rev. 317, 317–321, 322–24 (1987).*

It is 1948. I am sitting in a kindergarten classroom at the Dalton School, a fashionable and progressive New York City private school. My parents, both products of a segregated Mississippi school system, have come to New York to attend graduate and professional school. They have enrolled me and my sisters here at Dalton to avoid sending us to the public school in our neighborhood where the vast majority of the students are black and poor. They want us to escape the ravages of segregation, New York style.

It is circle time in the five-year old group, and the teacher is reading us a book. As she reads, she passes the book around the circle so that each of us can see the illustrations. The book's title is *Little Black Sambo*. Looking back, I remember only one part of the story, one illustration: Little Black Sambo is running around a stack of pancakes with a tiger chasing him. He is very black and has a minstrel's white mouth. His hair is tied up in many pigtails, each pigtail tied with a different color ribbon. I have seen the picture before the book reaches my place in the circle. I have heard the teacher read the "comical" text describing Sambo's plight and have heard the laughter of my classmates. There is a knot in the pit of my stomach. I feel panic and shame. I do not have the words to articulate my feelings—words like "stereotype" and "stigma" that might help cathart the shame and place it outside of me where it began. But I am slowly realizing that, as the only black child in the circle, I have some kinship with the tragic and ugly hero of this story—that my classmates are laughing at me as well as at him. I wish I could laugh along with my friends. I wish I could disappear.

I am in a vacant lot next to my house with black friends from the neighborhood. We are listening to *Amos and Andy* on a small radio and laughing uproariously. My father comes out and turns off the radio. He reminds me that he disapproves of this show that pokes fun at Negroes. I feel bad—less from my father's reprimand than from a sense that I have betrayed him and myself, that I have joined my classmates in laughing at us.

I am certain that my kindergarten teacher was not intentionally racist in choosing *Little Black Sambo*. I knew even then, from a child's intuitive sense, that she was a good, well-meaning person. A less benign combination of racial mockery and profit motivated the white men who produced the radio show and played the roles of Amos and Andy. But we who had joined their conspiracy by our laughter had not intended to demean our race.

A dozen years later I am a student at Haverford College. Again, I am a token black presence in a white world. A companion whose face and name I can't remember seeks to compliment me by saying, "I don't think of you as a Negro." I understand his benign intention and accept the compliment. But the knot is in my stomach again. Once again, I have betrayed myself.

This happened to me more than a few times. Each time my interlocutor was a good, liberal, white person who intended to express feelings of shared humanity. I did not yet understand the racist implications of the way in which the feelings were conceptualized. I am certain that my white friends did not either. We had not yet grasped the compliment's underlying premise: To be thought of as a Negro is to be thought of as less than human. We were all victims of our culture's racism. We had all grown up on *Little Black Sambo* and *Amos and Andy*.

Another ten years pass. I am thirty-three. My daughter, Maia, is three. I greet a pink-faced, four-year old boy on the steps of her nursery school. He proudly presents me with a book he has brought for his teacher to read to the class. "It's my favorite," he says. The book is a new edition of *Little Black Sambo*.

This article reconsiders the doctrine of discriminatory purpose that was established by the 1976 decision, *Washington v. Davis*. This now well-established doctrine requires plaintiffs challenging the constitutionality of a facially neutral law to prove a racially discriminatory purpose on the part of those responsible for the law's enactment or administration.

Davis has spawned a considerable body of literature treating its merits and failings. Minorities and civil rights advocates have been virtually unanimous in condemning *Davis* and its progeny. They have been joined by a significant number of constitutional scholars who have been equally disapproving, if more restrained, in assessing its damage to the cause of equal opportunity. These critics advance two principal arguments. The first is that a motive-centered doctrine of racial discrimination places a very heavy, and often impossible, burden of persuasion on the wrong side of the dispute. Improper motives are easy to hide. And because behavior results from the interaction of a multitude of motives, governmental officials will always be able to argue that racially neutral considerations prompted their actions. Moreover, where several decisionmakers are involved, proof of racially discriminatory motivation is even more difficult.

The second objection to the *Davis* doctrine is more fundamental. It argues that the injury of racial inequality exists irrespective of the decisionmakers' motives. Does the black child in a segregated school experience less stigma and humiliation because the local school board did not consciously set out to harm her? Are blacks less prisoners of the ghetto because the decision that excludes them from an all-white neighborhood was made with property values and not race in mind? Those who make this second objection reason that the "facts of racial inequality are the real problem." They urge that racially disproportionate harm should trigger heightened judicial scrutiny without consideration of motive.

Supporters of the intent requirement are equally adamant in asserting the doctrine's propriety. They echo the four main arguments that the Court itself set forth in *Davis*: (1) A standard that would subject all governmental action with a racially disproportionate impact to strict judicial scrutiny would cost too much; such a standard, the Court argues, would substantially limit legitimate legislative decisionmaking and would endanger the validity of a "whole range of [existing] tax, welfare, public service, regulatory and licensing statutes"; (2) a disproportionate impact standard would make innocent people bear the costs of remedying a harm in which they played no part; (3) an impact test would be inconsistent with equal protection values, because the judicial decision-maker would have to explicitly consider race; and (4) it would be inappropriate for the judiciary to choose to remedy the racially dispro-portionate impact of otherwise neutral governmental actions at the expense of other legitimate social interests.

* * * Traditional notions of intent do not reflect the fact that decisions about racial matters are influenced in large part by factors that can be characterized as neither intentional—in the sense that certain outcomes are self-consciously sought—nor unintentional—in the sense that the outcomes are random, fortuitous, and uninfluenced by the decisionmaker's beliefs, desires, and wishes.

Americans share a common historical and cultural heritage in which racism has played and still plays a dominant role. Because of this shared experience, we also inevitably share many ideas, attitudes, and beliefs that attach significance to an individual's race and induce negative feelings and opinions about nonwhites. To the extent that this cultural belief system has influenced all of us, we are all racists. At the same time, most of us are unaware of our racism. We do not recognize the ways in which our cultural experience has influenced our beliefs about race or the occasions on which those beliefs affect our actions. In other words, a large part of the behavior that produces racial discrimination is influenced by unconscious racial motivation.

There are two explanations for the unconscious nature of our racially discriminatory beliefs and ideas. First, Freudian theory states that the human mind defends itself against the discomfort of guilt by denying or refusing to recognize those ideas, wishes, and beliefs that conflict with what the individual has learned is good or right. While our historical experience has made racism an integral part of our culture, our society has more recently embraced an ideal that rejects racism as immoral. When an individual experiences conflict between racist ideas and the societal ethic that condemns those ideas, the mind excludes his racism from consciousness.

Second, the theory of cognitive psychology states that the culture—including, for example, the media and an individual's parents, peers, and authority figures—transmits certain beliefs and preferences. Because these beliefs are so much a part of the culture, they are not experienced as explicit lessons. Instead, they seem part of the individual's rational ordering of her perceptions of the world. The individual is unaware, for example, that the ubiquitous presence of a cultural stereotype has influenced her perception that blacks are lazy or unintelligent. Because racism is so deeply ingrained in our culture, it is likely to be transmitted by tacit understandings: Even if a child is not told that blacks are inferior, he learns that lesson by observing the behavior of others. These tacit understandings, because they have never been articulated, are less likely to be experienced at a conscious level.

* * * [T]his article proposes a new test to trigger judicial recogni-tion of race-based behavior. It posits a connection between unconscious racism and the existence of cultural symbols that have racial meaning. It suggests that the "cultural meaning" of an allegedly racially discriminatory act is the best available analogue for, and evidence of, a collective unconscious that we cannot observe directly. This test would thus evaluate governmental conduct to determine whether it conveys a symbolic message to which the culture attaches racial significance. A finding that the culture thinks of an allegedly discriminatory governmental action in racial terms would also constitute a finding regarding the beliefs and motivations of the governmental actors: The actors are themselves part of the culture and presumably could not have acted without being influenced by racial considerations, even if they are unaware of their racist beliefs. Therefore, the court would apply strict scrutiny.

Notes and Questions

1.   What is Lawrence's understanding of racism? Which of the theories we have read does it resemble most? What does he mean by "a collective unconscious that we cannot observe directly"?

Is the legal test Lawrence proposes workable? What kinds of experts might be called in to testify about whether "the culture thinks of an allegedly discriminatory government action in racial terms"?

2.   For the view that committed confrontation is necessary to cope with the permanence of American racism, see Derrick A. Bell, Jr., *Faces at the Bottom of the Well: The Permanence of Racism* (1992).

3.   For an analysis of pervasive microaggressions suffered by Blacks in daily life as well as in the legal system, see Peggy C. Davis, *Law as Microaggression*, 98 Yale L.J. 1559, 1565 (1989) (describing microaggressions as " 'subtle, stunning, often automatic, and non-verbal exchanges which are 'put downs' of blacks by offenders.' Psychiatrists who have studied black populations view them as 'incessant and cumulative' assaults on black self-esteem.") (citations omitted). Consider the extent to which members of other racialized communities are also subject to microaggressions.

4.   Does racism always entail stereotypes? Consider the readings that follow. Is racism a useful word to describe these problems? If so, how are the mechanisms that produce racism different in these contexts than the mechanisms that produce racial stereotyping?

EVELYN NAKANO GLENN

Cleaning Up/Kept Down: A Historical Perspective
on Racial Inequality in "Women's Work"
43 Stan. L. Rev. 1333, 1335, 1344–1353 (1991).*

* * * A careful reading of the history of Black, Hispanic, and Asian–American women workers reveals a persistent racial division of "women's work." This division of labor has subjected women of color to special forms of exploitation, subordinating them to White women and ensuring that their labor benefits White women and their families. * * *

* * * White middle-class women have entered the labor market in such large numbers that the "double day" has become a universal

phenomenon. Furthermore, women of color have made great gains in the labor market since World War II, with the most dramatic progress coming after the mid–1960s. The struggles of the civil rights movement contributed to growing Black political and economic strength. Ultimately, these efforts led to legislation which barred discrimination and broke down the blatant color barriers that excluded even well-educated people of color from white-collar jobs. Today, Black, Hispanic and Asian–American women work in formerly White female preserves, including clerical and administrative services, retail sales, and the professions. (See Table 2). The exodus of women of color from domestic service signals these changes most dramatically. As recently as 1960, 888,206 Black women, or 36.2 percent of all Black women workers, were private household workers. By 1980, only 233,024, or 5.0 percent of all Black women workers, were similarly employed. Even in the traditional Southwestern cities of El Paso and San Antonio, the percentage of Mexican women employed as domestic workers had fallen to 2.1 percent and 1.6 percent, respectively, by 1980. Most of those remaining in domestic work are older; there are few new recruits, except among recent immigrants. White women continue to shun domestic service, however. In 1980, less than one percent of employed White women worked in private households.

The collapse of color barriers has also been marked in white-collar occupations, which were largely White preserves before World War II. In 1960, less than 9 percent of Black female workers were in clerical and kindred occupations. By 1987, the percent had climbed to 28.0 percent. Comparable data on Hispanic women for 1960 are not available, but by 1989, 38.4 percent of employed Hispanic women worked in clerical, sales and technical positions. By 1987, 14.7 percent of all employed Hispanic women held managerial or professional jobs—a 61.2 percent increase from just four years earlier. Asian–American women made even greater gains during this period. By 1960, for example, 30 percent of Chinese–American women were employed in clerical positions, and by 1970, a greater proportion of Chinese– and Japanese–American women than White women were employed as professionals. Thus, at least at the level of broad occupational categories, women of color were increasingly integrated into all levels.

Table 2

Occupation	Black	Asian & Pacific Islander	Spanish–Origin[a]	White
Managerial	4.7	7.6	4.9	7.8
Professional	11.8	16.2	7.6	14.6
Technical	3.3	4.7	2.1	3.1
Sales	6.1	9.4	9.4	12.0

Occupations of Employed Black, Asian–American, Spanish–Origin, and White Women, Sixteen Years and Over, 1980 (percentages)

Occupation	Black	Asian & Pacific Islander	Spanish–Origin[a]	White
Administrative Support	25.8	26.2	27.5	32.2
Service	29.3	17.3	20.8	16.3
Farm/Forestry	0.5	0.9	1.8	1.0
Craft	2.3	3.6	3.9	2.3
Operatives/Laborers	16.1	14.2	22.0	10.8
Total	100.1[b]	100.1[b]	100.0	100.0

a. Spanish–Origin can be of any race.
b. Due to rounding.

Source: Computed from U.S. Bureau of the Census, *1980 Census of Population, Volume 1, Characteristics of the Population, Chapter C, General Social and Economic Characteristics, Part 1: United States Summary* (Washington, D.C.: U.S. Government Printing Office, 1983) (Tables 145 and 155).

The wage gap between White women and women of color also shrank significantly during this period. Whereas White women earned 34 percent more than Black women just after World War II, by 1990, * * * the wage differential between Black and White women employed full-time year-round was approximately 10 percent. Similarly, by 1990, the gap between Hispanic and White women was approximately 20 percent. Asian–American women gained the most during this period. Currently, Asian–American women earn slightly more than White women. Some commentators have interpreted these trends as signifying that gender, rather than race, is the most significant factor adversely affecting the economic achievement of women of color.

While these gains are dramatic and real, they do not tell the whole story. The impact of postwar economic changes has been complex, with some encouraging signs of decreasing racial and gender divisions accompanying more ominous indications of new forms of inequality. Three trends in particular—new forms of segregation in the women's job market, continuing wage inequity among racial groups, and the recent boom in non-domestic "social reproduction" jobs such as food service—all suggest that White women will continue to benefit from the subordination of women of color.

A. New Forms of Occupational Segregation

The growing similarity in the distribution of White women and women of color among broad occupational categories disguises the continuing segregation within these categories. Broad groupings, such as "administrative support," comprise jobs varying widely in skill, discretion, authority, and technological interaction. Many of the specific jobs within each grouping remain segregated. For example, while Blacks make up 11.4 percent of those in "administrative support" positions, they are not evenly distributed across specialties within that grouping: Black women comprise 14 percent of file clerks, 19.5 percent of data entry keyers, and 15.1 percent of typists, but only 7.67 percent of secretaries, 8.1 percent of receptionists, and 6.2 percent of bookkeepers. Hispanic women are also overrepresented as file clerks, data-entry keyers, and typists and are underrepresented among secretaries and bookkeepers. In short, a disproportionately large number of women of color work in more routine back-room jobs and in those being "de-skilled" by automation or phased out by technological advances. At the same time, women of color are underrepresented in jobs which allow greater discretion, require client contact, or involve face-to-face interaction with management.

Furthermore, even within a given job, women of color do not necessarily work in the same settings as White women because of sectoral segregation. For example, professional Black women are more likely to be employed in government or non-profit agencies that provide services to the Black community. They remain underrepresented in corporate America. Similarly, Natalie Sokoloff has found that the advances of Black women have not been distributed equally among the three groups of professions: those that are traditionally male-dominated, such as medicine; those that are mixed-sex, such as pharmacy; and those that are female-dominated, such as social work. She found that Black women have increased their representation mostly in the latter two categories, which tend to be the lowest paid, least autonomous, and which are more likely to be located in the public sector. Asian–American women workers also tend to be overrepresented in the government sector. Thus, even though Asian–Americans have apparently "made it" in the professions, they continue to be concentrated in less prestigious settings. For example, Asian–American health care professionals tend to be disproportionately employed in state institutions as opposed to private health care facilities. Thus, although minority women appear to have achieved professional integration, they remain segregated within particular specialties and settings.

B. Continuing Wage Inequity

While the wage gap between White women and women of color has narrowed,* * * the earnings advantage of White men, compared to all other groups, still persists. Two other points emerge * * *. First, although women of each race earn less than men of the same race, the relative disadvantage differs from group to group. While White women earn 69.1 percent of what White men earn, Black women earn 86.5 percent of what Black men earn, and Hispanic women earn 85.4 percent of what Hispanic men do. Second, and most striking, is that White women's 1989 median weekly income actually exceeded that of Hispanic men and almost equaled that of Black men. These data belie the cliche that women earn 59 cents for every dollar that men earn. The actual ratio depends upon the racial groups compared.

Hispanic men, Hispanic women, and Black women earn even less than White women * * * Thus, only White men have a reasonable chance of earning a wage sufficient to support a household. So, although it may be true that "all women are one man away from poverty," it is also true that White women are more likely to enjoy a high standard of living by virtue of their more frequent connections, marital and otherwise, to White men. * * *

C. The Commodification of Services

Due to a variety of circumstances—the aging of the American population, the fragmentation of families, the breakdown of extended kin and community ties, and the squeeze on women's time as they moved into the labor market—the post-World War II era has seen the expansion of commodified services to replace the "social reproduction" labor women formerly performed in the home. The fastest-growing occupations in the 1970s and 1980s were service occupations, which include health care, food service, and personal services, and they are projected to be among the fastest growing over the next decade. Health care occupations, in particular, will see tremendous growth through the year 2000, and more food preparation and service jobs (such as waitresses, cooks, and food counter workers) will be created than jobs of any other type. Women are the main labor force in these industries. Within this new realm of "public reproductive labor," we find a clear racial division of labor. Women of color are disproportionately assigned to do the dirty work: as nurses' aides in hospitals, as kitchen workers in restaurants and cafeterias, as maids in hotels, and as cleaners in office buildings. In the category of service occupations, except protective and household, all major minority groups (Spanish-origin, Black, Native American, and Asian and Pacific Islander) were overrepresented as of 1980. All of these groups were more likely to be employed in cleaning and building services than White women. For example, 1.7% of White women were employed in cleaning and building services, compared to 4.2% of Spanish-origin, 6.2% of Blacks, 4.1% of Native American, and 2.8% of Asian Americans. Black and Native–American women were strikingly overrepresented among nursing aides. In these same institutional settings, White women were disproportionately employed as supervisors, professionals, and administrative support staff. This division parallels the earlier division between domestic servants and White housewives. And just as in the household, White women benefit from the "dirty work" performed by women of color. They get to do more skilled, more fulfilling, less demeaning, and less onerous jobs.

As was true of domestic service earlier in this century, the allocation of lower level service occupations follows racial/ethnic caste lines in regions with substantial minority populations. Census data for 1980 show that Black and Latina women were overrepresented among service workers in cities in which they were a significant part of the population. Black women were between one and one-half to two times more likely to be employed in service occupations in northeastern and southern cities than White women. For example, in Atlanta in 1980, 20.9 percent of Black women were employed in service occupations, compared to only 10.5 percent of White women; in Memphis, the figures were 25.9 percent versus 10.2 percent; in New York, 21.5 percent versus 8.9 percent; and in Chicago, 16.4 percent versus 11.6 percent. In Southwestern cities with large Mexican–American populations, Spanish-origin women were much more likely to be service workers than Anglo women. In San Antonio, 21.9 percent of Spanish-origin women were service workers, compared to 15.4 percent of non-Spanish-origin White women; in El Paso, the percentages were 16.9 percent versus 13.5 percent; and in Los Angeles, 14.8 percent versus 11.8 percent. In 1980, Asian and Pacific Islander women accounted for 21.6 percent of service occupation employees in Honolulu, while White, non-Spanish-origin women accounted for only 13.7 percent.

Whether the shift from domestic service to service industry work represents an improvement is debatable. In many ways, minority women are performing the same kinds of unskilled or onerous work they did before, only in a new setting. Service work (again, referring to non-household, non-protective services) occupies a similarly low position in the occupational hierarchy and is, aside from private household work, the lowest paid category of work. In 1986, service workers made up nearly two-thirds of all workers earning less than minimum wage. Because their wages are so low, many service workers moonlight. For example, Timothy Diamond found that nursing aides typically have to hold second jobs to make ends meet. The service sector is largely non-union, and in many cases employers are subcontractors who do not provide any health or retirement benefits. Illness or aging thus exacts a heavier-than-normal toll among these workers.

Still, although the specific tasks performed in institutional service jobs resemble those performed in private domestic jobs, women of color clearly prefer service work in institutional settings to domestic service in White peoples' homes. The subordination is not so personal, and there are clearer contractual limits to tasks and hours. More explicit rules protect workers to some extent, from arbitrary discipline, and the presence of other workers makes it easier to resist unreasonable demands and demeaning treatment.

In many ways the impersonal structure of service work obscures the extent to which service workers's mental and emotional labor is exploited, often to the benefit of White women. Much service work is organized to be hidden from view: behind institutional walls, in kitchens and other back room settings, and during hours when clients and professional staff are gone. Both the work and the people who do it become "invisible."

SHEILA FOSTER

Justice from the Ground Up: Distributive Inequities, Grassroots Resistance, and the Transformative Politics of the Environmental Justice Movement
86 Calif. L.Rev. 775, 793–98 (1998).*

[C]ommentators note that studies charting the racially disparate outcomes [of siting decisions regarding environmentally polluting facilities] fail to compare the demographics of the neighborhoods at the time the facilities were sited with demographics at the time measured by the studies. This failure "leaves open the possibility that [the facilities] were not disparately sited in poor and minority neighborhoods," but that "market dynamics" led people of color and the poor to "come to the nuisance," that is, to move to areas surrounding waste facilities because those neighborhoods offered the cheapest available housing. If this is the case, then such post-siting "market dynamics" would be responsible for the distributive outcomes, not environmental decision-making processes.

Vicki Been, for instance, describes two factors which influence the poor to move to neighborhoods which may be otherwise undesirable to most people. The first factor is the cost of housing; the second is the characteristics of a neighborhood. Noting that the housing market in the United States is "extremely dynamic," Been explains that regardless of whether Locally Undesirable Land Uses (LULUs) were sited fairly originally, it could well be that neighborhoods surrounding LULUs became poorer and thus home to a greater percentage of people of color in the years following the siting. A LULU "may cause those who can afford to move to become dissatisfied and leave the neighborhood," or it "may decrease the value of the neighborhood's property, making the housing more available to lower income households and less attractive to higher income households."

Since the market is the realm of private transactions, where goods, services, and information are exchanged in accordance with the ability to pay, it predictably allocates to the poor the least desirable neighborhoods—including those containing a hazardous waste facility. As Been explains, "[a]s long as the market allows the existing distribution of wealth to allocate goods and services, *it would be surprising indeed if, over the long run, LULUs did not impose a disproportionate burden* upon the poor." It is the market, she concludes, that may ultimately lead the poor to "come to the nuisance," to move to neighborhoods that host LULUs.

Market theories, however, are notoriously incomplete. As others have argued persuasively, markets are social institutions shaped by various levels of state and private control. The historical and present reality of race discrimination inevitably, and not surprisingly, affects individual preferences and mobility in the housing arena. Been is careful not to overlook its influence. As she notes, the existence of a LULU, in addition to attracting lower income residents and deterring higher income households, ensures that "[t]he neighborhood also is likely to become home to more people of color." She acknowledges that the impact of "[r]acial discrimination in the sale and rental of housing relegates people of color (especially African–Americans) to the least desirable neighborhoods, regardless of their income level." Moreover, even after a neighborhood becomes predominantly composed of people of color, Been recognizes that "racial discrimination in the promulgation and enforcement of zoning and environmental protection laws, the provision of municipal services, and the lending practices of banks, may cause neighborhood quality to decline further" and that "[the] additional decline . . . will induce those who can leave the neighborhood—the least poor and those least subject to discrimination—to do so." She concludes that, "[a]s long as the market discriminates on the basis of race, *it would be remarkable if LULUs did not eventually impose a disproportionate burden upon people of color."*

* * * The question underlying environmental justice research is normative. It asks, "What do we mean when we call an outcome racist or evidence of injustice?" The chicken or egg inquiry posed by commentators such as Been is empirical. It asks, "Which came first: the waste facilities or the poor people of color?" Answering the second question does not necessarily answer the first, that is, the normative claim embedded in environmental justice research is not answered simply by a descriptive analysis of forces underlying a particular distributional pattern.

* * * [I]f existing racially discriminatory processes in the housing market, for instance, contribute to the distribution of environmental hazards, then it is entirely appropriate to call such outcomes unjust, and even racist. * * * So long as the distribution of environmental hazards is produced, even in part, by a discriminatory social structure, environmental injustice exists.

Notes and Questions

1. What role does racism play in the phenomena described in the Glenn and Foster articles? Is the tendency for people of color to end up in low-paying service jobs and environmentally polluted neighborhoods the result of racism or simply "market forces"? What is the connection between the two?

2. What role does racism play in the exploitation of undocumented workers, many of whom are from Mexico? Consider the comments of Linda Bosniak:

> [I]n spite of * * * [legal] protections, undocumented entrants suffer serious abuses at the hands of the Immigration and Naturalization Service [INS], as well as the courts. The INS and Border Patrol often resort to extreme and violent tactics to round up suspected border violators. Reports abound of "militaristic sweeps" and "terrorization" at the border and in the interior. At least fourteen farmworkers have drowned while attempting to escape apprehension during INS Border Patrol field operations during the last decade. The INS has also detained children of undocumented persons, conditioning their release on bail on the surrender of their parents to INS agents for interrogation and deportation. Detention conditions for undocumented persons (both children and adults) awaiting hearings or contesting deportation are often abominable. Aliens' rights organizations have filed lawsuits alleging, among other things, that detainees are subject to inhumane treatment, including strip searches, beatings, hours of unprotected exposure to desert sun, lack of medical attention, lack of any reading materials other than the Bible, lack of recreational activities, lack of visitation with family members, and denial of access to counsel. Many new detention centers are located far from urban areas where legal support for immigrants and refugees is more often available.

Linda S. Bosniak, *Exclusion and Membership: The Dual Identity of the Undocumented Worker under United States Law*, 1988 Wis. L. Rev. 955, 974–

76.*

Bosniak notes that undocumented persons have certain legal rights: they may sue in tort and contract; they may own property; and they are protected by certain constitutional provisions, such as the Due Process and Equal Protection Clauses of the Fifth and Fourteenth Amendments. Undocumented persons also have rights to some government benefits and to federal labor protection. However:

> While it is important to recognize the existence of this sphere of protected membership for undocumented aliens, the denial to them of a broad range of other membership rights and their subjection to the state's exclusionary project directly and indirectly nullify many of the protections they formally enjoy. Although undocumented aliens may be persons within the protection of the Due Process and Equal Protection Clauses, courts have permitted the federal and state governments to discriminate against all aliens for some purposes and to distinguish between permanent resident aliens and undocumented aliens for others. * * *

> Finally, even where formal rights exist, the ability of the undocumented to exercise these rights in practice is limited. Undocumented aliens often fear exposing themselves to the exclusionary powers of the state and will often forego the exercise of membership rights in order to avoid such an eventuality. Undocumented immigrants commonly decline to report private or official abuse and are frequently unwilling to pursue civil claims in court or to step forward to receive benefits to which they are entitled. The undocumented are also part of a larger group of Americans whose lack of access to power in the form of money and information severely constrains their ability to obtain the protections and benefits to which they are formally entitled. * * *

> Ironically, the community's unwillingness to extend membership to outsiders within our borders may sometimes serve to undermine the very boundaries it seeks to sustain. To the extent that the undocumented immigrants' lack of complete membership increases their desirability to employers, the demand for their labor increases. Under current conditions, undocumented workers are more, not less, likely to enter this country to meet that demand. * * *

Bosniak *supra* at 983–84, 986–87, 1004.

Is this racism? If so, which theorist we have read best describes its operation?

3. Consider the Glenn, Foster, and Bosniak readings in light of Iris Young's "five faces of oppression." Is Young's framework helpful in examining the relationship between these forms of injustice and racism?

4. In 1994, voters in the state of California passed Proposition 187, which read in part:

> The People of California find and declare as follows:

> That they have suffered and are suffering economic hardship caused by the presence of illegal aliens in this state.

* Copyright © 1988 by the University of Wisconsin Law Review.
Wisconsin. Reprinted by permission of the

That they have suffered and are suffering personal injury and damage caused by the criminal conduct of illegal aliens in this state.

That they have a right to the protection of their government from any person or persons entering this country unlawfully.

Therefore, the People of California declare their intention to provide for cooperation between their agencies of state and local government with the federal government, and to establish a system of required notification by and between such agencies to prevent illegal aliens in the United States from receiving benefits or public services in the State of California.

Proposition 187 made it illegal for undocumented workers to receive any public social services, including health care, except for "emergency medical care as required by federal law." It excluded children who were undocumented from attending public elementary or secondary schools. And, it required hospital and clinic workers and elementary and secondary school officials to report any suspected undocumented children to the INS. See Linda S. Bosniak, *Opposing Prop. 187: Undocumented Immigrants and the National Imagination*, 28 Conn. L. Rev. 555, 556 n.3 (1996); John SW Park, *Race Discourse and Proposition 187*, 2 Mich. J. Race & L. 175 (1996); Kevin R. Johnson, *An Essay on Immigration Politics, Popular Democracy, and California's Proposition 187: The Political Relevance and Legal Irrelevance of Race*, 70 Wash. L.Rev. 629 (1995). Several provisions of Proposition 187 were held unconstitutional in *League of United Latin American Citizens v. Wilson*, 908 F. Supp. 755 (C.D.Cal.1995).

SECTION 2.   DEFINING RACE

CHRISTOPHER A. FORD

Administering Identity: The Determination of "Race" in Race–Conscious Law
82 Calif. L. Rev. 1231, 1232–34, 1239–40, 1257–62 (1994).*

This article attempts to address two closely related questions. How is the law to define the nature and boundaries of the groups utilized in the administration of remedial preferences for persons "on the basis of * * * their membership in a specified group or groups"? How can the law accurately sort individuals into these categories? * * *

The case of *Malone v. Haley*,[3] an unreported single-justice opinion of the Supreme Judicial Court of Massachusetts, illustrates some of these conundrums. Paul and Philip Malone, twin brothers who lived in Milton, Massachusetts, took part in 1975 in a city civil service competition for jobs with the Boston Fire Department. They scored poorly and were not accepted. The twins, who were fair-haired and light-skinned, had identified themselves as White in the 1975 test application. In 1977 they tried again, this time identifying themselves as Black. The Boston Fire Department had by that time become subject to a court-ordered affirmative action program, under which the city maintained separate minority candidate lists for firefighter vacancies. The twins' 1977 test scores of 57 and 69, respectively, would not have qualified them for the job as White

* Copyright © 1994 by the California Law Review. Reprinted by permission.

3. No. 88–339 (Sup. Jud. Ct. Suffolk County, Mass. July 25, 1989).

candidates, but based upon their self-identification as Black they were hired and served on the force for ten years. The Malones' troubles began in 1987 when they sought promotion to lieutenant, and the Fire Commissioner noticed that the twins were classified as being "Black." A hearing officer declared that the Malones were not Black and had therefore falsified their 1977 application and examination materials, in violation of state Personnel Administration Rule 3(4)(c). The state's personnel administrator promptly fired the brothers. Noting that the Department had required only racial "self-identification" in 1977, the Malones appealed, arguing that they should still be considered Black by the Department.

Deferring to the "particular domain of the factfinder who had an opportunity to observe the witnesses and to judge their credibility," Judge Herbert Wilkins of the Supreme Judicial Court for Suffolk County, Massachusetts, followed the hearing officer's three-part test for adjudicating claims to racial identity.

> [T]he Malones might have supported their claim to be Black[:] (1) by visual observation of their features; (2) by appropriate documentary evidence, such as birth certificates, establishing Black ancestry; or (3) by evidence that they or their families hold themselves out to be Black and are considered to be Black in the community.

Neither Malone brother, Wilkins wrote, met any of these three criteria. To begin with, both had "fair skin, fair hair coloring, and Caucasian facial features." The personnel administrator had concluded that "they do not appear to be Black." The birth certificates of the Malone brothers and of their parents also showed the Malone family to have been "reported consistently to be White" for three generations.[12] "Finally, there was no evidence that the Malones identified themselves personally or socially as Blacks," except for the narrow purpose of claiming jobs and promotion in the Fire Department. Judge Wilkins also found substantial evidence that they "did not claim Black status honestly or in good faith," but did so only to take advantage of the Department's minority hiring program. * * *

The Malones' case created a stir in Boston. Fearing an epidemic of false racial claims, one city councilor asked the state attorney general to begin an investigation of the Fire Department. Mayor Raymond Flynn ordered an investigation into the Fire, Police, and School Departments, and by the time Judge Wilkins' opinion came down, eleven firefighters were under investigation on similar grounds. * * *

Assuming that identifying discrimination is unproblematic, what happens once discrimination has been found? Whatever the specific remedies adopted, we still require some coherent understanding of who precisely is to be helped, and why. * * *

---

12. * * * Against this evidence the Malones marshalled only a questionable and inconclusive photograph of a woman they claimed to be Sarah Carroll, their maternal great-grandmother.... [T]here was no reliable means of verifying the identity of the woman in the photograph. The Malones offered only their hearsay testimony that they had been told that this is a photograph of their great-grandmother. Moreover, even if the identity of the woman were accepted, the hearing officer found that the photograph itself was inconclusive on the issue of the race of the woman pictured.

There exist two basic approaches to this classificatory task:

(1) *Self-reported identity*—individuals are asked to assign themselves a racial identity based upon the particular group with which they most closely identify or of which they otherwise feel a part; and

(2) *"Other-ascribed" identity*—individuals are placed into categories according to the perceptions of their racial or ethnic identity held by a designated decision-making third party. An individual's membership in a particular group might thus be determined according either to

> (a) *Member reference*—whether or not members of that group (however defined) consider her to be a fellow member, or

> (b) *Nonmember reference*—whether or not nonmembers of that group consider her to be a member of that group.

It seems to be taken for granted in modern American racial jurisprudence that these categories are coterminous. For gender-based classification, this may be true: one would not, in most cases, expect divergence between someone's self-perceived identity as a male, on the one hand, and the agreement of either men or women about this fact of biological identity, on the other. With respect to racial and ethnic characterizations, however, this cannot so easily be said to be true. Therefore, these classification schemes may produce different results. If racial and ethnic identity is to remain a salient factor in the allocation of social benefits, we must be aware of how various procedural systems may differ; we must be willing to examine the degree to which the policy interests served by each such classification scheme map the contours of sociological identity. The proper procedure for "administering race" is the core dilemma of modern race-conscious law. * * *

[Eds. The author examines the criteria used for determining race in several American legal regimes, including the federal decennial census, the Equal Employment Opportunity Commission (EEO), electoral redistricting, and the FBI's Uniform Crime Reports.]

* * * Because birth certificate data include race, it may often be—as *Malone* illustrates—a tempting source of official "documentary evidence" for "double-checking" or "second-guessing" other methods of individual classification. This potential "official" status of vital statistics data, however, is especially worrisome because the origin of these data is even quirkier and more questionable than the data generated by the census or EEO systems.

The procedures generally used in making birth certificate race-identification records are outlined in guidelines prepared for state and local governments by the National Center for Health Statistics (NCHS) in Washington. From 1950 to 1989, these federal guidelines included a procedure for determining the race of a child from the self-reported race of its parents. The mother and father were asked their respective races, to be coded as follows: White (comprising Mexican, Puerto Rican, and other Caucasian) 1; Black 2; Indian (North, Central, and South American Indian, and Eskimo and Aleut) 3; Chinese 4; Japanese 5; Hawaiian (including part-Hawaiian) 6; Filipino 7; Other Asian or Pacific Islander

8; Other races 0; Not classifiable 9. The race of the child was then determined according to a formula supplied by the NCHS:

> In cases of mixed parentage where only one parent was white, the child was assigned to the other parent's race. When neither parent was white, the child was assigned the race of the father, except if either parent was Hawaiian, the child was assigned to Hawaiian. If race was not reported for one parent, the child was assigned the race of the parent for whom race was given.

Nonresponses were coded "not-classifiable." Additionally, if the race of the mother was coded not classifiable, the mother's race was recorded as that of the father, if known. If neither parent's race was known, officials were to "impute mother's race as race of mother of the preceding record with known race of mother." State health officials generally followed this system with only minor modifications.

This coding algorithm embodied a number of curious assumptions. One notable characteristic is that any coupling between Whites and non-Whites was deemed to produce non-White children. White racial status could only be removed by inter-group parentage, never gained. The origins of this categorization are obscure, but it may reflect shopworn racist assumptions about race "pollution"—that White status may only be "lost" by admixture, forfeited by foreign "taint." By the formal logic of the system, no amount of breeding with Whites will confer "White" status to a "non-White." Standing in stark contrast to this attribute of "White" status, Hawaiian status was defined so as to include any conceivable degree of "part-Hawaiian" descent, so that a code 6 (Hawaiian) parent always produced code 6 (Hawaiian) offspring no matter what the race of the other parent. Thus, in a sense, the status of "Hawaiian" was the morphological polar opposite of that of "White." While "White" status could only be maintained through the most selective breeding with other Whites, it was definitionally impossible to shake a "Hawaiian" designation: a child with one Hawaiian parent by this system was always "Hawaiian"; so also was that child's child, and so on indefinitely. Something in Hawaiian "blood" was apparently so indelible that it could never be erased.

In practice, since this system was self-reported and no attempt was made to ensure that one's self-identification corresponded to prior birth certificates, each generation was effectively classified anew. This system, in other words, was effectively "re-started" with each generation. Nevertheless, this does not mean that classifications on prior birth certificates are meaningless. We should not forget that Judge Wilkins employed a sort of birth certificate-derived racial estoppel against Paul and Philip Malone by judging their racial status in part according to the designations of their parents and grandparents. However odd this system of classification may be, it is sometimes accorded probative value in individual cases.

This coding system was abandoned by NCHS in 1989 in part because it was felt that "the increasing incidence of interracial parentage" combined with "the growing proportion of births with race of father not stated" made it "more appropriate to tabulate births by the mother's race" than to use a "necessarily arbitrary combination of parental races." Since 1989, NCHS has required the following system:

> Birth data are tabulated by the race of the mother as reported directly on the birth certificate. If race of mother was not stated, it was imputed as that of the father, if known. If neither race was stated, race of mother was imputed as the race of the mother on the preceding record with known race.

The 1989 birth certificate revisions have also attempted to obtain more specific information on race. The new 1992 guidelines, for example, require several states to adopt an elaborate series of subcategories for Asian or Pacific Islander respondents. Additionally, the 1989 revision of standardized birth data guidelines also contained a question about the mother's Hispanic origin on birth certificates.

Despite these attempts to improve the system, the post–1989 system is in some ways as odd as its predecessor. The race of one's father is irrelevant unless the mother's race is simply unknown or not otherwise available. Racial status in this formal system is thus rigidly matrilineal. Within this system, race can never change or be escaped except by accident of sex-chromosomal inheritance: only through male children can race be "changed." A Black woman's female progeny would remain Black for indefinite generations even should they marry Whites or even Hawaiians. The new coding system, like the old, effectively "re-starts" with each matrimonial self-identification. Women are not required to self-identify according to their own birth classification, but the potential for certificate-based estoppel as applied in *Malone* remains. As a conceptual system, the new method is dauntingly peculiar, and at best has only an arguable connection to the sociological reality of race and discrimination. Irrespective of his self-perception, or society's perception of him, for example, the child of a Black man and a White woman would forever possess a birth certificate classifying him as White.

Since both NCHS reporting systems have relied heavily upon racial and ethnic self-identification by infants' parents, elaborate methods have been devised for dealing with nonresponses and with nonstandard write-in answers for "other" categories. Maternal nonresponses where the father's race is unknown, as we have seen, are assigned "the race of the mother on the preceding record with known race." Thus if a mother neglects to fill in the proper check-box on her hospital birth certificate "worksheet" while recuperating from childbirth, her child will be assigned a race according to the race indicated on the previous record encountered by the data-entry clerk. Where no race or Hispanic origin is recorded (because the mother could or would not self-report), "unknowns" are distributed randomly.

The NCHS office in Washington, D.C. promulgates guidelines governing how local health officials are to fold write-in "other" responses back into the standardized codes. Although generally no second-guessing of written "other" entries takes place, coding "Indian" with a recorded birthplace outside the Americas is re-classified as "Other API" (or "Asian Indian" where available). To help state officials compile standard-category data from the diverse responses received in "other" write-ins, the NCHS provides lists of common self-designations with instructions as to how each may be coded back into the standard categories. Thus, for example, racial identity responses of "Amerasian," "Indo–Aryan," "Ubontilian," or "Hindu" are to be coded as "Other API," while "Anglo–Saxon," "Afghanistan," "Hebrew," "Hispanic," "Mohammedan," and "Zoroastrian" are all considered "White." As can be seen, certain religious affiliations under this system are allotted racial characteristics: Hindus are presumptively Asian, Jews and Muslims presumptively White. Mysteriously, responses of "Nassau" (the capital of the Bahamas) result in an NCHS coding as "Black," while answers of "Bahamian" are coded merely as "Not Classifiable or Unknown." A similar list aids state officials in coding nonstandard responses to the Hispanic-origin question back into the primary categories: "Falkland Islands" or "Guatemalteco" is to be coded 4 (Central or South American), "Basque," "Valencian," or "La Raza" responses become code 5 answers ("Other Hispanic"), while "Amish," "Bahamian," "Jewish," or "White" are classified as 9 (non-Hispanic). Incongruously, for the Hispanic-origin question a written response of "White" is treated as "non-Hispanic," while for the racial-origin question a response of "Hispanic" is treated as "White."

This algorithmic folding of nonresponses or idiosyncratic responses like "Ubontilian" back into the standardized category codes does not occur merely at the aggregate level, when NCHS compiles its annual natality statistics. Astonishingly, this process also takes place for individual birth certificates. As part of their "quality assurance follow-up," Connecticut health officials, for example, endeavor to ensure that every individual birth certificate is given both a race and an ethnicity code. Where no responses are recorded or a 9 ("Not Classifiable") entry is given, this might consist of contacting local physicians and having them try to re-establish contact with mothers for the purpose of soliciting a self-categorization more intelligible to the bureaucrats. Nonstandard written responses, if they appear on the master NCHS lists of "alternative" group names, are accordingly re-coded as standardized categories. When these methods fail, the certificates might be left as "unknown"—a category of little use for estoppel or other later adjudicative purposes.

This is the sort of system upon which judges will have to rely for "documentary evidence" of the race of future "Malones." Ultimately, as with the self-reported information on U.S. Census forms, the system lacks any "reality" check: What if Mrs. Malone had grinned and said "Black" when so asked by the hospital orderly? Had the twins' parents had more of a sense of humor—or more foresight?—their boys' career in the Boston Fire Department might have had a different ending.

DICKHEAD HUMOR

Notes and Questions

1. How do you know what race you are? How would you prove your race, if such proof were demanded?

2. Suppose you think of yourself as White and one day discover you have Black ancestors. What is your race? See Gregory Williams, *Life on the Color Line: The True Story of a White Boy Who Discovered He Was Black* (1995); James McBride, *The Color of Water: A Black Man's Tribute to His*

White Mother (1996); Judy Scales–Trent, *Notes of a White Black Woman: Race, Color, Community* (1995). For the story of a woman who considered herself White but discovered her birth certificate categorized her as "Black," and who ended up in a lawsuit over the issue, see Lawrence Wright, *One Drop of Blood*, The New Yorker, July 25, 1994, at 46; Calvin Trillin, *American Chronicles: Black or White*, New Yorker, April 14, 1986, at 62–78.

3. How many races are there, and what are they? Is race a biological category, or something else? Contemporary American racial categories draw on the "race science" of the nineteenth century. Consider the following excerpt.

JOE R. FEAGIN & CLAIRECE BOOHER FEAGIN

Racial and Ethnic Relations
6–9 (5th ed. 1996).*

In the 1600s François Bernier was one of the first Europeans to sort human beings into distinct categories. Soon a hierarchy of physically distinct groups (but not yet termed *races*) came to be accepted, with white Europeans, not surprisingly, at the top. Africans were relegated by European observers to the bottom, in part because of (black) Africans' color and allegedly "primitive" culture, but also because Africans were often known to Europeans as slaves. Economic and political subordination resulted in a low position in the white classification system.

Immanuel Kant's use of the German phrase for "races of mankind" in the 1770s was one of the first explicit uses of the term in the sense of biologically distinct categories of human beings. Johann Blumenbach, a German anatomist, is the European scholar whose 1795 classification of all human beings into five racial groups was perhaps the most influential. He was the first influential European to arrange a variety of human groups into a clear racial hierarchy: in order, the Caucasians (Europeans), the Mongolians (Asians), the Ethiopians (Africans), the Americans (Native Americans), and the Malays (Polynesians). Indeed, it was Blumenbach who first coined the term *Caucasian*; he felt that the Europeans in the Caucasus mountains of Russia were "the most beautiful race of men." Ever since, Europeans have been called by a term that once applied only to a small and unrepresentative area of Europe. Blumenbach also used Caucasian because he felt that the earliest human beings probably came from there. (In the twentieth century archaeologists would find the earliest human remains in Africa.)

The concept of race as a biologically distinctive category was developed by northern Europeans who for much of their histories had been largely isolated from contact with people who differed from them physically or culturally. Before the development of large sailing ships in the late 1400s they had little contact with people from Asia, Africa, or the Americas. Soon, however, it was these northern Europeans who established slave systems in the Americas. The slave colonies were legitimated and rationalized by the northern Europeans, including the English, who classified African slaves as a lesser "race." The idea of race was not developed from close scientific observations of all human beings. Rather, "race was, from its inception, a folk classification, a product of popular beliefs about human differences that evolved from the sixteenth through the nineteenth centuries."

From the eighteenth century to the twentieth century the use of *race* by biologists, physical anthropologists, and other scientists usually drew on this folk classification of race in the sense of biologically distinctive groups. The scientists who used race in this sense only reflected their own racial prejudices or those of the general public. Thus, "the scientists themselves undertook efforts to document the existence of the differences that the European cultural worldview demanded and had already created." Basic to this increasingly prevalent view was the Blumenbach theory of a set number of biologically distinct "races" with differing physical characteristics and the belief that these characteristics were hereditary and thus created a natural hierarchy of groups. By the late nineteenth century numerous European and U.S. scientists and popular writers were systematically downgrading all peoples not of northern European origin, especially southern Europeans and Jewish Europeans, as inferior "races." * * *

The basic tenet of racist thinking is that physical differences such as skin color or nose shape are intrinsically and unalterably tied to meaningful differentials in basic intelligence or "civilization." Yet, in spite of periodic assertions of such a linkage by white supremacy groups and pseudoscientists, no scientific support for this assumed linkage exists.

Indeed, there is no distinctive biological reality called "race" that can be determined by objective scientific procedures. The social, medical, and physical sciences have demonstrated this fact. Given the constant blending and interbreeding of human groups over many centuries and in the present, it is impossible to sort human beings into unambiguously distinctive "races" on genetic grounds. There is simply too much overlapping of genetic characteristics across the variety of human populations. Two randomly selected individuals from the world's population would have in common, on average, about 99.8 percent of their genetic material. Most of the genetic variation in regard to human populations "occurs *within* populations, not *between* them." There are genetic differences between geographically scattered human populations, but these differences are slight. The racial importance of the slight dissimilarities is socially, not scientifically, determined.

Human populations singled out as "races" are simply groups with visible differences that Europeans and European Americans have decided to emphasize as important in their social, economic, and political relations. * * * [S]uch racial categorizing is neither objective nor scientific. Indeed, there are *many* different ways of classifying human populations in terms of genetic characteristics. * * * [A]ntimalarial genes * * * are not found among the light-skinned Swedes or dark-skinned southern African groups like the Xhosas, but are commonly found in northern African groups and among Europeans such as Italians and Greeks. These antimalarial genes may be more important for human beings than those determining skin color variations, yet they are not used by Europeans or Euro–Americans, including pseudoscientists, for their "racial" classifications. * * *

Today social scientists view race not as a given biological reality but as a socially constructed reality. Sociologist Oliver C. Cox, one of the first to underscore this perspective, defined race as "any people who are distinguished, or consider themselves distinguished, in social relations with other peoples, by their physical characteristics." From the social-definition perspective, characteristics such as skin color have no self-evident meaning; rather, they have *social* meaning. Similarly, a racial group has been defined by Pierre van den Berghe as a "human group that defines itself and/or is defined by other groups as different from other groups by virtue of innate and immutable physical characteristics."

TESSIE LIU

Teaching the Differences Among Women from a Historical Perspective:
Rethinking Race and Gender as Social Categories
14(4) Women's Studies International Forum 265, 270–71 (1991).*

[R]ace as a social category is intimately linked to one of the basic ways in which human beings have organized society, that is, by kinship. * * * [E]tymologically, at least in England and France, *race* as a kinship term, usually to denote the *patronymic* or *family name*—called literally, the name of the race or *le nom de race*—predated our current usage of the term, which denotes distinct large populations. * * *

* * * When kinship becomes the key element in a stratified social order, as in dynastic politics or caste systems, the concept of race becomes important. Thus, European society, before actual contact with peoples of different skin tones and different cultures and customs, was organized by racial principles. The operating definition of race was based not on external physical characteristics but on blood ties—or, more precisely, some common substance passed on by fathers. In early modern Europe, when patriarchal rule and patrilineal descent predominated, political power, social station, and economic entitlements were closely bound to blood ties and lineage. Thus, race also encapsulated the notion of class. But class in this society was an accident of birth: either according to birth order (determining which rights and privileges the child inherited) or, more generally, according to the family into which one was born (noble or common, propertied or not). The privileges or stigmas of birth, in this system, were as indelible and as discriminatory as any racial system based on skin color or some other trait. The notion of legitimate and illegitimate birth indicates that blood ties did not extend to all who shared genetic materials, but only those with a culturally defined "common substance" passed on by fathers.

Understanding race as an element of social organization directs our attention to forms of stratification. The centrality of reproduction, especially in the transmission of common substance through heterosexual relations and ultimately through birth as the differentiating mark of social entitlements, for example, allows us to see the gendered dimensions of the concept of race. For societies organized by racial principles, reproductive politics are closely linked to establishing the boundaries of lineages. In a male-dominated system, regulating social relationships through racial metaphors necessitates control over women. The reproduction of the system entails not only regulating the sexuality of women in one's own group, but also differentiating between women according to legitimate access and prohibition. Considered in these terms, race as a social category functions through controlling sexuality and sexual behavior.

Notes and Questions

1. Does "race" exist? If so, what sort of thing is it? Consider the following argument:

There is a continuous temptation to think of race as an *essence*, as something fixed, concrete, and objective. And there is also an opposite temptation: to imagine race as a mere *illusion*, a purely ideological construct which some ideal non-racist social order would eliminate. It is necessary to challenge both these positions * * *.

The effort must be made to understand race as an unstable and "decentered" complex of social meanings, constantly being transformed by political struggle. With this in mind, let us propose a definition: *Race is a concept which signifies and symbolizes social conflicts and interests by referring to different types of human bodies.* * * *

We define *racial formation* as the sociohistorical process by which racial categories are created, inhabited, transformed, and destroyed. * * * From a racial formation perspective, race is a matter of both social structure and cultural representation. * * * [T]he theory of racial formation suggests that society is suffused with racial projects, large and small, to which all are subjected. This racial "subjection" is quintessentially ideological. Everybody learns some combination, some version, of the rules of racial classification, and of her own racial identity, often without obvious teaching or conscious inculcation. Thus are we inserted in a comprehensively racialized social structure. Race becomes "common sense"—a way of comprehending, explaining, and acting in the world.

Michael Omi & Howard Winant, *Racial Formation in the United States* at 54.

2. What is the relationship between race and gender? Is one more "real" than the other? More fundamental?

3. Ariela Gross notes that the temptation today is to believe that racism arose as a kind of scientific error about the nature of race, and thus that racism can be combated with more accurate scientific knowledge. Her study of trials in the nineteenth-century South in which racial identity was a contested issue reveals, however, that the law itself played a crucial role in producing racial categories, and that questions of "performance" (did the litigant hold himself out as a white man? Was he treated as such within the community?) were as important as questions of "blood" or "color." Ariela J. Gross, *Litigating Whiteness: Trials of Racial Determination in the Nine-*

teenth–Century South, 108 Yale L.J. 109 (1998). What does this suggest about the persistence of racism? About the persistence of racial categories?

4. Nineteenth-century scientific racial categories were adopted by the United States legal system in a number of different contexts. For example, the Supreme Court relied upon anthropological race science when interpreting a federal naturalization law requiring candidates for naturalization to be "White." See Chapter 6 § 1, *infra.* More recently, the Court has held that when deciding whether a group can bring a legal claim for racial discrimination under 42 U.S.C.A. § 1981, the courts must look to nineteenth-century racial categories as an arbiter of congressional intent. See *St. Francis College v. Al–Khazraji,* 481 U.S. 604 (1987); *Shaare Tefila Congregation v. Cobb,* 481 U.S. 615 (1987).

5. What happens when minority ethnic groups that perceive themselves as different from one another are "lumped" together by the dominant culture under the same racial rubric? Yen Le Espiritu describes this phenomenon as "pan-ethnicity."

> Panethnicity—the generalization of solidarity among ethnic subgroups—is largely a product of categorization. An imposed category ignores subgroup boundaries, lumping together diverse peoples in a single, expanded "ethnic" framework. Individuals so categorized may have nothing in common except that which the categorizer uses to distinguish them. The Africans who were forcibly brought to the United States came not as "blacks" or "Africans" but as members of distinct and various ethnic populations. As a result of slavery, "the 'Negro race' emerged from the heterogeneity of African ethnicity." Diverse Native American tribes also have had to assume the pan-Indian label in order to conform to the perceptions of the American state. Similarly, diverse Latino populations have been treated by the larger society as a unitary group with common characteristics and common problems. And the term Asian American arose out of the racist discourse that constructs Asians as a homogenous group. Excessive categorization is fundamental to racism because it permits "whites to order a universe of unfamiliar peoples without confronting their diversity and individuality." * * *

> This is not to say that panethnicity is solely an imposed identity. Although it originated in the minds of outsiders, today the panethnic concept is a political resource for insiders, a basis on which to mobilize diverse peoples and to force others to be more responsive to their grievances and agendas. * * *

Yen Le Espiritu, *Asian American Panethnicity: Bridging Institutions and Identities* 6–7 (1992).

6. Under what conditions should "pan-ethnic" groupings be treated as "races" for purposes of antidiscrimination law? In *Hernandez v. New York,* 500 U.S. 352 (1991), the Supreme Court held that a prosecutor's use of peremptory challenges to remove bilingual Spanish- and English-speaking members of a criminal jury did not violate the Equal Protection Clause. The jury considered translated Spanish-language testimony during the trial, and the prosecutor argued that the jurors were removed because he feared they would rely on the untranslated testimony instead. Justice Kennedy, in a plurality opinion, mused:

Just as shared language can serve to foster community, language differences can be a source of division. Language elicits a response from others, ranging from admiration and respect, to distance and alienation, to ridicule and scorn. Reactions of the latter type all too often result from or initiate racial hostility. In holding that a race-neutral reason for a peremptory challenge means a reason other than race, we do not resolve the more difficult question of the breadth with which the concept of race should be defined for equal protection purposes. We would face a quite different case if the prosecutor had justified his peremptory challenges with the explanation that he did not want Spanish-speaking jurors. It may well be, for certain ethnic groups and in some communities, that proficiency in a particular language, like skin color, should be treated as a surrogate for race under an equal protection analysis.

500 U.S. at 371.

Should language ability be a valid reason to discriminate among jurors? Is language difference like race? Is it part of race? Does the answer depend on the language? For a detailed review of the *Hernandez* case, see Juan F. Perea, Hernandez v. New York: *Courts, Prosecutors and the Fear of Spanish,* 21 Hofstra L. Rev. 1 (1992) (dissecting the Court's reasoning); see also Deborah Ramirez, *Excluded Voices: The Disenfranchisement of Ethnic Groups from Jury Service,* 1993 Wis. L. Rev. 761.

What was the Court's understanding of race in the *Hernandez* case? Why should language be a "surrogate" for race, but not "race" itself?

NEIL GOTANDA

A Critique of "Our Constitution Is Color–blind"
44 Stan. L. Rev. 1, 2, 3–5 (1991),*

This article examines the ideological content of the claim that "our Constitution is color-blind" and argues that the U.S. Supreme Court's use of color-blind constitutionalism—a collection of legal themes functioning as a racial ideology—fosters white racial domination. * * *

The Supreme Court's color-blind constitutionalism uses race to cover four distinct ideas: status-race, formal-race, historical-race, and culture-race. Status-race is the traditional notion of race as an indicator of social status. While traditional status-race is now largely discredited, it remains important as the racial model for efforts aimed at eradicating intentional forms of racial subordination, with their implication of racial inferiority.

The second use of race, formal-race, refers to socially constructed formal categories. Black and white are seen as neutral, apolitical descriptions, reflecting merely "skin color" or region of ancestral origin. Formal-race is unrelated to ability, disadvantage, or moral culpability. Moreover, formal-race categories are unconnected to social attributes such as culture, education, wealth, or language; this "unconnectedness" is the defining characteristic of formal-race, and no other usage of "race" incorporates the concept.

Historical-race, however, does assign substance to racial categories. Historical-race embodies past and continuing racial subordination, and is the meaning of race that the Court contemplates when it applies "strict scrutiny" to racially disadvantaging government conduct. The state's use of racial categories is regarded as so closely linked to illegitimate racial subordination that it is automatically judicially suspect.

Finally, culture-race uses "black" to refer to African–American culture, community, and consciousness. Culture refers to broadly shared beliefs and social practices; community refers to both the physical and spiritual senses of the term; and African–American consciousness refers to black nationalist and other traditions of self-awareness, as well as to action based on that self-awareness. Culture-race is the basis for the developing concept of cultural diversity. * * *

The Supreme Court has used words such as "race," "black," and "white" without explanation or qualification. In doing so, it has disguised its own role in perpetuating racial subordination. The modern Court has moved away from the two notions of race which recognize the diverging historical experiences of black and white Americans—status-race and historical-race. In place of these concepts, the Court relies increasingly on the formal-race concept of race, a vision of race as unconnected to the historical reality of black oppression. * * *

This article's central claim is that modern color-blind constitutionalism supports the supremacy of white interests and must therefore be regarded as racist. There is no legitimate rationale for the automatic rejection of all governmental consideration of race. However, strict scrutiny should not be abandoned altogether, given its efficacy as a weapon against segregation in years past. * * * This section, therefore, suggests some minimal requirements for an alternative constitutional approach to race.

First, any revised approach to race and the Constitution must explicitly recognize that race is not a simple, unitary phenomenon. Rather, * * * race is a unique social formation with its own meanings, understandings, discourses, and interpretive frameworks. As a socially constructed category with multiple meanings, race cannot be easily isolated from lived social experience. Moreover, race cannot legitimately be described and understood according to legal discourse. Any effort to understand its nature must go beyond legal formalism.

Second, constitutional jurisprudence on race must accommodate legitimate government efforts to address white racial privilege. The Supreme Court must not only acknowledge the multiple dimensions of race in the abstract but also expressly permit the different aspects of race to be considered in judicial and legislative decisions. Further, any constitutional program must recognize the cultural genocide implicit in the development of a color-blind society and acknowledge the importance of black culture, community, and consciousness. * * *

Finally, a revised approach to race must recognize the systemic nature of subordination in American society. The Supreme Court's efforts to interpret the Equal Protection and Due Process Clauses have addressed race, gender, sexuality, and class. To date, the court has regarded these phenomena as distinct, but racial subordination is inherently connected to other forms of subordination. The deep social context in which they are interwoven has begun to draw increasing attention. * * *

The Free Exercise and Establishment Clause decisions provide a model for constitutional adjudication in the area of race to supplant the color-blind model. * * *

Culture-race, with its wide range of social and cultural references, makes possible a form of free exercise of the positive aspects of race—recognizing black and white cultures as legitimate aspects of the American social fabric. Further, free exercise of race would allow, within appropriate limits, open discussion and implementation of governmental remedies to address the historical legacy of racial discrimination. Also protected will be the culture, community, and consciousness of American racial minorities. European–American cultures would also be recognized and respected, of course, even though their exercise has not been challenged in the same manner as black culture. * * *

There is also an "establishment" analog for race. What is impermissible—what the government may not "establish"—is racial subordination and white supremacy: the use of either status-race or formal-race to establish domination, hierarchy, and exploitation.

The paired considerations of racial establishment and free exercise are mixed in our social existence. The free exercise of some aspects of a white culture may overlap or coincide with racial domination, as with the attachment of many white southerners to the Confederate flag. Efforts to abolish domination will, therefore, interfere with the free exercise of race in such instances. The suggestion from the religion cases about how to approach this conflict is that the two discussions—of racial subordination and of black culture—can be considered together. Any problem should be addressed in its particular context, without the doctrinal compulsion to satisfy all aspects of either racial subordination or respect for racial-ethnic culture.

Notes and Questions

1. Reconsider the essays in this chapter. Is the author using status-race, formal-race, culture-race or historical-race when writing about race? Consider how authors and courts use the term "race" as you continue reading this book.

2. Antidiscrimination law represents one important area of the law where racial categories become salient. The United States decennial census is another. Consider the excerpts that follow.

LUIS ANGEL TORO

"A People Distinct from Others": Race and Identity in Federal Indian Law and the Hispanic Classification in OMB Directive No. 15
26 Tex. Tech L. Rev. 1219, 1220, 1225–1228, 1252–53, 1260–61, 1271–73 (1995).*

The presence of a Mexican origin community north of the border has confounded the system of racial classification in U.S. law since the Treaty of Guadalupe Hidalgo transformed northern Mexico into the southwestern United States. Chicanos confound the system of racial classification because we tend to view ourselves as a mestizo people whose culture arises from both Spanish and indigenous American roots. U.S. law has not adjusted to the presence of this community and cannot classify persons who claim to exist at the intersection of the four classic "races." One hundred fifty years after the annexation of the southwestern states, the law of racial classification has not benefited from a Chicano critique. * * *

Directive No. 15 [promulgated by the Office of Management and Budget (OMB), which sets out the racial-ethnic categories to be used in the census] governs the collection of federal statistics regarding the implementation of a host of civil rights and other laws. OMB has announced that it will reconsider its racial/ethnic classification scheme but has not indicated that elimination of the "Hispanic" classification is under consideration. The agency's official announcement of proposed revision noted that the data collected under the format mandated by the directive is used to enforce laws regarding voting rights and legislative redistricting, federal and private sector affirmative action programs, school desegregation, minority business development, and fair housing. Of course, a mere listing of the official goals of Directive No. 15 cannot capture its importance as a guideline for nongovernmental entities who wish to collect culturally specific information, as well as its importance as a manifestation of the white privilege both to exclude others from their status and to define for others their own communities.

A brief overview of Directive No. 15 reveals several highly questionable assertions about race and identity embedded in the classification scheme. Directive No. 15 instructs agencies to prefer separate questions for "race" and "ethnicity," the latter term referring, as previously noted, only to whether or not a person is "Hispanic." This preferred method was utilized by the Census Bureau in the 1990 Census. Question four on the Census questionnaire, the "race" question, instructs the person filling out the form to choose "the race that the person considers himself/herself to be." The choices include "White," "Black," "Indian (Amer.)," "Eskimo," "Aleut," several choices grouped under the heading "Asian or Pacific Islander," and "Other race." Question seven asks, "Is this person of Spanish/Hispanic origin?" and requires a "yes" or "no" answer. If the answer is "yes," the person filling out the form must choose among four more specific categories: "Mexican, Mexican–American, Chicano," "Puerto Rican," "Cuban," and "Other Spanish/Hispanic."

Directive No. 15 also permits agencies to use a shorter form of the race and Hispanic origin questions by combining the two. The categories in the combined form are "American Indian or Alaskan Native," "Asian or Pacific Islander," "Black, not of Hispanic origin," "Hispanic," and "White, not of Hispanic origin." The Directive permits agencies to use more detailed categories than the ones listed, but cautions that the categories must be susceptible to aggregation into the "basic racial/ethnic categories" they represent.

The definitions of the racial categories make it clear that, with two prominent exceptions, the individual is supposed to look to genealogy as the source of racial identity. For example, a "White" person is one "having origins in any of the original peoples of Europe, North Africa, or the Middle East," while a "Black" person has "origins in any of the black racial groups of Africa." That "origin" means biological ancestry is made clear by comparison with the two groups defined at least in part by "culture": "American Indian[s] or Alaskan Native[s]," who must have both pre-Columbian American ancestry and "cultural identification through tribal affiliation or community recognition," and "Hispanics," who are identified as having either "Spanish culture or origin." Further, the widespread but erroneous belief that cultural identity is fixed and biologically inherited insures that "origin" will be interpreted by most respondents as referring to biological ancestry. Directive No. 15 thus reflects and reinforces the view that race is a fixed, inherited trait with no relationship to culture. Further, by neglecting any reference to the relationship of the respondent to members of other cultural groups, Directive No. 15 locates racial identity in the individual, rather than in the nature of that person's relationship to others.

Hispanics are defined in Directive No. 15 as the ethnic group whose "culture or origin" is Spanish, "regardless of race," and Mexican–Americans are specifically described as a "Spanish cultur[al]" subgroup. The combined format declares that Hispanics are either white or Black. Because a "Black" person, under Directive No. 15, is defined as "a person having origins in any of the black racial groups of Africa," it is clear that Directive No. 15 perceives Mexican–Americans as a white ethnic group. This perception is at odds with Chicano identity and the Chicano people's historical experience of racial oppression, as well as the present, ongoing racial discrimination against Mexican–Americans. The perception also differs from the determinations Congress made when it decided that Mexican–Americans needed to be covered under laws addressing racial discrimination. The classification of Mexican–Americans as white is consistent only with prior Census practice, which stopped counting "Mexicans" as a race with the 1930 Census and instructed Census takers to list Chicanos as whites when those persons were "definitely not Negro, Indian, or some other race."

Directive No. 15 describes Chicano difference from the white majority as an "ethnic" difference, rather than a racial one. In other words, it describes Chicanos as part of the "white" race, but a part that has yet to fully assimilate into the mainstream status enjoyed by members of that group. This construct, sometimes described as the "immigrant analogy," holds that minorities in American society will all progress down the path of assimilation taken by such white ethnic groups as the Irish, the Jews, and the Italians, at least to the extent that minorities work as hard as members of those groups worked to gain acceptance as deserving of white status. Few now believe that the immigrant analogy holds true for groups such as Chicanos or immigrant communities from Asia, whose difference from majority society is defined both in racial and ethnic terms. * * *

The problems caused by the poor fit between the "Hispanic" classification and the disadvantaged minority groups it attempts to describe are numerous and well documented. First, the conceptualization of the "Hispanic" classification as an "ethnic" rather than a "racial" group (the only "ethnic" group the federal government recognizes) reduces the usefulness of much federal data, along with data generated to conform to Directive No. 15. This occurs because many people who are actually members of racially subordinated minorities are labeled as "White, Hispanic." This affects data concerning both "Hispanics" and African–Americans. When data comparing "Whites" and "Blacks" are compiled, the presence of Mexican–Americans and others misidentified as "White Hispanics" in the "White" sample will create an illusion that the disparity in income and other measures of community vitality between the majority population and the African–American community is smaller than it is in reality, because the presence of persons in the "White" sample who do not in reality enjoy the societal benefits of "White" status will skew the results. Similarly, the presence of African–Americans in the "non-Hispanic" sample will skew the results, although a countervailing factor is the presence in the "Hispanic" sample of persons I maintain should be deemed either white or members of other groups. This factor may reduce the skew, but it does not create a realistic picture of an actual cultural subgroup.

This conceptualization also ignores the racial nature of anti-Mexican subordination in the United States and the Mexican–American people's own conception of their identity. Worse, by lumping together people on both sides of what W.E.B. Du Bois called the "color line," this concept betrays forgetfulness of the reasons why our government needs to continue taking notice of a person's cultural identity. When white persons are allowed to compete with members of racially subordinated minority groups for the extremely limited resources that have been reserved for programs addressing racial discrimination, the goals of the program are defeated. This is exactly what occurs when persons for whom the description "White Hispanic" might accurately apply, along with white persons who view the Hispanic classification as a loophole through which to claim benefits meant to address the problems associated with racism, are lumped together with Chicanos in programs using the federal standards for racial and ethnic recordkeeping. * * *

A Mexican couple immigrates to the United States and has children. They receive a Census form in the mail and set about determining their own and their children's racial identity. Looking at the racial categories, the couple sees none that describe them. They do not view themselves as American Indians but as mestizos, persons of mixed European and indigenous heritage. They are not enrolled members of a recognized tribe, nor are they identified as Indians in the community in which they live. By the same token, neither are they identified as whites. In the "Hispanic origin" question, the couple sees "Mexican, Mexican–American or Chicano" specifically listed as a "Hispanic" group. They identify themselves as part of that group and as being of "Other" race on the race question.

This couple might identify their children in the same manner. Alternatively, they might believe that a "Mexican or Mexican–American" is only someone who was born in Mexico. As immigrants, they may not be familiar with the north of the border term "Chicano." Since their children were born in the U.S., they answer the Hispanic origin question in the negative. Knowing that there are millions of people like their children in this country, and believing that there must be some place on the Census form for them, they think again about the race question. Obviously, their children are not white: Every day they face the avoidance behaviors and "microaggressions" exhibited by whites, designed to remind them that they are not part of that group. They do not believe that their children are part of the "Black" or "Asian/Pacific Islander" groups, so they think again about the American Indian category. Perhaps aware of the one drop rule that, at least culturally, defines as Black any person with any known African ancestor or trace of apparent African ancestry, they conclude that "community recognition" as Indian means being treated as nonwhite on the basis of apparent indigenous ancestry. Therefore, they mark their children as members of the "American Indian or Alaskan Native" race.

Now, suppose that a fourth generation Chicano is filling out a Census form. Spiritually uplifted by the cultural pride inherent in the concept of Aztlán, he identifies himself racially as "American Indian" but answers "yes" to the Hispanic origin question, marking the "Mexican, Mexican–American, or Chicano" box. To the respondent, this seems like a decent reflection of his mestizo identity. To the Census Bureau, it is a wrong answer.

Suppose now that this same fourth generation Chicano is responding to a question under the combined race/ethnic short format permitted under Directive No. 15. Choosing between the selections, "White, Hispanic" and "American Indian" is easy. The respondent selects "American Indian" as the response, because he has never been treated as a white person in his community, because "Hispanic" seems an inaccurate description of a Chicano culture that has a strong indigenous influence, and because in physical appearance, *i.e.*, "racially," the respondent is far closer to being a Native American than a European. * * *

Federal Indian law, or more accurately, the indigenous traditions that the law has addressed, provides the solution to the dilemma the OMB faces. By illustrating alternatives to bloodline as the touchstone of identity, and by recognizing "community identification," federal Indian law provides an alternate means of classifying cultural identity that does not depend on an inquiry into genealogy. The best solution to the dilemma revealed by the problems inherent in the "Hispanic" classification is for the government to abandon the outdated racial ideology embodied in Directive No. 15 and replace it with questions designed to determine an individual's membership in a socially constructed, cultural subgroup. These cultural subgroups, not defined by reference to a person's bloodline, would be familiar to most Americans: Chicanos or Mexican–Americans, Blacks or African–Americans, Korean–Americans, and so on. Members of these groups recognize each other as sharing a common history and vocabulary of experience, even as they remain internally divided by class, gender, sexual orientation, and political belief—factors that Directive No. 15 does not attempt to measure.

Since the agency cannot grant formal, political recognition * * *, the OMB would inquire into social interaction to determine whether the subgroup is generally recognized in society as a "people distinct from others." The agency would have to undertake a detailed survey of American culture to determine exactly how people identify themselves and how they are recognized by others in order to create a framework of socially recognized ethnic or cultural subgroups. The agency should give priority to group self-identification over outsider identification because outsiders may tend to lump together different groups based upon presumptions of shared characteristics of the groups. This tendency is illustrated by the way the Asian/Pacific Islander groups and the Hispanic groups are combined.

More would be gained than simply eradicating the classical scheme of racial hierarchy from U.S. law. When an individual's membership in a cultural subgroup is legally significant, the law should not be hindered by a classification scheme that misstates the person's cultural identity, nor should the collection of accurate statistics be hampered by a classification scheme that serves only to confuse and mislead those attempting to classify themselves on a government form. * * *

When necessary, the next inquiry would be to determine on which side of the "color line" that divides American society the subgroup exists. An appreciation of the goals set by Congress when it enacted the statute in question would aid this inquiry. An examination of judicial findings when such data is used to assist compliance with court orders would also help. In the case of Chicanos, the historical record shows a long history of treatment as a racial minority. Because this does not hold true for all so-called "Hispanics," each group must be evaluated separately to determine the following: (1) whether or not they exist in a relationship of racial subordination to the mainstream population; and (2) why they might be considered a group needing assistance to combat racial harm.

In cases of box checking, the ideal solution would be to empower members of the target groups to determine whether the community recognizes the alleged phony minority as one of its members. The test would be whether the person is commonly recognized by persons in that group as one of their own—not whether some trait presumed to be shared by all members of the group is or is not present. In cases of doubt, outsider identification can be examined. If the claimant is generally identified as a member of a racially subordinated group, his or her self-identification should be upheld if a significant portion of the group also recognizes the claimant as a member.

TANYA KATERI HERNÁNDEZ

*"Multiracial" Discourse: Racial Classifications
in an Era of Color–Blind Jurisprudence*
57 Md. L. Rev. 97, 98–103, 107–112, 117–119, 121–
29, 130–31, 133–34, 165–170 (1998).*

For the past several years, there has been a Multiracial Category Movement (MCM) promoted by some biracial persons[3] and their parents for the addition of a "multiracial" race category on the decennial census. The stated aim of such a new category is to obtain a more specific count of the number of mixed-race persons in the United States and to have that tallying of mixed-race persons act as a barometer and promoter of racial harmony. As proposed, a respondent could choose the "multiracial" box in lieu of the presently listed racial classifications * * * On October 29, 1997, the U.S. Office of Management and Budget (OMB) adopted a federal Interagency Committee recommendation to reject the multiracial category in favor of allowing individuals to check more than one racial category. Some MCM proponents are not satisfied with the OMB's decision, because multiple box checking does not directly promote a distinct multiracial identity. These MCM proponents are committed to continue lobbying for a multiracial category on the 2010 Census. Further, an OMB official has indicated that the issue of a multiracial category might be reconsidered with an increase in mixed-race persons. Yet, the significance of the MCM extends beyond the actual decision of whether and how mixed-race persons should be counted. * * *

Multiracial discourse contends that a mixed-race census count is necessary because race has become too fluid to monitor. The theory posits that the inability to identify psychologically with just one racial category is inherent to mixed-race persons alone and that the growing number of mixed-race persons demonstrates the futility of racial categorization as a practice. For instance, MCM proponents often refer to the growing numbers of persons who choose the "Other Race" category to support the premise that the racial categories are inadequate for mixed-race persons. The multiracial narrative of modern race being more fluid than in the past corresponds with and reinforces the color-blind jurisprudence presentation of race as devoid of meaning. Thus, "multiracial discourse" has an immediate meaning as the rhetoric deployed in the campaign for a specific count of mixed-race persons, and a more expansive meaning as the approach to race that views the increasing diversity of society as deconstructing and transcending race. Multiracial discourse misconstrues the meaning of race used in the group measurement of

3. "Biracial" is used in this Article to refer to those individuals who claim a social identity based on their status as mixed-race persons. In contrast, the term "mixed-race" refers to the entire population of persons with parents of different races irrespective of biracial identity.

racial disparity, with an individual-focused assessment of fluid cultural identity. Such a view of race negates its sociopolitical meaning and thereby undermines effective legal mechanisms to ameliorate racial discrimination. In fact, the MCM can be viewed as a metonym for the more general color-blind approach to race evident in recent Supreme Court cases. * * *

The initial impetus for the MCM was the discomfort many White–Black interracial couples felt when choosing racial classifications for their mixed-race children on educational data collection forms. Yet, the MCM demand for a multiracial category is usually presented in terms of its disapproval of all forms of racial classification. For example, Susan Graham—a White mother of two Black–White biracial children, the Executive Director of Project RACE (a national organization advocating on behalf of multiracial children), and one of the principal advocates for the availability of a multiracial category—states that true progress would be the eradication of all racial classifications. Similarly, Carlos Fernandez, former President of the Association of MultiEthnic Americans, has also argued that his preference is that "racial and ethnic classifications should be done away with entirely." These statements reflect the general view among multiracial-category proponents that the use of current or any racial classifications is a form of discrimination in that the focus it places upon race diminishes the humanity of the individuals it purports to represent. The MCM advocates describe their movement as an instrumental step toward the "dream of racial harmony," as opposed to the creation of "one more divisive category." The MCM frequently posits that multiracial persons are a "unifying force" on the theory that multiracial persons "as a group may be the embodiment of America's best chance to clean up race relations." Thus, proponents value a multiracial category for its perceived shift away from the rigidity of racial classifications, which some perceive as a cause of racial hostility. The hope is that the multiracial category will act as an acknowledgement of the fluid and nebulous character of race and hence its meaninglessness as a grouping of persons. In effect, MCM proponents implicitly wish to use the multiracial category as a mechanism for moving toward a color-blind society that will effectuate racial equality. Thus, the demand for a multiracial category is less a race-conscious recognition of all the races with which a particular person identifies, than it is a mechanism for questioning the use of any system of racial classification.[55]

The implicit color-blind vision of the MCM is also reflected in what I term the "symmetrical identity demands" of the White parents who predominate among the MCM's spokespersons. The "symmetrical identity demand" is the appeal for all racial aspects of a child to be acknowledged in that child's public assertion of racial identity: "I'm part of this kid, too, no matter who he looks like." As one parent of multiracial

---

55. Consider one MCM proponent's assertion:

I contend that society should embrace, as a transitory vehicle, multiple racial categories that expressly recognize and acknowledge products of mixed-race unions as distinct from both blacks and whites. I assert that this will have the effect of creating a type of "shade confusion" which will eventually destroy the black/white dichotomy that currently exists, ultimately reducing race to a meaningless category, as it should be.

children testified in a recent congressional hearing, without a multiracial category, biracial children are forced to "choose one parent over the other." One can empathize with the parental impulse to have their familial connection to their children publicly reflected in the collection of racial data. However, claims to different racial ancestries are not socially symmetrical in effect. That is to say, what the parents of biracial children may fail to perceive is that while the political acknowledgment of White racial ancestry can be beneficial to the individual child, it also unfortunately reinforces societal White supremacy when society places greater value on White ancestral connections than on non-White connections. "Whiteness is an aspect of racial identity surely, but it is much more; it remains a concept based on relations of power, a social construct predicated on white dominance and Black subordination." Thus, the symmetrical identity demand can also function as a claim to having biracial children inherit all of the privileges of White status, which White parents logically would like to extend to their children as protection from racism against non-Whites. In short, the insistence on symmetry in racial categorization is color-blind in its refusal to acknowledge the sociopolitical nature of race.

In demanding a separate mixed-race category, the MCM misconstrues race as solely a cultural identification. Specifically, such a demand presupposes that there are "pure-Black" experiences, which make a person authentically Black, and inversely, that the lack of such authenticating cultural experiences makes a person "less Black." Part of what drives the push for a separate racial category is the desire to reflect more accurately the cultural experiences of biracial Blacks living in an interracial context. Although there may be a cultural component to the identification of persons who have been socially segregated into insular communities and who have a history of varied cultural ties to different African countries and tribes, such cultural manifestations are not uniform across the African diaspora. For instance, the cultural attributes of the insular Black community in New York are not equivalent to the cultural attributes of insular Black communities in Oaxaca, Mexico or in Loiza, Puerto Rico. The uniformity of Black social identification throughout the Black diaspora is by virtue of the fact that a Black person is viewed as distinct because of appearance, ancestry, or both, and not because of any commonality in culture. The OMB's recent decision allowing mixed-race persons to be counted with a "check-all-that-apply" system of racial classification also mistakenly construes race as cultural identification. If race were primarily a form of cultural identification, then an option to check more than one box would be appropriate for those persons reared within a mixed-cultural context. But race is a group-based experience of social differentiation that is not diminished by a diverse ancestral heritage. Further, the OMB decision may result in the division of a multiple-race response into shares; therefore, it is ill-suited to a collection of race data for measuring social differentiation. * * *

Social standing continues to be a significant benefit of whiteness, regardless of one's socioeconomic level. Whites have been "given public deference and titles of courtesy because they ... [are] white." After controlling for differences in education and job training, Whites continue to earn higher wages than Blacks. From an institutional perspective, the supremacy accorded White status in a racial hierarchy also benefits industry by defusing class tensions amongst Whites. W.E.B. Du Bois observed seventy years ago that "the white group of laborers, while they received a low wage, were compensated in part by a sort of public and psychological wage." Movements for formal racial equality have done little to diminish this hierarchy. In fact, even as standards of legal equality have been erected, the intangible object of whiteness has continued to be valued. Thus, the ability of Whites not to think of themselves in racial terms at all is another benefit of whiteness, in that whiteness is cognitively viewed as the norm and hence not a race. This is, in effect, another benefit that multiracial-category proponents logically want to pass on to their children—the leisure of not having to think about race at all.

Given this ongoing privilege of White racial status, it is important to examine the role that a mixed-race census count would have in reinforcing the estimation of whiteness. To be sure, the value placed on whiteness is not one which exists in a vacuum. Rather, it is an intrinsic part of an institutional racial hierarchy in which the closer one can approximate whiteness, the better off one is economically and socially. This racial hierarchy, which denigrates all connections to blackness in order to maintain the White ideal, evidences itself perhaps most starkly in the selection of adoptive children. In the adoptions market, White babies are highly prized, followed by mixed-race babies, with Black babies the least preferred. History demonstrates that, in such a racial hierarchy, those who are mixed-race will logically assert their White ancestry, while downplaying their African ancestry, in order to further themselves in the social structure and flee repression. Similarly, White parents will seize opportunities to extend their privilege of whiteness to non-White persons they care about. * * *

Color-blind platforms for such protective efforts permit concerned White parents to extend the supremacist system privilege to those who are viewed as "practically-all-White" without actually dismantling the racial hierarchy itself.

Accordingly, the demand for statistical recognition of mixed-race persons—and acknowledgment of all aspects of an individual's racial identity—is occurring within a sociopolitical context that values White ancestry and denigrates non-White ancestry. In such a racial caste system, it is impossible to acknowledge mixed-race persons officially without actually elevating the status of those who can claim to be other than "pure" Black, no matter how egalitarian the intent of the MCM. This same elevation of mixed-race classes is evident in various Latin American countries and in apartheid South Africa in ways that powerfully illuminate the implications of furthering multiracial discourse in the United States. * * *

In those Latin American countries such as Brazil, Cuba, Colombia, Panama, Venezuela, and Nicaragua, where sizable communities of Blacks reside, and where Whites are a numerical minority, a favored "Mulatto" class has long been recognized as distinct from the subor-

dinate Black population. Historian Carl Degler has termed this phenomenon as the "mulatto escape hatch," which he defines as the "recognition of a special place for mixed bloods." Mulattoes are accorded greater
favors than Blacks, but fewer privileges than the numerical minority of
empowered Whites: "The top jobs in business, politics and academia are
held by those with light skin. * * * Studies show that blacks are poorer,
less educated and less respected than whites and mulattoes." In turn,
the greater opportunities available to Mulattoes encourage them to
dissociate themselves from their African ancestry. Similar to lower class
Whites in the United States, Mulattoes in much of Latin America act as
a buffer class between elite Whites and economically exploited Blacks.
This buffer effectively maintains a system of White supremacy. It is this
temptation to dissociate from racial subordination that concerns many
about a mixed-race census count. * * *

The censuses in countries with middle-tier racial categories reflects
the distinct racial structure and demographic pattern of small White
populations with large Black populations. In Brazil, for example, in the
last four census schedules that included questions regarding color, race,
or both, the color terms used ranged from White, Yellow, Brown, and
Black. Although the Brazilian census schedules used the term "color"
categories, the color categories utilized corresponded directly with racial
categories. The Yellow category represented the inclusion of citizens of
Asian descent in Brazil's population, while "Black" represented persons
with African ancestry, and "Brown" represented persons with mixed
Black and White ancestry. The Brown category is somewhat akin to the
current United States proposal for a multiracial category in that it is
viewed as an umbrella for counting the many different shades of mixed
persons within the Brazilian population. In fact, the number of shades
included within the Brown category is extensive. In the 1976 Brazilian
census, a supplementary household survey included an open-ended color
question. Respondents described themselves with 136 different colors.

Ironically enough, after decades of utilizing mixed-race categories,
the 1991 Brazilian census was subject to a campaign for the elimination
of the Brown mixed-race color category in favor of a specific African-
ancestry race question. Although the request to eliminate the mixed-race
category did not prevail, the organizers also mounted a publicity campaign to encourage respondents to move away from the mixed-race
category by checking the Black category instead. This campaign was
entitled "Don't Let Your Color Pass into White: Respond with Good
Sense." The campaign was motivated by the concern that Brazilians
often lie about their color by selecting a lighter color because they are
embarrassed to have African origins. The campaign for greater numbers
of persons to accurately check the Black category was mounted to
produce more reliable socioeconomic data on Blacks and thereby assist in
mobilizing a racial justice movement. This is the insidious aspect of
middle-tier categories—the detachment of subordinated persons from
concern with racial justice out of a psychological sense of superiority,
notwithstanding their own consistent experiences of discrimination and
prejudice. Middle-tier census categories in racially stratified societies
thus present an inherent threat to racial justice efforts. Merely checking

the box has a political effect, despite the fact that an individual's phenotype will continue to determine her daily experiences of racism. This problem is further exacerbated when Whites feel pressure to accord tangible benefits to those occupying the middle tier, as occurred in apartheid South Africa.

Similar to the Brazilian White minority's use of the mixed-race Brown color category, apartheid South Africa's White minority utilized a middle-tier category for mixed-race persons known as "Coloured." The four South African census classifications have traditionally been White, Bantu (Black Africans), Coloured, and Asiatic (East Indians). The South African government historically accorded Coloureds greater material advantages than Bantus, such as higher wages, access to employment positions of higher status, and admission to White universities. However, Coloureds received fewer material benefits than Whites. Accordingly, a stratified value system accompanied the racial hierarchy. The Coloureds internalized notions of the racial hierarchy, *i.e.*, that lighter-skinned Coloureds were presumed to be smarter than darker-skinned Coloureds. Similar to the Brazilian and United States experience of racial hierarchy, lighter-skinned South African Coloureds often passed into the White community with greater access to employment and educational opportunities. As long as the Coloureds were receiving these material gains, there generally prevailed among them an acquiescence to apartheid. It was not until the apartheid system began to deny Coloureds their intermediary-status privileges that they became interested, as a group, in aligning themselves with the Bantus and the East Indians. This helped to successfully undermine the foundation of the apartheid system.

The South African departure from the privileging of middle-tier Coloureds was directly connected to the purposeful increase in the size of the White population. The 1970 census showed that the increase in the Coloured population was almost double that of the increase in the White population, and demographic projections indicated that by the end of the century, there would be as many Coloureds as Whites in South Africa. Following the release of these demographic projections, there was a relaxation of immigration controls for White European workers, which, in turn, allowed South Africa to increase its White population. The transformation of Whites into a numerical majority, and the use of White working-class immigrants as a new middle-tier community, diminished the need to favor mixed-race persons as a buffer class between the White elite and the economically exploited Bantus.

In contrast, Whites in the United States never needed to create a biracial middle tier, because Whites always far outnumbered persons of color relegated to the bottom of the racial hierarchy. The U.S. use of the "multiracial-type" categories of octoroon, quadroon, and Mulatto in the censuses of 1850–1920 has been described more as a reflection of the growth of the eugenics movement's ranking of genetic intelligence than as a serious attempt to institutionalize a mixed-race, middle-tier buffer class. Rather, the United States has periodically imported White immigrants who effectively served as a working-class buffer between its own White elite and the non-White underclass. For instance, when national concern grew about the increasing number of Mulattoes, appeals for immigrants from Europe were quickly made. Once here, these White immigrants were encouraged to support the maintenance of slavery and the racial caste system it enforced. From 1820 to 1920, exactly 29,656,589 Europeans legally immigrated to the United States, constituting anywhere from 70% to 96% of all legal immigrants admitted. * * *

Between 1911 and 1950, the systemic desire for greater numbers of White immigrants informed immigration legislation. The Immigration Act of 1924 institutionalized quotas that favored immigrants from northern and western European nations and barred Blacks. Blacks were barred as immigrants despite the fact that the 1924 quota system was established with the rationale that preference should be given to persons whose origins matched this nation's "native born" population for easier assimilation. In 1929, eighty-two percent of the immigrants allowed into the United States were from northern and western Europe. The use of European immigrants as a middle tier in the United States relegated non-White immigrants such as the Chinese—who themselves were completely excluded by the Immigration Act of 1917—to the lower status of Blacks.

In contrast, the persistent recognition of mixed-race classes in countries such as Brazil paralleled the continued demographic pattern of poor Blacks generally outnumbering Whites. Consequently, there has been an enduring need in Brazil for mixed-race persons to act as a buffer between these two classes in order to maintain the supremacy of a White minority. It is this same fear of demographic suffusion in the United States that partially drives the burgeoning White interest in the multiracial category. * * *

Yet, Latin American race relations are a poor model to emulate. The recognition of a separate class of mixed-race persons in Brazil has not led to a genuinely color-blind society, because the desire to avoid being categorized with a denigrated Black populace has resulted in a hyper-consciousness of color gradations and phenotypical traces of African ancestry. In fact, some Brazilians describe their race relations as "veiled apartheid." Brazilian commentators have noted that the country's Mulatto buffer class is a " 'much more intelligent [mechanism] for subjugating a race than South Africa, which used guns.' " This description is particularly apt when one considers that the promotion of a mixed-race class was motivated by the desire to "whiten" the country by having Blacks disappear through a mixing of the races, and that the census colors are ranked hierarchically from the most positively valued color of White to the pejoratively viewed color of Black. The whitening ideal "remains encoded and enmeshed in the language of 'a mixed people' which is generally taken to mean, a 'lighter' if not 'whiter' people." Thus, color-blindness has not led to a transcendence of race but instead to a reinforcement of a racial caste system in the one region long touted as a racial democracy. * * *

This Article proposes an openly race-conscious, single-box-checking census classification system. Such a system is needed because of the manner in which the hypo-descent rule seemingly pertains to all non-Whites in varying degrees, due to the fact that all forms of nonwhiteness are deemed inferior to whiteness. In fact, acknowledging the political meaning of race is crucial in working toward the MCM's goal of racial equality, which has thus far been missing from the discourse of the movement itself. * * *

I propose a Race–Conscious Racial Classification System that modifies government data collection forms by dispensing with such vacuous pseudoscientific racial definitions and, instead, employs an approach rooted in the sociopolitical meanings of race. This proposal is asserted not as the definitive classification scheme, but merely as an invitation for developing a classification system organized around the political meaning of race for more effective use of racial data. By focusing upon the political meaning of race, a race-conscious classification system can avoid the distortions of a race-as-culture focus. The race-as-culture focus invites responses about personal identity rather than monitoring social differentiation based on racial ancestry. The following proposal is set forth primarily as a vehicle for initiating the discussion of the importance of race-conscious racial classifications, rather than being a concrete model for statistical data collection. The current list of racial classifications should be accompanied by the following explanation (exclusive of footnotes):

> Recognizing that there are no such things as scientifically pure races or ethnicities, and that a person's individual identity can never be reduced to a single box, this form requests that you indicate which single race and/or ethnicity you find most politically and socially meaningful. Because the collection of racial and ethnic data is utilized and compiled for the specific purpose of monitoring discrimination in society (see attached list of civil rights statutes which rely upon the Census Bureau collection of racial data), this classification system focuses upon the ways in which your appearance and assertion of race affect your treatment by others in society

> In order to assess the political role of your racial background you may reflect upon the following questions. When first interacting with others, in what ways does your appearance affect the interaction? For instance, an individual who in his or her daily interactions in society finds that others consistently react to him or her as White or Black, and modify their behavior based upon that physical assessment, can conclude that his or her White or Black phenotype determines the sociopolitical role of his or her racial background, regardless of how diverse that particular individual's ancestry actually is. Alternatively, when you share the details of your racial ancestry, how does that revelation affect your treatment by others? For instance, where an individual may phenotypically appear White, but when sharing his or her background with others discloses that his or her ancestry also includes Blacks and then finds that the listener is fixated only on the person's Black ancestry, then it would be appropriate for such an individual who personally identifies as White and Black to conclude that the "Black" racial classification reflects the sociopolitical role of his or her diverse racial background.

The goal of the proposed race-conscious classification system is to cultivate a more precise understanding of the ways in which race is socially and politically significant, apart from its role as one of many factors in personal identity formation. By designing a classification system that interrogates the political content of race, the collection of racial data can more closely correspond with the social dynamic such data seek to measure. Furthermore, the proposal's disjunction of the political meaning of race from the cultural approach to race also preserves an individual's ability to assert a varied personal identity. Specifically, the frank explanation of the reasons for a public inquiry into political race may assure the respondent that the complex and varied ways individuals construct and restructure their personal identities are not being called into question or challenged by the Census Bureau.

Notes and Questions

1. Toro and Hernández disagree on the role that "culture-race" should play in determining census categories. Who has the stronger argument? Are they using "culture" to mean the same thing?

Are the classification systems that Toro and Hernández propose workable?

For another perspective on the multiracial movement, see the excerpt from Lisa Jones in Chapter 11, § 3.

2. How do you feel when you are asked to "check a box"? Which box or boxes do you check? Is box-checking a necessary evil or a positive good?

3. How should American law and society respond to the greater recognition that race is fluid, rather than fixed, and the increasing number of openly multiracial people? Should racial categories ultimately be abolished? Is requiring people to declare themselves a member of a racial group for legal purposes in tension with the goal of eliminating racism?

4. In an ideal world, would "race" exist? In a future American society, should "race" cease to be important? Will it?

5. In the meantime, courts continue to struggle with the problem of categorizing groups and individuals. As you read the following case, consider the readings that have come before. Would they have helped the judge in making his decision?

ARTHUR PERKINS v. LAKE COUNTY DEPARTMENT OF UTILITIES
860 F. Supp. 1262 (N.D.Ohio 1994).

This action, brought pursuant to the Civil Rights Act of 1964, 42 U.S.C.A. § 2000e (Title VII), was filed on April 10, 1992, alleging disparate treatment in the workplace due to Plaintiff's status as an American Indian. Plaintiff, Arthur Perkins, is employed as a Laborer for the Lake County Department of Utilities (hereinafter the Department). Defendants are the Department and three of its commissioners. * * *

Plaintiff alleges in his complaint that: * * *

During the course of his employment Plaintiff was continually subjected to racial comments and discrimination by not being allowed to work overtime, only work the worse [sic] type of positions and not being promoted or allowed to test for promotions because of his race. Plaintiff's submission to this racial discrimination was imposed as a term or condition of employment. * * *

* * * Plaintiff was denied a promotion and a white male was given a supervisory position for which Plaintiff was qualified. This opening was available for white males but he was never given an opportunity to be considered for the position and he is the only minority of American Indian descent in the Lake County Utilities Department. * * *

Defendants have filed two motions for summary judgment. The first seeks partial summary judgment on Plaintiff's allegations that he was unlawfully denied promotions and promotion opportunities by reason of his national origin, on the basis that under Ohio law he is disqualified from holding the positions he sought.

Defendants' second motion for summary judgment * * * attacks Plaintiff's Title VII claims on the ground that Plaintiff is not, in fact, an American Indian and, therefore, not being a member of a class protected by Title VII cannot make out a *prima facie* case of discrimination thereunder. It is this motion which will be first addressed in this ruling. * * *

Title VII provides in part:

(a) It shall be an unlawful employment practice for an employer—

(1) to * * * discriminate against any individual with respect to his compensation, terms, conditions, or privileges of employment, because of such individual's race, color, religion, sex, or national origin[.]

Plaintiff seeks relief under Title VII on the basis of alleged discrimination by reason of national origin. Under the standards articulated in *McDonnell Douglas Corp. v. Green,* 411 U.S. 792 (1973), in order to proceed on such a claim Plaintiff must make out a *prima facie* case of discrimination, which includes evidence that he is a member of a protected class within the reach of Title VII.

Defendant's motion presents this Court with two questions: (1) whether Plaintiff is an American Indian, for Title VII purposes; and, (2) if not, whether he can nevertheless obtain Title VII relief for discrimination based upon his and his employer's mistaken belief that he is an American Indian.

Defendants offer as proof of their contention that Plaintiff is not a member of the class for which he seeks Title VII protection the affidavit of Paula Shepherd in which Ms. Shepherd avers in pertinent part:

1. Affiant is a resident of Burton, Ohio and is expert in the field of tracing family ancestry and race. * * *

4. Affiant was retained by the Lake County Board of Commissioners and Lake County Department of Utilities to research the ancestry and racial composition of Arthur Perkins, Jr. * * *

5. Affiant performed exhaustive research of said ancestry and racial composition through the U.S. census, birth and death records, Bureau of Indian Affairs documentation, Smithsonian Institute documentation and literature, United States of America documentation, funeral home records, National Genealogical Society Quarterly literature, Goins family newsletters and records, Cherokee Nation research, tombstone information, Salt Lake City Mormon records, United States National Archives records, and many other sources.

6. Affiant prepared a pedigree chart for Arthur Perkins, Jr., attached hereto as Exhibit 2.

7. The birth record of Arthur Perkins, Jr. indicates that he is white, and that his parents, Rosa Ashworth Perkins and Arthur Perkins, Sr., are both white.

8. Arthur Perkins, Sr.'s (Perkins' father) two parents were Joshua Perkins and Elizabeth Betty Perkins. Joshua and Elizabeth were first cousins. According to the death certificates of both they were white.

9. Affiant has made a study of the United States census and its various components and changes through the decades. References are to "200 Years of U.S. Census Taking: Population and Housing Questions, 1790–1990," U.S. Dept. of Commerce (1989). In the 1830 and 1840 censuses, the choice for race included only "Free White Persons," "Slaves," and "Free Colored Persons." *Id.* at 20. The purpose of the census up to and including 1840 was to determine who should be paying taxes. Indians were not included on the census since they did not pay taxes. It would have been wise, in a fashion, for a person to claim Indian heritage on the census since that person would not be required to pay taxes. In 1870, the census added the category of "Mulatto." "Be particularly careful in reporting the class Mulatto. The word here is generic, and includes quadroons, octoroons, and all persons having any perceptible trace of African blood." *Id.* at 26.[4] In 1880, the census was altered to allow for the following races: White, Black, Mulatto, Chinese and Indian. The 1890 census included various degrees of Mulatto, such as "Octoroon" and "Quadroon." The 1900 census did not include a Mulatto classification. The 1910 census classified Mulatto as "Other." The 1920 census stated that "A person of mixed White and Indian blood was to be returned as an Indian, except where the percentage of Indian blood was very small or where he or she was regarded as White in the community." There was even a column to indicate the percentage of Indian blood and tribe. *Id.* at 60.

10. The parents of Joshua Perkins (Perkins' paternal grandfather) were Isaac Perkins and Frances Goins. According to the 1840 census, Isaac Perkins was "Free colored." Mulatto was not a choice in the 1840 census. The 1850, 1860, 1870 and 1880 censuses indicated that Joshua Perkins was a Mulatto. Similarly, Frances "Fanny" Goins, in the 1850, 1860 and 1870 censuses, was listed as

---

4. "Mulatto" is presently defined as "a person of mixed white and Black ancestry." *The American Heritage Dictionary of the English Language* (3rd ed. 1992).

Mulatto. Eleven children were all also listed as Mulatto. Affiant can find no provable prior family link to Goins. * * *

12.   The parents of Isaac Perkins were George Perkins and Mary Ashworth. George Perkins was listed as "Free Colored" in the 1810 and 1830 censuses. In 1850 he was censused as Mulatto. In the 1830 census, Mary Ashworth was listed as "Free Colored," while in 1850 she was listed as Mulatto. Available racial data by census for their thirteen children indicates Mulatto. * * *

16.   This concluded the family history, back through 1/32 composition, and there is no indication from this information, or other family history collected through various treaties written on these families that there is any perceptible degree of Indian blood.

17.   Since Arthur Perkins, Jr. claimed in his deposition that he was Cherokee Indian on his mother's side, this side will be further examined.

18.   As stated earlier, Perkins' mother is Rosa Ashworth. In the 1920 census, the most current available census, Rosa Ashworth was listed as White. * * *

20.   Henderson Ashworth's parents were Napoleon Ashworth and Elizabeth Howard. In 1860 through 1880, Napoleon Ashworth was classified as Mulatto. In 1900 he was classified as White. There was no classification for Mulatto in 1900. In 1910 he was classified as White. There was a 1910 classification for Mulatto, but the definition did not require merely a "perceptible trace of African blood." Napoleon Ashworth was most likely more White than Black. Elizabeth Howard was listed as Mulatto in 1880, and White in 1900 and 1920. The three children are also all listed as White for 1900 and thereafter.

21.   Napoleon Ashworth homesteaded on June 4, 1891 in Louisiana. The appropriate certified documentation is attached hereto as Exhibit 7. Historically, an Indian could not legally homestead at that time, therefore, Napoleon Ashworth could not have been an Indian.

22.   The parents of Napoleon Ashworth were Isaiah Ashworth and Hannah Perkins. Isaiah Ashworth and Hannah Perkins were both censused as Mulatto in 1860, 1870 and 1880. Their twelve children were all also listed as Mulatto. * * *

29.   Affiant submitted all of these available names to Genealogical Research, which performed research on the issue of whether any of these names appeared on any of the federally recognized rolls for the Cherokee Nation. A copy of their affidavit summarizing their findings is attached hereto indicating that none of these individuals, including Arthur Perkins, Jr., was an enrolled member of any tribe of the Cherokee Nation, his claimed ancestry.

30.   Attached hereto as Exhibits 11 and 12 are pertinent sections of Volumes I and II of the Preliminary Inventories from the National Archives of the United States, Records of the Bureau of Indian Affairs. These records list the recognized tribes and reservations of native american Indians. There is no listing for "Redbones."

31.   Attached Exhibits 13 through 38, inclusive, are certified copies from the National Archives and Records Commission illustrating the records searched for the five recognized Indian Nations for all available ancestors of Arthur Perkins, Jr.

32.   None of the Exhibits 13 through 38, inclusive, indicate that any of the ancestors of Arthur Perkins, Jr. was a member of any of said Nations or tribes thereof. * * *

34.   After reviewing all of the research enumerated herein, and applying my skills as a genealogical researcher, it is my expert opinion to a reasonable degree of professional and expert certainty that Arthur Perkins, Jr. has no provable ancestral ties to any of the recognized Indian Nations. * * *

36.   Finally, it is my expert opinion that Arthur Perkins, Jr. has no significant percentage of Indian blood.

The documentation upon which Ms. Shepherd bases her conclusions is attached to Defendants' brief, including the birth and death certificates cited by Ms. Shepherd in her affidavit in which Plaintiff's race and those of his immediate relatives are listed as "white." No member of Plaintiff's family tree is designated "Indian" on any documents before this Court.

Defendants also submit various documents including certificates of homesteading referred to in Ms. Shepherd's affidavit, as well as Indices and Rolls listing members of various tribes. Although a number of "Perkins" and some other family names are listed on the Rolls Ms. Shepherd avers that there is no indication that any of them are ancestors of Plaintiff.[5]

Defendants additionally direct this Court's attention to a number of cases in which the term "Indian" has been defined in various contexts. Defendant's assert that these cases preclude a finding that Plaintiff falls into that racial category.

In response, Plaintiff has submitted a number of affidavits, including his own in which he avers in part "affiant is an American Indian and his parents have always told him of his Indian heritage and they have acknowledged their Indian heritage all their life." Plaintiff has additionally submitted affidavits from his mother, Rosa Perkins; his brothers, George, Tony and James Perkins; his sisters, Hazel Cormier, Billie Mae Courts and Anna Faye Jones; and his brothers-in-law, Lee Roy Baily, Carson Jones and Donald L. Courts.

In her affidavit Plaintiff's mother avers: * * *

5. Although the exhibits submitted in support of Ms. Shepherd's affidavit are imposing, it is difficult for this Court to fully determine their significance, particularly with respect to the tribal Indices and Rolls. For instance, several of the copied pages of the Rolls submitted to this Court do not cover the portion of the alphabet which would include some of Plaintiff's relatives who do not have the name Perkins. The inherent difficulty of proving a negative, as well as this Court's ignorance concerning tribal membership and enrollment, make it unclear whether all relevant Indices and Rolls were examined and submitted. This Court does not impugn Ms. Shepherd's study, but merely wonders, is there more?

4. Affiant knows thru [sic] the Perkins family history that Arthur Perkins, Jr. is a descendant of an American Indian and that Arthur Perkins, Jr. can rightfully claim to be an American Indian.

5. The Perkins family has claimed American Indian heritage and Arthur Perkins, Sr. has publicly claimed his American Indian heritage during his lifetime.

6. Affiant states that Arthur Perkins, Jr. is an American Indian according to his family history.

The remaining affidavits of family members are identical to that of Rosa Perkins, except as to the names and residences of the affiants.

Plaintiff also points to the deposition of Melton Fletcher in support of his contention that he is a Native American.

Mr. Fletcher described himself as a licensed social worker and "the program coordinator for the North American Indian Cultural Center." He testified that he had worked as an Indian Affairs Specialist since 1957. He further stated that he was familiar with a "Perkins" family from Singer, Louisiana, with whom he had lived for a short period of time when he was child and who were Native Americans. Under cross-examination Mr. Fletcher acknowledged that he did not know if Plaintiff was related to the Perkins family that he knew in Louisiana.

Mr. Fletcher testified that Native Americans in the area of Singer, Louisiana called themselves "Redbones," and that when he first met Plaintiff in connection with this lawsuit and learned that Plaintiff was from Singer Mr. Fletcher said "Well, you are a Redbone." With respect to the term "Redbone" Mr. Fletcher offered the following explanation of its meaning:

Q. And where did that term, "Redbone" come from?

A. Well, I really don't know. That was before my time, but I do know what happened there.

Q. What did happen?

A. Well, it was two brothers and one married a black lady and the other one married another Indian. And one Indian went on one side of the road, on Bear Creek, and they settled on that side. And the black Indian went on the other side and they settled on that.

Q. And they were called Redbones?

A. They were called Redbones.

He testified that the term "Redbone" was a "derogatory remark" and that he considered it a racial slur. It is undisputed that "Redbone" is not a federally registered Indian tribe.

As to Plaintiff's personal appearance Mr. Fletcher stated that there was no doubt in his mind that Plaintiff is a Native American. While acknowledging that although himself an American Indian he had been mistaken on a number of occasions for an Italian or a Mexican, Mr. Fletcher reiterated on cross-examination that:

A. I said that he appeared to look like an Indian to me. He certainly—I've been around a lot of native people, and him walking in my door, I—it would be very hard for me to mistake him for anything else.

Q. Okay. Any specific features that indicate that to you?

A. Well, yes. You could tell by his facial structure, is one thing.

Q. Okay.

A. The other thing, he just—Indians look Indians. They have facial features, you know, about them and the complexion, that it would be hard to discern. They'd either have, number one, the facial features or the complexion.

* * *

A. You know, but I'm around Indians every day, every day, and you just can't hardly miss some feature in them, regardless of how much they've been mixed.

With respect to his physical characteristics and the perceptions of his employers and co-workers Plaintiff submitted affidavits of co-workers * * * in which the affiants signed substantially (not to mention suspiciously) identical affidavits stating in part that Plaintiff "appears to be an American Indian and he always claimed to be an American Indian[.]"

It is undisputed by Defendants that, without regard to whether Plaintiff is or is not demonstrably an American Indian, he considers himself and holds himself out to be such. Moreover, it appears that at least until institution of this action Defendants considered him to be such. This is evident by the fact that it was not until well into the litigation of this action that Defendants challenged his membership in that class. Additionally, Plaintiff was apparently listed in Defendants' records as an American Indian. Although the statistical records kept by Defendants do not list the racial background or nationality of its employees by name, Defendants' records include only one American Indian, and there is no indication that the employee so listed was other than Plaintiff.

Upon this evidentiary background this Court addresses the first question—Is Plaintiff an American Indian?

While this question is simple and would seem to be amenable to a straightforward answer, this Court has discovered that the issue of membership in a given racial classification is deceptively complex. It is complicated first by the amorphous definition of the term "race," and second by the difficulty of categorizing individuals with varied and/or unclear ancestry within a particular racial grouping.

The issue of who belongs in what racial classification has occupied the minds of Americans throughout the history of this country.

Regrettably, racial classifications may be, and traditionally have been, used to justify the exploitation of certain groups. Ashley Montagu, *Man's Most Dangerous Myth: The Fallacy of Race 38* (1964) ("It was only among peoples who had themselves for centuries been emancipated from serfdom and slavery, but who themselves kept slaves, that the hereditary or biological conception of race differences was developed.") More recently, racial classifications have been used as a method of determining entitlement to certain government subsidized benefits. Consequently, the incentive or disincentive to categorize oneself as a member of a particular minority class has varied over the years.

The traditional racial categorizations of Negroid, Caucasoid, and Mongoloid have been narrowed, expanded, and/or reconfigured by various social scientists and other disciplines over the years to the point that the very notion of "race" may be deemed illusory. * * *

Historically, racial classification in America arises out of what is apparently a uniquely "American institution known informally as 'the one-drop rule,' which defines as black a person with as little as a single drop of 'black blood.' This notion derives from a long-discredited belief that each race had its own blood type, which was correlated with physical appearance and social behavior." Lawrence Wright, *One Drop of Blood*, The New Yorker, July 25, 1994, 46, 48.

With the "one-drop rule" failing into deserved disrepute no easy classification system has taken its place, and issues of membership in a particular racial classification have been ill-defined and subjective.

> Whatever the word "race" may mean elsewhere in the world, or to the world of science, it is clear that in America the categories are arbitrary, confused, and hopelessly intermingled. In many cases, Americans don't know who they are racially speaking. A National Center for Health Statistics study found that 5.8 percent of the people who called themselves Black were seen as White by a census interviewer. Nearly a third of the people identifying themselves as Asian were classified as White or Black by independent observers. That was also true of seventy percent of people who identified themselves as American Indians. Robert A. Hahn, an epidemiologist at the Centers for Disease Control and Prevention, analyzed deaths of infants born from 1983 through 1985. In an astounding number of cases, the infant had a different race on its death certificate from the one on its birth certificate[.]

L. Wright, *supra*, at 53.

As early as 1934 the United States Supreme Court recognized that there was no strict formula for determining racial class. In a general discussion concerning naturalization the Supreme Court inserted an elastic element into the determination of race, explaining, "men are not white if the strain of colored blood in them is a half or a quarter, or, not improbably, even less, the governing test always being that of common understanding." *Morrison v. California*, 291 U.S. 82, 86 (1934). More recently, the Supreme Court recognized the problematic nature of racial categorization in *St. Francis College v. Al–Khazraji*, 481 U.S. 604 (1987) as follows:

> Many modern biologists and anthropologists, however, criticize racial classifications as arbitrary and of little use in understanding the variability of human beings. It is said that genetically homogeneous populations do not exist and traits are not discontinuous between populations; therefore, a population can only be described in terms of relative frequencies of various traits. Clear-cut categories do not

exist. The particular traits which have generally been chosen to characterize races have been criticized as having little biological significance. It has been found that differences between individuals of the same race are often greater than the differences between the "average" individuals of different races. These observations and others have led some, but not all, scientists to conclude that racial classifications are for the most part sociopolitical, rather than biological, in nature.

Id. at 610 n.4. See also *McCleskey v. Kemp,* 481 U.S. 279, 316 n.39, (1987) ("in our heterogeneous society the lower courts have found the boundaries of race and ethnicity increasingly difficult to determine.")

Lower courts have also questioned the efficacy of racial classification. * * *

The terms "race" and "racial discrimination" may be of such doubtful sociological validity as to be scientifically meaningless, but these terms nonetheless are subject to a commonly-accepted, albeit sometimes vague, understanding. Those courts which have extended the coverage of § 1981 have done so on a realistic basis, within the framework of this common meaning and understanding. On this admittedly unscientific basis, whites are plainly a "race" susceptible to "racial discrimination;" Hispanic persons and Indians, like blacks, have been traditional victims of group discrimination, and, however inaccurately or stupidly, are frequently and even commonly subject to a "racial" identification as "non-whites." *Budinsky v. Corning Glass Works*, 425 F. Supp. 786, 788 (W.D.Pa.1977). The thread running through such cases is that "race" is not a static concept. It lives and changes according to popular beliefs.

"Race," it should always be remembered is a human grouping which is culturally defined in a given society. "Race prejudice" is a system of reciprocal relations of stereotyping, discrimination, and segregation existing between human groupings which are considered as "races."

Montagu, *supra* at 137 (footnotes omitted).

The difficulty of placing individuals into racial categories is compounded in Title VII, because Title VII further categorizes and distinguishes national origin as a category presumably different from that of race. This very distinction between classifications based upon race and nationality illustrates the perception-oriented nature of the term "race."

This race-versus-national-origin complication is reflected in cases involving 42 U.S.C.A. § 1981, which has been held to protect individuals from racial discrimination. Many courts, when deciding § 1981 cases, have faced the challenge of determining whether a plaintiff was discriminated against due to his or her race, which is prohibited, or, rather, as a result of his or her national origin, which, arguably, is not prohibited by that statute. In engaging in the mental gymnastics arising out of this distinction courts have strived to define and distinguish the two terms with varying degrees of success.

This issue was addressed in *Ortiz v. Bank of America*, 547 F. Supp. 550 (E.D.Cal.1982), in which the court stated:

> As I will discuss more fully later in this opinion, I have serious doubt that race can be defined in contradistinction from national origin in any meaningful fashion. The difficulties in defining race often present themselves in attempting to define such terms as "Hispanic." For instance, is someone of native Indian descent who comes from present day Mexico a Hispanic? Even more importantly, should the government or the courts be in the business of "certifying" bloodlines and races?

Id. at 559 n.16. That court went on to question whether there is even an articulable distinction between the concepts of "race" and "national origin." *Id.* at 560 ("the notion of 'race' as contrasted with national origin is highly dubious"). See also, *Aponte v. National Steel Service Ctr.*, 500 F. Supp. 198 (N.D.Ill.1980) (distinguishing between "white" and "non-whites" rather than "race" and "national origin" for § 1981 purposes).[7]

In *Anooya v. Hilton Hotels Corp.*, 733 F.2d 48 (7th Cir.1984) the concurring opinion concluded that the plaintiff had no § 1981 action as a result of discrimination against him due to his national origin of Iraqi, but suggested that had the plaintiff plead [*sic*] discrimination on the basis of skin color the action would have been one under race discrimination. See also *Abdulrahim v. Gene B. Glick Co.*, 612 F. Supp. 256, 263 (N.D.Ind.1985) (discrimination based on skin color creates action based on race.)

Implicit in the holdings that discrimination on the basis of skin color amounts to racial discrimination is that a plaintiff's skin color, rather than indicating in positive terms what the race of the plaintiff is, appears merely to indicate the negative, that he or she is not white, thus, essentially breaking race down into two categories, white and non-white. *Gonzalez v. Stanford Applied Engineering*, 597 F.2d 1298, 1300 (9th Cir.1979). It is the skin color leading to the perception that the person is "different" from the white majority that leads to discrimination.

That such perception plays an important role in determining who is a member of a minority group for purposes of Title VII is illustrated in the Code of Federal Regulations of national origin discrimination. C.F.R. § 1606.1 provides in part:

> The Commission defines national origin discrimination broadly as including, but not limited to, the denial of equal employment opportunity because of an individual's, or his or her ancestor's, place of

---

7. It is noted that with respect to Native Americans it is not always clear whether a particular court categorizes them according to racial classifications or by national origin. See *e.g., Toledo v. Nobel–Sysco, Inc.*, 892 F.2d 1481 (10th Cir.), *cert.* denied, 495 U.S. 948 (1990) (addressing discrimination against American Indians in terms of both national origin and race); *Maier v. Police & Fire Federal Credit Union*, 813 F. Supp. 326 (E.D.Pa.1993) (same); *Scott v. Eversole Mortuary*, 522 F.2d 1110 (9th Cir.1975) (al- though court did not address issue of whether discrimination against Native American constituted racial or nationality discrimination it held that American Indian could state a claim under 42 U.S.C.A. § 1981 which arguably protects only on the basis of race); *Gonzalez v. Stanford Applied Engineering Inc.*, 597 F.2d 1298, 1300 (9th Cir.1979) (suggesting that discrimination on the basis of skin color is racial discrimination without regard to any scientific distinction between races).

origin; or because an individual has the physical, cultural or linguistic characteristics of a national origin group.

Under this definition physical characteristics associated with a particular nationality may be all that is necessary to show membership in a class, without regard to percentage of blood traceable to that nation.

Likewise, subjective perception of an individual's race clearly plays an important role in racial classification where discrimination is involved. This Court has never encountered an instance in which an employer admittedly first checked the pedigree of an employee before engaging in discriminatory conduct. "Historically, common notions of race divided people either along national lines or the perceiver's subjective evaluation of skin pigmentation. * * * The idea of race as an element of the history of ideas in this country has frequently been no more than a vehicle for racism, *i.e.*, a presumed inherited defect in those who are not of the racist's kind, however he defines his kind." *Ortiz,* 547 F. Supp. at 567.

Having considered the amorphous and subjective nature of racial classification in general, this Court must examine the subsidiary issue of categorizing an individual within a particular race.

As far as designation of individuals as Native Americans is concerned, there is no hard and fast rule.

"The term 'Indian' is used in several contexts including biological descent, cultural identity and legal status." *United States v. State of Washington,* 476 F. Supp. 1101, 1103 (W.D.Wash.1979). It is said that:

> From a legal standpoint, then, the biological question of race is generally pertinent, but not conclusive. Legal status depends not only upon biological, but also upon social factors, such as the relation of the individual concerned to a white or Indian community. This relationship, in turn, has two ends—an individual and a community. The individual may withdraw from a tribe or be expelled from a tribe; or he may be adopted by a tribe. He may or may not reside on an Indian reservation. He may or may not be subject to the control of the Federal Government with respect to various transactions. All these social or political factors may affect the classification of an individual as an "Indian" or a "non-Indian" for legal purposes, or for certain legal purposes. Indeed, in accordance with a statute reserving jurisdiction over offenses between tribal members to a tribal court, a white man adopted into an Indian tribe has been held to be an Indian, and the decided cases do not foreclose the argument that a person of entirely Indian ancestry who has never had any relations with any Indian tribe or reservation may be considered a non-Indian for most legal purposes.

> What must be remembered is that legislators, when they use the term "Indian" to establish special rules of law applicable to "Indians," are generally trying to deal with a group distinguished from "non-Indian" groups by public opinion, and this public opinion varies so widely that on certain reservations it is common to refer to a person as an Indian although 15 of his 16 ancestors, 4 generations

back, were white persons; while in other parts of the country, as in the Southwest, a person may be considered a Spanish–American rather than an Indian although his blood is predominantly Indian.

Felix S. Cohen, *Handbook of Federal Indian Law* 2 (1971).

Individual tribes frequently have constitutions defining who can be considered a member of that tribe. See *State of Washington*, 476 F. Supp. at 1104–1110 (Duwamish Tribe constitution requires Indian blood, although something less than full-blood, and descent from Duwamish tribe; Samish Tribe requires Indian blood of as little as 1/32nd, and name on official membership roll; Snohomish Tribe—Indian blood with no minimum amount, and listing on specified rolls; Snoqualmie—1/8th blood; Steilacoom—enrollment in Tribe and descent from Indian.)

There being no definitive test for labeling an individual as "Indian" or "non-Indian," this Court has reviewed the cases cited by Defendants and surveyed cases from other federal courts in search of criteria for such determination. Although this Court was unable to locate any cases in which an individual's status as a Native American was challenged within the context of a statute prohibiting racial discrimination it has arisen in other contexts, and a brief review of some of those cases may be instructive here. * * *

* * * Title VII does not single out Indians for special benefits or treatment, but, rather, attempts to equalize the position of all employees, be they Native American, African–American, Hispanic, Asian or white. The statute addresses perceived differences which do not have a basis in fact between races and ethnic groups. For example, when bringing an action under Title VII African–Americans do not have to demonstrate that their relatives lived in Africa, or that they visit the site of their roots, or that they are involved in any kind of cultural activities associated with Africa. They only have to appear to be African–Americans to be deemed members of that protected class.

It is because Title VII is in force to equalize rather than separate that this Court finds that membership in a given protected class carries a lower threshold of proof than would be the case under entitlement legislation. With this in mind, this Court turns to the evidence before it for a determination of whether Plaintiff has demonstrated a genuine issue as to whether he belongs in a protected category.

In addressing this question, this Court is mindful of the holding in *Bennun v. Rutgers State University*, 941 F.2d 154 (3d Cir. 1991), in which the court found that the trial court did not err in finding that the plaintiff was Hispanic, for purposes of making out a *prima facie* case of employment discrimination in the context of Title VII.[13] The court's finding was based not upon the plaintiff's ancestry but, rather, "his birth in Argentina, his belief that he is Hispanic, identifies with and continues to adopt Spanish culture in his life and speaks Spanish in his

---

13. Because the district court had found that the plaintiff had made out a *prima facie* case on the basis of race, Hispanic, rather than national origin, Argentinean, the court of appeals only addressed whether the plaintiff had demonstrated membership in that racial classification, such as it is. The *Bennun* decision is the closest in point to this case which this Court has been able to find.

home." *Id.* at 173. The court of appeals also noted that the district court had had an opportunity to observe the plaintiff's appearance, speech and mannerisms in determining his race.

This Court recognizes that in this case Defendants have submitted evidence suggesting that neither Plaintiff nor his immediate family are members of any tribe, live in an Indian community, or participate in Indian cultural events.

On the other hand, there is also evidence before this Court that Plaintiff has the physical appearance of an Indian, that he believes himself to be an Indian and has represented himself as such, and that heretofore Defendants apparently believed him to be an Indian. Moreover, Defendants concede that he may have some Native American blood, albeit less than 1/16th.

This Court is not prepared to hold as a matter of law that one-sixteenth Indian blood, which Defendants seemingly concede Plaintiff may have, is insufficient to establish membership in a protected class, based upon national origin, as an American Indian.

Further, the evidence relied upon by Defendants in support of the contention that Plaintiff is not an American Indian is not, in this Court's opinion, sufficient to conclusively establish the accuracy of that proposition.

The fact that Plaintiff and members of his family have been listed on birth and death certificates as "white" is not dispositive.[15] In an essay submitted by Defendants as part of Ms. Shepherd's research the inaccuracy of such certificates, especially where "verry slitly mixt" tri-racial persons are involved, is not unheard of. Virginia Easley DeMarce, *"Verry Slitly Mixt": Tri-racial Isolate Families of the Upper South—A Genealogical Study* 80 Nat'l Genealogical Soc'y 5, 7 (1992). Unions between Indian and English descendants tend to be disguised by the assumption of English names. *Id.* at 11. Moreover, seventy percent of American Indians marry outside their racial class, thereby making racial classification difficult. L. Wright, *supra*, at 49.

Defendants' showing of census listings is also not dispositive. Racial categorizations in the census have historically been dubious. *Id.* at 47 ("How unsettled this country has always been about its racial categories is evident in the fact that nearly every census since [1790] has measured race differently.")[16] The census does not require proof of ancestry. A person is listed on the census according to how he labels himself. See *Morton v. Ruiz*, 415 U.S. 199, 224 (1974).

---

15. The possibility that American Indians may not have always clamored to be recognized as members of that society is not a great surprise. "In assessing the impact of science upon eighteenth-and nineteenth-century views of race, we must first recognize the cultural milieu of a society whose leaders and intellectuals did not doubt the propriety of racial ranking—with Indians below whites, and blacks below everybody else." Gould, *supra*, at 31.

16. In 1960 Latin–Americans were listed on the census as "white." When Hispanics became a protected class, however, the question of classifying within that group became troublesome. In 1970 there was a category for people from Central or South America. That category was often checked by people from central or south United States, causing a statistical nightmare. L. Wright, *supra*, at 52.

As this Court believes that on the present record a jury issue exists on the factual issue of Plaintiffs heritage, it follows that Defendants' motion for summary judgment must be denied.

Notes and Questions

1.   Is Arthur Perkins an Indian? What facts are necessary to answer that question? Is his Indian identity a "factual" question at all? Is it a legal question? A racial question? A cultural question?

2.   Was Arthur Perkins, assuming his allegations to be true, discriminated against on the basis of "race"? On the basis of "national origin"? On some other ground? Why does it matter? Why should it matter? Suppose he was trying to gain a benefit, such as a preference in university admissions, rather than avoiding or gaining redress for an evil, such as discrimination?

3.   Should the belief of the employer be relevant to the determination of protected class status under Title VII? In an omitted part of the opinion, the court holds, "it is the employer's reasonable belief that a given employee is a member of a protected class that controls this issue." Should an employer's belief or an employee's identification control?

4.   Are "Latinos" a race? In *Hernandez v. Texas*, 347 U.S. 475 (1954), the Supreme Court, without treating Mexican Americans as a race, nevertheless held that discrimination against Mexican Americans violated the Equal Protection Clause. See Chapter 7 § 1, Chapter 4 § 1, and Ian F. Haney López, *Race and Erasure: The Salience of Race to LatCrit Theory*, 85 Calif. L. Rev. 1143 (1997); 10 La Raza L.J. 57 (1998).

Chapter 2

AFRICAN AMERICANS

The struggle of African Americans against slavery and racial oppression has been central in the struggle for civil rights for all Americans. Political debates and compromises on the issue of slavery were central in the formation of the Constitution. The oppression and cruelty of slavery, which we explore below, may encourage a tendency to see African Americans solely as victims of white oppression. While they certainly were so victimized, African Americans also resisted their oppression and fought for their freedom by every means available to them under extreme circumstances. Consider Herbert Aptheker's comments on why violence and cruelty against slaves was necessary:

> History certainly teaches us, if it teaches anything at all, that human beings have the glorious urge to be something better than they are at any moment, or to do something new, or to provide their offspring with greater advantages and a happier world than they themselves possess. People who are degraded and despised and sold and bought and arbitrarily separated from all that is familiar and dear will be unhappy. They will be discontented and will *think, at least, of bettering their conditions.* This last idea, if persisted in, was death to the slave institution, and it was precisely because the slaves were property, precisely because they were valuable and profitable, *but rational*, instruments of production, that cruelty was necessary.

See Herbert Aptheker, *Essays in the History of The American Negro* 8 (1973). In reading the materials that follow, it is crucial to maintain the sense of the constant, rational struggle of African Americans against the oppression imposed upon them. See Aldon D. Morris, *The Origins of the Civil Rights Movement* x (1984).

SECTION 1.   EARLY HISTORY

The literature on the history of, first, Africans, and, later, African Americans in the United States is vast. One of the first questions to confront any writer on this subject is where to start. Many historians of Africans in the United States begin with the arrival, in 1619, of a ship in Jamestown carrying twenty black persons, likely slaves, although possibly indentured servants. See A. Leon Higginbotham, Jr., *In the Matter of Color* 20–21 (1980); Winthrop D. Jordan, *White Over Black* 73–75 (1971).

One could begin the story earlier, with Estebanico, a Black who accompanied the Spanish explorer Cabeza de Vaca and who later led expeditions into the Southwest. Well before the American version of slavery was established in the United States, Estebanico explored the Southwest. Or one could begin the story even earlier, in Africa, before Europeans—Portuguese and Spanish first, and soon after the English—began commerce in black slaves that would shape profoundly the history of the United States. Consider the following excerpt from Howard Zinn.

HOWARD ZINN

A People's History of the United States: 1492–Present
23–38 (1995).*

* * *

There is not a country in world history in which racism has been more important, for so long a time, as the United States. And the problem of "the color line," as W.E.B. Du Bois put it, is still with us. So it is more than a purely historical question to ask: How does it start?—and an even more urgent question: How might it end? Or, to put it differently: Is it possible for whites and blacks to live together without hatred?

If history can help answer these questions, then the beginnings of slavery in North America—a continent where we can trace the coming of the first whites and the first blacks—might supply at least a few clues.

Some historians think those first blacks in Virginia were considered as servants, like the white indentured servants brought from Europe. But the strong probability is that, even if they were listed as "servants" (a more familiar category to the English), they were viewed as being different from white servants, were treated differently, and in fact were slaves. In any case, slavery developed quickly into a regular institution, into the normal labor relation of blacks to whites in the New World. With it developed that special racial feeling—whether hatred, or contempt, or pity, or patronization—that accompanied the inferior position of blacks in America for the next 350 years—that combination of inferior status and derogatory thought we call racism.

Everything in the experience of the first white settlers acted as a pressure for the enslavement of blacks. * * *

The Virginians needed labor, to grow corn for subsistence, to grow tobacco for export. They had just figured out how to grow tobacco, and in 1617 they sent off the first cargo to England. Finding that, like all pleasurable drugs tainted with moral disapproval, it brought a high price, the planters, despite their high religious talk, were not going to ask questions about something so profitable.

They couldn't force Indians to work for them, as Columbus had done. They were outnumbered, and while, with superior firearms, they could massacre Indians, they would face massacre in return. They could not capture them and keep them enslaved; the Indians were tough, resourceful, defiant, and at home in these woods, as the transplanted Englishmen were not.

White servants had not yet been brought over in sufficient quantity. Besides, they did not come out of slavery, and did not have to do more than contract their labor for a few years to get their passage and a start in the New World. * * *

Black slaves were the answer. And it was natural to consider imported blacks as slaves, even if the institution of slavery would not be regularized and legalized for several decades. Because, by 1619, a million blacks had already been brought from Africa to South America and the Caribbean, to the Portuguese and Spanish colonies, to work as slaves. Fifty years before Columbus, the Portuguese took ten African blacks to Lisbon—this was the start of a regular trade in slaves. African blacks had been stamped as slave labor for a hundred years. So it would have been strange if those twenty blacks, forcibly transported to Jamestown, and sold as objects to settlers anxious for a steadfast source of labor, were considered as anything but slaves.

Their helplessness made enslavement easier. The Indians were on their own land. The whites were in their own European culture. The blacks had been torn from their land and culture, forced into a situation where the heritage of language, dress, custom, family relations, was bit by bit obliterated except for the remnants that blacks could hold on to by sheer, extraordinary persistence.

Was their culture inferior—and so subject to easy destruction? Inferior in military capability, yes—vulnerable to whites with guns and ships. But in no other way—except that cultures that are different are often taken as inferior, especially when such a judgment is practical and profitable. Even militarily, while the Westerners could secure forts on the African coast, they were unable to subdue the interior and had to come to terms with its chiefs.

The African civilization was as advanced in its own way as that of Europe. In certain ways, it was more admirable; but it also included cruelties, hierarchical privilege, and the readiness to sacrifice human lives for religion or profit. It was a civilization of 100 million people, using iron implements and skilled in farming. It had large urban centers and remarkable achievements in weaving, ceramics, sculpture. * * *

Africa had a kind of feudalism, like Europe based on agriculture, and with hierarchies of lords and vassals. But African feudalism did not come, as did Europe's, out of the slave societies of Greece and Rome, which had destroyed ancient tribal life. In Africa, tribal life was still powerful, and some of its better features—a communal spirit, more kindness in law and punishment—still existed. And because the lords did not have the weapons that European lords had, they could not command obedience as easily.

* * *

Slavery existed in the African states, and it was sometimes used by Europeans to justify their own slave trade. But, as Davidson points out, the "slaves" of Africa were more like the serfs of Europe—in other words, like most of the population of Europe. It was a harsh servitude, but they had rights which slaves brought to America did not have, and they were "altogether different from the human cattle of the slave ships and the American plantations." In the Ashanti Kingdom of West Africa, one observer noted that "a slave might marry; own property; himself own a slave; swear an oath; be a competent witness and ultimately become an heir to his master.... An Ashanti slave, nine cases out of ten, possibly became an adopted member of the family, and in time his descendants so merged and intermarried with the owner's kinsmen that only a few would know their origin."

One slave trader, John Newton (who later became an antislavery leader), wrote about the people of what is now Sierra Leone:

> The state of slavery, among these wild barbarous people, as we esteem them, is much milder than in our colonies. For as, on the one hand, they have no land in high cultivation, like our West India plantations, and therefore no call for that excessive, unintermitted labour, which exhausts our slaves: so, on the other hand, no man is permitted to draw blood even from a slave.

African slavery is hardly to be praised. But it was far different from plantation or mining slavery in the Americas, which was lifelong, morally crippling, destructive of family ties, without hope of any future. African slavery lacked two elements that made American slavery the most cruel form of slavery in history: the frenzy for limitless profit that comes from capitalistic agriculture; the reduction of the slave to less than human status by the use of racial hatred, with that relentless clarity based on color, where white was master, black was slave.

* * *

First the Dutch, then the English, dominated the slave trade. (By 1795 Liverpool had more than a hundred ships carrying slaves and accounted for half of all the European slave trade.) Some Americans in New England entered the business, and in 1637 the first American slave ship, the *Desire*, sailed from Marblehead. Its holds were partitioned into racks, 2 feet by 6 feet, with leg irons and bars.

By 1800, 10 to 15 million blacks had been transported as slaves to the Americas, representing perhaps one-third of those originally seized in Africa. It is roughly estimated that Africa lost 50 million human beings to death and slavery in those centuries we call the beginnings of modern Western civilization, at the hands of the slave traders and plantation owners in Western Europe and America, the countries deemed the most advanced in the world.

* * *

This unequal treatment, this developing combination of contempt and oppression, feeling and action, which we call "racism"—was this the result of a "natural" antipathy of white against black? The question is important, not just as a matter of historical accuracy, but because any emphasis on "natural" racism lightens the responsibility of the social system. If racism can't be shown to be natural, then it is the result of certain conditions, and we are impelled to eliminate those conditions.

We have no way of testing the behavior of whites and blacks toward one another under favorable conditions—with no history of subordination, no money incentive for exploitation and enslavement, no desperation for survival requiring forced labor. All the conditions for black and white in seventeenth-century America were the opposite of that, all powerfully directed toward antagonism and mistreatment. Under such conditions even the slightest display of humanity between the races might be considered evidence of a basic human drive toward community.

* * *

In spite of [such] preconceptions about blackness, in spite of special subordination of blacks in the Americas in the seventeenth century, there is evidence that where whites and blacks found themselves with common problems, common work, common enemy in their master, they behaved toward one another as equals. As one scholar of slavery, Kenneth Stampp, has put it, Negro and white servants of the seventeenth century were "remarkably unconcerned about the visible physical differences."

Black and white worked together, fraternized together. The very fact that laws had to be passed after a while to forbid such relations indicates the strength of that tendency. In 1661 a law was passed in Virginia that "in case any English servant shall run away in company of any Negroes" he would have to give special service for extra years to the master of the runaway Negro. In 1691, Virginia provided for the banishment of any "white man or woman being free who shall intermarry with a negro, mulatto, or Indian man or woman bond or free."

There is an enormous difference between a feeling of racial strangeness, perhaps fear, and the mass enslavement of millions of black people that took place in the Americas. The transition from one to the other cannot be explained easily by "natural" tendencies. It is not hard to understand as the outcome of historical conditions.

Slavery grew as the plantation system grew. The reason is easily traceable to something other than natural racial repugnance: The number of arriving whites, whether free or indentured servants (under four to seven years contract), was not enough to meet the need of the plantations. By 1700, in Virginia, there were 6,000 slaves, one-twelfth of the population. By 1763, there were 170,000 slaves, about half the population.

Blacks were easier to enslave than whites or Indians. But they were still not easy to enslave. From the beginning, the imported black men and women resisted their enslavement. Ultimately their resistance was controlled, and slavery was established for 3 million blacks in the South. Still, under the most difficult conditions, under pain of mutilation and death, throughout their two hundred years of enslavement in North America, these Afro–Americans continued to rebel. Only occasionally was there an organized insurrection. More often they showed their refusal to submit by running away. Even more often, they engaged in sabotage, slowdowns, and subtle forms of resistance which asserted, if only to themselves and their brothers and sisters, their dignity as human beings.

* * *

Fear of slave revolt seems to have been a permanent fact of plantation life. William Byrd, a wealthy Virginia slaveowner, wrote in 1736:

We have already at least 10,000 men of these descendants of Ham, fit to bear arms, and these numbers increase every day, as well by birth as by importation. And in case there should arise a man of desperate fortune, he might with more advantage than Cataline kindle a servile war ... and tinge our rivers wide as they are with blood.

It was an intricate and powerful system of control that the slaveowners developed to maintain their labor supply and their way of life, a system both subtle and crude, involving every device that social orders employ for keeping power and wealth where it is. As Kenneth Stampp puts it:

A wise master did not take seriously the belief that Negroes were natural-born slaves. He knew better. He knew that Negroes freshly imported from Africa had to be broken into bondage; that each succeeding generation had to be carefully trained. This was no easy task, for the bondsman rarely submitted willingly. Moreover, he rarely submitted completely. In most cases there was no end to the need for control—at least not until old age reduced the slave to a condition of helplessness.

The system was psychological and physical at the same time. The slaves were taught discipline, were impressed again and again with the idea of their own inferiority to "know their place," to see blackness as a sign of subordination, to be awed by the power of their master, to merge their interest with the master's, destroying their own individual needs. To accomplish this there was discipline of hard labor, the breakup of the slave family, the lulling effects of religion (which sometimes led to "great mischief," as one slaveholder reported), the creation of disunity among slaves by separating them into field slaves and more privileged house slaves, and finally the power of law and the immediate power of the overseer to invoke whipping, burning, mutilation, and death. Dismemberment was provided for in the Virginia Code of 1705. Maryland passed a law in 1723 providing for cutting off the ears of blacks who struck whites, and that for certain serious crimes, slaves should be hanged and the body quartered and exposed. * * *

Only one fear was greater than the fear of black rebellion in the new American colonies. That was the fear that discontented whites would join black slaves to overthrow the existing order. In the early years of slavery, especially, before racism as a way of thinking was firmly ingrained, while white indentured servants were often treated as badly as black slaves, there was a possibility of cooperation. As Edmund Morgan sees it:

There are hints that the two despised groups initially saw each other as sharing the same predicament. It was common, for example, for servants and slaves to run away together, steal hogs together, get drunk together. It was not uncommon for them to make love together. In Bacon's Rebellion, one of the last groups to surrender was a mixed band of eighty negroes and twenty English servants.

As Morgan says, masters, "initially at least, perceived slaves in much the same way they had always perceived servants ... shiftless, irresponsible, unfaithful, ungrateful, dishonest...." And "if freemen with disappointed hopes should make common cause with slaves of desperate hope, the results might be worse than anything Bacon had done."

And so, measures were taken. About the same time that slave codes, involving discipline and punishment, were passed by the Virginia Assembly,

> Virginia's ruling class, having proclaimed that all white men were superior to black, went on to offer their social (but white) inferiors a number of benefits previously denied them. In 1705 a law was passed requiring masters to provide white servants whose indenture time was up with ten bushels of corn, thirty shillings and a gun, while women servants were to get 15 bushels of corn and forty shillings. Also, the newly freed servants were to get 50 acres of land.

Morgan concludes: "Once the small planter felt less exploited by taxation and began to prosper a little, he became less turbulent, less dangerous, more respectable. He could begin to see his big neighbor not as an extortionist but as a powerful protector of their common interests."

We see now a complex web of historical threads to ensnare blacks for slavery in America: the desperation of starving settlers, the special helplessness of the displaced African, the powerful incentive of profit for slave trader and planter, the temptation of superior status for poor whites, the elaborate controls against escape and rebellion, the legal and social punishment of black and white collaboration.

The point is that elements of this web are historical, not "natural." This does not mean that they are easily disentangled, dismantled. It means only that there is a possibility for something else, under historical conditions not yet realized. And one of these conditions would be the elimination of that class exploitation which has made poor whites desperate for small gifts of status, and has prevented that unity of black and white necessary for joint rebellion and reconstruction.

* * *

Notes and Questions

1. Consider the various political ramifications of beginning the story of African Americans at different historical moments: Africa prior to European slavery; Estebanico; and in 1619, with the arrival of the first Blacks in Virginia.

2.   As Zinn suggests, the development of white racism against Blacks as a justification for slavery also served an important political function. If Whites could adopt racism and learn to see Blacks as their inferiors, this would interfere with the recognition of shared interests among lower-class white servants and black slaves. As Edmund Morgan wrote:

> In Virginia too, before 1660, it might have been difficult to distinguish race prejudice from class prejudice. * * * But Virginians had always felt threatened by the danger of a servile insurrection, and their fears increased as the labor force grew larger and the proportion of blacks in it rose. * * * If freemen with disappointed hopes should make common cause with slaves of desperate hope, the results might be worse [than prior servant and slave revolts, such as Bacon's Rebellion of 1676].
>
> The answer to the problem, obvious if unspoken and only gradually recognized, was racism, to separate dangerous free whites from dangerous slave blacks by a screen of racial contempt.

Edmund S. Morgan, *American Slavery, American Freedom* 327–28 (1975).

Does this divisive function of racism survive today?

3.   Does Zinn's analysis suggest that anti-black racism was, though not "natural," inevitable in some way? Could the American slave society have flourished without it?

SECTION 2.   THE VIEWS OF THE FRAMERS

The views of American statesmen on Blacks and their role in society are important because they were influential men whose views on the races shaped the views of others and the development of American law and institutions. The views of Benjamin Franklin and Thomas Jefferson are presented here. For comprehensive treatments of the views of American leaders on slavery and Blacks, see Nathaniel Weyl & William Marina, *American Statesmen on Slavery and the Negro* (1971); Winthrop Jordan, *White Over Black* (1968); Paul Finkelman, *Slavery and the Founders: Race and Liberty in the Age of Jefferson* (1996).

BENJAMIN FRANKLIN

Observations Concerning the Increase of Mankind
(1755).*

* * *

The Introduction of Slaves. The Negroes brought into the English Sugar Islands, have greatly diminish'd the Whites there; the Poor are by this Means Depriv'd of Employment, while a few Families acquire vast Estates; which they spend on Foreign Luxuries, and educating their Children in the Habit of those Luxuries; the same Income is needed for the Support of one that might have maintain'd 100. The Whites who have Slaves, not labouring, are enfeebled, and therefore not so generally prolific; the Slaves being work'd too hard, and ill fed, their Constitutions are broken, and the Deaths among them are more than Births; so that a

* *The Papers of Benjamin Franklin*, pp. 229–31, 233–4 (Leonard Labaree et. al., eds). New Haven: Yale University Press 1961.

continual Supply is needed from Africa. The Northern Colonies having few Slaves increase in Whites. Slaves also pejorate the Families that use them; the white Children become proud, disgusted with Labor, and being educated in Idleness, are rendered unfit to get a Living by Industry. * * *

And since Detachments of English from Britain sent to America, will have their Places at Home so soon supply'd and increase so largely here; why should the Palatine Boors [Germans] be suffered to swarm into our Settlements, and by herding together establish their Language and Manners to the Exclusion of ours? Why should Pennsylvania, founded by the English, become a Colony of *Aliens*, who will shortly be so numerous as to Germanize us instead of our Anglifying them, and will never adopt our Language or Customs, any more than they can acquire our Complexion.

Which leads me to add one Remark: That the Number of purely white People in the World is proportionably very small. All Africa is black or tawny. Asia chiefly tawny. America (exclusive of the new Comers) wholly so. And in Europe, the Spaniards, Italians, French, Russians and Swedes, are generally of what we call a swarthy Complexion; as are the Germans also, the Saxons only excepted, who with the English, make the principal Body of White People on the Face of the Earth. I could wish their Numbers were increased. And while we are, as I may call it, *Scouring* our Planet, by clearing America of Woods, and so making this Side of our Globe reflect a brighter Light to the Eyes of Inhabitants in Mars or Venus, why should we in the Sight of Superior Beings, darken its People? Why increase the Sons of Africa, by Planting them in America, where we have so fair an Opportunity, by excluding all Blacks and Tawneys, of increasing the lovely White and Red? But perhaps I am partial to the Complexion of my Country, for such kind of Partiality is natural to Mankind.

Notes and Questions

1. Note Franklin's early expression of the view, or the wish, that America be a country for white Anglo–Saxons only. This view came to be commonly held by many American leaders.

2. Note that Franklin's way of dealing with the presence of black people is to suggest excluding them altogether from the country. As we shall see, this view also came to have many adherents. Was Franklin racist?

3. Franklin makes very interesting observations on the harmful effects of black slavery upon white slave owners. The slave owners themselves saw things very differently: In their view, black slavery enabled a white society based on principles of chivalry and nobility to flourish. Tensions between the North's emerging culture of self-denial and capitalist "industry" and the South's emerging culture of gentility and semi-feudal agriculture fueled the conflicts that eventually led to the Civil War.

4. Notice Franklin's apparent disdain for the Germans in colonial Pennsylvania. Does he perceive them as a different race? If so, what does that fact reveal about the evolution of "Whiteness" as a concept and as a race? For a full discussion of this issue, see Chapter 6 *infra*.

5. To what extent does Franklin's concern about the potential assimilation of Germans in Pennsylvania remain a concern today with respect to recent immigrants? Do similar concerns about race, assimilation, and language difference underlie concerns about recent Latino/a immigrants?

6. Franklin, later in his career, became an advocate for education for Blacks, a strong opponent of slavery and a leading abolitionist. Late in his life, Franklin was elected President of the Pennsylvania Society for Promoting the Abolition of Slavery and Relief of Free Negroes Unlawfully held in Bondage and for Improving the Condition of the African Race.

THOMAS JEFFERSON

Notes on the State of Virginia, Query XIV
(1787).*

[In this section of his *Notes*, Jefferson describes proposed revisions to existing Virginia laws; one proposal addressing the emancipation and removal of slaves from the colony.]

To emancipate all slaves born after passing the act. * * * that they should continue with their parents to a certain age, then be brought up, at the public expence, to tillage, arts or sciences, according to their geniuses till the females should be eighteen, and the males twenty-one years of age, when they should be colonized to such place as the circumstances of the time should render most proper * * * . It will probably be asked, Why not retain and incorporate the blacks into the state, and thus save the expence of supplying; by importation of white settlers, the vacancies they will leave? Deep rooted prejudices entertained by the whites; ten thousand recollections, by the blacks, of the injuries they have sustained; new provocations; the real distinctions which nature has made; and many other circumstances, will divide us into parties, and produce convulsions which will probably never end but in the extermination of one or the other race.—To these objections, which are political, may be added others, which are physical and moral. The first difference which strikes us is that of colour. Whether the black or the negro resides in the reticular membrane between the skin and scarf-skin, or in the scarf-skin itself; whether it proceeds from the colour of the blood, the colour of the bile, or from that of some other secretion, the difference is fixed in nature, and is as real as if its seat and cause were better known to us. And is this difference of no importance? Is it not the foundation of a greater or less share of beauty in the two races? Are not the fine mixtures of red and white, the expressions of every passion by greater or less suffusions of colour in the one, preferable to that eternal monotony, which reigns in the countenances, that immoveable veil of black which covers all the emotions of the other race? Add to these, flowing hair, a more elegant symmetry of form, their own judgment in favour of the whites, declared by their preference of them, as uniformly as is the preference of the Oranootan for the black women over those of his own species. The circumstance of superior beauty, is

* Thomas Jefferson, *Writings*. New York: The Library of America, 1984. Reprinted by permission of the publisher.

thought worthy of attention in the propagation of our horses, dogs, and other domestic animals; why not in that of man? Besides those of colour, figure, and hair, there are other physical distinctions proving a difference of race. * * * A black, after hard labour throughout the day, will be induced by the slightest amusements to sit up till midnight, or later, though knowing he must be out with the first dawn of the morning. They are at least as brave, and more adventuresome. But this may perhaps proceed from a want of forethought, which prevents their seeing a danger till it be present. When present, they do not go through it with more coolness or steadiness than the whites. They are more ardent after their female; but love seems with them to be more an eager desire, than a tender delicate mixture of sentiment and sensation. Their griefs are transient. Those numberless afflictions, which render it doubtful whether heaven has given life to us in mercy or in wrath, are less felt, and sooner forgotten with them. In general, their existence appears to participate more of sensation than reflection. * * * Comparing them by their faculties of memory, reason, and imagination, it appears to me, that in memory they are equal to the whites; in reason much inferior, as I think one could scarcely be found capable of tracing and comprehending the investigations of Euclid; and that in imagination they are dull, tasteless, and anomalous. It would be unfair to follow them to Africa for this investigation. We will consider them here, on the same stage with the whites, and where the facts are not apocryphal on which a judgment is to be formed. It will be right to make great allowances for the difference of condition, of education, of conversation, of the sphere in which they move. * * * But never yet could I find that a black had uttered a thought above the level of plain narration; never see even an elementary trait of painting or sculpture. * * * The improvement of the blacks in body and mind, in the first instance of their mixture with the whites, has been observed by every one, and proves that their inferiority is not the effect merely of their condition of life. * * * Let me add too, as a circumstance of great tenderness, where our conclusion would degrade a whole race of men from the rank in the scale of beings which their Creator may perhaps have given them. To our reproach it must be said, that though for a century and a half we have had under our eyes the races of black and of red men, they have never yet been viewed by us as subjects of natural history. I advance it therefore as a suspicion only, that the blacks, whether originally a distinct race, or made distinct by time and circumstances, are inferior to the whites in the endowments both of body and mind. It is not against experience to suppose, that different species of the same genus, or varieties of the same species, may possess different qualifications. Will not a lover of natural history then, one who views the graduations in all the races of animals with the eye of philosophy, excuse an effort to keep those in the department of man as distinct as nature has formed them? This unfortunate difference of colour, and perhaps of faculty, is a powerful obstacle to the emancipation of these people. Many of their advocates, while they wish to vindicate the liberty of human nature, are anxious also to preserve its dignity and beauty. Some of these, embarrassed by the question "What further is to be done with them?" join themselves in opposition with those who are actuated by sordid avarice only. Among the Romans emancipation required but one effort. The slave, when made free, might mix with, without staining the blood of his master. But with us a second is necessary, unknown to history. When freed, he is to be removed beyond the reach of mixture.

* * *

Notes and Questions

1. Notice Jefferson's concern about interracial marriage and sex, and hence his admonition that Blacks had to be "removed beyond the reach of mixture." Like Franklin, Jefferson too was concerned with creating a racially pure, white nation. In a subsequent letter, Jefferson wrote that "Their [Blacks'] amalgamation with the other color produces a degradation to which no lover of his country, no lover of excellence in the human character can innocently consent." See Jefferson to Edward Coles, August 25, 1814. Is this genetic view of racial inferiority reviving today?

THOMAS JEFFERSON TO JARED SPARKS
February 4, 1824.*

In the disposition of these unfortunate people, there are two rational objects to be distinctly kept in view. First. The establishment of a colony on the coast of Africa, which may introduce among the aborigines the arts of cultivated life, and the blessings of civilization and science. By doing this, we may make to them some retribution for the long course of injuries we have been committing on their population. * * * To fulfill this object, the colony of Sierra Leone promises well, and that of Mesurado adds to our prospect of success. * * *

The subject object, and the most interesting to us, as coming home to our physical and moral characters, to our happiness and safety, is to provide an asylum to which we can, by degrees, send the whole of that population from among us, and establish them under our patronage and protection, as a separate, free and independent people, in some country and climate friendly to human life and happiness. That any place on the coast of Africa should answer the latter purpose, I have ever deemed entirely impossible. * * * There are in the United States a million and a half of people of color in slavery. To send off the whole of these at once, nobody conceives to be practical for us, or expedient for them. Let us take twenty-five years for its accomplishment[.] * * * There is, I think, a way in which it can be done; that is, by emancipating the after-born, leaving them, on due compensation, with their mothers, until their services are worth their maintenance, and then putting them to industrious occupations, until a proper age for deportation. This was the result of my reflections on the subject five and forty years ago, and I have never yet been able to conceive any other practicable plan. It was sketched in the *Notes on Virginia*, under the fourteenth query. * * *

In the plan sketched in the *Notes on Virginia*, no particular place of asylum was specified; because it was thought possible, that in the

* Thomas Jefferson, *Writings*. New York: permission of the publisher.
The Library of America, 1984. Reprinted by

revolutionary state of America, then commenced, events might open to us some one within practicable distance. This has now happened. St. Domingo has become independent, and with a population of that color only; and if the public papers are to be credited, their Chief offers to pay their passage, to receive them as free citizens, and to provide them employment. This leaves, then, for the general confederacy, no expense but of nurture with the mother a few years, and would call, of course, for a very moderate appropriation of the vacant lands. * * *

I am aware that this subject involves some constitutional scruples. But a liberal construction, justified by the object, may go far, and an amendment of the constitution, the whole length necessary. The separation of infants from their mothers, too, would produce some scruples of humanity. But this would be straining at a gnat, and swallowing a camel.

    * * *

Notes and Questions

1. Are these comments on racial differences by Franklin and Jefferson important today? Why or why not?

2. Are Franklin and Jefferson "racist," in the current meaning of the term? Is it anachronistic to judge them by twenty-first-century standards?

3. Have you heard or read these comments before in your study of history? If not, consider why you have not learned this aspect of these framers' views until now.

SECTION 3. SLAVERY

A. THE CONSTITUTION AND SLAVERY

The centrality of black slavery in the development of American law and institutions is nowhere more evident than in the accommodation and protection of slavery in the Constitution. Several provisions of the Constitution sanction or protect slavery. Article I, § 2, Cl. 3 provides that representatives and direct taxes shall be apportioned "by adding to the whole Number of free Persons, including those bound to Service for a Term of Years, and excluding Indians not taxed, three fifths of all other Persons." This clause increased the representation of the southern states by including three fifths of slaves held as a basis for representation.

Article I, § 9, Cl. 1 limits the power of Congress to restrict the slave trade, an important protection for slavery: "The Migration or Importation of such Persons as any of the States now existing shall think proper to admit, shall not be prohibited by the Congress prior to the Year one thousand eight hundred and eight." This clause is striking as it is a direct limitation on Congress's otherwise plenary commerce powers. See, *e.g., Gibbons v. Ogden*, 22 U.S. (9 Wheat.) 1 (1824) (finding Congress's interstate commerce power to be plenary and subject to few limitations).

Article IV, § 2, Cl. 3 provides that "No Person held to Service or Labour in one State, under the Laws thereof, escaping into another, shall, in Consequence of any Law or Regulation therein, be discharged from such Service or Labour, but shall be delivered up on Claim of the Party to whom such Service or Labour may be due." This is the Fugitive Slave Clause, which preserves a slave's status as recoverable property even if a slave could escape to "free" states where slavery was prohibited or not extensive.

Despite the protections of slavery in the Constitution, its drafters were careful not to use the word "slave" at all, despite language that was understood by all to refer to slaves. The drafters of the Constitution did not want to "stain" the document by making any direct reference to slavery. The following excerpt from a debate in the House of Representatives on the wording of Article I, § 9, prohibiting the importation of persons after 1808, illustrates the point:

> [Mr. Dayton, (the Speaker)] recollected also, that in the discussion of its merits, no question arose, or was agitated respecting the admission of foreigners, but, on the contrary, that it was confined simply to slaves, and was first voted upon and carried with that word expressed in it, which was afterwards upon reconsideration changed for "*such persons*," as it now stands.... The sole reason assigned for changing it was that it would be better not to stain the Constitutional code with such a term, since it could be avoided by the introduction of other equally intelligible words, as had been done in the former part of the same instrument, where the same sense was conveyed by the circuitous expression of 'three fifths of all other persons'.

III *The Records of the Federal Convention of 1787* at 377 (Max Farrand ed. 1966, reproducing debate in the House of Representatives, June 16–20, 1798). Some of the drafters of the Constitution had been ashamed to use the word "slave" in the document, despite its ultimate sanction of the institution. See Staughton Lynd, *Slavery and the Founding Fathers*, in *Black History* 117, 128 (M. Drimmer ed. 1969); Derrick A. Bell, Jr., *Race, Racism, and American Law* 27 (3rd ed. 1992).

Some of the framers were ambivalent about supporting and adhering to the slave regime that ultimately was adopted. Maryland delegate Luther Martin, for example, made the following remarks addressing the legislature of Maryland:

> This report was adopted by a majority of the convention, but not without considerable opposition. It was said, that we had just assumed a place among independent nations, in consequence of our opposition to the attempts of Great Britain to enslave us; that this opposition was grounded upon the preservation of those rights to which God and nature had entitled us, not in particular, but in common with all the rest of mankind; that we had appealed to the Supreme Being for his assistance, as the God of freedom, who could not but approve our efforts to preserve the rights which he had thus imparted to his creatures; that now, when we scarcely had risen from our knees, from supplicating his aid and protection, in forming our government over a free people, a government formed pretendedly on the principles of liberty and for its preservation,—in that government, to have a provision not only putting it out of its power

to restrain and prevent the slave-trade, but even encouraging that most infamous traffic, by giving the States power and influence in the Union, in proportion as they cruelly and wantonly sport with the rights of their fellow creatures, ought to be considered as a solemn mockery of, and insult to that God whose protection we had then implored, and could not fail to hold us up in detestation, and render us contemptible to every true friend of liberty in the world. It was said, it ought to be considered that national crimes can only be, and frequently are punished in this world, by national punishments; and that the continuance of the slave-trade, and thus giving it a national sanction and encouragement, ought to be considered as justly exposing us to the displeasure and vengeance of Him, who is equally Lord of all, and who views with equal eye the poor African slave and his American master.

Luther Martin: *Genuine Information*, reprinted in III *The Records of the Federal Convention* 211 (Max Farrand ed. 1966) (italics omitted).

Slavery and the liberating, natural-law ideology of the Declaration of Independence thus stood in profound contradiction. The framers' willingness to reach a compromise that sacrificed liberty for black slaves in order to preserve their union and their property interests set a principle that continues today.

Notes and Questions

1. Going back in time to interrogate the framers, Geneva Crenshaw, a fictional character invented by Derrick Bell, comments, "The stark truth is that the racial grief that persists today ... originated in the slavery institutionalized in the [Constitution]. Is this, gentlemen, an achievement for which you wish to be remembered?" Crenshaw also recognizes that the benefits of slavery were desired by the North as well as the South: "But if a record be made, that record should show that the economic benefits of slavery do not accrue only to the South. Plantation states provide a market for Northern factories, and the New England shipping industry and merchants participate in the slave trade. Northern states, moreover, utilize slaves in the fields, as domestics, and even as soldiers to defend against Indian raids." Geneva Crenshaw continues: "Here you are then! Representatives from large and small states, slave states and those that have abolished slavery, all of you are protecting your property interests at the cost of your principles." For a further exposition of this constitutional contradiction, expressed through a dialogue between the fictional Geneva Crenshaw and the framers at the Constitutional Convention, see Derrick A. Bell, Jr., *The Real Status of Blacks Today: The Chronicle of the Constitutional Contradiction*, in *And We Are Not Saved* 26–42 (1987). See also Derrick A. Bell, Jr., *Race, Racism, and American Law* 26–36 (3rd ed. 1992).

2. As legal historians have noted, the Framers were concerned to protect the rights of property owners, not only against black slaves, but against property-less Whites. Fear that the emerging state would be destabilized or destroyed by "the mob" were common. Thus, for example, states frequently restricted the franchise to property owners.

3. Are the equality interests of Blacks, and other people of color, being sacrificed today for the sake of preserving white interests in property and

power? Or are the interests of all property-less persons of all racial back-grounds regularly sacrificed?

4. Why have the slavery compromises not been expunged from the Constitution? What are the ramifications, both positive and negative, of keeping this language in the Constitution?

Fifty years after the ratification of the Constitution, Frederick Douglass provided eloquent testimony to the development of the cruel paradox generated by the Framers' compromises.

FREDERICK DOUGLASS

The Meaning of July Fourth for the Negro, Rochester, NY
(July 5, 1852).*

* * *

Fellow citizens, pardon me, allow me to ask, why am I called upon to speak here to-day? What have I, or those I represent, to do with national independence? Are the great principles of political freedom and of natural justice, embodied in that Declaration of Independence, extended to us? and am I, therefore, called upon to bring our humble offering to the national altar, and to confess the benefits and express devout gratitude for the blessings resulting from your independence to us?

Would to God, both for your sakes and ours, that an affirmative answer could be truthfully returned to these questions! * * *

But such is not the state of the case. I say it with a sad sense of the disparity between us. I am not included within the pale of this glorious anniversary! Your high independence only reveals the immeasurable distance between us. The blessings in which you, this day, rejoice, are not enjoyed in common.—The rich inheritance of justice, liberty, prosperity and independence, bequeathed by your fathers, is shared by you, not by me. The sunlight that brought light and healing to you, has brought stripes and death to me. This Fourth of July is *yours*, not *mine*. *You* may rejoice, *I* must mourn. To drag a man in fetters into the grand illuminated temple of liberty, and call him to join you in joyous anthems, were inhuman mockery and sacrilegious irony. Do you mean, citizens, to mock me, by asking me to speak today? * * *

Fellow citizens, above your national, tumultuous joy, I hear the mournful wail of millions! whose chains, heavy and grievous yesterday, are, to-day, rendered more intolerable by the jubilee shouts that reach them. * * *

What, to the American slave, is your 4th of July? I answer; a day that reveals to him, more than all other days in the year, the gross injustice and cruelty to which he is the constant victim. To him, your celebration is a sham; your boasted liberty, an unholy license; your national greatness, swelling vanity; your sounds of rejoicing are empty and heartless; your denunciation of tyrants, brass fronted impudence;

* *The Life and Writings of Frederick Douglass*, Vol. 2: *The Pre–Civil War Decade, 1850–1860* at 188–92, 201. (Philip S.   Foner ed. 1950). Reprinted by permission of International Publishers Co.

your shouts of liberty and equality, hollow mockery; your prayers and
hymns, your sermons and thanksgivings, with all your religious parade
and solemnity, are, to Him, mere bombast, fraud, deception, impiety, and
hypocrisy—a thin veil to cover up crimes which would disgrace a nation
of savages. There is not a nation on the earth guilty of practices more
shocking and bloody than are the people of the United States, at this
very hour.

* * *

Fellow citizens, I will not enlarge further on your national inconsistencies. The existence of slavery in this country brands your republicanism as sham, your humanity as a base pretense, and your Christianity as
a lie. It destroys your moral power abroad; it corrupts your politicians at
home. It saps the foundation of religion; it makes your name a hissing
and bye-word to a mocking earth. It is the antagonistic force in your
government, the only thing that seriously disturbs and endangers your
Union. It fetters your progress; it is the enemy of improvement; the
deadly foe of education; it fosters pride; it breeds insolence; it promotes
vice; it shelters crime; it is a curse to the earth that supports it; and yet
you cling to it as if it were the sheet anchor of all your hopes. Oh! be
warned! be warned! a horrible reptile is coiled up in your nation's bosom;
the venomous creature is nursing at the tender breast of your youthful
republic; *for the love of God, tear away*, and fling from you the hideous
monster, and *let the weight of twenty millions crush and destroy it
forever!*

* * *

Notes and Questions

1. Notice how our holidays and other national symbols can have
radically different meaning for different people depending on their lived
experiences and histories. In addition to the Independence Day holiday on
July 4, what other national symbols might evoke different reactions among
different groups? For example, consider the continuing debate over the
Confederate battle flag as a state flag. How would you understand the
different responses to that symbol?

2. Many people celebrate the Constitution and its role in our nation.
Because of its protection of slavery and the numerous amendments required
to make it more just, the framers' Constitution can be considered a flawed
document. Consider Justice Thurgood Marshall's view of the Constitution.
Commenting on its meaning, Marshall wrote:

> Nor do I find the wisdom, foresight and sense of justice exhibited by the
> Framers particularly profound. To the contrary, the government they
> devised was defective from the start, requiring several amendments, a
> civil war, and momentous social transformation to attain the system of
> constitutional government, and its respect for the individual freedoms
> and human rights, we hold as fundamental today. When contemporary
> Americans cite "The Constitution," they invoke a concept that is vastly
> different from what the Framers barely began to construct two centuries
> ago.

Thurgood Marshall, *Reflections on the Bicentennial of the United States Constitution,* 101 Harv. L. Rev. 1, 2 (1987).

B. LEGAL AND SOCIAL SUPPORT FOR SLAVERY

By 1715, almost all the colonies had statutes permitting slavery. Once slavery developed, each colony had different variations on the extent and meaning of black slavery. The southern colonies were typically more brutal in their implementation of slavery and slave laws than the northern colonies. Virginia, South Carolina, and Georgia were among the cruelest colonies, while slavery was administered in a more moderate manner in colonies like Massachusetts and Pennsylvania. In part this can be attributed to the much lesser economic dependence on slaves and therefore the much smaller number of slaves needed in Massachusetts compared with the southern colonies. In Massachusetts, for example, Blacks "never lost the right and ability to seek judicial determination of the legitimacy of their individual enslavement," an ability generally denied in the southern colonies. And Pennsylvania became the first colony to pass "An Act for the Gradual Abolition of Slavery." See A. Leon Higginbotham, Jr., *In the Matter of Color* 60, 98, 198–99, 299, 305–310 (1978) (containing an excellent and detailed study of the different character of slavery in various colonies).

Far more typical, however, was the cruelty inherent in the slave codes developed in the slave states. Virginia was the leader in drafting slave codes. Beginning in 1680, Virginia enacted laws of increasing harshness that sought to deny Blacks their humanity and ability to participate in society. See Higginbotham, *supra*, at 38–60 for a detailed discussion of the development of slave codes in colonial Virginia. Consider the following excerpt from the slave laws of Virginia enacted in 1723.

SLAVE LAWS OF THE STATE OF VIRGINIA
Laws of Virginia, Ch. 4 (May, 1723).

An Act directing the trial of Slaves, committing capital crimes; and for the more effectual punishing conspiracies and insurrections of them; and for the better government of Negros, Mulattos, and Indians, bond or free.

I. Whereas the laws now in force, for the better ordering and governing of slaves, and for the speedy trial of such of them as commit capital crimes, are found insufficient to restrain their tumultuous and unlawful meetings, or to punish the secret plots and conspiracies carried on amongst them, and known only to such, as by the laws now established, are not accounted legal evidence: And it being found necessary, that some further provision be made, for detecting and punishing all such dangerous combinations for the future.

II. *Be it enacted* * * * That if any number of negros, or other slaves, exceeding five, shall at any time hereafter consult, advise, or conspire, to rebel or make insurrection, or shall plot or conspire the murder of any person or persons whatsoever, every such consulting, plotting, or conspiring shall be adjudged and deemed felony; and the slave or slaves convicted thereof, in manner herein after directed, shall suffer death, and be utterly excluded the benefit of clergy, and of all laws made concerning the same.

III. *And be it further enacted* * * * That every slave committing such offence, as, by the laws, ought to be punished with death, or loss of member, shall be forthwith committed to the common goal [jail] of the county, within which the said offence shall be committed, there to be safely kept; * * * the offender [shall] be publicly arraigned and tried, at the court-house of the said county, and to take for evidence, the confession of the offender, the oath of one or more credible witnesses, or such testimony of Negros, Mulattos, or Indians, bond or free, with pregnant circumstances, as to them shall seem convincing, without the solemnity of a jury * * * .

IV. And to the end, such Negros, Mulattos, or Indians, not being christians, as shall hereafter be produced as evidences, on the trial of any slave for capital crimes, may be under the greater obligation to declare the truth, *Be it enacted*, That where any such Negro, Mulatto, or Indian, shall upon due proof made, or pregnant circumstances appearing before any county court within this colony, be found to have given a false testimony, every such offender shall, without further trial, be ordered by the said court to have one ear nailed to the pillory, and there to stand for the space of one hour, and then the said ear to be cut off; and thereafter, the other ear nailed in like manner, and cut off, at the expiration of one other hour; and moreover, to order every such offender thirty-nine lashes, well laid on, on his or her bare back, at the common whipping-post. * * *

VII. *And be it further enacted* * * * That when any slave shall be convicted, by virtue of this act, the commissioners that shall sit on trial, shall put a valuation in money, upon such slave so convicted, and certify such valuation to the next assembly, that the said assembly may be enabled to make a suitable allowance thereupon to the master or owner of such slave.

VIII. And whereas many inconveniences have arisen, by the meetings of great numbers of negros and other slaves: For prevention thereof, *Be it enacted* * * * That from henceforth no meetings of negros, or other slaves, allowed, on any pretence whatsoever, (except as is hereafter excepted.)* * *

IX. *Provided always,* That nothing herein contained, shall be construed to restrain the negros, or other slaves, belonging to one and the same owner, and seated at distinct quarters or plantations, to meet, by the license of such owner, or his or her overseer, at any of the quarters or plantations to such owner belonging; nor to restrain the meeting of any number of slaves, on their owner's or overseer's business, at any public mill, so as such meeting be not in the night, or on a Sunday; nor to restrain their meeting on any other lawful occasion, by the license, in writing, of their master, mistress, or overseers; nor to prohibit any slaves repairing to and meeting at church to attend divine service, on the lord's day, or at any other time set apart by lawful authority, for public worship: But that all and every such meetings, shall be accounted lawful

meetings; any thing in this act contained to the contrary thereof notwithstanding.

X. *And be it further enacted* * * * That if any white person, free
negro, mulatto or Indian, shall at any time hereafter be found in
company with any such slaves, at any such unlawful meetings, as
aforesaid, or harbor or entertain any negro, or other slave whatsoever,
without the consent of their owners, he, she, or they, so offending, upon
being thereof lawfully convicted, shall forfeit and pay the sum of fifteen
shillings, or one hundred and fifty pounds of tobacco, to the informer.
* * *

XIII. *And be it further enacted* * * * That if any negro, mulatto, or
Indian slave, shall at any time hereafter presume to come and be upon
the plantation of any person or persons whatsoever, without the leave or
consent, in writing, of his or her master, owner, or overseer, and without
the consent and approbation of the owner or overseer of such plantation,
it shall and may be lawful to and for the master, owner, or overseer of
any such plantation or quarter, to correct and give such slave or slaves
ten lashes, well laid on, on his or her bare back, for every such offence.

XIV. *And be it further enacted* * * * That no negro mulatto or
Indian whatsoever; (except as is hereafter excepted,) shall hereafter
presume to keep, or carry any gun, powder, shot or any club, or other
weapon whatsoever, offensive or defensive; but that every gun, and all
powder and shot, and every such club or weapon[,] as aforesaid, found or
taken in the hands, custody, or possession of any such negro, mulatto, or
Indian, shall be taken away; and upon due proof thereof made, before
any justice of the peace of the county where such offence shall be
committed, be forfeited to the seisor and informer, and moreover, every
such negro, mulatto, or Indian, in whose hands, custody, or possession,
the same shall be found, shall, by order of the said justice, have and
receive any number of lashes, not exceeding thirty-nine, well laid on, on
his or her bare back, for every such offence.

　　　* * *

XVI. *And be it further enacted* * * * That if in the dispersing of
any unlawful assemblies, pursuit of rebels or conspirators, or seizing the
arms and ammunition of such as are prohibited by this act, to keep the
same, any slave shall happen to be killed or destroied, the court of the
county where such slave shall be killed, upon application of the owner of
such slave, and due proof thereof made, shall put a valuation in money,
upon such slave so killed, and certify such valuation to the next session
of assembly, that the said assembly may be enabled to make a suitable
allowance thereupon to the master or owner of such slave,

XVII. *And be it further enacted* * * * That no negro, mullatto, or
indian slaves, shall be set free, upon any pretence whatsover, except for
some meritorious services, to be adjudged and allowed by the governor
and council, for the time being, and a licence thereupon first had and
obtained. * * *

XVIII. And forasmuch, as the act passed in the fourth year of the
reign of her late Majesty Queen Anne, intituled, *An act concerning*

servants and slaves, whereby power is given to the county court, to order the dismembering of incorrigible runaways and other slaves, hath not had the intended effect, by reason of some misconstructions of the powers thereby granted, *Be it enacted,* That where any slaves shall hereafter be found notoriously guilty of going abroad in the night, or running away, and lying out, and cannot be reclaimed from such disorderly courses, by the common methods of punishment, it shall and may be lawful, to and for the court of the county, upon complaint and proof thereof to them made, by the owner of such slave, to order and direct every such slave to be punished, by dismembering, or any other way, not touching life, as the said county court shall think fit.

XIX.   And, for preventing all doubts which may arise, upon the construction of this, or any other act of assembly of this colony, touching the death of slaves under correction, or lawful punishment, *Be it enacted, by the authority aforesaid,* That if any slave shall happen to die by means of such dismembering, by order of the county court, or for or by reason of any stroke or blow given, during his or her correction; by his or her owner, for any offence by such slave committed, or for or by reason of any accidental blow whatsoever, given by such owner; no person concerned in such dismembering correction, or accidental homicide, shall undergo any prosecution or punishment for the same; unless upon examination before the county court, it shall be proved, by the oath of one lawful and credible witness, at the least, that such slave was killed wilfully, maliciously, or designedly; neither shall any person whatsoever, who shall be indicted for the murder of any slave, and upon trial, shall be found guilty only of manslaughter, incur any forfeiture or punishment for such offence or misfortune.

XX.   *Provided always,* That nothing herein contained, shall be construed, deemed, or taken, to defeat or barr the action of any person or persons, whose slave or slaves shall happen to be killed by any other person whatsoever, or whose slaves shall happen to die thro' the negligence of any surgeon, or other person, undertaking the dismembering or cure of such slave, liable to such punishment by this act: But that all and every owner or owners of such slave or slaves, shall and may bring his or her action, for recovery of damages for such slave or slaves so killed or dying, as if this act had never been made.

    * * *

XXIII.   *And be it further enacted, by the authority aforesaid, and it is hereby enacted and declared,* That no free negro, mullato, or indian whatsoever, shall hereafter have any vote at the election of burgesses, or any other election whatsoever.

William W. Hening, IV Laws of Virginia 126–34 (1820) (Chap. IV, May, 1723).

Notes and Questions

1.   Consider the purposes served by each of the restrictive provisions cited above in the Virginia slave law of 1723. Were these provisions necessary in some way? Were they compelled by the "peculiar institution" itself? What were the implications of these laws for Whites?

2.   Consider the extreme degree to which slave owners were concerned about possible slave insurrections and resistance. Doesn't this concern demonstrate that resistance against the slave regime was always present, in some form?

Brutality towards Slaves

No text, including this one, can possibly capture the violence and cruelty inflicted upon black slaves by their white masters and overseers. And although many court cases dealt with the subject of excessive cruelty to slaves, courts were reluctant to report the full extent of that brutality. For example, the "Supreme Court of Louisiana had an unspoken policy of underreporting or omitting entirely from its official reports certain kinds of cases involving cruelty to slaves. Cases of flagrant sexual abuse were one category that made the justices reticent." See Judith Kelleher Schafer, "Details Are of a Most Revolting Character": Cruelty to Slaves as Seen in Appeals to the Supreme Court of Louisiana, in Slavery & the Law 241, 257 (Paul Finkelman ed. 1997).

Accordingly, to avoid the problem of judicial reticence to describe the conditions of slavery, we begin this discussion with a Canadian newspaper account from a slave named Lavinia Bell. The following interview with Lavinia Bell was published in the Montreal [Canada] Gazette on January 31, 1861.

Interview with Lavinia Bell (interviewed, 1861, Canada)*

When, some years ago, Mrs. Stowe wrote "Uncle Tom's Cabin," and the whole world read the story of the wrongs of the black man, some there were who did not hesitate to say that though such things might exist in the brain of the novelist, they could nowhere else be found. We lay before our readers to-day a brief account of the sufferings of a poor negro woman, caused by the brutality of a master, which for hideous malignity and fiendish cruelty were beyond the imagination even of a Legree; * * * We have the account from the lips of the woman herself, who arrived in this city on Monday last; and we have also the statement, over his own signature, of Doctor Reddy, under whose treatment she now is, which fully bears out every word of hers regarding the cruelty to which she had been subjected. Her history, in brief, is as follows:—

Born in Washington of free parents, she was while yet an infant stolen from there, with two or three coloured men and thirty or forty other "cattle," * * *. She was taken down to the neighbourhood of Galveston, Texas, as the property of William Whirl, and whose wife, Polly, performed to her the part of a mother. It was from Polly Whirl she learned all these particulars, she being of course too young to know anything. * * *

After [she was thirteen or fourteen] she was sent into the cotton field with the other field hands, where the treatment was cruelly severe. No clothes whatever were allowed them, their hair was cut off close to their head, and thus were exposed to the glare of a southern sun from early morn until late at night. Scarcely a day passed without their receiving fifty lashes, whether they worked or whether they did not. They were also compelled to go down on their knees, and harnessed to a plough, to plough up the land, with boys for riders, to whip them when they flagged in their work. At other times, they were compelled to walk on hackles, used for hackling flax. Her feet are now dotted over with scars, caused by this brutality. She often, over and over again, attempted to escape, but, having no knowledge of the way, was easily overtaken and brought back. On one occasion, she and her husband, (if he could be called so) made an unsuccessful attempt to fly. The poor man had had on his legs for two years irons which had grown into the flesh; these impeded him in his flight, and caused their capture. He was then shockingly beaten, and otherwise cruelly ill-used, so that he died under the treatment, and she was brought back.

Her mistress, Polly Whirl, a Dutch woman, had always been a friend to the poor negress, who went by the name of "Captain Bull," and at last told her of Canada, that refuge for the hunted fugitive, and pointed out to her the North Star as her guide by night. [Lavinia attempted unsuccessfully to escape again]. * * * On her return to Texas, her master having had some difficulty in proving her identity, swore that he would mark her in such a manner that hereafter there would be no such trouble. He slit both her ears, then branded her on the back of her left hand with a hot iron, cut off with an axe the little finger and bone connecting therewith of her right hand, searing the wound with a hot iron, and also branded her on the stomach with a letter.

He heard she had tried to incite more of the slaves to escape to Canada, and tried to force her to tell who had told her anything about Canada, promising not to whip her if she did so. She, with the spirit of a martyr, refused to give any information, whereupon he had her fixed in what is there technically termed a 'buck.' This was doubling her in two, until her legs were passed over her head, where they were kept by a stick passed across the back of her neck. * * * While in this position, several panels of a board fence were raised, a notch cut in the boards, and her neck placed in the notch. She was then whipped to such a degree that the overseer, more humane than the master, interfered to prevent a murder. The wounds caused by the lash were rubbed with salt and water, and pepper, to keep away the green flies. After this, on one occasion, Whirl struck her on the head with a hoe-handle a number of times, and actually broke her skull. She says herself that a silver plate had to be put in, and that her master afterwards told her, cursing her, that she had 'a dollar in her head to pay her way to purgatory.' At another time she was left for a number of days without any thing to eat or drink. She says she tried to tear her eyes out to eat them, she was so hungry. Still later, for some disobedience on her part, they hoisted her into a tree, locked a chain round her neck, and hand-cuffed her wrists, the marks being yet visible. There she was left for two days and nights, without a morsel to eat, being taunted with such questions as to whether she was hungry, and would like something to eat, &c. &c., she never giving the satisfaction of answering a word. She succeeded at length, by spitting on her hands, in slipping off her cuffs, with which she wrenched asunder the locks of the chains around her neck and then fell exhausted on the ground. At another time, several of her teeth were knocked out by a hammer, she having bitten off a part of her master's nose, and at another time she was knocked down with a whip, leaving a scar of more than three inches in length on her cheek.

>   * * *

Slave Testimony 341–43 (John W. Blassingame ed. 1977).

Blassingame's book is an invaluable collection of first-person and reported accounts of slaves regarding all aspects of their lives. See Blassingame's Introduction for a valuable discussion of the value of different historical sources of knowledge about the lives of slaves. See also Theodore D. Weld, *American Slavery As It Is: Testimony of a Thousand Witnesses* (1968) (reprint of original 1839 edition).

Notes and Questions

1. Compare the treatment of Lavinia Bell to the excerpt from the Slave Laws of Virginia. What purposes were served by the violence against her? Was the violence against her necessary in some way? Were there any implications of this treatment of Blacks for Whites?

2. How can the United States atone today for slavery? Should the country try?

C. SLAVERY AND THE JUDICIARY

Courts played an important role in defining the relationships between masters and slaves. In the following cases, courts consider the liability of third parties who injured slaves owned by another. More importantly, these cases illustrate how violence and cruelty were used to enforce the subordination of slaves.

STATE v. JOHN MANN
13 N.C. 167 (1830).

RUFFIN, J. A Judge cannot but lament when such cases as the present are brought into judgment. It is impossible that the reasons on which they go can be appreciated, but where institutions similar to our own exist and are thoroughly understood. The struggle, too, in the Judge's own breast between the feelings of the man and the duty of the magistrate is a severe one, presenting strong temptation to put aside such questions, if it be possible. It is useless, however, to complain of things inherent in our political state. And it is criminal in a Court to avoid any responsibility which the laws impose. With whatever reluctance, therefore, it is done, the Court is compelled to express an opinion upon the extent of the dominion of the master over the slave in North Carolina.

The indictment charges a battery on Lydia, a slave of Elizabeth Jones. * * * Here the slave had been hired by the defendant, and was in his possession; and the battery was committed during the period of hiring. With the liabilities of the hirer to the general owner for an injury permanently impairing the value of the slave no rule now laid down is intended to interfere. That is left upon the general doctrine of bailment. The inquiry here is whether a cruel and unreasonable battery on a slave by the hirer is indictable. * * *

* * * Our laws uniformly treat the master or other person having the possession and command of the slave as entitled to the same extent of authority. * * * But upon the general question whether the owner is answerable *criminaliter* for a battery upon his own slave, or other exercise of authority or force not forbidden by statute, the Court enter-

tains but little doubt. That he is so liable has never yet been decided; nor, as far as is known, been hitherto contended. There have been no prosecutions of the sort. The established habits and uniform practice of the country in this respect is the best evidence of the portion of power deemed by the whole community requisite to the preservation of the master's dominion. * * * This had indeed been assimilated at the bar to the other domestic relations; and arguments drawn from the well-established principles which confer and restrain the authority of the parent over the child, the tutor over the pupil, the master over the apprentice, have been pressed on us. The Court does not recognize their application. There is no likeness between the cases. They are in opposition to each other, and there is an impassable gulf between them. The difference is that which exists between freedom and slavery—and a greater cannot be imagined. In the one, the end in view is the happiness of the youth, born to equal rights with that governor, on whom the duty devolves of training the young to usefulness in a station which he is afterwards to assume among freemen. To such an end, and with such a subject, moral and intellectual instruction seem the natural means; and for the most part they are found to suffice. Moderate force is superadded only to make the others effectual. If that fail it is better to leave the party to his own headstrong passions and the ultimate correction of the law than to allow it to be immoderately inflicted by a private person. With slavery it is far otherwise. The end is the profit of the master, his security and the public safety; the subject, one doomed in his own person and his posterity, to live without knowledge and without the capacity to make anything his own, and to toil that another may reap the fruits. What moral considerations shall be addressed to such a being to convince him what it is impossible but that the most stupid must feel and know can never be true—that he is thus to labor upon a principle of natural duty, or for the sake of his own personal happiness, such services can only be expected from one who has no will of his own; who surrenders his will in implicit obedience to that of another. Such obedience is the consequence only of uncontrolled authority over the body. There is nothing else which can operate to produce the effect. The power of the master must be absolute to render the submission of the slave perfect. I most freely confess my sense of the harshness of this proposition; I feel it as deeply as any man can; and as a principle of moral right every person in his retirement must repudiate it. But in the actual condition of things it must be so. There is no remedy. This discipline belongs to the state of slavery. They cannot be disunited without abrogating at once the rights of the master and absolving the slave from his subjection. It constitutes the curse of slavery to both the bond and free portion of our population. But it is inherent in the relation of the master and slave. * * *

* * * We cannot allow the right of the master to be brought into discussion in the courts of justice. The slave, to remain a slave, must be made sensible that there is no appeal from his master; that his power is in no instance usurped; but is conferred by the laws of man at least, if not by the law of God. The danger would be great, indeed, if the tribunals of justice should be called on to graduate the punishment appropriate to every temper and every dereliction of menial duty. No

man can anticipate the many and aggravated provocations of the master which the slave would be constantly stimulated by his own passions or the instigation of others to give; or the consequent wrath of the master, prompting him to bloody vengeance upon the turbulent traitor—a vengeance generally practiced with impunity by reason of its privacy. The Court, therefore, disclaims the power of changing the relation in which these parts of our people stand to each other.

We are happy to see that there is daily less and less occasion for the interposition of the Courts. The protection already afforded by several statutes, that all-powerful motive, the private interest of the owner, the benevolences towards each other, seated in the hearts of those who have been born and bred together, the frowns and deep execrations of the community upon the barbarian who is guilty of excessive and brutal cruelty to his unprotected slave, all combined, have produced a mildness of treatment and attention to the comforts of the unfortunate class of slaves, greatly mitigating the rigors of servitude and ameliorating the condition of the slaves. The same causes are operating and will continue to operate with increased action until the disparity in numbers between the whites and blacks shall have rendered the latter in no degree dangerous to the former, when the policy now existing may be further relaxed. This result, greatly to be desired, may be much more rationally expected from the events above alluded to, and now in progress, than from any rash expositions of abstract truths by a judiciary tainted with a false and fanatical philanthropy, seeking to redress an acknowledged evil by means still more wicked and appalling than even that evil.

I repeat that I would gladly have avoided this ungrateful question. But being brought to it the Court is compelled to declare that while slavery exists amongst us in its present state, or until it shall seem fit to the legislature to interpose express enactments to the contrary, it will be the imperative duty of the Judges to recognize the full dominion of the owner over the slave, except where the exercise of it is forbidden by statute. And this we do upon the ground that this dominion is essential to the value of slaves as property, to the security of the master, and the public tranquility, greatly dependent upon their subordination; and, in fine, as most effectually securing the general protection and comfort of the slaves themselves.

KENNEDY v. MASON

10 La. Ann. 519 (1855).

[Kennedy was the overseer of slaves on Mason's plantation. Kennedy mistreated and killed a slave, Jim Crack, as described below. The issue in the case is whether Kennedy owes to Mason an amount equal to the value of the slave because of Kennedy's mistreatment.]

VOORHIES, J.

* * *

The question then to be considered, in order to fix the liability of the plaintiff, is, whether the death of the slave Jim Crack was caused by any improper treatment or imprudence on the part of the plaintiff. * * *

We think it may be safely assumed that the record exhibits the following state of facts: The slave Jim Crack had run away and been absent for some time from the plantation, when he was captured and brought back on the 5th of January, 1852, about seven o'clock in the evening, the weather being extremely cold. He was shortly afterwards stripped of his clothes, tied down with his belly to the cold ground, and beaten with a hand-saw and whip; he remained in that position at least an hour and a half during which the beating continued with short intermissions. He was then rubbed with a mixture called No. 6, and a dose of castor oil was administered to him. * * *

It appears he was then conducted to his cabin, and about four hours after, found dead in his bed. Dr. Roane, who made a post mortem examination of his body the next day, about sixteen or eighteen hours after his death, says:

I saw that he had been whipped and considerably bruised on his buttock, and each side of his shoulders. The buttock and sides of the shoulders did not appear much cut, but considerably bruised, from which the blood oozed and stuck to the shirt in a few places. That amount of whipping under ordinary circumstances, would not produce death. I thought it imprudent to whip the boy at that time and under the circumstances. From internal and external indications, I think it more likely that death was caused by a congestive chill, than by the whipping; but more likely death in this case was caused by a combination of all the circumstances.

Under this state of facts we do not think it is unreasonable to infer that the slave's death was caused by the severity of the punishment inflicted upon him, combined with his exposure to the weather. Had the plaintiff taken proper care of him after he retired to his cabin, he might have averted the unfortunate consequence: but he did not. This was gross negligence on his part. * * *

We therefore conclude that [Kennedy, the overseer,] is liable to [the owner] for the value of the slave in question * * *.

     * * *

Notes and Questions

1. Notice that these cases, though involving violence committed by one person upon another, are legally about the existence and the extent of liability owed to a property owner for damage to his slave property.

2. What does Judge Ruffin mean by his remark that "there is daily less and less occasion for the interposition of the Courts"? What do you imagine he is referring to by a "false and fanatical philanthropy, seeking to redress an acknowledged evil by means still more wicked and appalling than even that evil"?

———

Courts played a key role in upholding slavery prior to the Civil War. See G. Stone, L. Seidman, C. Sunstein & M. Tushnet, *Constitutional Law* 500 (3rd ed. 1996). In *Prigg v. Pennsylvania*, 41 U.S. (16 Pet.) 539 (1842), the

Supreme Court declared unconstitutional a Pennsylvania law that punished the seizure and removal of a slave from the state by his master. The Court wrote:

Historically, it is well known, that the object of [the Fugitive Slave Clause] was to secure to the citizens of the slave-holding states the complete right and title of ownership in their slaves, as property, in every state in the Union into which they might escape from the state where they were held in servitude. The full recognition of this right and title was indispensable to the security of this species of property in all the slave-holding states; and, indeed, was so vital to the preservation of their domestic interests and institutions, that it cannot be doubted, that it constituted a fundamental article, without the adoption of which the Union could not have been formed. Its true design was to guard against the doctrines and principles prevalent in the non-slave-holding states, by preventing them from intermeddling with, or obstructing, or abolishing the rights of the owners of slaves. * * *

It is manifest, from this consideration, that if the constitution had not contained this clause, every non-slave-holding state in the Union would have been at liberty to have declared free all runaway slaves coming within its limits, and to have given them entire immunity and protection against the claims of their masters; a course which would have created the most bitter animosities, and engendered perpetual strife between the different states. The clause was, therefore, of the last importance to the safety and security of the southern states, and could not have been surrounded by them, without endangering their whole property in slaves. The clause was accordingly adopted into the constitution, by the unanimous consent of the framers of it; a proof at once of its intrinsic and practical necessity. * * *

We have said, that the clause contains a positive and unqualified recognition of the right of the owner in the slave, unaffected by any state law or legislation whatsoever, because there is no qualification or restriction of it to be found therein; and we have no right to insert any, which is not expressed, and cannot be fairly implied.... Upon this ground, we have not the slightest hesitation in holding, that under and in virtue of the constitution, the owner of a slave is clothed with entire authority, in every state in the Union, to seize and recapture his slave, wherever he can do it, without any breach of the peace or any illegal violence. In this sense, and to this extent, this clause of the constitution may properly be said to execute itself, and to require no aid from legislation, state or national.

Notes and Questions

1. Robert Cover, in *Justice Accused* (1975), explores the jurisprudence of anti-slavery southern judges. He argues that in order to reconcile their moral beliefs with their legal rulings, the judges resorted to several rhetorical strategies, including exaggerating the legal inevitability of their rulings and the political implications of a contrary ruling. Might some of these strategies be visible in the opinions reproduced above?

D. RESISTANCE TO SLAVERY

As Howard Zinn notes in an excerpt earlier in this chapter, slaves resisted enslavement in every way that they could, including rebellion and escape. Recall Lavinia Bell's escape to freedom in Canada, or the slave killed in *Kennedy v. Mason*. *State v. Mann* demonstrates the terror white slaveowners felt and their use of violence and cruelty to suppress the constant threat of rebellion.

Consider the following excerpt from Herbert Aptheker on slave resistance.

HERBERT APTHEKER

Negro Slave Revolts in the United States, 1526–1860,
in *Essays in the History of the American Negro*
10–69 (1973).*

WHY THE REVOLTS

Vengeance did not sleep. Bourbon historians, who have made slavery idyllic and the slaves an inferior people, have little place in their works for accounts of this vengeance—this heroic anti-slavery struggle of the Negroes. Thus, for example, Phillips in his latest work, published after his death, declared that "slave revolts and plots were very seldom in the United States"; and two other eminent historians recently said the same thing—John D. Hicks:"Attempts at insurrection were extremely rare"; James G. Randall: "Surprisingly few instances of slave insurrections."

The history of American slavery is marked by at least two hundred and fifty *reported* Negro conspiracies and revolts. This certainly demonstrates that organized efforts at freedom were neither "seldom" nor "rare," but were rather a regular and ever-recurring phenomenon in the life of the old South.

Considerable explanation of this rebellious activity has already been given. We have seen that cruelty—that is, actual physical maltreatment—was an essential part of slavery. We have seen that the system, in so-called normal times, provided a bare animal sustenance to its victims. And we have observed the fact that economic disaster seriously depressed the already miserably low standards of the Negroes.

Economic depression had other results of a disturbing nature. It would naturally sharpen the tempers of the slaveowners or of their overseers, whose incomes depended upon the value of the crop they could force the slaves to produce. Bankruptcy and liquidation are, moreover, concomitants of depression and, when property was human beings, its liquidation carried many stories of woe. For it entailed an increase in the leasing or sale of thousands of slaves, which meant the forced separation of brother from sister, child from mother, husband from wife. Surely it is more than a coincidence that the years of severe economic depression coincide with the periods of greatest rebellious activity.

Another factor of considerable importance in arousing concerted slave unrest was the occurrence of an exciting or unusual event. Thus, the landing of a new provincial governor from England in one of the colonies here might lead to a belief on the part of the slaves that they were to be freed, and thereby cause the masters trouble, as occurred in

* Herbert Aptheker, *Essays in the History of the American Negro* 10–16, 69 (1973). Reprinted by permission of International Publishers Co.

Virginia during 1730. Again, the prevalence of revolutionary philosophy and activity, as from 1770 to 1783, or the rapid spread and growth of an equalitarian religion, as Methodism from 1785 to 1805, or a war against a foreign power, as against Great Britain from 1812 to 1815, or stirring debates in Congress over the question of slavery, as in 1820, or particularly exciting Presidential campaigns as those of 1840 and 1856—all clearly aroused subversive activity on the part of the slaves. The actual outbreak of a slave revolt seems also to have had a contagious effect, so that, for instance, the tremendous struggles for liberation of the slaves of the French West Indies (especially St. Domingo or Haiti) in the 1790s and early 1800s certainly inspired similar attempts in the United States. It is to be noted, too, that attempts at revolt evoked more stringent measures of repression, and the added pinch these created was at times probably important in causing new conspiracies or rebellions.

The more rapid growth of the Negro population as compared to that of the white was also a disturbing factor. This occurred for various reasons. When, in the late seventeenth and early eighteenth centuries, Negro slavery was found to be profitable in certain regions, greed led to an enormous spurt in the importation of slaves. This undoubtedly is an explanation for the considerable slave unrest in South Carolina in the 1730s. The settlement of new and fertile slave areas was likewise followed by a disproportionate growth of the Negro population and consequent slave unrest, as in Mississippi in 1835. Depression, on the other hand, in the great staple producing areas caused them to import less slaves. This meant a severe blow to the prosperity of the slave-raising and slave-exporting regions of the South, with a resultant rapid rise in their slave populations and a more dangerous social condition. This state of affairs prevailed, for instance, from about 1820 to 1831 in eastern Virginia and eastern North Carolina.

Urbanization and industrialization—which were occurring to some extent in the South from about 1840 to 1860—and their creation of a proletarian Negro were also exceedingly dangerous to a slave society. These phenomena were probably important in accounting for some slave outbreaks, especially those of the late 1850's.

SAFEGUARDS OF THE SLAVOCRATS

While the propaganda mill of the slavocratic oligarchy incessantly ground out its falsehoods concerning the innate cowardice and stupidity of the Negro and the delights of being a slave, the same group nevertheless maintained a whole series of devices and laws which it knew was necessary to keep the Negro in bondage.

Armed might was the main instrument of suppression. This comprised large detachments of regular troops of the United States Army, the efficient militia of each of the Southern states, the patrols or mounted bodies of armed men who scoured every piece of land in every county of the South at various intervals from one week to four weeks, the considerable bodies of guards present and active in every Southern city, volunteer military organizations in numerous areas of the South, and the continual presence of at least one armed white, master or overseer, on every plantation.

The activities of the slaves were severely limited. None might possess arms. It was illegal to teach a slave how to read or write. Writing or saying anything with a "tendency" to create unrest among the slaves was a serious crime. No slave might buy or sell or trade anything without his master's permission. Slaves might not assemble without the presence of whites. They could not testify in any court in any case involving whites. Legal restrictions also hit free Negroes, so that their movements from county to county or from state to state were regulated or totally forbidden. They, too, could not testify in any court against a white person. They, as a rule, could not vote, and even their business activities were closely regulated and limited. In the two years immediately preceding the Civil War laws were passed in several Southern states having as their purposes the re-enslavement of free Negroes or their forced evacuation.

Numerous non-legal regulations and customs were important, too, in maintaining subordination. The opinion of a North Carolina judge rendered in 1852 indicated some of these:

What acts in a slave towards a white person will amount to insolence, it is manifestly impossible to define—it may consist in a look, the pointing of a finger, a refusal or neglect to step out of the way when a white person is seen to approach. But each of such acts violates the rules of propriety, and if tolerated, would destroy that subordination, upon which our social system rests.

A carefully nursed policy of division between the poor whites and the slaves on the basis of race hatred was another very important Bourbon device for retaining his power. Divisions amongst the slaves themselves were also fostered. Thus the domestic slaves were, generally, better treated than the field slaves. It was from this favored group that the slaveholders recruited spies and traitors to whom they gave considerable financial rewards together, often, with freedom—the greatest gift in the power of the "patriarchal" slaveholders!

The slaveholders' religion had, so far as the slave was concerned, one message—be meek. In the words of the Rev. Dr. Nelson, who lived for many years in North Carolina:

I have been intimately acquainted with the religious opportunities of the slaves,—in the constant habit of hearing the sermons which are preached to them. And I solemnly affirm that during the forty years of my residence and observation in this line, I never heard a single one of these sermons but what was taken up with the obligations and duties of slaves to their masters. Indeed, I never heard a sermon to slaves but what made obedience to masters by the slaves the fundamental and supreme law of religion.

But the slaves had a different religion. Their God had declared that all men were created of one blood, and that the divine rule of doing unto others as one would have others do unto you was the true guide for religious behavior. Their God had cursed man-stealers and had himself taken slaves out of their bondage. Their God had denounced the oppressors and had praised the humble. Their God had declared that the first would be the last and the last would be the first.

THE REVOLTS AND CONSPIRACIES

Before discussing the slave revolts themselves it is important that it be understood that they form but one manifestation of the discontent of the Negro. Revolt was merely one method by which the slaves hoped to obtain their liberty. There were others, each of which merits extensive treatment. One of the most important of these was flight. In the history of slavery many tens of thousands of slaves *succeeded* in escaping from their enslavers. They fled wherever freedom loomed—the destinations varying with the different times and places—to the Dutch, the Indians, the Mexicans, the British armies, the Canadians, the French, the Spanish, to the Northern states and to the swamps and mountains and forests of the South.

Other slaves, particularly those who were leased by their masters for work in towns and cities, were able, by working in their spare time, to accumulate enough money to purchase their freedom (this was possible, of course, only if the master were willing and honest). There is considerable evidence to indicate that this was by no means infrequent, especially in the more northern of the slave states, like Tennessee, Kentucky and Missouri.

Enlistment and faithful service in the armed forces of the nation was another method whereby Negroes at times gained their freedom. Several hundreds, for example, became free in this manner in the two wars against Great Britain. Individual acts of terrorism, self-mutilation and self-destruction (sometimes, as in Charleston, in 1807, mass suicides), sabotage, as shamming illness, "careless" work, destruction of tools and occasionally strikes were other forms of protest against enslavement.

It is, finally, not to be forgotten that Negroes were leaders in the agitational and political movement against slavery, none being more important in these respects than Allen, Jones, Hall, Truth, Purvis, Remond, Garnet, Ruggles, Wright, Still, Tubman, Walker, Ray, Douglass and a host of others. * * *

American slavery was a barbarous tyranny . It impoverished the land and the common people, Negro and white, of the South, tore away their freedom and attempted to destroy the liberty of all American citizens.

Its history, however, is not merely one of impoverishment, deprivation, and oppression. For imbedded in the record of American slavery is the inspiring story of the persistent and courageous efforts of the Negroes (aided, not infrequently, by the poor whites) to regain their heritage of liberty and equality, to regain their right to the elemental demands of human beings.

Notes and Questions

1. Herbert Aptheker provides a detailed account of slave revolts that were frequent and consistent. Interested readers should also consult his classic *American Negro Slave Revolts* (6th ed. 1993), documenting the extensive history of slave rebellions, large and small. Aptheker concludes that "[t]he material accumulated in the half century since [the first appear-

ance of his book] has further substantiated its thesis, namely, that the African–American people, in slavery, forged a record of discontent and of resistance comparable to that marking the history of any other oppressed people." *Id.* at xi. Eugene D. Genovese has also described the myriad forms of daily slave resistance to the slave regime, resistance which included stealing from slave owners, lying to and deceiving white owners, refusing to submit to whippings, disrupting work schedules, reacting with apathy to the owners' concerns, and running away. See Eugene D. Genovese, *Roll, Jordan, Roll: The World the Slaves Made* 597–660 (1974). See also Eugene D. Genovese, *From Rebellion to Revolution: Afro–American Slave Revolts in the Making of the Modern World* (1979).

E. SLAVERY AND CITIZENSHIP

DRED SCOTT v. SANDFORD
60 U.S. 393 (1856).

[Dred Scott was a slave. In 1834, Scott's owner, Dr. Emerson, took him from Missouri to Illinois, where they lived until 1836. Then Emerson took him from Illinois to the Louisiana territory, where they lived until 1838. Emerson then moved back to Missouri and sold Scott, his wife Harriet, and their daughters Eliza and Lizzie as slaves to the defendant, John Sandford.

Scott sued Sandford for his freedom and the freedom of his family. Scott brought his lawsuit in the federal Circuit Court for the District of Missouri. Scott based his suit on the diversity jurisdiction available in federal court. Scott claimed to be a citizen of Missouri, and Sandford was a citizen of New York. Scott argued that his residency in Illinois and in the Louisiana territory made him a free man. Sandford challenged Scott's claim to be a citizen of Missouri and argued that the federal courts lacked diversity jurisdiction under Article III of the Constitution. The Supreme Court thus considered whether Scott was a state citizen for purposes of suing in federal court and invoking diversity jurisdiction. The Supreme Court also considered the constitutionality of the Missouri Compromise, which prohibited slavery in the Louisiana territory.]

CHIEF JUSTICE TANEY delivered the opinion of the court.

* * * And it becomes, therefore, our duty to decide whether the facts stated in the plea are or are not sufficient to show that the plaintiff is not entitled to sue as a citizen in a court of the United States. * * *

The question is simply this: Can a negro, whose ancestors were imported into this country, and sold as slaves, become a member of the political community formed and brought into existence by the Constitution of the United States, and as such become entitled to all the rights, and privileges, and immunities, guarantied by that instrument to the citizen? One of which rights is the privilege of suing in a court of the United States in the cases specified in the Constitution.

It will be observed, that the plea applies to that class of persons only whose ancestors were negroes of the African race, and imported into this country, and sold and held as slaves. The only matter in issue before the

court, therefore, is, whether the descendants of such slaves, when they
shall be emancipated, or who are born of parents who had become free
before their birth, are citizens of a State, in the sense in which the word
citizen is used in the Constitution of the United States. * * *

The situation of this population was altogether unlike that of the
Indian race. The latter, it is true, formed no part of the colonial
communities, and never amalgamated with them in social connections or
in government. But although they were uncivilized, they were yet a free
and independent people, associated together in nations or tribes, and
governed by their own laws. Many of these political communities were
situated in territories to which the white race claimed the ultimate right
of dominion. But that claim was acknowledged to be subject to the right
of the Indians to occupy it as long as they thought proper, and neither
the English nor colonial Governments claimed or exercised any dominion
over the tribe or nation by whom it was occupied, nor claimed the right
to the possession of the territory, until the tribe or nation consented to
cede it. These Indian Governments were regarded and treated as foreign
Governments, as much so as if an ocean had separated the red man from
the white; and their freedom has constantly been acknowledged, from
the time of the first emigration to the English colonies to the present
day, by the different Governments which succeeded each other. Treaties
have been negotiated with them, and their alliance sought for in war;
and the people who compose these Indian political communities have
always been treated as foreigners not living under our Government. It is
true that the course of events has brought the Indian tribes within the
limits of the United States under subjection to the white race; and it has
been found necessary, for their sake as well as our own, to regard them
as in a state of pupilage, and to legislate to a certain extent over them
and the territory they occupy. But they may, without doubt, like the
subjects of any other foreign Government, be naturalized by the authority of Congress, and become citizens of a State, and of the United States;
and if an individual should leave his nation or tribe and take up his
abode among the white population, he would be entitled to all the rights
and privileges which would belong to an emigrant from any other foreign
people.

> * * *

The words "people of the United States" and "citizens" are synonymous terms, and mean the same thing. They both describe the political
body who, according to our republican institutions, form the sovereignty,
and who hold the power and conduct the Government through their
representatives. They are what we familiarly call the "sovereign people,"
and every citizen is one of this people, and a constituent member of this
sovereignty. The question before us is, whether the class of persons [the
descendants of African slaves] compose a portion of this people, and are
constituent members of this sovereignty? We think they are not, and
that they are not included, and were not intended to be included, under
the word "citizens" in the Constitution, and can therefore claim none of
the rights and privileges which that instrument provides for and secures
to citizens of the United States. On the contrary, they were at that time
considered as a subordinate and inferior class of beings, who had been

subjugated by the dominant race, and, whether emancipated or not, yet remained subject to their authority, and had no rights or privileges but such as those who held the power and the Government might choose to grant them. * * *

In the opinion of the court, the legislation and histories of the times, and the language used in the Declaration of Independence, show, that neither the class of persons who had been imported as slaves, nor their descendants, whether they had become free or not, were then acknowledged as a part of the people, nor intended to be included in the general words used in that memorable instrument.

It is difficult at this day to realize the state of public opinion in relation to that unfortunate race, which prevailed in the civilized and enlightened portions of the world at the time of the Declaration of Independence, and when the Constitution of the United States was framed and adopted. But the public history of every European nation displays it in a manner too plain to be mistaken.

They had for more than a century before been regarded as beings of an inferior order, and altogether unfit to associate with the white race, either in social or political relations; and so far inferior, that they had no rights which the white man was bound to respect; and that the negro might justly and lawfully be reduced to slavery for his benefit. He was bought and sold, and treated as an ordinary article of merchandise and traffic, whenever a profit could be made by it. This opinion was at that time fixed and universal in the civilized portion of the white race. It was regarded as an axiom in morals as well as in politics, which no one thought of disputing, or supposed to be open to dispute; and men in every grade and position in society daily and habitually acted upon it in their private pursuits, as well as in matters of public concern, without doubting for a moment the correctness of this opinion. * * *

[Laws prohibiting intermarriage in the colonies] show that a perpetual and impassable barrier was intended to be erected between the white race and the one which they had reduced to slavery, and governed as subjects with absolute and despotic power, and which they then looked upon as so far below them in the scale of created beings, that intermarriages between white persons and negroes or mulattoes were regarded as unnatural and immoral, and punished as crimes, not only in the parties, but in the person who joined them in marriage. And no distinction in this respect was made between the free negro or mulatto and the slave, but this stigma, of the deepest degradation, was fixed upon the whole race.

[Having decided that Dred Scott was not a federal citizen for purposes of diversity jurisdiction, the Court then invalidated the Missouri Compromise, holding that Congress lacked power to enact it.]

Notes and Questions

1. *Dred Scott* is one of the most reviled cases in American constitutional law. Is Taney accurate in his assertions about the Framers' intent? For an extensive discussion of the opinion and its historical context, see Don E.

Fehrenbacher, *The Dred Scott Case* (1978). See also Stanley I. Kutler, *The Dred Scott Decision* (1967).

2. Is Taney accurate that Blacks had "no rights"? What about free Blacks or Indians?

FREDERICK DOUGLASS

The Dred Scott Decision
Speech delivered before American Anti–Slavery Society, New York
(May 11, 1857).*

* * *

This infamous decision of the Slaveholding wing of the Supreme Court maintains that slaves are within the contemplation of the Constitution of the United States, property; that slaves are property in the same sense that horses, sheep, and swine are property; that the old doctrine that slavery is a creature of local law is false; that the right of the slaveholder to his slave does not depend upon the local law, but is secured wherever the Constitution of the United States extends; that Congress has no right to prohibit slavery anywhere; that slavery may go in safety anywhere under the star-spangled banner; that colored persons of African descent have no rights that white men are bound to respect; that colored men of African descent are not and cannot be citizens of the United States.

You will readily ask me how I am affected by this devilish decision—this judicial incarnation of wolfishness? My answer is, and no thanks to the slaveholding wing of the Supreme Court, my hopes were never brighter than now.

I have no fear that the National Conscience will be put to sleep by such an open, glaring, and scandalous tissue of lies as that decision is, and has been, over and over, shown to be.

The Supreme Court of the United States is not the only power in this world. It is very great, but the Supreme Court of the Almighty is greater. Judge Taney can do many things, but he cannot perform impossibilities. He cannot bale out the ocean, annihilate the firm old earth, or pluck the silvery star of liberty from our Northern sky. He may decide, and decide again; but he cannot reverse the decision of the Most High. He cannot change the essential nature of things—making evil good, and good evil.

Happily for the whole human family, their rights have been defined, declared, and decided in a court higher than the Supreme Court. "There is a law," says Brougham, "above all the enactments of human codes, and by that law, unchangeable and eternal, man cannot hold property in man."

Your fathers have said that man's right to liberty is self-evident. * * * To decide against this right in the person of Dred Scott, or the

* *The Life and Writings of Frederick Douglass*, Vol. 2: *The Pre–Civil War Decade, 1850–1860* at 410–12, 417–21 (Philip S. Foner ed. 1950). Reprinted by permission of International Publishers Co.

humblest and most whip-scarred bondman in the land, is to decide against God. It is an open rebellion against God's government. It is an attempt to undo what God has done, to blot out the broad distinction instituted by the *Allwise* between men and things, and to change the image and superscription of the everliving God into a speechless piece of merchandise.

Such a decision cannot stand. God will be true though every man be a liar. We can appeal from this hell-black judgment of the Supreme Court, to the court of common sense and common humanity. We can appeal from man to God. If there is no justice on earth, there is yet justice in heaven. You may close your Supreme Court against the black man's cry for justice, but you cannot, thank God, close against him the ear of a sympathising world, nor shut up the Court of Heaven. All that is merciful and just, on earth and in Heaven, will execrate and despise this edict of Taney.

If it were at all likely that the people of these free States would tamely submit to this demoniacal judgment, I might feel gloomy and sad over it, and possibly it might be necessary for my people to look for a home in some other country. But as the case stands, we have nothing to fear.

In one point of view, we, the abolitionists and colored people, should meet this decision, unlooked for and monstrous as it appears, in a cheerful spirit. This very attempt to blot out forever the hopes of an enslaved people may be one necessary link in the chain of events preparatory to the downfall and complete overthrow of the whole slave system. * * *

* * * While men thus respect law, it becomes a serious matter so to interpret the law as to make it operate against liberty. I have a quarrel with those who fling Supreme Law of this land between the slave and freedom. It is a serious matter to fling the weight of the Constitution against the cause of human liberty, and those who do it, take upon them a heavy responsibility. Nothing but absolute necessity, shall, or ought to drive me to such a concession to slavery. * * *

Now let us approach the Constitution from the standpoint thus indicated, and instead of finding it in a warrant for the stupendous system of robbery, comprehended in the term slavery, we shall find it strongly against the system.

"We the people of the United States, in order to form a more perfect Union, establish justice, insure domestic tranquility, provide for the common defence, promote the general welfare, and secure the blessings of liberty to ourselves and our posterity, do ordain and establish this Constitution for the United States of America."

Such are the objects announced by the instrument itself, and they are in harmony with the Declaration of Independence, and the principles of human well-being. * * *

Neither in the preamble nor in the body of the Constitution is there a single mention of the term *slave* or *slave holder, slave master,* or *slave state,* neither is there any reference to the color, or the physical peculiarities of any part of the people of the United States. Neither is there anything in the Constitution standing alone, which would imply the existence of slavery in this country.

"We, the people"—not we, the white people—not we, the citizens, or the legal voters—not we, the privileged class, and excluding all other classes but we, the people; not we, the horses and cattle, but we the people—the men and women, the human inhabitants of the United States, do ordain and establish this Constitution, &c.

I ask, then, any man to read the Constitution, and tell me where, if he can, in what particular that instrument affords the slightest sanction of slavery?

Where will he find a guarantee for slavery? Will he find it in the declaration that no person shall be deprived of life, liberty, or property, without the due process of law? Will he find it in the declaration that the Constitution was established to secure the blessing of liberty? Will he find it in the right of the people to be secure in their persons and papers, and houses, and effects? Will he find it in the clause prohibiting the enactment by any State of a bill of attainder?

These all strike at the root of slavery, and any one of them, but faithfully carried out, would put an end to slavery in every State in the American Union.

Take, for example, the prohibition of a bill of attainder. That is a law entailing on the child the misfortunes of the parent. This principle would destroy slavery in every State of the Union.

The law of slavery is a law of attainder. The child is property because its parent was property, and suffers as a slave because its parent suffered as a slave.

Thus the very essence of the whole slave code is in open violation of a fundamental provision of the Constitution, and is in open and flagrant violation of all the objects set forth in the Constitution. * * *

How is the constitutionality of slavery made out, or attempted to be made out?

First, by discrediting and casting away as worthless the most beneficent rules of legal interpretation; by disregarding the plain and common sense reading of the instrument itself; by showing that the Constitution does not mean what it says, and says what it does not mean, by assuming that the written Constitution is to be interpreted in the light of a secret and unwritten understanding of its framers, which understanding is declared to be in favor of slavery. It is in this mean, contemptible, underhand method that the Constitution is pressed into the service of slavery. * * *

The argument here is, that the Constitution comes down to us from a slaveholding period and a slaveholding people; and that, therefore, we are bound to suppose that the Constitution recognizes colored persons of African descent, the victims of slavery at that time, as debarred forever from all participation in the benefit of the Constitution and the Declaration of Independence, although the plain reading of both includes them in their beneficent range.

As a man, an American, a citizen, a colored man of both Anglo–Saxon and African descent, I denounce this representation as a most scandalous and devilish perversion of the Constitution, and a brazen misstatement of the facts of history.

* * *

Notes and Questions

1.   Consider Douglass's refutation of the *Dred Scott* opinion. What arguments can be made for and against his interpretation?

2.   The abolitionist movement had long denounced slavery. Abolitionists, both black and white, were outraged by the *Dred Scott* decision and its reinforcement of southern attitudes towards black slavery. See, *e.g.*, Leon F. Litwack, *North of Slavery* 6–19, 63 (1961); John Hope Franklin & Alfred A. Moss, Jr., *From Slavery to Freedom* 79–81, 171–83, 195 (7th ed. 1994); David A.J. Richards, *Women, Gays, and the Constitution* (1998) (discussing abolitionist feminists).

F. THE CIVIL WAR

Despite the hopes of many, the *Dred Scott* decision did nothing to settle the issue of slavery. If anything, it created instability regarding the status of the "peculiar institution" and so fueled the tensions that escalated into the Civil War. President Lincoln's attitude towards slavery and Blacks can best be characterized as ambivalent and expedient. Although he enjoys a reputation as the great emancipator of slaves, the historical record is mixed.

Lincoln, although morally opposed to slavery, believed in white supremacy and the inferiority of Blacks. In the first of his famous debates with Stephen Douglas, on August 21, 1858, Lincoln stated that

> [I] have no purpose directly or indirectly to interfere with the institution of slavery in the States where it exists. I believe I have no lawful right to do so, and I have no inclination to do so. I have no purpose to introduce political and social equality between the white and the black races. There is a physical difference between the two, which in my judgment will probably forever forbid their living together upon the footing of perfect equality * * * I, as well as Judge Douglas, am in favor of the race to which I belong, having the superior position.

First Lincoln–Douglas Debate, reprinted in *The Portable Abraham Lincoln* 115 (Andrew Delbanco ed. 1992). At the same time, Lincoln professed his belief that "there is no reason in the world why the negro is not entitled to all the natural rights enumerated in the Declaration of Independence." *Id.*

Lincoln advocated the emancipation of Blacks, but like Jefferson he could not tolerate nor envision a large black presence within the United States. Indeed, he was willing to emancipate the slaves, but only on the condition that they be removed from the country, to Liberia, to Haiti, to

Panama, and, in at least one proposal, to Texas. On August 15, 1862, Lincoln addressed a delegation of black men and pleaded with them that they consider leaving the United States for Liberia or a colony in Central America. See Nathaniel Weyl & William Marina, *American Statesmen on Slavery and the Negro* 194–234 (1971). Lincoln argued that "it is better for us both ... to be separated." Also in 1862, Lincoln proposed to Congress a constitutional amendment "to enable Congress to appropriate money and otherwise provide for colonizing free colored persons, with their own consent, at any place or places without the United States." Herman Ames, *The Proposed Amendments to the Constitution of the United States* 207 (1896, reprint 1970).

As expressed in the following letter, President Lincoln would do whatever he had to do, regardless of the freedom of Blacks, to preserve the Union.

ABRAHAM LINCOLN TO HORACE GREELEY
August 22, 1862.*

I would save the Union. I would save it the shortest way under the Constitution. The sooner the national authority can be restored; the nearer the Union will be "the Union as it was." If there be those who would not save the Union, unless they could at the same time *save* slavery, I do not agree with them. If there be those who would not save the Union unless they could at the same time *destroy* slavery, I do not agree with them. My paramount object in this struggle *is* to save the Union, and is *not* either to save or to destroy slavery. If I could save the Union without freeing *any* slave I would do it, and if I could save it by freeing *all* the slaves I would do it; and if I could save it by freeing some and leaving others alone I would also do that. What I do about slavery, and the colored race, I do because I believe it helps to save the Union; and what I forbear, I forbear because I do *not* believe it would help to save the Union. I shall do *less* whenever I shall believe what I am doing hurts the cause, and I shall do *more* whenever I shall believe doing more will help the cause. I shall try to correct errors when shown to be errors; and I shall adopt new views so fast as they shall appear to be true views.

I have here stated my purpose according to my view of *official* duty; and I intend no modification of my oft-expressed *personal* wish that all men every where could be free.

Notes and Questions

1. As Derrick Bell has written, "Lincoln's response to Greeley is significant for more than its candor. Here was, for perhaps the first and last time, a President of the United States acknowledging that the civil rights of blacks, even the basic right not to be a slave in a society dedicated to individual liberty, must take a lower priority to the preservation of the Union." See Derrick A. Bell, Jr., *Race, Racism, and American Law* 10 (3d ed. 1992).

* Reprinted in *The Portable Abraham Lincoln*, Andrew Delbanco ed. 239–40 (Viking Penguin, 1992).

2. On January 1, 1863, President Lincoln issued the Emancipation Proclamation, which provided that:

> all persons held as slaves within any State or designated part of the State the people whereof shall then be in rebellion against the United States, shall be then, thenceforward, and forever free; and the executive government of the United States * * * will recognize and maintain the freedom of such persons and will do no act or acts to repress such persons, or any of them, in any efforts they may make for their actual freedom.

The Emancipation Proclamation freed the slaves in the rebellious slave states, but did not free approximately 800,000 slaves in the border states not in rebellion. See John Hope Franklin & Alfred A. Moss, Jr. *From Slavery to Freedom* 198–219 (7th ed. 1994) (describing the Civil War, the military service of Blacks during the War, and the responses to the Emancipation Proclamation).

Derrick Bell's discussion of the Emancipation Proclamation and its teaching, that "blacks are more likely to obtain relief for even acknowledged racial injustice when that relief also serves, directly or indirectly, to further ends which policymakers perceive are in the best interests of the country," is well worth reading. Bell, *supra* at 12.

3. Even after the war had ended, Lincoln sought the voluntary deportation of Blacks, which was ultimately abandoned because of its cost. Lerone Bennett, *Before the Mayflower* 217 (5th ed. 1982). On Lincoln's efforts to both emancipate the slaves and to colonize them, see Franklin & Moss *supra* at 205–07 ("Colonization seemed almost as important to Lincoln as emancipation.").

4. Historians disagree about whether the Civil War was fought primarily over the issue of slavery or something else. Initially, Lincoln acted to preserve the unity of the nation threatened by the secession of southern states. By the time of his inauguration, seven southern states had seceded. "Even before his inauguration Lincoln perceived that his most important and difficult task was stemming the tide of national disintegration." Franklin & Moss, *supra* at 198.

SECTION 4. THE ERA OF RECONSTRUCTION, 1865–1877

Following the Civil War, the period of Reconstruction resulted in lasting changes to the Constitution and the relationship between the federal government and the states. Historian Eric Foner has described themes crucial to a contemporary understanding of Reconstruction. According to Foner, "[t]he first is the centrality of the black experience. Rather than passive victims of the actions of others or simply a 'problem' confronting white society, blacks were active agents in the making of Reconstruction. During the Civil War, their actions helped force the nation down the road to emancipation, and in the aftermath of that conflict, their quest for individual and community autonomy did much to establish Reconstruction's political and economic agenda. Although thwarted in their bid for land, blacks seized the opportunity created by the end of slavery to establish as much independence as possible in their working lives, consolidate their families and communities, and stake a claim to equal citizenship. Black participation in Southern public life after 1867 was the most radical development of the Reconstruction years, a massive experiment in interracial democracy without precedent in the history of this or any other country that abolished slavery in the nineteenth century. [Readers should] pay special attention both to the political mobilization of the black community and to the emergence and changing composition of a black political leadership that seized upon America's republican values as a weapon for attacking the nation's racial caste system * * * Reconstruction produced enduring changes in the laws and Constitution that fundamentally altered federal-state relations and re-defined the meaning of American citizenship. Yet because it threatened traditions of local autonomy, produced political corruption and rising taxes, and was so closely associated with the new rights of blacks, the rise of the state inspired powerful opposition, which, in turn, weakened support for Reconstruction." Eric Foner, *Reconstruction: America's Unfinished Revolution* xxiv-xxvi (1988).

Among the great legacies of the Civil War era and the era of Reconstruction that followed the war are the Reconstruction Amendments to the Constitution, Amendments XIII, XIV, and XV. As historian Kenneth Stampp has written, "[t]he fact that these amendments could not have been adopted under any other circumstances, or at any other time, before or since, may suggest the crucial importance of the Reconstruction era in American history." *Reconstruction: An Anthology of Revisionist Writings* 11–12 (Kenneth Stampp & Leon F. Litwack eds. 1969).

THE RECONSTRUCTION AMENDMENTS

Amendment XIII (1865)

Section 1. Neither slavery nor involuntary servitude, except as a punishment for crime whereof the party shall have been duly convicted, shall exist within the United States, or any place subject to their jurisdiction.

Section 2. Congress shall have power to enforce this article by appropriate legislation.

Amendment XIV (1868)

Section 1. All persons born or naturalized in the United States, and subject to the jurisdiction thereof, are citizens of the United States and of the State wherein they reside. No state shall make or enforce any law which shall abridge the privileges or immunities of citizens of the United States; nor shall any State deprive any person of life, liberty, or property, without due process of law; nor deny to any person within its jurisdiction the equal protection of the laws * * *

Section 5. The Congress shall have power to enforce, by appropriate legislation, the provisions of this article.

Amendment XV (1870)

Section 1. The right of citizens of the United States to vote shall not be denied or abridged by the United States or by any State on account of race, color, or previous condition of servitude.

Section 2. The Congress shall have power to enforce this article by appropriate legislation.

————

The events, meanings, and legacy of the Reconstruction era are complex and remain contested. The most controversial aspect of radical Reconstruction was black suffrage, guaranteed by the Fifteenth Amendment. As W.E.B. Du Bois put it: "One fact, and one alone, explains the attitude of most recent writers toward Reconstruction; they cannot conceive of Negroes as men." See W.E.B. Du Bois, *Black Reconstruction in America* 726 (1964). Du Bois wrote the following assessment of issues and outcomes in Reconstruction, including the legacy of black suffrage.

W.E.B. Du BOIS

Reconstruction and Its Benefits
(1910).*

There is danger to-day that between the intense feeling of the South and the conciliatory spirit of the North grave injustice will be done the negro American in the history of Reconstruction. Those who see in negro suffrage the cause of the main evils of Reconstruction must remember that if there had not been a single freedman left in the South after the war the problems of Reconstruction would still have been grave. Property in slaves to the extent of perhaps two thousand million dollars had suddenly disappeared. One thousand five hundred more millions, representing the Confederate war debt, had largely disappeared. Large amounts of real estate and other property had been destroyed, industry had been disorganized, 250,000 men had been killed and many more maimed. With this went the moral effect of an unsuccessful war with all its letting down of social standards and quickening of hatred and discouragement—a situation which would make it difficult under any circumstances to reconstruct a new government and a new civilization. Add to all this the presence of four million freedman and the situation is further complicated. But this complication is very largely a matter of well-known historical causes. Any human being "doomed in his own person, and his posterity, to live without knowledge, and without the capacity to make anything his own, and to toil that another may reap the fruits," is bound, on sudden emancipation, to loom like a great dread on the horizon.

How to train and treat these ex-slaves easily became a central problem of Reconstruction, although by no means the only problem.

* W.E.B. Du Bois, *Reconstruction and Its Benefits*, 15 American Historical Review 781–799 (July 1910).

Three agencies undertook the solution of this problem at first and their influence is apt to be forgotten. Without them the problems of Reconstruction would have been far graver than they were. These agencies were: (a) the negro church, (b) the negro school, and (c) the Freedmen's Bureau. After the war the white churches of the South got rid of their negro members and the negro church organizations of the North invaded the South. The 20,000 members of the African Methodist Episcopal Church in 1856 leaped to 75,000 in 1866 and 200,000 in 1876, while their property increased sevenfold. The negro Baptists with 150,000 members in 1850 had fully a half million in 1870. There were, before the end of Reconstruction, perhaps 10,000 local bodies touching the majority of the freed population, centering almost the whole of their social life, and teaching them organization and autonomy. They were primitive, ill-governed, at times fantastic groups of human beings, and yet it is difficult to exaggerate the influence of this new responsibility—the first social institution fully controlled by black men in America, with traditions that rooted back to Africa and with possibilities which make the 35,000 negro American churches today, with their three and one-half million members, the most powerful negro institutions in the world.

With the negro church, but separate from it, arose the school as the first expression of the missionary activity of Northern religious bodies. Seldom in the history of the world has an almost totally illiterate population been given the means of self-education in so short a time. The movement started with the negroes themselves and they continued to form the dynamic force behind it. "This great multitude rose up simultaneously and asked for intelligence." The education of this mass had to begin at the top with the training of teachers, and within a few years a dozen colleges and normal schools started; by 1877, 571,506 negro children were in school. There can be no doubt that these schools were a great conservative steadying force to which the South owes much. * * *

The Freedmen's Bureau was an attempt to establish a government guardianship over the negroes and insure their economic and civil rights. Its establishment was a herculean task both physically and socially, and it not only met the solid opposition of the white South, but even the North looked at the new thing as socialistic and over-paternal. It accomplished a great task but it was repudiated. Carl Schurz* in 1865 felt warranted in saying

> that not half of the labor that has been done in the south this year, or will be done there next year, would have been done or would be done but for the exertions of the Freedman's Bureau.... No other agency, except one placed there by the national government, could have wielded that moral power whose interposition was so necessary to prevent the southern society from falling at once into the chaos of a general collision between its different elements.

* [Eds. Carl Schurz was an abolitionist before the Civil War. After the war, he surveyed the South and observed and described the reign of terror experienced by former black slaves at the hands of their former masters. Eventually he became Secretary of the Interior in the administration of President Hayes. See Lerone Bennett, Jr., *Before the Mayflower* 225–26 (5th ed. 1982); Eric Foner, *Reconstruction* 5, 581 (1988); John Hope Franklin, *Race and History* 29 (1989)]

Notwithstanding this the Bureau was temporary, was regarded as a makeshift and soon abandoned. * * *

Meantime the negroes themselves began to ask for the suffrage—the Georgia Convention in Augusta, 1866, advocating "a proposition to give those who could write and read well, and possessed a certain property qualification, the right of suffrage." The reply of the South to these suggestions was decisive. In Tennessee alone was any action attempted that even suggested possible negro suffrage in the future, and that failed. In all other states the "Black Codes" adopted were certainly not reassuring to friends of freedom. To be sure it was not a time to look for calm, cool, thoughtful action on the part of the white South. Their economic condition was pitiable, their fear of negro freedom genuine; yet it was reasonable to expect from them something less than repression and utter reaction toward slavery. To some extent this expectation was fulfilled: the abolition of slavery was recognized and the civil rights of owning property and appearing as a witness in cases in which he was a party were generally granted the negro; yet with these went in many cases harsh and unbearable regulations which largely neutralized the concessions and certainly gave ground for the assumption that once free the South would virtually reenslave the negro. * * *

The Codes spoke for themselves. They have often been reprinted and quoted. No open-minded student can read them without being convinced that they meant nothing more nor less than slavery in daily toil. Not only this but as Professor Burgess (whom no one accuses of being negrophile) says:

> Almost every act, word or gesture of the Negro, not consonant with good taste and good manners as well as good morals, was made a crime or misdemeanor, for which he could first be fined by the magistrates and then be consigned to a condition of almost slavery for an indefinite time, if he could not pay the bill.

These laws might have been interpreted and applied liberally, but the picture painted by Carl Schurz does not lead one to anticipate this:

> Some planters held back their former slaves on their plantations by brute force. Armed bands of white men patrolled the country roads to drive back the negroes wandering about. Dead bodies of murdered negroes were found on and near the highways and by-paths. Gruesome reports came from the hospitals—reports of colored men and women whose ears had been cut off, whose skulls had been broken by blows, whose bodies had been slashed by knives or lacerated with scourges. A number of such cases I had occasion to examine myself. The negro found scant justice in the local courts against the white man. He could look for protection only to the military forces of the United States still garrisoning the "States lately in rebellion" and to the Freedmen's Bureau.

All things considered, it seems probable that if the South had been permitted to have its way in 1865 the harshness of negro slavery would have been mitigated so as to make slave-trading difficult, and to make it possible for a negro to hold property and appear in some cases in court;

but that in most other respects the blacks would have remained in slavery. * * *

[T]here was ground for the conclusion in the Reconstruction report of June 18, 1866, that so far as slavery was concerned "the language of all the provisions and ordinances of these States on the subject amounts to nothing more than an unwilling admission of an unwelcome truth." This was of course natural, but was it unnatural that the North should feel that better guarantees were needed to abolish slavery? Carl Schurz wrote:

> I deem it proper, however, to offer a few remarks on the assertion frequently put forth, that the franchise is likely to be extended to the colored man by the voluntary action of the Southern whites themselves. My observation leads me to a contrary opinion. Aside from a very few enlightened men, I found but one class of people in favor of the enfranchisement of the blacks: it was the class of Unionists who found themselves politically ostracized and looked upon the enfranchisement of the loyal negroes as the salvation of the whole loyal element.... The masses are strongly opposed to colored suffrage; anybody that dares to advocate it is stigmatized as a dangerous fanatic.

> The only manner in which, in my opinion, the southern people can be induced to grant to the freedman some measure of self-protecting power in the form of suffrage, is to make it a condition precedent to "readmission" [of the Southern states that seceded from the Union]. * * *

[T]he arguments for universal negro suffrage from the start were strong and are still strong, and no one would question their strength were it not for the assumption that the experiment failed. Frederick Douglass said to President Johnson: "Your noble and humane predecessor placed in our hands the sword to assist in saving the nation, and we do hope that you, his able successor, will favorably regard the placing in our hands the ballot with which to save ourselves." And when Johnson demurred on account of the hostility between blacks and poor whites, a committee of prominent colored men replied:

> Even if it were true, as you allege, that the hostility of the blacks toward the poor whites must necessarily project itself into a state of freedom, and that this enmity between the two races is even more intense in a state of freedom than in a state of slavery, in the name of Heaven, we reverently ask, how can you, in view of your professed desire to promote the welfare of the black man, deprive him of all means of defense, and clothe him whom you regard as his enemy in the panoply of political power? * * *

The granting of full negro suffrage meant one of two alternatives to the South: (a) the uplift of the negro for sheer self-preservation; this is what Schurz and the saner North expected; as one Southern superintendent said: "the elevation of this class is a matter of prime importance since a ballot in the hands of a black citizen is quite as potent as in the hands of a white one." Or (b) a determined concentration of Southern effort by actual force to deprive the negro of the ballot or nullify its use.

This is what happened, but even in this case so much energy was taken in keeping the negro from voting that the plan for keeping him in virtual slavery and denying him education failed. It took ten years to nullify negro suffrage in part and twenty years to escape the fear of federal intervention. In these twenty years a vast number of negroes had risen so far as to escape slavery forever. Debt peonage could be fastened on part of the rural South, and was, but even here the new negro landholder appeared. Thus despite everything the Fifteenth Amendment and that alone struck the death knell of slavery.

The steps that ended in the Fifteenth Amendment were not, however, taken suddenly. The negroes were given the right by universal suffrage to join in reconstructing the state governments and the reasons for it were cogently set forth in the report of the Joint Committee of Reconstruction in 1866, which began as follows:

A large proportion of the population had become, instead of mere chattels, free men and citizens. Through all the past struggle these had remained true and loyal, and had, in large numbers, fought on the side of the Union. It was impossible to abandon them without securing them their rights as free men and citizens. The whole civilized world would have cried out against such base ingratitude, and the bare idea is offensive to all right-thinking men. Hence it became important to inquire what could be done to secure their rights, civil and political.

The report then proceeded to emphasize the increased political power of the South and recommended the Fourteenth Amendment since

it appeared to your committee that the rights of these persons by whom the basis of representation had been thus increased should be recognized by the General Government. While slaves, they were not considered as having any rights, civil or political. It did not seem just or proper that all the political advantages derived from their becoming free should be confined to their former masters, who had fought against the Union, and withheld from themselves, who had always been loyal.

It was soon seen that this expedient of the Fourteenth Amendment was going to prove abortive and that determined and organized effort would be used to deprive the freedmen of the ballot. Thereupon the United States said the final word of simple justice, namely: the states may still regulate the suffrage as they please but they may not deprive a man of the right to vote simply because he is a negro.

For such reasons the negro was enfranchised. What was the result? No language has been spared to describe these results as the worst imaginable. Nor is it necessary to dispute for a moment that there were bad results, and bad results arising from negro suffrage; but it may be questioned if the results were as bad as painted or if negro suffrage was the prime cause.

Let us not forget that the white South believed it to be of vital interest to its welfare that the experiment of negro suffrage should fail ignominiously, and that almost to a man the whites were willing to insure this failure either by active force or passive acquiescence; that beside this there were, as might be expected, men, black, and white, Northern and Southern, only too eager to take advantage of such a situation for feathering their own nests. The results in such case had to be evil but to charge the evil to negro suffrage is unfair. It may be charged to anger, poverty, venality, and ignorance; but the anger and poverty were the almost inevitable aftermath of war; the venality was much greater among whites than negroes, and while ignorance was the curse of the negroes, the fault was not theirs, and they took the initiative to correct it.

The chief charges against the negro governments are extravagance, theft, and incompetency of officials. There is no serious charge that these governments threatened civilization or the foundation of social order. The charge is that they threatened property, and that they were inefficient. These charges are in part undoubtedly true, but they are often exaggerated. * * *

[T]he greatest stigma of the white South is not that it opposed negro suffrage and resented theft and incompetence, but that when it saw the reform movement growing and even in some cases triumphing, and a larger and larger number of black voters learning to vote for honesty and ability, it still preferred a Reign of Terror to a campaign of education, and disfranchised negroes instead of punishing rascals. * * * But unfortunately there was one thing that the white South feared more than negro dishonesty, ignorance, and incompetency, and that was negro honesty, knowledge, and efficiency.

In the midst of all these difficulties the negro governments in the South accomplished much of positive good. We may recognize three things which negro rule gave to the South:

1. Democratic government.

2. Free public schools.

3. New social legislation.

We are apt to forget that in all human probability the granting of negro manhood suffrage and the passage of the Fifteenth Amendment were decisive in rendering permanent the foundation of the negro common school. Even after the overthrow of the negro governments, if the negroes had been left a servile caste, personally free, but politically powerless, it is not reasonable to think that a system of common schools would have been provided for them by the Southern States. Serfdom and education have ever proven contradictory terms. But when Congress, backed by the nation, determined to make the negroes full-fledged voting citizens, the South had a hard dilemma before her: either to keep the negroes under as an ignorant proletariat and stand the chance of being ruled eventually from the slums and jails, or to join in helping to raise these wards of the nation to a position of intelligence and thrift by means of a public-school system. The "carpet-bag" governments hastened the decision of the South, and although there was a period of hesitation and retrogression after the overthrow of negro rule in the early seventies, yet the South saw that to abolish negro schools in addition to nullifying the negro vote would invite Northern interference;

and thus eventually every Southern state confirmed the work of the negro legislators and maintained the negro public schools along with the white.

Paint the "carpet-bag" governments and negro rule as black as may be, the fact remains that the essence of the revolution which the overturning of the negro governments made was to put these black men and their friends out of power. Outside the curtailing of expenses and stopping of extravagance, not only did their successors make few changes in the work which these legislatures and conventions had done, but they largely carried out their plans, followed their suggestions, and strengthened their institutions. Practically the whole new growth of the South has been accomplished under laws which black men helped to frame thirty years ago. I know of no greater compliment to negro suffrage.

Notes and Questions

1. Historian Garry Wills argues that Lincoln's Gettysburg Address introduced a new principle into American political life: equality. See Garry Wills, *Lincoln at Gettysburg: The Words that Remade America* (1992). As a constitutional principle, equality entered the American judicial discourse through the Reconstruction Amendments.

But "equality" is a word of many meanings. In the discourse of the day, Radical Republicans argued that the freed slaves should have equality in political rights; a smaller group argued for equality of civil rights. Hardly anyone would argue, however, that African Americans were entitled to equality in "social rights," chief among which were the right to marry and socialize freely with Whites. See generally Reva Siegel, *Why Equal Protection No Longer Protects: The Evolving Forms of Status-Enforcing State Action*, 49 Stan. L. Rev. 1111 (1997).

2. In addition to introducing the principle of equality into constitutional jurisprudence, the Reconstruction Amendments had a profound effect on American federalism, shifting power from the states to the national government. Much of the constitutional jurisprudence following the passage of these amendments concerned the struggle to find a new equilibrium between state and federal power. In this struggle, the courts frequently sided with "states' rights," a phrase that for African Americans soon became synonymous with racial oppression.

3. The Fifteenth Amendment, which prohibits racial discrimination in allocating the right to vote, had a dramatic effect on American politics, especially during the era of Reconstruction. Sixteen black legislators were elected to Congress during Reconstruction, many from states that would not see another black person in elected office until the 1980s and 1990s, over one hundred years after Reconstruction. See Eric Foner, *Reconstruction: America's Unfinished Revolution 1863–1877* at 352 & n.12 (1988).

4. Why is it that the Civil War is commemorated so extensively through re-enactments, movies, television documentaries, national parks, and other media? What are the racial implications of such commemoration?

5. Contrast this commemoration with the relative obscurity of the Reconstruction era. Was the Reconstruction era less important than the Civil War? Should it be considered less important? On the obscure legacy of Reconstruction, see Kenneth M. Stampp, *The Era of Reconstruction 1865–*

1877 (1965) (especially Chapter 1, *The Tragic Legend of Reconstruction*). W.E.B. Du Bois, *Black Reconstruction in America* (1964) (Chapter 17, *The Propaganda of History* describes the racist attitudes that led many historians to condemn Reconstruction as a failure.)

THE COURTS AND THE LEGACY OF RECONSTRUCTION

The Courts, interpreting the new Reconstruction amendments and statutes which were passed during this period, were hostile to the program of Radical Reconstruction and tended to limit the scope of these enactments, often in the name of federalism or "states' rights." In *The Slaughter–House Cases*, 83 U.S. (16 Wall.) 36 (1873)—the first Supreme Court interpretation of the Fourteenth Amendment—the Court interpreted the Privileges and Immunities Clause of the Amendment extremely narrowly so as to render it almost completely ineffective in the protection of the civil rights of the freedmen (and anyone else, for that matter). As noted by one commentator, "Unique among constitutional provisions, the privileges and immunities clause of the Fourteenth Amendment enjoys the distinction of having been rendered a 'practical nullity' by a single decision of the Supreme Court within five years after its ratification." See G. Stone, L. Seidman, C. Sunstein, M. Tushnet, *Constitutional Law* 801 (3rd ed. 1996) (quoting E. Corwin, *The Constitution of the United States of America* 965 (1953)).

In another early case, *Strauder v. West Virginia*, 100 U.S. (10 Otto) 303 (1879), the Court interpreted the Fourteenth Amendment and found that West Virginia had denied equal protection to its black citizens by enacting a statute that limited jury service to "white male persons who are twenty-one years of age and who are citizens of this State." This decision adhered to one of the principal purposes underlying the Fourteenth Amendment, to "assure to the colored race the enjoyment of all the civil rights that under the law are enjoyed by white persons, and to give to that race the protection of the general government, in that enjoyment, whenever it should be denied by the States." See generally Kenneth B. Nunn, *Rights Held Hostage: Race, Ideology and the Peremptory Challenge,* 28 Harv. C.R.-C.L. L. Rev. 63, 82–84 (1993). However, the *Strauder* decision was one of very few instances, until the equal protection cases culminating in *Brown v. Board of Education*, 347 U.S. 483 (1954), in which the Reconstruction Amendments were applied for the benefit of Blacks and the vindication of civil rights.

The most important and potentially far-reaching statute enacted by the Reconstruction Congress to promote and protect equality for Blacks was the Civil Rights Act of 1875. This Act provided that "all persons within the jurisdiction of the United States shall be entitled to the full and equal enjoyment of the accommodations, advantages, facilities, and privileges of inns, public conveyances on land or water, theaters, and other places of public amusement; subject only to the conditions and limitations established by law, and applicable alike to citizens of every race and color, regardless of any previous condition of servitude." In its essence, the Act sought to accomplish the same equality of treatment for

Blacks that was not achieved until Title II of the Civil Rights Act of 1964 was enacted nearly a century later.

When the Civil Rights Act of 1875 was considered by the Supreme Court in *The Civil Rights Cases*, 109 U.S. 3 (1883), the Court ruled that the Act was unconstitutional because it was beyond the powers of Congress to enact under both the Thirteenth and Fourteenth Amendments. The Court held that private discrimination of the kind addressed in the Act was not a "badge of slavery," and so Congress lacked power to reach this discrimination under the Thirteenth Amendment. Further, Congress could not regulate this private behavior under the Fourteenth Amendment because that Amendment was addressed as a limitation on State action, not private conduct.

According to Bernard Schwartz, "the Supreme Court decisions were but an indication of the general disenchantment with the Reconstruction program * * * By the turn of the century, 'equal protection' had become reduced to the status of a mere slogan for the Negro * * * The paradoxical result was that, though the post-Civil War amendments did work a veritable constitutional revolution, until recently they had little effect upon civil rights." The Supreme Court's Fourteenth Amendment decisions limited the states principally with respect to state interference with property rights and private economic interests. "The result was that the Fourteenth Amendment was converted into a Magna Carta for business, in place of the Great Charter for civil rights which its framers had intended." Bernard Schwartz, I *Statutory History of the United States* 10–11 (1970).

SECTION 5. THE JIM CROW ERA

The post-Reconstruction relationship between Blacks and Whites was regulated by the harsh regime of Jim Crow segregation laws. "What the new status of the Negro would be was not at once apparent, nor were the Southern white people themselves so united on that subject at first as has been generally assumed. The determination of the Negro's 'place' took shape gradually under the influence of economic and political conflicts among divided white people—conflicts that were eventually resolved in part at the expense of the Negro." C. Vann Woodward, *The Strange Career of Jim Crow* 6 (2d rev. ed. 1966).

The segregation imposed by Jim Crow laws was foreshadowed by the treatment of free Blacks throughout the country. Free Blacks in the South faced restrictions in their freedoms to move and to assemble and in other denials of full equality. In the North, lacking slavery as a means of white control over Blacks, segregation developed early and extensively. As one scholar described the segregation faced by most northern Blacks,

> [i]n virtually every phase of existence, Negroes found themselves systematically separated from whites. They were either excluded from railway cars, omnibuses, stagecoaches, and steamboats or assigned to special "Jim Crow" sections; they sat, when permitted, in secluded and remote corners of theaters and lecture halls; they could not enter most hotels, restaurants, and resorts, except as

servants; they prayed in "Negro pews" in the white churches, and if partaking of the sacrament of the Lord's Supper, they waited until the whites had been served the bread and wine. Moreover, they were often educated in segregated schools, punished in segregated prisons, nursed in segregated hospitals, and buried in segregated cemeteries.

Leon F. Litwack, *North of Slavery* 97 (1961). Segregated schools were upheld in the northern courts. In *Roberts v. City of Boston*, 59 Mass. 198 (1850), for example, the Supreme Judicial Court of Massachusetts upheld decisions of local school authorities to maintain separate primary schools for white and black children and to exclude a black child from a white school. Accordingly, there was ample basis in the customs and practices of both the South and North, and judicial precedent, for the Supreme Court's decision in *Plessy v. Ferguson*.

PLESSY v. FERGUSON

163 U.S. 537 (1896).

JUSTICE BROWN delivered the opinion of the court.

This case turns upon the constitutionality of an act of the general assembly of the state of Louisiana, passed in 1890, providing for separate railway carriages for the white and colored races. * * *

The first section of the statute enacts "that all railway companies carrying passengers in their coaches in this state, shall provide equal but separate accommodations for the white, and colored races, by providing two or more passenger coaches for each passenger train, or by dividing the passenger coaches by a partition so as to secure separate accommodations: provided, that this section shall not be construed to apply to street railroads. No person or persons shall be permitted to occupy seats in coaches, other than the ones assigned to them, on account of the race they belong to."

The information filed in the criminal district court charged, in substance, that Plessy, being a passenger between two stations within the state of Louisiana, was assigned by officers of the company to the coach used for the race to which he belonged, but he insisted upon going into a coach used by the race to which he did not belong. Neither in the information nor plea was his particular race or color averred.

The petition for the writ of prohibition averred that petitioner was seven-eighths Caucasian and one-eighth African blood; that the mixture of colored blood was not discernible in him; and that he was entitled to every right, privilege, and immunity secured to citizens of the United States of the white race; and that, upon such theory, he took possession of a vacant seat in a coach where passengers of the white race were accommodated, and was ordered by the conductor to vacate said coach, and take a seat in another, assigned to persons of the colored race, and, having refused to comply with such demand, he was forcibly ejected, with the aid of a police officer, and imprisoned in the parish jail to answer a charge of having violated the above act.

The constitutionality of this act is attacked upon the ground that it conflicts both with the Thirteenth Amendment of the constitution, abolishing slavery, and the Fourteenth Amendment, which prohibits certain restrictive legislation on the part of the states.

That it does not conflict with the Thirteenth Amendment, which abolished slavery and involuntary servitude, except as a punishment for crime, is too clear for argument. * * *

A statute which implies merely a legal distinction between the white and colored races—a distinction which is founded in the color of the two races, and which must always exist so long as white men are distinguished from the other race by color—has no tendency to destroy the legal equality of the two races, or re-establish a state of involuntary servitude. * * *

The object of the [Fourteenth] Amendment was undoubtedly to enforce the absolute equality of the two races before the law, but, in the nature of things, it could not have been intended to abolish distinctions based upon color, or to enforce social, as distinguished from political, equality, or a commingling of the two races upon terms unsatisfactory to either. Laws permitting, and even requiring, their separation, in places where they are liable to be brought into contact, do not necessarily imply the inferiority of either race to the other, and have been generally, if not universally, recognized as within the competency of the state legislatures in the exercise of their police power. The most common instance of this is connected with the establishment of separate schools for white and colored children, which have been held to be a valid exercise of the legislative power even by courts of states where the political rights of the colored race have been longest and most earnestly enforced.

One of the earliest of these cases is that of *Roberts v. City of Boston*, 59 Mass. 198, in which the supreme judicial court of Massachusetts held that the general school committee of Boston had power to make provision for the instruction of colored children in separate schools established exclusively for them, and to prohibit their attendance upon the other schools. * * * It was held that the powers of the committee extended to the establishment of separate schools for children of different ages, sexes and colors, and that they might also establish special schools for poor and neglected children, who have become too old to attend the primary school, and yet have not acquired the rudiments of learning, to enable them to enter the ordinary schools. Similar laws have been enacted by congress under its general power of legislation over the District of Columbia as well as by the legislatures of many of the states, and have been generally, if not uniformly, sustained by the courts.

Laws forbidding the intermarriage of the two races may be said in a technical sense to interfere with the freedom of contract, and yet have been universally recognized as within the police power of the state. * * *

It is claimed by the plaintiff in error that, in any mixed community, the reputation of belonging to the dominant race, in this instance the white race, is 'property,' in the same sense that a right of action or of inheritance is property. Conceding this to be so, for the purposes of this case, we are unable to see how this statute deprives him of, or in any way affects his right to, such property. If he be a white man, and assigned to a colored coach, he may have his action for damages against the company for being deprived of his so-called 'property.' Upon the other hand, if he be a colored man, and be so assigned, he has been deprived of no property, since he is not lawfully entitled to the reputation of being a white man.

In this connection, it is also suggested by the learned counsel for the plaintiff in error that the same argument that will justify the state legislature in requiring railways to provide separate accommodations for the two races will also authorize them to require separate cars to be provided for people whose hair is of a certain color, or who are aliens, or who belong to certain nationalities, or to enact laws requiring colored people to walk upon one side of the street, and white people upon the other, or requiring white men's houses to be painted white, and colored men's black, or their vehicles or business signs to be of different colors, upon the theory that one side of the street is as good as the other, or that a house or vehicle of one color is as good as one of another color. The reply to all this is that every exercise of the police power must be reasonable, and extend only to such laws as are enacted in good faith for the promotion of the public good, and not for the annoyance or oppression of a particular class.

So far, then, as a conflict with the Fourteenth Amendment is concerned, the case reduces itself to the question whether the statute of Louisiana is a reasonable regulation, and with respect to this there must necessarily be a large discretion on the part of the legislature. In determining the question of reasonableness, it is at liberty to act with reference to the established usages, customs, and traditions of the people, and with a view to the promotion of their comfort, and the preservation of the public peace and good order. Gauged by this standard, we cannot say that a law which authorizes or even requires the separation of the two races in public conveyances is unreasonable, or more obnoxious to the Fourteenth Amendment than the acts of congress requiring separate schools for colored children in the District of Columbia, the constitutionality of which does not seem to have been questioned, or the corresponding acts of state legislatures.

 We consider the underlying fallacy of the plaintiff's argument to consist in the assumption that the enforced separation of the two races stamps the colored race with a badge of inferiority. If this be so, it is not by reason of anything found in the act, but solely because the colored race chooses to put that construction upon it. The argument necessarily assumes that if, as has been more than once the case, and is not unlikely to be so again, the colored race should become the dominant power in the state legislature, and should enact a law in precisely similar terms, it would thereby relegate the white race to an inferior position. We imagine that the white race, at least, would not acquiesce in this assumption. The argument also assumes that social prejudices may be overcome by legislation, and that equal rights cannot be secured to the negro except by an enforced commingling of the two races. We cannot accept this proposition. If the two races are to meet upon terms of social equality, it must be the result of natural affinities, a mutual appreciation of each other's merits, and a voluntary consent of individuals. * * * Legislation is powerless to eradicate racial instincts, or to abolish distinctions based upon physical differences, and the attempt to do so can only result in accentuating the difficulties of the present situation. If the civil and political rights of both races be equal, one cannot be inferior to the other civilly or politically. If one race be inferior to the other socially, the constitution of the United States cannot put them upon the same plane.

It is true that the question of the proportion of colored blood necessary to constitute a colored person, as distinguished from a white person, is one upon which there is a difference of opinion in the different states; some holding that any visible admixture of black blood stamps the person as belonging to the colored race; others, that it depends upon the preponderance of blood; and still others, that the predominance of white blood must only be in the proportion of three-fourths. But these are questions to be determined under the laws of each state, and are not properly put in issue in this case. Under the allegations of his petition, it may undoubtedly become a question of importance whether, under the laws of Louisiana, the petitioner belongs to the white or colored race.

JUSTICE HARLAN dissenting.

* * * In respect of civil rights, common to all citizens, the constitution of the United States does not, I think, permit any public authority to know the race of those entitled to be protected in the enjoyment of such rights. Every true man has pride of race, and under appropriate circumstances, when the rights of others, his equals before the law, are not to be affected, it is his privilege to express such pride and to take such action based upon it as to him seems proper. But I deny that any legislative body or judicial tribunal may have regard to the race of citizens when the civil rights of those citizens are involved. Indeed, such legislation as that here in question is inconsistent not only with that equality of rights which pertains to citizenship, national and state, but with the personal liberty enjoyed by every one within the United States. * * *

It was said in argument that the statute of Louisiana does not discriminate against either race, but prescribes a rule applicable alike to white and colored citizens. But this argument does not meet the difficulty. Every one knows that the statute in question had its origin in the purpose, not so much to exclude white persons from railroad cars occupied by blacks, as to exclude colored people from coaches occupied by or assigned to white persons. * * * If a white man and a black man choose to occupy the same public conveyance on a public highway, it is their right to do so; and no government, proceeding alone on grounds of race, can prevent it without infringing the personal liberty of each.

It is one thing for railroad carriers to furnish, or to be required by law to furnish, equal accommodations for all whom they are under a legal duty to carry. It is quite another thing for government to forbid citizens of the white and black races from traveling in the same public conveyance, and to punish officers of railroad companies for permitting persons of the two races to occupy the same passenger coach. If a state can prescribe, as a rule of civil conduct, that whites and blacks shall not travel as passengers in the same railroad coach, why may it not so regulate the use of the streets of its cities and towns as to compel white citizens to keep on one side of a street, and black citizens to keep on the other? Why may it not, upon like grounds, punish whites and blacks who ride together in street cars or in open vehicles on a public road or street? Why may it not require sheriffs to assign whites to one side of a court room, and blacks to the other? And why may it not also prohibit the commingling of the two races in the galleries of legislative halls or in public assemblages convened for the consideration of the political questions of the day? Further, if this statute of Louisiana is consistent with the personal liberty of citizens, why may not the state require the separation in railroad coaches of native and naturalized citizens of the United States, or of Protestants and Roman Catholics?

The white race deems itself to be the dominant race in this country. And so it is, in prestige, in achievements, in education, in wealth, and in power. So, I doubt not, it will continue to be for all time, if it remains true to its great heritage, and holds fast to the principles of constitutional liberty. But in view of the constitution, in the eye of the law, there is in this country no superior, dominant, ruling class of citizens. There is no caste here. Our constitution is color-blind, and neither knows nor tolerates classes among citizens. In respect of civil rights, all citizens are equal before the law. The humblest is the peer of the most powerful. The law regards man as man, and takes no account of his surroundings or of his color when his civil rights as guarantied by the supreme law of the land are involved. It is therefore to be regretted that this high tribunal, the final expositor of the fundamental law of the land, has reached the conclusion that it is competent for a state to regulate the enjoyment by citizens of their civil rights solely upon the basis of race.

In my opinion, the judgment this day rendered will, in time, prove to be quite as pernicious as the decision made by this tribunal in the Dred Scott Case. * * *

But it seems that we have yet, in some of the states, a dominant race,—a superior class of citizens,—which assumes to regulate the enjoyment of civil rights, common to all citizens, upon the basis of race. The present decision, it may well be apprehended, will not only stimulate aggressions, more or less brutal and irritating, upon the admitted rights of colored citizens, but will encourage the belief that it is possible, by means of state enactments, to defeat the beneficent purposes which the people of the United States had in view when they adopted the recent amendments of the constitution, by one of which the blacks of this country were made citizens of the United States and of the states in which they respectively reside, and whose privileges and immunities, as citizens, the states are forbidden to abridge. Sixty millions of whites are in no danger from the presence here of eight millions of blacks. The destinies of the two races, in this country, are indissolubly linked together, and the interests of both require that the common government of all shall not permit the seeds of race hate to be planted under the sanction of law. What can more certainly arouse race hate, what more certainly create and perpetuate a feeling of distrust between these races, than state enactments which, in fact, proceed on the ground that colored citizens are so inferior and degraded that they cannot be allowed to sit in public coaches occupied by white citizens? That, as all will admit, is the real meaning of such legislation as was enacted in Louisiana. * * *

There is a race so different from our own that we do not permit those belonging to it to become citizens of the United States. Persons belonging to it are, with few exceptions, absolutely excluded from our country. I allude to the Chinese race. But, by the statute in question, a Chinaman can ride in the same passenger coach with white citizens of the United States, while citizens of the black race in Louisiana, many of whom, perhaps, risked their lives for the preservation of the Union, who are entitled, by law, to participate in the political control of the state and nation, who are not excluded, by law or by reason of their race, from public stations of any kind, and who have all the legal rights that belong to white citizens, are yet declared to be criminals, liable to imprisonment, if they ride in a public coach occupied by citizens of the white race. * * *

If evils will result from the commingling of the two races upon public highways established for the benefit of all, they will be infinitely less than those that will surely come from state legislation regulating the enjoyment of civil rights upon the basis of race. We boast of the freedom enjoyed by our people above all other peoples. But it is difficult to reconcile that boast with a state of the law which, practically, puts the brand of servitude and degradation upon a large class of our fellow citizens,—our equals before the law. The thin disguise of 'equal' accommodations for passengers in railroad coaches will not mislead any one, nor atone for the wrong this day done.

Notes and Questions

1. The *Plessy* decision gave the Supreme Court's sanction to the separate-but-equal Jim Crow laws of the late nineteenth century and probably fueled a dramatic expansion in the use of these laws during the early decades of the twentieth. The gradual hardening of white racism that occurred during the late nineteenth century was primarily due to a relaxation in the opposition to this racism. The reconciliation of southern and northern Whites, and between different classes of Whites in the South, was achieved through an increase in racism against Blacks. "Just as the Negro gained his emancipation and new rights through a falling out between white men, he now stood to lose his rights through the reconciliation of white men." Woodward, *supra* at 70.

2. The first and crucial step in establishing more rigid and extensive Jim Crow regulations of Blacks was the total disfranchising of Blacks, which began in Mississippi, then spread quickly to other states. Among the techniques for disfranchisement were property or literacy qualifications (with exceptions to accommodate lower-class Whites), poll taxes, and the white primary. These restrictive techniques were enormously effective. For example, the number of black voters in Louisiana in 1896 was 130,344. By 1904, this number had been curtailed to 1,342. See Woodward, *supra* at 83–85.

3. Jim Crow laws proliferated in the early decades of the twentieth century, spreading to regulate nearly every aspect of life. But it is important to recognize that "laws are not an adequate index of the extent and

prevalence of segregation and discriminatory practices in the South." Woodward, *supra* at 102. Jim Crow operated informally, pervasively, with or without statutes to yield virtually the complete isolation and degradation of the black American.

As just one example of a Jim Crow law in education, typical for its time, Tennessee passed a law in 1901 entitled "An act to prohibit the co-education of the white and colored races and to prohibit the white and colored races from attending the same schools, academies, colleges, or other places of learning in this State":

> Section 1. *Be it enacted by the General Assembly of the State of Tennessee,* That hereafter it shall be unlawful for any school, academy, college or other place of learning to allow white and colored persons to attend the same school, academy, college or other place of learning.
>
> Section 2. *Be it further enacted,* That it shall be unlawful for any teacher, professor, or educator in this State, in any college, academy, or school of learning, to allow the white and colored races to attend the same school or for any teacher or educator, or other person to instruct or teach both the white and colored races in the same class, school or college building, or in any other place or places of learning, or allow or permit the same to be done with their knowledge, consent, or procurement.
>
> Section 3. *Be it further enacted,* That any person or persons violating this Act or any of its provisions, when convicted shall be fined for each offense fifty ($50) dollars and imprisoned not less than thirty days nor more than six months at the discretion of the Court.
>
> * * *

Laws of Tennessee, 1901, Ch.7, House Bill No. 7, p. 9 (March 13, 1901). In addition to similar provisions, Florida went further, requiring the separation of public-school textbooks used by black children from those used by white children, even when the books were in storage. With painstaking specificity, a Birmingham, Alabama ordinance of 1930 made it "unlawful for a Negro and a white person to play together or in company with each other" either dominoes or checkers. Woodward, *supra* at 118.

Although Jim Crow was justified as adherence to the social customs of the South, in fact segregation was imposed even on Whites willing to live in equality with Blacks. See, *e.g., Berea College v. Kentucky,* 211 U.S. 45 (1908) (upholding statute prohibiting interracial educational facility).

LYNCHING

The period of the late nineteenth to the early and mid-twentieth century was a time of great poverty, violence, and educational and political deprivation for black Americans. It was also a time during which mob violence and lynching were freely inflicted upon black people. Between 1882 and 1968, records at the Tuskegee Institute show 4,743 persons lynched. This number cannot be the full total, since it reflects only those lynchings in some way recorded. Nearly seventy-three percent of these recorded victims of lynchings were Black. See Robert L. Zangrando, *The NAACP Crusade Against Lynching, 1909–1950* 4 (1980). Consider the following excerpt on lynching.

BARBARA HOLDEN–SMITH

Lynching, Federalism, and the Intersection of
Race and Gender in the Progressive Era
8 Yale J. L. & Feminism 31, 35–37, 39–40, 77–78 (1996).*

In 1904, a lynch mob of more than 1,000 white people burned Luther Holbert, a black Mississippi sharecropper, and his wife to death. A Vicksburg, Mississippi newspaper gave the following eye-witness account of the lynching:

[T]he two Negroes . . . were tied to trees and while the funeral pyres were being prepared, they were forced to hold out their hands while one finger at a time was chopped off. The fingers were distributed as souvenirs. The ears . . . were cut off. Holbert was beaten severely, his skull fractured and one of his eyes, knocked out with a stick, hung by a shred from the socket. Some of the mob used a large corkscrew to bore into the flesh of the man and woman. It was applied to their arms, legs and body, then pulled out, the spirals tearing out big pieces of . . . flesh every time it was withdrawn.[2]

* * *

A. THE LYNCHING PHENOMENON

During and immediately after the Revolutionary War, lynching was practiced primarily in the East, where it was used as an extralegal means by which private citizens' groups carried out their own enforcement of the criminal law. As the nation's frontier expanded, however, the practice of lynching spread west and south and became a popular means of enforcing local mores as well as of punishing suspected law-breakers. So pervasive was the practice that by 1918 lynchings had occurred in all but six states. The Department of Archives and Records of the Tuskegee Institute, which began gathering lynching accounts from newspapers during the 1880s, reports that from 1882 until 1968, 4,743 persons were lynched in the United States. Tuskegee stopped gathering statistics in 1968. By then the number of reported annual lynchings had been zero since 1965, and had not been more than three since 1947.

In the early 1880s, white victims outnumbered black victims, with most of the lynchings of whites occurring in the West. The white targets were often members of groups seen as outsiders by local citizens, such as Mormons in Indiana and Italian immigrants in the West and South. Native Americans, Chinese immigrant laborers, and Mexicans were also lynching victims. By the twentieth century, however, lynching had taken on a decidedly racial character and had become concentrated in the South. Thus, during the Progressive Era and afterwards, lynching was inflicted almost exclusively by white Southerners upon black Southerners. Of the 4,743 reported lynchings that had taken place by 1968, 3,445 of the victims were black.

As lynchings became concentrated in the South, their brutality increased. The mass mob began to dominate lynchings in some Southern

---

* Reprinted by permission of the Yale Journal of Law and Feminism. **2.** Ralph Ginzburg, *100 Years of Lynching* 63 (1969).

states, accounting, for example, for 35% of black lynchings in Georgia and 49% in Virginia from 1880 to 1930. These mass-mob lynchings were open affairs in which scores, and sometimes thousands, of whites participated. Members of the mob would often riddle the victim's body with thousands of bullets, or burn him (or her) alive. Although whites were murdered as a form of summary justice, mass mobs confined their killings largely to blacks. Frequently, the leaders of the mob would sever the victim's body parts before his (or her) execution. These parts, along with what remained of the victim after death, were fought over by enthusiastic mob members, who had come from miles around to attend the lynching. Newspapers, after announcing the lynching in advance, sent reporters and photographers to capture the actions of the mob. Mob members could then enjoy seeing pictures of themselves beside the victim's charred remains as they read the newspapers' accounts of the incident.

Mass mobs acted with community approval and regularly included some of the community's leading citizens. Men constituted the majority of the actual lynchers, but women and children often attended. They took an active role in the murders by cheering on the lynchers, "providing fuel for the execution pyre, and scavenging for souvenirs after the lynchings."

It is astonishing, given the barbarity of many Southern lynchings, just how commonplace and how acceptable they were, and how ordinary were the Americans who participated in such extreme violence. Southern apologists for lynching often claimed that only uneducated persons, persons of a lower class, or persons "outside the reach of modern agencies affecting group morals and public opinion," participated in lynchings. The actual portrait of lynchers belies these notions. In Georgia in 1922, for example, indictments for lynching were returned against a grocer, a loan agent, an insurance salesman, and a hotel clerk. In 1911, a South Carolina state legislator and his son were charged with having led a lynch mob. * * *

Whatever the cause of lynching's demise, the law had little or nothing to do with it. Throughout the Progressive Era, lynching remained a brutal crime that went largely uninvestigated, unprosecuted, unpunished, and undeterred by the agents of law at every level of government. State and local officials did not enforce existing law, and federal officials failed to enact any new legislation. Thus, lynchers never faced any serious deterrent from the government and could murder black people openly, notoriously, and boldly, without fear of reprisal. [Federal legislation was needed] as evidenced by the systematic failure of the Southern states—either from intention, indifference, or inability—to punish the crime of lynching. By the 1930s, most of the Southern states had specifically outlawed lynching. The first surge of such legislation occurred in the 1890s, partially in response to the threat of interracial unity posed by the Democratic Party. The second surge, in the 1920s, was probably prompted by the mass migration of African Americans from the South, as well as the increased militancy of African Americans after World War I. In addition, the 1920s legislation may partially have been a response to the near-passage of a federal anti-lynching statute in

1922, which generated fears among Southern whites that next time Congress might in fact succeed. Most of the statutes passed in the 1890s and the 1920s were weak. For example, none of them sought to prevent or punish the lynchings of persons who had not been accused of a crime. Instead, they sought only to deter or punish lynchings undertaken by mobs that seized prisoners from the custody of local sheriffs.

The near-total ineffectiveness of these laws during the Progressive Era requires no complex explanation: They were simply not enforced. Local officials rarely even arrested whites for lynching black people. Moreover, although the local community often knew the identities of lynchers, coroner's juries usually found that either no crime had been committed or that the identities of the perpetrators were unknown. In the rare instance where an indictment was issued, juries would not convict. The Tuskegee Institute records for the period between 1900 and 1930 reveal twelve instances in which a total of sixty-seven individual convictions were secured. Thus, only about eight-tenths of one percent of the lynchings in the United States since 1900 have been followed by convictions of the lynchers. Meanwhile, convictions for regular homicides during the same period ran at forty-four percent. * * *

Lynching was an open, notorious crime that the states allowed to continue unchecked by any agents of law enforcement. This wholesale failure of the states to protect the lives of their black citizens cried out for federal action. But throughout most of the history of lynching, the national government stood idly by. In addition to the pervasive racism of the times, the failure of Congress to enact an anti-lynching statute during the Progressive Era was due in substantial part to a prevailing and intense cultural aversion to sexual relations between black men and white women. This aversion was at the center of a number of social apprehensions during the Progressive Era, and certainly informed both the persistence of the phenomenon of lynching throughout the period and the federal government's failure to do anything to curb the practice.

This failure of the state and federal governments to protect blacks from lynching is part of a larger and more persistent failure of American law to find sufficient ways to defend black life and to ensure the promise of the Reconstruction Amendments to make African Americans full citizens. As the nation rushes forward to embrace a "new federalism" that returns social welfare responsibility to the states, the history of the failed federal anti-lynching legislative effort should provide a cautionary tale about the inadequacy of extreme deference to states' rights where the protection of minority communities is at stake. Indeed, this history should provide the necessary skepticism toward those legislators today who wrap themselves in the cloak of federalism so as to obscure the more distasteful, politically unpopular reasons for failing to take federal action.

Notes and Questions

1. Many black leaders struggled against the outrage of lynching. Ida B. Wells, teacher, journalist, and leading spokesperson against lynchings, reported on lynchings happening largely in the South in her newspaper *Free Speech*, published in Memphis, Tennessee. Wells published books, such as

Southern Horrors, and delivered many speeches as part of the campaign against lynching. See Jacqueline Jones Royster, *Southern Horrors and other Writings, The Anti–Lynching Campaign of Ida B. Wells, 1892–1900* (1997) (reproducing Wells' major writings and describing her fight against lynching).

Federal legislation was proposed continually through the first half of the twentieth century, yet Congress refused to enact any such legislation. It was not until the ineffective Civil Rights Act of 1957, creating a Commission on Civil Rights, that Congress passed the first civil rights legislation since Reconstruction. The NAACP also took up the fight against lynching, documented in Robert L. Zangrando, *The NAACP Crusade Against Lynching, 1909–1950* (1980). See also Bernard Schwartz, II *Statutory History of the United States* 935 (1970). See also Arthur F. Raper, *The Tragedy of Lynching* (1969) (discussing the disparity between alleged causes of reported lynchings and actual reported causes).

2. Holden–Smith says that before 1900 Native Americans, Chinese immigrants and Mexicans were lynched, but that "By the twentieth century * * * lynching had taken on a decidedly racial character." Does this mean that Indians, Mexicans and Chinese were lynched not because of race but for some other reason? What does the author mean?

RACISM AND THE MILITARY

Military service for the United States has often been seen by leaders and members of racial minority groups as a path to full and equal citizenship. Although Blacks have served in all American wars, their full citizenship has been denied and delayed notwithstanding military service. As described *infra*, the military was one of the first institutions forced to desegregate by President Truman's order in 1948.

In 1861, Frederick Douglass had urged Blacks to enlist in the army as a way to earn full citizenship: "He who fights the battles of America may claim America as his country and have that claim respected." See Mary F. Berry, *Toward Freedom and Civil Rights for the Freedmen: Military Policy Origins of the Thirteenth Amendment and the Civil Rights Act of 1866* 19 (1975). In the early twentieth century during the time of World War I, W.E.B. Du Bois also urged Blacks to fight, "while the war lasts, to forget our special grievances and close our ranks shoulder to shoulder with our own white fellow citizens and the allied nations that are fighting for democracy." Other black leaders were less optimistic. A. Philip Randolph, who would play an essential role in achieving this nation's first antidiscrimination laws during World War II, argued that despite the military service of Blacks in every war since Crispus Attucks in the Revolutionary War, these efforts had not brought full citizenship for Blacks. See Bernard C. Nalty, *Strength for the Fight: A History of Black Americans in the Military* 107 (1986).

During World War I white racism against black soldiers frustrated the efforts of Blacks to attain equal treatment. Black soldiers still faced the racism of their white colleagues abroad, and they faced the racism of the American public when they returned home. A remarkable example of American racism was the reaction of white officers and enlisted men to the favorable treatment that black soldiers received from French military commanders and citizens. American Whites objected strenuously, leading a French military commander to issue the following confidential directive on ways the French should treat black American soldiers in order to keep white American troops comfortable. See Nalty, *supra*, at 113–14, 120, 122–23.

The following confidential directive was collected by W.E.B. Du Bois and printed in *The Crisis*, the newspaper of the NAACP.

THE FRENCH DIRECTIVE

The Crisis, pp. 16–18 (May, 1919).*

The following documents have come into the hands of the Editor. He has absolute proof of their authenticity. The first document was sent out last August at the request of the American Army by the French Committee which is the official means of communication between the American forces and the French. It represents American and not French opinion and we have been informed that when the French Ministry heard of the distribution of this document among the Prefects and Sous-Prefects of France, they ordered such copies to be collected and burned.

FRENCH MILITARY MISSION

Stationed with the American Army, August 7, 1918.

SECRET INFORMATION CONCERNING BLACK AMERICAN TROOPS

1.   It is important for French officers who have been called upon to exercise command over black American troops, or to live in close contact with them, to have an exact idea of the position occupied by Negroes in the United States. The information set forth in the following communication ought to be given to these officers and it is to their interest to have these matters known and widely disseminated. It will devolve likewise on the French Military Authorities, through the medium of the Civil Authorities, to give information on this subject to the French population residing in the cantonments occupied by American colored troops.

2.   The American attitude upon the Negro question may seem a matter for discussion to many French minds. But we French are not in our province if we undertake to discuss what some call "prejudice." American opinion is unanimous on the "color question," and does not admit of any discussion.

The increasing number of Negroes in the United States (about 15,000,000) would create for the white race in the Republic a menace of degeneracy were it not that an impassable gulf has been made between them.

As this danger does not exist for the French race, the French public has become accustomed to treating the Negro with familiarity and indulgence.

* The authors wish to thank The Crisis Publishing Co., Inc., the publisher of the magazine of the National Association for the Advancement of Colored People, for authorizing the use of this work. Reproduced by permission of The Crisis Publishing Co.

This indulgence and this familiarity are matters of grievous concern to the Americans. They consider them an affront to their national policy. They are afraid that contact with the French will inspire in black Americans aspirations which to them [the whites] appear intolerable. It is of the utmost importance that every effort be made to avoid profoundly estranging American opinion.

Although a citizen of the United States, the black man is regarded by the white American as an inferior being with whom relations of business or service only are possible. The black is constantly being censured for his want of intelligence and discretion, his lack of civic and professional conscience and for his tendency toward undue familiarity.

The vices of the Negro are a constant menace to the American who has to repress them sternly. For instance, the black American troops in France have, by themselves, given rise to as many complaints for attempted rape as all the rest of the army. And yet the [black American] soldiers sent us have been the choicest with respect to physique and morals, for the number disqualified at the time of mobilization was enormous.

CONCLUSION

1. We must prevent the rise of any pronounced degree of intimacy between French officers and black officers. We may be courteous and amiable with these last, but we cannot deal with them on the same plane as with the white American officers without deeply wounding the latter. We must not eat with them, must not shake hands or seek to talk or meet with them outside of the requirements of military service.

2. We must not commend too highly the black American troops, particularly in the presence of [white] Americans. It is all right to recognize their good qualities and their services, but only in moderate terms strictly in keeping with the truth.

3. Make a point of keeping the native cantonment population from "spoiling" the Negroes. [White] Americans become greatly incensed at any public expression of intimacy between white women with black men. They have recently uttered violent protests against a picture in the "Vie Parisian" entitled "The Child of the Desert" which shows a [white] woman in a "cabinet particulier" with a Negro. Familiarity on the part of white women with black men is furthermore a source of profound regret to our experienced colonials who see in it an overweening menace to the prestige of the white race.

Military authority cannot intervene directly in this question, but it can through the civil authorities exercise some influence on the population.

(signed) LINARD

Notes and Questions

1. Consider the strength of white racism against black members of the armed forces. Suppose you are living temporarily in a different country where Blacks are treated with more equality. What would it take for you to

complain to government officials in that country about their more egalitarian treatment of Blacks? What does the French directive teach us about
American racism?

2. Consider whether there are other present-day exportations of American racism, as illustrated by the French directive.

3. For an account of Charles Hamilton Houston's encounter with white
racism in the military in France during World War I, see Genna Rae McNeil,
Groundwork: Charles Hamilton Houston and the Struggle for Civil Rights
43–45 (1983).

Segregation and racism against Blacks continued to be the rule during
the Depression and during World War II. Jim Crow ruled in the military as
elsewhere. Black aviators, such as the Tuskegee airmen, and soldiers served
in segregated units, with the exception of a few black fliers who flew with
white units that consented to have them notwithstanding the violation of the
rules enforcing segregation. Segregation was taken to fairly absurd extremes.
In the Arizona wilderness, Fort Huachuca "boasted not only separate
officers' clubs but two hospitals, one staffed by blacks for blacks and the
other operated by whites for white patients." The Red Cross, initially
reluctant even to accept blood from black donors, carefully separated the
blood donated by Blacks from blood donated by Whites. The rationale was
that Whites who needed transfusions of blood to survive might refuse if the
blood was from a black donor. As had happened during World War I with the
French, American forces tried to indoctrinate the British regarding how to
treat black servicemen in a racist fashion. According to a British RAF flier,
"at an indoctrination course addressed by an American lieutenant, the
lecture consisted of an 'explanation' of why British white troops should not
associate with Negro Americans." Some British bar and restaurant owners
responded by prohibiting *white* American soldiers from entering their estab-
lishments. See C.L.R. James, et. al., *Fighting Racism in World War II* 148–
49, 312 (1991); See Nalty, *supra* at 164, 181.

It was the racist treatment and violence inflicted upon returning black
veterans that finally captured the attention of President Harry Truman and
led to long-overdue efforts to end segregation in the military. At the end of
World War II, Isaac Woodard was discharged from the Army. Still in
uniform, he made a bus trip from Fort Gordon, Georgia, to return to his
home in North Carolina. In South Carolina, the bus driver, annoyed with
Woodard for taking too long to use a "colored only" rest room, called the
local sheriff and demanded that Woodard be arrested. Woodard was charged
with drunkenness, even though he did not drink. During his arrest, the
sheriff beat Woodard with a blackjack and someone, either the sheriff or a
policeman assisting him, plunged the end of a nightstick into Woodard's
eyes. Severely injured, Woodard spent the night in jail and received no
medical care. By the time he reached an Army hospital, he was blind. Due to
the efforts of the NAACP, Woodard's blinding received wide publicity. When
President Harry Truman was informed, he said, "My God! I had no idea it
was as terrible as that. We've got to do something." See Nalty, *supra* at 204–
205.

Notes and Questions

1. Is the military a haven of relative equality for people of color today?
Consider again the comments of Joel Kovel regarding the military in
Chapter 1, *supra*.

2. Why do you think President Truman began to desegregate the military? Because of compassion for Blacks? Because of white self-interest in not presenting the United States on the world stage as a bloody battleground divided by racial lines, most visibly in the South? Because of both?

SECTION 6. THE NAACP AND THE STRUGGLE FOR CIVIL RIGHTS

The National Association for the Advancement of Colored People (NAACP) was founded in 1909, quickly becoming the most prominent organization to use the courts in the ultimately successful attempt to overthrow segregation and Jim Crow laws. Many illustrious figures in the black struggle for civil rights were associated with the NAACP, among them W.E.B. Du Bois, its first director of research and publicity, Charles Hamilton Houston, architect of the NAACP's legal campaign against segregation and discrimination, Thurgood Marshall, Walter White, Robert Carter, Spottswood Robinson III, and Constance Baker Motley, among others. Houston and Marshall, most prominently, planned and implemented the extensive campaign of litigation that challenged race discrimination in many areas of life.

Charles Hamilton Houston, principal architect of the NAACP's attack on racial discrimination, remains under-recognized for his crucial role in the development of American civil rights law. Houston was one of the few black students admitted to Harvard Law School, where he began his studies in 1919. He made very high grades and was elected a member of the editorial board of the Harvard Law Review, the first black student to earn this honor. He also earned the admiration of his professors at Harvard, including Dean Roscoe Pound and then professor Felix Frankfurter. After earning his law degree, Houston earned the advanced S.J.D. degree from Harvard. See Genna Rae McNeil, *Groundwork: Charles Hamilton Houston and the Struggle for Civil Rights* 32–33, 49–54 (1983). Consider the following excerpt on Houston's strategy for the NAACP's litigation efforts.

GENNA RAE McNEIL

Groundwork: Charles Hamilton Houston and the Struggle for Civil Rights
132–33, 134–35 (1983).*

As Special Counsel, [Houston's] purpose was to carry out a planned legal campaign against discrimination in education and transportation. The "more acute" issue of discrimination in education received the greater portion of his time and attention. Although he had observed the evils resulting from discrimination in transportation and did not wish to minimize them, Houston had also seen the pressure of an economic depression lead to the sacrifice of black education in order to preserve white education. Houston insisted that black people could not let this continue. "Since education is a preparation for the competition of life," he noted, a poor education handicaps black youth who with "all elements of American people are in economic competition."

* Reprinted by permission of University of Pennsylvania Press.

From 1935 to 1940, Charles Houston established himself as the "architect and dominant force of [this] legal program" of the NAACP. He devised the legal strategy, charted the course, began a program of political education for the masses, and handled the civil rights cases. He called on former students to accept the challenge of civil rights law and brought into the campaign eager, alert, and astute lawyers. He advised and directed black lawyers throughout the nation about their local campaigns against discrimination in education, transportation, jury exclusion, and denial of the vote. With his philosophy of social engineering, Houston was confident of his cause, his strategy, and of his ability and that of his cohorts to engage in meaningful and successful struggle against segregation and inequality.

* * *

Houston was persuaded that failure to eradicate inequality in the education of black youth would condemn the entire race to an inferior position within American society in perpetuity. The white man claims black Americans' slowness, backwardness, and lesser intelligence to justify "poorer teachers, wretched schools, shorter terms and an inferior type of education" for blacks, Houston declared, but the reason for such treatment has nothing to do with alleged black inferiority.

Discrimination in education is symbolic of all the more drastic discriminations which Negroes suffer in American life. And these apparent senseless discriminations in education against Negroes have a very definite objective on the part of the ruling whites to curb the young [Blacks] and prepare them to accept an inferior position in American life without protest or struggle. In the United States the Negro is economically exploited, politically ignored and socially ostr[a]cized. His education reflects his condition; the discriminations practiced against him are no accident.

This assessment of American conditions and the black American reality informed Houston as he sought to determine limited objectives and the ultimate goal of the NAACP campaign against unequal, discriminatory, segregated public education. Clearly, he asserted, "equality of education is not enough. There can be no true equality under a segregated system. No segregation operates fairly on a minority group unless it is a d[o]minant minority.... The American Negro is not a dominant minority; therefore he must fight for complete elimination of segregation as his ultimate goal."

Having set this goal, the Special Counsel, understanding that the "[l]aw [is] ... effective ... always within its limitations," selected as his second task devising "positionary tactics" or "the steps [one] takes to move from one position to another"—and clearly articulating the rationale for these tactics. Houston had accepted the position on the condition that the program of litigation be conducted as a protracted legal struggle based on the planned, deliberate prosecution of test cases to secure favorable legal precedents, and thereby lay a foundation for subsequent frontal attacks against racial discrimination and segregation. He developed a plan of attack in accordance with this view.

After a great deal of thought and study, Houston committed himself to this action, for he was very aware of the degree to which it differed from ideas of other civil rights/civil liberties lawyers. His white predecessor, Nathan Margold, had suggested in his "Preliminary Report to the Joint Committee" that an immediate and direct attack on segregation be made, since it was unconstitutional when it involved inequality.

Nevertheless, Houston believed the step-by-step process would have greater long-range effects, first because it would take into account the lack of tradition for equality within the American system. Addressing the National Bar Association, Houston indicated that it was not realistic to expect that an immediate, direct attack on segregation would be sympathetically heard by judges.

> We must never forget that the public officers, elective or appointive, are servants of the class which places them in office and maintains them there. It is too much to expect the court to go against the established and crystallized social customs, when to do so would mean professional and political suicide.... We cannot depend upon the judges to fight ... our battles.

Second, Houston preferred the protracted struggle because he did not view the campaign as an exercise in "legal hand[i]work." An effective program must involve the masses of blacks with their role being the initiation of action against inequalities and discrimination in education subsequent to the exposure of the evils. Yet in the course of his work Houston found many black people fearful of militant action within their own communities, and others, who were not directly facing debilitating discrimination, seemed apathetic about struggle. "This means that we have to ... slow down until we have developed a sustaining mass interest behind the programs.... The social and public factors must be developed at least along with and, if possible, before the actual litigation commences," Houston reported to the Joint Committee.

Third, Houston sought to proceed slowly building precedents to support equality because to his mind it was also important to neutralize the poor white masses and persuade them of the logic and justice of the NAACP position. There would be no true educational equality until racial discrimination in mixed schools also was attacked and eliminated, for it was racial prejudice bolstered by inequalities which in part caused poor whites to be blinded to mutual interests with blacks. It was Houston's position that the achievement of democracy, equality, and justice in education, as in other areas, required the recognition that poor whites and most blacks were in the same economic condition and that unified action could advance their common interests.

* * *

In 1940, after resigning as Special Counsel for the NAACP, but while remaining on its National Legal Committee, Houston dedicated most of his time and energy to fighting, through the courts, the racism endemic in American life. See also Mark V. Tushnet, *The NAACP's Legal Strategy against Segregated Education 1925–1950* (1987).

One of Houston's students at Howard Law School was Thurgood Marshall, who eventually joined the NAACP staff and became Director-counsel of the NAACP Legal Defense Fund, Inc., and Special Counsel to the NAACP. Marshall became the dominant figure in the NAACP's legal efforts. "[I]n the end, Marshall became the central figure in the NAACP's legal activities because he knew what to do, and everyone else knew he knew it." Mark V. Tushnet, *Making Civil Rights Law: Thurgood Marshall and the Supreme Court, 1936–1961,* 67 (1994). Beginning in the 1940s and over the next decades Marshall and his associates would "mount[] a comprehensive attack on racial discrimination and its consequences. They challenged discrimination in employment, in housing, in criminal procedure, in transportation and in education. The precise issues the lawyers raised changed as the law developed in directions no one had foreseen, but the project of attacking racial discrimination comprehensively remained the same." *Id.* at 47, 67. It was in the school desegregation cases that these lawyers made their most powerful impact. Consider the following excerpt:

MARK V. TUSHNET

Making Civil Rights Law: Thurgood Marshall and the Supreme Court
1936–1961 at 116, 151–52 (1994).*

Attacking the separate but equal doctrine of *Plessy v. Ferguson* in education was probably the center of the NAACP's efforts. Achieving voting rights and eliminating kangaroo courts were important, of course, but segregated education was different. Every African American in the South was subjected to segregated education in grossly inadequate schools. Segregated schools were the central symbol of African–American subordination, a visible and daily demonstration to children as they were growing up that whites did not consider them fit to associate with. Although it was not inevitable that Marshall's triumph came in cases challenging segregated education, it was certainly appropriate.

From 1935 to 1950, the NAACP's lawyers attacked unequal salaries for school teachers and challenged segregated universities. By the late 1940s they were confident that the time had come for a broader attack on segregation. As they saw it, the salary and university cases were successes, and their attachment to the Constitution led them to believe that, once they persuaded the courts that school segregation was unconstitutional, desegregation would also succeed. In the end, their success was limited by others in "Judge and Company." The Supreme Court's justices were unwilling to order immediate desegregation, and the NAACP's opponents evaded the Supreme Court's mandate and, ultimately, simply resisted the Court's interpretation of the Constitution.

    * * *

By 1950, the NAACP's lawyers had made it clear to their constituents that they were ready for the next stage. Many communities were ready. African Americans, aware of the NAACP's position but acting independently, initiated numerous student strikes to challenge the inequalities of school segregation. After taking the first steps, they approached the NAACP, and, as in Farmville, often enthusiastically agreed to change their focus from equalization to desegregation. As Marshall put it in a 1949 letter to [Spottswood] Robinson, "Some of our branches are hell-bent on getting cases started concerning elementary and high school education."

Marshall gradually reached the decision on desegregation rather than equalization before the Court's 1950 opinions, but even toward the end of the 1940s he was willing to devote resources to equalization suits. Attacking segregation directly was a bold step, and not all his constituents were ready for it. Desegregation had some obvious costs. Many believed it would threaten the jobs of African-American teachers. Admittedly, if desegregation occurred, districts would still need teachers for the same total number of students. Despite the fact that, as Marshall told a national radio audience, "Negroes have been disciplining and teaching white children in the homes where they work," many feared that whites would not allow African Americans to teach their children.

In addition, many African Americans believed that whites would resist desegregation violently. Their children would have to run the gauntlet, and the educational advantages of desegregation under such conditions were no obviously larger than the educational advantages of forcing the South to invest money to make the segregated schools more nearly equal. Finally, one strand of African–American thought on racial issues was gradualist and accommodationist. According to accommodationist thought, as whites came to understand the inequities of segregation, they would voluntarily modify it, gradually improving conditions. A gradual evolution to integration was, on this view, more likely to stick than desegregation forced on the South through litigation.

No one could fairly dismiss these concerns as unfounded, but Marshall and his staff disagreed with the accommodationists.

* * *

The NAACP litigated and won many crucial Supreme Court cases in the struggle for equality. *Shelley v. Kraemer*, 334 U.S. 1 (1948) made racially restrictive housing covenants unenforceable. In *Smith v. Allwright*, 321 U.S. 649 (1944), the NAACP successfully challenged the white primary system in Texas. And in the field of education, the NAACP litigated and won a series of important cases that challenged segregation in higher and primary education and ultimately reversed the doctrine of *Plessy v. Ferguson* in the field of education. These cases included *Missouri* ex rel *Gaines v. Canada*, 305 U.S. 337 (1938) (holding that Mississippi violated equal protection by not offering an in-state opportunity for Blacks to study law); *Sipuel v. Board of Regents*, 332 U.S. 631 (1948) (reaffirming *Gaines*, and holding that the State must offer the plaintiff an equal legal education); *Sweatt v. Painter*, 339 U.S. 629 (1950) (holding that a hastily established law school was unequal, and ordering the plaintiff admitted to the University of Texas Law School), and culminated in *Brown v. Board of Education*, 347 U.S. 483

(1954), in which the Court held that segregation in public education was inherently unequal and therefore violated the Equal Protection Clause, thereby overturning *Plessy*. These cases will be discussed at greater length *infra* in Chapter 9, on race and education.

Thurgood Marshall, upon reargument of the case in *Brown v. Board of Education*, closed his argument with an eloquence that made clear the bottom line of what he felt was at stake in the Court's decision:

> He ended by talking about reasonableness again. The only way to defend segregation "is to find that for some reason Negroes are inferior to all other human beings." But "nobody will stand in the Court and urge that," yet "the only thing [it] can be is an inherent determination that the people who were formerly kept in slavery ... shall be kept as near that stage as is possible; and now is the time, we submit, that this Court should make it clear that that is not what our Constitution stands for."

Tushnet, *supra*, at 207. Thurgood Marshall, after service as a Circuit Judge on the United States Court of Appeals for the Second Circuit and as Solicitor General of the United States, in 1967, became the first African American appointed to the Supreme Court. After serving for 24 years, Justice Marshall retired from the Supreme Court in 1991 due to his declining health; he died in 1993.

SECTION 7. THE CIVIL RIGHTS MOVEMENT OF THE 1950s–1960s

After the NAACP's legal victories, the civil rights movement began to shift from the courtroom towards collective action. Its leadership emerged from those engaged in those groups. A bureaucratic organization founded in the North by prominent intellectuals such as W.E.B. Du Bois and Walter White, the NAACP did not achieve leadership in the black community in the South because it lacked both the organizational resources and tradition from which to mobilize thousands of black protesters. Another factor in the NAACP's limited role in the South was popular dissatisfaction with the slow pace of change that could be accomplished through the legal system, at which the NAACP had excelled and to which it was largely limited. While most black grass roots organizations maintained respect for what the NAACP had achieved in the courts, the movement for black civil rights and equality in the South grew from within the black church and the black community. In addition, as the NAACP won court victories it began to attract the hostility of southern states, some of which, like Alabama, prohibited its existence within the state. This development actually facilitated the development of leadership from within well-established black churches. Aldon D. Morris, *The Origins of the Civil Rights Movement* 37–39 (1984).

Organized, collective black protest against racial injustice grew from important, crucial traditions. Some, such as slave revolts, as well as the individual resistance of countless individuals, have been described above. A. Philip Randolph, in one of the most important events foreshadowing the civil rights movement, organized the March on Washington movement. Randolph threatened to have 100,000 black Americans march in Washington D.C. as a protest against racial discrimination, a threat that President Roosevelt did not ignore. In response to Randolph's threatened action, Roosevelt signed the first executive order prohibiting discrimination in wartime industries—the first step towards the Civil Rights Act of 1964. See Herbert Garfinkel, *When Negroes March* 53–61 (1959). Furthermore,

> [t]he modern civil rights movement broke from the protest tradition of the past in at least two crucial ways. One, it was the first time that large masses of blacks directly confronted and effectively disrupted the normal functioning of groups and institutions thought to be responsible for their oppression. The hallmark of the modern civil rights movement is that these mass confrontations were widespread and sustained over a long period of time in the face of heavy repression. Two, this was the first time in American history that blacks adopted nonviolent tactics as a mass technique for bringing about social change. For these reasons the modern civil rights movement demands attention on its own terms.

Aldon D. Morris, *The Origins of the Civil Rights Movement* xi (1984).*

The "black church functioned as the institutional center of the modern civil rights movement." Morris, *supra,* at 4. Although the NAACP and the leadership emerging from the black church in the South often disagreed over tactics, close links united them. For example, many church leaders had also been officers in the NAACP branches in their respective regions. Morris, *supra*, at 37. In 1957, the Southern Christian Leadership Conference (SCLC) was formed through the collective efforts of a large coalition of leaders, including Martin Luther King, Fred Shuttlesworth, C.K. Steele, Ralph Abernathy, and Northern leaders such as A. Philip Randolph and Ella Baker. Morris, *supra* at 83. The SCLC, the "decentralized political arm of the black church," "was closely related to two enduring institutions of the black community—the NAACP and the church—and it was rooted in the black protest tradition." Morris, *supra* at 87, 91. Although closely related to these two organizations, there is little question that the tactics of the SCLC would be profoundly different from those of the NAACP. One of the SCLC's early working papers states as much:

> We must recognize in this new period that direct action is our most potent political weapon. We must understand that our refusal to accept Jim Crow in specific areas challenges the entire social, political and economic order that has kept us second class citizens since 1876.

See Morris, *supra* at 84 (quoting *Working Paper No. 7* of the SCLC).

Martin Luther King, Jr., emerged as the most prominent leader of the SCLC. King became the charismatic leader of the grass roots civil rights movement, well qualified by education, background and experience to lead. "King had the ability to convey in folksy language the commonalities that the contemporary black movement shared with great liberation movements of biblical times. That message was clearly felt among the masses: Protest was right and even divine, and Martin Luther King was the moral figure and prophet divinely inspired to lead the movement. The fact that the masses associated King with Jesus, Moses, and other biblical leaders strengthened King's charismatic appeal." Morris, *supra* at 60.

It is beyond the scope of this chapter to give detailed accounts of all the achievements of the black civil rights movement. But among its greatest achievements, one would have to list the Montgomery, Alabama bus boycott and the direct challenge to segregation in Birmingham, both of which were meticulously planned and courageously executed under the leadership of the SCLC. For detailed descriptions of these key events, consult the following sources: on the Montgomery bus boycott, see Aldon Morris, *The Origins of the Civil Rights Movement* 40–63 (1984); on the Birmingham protests, see Morris, *supra*, at 229–74, Harvard Sitkoff, *The Struggle for Black Equality 1954–1980* at 144 (1981).

The student sit-in movement that began in Greensboro, North Carolina in 1960, was another key set of events. The sit-ins eventually gave rise to the Student Non–Violent Co-ordinating Committee (SNCC). Clayborne Carson describes the evolution of the radicalism for which SNCC came to be known:

> This process involved conflict as well as consensus, for SNCC was not a homogeneous sect organized around a single set of beliefs. Staff members questioned not only the assumptions which underlay the status quo but also those that underlay their own rebellion against authority. They agreed that the goal of their struggle was to enhance human freedom, but they became increasingly aware of the inherent limitations of individualistic values as a guide for movements seeking collective goals. Although a belief in the emergence of new and better leaders from the militant black struggles prevailed within SNCC during most of the 1960s, an increasing number of staff members argued that strong, lasting institutions were also needed if SNCC were to move beyond the goal of civil rights reforms and change the American political structure. The uncompromising tone of SNCC's criticisms of the federal government and American liberalism obscured the vigorous debates within SNCC regarding tactics, strategy, and goals. In the course of their discussions, SNCC workers acquired insights regarding a question faced by idealistic reformers and revolutionaries throughout history: whether it is possible to help powerless people make political gains without creating new sources of oppression.

Clayborne Carson, *In Struggle: SNCC and the Black Awakening of the 1960s* at 2 (1981)*. SNCC leaders such as James Lawson, Robert Moses, John Lewis, and Stokely Carmichael played key roles in organizing the

Freedom Rides through the deep South and in registering black voters. See Carson, *supra*.

The legislative achievements of this era of the civil rights movement were the most impressive since the Reconstruction era. Indeed, this period is often referred to as the "Second Reconstruction." Pressured by the manifest and televised injustice of white violence inflicted upon nonviolent black protesters, Congress passed the broad-ranging Civil Rights Act of 1964 and the Voting Rights Act of 1965. Yet despite the equality and political participation promised by these statutes, the legacy of this legislation is quite ambiguous.

An important reason for the ambiguous legacy and the disappointment surrounding the Civil Rights Act may be the inherent limitations of law as a vehicle for transformative social change. As Professor Kimberlé Crenshaw has pointed out, antidiscrimination laws are capable of both expansive and restrictive interpretations, with very different consequences for Blacks. The expansive view defines equality as equality of result, and thus embodies a vision calling for substantive redistribution of opportunities that would alleviate the material deprivations caused by racism. On the other hand, the restrictive interpretation, which seems the prevailing ideology today, focuses on equality as a formal process, with remedies available only against isolated individual offenders. Once colorblind, formally equal processes are in place, law should do no more, under this view. According to Professor Crenshaw, the removal of the formal indicia of white supremacy, such as *de jure* segregation, now replaced by race neutral laws, has failed to eliminate racial inequality:

> Racial hierarchy cannot be cured by the move to facial race-neutrality in the laws that structure the economic, political, and social lives of Black people. * * *

> The end of Jim Crow has been accompanied by the demise of an explicit ideology of white supremacy. The white norm, however, has not disappeared; it has only been submerged in popular consciousness. It continues in an unspoken form as a statement of the positive social norm, legitimating the continuing domination of those who do not meet it. Nor have the negative stereotypes associated with Blacks been eradicated. The rationalizations once used to legitimate Black subordination based on a belief in racial inferiority have now been reemployed to legitimate the domination of Blacks through reference to an assumed cultural inferiority.

See Kimberlé Williams Crenshaw, *Race, Reform, and Retrenchment: Transformation and Legitimation in Antidiscrimination Law*, 101 Harv. L. Rev. 1331, 1378–79 (1988). We defer detailed discussion of the ultimate effectiveness of the Civil Rights Act of 1964 and the Voting Rights Act of 1965 to Chapters 7 and 8, on equality and voting rights, respectively.

SECTION 8. CONTEMPORARY RACISM

Today it is popular to argue that prosperity among some middle class Blacks demonstrates that racism is no longer a problem, and that today, with fair employment laws in place, all are judged by their merit. Indeed, the argument is made that Whites are currently disadvantaged by widespread favoritism towards Blacks in employment, education, and other important arenas. Consider the validity of these arguments in light of the following materials.

JOE R. FEAGIN & MELVIN P. SIKES

Living With Racism vi-x
15–18, 169–72 (1994).*

"What is it like to be a black person in white America today? One step from suicide! What I'm saying is—the psychological warfare games that we have to play everyday just to survive. We have to be one way in our communities and one way in the workplace or in the business sector. We can never be ourselves all around. I think that may be a given for all people, but us particularly; it's really a mental health problem. It's a wonder we haven't all gone out and killed somebody or killed ourselves."

Our interviews began with this statement from a successful black entrepreneur, the first respondent of 209 African Americans we interviewed in a number of cities across the United States. She challenges us to see the personal and family losses that have resulted from decades of dealing with prejudiced whites. She summons us to understand the great tension between conforming to white standards and trying to maintain personal integrity and black identity. She dares us to look beyond the statistics of inequality conventionally provided by scholars and journalists to experience the reality and pain of recurring racial discrimination, raising the questions: How are the unique vicissitudes of my life defined? How have I survived? And at what price?

A common white credo about racial relations today holds that discrimination is no longer a serious and widespread problem and that whatever blatant antiblack hostility remains is mostly that of isolated white bigots and Klan-type groups. In particular, middle-class African Americans are not viewed as victims of discrimination, but are seen as prosperous examples of the success of equal opportunity and affirmative action programs. Indeed, middle-class black Americans are thought by many whites to be the beneficiaries of racial quotas that have gone too far, to the point of "reverse discrimination."

Middle-class black Americans appear to most whites to have secured the promises of the American dream. They and their families have sacrificed to get a good education; they have worked very hard; and they have done everything said to be required to achieve the American dream.

All have achieved or will soon achieve some signs of material success—the good income, the credit cards, the nice car. They appear to be well integrated into middle-class America, and from a white perspective they have no real reason to link problems in their lives to skin color.

Yet when one engages in extended conversations with middle-class African Americans about their efforts, achievements, and obstacles, their often vivid accounts of the white hostility and discrimination they have experienced tell a different story. In this book we hope to show the image of untrammeled black middle-class prosperity and integration to be a white illusion, quite out of touch with the daily reality.

Our in-depth interviews provide windows into the black middle-class world, one not only of determination and hard work but also of frustration and rage over persisting discrimination. These African Americans show in their personal accounts that they have not been accepted as equals by many of the working class and middle-class whites they encounter in their daily lives. In our analysis we address the character of the hostility and discrimination these middle-class respondents have experienced in public places and in traditionally white workplaces, business arenas, residential complexes and neighborhoods, and schools and colleges. They present a tragic and terrible portrait of recent and continuing experiences with white racism.

But there is more to our argument than the contention that middle-class African Americans face serious discrimination. Our data say something even more profound about the state of this nation. Clearly, no amount of hard work and achievement, no amount of money, resources, and success, can protect black people from the persisting ravages of white racism in their everyday lives. Our respondents are alternately baffled, frustrated, shocked, and outraged that the strong evidence of their hard work and personal achievements does not protect them from white discrimination. Moreover, while they may have greater resources with which to respond to discrimination than less affluent black Americans, the presence and use of these resources appear to have had little lasting effect on the magnitude of white racism in the United States today. Racial stereotyping, prejudice, and hostility still operate indiscriminately, despite the actual identities and achievements of the black individuals discriminated against. In the everyday experience of our black middle-class respondents the full attainment of the American dream is "for whites only." The implications of this continuing racism for the fundamental democratic values of this society are far-reaching. The classic American creed promises the inalienable rights of "life, liberty, and the pursuit of happiness" today for all citizens of this democratic nation. Yet after several centuries of struggle these rights are not even close to being secured for black Americans, including middle-class black Americans. Perhaps the greatest tragedy in our findings of wide-spread racism is that they reveal the much-celebrated American creed to be little more than hollow words.

RACISM AS EVERYDAY EXPERIENCE

Much of the analysis * * * is shaped by several theoretical propositions derived substantially from close readings of our interviews with middle-class African Americans. We have found existing theories useful for interpretive purposes, but we have relied heavily on the many theoretical insights provided by our respondents. As a group, they are deeply reflective about their lives as African Americans and have constructed their own insightful theoretical frames.

The first of these general propositions is that modern racism must be understood as *lived experience*. The recurring experiences of middle-class and other black Americans with whites who discriminate are the heart of the racial problem in this nation. When our respondents talk about being black in a country dominated by whites, they do not speak in abstract concepts of discrimination or racism learned only from books, but tell of mistreatment encountered as they traverse traditionally white places. Most reflect on their trials, and their interpretations of the black middle-class experience are theories grounded in their everyday lives.
* * *

A second proposition gleaned from the interviews is that experiences with serious discrimination not only are very painful and stressful in the immediate situation and aftermath but also have a *cumulative* impact on particular individuals, their families, and their communities. A black person's life is regularly disrupted by the mistreatment suffered personally or by family members. The presence of the pronoun "we" in many black accounts of encounters with whites often suggests the collective character of the African American experience. Recurring encounters with white racism can be viewed as a series of "life crises," often similar to other serious life crises, such as the death of a loved one, that disturb an individual's life trajectory. Sympathetic whites may have an intellectual understanding of the consequences of racial discrimination. Profound understanding or empathy, however, involves feeling the pain and comprehending that discrimination is a series of unforgettable life crises.

The cumulative impact on an individual of repeated personal encounters with racial hostility is greater than the sum of these encounters might appear to be to a casual observer. In addition, discrimination is seldom just a personal matter. A black victim frequently shares the account with family and friends, often to lighten the burden, and this sharing creates a domino effect of anguish and anger rippling across an extended group. An individual's discrimination becomes a family matter. Another aspect of the cumulative effect of discrimination is, of course, historical, for discriminatory incidents are freighted with centuries of racial oppression of which the black victims are consciously or unconsciously aware. Memory is a key factor. Experiences with serious discrimination are stored not only in individual memories but also in family stories and group recollections. As a result, in discussing their negative encounters with whites many respondents move easily from the "I" of their own experiences to the "we" that indicates both a broad racial consciousness and a sense of group solidarity.

The third generalization we suggest is that the repeated experience of racism significantly affects a black person's behavior and understanding of life. It shapes both one's way of living—as family members, as church members, as employees, and as citizens—and one's life perspective. By life perspective we mean one's model, one's paradigmatic assumptions about and understandings of life and of the social world. A black American's life perspective comes to embed a repertoire of responses to hostile and racist acts by whites. Like other black Americans, those we interviewed have learned to cope and contend with racial mistreatment in a variety of creative ways and somehow to maintain their equilibrium.

A fourth proposition we offer is that the daily experiences of racial hostility and discrimination encountered by middle-class and other African Americans are the constituent elements of the interlocking societal structures and processes called "institutionalized racism." Our interviews reveal much about how this discrimination works. Particular encounters with whites often hint at or reveal the influence of the larger context of institutionalized racism, for racial hostility is not inborn but learned. The reflections on black experiences and the incidents recounted in the interviews add together to show the web of intentional and unconscious discrimination across traditionally white spaces. Individual black Americans soon come to see that no amount of hard work or achieved status can protect them from racial oppression across numerous institutional arenas of this society. White discriminators typically see only the color of their skins and not their great efforts, sacrifices, and personal achievements. Moreover, through institutionalized discrimination whites not only restrict individual mobility but also social, economic, and political mobility for black Americans as a group. Indeed, to limit group mobility, to protect white privilege and power, seems to be the underlying reason for institutionalized racism. * * *

A young lawyer in an East Coast law firm commented about the presumptions many of her coworkers make:

They look at me as a young black, and they can't believe I'm an attorney. They still open their mouths like, "Oh, that's who the new attorney is!" And then it's, "I didn't know you were a (pause) woman." Well, my name is Judy, how many men named Judy do you know? So, that's not the surprise. I've had more than a number of them submit reports to my office and then call to ask me if I understand. And my response to that is, "I understand English. Did you write what you meant? Well then, yes, I understand." And I know, like with my predecessor, that did not happen ... By the same token, it's presumed that I can't read a clear sentence, or interpret a clear sentence, or I need some extra help. They also want to have a lot of meetings to make sure I understand. They don't like my making decisions. If I tell them that I don't think their case will win in court, or it doesn't meet the legal standard, then they tell me I don't understand law.... I think that a lot of white people are very intimidated by black people, especially black men who are successful, and who have degrees and goals and strength about them, and know who they are, and don't try to abuse their identity. I think it's known throughout the agency that I'm [aggressive]. One of the problems that I have is I'll say, "How ya doin'?" If I'm in the mood to say, "How ya doin'?" instead of, "Good morning, how are you?" that's part of who I am, and who I grew up to be. And I don't want to change that. By the same token, I play my music in my office, whether it insults them or not.... They see a problem with that.

Research has shown that high-level (usually white) women employees must carry out their jobs under greater corporate scrutiny than their male counterparts. In addition to being patronized, this attorney is quite conscious of the prevailing notions of propriety in the white corporate culture, which she resists.

In the late 1980s the *National Law Journal* reported that blacks accounted for less that 2 percent of the lawyers and less than 1 percent of the partners of the nation's 250 largest law firms. Black lawyers and judges are rare in most courtrooms. For those whose workplace is the courtroom, however, discrimination can still be a problem, as a law professor at an eastern university explained:

I was an attorney with the Justice Department. And I tried cases; I met judges [who] were incredulous that a black man could try a case before them, or be a lawyer even, and certainly be one that represented the United States government in court. And often the discrimination took the form of their trying to get me to do things that would compromise my case: "Well, counselor, you don't need to interview any witnesses, do you? We can just move on; you can just chat with them; you don't have to interview them under oath do you?" [I said] "Well, your honor, you have to have them under oath because that way they may be more likely to tell the truth. Or if they don't, then we have some way of having sanctions apply." Well, that's one example. As a lawyer, I dealt with judges a lot, and some of their discrimination was relatively overt.

This lawyer displayed considerable patience while standing his ground vis-a-vis the harassment of a white judge.

Coworkers' and associates' discrimination can be blatant. A young manager of a service firm recounted numerous experiences with racial hostility:

Probably the most racism I've ever felt has been in the workplace. One company that I worked for, I was the regional manager for five of their branches. I traveled back and forth to the different branches to make sure that everything was OK. This one particular branch that I got was in a southwestern city. The demographics for this branch were bad ... When I went to the branch, the branch manager, his face dropped as soon as he saw me, he didn't know that I was black. The other people in the office couldn't deal with the fact that they would have to take instructions from a black person. I think that I was probably one of two black people in that city, because I never saw any black people there. I remember one time, one supervisor, we became fast friends. He was white. We got along very well. And he would always tell me all the horrible things said about me, and they were primarily because I was black. I remember the second day that I was there he told me that the installation manager, of all people—he has absolutely nothing to do with my job—told him [that] he didn't understand why he was so attentive to me, so concerned about what I thought about his job. And he said, "Well, she's my supervisor. I should be concerned about what she thinks." He said, "Well, I wouldn't worry about it. Don't worry about it. She's just a black woman. It's not a big deal. I'm sure they're going to get her out of here soon. It's no problem. Don't worry about it." But that was just one of so many crazy things.... Everybody was so conscious of the fact that I was black, and they just couldn't deal with me being somebody that they had to take instructions from. I guess if I had been the maid I would've gotten more respect. But it was just that constant struggle, constantly dealing with those people.

As the first black person to hold a supervisory position in this local firm, she was treated as a temporary aberration by whites who were unwilling to abandon their stereotypes and feelings of racial superiority.

"BLACK MAN FATALLY DRAGGED IN A POSSIBLE RACIAL KILLING"

by Carol Marie Cropper
The New York Times, June 10, 1998.*

DALLAS, June 9—A black man was dragged to his death from the back of a pickup truck in a rural section of Texas known for racist and Klan activity, and today three white men were charged with the murder.

The broken body of James Byrd Jr., 49, was discovered on Sunday morning by residents of an area just outside the East Texas town of Jasper, population 8,000. As he walked home from his parents' house on Saturday night, Mr. Byrd was apparently picked up by the men sometime after midnight and taken to woods, where he was beaten, then chained to the truck and dragged for two miles.

Guy James Gray, the Jasper County District Attorney, called the killing "probably the most brutal I've ever seen" in 20 years as a prosecutor. Mr. Byrd's torso was found at the edge of a paved road, his head and an arm in a ditch about a mile away, according to an affidavit.

The police charged Shawn A. Berry, 23, Lawrence R. Brewer, 31, and John W. King, 23, with murder. The District Attorney said Mr. Brewer and Mr. King had racist tattoos and were Ku Klux Klan supporters, leading investigators to believe the killing was racially motivated.

The three were apparently roommates in a Jasper apartment.

R. C. Horn, Mayor of Jasper, said the victim came from a "beautiful family." Mr. Byrd's sisters said he had been on disability and did not have a car but often accepted rides from acquaintances or walked around Jasper, where the number of blacks almost equals that of whites.

Mayor Horn said there had been no unusual racial problems in the town, built on the timber industry. "Jasper is a city that has a strong bind together, both black and white," said Mr. Horn, who is black.

But Gary Bledsoe, president of the state chapter of the National Association for the Advancement of Colored People, said the eastern part of Texas, which includes Jasper, has been considered a problem area and a hotbed of Klan activity for years. He pointed to problems in 1993 integrating a housing project in nearby Vidor, for decades an all-white town, where an avowed white supremacist threatened the first black residents, and teen-agers dressed in sheets confronted black newcomers.

Mr. Bledsoe called for adding kidnapping charges, making the killing a capital crime. He said that he planned to go to Jasper to help the authorities with the investigation and that the N.A.A.C.P. wanted to help organize a community response, like a march or rally.

Mayor Horn said local church leaders were planning a prayer meeting at the courthouse square for Monday night.

According to the police affidavit, items left in the woods and along the dirt logging road where Mr. Byrd was first dragged led officials to the three men charged. One item was a cigarette lighter inscribed with a Klan symbol that the police said they believed belonged to one of the men.

Mr. Berry told the police he had been riding around with the other two men when he saw Mr. Byrd walking and offered him a ride, according to the affidavit. Mr. Byrd and Mr. Berry might have known each other because they had the same parole officer, The Associated Press reported. Mr. Byrd served six years in prison for theft and violating parole. All three suspects have criminal records for offenses including burglary and drug possession and served jail time together.

After Mr. Byrd was picked up, Mr. King became upset and began cursing, Mr. Berry is quoted as saying in the affidavit. The men stopped at a convenience store and then Mr. King drove to the dirt road, saying he was about to scare Mr. Byrd. The other two began to beat the victim, Mr. Berry told the police.

The Federal Bureau of Investigation may charge the three with violating the victim's civil rights, said Al Tribble, an F.B.I. special agent in Houston.

The national N.A.A.C.P. is also watching the case, said Jean Hitchcock, acting chief operating officer for the organization. "We call upon all Americans to stand up and be counted and to condemn this for the heinous crime that it is."

Notes and Questions

1. How do you evaluate the violence against James Byrd, Jr.? Is it merely an isolated instance of violence by racist extremists? Is it consistent with our history? Made possible by that history? What specific material presented in this chapter contributes to an understanding of this incident?

2. Consider whether you would feel differently if the victim had been white. Would the meaning of these events vary if the victim's race had been different? If so, how?

3. If the meaning would vary depending on the victim's race, what does this teach us about the significance of history in the meaning of current

events? Can we ever ignore history in understanding the meaning of those events? Can we ever ignore race in understanding current events?

4.   Do middle-class and professional Blacks suffer more, less, or different racism than Blacks employed in blue collar jobs? Does it seem reasonable to assume that middle-or upper-class Blacks do not suffer from racism because of their economic positions? See generally Ellis Cose, *The Rage of a Privileged Class (1993).*

Chapter 3

AMERICAN INDIANS

Before Columbus and other European explorers "discovered" them, Indians inhabited the American continent. Columbus's initial contacts occurred with the Arawaks, of the Bahama Islands, and with other Indians on Hispaniola (now Haiti and the Dominican Republic) and Cuba. His subsequent clashes with Indians, during later voyages to these areas, as well as the voyages of discovery of other explorers, can fairly be characterized as murderous, genocidal. The Spanish explorers killed, maimed and enslaved countless Indian peoples. And "[w]hat Columbus did to the Arawaks of the Bahamas, Cortes did to the Aztecs of Mexico, Pizarro to the Incas of Peru, and the English settlers of Virginia and Massachusetts to the Powhatans and the Pequots." Howard Zinn, *A People's History of the United States* 11 (1995).

While it is impossible to do justice to the particularity of all of the Indian nations that populated the lands we now know as the United States, we can at least emphasize their diversity. Indians have never been homogeneous. By one scholar's estimate, approximately 75 million Indians populated the entire American continent by the time of Columbus's arrival, approximately 25 million in North America alone. "Responding to the different environments of soil and climate, they developed hundreds of different tribal cultures, perhaps two thousand different languages." Zinn, *supra*, at 18. For more extensive descriptions of native peoples before contact with Europeans, consult Gary B. Nash, *Red, White, & Black: The Peoples of Early North America* 7–27 (3rd. ed. 1992); Angie Debo, *A History of the Indians of the United States* 3–18 (1970).

According to the 1990 Census, the number of persons identifying themselves as Native Americans in the United States was about 1,959,000 persons. This number includes approximately 80,000 Eskimos and Aleuts and almost 139,000 Native Hawaiians. These aggregate numbers conceal the great variety of Indian tribes that have survived. The largest tribes or groups of native peoples, according to the 1990 Census, were:

Tribal/Ethnic Grouping	Population
Cherokee	308,132
Navajo	219,198
Native Hawaiians	138,742

173

Tribal/Ethnic Grouping	Population
Chippewa	103,826
Sioux	103,255
Choctaw	82,299
Eskimo	57,152
Pueblo	52,939
Apache	50,051
Iroquois	49,038
Lumbee	48,444
Creek	43,550
Blackfoot	32,234
Aleut	23,797
Chickasaw	20,631
Potawatomi	16,763
Tohono O'Odham	16,041
Pima	14,431
Tlingit	13,925
Seminole	13,797
Alaskan Athabascans	13,738
Cheyenne	11,456
Comanche	11,322
Paiute	11,142
Puget Sound Salish	10,246

Source: Bureau of the Census, American Tribes with 1,000 or More American Indians for the United States: 1990.

See D. Getches, C. Wilkinson, & R. Williams, Jr., *Federal Indian Law* 7–30 (3d ed. 1993), for a good introduction to the status of American Indians today.

SECTION 1. THE CONQUEST AND THE DOCTRINE OF DISCOVERY

Europeans crossed the ocean believing that lands inhabited by "heathens and infidels" should be possessed by Europeans. The Spanish justified their conquests by proclaiming their mission to spread Christianity everywhere through the conversion of native peoples. J.H. Parry, *The Spanish Theory of Empire in the Sixteenth Century* 5–6 (1978). Columbus is reported to have stated: "I hope in Our Lord to be able to propagate His holy name and His Gospel throughout the universe." Tzvetan Todorov, *The Conquest of America* 10 (1992). The Spanish demanded that Indians accept the *Requerimiento,* a pronouncement that obligated them to submit peacefully to the Spanish and to accept the Catholic faith. As Robert Williams, Jr. describes it, "[t]he Requerimiento was intended as a charter of conquest. Accordingly, it informed the Indians in the simplest terms that they could either accept Christian missionaries and Spanish imperial hegemony or be annihilated." Robert A. Williams, Jr., *The American Indian in Western Legal Thought* 91 (1990).

The English had their own version of this doctrine. Lord Coke wrote in *Calvin's Case,* decided in 1608, that "if a Christian King should conquer a kingdom of an infidel, and bring them under his subjection, there *ipso facto* the laws of the infidel are abrogated, for that they be not only against Christianity, but against the law of God and of nature * * *." *Calvin's Case,* 77 Eng. Rep. 377, 398 (K.B. 1608). This ideology provided important groundwork for Chief Justice Marshall's exposition of the Doctrine of Discovery in *Johnson v. McIntosh,* in which the Supreme Court ruled that conquest justifies the conqueror's assertion of dominion and title to lands formerly possessed by Indians: "This principle was that discovery gave title to the government by whose subjects, or by whose authority, it was made, against all other European governments, which title might be consummated by possession." *Johnson v. McIntosh,* 21 U.S. (8 Wheat.) 543, 573 (1823). Indian possession of desirable lands, according to Justice Story, "was not treated as a right of property and dominion, but as a mere right of occupancy. As infidels, heathens, and savages, they were not allowed to possess the prerogatives belonging to absolute, sovereign, and independent nations." Joseph Story, *Commentaries,* § 152, quoted in Williams, *The American Indian In Western Legal Thought* 316 (1990).

JOHNSON v. McINTOSH

21 U.S. (8 Wheat.) 543 (1823).

CHIEF JUSTICE MARSHALL delivered the opinion of the Court.

The plaintiffs in this cause claim the land, in their declaration mentioned, under two grants, purporting to be made, the first in 1773, and the last in 1775, by the chiefs of certain Indian tribes, constituting the Illinois and the Piankeshaw nations; and the question is, whether this title can be recognised in the Courts of the United States?

The facts, as stated in the case agreed, show the authority of the chiefs who executed this conveyance, so far as it could be given by their own people; and likewise show, that the particular tribes for whom these chiefs acted were in rightful possession of the land they sold. The inquiry, therefore, is, in a great measure, confined to the power of Indians to give, and of private individuals to receive, a title which can be sustained in the Courts of this country.

As the right of society, to prescribe those rules by which property may be acquired and preserved is not, and cannot be drawn into question; as the title to lands, especially, is and must be admitted to depend entirely on the law of the nation in which they lie; it will be necessary, in pursuing this inquiry, to examine, not singly those principles of abstract justice, which the Creator of all things has impressed on the mind of his creature man, and which are admitted to regulate, in a great degree, the rights of civilized nations, whose perfect independence is acknowledged; but those principles also which our own government has adopted in the particular case, and given us as the rule for our decision.

On the discovery of this immense continent, the great nations of Europe were eager to appropriate to themselves so much of it as they could respectively acquire. Its vast extent offered an ample field to the ambition and enterprise of all; and the character and religion of its inhabitants afforded an apology for considering them as a people over whom the superior genius of Europe might claim an ascendency. The potentates of the old world found no difficulty in convincing themselves that they made ample compensation to the inhabitants of the new, by bestowing on them civilization and Christianity, in exchange for unlimited independence. But, as they were all in pursuit of nearly the same object, it was necessary, in order to avoid conflicting settlements, and consequent war with each other, to establish a principle, which all should acknowledge as the law by which the right of acquisition, which they all asserted, should be regulated as between themselves. This principle was, that discovery gave title to the government by whose subjects, or by whose authority, it was made, against all other European governments, which title might be consummated by possession.

The exclusion of all other Europeans, necessarily gave to the nation making the discovery the sole right of acquiring the soil from the natives, and establishing settlements upon it. It was a right with which no Europeans could interfere. It was a right which all asserted for themselves, and to the assertion of which, by others, all assented.

Those relations which were to exist between the discoverer and the natives, were to be regulated by themselves. The rights thus acquired being exclusive, no other power could interpose between them.

In the establishment of these relations, the rights of the original inhabitants were, in no instance, entirely disregarded; but were necessarily, to a considerable extent, impaired. They were admitted to be the rightful occupants of the soil, with a legal as well as just claim to retain possession of it, and to use it according to their own discretion; but their rights to complete sovereignty, as independent nations, were necessarily diminished, and their power to dispose of the soil at their own will, to whomsoever they pleased, was denied by the original fundamental principle, that discovery gave exclusive title to those who made it.

While the different nations of Europe respected the right of the natives, as occupants, they asserted the ultimate dominion to be in themselves; and claimed and exercised, as a consequence of this ultimate dominion, a power to grant the soil, while yet in possession of the natives. These grants have been understood by all, to convey a title to the grantees, subject only to the Indian right of occupancy. * * *

No one of the powers of Europe gave its full assent to this principle, more unequivocally than England. The documents upon this subject are ample and complete. So early as the year 1496, her monarch granted a commission to the Cabots, to discover countries then unknown to Christian people, and to take possession of them in the name of the king of England. Two years afterwards, Cabot proceeded on this voyage, and discovered the continent of North America, along which he sailed as far south as Virginia. To this discovery the English trace their title.

In this first effort made by the English government to acquire territory on this continent, we perceive a complete recognition of the principle which has been mentioned. The right of discovery given by this commission, is confined to countries "then unknown to all Christian people;" and of these countries Cabot was empowered to take possession in the name of the king of England. Thus asserting a right to take possession notwithstanding the occupancy of the natives, who were heathens, and, at the same time, admitting the prior title of any Christian people who may have made a previous discovery. * * *

Thus, all the nations of Europe, who have acquired territory on this continent, have asserted in themselves, and have recognised in others, the exclusive right of the discoverer to appropriate the lands occupied by the Indians. Have the American States rejected or adopted this principle? By the treaty which concluded the war of our revolution, Great Britain relinquished all claim, not only to the government, but to the "propriety and territorial rights of the United States," whose boundaries were fixed in the second article. By this treaty, the powers of government, and the right to soil, which had previously been in Great Britain, passed definitively to these States. We had before taken possession of them, by declaring independence; but neither the declaration of independence, nor the treaty confirming it, could give us more than that which we before possessed, or to which Great Britain was before entitled. It has never been doubted, that either the United States, or the several States, had a clear title to all the lands within the boundary lines described in the treaty, subject only to the Indian right of occupancy, and that the exclusive power to extinguish that right, was vested in that government which might constitutionally exercise it. * * *

The United States, then, have unequivocally acceded to that great and broad rule by which its civilized inhabitants now hold this country. They hold, and assert in themselves, the title by which it was acquired. They maintain, as all others have maintained, that discovery gave an exclusive right to extinguish the Indian title of occupancy, either by purchase or by conquest; and gave also a right to such a degree of sovereignty, as the circumstances of the people would allow them to exercise.

* * *

We will not enter into the controversy, whether agriculturists, merchants, and manufacturers, have a right, on abstract principles, to expel hunters from the territory they possess, or to contract their limits. Conquest gives a title which the Courts of the conqueror cannot deny, whatever the private and speculative opinions of individuals may be, respecting the original justice of the claim which has been successfully asserted. The British government, which was then our government, and whose rights have passed to the United States, asserted title to all the lands occupied by Indians, within the chartered limits of the British colonies. It asserted also a limited sovereignty over them, and the exclusive right of extinguishing the title which occupancy gave to them. These claims have been maintained and established as far west as the river Mississippi, by the sword. The title to a vast portion of the lands we now hold, originates in them. It is not for the Courts of this country to question the validity of this title, or to sustain one which is incompatible with it.

Although we do not mean to engage in the defence of those principles which Europeans have applied to Indian title, they may, we think, find some excuse, if not justification, in the character and habits of the people whose rights have been wrested from them. * * *

[T]he tribes of Indians inhabiting this country were fierce savages, whose occupation was war, and whose subsistence was drawn chiefly from the forest. To leave them in possession of their country, was to leave the country a wilderness; to govern them as a distinct people, was impossible, because they were as brave and as high spirited as they were fierce, and were ready to repel by arms every attempt on their independence. * * *

However extravagant the pretension of converting the discovery of an inhabited country into conquest may appear; if the principle has been asserted in the first instance, and afterwards sustained; if a country has been acquired and held under it; if the property of the great mass of the community originates in it, it becomes the law of the land, and cannot be questioned. So, too, with respect to the concomitant principle, that the Indian inhabitants are to be considered merely as occupants, to be protected, indeed, while in peace, in the possession of their lands, but to be deemed incapable of transferring the absolute title to others. However this restriction may be opposed to natural right, and to the usages of civilized nations, yet, if it be indispensable to that system under which the country has been settled, and be adapted to the actual condition of the two people, it may, perhaps, be supported by reason, and certainly cannot be rejected by Courts of justice. * * *

ROBERT A. WILLIAMS, JR.

Columbus's Legacy: The Rehnquist Court's Perpetuation of European Cultural Racism against American Indian Tribes
39 Fed. Bar News & Journal 358, 362–63 (1992).*

The Christian European legal tradition of cultural racism and discrimination against non-Christian peoples, first brought to the New World by Columbus, and translated and adapted by English Protestant monarchs in North America, was formally incorporated into United States Federal Indian law by Chief Justice John Marshall in 1823, in the Supreme Court's first major decision on American Indian tribes' self-determining rights and status *Johnson v. McIntosh.* * * *

In holding that American Indian tribes had no power to give title to lands to private individuals recognizable in a United States court, Marshall's opinion in *Johnson* relied exclusively and directly upon the medievally-derived legal tradition of Christian European crusading conquest and denial of non-Christian infidel peoples' rights brought to the New World by Columbus. * * *

Of necessity, the Discovery Doctrine's foundational principle of superior sovereign rights in Christian Europeans to the territories occupied by indigenous tribal peoples denied American Indian tribes equal rights to self-determination. * * *

* Copyright © by Robert A. Williams, Jr.,   thor.
1992. Reprinted by permission of the au-

The *Johnson* Court was well aware of the racist legacy of this legal principle now incorporated as the conqueror's law of the land by the United States Supreme Court. As Marshall's opinion itself had conceded in its opening discussion of the historical basis of the Discovery Doctrine, the American Indians' "character and religion . . . afforded an apology for considering them as a people over whom the superior genius of Europe might claim an ascendancy."

Johnson's candid acknowledgment of the racist assumptions supporting the Doctrine of Discovery illuminates how deeply embedded European cultural racism is in the foundations of United States Federal Indian Law. A medievally-derived assumption of European cultural superiority justifies the diminished legal status of American Indian tribes under United States law. From the Discovery Doctrine's racist assumptions of a presumed superior sovereignty in a European-derived government over the territory occupied by indigenous tribal peoples, subsequent Supreme Court decisions constructed the principle of Congressional plenary power in Indian affairs. The Doctrine's impairment of rights to self-rule and property for American Indian tribes determined the diminished sovereign status of tribes in United States Federal Indian law. The Doctrine's institutionalization of Christian European cultural racism against normatively divergent and deficient non-Christian peoples was subsequently fashioned into the Trust doctrine's concept of a guardian-ward relationship between the United States and American Indian tribes by the Supreme Court. * * *

SECTION 2. VIEWS OF THE FRAMERS AND THE BEGINNINGS OF EARLY FEDERAL INDIAN POLICY

After the Revolutionary War, relationships between the colonists and the "savage" Indian nations remained unsettled in part because the Indian nations had not participated at the Peace of Paris, which settled the war with Great Britain. In the following letter and in his Third Annual Message to Congress, George Washington expresses his concerns about non-governmental dealings with the Indians and sets out principles that influenced the development of federal policy toward the Indian nations.

GEORGE WASHINGTON TO JAMES DUANE
September 7, 1783.

* * *

To suffer a wide extended Country to be over run with Land Jobbers, Speculators, and Monopolisers or even with scatter'd settlers, is, in my opinion, inconsistent with that wisdom and policy which our true interest dictates, or that an enlightened People ought to adopt and, besides, is pregnant of disputes both with the Savages, and among ourselves, the evils of which are easier, to be conceived than described; and for what? but to aggrandize a few avaricious Men to the prejudice of many, and the embarrassment of Government. [F]or the People engaged in these pursuits without contributing in the smallest degree to the support of Government, or considering themselves as amenable to its Laws, will involve it by their unrestrained conduct, in inextricable perplexities, and more than probable in a great deal of Bloodshed.

My ideas therefore of the line of Conduct proper to be observed not only towards the Indians, but for the government of the Citizens of America, in their Settlement of the Western Country (which is intimately connected therewith) are simply these. * * *

That the Indians should be informed, that after a Contest of eight years for the Sovereignty of this Country G[reat] Britain has ceded all the Lands of the United States within the limits described by the [article] of the Provisional Treaty.

That as they (the Indians) maugre all the advice and admonition which could be given them at the commencement; and during the prosecution of the War could not be restrained from acts of Hostility, but were determined to join their Arms to those of G[reat] Britain and to share their fortune; so, consequently, with a less generous People than Americans they would be made to share the same fate; and be compell[e]d to retire along with them beyond the Lakes. But as we prefer Peace to a state of Warfare, as we consider them as a deluded People; as we perswade ourselves that they are convinced, from experience, of their error in taking up the Hatchet against us, and that their true Interest and safety must now depend upon our friendship. As the Country, is large enough to contain us all; and as we are disposed to be kind to them and to partake of their Trade, we will from these considerations and from motives of Compn., draw a veil over what is past and establish a boundary line between them and us beyond which we will *endeavor* to restrain our People from Hunting or Settling, and within which they shall not come, but for the purposes of Trading, Treating, or other business unexceptionable in its nature. * * *

The limits being sufficiently extensive (in the New Ctry.) to comply with all the engagements of Government and to admit such emigrations as may be supposed to happen within a given time not only from the several States of the Union but from Foreign Countries, and moreover of such magnitude as to form a distinct and proper Government; a Proclamation in my opinion, should issue making it Felony (if there is power for the purpose and if not imposing some very heavy restraint) for any person to Survey or Settle beyond the Line; and the Officers Commanding the Frontier Garrison should have pointed and peremptory orders to see that the Proclamation is carried into effect.

* * *

Every advantage that could be expected or even wished for would result from such a mode of procedure our Settlements would be compact, Government well established, and our Barrier formidable, not only for ourselves but against our Neighbours, and the Indians as has been observed in Genl Schuylers Letter will ever retreat as our Settlements advance upon them and they will be as ready to sell, as we are to buy; That it is the cheapest as well as the least distressing way of dealing with them, none who are acquainted with the Nature of Indian warfare, and has ever been at the trouble of estimating the expence of one, and comparing it with the cost of purchasing their Lands, will hesitate to acknowledge.

* * *

At first view, it may seem a little extraneous, when I am called upon to give an opinion upon the terms of a Peace proper to be made with the Indians, that I should go into the formation of New States; but the Settlemt. of the Western Country and making a Peace with the Indians are so analogous that there can be no definition of the one without involving considerations of the other. [F]or I repeat it, again, and I am clear in my opinion, that policy and oeconomy point very strongly to the expediency of being upon good terms with the Indians, and the propriety of purchasing their Lands in preference to attempting to drive them by force of arms out of their Country; which as we have already experienced is like driving the Wild Beasts of the Forest which will return us soon as the pursuit is at an end and fall perhaps on those that are left there; when the gradual extension of our Settlements will as certainly cause the Savage as the Wolf to retire; both being beasts of prey tho' they differ in shape. In a word there is nothing to be obtained by an Indian War but the Soil they live on and this can be had by purchase at less expence, and without that bloodshed, and those distresses which helpless Women and Children are made partakers of in all kinds of disputes with them. * * *

27 *The Writings of George Washington* 133–40 (John C. Fitzpatrick ed. 1938).

PRESIDENT GEORGE WASHINGTON

Third Annual Address to Congress
October 25, 1791.

* * *

Among the most important of these [objects] is the defense and security of the Western frontiers. To accomplish it on the most humane principles was a primary wish.

Accordingly, at the same time that treaties have been provisionally concluded and other proper means used to attach the wavering and to confirm in their friendship the well-disposed tribes of Indians, effectual measures have been adopted to make those of a hostile description sensible that a pacification was desired upon terms of moderation and justice.

These measures having proved unsuccessful, it became necessary to convince the refractory of the power of the United States to punish their depradations. Offensive operations have therefore been directed, to be conducted, however, as consistently as possible with the dictates of humanity. * * *

Overtures of peace are still continued to the deluded tribes, and considerable numbers of individuals belonging to them have lately renounced all further opposition, removed from their former situations, and placed themselves under the immediate protection of the United States.

It is sincerely to be desired that all need of coercion in future may cease and that an intimate intercourse may succeed, calculated to advance the happiness of the Indians and to attach them firmly to the United States.

In order to this it seems necessary—

That they should experience the benefits of an impartial dispensation of justice.

That the mode of alienating their lands, the main source of discontent and war, should be so defined and regulated as to obviate imposition and as far as may be practicable controversy concerning the reality and extent of the alienations which are made.

That commerce with them should be promoted under regulations tending to secure an equitable deportment toward them, and that such rational experiments should be made for imparting to them the blessings of civilization as may from time to time suit their condition.

That the Executive of the United States should be enabled to employ the means to which the Indians have been long accustomed for uniting their immediate interests with the preservation of peace.

And that efficacious provision should be made for inflicting adequate penalties upon all those who, by violating their rights, shall infringe the treaties and endanger the peace of the Union.

A system corresponding with the mild principles of religion and philanthropy toward an unenlightened race of men, whose happiness materially depends on the conduct of the United States, would be as honorable to the national character as conformable to the dictates of sound policy.

* * *

I *Messages and Papers of the Presidents 1789–1897* at 104–105 (James D. Richardson ed. 1899).

Notes and Questions

1. Describe Washington's attitude toward the Indians. Does Washington harbor much doubt about the inevitability of the expansion of white settlements and the displacement of Indians?

2. Note Washington's attitude towards "hostile," "refractory," and "deluded" tribes. From an Indian point of view, didn't resistance to white settlements and military force make sense? What would you do if newcomers started taking over your land?

———

President Jefferson's letter to William Henry Harrison contains an early exposition of the principal strategies for dealing with Indians: either coerced assimilation or removal from desirable lands. Both strategies facilitated acquisition by Whites of desirable Indian lands. Ronald Takaki, *Iron Cages: Race and Culture in Nineteenth–Century America* 62–63 (1979).

PRESIDENT JEFFERSON TO WILLIAM HENRY HARRISON

February 27, 1803.

* * *

[F]rom the Secretary of War you receive from time to time information and instructions as to our Indian affairs. These communications being for the public records, are restrained always to particular objects and occasions; but this letter being unofficial and private, I may with safety give you a more extensive view of our policy respecting the Indians, that you may the better comprehend the parts dealt out to you in detail through the official channel, and observing the system of which they make a part, conduct yourself in unison with it in cases where you are obliged to act without instruction. Our system is to live in perpetual peace with the Indians, to cultivate an affectionate attachment from them, by everything just and liberal which we can do for them within the bounds of reason, and by giving them effectual protection against wrongs from our own people. The decrease of game rendering their subsistence by hunting insufficient, we wish to draw them to agriculture, to spinning and weaving. The latter branches they take up with great readiness, because they fall to the women, who gain by quitting the labors of the field for those which are exercised within doors. When they withdraw themselves to the culture of a small piece of land, they will perceive how useless to them are their extensive forests, and will be willing to pare them off from time to time in exchange for necessaries for their farms and families. To promote this disposition to exchange lands, which they have to spare and we want, for necessaries, which we have to spare and they want, we shall push our trading uses, and be glad to see the good and influential individuals among them run in debt, because we observe that when these debts get beyond what the individuals can pay, they become willing to lop them off by a cession of lands. At our trading houses, too, we mean to sell so low as merely to repay us cost and charges, so as neither to lessen nor enlarge our capital. This is what private traders cannot do, for they must gain; they will consequently retire from the competition, and we shall thus get clear of this pest without giving offence or umbrage to the Indians. In this way our settlements will gradually circumscribe and approach the Indians, and they will in time either incorporate with us as citizens of the United States, or remove beyond the Mississippi. The former is certainly the termination of their history most happy for themselves; but, in the whole course of this, it is essential to cultivate their love. As to their fear, we presume that our strength and their weakness is now so visible that they must see we have only to shut our hand to crush them, and that all our liberalities to them proceed from motives of pure humanity only. Should any tribe be foolhardy enough to take up the hatchet at any time, the seizing the whole country of that tribe, and driving them across the

Mississippi, as the only condition of peace, would be an example to others, and a furtherance of our final consolidation .

* * *

10 *Writings of Thomas Jefferson* 369–71 (Andrew A. Lipscomb ed. 1904).

Jefferson sought to compel the Indian nations to give up their traditional ways in order to reduce their dependence on hunting and increase their dependence on agriculture, commerce, and their indebtedness to white people. In this way, he anticipated that Indians would sell their lands willingly. These points are especially clear in Jefferson's Confidential Message to Congress of January 18, 1803.

THOMAS JEFFERSON

Confidential Message Recommending a Western Exploring Expedition
January 18, 1803.

* * *

The Indian tribes residing within the limits of the United States have for a considerable time been growing more and more uneasy at the constant diminution of the territory they occupy, although effected by their own voluntary sales, and the policy has long been gaining strength with them, of refusing absolutely all further sale on any conditions, insomuch that at this time it hazards their friendship and excites dangerous jealousies and perturbations in their minds to make any overture for the purchase of the smallest portions of their land. A very few tribes only are not yet obstinately in these dispositions. In order peaceably to counteract this policy of theirs and to provide an extension of territory which the rapid increase of our numbers will call for, two measures are deemed expedient. First. To encourage them to abandon hunting, to apply to the raising stock, to agriculture, and domestic manufacture, and thereby prove to themselves that less land and labor will maintain them in this better than in their former mode of living. The extensive forests necessary in the hunting life will then become useless, and they will see advantage in exchanging them for the means of improving their farms and of increasing their domestic comforts. Secondly. To multiply trading houses among them, and place within their reach those things which will contribute more to their domestic comfort than the possession of extensive but uncultivated wilds. Experience and reflection will develop to them the wisdom of exchanging what they can spare and we want for what we can spare and they want. In leading them thus to agriculture, to manufactures, and civilization; in bringing together their and our sentiments, and in preparing them ultimately to participate in the benefits of our Government, I trust and believe we are acting for their greatest good. * * *

I *Messages and Papers of the Presidents 1789–1897* 352 (James D. Richardson ed. 1899). See also Ronald Takaki, *Iron Cages* 61 (1979).

Notes and Questions

1. What assumptions does Jefferson make regarding Indians' desire for lands and goods as possessed by Whites? Are these assumptions informed at

all by knowledge of Indians' desires, or by expressions by them of what they wanted? Or do these assumptions merely justify what Jefferson and other Whites already wanted?

2.   Notice Jefferson's readiness to use force and seize the lands of any Indian tribe that resisted the advance of white settlements.

3.   To what extent should Indian sales of land be considered "voluntary" under the circumstances?

Jefferson viewed Indians and Blacks differently, and suggested that Indians were, or could be, equal to Whites and superior to Blacks. He wrote the following:

THOMAS JEFFERSON TO THE MARQUIS DE CHASTELLUX

(June 7, 1785).

* * *

I am safe in affirming, that the proofs of genius given by the Indians of North America, place them on a level with whites in the same uncultivated state. The North of Europe furnishes subjects enough for comparison with them, and for a proof of their equality. I have seen some thousands myself, and conversed much with them, and have found in them a masculine, sound understanding. * * * I believe the Indian, then, to be in body and mind equal to the white man. I have supposed the black man, in his present state, might not be so; but it would be hazardous to affirm, that, equally cultivated for a few generations, he would not become so.

Thomas Jefferson: Writings 801 (Merrill D. Peterson ed. 1984).

Notes and Questions

1.   Historian Ronald Takaki explains Jefferson's radically different conceptions of Indians and Blacks in terms of their differing relations to the process of production. Since black slaves did not own land, only their slave labor was needed for accumulation of wealth by Whites. Since Indians possessed desirable lands, and since they were not enslaved, only their lands, and not their labor, was needed. Thus Indians were conceived as unwelcome occupants who had to be displaced, bounded in reservations or removed to make room for white agriculture. See Takaki, *supra* at 62–63.

SECTION 3.   THE DEVELOPMENT OF FEDERAL INDIAN POLICY

The formation of treaties between the federal government and Indian nations, of federal statutes, and the concept of Indian reservations were "means of confining Indian occupancy and use of land to specific territory." Many treaties settled the acquisition of Indian lands. Treaties also "defined the nature of Indian tribes as governments relative to the other sovereigns in the United States—the federal government and the states." Getches, Wilkinson, & Williams, *Federal Indian Law* 83, 167 (3d ed. 1993). The federal government made treaties with many Indian tribes until 1871 when Congress declared that it would no longer enter treaties with Indian nations.

One early treaty, referred to *infra* in discussing the Cherokee cases, was the Treaty of Hopewell, of November 28, 1785, which attempted to settle persistent conflicts between the Cherokee nation and white settlers in Georgia who intruded upon the Cherokees' land and which grew directly out of George Washington's policy recommendations excerpted *supra*. The treaty was intended to "give peace to all the Cherokees, and receive them into the favour and protection of the United States of America." The treaty thus attempted to create federal protection for the Cherokees against hostile white intruders and against the state of Georgia, which insisted upon its sovereignty and refused to acknowledge superior federal sovereignty. The provisions of the treaty settled the boundary separating the Cherokees from others, called for an exchange of prisoners, withdrew federal protection from non-Indian settlers who entered or remained on Cherokee lands, and acknowledged "the Cherokees to be under the protection of the United States of America, and of no other sovereign whatsoever." See 7 Stat. 18–21 (1785). The treaty did not succeed in creating peace, however, because of repeated incursions by intruders into Cherokee territory and because of the difficulty encountered by the federal government in enforcing its provisions. See Francis Paul Prucha, *American Indian Treaties: The History of a Political Anomaly* 59–66 (1994).

After ratification of the Constitution, Congress and the federal government had two principal sources of power which enabled the enactment of treaties and statutes regulating the Indian tribes. The Treaty power, Art. II, § 2, Cl. 2, provided that the President "shall have Power, by and with the Advice and Consent of the Senate, to make Treaties." And among the enumerated powers of Congress, the Indian Commerce Clause, Art. I, § 8, Cl. 3, empowered Congress to "regulate Commerce * * * with the Indian Tribes." Pursuant to this power, Congress enacted statutes regulating trade with Indians. Among the most important statutes which defined the relationship between Indian sovereignty and the federal government were the several Indian Trade and Intercourse Acts of 1790–1834.

FRANCIS PAUL PRUCHA

American Indian Policy in the Formative Years: The
Indian Trade and Intercourse Acts, 1790–1834
1–3 (1962).*

The basic Indian policy of the United States was formulated during the first decades of our national existence, as the federal government sought solutions to the problems caused by the presence of the Indians. * * *

The immediate difficulty facing the United States after the Revolution was the establishment of peace with the tribes, who had been allies of the British, but there were also other basic problems: determining the precise authority of the states and of the national government in managing Indian affairs, extinguishing in an orderly way the Indian title to the land so that the expanding settlements might find unencumbered room, restraining aggressive frontiersmen from encroaching upon country still claimed by the Indians, regulating the contacts between the two races that grew out of trade, providing adequate means to protect the rights of the red man, and fulfilling the responsibility that the Christian whites had to aid the savage pagans along the path toward civilization.

For the management of these Indian affairs the United States by the 1830s had determined a set of principles which became the standard base lines of American Indian policy. The fundamental elements of the federal program were the following:

(1) Protection of Indian rights to their land by setting definite boundaries for the Indian Country, restricting the whites from entering the area except under certain controls, and removing illegal intruders.

(2) Control of the disposition of Indian lands by denying the right of private individuals or local governments to acquire land from the Indians by purchase or by any other means.

(3) Regulation of the Indian trade by determining the conditions under which individuals might engage in the trade, prohibiting certain classes of traders, and actually entering into the trade itself.

(4) Control of the liquor traffic by regulating the flow of intoxicating liquor into the Indian Country and then prohibiting it altogether.

(5) Provision for the punishment of crimes committed by members of one race against the other and compensation for damages suffered by one group at the hands of the other, in order to remove the occasions for private retaliation which led to frontier hostilities.

(6) Promotion of civilization and education among the Indians, in the hope that they might be absorbed into the general stream of American society.

This Indian policy of the government was expressed in the formal treaties made with the Indian tribes, but it took shape primarily in a series of federal laws "to regulate trade and intercourse with the Indian tribes, and to preserve peace on the frontier." The first of these laws was passed in 1790, the final and enduring one in 1834. In them appeared the legislative statement of the decisions made by the United States as it was feeling its way toward satisfactory solutions to the problems resulting from the presence of uncultured tribesmen in the path of aggressive and land-hungry whites. * * *

The goal of American statesmen was the orderly advance of the frontier. To maintain the desired order and tranquility it was necessary to place restrictions on the contacts between the whites and the Indians. The intercourse acts were thus restrictive and prohibitory in nature— aimed largely at restraining the actions of the whites and providing justice to the Indians as the means of preventing hostility. But if the goal was an *orderly* advance, it was nevertheless *advance* of the frontier, and in the process of reconciling the two elements, conflict and injustice were often the result.

The policy that the United States set forth in the Indian intercourse acts was not the total expression of American attitudes toward the Indians. Behind the laws on the statute books there were deep-running and divergent currents of thought about the character of the Indian and his rights. One of these currents was represented by official government policy; it found expression in the laws passed by Congress, which in large part followed the recommendations and reports of the presidents, the secretaries of war, and other executive officials, in the directives and regulations issued by the War Department and in the decisions of the courts. The other was the frontiersmen's position, a popular attitude of hostility toward the red man, which spurred the ruthless drive against the Indians and made it impossible for the government to carry out its policy with anything like complete effect. The full history of Indian relations in the United States is the history of the interaction of these two currents. * * *

Notes and Questions

1. Consider how Washington's and Jefferson's attitudes towards Indians are reflected in legislative and policy initiatives such as the Trade and Intercourse Acts.

SECTION 4. INDIAN REMOVAL

As seen in his letter to William Henry Harrison, *supra,* President Jefferson was among the first prominent leaders to suggest removal of Indians "beyond the Mississippi." After the Louisiana Purchase in 1803, the possibility of Indian removal west of the Mississippi was much more realistic and was soon embraced by President Andrew Jackson. A veteran of combat against the Indians prior to his election as President, Jackson was predisposed to favor the prerogatives of white citizens and the States containing Indians. Jackson clearly expresses his support for Indian removal in the following message to the Senate in 1829.

PRESIDENT ANDREW JACKSON

First Annual Message to Congress
December 8, 1829.

* * *

The condition and ulterior destiny of the Indian tribes within the limits of some of our States have become objects of much interest and importance. It has long been the policy of Government to introduce among them the arts of civilization, in the hope of gradually reclaiming them from a wandering life. This policy has, however, been coupled with another wholly incompatible with its success. Professing a desire to civilize and settle them, we have at the same time lost no opportunity to purchase their lands and thrust them farther into the wilderness. By this means they have not only been kept in a wandering state, but been led to look upon us as unjust and indifferent to their fate. Thus, though lavish in its expenditures upon the subject, Government has constantly defeated its own policy, and the Indians in general, receding farther and farther to the west, have retained their savage habits. A portion, however, of the Southern tribes, having mingled much with the whites and made some progress in the arts of civilized life, have lately attempted to erect an independent government within the limits of Georgia and Alabama. These States, claiming to be the only sovereigns within their territories, extended their laws over the Indians, which induced the latter to call upon United States for protection.

Under these circumstances the question presented was whether the General Government had a right to sustain those people in their pretensions. The Constitution declares that "no new State shall be formed or erected within the jurisdiction of any other State" without the consent of its legislature. If the General Government is not permitted to tolerate the erection of a confederate State within the territory of one of the members of this Union against her consent, much less could it allow a foreign and independent government to establish itself there. Georgia became a member of the Confederacy which eventuated in our Federal Union as a sovereign State, always asserting her claim to certain limits, which, having been originally defined in her colonial charter and subsequently recognized in the treaty of peace, she has ever since continued to enjoy, except as they have been circumscribed by her own voluntary transfer of a portion of her territory to the United States in the articles of cession of 1802. * * *

Actuated by this view of the subject, I informed the Indians inhabiting parts of Georgia and Alabama that their attempt to establish an independent government would not be countenanced by the Executive of the United States, and advised them to emigrate beyond the Mississippi or submit to the laws of those States.

Our conduct toward these people is deeply interesting to our national character. Their present condition, contrasted with what they once were, makes a most powerful appeal to our sympathies. Our ancestors found them the uncontrolled possessors of these vast regions. By persuasion and force they have been made to retire from river to river and from mountain to mountain, until some of the tribes have become extinct and others have left but remnants to preserve for awhile their once terrible names. Surrounded by the whites with their arts of civilization, which by destroying the resources of the savage doom him to weakness and decay, the fate of the Mohegan, the Narragansett, and the Delaware is fast overtaking the Choctaw, the Cherokee, and the Creek. That this fate surely awaits them if they remain within the limits of the States does not admit of a doubt. Humanity and national honor demand that every effort should be made to avert so great a calamity. It is too late to inquire whether it was just in the United States to include them and their territory within the bounds of new States, whose limits they could control. That step cannot be retraced. A State can not be dismembered by Congress or restricted in the exercise of her constitutional power. But the people of those States and of every State, actuated by feelings of justice and a regard for our national honor, submit to you the interesting questions whether something can not be done, consistently with the rights of the States, to preserve this much-injured race.

As a means for effecting this end I suggest for your consideration the propriety of setting apart an ample district west of the Mississippi, and without the limits of any State or Territory now formed, to be guaranteed to the Indian tribes as long as they shall occupy it, each tribe having a distinct control over the portion designated for its use. * * *

This emigration should be voluntary, for it would be as cruel as unjust to compel the aboriginies to abandon the graves of their fathers and seek a home in a distant land. But they should be distinctly informed that if they remain within the limits of the States they must be subject to their laws. * * *

II *Messages and Papers of the Presidents 1789–1902* 456–59 (James D. Richardson ed. 1903).

Congress implemented Jackson's proposal with the Indian Removal Act of 1830:

INDIAN REMOVAL ACT
4 Stat. 411–12 (May 28, 1830).

An Act to provide for an exchange of lands with the Indians residing in any of the states or territories, and for their removal west of the river Mississippi.

*Be it enacted * * *,* That it shall and may be lawful for the President of the United States to cause so much of any territory belonging to the United States, west of the river Mississippi, not included in any state or organized territory, and to which the Indian title has been extinguished, as he may judge necessary, to be divided into a suitable number of districts, for the reception of such tribes or nations of Indians as may choose to exchange the lands where they now reside and remove there * * *.

Sec. 2. * * * [I]t shall and may be lawful for the President to exchange any or all of such districts, so to be laid off and described, with any tribe or nation of Indians now residing within the limits of any of the states or territories, and with which the United States have existing treaties, for the whole or any part or portion of the territory claimed and occupied by such tribe or nation, within the bounds of any one or more of the states or territories, where the land claimed and occupied by the Indians, is owned by the United States, or the United States are bound to the state within which it lies to extinguish the Indian claim thereto.

Sec. 3 * * * [I]t shall and may be lawful for the President solemnly to assure the tribe or nation with which the exchange is made, that the United States will forever secure and guaranty to them, and their heirs or successors, the country so exchanged with them; * * * *Provided always*, That such lands shall revert to the United States, if the Indians become extinct, or abandon the same.

* * *

Notes and Questions

1.   Notice Jackson's sympathy for the positions of Georgia with respect to state sovereignty and law being enforceable even on the lands of the Cherokee. Jackson's *Message to Congress* anticipates his apparent refusal to enforce the Supreme Court's decision in *Worcester v. Georgia, infra.*

2.   Note that Jackson shares certain assumptions with the earlier generation of white policymakers on Indian rights such as Washington and Jefferson. What are some of the shared assumptions about the Indian people and their rights?

3.   How different was Indian removal from the "ethnic cleansing" in Bosnia, Kosovo, and other parts of former Yugoslavia? How do you explain the United States's very different roles in these removals of undesired peoples?

———

Several justifications were offered for the removal of Indians from the Southeast to west of the Mississippi. Indians were regarded as unassimilable and incompatible with the white people settling the eastern states. Indians were deemed an inferior and savage race by politicians and the settlers. White settlers coveted the desirable lands possessed by the Indians prior to their removal. In addition, as President Jackson mentioned in his message, states objected to the presence of Indian nations with even limited sovereignty within their borders. This limited Indian sovereignty meant that Indians, while subject to federal law, were not subject to the laws of any state within which their nations were located. Even advocates of Indian welfare came to support the removal policy as a way of guaranteeing the survival of the Indians and time for their more gradual "civilization." "The promoters of the program argued with great sincerity that only if the Indians were removed beyond contact with Whites could the slow process of education, civilization, and Christianization take place. Insofar as removal was necessary to safeguard the Indian, to that extent the intercourse acts had failed." Francis Paul Prucha, *American Indian Policy in the Formative Years: Indian Trade and Intercourse Acts, 1790–1834* 225 (1962). It is important to recognize that although removal is usually associated just with the forced migration of the "Five Civilized Tribes," the Cherokees, Choctaws, Creeks, Chickasaws, and Seminoles, from the Southeast to Indian territory in Oklahoma, many more Indians nations were affected. "[T]he practice of transferring tribes from ancestral lands to reservations in other areas was far more widespread: removals occurred in most parts of the country during the entire 19th Century." Getches, Wilkinson, & Williams, *supra* at 154.

SECTION 5.   THE CHEROKEE CASES

The Cherokees were one of the "Southern tribes" that intermingled extensively with southern Whites and actively sought to assimilate and become a part of white society. They succeeded to a remarkable degree, well described by William McLoughlin:

[The Cherokees] were the test case for a major re-examination of the "Indian question." They were the prime example of how far a tribe of heathen hunters could progress under benevolent guidance within one generation. Their nation contained more mission churches, more schools, more farms, more Christians than any other. They had the most stable and republican form of government. They were the most prosperous and economically self-sufficient. If one needed proof of the potential of the Indian to become a white American in everything but the color of his skin, the Cherokees provided it. For the people of Georgia, the Cherokees were a test case precisely because they were so successful.

William G. McLoughlin, *Cherokees and Missionaries, 1789–1839* 245 (1995).

RENNARD STRICKLAND

Fire and the Spirit—Cherokee Law from Clan to Court
65–67 (1975).*

* * *

The euphoria resulting from the adoption of the Cherokee Constitution of 1827 was perhaps best shown in an editorial in the *New York Observer,* which noted that "their laws . . ., if we judge from what we have seen, are superior to the wisdom of Lycurgus or Solon." The adoption of a written constitution seemed the ultimate step in civilization. The Cherokee Constitution was copied in most respects from the Constitution of the United States. The Preamble, for example, began: "We, the Representatives of the people of the Cherokee Nation, in Convention assembled, in order to establish justice, ensure tranquility, promote our common welfare, and secure to ourselves and our prosterity [*sic*] the blessings of liberty."

The document created three branches of government and enumerated their powers. The dual legislative bodies of national committee and national council were retained with a provision for joint sessions. The executive power was entrusted to the principal chief, assistant principal chief, treasurer, and national marshal. A three-member council, appointed by the legislative committee and council, was to advise and meet with the chiefs. The judicial system was not significantly modified.

Personal liberties and safeguards were borrowed from the United States Constitution. Yet surely the most important provisions, from the standpoint of the laws of the Cherokees, were those which were not a part of the United States Constitution. Absolutely essential to the maintenance of the Cherokee Nation were the restrictions making all land the "common property of the Nation." * * *

The Cherokee Constitutional Convention was called by a resolution of the committee and council in October, 1826, and met in July of 1827. Much fanfare attended the adoption of the new articles of government, but the constitution was, in effect, stillborn. During much of the next decade the Cherokees fought to retain the constitution while living under control of the Georgia militia and the martial law of the United States Army. Yet all the while the Cherokee Nation proclaimed that its constitution remained its supreme law.

The discovery of gold on Cherokee land coincided almost exactly with the Constitutional Convention. While the Cherokees viewed the formation of the constitutional government as an important step in the preservation of their tribal lands, ironically it was the very success of the Cherokees in adopting a constitution and written code which convinced the "land hungry Georgians" of the necessity of Indian removal. Therefore, in 1828 the Georgia legislature prevented the Cherokees, whose land was within the boundaries of the state of Georgia, from acting as an independent government and extended state laws into the Indian country.

The struggle between the Cherokees and Georgia was climaxed in 1838 by the forcible removal of more than 16,000 Cherokees over a Trail of Tears to what became the state of Oklahoma. The years between 1828 and 1838 were years of chaos in which the Cherokees fought to retain tribal land and law. John Marshall's decisions in *Cherokee Nation v. Georgia* and *Worcester v. Georgia* provided disappointment and then hope, but ultimately it became clear that Marshall might make the law but Jackson enforced the law.

* * *

————

The conflict between Georgia and the Cherokees and other Indians had a long history. In 1802 Georgia and the federal government signed an agreement in which Georgia agreed to cede its claims to Western lands, which eventually became the states of Mississippi and Alabama. In exchange, the federal government agreed that "the United States shall, at their own Expense, extinguish for the Use of Georgia, as early as the same can be peacably obtained on reasonable terms * * * the indian Title to all the other Lands within the State of Georgia." See V *The Territorial Papers of the United States* 142–46 (Clarence E. Carter ed. 1937). Georgia thus had a basis for asserting its sovereignty and denying Indian sovereignty within the limits of the state. The compact between Georgia and the federal government also foreshadows the removal of the Cherokee from the state. See Francis Paul Prucha, *American Indian Treaties* 156–82 (1994); Getches, Wilkinson & Williams, *supra* at 122.

In 1828 the Georgia legislature passed laws making the Cherokee nation subject to its state law and sovereignty. The clash between Georgia and the Cherokees led to landmark litigation in the Supreme Court in the cases of *Cherokee Nation v. Georgia* and *Worcester v. Georgia*. Consider the following excerpts:

CHEROKEE NATION v. GEORGIA

30 U.S. (5 Pet.) 1 (1831).

CHIEF JUSTICE MARSHALL delivered the opinion of the Court.

This bill is brought by the Cherokee nation, praying an injunction to restrain the state of Georgia from the execution of certain laws of that state, which, as is alleged, go directly to annihilate the Cherokees as a political society, and to seize, for the use of Georgia, the lands of the nation which have been assured to them by the United States in solemn treaties repeatedly made and still in force.

If courts were permitted to indulge their sympathies, a case better calculated to excite them can scarcely be imagined. A people once numerous, powerful, and truly independent, found by our ancestors in the quiet and uncontrolled possession of an ample domain, gradually sinking beneath our superior policy, our arts and our arms, have yielded their lands by successive treaties, each of which contains a solemn guarantee of the residue, until they retain no more of their formerly extensive territory than is deemed necessary to their comfortable subsistence. To preserve this remnant, the present application is made.

Before we can look into the merits of the case, a preliminary inquiry presents itself. Has this court jurisdiction of the cause?

The third article of the constitution describes the extent of the judicial power. The second section closes an enumeration of the cases to which it is extended, with "controversies" "between a state or the citizens thereof, and foreign states, citizens, or subjects." A subsequent clause of the same section gives the supreme court original jurisdiction in all cases in which a state shall be a party. The party defendant may then unquestionably be sued in this court. May the plaintiff sue in it? Is the Cherokee nation a foreign state in the sense in which that term is used in the constitution?

The counsel for the plaintiffs have maintained the affirmative of this proposition with great earnestness and ability. So much of the argument as was intended to prove the character of the Cherokees as a state, as a distinct political society, separated from others, capable of managing its own affairs and governing itself, has, in the opinion of a majority of the judges, been completely successful. They have been uniformly treated as a state from the settlement of our country. The numerous treaties made with them by the United States recognize them as a people capable of maintaining the relations of peace and war, of being responsible in their political character for any violation of their engagements, or for any aggression committed on the citizens of the United States by any individual of their community. Laws have been enacted in the spirit of these treaties. The acts of our government plainly recognize the Cherokee nation as a state, and the courts are bound by those acts.

A question of much more difficulty remains. Do the Cherokees constitute a foreign state in the sense of the constitution?

The counsel have shown conclusively that they are not a state of the union, and have insisted that individually they are aliens, not owing allegiance to the United States. An aggregate of aliens composing a state must, they say, be a foreign state. Each individual being foreign, the whole must be foreign.

This argument is imposing, but we must examine it more closely before we yield to it. The condition of the Indians in relation to the United States is perhaps unlike that of any other two people in existence. In the general, nations not owing a common allegiance are foreign to each other. The term foreign nation is, with strict propriety, applicable by either to the other. But the relation of the Indians to the United States is marked by peculiar and cardinal distinctions which exist no where else.

     * * *

Though the Indians are acknowledged to have an unquestionable, and, heretofore, unquestioned right to the lands they occupy, until that right shall be extinguished by a voluntary cession to our government; yet it may well be doubted whether those tribes which reside within the acknowledged boundaries of the United States can, with strict accuracy, be denominated foreign nations. They may, more correctly, perhaps, be denominated domestic dependent nations. They occupy a territory to which we assert a title independent of their will, which must take effect in point of possession when their right of possession ceases. Meanwhile they are in a state of pupilage. Their relation to the United States resembles that of a ward to his guardian.

They look to our government for protection; rely upon its kindness and its power; appeal to it for relief to their wants; and address the president as their great father. They and their country are considered by foreign nations, as well as by ourselves, as being so completely under the sovereignty and dominion of the United States, that any attempt to acquire their lands, or to form a political connexion with them, would be considered by all as an invasion of our territory, and an act of hostility.

These considerations go far to support the opinion, that the framers of our constitution had not the Indian tribes in view, when they opened the courts of the union to controversies between a state or the citizens thereof, and foreign states.

     * * *

* * * [T]he peculiar relations between the United States and the Indians occupying our territory are such, that we should feel much difficulty in considering them as designated by the term *foreign state*, were there no other part of the constitution which might shed light on the meaning of these words. But we think that in construing them, considerable aid is furnished by that clause in the eighth section of the third article; which empowers congress to "regulate commerce with foreign nations, and among the several states, and with the Indian tribes."

In this clause they are as clearly contradistinguished by a name appropriate to themselves, from foreign nations, as from the several states composing the union. They are designated by a distinct appellation; and as this appellation can be applied to neither of the others, neither can the appellation distinguishing either of the others be in fair construction applied to them. The objects, to which the power of regulating commerce might be directed, are divided into three distinct classes— foreign nations, the several states, and Indian tribes. When forming this article, the convention considered them as entirely distinct. * * *

* * * We perceive plainly that the constitution in this article does not comprehend Indian tribes in the general term "foreign nations;" not we presume because a tribe may not be a nation, but because it is not foreign to the United States. When, afterwards, the term "foreign state" is introduced, we cannot impute to the convention the intention to desert its former meaning, and to comprehend Indian tribes within it, unless the context force that construction on us. We find nothing in the context, and nothing in the subject of the article, which leads to it.

The court has bestowed its best attention on this question, and, after mature deliberation, the majority is of opinion that an Indian tribe or nation within the United States is not a foreign state in the sense of the constitution, and cannot maintain an action in the courts of the United States.

* * *

If it be true that the Cherokee nation have rights, this is not the tribunal in which those rights are to be asserted. If it be true that wrongs have been inflicted, and that still greater are to be apprehended, this is not the tribunal which can redress the past or prevent the future.

MR. JUSTICE JOHNSON [concurring:]

* * *

I cannot but think that there are strong reasons for doubting the applicability of the epithet state, to a people so low in the grade of organized society as our Indian tribes most generally are. I would not here be understood as speaking of the Cherokees under their present form of government; which certainly must be classed among the most approved forms of civil government. Whether it can be yet said to have received the consistency which entitles that people to admission into the family of nations is, I conceive, yet to be determined by the executive of these states. Until then I must think that we cannot recognize it as an existing state, under any other character than that which it has maintained hitherto as one of the Indian tribes or nations.

* * *

In the very treaty of Hopewell, the language or evidence of which is appealed to as the leading proof of the existence of this supposed state, we find the commissioners of the United States expressing themselves in these terms. "The commissioners plenipotentiary of the United States give peace to all the Cherokees, and receive them into the favour and protection of the United States on the following conditions." This is certainly the language of sovereigns and conquerors, and not the address of equals to equals. And again, when designating the country they are to be confined to, comprising the very territory which is the subject of this bill, they say, "Art. 4. The boundary allotted to the Cherokees for their hunting grounds" shall be as therein described. Certainly this is the language of concession on our part, not theirs; and when the full bearing and effect of those words, "for their hunting grounds," is considered, it is difficult to think that they were then regarded as a state, or even intended to be so regarded. It is clear that it was intended to give them no other rights over the territory than what were needed by a race of hunters; and it is not easy to see how their advancement beyond that state of society could ever have been promoted, or, perhaps, permitted, consistently with the unquestioned rights of the states, or United States, over the territory within their limits. * * *

But it is said, that we have extended to them the means and inducement to become agricultural and civilized. It is true: and the immediate object of that policy was so obvious as probably to have intercepted the view of ulterior consequences. Independently of the general influence of humanity, these people were restless, warlike, and signally cruel in their irruptions during the revolution. The policy, therefore, of enticing them to the arts of peace, and to those improvements which war might lay desolate, was obvious; and it was wise to prepare them for what was probably then contemplated, to wit, to incorporate them in time into our respective governments: a policy which their inveterate habits and deep seated enmity has altogether baffled. But the project of ultimately organizing them into states, within the limits of those states which had not ceded or should not cede to the United States the jurisdiction over the Indian territory within their bounds, could not possibly have entered into the contemplation of our government. Nothing but express authority from the states could have justified such a policy, pursued with such a view.

* * *

There is one consequence that would necessarily flow from the recognition of this people as a state, which of itself must operate greatly against its admission.

Where is the rule to stop? Must every petty kraal of Indians, designating themselves a tribe or nation, and having a few hundred acres of land to hunt on exclusively, be recognized as a state? We should indeed force into the family of nations, a very numerous and very heterogeneous progeny. * * *

[B]y what attributes is the Cherokee nation identified with other states?

The right of sovereignty was expressly assumed by Great Britain over their country at the first taking possession of it; and has never since been recognized as in them, otherwise than as dependent upon the will of a superior.

The right of legislation is in terms conceded to congress by the treaty of Hopewell, whenever they choose to exercise it. And the right of soil is held by the feeble tenure of hunting grounds, and acknowledged on all hands subject to a restriction to sell to no one but the United States, and for no use but that of Georgia.

They have in Europe sovereign and demi-sovereign states and states of doubtful sovereignty. But this state, if it be a state, is still a grade below them all: for not to be able to alienate without permission of the remainder-man or lord, places them in a state of feudal dependence.

However, I will enlarge no more upon this point; because I believe, in one view and in one only, if at all, they are or may be deemed a state, though not a sovereign state, at least while they occupy a country within our limits. Their condition is something like that of the Israelites, when inhabiting the deserts. Though without land that they can call theirs in the sense of property, their right of personal self government has never been taken from them; and such a form of government may exist though the land occupied be in fact that of another. The right to expel them may exist in that other, but the alternative of departing and retaining the right of self government may exist in them. And such they certainly do possess; it has never been questioned, nor any attempt made at subjugating them as a people, or restraining their personal liberty except as to their land and trade.

But in no sense can they be deemed a foreign state, under the judiciary article. * * *

The argument is that they were states; and if not states of the union, must be foreign states. But I think it very clear that the constitution neither speaks of them as states or foreign states, but as just what they were, Indian tribes; an anomaly unknown to the books that treat of states, and which the law of nations would regard as nothing more than wandering hordes, held together only by ties of blood and habit, and having neither laws or government, beyond what is required in a savage state. The distinction is clearly made in that section which vests in congress power to regulate commerce between the United States with foreign nations and the Indian tribes.

* * *

Mr. Justice Baldwin [concurring:]

* * *

In my opinion there is no plaintiff in this suit; and this opinion precludes any examination into the merits of the bill, or the weight of any minor objections. * * *

* * *

My view of the plaintiffs being a sovereign independent nation or foreign state, within the meaning of the constitution, applies to all the tribes with whom the United States have held treaties: for if one is a foreign nation or state, all others in like condition must be so in their aggregate capacity; and each of their subjects or citizens, aliens, capable of suing in the circuit courts. This case then is the case of the countless tribes, who occupy tracts of our vast domain; who, in their collective and individual characters, as states or aliens, will rush to the federal courts in endless controversies, growing out of the laws of the states or of congress. * * *

* * * It is clear then, that neither the old or new government did ever consider Indian affairs, the regulation of our intercourse or treaties

with them, as forming any part of our foreign affairs or concerns with foreign nations, states, or princes.

* * *

[The Treaty of Hopewell] is in the beginning called "Article:" the word "treaty" is only to be found in the concluding line, where it is called "this definitive treaty." But article or treaty, its nature does not depend upon the name given it. It is not negotiated between ministers on both sides representing their nations; the stipulations are wholly inconsistent with sovereignty; the Indians acknowledge their dependent character; hold the lands they occupy as an allotment of hunting grounds; give to congress the exclusive right of regulating their trade and managing all their affairs as they may think proper. So it was understood by congress * * * and so understood at the adoption of the constitution.

* * *

* * * There can be no dependence so antinational, or so utterly subversive of national existence as transferring to a foreign government the regulation of its trade, and the management of all their affairs at their pleasure. The nation or state, tribe or village, head men or warriors of the Cherokees, call them by what name we please, call the articles they have signed a definitive treaty or an indenture of servitude; they are not by its force or virtue a foreign state capable of calling into legitimate action the judicial power of this union, by the exercise of the original jurisdiction of this court against a sovereign state, a component part of this nation. Unless the constitution has imparted to the Cherokees a national character never recognized under the confederation; and which if they ever enjoyed was surrendered by the treaty of Hopewell; they cannot be deemed in this court plaintiffs in such a case as this.

In considering the bearing of the constitution on their rights, it must be borne in mind, that a majority of the states represented in the convention had ceded to the United States the soil and jurisdiction of their western lands, or claimed it to be remaining in themselves; that congress asserted as to the ceded, and the states as to the unceded territory, their right to the soil absolutely and the dominion in full sovereignty, within their respective limits, subject only to Indian occupancy, not as foreign states or nations, but as dependent on and appendant to the state governments: that before the convention acted, congress had erected a government in the north western territory containing numerous and powerful nations or tribes of Indians, whose jurisdiction was continued and whose sovereignty was overturned, if it ever existed, except by permission of the states or congress, by ordaining that the territorial laws should extend over the whole district; and directing divisions for the execution of civil and criminal process in every part; that the Cherokees were then dependants, having given up all their affairs to the regulation and management of congress, and that all the regulations of congress, over Indian affairs were then in force over an immense territory, under a solemn pledge to the inhabitants, that whenever their population and circumstances would admit they should form constitutions and become free, sovereign and independent states on equal footing with the old component members of the confederation; that by the existing regulations and treaties, the Indian tenure to their lands was their allotment as hunting grounds without the power of alienation, that the right of occupancy was not individual * * *.

To correctly understand the constitution, then, we must read it with reference to this well known existing state of our relations with the Indians; the United States asserting the right of soil, sovereignty, and jurisdiction, in full dominion; the Indians occupant, of allotted hunting grounds.

* * *

MR. JUSTICE THOMPSON, dissenting.

* * *

That a state of this union may be sued by a foreign state, when a proper case exists and is presented, is too plainly and expressly declared in the constitution to admit of doubt; and the first inquiry is, whether the Cherokee nation is a foreign state within the sense and meaning of the constitution.

The terms state and nation are used in the law of nations, as well as in common parlance, as importing the same thing; and imply a body of men, united together, to procure their mutual safety and advantage by means of their union. Such a society has its affairs and interests to manage; it deliberates, and takes resolutions in common, and thus becomes a moral person, having an understanding and a will peculiar to itself, and is susceptible of obligations and laws. Nations being composed of men naturally free and independent, and who, before the establishment of civil societies, live together in the state of nature, nations or sovereign states; are to be considered as so many free persons, living together in a state of nature. Every nation that governs itself, under what form soever, without any dependence on a foreign power, is a sovereign state. Its rights are naturally the same as those of any other state. Such are moral persons who live together in a natural society, under the law of nations. It is sufficient if it be really sovereign and independent: that is, it must govern itself by its own authority and laws. We ought, therefore, to reckon in the number of sovereigns those states that have bound themselves to another more powerful, although by an unequal alliance. The conditions of these unequal alliances may be infinitely varied; but whatever they are, provided the inferior ally reserves to itself the sovereignty or the right to govern its own body, it ought to be considered an independent state. Consequently, a weak state, that, in order to provide for its safety, places itself under the protection of a more powerful one, without stripping itself of the right of government and sovereignty, does not cease on this account to be placed among the sovereigns who acknowledge no other power. Tributary and feudatory states do not thereby cease to be sovereign and independent states, so long as self government, and sovereign and independent authority is left in the administration of the state.

Testing the character and condition of the Cherokee Indians by these rules, it is not perceived how it is possible to escape the conclusion, that they form a sovereign state. They have always been dealt with as such by the government of the United States; both before and since the adoption of the present constitution. They have been admitted and treated as a people governed solely and exclusively by their own laws, usages, and customs within their own territory, claiming and exercising exclusive dominion over the same; yielding up by treaty, from time to time, portions of their land, but still claiming absolute sovereignty and self government over what remained unsold. And this has been the light in which they have, until recently, been considered from the earliest settlement of the country by the white people. And indeed, I do not understand it is denied by a majority of the court, that the Cherokee Indians form a sovereign state according to the doctrine of the law of nations; but that, although a sovereign state, they are not considered a foreign state within the meaning of the constitution. * * *

That numerous tribes of Indians, and among others the Cherokee nation, occupied many parts of this country long before the discovery by Europeans, is abundantly established by history; and it is not denied but that the Cherokee nation occupied the territory now claimed by them long before that period. * * *

       * * *

They have never been, by conquest, reduced to the situation of subjects to any conqueror, and thereby lost their separate national existence, and the rights of self government, and become subject to the laws of the conqueror. * * *

In this view of their situation, there is as full and complete recognition of their sovereignty, as if they were the absolute owners of the soil. The progress made in civilization by the Cherokee Indians cannot surely be considered as in any measure destroying their national or foreign character, so long as they are permitted to maintain a separate and distinct government; it is their political condition that constitutes their foreign character, and in that sense must the term foreign, be understood as used in the constitution. It can have no relation to local, geographical, or territorial position. It cannot mean a country beyond sea. Mexico or Canada is certainly to be considered a foreign country, in reference to the United States. It is the political relation in which one government or country stands to another, which constitutes it foreign to the other. The Cherokee territory being within the chartered limits of Georgia, does not affect the question. When Georgia is spoken of as a state, reference is had to its political character, and not to boundary; and it is not perceived that any absurdity or inconsistency grows out of the circumstance, that the jurisdiction and territory of the state of Georgia surround or extend on every side of the Cherokee territory. It may be inconvenient to the state, and very desirable, that the Cherokees should be removed; but it does not at all affect the political relation between Georgia and those Indians. Suppose the Cherokee territory had been occupied by Spaniards or any other civilized people, instead of Indians, and they had from time to time ceded to the United States portions of their lands precisely in the same manner as the Indians have done, and in like manner retained and occupied the part now held by the Cherokees, and having a regular government established there: would it not only be considered a separate and distinct nation or state, but a foreign nation, with reference to the state of Georgia or the United States. If we look to lexicographers, as well as approved writers, for the use of the term foreign, it may be applied with the strictest propriety to the Cherokee nation. * * *

Notes and Questions

1. Notice that while Chief Justice Marshall's opinion in *Cherokee Nation v. Georgia* is most often cited as the opinion of the Court, in fact it was just an opinion on behalf of only Marshall and one other justice. The Court was deeply divided as to the status of Indian "nations" and the meaning of Indian sovereignty. "The Court had seven members, and Justice Duvall was absent, leaving a 2–2–2 split: Marshall and McLean seeing tribes as 'domestic dependent nations'; Johnson and Baldwin viewing them as possessing no sovereignty at all; and Thompson and Story concluding that the Cherokee Nation was a foreign nation possessing sovereignty in the international sense." See Getches, Wilkinson & Williams, *supra*, at 137.

2. Consider the implications of the different views of Indian sovereignty as described in each of the opinions in *Cherokee Nation v. Georgia*.

———

Samuel A. Worcester and several other missionaries worked with the Cherokee and were convicted and sentenced to four years at hard labor for violating a Georgia state law that made it a crime for "all white persons" to reside on Cherokee lands without a license from the governor and without taking a prescribed oath. Worcester appealed his conviction to the Supreme Court.

WORCESTER v. GEORGIA

31 U.S. (6 Pet.) 515 (1832).

CHIEF JUSTICE MARSHALL, delivered the opinion of the Court.

* * *

The defendant is a state, a member of the union, which has exercised the powers of government over a people who deny its jurisdiction, and are under the protection of the United States.

The plaintiff is a citizen of the state of Vermont, condemned to hard labour for four years in the penitentiary of Georgia; under colour of an act which he alleges to be repugnant to the constitution, laws, and treaties of the United States.

The legislative power of a state, the controlling power of the constitution and laws of the United States, the rights, if they have any, the political existence of a once numerous and powerful people, the personal liberty of a citizen, are all involved in the subject now to be considered.

* * *

The indictment charges the plaintiff in error, and others, being white persons, with the offence of "residing within the limits of the

Cherokee nation without a license," and "without having taken the oath to support and defend the constitution and laws of the state of Georgia." * * *

The plea avers, that [Worcester's residence among the Cherokee], charged in the indictment, was under the authority of the president of the United States, and with the permission and approval of the Cherokee nation. That the treaties, subsisting between the United States, and the Cherokees, acknowledge their right as a sovereign nation to govern themselves and all persons who have settled within their territory, free from any right of legislative interference by the several states composing the United States of America. That the act under which the prosecution was instituted is repugnant to the said treaties, and is, therefore, unconstitutional and void. That the said act is, also, unconstitutional; because it interferes with, and attempts to regulate and control, the intercourse with the Cherokee nation, which belongs, exclusively, to congress; and, because, also, it is repugnant to the statute of the United States, entitled "an act to regulate trade and intercourse with the Indian tribes, and to preserve peace on the frontiers." * * *

The indictment and plea in this case draw in question, we think, the validity of the treaties made by the United States with the Cherokee Indians; if not so, their construction is certainly drawn in question; and the decision has been, if not against their validity, "against the right, privilege or exemption, specially set up and claimed under them." They also draw into question the validity of a statute of the state of Georgia, "on the ground of its being repugnant to the constitution, treaties and laws of the United States, and the decision is in favour of its validity." * * *

It has been said at the bar, that the acts of the legislature of Georgia seize on the whole Cherokee country, parcel it out among the neighbouring counties of the state, extend her code over the whole country, abolish its institutions and its laws, and annihilate its political existence.

If this be the general effect of the system, let us inquire into the effect of the particular statute and section on which the indictment is founded.

It enacts that "all white persons, residing within the limits of the Cherokee nation on the 1st day of March next, or at any time thereafter, without a license or permit from his excellency the governor, or from such agent as his excellency the governor shall authorise to grant such permit or license, and who shall not have taken the oath hereinafter required, shall be guilty of a high misdemeanour, and, upon conviction thereof, shall be punished by confinement to the penitentiary, at hard labour, for a term not less than four years." * * *

The extra-territorial power of every legislature being limited in its action, to its own citizens or subjects, the very passage of this act is an assertion of jurisdiction over the Cherokee nation, and of the rights and powers consequent on jurisdiction. * * *

But power, war, [and] conquest, give rights, which, after possession, are conceded by the world; and which can never be controverted by those on whom they descend. * * *

The charters [from the British crown to several states] contain passages showing one of their objects to be the civilization of the Indians, and their conversion to Christianity—objects to be accomplished by conciliatory conduct and good example; not by extermination. * * * Certain it is, that our history furnishes no example, from the first settlement of our country, of any attempt on the part of the crown to interfere with the internal affairs of the Indians, farther than to keep out the agents of foreign powers, who, as traders or otherwise, might seduce them into foreign alliances. The king purchased their lands when they were willing to sell, at a price they were willing to take; but never coerced a surrender of them. He also purchased their alliance and dependence by subsidies; but never intruded into the interior of their affairs, or interfered with their self government, so far as respected themselves only. * * *

During the war of the revolution, the Cherokees took part with the British. After its termination, the United States, though desirous of peace, did not feel its necessity so strongly as while the war continued. Their political situation being changed, they might very well think it advisable to assume a higher tone, and to impress on the Cherokees the same respect for congress which was before felt for the king of Great Britain. This may account for the language of the treaty of Hopewell. There is the more reason for supposing that the Cherokee chiefs were not very critical judges of the language, from the fact that every one makes his mark; no chief was capable of signing his name. It is probable the treaty was interpreted to them.

The treaty is introduced with the declaration, that "the commissioners plenipotentiary of the United States give peace to all the Cherokees, and receive them into the favour and protection of the United States of America, on the following conditions." * * *

The third article acknowledges the Cherokees to be under the protection of the United States of America, and of no other power.

This stipulation is found in Indian treaties, generally. It was introduced into their treaties with Great Britain; and may probably be found in those with other European powers. Its origin may be traced to the nature of their connexion with those powers; and its true meaning is discerned in their relative situation. * * *

The same stipulation entered into with the United States, is undoubtedly to be construed in the same manner. They receive the Cherokee nation into their favor and protection. The Cherokees acknowledge themselves to be under the protection of the United States, and of no other power. Protection does not imply the destruction of the protected. The manner in which this stipulation was understood by the American government, is explained by the language and acts of our first president. * * *

The ninth article is in these words: "for the benefit and comfort of the Indians, and for the prevention of injuries or oppressions on the part of the citizens or Indians, the United States, in congress assembled, shall have the sole and exclusive right of regulating the trade with the Indians, and managing all their affairs, as they think proper."

To construe the expression "managing all their affairs," into a surrender of self-government, would be, we think, a perversion of their necessary meaning, and a departure from the construction which has been uniformly put on them. The great subject of the article is the Indian trade. The influence it gave, made it desirable that congress should possess it. The commissioners brought forward the claim, with the profession that their motive was "the benefit and comfort of the Indians, and the prevention of injuries or oppressions." This may be true, as respects the regulation of their trade, and as respects the regulation of all affairs connected with their trade, but cannot be true, as respects the management of all their affairs. The most important of these, are the cession of their lands, and security against intruders on them. Is it credible, that they should have considered themselves surrendering to the United States the right to dictate their future cessions, and the terms on which they should be made? or to compel their submission to the violence of disorderly and licentious intruders? It is equally inconceivable that they could have supposed themselves, by a phrase thus slipped into an article, on another and most interesting subject, to have divested themselves of the right of self-government on subjects not connected with trade. Such a measure could not be "for their benefit and comfort," or for "the prevention of injuries and oppression." Such a construction would be inconsistent with the spirit of this and of all subsequent treaties; especially of those articles which recognise the right of the Cherokees to declare hostilities, and to make war. It would convert a treaty of peace covertly into an act, annihilating the political existence of one of the parties. Had such a result been intended, it would have been openly avowed. * * *

The treaty of Hopewell seems not to have established a solid peace. To accommodate the differences still existing between the state of Georgia and the Cherokee nation, the treaty of Holston was negotiated in July 1791. The existing constitution of the United States had been then adopted, and the government, having more intrinsic capacity to enforce its just claims, was perhaps less mindful of high sounding expressions, denoting superiority. We hear no more of giving peace to the Cherokees. The mutual desire of establishing permanent peace and friendship, and of removing all causes of war, is honestly avowed, and, in pursuance of this desire, the first article declares, that there shall be perpetual peace and friendship between all the citizens of the United States of America and all the individuals composing the Cherokee nation.

The second article repeats the important acknowledgement, that the Cherokee nation is under the protection of the United States of America, and of no other sovereign whosoever. * * *

From the commencement of our government, congress has passed acts to regulate trade and intercourse with the Indians; which treat them as nations, respect their rights, and manifest a firm purpose to afford that protection which treaties stipulate. All these acts, and especially that of 1802, which is still in force, manifestly consider the several Indian nations as distinct political communities, having territorial boundaries, within which their authority is exclusive, and having a right to all the lands within those boundaries, which is not only acknowledged, but guarantied by the United States. * * *

[The Civilization Fund Act of 1819, 3 Stat. 516 (1819)] avowedly contemplates the preservation of the Indian nations as an object sought by the United States, and proposes to effect this object by civilizing and converting them from hunters into agriculturists. Though the Cherokees had already made considerable progress in this improvement, it cannot be doubted that the general words of the act comprehend them. Their advance in the "habits and arts of civilization," rather encouraged perseverance in the laudable exertions still farther to meliorate their condition. This act furnishes strong additional evidence of a settled purpose to fix the Indians in their country by giving them security at home.

The treaties and laws of the United States contemplate the Indian territory as completely separated from that of the states; and provide that all intercourse with them shall be carried on exclusively by the government of the union. * * *

The Cherokee nation, then, is a distinct community occupying its own territory, with boundaries accurately described, in which the laws of Georgia can have no force, and which the citizens of Georgia have no right to enter, but with the assent of the Cherokees themselves, or in conformity with treaties, and with the acts of congress. The whole intercourse between the United States and this nation, is, by our constitution and laws, vested in the government of the United States. * * *

If the review which has been taken be correct, and we think it is, the acts of Georgia are repugnant to the constitution, laws, and treaties of the United States.

They interfere forcibly with the relations established between the United States and the Cherokee nation, the regulation of which, according to the settled principles of our constitution, are committed exclusively to the government of the union. * * *

MR. JUSTICE McLEAN, [concurring:]

If a tribe of Indians shall become so degraded or reduced in numbers, as to lose the power of self-government, the protection of the local law, of necessity, must be extended over them. * * *

The exercise of the power of self-government by the Indians, within a state, is undoubtedly contemplated to be temporary. This is shown by the settled policy of the government, in the extinguishment of their title, and especially by the compact with the state of Georgia. It is a question, not of abstract right, but of public policy. I do not mean to say, that the same moral rule which should regulate the affairs of private life, should not be regarded by communities or nations. But, a sound national policy does require that the Indian tribes within our states should exchange their territories, upon equitable principles, or, eventually, consent to become amalgamated in our political communities.

At best they can enjoy a very limited independence within the boundaries of a state, and such a residence must always subject them to encroachments from the settlements around them; and their existence within a state, as a separate and independent community, may seriously embarrass or obstruct the operation of the state laws. If, therefore, it would be inconsistent with the political welfare of the states, and the social advance of their citizens, that an independent and permanent power should exist within their limits, this power must give way to the greater power which surrounds it, or seek its exercise beyond the sphere of state authority. * * *

But, if it shall be the policy of the government to withdraw its protection from the Indians who reside within the limits of the respective states, and who not only claim the right of self government, but have uniformly exercised it; the laws and treaties which impose duties and obligations on the general government should be abrogated by the powers competent to do so. So long as those laws and treaties exist, having been formed within the sphere of the federal powers, they must be respected and enforced by the appropriate organs of the federal government. * * *

Notes and Questions

1. For an excellent study of the relationships between the Cherokee and Christian missionaries of various sects, including detailed discussion of the events surrounding *Worcester v. Georgia*, see William G. McLoughlin, *Cherokees and Missionaries 1789–1839* (1995).

2. Andrew Jackson stated, in his *First Annual Message to Congress*, *supra*, that States should be able to extend their sovereignty and their laws to govern Indian nations. Thus, despite the Supreme Court decision in *Worcester v. Georgia*, Jackson refused to enforce the decision and Georgia was able to ignore the decision.

3. The Court's decision generated a constitutional crisis. The Supreme Court had declared Georgia's law null and void. Yet the State, which had refused to appear in the Supreme Court proceedings, refused to comply with the Court's decision. Samuel Worcester, who had won the case, remained in prison under the void Georgia law. Felix S. Cohen, *Handbook of Federal Indian Law* 123 (1945). Because of procedural difficulties, a Court order directing federal marshals to release Worcester could not be obtained until the Court's next session in 1833. Ultimately, Worcester and Elizur Butler, who had been imprisoned with him, refused to pursue further legal action and accepted pardons, which ended the legal proceedings in the case. See Getches, Wilkinson, & Williams, *Federal Indian Law* at 149. McLoughlin, *supra*, at 297–99.

4. Unlike *Marbury v. Madison*, which only threatened a constitutional crisis, this case presented the actual refusal of a state, with presidential support, to comply with a Supreme Court decision. What do these events

teach about the Supreme Court's power? *Worcester v. Georgia* is not taught routinely in classes and casebooks on constitutional law. Should it be?

SECTION 6. THE ALLOTMENT POLICY AND THE AMERICANIZATION OF THE INDIAN

After the period of removal, many Indians lived on reservations located west of the Mississippi river. Before 1850, almost all Indian land was held communally by all members of a tribe or nation. During the 1870s, Congress began increasing its control over Indian life for the purposes of ending the unique political status of Indian nations and absorbing Indians into the mainstream of American life. "[S]entiment against treaty making had been steadily growing in the United States. There was a deepening appreciation of the anomaly, a conviction that the Indian tribes no longer possessed the attributes of sovereign nations necessary to make new treaties between themselves and the United States reasonable and acceptable contracts." Francis Paul Prucha, *American Indian Treaties* 289 (1994).

Congress decided to end future treaty-making unilaterally. In the Indian Appropriations Act of 1871, Congress provided that "hereafter no Indian nation or tribe within the territory of the United States shall be acknowledged or recognized as an independent nation, tribe, or power with whom the United States may contract by treaty: *Provided, further,* That nothing herein contained shall be construed to invalidate or impair the obligation of any treaty heretofore lawfully made and ratified with any such Indian nation or tribe * * *." 16 Stat. 566 (1871). For a discussion of the legislative history of this statute see Prucha, *American Indian Treaties* at 289–310.

As Congress sought to expand its power over Indian nations, the Supreme Court issued its landmark decision in the case of *Ex Parte Crow Dog. Crow Dog* stands as one of the Supreme Court's strongest affirmations of tribal sovereignty.

EX PARTE CROW DOG

109 U.S. 556 (1883).

Justice Matthews delivered the opinion of the court.

The petitioner is in the custody of the marshal of the United States for the territory of Dakota, imprisoned in the jail of Lawrence county, in the first judicial district of that territory, under sentence of death, adjudged against him by the district court for that district, to be carried into execution January 14, 1884. That judgment was rendered upon a conviction for the murder of an Indian of the Brule Sioux band of the Sioux nation of Indians, by the name of Sin-ta-ge-le-Scka, or in English, Spotted Tail, the prisoner also being an Indian of the same band and nation, and the homicide having occurred, as alleged in the indictment, in the Indian country, within a place and district of country under the exclusive jurisdiction of the United States and within the said judicial district. The judgment was affirmed on a writ of error, by the supreme court of the territory. It is claimed on behalf of the prisoner that the crime charged against him, and of which he stands convicted, is not an offense under the laws of the United States; that the district court had no jurisdiction to try him, and that its judgment and sentence are void. It therefore prays for a writ of habeas corpus, that he may be delivered from an imprisonment which he asserts to be illegal.

The indictment is framed upon section 5339 of the Revised Statutes. That section is found in title 70, on the subject of crimes against the United States, and in chapter 3, which treats of crimes arising within the maritime and territorial jurisdiction of the United States. It provides that "every person who commits murder, * * * within any fort, arsenal, dock-yard, magazine, or in any other place or district of country under the exclusive jurisdiction of the United States, * * * shall suffer death."

Title 28 of the Revised Statutes relates to Indians, and the sub-title of chapter 4 is, "Government of Indian Country." It embraces many provisions regulating the subject of intercourse and trade with the Indians in the Indian country, and imposes penalties and punishments for various violations of them. * * * The next two sections [of Title 28] are as follows:

Sec. 2145. Except as to crimes, the punishment of which is expressly provided for in this title, the general laws of the United States as to the punishment of crimes committed in any place within the sole and exclusive jurisdiction of the United States, except the District of Columbia, shall extend to the Indian country.

Sec. 2146. The preceding section shall not be construed to extend to [crimes committed by one Indian against the person or property of another Indian, nor to] any Indian committing any offense in the Indian country who has been punished by the local law of the tribe, or to any case where by treaty stipulations the exclusive jurisdiction over such offenses is or may be secured to the Indian tribes respectively.

* * *

The argument in support of the jurisdiction and conviction is, that the exception contained in section 2146 is repealed by the operation and legal effect of the treaty with the different tribes of the Sioux Indians of April 29, 1868 (15 St. 635) and an act of congress, approved February 28, 1877, to ratify an agreement with certain bands of the Sioux Indians.

The following provisions of the treaty of 1868 are relied on:

"Article 1. From this time forward all war between the parties to this agreement shall forever cease. The government of the United States desires peace, and its honor is hereby pledged to keep it. The Indians desire peace, and they now pledge their honor to maintain it.

"If bad men among the whites, or among other people subject to the authority of the United States, shall commit any wrong upon the person or property of the Indians, the United States will, upon proof made to the agent and forwarded to the commissioner of Indian affairs at Washington city, proceed at once to cause the offender to be arrested and punished according to the laws of the United States, and also reimburse the injured person for the loss sustained.

"If bad men among the Indians shall commit a wrong or depredation upon the person or property of any one, white, black, or Indian, subject to the authority of the United States and at peace therewith, the Indians herein named solemnly agree that they will, upon proof made to their agent and notice by him, deliver up the wrong-doer to the United States, to be tried and punished according to its laws. And in case they wilfully refuse so to do, the person injured shall be reimbursed for his loss from the annuities or other moneys due or to become due to them under this or other treaties made with the United States. * * *"

* * *

But it is quite clear from the context that this does not cover the present case of an alleged wrong committed by one Indian upon the person of another of the same tribe. The provision must be construed with its counterpart, just preceding it, which provides for the punishment by the United States of any bad men among the whites, or among other people subject to their authority, who shall commit any wrong upon the person or property of the Indians. Here are two parties, among whom, respectively, there may be individuals guilty of a wrong against one of the other—one is the party of whites and their allies, the other is the tribe of Indians with whom the treaty is made. In each case the guilty party is to be tried and punished by the United States, and in case the offender is one of the Indians who are parties to the treaty, the agreement is that he shall be delivered up. In case of refusal, deduction is to be made from the annuities payable to the tribe, for compensation to the injured person, a provision which points quite distinctly to the conclusion that the injured person cannot himself be one of the same tribe. Similar provisions for the extradition of criminals are to be found in most of the treaties with Indian tribes, as far back, at least, as that concluded at Hopewell with the Cherokees.

The second of these provisions, that are supposed to justify the jurisdiction asserted in the present case, is the eighth article of the agreement, embodied in the act of 1877, in which it is declared:

"And congress shall, by appropriate legislation, secure to them an orderly government; they shall be subject to the laws of the United States, and each individual shall be protected in his rights of property, person, and life."

It is equally clear, in our opinion, that these words can have no such effect as that claimed for them. The pledge to secure to these people, with whom the United States was contracting as a distinct political body, an orderly government, by appropriate legislation thereafter to be framed and enacted, necessarily implies, having regard to all the circumstances attending the transaction, that among the arts of civilized life, which it was the very purpose of all these arrangements to introduce and naturalize among them, was the highest and best of all,—that of self-government, the regulation by themselves of their own domestic affairs, the maintenance of order and peace among their own members by the administration of their own laws and customs. They were nevertheless to be subject to the laws of the United States, not in the sense of citizens, but, as they had always been, as wards, subject to a guardian; not as individuals, constituted members of the political community of the United States, with a voice in the selection of representatives and the framing of the laws, but as a dependent community who were in a state of pupilage, advancing from the condition of a savage tribe to that of a people who, through the discipline of labor, and by education, it was hoped might become a self-supporting and self-governed society. The laws to which they were declared to be subject were the laws then existing, and which applied to them as Indians, and, of course, included the very statute under consideration, which excepted from the operation of the general laws of the United States, otherwise applicable, the very case of the prisoner. * * * The expressions contained in these clauses must be taken in connection with the entire scheme of the agreement as framed, including those parts not finally adopted, as throwing light on the meaning of the remainder; and looking at the purpose, so clearly disclosed in that, of the removal of the whole body of the Sioux nation to the Indian territory proper, which was not consented to, it is manifest that the provisions had reference to their establishment as a people upon a defined reservation as a permanent home, who were to be urged, as far as it could successfully be done, into the practice of agriculture, and whose children were to be taught the arts and industry of civilized life, and that it was no part of the design to treat the individuals as separately responsible and amenable, in all their personal and domestic relations with each other, to the general laws of the United States, outside of those which were enacted expressly with reference to them as members of an Indian tribe.

It must be remembered that the question before us is whether the express letter of section 2146 of the Revised Statutes, which excludes from the jurisdiction of the United States the case of a crime committed in the Indian country by one Indian against the person or property of another Indian, has been repealed. If not, it is in force and applies to the present case. The treaty of 1868 and the agreement and act of congress of 1877, it is admitted, do not repeal it by any express words. What we have said is sufficient at least to show that they do not work a repeal by necessary implication. * * *

        * * *

The nature and circumstances of this case strongly reinforce this rule of interpretation in its present application. It is a case involving the judgment of a court of special and limited jurisdiction, not to be assumed without clear warrant of law. It is a case of life and death. It is a case where, against an express exception in the law itself, that law, by argument and inference only, is sought to be extended over aliens and strangers; over the members of a community, separated by race, by tradition, by the instincts of a free though savage life, from the authority and power which seeks to impose upon them the restraints of an external and unknown code, and to subject them to the responsibilities of civil conduct, according to rules and penalties of which they could have no previous warning; which judges them by a standard made by others, and not for them, which takes no account of the conditions which should except them from its exactions, and makes no allowance for their inability to understand it. It tries them not by their peers, nor by the customs of their people, nor the law of their land, but by superiors of a different race, according to the law of a social state of which they have an imperfect conception, and which is opposed to the traditions of their history, to the habits of their lives, to the strongest prejudices of their savage nature; one which measures the red man's revenge by the maxims of the white man's morality. * * *

To give to the clauses in the treaty of 1868 and the agreement of 1877 effect, so as to uphold the jurisdiction exercised in this case, would be to reverse in this instance the general policy of the government towards the Indians, as declared in many statutes and treaties, and recognized in many decisions of this court, from the beginning to the present time. To justify such a departure, in such a case, requires a clear expression of the intention of congress, and that we have not been able to find. It results that the first district court of Dakota was without jurisdiction to find or try the indictment against the prisoner; that the conviction and sentence are void, and that his imprisonment is illegal.

Notes and Questions

1. The *Crow Dog* decision incited reformers to seek expansion of federal criminal jurisdiction over Indian reservations. Congress passed the Major Crimes Act of 1885, which expanded the jurisdiction of federal courts to consider seven serious crimes committed in Indian Country by Indians. The Major Crimes Act provided that

> all Indians, committing against the person or property of another Indian or other person any of the following crimes, namely, murder, man-slaughter, rape, assault with intent to kill, arson, burglary, and larceny, within any Territory of the United States, and either within or without an Indian reservation, shall be subject therefor to the laws of such Territory relating to said crimes, and shall be tried therefor in the same courts and in the same manner and shall be subject to the same penalties as are all other persons charged with the commission of said crimes, respectively * * *.

23 Stat. 385 (1885).

This Act was another step in the trend of federal policy towards increasing control of Indian nations by Congress and the federal government and diminishing tribal sovereignty. As stated by one commentator, "[T]he Major Crimes Act of 1885 is not difficult to understand. While it was a clear departure from existing practice, it was consistent with the whole general trend of Indian policy, the move from a policy based on treaty rights recognizing Indian sovereignty to one of dependency and forced assimilation." See Sidney L. Harring, *Crow Dog's Case: A Chapter in the Legal History of Tribal Sovereignty*, 14 Am. Indian L. Rev. 191, 230 (1989).

———

In the following case, decided just three years after *Crow Dog*, the Supreme Court considered the constitutionality of the Major Crimes Act:

UNITED STATES v. KAGAMA

118 U.S. 375 (1886).

JUSTICE MILLER delivered the opinion of the Court.

* * *

The indictment sets out in two counts that Kagama, alias Pactah Billy, an Indian, murdered Iyouse, alias Ike, another Indian, at Humboldt county, in the state of California, within the limits of the Hoopa Valley reservation, and it charges Mahawaha, alias Ben, also an Indian, with aiding and abetting in the murder.

* * *

The mention of Indians in the constitution which has received most attention is that found in the clause which gives congress "power to regulate commerce with foreign nations, and among the several states, and with the Indian tribes."

This clause is relied on in the argument in the present case, the proposition being that the statute under consideration is a regulation of commerce with the Indian tribes. But we think it would be a very strained construction of this clause that a system of criminal laws for Indians living peaceably in their reservations, which left out the entire code of trade and intercourse laws justly enacted under that provision, and established punishments for the common-law crimes of murder, manslaughter, arson, burglary, larceny, and the like, without any reference to their relation to any kind of commerce, was authorized by the grant of power to regulate commerce with the Indian tribes. * * *

But these Indians are within the geographical limits of the United States. The soil and the people within these limits are under the political control of the government of the United States, or of the states of the Union. There exists within the broad domain of sovereignty but these two. * * * [The] power of congress to organize territorial governments, and make laws for their inhabitants, arises, not so much from the clause in the constitution in regard to disposing of and making rules and regulations concerning the territory and other property of the United States, as from the ownership of the country in which the territories are, and the right of exclusive sovereignty which must exist in the national government, and can be found nowhere else.

* * *

The Indian reservation in the case before us is land bought by the United States from Mexico by the treaty of Guadaloupe Hidalgo, and the whole of California, with the allegiance of its inhabitants, many of whom were Indians, was transferred by that treaty to the United States.

The relation of the Indian tribes living within the borders of the United States, both before and since the Revolution, to the people of the United States, has always been an anomalous one, and of a complex character.

Following the policy of the European governments in the discovery of America, towards the Indians who were found here, the colonies before the Revolution, and the states and the United States since, have recognized in the Indians a possessory right to the soil over which they roamed and hunted and established occasional villages. But they asserted an ultimate title in the land itself, by which the Indian tribes were forbidden to sell or transfer it to other nations or peoples without the consent of this paramount authority. When a tribe wished to dispose of its land, or any part of it, or the state or the United States wished to purchase it, a treaty with the tribe was the only mode in which this could be done. The United States recognized no right in private persons, or in other nations, to make such a purchase by treaty or otherwise. With the Indians themselves these relations are equally difficult to define. They were, and always have been, regarded as having a semi-independent position when they preserved their tribal relations; not as States, not as nations, not as possessed of the full attributes of sovereignty, but as a separate people, with the power of regulating their internal and social relations, and thus far not brought under the laws of the Union or of the state within whose limits they resided.

* * *

It will be seen at once that the nature of the offense (murder) is one which in most all cases of its commission is punishable by the laws of the States, and within the jurisdiction of their courts. The distinction is claimed to be that the offense under the statute is committed by an Indian, that it is committed on a reservation set apart within the state for residence of the tribe of Indians by the United States, and the fair inference is that the offending Indian shall belong to that or some other tribe. It does not interfere with the process of the state courts within the reservation, nor with the operation of state laws upon white people found there. Its effect is confined to the acts of an Indian of some tribe, of a criminal character, committed within the limits of the reservation.

It seems to us that this is within the competency of congress. These Indian tribes are the wards of the nation. They are communities dependent on the United States,—dependent largely for their daily food; dependent for their political rights. They owe no allegiance to the states, and receive from them no protection. Because of the local ill feeling, the people of the states where they are found are often their deadliest enemies. From their very weakness and helplessness, so largely due to the course of dealing of the federal government with them, and the treaties in which it has been promised, there arises the duty of protection, and with it the power. This has always been recognized by the executive, and by congress, and by this court, whenever the question has arisen.

* * *

The power of the general government over these remnants of a race once powerful, now weak and diminished in numbers, is necessary to their protection, as well as to the safety of those among whom they dwell. It must exist in that government, because it never has existed anywhere else; because the theater of its exercise is within the geographical limits of the United States; because it has never been denied; and because it alone can enforce its laws on all the tribes.

* * *

Notes and Questions

1. Is *Kagama* consistent with *Crow Dog*? What might account for the difference in these decisions, rendered only three years apart?

———

The single most destructive achievement of the nineteenth century movement to break the structure and sovereignty of Indian tribes was Congress's passage of the General Allotment Act of 1887, also known as the Dawes Act, which provided that:

> [I]n all cases where any tribe or band of Indians has been, or shall hereafter be, located upon any reservation created for their use either by treaty stipulation or by virtue of an act of Congress or executive order setting apart the same for their use, the President of the United States be, and hereby is, authorized, whenever in his opinion any reservation or any part thereof of such Indians is advantageous for agricultural and grazing purposes, to cause said reservation, or any part thereof, to be surveyed * * * and to allot the lands in said reservation in severalty to any Indian located thereon * * *.

24 Stat. 388 (1887). The Allotment Act broke up lands held jointly by tribes and reallocated them in separate parcels to individual tribal members.

According to leading scholars of Indian law:

Shrinking the Indian reservation land base was designed to serve dual goals: to open more land for settlement and to end tribalism. The Allotment policy of the late 19th Century Expansion Era was supposed to turn reservations into campuses for training Indians in the "arts of civilization." The Bureau of Indian Affairs took unprecedented control of everyday Indian life, seeking to squeeze out Indian government, religion, and culture. Tribal lands were carved up and parceled to individual Indians who were to be converted from hunters to farmers. "Surplus" lands were sold for non-Indian settlement; the result was a loss of about two-thirds of all the Indians' lands. * * *

Getches, Wilkinson & Williams, *Federal Indian Law* 168 (3d ed. 1993). Teddy Roosevelt described the General Allotment Act as "a mighty pulverizing engine to break up the tribal mass." Quoted in Getches, Wilkinson & Williams, *supra* at 215.

In addition to Congress's efforts to destroy the special relationship between Indian tribes and the federal government, the Supreme Court supported these efforts by affirming Congress's plenary power over Indian affairs in *Lone Wolf v. Hitchcock*.

LONE WOLF v. HITCHCOCK

187 U.S. 553 (1903).

[This case dealt with a dispute between Kiowa, Comanche, and Apache Indians over the ability of Congress to enact Allotment-era statutes that divided and allocated the tribes' lands in severalty, contrary to the provisions of an 1867 Treaty establishing a reservation for the three tribes. The Court relied on the plenary power of Congress in regulating Indian affairs in deciding that the issue was a non-justiciable political question.]

Plenary authority over the tribal relations of the Indians has been exercised by Congress from the beginning, and the power has always been deemed a political one, not subject to be controlled by the judicial department of the government. Until the year 1871 the policy was pursued of dealing with the Indian tribes by means of treaties, and of course, a moral obligation rested upon Congress to act in good faith in performing the stipulations entered into on its behalf. But as with treaties made with foreign nations (*Chinese Exclusion Case*, 130 U.S. 581) the legislative power might pass laws in conflict with treaties made with the Indians. * * *

The power exists to abrogate the provisions of an Indian treaty, though presumably such power will be exercised only when circumstances arise which will not only justify the government in disregarding the stipulations of the treaty, but may demand, in the interest of the country and the Indians themselves, that it should do so. When, therefore, treaties were entered into between the United States and a tribe of Indians it was never doubted that the power to abrogate existed in Congress, and that in a contingency such power might be availed of from considerations of governmental policy, particularly if consistent with perfect good faith towards the Indians. * * *

[handwritten marginal note: P.S. we can fuck you anytime we want pose]

SECTION 7. INDIAN REORGANIZATION (1928–1945)

In response to the decimation of tribal lands and culture wrought by the General Allotment Act, progressive reformers such as Felix S. Cohen, renowned Indian law scholar, and John Collier, Commissioner of the Bureau of Indian Affairs during the administration of President Franklin Roosevelt, sought to restore tribal sovereignty and governance. The Meriam report of 1928, which chronicled in great detail Indian poverty and the poor state of Indian health and education engendered by the government's implementation of the Allotment Act, provided impetus for Congressional reconsideration of federal Indian policy.

In 1934, Congress passed the Indian Reorganization Act (IRA), 48 Stat. 984 (1934), which sought to reestablish tribal forms of governance and to increase Indian control over tribal affairs. Section 1 of the IRA stated that "hereafter no land of any Indian reservation, created or set apart by treaty or agreement with the Indians, Act of Congress, Executive order, purchase, or otherwise, shall be allotted in severalty to any Indian," abolishing the prior policy of allotment. Section 4 of the Act prohibited sales or transfers of Indian lands; such lands could only be transferred to other Indians with the approval of the Secretary of the Interior. Section 16 of the Act provided for the tribal adoption of constitutions for governance and for the vesting of particular rights within the tribe, subject to the approval of the Secretary of the Interior. Although the IRA represented an improvement over the past policy of allotment and outright destruction of tribal governance, the statute was only a partial improvement that left an ambiguous legacy. Consider the following excerpt:

VINE DELORIA, JR. AND CLIFFORD M. LYTLE

American Indians, American Justice
14–15 (1983).*

From the standpoint of government organization, the IRA enabled tribes to organize for their common welfare and to adopt federally approved constitutions and bylaws. It permitted the employment of legal counsel of the tribe's own choice and authorized tribal councils established under the act to negotiate with federal, state and local governments. The major thrust of the act was to minimize the enormous discretion and power exercised by the Department of the Interior and the Office of Indian Affairs. The focus of power was to be decentralized and moved from the Indian bureaucracy in Washington to the reservation governments. Formal tribal government was expected to become the rule rather than the exception.

The opportunities made available to the tribes under this act were immense. While the act did not provide them with powers they had not previously possessed, it did recognize these powers as inherent in their status and resurrected them in a form in which they could be used at the discretion of the tribe. This recognition, coupled with the promise of expanded social programs and federal funding of projects, was an exciting prospect. Before the IRA could be made applicable to a tribe, however, the enrolled members had to vote within a two-year period to accept it. Within the time allocated, 358 elections were held in which 181 tribes [129,750 Indians] voted to accept the IRA provisions. Seventy-seven tribes rejected the act (86,365 Indians, including the large Navajo tribe of approximately 45,000 people). Some tribes voted to accept the act and then refused to organize under it * * *.

While a number of opportunities for Indian revitalization were initiated under the IRA, its promise was never fully realized. The era of allotment had taken a heavy toll on the tribes. Many of the old customs and traditions that could have been restored under the IRA climate of cultural concern had vanished during the interim period since the tribes had gone to the reservations. The experience of self-government according to Indian traditions had eroded and, while the new constitutions were akin to the traditions of some tribes, they were completely foreign to others. The new constitutions called for election of council members and were based upon the old "boss farmer" districts, which had been

* From American Indians, American Justice by Vine Deloria, Jr. and Clifford M. Lytle, Copyright © 1983. Reprinted by permission of the University of Texas Press.

drawn when the allotment policy dictated that the Indians would be taught to farm. Familiar cultural groupings and methods of choosing leadership gave way to the more abstract principles of American democracy, which viewed people as interchangeable and communities as geographical marks on a map.

Although there were some variations, in general the new tribal constitutions and bylaws were standardized and largely followed the Anglo–American system of organizing people. Traditional Indians of almost every tribe strongly objected to this method of organizing and criticized the IRA as simply another means of imposing white institutions on the tribes. In some of the constitutions the traditional Indians were able to protect themselves by insisting that the tribal government derive from the more ancient form of government and be subjected in its operation to the powers that the people had allocated to it. Other tribes rejected the idea of a formal, and small, tribal council governing them and demanded that the tribal council consist of the whole tribe meeting in concert. Experience proved this approach to have its merits and its shortcomings.

———

Felix S. Cohen is one of the great scholars of Indian law and one of the architects of Indian reorganization. The following excerpt from his *Handbook of Federal Indian Law*, in which Cohen describes the nature of Indian sovereignty and the relationship of Indians to the federal government, has been characterized as "without question, the single most influential passage ever written by an Indian law scholar." Getches, Wilkinson & Williams, *supra*, at 227.

FELIX S. COHEN

Handbook of Federal Indian Law
122–23 (1945).

* * *

Perhaps the most basic principle of all Indian law, supported by a host of decisions * * * is the principle that *those powers which are lawfully vested in an Indian tribe are not, in general, delegated powers granted by express acts of Congress, but rather inherent powers of limited sovereignty which has never been extinguished.* Each Indian tribe begins its relationships with the Federal Government as a sovereign power, recognized as such in treaty and legislation. The powers of sovereignty have been limited from time to time by special treaties and laws designed to take from the Indian tribes control of matters which, in the judgement of Congress, these tribes could no longer be safely permitted to handle. The statutes of Congress, then, must be examined to determine the limitations of tribal sovereignty rather than to determine its sources or its positive content. What is not expressly limited remains within the domain of tribal sovereignty.

The acts of Congress which appear to limit the powers of an Indian tribe are not to be unduly extended by doubtful inference. * * *

From the earliest years of the Republic the Indian tribes have been recognized as "distinct, independent, political communities," and, as such, qualified to exercise powers of self-government, not by virtue of any delegation of powers from the Federal Government, but rather by reason of their original tribal sovereignty. Thus treaties and statutes of Congress have been looked to by the courts as limitations upon original tribal powers, or, at most, evidences of recognition of such powers, rather than as the direct source of tribal powers. This is but an application of the general principle that "It is only by positive enactments, even in the case of conquered and subdued nations, that their laws are changed by the conqueror."

* * *

The earliest complete expression of these principles is found in the case of *Worcester v. Georgia*.... John Marshall's analysis of the basis of Indian self-government in the law of nations has been consistently followed by the courts for more than a hundred years. * * *

The whole course of judicial decision on the nature of Indian tribal powers is marked by adherence to three fundamental principles: (1) An Indian tribe possesses, in the first instance, all the powers of any sovereign state. (2) Conquest renders the tribe subject to the legislative power of the United States and, in substance, terminates the external powers of sovereignty of the tribe, *e.g.*, its power to enter into treaties with foreign nations, but does not by itself affect the internal sovereignty of the tribe, *i.e.*, its powers of local self-government. (3) These powers are subject to qualification by treaties and by express legislation of Congress, but, save as thus expressly qualified, full powers of internal sovereignty are vested in the Indian tribes and in their duly constituted organs of government.

Notes and Questions

1. Note how much of Cohen's analysis builds upon Chief Justice Marshall's discussion of Indian rights in *Worcester v. Georgia, supra.*

2. What is the nature of the inherent tribal sovereignty and the doctrine of reserved rights described by Cohen and Marshall?

SECTION 8.   TERMINATION PERIOD (1945–1961)

In an equal and opposite reaction to the reforms of the Indian Reorganization Act and the more progressive Bureau of Indian Affairs, Congress soon sought to terminate the federal relationship with Indian tribes and to terminate many of the tribes themselves. This period is thus called the "termination period," which spawned legislation designed to end tribal identity as it had existed. The first legislative act was House Concurrent Resolution 108, which expressed the sense of Congress to end the historic federal supervision of Indian tribes.

House Concurrent Resolution 108, 83rd Cong.,
67 Stat. B132 (August 1, 1953)

Whereas it is the policy of Congress, as rapidly as possible, to make the Indians within the territorial limits of the United States subject to the same laws and entitled to the same privileges and responsibilities as are applicable to other citizens of the United States, to end their status as wards of the United States, and to grant them all of the rights and prerogatives pertaining to American citizenship; and

Whereas the Indians within the territorial limits of the United States should assume their full responsibilities as American citizens. * * *

[I]t is declared to be the sense of Congress that, at the earliest possible time, all of the Indian tribes and the individual members thereof located within the States of California, Florida, New York, and Texas, and all of the following named Indian tribes and the individual members thereof should be freed from Federal supervision and control and from all disabilities and limitations specially applicable to Indians * * *.

In support of the concurrent resolution, Congress passed legislation terminating individual tribes between 1954–1962. Congress also carried forward the termination program by making state criminal laws applicable within Indian reservations in Public Law 280, enacted in 1953:

Each of the States listed * * * shall have jurisdiction over offenses committed by or against Indians in the areas of Indian country * * * to the same extent that such State has jurisdiction over offenses committed elsewhere within the State, and the criminal laws of such State shall have the same force and effect within such Indian country as they have elsewhere within the State * * *.

See 67 Stat. 588 (1953). This statute abrogated a major aspect of Indian tribal sovereignty, and was thus fully consistent with the ideals of the termination program.

The termination program generated a strong response, raising Indian consciousness and fueling an intellectual resistance movement. "The termination policy adopted by the federal government * * * had a defining impact on the minds of the present generation of Indian leadership. Though now formally repudiated by the federal government, the memory of Congressional committees and bureaucrats in Washington 'terminating' the existence of hundreds of tribes across Indian country still lingers threateningly for Indian leaders even today. Termination stands as a chilling reminder to Indian peoples that Congress can unilaterally decide to extinguish the special status and rights of tribes without Indian consent and without even hearing Indian views." Getches, Wilkinson & Williams, *Federal Indian Law* at 229–30.

SECTION 9. THE PERIOD OF SELF–DETERMINATION

Indians responded to the threat posed by the termination policy with strong organized opposition. The National Congress of American Indians held an emergency conference in 1954 to protest the termination policy. An important conference of American Indian leaders convened at the University of Chicago in June, 1961. This conference produced a Declaration of Indian Purpose which stated the aspirations of Indian people as well as specific legislative proposals designed to improve and restore the condition of Indians in the United States.

DECLARATION OF INDIAN PURPOSE
(June, 1961).*

WE BELIEVE in the inherent right of all people to retain spiritual and cultural values, and that the free exercise of these values is necessary to the normal development of any people. Indians exercised this inherent right to live their own lives for thousands of years before the white man came and took their lands. It is a more complex world in which Indians live today, but the Indian people who first settled the New World and built the great civilizations which only now are being dug out of the past, long ago demonstrated that they could master complexity.

WE BELIEVE that the history and development of America show that the Indian has been subjected to duress, undue influence, unwarranted pressures, and policies which have produced uncertainty, frustration, and despair. Only when the public understands these conditions and is moved to take action toward the formulation and adoption of sound and consistent policies and programs will these destroying factors be removed and the Indian resume his normal growth and make his maximum contribution to modern society.

WE BELIEVE in the future of a greater America, an America which we were first to love, where life, liberty, and the pursuit of happiness will be a reality. In such a future, with Indians and all other Americans cooperating, a cultural climate will be created in which the Indian people will grow and develop as members of a free society.

LEGISLATIVE AND REGULATORY PROPOSALS

In order that basic objectives may be restated and that action to accomplish these objectives may be continuous and may be pursued in a spirit of public dedication, it is proposed that recommendations be adopted to strengthen the principles of the Indian Reorganization Act and to accomplish other purposes. These recommendations would be comparable in scope to the Indian Trade and Intercourse Act of June 30, 1834, the Act of the same date establishing the Bureau of Indian Affairs, and the Indian Reorganization Act of June 18, 1934, which recognized the inherent powers of Indian Tribes.

The recommendations we propose would redefine the responsibilities of the United States toward the Indian people in terms of a positive national obligation to modify or remove the conditions which produce the poverty and lack of social adjustment as these prevail as the outstanding attributes of Indian life today. Specifically, the recommendations would:

1. Abandon the so-called termination policy of the last administration by revoking House Concurrent Resolution 108 of the 83rd Congress.

* Reprinted from *Documents of United States Indian Policy* 244–46, 2d ed, expanded, edited by Francis Paul Prucha, by permission of the University of Nebraska Press. Copyright © 1975, 1990 by the University of Nebraska Press.

2. Adopt as official policy the principle of broad educational process as the procedure best calculated to remove the disabilities which have prevented Indians from making full use of their resources.

It has long been recognized that one Commissioner cannot give the personal attention to all tribal matters which they deserve. He cannot meet all callers to his office, make necessary visits to the field, and give full attention to the review of tribal programs and supporting budget requests. In view of these conditions, we most urgently recommend that the present organization of the Bureau of Indian Affairs be reviewed and that certain principles be considered no matter what the organizational change might be.

The basic principle involves the desire on the part of Indians to participate in developing their own programs with help and guidance as needed and requested, from a local decentralized technical and administrative staff, preferably located conveniently to the people it serves. Also in recent years certain technical and professional people of Indian descent are becoming better qualified and available to work with and for their own people in determining their own programs and needs. The Indians as responsible individual citizens, as responsible tribal representatives, and as responsible Tribal Councils want to participate, want to contribute to their own personal and tribal improvements and want to cooperate with their Government on how best to solve the many problems in a business-like, efficient and economical manner as rapidly as possible.

It is therefore recommended that:

1.   Area offices be abolished and their authority be given to the agency superintendents.

2.   The position of reservation Superintendent be strengthened to permit broader exercise of responsibility and authority to act on significant and important matters of daily operations of Indian problems, preventing undue delays.

3.   Position qualifications require the employment of Superintendents with courage and determination, among other qualities, to help with local problems and be willing to make without further referral to higher levels, decisions commensurate with the delegated authorities.

4.   The Superintendent be charged with the responsibilities of cooperating with the local tribal governing bodies in developing the Federal Program and Budget for that particular tribe or reservation. * * *

CONCLUDING STATEMENT

To complete our Declaration, we point out that in the beginning the people of the New World, called Indians by accident of geography, were possessed of a continent and a way of life. In the course of many lifetimes, our people had adjusted to every climate and condition from the Arctic to the torrid zones. In their livelihood and family relationships, their ceremonial observances, they reflected the diversity of the physical world they occupied.

The conditions in which Indians live today reflect a world in which every basic aspect of life has been transformed. Even the physical world is no longer the controlling factor in determining where and under what conditions men may live. In region after region, Indian groups found their means of existence either totally destroyed or materially modified. Newly introduced diseases swept away or reduced regional populations. These changes were followed by major shifts in the internal life of tribe and family.

The time came when the Indian people were no longer the masters of their situation. Their life ways survived subject to the will of a dominant sovereign power. This is said, not in a spirit of complaint; we understand that in the lives of all nations of people, there are times of plenty and times of famine. But we do speak out in a plea for understanding. When we go before the American people, as we do in this Declaration, and ask for material assistance in developing our resources and developing our opportunities, we pose a moral problem which cannot be left unanswered. For the problem we raise affects the standing which our nation sustains before world opinion.

Our situation cannot be relieved by appropriated funds alone, though it is equally obvious that without capital investment and funded services, solutions will be delayed. Nor will the passage of time lessen the complexities which beset a people moving toward new meaning and purpose.

The answers we seek are not commodities to be purchased, neither are they evolved automatically through the passing of time.

The effort to place social adjustment on a money-time interval scale which has characterized Indian administration, has resulted in unwanted pressure and frustration.

When Indians speak of the continent they yielded, they are not referring only to the loss of some millions of acres in real estate. They have in mind that the land supported a universe of things they knew, valued, and loved.

With that continent gone, except for the few poor parcels they still retain, the basis of life is precariously held, but they mean to hold the scraps and parcels as earnestly as any small nation or ethnic group was ever determined to hold to identity and survival.

What we ask of America is not charity, not paternalism, even when benevolent. We ask only that the nature of our situation be recognized and made the basis of policy and action.

In short, the Indians ask for assistance, technical and financial, for the time needed, however long that may be, to regain in the America of the space age some measure of the adjustment they enjoyed as the original possessors of their native land.

———

The termination policy was abandoned gradually during the Kennedy and Johnson administrations. During the Kennedy administration, there was no active enforcement of the termination policy. President Lyndon B. Johnson supported Indian tribes and made significant investments to improve social programs and infrastructure on tribal reservations.

President Johnson articulated a forceful vision of self-determination for Indian tribes, with the support of the federal government, in his Special Message to Congress on the Problems of the American Indian: "The Forgotten American," March 6, 1968:

I propose a new goal for our Indian programs: A goal that ends the old debate about "termination" of Indian programs and stresses self-determination; a goal that erases old attitudes of paternalism and promotes partnership self-help.

Our goal must be:

—A standard of living for the Indians equal to that of the country as a whole.

—Freedom of Choice: An opportunity to remain in their homelands, if they choose, without surrendering their dignity; an opportunity to move to the towns and cities of America, if they choose, equipped with the skills to live in equality and dignity.

—Full participation in the life of modern America, with a full share of economic opportunity and social justice.

I propose, in short, a policy of maximum choice for the American Indian: a policy expressed in programs of self-help, self-development, self-determination.

See *Public Papers of the Presidents of the United States: Lyndon B. Johnson, 1968–69*, Vol. 1, p. 336 (March 6, 1968).

Following and expanding the vision of Indian self-determination, President Richard M. Nixon issued a landmark message to Congress on July 8, 1970, rejecting the legacy of the termination policy and recommending a policy of self-determination. Nixon wrote:

This policy of forced termination is wrong, in my judgment, for a number of reasons. * * * The special relationship between Indians and the Federal government is the result * * * of solemn obligations which have been entered into by the United States Government. [T]hrough written treaties and through formal and informal agreements, our government has made specific commitments to the Indian people. * * * [T]he special relationship between the Indian tribes and the Federal government which arises from these agreements continues to carry immense moral and legal force. To terminate this relationship would be no more appropriate than to terminate the citizenship rights of any other American. * * * Federal termination errs in one direction, Federal paternalism errs in the other. Only by clearly rejecting both of these extremes can we achieve a policy which truly serves the best interests of the Indian people. Self-determination among Indian people can and must be encouraged without the threat of eventual termination. * * *

Public Papers of the Presidents of the United States, Richard M. Nixon, *Special Message to the Congress on Indian Affairs* 565–66 (July 8, 1970).

Nixon's message also contained specific proposals for legislation to improve Indian control over resources and self determination. Several proposals were enacted by Congress, including legislation to improve Indian education, to increase Indian participation in self-determination and education, and to finance Indian economic development. See Getches, Wilkinson & Williams, *Federal Indian Law* at 254–56.

According to Vine Deloria, Jr., "[t]he biggest policy change in these intervening years, contained in President Richard M. Nixon's July, 1970 *Message to Congress*, was the official disavowal of termination as a formal goal of the federal government. Indeed, while Nixon may have failed in spectacular fashion in other aspects of his presidency, in retrospect his administration must be granted very high marks for its Indian policy. In responsiveness to Indian aspirations, it will probably be seen as the best administration in American history, and in terms of its accomplishments it should be ranked close to the New Deal, which radically turned the tide in favor of Indians." Vine Deloria, Jr., *Custer Died for Your Sins* viii (1988 edition).

The unique political status of Indians relative to the federal government was discussed, and approved, by the Supreme Court in *Morton v. Mancari*.

MORTON v. MANCARI

417 U.S. 535 (1974).

JUSTICE BLACKMUN delivered the opinion of the Court.

[Non–Indian employees of the Bureau of Indian Affairs (BIA) brought a class action lawsuit alleging that the preference for employing Indians at the BIA constituted race discrimination, violating both Title VII of the Civil Rights Act of 1964 and the Due Process Clause of the Fifth Amendment.]

* * *

The federal policy of according some hiring preference to Indians in the Indian service dates at least as far back as 1834. Since that time, Congress repeatedly has enacted various preferences of the general type here at issue. The purpose of these preferences, as variously expressed in the legislative history, has been to give Indians a greater participation in their own self-government, to further the Government's trust obligation toward the Indian tribes; and to reduce the negative effect of having non-Indians administer matters that affect Indian tribal life.

The preference directly at issue here was enacted as an important part of the sweeping Indian Reorganization Act of 1934. The overriding purpose of that particular Act was to establish machinery whereby Indian tribes would be able to assume a greater degree of self-government, both politically and economically. Congress was seeking to modify the then-existing situation whereby the primarily non-Indian-staffed BIA had plenary control, for all practical purposes, over the lives and destinies of the federally recognized Indian tribes. * * *

One of the primary means by which self-government would be fostered and the Bureau made more responsive was to increase the participation of tribal Indians in the BIA operations. * * *

Congress was well aware that the proposed preference would result in employment disadvantages within the BIA for non-Indians. Not only was this displacement unavoidable if room were to be made for Indians, but it was explicitly determined that gradual replacement of non-Indians with Indians within the Bureau was a desirable feature of the entire program for self-government. Since 1934, the BIA has implemented the preference with a fair degree of success. The percentage of Indians employed in the Bureau rose from 34% in 1934 to 57% in 1972. This reversed the former downward trend * * * and was due, clearly, to the presence of the 1934 Act. The Commissioner's extension of the preference in 1972 to promotions within the BIA was designed to bring more Indians into positions of responsibility and, in that regard, appears to be a logical extension of the congressional intent.

It is against this background that we encounter the first issue in the present case: whether the Indian preference was repealed by the Equal Employment Opportunity Act of 1972. Title VII of the Civil Rights Act of 1964 was the first major piece of federal legislation prohibiting discrimination in private employment on the basis of "race, color, religion, sex, or national origin." Significantly, §§ 701(b) and 703(i) of that Act explicitly exempted from its coverage the preferential employment of Indians by Indian tribes or by industries located on or near Indian reservations. This exemption reveals a clear congressional recognition, within the framework of Title VII, of the unique legal status of tribal and reservation-based activities. * * *

The 1964 Act did not specifically outlaw employment discrimination by the Federal Government. * * * In order to remedy this, Congress, by the 1972 Act, amended the 1964 Act and proscribed discrimination in most areas of federal employment. In general, it may be said that the substantive anti-discrimination law embraced in Title VII was carried over and applied to the Federal Government. * * *

The above-mentioned affirmative provisions in the 1964 Act [exclude] coverage of tribal employment and of preferential treatment by a business or enterprise on or near a reservation. These 1964 exemptions as to private employment indicate Congress' recognition of the long-standing federal policy of providing a unique legal status to Indians in matters concerning tribal or "on or near" reservation employment. The exemptions reveal a clear congressional sentiment that an Indian preference in the narrow context of tribal or reservation-related employment did not constitute racial discrimination of the type otherwise proscribed. In extending the general anti-discrimination machinery to federal employment in 1972, Congress in no way modified these private employment preferences built into the 1964 Act, and they are still in effect. It would be anomalous to conclude that Congress intended to eliminate the longstanding statutory preferences in BIA employment, as being racially discriminatory, at the very same time it was reaffirming the right of tribal and reservation-related private employers to provide Indian preference. Appellees' assertion that Congress implicitly repealed the preference as racially discriminatory, while retaining the 1964 preferences, attributes to Congress irrationality and arbitrariness, an attribution we do not share. * * *

In light of the factors indicating no repeal, we simply cannot conclude that Congress consciously abandoned its policy of furthering Indian self-government when it passed the 1972 amendments. * * *

We still must decide whether, as the appellees contend, the preference constitutes invidious racial discrimination in violation of the Due Process Clause of the Fifth Amendment. * * *

As discussed above, Congress in 1934 determined that proper fulfillment of its trust required turning over to the Indians a greater control of their own destinies. The overly paternalistic approach of prior years had proved both exploitative and destructive of Indian interests. Congress was united in the belief that institutional changes were required. An important part of the Indian Reorganization Act was the preference provision here at issue.

Contrary to the characterization made by appellees, this preference does not constitute "racial discrimination." Indeed, it is not even a "racial" preference.[24] Rather, it is an employment criterion reasonably designed to further the cause of Indian self-government and to make the BIA more responsive to the needs of its constituent groups. It is directed to participation by the governed in the governing agency. The preference is similar in kind to the constitutional requirement that a United States Senator, when elected, be "an Inhabitant of that State for which he shall be chosen," Art. I, § 3, Cl. 3, or that a member of a city council reside within the city governed by the council. Congress has sought only to enable the BIA to draw more heavily from among the constituent group in staffing its projects, all of which, either directly or indirectly, affect the lives of tribal Indians. The preference, as applied, is granted to Indians not as a discrete racial group, but, rather, as members of quasi-sovereign tribal entities whose lives and activities are governed by the BIA in a unique fashion. In the sense that there is no other group of people favored in this manner, the legal status of the BIA is truly *sui generis*. Furthermore, the preference applies only to employment in the Indian service. The preference does not cover any other Government agency or activity, and we need not consider the obviously more difficult question that would be presented by a blanket exemption for Indians from all civil service examinations. Here, the preference is reasonably and directly related to a legitimate, nonracially based goal. This is the

24. The preference is not directed towards a "racial" group consisting of "Indians"; instead, it applies only to members of "federally recognized" tribes. This operates to exclude many individuals who are racially to be classified as "Indians." In this sense, the preference is political rather than racial in nature. * * *

principal characteristic that generally is absent from proscribed forms of racial discrimination. * * *

We cannot say that Congress' classification violates due process.

Notes and Questions

1. Notice the Court's discussion of whether or not the BIA's hiring preference for Indians was racial or political. This illustrates the concept that Indians constitute a political minority, with a unique historical relationship to the federal government.

2. Does the reasoning in *Morton v. Mancari* survive the recent Supreme Court opinion in *Adarand Constructors, Inc. v. Pena*, 515 U.S. 200 (1995) (See Chapter 7 § 3 *infra*), which holds that all racial classifications will be analyzed using strict scrutiny? Is there any basis for distinguishing the two cases?

SECTION 10. CONTEMPORARY RACISM AND ISSUES

LAC du FLAMBEAU BAND OF LAKE SUPERIOR CHIPPEWA INDIANS v. STOP TREATY ABUSE—WISCONSIN, INC.

759 F. Supp. 1339 (W.D.Wis.1991).

CRABB, CHIEF JUDGE.

[The plaintiffs, Chippewa Indians, sued to enjoin interference by protesters and local police with their rights, guaranteed by federal treaty, to fish for walleye off their reservation. They prevail only against the individual protesters.]

The Lake Superior Chippewa Indians are a tribe recognized by the United States government. In 1837 and 1842, the tribe entered into treaties with the United States under which they gave up hundreds of thousands of acres of land in what is now Wisconsin but reserved their right to hunt, fish and gather food in the territory they had ceded. Pursuant to the treaties, members of the plaintiff Lac du Flambeau band have a treaty-guaranteed right to fish off the reservation. * * *

The walleye spearing season begins in April or May, shortly after the ice breaks up and the lakes open and the fish come up out of the depths of the lake to spawn in the shallow water near the shore. The season lasts about fifteen days and is open only to members of the Lake Superior Chippewa. State law prohibits open water spearing by non-Indians.

Spearers fish after dark when the fish have moved onto the spawning beds. They spear from a standing position in the front of a slowly moving shallow draft boat, using a ten foot long metal spear. Light is provided by a large lamp mounted on the spearer's headgear.

Spearing is an important part of the cultural and religious heritage of the Chippewa. The fish that plaintiffs and other tribal spearers take are an important source of food for the spearers and for others in the tribe who are needy and unable to fish.

Plaintiffs Maulson, Martin, Hockings and Chapman have been spearers since childhood and have been exercising their right to spear off the reservation since the courts confirmed that the Chippewa retained this right. When they and other tribal members began exercising their off-reservation fishing rights, they met with little opposition. Beginning in 1986 and 1987, however, more and more people began to demonstrate against spearing at the boat landings on lakes where spearing was taking place, and local police and sheriffs found it difficult to control the demonstrations. * * *

Despite the presence of large numbers of law enforcement officials, members of defendant STA [Stop Treaty Abuse—Wisconsin, Inc.] have subjected plaintiffs, other tribal spearers and the families of spearers to stone throwing, threats of harm, racial and sexual insults, minor batteries, and damage to their vehicles. It is the intent of STA and the other private defendants to minimize the number of fish that plaintiffs can take during spawning season, by blocking the landings, creating wakes, planting concrete walleye decoys, and gathering large numbers of persons at the boat landings to harass the spearers and their families and friends with threats, taunts, racial insults, obscene comments, air raid sirens, whistles, and derogatory songs and chants.

STA members have endangered the lives of spearers by intentionally creating wakes to make it more difficult for spearers to fish. High wakes interfere with a spearer's ability to see and to spear fish and they create the risk that the spearer will fall from the boat into the recently thawed water.

* * *

Protesters have dragged heavy objects through the spawning beds to stir up the lake bottom and make it difficult to see fish. Also they have played "leapfrog" with spearing boats, blocking the path of a boat by pretending to fish by hook-and-line so that the spearer has to go around the protester boat, and then moving quickly in front of the spearing boat again. Another protest tactic is shining boat lights into the faces of spearers so that they cannot see to fish or into the eyes of the boat driver so that he cannot guide the boat. At some boat landings STA members launch boats and remain close to the landing so that they can verbally harass plaintiffs and other spearers and impede their progress as they try to move their boats out to the spawning areas.

On posters and in verbal taunts, STA members and other protesters have expressed racial insults to plaintiffs, their family members and their friends, such as "Timber nigger"; "Save a walleye; spear a squaw"; "Spear a pregnant squaw; save two walleye"; "Custer had the right idea"; "Scalp 'em"; "Tom Maulson is a fucking Jew; he needs a Hitler"; "You're a conquered nation; go home to the reservation"; "wagonburners" and "diarrhea face." Defendant David Worthen has a poster in his bar that reads, "Help Wanted: Small Indians for mud flaps. Must be willing to travel."

Spearers have been threatened with violence. Protesters have told Tom Maulson, "We'll be waiting for you; you'll never get back to

Flambeau"; "We know where your wife is"; "Do you think you'll see your wife again?"; "This is your night tonight." A common STA song at the landings is "Hang down your head, Tom Maulson, poor boy, you're going to die." Protesters have made similar threats to plaintiffs Robert Martin, Nick Hockings and Gilbert Chapman. STA members have told spearers, "We hope you brought your body bags," and have chanted, "Drown them, drown them."

Families and friends of spearers have been threatened with violence and assaulted and battered. During the 1990 spearing season, protesters began the practice of blowing whistles loudly, often directly in the ears of spearing supporters. Protesters have encircled spearing supporters, causing them great anxiety. Also, protesters have hit and shoved spearers' family members and friends and yelled racial and sexual insults at them. One seventeen-year-old boy was told by a protester, "I'm going to remember you. I'm going to get you, you motherfucker."

The activities of the private defendants and others have caused spearers concern for their physical safety and have deterred them from bringing their wives, children and young nieces and nephews with them when they spear. * * *

The private defendants' argument [that their behavior was not racially motivated] ignores the posters labeling spearers as "timberniggers" or "mud flaps" and the taunts of "Custer had the right idea" or "Scalp 'em" or "Go home to the reservation; you're a conquered nation." The private defendants' own statements leave no doubt that much of the anti-spearing campaign is driven by racial hostility toward Indians. * * *

[The court granted the Indians a preliminary injunction prohibiting the private individual defendants from interfering with the Chippewas' spearing of walleye.]

Notes and Questions

1. After *Lac du Flambeau*, are you persuaded that that Indians are just a political minority? Aren't they subject to racism too, and thus also a racial minority?

2. Another problem arises when the tribal identity of Indians is not recognized appropriately. For example, in *Mashpee Tribe v. Town of Mashpee*, 447 F. Supp. 940 (D.Mass.1978), the court decided, despite evidence of the centuries-long existence of the Mashpees, that they were not a tribe for purposes of invoking the Indian Nonintercourse Act, which would have invalidated certain real estate transactions in which the tribe lost some of its ancestral lands. For critiques of the court's decision and insightful discussions of the issues raised by the case concerning tribal identity, see Jo Carrillo, *Identity as Idiom:* Mashpee *Reconsidered,* 28 Ind. L. Rev. 511 (1995), and Gerald Torres & Kathryn Milun, *Translating* Yonnondio *by Precedent and Evidence: The Mashpee Indian Case*, 1990 Duke L. J. 625.

ROBERT A. WILLIAMS, JR.

Columbus's Legacy: The Rehnquist Court's Perpetuation of European
Cultural Racism against American Indian Tribes
39 Fed. Bar News & Journal 358, 359 (1992).*

The law brought to the New World by Columbus and the Europeans who followed him in his quest for colonial empire was irretrievably and irredeemably racist in its origins and application respecting the rights of self-determination belonging to the New World's indigenous tribal peoples. "Racism," in the colonial context, is regarded by most of contemporary United States society as alien or no longer immediately relevant to an historical understanding of itself. Most Americans of European heritage associate "racism" with the oppressions of slavery and subsequent "Jim Crow" forms of *de facto* and *de jure* racial discrimination directed against African Americans. It is important, therefore, in order to understand the continuing legacy of European cultural racism against indigenous tribal peoples in contemporary United States society, to define the unique forms of racial discrimination applied in the colonial context by Europeans in the New World.

Historically, in the United States, the legalized forms of racial discrimination aimed at African Americans were designed generally to prevent systematically the assimilation of the individual African American into the dominant European-derived society. The quaint but insidious racialized caste system of the Old South, with its institutionalized classifications of "quadroon" and "octoroon," by which any "Negro" blood was regarded as tainted, reflected a racist need for keeping African Americans "in their place" as a lower order of humanity serving the needs of the dominant "white" society.

Historically, however, the racism directed against indigenous peoples in the United States has been aimed at *displacing* tribalism as a way of life on lands desired by the dominant European-derived society. Perceived deficiencies in culture, rather than biology and genetics, have served to justify the denial of equal rights of self-determination to indigenous peoples in the New World as cultural groups.

* * *

VINE DELORIA, JR.

Custer Died for Your Sins
168–74 (1988 ed.).*

THE RED AND THE BLACK

Civil rights has been the most important and least understood movement of our generation. To some it has seemed to be a simple matter of fulfilling rights outlined by the Constitutional Amendments after the Civil War. To others, particularly church people, Civil Rights has appeared to be a fulfillment of the brotherhood of man and the determination of humanity's relationship to God. To those opposing the movement, Civil Rights has been a foreign conspiracy which has threatened the fabric of our society.

For many years the movement to give the black people rights equal to those of their white neighbors was called Race Relations. The preoccupation with race obscured the real issues that were developing and meant that programs devised to explore the area of race always had a black orientation.

To the Indian people it has seemed quite unfair that churches and government agencies concentrated their efforts primarily on the blacks. By defining the problem as one of race and making race refer solely to black, Indians were systematically excluded from consideration. National church groups have particularly used race as a means of exploring minority-group relations. Whatever programs or policies outlined from national churches to their affiliates and parishes were generally black-oriented programs which had been adapted to include Indians.

There was probably a historical basis for this type of thinking. In many states in the last century, Indians were classified as white by laws passed to exclude blacks. So there was a connotation that Indians might in some way be like whites. But in other areas, particularly marriage laws, Indians were classified as blacks and this connotation really determined the role into which the white man forced the red man. Consequently, as far as most Race Relations were concerned, Indians were classified as non-whites.

There has been no way to positively determine in which category Indians belong when it comes to federal agencies. The Bureau of Indian Affairs consistently defined Indians as good guys who have too much dignity to demonstrate, hoping to keep the Indian people separate from the ongoing Civil Rights movement. Other agencies generally adopted a semi-black orientation. Sometimes Indians were treated as if they were blacks and other times not.

The Civil Rights Commission and the Community Relations Service always gave only lip service to Indians until it was necessary for them to write an annual report. At that time they always sought out some means of including Indians as a group with which they had worked the previous fiscal year. That was the extent of Indian relationship with the agency: a paragraph in the annual report and a promise to do something next year.

Older Indians, as a rule, have been content to play the passive role outlined for them by the bureau. They have wanted to avoid the rejection and bad publicity given activists.

The Indian people have generally avoided confrontation between the different minority groups and confrontations with the American public at large. They have felt that any publicity would inevitably have bad results and since the press seemed dedicated to the perpetuation of sensationalism rather than straight reporting of the facts, great care has been taken to avoid the spotlight. Because of this attitude, Indian people have not become well known in the field of inter-group and race relations. Consequently they have suffered from the attitudes of people who have only a superficial knowledge of minority groups and have attached a certain stigma to them.

The most common attitude Indians have faced has been the unthoughtful Johnny-come-lately liberal who equates certain goals with a dark skin. This type of individual generally defines the goals of all groups by the way he understands what he wants for the blacks. Foremost in this category have been younger social workers and clergymen entering the field directly out of college or seminary. For the most part they have been book-fed and lack experience in life. They depend primarily upon labels and categories of academic import rather than on any direct experience. Too often they have achieved positions of prominence as programs have been expanded to meet needs of people. In exercising their discretionary powers administratively, they have run roughshod over Indian people. They have not wanted to show their ignorance about Indians. Instead, they prefer to place all people with darker skin in the same category of basic goals, then develop their programs to fit these preconceived ideas.

Since the most numerous group has been the blacks, programs designed for blacks were thought adequate for all needs of all groups. When one asks a liberal about minority groups, he unconsciously seems to categorize them all together for purposes of problem solving. Hence, dark-skinned and minority group as categorical concepts have brought about the same basic results—the Indian is defined as a subcategory of black.

Cultural differences have only seemed to emphasize the white liberal's point of view in lumping the different communities together. When Indians have pointed out real differences that do exist, liberals have tended to dismiss the differences as only minor aberrations which distinguish different racial groups.

At one conference on education of minority groups, I once mentioned the existence of some three hundred Indian languages which made bicultural and bilingual education a necessity. I was immediately challenged by several white educators who attempted to prove that blacks also have a language problem. I was never able to make the difference real to them. For the conference people the point had again been established that minority groups all had the same basic problems.

Recently, blacks and some Indians have defined racial problems as having one focal point—the White Man. This concept is a vast oversimplification of the real problem, as it centers on a racial theme rather than on specific facts. And it is simply the reversal of the old prejudicial attitude of the white who continues to define minority groups as problems of his—that is, Indian problem, Negro problem, and so on.

Rather than race or minority grouping, non-whites have often been defined according to their function within the American society. Negroes, as we have said, were considered draft animals, Indians wild animals. So too, Orientals were considered domestic animals and Mexicans humorous lazy animals. The white world has responded to the non-white groups in a number of ways, but primarily according to the manner in which it believed the non-whites could be rescued from their situation.

Thus Orientals were left alone once whites were convinced that they preferred to remain together and presented no basic threat to white social mores. Mexicans were similarly discarded and neglected when whites felt that they preferred to remain by themselves. In both cases there was no direct confrontation between whites and the two groups because there was no way that a significant number of them could be exploited. They owned little; they provided little which the white world coveted.

With the black and the Indian, however, tensions increased over the years. Both groups had been defined as animals with which the white had to have some relation and around whom some attitude must be formed. Blacks were ex-draft animals who somehow were required to become non-black. Indeed, respectability was possible for a black only by emphasizing characteristics and features that were non-black. Indians were the ex-wild animals who had provided the constant danger for the civilizing tendencies of the invading white. They always presented a foreign aspect to whites unfamiliar with the western hemisphere.

The white man adopted two basic approaches in handling blacks and Indians. He systematically excluded blacks from all programs, policies, social events, and economic schemes. He could not allow blacks to rise from their position because it would mean that the evolutionary scheme had superseded the Christian scheme and that man had perhaps truly descended from the ape.

With the Indian the process was simply reversed. The white man had been forced to deal with the Indian in treaties and agreements. It was difficult, therefore, to completely overlook the historical antecedents such as Thanksgiving, the plight of the early Pilgrims, and the desperate straits from which various Indian tribes had often rescued the whites. Indians were therefore subjected to the most intense pressure to become white. Laws passed by Congress had but one goal—the Anglo-Saxonization of the Indian. The antelope had to become a white man.

Between these two basic attitudes, the apelike draft animal and the wild free-running antelope, the white man was impaled on the horns of a dilemma he had created within himself.

It is well to keep these distinctions clearly in mind when talking about Indians and blacks. When the liberals equate the two they are overlooking obvious historical facts. Never did the white man systematically exclude Indians from his schools and meeting places. Nor did the white man ever kidnap black children from their homes and take them off to a government boarding school to be educated as whites. The white man signed no treaties with the black. Nor did he pass any amendments to the Constitution to guarantee the treaties of the Indian.

The basic problem which has existed between the various racial groups has not been one of race but of culture and legal status. The white man systematically destroyed Indian culture where it existed, but separated blacks from his midst so that they were forced to attempt the creation of their own culture.

The white man forbade the black to enter his own social and economic system and at the same time force-fed the Indian what he was denying the black. Yet the white man demanded that the black conform to white standards and insisted that the Indian don feathers and beads periodically to perform for him.

The white man presented the *problem* of each group in contradictory ways so that neither black nor Indian could understand exactly where the problem existed or how to solve it. The Indian was always told that his problem was one of conflicting cultures. Yet, when solutions were offered by the white man, they turned out to be a reordering of the legal relationship between red and white. There was never a time when the white man said he was trying to help the Indian get into the mainstream of American life that he did not also demand that the Indian give up land, water, minerals, timber, and other resources which would enrich the white men.

The black also suffered from the same basic lie. Time after time legislation was introduced which purported to give the black equal rights with the white but which ultimately restricted his life and opportunities, even his acceptance by white people. The initial Civil Rights Act following the thirteenth, fourteenth and fifteenth amendments was assumed to give the blacks equal rights with "white citizens." In fact, it was so twisted that it took nearly a century to bring about additional legislation to confirm black rights.

In June of 1968 the Supreme Court finally interpreted an ancient statute in favor of blacks in the matter of purchasing a house. Had the right existed for nearly a century without anyone knowing it? Of course not, the white had simply been unwilling to give in to the black. Can one blame the black athletes at the recent Olympic Games for their rebellion against the role cast for them by white society? Should they be considered as specially trained athletic animals suitable only for hauling away tons of gold medals for the United States every four years while equality remains as distant as it ever was?

It is time for both black and red to understand the ways of the white man. The white is after Indian lands and resources. He always has been and always will be. For Indians to continue to think of their basic conflict with the white man as cultural is the height of folly. The problem is and always has been the adjustment of the legal relationship between the Indian tribes and the federal government, between the true owners of the land and the usurpers.

The black must understand that whites are determined to keep him out of their society. No matter how many Civil Rights laws are passed or how many are on the drawing board, the basic thrust is to keep the black out of society and harmless. The problem, therefore, is not one of legal status, it is one of culture and social and economic mobility. It is foolish for a black to depend upon a law to make acceptance of him by the white possible. Nor should he react to the rejection. His problem is social, and economic, and cultural, not one of adjusting the legal relationship between the two groups.

When the black seeks to change his role by adjusting the laws of the nation, he merely raises the hope that progress is being made. But for the majority of blacks progress is not being made. Simply because a middle-class black can eat at the Holiday Inn is not a gain. People who can afford the best generally get it. A socio-economic, rather than legal adjustment, must consequently be the goal.

Notes and Questions

1. Both Williams and Deloria make a point about the difference in the racism experienced by Blacks and Indians. How would you describe the difference?

2. Is Deloria too harsh in his description of Blacks, Indians, "Orientals," and Mexicans as different types of animals? Or is he describing a certain truth about the way white society racializes each group?

3. Consider Deloria's critique of the reliance of Blacks on changes in civil rights laws. Is he too dismissive of the possibilities of transformation through legal change, or appropriately skeptical? What does historical context teach about the usefulness of law in changing the relative statuses of the races?

4. Reconsider Jefferson's letter to the Marquis de Chastellux, *supra*, and the excerpt from *Notes on the State of Virginia*, in Chapter 2, in which Jefferson seems to view Indians and Blacks differently. How do Jefferson's views compare with the roles Deloria claims that white society assigns to Blacks and Indians? How much has changed in the perception of these two peoples in the roughly two hundred years separating the two documents?

5. Describe the differential constructions or racializations of Indians and Blacks. How do you understand the groups to be different or alike?

INTERNATIONAL HUMAN RIGHTS STRATEGIES FOR INDIGENOUS PEOPLES

One of the most recent civil rights strategies of indigenous peoples is advocacy for development of international norms of human rights that recognize their unique histories and needs. These norms support important arguments regarding self-determination for native peoples. Consider the following excerpt, which gives both a historical introduction to Native Hawaiians and a survey of international human rights norms supporting the claims of indigenous peoples generally.

S. JAMES ANAYA

The Native Hawaiian People and International Human Rights
Law: Toward a Remedy for Past and Continuing Wrongs
28 Ga. L. Rev. 309, 311–20, 336–57, 359–62 (1994).*

Foreign influence has weighed heavily on indigenous Hawaiians since the British explorer James Cook landed there in 1778. At that time, several hundred thousand people populated the Islands.

Their modern-day descendants, the indigenous or Native Hawaiians, trace their origins through oral tradition to early Polynesians and beyond them to the forces of nature. As recounted by the Hawaiian historian Davianna Pomaika'i McGregor,

> [t]he Hawaiian people are the living descendants of Papa, the earth mother and Wakea, the sky father. They also trace their origins through Kane of the living waters found in streams and springs; Lono of the winter rains and the life force for agricultural crops; Kanaloa of the deep foundation of the earth, the ocean and its currents and winds; Ku of the thunder, war, fishing and planting; Pele of the volcano; and thousands of deities of the forest, the ocean, the winds, the rains and the various other elements of nature. . . . This unity of humans, nature and the gods formed the core of the Hawaiian people's philosophy, world view, and spiritual belief system.[6]

The Hawaiian world view shaped political and social institutions in existence at the time of Western contact. Hawaiians lived within a system of interrelated chiefdoms and communal land tenure. The basic land unit was the communal *ahupua'a*, which typically included irrigated agricultural land and access to the sea. The cultivation of taro and fishing were at the center of an abundant economy that supported a social structure integrating the entire archipelago. As foreigners arrived in greater numbers in the early nineteenth century, the Islands became unified under a single high chief or king, Kamehameha I. Political unification was instrumental both in preserving the indigenous land tenure system in the face of the onslaught of foreigners and in providing central leadership with which foreigners could deal.

It was not long before substantial foreign influence came to bear upon the Hawaiian people and their government. Traders seeking commercial advantage and proselytizing missionaries were the first to attempt aggressively to reshape Hawaiian cultural, economic and political life. The Hawaiian land tenure system came under heightened pressure as foreigners sought land for themselves and settled in Hawaii in increasing numbers. Ka Mahele (The Land Division) of 1848 was the transformation of traditional Hawaiian land tenure into a property regime that facilitated the alienation of lands and hence was more suited to Western economic interests. By the late nineteenth century, foreigners, mostly American, owned over a million acres in Hawaii and leased another three-quarters of a million acres of government, or Crown lands, at near nominal rates.

In 1887, a group of American residents with United States military support forced the Hawaiian monarch, King Kalakaua, to sign what has become known as the "Bayonet Constitution." Under the 1887 Constitution, the King was reduced to a figurehead, and the Hawaiian government was placed in the hands of a United States-dominated cabinet. Any pretense of constitutional regularity was disregarded in 1893 when United States troops invaded Hawaii and helped depose the King's successor, Queen Liliuokalani, and replace her with a provisional govern-

6. Davianna McGregor, *Hawaiians Organizing in the 1970's*, 7 Amerasia J. 3 (1980).

ment. American residents subsequently established the short-lived "Republic of Hawaii" and forced the imprisoned Queen to abdicate officially. The United States formally annexed Hawaii in 1898, despite a petition to Congress, signed by about 29,000 Hawaiians, protesting the annexation.

Thus, Hawaii became a territory of the United States, joining the ranks of colonial territories of other Western powers driven by the forces of empire. The Organic Act of 1900 set up a territorial government headed by a governor appointed by the United States. Under it, the remnants of Hawaiian land tenure, other traditional or customary institutions, and cultural practices, including the use of the Hawaiian language, were suppressed. This was in keeping with Western thinking, which regarded non-Western cultures as inferior, coupled with an official policy of assimilating the indigenous Hawaiians into American cultural life. With annexation, furthermore, the Hawaiian Crown and government lands, in which the Hawaiian people were to have an interest following the Mahele, passed to the United States, and the private acquisitive forces of American Manifest Destiny were altogether unleashed. In the process of Western encroachment culminating in the 1898 annexation,

> many Hawaiians found they no longer could farm or gain access to the traditional gathering areas in the mountains and the ocean that once supported them. Other Hawaiians were left landless. As a result, many were forced to move to urban areas to seek employment. They abandoned traditional subsistence living, which had supported the Hawaiian culture for centuries. Many Hawaiians became members of the "floating population crowding into the congested tenement districts of the larger towns and cities of the Territory" under conditions which many believed would "inevitably result in the extermination of the race."

> Stripped of their resource base, Hawaiians faced a cultural crisis and the decimation of their population. In the century following Western contact, hundreds of thousands of Hawaiians died from a variety of infectious diseases introduced by the white man. Ailments seldom fatal to foreigners were deadly for Hawaiians who had acquired no immunity to these diseases. Under conservative estimates, from 1778 to 1893, the Hawaiian population dropped by at least 87 percent, from approximately 300,000 to less than 40,000. More recent theorists believe that this population decline has been grossly understated.[8]

In 1910, recognizing deteriorating social and economic conditions among indigenous Hawaiians, the United States Congress amended the Organic Act to facilitate homesteading. The 1910 amendment was followed by the Hawaiian Homes Commission Act of 1920, which set aside approximately 200,000 acres of public lands for Native Hawaiian homesteads. Neither piece of legislation, however, had much effect on the overall conditions of indigenous Hawaiians. Despite a backlog of homestead applicants, most of the land set aside by the 1920 Act has yet to be

---

8. *Native Hawaiian Rights Handbook* 44 (Melody Kapilialoha MacKenzie ed.   1991)(quoting S. Cong. Rec.2, 10th Leg. of Territory of Hawaii, 1919 Senate J. 25–26).

distributed, and what has been is largely unsuitable for agriculture. Observers surmise that the legislation was mostly calculated to benefit large agricultural business by limiting the availability of land necessary to meet the needs of Hawaiian homesteaders and by terminating homesteading by the general public. Subsequent legislation similarly has failed to raise Native Hawaiians from their severely disadvantaged condition.

The 1959 Statehood Admission Act, by which Hawaii gained statehood, transferred to the State of Hawaii most of the lands that had been ceded to the United States at annexation in 1898. The State, however, failed for years to act effectively on its trust obligation specified in the Act to hold the lands in part "for the betterment of the conditions of Native Hawaiians." The State amended its constitution in 1978 in what is generally considered a meager step toward addressing Native Hawaiian concerns over the ceded lands trust. The 1978 constitutional amendments created the Office of Hawaiian Affairs, which is managed by a Native Hawaiian board of trustees elected by Native Hawaiians in a special election. The board receives and expends the portion of income from the trust lands that is allocable to Native Hawaiians.

Plundered by two centuries of Western encroachment and left virtually landless, Native Hawaiians living on the Islands today number around 204,000—about one fifth of the Islands' population. As a group, Native Hawaiians comprise the most economically disadvantaged sector of the Islands' population, overrepresented among the ranks of welfare recipients and prison inmates and underrepresented among high school and college graduates, professionals, and political officials. * * *

Without an effective land base, surviving Native Hawaiian customs—intertwined with land use and stewardship patterns—are suppressed. Access to and protection of sacred sites, including the volcano deity Pele, have been matters of particularly intense struggle for Native Hawaiians. Other remaining aspects of Native Hawaiian culture are subsumed within a majority settler population with its cultural roots elsewhere. Native Hawaiians are governed by Western-oriented institutions that, while essentially democratic, scarcely reflect Native Hawaiians' own distinctive values and traditions and are dominated by the majority settler population. * * *

THE PRINCIPLE OF SELF-DETERMINATION

* * *

[S]elf-determination is a universe of human rights precepts concerned broadly with peoples, including the Native Hawaiian people, and grounded in the idea that all are equally entitled to be in control of their own destinies. * * * Self-determination includes two strains: first, that the governing institutional order substantially be the creation of constitutional processes guided by the will of the people, or peoples, governed; second, that the governing institutional order, independently of the processes leading to its creation or alteration, be one under which people may live and develop freely on a continuous basis. Self-determination gives rise to remedies that tear at the legacies of empire, discrimination, suppression of democratic participation, and cultural suffocation.

* * *

The latest U.N. Working Group draft declaration on indigenous peoples' rights contains specific recognition of the right of indigenous peoples to self-determination. The 1993 draft, borrowing from the self-determination language of the International Human Rights Covenants, declares: Indigenous peoples have the right of self-determination. By virtue of that right they freely determine their political status and freely pursue their economic, social and cultural development.[87]

* * *

Insofar as indigenous peoples have been denied self-determination, the international indigenous rights regime prescribes remedial measures, that may involve changes in the political order, [that] are to be developed in accordance with the aspirations of indigenous peoples themselves. Thus, ILO Convention No. 169 requires the development of "special measures" to safeguard indigenous "persons, institutions, property, labour, cultures and environment," and specifies that the measures be consistent with "the freely-expressed wishes of the peoples concerned."[90] Also, the Convention requires that consultations with indigenous peoples "be undertaken, in good faith...with the objective of achieving agreement or consent."

* * *

The international norms concerning indigenous peoples, which elaborate upon the requirements of self-determination, generally fall within the following categories: cultural integrity, lands and resources, social welfare and development, and self-government. * * *

1. Cultural Integrity. A central aspect of self-determination is the ability of groups to maintain and freely develop their cultural identities. The notion of respect for cultural determinism has long been a feature of bilateral as well as multilateral treaties. For example, Article 27 of the United States-ratified International Covenant on Civil and Political Rights[101] affirms in universalist terms the right of persons belonging to "ethnic, religious or linguistic minorities ... to enjoy their own culture, to profess and practice their own religion, (and) to use their own language."

* * *

* * * As the international community has come to consider indigenous cultures as equal in value to all others, the cultural integrity norm has developed to entitle indigenous groups like the Native Hawaiian people to affirmative measures to remedy the past undermining of their

87. Draft Declaration on the Rights of Indigenous Peoples as Agreed Upon by the Members of the Working Group at its Eleventh Session, Art. 3, U.N. Doc. E/CN.4/Sub.2/1993/29, Annex I (1993).

90. *Convention Concerning Indigenous and Tribal Peoples in Independent Countries* (No. 169), International Labour Conference, June 27, 1989 (entered into force Sept. 5, 1991), Art. 4.

101. *International Covenant on Civil and Political Rights*, Art. 27, Section 1, G.A. Res. 2200, U.N. GAOR, 21st Sess., Supp. No. 16, U.N. Doc A/6316 (1966).

cultural survival and to guard against continuing threats. It is not sufficient, therefore, that states simply refrain from coercing assimilation of indigenous peoples or abandonment of their cultural practices. ILO Convention No. 169 provides:

> Governments shall have responsibility for developing, with the participation of the peoples concerned, coordinated and systematic action to protect the rights of these peoples and to guarantee respect for their integrity.

* * *

2. Lands and Natural Resources. The importance of lands and resources to the survival of indigenous cultures is widely acknowledged. * * * [A] self-determination provision common to the International Human Rights Covenants affirms: "In no case may a people be deprived of its own means of subsistence."

* * *

* * * Article 14(1) of ILO Convention No. 169 affirms:

> The rights of ownership and possession of (indigenous peoples) over the lands which they traditionally occupy shall be recognised. In addition, measures shall be taken in appropriate cases to safeguard the right of the peoples concerned to use lands not exclusively occupied by them, but to which they have traditionally had access for their subsistence and traditional activities. Article 15, furthermore, specifies the right "to participate in the use, management and conservation" of the natural resources pertaining to their lands.

The land rights provisions of Convention No. 169 are framed by article 13(1), which states:

> In applying the provisions of this Part of the Convention governments shall respect the special importance for the cultures and spiritual values of the peoples concerned of their relationship with the lands or territories, or both as applicable, which they occupy or otherwise use, and in particular the collective aspects of this relationship.

* * *

Consider also Article 14(3), which mandates "(a)dequate procedures ... within the national legal system to resolve land claims by" indigenous peoples. This provision is without any temporal limitation and thus empowers claims originating well in the past. Article 14(3) is a response to the historical processes that have afflicted indigenous peoples, including the Native Hawaiians, by trampling on their cultural attachment to ancestral lands, disregarding or minimizing their legitimate property interests, and leaving them without adequate means of subsistence. In light of the acknowledged centrality of lands and resources to indigenous cultures and economies, the requirement to provide meaningful redress for indigenous land claims implies an obligation on the part of states to provide remedies that include the option of regaining lands and access to natural resources.

* * *

3. Social Welfare and Development. Indigenous peoples' interests in a secure land base are both cultural and economic. Related to these interests are entitlements of social welfare and development, entitlements also grounded in the U.N. Charter and the principle of self-determination.[†]

Building upon the Charter provisions, the International Covenant on Economic, Social, and Cultural Rights affirms an array of social welfare rights and corresponding state obligations that are to benefit "everyone," including rights to health, education, and an adequate standard of living. * * *

* * * In December of 1986, the U.N. General Assembly adopted by an overwhelming majority the "Declaration on the Right to Development"—"an inalienable human right by virtue of which every human person and all peoples are entitled to participate in, contribute to, and enjoy economic, social, cultural and political development, in which all human rights and fundamental freedoms can be fully realized."

* * * These norms are aimed at remedying two distinct but related historical phenomena that result in most indigenous communities living in an economically disadvantaged condition. The first such phenomenon entails the progressive plundering of indigenous peoples' lands and resources over time, processes that have impaired or, as in the case of Native Hawaiians, devastated indigenous economies and subsistence life and left indigenous people among the poorest of the poor. The second corresponds with patterns of discrimination that have tended to exclude members of indigenous communities from enjoyment of the social welfare benefits generally available in the states within which they live.

In response to these historical phenomena, ILO Convention No. 169 establishes "as a matter of priority" the "improvement of the conditions of life and work and levels of health and education of (indigenous) peoples," and it mandates "(s)pecial projects ... to promote such improvement." The Convention, furthermore, specifies duties on the part of states to ensure the absence of discriminatory practices and effects in areas of employment, vocational training, social security and health, education, and means of communication. The Convention emphasizes that the special programs devised to ensure the social welfare and development of indigenous peoples are to be established in cooperation with the indigenous peoples concerned and in accordance with their own collectively formulated priorities.

* * *

† [Editors' Footnote] Chapter IX of the Charter, under the heading "International Economic and Social Co-operation," states in part:

Article 55

With a view to the creation of conditions of stability and well-being which are necessary for peaceful and friendly relations among nations based on respect for the principle of equal rights and self-determination of peoples, the United Nations shall promote:

a. higher standards of living, full employment, and conditions of economic and social progress and development;

b. solutions of international economic, social, health, and related problems; and international cultural and educational co-operation....

Article 56

All members pledge themselves to take joint and separate action in co-operation with the Organization for the achievement of the purposes set forth in Article 55.

4. Self–Government. Self-government consists of the idea that government is to function according to the will of the people governed. * * *

In the particular context of indigenous peoples, notions of democracy (including decentralized government) join with precepts of cultural integrity to create a *sui generis* self-government norm. The norm upholds the accommodation of spheres of governmental or administrative autonomy for indigenous communities, while at the same time upholding measures to ensure their effective participation in all decisions affecting them left to the larger institutions of government.

ILO Convention No. 169 upholds the right of indigenous peoples to "retain their own customs and institutions"; and requires that "the methods customarily practised by the peoples concerned for dealing with offences committed by their members shall be respected." Similarly, the 1993 Working Group Draft Declaration states: "Indigenous peoples have the right to promote, develop and maintain their institutional structures and their distinctive juridical customs, traditions, procedures and practices, in accordance with internationally recognized human rights standards."

* * * In the context of Native Hawaiians, Michael Dudley and Keoni Agard echo the demand for "nationhood" and "sovereignty"—that is, some form of autonomous political status for Native Hawaiians—as a means of securing the education of children in Hawaiian ways, for the revitalization of the Hawaiian language, for the reclaiming of the Native Hawaiian spiritual heritage and connection with the natural world, and, in general, for the natural evolution of Hawaiian culture cushioned from the onslaught of outside influences that have thus far had devastating effects.

* * *

The dual thrust of the normative regime concerning indigenous peoples' self-government—on the one hand autonomy and on the other participatory engagement—reflects the view, apparently held by indigenous peoples themselves, that they are not to be considered a priori unconnected from larger social and political structures. Rather, indigenous groups—whether characterized as communities, peoples, nations or other—are appropriately viewed as simultaneously distinct yet parts of larger units of social and political interaction, units which may include indigenous federations, the states within which they live, and the global community itself. This view challenges traditional Western conceptions of mutually exclusive states and promotes a political order that is less state-centered and more centered on people living in a world of distinct yet increasingly integrated and overlapping spheres of community and authority.

* * *

The norms just discussed and the underlying principle of self-determination are binding upon the United States. The United States is party to the U.N. Charter and the International Covenant on Civil and Political Rights, both of which expressly affirm the principle of self-determination. The Charter, the Covenant, and other international treaties to which the United States is a party include related human rights norms. Particularly relevant are the cultural rights guarantees expressed in Article 27 of the Covenant and developed through authoritative interpretive processes. The United States is bound to uphold new and developing international norms concerning indigenous peoples, insofar as those norms form part of the principle of self-determination or are derivative of related treaty norms. The United States is furthermore bound insofar as the norms concerning indigenous peoples are part of general or customary international law. Customary norms are binding upon the constituent units of the world community regardless of any formal act of assent to those norms.

* * *

Notes and Questions

1.   In 1993, Congress passed the following joint resolution: * * *

Whereas the health and well-being of the Native Hawaiian people is intrinsically tied to their deep feelings and attachment to the land;

Whereas the long-range economic and social changes in Hawaii over the nineteenth and early twentieth centuries have been devastating to the population and to the health and well-being of the Hawaiian people;

Whereas the Native Hawaiian people are determined to preserve, develop and transmit to future generations their ancestral territory, and their cultural identity in accordance with their own spiritual and traditional beliefs, customs, practices, language, and social institutions;

* * *

Whereas it is proper and timely for the Congress on the occasion of the impending one hundredth anniversary of the event, to acknowledge the historic significance of the illegal overthrow of the Kingdom of Hawaii, to express its deep regret to the Native Hawaiian people, and to support the reconciliation efforts of the State of Hawaii and the United Church of Christ with Native Hawaiians;

* * *

Section 1. Acknowledgement and Apology.

The Congress—

(1) on the occasion of the 100th anniversary of the illegal overthrow of the Kingdom of Hawaii on January 17, 1893, acknowledges the historical significance of this event which resulted in the suppression of the inherent sovereignty of the Native Hawaiian people;

(2) recognizes and commends efforts of reconciliation initiated by the State of Hawaii and the United Church of Christ with Native Hawaiians;

(3) apologizes to Native Hawaiians on behalf of the people of the United States for the overthrow of the Kingdom of Hawaii on January 17, 1893 with the participation of agents and citizens of the United States, and the deprivation of the rights of Native Hawaiians to self-determination;

(4) expresses its commitment to acknowledge the ramifications of the overthrow of the Kingdom of Hawaii, in order to provide a proper foundation for

reconciliation between the United States and the Native Hawaiian people; and

(5) urges the President of the United States to also acknowledge the ramifications of the overthrow of the Kingdom of Hawaii and to support reconciliation efforts between the United States and the Native Hawaiian people.

S.J. Res. 19, 103d Cong., 1st Sess., 107 Stat. 1510 (1993).

2. What else, if anything, should Congress do to conform to norms of international human rights in its treatment of Native Hawaiians?

3. What should Congress do to conform to these norms in the treatment of other Indian peoples?

4. Notice that Congress has passed no resolution like Joint Resolution 19 for African Americans. Why not? Indeed, there was so much controversy over President Clinton uttering an apology for slavery that he never made one. Why is it easier to pass a joint resolution apologizing for the treatment of Native Hawaiians than for the treatment of Africans and African Americans?

5. How would you draft a resolution, addressed to African Americans, apologizing for slavery? What else, if anything, would constitute a just remedy?

6. For another source on the move by indigenous peoples to assert claims based on the law of international human rights, see Robert A. Williams, Jr., *Encounters on the Frontiers of International Human Rights Law: Redefining the Terms of Indigenous Peoples' Survival in the World*, 1990 Duke L.J. 660.

7. For additional sources on the status and legal rights of native Hawaiians, see Jon M. Van Dyke, *The Political Status of the Native Hawaiian People*, 17 Yale L. & Pol'y Rev. 95 (1998) (demonstrating comprehensively that the "Native Hawaiian people have their own unique 'special relationship' with the United States and the State of Hawai'i," justifying special treatment under U.S. and international law; criticizing Benjamin article, cited *infra* this note); Mililani B. Trask, *Historical and Contemporary Hawaiian Self–Determination: A Native Hawaiian Perspective*, 8 Ariz. J. Int'l & Comp. L. 77 (1991); Maivan Clech Lam, *The Kuleana Act Revisited: The Survival of Traditional Hawaiian Commoner Rights in Land*, 64 Wash. L. Rev. 233 (1989).

For a controversial interpretation of the status of Native Hawaiians, see Stuart Minor Benjamin, *Equal Protection and the Special Relationship: The Case of Native Hawaiians*, 106 Yale L.J. 537 (1996) (arguing that because native Hawaiians are not organized as an Indian tribe, the *Adarand* decision [discussed in Chapter 7, § 3] will likely subject programs for native Hawaiians to strict scrutiny review). But see Philip P. Frickey, *Adjudication and its Discontents: Coherence and Conciliation in Federal Indian Law*, 110 Harv. L. Rev. 1754, 1757 (1997) (commenting on Benjamin article: "Benjamin's analysis of the constitutional issues concerning the special treatment of Hawaiian natives exposes a different, but more fundamental problem: Unless injected with a heavy dose of historical perspective and legal realism, formal lawyerly analysis not only often fails to illuminate the issues in federal Indian law, but can also result in deceiving conclusions.").

Chapter 4

LATINOS/AS

The experience of Latinos/as, particularly Mexican Americans and Puerto Ricans, is one of struggle, conquest and the ramifications of conquest. Both populations endured a double conquest, an early conquest and governance by the Spanish, followed by conquest and governance by the United States. Both conquests continue to exert powerful influence on American life.

We are taught little about the conquest of Mexico, and the later invasion of Puerto Rico. The relative lack of widely disseminated knowledge about the history of Latino people in the United States contrasts with our much greater knowledge of the experience of African Americans. We do not mean to suggest that public knowledge of African Americans and their history is in any way adequate. Rather, as inadequate as our knowledge of African Americans may be, that knowledge far exceeds public knowledge and recognition of the history of Latinos in the United States. Readers should ask themselves why this is so. Is there anything inherent in conquest that produces this result? As historian Patricia Limerick has observed:

> Like slavery, conquest tested the ideals of the United States. Conquest deeply affected both the conqueror and the conquered, just as slavery shaped slaveholder and slave. Both historical experiences left deep imprints on particular regions and on the nation at large. The legacy of slavery and the legacy of conquest endure, shaping events in our own time.

> Here, however, we reach a principal difference: To most twentieth-century Americans, the legacy of slavery was serious business, while the legacy of conquest was not. Southern historians successfully fought through the aura of moonlight and magnolias, and established slavery, emancipation, and black/white relations as major issues in American history. The Civil War, Reconstruction, the migration of Southern blacks into other regions, and the civil rights movement all guaranteed that the nation would recognize the significance of slavery and the South.

Patricia Nelson Limerick, *The Legacy of Conquest* 18–19 (1987).

Given the importance of conquest, why do we know so little about it? In particular, why do we know so little about the significance of conquest in the legal history of Mexican Americans and other Latinos/as? Mexicans were subject to a double conquest: first by Spain, and then by Anglo Americans, through the annexation of Texas and the United States' War with Mexico of 1846–48. The experience and legacy of Spanish conquest are one of the links between the histories of Latinos and Indians in the United States. Another is the ultimate conquest of both groups by the United States. The notion of overlapping conquests is well described by Edward Spicer:

> The frontiers of the Spanish and the English conquests on North America met and overlapped in the arid southwestern part of the continent. The Spanish conquest, after two hundred years of steady advance northward from the Valley of Mexico, faltered during the last half of the 1700s and, in the face of the uncontrollable Apaches in what is now Sonora, began to recede a little southward. The English conquest, some two hundred years behind the Spanish, had by this time reached only into the Plains states and Texas; but by the early 1800s Anglo–American trappers were venturing into the already Spanish-explored provinces of New Mexico, New Biscay, and Sonora. Then in 1848, with the Treaty of Guadalupe Hidalgo closing the war between Mexico and the United States, the latter took over the frontier which Spain had never quite been able to control. As the region was partitioned into the modern states of Chihuahua, Sonora, New Mexico, and Arizona, the two new nations of Mexico and the United States resumed Spain's wavering efforts to conquer and make over the Indians.

Edward H. Spicer, *Cycles of Conquest* 4–5 (1962). Spicer is also careful to mention the role of independent Mexico in conquering Indians subject to its jurisdiction, so with regard to Indians, there is yet another layer to the conquests.

The population of areas originally conquered by Spain became racially varied and mixed through intermarriage between Spaniards and Indians, as well as rape and the Spanish importation of black slaves, who also intermarried with Indians. Contrary to the myths of a pure Spanish population of the northern regions of Mexico (which came to form part of the United States upon the independence of Texas and at the conclusion of the Mexican–American war), the first census of Los Angeles, in 1781, reveals a racially mixed Mexican population. Only two of 47 persons counted were identified as Spanish; the majority were identified as mulatto/a, mestizo/a, Indian, and Black. *Foreigners in Their Native Land* 33–35 (David Weber ed. 1973). According to one estimate of the population of South and Central America in 1823, Whites were only about twenty percent of the total population, with far larger proportions of mestizos and Indians and a smaller number of Blacks. See Charles Edward Chapman, *Colonial Hispanic America* 189 (1933).

An important reason to describe the Spanish conquest, as well as the United States', is that we still live, to a greater or lesser extent, with the consequences of that conquest. The Spanish imperatives of conquest called for civilizing the native peoples by teaching them the Spanish language and by converting them to the Roman Catholic religion. Spicer, *supra* at 5. Thus the current importance of Spanish and Catholicism to many, but certainly not all, Latinos stems fairly directly from the objectives of the Spanish conquest. Furthermore, past and current controversies over Official English, Spanish, and bilingual education have roots in the Spanish conquest followed by the American conquest, which we explore below.

Much of the material readers will encounter in these pages is not widely known. The omission of this material, which includes treaties, state constitutions, federal legislation and Supreme Court decisions, from standard histories may shed some light on the nature of conquest. Perhaps historians and textbook writers unconsciously need to forget that the United States engaged in aggressive military conquest of Mexico, and later the military invasion and subsequent annexation of Puerto Rico. Perhaps the facts of these conquests, and ensuing developments, were too inconsistent with the image of a peaceful, benevolent United States spreading freedom throughout the world. Consider, for example, the contrast between the tradition of celebration of World War II, in which the United States could more legitimately claim to be fighting in the interests of freedom, and the intellectual and historical oblivion reserved for the War with Mexico. Was the War with Mexico unimportant? Today, approximately one-third of the continental United States consists of land acquired or annexed from Mexico, including California, Texas, New Mexico, Arizona, Nevada and parts of Colorado, Utah, and Kansas. This amount of land and its importance to the present-day United States can hardly be considered unimportant, yet we know very little about how this land came to belong to the United States. The story of how Latinos came to be incorporated in the United States has yet to be told and included as part of United States history.

Consider the following excerpt on the different groups that constitute the Latino/a population of the United States.

BERTA ESPERANZA HERNÁNDEZ-TRUYOL

Building Bridges—Latinas and Latinos at the Crossroads:
Realities, Rhetoric and Replacement
25 Colum Hum. Rts. L. Rev. 369, 383–393 (1994).*

DEMOGRAPHICS OF THE HISPANIC POPULATION

Since the early 1800s persons of latina/o origin have been a substantial presence in the United States. The 1980 census, however, represents the first time that a serious effort was made to improve the coverage of the latina/o population. Social scientists consider the "most significant change" in the 1980 census the inclusion of a question that "required all households to indicate whether their members were of Spanish/Hispanic origin or descent." If the response was affirmative, the households were asked specifically whether the origin was Mexican, Puerto Rican, Cuban or other. This inquiry resulted in the largest count of people of latina/o origin in the United States: approximately 14,600,000, comprising approximately 6.54% of the country's population. Demographers estimated that 97% of all persons identifying themselves as latina/o at that time were white, most likely because latinas/os' concept of whiteness differs greatly from the NLW [Non–Latino White] idea of whiteness.

Since this first attempt at a comprehensive count, the latina/o population in the United States has increased by 53%. By 1991 it had grown to approximately twenty-two million, constituting about 9% of the total United States population. [Eds. This percentage now stands at about 11%. See *The Latino/a Condition: A Critical Reader* xvii (R. Delgado & J. Stefancic eds. 1998).] At this rate of growth, it is predicted that the latina/o population of the United States will double in size by the year 2020. If these prognostications are accurate, latinas/os will soon become the nation's largest ethnic group.

Considering latinas/os' exponentially increasing presence and concomitant ability to make their voices heard, it is surprising that their potential roar remains a mere whisper. The explanation could lie, in part, in our diversity. Notwithstanding the uniform label, latinas/os speak in many different voices. In fact, although the generic term "latina/o" is used to designate a class, as is shown below, the term really classifies an "outsider" ethnic group that is far from homogeneous. Consequently, because of the diversity within the classification, no single issue or agenda around latina(*o*)ness has caught fire.

A review of the make-up of the latina/o population in the United States reveals four major latina/o-origin subgroups: (1) Mexican, 12.6 million persons, constituting 62.6% of all latinas/os—well over half of the latina/o population; (2) Puerto Rican, numbering 2.5 million, or 13% of the latina/o population; (3) Central or South American, also totalling 2.5 million, or 13% of the latina/o population; and (4) Cuban, 1.1 million, or 5.3% of the latinas/os in the United States. The balance of the population is classified as "other hispanic origins"—those whose origins are in Spain and those who identify themselves as "hispanic," Spanish, Spanish–American, or latina/o. This catch-all category is made up of 1.6 million, or 7.8% of the latina/o population.

The migration history of these groups illustrates their varied roots. It promotes understanding about the diversity of latinas/os, and also the differences in their origins as they relate to the "majority" group. The following paragraphs briefly describe the circumstances surrounding these migrations—when and from where the flow came.

Prior to 1900, the number of people who migrated to the United States from Mexico was small. In fact, the first Mexican–American presence in the United States resulted not from migration of people from Mexico to the United States, but rather from the shifting of the United States borders south—to include approximately 50% of Mexico's territory—as a result of the United States' victory in war. The Treaty of Guadalupe Hidalgo ended the Mexican–American War and created the Mexican–American peoples as it "gave the 75,000 Mexicans living in what later became the states of California, Arizona, New Mexico, and Colorado . . . the option of moving south to Mexico or staying put and automatically becoming American Citizens." Given "19th century reality, a distant federal government, whether Mexican or American, probably made little difference to the residents of the region," with the consequence that very few persons in the newly annexed territory—estimated at only 2000—opted to leave their homes and move south to the land that was still Mexico. During the period of annexation, a Mexican–American ethnic identity probably did not exist. However, social scientists posit that an identity emerged soon thereafter because "[f]ollowing incorporation of the Southwest into the United States in the mid–1800s there developed the experience of economic subjugation, followed by race and ethnic prejudice."[73]

Between 1900 and 1940, however, the numbers of Mexicans journeying to the United States began to increase and the "creation generation" gave way to the "migration generation." Some reasons for this increase were the Mexican Revolution, poor economic conditions, and a rapid increase in the size of the Mexican population already within the United States. Another reason for this new migration northward was the desire for higher wages associated with the need for manual labor in farms and ranches of the Southwest. The dramatic increase of Mexicans coming north to the United States resulted in Mexican–Americans being the smaller of the Mexican-origin populations in the United States.

Historians and sociologists saw a change in Mexican–American ethnic identity in the post-World War II through 1965 period. This "Mexican–American" or "Chicano" generation, while identifying itself culturally with the United States, lagged behind American society demographically in such areas as economics, years of education and annual income. By the 1960s most of the Mexican–Americans were second or third generation, with a heightened consciousness about the desire to change the status of their community in the United States and fight discrimination in all areas of life. Today, Mexicans still account for the largest number of latina/o immigrants to the United States, both legally and illegally. The singular largest factor for the continued rate of immigration is the demand for cheap labor. The majority of Mexican-origin latinas/os settled in the Southwest, particularly in Texas, New Mexico, Colorado, Arizona, and California.

The migrations from both Puerto Rico and Cuba, like the Mexican presence, originated from United States victories in war. As a result of the Spanish–American War, Puerto Rico and Cuba became possessions of the United States. In 1902, Cuba achieved independence. Fifty years later, Puerto Rico obtained commonwealth status, the benefits and desirability of which are still hotly debated.

The Treaty of Paris, ratified the year after Puerto Rico's annexation, provided that Congress would define the political and civil rights of the people of the island. Congress did not make any determination until 1917. In that year, Congress made the Puerto Rican peoples United States citizens through the Second Organic Act of 1917, known as the Jones Act. Puerto Rico's colonial status, Puerto Ricans' United States

73. Rodolfo Alvarez, *The Psycho–Historical and Socioeconomic Development of the* *Chicano Community in the United States* 53(4) Soc. Sci. Q. 920, 924 (1973).

citizenship, and escalating economic relations between Puerto Rico and the United States, stimulated the first migrant wave of Puerto Ricans to the United States' mainland. Once again, economic motives were at the root of this migration.

The largest wave of Puerto Rican migration occurred after World War II, when the economy of Puerto Rico began to deteriorate. At present, the flow to and from Puerto Rico has steadied, unlike the continuing influx of immigrants from Mexico. The United States citizenship status of Puerto Ricans facilitates their movement between the island and the mainland. As a result, a large percentage of Puerto Ricans return to the island.

Like Mexican–Americans, Puerto Ricans have been the targets of ethnic and cultural attitudes of NLWs [Eds. Non–Latino Whites]. They encounter racial prejudice as it is defined by the United States, even though the latina/o perception of race differs:

> [T]oo often the Puerto Rican who regards himself at home as white rapidly discovers to his horror that the American scheme of ethnic identification classifies him as Negro; and his own fatal ambiguity in relation to the color problem receives a new emphasis by the shame and degradation he experiences.[98]

Like other migrant "outsider" groups, "puertorriquenas/os" also lag behind their NLW counterparts in social indicators of success such as education and income.

Finally, the Cuban migration, the most recent of the latina/o migrations, was driven by factors quite different from the Mexican and Puerto Rican migrations. Although some Cuban presence in Florida and New York dates to 1870, Cubans have come to the United States as refugees mainly to flee the socialist revolutionary regime of Fidel Castro. The reasons for the flight were political and economic: The first to flee were the educated, professional, and wealthy classes who had the most to lose economically from the imposition of a socialist economic regime. In this sense, the Cuban influx is unique. In addition, as refugees, their entry is radically different from that of other latinas/os. Their presence has not been subject to quotas. Particularly during the cold war years, Cubans have received substantial government assistance and preferential treatment as they have been used as part of the war against communism.

The recent and significant Cuban influx occurred in three identifiable stages, the first being in 1959 and the latest in 1980. This twenty year period accounted for a migration equivalent to approximately 10% of the total population of the island.

The first large exodus from Cuba, comprising slightly over one-third of the Cuban migration, took place between 1959 and 1962—a direct reaction to Castro's overthrow of the Fulgencio Batista dictatorship and subsequent declaration that Cuba was a socialist state. The majority of these refugees were middle or upper class, educated professionals and skilled technicians, as well as high level functionaries of the overthrown government and other dissidents. A second wave of Cubans, comprising

98. Gordon K. Lewis, *Puerto Rico: Freedom and Power in the Caribbean* 2 (1965).

(1965– 1973) approximately 46% of the total Cuban migration, came to the United States between 1965 and 1973. Although this group was more representative of a cross-section of the Cuban population in terms of class, race and education than the first wave, it too left for political reasons.

(1980's.) The third and the final wave of Cubans migrated to the United States in the early 1980s. It constituted 17% of the Cuban migration. This stage commenced when the Cubans took advantage of the withdrawal from the Peruvian embassy of the military guard that was in charge of protecting diplomatic missions. A bus-load of Cubans crashed through the gates of the embassy in Havana and over 11,000 Cubans seeking asylum entered the embassy grounds in a period of forty-eight hours. Thereupon Castro, whose policy was to permit only very regulated emigration, declared that whomever wanted to leave could do so. Acting upon such declaration, Miami Cubans organized flotillas that, over a five month period, brought 125,000 Cubans to the United States. This last group of Cubans, known as "Marielitos" because the flotilla converged on Mariel Harbor, was a very different group from the first wave. Unlike the very educated, professional 1959–1962 group, the 1980 Cubans were from the working class. The class difference, and probably the circumstances of their departure, resulted in the "Marielitos" not being as welcome or as well treated—either by the United States or by their first-wave compatriots—as the first migration.

Like their Mexican and Puerto Rican counterparts, Cubans have settled in a concentrated geographic location, mostly in Florida. Notwithstanding these initial geographic distribution patterns, all three of these latino/a groups are now spreading out from their original places of concentration. Mexicans are moving to the Midwest, the Pacific Northwest, and recently to Florida and the East Coast; Puerto Ricans are moving beyond New York, and Cubans are relocating to places other than Miami.

In addition to these three main groups of latina/o migrants, Central and South American immigrants from states such as Guatemala, Nicaragua, and Peru began entering the United States in large numbers in the 1960s and 1970s to escape social and political unrest in their home countries. Initially, these immigrants were concentrated in California and New York, but like the three major latina/o groups they too are dispersing.

Notes and Questions

1. Having described briefly the principal groups of Latinos/as in the United States, one can ask the question "What is a Hispanic or Latino/a?" For a good discussion of the terminology, see Angel Oquendo, *Re-imagining the Latino/a Race*, 12 Harv. BlackLetter L.J. 93 (1995).

2. The excerpt above states that given "19th century reality, a distant federal government, whether Mexican or American, probably made little difference to the residents of the region." Consider whether this statement is true in light of the materials that follow.

SECTION 1.   MEXICAN AMERICANS

A.   THE UNITED STATES' CONQUEST OF MEXICO

In a peaceful revolution in 1821, Mexico became independent from Spain. At that time, Mexico was approximately twice its current size, and included present-day Texas, California, Arizona, New Mexico, Nevada, and parts of Utah, Colorado, and Kansas. After Mexican independence, American settlers began arriving in the Texas territories. During these early years of Mexican independence, Mexicans were concerned about United States aggression and expansionism, fears which were to prove true.

By 1836, Anglo immigrants and Tejanos (former Mexicans living in Texas) had successfully fought for independence from Mexico. However, Mexico did not recognize Texas' claim to independence. In December 1845, Texas became a state under a joint resolution of Congress. For a more detailed explanation of the heavily United States-influenced move for Texan independence, see Rodolfo Acuña, *Occupied America: A History of Chicanos* 6–12 (3d ed. 1988).

THE UNITED STATES WAR WITH MEXICO

United States President James K. Polk was a strong advocate for the annexation of Texas and, generally, for expansion through acquisition of Mexican territory. On the night Polk was inaugurated, he expressed desire to acquire California, which was part of Mexico at the time. In 1845, Polk ordered General Zachary Taylor to move American troops to the Rio Grande, a maneuver calculated to provoke Mexico. Although the actual boundary was uncertain, the line between the United States and Mexico was understood, historically, to be at the Nueces River, 150 miles north of the Rio Grande. Polk had sent troops into an area understood to be Mexican territory. At least since Jefferson's presidency, the United States had wanted the Rio Grande and its valuable port Matamoros, which provided full access to the Gulf of Mexico. In 1846, Taylor's army advanced to the Rio Grande, much closer to Mexican territory but still within the arguably disputed zone between the two rivers. See Howard Zinn, *A People's History of the United States* 147–51 (1995).

"All that was needed in the spring of 1846," according to Howard Zinn, "was a military incident to begin the war that Polk wanted." Polk received *two* incidents, the murder of General Taylor's quartermaster, and an attack by Mexicans upon one of Taylor's patrols that left sixteen Americans dead, and the rest wounded and captured. Polk immediately sought war, declaring that "now, after reiterated menaces, Mexico has passed the boundary of the United States, has invaded our territory and shed American blood upon the American soil." Howard Zinn, *supra* 149–50 (1995); Rodolfo Acuña, *Occupied America* 13 (1988). According to Howard Zinn,

> The Mexicans had fired the first shot. But they had done what the American government wanted, according to Colonel Hitchcock [who

served in Taylor's army], who wrote in his diary, even before those first incidents:

I have said from the first that the United States are the aggressors.... We have not one particle of right to be here.... It looks as if the government sent a small force on purpose to bring on a war, so as to have a pretext for taking California and as much of this country as it chooses, for, whatever becomes of this army, there is no doubt of a war between the United States and Mexico....

Zinn, *supra* at 149.

Historian Rodolfo Acuña summarizes the ensuing course of the war, which accomplished United States aims of expansion:

The poorly equipped and poorly led Mexican army stood little chance against the expansion-minded Anglos. Even before the war Polk planned the campaign in stages: (1) Mexicans would be cleared out of Texas; (2) Anglos would occupy California and New Mexico; and (3) U.S. forces would march to Mexico City to force the beaten government to make peace on Polk's terms. And that was the way the campaign basically went. In the end, at a relatively small cost in men and money, the war netted the United States huge territorial gains. In all, the United States took over 1 million square miles from Mexico.

Acuña, *supra* at 13.

White supremacy and the racism of Whites toward dark-skinned Mexicans played a major role in the War with Mexico. Consider the following excerpt.

REGINALD HORSMAN

Race and Manifest Destiny
208–213 (1981).*

The Anglo–Saxon blood could never be subdued by anything that claimed Mexican origin.

James Buchanan, February 14, 1845

The decisive years in the creation of a new Anglo–Saxon political ideology were from the mid–1830s to the mid 1840s. In these years American politicians and the American population were overwhelmed by a variety of influences, both practical and theoretical, which inspired a belief that the American Anglo–Saxons were destined to dominate or penetrate the American continents and large areas of the world. Americans had faith that they would increase in such numbers that they would personally shape the destiny of other areas.

The catalyst in the overt adoption of a racial Anglo–Saxonism was the meeting of Americans and Mexicans, in the Southwest, the Texas Revolution, and the war with Mexico. In confronting the Mexicans the

Americans clearly formulated the idea of themselves as an Anglo–Saxon race. The use of *Anglo-Saxon* in a racial sense, somewhat rare in the political arguments of the early 1830s, increased rapidly later in the decade and became commonplace by the mid 1840s. The manner in which the Anglo–Saxon race was being isolated from other peoples was stated with clarity by Senator Benjamin Leigh of Virginia in January 1836 when opposing the abolitionist petitions. After pointing out that his fellow Congressmen had only to remember how the mobs of Cincinnati, Philadelphia, and New York had dealt with the few free Negroes in their midst to appreciate what would follow general emancipation, he candidly sketched the problem: "It is peculiar to the character of this Anglo–Saxon race of men to which we belong, that it has never been contented to live in the same country with any other distinct race, upon terms of equality; it has, invariably, when placed in that situation, proceeded to exterminate or enslave the other race in some form or other, or, failing in that, to abandon the country."

The idea of the Anglo–Saxon race as a distinct, all-encompassing force was expressed with increasing frequency in the late 1830s. In February 1837 William Gilpin wrote to his father from New Orleans that while the town was still Gallic in character the "Anglo–Saxon is pushing aside the Frenchman and eating him up. The big steamers ... are Anglo–Saxon, the huge stores and warehouses into which [goods] are piled have an Anglo–Saxon look and an Anglo–Saxon ship bears them hence. [Of] all the new part of the city, the only decent part is English." When Horace Bushnell, in August 1837, delivered an oration on the principles of national greatness, he used old and familiar arguments concerning America as a land saved for events of world significance; however, he used a new precision in writing of the origin of the people for whom the New World had been preserved. "Out of all the inhabitants of the world," he said, "... a select stock, the Saxon, and out of this the British family, the noblest of the stock, was chosen to people our country." In contrast, the Mexican state, he said, had started with fundamental disadvantages in the character of its immigrants. If the quality of the British people was changed into that of the Mexican, "five years would make their noble island a seat of poverty and desolation." For Bushnell, God had reserved America for a special people of Saxon blood.

By the 1830s the Americans were eagerly grasping at reasons for their own success and for the failure of others. Although the white Americans of Jacksonian America wanted personal success and wealth, they also wanted a clear conscience. If the United States was to remain in the minds of its people a nation divinely ordained for great deeds, then the fault for the suffering inflicted in the rise to power and prosperity had to lie elsewhere. White Americans could rest easier if the sufferings of other races could be blamed on racial weakness rather than on the whites' relentless search for wealth and power. In the 1830s and 1840s, when it became obvious that American and Mexican interests were incompatible and that the Mexicans would suffer, innate weakness was found in the Mexicans. Americans, it was argued, were not to be blamed for forcibly taking the northern provinces of Mexico, for Mexicans, like Indians, were unable to make proper use of the land. The Mexicans had failed because they were a mixed, inferior race with considerable Indian and some black blood. The world would benefit if a superior race shaped the future of the Southwest.

By the time of the Mexican War, America had placed the Mexicans firmly within the rapidly emerging hierarchy of superior and inferior races. While the Anglo–Saxons were depicted as the purest of the pure— the finest Caucasians—the Mexicans who stood in the way of southwestern expansion were depicted as a mongrel race, adulterated by extensive intermarriage with an inferior Indian race. Travelers delighted in depicting the Mexicans as an unimprovable breed and were particularly scathing about the inhabitants of Mexico's northern provinces. T. J. Farnham in 1840 wrote of the Californians as "an imbecile, pusillanimous, race of men, and unfit to control the destinies of that beautiful country." No one who knew "the indolent, mixed race of California," he argued, could believe they would long populate much less govern, the region. The mixed white and Indian races of California and Mexico "must fade away; while the mingling of different branches of the Caucasian family in the States" would produce a race which would expand to cover all the northern provinces of Mexico. "The old Saxon blood must stride the continent," wrote Farnham, "must command all its northern shores ... and ... erect the altar of civil and religious freedom on the plains of the Californias."

The Mexican Californians were constantly attacked as shiftless and ineffective. Richard Dana thought them "an idle, thriftless people" and asserted that nothing but the character of the population prevented Monterey from becoming a large town. "In the hands of an enterprising people," he said, "what a country this might be!" Lansford Hastings, in his famous emigrants' guide of 1845, characterized the Mexican inhabitants of California as "scarcely a visible grade, in the scale of intelligence, above the barbarous tribes by whom they are surrounded." This was not surprising, said Hastings. There had been extensive intermarriage and "as most of the lower order of Mexicans, are Indians in fact, whatever is said in reference to the one, will also be applicable to the other." Stereotypes that were to persist in American thinking long after the 1840s were firmly fixed in Hastings's work. A Mexican, he said, "always pursues that method of doing things, which requires the least physical or mental exorcise [sic], unless it involves some danger, in which case, he always adopts some other method." Writing of soldiers who were brought into California in 1842, he commented that they were "mere Indians," and that it was "with these wild, shirtless, earless and heartless creatures, headed by a few timid, soulless, brainless officers, that these semi-barbarians, intend to hold this delightful region, as against the civilized world." The process of dehumanizing those who were to be misused or destroyed proceeded rapidly in the United States in the 1840s. To take lands from inferior barbarians was no crime; it was simply following God's injunctions to make the land fruitful.

In the Southwest there was even a tendency for American travelers to praise the Pueblo Indians in order further to debase the "mongrel" Mexicans. George Kendall, who was on the Texas–Santa Fe expedition, commented in his account of that sorry affair that "the *pueblos,* or town Indians of New Mexico, are by far the better part of the population." Most Mexicans, he said, were content if they could satisfy their animal wants, "and so they will continue to be until the race becomes extinct or amalgamated with Anglo–Saxon stock." Rufus Sage echoed Kendall: "There are no people on the continent of America, whether civilized or uncivilized, with one or two exceptions, more miserable in condition or despicable in morals than the mongrel race inhabiting New Mexico."

The scathing denunciations of the Mexican race encompassed the inhabitants of central Mexico as well as its outlying provinces, and these denunciations were not confined to writers from any one party or one region in the United States. Waddy Thompson of South Carolina, who went to Mexico in 1842 as minister for the Whig administration, advanced the familiar stereotype in his *Recollections,* which was published in 1847. While condemning aggressive expansionism and the rapacious spirit of acquisition which was developing in the United States, Thompson had no doubt at all of the ultimate result of the meeting of the Anglo–Saxon and the Mexican races. He objected to the means, not to the end. "That our language and laws are destined to pervade this continent," he wrote, "I regard as more certain than any other event which is in the future. Our race has never yet put its foot upon a soil which it has not only kept but has advanced. I mean not our English ancestors only, but that great Teuton race from which we have both descended."

To Thompson an essential element in Mexican weakness was the mixed population. Of seven million inhabitants, he wrote, only one million were white Europeans or their descendants. Of the others there were some four to four and one-half million pure-blooded Indians, and the rest of mixed blood. Thompson, like many others at this time, was easily able to envisage a mysterious disappearance of millions of people. "That the Indian race of Mexico must recede before us," he wrote, "is quite as certain as that that is the destiny of our own Indians." Negroes in Mexico Thompson characterized as "the same lazy, filthy, and vicious creatures that they inevitably become where they are not held in bondage." The general Mexican population Thompson characterized as "lazy, ignorant, and, of course, vicious and dishonest."

The American dismissal of the Mexicans as an inferior, largely-Indian race did not pass unnoticed in Mexico. Mexican ministers in the United States warned their government that the Americans considered the Mexicans an inferior people. The Mexicans realized both that their neighbors to the north were likely to invade their northern provinces, and that they would claim that this was justified because they could make better use of the lands. Mexicans who served as diplomatic representatives in the United States were shocked at the rabid anti-Mexican attitudes and at the manner in which Mexicans were lumped together with Indians and blacks as an inferior race.

The Texas Revolution was from its beginnings interpreted in the United States and among Americans in Texas as a racial clash, not simply a revolt against unjust government or tyranny. Thomas Hart

Benton said that the Texas revolt "has illustrated the Anglo–Saxon character, and given it new titles to the respect and admiration of the world. It shows that liberty, justice, valour—moral, physical, and intellectual power—discriminate that race wherever it goes." Benton asked "old England" to rejoice that distant Texas streams had seen the exploits of "a people strung from their loins, and carrying their language, laws, and customs, their *magna charta* and all its glorious privileges, into new regions and far distant climes."

In his two terms as president of Texas, Sam Houston consistently thought of the struggle in his region as one between a glorious Anglo–Saxon race and an inferior Mexican rabble. Victory for the Texans and the Americans in the Southwest would mean that larger areas of the world were to be brought under the rule of a race that could make best use of them. Houston was less imbued with the harsh scientific racial theories that carried most Americans before them in the 1840s than with the romantic exaltation of the Saxons given by Sir Walter Scott and his followers.

The racial character of the War with Mexico is made clearer by the reluctance of the United States to fight Britain over the Oregon territory. While a war with Mexico would be fought against a people presumed racially inferior, a war with Britain would require Anglo–Saxons to fight Anglo–Saxons. While the War with Mexico resulted in a conquest in which Americans could claim racial dominion, the latter confrontation resulted in an affirmation of shared Anglo–Saxon origins and a negotiated settlement. Horsman, *supra* at 220–221, 224–25.

B. SOME VIEWS OF AMERICAN POLITICIANS ON THE ANNEXATION OF MEXICO AND MEXICANS

Before Mexico had gained its independence, and long before the war with Mexico, American statesmen and commentators had expressed the wish for Mexican lands. In 1767, Benjamin Franklin had identified Mexico and Cuba as targets for future American expansion. The adjacent Louisiana Purchase stimulated thoughts of further expansion. President Jefferson had attempted unsuccessfully to claim the Rio Grande as the southern boundary of Louisiana. President John Quincy Adams expressed his desire for one of the important Texas rivers, particularly the Rio Grande. In 1826, Mexico rejected Adams' offer to buy Texas for $1 million. By 1821, Anglo Americans had pushed into New Mexico and Texas. See Rodolfo Acuña, *Occupied America* 6–7 (1988); David J. Weber, *The Mexican Frontier 1821–1846: The American Southwest Under Mexico* 1–14 (1982).

Once American armies had conquered the Mexican territory that Polk wanted, American politicians faced a serious dilemma. Given the commitment of many politicians to white supremacy, the annexation of former Mexican lands, populated by Mexicans, posed a severe threat to the cherished white racial integrity of the United States. The prospect of incorporating undesirable, mixed-race Mexicans into the United States was revolting to many politicians forced to consider annexing Mexican lands and people.

Senator John C. Calhoun objected to Polk's war and to the conquest of Mexico, because the United States would have to deal with "eight or nine millions of Mexicans, without a government, on [our] hands." *Cong. Globe*, 30th Cong., 1st Sess. 53 (1848). Calhoun may have been interested in Mexican lands, but only if they contained no Mexicans: "[O]ur army has ever since held all that it is desirable to hold—that portion whose population is sparse, and on that account the more desirable to be held. For I hold it in reference to this war a fundamental principle, that when we receive territorial indemnity, it shall be unoccupied territory." *Cong. Globe*, 30th Cong., 1st Sess. 96 (Jan.4, 1848).

During the same speech, on January 4, 1848, Calhoun expressed his fear that annexing Mexico would disrupt white racial purity and political control:

> The next reason which my resolutions [opposing the conquest of Mexico] assign, is, that it is without example or precedent, either to hold Mexico as a province, or to incorporate her into our Union. No example of such a line of policy can be found. We have conquered many of the neighboring tribes of Indians, but we never thought of holding them in subjection—never of incorporating them into our Union. They have either been left as an independent people amongst us, or been driven into the forests.

> I know further, sir, that we have never dreamt of incorporating into our Union any but the Caucasian race—the free white race. To incorporate Mexico, would be the very first instance of the kind of incorporating an Indian race; for more than half of the Mexicans are Indians, and the other is composed chiefly of mixed tribes. I protest against such a union as that! Ours, sir, is the Government of a white race. The greatest misfortunes of Spanish America are to be traced to the fatal error of placing these colored races on an equality with the white race. That error destroyed the social arrangement which formed the basis of society. * * * And yet it is professed and talked about to erect these Mexicans into a Territorial Government and place them on an equality with the people of the United States. I protest utterly against such a project. * * *

> Are we to associate with ourselves as equal, companions and fellow citizens, the Indians and mixed race of Mexico? Sir, I should consider such a thing as fatal to our institutions.

Cong. Globe, 30th Cong., 1st Sess. 96–98 (Jan. 4, 1848). Calhoun argued for ending the Mexican campaign and keeping only the sparsely populated lands already won.

Henry Clay also opposed the war on racial grounds. Like Calhoun, he was appalled by the prospect of annexing Mexico:

> Does any considerable man believe it possible that two such immense countries, with territories of nearly equal extent, with populations so incongruous, so different in race, language, in religion and

in laws, could be blended together in one harmonious mass, happily governed by one common authority?

Philip Anthony Hernández, *The Other North Americans: The American Image of Mexico and Mexicans, 1550–1850* at 246–47 (Ph.D. Diss. U. Cal. Berkeley 1974) (quoting speech of Henry Clay of Nov. 13, 1847 in Lexington, Kentucky).

The outbreak of the war had provided the opportunity for many more Americans to acquire negative attitudes toward Mexicans. "Mexicans remained in the eyes of Americans what they were before the outbreak of hostilities—a distinctly inferior people whose racial characteristics offended the deeply held American assumptions on racial purity." Hernández, *supra* at 203. Ultimately, these racial concerns were resolved by the annexation of only the northernmost, most sparsely populated parts of Mexico and by the Treaty of Guadalupe Hidalgo.

C. THE TREATY OF GUADALUPE HIDALGO (1848)

The Treaty of Guadalupe Hidalgo of 1848 settled the war between the United States and Mexico, drawing the boundary line between the two countries at the Rio Grande and providing for the transfer of conquered territory from Mexico to the United States. Mexico transferred to the United States long-coveted California, including the desirable port of San Diego, and a huge territory that included present day Nevada, Arizona, New Mexico, and parts of Colorado and Utah. The United States paid $15 million indemnity for the former Mexican lands. In addition, Mexico was concerned about the fate of Mexicans remaining in the conquered territories, and bargained for protections for them and their property in what eventually became Articles VIII and IX of the Treaty. See Richard Griswold del Castillo, *The Treaty of Guadalupe Hidalgo: A Legacy of Conflict* 38–42 (1990); Fernando Chacon Gomez, *The Intended and Actual Effect of Article VIII of the Treaty of Guadalupe Hidalgo: Mexican Treaty Rights Under International and Domestic Law* 22–38 (Ph.D. Diss. U. Mich. 1977).

Notwithstanding its importance in legal history, the Treaty of Guadalupe Hidalgo remains largely unknown and ignored. As historian David Weber has written.

> The Treaty of Guadalupe Hidalgo is the key document of Mexican American history, for through it Mexicans living in the Southwest became Americans and were guaranteed "all the rights of citizens of the United States." Yet the treaty remains relatively unknown in the United States. In Mexico, on the other hand, since losers have a longer memory than victors, the treaty is still remembered with bitterness.

David J. Weber, *Foreigners in Their Native Land* 141 (1973).

The history of the amendment and ratification of the Treaty of Guadalupe Hidalgo reveals Presidential and Senatorial unwillingness to deal with Mexicans on terms of equal citizenship, despite treaty language suggesting otherwise, and the United States' desire to facilitate the transfer of Mexican-owned lands to Whites. It must be borne in mind that in negotiating and later ratifying this treaty, the parties were not in an equal bargaining position: The United States had a much stronger position because of its successful military conquest; the Mexicans could bargain only to save face and for whatever concessions the United States was willing to give. See Weber, *supra* at 141–42.

President Polk, when he first transmitted the draft treaty to the Senate, wrote that:

> To the tenth article of the treaty there are serious objections, and no instructions given to Mr. Trist contemplated or authorized its insertion. The public lands within the limits of Texas belong to that State, and this Government has no power to dispose of them or to change the conditions of grants already made. All valid titles to land within the other territories ceded to the United States will remain, unaffected by the change of sovereignty; and I therefore submit that this article should not be ratified as a part of the treaty.

V *Treaties and Other International Acts of the United States of America* 248 (Hunter Miller ed. 1937).

Article X, as drafted, provided that:

> All grants of land made by the Mexican government or by the competent authorities, in territories previously appertaining to Mexico, and remaining for the future within the limits of the United States, shall be respected as valid, to the same extent that the same grants would be valid, if the said territories had remained within the limits of Mexico.

The Senate followed Polk's recommendation and struck Article X from the Treaty. To quiet the ensuing protests of Mexicans, who presumably feared that pre-existing land titles would not be honored in the absence of Article X, the United States issued a Statement of Protocol which provided the following:

> The American government by suppressing the Xth article of the Treaty of Guadalupe Hidalgo did not in any way intend to annul the grants of lands made by Mexico in the ceded territories. These grants . . . preserve the legal value which they may possess, and the grantees may cause their legitimate (titles) to be acknowledged before the American tribunals.
>
> Conformable to the law of the United States, legitimate titles to every description of property, personal and real, existing in the ceded territories, are those which were legitimate titles under the Mexican law of California and New Mexico up to the 13th of May, 1846 and in Texas up to the 2nd of March, 1836.

Rodolfo Acuña, *Occupied America* 19–20 (3d ed. 1988) (quoting *Compilation of Treaties in Force* 402 (1899)).

It is apparent, however, that deleting Article X would undermine the legitimacy of Mexican land grants both by denying explicit recognition of the validity of Mexican grants made before the War and by refusing to acknowledge outright the validity of Mexican practices and customs for designating land grants. Later, during litigation over contested claims to land, the customs and practices of Mexican authorities in designating land grants were often held to be too vague to be enforceable under very different United States standards. Thus, by deleting Article X, Polk and the Senate made it much easier to deprive Mexicans of their lands by making United States law and practice determinative and by refusing to acknowledge Mexican law and custom as the appropriate reference doctrines for ascertaining the validity of land claims. Thus the potential legal impediment wrought by Article X to the taking of Mexican land was easily disposed.

Articles VIII and IX of the Treaty contain important provisions regarding citizenship. Under Article VIII, both as drafted and as ratified, Mexicans in the conquered territories had the right to remain in the United States and, either by election within one year or by continued residence within the United States, they "shall be considered to have elected to become citizens of the United States."

Revisions to Article IX of the draft treaty show the limited meaning of federal citizenship at the time and the resolution of Congress's concerns about diminishing the racial purity of the United States. Under the original draft Article IX, those Mexicans who became United States citizens

> shall be incorporated into the Union of the United States, and admitted as soon as possible, according to the principles of the Federal Constitution, to the enjoyment of all the rights of citizens of the United States. In the meantime, they shall be maintained and protected in the enjoyment of their liberty, their property, and the civil rights now vested in them according to the Mexican laws.

The Senate amended the Treaty so that the final ratified version read:

> The Mexicans * * * shall be incorporated into the Union of the United States and be admitted, *at the proper time (to be judged of by the Congress of the United States) to the enjoyment of all the rights of citizens of the United States according to the principles of the Constitution.*

See V *Treaties and other International Acts of the United States of America* 219 (Hunter Miller ed. 1937) (emphasis added).

Rather than admit Mexicans into the Union "as soon as possible," the Senate made their admission more discretionary, "at the proper time," to be judged by Congress. The original language raised the scary (to Anglos) prospect of Mexicans on an equal legal footing with whites. To avoid equality, the Senate gave Congress discretion to admit states containing Mexicans whenever Congress deemed it "proper."

1. Articles VIII and IX of the Treaty of Guadalupe Hidalgo (1848)

Article VIII:

Mexicans now established in territories previously belonging to Mexico, and which remain for the future within the limits of the United States, as defined by the present Treaty, shall be free to continue where they now reside, or to remove at any time to the Mexican Republic, retaining the property which they possess in the said territories, or disposing thereof and removing the proceeds wherever they please; without their being subjected, on this account, to any contribution, tax or charge whatever.

Those who shall prefer to remain in the said territories, may either retain the title and rights of Mexican citizens, or acquire those of citizens of the United States. But, they shall be under the obligation to make their election within one year from the date of the exchange of ratifications of this treaty: and those who shall remain in the said territories, after the expiration of that year, without having declared their intention to retain the character of Mexicans, shall be considered to have elected to become citizens of the United States.

In the said territories, property of every kind, now belonging to Mexicans not established there, shall be inviolably respected. The present owners, the heirs of these, and all Mexicans who may hereafter acquire said property by contract, shall enjoy with respect to it, guaranties equally ample as if the same belonged to citizens of the United States.

Article IX:

The Mexicans who, in the territories aforesaid, shall not preserve the character of citizens of the Mexican Republic, conformably with what is stipulated in the preceding article, shall be incorporated into the Union of the United States and be admitted, at the proper time (to be judged of by the Congress of the United States) to the enjoyment of all the rights of citizens of the United States according to the principles of the Constitution; and in the mean time shall be maintained and protected in the free enjoyment of their liberty and property, and secured in the free exercise of their religion without restriction.

See V *Treaties and other International Acts of the United States of America* 207–428 (Hunter Miller ed. 1937) for the complete text of the Treaty and a detailed description of its negotiation and ratification history.

The final, revised language quieted the racial fears of Senator John Calhoun, concerned over the Mexican racial threat to white rule in the United States. *Senate Executive Documents,* 30th Cong., 1st Sess., No. 52 at 27. The revised language also relieved public angst over possible political participation by Mexicans. As stated in the *New Orleans Picayune:*

> In the annexation of New Mexico and California the United States will incur none of the danger which have been predicted of admitting a race of men, differing from us in language, religion, descent, laws, manners, and social condition to an equal participation in the benefits and responsibilities of free government. The country thus acquired is comparatively unsettled, and by the time it has a population enough to send a member of Congress, will be thoroughly Americanized. So all of the forebodings concerning the appearance in the Senate or House of Representatives of a thorough-bred Mexican or half-breed Mexican will be dissipated.

New Orleans Picayune, February 15, 1848, quoted in Philip Hernández, *supra* at 268–69. Congress used its discretion under the revised Article IX to deny statehood to New Mexico for sixty-two years, the longest period in American history, despite recurrent petitions from the territory. Among the principal reasons for denying statehood to New Mexico were its Mexican-ancestry, Spanish-speaking population, which constituted a majority until 1912.

Notes and Questions

1. What was the meaning of the federal citizenship granted in the Treaty? Consider the relative importance of state, as opposed to federal, citizenship prior to the Reconstruction Amendments. See Gerald L. Neuman, *Strangers to the Constitution* 63–66 (1996).

2. Texas, although formerly part of Mexico, first become independent and then was annexed as a state by the United States in 1845, before the war with Mexico. Occasionally questions arose about the applicability of the Treaty in Texas, questions which were resolved by the Supreme Court in *McKinney v. Saviego*, 59 U.S. (18 How.) 235, 240 (1855):

> We think it clear that [Section VIII of the Treaty] did not refer to any portion of the acknowledged limits of Texas. The territories alluded to are those which had, previously to the treaty, belonged to Mexico, and which, after the treaty, should remain within the limits of the United States. The republic of Texas had been many years before acknowledged by the United States as existing separately and independently of Mexico; and as a separate and independent State it had been admitted to the Union. The government of the United States, by that act, had conferred upon the population established there all the privileges within their constitutional competency to grant.

Therefore, whatever rights were created by the Treaty did not necessarily apply to Mexicans living in Texas.

3. Compare the denial of federal citizenship to Blacks in the *Dred Scott* opinion with the granting of such citizenship to Mexicans who remained within the territories. What conclusions do you draw? What would have been the outcome for Mexicans of an application of Chief Justice Taney's reasoning in *Dred Scott*?

4. Consider the views of Justice McLean, dissenting in *Dred Scott*, who refuted Chief Justice Taney's assertions that citizenship was not available to peoples of color by citing the Treaty of Guadalupe Hidalgo and other treaties to demonstrate that Mexicans, Blacks and some Indians had in fact been granted federal or state citizenship:

> In the argument, it was said that a colored citizen would not be an agreeable member of society. This is more a matter of taste than of law. Several of the States have admitted persons of color to the right of suffrage, and in this view have recognized them as citizens; and this has been done in the slave as well as the free States. On the question of citizenship, it must be admitted that we have not been very fastidious. Under the late treaty with Mexico, we have made citizens of all grades, combinations and colors. The same was done in the admission of Louisiana and Florida. No one ever doubted, and no court ever held, that the people of these Territories did not become citizens under the

treaty. They have exercised all the rights of citizens, without being naturalized under the acts of Congress.

Dred Scott, 60 U.S.(19 How.) at 533 (McLean, J., dissenting).

5.   Have you encountered any of this material before in your legal or other education? If not, why not? Consider the significance of leaving the conquest of Mexico out of traditional narratives of United States history. Is it appropriate to ignore a series of events that accounts for fully one-third of the United States land mass and for a significant percentage of its population?

2.   *The Treaty of Guadalupe Hidalgo and Citizenship*

The Treaty and its aftermath left many questions unanswered about the actual status of Mexicans remaining in the now-United States territories that had been Mexico. Fundamental questions arose about the meaning of the citizenship and the property rights granted by the Treaty to Mexicans who either remained in the United States or elected to become United States citizens. The federal citizenship of Mexicans of mixed Indian, Spanish and black ancestry did not mean that they would be allowed to participate politically on an equal basis with Whites:

> When the United States acquired Mexico's northern frontier, the mestizo ancestry of the conquered Mexicans placed them in an ambiguous social and legal position. In the U.S. government bureaucracy, it became unclear whether Mexicans were to be accorded the citizenship rights of white citizens or were to be treated as Indian inhabitants. Most government officials argued that Mexicans of predominantly Indian descent should be extended the same legal status as the detribalized American Indians. Mexicans, on the other hand, argued that under the Treaty of Guadalupe Hidalgo and international laws, the U.S. Government agreed to extend [to] all Mexican citizens—regardless of their race—the political rights enjoyed by white citizens. These rights were accorded to them on the basis of the international principle guaranteeing inhabitants of ceded territories the nationality of the successor state unless other provisions are made in the treaty of peace.

See Martha Menchaca, *Chicano Indianism: A Historical Account of Racial Repression in the United States*, 20 American Ethnologist 583, 584 (1993). Since 1812, when it became an independent nation, Mexico granted full citizenship and political rights to Indians. Thus, at the time of this conquest, Mexico had no formal racial restrictions on who could be a full citizen.

Once the northern half of Mexico was annexed by the United States, however, the meaning of the grant of citizenship in the Treaty to Mexicans was largely contingent on the Anglo–American perception of the race of particular Mexicans. Dark-skinned mestizos, the mixed-race Mexicans of Spanish and Indian ancestry so despised by white Anglo–Americans, were denied citizenship and meaningful political participation. The American treatment of Indians furnished a paradigm for the treatment of apparently Indian Mexicans. Lighter-skinned Mexicans were treated as white and were granted more political and citizenship rights. "Given the nature of the U.S. racial system and its laws, the conquered Mexican population learned that it was politically expedient to assert their Spanish ancestry; otherwise, they were susceptible to being treated as American Indians." See Menchaca, *supra*, 587–89. Although the Treaty granted federal citizenship to all Mexicans who either elected it or who remained in the territories acquired by the United States, it was state citizenship that was significant for purposes of political participation, since the states defined qualifications for voting and access to education.

State and territorial legislatures discriminated against Mexicans who looked Indian and in favor of Mexicans who looked white. The California state constitution of 1849 granted the right to vote only to Whites, consequently disenfranchising the vast majority of Mexicans, mestizos whose appearance revealed their Indian ancestry.

CALIFORNIA CONSTITUTION OF 1849 (ARTICLE II)

The debates of the Constitutional Convention made clear that "savage" Indians and Blacks were to be denied the right to vote:

It was evident from the start of the convention that the Negro was not wanted in the new territory. At all events, it was agreed overwhelmingly that those Negroes already in the territory should not vote. The Indian was already in the state, but he should not be either a citizen or a voter. * * *

The delegates at Monterey in 1849 remained firm in their convictions that no persons other than whites should play any part in the governing of the state and proceeded to disenfranchise many of those individuals who had originally cast their ballots in the special election that put these very same delegates in their convention seats. Even an amendment that proposed to grant the right to vote to those Indians who had been citizens of Mexico and were taxed as owners of real estate, and expressly excepted all Negroes, was defeated by a vote of 22 to 21.

Robert F. Heizer & Alan F. Almquist, *The Other Californians* 96 (1971).

Which Californians would have the privilege of voting was a major subject of debate at the convention. At this time, it was within the province of state power to determine voter qualifications. Accordingly, while the United States citizenship granted by the Treaty of Guadalupe Hidalgo might include federal citizenship for Mexicans of mixed Indian and Spanish ancestry, the Treaty's guarantee of federal citizenship offered no guarantee of voting rights or political participation, which were matters left to the states. See Robert F. Heizer & Alan F. Almquist, *The Other Californians* 92–119 (1971). The convention ultimately agreed upon the following provision regarding suffrage:

Section 1. Every white male citizen of the United States, *and every white male citizen of Mexico*, who shall have elected to become a citizen of the United States, under the treaty of [Guadalupe Hidalgo], * * * of the age of twenty-one years who shall have been a resident of the state six months next preceding the election * * * shall be entitled to vote at all elections which are now or hereafter may be authorized by law: *Provided*, That nothing herein contained, shall be construed to prevent the Legislature, by a two-thirds concurrent vote, from admitting to the right of suffrage, Indians or the descendants of Indians, in such special cases as such a proportion of the legislative body may deem just and proper.

Cal Const. Art. II, § 1 (1849) (emphasis added).

Notes and Questions

1. Consider *People v. Hall*, 4 Cal. 399 (1854), in which the California Supreme Court ruled that the testimony of Chinese witnesses was not admissible against a white defendant. This decision is reproduced in Chapter 5, § 1. The same principles articulated in *People v. Hall* applied to Mexican–American mestizos.

In April, 1857, Manuel Domínguez, a mestizo, attempted to testify as a defense witness in a San Francisco courtroom. One of the most distinguished citizens of California, Domínguez had been a delegate to the Constitutional Convention and had signed the Constitution of 1849. By 1857, he was supervisor of Los Angeles County and a wealthy landowner. Notwithstanding his prominence, the presiding judge dismissed him as a witness when the plaintiff's lawyer argued that Domínguez's Indian blood rendered his testimony inadmissible. See Heizer & Almquist, *supra* at 131; Leonard Pitt, *Decline of the Californios* 202 (1966).

Article II of the California Constitution raised intriguing questions about who would be considered a "white Mexican male" entitled to vote. And who would decide who was white enough to be a "white Mexican male"? In an early case, the California Supreme Court was required to answer this question with respect to an elected California judge.

Pablo de la Guerra came from an influential family and was a delegate to the 1849 Constitutional Convention. De la Guerra also served in the California Senate, and later in his career was elected to a judgeship. See Pitt, *supra* at 43–46, 116–17, 234–39. De la Guerra objected to the limitation of suffrage to white males: "[He] arose to argue that many Californios were dark-skinned, and that to disfranchise them would be tantamount to denying them a part of their citizenship as granted by the Treaty of Guadalupe Hidalgo." Pitt, *supra*, at 45. It may have been predictable, then, that someone would challenge the validity of his judgeship by questioning his citizenship.

PEOPLE v. DE LA GUERRA
40 Cal. 311 (1870).

TEMPLE, J. delivered the opinion of the Court, WALLACE, J., and CROCKETT, J., concurring:

The respondent was born at Santa Barbara, in 1819, and has ever since resided at that place, and is admitted to have been a white male citizen of Mexico at the date of the Treaty of Guadalupe Hidalgo. After the ratification of that treaty he elected to become a citizen of the United States in the mode provided in the treaty. He was a member of the Constitutional Convention which framed the Constitution of California, and has almost continuously, since the adoption of that instrument, held office under its provisions. At the judicial election, held in 1869, he was elected Judge of the First Judicial District, and the relator in this proceeding contests his right to the office, on the ground that he is not a citizen of the United States, as by an Act passed April 20, 1863, it is provided that "no person shall be eligible to the office of District Judge, who shall not have been a citizen of the United States and a resident of this State for two years." * * *

It is contended on the part of the relator that Mexicans who were resident in California at the date of the [Treaty of Guadalupe Hidalgo], and who elected in the mode provided to become citizens of the United States, did not acquire the right of citizenship by the terms of the treaty, but an Act of Congress admitting them to such rights is necessary, and that no such Act having been passed, the respondent is not a citizen.

The question raised would be of very grave import to the people of this State, were it not for the fact that its solution is quite obvious. By the eighth article of the treaty it is provided that the Mexicans who were resident in the ceded territory might either remain or remove to the Mexican Republic, and should be protected in their property. * * *

The natural consequence of the cession of the Territory by Mexico, and its acquisition by the United States, would be that the allegiance of the inhabitants who remained in it would be transferred to the new sovereign. By the stipulation of the treaty, however, three courses were left open to inhabitants. One was to remove to the Republic of Mexico; in which event they would of course, continue to be citizens of Mexico; the second was to remain in the ceded Territory and retain the title and rights of Mexicans citizens; the third, to become citizens of the United States.

That the treaty was intended to operate directly, and of itself to fix the status of those inhabitants, does not admit of a doubt. That it had that effect, so far as those who elected to remain citizens of Mexico are concerned, is obvious, and there is no reason for a different construction as to those who elected to become citizens of the United States. In fact, this would have been the natural consequence of the treaty (so far as was possible under our form of Government), and it required this special treaty stipulation to enable the inhabitants to remain in the ceded territory and owe no allegiance to the new Government. But for this provision the Mexicans who remained would not have been considered aliens, but would have been vested with such rights of citizenship as can be conferred upon the inhabitants of a Territory who are not citizens of any of the States of the Union. But, by the terms of the treaty, those who did not elect to remain citizens of Mexico, lost their rights as Mexican citizens, at least as soon as the election was made, and the conclusion is irresistible that they acquired (so far as was possible) the rights of citizens of the United States at the time they lost those of Mexican citizens; otherwise they remained a people without a country.

This article of the treaty would probably never have received a different construction from that here given, were it not for the following article, which has been strangely misconstrued. It provides that these

Mexicans in the ceded Territories, who do not retain the character of Mexican citizens, shall be incorporated into the Union of the United States, and be admitted at the proper time (to be judged of by the Congress of the United States), to the enjoyment of all the rights of citizens of the United States, according to the principles of the Constitution. The Union with which they are to be incorporated is, of course, the Union of the States composing the United States, and by which Union that Government is created. They can be incorporated into this Union only as a State, and the admission of the people to the full rights as citizens of the United States follows as the consequence of that act; and this is the only way in which it was possible for Congress to confer upon them all the rights of citizens of the United States. For this purpose it [is] not necessary to inquire whether, under our form of Government, there can be a citizen of the United States who is not a citizen of one of the States. I have no doubt that those born in the Territories, or in the District of Columbia, are so far citizens as to entitle them to the protection guaranteed to citizens of the United States in the Constitution, and to the shield of nationality abroad; but it is evident that they have not the political rights which are vested in citizens of the States. They are not constituents of any community in which is vested any sovereign power of government. Their position partakes more of the character of subjects than of citizens. They are subject to the laws of the United States, but have no voice in its management. If they are allowed to make laws, the validity of these laws is derived from the sanction of a Government in which they are not represented. Mere citizenship they may have, but the political rights of citizens they cannot enjoy until they are organized into a State, and admitted into the Union. * * *

Having admitted into the Union a State, of which these inhabitants were constituent members, Congress could do no more. It has conferred upon them all the rights of citizens, or rather it has recognized these rights in the only mode provided by the Constitution which was applicable to them. * * *

But it is suggested by counsel for relator, that if this construction be correct, then the Constitution of California is in conflict with the ninth article of the [Treaty of Guadalupe Hidalgo], for that article provides that all Mexican citizens who elect to become citizens of the United States shall be admitted to all the rights of citizens, while the Constitution discriminates. It declares that white male citizens of Mexico, who have elected to become citizens of the United States, shall be electors, while all, without distinction of color, including Indians, were Mexican citizens, and entitled to vote by the laws of Mexico.

If this be so, it does not follow that the respondent is not a citizen of the United States, but that the elective franchise is denied to certain persons who had been entitled to its exercise under the laws of Mexico. The possession of all political rights is not essential to citizenship. When Congress admitted California as a State, the constituent members of the State, in their aggregate capacity, became vested with the sovereign powers of government, "according to the principles of the Constitution." They then had the right to prescribe the qualifications of electors, and it is no violation of the treaty that these qualifications were such as to exclude some of the inhabitants from certain political rights. They were excluded in accordance with the principles of the Constitution.

The respondent is clearly a citizen of the United States, and the judgement should be affirmed.

Notes and Questions

1. Notice the significance of the racial mixture of mestizos in determining the political rights of Mexicans. Who would decide whether a Mexican was white enough to be "white" for purposes of voting? See Fernando Padilla, *Early Chicano Legal Recognition, 1846–1897*, 13 J. of Popular Culture 564–74 (1979). See also Luis Angel Toro, *supra*, Chapter 1.

2. What are the implications of these early political and social benefits of being a "white Mexican," as defined by Anglo–American laws? What do you think the effect would be upon the unity of the Mexican community? Then? Now?

3. Note that this case was decided the same year as the Fifteenth Amendment was enacted, 1870. That Amendment provides that the right of United States citizens "to vote shall not be denied or abridged by the United States or by any State on account of race, color, or previous condition of servitude." U.S. Const. Am. 15 (1870). What difference should the Fifteenth Amendment make in California's denial of suffrage to Blacks, mestizos and Indians?

4. Note the court's discussion of state citizenship, and admission by Congress as a state, as the form of citizenship that guarantees political participation.

5. In In Re *Rodriguez*, 81 Fed. 337 (W.D.Tex.1897), the court decided that a mestizo Mexican, who was neither a "free white person" nor a person of "African nativity" or "African descent" was nonetheless eligible for naturalization. For a detailed discussion of the racial requirements for naturalized citizenship, and Supreme Court decisions on the subject, see Chapter 6 § 1. See Ian F. Haney López, *White By Law: The Legal Construction of Race* (1996) (discussing extensively the Supreme Court decisions on who was "White" and who was not).

3. The Treaty of Guadalupe Hidalgo and Land Ownership

Like the meaning of the federal citizenship promised in the Treaty of Guadalupe Hidalgo, another set of fundamental questions arose under the Treaty. What would be the status of Mexican-owned real property after the transfer of sovereignty to the United States? How did approximately half of Mexico, owned by Mexicans through land grants made under Spanish and Mexican law, come to be owned by and integrated into the United States?

There were many ways in which this massive transfer of land occurred. In Texas, many Mexicans were simply run off their lands by Anglos angered by their presence. The Treaty of Guadalupe Hidalgo did not apply to Texas, except to settle its southern boundary at the Rio Grande. See Article V, Treaty of Guadalupe Hidalgo, in V *Treaties and Other International Acts of the United States of America* 213, 315–16 (Hunter Miller ed. 1937). Texas had became a state in 1845, preceding the war and the Treaty. Describing the post-war situation in Texas, David Montejano writes:

> The American settlers, in speaking of Mexicans, constantly distinguished themselves as "white folks." Newcomers were sometimes surprised at the rights of Mexicans. Olmsted overheard one newcomer informing another American that he had seen a Mexican with a revolver and stating that they shouldn't be allowed to carry firearms. The other replied that it would be difficult to prevent it— "they think themselves just as good as white men." Around the Victoria area, Anglo-Americans had sharply distinct views of Germans and Mexicans: "They always employed German mechanics, and spoke well of them. Mexicans were regarded in a somewhat unchristian tone, not as heretics or heathen to be converted with flannel and tracts, but rather as vermin to be exterminated. The lady was particularly strong in her prejudices. White folks and Mexicans were never made to live together, anyhow, and the Mexicans had no business here. They were getting so impertinent, and were so well protected by the laws, that the Americans would just have to get together and drive them all out of the country."

David Montejano, *Anglos and Mexicans in the Making of Texas 1836–1986* at 29 (1987)* (quoting Frederick Law Olmsted, *A Journey Through Texas; or, a Saddletrip on the Southwestern Frontier* 164, 245 (1860, reprinted 1969)).

Anglo Americans acquired Mexican lands in other ways as well. Anglo men would marry Mexican women from wealthy, land-owning families and so become entitled to part of the Mexican family's land holdings. In addition, Mexican-owned lands were sold, usually at steep discounts, to cover taxes enacted by the new Anglo governors. See Montejano, *supra* at 35, 37, 52; Arnoldo De León, *The Tejano Community* 1836–1900 at 14, 17 (1982).

Major losses of Mexican lands occurred as a direct result of actions of the United States government. Congress established tribunals that placed into question lands claimed under Mexican and Spanish grants preceding the war and the Treaty of Guadalupe Hidalgo. Congress established the California Land Claims Commission, a Surveyor General's office, and the Court of Private Land Claims to resolve previously undisputed land grants that were put into dispute by Congress after the war. The California Land Claim Act of 1851 established a commission, consisting of three appointed commissioners, whose purpose it was to ascertain the validity of private land claims in California. 9 Stat. 631 (1851). Congress then established the office of Surveyor General of New Mexico, Kansas, and Nebraska. 10 Stat. 308 (1854). In 1891, Congress created the Court of Private Land Claims which eventually had jurisdiction to resolve land claims in the entire region acquired from Mexico during the war. See 26 Stat. 854 (1891); 27 Stat. 470 (1893). Consider the following excerpt, describing these government tribunals and their effect on the Mexicans populating the territories newly acquired by the United States.

MALCOLM EBRIGHT

Land Grants and Lawsuits in Northern New Mexico
34, 38–39, 45–50 (1994).*

The only part of the [Treaty of Guadalupe Hidalgo] protecting land grant property rights after the Senate amendments was Article 8, which provided that "property of every kind now belonging to Mexicans ... shall be inviolably respected." Questions were left unanswered by Article 8 that had been resolved by Article 10, like the standard to be used in land grant adjudication * * *. The [law creating the California Land Claims Commission] placed the burden on the land grant owner to file a claim with the land board by 1853 or have his or her property declared public domain of the United States. This burden of initiating and proving a claim required the claimant to hire an attorney and to gather all the documents and testimony needed to support that claim. After the initial hearing, the land board's decision could be appealed to the federal district court where a new trial would take place. The district court's decision could also be appealed to the U.S. Supreme Court. If the claimant was finally successful there, they still had the burden of paying the cost of surveying their land and defending their survey before the Surveyor General's office.

This procedure transformed land grant owners into claimants who had to jump through numerous costly hoops before their property rights under the treaty were recognized. * * *

THE SURVEYOR GENERAL OF NEW MEXICO

The surveyor general's primary duty was to extend the federal public land survey system that provided for a checkerboard of townships, each containing thirty-six 640–acre sections. Once public land had been surveyed under this system, ownership could be obtained under the homestead and other laws that the surveyor general administered. The boundaries of land grants were not to be surveyed until after they were confirmed; even today large areas within land grants have not been surveyed. The American surveying system did not fit the arid Southwest, and Anglo property law was not understood by most Hispanos. Corruption of public officials and dishonesty of claimants under the United States land laws were additional factors preventing Hispanic land grant heirs from obtaining title to the land grants they occupied under the homestead and other similar laws. It was not unusual for enterprising Anglos to wrest from Hispanos their land grant property through fraud or manipulation of the land laws.

In addition to these problems, the scheme for adjudicating land grants under the surveyor general system was badly flawed. Hispanos did not understand or have any trust in the American system of land

ownership. Although written evidence of title was not without importance under the Spanish and Mexican land systems, for Hispanos,
possession was indeed nine-tenths of the law. Their use of the land was
more important in establishing their ownership than were any documents. When called upon to bring their documents to Santa Fe and file
claims with the surveyor general, most Hispanos demurred. Some feared
that they would lose their documents if they turned them over to the
surveyor general, while others felt they were adequately protected by the
Treaty of Guadalupe Hidalgo and didn't need to file a claim. Most
Hispanos never conceived of the possibility that the common lands of
their community grants were in jeopardy because under their laws and
customs, the common lands could never be sold. Since filing a claim
entailed considerable expense, it was the questionable claim held by the
speculator that was often filed first.

The surveyor general's responsibility concerning land grants was to
report to Congress his recommendation as to whether claims should be
confirmed or rejected by that body. * * *

THE COURT OF PRIVATE LAND CLAIMS

    * * *

The statute setting up the Court of Private Land Claims was not in
itself a radical departure from the procedure followed in California to
adjudicate land titles there, but differences in language between the two
statutes were later used by the courts to justify a stricter, more technical
approach under the 1891 Act. For example, the 1891 Act did not
specifically mention custom as a factor to be considered by the court in
making its decisions although custom would be implied under international law, a factor that was mentioned. Additionally the act required
proof that every condition of a grant was performed within the time
allowed and only a grant "lawfully and regularly derived from the
Government of Spain or Mexico" was entitled to confirmation. * * *

The procedure in the Court of Private Land Claims heavily favored
the government, resulting in numerous unjust decisions. As with the
surveyor general system, the claimant before the land claims court had
the burden of proving the existence of the grant and the performance of
all its conditions. Previously, however, the claimant was aided by certain
presumptions that eased the burden of proof, such as the presumption of
the existence of a community grant from the existence of a settlement on
the grant in 1846, the presumption of regularity of a grant, and the
presumption of authority of a granting official. Under the Court of
Private Land Claims, all three of these presumptions were eliminated.
* * *

Although the adversarial climate favored the government in the
Court of Private Land Claims, the decisions of the land claims court
occasionally displayed a balanced approach that yielded a result favorable to the claimants. But in several instances, when the U.S. attorney
appealed these decisions, the U.S. Supreme Court reversed, siding with
the government and against the claimant. The most famous of these
decisions concerned the ownership of the common lands of the San
Miguel del Bado grant in San Miguel County. [Eds. The Supreme Court

considered this grant in *United States v. Sandoval*, 167 U.S. 278 (1897). Contrary to Spanish and Mexican law, the Court decided that the common lands of a community grant were owned not by the community but by the Spanish or Mexican governments, such that title to such lands passed to the United States after 1848.] * * *

After the 1897 *Sandoval* decision, the land claims court rejected the common lands of every community grant that came up for adjudication. This vast acreage acquired by the United States now comprises most of the Carson and Santa Fe National Forests in northern New Mexico. But since the Court of Private Land Claims refused to apply the *Sandoval* decision retroactively, community grants confirmed before the *Sandoval* decision were able to retain their common lands.

Several other grounds were used by the Supreme Court and by the Court of Private Land Claims to reject perfectly valid grants. These included requirements that the grant be recorded in the Spanish or Mexican archives of New Mexico, that the grant be approved by the territorial deputation if made during the Mexican Period, and that there be strict compliance with each of the procedural steps of the grant: the petition, the grant, and the act of possession. But these technical reasons were seldom if ever the basis for a land grant rejection by Spain or Mexico. One situation in which Spanish or Mexican officials did reject a land grant due to a procedural defect was where notice to adjacent landowners, giving them the opportunity to object to the grant, had not been given. But United States courts rarely looked to see how the Spanish and Mexican governments had treated land grants in Hispanic New Mexico, despite the availability of numerous cases involving land grant disputes in the archives of New Mexico.

There were several grounds that did justify the rejection of land grants by Spanish and Mexican authorities. These included: (1) forgery of the documents, (2) insufficient proof that a grant had been made, (3) failure to notify owners of land adjoining the grant, (4) failure to meet a condition of the grant, (5) revocation of the grant by Spanish or Mexican officials, and (6) failure to settle the land four years after the grant was made, with continuous possession thereafter. These were grounds that would also justify United States courts in rejecting grants. For under international law, United States courts should have adjudicated land grants in the same manner as Spain and Mexico would have done. But instead, these courts often found it more expedient to rely on an obscure Spanish or Mexican law or commentary on Hispanic Law as the basis for a decision rather than seek the benefit of expert testimony on questions of Spanish and Mexican law.

* * *

Under the Mexican Colonization Law of 1824, individuals could receive grants of up to eleven leagues of land, about 48,000 acres. Yet many non-Mexican Americans found the size of such grants shocking. When Congressman William Carey Jones was sent to investigate the land situation in California in 1849, Jones's report on the size of such grants was astounding to many:

> When the immigration [into California] began, the Americans, used to the freedom of the boundless west, looked with incredulous surprise at the great stretches of the best land in California owned by single individuals, grantees of the Mexican and Imperial Spanish Governments. The United States population had a poor opinion of the native Californians anyway and were not at all sure that the latter were anything but aliens with rights little better than the native Indians.

George Cosgrave, *Early California Justice* 25 (1948). Anglo–American squatters regularly staked out claims on Mexican-settled and owned land. Later, in litigations about the validity of Mexican land grants, the "avaricious squatters in their endless harassing of grant holders, had as their chief ally none other than the Government of the United States." Cosgrave, *supra* at 27. So the large size, by United States standards, of individual Mexican land holdings also became a problem. Ebright, *supra* at 33. Consider the following cases, bearing in mind that there were many land grant cases which resulted in decisions by the United States Supreme Court.

LAND GRANT CASES

The conquest of California began with the short-lived "Bear Flag Rebellion," led by John C. Frémont, on June 6, 1846. Armed men under Frémont's command arrested and imprisoned Mexican General Mariano Vallejo. These acts have been interpreted by historians of California as a provocation intended to goad the Californios, the Mexicans populating California, into military retaliation that would, in turn, justify all-out war against them. Later, Frémont was appointed commander of the California Battalion of Volunteers, which waged unsuccessful guerilla warfare in South California. Frémont was eventually court-martialed for calling himself military governor. He rehabilitated himself as the population of California became predominantly Anglo in the wake of the Gold Rush, winning election to the United States Senate and later running for President as a Republican. See Leonard Pitt, *supra* at 26–37, 85, 198–202.

In 1847, José Alvarado sold off his assets to pay off insistent creditors. He sold Rancho Mariposa ("Butterfly Ranch") to John Frémont. See Pitt, *supra* at 36. The validity of Alvarado's (and, derivatively, Frémont's) claim were decided first by the California land claims commission, then by the United States district court and, ultimately, in the following decision by the United States Supreme Court.

JOHN CHARLES FREMONT v. UNITED STATES
58 U.S. (17 How.) 542 (1854).

CHIEF JUSTICE TANEY delivered the opinion of the Court.

The court have considered this case with much attention. It is not only important to the claimant and the public, but it is understood that many claims to land in California depend upon the same principles, and will, in effect, be decided by the judgment of the court in this case. * * *

There can be no question as to the power of the governor of California to make the grant [to Alvarado, from whom Fremont purchased the land at issue]. And it appears to have been made according to the regular forms and usages of the Mexican law. It has conditions attached to it; but these are conditions subsequent. And the first point to be decided is, whether the grant vested in Alvarado any present and immediate interest; and, if it did, then, secondly, whether any thing done or omitted to be done by him, during the existence of the Mexican government in California, forfeited the interest he had acquired, and revested it in the government? For if, at the time the sovereignty of the country passed to the United States, any interest, legal or equitable, remained vested in Alvarado or his assigns, the United States are bound in good faith to uphold and protect it. * * *

[T]he grant, after reciting that Alvarado was worthy, for his patriotic services, to be preferred in his pretension for his personal benefit, and that of his family, for the tract of land known by the name of Mariposas, to the extent of ten square leagues, within certain limits mentioned in the grant; and that the necessary requirements, according to the provisions of the laws and regulations, had been previously complied with, proceeds, in the name of the Mexican nation, to grant him the aforesaid tract, declaring the same, by that instrument, to be his property in fee, subject to the approbation of the departmental assembly and the conditions annexed to the grant.

The words of the grant are positive and plain. They purport to convey to him a present and immediate interest. And the grant was not made merely to carry out the colonization policy of the government, but in consideration of the previous public and patriotic services of the grantee. This inducement is carefully put forth in the title papers. And, although this cannot be regarded as a money consideration, making the transaction a purchase from the government, yet it is the acknowledgment of a just and equitable claim; and, when the grant was made on that consideration, the title in a court of equity ought to be as firm and valid as if it had been purchased with money on the same conditions.

It is argued that the description is so vague and uncertain that nothing passed by the grant; and that he had no vested interest until the land was surveyed, and the part intended to be granted severed by lines or known boundaries from the public domain. But this objection cannot be maintained. * * * [As] between him and the government, he had a vested interest in the quantity of land mentioned in the grant. The right to so much land, to be afterwards laid off by official authority, in the territory described, passed from the government to him by the execution of the instrument granting it. * * *

Regarding the grant to Alvarado, therefore, as having given him a vested interest in the quantity of land therein specified, we proceed to inquire whether there was any breach of the conditions annexed to it, during the continuance of the Mexican authorities, which forfeited his right and revested the title in the government.

The main objection on this ground is the omission to take possession, to have the land surveyed, and to build a house on it, within the time limited in the conditions. It is a sufficient answer to this objection to say, that negligence in respect to these conditions and others annexed to the grant does not, of itself, always forfeit his right. It subjects the land to be denounced by another, but the conditions do not declare the land forfeited to the State, upon the failure of the grantee to perform them. * * *

Now, it is well known that Mexico, and California as a part of it, had, for some years before, been in a disturbed and unsettled state, constantly threatened with insurrectionary and revolutionary movements; and in this state of things, the uncivilized Indians had become more turbulent, and were dangerous to the frontier settlements, which were not strong enough to resist them. * * * Now, it is very clear, from the evidence, that during the continuance of the Mexican power it was impossible to have made a survey, or to have built a house on the land, and occupied it for the purposes for which it was granted. * * *

Two other objections on the part of the United States to the confirmation of this title remain to be noticed. The first condition annexed to the grant prohibits grantee from selling, alienating, or mortgaging the property, or subjecting it to taxes, entail, or any other incumbrances. And by the laws of Mexico, the grantee could not, it is said, sell or convey the land to any one but a Mexican citizen, and that Fremont was not a Mexican citizen at the time of the conveyance under which he claims. * * *

But if this condition was valid by the laws of Mexico, and if any conveyance made by Alvarado would have forfeited the land under the Mexican government as a breach of this condition, or if it would have been forfeited by a conveyance to an alien, it does not by any means follow that the same penalty would be incurred by the conveyance to Fremont. * * *

California was at that time in possession of the American forces, and held by the United States as a conquered country, subject to the authority of the American government. The Mexican municipal laws, which were then administered, were administered under the authority of the United States, and might be repealed or abrogated at their pleasure; and any Mexican law inconsistent with the rights of the United States, or its public policy, or with the rights of its citizens, were annulled by the conquest. Now, there is no principle of public law which prohibits a citizen of a conquering country from purchasing property, real or personal, in the territory thus acquired and held; nor is there any thing in the principles of our government, in its policy or its laws, which forbids it. The Mexican government, if it had regained the power, and it had been its policy to prevent the alienation of real estate, might have treated the sale by Alvarado as a violation of its laws; but it becomes a very different question when the American government is called on to execute the Mexican law. And it can hardly be maintained that an American citizen, who makes a contract or purchases property under such circumstances, can be punished in a court of the United States with the penalty of forfeiture, when there is no law of congress to inflict it. The purchase was perfectly consistent with the rights and duties of Colonel Fremont, as an American officer and an American citizen; and the country in which he made the purchase was, at the time, subject to the authority and dominion of the United States.

Still less can the fact that he was not a citizen of Mexico impair the validity of the conveyance. Every American citizen who was then in California had at least equal rights with the Mexicans; and any law of the Mexican nation which had subjected them to disabilities, or denied to them equal privileges, were necessarily abrogated without a formal repeal. * * *

Upon the whole, it is the opinion of the court that the claim of the petitioner is valid, and ought to be confirmed.

[Eds. Dissenting opinions by Justices Catron and Campbell are omitted].

DE ARGUELLO v. UNITED STATES
59 U.S. 539 (1855).

[The claimants in this case sought to have their title confirmed to a tract of land called the "Rancho de las Pulgas." The Arguello family alleged that this tract contained twelve square leagues of land, having a front on the bay of San Francisco of four leagues, bounded southerly by a creek called San Francisquito, and northerly by the San Mateo, and extending back from the bay some three leagues to the sierra or range of mountains, including a valley called Canada de Raymundo.

Justice Grier, writing for the majority, decided that the Arguellos had a valid claim to the ranch "Las Pulgas." The court determined the grant to be four leagues long and one league wide, not including the Canada de Raymundo. Thus, although affirming the grant, the majority trimmed it down considerably, despite evidence that the Arguello family had possessed and asserted claim to the entire tract apparently continuously since 1820. One controversial aspect of Justice Grier's opinion was that the grant was approved despite the fact that it violated a Mexican law prohibiting land grants within ten leagues of the sea coast, the "littoral leagues."]

JUSTICE DANIEL, dissenting.

From the decision of the court in each of these causes, (as I have done in that of the *United States v. Reading*, during the present term, and as I should have done in those of the *United States v. Ritchie*, 17 How. 525, and of the *United States v. Fremont*, had I sat in the causes last mentioned,) I am constrained to declare my dissent.

The decisions in all the causes above enumerated have, according to my apprehension, been made in violation of the acknowledged laws and authority of that government which should have controlled those decisions and the subjects to which they relate; are subversive alike of justice and of the rights and the policy of the United States in the distribution and seating of the public lands—of the welfare of the people of, California, by inciting and pampering a corrupt and grasping spirit of speculation and monopoly—subversive, likewise, of rules and principles of adjudication heretofore asserted by this court in relation to claims to lands within the acquired domain of the United States.

It has by this court been repeatedly and expressly ruled, with respect to the territories acquired by the United States, either by purchase or conquest, that the laws and institutions in force within those territories at the time of the acquisition, were not from thence to be regarded as foreign laws, and in that aspect to be proved as matters of fact, but that the courts of the United States were authorized and bound to take the same judicial cognizance and notice of these laws which they were authorized and bound to extend to the laws of the several States. * * *

Amongst the laws and ordinances here referred to, are those by which the authority of the provincial commanders of governors to originate the titles to lands was conferred and limited. The prerequisites indispensable for the consummation of titles—the immunity from the power of the provincial governors, or from grants or alienations by them, of lands belonging to the Missions; the prohibition of colonization and settlement within twenty leagues of a foreign territory, and within what have been denominated the littoral leagues, or ten leagues from the sea-coast; and the necessity for a sanction by the departmental assemblies to give validity to private or individual titles, were all, by the same system or body of laws, established and proclaimed. * * *

An attempt is made, however, to escape from the authority and effect of those public laws [of Mexico] by setting up a practice in violation of them, and, from the proof of this practice, to establish a different code or system by which the former, regularly adopted and promulgated, and never directly repealed, has been abrogated and disannulled. The results of this attempt, if successful, (and by this court it has been thus far rendered successful,) are these—that the laws and institutions of the republic of Mexico, inscribed in her archives, are not to be received and judicially noticed by this court. * * *

How a proceeding like this is to be reconciled with the decisions of this court already cited, or how indeed it can be reconciled with uniformity or with the safety either of property or person, passes my comprehension to conceive. It can hardly admit of a rational doubt in the mind of any man who considers the character of much of the population of the late Spanish dominions in America—sunk in ignorance, and marked by the traits which tyranny and degradation, political and moral, naturally and usually engender—that proofs, or rather statements, might be obtained, as to any fact or circumstance which it might be deemed desirable or profitable to establish. And it will very probably be developed in the progress of the struggle or scramble for monopoly of the public domain, that many of the witnesses upon whose testimony the novel and sturdy Mexican code of practice or seizure is to be established, in abrogation of the written law, are directly or intermediately interested in the success of a monopoly by which, under the countenance of this court, PRINCIPALITIES are won by AN AFFIDAVIT, and conferred upon the unscrupulous few, to the exclusion and detriment of the many, and by the sacrifice of the sovereign rights of the United States. * * *

Turning our attention next to the grants themselves, they are, without an exception,—deficient in the requisites prescribed by the established written laws of the country, as indispensable to impart to them validity—but rest solely upon the circumstances * * * that they have originated in practical and temporary usurpations of power; and that, amidst scenes of violence and disorder, have been either maintained or acquiesced in, in defiance of the known public law. * * *

Upon such a foundation, such a pretence, or rather such a defiance of authority, I will not, by an abuse of language, call it even a pretence of right. I cannot consent to impair or destroy the sovereign rights and the financial interests of the United States in the public domain. I can perceive no merit, no claim whatsoever, to favor, on the part of the grasping and unscrupulous speculator and monopolist; no propriety in retarding, for his advantage or profit, the settlement and population of new States, by excluding therefrom the honest citizen of small means, by whose presence and industry the improvement and wealth, and social and moral health, and advancement of the country are always sure to be promoted.

Notes and Questions

1. Notice that Chief Justice Taney in the *Fremont* case reasons his way around several requirements of Mexican land grant law in order to uphold Frémont's claim. Despite the apparent invalidity of the grant under Mexican law, which was argued forcefully by the United States attorney in the case, the Court upholds the validity of the grant to Frémont of ten square leagues of land, with no one knowing quite where the land was. Judge Hoffman of the United States district court denied the validity of Frémont's claim because of the vagueness of its boundaries and because of Alvarado's failure to meet the conditions stipulated under Mexican law. See *United States v. Fremont*, 25 Fed.Cas. 1214 (N.D.Cal.1853), rev'd, 58 U.S. (17 How.) 542 (1854). Is Justice Daniel's dissent in *De Arguello*, in which he explicitly objects to the result in the *Fremont* case, correct?

2. Chief Justice Murray of the California Supreme Court made the following comments about the reasoning in the *Fremont* case:

> At the risk of exposing myself to the ridicule or censure of many, for what may be considered temerity on my part in questioning the soundness of these decisions [the *Ritchie* and *Fremont* decisions], I cannot refrain from the opinion that in these cases the Supreme Court [has] taken a new departure, and entirely disregarded their previous decisions. It is, however, a matter of congratulation to myself to know that this wholesale abandonment of principles, so long and satisfactorily settled, was not unanimous, and that [Justices Catron and Campbell] ... both dissented from the opinions in the case of *Fremont*, and for reasons substantially the same as those which influenced the decisions of this Court.

See *Gunn v. Bates*, 6 Cal. 263, 270 (1856). Chief Justice Murray's criticism of the Supreme Court suggests that the Court was not adhering to the accepted ways of deciding these cases. Why do you think the Supreme Court decided as it did in Fremont's case?

3. Why is Justice Daniel dissenting in these cases? Is he concerned about the enforcement of the Mexican law of land grants? Or does his dissent reveal a different concern? Is it significant that if the Supreme Court denies the validity of any land claim, it automatically reverts to the public domain of the United States for other disposition?

4. Would the outcome have been the same in the *Fremont* case if the ultimate owner of Alvarado's grant had been a Mexican, rather than Colonel Frémont? Recall that Alvarado had failed to meet several requirements of Mexican law, including the failure to include a survey of the land grant. See, *e.g.*, *United States v. Vallejo*, 63 U.S. (22 How.) 416 (1859) (Court reverses a grant of title where the grant is not found in original Mexican records); *United States v. Pico*, 27 Fed. Cas. 532 (1859) (claim of Mexican title rejected where unsupported by evidence from the Mexican archives; the reasoning resting on a significant number of assumptions by the district judge).

5. Why does the United States Attorney challenge these claims so vigorously and so often? What happens when he wins?

6. Malcolm Ebright's assessment of the *Fremont* decision was that

Taney treated the issue as one of vesting of title and found in favor of the Frémont claim, saying that when the grant was first made title was vested even though the condition [Alvarado's failure to occupy the grant within a year] had not been performed. This was a typical Anglo–American way to view the problem, not a Hispanic one. The *Fremont* case was liberal for the wrong reasons and resulted in a backlash of stricter Supreme Court decisions regarding California land grants. Ironically, a similar pattern occurred later in Supreme Court decisions dealing with New Mexico land grants: liberal decisions favoring speculators initially, yielding to overly strict rulings later that hurt legitimate grantees living on the land.

M. Ebright, *supra* at 37.

7. The Supreme Court's decision in *Fremont* was influential, prompting Judge Hoffman, who had decided the lower court case, and who decided many of the California land grant cases, to write:

The case of *Fremont v. United States* was among the earliest of the cases decided by the United States district court on appeal from the board of commissioners. It was the first in which the Supreme Court announced the principles by which this class of cases was to be decided. It has, therefore, remained the most important and the leading case on this branch of the law, and has exercised a controlling influence on all subsequent decisions of this court.

United States v. Cambuston, 25 Fed. Cas. 266, 273 (D.Cal.1859).

8. Mexican claimants won some of their cases. The *De Arguello* case is one example, although the court reduces the size of the land grant. See also *United States v. Peralta*, 60 U.S. (19 How.) 343 (1856), affirming a land grant held by Mexicans, with a dissent from Justice Daniels, who dissented in *De Arguello* and objected to the *Fremont* decision.

BOTILLER v. DOMÍNGUEZ

130 U.S. 238 (1889).

[Domínguez attempted to eject Botiller from the "Rancho Las Virgenes." The title of the plaintiff was a grant claimed to have been made by the government of Mexico to Domínguez, but no claim under this grant had ever been presented for confirmation to the board of land commissioners, appointed under the Act of Congress of March 3, 1851, (9 St. 631) "to ascertain and settle the private land claims in the state of California."

The California Supreme Court had decided that the federal statute creating the California Land Claims Commission was invalid.]

JUSTICE MILLER delivered the opinion of the court.

* * *

The question presented is an important one in reference to land titles in the state of California, and is entitled to our serious consideration. Although it has been generally supposed that nearly all the private claims to any of the lands acquired by the United States from Mexico, by the treaty of peace made at the close of the Mexican war, have been presented to and passed upon by the board of commissioners appointed for that purpose by the act of 1851, yet claims are now often brought forward which have not been so passed upon by that board, and were never presented to it for consideration. And if the proposition on which the Supreme Court of California decided this case is a sound one, namely, that the board constituted under that act had no jurisdiction of, and could not by their decree affect in any manner, a title which had been perfected under the laws of the Mexican government prior to the transfer of the country to the United States, it is impossible to tell to what extent such claims of perfected titles may be presented, even in cases where the property itself has by somebody else been brought before that board and passed upon. * * *

Two propositions under this statute are presented by counsel in support of the decision of the Supreme Court of California. The first of these is, that the statute itself is invalid, as being in conflict with the provisions of the [Treaty of Guadalupe Hidalgo], and violating the protection which was guaranteed by it to the property of Mexican citizens, owned by them at the date of the treaty; and also in conflict with the rights of property under the constitution and laws of the United States, so far as it may affect titles perfected under Mexico. The second proposition is, that the statute was not intended to apply to claims which were supported by a complete and perfect title from the Mexican government, but, on the contrary, only to such as were imperfect, inchoate, and equitable in their character, without being a strict legal title.

With regard to the first of these propositions it may be said, that so far as the act of Congress is in conflict with the treaty with Mexico, that is a matter in which the court is bound to follow the statutory enactments of its own government. If the treaty was violated by this general statute enacted for the purpose of ascertaining the validity of claims derived from the Mexican government, it was a matter of international concern, which the two states must determine by treaty, or by such other means as enables one State to enforce upon another the obligations of a treaty. This court, in a class of cases like the present, has no power to set itself up as the instrumentality for enforcing the provisions of a treaty with a foreign nation which the government of the United States, as a sovereign power, chooses to disregard. * * *

There is nothing in the language of the statute to imply any exclusion of [claims perfected under Mexican law] from the jurisdiction of the commission. * * *

Nor can it be said that there is anything unjust or oppressive in requiring the owner of a valid claim, in that vast wilderness of lands unclaimed and unjustly claimed, to present his demand to a tribunal possessing all the elements of judicial functions, with a guarantee of judicial proceedings, so that his title could be established if it was found to be valid, or rejected if it was invalid.

We are unable to see any injustice, any want of constitutional power, or any violation of the treaty, in the means by which the United States undertook to separate the lands in which it held the proprietary interest from those which belonged, either equitably or by a strict legal title, to private persons. Every person owning land or other property is at all times liable to be called into a court of justice to contest his title to it. This may be done by another individual, or by the government under which he lives. * * *

[T]here can be no doubt of the proposition, that no title to land in California, dependent upon Spanish or Mexican grants can be of any validity which has not been submitted to and confirmed by the board provided for that purpose in the act of 1851, or, if rejected by that board, confirmed by the District or Supreme Court of the United States.

Notes and Questions

1. Note the Court's holding that, even if the statute creating the California Land Claims Commission violated the Treaty of Guadalupe Hidalgo, the courts were bound to enforce only the statute. What effect would you expect this to have with respect to subsequent acts of Congress dealing with the lands ceded under the Treaty of Guadalupe Hidalgo? Recall that one such subsequent act is the congressional act creating the Court of Private Land Claims, passed shortly after this decision in 1891. What effect would you expect this decision to have on enforcement of the Treaty's guarantees by Congress? By the Courts?

2. Consider the following assessment of the *Fremont* and *Domínguez* cases:

> Moreover, the key example offered by Professor [Paul] Gates to support the notion that the judiciary "leaned so far in the direction of leniency" so as to demonstrate "the greatest readiness ... to accept any substantial evidence" to confirm Mexican grants—the case of American pioneer and Bear Flag revolt leader John C. Frémont—supports rather

than undermines the notion that Mexican grantees suffered discrimination in tribunals adjudicating Treaty rights. On the one hand were claimants like Frémont, an Anglo who possessed questionable papers documenting dubious title. Still the Supreme Court gave him the benefit of the doubt and confirmed his patent. On the other hand were claimants like Dominga Domínguez, a Mexican who possessed unquestionable papers documenting perfect title. Yet the Court brushed aside her claim because she had failed to make a timely application for a patent with the board of land commissioners, and refused to eject the French and Anglo squatters who had overrun her lands east of Mission San Gabriel, California.

In short, the indeterminate nature of the Treaty, and U.S. laws purporting to implement it, could be manipulated to promote the claims of grant holders when it suited the courts and to extinguish them when it did not.

Christopher David Ruiz Cameron, *One Hundred Fifty Years of Solitude: Reflections on the End of the History Academy's Dominance of Scholarship on the Treaty of Guadalupe Hidalgo*, 5. Sw. J.L. & Trade Am. 83, 97 (1998) (interesting observations on historical interpretations of the Treaty and the need for new interpretation and analysis by legal scholars).

One of the aspects of Spanish and Mexican land grant law frequently misunderstood was the community ownership of lands in a community land grant. Consider the following case.

UNITED STATES v. SANDOVAL

167 U.S. 278 (1897).

[Julian Sandoval petitioned the Court of Private Land claims for the confirmation of the San Miguel del Bado Grant, in the New Mexico territory, containing 315,300 acres. This grant contained both individual grants to approximately 51 settlers in the town of San Miguel del Bado, as well as a substantial amount of land held in common by the town. The United States attorney argued that only the grants to the individual settlers could be confirmed, and that the lands held in common passed directly from Mexico to the United States with the change in sovereignty after the war.]

Chief Justice Fuller delivered the opinion of the court.

By article 8 of the Treaty of Guadalupe Hidalgo of February 2, 1848 (and we are not concerned here with the treaty of December 30, 1853), Mexicans established in territories previously belonging to Mexico, and remaining for the future within the limits of the United States as defined by the treaty, were free to continue where they then resided, or to remove at any time to Mexico, "retaining the property which they possessed in said territories or disposing thereof or removing the proceeds wherever they pleased," and "in the said territories property of every kind now belonging to Mexicans now established there shall be inviolably respected. The present owners, the heirs of these, and all Mexicans who may acquire said property by contract, shall enjoy, with respect to it, guarantees equally ample as if the same belonged to citizens of the United States."

The mode in which private rights of property may be secured, and the obligations imposed upon the United States by treaties fulfilled, belongs to the political department of the government to provide. In respect to California, this was done through the establishment of a judicial tribunal; but, in respect of the adjustment and confirmation of claims under grants from the Mexican government in New Mexico and in Arizona, congress reserved to itself, prior to the passage of the act of March 3, 1891, creating the court of private land claims, the determination of such claims.

By the act of March 3, 1851, ch. 41 (9 Stat. 631), congress created a board of land commissioners to determine claims to land in California asserted "by virtue of any right, or title, derived from the Spanish or Mexican government."

Section 11 of the act provided that the board of commissioners thereby created, the district court, and this court, "in deciding on the validity of any claim brought before them under the provisions of this act, shall be governed by the Treaty of Guadalupe Hidalgo, the law of nations, the laws, usages, and customs of the government from which the claim is derived, the principles of equity, and the decisions of the supreme court of the United States, so far as they are applicable"; that is, the decisions theretofore given in relation to titles in Louisiana and Florida, which were derived from the French or Spanish authorities previous to the cession to the United States. *Fremont v. U. S.*, 17 How. 542, 553.

Section 14 permitted the claims of lot holders in a city, town, or village to be presented in the name thereof, and authorized the presumption of a grant to such city, town, or village, when shown to have been in existence on the day named.

The act of March 3, 1891, is couched in different phraseology.

Section 6 authorizes any person or persons or corporation, or their legal representatives, claiming lands within the limits of the territory derived by the United States from the republic of Mexico, "by virtue of any such Spanish or Mexican grant, concession, warrant, or survey as the United States are bound to recognize and confirm by virtue of the treaties of cession of said country by Mexico to the United States which at the date of the passage of this act have not been confirmed by act of congress, or otherwise finally decided upon by lawful authority, and which are not already complete and perfect," to file a petition in the court of private land claims praying that "the validity of such title or claim may be inquired into and decided." * * *

The seventh subdivision of [Section 13 of the Act of March 3, 1891] reads thus:

"No confirmation in respect of any claims or lands mentioned in section six of this act or in respect of any claim or title that was not complete and perfect at the time of the transfer of sovereignty to the United States as referred to in this act, shall in any case be made or patent issued for a greater quantity than eleven squares leagues of land to or in the right of any one original grantee or claimant, or in the right of any one original grant to two or more persons jointly, nor for a greater quantity than was authorized by the respective laws of Spain or Mexico applicable to the claim. * * *

"The difference between the act of 1891 and the California act of 1851, hitherto referred to, accentuates the intention of congress to confine the authority conferred by the later act to narrower limits than those fixed by the act of 1851. The act of 1851 authorized the adjudication of claims to land by virtue of any 'right' or 'title' derived from the Spanish government, and conferred the power in express language on the board and court to presume a grant in favor of a town. The act of 1891 not only entirely omits authority to invoke this presumption, but, as we have seen, excludes by express terms any claim, the completion of which depended upon the mere grace or favor of the government of Spain or Mexico, and of the United States as the successor to the rights of these governments."

The contention on behalf of the United States is that the court of private land claims had no power to confirm lands [situated] as these were, within the outboundaries, that had not been allotted prior to the date of the treaty, because under the laws of Spain and Mexico the *jus disponendi* of all unassigned lands remained in the government, and passed to the United States.

The papers in the *expediente* show that it was the intention that a town or pueblo should be, and that it was, established. The application stated that the land asked for was intended, not only for the 51 petitioners, "but also for every one in the province not supplied." The Alcalde Ortiz was directed to execute the grant on "the conditions and requisites required in such cases to be observed." The conditions are set out by the alcalde in his report as all agreed to by petitioners; among them being the provision that the tract was to "be in common, not only in regard to themselves, but also to all the settlers who may join them in the future."

In 1803 the Alcalde Pino, under instructions from the governor, went upon the grant, and divided the lands which had been occupied and cultivated among the original petitioners and some others, and put each one in the possession of the lot drawn by him; notifying them that no one should have the right to sell the land allotted to him until the expiration of 10 years from that date, as directed by the governor. The grant purported to convey only the use of the land, with the right to acquire the legal title to such portion of it as might be allotted to each in severalty, on condition that they remained on it and cultivated it for 10 years, while the unoccupied or common lands were declared to be for the benefit of the original grantees and all other persons who might desire to settle on the grant, and who complied with the terms in regard to settlement and cultivation.

Did the fee to lands embraced within the limits of the pueblo, and intended for community use, continue to remain in the sovereign, or did it pass to the pueblo? * * *

The existence of [the] power of control and disposition as to municipal lands in the supreme Spanish and then Mexican authority was shown by * * * references, and various acts of congress were cited as enacted in view "of this state of the Spanish law, and the unquestioned power lodged in the king of Spain to exercise unlimited authority over the lands assigned to a town, and undisposed of, and not the subject of private grant, to all of which rights the United States succeeded as successor of the king of Spain and the government of Mexico."

"So, also," said the court, "it may well be supposed that it was upon this aspect of the imperfect nature of right in land claimed by towns in territory formerly owned by Spain and Mexico, and the long-established construction of such rights evidenced by the foregoing acts of congress, which caused this court, speaking through Mr. Justice Field in *Grisar v. McDowell*, 6 Wall. at 373, to say: 'Even after the assignment the interest acquired by the pueblo was far from being an indefeasible estate such as is known to our laws. The purposes to be accomplished by the creation of pueblos did not require their possession of the fee. The interest * * * amounted to little more than a restricted and qualified right to alienate portions of the land to its inhabitants for building or cultivation, and to use the remainder for commons, for pasture lands, or as a source of revenue, or for other public purposes. And this limited right of disposition and use was in all particulars subject to the control of the government of the country.' " * * *

Under the laws of the Indies, lands not actually allotted to settlers remained the property of the king, to be disposed of by him, or by those on whom he might confer that power. As Mr. Hall says (chapter 7, § 122): "The fee of the lands embraced within the limits of pueblos continued to remain in the sovereign, and never in the pueblo as a corporate body." Subsequent decrees, orders, and laws did not change the principle.

Towns were established in two ways: By their formation by *empresarios* or contractors, the title to the lands granted vesting in the contractors and settlers, minute provisions being made in relation thereto. By individuals associating themselves together for that purpose, and applying to the governor of the province, through whose action a city, villa, or place was established. These municipalities appear to have been quasi corporations, corporations *sub modo*, and their *ayuntamientos* exercised political control over the pueblos, and over surrounding country attached to their jurisdiction. The alcalde made allotments subject to the orders of the ayuntamiento, and they, again, were apparently subject to the provincial deputation, or an equivalent superior body. At all events, unallotted lands were subject to the disposition of the government.

At the date of the Treaty of Guadalupe Hidalgo, neither these settlers nor this town could have demanded the legal title to such lands of the former government, and the court of private land claims was not empowered to pass the title to either. It is for the political department to deal with the equitable rights involved.

Notes and Questions

1.　In *Sandoval*, the Court confirms only the portions of the San Miguel del Bado grant that were allotted to individual landowners and excludes the common lands, which constituted the vast majority of the grant.

In a subsequent decision, *Rio Arriba Land & Cattle Co. v. United States*, 167 U.S. 298 (1897), the Court relied on *Sandoval* and disallowed the community-owned common lands of the San Joaquin land grant. In *Rio Arriba*, the Court wrote: "We have just held in *United States v. Sandoval*, 167 U.S. 278, that as to all unallotted lands, within exterior boundaries, where towns or communities were sought to be formed, as in this instance, the title remained in the government, for such disposition as it might see proper to make." As a result of this decision, the common lands of the San Joaquin grant were transferred to the United States government. Eventually these common lands became part of the Kit Carson National Forest. Reies Tijerina and his followers later claimed that these lands still belonged to the community and not to the United States government. See *infra*.

2. Commenting on the *Rio Arriba Land & Cattle Co.* decision, Malcolm Ebright writes:

> The Supreme Court's decision was based on scanty Spanish legal authorities and did not take into account either the long history of the Castilian land-owning pueblo or Mexican Period New Mexico cases concerning common land ownership. This and other legal and historical authority not brought to the Supreme Court's attention, indicate that the New Mexico community land grant itself owned its common lands.

Ebright, *supra* at 105. See Ebright at 105–123 for a detailed discussion of the Supreme Court's erroneous disposition of the San Joaquin land grant.

3. Judges were not insulated from the popular opinions of the times towards Mexicans and Indians. Justice Daniel, dissenting in *De Arguello*, described the character of Mexicans as "sunk in ignorance, and marked by the traits which tyranny and degradation, political and moral, naturally and usually engender." Consider the following comments from the Honorable Wilbur F. Stone, an Associate Justice of the Court of Private Land Claims. Justice Stone wrote a history of that Court and its work, in which he remarked on one occasion during which an Indian witness appeared before the court:

> Occasionally the court room at Santa Fe would be enlivened by a squad of Indians who had journeyed thither from their distant pueblos as witnesses for their grant. These delegations were usually headed by the governor of their tribe, who exhibited great pride in striding up to the witness stand and being sworn on the holy cross: wearing a badge on his breast, a broad red sash round his waist, and clad in a white shirt, the full tail of which hung about his Antarctic zone like the skirt of a ballet dancer and underneath which depended his baggy white muslin trousers, a la Chinese washee-washee.

> The grave and impurturbable [*sic*] bow which the governor gave to the judges on the bench, in recognition of their equality with himself as official dignitaries, arrayed in that grotesque fashion, was enough to evoke a hilarious bray from a dead burro.

Journal of the New Mexico Bar Association (1904), reprinting a brief history of the Public Claims Court by the Hon. Wilbur F. Stone. What were the chances that a judge expressing such attitudes would credit the testimony of American or Mexican Indian witnesses appearing before him?

The procedures of the California commission, and later the Public Land Claims court, were administered in a way that often denied the validity of

Mexican land grants and either affirmed the land titles of new Anglo–American owners of such lands or placed the land in trust for ultimate distribution or ownership by the United States government. There were many ways in which the commission or court exercised discretion to deny the validity of Mexican land grants. A judge might conclude that the Mexican authority granting a land claim lacked authority to do so, or question the validity of Indian land claims under Mexican law (under Mexican law, Indians were citizens and entitled to land grants). Mexican landowners were required to verify their ownership through detailed and extensive archival documents, which were often unavailable because of the destruction of crucial documents during the war or by fires. Documents were also destroyed by government officials. In addition, Mexican usage and custom were not respected, so that the descriptions of Mexican land grants were found to be "too vague" or "imprecise" when compared to Anglo–American land surveys. Finally, Mexicans who contested adverse rulings either initially or on appeal incurred heavy legal fees, which were regularly settled by giving their lawyer one-third to one-half of the original land grant. Through all of these means, Mexicans were deprived of their lands, despite the promise in the Treaty of Guadalupe Hidalgo that the property of Mexicans remaining in the territories ceded to the United States would be "inviolably respected." See generally W.A. Keleher, *Law of the New Mexico Land Grant*, 4 New Mexico Historical Review 350–71 (1929); J. of the New Mexico Bar Association 5–26 (1904) (containing a brief history of the Court of Public Land Claims by the Hon. Wilbur F. Stone, Associate Justice of the Court of Public Land Claims); George Cosgrave, *Early California Justice* 25–32 (1948); Robert J. Rosenbaum, *Mexicano Resistance in the Southwest* 41 (1981).

In many ways, the results of the California commission and the Court of Private Land Claims speak for themselves. In California, of 848 land grant cases filed, 613 grants were upheld and 200 rejected, with the remainder disposed on other grounds. These outcomes, while not appearing devastating in terms of the invalidation of Mexican land grants, do not reflect the enormous costs involved in securing them through litigation of multiple appeals. Describing the California outcomes, one commentator wrote that "[t]he land grant procedure was a measure of oppression." Cosgrave, *supra* at 32. As described by another commentator:

Two effects of the California Land Claims Act had a catastrophic impact on the original California landholders. First, the imposition of the law called all land title in the state into question. During the years that it took to have claims considered and confirmed by the Land Claims Commission and the courts, landholders had no legal remedy against an army of "settlers" who staked claims on their rangeland. By the time some grantholders received patents to protect their lands, they had little left to protect. Second, the process of title confirmation under the California Land Claims Act placed an enormous financial burden on the claimants. Many lost their holdings as a result of the costs of litigation.

See Frederico M. Cheever, Comment, *A New Approach to Spanish and Mexican Land Grants and the Public Trust Doctrine: Defining the Property Interest Protected by the Treaty of Guadalupe Hidalgo*, 33 UCLA L. Rev. 1364, 1401–1402 (1986). See also Ebright, *supra* at 37.

In the Court of Private Land Claims, the results were devastating. According to Justice Stone, 301 land grant cases were filed before the court, involving 36 million acres of land. Eighty-seven grants were confirmed, totalling about 3 million acres. Of 36 million acres claimed under original Mexican or Spanish grants, only 3 million acres, or one-twelfth of the total, remained under the control of Mexican grantees or their heirs. The remaining 33 million acres of land reverted to the public domain of the United States for disposal by the government. Commenting on the work of the court, Justice Stone wrote that "In addition to the benefits mentioned [greater stability in investment and finality of land titles], the reversion to the public domain of the general government of more than 30,000,000 acres of land comes like new cession of country to the United States—a region illimitible in the undeveloped wealth of its coal, metals, agriculture and health-giving climate." Stone, *supra* at 26. It is little wonder, then, that "[t]he work of the land court, from its beginning until now, has received the highest commendation as well from the department of justice at Washington as from the Bar, the press and the people within its jurisdiction, whose interests are directly affected by its adjudications." *Id.*

Notes and Questions

1.   Given the ideology of Manifest Destiny, which sought Anglo–Saxon dominion over the desirable lands of Mexico and provided the rationale for the war against Mexico, are these outcomes of the work of the California commission and the Court of Private Land Claims surprising? Are these outcomes fairly inevitable? Could these judicial bodies have ruled differently?

2.   Consider, in this regard, that the United States paid 15 million dollars for the territories ceded in the Treaty of Guadalupe Hidalgo. "[T]he United States looked at the treaty as an enormous real estate deal; it expected to get clear title to most of the land it was paying for regardless of the property rights of Mexicans." Ebright, *supra* at 30.

3.   For a comprehensive analysis and interpretation of the Mexican land grant adjudications and the alienation of Chicana/o property interests, see Guadalupe T. Luna, *Chicana/Chicano Land Tenure in the Agrarian Domain: On the Edge of a "Naked Knife,"* 4 Mich. J. Race & Law 39 (1998). Professor Luna comments on the importance of study of the land grant cases, not just because of the story they tell with respect to the dispossession of Mexican property owners, but because of their historical significance:

> From the time the Founders signed the United States Constitution to the present, considerations of race have governed the agricultural agenda and the resulting control of the nation's natural resources. The counter-story presented here reveals that throughout most of American legal history, biased interpretations of the law created a system that dispossessed and disenfranchised individuals of Mexican background. Moreover, Constitutional directives protecting property rights were held hostage to the whims of the interpreters of law. Alienated from their property, Chicanas/Chicanos were treated as foreigners and disallowed full citizenship status. In the aggregate, their stories present complex analytical issues. The governmental practices involved in their dispossession played a significant role in determining their current economic status in ways that are difficult to reconcile with present understandings in property law.

This Article began with the observation that Chicanas/Chicanos have long held an invisible status within the study of law. While scholars outside of legal academia continue to ascribe the alienation of grantees from their property interests to various causes, land dispossession and its origins remain excluded from legal scholarship. By exploring the application of the Treaty of Guadalupe Hidalgo to the claims of Mexican land grantees, this Article urges continued study of Chicana/Chicano legal history to offset simplistic readings of the country's historical past, promote greater intellectual exercise for students, and help diminish Chicanas'/Chicanos' subordinate legal status.

Id. at 142–44.

4. For recent scholarship on the Treaty of Guadalupe Hidalgo, see *Symposium: Understanding the Treaty of Guadalupe Hidalgo on its 150th Anniversary*, 5 Sw. J.L. & Trade Am. 5–207 (1998).

D. THE MEXICAN RESISTANCE TO THE CONQUEST IN THE SOUTHWEST

The struggles over the former land and people of Mexico were not waged solely in the courts. Mexicans who had been routed or later displaced from their lands mounted armed, violent resistance. Much of this resistance can be understood as guerilla warfare against an oppressor. Much of it took place on the newly created border of the Rio Grande now dividing former Mexico in two. Consider the following excerpt.

ROBERT J. ROSENBAUM

Mexicano Resistance in the Southwest
15–17 (1981).*

VIOLENT RESISTANCE

When seen as a whole, the nineteenth century landscape of the Southwest appears dotted with brushfire conflicts between *mexicanos* and *americanos*. Some flared sharply and threatened to engulf whole towns and the surrounding countryside; isolated flashes of outrage, of just having had enough, left scorched spots like those along railroad tracks started by the hotboxes from passing trains. And in some places, violence smoldered constantly, leaving a perpetual atmospheric haze like the smog over Los Angeles.

Violence is not new to human societies; in fact, it seems to be a constant of the human condition. As political scientist Ted Robert Gurr observes, European states and empires through the past twenty-four centuries have averaged one year of violent disturbance in five, counting "important" disturbances only, and since 1945 violent attempts to overthrow governments have been more frequent than elections throughout the world.

The fact that mexicanos violently resisted Anglo American domination may come as a surprise. Resistance does not fit the myth of the speedy conquest; neither does it square with the stereotype of cowardly

* Copyright © by Robert J. Rosenbaum.   Reprinted by permission of the author.

and inferior "meskins" nor the comforting belief in the benevolence and general attractiveness of the American way of life.

Equally important, however, in accounting for the omission of mexicano resistance from Anglo-American historic consciousness is the fact that uprisings never fundamentally threatened Anglo-American control; they never achieved a sufficient size or posed a severe enough threat to be recognized as revolutions.

Most of the literature about civil disorder and internal violence focuses on revolutions, the large-scale attempt to overthrow government, and either ignores urban riots and rural uprisings or dismisses them as insignificant expressions of frustration by the oppressed. Only recently have historians, anthropologists, and political scientists begun to examine these expressions of popular discontent as political activity—attempts by social groups to influence and determine matters that affect their common welfare.

During the course of the nineteenth century, mexicanos employed violence as one means for retaining some measure of self-determination in the face of an increasingly oppressive new regime. All incidents of political violence fall within the general category that Hobsbawm terms "peasant" or "primitive" rebellions, although several cases carried hints of other possibilities. The outbreaks divide into five types within Hobsbawm's "peasant" framework: Border Warfare, where the locale provided a unifying theme to all of the resistance even though each of the other types appeared; Social Banditry, the most basic and constant expression of hostility that was carried out by individuals who refused to submit and who enjoyed the support of their general communities; Community Upheavals, when tensions became sufficiently high and widespread to precipitate a "spontaneous" outbreak; Long–Term Skirmishing, where violent set-tos occurred at a low level of intensity but over a long period of time and Coordinated Rebellions.

LAW AND LAND

Friction between mexicano and americano involved race, language, religion, food, sex and almost every other conceivable cultural distinction. But the points where friction usually provoked violent resistance were law and land.

Anglo Americans brought their version of the English common law to the conquered territory. Mexicanos, particularly *los pobres*, accustomed to the more personalized and traditional procedures of the *alcaldes*, found Anglo law confusing. It was in English, in itself a problem, and the fact that Anglos blatantly manipulated legal codes and court procedures added to the mexicano's resentment. Law enforcement contributed a more pronounced level of anger. Mexicanos perceived their treatment by Anglo peace officers as capricious and unjust; the number of unpunished lynchings and killings of mexicanos by americanos gave stark evidence for the accuracy of this perception.

Land provided the other major stimulus for violence. Both Anglo and Hispanic competed for it. Fundamental differences in practices of land tenure and conceptions about proper land use, particularly the tensions inherent in the transformation of land into a saleable commodity, complicated the fundamental competition. And the terms of the Treaty of Guadalupe Hidalgo, guaranteeing property rights but not specifying how traditional Hispanic forms of land ownership were to be translated into modes compatible with American law, added to the confusion and increased distrust and hostility.

Thus, the confrontation between mexicano and americano is a history of conflict. The conflict was between cultures, and it occurred on two levels: Often conflict grew out of misunderstanding, as neither group understood the other's socially established structures of meaning; at least as often, however, conflict was between meanings—each understood the other well enough and that was precisely the problem. They didn't want the same things.

Western expansion and the frontier experience are often cited as the most distinctive feature about the United States and the source of the qualities that are identified as uniquely American. How accurate that interpretation is, is a matter of debate. But the history of the mexicano peoples in the Southwest leads to a somewhat different characterization. Because mexicanos followed an essentially peasant culture in their traditional homelands and were but recently severed from their mother country, the conflict between mexicano and americano emerges as the most European occurrence in the history of the trans-Mississippi West.

THE CORTINA WARS AND GREGORIO CORTEZ

While too many conflicts broke out to list here, at least a few deserve mention. The Cortina War, the saga of Gregorio Cortez, and Reies Tijerina and the New Mexico Land Grant War of 1967 are among the most significant acts of resistance following the United States War with Mexico. These and other conflicts grow directly out of the treatment of Mexicans at the hands of United States authorities and courts.

ROBERT J. ROSENBAUM
Mexicano Resistance in the Southwest
42–49 (1981).*

THE CORTINA WAR

Thirty-five years old in 1859, Juan Cortina was a man of mature vigorous years, from a prominent family, experienced in military affairs, and with a history of opposition to Anglo Americans. He was, in short, a natural leader of the society split by the new border. His family's property, the Espíritu Santo land grant, had been diminished by the Anglo courts. Cortina's pride rebelled against the gringo law officers whose arrogance rose as Anglo merchants and lawyers increased their inroads in the Valley. Twelve years under Anglo domination had built a volatile fund of anger and resentment in Cortina and his people that needed only a spark to ignite it into open war.

A law officer struck the spark. On July 13, 1859, in Brownsville, Cortina saw city marshal Bob Spears pistol-whipping a drunken vaquero who worked for Cortina's mother. He shot Spears and left town with the vaquero. Two months later, Cortina led an estimated sixty riders into Brownsville, where they released all of the mexicano prisoners in the jail, sacked the stores of particularly obnoxious merchants, and executed four Americans who had killed mexicanos and had gone unpunished.

Influential citizens, including the Mexican consul in Brownsville and Cortina's cousin, persuaded him to leave the city. Two days later, however, Cortina issued a proclamation that enumerated the grievances of his band and vowed that they would continue to fight for justice. Apparently, further pleas from mexicano residents of Brownsville convinced him to disband; in any event, Cortina did not strike again until Brownsville police captured one of his lieutenants, Tomás Cabrera. Regrouping, Cortina threatened to destroy the city if his man was not released. A joint force made up of Anglos and Mexican national guardsmen lent by the Liberal government, which did not want to disrupt U.S.-Mexican harmony, attacked Cortina on October 22. They suffered a resounding defeat. Cortina controlled the countryside and kept Brownsville under siege.

The arrival of the Texas Rangers inflamed the situation. In exasperation, the Rangers hanged Cabrera, despite earlier promises from Brownsville leaders that he would receive a fair trial. Cortina responded with a second proclamation and renewed his attacks. Mexicano riders swelled the size of his army. Noncombatants refused to help state officials and volunteered supplies to Cortina instead. Cortina's statements and actions won widespread approval from the people of the Border, and the combination of popular support and successful skirmishes kept Cortina master of the Rio Grande for the remainder of the year.

It took the U.S. Army to defeat the insurgents. Troops under Major S.P. Heintzelman accompanied by a force of Texas Rangers under Colonel John S. Ford defeated the rebels at Rio Grande City on December 27, 1859. Sporadic fighting continued into the new year, but Cortina was now confined to sniping and harassing actions as he moved along both sides of the border pursued by American and Mexican troops. The aftermath of the rebellion saw Anglos, principally the Rangers, retaliate indiscriminately against all mexicanos in a fit of bloody terrorism.

Gringos called Cortina a bandit and attributed the uprising to the inherent characteristics of a vicious race who wanted plunder and the chance to "execute summary vengeance on all towards whom [they] had *private* grudges" (emphasis added). Americans on the Border were acutely conscious of being in the minority—numbering only three hundred against twelve thousand according to one contemporary estimate—and conscious of their disproportionate economic and political power. People occupying a privileged status often find it necessary to justify themselves in terms of the "natural" order of things and to attribute any signs of discontent to a biological or moral flaw of the complainers. But contemporary Anglo accounts of the uprising sometimes allowed traces of guilt or glimmerings of awareness of oppression to show through. Accounts of the Brownsville raid said that Cortina's raiders had shouted "Death to Americans; *viva la republica Mexicana;* and threatened to hold the Mexican flag on the staff of our deserted garrison," clearly attributing a political motive to the raiders. Another account explained the raid by saying: " . . . under a polite exterior, the deepest, settled hatred exists in the Mexican mind towards us," an expression suggesting that there might be legitimate grievances against the newcomers.

Anglos made occasional lapses which hinted that Cortina and his followers were something other than bandits; Cortina asserted unequivocally that the movement aimed to bring justice to his people. The first proclamation, issued two days after the Brownsville raid, explained that in the name of "the sacred right of self-preservation" Cortina and his men were trying to "put an end to our misfortunes." Cortina laid the blame on a "secret conclave . . . [that] persecute[s] and rob[s] for no other crime than that of being of Mexican origin." Cortina described the Brownsville raiders as "clothed in the imposing aspect of our exasperation" and went on to warn that though they might have to lead a "wandering life . . . our personal enemies shall not possess our lands until they have fattened it with their own gore."

Cortina's two proclamations emphasize three major complaints: loss of land either through legal manipulation or through intimidation; the impunity with which Anglos killed Mexicans; and the arrogance of Anglo–American racism, "so ostentatious of its own qualities." While the grievances against the Anglos are expressed long and eloquently, the remedies are brief and vague. Beyond swearing to correct injustices and exterminate the "tyrants," the only specific proposal suggests that mexicanos "repose their lot under the good sentiments of the governor elect of the State, General Houston." A tragic aura, arising from phrases like "a wandering life" and "I am ready to offer myself as a sacrifice to your happiness," joins with the ill-defined proposals to give a hopeless quality to the undertaking. The grievances and the anger are real and powerful, but there is no corresponding conviction of hope for the future.

The Cortina War was planned and coordinated, widespread and momentarily effective: For three of the seven months that it lasted, Cortina controlled the Lower Rio Grande Border. It was a resistance movement that grew out of Border culture and was limited by Border culture as well. * * *

Many others also tried. Cortina was joined by other Border fighters who combined the dual roles of *enganchado* and *juarista* (a Benito Juárez supporter), and this double activity continued through the century, underscoring the regional sentiment in Border culture. But before there can be resistance movements, there must be people who are willing to resist. The essential materials for any form of resistance are individuals who refuse to submit, who will "break before they bend." The Border sheltered many proud people, and the most outstanding were remembered in ballads called *corridos*. The saga of Gregorio Cortez provides a good picture of the values and attributes that formed the basis for the resistance that came out of nineteenth-century Border culture.

The Saga of Gregorio Cortez

The story of Gregorio Cortez, who "defended his right with his pistol in his hand," captures much of the mexicanos' situation in Texas at the turn of the century. It began in 1901 with a brief flurry of gunfire and ended in 1913 after a legal fight waged by Hispanic Texans. The battle grew out of a confrontation between Anglo lawmen and a mexicano farmer. Set in a context of mutual mistrust and hostility, specific cultural problems—three errors in translation by a "bilingual" deputy named Boone Choate—touched off ten days of turmoil that reached epic proportions.

On June 12, 1901, Karnes County Sheriff W.T. (Brack) Morris, an experienced Texas peace officer, set out with two deputies in search of a "Mexican" horsethief. They were armed but unencumbered with a warrant. The lawmen learned that Gregorio Cortez, a rancher and farmer who had lived in the county for some eleven years, had recently traded a horse to a neighbor. Morris and his party went to question him, arriving as Cortez, his brother Romaldo, and their families were resting after the noon meal.

Whether Morris actually suspected Cortez or merely wanted information is not clear. Three mistakes by Choate, the translator, rendered the question academic.

The officers first spoke to Romaldo, asking if Gregorio was there. Romaldo turned, saying, *"Te quieren,"* literally, "You are wanted." In Spanish, this is a common way of saying "Somebody wants to talk to you." To a barely fluent Anglo deputy, it sounded very close to an admission of guilt.

Morris then asked, through Choate, if Cortez had traded a horse (*caballo*) to a man named Villarreal. Cortez said no, meaning that he had not traded a caballo but a mare, a *yegua*. Hearing the negative, Morris then told Choate to tell Cortez that he was going to arrest him and moved closer, drawing his gun. After Choate's translation, Cortez answered, "You can't arrest me for nothing," which Choate took to mean "No one can arrest me." Gunplay followed that left Morris dead on the spot and Romaldo fatally wounded.

Cortez became a hunted man. At first on foot, later mounted, he eluded posse after posse—some numbering over three hundred men—leading Texas authorities on a ten-day, five-hundred-mile chase toward Laredo—the border and safety. The lone Cortez almost made it; a vaquero betrayed him to the Texas Rangers as he rested, preparing to cross the Rio Grande at night.

A series of trials ensued that lasted almost four years. Cortez was charged with horse stealing and three counts of murder (Morris and two other lawmen). He was found not guilty by reason of self-defense for killing Morris, not guilty of horse theft, and not guilty of killing a posse member named Schnaebel. The Court of Criminal Appeals upheld his conviction for the murder of a man named Glover, however, and on January 2, 1905, Cortez entered Huntsville to serve a life sentence. Governor O.B. Colquitt pardoned him in 1913, and Cortez returned to the Border where he was born. He died in 1916, probably of natural causes, although both legend and family tradition maintained he was poisoned.

The saga of Gregorio Cortez is remarkable not only because it tells how one mexicano responded to a serious threat, but also because of the folklore that developed about him. * * *

Anglo Texans divided in their attitudes toward Cortez after his capture. Grudging admiration surfaced amidst the vituperative outpourings during the chase, and his conduct during the trial won many Anglos, including many of his pursuers, to his side. And Cortez was found not guilty of killing Morris, indicating that Anglos, too, thought that he had a right to defend himself.

On the other hand, many Anglos saw Cortez as a vicious specimen of a corrupt and inferior race. They called for his lynching, trumped up charges against him, abused and terrorized his family and other mexicanos. This sentiment remained alive throughout the era. One newspaper responded to the pardon with a vehement attack against the "chicken-hearted Governor" who had freed a "Mexican who took the lives of American citizens." * * *

Notes and Questions

1. See Américo Paredes, *"With His Pistol In His Hand"* (1994), for a definitive study of Gregorio Cortez and his significance in Border folklore. As Paredes has written, "[i]t was almost as if the Border people had dreamed Gregorio Cortez before producing him, and had sung his life and his deeds before he was born." Gregorio Cortez's story was eventually made into a major motion picture entitled *The Ballad of Gregorio Cortez*. As one might expect, Juan Cortina also has a *corrido*, or ballad. See Américo Paredes, *Folklore and Culture on the Texas–Mexican Border* 27 (R. Bauman ed. 1993). See also R. Acuña, *Occupied America: A History of Chicanos* 43–47 (3d ed. 1988). For another account of the Cortina war, characterizing Cortina as a lawless bandit, see Walter Prescott Webb, *The Texas Rangers* 175–93 (1995 ed.) (The first edition appeared in 1935).

REIES TIJERINA AND THE NEW MEXICO LAND GRANT WARS

The tradition of Mexican–American resistance to the conquest has continued well into the twentieth century. As discussed above, in the *Rio Arriba Land Company* decision, the Court of Private Land Claims, affirmed by the Supreme Court, concluded that the common lands of the San Joaquin land grant belonged in the public domain of the United States and not to the community. This decision resulted in the loss of many thousands of acres which are now contained within the Kit Carson and the Sangre de Cristo national forests. In the 1960s, Reies Tijerina established himself as a Chicano activist and leader when he mounted a major protest against the United States' seizure of these lands.

RODOLFO ACUÑA

Occupied America: A History of Chicanos
340–41 (3d ed. 1988).*

REIES LÓPEZ TIJERINA

Reies López Tijerina, or *El Tigre,* was the most charismatic of the Chicano leaders. Born in 1926, in farm fields close to Fall City, Texas, he lived a marginal existence. The young man soon learned to hate his oppressors, especially Texas Rangers.

Tijerina became a preacher. He wandered into northern New Mexico, witnessing the poverty of the people there. [Tijerina] became interested in the land-grant question. He studied the Treaty of Guadalupe Hidalgo and became convinced that the national forest in Tierra Amarilla belonged to the *Pueblo de San Joaquín de Chama.* This was *ejido* land (communal or village land) that, according to Hispano–Mexican law, could not be sold and was to be held in common by the people. Villagers had the right to graze their animals and cut and gather timber in these forest lands. According to Tijerina, the U.S. government participated in frauds that deprived the people of the ejido lands. He got involved with the *Albiquiu* Corporation, an organization committed to the return of land grants to the New Mexicans.

In 1963 he incorporated *La Alianza Federal de Mercedes* (The Federal Alliance of Land Grants). It appealed to poor New Mexicans and to their lost dreams. The *Alianza* led marches on the state capital. On October 15, 1966, Tijerina and 350 members occupied the national forest campgrounds known as the Echo Amphitheatre and asserted the revival of the ejido rights of the Pueblo de San Joaquin de Chama, whose 1,400 acres lay mainly within the confines of the Kit Carson National Forest. In less than a week state police, sheriff's deputies, and Rangers moved in. On October 22 Alianza members took two Rangers into custody and tried them for trespassing and being a public nuisance. The Alianza court fined them and sentenced them to 11 months and 22 days in jail, and then "mercifully" suspended the sentence.

On November 6, 1967, Tijerina stood trial for the Amphitheatre affair. Original charges included conspiracy, but the jury threw it out. It did convict him of two counts of assault and he was sentenced to two years in a state penitentiary, with five years' probation.

Meanwhile, as the sentence was being appealed, Tijerina's actions alienated the establishment under the leadership of U.S. Senator Joseph Montoya. His support dwindled in New Mexico. Many followers were frightened by his growing militancy. Tijerina now entered Tierra Amarilla with the intention of making a citizen's arrest of District Attorney Alfonso Sánchez. A running gun battle followed and Tijerina was arrested. While on bail, he appeared at numerous protest rallies. Tijerina's uncompromising tactics gained him the admiration of militants and activists throughout the United States. In May and June 1968, Tijerina participated in the Poor People's Campaign, threatening to pull the Chicano contingent out if Black organizers did not treat them as equals. In the fall he ran for governor of New Mexico on the People's Constitutional party ticket.

Tijerina stood trial in late 1968 for the Tierra Amarilla raid. A key witness for the prosecution had been murdered. Tijerina defended himself. Much of the trial centered on the right to make a citizen's arrest. Tijerina proved his points, and the jury entered a verdict of not guilty.

In mid-February 1969 the Court of Appeals for the Tenth Circuit upheld the Amphitheatre conviction; Tijerina's lawyer immediately appealed to the Supreme Court. On June 5, 1969, *El Tigre* again attempted to occupy Kit Carson National Forest at the Coyote Campsite. His wife, Patsy, and some of the participants burned a few signs. Two days later the Rangers and police arrested several of the liberators. Tijerina allegedly pointed a carbine at one of the Rangers, when deputies threatened his wife. Authorities charged him with aiding and abetting the destruction of U.S. Forest Service signs and assaulting and threatening a federal agent. The court sentenced him to three years in the federal penitentiary. On October 13, Chief Justice Warren Burger refused to hear his appeal on the Amphitheatre case, and Tijerina went to prison. For seven months prison authorities isolated him from the other prisoners. Tijerina became a symbol, convicted of political crimes, rather than of crimes against "society." Tijerina was released in the summer of 1971.

Notes and Questions

1. For additional accounts of Tijerina's activism, see Richard Gardner, *Grito! Reies Tijerina and the New Mexico Land Grant War of 1967* (1970); Peter Nabakov, *Tijerina and the Courthouse Raid* (2d ed. 1970).

E. THE LINGUISTIC HERITAGE OF THE SOUTHWEST

One of the significant, and largely ignored, aspects of the conquest of Mexico is the linguistic heritage, predominantly in Spanish, retained by the conquered peoples who remained. Indeed, during long periods of the nineteenth century and well into the twentieth. California and New Mexico were officially bilingual in Spanish and English, reflecting the bilingual character of the citizens of these areas. The following excerpt documents this legal history.

JUAN F. PEREA

Demography and Distrust: An Essay on American Languages,
Cultural Pluralism and Official English
72 Minn. L. Rev. 269, 316–323 (1992).*

The Spanish language was introduced into Mexico in 1519, when explorers and conquerors from Spain arrived and claimed Mexico for the Spanish crown. Over the next three centuries, Spanish-speaking people migrated northward into the area which later became Arizona, California, New Mexico, and Texas. By 1790, approximately 23,000 Spanish-speaking persons populated these areas. * * *

After brief rule under two American military governors, a constitutional convention was held in 1849 in Monterey, which ultimately led to statehood. Within a short time democracy unleashed the hostility of the new English-speaking immigrants against the native Spanish-speaking *Californios*. The first California State Constitution, however, was drafted in a "context of linguistic equality."[249] Eight of the forty-eight delegates to the California Constitutional Convention were Spanish-speaking Californios. An official translator was present.

The Californios arrived at the convention anxious to protect their civil rights and land titles, which were at risk under the Treaty of Guadalupe Hidalgo and because of the influx of English-speaking Anglo gold-rushers. The Californios shaped several features of the 1849 Constitution, including provisions on voting qualifications, taxation, boundaries, and publication of the laws. All resolutions and articles the convention considered were translated prior to any vote. The Constitution was published in both Spanish and English.

One provision of California's first Constitution, adopted unanimously by the convention, provided for official recognition of Spanish and English through the promulgation of the laws in both languages: "All laws, decrees, regulations, and provisions, which from their nature require publication, shall be published in English and Spanish." The United States Congress approved this constitution, containing this provision, when it admitted California as a state on September 9, 1850. Implementing the constitutional provision, the California legislature provided for a state translator.

In 1850, the legislature enacted a statute that authorized the dissemination of statutes, legislative journals, supreme court decisions, and other government documents in Spanish and English. During that session, the legislature ordered the printing of 1,050 English copies and 350 Spanish copies of all laws passed that year. During the 1851 and 1852 legislative sessions, the legislature authorized the printing of the California laws and other documents in English and Spanish. The 1852 legislature authorized 700 English copies and 300 Spanish copies of laws passed that session. Some of the Spanish editions of the California laws were abridged versions of the English editions. A series of legislative enactments during the period from 1852 to 1863 established procedures for the translation of the laws into Spanish, including the selection of laws to be translated, the selection of a qualified translator, the administration of an oath promising faithful and correct translation, and a bidding procedure for choosing the least expensive translator.

At the same time, there was much ambivalence toward the Californios and their Spanish language. The 1855 legislature, gripped by "Hispanophobia," among other factors, defied the California Constitution and refused to provide for a Spanish translation of the laws. By the 1870s, the political climate had changed with the demographics of the state,

249. Arnold H. Leibowitz, *The Imposition of English as the Language of Instruction in American Schools*, 10 Revista de Derecho Puertorriqueno 175, 200 (1970).

which had experienced a huge influx of English speakers during the years of the gold rush, 1849 and beyond.

In 1848, approximately half of California's 15,000 residents were of Mexican descent and presumably Spanish-speaking. In the wake of the gold rush, in 1849 alone the population grew by about 100,000, including 80,000 new Anglo English speakers. Initially, the Californios participated in the gold rush. They were, however, met with tremendous hostility from the new Yankee immigrants who, ironically, labeled the Californios "foreigners" in their own land. With a new political majority of English speakers, and a diminishing minority of Spanish speakers, the perceived necessity for and the perceived utility of laws published in Spanish deteriorated gradually.

The Californios eventually lost the political clout that they had had during the Constitutional Convention of 1849 because of several factors: The hostility and violence of the Anglo immigrants to California; the administration of property laws that non-English speakers did not understand; and the sudden transformation of the Californios into a political minority. The last official edition of the California laws in Spanish appeared in 1878.

The next year, the California Constitution of 1879 prohibited the publication of the laws in any language other than English: the laws and proceedings of government were to be published in "no other than the English language." Despite this change in the Constitution, certain regions, such as southern California, remained Spanish-speaking during and after the 1870s. In 1894, an amendment to the California Constitution provided that the laws were to be published in "no other than the English language" and imposed an English literacy requirement for eligibility to vote. Subsequently, in 1897, the legislature repealed laws authorizing publication of the California laws in Spanish. In 1986, nearly 100 years later, California voters, by referendum, amended the state constitution to make English the official language of the state.

NEW MEXICO

The immigration of English-speakers to New Mexico had "an entirely different character, in quality and quantity, from the immigration that so quickly engulfed the Spanish-speaking in ... California."[277] This difference accounts, perhaps, for the greater longevity of official bilingualism in New Mexico and for the greater acceptance and recognition of New Mexico's Spanish and English linguistic traditions that continues today. Prior to 1846, there were only about 100 English-speaking settlers in New Mexico. It took many more years for English speakers to become a politically dominant group.

The organic laws of the territory of New Mexico were published in a bilingual, Spanish-and-English edition on October 7, 1846. The first page announces its title, "Leyes del Territorio de Nuevo Méjico," "Laws of the Territory of New Mexico," in both languages. Each subsequent page of this edition contains the laws printed in Spanish on the left side of the page and in English on the right, a reflection of linguistic and cultural

277. Carey McWilliams, *North from Mexico* 116 (1968).

parity. In December, 1847, the first laws enacted by the territorial general assembly were published in both Spanish and English, with the Spanish version on one page and the English version on the opposite page of the same volumes. This manner of publishing the laws continued until 1867, after which separate Spanish and English editions of the New Mexico laws were usually published. The laws of the New Mexico territory enacted during the session held in June, 1851, were published in Spanish and English as a United States Senate document, the only session laws to be published as a federal document.

The laws enacted during the 1868–69 session were translated into English from the original enactment in Spanish. This was typical at the time. Until 1870, the laws were usually enacted in Spanish and then translated into English. After 1870, the opposite order became prevalent, with enactment in English followed by translation into Spanish.

Between 1870 and 1907, the legislature routinely authorized the publication of "bills, rules, reports" and other documents in Spanish. In 1874, the legislature passed an act requiring that "in the construction of the statutes of this Territory . . . the language in which the said law was originally passed, shall govern, whether it be in Spanish or English." The legislature apparently concluded that statutory meaning was rendered more faithfully in the original language of enactment, rather than the language of translation.

New Mexico's bilingual identity was also recognized in its educational system. In 1909, the state legislature created the "New Mexico Spanish-American Normal School." The school was deemed necessary because "[o]ver 400 country public schools in New Mexico are composed principally of scholars whose native language is Spanish, and who consequently can only be taught English and other studies effectively by teachers acquainted with the Spanish language." The state created the school to train Spanish-speaking teachers in the art of instructing Spanish-speaking students to speak English.

Despite repeated attempts at statehood beginning in 1850, New Mexico did not became a state until 1912, when a majority of its population was English-speaking for the first time. The reason for this delay was Congress's unwillingness to grant statehood to a predominantly Spanish-speaking territory. Congress also expressed its bias in favor of English in the New Mexico Enabling Act, which made New Mexico a state. The Enabling Act required that the public "schools shall always be conducted in English" and that "ability to read, write, speak and understand the English language without an interpreter shall be a necessary qualification for all state officers and members of the state legislature." Congress, bowing to pressure from Hispanic citizens of the state, withdrew the English literacy requirement for state elective offices in the next year.

New Mexico adopted a constitution in 1911. Perhaps in response to the segregation of black children in public schools, the constitution prohibited such treatment for Hispanic children:

> Children of Spanish descent in the State of New Mexico shall never be denied the right and privilege of admission and attendance

in the public schools or other public educational institutions of the State, and they shall never be classed in separate schools, but shall forever enjoy perfect equality with other children in all public schools and educational institutions of the State, and the legislature shall provide penalties for the violation of this section.

The constitution required official bilingualism, stating that for twenty years after its adoption, all laws "shall be published in both the English and Spanish languages." Two legislative acts extended this period by twenty years, until early in 1953.

Beginning with the organic laws of 1846 and continuing for over 100 years, the laws of New Mexico were published in official Spanish and English editions. State-sponsored official bilingualism, therefore, enjoyed unusual longevity in New Mexico. More recently, in 1989, New Mexico officially endorsed the preservation of its bilingual linguistic heritage:

[The New Mexico legislature] reaffirms its advocacy of the teaching of other languages in the United States and its belief that the position of English is not threatened. Proficiency on the part of our citizens in more than one language is to the economic and cultural benefit of our state and the nation.... Proficiency in English plus other languages should be encouraged throughout the state.

Notes and Questions

1.   Other states in addition to California and New Mexico were officially bilingual for significant periods of their histories. Pennsylvania was officially bilingual in German and English and Louisiana was officially bilingual in French and English during extended periods of the nineteenth century. Bilingual education is well-documented in Pennsylvania with the founding of Lancaster College (now Franklin & Marshall College) in 1787 as a bilingual, German–English institution of higher learning. In addition, during Pennsylvania's constitutional convention of 1837–38, bilingual education in German and English was a significant topic of debate. In 1837, the Pennsylvania legislature authorized the establishment of German-language and English-language schools on an equal basis. See Perea, *supra*, at 291–92, 310–15, 323–26.

2.   Does this history cast any different light on current controversies over Official English and bilingual education? Is it appropriate to consider bilingual education as an issue of recent origin completely outside of its extensive historical context?

3.   What does this history suggest about the Official English movement's insistence that one language is a requirement of national unity? Did the country disintegrate when some states were officially bilingual? Conversely, consider that our most significant political divisions, the Revolutionary War and the Civil War, were fought predominantly by English speakers sharing linguistic and many cultural ties. Is language, therefore, a good or a poor guarantee of national unity?

Unresolved struggles over language, especially the Spanish language, are directly the result of the conquest of Mexico and the later conquest of Puerto Rico. The Official English movement and struggles over bilingual education should be understood as part of the continuing struggle for identity that dates back to the conquest. These current struggles over language are primary evidence of the unresolved issues of the conquest. These issues cannot be adequately understood nor appreciated outside of this context.

4. For a thorough analysis of contemporary bilingual education, see Rachel F. Moran, *Bilingual Education as a Status Conflict*, 75 Calif. L. Rev. 321 (1987).

F. MEXICAN AMERICANS AND THE STRUGGLE AGAINST SEGREGATION

The preceding passages describe resistance to the enormous loss of Mexican-owned land which was perceived, correctly in many cases, to have been unfair and in violation of the Treaty of Guadalupe Hidalgo. Mexican Americans and Puerto Ricans also faced racism and segregation in the areas where they lived. Jim Crow, in addition to targeting Blacks, also took aim at Latinos/as through segregated schools and other public facilities. Latinos/as, particularly Mexican Americans, used the courts to struggle against this widespread segregation. Most people do not realize the extent to which Mexican Americans were subject to segregation and resisted that segregation in the courts. Consider the following excerpt.

JUAN F. PEREA

*The Black/White Binary Paradigm of Race: The "Normal
Science" of American Racial Thought*
85 Calif. L. Rev. 1213, 1242–51 (1997); 10 La Raza L.J. 127 (1998).*

* * *

Mexican Americans suffered from a long tradition of segregation in public schools throughout the Southwest, both before and after the Supreme Court's decision in *Brown v. Board of Education*. Carey McWilliams described the segregated schools in Westminster, Orange County, California:

> There are two schools in Westminster: a handsomely equipped school with green lawns and shrubs for the Anglo–Americans; and a Mexican school whose meager equipment matches the inelegance of its surroundings. It was not the discrepancy between the two schools, however, that annoyed Gonzalo Mendez. Rather it was the fact, so he said, that he didn't like the idea of his Sylvia, Gonzalo Jr., and Geronimo, growing up with hatred in their hearts for the children who went to the beautiful school. In the nearby community of El Modeno, the two schools were side by side; but the Mexican youngsters were always served lunch at a different hour from the Anglo–American students.[141]

* * *

Chicanos played an important role in fighting and ultimately overturning school segregation. In *Mendez v. Westminster School District of Orange County*, [64 F. Supp. 544 (S.D.Cal.1946), aff'd, 161 F.2d 774 (9th Cir.1947)] Gonzalo Mendez and several other Mexican–American parents challenged the long-standing and pervasive segregation of Mexican–

---

* Copyright © 1997 by the California Law Review, Inc. Reprinted by permission.

141. Carey McWilliams, *North from Mexico* 280–81 (1949).

American children in Orange County. California's segregation statutes permitted school boards to establish separate schools for "Indian children ... and for children of Chinese, Japanese, or Mongolian parentage." Despite the absence of Mexican Americans from the statutory list, the parties "admitted that segregation *per se* is practiced in the above-mentioned school districts as the Spanish-speaking children enter school life and as they advance through the grades in the respective school districts." One commentator found it ironic that "the Code did not mention the group that was most commonly segregated by 1945: children of Mexican descent."[146]

One of the State's arguments in *Mendez* was that the Supreme Court had authorized the segregation of the races under the "separate but equal" doctrine of *Plessy v. Ferguson*. District Judge McCormick found that the physical facilities, teachers and curricula of the segregated school for Mexican children were "identical and in some respects superior to those in the other schools." Accordingly, unlike many of the pre-*Brown* Black segregation cases, this case did not focus on the inequality of separate facilities, but rather on the inherent evil of state-sponsored segregation itself.

After concluding that segregation of Mexican–American children was inconsistent with California's Education Code, Judge McCormick considered the federal constitutional question. Relying on a prescient interpretation of equal protection and on the stigmatizing effects of segregation on children subject to it, he concluded that California's segregation of Mexican–American pupils violated the Equal Protection Clause. The judge wrote:

> "The equal protection of the laws" pertaining to the public school system in California is not provided by furnishing in separate schools the same technical facilities, text books and courses of instruction to children of Mexican ancestry that are available to the other public school children regardless of their ancestry. A paramount requisite in the American system of public education is social equality. It must be open to all children by unified school association regardless of lineage.

In this remarkable paragraph, the court rejects the entire underpinning of the Supreme Court's opinion in *Plessy v. Ferguson* and foreshadows the reasoning of the Court in *Brown v. Board of Education*. Where *Plessy* had reified segregation by disclaiming the Court's power to act to remedy social inequality, the *Mendez* opinion conveys a powerfully different understanding of equality that ultimately prevails in *Brown*.

The *Mendez* court also anticipated *Brown*, and rejected *Plessy*, in its understanding of the role of public education and the stigmatizing meaning and purpose of segregation:

> The evidence clearly shows that Spanish-speaking children are hindered impeded in learning English by lack of exposure to its use because of segregation, and that commingling of the entire student

146. See Charles Wollenberg, *Mendez v. Westminster: Race, Nationality and Segre-* *gation in California Schools*, 53 Cal. Hist. Q. 317 (1974).

body instills and develops a common cultural attitude among the school children which is imperative for the perpetuation of American institutions and ideals. It is also established by the record that the methods of segregation prevalent in the defendant school districts foster antagonisms in the children and suggest inferiority among them where none exists.

The United States Court of Appeals for the Ninth Circuit upheld Judge McCormick's decision on narrower statutory grounds.

Legal scholars and the general public recognized the importance of the Mendez decision. A Note on the *Mendez* case in the *Yale Law Journal* commented, regarding *Plessy's* "separate but equal" doctrine, that:

a recent district Court decision [*Mendez*] . . . has questioned the basic assumption of the *Plessy* case and may portend a complete reversal of the doctrine. . . . Modern sociological and psychological studies lend much support to the District Court's views. A dual school system, even if "equal facilities" were ever in fact provided, does imply social inferiority.[159]

Another Note on the *Mendez* case, in *Columbia Law Review*, commented on its significance:

The segregation of races has not previously been considered a denial of equal protection so long as equal facilities were made available to the members of both groups. . . .

Attacks on segregation based on the equal protection clause of the Fourteenth Amendment have been equally unsuccessful. If the physical facilities available to each group are substantially equal, the courts have followed the traditional view that the humiliation engendered by relegation to an inferior social status is not in itself indicative of discrimination. The court in the instant case breaks sharply with this approach and finds that the Fourteenth Amendment requires "social equality" rather than equal facilities.[160]

Both of these notes, but particularly the former, recognize the importance of *Mendez* in furthering the cause of racial justice and desegregation for Blacks. On appeal, Thurgood Marshall, Robert L. Carter, and Loren Miller filed an *amicus* brief on behalf of the NAACP urging the desegregation of Orange County's schools. Robert L. Carter, Assistant Special Counsel of the NAACP, apparently used this brief as a dry run of the argument that segregation was unconstitutional *per se*.[163] Carter noted that cases pending in Oklahoma, Texas, Louisiana and South Carolina involving segregated schools "may require a Supreme Court ruling in the near future on the constitutional issue of the *Mendez* case."[164] The NAACP's efforts in support of the Mexican–American

---

159. Note, *Segregation in the Public Schools—A Violation of "Equal Protection of the Laws"*, 56 Yale. L.J. 1059, 1060 (1947).

160. Note, *Segregation in Schools as a Violation of the XIVth Amendment*, 47 Colum. L. Rev. 325, 326–27 (1947).

163. See Richard Kluger, *Simple Justice* 399–400 (1975).

164. Note, *supra* note 159, at 1060 n.12 (communication to Yale Law Journal from Robert L. Carter, Ass't Special Counsel NAACP).

plaintiffs in these cases provide an example of early coalition between Blacks and Latinos/as to defeat white racism and Jim Crow as inflicted upon Latinos/as. Mexican–American plaintiffs also sued to desegregate the Texas schools in the *Delgado v. Bastrop*[165] litigation, the first step leading to the defeat of school segregation in Texas.

Significantly, it was the *Mendez* decision that led to California's repeal of its school segregation statutes. Then Governor Earl Warren signed legislation repealing California's segregation statutes on June 14, 1947.[168] This was, of course, the same Earl Warren who, as Chief Justice of the United States, would later pen the opinions in *Brown v. Board of Education* and *Hernandez v. Texas*. The sequence of events following *Mendez* might have provided a clue about what was to come when school segregation reached the Supreme Court.

Other segregation-era cases tell a powerful story of white racism against Mexican Americans and strong Mexican–American resistance in the courts. In *Lopez v. Seccombe*, [71 F. Supp. 769 (S.D.Cal.1944)], for example, several leading Mexican–American and Puerto Rican citizens of San Bernardino, California, representing a class of 8,000 Mexican Americans, sued officials of San Bernardino to gain simple access to a public park. All persons of Mexican or Latin descent, including the plaintiffs, had "been excluded, barred and precluded" for several years from using a public park, playground, swimming pool, bathhouse and other facilities solely because of their Mexican and Puerto Rican ancestry. Apparently in response to contrary arguments by counsel for San Bernardino, the trial judge found it necessary to make a specific finding that the plaintiffs "are of clean and moral habits not suffering any disability, infectious disease, nor have they any physical or mental defect" that might justify the discrimination against them. The court concluded that segregation of San Bernardino's public park violated the Equal Protection Clause and issued a permanent injunction prohibiting the segregation of persons of Mexican and Latin ancestry.

The Supreme Court finally considered discrimination against Mexican Americans in *Hernandez v. Texas*, [347 U.S. 475 (1954)], decided two weeks before *Brown v. Board of Education*. In Jackson County, Texas, grand and petit jurors were chosen by jury commissioners sworn to "not knowingly select a grand juror they believe unfit or unqualified." The state agreed to a stipulation that qualified male Mexican–American freeholders who lived in Jackson County were fully qualified to serve on grand juries. Between six and seven percent of the freeholders in Jackson County, Texas were Mexican American, but not a single Mexican American had served on a Jackson County jury in the last 25 years. The Court concluded that "the result bespeaks discrimination, whether or not it was a conscious decision on the part of any individual jury commissioner." Accordingly, the Court decided that the discriminatory application of ostensibly neutral jury selection procedures violated the Equal Protection Clause.

165. Civil No. 388 (W.D.Tex. June 15, 1948) (unpublished order).

168. See Charles Wollenberg, Mendez v. Westminster: *Race, Nationality and Segre-* *gation in California Schools*, 53 Cal. Hist. Q. at 329.

The *Hernandez* decision is important in constitutional law for several reasons. It was the first case to recognize that Mexican Americans constitute a "cognizable minority group for equal protection purposes in areas where they are subject to local discrimination." The Warren Court was able to transcend, at least to a limited extent, the black/white binary paradigm. The Court wrote that the "Fourteenth Amendment is not directed solely against discrimination due to a 'two-class theory'—that is, based upon differences between 'white' and Negro."

Second, like *Yick Wo v. Hopkins* [118 U.S. 356 (1886)], the *Hernandez* decision stands for the proposition that the discriminatory application of a neutrally worded standard against a minority defined by race and national origin (persons of Mexican ancestry) violates the Equal Protection Clause. Furthermore, the decision is tied directly to the Court's early interpretation of the Fourteenth Amendment in *Strauder v. West Virginia* [100 U.S. 303 (1879)]. In *Strauder*, the Court declared that the statutory exclusion of Blacks from jury service violated the Equal Protection Clause. The Court also foresaw the eventual extension of equal protection doctrine to national origin classifications, a move finally accomplished in *Hernandez*. In *Strauder*, the Court wrote: "Nor if a law should be passed excluding all naturalized Celtic Irishmen, would there be any doubt of its inconsistency with the spirit of the amendment." Given these links to *Strauder*, casebook authors should cite *Hernandez*, as well as the *Yick Wo* opinion, for the principle that they both articulate.

Finally, *Hernandez* is also important for the snapshot it gives of the application of Jim Crow laws against Mexican Americans in Texas and throughout the Southwest. Describing conditions faced by Mexican Americans in Jackson County, the Court wrote:

[T]he testimony of responsible officials and citizens contained the admission that residents of the community distinguished between "white" and "Mexican." The participation of persons of Mexican descent in business and community groups was shown to be slight. Until very recent times, children of Mexican descent were required to attend a segregated school for the first four grades. [Most of the children of Mexican descent left school by the fifth or sixth grade.] At least one restaurant in town prominently displayed a sign announcing "No Mexicans Served." On the courthouse grounds at the time of the hearing, there were two men's toilets, one unmarked, and the other marked "Colored Men" and "Hombres Aquí" ("Men Here"). No substantial evidence was offered to rebut the logical inference to be drawn from these facts.

* * *

In the context of constitutional law, the paradigmatic presentation of the evolution of equality jurisprudence virtually guarantees that students will learn nothing about the history of racism and "separate but equal" segregation against Mexican Americans nor about the federal cases in which the courts found such segregation unconstitutional. How many of my present readers are aware that Mexican Americans were lynched frequently? Mexican Americans were segregated in separate but unequal schools, were kept out of public parks by law, were refused service in restaurants, were prohibited from attending "white" churches on Sundays, and were denied burial in "white" cemeteries, among all of the other horrors of the separate but equal scheme.[200]

The paradigmatic, truncated presentation of racial and legal history that results from the black/white binary paradigm ensures that most readers will never learn anything about Mexican American struggles for equality. A presentation of this omitted history, on the other hand, would present law students with a more complex and accurate sense of the scope of racism and the multiple struggles mounted against it. Cases such as *Lopez*, *Mendez* and *Hernandez* should be included in every book that discusses racism and segregation, especially books on constitutional law. Omit these cases, omit this history, and the vast majority of law students (and many law teachers) will have no clue that the Mexican–American struggle against segregation has been long and hard-fought in the courts. Omit these cases and most law students will have no clue that the Mexican–American struggle against segregation has a place in our constitutional history.

* * *

Robert Blauner describes more generally the omission of Chicano history by white scholars, which leads directly to reproduction of the black/white paradigm and public ignorance about Latinos/as:

> Even informed Anglos [and Blacks] know almost nothing about La Raza, its historical experience, its present situation, its collective moods. And the average citizen doesn't have the foggiest notion that Chicanos have been lynched in the Southwest and continue to be abused by the police, that an entire population has been exploited economically, dominated politically, and raped culturally. In spite of the racism that attempts to wipe out or, failing that, distort and trivialize the history and culture of the colonized, both expert and man in the street are far more aware of the past and present oppression suffered by blacks.[201]

Blauner refers to this continuing omission as "academic colonialism" by white scholars who persist in ignoring the history and problems encountered by Mexican Americans.

Notes and Questions

1. At this point, it is worth considering again the extent to which readers have been aware of this history. If you have been unaware of it, why have you been unaware? Consider all of your years of education and your prior study of American history. Assuming that much of this material is new to you, why are the materials presented in this chapter not taught routinely as part of our history, nor as part of our civil rights history? Would inclusion

200. Rodolfo Acuña, *Occupied America: A History of Chicanos* 34, 119–21, 254 (3d ed. 1988); Carey McWilliams, *North From Mexico* 272–74 (1949). [Eds. Relocated footnote].

201. Robert Blauner, *Racial Oppression in America* 166 (1972).

of this material necessarily displace other material, or does it constitute part of a comprehensive narrative?

2. For discussions of the history of school segregation against Mexican Americans, see George A. Martinez, *Legal Indeterminacy, Judicial Discretion and the Mexican–American Litigation Experience, 1930–1980*, 27 U.C. Davis L. Rev. 555, 574–602 (1994); Jorge C. Rangel & Carlos M. Alcala, *Project Report: De Jure Segregation of Chicanos in Texas Schools*, 7 Harv. C.R.-C.L. L. Rev. 307 (1972). See also Gilbert G. Gonzalez, *Chicano Education in the Era of Segregation* (1990).

3. The *Mendez v. Westminster* opinion is reproduced in Ch. 9, § 2 *infra*. For further discussion of *Hernandez v. Texas*, see Chapter 7, § 1 *infra*, reproducing the case.

G. MEXICAN LABOR AND THE BRACERO PROGRAMS

In the United States, the story of Mexican Americans is also a story of back-breaking farm labor. Poor Mexicans had often labored on farms, whether owned by rich Mexicans or, after the conquest, by wealthy white Americans. In the 1920s, when national origins quotas were actively debated and enacted in order to end the immigration of peoples presumed to be racially inferior to the dominant Anglo–Saxon stock, Mexicans were always exempted from the quotas, despite popular hostility toward their mestizo racial heritage. Large agriculturalists, dependent on their labor to get the crops picked, lobbied hard and successfully to make sure the supply of Mexican immigrant labor was uninterrupted. And so began a continuing alternating cycle of need for and abandonment of Mexicans, well described in the following excerpt.

GILBERT PAUL CARRASCO

Latinos in the United States: Invitation and Exile, in Immigrants Out!: The New Nativism and the Anti–Immigrant Impulse in the United States 190–200 (Juan F. Perea, ed.) (1997).*

Throughout the history of the United States, there have been periods of labor shortage and labor surplus. In times of labor shortage, the United States has enthusiastically welcomed immigrants to fill gaps in the labor pool. More often than not, however, available employment has been characterized by harsh working conditions, enormous amounts of physical labor, and minimal remuneration. In addition to abject working conditions, immigrants have also faced discrimination and resentment.

During periods of labor surplus or economic stress, immigrants in the United States have been subjected to particular cruelty. Americans, led by various nativist organizations and movements such as the Know–Nothing Party in the 1850s or, more recently, U.S. English or California's "Save Our State" campaign, have blamed immigrants for the country's economic woes. Such xenophobic bigotry has resulted in calls for anti-immigrant legislation (including restrictions on immigration for whichever immigrant group was targeted at the time), attempts to deny public services (including elimination of bilingual education for school-aged immigrants and the American citizen children of undocumented immigrants), and, ultimately, deportation.

Mexican immigrants have usually been the subject of these seesaw trends. One reason for this is that Mexico and the United States share a common border. The border between the two countries stretches for two thousand miles and is evidenced in some places by a fence, but at most points merely by an imaginary line in the sand or by the Rio Grande River. A border that has historically been easy to traverse, this proximity facilitates immigration, both legal and illegal, as well as expulsion.

Due to their great distance from the United States, Europeans historically could not make the journey to where their labor was needed (typically the southwestern United States) before the need was met. The only immigrants left within reach of the American Southwest were Mexicans and Asians. The Chinese and the Japanese have their own regrettable history of discrimination in the United States. The laws and policies that temporarily ended immigration from Japan and China left Mexico as the only source to fill the labor vacuum. Mexican laborers have since become the United States' disposable labor force, brought in when needed, only to fulfill their use and be unceremoniously discarded, a trend that has been recurring for over 150 years.

FROM THE GOLD RUSH TO WORLD WAR I

Early migration into the United States was aided by negligible border restrictions and virtually no immigration laws. The first wave of Mexican laborers was drawn to California by the Gold Rush shortly after Mexico ceded California to the United States under the terms of the Treaty of Guadalupe Hidalgo in 1848. The Gold Rush drew people from all over the world, triggering rapid population growth. Because most people who flocked to California wanted to strike it rich in their own mines, unskilled manual labor was scarce and laborers were needed to work not only in Anglo-owned mines but also to construct the railroads and to farm in agricultural areas. The work was backbreaking, low-paying, and often dangerous, so it was difficult to find Anglos who would do it.

In addition to fulfilling labor demands Mexicans brought with them the knowledge of mining. Anglos came to California with dreams of striking it rich but had little practical experience or knowledge of how to do it. Anglos, however, soon acquired the knowledge, tools, and techniques of Latino miners.

Unfortunately for Latinos, a need for their labor and knowledge did not translate into good attitudes toward them. Popular accounts of Latinos during that period were influenced by manifest destiny, "scientific" theories of racial miscegenation, and the Mexican War. These accounts provided the Anglo miner with a negative stereotype of the Latino that led to discrimination and hostility. These hostilities took the form of threats, violence, and restrictive legislation directed against Mexicans and Mexican Americans. Examples of these hostilities include posters appearing in mining areas threatening violence to any "foreigners" who remained where "they had no right to be," vigilante groups expelling Latinos from mines claiming that mineral rights and wealth in America were reserved for "Americans," the imposition of a Foreign Miners' Tax Law, assaults and lynchings.

In addition to the negative stereotypes and misconceptions, anti-Latino attitudes were also fueled by greed for the much coveted gold. Latinos who labored in the fields, on the railroads, or in the mines of Anglos were not as persecuted and discriminated against as those who sought their own fortunes in the mines. Nevertheless, although nonminers were not as persecuted as miners, there are recorded incidents of whole towns being put to the torch, rioters shooting any Mexican in sight, random murders, and other vigilante actions throughout this period.

Even while Latinos were being persecuted, their labor was needed, especially in jobs that were low-paying and labor-intensive. Such jobs included ranching, agriculture (especially for crops such as cotton and sugar beets), laying the rails that traverse the Southwest (a task made harder because most of the terrain is desert, semidesert, and/or mountainous), and mining (where, although their knowledge of mining techniques proved invaluable, they received lower wages for the same work that their unskilled Anglo counterparts did).

There was such a demand for Mexican labor in some labor-intensive occupations that employers held Mexicans captive. One such industry was the Colorado sugar beet industry. Sugar beets require attention almost year-round and, therefore, need a semipermanent labor force. When farmers could not persuade Mexican laborers to stay year-round to perform the arduous labor, they resorted to coercion. Coercive tactics employed by farmers took different forms. One such tactic was to refuse to make final wage payments to their employees so that they were unable to leave; thus, they had to remain in the area until the following season to collect their pay. Essentially, farmers had a captive work force without rights of citizenship or the ability to leave.

WORLD WAR I THROUGH THE GREAT DEPRESSION

Although there were periods of economic trouble in 1907 and 1921 when immigrants were blamed for many of the problems, Mexican immigrants were generally welcomed into the United States until the 1930s and the Great Depression. Prior to the Depression, U.S. immigration policies were aimed mainly at keeping out Asians and southern and eastern Europeans, while allowing Mexican laborers to immigrate. For example, within a year of the enactment of the most restrictive immigration legislation in U.S. history—the Immigration Act of 1917—the first foreign labor program was initiated.

In response to pressure from agricultural employers in the Southwest, Congress included provisions in the law that allowed entry into the United States of "temporary" workers who would otherwise be inadmissible under the Act. This temporary worker program, or the first *bracero* program as Kiser and Kiser called it, was enacted for the duration of World War I and was extended until 1922, four years after the war ended. Although this program did not include the Mexican government's proposals to guarantee the contracts of immigrant workers as did later bracero agreements, it was the blueprint upon which the later programs were based.

After the Depression began, Latinos found themselves unemployed and unwanted. Jobs that Latinos had been doing for years were no longer available, either because the jobs were no longer there or because they were being performed by Anglos who were forced to resort to that type of labor. Because Latinos were historically ill-paid, many had little or no financial reserves and had no choice but to go on welfare or other relief programs. Another result of the Depression was that Mexican workers and immigrants were no longer welcomed. In fact, they were so unpopular that many were driven from the country. For example, Latinos in Oklahoma were threatened with being burned out of their homes, in Indiana a mob forced railworkers to "give up their jobs," and in Texas signs were displayed warning Mexicans to get out of town.

As the Depression lingered and county, state, and federal budgets dwindled, governments sought ways to cut welfare costs. One method used was to deny welfare benefits to Mexican laborers. This action, labeled "fair and humane" by government agents, was a move to reduce the labor surplus and at the same time to reduce welfare rolls. No longer welcome in the United States, and with no way to sustain themselves, many Mexicans began a mass exodus to Mexico.

The Mexican migration was heralded by governments of various jurisdictions. They decided to expedite this process by sending lawful resident Mexican workers back to Mexico rather than carry them on the public welfare rolls; however, this decision was problematic for a variety of reasons. Legally, to expel Mexicans from the United States was as costly as keeping them afloat when their funds were depleted. Consequently, instead of using costly legal maneuvers such as public hearings and formal deportation proceedings, social workers resorted to betraying Mexicans by telling officials that they wanted to return to Mexico. This duplicitous tactic, of course, lowered the cost of expulsion considerably. It also, however, effectively deprived many of due process.

This treachery toward Latinos continued throughout the Depression. Tragically, some, if not most, of the repatriated Latinos were lawful permanent residents of the United States. They had lived in the United States for decades, establishing homes and roots. Another result of repatriation was that many families were separated. In some instances, either one or both parents was an "alien," but children, having been born and raised in the United States, were American citizens. In some cases, the children were allowed to stay in the United States while their parents were repatriated, but in many other cases such U.S. citizens were themselves "repatriated." By the end of the Depression, over 400,000 Latinos were "repatriated" to Mexico without any formal deportation proceedings, including thousands of American citizens.

These repatriation programs naturally sparked protest from the Mexican government. In response to the protests, the Los Angeles Chamber of Commerce issued a statement assuring Mexican authorities that the city was in no sense unfriendly to Mexican labor. The communique stated further that the repatriation policy was designed solely to help the destitute. This was supposedly the case when invalids were removed from County Hospital in Los Angeles and shipped across the border.

WORLD WAR II AND THE *BRACERO* PROGRAM

When the Great Depression ended at the onset of World War II, so did the labor surplus that the Depression had created. Agricultural growers in the Southwest, however, began as early as 1940 to petition agencies of the United States for permission to use foreign labor to fill labor shortages, a precedent established during World War I. Shortly after Mexico declared war on the Axis powers on June 1, 1942, the Department of State contacted it about the importation of labor. The Mexican government doubted that the labor shortage really existed and viewed the efforts of the State Department as a way of obtaining cheap labor.

Cognizant of the deportation and repatriation of Latinos during the Great Depression, the Mexican government, to protect its citizens from harsh treatment and discrimination, entered into a formal agreement with the United States. This protection was provided by a government-to-government accord signed on July 23, 1942. The Mexican Labor Program, or the Bracero Program as it is more commonly known, was first implemented on August 4, 1942 and was funded by the U.S. President's emergency fund. The Bracero Program was renewed on April 26, 1943.

Under the Bracero agreement, Mexico would permit its citizens to work in the United States for temporary, renewable periods under agreed-upon conditions. The conditions stipulated methods of recruitment, transportation, standards of health care, wages, housing, food, and the number of hours the braceros were allowed to work. There was even a stipulation that there should be no discrimination against braceros. A violation of these conditions was supposed to have resulted in the suspension of braceros' availability for the violating area. Unfortunately, the conditions were, for the most part, ignored by both the growers and the U.S. government; thus, migrant laborers were subjected to most oppressive working environments.

Braceros across the country were compelled to endure poor food, excessive charges for board, substandard housing, discrimination, physical mistreatment, inappropriate deductions from their wages, and exposure to pesticides and other dangerous chemicals. Although Texas was not the only state that violated the conditions of the agreement, discrimination toward braceros there was so bad that Texas lost its privilege to utilize bracero labor until after the war.

To illustrate how important bracero labor was, we need only look at the impact on Texas of losing braceros. To fill its labor needs, Texas was forced to recruit local Mexican Americans, college students, school children, and prisoners of war. As a result, the cotton wages in Texas rose 236 percent during the war years, contrasted with California, where cotton wages increased 136 percent.

The upshot of the Bracero Program was that the U.S. government provided growers with cheap labor. Agricultural growers preferred hiring braceros to American citizens for two reasons. First, growers were able to set the wages that would be paid braceros instead of basing their remuneration on the principle of supply and demand or on collective bargaining agreements. Second, braceros tended to be males who traveled alone, while Americans had their families with them, thus making it easier to provide transportation and housing for braceros.

A secondary effect of the Bracero Program was that it provided the United States with soldiers to fight the war. Although braceros were initially brought in to replace Japanese Americans who were sent to internment camps and Americans who went into the armed services or the defense industry, braceros additionally freed up many Mexican Americans for the armed services. Deferments were given to those who held defense industry jobs, few of whom were Mexican American, while workers in the agricultural industry, heavily staffed by Mexican Americans, were eligible for the draft. In short, Mexican Americans in the agricultural industry were sent off to the war while braceros were imported to replace them.

While in the armed forces, Latinos distinguished themselves as fierce and reliable soldiers. Throughout the course of World War II, no Latino soldier was ever charged with desertion, treason, or cowardice. The bravery of Latino troops was recognized in the many medals awarded to Mexican Americans, including the Congressional Medal of Honor (the United States' highest honor), the Silver Star, the Bronze Star, and the Distinguished Service Cross. Seventeen Mexican Americans received the Congressional Medal of Honor for action in World War II and Korea. These seventeen Latino soldiers represent the highest proportion of Medal of Honor winners of any identifiable ethnic group. Because Mexican Americans seem to have gravitated to the most dangerous sections of the armed forces, they were overrepresented on military casualty lists.

Ironically, when the Mexican soldiers returned home, they were treated no better than they had been before they left. In Texas, a funeral parlor in Three Rivers refused to bury Félix Longoria, an American soldier decorated for heroism, because he was of Mexican descent. This obviously racist action sparked a storm of controversy that ended with the intervention of then Texas Senator Lyndon B. Johnson, who secured burial for Longoria in Arlington National Cemetery. Sergeants José Mendoza López and Macario García, each awarded the Congressional Medal of Honor, were refused service in restaurants and diners because of their Mexican heritage.

Sergeant García, however, decided to challenge such discrimination against Latinos. García, after being told that he would not be served because he was a "Mexie," admonished the proprietor to serve him, declaring, "[if I am] good enough to fight your war for you, I'm good enough for you to serve a cup of coffee to." The merchant in charge of the diner refused to serve García and went so far as to attempt physically to remove García from the diner. García defended himself.

The altercation ended with the arrival of the police. The police sent everyone home and ordered the diner closed for the night to end the incident. Later, after the incident was recounted over the national news, Sergeant García was arrested and charged with aggravated assault in an attempt by the city to save face.

After the war, American soldiers returned to work, ending the labor shortage. Growers in the agricultural industry were, nonetheless, reluctant to give up bracero labor. Under the influence of agribusiness, Congress kept the program alive. The pressure they brought to bear was not enough to keep the program going on indefinitely, however, and the Bracero Program came to an end in December of 1947. Nonetheless, despite the termination of the Bracero Program, the use of Mexican labor did not end.

For nine months after the end of the Bracero Program, while no agreement existed between the United States and Mexico, the number of undocumented workers in the United States increased dramatically. Both governments became concerned with the increase and pushed for renewed labor negotiations. These negotiations led to a new bracero agreement in August of 1949. In addition to providing labor to the United States, the new bracero agreement stressed a reduction in the flow of undocumented workers from Mexico and the legalization of undocumented workers already in the United States. The program resulted in 238,439 undocumented workers being recruited into the work force between 1947 and 1951, when mass legalization ended. Mass legalization ended for two reasons. First, it was ineffective in stemming the tide of undocumented workers coming into the country. Most importantly, the enactment of Public Law 78 on July 12, 1951, in response to the outbreak of the Korean War, created a new bracero program.

Under the new program, the U.S. Department of Labor was given administrative control of migration and essentially became a labor contractor. Public Law 78 conferred on the Secretary of Labor the responsibility for the certification of the need for the braceros, for authorization of their recruitment in Mexico, for transportation of the braceros to the labor camps, for guaranteeing the terms of their labor contracts, and for setting the prevailing wage. The new bracero agreement also rectified some problems of the prior agreements. The braceros were to enter contracts for periods of time ranging from six weeks to six months instead of year-long contracts. The braceros were also guaranteed work for at least 75 percent of the time for which they had contracted, as well as being paid the wages set by the Secretary of Labor.

FROM THE KOREAN WAR TO "OPERATION WETBACK"

Public Law 78 did not stem the tide of undocumented workers. Further, immigration authorities started finding undocumented workers in industrial jobs, causing labor unions to proclaim undocumented traffic as destructive to their welfare. As a result of these complaints, on June 17, 1954, Herbert Brownell, Jr., the U.S. Attorney General, ordered a crackdown on illegal immigration and a massive deportation drive, "Operation Wetback."

This crackdown on illegal immigration and the ensuing process of deportation were left to the Commissioner of Immigration, Joseph P. Swing. Swing, a retired army general and reputed "professional, long-time Mexican hater," developed "Operation Wetback" along the lines of a military campaign. "Operation Wetback" was a two-fold plan that coordinated the border patrol to prevent undocumented aliens from getting into the United States while rounding up and deporting those who were already here.

"Operation Wetback" went beyond its scope, however, and Americans of Mexican descent were also deported, stirring up memories of the mass deportations of the 1930s. Many of those deported were denied the opportunity to present evidence that would have prevented their deportation. Between 1954 and 1959, "Operation Wetback" was responsible for over 3.7 million Latinos being deported. Of that number, an unknown amount were American citizens. In their haste to deport "illegals," only 63,500 persons were removed through formal deportation proceedings. The rest of the deportees left the United States "voluntarily."

In addition to violating the civil liberties of American citizens via questionable expulsions, "Operation Wetback" violated the human rights of the people being deported. Deportations were characterized by disrespect, rudeness, and intimidation. There were even reports of immigration officers "collecting fares" from persons being deported.

Ironically, the bracero program was in effect while "Operation Wetback" was being executed. Public Law 78 was extended until it finally was allowed to lapse in December of 1964. Although the bracero program was originally intended to be an emergency remedy for labor shortages during World War II, it survived the war by almost twenty years. Further, more braceros were hired in single years after the war than were hired during all of the years of the war combined.

Modern Labor Programs

Even after the bracero program ended, importation of Mexican labor continued under the McCarran–Walter Immigration Act of 1952. Under the Act, immigrants from Mexico were permanently admitted to the United States to ensure there would be enough laborers. To guarantee there would be a sufficient labor force available under the Act, the Department of Labor lowered the admission standards for Mexican workers just days before the expiration of Public Law 78 and the Bracero Program.

Although many Mexican citizens were issued visas, or "green cards," that would allow them to live and work in the United States, most preferred to reside in Mexico. These people, known as commuters because they traversed the border regularly to get to work, maintained the bracero lifestyle by working in the United States for days, weeks, or even months at a time, only to return to Mexico. As well as emulating bracero work patterns, these migrant workers performed similar jobs to the braceros' (i.e., low-skilled or service oriented). In 1977, there were approximately one million Mexican resident aliens in the United States, according to the Immigration and Naturalization Service. The actual number of commuters is unknown due to inaccurate records and varying numbers of commuters from day to day.

The McCarran–Walter Act also established a fallback Bracero Program. The "H–2 program" revived all the worst parts of the Bracero Program. Under the "H–2 program," the U.S. Department of Labor has power to admit foreign labor for temporary jobs if able, willing, and qualified domestic workers can not be found at the time and place where they are needed. Similar to the mistreatment suffered by workers in the Bracero Program, these migrants are totally dependent on the growers for employment. If the worker proves himself to be hard-working and faithful, he might be asked to return again the following year; if not, he can be deported without an appeal.

In 1986 the United States went through its most recent mass legalization program. The Immigration Reform and Control Act of 1986 (IRCA) gave legal status to undocumented persons who had been in the United States from January 1, 1982 to the time of application (between May 5, 1987 and May 4, 1988). Like the McCarran–Walter Act, the IRCA provided special status to migrant farmworkers. The IRCA offered legal status to special agricultural workers who could prove that they spent at least ninety "man-days" during a qualifying period doing agricultural work on specified crops. The end result of the IRCA was to legalize millions of undocumented workers and fill a labor shortage caused by the most recent immigrant expulsion, "Operation Jobs."

Another method of obtaining Mexican labor has been accomplished through the exportation of jobs. This phenomenon is euphemistically called the Border Industrialization Program or, as it is more familiarly known, the *Maquiladora* Program. The program is a system of concessions vis-à-vis Mexico that allows manufacturing and assembly plants or *maquilas* to be located in border towns in northern Mexico and exportation of their products directly to the United States. Other concessions granted by Mexico have included exemptions from labor and environmental regulations.

The exemptions granted by Mexico do more than help American companies enter Mexico; they help American companies exploit Mexican labor. The maquilas have proven to be a financial success, but only at the expense of Mexican laborers suffering under poor working conditions, inadequate wages, deteriorating environmental conditions, and the inability to take any legal actions against their employers.

History shows that whenever labor is needed, it is sought out in Mexico and discarded when the need is over, with little regard for Mexican Americans who are often ensnared in the same net. This was true with the U.S. repatriation programs during the Depression in the 1930s and "Operation Wetback" in the 1950s.

Due to intense exploitation suffered by migrant workers, their productive capacities are used up early in their lives and they have to be replaced by new waves of younger immigrants. For the United States, employment of migrant workers represents a significant savings in producing and reproducing "human capital" because they stay in the United States only temporarily. Even though the United States needs

Mexican labor, migrant laborers arrive to face more than exploitation and brutal working conditions. They face racism, xenophobia, and discrimination. Although Latinos both within and outside the United States have come to recognize the American perspective that they are dispensable and disposable when the need for their labor diminishes, their struggle for human dignity continues, notwithstanding the seemingly inexorable cycle of invitation and exile.

Notes and Questions

1. Agriculturalists who have employed Mexican and Mexican–American laborers have always sought to maximize the usefulness of Mexicans as physical laborers while minimizing their political participation and their claims upon society. As Professor Michael A. Olivas described the situation:

> Most crucial to the agricultural growers was the need for a reserve labor pool of workers who could be imported for their work, displaced when not needed, and kept in subordinate status so they could not afford to organize collectively or protest their conditions. Mexicans filled this bill perfectly, especially in the early twentieth century Southwest, where Mexican poverty and the Revolution forced rural Mexicans to come to the United States for work. This migration was facilitated by United States growers' agents, who recruited widely in Mexican villages, by the building of railroads (by Mexicans, not Chinese) from the interior of Mexico to El Paso, and by labor shortages in the United States during World War I.

Michael A. Olivas, *The Chronicles, My Grandfather's Stories, and Immigration Law: The Slave Traders Chronicle as Racial History*, 34 St. Louis U. L.J. 425, 436 (1990). Similar motivations continued during subsequent periods of importation of Mexican labor. As Professor Olivas describes the Bracero program, he notes that it was "cynically employed to create a reserve pool of temporary laborers who had few rights and no vesting of equities." *Id*. at 438.

Do you think anything fundamental has changed in the perception of and use of Mexican labor today? Consider the implications of Proposition 187 in California, which sought to deny medical care and public education to undocumented Mexicans within the country. See generally *Immigrants Out! The New Nativism and the Anti–Immigrant Impulse in the United States* (Juan F. Perea ed.1997).

2. If Carrasco's figures are right, the U.S. deported almost four million Mexicans in two xenophobic waves in a 20–year period—a total rivaling in extent (if not in savagery) other, better-known atrocities such as Indian relocation, the Turks' extermination of Armenians, or Hitler's execution of Jews during the Third Reich. The U.S. has never admitted fault, however, and indeed tolerates continued measures against Latinos, such as California's Proposition 187 and various English-only measures. If you were in charge of a Latino/a advocacy-litigation organization, what would you do? See generally Michael A. Olivas, *supra* (describing the history of Cherokee removal, Chinese exclusion, and the Mexican Bracero Program and Operation Wetback as historical examples illustrating the thesis of Derrick Bell's slave traders' Chronicle).

3. Does the cyclical use and expulsion of immigrant labor help explain the persistent attribution of "foreignness" or "un-American" status imputed

to many Mexican–American citizens? For a discussion of the impact of Mexican immigration on Mexican Americans, and differing poles of opinion regarding immigration, see David G. Gutiérrez, *Walls and Mirrors* (1995).

4. The exclusion of Mexican immigrants has pernicious effects on citizens of Mexican ancestry. As Professor Kevin Johnson writes:

> Racial exclusion of noncitizens under the immigration laws, be they express or covert, reveals to domestic minorities how they are viewed by society. The unprecedented efforts to seal the U.S.-Mexico border combined with the increased efforts to deport undocumented Mexicans, for example, tell much about how a majority of society views Mexican Americans and suggests to what lengths society might go, if permitted under color of law, to rid itself of domestic Mexican Americans. In fact, during the New Deal, Mexican-American citizens, as well as Mexican immigrants, were "repatriated" to Mexico. It therefore is no surprise that the organized Mexican-American community consistently resists the harsh attacks on immigration and immigrants. This is true despite sentiment among some Mexican Americans to restrict immigration because of perceived competition with immigrants in the job market.

Kevin R. Johnson, *Race, the Immigration Laws, and Domestic Race Relations: A "Magic Mirror" into the Heart of Darkness*, 73 Ind. L. J. 1111, 1152 (1998).

Wouldn't the principle expressed by Professor Johnson apply to any racial or national origin group targeted in the immigration laws? Doesn't this counsel vigilance on the part of any groups vulnerable to attack under the immigration laws?

5. While Mexican labor is most frequently associated with the southwestern United States, Mexican and Puerto Rican agricultural laborers have also been prominent in other parts of the country, including the midwest. See Dennis Nodin Valdes, *Al Norte: Agricultural Workers in the Great Lakes Region, 1917–1970* (1991).

6. For additional analysis of Mexican migration, see Gerald P. López, *Undocumented Mexican Migration: In Search of a Just Immigration Law and Policy*, 28 UCLA L. Rev. 615 (1981).

7. For other references on the Bracero Program and Operation Wetback, consult the following books: Ernesto Galarza, *Merchants of Labor* (1964); Julian Samora, Los Mojados: *The Wetback Story* (1971); Francisco E. Balderrama & Raymond Rodriguez, *Decade of Betrayal, Mexican Repatriation in the 1930s* (1995); Abraham Hoffman, *Unwanted Mexican Americans in the Great Depression* (1974); Kitty Calavita, *Inside the State: The Bracero Program, Immigration and the I.N.S.* (1992).

For references on Mexican labor, see Juan Gómez-Quiñones, *Mexican American Labor* (1994); *Mexican Workers In the United States* (George C. Kiser & Martha Woody Kiser eds. 1979). See Guadalupe T. Luna, *An Infinite Distance?: Agricultural Exceptionalism and Agricultural Labor*, 1 U. Pa. J. Labor & Emp. L. 487 (1998) (criticizing the doctrine of "agricultural exceptionalism," which produces unfair and unequal treatment of agricultural workers).

CÉSAR CHÁVEZ AND THE UNITED FARMWORKERS

The struggles of Mexican and Filipino farmworkers of the 1960s, and the emergence of César Chávez as a prominent national Latino leader, must be understood within the broad context of the essential and consistent role played by Mexican labor in the Southwest, as described by Professor Carrasco. But Chávez also emerges as an important figure in the history of Mexican-American protest and resistance to oppression, in this case oppressive working conditions in the fields of California. Consider the importance of Mexicans' relationship to land in the Southwest, both as former owners and workers of the land, and later as cyclical laborers for hire.

RODOLFO ACUÑA

Occupied America: A History of Chicanos
324–27 (3d ed. 1988).*

THE ROAD TO DELANO: CREATING A MOVEMENT

Many Chicanos have incorrectly labeled the second half of the 1960s as the birth of the Chicano movement. As witnessed in preceding chapters, Mexicans in the United States have responded to injustice and oppression since the U.S. wars of aggression that took Texas and the Southwest from Mexico. Middle-class organizations generally spoke for the community, since its members had the education, money, and stability to maintain more or less permanent associations. Established Anglo power brokers also recognized these organizations.

By the mid–1960s, traditional groups such as LULAC [League of United Latin American Citizens] and the G.I. Forum, along with recently formed political groups such as MAPA [Mexican American Political Association] and PASSO [Political Association of Spanish–Speaking Organizations], were challenged. For better or worse, the established Mexican–American associations had served as agents of social control, setting the norm for conduct. The rise of cultural nationalism challenged the acceptance of assimilation as a goal. Sectors of youth, women, and more militant activists were skeptical of traditional methods of struggle and advocated direct action. They also questioned the legitimacy of established leaders.

For the most part, LULAC and Forum leaders at first rejected "street politics"—marches, walkouts, confrontations, civil disobedience, and so on. Over the years their ties with the system tightened. At the same time, the civil rights, antinuclear, and anti-Vietnam movements, along with community action programs, legitimated an ideology of confrontation, creating a new awareness among Chicanos that resulted in a demand for self-determination by *los de abajo* (the underdogs) and youth. Also important was that sectors of the North American left, as well as government agencies, no longer dealt with established groups exclusively but recognized more militant Chicano organizations. This, for a time, broke the monopoly of the Mexican American middle class. Moreover, rank and file members of LULAC and the Forum grew closer to the new Chicano agenda.

César Chávez and the United Farm Workers

César Chávez gave the Chicano movement a national leader. In all probability Chávez was the only Mexican American to be so recognized by the mainstream civil rights and antiwar movements. Chávez and farm workers were also supported by the center Mexican American organizations along with the left.

On September 8, 1965, the Filipinos in the Agricultural Workers Organizing Committee (AWOC) struck the grape growers of the Delano area in the San Joaquín Valley. Filipino workers had been encouraged by a victory in the spring of 1965 in the Coachella Valley, where the U.S. Labor Department announced the *braceros* would be paid $1.40 an hour. The domestic pickers received 20¢ to 30¢ an hour less. Joined by Mexicans, the Filipinos walked out, and ten days later they received a guarantee of equivalent pay with braceros. When the Filipinos requested the same guarantee in the San Joaquín Valley, growers refused, and led by Larry Itlong, they voted to strike. The strike demands were simple: $1.40 an hour or 25¢ a box. The Di Giorgio Corporation became the major target. The rank and file of the National Farm Workers Association (NFWA) voted on September 16 to join the Filipinos. The termination at the end of 1964 of Public Law 78 significantly strengthened the union's position.

Chávez emerged as the central figure in the strike. Born in Yuma, Arizona, in 1927, he spent his childhood as a migrant worker. His father had belonged to farm labor unions and Chávez himself had been a member of the National Farm Labor Union. In the 1940s he moved to San Jose, California, when he married Helen Fávila. In San Jose Chávez met Father Donald McDonnell, who tutored him in *Rerum Novarum*, Pope Leo XIII's encyclical which supported labor unions and social justice. Through Father McDonnell Chávez met Fred Ross of the Community Service Organization (CSO). He became an organizer for the CSO and learned grass-roots strategies. Chávez rose to the position of general director of the national CSO, but in 1962 he resigned, moving to Delano, where he began to organize his union. Chávez went door to door visiting farm workers. Delano was chosen because of its substantial all-year farm-worker population; in 1968, 32 percent of the 7,000 harvest workers lived and worked in the Delano area year round.

Chávez concentrated his efforts on the Mexican field hands, for he knew the importance of nationalism in solidifying an organization. He carefully selected a loyal cadre of proven organizers, such as Dolores Huerta and Gil Padilla, whom he had met in the CSO. By the middle of 1964 the NFWA was self-supporting.

A year later the NFWA had some 1,700 members. Volunteers, fresh from civil rights activities in the South, joined the NFWA at Delano. Protestant groups, inspired by the civil rights movement, championed the cause of the workers. A minority of Catholic priests, influenced by Vatican II, joined Chávez. Anglo–American labor belatedly jumped on the bandwagon. In Chávez's favor was the growing number of Chicano workers living in the United States. Over 80 percent lived in cities, and many belonged to unions. Many, in fact, belonged to big labor such as the United Auto Workers (UAW).

The times allowed Chávez to make his movement a crusade. The stabilization of a large part of the Mexican American workforce made the forging of an organization possible. And, finally, the end of the bracero program took a lethal weapon from the growers.

The most effective strategy was the boycott. Supporters were urged not to buy Schenley products or Di Giorgio grapes. The first breakthrough came when the Schenley Corporation signed a contract in 1966. The Teamsters unexpectedly refused to cross picket lines in San Francisco. Rumors of a bartenders' boycott reached 75–year-old Lewis Solon Rosenstiel, Schenley's president, who decided that a settlement was advisable. Soon afterward Gallo, Christian Brothers, Paul Masson, Almaden, Franzia Brothers, and Novitiate signed contracts.

The next opponent was the Di Giorgio Corporation, one of the largest grape growers in the central valley. In April 1966, Robert Di Giorgio unexpectedly announced he would allow his workers at Sierra Vista to vote on whether they wanted a union and who would represent them. Di Giorgio did not act in good faith and his agents set out to intimidate the workers.

With the support of Di Giorgio the Teamsters opposed the farm workers and bid to represent the workers. Di Giorgio, without consulting the NFWA, set the date for the election. The NFWA urged its followers not to vote, since it did not have time to campaign or to participate in establishing the ground rules. It needed enough time to return eligible voters to the Delano area. Out of 732 eligible voters only 385 voted; 281 voters specified that they wanted the Teamsters as their union agent. The NFWA immediately branded the election as fraudulent and pressured Governor Edmund G. Brown, Sr., a friend of Di Giorgio, to investigate the election. Brown needed the Chicano vote as well as that of the liberals who were committed to the farm workers. The governor's investigator recommended a new election, and the date was set for August 30, 1966.

That summer an intense campaign took place between the Teamsters and the NFWA. A state Senate committee investigated charges of communist infiltration of the NFWA; the committee found nothing to substantiate charges. As the election neared, Chávez became more somber. He had to keep the eligible voters in Delano, and he had the responsibility of feeding them and their families as well as the army of strikers and volunteers. The Di Giorgio campaign drained the union's financial resources. Some weeks before the strike vote, Chávez reluctantly merged the NFWA and AWOC into the United Farm Workers Organizing Committee (UFWOC).

Teamsters red-baited the UFWOC and circulated free copies of Gary Allen's John Birch Society pamphlet. The UFWOC passed out excerpts from *The Enemy Within*, in which Robert Kennedy indicted James Hoffa and the Teamsters in scathing terms; association with the Kennedy named helped. Finally the vote was taken. The UFWOC won the election, 573 votes to the Teamsters' 425. Field workers voted 530 to 331 in favor of the UFWOC. Soon afterward the Di Giorgio Corporation and the UFWOC signed a contract.

Other growers proved to be more difficult. In 1967 the Giumarra Vineyards Corporation, the largest producer of table grapes in the United States, was targeted. When Guimarra used other companies' labels to circumvent the boycott, in violation of the Food and Drug Administration rules, the union boycotted all California table grapes. Boycott activities spread into Canada and Europe. Grape sales decreased significantly. Some of the slack was taken up by the U.S. Defense Department. In 1966 U.S. troops in Vietnam were shipped 468,000 pounds of grapes; in 1967, 555,000 pounds; in 1968, 2 million pounds; and by 1969, more than 4 million pounds. Later the U.S. Defense Department spent taxpayers' money to buy large quantities of lettuce when the union boycotted this product. In the summer of 1970 the strike approached its fifth year. In June 1970 a group of Coachella Valley growers agreed to sign contracts, as did a majority of growers. Victories in the San Joaquin Valley followed.

After this victory the union turned to the lettuce fields of the Salinas Valley, where growers were among the most powerful in the state. During July 1970 the Growers–Shippers Association and 29 of the largest growers in the valley entered into negotiations with the Teamsters. Agreements signed with the truckers' union in Salinas were worse than sweetheart contracts: They provided no job security, no seniority rights, no hiring hall, and no protection against pesticides.

Many growers, like the Bud Antle Company (a partner of Dow Chemical), had dealt with the Teamsters since the 1950s. In 1961, in return for a $1 million loan, Antle signed a contract with the truckers. By August 1970 many workers refused to abide by the Teamster contracts and 5,000 walked off the lettuce fields. The growers launched a campaign of violence. Jerry Cohen, a farm-worker lawyer, was beaten unconscious. On December 4, 1970, Judge Gordon Campbell of Monterey County jailed Chávez for refusing to obey an injunction and held him without bail. This arbitrary action gave the boycott needed publicity. Dignitaries visited Chávez in jail; he was released on Christmas Eve.

By the spring of 1971 Chávez and the Teamsters signed an agreement that gave the UFWOC sole jurisdiction in the lettuce fields and that allowed George Meany, president of the AFL, and the Teamsters president, Frank Fitzsimmons to arbitrate the situation. Throughout the summer and into the fall, however, growers refused to disqualify Teamster contracts and gradually the situation became stalemated.

The fight with the Teamsters hurt the UFWOC since it turned its attention from servicing contracts. Chávez refused help from the AFL for professional administrators, believing that farm workers had to learn from their own mistakes. According to *Fresno Bee* reporter Ron Taylor, although Chávez was a patient teacher, he did not delegate authority and involved himself with too much detail. Farm workers had never had the opportunity to govern themselves and Chávez had to build "ranch committees" from the bottom up. This took time and the corporate ranchers who ran agribusiness had little tolerance for democracy.

Notes and Questions

1. For additional works on César Chávez and the Farmworkers' movement, see Susan Ferris & Ricardo Sandoval, *The Fight in the Fields: César Chávez and the Farmworkers Movement* (Diana Hembree ed. 1997); Richard Griswold del Castillo & Richard A. Garcia, *César Chávez: A Triumph of Spirit* (1995); Peter Matthiessen, *Sal Si Puedes: César Chávez and the New American Revolution* (1969); Jacques E. Levy, *César Chávez: Autobiography of La Causa* (1975).

————

As we close these materials on Mexican Americans, consider how long they have struggled, in one way or another, for their relationship to their former lands. Their early, mostly futile battles were in courts and commissions to establish the legitimacy of their previously unquestioned claims to land. They engaged in armed resistance to protest the usurpation of their lands. Ultimately, deprived of land, they struggled for the right to work their former lands at a decent wage and under decent working conditions. Consider the complex relationship between present-day Mexican Americans and the lands previously owned by the ancestors of some prior to the Treaty of Guadalupe Hidalgo.

Notes and Questions

1. How would you feel, if you were Mexican American, about the lands that were formerly Mexican?

2. Is it appropriate to attribute foreignness to Mexican Americans and their culture, or to the Spanish language in the Southwest?

3. Consider the similarities and differences between Indians and Mexican Americans with regard to their relationship to the lands of the West. What do the two groups have in common? How was law used to deprive each of lands formerly possessed by members of each group?

4. Consider the role of law in facilitating the desire of the white majority to possess land. What does history teach about the meaning and use of ostensibly neutral or protective laws or treaties?

5. For a contemporary analysis of Mexican–American identity, see Kevin R. Johnson, *How Did You Get to Be Mexican? A White/Brown Man's Search for Identity* (1999). For an exploration of the complexities of assimilation for Mexican Americans, see Kevin R. Johnson, *"Melting Pot" or "Ring of Fire"?: Assimilation and the Mexican–American Experience*, 85 Calif. L. Rev. 1259 (1997); 10 La Raza L.J. 173 (1998).

6. For an analysis of how immigration law, official language policy and rhetoric stigmatize Latino/a identity, and on the ambivalence surrounding Mexican–American identification with the United States, see Yxta Maya Murray, *The Latino–American Crisis of Citizenship*, 31 U.C. Davis L. Rev. 503 (1998).

SECTION 2. PUERTO RICO AND PUERTO RICANS

As a result of the Spanish–American War of 1898, approximately one million Puerto Ricans came under the jurisdiction of the United States. The United States has maintained an ambiguous colonial relationship with Puerto Rico. One of its foremost historians has named Puerto Rico the "oldest colony," an apt description of its political relationship to the United States. See generally José Trías Monge, *Puerto Rico: The Trials of the Oldest Colony in the World* (1997).

Although the war began in Cuba, United States politicians did not want the war to end until they had expelled Spain from Puerto Rico and annexed the island. In May, 1898, before the invasion of Puerto Rico in July of that year, the following exchange occurred:

> Assistant Secretary of the Navy Theodore Roosevelt, in a personal letter to Senator Henry Cabot Lodge, wrote: "give my best love to Nannie, and *do not make peace until we get Porto Rico.*" Lodge replied: "Porto Rico is not forgotten and we mean to have it. Unless I am utterly . . . mistaken, the administration is now fully committed to the large policy that we both desire."

Selections from the Correspondence of Theodore Roosevelt and H.C. Lodge, 1884–1918 (1925) quoted in *The Puerto Ricans: A Documentary History* 89 (Kal Wagenheim & Olga Jimenez de Wagenheim eds. 1994).

The United States wanted Puerto Rico for a number of reasons. The ideology of Manifest Destiny, which had played such an important role in the conquest of Mexico, continued to fuel United States expansionism in 1898. Puerto Rico was seen as an important location for military reasons, as an important way to control the Gulf of Mexico and the canal connecting the Gulf to the Pacific. There were also important business reasons for the conquest. The war occurred during a time of economic hardship, and the United States sought new markets for its increasing surpluses of goods. The purpose of expanding markets was amply fulfilled, as today Puerto Rico is a major overseas trading partner of the United States. See Ediberto Roman, *Empire Forgotten: The United States's Colonization of Puerto Rico*, 42 Vill. L. Rev. 1119, 1149 (1997).

Prior to the invasion, Puerto Ricans recognized the threat posed by their "dangerous neighbor":

> The American nation is a dangerous neighbor, especially for Cuba, the Dominican Republic, and Puerto Rico. We must trust very little in her statements. We must not fall asleep, and must keep watchful eyes on the Florida Channel. Anglo–American traditions are not the most reassuring.

> There you have Mexico, invaded and dismembered, due to the greed of the Colossus. There you have Nicaragua, where they arrived one day, stirring troubles and difficulties. The North American Republic is too powerful to relax her pressure on the weak Latin American Republics.

On the alert, then ... the United States urgently needs to establish a position in the Antilles. In 1891, they talked and acted in this direction, without beating about the bush.

Translated from *La Democracia, 1894, No. 1030*, quoted in Wagenheim & Jimenez de Wagenheim, *supra* at 85.

The Spanish–American War was settled in the Treaty of Paris of 1898. This treaty ceded Puerto Rico and the Philippines to the United States.

A. THE TREATY OF PARIS (1898)

Article I:

Spain relinquishes all claim of sovereignty over and title to Cuba. * * *

Article II:

Spain cedes to the United States the island of Porto Rico and other islands now under Spanish sovereignty in the West Indies, and the island of Guam in the Marianas or Ladrones.

Article III:

Spain cedes to the United States the archipelago known as the Philippine Islands * * *.

The United States will pay to Spain the sum of twenty million dollars ($20,000,000) within three months after the exchange of the ratifications of the present treaty. * * *

Article IX:

Spanish subjects, natives of the Peninsula, residing in the territory over which Spain by the present treaty relinquishes or cedes her sovereignty, may remain in such territory or may remove therefrom, retaining in either event all their rights of property, including the right to sell or dispose of such property or of its proceeds; and they shall also have the right to carry on their industry, commerce and professions, being subject in respect thereof to such laws as are applicable to other foreigners. In case they remain in the territory they may preserve their allegiance to the Crown of Spain by making, before a court of record, within a year from the date of the exchange of ratifications of this treaty, a declaration of their decision to preserve such allegiance; in default of which declaration they shall be held to have renounced it and to have adopted the nationality of the territory in which they may reside.

The civil rights and political status of the native inhabitants of the territories hereby ceded to the United States shall be determined by the Congress.

   * * *

Treaty of Paris, reprinted in 11 *Treaties and Other International Agreements of the United States of America 1776–1949* at 615–19 (Charles I. Bevans ed. 1974).

Notes and Questions

1. Notice the change in language from Article IX of the Treaty of Guadalupe Hidalgo to Article IX of the Treaty of Paris. Is the difference significant? Why? Judge José Cabranes has commented that, "For the first time in American history, in a treaty acquiring territory for the United States, there was no promise of citizenship . . . [nor any] promise, actual or implied, of statehood. The United States thereby acquired not 'territories' but possessions or 'dependencies' and became, in that sense, an 'imperial' power." José A. Cabranes, *Citizenship and the American Empire* 20 (1979) (quoting J. Pratt, *America's Colonial Experiment* 68 (1950)). Do you agree with this comment? In light of New Mexico's 62–year struggle for statehood?

2. Note the distinction that Article IX makes between "Spanish subjects, natives of the [Iberian] Peninsula," and "native inhabitants of the territories." Only the Spanish could elect to retain their Spanish citizenship, not the predominantly *criollos* (creoles) who were citizens under the former Spanish rule. Thus the "native inhabitants" lost their Spanish citizenship and became subject to the will of Congress in defining their "civil rights and political status."

3. Consider the views of Rubin Francis Weston:

Those who advocated overseas expansion faced this dilemma: What kind of relationship would the new peoples have to the body politic? Was it to be the relationship of the Reconstruction period, an attempt at political equality for dissimilar races, or was it to be the Southern "counterrevolutionary" point of view which denied the basic American constitutional rights to people of color? The actions of the federal government during the imperial period and the relegation of the Negro to a status of second-class citizenship indicated that the Southern point of view would prevail. The racism which caused the relegation of the Negro to a status of inferiority was to be applied to the overseas possessions of the United States.

Rubin Francis Weston, *Racism in U.S. Imperialism* 15 (1972).

B. THE PUERTO RICO TERRITORY: CONSTRUCTING STATUS

Consider the following excerpt, which describes the ideological background of the *Insular* cases, which were crucial in defining the current status of Puerto Rico.

EFRÉN RIVERA RAMOS

The Legal Construction of American Colonialism: The Insular Cases (1901–1922)
65 Revista Jurídica U. P. R. 225, 226–27, 284–89 (1996).*

* * *

From the earliest stages of the overseas expansionist movement, law would be called upon to play an important role in the construction of the new American colonial venture. This role would assume multiple forms. For example, the American ideology of the rule of law and the particular place that courts had come to occupy in American political life would soon require that the policy of expansion be tested for its constitutional legitimacy within the judicial process. The legal justification of that policy would be eventually provided by principles developed by the Supreme Court as the final arbiter of constitutional controversy within the United States. * * *

The discourse elaborated in the lengthy discussions carried out by the Justices in the *Insular Cases* was permeated by wider conceptions and values whose analysis is necessary in order to understand properly the import of the legal doctrine established by the decisions. It is in this sense that the term "ideology" is used in this section.

RACISM, MANIFEST DESTINY, SOCIAL DARWINISM, AND THE CONSTRUCTION OF THE "OTHER"

A certain rhetoric, a particular discourse of power, distinctive notions of history, society, order, progress, and of the relations among peoples served as justifications and contributed to provide impetus to the United States' expansionist drive at the end of the nineteenth century. * * *

One very important implicit assumption that can be extricated from the variety of arguments for continued expansion, and that seems to have been a fundamental feature of the ethos of the times, was a certain ingrained notion of an inherent "right" to expand that had accrued to the American people. This was probably rooted in a perceived "tradition of expansion," developed through a century of an almost continuous practice of territorial enlargement throughout the continent. * * *

This "right to expand" was in turn predicated on a very strong belief in the principle of the inequality of peoples.[232] A belief that many thought was buttressed by History itself. After all, was not the world replete with contemporary examples of peoples living in patent conditions of inequality, and were not the Anglo–Saxon Americans one of the few privileged groups who, through hard work, dedication, special "natural" endowments and, above all, divine design, were enjoying the blessings of the most advanced economic and political institutions? The dominant view was articulated in a series of binary oppositions: the civilized and the barbarous, the prosperous and the stagnant, the rational and the irrational, the hardworking and the indolent, the self-disciplined and the disorderly, the meritorious and the undeserving. The categories were constructed in direct reference to race: The white, Anglo–Saxon race was the privileged pole in the discourse of power; the "others," the non-white and non-Europeans, those of mixed races, were to be in the receiving end of the exercise of that power. Those "others" were the barbarous, the stagnant, the irrational, the indolent, the disorderly and the undeserving, more fit to be governed than to govern. There was also a geography of power. Whereas the template zones were thought to be more conducive to hard work, self-discipline and, therefore, capacity for self-government and economic and scientific progress, the "tropics" were considered to be breeders of lazy, ignorant and

232. See David Healy, *Drive to Hegemony: The United States in the Caribbean 1898–1917* 288 (1988).

inferior populations incapable of self-government and condemned to be governed from outside in order for progress and civilization ever to flourish in their midst.

The notion of racial superiority had been present in American life since colonial times. The male, white, Anglo–Saxon ruling elites had ample occasion to put in practice domestically what was later to become the guiding ideology of the nation's imperial career. As Rubin Weston has pointed out, the attitude that would permeate the metropolitan state's dealings with the peoples of its insular possessions after 1898 had been shaped through white America's experience with, and treatment of, the Native Americans, the Chinese, the Japanese, the African Americans and, we may add, the Mexicans and, with varying degrees, the non-Anglo–Saxon European immigrants of working class and peasant origin. Furthermore, in a convenient interplay of dialectical reenforcement, the policies sustained abroad would, in turn, be used as justification for the continued subjugation, on racial, ethnic and social grounds, of the various subordinated groups at home.

John W. Burgess, a leading political and constitutional theorist of the times, whose classes at Columbia University were attended, among others, by Theodore Roosevelt, would express it patently:

> The North is learning every day by valuable experiences that there are vast differences in political capacity between the races, that it is the white man's mission, his duty, and his right to hold the reins of political power in his own hands for the civilization of the world and the welfare of mankind.

For Burgess, "the Teutonic nations" were "intrusted, in the general economy of history, with the mission of conducting the political civilization of the modern world," by taking that civilization "into those parts of the world inhabited by unpolitical and barbaric races; *i.e.,* they must have a colonial policy."

"Right," "duty," "mission," those were the key concepts in the ideology of Manifest Destiny, that special calling of the "superior Anglo–Saxon race" to spread the gospel and practices of civilization throughout the world.

Social Darwinism added a new philosophical base to the discourse of imperial power. The "survival of the fittest" was not only the inescapable law of the natural world, but of social and international life as well. * * * Darwin himself had encouraged the notion with his characterization of the American as "the heir of all the ages, in the foremost files of time" and with his statement in *The Descent of Man* that: "There is apparently much truth in the belief that the wonderful progress of the United States, as well as the character of the people, are the results of natural selection". The competition for new markets and territories that was the hallmark of the "new imperialism" of the end of the century provided a material justification to the Social Darwinists of the day. The United States must do as the other imperial powers, they argued, lest it become a second rate nation threatened with eventual extinction. * * *

Present throughout, particularly among the new industrial, commercial and financial elites and the intellectuals closely associated to those interests was the economic ideology of liberal capitalism: the unquestioned belief in "free enterprise" and the promotion of the idea that investment in foreign lands would be necessarily beneficial for the investor and the "host" country alike. Experience would later refute this axiom, as it would become more and more evident that in the case of the poorer countries of Latin America and other regions the greatest beneficiaries by far would almost invariably be the foreign capitalists and, to a lesser degree perhaps, the local ruling classes. * * * The ideology of expansion at this stage was predicated on a certain vision of order, tied to the rationality of capital and the market and to the institutions of liberal government, a vision obsessed with stability as the cornerstone of progress, but stability conceived as the unquestioned acceptance of hierarchy and subordination under the normalizing control of the institutions of capital, patriarchy, racism, and elitist representative politics. This vision of order would be used repeatedly as a justification for outright intervention in the internal affairs of the Caribbean and Central America and even for the establishment of diverse forms of prolonged political and military control. * * *

The discourse of the *Insular Cases* incorporated many of the notions that constituted what I have termed the "ideology of expansion".

THE FORAKER ACT OF 1900 AND THE *INSULAR CASES*

As with the Treaty of Guadalupe Hidalgo, treaties answer only the most basic questions of national sovereignty over disputed territory and raise many questions of meaning. In the case of Puerto Rico, the Treaty of Paris says only that the civil and political rights of Puerto Ricans would be determined by Congress. Congress enacted important legislation establishing governance and regulation in Puerto Rico.

In 1900, Congress passed the Foraker Act, 31 Stat. 79 (1900), entitled "An Act Temporarily to provide revenues and a civil government for Porto Rico, and for other purposes." Arnold Leibowitz describes the Act as follows:

President McKinley's Puerto Rican policy, which was incorporated in the Foraker Act of 1900, established a civil government in which the key roles would be given to Americans appointed by the President. There would be a Governor appointed by the President, an 11-man Executive Council (with a majority being Statesiders), 35 elected Puerto Ricans in the House of Delegates (whose laws were subject to Congressional veto), and an elected Resident Commissioner who spoke for Puerto Rico in the U.S. House of Representatives but who had no vote there.

Arnold H. Leibowitz, *Defining Status: A Comprehensive Analysis of United States Territorial Relations* 141–42 (1989).

In an important series of cases now referred to as the *Insular Cases,** the Supreme Court wrestled with the issue of the status of the Puerto

* *DeLima v. Bidwell*, 182 U.S. 1 (1901); *Downes v. Bidwell*, 182 U.S. 244 (1901); *Dooley v. United States*, 182 U.S. 222 (1901); and *Armstrong v. United States*, 182 U.S. 243 (1901). See Leibowitz, *supra* at 143 n.66.

Rico territory. *Downes v. Bidwell* was one of the major cases, concerning the constitutionality of the Foraker Act's tax provisions. More importantly, the court's discussion of the status of Puerto Rico and its relationship to the United States had, and continues to have, enormous significance.

DOWNES v. BIDWELL

182 U.S. 244 (1901).

[This was an action by Downes against the collector of the port of New York to recover taxes of $659.35 paid on oranges imported from Puerto Rico in November, 1900, after passage of the Foraker Act.]

JUSTICE BROWN announced the conclusion and judgment of the court:

This case involves the question whether merchandise brought into the port of New York from Porto Rico since the passage of the Foraker act is exempt from duty, notwithstanding the 3d section of that act which requires the payment of "15 per centum of the duties which are required to be levied, collected, and paid upon like articles of merchandise imported from foreign countries." * * *

In the case of *De Lima v. Bidwell* just decided, we held that, upon the ratification of the treaty of peace with Spain, Porto Rico ceased to be a foreign country, and became a territory of the United States, and that duties were no longer collectible upon merchandise brought from that island. We are now asked to hold that it became a part of the United States within that provision of the Constitution which declares that "all duties, imposts, and excises shall be uniform throughout the United States." Art. 1, § 8. If Porto Rico be a part of the United States, the Foraker act imposing duties upon its products is unconstitutional, not only by reason of a violation of the uniformity clause, but because by § 9 "vessels bound to or from one state" cannot "be obliged to enter, clear, or pay duties in another."

The case also involves the broader question whether the revenue clauses of the Constitution extend of their own force to our newly acquired territories. The Constitution itself does not answer the question. * * *

[I]t can nowhere be inferred that the territories were considered a part of the United States. The Constitution was created by the people of the United States, as a union of states, to be governed solely by representatives of the states; and even the provision relied upon here, that all duties, imposts, and excises shall be uniform "throughout the United States," is explained by subsequent provisions of the Constitution, that "no tax or duty shall be laid on articles exported from any state," and "no preference shall be given by any regulation of commerce or revenue to the ports of one state over those of another; nor shall vessels bound to or from one state be obliged to enter, clear, or pay duties in another." In short, the Constitution deals with states, their people, and their representatives.

* * *

It is sufficient to say that * * * Congress has been consistent in recognizing the difference between the states and territories under the Constitution. * * *

Indeed, the practical interpretation put by Congress upon the Constitution has been long continued and uniform to the effect that the Constitution is applicable to territories acquired by purchase or conquest, only when and so far as Congress shall so direct. * * *

We are also of opinion that the power to acquire territory by treaty implies, not only the power to govern such territory, but to prescribe upon what terms the United States will receive its inhabitants, and what their status shall be in what Chief Justice Marshall termed the "American empire." There seems to be no middle ground between this position and the doctrine that if their inhabitants do not become, immediately upon annexation, citizens of the United States, their children thereafter born, whether savages or civilized, are such, and entitled to all the rights, privileges and immunities of citizens. If such be their status, the consequences will be extremely serious. Indeed, it is doubtful if Congress would ever assent to the annexation of territory upon the condition that its inhabitants, however foreign they may be to our habits, traditions, and modes of life, shall become at once citizens of the United States. * * *

[I]n *Johnson v. McIntosh*, 8 Wheat. 543, 583, it was said by [Chief Justice Marshall]:

"The title by conquest is acquired and maintained by force. The conqueror prescribes its limits. Humanity, however, acting on public opinion, has established, as a general rule, that the conquered shall not be wantonly oppressed, and that their condition shall remain as eligible as is compatible with the objects of the conquest. Most usually they are incorporated with the victorious nation and become subjects or citizens of the government with which they are connected. The new and old members of the society mingle with each other; the distinction between them is gradually lost, and they make one people. Where this incorporation is practicable humanity demands, and a wise policy requires, that the rights of the conquered to property should remain unimpaired; that the new subjects should be governed as equitably as the old; and that confidence in their security should gradually banish the painful sense of being separated from their ancient connections and united by force to strangers.

"When the conquest is complete, and the conquered inhabitants can be blended with the conquerors, or safely governed as a distinct people, public opinion, which not even the conqueror can disregard, imposes these restraints upon him; and he cannot neglect them without injury to his fame and hazard to his power." * * *

It is obvious that in the annexation of outlying and distant possessions grave questions will arise from differences of race, habits, laws, and customs of the people, and from differences of soil, climate, and production, which may require action on the part of Congress that would be quite unnecessary in the annexation of contiguous territory inhabited only by people of the same race, or by scattered bodies of native Indians.

     * * *

Whatever may be finally decided by the American people as to the status of these islands and their inhabitants,—whether they shall be introduced into the sisterhood of states or be permitted to form independent governments,—it does not follow that in the meantime, awaiting that decision, the people [of Puerto Rico] are in the matter of personal rights unprotected by the provisions of our Constitution and subject to the merely arbitrary control of Congress. Even if regarded as aliens, they are entitled under the principles of the Constitution to be protected in life, liberty, and property. This has been frequently held by this court in respect to the Chinese, even when aliens, not possessed of the political rights of citizens of the United States. * * * We do not desire, however, to anticipate the difficulties which would naturally arise in this connection, but merely to disclaim any intention to hold that the inhabitants of these territories are subject to an unrestrained power on the part of Congress to deal with them upon the theory that they have no rights which it is bound to respect.

Large powers must necessarily be intrusted to Congress in dealing with these problems, and we are bound to assume that they will be judiciously exercised. That these powers may be abused is possible. But the same may be said of its powers under the Constitution as well as outside of it. Human wisdom has never devised a form of government so perfect that it may not be perverted to bad purposes. It is never conclusive to argue against the possession of certain powers from possible abuses of them. It is safe to say that if Congress should venture upon legislation manifestly dictated by selfish interests, it would receive quick rebuke at the hands of the people. * * *

Patriotic and intelligent men may differ widely as to the desireableness of this or that acquisition, but this is solely a political question. We can only consider this aspect of the case so far as to say that no construction of the Constitution should be adopted which would prevent Congress from considering each case upon its merits, unless the language of the instrument imperatively demand it. A false step at this time might be fatal to the development of what Chief Justice Marshall called the American empire. Choice in some cases, the natural gravitation of small bodies towards large ones in others, the result of a successful war in still others, may bring about conditions which would render the annexation of distant possessions desirable. If those possessions are inhabited by alien races, differing from us in religion, customs, laws, methods of taxation, and modes of thought, the administration of government and justice, according to Anglo–Saxon principles, may for a time be impossible; and the question at once arises whether large concessions ought not to be made for a time, that ultimately our own theories may be carried out, and the blessings of a free government under the

Constitution extended to them. We decline to hold that there is anything in the Constitution to forbid such action.

We are therefore of opinion that the island of Porto Rico is a territory appurtenant and belonging to the United States, but not a part of the United States within the revenue clauses of the Constitution; that the Foraker act is constitutional, so far as it imposes duties upon imports from such island, and that the plaintiff cannot recover back the duties exacted in this case.

JUSTICE WHITE, with whom concurred JUSTICE SHIRAS and JUSTICE McKENNA, uniting in the judgment of affirmance:

* * *

While * * * there is no express or implied limitation on Congress in exercising its power to create local governments for any and all of the territories, by which that body is restrained from the widest latitude of discretion, it does not follow that there may not be inherent, although unexpressed, principles which are the basis of all free government which cannot be with impunity transcended. But this does not suggest that every express limitation of the Constitution which is applicable has not force, but only signifies that even in cases where there is no direct command of the Constitution which applies, there may nevertheless be restrictions of so fundamental a nature that they cannot be transgressed, although not expressed in so many words in the Constitution. * * *

In the case of the territories, as in every other instance, when a provision of the Constitution is invoked, the question which arises is, not whether the Constitution is operative, for that is self-evident, but whether the provision relied on is applicable. * * *

From these conceded propositions it follows that Congress in legislating for Porto Rico was only empowered to act within the Constitution and subject to its applicable limitations, and that every provision of the Constitution which applied to a country situated as was that island was potential in Porto Rico.

* * *

There is in reason, then, no room in this case to contend that Congress can destroy the liberties of the people of Porto Rico by exercising in their regard powers against freedom and justice which the Constitution has absolutely denied. There can also be no controversy as to the right of Congress to locally govern the island of Porto Rico as its wisdom may decide, and in so doing to accord only such degree of representative government as may be determined on by that body. There can also be no contention as to the authority of Congress to levy such local taxes in Porto Rico as it may choose, even although the amount of the local burden so levied be manifold more onerous than is the duty with which this case is concerned. * * *

It may not be doubted that by the general principles of the law of nations every government which is sovereign within its sphere of action possesses as an inherent attribute the power to acquire territory by discovery, by agreement or treaty, and by conquest. It cannot also be gainsaid that, as a general rule, wherever a government acquires territory as a result of any of the modes above stated, the relation of the territory to the new government is to be determined by the acquiring power in the absence of stipulations upon the subject. * * *

The general principle of the law of nations, already stated, is that acquired territory, in the absence of agreement to the contrary, will bear such relation to the acquiring government as may be by it determined. To concede to the government of the United States the right to acquire, and to strip it of all power to protect the birthright of its own citizens and to provide for the well being of the acquired territory by such enactments as may in view of its condition be essential, is, in effect, to say that the United States is helpless in the family of nations, and does not possess that authority which has at all times been treated as an incident of the right to acquire. Let me illustrate the accuracy of this statement. Take a case of discovery. Citizens of the United States discover an unknown island, peopled with an uncivilized race, yet rich in soil, and valuable to the United States for commercial and strategic reasons. Clearly, by the law of nations, the right to ratify such acquisition and thus to acquire the territory would pertain to the government of the United States. *Johnson v. McIntosh*, 8 Wheat. 543, 595, * * *. Can it be denied that such right could not be practically exercised if the result would be to endow the inhabitants with citizenship of the United States and to subject them, not only to local, but also to an equal proportion of national, taxes, even although the consequence would be to entail ruin on the discovered territory, and to inflict grave detriment on the United States, to arise both from the dislocation of its fiscal system and the immediate bestowal of citizenship on those absolutely unfit to receive it? * * *

When the various treaties by which foreign territory has been acquired are considered in the light of the circumstances which surrounded them, it becomes to my mind clearly established that the treaty-making power was always deemed to be devoid of authority to incorporate territory into the United States without the assent, express or implied, of Congress, and that no question to the contrary has ever been even mooted. * * *

It is, then, as I think, indubitably settled by the principles of the law of nations, by the nature of the government created under the Constitution, by the express and implied powers conferred upon that government by the Constitution, by the mode in which those powers have been executed from the beginning, and by an unbroken line of decisions of this court, first announced by Marshall and followed and lucidly expounded by Taney, that the treaty-making power cannot incorporate territory into the United States without the express or implied assent of Congress, that it may insert in a treaty conditions against immediate incorporation, and that on the other hand, when it has expressed in the treaty the conditions favorable to incorporation they will, if the treaty be not repudiated by Congress, have the force of the law of the land, and therefore by the fulfillment of such conditions cause incorporation to result. It must follow, therefore, that where a treaty contains no conditions for incorporation, and, above all, where it not only has no such conditions, but expressly provides to the contrary, that incorporation does not arise until in the wisdom of Congress it is deemed that the acquired territory has reached that state where it is proper that it should enter into and form a part of the American family.

Does, then, the treaty [of Paris] contain a provision for incorporation, or does it, on the contrary, stipulate that incorporation shall not take place from the mere effect of the treaty and until Congress has so determined?—is then the only question remaining for consideration. * * *

It is to me obvious that [Articles II, IX, and X of the Treaty of Paris] do not stipulate for incorporation, but, on the contrary, expressly provide that the "civil rights and political status of the native inhabitants of the territories hereby ceded" shall be determined by Congress. * * *

The result of what has been said is that while in an international sense Porto Rico was not a foreign country, since it was subject to the sovereignty of and was owned by the United States, it was foreign to the United States in a domestic sense, because the island had not been incorporated into the United States, but was merely appurtenant thereto as a possession. * * *

Conceding, then, for the purpose of the argument, it to be true that it would be a violation of duty under the Constitution for the legislative department, in the exercise of its discretion, to accept a cession of and permanently hold territory which is not intended to be incorporated, the presumption necessarily must be that that department, which within its lawful sphere is but the expression of the political conscience of the people of the United States, will be faithful to its duty under the Constitution, and therefore, when the unfitness of particular territory for incorporation is demonstrated, the occupation will terminate. * * *

[Eds. A concurring opinion by Justice Gray and a dissenting opinion by Justice Harlan have been omitted].

Notes and Questions

1. What exactly was the status of Puerto Ricans after *Downes v. Bidwell*?

2. Is the Court correct that the general public would necessarily "rebuke" invasive legislation taken by Congress in a territory? What if the general public didn't care, especially after time passed? How much does the general public know about Puerto Rico and its continuing status? Consider these points when you read the more modern cases reproduced *infra*.

3. "Former President Harrison pointed out that the perplexing question was related to the status of the new possessions 'and to the rights of their civilized inhabitants who have elected to renounce their allegiance to the Spanish Crown, and either by choice or operation of law have become American—somethings—what? Subject or citizen? There is no other status since they are not aliens any longer, unless a newspaper heading that recently attracted my attention offers another. It ran thus: 'Porto Ricans not citizens of the United States *proper*.' Are they citizens of the United States *improper*, or improper citizens of the United States?'" Weston, *supra*, at 190–91.

4. Reflect upon the opinions in *Downes* and consider the ways in which these opinions reflect what Efren Rivera Ramos terms the "ideology of expansion." Consider, for instance, the majority's reliance on the language of conquest from *Johnson v. McIntosh*.

The position articulated by Justice White, in his concurring opinion in *Downes v. Bidwell* ultimately became the controlling view, as expressed in the following case.

BALZAC v. PEOPLE OF PORTO RICO
258 U.S. 298 (1922).

CHIEF JUSTICE TAFT delivered the opinion of the Court.

These are two prosecutions for criminal libel, brought against the same defendant, Jesus M. Balzac, on informations filed in the district court for Arecibo, Porto Rico, by the district attorney for that district. Balzac was the editor of a daily paper published in Arecibo, known as "El Baluarte," and the articles upon which the charges of libel were based were published on April 16 and April 23, 1918, respectively. In each case the defendant demanded a jury. The Code of Criminal Procedure of Porto Rico grants a jury trial in cases of felony, but not in misdemeanors. The defendant, nevertheless, contended that he was entitled to a jury in such a case, under the Sixth Amendment to the Constitution, and that the language of the alleged libels was only fair comment, and their publication was protected by the First Amendment. His contentions were overruled; he was tried by the court, and was convicted in both cases and sentenced to five months' imprisonment in the district jail in the first, and to four months in the second, and to the payment of the costs in each. The defendant appealed to the Supreme Court of Porto Rico. That court affirmed both judgments. * * *

[The Court decided that, based on federal statute, it had jurisdiction over appeals from the Supreme Court of Puerto Rico.]

We have now to inquire whether that part of the Sixth Amendment to the Constitution, which requires that in all criminal prosecutions, the accused shall enjoy the right to a speedy and public trial, by an impartial jury of the state and district wherein the crime shall have been committed, which district shall have been previously ascertained by law, applies to Porto Rico. Another provision on the subject is in Article 3 of the Constitution providing that the trial of all crimes, except in cases of impeachment, shall be by jury; and such trial shall be held in the state where the said crimes shall have been committed; but when not committed within any state, the trial shall be at such place or places as the Congress may by law have directed. The Seventh Amendment of the Constitution provides that in suits at common law, when the value in controversy shall exceed twenty dollars, the right of trial by jury shall be preserved. It is well settled that these provisions for jury trial in criminal and civil cases apply to the Territories of the United States. * * * But it is just as clearly settled that they do not apply to territory belonging to the United States which has not been incorporated into the Union. It was further settled in *Downes v. Bidwell*, 182 U. S. 244, and confirmed by *Dorr v. United States*, 195 U. S. 138, that neither the Philippines nor Porto Rico was territory which had been incorporated in the Union or become a part of the United States, as distinguished from merely belonging to it; and that the acts giving temporary governments to the Philippines and to Porto Rico had no such effect. The *Insular Cases* revealed much diversity of opinion in this Court as to the constitutional status of the territory acquired by the Treaty of Paris ending the Spanish War, but the *Dorr* case shows that the opinion of Mr. Justice White of the majority, in *Downes v. Bidwell*, has become the settled law of the court. The conclusion of this court in the *Dorr* case, 195 U. S. at 149, was as follows:

"We conclude that the power to govern territory, implied in the right to acquire it, and given to Congress in the Constitution in Article 4, § 3, to whatever other limitations it may be subject, the extent of which must be decided as questions arise, does not require that body to enact for ceded territory, not made part of the United States by congressional action, a system of laws which shall include the right of trial by jury, and that the Constitution does not, without legislation and of its own force, carry such right to territory so situated."

The question before us, therefore, is: Has Congress, since the Foraker Act of April 12, 1900 (31 Stat. 77), enacted legislation incorporating Porto Rico into the Union? Counsel for the plaintiff in error give, in their brief, an extended list of acts, to which we shall refer later, which they urge as indicating a purpose to make the island a part of the United States, but they chiefly rely on the Organic Act of Porto Rico of March 2, 1917, known as the Jones Act.

* * *

The section of the Jones Act which counsel press on us is section 5. This in effect declares that all persons who under the Foraker Act were made citizens of Porto Rico and certain other residents shall become citizens of the United States. * * * Unaffected by the considerations already suggested, perhaps the declaration of section 5 would furnish ground for an inference such as counsel for plaintiff in error contend, but under the circumstances we find it entirely consistent with nonincorporation. When Porto Ricans passed from under the government of Spain, they lost the protection of that government as subjects of the king of Spain, a title by which they had been known for centuries. They had a right to expect, in passing under the dominion of the United States, a status entitling them to the protection of their new sovereign. In theory and in law, they had it as citizens of Porto Rico, but it was an anomalous status, or seemed to be so in view of the fact that those who owed and rendered allegiance to the other great world powers were given the same designation and status as those living in their respective home countries so far as protection against foreign injustice went. It became a yearning of the Porto Ricans to be American citizens, therefore, and this act gave them the boon. What additional rights did it give them? It enabled them to move into the continental United States and becoming residents of any State there to enjoy every right of any other citizen of the United States, civil, social and political. A citizen of the Philippines must be naturalized before he can settle and vote in this country. Not so the Porto Rican under the Organic Act of 1917.

In Porto Rico, however, the Porto Rican can not insist upon the right of trial by jury, except as his own representatives in his legislature shall confer it on him. The citizen of the United States living in Porto Rico cannot there enjoy a right of trial by jury under the federal Constitution, any more than the Porto Rican. It is locality that is determinative of the application of the Constitution, in such matters as judicial procedure, and not the status of the people who live in it. * * *

The jury system needs citizens trained to the exercise of the responsibilities of jurors. In common-law countries centuries of tradition have prepared a conception of the impartial attitude jurors must assume. The jury system postulates a conscious duty of participation in the machinery of justice which it is hard for people not brought up in fundamentally popular government at once to acquire. One of its greatest benefits is in the security it gives the people that they, as jurors, actual or possible, being part of the judicial system of the country, can prevent its arbitrary use or abuse. Congress has thought that a people like the Filipinos, or the Porto Ricans, trained to a complete judicial system which knows no juries, living in compact and ancient communities, with definitely formed customs and political conceptions, should be permitted themselves to determine how far they wish to adopt this institution of Anglo–Saxon origin, and when. Hence the care with which * * * the United States has been liberal in granting to the islands acquired by the Treaty of Paris most of the American constitutional guaranties, but has been sedulous to avoid forcing a jury system on a Spanish and civil law country until it desired it. We cannot find any intention to depart from this policy in making Porto Ricans American citizens, explained as this is by the desire to put them as individuals on an exact equality with citizens from the American homeland, to secure them more certain protection against the world, and to give them an opportunity, should they desire, to move into the United States proper, and there without naturalization to enjoy all political and other rights.

* * * The Constitution of the United States is in force in Porto Rico as it is wherever and whenever the sovereign power of that government is exerted. This has not only been admitted, but emphasized, by this court in all its authoritative expressions upon the issues arising in the *Insular Cases*, especially in the *Downes v. Bidwell* and the *Dorr* cases. The Constitution, however, contains grants of power, and limitations which in the nature of things are not always and everywhere applicable and the real issue in the *Insular Cases* was not whether the Constitution extended to the Philippines or Porto Rico when we went there, but which ones of its provisions were applicable by way of limitation upon the exercise of executive and legislative power in dealing with new conditions and requirements. * * *

On the whole, therefore, we find no features in the Organic Act of Porto Rico of 1917 from which we can infer the purpose of Congress to incorporate Porto Rico into the United States with the consequences which would follow. * * *

The judgments of the Supreme Court of Porto Rico are affirmed.

Notes and Questions

1. For a detailed and insightful analysis of both the *Insular Cases* and *Balzac*, see the full article by Efrén Rivera Ramos, excerpted *supra*.

C. PUERTO RICAN CITIZENSHIP

In the Jones Act of 1917, Congress enacted a bill of rights for Puerto Rico and granted United States citizenship to Puerto Ricans. In Section 5 of the Jones Act, "all citizens of Porto Rico, as defined by [the Foraker Act] ... are hereby declared, and shall be deemed and held to be, citizens of the United States." However, this grant of citizenship was never intended to be a grant of full citizenship as we know it. According to Senator Foraker, the United States citizenship of Puerto Ricans was not granted to recognize any individual rights they might have, but rather to "recognize that Puerto Rico belongs to the United States of America." Foraker also commented:

> We considered very carefully what status in a political sense we would give to the people of [Puerto Rico], and we reported that provision not thoughtlessly.... We concluded ... that the inhabitants of that island must be either citizens or subjects or aliens. We did not want to treat our own as aliens, and we do not propose to have any subjects. Therefore, we adopted the term "citizens." *In adopting the term "citizens" we did not understand, however, that we were giving to those people any rights that the American people do not want them to have.* "Citizens" is a word that indicates, according to Story's work on the Constitution of the United States, allegiance on the one hand and protection on the other.

See Cabranes, *supra* at 37 (quoting 33 *Cong. Rec.* 2473–74 (1900) (remarks of Sen. Foraker)).

Consider the role that race and racism played in defining the meaning of United States citizenship for Puerto Ricans, as discussed in the following excerpt:

RUBIN FRANCIS WESTON

Racism in U.S. Imperialism
194–201, 204 (1972).*

DEMOCRATS AND PUERTO RICAN CITIZENSHIP

During fourteen years of Republican administration, American citizenship for the Puerto Ricans was denied. When the Democrats gained control of the House in 1912, they immediately started to act on various proposals to give American citizenship to the Puerto Ricans. A report on a bill to provide citizenship to the Puerto Ricans pointed out that under the Foraker Act of 1900 it was sometimes argued that Puerto Ricans were citizens of the United States. The basis of the argument was Section 1891 of the Revised Statutes which declares that "the Constitution and all laws of the United States which are not locally inapplicable shall have the same force and effect within all the organized territories and in every territory hereafter organized or elsewhere within the United States." Some Americans, however, contended that in the meaning of Section 1891 the Puerto Ricans were not citizens and "that the extension of the Constitution and laws over the island would not of itself have the effect of constituting the inhabitants thereof citizens of the United States." Many inhabitants of the states under the Constitution were not citizens, "as for instance Chinese, Indians, and others." Although the argument in favor of Puerto Rican citizenship had been presented, the Supreme Court had refused to "hold either that the Constitution of the United States extends over the island of Puerto Rico in all respects and for all purposes, or that the inhabitants thereof are citizens of the United States." It was the purpose of the proposed bill to confer American citizenship upon the Puerto Ricans collectively, "subject only to the condition that each take the oath of allegiance and receive a certificate." Those who did not wish American citizenship would not be forced to become citizens.

The debates in the House of Representatives on the question of American citizenship for the Puerto Ricans revolved around the racial questions. "Considering all the conditions with Haiti, Santo Domingo, Central America and elsewhere," Representative Joseph G. Cannon did not believe that Puerto Ricans were competent for self-government. The United States already had her hands full in taking care of all the aforementioned countries. The Illinois congressman felt that the Puerto Ricans did not "understand, as we understand it, government of the people, and by the people," because they had a different language. He contended that "75 or 80 per cent of those people are mixed blood in part and are not the equal to the full-blooded Spaniard and not equal, in my judgement, to the unmixed African, and yet they were to be made citizens of the United States."

Representative James L. Slayden of Texas opposed the bill on grounds similar to those expressed by Representative Cannon. He took exception to the view that the hybrid, a cross between the blacks and whites or between the brown and whites, was "less well fitted for self-government than the full-blooded African Negro." According to his observations, the Negro had not shown any moderate success in government "hybrid or thoroughbred." Haiti was used as an example of an almost completely black country not able to govern itself successfully. Cuba and the Dominican Republic were cited as countries of hybrids unable to sustain republican forms of government. Slayden believed that the problem was not in language but in color, and that Representative Cannon would certainly have been more accurate if he had said that "as a whole, they have a different color." That would better have explained what he conceived to be their incapacity, for "color in this matter is more important than language." The representative declared that the climate and geography of Puerto Rico were not conducive to Anglo–Saxon government because "the Tropics seem to heat the blood while enervating the people who inhabit them." According to Slayden, the United States was already in "an awkward situation with reference to

... Porto Rico ... and every member of the House" knew it. They were charging the United States "with inconsistency and worse ... they prove it." He continued, "They know that we tax them without permitting representation in our Congress, something that was a crime when done by the British Parliament, but which does not appear so wicked when we play the role of King George and his Parliamentarians." Representative Slayden concluded by saying that "many people in this country who want to sever the tie that binds us to tropical and alien people take that position, because they see in it danger for us." They agreed that people inhabiting lands within 20 degrees of the equator could "neither comprehend nor support representative government constructed on the Anglo–Saxon plan."

Representative James Mann of Illinois observed that if the Puerto Ricans were made citizens, they could "demand admission into the Union with greater force and with better logic." To admit into the Union as a state with the "deciding power in the Senate if not in the House a people who were somewhat ... strange" to the internal problems of the United States and its civilization was not to be desired.

Outside Congress influential persons expressed similar views to those expressed on the floor of the House. The former governor of Puerto Rico, R.H. Post, said, "The granting of citizenship to all of the inhabitants of Porto Rico, although but a step in the direction of complete assimilation, is still a step, and would tend to commit us to eventual statehood for Porto Rico, and might be construed as indicating that it was the policy of the United States that extraneous territory occupied by foreign races falling under the influence of the United States will eventually be admitted as sovereign States of the Union."

Outlook in its editorial policy agreed that the Puerto Ricans had legitimate grievances but asserted, "Statehood would not be of advantage to the United States and of doubtful advantage to Porto Rico." It was opposed to blanket naturalization because "it puts Porto Rico in the line to become first an organized territory and eventually a State in the Union, and raises hope of this ultimate statehood ... a consummation very undesirable both for them and for us ...."

William Hayes Ward, editor of the *Independent,* wrote that he could not sympathize with a nation "which demands a special racial," intellectual, or educational "standard for citizenship or the ballot." The doctrine was aristocratic, and full democracy was "safer than aristocracy" since democracy always had the future. "Give the ballot to the ignorant and you will educate them, for you will have to. The ballot to the negro in the South gave the South the public school system, and so justified all the risk we took in the act." Ward supported unconditional statehood for Puerto Rico.

Supporters of the bill, such as Representative Henry A. Cooper of Wisconsin, believed that the people of Puerto Rico were civilized and entitled to citizenship in the United States. As evidence of their civilization, Cooper pointed to the fact that they voluntarily freed their slaves, taxing themselves $30,000,000 to compensate the owners. They were entitled to citizenship because under the Constitution the United States could not hold people in subjection to its laws for an indefinite period unless they were citizens. Since the United States was committed to hold Puerto Rico forever because of the Panama Canal, citizenship was the only logical status for the inhabitants of the island.

Representative Elmer A. Morse, also of Wisconsin, noted that the Negro population was not much larger, if any, "in Puerto Rico than in the great State of South Carolina." It was his belief that "while the quality of citizenship" was not as high as it should be, the people should be given the privilege of American citizenship.

The Senate failed to act on this bill in 1912. In 1913 Resident Commissioner Louis Muñoz Rivera observed, "My countrymen, having waited since 1898 for a measure of absolute and ample self-government, do expect today more than ever before that their hopes will soon be realized, Congress granting them American citizenship together with a law creating two elective houses, and investing them, through their representatives in both chambers, with power to make their laws and to regulate all their local matters."

It was with a degree of renewed hope that the Puerto Ricans welcomed the success of the Democrats at the polls in 1912. Democratic control of Congress and the Executive Department suggested that the concept of democratic expansion, long advocated by the party, would be applied to Puerto Rico.

President-elect Woodrow Wilson seemed to agree with the resident commissioner when he said, "No doubt we shall successfully enough bind Porto Rico ... to ourselves by ties of justice and interest and affection ... We can satisfy the obligation of generous justice toward the people of Porto Rico by giving them ample and familiar rights and privileges accorded our own citizens in our own territories...."

The Congress has never been noted for haste in its actions on civil and political rights, and Puerto Rican citizenship was no exception. When Congress took up the question of civil government for Puerto Rico, it was acting to replace a fourteen-year-old "Act Temporarily to Provide Revenue and Civil Government for Porto Rico and for Other Purposes." Serious debate on the bill, however, was not begun until 1916. Resident Commissioner Rivera, speaking in support of the citizenship bill before the House of Representatives, observed that the Republican party by decreeing independence for Cuba had gained glory for itself. The Democratic party was bound by the "principles written into its platforms and by recorded speeches of its leaders to decree liberty for Porto Rico." The bill under consideration could not "meet the earnest aspirations" of Puerto Ricans because it was "not a measure of self-government ample enough to solve definitely" the basic political problems or to match the national reputation of the United States—a reputation which had been established by "successful championship for liberty and justice throughout the world." From this viewpoint, the Puerto Ricans were willing to accept statehood as a step in the right direction and as "a reform paving the way for others more acceptable and satisfactory," which should come later provided the Puerto Ricans could demonstrate the capacity to govern themselves. To that capacity it was his "pleasant duty to assure

Congress that the Porto Ricans" would "endeavor to prove their intelligence, their patriotism and their full preparation to enjoy and exercise a democratic regime."

The commissioner supported the measure only because he felt that it was the best that could be hoped for at that time. It was his opinion that Puerto Rico deserved better treatment. He pointed out that the behavior of the Puerto Ricans in the past was a testimony in favor of good behavior in the future. In spite of the Latin blood that predominated, there had never been a revolution or "an attack against the majesty of law." There was not sufficient reason to justify "American statesmen in denying self-government" to Puerto Rico and thereby compromise the basic American principle of popular sovereignty:

> ... My countrymen ... refuse to accept a citizenship of an inferior order, a citizenship of the second class, which does not permit them to dispose of their own resources nor to live their own lives nor to send to this Capital their proportional representation ... Give us statehood and your glorious citizenship will be welcome to us and to our children. If you deny us statehood, we decline your citizenship, frankly, proudly, as befits a people who can be deprived of their civil liberties, but who, although deprived of their civil liberties, will preserve their conception of honor....

Commissioner Rivera observed that the bill "authorized those who do not accept American citizenship to so declare before a court of justice, and thus retain Porto Rican citizenship." The bill further provided that "no person shall be allowed to register as a voter in Porto Rico who is not a citizen of the United States." Rivera objected to this provision:

> My compatriots are generously permitted to be citizens of the only country they possess, but they are eliminated from the body politic; the exercise of political rights is forbidden them; by a single stroke of the pen they are converted into pariahs and there is established in America on American soil, protected by the Monroe Doctrine, a division into castes like the Brahamans and Sudras of India. The Democratic platform of Kansas City declared 14 years ago, "A nation can not long endure half empire and half republic, and imperialism abroad will lead rapidly and irreparably to despotism at home." These are not Porto Rican phrases reflecting our Latin impressionability; they are American phrases, reflecting the Anglo–Saxon spirit, calm in its attitude and jealous—very jealous—of its privileges.

Inquiring into some of the probable reasons why Puerto Rico had not been given self-government, he found it could not be the fact that two races coexisted on the island of Puerto Rico because "in America more than ten states had a higher percentage of Negroes in their population than Porto Rico." It was not the lack of adequate numbers, for Puerto Rico was more populous than eighteen other states. After examining the probable reasons, he concluded that the reason behind the denial of self-government was based on the desire of office seekers "determined to report to their superiors that the Porto Ricans were unprepared for self-government."

The resident commissioner could not conceive of a people being denied the rights of self-government on purely racial grounds. His efforts to compare the racial situation in Puerto Rico with the situation in several of the Southern states was not a valid comparison. In Puerto Rico there had been considerable racial interbreeding while in the United States this practice was kept at a minimum, and in many areas by law. The incorporation of a large population of mixed races was potentially dangerous to existing racial patterns in the United States.

The importance of these racial implications was pointed up by Representative Joseph Cannon, who felt that

> when you talk about a people competent for self-government, certain things are to be taken into consideration. One is the racial question ... Porto Rico is populated by a mixed race. About 30 per cent pure African. I was informed by the army officers when I was down there that when the census was taken every man that was a pure African was listed and counted as such, but that there was 75 to 80 per cent of the population that was pure African or had an African strain in their blood ... Will anybody say that I am abusing the African. I am not any more than I am abusing the Filipino or the Moros; and I am certainly not abusing the African in the United States ... But the Commissioner from Porto Rico said that this bill is not as liberal as he wanted it, and he hoped more and more would be given, and as I listened to his remarks I thought he was referring to Statehood. God forbid that in his time or my time, there should be statehood for Porto Rico as one of the United States.

Cannon hoped that Puerto Rico would not be admitted to statehood within the next three generations because the "people of Porto Rico did not have the slightest conception of self-government." He would vote against the pending bill because in the two hundred or three hundred years that the British had been in Jamaica, where there was also a large percentage of African blood, they had not been able to prepare the natives for self-government. In the United States the situation was reversed, for there were "10,000,000 people lately enslaved, who have made very great progress, but they were in contact with 90,000,000 of people who have proved their competency for self-government of the Caucasian race...."

Commissioner Rivera replied that Puerto Rico

> deprived of its national sovereignty depends upon the generosity and chivalry of the American lawmakers ... It is very unfortunate that a Porto Rican is obliged to hear on this floor remarks offensive to the dignity of his native land.... It is not our fault that we are compelled to come here and ask for the enactment of legislation, of a constitution, which, should be our undeniable right to make, according to American principles ourselves. I must conclude, declaring emphatically that I am as proud to be Porto Rican as the gentlemen from Illinois is proud of being an Illinoisan, and as every gentleman on this floor is proud to be an American.

Representative Simeon D. Fess of Ohio saw in the Puerto Rican bill an attempt to do for Puerto Rico something that had not been done previously by Anglo–Saxons for non-Anglo–Saxons—giving them "the best form of local government" that the United States could outline for them and at the same time giving them United States citizenship. * * *

Americans in positions to influence or to establish policy were not very generous in giving to the Puerto Ricans rights usually given to Americans. For the first third of the twentieth century they rationalized the inconsistency of their treatment of the Puerto Ricans on the basis of cultural differences. In the final analysis, race emerged as the determining factor in establishing policy. That policy assumed that the Puerto Ricans were radically different from the Anglo–Saxons and were unassimilable into the American body politic. To the Puerto Ricans, the frustrations caused by this policy created a reciprocal dislike for Americans who gave out their culture and democracy in "a most patronizing manner." America's treatment of Puerto Rico was observed in Latin America and had some effect on attitudes toward the United States. According to one observer, the American treatment of Puerto Rico resulted from the concept of harmonious racial interbreeding brought by the Spanish to their American colonies, a concept completely alien to Anglo–Saxons. The term *Latin America* connoted cultural fraternity, and this did not serve to weaken the wall separating the United States from Latin America in general and Puerto Rico in particular. The difference in concepts added new buttresses to the wall in the form of factors unassimilable for the United States and recalcitrant to all absorption.

Notes and Questions

1. Note that the United States citizenship of Puerto Ricans did not (and does not) include the right to vote or the right to voting representation in Congress since Puerto Rico was and is not a state. As stated in *Balzac*, however, Puerto Ricans have the right to move to a state and, once they achieve residency there, they can exercise all the rights of any state citizen, including voting.

In *Sanchez v. United States*, 376 F. Supp. 239 (D.P.R.1974), the plaintiff, Ada Flores Sanchez, a resident of Puerto Rico, attempted to challenge her ineligibility, despite her United States citizenship, to vote in elections for the President and Vice President of the United States. The judge held that:

> The constitutional challenge in this instance is plainly without merit. Although plaintiff is a U.S. citizen, under the Constitution of the United States the President is not chosen directly by the citizens, but by the electoral colleges in the States and the District of Columbia. * * *

> Today, electors are chosen by popular vote on State-wide tickets and State legislatures generally determine the qualifications for presidential electors. * * * [T]he Constitution does not, by its terms, grant citizens the right to vote, but leaves the matter entirely to the States.

> Although citizenship may be a prerequisite of voting, the right to vote is not an essential right of citizenship. * * *

> This Court * * * is of the opinion that it is inexcusable that there still exists a substantial number of U.S. citizens who cannot legally vote for the President and Vice President of the United States. However, until the Commonwealth votes for Statehood, or until a constitutional amend-

ment is approved which extends the presidential and vice presidential vote to Puerto Rico, there is no substantial constitutional question raised by plaintiff. * * *

See also Leibowitz, *Defining Status,* at 149.

2. Consider the future implications of such diluted citizenship for Puerto Ricans. How would you expect Congress to treat Puerto Ricans resident on the island, who have no voting representation in Congress and no vote for the President?

D. THE DEVELOPMENT OF COMMONWEALTH STATUS FOR PUERTO RICO

In 1950, Congress passed Public Law 600, which created a "compact" with Puerto Rico and which granted limited powers to Puerto Rico. Public Law 600, and its implementation, culminated in Puerto Rico's current status as a "Commonwealth." Consider the following excerpt.

EDIBERTO ROMAN

Empire Forgotten: The United States' Colonization of Puerto Rico
42 Vill. L. Rev. 1119, 1151–56 (1997).*

THE CREATION OF THE COMMONWEALTH

In 1943, forty-five years after the initial occupation, the first major legal efforts were made to address the Puerto Rican people's lack of autonomy. Here again, the United States, uncomfortable with the role of colonizer, continued its denial and eventually developed a new euphemism for the term "colony": "commonwealth" status.

During the same period that the United States was endorsing self-determination principles in the Atlantic Charter, the Puerto Rican people cried out for an end to colonialism. After fifty years of U.S. control, the Puerto Rican legislature, relying upon the United States's declarations in the Atlantic Charter, demanded that Congress terminate "the colonial system of government ... totally and definitely." Shortly after that demand, President Roosevelt initiated the first of what was to become the trademark U.S. response to the Puerto Rican plea for autonomy—congressional or executive department hearings to review the status issue. President Roosevelt's committee proposed amendments to the Jones Act and forwarded a proposed bill to Senator Tydings for introduction before Congress. Tydings had sympathetically observed:

> [I]f you are willing to have help of a kind and have no real voice in the government of the nation to which you are appended, why, then, that is one thing.
>
> * * *
>
> If I were a Puerto Rican that would not satisfy me, just as it did not satisfy George Washington, Thomas Jefferson, and Simon Bolivar.

Roosevelt's initiative resulted in the enactment of laws that would produce the next changes in Puerto Rico's governmental structure, but which ultimately amounted to only a modicum of autonomy for the Puerto Rican people. In 1947, a year after the Philippines was given independence, Congress passed legislation that granted the Puerto Rican people the right to select a governor of their own choosing and empowered the governor to appoint executive officials.

In 1950, Congress enacted Public Law 600, which, in the form of a "compact" between the United States and Puerto Rico, granted the people of Puerto Rico further powers, including the right to organize a government and adopt a constitution. As will be addressed below, the use of the term "compact" assisted the United States in appeasing Puerto Rican and international calls to end the colonial status of Puerto Rico. Unfortunately, the use of "compact," and the representations by U.S. officials concerning the new status, left both the international community and the Puerto Rican political spectrum in a state of turmoil concerning the true status of the territory, an occurrence that has fostered the maintenance of the status quo.

Sections 1 and 2 of Public Law 600 provided that a referendum would be submitted to the Puerto Rican people to determine if they wished to organize their own government pursuant to a constitution of their own choosing. Although these provisions suggest that Puerto Rico was to be granted autonomy, the rest of the act made clear that Puerto Rico was not free from U.S. control. Specifically, Public Law 600 provided that if the Puerto Rican people adopted a constitution, the President would transmit it to Congress "if [the President found] that such constitution conform[ed] with the applicable provisions of this Act and of the Constitution of the United States." Further, House Report 2275 on Public Law 600 confirms Congress's intent to keep Puerto Rico a U.S. possession:

This bill does not commit the Congress, either expressly or by implication, to the enactment of statehood legislation for Puerto Rico in the future. Nor will it in any way preclude a future determination by the Congress of Puerto Rico's ultimate political status.

       * * *

The United States has never made any promises to the people of Puerto Rico, or to Spain from whom Puerto Rico was acquired, that Puerto Rico would eventually be admitted into the Union.

Consistent with its intended imperialistic tenor, Public Law 600's proposed referendum failed to provide the Puerto Rican people with options other than colonial or commonwealth status, as the choice of "permanent" association with a "federal union" was posed in a yes-or-no referendum. The referendum was thus not a statement of the Puerto Rican peoples' freely expressed will. In any event, in 1951 a referendum was held in Puerto Rico to approve Public Law 600. A second referendum was held to approve the constitution. In March of 1952, by virtue of Public Law 447, Congress, after amending portions, approved the Puerto Rican Constitution and revoked inconsistent provisions of the Jones Act.

In the summer of 1952, the Puerto Rican Constitution and the Commonwealth of Puerto Rico were born. The first popularly elected

Puerto Rican governor, Luis Muñoz Marin, attempted to give some real teeth to Puerto Rico's new status. Tracking the introductory remarks of the law, Muñoz Marin argued that Public Law 600 transformed the relationship between the Puerto Rican people and Congress to one which could not be altered without the consent of each of the contracting parties. By virtue of this so-called compact, the Puerto Rican people acquired a certain amount of local autonomy. The autonomy bestowed upon Puerto Rico by its parent state, however, was unquestionably limited and revocable, as is the case in a classic colonial relationship. In fact, all of the parties involved, including Muñoz Marin, accepted that the United States maintained complete control over Puerto Rico and could even revoke the Puerto Rican Constitution.

Public Law 600's use of the term "compact" also allowed the United States to address a potential international embarrassment that it might soon face concerning Puerto Rico. As a signatory to the U.N. Charter, which specifically endorsed self-determination, the United States faced the potential of increasing international scrutiny. Specifically, the United States faced the dilemma of being a member of an international organization that promoted self-determination and could therefore criticize the United States concerning Puerto Rico. The United States responded by ingeniously using the compact language of Public Law 600 and the territory's new status to avoid international condemnation. * * * Puerto Rico's political status remained unchanged as a result of the creation of the commonwealth status despite the United States's statements to the international community concerning Puerto Rico.

* * *

E.   THE CURRENT STATUS OF PUERTO RICANS

Bearing in mind the status of Puerto Rico as defined by the *Insular Cases*, *Balzac*, and subsequent developments, consider the following cases. How has Congress treated United States citizens from Puerto Rico?

CALIFANO v. TORRES
435 U.S. 1 (1978).

PER CURIAM.

Certain benefits under the Social Security Act, as amended in 1972, are payable only to residents of the United States, defined as the 50 States and the District of Columbia. The District Court for the District of Puerto Rico held in these cases that this geographic limitation is unconstitutional as applied to persons who upon moving to Puerto Rico lost the benefits to which they were entitled while residing in the United States. The Secretary of Health, Education, and Welfare, responsible for the administration of the Social Security Act, has appealed.

One of the 1972 amendments to the Social Security Act created a uniform program, known as the Supplemental Security Income (SSI) program, for aid to qualified aged, blind, and disabled persons. * * *

The exclusion of Puerto Rico in the amended program is apparent in the definitional section. Section 1611(f) of the Act * * * states that no individual is eligible for benefits during any month in which he or she is outside the United States. The Act defines "the United States" as "the 50 States and the District of Columbia." The repeal of the pre-existing programs did not apply to Puerto Rico. Thus persons in Puerto Rico are not eligible to receive SSI benefits, but are eligible to receive benefits under the pre-existing programs. [The SSI benefits are significantly larger.]

Appellee Torres received SSI benefits while residing in Connecticut; the benefits were discontinued when he moved to Puerto Rico. Similarly, appellees Colon and Vega received benefits as residents of Massachusetts and New Jersey, respectively, but lost them on moving to Puerto Rico.

Torres filed a complaint in the District Court of Puerto Rico claiming that the exclusion of Puerto Rico from the SSI program was unconstitutional, and a three-judge court was convened to adjudicate the suit. Viewing the geographic limitations in the law as an interference with the constitutional right of residents of the 50 States and the District of Columbia to travel, the court searched for a compelling governmental interest to justify such interference. Finding none, the court held [the statutes] unconstitutional as applied to Torres. *Torres v. Mathews*, 426 F. Supp. 1106.[4] Soon after that decision, appellees Colon and Vega also sued in the Puerto Rico District Court. Relying on the *Torres* decision, a single judge enjoined the Social Security Administration from discontinuing their SSI benefits on the basis of their change of residency to Puerto Rico.

In *Shapiro v. Thompson*, 394 U.S. 618 (1969) and *Memorial Hospital v. Maricopa County*, 415 U.S. 250 (1974), this Court held that laws prohibiting newly arrived residents in a State or county from receiving the same vital benefits as other residents unconstitutionally burdened the right of interstate travel. As the Court said in *Memorial Hospital*, "the right of interstate travel must be seen as insuring new residents the same right to vital governmental benefits and privileges in the States to which they migrate as are enjoyed by other residents." *Id.* at 261.

In the present cases the District Court altogether transposed that proposition. It held that the Constitution requires that a person who travels to Puerto Rico must be given benefits superior to those enjoyed by other residents of Puerto Rico if the newcomer enjoyed those benefits in the State from which he came. This Court has never held that the constitutional right to travel embraces any such doctrine, and we decline to do so now. Such a doctrine would apply with equal force to any

---

4. The complaint had also relied on the equal protection component of the Due Process Clause of the Fifth Amendment in attacking the exclusion of Puerto Rico from the SSI program. Acceptance of that claim would have meant that all otherwise qualified persons in Puerto Rico are entitled to SSI benefits, not just those who received such benefits before moving to Puerto Rico. But the District Court apparently acknowl-edged that Congress has the power to treat Puerto Rico differently, and that every federal program does not have to be extended to it. Puerto Rico has a relationship to the United States "that has no parallel in our history." *Examining Board v. Flores de Otero*, 426 U.S. 572, 596 (1976). Cf. *Balzac v. Porto Rico*, 258 U.S. 298 (1922); *Dorr v. United States*, 195 U.S. 138 (1904); *Downes v. Bidwell*, 182 U.S. 244 (1901). * * *

benefits a State might provide for its residents, and would require a State to continue to pay those benefits indefinitely to any persons who had once resided there. And the broader implications of such a doctrine in other areas of substantive law would bid fair to destroy the independent power of each State under our Constitution to enact laws uniformly applicable to all of its residents.

If there ever could be a case where a person who has moved from one State to another might be entitled to invoke the law of the State from which he came as a corollary of his constitutional right to travel, this is surely not it. For we deal here with a constitutional attack upon a law providing for governmental payments of monetary benefits. Such a statute "is entitled to a strong presumption of constitutionality." "So long as its judgments are rational, and not invidious, the legislature's efforts to tackle the problems of the poor and the needy are not subject to a constitutional straitjacket." *Jefferson v. Hackney*, 406 U.S. 535, 546 (1972).[7]

The judgments are reversed.

JUSTICE BRENNAN would affirm.

JUSTICE MARSHALL would note probable jurisdiction and set these cases for oral argument.

HARRIS v. ROSARIO

446 U.S. 651 (1980).

PER CURIAM.

The Aid to Families with Dependent Children program (AFDC) provides federal financial assistance to States and Territories to aid families with needy dependent children. Puerto Rico receives less assistance than do the States. Appellees, AFDC recipients residing in Puerto Rico, filed this class action against the Secretary of Health, Education, and Welfare (now the Secretary of Health and Human Services) in March 1977 in the United States District Court for the District of Puerto Rico; they challenged the constitutionality of 42 U.S.C.A. §§ 1308 and 1396d(b), claiming successfully that the lower level of AFDC reimbursement provided to Puerto Rico violates the Fifth Amendment's equal protection guarantee.

We disagree. Congress, which is empowered under the Territory Clause of the Constitution, U.S.Const., Art. IV, § 3, cl. 2, to "make all needful Rules and Regulations respecting the Territory ... belonging to the United States," may treat Puerto Rico differently from States so long as there is a rational basis for its actions. In *Califano v. Torres*, 435 U.S. 1 (1978) (*per curiam*), we concluded that a similar statutory classification was rationally grounded on three factors: Puerto Rican residents do not contribute to the federal treasury; the cost of treating

---

7. At least three reasons have been advanced to explain the exclusion of persons in Puerto Rico from the SSI program. First, because of the unique tax status of Puerto Rico, its residents do not contribute to the public treasury. Second, the cost of including Puerto Rico would be extremely great— an estimated $300 million per year. Third, inclusion in the SSI program might seriously disrupt the Puerto Rican economy. * * *

Puerto Rico as a State under the statute would be high; and greater benefits could disrupt the Puerto Rican economy. These same considerations are forwarded here in support of §§ 1308 and 1396d(b)* and we see no reason to depart from our conclusion in *Torres* that they suffice to form a rational basis for the challenged statutory classification.

We reverse.

JUSTICE BRENNAN and JUSTICE BLACKMUN, not now being persuaded that the Court's summary disposition in *Califano v. Torres*, 435 U.S. 1 (1978), so clearly controls this case, would note probable jurisdiction and set the case for oral argument.

JUSTICE MARSHALL, dissenting.

The Court today rushes to resolve important legal issues without full briefing or oral argument. The sole authority cited for the majority's result is another summary decision by this Court. The need for such haste is unclear. The dangers of such decisionmaking are clear, however, as the Court's analysis is, in my view, ill-conceived in at least two respects.

The first question that merits plenary attention is whether Congress, acting pursuant to the Territory Clause of the Constitution, U.S. Const., Art. IV, § 3, cl. 2, "may treat Puerto Rico differently from States so long as there is a rational basis for its actions." No authority is cited for this proposition. Our prior decisions do not support such a broad statement.

It is important to remember at the outset that Puerto Ricans are United States citizens and that different treatment to Puerto Rico under AFDC may well affect the benefits paid to these citizens. While some early opinions of this Court suggested that various protections of the Constitution do not apply to Puerto Rico, see, *e.g. Downes v. Bidwell*, 182 U.S. 244 (1901); *Balzac v. Porto Rico*, 258 U.S. 298 (1922), the present validity of those decisions is questionable. We have already held that Puerto Rico is subject to the Due Process Clause of either the Fifth or Fourteenth Amendment and the equal protection guarantee of either the Fifth or the Fourteenth Amendment. The Fourth Amendment is also fully applicable to Puerto Rico, either directly or by operation of the Fourteenth Amendment. At least four Members of this Court are of the view that all provisions of the Bill of Rights apply to Puerto Rico.

Despite these precedents, the Court suggests today, without benefit of briefing or argument, that Congress needs only a rational basis to support less beneficial treatment for Puerto Rico, and the citizens residing there, than is provided to the States and citizens residing in the States. Heightened scrutiny under the equal protection component of the Fifth Amendment, the Court concludes, is simply unavailable to protect Puerto Rico or the citizens who reside there from discriminatory legislation, as long as Congress acts pursuant to the Territory Clause. Such a

---

* For example, the Secretary estimates that the additional cost of treating Puerto Rico as a State for AFDC purposes alone would be approximately $30 million per year, and, if the decision below were to apply equally to various other reimbursement programs under the Social Security Act, the total annual cost could exceed $240 million.

proposition surely warrants the full attention of this Court before it is made part of our constitutional jurisprudence.

Califano v. Torres, 435 U.S. 1 (1978) (*per curiam*), the only authority upon which the majority relies, does not stand for the proposition the Court espouses today. * * * While the plaintiffs in that case had also challenged the provision on equal protection grounds, the District Court relied entirely on the right to travel, and therefore no equal protection question was before this Court. The Court merely referred to the equal protection claim briefly in a footnote. * * * Observing that Puerto Rico's relationship with the United States was unique, the Court simply noted that the District Court had "apparently acknowledged that Congress has the power to treat Puerto Rico differently, and that every federal program does not have to be extended to it." That Puerto Rico has an unparalleled relationship with the United States does not lead ineluctably to the legal principle asserted here. At most, reading more into that single footnote of dictum than it deserves, *Califano v. Torres* may suggest that under the equal protection component of the Due Process Clause of the Fifth Amendment, Puerto Rico may be treated differently from the States if there is a rational basis for the discrimination when Congress enacts a law providing for governmental payments of monetary benefits. That is a more limited view than is asserted in this case, but even that position should be reached only after oral argument and full briefing.

I also object to the Court's reliance on the effect greater benefits could have on the Puerto Rican economy. This rationale has troubling overtones. It suggests that programs designed to help the poor should be less fully applied in those areas where the need may be the greatest, simply because otherwise the relative poverty of recipients compared to other persons in the same geographic area will somehow be upset. Similarly, reliance on the fear of disrupting the Puerto Rican economy implies that Congress intended to preserve or even strengthen the comparative economic position of the States vis-a-vis Puerto Rico. Under this theory, those geographic units of the country which have the strongest economies presumably would get the most financial aid from the Federal Government since those units would be the least likely to be "disrupted." Such an approach to a financial assistance program is not so clearly rational as the Court suggests, and there is no citation by the Court to any suggestion in the legislative history that Congress had these economic concerns in mind when it passed the portion of the AFDC program presently being challenged. Nor does appellant refer to any evidence in the record supporting the notion that such a speculative fear of economic disruption is warranted. In my view it is by no means clear that the discrimination at issue here could survive scrutiny under even a deferential equal protection standard.

Ultimately this case raises the serious issue of the relationship of Puerto Rico, and the United States citizens who reside there, to the Constitution. An issue of this magnitude deserves far more careful attention than it has received in *Califano v. Torres* and in the present case. I would note probable jurisdiction and set the case for oral argument. Accordingly, I dissent from the Court's summary disposition.

Notes and Questions

1.   Consider the significance of the Court's disposition of these important issues in brief *per curiam* opinions, together with the District Court decision that Puerto Ricans resident on the island are ineligible to vote for President and Vice President. Do the Courts and Congress treat the people of Puerto Rico fairly? Do the issues presented justify more thorough consideration, and possible reconsideration by Congress? Why has that not happened?

2.   Does the Court's use of the permissive rational basis standard of review in reviewing the unequal treatment of Puerto Rican residents by Congress make sense? How can Congress treat an entire group of people defined by Puerto Rican ancestry less generously and differently from other Americans? The Court has held that classifications based on national origin will be subject to strict scrutiny. See *Hernandez v. Texas*, 347 U.S. 475 (1954). Cf. *Korematsu v. United States*, 323 U.S. 214 (1944); *Hernandez v. New York*, 500 U.S. 352, 371 (1991). Is it tolerable under equal protection principles for Congress to treat Puerto Ricans less favorably than other Americans?

3.   If you were Puerto Rican, living on the island, what would you do? What are your choices in order to get representation?

SECTION 3.   CURRENT ISSUES AND RACISM AGAINST LATINOS/AS

BERTA ESPERANZA HERNÁNDEZ–TRUYOL

Building Bridges—Latinas and Latinos at the Crossroads:
Realities, Rhetoric and Replacement
25 Colum. Hum. Rts. L. Rev. 369, 404–412, 423–431 (1994).*

A critical factor that repeatedly is ignored by lumping persons in a generic "hispanic" category that purports to constitute latinas/os is the diversity of the latina/o population. For example, the federal forms that request information about a person's racial and ethnic identity usually provide the following options: black (not of hispanic origin); white (not of hispanic origin); hispanic. As the forms seek information in the conjunctive, implicitly recognizing that ethnic identity and racial identity are two separate, co-existing traits, it is particularly ironic that latinas/os are deprived of the opportunity to identify as ethnic, *i.e.*, latina/o, including subcategory identification such as Cuban, Mexican, Puerto Rican, as well as to identify by race. As multiple-layered selves we are denied part of our personhood when we have to deny part of who we are. Our experience simply cannot be sanitized to fit a mold in the creation of which we were not considered.

Two specific points are noteworthy with respect to the consequences of the existing classification scheme. First, and of critical importance, the disjunctive nature of the categories with which latinas/os are expected to identify collapses and simultaneously excises latina/o ethnicity from the black or white races and places latinas/os as separate from both. Second, such myopic categorization not only proscribes latinas/os from claiming their racial identification, be it black or white, but also, by virtue of listing only black and white as "not of hispanic origin," renders invisible latinas/os of other racial and ethnic backgrounds such as Asian, Indios, Mestizos and so on.

Certainly, the insensitivity and the under-and over-inclusiveness of any generic latina/o categorization, the invisibility in which it results, and the homogenization it engenders further the myth of a monolithic latina/o identity. What is tragically wrong with this picture is that latinas/os, in reality, are a racially and culturally diverse group. * * *

This schism in which latinas/os fall is everywhere. Language is harmful when it stereotypes in a destructive and isolating way. The poisonous nature of this "you do not belong there" is exacerbated because it comes not in terms of a dichotomy of black-white relations but rather in terms that touch deeply on latinas/os' multi-dimensionality. Latinas/os are continually bombarded with the "you are not *us*" message. The myth tells latinas/os: you are not white, not black, not Asian, not Indian. The reality is that latinas/os can be *all* of the above.

The result of the complete "otherness" perspective is a silencing of latina/o voices by all, a total banishment. On the one hand, so-called NLWs [non-Latina/o whites] perceive latinas/os as "minorities"—the "other," an "other" who speaks a different language to boot.

On the other hand, non-latina/o blacks see latinas/os as "not black," and perhaps even as white. Professor Derrick Bell clearly articulated this view in a recent address in which he noted that "there is every reason to believe that Spanish-speaking ... immigrants, *like their European predecessors*, will move beyond the bottom of the society and leave blacks in the role society has designated for them...." Certainly Professor Bell does not, as he cannot, believe the myth that all latinas/os are of European heritage or that they are all white. The history of intermarriages in, for example, the Southwestern states, Puerto Rico, Cuba, and the Republica Dominicana attest otherwise. It is plain that there are many latinas/os of African heritage, Asian heritage and Indian heritage. Nor can, or should, recent latina/o immigrants be likened to "their European predecessors" even if they are of distant European heritage. * * * [D]ramatically different issues are at play today than there existed in the colonial period or the earlier twentieth century European immigrations. Nevertheless, the perception exists that because latinas/os are not black, there is a dissonance, a lack of sharing of issues and concerns between latinas/os and blacks. In reality, this is a great misperception. For example, employment and education are two major concerns shared by the black and the latina/o communities. Nevertheless, the existence of the misperception as a reality—the view that these communities do not share issues and concerns—strengthens oppositionality.

A June 27, 1993 *New York Times* article provides a specific example of the tensions engendered by the scripting of latinas/os as adversaries of blacks. The piece, entitled *As Hispanic Presence Grows, So Does Black Anger* noted the growing resentment of blacks in Miami against latinas/os who "take their jobs." The article suggests that the tension is aggravated as the city's latina/o population grows to dominate the economic and political life. As one black woman interviewed put it, "[t]hey are taking over, and I am a victim of that...." This echoes the complaints of her white counterparts about the evils of "affirmative action programs" (code: "minorities" meaning blacks *and* latinas/os) because they take jobs away from deserving whites.

This rivalry perspective can create differences that do not exist, exacerbate differences that might exist, and eclipse the existence of similarities and shared concerns. The created images reinforce the vision of latinas/os as foes of both whites and blacks.

The tragic flaw of the approach that drives the normative-driven oppositionality is that rather than trying to find a novel solution for a new dilemma—the existence of peoples in this society who do not fit squarely into the dichotomous black-white model's structure—it merely seeks to utilize the pre-existing model. The black or white model does not fit the latinas/os, just like the black or woman model does not fit the black woman. Simply to throw latinas/os into the pot and stir is simplistic, inappropriate, and naive.

Latinas/os bring different issues into play than the black-white polarity that gave rise to the civil rights movement. Here slavery is not the issue; that was theoretically solved by the Thirteenth Amendment. Nor is the problem the consequence of slavery, a problem that still lacks a solution. Nor is formal equal access to public accommodations, housing, employment and education the issue. Technically, the 1964 Civil Rights Act crafted the tools to solve that problem, although making these wonderful paper rights a reality is a struggle latinas/os share with the black community. On the other hand, latinas/os need to grapple with the present-day issues of language and immigration. Latinas/os must do battle in order to work—either prove you have a green card when you are a citizen/legal resident or find a way to live without one and still be labelled lazy or a welfare cheat. Additionally, we must face the problems caused by the inhuman conditions in which migrant workers live as well as the problems that result from the creation of an uninsured, under-class of persons who provide domestic help, such as nannies, housekeepers, and gardeners. To be sure, this is not an issue unique to latinas/os as we may well see analogous problems arise among some of the new groups of immigrants to the United States; so much the more important it becomes that latinas/os who have a long history in this country start working on building bridges.

Latinas/os' racial diversity also presents a novel issue, often unspoken, certainly as unresolved and complicated as the dilemma involving the intersection of race and gender. Their racial diversity injects yet another layer to the essentialism/intersectionality discourse. Latina/o blacks, for example Afro–Cubans, may identify more with the racially mixed Cuban population than with racially homogeneous (but culturally diverse) English-speaking black population. Rather than identify solely on the basis of race, Afro–Cubans also identify with their linguistic and cultural heritage. This identification, however does not, as it can not, render Afro–Cubans "not black."

Yet another angle to latinas/os as "others" is that some appear "white" in the "Anglo" sense. These particular traits inform some latinas/os of what it feels to look like the privileged normativa/o. Of course, this "white look" does not make one bit of difference if the initial interaction is on paper, as are most applications for employment or to institutions of higher education. Given that there appears to be a very clear image in our society of what a latina/o looks like, such initial paper contact may well conjure up the stereotypic images of what an applicant should look like. * * *

These are particularly difficult issues without easy answers. If the law has difficulty understanding the concept of a "blackwoman," what can it do with a "blackCubanwoman" concept? Or a *Puertorriqueña trigueña*? By restricting analysis to a single-trait approach, the law isolates and disempowers latinas/os by creating a landscape where both NLWs and (non-latina/o) blacks see latinas/os as "other." Such an exclusionary approach misinforms as it induces misperceptions, creates expectations, and generates images that are, at best incomplete and at worst false. Yet the myth—the sham images—proliferates. Latinas/os are reduced to race-less homogeneity belonging nowhere. The reality of a culturally and racially diverse people is invisible.

* * *

JUDGE ORDERS AMARILLO MOTHER TO SPEAK ENGLISH TO DAUGHTER: NOT DOING SO IS "ABUSING" CHILD, HE RULES IN CUSTODY CASE

by Diane Jennings.
Dallas Morning News (August 29, 1995).*

A West Texas judge has created an uproar in Amarillo by ordering a bilingual mother to speak English to her child to better prepare her for school.

To do otherwise is "abusing that child" and "relegating her to the position of a housemaid," state District Judge Samuel C. Kiser told the naturalized U.S. citizen, according to the transcript of a child custody hearing this summer.

"When he was telling me I was raising a housemaid, I felt like I was out of Earth, like I was floating in space," the mother, Martha Laureano, said Monday afternoon.

Ms. Laureano, 29, was born in Mexico and moved to the United States at age 14.

The office clerk is fluent in Spanish and English. She wanted her five children to be bilingual, and when her 5–year-old daughter was younger, she and her then-husband, Timothy Garcia, agreed that he would speak English to her and she would speak Spanish, Ms. Laureano said.

The couple have divorced, and in a child custody hearing in which Mr. Garcia was seeking unsupervised visits with his daughter, he complained that the only English the child was learning was what he taught her.

Neither Mr. Garcia nor his attorney could be reached for comment Monday. Earlier, Mr. Garcia defended Judge Kiser.

"He was fair. He was fair to both of us," he said.

Judge Kiser also could not be reached for comment Monday.

At the hearing, Judge Kiser ordered unsupervised visits with the child and said, "The child will only hear English."

The judge's decision offended people throughout Amarillo, said Dr. Ramon Godoy, publisher of *El Mensajero*, a weekly Spanish-language newspaper. They are insulted by the reference to domestic workers, he said, and afraid that anyone who speaks another language is open to child abuse charges.

"What the judge is telling us is it's not all right to speak any language [other than English] at home," Dr. Godoy said.

Judge Kiser based his remarks on the need to prepare the child to compete in a primarily English-speaking educational system.

"If she starts first grade with the other children and cannot even speak the language that the teachers and the other children speak, and she's a full-blood American citizen, you're abusing that child," he said, according to the transcript.

"You start speaking English to that child because if she doesn't do good in school, then I can remove her because it's not in her best interest to be ignorant," he told Ms. Laureano.

In the transcript, the judge said the girl "is not bilingual. She only speaks Spanish...."

Ms. Laureano said the 5–year-old "is not completely bilingual, but I would say she understands most of the English." Her four school-age children do well in school, she said.

Mark Tabaoda, Ms. Laureano's new attorney, who said he speaks Spanish to his children, said he will ask for a new trial on the basis of "prejudice on the part of the judge" or appeal the decision.

In a written order, the judge "toned down," Mr. Tabaoda said, "saying that the mother will make every effort to make sure the child speaks the English language."

Judge Kiser studied in South America as a college student and has said he occasionally speaks Spanish to his children.

Although Mr. Tabaoda said he is afraid that his client may be held in contempt, Ms. Laureano said she is still speaking Spanish to her children.

"That's just natural," she said. "If I was to speak all English, I would be forcing myself."

Luis de la Garza, president of Grupo de Apoyo a Inmigrantes Latino Americano, a Dallas support organization for immigrants, said his group was contacted about the incident by Dr. Godoy and plans to send a delegation to Amarillo soon to demonstrate its support for Ms. Laureano and Amarillo's Hispanic residents.

"We're going to try to speak to the judge and see what's going on there," Mr. de la Garza said.

He said the judge's actions and comments are part of what he called a national anti-immigration sentiment that some say has been growing since the passage of Proposition 187 in California last year. The measure, which has yet to be implemented because of legal challenges, would restrict access to certain benefits by undocumented immigrants.

Mauro E. Mujica, chairman of the board of U.S. English, in Washington D.C., said, "While I certainly agree with the judge that it would be better for the child to learn English, we don't advocate becoming involved in personal matters."

"I think it would be the same case if they (the child's parents) had a problem with religion," Mr. Mujica said. "If, say, a mother wants to raise a child Jewish and a judge is telling the mother to also teach the kid the Catholic religion, I would have the same problem."

Mr. Mujica said his organization is interested in trying to get English adopted as the official language of government, but not in private matters.

LOPEZ v. UNION TANK CAR CO.

8 F. Supp.2d 832 (N.D.Ind.1998).

MOODY, DISTRICT JUDGE.

* * *

Plaintiff Robert Lopez was 46 years old at the time of his discharge on July 12, 1995. Lopez is of Hispanic descent, and suffers from polio and post-polio syndrome. At the time of his discharge Lopez was employed as a "layout draftsman/CAD operator" in Union's drafting department. Lopez had been employed by Union since October, 1977.

The person with overall supervisory responsibility for the drafting department is known as the Chief Draftsman. Beginning March 3, 1992, the Chief Draftsman was Dennis Chansler. According to Union, the Chief Draftsman is the "sole supervisor" in the drafting department and the only individual authorized to make hiring/firing decisions.

* * *

On [Lopez's employment] evaluation covering 1992, prepared by group leader Richard Benak, Lopez was rated 4.0 on a five-point scale. The form describes a 4.0 rating as "SUPERIOR (Far above expected performance.)" Prior to preparing that evaluation, Benak recommended to Chansler that Lopez be promoted to the designer position, but Chansler disagreed. On his evaluation covering 1993, also prepared by Benak, Lopez was rated 3.7. Benak had rated Lopez 3.96, but Chansler modified the rating. A 3.0 rating is "COMMENDABLE" (Achieves all key responsibilities.)

Lopez worked for Benak during the first six months of 1994, then for other group leaders. Chansler prepared Lopez's evaluation for 1994, and rated Lopez 2.82. A rating of 2.0 is "MARGINAL" (Performance acceptable but should improve).

In preparing the evaluation for 1994, Chansler deviated from his normal practice by not soliciting input from Benak. According to Chansler, he did not consult with Benak at least in part because Chansler believed that Benak had rated Lopez too highly in the past. The group leaders Chansler did consult with included Carl Carney, who regularly referred to Lopez as a "wetback" and who, in a June 1994 meeting including Chansler and other group leaders, announced "no spics allowed" when he entered the room and observed that Lopez was present.

On March 14, 1995, Lopez sent a memo to Philip Daum, Union's Chief Engineer, and Benjamin Damiani, Union's Vice President of Engineering, complaining that Chansler's evaluation was "not objective," "demeaning," and "meant to defame my ability as a layout draftsman." Daum and Lopez met and discussed the review on March 20, 1995. On March 21, 1995, a confidential memo written by Daum detailing "plans to achieve the Plant 1 staffing reduction goals" recommended reducing the drafting staff by two, including Lopez.

On April 8, 1995, Lopez filed a charge with the Equal Employment Opportunity Commission (EEOC) concerning Chansler's evaluation covering 1994. In or around May 1995, Chansler and Daum discussed reducing the size of the drafting department. Chansler decided to discharge four people, and identified eight candidates for discharge, one of whom was Lopez. Although Lopez initially was not one of the more likely candidates, by late May Chansler had decided to discharge Lopez. * * *

Lopez complained to Benak about harassing conduct directed at him by group leaders and other employees. Benak witnessed harassment of Lopez, including slurs such as "cockroach," "fucking Mexican" and "fucking spic." Benak observed numerous occasions when Lopez was criticized about his physical handicap, including comments about his arms. * * *

A plaintiff attempting to prove discrimination based upon a racially or ethnically hostile environment must establish not only the existence of harassment so severe and pervasive that it alters the terms and conditions of plaintiff's employment, from both a subjective and objective view, but also that plaintiff's employer acted negligently with respect to the harassment; that is, knew or should have known that it was taking place, and failed to take reasonable remedial action.

Union's motion for summary judgment is based on one ground: that because Lopez's supervisor, Dennis Chansler, denies any knowledge that "any employee made any comments regarding Plaintiff's age, disability and/or race/national origin," and Lopez admits that he never reported any derogatory comments to Chansler, Union had no knowledge of harassment and so cannot be found negligent in failing to act remedially.

* * *

Nevertheless, the court believes that Lopez has demonstrated that a question of fact exists whether Chansler had knowledge that Lopez's co-employees verbally abused Lopez. First, Lopez testified in his deposition that in 1987 or 1988 Chansler himself asked Lopez if he "was good at picking lettuce."[4] Although this occurred before Chansler was promoted to the position where he had hiring/firing authority over Lopez, it occurred after Chansler became Lopez's group leader, a position where he had some authority to direct Lopez's work activities. This comment, in and of itself, is evidence of a hostile environment.

But more importantly, the "lettuce-picking" comment considered in conjunction with other evidence casts doubt on the credibility of Chansler's denial that he was not aware of any derogatory comments made by Lopez's co-employees. For example, Lopez also testified that at a meeting of group leaders called by Chansler after Chansler's promotion, a group leader named Carl Carney arrived late for the meeting and announced "no spics allowed." Lopez "waited for Mr. Chansler to say something. He did not say a word." In addition, before Chansler was promoted and obtained his own office, he worked "out in the open" with the others making it possible for him to hear any one of a number of racial slurs and other derogatory comments directed at Lopez.

Viewing the evidence in the light most favorable to Lopez, as the court must, there is a question of fact whether Chansler was aware of harassment directed at Lopez. As a result, Union is not entitled to summary judgment on this aspect of Lopez's suit.

* * *

MACHADO v. GOODMAN MANUF. CO.

10 F. Supp. 2d 709 (1997).

ATLAS, DISTRICT JUDGE.

Plaintiff Eduardo Machado (Plaintiff) has brought this action against Defendants Goodman Manufacturing Company, L.P. and Goodman Holding Company, alleging that he was discriminated against on account of his national origin in violation of Title VII of the Civil Rights Act of 1964 * * *.

Eduardo Machado began working for Defendant Goodman Manufacturing Company, L.P., a manufacturer and distributor of air conditioning equipment, in January 1991 in the position of Regional Sales Manager for Mexico, Latin America, and the Caribbean. For four years, Plaintiff remained in this position, working out of his home in Miami, Florida.

---

4. Although Union's attorney expressed surprise in the deposition that Lopez perceived this comment to be related to his national origin, the court believes that anyone with any awareness of César Chávez and the plight of migrant farmworkers, and who was not raised in a cocoon, would understand the comment to be directed at Lopez's national origin.

During this period, while he was based in Miami, Plaintiff claims that he was never subject to discriminatory treatment in connection with his employment.

In March 1995, Plaintiff was promoted to the position of Vice President of International Sales, for which he was relocated to Houston, Texas. After his relocation, Plaintiff claims that he began to suffer discrimination on the basis of his national origin, Cuban. In particular, Plaintiff asserts that he was subject to discriminatory remarks by another Goodman Vice President, Barry Watson, and that Watson's and other Goodman executives' discriminatory treatment of him created a hostile environment that was severe enough to compel Plaintiff ultimately to resign his position.

Plaintiff claims that his work environment became so hostile that, in June 1995, he sought and received permission from Thomas Burkett, Goodman's President and CEO, to return to Miami to perform his duties as Vice President from his home office. However, even after Plaintiff returned to Miami, he claims that Watson, who was apparently at that point made Plaintiff's supervisor, continued his discriminatory harassing behavior which interfered with Plaintiff's ability to perform his job. After complaining fruitlessly to Burkett of Watson's behavior, Plaintiff resigned in August 1995. Subsequently, Plaintiff brought this action alleging that he was subject to national origin discrimination that led to his constructive discharge.

* * *

First, Plaintiff complains about his treatment in connection with his promotion to Vice President of International Sales. For instance, he testifies that although he had been promised the position by the outgoing Vice President, [Burkett] was hesitant about placing Plaintiff in that position. Plaintiff submits evidence that Burkett advertised for the position in trade journals and made Plaintiff go through an interview in order to obtain the position. After attaining the position, Plaintiff states that he received less compensation than his predecessor, who was not Cuban, and was given a substandard office.

Plaintiff contends that after his move to Houston, he "was faced with fellow VPs who were disrespectful, undermined his authority, embarrassed him in front of clients, and made discriminatory comments regarding his national origin." For example, Plaintiff testifies that when he was preparing for a business trip to Asia to determine what new products the company should buy, another Vice President, Peter Alexander, instructed him simply to "play dumb" and bring back brochures for the other managers to consider. In Thailand, one of the companies Plaintiff was scheduled to visit informed Plaintiff that, prior to his arrival, the company had received a phone call telling them that Plaintiff was not the decision maker for his company and that he was only there to look over equipment and pick up brochures.

Plaintiff submits evidence of several overtly discriminatory remarks made to him by Watson in front of other employees. On three separate occasions, Watson told Plaintiff that he did not want Cubans living in his neighborhood.[3]

In May 1995, Plaintiff tendered a letter of resignation to Burkett, informing Burkett of the discriminatory treatment he believed he had experienced, including Watson's remarks about not wanting Cubans in his neighborhood.[4]

Burkett convinced Plaintiff not to resign and initiated an investigation into the alleged discriminatory comments by Watson. Defendants claim that Burkett took prompt remedial action, including threatening Watson with termination if his discriminatory conduct continued. * * *

After Watson was reprimanded, Plaintiff claims that Watson made another offensive remark referring to Plaintiff's national origin[5] and that Watson continued to harass him by interfering with his ability to perform his job and slighting him on various occasions in front of clients.[6]

Because he found his work environment so hostile, Plaintiff sought and received permission from Burkett in June 1995 to return to Miami to perform his duties as Vice President from his home office. Despite Plaintiff's problems with Watson, Burkett assigned Watson to supervise Plaintiff after his return to Miami. * * *

3. Plaintiff testifies, "As I was looking for homes in the Houston area and getting information from my coworkers about different neighborhoods, [Watson] would jump into the conversation and say he did not want Cubans in his neighborhood." "He said, 'I don't want Cubans in my neighborhood, and I'm not going to tell you where I live.'" One of Machado's co-workers, James Plant, testifies that Watson told Machado that a subdivision they were discussing "didn't allow Cubans." Another co-worker wrote the following statement describing a similar incident:

> Ed Machado, Barry Watson and I were in my office discussing Ed's relocation to Houston. Ed inquired about the Woodlands and I provided some general information about housing, schools, etc. I told Ed that he should come out to the area and see what is available. I also told Ed that if he was considering a move to the north side of Houston there were other nice areas he should check such as Barry's subdivision. I asked Barry if he was aware of any houses for sale or lease in his neighborhood. Barry responded that he didn't want Cubans moving into the neighborhood. Barry then left my office. Ed shook his head and then left. Ed was very upset by Barry's remark, which I also perceived Barry's statement to be an ethnic slur.

4. In this letter, Plaintiff wrote the following:

> [I]t appears that the position [of Vice President] was in title only. In reality, not only have I not been allowed to make the decisions that the position calls for, I am no longer allowed the decision making authority of my previous position. To make matters worse, I have been looked down upon and treated with disrespect. I have had senior personnel make derogatory remarks such as "I don't want Cubans living in my neighborhood" and have been told to "shush" in the middle of an office meeting. Furthermore, prior to my departure to the Far East, I was told to "play dumb." During my visit in Thailand, I was told by the companies I visited that they were informed that I was not the decision maker and that I was only there to look over equipment and pick up brochures. As someone who has dedicated his whole life to this industry, this situation was not only very embarrassing, but extremely degrading.

5. Plaintiff testifies that at a dinner with clients at which Burkett was present, during a conversation about Cuban baseball, Watson remarked, "Don't talk about Cubans. Ed gets upset."

6. For example, Plaintiff testifies that Watson embarrassed him at a meeting with clients; Watson was sitting next to Plaintiff, but when photos of the client's product were being passed around the table, Watson reached around Plaintiff and passed the photos to the person sitting on the other side of Plaintiff. On another occasion, Watson agreed to attend a business lunch with Plaintiff and some clients, but Watson did not show up.

After his move back to Miami, Plaintiff testifies that Watson continued to humiliate him and interfere with Plaintiff's ability to perform his job. For example, Plaintiff testifies that Watson repeatedly intercepted faxes and international correspondence to and from Plaintiff and responded to letters addressed to Plaintiff. Plaintiff also presents evidence that Watson denied Plaintiff's expense report, in which Plaintiff sought reimbursement for expenses he incurred equipping his home office; Plaintiff claims that the company had reimbursed several non-Hispanic employees for such expenses. Watson also warned Plaintiff that his meal expenses for entertaining clients "far exceeded" the company limit; Plaintiff has submitted evidence that his expenses were no greater than those claimed by other employees, but that other employees did not receive the warning Watson gave Plaintiff.

Plaintiff complained repeatedly to Burkett about Watson's behavior, but Burkett dismissed his complaints as petty and denied that Watson's behavior continued to be discriminatory or prejudiced. Because he felt that, if he remained with the company, Watson would continue to subject him to a hostile work environment and Burkett would not take action to stop Watson's discriminatory behavior, in August 1995, Plaintiff resigned from the company. * * *

[The court denied the defendant's motion for summary judgment on the claim of harassment because of national origin, but granted it on the constructive discharge claim.]

Notes and Questions

1.   What view of Mexicans does the judge seem to hold when he concludes that teaching a child Spanish in the home "would relegate her to the position of a housemaid"? How widely shared is this view of Mexicans' role in society?

2.   Why is bilingualism seen as an impediment to success? Why is more knowledge treated as less? Note that speaking French—or English with British or French accents—confers high status. Why the difference? For more discussion of accent discrimination, see Chapter 7, *infra*.

3.   Do the judge's comments about the Spanish language suggest something about how society views the Spanish language? Would the comments have been the same if this mother were teaching her daughter French or Japanese? What does this incident teach us about the use of language to racialize Mexican Americans and others?

4.   Note that a "reasonable person" standard is used to consider the severity of harassment and whether a "constructive discharge" occurred. Of what race is the "reasonable person" assumed to be? Is it not likely that a reasonable Mexican American or Cuban American would react very differently to the insults in the preceding cases than a non-Latino White person? Yet who represents the norm of the "reasonable person"?

5.   In the *Machado* case, note that the plaintiff doesn't complain of discrimination initially in Miami, prior to his transfer to Houston. Some Cubans argue that there is no discrimination against Latinos in the United States. Since Miami has such a large Cuban population, is it possible that Cubans may experience little or no discrimination there, only to experience

anti-Latino discrimination once they leave that city? Does this suggest that racism may be, to some extent a regional phenomenon, or at least variable depending on the environment in which one finds oneself? For example, one would not ordinarily be treated in a racist fashion at home, by one's family. But what about the surrounding neighborhood, or the workplace?

6.   Does society differentiate among Latinos/as or merely lump them all together, as Professor Hernández suggests? What are your views of Cubans, Mexicans and Puerto Ricans? How do these views differ from each other? If you have differing views of each group, how do you explain the differences?

7.   What color do you assume members of each of these groups to be? If you view members of these groups differently, to what extent do your views depend on the color you assumed for members of each group? Does color end up being a primary factor in your evaluation of each group?

8.   For analysis of how the concepts of "Americanization," assimilation and the white ethnic immigrant narrative operate to privilege white identity and to exclude Latino/a identity, see Sylvia R. Lazos Vargas, *Deconstructing Homo[geneous] Americanus: The White Ethnic Immigrant Narrative and its Exclusionary Effect*, 72 Tul. L. Rev. 1493 (1998). See also Sylvia R. Lazos Vargas, *Democracy and Inclusion: Reconceptualizing the Role of the Judge in a Pluralist Polity*, 58 Md L. Rev. 150 (1999).

9.   For a comprehensive collection of scholarly articles on Latinos in the United States, see *Latinos in the United States: History, Law and Perspective* (Antoinette Sedillo Lopez ed. 1995). See also *The Latino/a Condition: A Critical Reader* (R. Delgado & J. Stefancic eds. 1998).

Chapter 5

ASIAN AMERICANS

Unlike Blacks, Indians, and Latinos/as, Asian Americans first arrived in the United States as immigrants. This becomes significant because, in addition to the usual sites of racial contestation, such as segregated education, segregated housing, voting and employment discrimination, much of the legal history of racism against Asian Americans is found in immigration law. Furthermore, the Chinese and Japanese governments occasionally played important roles in the destinies of Chinese and Japanese immigrants and Americans. Lastly, the persistent attribution of "foreignness" to Asian Americans is, perhaps, linked to the early discriminatory treatment of Asian peoples under the immigration laws, notwithstanding their subsequent attainment of citizenship.

The people grouped together under the label of "Asian American" are peoples of different national ancestries who differ widely in history, culture, languages and in every way that peoples of various national heritages differ from each other. Indeed, the only features that bring them together are origins somewhere in Asia and the externally-imposed perception that Asians share physical characteristics which allows outsiders to identify them as a "race." These are some of the groups that constitute "Asian Americans:" Chinese, Japanese, Koreans, Filipinos, Asian Indians, and, more recently, Vietnamese, Laotians, and Cambodians.

1990 Census on Composition of Asian American Population:

Asian or Pacific Islander
Asian

Chinese	1,645,472
Filipino	1,406,770
Japanese	847,562
Asian Indian	815,447
Korean	798,849
Vietnamese	614,547
Cambodian	147,411
Hmong	90,082
Laotian	149,014
Thai	91,275
Other Asian	302,209

Pacific Islander
    Polynesian
        Hawaiian   211,014
        Samoan   62,964
        Tongan   17,606
        Other Polynesian   4,561
    Micronesian
        Guamanian   49,345
        Other Micronesian   6,808
    Melanesian   7,195
    Pacific Islander, not specified   5,531

Source: *1990 Census of Population and Housing Summary* Tape File 1C

The following excerpt describes the effects of immigration law in shaping the current population of Asian Americans.

SUCHENG CHAN

Introduction to *Entry Denied: Exclusion and the
Chinese Community in America, 1882–1943*
vii–viii (Sucheng Chan ed. 1991).*

About half the people immigrating to the United States today are from Asia, but historically Asians represented only a tiny fraction of the nation's immigrants. Before 1965, of the more than fifty million people from other lands who came to the United States, Asians numbered only about one million. But since 1965, when Congress reformed the country's immigration laws, approximately five million Asians have arrived as quota and nonquota immigrants and as refugees.

One reason that relatively few Asian immigrants came before 1965 is that four of the major groups—the Chinese, Japanese, Asian Indians, and Filipinos—were each excluded by law two or three decades after their initial arrival. Chinese began coming in sizable numbers during the California gold rush, but as anti-Chinese sentiments and activities increased, Congress passed a series of exclusion laws between 1882 and 1904 to bar Chinese laborers. The manner in which these laws were implemented also made it well-nigh impossible for other occupational groups to enter. Japanese immigration began in 1885 and was curtailed in stages. Under the 1907 Gentlemen's Agreement reached between American and Japanese diplomats, Japan stopped issuing passports to laborers bound for the United States. The same year President Theodore Roosevelt signed Executive Order 589 making it illegal for Japanese with visas to Hawaii, Canada, and Mexico to re-migrate to the continental United States. In 1920, in response to agitation against the entry of "picture brides"—women whose marriage arrangements were facilitated by an exchange of photographs—Japan stopped issuing passports to these female emigrants. Finally, the 1924 Immigration Act, which prohibited "aliens ineligible to citizenship" from immigrating, virtually ended Japanese immigration. (The then-existing U.S. naturalization laws allowed only free white immigrants and people of African ancestry to become naturalized citizens.) Immigrants from India started arriving in 1908 but were barred by a clause in the 1917 Immigration Act denying entry to people living within a triangular area that included most of the Asian continent. Filipinos, whose homeland the United States acquired in 1898 from Spain and who were subsequently categorized as American "nationals," began showing up in numbers in 1909 but were reduced to fifty immigrants a year when Congress promised independence to the Philippines under the terms of the 1934 Tydings—McDuffie Act, thus making them aliens excludable by law.

The 1924 Immigration Act also limited the number of immigrants from central, eastern, and southern Europe—reducing the annual quota for each group to 2 percent of the number counted by the U.S. Census in 1890—but their immigration history was never truncated in the same drastic manner as was that of Asians. Asian immigration history consequently shows more distinct "breaks" than that of Europeans, periodized not so much by social developments within the immigrant communities as by the enactment of exclusion laws.

Notes and Questions

1. Consider the effect of exclusion laws and effective cessation of Asian immigration on the present composition of the population of the United States. How might the country be different, racially, linguistically, and culturally, if the number of Asians had not been legally limited and reduced?

2. As you read through the following materials, consider the importance of the theme of "exclusion," in many areas of life, in the history of Asian Americans in the United States.

SECTION 1.   CHINESE AMERICANS

Chinese laborers began to immigrate to the mainland United States in 1849–50. Initially they arrived as sojourners, hoping to work for three to five years, accumulate wealth, and return home. Largely during the middle and late nineteenth century, approximately 400,000 Chinese immigrants arrived in the United States. Many Chinese left China fleeing internal wars and seeking safety, but most were driven from China because of economic hardship. As news of the California gold rush reached China, fantasies and rumors of the possibility of great wealth in the United States encouraged migration. See Ronald Takaki, *Strangers from a Different Shore* 192–95 (1989).

A. EARLY RACISM AGAINST THE CHINESE

When the Chinese first arrived in California, they were welcomed as productive new members of the community. As the numbers of Chinese immigrants increased, however, Whites began to express increasing resentment against them. The reasons for this resentment were straightforward. As the Chinese were described by one writer:

As a class, [they] were harmless, peaceful and exceedingly industrious; but, as they were remarkably economical and spent little or none of their earnings except for the necessaries of life and this chiefly to merchants of their own nationality, they soon began to provoke the prejudice and ill-will of those who could not see any value in their labor to the country.

Charles J. McClain, *In Search of Equality: The Chinese Struggle Against Discrimination in Nineteenth–Century America* 10 (1994) (quoting Theodore Hittell, *History of California* (1898)). As Professor McClain comments, "In short, they worked too hard (often for less pay than others were willing to accept), saved too much, and spent too little. In addition, they looked and behaved differently from the majority population." McClain, *supra* at 10.

Many early Chinese immigrants worked in California's recently opened gold fields. Early hostility towards Chinese, Mexican, and Latin American miners found its way into statutes that imposed license taxes on all foreign miners. These statutes, enacted in 1852 and 1855, created license fees of $3 per month (subsequently increased to $6 per month) payable by foreign miners. Anyone who lacked a license was denied access to the courts. A "commutation tax," intended to discourage Chinese migration to California, was also enacted. Although Chinese district associations protested these discriminatory legislative burdens, the Chinese were met with more legislative hostility and increasing violence in the mining districts. McClain, *supra* at 12–20. The foreign miners' taxes were enforced with zeal. In 1861, the legislature amended the statute so that all foreigners ineligible to citizenship residing within a mining district would be considered miners for purposes of the tax. Thus Ah Pong, a Chinese laundryman, was convicted and imprisoned for failing to pay the miners' tax. Challenging his conviction through a writ of habeas corpus, however, the court found that application of the statute to Ah Pong "cannot be supported." See *Ex parte Ah Pong*, 19 Cal. 106 (1861).

In 1854, the California Supreme Court dealt a serious blow to the civil rights of Chinese immigrants and inscribed in law the racial prejudice faced by the Chinese when, in *People v. Hall,* the Court decided that Chinese testimony could not be used in a criminal trial against a white defendant.

PEOPLE v. HALL
4 Cal. 399 (1854).

The appellant, a free white citizen of this State, was convicted of murder upon the testimony of Chinese witnesses.

The point involved in this case, is the admissibility of such evidence.

The 394th section of the Act Concerning Civil Cases, provides that no Indian or Negro shall be allowed to testify as a witness in any action or proceeding in which a White person is a party.

The 14th section of the Act of April 16th, 1850, regulating Criminal Proceedings, provides that "No Black or Mulatto person, or Indian, shall be allowed to give evidence in favor of, or against a white man."

The true point at which we are anxious to arrive is, the legal signification of the words, "Black, Mulatto, Indian and White person," and whether the Legislature adopted them as generic terms, or intended to limit their application to specific types of the human species. * * *

At the period from which this legislation dates, those portions of Asia which include India proper, the Eastern Archipelago, and the countries washed by the Chinese waters, as far as then known, were denominated the Indies, from which the inhabitants had derived the generic name of Indians.

Ethnology, at that time, was unknown as a distinct science, or if known, had not reached that high point of perfection which it has since attained by the scientific inquiries and discoveries of the master minds of the last half century. Few speculations had been made with regard to the moral or physical differences between the different races of mankind. These were general in their character, and limited to those visible and palpable variations which could not escape the attention of the most common observer.

The general, or perhaps universal opinion of that day was * * * that there were but three distinct types of the human species, which, in their turn, were subdivided into varieties of tribes. * * *

We have adverted to these speculations [the Court had described its understanding of the migration of Asian peoples across the Bering Strait] for the purpose of showing that the name of Indian, from the time of Columbus to the present day, has been used to designate, not alone the North American Indian, but the whole of the Mongolian race, and that the name, though first applied probably through mistake, was afterwards continued as appropriate on account of the supposed common origin.

That this was the common opinion in the early history of American legislation, cannot be disputed, and, therefore, all legislation upon the subject must have borne relation to that opinion. * * *

It will not be disputed that "White" and "Negro" are generic terms, and refer to two of the great types of mankind. If these, as well as the word "Indian," are not to be regarded as generic terms, including the two great races which they were intended to designate, but only specific, and applying to those whites and Negroes who were inhabitants of this continent at the time of the passage of the Act, the most anomalous consequences would ensue. The European white man who comes here would not be shielded from the testimony of the degraded and demoralized caste, while the Negro, fresh from the coast of Africa, or the Indian of Patagonia, the Kanaka, South Sea Islander, or New Hollander, would be admitted, upon their arrival, to testify against white citizens in our courts of law.

* * *

To argue such a proposition would be an insult to the good sense of the Legislature.

The evident intention of the Act was to throw around the citizen a protection for life and property, which could only be secured by removing him above the corrupting influences of degraded castes.

It can hardly be supposed that any Legislature would attempt this by excluding domestic negroes and Indians, who not unfrequently have correct notions of their obligations to society, and turning loose upon the community the more degraded tribes of the same species, who have nothing in common with us, in language, country or laws.

We have, thus far, considered this subject on the hypothesis that the 14th section of the Act Regulating Criminal Proceedings and the 394th section of the Practice Act, were the same.

As before remarked, there is a wide difference between the two. The word "black" may include all negroes, but the term "negro" does not include all black persons.

By the use of this term in this connection, we understand it to mean the opposite of "white," and that it should be taken as contradistinguished from all white persons.

In using the words "no black or mulatto person, or Indian shall be allowed to give evidence for or against a white person," the Legislature, if any intention can be ascribed to it, adopted the most comprehensive terms to embrace every known class or shade of color, as the apparent design was to protect the white person from the influence of all testimony other than that of persons of the same caste. The use of these terms must, by every sound rule of construction, exclude every one who is not of white blood.

The Act of Congress, in defining what description of aliens may become naturalized citizens, provides that every "free white citizen," etc., etc. [sic] In speaking of this subject, Chancellor Kent says that "the Act confines the description to 'white' citizens, and that it is a matter of doubt, whether, under this provision, any of the tawny races of Asia can be admitted to citizenship."

We are not disposed to leave this question in any doubt. The word "white" has a distinct signification which * * * excludes black, yellow, and all other colors. It will be observed, by reference to the first section of the second Article of the Constitution of this State, that none but white males can become electors, except in the case of Indians, who may be admitted by special Act of the Legislature. On examination of the constitutional debates, it will be found that not a little difficulty existed in selecting these precise words, which were finally agreed upon as the most comprehensive that could be suggested to exclude all inferior races.

If the term "white," as used in the Constitution, was not understood in its generic sense as including the Caucasian race, and necessarily excluding all others, where was the necessity of providing for the admission of Indians to the privilege of voting, by special legislation?

We are of the opinion that the words, "white," "negro," "mulatto," "Indian," and "black person," wherever they occur in our Constitution and laws, must be taken in their generic sense, and that, even admitting the Indian of this continent is not of the Mongolian type, that the words "black person," in the 14th section, must be taken as contradistinguished from white, and necessarily excludes all races other than the Caucasian.

We have carefully considered all the consequences, resulting from a different rule of construction, and are satisfied that even in doubtful case, we would be impelled to this decision on grounds of public policy.

The same rule which would admit them to testify, would admit them to all the equal rights of citizenship, and we might soon see them at the polls, in the jury box, upon the bench, and in our legislative halls.

This is not a speculation which exists in the excited and over-heated imagination of the patriot and statesman, but it is an actual and present danger.

The anomalous spectacle of a distinct people, living in our community, recognizing no laws of this State, except through necessity, bringing with them their prejudices and national feuds, in which they indulge in open violation of law; * * * whose mendacity is proverbial; a race of people whom nature has marked as inferior, and who are incapable of progress or intellectual development beyond a certain point, as their history has shown; differing in language, opinions, color, and physical conformation; between whom and ourselves nature has placed an impassable difference, is now presented, and for them is claimed, not only the right to swear away the life of a citizen, but the further privilege of participating with us in administering the affairs of our Government. * * *

Notes and Questions

1. Subsequently, the California Supreme Court extended the ban on Chinese testimony from criminal cases to civil cases in *Speer v. See Yup Co.*, 13 Cal. 73 (1859). This ban on testimony in criminal and civil cases was later codified in 1863. See McClain, *supra* at 22.

2. The Chinese responded to *People v. Hall* with outrage. Lai Chun-chuen, a prominent merchant wrote:

> [Lately], your honorable people have established a new practice. They have come to the conclusion that we Chinese are the same as Indians and Negroes, and your courts will not allow us to bear witness. And yet these Indians know nothing about the relations of society; they know no mutual respect; they wear neither clothes nor shoes; they live in wild places and in caves.

McClain, *supra* at 22 (quoting *Lai Chun-chuen to John Bigler*, January, 1855).

3. Notice Lai Chun-chuen's attempt to distinguish Chinese civilization from that of Blacks and Indians. Is he persuasive? Obviously Chief Justice Hugh Murray, who wrote *Hall*, was not persuaded of any difference. What are the implications of Lai Chun–chuen's argument for future relations between Chinese and Blacks, Indians, and Whites? What would you expect the results to be of a civil rights strategy based on the notion that "my civilization is better than yours, and therefore more worthy of trust."

4. Until the ban on Chinese testimony was effectively reversed, the Chinese perceived this limitation as the most severe disability in the struggle to protect themselves and to gain some measure of equal treatment in the United States. For example, Chinese victims of crime were unable to testify, or to summon the testimony of Chinese witnesses, if the alleged defendants

were White or Black. Thus the Chinese community was in large measure rendered defenseless and unable to get redress for crimes against their lives and property. The California legislature eventually repealed the ban on Chinese testimony in both criminal and civil cases in 1872. See McClain, *supra* at 42.

THE BURLINGAME TREATY (1868)

In 1867, the government of China asked Anson Burlingame, then U.S. minister in Peking, to conduct a goodwill mission to the United States. This mission resulted in amendments to the Treaty of Tientsin, and has henceforth been known as the Burlingame Treaty. The Chinese government sought, and obtained, treaty protections for the civil rights of Chinese persons in the United States.

The treaty made between the United States and China on July 28, 1868, contained the following stipulations:

Art. 5. The United States of America and the emperor of China cordially recognize the inherent and inalienable right of man to change his home and allegiance, and also the mutual advantage of the free migration and emigration of their citizens and subjects, respectively, from one country to the other, for purposes of curiosity, of trade, or as permanent residents.

Art. 6. Citizens of the United States visiting or residing in China, * * * and, reciprocally, Chinese subjects visiting or residing in the United States, shall enjoy the same privileges, immunities, and exceptions, in respect to travel or residence, as may there be enjoyed by the citizens or subjects of the most favored nation. But nothing herein contained shall be held to confer naturalization upon citizens of the United States in China nor upon the subjects of China in the United States.

16 Stat. 740 (1868).

The Chinese government expressed its hope that, with these treaty modifications, "the Chinese in California will cease to be subjected to the ill treatment they have hitherto met with." See McClain, *supra* at 30–31 (quoting Chinese Foreign Office to Anson Burlingame, dated Peking, 1868, 4th Moon, 27th Day).

THE CIVIL RIGHTS ACT OF 1870

The Enforcement Act of 1870, also known as the Civil Rights Act of 1870, was enacted with two principal objects: "(1) protection of the right to vote, so recently guaranteed in the Fifteenth Amendment; (2) [addressing] the problem of violence aimed at keeping Negroes from the polls." 1 *Statutory History of the United States* 443 (Bernard Schwartz ed. 1970). However, its principal sponsor in the Senate, Senator William Stewart, introduced into this legislation provisions specifically designed to protect the Chinese. As ultimately enacted, Section 16 of the Civil Rights Act of 1870 provided:

That all persons within the jurisdiction of the United States shall have the same right in every State and Territory in the United

States to make and enforce contracts, to sue, be parties, give evidence, and to the full and equal benefit of all laws and proceedings for the security of person and property as is enjoyed by white citizens, and shall be subject to like punishment, pains, penalties, taxes, licenses, and exactions of every kind, and none other, any law, statute, ordinance, regulation, or custom to the contrary notwithstanding. No tax or charge shall be imposed or enforced by any State upon any person immigrating thereto from a foreign country which is not equally imposed and enforced upon every person immigrating to such State from any other foreign country; and any law of any State in conflict with this provision is hereby declared null and void.

On May 20, 1870, Senator Stewart explained that the purpose underlying Section 16 was to "protect Chinese aliens or any other aliens whom we allow to come here, and give them a hearing in our courts; let them sue and be sued; let them be protected by all the laws and the same laws that other men are." On a subsequent occasion, Stewart celebrated the provisions of the Civil Rights Act of 1870:

particularly those provisions which extend the strong arm of the Government to the protection of the Chinese; those provisions which protect those industrious, helpless people whom we have invited to our shores; those provisions which go at this late date to wipe out to some extent the infamy that rests upon this nation for having invited the Asiatics to come here, having made treaties for their protection, and then allowed a State in this Union to pass barbarous and cruel laws, to place upon them unjust and cruel burdens, to tax them differently from other people, and collect that tax in a brutal manner.

McClain, *supra* at 37–39 (quoting *Congressional Globe*, 41st Cong., 2d Sess., 3658, 3807) (May 20, 1870). Section 16 of this Act thus intended to abolish, for example, the foreign miners' taxes and the prohibition on Chinese testimony that had long plagued the Chinese in California. Unfortunately, despite passage of the Enforcement Act of 1870, including Section 16, state officials and judges continued to enforce the foreign miners' taxes and the ban on Chinese testimony. See McClain, *supra* at 41–42.

B. INTENSIFYING RACISM AGAINST THE CHINESE

By 1876, hatred of the Chinese had spread throughout California and spawned organized anti-Chinese hate groups. An Anti–Chinese Union formed, pledged " 'to unite, centralize and direct the anti-Chinese strength of our Country.' Each member of [an anti-Chinese] club was to be pledged to four things: to the constitution of the club, not to employ Chinese, not to purchase goods from the employer of Chinese, and not to sustain the Chinese or the employer of Chinese." Elmer Clarence Sandmayer, *The Anti–Chinese Movement in California* 57 (1991) (quoting Constitution and By–Laws of the Anti–Chinese Union of San Francisco).

Responding to a complex set of economic hardships, the California Workingmen's party was organized under the leadership of Dennis Kearney to improve labor conditions for white laborers. Although Chinese laborers were neither the sole nor the primary cause of the workingmen's distress, resentment against the Chinese unified the workingmen. Sandmeyer, *supra* at 65. Kearney expressed his views against the Chinese:

> We have made no secret of our intentions. We make none. Before you and before the world we declare that the Chinaman must leave our shores. We declare that white men, and women, and boys and girls, cannot live as the people of the great republic should and compete with the single Chinese coolie in the labor market. We declare that we cannot hope to drive the Chinaman away by working cheaper than he does. None but an enemy would expect it of us; None but an idiot would hope for success; none but a degraded coward and slave would make the effort. To an American, death is preferable to life on a par with the Chinaman.

Sandmeyer, *supra* at 65 (quoting Kearney's "manifesto").

In September of 1877, California voters approved a convention to revise the 1849 state constitution. Approximately one-third of the convention delegates were Workingmen, assuring that severe anti-Chinese provisions would be considered and adopted in the new constitution. Article XIX declared the Chinese a menace to California and urged the adoption of measures to discourage further Chinese immigration. During debate on the immigration provision, some participants expressed the view that the provision interfered with federal power over foreign commerce and was therefore unconstitutional. Despite expressed doubts about its constitutionality, Article XIX of the 1879 Constitution was adopted by the convention. Sandmeyer, *supra* at 69.

CALIFORNIA CONSTITUTION OF 1879: ARTICLE XIX

Article XIX of the California Constitution of 1879, otherwise known as the Article on the Chinese, provided the following:

Section 1.   The Legislature shall prescribe all necessary regulations for the protection of the State * * * from the burdens and evils arising from the presence of aliens, who are or may become vagrants, paupers, mendicants, criminals, or invalids afflicted with contagious or infectious diseases, and from aliens otherwise dangerous or detrimental to the well-being or peace of the State, and to impose conditions upon which such persons may reside in the State, and to provide the means and mode of their removal from the State, upon their failure or refusal to comply with such conditions; *provided* that nothing contained in this section shall be construed to impair or limit the power of the legislature to pass such police laws or other regulations as it may deem necessary.

Section 2.   No corporation now existing or hereafter formed under the laws of this State, shall, after the adoption of this Constitution, employ, directly or indirectly, in any capacity, any Chinese or Mongolian. The Legislature shall pass such laws as may be necessary to enforce this provision.

Section 3.   No Chinese shall be employed on any State, county, municipal, or other public work, except in punishment for crime.

Section 4. The presence of foreigners ineligible to become citizens of the United States is declared to be dangerous to the well-being of the State, and the Legislature shall discourage their immigration by all the means within its power. Asiatic coolieism is a form of human slavery, and is forever prohibited in this State, and all contracts for coolie labor shall be void. * * * The Legislature shall delegate all necessary power to the incorporated cities and towns of this State for the removal of Chinese without the limits of such cities and towns, or for their location within prescribed portions of those limits, and it shall also provide the necessary legislation to prohibit the introduction into this State of Chinese after the adoption of this Constitution. This section shall be enforced by appropriate legislation.

See McClain, *supra* at 79–83; Elmer Clarence Sandmeyer, *The Anti–Chinese Movement in California* 57–77 (1991).

Notes and Questions

1. The most vexing part of Article XIX was Section 2's prohibition on the employment of Chinese by California corporations. Both the Chinese, now rendered unemployable, and many corporations, now subject to criminal prosecution for employing them, could not long survive without challenging the constitutional provision. That challenge came quickly in In re *Tiburcio Parrott*, 1 Fed. 481 (C.C.D.Cal.1880), in which the federal circuit court invalidated the relevant provisions of the California Constitution on the grounds that the state lacked power to so regulate corporations and to invade the individual rights of Chinese laborers. See the discussion of the California constitution of 1879 and the *Parrott* case in Charles J. McClain, *In Search of Equality: The Chinese Struggle Against Discrimination in Nineteenth–Century America* 79–92 (1994).

2. Does it seem incredible that California barred Chinese workers from corporate jobs in the state's *constitution*? What made this restriction possible?

Part of the course

C. ECONOMIC DISCRIMINATION AND THE LAUNDRY ORDINANCES

Local legislators, determined to discourage Chinese immigration to California, attempted to make it impossible for Chinese business owners to earn a living. Chinese entrepreneurs had begun operating commercial laundries virtually since their arrival in California, and by 1870 they were dominant in the laundry industry. Ordinances making it effectively impossible to operate these laundries targeted Chinese laundrymen, "a logical and likely target for legislation of this sort since Chinese laundries constituted a highly visible symbol—perhaps the most visible symbol—of the Chinese presence in the local economy." See McClain, *supra* at 47.

San Francisco ordinances sought to regulate different aspects of commercial laundries, but all sought to put the Chinese out of business. An early ordinance was proposed that charged the highest laundry license fees for laundries that used no horse-drawn vehicles. Since the Chinese laundries were modest and used no such vehicles, they would bear the heaviest license fees. These laundry license fee ordinances were struck down by San Francisco courts.

Several neutrally worded ordinances were passed in 1880 that also targeted the Chinese. One required that all laundries "shall be constructed but one story in height, with brick or stone walls, not less than twelve inches in thickness." A subsequent ordinance made it unlawful to operate a laundry without the consent of the board of supervisors unless it was contained in a brick or stone building. Another ordinance required all laundries within designated parts of San Francisco to obtain the consent of the board of supervisors, upon the recommendation of twelve "citizens and taxpayers" living in the block where the laundry operated. The requirement of recommendations from citizens prevented the Chinese laundrymen from obtaining recommendations from other Chinese.

Since the Chinese laundries were housed in wood-frame buildings, the ordinance requiring brick or stone construction presented an insurmountable obstacle. To comply with the ordinances, they would either have to relocate or rebuild, both of which were prohibitively expensive. Alternatively, they would have to rely on the discretion of the San Francisco board of supervisors. Unsurprisingly, this discretion was routinely exercised to turn down the applications of Chinese laundrymen for exemption from the requirements of the building ordinance. See McClain, *supra* at 47–48, 98–101.

Chinese businessmen protested vigorously against the ordinances, continued operating in defiance of them, and litigated many cases challenging their constitutionality. See McClain, *supra* 98–132. The most famous case is the Supreme Court decision in *Yick Wo v. Hopkins*, 118 U.S. 356 (1886).

YICK WO v. HOPKINS

118 U.S. 356 (1886).

[This decision involved two companion cases raising similar issues, the cases of *Yick Wo* and *Wo Lee*]

The plaintiff in error, Yick Wo, on August 24, 1885, petitioned the supreme court of California for the writ of *habeas corpus*, alleging that he was illegally deprived of his personal liberty by the defendant as sheriff of the city and county of San Francisco. [The petitioner had been] found guilty of a violation of certain ordinances of the board of supervisors of that county, and adjudged to pay a fine of $10, and, in default of payment, be imprisoned in the county jail at the rate of one day for each dollar of fine until said fine should be satisfied; and a commitment in consequence of non-payment of said fine.

The ordinances for the violation of which he had been found guilty are set out as follows: Order No. 1,569, passed May 26, 1880, prescribing the kind of buildings in which laundries may be located.

The people of the city and county of San Francisco do ordain as follows:

Section 1. It shall be unlawful, from and after the passage of this order, for any person or persons to establish, maintain, or carry on a laundry, within the corporate limits of the city and county of San Francisco, without having first obtained the consent of the board of supervisors, except the same be located in a building constructed either of brick or stone. * * *

Sec. 3. Any person who shall violate any of the provisions of this order shall be deemed guilty of a misdemeanor, and upon conviction thereof shall be punished by a fine of not more than one thousand dollars, or by imprisonment in the county jail not more than six months, or by both such fine and imprisonment.

Order No. 1,587, passed July 28, 1880, [stated]:

Sec. 68. It shall be unlawful, from and after the passage of this order, for any person or persons to establish, maintain, or carry on a laundry within the corporate limits of the city and county of San Francisco without having first obtained the consent of the board of supervisors, except the same be located in a building constructed either of brick or stone.

The following facts are also admitted on the record: That petitioner is a native of China, and came to California in 1861, and is still a subject of the emperor of China; that he has been engaged in the laundry business in the same premises and building for 22 years last past; that he had a license from the board of fire-wardens, dated March 3, 1884, from which it appeared "that the above-described premises have been inspected by the board of fire-wardens, and upon such inspection said board found all proper arrangements for carrying on the business; that the stoves, washing and drying apparatus, and the appliances for heating smoothing-irons, are in good condition, and that their use is not danger-ous to the surrounding property from fire, and that all proper precau-tions have been taken * * *; that he had a certificate from the health officer that the same premises had been inspected by him, and that he found that they were properly and sufficiently drained, and that all proper arrangements for carrying on the business of a laundry, without injury to the sanitary condition of the neighborhood, had been complied with; that the city license of the petitioner was in force, and expired October 1, 1885; and that the petitioner applied to the board of supervi-sors, June 1, 1885, for consent of said board to maintain and carry on his laundry, but that said board on July 1, 1885, refused said consent." It is also admitted to be true, as alleged in the petition, that on February 24, 1880, "there were about 320 laundries in the city and county of San Francisco, of which about 240 were owned and conducted by subjects of China, and of the whole number, *viz.*, 320, about 310 were constructed of wood, the same material that constitutes nine tenths of the houses in the city of San Francisco. * * *"

It is also admitted "that petitioner and 200 of his countrymen similarly situated petitioned the board of supervisors for permission to continue their business in the various houses which they had been occupying and using for laundries for more than twenty years, and such petitions were denied, and all the petitions of those who were not Chinese, with one exception of Mrs. Mary Meagles, were granted." * * *

MATTHEWS, J.

[The laundry ordinances] seem intended to confer, and actually to confer * * * but a naked and arbitrary power to give or withhold consent, not only as to places, but as to persons; so that, if an applicant for such consent, being in every way a competent and qualified person, and having complied with every reasonable condition demanded by any public interest, should, failing to obtain the requisite consent of the supervisors to the prosecution of his business, apply for redress by the judicial process of *mandamus* to require the supervisors to consider and act upon his case, it would be a sufficient answer for them to say that the law had conferred upon them authority to withhold their assent, without reason and without responsibility. The power given to them is not confided to their discretion in the legal sense of that term, but is granted to their mere will. It is purely arbitrary, and acknowledges neither guidance nor restraint. Class legislation, discriminating against some and favoring others, is prohibited; but legislation which, in carrying out a public purpose, is limited in its application, if, within the sphere of its operation, it affects alike all persons similarly situated, is not [prohibited by the Fourteenth Amendment].

        * * *

The rights of the petitioners, as affected by the proceedings of which they complain, are not less because they are aliens and subjects of the emperor of China. By the third article of the treaty between this government and that of China, concluded November 17, 1880, (22 Stat. 827), it is stipulated: "If Chinese laborers, or Chinese of any other class, now either permanently or temporarily residing in the territory of the United States, meet with ill treatment at the hands of any other persons, the government of the United States will exert all its powers to devise measures for their protection, and to secure to them the same rights, privileges, immunities, and exemptions as may be enjoyed by the citizens or subjects of the most favored nation, and to which they are entitled by treaty." The Fourteenth Amendment to the constitution is not confined to the protection of citizens. It says: "Nor shall any state deprive any person of life, liberty, or property without due process of law; nor deny to any person within its jurisdiction the equal protection of the laws." These provisions are universal in their application, to all persons within the territorial jurisdiction, without regard to any differences of race, of color, or of nationality; and the equal protection of the laws is a pledge of the protection of equal laws. * * * The questions we have to consider and decide in these cases, therefore, are to be treated as involving the rights of every citizen of the United States equally with those of the strangers and aliens who now invoke the jurisdiction of the court.

It is contended on the part of the petitioners that the ordinances for violations of which they are severally sentenced to imprisonment are void on their face, as being within the prohibitions of the Fourteenth Amendment, and, in the alternative, if not so, that they are void by reason of their administration, operating unequally, so as to punish in the present petitioners what is permitted to others as lawful, without any distinction of circumstances,—an unjust and illegal discrimination, it is claimed, which, though not made expressly by the ordinances, is made possible by them. * * *

[T]he cases present the ordinances in actual operation, and the facts shown establish an administration directed so exclusively against a particular class of persons as to warrant and require the conclusion that, whatever may have been the intent of the ordinances as adopted, they are applied by the public authorities charged with their administration, and thus representing the state itself, with a mind so unequal and oppressive as to amount to a practical denial by the state of that equal protection of the laws which is secured to the petitioners, as to all other persons, by the broad and benign provisions of the Fourteenth Amendment to the constitution of the United States. Though the law itself be fair on its face, and impartial in appearance, yet, if it is applied and administered by public authority with an evil eye and an unequal hand so as practically to make unjust and illegal discriminations between persons in similar circumstances, material to their rights, the denial of equal justice is still within the prohibition of the constitution. * * *

The present cases, as shown by the facts disclosed in the record, are within this class. It appears that both petitioners have complied with every requisite deemed by the law, or by the public officers charged with its administration, necessary for the protection of neighboring property from fire, or as a precaution against injury to the public health. No reason whatever, except the will of the supervisors, is assigned why they should not be permitted to carry on, in the accustomed manner, their harmless and useful occupation, on which they depend for a livelihood; and while this consent of the supervisors is withheld from them, and from 200 others who have also petitioned, all of whom happen to be Chinese subjects, 80 others, not Chinese subjects, are permitted to carry on the same business under similar conditions. The fact of this discrimination is admitted. No reason for it is shown, and the conclusion cannot be resisted that no reason for it exists except hostility to the race and nationality to which the petitioners belong, and which, in the eye of the law, is not justified. The discrimination is therefore illegal, and the public administration which enforces it is a denial of the equal protection of the laws, and a violation of the Fourteenth Amendment of the constitution. The imprisonment of the petitioners is therefore illegal, and they must be discharged. * * *

Notes and Questions

1. The *Yick Wo* decision represented an important victory for Chinese litigants against discrimination and an important interpretation of the Fourteenth Amendment. However, in light of both the preceding materials and those that follow on Chinese exclusion, it can be seen as a very limited victory. Constitutional law casebooks routinely discuss the *Yick Wo* decision but fail to discuss the Chinese Exclusion cases and the anti-Chinese movement that provides the context for these court challenges. Why do you think some casebook authors would discuss only the *Yick Wo* decision, and not the full context?

D. CHINESE EXCLUSION

Californians had long wanted to end Chinese immigration. Since the constitutionality of state laws limiting Chinese immigration, such as

Article XIX of the California Constitution, was in doubt, Californians had also sought federal laws to accomplish the same object. As early as 1867, Congressman Johnson of California had introduced a resolution inquiring whether Congress could prohibit "the Chinese and other inferior races" from immigrating to the United States. McClain, *supra* at 147. American desire to limit Chinese immigration led to renegotiation of some terms of the Burlingame Treaty in 1880, to allow the suspension of immigration of Chinese laborers to the United States. Congress then passed the "Act to Execute Certain Treaty Stipulations Relating to Chinese," which would come to be known as the Chinese Exclusion Act. As Professor McClain writes, the Chinese Exclusion Act was "the first federal immigration statute to single out an ethnic group by name for invidious treatment. It represented, to say the least, a dramatic reversal in the historic American policy of open immigration." McClain, *supra* at 149.

THE CHINESE EXCLUSION ACT
(May 6, 1882).

Whereas, in the opinion of the Government of the United States the coming of Chinese laborers to this country endangers the good order of certain localities within the territory thereof: Therefore * * * until the expiration of ten years next after the passage of this act, the coming of Chinese laborers to the United States be, and the same is hereby, suspended; and during such suspension it shall not be lawful for any Chinese laborer to come [to or] remain within the United States.

SEC. 2. That the master of any vessel who shall knowingly bring within the United States on such vessel, and land or permit to be landed, any Chinese laborer, from any foreign port or place, shall be deemed guilty of a misdemeanor, and on conviction thereof shall be punished by a fine of not more than five hundred dollars for each and every such Chinese laborer so brought, and may be also imprisoned for a term not exceeding one year.

SEC. 3. That the two foregoing sections shall not apply to Chinese laborers who were in the United States on the seventeenth day of November, eighteen hundred and eighty, or who shall have come into the same before the expiration of ninety days next after the passage of this act * * *

SEC. 4. That for the purpose of properly identifying Chinese laborers who were in the United States on the seventeenth day of November, eighteen hundred and eighty, or who shall have come into the same before the expiration of ninety days next after the passage of this act, and in order to furnish them with the proper evidence of their right to go from and come to the United States of their free will and accord * * * the collector of customs [shall] go on board each vessel having on board any such Chinese laborer and cleared or about to sail from his district for a foreign port, and on such vessel make a list of all such Chinese laborers, which shall be entered in registry-books to be kept for that purpose, in which shall be stated the name, age, occupation, last place of residence, physical marks or peculiarities, and all facts necessary for the identification of each of such Chinese laborers, which books shall be safely kept in the custom-house; and every such Chinese laborer so departing from the United States shall be entitled to, and shall receive * * * a certificate * * * [which] shall contain a statement of the name, age, occupation, last place of residence, personal description, and facts of identification of the Chinese laborer to whom the certificate is issued, corresponding with the said list and registry in all particulars. * * * The certificate herein provided for shall entitle the Chinese laborer to whom the same is issued to return to and re-enter the United States upon producing and delivering the same to the collector of customs * * *.

SEC. 6. [E]very Chinese person other than a laborer who may be entitled by [the Burlingame] Treaty and this act to come within the United States * * * shall be identified as so entitled by the Chinese Government in each case, such identity to be evidenced by a certificate issued under the authority of said government, which certificate shall be in the English language or (if not in the English language) accompanied by a translation into English, stating such right to come, and which certificate shall state the name, title, or official rank, if any, the age, height, and all physical peculiarities, former and present occupation or profession, and place of residence in China of the person to whom the certificate is issued and that such person is entitled comfortably to the treaty in this act mentioned to come within the United States. * * *

SEC. 9. That before any Chinese passengers are landed from any such vessel, the collector, or his deputy, shall proceed to examine such passengers, comparing the certificates with the list and with the passengers; and no passenger shall be allowed to land in the United States from such vessel in violation of law.

SEC. 10. That every vessel whose master shall knowingly violate any of the provisions of this act shall be deemed forfeited to the United States, and shall be liable to seizure and condemnation in any district of the United States into which such vessel may enter or in which she may be found. * * *

SEC. 14. That hereafter no State court or court of the United States shall admit Chinese to citizenship; and all laws in conflict with this act are hereby repealed.

SEC. 15. That the words "Chinese laborers", wherever used in this act, shall be construed to mean both skilled and unskilled laborers and Chinese employed in mining.

22 Stat. 58 (1882).

In 1884, Congress passed amendments to the Exclusion Act that were meant to eliminate perceived "loopholes" that had permitted some Chinese to enter the United States. These amendments stiffened the documentary requirements for the entry of laborers into the United States and defined the Section 4 certificate as the only evidence that established a laborer's right of re-entry. These changes provoked angry protest from the Chinese legation to the United States, who claimed the United States was going far beyond the 1880 treaty.

The early federal court decisions on the Exclusion Act "suggested that the courts were on the whole prepared to give the exclusion legislation a reasonable, even liberal interpretation, one that would not impose unnecessary hardship on the Chinese." See McClain, *supra* at 150–72. However, the seeming reasonableness of the federal courts was far out of step with public opinion and legislative and judicial developments to follow.

Under the Burlingame Treaty as amended in 1880, the United States could "suspend" the coming of Chinese laborers but could not absolutely prohibit them from entering. In 1888 Congress passed the Scott Act, which legislated the permanent exclusion of Chinese laborers and declared certificates issued under the old act to be null and void. While the executive branch was trying to negotiate changes in the Treaty, Congress passed this law which abrogated directly provisions of the Burlingame Treaty.

THE SCOTT ACT
(1888).

Be it enacted by the senate and house of representatives of the United States of America, in congress assembled, that from and after the passage of this act it shall be unlawful for any Chinese laborer who shall at any time heretofore have been, or who may now or hereafter be, a resident within the United States, and who shall have departed, or shall depart, therefrom, and shall not have returned before the passage of this act, to return to or remain in the United States.

Sec. 2. That no certificates of identity . . . shall hereafter be issued; and every certificate heretofore issued . . . is hereby declared void and of no effect, and the Chinese laborer claiming admission by virtue thereof shall not be permitted to enter the United States.

25 Stat. 504 (1888).

———

Californians celebrated this most forceful exclusion of Chinese to date. The effect of this act was to make it impossible for any Chinese laborer to leave the United States and then to return. Chinese laborers had to choose between abandoning their families in China or in the United States. The Scott Act was promptly challenged.

CHAE CHAN PING v. UNITED STATES
130 U.S. 581 (1889).

FIELD, J.

This case comes before us on appeal from an order of the circuit court of the United States for the Northern district of California, refusing to release the appellant, on a writ of *habeas corpus*, from his alleged unlawful detention by Capt. Walker, master of the steam-ship Belgic, lying within the harbor of San Francisco. The appellant is a subject of the emperor of China, and a laborer by occupation. He resided at San Francisco, Cal., following his occupation, from some time in 1875 until June 2, 1887, when he left for China on the steam-ship Gaelic, having in his possession a certificate in terms entitling him to return to the United States, bearing date on that day, duly issued to him by the collector of customs of the port of San Francisco, pursuant to [Section 4 of the Chinese Exclusion Act]. On the 7th of September, 1888, the appellant, on his return to California, sailed from Hong Kong in the steam-ship Belgic, which arrived within the port of San Francisco on the 8th of October following. On his arrival he presented to the proper custom-house officers his certificate, and demanded permission to land. The collector of the port refused the permit, solely on the ground that under the [Scott Act of 1888], the certificate had been annulled, and his right to land abrogated, and he had been thereby forbidden again to enter the United States. The captain of the steam-ship, therefore, detained the appellant on board the steamer. * * *

The appeal involves a consideration of the validity of the act of congress of October 1, 1888, prohibiting Chinese laborers from entering the United States who had departed before its passage, having a certificate issued under the act of 1882 as amended by the act of 1884, granting them permission to return. The validity of the act is assailed as being in effect an expulsion from the country of Chinese laborers, in violation of existing treaties between the United States and the government of China, and of rights vested in them under the laws of congress. * * *

But notwithstanding these strong expressions of friendship and good will [found in the treaties between the United States and China, including the Burlingame Treaty], and the desire they evince for free intercourse, events were transpiring on the Pacific coast which soon dissipated the anticipations indulged as to the benefits to follow the immigration of Chinese to this country. The previous treaties of 1844 and 1858 were confined principally to mutual declaration of peace and friendship, and to stipulations for commercial intercourse at certain ports in China, and for protection to our citizens while peaceably attending to their affairs. It was not until the additional articles of 1868 were adopted that any public declaration was made by the two nations that there were advantages in the free migration and emigration of their citizens and subjects, respectively, from one country to the other, and stipulations given that each should enjoy in the country of the other, with respect to travel or residence, the "privileges, immunities, and exemptions" enjoyed by citizens or subjects of the most favored nation. Whatever modifications have since been made to these general provisions have been caused by a well-founded apprehension—from the experience of years—that a limitation to the immigration of certain classes from China was essential to the peace of the community on the Pacific coast, and possibly to the preservation of our civilization there. A few words on this point may not be deemed inappropriate here, they being confined to matters of public notoriety, which have frequently been brought to the attention of congress.

The discovery of gold in California in 1848, as is well known, was followed by a large immigration thither from all parts of the world, attracted not only by the hope of gain from the mines, but from the great prices paid for all kinds of labor. The news of the discovery penetrated China, and laborers came from there in great numbers, a few with their own means, but by far the greater number under contract with employers, for whose benefit they worked. These laborers readily secured employment, and, as domestic servants, and in various kinds of outdoor work, proved to be exceedingly useful. For some years little opposition was made to them, except when they sought to work in the mines, but, as their numbers increased, they began to engage in various mechanical pursuits and trades, and thus came in competition with our artisans and mechanics, as well as our laborers in the field. The competition steadily increased as the laborers came in crowds on each steamer that arrived from China, or Hong Kong, an adjacent English port. They were generally industrious and frugal. Not being accompanied by families, except in rare instances, their expenses were small; and they were content with the simplest fare, such as would not suffice for our laborers and artisans. The competition between them and our people was for this reason altogether in their favor, and the consequent irritation, proportionately deep and bitter, was followed, in many cases, by open conflicts, to the great disturbance of the public peace. The differences of race added greatly to the difficulties of the situation. Notwithstanding the favorable provisions of the new articles of the treaty of 1868, by which all the privileges, immunities, and exemptions were extended to subjects of China in the United States which were accorded to citizens or subjects of the most favored nation, they remained strangers in the land residing apart by themselves, and adhering to the customs and usages of their own country. It seemed impossible for them to assimilate with our people, or to make any change in their habits or modes of living. As they grew in numbers each year the people of the coast saw, or believed they saw, in the facility of immigration, and in the crowded millions of China, where population presses upon the means of subsistence, great danger that at no distant day that portion of our country would be overrun by them, unless prompt action was taken to restrict their immigration. The people there accordingly petitioned earnestly for protective legislation.

In December, 1878, the convention which framed the present constitution of California, being in session, took this subject up, and memorialized congress upon it, setting forth, in substance, that the presence of Chinese laborers had a baneful effect upon the material interests of the state, and upon public morals; that their immigration was in numbers approaching the character of an Oriental invasion, and was a menace to our civilization; that the discontent from this cause was not confined to any political party, or to any class or nationality, but was well nigh universal; that they retained the habits and customs of their own country, and in fact constituted a Chinese settlement within the state, without any interest in our country or its institutions; and praying congress to take measures to prevent their further immigration. This memorial was presented to congress in February, 1879. So urgent and constant were the prayers for relief against existing anticipated evils, both from the public authorities of the Pacific coast and from private individuals, that congress was impelled to act on the subject. * * *

The validity of [the Scott Act], as already mentioned, is assailed, as being in effect an expulsion from the country of Chinese laborers, in violation of existing treaties between the United States and the government of China, and of rights vested in them under the laws of congress. * * * Here the objection made is that the act of 1888 impairs a right vested under the treaty of 1880, as a law of the United States, and the statutes of 1882 and of 1884 passed in execution of it. It must be conceded that the act of 1888 is in contravention of express stipulations of the treaty of 1868, and of the supplemental treaty of 1880, but it is not on that account invalid, or to be restricted in its enforcement. The treaties were of no greater legal obligation than the act of congress. By the constitution, laws made in pursuance thereof, and treaties made under the authority of the United States, are both declared to be the supreme law of the land, and no paramount authority is given to one over the other. A treaty, it is true, is in its nature a contract between nations, and is often merely promissory in its character, requiring legislation to carry its stipulations into effect. Such legislation will be open to future repeal or amendment. If the treaty operates by its own force, and relates to a subject within the power of congress, it can be deemed in that particular only the equivalent of a legislative act, to be repealed or modified at the pleasure of congress. In either case the last expression of the sovereign will must control. * * *

[I]f congress has this power it is wholly immaterial to inquire whether it has, by the statute complained of, departed from the treaty or not; or, if it has, whether such departure was accidental or designed; and, if the latter, whether the reasons therefor were good or bad. * * * if the power mentioned is vested in congress, any reflection upon its motives, or the motives of any of its members in exercising it, would be entirely uncalled for. This court is not a censor of the morals of other departments of the government; it is not invested with any authority to pass judgment upon the motives of their conduct. When once it is established that congress possesses the power to pass an act, our province ends with its construction and its application to cases as they are presented for determination. * * *

There being nothing in the treaties between China and the United States to impair the validity of the act of congress of October 1, 1888, was it on any other ground beyond the competency of congress to pass it? If so, it must be because it was not within the power of congress to prohibit Chinese laborers who had at the time departed from the United States, or should subsequently depart, from returning to the United States. Those laborers are not citizens of the United States; they are aliens. That the government of the United States, through the action of the legislative department, can exclude aliens from its territory is a proposition which we do not think open to controversy. Jurisdiction over its own territory to that extent is an incident of every independent nation. It is a part of its independence. If it could not exclude aliens it would be to that extent subject to the control of another power. * * *

To preserve its independence, and give security against foreign aggression and encroachment, is the highest duty of every nation, and to attain these ends nearly all other considerations are to be subordinated. It matters not in what form such aggression and encroachment come, whether from the foreign nation acting in its national character, or from vast hordes of its people crowding in upon us. * * * If, therefore, the government of the United States, through its legislative department, considers the presence of foreigners of a different race in this country, who will not assimilate with us, to be dangerous to its peace and security, their exclusion is not to be stayed because at the time there are no actual hostilities with the nation of which the foreigners are subjects. The existence of war would render the necessity of the proceeding only more obvious and pressing. The same necessity, in a less pressing degree, may arise when war does not exist, and the same authority which adjudges the necessity in one case must also determine it in the other. In both cases its determination is conclusive upon the judiciary. If the government of the country of which the foreigners excluded are subjects is dissatisfied with this action, it can make complaint to the executive head of our government, or resort to any other measure which, in its judgment, its interests or dignity may demand; and there lies its only remedy.

* * *

The power of exclusion of foreigners being an incident of sovereignty belonging to the government of the United States as a part of those sovereign powers delegated by the constitution, the right to its exercise at any time when, in the judgment of the government, the interests of the country require it, cannot be granted away or restrained on behalf of any one.

Chae Chan Ping settled the plenary power of Congress to regulate the status of Chinese laborers (and other aliens), regardless of extant treaty provisions. Congress, still seized with the Sinophobia of the West Coast, went further still in its legislative policing of the Chinese. The Geary Act represented the nadir in imposing humiliating conditions upon the Chinese.

AN ACT TO PROHIBIT THE COMING OF CHINESE PERSONS INTO THE UNITED STATES

(1892) (The Geary Act).

Be it enacted by the senate and house of representatives of the United States of America in congress assembled, that all laws now in force prohibiting and regulating the coming into this country of Chinese persons and persons of Chinese descent are hereby continued in force for a period of ten years from the passage of this act.

Sec. 2. That any Chinese person or person of Chinese descent, when convicted and adjudged under any of said laws to be not lawfully entitled to be or remain in the United States, shall be removed from the United States to China, unless he or they shall make it appear to the justice, judge, or commissioner before whom he or they are tried that he or they are subjects or citizens of some other country, in which case he or they shall be removed from the United States to such country. * * *

Sec. 4. That any such Chinese person or person of Chinese descent convicted and adjudged to be now lawfully entitled to be or remain in the United States shall be imprisoned at hard labor for a period of not exceeding one year, and thereafter removed from the United States, as hereinbefore provided. * * *

Sec. 6. And it shall be the duty of all Chinese laborers within the limits of the United States * * * to apply to the collector of internal revenue of their respective districts * * * for a certificate of residence; and any Chinese laborer * * * who shall neglect, fail, or refuse to comply with the provisions of this act * * * shall be deemed and adjudged to be unlawfully within the United States, and may be arrested * * * and taken before a United States judge, whose duty it shall be to order that he be deported from the United States * * * unless he shall establish clearly * * * that by reason of accident, sickness, or other unavoidable cause he has been unable to procure his certificate, and to the satisfaction of the court, *and by at least one credible white witness*, that he was resident of the United States at the time of the passage of this act * * *

Sec. 7. That immediately after the passage of this act the secretary of the treasury shall make such rules and regulations as may be necessary for the efficient execution of this act, and shall prescribe the necessary forms and furnish the necessary blanks to enable collectors of internal revenue to issue the certificates required hereby, and make such provisions that certificates may be procured in localities convenient to the applicants. Such certificates shall be issued without charge to the applicant, and shall contain the name, age, local residence, and occupation of the applicant, and such other description of the applicant as shall be prescribed by the secretary of the treasury * * *.

27 Stat. 25 (1892) (emphasis added).

———

The Geary Act established the first internal passport system based on race in United States history. It also required testimony from a white witness for a Chinese laborer, lacking and unable to produce a requisite certificate, to establish residence. This imposed a difficult requirement for most Chinese to meet. A Chinese laborer, arrested because he lacked a certificate, might well be deported unless he could produce a white witness to testify regarding his residence.

The Chinese were quick to express their outrage and to challenge the legislation in court. The minister of the Chinese legation in Washington expressed his revulsion, and labeled the legislation as "a violation of every principle of justice, equity, reason and fair dealing between two friendly powers," and urged its repeal. McClain, *supra* at 203 (quoting Note from Minister Tsui to Secretary Blaine, Nov. 7, 1892, *Notes from the Chinese Legation*). Chinese were urged by their leaders to disobey the law, and to contribute to a massive legal defense fund with which to challenge the Act. The following challenges soon ensued.

FONG YUE TING v. THE UNITED STATES ET. AL.
149 U.S. 698 (1893).

[This important decision included three companion cases, all stemming from violations of the Geary Act. In the first two cases Chinese laborers were arrested for not having certificates of residence as required by Section 6 of the Act. In the third a Chinese laborer had applied for a certificate, but the inspector refused to give him one because his witnesses "were [only] persons of the Chinese race, and not credible," and he was unable to produce any white witness. Unable to procure a certificate of residence he was arrested and ordered deported.]

JUSTICE GRAY delivered the opinion of the court.

In the recent case of *Nishimura Ekiu v. U.S.*, 142 U.S. 651, 659, the court, in sustaining the action of the executive department, putting in force an act of congress for the exclusion of aliens, said: "It is an accepted maxim of international law that every sovereign nation has the power, as inherent in sovereignty, and essential to self-preservation, to forbid the entrance of foreigners within its dominions, or to admit them only in such cases and upon such conditions as it may see fit to prescribe. In the United States this power is vested in the national government, to which the constitution has committed the entire control of international relations, in peace as well as in war. It belongs to the political department of the government, and may be exercised either through treaties made by the president and senate or through statutes enacted by congress."

The same views were more fully expounded in the earlier case of *Chae Chan Ping v. U.S.*, 130 U.S. 581, in which the validity of a former act of congress, excluding Chinese laborers from the United States, under the circumstances therein stated, was affirmed. * * *

The right of a nation to expel or deport foreigners who have not been naturalized, or taken any steps towards becoming citizens of the country, rests upon the same grounds, and is as absolute and unqualified, as the right to prohibit and prevent their entrance into the country. * * *

The right to exclude or to expel all aliens, or any class of aliens, absolutely or upon certain conditions, in war or in peace, being an inherent and inalienable right of every sovereign and independent nation, essential to its safety, its independence, and its welfare, the question now before the court is whether the manner in which congress has exercised this right in sections 6 and 7 of the [Geary Act] is consistent with the constitution. * * *

Congress, having the right, as it may see fit, to expel aliens of particular class, or to permit them to remain, has undoubtedly the right to provide a system of registration and identification of the members of that class within the country, and to take all proper means to carry out the system which it provides. * * *

Chinese laborers * * * like all other aliens residing in the United States for a shorter or longer time are entitled, so long as they are permitted by the government of the United States to remain in the country, to the safeguards of the constitution, and to the protection of the laws, in regard to their rights of person and of property, and to their civil and criminal responsibility. But they continue to be aliens, having taken no steps towards becoming citizens, and incapable of becoming such under the naturalization laws; and therefore remain subject to the power of congress to expel them, or to order them to be removed and departed from the country, whenever, in its judgment, their removal is necessary or expedient for the public interest. * * *

The manifest objects of [Sections 6 and 7 of the Geary Act] are to provide a system of registration and identification of such Chinese laborers, to require them to obtain certificates of residence, and, if they do not do so within a year, to have them deported from the United States. * * *

For the reasons stated in the earlier part of this opinion, congress, under the power to exclude or expel aliens, might have directed any Chinese laborer found in the United States without a certificate of residence to be removed out of the country by executive officers, without judicial trial or examination, just as it might have authorized such officers absolutely to prevent his entrance into the country. But congress has not undertaken to do this.

The effect of [Section 6 of the Act] is that, if a Chinese laborer, after the opportunity afforded him to obtain a certificate of residence within a year, at a convenient place, and without costs, is found without such a certificate, he shall be so far presumed to be not entitled to remain within the United States that an officer of the customs, or a collector of internal revenue, or a marshal, or a deputy of either, may arrest him, not with a view to imprisonment or punishment, or to his immediate deportation without further inquiry, but in order to take him before a judge, for the purpose of a judicial hearing and determination of the only facts which, under the act of congress, can have a material bearing upon the question whether he shall be sent out of the country, or be permitted to remain. * * *

The provision which puts the burden of proof upon him of rebutting the presumption arising from his having no certificate, as well as the requirement of proof "by at least one credible white witness that he was a resident of the United States at the time of the passage of this act," is within the acknowledged power of every legislature to prescribe the evidence which shall be received, and the effect of that evidence, in the courts of its own government. * * * The competency of all witnesses, without regard to their color, to testify in the courts of the United States, rests on acts of congress, which congress may, at its discretion, modify or repeal. The reason for requiring a Chinese alien, claiming the privilege of remaining in the United States, to prove the fact of his residence here at the time of the passage of the act "by at least one credible white witness," may have been the experience of congress, as mentioned by Mr. Justice Field in Chae Chan Ping's Case, that the enforcement of former acts under which the testimony of Chinese persons was admitted to prove similar facts, "was attended with great embarrassment, from the suspicious nature, in many instances, of the testimony offered to establish the residence of the parties, arising from the loose notions entertained by the witnesses of the obligation of an oath."

* * *

The question whether, and upon what conditions, these aliens shall be permitted to remain within the United States being one to be determined by the political departments of the government, the judicial department cannot properly express an opinion upon the wisdom, the policy, or the justice of the measures enacted by congress in the exercise of the powers confided to it by the constitution over this subject. * * *

Upon careful consideration of the subject, the only conclusion which appears to us to be consistent with the principles of international law, with the constitution and laws of the United States, and with the previous decisions of this court, is that in each of these cases the judgment of the circuit court dismissing the writ of habeas corpus is right, and must be affirmed.

[Justice Brewer, after a lengthy dissent arguing that Chinese resident aliens were entitled to full constitutional protections and that the Geary Act was unconstitutional, ended his dissent with a pithy question: "In view of this enactment of the highest legislative body of the foremost Christian nation, may not the thoughtful Chinese disciple of Confucius fairly ask, 'Why do they send missionaries here?' "]

JUSTICE FIELD, dissenting.

* * *

I had the honor to be the organ of the court in announcing [the] opinion and judgment [in *Chae Chan Ping*]. I still adhere to the views there expressed, in all particulars; but between legislation for the exclusion of Chinese persons,—that is, to prevent them from entering the country,—and legislation for the deportation of those who have acquired a residence in the country under a treaty with China, there is a wide and essential difference. The power of the government to exclude foreigners from this country,—that is, to prevent them from entering it,—whenever the public interests, in its judgment, require such exclusion, has been repeatedly asserted by the legislative and executive departments of our government, and never denied; but its power to deport from the country persons lawfully domiciled therein by its consent, and engaged in the ordinary pursuits of life, has never been asserted by the legislative or executive departments, except for crime, or as an act of war, in view of existing or anticipated hostilities, unless the alien act of 1798 can be considered as recognizing that doctrine. * * *

In no other instance, until the law before us was passed, has any public man had the boldness to advocate the deportation of friendly aliens in time of peace. I repeat the statement that in no other instance has the deportation of friendly aliens been advocated as a lawful measure by any department of our government. And it will surprise most people to learn that any such dangerous and despotic power lies in our government,—a power which will authorize it to expel at pleasure, in time of peace, the whole body of friendly foreigners of any country domiciled herein by its permission; a power which can be brought into exercise whenever it may suit the pleasure of congress, and be enforced without regard to the guaranties of the constitution intended for the protection of the rights of all persons in their liberty and property. Is it possible that congress can, at its pleasure, in disregard of the guaranties of the constitution, expel at any time the Irish, German, French, and English who may have taken up their residence here on the invitation of the government, while we are at peace with the countries from which they came, simply on the ground that they have not been naturalized? * * *

The purpose of [Section 6] was to secure the means of readily identifying the Chinese laborers present in the country, and entitled to remain, from those who may have clandestinely entered the country in violation of its laws. Those entitled to remain, by having a certificate of their identification, would enable the officers of the government to readily discover, and bring to punishment, those not entitled to enter, but who are excluded. To procure such a certificate was not a hardship to the laborers, but a means to secure full protection to them, and at the same time prevent an evasion of the law.

This object being constitutional, the only question for our consideration is the lawfulness of the procedure provided for its accomplishment; and this must be tested by the provisions of the constitution and laws intended for the protection of all persons against encroachment upon their rights. Aliens from countries at peace with us, domiciled within our country by its consent, are entitled to all the guaranties for the protection of their persons and property which are secured to native-born citizens. The moment any human being from a country at peace with us comes within the jurisdiction of the United States, with their consent,— and such consent will always be implied when not expressly withheld, and, in the case of the Chinese laborers before us, was, in terms, given by [the Burlingame Treaty],—he becomes subject to all their laws, is amenable to their punishment, and entitled to their protection. Arbitrary and despotic power can no more be exercised over them, with reference to their persons and property, than over the persons and property of native-born citizens. They differ only from citizens in that they cannot vote, or hold any public office. As men having our common humanity, they are protected by all the guaranties of the constitution. To hold that they are subject to any different law, or are less protected in any particular, than other persons, is, in my judgment, to ignore the teachings of our history, the practice of our government, and the language of our constitution. * * *

I utterly dissent from, and reject, the doctrine expressed in the opinion of the majority, that "congress, under the power to exclude or expel aliens, might have directed any Chinese laborer found in the United States without a certificate of residence to be removed out of the country by executive officers, without judicial trial or examination, just as it might have authorized such officers absolutely to prevent his entrance into the country." [Eds. These words were originally printed in the opinion of the Court, to which the dissent was directed. In the revision of the opinion the phraseology is changed]. * * *

The punishment is beyond all reason in its severity. It is out of all proportion to the alleged offense. It is cruel and unusual. As to its cruelty, nothing can exceed a forcible deportation from a country of one's residence, and the breaking up of all the relations of friendship, family, and business there contracted. The laborer may be seized at a distance from his home, his family, and his business, and taken before the judge for his condemnation, without permission to visit his home, see his family, or complete any unfinished business. * * *

Again, when taken before a United States judge, he is required, in order to avoid the doom declared, to establish clearly, to the satisfaction of the judge, that by reason of accident, sickness, or other unavoidable cause he was unable to secure his certificate, and that he was a resident of the United States at the time, by at least one credible white witness. Here the government undertakes to exact of the party arrested the testimony of a witness of a particular color, though conclusive and incontestable testimony from others may be adduced. The law might as well have said that unless the laborer SHOULD ALSO PRESENT A PARTICULAR PERSON as a witness, who could not be produced, from sickness, absence, or other cause, such as the archbishop of the state, to establish the fact of residence, he should be held to be unlawfully within the United States.

There are numerous other objections to the provisions of the act under consideration. Every step in the procedure provided, as truly said by counsel, tramples upon some constitutional right. * * *

I will not pursue the subject further. The decision of the court, and the sanction it would give to legislation depriving resident aliens of the guaranties of the constitution, fill me with apprehensions. Those guaranties are of priceless value to every one resident in the country, whether citizen or alien. I cannot but regard the decision as a blow against constitutional liberty, when it declares that congress has the right to disregard the guaranties of the constitution intended for the protection of all men domiciled in the country with the consent of the government, in their rights of person and property. How far will its legislation go? The unnaturalized resident feels it to-day, but if congress can disregard the guaranties with respect to any one domiciled in the country with its consent, it may disregard the guaranties with respect to naturalized citizens. What assurance have we that it may not declare that naturalized citizens of a particular country cannot remain in the United States after a certain day, unless they have in their possession a certificate that they are of good moral character, and attached to the principles of our constitution, which certificate they must obtain from a collector of internal revenue upon the testimony of at least one competent witness of a class or nationality to be designated by the government?

* * *

Notes and Questions

1. Why does Justice Field take seemingly inconsistent positions in *Chae Chan Ping* and *Fong Yue Ting*?

2. The *Chae Chan Ping* and *Fong Yue Ting* decisions are important building blocks of the plenary power that Congress is thought to have over immigration. See Stephen H. Legomsky, *Immigration and Refugee Law and Policy* 46–47 (2d ed. 1997).

3. For a detailed examination of the administration of the Chinese exclusion laws, see Lucy E. Salyer, *Laws Harsh as Tigers: Chinese Immigrants and the Shaping of Modern Immigration Law* (1995).

4. Does the history of legislation and Supreme Court decisions hostile to the Chinese help us understand the current anti-immigrant atmosphere in the United States? Reflect upon the relevance of this history in understanding Proposition 187 and other legislation hostile to Latino/a and Asian immigrants.

5. Derrick Bell believes that white self-interest explains the rise and fall of black fortunes in the United States. Do the needs of the labor market explain some of the virulent anti-Asian actions you have just read about?

6. For an insightful critique of the limits of Justice Harlan's celebrated racial ideology, see Gabriel J. Chin, *The Plessy Myth: Justice Harlan and the Chinese Cases*, 82 Iowa L. Rev. 151 (1996) (Harlan "was a faithful opponent of the constitutional rights of Chinese for much of his career on the Court.").

7. For an analysis linking the nineteenth-century Chinese cases to the development of substantive due process, see Thomas Wuil Joo, *New "Conspiracy Theory" of the Fourteenth Amendment: Nineteenth Century Chinese Civil Rights Cases and the Development of Substantive Due Process Jurisprudence*, 29 U.S.F. L. Rev. 353 (1995).

E. THE SIGNIFICANCE OF CHINESE LEGAL HISTORY IN THE UNITED STATES

CHARLES J. McCLAIN

In Search of Equality: The Chinese Struggle Against Discrimination In Nineteenth–Century America
1–4 (1994).*

The Chinese, I think it is safe to say, occupy at best an obscure niche in the historical consciousness of the average educated American. Most know that thousands of Chinese immigrants came to the West Coast in the second half of the nineteenth century—initially to work California's newly opened gold fields, later to labor on the construction of the trans-continental railroad and in other trades. Most know as well that their presence came to arouse hostility in the white population and that this hostility was eventually translated into discriminatory local and national legislation. But there general familiarity ends. This is not at all surprising. Most accounts of the great Chinese immigration to the

United States in the nineteenth century have concentrated almost exclusively on the reaction it provoked in the white population. They have tended to ignore the Chinese and their perception of their experience in this country. As one of the leading historians of anti-Orientalism in California, Roger Daniels, has put it, "Other immigrant groups were celebrated for what they had accomplished; Orientals were important for what was done to them."

Those relatively few scholarly writings that have focused on the Chinese community, until very recently at any rate, have tended to be deprecatory, emphasizing what is usually described as the authoritarian structure of Chinese–American society; the corruption or ineptitude of the leadership; and the passivity, docility, and otherworldliness of the Chinese masses. These writings make much of what they see as the unique character of the Chinese immigration. The Chinese who came to this country, so the argument goes, had no desire to settle or assimilate, wishing only to accumulate a quick fortune and return home. One historian, Gunther Barth, even suggests that it was this feature of their immigration that was most responsible for the misfortunes that were visited upon them. According to this thesis—one which, I hasten to add, I view as untenable—white Californians offered the hand of welcome to the newcomers from Asia but saw their overtures of goodwill rebuffed. They then turned on the Chinese and determined to exclude them from the privileges and obligations they extended to other immigrants.

Two related views are that the nineteenth-century Chinese immigrants were utterly unacquainted with American political institutions and that they passively submitted to discrimination. U.S. Supreme Court Justice Stephen Field, who, as we shall see, should have known better, observed in 1884, "Our institutions have made no impression on [the Chinese] during the more than thirty years they have been in this country." And Barth argues that the Chinese community failed to appreciate the severity of the legal restrictions under which it operated or to respond to them in any significant way. On this view the Chinese were, in the words of the early twentieth-century historian of California, Robert Glass Cleland, a group of people "who suffered with helpless stoicism whatever indignities were thrust upon [them]."

But *Yick Wo* could hardly be seen as an instance of a people suffering indignities with helpless stoicism. It was clearly an example of resistance to perceived discrimination. Furthermore, it took little rummaging around in the federal and state case reports to realize that it was but one of many cases brought by the Chinese during the nineteenth century. Indeed between 1880 and 1900 Chinese litigants carried some twenty appeals to the Supreme Court of the United States. Furthermore, I discovered one could find examples of the Chinese protesting discriminatory treatment dating back to the very infancy of the immigration. Knowing that the Presbyterians had been active in the San Francisco Chinese community, I visited the San Francisco Theological Seminary, a Presbyterian institution in San Anselmo, California. There I found an extraordinary series of letters, indicating that the leaders of the Chinese community had in 1860 asked a churchman to help them find a lobbyist to speak on their behalf against anti-Chinese legislation then being considered by the state legislature. * * * *Yick Wo*, in fine, was but the small tip of a very large iceberg. * * *

[The] conventional wisdom concerning the Chinese and their supposed political backwardness needs to be stood on its head. The nineteenth-century Chinese–American community may, because of language, have been more isolated from mainstream society than other immigrant groups in certain respects, but lack of political consciousness was not one of its distinguishing characteristics. As this account will demonstrate, there is abundant evidence that the leaders of the nineteenth-century Chinese community—and many other Chinese as well—were thoroughly familiar with American governmental institutions, the courts in particular, and knew how to use those institutions to protect themselves. Far from being passive or docile in the face of official mistreatment, they reacted with indignation to it and more often than not sought redress in the courts. Indeed during the second half of the nineteenth century, the Chinese mounted court challenges to virtually every governmentally imposed disability under which they labored. Why a fact so obvious and so important as this should have been so largely ignored by American historiography shall always remain to be something of a mystery. The Chinese readiness to resort to the courts to remedy perceived wrongs is an aspect of their experience in the United States barely touched on in the published literature. Yet it is surely one of the most salient and defining features of that experience. To ignore it would be comparable to ignoring the many legal contests of black Americans. It would be as if an historian of African America should, after surveying the long, shameful treatment of blacks, ask why, in the midst of so much persecution did these people never think of going to court to defend themselves.

To ignore Chinese legal initiatives is, as well, to ignore an important facet of U.S. constitutional history in general. The cases brought by the Chinese raised immensely interesting questions of constitutional and statutory interpretation. Many of them contributed significantly to the molding of American constitutional jurisprudence.

Notes and Questions

1. Why do you think so much Chinese and Chinese–American legal history has been ignored both as legal history and as racial history? Is the treatment suffered by the Chinese irrelevant in American history?

2. What does this history teach us about the United States during the nineteenth century? What does it teach us about the United States today?

SECTION 2. JAPANESE AMERICANS

Japanese began immigrating in significant numbers to the United States in 1885, when the Japanese government made emigration legal. Approximately 200,000 Japanese were admitted to the United States between 1891 and 1924, when American immigration legislation terminated Japanese immigration. See Harry H.L. Kitano, *Japanese Americans* 8 n.7 (2d ed. 1976).

Japanese emigrated to the United States for several reasons. Since wage rates for labor were much higher in the United States than in

Japan, immigrants were attracted by seemingly greater possibilities for prosperity. Initially, Japanese labor was sought (as was Black, Mexican, and Puerto Rican labor) to alleviate a labor shortage caused in part by the successful legal exclusion of the Chinese. Raymond Leslie Buell, *The Development of Anti–Japanese Agitation in the United States*, reprinted in Charles McClain, *Japanese Immigrants and American Law* 25 (1994).

In the wake of California's violent, hostile campaign against the Chinese, the Japanese, first desired for their labor, immigrated into a situation that was ripe for hostility against them. As the Japanese became successful and sought upward mobility, white workers perceived them as an economic threat which they sought to eliminate. As expressed in the *San Francisco Chronicle*:

> Had the Japanese laborer throttled his ambition to progress along the lines of American citizenship and industrial development, he probably would have attracted small attention of the public mind. Japanese ambition is to progress beyond mere servility to the plane of the better class of American workman and to own a home with him. The moment that this position is exercised, the Japanese ceases to be an ideal laborer.

San Francisco Chronicle, quoted in Kitano, *supra* p. 18. As early as 1905, a Japanese and Korean Exclusion League formed, seeking to shut out Japanese and Korean laborers, to boycott Japanese businesses, to segregate Japanese from white children, and to focus national attention on the Japanese "menace." In response to anti-Japanese sentiment in California, the Japanese and United States governments entered into a "Gentleman's Agreement" in 1907–08. Under its terms, Japan agreed to restrict the emigration of Japanese laborers by denying passports to most persons of the laboring class. Raymond Leslie Buell, *The Development of Anti–Japanese Agitation in the United States*, reprinted in McClain, *Japanese Immigrants, supra* at 54–56.

A. THE ALIEN LAND LAWS

Many of the Japanese who immigrated to the United States were farmers and farm laborers. They were able to take up these occupations easily in California. Over time the Japanese significantly increased their acreage, whether owned or leased. For example, the amount of Japanese agricultural farmland in California increased between 1905 and 1913 from 61,858 acres to 281,687 acres. See Yuji Ichioka, *Japanese Immigrant Response to the 1920 California Land Law*, reprinted in McClain, *Japanese Immigrants, supra* at 230. As the Japanese established a presence in agriculture, Californians acted to deprive them of their success by enacting the Alien Land Law of 1913, which, despite its seemingly neutral title, aimed directly at the Japanese.

THE CALIFORNIA ALIEN LAND LAW (1913)

SEC. 1. All aliens eligible to citizenship under the laws of the United States may acquire, possess, enjoy, transmit and inherit real property, or any interest therein, in this state, in the same manner and to the same extent as citizens of the United States, except as otherwise provided by the laws of this state.

SEC. 2. All aliens other than those mentioned in section one of this act may acquire, possess, enjoy and transfer real property, or any interest therein, in this state, in the manner and to the extent and for the purposes prescribed by any treaty now existing between the government of the United States and the nation or country of which such alien is a citizen or subject, and not otherwise, and may in addition thereto lease lands in this state for agricultural purposes for a term not exceeding three years.

SEC. 3 Any company, association or corporation organized under the laws of this or any other state or nation, of which a majority of the members are aliens other than those specified in section one of this act, or in which a majority of the issued capital stock is owned by such aliens, may acquire, possess, enjoy and convey real property, or any interest therein, in this state, in the manner and to the extent and for the purposes prescribed by any treaty now existing between the government of the United States and the nation or country of which such members or stockholders are citizens or subjects, and not otherwise, and may in addition thereto lease lands in this state for agricultural purposes for a term not exceeding three years.

SEC. 4. Whenever it appears to the court in any probate proceeding that by reason of the provisions of this act any heir or devisee can not take real property in this state which, but for said provisions, said heir or devisee would take as such, the court, instead of ordering a distribution of such real property to such heir or devisee, shall order a sale of said real property to be made in the manner provided by law for probate sales of real property, and the proceeds of such sale shall be distributed to such heir or devisee in lieu of such real property.

SEC. 5. Any real property hereafter acquired in fee in violation of the provisions of this act by any alien mentioned in section two of this act, or by any company, association or corporation mentioned in section three of this act, shall escheat to, and become and remain the property of the State of California. * * *

SEC. 6. Any leasehold or other interest in real property less than the fee, hereafter acquired in violation of the provisions of this act by any alien mentioned in section two of this act, or by any company, association or corporation mentioned in section three of this act, shall escheat to the State of California. * * *

Statutes of California, 40th Sess., Ch. 113, pp. 206–208.

————

Because, at this time, Japanese were ineligible for naturalized citizenship since they were neither white nor of African descent, this law applied directly to them. Japanese farmers were able to find ways around the law, for example by forming landholding corporations whose stock was owned by citizens, including their citizen children; by paying Americans to hold the land in trust for them or their children; or by guardianship, when Japanese parents would purchase land in the names of their citizen children, while the parents would act as guardians and farm the land. See Buell, in McClain, *Japanese Immigrants, supra* at 67–68.

Although their landholdings increased between 1913 and 1920, the Alien Land Law was costly and damaging to the Japanese. The land of Japanese farmers, who died without transferring ownership of their lands, sold at a substantial discount. The three-year leasing limitation encouraged cultivation of speculative, short-term crops and discouraged investment in longer-term crops. The law made many Japanese uncertain about their future in the United States, and so encouraged their return to Japan. Most importantly, "the 1913 Alien Land Law forced all Japanese to live with the stigma of being aliens ineligible to citizenship and subject to discriminatory treatment." Ichioka, in McClain, *Japanese Immigrants, supra* at 234–35. Following California's lead, eleven other states enacted alien land laws: "Arizona in 1917; Louisiana, 1921; [Eds. Washington, 1921]; New Mexico, 1922; Idaho, 1923; Montana, 1923; Oregon, 1923; Kansas, 1925 and Utah, 1943." Wyoming and Arkansas joined their predecessors in 1943. See Dudley O. McGovney, *The Anti-Japanese Land Laws of California and Ten Other States*, 35 Cal. L. Rev. 7, 8 (1947), reprinted in McClain, *Japanese Immigrants, supra* at 277–78.

In 1920, Californians, concerned about the increase in Japanese farming even after the Alien Land Law, decided to make the law more restrictive. As Yuji Ichioka describes it:

> Designed to plug up the loopholes in the 1913 law, the 1920 California Alien Land Law had the undisguised purpose of driving Japanese farmers out of California agriculture. This law prohibited aliens ineligible to citizenship not only from purchasing but also from leasing agricultural land. It also denied them the right of buying and selling stock in land companies which owned or leased agricultural land and disqualified them from being appointed guardians of minors who had interest in such land.

Ichioka, in McClain, *Japanese Immigrants, supra* at 235.

Notes and Questions

1. Why were states like Louisiana and Kansas inspired to pass anti-Japanese laws? Why do you think Arkansas enacted its law in 1943?

———

Supported by a coalition of Japanese citizen organizations, Japanese immigrants challenged the alien land laws in a series of cases decided by the Supreme Court. The lead case was *Terrace v. Thompson*, 263 U.S. 197 (1923), in which Terrace challenged the constitutionality of Washington's Alien Land Law, which was substantially similar to California's law.

TERRACE v. THOMPSON

263 U.S. 197 (1923).

JUSTICE BUTLER delivered the opinion of the Court.

[Terrace was a white landowner who wanted to lease his agricultural land to Nakatsuka, a Japanese farmer, for five years.]

Appellants brought this suit to enjoin the Attorney General of Washington from enforcing the Anti–Alien Land Law of that state (Chapter 50, Laws 1921), on the grounds that it is in conflict with the Due Process and Equal Protection Clauses of the Fourteenth Amendment, with the treaty between the United States and Japan, and with certain provisions of the Constitution of the state.

The appellants are residents of Washington. The Terraces are citizens of the United States and of Washington. Nakatsuka was born in Japan of Japanese parents and is a subject of the emperor of Japan. The Terraces are the owners of a tract of land in King county which is particularly adapted to raising vegetables, and which for a number of years had been devoted to that and other agricultural purposes. The complaint alleges that Nakatsuka is a capable farmer and will be a desirable tenant of the land, that the Terraces desire to lease their land to him for the period of five years, that he desires to accept such lease, and that the lease would be made but for the act complained of; and it is alleged that the defendant, as Attorney General, has threatened to and will take steps to enforce the act against the appellants if they enter into such lease, and will treat the leasehold interest as forfeited to the state, and will prosecute the appellants criminally for violation of the act; that the act is so drastic and the penalties attached to its violation are so great that neither of the appellants may make the lease even to test the constitutionality of the act; and that, unless the court shall determine its validity in this suit, the appellants will be compelled to submit to it, whether valid or invalid, and thereby will be deprived of their property without due process of law and denied the equal protection of the laws.

Section 33 of Article 2 of the Constitution of Washington prohibits the ownership of land by aliens other than those who in good faith have declared intention to become citizens of the United States, except in certain instances not here involved. The act provides in substance that any such alien shall not own, take, have or hold the legal or equitable title, or right to any benefit of any land as defined in the act, and that land conveyed to or for the use of aliens in violation of the state constitution or of the act shall thereby be forfeited to the state, and it is made a gross misdemeanor, punishable by fine or imprisonment or both, knowingly to transfer land or the right to the control, possession or use of land to such an alien. It is also made a gross misdemeanor for any such alien having title to such land or the control, possession or use thereof, to refuse to disclose to the Attorney General or the prosecuting attorney the nature and extent of his interest in the land. The Attorney General and the prosecuting attorneys of the several counties are charged with the enforcement of the act.

* * *

The Terraces' property rights in the land include the right to use, lease and dispose of it for lawful purposes * * *, and the Constitution protects these essential attributes of property * * *, and also protects Nakatsuka in his right to earn a livelihood by following the ordinary occupations of life * * *.

Appellants contend that the act contravenes the due process clause in that it prohibits the owners from making lawful disposition or use of their land, and makes it a criminal offense for them to lease it to the alien, and prohibits him from following the occupation of farmer; and they contend that it is repugnant to the Equal Protection Clause in that aliens are divided into two classes,—those who may and those who may not become citizens, one class being permitted, while the other is forbidden, to own land as defined. * * *

And, while Congress has exclusive jurisdiction over immigration, naturalization and the disposal of the public domain, each state, in the absence of any treaty provision to the contrary, has power to deny to aliens the right to own land within its borders. * * *

State legislation applying alike and equally to all aliens, withholding from them the right to own land, cannot be said to be capricious or to amount to an arbitrary deprivation of liberty or property, or to transgress the Due Process Clause.

This brings us to a consideration of appellants' contention that the act contravenes the Equal Protection Clause. That clause secures equal protection to all in the enjoyment of their rights under like circumstances. * * * But this does not forbid every distinction in the law of a state between citizens and aliens resident therein. * * *

By the statute in question all aliens who have not in good faith declared intention to become citizens of the United States, as specified in section 1(a), are called "aliens," and it is provided that they shall not "own" land, as defined in clauses (d) and (b) of section 1 respectively. The class so created includes all, but is not limited to, aliens not eligible to become citizens. Eligible aliens who have not declared their intention to become citizens are included, and the act provides that unless declarants be admitted to citizenship within seven years after the declaration is made, bad faith will be presumed. This leaves the class permitted so to own land made up of citizens and aliens who may, and who intend to, become citizens, and who in good faith have made the declaration required by the naturalization laws. The inclusion of good faith declarants in the same class with citizens does not unjustly discriminate against aliens who are ineligible or against eligible aliens who have failed to declare their intention. The classification is based on eligibility and purpose to naturalize. Eligible aliens are free white persons and persons of African nativity or descent. Congress is not trammeled, and it may grant or withhold the privilege of naturalization upon any grounds or without any reason, as it sees fit. But it is not to be supposed that its acts defining eligibility are arbitrary or unsupported by reasonable consideration of public policy.

The state properly may assume that the considerations upon which Congress made such classification are substantial and reasonable. Generally speaking, the natives of European countries are eligible. Japanese, Chinese and Malays are not. Appellants' contention that the state act discriminates arbitrarily against Nakatsuka and other ineligible aliens because of their race and color is without foundation. All persons of whatever color or race who have not declared their intention in good faith to become citizens are prohibited from so owning agricultural lands. Two classes of aliens inevitably result from the naturalization laws—those who may and those who may not become citizens. The rule established by Congress on this subject, in and of itself, furnishes a reasonable basis for classification in a state law withholding from aliens the privilege of land ownership as defined in the act. We agree with the court below that:

> It is obvious that one who is not a citizen and cannot become one lacks an interest in, and the power to effectually work for the welfare of, the state, and, so lacking, the state may rightfully deny him the right to own and lease real estate within its boundaries. If one incapable of citizenship may lease or own real estate, it is within the realm of possibility that every foot of land within the state might pass to the ownership or possession of noncitizens.

And we think it is clearly within the power of the state to include nondeclarant eligible aliens and ineligible aliens in the same prohibited class. Reasons supporting discrimination against aliens who may but who will not naturalize are obvious. * * *

In the case before us, the thing forbidden is very different [from an alien's right to work for a living]. It is not an opportunity to earn a living in common occupations of the community, but it is the privilege of owning or controlling agricultural land within the state. The quality and allegiance of those who own, occupy and use the farm lands within its borders are matters of highest importance and affect the safety and power of the state itself.

The Terraces, who are citizens, have no right safeguarded by the Fourteenth Amendment to lease their land to aliens lawfully forbidden to take or have such lease. The state act is not repugnant to the Equal Protection Clause and does not contravene the Fourteenth Amendment.

The state act, in our opinion, is not in conflict with the treaty between the United States and Japan. * * *

The only [treaty] provision that relates to owning or leasing land is in the first paragraph of Article I, which is as follows:

> The citizens or subjects of each of the High Contracting Parties shall have liberty to enter, travel and reside in the territories of the other to carry on trade, wholesale and retail, to own or lease and occupy houses, manufactories, warehouses and shops, to employ agents of their choice, to lease land for residential and commercial purposes, and generally to do anything incident to or necessary for trade upon the same terms as native citizens or subjects, submitting themselves to the laws and regulations there established.

For the purpose of bringing Nakatsuka within the protection of the treaty, the amended complaint alleges that, in addition to being a capable farmer, he is engaged in the business of trading, wholesale and retail, in farm products and shipping the same in intrastate, interstate and foreign commerce, and, instead of purchasing such farm products, he has produced, and desires to continue to produce, his own farm products for the purpose of selling them in such wholesale and retail trade, and if he is prevented from leasing land for the purpose of producing farm products for such trade he will be prevented from engaging in trade and the incidents to trade, as he is authorized to do under the treaty.

To prevail on this point, appellants must show conflict between the state act and the treaty. Each State, in the absence of any treaty provision conferring the right, may enact laws prohibiting aliens from owning land within its borders. Unless the right to own or lease land is given by the treaty, no question of conflict can arise. We think that the treaty contains no provision giving Japanese the right to own or lease land for agricultural purposes, but when viewed in the light of the negotiations leading up to its consummation, the language shows that the high contracting parties respectively intended to withhold a treaty grant of that right to the citizens or subjects of either in the territories of the other. That right to "carry on trade" or "to own or lease and occupy houses, manufactories, warehouses and shops", or "to lease land for residential and commercial purposes", or "to do anything incident and necessary for trade" cannot be said to include the right to own or lease or to have any title to or interest in land for agricultural purposes. The enumeration of rights to own or lease for other specified purposes impliedly negatives the right to own or lease land for these purposes. A careful reading of the treaty suffices in our opinion to negative the claim asserted by appellants that it conflicts with the state act.

* * *

[The Court thus upheld the Washington Alien Land Law in its entirety.]

Notes and Questions

1. Is the Court correct in stating that the right "to lease land for residential and commercial purposes * * * cannot be said to include the right to own or lease or to have any title to or interest in land for agricultural purposes?" Is a contrary interpretation possible? Likely? Why did the Court interpret the treaty language as it did?

———

In California, the Japanese won an early victory in the case of *Tetsubumi Yano,* 188 Cal. 645, 206 P. 995 (1922), in which the California Supreme Court, sitting *en banc,* upheld the right of a Japanese father to act as a guardian for property owned in the name of his minor daughter, even if the father's intent was to evade the intent of the 1913 Alien Land Law. One of the 1920 amendments to the 1913 law made it illegal for a Japanese alien to act as a guardian, but the father, Hayao Yano, had acted before the 1920 amendments were enacted. Subsequent Supreme Court decisions, however, relying on *Terrace v. Thompson,* consistently upheld the provisions of California's Alien Land Law and dealt bitter defeats to the Japanese who struggled to preserve their farms. The first of these decisions, *Porterfield v. Webb*, 263 U.S. 225 (1923), summarily upheld the California provision prohibiting the leasing of land to aliens ineligible for citizenship (the Japanese) on the authority of *Terrace*. In *Webb v. O'Brien*, 263 U.S. 313 (1923), the Supreme Court upheld the Alien Land Law as it applied to prohibit a cropping contract between a citizen (O'Brien) and a Japanese farmer named Inouye, who would farm the land, live on it and receive half of the crop in exchange for protection by O'Brien against anyone who would interfere with operation of the farm. In *Frick v. Webb*, 263 U.S. 326 (1923), the Court upheld California's ban on the sale to aliens of shares in a landholding corporation. "By upholding the constitutionality of the alien land laws, the Supreme Court decisions had destroyed the economic foundations of Japanese immigrant society." Yuji Ichioka, *The Issei* 234 (1988).

B.   THE JAPANESE QUEST FOR CITIZENSHIP

Despite the assumption that Japanese were ineligible for citizenship in the Alien Land Laws (because they were neither "free white persons" nor of African ancestry), the naturalization status of Japanese had not been settled definitively. According to the 1910 census four hundred twenty Japanese had been naturalized. See Yuji Ichioka, *The Early Japanese Immigrant Quest for Citizenship: The Background of the 1922 Ozawa Case*, reprinted in McClain, *Japanese Immigrants, supra* at 398. The Supreme Court settled the eligibility of Japanese for naturalization definitively in *Ozawa v. United States*, 260 U.S. 178 (1922). In *Ozawa*, the Court concluded that Ozawa Takao, born in Japan, was ineligible to be naturalized under the federal naturalization statute, which allowed naturalization only to "free white persons and to aliens of African nativity and to persons of African descent." The important *Ozawa* case and is excerpted and discussed at length *infra* in Chapter 6, on the construction of whiteness.

YUJI ICHIOKA

The Early Japanese Immigrant Quest for Citizenship:
The Background of the 1922 Ozawa Case
4 Amerasia J. 1–2, 17–18 (1977).*

Denied the right of naturalization, Japanese immigrants were so-called "aliens ineligible to citizenship" for decades. In the noted case of Ozawa Takao, the United States Supreme Court upheld the ineligibility of the Japanese in a 1922 landmark decision that stood unchallenged until the McCarran Act of 1952 altered their legal status and finally admitted them into citizenship. The literature in English on the early history of the immigrants is one-sided. Principally devoted to the movement to exclude the Japanese from the United States in the first quarter of the twentieth century, it covers the origins, causes, and development of the exclusion movement and the averse repercussions it had on United States–Japan relations. Highlighting the *excluders* rather then the *excluded*, the literature rarely touches on how the immigrants felt, thought, and reacted to being excluded. Slighting them, past studies give

every childhood story

* Reprinted by permission of Amerasia Journal.

at best the false impression of their having been merely a victimized mass. Japanese immigrants were anything but passive victims; on the contrary, they actively fought the exclusion movement. As a part of their long and bitter struggle, they supported the *Ozawa* case in the hope of gaining the right of naturalization. * * *

To grasp the full meaning of the *Ozawa* case, the larger historical context must be taken into account. The term *kimin* often appears in the writings of Japanese immigrants. Meaning "an abandoned people," this special term stems from the immigrants' profound sense of rejection. It refers, on the one hand, to the failure of the Japanese government to come to their aid in times of need. Japanese diplomats usually sacrificed the immigrants' welfare for the sake of what they perceived as diplomatic necessity. An instance was their reluctance to negotiate naturalization rights for the immigrants. Prejudiced by class and bureaucratic biases, many Japanese officials and prominent persons in Japan indeed looked down with arrogant contempt upon their uprooted countrymen as an uneducated, ignorant lot and blamed them for the animosity of white Americans. Such individuals felt that the immigrants, by their own conduct in the United States, were responsible for causing the exclusion movement.

On the other hand, kimin refers to the American repudiation of the immigrants, especially after 1922. Parallel to the *Ozawa* case, the immigrants instituted land litigation to contest the 1920 California and 1921 Washington alien land laws. Three types of cases pended before the Supreme Court in 1922 which tempered the immigrant response to the *Ozawa* decision. For the prevailing opinion among immigrant leaders was that they would win the separate land cases, even if they lost the naturalization test cases. To their utter dismay, the immigrants suffered total defeat in the land cases in 1923 which undermined the livelihood of many tenant farmers. Terminating all Japanese immigration to the United States, the Immigration Act of 1924 was the culminating event. Prohibiting the entry of all aliens ineligible to citizenship, the immigrants interpreted this enactment as America's final rejection of them. The *Ozawa* decision was rendered within this broad historical context. Viewed from the vantage of the immigrants themselves, it was one of many events that contributed to their sense of having been reduced to "an abandoned people" forsaken by both the mother country and the immigrant land.

C. WORLD WAR II AND JAPANESE INTERNMENT

For Japanese immigrants and their citizen children, their sense of *kimin,* of being an abandoned people, could only deepen with the events of World War II. The bombing of Pearl Harbor on December 7, 1941 plunged the United States into a declared war against Japanese combatants, and an undeclared war against citizens and aliens of Japanese ancestry resident in the United States. Consider the following excerpt.

RONALD TAKAKI

Strangers From a Different Shore
392–96 (1989).*

President Roosevelt had signed a blank check, giving full authority to General DeWitt to evacuate the Japanese and place them in assembly centers and eventually in internment camps. And so it happened, tragically for the Japanese and for the U.S. Constitution, for there was actually no "military necessity."

Under General DeWitt's command, the military ordered a curfew for all enemy aliens and all persons of Japanese ancestry and posted orders for evacuation: "Pursuant to the provisions of Civilian Exclusion Order No. 27, this Headquarters, dated April 30, 1942, all persons of Japanese ancestry, both alien and non-alien, will be evacuated from the above area by 12 o'clock noon, P. W. T., Thursday May 7, 1942." The evacuees were instructed to bring their bedding, toilet articles, extra clothing, and utensils. "No pets of any kind will be permitted." Japanese stood in silent numbness before the notices. Years later, Congressman Robert Matsui, who was a baby in 1942, asked: "How could I as a 6–month-old child born in this country be declared by my own Government to be an enemy alien?" But the order applied to everyone, including children. An American birthright made absolutely no difference. "Doesn't my citizenship mean a single blessed thing to anyone?" asked Monica Sone's brother in distress. "Several weeks before May, soldiers came around and posted notices on telephone poles," said Takae Wahizu. "It was sad for me to leave the place where I had been living for such a long time. Staring at the ceiling in bed at night, I wondered who would take care of my cherry tree and my house after we moved out."

> *Notice of evacuation*
> *One spring night*
> *The image of my wife*
> *Holding the hands of my mother.*

Believing the military orders were unconstitutional, Minoru Yasui of Portland refused to obey the curfew order: "It was my belief that no military authority has the right to subject any United States citizen to any requirement that does not equally apply to all other U.S. citizens. If we believe in America, if we believe in equality and democracy, if we believe in law and justice, then each of us, when we see or believe errors are being made, has an obligation to make every effort to correct them." Meanwhile Fred Korematsu in California and Gordon Hirabayashi in Washington refused to report to the evacuation center. "As an American citizen," Hirabayashi explained, "I wanted to uphold the principles of the Constitution, and the curfew and evacuation orders which singled out a group on the basis of ethnicity violated them. It was not acceptable to me to be less than a full citizen in a white man's country." The three men were arrested and convicted; sent to prison, they took their cases to the Supreme Court, which upheld their convictions, saying the government's policies were based on military necessity. Most Japanese, however, felt they had no choice but to comply with the evacuation orders.

Instructed they would be allowed to take only what they could carry, evacuees had to sell most of their possessions—their refrigerators, cars, furniture, radios, pianos, and houses. "I remember how agonizing was my despair," recounted Tom Hayase, "to be given only about six days in which to dispose of our property." "It is difficult to describe the feeling of despair and humiliation experienced by all of us," said another evacuee, "as we watched the Caucasians coming to look over our possessions and offering such nominal amounts knowing we had no recourse but to accept whatever they were offering because we did not know what the future held for us."

At the control centers, the evacuees were registered and each family was given a number. "Henry went to the Control Station to register the family," remembered Monica Sone. "He came home with twenty tags, all numbered '10710', tags to be attached to each piece of baggage, and one to hang from our coat lapels. From then on, we were known as Family #10710." When they reported at the train stations, they found themselves surrounded by soldiers with rifles and bayonets.

> Like a dog
> I am commanded
> At a bayonet point.
> My heart is inflamed
> With burning anguish.

From there they were taken to the assembly centers. "I looked at Santa Clara's streets from the train over the subway," wrote Norman Mineta's father in a letter to friends in San Jose. "I thought this might be the last look at my loved home city. My heart almost broke, and suddenly hot tears just came pouring out...." They knew that more than their homes and possessions had been taken from them. "On May 16, 1942, my mother, two sisters, niece, nephew, and I left ... by train," said Teru Watanabe. "Father joined us later. Brother left earlier by bus. We took whatever we could carry. So much we left behind, but the most valuable thing I lost was my freedom."

When they arrived, the evacuees were shocked to discover that they were to be housed at stockyards, fairgrounds, and race tracks. "The assembly center was filthy, smelly, and dirty. There were roughly two thousand people packed in one large building. No beds were provided, so they gave us gunny sacks to fill with straw, that was our bed." Stables served as housing. "Where a horse or cow had been kept, a Japanese American family was moved in." "Suddenly you realized that human beings were being put behind fences just like on the farm where we had horses and pigs in corrals."

> If you live in a
> Horse stable
> The wind of cities
> Blow through.

Conditions were crowded and noisy. "There was a constant buzzing—conversations, talk. Then, as the evening wore on, during the still of the night, things would get quiet, except for the occasional coughing, snoring, giggles. Then someone would get up to go to the bathroom. It was like a family of three thousand people camped out in a barn." Everywhere there were lines. "We lined up for mail, for checks, for meals, for showers, for washrooms, for laundry tubs, for toilets, for clinic service, for movies." There were curfews and roll calls, and "day and night camp police walked their beats within the center."

After a brief stay in the assembly centers, the evacuees were herded into 171 special trains, five hundred in each train.

Snow in mountain pass
Unable to sleep
The prison train.

They had no idea where they were going. In their pockets, some carried photographs of themselves and the homes they had left behind, and they occasionally turned their gaze away from the landscape whizzing by them and pulled out their pictures.

Falling asleep with
A photograph,
Awakened by a dream,
Cold snowy wind of
Missoula.

The trains took them to ten internment camps—Topaz in Utah, Poston and Gila River in Arizona, Amache in Colorado, Jerome and Rohwer in Arkansas, Minidoka in Idaho, Manzanar and Tule Lake in California, and Heart Mountain in Wyoming.

Most of the camps were located in remote desert areas. "We did not know where we were," remembered an internee. "No houses were in sight, no trees or anything green—only scrubby sagebrush and an occasional low cactus, and mostly dry, baked earth." They looked around them and saw hundreds of miles of wasteland, "beyond the end of the horizon and again over the mountain—again, more wasteland." They were surrounded by dust and sand. At Minidoka, Monica Sone recalled, "we felt as if we were standing in a gigantic sand-mixing machine as the sixty-mile gale lifted the loose earth up into the sky, obliterating everything. Sand filled our mouths and nostrils and stung our faces and hands like a thousand darting needles."

In the camps, the internees were assigned to barracks, each barrack about twenty by 120 feet, divided into four or six rooms. Usually a family was housed in one room, twenty by twenty feet. The room had "a pot bellied stove, a single electric light hanging from the ceiling, an Army cot for each person and a blanket for the bed."

Birds,
Living in a cage,
The human spirit.

The camp was linear, its barracks lined in orderly rows; barbed-wire fences with guard towers defined space for the internees. Some tried to resist the strictures of the new form of "necessity" by creating rock gardens with bonsai outside their drab barracks.

Their little gardens provided relief in a world of military-like routine. "Camp life was highly regimented and it was rushing to the wash basin to beat the other groups, rushing to the mess hall for breakfast, lunch and dinner." Every morning at 7 A.M., the internees were awakened by a siren blast. After eating breakfast in a cafeteria, the children went to school, where they began the day by saluting the flag of the United States and then singing "My country, 'tis of thee, sweet land of liberty." Looking beyond the flagpole, they saw the barbed wire, the watchtowers, and the armed guards. "I was too young to understand," stated George Takei years later, "but I remember soldiers carrying rifles, and I remember being afraid."

[handwritten marginal note: irony cruelty]

——————

The war itself, and particularly the curfew and exclusion orders imposed upon the Japanese living along the West coast, provoked a crisis within the Japanese community. Leaders of the Japanese American Citizens League, the most prominent organization of Japanese Americans, debated whether to comply or not with these orders. In the end, the organization concluded that they could demonstrate the greatest amount of loyalty to the United States by cooperating with these governmental orders, however harsh. Roger Daniels, *Prisoners Without Trial* 50 (1993); Peter Irons, *Justice at War* 78–81 (1983).

Some Japanese Americans, however, felt that these orders were unconstitutional and that, as loyal American citizens they should challenge their adverse treatment in court. Gordon Hirabayashi, for example, was a United States citizen by virtue of his birth in Seattle, Washington, and was 24 years old at the time of his incarceration. A senior at the University of Washington, he was a student officer of the YMCA and joined the University Quaker meeting. Hirabayashi dropped out of school when the Civilian Exclusion Order was issued on March 29, 1942. Hirabayashi figured he would not be around very long. After months of complying with curfew orders, eventually he resented the demand it placed on his life. In his words: "I expected like every citizen to obey the law, and I did * * * There were twelve of us living in the YMCA dorm, and they all became my volunteer timekeepers—'Hey, it's five minutes to eight, Gordy'—and I'd dash back from the library or the coffee shop. One of the times I stopped and said, 'Why the hell am I running back? Am I a American or not? Why am I running back and nobody else is?'" Peter Irons, *Justice at War* 90 (1983).

Hirabayashi challenged the curfew orders in a case that was decided eventually by the Supreme Court. The Court upheld the curfew orders in *Hirabayashi v. United States*, 320 U.S. 81 (1943), reasoning that Congress and General DeWitt (who issued the curfew and exclusion orders), had acted within their respective powers and had used reasonable judgment in responding to the potential threat posed by persons possibly loyal to Japan within the United States:

There is support for the view that social, economic and political conditions which have prevailed since the close of the last century, when the Japanese began to come to this country in substantial numbers, have intensified their solidarity and have in large measure prevented their assimilation as an integral part of the white population. In addition, large numbers of children of Japanese parentage are sent to Japanese language schools outside the regular hours of public schools in the locality. Some of these schools are generally believed to be sources of Japanese nationalistic propaganda, cultivating allegiance to Japan. Considerable numbers, estimated to be approximately 10,000, of American-born children of Japanese parentage have been sent to Japan for all or a part of their education. * * *

As a result of all these conditions affecting the life of the Japanese, both aliens and citizens, in the Pacific Coast area, there has been relatively little social intercourse between them and the white population. The restrictions, both practical and legal, affecting the privileges and opportunities afforded to persons of Japanese extraction residing in the United States, have been sources of irritation and may well have tended to increase their isolation, and in many instances their attachments to Japan and its institutions.

Viewing these data in all their aspects, Congress and the Executive could reasonably have concluded that these conditions have encouraged the continued attachment of members of these groups to Japan and Japanese institutions. * * * Whatever views we may entertain regarding the loyalty to this country of the citizens of Japanese ancestry, we cannot reject as unfounded the judgment of the military authorities and of Congress that there were disloyal members of that population, whose number and strength could not be precisely and quickly ascertained.

320 U.S. at 96–99.

After Hirabayashi's challenge to the curfew orders had been rejected, another Japanese–American citizen challenged the more disruptive exclusion orders, which required persons of Japanese ancestry to gather at designated assembly centers and ultimately to reside at "relocation centers." Fred Korematsu was a welder who attempted to volunteer for service in the Navy in June 1941. Because of medical problems he was classified 4–F and was unable to serve. Imprisoned when he refused to comply with the exclusion orders, he challenged these orders in court. His internment was upheld by the Supreme Court in *Korematsu v. United States*, 323 U.S. 214 (1944), reproduced *infra* in Chapter 7 § 1, on equality.

Notes and Questions

1.   Due to the activism of advocates for the interned Japanese–American families, the survivors and descendants of persons interned during the war ultimately received official letters of apology from the United States Government, signed by President George Bush, and payments of $20,000 per

survivor in partial reparations. See Yasuko I. Takezawa, *Breaking the Silence: Redress and Japanese American Ethnicity* 51–59 (1995).

2. Should the United States pay reparations to other peoples of color harmed by governmental action? What other harmful governmental actions should be redressed? Should reparations or any other form of redress go only to the immediate victims, or also to their descendants? What happens when the immediate victims are all or mostly dead by the time the government decides to make reparations? See *When Sorry Isn't Enough: The Controversy Over Apologies and Reparations for Human Injustice* (Roy Brooks ed. 1999).

3. Japanese and Japanese American civilians were not the only ones affected by U.S. policies in World War II and its aftermath. Over 100,000 Filipinos joined the U.S. army in fighting to defend the U.S. territory. Approximately 22,000 of the 75,000 survivors live in the continental United States today. Many emigrated following the Immigration Act of 1990 which granted them citizenship.

> Many vets have difficulty finding jobs because of their age. * * * Many live in transitional housing while they wait for welfare benefits to kick in. Some are homeless. Others live in groups of four or five to a room. It's a very sad situation for these veterans who fought so courageously for this country.

Emelyn Cruz Lat, *Forgotten Vets: Aging Filipinos Who Fought for U.S. Live Lonely Lives Waiting for Promises to Be Kept*, S.F. Examiner, May 25, 1997 at C1.

Advocacy groups continue to seek veterans benefits for survivors including medical treatment and pensions. Nicole Tsong, *Filipino WWII Vets Seek U.S. Benefits*, S.F. Examiner, July 23, 1998 at A21. For the story of one Filipino veteran, Manuel Fragante, and his struggle against discrimination because of his accent, see Chapter 7, § 2 *infra*.

SECTION 3. CURRENT ISSUES AND VIOLENCE AGAINST ASIAN AMERICANS

THE MYTH OF THE "MODEL MINORITY"

Asian Americans are widely regarded as a "model minority" because some members of this community have achieved outstanding success in the academic arena and other areas. Consider the meaning and deployment of the "model minority" concept in light of the following excerpt.

ROBERT S. CHANG

Toward an Asian American Legal Scholarship: Critical Race Theory, Post–Structuralism, and Narrative Space
81 Cal. L. Rev. 1241, 1258–65, 1308–12 (1993); 1 Asian L.J. 1 (1994).*

THE MODEL MINORITY MYTH

This history of discrimination and violence, as well as the contemporary problems of Asian Americans, are obscured by the portrayal of Asian Americans as a "model minority." Asian Americans are portrayed as "hardworking, intelligent, and successful." This description represents a sharp break from past stereotypes of Asians as "sneaky, obsequious, or inscrutable."

But, the dominant culture's belief in the "model minority" allows it to justify ignoring the unique discrimination faced by Asian Americans. The portrayal of Asian Americans as successful permits the general public, government officials, and the judiciary to ignore or marginalize the contemporary needs of Asian Americans.

An early articulation of the model minority theme appeared in *U.S. News & World Report* in 1966:

> At a time when Americans are awash in worry over the plight of racial minorities—
>
> One such minority, the nation's 300,000 Chinese Americans, is winning wealth and respect by dint of its own hard work.
>
> In any Chinatown from San Francisco to New York, you discover youngsters at grips with their studies . . .
>
> Still being taught in Chinatown is the old idea that people should depend on their own efforts—not a welfare check—in order to reach America's "promised land."
>
> Visit "Chinatown U.S.A." and you find an important racial minority pulling itself up from hardship and discrimination to become a *model* of self-respect and achievement in today's America.[77]

This "model minority" theme has become a largely unquestioned assumption about current social reality.

At its surface, the label "model minority" seems like a compliment. However, once one moves beyond this complimentary facade, one can see the label for what it is—a tool of oppression which works a dual harm by denying the existence of present-day discrimination against Asian Americans and the present-day effects of past discrimination, and legitimizing the oppression of other racial minorities and poor whites.

That Asian Americans are a "model minority" is a myth. But the myth has gained a substantial following, both inside and outside the Asian–American community. The successful inculcation of the model minority myth has created an audience unsympathetic to the problems of Asian Americans. Thus, when we try to make our problems known, our complaints of discrimination or calls for remedial action are seen as unwarranted and inappropriate. They can even spark resentment. For example, Professor Mitsuye Yamada tells a story about the reactions of her Ethnic American Literature class to an anthology compiled by some outspoken Asian–American writers:

> [One student] blurted out that she was offended by its militant tone and that as a white person she was tired of always being blamed for the oppression of all the minorities. I noticed several of her classmates' eyes nodding in tacit agreement. A discussion of the "mili-

---

77. *Success Story of One Minority Group in U.S.*, U.S. News & World Rep., Dec. 26, 1966, at 73, 73, *reprinted in Roots: An Asian American Reader* 6 (Amy Tachiki et al. eds. 1971) (emphasis added).

tant" voices in some of the other writings we had read in the course ensued. Surely, I pointed out, some of these other writings have been just as, if not more, militant as the words in this introduction? Had they been offended by those also but failed to express their feelings about them? To my surprise, they said they were not offended by any of the Black American, Chicano or Native American writings, but were hard-pressed to explain why when I asked for an explanation. A little further discussion revealed that they "understood" the anger expressed by the Blacks and Chicanos and they "empathized" with the frustrations and sorrow expressed by the Native American. But the Asian Americans??

Then finally, one student said it for all of them "It made me angry. *Their* anger made *me* angry, because I didn't even know the Asian Americans felt oppressed. I didn't expect their anger."[80]

This story illustrates the danger of the model minority myth: it renders the oppression of Asian Americans invisible. This invisibility has harmful consequences, especially when those in positions of power cannot see:

> To be out of sight is also to be without social services. Thinking Asian Americans have succeeded, government officials have sometimes denied funding for social service programs designed to help Asian Americans learn English and find employment. Failing to realize that there are poor Asian families, college administrators have sometimes excluded Asian–American students from Educational Opportunity Programs, which are intended for all students from low-income families.[81]

In this way, the model minority myth diverts much-needed attention from the problems of many segments of the Asian American community, particularly the Laotians, Hmong, Cambodians, and Vietnamese who have poverty rates of 67.2%, 65.5%, 46.9% and 33.5%, respectively. These poverty rates compare with a national poverty rate of 9.6%.

In addition to government officials, this distorted view of the current status of Asian Americans has infected at least one very influential member of the judiciary and legal academy. At a recent conference of the Association of American Law Schools, Judge Richard Posner asked two rhetorical questions: "Are Asians an oppressed group in the United States today? Are they worse off for lacking sizable representation on the faculties of American law schools?" His questions are rhetorical because he already has answers, with figures to back them up: "In 1980, Japanese Americans had incomes more than 32% above the national average income, and Chinese Americans had incomes more than 12% above the national average; Anglo Saxons and Irish exceeded the average by 5% and 2%, respectively." He also points out that "in 1980, 17.8% of the white population aged 25 and over had completed four or more years of college, compared to 32.9% of the Asian–American population."

---

80. Mitsuye Yamada, *Invisibility is an Unnatural Disaster: Reflections of an Asian American Woman*, in *This Bridge Called My Back: Writings By Radical Women of Color* 35, 35 (Cherríe Moraga & Gloria Anzaldúa eds. 1981).

81. Ronald Takaki, *Strangers from a Different Shore: A History of Asian Americans* 478 (1989).

The unspoken thesis in Judge Posner's comments, which has been stated by other proponents of meritocracy, is "that, when compared to Whites, there are equal payoffs for qualified and educated racial minorities; education and other social factors, but not race, determine earnings." If Posner is right, Asian Americans should make as much as their white counterparts, *taking into account* "education and other social factors, but not race." Yet when we look more carefully at the statistics, we find some interesting anomalies which belie the meritocratic thesis.

First, Posner's reliance on median family income as evidence for lack of discriminatory effects in employment is misleading. It does not take into account the fact that Asian–American families have more workers per household than do white families; in fact, "more Asian–American women are compelled to work because the male members of their families earn such low wages." Second, the use of national income averages is misleading because most Asian Americans live in geographical locations which have both higher incomes and higher costs of living. Wage disparities become apparent when geographic location is considered. Third, the fact that Asian Americans have a higher percentage of college graduates does not mean that they have economic opportunities commensurate to their level of education. Returns on education rather than educational level provide a better indicator of the existence of discrimination. Many Asian Americans have discovered that they, like other racial minorities, do not get the same return for their educational investment as do their white counterparts.

A closer look, then, at Japanese Americans, Posner's strongest case, reveals flaws in his meritocratic thesis when individual income, geographic location, educational attainment, and hours worked are considered. In 1980, Japanese–American men in California earned incomes comparable to those of white men, but "they did so only by acquiring more education (17.7 years compared to 16.8 years for white men twenty-five to forty-four years old) and by working more hours (2,160 hours compared to 2,120 hours for white men in the same age category)." The income disparities for men from other Asian–American groups are more glaring.

Thus, the answer to Posner's first question is yes—Asian Americans are an oppressed group in America. To accept the myth of the model minority is to participate in the oppression of Asian Americans.

In addition to hurting Asian Americans, the model minority myth works a dual harm by hurting other racial minorities and poor whites who are blamed for not being successful like Asian Americans. "African Americans and Latinos and poor whites are told, 'look at those Asians— anyone can make it in this country if they really try.'" This blame is justified by the meritocratic thesis supposedly proven by the example of Asian Americans. This blame is then used to campaign against government social services for these "undeserving" minorities and poor whites and against affirmative action. To the extent that Asian Americans accept the model minority myth, we are complicitous in the oppression of other racial minorities and poor whites.

This blame and its consequences create resentment against Asian Americans among African Americans, Latino, and poor whites. This resentment, fueled by poor economic conditions, can flare into anger and violence. Asian Americans, the "model minority," serve as convenient scapegoats, as Korean Americans in Los Angeles discovered during the 1992 riots. Many Korean Americans "now view themselves as 'human shields' in a complicated racial hierarchy," caught between "the racism of the white majority and the anger of the black minority." The model minority myth plays a key role in establishing a racial hierarchy which denies the oppression of Asian Americans while simultaneously legitimizing the oppression of other racial minorities and poor whites. * * *

THE NOT SO MODEL MINORITY

While Japanese Americans may enjoy some apparent economic advantages compared to other Asian–American groups, the reality is that many Asian Americans, particularly recent immigrants, are neither economically well-off nor politically empowered. Because the problems of these "not so model minorities" are rarely given voice, I will tell the stories of one such Asian–American subgroup—Asian immigrant garment workers.

* * *

After sewing, laundry, cleaning and cooking, I have no breath left to sing.[342]

In China, Chan Wai Fun (not her real name) worked as an office manager and sang Chinese opera. She immigrated to the United States in 1985, and, like many other Asian immigrant women who have recently arrived in America, she entered the garment industry. Like other immigrant women, Chan desperately wants to learn English in order to get a better job, but also like these other immigrants, she is trapped in her job because she does not have the time or energy to study English. One commentator describes the cycle of poverty reinforced by the garment and restaurant industries in Chinatown:

> They come over, they don't speak English, the man gets a job in a restaurant and the woman in a garment factory down here. In a few years, they think they'll learn English, save some money, and move out. Everyone talks about that. But ... they've lived in Chinatown all ten or twenty years. They earn just enough to keep going, they've hardly saved at all. They don't get exposed to English at work, they're too tired to study at night. The job they got to tide over ends up as a life-time occupation. It's like a vicious cycle. If they didn't have the garment industry, or those restaurant jobs, a lot of people in Chinatown wouldn't make it. But as long as they have those jobs, they'll never get out of here.[348]

342. Miriam C. Louie, *Immigrant Asian Women in Bay Area Garment Sweatshops: "After Sewing, Laundry, Cleaning and Cooking, I Have No Breath Left to Sing,"* 18 Amerasia J. 1, 10 (1992) (quoting a garment worker).

348. Harold P. Dygert III & David Shibata, Note, *Chinatown Sweatshops: Wage Law Violations in the Garment Industry*, 8 U.C. Davis L. Rev. 63, 83 (1975) (quoting B. De Nee & V. De Nee, *Longtime Californ': A*

Although Wai Fun has "no breath left to sing," she is one of the lucky few in that she earns five dollars an hour for her labor. Many garment workers receive less than half the federal minimum wage. The truly unfortunate workers receive nothing at all.

Four hundred fifty garment workers in San Francisco and Oakland almost learned this harsh lesson when they showed up for work on July 17, 1991, only to find their workplace doors padlocked. Their employers, Raymond and Yee Nor Kong, disappeared, leaving the workers with problems far greater than the immediate loss of their jobs:

> The Kongs had not paid them for two months, claiming that money was tight and that compensation would follow when cash became available. The Kongs had borrowed substantial sums from their employees, threatening to terminate workers who would not lend them money. Furthermore, the Kongs had ceased paying health insurance premiums, despite having deducted money from employees' paychecks for this purpose.[353]

Fortunately for these workers, most of whom were Southeast Asian immigrants who spoke little English and did not understand their rights as employees, a total loss was averted:

> [T]he International Ladies Garment Workers Union provided help in filing claims for lost wages and in preventing large creditors from seizing the Kongs' assets before the lost wages were paid. Furthermore, Byer California, a clothing manufacturer which held production contracts with the Kongs, paid $200,000 to the State Labor Commissioner's Office to help cover the unpaid wages of the workers in an act of apparent goodwill.[354]

Twelve women who worked for the Lucky Sewing Company in Oakland's Chinatown discovered, though, that one cannot depend on the generosity of manufacturers. In May of 1992, these women found themselves unemployed; without any notice, their employer, like many other garment shop owners, had closed down the sweatshop and filed for bankruptcy. These twelve workers were owed approximately $15,000 in back wages.

Since these women knew that they had sewn dresses for San Francisco fashion designer Jessica McClintock, several of them visited the Jessica McClintock boutique in San Francisco in August. The workers were shocked to find dresses like the ones they had sewn selling for $175. One seamstress with seven years' experience commented, "I was angry. I didn't expect our dresses to sell for such a high price." This worker, who was owed $3,000 for approximately two and a half months' of work, had worked seven days a week, ten hours a day, and had not

Documentary Study of an American Chinatown 317 (1972)).

353. Dennis Hayashi, *Preventing Human Rights Abuses in the U.S. Garment Industry: A Proposed Amendment to the Fair Labor Standards Act*, 17 Yale J. Int'l L. 195, 195 (1992).

354. Leo L. Lam, Note, *Designer Duty: Extending Liability to Manufacturers for Violations of Labor Standards in Garment Industry Sweatshops*, 141 U. Pa. L. Rev. 623, 626 (1992).

received even the $5 that she should have been paid for sewing that $175 dress.

With the help of community activists, the workers asked Jessica McClintock to compensate them for approximately $2,000 of the $15,000, but McClintock refused. A national media campaign and boycott against her goods ensued, but the garment workers remain unpaid.

Jessica McClintock is at present not legally liable for the workers' back wages, but garment manufacturers should be held liable for the labor law violations of their subcontractors in order to improve working conditions in the industry. Others have set forth the legal basis for manufacturer liability; the narrative accounts of the garment workers' experiences provide moral force for bringing about such a change. Because many Asian–American problems are clouded and silenced by such misperceptions as the model minority myth, change will occur only when voice is given to the stories of the disempowered. Stories such as that of Chan Wai Fun caught in a cycle of poverty, or of the workers abandoned by the Kongs, or of the woman who does not receive $5 in wages for work on a dress retailing for $175, provoke the sense of moral outrage that is often a necessary precursor for change.

* * *

Notes and Questions

1. For further analysis of the paradoxical assumptions made about Asian Americans, see Pat K. Chew, Asian Americans: The "Reticent" Minority and Their Paradoxes, 36 Wm. & Mary L. Rev. 1 (1994) (debunking widely-held stereotypes of Asian Americans).

THE PROBLEM OF ATTRIBUTED "FOREIGNNESS"

One of the problems faced by Asian Americans (and Latinos/as) is that they are constantly presumed to be foreign and un-American regardless of their, and their ancestors', United States citizenship and residency within the country. Neil Gotanda has described this phenomenon eloquently:

> [W]ithin the United States, if a person is racially identified as African American or white, that person is presumed to be legally a U.S. citizen and socially an American.

> * * * [T]hese presumptions are not present for Asian Americans, Latinos, Arab Americans, and other non-Black racial minorities. Rather, there is the opposite presumption that these people are foreigners; or, if they are U.S. citizens, then their racial identity includes a foreign component.

Neil Gotanda, Asian American Rights and the "Miss Saigon Syndrome" in Asian Americans and the Supreme Court 1087, 1096 (Hyung-chan Kim ed. 1992). Consider the meaning and results of this attributed foreignness as you read the next excerpt:

NATSU TAYLOR SAITO

Alien and Non–Alien Alike: Citizenship, "Foreignness,"
and Racial Hierarchy in American Law
76 Or. L. Rev. 261, 294–99, 301–302, 307–308 (1997).*

* * *

[J]ust as the black/white distinction was created by the desire to reinforce slavery, a similar, if less stark, desire to maintain sociopolitical and economic boundaries created the category identified as "yellow," Mongolian, Oriental, or Asian. It has been a less stable classification—often encoded in terms of nationality or ethnicity—but clearly a racial categorization nonetheless. Gotanda describes this in the context of model minority imagery:

> The image of Asians as model minority is a distinctly racial concep-
> tualization. The perception of economic gains of Asian American
> small businesses (especially the image of the "Korean grocer"), the
> dramatic presence of Asians at U.S. colleges and universities, and
> Japanese automobile sales are blended together in a confusing mix.
> These various images of the successful Asian have only the Asian
> racial image in common.[180]

Yet Asians have not just formed a "yellow" layer between black and white. Part of the distinct identity of Asian Americans is that they are simultaneously outsiders as well. The court in In re *Camille* contrasted the "savage and strange inhabitants of the 'dark continent'" with the "intermediate and much-better-qualified red and yellow races," yet found that these "intermediate" races were not eligible for naturalization.[182] Perhaps because Asian immigrants were excluded from citizenship for so long, or perhaps because the imagery slips from race to nationality so easily, foreignness is a deeply ingrained aspect of the racial identification of Asian Americans.

* * *

ASIANS ARE RACED AS "FOREIGN"

From the ugly "Go back to where you came from" to the purportedly neutral "Where are you from?" or the intended-to-be-complimentary "You speak such good English," Asian Americans are confronted daily with the presumption that they are not really Americans. Where does this presumption come from? Why is it so pervasive and so apparently acceptable?

With respect to Asian Americans, there is ongoing conflation of the domestic and the international. This confusion is rooted in the ways in which we have constructed our ideas of race and of nationality. Much of the related negative imagery is not really about foreignness, but reflects

---

* Reprinted by permission. Copyright © 1997 by the University of Oregon; Natsu Taylor Saito.

180. Neil Gotanda, *Asian American Rights and the "Miss Saigon Syndrome"* in *Asian Americans and the Supreme Court* 1087, 1089 (Hyung-chan Kim ed., 1992).

182. In re *Camille*, 6 F. 256, 258–59 (D. Or. 1880).

an imagined foreignness that says more about anti-Asian racism in the United States than it says about Asian cultures. Drawing on Edward Said's work, Keith Aoki defines "orientalism" as "that process whereby Eurocentric nation-states for the past five centuries (at least) have defined themselves in opposition to 'Oriental' others."[187] He notes:

> The position occupied by Asian Americans reflects this tension between global "Orientalism" and domestic U.S. understandings of "race." In addition to being "race-ed" as "non-whites," Asian Americans are also "race-ed" as "foreign"—the palimpsest of Asian origin is never fully erased in the U.S., but acquires a racialized charge.[188]

The attribution of foreignness takes on both ostensibly positive and negative forms. Positive portrayals generally include images of Asians as hardworking, industrious, thrifty, family-oriented and, for women, seductively mysterious and exotic. The negative images are almost invariably the same traits, simply portrayed with different connotations. Gary Okihiro notes:

> The Asian work ethic, family values, self-help, culture and religiosity, and intermarriage—all elements of the model minority—can also be read as components of the yellow peril. . . . [T]he yellow peril and the model minority are not poles, denoting opposite representations along a single line, but in fact form a circular relationship that moves in either direction.[189]

Hardworking and industrious becomes unfairly competitive; family-oriented becomes clannish; mysterious becomes dangerously inscrutable. Nonetheless, both the positive and negative forms of foreignness are portrayals of outsiders, of the "other."

Part of what allows for this fluidity, this right-before-your-eyes magical transformation from model minority to yellow peril and back to model minority again is the construct of foreignness. Each of the images has been painted with the brush of foreignness, and it is this tinting that provides the continuity behind the changing value-attribution. This attribution of both purportedly positive and negative images of foreignness to Asian Americans has been consistent in U.S. history, from the importation of Chinese labor in the mid–1800s to the present. That these characterizations are so fluid and persistent indicates that they further some significant purposes in American society.

* * *

USES OF "FOREIGNNESS": CHEAP LABOR AND READY ENEMIES

Asian immigration was initially encouraged as a source of cheap and relatively easily controlled labor. In using Asian labor, there were several advantages to keeping the workers clearly identified as foreign. One advantage was that the labor force was more easily controlled when it

187. Keith Aoki, *"Foreign-ness" & Asian American Identities: Yellowface, World War II Propaganda, and Bifurcated Racial Stereotypes*, 4 U.C.L.A. Asian Am. Pac. Islands L.J. (forthcoming).

188. *Id.*

189. Gary Y. Okihiro, *Margins and Mainstreams: Asians in American History and Culture* 141 (1994).

was composed of different groups which could be played off against each other. For example, the planters in Hawaii began importing Portuguese workers in the 1880s for this reason:

> "We need them," they explained, "especially as an offset to the Chinese. . . . We lay great stress on the necessity of having our labor mixed. By employing different nationalities, there is less danger of collusion among laborers, and the employers [are able to] secure better discipline." Meanwhile, planters initiated the importation of Japanese laborers as "the principle check upon the Chinese, in keeping down the price of labor."[194]

A second advantage of utilizing foreign labor was that the workers could be pitted against American labor, driving down wages and preventing unification of the American working class. In 1871 Calvin Sampson, the owner of a North Adams, Massachusetts shoe factory, responded to the demands of his newly organized workers for higher wages and better working conditions by firing the striking workers and bringing in Chinese workers from San Francisco.

> Sampson's daring action had sobering effects on white workers in other North Adams shoe factories. Ten days after the arrival of Sampson's "Mongolian battery," Parker Brothers, Cady Brothers, Millard and Whitman, and E. R. and N. L. Millard forced laborers to return to work with a 10 percent wage reduction. . . . [A] writer for *Scribner's Monthly* wrote: "If for no other purpose than the breaking up of the incipient steps toward labor combinations and 'Trade Unions' . . . the advent of Chinese labor should be hailed with warm welcome." The "heathen Chinee," he concluded, could be the "final solution" to the labor problem in America.[197]

A third advantage to labor identified as foreign was that the supply could be more readily matched to changing needs. As with migrant labor today, when labor was scarce, workers could be easily imported. When the need was filled, the employers could easily dispose of the workers. The supply could be shut off and the workers deported, or if immigration laws prevented family unification, as in the case of the Chinese bachelors, they would die without reproducing.

　　　　* * *

A second significant function served by the attribution of foreignness to Asian Americans is the ability to turn them into enemies on a moment's notice. This has been true both metaphorically, as enemies in trade wars, and in a literal sense. Asians have been identified as the enemy in the most significant armed conflicts involving the United States within the memory of most Americans—World War II, the Korean War, and the war in Vietnam, as well as the Cold War. Racial stereotypes

194. Ronald Takaki, *Strangers From a Different Shore: A History of Asian Americans* 25 (1989) (quoting *Planters' Monthly*, vol. 2, no. 11, Nov. 1883, at 177, 245–47; A.S. Cleghorn in Republic of Hawaii, *Report of the Bureau of Immigration* 256–57 (Honolulu, 1895)).

197. Takaki, *Strangers From a Different Shore* at 98–99 (quoting Frank Norton, Our Labor System and the Chinese, *Scribner's Monthly*, May 1871, at 70).

of Asians have been used to make them appear evil and inhuman and perhaps, thus, easier to kill. In addition to affecting how these wars have been portrayed and perceived, this imagery has contributed to the perception of Asian Americans as foreign.

That Asian Americans have served in the U.S. military and that Asians have been allies in each of these wars does not seem to affect these perceptions. However, it illustrates how having a racial identity that is linked to certain national origins can be used. Groups within the Asian racial classification can be distinguished on the basis of national origin, with one group praised and another vilified through racialized stereotypes. Those same stereotypes, because they are race-based, can then be turned against any of the other subgroups. This is illustrated by how easily the portrayal of Chinese as good and Japanese as evil during World War II was reversed during the Cold War.

* * *

Justice Harlan, in his famous dissent in *Plessy v. Ferguson*, said of the Chinese, "[t]here is a race so different from our own that we do not permit those belonging to it to become citizens of the United States."[241] If one substitutes "Americans" for "citizens of the United States," this attitude toward Asian Americans is still common today.

The publicity surrounding the 1995 murder trial of O.J. Simpson brought to public attention comments of the sort that Asian Americans find commonplace. In one incident, U.S. Senator Alfonse D'Amato publicly "imitated" Judge Lance Ito, ascribing to Ito, a third generation Japanese American, a pseudo-Japanese accent. A popular spoof depicted Judge Ito, whose family had been interned, as a Japanese soldier in World War II, being attacked by U.S. planes and bombs. One caricature was accompanied by the following text:

Ito, Ito, bag of fritos

Hiroshima, nuke Judge Ito

Banzai, banzai, Nagasaki

Use his head for backyard hockey![244]

That the judge in such a visible trial would be mocked is not surprising. However, he was not mocked as a judge or even as a Japanese American: he was mocked as a foreigner. Cynthia Lee notes that "the recurring racialization of Asian Americans associated with the Simpson case serves as a sobering reminder of the ease with which Asian Americans are portrayed as 'foreign.' This portrayal suggests that Asian Americans are the enemy, or that we are 'different'.... "[245]

* * *

Notes and Questions

1. For further analysis of the relationship of Asian Americans to national identity, see Robert S. Chang, *Disoriented: Asian Americans, Law, and the Nation–State* (1999).

241. *Plessy v. Ferguson*, 163 U.S. 537, 561 (1896).

244. Henry Beard & John Boswell, *O.J.'s Legal Pad* 5 (1995).

245. Cynthia Kwei Yung Lee, *Beyond Black and White: Racializing Asian Americans in a Society Obsessed with O.J.*, 6 Hastings Women's L.J. 165, 203 (1995).

2.　For another analysis of the foreignness attributed to Asian Americans, see Margaret (H.R.) Chon, *On the Need for Asian American Narratives in Law: Ethnic Specimens, Native Informants, Storytelling and Silences*, 3 Asian Pac. Am. L.J. 4, 24 (1995) ("Asian American responses to being an 'ethnic specimen' are problematic precisely because of the foreignness that is imposed upon us in the racialization process. American Orientalism immediately displaces and decenters racial representations by placing us literally outside the national body, complicating the response to race.")

VIOLENCE AGAINST ASIAN AMERICANS

U.S. Commission on Civil Rights: Civil Rights Issues
Facing Asian–Americans in the 1990s
25–31 (February 1992).

RECENT INCIDENTS OF BIGOTRY AND VIOLENCE AGAINST ASIAN AMERICANS

* * *

Two racially motivated murders of Asian Americans in the 1980s have been etched into the national consciousness as examples of racism against Asian Americans: the murder of Vincent Chin in 1982 and the murder of Jim (Ming Hai) Loo in 1989. These killings are prominent examples of racially motivated violence against Asian Americans, but are not isolated incidents. Racially motivated violence leading to injury and sometimes to death occurs with disturbing frequency across the country and affects many different Asian groups. This section discusses five examples of anti-Asian violence: the murders of Vincent Chin, Jim Loo, Navroze Mody, and Hung Truong, and the mass killing of Indochinese school children in Stockton, California.

Vincent Chin—The racially motivated murder of Vincent Chin and the inability of the American judicial system to bring his murderers to justice became a vivid symbol and source of outrage during the mid–1980s. The facts of the case are as follows.

On the evening of June 19, 1982, Vincent Chin, a 27–year-old Chinese American, met with some friends in a Detroit bar to celebrate his upcoming wedding. He was accosted by Ronald Ebens and Michael Nitz, two white automobile factory workers, who reportedly called him a "Jap" and blamed him for the loss of jobs in the automobile industry. Ebens and Nitz chased Chin out of the bar, and when they caught up with him, Nitz held Chin while Ebens beat him "numerous times in the knee, the chest, and the head" with a baseball bat. Chin died of his injuries four days later.

Ebens and Nitz were initially charged with second-degree murder but subsequently allowed to plead guilty to manslaughter. In March 1983 the defendants were each sentenced to three years' probation and fined $3,780 by Wayne Circuit County Judge Charles Kaufman, who reasoned that the defendants had no previous history of violence and were unlikely to violate probation.

The U.S. Department of Justice brought federal civil rights charges against Ebens and Nitz to a federal grand jury, which indicted them on November 2, 1982. On June 18, 1984, Ebens was found guilty of interfering with Chin's civil rights, and on September 18, 1994, he was sentenced to 25 years in prison. However, Nitz was acquitted of the federal civil rights charges.

Ebens' conviction was overturned by the Sixth Circuit Court of Appeals in September 1986 for technical reasons, including issues pertaining to the admissibility of audio tapes and prosecutorial misconduct (overzealousness) in preparing witnesses. When Ebens came up for retrial in the Eastern District of Michigan, the defense moved for a change of venue on the grounds that Ebens could not get a fair trial in Detroit. The defense motion was granted, and the trial was moved to Cincinnati. The case was retried during the month of April 1987, and this time Ebens was acquitted.

The acquittal of Ebens in the second federal trial means that neither Ebens nor Nitz ever went to prison for Vincent Chin's killing.

Some have speculated that the main reason that the Cincinnati jury acquitted Ebens is that the jury could not comprehend the reality of anti-Asian bias as it existed in Detroit in the early 1980s. Whereas Detroit in the early 1980s was the scene of a massive media campaign against foreign imports, especially those from Japan, a campaign that inflamed anti-Asian sentiments in that city, there had not been the same type of campaign in Cincinnati. Also, there were very few Asians in Cincinnati, and anti-Asian sentiments were not widespread.

Others contend that the Cincinnati jury's acquittal of Ebens reflects a fundamental problem with current federal civil rights laws. Ebens was charged under federal criminal civil rights law section 245(b), which prohibits (among other things) the racially motivated interference by force or threat of force with a person's use of public facilities, such as restaurants and bars. Some experts argue that the jury may have been confused about what had to be shown for there to be a civil rights violation under section 245(b): even though the jury may have felt that the attack was indeed racially motivated, it might not have thought that Ebens specifically intended to interfere with Chin's use of a public facility (the bar).

Jim (Ming Hai) Loo—Seven years after Vincent Chin's killing, another Chinese American was killed in Raleigh, North Carolina under similar circumstances.

Jim (Ming Hai) Loo, 24, had immigrated to the United States from China 13 years before, was working in a Chinese restaurant, and was saving money so that he could attend college. On the evening of Saturday, July 29, 1989, during an altercation that began in a nearby pool hall, Loo was hit on the back of the head by a handgun held by Robert Piche. He fell onto a broken beer bottle, which pierced his eye and caused a bone fragment to enter his brain, resulting in his death on July 31.

Loo and several Vietnamese friends had been playing pool in the pool hall, when Robert Piche, 35, and his brother, Lloyd Piche, 29, began calling them "gooks" and "chinks" and blaming them for American deaths in Vietnam. Lloyd Piche said, "I don't like you because you're

Vietnamese. Our brothers went over to Vietnam, and they never came back," and "I'm gonna finish you tonight," Although the manager forced the Piche brothers to leave the pool hall, they waited outside for Loo and his friends, and attacked them as they left the pool hall. Robert Piche and his brother first attacked one of Loo's friends, Lahn Tang, with a shotgun, but when Tang escaped, Robert swung a pistol at another of Loo's friends, Jim Ta. He missed his intended victim and hit Loo on the head instead.

Although Lloyd Piche made most of the racial remarks, he did not strike the fatal blow. He was sentenced to six months in prison for disorderly conduct and simple assault (on Tang), both of which are misdemeanor. In March 1990, Robert Piche was found guilty of second-degree murder and assault with a deadly weapon and sentenced to a total of 37 years in prison. He will be eligible for parole after serving four and a half years. Although Judge Howard E. Manning Jr. gave Piche a stiff lecture, the sentence was less than he could have meted out: under North Carolina law Piche could have been given life in prison.

Many Asian–American community leaders, struck by the similarities between Loo's murder and Chin's, pressed the U.S. Department of Justice to bring federal civil rights charges against Robert and Lloyd Piche. They were particularly anxious to see a prosecution of Lloyd Piche, who received a minimal sentence despite being the chief instigator of the incident. After a lengthy investigation, the Justice Department announced on March 29, 1991, that it had indicted Lloyd Piche on federal civil rights charges, but it did not indict Robert Piche.

In making the announcement, Attorney General Thornburgh said:

This is a heinous crime committed against innocent patrons of a public facility. Such egregious behavior, especially with death resulting, cannot go unpunished.

This country was built on the freedom to enjoy life, liberty, and the pursuit of happiness. When innocent patrons of a public facility are harassed and ultimately killed simply because of their race, religion, or national origin, the government has a moral and legal obligation to step in and prosecute.

Lloyd Piche was indicted on eight counts of violating federal civil rights laws. On July 15, 1991, in a federal district court in Wilmington, North Carolina, Lloyd Piche was found guilty on all eight counts. On October 15, 1991, Lloyd Piche was sentenced to four years in prison and ordered to pay over $28,000 in restitution to the Loo family. Although the Justice Department had sought the maximum sentence under federal sentencing guidelines, Piche's sentence was less than the minimum sentence (six to seven and a half years) under the federal guidelines.

There are many similarities between the Loo and the Chin murders. In each case, the victim was a young man spending an evening relaxing with friends in a public facility (a bar in Chin's case, a pool hall in Loo's). In each case, an altercation began inside the public facility, and violence leading to murder erupted outside of the facility. In each case, the victim was killed after being mistaken for or associated with Asians of other nationalities. In Chin's case, his killers were venting hostility against foreign Japanese, and in Loo's case, his murderers apparently mistook him for a Vietnamese. Thus, both Chin and Loo became victims simply because they were of Asian descent.

Together, the Chin and Loo murders underscore the harsh reality of racially motivated violence against Asians. They also signal in differing ways the general public's lack of awareness of and to some extent indifference towards anti-Asian discrimination. The three-year probation and almost nominal fines imposed by Judge Kaufman on Chin's murderers are suggestive of very little value being placed on an Asian–American life. The ultimate failure of the American justice system to convict Ebens of civil rights charges, perhaps partly because of the Cincinnati jury's difficulty in believing in the existence of anti-Asian hatred, also implies that many Americans view racial hatred purely as a black-white problem and are unaware that Asian Americans are also frequently targets of hate crimes. Finally, neither murder was given much national prominence. Chin's killing did receive some national attention, but Loo's killing (in stark contrast to the murder of a young black man in Bensonhurst that occurred at roughly the same time) was hardly covered by the national media and raised no national sense of outrage.

Unlike the Vincent Chin case, Loo's murder resulted in a successful federal prosecution—the first ever successful federal civil rights prosecution where the victim was Asian American. If given sufficient attention, the federal civil rights trial of Lloyd Piche could do much to highlight the racial aspect of Loo's killing and will send a message that anti-Asian racism will not be tolerated by the United States government.

Navroze Mody—The 1987 killing of Navroze Mody shows that Asians, like other minorities, are potential targets of organized hate campaigns and that anti-Asian violence can be the outcome of such campaigns.

In early September 1987 the *Jersey Journal* published a letter from a group, called the Dotbusters, whose avowed purpose was to rid Jersey City of Asian Indians. There followed numerous racial incidents against Asian Indians ranging from vandalism to assault.

On September 27, 1987, Navroze Mody, an Indian, was "bludgeoned with bricks, punched, and kicked into a coma" by a gang of 11 youths, while his white friend remained unharmed. In April 1989 three of his assailants were convicted of assault, and one was convicted of aggravated assault. Murder charges were not brought against any of the assailants.

Although many in the New Jersey Indian community felt that the crime was racially motivated, no bias charges were brought, and prosecutors denied that Mody's killers were Dotbusters. There were reports, however, that two of the youths involved in the Mody killing had attacked some Indian students at Stevens Institute of Technology two weeks previously, but that the police had not filed a report in that incident. Whether or not Mody's killing was racially motivated, coming as it did in the wake of an organized outbreak of bigotry and violence against Asian Indians in Jersey City, it added significantly to the fears of Asian Indians throughout the country. Anti–Indian incidents continued to occur frequently in the Jersey City area for at least a year after Mody's killing.

Hung Truong—A more recent killing of a 15–year-old Vietnamese boy in Houston, Texas, illustrates the threat posed to Asian Americans along with other minorities by skinheads. Hung Truong moved to the Houston area from Vietnam with his father in 1980. His mother and three brothers remained in Vietnam. On August 9, 1990 at 2 a.m., Truong was walking down the street with three friends, when they were accosted by persons in two cars that stopped alongside them. Several minutes later, one of the cars followed them, stopped, and two 18–year-old men, Derek Hilla and Kevin Michael Allison, came out of the car, one of them carrying a club. One of Truong's friends later testified that the two men had shouted "White Power." They chased Truong, who became separated from his friends, and kicked and beat him with their feet and hands. Allison later testified that Truong had begged them to stop, saying, "God forgive me for coming to this country. I'm so sorry." After Hilla and Allison had left the scene, Truong's friends caught up with Truong, finding him lying on the ground bleeding. Truong's friends went for help, but when the paramedics arrived, Truong seemed okay, and they let him go home with a friend. The following morning at 7:15 a.m. paramedics were called to Truong's friend's apartment. Truong died shortly after arrival at the hospital. Hilla and Allison were arrested and charged with Truong's murder the following day.

Hilla was well known to have racist views and to have skinhead ties. During the January 1991 trial, witnesses described him as a violent man. Although denying that he was a racist, Allison admitted during the trial that he had participated in a couple of fights with skinhead friends and that his parents had kicked him out of the house when they discovered a swastika in his room. He also admitted that the only reason he and Hilla had attacked Truong was because he was Vietnamese.

On January 23, 1991, a Houston jury convicted Hilla of murder and Allison of involuntary manslaughter in Truong's killing. The jury sentenced Hilla to 45 years in prison and gave him a $10,000 fine. The jury also found that Hilla had used his feet as a deadly weapon, which means that he will be required to serve at least one-fourth of his sentence before becoming eligible for parole. Allison was sentenced to ten years in prison (the maximum allowable prison sentence for involuntary manslaughter) and also was assessed a $10,000 fine.

Although the prosecutor presented the case as a racial killing, neither Hilla nor Allison were tried on a civil rights charge, because Texas law does not provide for additional penalties for racially motivated crimes against persons. Truong's killing has added momentum to a movement to pass legislation that would provide stronger sentencing provisions for hate crimes.

Stockton Schoolyard Massacre—A chilling massacre of school children in Stockton, California, illustrates the tragic consequences of racial hatred.

On January 17, 1989, a gunman dressed in military garb entered the schoolyard at Cleveland Elementary school in Stockton and repeatedly fired an AK–47 assault rifle, killing five Indochinese children and wounding 30 others. The gunman, Patrick Edward Purdy, then turned the rifle on himself. The children who died were identified as Raphanar Or, 9; Ram Chun, 8; Thuy Tran, 6; Sokhim An, 6; and Ocun Lim, 8. Four of the dead children were Cambodian, and one was Vietnamese. Almost 60 percent of the pupils at Cleveland Elementary were from Southeast Asian families.

In the days following the massacre, news coverage focused in large part on the rifle used by Purdy, and the incident was a powerful force behind gun control initiatives across the country. Purdy was described as a "deranged young man ... who nursed an obsession with guns and the military." The possibility that the killings were racially motivated was hardly addressed in the national press. Almost ten months later, however, California Attorney General John Van de Kamp issued a report on the incident concluding that the killings were driven by a hatred of racial and ethnic minorities. The report observed, "Purdy was filled with hate and anger toward many groups of people, including virtually all identifiable ethnic minorities." It then concluded:

> It appears highly probable that Purdy deliberately chose Cleveland Elementary School as the location for his murderous assault in substantial part because it was heavily populated by Southeast Asian children. His frequent resentful comments about Southeast Asians indicates a particular animosity against them.

Notes and Questions

1. Do these repeated incidents of anti-Asian violence surprise you? If so, why did you not know more about them? For another analysis of the racialization of Asian Americans, see Cynthia Kwei Yung Lee, *Beyond Black and White: Racializing Asian Americans in a Society Obsessed with O.J.*, 6 Hastings Women's L. J. 165 (1995).

2. How do you reconcile the simultaneous "model minority" myth surrounding Asian Americans with the violence against them? Does the myth hide some of the reality? Does the myth help cause the violence?

3. Affirmative action for Blacks and Latinos/as sometimes ends up hurting Asians, as in competition for admission to elite programs such as the University of California at Berkeley and Lowell High School in San Francisco. Do Asians who raise these issues have a valid point? For a more extended discussion of affirmative action in education, see Chapter 9 § 2D, *infra*.

4. On media stereotypes of Asians as hapless, sneaky, pidgin-speaking, or driven, see Chapter 12 § 1, *infra*.

Chapter 6

RACE, RACISM, AND WHITES: THE CASE OF WHITENESS

Today, any serious study of race must take into account the growing movement that focuses on Whites, whiteness, and the white race. Sometimes called Critical White Studies (see, e.g., *Critical White Studies: Looking Behind the Mirror* (R. Delgado & J. Stefancic eds. 1997)) or, simply, whiteness studies, this movement focuses on such issues as:

- How the law helped define and create "the white race"
- Color imagery in literature and popular media
- Whiteness as the baseline for discussions of race
- White transparency and invisibility
- White privilege
- Underprivileged Whites and "white trash"
- Upward mobility of immigrant groups, such as Italians and Jews who, when they first arrived, were seen as nonwhite but became White over time
- Multiracial people and "passing for White"
- White consciousness, white power, and white supremacist groups
- A role for Whites in the civil rights movement

The following materials examine some of these questions. The suggested readings and notes offer further resources for the reader wishing to explore whiteness studies more deeply. As the reader will see, many of the same lessons of critical race theory and conventional civil rights analysis can be gained from a study of Whites and whiteness.

SECTION 1. HOW THE LEGAL SYSTEM CONTRIBUTED TO THE DEFINITION OF WHITENESS

For nearly a century, the 1790 Naturalization Act expressly limited acquisition of U.S. citizenship to persons of the white race. ("Persons of African nativity ... or descent" were not added until 1870). During this time, the federal courts had dozens of occasions to tackle such weighty problems as whether an Iranian, or a person of mixed German and Japanese ancestry, was White. A handful of such cases even reached the Supreme Court. Reading the confused, opinionated, result-driven jurisprudence developed during this period does much to dispel any image the reader might have of U.S. courts as socially wise or sensitive. Sometimes, courts relied on a "common understanding" test, according to which, for example, Japanese, despite light skins, were not White. At other times, they adhered to an outmoded and simplistic biological theory, according to which the human race came divided into four (or more, or a vague number) genetically marked races, laid down by evolution or the Creator. See Ian F. Haney López, *White by Law: The Legal Construction of Race* (1996).

Many of the cases contain thinly disguised overtones of white supremacist thinking and describe would-be immigrants in tones of scorn. Is this an anomaly, an embarrassing blip in legal history—or were the judges busily engaged in relegating foreign nationals and persons of color to an outer reach of purgatory actually acting in accord with original intent and, thus, technically, doing the right thing? For the view that the Framers intended the U.S. to be a basically white nation, see Derrick Bell, *Race, Racism, and American Law* (3d ed. 1992). See also Ronald Takaki, *Iron Cages* (1979), and Rogers Smith, *Civic Ideals* (1997). As the reader goes through these materials, he or she should ponder whether a society founded on white supremacist assumptions can ever change those foundations, and, if so, how.

IN RE AH YUP

1 Fed.Cas. 223 (D.Cal.Cir.Ct.1878).

Ah Yup, a native and citizen of the empire of China, of the Mongolian race, presented a petition in writing, praying that he be * * * admitted as a citizen of the United States. * * * This being the first application made by a native Chinaman for naturalization, * * * the only question is, whether the statute authorizes the naturalization of a native of China of the Mongolian race. * * *

In all the acts of congress relating to the naturalization of aliens, from that of April 14, 1802, down to the Revised Statutes, the language has been "that any alien, being a free white person, may be admitted to become a citizen," etc. After the adoption of the Thirteenth and Fourteenth amendments to the national constitution; the former prohibiting slavery, and the latter declaring who shall be citizens, congress ... amended [the statute] "to correct errors and to supply omissions in the Revised Statutes of the United States," of February 18, 1875, so as to read: "The provisions of this title shall apply to aliens being free white persons, and to aliens of African nativity, and to persons of African descent." Rev. St. (1st Ed.) p. 1435; 18 Stat. 318. And so the statute now stands.

The questions are: 1. Is a person of the Mongolian race a "white person" within the meaning of the statute? 2. Do these provisions exclude all but white persons and persons of African nativity or African descent? Words in a statute, other than technical terms, should be taken in their ordinary sense. The words "white person" ... constitute a very indefinite description of a class of persons, where none can be said to be literally white, and those called white may be found of every shade from the lightest blonde to the most swarthy brunette. But these words in this country, at least, have undoubtedly acquired a well settled meaning in common popular speech, and they are constantly used in the sense so acquired in the literature of the country, as well as in common parlance. As ordinarily used everywhere in the United States, one would scarcely fail to understand that the party employing the words "white person" would intend a person of the Caucasian race.

In speaking of the various classifications of races, Webster in his dictionary says, "The common classification is that of Blumenbach, who makes five. 1. The Caucasian, or white race, to which belong the greater part of the European nations and those of Western Asia; 2. The Mongolian, or yellow race, occupying Tartary, China, Japan, etc.; 3. The Ethiopian or Negro (black) race, occupying all Africa, except the north; 4. The American, or red race, containing the Indians of North and South America; and, 5. The Malay, or Brown race, occupying the islands of the Indian Archipelago," etc. This division was adopted from Buffon, with some changes in names, and is founded on the combined characteristics of complexion, hair and skull. * * * "Others make many more [divisions], but no one includes the white, or Caucasian, with the Mongolian or yellow race; and no one of those classifications recognizing color as one of the distinguishing characteristics includes the Mongolian in the white or whitish race." See New American Cyclopedia, tit. "Ethnology."

Neither in popular language, in literature, nor in scientific nomenclature, do we ordinarily, if ever, find the words "white person" used in a sense so comprehensive as to include an individual of the Mongolian race. Yet, in all, color, notwithstanding its indefiniteness as a word of description, is made an important factor in the basis adopted for the distinction and classification of races. I am not aware that the term "white person," as used in the statutes as they have stood from 1802 till the late revision, was ever supposed to include a Mongolian. * * * I do find much in the proceedings of congress to show that it was universally understood in that body, in its recent legislation, that it excluded Mongolians. At the time of the amendment, in 1870, extending the naturalization laws to the African race, Mr. Summer made repeated and strenuous efforts to strike the word "white" from the naturalization laws, or to accomplish the same object by other language. It was opposed on the sole ground that the effect would be to authorize the admission of Chinese to citizenship. Every senator, who spoke upon the subject, assumed that they were then excluded by the term "white person," and that the amendment would admit them, and the amendment was advocated on the one hand, and opposed on the other, upon that single idea. * * * It was finally defeated, and the amendment cited, extending the right of naturalization to the African only, was adopted. It is clear, from these proceedings that congress retained the word "white" in the naturalization laws for the sole purpose of excluding the Chinese from the right of naturalization. * * * Thus, whatever latitudinarian construction might otherwise have been given to the term "white person," it is entirely clear that congress intended by this legislation to exclude Mongolians from the right of naturalization. I am, therefore, of the opinion that a native of China, of the Mongolian race, is not a white person within the meaning of the act of congress.

The second question is answered in the discussion of the first. The amendment is intended to limit the operation of the provision as it then stood in the Revised Statutes. * * * It was certainly intended to have some operation, or it would not have been adopted. The purpose undoubtedly was to restore the law to the condition in which it stood before the revision, and to exclude the Chinese. It was intended to exclude some classes, and as all white aliens and those of the African race are entitled to naturalization under other words, it is difficult to perceive whom it could exclude unless it be the Chinese. It follows that the petition must be denied, and it is so ordered.

Notes and Questions

1.   Do you agree with the decision of the Court that Ah Yup was not "White"? Today we classify those of Asian ancestry as minorities, so why is the Court's recognition of this classification troubling? Or is *Ah Yup*, despite its peculiar reasoning, a sound ruling?

2.   The Court's ruling was based on the meaning of a "white person" in 1875 when the naturalization statute was revised. How would you define a "white person" today? Would your definition change the outcome of this case? Would it change the outcome if Ah Yup were Latino?

3.   In *Ex parte Shahid*, a federal district court in South Carolina complained of the lack of clarity in the federal statute limiting naturalization to persons who are "White." Frustrated, it resorted to history, ruling that "White" meant "such persons [who] in 1790 were known as white Europeans, with their descendants, including as their descendants their descendants in other countries to which they have emigrated." *Ex parte Shahid*, 205 Fed. 812 (E.D.S.C.1913). The circularity is patent: a person is White if he or she is known as such.

4.   And in In re *Najour*, 174 Fed. 735 (C.C.N.D.Ga.1909), another federal district court articulated a different test—a person is White if science declares him or her so. The language in the federal naturalization statute should be taken as referring to "race, rather than color" so that a person is White if he or she "comes within the classification of the white or Caucasion race, and I consider the Syrians as belonging to what we now recognize, and what the world recognizes, as the white race." The court went on to cite *The World's People*, a reference book written by Dr. A.H. Keane.

Najour introduced a hopeless split among the federal courts, about half adhering to a biological, the others holding to a general knowledge ("I know one when I see one") test. Haney López, *White by Law, supra*.

GEORGE A. MARTINEZ

The Legal Construction of Race: Mexican Americans and Whiteness
2 Harv. Latino L. Rev. 321, 325–28, 335–39 (1997).*

* * * During slavery, the racial divide between black and white became a line of protection from the threat of commodification: White-

* Used by permission of the author and the Harvard Latino Law Review.

ness protected one against being an object of property. Even after slavery ended, the status of being white continued to be a valuable asset, carrying with it a set of assumptions, privileges and benefits. In light of the privileged status of whiteness, it is instructive to examine how legal actors—courts and others—constructed the race of Mexican Americans. In *Inland Steel Co. v. Barcelona*,[19] an Indiana appellate court addressed the question of whether Mexicans were white. The court noted that the *Encyclopaedia Britannica* stated that approximately one-fifth of the inhabitants of Mexico are whites, approximately two-fifths Indians and the balance made up of mixed bloods, blacks, Japanese and Chinese. Given this, the court held that a "Mexican" should not necessarily be found to be a white person.

The Texas courts also considered the same question. In In re *Rodriguez*,[21] a Texas federal court addressed whether Mexicans were white for purposes of immigration. At that time, the federal naturalization laws required that an alien be white in order to become a citizen of the United States. The court stated that Mexicans would probably be considered non-white from an anthropological perspective, but went on to note that the United States had entered into certain treaties with Mexico. [*e.g.*, the Treaty of Guadalupe Hidalgo.] Those treaties expressly allowed Mexicans to become citizens of the United States. Thus, the court held that Congress must have intended that Mexicans were white within the meaning of the naturalization laws. In re *Rodriguez* reveals how racial categories can be constructed through the political process. Through the give and take of treaty making, Mexicans became "white."

Other cases show how politics operated to turn persons of mixed blood into whites or the opposite. In immigration cases, mixed race applicants often failed to establish their whiteness. For example, in In re *Camille*,[27] the court held that the son of a white Canadian father and an Indian mother was non-white, and therefore not entitled to naturalization. Similarly, in In re *Young*,[28] the son of a German father and a Japanese mother was not a white person within the meaning of the immigration laws. If these cases stand for the proposition that mixed race persons were not white, Mexicans—a mixture of Spanish and Indian—should not have counted as white. The treaties nevertheless operated to turn them into whites.

The issue of the race of Mexican Americans also arose in connection with school segregation. In *Independent School District v. Salvatierra*,[30] plaintiffs sought to enjoin segregation of Mexican Americans in the city of Del Rio, Texas. There, the court treated Mexican Americans as white, holding that Mexican Americans could not be segregated from children of "other white races, merely or solely because they are Mexicans."[31] Significantly, the court did permit segregation of Mexican Americans on the basis of linguistic difficulties and migrant farming patterns.

19. 39 N.E.2d 800 (Ind.1942).

21. 81 F. 337 (W.D.Tex.1897).

27. 6 F. 256 (1880).

28. 198 F. 715 (1912).

30. 33 S.W.2d 790 (Tex.Civ.App.1930). *Salvatierra* was the first case to decide the issue of whether segregation of Mexican Americans in public schools was permissible.

31. *Id.* at 795.

Mexican–American jury participation and exclusion also show how the race of Mexican Americans is constructed. For example, in *Hernandez v. State*, a Mexican American had been convicted of murder. He sought to reverse his conviction on the ground that Mexican Americans had been excluded from the grand and the petit juries. He relied on cases holding that exclusion of blacks from jury service violated due process and equal protection. The court recognized only two classes as falling within the guarantee of the Fourteenth Amendment: the white and the black races. It went on to hold that Mexican Americans are white for purposes of the Fourteenth Amendment. The court reasoned that to say that the members of the various groups comprising the white race must be represented on grand and petit juries would destroy the jury system.[37] Since the juries that indicted and convicted the defendant were composed of members of his race—white persons—he had not been denied the equal protection of the laws.

* * *

White identity traditionally has served as a source of privilege and protection. Since the law usually recognized Mexican Americans as white, one might have expected that social action would have reflected the Mexican American's privileged legal status as white. That, however, was not the case. Legal recognition of the Mexican American as white had only a slight impact on private conduct. Far from having a privileged status, Mexican Americans faced discrimination very similar to that experienced by African Americans. Excluded from public facilities and neighborhoods and the targets of racial slurs, Mexican Americans typically lived in one section of town because they were not permitted to rent or own property anywhere except in the "Mexican Colony." Segregated in public schools, Mexican Americans also faced significant discrimination in employment. Mexican Americans were earmarked for exclusive employment in the lowest brackets of employment and paid less than Anglo Americans for the same jobs. Moreover, law enforcement officials have committed widespread discrimination against Mexican Americans, arresting them on pretexts and meting out harassment and penalties disproportionately severe compared to those imposed on Anglos for the same acts. In all these respects actual social behavior failed to reflect the legal norms that defined Mexican Americans as white. Although white as a matter of law, that law failed to provide Mexican Americans with a privileged status.

* * *

The legal construction of Mexican Americans as white thus stands as an irony—thoroughly at odds with the colonial discourses that developed in the American Southwest. As happened in other regions of the world the colonizers engaged in epistemic violence—*i.e.*, produced modes of knowing that enabled and rationalized colonial domination from the standpoint of the West. Through this discourse on the Mexican American, Anglo Americans also reformulated their white selves. Anglo judges, as we have seen, did the same, ruling that Mexicans were co-whites

37. 251 S.W.2d 531, 532, 535 (Tex. 1952).

when this suited the dominant group—and nonwhite when necessary to protect Anglo privilege and supremacy.

TAKAO OZAWA v. UNITED STATES

260 U.S. 178 (1922).

The appellant is a person of the Japanese race born in Japan [who] applied to the United States District Court for the Territory of Hawaii to be admitted as a citizen of the United States. His petition was opposed by the United States District Attorney for the District of Hawaii. Including the period of his residence in Hawaii appellant had continuously resided in the United States for 20 years. He was a graduate of the Berkeley, Cal., high school, had been nearly three years a student in the University of California, had educated his children in American schools, his family had attended American churches and he had maintained the use of the English language in his home. That he was well qualified by character and education for citizenship is conceded.

The District Court of Hawaii, however, held that, having been born in Japan and being of the Japanese race, he was not eligible to naturalization under section 2169 of the Revised Statutes (Comp. St. § 4358), and denied the petition. Thereupon the appellant brought the cause to the Circuit Court of Appeals for the Ninth Circuit and that court has certified the following questions, upon which it desires to be instructed: * * *

1. Is the Naturalization Act of June 29, 1906 (Comp. St. § 4351 *et seq*.), limited by the provisions of section 2169 of the Revised Statutes of the United States?

2. If so limited, is the appellant eligible to naturalization under that section?

First. Section 2169 is found in title XXX of the Revised Statutes, under the heading "Naturalization," and reads as follows:

"The provisions of this title shall apply to aliens, being free white persons and to aliens of African nativity and to persons of African descent."

* * *

There is nothing in section 2169 which is repugnant to anything in the act of 1906. Both may stand and be given effect. It is clear, therefore, that there is no repeal by implication.

But it is insisted by appellant that section 2169, by its terms is made applicable only to the provisions of title XXX, and that it will not admit of being construed as a restriction upon the act of 1906. Since section 2169, it is in effect argued, declares that "the provisions of this title shall apply to aliens being free white persons, . . ." it should be confined to the classes provided for in the unrepealed sections of that title, leaving the act of 1906 to govern in respect of all other aliens, without any restriction except such as may be imposed by that act itself.

It is contended that, thus construed, the act of 1906 confers the
privilege of naturalization without limitation as to race, since the general
introductory words of section 4 (Comp. St. § 4352) are:

"That an alien may be admitted to become a citizen of the United
States in the following manner, and not otherwise."

But, obviously, this clause does not relate to the subject of eligibility
but to the "manner," that is, the procedure, to be followed. Exactly the
same words are used to introduce the similar provisions contained in
section 2165 of the Revised Statutes. * * *

In all of the naturalization acts from 1790 to 1906 the privilege of
naturalization was confined to white persons (with the addition in 1870
of those of African nativity and descent), although the exact wording of
the various statutes was not always the same. If Congress in 1906
desired to alter a rule so well and so long established it may be assumed
that its purpose would have been definitely disclosed and its legislation
to that end put in unmistakable terms.

　　　* * *

Second. This brings us to inquire whether, under section 2169, the
appellant is eligible to naturalization. The language of the naturalization
laws from 1790 to 1870 had been uniformly such as to deny the privilege
of naturalization to an alien unless he came within the description "free
white person." ... Is appellant, therefore, a "free white person," within
the meaning of that phrase as found in the statute?

On behalf of the appellant it is urged that we should give to this
phrase the meaning which it had in the minds of its original framers in
1790 and that it was employed by them for the sole purpose of excluding
the black or African race and the Indians then inhabiting this country. It
may be true that those two races were alone thought of as being
excluded, but to say that they were the only ones within the intent of the
statute would be to ignore the affirmative form of the legislation. The
provision is not that Negroes and Indians shall be excluded, but it is, in
effect, that only free white persons shall be included. The intention was
to confer the privilege of citizenship upon that class of persons whom the
fathers knew as white, and to deny it to all who could not be so
classified. It is not enough to say that the framers did not have in mind
the brown or yellow races of Asia. It is necessary to go farther and be
able to say that had these particular races been suggested the language
of the act would have been so varied as to include them within its
privileges.

　　　* * *

Beginning with the decision of Circuit Judge Sawyer, In re *Ah Yup*,
5 Sawy. 155, Fed. Cas. No. 104 (1878), the federal and state courts, in an
almost unbroken line, have held that the words "white person" were
meant to indicate only a person of what is popularly known as the
Caucasian race. * * * With the conclusion reached in these several
decisions we see no reason to differ. Moreover, that conclusion has
become so well established by judicial and executive concurrence and
legislative acquiescence that we should not at this late day feel at liberty

to disturb it, in the absence of reasons far more cogent than any that have been suggested. *United States v. Midwest Oil Co.*, 236 U. S. 459, 472.

* * *

The appellant, in the case now under consideration, however, is clearly of a race which is not Caucasian.

Notes and Questions

1. *Ozawa* was decided almost fifty years after In re *Ah Yup*. Has the Court's treatment of this issue changed? If so, how?

2. With George A. Martinez's *Mexican–Americans and Whiteness* in mind, how would a person of Mexican heritage be treated by the *Ozawa* Court?

3. Since courts consider Mexican Americans White, for some purposes, should we no longer consider them a minority? Note that the census considered Mexicans and other Hispanics White for much of our history.

4. If, to some members of the majority group at least, Mexicans are of dubious whiteness (see also Chapter 12 on popular images of this group), how are they seen by Blacks?

5. Note the evidence of Ozawa's assimilation in the first paragraph of the opinion. Did his conformity to social norms make any difference to the Court? How much does it make now? See *Korematsu v. United States*, 323 U.S. 214 (1944).

UNITED STATES v. BHAGAT SINGH THIND

261 U.S. 204 (1923).

This cause is here upon a certificate from the Circuit Court of appeals requesting the instruction of this Court in respect of the following questions:

1. Is a high-caste Hindu, of full Indian blood, born at Amritsar, Punjab, India, a white person within the meaning of section 2169, Revised Statutes?

2. Does the Act of February 5, 1917 (39 Stat. 875, § 3), disqualify from naturalization as citizens those Hindus now barred by that act, who had lawfully entered the United States prior to the passage of said act?

* * *

Section 2169, Revised Statutes (Comp. St. § 4358), provides that the provisions of the Naturalization Act "shall apply to aliens being free white persons and to aliens of African nativity and to persons of African descent."

If the applicant is a white person, within the meaning of this section, he is entitled to naturalization; otherwise not. In *Ozawa v. United States*, 260 U.S. 178, we had occasion to consider the application of these words to the case of a cultivated Japanese and were constrained to hold that he was not within their meaning. As there pointed out, the provision is not that any particular class of persons shall be excluded, but it is, in effect, that only white persons shall be included within the privilege of the statute. * * * Following a long line of decisions of the lower Federal courts, we held that the words imported a racial and not an individual test and were meant to indicate only persons of what is popularly known as the Caucasian race. But, as there pointed out, the conclusion that the phrase "white persons" and the word "Caucasian" are synonymous does not end the matter. It enabled us to dispose of the problem as it was there presented, since the applicant for citizenship clearly fell outside the zone of debatable ground on the negative side; but the decision still left the question to be dealt with, in doubtful and different cases, by the "process of judicial inclusion and exclusion." Mere ability on the part of an applicant for naturalization to establish a line of descent from a Caucasian ancestor will not *ipso facto* to and necessarily conclude the inquiry. * * *

In the endeavor to ascertain the meaning of the statute we must not fail to keep in mind that it does not employ the word "Caucasian," but the words "white persons," and these are words of common speech and not of scientific origin. * * * It is in the popular sense of the word, therefore, that we employ it as an aid to the construction of the statute, for it would be obviously illogical to convert words of common speech used in a statute into words of scientific terminology when neither the latter nor the science for whose purposes they were coined was within the contemplation of the framers of the statute or of the people for whom it was framed. The words of the statute are to be interpreted in accordance with the understanding of the common man from whose vocabulary they were taken. See *Maillard v. Lawrence*, 16 How. 251, 261.

They imply, as we have said, a racial test; but the term "race" is one which, for the practical purposes of the statute, must be applied to a group of living persons now possessing in common the requisite characteristics, not to groups of persons who are supposed to be or really are descended from some remote, common ancestor, but who, whether they both resemble him to a greater or less extent, have, at any rate, ceased altogether to resemble one another. It may be true that the blond Scandinavian and the brown Hindu have a common ancestor in the dim reaches of antiquity, but the average man knows perfectly well that there are unmistakable and profound differences between them to-day; and it is not impossible, if that common ancestor could be materialized in the flesh, we should discover that he was himself sufficiently differentiated from both of his descendants to preclude his racial classification with either. The question for determination is not, therefore, whether by the speculative processes of ethnological reasoning we may present a probability to the scientific mind that they have the same origin, but whether we can satisfy the common understanding that they are now the same or sufficiently the same to justify the interpreters of a statute— written in the words of common speech, for common understanding, by unscientific men—in classifying them together in the statutory category as white persons. * * *

The eligibility of this applicant for citizenship is based on the sole fact that he is of high-caste Hindu stock, born in Punjab, one of the extreme northwestern districts of India, and classified by certain scientific authorities as of the Caucasian or Aryan race. The Aryan theory as a racial basis seems to be discredited by most, if not all, modern writers on the subject of ethnology. * * *

The term "Aryan" has to do with linguistic, and not at all with physical, characteristics, and it would seem reasonably clear that mere resemblance in language, indicating a common linguistic root buried in remotely ancient soil, is altogether inadequate to prove common racial origin. There is, and can be, no assurance that the so-called Aryan language was not spoken by a variety of races living in proximity to one another. Our own history has witnessed the adoption of the English tongue by millions of negroes, whose descendants can never be classified racially with the descendants of white persons, notwithstanding both may speak a common root language.

The word "Caucasian" is in scarcely better repute.[1] It is at best a conventional term, with an altogether fortuitous origin,[2] which under scientific manipulation, has come to include far more than the unscientific mind suspects.

* * *

It does not seem necessary to pursue the matter of scientific classification further. We are unable to agree with the District Court, or with other lower federal courts, in the conclusion that a native Hindu is eligible for naturalization under section 2169. The words of familiar speech, which were used by the original framers of the law, were intended to include only the type of man whom they knew as white. The immigration of that day was almost exclusively from the British Isles and Northwestern Europe, whence they and their forebears had come. When they extended the privilege of American citizenship to "any alien being a free white person" it was these immigrants—bone of their bone and flesh of their flesh—and their kind whom they must have had affirmatively in mind. * * *

What, if any, people of Primarily Asiatic stock come within the words of the section we do not deem it necessary now to decide. There is much in the origin and historic development of the statute to suggest that no Asiatic whatever was included. * * *

What we now hold is that the words "free white persons" are words of common speech, to be interpreted in accordance with the understanding of the common man, synonymous with the word "Caucasian" only as that word is popularly understood. As so understood and used, whatever

1. *Dictionary of Races*, S. Doc. No. 61–662, at 31 (3d Sess. 1910–11).

2. 2 *Encyclopaedia Britannica* (11th ed.) p. 113: "The ill-chosen name of Caucasian, invented by Blumenbach in allusion to a South Caucasian skull of specially typical proportions, and applied by him to the so-called white races, is still current; it brings into one race peoples such as the Arabs and Swedes, although these are scarcely less different than the Americans and Malays, who are set down as two distinct races. Again, two of the best marked varieties of mankind are the Australians and the Bushmen, neither of whom, however, seems to have a natural place in Blumenbach's series."

may be the speculations of the ethnologist, it does not include the body of people to whom the appellee belongs. It is a matter of familiar observation and knowledge that the physical group characteristics of the Hindus render them readily distinguishable from the various groups of persons in this country commonly recognized as white. The children of English, French, German, Italian, Scandinavian, and other European parentage, quickly merge into the mass of our population and lose the distinctive hallmarks of their European origin. On the other hand, it cannot be doubted that the children born in this country of Hindu parents would retain indefinitely the clear evidence of their ancestry. It is very far from our thought to suggest the slightest question of racial superiority or inferiority. What we suggest is merely racial difference, and it is of such character and extent that the great body of our people instinctively recognize it and reject the thought of assimilation.

what clear evidence?

oh diff. but equal. See Brown

* * *

It follows that a negative answer must be given to the first question, which disposes of the case and renders an answer to the second question unnecessary, and it will be so certified.

Answer to question No. 1, No.

Notes and Questions

1. If courts found Indians, Japanese, and Chinese persons not "White," why was a Mexican American treated differently? Has this difference in treatment led to Mexican Americans having a higher status than other minorities?

2. Having read In re *Ah Yup, Ozawa,* and *Bhagat Singh Thind,* do you agree with these decisions? Were they technically correct? If not, do you think the Congress in 1875 meant to include Indians and Asians as "white persons?" If not, is the court's treatment of Mexican Americans contrary to the intent of the revised naturalization statute?

3. Despite a little uncertainty at the edges, in the line of cases you read, the Court remained relatively consistent in its definition of "White." Do you think the present Supreme Court would continue to use that definition? Does the increasing number of biracial people complicate things? Who should decide what race a person is—the court, the legislature, the person himself or herself? In light of intermarriage, does racial purity exist anymore, except perhaps in the most isolated regions of the world?

4. Other measures have attempted to restrict the grant of citizenship to nonwhites. Currently persons born in the United States are automatically citizens regardless of the legality or illegality of their parents' status. Some, concerned that pregnant women are crossing the border to give birth on U.S. soil and thereby attain citizenship for their children, have campaigned for an amendment to the Fourteenth Amendment to the United States Constitution limiting citizenship to persons born in the United States of mothers who are citizens, legal residents, or naturalized citizens. This would be the first time the Fourteenth Amendment has been amended in its entire history. See *Immigrants Out!* (Juan F. Perea ed. 1997). Do you agree that such an amendment is called for? Do you think the framers of the Constitution foresaw transient border crossings to give birth and attain citizenship? Can you see how such an amendment could affect other laws which rely on the

word "born"? For the argument that American citizenship should be based on consent, see Peter Schuck & Rogers Smith, *Citizenship Without Consent: Illegal Aliens in the American Polity* (1985).

5. In Philip Sterling's *Laughing on the Outside* (1965) comedian Dick Gregory points out that Whites and Blacks often view historical events and celebrations, such as the Civil War Centennial, quite differently. (Whites tend to celebrate more, considering that slavery and unfair treatment of Blacks lie in the distant past). He points out:

I went to one of those separate but equal schools down South. I don't know how old the textbooks were, but they sure kept me out of the Navy. If people wanted to sail off the edge of the earth—I sure wasn't gonna be one of them. . . . And those Southern history books! Do you realize I was twenty-two before I learned that Lincoln freed the slaves? I always figured that Jefferson Davis had us out on probation.

In other situations, however:

People keep talking about the white race and the black race and it really doesn't make sense. When I played Miami, I met a fellow two shades darker than me—and his name was Ginsberg! He took my place in two sit-in demonstrations—nobody knew the difference. Then he tried for a lunch counter and blew the whole bit . . . Asked for blintzes.

On African Americans' success in sports, he comments:

Isn't it funny, the more we get harassed, the more we seem to make of it? Like lynch mobs. You might ask, what do we have to be thankful to lynch mobs for? Well, I've got a brother who can run a half-mile faster than any white boy in the world! . . . Same thing with wade-ins. They keep pushin' us—Australia better watch out. We already got one fella swims the hundred yards in fourteen seconds flat. And carrying a picket sign. That ain't bad!

Is Gregory right that whiteness is in the eye of the beholder, and may mean everything—or nothing? What about a dark-skinned Italian who points out that his skin color is lighter than that of a light-skinned African American? On minorities' gravitation toward athletics, see Chapter 12 § 2.

U.S. mixed-race people and foreigners trying to immigrate or naturalize are not the only ones left in legal limbo. Consider the plight of children of U.S. servicemen and Vietnamese mothers, the Amerasians left behind in the wake of the Vietnam War:

BONNIE KAE GROVER

Aren't These Our Children? Vietnamese Amerasian Resettlement and Restitution
2 Va. J. Soc. Pol'y & L. 247, 248–49, 253–62 (1995).*

The thought first came to me on my wedding day in 1967, that American servicemen who went to Vietnam did not just fight, go on R & R, get drunk, have sex when available, and do drugs. Some of them fell in love. My soon to be brother-in-law had just come home from his second tour of duty, and his wife was devastated by the picture she found in his wallet. "She is so petite, so pretty and so young, and she has hair down to here. He says she was just a good friend, but what would you think?" What would I think, indeed? What I would—and did—think, was that my dashing brother-in-law, the adventurer, the spy, had fallen deeply in love.

My wedding day was also the day I realized, love or not, that there had to be a lot of babies with American fathers and Vietnamese mothers. What was going to happen to all those American babies in Vietnam? What was my brother-in-law planning to do if he had left a child there?

As it turned out, most of America forgot its Amerasian children in Vietnam, just as America has forgotten its other children around the world and at home. In the United States, half of all children at some time have an absent father, less than half of those children receive any court-ordered child support, and one of five children lives in poverty. It is thus disheartening, but not surprising, that government and military policies demonstrate so little regard for the "half-American" children left in a foreign land, half a world away. * * *

The United States is not alone in its legacy of neglect. Many governments, but not all, take a "boys will be boys" attitude toward the people of countries in which they conduct military actions, ignoring the magnitude of changes and problems those countries and their people find themselves left with long after foreign armed forces have gone. * * *

By conservative estimates, tens of thousands of Amerasian children were born to Vietnamese mothers during and immediately after the United States–Vietnam war. In contrast to the Eurasians, these Amerasian children have had far less satisfactory resettlement options and the conditions under which they live are, in most cases, much worse than those of their French counterparts. Until 1982, Amerasian children had no options at all. Because they were born in Vietnam, they did not acquire United States citizenship by birth, nor did they acquire it through their fathers. United States immigration law does not generally—and did not then—confer citizenship on an illegitimate child who is born abroad and whose father is a United States citizen.

Ordinary avenues for relocation—student or refugee status, green cards, and guest worker programs—are foreclosed as well. Most Amerasians were born to working class women and thus lack the education and resources to relocate to the United States or even make contact with their fathers. Many of them look strikingly occidental, but far from conferring an advantage, their Western appearance subjects them to scorn and derision. Vietnam is a relatively homogeneous society in which Amerasians cannot hide that their mothers consorted with a hated enemy. Some mothers abandoned their children, placed them in orphanages, or gave them to relatives to raise. Subject to intense discrimination, most cannot find jobs and live on the streets or lead lives of crime and prostitution. Many live in official compounds built for their protection or otherwise depend on the government for safety.

There has been little public pressure to make amends and little hue and cry in the United States to try to relieve the conditions under which these children live. For nearly twenty years, the United States had virtually no diplomatic relations with Vietnam. Economic sanctions, which lasted until the early 1990s, seriously restricted travel to that country, so Americans' general knowledge of conditions there was extremely limited and frequently inaccurate. Americans seemed to push the children, like the war, out of their consciousness. They, too, were part of the war America wanted to forget. * * *

Although official policy forbade United States servicemen from marrying Vietnamese women without the consent of their commanding officers, common law relationships were tacitly approved. If a serviceman insisted on marrying a Vietnamese woman, most commanding officers would delay giving consent until the soldier had returned home and lost communication with the woman. Once the serviceman had returned to the United States without his Vietnamese family or proof of a legal marriage, the barriers to having the family join him proved insurmountable. As a result, many fathers who once wanted and actively sought their Vietnamese families have given up hope and gone on with their lives. But even after many years with an American wife and family, a surprising number of former servicemen traveling to Vietnam are fathers, husbands, and lovers returning, at least in part, to search for the families they left behind.

Some servicemen never knew they had fathered children. Perhaps many of them would not have wished to assume responsibility. Forming sexual liaisons and patronizing prostitutes are generally winked at by the United States military establishment, which has shown little regard for such concepts as birth control or responsible sex, preferring to concentrate its efforts on social and medical concerns such as AIDS, sporadic distribution of condoms, and even setting parameters within which local prostitutes are expected to operate. Sexual adventures have long been considered an unwritten fringe benefit of what is an otherwise dangerous, dreary, and underpaid job. * * *

When the United States evacuated the last of its forces from Vietnam in 1975, the press was silent about the fate of the Amerasian children left behind. The United States government offered Operation Babylift to show the wonderful, last-ditch heroics of America—the "rescue" of "Vietnamese orphans," portrayed as the most helpless, most precious little people of all, snatched from the hands of the rapidly advancing North Vietnamese forces and evacuated at great risk even as Saigon fell. Undoubtedly a few of these children were Amerasians, but they were not represented to the American public as children of American servicemen. It was not until many years after the fall of Saigon, not even until after the great fanfare as the last of the United States prisoners of war known to be alive stepped off planes onto American soil, that the deplorable circumstances in which the United States had abandoned its Vietnamese Amerasian children were brought before the public with any degree of sustained vigor.

When stories and pictures of the desperate children left behind in Vietnam finally reached the pages of *Life* and the Sunday supplements, it seemed obvious to many Americans that these children must somehow be United States citizens, and that, even if they were not, a determined effort could reunite the children with their anxiously awaiting fathers. But this was not so. Because of their appearance and ancestry, the Amerasians had no home country. They did not belong in Vietnam and under United States immigration law they could not easily be brought home to America. The same government, which sent hundreds of thousands of young male troops to Vietnam and did little in the way of instilling in them a sense of social responsibility, had created during the previous two hundred years a complicated morass of citizenship and naturalization laws whose effect was to deny citizenship to many of the persons who most desperately needed it. With certain limited exceptions, any person born within the United States or its territories is a United States citizen. This is the principle of *jus soli*—citizenship by country of birth. Since 1790, the United States has also allowed for citizenship in a very limited fashion based on *jus sanguinis* or descent. The United States Supreme Court, however, has not found this latter type of citizenship to be either expressly or impliedly guaranteed by the Constitution. Of course, Congress is free to change the requirements for citizenship, or to eliminate them altogether. The lack of a constitutional grant of citizenship by descent, coupled with what the Supreme Court regards as the absolute or plenary powers of Congress to determine the laws of immigration and nationality, has created an area of legislative and administrative discretion that commands a very low level of judicial scrutiny. * * *

An illegitimate child born abroad of a United States citizen father must be legitimated by the father before the age of eighteen in order to be a United States citizen. In contrast, an illegitimate child born abroad to a United States citizen mother is automatically regarded as a United States citizen. The Supreme Court has held that such strange and seemingly contradictory definitions of "child" for purposes of determining citizenship are permissible. Not until the Immigration Reform and Control Act of 1986 did Congress add fathers of illegitimate children with "a bona fide parent-child relationship" to the roster of those eligible to pass citizenship by descent. This provision, even when generously applied, is of little use to a father and child who are separated for many years by great distances and inadequate communication, who may not know if the other is alive or dead, and whose governments do not even recognize each other. Unless broadly and generously applied, the provision is even more useless to a man who is unaware that he has in fact fathered a child and to a child who has no means of identifying his or her father. Unfortunately, most of these limitations apply with full force to Amerasian children of United States servicemen who served in Vietnam.

Notes and Questions

1. For readings on the social and legal construction of Whiteness, see Ian F. Haney López, *White by Law: The Legal Construction of Race* (1996); *Critical White Studies: Looking Behind the Mirror* (R. Delgado & J. Stefancic eds. 1997); Theodore Allen, *The Invention of the White Race* Vols. 1–2 (1994, 1997); Alexander Saxton, *The Rise and Fall of the White Republic* (1990);

David Roediger, *The Wages of Whiteness: Race and the Making of the American Working Class* (Rev. ed. 1999); David Roediger, *Towards the Abolition of Whiteness* (1994).

SECTION 2.　BECOMING WHITE: HOW THE IRISH, ITALIANS, AND JEWS BECAME WHITE

In *Old Poison in New Bottles: The Deep Roots of Modern Nativism,* in *Immigrants Out!* (Juan F. Perea ed. 1997), Joe Feagin shows how today's anti-immigrant sentiments, exemplified by a series of referenda in California, bills in Congress, and calls to shut down the border with Mexico, have roots in older, more virulent forms of white supremacy dating to the eighteenth century. Americans of English or Northern European stock have always resisted newcomers of darker hues:

> Over the entire course of U.S. history we can see that one-way assimilation to an Anglo–Protestant core culture—consisting of an Anglo–British legal system, Anglo–Protestant religious values and English language, and an Anglo-capitalist economic system—has been both the norm and the reality for new immigrants.

In the same essay, Feagin also points out how early American industrialists, such as Henry Ford, maintained "Sociological Departments" with social workers who visited immigrants' homes, taught English, personal hygiene, and other American values, all leading up to a ceremony in which the newly graduated workers shed their native garb, put on American clothes, and walked through a large melting pot holding American flags.

JAMES R. BARRETT AND DAVID ROEDIGER
How White People Became White.[*]

In 1980, Joseph Loguidice, an elderly Italian American from Chicago, sat down to give his life story to an interviewer. His first and most vivid childhood recollection was of a race riot that had occurred on the city's near north side. Wagons full of policemen with "peculiar hats" streamed into his neighborhood. But the "one thing that stood out in my mind," Loguidice remembered after six decades, was "a man running down the middle of the street hollering ... 'I'm White, I'm White!' After first taking him for an African American, Loguidice soon realized that the man was a white coal handler covered in dust. He was screaming for his life, fearing that 'people would shoot him down.' He had, Loguidice concluded, 'got caught up in ... this racial thing.' "[1]

Joseph Loguidice's tale might be taken as a metaphor for the situation of millions of "new immigrants" from Eastern and Southern

* Copyright 1996 by James R. Barrett and David Roediger. Used by permission. This material appears in a different form as *Inbetween Peoples: Race, Nationality and the "New Immigrant" Working Class,* in *Against Exceptionalism,* edited by Rick Halpern and Jonathan Morris, London: Macmillan, 1997.

1. Joe Sauris, *Interview with Joseph Loguidice,* July 25, 1980, Italians in Chicago Project, copy of transcript, Box 6, Immigration History Research Center, University of Minnesota, St. Paul, Minn.

Europe who arrived in the United States between the end of the nineteenth century and the early 1920s. That this episode made such a profound impression is in itself significant, suggesting both that this was a strange, new situation and that thinking about race became an important part of the consciousness of immigrants like Loguidice. How did this racial awareness and increasingly racialized worldview develop among new immigrant workers? Most did not arrive with conventional U.S. attitudes regarding "racial" difference, let alone its significance and implications in industrial America. Yet most, it seems, "got caught up in . . . this racial thing." How did this happen? If race was indeed socially constructed, then what was the raw material that went into the process?

How did these immigrant workers come to be viewed in racial terms by others—employers, the state, reformers, and other workers? Like the coal handler in Loguidice's story, their own ascribed racial identity was not always clear. A whole range of evidence—laws; court cases; formal racial ideology; social conventions; popular culture in the form of slang, songs, films, cartoons, ethnic jokes, and popular theatre—suggests that the native born and older immigrants often placed the new immigrants not only *above* African and Asian Americans, for example, but also *below* "white" people. Indeed, many of the older immigrants and particularly the Irish had themselves been perceived as "nonwhite" just a generation earlier. As labour historians, we are interested in the ways in which Polish, Italian, and other European artisans and peasants became American workers, but we are equally concerned with the process by which they became "white." Indeed, in the United States the two identities merged and this explains a great deal of the persistent divisions within the working-class population. How did immigrant workers wind up "inbetween"? * * *

We aim to capture the confusion, inbetweenness and flux in the minds of native-born Americans and the immigrants themselves. Untangling the processes of Americanization and of whitening, we offer a two-sided experience: new immigrants underwent racial categorizing at the same time they developed new identities, and the two sides of the process cannot be understood apart from the other. Similarly, the categories of state, class and immigrant self-activity can be separated at best arbitrarily and inconsistently. * * *

INBETWEEN IN THE POPULAR MIND

Italians, involved in a spectacular international diaspora in the early twentieth century, were racialized as the "Chinese of Europe" in many lands. But in the United States their racialization was pronounced and more likely to connect Italians with Africans. During the debate at the Louisiana state constitutional convention of 1898 over how to disfranchise blacks, and over which whites might lose the vote, some acknowledged that the Italian's skin "happens to be white" even as they argued for his disfranchisement. But others held that "according to the spirit of our meaning when we speak of 'white man's government,' [the Italians] are as black as the blackest negro in existence."[13] More than metaphor

13. George E. Cunningham, *The Italian: A Hindrance to White Solidarity in* *Louisiana*, 1890–1898, Journal of Negro History, 50 (January 1965): 34, includes the quotes.

intruded on this judgment. At the turn of the century, a West Coast construction boss was asked, "You don't call the Italian a white man?" The negative reply assured the questioner that the Italian was "a dago." Recent studies of Italian and Greek Americans make a strong case that racial, not just ethnic, oppression long plagues "nonwhite" immigrants from Southern Europe. * * *

The equation between legal whiteness and fitness for naturalizable citizenship helps to predict which groups would *not* be made non white in an ongoing way. Not only did the Irish, whose whiteness was under sharp question in the 1840s and 1850s, and later the new immigrants, gain the powerful symbolic argument that the law declared them white and fit. They also had the power of significant numbers of votes, although naturalization rates for new immigrants were not always high. During Louisiana's disfranchising constitutional convention of 1898, for example, the bitter debate over Italian whiteness ended with a provision passed extending to new immigrants protections comparable, even superior, to those which the "grandfather clause" gave to native white voters. New Orleans' powerful Choctaw Club machine, already the beneficiary of Italian votes, led the campaign for the plank. When Thomas Hart Benton and Stephen Douglas argued against Anglo–Saxon superiority for a pan-white "American race" in the 1850s, they did so before huge blocs of Irish voters. When Theodore Roosevelt extolled the "mixture of blood" making the American race, a "new ethnic type in this melting pot of the nations," he emphasized to new immigrant voters his conviction that each of their nationalities would enrich America by adding "its blood to the life of the nation." Woodrow Wilson also tailored his thinking about racial desirability of the European new immigrants in the context of an electoral campaign in which the "foreign" vote counted heavily. * * *

One Italian American remembered the early twentieth century as a time when "he and his family had been badly mistreated by a French plantation owner near New Roads where he and his family were made to live among the Negroes and were treated in the same manner. At first he did not mind because he did not know any difference, but when he learned the position that the Negroes occupied in this country, he demanded that his family be moved to a different house and be given better treatment." In denouncing all theories of white supremacy, the Polish language Chicago-based newspaper *Dziennik Chicagoski* editorialized, " . . . if the words 'superior race' are replaced by the words 'Anglo-Saxon' and instead of 'inferior races' such terms as Polish, Italian, Russian and Slavs in general—not to mention the Negro, the Chinese, and the Japanese—are applied, then we shall see the political side of the racial problems in the United States in stark nakedness."[75] In the first instance, consciousness of an inbetween racial status leads to a desire for

75. Jean Scarpaci, *Immigrants in the New South: Italians in Louisiana's Sugar Parishes, 1880–1910*, 16 Labor History 177 (Spring 1975); Thaddeus Radzialowski, *The Competition for Jobs and Racial Stereotypes: Poles and Blacks in Chicago*, Polish American Studies 33 (Autumn 1976): 17.

literal distance from nonwhites. In the second, inbetweenness leads to a sense of grievances shared in common with nonwhites. * * *

Both eager embraces of whiteness and, more rarely, flirtations with nonwhiteness characterized new immigrant racial identity. But to assume that new immigrants as a mass clearly saw their identity with nonwhites or clearly fastened on their differences is to miss the confusion of inbetweenness. The discussion of whiteness was an uncomfortable terrain for many reasons and even in separating themselves from African Americans and Asian Americans, immigrants did not necessarily become white. Indeed, often they were curiously indifferent to whiteness.

Models that fix on one extreme or the other of new immigrant racial consciousness—the quick choice of whiteness amidst brutal competition or the solidarity with nonwhite working people based on common oppression—capture parts of the new immigrant experience. At times Southern and Eastern Europeans were exceedingly apt, and not very critical, students of American racism. Greeks admitted to the Western Federation of Miners saw the advantage of their membership and did not rock the boat by demanding admission for the Japanese–American mine workers with whom they had previously allied. Greek Americans sometimes battled for racial status fully within the terms of white supremacy, arguing that classical civilization had established them as "the highest type of the caucasian race."[77] In the company town of Pullman and adjacent neighborhoods, immigrants who sharply divided on national and religious lines coalesced impressively as whites in 1928 to keep out African–American residents. Recently arrived Jewish immigrants on New York City's Lower East Side resented reformers who encouraged them to make a common cause with the "schwartzes." In New Bedford, "white Portuguese" angrily reacted to perceived racial slights and sharply drew the color line against "black Portuguese" Cape Verdeans, especially when preference in jobs and housing hung in the balance. Polish workers may have developed their very self-image and honed their reputation in more or less conscious counterpoint to the stereotypical *niggerscab*. Theodore Radzialowski reasons that "Poles who had so little going for them (except their white skin—certainly no mean advantage but more important later than earlier in their American experience), may have grasped this image of themselves as honest, honorable, non-scabbing workers and stressed the image of the black scab in order to distinguish themselves from ... the blacks with whom they shared the bottom of American society."[80]

Many new immigrants learned to deploy and manipulate white supremacist images from the vaudeville stage and the screens of Hollywood film where they saw "their own kind" stepping out of conventional racial and gender roles through blackface and other forms of cross-dress.

77. Ronald L. Lewis, *Black Coal Miners in America: Race, Class, and Community Conflict, 1780–1900*, at 110 (1987); Robert Allen & Pamela Allen, *Reluctant Reformers: Racism and Social Reform Movements in the United States* 180 (1974). For a recent expression of the common oppression argument, see Paul Berman, *The Other and the Almost the Same*, in *Blacks and Jews: Alliances and Arguments* 11–30 (P. Berman ed. 1994).

80. Radzialowski, *supra* note 75, at 14, n.20.

"Facing nativist pressure that would assign them to the dark side of the racial divide," Michael Rogin argues provocatively, new immigrants and entertainers like Al Jolson, Sophie Tucker and Rudolph Valentino, "Americanized themselves by crossing and recrossing the racial line."[81]
* * *

Examples pile up on both sides of the new immigrants' racial consciousness. But to see the matter largely in terms of which stack is higher misses the extent to which the exposed position of racial inbetweenness could generate both positions at once, and sometimes a desire to avoid the issue of race entirely. The best frame of comparison for discussing new immigrant racial consciousness is that of the Irish Americans in the mid-nineteenth century. Especially when not broadly accepted as such, Irish Americans insisted that politicians acknowledge them as part of the dominant race. Changing the political subject from Americanness and religion to race whenever possible, they challenged anti-Celtic Anglo Saxonism by becoming leaders in the cause of white supremacy. New immigrant leaders never approximated that path. With a large segment of both parties willing to vouch for the possibility of speedy, orderly Americanization and with neither party willing to vouch unequivocally for their racial character, Southern and Eastern Europeans generally tried to change the subject from whiteness to nationality and loyalty to American ideals. * * *

Both "becoming American" and "becoming white" could imply coercive threats to European national identities. The 1906 remarks of Luigi Villiari, an Italian government official investigating Sicilian sharecroppers in Louisiana, illustrate the gravity and inter-relation of both processes. Villiari found that "a majority of plantation owners cannot comprehend that ... Italians are white," and instead considered the Sicilian migrant "a white-skinned negro who is a better worker than the black-skinned negro." He patiently explained the "commonly held distinction ... between 'negroes,' 'Italians' and 'whites' (that is, Americans)." In the South, he added, the "American will not engage in agricultural, manual labour, rather he leaves it to the negroes. Seeing that the Italians will do this work, naturally he concludes that Italians lack dignity. The only way an Italian can emancipate himself from this inferior state is to abandon all sense of national pride and to identify completely with the Americans."[86]

One hundred percent whiteness and one hundred percent Americanism carried overlapping and confusing imperatives for new immigrants in and out of the South, but in several ways the former was even more

81. Michael Rogin, *Making America Home: Racial Masquerade and Ethnic Assimilation in the Transition to Talking Pictures,* 79 J. Amer. Hist. 1050, 1053 (1992); Robert W. Snyder, *The Voice of the City: Vaudeville and Popular Culture in New York* 120 (1989); Lewis Erenberg, *Steppin' Out: New York Nightlife and the Transformation of American Culture, 1890–1930,* at 195 (1981); Michael Rogin, *Blackface, White Noise: The Jewish Jazz Singer Finds His Voice,* 18 Critical Inquiry 420, 437–48

(1992); Harold David Brackman, *The Ebb and Flow of Race Relations: A History of Black–Jewish Relations Through 1900,* at 450 (unpublished Ph.D. dissertation, University of California, Los Angeles, 1997).

86. Luigi Villiari, *Relazione dell dott. Luigi Villiari gugli Italiana nel Distretto Consolare di New Orleans,* Bolletino dell Emigrazione (Italian Ministry of Foreign Affairs, Royal Commission on Emigration, 1907), 2439, 2499, 2532.

uncomfortable terrain than the latter. The pursuit of white identity, so tied to competition for wage labour and to political citizenship, greatly privileged male perceptions. But identity formation, as Americanizers and immigrant leaders realized, rested in great part on the activities of immigrant mothers, who entered discussions of nationality and Americanization more easily than those of race. More cast in determinism, the discourse of race produced fewer openings to inject class demands, freedom and cultural pluralism than did the discourse of Americanism. The modest strength of *herrenvolk* democracy, weakened even in the South at a time when huge numbers of white poor were disfranchised, paled in comparison to the opportunities to try to give progressive spin to the idea of a particularly freedom-loving "American race."

DAVID ROEDIGER

*Early Twentieth Century European Immigration and the First Word in Whiteness.**

A character in Chester Himes' 1945 novel, *If He Hollers Let Him Go*, has a "funny thought." He begins to "wonder when white people started to get white—or rather, when they started losing it." The narrower question of when new immigrants "started to get white" and of what they lost in doing it, has received passionate and varied treatment within African–American thought. That elaboration provides the best point of entry to the question of white identity among new immigrants to date.

The simplest and perhaps most celebrated answer to how the whiteness of new European immigrants came about appears in the epilogue to Malcolm X's *Autobiography*. His collaborator, Alex Haley, describes being in a U.S. airport with Malcolm and admiring an arriving family of European immigrants. They are, Malcolm predicts, about to learn their first word of English: *nigger*. Malcolm's one-liner, which recalls images of the Gads Hill minstrel show, is so precisely repeated (without credit) in the works of black artists from John Oliver Killens to Richard Pryor—and Toni Morrison counts *nigger* as the second word in the immigrant's English vocabulary with only *okay* coming before—as to raise the possibility that each teller of the joke drew it from black folk humor. Like the most enduring folklore, it distills a sharp point and operates on a variety of levels. Pessimistic to the point of rancor, the joke's logic resembles that of African–American usages of *hunky* and *honky*, the mixing up and evolution of which imply that the new Eastern European immigrants slurred by the former term could come to exemplify the white oppressors identified by the latter in a remarkably short time. But however bitter, the joke does not make immigrant racism a product of the essential "white" characteristics of the newcomers. The weight of U.S. racial division must be learned—and the immigrants' beauty, or as Baldwin has it, "soul," lost—on this view. The tragedy arises from the knowledge that American realities were such brutal and effective teachers of that division and that immigrants were such apt and ready learners of it.

Coexisting with the bitterness of Malcolm's joke is a much more lyrical tradition of black commentary on new immigrant whiteness—a tradition which is, however, equally premised on a deep sense of tragedy. In William Attaway's soon-to-be canonical 1941 proletarian novel, *Blood On The Forge,* Melody and his half-brother, Chinatown, disagreed on the merits of the music made by Slavic immigrants with whom they worked in Pittsburgh's steel mills. Chinatown heard nothing in it but a "yowl," adding that "a man can't understand one word they yowlin'." But Melody, who lived to play the blues and who could "hear music in a snore," knew better. He had heard some of these people from the Ukraine singing. He hadn't understood one word. Yet he didn't have to know the words to understand what they were wailing about. Words didn't count when the music had a tongue. The field hands of the sloping red-hill country in Kentucky sang that same tongue. Hearing the wails of his (and Chinatown's) old Kentucky home in Ukrainian music, Melody echoed Frederick Douglass' observations of almost a century earlier. During his 1845–46 tour of Ireland, Douglass heard the "wailing notes" of the music of the oppressed and famished Irish people as close kin of the "wild notes" of the slaves' sorrow songs.

For the jazz musician Mezz Mezzrow, it was weeping and wailing that united black and new immigrant musics. In a remarkable section of his autobiographical *Really the Blues*, Mezzrow recalled a prison term he served for selling drugs. Having convinced himself that, despite Jewish–American origins, he was in fact black, Mezzrow likewise convinced prison officials, who allowed him to be confined in the segregated African–American section of the prison. Nonetheless, when white Catholic prisoners organized Christmas caroling, the response of Jewish inmates was to ask Mezzrow to lead them in song. Professing surprise that he, "a colored guy," would be chosen to direct a Jewish chorus, Mezzrow learned "once more how music of different oppressed peoples blends together." He did not "know the Hebrew chants," but a "weepy blues inflection" made his interpretation of their "wailing and lament" a huge success.

On one level, these African–American commentaries on the soul of the music of oppressed Europeans underline the affinities of blacks and "inbetween" immigrants. But Mezzrow, Douglass, and Attaway all were as intent to invoke tragedy as possibility in discussing new immigrant relations with nonwhite Americans. Mezzrow disdained appeals to Jewish "racial" solidarity in the entertainment world, seeing such "jive" as a betrayal of "colored musicians" who were his "real brothers." Douglass lingered over the wails of the Irish to emphasize the tragedy of Irish–American racism, seconding Irish nationalist leader Daniel O'Connell's longstanding point that this was "cruelty" not learned in Ireland and was utterly inappropriate to the Irish experience. Attaway portrayed common oppression at every turn. Blacks and Bohunks shared a wrenching from the land, lived in comparable squalor and died in the same industrial accidents.

James Baldwin's indispensable essays on the whitening of new immigrants bring together the acerbity of Malcolm's joke and the attuned-to-tragedy humanism of Attaway and Douglass. Especially in "'On

Being White' and Other Lies" and in "White Man's Guilt," Baldwin pairs the embrace of whiteness with the immigrants' losses of contact with land and with community. Reminding readers that folks in Norway did not preen themselves on how white they were, Baldwin makes the taking up of whiteness a product and cause of the new immigrants' "losing it" in terms of humanity. As insistently (and far less wrongheadedly) as Stanley Elkins wrote of the slave trade's devastation of the African's personality, Baldwin saw a loss of humanity among those wrenched from European villages and then whitened. Regimented by necessity into industrial work, these new immigrants also chose to enter the imprisoning confines of whiteness, which Baldwin suggestively terms a "factory." At times Baldwin posits an almost immediate sea change to a white identity. Elsewhere he describes a process which "took generations and a vast amount of coercion." In that process he emphasizes that the joining in racial victimization and the committing of atrocities against nonwhites affirmed the immigrants' whiteness over time. Deep empathy and disquiet run through every line of Baldwin's writings as he shouts out to those in the factory: "So long as you think you are white, there's no hope for you."

Attaway, Killens, Pryor, Malcolm X, and Douglass were not commenting principally on the European immigrant experience, and when Baldwin did so he did not write more than a few thousand words. Even so, their work poses the drama and importance of race within the new immigrant experience in ways in which even the best of immigration history has only begun to approach. For that reason, the best reaction to their insights is not to quibble about what is mistaken or omitted in the ground they cover. Rather, it is to address urgently the issues that are raised but not settled in their remarks. These include the question of when and how whiteness was learned, of who taught it, of whether learning to call others *nigger* meant being ready or able to call oneself white, of why those whose musical wails were close cousins of African–American sorrow songs came to march to the tune of whiteness.

Notes and Questions

1. When is whiteness learned, and how? Did "learning to call others *nigger* [mean] being ready or able to call oneself white," as Roediger writes, so that immigrants almost literally rose on the backs of Blacks as Toni Morrison wrote? Or could one learn, almost as a curiosity or matter of side interest, that one is white (or black or brown or red or yellow) without putting any value construction on it?

2. Could you easily imagine Snow White, Jesus, the Virgin Mary, Moses, or Joan of Arc as black?

3. Did the white race not exist until it was invented? Who did the inventing, and why? Can one identify oneself as belonging to any race, White or nonwhite, without buying into narrow nationalism, supremacist thought, or outmoded pseudoscience?

4. Suppose that global environmental conditions change so that it is a serious disadvantage to be White. Whites are sickly, weak, and die young in

comparison to members of other groups. Would everyone now want to be nonwhite, "pass for black (or brown etc.)" and conceal their white ancestry?

————

In *How the Irish Became White* (1995), labor historian Noel Ignatiev describes how the first Irish immigrants to the United States were looked down upon and treated as a new kind of Black. Karl Marx observed that the average English worker looked upon them roughly the way poor Whites in the U.S. South regarded Negroes. Ignatiev reviews the Irish's struggle for acceptance, for upward mobility in work, and ultimately for admission into the white race. After immigrating to U.S. shores, the Irish became White by achieving the vote, by supporting the Democratic Party, and by preventing free African Americans from competing with them for jobs. For an intriguing analysis of "How Did Jews Become White Folks?" see Karen Sacks' article by that title, excerpted in *Critical White Studies*, *supra* at 395, discussing how Anglo–Saxon concern over the masses of European immigrants arriving on our shores in the late 1880s and clustering in our cities, coupled with the advent of eugenic racism in the early twentieth century and Red Scares, produced the notion of European races. When the first Jewish immigrant groups sought to enter colleges, the Protestant elite complained that they were loud, brash, and pushy. Jewish quotas soon followed. "Compared with other immigrants, Jews were upwardly mobile. But compared with . . . nonimmigrant whites, their ability was . . . circumscribed."

————

Can "reverse immigration" take place, so that a person who considered himself or herself white and was regarded that way by others undergoes a change and becomes nonwhite? In a 1995 book, law dean Gregory Howard Williams describes his own life as a white-black. A mixed-race man who looks outwardly white, Williams was first raised by the white side of his family (his mother's). Then, when family circumstances changed, he went to live with black relatives in a black neighborhood, where he was raised as a black and came to see himself as such. He describes the transition as follows:

GREGORY WILLIAMS
Life On The Color Line
32–36 (1995).*

I didn't understand Dad. I knew I wasn't colored, and neither was he. My skin was white. All of us are white, I said to myself. But for the first time, I had to admit Dad didn't exactly look white. His deeply tanned skin puzzled me as I sat there trying to classify my own father. Goose bumps covered my arms and I realized that whatever he was, I was.

* * *

He continued. "Life is going to be different from now on. In Virginia you were white boys. In Indiana you're going to be colored boys. I want you to remember that you're the same today that you were yesterday. But people in Indiana will treat you differently."

I refused to believe Dad. I looked at Mike. His skin, like mine, was a light, almost pallid, white. He had Dad's deep brown eyes, too, but our hair was straight. Leaning toward Dad, I examined his hands for a sign, a black mark. There was nothing. * * *

"I don't wanta be colored," Mike whined.... "We can't go swimmin' or skatin'." * * *

The rest of the book chronicles his teenage years, relations with young women, and treatment at the hands of schoolteachers and other adults. Highly engrossing, it may be considered a modern-day version of the celebrated *Black Like Me*, discussed in Chapter 12.

Hypothetical

As a thought exercise, imagine that you wake up one morning to discover that you are not a member of the race you always thought you were. Your father or mother informs you that you really are a _____ and, because of a divorce or separation, you will have to go live in another city with your relatives, whom you have never met or heard of, and who are of a radically different race. They listen to different music, follow a lifestyle completely different from your own, eat unfamiliar foods, and send their children to an all-_____ school. Would you accept your new fate with interest? Trepidation? Run away? Does it depend on the new racial identity you will have to assume, and if so, why?

Notes and Questions

1. If you are Jewish, Irish, or Greek, do you consider yourself White? Did your parents or grandparents?

2. In the 1996 film, *A Family Thing*, actor Robert Duvall discovers that his brother, whom he has never seen, is Black and that he, Duvall, has the same black mother. In the film, he must deal with his own consternation at this discovery and come to terms with his brother and his blackness.

3. In 1983 Susie Phipps lost a five-year-long battle to have her official birth certificate changed to show that she was born White. She had gone through life to that point as a Black. Her home state, Louisiana, was the only one to provide a legislative definition of "Black." Six years later in a Colorado court, a different plaintiff, Mary Walker, succeeded in getting herself declared a Black; to that point she had been regarded as White.

Why would anyone want to change their legal classification, and why would courts make it harder to change in one direction than the opposite one? See Luther Wright, Jr., *Who's Black, Who's White, and Who Cares*, 48 Vand. L. Rev. 513 (1995).

4. See Adrian Piper, *Passing for White, Passing for Black*, 58 Transitions 4 (1992):

No reflective ... white person ... wants to admit to instinctively recoiling at the thought of being identified as black.... But if you want to see such a ... person do this, just peer at the person's facial features and tell her, in a complimentary tone of voice, that she looks as though she might have some black ancestry.... The ultimate test of a person's repudiation of racism is not what she can contemplate doing for or on behalf of black people, but whether she herself can contemplate calmly the likelihood of being black.

See also Jerome Culp, *The Michael Jackson Pill*, 92 Mich. L. Rev. 2613 (1994).

5.   Suppose a government official knocked at your door and announced that a terrible mistake had been made. You (a white person) were supposed to have been born Black. It will be necessary now to correct this error by a painless operation that will change you into a Black. The government is prepared to pay for the operation and compensate you for your damages in having to go through the rest of your life as a Black. (Your personality, thoughts, and memories will remain the same—you will be the same person as before, except that you will look black.)

How much money would you want? See Andrew Hacker, *Two Nations* (1992) (reporting that his students answer: one million dollars a year for life).

SECTION 3.   WHITE TRANSPARENCY
BARBARA J. FLAGG

*"Was Blind, But Now I See:" White Race Consciousness
and the Requirement of Discriminatory Intent*
91 Mich. L. Rev. 953, 969–70, 973–74, 976–82 (1993).*

THE TRANSPARENCY PHENOMENON

In this society, the white person has an everyday option not to think of herself in racial terms at all. In fact, whites appear to pursue that option so habitually that it may be a defining characteristic of whiteness: To be white is not to think about it. I label the tendency for whiteness to vanish from whites' self-perception the transparency phenomenon. * * * Because transparency is such a pervasive fact of whites' conceptualization of ourselves we have reason to be skeptical of ostensibly race-neutral decisionmaking by white decisionmakers. * * * I propose that white decisionmakers adopt that deliberate skepticism as well regarding their own criteria of decision.

On a recent trip to Washington, D.C. my life partner, who is white, was visiting a white friend and bringing her up to date on family events and activities. When she mentioned that I have been teaching a new course on Critical Race Theory, her friend appeared puzzled and surprised. "But," said the friend, "isn't she white?"

      * * *

RACE–NEUTRAL DECISIONMAKING

Transparency casts doubt on the concept of race-neutral decision-making. Facially neutral criteria of decision formulated and applied by whites may be as vulnerable to the transparency phenomenon as is the

* Originally published in the Michigan Law Review. Used by permission.

race of white people itself. I suggest that whites should respond to the transparency phenomenon with a deliberate skepticism concerning race neutrality. At a minimum, transparency counsels that we not accept seemingly neutral criteria of decision at face value. Whites rely on primarily white referents in formulating the norms and expectations that become criteria of decision for white decisionmakers. Given whites' tendency not to be aware of whiteness, it's unlikely that white decisionmakers do not similarly misidentify as race-neutral personal characteristics, traits, and behaviors that are in fact closely associated with whiteness. The ways in which transparency might infect white decisionmaking are many and varied. * * *

Three considerations, however, counsel against attempting to formulate a "rule" to distinguish transparent from authentically race-neutral criteria of decision. First, transparency is often difficult to recognize and analyze. * * * Whites as a group lack the experiential foundation necessary even to begin to construct the analytic tools that would ground a comprehensive theory of transparency.

Second, transparency probably attaches more to word usages than to the words themselves. For example, *hostility* may not have a race-laden connotation in every instance in which a white decisionmaker employs it. The context of use—the combination of speaker, audience, decisionmaking process, and purpose—more likely supplies the racial content of the term *hostile* as applied. Thus, a general analysis of transparency might have to be, paradoxically, situation specific, with a concomitant exponential increase in the difficulty of the theoretical project.

Finally, the assumption that we can get better at identifying genuinely race-neutral decisionmaking presupposes that such a thing is possible. However, to repose any confidence in the concept of race neutrality is premature at best, because little supports it other than whites' subjective experience, itself subject to the transparency phenomenon. The available empirical evidence points in the opposite direction. Social scientists' work shows that race nearly always influences the outcomes of discretionary decisionmaking processes, including those in which the decisionmaker relies on criteria thought to be race-neutral. There is, of course, no conclusive evidence that no instances of genuine race neutrality exist, but neither is there conclusive evidence to the contrary. The pervasiveness of the transparency phenomenon militates against an unsupported faith by whites in the reality of race-neutral decisionmaking.

I recommend instead that whites adopt a deliberate and thoroughgoing skepticism regarding the race neutrality of facially neutral criteria of decision. This stance has the potential to improve the distribution across races of goods and power that whites currently control. In addition, skepticism may help to foster the development of a positive white racial identity that does not posit whites as superior to blacks. * * *

Even when he looks for it, however, the white decisionmaker may not always be able to uncover the hidden racial content of the criteria he employs. In those instances, the skeptical stance may function to promote distributive justice in two different ways. First, the skeptical decisionmaker may opt to temper his judgment with a simultaneous acknowledgment of his uncertainty concerning nonobvious racial specificity. * * * Second, white decisionmakers might choose to develop pluralistic criteria of decision as a guard against covert white specificity. * * *

The skeptical stance may contribute to the development of a positive white racial identity by relativizing white norms. Even whites who do not harbor any conscious or unconscious belief in the superiority of white people participate in the maintenance of white supremacy whenever we impose white norms without acknowledging their whiteness. Any serious effort to dismantle white supremacy must include measures to dilute the effect of whites' dominant status, which carries with it the power to define as well as to decide. Because the skeptical stance prevents the unthinking imposition of white norms, it encourages white decisionmakers to consider adopting nonwhite ways of doing business, so that the formerly unquestioned white-specific criterion of decision becomes just one option among many. The skeptical stance thus can help develop a relativized white race consciousness, in which the white decisionmaker is conscious of the whiteness and contingency of white norms. * * *

A LOOK AT THE DISCRIMINATORY INTENT RULE

The threshold requirement in most of antidiscrimination laws that the plaintiff prove discriminatory intent draws a sharp distinction between facially neutral but unconsciously race-specific white decisionmaking, on the one hand, and the deliberate use of race, whether overt or covert, on the other; only the latter is constitutionally impermissible. Relying on a distinction among discriminators' states of mind seems a curious strategy for curbing racist decisionmaking, because a racial criterion is equally present in either case. Indeed, the current rule appears more suited to drive the race specificity of white decisionmaking underground—out of whites' awareness—than to eradicate it altogether. However, the intent requirement might rest on either of two assumptions that, coupled with the perceived institutional costs of heightened scrutiny, provide ostensible justification for the decision to disapprove only the *purposeful* use of race in government decisionmaking. These foundational assumptions are, first, that unconsciously race-specific decisionmaking is relatively rare, or, second, that the conscious use of race as a factor in decisionmaking is more blameworthy than its unconscious use. * * *

The transparency phenomenon counsels skepticism regarding the belief that truly race-neutral decisionmaking is the norm. In addition, the social science literature provides further evidence that unconscious race-specific decisionmaking is in fact relatively common, and the potential impact of transparency upon the research itself strengthens that conclusion. * * *

The Court's decision [in *Washington v. Davis*, 426 U.S. 229 (1976), which held that a plaintiff in a racial discrimination case must show that the defendant intended to discriminate against him or her on grounds of race; a mere showing that a defendant's *policy*—for example, insisting on a college diploma—has a disproportionate impact on minorities does not suffice] to adopt a discriminatory intent rule that does not reach unconscious race-specific decisionmaking might rest on a belief that such discrimination does not commonly occur. Such a belief is, perhaps, the natural corollary of whites' widespread faith in the pervasiveness of race-neutrality. This faith views Klan and other overtly white supremacist attitudes as extreme, perhaps pathological, deviations from the norm of white racial thinking, as if those attitudes can be comprehended in complete isolation from the culture in which they are embedded. Similarly, whites tend to adopt the "things are getting better" story of race relations, which allows us to suppose that our unfortunate history of socially approved race discrimination is largely behind us. This white confidence in race neutrality might dictate that the law should treat the unconscious use of nonobviously race-specific criteria of decision as nothing more than an occasional deviation from the prevailing practice of race-neutral government decisionmaking. From this perspective, given that significant institutional costs are associated with judicial intervention, unconscious race specificity seems too rare to justify heightened review.

The transparency phenomenon provides two arguments against this view. At a minimum, it counsels that we distrust any view that accepts race neutrality at face value, whether as a matter of fact or of frequency of occurrence. Second, transparency supports the stronger, affirmative argument that unconscious race-specific decisionmaking is so common that it is in fact the norm for white decisionmakers.

The belief that race-neutral decisionmaking is relatively common and unconsciously race-specific decisionmaking relatively uncommon stands analytically distinct from the belief that any particular instance of facially neutral decisionmaking is in fact what it seems. Even if the unconscious use of race were extremely rare, whites could still misperceive the true character of every one of the few instances in which race was a factor in the decision. Conversely, that whites frequently are unaware of the white-specific factors that may be used in white decisionmaking does not dictate one conclusion or another regarding the frequency with which such factors actually are employed. This analytic distinction notwithstanding, transparency counsels skepticism with respect to the frequency of race-neutral decisionmaking as well.

Because the transparency phenomenon creates a risk that whites will misapprehend the race-specific nature of apparently race-neutral decisionmaking, it simultaneously creates a risk that we will systematically underestimate the incidence of such decisionmaking. Each circumstance in which we fail to perceive accurately the racial content of our decisions contributes to the overall perception that race neutrality is the more common way of doing business. Thus, even though the conclusion that race specificity is the norm does not necessarily follow from transparency alone, we ought to adopt a healthy skepticism toward, rather than a blind faith in the pervasiveness of, race neutrality if we wish to be able more accurately to assess the role of race in white decisionmaking.

Notes and Questions

1. Does white continue to be the legal baseline today? Note that various federal civil rights laws provide that Blacks and other nonwhites are to be afforded the same rights as Whites. See 48 U.S.C.A. § 1981, guaranteeing to all the civil rights "as enjoyed by white persons."

2. Does this mean that the law first decides what the aspects of dignified personhood mean with reference to Whites, that is, what a white person ought to have in life? Then, in a spasm of conscience, it decides, after the fact, that Blacks and browns should maybe have some of them too?

3. If so, does this mean that protecting Whites from injury, insult, and rude treatment comes first and that other groups are an afterthought?

WHITE PRIVILEGE AND WHITE TRANSPARENCY

In *Making Systems of Privilege Visible*, in *Privilege Revealed* 11–20 (1996), Stephanie Wildman and Adrienne Davis point out that much privileging operates outside of consciousness. Moreover, it is easier to deny that one is a racist than to admit that one goes about one's life as the beneficiary of a privilege:

> First, calling someone a racist individualizes the behavior and veils * * * that racism can occur only where it is culturally, socially, and legally supported. It lays the blame on the individual rather than the systemic forces that have shaped that individual and his or her society. Whites know they do not want to be labeled racist; they become concerned with how to avoid that label, rather than worrying about systemic racism and how to change it. * * *

Moreover:

> [T]he very vocabulary we use to talk about discrimination hides * * * power systems and the privilege that is their natural companion. * * *
>
> For me, the struggle to visualize privilege has most often taken the form of the struggle to see my white privilege. Even as I write about this struggle, I fear that my own racism will make things worse, causing me to do more harm than good. Some readers may be shocked to see a white person contritely acknowledge that she is racist. I do not say this with pride. I simply believe that no matter how hard I work at not being racist, I still am. Because part of racism is systemic, I benefit from the privilege that I am struggling to see.

Notes and Questions

1. If one lives in a society that systematically submerges the chances of group X, then anyone not in group X benefits—the rule cuts down the competition. Is such a person privileged, and if so, what follows from this? What should he or she do?

2. In *White Privilege and Male Privilege: A Personal Account of Coming to See Correspondences through Work in Women's Studies*, Peggy McIntosh identifies 46 varieties of privilege that she enjoys by reason of her white skin, including:

1. I can if I wish arrange to be in the company of people of my race most of the time.

6. I can turn on the television or open to the front page of the paper and see people of my race widely represented.

8. I can be sure that my children will be given curricular materials that testify to the existence of their race.

13. Whether I use checks, credit cards, or cash, I can count on my skin color not to work against the appearance of financial reliability.

20. I can do well in a challenging situation without being called a credit to my race.

29. I can be pretty sure that if I argue for the promotion of a person of another race ... this is not likely to cost me heavily within my present setting.

46. I can choose a blemish cover or bandages in "flesh" color and have them more or less match my skin.

3. For each of Professor McIntosh's instances of privilege, consider the likely experience of a black, brown, or Native American person in that situation.

4. Is there such a thing as black privilege? Brown privilege? Christian privilege?

CALVIN TRILLIN

Doing the White Male Kvetch*
(A Pale Imitation of a Rag).

You're not allowed to give the wife a smack.
And people get their jobs because they're black.
Reverse discrimination's just not right.
We earned our jobs, by God, by being white.

(Chorus)

You put your right wing out.
You pop a can of brew.
You jiggle—just a bit,
Not like those black guys do.
You settle on the couch,
And then you yawn and stretch.
You're doin' paleface jive.
It's called the white male kvetch.

The Brady bill is flat unfair to shooters.
A guy these days can't even mention hooters—
A word the femiNazis now forbid.
You're also not allowed to smack your kid.

(Repeat chorus)

The welfare queens with Cadillacs eat steaks.
It's true: these colored folks get all the breaks.
They've got a right to sing the blues? Our rights
Should sure include the right to whine the whites.

(Repeat chorus, to distraction)

JOSHUA SOLOMON

Skin Deep; Reliving "Black Like Me": My Own Journey
into the Heart of Race–Conscious America
Washington Post, Sunday, October 30, 1994.*

What I noticed at the start of it, my first few days living as a black man, were the small things, the differences in the way people treated me. The doorman at my brother's apartment, a man I'd walked past every day for a month, stopped me, asked my name and where I was staying. * * * The hostess at a restaurant told me there would be a long wait, even though there were several empty tables. I'd thought about the idea of living as a black person ever since I read John Howard Griffin's *Black Like Me* in high school. In 1959, Griffin, a white journalist, disguised himself as a black man and traveled through the rural South. * * *

I picked up Griffin's book by chance one morning at the Springbrook High School library; I sat there all day reading it, oblivious to everything else, to the end of the school day. Then and there I decided that sometime soon I, too, would become black. It's as simple as this—I wanted to know what it was like. So it was that, in February of this year, I talked with Aaron B. Lerner, a physician who heads the department of dermatology at Yale University. I told him that I, a white, 20–year-old University of Maryland sophomore, had dropped out of school for a semester to live as a black man. And I wanted his help. Lerner was surprisingly nonchalant. Unlike others I'd told, he didn't dismiss me. Instead he explained that Griffin had used a derivative of the drug Psorlen to change his skin from white to brown. He also explained that it was suspected that Griffin's early death in 1980 was partially due to liver damage caused by the medication. I told the doctor that I'd had a heart condition since birth, that I was used to the dangers of potent medication and to life-and-death choices.

"Why," Lerner asked. "Why are you doing this?"

I had prepared a neat answer. Now I stammered and forgot what I'd planned to say. "I don't know," I finally said. "It's just, growing up in Silver Spring, I've always had a lot of black friends. Whenever something went down, they always said it was racism. Education, jobs, crime, poverty, social misunderstandings—they blamed everything on color. 'It's a white man's world,' they would say." That's what I told Lerner.

But there was something else—I'd sympathized with my friends, and I wanted to support them, but secretly, inside, I'd always felt that many black people used racism as a crutch, an excuse. Couldn't they just shrug off the rantings of ignorant people? * * *

In early April I decided my complexion had changed enough for me to pass. Over two months the color of my skin had changed from olive to reddish-brown. Someone said that, with my straight nose and full lips, I looked Haitian. On the steps outside our house, my brother shaved my head. I'd had my hair cut pretty short already, and my scalp was tan. Still, just for good measure, Jon rubbed some theatrical skin stain over my head to even the color. When he'd finished I looked in the mirror. It was scary. I wasn't me anymore. I was black. It was time to go.

I was going to make Atlanta my first stop. Waiting at Dulles for my flight, I noticed for the first time how few of the travelers in the airport were black. Most of the black people were working behind metal detectors or pushbrooms. When we boarded the shuttle to go to the plane, I took the first available seat. It was next to a white woman. I smiled at her, the way I usually do. She cut her eyes to the ground. A white man placed a bag on the vacant seat next to me and continued to stand. I wondered why he didn't sit. And then I asked myself if I was looking for things that weren't really there. Nonetheless, during that short ride, I couldn't help noticing something—the moment I met a white person's eyes, that person immediately turned away. * * *

The next morning when I went to a nearby drugstore, a white employee followed me around the store. At the drink refrigerator, I turned suddenly and stared right at her, letting her know that I knew what she was doing—shadowing me as if I were a potential thief. I'd hoped to embarrass her, but she didn't flinch. She stared right back, hands on her hips.

"Are you gonna buy something or not?" she asked.

I grabbed some orange juice.

"That'll be $1.94," said the woman behind the counter.

"Pretty expensive o.j." I said. "Then don't buy it," she countered.

I checked out of my room, went to the bus station. My destination was Gainesville, Ga., the closest bus station to Forsyth County, which I had chosen because no blacks live there. Following the rape of a young white girl in 1912, two black men were convicted. Several lynchings were recorded following the verdict; the accused were eventually hanged. Using force and intimidation, the white community drove all black residents from the county. The 1990 census statistics on Forsyth County today show "N/A" under all categories for black people.

A light-skinned black man called me "brother" and asked where I was going. (I told him.) "Man!" he said, shocked. "You don't want to go to Forsyth. They got old ways down there, the lynching mentality. You should stay in the city." * * *

After checking into the Ramada Inn, I went out to explore. From what I could see, walking through the north side of the city, it was like a movie set for an old Southern town, complete with a statue of a Confederate soldier in the square. Three churches within two blocks, some store fronts, few people in evidence. Continuing up Green Avenue, the residential area began, a beautiful neighborhood, the sidewalks shaded with majestic boxwoods. On one porch, two ladies chatted. As I passed, their conversation stopped. I kept walking. When I looked back, they were still watching me.

I circled back to my room, called everyone I could think of, needing somebody to talk to. Finally I got through to Earnest Sharpe, a reporter who had written the most recent article on John Howard Griffin. He'd been supportive when I'd called him before. I was confused and angry about the intense emotions that petty indignities stirred in me. I'd hardly started on my journey, but I was already furious, almost to the point of paralysis. I began to cry as I recounted the events of the last two days, the drip-drop of indifference and fear from the white people I had encountered. Their lack of patience, their downright contempt. He gave me the number of some of his friends in Atlanta. He told me that if things got bad, I could go there. I asked if they were white. I would stay with white people if they knew I wasn't really black. * * *

I headed for a diner I had seen the day before. All of the tables were occupied by white customers. There was one black patron at the counter, I took a seat next to him [and we began to talk]. * * *

"Look, you're here cause you heard about the New South, right? You've heard we've come a long way and you want to find a new place to start. Well, let me tell you. Atlanta might be the New South, but here in Gainesville, in all these little towns, this is still the Old South," he said. "What do you think happened to all those fellows who used to tell me and your daddy to sit in the back of the bus or to go around back to find the black bathroom? You think all those people died when they killed Mister Crow?" * * *

A few blocks farther a police car passed, made a U-turn, stopped directly in my path. The cop waved me over. I walked to the car, put my hand on the roof of his cruiser.

"Get your hands off my cruiser," he said. (I put them in my pockets.) "You don't want to do that either."

I folded my fingers in front of my chest like a choirboy. He regarded me a moment. "You're new in town, aren't you?" he asked. His breath stank. "Well, we've had plenty of trouble down here. I hope you don't have any more in mind."

"No way. No, sir," I assured him. I prayed that he wouldn't ask for my ID. How would I explain this white man's driver's license in my pocket? Visions of Rodney King flashed through my head.

"Okay," he said, "Stay out of trouble now, you hear?" * * *

When I got to the room, it hit me. I was sick of being black. I couldn't take it anymore. I wanted to throw up. Enough is enough, I thought. I didn't need to be hit over the head with a baseball bat to understand what was going on here. Usually, I'd made friends pretty easily. I was nice to them and they were nice to me. Now people acted like they hated me. Nothing had changed but the color of my skin.

I went to the closet, pulled out my suitcase. After all of two days, the experiment was over. Maybe I was weak, maybe I couldn't hack it. I didn't care. This anger was making me sick and the only antidote I knew was a dose of white skin. I called my mother and told her I was finished with my journey. All the hurt, all the anger, all the inhumanity. I started to cry. . . .

The bus came into Gainesville at about 3 p.m. The quiet ride ended in Atlanta at about 4:30. I took the subway back to the airport. A young black woman leaned against the seat next to me. She dozed off occasionally. In her arms she cradled a sack of books. Around her neck hung a stethoscope. Why hadn't she given up? I could return home to my comfortable world. I could wait for my skin to turn white again. She would have to endure.

Joshua Solomon is a University of Maryland student.

[For an excerpt from *Black Like Me*, see Chapter 12, § 2.]

Notes and Questions

1. Are you surprised that Joshua Solomon only lasted a few short days as a Black? Suppose a black college student reversed the experiment and went about the world made up to look perfectly white. What feelings and experiences might she confront? Would people treat her differently? How would she feel when she went back to her former identity?

2. Are white people privileged? Unprivileged? Privileged at some times and in some situations, and not others? Is it a privilege not to have to think about your privilege most of the time? When you take a road trip, do you carefully plan every detail in advance, including where you will fill up with gas or where you will spend every night? Many people of color do, especially when traveling in the South or in rural areas. Are light-skinned Chicanos or Blacks privileged vis-a-vis darker members of their groups? Is it possible for a Black to be racist, or to lord privilege, over another Black?

3. For further reading on racial privilege and transparency, see Jerome Culp, *Posner on Duncan Kennedy and Racial Difference*, 41 Duke L.J. 1095 (1992); Barbara Flagg, *Was Blind, But Now I See: White Race Consciousness and the Law* (1998); Ruth Frankenberg, *Growing Up White*, 45 Feminist Rev. 51 (1993); Marlee Kline, *Race, Racism, and Feminist Theory*, 12 Harv. Women's L.J. 115 (1989); Vron Ware, *Beyond the Pale: White Women, Racism, and History* (1991); Stephanie Wildman, et al., *Privilege Revealed: How Invisible Preference Undermines America* (1996).

SECTION 4. COLOR IMAGERY AND "SNOW WHITE"

SNOW WHITE

In the fairy tale by the brothers Grimm, a princess with skin "as white as snow, lips as red as blood, and hair as black as ebony" had a psychologically rocky relationship with her stepmother following the death of her mother, the Queen:

Now Snow White was growing prettier and prettier, and when she was seven years old she was as beautiful as day, far more so than the Queen herself. So one day when the Queen went to her mirror and said:

> Looking glass upon the wall,
>
> Who is fairest of us all?

It answered:

> Queen, you are full fair, 'tis true,
>
> But Snow White fairer is than you.

This made the Queen furious; she sent Snow White away to be killed; Snow White escaped and went to live with seven dwarfs in the woods. More mirrors, poisoned apples, and escapes later, Snow White is rescued by a prince who comes upon her seemingly lifeless body, awakens her and takes her to his castle. The wicked Queen is dispatched, and the two live happily ever after. See *Grimms' Fairy Tales* (E.V. Lucas, L. Crane & M. Edwardes, trans. 1945).

Notes and Questions

1. The fairy tale equates "fair" with "white" (indeed, very white), and "white" with "pretty." Could an extremely attractive Asian, Latino, or black girl play the role of Snow White, in literature and myth? The Grimm brothers were writing, of course, against a background of European nobility and its times, when very few princesses were nonwhite. But a century later, Western folklore still contains few, if any, children's tales celebrating nonwhite beauty. Is this accidental? Could it be otherwise? If not, what does this say about color, beauty, and the social and literary regulation of caste?

2. The illustrations for a widely sold volume of Grimm's fairy tales show children and young heroes and heroines as Aryan and noble-looking; dwarfs as working-class people, and the aged as ugly and deformed. When a society, like nineteenth-century Europe, lacks racial outcasts, does it simply create them in another form?

3. For a detailed treatment of racial imagery in materials for adults, see Chapter 12.

THOMAS ROSS

The Rhetorical Tapestry of Race: White Innocence and Black Abstraction
32 Wm. & Mary L. Rev. 1, 34–39 (1990).*

To understand the power of white innocence, one must begin with the power of the cultural conception. To be innocent is important everywhere in our culture. The argument for the white person's innocence in matters of race connects with the cultural ideas of innocence and defilement. The very contrast between the colors, white and black, often symbolizes the contrast between innocence and defilement. Thus, the theme of white innocence in the legal rhetoric of race draws its power from more than the obvious advantage of pushing away responsibility. It takes power from the cultural, religious, and sexual themes its terms suggest.

* Originally published in the William and Mary Law Review. Used by permission.

White and black often symbolize some form of good and bad. Black or darkness has been the symbol of evil for many Western cultures. Darkness is a symbol of the anti-God, Satan by any name. "Black magic" is often used to describe a perverse form of magic and worship. In Christian sects, darkened churches symbolize Lent, whereas the glory of Easter is a time to throw open the windows and let in the light. The sexual connotations of white innocence are many and complex. White often symbolizes innocence as chaste, whereas black symbolizes noninnocence, as in the defiled and the defiler. The white wedding dress is a double symbol of the connection between white and innocence and the significance of sexual innocence of women.

The black person is often depicted as the sexual defiler. Shakespeare's depiction of Othello, although an uncommonly rich portrait of a black person in literature, expressed the idea of the black as sexually wanton. * * * As a result of early contacts with Africa, Englishmen tended to associate blackness with savagery, heathenism, and general failure to conform to European standards of civilization and propriety. Contributing to this predisposition were the conscious and unconscious connotations of the color black. The association of black with evil was of course deeply rooted in Western and Christian mythology; it was natural to think of Satan as the Prince of Darkness and of witchcraft as black magic. On the unconscious level, twentieth-century psychoanalysts have suggested, blackness or darkness can be associated with suppressed libidinous impulses. Carl Gustav Jung has even argued that the Negro became for European whites a symbol of the unconscious itself—of what he calls "the shadow"—the whole suppressed or rejected side of the human psyche. * * *

The contrast between black and white in its sexual context is most vividly captured in miscegenation statutes, always accompanied by images of the black man's defilement of the white woman. Commentators on southern culture have noted the recurring mythology of the black man as the oversexed, large, would-be defiler of the innocent white woman. Griffith's epic motion picture, *Birth of a Nation*, depicts the suicide of the innocent white woman seeking to avoid the touch of the black man, portrayed as a slobbering beast.

Our media's obsession with the violent sexual assault of a white woman by a group of blacks in the "Central Park jogger" case suggests that the sexual connotation of white innocence persists. The notion of the black person as oversexed and dirty is part of our cultural stereotypes. The unconscious racism which our culture continues to teach expresses the terror of the black defiler of the innocent white. In 1967, *Loving v. Virginia* finally declared unconstitutional our most vivid legal expression of this form of racism, the miscegenation statutes, although the Court's opinion lacked any real expression of outrage.

The rhetorical theme of white innocence thus connects with the cultural, religious, and sexual notions of innocence, sin, and defilement. The power of the rhetoric comes in part from its ability to conjure in us at some unconscious level the always implied contrast to white innocence—the black one who is both defiled and the potential defiler. * * *

The irony is that the rhetoric of white innocence was arguably less powerful in its nineteenth-century version because these cultural connections and images were part of accepted public ideology and discourse. People spoke publicly of blacks as degenerate, dirty, and beast-like. The rhetoric of white innocence thus might have been merely an alternative way of expressing a widely accepted vision of blacks and whites—the vision of blunt and explicit racism. On the other hand, the rhetoric of white innocence in its contemporary form may be rhetorically more powerful. Our public ideology and discourse are ones of nonracism. Judges cannot say out loud that blacks are inferior, nor can lawyers make arguments with the explicit premises of racism. When the contemporary rhetoric of white innocence invites the cultural connections and images, we may be tapping into a repressed vein of unconscious racism which cannot be expressed in any way but indirectly and metaphorically. We ought to set aside the rhetoric of white innocence for several reasons. First, its family resemblance to the rhetoric of cases we now disavow makes it suspect. Second, when we consider the implicit premises of our claim to innocence, we see a much more complicated set of circumstances. Finally, when we consider the cultural connections that the rhetoric invites and the fact that those connections are part of the unconscious racism that persists in our culture, we have the most powerful reason of all to stop talking this way. * * *

[Consider, now, the correlate of white innocence, namely,] black abstraction. In various ways, legal rhetoric denied, or obscured, the full humanness of the black person. By doing so, we made legally coherent the nineteenth-century legal choices first to enslave and thereafter to segregate blacks. Slavery became legally coherent when the subject was not human. *De jure* segregation became legally coherent when whites supposed that blacks suffered no harm and experienced no stigma. * * * The denial of the full humanness of the black person has been a central and tragic part of our discourse. Black abstraction functioned as a lens through which we remade the setting in which our choices were played out. We abstracted away the pieces of reality that might have made those choices less comfortable.

Black abstraction also worked in another equally tragic way. * * * In law and elsewhere, black abstraction makes more difficult the empathic response of the white person to the suffering of the black. Empathy connotes the capacity to share, in some imperfect way, in the suffering of others. We easily can achieve some degree of empathy for the suffering of those whom we think of as familiar. * * * We have a more difficult time achieving empathy for the suffering of people we think of as unfamiliar. We can separate ourselves more easily from their circumstances; we can simply not imagine that they suffer; we can suppose some sense of justice in whatever suffering we are forced to see. * * * White innocence and black abstraction comfort us in our choices. They provide a source of shelter that we should struggle to give up. We should try to see the problematic quality of white innocence and the "make believe" world depicted through black abstraction.

Changing the way we talk about race is not simply a matter of resolve. We cannot slough off the assumptions and attitudes that determine in part the language we use. White innocence and black abstraction never have been simply rhetorical structures that we made up by ourselves. They always have been a product of both the imagination of the rhetorician and the influences of history and culture. To change truly the way we talk about race requires a parallel change in attitudes and assumptions. As language and rhetoric shape assumptions and ideas, so do they shape language and rhetoric.

LINDA L. AMMONS

Mules, Madonnas, Babies, Bathwater, Racial Imagery and Stereotypes
1995 Wis. L. Rev. 1003, 1046–56.*

By the time a child is four or five, he or she has learned the significance of skin color and racial membership.... Whites have been taught either expressly or implicitly that they are better than blacks. Kimberlé Crenshaw has provided the following chart illustrating how the negative image of blacks corresponds with the images of whites:

White Images	Black Images
Industrious	Lazy
Intelligent	Unintelligent
Moral	Immoral
Knowledgeable	Ignorant
Enabling Culture	Disabling Culture
Law-abiding	Criminal
Responsible	Shiftless
Virtuous/Pious	Lascivious[164]

Even when adults conform their public behavior to what is socially acceptable because of the changing laws and/or mores, the indoctrination of childhood can create psychological conflicts.... For example, two black women, interviewed by sociologist Joe Feagin, recounted: "[I have faced] harassment in stores, being followed around, being questioned about what are you going to purchase here.... [A] few ... white people ... won't put change in your hand, touch your skin."[180] When African Americans are brought to trial the question of how extra-legal factors alter their ability to get a fair trial linger on, raising the possibility that different standards of justice exist for people who are of European descent and those who are not. Racial bias in the courtroom is *de jure* illegal, but *de facto* bias exercises its malevolent sway nevertheless.

* Originally published in the Wisconsin Law Review. Copyright 1995 by the Board of Regents of the University of Wisconsin System. Reprinted by permission of the Wisconsin Law Review.

164. Kimberlé Crenshaw, *Race, Reform and Retrenchment: Transformation and Legitimation in Antidiscrimination Law*, 101 Harv. L. Rev. 1331, 1373 (1988). Crenshaw also explains how racism and oppression work. "Racism serves to single out Blacks as one of these groups 'worthy' of suppression.... The most significant aspect of Black oppression seems to be what is believed about Black Americans not what Black Americans believe." *Id*. at 1358.

180. Joe R. Feagin, *The Continuing Significance of Race: Antiblack Discrimination in Public Places*, 56 Am. Soc. Rev. 101, 107 (1991).

D. MARVIN JONES
Darkness Made Visible: Law, Metaphor, and the Racial Self
82 Geo. L.J. 437, 471–73 (1993).*

Society has created a connection between color and meaning. But what of black and white?

> Black is ... the *total absence of color*, due to the absence or total *absorption* of light.... "White" is "fully luminous and devoid of any distinctive hues." That void is the point where white and black meet and reverse; for if white is an empty fullness (fully luminous but *void*), then black is a full emptiness (*total* absence).[133] * * *

Western culture has fixed blackness within the structure of language, firmly entrenching blackness as a symbol of negation. Frantz Fanon writes:

> In Europe ... the Torturer is the black man, Satan is black, one talks of the shadow, when one is dirty one is black—whether one is thinking of physical dirtiness or moral dirtiness ... Blackness, darkness, shadow, shades, night, and the labyrinths of earth, abysmal depths, blacken someone's reputation; and on the other side, the bright look of innocence, the white dove of peace, magical, heavenly light.[138]

The root of this negative image of blackness in the English language is traceable to a religio-ethical tradition of associating whiteness with purity and blackness with sin.

The imagery of blackness as sin continues today, in songs that are presently sung:

> On the Cross at Cavalry,
> Jesus died for you and me
> There he shed His precious blood
> That from sin we might be free
> O cleansing stream does flow
> And it washes *white* as snow[142]

This symbolic framework, which drew together notions of spiritual equality and secular inferiority, was instrumental throughout the slave and colonial regimes in reconciling religious equalitarianism with colonial domination and slavery. A variation on this theme of blackness as the absence of virtue is the idea that blackness represents the absence of intelligence. As a color, black does not reflect. As such it was an easy, if illogical, step to extend Gobineau's "Le noir ne reflechit pas" (the color of black does not reflect) to the notion that the black man does not "reflect" (*i.e.*, think). Consequently, Hume could posit a fundamental identity between color, intellectual achievement, and intelligence:

> I am apt to suspect the negroes, and in general all the other species of men (for there are four or five different kinds) to be naturally

---

* Copyright 1993 by D. Marvin Jones. Originally published in the Georgetown Law Journal. Used by permission of the author.

133. Christopher Miller, *Blank Darkness* 30–31 (1985).

138. Frantz Fanon, *Black Skin, White Masks* 188–89 (C. Lammarkman trans., 1967).

142. *On the Cross of Calvary*, in *Song Book of the Salvation Army* 33 (1963) (emphasis added).

inferior to the whites. There never was a civilized nation of any other complexion than white, nor even any individual eminent either in action or speculation. No ingenious manufactures amongst them, no arts, no sciences. . . . Such a uniform and constant difference could not happen, in so many countries and ages, if nature had not made an original distinction betwixt these breeds of men. Not to mention our colonies, there are NEGROE slaves dispersed all over EUROPE, of which none ever discovered any symptoms of ingenuity. . . . In JAMAICA indeed they talk of one negroe as a man of parts and learning; but 'tis likely he is admired for very slender accomplishments, like a parrot, who speaks a few words plainly.[144]

Notes and Questions

1. Is color imagery like Snow White pernicious, or just harmless children's fun? Can jurors disregard media and other images of Blacks, Asians, and Mexicans and presume innocence? James Baldwin, in *The Fire Next Time* (1963), writes that God is black, but this information is almost unthinkable to most Christians. Why should that be, any more so than the presumption that God is white is for nonwhites?

2. Toni Morrison, in *The Bluest Eye* (1979), writes of the chagrin of a sensitive black character over the realization that she will never measure up to white standards of beauty:

> Pretty eyes. Pretty blue eyes. Big blue pretty eyes. . . . Alice has blue eyes. Jerry has blue eyes. . . . Four pretty blue eyes. Blue-sky eyes. Blue-like-Mrs. Forrest's-blue-blouse eyes. Morning-glory-blue eyes. Alice-and-Jerry-blue-storybook eyes.

> Each night, without fail she prayed for blue eyes. Fervently, for a year she had prayed. . . . To have something as wonderful as that happen would take a long, long time.

Is this sense of inadequacy any different from that of a person unhappy with his or her weight or physique? Consider, by the same author, *Playing in the Dark* (1992), discussing the way society "abstracts" Blacks as a rhetorical foil for white power.

3. In an essay, *Language and Prejudice Toward Negroes*, in *White Racism* (Barry Schwartz & Robert Disch eds. 1970), Simon Podair offers the following examples of the way language encodes color imagery:

blackball—to exclude another from membership

black book—containing names of persons who are out of favor

blacken—to sully or defame

blackguard—one who uses foul or abusive language

blacklist—containing names of persons suspected of evildoing

blackmail—distortion

black market—illegal sales

black mood—deep gloom

Podair writes:

144. David Hume, *Of National Characters*, in 1 *The Philosophical Works* 252 n.1 (Thomas H. Green & Thomas H. Grose eds. 1964).

Language is the mirror of society, reflecting its attitudes and thinking. As a society changes . . . its language patterns may be modified. Thus, in years to come, the symbols "black" and "white" may no longer take on divergent meanings. . . . [T]here may be substituted a more honest appraisal of color, with a resultant favorable effect upon race relations. See Podair, *supra* at 391.

Has the hoped-for improvement taken place?

CHILDREN'S STORIES

Readers interested in understanding how children's stories reinforce racial and color lines may wish to see Harold Isaacs' classic *Blackness and Whiteness* (*Encounter*, Aug. 1963, at 12) and David Milner's *Children and Race* (1983). Isaacs shows how the terms for African Americans changed as the status of this group vis-a-vis Whites waxed and waned. The author shows how races are depicted in classic texts such as the Bible, children's stories like "Dr. Doolittle," and in *Othello* and other works by Shakespeare. According to one author he discusses:

The Anglo–Saxon civilisation is the highest and best yet evolved in the history of the human race. . . . The word "Negro" originally referred to a native African black, who was a barbarian and a savage. . . . "Negro" calls up a black, kinky-haired and heavy-featured being. . . . [It] suggests physical and spiritual kinship to the ape. (*id.* at 12)

Milner examines the treatment of race in children's stories, including who these stories assign to the role of hero and who to that of villain, concluding:

It would be easy indeed to emerge from a childhood spent with some of these books believing that Africans seldom come out of the jungle, Chinese men wear pigtails, and French men . . . dine exclusively on frogs and snails.

Milner quotes one children's book whose heroine was "a beauty . . . Marusia the Fair they called her. Her skin was as white as milk . . . [she] was kind and good-natured as she was pretty."

Do these stories and tales cause children to value races differently? Some polls show that children do so, as young as three. Are stories like these part of the reason? See Milner, *supra* at 100.

JUAN F. PEREA
The Black/White Binary Paradigm of Race: The "Normal Science" of American Racial Thought
85 Calif. L.Rev. 1213, 1214, 1216–17, 1219–27 (1997).*

Much writing on racism is structured by a paradigm that is widely held but rarely recognized. This paradigm shapes our understanding of what race and racism mean and the nature of our discussions about race.

It is crucial, therefore, to identify and describe this paradigm and to demonstrate how it binds and organizes racial discourse, limiting both the scope and the range of legitimate viewpoints in that discourse. I mean, of course, one of the most salient features of past and current discourse about race in the United States, the Black/White binary paradigm of race. * * *

Thomas Kuhn, in *The Structure of Scientific Revolutions*, describes the properties of paradigms and their power in structuring scientific research and knowledge. A paradigm is a shared set of understandings or premises which permits the definition, elaboration, and solution of a set of problems defined within the paradigm. A paradigm is an accepted model or pattern that, "like an accepted judicial decision in the common law ... is an object for further articulation and specification under new or more stringent conditions."[6] Paradigms exist, therefore, not just in the sciences but also in law and other disciplines. Thus, a paradigm is the set of shared understandings that permits us to distinguish those facts that matter in the solution of a problem from those that do not. As Kuhn writes,

> [i]n the absence of a paradigm or some candidate for paradigm, all of the facts that could possibly pertain to the development of a given science are likely to seem equally relevant. As a result, early fact-gathering is a far more nearly random activity than the one that subsequent scientific development makes familiar.[8]

Paradigms thus define relevancy. In so doing, they control fact-gathering and investigation. Data-gathering efforts and research are focused on understanding the facts and circumstances that the relevant paradigm teaches us are important.

Paradigms are crucial in the development of * * * knowledge because, by setting boundaries within which problems can be understood, they permit detailed inquiry into these problems. In Kuhn's words, a "paradigm forces scientists to investigate some part of nature in a detail and depth that would otherwise be unimaginable."[10] However, as a paradigm becomes the widely accepted way of thinking and of producing knowledge on a subject, it tends to exclude or ignore alternative facts or theories that do not fit the expectations produced by the paradigm.

Kuhn uses the concept of "normal science" to describe the elaboration of the paradigm and the solution of problems that the paradigm allows us to perceive. Scientists and researchers spend almost all of their time engaged in normal science, conducting their research under the rules prescribed by the paradigm and attempting to solve problems cognizable and derivable from it. However, normal science "often suppresses fundamental novelties because they are necessarily subversive of its basic commitments."[13] As Kuhn describes, normal science "seems an attempt to force nature into the performed and relatively inflexible box that the paradigm supplies. No part of the aim of normal science is to

---

6. Thomas S. Kuhn, *The Structure of Scientific Revolutions* 23 (2d ed. 1970).

8. Kuhn, *supra*, at 15.

10. *Id.* at 24.

13. *Id.* at 5.

call forth new sorts of phenomena; indeed those that will not fit the box are often not seen at all."[14] * * *

In similar fashion, paradigms of *race* shape our understanding of race and our definition of racial problems. The most pervasive and powerful such paradigm in the United States is the Black/White binary paradigm—the conception that race in America consists, either exclusively or primarily, of only two constituent racial groups, the Black and the White. Many scholars of race reproduce this paradigm when they write and act as though only the Black and the White races matter for purposes of discussing race and social policy. The mere recognition that "other people of color" exist, without careful attention to their voices, their histories, and their real presence, is merely a reassertion of the Black/White paradigm. If one conceives of race and racism as primarily of concern only to Blacks and Whites, and understands "other people of color" only through some unclear analogy to the "real" races, this just restates the binary paradigm with a slight concession to demographics.

My assertion is that our shared understanding of race and racism is essentially limited to this Black/White binary paradigm. This paradigm defines, but also limits, the set of problems that may be recognized in racial discourse. Kuhn's notion of "normal science," which further articulates the paradigm and seeks to solve the problems perceivable because of the paradigm, also applies to "normal research" on race.

Given the Black/White paradigm, we would expect to find that much research on race is concerned with understanding the dynamics of these two races and attempting to solve the problems between Blacks and Whites. Within the paradigm, the relevant facts are ones about Blacks and Whites. In addition, the paradigm dictates that all other racial identities and groups in the United States are best understood through the Black/White binary paradigm. Only a few writers even recognize that they use a Black/White paradigm as the frame of reference through which to understand racial relations. Most simply assume the importance and correctness of the paradigm, and leave the reader grasping for whatever significance descriptions of the Black/White relationship have for other people of color. Because the Black/White binary paradigm is so widely accepted, other racialized groups like Latinos/as, Asian Americans, and Native Americans are often marginalized or ignored altogether. As Kuhn writes, "those that will not fit the box are often not seen at all."[29] * * *

Andrew Hacker's famous book, *Two Nations: Black and White, Separate, Hostile, Unequal*, provides an excellent example.[32] Its title, proclaiming two nations, Black and White, boldly professes that paradigm. Although Hacker recognizes explicitly that a full perspective on race in America requires inclusion of Latinos/as and Asians, this recognition is, in the context of the entire book, insignificant and underdevel-

14. *Id.* at 24.

29. Kuhn, *supra* note 6, at 24; see also Juan F. Perea, *Los Olvidados: On the Making of Invisible People*, 70 N.Y.U. L. Rev. 965 (1995); Anne Sutherland, *Gypsies: The Hidden Americans* (1986).

32. Andrew Hacker, *Two Nations: Black and White, Separate, Hostile, Unequal* (1992).

oped. His almost exclusive focus on Blacks and Whites is clearly intentional: *"Two Nations* will adhere to its title by giving central attention to black and white Americans."[34] Hacker's justification for this focus is that "[i]n many respects, other groups find themselves sitting as spectators, while the two prominent players try to work out how or whether they can coexist with one another."[35] This justification perpetuates the marginalization of the already marginalized. Hacker and so many other writers on race decline to understand that, by focusing only on Blacks and Whites, they both produce and replicate the belief that only "two prominent players," Black and White, count in debates about race. These writers thus render other nonwhite groups invisible and implicitly characterize them as passive, voluntary spectators. Such characterization is contrary to the history of these groups.

Hacker describes in detail only conditions experienced by White or Black Americans:

America is inherently a "white" country: in character, in structure, in culture. Needless to say, black Americans create lives of their own. Yet, as a people, they face boundaries and constrictions set by the white majority. America's version of apartheid, while lacking overt legal sanction, comes closest to the system even now being reformed in the land of its invention.[37]

Of course, Latinos/as, Asian Americans, Native Americans, Gypsies, and all nonWhite Americans face "boundaries and constrictions set by the white majority," but the vision Hacker advances considers only Blacks as significantly disadvantaged by White racism.

Similarly, Hacker describes Blackness as uniquely functional for Whites:

As James Baldwin has pointed out, white people need the presence of black people as a reminder of what providence has spared them from becoming.... In the eyes of white Americans, being black encapsulates your identity. No other racial or national origin is seen as having so pervasive a personality or character.[38]

According to Hacker, then, Blackness serves a crucial function in enabling Whites to define themselves as privileged and superior, and racial attributes of other minorities do not serve this function. * * *

The greatest danger in Hacker's vision is its suggestion that non-White groups other than Blacks are not really subject to racism. Hacker seems to adopt the deservedly criticized ethnicity theory, which posits that nonWhite immigrant ethnics are essentially Whites-in-waiting who will be permitted to assimilate and become White. This is illustrated best in Chapter 8, "On Education: Ethnicity and Achievement," which offers the book's only significant discussion of nonWhite groups other than Blacks. Hacker describes Asians in "model minority" terms, because of high standardized test scores as a group. He portrays Latinos/as as below standard, because of low test scores and graduation rates, and as

34. *Id.* at xii.
35. *Id.*

37. *Id.* at 4.
38. *Id.* at 30, 32

aspiring immigrants. Describing Asian Americans, Latinos/as and other immigrant groups, Hacker writes:

> Members of all these "intermediate groups" have been allowed to put a visible distance between themselves and black Americans. Put most simply, none of the presumptions of inferiority associated with Africa and slavery are imposed on these other ethnicities.[45]

While a full rebuttal of this proposition is beyond the scope of this article, its inaccuracy can be quickly demonstrated. Consider, for instance, the observations of historian David Weber, who described early Anglo perceptions of Mexican people: "American visitors to the Mexican frontier were nearly unanimous in commenting on the dark skin of Mexican mestizos who, it was generally agreed, had inherited the worst qualities of Spaniards and Indians to produce a 'race' still more despicable than that of either parent."[46] Rufus B. Sage expressed the common view of Mexicans in 1846:

> There are no people on the continent of America, whether civilized or uncivilized, with one or two exceptions, more miserable in condition or despicable in morals than the mongrel race inhabiting New Mexico.... To manage them successfully, they must needs be held in continual restraint, and kept in their place by force, if necessary,—else they will become haughty and insolent. As servants, they are excellent, when properly trained, but are worse than useless if left to themselves.[47]

More briefly, the common perception of Mexican Americans was that "They are an inferior race, that is all."[48]

Incredibly, and without any supporting evidence, Hacker writes that "[m]ost Central and South Americans can claim a strong European heritage, which eases their absorption into the 'white' middle class."[49] Hacker continues, "[w]hile immigrants from Colombia and Cyprus may have to work their way up the social ladder, they are still allowed as valid a claim to being 'white' as persons of Puritan or Pilgrim stock."[50] Hacker's comments are simply incredible for their blithe lack of awareness of how racism burdens the lives of Latino/a, Asian–American and other racialized immigrant groups. While some Latinos/as may look White and may act Anglo (the phenomenon of passing for White is not limited to Blacks), Hacker's statement is certainly false for millions of others. Current anti-immigrant initiatives targeted at Latinos/as and Asians, such as California's Proposition 187 and similar federal legislation targeting legal and illegal immigrants, California's Proposition 209, and unprecedented proposals to deny birthright citizenship to the United

45. *Id.* at 16.

46. David J. Weber, *Editor's Introduction to Chaper II,* in *Foreigners in Their Native Land: Historical Roots of the Mexican Americans* 59 (David J. Weber ed. 1973).

47. *Id.* at 72, 74 (quoting 2 *Rufus B. Sage: His Letters and Papers, 1836–1847* (LeRoy R. & Ann W. Hafen eds. 1956)).

48. Texas school officials offered this justification for segregating Mexican Americans in 1929. See Jorge C. Rangel & M. Alcala, *Project Report: De Jure Segregation of Chicanos in Texas Schools,* 7 Harv. C.R.-C.L. L. Rev. 307, 307 (1972) (quoting Paul Schuster Taylor, *An American Mexican Frontier* 219 (1934)).

49. Hacker, *supra* note 32, at 10.

50. *Id.* at 12.

States-born children of undocumented persons, debunk any notion that the White majority tolerates easily the presence of Latino/a or Asian people. * * *

Nor is Hacker alone in perpetuating the Black/White binary paradigm. Cornel West is one of the most well-known and well-regarded philosophers and commentators on race in the nation. While West writes with more insight than Hacker, his recent book *Race Matters* also reproduces the Black/White binary paradigm of race.[57] Several of the essays seem addressed chiefly to the Black community, and some to the Black and White communities. His critiques of Black leadership, intellectuals, and conservatism are powerful, unflinching, and persuasive.

To a large extent, however, West adopts the Black/White binary paradigm by addressing only the relationship between Blacks and Whites (and, in one essay, Blacks and Jews). West writes as though "race" means only the Black race. His remarks confine the discussion of race and antiracism to the need to struggle against Black oppression, rather than a broader antisubordination agenda that would include all people of color and antiracist Whites in confronting patriarchy and racism in all their manifestations.

West correctly recognizes, in one sentence, the "multiracial, transclass, and largely male display of justified social rage" that occurred during the Los Angeles riots of 1992.[58] West notes that only 36 percent of those arrested were Black (51 percent were Latino, making the riots and looting prominently Latino). But rather than discuss the multiracial rage and despair that fueled the riots, West discusses the inadequacy of our racial discourse in binary, Black/White terms. West describes the kind of discussions that we need to have about race in terms suggesting that only Blacks and Whites need to participate in the discussion:

> To engage in a serious discussion of race in America, we must begin not with the problems of black people but with the flaws of American society—flaws rooted in historic inequalities and long-standing cultural stereotypes. How we set up the terms for discussing racial issues shapes our perception and response to these issues. As long as black people are viewed as a "them," the burden falls on blacks to do all the "cultural" and "moral" work necessary for healthy race relations.

> ... [W]e confine discussions about race in America to the "problems" black people pose for whites rather than consider what this way of viewing black people reveals about us as a nation.... Both [liberals and conservatives] fail to see that the presence and predicaments of black people are neither additions to nor defections from American life, but rather *constitutive elements of that life*.[60]

West's statements are accurate, and I would fault him only for not recognizing that exactly the same statements apply to Latinos/as, Asian Americans and Native Americans. If the "terms for discussing racial issues" include only Blacks and Whites, this fact will indeed shape

---

57.   Cornel West, *Race Matters* (1993).   **60.**   *Id*. at 2–3.
58.   *Id*. at 1.

everyone's perception of who belongs in the discussion, and Latinos/as, Asian Americans and Native Americans will promptly disappear. Any serious discussion of race requires incorporating the multiple points of view of all racialized peoples. Like Blacks, Latinos/as, Asian Americans, and Native Americans are all constitutive of American life and identity to a degree that has not been fully recognized and is, in fact, actively resisted.

Notes and Questions

1.   Ralph Ellison, in *Invisible Man* 7–8 (1952, reprinted 1982), writes:

"Brothers and sisters, my text this morning is the 'Blackness of Blackness.'"

And a congregation of voices answered: "That blackness is most black, brother, most black ..."

"In the beginning ..."

"At the very start," they cried.

" ... there was blackness ..."

"Preach it ..."

" ... and the sun ..."

"The sun, Lawd ..."

" ... was bloody red ..."

"Red ..."

"Now black is ..." the preacher shouted.

"Bloody ..."

"I said black is ..."

"Preach it, brother ..."

" ... an' black ain't ..."

"Black will git you ..."

"Red, Lawd, red: He said it's red!"

"Amen, brother ..."

"Yes it will ..."

" ... an, black won't ..."

"Black will make you ..."

"Black ..."

" ... or black will un-make you."

"Ain't it the truth Lawd?"

Ellison's title and the short excerpt, taken together, suggest that black people are "invisible"—*i.e.*, ignored—by others, but very visible to themselves and each other. Are things sometimes the other way around?

2.   Is Christmas white, and, if so, is this a metaphor for how the majority race sees those who embrace a different religion or are of a nonwhite race?

3.   Consider the words of a classic Christmas carol, "White Christmas" by Irving Berlin:

I'm dreaming of a white Christmas just like the ones I used to know,

Where the treetops glisten and children listen to hear sleighbells in the snow.

I'm dreaming of a white Christmas. With every Christmas card I write,

"May your days be merry and bright, and may all your Christmases be white."

Does this carol harken nostalgically to a time when the U.S. population was dominantly white? Is that the author's dream? Or, do the lyrics merely refer to snow and snowflakes? But, if so, snow is white today—so why the need to dream? And, what about regions of the country, such as the South, where snow rarely falls—why is snow a powerful metaphor there?

4.   In the black-white paradigm of which Juan Perea writes, everyone is either Black or White—others are irrelevant or come into the equation only insofar as they are near-Whites or near-Blacks. Is this much of an improvement over the society of myth, song, and legend, in which all the holidays and standards of beauty are of one color only, namely white?

5.   For suggested readings on color imagery, see Thomas Ross, *White Innocence, Black Abstraction,* in *Critical White Studies, supra* at 263; D. Marvin Jones, *The Curse of Ham,* in *id.* at 255; David Theo Goldberg, *The Semantics of Race,* 15 Ethnic & Racial Stud. 543 (1992); Marlon Riggs, *Ethnic Notions* (California Newsreel [video] 1987); George Fredrickson, *The Arrogance of Race* (1988).

6.   On the black-white binary, see Juan Perea, *Ethnicity and the Constitution: Beyond the Black and White Binary Constitution,* 36 Wm. & Mary L. Rev. 571 (1995); Richard Delgado, *Rodrigo's Fifteenth Chronicle: Racial Mixture, Latino-Critical Scholarship, and the Black–White Binary,* 75 Tex. L. Rev. 1181 (1997).

SECTION 5. WHITE POWER

See *Hatelines,* Week of Sunday, April 7, 1996. Compiled by the Center for Democratic Renewal:

April is a big month for Aryans, including Uncle Adolph's birthday on April 20th. April is recognized by many as Aryan, or white, history month. . . .

[Springtime is] a time of renewal, as the sun moves back towards the northern hemisphere, giving more light and warmth to our native northland. The rebirth of the sun was celebrated by our ancient Aryan ancestors. The cross that Christians use today is the ancient Aryan cross, or sunwheel—another form of swastika. . . .

[Breaks to answer questions left by callers.]

Q.   How do I pursue a restaurant or any public establishment that discriminates against me just for wearing racial symbols?

A.   Tom again advises callers to carry a small tape player at all times to record such encounters. * * *

Q. Is Ralph Nader a Jew?

A. I think he is but do not have evidence at this time. I must say, however, Nader lives a very austere lifestyle and he does champion several issues ... that are good for white working people.

* * *

Q. Does WAR [White Aryan Resistance] have a solution to the mestizo problem? Otherwise known as the invasion from Mexico and "Points South"?

A. Encourage as much frustration as possible among the general public.... Because even the dumbest whites know something's wrong. A pressure cooker with no escape valve must explode sooner or later....

Q. What if there is no upheaval or white revolution? Then what do we do?

A. Then our race is doomed in North America and eventually Europe. It is as simple as that. * * *

ELINOR LANGER

The American Neo–Nazi Movement Today; Special Report.*

* * *

In writing about a subject that carries with it the automatic weight of its association with Nazi Germany, I find myself uncomfortable, * * * suspended between caution and alarm. Especially about a movement as underreported as this one, you do not write, in the first place, merely to observe "this too will pass away"; you write to sound an alert. At the same time, you know that the tests of time are different and that historians of another generation will consider the evidence and say either that it was all simply part of another "Brown Scare" in which people, as usual, lost their heads, and some their civil liberties, or that a dangerous movement was on the rise and that we failed to discern it early enough and help stamp it out. I do not know where along that spectrum the truth of the neo-Nazi movement lies. I do know that it is among us, that it is violent and mean, and that it is time to open up the subject for further investigation and discussion so that out of a broader base of information and a variety of perspectives there can possibly be fashioned a sound response.

In using the term neo-Nazi, I am referring roughly to an array of groups and individuals, including:

· Nazis: old-line groups principally descended from the American Nazi Party [ANP] founded by George Lincoln Rockwell in 1959, whose members still appear in uniform, as well as other small Nazi-identified parties and groupings whose members usually do not.

* Copyright 1990 by Elinor Langer. Reprinted by permission of Georges Borchardt, Inc. for the author. Research for the essay (originally published in *The Nation*) was supported, in part, by grants from the Fund for Investigative Journalism and the Dick Goldensohn Fund.

· The skinheads: youth gangs in various cities with names like Youth of Hitler and the Confederate Hammerskinssome, like San Francisco's American Front, openly connected with Metzger's WAR [White Aryan Resistance], and some not; skinheads are the fastest-growing wing of the movement today.

· The Ku Klux Klan: no longer the centralized Klan of previous eras, but three separate and rival Klan federations and innumerable splinter groups; it is a government-infiltrated and at times government-manipulated Klan, a shadow of its former self, many of whose units are, however, "Nazified" in that they cooperate freely with the Nazi groups (something that was unthinkable in the past, when the Klan's patriotism and the Nazi's Germanophilism invariably clashed) and share many of the same ideas.

· The Posse Comitatus: a decentralized, antistate and largely rural movement, which also appears as the Christian Patriots or American Freemen Association, whose adherents believe, among other things, that all government should be rooted at the county level and that cooperating with any higher authority, including the I.R.S. or, indeed, even the state Department of Motor Vehicles, is wrong.

· The Christian Identity movement: an Aryan-inspired religious denomination descended from a nineteenth-century movement known as Anglo–Israelism or British Israelism, which holds that the "chosen people" of the Bible are white Anglo–Saxons, that Jews are descended from Satan and that all nonwhites are "pre-Adamic" "mud people'" a lower species than whites; it is a religious movement that, as in the case of Idaho's Aryan Nations-church of Jesus Christ, Christian (as opposed to Jesus Christ, Jew), is often indistinguishable from a political one.

THE NATURE OF THE MOVEMENT

In the phrase "neo-Nazi movement:" both the terms "neo-Nazi" and "movement" require further discussion, and they have to be argued together. The Klanwatch Project of the Southern Poverty Law Center (S.P.L.C.) in Montgomery, Alabama includes the categories listed above, but uses the overall heading "white supremacist" and reserves "neo-Nazi" for the groups that had their genesis with [the ANP]. The term "white supremacist" is also used by another major monitoring organization, the Center for Democratic Renewal in Atlanta. The problem with this usage, it seems to me, is not that it is wrong but that it does not go far enough, retaining an old-fashioned, unduly Southern and narrowly political flavor that fails to reflect the modern racialism that comes to us directly from the Nazi era and that I think is the essential characteristic these groups share. The neo-Nazi label does have varying degrees of applicability. James Farrands, Imperial Wizard of The Invisible Empire, Knights of the Ku Klux Klan, with whom I spoke a few months ago, was indignant at being associated with neo-Nazis and at pains to assure me that "you don't have to be a Nazi to be an anti-semite:" and to find a member of the Posse Comitatus with the same revulsion would not be difficult. But for the most part these organizations have no enemies to the right. If there are those within the movement who object to their Nazi bedfellows, they do not generally make themselves heard.

More important than any differences among the groups is that the individuals within them function together as a movement and know that they are one—a point on which the two monitoring organizations mentioned above, as well as the Anti-Defamation League of B'nai B'rith (A.D.L.), largely agree. Klan and Nazi units have worked together at least since their combined assault on anti-Klan demonstrators at a rally in Greensboro, North Carolina, in 1979, in which five were killed, three of them members of the Communist Workers Party. Klan/Neo–Nazi joint appearances on occasions such as an annual gathering in Pulaski, Tennessee, honoring the founding of the Klan—this year also attended by Aryan Nations pastor Richard Butler—have become routine. * * *

The mail-order catalogues of the Christian Patriots, a Posse group, and of the National Vanguard, a West Virginia Nazi group begun by Rockwell-follower William Pierce, not only offer many selections in their specialized areas (roughly, European prehistory and myth, in the case of the Nazis; the monetary system, in the case of the Patriots) but often overlap, featuring not only such classics as Carleton Putnam's *Race and Reason* (which is still winning converts) and Henry Ford's *The International Jew* but such newer and highly influential tracts as *The Hoax of the Twentieth Century* by Arthur Butz and *Did Six Million Really Die?* by Richard Harwood. If there is a household of an adherent of any wing of the movement that does not have a copy of *The Turner Diaries*, Pierce's fantasy of the violent overthrow of the U.S. government by patriotic guerrillas, I would be surprised.

To the readers of these books, Jews are the force controlling your life, blacks are genetically inferior and race mixing is the nearest thing to the end of the world this side of Armageddon. Although one group may start with the Jews and end with the blacks and another may start with the blacks and end with the Jews, they are linked by the newer idea that blacks are the latest woe that the Jews are heaping on the world. These are not the only convictions held in common, of course. Hostility to homosexuals and aliens, to name only two other groups, is also universal, though reflected less in the current ideological libraries than in the streets. But it is above all else the centrality of the Jew, even in the wake of the Holocaust, that makes me believe that "neo-Nazi" is the proper label for the movement in question. The quality of its hate and the direction of its intentions go beyond what we have seen in America before. As anomalous as it seems in a country in which blacks are not only the primary historical but also the primary daily victims of racism of every description, the Jew is, increasingly, the ultimate target; and lest the logic elude you, it is that, out of fear of being recognized as a race themselves, the Jews have conceived and implemented a variety of political strategies, of which integration is only the most offensive, designed to minimize racial differences in general. The significance of the historic shift on the far right from the dominance of the Klan to the dominance of the Nazi-influenced skinheads and others is in fact precisely the linkage of blacks and Jews in an explicitly genocidal context. A WAR video that opens with a laugh track over a scene of bulldozers burying bodies at Auschwitz, the words of Rick Cooper ("When the people can no longer tolerate the Jews, those people who don't believe in the Holocaust will want one; and those who do believe in the Holocaust will want another one.... The next Holocaust won't be a hoax"), all emanating from the same source, have got to give one pause. However much some Jews, and some blacks, may now wish to part company, from the neo-Nazi viewpoint they are part of the same problem, as are gays and every other minority as well.

The reader would undoubtedly like to know how many people are involved, a point on which the available data are unfortunately not very good. Estimates made by the three monitoring organizations mentioned above range from about 10,000 to about 20,000 members of these groups nationally, with the organizations agreeing on a rule of thumb of about ten passive supporters for every hard-core member—and thus a possible total of up to 200,000—and agreeing as well that the numbers are conservative.   * *   As uncertain as the number of adherents is the number of incidents of hate-motivated violence that we read about in our papers every day; everyone agrees they are dramatically increasing, but there are no reliable figures. With the exception of the A.D.L., which issues an annual audit of anti-semitic incidents (1,432 in 1989, a 12 percent increase over the previous year), most national organizations prefer not to quantify, believing that with the violence and the reporting apparently increasing simultaneously, the situation is not only a social but also a statistical mess; and with a monitoring agency in the Northwest alone reporting a 400 percent overall increase during the same year, this seems a reasonable inference. * * *

More important than the number either of members or of incidents, however, is the relationship between the two—a matter that has scarcely begun to be discussed. While it appears that most hate crimes are committed by individuals who are not associated with any organized group, the impulses of the member and the nonmember appear to be much the same. If it is an exaggeration to say that every hate criminal is a potential neo-Nazi, certainly they give the leaders reason to hope. At the least, there appears to be a kind of multiplier effect whereby one thing leads to another, and the mere existence of the movement acts as an enabling force for the open expressions of racism that, until recently, have tended to be underground. There is a dynamism at work here that any static accounting, whether of "members" or incidents'" cannot reflect. Tom Metzger is one of the principal sources of that dynamism, as his television program makes clear.

"Hi, this is Tom Metzger, your host for Race and Reason, the longest-running show of its type on cable access TV, seen in approximately fifty cities across the United States, blazing a trail of real free speech, free speech for white working people for a change. Race and Reason is an island of free speech in a sea of managed and controlled news ..."

The suit is brown, the shirt is blue, the tie is polka-dot, the voice is mellow and the guest tonight is "Baxter the Pagan," a skinhead leader and mainstay of the WAR organization who takes the "Pagan" from the ancient Germanic tribal religion of Odinism, of which he, like many neo-Nazis, is a follower.

"It must have been tough, a white boy in New York,'" Metzger begins. "How does it work?"

"I grew up in a predominantly white neighborhood:" Baxter replies. "The only blacks around were in an orphanage that was very large at one time, but the race riots of the sixties took care of that—a couple of white victories here and there."

Metzger does not question this logic, but continues:

"But you gradually got out into the streets of New York?"

"Yeah. The suburbs become boring. Especially to someone with an adventurous spirit. Someone not held back by the Christian lie."

What did he find in the city? Metzger wants to know.

"Gangs," says Baxter. "Your drug gangs, your race mixers, your white gangs who don't know that they're supremists [*sic*], but they are."

They discuss the Guardian Angels, who have interposed themselves between skinheads and antiracist protesters on occasions such as the gathering known as the Aryan Woodstock, which Metzger sponsored in Napa, California, in the spring of 1989, not long before this television session took place.

"Is it true the Angels don't encourage white boys and white girls to work together in a group?" Metzger asks.

"It seemed that way to me," Baxter agrees. "The white girls, they talk like Puerto Rican girls, they always have black boyfriends, it seemed like in a white couple the woman would receive so much guff from the black guys about how much of a racist she is not to let their black slime between her legs, and the white guy would just be too much of a wimp to do anything about it."

What about Italians, Metzger wonders. "Did you ever go around Little Italy?"

"Oh, Mott Street, sure," says Baxter. "The Italians are very racially motivated people."

"Racially motivated"—sometimes either just "racial" or "motivated"—is a phrase that recurs throughout the broadcast, once in relation to Baxter's suburb ("the town I come from is still pretty racially motivated"), once in relation to Howard Beach ("the white people in New York are pretty racially motivated if not totally insane") and once in relation to the Russians, thus:

Metzger: "We get a lot of mail from young people thinking the military is going to make a man of them, but when they find this tremendous leaning over for blacks most of them want to get out as soon as they get in. What kind of defense is this mongrelized army going to give us? I mean, if the Russians really did try to invade the US...."

Baxter: "If the Russians really did try to invade the US, I'd probably be fighting with them."

Metzger: "That just lost us the V.F.W. vote. But when you see a Russian submarine or ship coming in, they're almost all white. You might see a Mongol."

Baxter: "Or throw in an Armenian."

Metzger: "But you never see a nonwhite on a Russian sub."

Baxter: "Sure, he'd be bilged before the day was up. The Russians are pretty motivated people, from what I understand."

The conversation with Baxter identifies many of Metzger's immediate enemies and highlights some of his long-range themes—"skinheads who claim they're white power but yet they'll screw a beaner chick or a half-breed gook or some epitome like that"; the conservative whites in Napa County who "technically conspired with the Marxists and lesbians and homosexuals from San Francisco" to stop the Napa concert; "cops on the front lines that are the ones giving us the most trouble ... so aren't we really in a white civil war?"—but there are many others.

Notes and Questions

1. Is it possible to be proud of being a member of the white race, without risking lapsing into white supremacist ideas? What about being a black, Chicano, Asian, or Native American nationalist—does one face the same risk if one is "black and proud"?

2. What is wrong with being proud of your country? If America is (still) dominantly a white country, with white institutions and leadership, is pride in America a form of racial jingoism?

3. Germany has banned neo-Nazi groups. Should the U.S. do likewise?

4. Throughout history, the black community has received poor protection at the hands of the police—and a certain degree of outright harassment. Should African Americans, then, purchase and carry guns, as white militia have done? See Robert Cottrol & Raymond Diamond, *The Second Amendment: Toward an Afro–Americanist Reconsideration*, 80 Geo. L.J. 309 (1991).

In *The Racist Mind* (1995), professor Raphael S. Ezekiel describes his studies of and interviews with American neo-Nazis and Klansmen. After examining their literature, attending their meetings, and meeting their leaders and followers, he concluded that a feature of the belief system of such groups is essentialism, the idea that race singles out a single, identifying quality, and that the white version is superior to the others. He also found that most white Americans hold this belief to some extent. Supremacists see the world in terms of power and authority. Looking around them, they see that in our society white people hold most of the power and occupy the most authoritative jobs. They infer that this is because Whites are superior in nature and that this superiority grants them the right to rule others. Militant white racist movements count about 25,000 members; have 150,000 sympathizers who buy literature and attend meetings; and 450,000 who do not buy the literature but read it. He describes the militant movement as a "loose confederation of small groups" whose coordination "comes from the constant circuit riding of the leaders." The overarching idea is white specialness, and the special role of power in human relations.

MARK MUELLER

Hate Groups Spewing Venom on Net
Boston Herald, September 15, 1996.*

Once banished to society's fringes, race-baiting hate groups have found new life and a new link to mainstream culture through the Internet. From traditional agitators like the Ku Klux Klan to the more obscure but similarly racist Aryan Crusaders, hate groups are trolling for apostles with polished, splashy sites on the World Wide Web and flooding other areas of the Internet with propaganda dressed as fact. "The Internet is allowing hate groups who promote racism, anti-Semitism and overall bigotry the kind of forum they've never before enjoyed," said Sally Greenberg, civil rights counsel for the Anti–Defamation League. "They can literally reach millions of people, many of them young, in a way that's unprecedented."

The Los Angeles-based Simon Wiesenthal Center, a human rights organization that has been at the forefront of tracking Internet hate, said the number of racist sites on the World Wide Web has jumped from about 50 nine months ago to more than 200 today.

"For the first time, the extremists, the militias, the angry anarchists have the immediate capability to go mainstream," said Rabbi Abraham Cooper, an associate dean at the center. "They've embraced the technology, and they're out there growing in numbers and sophistication, developing a subculture that promotes hate and violence."

Encountering racist material on the Internet is no difficult matter. Punch in the words "Jewish" or "African-American" on one of the World Wide Web's search engines, for example, and of the hundreds or thousands of sites listed, dozens are hate-related. Some examples:

"Stormfront: the White Nationalist Resource Page," bills itself as "a resource for those courageous men and women fighting to preserve their White Western culture, ideals and freedom of speech and association—a forum for planning strategies and forming political and social groups to ensure victory."

The page provides skewed versions of history and links to other racist Web pages. The site's founder, Don Black, is a former leader of the Knights of the Ku Klux Klan, according to "The Web of Hate," an ADL report on Internet hate activities.

"W.A.R.," a self-described "White Racist Web Page," invites people to enter the "hate room," where racial epithets are freely used and where cartoons depict Jews as insects dying under a cloud of "Berg spray." Such talk is just as widespread among Internet newsgroups, where users leave messages for one another in forums devoted to "white power," "skinheads" and "revisionism." A frequent topic is the denial of the Holocaust. Most terrifying to groups like the Wiesenthal Center and the ADL is the potential for children to stumble across the unfiltered messages. * * *.

"The haters, the bigots are just looking for a few gullible young people to help them carry out their plans," Cooper said.

The Wiesenthal Center also mailed letters to 600 Internet providers, pressuring them to set guidelines for their clients like the decency standards newspapers use in accepting advertising.

The issue has become enough of a concern for the United Nations to address it. Cooper recently appeared before the U.N.'s Human Rights Commission, giving a three-hour presentation on Internet hate. Cooper said he presented the same information to President Clinton at a White House breakfast. But while the government has taken steps to curb pornography on the Internet, speech—even bigoted speech—is strictly protected by the Constitution and its stewards, the judiciary.

A broader concern than children's access, however, is the effect the Internet's hate offerings will have on race relations in America.

"It represents a form of electronic terrorism," the Rev. Charles Stith, president of the Organization for New Equality, said. "It helps create a climate of physical terrorism. Fanning the flames of ethnic and racial hatred is akin to hollering fire in a crowded theater."

RACIAL PARANOIA ON–LINE

Consider the following excerpts from various on-line newsgroups. Some parts of their messages are reasonable, or at least plausible (indeed, that is part of their appeal); others are not. At what point do you "jump ship"?

1. If you intend to live in N. America, you have no choice but to accept a society headed for racelessness. In several generations virtually

everyone will be of mixed race. Accept it, fighting against it will only lead to bad health for you.

I doubt a mulatto, Brazilian style, population will do well in the harsh North American climate (without welfare, which will end).

It is your subjective opinion that the Brazilian population mix is undesirable.

Well, it's suitable for the equator.

Your assertion that non-whites in general will not survive in a welfareless continent is questionable. Here are the ethnic groups by income:

Jews

Japanese

Chinese

Asian Indian

White

Hispanic

African–American

American Indian

Why do you equate income with the ability to live in a harsh climate? Just because a lot of Jewish and Asian parasites can manipulate the white race into providing them with dollars doesn't mean they could survive a Minnesota winter on their own. I'd just LOVE to see a bunch of Jew schister [sic] lawyers try it.

* * *

2. Now all you half ass skinheads throwing your business all over the internet get some act-right about yourselves!

I'm a u.s. skin from way back, when being a skin was living a clean, hard-working life and keeping the trash out of our neighborhoods. We might have had a little reputation for violence, we didn't have a whole lot of money, and we weren't the prettiest bunch of kids, either. We sure didn't know how to sit in front of a computer and argue with some Jewish intellectuals about race relations in our country. But we took a whole lot of pride in who we were and what we stood for. And even though we couldn't quote statistics or argue archeology, we just knew there was something special to having a solid white bloodline, and that's all that mattered.

* * *

3. H–K USP .40 CALIBER SEMI–AUTOMATIC

This baby ain't no World War I Colt .45. It's made by Heckler & Koch right now in the 90's, out of space-age plastic, steel, and other goodies. It's a whole new mindset—it's lighter, fires quicker, the trigger is smoother, and it packs one hell of a lot more stopping power, and benefits from 100 years of Aryan engineering thought. This unit really puts your Glocks and S & W's to shame on the gun range, just thru its operating feel. This thing becomes an extension of your own body. Expect to be set back roughly $600–$650 at most gun shops.

H–K really has thought out everything. Let's look at the safety. It's a unique lever over on the left side, EXACTLY NEXT TO YOUR RIGHT THUMB. Presuming you're shoulder holstered on the left, when that nigger marches into McDonald's spraying his AK–47, you reach into your coat with the right hand, pull outwards and extend into firing position. Simultaneously your thumb, which is immediately over the safety, throws down to release you for action. Now you pull the trigger again and again, spraying them nigger brains all over those golden arches. Total elapsed time can be 2–4 seconds.

How many bullets to drop that nigger? My personal USP .40 caliber was bought just before faggot Bill's great gun control law back around '94, so MY USP has 13 rounds in the clip plus 1 more in the chamber. I don't care how thick the bones are on that coon, this sweet little machine will put your monkey onto the floor tiles.

* * *

4. You're obviously an ugly, pissed off black bitch who's too ugly to get someone of your own kind to date you. I don't know where you get your figures from but my white women loves my white d___, and woudn't [sic] touch a "foreigner" for all the money in your crack infested neighborhoods! So I guess you've got nothing to worry about, huh.

Notes and Questions

1. Should hate messages on-line be banned? Screened out of university or other proprietary systems? See Chapter 10 for a discussion of hate speech and the First Amendment.

2. Some purveyors of on-line hate are down-and-out Whites working at dead-end, marginal jobs. Why do they displace resentment onto Blacks and other people of color, instead of joining with them in demanding concessions from the corporate elite that oppresses them both?

3. See Andrew MacDonald (William Pierce), Turner Diaries (National Vanguard, 2d ed. 1980), a futuristic novel set during a race war between Whites and Blacks:

> September 15, 1991. Today it finally began! After all these years of talking—and nothing but talking—we have finally taken our first action. We are at war with the System, and it is no longer a war of words....
>
> ... I'll never forget that terrible day: November 8, 1989. They knocked on my door at five in the morning. I was completely unsuspecting as I got up to see who it was.

I opened the door, and four Negroes came pushing into the apartment.... One was carrying a baseball bat, and two had long kitchen knives thrust into their belts. The one with the bat shoved me back into a corner and stood guard ... while the other three began ransacking my apartment. (*id*. at 1)

Chapters describe the bombing of an FBI building (*id*. at 32) employing homemade explosives, a flood of Mexican immigrants swarming across the border (*id*. at 33), the government's enactment of a law forbidding white resistance (*id*. at 1, 34), and roving gangs of Blacks who clash with Whites trying to protect civilization. The novel has become a mainstay of white supremacist groups.

4. For further readings on white supremacy, see David Chalmers, *Hooded Americanism: The History of the Ku Klux Klan* (1981); James Corcoran, *Bitter Harvest—Gordon Kahl and the Posse Comitatus* (1990); Wyn C. Wade, *The Fiery Cross: The Ku Klux Klan in America* (1987); James Ridgeway, *Blood in the Face: The Ku Klux Klan, Aryan Nations, Nazi Skinheads, and the Rise of a New White Culture* (2d ed. 1995); Michael Novick, *White Lies, White Power: The Fight Against White Supremacy and Reactionary Violence* (1995).

SECTION 6.   WHAT THEN SHALL WE DO? A ROLE FOR WHITES

TREASON TO WHITENESS IS LOYALTY TO HUMANITY

An interview with Noel Ignatiev of Race Traitor Magazine
The Blast! (June/July 1994).*

What is a race traitor anyway?

A traitor to the white race is someone who is nominally classified as white, but who defies the rules of whiteness so flagrantly as to jeopardize his or her ability to draw upon the privileges of the white skin.

As Theodore Allen points out * * *, the white race meant not only that no European–Americans were slaves, but also that all European Americans, even laborers, were by definition enforcers of slavery. In the Chesapeake Bay Colony (Virginia and Maryland), people from Africa and people from Europe worked together in the tobacco fields. They mated with each other, ran away and rebelled together, at first. At the end of the 1600s, people of African descent, even those who were free, lost certain rights they had had before and that even the poorest and most downtrodden person of European descent continued to enjoy. In return for these privileges, European Americans of all classes came to be part of the apparatus that maintained Afro Americans in chattel slavery (and themselves in unfreedom). That was the birth of "race," as we use the term. * * *

* Reprinted by permission of the author.

Can you provide an example of a people suddenly becoming "white"?

The Irish are as clear an example as any. In Ireland, under the Protestant Ascendancy, Catholic Irish were the victims of discrimination identical to what we in America call racial, and were even referred to as a "race." Karl Marx, writing from England, reported that the average English worker looked down on the Irish the way poor whites in the American South looked upon Afro Americans. Yet over here the Irish became "whites," by gaining the right to vote while free Negroes were losing it, by supporting the Democratic Party (the party of the slaveholders), and by preventing free Afro Americans from competing with them for jobs. The overcoming of anti-Irish prejudice meant that the Irish were admitted to the privileges of whiteness.

What do you mean by the "new abolitionism"?

We believe that so long as the white race exists, all movements against what is called "racism" will fail. Therefore, our aim is to abolish the white race.

How does your position on race and whiteness differ from the standard political stance of antiracism?

Racism is a pretty vague term. It has come to mean little more than a tendency to dislike people for the color of their skin. Most antiracists, even while they oppose discrimination, believe that racial status is fixed and eternal. We hold that without social distinctions, "race" is a fiction. The only race is the human race.

Even if a person declares him/herself a "race traitor" to the vast majority of people in this society, s/he is still white and therefore allowed all the privileges of the "white club." Is it possible to abolish the white race, ironically, only as white people?

The white race does not like to relinquish a single member, so that even those who step out of it in one situation find it virtually impossible not to rejoin it later, if only because of the assumptions of others— unless, like John Brown, they have the good fortune to be hanged before that happens. So-called whites have special responsibilities to abolition that only they can fulfill. Only they can dissolve the white race from within, by rejecting the poisoned bait of white-skin privileges. If that is what you mean by abolishing the white race "as whites," then we have no quarrel.

Is there such a thing as a "white culture"?

No. There is Italian culture, and Polish, Irish, Yiddish, German, and Appalachian culture: there is youth culture and drug culture and queer culture; but there is no "white" culture—unless you mean Wonder bread and television game shows. Whiteness is nothing but an expression of race privilege. It has been said that the typical "white" American male spends his childhood as an Indian, his adolescence as an Afro American, and only becomes white when he reaches the age of legal responsibility.

In an autobiographical essay, Joel Gilbert says that most of his whiteness has washed away and that he has "plenty of black inside." How is it possible for a white person to have "plenty of black" inside? How is it possible for whites to wash away their whiteness? Should a black person accept a white person's claim to have "a lot of black inside"?

Politically, whiteness is the willingness to seek a comfortable place within the system of race privilege. Blackness means total, implacable, and relentless opposition to that system. To the extent so-called whites oppose the race line, repudiate their own race privileges and jeopardize their own standing in the white race, they can be said to have washed away their whiteness and taken in some blackness. Probably a black person should not accept a white person's claim to have done that, but should watch how that person acts.

How does wanting to abolish racial classifications avoid doing away with cultural differences, which is what most liberal attempts to "confront racism" do?

For us, black and white are political categories, separate from, although not unrelated to, culture. One of the effects of white supremacy is that it represses the cultures of Afro Americans and other peoples of color. If that repression were removed, who knows how they would flourish. Moreover, American culture is, as Albert Murray has pointed out, incontestably mulatto. Without race prejudice, Americans might discover that culturally they are all Afro American, as well as Native American, and so forth.

In being a race traitor, to whom do you announce your treason—fellow so-called whites? Is it ever appropriate to tell a person of color that you have abandoned your whiteness?

I would never say that, although I might say I was working on it.

What kinds of relations with people of color are implied when one becomes a race traitor? How does a race traitor act politically with people of color?

Relations must be based on solidarity. People of color have a wealth of experience with white supremacy from which others can learn, but the fight against white supremacy is not something to engage in as a favor to anyone. All people who wish to be free have an equal stake—yes, an equal stake—in overturning the system of white supremacy. I'm reminded of the old IWW [Industrial Workers of the World, the "Wobblies"] slogan, "An injury to one is an injury to all." Decades of distortion have reduced the message of those words to the idea that you should oppose injustice against others today because if you don't it will come your way tomorrow. We believe in the original intent of the slogan. The Bible offers the same instruction: "Remember them that are in bonds as bound with them."

How do we, collectively, abolish the white race?

For the white race to be effective, it must be unanimous, or nearly so. The reason is that if the cops and the courts and so forth couldn't be sure that every person who looked white was loyal to the system, then what would be the point of extending race privileges to whites? And if they stopped extending race privileges, what would happen to the white race? Our strategy seeks to bring together a determined minority, willing to defy white rules so flagrantly they make it impossible to pretend that all those who look white are loyal to the system of racial oppression.

We wish we could cite more examples of collective resistance. The whites who joined the rebellions in Los Angeles and elsewhere were a good example. The Attica prison rebellion was another. The initiative by Love and Rage to launch a campaign culminating in a day of action against immigration controls and anti-immigrant violence was a good project, but unfortunately it never got off the ground. Collective struggle is crucial, but at some point every white person has to choose, like Huck Finn, between being white and striking out for freedom.

It seems from your journal and from thinking about your ideas that abolishing the white race would bring about widespread, radical changes in other aspects of social life. Is race treason necessarily revolutionary in that it threatens not only white supremacy but class rule as well?

It would be good if people could forget that they are white and pursue their interests as workers, or women, or whatever else moves them. The problem is that American society does not allow anyone to forget, but injects race into every political controversy. For those in power, the privileges granted whites are a small price to pay for the stability of an unjust social system. While not all forms of injustice can be collapsed into whiteness, undermining white race solidarity opens the door to fundamental social change in other areas. For so-called whites, treason to the white race is the most subversive act I can imagine.

For further discussion of the race traitor idea, see *Race Traitor* (Noel Ignatiev & John Garvey eds. 1996).

NOEL IGNATIEV

How To Be a Race Traitor*
Six ways to fight being white.

* Identify with the racially oppressed; violate the rules of whiteness in ways that can have a social impact.

* Answer an anti-black slur with, "Oh, you probably said that because you think I'm white. That's a mistake people often make because I look white." Reply "me, too" to charges that "people on welfare don't want to work, they just want to stay home and have babies."

* Oppose tracking in the schools, oppose all mechanisms that favor whites in the job market, and oppose the police and courts, which define black people as a criminal class.

* Do not merely oppose these things but seek to disrupt their normal functioning.

* The color line is not the work of the relatively small number of hard-core "racists"; target not them but the mainstream institutions that reproduce it.

* Finally, do not reject in advance any means of attaining the goal of abolishing the white race; indeed, the willingness to go beyond socially acceptable limits of protest is a dividing line between "good whites" and traitors to the white race.

Notes and Questions

1. What *is* the role for Whites in the struggle for equality? Is the race traitor tactic tenable? For large numbers of Whites?

2. Consider *Taxman v. Piscataway Township Board of Education*, 91 F.3d 1547 (3d Cir.1996), *cert. dismissed* 522 U.S. 1010 (1997), in which a school board was faced with having to cut one teacher. Two were supposedly equally qualified: one White, the other Black. To promote the goal of a diversified faculty, the board cut the White, who sued and won. Should she have stepped meekly aside? How would Ignatiev analyze this case? Note that the black teacher had an M.A. degree, which the white teacher lacked, yet the school board "equalized" their credentials. Does a black teacher have to be a superstar to get a job?

3. For further analysis of the race traitor idea, including how it might conceivably cause the system to trip on its own gears—and of a second role for white fellow travelers—see the selection from a recent "Rodrigo's Chronicle," by Richard Delgado in Chapter 14 *infra*.

FRANCES LEE ANSLEY

A Civil Rights Agenda for The Year 2000: Confessions of an Identity Politician
59 Tenn. L. Rev. 593, 600–09 (1992).*

I want to draw your attention to two problems with the way identity politics handles multiple categories. First, it tends to treat the different

---

* Used by permission of the author.   * Reprinted by permission of the author and Tennessee Law Review Association, Inc.

"identities" a person has as somehow separable from all their other possible identities and also from some generic humanness we all have in common. This is the kind of thinking that leads to questions like, "Which is more important to you, that you are black, or that you are a woman?" I sometimes think of this as my File Drawer Problem. I have one drawer in my filing cabinet labeled "WOMEN" and another labeled "RACE." This makes a certain amount of sense, but I run into all kinds of problems when I file things. Where should I put information relating to the problems of Latina women in South Texas, for instance? Should I create a Latina file for my WOMEN drawer or file the information in the Latino file in my RACE drawer? If I file it in the RACE drawer, am I not implicitly saying that the problems of Latinas at the border are best thought of as racial? Isn't that also inaccurate and misleading, because I know many of their problems are directly tied to their identity as women? If I put the information in the WOMEN drawer, am I not muting that incredibly important part of the problems of Chicana women that springs from their identity as brown people?

Furthermore, if, for example, I put the Latinas in my WOMEN drawer, that leaves me with a Latino file in the RACE drawer. What am I supposed to put there? If I put in it anything that relates to Latinos that is not explicitly related to women, am I not giving basic humanity to the men while reserving some special, different-from-plain-old-Latin status for women? * * *

Those of us trying to think about, reason about, and act on these matters of identity need to be aware of the distortions of categorization that may occur when we try to build a civil rights vision based on identity politics. We do violence to people's multipleness and complexity. We blind ourselves to cases that do not fit our categories and that are obscured when we look at a situation with only one lens. * * *

A second and related problem with categories of identity is the tendency for each category to carry within itself an unstated norm, and for that norm to reinforce and mirror some of the very inequities that the civil rights movement set out to overcome. For example, at one point in the development of the feminist movement, white feminists launched a campaign against rape. The idea was to tell the story of sexual violence from a woman's point of view, to redefine the law of rape in a way that was mindful of women's welfare. However, we white feminists left three things out of our early accounts of rape:

— We did little investigation, and spoke very little, of the long and special history of sexual abuse of black women at the hands of white men. This is an important part of the history and dynamics of rape, and the early white feminist account was impoverished by its relative absence.

— Neither did we explore the racist use of the rape charge against black men as an instrument of racist terror during long stretches of our national history: a practice in which white women were often complicit, and a setting in which those women could hardly be described as the victims of a prosecutorial process biased against conviction.

— We also ignored the sexual abuse of black women at the hands of black men, therefore missing entirely an additional burden and constraint often borne by black rape victims seeking security and redress. These victims often experience deep ambivalence about invoking law enforcement authority against a black man because of what they know about racial politics and about the police.

In other words, white women confidently spoke of "We women." Upon closer examination, however, the "we" of those initial analyses was not really "we women," it was "we white women." The unstated norm hidden in the term "woman" was in that case "white." Black women's experiences were left out of this account, and the resulting parochialism weakened it for everyone. Fortunately, black feminists have provoked an extremely productive reassessment of this issue, at least in many quarters of the women's movement. * * *

In addition to the problem with boundaries, and in addition to the difficulty in accounting for the multiple identities which people actually do have, the turn to identity politics as a solution to the civil rights crisis can set different groups against each other—groups who ought to be making common cause. It can divide the large group of people whose interests lie in serious change into warring factions resentful and distrustful of each other, worried that any attempt to empathize with the situation of another may threaten the sense of their own identity they have worked so hard to build. * * *

The structure of civil rights law has promoted identity politics in ways that sometimes have been very positive, but at other times [not]. Our civil rights law is centrally built around the notion of membership in a victim group—what we call a "protected group" in Title VII doctrine and a "suspect class" in Fourteenth Amendment lingo. To have a cause of action under much of our civil rights law, one must assert a cognizable "identity," and beyond these special categories of recognized victimhood, one has no grievance.

I first began to appreciate this situation as a limit and a contradiction in the area of employment law. When I had just begun to work for legal services years ago, a worker came in for an interview one day. This worker was convinced by her own astute reading of the signs that she was about to be fired. Her supervisor (a female) had begun criticizing her publicly in ways that seemed both unwarranted and calculated to make her lose her temper. I felt she was right to be concerned about losing her job. * * *

The trouble was that the experiences of this black woman didn't really fit a race discrimination or sex discrimination mold. We could have perhaps made out a case, but she didn't believe her experiences resulted from race or gender animus. She felt they were individually and personally motivated, arbitrary, and unfair. She felt she should have some recourse and basic job security, and she could not fathom why the law would protect her from one type of arbitrary treatment and not from the others. * * *

Many arbitrary irrational classifications based on race and sex still remain. Even if those were eradicated, plenty of arbitrariness would be left. How do we explain who gets born to a college professor, and who to a coal miner? Who is born to a family lucky enough to have a miner at work and who to a single mother struggling to stretch a welfare check? Who is born to a Charleston chemical company executive and who to someone in McDowell County hoping for a job in one of Appalachia's new industries: perhaps burying garbage shipped in from New Jersey or guarding prisoners shipped in from Washington, D.C.? These inequities remain untouched by American anti-discrimination law.

I am not blaming the persistence of these non-racial, non-sexual inequities on the selfishness of identity politicians, although those who complain that race and gender issues are the provenance of "special interest groups," or those who oppose affirmative action sometimes seem to suggest as much. Quite the contrary. For example, people of color frequently have litigated to expand the law beyond the suspect-classification, identity-politics branch of equal protection and to strengthen the other, "non-identity" branch of Fourteenth Amendment equality, which is rooted in fundamental rights. Likewise they have lobbied repeatedly for legislation that would benefit more whites than blacks, such as increases in AFDC benefits, food stamps, and the like. Far too often they have enjoyed far too few allies in these endeavors.

If we are searching for causes of "non-racial" problems that beset disadvantaged groups in America, we might ironically conclude that the stubborn racism of large segments of the white electorate has been the most crucial one, a racism that has prevented those segments from making common cause with people of color. This deep racial divide has been a major reason why the United States lags astoundingly behind other industrialized countries in basic indices of human welfare, such as infant mortality, universal availability of health care, employment security, and adequate education. So I do not blame us identity politicians for these other kinds of inequities. But I do want to exhort us to action. Identity politicians, and I include myself in that category, must see beyond the lens of their own group identification. * * *

One approach would not require the discarding or transcending of one's own identity, but rather the deepening of it. Here is my proposal: all ... should consciously consider the political needs of those members of our group who are least privileged. We should conceive of our problems and design our reform strategies with their needs and perspectives firmly in mind. In other words, a woman like me (a self-identified feminist, white, employed, presently-abled, American, heterosexual, and in a two-parent, two-wage-earner family) needs to investigate the points of view of women who are, for instance, black, brown, poor, alien, ill, single, lesbian, third-world, battered, unemployed, or all of the above. Viewing women's problems from those perspectives, I believe, will complicate matters but it will often suggest fruitful answers to strategic questions. Seen from this vantage point, for instance, the goal of helping my sister attorneys crash the glass ceilings at their law firms seems less compelling than universal health insurance, free day care centers, battered women's shelters, and family leave, not to mention development of a responsible industrial policy that aims at sustainable growth both in the United States and for our neighbors in the South.

Certain groups of women have less access to resources, fewer ways to make themselves heard or felt by others, more chances of being marginalized as deviant from a presumed norm, and more likelihood of suffering material deprivations. It is these women I am suggesting we feminists should place at the center in our visions and strategies. This suggestion that identity politicians should privilege the least privileged among them also suggests coalitions beyond the original identity circle and therefore an expansion beyond the particular identity group in which the project began and in which it remains rooted.

I invite you to think about your own identity and about the categories of belonging and exclusion that have helped to define you. Think about those who share some aspects of your identity but not others, and think especially about those "at the bottom" of whatever category you have chosen for your focus or whatever efforts and institutions in which you find yourself. How might the world look from their perspective?

BARBARA J. FLAGG

"Was Blind, But Now I See": White Race Consciousness
and the Requirement of Discriminatory Intent
91 Mich. L. Rev. 953, 957–59, 968–69 (1993).*

Reconceptualizing white race consciousness means doing the hard work of developing a positive white racial identity, one neither founded on the implicit acceptance of white racial domination nor productive of distributive effects that systematically advantage whites. This work can be highly beneficial. According to psychologist Janet Helms, a leading author on racial identity theory, the development of a healthy white racial identity requires the individual to overcome those aspects of racism—whether individual, institutional, or cultural—that have become a part of that person's identity, and in addition to "accept his or her own whiteness, the cultural implications of being white, and define a view of Self as a racial being that does not depend on the perceived superiority of one racial group over another."[20] One step in that process is the deconstruction of transparency in white decisionmaking. [Eds. See also *supra* § 3, this chapter.] We can work to make explicit the unacknowledged whiteness of facially neutral criteria of decision, adopting strategies that counteract the influence of unrecognized white norms. These approaches permit white decisionmakers to incorporate pluralist means of achieving our aims, and thus to contribute to the dismantling of white supremacy. Making nonobvious white norms explicit, and thus exposing their contingency, can begin to define for white people a coequal role in a racially diverse society. * * *

The imposition of transparently white norms is a unique form of unconscious discrimination, one that cannot be assimilated to the notion of irrationalism that is central to the liberal ideology of racism. While

* Originally published in the Michigan Law Review. Used by permission.

20. Janet E. Helms, *Toward a Model of White Racial Identity Development,* in *Black and White Racial Identity* 49 (Janet E. Helms ed. 1990).

racial stereotyping can be condemned as the failure accurately to perceive the individual for who he really is, and bias as the inability to exclude subjective misconceptions or hostilities, or both, from one's decisionmaking processes, transparency exemplifies the structural aspect of white supremacy. Beyond the individual forms of racism that stereotyping, bias, and hostility represent lie the vast terrains of institutional racism—the maintenance of institutions that systematically advantage whites—and cultural racism—the usually unstated assumption that white culture is superior to all others. Because the liberal gravitates toward abstract individualism and its predicates, she generally fails to recognize or to address the more pervasive harms that institutional and cultural white supremacy inflict. The exercise of focusing exclusively on the transparency phenomenon as an example of structural racism, then, has transformative potential for the white liberal, both on the personal level and as a springboard for reflection on what it means for government genuinely to provide the equal protection of the laws.   * * *

White people tend to view intent as an essential element of racial harm; nonwhites do not. The white perspective can be, and frequently is, expressed succinctly and without any apparent perceived need for justification: "[W]ithout concern about past and present intent, racially discriminatory effects of legislation would be quite innocent."[70] For black people, however, the fact of racial oppression exists largely independent of the motives or intentions of its perpetrators. Whites' level of confidence in race neutrality is much greater than nonwhites'; a skeptic (nonwhite, more likely than not) would not adopt a rule that presumes the neutrality of criteria of decision absent the specific intent to do racial harm. Finally, retaining the intent requirement in the face of its demonstrated failure to effectuate substantive racial justice reveals a complacency concerning, or even a commitment to, the racial status quo that can only be enjoyed by those who are its beneficiaries—by white people.

A raised white consciousness of race would produce a very different rule in disparate impact cases. In particular, white people who take seriously the transparency phenomenon, and who want to foster racial justice, will look for ways to diffuse transparency's effects and to relativize previously unrecognized white norms. Existing doctrinal tools are adequate, in large measure, to accomplish these goals, if they are tailored to correct the evil of transparency.

Notes and Questions

1. Does identity politics obscure the role of class? Vice versa?

2. If whiteness is transparent, what happens when Whites are beleaguered, or in a minority, as they might be in certain social settings, or in sports?

3. In a landmark article, *Obscuring the Importance of Race: The Implications of Making Comparisons Between Racism and Sexism (or Other–isms)*, 1991 Duke L.J. 397, Trina Grillo and Stephanie M. Wildman point out that Whites who struggle to understand racism may end up making matters

---

70. Robert W. Bennett, *"Mere" Rationality In Constitutional Law: Judicial Re-* view and Democratic Theory, 67 Cal. L. Rev. 1049, 1076 (1979).

worse. Often the speaker, trying to understand "what it's like to be black (brown, etc.)," fastens upon an analogy or comparison to something within his or her experience.

> When a speaker compared sexism and racism, the significance of race was marginalized and obscured, and the different role that race plays in the lives of people of color and of whites was overlooked. The concerns of whites became the focus of discussion, even when the conversation supposedly had been centered on race discrimination.

The discussion, in short, ended up being about Whites; the nonwhites in the audience fell silent and had to endure a discussion of how the speaker felt over being too short for her age, having straight, lank hair, an adolescent eating disorder, or parents who didn't understand her.

4.   But do not metaphors and analogies constitute inevitable—sometimes the only—bridges to understanding, by which one person can come to understand what it is like to be another?

5.   Suggested readings about whiteness include: bell hooks, *Overcoming White Supremacy*, in *Talking Back: Thinking Feminist, Thinking Black* (1989); Derrick Bell, *White Superiority in America: Its Legacy, Its Economic Costs*, 33 Vill. L. Rev. 767 (1988); Judy Scales-Trent, *Commonalities: On Being Black and White, Different and the Same*, 2 Yale J.L. & Feminism 305 (1990).

Chapter 7

RACE AND DEVELOPING NOTIONS OF EQUALITY

WHAT IS EQUALITY?

"Equal Justice Under Law" is so important a promise of our legal order that these words are sculpted above the entrance to the U.S. Supreme Court building. But equality is a relatively recent constitutional value. The message of equality was incorporated into the U.S. Constitution in 1868 by the passage of the Fourteenth Amendment, which provides in relevant part: "No State shall ... deny to any person within its jurisdiction the equal protection of the laws." The Due Process Clause of the Fifth Amendment extends the protection of the Fourteenth Amendment to equal protection claims against the federal government. *Bolling v. Sharpe*, 347 U.S. 497, 500 (1954). Thus the concept of equality, embodied in the Fourteenth Amendment, applies to both the state and federal governments. Federal and state antidiscrimination laws also promise equal opportunity. But what does this concept of equality mean?

The prevalent notion of equality requires comparing individuals, ensuring that likes are treated alike. Each person is considered an atomistic individual, viewed absent any relation to others. Under this view of equality, the harm of racism occurs to disparate individuals, who are unconnected by race or by the other categories that identify and connect people. Yet the harm of racism encompasses all of the group. When Vincent Chin was murdered by out-of-work auto workers in Detroit, who screamed anti-Japanese epithets as they assaulted him, he was not being treated as the individual Chinese American he was, but as a member of the group of Asian Americans targeted as victims. See Robert S. Chang & Keith Aoki, *Centering the Immigrant in the Inter/National Imagination*, 85 Calif. L. Rev. 1395, 1415 (1997) (describing the murder of Vincent Chin as an example of nativistic racism expressing itself through violent attack). When hundreds of sports fans in Atlanta perform the tomahawk chop to cheer the Atlanta Braves, they are not treating Native Americans as individuals with dignity, but subjecting many people to a stereotype. See Daniel J. Trainor, Note: *Native American Mascots, Schools, and the Title VI Hostile Environment Analysis*, 1995 U. Ill. L. Rev. 971, 974 (describing Native–American mascots as portraying a monolithic group, ignoring cultural diversity). Do these examples of racism's failure to discern individuals lend support for or cast doubt on the emphasis upon the individual in evolving a notion of equality?

The post-modern vision of the person recognizes that individuals are more complex than an identifying trait. Individuals exist as part of larger groups—races, families, genders, sexual orientations, and many other vectors that comprise identity. Declining to see both the individual and the connections results in unfair treatment, a failure of equality.

Whether equality doctrine applies to individuals or groups remains contested. This struggle over the meaning of equality is taking place in constitutional doctrine as well as in statutory law governing equality in the workplace. This struggle is also visible in the debate about affirmative action in the workplace and in educational institutions. Consider the different uses of the words "equal" or "equality" as you read the materials in this chapter.

SECTION 1. EVOLVING NOTIONS OF EQUALITY UNDER THE FOURTEENTH AMENDMENT EQUAL PROTECTION CLAUSE

The reach of the Equal Protection Clause was debated soon after its passage and was contested in a series of early decisions. Even as the protection of the Clause was broadened beyond African Americans, the question of group, as opposed to individual, protection remained. See Owen Fiss, *Groups and the Equal Protection Clause*, 5 Phil. & Pub. Aff. 107 (1976). See also Aviam Soifer, *Law and the Company We Keep* (1995) (urging recognition of the crucial role of identity groups within the larger national community).

Native Americans are remarkably absent from the case law canon that marks the development of equal protection doctrine. See Chapter 3, *supra*, reciting that history. What can constitutional equality mean when it ignores many nations of indigenous peoples? Does this absence of Native Americans from equality doctrine suggest that the doctrine is flawed? Does it indicate that Native Americans are not interested in equality, but rather in sovereignty and self-determination?

JUAN F. PEREA

Ethnicity and the Constitution: Beyond the Black and White Binary Constitution
36 Wm. & Mary L. Rev. 571, 579–81 (1995).*

In *The Slaughter–House Cases*, 83 U.S. (16 Wall.) 36 (1873), the Supreme Court interpreted the Reconstruction Amendments for the first time. The Court stated that the primary purpose underlying the Thirteenth, Fourteenth and Fifteenth Amendments was to secure the freedoms of newly freed African–American citizens. Construing the Equal

Protection Clause, the Court "doubt[ed] very much whether any action of a State not directed by way of discrimination against the negroes as a class, or on account of their race, will ever be held to come within the purview of this provision." The Court also suggested, however, a broader reach for these amendments:

> We do not say that no one else but the negro can share in this protection.... Undoubtedly while negro slavery alone was in the mind of the Congress which proposed the thirteenth article, it forbids any other kind of slavery, now or hereafter. If Mexican peonage or the Chinese coolie labor system shall develop slavery of the Mexican or Chinese race within our territory, this amendment may safely be trusted to make it void. And so if other rights are assailed by the States which properly and necessarily fall within the protection of these articles, that protection will apply, though the party interested may not be of African descent.

The Court acknowledged, therefore, that the amendments could apply to classifications based on ancestry or national origin.

In *Strauder v. West Virginia*, 100 U.S. 303 (1879), the Court again stated that the purpose of the Fourteenth Amendment was to prohibit "discrimination because of race or color" against the African–American citizens of the nation. The Court concluded that the West Virginia law at issue, which limited eligibility for jury service to "white male persons," was just such a prohibited discrimination. Having found that the primary purpose underlying the Fourteenth Amendment was to protect blacks, the Court, in dicta, somewhat contradictorily stated that the Equal Protection Clause would be violated equally by a law excluding white men from jury service—an extremely unlikely hypothetical.

In *Strauder*, the Court suggested a broader reach for the Equal Protection Clause than its statement from *The Slaughter–House Cases* quoted above. In dicta, the Court wrote: "Nor if a law should be passed excluding all naturalized Celtic Irishmen, would there be any doubt of its inconsistency with the spirit of the amendment." In the Court's view, a classification based on ethnicity and national origin excluding naturalized Celtic Irishmen would also violate the Equal Protection Clause. Perhaps acknowledging some departure from the primary purpose of the amendment, the Court characterized such a classification as inconsistent with the spirit of the amendment, not the amendment itself. The Court thus recognized early that the Equal Protection Clause prohibited discrimination based on national origin, but the prohibition was based only on some unstated analogy between race and national origin.

Notes and Questions

1. Is the Court decision in *Strauder* clear about whether the individual or the group is the focus of constitutional protection under the Equal Protection Clause?

2. The notion that "all persons, whether colored or white, shall stand equal before the laws of the states" was unthinkable to the Court just thirty years earlier when Justice Taney wrote that, at the time of the founding of the Republic, the "negro African race" had been "regarded as beings ... so

far inferior, that they had no rights which the white man was bound to respect." Justice Taney explained:

> [T]he legislation and histories of the [late eighteenth century], and the language used in the Declaration of Independence, show, that neither the class of persons who had been imported as slaves, nor their descendants, whether they had become free or not, were then acknowledged as a part of the people, nor intended to be included in the general words used in that memorable instrument. * * *

> [African Americans] had for more than a century before been regarded as beings of an inferior order, and altogether unfit to associate with the white race, either in social or political relations; and so far inferior, that they had no rights which the white man was bound to respect; and that the negro might justly and lawfully be reduced to slavery for his benefit. He was bought and sold, and treated as an ordinary article of merchandise and traffic, whenever a profit could be made by it. This opinion was at that time fixed and universal in the civilized portion of the white race. It was regarded as an axiom in morals as well as in politics, which no one thought of disputing, or supposed to be open to dispute; and men in every grade and position in society daily and habitually acted upon it in their private pursuits, as well as in matters of public concern, without doubting for a moment the correctness of this opinion.

Dred Scott v. Sandford, 60 U.S. (19 How.) 393, 407 (1857). See discussion of *Dred Scott*, Chapter 2 § 3 *supra*.

3.   The *Strauder* court asks: "[H]ow can it be maintained that compelling a colored man to submit to a trial for his life by a jury drawn from a panel from which the State has expressly excluded every man of his race, because of color alone, however well qualified in other respects, is not a denial to him of equal legal protection?" Substitute "woman of color" for "colored man" in this sentence and change the pronouns. For women of color the gendering of the question as female means it is not race alone that is causing their exclusion from juries, it is race and gender. Yet evidently the exclusion from jury service based on gender remained no affront to equality. As recently as 1961 the Court upheld a Florida statute that kept women from jury service unless they registered with the court clerk. The Court observed that "woman is still the center of home and family life," concluding that the treatment of women did not violate the constitution. *Hoyt v. Florida*, 368 U.S. 57, 62 (1961). *Hoyt* was overruled in *Taylor v. Louisiana*, 419 U.S. 522 (1975).

This example illustrates that the comparison mode of analysis, prevalent in equality analysis, does not work for women of color. See *Rogers v. American Airlines* (Chapter 7 § 2). Does this failure of the comparison mode suggest it may be inadequate for other identity categories as well?

4.   In *Strauder*, the Court noted the plaintiff's race. The opinion begins "The plaintiff in error, a colored man, was indicted for murder." Do the cases of the same era notice the race of white litigants? Would an approach of *not noticing* race be preferable? Does an approach of *not noticing* race promote equality?

5.   Review *Plessy v. Ferguson* (Chapter 2, § 5) holding that the doctrine of "separate but equal" treatment in public accommodations does not violate

the constitutional command of equal protection. *Plessy* is widely cited for the proposition, urged by Justice Harlan in his dissent, that "the Constitution is color-blind." Yet reading Harlan's language makes clear that he is not color-blind, but rather adheres to the prevalent view of white racial superiority. Reconsider Neil Gotanda's thesis that the use of this metaphor maintains white advantage:

> [T]he metaphor "Our Constitution is color-blind," * * * fosters white racial domination. * * * A color-blind interpretation of the Constitution legitimates, and thereby maintains, the social, economic, and political advantages that whites hold over other Americans. * * *

> The Supreme Court's color-blind constitutionalism uses race to cover four distinct ideas: status-race, formal-race, historical-race, and culture-race. Status-race is the traditional notion of race as an indicator of social status. While traditional status-race is now largely discredited, it remains important as the racial model for efforts aimed at eradicating intentional forms of racial subordination with their implication of racial inferiority.

> The second use of race, formal-race, refers to socially constructed formal categories. Black and white are seen as neutral, apolitical descriptions, reflecting merely "skin color" or country of ancestral origin. Formal-race is unrelated to ability, disadvantage, or moral culpability. Moreover, formal-race categories are unconnected to social attributes such as culture, education, wealth, or language. This "unconnectedness" is the defining characteristic of formal-race, and no other usage of "race" incorporates the concept.

> Historical-race does assign substance to racial categories. Historical-race embodies past and continuing racial subordination, and is the meaning of race that the Court contemplates when it applies "strict scrutiny" to racially disadvantaging government conduct. The state's use of racial categories is regarded as so closely linked to illegitimate racial subordination that it is automatically judicially suspect.

> Finally, culture-race uses "Black" to refer to African–American culture, community, and consciousness. Culture refers to broadly shared beliefs and social practices; community refers to both the physical and spiritual senses of the term; and African–American consciousness refers to Black Nationalist and other traditions of self-awareness and to action based on that self-awareness. Culture-race is the basis for the developing concept of cultural diversity. * * *

> The Court has used words such as "race," "Black," and "white" without explanation or qualification. In doing so, they have disguised their own role in perpetuating racial subordination. The modern Court has moved away from the two notions of race that recognize the diverging historical experiences of Black and white Americans: status-race and historical-race. In place of these concepts, the Court relies increasingly on the formal-race concept of race, a vision of race as unconnected to the historical reality of Black oppression.

Neil Gotanda, *A Critique of "Our Constitution Is Color-blind,"* 44 Stan. L. Rev. 1, 2–5, 36–37 (1991).* For further discussion of this excerpt, see Chapter 1 § 2 *supra*.

6. Gotanda points out that the formal-race, color-blind approach embodied by *Plessy* "assumes 'equal protection of the law' based on common 'citizenship.'" Thus, "racial segregation is simply a legislative differentiation which must be considered to have no inherent social meaning." *Id.* at 38.

7. Gotanda comments that Justice Harlan's dissent in *Plessy* utilized historical-race:

> Justice Harlan recognized that segregation based on race is inherently subordinating. By rejecting the majority's view that racial segregation is unconnected to oppression and by refusing to adopt the rigid legalism of formal-race Justice Harlan anticipated by a half-century the spirit of *Brown v. Board of Education.*

Justice Harlan was advocating a peculiar mix of historical-race and formal-race. Government acts were required to be genuinely neutral; therefore judicial review of race-based legislation should recognize the historical content of race. *Id.* at 39.

Gotanda continues:

> The assimilationist color-blind society ignores, and thereby devalues, culture-race. Culture-race includes all aspects of culture, community, and consciousness. The term includes, for example, the customs, beliefs, and intellectual and artistic traditions of Black America, and institutions such as Black churches and colleges. [For the most part] * * * the Court has devalued or ignored Black culture, community, and consciousness. Its opinions use the same categorical name—Black—to designate reified systemic subordination (what I have termed historical-race) as well as the cultural richness that defines culture-race. Only by treating culture-race as analytically distinct from other usages of race can one begin to address the link between the cultural practices of Blacks and the subordination of Blacks, elements that are, in fact, inseparable in the lived experience of race.

Id. at 56. Are Gotanda's categories useful as a description of the different uses of race? How might *Plessy* be decided under a culture-race analysis?

8. The Court's conflation of different meanings of race created difficulty in clarifying the evolving notion of equality. Legal commentators attempted to articulate the tests used by the Court when equal protection of the laws was at issue.

Justice Holmes described the Equal Protection Clause as the "last resort" of constitutional argument. *Buck v. Bell*, 274 U.S. 200, 208 (1927). See Richard Delgado & Jean Stefancic, *Norms and Narratives: Can Judges Avoid Serious Moral Error?*, 69 Tex. L. Rev. 1929, 1949 (1991) (commenting that Holmes treated Ms. Buck's "equal protection argument like an unreasonable citizen's demand that the state justify its practice of fixing potholes on the west side of town first, those on the east side later."). Yet interpretation of the Fourteenth Amendment Equal Protection Clause has significantly influenced notions of equality. John Hart Ely described the ambiguous wording of the clause, referring to the language "the equal protection of the laws" as "delphic." John Hart Ely, *Standing to Challenge Pro–Minority Gerrymanders*, 111 Harv. L. Rev. 576, 578, n.8 (1997). The language of the Clause created an interpretive dilemma, explained by Professors Joseph Tussman and Jacobus tenBroek as follows:

The equal protection of the laws is a "pledge of the protection of equal laws." But laws may classify. And "the very idea of classification is that of inequality." In tackling this paradox the Court has neither abandoned the demand for equality nor denied the legislative right to classify. It has taken a middle course. It has resolved the contradictory demands of legislative specialization and constitutional generality by a doctrine of reasonable classification.

The essence of that doctrine can be stated with deceptive simplicity. The Constitution does not require that things different in fact be treated in law as though they were the same. But it does require, in its concern for equality, that those who are similarly situated be similarly treated. The measure of the reasonableness of a classification is the degree of its success in treating similarly those similarly situated. * * *

[W]here are we to look for the test of similarity of situation which determines the reasonableness of a classification? The inescapable answer is that we must look beyond the classification to the purpose of the law. A reasonable classification is one which includes all persons who are similarly situated with respect to the purpose of the law.

The purpose of a law may be either the elimination of a public "mischief" or the achievement of some positive public good.

Joseph Tussman & Jacobus tenBroek, *The Equal Protection of the Laws*, 37 Cal. L. Rev. 341, 344, 346 (1949).*

The use of this reasonableness or rational basis test in the modern era is illustrated by the following case.

KOTCH v. BOARD OF RIVER PORT PILOT COMMISSIONERS

330 U.S. 552 (1947).

JUSTICE BLACK delivered the opinion of the Court.

Louisiana statutes provide in general that all seagoing vessels moving between New Orleans and foreign ports must be navigated through the Mississippi River approaches to the port of New Orleans and within it, exclusively by pilots who are State Officers. New State pilots are appointed by the governor only upon certification of a State Board of River Pilot Commissioners, themselves pilots. Only those who have served a six month apprenticeship under incumbent pilots and who possess other specific qualifications may be certified to the governor by the board. Appellants here have had at least fifteen years experience in the river, the port, and elsewhere, as pilots of vessels whose pilotage was not governed by the State law in question. Although they possess all the statutory qualifications except that they have not served the requisite six months apprenticeship under Louisiana officer pilots, they have been denied appointment as State pilots. Seeking relief in a Louisiana state court, they alleged that the incumbent pilots, having unfettered discretion under the law in the selection of apprentices, had selected with occasional exception, only the relatives and friends of incumbents; * * * that since "membership * * * is closed to all except those having the favor of the pilots" the result is that only their relatives and friends have and can become State pilots. * * *

The constitutional command for a state to afford "equal protection of the laws" sets a goal not attainable by the invention and application of a precise formula. This Court has never attempted that impossible task. A law which affects the activities of some groups differently from the way in which it affects the activities of other groups is not necessarily banned by the Fourteenth Amendment. Otherwise, effective regulation in the public interest could not be provided, however essential that regulation might be. For it is axiomatic that the consequence of regulating by setting apart a classified group is that those in it will be subject to some restrictions or receive certain advantages that do not apply to other groups or to all the public. This selective application of a regulation is discrimination in the broad sense, but it may or may not deny equal protection of the laws. Clearly, it might offend that constitutional safeguard if it rested on grounds wholly irrelevant to achievement of the regulation's objectives. An example would be a law applied to deny a person a right to earn a living or hold any job because of hostility to his particular race, religion, beliefs, or because of any other reason having no rational relation to the regulated activities.

The case of *Yick Wo v. Hopkins*, relied on by appellants, is an illustration of a type of discrimination which is incompatible with any fair conception of equal protection of the laws. Yick Wo was denied the right to engage in an occupation supposedly open to all who could conduct their business in accordance with the law's requirements. He could meet these requirements, but was denied the right to do so solely because he was Chinese. And it made no difference that under the law as written Yick Wo would have enjoyed the same protection as all others. Its unequal application to Yick Wo was enough to condemn it. * * * So here, we must consider the relationship of the method of appointing pilots to the broad objectives of the entire Louisiana pilotage law. In so doing we must view the appointment system in the context of the historical evolution of the laws and institution of pilotage in Louisiana and elsewhere. And an important factor in our consideration is that this case tests the right and power of a state to select its own agents and officers.

Studies of the long history of pilotage reveal that it is a unique institution and must be judged as such. In order to avoid invisible hazards, vessels approaching and leaving ports must be conducted from and to open waters by persons intimately familiar with the local waters. The pilot's job generally requires that he go outside the harbor's entrance in a small boat to meet incoming ships, board them and direct their course from open waters to the port. The same service is performed for vessels leaving the port. Pilots are thus indispensable cogs in the transportation system of every maritime economy. Their work prevents traffic congestion and accidents which would impair navigation in and to the ports. It affects the safety of lives and cargo, the cost and time expended in port calls, and in some measure, the competitive attractiveness of particular ports. Thus, for the same reasons that governments of most maritime communities have subsidized, regulated, or have themselves operated docks and other harbor facilities and sought to improve the approaches to their ports, they have closely regulated and often operated their ports' pilotage system.

The history and practice of pilotage demonstrate that, although inextricably geared to a complex commercial economy, it is also a highly personalized calling. A pilot does not require a formalized technical education so much as a detailed and extremely intimate, almost intuitive, knowledge of the weather, waterways and conformation of the harbor or river which he serves. This seems to be particularly true of the approaches to New Orleans through the treacherous and shifting channel of the Mississippi River. Moreover, harbor entrances where pilots can most conveniently make their homes and still be close to places where they board incoming and leave outgoing ships are usually some distance from the port cities they serve. These "pilot towns" have begun, and generally exist today, as small communities of pilots perhaps near, but usually distinct from the port cities. In these communities young men have an opportunity to acquire special knowledge of the weather and water hazards of the locality and seem to grow up with ambitions to become pilots in the traditions of their fathers, relatives, and neighbors. We are asked, in effect, to say that Louisiana is without constitutional authority to conclude that apprenticeship under persons specially interested in a pilot's future is the best way to fit him for duty as a pilot officer in the service of the State. * * *

The practice of nepotism in appointing public servants has been a subject of controversy in this country throughout our history. Some states have adopted constitutional amendments or statutes, to prohibit it. These have reflected state policies to wipe out the practice. But Louisiana and most other states have adopted no such general policy. We can only assume that the Louisiana legislature weighed the obvious possibility of evil against whatever useful function a closely knit pilotage system may serve. Thus the advantages of early experience under friendly supervision in the locality of the pilot's training, the benefits to morale and esprit de corps which family and neighborly tradition might contribute, the close association in which pilots must work and live in their pilot communities and on the water, and the discipline and regulation which is imposed to assure the State competent pilot service after appointment, might have prompted the legislature to permit Louisiana pilot officers to select those which whom they would serve.

The number of people, as a practical matter, who can be pilots is very limited. No matter what system of selection is adopted, all but the few occasionally selected must of necessity be excluded. We are aware of no decision of this Court holding that the Constitution requires a state governor * * * to select state public servants by competitive tests or by any other particular method of selection. The object of the entire pilotage law, as we have pointed out, is to secure for the State and others interested the safest and most efficiently operated pilotage system practicable. We cannot say that the method adopted in Louisiana for the selection of pilots is unrelated to this objective * * *[or] the practice appellants attack is the kind of discrimination which violates the equal protection clause of the Fourteenth Amendment.

Affirmed.

Justice Rutledge, dissenting.

* * * Blood is, in effect, made the crux of selection. That, in my opinion, is forbidden by the Fourteenth Amendment's guaranty against denial of the equal protection of the laws. The door is thereby closed to all not having blood relationship to presently licensed pilots. Whether the occupation is considered as having the status of "public officer" or of highly regulated private employment, it is beyond legislative power to make entrance to it turn upon such a criterion. * * *

It is not enough to avoid the Amendment's force that a familial system may have a tendency or, as the Court puts it, a direct relationship to the end of securing an efficient pilotage system. Classification based on the purpose to be accomplished may be said abstractly to be sound. But when the test adopted and applied in fact is race or consanguinity, it cannot be used constitutionally to bar all except a group chosen by such a relationship from public employment. That is not a test; it is a wholly arbitrary exercise of power.

Conceivably the familial system would be the most effective possible scheme for training many kinds of artisans or public servants, sheerly from the viewpoint of securing the highest degree of skill and competence. Indeed, something very worth while largely disappeared from our national life when the once prevalent familial system of conducting manufacturing and mercantile enterprises went out and was replaced by the highly impersonal corporate system for doing business.

But that loss is not one to be repaired under our scheme by legislation framed or administered to perpetuate family monopolies of either private occupations or branches of the public service. It is precisely because the Amendment forbids enclosing those areas by legislative lines drawn on the basis of race, color, creed, and the like, that, in cases like this, the possibly most efficient method of securing the highest development of skills cannot be established by law. Absent any such bar, the presence of such a tendency or direct relationship would be effective for sustaining the legislation. It cannot be effective to overcome the bar itself. The discrimination here is not shown to be consciously racial in character. But I am unable to differentiate in effects one founded on blood relationship. * * *

Notes and Questions

1. Did the majority's reasoning convince you that Louisiana had a rational basis for regulating river port pilots as it traditionally had done? Who will usually be selected if "membership of pilot associations is limited to persons agreeable to those already members?" What relation does nepotism bear to race? Is the process of grooming the next generation for jobs much different in other professions in the modern era? Did you change your mind about the majority's reasonableness when you read the dissent? What scrutiny should be given to modern justifications for "the way things are" that perpetuate racially inequitable practices?

2. In *Quong Wing v. Kirkendall*, 223 U.S. 59 (1912), plaintiff challenged a license fee imposed on "all persons engaged in the laundry business," but exempting women. Justice Holmes wrote:

> A state does not deny the equal protection of the laws merely by adjusting its revenue laws and taxing system in such a way as to favor certain industries or forms of industry. * * * It may make discriminations, if founded on distinctions that we cannot pronounce unreasonable and purely arbitrary. * * * If Montana deems it advisable to put a lighter burden upon women than upon men with regard to an employment that our people commonly regard as more appropriate for the former, the Fourteenth Amendment does not interfere by creating a fictitious equality where there is a real difference. The particular points at which that difference shall be emphasized by legislation are largely in the power of the state.
>
> Another difficulty suggested by the statute is that it is impossible not to ask whether it is not aimed at the Chinese, which would be a discrimination that the Constitution does not allow. It is a matter of common observation that hand laundry work is a widespread occupation of Chinamen in this country, while, on the other hand, it is so rare to see men of our race engaged in it that many of us would be unable to say that they ever had observed a case.

The tax was upheld.

3. The *Kotch* and *Quong Wing* courts articulated what has come to be called the rational basis test presumptively applied in interpreting the Equal Protection Clause.

4. Tussman & tenBroek explain that the rational basis test does not describe the full landscape of the Equal Protection Clause. Some classifications must be strictly scrutinized:

> The bearing of the Equal Protection Clause on the problem of classification is not exhausted by the reasonable classification requirement. The assertion of human equality is closely associated with the denial that differences in color or creed, birth or status, are significant or relevant to the way in which men should be treated. These factors, the egalitarian asserts, are irrelevant accidents in the face of our common humanity. To these differences in the supplicants before her bar, Justice must be blind. Laws which classify men by color or creed or blood accordingly, are repugnant to the demand for equality, and therefore, such traits should not be made the basis for the classification of individuals in laws. Speaking of "indigence," for example, Mr. Justice Jackson has said, "The mere state of being without funds is a neutral fact—constitutionally an irrelevance, like race, creed, or color." [citing *Edwards v. California*, 314 U.S. 160, 184 (1941)]

Joseph Tussman & Jacobus tenBroek, *The Equal Protection of the Laws*, 37 Cal. L. Rev. 341, 353 (1949).*

5. The Court cites *Yick Wo v. Hopkins*, 118 U.S. 356 (1886) (Chapter 5, § 1C) in which plaintiff had been fined for violating a local ordinance making it unlawful to conduct a laundry business in a wooden building. Yick Wo alleged "eighty odd laundries under similar conditions are left unmolest-

* Copyright ©1949 by the California Law Review, Inc. Reprinted by permission.

ed and free to enjoy the enhanced trade and profits arising from this hurtful and unfair discrimination." The Supreme Court found "a denial of the equal protection of the laws, and a violation of the Fourteenth Amendment of the constitution."

Today most dry cleaners in San Francisco are small businesses owned by Asian Americans, many of whom are non-English speakers, who live in the buildings that house the business. In 1994 the state air quality agency adopted Rule 1116, requiring all dry cleaners located underneath residences to "either retrofit or install new equipment to reduce the amount of [a commonly used carcinogenic cleaning chemical] released into the air. The upgrade can cost as much as $60,000." Litigation challenging this statute exposed information, withheld by the air quality board, about another non-carcinogenic cleaning compound that could have avoided the retrofit costs. "A hundred years after the original discriminatory practices, Chinese laundries are still looking for a level playing field." Leland Y. Yee, *Chinese Laundries See Renewed Bias*, S.F. Chron., May 26, 1998, at A17, col. 2. Is there value in an equality doctrine that requires continued litigation?

KOREMATSU v. UNITED STATES
323 U.S. 214 (1944).

Justice Black delivered the opinion of the Court.

The petitioner [Fred Toyosaburo Korematsu], an American citizen of Japanese descent, was convicted in a federal district court for remaining in San Leandro, California, a "Military Area," contrary to Civilian Exclusion Order No. 34 of the Commanding General of the Western Command, U.S. Army, which directed that after May 9, 1942, all persons of Japanese ancestry should be excluded from that area. No question was raised as to petitioner's loyalty to the United States. * * *

It should be noted, to begin with, that all legal restrictions which curtail the civil rights of a single racial group are immediately suspect. That is not to say that all such restrictions are unconstitutional. It is to say that courts must subject them to the most rigid scrutiny. Pressing public necessity may sometimes justify the existence of such restrictions; racial antagonism never can. * * *

Exclusion Order No. 34, which the petitioner knowingly and admittedly violated was one of a number of military orders and proclamations, * * * issued after we were at war with Japan. * * *

[One of these proclamations was a prior curfew order] designed as a "protection against espionage and against sabotage." In *Kiyoshi Hirabayashi v. United States*, 320 U.S. 81, we sustained a conviction obtained for violation of the curfew order. The Hirabayashi conviction and this one thus rest on the same 1942 Congressional Act and the same basic executive and military orders, all of which orders were aimed at the twin dangers of espionage and sabotage.

The 1942 Act was attacked in the *Hirabayashi* case as an unconstitutional delegation of power; it was contended that the curfew order and other orders on which it rested were beyond the war powers of the Congress, the military authorities and of the President, as Commander in Chief of the Army; and finally that to apply the curfew order against none but citizens of Japanese ancestry amounted to a constitutionally prohibited discrimination solely on account of race. To these questions, we gave the serious consideration which their importance justified. We upheld the curfew order as an exercise of the power of the government to take steps necessary to prevent espionage and sabotage in an area threatened by Japanese attack.

In the light of the principles we announced in the *Hirabayashi* case, we are unable to conclude that it was beyond the war power of Congress and the Executive to exclude those of Japanese ancestry from the West Coast war area at the time they did. True, exclusion from the area in which one's home is located is a far greater deprivation than constant confinement to the home from 8 p.m. to 6 a.m. Nothing short of apprehension by the proper military authorities of the gravest imminent danger to the public safety can constitutionally justify either. But exclusion from a threatened area, no less than curfew, has a definite and close relationship to the prevention of espionage and sabotage. The military authorities, charged with the primary responsibility of defending our shores, concluded that curfew provided inadequate protection and ordered exclusion. * * *

Here, as in the *Hirabayashi* case, " * * * we cannot reject as unfounded the judgment of the military authorities and of Congress that there were disloyal members of that population, whose number and strength could not be precisely and quickly ascertained. We cannot say that the war-making branches of the Government did not have ground for believing that in a critical hour such persons could not readily be isolated and separately dealt with, and constituted a menace to the national defense and safety, which demanded that prompt and adequate measures be taken to guard against it."

Like curfew, exclusion of those of Japanese origin was deemed necessary because of the presence of an unascertained number of disloyal members of the group, most of whom we have no doubt were loyal to this country. It was because we could not reject the finding of the military authorities that it was impossible to bring about an immediate segregation of the disloyal from the loyal that we sustained the validity of the curfew order as applying to the whole group. In the instant case, temporary exclusion of the entire group was rested by the military on the same ground. * * *

We uphold the exclusion order as of the time it was made and when the petitioner violated it. In doing so, we are not unmindful of the hardships imposed by it upon a large group of American citizens. But hardships are part of war, and war is an aggregation of hardships. All citizens alike, both in and out of uniform, feel the impact of war in greater or lesser measure. Citizenship has its responsibilities as well as its privileges, and in time of war the burden is always heavier. Compulsory exclusion of large groups of citizens from their homes, except under circumstances of direst emergency and peril, is inconsistent with our basic governmental institutions. But when under conditions of modern warfare our shores are threatened by hostile forces, the power to protect must be commensurate with the threatened danger. * * *

It is said that we are dealing here with the case of imprisonment of a citizen in a concentration camp solely because of his ancestry, without evidence or inquiry concerning his loyalty and good disposition towards the United States. Our task would be simple, our duty clear, were this a case involving the imprisonment of a loyal citizen in a concentration camp because of racial prejudice. Regardless of the true nature of the assembly and relocation centers—and we deem it unjustifiable to call them concentration camps with all the ugly connotations that term implies—we are dealing specifically with nothing but an exclusion order. To cast this case into outlines of racial prejudice, without reference to the real military dangers which were presented, merely confuses the issue. Korematsu was not excluded from the Military Area because of hostility to him or his race. He was excluded because we are at war with the Japanese Empire, because the properly constituted military authorities feared an invasion of our West Coast and felt constrained to take proper security measures, because they decided that the military urgency of the situation demanded that all citizens of Japanese ancestry be segregated from the West Coast temporarily, and finally, because Congress, reposing its confidence in this time of war in our military leaders—as inevitably it must—determined that they should have the power to do just this. There was evidence of disloyalty on the part of some, the military authorities considered that the need for action was great, and time was short. We cannot—by availing ourselves of the calm perspective of hindsight—now say that at that time these actions were unjustified.

Affirmed. * * *

JUSTICE ROBERTS, [dissenting]

I dissent, because I think the indisputable facts exhibit a clear violation of Constitutional rights.

This is not a case of keeping people off the streets at night as was *Kiyoshi Hirabayashi v. United States*, nor a case of temporary exclusion of a citizen from an area for his own safety or that of the community, nor a case of offering him an opportunity to go temporarily out of an area where his presence might cause danger to himself or to his fellows. On the contrary, it is the case of convicting a citizen as a punishment for not submitting to imprisonment in a concentration camp, based on his ancestry, and solely because of his ancestry, without evidence or inquiry concerning his loyalty and good disposition towards the United States. If this be a correct statement of the facts disclosed by this record, and facts of which we take judicial notice, I need hardly labor the conclusion that Constitutional rights have been violated. * * *

The petitioner, a resident of San Leandro, Alameda County, California, is a native of the United States of Japanese ancestry who, according to the uncontradicted evidence, is a loyal citizen of the nation. * * *

[The facts] show that the exclusion was but a part of an over-all plan for forceable detention. * * *

JUSTICE MURPHY, dissenting.

This exclusion of "all persons of Japanese ancestry, both alien and non-alien," from the Pacific Coast area on a plea of military necessity in the absence of martial law ought not to be approved. Such exclusion goes over "the very brink of constitutional power" and falls into the ugly abyss of racism. * * *

That this forced exclusion was the result in good measure of this erroneous assumption of racial guilt rather than bona fide military necessity is evidenced by the Commanding General's Final Report on the evacuation from the Pacific Coast area. In it he refers to all individuals of Japanese descent as "subversive," as belonging to "an enemy race" whose "racial strains are undiluted," and as constituting "over 112,000 potential enemies * * * at large today" along the Pacific Coast. In support of this blanket condemnation of all persons of Japanese descent, however, no reliable evidence is cited to show that such individuals were generally disloyal, or had generally so conducted themselves in this area as to constitute a special menace to defense installations or war industries, or had otherwise by their behavior furnished reasonable ground for their exclusion as a group. * * *

Individuals of Japanese ancestry are condemned because they are said to be "a large, unassimilated, tightly knit racial group, bound to an enemy nation by strong ties of race, culture, custom and religion." They are claimed to be given to "emperor worshipping ceremonies" and to "dual citizenship." Japanese language schools and allegedly pro-Japanese organizations are cited as evidence of possible group disloyalty, together with facts as to certain persons being educated and residing at length in Japan. It is intimated that many of these individuals deliberately resided "adjacent to strategic points," thus enabling them "to carry into execution a tremendous program of sabotage on a mass scale should any considerable number of them have been inclined to do so." The need for protective custody is also asserted. The report refers without identity to "numerous incidents of violence" as well as to other admittedly unverified or cumulative incidents. From this, plus certain other events not shown to have been connected with the Japanese Americans, it is concluded that the "situation was fraught with danger to the Japanese population itself" and that the general public "was ready to take matters into its own hands." Finally, it is intimated, though not directly charged or proved, that persons of Japanese ancestry were responsible for three minor isolated shellings and bombings of the Pacific Coast area, as well as for unidentified radio transmissions and night signalling.

The main reasons relied upon by those responsible for the forced evacuation, therefore, do not prove a reasonable relation between the group characteristics of Japanese Americans and the dangers of invasion, sabotage and espionage. The reasons appear, instead, to be largely an accumulation of much of the misinformation, half-truths and insinuations that for years have been directed against Japanese Americans by people with racial and economic prejudices—the same people who have been among the foremost advocates of the evacuation. * * *

The military necessity which is essential to the validity of the evacuation order thus resolves itself into a few intimations that certain individuals actively aided the enemy, from which it is inferred that the entire group of Japanese Americans could not be trusted to be or remain loyal to the United States. No one denies, of course, that there were some disloyal persons of Japanese descent on the Pacific Coast who did all in their power to aid their ancestral land. Similar disloyal activities have been engaged in by many persons of German, Italian and even more pioneer stock in our country. But to infer that examples of individual disloyalty prove group disloyalty and justify discriminatory action against the entire group is to deny that under our system of law individual guilt is the sole basis for deprivation of rights. * * *

No adequate reason is given for the failure to treat these Japanese Americans on an individual basis by holding investigations and hearings to separate the loyal from the disloyal, as was done in the case of persons of German and Italian ancestry. * * *

I dissent, therefore, from this legalization of racism. Racial discrimination in any form and in any degree has no justifiable part whatever in our democratic way of life. It is unattractive in any setting but it is utterly revolting among a free people who have embraced the principles set forth in the Constitution of the United States. All residents of this nation are kin in some way by blood or culture to a foreign land. Yet they are primarily and necessarily a part of the new and distinct civilization of the United States. They must accordingly be treated at all times as the heirs of the American experiment and as entitled to all the rights and freedoms guaranteed by the Constitution.

JUSTICE JACKSON, dissenting.

Korematsu was born on our soil, of parents born in Japan. The Constitution makes him a citizen of the United States by nativity and a citizen of California by residence. No claim is made that he is not loyal to this country. There is no suggestion that apart from the matter involved here he is not law-abiding and well disposed. Korematsu, however, has been convicted of an act not commonly a crime. It consists merely of being present in the state whereof he is a citizen, near the place where he was born, and where all his life he has lived. * * *

A citizen's presence in the locality, however, was made a crime only if his parents were of Japanese birth. Had Korematsu been one of four— the others being, say, a German alien enemy, an Italian alien enemy, and a citizen of American-born ancestors, convicted of treason but out on parole—only Korematsu's presence would have violated the order. The difference between their innocence and his crime would result, not from anything he did, said, or thought, different than they, but only in that he was born of different racial stock.

Now, if any fundamental assumption underlies our system, it is that guilt is personal and not inheritable. Even if all of one's antecedents had been convicted of treason, the Constitution forbids its penalties to be visited upon him * * *. But here is an attempt to make an otherwise innocent act a crime merely because this prisoner is the son of parents as to whom he had no choice, and belongs to a race from which there is no way to resign.

Notes and Questions

1. The majority states "all legal restrictions which curtail the civil rights of a single racial group are immediately suspect" and should be subjected to "the most rigid scrutiny." What kind of scrutiny does the majority use to evaluate the exclusion order? How does the majority's analysis compare with the scrutiny of the dissenters?

2. What should be the nature of judicial examination of government actions "which curtail civil rights of a single racial group?" Should any such classification be unconstitutional? Should the intent of the action be significant in making this determination?

3. Does this decision argue for an emphasis upon the individual, without regard for context, in evaluating equal protection claims?

4. Fred Korematsu was vindicated on April 19, 1984 when his conviction was vacated on grounds of governmental misconduct. "[T]here is substantial support in the record that the government deliberately omitted relevant information and provided misleading information* * *." *Korematsu v. United States*, 584 F. Supp. 1406, 1420 (N.D.Cal.1984). The development of the case leading to "Righting a Great Wrong" is reported in Peter Irons, *Justice Delayed: The Record of the Japanese American Internment Cases* (1989).

5. Natsu Taylor Saito describes how as a law student she followed the vindication of Fred Korematsu and Gordon Hirabayashi. But she says, "I always felt that something was missing in the legal and historical explanations of the internment." Natsu Taylor Saito, *Model Minority, Yellow Peril: Functions of "Foreignness" in the Construction of Asian American Legal Identity*, 4 Asian L.J. 71, 73 (1997) (symposium in honor of Neil Gotanda describing how "foreignness" has been used to mask discrimination against Asian Americans).*

She continues:

> In 1980, Congress established the Commission on Wartime Relocation and Internment of Civilians which held nationwide hearings. Its final report concluded, "The promulgation of Executive Order 9066 was not justified by military necessity, and the decisions which followed from it ... were not driven by analysis of military conditions. The broad historical causes which shaped these decisions were race prejudice, war hysteria and a failure of political leadership." Based on this report, the President issued an official apology and Congress passed legislation providing for at least symbolic redress. These, too, imply that the experience was an unfortunate detour in an otherwise honorable history of respect for the rights of citizens.
>
> Ruling in 1986 on motions for reconsideration in the *Hirabayashi* case, Judge Voorhees stated, "It is now considered by almost everyone that the internment of Japanese Americans during World War II was simply a tragic mistake for which American society as a whole must

---

* Copyright © 1997 by Natsu Taylor Saito and the Asian Law Journal. Used by   permission.

accept responsibility." However, it is not clear to me that the internment and the judicial decisions upholding it were aberrations, or a "tragic mistake." They are a quite logical extension of a history of law that tended, on the whole, to exclude those of Asian descent from mainstream society. They fit in quite well with the Chinese Exclusion Act, the "Gentlemen's Agreement" of 1908 excluding Japanese immigrants, the laws prohibiting the naturalization of persons of Asian descent, license and head taxes on immigrants, and laws which prohibited the ownership of land by aliens ineligible to citizenship. They also comport with a social history of discrimination, segregation, exclusion and race-based violence against Asian Americans. Yet this history is rarely discussed in the legal analyses of the internment cases.

Id. at 74–75.

HERNANDEZ v. TEXAS

347 U.S. 475 (1954).

CHIEF JUSTICE WARREN delivered the opinion of the Court.

The petitioner, Pete Hernández, was indicted for the murder of one Joe Espinosa by a grand jury in Jackson County, Texas. He was convicted and sentenced to life imprisonment. * * * [T]he petitioner, by his counsel, offered timely motions to quash the indictment and the jury panel. He alleged that persons of Mexican descent were systematically excluded from service as jury commissioners, grand jurors, and petit jurors, although there were such persons fully qualified to serve residing in Jackson County. The petitioner asserted that exclusion of this class deprived him, as a member of the class, of the equal protection of the laws guaranteed by the Fourteenth Amendment of the Constitution. * * *

In numerous decisions, this Court has held that it is a denial of the equal protection of the laws to try a defendant of a particular race or color under an indictment issued by a grand jury, or before a petit jury, from which all persons of his race or color have, solely because of that race or color, been excluded by the State, whether acting through its legislature, its courts, or its executive or administrative officers. * * * The State of Texas would have us hold that there are only two classes—white and Negro—within the contemplation of the Fourteenth Amendment. The decisions of this Court do not support that view. And, except where the question presented involves the exclusion of persons of Mexican descent from juries, Texas courts have taken a broader view of the scope of the Equal Protection Clause.

Throughout our history differences in race and color have defined easily identifiable groups which have at times required the aid of the courts in securing equal treatment under the laws. But community prejudices are not static, and from time to time other differences from the community norm may define other groups which need the same protection. Whether such a group exists within a community is a question of fact. When the existence of a distinct class is demonstrated, and it is further shown that the laws, as written or as applied, single out that class for different treatment not based on some reasonable classification, the guarantees of the Constitution have been violated. The Fourteenth Amendment is not directed solely against discrimination due to a "two-class theory"—that is, based upon differences between "white" and Negro.

As the petitioner acknowledges, the Texas system of selecting grand and petit jurors by the use of jury commissions is fair on its face and capable of being utilized without discrimination. But as this Court has held, the system is susceptible to abuse and can be employed in a discriminatory manner. The exclusion of otherwise eligible persons from jury service solely because of their ancestry or national origin is discrimination prohibited by the Fourteenth Amendment. The Texas statute makes no such discrimination, but the petitioner alleges that those administering the law do.

The petitioner's initial burden in substantiating his charge of group discrimination was to prove that persons of Mexican descent constitute a separate class in Jackson County, distinct from "whites." One method by which this may be demonstrated is by showing the attitude of the community. Here the testimony of responsible officials and citizens contained the admission that residents of the community distinguished between "white" and "Mexican." The participation of persons of Mexican descent in business and community groups was shown to be slight. Until very recent times, children of Mexican descent were required to attend a segregated school for the first four grades. At least one restaurant in town prominently displayed a sign announcing "No Mexicans Served." On the courthouse grounds at the time of the hearing, there were two men's toilets, one unmarked, and the other marked "Colored Men" and "Hombres Aqui" ("Men Here"). No substantial evidence was offered to rebut the logical inference to be drawn from these facts, and it must be concluded that petitioner succeeded in his proof.

Having established the existence of a class, petitioner was then charged with the burden of proving discrimination. To do so, he relied on the pattern of proof established by *Norris v. State of Alabama*, 294 U.S. 587. In that case, proof that Negroes constituted a substantial segment of the population of the jurisdiction, that some Negroes were qualified to serve as jurors, and that none had been called for jury service over an extended period of time, was held to constitute *prima facie* proof of the systematic exclusion of Negroes from jury service. This holding, sometimes called the "rule of exclusion," has been applied in other cases, and it is available in supplying proof of discrimination against any delineated class.

The petitioner established that 14% of the population of Jackson County were persons with Mexican or Latin American surnames, and that 11% of the males over 21 bore such names. The County Tax Assessor testified that 6 or 7% of the freeholders on the tax rolls of the County were persons of Mexican descent. The State of Texas stipulated that "for the last twenty-five years there is no record of any person with a Mexican or Latin American name having served on a jury commission, grand jury or petit jury in Jackson County." The parties also stipulated that "there are some male persons of Mexican or Latin American descent in Jackson County who, by virtue of being citizens, freeholders, and having all other legal prerequisites to jury service, are eligible to serve as members of a jury commission, grand jury and/or petit jury."

The petitioner met the burden of proof imposed in *Norris v. Alabama, supra.* To rebut the strong *prima facie* case of the denial of the equal protection of the laws guaranteed by the Constitution thus established, the State offered the testimony of five jury commissioners that they had not discriminated against persons of Mexican or Latin American descent in selecting jurors. They stated that their only objective had been to select those whom they thought were best qualified. This testimony is not enough to overcome the petitioner's case. * * *

Circumstances or chance may well dictate that no persons in a certain class will serve on a particular jury or during some particular period. But it taxes our credulity to say that mere chance resulted in their being no members of this class among the over six thousand jurors called in the past 25 years. The result bespeaks discrimination, whether or not it was a conscious decision on the part of any individual jury commissioner. The judgment of conviction must be reversed.

a small one for the good guys.

Notes and Questions

1. What vision of the Equal Protection Clause is proposed by the *Hernandez* court which says, "Throughout our history differences in race and color have defined easily identifiable groups which have at times required the aid of the courts in securing equal treatment under the laws. But community prejudices are not static, and from time to time other differences from the community norm may define other groups which need the same protection"? What role does the court think race plays in defining Mexican Americans as a group entitled to equal protection? See Ian F. Haney López, *Race and Erasure: The Salience of Race to LatCrit Theory*, 85 Calif. L. Rev. 1143 (1997) (arguing that a racial understanding of the group Latinos may be preferable and should at least be evaluated). See also Juan F. Perea, *The Black/White Binary Paradigm of Race: The "Normal Science" of American Racial Thought*, 85 Calif. L. Rev. 1213 (1997) (discussing prevalent binary conception of race as Black or White).

2. In *McLaughlin v. Florida*, 379 U.S. 184 (1964), the Court overturned a conviction that criminalized only conduct by an interracial couple, again emphasizing the special scrutiny that should be turned to a race-based classification. The Court commented:

Judicial inquiry under the Equal Protection Clause, therefore, does not end with a showing of equal application among the members of the class defined by the legislation. The courts must reach and determine the question whether the classifications drawn in a statute are reasonable in light of its purpose—in this case, whether there is an arbitrary or invidious discrimination between those classes covered by [the legislation] and those excluded. * * * Normally, the widest discretion is allowed the legislative judgment in determining whether to attack some, rather than all, of the manifestations of the evil aimed at; and normally that judgment is given the benefit of every conceivable circumstance which might suffice to characterize the classification as reasonable rather than arbitrary and invidious. But we deal here with a classification based upon the race of the participants, which must be viewed in light of the historical fact that the central purpose of the Fourteenth Amendment was to eliminate racial discrimination emanating from official sources in the States. This strong policy renders racial classifications "constitutionally suspect," and subject to the "most rigid scrutiny," and "in most circumstances irrelevant" to any constitutionally acceptable legislative purpose.

Id. at 191–92, 288.

3. In *Loving v. Virginia*, 388 U.S. 1 (1967), the Court revisited the issue of interracial marriage, again finding that the state statutory prohibition violated the Fourteenth Amendment. The state court had upheld the legislation, concluding, "that the State's legitimate purposes were 'to preserve the racial integrity of its citizens,' and to prevent 'the corruption of blood,' 'a mongrel breed of citizens,' and 'the obliteration of racial pride.' " Seeking to support this holding on appeal the state contended that because its miscegenation statutes punished "equally both the white and the Negro participants in an interracial marriage, these statutes, despite their reliance on racial classifications do not constitute an invidious discrimination based upon race."

The Court disagreed: "At the very least, the Equal Protection Clause demands that racial classifications, especially suspect in criminal statutes, be subjected to the 'most rigid scrutiny,' and, if they are ever to be upheld, they must be shown to be necessary to the accomplishment of some permissible state objective, independent of the racial discrimination which it was the object of the Fourteenth Amendment to eliminate. * * * The fact that Virginia prohibits only interracial marriages involving white persons demonstrates that the racial classifications must stand on their own justification, as measures designed to maintain White Supremacy."

See Chapter 11 for further discussion of inter-racial marriage.

4. In addition to the rational basis and strict scrutiny standard of judicial review, the Court has fashioned a third standard, intermediate scrutiny. Intermediate scrutiny typically requires that a classification serve " 'important governmental objectives and that the discriminatory means employed' are 'substantially related to the achievement of those objectives.' " *United States v. Virginia*, 518 U.S. 515, 533 (1996). Courts use intermediate scrutiny most frequently in reviewing classifications that discriminate on the basis of sex. See also *Plyler v. Doe*, 457 U.S. 202 (1982) (applying a variant of intermediate scrutiny to invalidate a Texas statute that required the children of undocumented immigrants to pay a "tuition fee" to attend public school, which was free to others).

REVA SIEGEL

Why Equal Protection No Longer Protects: The Evolving
Forms of Status–Enforcing State Action
49 Stan. L. Rev. 1111, 1112–1147 (1997).*

* * *

In our constitutional culture, we often express judgments about subordinating practices of the past as if they were timeless truths.

Speaking in this tradition, the Supreme Court recently asserted that "we think *Plessy* was wrong the day it was decided." This manner of speaking about past practices aspires to transcontextual moral certainty. * * * Thus, even if *Plessy* was wrong the day it was decided, the decision was surely wrong in 1896 in a different sense than it would be "wrong" if announced by the Court today.

Why examine the ways in which earlier generations of Americans justified the subordinating practices of their day? Is the point of such an exercise to make excuses for our predecessors? To the contrary: it is to discuss the practices of our predecessors in terms that more deeply implicate us in the present. It is now commonplace to condemn slavery and segregation—a rhetorical practice presumably intended to bind Americans ever more closely to principles of equality. But repeated condemnation of slavery and segregation may have just the opposite effect. We have demonized subordinating practices of the past to such a degree that condemning such practices may instead function to exonerate practices contested in the present, none of which looks so unremittingly "evil" by contrast. That which we retrospectively judge evil was once justified as reasonable. If we reconstruct the grounds on which our predecessors justified subordinating practices of the past, we may be in a better position to evaluate contested practices in the present.

This essay begins from a simple proposition: The ways in which the legal system enforces social stratification are various and evolve over time. Efforts to reform a status regime bring about changes in its rule structure and justificatory rhetoric—a dynamic I have elsewhere called "preservation-through-transformation." In short, status-enforcing state action evolves in form as it is contested.

This, of course, is not the prevailing view in our constitutional culture. Contemporary equal protection law is premised on a formal and historically static conception of "discrimination." Race or sex discrimination occurs when the state regulates on the basis of race- or sex-based classifications; heightened scrutiny of such state action is necessary for the nation to transcend a "history of classification"—the Court's summary referent for the history of race- and gender-subordinating state action. This concept of classification defines understandings of discrimination, both historical and contemporary. When the state regulates on the basis of "facially neutral" criteria that have injurious effects on minorities or women, the Court presumes the regulation is constitutional and reviews it in a highly deferential manner. The Court will only strike down such regulation if it is shown to be adopted with discriminatory purpose—a concept the Court has defined as tantamount to malice.

Over the last several decades, this body of equal protection doctrine has abolished many traditional forms of race and gender status regulation, and so has transformed the face of the American legal system. But has it ended the state's role in enforcing race and gender stratification— or instead caused such regulation to assume new form? Viewed historically, this question might be recast in the following terms. The body of equal protection law that sanctioned segregation was produced as the legal system endeavored to disestablish slavery; the body of equal protection law we inherit today was produced as the legal system endeavored to disestablish segregation. Are we confident that the body of equal protection law we inherit today is "true" equal protection, or might it stand in relation to segregation as *Plessy* and its progeny stood in relation to slavery?

So long as we view status law in static and homogenous terms—as we do when we equate "discrimination" with "classification"—it is plausible to imagine ourselves at the end of history, finally and conclusively repudiating centuries of racial and gender inequality. But if we consider the possibility that the kinds of rules and reasons employed to enforce status relationships change as they are contested, then it is possible to see contemporary equal protection law in a different light.
* * *

For centuries, the Anglo–American common law situated persons in explicitly hierarchical relationships. Thus, the common law organized the "domestic" relations of husband/wife and master/servant as relations of governance and dependence, with the law specifying the rights and obligations of superior and inferior parties. The American common law modeled chattel slavery on this "domestic" analogue as well.

It is conventionally asserted that status law of this sort died out with the growth of capitalism and the spread of liberal conceptions of citizenship. Various accounts of modernization posit a movement during the nineteenth century from "status to contract," resulting in the break up of status hierarchies and the redefinition of juridical persons as equal in capacity and entitlement.

These traditional assumptions about the form and developmental trajectory of status law do not bear up well under historical scrutiny.
* * *

There is no doubt that by the second half of the nineteenth century the American legal system began to address the old status relations of the common law in new ways. In this period, the legal system began to eschew overt relations of hierarchy, and to assert the juridical equality of persons formerly related in hierarchical terms. But as one begins to scrutinize particular bodies of nineteenth-century law, it becomes clear that such changes did not eradicate foundational status structures: In gender, race, and class relationships, the legal system continued to allocate privileges and entitlements in a manner that perpetuated former systems of express hierarchy. Analyzed from this vantage point, the rise of liberal and capitalist systems of social organization did not result in the dismantlement of status relationships, but instead precipitated their evolution into new forms.

This process of transformation is well worth examining. In the middle decades of the nineteenth century, the American legal system sought, as it never had before, to repudiate bodies of law that for centuries had defined African Americans and white women as subordinate members of the polity. That this effort to disestablish entrenched bodies of status law was fitfully pursued, energetically resisted, and soon abandoned does not detract from its significance. For in this period of sweeping sociolegal change, we can examine the disestablishment dynamic as it actually unfolds in history. In the tug and haul of politics, the process of dismantling an entrenched system of status relations may well transform the regime without abolishing it. * * *

The concept of preservation-through-transformation provides a framework for thinking about the evolution of racial status law during the Reconstruction era. The regime of segregation sanctioned in *Plessy* was, after all, the result of efforts to disestablish slavery. Though today we tend to think about the transition from slavery to segregation as a seamless episode of invidious racial classification, white Americans in the nineteenth century viewed the changes in racial status law of their day in very different terms: as elevating African Americans from subordination in slavery to equality at law. In the nineteenth century, at a time when the state still openly drew distinctions in the rights and disabilities of diverse groups of citizens, equality at law was an ill-defined concept, fraught with contradictions and subject to contestation.

White Americans who emphatically opposed slavery regularly disagreed about what it would mean to emancipate African Americans. Some defined freedom from slavery as equality in civil rights; others insisted that emancipating African Americans from slavery entailed equality in civil and political rights; but most white Americans who opposed slavery did not think its abolition required giving African Americans equality in "social rights." Distinctions among civil, political, and social rights functioned more as a framework for debate than a conceptual scheme of any legal precision. But it was generally understood that civil rights were those rights exercised by economic man, such as the capacity to hold property and enter into contracts, and to bring suit to defend those rights in the legal system. Voting was the core political right. [Political rights were often said to include voting, office holding, jury service, and militia service.] Social rights were those forms of association that, white Americans feared, would obliterate status distinctions and result in the "amalgamation" of the races.

White Americans reasoning about the fate of the emancipated slaves drew such distinctions precisely because their commitment to abolish slavery was not a commitment to recognize African Americans as equals in all spheres of social life; in the years before and after the Civil War, white Americans of widely varying political views reiterated their conviction that emancipating African Americans entailed granting the freedmen some form of legal equality, but assuredly did not require granting them "social equality." Abolishing slavery thus entailed a struggle over the shape of racial status law, one that would ultimately transform its rule structure and justificatory rhetoric. The triadic distinction among civil, political, and social rights created a discursive field in which we can see the dynamic of preservation-through-transformation at work.

From this perspective, the successive waves of federal legislation enacted in the aftermath of the Civil War make conceptual sense. When southern states adopted Black Codes constricting land ownership and employment of freedmen in such a way as to tie the emancipated slaves to their former owners, Congress passed the 1866 Civil Rights Act, providing that:

[c]itizens of every race ... shall have the same right ... to make and enforce contracts, to sue, be parties, and give evidence, to inherit, purchase, lease, sell, hold, and convey real and personal property, and to full and equal benefit of all laws and proceedings for the security of person and property, as is enjoyed by white citizens, and shall be subject to like punishment. [Act of Apr. 9, 1866, ch. 31, § 1, 14 Stat. 27 (current version at 42 U.S.C.A. §§ 1981, 1982 (1996)).]

Because there was dispute about whether the Thirteenth Amendment's prohibition of slavery vested Congress with the power to define and protect civil rights in this fashion, Congress began work on the drafting and ratification of the Fourteenth Amendment, and soon thereafter reinacted the substance of the 1866 statute in the Civil Rights Act of 1870. When similar disputes arose over scope of rights protected by the Fourteenth Amendment, Congress vested the emancipated slaves with the political right of voting through the Fifteenth Amendment.

As white Americans argued about the kinds of reform that would be required to disestablish slavery, their conflicts were expressed in struggles over constitutional amendments and various pieces of civil rights legislation, as well as in debates about their interpretation. These disputes in turn progressively reshaped the rules and rhetoric of racial status law. * * *

In the aftermath of the war, when states moved to enact or enforce legislation barring interracial marriage, the question immediately arose: Was marriage a contract protected by the 1866 Civil Rights Act? As opponents of the 1866 Act had feared, a few courts initially ruled that it was. But other courts moved rapidly to restrict the meaning of the federal statute, by construing its antidiscrimination provision to apply to contracts involving "civil" rather than "social" rights. In this view, the right to marry was a "social right," not governed by the federal law. * * *

Courts upholding antimiscegenation statutes relied upon the distinction between civil and social rights until they were confident enough—which they were not initially—simply to assert that regulating marriage lay beyond the scope of federal power.

Disputes over the legality of miscegenation laws illustrated that distinctions between civil and social rights were not fixed, but instead were forged in the struggle over the scope of Reconstruction legislation. This dynamic is especially evident in disputes over the legality of segregation in transportation and accommodations. When Republicans in Congress first attempted to enact antidiscrimination legislation to cover common carriers and public accommodations, they asserted that long-standing common law traditions made equal access to such institutions a basic civil right. But the initial bill addressing these matters also covered schools, churches, cemeteries, theaters, and other institutions, and elicited vehement and continuing objections that Congress was attempting to regulate private associations and thereby to legislate social equality. When Congress finally enacted a much narrower version of the statute in the Civil Rights Act of 1875, which prohibited race discrimination in public transportation, accommodations, and theaters, the charge that Congress was impermissibly regulating social rights continued to inform the statute's interpretation and application. As historians have demonstrated, courts generally construed the federal statute to forbid race-based exclusions from covered institutions, but to allow segregation so long as blacks were provided substantially equal facilities with whites.

In rationalizing this result, courts invoked social rights discourse. As one court put it, the 1875 Act did not intend "to affect social rights through civil and legal rights." Another court adopting this interpretation of the Act justified it on the grounds that segregation in the covered institutions was necessary to preserve status relations of inequality which originated in slavery. * * *

In this interpretive framework, equality of access to public transportation was a civil right, but integrated access raised questions of social rights, and was unacceptable because it threatened status relations forged in the institution of slavery.

The Supreme Court employed the language of social rights to interpret the Constitution, but, as it did so, it suppressed reference to many of the social understandings informing the discourse. For example, when the Court struck down the Civil Rights Act of 1875 in *The Civil Rights Cases*, it declared that Congress lacked power under the Thirteenth Amendment to enact the 1875 statute because—unlike the 1866 Civil Rights Act—the 1875 Act regulated "social rights" that had "nothing to do with slavery."

Detached from its reference to slavery, social rights discourse played an even more prominent role in the *Plessy* decision, where it was invoked by the Court to explain why laws mandating racial segregation of public transportation were permissible under the Fourteenth Amendment:

> The object of the amendment was undoubtedly to enforce the absolute equality of the two races before the law, but in the nature of things it could not have been intended to abolish distinctions based upon color, or to enforce social, as distinguished from political equality, or a commingling of the two races upon terms unsatisfactory to either.

The Court pointed to its decision in *Strauder v. West Virginia* holding that states could not exclude blacks from jury service in order to emphasize "[t]he distinction between laws interfering with the political equality of the negro and those requiring the separation of the two races in schools, theaters and railway carriages." In *Plessy*, the Court again denied "that the enforced separation of the two races stamps the colored race with a badge of inferiority"—even as the very language of its opinion discussed the "commingling of the two races" as an objectionable form of "social equality." To resolve this contradiction, the opinion attempted to characterize questions of equality as questions of liberty, and to describe status discriminations as expressions of taste and sensibility. Rejecting the plaintiff's argument that segregation connoted inferiority, the Court responded that:

[t]he argument ... assumes that social prejudices may be overcome by legislation, and that equal rights cannot be secured to the negro except by an enforced commingling of the two races. We cannot accept this proposition. If the two races are to meet upon terms of social equality, it must be the result of natural affinities, a mutual appreciation of each other's merits and a voluntary consent of individuals.... If the civil and political rights of both races be equal one cannot be inferior to the other civilly or politically. If one race be inferior to the other socially, the Constitution of the United States cannot put them upon the same plane.

Thus, in *Plessy*, the Court contended that segregation did not connote inferiority, but conceded that if it did, it was inferiority of a sort that was beyond the power of law to rectify.

Justice Harlan's famous dissent in *Plessy* repeatedly chided the majority for denying what he called the "real meaning" of segregation: that "colored citizens are so inferior and degraded that they cannot be allowed to sit in public coaches occupied by white citizens." But Justice Harlan did not assert that "colored citizens" were the social equals of white citizens, or that the law should make them so; indeed, passages of his dissent—including the famous color-blindness argument—continue to emphasize distinctions between legal and "social" equality. Justice Harlan broke with the majority because he, like the Congress that enacted the 1875 Civil Rights Act, viewed equal access to public transportation as a civil right which, accordingly, could not be the subject of racially discriminatory regulation: "In respect of civil rights, all citizens are equal before the law." However, by the time Justice Harlan wrote his dissent in *Plessy* (two decades after passage of the 1875 Act), the discourse of social rights had largely displaced the language of civil rights in public accommodations law, facilitating the justification of segregation in terms that the architects of Reconstruction would have wholly repudiated. * * *

Thus, considered in retrospect, the distinction between civil and political rights on the one hand, and social rights on the other, helps explain juridical differences in the rule structure of racial status regulation enacted in the decades following the Civil War. In matters deemed to concern civil and political rights, states over time came to regulate race relations by means of statutes that employed no express racial distinctions on their face. Thus, states seeking to disenfranchise African Americans successively experimented with the grandfather clause, residency and literacy requirements, and "privatization" through the white primary, as well as the familiar tactics of racist intimidation and discriminatory administration of facially neutral registration statutes. It was in the sphere of so-called social rights (a sphere which ultimately was to include marriage, education, public transportation, and accommodation) that states openly employed race-based distinctions to enforce racial segregation.

The regime of segregation authorized by the social rights concept lasted well into the twentieth century, until the Court began its dismantlement in *Brown*. In this era, the discourse of social rights supplied a basis for opposing *Brown*. For example, Herbert Wechsler drew upon this tradition to advance his prominent critique of the *Brown* decision:

> But if the freedom of association is denied by segregation, integration forces an association upon those for whom it is unpleasant or repugnant. . . . Given a situation where the state must practically choose between denying the association to those individuals who wish it or imposing it on those who would avoid it, is there a basis in neutral principles for holding that the Constitution demands that the claims for association should prevail? [Herbert Wechsler, *Toward Neutral Principles of Constitutional Law*, 73 Harv. L. Rev. 1, 34 (1959).]

In this period, similar arguments were advanced against civil rights legislation that would require businesses to deal with the public on a nondiscriminatory basis. So strong was the tradition of protecting white "associational" liberties that it was not until 1967, thirteen years after *Brown* was decided, that the Court was willing to declare that antimiscegenation statutes violated the Equal Protection Clause. Only after the Court's decision in *Loving* struck down Virginia's antimiscegenation statute as an expression of "White Supremacy" could it be confidently asserted that the Court had adopted a categorical presumption against race-based regulation. * * *

Viewed retrospectively, the civil-political-social rights distinction may strike us as profoundly misguided, or worse. Yet for generations of white Americans this conceptual framework offered an entirely reasonable way of understanding the Fourteenth Amendment's guarantee of "equal protection of the laws." For these Americans, *Plessy* was not "wrong the day it was decided"; to the contrary, the decision conformed with "common sense" intuitions about the meaning of equality in a constitutional democracy. The Fourteenth and Fifteenth Amendments guaranteed African Americans equality in civil and political rights; equality in "social rights" was not to be enforced by law. Thus, constitutional scholars as eminent as Herbert Wechsler worried that the Court's decision in *Brown* lacked a basis in neutral principles because it protected the associational preferences of African Americans at the expense of whites who might find association with African Americans "unpleasant or repugnant." In raising such objections, Wechsler and others who defended the constitutional liberties of white Americans to choose their associations were speaking in "good faith," invoking principles that had governed the meaning of equal protection for generations.

The civil-political-social rights distinction thus offered a framework within which white Americans could disestablish slavery, guarantee the emancipated slaves equality at law, and yet continue to justify policies and practices that perpetuated the racial stratification of American society. Once we appreciate how conflicts over the disestablishment of slavery produced the constitutional framework authorizing segregation, we are in a better position to think about the ways in which the Court interprets the Equal Protection Clause today.

Just as the interpretation of equal protection offered in *Plessy* emerged from the Court's efforts to disestablish slavery, the interpretation of equal protection we inherit today emerged from the Court's efforts to disestablish segregation. Has the body of equal protection law that disestablished segregation prohibited all forms of state action that perpetuate the racial stratification of American society? Quite plainly, it has not. Equal protection doctrine currently constrains explicitly race-based forms of state action; but, as the Court has repeatedly held, the state may enforce "facially neutral" policies and practices with a disparate impact on minorities or women so long as such policies or practices are not enacted for discriminatory purposes.

In the nineteenth century, the Court was confident that it had abolished slavery and granted African Americans equal protection of the laws. In this period, doctrines concerning social rights authorized certain forms of state action that perpetuated racial stratification as consistent with constitutional guarantees of equal protection. Today, the Court is confident that it has abolished segregation and granted African Americans equal protection of the laws. Now, doctrines concerning discriminatory purpose authorize certain forms of state action that perpetuate racial stratification as consistent with constitutional guarantees of equal protection. * * *

The Court's decision to apply strict scrutiny to race-based state action in the 1950s and 1960s was momentous, given the wide variety of circumstances in which the Court had previously sanctioned explicit discrimination under the Equal Protection Clause. Once *Brown* and *Loving* demonstrated that the Court had definitively repudiated the old distinction between civil and social rights, there was no longer a tenable basis for defending the constitutionality of overtly race-based regulation. State regulation of matters once held to concern social rights thus assumed the facially neutral form that had generally characterized regulation of matters deemed to concern civil and political rights since the Reconstruction era.

Collapse of the distinction between civil and social rights shifted the terrain of conflict. * * * [T]he Court embraced the concept of discriminatory purpose as the touchstone for determining the constitutionality of facially neutral state action alleged to discriminate on the basis of race.

It was in no sense natural, inevitable, or necessary for the Court to interpret the Equal Protection Clause this way. In the years after *Brown*, prominent legal process scholars such as Alexander Bickel and Herbert Wechsler suggested that it was inappropriate for judges to inquire into the motives of legislators in determining whether statutes comported with constitutional requirements. And the Court itself asserted as much in several of its opinions in the late 1960s and early 1970s. Although in 1960 the Court in *Gomillion v. Lightfoot* [364 U.S. 339 (1960)] stated that "[a]cts generally lawful may become unlawful when done to accomplish an unlawful end," by 1968, the Court cast aspersion on the propriety of reviewing legislative motivation in a First Amendment opinion that announced: "The decisions of this court from the beginning lend no support whatever to the assumption that the judiciary may restrain the exercise of lawful power on the assumption that a wrongful purpose or motive has caused the power to be exerted." The

Court again emphasized this view in *Palmer v. Thompson*, [403 U.S. 217 (1971)] a race discrimination case decided in 1971, which held that a city's decision to close segregated public swimming pools rather than integrate them could not be impugned on the basis of legislative motivation alone. In *Palmer*, the Court announced that "no case in this Court has held that a legislative act may violate equal protection solely because of the motivations of the men who voted for it," and proceeded to rehearse again the reasons why it deemed this form of review inappropriate. That same year, in *Griggs v. Duke Power Co.*, [401 U.S. 424 (1971)] the Court held that, under Title VII of the Civil Rights Act of 1964, plaintiffs could prove claims of employment discrimination on a showing of disparate impact evidence alone.

A period of uncertainty about constitutional standards ensued. In this period, second-generation legal process scholars, who were critical of the Court's decision in *Palmer*, began to defend motive review as important in determining the forms of legislative action to which courts should properly defer, while other constitutional commentators began openly to worry about the practical consequences of allowing plaintiffs to challenge facially neutral laws with racially disparate impacts. A number of federal courts were deciding equal protection challenges to facially neutral state action on the basis of evidence of racial impact alone, and the Court moved sharply to curb this practice. Reversing one such case in 1976, the Court in *Washington v. Davis* [426 U.S. 229 (1976)] announced that there was an important distinction between equal protection and Title VII standards, and drew upon the school segregation cases to assert the general principle that plaintiffs challenging facially neutral state action would have to demonstrate that the state acted with discriminatory purpose in order to make out an equal protection violation. *Davis* repudiated the Court's prior statements that impugned motive analysis as "dicta," and expressly criticized the many appellate court opinions that had found equal protection violations on the basis of impact evidence alone. Thus, in *Davis*, a case involving a challenge to an employment exam that excluded four times as many African Americans as whites applying for a position on the District of Columbia police force, and a year later in *Village of Arlington Heights v. Metropolitan Housing Development Corp.*, a case involving a challenge to a zoning ordinance prohibiting the construction of low and moderate income housing, the Court made clear that proving discriminatory purpose was now not only permitted, but required in all cases challenging facially neutral state action having a disparate impact on protected classes. * * *

[T]he Court defined discriminatory purpose in terms that are extraordinarily difficult to prove in the constitutional culture its modern equal protection opinions have created—a culture that now embraces "equal opportunity" and "nondiscrimination" as a form of civic religion. Because doctrines of heightened scrutiny now require legislators enacting race- or sex-based programs to articulate legitimate, nondiscriminatory reasons for their policy choices, legislators do not make a practice of justifying legislation on the grounds that it will adversely affect groups that have historically been subject to discrimination. To the contrary, doctrines of heightened scrutiny have created incentives for legislators to explain their policy choices in terms that cannot be so impugned.

The Court has thus adopted a working definition of discriminatory purpose that raises a substantial barrier to suits challenging facially neutral state action. The Court itself has acknowledged as much, observing that "[p]roving the motivation behind official action is often a problematic undertaking," and more bluntly still, "[t]he distinction between being aware of racial considerations and being motivated by them may be difficult to make." Because it is so hard to prove discriminatory purpose under the Equal Protection Clause, most institutions, practices, and values will be constitutionally characterized as race- or sex-neutral. * * *

For these reasons, the discriminatory purpose requirement now insulates many, if not most, forms of facially neutral state action from equal protection challenge. Indeed, a recent study hypothesizes that "[t]he intent standard's demands might discourage plaintiffs from bringing intent-based claims," offering statistics suggesting that on average, just one or two intent claims are filed per federal district per year. What concerns justify the * * * framework?

In defining discriminatory purpose, the Court did not consult sociological or psychological studies of racial bias. Had it done so, it would have encountered surveys and polls documenting that the majority of white Americans repudiate "dominative" racism. * * * At the same time, the empirical literature on racial bias demonstrates that there is a significant difference between the principles that white Americans espouse in such polls and their actual attitudes in matters of race. These studies demonstrate that many white Americans now view overt racism as socially unacceptable and mute expression of their racially biased opinions in public settings—even settings as relatively anonymous as an opinion poll or survey. And an even larger body of literature demonstrates that white Americans who embrace principles of racial equality manifest unconscious forms of racial bias in diverse spheres of social life. In sum, the sociological and psychological literature demonstrates that (1) racial bias remains the norm among white Americans; but that (2) they are strongly inhibited in expressing the racial attitudes they consciously hold, and often are wholly unaware of the extent to which their conscious judgments are unconsciously race based. Thus, the form of discriminatory purpose the Court asked plaintiffs to prove * * * ("that the decisionmaker ... selected or reaffirmed a particular course of action at least in part 'because of,' not merely 'in spite of,' its adverse effects upon an identifiable group") is one that the sociological and psychological studies of racial bias suggest plaintiffs will rarely be able to prove. In short, the empirical literature on racial bias suggests that, under the * * * framework, most race-dependent governmental decisionmaking will elude equal protection scrutiny. * * *

In the very same era that the Court adopted the highly deferential * * *[discriminatory purpose] framework, it began steadily to increase its scrutiny of affirmative action policies—recently subjecting such policies to strict scrutiny. Considered together, these two bodies of law create an interesting study in contrasts. When plaintiffs challenge facial-ly neutral policies that have a disparate impact on minorities or women, the Court adopts a highly deferential stance towards a legislature's judgments. But when white plaintiffs challenge affirmative action poli-cies that increase the institutional representation of minority groups, the Court has, with increasing insistence, warned that it will review and restrict the ambit of legislative action. Today, when legislatures employ race-based criteria primarily for the purpose of remedying past discrimi-nation, the Court applies strict scrutiny to such programs, intervening in the legislative process to protect the interests of whites in ways that it will not when plaintiffs challenge legislation having a disparate impact on minorities or women.

Of course, the Court would justify its discrepant response to these two forms of discrimination claims by insisting that it only applies doctrines of heightened scrutiny to facially explicit race- or sex-based state action. But, we might very well ask why this is so. When first adopted, doctrines of heightened scrutiny invalidated many traditional forms of race- and gender-status legislation, but regulatory bodies re-sponded by abandoning the use of race- and most forms of gender-specific criteria. The Court never revised doctrines of heightened scruti-ny so that judicial review could detect latent bias in the forms of facially neutral state action that resulted. Thus, today, especially in the area of race, doctrines of heightened scrutiny are functioning primarily as a check on affirmative action programs. By their terms, doctrines of heightened scrutiny do not apply to facial neutral laws like the sentenc-ing guidelines, decisions concerning education and zoning, or policies concerning spousal assault and child support, whose incidence falls primarily on minorities or women. The Court assumes these policies were enacted in good faith—even as it applies "skeptical scrutiny" to policies that attempt to rectify centuries of discrimination against minor-ities and women.

The Court invokes history to justify applying strict scrutiny to race-conscious remedies, emphasizing, on more than one occasion, that "[t]he history of racial classifications in this country suggests that blind judicial deference to legislative or executive pronouncements of necessity has no place in equal protection analysis." But the historical narrative the Court invokes to justify its current use of strict scrutiny doctrine is highly abstracted, depicting centuries of racial status regulation as a "history of racial classifications." When the Court presents the history of racial status regulation as a "history of racial classifications," it can equate racial classifications used to promote integration with racial classifications used to promote segregation, and equate regulation seek-ing to alleviate racial stratification with regulation seeking to perpetuate racial stratification. At the same time, by abstracting the history of racial status regulation into a narrative of "racial classifications," the Court obscures the multiple and mutable forms of racial status regulation that have subordinated African Americans since the Founding—including the facially neutral forms of state action that, since Reconstruction, have regulated racial status in matters of employment, political participation, and criminal justice. From this highly abstracted standpoint—one that is inattentive to the social meaning of racial status regulation or the various and evolving forms it has assumed over the course of American history—it "makes sense" to apply "skeptical scrutiny" to race-conscious remedies, while reviewing facially neutral regulation deferentially, on the premise that it is enacted in good faith.

Of course, contemporary equal protection law looks quite different from the analytical standpoint of this essay—which does not equate discrimination with "classification," but begins instead from the premise that status-enforcing state action is mutable in form, evolving in rule structure and justificatory rhetoric as it is contested. When considered from this vantage point, the Court's "fidelity" to doctrines of heightened scrutiny can most charitably be characterized as inflexibility—a failure to adapt its practices of review to changing regulatory circumstances. The Court adopted doctrines of heightened scrutiny to strike down certain forms of race and gender status regulation dating from the nineteenth century. As we know, doctrines of heightened scrutiny disestablished much of this legislation and prompted state actors to abandon the use of group-based classifications and traditional status-based rationales in most regulatory contexts, while reserving regulatory use of group-based classifications for remedial purposes (a response in keeping with the normative concerns initially prompting heightened scrutiny). But once equal protection doctrine had produced these changes, the Court did not modify doctrines of heightened scrutiny so that courts could detect race or gender bias in the legal culture that heightened scrutiny produced: a legal culture in which state actors regulate by facially neutral means, and for reasons which they assert to be, and generally understand to be, legitimate and nondiscriminatory. Instead, the Court adopted a doctrine of discriminatory purpose for reviewing facially neutral regulation that is explicitly premised on the assumption that courts should defer to the work of coordinate branches of government, and which sanctions facially neutral regulation so long as it is justified in terms that do not sound in discredited forms of status-based reasoning. The Court then began to use doctrines of heightened scrutiny to review and restrict race-based remedial regulation—insisting that affirmative action policies could not rectify "societal discrimination" or promote proportional representation or otherwise engage in what some have called "social engineering." (Note how justifications for constitutional restrictions on affirmative action resemble the nineteenth-century claim that civil rights measures should not legislate "social equality.") Thus, today doctrines of heightened scrutiny function primarily to constrain legislatures from adopting policies designed to reduce race and gender stratification, while doctrines of discriminatory purpose offer only weak constraints on the forms of facially neutral state action that continue to perpetuate the racial and gender stratification of American society.

Just as importantly, this body of equal protection doctrine supplies a language and a perceptual framework that shapes popular debates about race and gender equality. The governing equal protection framework identifies race- and gender-conscious remedies as pernicious "discrimination," while deflecting attention from the many ways that the state continues to regulate the social status of minorities and women, thereby constructing discrimination against minorities and women as a practice of the (distant) past. The social position of minorities and women thus appears to be a legacy of past discrimination—or the product of culture, choice, and ability—while the state's continuing role in shaping the life prospects of minorities and women disappears from view. * * *

It is not difficult for us to imagine alternatives to the current constitutional framework. * * * Today, government rarely classifies by race or gender, but it conducts a "war on drugs," regulates education and residential zoning, responds to "sexual assault" and "domestic violence," and makes policy concerning "child care," "family leave," "child support," and the "welfare" of "single-headed households" in ways that often perpetuate, or aggravate, historic patterns of race and gender inequality. We might construe equal protection guarantees to require heightened scrutiny of the justifications for the design and administration of some or all of these facially neutral policies, yet we do not. As we condemn the ways in which past generations of Americans interpreted the meaning of equal protection, we might also consider how future generations of Americans will judge our own. * * *

Notes and Questions

1. Have the latter day rationales for denying equality that we condemn today been recycled in the modern era? Does Siegel's analysis suggest arguments for critiquing current interpretations of equality?

2. Reflect upon how notions of equality have changed since the passage of the Fourteenth Amendment. What view of equality existed when the Equal Protection Clause was written? Has modern doctrine moved away from the distinctions between equality of social rights, political rights, and civil rights?

3. Is equality perceived as a right today? If so, what does it mean? Peter Westen has suggested that the idea of equality is empty. Peter Westen, *The Empty Idea of Equality*, 95 Harv. L. Rev. 537 (1982) (explaining that the notion of equality must incorporate external values to decide which persons and treatments are alike; equality itself is contentless). If equality is a right that has content, what has been the role of subordinated groups in defining that right? See Celeste Michelle Condit & John Louis Lucaites, *Crafting Equality: America's Anglo–African Word* (1993) (arguing that African–American struggles have given content to the word) and Patricia J. Williams, *The Alchemy of Race and Rights* 163 (1991) (describing rights made alchemically out of nothing.). See also Sumi K. Cho, *Multiple Consciousness and the Diversity Dilemma*, 68 U. Colo. L. Rev. 1035 (1997) (arguing that the Fourteenth Amendment represents a "survival covenant necessitated by a history of genocide, slavery, conquest * * * and other forms of racial subjugations").

4. What competing views of equality exist now? Does a distinction based on social rights still justify racial exclusion today? How has the evolution of ideas about equality occurred? Siegel describes the use of racially neutral language to regulate civil and political rights in the modern era. Does this shift suggest that the use of "neutrality" in adjudicating racial issues is not truly neutral?

SECTION 2.   EVOLVING NOTIONS OF EQUALITY
IN THE WORKPLACE UNDER TITLE VII OF
THE 1964 CIVIL RIGHTS ACT

The meaning of equality is contested in the workplace under equal employment laws such as Title VII of the Civil Rights Act of 1964. Title VII forbids an employer to "fail or refuse to hire or to discharge any individual, or *otherwise to discriminate* against any individual with respect to his compensation, terms, conditions, or privileges of employment," or to "limit, segregate, or classify his employees or applicants for employment *in any way* which would deprive or tend to deprive any individual of employment opportunities or otherwise adversely affect his status as an employee, because of such individual's race, color, religion, sex, or national origin." 42 U.S.C.A. § 2000e–2(a)(1), (2) (emphasis added). [Eds. Notice that in the fair-employment statute just quoted, employers and employees are referred to persistently as male-gendered— *e.g.*, "*his* compensation," "*his* employees," "*his* status." Did Congress intend to exclude female employers and employees from the ambit of the statute? See Jo Freeman, *How "Sex" Got into Title VII: Persistent Opportunism as a Maker of Public Policy*, 9 Law & Ineq. J. 163 (1991).]

The popular interpretation of such laws has been a focus on ending discrimination, rather than an elimination of bias or support for equality. What is missing from a vision of antidiscrimination law that focuses upon discrimination?

STEPHANIE M. WILDMAN
Privilege in the Workplace: The Missing Element in Antidiscrimination Law
in Stephanie M. Wildman with Margalynne Armstrong, Adrienne
D. Davis & Trina Grillo, *Privilege Revealed: How Invisible
Preference Undermines America* 27–30 (1996).*

Whiteness, heterosexuality, and middle class values are all privileged in the workplace, as they are privileged in our culture. * * *

Title VII law has missed the systemic nature of the discrimination it seeks to combat, and, therefore, failed to provide a remedy. In naming sex, race, national origin, color, and religion, Title VII articulates categories to be particularly scrutinized in a search for unfair treatment in the workplace. Case law development under Title VII has focused on discrimination based upon these categories, but not on the power systems that operate within and across each category to discriminate against some and to privilege many. This deficiency in Title VII doctrine, ignoring the operation of privilege, has handicapped antidiscrimination law and doomed it to failure.

Privilege * * * is the systemic conferral of benefit and advantage. Members of a privileged group gain this status by affiliation, conscious or not and chosen or not, to the dominant side of a power system. The Title VII categories identify power systems. At a recent conference, Professor Fran Ansley drew a horizontal line, labeled the power line, and asked participants to imagine where they were situated in terms of race, gender, sexual orientation, and other categories. Everyone knew what she meant by the power line, which divided those attributes that are privileged from those that are not. Those above the power line shared privileged characteristics.

Affiliation with the dominant side of the power line is often defined as merit and worthiness. Characteristics and behaviors shared by those on the dominant side of the power line often delineate the societal norm. For example, white skin color is often called "flesh-colored"; women's hosiery colors labeled "nude" are also a pale tone. Human skin comes in many different colors and shades, but whiteness is privileged to have the definition of human color associated with it. Hiring someone with an English or German accent, who is difficult to understand, may be acceptable; the accent is associated with upper class and European privilege. But hiring someone with a Filipino accent may bring the criticism that the person cannot speak English. A loud, deep voice is privileged in public speaking, such as in law school teaching. One law professor I know was told on her evaluations that she would be a better teacher if she lowered her voice an octave. Women's voices are often described pejoratively as "high and squeaky," but we do not have negative words to describe a low-pitched voice. Even "booming" is complimentary. * * *

Perhaps most important, privilege is not visible to the holder of the privilege; privilege appears as part of the normal fabric of daily life, not as something special. Privilege often bestows a higher comfort level in social interaction; the holder of the privilege need not feel excluded when the norm describes her own actuality. One diversity consultant I know uses this example:

> Suppose you as a human are told to live in the ocean in a society of fish. You find it difficult to breathe. When you complain that oxygen is a problem, the fish would say this is simply the way the world is, and you should adjust. The fish might even feel beleaguered as you gasp. "You are getting tiresome," they say, "can't you think of *anything* besides oxygen?" Water is the only world they know, even though the fish did not create it.

People of color and white women must learn the workplace world of white male supremacy, which they did not create, and master how to live in it, even though it deprives them of the equivalent of oxygen. Well-meaning people who function in that world as white males, like the fish, think that their world is normal, the way things are. For the most part, they do not mean to discriminate or disadvantage.

Notes and Questions

1. Suppose a large company hires exclusively through a network of "people who know people" and therefore chooses a disproportional number of children of current executives and their friends. Is Title VII's language, quoted *supra* at 534, broad enough to include an analysis of invisible systems of privilege and power? Could the statutory language that makes it illegal to "otherwise discriminate" or to "limit ... employees ... in any way" include

an analysis of invisible systems of privilege and power, which operate based on sex, race, national origin, color, or religion to deprive individuals of employment opportunities?

2.   Would it be possible to draft an equal opportunity statute that did not rely on the use of categories? As you read the next case, consider how the treatment of a plaintiff, like Ms. Rogers who exists at the juncture of categories, can be addressed in order to promote equality?

ROGERS v. AMERICAN AIRLINES
527 F. Supp. 229 (S.D.N.Y.1981).

Plaintiff is a black woman who seeks $10,000 damages, injunctive, and declaratory relief against enforcement of a grooming policy of the defendant American Airlines that prohibits employees in certain employment categories from wearing an all-braided hairstyle. Plaintiff has been an American Airlines employee for approximately eleven years, and has been an airport operations agent for over one year. Her duties involve extensive passenger contact, including greeting passengers, issuing boarding passes, and checking luggage. She alleges that the policy violates her rights under * * * Title VII of the Civil Rights Act and under 42 U.S.C.A. § 1981 (1976), in that it discriminates against her as a woman, and more specifically as a black woman. She claims that denial of the right to wear her hair in the "corn row" style intrudes upon her rights and discriminates against her. * * *

The motion [by defendant to dismiss is] meritorious with respect to the statutory claims insofar as they challenge the policy on its face. The statutory bases alleged, Title VII and section 1981, are indistinguishable in the circumstances of this case, and will be considered together. The policy is addressed to both men and women, black and white. Plaintiff's assertion that the policy has practical effect only with respect to women is not supported by any factual allegations. Many men have hair longer than many women. Some men have hair long enough to wear in braids if they choose to do so. Even if the grooming policy imposed different standards for men and women, however, it would not violate Title VII. It follows, therefore, that an even-handed policy that prohibits to both sexes a style more often adopted by members of one sex does not constitute prohibited sex discrimination. This is because this type of regulation has at most a negligible effect on employment opportunity. It does not regulate on the basis of any immutable characteristic of the employees involved. It concerns a matter of relatively low importance in terms of the constitutional interests protected by the Fourteenth Amendment and Title VII, rather than involving fundamental rights such as the right to have children or to marry. The complaint does not state a claim for sex discrimination.

The considerations with respect to plaintiff's race discrimination claim would clearly be the same, except for plaintiff's assertion that the "corn row" style has a special significance for black women. She contends that it "has been, historically, a fashion and style adopted by Black American women, reflective of cultural, historical essence of the Black women in American society." "The style was 'popularized' so to speak, within the larger society, when Cicely Tyson adopted the same for an appearance on a nationally viewed Academy Awards presentation several years ago.... It was and is analogous to the public statement by the late Malcolm X regarding the Afro hair style.... At the bottom line, the completely braided hair style, sometimes referred to as corn rows, has been and continues to be part of the cultural and historical essence of Black American women." "There can be little doubt that, if American adopted a policy which foreclosed Black women/all women from wearing hair styled as an 'Afro/bush,' that policy would have very pointedly racial dynamics and consequences reflecting a vestige of slavery unwilling to die (that is, a master mandate that one wear hair divorced from one's historical and cultural perspective and otherwise consistent with the 'white master' dominated society and preference thereof)."

Plaintiff is entitled to a presumption that her arguments, largely repeated in her affidavit, are true. But the grooming policy applies equally to members of all races, and plaintiff does not allege that an all-braided hair style is worn exclusively or even predominantly by black people. Moreover, it is proper to note that defendants have alleged without contravention that plaintiff first appeared at work in the all-braided hairstyle on or about September 25, 1980, soon after the style had been popularized by a white actress in the film "10.". Plaintiff may be correct that an employer's policy prohibiting the "Afro/bush" style might offend Title VII and section 1981. But if so, this chiefly would be because banning a natural hairstyle would implicate the policies underlying the prohibition of discrimination on the basis of immutable characteristics. In any event, an all-braided hairstyle is a different matter. It is not the product of natural hair growth but of artifice. An all-braided hair style is an "easily changed characteristic," and, even if socioculturally associated with a particular race or nationality, is not an impermissible basis for distinctions in the application of employment practices by an employer. The Fifth Circuit recently upheld, without requiring any showing of business purpose, an employer's policy prohibiting the speaking of any language but English in the workplace, despite the importance of Spanish to the ethnic identity of Mexican Americans. *Garcia v. Gloor*, 618 F.2d 264, 267–69. The court stated that Title VII

> is directed only at specific impermissible bases of discrimination-race, color, religion, sex, or national origin. National origin must not be confused with ethnic or sociocultural traits.... Save for religion, the discriminations on which the Act focuses its laser of prohibition are those that are either beyond the victim's power to alter, or that impose a burden on an employee on one of the prohibited bases....
> "(A) hiring policy that distinguishes on some other ground, such as grooming codes or length of hair, is related more closely to the employer's choice of how to run his business than to equality of employment opportunity."

Id. at 269.

Although the Act may shield "employees' psychological as well as economic fringes" from employer abuse, plaintiff's allegations do not amount to charging American with "a practice of creating a working environment heavily charged with ethnic or racial discrimination," or one "so heavily polluted with discrimination as to destroy completely the emotional and psychological stability of minority group workers...." *Id.* If an even-handed English-only policy that has the effect of prohibiting a Mexican American from speaking Spanish during working hours is valid without a showing of business purpose, the policy at issue here, even if ill-advised, does not offend the law.

Moreover, the airline did not require plaintiff to restyle her hair. It suggested that she could wear her hair as she liked while off duty, and permitted her to pull her hair into a bun and wrap a hairpiece around the bun during working hours. * * * Plaintiff has done this, but alleges that the hairpiece has caused her severe headaches. A larger hairpiece would seem in order. But even if any hairpiece would cause such discomfort, the policy does not offend a substantial interest.

Plaintiff has failed to allege sufficient facts to require defendants to demonstrate that the policy has a bona fide business purpose. In this regard, however, plaintiff does not dispute defendant's assertion that the policy was adopted in order to help American project a conservative and business-like image, a consideration recognized as a bona fide business purpose. Rather she objects to its impact with respect to the "corn row" style, an impact not protected against by Title VII or section 1981.

Plaintiff also asserts in her complaint that the regulation has been applied in an uneven and discriminatory manner. She claims that white women in particular have been permitted to wear pony tails and shag cuts. She goes on to claim, in fact, that some black women are permitted to wear the same hairstyle that she has been prohibited from wearing. These claims seriously undercut her assertion that the policy discriminates against women, and her claim that it discriminates against black women in particular. Conceivably, however, the complaint could be construed as alleging that the policy has been applied in a discriminatory manner against plaintiff because she is black by some representative of the defendant. * * *

This action is dismissed, except for plaintiff's claim of discriminatory treatment in the application of the grooming policy. * * *

So ordered.

Notes and Questions

1. Does an employment policy directed at braided hair relate to an "employer's choice of how to run his business" rather than to equal treatment in the workplace?

2. Consider Paulette M. Caldwell, *A Hair Piece: Perspectives on the Intersection of Race and Gender*, 1991 Duke L.J. 365, 365–66*:

> I want to know my hair again, to own it, to delight in it again, to recall my earliest mirrored reflection when there was no beginning and I first knew that the person who laughed at me and cried with me and stuck out her tongue at me was me. I want to know my hair again, the way I knew it before I knew that my hair is me, before I lost the right to

me, before I knew that the burden of beauty—or lack of it—for an entire race of people could be tied up with my hair and me.

I want to know my hair again, the way I knew it before I knew Sambo and Dick, Buckwheat and Jane, Prissy and Miz Scarlett. Before I knew that my hair could be wrong—the wrong color, the wrong texture, the wrong amount of curl or straight. Before hot combs and thick grease and smelly-burning lye, all guaranteed to transform me, to silken the coarse, resistent wool that represents me. I want to know once more the time before I denatured, denuded, denigrated, and denied my hair and me, before I knew enough to worry about edges and kitchens and burrows and knots, when I was still a friend of water—the rain's dancing drops of water, a swimming hole's splashing water, a hot, muggy day's misty invisible water, my own salty, sweaty, perspiring water.

When will I cherish my hair again, the way my grandmother cherished it, when fascinated by its beauty, with hands carrying centuries-old secrets of adornment and craftswomanship, she plaited it, twisted it, cornrowed it, finger-curled it, olive-oiled it, on the growing moon cut and shaped it, and wove it like fine strands of gold inlaid with semiprecious stones, coral and ivory, telling with my hair a lost-found story of the people she carried inside her?

Mostly, I want to love my hair the way I loved hers, when as granddaughter among grandsons I stood on a chair in her room—her kitchen-bed-living-dining room—and she let me know her hair, when I combed and patted it from the crown of her head to the place where her neck folded into her shoulders, caressing steel-gray strands that framed her forehead before falling into the soft, white, cottony temples at the border of her cheekbones. * * *

I discovered *Rogers* while reading a newspaper article describing the actual or threatened firing of several black women in metropolitan Washington, D.C. solely for wearing braided hairstyles. The article referred to *Rogers* but actually focused on the case of Cheryl Tatum, who was fired from her job as a restaurant cashier in a Hyatt Hotel under a company policy that prohibited "extreme and unusual hairstyles."

The newspaper description of the Hyatt's grooming policy conjured up an image of a ludicrous and outlandishly-coiffed Cheryl Tatum, one clearly bent on exceeding the bounds of workplace taste and discipline. But the picture that accompanied the article revealed a young, attractive black woman whose hair fell neatly to her shoulders in an all-American, common, everyday pageboy style, distinguished only by the presence of tiny braids in lieu of single strands of hair.

Whether motivated by politics, ethnic pride, health, or vanity, I was outraged by the idea that an employer could regulate or force me to explain something as personal and private as the way that I groom my hair. I resented the implication that I could not be trusted to choose standards appropriate for the workplace and that my right to work could be conditioned on my disassociation with my race, gender, and culture. Mostly, I marveled with sadness that something as simple as a black woman's hair continues to threaten the social, political, and economic fabric of American life. * * *

Hair seems to be such a little thing. Yet it is the little things, the small everyday realities of life, that reveal the deepest meanings and values of a culture, give legal theory its grounding, and test its legitimacy. * * *

My initial outrage notwithstanding, *Rogers* is an unremarkable decision. Courts generally protect employer-mandated hair and dress codes, and they often accord the greatest deference to codes that classify individuals on the basis of socially-conditioned rather than biological differences. And although *Rogers* rests on one line of authority without acknowledging the existence of another, grooming codes are governed by decisional law that clearly lacks conceptual coherence. All in all, such cases are generally considered only marginally significant in the battle to secure equal employment rights.

But *Rogers* is regrettably unremarkable in an important respect. It rests on suppositions that are deeply imbedded in American culture— assumptions so entrenched and so necessary to the maintenance of interlocking, interdependent structures of domination that their mythological bases and political functions have become invisible, especially to those to whom their existence is most detrimental. *Rogers* proceeds from the premise that, although racism and sexism share much in common, they are nonetheless fundamentally unrelated phenomena—a proposition proved false by history and contemporary reality. Racism and sexism are interlocking, mutually-reinforcing components of a system of dominance rooted in patriarchy. No significant and lasting progress in combatting either can be made until this interdependent aspect of their relation is acknowledged, and until the perspectives gained from considering their interaction are reflected in legal theory and public policy.

3.   Does the comparison implicitly made when equality is at issue contribute to the failure of legal analysis in achieving equality? Consider this critique of the comparison mode:

The comparison mode * * * [needed to prove discrimination] veils the operation of privilege. Many cases involving discrimination based on gender, race, and other Title VII categories will never be brought because the Title VII analysis has been based on a comparison mode. * * * The comparison mode has been used by an individual claiming disparate, disadvantaging treatment by comparing the treatment of the individual to treatment received by those in another social group. For example, a woman barred from the practice of law claimed that men could practice law and, therefore, she should be admitted to practice. * * *

[Similarly] in employment discrimination cases, a plaintiff claiming discrimination based on sex must show how men were treated differently in the workplace. For example, one court has said, "It is significant to note that instances of complained of sexual conduct that prove equally offensive to male and female workers would not support a Title VII sexual harassment charge because both men and women were accorded like treatment." Yet offensive sexual conduct in the workplace supports a system of subordination of women by men that contravenes the goal of equal employment embodied in Title VII.

Privileging of whiteness in the workplace can occur even when all participants are African American. This privileging will remain invisible under the comparison mode. One litigator I know described a case that settled in which the African–American female plaintiff sued for discrimination under Title VII. Her supervisor was a white woman, but the other co-workers in her department were also African–American women.

The plaintiff was a large, dark, and loud woman. The supervisor was small and demure. The plaintiff could not prove discrimination under Title VII, which would compare her situation to others. The evidence of other African–American women in the workplace would dispel her claim of race discrimination. That she was the "wrong kind" of African–American woman, because of societal preference for certain characteristics, could not be remedied under the statutory framework without an analysis of privilege. * * *

Stephanie M. Wildman, *Privilege in the Workplace: The Missing Element in Antidiscrimination Law*, in Stephanie M. Wildman with Margalynne Armstrong, Adrienne D. Davis & Trina Grillo, *Privilege Revealed: How Invisible Preference Undermines America* 35–36 (1996).* Surely, Title VII's drafters did not intend to leave out discrimination against women of color from the reach of the statute. Yet the comparison logic renders women of color invisible. See Elizabeth M. Iglesias, *Structures of Subordination:Women of Color at the Intersection of Title VII and the NLRA. Not!*, 28 Harv. C.R.-C.L. L. Rev. 395 (1993).

4. Does an employer English-only policy provide useful precedent? Consider the next case.

GARCIA v. SPUN STEAK COMPANY

998 F.2d 1480 (9th Cir.1993).

O'SCANNLAIN, CIRCUIT JUDGE.

We are called upon to decide whether an employer violates Title VII of the Civil Rights Act of 1964 in requiring its bilingual workers to speak only English while working on the job.

Spun Steak Company ("Spun Steak") is a California corporation that produces poultry and meat products in South San Francisco for wholesale distribution. Spun Steak employs thirty-three workers, twenty-four of whom are Spanish-speaking. Virtually all of the Spanish-speaking employees are Hispanic. While two employees speak no English, the others have varying degrees of proficiency in English. Spun Steak has never required job applicants to speak or to understand English as a condition of employment.

Approximately two-thirds of Spun Steak's employees are production line workers or otherwise involved in the production process. Appellees García and Buitrago are production line workers; they stand before a conveyor belt, remove poultry or other meat products from the belt and place the product into cases or trays for resale. Their work is done individually. Both García and Buitrago are fully bilingual, speaking both English and Spanish.

Appellee Local 115, United Food and Commercial Workers International Union, AFL–CIO ("Local 115"), is the collective bargaining agent representing the employees at Spun Steak.

* Copyright © 1996 by New York University Press. Used by permission.

Prior to September 1990, these Spun Steak employees spoke Spanish freely to their co-workers during work hours. After receiving complaints that some workers were using their bilingual capabilities to harass and to insult other workers in a language they could not understand, Spun Steak began to investigate the possibility of requiring its employees to speak only English in the workplace. Specifically, Spun Steak received complaints that García and Buitrago made derogatory, racist comments in Spanish about two co-workers, one of whom is African American and the other Chinese American.

The company's president, Kenneth Bertelson, concluded that an English-only rule would promote racial harmony in the workplace. In addition, he concluded that the English-only rule would enhance worker safety because some employees who did not understand Spanish claimed that the use of Spanish distracted them while they were operating machinery, and would enhance product quality because the U.S.D.A. inspector in the plant spoke only English and thus could not understand if a product-related concern was raised in Spanish. Accordingly, the following rule was adopted:

[I]t is hereafter the policy of this Company that only English will be spoken in connection with work. During lunch, breaks, and employees' own time, they are obviously free to speak Spanish if they wish. However, we urge all of you not to use your fluency in Spanish in a fashion which may lead other employees to suffer humiliation.

In addition to the English-only policy, Spun Steak adopted a rule forbidding offensive racial, sexual, or personal remarks of any kind.

It is unclear from the record whether Spun Steak strictly enforced the English-only rule. According to the plaintiffs-appellees, some workers continued to speak Spanish without incident. Spun Steak issued written exceptions to the policy allowing its clean-up crew to speak Spanish, allowing its foreman to speak Spanish, and authorizing certain workers to speak Spanish to the foreman at the foreman's discretion. One of the two employees who speak only Spanish is a member of the clean-up crew and thus is unaffected by the policy.

In November 1990, García and Buitrago received warning letters for speaking Spanish during working hours. For approximately two months thereafter, they were not permitted to work next to each other. Local 115 protested the English-only policy and requested that it be rescinded but to no avail.

On May 6, 1991, García, Buitrago, and Local 115 filed charges of discrimination against Spun Steak with the U.S. Equal Employment Opportunity Commission ("EEOC"). The EEOC conducted an investigation and determined that "there is reasonable cause to believe [Spun Steak] violated Title VII of the Civil Rights Act of 1964, as amended, with respect to its adoption of an English-only rule and with respect to retaliation when [García, Buitrago, and Local 115] complained."

García, Buitrago, and Local 115, on behalf of all Spanish-speaking employees of Spun Steak, (collectively, "the Spanish-speaking employees") filed suit, alleging that the English-only policy violated Title VII.

On September 6, 1991, the parties filed cross-motions for summary judgment. The district court denied Spun Steak's motion and granted the Spanish-speaking employees' motion for summary judgment, concluding that the English-only policy disparately impacted Hispanic workers without sufficient business justification, and thus violated Title VII.

[The court decided that Local 115 had standing to sue on behalf of the Spanish-speaking employees at Spun Steak.]* * * It is well-settled that Title VII is concerned not only with intentional discrimination, but also with employment practices and policies that lead to disparities in the treatment of classes of workers. See, *e.g.*, *Griggs v. Duke Power Co.*, 401 U.S. 424, 430–31 (1971). Thus, a plaintiff alleging discrimination under Title VII may proceed under two theories of liability: disparate treatment or disparate impact. While the disparate treatment theory requires proof of discriminatory intent, intent is irrelevant to a disparate impact theory. * * *

The Spanish-speaking employees do not contend that Spun Steak intentionally discriminated against them in enacting the English-only policy. Rather, they contend that the policy had a discriminatory impact on them because it imposes a burdensome term or condition of employment exclusively upon Hispanic workers and denies them a privilege of employment that non-Spanish-speaking workers enjoy. Because their claim focuses on disparities in the terms, conditions, and privileges of employment, and not on barriers to hiring or promotion, it is outside the mainstream of disparate impact cases decided thus far. * * *

[The Court concludes that "a disparate impact claim may be based upon a challenge to a practice or policy that has a significant adverse impact on the 'terms, conditions, or privileges' of the employment of a protected group under section 703(a)(1)."]

To make out a prima facie case of discriminatory impact, a plaintiff must identify a specific, seemingly neutral practice or policy that has a significantly adverse impact on persons of a protected class. If the prima facie case is established, the burden shifts to the employer to "demonstrate that the challenged practice is job related for the position in question and consistent with business necessity." 42 U.S.C.A. § 2000e–2(k)(1)(A) (Supp.1992). In this case, the district court granted summary judgment in favor of the Spanish-speaking employees, concluding that, as a matter of law, the employees had made out the prima facie case and the justifications offered by the employer were inadequate. * * *

It is beyond dispute that, in this case, if the English-only policy causes any adverse effects, those effects will be suffered disproportionately by those of Hispanic origin. The vast majority of those workers at Spun Steak who speak a language other than English—and virtually all those employees for whom English is not a first language—are Hispanic. It is of no consequence that not all Hispanic employees of Spun Steak speak Spanish; nor is it relevant that some non-Hispanic workers may speak Spanish. If the adverse effects are proved, it is enough under Title VII that Hispanics are disproportionately impacted.

The crux of the dispute between Spun Steak and the Spanish-speaking employees, however, is not over whether Hispanic workers will disproportionately bear any adverse effects of the policy; rather, the dispute centers on whether the policy causes any adverse effects at all, and if it does, whether the effects are significant. The Spanish-speaking employees argue that the policy adversely affects them in the following ways: (1) it denies them the ability to express their cultural heritage on the job; (2) it denies them a privilege of employment that is enjoyed by monolingual speakers of English; and (3) it creates an atmosphere of inferiority, isolation, and intimidation. We discuss each of these contentions in turn.

The employees argue that denying them the ability to speak Spanish on the job denies them the right to cultural expression. It cannot be gainsaid that an individual's primary language can be an important link to his ethnic culture and identity. Title VII, however, does not protect the ability of workers to express their cultural heritage at the workplace. Title VII is concerned only with disparities in the treatment of workers; it does not confer substantive privileges. See, e.g., *Garcia v. Gloor*, 618 F.2d 264, 269 (5th Cir.1980), *cert.* denied, 449 U.S. 1113 (1981). It is axiomatic that an employee must often sacrifice individual self-expression during working hours. Just as a private employer is not required to allow other types of self-expression, there is nothing in Title VII which requires an employer to allow employees to express their cultural identity.

Next, the Spanish-speaking employees argue that the English-only policy has a disparate impact on them because it deprives them of a privilege given by the employer to native-English speakers: the ability to converse on the job in the language with which they feel most comfortable. It is undisputed that Spun Steak allows its employees to converse on the job. The ability to converse—especially to make small talk—is a privilege of employment, and may in fact be a significant privilege of employment in an assembly-line job. It is inaccurate, however, to describe the privilege as broadly as the Spanish-speaking employees urge us to do.

The employees have attempted to define the privilege as the ability to speak in the language of their choice. A privilege, however, is by definition given at the employer's discretion; an employer has the right to define its contours. Thus, an employer may allow employees to converse on the job, but only during certain times of the day or during the performance of certain tasks. The employer may proscribe certain topics as inappropriate during working hours or may even forbid the use of certain words, such as profanity.

Here, as is its prerogative, the employer has defined the privilege narrowly. When the privilege is defined at its narrowest (as merely the ability to speak on the job), we cannot conclude that those employees fluent in both English and Spanish are adversely impacted by the policy. Because they are able to speak English, bilingual employees can engage in conversation on the job. It is axiomatic that "the language a person who is multi-lingual elects to speak at a particular time is ... a matter of choice." *Garcia*, 618 F.2d at 270. The bilingual employee can readily comply with the English-only rule and still enjoy the privilege of speaking on the job. "There is no disparate impact" with respect to a privilege of employment "if the rule is one that the affected employee can readily observe and nonobservance is a matter of individual preference."

This analysis is consistent with our decision in *Jurado v. Eleven–Fifty Corporation*, 813 F.2d 1406, 1412 (9th Cir.1987). In *Jurado*, a bilingual disc jockey was fired for disobeying a rule forbidding him from using an occasional Spanish word or phrase on the air. We concluded that Jurado's disparate impact claim failed "because Jurado was fluently bilingual and could easily comply with the order" and thus could not have been adversely affected.

The Spanish-speaking employees argue that fully bilingual employees are hampered in the enjoyment of the privilege because for them, switching from one language to another is not fully volitional. Whether a bilingual speaker can control which language is used in a given circumstance is a factual issue that cannot be resolved at the summary judgment stage. However, we fail to see the relevance of the assertion, even assuming that it can be proved. Title VII is not meant to protect against rules that merely inconvenience some employees, even if the inconvenience falls regularly on a protected class. Rather, Title VII protects against only those policies that have a significant impact. The fact that an employee may have to catch himself or herself from occasionally slipping into Spanish does not impose a burden significant enough to amount to the denial of equal opportunity. This is not a case in which the employees have alleged that the company is enforcing the policy in such a way as to impose penalties for minor slips of the tongue. The fact that a bilingual employee may, on occasion, unconsciously substitute a Spanish word in the place of an English one does not override our conclusion that the bilingual employee can easily comply with the rule. In short, we conclude that a bilingual employee is not denied a privilege of employment by the English-only policy.

By contrast, non-English speakers cannot enjoy the privilege of conversing on the job if conversation is limited to a language they cannot speak. As applied "[t]o a person who speaks only one tongue or to a person who has difficulty using another language than the one spoken in his home," an English-only rule might well have an adverse impact. *Garcia*, 618 F.2d at 270. * * *

Finally, the Spanish-speaking employees argue that the policy creates an atmosphere of inferiority, isolation, and intimidation. Under this theory, the employees do not assert that the policy directly affects a term, condition, or privilege of employment. Instead, the argument must be that the policy causes the work environment to become infused with ethnic tensions. The tense environment, the argument goes, itself amounts to a condition of employment.

The Supreme Court in *Meritor Savings Bank v. Vinson*, 477 U.S. at 66, held that an abusive work environment may, in some circumstances, amount to a condition of employment giving rise to a violation of Title VII. The Court quoted with approval the decision in *Rogers v. EEOC*, 454 F.2d 234, 238 (5th Cir.1971):

[T]he phrase "terms, conditions or privileges of employment" in [Title VII] is an expansive concept which sweeps within its protective ambit the practice of creating a working environment heavily charged with ethnic or racial discrimination.... One can readily envision working environments so heavily polluted with discrimination as to destroy completely the emotional and psychological stability of minority group workers.

Although *Vinson* is a sexual harassment case in which the individual incidents involved behavior that was arguably intentionally discriminatory, its rationale applies equally to cases in which seemingly neutral policies of a company infuse the atmosphere of the workplace with discrimination. The *Vinson* Court emphasized, however, that discriminatory practices must be pervasive before an employee has a Title VII claim under a hostile environment theory.

Here, the employees urge us to adopt a *per se* rule that English-only policies always infect the working environment to such a degree as to amount to a hostile or abusive work environment. This we cannot do. Whether a working environment is infused with discrimination is a factual question, one for which a *per se* rule is particularly inappropriate. The dynamics of an individual workplace are enormously complex; we cannot conclude, as a matter of law, that the introduction of an English-only policy, in every workplace, will always have the same effect.

The Spanish-speaking employees in this case have presented no evidence other than conclusory statements that the policy has contributed to an atmosphere of "isolation, inferiority or intimidation." The bilingual employees are able to comply with the rule, and there is no evidence to show that the atmosphere at Spun Steak in general is infused with hostility toward Hispanic workers. Indeed, there is substantial evidence in the record demonstrating that the policy was enacted to prevent the employees from intentionally using their fluency in Spanish to isolate and to intimidate members of other ethnic groups. In light of the specific factual context of this case, we conclude that the bilingual employees have not raised a genuine issue of material fact that the effect is so pronounced as to amount to a hostile environment.

We do not foreclose the prospect that in some circumstances English-only rules can exacerbate existing tensions, or, when combined with other discriminatory behavior, contribute to an overall environment of discrimination. Likewise, we can envision a case in which such rules are enforced in such a draconian manner that the enforcement itself amounts to harassment. In evaluating such a claim, however, a court must look to the totality of the circumstances in the particular factual context in which the claim arises.

In holding that the enactment of an English-only while working policy does not inexorably lead to an abusive environment for those whose primary language is not English, we reach a conclusion opposite to the EEOC's long standing position. The EEOC Guidelines provide that an employee meets the *prima facie* case in a disparate impact cause of action merely by proving the existence of the English-only policy. See 29 C.F.R. § 1606.7(a) & (b) (1991). Under the EEOC's scheme, an employer must always provide a business justification for such a rule. The EEOC enacted this scheme in part because of its conclusion that English-only rules may "create an atmosphere of inferiority, isolation and intimidation based on national origin which could result in a discriminatory working environment." 29 C.F.R. § 1606.7(a).

We do not reject the English-only rule Guideline lightly. We recognize that "as an administrative interpretation of the Act by the enforcing agency, these Guidelines ... constitute a body of experience and informed judgment to which courts and litigants may properly resort for guidance." *Meritor*, 477 U.S. at 65. But we are not bound by the Guidelines. We will not defer to "an administrative construction of a statute where there are 'compelling indications that it is wrong.'"

We have been impressed by Judge Rubin's pre-Guidelines analysis for the Fifth Circuit in *Garcia*, which we follow today. Nothing in the plain language of section 703(a)(1) supports EEOC's English-only rule Guideline. * * * It is clear that Congress intended a balance to be struck in preventing discrimination and preserving the independence of the employer. In striking that balance, the Supreme Court has held that a plaintiff in a disparate impact case must prove the alleged discriminatory effect before the burden shifts to the employer. The EEOC Guideline at issue here contravenes that policy by presuming that an English-only policy has a disparate impact in the absence of proof. We are not aware of, nor has counsel shown us, anything in the legislative history to Title VII that indicates that English-only policies are to be presumed discriminatory. Indeed, nowhere in the legislative history is there a discussion of English-only policies at all. * * *

In sum, we conclude that the bilingual employees have not made out a *prima facie* case and that Spun Steak has not violated Title VII in adopting an English-only rule as to them. Thus, we reverse the grant of summary judgment in favor of García, Buitrago, and Local 115 to the extent it represents the bilingual employees, and remand with instructions to grant summary judgment in favor of Spun Steak on their claims. * * *

Reversed and Remanded.

BOOCHEVER, CIRCUIT JUDGE, dissenting in part:

I agree with most of the majority's carefully crafted opinion. I dissent, however, from the majority's rejection of the EEOC guidelines. The guidelines provide that an employee establishes a *prima facie* case in a disparate impact claim by proving the existence of an English-only policy, thereby shifting the burden to the employer to show a business necessity for the rule. See 29 C.F.R. § 1606.7(b) (1991) ("An employer may have a rule requiring that employees speak only in English at certain times where the employer can show that the rule is justified by business necessity."). I would defer to the Commission's expertise in construing the Act, by virtue of which it concluded that English-only rules may "create an atmosphere of inferiority, isolation and intimidation based on national origin which could result in a discriminatory working environment." *Id.* § 1606.7(a).

As the majority indicates, proof of such an effect of English-only rules requires analysis of subjective factors. It is hard to envision how the burden of proving such an effect would be met other than by conclusory self-serving statements of the Spanish-speaking employees or possibly by expert testimony of psychologists. The difficulty of meeting such a burden may well have been one of the reasons for the promulgation of the guideline. On the other hand, it should not be difficult for an employer to give specific reasons for the policy, such as the safety reasons advanced in this case.

It is true that EEOC regulations are entitled to somewhat less weight than those promulgated by an agency with Congressionally delegated rulemaking authority. Nevertheless, the EEOC guideline is entitled to "great deference" in the absence of "compelling indications that it is wrong." *Espinoza v. Farah Mfg. Co.*, 414 U.S. 86, 94–95 (1973). While one may reasonably differ with the EEOC's position as a matter of policy, I can find no such "compelling indications" in this case. The lack of directly supporting language in § 703(a)(1) or the legislative history of Title VII, relied on by the majority, does not in my opinion make the guideline "inconsistent with an obvious congressional intent not to reach the employment practice in question." *Id.*

I conclude that if appropriate deference is given to the administrative interpretation of the Act, we should follow the guideline and uphold the district court's decision that a *prima facie* case was established. I believe, however, that triable issues were presented whether Spun Steak established a business justification for the rule, and I would remand for trial of that issue.

Notes and Questions

1. Who has the better of the arguments concerning the EEOC guidelines, the majority or the dissent?

2. The United States currently contains the fourth or fifth largest Spanish-speaking population in the world. Estimates of the Latino/a population in the United States range between 18 million and 30 million. Early in the next millenium, perhaps as soon as 2005, Latinos/as will be the largest ethnic minority group in the country. Juan F. Perea, *English-Only Rules and the Right to Speak One's Primary Language in the Workplace*, 23 U. Mich. J.L. Ref. 265, 317 (1990) (arguing that English-only rules have an exclusive adverse impact on language minority groups, which supports an analysis based on disparate treatment).

In the early 1920s, Robert Meyer was convicted of violating a Nebraska statute forbidding the teaching of any language other than English to students who had not passed the eighth grade. Meyer, an instructor at the Zion Evangelical Lutheran Congregation's parochial school, had read biblical stories in the German language to a ten-year-old student. "In *Meyer v. Nebraska*, 262 U.S. 390 (1923), the United States Supreme Court reversed, finding that the statute interfered with the profession of modern language teachers, with the acquisition of knowledge by students, and with the prerogative of parents to control the education of their children. The Court concluded that the statute violated the due process clause of the Fourteenth Amendment, noting that 'the individual has certain fundamental rights which must be respected. The protection of the Constitution extends to all, to those who speak other languages as well as to those born with English on the tongue.' " *Id.* at 365–66.

Should the Court's recognition of a "fundamental right' " to language influence an employee's right to speak his primary language in the workplace?

3. What effect does an English-only rule have on those for whom English is not a native language? Why might those whose first language is English care whether conversations occur in other languages? Juan Perea comments:

> In his recent book, *Latinos* [: *A Biography of the People* (1992)], Earl Shorris poignantly describes Bienvenida Petilón, a Jewish Latino immigrant, who clings to her language and culture "as if they were life itself." When Bienvenida dies, it is "not of illness, but of English." Bienvenida dies of English when she is confined to a nursing home where no one speaks Spanish, an environment in which she cannot communicate and in which no one cares about her language and culture.

> "Death by English" is a death of the spirit, the slow death that occurs when one's own identity is replaced, reconfigured, overwhelmed, or rejected by a more powerful, dominant identity not one's own. For Latinos, illness by English of varying degree, even death by English, is a common affliction, without known cure. It may be identified, however, by some of its symptoms.

> The mere sound of Spanish offends and frightens many English-only speakers, who sense in the language a loss of control over what they regard as "their" country. Spanish also frightens many Latinos, for it proclaims their identity as Latinos, for all to hear. The Latino's fear is rational. Spanish may subject Latinos to the harsh price of difference in the United States: the loss of a job, instant scapegoating, and identification as an outsider. Giving in to this fear and denying one's own identity as a Latino is, perhaps, to begin to die of English.

> Latino invisibility is, I believe, the principal cause of illness by English. When I write of Latino invisibility, I mean a relative lack of positive public identity and legitimacy. I believe invisibility in this sense is created in several ways. Sometimes we are rendered invisible through the absence of public recognition and portrayal. Sometimes we are silenced through prohibitions on the use of Spanish. Sometimes we are rendered politically invisible, or nearly invisible, through the attribution of foreignness, what I shall call "symbolic deportation." I do not claim that Latinos are the only American people rendered invisible in America. In many respects the processes of invisibility have more general application.

Juan F. Perea, *Los Olvidados: On the Making of Invisible People*, 70 N.Y.U. L. Rev. 965, 965–66 (1995).* See also Christopher David Ruiz Cameron, *How the García Cousins Lost Their Accents: Understanding the Language of Title VII Decisions Approving English–Only Rules as the Product of Racial Dualism, Latino Invisibility, and Legal Indeterminacy*, 85 Calif. L. Rev. 1347 (1997) (demonstrating how the majority culture's ignorance of Spanish, as well as the perceptions of Latinos/as in subordinate roles, render Latinos/as invisible and their claims illegitimate).

4. Why does the cultural definition of merit not reward those who are bi-or tri-lingual? "What if we required knowledge of a non-English language as part of [law school] graduation requirements, so students could serve a wider client base? Who would then be the experts sought after in study groups?" Stephanie M. Wildman, *Reflections on Whiteness and Latina/o Critical Theory*, 2 Harv. Latino L. Rev. 307, 315 (1997).

5. *Griggs v. Duke Power*, cited by the court for the notion that intent to discriminate need not be proven under Title VII, held the act prohibited an employer from requiring a high school diploma or passing of a standardized general intelligence test as a condition of employment, where neither criteria was significantly related to job performance. These job requirements had operated to disqualify African Americans at a substantially higher rate than white job-seekers, and "the jobs in question formerly had been filled only by white employees as part of a long-standing practice of giving preference to whites." 401 U.S. at 426. See also Charles R. Lawrence III, *The Id, the Ego, and Equal Protection: Reckoning with Unconscious Racism*, 39 Stan. L. Rev. 317 (1987) (criticizing the intent requirement for proof of discrimination under the Equal Protection Clause).

6. The *Garcia v. Spun Steak* court uses *Rogers* to support its reasoning. *Rogers* used another English-only case, *Garcia v. Gloor* to justify its holding. Consider Paulette Caldwell's view:

> To narrow the concept of race further—and, therefore, racism and the scope of legal protection against it—the *Rogers* court likened the plaintiff's claim to ethnic identity in the wearing of braids to identity claims based on the use of languages other than English. The court sought refuge in *Garcia v. Gloor*, a decision that upheld the general right of employers to prohibit the speaking of any language other than English in the workplace without requiring employers to articulate a business justification for the prohibition. By excising the cultural component of racial or ethnic identity, the court reinforces the view of a homogenous, unicultural society, and pits blacks and other groups against each other in a battle over minimal deviations from cultural norms. Black women cannot wear their hair in braids because Hispanics cannot speak Spanish at work. The court cedes to private employers the power of family patriarchs to enforce a numbing sameness, based exclusively on the employers' whim, without the obligation to provide a connection to work performance or business need, and thus deprives employees of the right to be judged on ability rather than on image or sound.

> Like *Rogers*, the *Garcia* case is a fascinating study of the extent to which antidiscrimination law perpetuates the allocation to employers of a kind of property right in the persons of women and minority employees. Out of business necessity, thirty-one of the thirty-nine employees of the company in *Garcia* were Hispanic because the population in the area served by the business was seventy-five percent Hispanic. Most of the employees were bilingual because many of the company's customers wanted to be waited on by a Spanish-speaking person. The employer prohibited employees from speaking Spanish on the job unless they were speaking to Spanish-speaking customers. Hector García, a Mexican–

American employee, was fired for responding in Spanish to a question from another Mexican–American employee about the availability of an item requested by a customer. The use of Spanish is thus a virtue when the employer benefits, a vice when the employee does.

Paulette M. Caldwell, *A Hair Piece: Perspectives on the Intersection of Race and Gender*, 1991 Duke L.J. 365, 380–381.*

7.   English-only rules lead logically to the question, "If everyone may be forced to speak English, without violating an equality principle, then shouldn't discrimination based on accent be illegal?"

MARI J. MATSUDA

*Voices of America: Accent, Antidiscrimination Law, and
a Jurisprudence For the Last Reconstruction*
100 Yale L.J. 1329, 1329–1404 (1991).**

Every person who reads this article has an accent. Your accent carries the story of who you are—who first held you and talked to you when you were a child, where you have lived, your age, the schools you attended, the languages you know, your ethnicity, whom you admire, your loyalties, your profession, your class position: Traces of your life and identity are woven into your pronunciation, your phrasing, your choice of words. Your self is inseparable from your accent. Someone who tells you they don't like the way you speak is quite likely telling you that they don't like you.

Every person has an accent—even those who do not communicate with voice. The deaf have an accent in the way they use American Sign Language. An observer familiar with deaf culture can identify Black signing, upper-class signing, "hearie" signing, regional signing, teenage signing, "heavy" signing, and signing associated with certain residential schools. Every person has an accent. Yet, in ordinary usage, we say a person "has an accent" to mark difference from some unstated norm of non-accent, as though only some foreign few have accents.

* * *

Horatio Alger gained fame writing about men like Manuel Fragante, who faced adversity with resilience, self-reliance, intelligence, and hard work. While Fragante shares those traits with Alger's heroes, his story ends in Title VII litigation, not in the triumphant recognition of his talents by the free market.

In 1981 Manuel Fragante took a civil service examination along with over 700 other applicants. He is an intelligent and educated man, and he was not surprised when he received the highest score of all applicants who took the test. Fragante was ranked first on the list of eligibles, but, after a brief interview, he was turned down for the job of clerk in the Division of Motor Vehicles. When he asked why, he learned that he was rejected because of his Filipino accent. Manuel Fragante, combat veteran of two wars and true believer in the rhetoric of equality, promptly contacted a Filipino American state legislator, who in turn recommended that Fragante visit the run-down office of a neighborhood public interest law firm.

The lawyers advised Mr. Fragante that Title VII litigation is costly and difficult, that money damages in a case such as his are often nominal, and that although he was treated unfairly, discrimination is difficult to prove. Mr. Fragante listened carefully and replied that his case was a strong one, and that discrimination is not allowed under American law. He was prepared for a fight, even a long and bitter one, in order to show the truth about his case.

The lawyers were impressed. Here was an articulate and passionate plaintiff, unquestionably qualified in every respect for the job, turned down because of his accent. The issues were clean. The client was committed. The lawyers realized they would never get another plaintiff as good as Mr. Fragante to test the application of Title VII to accent cases. They agreed to fight the case to the end. And so they did, losing at every level before the federal courts.

Manuel Fragante was born and raised in the Philippines, during a time of heavy American influence there. He is an educated man, with a university degree in law. The Philippines is a land of many languages, including Ilocano, Ilongo, Visayan, Cebuano Visayan, Tagalog, and English—the last four of which Mr. Fragante speaks. In part because of this diversity, and in part because of the influence of the United States, English is the language used in many Filipino schools, universities, businesses, and media. All of Manuel Fragante's schooling was in English, and his command of the English language—given the strict, no-nonsense, prewar style of his early teachers—exceeds that of many Americans.

Manuel Fragante loves two countries: the Philippines, his birth home, and the United States, his adopted home. When Japan occupied the Philippine Islands, Fragante was one of thousands of young men who took to the hills to join the resistance. As a guerilla fighter, he swore to outlast the occupation, predicting the eventual liberation of his homeland. He fought for three years, surviving several bouts of malaria. After the war, like veterans of many nations of that time, Fragante started a family, furthered his education, and made modest economic gains as he continued to work in the military and in civilian enterprises. He believed in self-reliance, hard work, and respect for authority—the kind of ideas questioned and ridiculed by the generation that followed his. Fragante's loyalty to the United States, liberator of the Philippines, was solid. He volunteered from Manila to serve on the American side for a twenty-three-month tour of duty in the Vietnam War, and he continued military training in places like Fort Harrison, Indiana, and Fort Leavenworth, Kansas. He is particularly proud of his performance in U.S. military schools, where his intellectual skills frequently put him ahead of American officers in test scores.

In all his years of service to the American military, he says, no one ever complained of his accent. His military superiors repeatedly rated his

English language ability "excellent." His acceptance in the military made him think more and more often of emigrating. His daughter was already settled in Honolulu. As he approached retirement age, he moved to Hawaii and became a naturalized citizen. Having worked all his life, he could not imagine remaining idle. He knew enough about American prejudice to guess that businesses might not welcome an older immigrant as an employee. The civil service system, with its tests and constant demand for clerical workers, seemed a better prospect.

The Division of Motor Vehicles (DMV) of the City and County of Honolulu is much like similar departments all over the United States. Clerks dispense forms, administer tests, and take pictures for driver's licenses. Lines of waiting citizens move slowly throughout the day. Dog licenses, bicycle tags, car registration, driver permits—the bureaucratic necessities of modern life are doled out for the price of patience, paperwork, and the proper fee. Teenagers wait with parents for first driving tests, immigrants anxiously scan test preparation booklets, young soldiers complain that they can't possibly pay this tax on top of that fee and those insurance premiums. The Honolulu DMV differs from others only in the astonishing array of races among people who go there with their colorful dress and their many languages.

It is in the nature of such places that people are not always at their best. Some customers become impatient and demanding. The job of motor vehicle clerk is the lowest paying job in the city employment hierarchy. It has the highest turnover. Employees rarely last over a year, and the city is constantly looking for new clerks.

Because the DMV creates constant demand for new employees, the personnel department sent a specialist to study the job and devise a screening test to help identify a large pool of prospective clerks. This is a well-established procedure used by large employers. The specialist observed clerks on the job. The key skills she identified included alphabetizing, reproducing numbers and letters with accuracy, making change, exhibiting courtesy, and other routine clerical skills. A test was devised to measure these skills.

In these days of skepticism toward standardized tests, this particular type of test is still highly regarded by employment specialists. Clerical skills are measurable with considerable accuracy, and performance in tasks such as accurately addressing large numbers of envelopes is largely predictable from test results. If such a test is devised with actual job functions in mind, it tends to predict fairly, and is less susceptible to racial or cultural bias than other tests. While general intelligence tests, personality tests, and scholastic aptitude tests are increasingly suspect because of their bias in favor of upper-class white men, tests of skills like alphabetizing and typing speed are biased in the good way: They favor only those with superior job skills. It is no accident that tests like these form the backbone of the civil service system—a system historically supported by Jews, African Americans, and other outsiders to the old spoils system that handed out jobs in exchange for votes, rather than as the reward for ability.

This was the premise Manuel Fragante relied on when he took the civil service examination and out-tested his 700 competitors. He was proud of his score and felt assured of the job. While others thought the job was beneath him given his age and experience, he was looking forward to the simplicity of its tasks, to the official feel of working for the government in an air-conditioned building, and to the chance to earn some spending money instead of wasting his time in boring idleness. He found warnings that the job was stressful mildly amusing. Having lived through invasion, war, and economic uncertainty, Manuel Fragante figured he could handle an irate taxpayer complaining about a long wait in line. He thus walked in for his interview with a calm and assured dignity. He knew the job was his.

The interviewers were other employees of the DMV: a supervisor and a secretary. The interview surprised Mr. Fragante. It was less of an interview than a brief conversation, lasting ten to fifteen minutes. The interviewers had no list of standard questions. They did have a rating sheet devised by one of the interviewers. After Mr. Fragante left, the interviewers conferred and entered scores on the rating sheet.

An expert in employment practices would later state that the rating sheet was the "worst" he had seen in his thirty-five years of experience in the field. It rated on a scale of one to ten, with no indication of what the numerical gradations stood for. It listed various oddly matched traits, such as "inarticulate" as the opposite of "convincing." Fragante was rated low in speech. The interviewers made these comments:

"Difficult manner of pronunciation."

"Pronounced" and "Heavy Filipino" accent.

Manuel Fragante was passed over for the job. The administrator in charge of hiring recommendations stated, "because of his accent, I would not recommend him for this position." The interviewers heard what any listener would hear in a brief conversation with Mr. Fragante: He speaks with a heavy Filipino accent, one that he is unlikely to lose at his age.

At the trial in the Fragante case, a linguist who studies Filipino and non-Filipino interactions stated that Mr. Fragante speaks grammatically correct, standard English, with the characteristic accent of someone raised in the Philippines. There is a history, in Hawaii and elsewhere, of prejudice against this accent, the linguist explained, that will cause some listeners to "turn off" and not comprehend it. The degree of phonological—or sound—deviation in Fragante's speech was not, however, so far afield from other accents of English-speakers in Hawaii that he would not be understood. Any nonprejudiced speaker of English would have no trouble understanding Mr. Fragante, the linguist concluded.

The defendant's witnesses testified otherwise. They explained that the DMV is a place of high-stress, short-term interactions with an often unreasonable public. Communication is the essence of the job. They insisted they bore no prejudice against Filipinos. Mr. Fragante's degree of accent would simply not work in the job. At no time did any of the defendant's witnesses state that they could not understand Mr. Fragante.

The linguist sat through the trial and noted the proceedings with interest. Attorneys for both sides suffered lapses in grammar and sentence structure, as did the judge. Mr. Fragante's English, a review of the transcript confirmed, was more nearly perfect in standard grammar and syntax than any other speaker in the courtroom. Mr. Fragante testified for two days, under the stress of both direct and cross-examination. The judge and the examiners spoke to Fragante in English and understood his answers. A court reporter understood and took down his words verbatim. In the functional context of the trial, everyone understood Manuel Fragante's speech. Yet the defendant's interviewers continued to claim Fragante could not be understood well enough to serve as a DMV clerk. * * *

The judge was on assignment from Arizona. He listened to four days of testimony and concluded that Manuel Fragante was denied the job not because of national origin, but because of legitimate difficulties with his accent. The opinion was somewhat of a puzzle. The judge found, as fact, that Manuel Fragante "has extensive verbal communication skill in English," but paradoxically that he has a "difficult manner of pronunciation" and a "military bearing," and that some listeners would "stop listening" when they hear a Filipino accent. The court made much of the high-stress communication required for the job, and found that speech was a bona fide occupational qualification. Finally, the court applied the McDonnell Douglas test, and found no proof of discriminatory intent or subterfuge.

Manuel Fragante was upset by the opinion. Soon after losing out on the DMV job, he was hired by the State of Hawaii as a statistician. Much of his work involved telephone interviews. Fragante felt his employment with the State proved his claim that the city misjudged his accent. He told his attorneys he wanted to press forward with his case.

Fragante lost on appeal before the Ninth Circuit although he did gain the symbolic victory of the court's sympathetic recognition that accent discrimination could violate Title VII. [*Fragante v. City and County of Honolulu*, 888 F.2d 591, 594–95 (1989).] The U.S. Supreme Court denied certiorari.

Manuel Fragante met his pledge to take his case as far as he could. His case has brought him a notoriety he is proud of, and he continues to argue against accent discrimination to community groups. Manuel Fragante, denied a job because of the way he speaks, has been interviewed on radio and television. He has spoken at fundraisers in California and Hawaii. He has campaigned actively, speaking in his own voice, against accent discrimination. * * *

THE DOCTRINAL PUZZLE OF ACCENT AND ANTIDISCRIMINATION LAW

* * * The puzzle in accent cases is that accent is often derivative of race and national origin. Only Filipino people speak with Filipino accents. Yet, within the range of employer prerogatives, it is reasonable to require communication skills of employees. The claim that accent impedes job ability is often made with both sincerity and economic rationality. How, then, should Title VII squeeze between the walls of accent as protected trait and speech as job requirement?

This puzzle is evident in every reported case considering accent and Title VII. The courts recognize that discrimination against a trait that is a stand-in for a protected category is prohibited. An employer who says, "I'm not discriminating against people of color, I just don't want to hire people with dark skin," is in violation of Title VII. The EEOC has found that discrimination against an accent associated with foreign birth is the equivalent of discrimination against foreign birth, relying in part on evidence that it is nearly impossible for an adult to eliminate their natural accent. Even the skilled mimics of new accents frequently overcorrect. That is, they blanketly apply stereotypical traits of the acquired accent, even in circumstances in which native speakers would drop the trait. To acquire natural, unself-conscious, and native-sounding speech with a new accent is a feat accomplished easily only by young children, who are still in the process of language acquisition. Given this near-immutability, discrimination against accent is the functional equivalent of discrimination against foreign origin.

The Ninth Circuit, in the *Fragante* case, agreed with the EEOC position that denial of employment opportunity because of a person's "linguistic characteristics of a national origin group" constitutes prohibited discrimination. The court added:

> Accent and national origin are obviously inextricably intertwined in many cases. It would therefore be an easy refuge in this context for an employer unlawfully discriminating against someone based on national origin to state falsely that it was not the person's national origin that caused the employment or promotion problem, but the candidate's inability to measure up to the communications skills demanded by the job. We encourage a very searching look by the district courts at such a claim.

The court accepted this proposition, but went on to hold that it was not Fragante's accent, but rather the "effect of his Filipino accent on his ability to communicate" that resulted in the selection of employees with "superior qualifications." The court went on to find "no proof whatsoever of pretext," and therefore no Title VII violation.

Once courts accept the proposition that accent discrimination can violate Title VII, they are in a difficult position when an employer comes to court saying, "I have nothing against Filipinos, but I can't hire someone with a heavy Filipino accent. None of my customers will understand them." In the daily work lives of most people, communication is an essential part of the job. The employer's plea seems, on its face, reasonable.

The problem is that in every accent case the employer will raise the "can't understand" defense, and in almost every reported case, the courts have accepted it. The rule that trait-based discrimination against accent is prohibited national origin discrimination dissolves in application, when the courts are faced with the employer's efficiency-based complaint that accent impedes job function. * * *

What kind of people demand uniformity of accent? The demand for speech uniformity suggests preference for conformity, distrust of difference, and attachment to a large, looming notion of "we." The demand for speech uniformity is scary, in the scary sense of statism, nationalism, territorial acquisitiveness, and purist conceptions of race.

The nations—including ours, in its worst moments—that have humiliated school children for speaking "the wrong way" have been the imperial ones, the bullies, the takers without right, and the teachers of intolerance. Given this history, linguistic pluralism represents our better self: the generous and tolerant self that marvels at difference and feels no need to destroy individual variability in the process of self-definition. The presence of a variety of accents in schools, in the workplace, in the media, in all public spaces, promotes the value of tolerance. It makes variability commonplace and unfrightening. It remembers that we can be our best, welcoming, unafraid self. * * *

Self-worth, identity, integrity, and autonomy are the words academics use to express an idea that infuses the core of our Constitution and creed: People have a right to be what they are. The popular notion of the Constitution distills to that idea—"it's a free country," children yell back at bossy elders. This core notion of individual freedom is understood by millions of Americans who could not recite a line from the Bill of Rights.

The way we talk, whether it is a life choice or an immutable characteristic, is akin to other attributes of the self that the law protects. In privacy law, due process law, protection against cruel and unusual punishment, and freedom from inquisition, we say the state cannot intrude upon the core of you, cannot take away your sacred places of the self. A citizen's accent, I would argue, resides in one of those places. * * *

There are, however, serious pitfalls in using liberal values without attention to history and context. * * *

ACCENT AND ANTISUBORDINATION: A RADICAL CRITIQUE

* * *

What employers purport to do when they identify an accent and declare it unintelligible is to apply neutral standards of evaluation to objective reality. This familiar process, critical scholars have argued, is often what disguises value as fact. In looking at the accent cases, what emerges is not the "fact" that Asian or Latino or African–American accents are unintelligible, but the hidden assumption of an Anglo accent at the center. The Anglo speech is normal, everything else is different, and acceptability of any given speech depends upon its closeness to Anglo speech. * * *

Which accent is seen as normal, intelligent, most-likely-to-succeed is a function of power distribution. Thus the key inquiry in understanding accent cases is "what are the power distributions." Attempting to apply Title VII without asking that question is what allows courts to suggest that employers can pick the best accent out of many, without seeing that "best" points up the racial hierarchy. Unmasking the hidden center reveals accent evaluation for what it is: an exercise in power.

Seeing accent evaluation as an exercise of power helps refute the typical justifications for excluding or repressing certain accents, which include:

1.   The inherent superiority of the standard accent. The claim here is that the standard accent is more pure, more eloquent, more expressive, more valuable.

2.   The universality of the standard accent. Most people speak it and everyone understands it, therefore it is reasonably designated the national standard.

3.   Standardization is efficient. Even if the standard is somewhat arbitrary, having a standard increases communication among diverse speakers. It reduces misunderstanding and saves time.

4.   The standard is unifying. Having a standard helps forge a national identity and avoids the balkanizing disarray that comes with language variation.

The concept of positioned perspective, developed by feminists and critical race theorists, and the critique of neutrality associated with Foucault and the critical legal theorists, rejects the idea of a universal measure of accent quality. Add to this critique the empirical work of sociolinguists, and the argument that standard pronunciation is inherently superior and universal disappears. While most people in power speak the standard, the critical technique of challenging false norms as creations of power helps show how the seemingly absolute universality of standard pronunciation is actually an imposed universality.

This leaves the final two arguments of efficiency and unity. The argument that uniformity is efficient presumes that uniformity is attainable and that variability impedes communication. Both claims are historically and empirically false. Uniformity never has been, and by all indications never will be, the reality of spoken English. Language is a living, moving thing. Linguistic geographers show this graphically in an obscure but fascinating form of cartography that charts the journeys of words and pronunciation over space and time. The names we call things by are born, expand outward gathering more speakers of those names, and die, as other names take over. The word "orts" for scraps of garbage traveled from England to Massachusetts in the time of the colonies, where it thrived and then faded until only one informant in Bar Harbor and one in New Bedford could tell field researchers what it meant. Similarly, "standard pronunciation" varies both regionally in our time and historically over time. The teachers of "correct enunciation" of fifty years ago would hang their heads in sorrow over what passes for correct on Cable News Network today.

The standard and the nonstandard interact in a dynamic way. Like two human beings forging a true friendship, neither is exactly the same as before the influence of the other. Through and across the change, interaction, and variation that is our living language, we still speak and understand. * * *

The process of unmasking hidden centers and false objectivity is an important first step in producing a counter-ideology of antisubordination, as is acknowledging the psychology of dominance that accompanies subordination. * * *

The accent cases illustrate some of what we know about subordination. We know that subordination has material and ideological dimensions. In the case of accent, the material dimensions include the real denial of life chances: Jobs, housing, and educational opportunity may depend on talking the right way. Whether one can speak persuasively before the law—before a police officer or a judge or a legislature or a jury—may determine life or death, freedom or jail, protection or neglect. The ideological dimension of accent discrimination is the creation and maintenance of a belief system that sees some as worthy and others as unworthy based on accent, such that disparities in wealth and power are naturalized.

Much of the system of thinking that justifies subordination depends on such in/out sorting. Some people deserve degraded status because they are lazy, stupid, ill-mannered, latecomers without vested rights, outside the circle of those we care about. Other people deserve privileged status because they are smarter, more hardworking, more like us, more like the entitled insiders. An interesting opening in the sacred circle of the entitled is made for those who are seen to have fallen from the circle through no fault of their own—those who are enough like us that we can give them charity. The concept of the deserving poor, the psychological identification with earthquake victims, and the outpouring of care for children who fall into wells, suggest this. After the California earthquake, many emergency shelters made a distinction between the new homeless, who were welcome in the shelters, and the old homeless, who were not. In order to stay in an earthquake relief shelter, one had to prove they had a home before the earthquake.

The sympathy generated by natural disaster together with the implied lack of human agency behind earthquake-generated homelessness, raises the issue of immutability as a justification for favored treatment under law. Ever since the famous footnote four, the idea of difference-by-act-of-God has fed our notions of equal protection and deservedness. People can't help it if they are born Black, or female, or foreign, therefore it is unfair to disadvantage them based on an "unfortunate accident of birth." The widespread generosity of ordinary Americans toward the handicapped and afflicted is a proud fact of our national culture. Millions contribute to telethons, walkathons, blood drives, and other charitable activities for various illnesses and disabilities. Overcoming handicap is a significant theme in books devoured by young readers.

Our discomfort when disadvantage is somehow linked to choice stands in contrast to this passion for the faultless victim. For this reason many gay rights activists, and sympathizers in the popular media, emphasize the immutability of sexual orientation: We can't help it if we were born gay. Growing numbers of gay and lesbian activists are dissatisfied by the immutability argument. Lesbians in particular often see woman-to-woman sexuality as a choice—a political, prideful, and joyous choice determined not by biology but by love of womankind.

Similarly, many religious and ethnic groups choose to live a certain way—to speak, act, eat, dance or not dance according to custom and meaning deliberately constructed to define separation from the dominant culture. If immutability determines when the law cares about our differences, the logical corollary is that difference by choice is not protected.

Thus in a range of distinctions we divide "innocent victims of AIDS" from those who somehow deserve what they got. We separate the "deserving" welfare recipients from the lazy poor. We call out the "typical Jews" from the assimilated ones, ever sorting between those who can enter the circle of public power and care and those who are rightfully left outside. The core group of the entitled will, through beneficence, let in the anointed few whose difference does not offend.

Immutability arguments feed into this hierarchical ideology. In arguing for accent tolerance, the rationale of accent as immutable is thus a dangerous one. A more progressive argument is that even if accent is changeable, no citizen should have to alter core parts of identity in order to participate in society. A true antisubordination agenda would apply reasonable accommodation to all differences, whether chosen or immutable, that are historically subject to exploitation or oppression by dominant groups. * * *

In summary, the antisubordination rationale for accent tolerance suggests a radically pluralistic re-visioning of national identity. The only center, the only glue, that makes us a nation is our many-centered cultural heritage. Just as our use of language is rich, varied, interactive, and changeable, so is our national culture. We are the only country in which an Okinawan vendor serves Kosher pastrami and stir-fried vegetables wrapped in a tortilla to young white punk rockers at 3:00 a.m. in the morning. We are the only country in which a white child sleeps blissfully under a quilt lovingly stitched by his aunt, emblazoned with a life-sized portrait of an African–American basketball star. We are the only country in which a group of parents planning a Little League fundraiser around a transvestite beauty contest would call the ACLU to defend their right to use a public park for the event, and convince a mayor named Hannibal Tavares to change his mind about a permit. From the oversized plaster chickens and donuts that mark our highways to the exquisite wisps of nouvelle Franco–Latin–Japanese cuisine set before our expense-account diners, we are a nation fantastic and wide-ranging in our vernacular and our juxtapositions. From the Grand Ole Opry to neo-metal, from zydeco to the Met, we are a range of tastes and sounds wider than ever before known to the nations of this planet. That is the defining centrality of the American culture I grew up in and love: a broad and delightfully incongruous coming together of difference. In acknowledging plural culture as a strength, and in recognizing and dismantling the false hierarchies that place one culture over another, it may come to pass that we live together in celebration and peace. * * *

* * * I believe the antisubordination principle is a principle, and that it can inform our law in a way that is as principled and as disciplined as the ideas of property, equality, and due process that are

our constitutional legacy. I have tried to show that accent discrimination is rooted in a culture of dominance fundamentally at odds with the creed of this nation—at odds both with the Enlightenment ideals of liberalism that attended our national birth and the ideal of antisubordination that has constituted the core of our defining struggles against slavery, against fascism, against Jim Crow.

The many brilliant scholars who caution against overreliance on law or logic, claims of truth or absolute normative priority, legalism and constitutionalism, present challenges I wish to hear. In meeting the goal of true equality—of ending all forms of subordination—I continue to see claims of logic, legality, and justice as both useful and true.

Notes and Questions

1. Is Matsuda's faith in an antisubordination principle justified? Should equality be defined by an antisubordination principle? Can an antisubordination principle be reconciled with race-consciousness? Wouldn't many who oppose affirmative action claim that they are trying to end subordination by making racial categorization of any kind illegal?

2. The Supreme Court set forth the elements and burdens of proof for a *prima facie* case of disparate treatment (cases requiring proof of an employer's discriminatory intent) under Title VII in *McDonnell Douglas Corp. v. Green*, 411 U.S. 792 (1973). A plaintiff establishes a *prima facie* case by proving four elements: "i) that he belongs to a racial minority; ii) that he applied and qualified for a job for which the employer was seeking applicants; iii) that, despite his qualifications, he was rejected; and iv) that, after his rejection, the position remained open and the employer continued to seek applicants from persons of complainant's qualifications." The burden of production then shifts to the employer, who must "articulate some legitimate, nondiscriminatory reason for the employee's rejection." The burden of proof remains with the plaintiff (employee), who must prove that the employer's proffered reason was a pretext for discrimination. In *St. Mary's Honor Center v. Hicks*, 509 U.S. 502 (1993), the Supreme Court clarified that mere proof of pretext, proof that the employer gave a false reason for a discriminatory action was insufficient. A plaintiff always carries the burden of proving that the employer intentionally discriminated against him or her.

Distinguish disparate treatment cases from cases based on discriminatory impact, involving facially neutral employment practices that "fall more harshly on one group than another and cannot be justified by business necessity." *International Broth. of Teamsters v. United States*, 431 U.S. 324, 334–36, n.15 (1977).

3. Consider this hypothetical suit, posed by Matsuda, *id.* at 1353:

Tran is a [university] lecturer in computer science. Approximately one-fourth of her time is spent in communication with students, either in class or in conference. The rest of her time is spent reviewing and grading papers, engaging in research and writing, and administering the computer lab. She excels at these tasks by all accounts. She has a heavy Vietnamese accent. Most of her students are white. There is evidence of strong prejudice in the community against Vietnamese, including acts of hate violence. Tran gets poor teaching evaluations in which students claim she "can't speak English" and that "we aren't learning a thing in class." Asian–American students report no difficulty in understanding Tran. Some of the evaluations also contain racist and sexist slurs and obscenities. "Why can't we get real American teachers," one student complains. Tran is denied contract renewal, and she sues.

Should the racial slurs be relevant to her employment discrimination claim? The claims of difficulty in understanding Tran? Matsuda comments, "Communication is essential to the job of teaching. Inability to communicate clearly should disqualify the candidate from classroom teaching. The reality of significant anti-Asian sentiment, however, gives one pause in determining whether to take the student complaints at face value." *Id.*

SECTION 3.   AFFIRMATIVE ACTION AND THE DEBATE ABOUT EQUALITY

The concern whether the Fourteenth Amendment guarantee of equal protection of the laws protects groups or individuals comes clearly into focus when we turn to the issue of affirmative action. Courts and commentators have struggled to define affirmative action. See David Benjamin Oppenheimer, *Distinguishing Five Models of Affirmative Action*, 4 Berkeley Women's L.J. 42 (1988).

Nowhere is the definitional issue more visible than in the effort to translate the term from English to Chinese for Sharon K. Hom & Xin Chunying, *English-Chinese Lexicon of Women and Law (Yinghan Funnu Yu Falu Cehuishiyi)* (1995). Sharon Hom explains:

> I had seen affirmative action once literally translated in Chinese as affirmative action, *jiji* (積極), as in affirmatively to act. But without any social, historical context to support this phrase in translation, this term was meaningless and conveyed to me a bizarre image of hyperactive people. Another more common translation is *chabie duidai yuanze* (差别对待原则), "the principle of dealing with difference." Both translations needed the invocation of situated civil rights struggle, culturally specific notions of rights, equality and equity, private and public spheres of action, and assumptions regarding the role of government and law. In the end, instead of the more common translation, we adopted a fairly long winded phrase, *weile shixian pingdeng er shixing de chabie duidai yuanze* (为了实现平等而实行的差别对待原则), clearly not a Chinese "translation," but Chinglish.
>
> The entry reads: "Affirmative Action originally referred to the policy adopted by the U.S. federal government requiring all companies, universities, and other institutions that do business with the government, or receive federal funding, to 'take affirmative action to ensure that applicants are employed, and that employees are treated during their employment, without regard to their race, color, religion, sex, or national origin.' " The term has since come to refer to programs designed to remedy effects of past and continuing discriminatory practices in the recruiting, selecting, developing, and promoting of minority group members. It seeks to create systems and

procedures to prevent future discrimination and is commonly based on population percentages of minority groups in a particular area. * * * Opponents of affirmative action have charged that these policies can only be achieved by "reverse discrimination" against white males.

Sharon K. Hom, *Lexicon Dreams and Chinese Rock and Roll: Thoughts on Culture, Language, and Translation as Strategies of Resistance and Reconstruction*, talk at LatCrit III Conference, Miami, Florida, May 1998.*

What meaning do you give to the term affirmative action? How does your definition relate to your view of equality as offering protection to individuals or to groups?

Given the controversy surrounding affirmative action, litigators have pressed the Supreme Court for clarification. After declining to give the issue full hearing in *DeFunis v. Odegaard*, 416 U.S. 312 (1974) (concerning admission to the University of Washington Law School), the U.S. Supreme Court faced the issue in *Regents of the University of California v. Bakke*, 438 U.S. 265 (1978). Alan Bakke, denied admission to the University of California at Davis Medical School, alleged in his complaint that

> a special admissions committee composed of racial minority members evaluated applications of a special group of persons purportedly from economic[ally] and educationally disadvantaged backgrounds; that from this group, a quota of 16 percent, or 16 out of 100 first-year class members, was selected; that, in fact, all applicants admitted to said medical school as members of this group were members of racial minorities, that under this admission program racial minority and majority applicants went through separate segregated admission procedures with separate standards for admissions; that the use of such separate standards resulted in the admission of minority applicants less qualified than plaintiff and other non-minority applicants who were therefore rejected.

Joel Dreyfuss & Charles Lawrence III, *The Bakke Case: The Politics of Inequality* 37–38 (1979).

Explaining his theory of the case Mr. Bakke's attorney said that his client was in court as an individual. Dreyfuss and Lawrence comment: "Whenever the case threatened to become too abstract, [the attorney] would focus attention on his client. The case would no longer involve an amorphous white person deprived for the public good. It would become a case about Allan Bakke, Vietnam veteran, aerospace engineer, and a man with a strong commitment to medicine." *Id*.

The *Bakke* case is discussed in greater detail in *Hopwood*, Chapter 9 *infra*, in the context of affirmative action and education. The Supreme Court's more recent pronouncements about affirmative action have appeared in the area of employment.

ADARAND CONSTRUCTORS, INC. v. PENA
515 U.S. 200 (1995).

JUSTICE O'CONNOR. * * *

Petitioner Adarand Constructors, Inc., claims that the Federal Government's practice of giving general contractors on government projects a financial incentive to hire subcontractors controlled by "socially and economically disadvantaged individuals," and in particular, the Government's use of race-based presumptions in identifying such individuals, violates the equal protection component of the Fifth Amendment's Due Process Clause. * * *

[The Court describes the statutes and regulations that govern bidding for government contracts, including the race-based presumption found in the Small Business Act, which "presumes that Black, Hispanic, Asian Pacific, Subcontinent Asian, and Native Americans, as well as 'members of other groups designated from time to time by SBA,' are 'socially disadvantaged.' "]

The Court of Appeals upheld the use of subcontractor compensation clauses, interpreting past decisions as having "adopted 'a lenient standard, resembling intermediate scrutiny, in assessing' the constitutionality of federal race-based action."] * * *

The Government urges that "[t]he Subcontracting Compensation Clause program is ... a program based on disadvantage, not on race," and thus that it is subject only to "the most relaxed judicial scrutiny." To the extent that the statutes and regulations involved in this case are race neutral, we agree. The Government concedes, however, that "the race-based rebuttable presumption used in some certification determinations under the Subcontracting Compensation Clause" is subject to some heightened level of scrutiny. The parties disagree as to what that level should be. (We note, incidentally, that this case concerns only classifications based explicitly on race, and presents none of the additional difficulties posed by laws that, although facially race neutral, result in racially disproportionate impact and are motivated by a racially discriminatory purpose.) * * *

Our action today makes explicit what Justice Powell thought implicit in the *Fullilove* lead opinion: Federal racial classifications, like those of a State, must serve a compelling governmental interest, and must be narrowly tailored to further that interest. See *Fullilove*, 448 U.S. at 496 (concurring opinion). * * * Of course, it follows that to the extent (if any) that *Fullilove* held federal racial classifications to be subject to a less rigorous standard, it is no longer controlling. But we need not decide today whether the program upheld in *Fullilove* would survive strict scrutiny as our more recent cases have defined it.

Some have questioned the importance of debating the proper standard of review of race-based legislation. But we agree with Justice Stevens that, "[b]ecause racial characteristics so seldom provide a relevant basis for disparate treatment, and because classifications based on race are potentially so harmful to the entire body politic, it is especially important that the reasons for any such classification be clearly identified and unquestionably legitimate," and that "[r]acial classifications are simply too pernicious to permit any but the most exact connection between justification and classification." *Fullilove* at 533–535, 537 (dissenting opinion). We think that requiring strict scrutiny is the best way to ensure that courts will consistently give racial classifications that kind of detailed examination, both as to ends and as to means. *Korematsu* demonstrates vividly that even "the most rigid scrutiny" can sometimes fail to detect an illegitimate racial classification, compare *Korematsu*, 323 U.S. at 223 ("To cast this case into outlines of racial prejudice, without reference to the real military dangers which were presented, merely confuses the issue. Korematsu was not excluded from the Military Area because of hostility to him or his race"), with Pub.L. 100–383, § 2(a), 102 Stat. 903–904 ("[T]hese actions [of relocating and interning civilians of Japanese ancestry] were carried out without adequate security reasons . . . and were motivated largely by racial prejudice, wartime hysteria, and a failure of political leadership"). Any retreat from the most searching judicial inquiry can only increase the risk of another such error occurring in the future.

Finally, we wish to dispel the notion that strict scrutiny is "strict in theory, but fatal in fact." *Fullilove* at 519 (Marshall, J., concurring in judgment). The unhappy persistence of both the practice and the lingering effects of racial discrimination against minority groups in this country is an unfortunate reality, and government is not disqualified from acting in response to it. As recently as 1987, for example, every Justice of this Court agreed that the Alabama Department of Public Safety's "pervasive, systematic, and obstinate discriminatory conduct" justified a narrowly tailored race-based remedy. See *United States v. Paradise*, 480 U.S. at 167 (plurality opinion of Brennan, J.). When race-based action is necessary to further a compelling interest, such action is within constitutional constraints if it satisfies the "narrow tailoring" test this Court has set out in previous cases.

Because our decision today alters the playing field in some important respects, we think it best to remand the case to the lower courts for further consideration in light of the principles we have announced. * * *

JUSTICE SCALIA, concurring in part and concurring in the judgment.

I join the opinion of the Court, * * * except insofar as it may be inconsistent with the following: In my view, government can never have a "compelling interest" in discriminating on the basis of race in order to "make up" for past racial discrimination in the opposite direction. Individuals who have been wronged by unlawful racial discrimination should be made whole; but under our Constitution there can be no such thing as either a creditor or a debtor race. That concept is alien to the Constitution's focus upon the individual, and its rejection of dispositions based on race, or based on blood. To pursue the concept of racial entitlement—even for the most admirable and benign of purposes—is to reinforce and preserve for future mischief the way of thinking that produced race slavery, race privilege and race hatred. In the eyes of government, we are just one race here. It is American.

It is unlikely, if not impossible, that the challenged program would survive under this understanding of strict scrutiny, but I am content to leave that to be decided on remand.

JUSTICE THOMAS, concurring in part and concurring in the judgment.

I agree with the majority's conclusion that strict scrutiny applies to all government classifications based on race. I write separately, however, to express my disagreement with the premise underlying Justice Stevens' and Justice Ginsburg's dissents: that there is a racial paternalism exception to the principle of equal protection. I believe that there is a "moral [and] constitutional equivalence," between laws designed to subjugate a race and those that distribute benefits on the basis of race in order to foster some current notion of equality. Government cannot make us equal; it can only recognize, respect, and protect us as equal before the law.

That these programs may have been motivated, in part, by good intentions cannot provide refuge from the principle that under our Constitution, the government may not make distinctions on the basis of race. As far as the Constitution is concerned, it is irrelevant whether a government's racial classifications are drawn by those who wish to oppress a race or by those who have a sincere desire to help those thought to be disadvantaged. There can be no doubt that the paternalism that appears to lie at the heart of this program is at war with the principle of inherent equality that underlies and infuses our Constitution. See Declaration of Independence ("We hold these truths to be self-evident, that all men are created equal, that they are endowed by their Creator with certain unalienable Rights, that among these are Life, Liberty, and the pursuit of Happiness").

These programs not only raise grave constitutional questions, they also undermine the moral basis of the equal protection principle. Purchased at the price of immeasurable human suffering, the equal protection principle reflects our Nation's understanding that such classifications ultimately have a destructive impact on the individual and our society. Unquestionably, "[i]nvidious [racial] discrimination is an engine of oppression." It is also true that "[r]emedial" racial preferences may reflect "a desire to foster equality in society." But there can be no doubt that racial paternalism and its unintended consequences can be as poisonous and pernicious as any other form of discrimination. So-called "benign" discrimination teaches many that because of chronic and apparently immutable handicaps, minorities cannot compete with them without their patronizing indulgence. Inevitably, such programs engender attitudes of superiority or, alternatively, provoke resentment among those who believe that they have been wronged by the government's use of race. These programs stamp minorities with a badge of inferiority and may cause them to develop dependencies or to adopt an attitude that they are "entitled" to preferences. * * *

In my mind, government-sponsored racial discrimination based on benign prejudice is just as noxious as discrimination inspired by malicious prejudice. In each instance, it is racial discrimination, plain and simple.

JUSTICE STEVENS, with whom JUSTICE GINSBURG joins, dissenting.

Instead of deciding this case in accordance with controlling precedent, the Court today delivers a disconcerting lecture about the evils of governmental racial classifications. For its text the Court has selected three propositions, represented by the bywords "skepticism," "consistency," and "congruence." I shall comment on each of these propositions, then add a few words about *stare decisis*, and finally explain why I believe this Court has a duty to affirm the judgment of the Court of Appeals.

The Court's concept of skepticism is, at least in principle, a good statement of law and of common sense. Undoubtedly, a court should be wary of a governmental decision that relies upon a racial classification. * * *

The Court's concept of "consistency" assumes that there is no significant difference between a decision by the majority to impose a special burden on the members of a minority race and a decision by the majority to provide a benefit to certain members of that minority notwithstanding its incidental burden on some members of the majority. In my opinion that assumption is untenable. There is no moral or constitutional equivalence between a policy that is designed to perpetuate a caste system and one that seeks to eradicate racial subordination. Invidious discrimination is an engine of oppression, subjugating a disfavored group to enhance or maintain the power of the majority. Remedial race-based preferences reflect the opposite impulse: a desire to foster equality in society. * * *

To illustrate the point, consider our cases addressing the Federal Government's discrimination against Japanese Americans during World War II, *Hirabayashi v. United States*, 320 U.S. 81 (1943), and *Korematsu v. United States*, 323 U.S. 214 (1944). The discrimination at issue in those cases was invidious because the Government imposed special burdens—a curfew and exclusion from certain areas on the West Coast—on the members of a minority class defined by racial and ethnic characteristics. Members of the same racially defined class exhibited exceptional heroism in the service of our country during that War. Now suppose Congress decided to reward that service with a federal program that gave all Japanese–American veterans an extraordinary preference in Government employment. If Congress had done so, the same racial characteristics that motivated the discriminatory burdens in *Hirabayashi* and *Korematsu* would have defined the preferred class of veterans. Nevertheless, "consistency" surely would not require us to describe the incidental burden on everyone else in the country as "odious" or "invidious" as those terms were used in those cases. We should reject a concept of "consistency" that would view the special preferences that the National Government has provided to Native Americans since 1834[3] as compara-

3. See *Morton v. Mancari*, 417 U.S. 535, 541 (1974). To be eligible for the preference in 1974, an individual had to " 'be one fourth or more degree Indian blood and be

ble to the official discrimination against African Americans that was prevalent for much of our history.

The consistency that the Court espouses would disregard the difference between a "No Trespassing" sign and a welcome mat. It would treat a Dixiecrat Senator's decision to vote against Thurgood Marshall's confirmation in order to keep African Americans off the Supreme Court as on a par with President Johnson's evaluation of his nominee's race as a positive factor. It would equate a law that made black citizens ineligible for military service with a program aimed at recruiting black soldiers. An attempt by the majority to exclude members of a minority race from a regulated market is fundamentally different from a subsidy that enables a relatively small group of newcomers to enter that market. An interest in "consistency" does not justify treating differences as though they were similarities.

The Court's explanation for treating dissimilar race-based decisions as though they were equally objectionable is a supposed inability to differentiate between "invidious" and "benign" discrimination. But the term "affirmative action" is common and well understood. Its presence in everyday parlance shows that people understand the difference between good intentions and bad. As with any legal concept, some cases may be difficult to classify, but our equal protection jurisprudence has identified a critical difference between state action that imposes burdens on a disfavored few and state action that benefits the few "in spite of" its adverse effects on the many. *Feeney.* * * *

JUSTICE GINSBURG, with whom JUSTICE BREYER joins, dissenting.

For the reasons stated by Justice Souter, and in view of the attention the political branches are currently giving the matter of affirmative action, I see no compelling cause for the intervention the Court has made in this case. I further agree with Justice Stevens that, in this area, large deference is owed by the Judiciary to "Congress' institutional competence and constitutional authority to overcome historic racial subjugation." I write separately to underscore not the differences the several opinions in this case display, but the considerable field of agreement—the common understandings and concerns—revealed in opinions that together speak for a majority of the Court.

The statutes and regulations at issue, as the Court indicates, were adopted by the political branches in response to an "unfortunate reality": "[t]he unhappy persistence of both the practice and the lingering effects of racial discrimination against minority groups in this country." The United States suffers from those lingering effects because, for most of our Nation's history, the idea that "we are just one race," was not embraced. For generations, our lawmakers and judges were unprepared to say that there is in this land no superior race, no race inferior to any other. In *Plessy v. Ferguson*, 163 U.S. 537 (1896), not only did this Court endorse the oppressive practice of race segregation, but even Justice Harlan, the advocate of a "color-blind" Constitution, stated:

a member of a Federally-recognized tribe.'" We concluded that the classification was not "racial" because it did not encompass all Native Americans. 417 U.S. at 553–554. * * * [Eds. Morton v. Mancari is reproduced in Chapter 3 *supra*.]

"The white race deems itself to be the dominant race in this country. And so it is, in prestige, in achievements, in education, in wealth and in power. So, I doubt not, it will continue to be for all time, if it remains true to its great heritage and holds fast to the principles of constitutional liberty."

Not until *Loving v. Virginia*, 388 U.S. 1 (1967), which held unconstitutional Virginia's ban on interracial marriages, could one say with security that the Constitution and this Court would abide no measure "designed to maintain White Supremacy."

The divisions in this difficult case should not obscure the Court's recognition of the persistence of racial inequality and a majority's acknowledgment of Congress' authority to act affirmatively, not only to end discrimination, but also to counteract discrimination's lingering effects. Those effects, reflective of a system of racial caste only recently ended, are evident in our workplaces, markets, and neighborhoods. Job applicants with identical resumes, qualifications, and interview styles still experience different receptions, depending on their race. White and African–American consumers still encounter different deals. People of color looking for housing still face discriminatory treatment by landlords, real estate agents, and mortgage lenders. Minority entrepreneurs sometimes fail to gain contracts though they are the low bidders, and they are sometimes refused work even after winning contracts. Bias both conscious and unconscious, reflecting traditional and unexamined habits of thought, keeps up barriers that must come down if equal opportunity and nondiscrimination are ever genuinely to become this country's law and practice.

Given this history and its practical consequences, Congress surely can conclude that a carefully designed affirmative action program may help to realize, finally, the "equal protection of the laws" the Fourteenth Amendment has promised since 1868.

The lead opinion uses one term, "strict scrutiny," to describe the standard of judicial review for all governmental classifications by race. But that opinion's elaboration strongly suggests that the strict standard announced is indeed "fatal" for classifications burdening groups that have suffered discrimination in our society. That seems to me, and, I believe, to the Court, the enduring lesson one should draw from *Korematsu v. United States*; for in that case, scrutiny the Court described as "most rigid," nonetheless yielded a pass for an odious, gravely injurious racial classification. A *Korematsu*-type classification, as I read the opinions in this case, will never again survive scrutiny: such a classification, history and precedent instruct, properly ranks as prohibited.

For a classification made to hasten the day when "we are just one race," however, the lead opinion has dispelled the notion that "strict scrutiny" is " 'fatal in fact.' " Properly, a majority of the Court calls for review that is searching, in order to ferret out classifications in reality malign, but masquerading as benign. The Court's once lax review of sex-based classifications demonstrates the need for such suspicion. Today's decision thus usefully reiterates that the purpose of strict scrutiny "is precisely to distinguish legitimate from illegitimate uses of race in governmental decisionmaking," "to 'differentiate between' permissible and impermissible governmental use of race," to distinguish " 'between a "No Trespassing" sign and a welcome mat.' "

Close review also is in order for this further reason. As Justice Souter points out, and as this very case shows, some members of the historically favored race can be hurt by catch-up mechanisms designed to cope with the lingering effects of entrenched racial subjugation. Court review can ensure that preferences are not so large as to trammel unduly upon the opportunities of others or interfere too harshly with legitimate expectations of persons in once-preferred groups.

* * *

While I would not disturb the programs challenged in this case, and would leave their improvement to the political branches, I see today's decision as one that allows our precedent to evolve, still to be informed by and responsive to changing conditions.

Notes and Questions

1. Is *Adarand*'s holding limited to employment? Or does the same rule apply in cases involving education?

2. Is the *Adarand* court's use of *Korematsu*, in effect admitting that decision was incorrect, persuasive as an argument for using strict judicial scrutiny for racial classifications? Is the court's result dictated by the rhetoric of liberalism that Matsuda described, *supra*? Would an antisubordination analysis provide a different result? How could such an argument be framed in language that a court could understand?

3. Consider Justice Scalia's use of race in his concurring opinion, claiming, "In the eyes of government, we are just one race here. It is American." What are the implications of using race in this manner?

4. Consider Robin West's observations about the notion of equality:

> It is by now an open secret that current interpretations of the meaning of the Equal Protection Clause of the Fourteenth Amendment, and of its relevance and mandate for contemporary problems of racial, gender, and economic justice, are deeply and, in a sense, hopelessly conflicted. The conflict, simply stated, is this: To the current Supreme Court, and to a sizeable and influential number of constitutional theorists, the "equal protection of the laws" guaranteed by the Constitution is essentially a guarantee that the categories delineated by legal rules will be "rational" and will be rationally related to legitimate state ends. To this group of jurists, the relevance of the Equal Protection Clause to issues of racial justice rests on the important complementary minor premise to this guarantee of rationality: The claim, both descriptive and normative, that legislative distinctions based upon race can simply never be rational because there are no differences between the races that can in any way be relevant to state purposes, and, consequently, racial differentiation in any context cannot be a legitimate state goal.

> On this view, the Equal Protection Clause is historically rooted in a constitutional and federal response to the pernicious slave laws, black codes, Jim Crow laws, and segregation mandates of southern states, all of which rested upon a specious and false theory of racial difference and

hence upon presumably "natural" distinctions between the slave and the freeman, the black man, and the white man to justify the different legal treatment and protections accorded them. From the historic repudiation of this false theory of racial difference and white superiority culminating in passage of the Fourteenth Amendment—and from the further constitutional premise that categories must be rational—follows the important ethical and constitutional mandate that the central meaning of the Equal Protection Clause, and indeed of the Fourteenth Amendment in its entirety, is that the law must be colorblind.

For a second group of jurists, including the liberal dissenters on the Court and a sizeable number of constitutional theorists in law schools, the "equal protection" clause of the Fourteenth Amendment requires not "rationality" in legislation but, rather, substantive justice. For this group the guarantee of equal protection is a constitutional imperative for the states and Congress to take substantive steps toward the eradication of the unjust subordination of one group of citizens by another, including African Americans and other peoples of color by whites, women by men, and gays and lesbians by heterosexuals. On this view, the equal protection mandate and the Fourteenth Amendment are historically grounded not in the pernicious idea of racial difference but, rather, in the pernicious practice of racial subordination: the willful and continuing attempt of white people, with the willing acquiescence of state governments, to subordinate, deny, oppress, and use black people for their own ends. That subordination began with the enslavement of blacks by whites and their oppression through black codes and Jim Crow laws. The subordination continues in our time through the use of purportedly "neutral" but in fact unjustified and exclusionary criteria that precludes entry of not only blacks, but also women and other people of color into the higher echelons of political, professional, educational, and economic life. The equal protection mandate for these theorists is a guarantee that either the states or, in the breach, Congress will act to reverse these patterns of subordination.

On this view, it most assuredly does not follow that the law must be "colorblind." Rather, the law must be sensitive and responsive to the very real and relevant differences that exist between both blacks and whites, women and men: differences in power, differences in status, and differing positions on the economic, social, and political hierarchies that comprise our public and private lives. The mandate of equal protection is minimally not to exacerbate those inequalities but, understood generously, the Fourteenth Amendment in general, and equal protection in particular, is a mandate to eradicate them.

Robin West, *Toward an Abolitionist Interpretation of the Fourteenth Amendment*, 94 W. Va. L. Rev. 111, 111–13 (1991).*

Is there any middle ground between the positions West describes or will the notion of equality necessarily remain contested?

5.   Who benefits from a policy of acting affirmatively to increase multiracial representation at work? Consider this commentary by Richard Delgado:

Scholars of color have grown increasingly skeptical about both the way in which affirmative action frames the issue of minority representation and the effects that it produces in the world. Affirmative action, I have noticed, generally frames the question of minority representation in an interesting way: Should we as a society admit, hire, appoint, or promote some designated number of people of color in order to promote certain policy goals, such as social stability, an expanded labor force, and an integrated society? These goals are always forward-looking; affirmative action is viewed as an instrumental device for moving society from state A to state B. The concept is neither backward-looking nor rooted in history. * * * Minorities are hired or promoted not because we have been unfairly treated, denied jobs, deprived of our lands, or beaten and brought here in chains. Affirmative action neatly diverts our attention from all those disagreeable details and calls for a fresh start. Well, where are we now? So many Chicano bankers and chief executive officers, so many black lawyers, so many Native American engineers, and so many women physicians. What can we do to increase these numbers over the next ten or twenty years? The system thus bases inclusion of people of color on principles of social utility, not reparations or rights. When those in power decide the goal has been accomplished, or is incapable of being reached, what logically happens? Naturally, the program stops. At best, then, affirmative action serves as a homeostatic device, assuring that only a small number of women and people of color are hired or promoted. Not too many, for that would be terrifying, nor too few, for that would be destabilizing. Just the right small number, generally those of us who need it least, are moved ahead.

Affirmative action also neatly frames the issue so that even these small accomplishments seem troublesome, requiring great agonizing and gnashing of teeth. Liberals and moderates lie awake at night, asking how far they can take this affirmative action thing without sacrificing innocent white males. Have you ever wondered what that makes us—if not innocent, then ...? Affirmative action enables members of the dominant group to ask, "Is it fair to hire a less-qualified Chicano or black over a more-qualified white?" This is a curious way of framing the question, as I will argue in a moment, in part because those who ask it are themselves the beneficiaries of history's largest affirmative action program. This fact is rarely noticed, however, while the question goes on causing the few of us who are magically raised by affirmative action's unseen hand to feel guilty, undeserving, and stigmatized.

Affirmative action, as currently understood and promoted, is also ahistorical. For more than 200 years, white males benefitted from their own program of affirmative action, through unjustified preferences in jobs and education resulting from old-boy networks and official laws that lessened the competition. Today's affirmative action critics never characterize that scheme as affirmative action, which of course it was. By labeling problematic, troublesome, and ethically agonizing a paltry system that helps a few of us get ahead, critics neatly take our eyes off the system of arrangements that brought and maintained them in power, and enabled them to develop the rules and standards of quality and merit that now exclude us, make us appear unworthy, dependent (naturally) on affirmative action.

Well, if you were a member of the majority group and invented something that cut down the competition, made you feel good and virtuous, made minorities grateful and humble, and framed the "minority problem" in this wondrous way, I think you would be pretty pleased with yourself. Moreover, if you placed the operation of this program in the hands of the very people who brought about the situation that made it necessary in the first place, society would probably reward you with prizes and honors.

Please do not mistake what I am saying. As marginalized people we should strive to increase our power, cohesiveness, and representation in all significant areas of society. We should do this, though, because we are entitled to these things and because fundamental fairness requires this reallocation of power. We should reformulate the issue. Our acquiescence in treating it as "a question of standards" is absurd and self-defeating when you consider that we took no part in creating those standards and their fairness is one of the very things we want to call into question.

Affirmative action, then, is something no self-respecting attorney of color ought to support. We could, of course, take our own program, with our own goals, our own theoretical grounding, and our own managers and call it "Affirmative Action." But we would, of course, be talking about something quite different. My first point, then, is that we should demystify, interrogate, and destabilize affirmative action. The program was designed by others to promote their purposes, not ours.

Richard Delgado, *Affirmative Action as a Majoritarian Device: Or, Do You Really Want to Be a Role Model?*, 89 Mich. L. Rev. 1222, 1223–26 (1991).* See also Gabriel J. Chin, Bakke *to the Wall: The Crisis of Bakkean Diversity*, 4 Wm. & Mary Bill Rts. J. 881 (1996) (criticizing *Bakke* for not explaining whether the permissible diversity is cultural or racial).

Does characterizing affirmative action as substantive justice ignore the realities that Delgado describes?

6. For additional analysis of the issue of affirmative action, see Bryan K. Fair, *Notes of a Racial Caste Baby: Color Blindness and the End of Affirmative Action* (1997).

7. Affirmative action is often posed as an issue of special treatment. Reconsider *Morton v. Mancari*, Chapter 3 *supra*, characterizing "the preference [granted to Native Americans] as political rather than racial in nature." This statement appears in the location where the Supreme Court puts many of its important proclamations, in a footnote. Is this decision changed by *Adarand*? Should it be? Does the classification as political rather than racial favor Native peoples?

Consider the view expressed by David Williams, *The Borders of the Equal Protection Clause: Indians as Peoples*, 38 UCLA L. Rev. 759, 830–31 (1991):**

The primary error that the Court has made in analyzing the status of Indians under the Equal Protection Clause is to assert that the Clause applies to Indians in the same way and to the same extent that it applies to everyone else. A more honest approach would begin from a very different point: Reservation Indians are simply a categorical exception to the requirements of the Equal Protection Clause. This position is more consistent with what the Court actually does, with the historical underpinnings of the Clause, and with the moral intuitions of many of those who believe in the right of Indian separatism.

Any such view must answer at least two substantial objections. First, as a matter of positive law, how can one say that the Clause—with its apparently universal language—does not prohibit discrimination based on Indian ancestry, as it does every other kind of racial classification? And second, as a theoretical matter, does not removing the Indians from the protection of the Clause raise all the same concerns that a removal of any other group would? Does it not expose the Indians to even more of the kind of governmental racial hostility with which they are already too familiar? And, on the other hand, does it not allow the possibility for rank racial preference for the Indians to the detriment of the "the majority"?

The answer to the positive law challenge begins with a fact that the Court has almost willfully overlooked in its opinions dealing with Indians and the Equal Protection Clause: The Fourteenth Amendment itself says some specific things, both explicitly and implicitly, about the Indians. In particular, the Amendment plainly contemplates that the protections of the Amendment would not extend to Indians who owed at least partial allegiance to a tribal government. The Indians, under the Amendment, are in a profound sense still subjects of a semiforeign government and so may be treated differently from other inhabitants of the United States. And, importantly, nothing in the Amendment is meant to prevent Congress from continuing that pattern: As long as—but only as long as—Indians are subjects of sovereign tribal governments, Congress may single them out for special treatment, even if that treatment incorporates racial classifications.

8. As the court moves in the direction of emphasizing individuals and considering race only as an individual characteristic, forbidden to be used, consider the role of discrimination based on characteristics such as language, not routinely considered part of race, as raised by Juan Perea, discussing *Hernandez v. New York*, 500 U.S. 352 (1991).

In that case, the Court concluded that there was no equal protection violation when a prosecutor used peremptory challenges to exclude two bilingual Latino jurors from a jury that was expected to consider Spanish-language testimony. Because the discrimination in *Hernandez v. New York* was based on bilingualism, an ethnic characteristic of approximately two-thirds of American Latinos, *Hernandez* provides a good vehicle for assessing the current Court's ability to recognize and deal appropriately with discrimination because of ethnic characteristics.
* * *

The plurality opinion in *Hernandez v. New York*, authored by Justice Kennedy, uses the words "race" and "ethnicity" as though they were interchangeable. The opinion begins with the proposition that discrimination against two Latino jurors "by reason of their ethnicity" would violate the Equal Protection Clause. In the next sentence, Kennedy writes that the Court must determine whether the prosecutor offered a "race-neutral" reason for excluding the two Latino jurors. If the Court is considering potential discrimination because of ethnicity, as the plurality appears to recognize, then it should be determining whether the prosecutor's reason was "ethnicity-neutral," not "race-neutral." This distinction is more than a semantic difference because many reasons that can be deemed "race-neutral"—meaning "not race"—such as bilingualism, accent, or Latino surname, may not be "ethnicity-neutral."

The plurality acknowledged ambiguity in its conception of race:

> [W]e do not resolve the more difficult question of the breadth with which the concept of race should be defined for equal protection purposes.... [I]t may well be, for certain ethnic groups and in some communities, that proficiency in a particular language, like skin color, should be treated as a surrogate for race under an equal protection analysis.

Similarly, the plurality suggested that excluding jurors because they are Spanish-speaking, an ethnic characteristic of many Latinos, would violate the Equal Protection Clause.

The plurality's reference to the breadth, possibly expanding, possibly contracting, of its "concept of race" demonstrates that the plurality conceives of race as the only relevant characteristic protected under the Equal Protection Clause. The problem with grouping ethnic characteristics under the label "race" is that the single concept makes it harder to identify and redress discrimination because of ethnic characteristics. The Court can only consider the languages of ethnic groups as part of its concept of race and not on their own terms as targets of unconstitutional discrimination. By submerging the distinctive traits of language difference and bilingualism into race, the Court confuses ethnicity with race.

Although the plurality acknowledges that language may be a "surrogate" for race, it ignores the many other perceptible ethnic traits that elicit discrimination and that should also be subjects of heightened judicial scrutiny when used as the basis for state classifications. Professor Allport has listed many of the traits that elicit prejudice and discrimination. These include, among others, skin color, physical features, gestures and mannerisms, speech and accent, dress, religious practices, food habits, names and surnames, places of residence, and ethnic insignia. By collapsing all perceptible manifestations of ethnicity into its ambiguous "concept of race," the plurality makes it easy to ignore the discrimination that can occur because of any of these ethnic traits.

By creating a "concept of race" that it can expand or contract at will, the Court dilutes the meaning and proper analysis of race and ethnicity under the Constitution. A pliable "concept of race" leads easily to non-recognition of discrimination based on ethnic characteristics whenever the Court decides that certain traits, such as bilingualism, language difference, or accent do not belong within the boundaries it defines for race. Recognizing the capricious nature of the Court's concept of race is one way to understand the result in *Hernandez*: A majority of the Court decided that bilingualism, despite constituting part of Latino ethnicity, was not the same as race. Because language difference is not the same as race, the argument goes, discrimination because of language difference does not violate the Equal Protection Clause.

The plurality's apparent willingness to allow certain ethnic characteristics to be treated as "surrogates for race" illustrates what I shall call the correlation problem. This problem is created for advocates and litigants who must persuade a court that an ethnic characteristic is sufficiently linked to race or national origin to function as a "surrogate" for the recognized protected categories of race or national origin. One correlation problem is that courts retain discretion to decide which ethnic traits can, as a threshold matter, properly function as proxies for the "real" protected category of race. This formulation seems inconsistent with the Court's recognition that discrimination because of ethnicity violates the Equal Protection Clause. If the Court neither recognizes that language difference is an aspect of ethnicity nor that discrimination because of bilingualism raises an equal protection issue, then it has turned ethnicity into a meaningless abstraction.

In the absence of constitutional recognition that it is ethnicity itself, in its manifold aspects, that deserves constitutional protection, judges will make arbitrary and inconsistent decisions regarding which characteristics are "surrogates" for race. In applying the *Batson* standard of "race neutrality," for example, courts have differed widely on whether identical ethnic traits can function as proxies for race. Bilingualism and Spanish surname have been found, by different courts, to be both "race-neutral," and not "race-neutral." Courts have also rejected class certification for Mexican Americans by rejecting the significance of ethnic traits such as self identification, Spanish surname, Mexican or Spanish ancestry, and Spanish language.

Another correlation problem is the uncertain degree of correlation one must prove. What level of correlation would establish that an ethnic characteristic is actually a proxy for prohibited race or national origin discrimination? Would the fact that two-thirds of American Latinos are bilingual establish Spanish/English bilingualism as a proxy for Latino ethnicity? Is ninety percent required? Because there are no guidelines to establish the sufficiency of a correlation for legal purposes, judges will make arbitrary and inconsistent choices as to what degree of correlation is "sufficient" for the purposes of establishing discrimination. The correlation problem forces advocates to make the weak and potentially unpersuasive legal argument that some degree of correlation is sufficient for an ethnic trait to be considered a proxy for race or national origin.

By collapsing the traits of ethnicity into an ambiguous and pliable notion of "surrogacy for race," the plurality ignores the independent significance that ethnicity should have in equal protection analysis. Courts protecting solely against race or national origin discrimination do not protect enough. Discrimination because of ethnicity often will not be redressed because of correlations or surrogacy deemed insufficient.
* * *

In a concurring opinion in *Hernandez v. New York*, Justice O'Connor, joined by Justice Scalia, took a narrower view of race that would not permit its extension to encompass any ethnic characteristics. To prevail, the Justice wrote, the defendant must prove that the prosecutor "intentionally discriminated against Hispanic jurors on the basis of their race." O'Connor also rejected the significance of the correlation between ethnic characteristics, race, and presumably national origin:

> No matter how closely tied or significantly correlated to race the explanation for a peremptory strike may be, the strike does not implicate the Equal Protection Clause unless it is based on race. That is the distinction between disproportionate effect, which is not sufficient to constitute an equal protection violation, and intentional discrimination, which is.

The approach taken by O'Connor generates major problems for advocates attempting to argue that a classification based on "national origin" violates the Equal Protection Clause. O'Connor tells us that only discrimination because of race, and presumably national origin, matters; discrimination for any other reason does not violate equal protection. If this approach gains popularity among the Justices, then invidious discrimination because of ethnic characteristics, like language, accent, surname, religion, and certain physical characteristics will always be "race-neutral" in the sense that these traits are not race.

The concurrence's approach grants prosecutors free license to discriminate for many reasons that have been found to be discriminatory in other, related contexts. Under the Equal Employment Opportunity Commission's Guidelines on National Origin Discrimination, for example, the Commission has recognized that ethnic traits such as surname, accent, language difference, and other characteristics may be reasons for discrimination. Some courts, interpreting the prohibition against "national origin" discrimination in Title VII of the Civil Rights Act of 1964, have found that these ethnic traits can be the basis for prohibited discrimination.

Furthermore, prosecutors and other governmental actors have learned to avoid overt expressions of discrimination because of national origin or race. As Justice Thurgood Marshall recognized some time ago, "[a]ny prosecutor can easily assert facially neutral reasons for striking a juror, and trial courts are ill equipped to second-guess those reasons." The narrow conception of race expressed in the concurrence facilitates an enormous amount of discrimination.

Furthermore, applying a narrow concept of race to Latinos makes no sense. Latinos constitute a heterogenous group composed of people of many races and nationalities but with a high degree of commonality in culture, language, history, and tradition. For this group, equal protection defined narrowly by race really constitutes little or no protection because much discrimination suffered by Latinos does not depend on racial difference. * * *

In a dissenting opinion joined by Justice Marshall, Justice Stevens reiterated his view that a significant disproportionate impact is itself evidence of discriminatory purpose. Justice Stevens would have found a violation of equal protection in *Hernandez v. New York* for three reasons: (1) because of the inevitable disproportionate impact of the prosecutor's exclusion of bilinguals upon Spanish-speaking prospective jurors, (2) because "[a]n explanation that is 'race-neutral' on its face is nonetheless unacceptable if it is merely a proxy for a discriminatory practice," and (3) because less drastic means could have satisfied the prosecutor's interests.

While Justice Stevens' approach, if followed, holds more potential for redressing discrimination than the approaches described in the other opinions, his approach is flawed because he concedes the facial neutrality of governmental action that is not neutral. There is nothing neutral about a governmental peremptory challenge that, on its face, excludes mostly Latino people because of their bilingualism. The absence of neutrality is easily shown by considering the prosecutor's question at issue in *Hernandez v. New York.*

The prosecutor asked the jurors "whether or not they could accept the translation" of Spanish-language testimony. Monolingual English-speaking jurors, who will understand only the English interpretation of testimony, have no choice but to accept the interpreter's translation. Their response to the question was an easy "yes." Bilingual jurors, who will understand both the Spanish-language source testimony as well as the interpreted version, will be aware of discrepancies between the testimony and its interpretation. Such discrepancies occur routinely in interpreted testimony. Suppose that the interpreter makes errors in the interpretation. Bilingual jurors will then be forced into the dilemma of accepting an inaccurate translation or relying on their understanding of what the testimony actually was, an intellectual dilemma not confronted by monolingual English speakers. Why should bilingual jurors promise under oath to accept a potentially erroneous interpretation? If a bilingual juror promises to accept an interpretation of unknown accuracy, is the juror possibly violating her duty to find the facts to the best of her ability? These are inevitable issues for bilingual jurors, which demonstrate that the prosecutor's question is not facially neutral.

In the United States, most persons become bilingual by being born into a family whose primary language is not English and subsequently growing up in that family. Many such persons claim Spanish as their first language, and then learn English in order to adapt to the dominant English-speaking culture.

Justice Stevens' approach transforms an unstated norm of the dominant culture, English-speaking monolingualism, into a baseline for facial neutrality. Facial neutrality, thus constructed, becomes no more than the means for the enforcement of the norms of the dominant culture for assessing social deviance and constitutionality. The Court has erred as badly in the context of gender, with its holdings that discrimination on the basis of pregnancy did not constitute sex discrimination. In both the bilingualism and pregnancy cases, the Court concluded that discrimination with an exclusive adverse impact upon a historically disadvantaged group was not discrimination, transforming dominant cultural norms of English-speaking monolingualism and male gender into "facially neutral" baselines against which social and constitutional deviance are measured. But there is no facial neutrality when a rule or practice will burden only historically disempowered groups. The lack of neutrality in other so-called facially neutral standards, such as objective tests like the LSAT, have come under increasing criticism.

Together, the plurality and concurring opinions demonstrate much about the current Court's flawed approach to questions of discrimination because of ethnicity. First, both opinions treat race as the only relevant prohibited basis for discrimination under the Equal Protection

Clause. By focusing exclusively on race, the Court will not recognize, either by design or through error, many equally pernicious forms of discrimination because of ethnic traits. The Court's exclusive focus on race, either broadly or narrowly conceived, reinforces the tendency to consider all issues of discrimination and racism in the binary terms of only two communities, the African American and the white. The Court's use of only race oversimplifies grossly the complexity in our ethnically diverse country. The dissent's approach also over-simplifies by defining facial neutrality to correspond to unstated majoritarian norms when in fact such norms are inherently discriminatory in certain cases. §*Hernandez* presents one such case—a norm of English monolingualism is inherently discriminatory against bilingual persons. Rather than over-simplification, our ethnic diversity requires much greater nuance in the analysis of problems of discrimination under the Constitution.

Juan F. Perea, *Ethnicity and the Constitution: Beyond the Black and White Binary Constitution*, 36 Wm. & Mary L. Rev. 571, 594–603 (1995).* See also Miguel A. Méndez, Hernandez: *The Wrong Message at the Wrong Time*, 4 Stan. L. & Pol'y Rev. 193 (1993); Deborah A. Ramirez, *Excluded Voices: The Disenfranchisement of Ethnic Groups from Jury Service,* 1993 Wis. L. Rev. 761.

9.   Professor Perea has advocated expanding our notion of "race" such that it encompasses all characteristics used as the basis for invidious discrimination. Thus traits such as language, accent, hair style, and dress, in addition to skin color and other phenotypical features, should be understood as constitutive parts of the social construction of race. Cf., *e.g.*, Juan F. Perea, *The Black/White Binary Paradigm of Race*, excerpted *supra* in Chs. 4 and 6. Would this broadening of the notion of race further the evolution of notions of equality? On the important concept of the social construction of race, see Ian F. Haney López, *The Social Construction of Race: Some Observations on Illusion, Fabrication, and Choice*, 29 Harv. C.R.-C.L. L. Rev. 1 (1994); *Race and Erasure: The Salience of Race to LatCrit Theory*, 85 Calif. L. Rev. 1143 (1997).

10.   Most of the cases addressed in this chapter which shed light on developing notions of equality have originated in an employment setting. "The subject matter addressed by Title VII—employment and the antidiscrimination principle—is the back end of and the last step on a linear progression that begins with housing and education and ends with the acquisition of human capital and competitive skills that individuals will use to enter the labor market and seek employment. To the extent that the anticompetitive effects of racism at the first steps of the progression (housing and education) negatively affect the acquisition of indispensable human capital, blacks and others who are adversely affected will have no or relatively fewer job skills * * *." Ronald Turner, *Thirty Years of Title VII's Regulatory Regime: Rights, Theories, and Realities*, 46 Ala. L. Rev 375, 381–82 (1995). We turn in Chapter 9 to issues relating to race and housing and education.

Chapter 8

RACE, VOTING, AND PARTICIPATION IN DEMOCRACY

SECTION 1. VOTING MATTERS

Perhaps no issue is more central to the notion of democracy than the election of public officials by the citizenry. "Undoubtedly, the right of suffrage is a fundamental matter in a free and democratic society. Especially since the right to exercise the franchise in a free and unimpaired manner is preservative of other basic civil and political rights, any alleged infringement of the right of citizens to vote must be carefully and meticulously scrutinized." *Reynolds v. Sims*, 377 U.S. 533, 561–62 (1964). A government based on democratic norms must, by definition, provide for the participation of its citizens. But who is a citizen? What does participation mean? Lenore Look puts a personal face on these issues:

LENORE LOOK
My Mother's Vote
Princeton Alumni Weekly, Mar. 19, 1997 at 56.*

My mother never wastes anything. She eats fish eyes, chicken butts, bone marrow. She saves wrapping paper and margarine containers, and endlessly recycles cellophane wrap and aluminum foil. In the same spirit of economy, she leaves lamp shades in their plastic wraps and covers her furniture with bedsheets. She keeps Christmas candy and rum cakes forever. And for reasons beyond my understanding until now, she saved, untouched for nearly 30 years, her right to vote.

It never made sense to me, as a second-generation American, why my mother worked so hard at getting her U.S. Citizenship, then shunned its most basic duty. When I was a child she spent long hours taking language and civics lessons from an older Chinese woman who tutored recent immigrants for their citizenship exams. I remember my mother cramming for her exam and asking me for help, though I was barely in school myself. She completely covered her workbook pages with nota-

* Copyright © 1997 by Lenore Look. Used by permission.

580

tions in Chinese as she flipped back and forth between her Chinese/English dictionary and her text, searching for the key that would unlock America for her. It was a painful trip through basic American history and simple conversational English, taken word by word through a slow multi-step process that began with deciphering letters and syllables and ended in tears. She faced formidable obstacles to citizenship, including my uncle, who admonished her for being a "traitor." She persevered, but when she finally obtained her citizenship, in 1967, there was no celebration or even acknowledgment of what she had accomplished.

Sometime after my mother took her oath of citizenship, we were joined by other members of her family—her mother, three brothers, a sister-in-law, and an infant nephew. Penniless immigrants, they had come to live with us in our modest three-bedroom, one-bath house on Beacon Hill, a deteriorating neighborhood on Seattle's south side, where Chinese were allowed to buy real estate. Their arrival turned our home into a noisy, crowded place of perpetual activity and endless chatter, an atmosphere that must have resembled at once a carnival and a cocktail party.

I remember my mother as particularly happy during that time; her aura was like that of a triumphant athlete. She had moved a mountain; she had obtained the golden ticket—citizenship—that had brought her family to the States. But with her duty done, she began to lose most of what little English she had learned and any interest in her adopted country.

It was during this period that she started working as a seamstress in a sporting goods factory. Almost all the workers were Chinese immigrants, and few if any spoke more than rudimentary English. Despite the low wages and crippling work, my mother preferred this world, which allowed her to remain an outsider; she saw no point in adopting the language and culture of her new country. She continued to speak only Chinese, to surround herself with Chinese coworkers and friends, and to shop mostly at Chinese stores. She loathed having to use any of her fading English, and she hated American food, American TV, and most of all the rebelliousness of her American children.

In the 1970s, a Chinese–American woman who owned a restaurant ran for the Seattle City Council. In our Toisan patois my mother called her despicable. "Look at her," she said. "Has she no shame? Showing herself like that!" In her eyes, running for office was tantamount to being a prostitute.

My mother's aversion to politics was my attraction to it. As a teenager, I was dismissive and resentful about everything my mother stood for, everything she symbolized: tradition, filial piety, invisibility. When I began to push beyond the boundaries of our home, I was arrogant enough to determine that my life would count for more than hers. I would embrace all that she feared, all that she was not. To her chagrin, I joined the staff of my high-school newspaper. I wrote stories about local politicians and essays about political issues. * * * When I cast my first vote (for Jimmy Carter), it became an opportunity to harangue my mother about her civic duty. * * *

Four years later, while working as a reporter at the *Los Angeles Times*, I reminded her again of her obligation. "Your dad voted," she said, as though his ballot alone was sufficient for the two of them. Four years later she had another excuse.

Somewhere between the 1988 election and last year's, I grew increasingly cynical about my own civic duty and stopped hounding my mother about hers. My interest in politics waned as one election after another seemed to offer up the same uninspiring choices. My years of preaching political involvement were over.

Then, last November, my mother called me at my home in New Jersey for one of our weekly chats.

"Do you remember that family who lived in that house three blocks from us on Beacon Hill?" she asked in Chinese.

"Which one?"

"You went to school with their younger son, and his sister beat up your brother once.... Their eldest son just became governor."

In the *New York Times* I had read with mild interest about Gary Locke's victory. His family and ours had attended the same Chinese Baptist Church, and I remembered him as a counselor at summer Bible camp.

"I voted for him," she let drop.

"You voted?"

"I had to. Everyone voted," she said, referring to her Chinese friends.

"But you never voted before."

"His mother sewed, and his father worked like yours."

I understood. Her voice was clear, and for the first time she sounded proud of their immigrant life of bent-back labor.

So nearly three decades after gaining her citizenship, my mother, the political outsider, stepped in from the margin of society to add her vote to the landslide victory for our nation's first Chinese–American governor.

My mother voted because she saw, for the first time, a choice. An Asian–American governor would mean less discrimination, she said. It was a victory that she hoped would give Asian Americans some sway over issues that concern them, like immigration and bilingual education, a victory that would give them respect.

From its periphery, she had entered a society that until now had seemed to her indifferent and unalterable. To me, her vote revealed that in our country there are no centers or certain names around which we must arrange ourselves; instead, as Emerson said of American politics, "Any particle may suddenly become the center of the movement and compel the system to gyrate around it."

My mother never wastes anything, and she didn't waste her vote. I hope she finds reason to cast it again.

Notes and Questions

1. Did you have an emotional reaction when Ms. Look's mother said she had finally voted? Positive or negative? What meanings are imbedded in the idea of voting?

2. Do members of your extended family talk about elections? Do they vote? Do you? Why or why not? Do you believe that your vote matters? Might the significance of voting to you and your classmates vary according to race?

3. Is the issue of voting gendered? Why didn't Ms. Look's mother vote when a Chinese–American woman ran for city council? Are men who run for office like prostitutes? Is your answer different if the candidate is a member of a racial minority, like Governor Locke?

4. What concerns are implicated by the act of voting besides simply going to the polling place and filling out a ballot? Derrick Bell has identified three prerequisites for effective voting: (1) access to the ballot, (2) availability of political power, and (3) motivation to participate in the political process. Derrick Bell, *Race, Racism, and American Law* (3d ed. 1992). After this nation's history of exclusion from the franchise based on race, the Voting Rights Act with its amendments sought to enable everyone to achieve the first condition, access to the ballot. The use of the Voting Rights Act to achieve political power remains controversial. Motivation to participate in the political process remains tied to the pervasive problem of societal racism, particularly in areas of education and employment. This Chapter examines voting issues in each of these three areas, exclusion from voting, the availability of political power, and motivation to participate, concluding with reflections on the connection between voting and democracy.

SECTION 2. EXCLUSION FROM VOTING

Although today most Americans take this right to vote for granted, in the infancy of the United States this basic democratic right was denied, based on race. This exclusion from the right to vote continued throughout this nation's history.

The founders excluded nonwhites from eligibility for naturalized citizenship. The first condition for naturalization in the Naturalization Act of 1790 was that one be a "free white person." Describing the reasons why access to citizenship was restricted, Ronald Takaki writes that "[t]he Founding Fathers needed to define political membership for the new republic. In Congress, they enacted the Naturalization Act of 1790. In supporting this law, they affirmed their commitment to the 'pure principles of Republicanism' and their determination to develop a citizenry of good and 'useful' men. Only the 'worthy part of mankind' would be encouraged to settle in the new republic and be eligible for citizenship. * * * Applicants for naturalized citizenship were required to reside in the United States for two years as well as provide 'proof' of good character in court and document their republican fitness. They also had to be 'white.' This law reflected what Thomas Jefferson envisioned as a society composed of 'a people speaking the same language, governed in similar forms, and by similar laws.' The Naturalization Act excluded from citizenship not only nonwhite immigrants but also a group of people already here—Indians. Though they were born in the United States, they were regarded as members of tribes, or as domestic subjects; their status was considered analogous to children of foreign diplomats born here. As domestic 'foreigners,' Native Americans could not seek naturalized citizenship, for they were not 'white.'" Ronald Takaki, *A Different Mirror* 79–80 (1993) (footnotes omitted).

Passage of the Fourteenth Amendment in 1868 legally changed the notion of citizenship and confirmed the democratic notion of inclusion: "All persons born or naturalized in the United States, and subject to the jurisdiction thereof, are citizens of the United States and of the State wherein they reside." U.S. Const. Amend. XIV, § 1. The Fifteenth Amendment, passed in 1870, provided that "the rights of citizens of the United States to vote shall not be denied or abridged by the United States or by any State on account of race, color, or previous condition of servitude." U.S. Const. Amend. XV. Women of all races remained citizens without the right to vote, until the Nineteenth Amendment passed in 1920. U.S. Const. Amend. XIX.

Conferral of the right to vote for men of all races by the Fifteenth Amendment did not change voting patterns in many places. State officials and vigilante groups used an arsenal of weapons to ensure the continuity of the white ballot box and to deny the franchise to men of color. These means of limiting suffrage included multiple box laws (requiring voters to place ballots in the appropriate boxes), secret ballots, literacy tests, poll taxes, disqualifications from eligibility to vote for certain crimes, white primaries, and grandfather clauses.

Enactment of the post-Civil War amendments did give legal fodder for challenging these exclusionary practices, as in the following case, an indictment against Abraham Elm, for illegal voting.

UNITED STATES v. ELM

25 Fed.Cas. 1006 (N.D.N.Y.1877).

WALLACE, District Judge.

The defendant, an Oneida Indian, who was born and had always resided within the town of Lenox, Madison county, voted for representative in congress at the election of 1876, claiming to be a citizen of the United States. He was indicted for illegal voting, tried, and convicted in this court. * * * [T]he question is now presented whether or not the Oneida Indians are citizens of the United States, and, as such, entitled to vote.

If the defendant was a citizen of the United States, he was entitled to exercise the right of suffrage. The right to vote is conferred by the state, not by the United States, and it has been conferred in New York upon "every male citizen of the age of twenty-one years who shall have been a citizen for ten days and an inhabitant of this state one year next preceding an election, and for the last four months a resident of the county, and for the last twenty days a resident of the election district in which he may offer his vote." By the Fourteenth Amendment to the constitution it is declared that "all persons born or naturalized in the

United States and subject to the jurisdiction thereof are citizens of the United States and of the state wherein they reside," and by force of this language every citizen of the United States is a citizen of the state wherein he resides. It is not enough to confer citizenship on the defendant that he was born in the United States. It must also appear that he was "subject to the jurisdiction thereof," within the meaning of the Fourteenth Amendment.

In a general sense every person born in the United States is within the jurisdiction thereof while he remains in the country. Aliens, while residing here, owe a local allegiance, and are equally bound with citizens to obey all general laws for the maintenance of peace and order which do not relate specially to our own citizens, and they are amenable to the ordinary tribunals of the country. But there are classes of residents who, though they may be born here, are not subject to the exercise of those prerogatives of sovereignty which a government has the right to enforce over its own citizens, and over them alone, and it is to these that the language of the Amendment applies. Within this sense, those persons who, though born here, are born within the allegiance of a foreign sovereign, or of another government, are not subject to the jurisdiction of the United States. The children of ambassadors, though in fact born here, are, in the theory of the law, born within the allegiance of the foreign power the parent represents.

Indians who maintain their tribal relations are the subjects of independent governments, and, as such, not in the jurisdiction of the United States, within the meaning of the Amendment, because the Indian nations have always been regarded as distinct political communities, between which and our government certain international relations were to be maintained. These relations are established by treaties to the same extent as with foreign powers. They are treated as sovereign communities, possessing and exercising the right of free deliberation and action, but, in consideration of protection, owing a qualified subjection to the United States.

If defendant's tribe continued to maintain its tribal integrity, and he continued to recognize his tribal relations, his status as a citizen would not be affected by the Fourteenth Amendment; but such is not his case. His tribe has ceased to maintain its tribal integrity, and he has abandoned his tribal relations, as will hereafter appear; and because of these facts, and because Indians in this state are subject to taxation, he is a citizen, within the meaning of the Fourteenth Amendment. This conclusion is sanctioned not only by the language of the Fourteenth Amendment, but is fortified by other legislation by congress concerning citizenship.

By [the Civil Rights Acts of 1866] all persons born in the United States and not subject to any foreign power, excluding Indians not taxed, are declared to be citizens of the United States. Native Indians in this state are taxed. By an act of the legislature passed in 1843, native Indians are authorized to purchase, take, hold, and convey real estate, and, when they become freeholders to the value of $100, "are subject to taxation and to the civil jurisdiction of courts of law and equity in the same manner and to the same extent as citizens." When by the civil rights bill Indians not taxed were excluded from the classes upon which citizenship was conferred, upon well-settled rules of construction those who were taxed were by implication included in the grant. In other words, those Indians who were taxed were not excepted from the class who were declared to be citizens. * * *

While, primarily, these measures [the Fourteenth Amendment and another Congressional act], originated for the protection of natives of African descent, who, by the decision in the case of *Scott v. Sandford*, [19 How. [60 U.S.] 393,] were held not to be citizens of the United States, within the meaning of the constitution, it is not to be doubted that they were intended to confer the rights of citizenship upon such others as, owing to the peculiar condition of our national development, were not citizens in legal contemplation, though by birth and by allegiance they were or might become entitled to recognition as such.

The phraseology employed is sufficiently broad to include Indians who have abandoned their tribes and become so far integrated with the general body of citizens that the states in which they reside have subjected them to the duties of citizens and enforced over them the prerogatives of sovereignty. Prior to the adoption of the Fourteenth Amendment, many of the Indian tribes had become disintegrated, and the members had abandoned their tribal relations, and were distributed among and assimilated with the general body of citizens of the state in which they lived, conforming to the same usages, and their rights of person and property regulated by the same laws, which controlled the rest of the inhabitants of the state. They were natives by birth, and were not aliens in allegiance. Their status had been defined, sometimes, as that of alien residents; sometimes, as that of domestic subjects. In the case of *Scott v. Sandford*, 19 How. [60 U.S.] at 404, Chief Justice Taney said: "If an individual Indian should leave his tribe, and take up his abode among the white population, he would be entitled to all the rights and privileges which would belong to an emigrant from any other foreign people." Accepting this as a correct statement of the law, it would follow that such an Indian was not, and in the absence of special legislation could not become, a citizen. He could not be naturalized, because the naturalization laws only apply to persons born out of the United States. The remarks of Chief Justice Taney were applicable to that class of Indians who had left their tribes, and thus abandoned their tribal relations; but instances were extant, in the history of the Indian tribes, where the tribal organization had become defunct, and where the individual Indians had so far been recognized as citizens of the state that they had been authorized to acquire and hold real estate, and subjected to taxation and to the civil jurisdiction of the courts. It had never been authoritatively decided whether or not such Indians were citizens.

In 1822 the supreme court of this state decided, in *Jackson v. Goodell*, 20 Johns. 188, that the Indians resident in this state were citizens, but that decision was reversed by the court of errors. Since that decision, however, great changes have taken place in the social and political relations between the Indians and the body of citizens at large, as is well illustrated by the history of the Oneidas. By treaties between the United States and the Six Nations, the Menomonies, and Winnebagoes in 1831 and 1838, the Six Nations acquired extensive cessions of lands in Wisconsin near Green Bay; and about that time the main body of the Oneidas removed to these lands. Since then, the tribal government has ceased as to those who remained in this state. It is true those remaining here have continued to designate one of their number as chief, but his sole authority consists in representing them in the receipt of an annuity which he distributes among the survivors. The 20 families which constitute the remnant of the Oneidas reside in the vicinity of their original reservation. They do not constitute a community by themselves, but their dwellings are interspersed with the habitations of the whites. In religion, in customs, in language, in everything but the color of their skins, they are identified with the rest of the population. In 1843, by an act of the legislature of this state, they were authorized to hold their lands in severalty, according to a partition which had theretofore been made. Reference has already been made to the general law of this state, passed in 1843, subjecting them to taxation and to the jurisdiction of the courts in the same manner and to the same extent as other citizens. In view of the changes which have intervened in the social and political relations of the Indians of this state since the decision of *Jackson v. Goodell*, there is certainly fair reasons to assume that, irrespective of the Fourteenth Amendment, they would now be held to be citizens of the state. However that might be, those who, like the defendant, have no tribe, and are taxed, are, within the language of the Fourteenth Amendment, subject to the jurisdiction of the United States, as that language should be interpreted in the light of the civil rights bill. They are natives, they owe no allegiance other than to the government of the United States, and they have been placed by the state upon an equality with its citizens respecting important rights denied to aliens. As the state and the United States can impose upon them all the duties and obligations of subjects, they are entitled to the corresponding rights which spring from relation. These are the rights which a government owes to its citizens.

For these reasons, my conclusion is the defendant was entitled to vote, and was improperly convicted. The motion for a new trial is granted.

Notes and Questions

1. Why does the court need to make so many arguments that Indians are citizens? How does the "peculiar condition of our national development" have bearing on the court's reasoning?

2. The court comments, "In religion, in customs, in language, in everything but the color of their skins, they are identified with the rest of the population." Notice that Indians are deemed citizens only if they have abandoned their tribes. Should such assimilation be required in order to vote or be viewed as part of the fabric of democratic life? See Bill Ong Hing, *To Be an American: Cultural Pluralism and the Rhetoric of Assimilation* 20–22 (1997) (describing the Americanization movement directed at "every facet of Native American life: language, appearance, religion, economic structure, political models, value, and philosophy").

3. For the origin of the phrase "Indians, not taxed," see United States Constitution, Art. I, § 2, which provides that "Indians, not taxed" be excluded from the population count used to determine Congressional representatives. Congress did not grant citizenship to Indians until it passed the Citizenship Act of 1924, codified as amended at 8 U.S.C.A. § 1401(b) (1998) (granting citizenship to "all non-citizen Indians born within the territorial limits of the United States" regardless of whether they wanted to be considered citizens or not).

4. The role of law as an important avenue for vindicating legal rights is quite evident in the voting arena. A series of cases successfully challenged the pervasive exclusionary practices used to deny the franchise to citizens of color.

In *Terry v. Adams*, 345 U.S. 461 (1953), African–American citizens challenged the white primary, in which a political group limited to white members held its own primary election prior to the Democratic primary. The Supreme Court held such primaries unconstitutional, finding that they produced candidates who were simply ratified by white voters in the following primary and general election, effectively denying African–American citizens any voice in electing county officials.

The requirement that voters pay poll taxes could also subvert the Fifteenth Amendment. The U.S. Supreme Court first upheld this practice in *Breedlove v. Suttles*, 302 U.S. 277 (1937) observing, "The Equal Protection Clause does not require absolute equality." 302 U.S. at 281. In *Harper v. Virginia Bd. of Elections*, 383 U.S. 663 (1966), the Supreme Court overruled *Breedlove* and declared the poll tax unconstitutional, finding an equal protection violation whenever a state "makes the affluence of the voter or payment of any fee an electoral standard." 383 U.S. at 666.

Guinn v. United States, 238 U.S. 347 (1915), established that the grandfather clause (allowing those of a certain age and their descendants a right to register without complying with literacy requirements) was invalid.

The Court ruled that Congress had the power to regulate literacy requirements for voting and to prohibit states from using them, in *Katzenbach v. Morgan*, 384 U.S. 641 (1966).

5. But even though law provided an avenue to secure voting rights in these cases and for Abraham Elm, the threat and intimidation of the possibility of prosecution, even one that might later be overturned, would deter many citizens of color from exercising those legal rights. Even with the victory in a case like this, many others might still be deterred from thinking about exercising the right to vote.

The history of voter registration drives in the South revealed many illegal abuses that led to the passage of the 1965 Voting Rights Act. This history is recounted in Taylor Branch, *Parting the Waters* 480–81 (1988),* who explains that U.S. Attorney General Robert Kennedy, in an effort to rechannel the Freedom Ride Coordinating Committee, originally promised federal support and protection if they would begin a voter registration drive aimed at registering African Americans. Robert Moses "labored to implant tiny registration projects in the core counties of the Mississippi Delta, north of Jackson. It was plantation country, where most of the potential Negro

---

voters lived on scattered farms amid unspeakable poverty and illiteracy, in a state of semifeudal dependence on the white planters." *Id.* at 634. Beginning in the town of McComb, Mississippi, Moses conducted voter registration classes. Branch describes the first effort to register voters in Amite County:

> On the morning of August 15, Moses and the first three Amite County volunteers drove to the county courthouse in the town of Liberty, some twenty-five miles from McComb. A plaque on the lawn proclaimed that it was the oldest courthouse in Mississippi, built in 1839, and boasted that Cecil Borden's condensed milk had been invented in Liberty, as had Dr. Tichener's antiseptic powder. The four Negroes passed the plaque and the Confederate memorial statue, entered the enormous white brick structure, and made their way to the office of the county registrar, who asked rather sternly what had brought them there.

> A very old Negro man waited helplessly for one of the two women volunteers to reply, but both of them also stood speechless with fear. Moses finally spoke up from behind, "They would like to try to register to vote," he said. The registrar questioned Moses about his interest in the matter and then told them all to wait. While they did, curious officials came by for silent looks at the oddities who were making themselves the chief topic of the day's conversation. The sheriff stopped in, followed by deputies, clerks from the tax office, and an examiner from the driver's license bureau. A Mississippi highway patrolman sauntered in and took a seat.

> Six hours later, Moses finally escaped the tension of the courthouse. His three volunteers knew they would be rejected as voters, but they were elated anyway, because they had been allowed to fill out the forms.

Id. at 494.

The jubilation waned as the group was followed by a highway patrolman for the entire drive home. "[T]he Amite county volunteers vowed never again to set foot in the registrar's office." *Id.* at 495. The officer arrested Moses when the group arrived in McComb.

6. The hard political organizing work of leaders like Robert Moses and unsung heroes like his band of volunteers created a sense of urgency in Congress about voting. The prevention of African Americans from voting by intimidating practices remained serious enough to lead Congress to pass the Voting Rights Act of 1965 with amendments in 1982, 42 U.S.C.A. § 1973. The Court described the Voting Rights Act in *South Carolina v. Katzenbach*:

> The Voting Rights Act of 1965 reflects Congress' firm intention to rid the country of racial discrimination in voting. The heart of the Act is a complex scheme of stringent remedies aimed at areas where voting discrimination has been most flagrant. Section 4(a)—(d) lays down a formula defining the States and political subdivisions to which these new remedies apply. The first of the remedies * * * is the suspension of literacy tests and similar voting qualifications for a period of five years from the last occurrence of substantial voting discrimination. Section 5 prescribes a second remedy, the suspension of all new voting regulations pending review by federal authorities to determine whether their use would perpetuate voting discrimination. The third remedy, covered in §§ 6(b), 7, 9, and 13(a), is the assignment of federal examiners on

certification by the Attorney General to list qualified applicants who are thereafter entitled to vote in all elections.

Other provisions of the Act prescribe subsidiary cures for persistent voting discrimination. [The Act] authorizes the appointment of federal poll-watchers in places to which federal examiners have already been assigned, * * * excuses those made eligible to vote by the Act from paying accumulated past poll taxes for state and local elections, * * * [and] provides for balloting by persons denied access to the polls in areas where federal examiners have been appointed.

The remaining remedial portions of the Act are aimed at voting discrimination in any area of the country where it may occur. Section 2 broadly prohibits the use of voting rules to abridge exercise of the franchise on racial grounds. [Other sections] strengthen existing procedures for attacking voting discrimination by means of litigation. [The Act] excuses citizens educated in American schools conducted in a foreign language from passing English-language literacy tests, * * * facilitates constitutional litigation challenging the imposition of all poll taxes for state and local elections, [and] authorize[s] civil and criminal sanctions against interference with the exercise of rights guaranteed by the Act.

383 U.S. 301, 316 (1966).

SECTION 3. THE AVAILABILITY OF POLITICAL POWER AND HAVING THE VOTE "COUNT"

An underlying issue in voting cases concerns the availability of political power. The notion that everyone's individual vote should matter in the political process is well established. "[T]he right to have one's vote counted is as open to protection . . . as the right to put a ballot in a box." *United States v. Mosley*, 238 U.S. 383, 386 (1915). What does having "one's vote counted" mean? Methods of representation, voter dilution, and gerrymandering cases all implicate the interpretation of having one's vote count.

A. METHODS OF REPRESENTATION AND VOTER DILUTION

Cases addressing methods of representation relate to political power. Most state legislatures draw elective districts so that voters elect one representative from that district. In a multimember district, residents elect more than one official. Use of the multimember district has been one method used to diminish the impact of minority votes. A minority group, which could elect at least one representative if its population were drawn to constitute one out of five districts, might be unable to elect anyone in a multimember district with five representatives.

Minority groups have used bullet voting as a means to avoid the potential disenfranchisement resulting from multimember districts. The Supreme Court explained bullet (single-shot) voting as follows:

Consider [a] town of 600 whites and 400 blacks with an at-large election to choose four council members. Each voter is able to cast four votes. Suppose there are eight white candidates, with the votes of the whites split among them approximately equally, and one black candidate, with all the blacks voting for him and no one else. The result is that each white candidate receives about 300 votes and the black candidate receives 400 votes. The black has probably won a seat. This technique is called single-shot voting. Single-shot voting enables a minority group to win some at-large seats if it concentrates its vote behind a limited number of candidates and if the vote of the majority is divided among a number of candidates.

Thornburg v. Gingles, 478 U.S. 30, 39 n.5 (1986).

Dilution of minority voting by multimember districts directly affects political power. The practice was attacked as unconstitutional and violative of the Voting Rights Act in *Thornburg v. Gingles*, 478 U.S. 30 (1986). In *Thornburg*, the Supreme Court interpreted the new legal standards created by the 1982 congressional amendments to the Voting Rights Act. The amendments were "largely a response to this Court's plurality opinion in *Mobile v. Bolden*, 446 U.S. 55 (1980), which had declared that, in order to establish a violation either of § 2 or of the Fourteenth or Fifteenth Amendments, minority voters must prove that a contested electoral mechanism was intentionally adopted or maintained by state officials for a discriminatory purpose. Congress substantially revised § 2 to make clear that a violation could be proved by showing discriminatory effect alone and to establish as the relevant legal standard the 'results test.' " 478 U.S. at 35. Under the results test, "plaintiffs could prevail by showing that, under the totality of the circumstances, a challenged election law or procedure had the effect of denying a protected minority an equal chance to participate in the electoral process. Under the 'results test,' plaintiffs are not required to demonstrate that the challenged electoral law or structure was designed or maintained for a discriminatory purpose." 478 U.S. at 44, n.8.

THORNBURG v. GINGLES

478 U.S. 30 (1986).

Justice Brennan delivered the opinion of the Court.

This case requires that we construe for the first time § 2 of the Voting Rights Act of 1965, as amended June 29, 1982. 42 U.S.C.A. § 1973. The * * * [district court] held that the use in a legislative redistricting plan of multimember districts in five North Carolina legislative districts violated § 2 by impairing the opportunity of black voters "to participate in the political process and to elect representatives of their choice." * * *

In April 1982, the North Carolina General Assembly enacted a legislative redistricting plan for the State's Senate and House of Representatives. Appellees, black citizens of North Carolina who are registered to vote, challenged seven districts, one single-member and six multimember districts, alleging that the redistricting scheme impaired black citizens' ability to elect representatives of their choice in violation of the Fourteenth and Fifteenth Amendments to the United States Constitution and of § 2 of the Voting Rights Act. * * *

Section 2, as amended, 96 Stat. 134, reads as follows:

"(a) No voting qualification or prerequisite to voting or standard, practice, or procedure shall be imposed or applied by any State or political subdivision in a manner which results in a denial or abridgement of the right of any citizen of the United States to vote on account of race or color, * * *

"(b) A violation of subsection (a) is established if, based on the totality of circumstances, it is shown that the political processes leading to nomination or election in the State or political subdivision are not equally open to participation by members of a class of citizens protected by subsection (a) in that its members have less opportunity than other members of the electorate to participate in the political process and to elect representatives of their choice. The extent to which members of a protected class have been elected to office in the State or political subdivision is one circumstance which may be considered: Provided, that nothing in this section establishes a right to have members of a protected class elected in numbers equal to their proportion in the population."

The Senate Judiciary Committee majority Report accompanying the bill that amended § 2, elaborates on the circumstances that might be probative of a § 2 violation, noting the following "typical factors":

1. the extent of any history of official discrimination in the state or political subdivision that touched the right of the members of the minority group to register, to vote, or otherwise to participate in the democratic process;

2. the extent to which voting in the elections of the state or political subdivision is racially polarized;

3. the extent to which the state or political subdivision has used unusually large election districts, majority vote requirements, anti-single-shot provisions, or other voting practices or procedures that may enhance the opportunity for discrimination against the minority group;

4. if there is a candidate slating process, whether the members of the minority group have been denied access to that process;

5. the extent to which members of the minority group in the state or political subdivision bear the effects of discrimination in such areas as education, employment and health, which hinder their ability to participate effectively in the political process;

6. whether political campaigns have been characterized by overt or subtle racial appeals;

7. the extent to which members of the minority group have been elected to public office in the jurisdiction.

Additional factors that in some cases have had probative value as part of plaintiffs' evidence to establish a violation are:

[1.] whether there is a significant lack of responsiveness on the part of elected officials to the particularized needs of the members of the minority group.

[2.] whether the policy underlying the state or political subdivision's use of such voting qualification, prerequisite to voting, or standard, practice or procedure is tenuous.

S.Rep., at 28–29, U.S.Code Cong. & Admin.News 1982, pp. 206–207.

The District Court applied the "totality of the circumstances" test set forth in § 2(b) to appellees' statutory claim, and, relying principally on the factors outlined in the Senate Report, held that the redistricting scheme violated § 2 because it resulted in the dilution of black citizens' votes in all seven disputed districts. * * *

Preliminarily, the court found that black citizens constituted a distinct population and registered-voter minority in each challenged district. The court noted that at the time the multimember districts were created, there were concentrations of black citizens within the boundaries of each that were sufficiently large and contiguous to constitute effective voting majorities in single-member districts lying wholly within the boundaries of the multimember districts. * * * The District Court then proceeded to find that the following circumstances combined with the multimember districting scheme to result in the dilution of black citizens' votes.

First, the court found that North Carolina had officially discriminated against its black citizens with respect to their exercise of the voting franchise from approximately 1900 to 1970 by employing at different times a poll tax, a literacy test, a prohibition against bullet (single-shot) voting and designated seat plans[6] for multimember districts. The court observed that even after the removal of direct barriers to black voter registration, such as the poll tax and literacy test, black voter registration remained relatively depressed; in 1982 only 52.7% of age-qualified blacks statewide were registered to vote, whereas 66.7% of whites were registered. The District Court found these statewide depressed levels of black voter registration to be present in all of the disputed districts and to be traceable, at least in part, to the historical pattern of statewide official discrimination.

Second, the court found that historic discrimination in education, housing, employment, and health services had resulted in a lower socioeconomic status for North Carolina blacks as a group than for whites. The court concluded that this lower status both gives rise to special group interests and hinders blacks' ability to participate effectively in the political process and to elect representatives of their choice.

Third, the court considered other voting procedures that may operate to lessen the opportunity of black voters to elect candidates of their choice. It noted that North Carolina has a majority vote requirement for primary elections and, while acknowledging that no black candidate for election to the State General Assembly had failed to win solely because of this requirement, the court concluded that it nonetheless presents a

6. Designated (or numbered) seat schemes require a candidate for election in multimember districts to run for specific seats, and can, under certain circumstances, frustrate bullet voting.

continuing practical impediment to the opportunity of black voting minorities to elect candidates of their choice. * * *

Fourth, the court found that white candidates in North Carolina have encouraged voting along color lines by appealing to racial prejudice. It noted that the record is replete with specific examples of racial appeals, ranging in style from overt and blatant to subtle and furtive, and in date from the 1890s to the 1984 campaign for a seat in the United States Senate. The court determined that the use of racial appeals in political campaigns in North Carolina persists to the present day and that its current effect is to lessen to some degree the opportunity of black citizens to participate effectively in the political processes and to elect candidates of their choice.

Fifth, the court examined the extent to which blacks have been elected to office in North Carolina, both statewide and in the challenged districts. It found, among other things, that prior to World War II, only one black had been elected to public office in this century. While recognizing that "it has now become possible for black citizens to be elected to office at all levels of state government in North Carolina," the court found that, in comparison to white candidates running for the same office, black candidates are at a disadvantage in terms of relative probability of success. It also found that the overall rate of black electoral success has been minimal in relation to the percentage of blacks in the total state population. For example, the court noted, from 1971 to 1982 there were at any given time only two-to-four blacks in the 120–member House of Representatives—that is, only 1.6% to 3.3% of House members were black. From 1975 to 1983 there were at any one time only one or two blacks in the 50–member State Senate—that is, only 2% to 4% of State Senators were black. By contrast, at the time of the District Court's opinion, blacks constituted about 22.4% of the total state population. * * *

Finally, the court considered the extent to which voting in the challenged districts was racially polarized. Based on statistical evidence presented by expert witnesses, supplemented to some degree by the testimony of lay witnesses, the court found that all of the challenged districts exhibit severe and persistent racially polarized voting.

Based on these findings, the court declared the contested portions of the 1982 redistricting plan violative of § 2 and enjoined appellants from conducting elections pursuant to those portions of the plan. * * * Appellants argue, first, that the District Court utilized a legally incorrect standard in determining whether the contested districts exhibit racial bloc voting to an extent that is cognizable under § 2. Second, they contend that the court used an incorrect definition of racially polarized voting and thus erroneously relied on statistical evidence that was not probative of polarized voting. Third, they maintain that the court assigned the wrong weight to evidence of some black candidates' electoral success. Finally, they argue that the trial court erred in concluding that these multimember districts result in black citizens having less opportunity than their white counterparts to participate in the political process and to elect representatives of their choice. * * *

SECTION 2 AND VOTE DILUTION THROUGH USE OF MULTIMEMBER DISTRICTS

An understanding both of § 2 and of the way in which multimember districts can operate to impair blacks' ability to elect representatives of their choice is prerequisite to an evaluation of appellants' contentions. First, then, we review amended § 2 and its legislative history in some detail. Second, we explain the theoretical basis for appellees' claim of vote dilution. * * *

Subsection 2(a) prohibits all States and political subdivisions from imposing any voting qualifications or prerequisites to voting, or any standards, practices, or procedures which result in the denial or abridgment of the right to vote of any citizen who is a member of a protected class of racial and language minorities. Subsection 2(b) establishes that § 2 has been violated where the "totality of the circumstances" reveal that "the political processes leading to nomination or election . . . are not equally open to participation by members of a [protected class] . . . in that its members have less opportunity than other members of the electorate to participate in the political process and to elect representatives of their choice." While explaining that "[t]he extent to which members of a protected class have been elected to office in the State or political subdivision is one circumstance which may be considered" in evaluating an alleged violation, § 2(b) cautions that "nothing in [§ 2] establishes a right to have members of a protected class elected in numbers equal to their proportion in the population."

* * * The "right" question, as the Report emphasizes repeatedly, is whether "as a result of the challenged practice or structure plaintiffs do not have an equal opportunity to participate in the political processes and to elect candidates of their choice."

In order to answer this question, a court must assess the impact of the contested structure or practice on minority electoral opportunities "on the basis of objective factors." * * * [The court reiterates the Senate Report factors listed in ¶ 3 of the opinion] The Report stresses, however, that this list of typical factors is neither comprehensive nor exclusive. While the enumerated factors will often be pertinent to certain types of § 2 violations, particularly to vote dilution claims, other factors may also be relevant and may be considered. Furthermore, the Senate Committee observed that "there is no requirement that any particular number of factors be proved, or that a majority of them point one way or the other." Rather, the Committee determined that "the question whether the political processes are 'equally open' depends upon a searching practical evaluation of the 'past and present reality,' " and on a "functional" view of the political process.

Although the Senate Report espouses a flexible, fact-intensive test for § 2 violations, it limits the circumstances under which § 2 violations may be proved in three ways. First, electoral devices, such as at-large elections, may not be considered *per se* violative of § 2. Plaintiffs must demonstrate that, under the totality of the circumstances, the devices result in unequal access to the electoral process. Second, the conjunction of an allegedly dilutive electoral mechanism and the lack of proportional representation alone does not establish a violation. Third, the results test does not assume the existence of racial bloc voting; plaintiffs must prove it. * * *

Appellees contend that the legislative decision to employ multimember, rather than single-member, districts in the contested jurisdictions dilutes their votes by submerging them in a white majority, thus impairing their ability to elect representatives of their choice.

The essence of a § 2 claim is that a certain electoral law, practice, or structure interacts with social and historical conditions to cause an inequality in the opportunities enjoyed by black and white voters to elect their preferred representatives. This Court has long recognized that multimember districts and at-large voting schemes may " 'operate to minimize or cancel out the voting strength of racial [minorities in] the voting population.' " The theoretical basis for this type of impairment is that where minority and majority voters consistently prefer different candidates, the majority, by virtue of its numerical superiority, will regularly defeat the choices of minority voters. Multimember districts and at-large election schemes, however, are not *per se* violative of minority voters' rights. Minority voters who contend that the multimember form of districting violates § 2, must prove that the use of a multimember electoral structure operates to minimize or cancel out their ability to elect their preferred candidates.

While many or all of the factors listed in the Senate Report may be relevant to a claim of vote dilution through submergence in multimember districts, unless there is a conjunction of the following circumstances, the use of multimember districts generally will not impede the ability of minority voters to elect representatives of their choice. Stated succinctly, a bloc voting majority must usually be able to defeat candidates supported by a politically cohesive, geographically insular minority group. These circumstances are necessary preconditions for multimember districts to operate to impair minority voters' ability to elect representatives of their choice for the following reasons. First, the minority group must be able to demonstrate that it is sufficiently large and geographically compact to constitute a majority in a single-member district. If it is not, as would be the case in a substantially integrated district, the multimember form of the district cannot be responsible for minority voters' inability to elect its candidates. Second, the minority group must be able to show that it is politically cohesive. If the minority group is not politically cohesive, it cannot be said that the selection of a multimember electoral structure thwarts distinctive minority group interests. Third, the minority must be able to demonstrate that the white majority votes sufficiently as a bloc to enable it—in the absence of special circumstances, such as the minority candidate running unopposed, usually to defeat the minority's preferred candidate. In establishing this last circumstance, the minority group demonstrates that submergence in a white multimember district impedes its ability to elect its chosen representatives.

Finally, we observe that the usual predictability of the majority's success distinguishes structural dilution from the mere loss of an occasional election.

RACIALLY POLARIZED VOTING

Having stated the general legal principles relevant to claims that § 2 has been violated through the use of multimember districts, we turn to the arguments of appellants and of the United States as *amicus curiae* addressing racially polarized voting. First, we describe the District Court's treatment of racially polarized voting. Next, we consider appellants' claim that the District Court used an incorrect legal standard to determine whether racial bloc voting in the contested districts was sufficiently severe to be cognizable as an element of a § 2 claim. Finally, we consider appellants' contention that the trial court employed an incorrect definition of racially polarized voting and thus erroneously relied on statistical evidence that was not probative of racial bloc voting. * * *

* * * The District Court found that blacks and whites generally preferred different candidates and, on that basis, found voting in the districts to be racially correlated.[21] * * * [T]he court found that in all but 2 of the 53 elections the degree of racial bloc voting was "so marked as to be substantively significant, in the sense that the results of the individual election would have been different depending upon whether it had been held among only the white voters or only the black voters."

The court also reported * * * that a high percentage of black voters regularly supported black candidates and that most white voters were extremely reluctant to vote for black candidates. The court then considered the relevance to the existence of legally significant white bloc voting of the fact that black candidates have won some elections. It determined that in most instances, special circumstances, such as incumbency and lack of opposition, rather than a diminution in usually severe white bloc voting, accounted for these candidates' success. The court also suggested that black voters' reliance on bullet voting was a significant factor in their successful efforts to elect candidates of their choice. Based on all of the evidence before it, the trial court concluded that each of the districts experienced racially polarized voting "in a persistent and severe degree." * * *

The purpose of inquiring into the existence of racially polarized voting is twofold: to ascertain whether minority group members constitute a politically cohesive unit and to determine whether whites vote sufficiently as a bloc usually to defeat the minority's preferred candidates. Thus, the question whether a given district experiences legally significant racially polarized voting requires discrete inquiries into minority and white voting practices. A showing that a significant number of minority group members usually vote for the same candidates is one way of proving the political cohesiveness necessary to a vote dilution claim, and, consequently, establishes minority bloc voting within the context of § 2. And, in general, a white bloc vote that normally will defeat the combined strength of minority support plus white "crossover"

---

21. The court used the term "racial polarization" to describe this correlation. It adopted Dr. Grofman's definition—"racial polarization" exists where there is "a consistent relationship between [the] race of the voter and the way in which the voter votes," or to put it differently, where "black voters and white voters vote differently." We, too, adopt this definition of "racial bloc" or "racially polarized" voting.

votes rises to the level of legally significant white bloc voting. The amount of white bloc voting that can generally "minimize or cancel," black voters' ability to elect representatives of their choice, however, will vary from district to district according to a number of factors, including the nature of the allegedly dilutive electoral mechanism; the presence or absence of other potentially dilutive electoral devices, such as majority vote requirements, designated posts, and prohibitions against bullet voting; the percentage of registered voters in the district who are members of the minority group; the size of the district; and, in multi-member districts, the number of seats open and the number of candidates in the field.

Because loss of political power through vote dilution is distinct from the mere inability to win a particular election, a pattern of racial bloc voting that extends over a period of time is more probative of a claim that a district experiences legally significant polarization than are the results of a single election. * * * [I]n a district where elections are shown usually to be polarized, the fact that racially polarized voting is not present in one or a few individual elections does not necessarily negate the conclusion that the district experiences legally significant bloc voting. Furthermore, the success of a minority candidate in a particular election does not necessarily prove that the district did not experience polarized voting in that election; special circumstances, such as the absence of an opponent, incumbency, or the utilization of bullet voting, may explain minority electoral success in a polarized contest.

As must be apparent, the degree of racial bloc voting that is cognizable as an element of a § 2 vote dilution claim will vary according to a variety of factual circumstances. Consequently, there is no simple doctrinal test for the existence of legally significant racial bloc voting. However, the foregoing general principles should provide courts with substantial guidance in determining whether evidence that black and white voters generally prefer different candidates rises to the level of legal significance under § 2. * * *

Appellants and the United States contend that the legal concept of "racially polarized voting" refers not to voting patterns that are merely correlated with the voter's race, but to voting patterns that are determined primarily by the voter's race, rather than by the voter's other socioeconomic characteristics.

The first problem with this argument is that it ignores the fact that members of geographically insular racial and ethnic groups frequently share socioeconomic characteristics, such as income level, employment status, amount of education, housing and other living conditions, religion, language, and so forth. See, e.g., Butler at 902 (Minority group "members' shared concerns, including political ones, are … a function of group status, and as such are largely involuntary.… As a group blacks are concerned, for example, with police brutality, substandard housing, unemployment, etc., because these problems fall disproportionately upon the group"). Where such characteristics are shared, race or ethnic group not only denotes color or place of origin, it also functions as a shorthand notation for common social and economic characteristics.

Appellants' definition of racially polarized voting is even more pernicious where shared characteristics are causally related to race or ethnicity. The opportunity to achieve high employment status and income, for example, is often influenced by the presence or absence of racial or ethnic discrimination. A definition of racially polarized voting which holds that black bloc voting does not exist when black voters' choice of certain candidates is most strongly influenced by the fact that the voters have low incomes and menial jobs—when the reason most of those voters have menial jobs and low incomes is attributable to past or present racial discrimination—runs counter to the Senate Report's instruction to conduct a searching and practical evaluation of past and present reality, S.Rep., at 30, and interferes with the purpose of the Voting Rights Act to eliminate the negative effects of past discrimination on the electoral opportunities of minorities.

Furthermore, under appellants' theory of racially polarized voting, even uncontrovertible evidence that candidates strongly preferred by black voters are always defeated by a bloc voting white majority would be dismissed for failure to prove racial polarization whenever the black and white populations could be described in terms of other socioeconomic characteristics. * * *

North Carolina's and the United States' suggestion that racially polarized voting means that voters select or reject candidates principally on the basis of the candidate's race is also misplaced.

First, both the language of § 2 and a functional understanding of the phenomenon of vote dilution mandate the conclusion that the race of the candidate *per se* is irrelevant to racial bloc voting analysis. Section 2(b) states that a violation is established if it can be shown that members of a protected minority group "have less opportunity than other members of the electorate to ... elect representatives of their choice." Because both minority and majority voters often select members of their own race as their preferred representatives, it will frequently be the case that a black candidate is the choice of blacks, while a white candidate is the choice of whites. Indeed, the facts of this case illustrate that tendency—blacks preferred black candidates, whites preferred white candidates. Thus, as a matter of convenience, we and the District Court may refer to the preferred representative of black voters as the "black candidate" and to the preferred representative of white voters as the "white candidate." Nonetheless, the fact that race of voter and race of candidate is often correlated is not directly pertinent to a § 2 inquiry. Under § 2, it is the status of the candidate as the chosen representative of a particular racial group, not the race of the candidate, that is important.

An understanding of how vote dilution through submergence in a white majority works leads to the same conclusion. The essence of a submergence claim is that minority group members prefer certain candidates whom they could elect were it not for the interaction of the challenged electoral law or structure with a white majority that votes as a significant bloc for different candidates. Thus, * * * the existence of racial bloc voting is relevant to a vote dilution claim in two ways. Bloc voting by blacks tends to prove that the black community is politically cohesive, that is, it shows that blacks prefer certain candidates whom they could elect in a single-member, black majority district. Bloc voting by a white majority tends to prove that blacks will generally be unable to elect representatives of their choice. Clearly, only the race of the voter, not the race of the candidate, is relevant to vote dilution analysis. * * *

Congress intended that the Voting Rights Act eradicate inequalities in political opportunities that exist due to the vestigial effects of past purposeful discrimination. Both this Court and other federal courts have recognized that political participation by minorities tends to be depressed where minority group members suffer effects of prior discrimination such as inferior education, poor employment opportunities, and low incomes. The Senate Report acknowledges this tendency and instructs that "the extent to which members of the minority group ... bear the effects of discrimination in such areas as education, employment and health, which hinder their ability to participate effectively in the political process," is a factor which may be probative of unequal opportunity to participate in the political process and to elect representatives. Courts and commentators have recognized further that candidates generally must spend more money in order to win election in a multimember district than in a single-member district. If, because of inferior education and poor employment opportunities, blacks earn less than whites, they will not be able to provide the candidates of their choice with the same level of financial support that whites can provide theirs. Thus, electoral losses by candidates preferred by the black community may well be attributable in part to the fact that their white opponents outspent them. But, the fact is that, in this instance, the economic effects of prior discrimination have combined with the multimember electoral structure to afford blacks less opportunity than whites to participate in the political process and to elect representatives of their choice. It would be both anomalous and inconsistent with congressional intent to hold that, on the one hand, the effects of past discrimination which hinder blacks' ability to participate in the political process tend to prove a § 2 violation, while holding on the other hand that, where these same effects of past discrimination deter whites from voting for blacks, blacks cannot make out a crucial element of a vote dilution claim. * * *

Finally, we reject the suggestion that racially polarized voting refers only to white bloc voting which is caused by white voters' racial hostility toward black candidates. To accept this theory would * * * prevent minority voters who have clearly been denied an opportunity to elect representatives of their choice from establishing a critical element of a vote dilution claim. * * *

In sum, we would hold that the legal concept of racially polarized voting, as it relates to claims of vote dilution, refers only to the existence of a correlation between the race of voters and the selection of certain candidates. Plaintiffs need not prove causation or intent in order to prove a *prima facie* case of racial bloc voting and defendants may not rebut that case with evidence of causation or intent. * * *

ULTIMATE DETERMINATION OF VOTE DILUTION * * *

The District Court in this case carefully considered the totality of the circumstances and found that in each district racially polarized voting; the legacy of official discrimination in voting matters, education, housing, employment, and health services; and the persistence of campaign appeals to racial prejudice acted in concert with the multimember districting scheme to impair the ability of geographically insular and politically cohesive groups of black voters to participate equally in the political process and to elect candidates of their choice. It found that the success a few black candidates have enjoyed in these districts is too recent, too limited, and, with regard to the 1982 elections, perhaps too aberrational, to disprove its conclusion. Excepting House District 23, with respect to which the District Court committed legal error, we affirm the District Court's judgment. We cannot say that the District Court, composed of local judges who are well acquainted with the political realities of the State, clearly erred in concluding that use of a multimember electoral structure has caused black voters in the districts other than House District 23 to have less opportunity than white voters to elect representatives of their choice.

The judgment of the District Court is affirmed in part and reversed in part. * * *

JUSTICE WHITE, concurring. * * *

Justice Brennan states * * * that the crucial factor in identifying polarized voting is the race of the voter and that the race of the candidate is irrelevant. Under this test, there is polarized voting if the majority of white voters vote for different candidates than the majority of the blacks, regardless of the race of the candidates. I do not agree. Suppose an eight-member multimember district that is 60% white and 40% black, the blacks being geographically located so that two safe black single-member districts could be drawn. Suppose further that there are six white and two black Democrats running against six white and two black Republicans. Under Justice Brennan's test, there would be polarized voting and a likely § 2 violation if all the Republicans, including the two blacks, are elected, and 80% of the blacks in the predominantly black areas vote Democratic. I take it that there would also be a violation in a single-member district that is 60% black, but enough of the blacks vote with the whites to elect a black candidate who is not the choice of the majority of black voters. This is interest-group politics rather than a rule hedging against racial discrimination. I doubt that this is what Congress had in mind in amending § 2 as it did. * * *

Notes and Questions

1. How is the concept "race" used in the language of the Voting Rights Act, as amended? How is it used by the court in *Thornburg*? Why does the *Thornburg* court believe that a candidate's race is not significant?

2. The court states that where characteristics of job status, education, and income are shared by racial group members, "race or ethnic group not only denotes color or place or origin, it also functions as a shorthand notation for common social and economic characteristics." Is the court

correct? Why would we denote color or place of origin? Can/should race be used as a shorthand for social and economic characteristics?

3. How does the court define racially polarized voting? How does Justice White, concurring, part company from the majority? Can one determine with certainty how election ballots were cast?

B. GERRYMANDERING

The drawing of legislative districts seriously implicated the question of whether an individual's vote would matter or be diluted. In *Reynolds v. Sims*, 377 U.S. 533, 567 (1964) the court acknowledged:

> The fact that an individual lives here or there is not a legitimate reason for overweighting or diluting the efficacy of his vote. The complexions of societies and civilizations change, often with amazing rapidity. A nation once primarily rural in character becomes predominantly urban. Representation schemes once fair and equitable become archaic and outdated. But the basic principle of representative government remains, and must remain, unchanged—the weight of a citizen's vote cannot be made to depend on where he lives.

In an early vote dilution case, *Gomillion v. Lightfoot*, 364 U.S. 339 (1960), the City of Tuskegee redrew its boundaries to exclude black voters. The Court observed: "The essential inevitable effect of this redefinition of Tuskegee's boundaries is to remove from the city all save only four or five of its 400 Negro voters while not removing a single white voter or resident. The result of the Act is to deprive the Negro petitioners discriminatorily of the benefits of residence in Tuskegee, including, *inter alia*, the right to vote in municipal elections." 364 U.S. at 341. Explaining *Gomillion* several decades later, Justice Ginsburg said, "This apportionment was unconstitutional not simply because it was motivated by race, but notably because it had a dilutive effect: It disenfranchised Tuskegee's black community." *Miller v. Johnson*, 515 U.S. 900, 939 n.2 (Ginsburg, J., dissenting). The city boundary drawn in *Gomillion* changed the city "from a square to an uncouth twenty-eight sided figure." 364 U.S. at 340.

The line drawing challenged in *Gomillion* had harmed the black community. In *Shaw v. Reno*, 509 U.S. 630 (1993), the Court struck down a district it viewed as prominority, drawn to assure that African Americans could be elected to Congress. The Court criticized the shape of the challenged district as "bizarre." 509 U.S. at 644. Characterizing *Shaw* as articulating this "bizarre shape test," John Hart Ely observed:

> Rather than simply reflecting what has undoubtedly been a general change in what it takes to shock Americans, the semantic move from "uncouth" [a reference to the court's description of the challenged district in *Gomillion*] to "bizarre" may also unconsciously reflect a difference in the Court's reaction to antiminority and prominority gerrymanders.

John Hart Ely, *Gerrymanders: The Good, the Bad, and the Ugly*, 50 Stan. L. Rev. 607, n.2 (1998). A few years later the court revisited the issue in the next case.

MILLER v. JOHNSON

515 U.S. 900 (1995).

JUSTICE KENNEDY delivered the opinion of the court.

The constitutionality of Georgia's congressional redistricting plan is at issue here. In *Shaw v. Reno*, 509 U.S. 630 (1993), we held that a plaintiff states a claim under the Equal Protection Clause by alleging that a state redistricting plan, on its face, has no rational explanation save as an effort to separate voters on the basis of race. The question we now decide is whether Georgia's new Eleventh District gives rise to a valid equal protection claim under the principles announced in *Shaw*, and, if so, whether it can be sustained nonetheless as narrowly tailored to serve a compelling governmental interest.

The Equal Protection Clause of the Fourteenth Amendment provides that no State shall "deny to any person within its jurisdiction the equal protection of the laws." U.S. Const. Am. 14, § 1. Its central mandate is racial neutrality in governmental decisionmaking. See, *e.g.*, *Loving v. Virginia*, 388 U.S. 1, 11 (1967); *McLaughlin v. Florida*, 379 U.S. 184, 191–192 (1964); see also *Brown v. Board of Education*, 347 U.S. 483 (1954). Though application of this imperative raises difficult questions, the basic principle is straightforward: "Racial and ethnic distinctions of any sort are inherently suspect and thus call for the most exacting judicial examination.... This perception of racial and ethnic distinctions is rooted in our Nation's constitutional and demographic history." *Regents of Univ. of California v. Bakke*, 438 U.S. 265, 291 (1978) (opinion of Powell, J.). This rule obtains with equal force regardless of "the race of those burdened or benefited by a particular classification." *Richmond v. J.A. Croson Co.*, 488 U.S. 469, 494 (1989) (plurality opinion). Laws classifying citizens on the basis of race cannot be upheld unless they are narrowly tailored to achieving a compelling state interest.

In *Shaw v. Reno*, we recognized that these equal protection principles govern a State's drawing of congressional districts, though, as our cautious approach there discloses, application of these principles to electoral districting is a most delicate task. Our analysis began from the premise that "[l]aws that explicitly distinguish between individuals on racial grounds fall within the core of [the Equal Protection Clause's] prohibition." This prohibition extends not just to explicit racial classifications, but also to laws neutral on their face but " 'unexplainable on grounds other than race.' " Applying this basic Equal Protection analysis in the voting rights context, we held that "redistricting legislation that is so bizarre on its face that it is 'unexplainable on grounds other than race,' ... demands the same close scrutiny that we give other state laws that classify citizens by race."

This case requires us to apply the principles articulated in *Shaw* to the most recent congressional redistricting plan enacted by the State of Georgia.

In 1965, the Attorney General designated Georgia a covered jurisdiction under § 4(b) of the Voting Rights Act. In consequence, § 5 of the Act requires Georgia to obtain either administrative preclearance by the Attorney General or approval by the United States District Court for the District of Columbia of any change in a "standard, practice, or procedure with respect to voting" made after November 1, 1964. The preclearance mechanism applies to congressional redistricting plans, and requires that the proposed change "not have the purpose and will not have the effect of denying or abridging the right to vote on account of race or color." "[T]he purpose of § 5 has always been to insure that no voting-procedure changes would be made that would lead to a retrogression in the position of racial minorities with respect to their effective exercise of the electoral franchise."

Between 1980 and 1990, one of Georgia's 10 congressional districts was a majority-black district, that is, a majority of the district's voters were black. The 1990 Decennial Census indicated that Georgia's population of 6,478,216 persons, 27% of whom are black, entitled it to an additional eleventh congressional seat, prompting Georgia's General Assembly to redraw the State's congressional districts. Both the House and the Senate adopted redistricting guidelines which, among other things, required single-member districts of equal population, contiguous geography, nondilution of minority voting strength, fidelity to precinct lines where possible, and compliance with §§ 2 and 5 of the Act. Only after these requirements were met did the guidelines permit drafters to consider other ends, such as maintaining the integrity of political subdivisions, preserving the core of existing districts, and avoiding contests between incumbents. * * *

[The Georgia legislature submitted a congressional redistricting plan for preclearance.] The legislature's plan contained two majority-minority districts, the Fifth and Eleventh, and an additional district, the Second, in which blacks comprised just over 35% of the voting age population. Despite the plan's increase in the number of majority-black districts from one to two and the absence of any evidence of an intent to discriminate against minority voters, the Department of Justice refused preclearance on January 21, 1992. The Department's objection letter noted a concern that Georgia had created only two majority-minority districts, and that the proposed plan did not "recognize" certain minority populations by placing them in a majority-black district.

The General Assembly returned to the drawing board. A new plan was enacted and submitted for preclearance. This second attempt assigned the black population in Central Georgia's Baldwin County to the Eleventh District and increased the black populations in the Eleventh, Fifth and Second Districts. The Justice Department refused preclearance again, relying on alternative plans proposing three majority-minority districts. One of the alternative schemes relied on by the Department was the so-called "max-black" plan, drafted by the American Civil Liberties Union (ACLU) for the General Assembly's black caucus. The key to the ACLU's plan was the "Macon/Savannah trade." The dense black population in the Macon region would be transferred from the Eleventh District to the Second, converting the Second into a majority-black district, and the Eleventh District's loss in black population would be offset by extending the Eleventh to include the black populations in Savannah. Pointing to the General Assembly's refusal to enact the Macon/Savannah swap into law, the Justice Department concluded that Georgia had "failed to explain adequately" its failure to create a third majority-minority district. * * *

Twice spurned, the General Assembly set out to create three majority-minority districts to gain preclearance. Using the ACLU's "max-black" plan as its benchmark, the General Assembly enacted a plan that "bore all the signs of [the Justice Department's] involvement: The black population of Meriwether County was gouged out of the Third District and attached to the Second District by the narrowest of land bridges; Effingham and Chatham Counties were split to make way for the Savannah extension, which itself split the City of Savannah; and the plan as a whole split 26 counties, 23 more than the existing congressional districts."

The new plan also enacted the Macon/Savannah swap necessary to create a third majority-black district. The Eleventh District lost the black population of Macon, but picked up Savannah, thereby connecting the black neighborhoods of metropolitan Atlanta and the poor black populace of coastal Chatham County, though 260 miles apart in distance and worlds apart in culture. In short, the social, political and economic makeup of the Eleventh District tells a tale of disparity, not community. * * *

The Almanac of American Politics has this to say about the Eleventh District: "Geographically, it is a monstrosity, stretching from Atlanta to Savannah. Its core is the plantation country in the center of the state, lightly populated, but heavily black. It links by narrow corridors the black neighborhoods in Augusta, Savannah and southern De-Kalb County." Georgia's plan included three majority-black districts, though, and received Justice Department preclearance on April 2, 1992.

Elections were held under the new congressional redistricting plan on November 4, 1992, and black candidates were elected to Congress from all three majority-black districts. On January 13, 1994, appellees, five white voters from the Eleventh District, filed this action * * * [alleging] that Georgia's Eleventh District was a racial gerrymander and so a violation of the Equal Protection Clause as interpreted in *Shaw v. Reno.* * * *

Finding that the "evidence of the General Assembly's intent to racially gerrymander the Eleventh District is overwhelming, and practically stipulated by the parties involved," the District Court held that race was the predominant, overriding factor in drawing the Eleventh District. Appellants do not take issue with the court's factual finding of this racial motivation. Rather, they contend that evidence of a legislature's deliberate classification of voters on the basis of race cannot alone suffice to state a claim under *Shaw.* They argue that, regardless of the legislature's purposes, a plaintiff must demonstrate that a district's shape is so bizarre that it is unexplainable other than on the basis of race, and that appellees failed to make that showing here. Appellants' conception of the constitutional violation misapprehends our holding in *Shaw* and the Equal Protection precedent upon which *Shaw* relied. * * *

[T]he essence of the equal protection claim recognized in *Shaw* is that the State has used race as a basis for separating voters into districts. Just as the State may not, absent extraordinary justification, segregate citizens on the basis of race in its public parks, *New Orleans City Park Improvement Assn. v. Detiege*, 358 U.S. 54 (1958) (*per curiam*), buses, *Gayle v. Browder*, 352 U.S. 903 (1956) (*per curiam*), golf courses, *Holmes v. Atlanta*, 350 U.S. 879 (1955) (*per curiam*), beaches, *Mayor and City Council of Baltimore v. Dawson*, 350 U.S. 877 (1955) (*per curiam*), and schools, *Brown, supra*, so did we recognize in *Shaw* that it may not separate its citizens into different voting districts on the basis of race. The idea is a simple one: "At the heart of the Constitution's guarantee of equal protection lies the simple command that the Government must treat citizens 'as individuals,' not as 'simply components of a racial, religious, sexual or national class.'" *Metro Broadcasting, Inc. v. FCC*, 497 U.S. 547, 602 (1990) (O'Connor, J., dissenting) When the State assigns voters on the basis of race, it engages in the offensive and demeaning assumption that voters of a particular race, because of their race, "think alike, share the same political interests, and will prefer the same candidates at the polls." Race-based assignments "embody stereotypes that treat individuals as the product of their race, evaluating their thoughts and efforts—their very worth as citizens—according to a criterion barred to the Government by history and the Constitution." They also cause society serious harm. As we concluded in *Shaw*:

> Racial classifications with respect to voting carry particular dangers. Racial gerrymandering, even for remedial purposes, may balkanize us into competing racial factions; it threatens to carry us further from the goal of a political system in which race no longer matters— a goal that the Fourteenth and Fifteenth Amendments embody, and to which the Nation continues to aspire. It is for these reasons that race-based districting by our state legislatures demands close judicial scrutiny. * * *

We recognized in *Shaw* that, outside the districting context, statutes are subject to strict scrutiny under the Equal Protection Clause not just when they contain express racial classifications, but also when, though race neutral on their face, they are motivated by a racial purpose or object. * * *

Appellants and some of their *amici* argue that the Equal Protection Clause's general proscription on race-based decisionmaking does not obtain in the districting context because redistricting by definition involves racial considerations. Underlying their argument are the very stereotypical assumptions the Equal Protection Clause forbids. It is true that redistricting in most cases will implicate a political calculus in which various interests compete for recognition, but it does not follow from this that individuals of the same race share a single political interest. The view that they do is "based on the demeaning notion that members of the defined racial groups ascribe to certain 'minority views' that must be different from those of other citizens," the precise use of race as a proxy the Constitution prohibits.

* * * Although race-based decisionmaking is inherently suspect, until a claimant makes a showing sufficient to support that allegation the good faith of a state legislature must be presumed. The courts, in assessing the sufficiency of a challenge to a districting plan, must be sensitive to the complex interplay of forces that enter a legislature's redistricting calculus. Redistricting legislatures will, for example, almost always be aware of racial demographics; but it does not follow that race predominates in the redistricting process. The distinction between being aware of racial considerations and being motivated by them may be difficult to make. This evidentiary difficulty, together with the sensitive nature of redistricting and the presumption of good faith that must be accorded legislative enactments, requires courts to exercise extraordinary caution in adjudicating claims that a state has drawn district lines on the basis of race. The plaintiff's burden is to show, either through circumstantial evidence of a district's shape and demographics or more direct evidence going to legislative purpose, that race was the predominant factor motivating the legislature's decision to place a significant number of voters within or without a particular district. To make this showing, a plaintiff must prove that the legislature subordinated traditional race-neutral districting principles, including but not limited to compactness, contiguity, respect for political subdivisions or communities defined by actual shared interests, to racial considerations. Where these or other race-neutral considerations are the basis for redistricting legislation, and are not subordinated to race, a state can "defeat a claim that a district has been gerrymandered on racial lines." These principles inform the plaintiff's burden of proof at trial. * * *

In our view, the District Court applied the correct analysis, and its finding that race was the predominant factor motivating the drawing of the Eleventh District was not clearly erroneous. The court found it was "exceedingly obvious" from the shape of the Eleventh District, together with the relevant racial demographics, that the drawing of narrow land bridges to incorporate within the District outlying appendages containing nearly 80% of the district's total black population was a deliberate attempt to bring black populations into the district. Although by comparison with other districts the geometric shape of the Eleventh District may not seem bizarre on its face, when its shape is considered in conjunction with its racial and population densities, the story of racial gerrymandering seen by the District Court becomes much clearer. Although this evidence is quite compelling, we need not determine whether it was, standing alone, sufficient to establish a *Shaw* claim that the Eleventh District is unexplainable other than by race. The District Court had before it considerable additional evidence showing that the General Assembly was motivated by a predominant, overriding desire to assign black populations to the Eleventh District and thereby permit the creation of a third majority-black district in the Second.

The court found that "it became obvious," both from the Justice Department's objection letters and the three preclearance rounds in general, "that [the Justice Department] would accept nothing less than abject surrender to its maximization agenda." It further found that the General Assembly acquiesced and as a consequence was driven by its overriding desire to comply with the Department's maximization demands. * * * Hence the trial court had little difficulty concluding that the Justice Department "spent months demanding purely race-based revisions to Georgia's redistricting plans, and that Georgia spent months attempting to comply." On this record, we fail to see how the District Court could have reached any conclusion other than that race was the predominant factor in drawing Georgia's Eleventh District; and in any event we conclude the court's finding is not clearly erroneous. * * *

Nor can the State's districting legislation be rescued by mere recitation of purported communities of interest. The evidence was compelling "that there are no tangible 'communities of interest' spanning the hundreds of miles of the Eleventh District." A comprehensive report demonstrated the fractured political, social, and economic interests within the Eleventh District's black population. It is apparent that it was not alleged shared interests but rather the object of maximizing the District's black population and obtaining Justice Department approval that in fact explained the General Assembly's actions. A State is free to recognize communities that have a particular racial makeup, provided its action is directed toward some common thread of relevant interests. "[W]hen members of a racial group live together in one community, a reapportionment plan that concentrates members of the group in one district and excludes them from others may reflect wholly legitimate purposes." But where the State assumes from a group of voters' race that they "think alike, share the same political interests, and will prefer the same candidates at the polls," it engages in racial stereotyping at odds with equal protection mandates.

Race was, as the District Court found, the predominant, overriding factor explaining the General Assembly's decision to attach to the Eleventh District various appendages containing dense majority-black populations. As a result, Georgia's congressional redistricting plan cannot be upheld unless it satisfies strict scrutiny, our most rigorous and exacting standard of constitutional review.

To satisfy strict scrutiny, the State must demonstrate that its districting legislation is narrowly tailored to achieve a compelling interest. There is a "significant state interest in eradicating the effects of past racial discrimination." The State does not argue, however, that it created the Eleventh District to remedy past discrimination, and with good reason: There is little doubt that the State's true interest in designing the Eleventh District was creating a third majority-black district to satisfy the Justice Department's preclearance demands. Whether or not in some cases compliance with the Voting Rights Act, standing alone, can provide a compelling interest independent of any interest in remedying past discrimination, it cannot do so here. As we suggested in *Shaw*, compliance with federal antidiscrimination laws cannot justify race-based districting where the challenged district was not reasonably necessary under a constitutional reading and application of those laws. The congressional plan challenged here was not required by the Voting Rights Act under a correct reading of the statute. * * *

We do not accept the contention that the State has a compelling interest in complying with whatever preclearance mandates the Justice Department issues. When a state governmental entity seeks to justify race-based remedies to cure the effects of past discrimination, we do not accept the government's mere assertion that the remedial action is required. Rather, we insist on a strong basis in evidence of the harm being remedied. Our presumptive skepticism of all racial classifications, prohibits us as well from accepting on its face the Justice Department's conclusion that racial districting is necessary under the Voting Rights Act. Where a State relies on the Department's determination that race-based districting is necessary to comply with the Voting Rights Act, the judiciary retains an independent obligation in adjudicating consequent equal protection challenges to ensure that the State's actions are narrowly tailored to achieve a compelling interest. Were we to accept the Justice Department's objection itself as a compelling interest adequate to insulate racial districting from constitutional review, we would be surrendering to the Executive Branch our role in enforcing the constitutional limits on race-based official action. We may not do so. * * *

The judgment of the District Court is affirmed.

JUSTICE GINSBURG, dissenting.

Legislative districting is highly political business. This Court has generally respected the competence of state legislatures to attend to the task. When race is the issue, however, we have recognized the need for judicial intervention to prevent dilution of minority voting strength. Generations of rank discrimination against African Americans, as citizens and voters, account for that surveillance. * * *

Today the Court expands the judicial role, announcing that federal courts are to undertake searching review of any district with contours "predominantly motivated" by race: "strict scrutiny" will be triggered not only when traditional districting practices are abandoned, but also when those practices are "subordinated to"—given less weight than—race. Applying this new "race-as-predominant-factor" standard, the Court invalidates Georgia's districting plan even though Georgia's Eleventh District, the focus of today's dispute, bears the imprint of familiar districting practices. Because I do not endorse the Court's new standard and would not upset Georgia's plan, I dissent.

At the outset, it may be useful to note points on which the Court does not divide. First, we agree that federalism and the slim judicial competence to draw district lines weigh heavily against judicial intervention in apportionment decisions; as a rule, the task should remain within the domain of state legislatures. Second, for most of our Nation's history, the franchise has not been enjoyed equally by black citizens and white voters. To redress past wrongs and to avert any recurrence of exclusion of blacks from political processes, federal courts now respond to Equal Protection Clause and Voting Rights Act complaints of state action that dilutes minority voting strength. Third, to meet statutory requirements, state legislatures must sometimes consider race as a factor highly relevant to the drawing of district lines. Finally, state legislatures may recognize communities that have a particular racial or ethnic makeup, even in the absence of any compulsion to do so, in order to account for interests common to or shared by the persons grouped together. See *Shaw* ("[W]hen members of a racial group live together in one community, a reapportionment plan that concentrates members of the group in one district and excludes them from others may reflect wholly legitimate purposes.").

Therefore, the fact that the Georgia General Assembly took account of race in drawing district lines—a fact not in dispute—does not render the State's plan invalid. To offend the Equal Protection Clause, all agree, the legislature had to do more than consider race. How much more, is the issue that divides the Court today. * * *

In contrast to the snake-like North Carolina district inspected in *Shaw*, Georgia's Eleventh District is hardly "bizarre," "extremely irregular," or "irrational on its face." Instead, the Eleventh District's design reflects significant consideration of "traditional districting factors (such as keeping political subdivisions intact) and the usual political process of compromise and trades for a variety of nonracial reasons." The District covers a core area in central and eastern Georgia, and its total land area of 6,780 square miles is about average for the State. The border of the Eleventh District runs 1,184 miles, in line with Georgia's Second District, which has a 1,243-mile border, and the State's Eighth District, with a border running 1,155 miles.

Nor does the Eleventh District disrespect the boundaries of political subdivisions. Of the 22 counties in the District, 14 are intact and 8 are divided. That puts the Eleventh District at about the state average in divided counties. By contrast, of the Sixth District's 5 counties, none are intact, and of the Fourth District's 4 counties, just 1 is intact. Seventy-one percent of the Eleventh District's boundaries track the borders of political subdivisions. Of the State's 11 districts, 5 score worse than the Eleventh District on this criterion, and 5 score better. Eighty-three percent of the Eleventh District's geographic area is composed of intact counties, above average for the State's congressional districts. And notably, the Eleventh District's boundaries largely follow precinct lines.

Evidence at trial similarly shows that considerations other than race went into determining the Eleventh District's boundaries. For a "political reason"—to accommodate the request of an incumbent State Senator regarding the placement of the precinct in which his son lived—the DeKalb County portion of the Eleventh District was drawn to include a particular (largely white) precinct. The corridor through Effingham County was substantially narrowed at the request of a (white) State Representative. In Chatham County, the District was trimmed to exclude a heavily black community in Garden City because a State Representative wanted to keep the city intact inside the neighboring First District. The Savannah extension was configured by "the narrowest means possible" to avoid splitting the city of Port Wentworth.

Georgia's Eleventh District, in sum, is not an outlier district shaped without reference to familiar districting techniques. Tellingly, the District that the Court's decision today unsettles is not among those on a statistically calculated list of the 28 most bizarre districts in the United States, a study prepared in the wake of our decision in *Shaw.* * * *

Along with attention to size, shape, and political subdivisions, the Court recognizes as an appropriate districting principle, "respect for . . . communities defined by actual shared interests." The Court finds no community here, however, because a report in the record showed "fractured political, social, and economic interests within the Eleventh District's black population."

But ethnicity itself can tie people together, as volumes of social science literature have documented—even people with divergent economic interests. For this reason, ethnicity is a significant force in political life. As stated in a classic study of ethnicity in one city of immigrants:

> "[M]any elements—history, family and feeling, interest, formal organizational life—operate to keep much of New York life channeled within the bounds of the ethnic group. . . .

> " . . . The political realm . . . is least willing to consider [ethnicity] a purely private affair. . . .

> . . .

> "[P]olitical life itself emphasizes the ethnic character of the city, with its balanced tickets and its special appeals. . . ." Nathan Glazer & Daniel Moynihan, *Beyond the Melting Pot* 19–20 (1963).

To accommodate the reality of ethnic bonds, legislatures have long drawn voting districts along ethnic lines. Our Nation's cities are full of districts identified by their ethnic character—Chinese, Irish, Italian, Jewish, Polish, Russian, for example. The creation of ethnic districts reflecting felt identity is not ordinarily viewed as offensive or demeaning to those included in the delineation.

To separate permissible and impermissible use of race in legislative apportionment, the Court orders strict scrutiny for districting plans "predominantly motivated" by race. No longer can a State avoid judicial oversight by giving—as in this case—genuine and measurable consideration to traditional districting practices. Instead, a federal case can be mounted whenever plaintiffs plausibly allege that other factors carried less weight than race. This invitation to litigate against the State seems to me neither necessary nor proper.

The Court derives its test from diverse opinions on the relevance of race in contexts distinctly unlike apportionment. The controlling idea, the Court says, is " 'the simple command [at the heart of the Constitution's guarantee of equal protection] that the Government must treat citizens as individuals, not as simply components of a racial, religious, sexual or national class.' " In adopting districting plans, however, States do not treat people as individuals. Apportionment schemes, by their very nature, assemble people in groups. States do not assign voters to districts based on merit or achievement, standards States might use in hiring employees or engaging contractors. Rather, legislators classify voters in groups—by economic, geographical, political, or social characteristics—and then "reconcile the competing claims of [these] groups."

That ethnicity defines some of these groups is a political reality. Until now, no constitutional infirmity has been seen in districting Irish or Italian voters together, for example, so long as the delineation does not abandon familiar apportionment practices. If Chinese Americans and Russian Americans may seek and secure group recognition in the delineation of voting districts, then African Americans should not be dissimilarly treated. Otherwise, in the name of equal protection, we would shut out "the very minority group whose history in the United States gave birth to the Equal Protection Clause."

Under the Court's approach, judicial review of the same intensity, i.e., strict scrutiny, is in order once it is determined that an apportionment is predominantly motivated by race. It matters not at all, in this new regime, whether the apportionment dilutes or enhances minority voting strength. As very recently observed, however, "[t]here is no moral or constitutional equivalence between a policy that is designed to perpetuate a caste system and one that seeks to eradicate racial subordination."

Special circumstances justify vigilant judicial inspection to protect minority voters—circumstances that do not apply to majority voters. A history of exclusion from state politics left racial minorities without clout to extract provisions for fair representation in the lawmaking forum. The equal protection rights of minority voters thus could have remained unrealized absent the Judiciary's close surveillance. *Cf. United States v. Carolene Products Co.*, 304 U.S. 144, 153, n.4 (1938) (referring to the "more searching judicial inquiry" that may properly attend classifications adversely affecting "discrete and insular minorities"). The majority, by definition, encounters no such blockage. White voters in Georgia do not lack means to exert strong pressure on their state legislators. The force of their numbers is itself a powerful determiner of what the legislature will do that does not coincide with perceived majority interests. * * *

Notes and Questions

1. Justice Kennedy, writing for the majority, cites *Loving v. Virginia*, 388 U.S. 1 (1967), and *McLaughlin v. Florida*, 379 U.S. 184 (1964), for the proposition that "racial neutrality" is the "central mandate" of government decisionmaking under the Fourteenth Amendment Equal Protection Clause. Do those cases sustain that view?

2. How does the *Miller* court view race? The term "majority-minority" district is used by the Court to describe districts where nonwhites have a voting majority. Why doesn't the Court use racially descriptive language such as "majority nonwhite" or "majority white" districts? Is it simply common understanding that majority means white? Note the General Assembly's Black Caucus called their plan the "max-black" plan. Why would they choose to utilize this racialized language?

3. The Court asserts the state may not segregate based on race in public parks, buses, golf courses, beaches, and schools. Is the purpose of government segregation in such facilities the same as government line drawing by race to create voting districts? What forces created the pockets of white and nonwhite residential communities seeking Congressional repre-

sentation in need of Voting Rights Act review? The Court concedes that "the distinction between being aware of racial considerations and being motivated by them may be difficult to make." 515 U.S. at 916. Is the Court making a distinction without a difference?

4. Does "treating citizens as individuals," which the court describes as constitutionally mandated, require ignoring "race, religion, sex, or national class"? Should legislatures view race differently from ethnicity for purpose of legislative districting? Justice Ginsburg suggests they should not. Is she correct? What about for other purposes than legislative districting?

5. The Court cites the *Shaw* language stating it is "offensive and demeaning" to assume that voters of a "particular race, because of their race, 'think alike, share the same political interests, and will prefer the same candidates at the polls.'" Do you agree? Did the *Thornburg* court agree? Does the *Miller* court make this assumption about white voters? Is making this assumption necessary in order to attend to how districts are drawn? Might such generalizations be used to empower people of color? *Cf.* E. J. Dionne, Jr., *The Minorities Vote*, Wash. Post Dec. 1, 1998, at A25 (noting that in the November 1998 elections African–American candidates were elected to both statewide and national office from predominantly white districts). Asked whether changing white attitudes made "majority minority" districts obsolete, Rep. Mel Watt, said no, emphasizing the question required a complicated answer. *Id.* What kind of complicated answer might be required and how might such complications be explained to a court reviewing a district under a Voting Rights Act challenge?

6. Does anything remain of *Thornburg* after *Miller*?

7. How useful is the "dominant purpose test" articulated in *Miller*? See John Hart Ely, *Gerrymanders: The Good, the Bad, and the Ugly*, 50 Stan. L. Rev. 607 (1998) (preferring the *Shaw* "bizarre shape test," but concluding that race should not be considered in configuring voting districts).

8. Should white voters have standing to challenge the Georgia redistricting plan, as the court assumes? See John Hart Ely, *Standing to Challenge Pro–Minority Gerrymanders*, 111 Harv. L. Rev. 576, 595 (1997)* where the author, discussing white voters such as the *Miller* plaintiffs, concludes:

> No more than anyone else have they a constitutional right to a representative of their own race, nor are their rights denied simply because the district they inhabit is configured so as to make that outcome unlikely. However, when the district is configured with the intention of making it unlikely—in the cases we're discussing, virtually unthinkable—they have at the least a nonfrivolous argument that it's unconstitutional. Perhaps the argument is one that ultimately should fail. But they have standing to make it.

Compare Stephanie M. Wildman with contributions by Margalynne Armstrong, Adrienne D. Davis & Trina Grillo, *Privilege Revealed: How Invisible Preference Undermines America* 170 (1996):

> I found myself trapped, not for the first time, in legal liberalism. Legal liberalism teaches us that all people should be treated equally, fairly, and the same. It is the solid underpinning of the notion of the

color-blind constitution * * * [which says] "Race shall play no part in American society." This is our ideal, and it is attractive.

The reality is that if we say race plays no part, then the invisible system of white privilege will inevitably continue. In this status quo of white privilege, [the African-American family who suffered racial harassment and were evicted] may now be without a place to live, while the evicted white family [the harasser] finds a new home easily. Even if the African–American tenants find a new home, they may be racially harassed and suffer eviction again. The system of white privilege means that the white family is not at risk in the same way.

Would a privilege lens, suggesting asymmetrical positioning based on race, lead to a different result in this case? Could it provide a meaningful way to evaluate legislative redistricting?

SECTION 4. MOTIVATION TO PARTICIPATE AND MEANINGFUL PARTICIPATION

Ensuring meaningful participation in a democratic life means developing democratic habits from an early age. Daily life in school should offer practice and training for democracy. The next chapter on education considers some of the issues that have arisen in relation to race and education, which greatly affect our concept of democracy. The many communities in which we live and work give us the opportunity to practice democracy. All too often these community environments, workplaces, and families do not embody democratic norms, but rather preserve hierarchy and the systemic privileges described earlier. Where democracy seems hollow, motivation to participate is low. Is democracy hollow for racial minorities and the poor?

Robert Chang describes his attendance at his first faculty meeting to illustrate the significance of meaningful participation.

ROBERT S. CHANG

Toward an Asian American Legal Scholarship: Critical Race Theory, Post-Structuralism, and Narrative Space
81 Cal. L. Rev. 1241, 1300–03 (1993), 1 Asian L.J. 1, 60–63 (1994).*

When I joined the faculty at my former school, the Dean told me that I could participate in faculty meetings. On the first Tuesday of September, I felt proud to attend my first faculty meeting. I did not know then that it would be the last meeting I would attend that semester. As issues came up for decision, I voted, just like the other faculty members. It was only after the meeting that I was told that, as a legal writing instructor, I was not allowed to vote. My face turned red. I did not return.

The Dean had not lied to me when he told me that I was allowed to participate in faculty meetings; we simply differed in our interpretation of "participation." From my perspective, the Dean's notion of "participation" was impoverished because I included "meaningful" as part of my definition of "participation."

To an outside observer, it might appear that I stopped going because I did not care about faculty meetings. But when you listen to my story, you will understand that this is not so.

Systemic disfranchisement—whether at the level of faculty meetings or national elections—discourages many Asian Americans from participating in the political process. This is reflected in the low voter registration statistics which show Asian Americans to be "grossly underrepresented in terms of their voting power in relation to their numbers in the population." This political silence has been attributed to "cultural differences, the difficulty of combining Asian Pacific American subgroups into a cohesive 'minority' group because of their diverse nationalities and generations, and their lack of interest in politics." These reasons, however, are largely myths created to prevent the enfranchisement of Asian Americans. The low voter registration figures can be attributed to several specific barriers that prevent Asian Americans from participating in a meaningful manner.

The greatest historical barrier to Asian–American participation in the political process was the fact that Asian Americans could not become naturalized and could therefore not vote since only citizens had that right. Some states even prohibited American-born Asians from voting.[296] This historical exclusion has an inertia that carries into the present. Yet the dominant culture, and in particular, the legislature and judiciary, do not understand because they are largely unaware of this pattern of formally excluding Asian Americans.

In fact, according to the Civil Rights Report, formal barriers to political participation still exist:

1) apportionment policies that dilute the voting strength of Asian–American voting blocks; 2) the unavailability of Asian-language ballots and other election materials; 3) problems with the implementation of the Census of Population; and 4) anti-Asian sentiments among non-Asian voters and the media and the consequent dearth of Asian–American political candidates (which may also be partly caused by political parties that ignore the Asian–American population and do not actively seek or promote Asian candidates).

I address the first two barriers examined by the Civil Rights Commission.[298]

Two current apportionment policies dilute Asian–American voting strength: (1) the splitting of the Asian–American population in an area

---

296. See, *e.g.*, Cal. Const. Art. II, § 1 (1911).

298. As for the third factor, the Census provides a barrier in two ways: (1) no forms use Asian languages, and (2) data on Asian Americans from the 1980 census were not released until 1988. The latter factor is important in establishing whether Asian Americans constitute a language minority for the purposes of the Voting Rights Language Assistance Act. The importance of the fourth factor can be seen in the results of exit polls which show that 71% of Asian–American voters would vote more often "if more Asian candidates ran for office."

into several voting districts,[299] and (2) the establishment of at-large election systems in areas of high Asian–American population.[300] Attempts to redress Asian–American vote dilution are hindered by a United States Supreme Court decision which requires that a minority group "be able to demonstrate that it is sufficiently large and geographically compact to constitute a majority in a single-member district."[301] One problem with this requirement is that it excludes Asian Americans, many of whom are geographically dispersed, at times involuntarily, through the will of the government.[302]

Another formal mechanism that prevents greater voter participation among Asian Americans is the use of English-only ballots. Congress, recognizing the problems with English-only ballots, amended the Voting Rights Act in 1975 and again in 1982 to provide language assistance to "language minorities."[303] However, these measures did not take into account the distinct problems facing Asian Americans. Congress, in establishing that a language minority must constitute at least five percent of the voting age population, did not consider the diversity of languages and cultures among Asian Americans. Thus, even if the Asian–American population in a given political subdivision were greater than the requisite five percent, no single Asian–American language minority constituted a large enough group to benefit from the Act's provisions.[304] As a result, no Asian–American groups were able to claim the status of a "language minority" under that amendment.

This did not change until the voices of Asian Americans spoke our distinct problems into existence. Because Asian Americans were unable to constitute language minorities for the purposes of the 1982 Voting Rights Act, members of the community began to voice concerns and to protest the 1982 Act. Many participated in Roundtable Conferences on

---

299. For example, the Los Angeles Koreatown, Chinatown, and Filipinotown areas are each split into multiple districts. U.S. Commission on Civil Rights, *Civil Rights Issues Facing Asian Americans in the 1990s*, at 159.

300. An example of at-large districts diluting the strength of Asian–American votes can be seen in Daly City, California, where Asian Americans (primarily Filipino Americans) constitute over 42% of the city's population. Yet the first Filipino American to serve on the city council was elected this year.

301. *Thornburg v. Gingles*, 478 U.S. 30, 50 (1986).

302. See Su Sun Bai, Comment, *Affirmative Pursuit of Political Equality for Asian Pacific Americans: Reclaiming the Voting Rights Act*, 139 U. Pa. L. Rev. 731, 757 n.125 (1991) (discussing the internment of Japanese Americans during World War II which destroyed many Japanese American communities and the government's appeals to Japanese Americans not to return to those communities in California, recent ur-

ban renewal programs which have forced many Asian Americans out of ethnic communities such as Chinatowns, and the purposeful dispersal of Southeast Asian refugees throughout the United States to lessen the burden on a particular community).

303. 42 U.S.C. § 1973aa–1a (1988); H.R. Rep. No. 655, 102d Cong., 2d Sess. 3 (1992). Congress found that through the use of various practices and procedures, citizens of language minorities have been effectively excluded from participation in the electoral process. Among other factors, the denial of the right to vote of such minority group citizens is ordinarily directly related to the unequal educational opportunities afforded them, resulting in high illiteracy and low voting participation.

42 U.S.C. § 1973aa–1a(a).

304. Other minority groups were able to establish themselves as language minorities under the act. H.R. Rep. No. 655, 102d Cong., 2d Sess. 3 (1992) at 4. In pointing this out, I do not mean to imply that all the voting barriers of other minority groups were removed. They were not.

Civil Rights sponsored by the United States Commission on Civil Rights. Their efforts led to the 1992 amendment to the Voting Rights Act, which led to the enfranchisement of many Asian Americans.

Achieving enfranchisement is only the first step toward meaningful political participation and social change. The next step is to elect legislators and appoint public officials who will address and respond to the unique needs of Asian Americans. In legislative halls, executive agencies, and judicial chambers, the law is made and implemented, but Asian Americans, perhaps more so than other disempowered groups, have not yet been able to enter these domains in a significant way. Nevertheless, the voting rights example shows how legal reform can be brought about when Asian Americans participate in the political process and give voice to our oppression and our needs.

Notes and Questions

1. Motivation to participate in the political process is tied to the pervasive problem of societal racism, particularly in areas of education and employment. This racism persists, even in the process of trying to address it in legal challenges. In *White v. Regester*, 412 U.S. 755 (1973), the Court observed:

> Surveying the historic and present condition of the Bexar County Mexican–American community, which is concentrated for the most part on the west side of the city of San Antonio, the court observed, based upon prior cases and the record before it, that the Bexar community, along with other Mexican Americans in Texas,[12] had long "suffered from, and continues to suffer from, the results and effects of invidious discrimination and treatment in the fields of education, employment, economics, health, politics and others." The bulk of the Mexican–American community in Bexar County occupied the Barrio, an area consisting of about 28 contiguous census tracts in the city of San Antonio. Over 78% of Barrio residents were Mexican Americans, making up 29% of the county's total population. The Barrio is an area of poor housing; its residents have low income and a high rate of unemployment. The typical Mexican American suffers a cultural and language barrier that makes his participation in community processes extremely difficult, particularly, the court thought, with respect to the political life of Bexar County. "(A) cultural incompatibility ... conjoined with the poll tax and the most restrictive voter registration procedures in the nation have operated to effectively deny Mexican Americans access to the political processes in Texas even longer than the Blacks were formally denied access by the white primary." The residual impact of this history reflected itself in the fact that Mexican–American voting registration remained very poor in the county and that, only five Mexican Americans since 1880 have served in the Texas Legislature from Bexar County. Of these, only two were from the Barrio area. The District Court also concluded from the evidence that the Bexar County legislative delegation in the House was insufficiently responsive to Mexican–American interests.

12. Mexican Americans constituted approximately 20% of the population of the State of Texas.

412 U.S. at 767–68.

Would the Mexican–American community describe the problem of meaningful participation this way? Do you think they believe they "suffer a cultural barrier?"

2. Asian Americans continue to have low voter registration rates and voter turnout. See Julie Chao, *Poll Finds Asians Lag Politically,* S.F. Examiner, Dec. 6, 1998, at C-1 (concluding "Asians lag behind other groups in political participation").

3. Even after passage of the Voting Rights Act, victories in drawing legislative districts and in determining methods of representation, members of previously disenfranchised groups faced new obstacles to having their votes count.

PRESLEY v. ETOWAH COUNTY COMMISSION

502 U.S. 491 (1992).

[Black newly elected county commissioners brought these consolidated cases alleging that their respective counties had violated § 5 of the Voting Rights Act by failing to obtain preclearance for resolutions altering the prior practice of allowing each commissioner full authority to determine how to spend funds allocated to his own road district or for a unit system abolishing individual road districts and transferring responsibility for all road operations to the county engineer appointed by commission. Section 5 of the Voting Rights Act of 1965 requires a covered jurisdiction to obtain either judicial or administrative preclearance before enforcing any new "voting qualification or prerequisite to voting, or standard, practice, or procedure with respect to voting." In two Alabama counties, voters elect members of county commissions whose principal function is to supervise and control county road maintenance, repair, and construction.

The Etowah County Commission, without seeking preclearance, passed its "Common Fund Resolution," which altered the prior practice of allowing each commissioner full authority to determine how to spend funds allocated to his own road district. The resolution was passed by the four holdover members of the commission shortly after appellant Presley, a black man, and another new member were elected.

The Russell County Commission adopted a "Unit System," which abolished individual road districts and transferred responsibility for all road operations to the county engineer, a commission appointee. Appellants Mack and Gosha were elected as Russell County's first black county commissioners in modern times. They, along with Presley, filed suit in the District Court, alleging, among other things, that Etowah and Russell Counties had violated § 5 by failing to obtain preclearance for, respectively, the Common Fund Resolution and the adoption of the Unit System.]

JUSTICE KENNEDY delivered the opinion of the court.

In various Alabama counties voters elect members of county commissions whose principal function is to supervise and control the maintenance, repair, and construction of the county roads. The consolidated appeals now before us concern certain changes in the decisionmaking authority of the elected members on two different county commissions, and the question to be decided is whether these were changes "with respect to voting" within the meaning of § 5 of the Voting Rights Act of 1965. These cases have significance well beyond the two county commissions; for the appellants, and the United States as *amicus curiae*, ask us to adopt a rule embracing the routine actions of state and local governments at all levels. We must interpret the provisions of § 5, which require a jurisdiction covered by the Act to obtain either judicial or administrative preclearance before enforcing any new "voting qualification or prerequisite to voting, or standard, practice, or procedure with respect to voting."

I

To determine whether there have been changes with respect to voting, we must compare the challenged practices with those in existence before they were adopted. Absent relevant intervening changes, the Act requires us to use practices in existence on November 1, 1964, as our standard of comparison.

A

We consider first the Etowah County Commission. On November 1, 1964, commission members were elected at large under a "residency district" system. The entire electorate of Etowah County voted on candidates for each of the five seats. Four of the seats corresponded to the four residency districts of the county. Candidates were required to reside in the appropriate district. The fifth member, the chairman, was not subject to a district residency requirement, though residency in the county itself was a requirement.

Each of the four residency districts functioned as a road district. The commissioner residing in the district exercised control over a road shop, equipment, and road crew for that district. It was the practice of the commission to vote as a collective body on the division of funds among the road districts, but once funds were divided each commissioner exercised individual control over spending priorities within his district. The chairman was responsible for overseeing the solid waste authority, preparing the budget, and managing the courthouse building and grounds. * * *

On August 25, 1987, the commission passed the "Road Supervision Resolution." It provided that each holdover [previously-elected] commissioner would continue to control the workers and operations assigned to his respective road shop, which, it must be remembered, accounted for all the road shops the county had. It also gave the four holdovers joint responsibility for overseeing the repair, maintenance, and improvement of all the roads of Etowah County in order to pick up the roads in the districts where the new commissioners resided. The new commissioners, now foreclosed from exercising any authority over roads, were given other functions under the resolution. Presley was to oversee maintenance of the county courthouse and Williams the operation of the engineering department. The Road Supervision Resolution was passed by a 4–to–2 margin, with the two new commissioners dissenting.

The same day the Road Supervision Resolution was passed, the commission passed a second, the so-called "Common Fund Resolution." It provides in part that

"all monies earmarked and budgeted for repair, maintenance and improvement of the streets, roads and public ways of Etowah County [shall] be placed and maintained in common accounts, [shall] not be allocated, budgeted or designated for use in districts, and [shall] be used county-wide in accordance with need, for the repair, maintenance and improvement of all streets, roads and public ways in Etowah County which are under the jurisdiction of the Etowah County Commission."

This had the effect of altering the prior practice of allowing each commissioner full authority to determine how to spend the funds allocated to his own district. The Etowah County Commission did not seek judicial or administrative preclearance of either the Road Supervision Resolution or the Common Fund Resolution. The District Court held that the Road Supervision Resolution was subject to preclearance but that the Common Fund Resolution was not. No appeal was taken from the first ruling, so only the Common Fund Resolution is before us in the Etowah County case.

B

We turn next to the background of the Russell County Commission. On November 1, 1964, it had three commissioners. Like the members of the Etowah County Commission before the consent decree change, Russell County Commissioners were elected at large by the entire electorate, subject to a requirement that a candidate for commissioner reside in the district corresponding to the seat he or she sought. A 1972 federal court order * * * required that the commission be expanded to include five members. The two new members were both elected at large from one newly created residency district for Phenix City, the largest city in Russell County. Following the implementation of the court order, each of the three rural commissioners had individual authority over his own road shop, road crew, and equipment. The three rural commissioners also had individual authority for road and bridge repair and construction within their separate residency districts. Although funding for new construction and major repair projects was subject to a vote by the entire commission, individual commissioners could authorize expenditures for routine repair and maintenance work as well as routine purchase orders without seeking approval from the entire commission.

Following the indictment of one commissioner on charges of corruption in Russell County road operations, in May 1979 the commission passed a resolution delegating control over road construction, maintenance, personnel, and inventory to the county engineer, an official appointed by the entire commission and responsible to it. * * * The parties refer to abolition of the individual road districts and transfer of responsibility for all road operations to the county engineer as the adoption of a "Unit System." Neither the resolution nor the statute which authorized the Unit System was submitted for preclearance under § 5.

Litigation involving the Russell County Commission led to a 1985 consent decree * * * that enlarged the commission to seven members and replaced the at-large election system with elections on a district-by-district basis. Without any mention of the Unit System changes, the consent decree was precleared by the Department of Justice under § 5. Following its implementation, appellants Mack and Gosha were elected in 1986. They are Russell County's first black county commissioners in modern times.

C

In May 1989, appellants in both cases now before us filed a single complaint in the District Court for the Middle District of Alabama, alleging racial discrimination in the operation of the Etowah and Russell County Commissions in violation of prior court orders, the Constitution, Title VI of the Civil Rights Act of 1964, 42 U.S.C.A. § 2000d, and § 2 of the Voting Rights Act. In a series of amended complaints, appellants added claims under § 5. The § 5 claims alleged that Etowah County had violated the Act by failing to obtain preclearance of the 1987 Road Supervision and Common Fund Resolutions, and that Russell County had failed to preclear the 1979 change to the Unit System. * * *

With respect to the issues now before us, a majority of the District Court held that neither the Common Fund Resolution of the Etowah County Commission nor the adoption of the Unit System in Russell County was subject to § 5 preclearance. The court held that changes in the responsibilities of elected officials are subject to preclearance when they "effect a significant relative change in the powers exercised by governmental officials elected by, or responsible to, substantially different constituencies of voters." Applying its test, the court found that the Common Fund Resolution in Etowah County did not effect a significant change and adoption of the Unit System in Russell County did not transfer authority among officials responsible to different constituencies. * * * We affirm the District Court but adopt a different interpretation of § 5 as the rationale for our decision.

II

* * *

After *South Carolina v. Katzenbach* upheld the Voting Rights Act against a constitutional challenge, it was not until we heard *Allen v. State Bd. of Elections*, 393 U.S. 544 (1969), that we were called upon to decide whether particular changes were covered by § 5. There we rejected a narrow construction, one which would have limited § 5 to state rules prescribing who may register to vote. We held that the section applies also to state rules relating to the qualifications of candidates and to state decisions as to which offices shall be elective. We observed that "[t]he Voting Rights Act was aimed at the subtle, as well as the obvious, state regulations which have the effect of denying citizens their right to vote because of their race." Our decision, and its rationale, have proved sound, and we adhere to both.

In giving a broad construction to § 5 in *Allen*, we noted that "Congress intended to reach any state enactment which altered the election law of a covered State in even a minor way." Relying on this language and its application in later cases, appellants and the United States now argue that because there is no *de minimis* exception to § 5, the changes at issue here must be subject to preclearance. This argument, however, assumes the answer to the principal question in the case: whether the changes at issue are changes in voting, or as we phrased it in *Allen*, "election law."

We agree that all changes in voting must be precleared and with *Allen*'s holding that the scope of § 5 is expansive within its sphere of operation. That sphere comprehends all changes to rules governing voting, changes effected through any of the mechanisms described in the statute. Those mechanisms are any "qualification or prerequisite" or any "standard, practice, or procedure with respect to voting."

The principle that § 5 covers voting changes over a wide range is well illustrated by the separate cases we considered in the single opinion for the Court in *Allen*. *Allen* involved four cases. The eponymous *Allen v. State Bd. of Elections* concerned a change in the procedures for the casting of write-in ballots. In *Whitley v. Williams*, there were changes in the requirements for independent candidates running in general elections. The challenged procedure in *Fairley v. Patterson* resulted in a change from single-district voting to at-large voting. The remaining case, *Bunton v. Patterson*, involved a statute which provided that officials who in previous years had been elected would be appointed. We held that the changes in each of the four cases were covered by § 5.

Our cases since *Allen* reveal a consistent requirement that changes subject to § 5 pertain only to voting. Without implying that the four typologies exhaust the statute's coverage, we can say these later cases fall within one of the four factual contexts presented in the *Allen* cases. First, we have held that § 5 applies to cases like *Allen v. State Bd. of Elections* itself, in which the changes involved the manner of voting. Second, we have held that § 5 applies to cases like *Whitley v. Williams*, which involve candidacy requirements and qualifications. Third, we have applied § 5 to cases like *Fairley v. Patterson*, which concerned changes in the composition of the electorate that may vote for candidates for a given office. Fourth, we have made clear that § 5 applies to changes, like the one in *Bunton v. Patterson*, affecting the creation or abolition of an elective office.

The first three categories involve changes in election procedures, while all the examples within the fourth category might be termed substantive changes as to which offices are elective. But whether the changes are of procedure or substance, each has a direct relation to voting and the election process.

III

A comparison of the changes at issue here with those in our prior decisions demonstrates that the present cases do not involve changes covered by the Act.

A

The Etowah County Commission's Common Fund Resolution is not a change within any of the categories recognized in *Allen* or our later cases. It has no connection to voting procedures: It does not affect the manner of holding elections, it alters or imposes no candidacy qualifications or requirements, and it leaves undisturbed the composition of the electorate. It also has no bearing on the substance of voting power, for it does not increase or diminish the number of officials for whom the electorate may vote. Rather, the Common Fund Resolution concerns the internal operations of an elected body.

Appellants argue that the Common Fund Resolution is a covered change because after its enactment each commissioner has less individual power than before the resolution. A citizen casting a ballot for a commissioner today votes for an individual with less authority than before the resolution, and so, it is said, the value of the vote has been diminished.

Were we to accept appellants' proffered reading of § 5, we would work an unconstrained expansion of its coverage. Innumerable state and local enactments having nothing to do with voting affect the power of elected officials. When a state or local body adopts a new governmental program or modifies an existing one it will often be the case that it changes the powers of elected officials. So too, when a state or local body alters its internal operating procedures, for example by modifying its subcommittee assignment system, it "implicate[s] an elected official's decisionmaking authority."

Appellants and the United States fail to provide a workable standard for distinguishing between changes in rules governing voting and changes in the routine organization and functioning of government. Some standard is necessary, for in a real sense every decision taken by government implicates voting. This is but the felicitous consequence of democracy, in which power derives from the people. Yet no one would contend that when Congress enacted the Voting Rights Act it meant to subject all or even most decisions of government in covered jurisdictions to federal supervision. Rather, the Act by its terms covers any "voting qualification or prerequisite to voting, or standard, practice, or procedure with respect to voting." 42 U.S.C.A. § 1973c. A faithful effort to implement the design of the statute must begin by drawing lines between those governmental decisions that involve voting and those that do not.

A simple example shows the inadequacy of the line proffered by appellants and the United States. Under appellants' view, every time a covered jurisdiction passed a budget that differed from the previous year's budget it would be required to obtain preclearance. The amount of funds available to an elected official has a profound effect on the power exercised. A vote for an ill-funded official is less valuable than a vote for a well-funded one.

No doubt in recognition of the unacceptable consequences of their views, appellants take the position that while "some budget changes may affect the right to vote and, under particular circumstances, would be subject to preclearance," most budget changes would not. Under their interpretation of § 5, however, appellants fail to give any workable standard to determine when preclearance is required. And were we to acknowledge that a budget adjustment is a voting change in even some instances, the likely consequence is that every budget change would be covered, for it is well settled that every voting change with a "potential for discrimination" must be precleared.

Confronting this difficulty, at oral argument the United States suggested that we draw an arbitrary line distinguishing between budget changes and other changes. There is no principled basis for the distinction, and it would be a marked departure from the statutory category of voting. If a diminution or increase in an elected official's powers is a change with respect to voting, then whether it is accomplished through an enactment or a budget shift should not matter. Even if we were willing to draw an unprincipled line excluding budgetary changes but not other changes in an elected official's decisionmaking authority, the result would expand the coverage of § 5 well beyond the statutory language and the intention of Congress.

Under the view advanced by appellants and the United States, every time a state legislature acts to diminish or increase the power of local officials, preclearance would be required. Governmental action decreasing the power of local officials could carry with it a potential for discrimination against those who represent racial minorities at the local level. At the same time, increasing the power of local officials will entail a relative decrease in the power of state officials, and that too could carry with it a potential for discrimination against state officials who represent racial minorities at the state level. The all but limitless minor changes in the allocation of power among officials and the constant adjustments required for the efficient governance of every covered State illustrate the necessity for us to formulate workable rules to confine the coverage of § 5 to its legitimate sphere: voting.

Changes which affect only the distribution of power among officials are not subject to § 5 because such changes have no direct relation to, or impact on, voting. The Etowah County Commission's Common Fund Resolution was not subject to the preclearance requirement.

B

We next consider Russell County's adoption of the Unit System and its concomitant transfer of operations to the county engineer. Of the four categories of changes in rules governing voting we have recognized to date, there is not even an arguable basis for saying that adoption of the Unit System fits within any of the first three. As to the fourth category, it might be argued that the delegation of authority to an appointed official is similar to the replacement of an elected official with an appointed one, the change we held subject to § 5 in *Bunton v. Patterson*. This approach, however, would ignore the rationale for our holding: "[A]fter the change, [the citizen] is prohibited from electing an officer formerly subject to the approval of the voters." In short, the change in *Bunton v. Patterson* involved a rule governing voting not because it effected a change in the relative authority of various governmental officials, but because it changed an elective office to an appointive one.

The change in Russell County does not prohibit voters "from electing an officer formerly subject to the[ir] approval." Both before and after the change the citizens of Russell County were able to vote for the members of the Russell County Commission. To be sure, after the 1979 resolution each commissioner exercised less direct authority over road operations, that authority having been delegated to an official answerable to the commission. But as we concluded with respect to Etowah County, the fact that an enactment alters an elected official's powers does not in itself render the enactment a rule governing voting.

It is a routine part of governmental administration for appointive positions to be created or eliminated and for their powers to be altered. Each time this occurs the relative balance of authority is altered in some way. The making or unmaking of an appointive post often will result in the erosion or accretion of the powers of some official responsible to the electorate, but it does not follow that those changes are covered by § 5. By requiring preclearance of changes with respect to voting, Congress did not mean to subject such routine matters of governance to federal supervision. Were the rule otherwise, neither state nor local governments could exercise power in a responsible manner within a federal system. * * *

IV

The United States urges that despite our understanding of the language of § 5, we should defer to its administrative construction of the provision. We have recognized that "the construction placed upon the [Voting Rights] Act by the Attorney General ... is entitled to considerable deference." But the principle has its limits. Deference does not mean acquiescence. * * *

V

Nothing we say implies that the conduct at issue in these cases is not actionable under a different remedial scheme. The Voting Rights Act is not an all-purpose antidiscrimination statute. The fact that the intrusive mechanisms of the Act do not apply to other forms of pernicious discrimination does not undermine its utility in combating the specific evils it was designed to address.

Our prior cases hold, and we reaffirm today, that every change in rules governing voting must be precleared. The legislative history we rehearsed in *South Carolina v. Katzenbach* was cited to demonstrate Congress' concern for the protection of voting rights. Neither the appellants nor the United States has pointed to anything we said there or in the statutes reenacting the Voting Rights Act to suggest that Congress meant other than what it said when it made § 5 applicable to changes "with respect to voting" rather than, say, changes "with respect to governance."

If federalism is to operate as a practical system of governance and not a mere poetic ideal, the States must be allowed both predictability and efficiency in structuring their governments. Constant minor adjustments in the allocation of power among state and local officials serve this elemental purpose.

Covered changes must bear a direct relation to voting itself. That direct relation is absent in both cases now before us. The changes in Etowah and Russell Counties affected only the allocation of power among governmental officials. They had no impact on the substantive question whether a particular office would be elective or the procedural question how an election would be conducted. Neither change involves a new "voting qualification or prerequisite to voting, or standard, practice, or procedure with respect to voting." 42 U.S.C.A. § 1973c.

The judgment of the District Court is affirmed.

JUSTICE STEVENS, with whom JUSTICE WHITE and JUSTICE BLACKMUN join, dissenting.

In 1986, an important event occurred in each of two Alabama counties with long histories of white-dominated political processes. In Etowah County, a black commissioner was elected to the county commission for the first time in recent history, and in Russell County, two black commissioners were elected to the county commission for the first time in "modern times." Because of the three resolutions at issue in these cases—two adopted in Etowah County after Commissioner Presley's election and one adopted in Russell County before the election of Commissioners Mack and Gosha—none of the three newly elected black commissioners was able to exercise the decisionmaking authority that had been traditionally associated with his office.

As I shall explain, this is a case in which a few pages of history are far more illuminating than volumes of logic and hours of speculation about hypothetical line-drawing problems. Initially, however, it is important to note that a different decision in these cases would not impose any novel or significant burden on those jurisdictions that remain covered under § 5 of the Voting Rights Act of 1965.

Prior to these cases, federal courts had uniformly agreed with the Attorney General's interpretation that § 5 covered transfers of decision-making power that had a potential for discrimination against minority voters. On at least eight occasions since 1975, the Department of Justice has refused to preclear changes in the power of elected officials that had a potentially discriminatory impact on black voters. The Department has routinely precleared numerous other transfers of authority after determining that they had no discriminatory purpose or effect. There is no evidence that the prevailing practice imposed any special burden on covered jurisdictions. For example, in this fiscal year the Attorney General has processed over 17,000 preclearance requests, and has approved over 99 percent of them without any undue delay. It is, therefore, simply hyperbole for the Court to suggest that if we adopted the Attorney General's position in this case "neither state nor local governments could exercise power in a responsible manner within a federal system."

In all of our prior cases interpreting § 5 of the Voting Rights Act, the Court has agreed with the Attorney General's construction of this important statute. I share the Court's view that the "considerable deference" to which the Attorney General's construction is entitled does not mean automatic "acquiescence;" however, I strongly disagree with the Court that our task in these cases is "to formulate workable rules to confine the coverage of § 5 to its legitimate sphere: voting." For reasons that I shall explain, even if the Attorney General, participating in these cases as *amicus curiae*, has asked the Court to adopt a broader rationale than is necessary or appropriate, a narrower basis for a decision is obviously available in the Etowah County case and, in my judgment, in the Russell County case as well.

I

The original enactment of § 5, the interpretations of the Act by this Court and by the Attorney General, and the reenactment of the statute by Congress in light of those interpretations reveal a continuous process of development in response to changing conditions in the covered jurisdictions.

The central purpose of the original Act was to eliminate the various devices, such as literacy tests, requirements of "good moral character," vouchers, and poll taxes, that had excluded black voters from the registration and voting process in the southern States for decades. As we explained in *McCain v. Lybrand*, 465 U.S. 236:

> "The Voting Rights Act of 1965 * * * was enacted by Congress as a response to the 'unremitting and ingenious defiance' of the command of the Fifteenth Amendment for nearly a century by state officials in certain parts of the Nation. Congress concluded that case-by-case litigation under previous legislation was an unsatisfactory method to uncover and remedy the systematic discriminatory election practices in certain areas: Such lawsuits were too onerous and time-consuming to prepare, obstructionist tactics by those determined to perpetuate discrimination yielded unacceptable delay, and even successful lawsuits too often merely resulted in a change in methods of discrimination. Congress decided 'to shift the advantage of time and inertia from the perpetrators of the evil to its victims,' and enacted 'stringent new remedies' designed to 'banish the blight of racial discrimination in voting' once and for all."

During the first few years after the enactment of § 5, the federal courts gave its text a narrow literal construction that confined its coverage to the political subdivisions that registered voters and to the practices that directly concerned the registration and voting process. Prior to the Court's decision in *Allen v. State Bd. of Elections*, 393 U.S. 544 (1969), only three States submitted any changes to the Attorney General for preclearance and a total of only 323 changes were submitted during the first five years of administration. At that time, the covered jurisdictions were able to respond to the increase in the number of black registered voters by means that prevented the newly registered minority voters from having a proportionate impact on the political process.

In *Allen* and its companion cases, however, the Court held that some of these responses, even if not described in the literal text of the Act, were nevertheless included within the scope of § 5. Relying heavily on the statutory definition of voting as encompassing " 'all action necessary to make a vote effective,' " and the broad remedial purposes of the Act, the Court held that a change from district to at-large voting for county supervisors, a change that made an important county office appointive rather than elective, and a change that altered the requirements for independent candidates, were all covered voting practices. Thus, § 5 was not limited to changes directly affecting the casting of a ballot. ("The right to vote can be affected by a dilution of voting power as well as by an absolute prohibition on casting a ballot. See *Reynolds v. Sims*, 377 U.S. 533, 555 (1964)"). Nothing in *Allen* implied that the Court had defined an exhaustive category of changes covered by the Act. On the contrary, the Court described § 5 as "aimed at the subtle, as well as the obvious, state regulations which have the effect of denying citizens their right to vote because of their race," and expressed, in no uncertain terms, that § 5 should be given "the broadest possible scope." Aware of the consequences of its decision, the Court gave its broad reading of the Act "only prospective effect."

The Court's construction of the Act in *Allen*, as requiring preclearance of changes in covered jurisdictions that were responsive to the increase in the number of black registered voters, was consistent with the concern that justified the extraordinary remedy set forth in § 5 itself, particularly the concern that recalcitrant white majorities could be expected to devise new stratagems to maintain their political power if not closely scrutinized.

* * *

Thus, § 5 was understood to be "a 'vital element' of the Act," and was designed to be flexible enough to ensure that " 'new subterfuges will be promptly discovered and enjoined.' " Section 5, as construed by the Court, was not limited to a "simple inventory of voting procedures," but rather, was understood to address "the reality of changed practices as they affect Negro voters."

In subsequent cases, this Court has reaffirmed the broad scope of § 5 coverage, as first articulated by the Court in *Allen*. The Court has interpreted § 5 expansively and has said in the context of candidate qualification that a statute requiring independent candidates to declare their intention to seek office two months earlier than under the previous procedures created a barrier to candidacy and required § 5 preclearance, and in other contexts, that preclearance is required when there is a change in polling places, an alteration in municipal boundaries, reapportionment and redistricting plans, and the introduction of numbered posts and staggered terms.

* * *

One Congressman who had supported the 1965 Act observed: "When I voted for the Voting Rights Act of 1965, I hoped that 5 years would be ample time. But resistance to progress has been more subtle and more effective than I thought possible. A whole arsenal of racist weapons has been perfected. Boundary lines have been gerrymandered, elections have been switched to an at-large basis, counties have been consolidated, elective offices have been abolished where blacks had a chance of winning, the appointment process has been substituted for the elective process, election officials have withheld the necessary information for voting or running for office, and both physical and economic intimidation have been employed."

"Section 5 was intended to prevent the use of most of these devices."

Since the decision in *Allen*, the debate on reenactment of § 5 in 1970, and the issuance of regulations by the Department of Justice, it has been recognized that the replacement of an elective office that might be won by a black candidate with an appointive office is one of the methods of maintaining a white majority's political power that § 5 was designed to forestall. As a practical matter, such a change has the same effect as a change that makes an elected official a mere figurehead by transferring his decisionmaking authority to an appointed official, or to a group of elected officials controlled by the majority. Although this type of response to burgeoning black registration may not have been prevalent during the early history of the Act, it has been an active concern of the Attorney General since 1976. In my judgment, such a change in the reallocation of decisionmaking authority in an elective office, at least in its most blatant form, is indistinguishable from, and just as unacceptable as, gerrymandering boundary lines or switching elections from a district to an at-large basis.

II

The two resolutions adopted by the Etowah County Commission on August 25, 1987, less than nine months after the county's first black commissioner took office, were an obvious response to the redistricting of the county that produced a majority black district from which a black commissioner was elected. In my view, it was wrong for the District Court to divorce the two parts of this consolidated response and to analyze the two resolutions separately. * * * Both resolutions diminished the decisionmaking authority of the newly elected black commissioner, and both were passed on the same day and in response to the districting changes effected by the consent decree.

At the very least, I would hold that the reallocation of decisionmaking authority of an elective office that is taken (1) after the victory of a black candidate, and (2) after the entry of a consent decree designed to give black voters an opportunity to have representation on an elective body, is covered by § 5. * * *

Although the test I propose here may not adequately implement § 5, it would certainly provide a workable rule that would result in the correct disposition of this case without opening the Pandora's box that the Court seems to fear.

III

The record indicates that the resolution challenged in the Russell County case may well have had a nondiscriminatory, anticorruption purpose. It would not be covered by the narrow standard that I have proposed as a "workable rule" for deciding the Etowah County case. I would, however, adopt a broader standard that would require preclearance in this case as well. The proper test, I believe, is suggested by the examples of resistance to the increase in black registration that were noted in our opinion in *Perkins v. Matthews, supra.*

Changes from district voting to at-large voting, the gerrymandering of district boundary lines, and the replacement of an elected official with an appointed official all share the characteristic of enhancing the power of the majority over a segment of the political community that might otherwise be adequately represented. A resolution that reallocates decisionmaking power by transferring authority from an elected district representative to an official, or a group, controlled by the majority, has the same potential for discrimination against the constituents in the disadvantaged districts. The Russell County Resolution satisfies that test, and therefore, like both Etowah County Resolutions, should have been precleared. To hold otherwise, as the Court does today, leaves covered States free to evade the requirements of § 5, and to undermine the purpose of the Act, simply by transferring the authority of an elected official, who happens to be black, to another official or group controlled by the majority.

The Court today rejects the Attorney General's position that transfers of authority are covered under § 5 when "they implicate the decisionmaking authority of elected officials." It does so because it fears that such a rule creates line-drawing problems and moves too far afield from "voting." Whether or not the rationale advocated by the Attorney General in this case is appropriate, his judgment concerning the proper disposition of these two cases is unquestionably correct.

I would therefore reverse in both cases.

Notes and Questions

1. Why should the majority and dissent conceptualize this case so differently? Isn't line-drawing a problem in most cases that are resolved by litigation? Who is more persuasive, the majority or the dissent?

2. Is denial of access to voting taking new forms? If so, are these new forms consistent with our history? Reconsider Reva Siegel, *Why Equal Protection No Longer Protects: The Evolving Forms of Status–Enforcing State Action*, [See Chapter 7 § 1].

Hunter v. Underwood, 471 U.S. 222 (1985), challenged an Alabama statute disqualifying voters for crimes of moral turpitude. The appellate court had found that ten times more Blacks than Whites had been disenfranchised. Although disparate impact would not be enough to show the intentional discrimination needed to sustain an equal protection challenge, Justice Rehnquist, writing for the majority, found racial motivation in the legislative speeches surrounding its enactment. "And what is it that we want to do? Why it is within the limits imposed by the federal constitution, to establish white supremacy in this state." 471 U.S. at 229. See also Alice E. Harvey, Comment, *Ex-Felon Disenfranchisement and Its Influence on the Black Vote: The Need for a Second Look*, 142 U. Pa. L. Rev. 1145 (1994) (noting that fifteen states permanently disenfranchise ex-felons) and Andrew L. Shapiro, Note, *Challenging Criminal Disenfranchisement Under the Voting Rights Act: A New Strategy*, 103 Yale L.J. 537, 538 (1993) (describing criminal disenfranchisement as "the most subtle method of excluding Blacks from the franchise").

During Senate Judiciary Committee Hearings to confirm his nomination as Chief Justice of the United States Supreme Court, Justice Rehnquist denied allegations that he had questioned or challenged voters about their qualifications in the early 1960s in Arizona. Stuart Taylor, Jr. *Rehnquist Says He Didn't Deter Voters in 60s*, N. Y. Times, July 31, 1986 at A1, col. 4. Melvin Mirkin, a Phoenix lawyer and Democratic poll-watcher, had said that he saw William Rehnquist at a polling place "loudly announcing that people who were not registered or were not literate would not be permitted to vote." *Id*. Mr. Mirkin said, "Some black and Mexican–American voters left the line, perhaps out of shame that they could read only haltingly, which would not disqualify them to vote but would cause them embarrassment." *Id*.

3. What practices can transform our notion of voting, ensuring access and preventing voter dilution, while sustaining democratic practice and meaningful participation? Consider the ideas described in this next article.

LANI GUINIER

More Democracy
1995 U. Chi. Legal F. 1.*

I want to suggest the extraordinary notion that democracy means that ordinary people should participate in making the decisions that affect their lives. I want to talk about how we can make democracy more participatory and less alienating. I want to describe a vision of democracy as engaged public communication, democracy that is less about winning a "game" and more about listening, responding, and working through the creative tension of difference. This is democracy in which we strive for a synthesis of component voices rather than the monolithic command of a single or homogeneous majority. This is democracy as participatory public conversation.

My husband and I were sitting around the kitchen table as I was preparing to give this talk. I was trying to explain the basic idea that people should be participating in the decisions that affect their lives. So I said, "What could I call this in order that people would understand what I am talking about?" My husband said, "Well, what you're really talking about, Lani, is participatory democracy." And I said, "Oh no, participatory democracy, that's too abstract a concept. I need something catchy." So my seven-year-old son, who was eavesdropping as he loaded magnets on the refrigerator door, exclaimed, "Oh, I know what you should call it." Curious, I asked, "What's that?" He announced, "Baseball!"

I paused. "Baseball?" I skeptically repeated his statement. Without missing a beat, my son responded, "Yeah, you know, you said 'catchy,' and when you're playing baseball, you go out into the field and you catch the ball." As any good law professor would, I questioned my son further. I asked, "Nikolas, do you know what we're talking about?" He answered proudly, "Yeah, democracy." I continued the Socratic interrogation. I asked, "Well, what is democracy?" He said, "It's this really weird thing where people raise their hands and vote. Now can you imagine doing that all day, just raising your hands and voting? Who would want to do that? That's really weird." I queried him further, "Well, why would people vote?" Nikolas replied, "Well, I guess you vote because otherwise the person who's President would be President for their whole life and that would be really boring."

I was intrigued. I starting thinking about a seven year old's version of democracy. I thought, "Is there some way to use Nikolas's notion that on the one hand, democracy is really weird if it is only about voting, and yet on the other hand, if you don't vote, you give up the chance to hold elected officials accountable? Voting is an essential aspect of democracy but it is 'weird' if it becomes the only condition of a genuine democracy."
* * *

PBS just produced a critically acclaimed television series about baseball. An African–American philosopher was interviewed. He predicted that in a thousand years the United States of America will probably be known for three things: its form of constitutional democracy, jazz, and baseball. So, you see, others unrelated to me have perceived some connection between baseball and democracy. Baseball, democracy, and jazz are authentic American pursuits that are part of the ongoing experiment we call the United States. I want to explore with you today another way of viewing the evolution and dynamic interaction of all three indigenous experiments: constitutional democracy, baseball, and jazz.

In one sense, my son was exactly right. Democracy and baseball have a lot in common. Baseball is a highly structured and open-ended game of strategy, skill, and luck. It is often reduced to a confrontation between a pitcher and a batter, but it takes an entire team to execute. Many people say that baseball is fun to play but boring to watch. The same can be said of democracy.

Both baseball and, unfortunately, democracy as we now practice it have become spectator sports. They are games in which the emphasis is on watching others play to win. Voters do not participate; they spectate. Elections in which voters are spectators are elections characterized by high levels of alienation and low levels of turnout. When voters merely spectate, they do not listen, learn, or engage. * * *

Jazz is different. You don't "win" at jazz; you collaborate in order to communicate. Jazz is highly structured—like baseball and American politics. Its goal, however, is not winning or losing but producing something of beauty that is shared as much among the musicians as it is between the musicians and the audience. Its beauty lies in the improvisation that exalts communication over mere performance. The best jazz artists are usually remembered for the way they function in a collaborative setting. The excitement might be generated by a soloist, but the soloist is almost always playing against, and with the support of, the rhythm section and the melodic themes of the piece. Dissonance, double time, improvisation, and extending the melody through different rhythmic ranges produce a new way of hearing and speaking that borrows from European as well as African roots.

I want to discuss whether democracy as we practice it in the United States could become less like a spectator sport and more like a jazz conversation. I want to talk about how we can make political participation less like a game of winners and losers and more like a medley of diverse voices working together to interpret a theme and to drive it forward. I want to explore whether democracy, like jazz music, can be an evolving experiment in public conversation.

I want to discuss the idea of reconceptualizing democracy as participatory, public conversation in the context of race. The question I ask is: How can we have a democracy in a multiracial society in which everyone feels that they have an opportunity to participate, in which everyone feels that they have access to the forum where the debate is taking place, and in which everyone feels not only that we are playing on a level playing field, but that they have a shot at getting a chance at bat?

Now, I'm talking about race in part because race is such an important political cue in our democracy. Race, in other words, still matters. Race, unfortunately, or fortunately, depending on your perspective, still defines the political interests of many Americans, and it should not surprise us that this is true given the fact that we live in such a racially defined world. * * *

Times Mirror did a study recently, a very extensive study, of American attitudes. One of the most interesting results was that 65 percent of white Americans now agree that it would be okay for a member of their family to date an African American. * * * That is a huge increase from just four years ago; in fact, it is a twenty point increase from just four years ago. And yet, of the same group of white respondents, 51 percent say that we have gone too far in pushing for equal rights in this country. So, on the one hand, people are willing to make exceptions for individuals who may be of a different race, but in terms of groups, in terms of equal rights for African Americans as a group, we're still thinking very much along different and racialized lines.

Now, in the legal academy, on the Supreme Court, and in public discourse, many people who are committed to contemporary equality jurisprudence and who believe that equal rights should matter nevertheless say that race should not matter. Many of those people committed to contemporary equality jurisprudence say that race should not matter and that government must be color-blind as a normative principal. They argue that if we recognize race, we inevitably advantage some and disadvantage others, and that to recognize race in the public sphere simply reinforces existing hostilities or provides a moment at which people who are feeling stigmatized will just feel more so.

Those who say that we have to pursue a color-blind jurisprudence also suggest that we must be color-blind not only as a normative matter, but as an empirical matter. They point out that not all members of a racial group think alike. People who are members of a particular racial group do not all think alike. People do not all think alike whether it is the white majority, the Latino minority, the Asian minority, or the African–American minority. These commentators point out that, indeed, there are a range of viewpoints within each group and that to recognize race ignores the shades and the nuances of differences within those groups. In addition, those who claim that the government should be color-blind suggest that race is socially constructed, that race is not a real category, and that we don't know what race is anymore when we have so many people who don't identify solely as a member of one race or another. They argue that what should matter—these critics of race-conscious policies—is the individual, not the group.

I am here to provide an alternative viewpoint. I believe that talking about race is important to encourage biracial cooperation. I believe that recognizing racial difference is an essential precondition to multiracial collaboration. I believe that in talking about race we must acknowledge the complexity of race, but that we cannot talk about democracy in a multiracial society without also talking about race.

I am not saying that race should matter always and I am not saying that race should matter always in the same way. But I am saying that race does matter. And I am saying that in the political sphere, if we are talking about participatory democracy, if we are talking about a democracy in which everyone feels that they have an opportunity to participate in making decisions about things that affect their lives, then we have to be aware of race. We have to be conscious of racial differences because those differences matter to many of the people that we want to participate in the political process. Racial pride, racial identity, and racial solidarity can, of course, be marginalizing "cul-de-sacs." But recognition of race can also be empowering, affirming, and energizing. Racial awareness among racial minority group members can mobilize political participation. And that political participation can become the basis for participation across, not just within, racial groups. Indeed, when racial minority-group members are confident that they are being respected, when they do not feel the need to "racialize" an issue just to be recognized, then they can participate vigorously and confidently in cross-racial majorities. Indeed, I have argued elsewhere that it is often the refusal to recognize race that highlights and cements its salience.

Now, when I argue that race matters, I am not saying that race is monolithic. I am not saying that we should redefine race as a fixed social category. I am not saying that we should reinforce arbitrary distinctions along racial lines. I am not saying that people who disagree or dissent from the prevailing or majority viewpoint of a particular racial group should be excommunicated and booted out of the racial category.

Race does matter. But that does not mean that we have to make race the only thing that matters or that we or any group of elites have to decide for other people how they should racially identify themselves. Nor does it mean that talking about race is a means of empowering only racial minorities. Talking about race and democracy does not mean gaining the opportunity for racial minorities to do to the racial majority what has been done to them. So what am I talking about then?

I am basically talking about a theory or a framework for democracy that respects racial groups, that respects racial-group identity as a matter of democratic community. I am talking about a theory or a framework for democracy which does not see democratic participation purely and exclusively as a matter of individuals, but respects and acknowledges the role that groups and group participation play in organizing the way people think about their public roles. I am talking about a theory of democracy that helps mobilize people to participate in public activity by giving them a genuine voice in the ongoing conversation. I am talking about a theory of democracy that recognizes that such a voice often requires the ability to act in concert, the ability to organize to participate with a group of like-minded individuals, the desire to participate in a genuinely collaborative political project, and a politics in which more people participate than stay home. I am talking about a philosophy of participatory democracy in which the individual gains stature and voice in community with other like-minded individuals. Finally, I am describing a vision of cross-racial collaboration in which individuals, empowered by the opportunity to participate as members of a group in the democratic conversation, engage and communicate across racial lines to solve real problems.

What I am saying is that democratic representation cannot be understood purely and exclusively in terms of one person, one vote. One person, one vote suggests that democracy is only about voting and that voting is merely an exercise in individual empowerment and individual scoring or winning. But individuals, meaning individual voters, don't "win." Individuals don't elect people, groups of individuals do. Representative democracy presumably rewards a group for mobilizing politically cohesive voters to participate and elect representatives who advocate their interests. The first question, then, is how do you aggregate individuals into groups to determine what groups of individuals are going to elect which representatives?

The way that we commonly aggregate individuals in this society, in terms of determining what groups of individuals can elect what representatives, is through something called geographic districting. We allocate representation by drawing physical communities of political representation and we call those physical or geographical communities "districts." And then we give each district one representative. It is a way of presumably assuring that local communities have a voice in our democratic conversation. Districts are geographic groups. Districting reflects the presumption that geography is a suitable proxy, on some level, for community. By community, we mean "community of interests," *i.e.*, territorially defined communities of political interests. We aggregate individuals into a group called a district and we then allow that group to choose a representative to represent them.

Political parties are also a form of group representation. Political parties are ideological groups more or less. Political parties are groups of people who organize along some kind of communal, cooperative, or congenial sense of what their interests are. In our democracy, we acknowledge group representation for at least these two kinds of collective aggregations: geographic collections of people in districts and partisan or ideological collections of people in political parties.

Two of the dominant concepts, at least twentieth-century dominant concepts, of democracy are communitarianism and pluralism. Both assume that groups play an important role. Therefore, in my view, these concepts are consistent with the idea that in a democracy individual rights can best be protected and acknowledged when groups of people are provided the opportunity to participate in our democratic conversation.

In communitarianism, the basic assumption is that community is fundamental to democracy. The idea of democracy depends upon a collection of individuals with a collective consciousness or a common cultural or social experience. That collection of people is the essence of democracy; that community is the primary site for citizen participation and involvement. Communitarians would argue that a sense of community and a shared set of values help to legitimate political authority, that democracy is most fruitful where intermediate groups or local communities help to generate a common fund of knowledge and information to facilitate productive and rational debate and promote interaction among citizens. In a sense, for communitarians, political groups become an alternative to neighborhood-based geographic communities, and especially in an era when modern technology permits rapid exchange of information without the constraints of space or physical proximity, voluntary interest groups function as a modern version of community.

As Americans become less tied to, and less identified with, a particular geographic locality, political groups or these voluntary interest groups become surrogate communities. Interest groups or associations of like-minded people are communities of interest or belief rather than communities of geography. Twenty percent of Americans move every year. In an age with that kind of mobility, many communitarians seek to enhance voluntary political groups or associations as a way to strengthen American democracy. Indeed, they argue that it is the absence of healthy political groups and parties that is at the root of much current apathy and skepticism about our democracy. So, communitarians say that communities or groups are the essence of political participation and involvement.

Pluralism, another important twentieth-century concept about democracy, also assumes that groups are an important unit in democratic functioning. In a pluralistic conception, democracy is based on free competition between groups. Individuals join groups based on their perceptions about their group interests. The democratic process becomes a clash among group interests, bargains, compromises, trade-offs, coalitions, and negotiations. Groups are natural competitors because one group's advancement occurs only at the expense of another. There is not an independent common good except the compromise between competing groups. Political life then, as pluralism sees it, is a game with group winners and group losers. And group competition may replicate, on a larger scale, the self-interested individual; or, as pluralism might assert, group solidarity can help individuals transcend their private or passive conceptions of self-interest. But, in any event, groups are an important part of the political process. They provide individuals with an opportunity to organize effectively with other individuals, and they give such groups an incentive to try and win over the majority through bargains and coalitions that promote familiarity with the viewpoints of others and a willingness to work with others, including those with whom one disagrees. So, we have these two conceptions of democracy, both of which enjoy, or at least embrace, the idea of group participation as important to democratic function.

Now, some people don't buy into that. They think that democracy is exclusively about giving individuals access to the ballot. These commentators have the conception that democracy is really about individual political competition, about individuals voting an individual political choice. When you think about democracy as purely an individualist form of participation, then the ideal form of democracy becomes the referendum, the initiative, or the public opinion survey poll. Right? Because direct democracy—democracy by referendum or initiative—is purely individualistic in the sense that one's voice can be heard based exclusively on how one votes without necessarily taking into account collective action or organization.

Direct democracy, in the form of referenda or initiatives, aggregates individual preferences. It does not lump voters into voting units or assign them representatives. Each voter speaks for himself or herself directly and exclusively by the way he or she casts a ballot. Direct democracy or democracy by public opinion poll is most closely aligned, therefore, with an individualistic view of political participation. All that voters enjoy is the right to have their opinion noted or tabulated.

I would argue that direct democracy by referenda or initiatives collapses democracy into its most crude, some would say its most primitive, form. Democracy becomes, in terms of the public opinion polls, simply an arithmetic exercise in which we count votes and award public-policy preferences to those with the most votes. And the public interest simply becomes the most popular individual interest. But this is a very passive version of democracy. It is a passive version of interest group pluralism with less incentive for interaction or for participation. You can just sit home and dial your vote.

Indeed, individualistic aggregation of opinion in my view undermines the interactive premise of representative democracy because representative democracy, which is what we in the United States presumably practice, believes that the representative can stand in for individuals because the representative has some kind of interactive relationship with those same individuals. The representative can act because the representative knows in fact what the individuals who have voted for him or her want. The individual voters also know what the representative is doing, supposedly on their behalf, and the individuals who are voting have the capacity to vote the representative in or out of office based on what that representative is doing. Representative democracy demands a concern for, and a familiarity with, the views of people other than oneself. In this sense, representative democracy demands a conversation between groups of individuals—called constituents—and their elected representative. It also suggests the need for a conversation between and among the constituents themselves so that the elected official can hear their message. It may not be a single message. They may not all agree, but the conversation is interactive; it requires speaking and listening. It is communication as engagement rather than performance. One participates in many more ways than merely raising one's hand and voting up or down on binary issues.

By contrast, individualized democracy or democracy by public opinion poll allows little room for interactive democratic conversation. So the metaphor that I am using for democracy—democracy as conversation, democracy as public collaboration, democracy as jazz music—really requires more than one person to be involved. And indeed, Hannah Arendt describes democracy as public conversation in a way that on some level tracks my son's version of why voting as the embodiment of democracy is so weird. She said, and I am paraphrasing, "Voting cannot be the essence of democracy. Because if voting is the essence of democracy, it is a very private, not a public, act. Because if you look at the voting booth as the ultimate metaphor for democracy, there is only room enough in that booth for one person. That can't be democracy."

If, as Hannah Arendt suggests, democracy is about people talking to each other and participating collectively in trying to decide public policy, then I would argue that group representation and group participation is essential to a functioning democracy. Group participation, assuming the group is a voluntary association of individuals, is a way of mobilizing individuals. It is a way of dispersing authority and it is a way of creating broad-based access to that conversation.

I would argue that if democracy is a public conversation in which we want broad-based public participation, then we should also ensure representation for racial groups if those groups feel politically congenial and if those groups act in a way that is similar to other voluntary political associations. Group participation or group representation is particularly important for disadvantaged racial groups who have been denied historical access to that democratic conversation. And indeed, in my view, that is what the Voting Rights Act has tried to remedy. The goal of the Voting Rights Act is to undo the exclusion of certain disadvantaged groups who have been denied access, who have been denied the opportunity to participate as equals in our democratic conversation. So the Voting Rights Act justifies intervention, it justifies court or legal intervention to correct certain political arrangements where the majority is hoarding power and not allowing minority groups to participate in the democratic conversation. It allows or promotes intervention where the majority is not acting as a representative of the whole but is acting as a representative of its own natural self-interest.

Now, what am I talking about when I say that the majority is not representing the whole? Well, when we think of democracy, some of us think that democracy is simply winner-take-all, majority rule. Some of us think that democracy simply means that 51 percent of the people get 100 percent of the power. That is democracy, right? You vote. Whoever gets the most votes gets all the power. Well, that is one version of democracy and it is a version of democracy that we assume is fair because we assume that those with the most votes are going to disperse their power not only to benefit themselves but to benefit everybody. We assume that the majority is really a majority or a collection of shifting coalitions. We assume that the majority is a shifting or fleeting collection of individuals, not a monolithic group that is hoarding power permanently.

I like to tell a story that again involves my son Nikolas. This time he was four years old and we were looking at a Sesame Street magazine. I was very excited because the headline on the magazine article stated, "Vote!" So I thought, "Ah, I get to teach a four year old about voting." The magazine pictured six kids and they were trying to decide what game to play. Four of the kids had their hands raised because they wanted to play tag, and two had their hands down because they wanted to play hide and seek. The magazine said to the reader, "What game will the children play? Count the number of hands raised, count the number of hands lowered, and answer the question." My son—the son of a law professor—bucked the hypo! Nikolas said, "First they will play tag, because four kids want to play tag, and then they will play hide and seek because there are two who want to play hide and seek."

Nikolas implicitly challenged the basic premise that those with the most votes should always decide each and every game. Nikolas did not assume that the preference of the majority, the four who wanted to play a particular game, should control every decision. Nikolas declined to award 66 percent of the kids 100 percent of the power. The magazine, by contrast, assumed that the majority should decide for everybody what game to play. The magazine assumed that two-thirds of the children could and should act on behalf of all of the children.

This assumption, that the four who wanted to play tag would be acting democratically by deciding for everybody what game to play, is based on two conditions. First, we assume that the majority is operating on the golden rule. We assume that the tag majority is going to treat the hide and seek players with some respect, that at some point they are going to say, "Okay, we will now play hide and seek because that is what you guys what to play." Second, we assume that the tag majority is not monolithic; we assume the tag majority is not homogeneous; we assume the tag majority is not permanent. We assume that the tag majority is a majority today, but that it has to worry about being a different minority tomorrow. The tag majority, we believe, worries about defectors. Some of those who want to play tag may join forces with the hide and seek players on a different issue to forge a new majority. We believe, therefore, that today's majority is going to treat today's minority fairly because today's majority does not want to be treated any differently when it becomes tomorrow's minority.

What if these two conditions are absent? What if the majority is disrespectful and monolithic? What if the majority of today is also the majority of yesterday and of the year before that and of the year before that and has every likelihood of being the majority of tomorrow? What if the majority of today is not treating the minority of today with respect; what if the majority is not worrying about what the minority thinks because the majority is assured permanent power. In this case, the majority does not have to worry about the minority because the majority is not a group of shifting individuals but is a single monolithic group. I have litigated cases in which that in fact was the problem.

I have litigated many such cases, including * * * a case in which the majority in Phillips County, Arkansas was a monolithic group hoarding power. Even though blacks were about 44 percent of the electorate in that community, they had never been able to elect a representative of their choice to any of the seven countywide governing positions in this century. Blacks were unsuccessful in county elections because voting in the county was racially polarized. Racially polarized voting meant that whites would vote for whites and blacks would vote for blacks. Voting in Phillips County was not only racially polarized, it was extremely polarized. Our expert witness testified that there were some precincts in which no whites voted for any black running for office. * * *

There was also testimony that in this particular community, whites would not publicly support black candidates for office even when they thought those black candidates were the most qualified. One of our witnesses testified that he ran several times without success for public office in Phillips County. Our witness was a black attorney. He described the time he ran in a three-person race. In the primary, the black attorney came in first but with less than 51 percent of the vote. Because there was a majority-vote requirement in Phillips County, whoever won had to get 51 percent of the vote. So, there had to be a run-off because none of the candidates got "a majority" of the vote. Prior to the second election, the majority-vote, run-off election, the losing candidate—the person who came in third in the first primary—came up to the black candidate and said, "You know, Mr. Whitfield, I believe you are the most qualified candidate, but I cannot say that publicly because I am a farmer and my wife is a school teacher and if we are going to continue to live in this community, and we are white—I cannot support you."

So, Phillips County, Arkansas represented a majority that is a self-centered, monolithic group. Because of racially polarized voting, winner-take-all majority rule is not working as we assume it should. It is in those instances that I believe the Voting Rights Act suggests that a court should intervene to protect the interests of a minority that is being ignored or excluded by the permanent majority. But, the question becomes, even if a court should intervene because the minority has been excluded and has been excluded because of racial prejudice, what is the remedy? How do you remedy that exclusion? And that is where the issue is joined right now in terms of the debate about group participation in voting and elections and the Voting Rights Act of 1965 as it has been amended in 1982.

It is at that stage—how do you remedy the violation?—that I proposed those remedies that got me into so much trouble. [O]ne of the remedies that I proposed is used in corporations to elect their boards of directors; it is called cumulative voting. It was also used in Illinois; it was called bullet voting. It was used in Illinois to elect members of the state legislature for many years in the middle of this century.

Where the majority is not functioning to protect and include the minority, I have proposed a system of nondistricted elections—basically, a system in which the voters district themselves by the way they cast their ballots. It is a system in which if you have, for example, a seven-person governing body, every voter gets seven votes. The conventional approach would be to divide that governing body into seven single-member electoral districts. The conventional approach would protect the excluded minority by giving that minority a district in which it is the majority. The conventional approach would protect the minority by carving out from control by the governing majority a special district in which the minority becomes the majority and can then elect its own, minority, representative. I have suggested [cumulative voting as] an alternative that does not involve districts. I have suggested giving each voter the same number of votes, in this case seven votes, and letting them district themselves by the way they cast their ballots. If they want to put all seven of their votes on one candidate because that person reflects their most preferred, most deeply held preferences, they can. If they want to put six on one candidate and one on another, they can. If they want to put seven on seven different candidates, they can. It is up to the voter to district him or herself by the way he or she casts or distributes the seven ballots.

Now what does this have to do with the idea of participatory democracy? Well, basically, I believe that if you give voters the choice to district themselves, if you give voters the means of deciding what is important to them, and if you give voters multiple votes to cast, it is a way of including more people in our democratic conversation. It is a way of telling voters, "Your votes do count." It is a way of ensuring a principle that I call "one vote, one value": Everyone's vote should count towards the election of someone who has a good chance of getting elected. Not just black voters' votes should count, not just Latino voters' votes should count—all voters' votes should count.

One vote, one value is based on three fundamental democratic principles: (1) all voters should be able to help elect someone; (2) members of self-identified groups should be able to participate in the democratic conversation as a group; and (3) self-identified groups should enjoy the opportunity to exercise a fair share of political power. Everyone should get a chance to vote for representatives of their choice, everyone who identifies with a common and significant set of interests (significant as measured by a locally defined threshold) should get to have those interests articulated and represented in the conversation we call democracy, and everyone should be represented commensurate to their ability to mobilize and organize political support. This principle applies not just to racial minorities, but to any politically cohesive minority; so women, gays, religious minorities, Republicans in Democratic cities, and Democrats in Republican suburbs all can use this approach to gain political representation. In this way, empowering racial minorities opens up democratic participation for many underrepresented groups.

One of the reasons that all voters' votes should count is because democracy is not just about the symbolic ritual of casting a ballot. It is not just about going into that secret space—that anonymous voting booth—and exercising private preferences. Political participation is about joining with other people with whom you have shared interests and trying to see those interests represented in public discourse, in that public space, in that public conversation that we call democracy.

Democracy is not just about voting; it is not just about winning. Democracy is about participating. Participation matters. It matters because the decisions that governments make affect everyone. Respect for those decisions, including those with which we disagree, demands meaningful participation in the decision making process. People have to be able to express their preferences, but more importantly, people have to participate in the formation and the implementation of preferences. In this project, voting is a necessary but hardly sufficient condition to achieve more democracy. * * *

[D]emocratic participation depends upon opportunities to communicate and opportunities to hear opposing points of view. * * * Cumulative voting may help us see that we may not want to lock people into a particular set of preferences—which we call districts—which must last for ten years between census enumerations. We may need a decision-making process that is more dynamic; we may need to consider a process that allows people to ascertain their preferences—and to organize in conjunction with like-minded other people—based on a full discussion of the issues that emerge at each election.

Many people, not all people, but many people think of their interests along racial lines. If that is true, and that is important to them, and they choose to vote along racial lines, then it is democratic, in my view, to allow them to participate as a racial group. But we must allow people to self-identify so that if they do not want to vote along racial lines, they don't have to. Nobody is forcing them. Cumulative voting or nondistricted elections provide exit opportunities for people who do not want to vote along with the majority of their particular racial-minority group. Cumulative voting provides racial "dissenters" the opportunity to form coalitions, biracial coalitions. But it also provides racial minority groups with a chance to reach out to other groups. Because it minimizes "wasted" votes, meaning votes cast for political losers, cumulative voting enables groups to reach out beyond their racial "cul-de-sac" and negotiate and bargain excess votes on particular issues or at particular elections.

Cumulative voting does not eliminate the need for compromise. It changes, however, the timing and the atmosphere of the compromise. Compromises are made in the open; compromises are made after open exchanges of views. Compromises are not hidden in order to confuse voters; compromises are not suppressed in order to pretend one is all things to all people.

Now some people might argue that the problem with cumulative voting, the problem with race-conscious districting, and the problem with any remedy for the exclusion of minorities from the democratic conversation is that it will balkanize the electorate. It will further divide us; it will fragment us. It will reinforce race as a meaningful interest when we should be erasing race.

My response to that is, they may be right. But maybe and are are not the same. They may be right, but in my view we are already balkanized. We are not watching the same television shows. We are not living next door to each other. We are not going to the same elementary and high schools together. So we are already balkanized. And the question is, how do you deal with that? Do you deny that the balkanization is there and pretend that everything is fine and that we are all color-blind; do you sacrifice the demonstrated virtues of a robust pluralism for fear of the potential excesses of unbounded factionalism; or do you acknowledge that there are differences, respect those differences, and then, having acknowledged, recognized, and respected those differences, invite everyone into that democratic conversation?

My view is that it is premature to deny those differences when they are so important to so many people. That is not to say that you want ultimately to reinforce those differences as our goal or as our vision. But it does mean that if you are going to get people to the point where they can converse together and communicate across these differences, the first thing that you have to do is respect and recognize those differences. And having respected and recognized those differences, in my experience, you will find that people are much more willing to engage in conversation about the common good and about our common interests because their differences don't become so key to their self-definition. You have already recognized and respected those differences, so every conversation doesn't have to be about those differences which you've already recognized and respected. It's a way of transcending race ultimately. But in order get there, you must first recognize race.

Thinking about democracy in terms of group participation is also important to revive our confidence in democracy as a public, not a private, activity. Group activity in a public space is a way of reclaiming democracy for all of its citizens. Group participation is necessary to overcome the profound alienation that many people observe among members of our electorate. Just as the term-limits movement reflects a desire to mobilize voters "to take back their government," alternative election systems can respond to the profound alienation that is corroding our public discourse. * * *

My focus on participatory democracy is, thus, part of an effort to take back the democratic space from which American citizens have been evacuated by the increasingly angry, bitter, and polarizing terms of talk radio, negative television ads during election campaigns, winner-take-all electoral politics, and gridlock governance. It is another way of looking at democracy—as a well-conducted conversation. But no conversation is interesting if we don't think we will get a chance to speak and be heard.

If we are going to be serious about public, participatory democracy, then we need to rethink the nature of democracy's conversation. We need not proceed in an entirely adversarial model in which we vote to determine the winners and losers. We need not showcase only the most extreme viewpoints on a subject in a flawed effort to get balance. Individuals, empowered by their association with other like-minded individuals, can be subjects rather than objects of democracy's conversation. Individuals, acting in concert, can transform our democratic project.

Ultimately, what participatory democracy means is that governance must be first and foremost about a well-conducted conversation—a conversation in which we all get a chance to speak, to listen, to be heard, and to collaborate to solve our problems. To local citizens, participatory democracy is not just insider talk about or among winners. To make America a genuine democracy, we must all be encouraged to partake actively in its conversation. The challenge is to imagine a democratic system that permits a range of views to be represented—not just in the streets or on talk radio, but in the sturdy halls of the legislatures and other public spaces constructed to house vigorous debate and true deliberation—in order to restore trust, overcome antagonism, regain government's legitimacy, and achieve our collective wisdom.

I am basically suggesting that the goals of the Voting Rights Act, as a matter of political philosophy, can and should be defended by framing them within a theory of group representation in which the claims of racial minorities are not resolved to benefit racial minorities alone. Empowering previously excluded racial minorities is important; empowering those minorities in a way that enhances democracy for all voters is transformative. This approach enables the Voting Rights Act to achieve its original objectives. It accomplishes Congress's goal to enfranchise victims of racial discrimination. But it also accomplishes an important secondary goal of answering the Act's critics. By potentially empowering politically cohesive and politically mobilized groups, a theory of democratic group representation suggests the possibility of transforming the political process to benefit all voters.

Like jazz music, this is an approach that originated within or on behalf of a racial-minority group. It is designed to empower that racial minority. But, like jazz music, it is also a distinctly and thoroughly American phenomena. Familiar melodies are reconstituted and disassembled, but not erased. It is not a mere collection of soloists, but of musicians who are deeply committed to integrating the contributions of other players. Individual musicians work together to produce a whole bigger than any of them could produce on their own. That is also the nature of successful governance. Participants learn to see nuance, to see complexity, and to respect differences, even with those with whom they disagree. We all may learn that where you sit determines what you see, but if we listen carefully, we may come to understand that those with whom we disagree may have a point, not just a point of view. Things that sound funny to ears trained to hear only one kind of music in fact can add to the way in which we all appreciate the beauty of our peculiar American form of constitutional democracy.

In other words, like jazz, democracy holds the promise of producing a system that respects individuals and groups, that doesn't lock people into a hierarchy of perpetual winners and losers, and that makes room for the tiniest voice to contribute to the composition. With a collaborative approach to the challenges of a multiracial democracy, we can implement the Voting Rights Act as it was intended—to achieve more democracy, not less.

Notes and Questions

1. Guinier's essay begins with this epigram by John Dewey: "The cure for the ailments of democracy is more democracy." Do her proposals provide

"more democracy?" See also Lani Guinier, *The Tyranny of the Majority: Fundamental Fairness in Representative Democracy* (1994).

2. What does Guinier mean when she says that "democratic representation cannot be understood purely and exclusively in terms of one person one vote?" Do you agree? Is Guinier persuasive in arguing that voting is a group activity? Reconsider the tension between the individual and group identification discussed earlier (Chapter 7).

3. Do you agree with Guinier that as a nation we are "already balkanized?" Why does that term have a negative connotation? Is there a fear that a balkanized country cannot be successfully democratic?

4. What are the component parts of a democracy? What forms of voting will best ensure democratic participation? Is equal voting power fundamental to democracy? Consider this response: "[E]qual voting power is an important part of what it means to be treated as a civic equal * * * [b]ecause equal voting power publicly expresses the idea of our civic equality." Amy Gutmann, *Responding to Racial Injustice*, in K. Anthony Appiah & Amy Gutmann, *Color Conscious: The Political Morality of Race* 156 (1996).

Does the redistricting plan in *Miller*, § 3 *supra*, deny to any citizens equal standing in democracy or would it promote that equal standing?

5. What exactly is cumulative voting? Will it work? Does it present any special risks?

6. In 1970 the number of African–American elected officials was 1,469. By 1993 that figure had grown to 7,984. Yet, the well-being of this group, measured by infant mortality rate, family income, family wealth, and many other indices is only slightly better. See, *e.g.*, 21 J. Blacks in Higher Ed. 46–49, 60–61 (Autumn 1998).

Why has democracy not improved these dismal statistics? Are voting and democratic participation myths used to legitimate a social regime that relegates minorities, over and over, to the margins of society? See Alan Freeman, *Legitimizing Racial Discrimination Through Antidiscrimination Law*, 62 Minn. L. Rev. 1049 (1978). See also Lani Guinier, *The Triumph of Tokenism: The Voting Rights Act and the Theory of Black Electoral Success*, 89 Mich. L. Rev. 1077 (1991) (pointing out that sometimes minorities who are elected to public office make little difference).

7. In *Department of Commerce v. United States House of Representatives*, 525 U.S. 316 (1999), the Supreme Court rejected the use of statistical sampling to determine official census figures for the year 2000 Census. This census taking, which will be used to apportion seats in the House of Representatives, must rely on the traditional head count method. The Clinton administration had urged statistical sampling as a means to ensure proper counting of disproportionately urban, racial, and ethnic minority group members, who are traditionally undercounted. The court did acknowledge that statistical adjustment could be made for other purposes, including state redistricting and the distribution of federal money to state programs.

Is the premise of democracy undermined when citizens concentrated in low-income, urban areas are undercounted for the purpose of assessing their right to representation? For a discussion anticipating reapportionment issues following the 2000 Census see Pamela S. Karlan, *The Fire Next Time: Reapportionment after the 2000 Census*, 50 Stan. L. Rev. 731 (1998).

Chapter 9

RESIDENTIAL SEGREGATION, EDUCATION, AND RACE

The history of segregation in residential housing patterns has profoundly influenced education in the United States, where education has been tied primarily to neighborhoods. "Parents, researchers, courts, and others interested in school desegregation for the last four decades have noted almost unanimously that school segregation and residential segregation are inextricably entwined." Nancy A. Denton, *The Persistence of Segregation: Links Between Residential Segregation and School Segregation*, 80 Minn. L. Rev. 795, 795 (1996). Recognizing the link between segregation and education, this chapter will first consider residential segregation and then turn to education.

SECTION 1. RESIDENTIAL SEGREGATION

Residential housing discrimination remains a pressing national problem. Margalynne Armstrong explains:

In a national housing discrimination study, the Department of Housing and Urban Development (HUD) concluded that African–American homeseekers who visit four real estate agents can expect to encounter discrimination seventy-two percent of the time when attempting to rent and forty-eight percent of the time when seeking to purchase housing. In one urban area of the United States, there is at best a nine percent chance that an African–American homebuyer who visits seven realtors will not encounter discrimination.

The impact of such widespread housing discrimination goes beyond depriving access to individual units of housing. The discriminator's refusal to consider the personal merit of the housing applicant denigrates the homeseeker's individual identity. Housing discrimination also denies African Americans access to the mainstream of American society and to the rewards of the American work ethic. Americans are supposed to be free to live wherever they can afford to live. By depriving free choice of housing, discrimination prevents individuals from reaping the rewards of their labor. In the words of one victim: "I don't think I should have to go through that in this day and age. We work hard every day. We figure we should be able to live anywhere we want."

Housing discrimination results in residential segregation and ultimately sustains segregated public education.

Margalynne Armstrong, *Desegregation Through Private Litigation: Using Equitable Remedies to Achieve the Purposes of the Fair Housing Act,* 64 Temp. L. Rev. 909, 909 (1991).

MARGALYNNE ARMSTRONG
Race and Property Values in Entrenched Segregation
in *Black Property* (forthcoming NYU Press).*

The United States enacted the Fair Housing Act (FHA), a comprehensive antidiscrimination statute, more than three decades ago. Yet housing discrimination is still extensive and the residential segregation of African Americans continues to be pervasive. Two recent studies of America's ten largest cities present desolate statistics: 69 percent of minority apartment-seekers who look at four different units will be subjected to discrimination at least once. Although fewer and fewer communities contain no African–American inhabitants, Blacks are continually under-represented in many areas where they would otherwise dwell if residence correlated to income and race were not a factor. Even though individual access has clearly increased, the 1990 census reported that nine million African Americans reside in neighborhoods that are at least 90 percent Black and that 68 percent of Whites live in virtually all-white neighborhoods.

Why do African Americans continue to experience disproportionately high levels of residential segregation when housing discrimination is ostensibly illegal? Why does integration often succumb to resegregation under the "tipping" phenomenon, where white residents flee a neighborhood when the percentage of non-white residents reaches a level deemed unacceptable to the Whites (often as small as between 10 and 20 percent)? Granted that *many* factors contribute to what Denton and Massey have evocatively termed "American Apartheid," one important piece of this complicated puzzle is that many white realtors, home-sellers and home-seekers cling to excuses not to integrate. One of the most commonly asserted, longstanding, and deeply entrenched excuses is that African–American land ownership or possession causes property values to decline.

Many people in the United States share a strongly held, but essentially irrational, idea that the black skin color of an occupant has the capacity to cause real property to lose some portion of its value or its ability to appreciate in value. Racial valuation and devaluation of property is undoubtedly tied to powerful beliefs. Although these convictions are inaccurate, the beliefs shape the reality in which we reside. This irrational proposition has created and sustains a shameful situation whereby black-owned real property appreciates at lower rates than comparable property owned by Whites and thus becomes less valuable than it would be if the owner were White. But in fact, any skin-color related decrease in value is attributable to withdrawal of white demand rather to any action on the part of the black land owner.

The concept that blackness has the ability to devalue property is a contemporary manifestation of America's tradition of questioning whether African Americans should even have a legal right to own property. Because laws denying ownership ability to Blacks could no longer be morally or legally justifiable, the devaluation fallacy reframes the issue to focus on an imagined injury to white interests and to place the blame on Blacks. In reality there is often no injury that is sustained by Whites. Blacks usually bear the subsequent decrease in value due to the behavior of Whites who refuse to purchase property in areas where there is any significant black presence.

The perception that Blacks devalue property has the additional pernicious effect of undermining the ability of the Fair Housing Act to achieve one of its legislative objectives, "truly integrated and balanced living patterns." [See *Jorman v. Veterans Administration*, 579 F. Supp. 1407 (1984) for a discussion of the FHA's legislative history and judicial interpretations of the Act's purposes]. The belief has enabled significant sectors of society to effectively resist the mandates of the FHA by obscuring prejudice and rationalizing defiance. Such intransigence presents another instance of the inability of positive law by itself, and without strong enforcement, to counteract a majority determined to undermine black rights.

Real property is a concrete, inanimate thing that has physical existence and tangible characteristics. The characteristics of a given parcel of land are not determined by its ownership; that is, the identity of the property's owner at any given moment does not change the property's physical characteristics. Logically, it follows that the identity of the property's owner should not affect the property's market value. But logic flies out the window when real property belongs to African Americans.

This phenomenon is illustrated in the book *Rage of a Privileged Class*. Author Ellis Cose describes the experience of Joseph Boyce, an African–American journalist who sought an assessment of his home:

> Because Time Inc. (his employer), has a policy of buying a transferred employee's current home at 105 percent of appraised value, it was in his interest to get a high appraisal. The first appraisal on his four-bedroom house came in significantly lower than expected, and Boyce ... wondered whether his race was blinding the realtors to its true value, so he summoned another team of realtors. On the appointed day, he moved out and had his white secretary move in. She replaced the photographs of his beaming family with hers, and when the appraiser arrived she waltzed around the house as if she had lived there all her life. The result was an appraised value nearly 15 percent above the prior assessment.

This narrative illustrates the irrationality of white perceptions about the effect of black ownership on property values. It was completely against the self-interests of the realtors to undervalue the property. Not only would the commission they received be based on a smaller figure, undervaluing property does not make one's services attractive to potential customers. Secondly, the purchaser of the property, Boyce's employers, certainly knew Boyce's race and were committed to purchasing the property. Any subsequent purchaser from Time Inc. would be purchasing from a white-identified corporation, rather than from a black home seller. The race of the house's previous occupant would likely be unknown to future purchasers.

The link between race and property devaluation is longstanding and deeply embedded in the fabric of American real estate transactions. Luigi Laurenti documented the evolution of theories about race and property values that appeared in real estate industry literature from the 1920s though the 1950s. Commenting on articles by "real estate and finance spokesmen, land economists and others," Laurenti noted "most of their conclusions are unaccompanied by supporting evidence, although such evidence may have been observed by the writers." The twenties and thirties saw flat statements such as: "It is a matter of common observation that the purchase of property by certain racial types is very likely to diminish the value of other property in the section" and "Neighborhoods populated by white persons have been invaded by colored families, and often aristocratic residential districts have suffered tremendous lessening of property values because of the appearance of a Negro resident."

Laurenti found that later writings on real estate and race became somewhat more sophisticated, in that they considered the impact of factors such as socio-economic status and the condition of the neighborhood prior to non-white entry. Nonetheless, as the following illustrative statements indicate, blackness was linked to property devaluation:

(F)amilies in any particular class who rise in economic status move to a better district. If they have a degree of inferiority they damage that community, displace the occupying class, and lower values.... Most of the variations and differences between people are slight and value declines therefore are gradual. But there is one difference in people, namely race, which can result in a very rapid decline.

Another commentator wrote:

It [the effect of Negroes on property values] has a most important bearing on future developments in our housing program. Appraisers are interested in the problem from many angles. In addition, they desire the problem to be considered objectively from one specific point; *i.e.*, does Negro occupancy have a tendency to blight only the area where it occurs, or does it blight the surrounding white area, with a corresponding decrease in valuation and loss of tenants ...?

Laurenti notes that by the 1950s there was considerable debate about the effects that black purchasers had on property values. Professional appraiser George W. Beehler presented an analysis of price behavior upon the in-migration of black occupants. Beehler predicted "an initial period of price stagnation followed by continued stagnation or slight price declines, but eventually reaching a period of higher prices." Beehler concluded that neighborhood values would continue to increase. In contrast to Beehler, another appraiser, Oscar I. Stern, believed that although pent-up demand for black occupied housing would cause a temporary price increase when formerly all-white housing became available, ultimately the value in a black neighborhood could be sustained but would not increase. Despite the divergence in the opinions of Beehler and Stern, they did, however, share the premise that regardless of the value of homes in neighborhoods where African Americans have moved in, the incoming purchasers in those neighborhoods would not be White.

Beliefs about race and property values, whether or not based on factual evidence, became reality through a number of mechanisms. The beliefs about race that appeared in the real estate industry's professional literature became industry standard through its professional code. For example, the 1934 Code of Ethics of the National Association of Real Estate Boards (now the National Association of Realtors) Article 34 read: "A Realtor should never be instrumental in introducing into a neighborhood a character of property or occupancy, members of any race or nationality, or any individual whose presence will clearly be detrimental to property values in that neighborhood."

More specific directions about race and property value were provided in a manual for real estate appraisers. An ethnic and racial ranking scale developed by University of Chicago economist Homer Hoyt appeared in the widely used McMichael's *Appraising Manual*. Predictably, "Negroes" and "Mexicans" received the lowest rankings. Racial rankings were not completely abandoned by the industry until 1977, when the Justice Department sued appraisers and lenders to discontinue use of the rankings. As a defense to this lawsuit the appraisers asserted that the First Amendment protected the continued use of the standards.

The federal government supported the real estate industry with programs that ensured that Blacks would bear the burden of Whites' beliefs that non-white race devalued property. The practice of redlining was initiated by the Home Owner's Loan Corporation (HOLC) a federal program designed to grant low interest loans to urban mortgagees in danger of default. The HOLC used rating procedures that "systematically undervalued central city neighborhoods that were racially or ethnically mixed.... black areas were invariably rated as fourth (the lowest) grade and 'redlined.'" From the 1930s until the 1950s several Federal Housing Authority policies tied valuation concerns to racial discrimination. Federal mortgage insurance underwriters were instructed to reject or give poor ratings to loan applications from neighborhoods inhabited by inharmonious racial or ethnic groups. Until 1950, two years after *Shelley v. Kraemer* [334 U.S. 1 (1948)] determined their enforcement unconstitutional, the FHA recommended the use of racially restrictive covenants to protect the value of property purchased with federally funded or insured loans. These loans fueled modern suburbanization, and the "evolution of overwhelmingly white suburbs surrounding increasingly black cities." * * *

Because racial biases remain powerful, realtors are likely to encounter prejudiced customers. A California study released in 1996 revealed that "racial prejudice, particularly against Blacks, remains the greatest cause of housing segregation in Los Angeles county—more powerful than costs or the desire to live among similar people." But because blatant biases garner social disapproval, buyers seek ways to deny their bigotry. Real estate professionals should be working to debunk, rather than affirm, prejudices. Instead, the real estate industry has long supplied a mechanism for concealing bias by disseminating and perpetuating the "popular wisdom" that black ownership degrades property values. Concerns about property values provide a rationalization that is almost impenetrable due to the great legal and social deference accorded economic concerns.

The view that African Americans lower property values has been used not only to mask bias but also to attack the analyses that have determined that entrenched segregation is a structural problem, rather than the cumulative effect of individual wrongdoing. Professor John Calmore has shown that the right-wing critique of the Douglas Massey and Nancy Denton *American Apartheid* analysis locates itself squarely in the bunker of property value. Calmore's article *Racialized Space and the Culture of Segregation* notes Nathan Glazer's accusation that liberal researchers were never quite honest about the effects of an increase in black population on property values and that property value concerns are justified by reference to the increased crime and declines in schools and services in black or transitional areas. Of course Glazer's accusation ignores the withdrawal of financial resources and infrastructure from the urban areas where Blacks remained and the redirection of these assets to the suburbs into which the white population fled. * * *

The conventional wisdom about race and property values conveniently omits the role of white market abandonment and resource withdrawal. White perceptions that black ownership adversely affects property values thus becomes a self-fulfilling prophecy that even today continues to harm African Americans as both purchasers and owners of real property. "Blacks . . . pay a disproportionate amount of their income for housing, are limited in the amount of equity accumulation and live in the poor quality residential environments." * * *

Solutions to entrenched residential segregation will require a multi-pronged attack. The first strategy should be a preventative one. It is necessary to foster integration by preventing the creation of new segregated enclaves. This is an area in which the existing law can be an effective tool. The Fair Housing Act should be vigorously enforced and any discrimination on the part of developers and real estate agents must be eliminated. Fair housing enforcement efforts should call for realtors and developers to reach out to African–American purchasers with advertising and affirmative marketing. Enforcement of prohibitions against the racial steering of Blacks must be vigorous. By integrating new developments with *multiple* families of color the environment will be more welcoming to black home seekers. Black homeowners in stable integrated neighborhoods will have access to a more comprehensive pool of buyers than if their homes were in exclusively black neighborhoods.

A second approach is to eradicate the steering of white property purchasers. Realtors must abandon the idea that black middle class suburbs are inevitably uninteresting to white purchasers. Some of the housing opportunities in these suburbs present excellent values, giving the purchaser "more house for the money." This strategy requires the real estate industry to portray predominantly black areas in a positive light and could begin to revise the industry's negative relationship with black communities. Increasing the market for homes that are currently owned by Blacks will increase the property's appreciation and decrease wealth disparities between otherwise comparable black and white home-owners. Care must be taken to preserve integration, avoiding gentrification, or the reclaiming of black residential neighborhoods by higher income Whites.

Finally, it is important to greatly improve conditions in currently hypersegregated urban neighborhoods. Following John Calmore's model of spatial equality (which has sometimes been mischaracterized as completely separatist), our society should direct attractive resources to improve the poorest of the nation's black segregated communities as a "*prelude* to integration." Modern, environmentally sound, sustainable urban planning should be targeted at our cities' most depressed areas. Planners should determine what facilities and features people want in the cities of the twenty-first century and make affirmative decisions to site those facilities in African-American neighborhoods, supporting them with superior infrastructure. In addition to making long needed improvements in the lives of poor African Americans, this is another strategy aimed at changing the minds of those who now invariably link black neighborhoods to decay and decline. Instead, black neighborhoods can be reconfigured to attract positive interest and serve as models to be replicated, rather than avoided. Environmental and racial coalitions should work together to achieve multiple goals of improving spatial conditions in black neighborhoods and beginning the needed widespread transition to sustainable cities. Because communities of color currently live in some of the most environmentally degraded neighborhoods in this country, environmentalist-minority coalitions already exist. The idea of creating new issues for coalition work can bring the members of these groups closer together and form new bases for community. It is to be hoped that some day such community will take the form of residential integration, achieving the Fair Housing Act's most elusive goal.

Notes and Questions

1.   The belief Armstrong describes that Blacks cause property values to decline appears to cross racial lines and to operate among other nonwhite groups, as well as among some African Americans. See Keith Aoki, *Direct Democracy, Racial Group Agency, Local Government Law, and Residential Racial Segregation: Some Reflections on Radical and Plural Democracy,* 33 Cal. W. L. Rev. 185, 192, 200 (1997) (describing how Asian Americans and Latinos/as may benefit from housing segregation when they are treated as non-Black).

2.   John O. Calmore, *Racialized Space and the Culture of Segregation: "Hewing a Stone of Hope from a Mountain of Despair,"* 143 U. Pa. L. Rev. 1233, 1235 (1995) explains the racialization of space as a "process by which residential location and community are carried and placed on racial identity." Calmore notes that while the racialization of space once was a black/white issue, it is now more complex "as Latinos and Asians enter the mix."

Id. at 1236. While he observes that "any strategy to transform local neighborhoods must be multiracial and multiethnic," *id.* at 1256, Calmore recognizes:

> It is hard to develop common agendas among grassroots groups because there is a reliance on a competing claims model of politics. Latino emphasize their large numbers and underrepresentation. Asians empha size their status as the fastest growing "minority" and their consequen need for greater attention being paid to them and their issues. Africa Americans emphasize the need to have historic subordination, disem powerment, and discrimination redressed. *Id.* at 1262–63.

Given the competing claims between groups affected by housing discrimin tion and a racialized view of space, can available legal remedies provi relief? See also John O. Calmore, *Race/ism Lost and Found: The Fa Housing Act at Thirty*, 52 U. Miami L. Rev. 1067 (1998).

3. Congressional legislation addresses housing discrimination und the Fair Housing Provisions (Title VIII) of the Civil Rights Act of 1968 [P L. No. 90–284, 82 Stat. 73, 81–89, (codified as amended at 42 U.S.C §§ 3601–3614(a)) (1988)]. Armstrong describes the reach of the act:

> Housing discrimination is prevalent across the United States spite of Congress's longstanding prohibition against such conduct. M than twenty years ago, Congress enacted the Fair Housing Provisi (Title VIII) of the Civil Rights Act of 1968 to bar racial discriminatio the sale or rental of real property. The Fair Housing Act's (FHA) g included fostering housing integration and the eradication of reside segregation in addition to outlawing discrimination. Title VIII is forced primarily through lawsuits initiated by individual victim discrimination or by fair housing organizations. The original Act lin punitive damages awards and the availability of attorney's fees. mentators frequently cited these limitations as the primary reasons Title VIII was not effective in eradicating housing discrimination. decades later, Congress responded by passing the Fair Housing A ments Act of 1988 (1988 Amendments) [Pub. L. No. 100–430, 102 1619 (codified as amended at 42 U.S.C.A. §§ 3601–3631 (1988))]. Amendments eliminated the restrictions on attorney's fees and pu damages and provided an administrative adjudication option for h discrimination complainants.

> Although the 1988 Amendments were designed to increase VIII's effectiveness in combating individual acts of housing discr tion, Congress failed to address the inherent limitations in using litigation as a means of correcting the public problem of h discrimination. The 1988 Amendments failed to address the fa individual causes of action have had little impact on residential s tion during Title VIII's twenty-two year history.

> The Civil Rights Act of 1968 and the Fair Housing Amendme of 1988 probably can never completely eradicate the national pro housing segregation because they fail to attack the evil in a sys manner. Using private litigation to address residential segrega sults in treating the problem as one of individual access rather illegal activity aimed at a segment of society. However, racial dis tion in housing access affects not only the individual who h denied a specific housing unit, but creates and maintains se

reas, and schools. Too often, an individual action
sing violation ignores the larger dynamics and conse-
liscrimination. Although a particular act of discrimina-
ectly upon the individual victim, the discrimination is
cts, the entire minority group to which the individual

*Desegregation Through Private Litigation: Using
Achieve the Purposes of the Fair Housing Act,* 64
-912 (1991)* (suggesting "group-oriented relief can
l cases in a manner that can be reconciled with
statutory and constitutional civil rights").

dies for housing discrimination repair the harm
remedies could be fashioned?

eflect the vested economic interests of the land
ons, issued by both state and federal courts, have
lerations can be used to justify exclusion of the
ct is borne primarily by racial minorities. See
ivilege in Residential Housing in Stephanie M.
Revealed: How Invisible Privilege Undermines

THA R. MAHONEY

Whiteness, And Transformation
659–63, 1666–67, 1669–74, 1677–79 (1995).**

s both cause and product in the processes
f race in America. The concept of race has
ent or meaning other than those meanings
f white privilege and racist domination.
eory helps understand residential segrega-
ial construction and whiteness as a racial
te product of notions of black inferiority
ted geographically through the exclusion
white neighborhoods and the concentra-
neighborhoods stigmatized by both race
gated world we inhabit comes to define
ed experience of people in a segregated
al quality of the world we inhabit with
ing the social construction of race a
and inevitable. Segregation therefore
ated concepts of blackness and white-
ocially constructed, and that its social
ralized feature of the physical world
in help us understand how to trans-
ege. * * *

listory of racial subordination, social
e formal legal equality with equality
segregation, this formalism leads to

de-emphasizing the ongoing existence and harms of segregation and to emphasizing legal and economic mechanisms that could theoretically correct it. * * * Civil rights scholars necessarily put a great deal of energy into revealing past and present structures of subordination. We prove (again and again) that subordination has happened and does happen, that segregation reflects and creates inequality, and that white privilege is real. The metaphor of a "property right in whiteness" helps emphasize that privilege exists and that law protects it. While necessarily repeated, the reiteration of the existence of subordination and privilege tends to take our eyes off the question of transformation. * * *

Race is a social construction, not "a natural division of humankind." As a concept or an ideology, however, race derives much of its power from seeming to be a natural or biological phenomenon or, at the very least, a coherent social category. For whites, residential segregation is one of the forces giving race a "natural" appearance: "good" neighborhoods are equated with whiteness, and "black" neighborhoods are equated with joblessness. The construction of race in America today allows whiteness to remain a dominant background norm, associated with positive qualities, for white people, and it allows unemployment and underemployment to seem like natural features of black communities. As I tell my Property students, when you wake up in the morning and go to the kitchen for coffee, you do not feel as if you hold partial interests or particular sticks in a bundle of rights in the structure you inhabit, nor does it feel as if land-use regulation shaped your structure, street, and community. This is home, where you roll out of bed, smell the coffee, reach for clothing, and inhabit the "reality" of the house. The physicality of home and community—that apparently natural quality from which Property professors must detach students to teach legal concepts—tends to make our lived experience appear natural. The appearance that this is "the way things are" in turn tends to make prevailing patterns of race, ethnicity, power, and the distribution of privilege appear as features of the natural world.

Race is a relational concept. It describes at least two social and cultural groups in relation to each other. The concept of race acquires meaning only in the context of historical development and existing race relations. Therefore, the construction of whiteness as "naturally" employed and employable, and blackness as "naturally" unemployed and unemployable, are both examples of the way in which concepts of whiteness and blackness imply whiteness as dominant and blackness as "other." Both become part of the way of thinking about race in America.

Race is a powerful concept, even though it is neither natural nor fixed. Social constructions acquire power because we inhabit their landscape and see through their lenses. Therefore, change cannot be achieved by a decision not to act racially, given the patterns of privilege and exclusion, dominance, and subordination that characterize individual and collective life in a racialized society. Large-scale patterns of urban development have shaped patterns of privilege for mostly white areas and subordination, including economic decline, for many mostly black areas and have made these patterns part of the space we inhabit. In the context of residential segregation and urban/suburban development, therefore, the challenge of ending subordination involves changing widespread patterns of residence and economic development and changing the social meanings attached to these patterns. * * *

Ruth Frankenberg divides whiteness into a set of "linked dimensions": a location of structural advantage and race privilege; a "standpoint" from which white people look at ourselves, at others, and at society; and a set of cultural practices that are usually unmarked and unnamed. Frankenberg explores the ways in which material existence and the way we understand and describe it are interconnected in the construction of whiteness. The interaction of the material world and the ways we explain and understand it "generates experience" and, therefore, the "experience" of lived whiteness is something continuously constructed, reconstructed, and transformed for white people. Frankenberg's description of the relationship between the material world and our understanding of our experience helps explain the ways in which urban segregation itself becomes a force in constructing social concepts of race. For whites, white neighborhoods become part of the "natural" world, helping to keep their whiteness unnoticed and undisturbed, and helping to equate whiteness with something that reflects positive values and feels like home.

Whites have difficulty perceiving whiteness, both because of its cultural prevalence and because of its cultural dominance. Anthropologist Renato Rosaldo describes "culture" as something perceived in someone else, something one does not perceive oneself as having. "Culture" is a feature that marks a community in inverse proportion with power, so that the less full citizenship one possesses, the more "culture" one is likely to have. What we ourselves do and think does not appear to us to be "culture," but rather appears to be the definition of what is normal and neutral, like the air we breathe, transparent from our perspective. * * *

Because the dominant norms of whiteness are not visible to whites, whites are free to see ourselves as "individuals," rather than as members of a culture. Individualism in turn becomes part of white resistance to perceiving whiteness and indeed to being placed in the category "white" at all. The shift in vision that makes whiteness perceptible is thus doubly threatening for whites: It places us in a category that our whiteness itself requires us to be able to ignore, and it asks us to admit into our perception of ourselves the perceptions of those defined outside the circle of whiteness.

Ruth Frankenberg identified discursive repertoires in the way white women were "thinking through race," essentialist racism, color and power evasion, and race cognizance. Color and power evasion are the key strategies in the colorblind ideology that characterizes most legal opinions and predominates in most areas of public discourse in the United States today. Color evasion is similar to what Neil Gotanda calls the myth of "non-recognition." Noticing a person's color, and noticing differences between another person's color and one's own, is equated with being "prejudiced." Whites are color evasive about people of color, often declining to identify the race of someone who is "other" than white in an effort to avoid appearing prejudiced. Notably, whites are also color evasive when describing a white self in relation to people of color. For whites, noticing race is not nice for whites because the meaning of "race" itself is "Other," inferior, and stigmatized. The colorblind approach, which is generally adopted by whites to avoid being racist, therefore implicitly preserves much of the power structure of essentialist racism. Power evasion, in Frankenberg's terms, is color evasion with a different edge. Whites notice difference but do not allow into consciousness those differences that threaten white self-perceptions or make whites feel bad.

Race cognizance, Frankenberg's third category, means recognizing difference on the basis of cultural autonomy and empowerment for people of color. Because white privilege and whiteness are not visible, whites can only recognize "racism" or animus—but we recognize this quality in others more than ourselves. Therefore, most whites perceive racism as something that a second party (the racist actor) does to a third party (the subordinated person of a minority race). For white Americans of middle-class and elite status—the people who write the books and do the social analysis—racism is something that working-class whites (particularly Southerners) do to blacks and other people of color. Although racism is capable of being recognized in this framework, it appears as an unchanging artifact that is assigned to a social location within the white working class. * * *

In the context of desegregation and urban development, the routine acceptance of whiteness as a dominant background norm is apparent in attitude surveys that inquire about the percentage of blacks whom whites would be willing to tolerate as neighbors. Whites are seldom asked how many whites they require as neighbors in order to feel comfortable. The accepted concept of "neighbors" or "area residents" is one that is white. On the other hand, defensive white self-awareness manifests itself quickly during times of racial transition in an area, or in relation to nearby groups in "other" neighborhoods. * * *

There is an interactive relationship between residential segregation and the reproduction of whiteness and white dominance. White choices are not only the aggregation of individual preferences regarding proximity to blacks. Rather, governmental and private forces—in interaction with each other—in the past created a racialized process of urban/suburban development in which "good" neighborhoods were defined as white and whiteness was defined as good, stable, employed, and employable.

Racial segregation was systematically promoted during the 1930s, 1940s, and 1950s by federal programs like the Home Owners Loan Corporation (HOLC), which made loans to homeowners, and the Federal Housing Authority (FHA), which insured private-sector loans. These programs refused to lend money to blacks. They also actively promoted systems of restrictive racial covenants. The greatest impact of these federal agencies in structuring the market, however, lay in the ranking system—the origins of redlining—that the government used to rank communities in their eligibility for federally-financed or federally-insured loans.

Using these guidelines, HOLC and FHA actually refused to lend money or underwrite loans for whites if whites moved to areas where people of color lived. Private lenders adopted policies in line with federal guidelines. These programs reduced housing opportunities for blacks. But they also went considerably further in the process of socially constructing whiteness and blackness in urban areas. Redlining causes decline in majority-black areas, and it prevents lending in majority-white areas where the presence of "inharmonious" racial groups causes lower rankings.

These federal policies, incorporated into private practices, enforced a system in which whiteness was both required and rewarded as a feature of development. Blacks had no choice to move to suburbia. Whites had no choice to move to integrated suburbia. Racism—prejudice against blacks—is so pervasive in America that the importance of the construction of whiteness is often overlooked in discussions of racial geography. Whites generally express preferences to live in neighborhoods shared with very low percentages of blacks. Blacks generally express preferences for living in neighborhoods that are more evenly racially mixed. Generally, these differences have been treated as creating a "natural" tendency to racial "tipping." In any community, if five percent of new residents are black, the story goes, those whites who would only tolerate two percent of black neighbors move out. These vacancies are filled by more blacks, and those whites who would only have tolerated five percent of black neighbors move out. In this vision, racial transition is a naturalized process, in which white preference for white neighbors is less examined than hostility to black neighbors. If the preference for whiteness is addressed at all, it is raised in examining whether the use of racial steering or quotas to prevent white flight is permissible. The construction of this white preference for whiteness is not examined at all. Racism is treated as a natural and unexamined force. * * *

The federal requirement of segregation, as the modern, suburban home-financing system developed, placed a stamp of approval on all private forms of discrimination as well. Both real estate brokers and private lenders pursued policies that promoted segregation. Federal action therefore helped to create racialized housing markets: Once racialized community development through control of the real estate finance market was institutionalized as federal policy, any private sector actor who went against the segregated norm would have compromised buyers and their neighbors. Both the ability of the current owners to sell to buyers with federally funded or insured mortgages on resale of the property, and the mortgage insurability of nearby properties, rested on maintaining whiteness in suburbia. Not only were white people socially reluctant to live near black people, but they were also economically rewarded for living near white people. Maintaining a white market paid. The incentives and preferences for maintaining whiteness were systemic, not merely individual.

The Kerner Commission on Civil Disorders, inquiring into the causes of the racial riots of the late 1960s, noted that they did not find whites moving to the suburbs primarily to avoid blacks. The "more basic" reason for white migration to the suburbs was the "rising mobility and affluence of middle-class families." The suburbs had better schools, living conditions, and affordable housing. But all those qualities of ease and comfort were associated with whiteness, and in turn these qualities increasingly defined whiteness. Jobs moved to the suburbs as well, following the white work force and attracting more white workers. Blacks incur higher time and money costs to commute; blacks possess less information about distant jobs; and suburban locations build employers' fear of white resentment if blacks arrive and remove pressures on employers to avoid discriminating. Some authors emphasize the primary role of housing discrimination in this process; other scholars have proposed that jobs may cause residential choice rather than the other way around. From this perspective, employer attitudes toward prospective employees are extremely important in determining both housing and job opportunities.

Government-sponsored segregation helped inscribe in American culture the equation of "good neighborhoods" with white neighborhoods. The close correlation between employment opportunity and residential segregation meant that "black" was increasingly linked with "inner-city" and with "unemployed or unemployable" in white consciousness; whiteness was identified with "employed or employable," stability and self-sufficiency. In this way, residential segregation was both product and cause of racial constructions that tended to promote further preferences for whites and further exclusion for black communities and individuals. White neighborhoods in this process of racial construction increasingly seem to be suitable sites for investment, while black neighborhoods seem unsuitable. * * *

In the context of residential segregation, antidiscrimination law is part of the attack on whiteness as a dominant norm. Whiteness has been constructed by excluding blacks, by defining white areas as superior, and by allocating to white areas the resources that reinforce privilege. Housing discrimination perpetuates segregation. It reflects the social construction of race—blacks as undesirable residents for white areas, whites as desirable residents for those areas—and perpetuates the processes that concentrate black poverty and continue to reproduce race and racism in America. A straight-forward attack on housing discrimination is therefore vital to break down walls of exclusion and begin the process of including people of color into formerly all-white or mostly white areas. Fighting housing discrimination is an important part of transforming whiteness in America.

Antidiscrimination law by itself, however, even when combined with a ban on employment discrimination, is insufficient to undo the processes by which residential life is segregated by race and racial concentration of blacks is linked with poverty. The many areas of selective investment and divestment that continue to reproduce segregation and exclusion and protect white privilege are larger social processes than can be attacked through antidiscrimination law. Therefore, the processes that reproduce whiteness and blackness must be deprived of their apparently natural quality, revealing the multiple forces and factors linking whiteness with access and economic development, and linking blackness with exclusion and impoverishment.

Land-use decisions affect the development of jobs and housing and the racialized allocation of resources and economic access—even when those decisions appear to have nothing to do with race. Decisions like highway planning, industrial-park location, bridge development, and other decisions should all be evaluated for their impact on the perpetuation of current patterns of racial segregation in housing and employment. All decisions should then be scrutinized for their effect on the racial reproduction of power and access in employment and on residence as well. Reports evaluating potential decisions would project the impact of any development on residential and employment segregation.

Notes and Questions

1.   What does Mahoney mean when she writes: "The lived experience of people in a segregated society links the perceived natural quality of the world we inhabit with its racialized characteristics. * * * Segregation therefore reflects and reinforces socially created concepts of blackness and whiteness."? Do you agree? Can you think of examples that prove her statement true or false?

2.   Mahoney explains how racial segregation comes to be perceived as the natural order, "the way things are." She explains that Whites, seeking to avoid appearing prejudiced, decline to notice race. Would encouraging Whites to notice race, including whiteness, be a positive step? Can noticing race help people to combat racially discriminatory impulses within themselves or will it reinforce such impulses?

3.   Cheryl Harris, *Whiteness as Property*, 106 Harv. L. Rev. 1709 (1993) suggests that whiteness itself has a value as property. What impact does residential segregation and the creation of a property value in whiteness have upon the education system?

SECTION 2.   EDUCATION

Because residential patterns of segregation are the norm, this segregation has been replicated in public schools. This section first examines segregation in education, including its pervasiveness and the systematic challenges to the exclusionary structure. Next it turns to quality of education, the desirability of integration, and the permissibility of using racial classifications in an educational setting.

A.   SEGREGATION IN EDUCATION

TUCKER v. BLEASE
97 S.C. 303, 81 S.E. 668 (1914).

[Members of the school board in South Carolina dismissed the Kirby children from school. Although "[t]hese children have the appearance of white children," they were regarded as mixed-race. School officials were concerned that if they admitted these children, they would also have to admit "others of the class." The children were dismissed "on account of their ancestry, associations [with Blacks], and reputation in the community." Testimony from witnesses about the family background of the children is omitted.]

GARY, C. J.

This is an application for a writ of *certiorari* for the purpose of determining by what authority the trustees summarily dismissed Herbert Kirby, Eugene Kirby, and Dudley Kirby from attending as pupils the Dalcho school, of Dillon county, for white children. * * *

[T]hese children had been attending the Dalcho school two sessions prior to the session during which they were dismissed; that objection had been made at various times to their presence in the school, but, as there were no others of that class attending, the trustees had been loath to take any action; that, shortly before they were dismissed, other children of the same class were attempting to enter the said school, and complaints were being made by its patrons; the trustees saw that, unless all children of that class were dismissed from the school, it would be materially injured. * * * [T]he trustees, in dismissing these children, were not actuated by any feeling of animosity towards them, but that their action was based upon what they deemed to be for the best interest of the school. They further alleged that they were ready and willing to provide a school for all children of this class in that district; that such a school had been provided in the past, but had been discontinued, because of friction among the patrons, and that, since the discontinuance of said school, the trustees had provided for the attendance of such children in other districts where they were allowed to enter the schools. The * * * [record] also contains the following language: "That respondents are informed and believe that the wards of petitioners are not of pure Caucasian blood, and that this fact is generally known to the citizens of the community, and that it would not be right or proper, or for the best interest of the schools in said district, for the children to attend the white public schools, and for the further reason that the environment and antecedents of the said children, and the knowledge of the public thereof, place them in a separate class from the white people of the community."

[The court examined the statutes of South Carolina, under which it was a crime for "any white man to intermarry with any woman of either the Indian or negro races, or any mulatto, mestizo, or half-breed, or for any white woman to intermarry with any other person than a white man, or for any mulatto, half-breed, negro, Indian, or mestizo to intermarry with a white woman." In addition, the South Carolina Constitution provided that "Separate schools shall be provided for children of the white and colored races, and no child of either race shall ever be permitted to attend a school provided for children of the other race."

Noting that the cut-off point at which marriage of a white person with a mulatto became illegal was "one-eighth or more of negro blood," the court reasoned that the child of such parents should be "entitled to exercise all the legal rights of a white person, except those arising from a proper classification, when equal accommodations are afforded."]

We therefore proceed to determine whether the law allows a proper classification to be made between those without negro blood and those with less than one-eighth, when there is a provision for equal accommodation.

The law recognizes that there is a social element, arising from racial instinct, to be taken into consideration between those with and those without negro blood. * * * The decisions prior to the abolition of slavery show that the classification between white and colored persons did not depend upon the extent of the mixed blood.

The rule was thus stated by Chancellor Harper * * *: "The status of the individual is not to be determined solely by the distinct and visible mixture of negro blood, but by reputation, by his reception into society, and his having commonly exercised the privileges of a white man. But his admission to these privileges, regulated by the public opinion of the community in which he lives, will very much depend on his own character and conduct; and it may be well and proper that a man of worth, honesty, industry, and respectability, should have the rank of a white man, while a vagabond of the same degree of blood should be confined to the inferior caste. It will be a stimulus to the good conduct of these persons, and security for their fidelity as citizens." * * *

"Among the citizens of South Carolina we have two distinct races. Before the law they are equal. The colored race, in our courts of justice, stand on the same plane as the white race. Our laws bear equally on all, without regard to race, color, or previous condition. Our social conditions, however, are very different. Friends, companions, and neighbors must be of our own choice. These relations and associations the law does not undertake to make or regulate for us. If we do not wish to associate with one class of society, there is no law that I know of which compels us to do so." * * *

[The opinion then quotes *Plessy v. Ferguson* (reproduced in Chapter 2, § 5 *supra*) as to the appropriateness of segregation as a legal recognition of social custom.]

While the testimony shows that the children are entitled to be classed as white nevertheless the action of the board of trustees was neither capricious nor arbitrary, as they are willing to provide equal accommodations for the Kirby children and those in the same class with them. The testimony also shows that the decided majority of the patrons would refuse to send their children to the Dalcho school if the Kirby children were allowed to continue in attendance. Tested by the maxim, "The greatest good to the largest number," it would seem to be far better that the children in question should be segregated than that the large majority of the children attending that school should be denied educational advantages. * * *

Petition dismissed.

Notes and Questions

1. Why is the court unconcerned about "educational advantages" to the Kirby children?

2. In *Gong Lum v. Rice*, 275 U.S. 78 (1927), the Mississippi Supreme Court construed § 207 of the state Constitution of 1890, which provided: "Separate schools shall be maintained for children of the white and colored races."

The court held that this provision of the Constitution divided the educable children into those of the pure white or Caucasian race, on the one hand, and the brown, yellow, and black races, on the other, and therefore that Martha Lum, of the Mongolian or yellow race, could not insist on being classed with the whites under this constitutional division. 275 U.S. at 82.

Plaintiff appealed, contending that state authorities had misapplied the equal protection doctrine by classifying her with Negro children and requiring her to attend a Negro school.

The case then reduces itself to the question whether a state can be said to afford to a child of Chinese ancestry, born in this country and a citizen of the United States, the equal protection of the laws, by giving her the opportunity for a common school education in a school which receives only colored children of the brown, yellow or black races. * * *

275 U.S. at 85. Citing *Plessy*, the Court observed: "the establishment of separate schools for white and colored children * * * has been held to be a valid exercise of the legislative power. * * * The decision is within the discretion of the state in regulating its public schools, and does not conflict with the Fourteenth Amendment." 275 U.S. at 86–87.

3. Segregation of Native American children as part of their educational experience was also the norm, as this essay describes:

MARGARET SZASZ

Education and the American Indian: The Road to Self-determination, 1928–1973
1–2, 4–5, 8–9, 10–15 (1974).*

The Bureau of Indian Affairs became involved in Indian education in the late nineteenth century when the United States government first accepted its responsibilities for educating the Native American. By 1928, the Indian Bureau's Education Division had been directing Indian schooling for almost fifty years. Bureau educators in this decade were optimistic about the new directions being taken by Indian Service education. Their optimism was not unfounded, for a number of conditions were in their favor. They had the support of John Collier, Commissioner of Indian Affairs from 1933 to 1945; they had the support of Congress; and they had adequate funds for experimentation. In short, they saw a bright future ahead.

Forty years later, in 1970, critics of the Indian Bureau charged that Indian education had not improved measurably during these four decades. There were more children in school, but the equality of their education was as inferior as it had been in 1928. * * *

In 1930, statistics suggested that Indian education was one of the most successful programs of the Indian Bureau. Almost 90 percent of all Indian children were enrolled in school. Approximately half of these children attended public school; a little over a third of them were in schools operated by the Indian Bureau; and almost 10 percent were in private or mission schools. Of those who attended Indian Bureau schools,

an equal number were enrolled in off-reservation and reservation boarding schools and a much smaller percentage were in day schools.

These statistics, however, were misleading. Although many children
started school, a large proportion of them dropped out in the early years.
On some reservations the average education level was fifth grade. Most
students who attended Bureau boarding schools returned to their reservation, where they were unable to apply the training they had received.
Course work in these schools was usually unrelated to the environment
and culture from which the student came; on the other hand, vocational
training was not sufficiently advanced to enable the student to find an
urban job. Physical conditions in boarding schools were notoriously
inadequate. Overcrowding, insufficient food, and improper treatment of
sick children led to frequent epidemics. Since congressional appropriations were meager, boarding-school pupils, including a significant percentage of preadolescent children, were forced to provide almost all
essentials by working long hours in the shops, the gardens, and the
kitchens. In addition, they were subjected to harsh discipline according
to the arbitrary will of the school superintendents. * * *

Between 1928 and 1973, the educational policies of the Indian
Bureau were formed under conditions that precluded any degree of
freedom. Perhaps the greatest barrier was the number of outside pressures that shaped Education Division policy. The first of these pressures
was federal Indian policy itself. Throughout the years of federal involvement in Indian education, the Education Division served as a barometer;
whenever federal policy changed course, Indian education also changed.
Thus, even during the late nineteenth century, education was a prominent feature of the policy of assimilation, which sought to absorb the
Indian into the mainstream culture. In the 1920s Indian education was
affected by the reform movement, which encouraged a return to Indian
culture. In the late 1940s, it was subject to the policy of termination (an
updated version of the old policy of assimilation). Finally, in the late
1960s, it responded to the movement for Indian self-determination by
recognizing that Indians should have a voice in their own educational
programs. The influence of federal Indian policy on the Education
Division determined in large part the shape of Indian education.

The second pressure on Bureau education was the national educational scene. As new trends permeated public and private schools, they
also affected Indian schooling. In the 1930s the Progressive Education
movement saw its ideas adapted to Indian Service schools through the
energetic efforts of directors Ryan and Beatty, both of whom were
Progressive Education leaders. In the postwar period, as this movement
declined in non-Indian education, it also lost strength in Indian Bureau
schools. The demise of the community-school concept exemplified this
change. In the 1950s, when the nation began to demand an educational
system suited to a technological society, the reorganized Branch of
Education shifted its high school curriculum toward academic rather
than vocational courses and encouraged post-high school training. The
early 1970s witnessed a renewed interest in Progressive Education
concepts, newly labeled "open education." As the experimental stage of

this movement began to affect public and private schools, it also reached into schools run by the Indian Bureau. * * *

In the fifty years before the publications of the Meriam Report, the federal government pursued a policy of total assimilation of the American Indian into the mainstream society. Recognizing the vast difficulties in achieving this goal, Congress and the Indian Bureau adopted a plan to remold the Indian's conception of life, or what came to be known as his "system of values." If this could be changed, assimilationists reasoned, the Indian would then become like the white man. The Indian's system of values was expressed in the education of his children and in his attitude toward the land. Consequently, the assimilationists chose to attack these two concepts as the major targets of their campaign.

The land issue was easily resolved. If the Indian owned his own land, they reasoned, he would assume a responsibility for taking care of it and would thus become a good citizen. Land allotment was secured through the passage of the Dawes Act (more commonly known as the Allotment Act) [See Chapter 3, § 6 *supra*] of 1887, which provided for the allotment of lands in severalty of Indians on the various reservations. The remolding of Indian education to conform to white cultural values could not be achieved by a single piece of legislation, but during this same decade the federal government began to assume responsibility for Indian education and provided the first significant federal funding for Indian schools.

During the first century of U.S. Indian policy the federal government had largely neglected Indian education. The negligible sums that Congress had allocated for "civilization" had had little effect. Although a number of Indian treaties, such as the 1855 treaty with the Yakimas, contained provisions for schools, few of these educational commitments had been fulfilled by the time the treaty period came to a close shortly after the Civil War. It is not surprising, therefore, that the bulk of Indian education before the 1880s was carried out by missionaries. However, a number of southeastern tribes developed their own highly successful education systems in the nineteenth century.

Although there had always been a small number of people who were convinced that the Indian could be civilized, the public generally believed that he was incapable of progress. This negative view was reinforced by attitudes on the frontier. Many frontiersmen were inveterate Indian haters, and as the frontier shrank in physical size this attitude seemed to intensify. Those who encountered the Indian under the often brutal frontier conditions had little respect for the humanitarian viewpoint of the easterner.

In the post-Civil War decades the public attitude began to shift, and within the space of a few years, in spite of the antagonism of westerners, assimilation became the popular approach. The impetus for this change of opinion was provided by reformers who responded to a national outcry against publicized incidents of white injustice. Events like the Nez Perce retreat, the Ponca removal, and the flight of the Northern Cheyenne, as well as the intrusion of white settlers into Indian Territory and the exposure of graft within the Indian Bureau, increased congressional concern and aided the reformers in their efforts to secure legislation to change the national Indian policy.

In this era of individual fortunes and economic dreams, the presence of idealistic reformers may seem somewhat strange. On the other hand, the American system had yet to be shaken by internal doubts. Consequently, these reformers, like many other Americans, held their society in such high esteem that they developed an almost imperialistic attitude toward cultures that responded to other values. Armed with this type of evangelistic fervor, the reformers stood a good chance of succeeding. By the late 1870s they had begun their campaign. * * *

[T]he off-reservation industrial boarding school became an entrenched form of federal Indian schooling during the assimilation period. Shortly before the turn of the century, however, other forms of education were introduced. The main alternatives were reservation boarding or day schools. Critics of off-reservation education supported this type of schooling because it offered several distinct advantages. In the first place, reservation schools were less expensive. Day schools required little transportation or boarding, and transportation to reservation boarding schools was much cheaper than to off-reservation schools. Second, reservation schools were more acceptable to parents, who were generally hostile to the idea of having their children taken any distance from home. Incidents of enforced seizure of children to fill the quotas of off-reservation schools during this period have been reported too frequently to be considered mere exaggeration. Although many parents objected to off-reservation schooling, opposition to education itself was by no means a universal phenomenon among Indians. However, those parents who did object may have "understood ... that it represented the most dangerous of all attacks on basic Indian values, the one most likely to succeed in the end because it aimed at the children, who had known little if any of the old life."

As an adjunct, then, to the off-reservation industrial boarding schools, the reservation schools were the second type of federal Indian education. Day schools in particular increased after the turn of the century. Many of those who promoted Indian assimilation, however, predicted that public schools would prove to be the best solution to the problems of Indian education. Early observers of the effects of public schooling on the Indian child concluded that separate Indian schools supported by the federal government would eventually become an anachronism.

With the exception of eastern Indians not under the jurisdiction of the federal government, the first tribes subject to public schooling were those whose reservations were allotted. As whites responded eagerly to the newly available leases and surplus lands of these reservations, they brought with them demands for public schools for their children. By 1902 Agent Jay Lynch wrote from the Yakima Reservation that there were "so many white people renting land on the reservation ... it was found necessary to have schools for white people renting Indian lands." On reservations that were not allotted (including most reservations in the Southwest), public schooling did not become an issue. Where it existed, it encouraged assimilation. As Agent Lynch wrote, "Indian children progress much faster when thus thrown in contact with white children than they do when they are all kept together with whites excluded."

By the turn of the century these three major forms of Indian education had become firmly established. A fourth form that should be mentioned was the mission school, the forerunner of both federal and public Indian education, which retained its foothold during this period. Although mission schools did not educate a significant proportion of Indian children, they were responsible for a consistently small percentage, with considerable variation from reservation to reservation. One of the reasons for their continued existence was simply that not enough schools were built to take their place. However, mission schools continued to exist even after the Indian Bureau was able to report that the majority of Indian children were enrolled in some other type of schooling. Another reason for their tenacity may have been that they had become established institutions.

At the beginning of the twentieth century the status of the Indian was not only bleak, it was hovering on the edge of disaster. The dual inheritance of the assimilation policies of education and land allotment had already given some indication of their potential ability to damage if not destroy a majority of the Indian people. During the next three decades (1900–1930) the unchecked pursuit of these policies led the Indian to a point of no return. By the end of World War I he was suffering increasingly from disease and a short life expectancy, malnutrition and starvation, a diminishing land base, and a stagnant, unrealistic school system. In the early 1920s federal Indian policy was a notorious example of bureaucratic inefficiency and ineffectiveness, and the possibility of change from within appeared to be hopeless. The time was ripe for reform.

The decade of the 1920s witnessed the movement for reform; the decade of the 1930s saw the rhetoric of reform transformed into action. Reformers of the 1920s uncovered extensive mismanagement within the Bureau, which gave them ready ammunition for their attack on the administrative walls of the structure. Failures of the education system provided some of the most lethal ammunition. The reformers dwelt on the "plight" of Indian children through a direct emotional appeal that drew immediate response from an increasingly irate public.

Reform in the 1920s followed a pattern not uncommon to other reform movements in the United States. It was triggered by a *cause celebre*, an incident that occurred when the climate of opinion was ready for reform. The Bursum bill of 1922, "an act to quiet title to lands within Pueblo Indian land grants," proposed to give potential legal rights to white men who had settled on Pueblo lands and force the Pueblo Indians to prove ownership of their lands. Establishing such proof would have been difficult if not impossible, for the Pueblos would have had to clarify ownership through three periods of occupation— Spanish, Mexican, and American. The Bursum bill and the Dawes, or Allotment, Act bore witness to the land hunger of those who lived near reservations. Although the Dawes Act had been encouraged in 1887 by reformers who were anxious for Indians to become independent, self-supporting citizens, it had also received a hearty push from westerners who were eager to acquire Indian land. However, in 1922 the Bursum bill served as a catalyst for change because it was proposed at a time when the increasingly disastrous effects of the Dawes Act had become apparent to advocates of Indian rights.

Serving as a target for these sympathizers, the controversial bill provided a focal point of discontent and thus led the reform movement to its second phase—development of dynamic leadership among the reformers themselves. During the 1920s a number of leaders emerged from Congress and from the new organizations formed to fight the Bursum bill. One man overshadowed all the rest. This was John Collier, the outspoken idealist whose life became intertwined with the fortunes and future of the Indians. Collier went on to become Commissioner of Indian Affairs from 1933 to 1945 under Franklin D. Roosevelt, holding that position longer than anyone else before or since.

Collier's interest in Indians dated from 1920, when he and his family came to Taos at the invitation of Mabel Dodge Luhan, a friend from New York City, where she had been best known for her salon. Like many other members of the "Lost Generation," Mabel Dodge Luhan had been depressed and dissatisfied with America after the war. Unlike her contemporaries who fled to Europe, she sought her new life in the American Southwest. For Collier, also, it was dissatisfaction that initially led him to the West, first to California and then to New Mexico. Among the Taos Indians he found a perfect example of the communal life he valued so highly. From these Indians his interest spread, first to the other Pueblos, then to tribes across the continent. The fight against the Bursum bill propelled him into the forefront of the reform movement.

As the principal spokesman for the reformers, Collier was pushed into the limelight when he became Executive Secretary of the American Indian Defense Association. This organization, formed in direct response to the Bursum bill, became the strongest and most outspoken of the Indian reform groups of the 1920s. Although its directives (many of them Collier's) came from the main office in New York, California claimed four of the seven chapters that formed between 1922 and 1927. Many of the California reformers were also active in the Division of Indian Welfare of the General Federation of Women's Clubs. The goals of the two organizations were complementary.

The American Indian Defense Association was determined to reach the public. It published its own bulletin, *American Indian Life,* in the muckraking tradition established at the turn of the century by men like Lincoln Steffens, and it also had ready access to the press. Liberal magazines like *The Nation, Survey Graphic,* and *The New Republic* turned a sympathetic ear to the popular topic of Indian reform, but the issue was also covered in prestigious journals like *Current History* and *The Forum.* The magazine that became the primary voice for the reformers, however, was *Sunset,* a popular California publication edited by Walter V. Wohlke. A prominent crusader, Wohlke wrote many of the articles that criticized the Bureau.

Through this publicity the reformers launched the third phase of the reform movement—public response and encouragement. The level of the appeal was emotional; the crusaders often contrasted the appalling extent of Indian poverty with the general prosperity of the 1920s. Reader reaction to this approach indicated its effectiveness. One *Sunset* reader wrote, "I have been shocked and pained at the revelations brought out by these articles. I feel that in the name of humanity and to keep our great country from blackening its fair name any further, something should be done and that right soon.... I want to know what I can do to help."

Public response led the reform movement into its final and most significant phase—action. In the 1920s, however, the action taken failed to satisfy the demands of the reformers, for it came primarily in the form of independent, private studies commissioned by the federal government. The twentieth-century reformer already had begun to learn that the results of such studies often lie neglected. This was what happened to the first study made in the 1920s, a report compiled by the Committee of One Hundred, a group of citizens who met in Washington, D.C., on December 12 and 13, 1923, to discuss the direction of Indian affairs and to make suggestions for their improvement. The recommendations of this committee, particularly in the area of education, were noteworthy, but they had little effect on the Bureau. Although the Indian Service began to encourage public-school enrollment and to reorganize its own schools in order to offer more advanced instruction, these steps did not radically alter its total education system. Few federal boarding schools had a high school curriculum, and none of those that did compared favorably in quality to the public schools. Vocational training in Bureau schools remained inferior, and other courses continued to be unrelated to the reservation life that the pupil generally returned to when he left school. Although the Bureau recognized the existence of the report, its overall effect was negligible and it served only to point out that the work of the reformers was far from finished.

Notes and Questions

1. Did the federal government *intend* to harm Native children by sending them to Indian schools?

2. Did the federal government intend to harm their culture? Did it succeed?

———

Mexican American plaintiffs challenged school segregation practices directed at them. Consider the following case:

MENDEZ v. WESTMINSTER SCHOOL DISTRICT OF ORANGE COUNTY*

64 F. Supp. 544 (S.D.Cal.1946), aff'd, 161 F.2d 774 (9th Cir.1947).

[Gonzalo Mendez, William Guzman, Frank Palomino, Thomas Estrada and Lorenzo Ramirez filed suit against the Westminster, Garden Grove and El Modeno School Districts, and the Santa Ana City Schools, all located in Orange County, California. The plaintiffs claimed that segregation practiced by these schools against Mexican–American children violated the Equal Protection Clause of the Fourteenth Amendment.]

McCORMICK, District Judge.

* * *

It is conceded by all parties that there is no question of race discrimination in this action. It is, however, admitted that segregation *per se* is practiced in the above-mentioned school districts as the Spanish-speaking children enter school life and as they advance through the grades in the respective school districts. It is also admitted by the defendants that the petitioning children are qualified to attend the public schools in the respective districts of their residences.

In the Westminster, Garden Grove and El Modeno school districts the respective boards of trustees had taken official action, declaring that there be no segregation of pupils on a racial basis but that non-English-speaking children (which group, excepting as to a small number of pupils, was made up entirely of children of Mexican ancestry or descent), be required to attend schools designated by the boards separate and apart from English-speaking pupils; that such group should attend such schools until they had acquired some proficiency in the English language.

The petitioners contend that such official action evinces a covert attempt by the school authorities in such school districts to produce an arbitrary discrimination against school children of Mexican extraction or descent and that such illegal result has been established in such school districts respectively. * * *

* * * The segregation exists in the elementary schools to and including the sixth grade in two of the defendant districts, and in the two other defendant districts through the eighth grade. The record before us shows without conflict that the technical facilities and physical conveniences offered in the schools housing entirely the segregated pupils, the efficiency of the teachers therein and the curricula are identical and in some respects superior to those in the other schools in the respective districts.

The ultimate question for decision may be thus stated: Does such official action of defendant district school agencies and the usages and practices pursued by the respective school authorities as shown by the evidence operate to deny or deprive the so-called non-English-speaking school children of Mexican ancestry or descent within such school districts of the equal protection of the laws?

* * *

---

* Eds. For reasons unknown to us, the court opinions in this case consistently misspell the name of the town of Westminster. We have decided to use the correct spelling in this volume.

[A] violation by a State of a personal right or privilege protected by the Fourteenth Amendment in the exercise of the State's duty to provide for the education of its citizens and inhabitants would justify the Federal Court to intervene. *State of Missouri ex rel. Gaines v. Canada*, 305 U.S. 337.

* * *

We therefore turn to consider whether under the record before us the school boards and administrative authorities in the respective defendant districts have by their segregation policies and practices transgressed applicable law and Constitutional safeguards and limitations and thus have invaded the personal right which every public school pupil has to the equal protection provision of the Fourteenth Amendment to obtain the means of education.

We think the pattern of public education promulgated in the Constitution of California and effectuated by provisions of the Education Code of the State prohibits segregation of the pupils of Mexican ancestry in the elementary schools from the rest of the school children.

Section 1 of Article IX of the Constitution of California directs the legislature to "encourage by all suitable means the promotion of intellectual, scientific, moral, and agricultural improvement" of the people. Pursuant to this basic directive by the people of the State many laws stem authorizing special instruction in the public schools for handicapped children. Such legislation, however, is general in its aspects. It includes all those who fall within the described classification requiring the special consideration provided by the statutes regardless of their ancestry or extraction. The common segregation attitudes and practices of the school authorities in the defendant school districts in Orange County pertain solely to children of Mexican ancestry and parentage. They are singled out as a class for segregation. Not only is such method of public school administration contrary to the general requirements of the school laws of the State, but we think it indicates an official school policy that is antagonistic in principle to §§ 16004 and 16005 of the Education Code of the State.

Obviously, the children referred to in these laws are those of Mexican ancestry. And it is noteworthy that the educational advantages of their commingling with other pupils is regarded as being so important to the school system of the State that it is provided for even regardless of the citizenship of the parents. We perceive in the laws relating to the public educational system in the State of California a clear purpose to avoid and forbid distinctions among pupils based upon race or ancestry except in specific situations[5] not pertinent to this action. Distinctions of

5. [Eds. This footnote reproduces California's school segregation statutes.]

Sec. 8003. "Schools for Indian children, and children of Chinese, Japanese, or Mongolian parentage: Establishment. The governing board of any school district may establish separate schools for Indian children, excepting children of Indians who are wards of the United States Government and children of all other Indians who are descendants of the original American Indians of the United States, and for children of Chinese, Japanese, or Mongolian parentage."

Sec. 8004. "Same: Admission of children into other schools. When separate schools are established for Indian children or children of Chinese, Japanese, or Mongo-

that kind have recently been declared by the highest judicial authority of the United States "by their very nature odious to a free people whose institutions are founded upon the doctrine of equality." They are said to be "utterly inconsistent with American traditions and ideals." *Hirabayashi v. United States*, 320 U.S. 81.

Our conclusions in this action, however, do not rest solely upon what we conceive to be the utter irreconcilability of the segregation practices in the defendant school districts with the public educational system authorized and sanctioned by the laws of the State of California. We think such practices clearly and unmistakably disregard rights secured by the supreme law of the land.

"The equal protection of the laws" pertaining to the public school system in California is not provided by furnishing in separate schools the same technical facilities, text books and courses of instruction to children of Mexican ancestry that are available to the other public school children regardless of their ancestry. A paramount requisite in the American system of public education is social equality. It must be open to all children by unified school association regardless of lineage.

We think that under the record before us the only tenable ground upon which segregation practices in the defendant school districts can be defended lies in the English language deficiencies of some of the children of Mexican ancestry as they enter elementary public school life as beginners. But even such situations do not justify the general and continuous segregation in separate schools of the children of Mexican ancestry from the rest of the elementary school population as has been shown to be the practice in the defendant school districts—in all of them to the sixth grade, and in two of them through the eighth grade.

The evidence clearly shows that Spanish-speaking children are retarded in learning English by lack of exposure to its use because of segregation, and that commingling of the entire student body instills and develops a common cultural attitude among the school children which is imperative for the perpetuation of American institutions and ideals. It is also established by the record that the methods of segregation prevalent in the defendant school districts foster antagonisms in the children and suggest inferiority among them where none exists. One of the flagrant examples of the discriminatory results of segregation in two of the schools involved in this case is shown by the record. In the district under consideration there are two schools, the Lincoln and the Roosevelt, located approximately 120 yards apart on the same school grounds, hours of opening and closing, as well as recess periods, are not uniform. No credible language test is given to the children of Mexican ancestry upon entering the first grade in Lincoln School. This school has an enrollment of 249 so-called Spanish-speaking pupils, and no so-called English-speaking pupils; while the Roosevelt, (the other) school, has 83 so-called English-speaking pupils and 25 so-called Spanish-speaking pupils. Standardized tests as to mental ability are given to the respective classes in the two schools and the same curricula are pursued in both

lian parentage, the Indian children or children of Chinese, Japanese, or Mongo-

lian parentage shall not be admitted into any other school."

schools and, of course, in the English language as required by State law. In the last school year the students in the seventh grade of the Lincoln were superior scholarly to the same grade in the Roosevelt School and to any group in the seventh grade in either of the schools in the past. It further appears that not only did the class as a group have such mental superiority but that certain pupils in the group were also outstanding in the class itself. Notwithstanding this showing, the pupils of such excellence were kept in the Lincoln School. It is true that there is no evidence in the record before us that shows that any of the members of this exemplary class requested transfer to the other so-called intermingled school, but the record does show without contradiction that another class had protested against the segregation policies and practices in the schools of this El Modeno district without avail.

* * *

* * * [I]t should be noted that the omnibus segregation of children of Mexican ancestry from the rest of the student body in the elementary grades in the schools involved in this case because of language handicaps is not warranted by the record before us. The tests applied to the beginners are shown to have been generally hasty, superficial and not reliable. In some instances separate classification was determined largely by the Latinized or Mexican name of the child. Such methods of evaluating language knowledge are illusory and are not conducive to the inculcation and enjoyment of civil rights which are of primary importance in the public school system of education in the United States.

It has been held that public school authorities may differentiate in the exercise of their reasonable discretion as to the pedagogical methods of instruction to be pursued with different pupils.[7] And foreign language handicaps may be to such a degree in the pupils in elementary schools as to require special treatment in separate classrooms. Such separate allocations, however, can be lawfully made only after credible examination by the appropriate school authority of each child whose capacity to learn is under consideration and the determination of such segregation must be based wholly upon indiscriminate foreign language impediments in the individual child, regardless of his ethnic traits or ancestry

* * *

There are other discriminatory customs, shown by the evidence, existing in the defendant school districts as to pupils of Mexican descent and extraction, but we deem it unnecessary to discuss them in this memorandum.

We conclude by holding that the allegations of the complaint (petition) have been established sufficiently to justify injunctive relief against all defendants, restraining further discriminatory practices against the pupils of Mexican descent in the public schools of defendant school districts.

* * *

7. See *Plessy v. Ferguson*, 163 U.S. 537 (1896).

Notes and Questions

1. The district court's decision was affirmed on narrower statutory grounds in *Westminster School Dist. v. Mendez,* 161 F.2d 774 (9th Cir.1947) (holding that since Mexicans were not included among the groups designated for segregated schools in California's school segregation statutes, it was contrary to the statute to segregate them).

2. What did the court mean in its opening sentence, "It is conceded by all parties that there is no question of race discrimination in this action"? Why might the parties concede this? Were they correct in doing so? Can discrimination because of alleged language deficiencies constitute race discrimination, or act as a proxy for race discrimination? Notice that the court's findings regarding standardized test scores at the exclusively Mexican–American school and the shoddy language testing procedures belie the "language deficiency" rationale.

3. Notice that some of the schools at issue were at least partially integrated. In a section of the opinion not reproduced, the court wrote that "26 pupils of Mexican descent * * * are permitted by the School Board to attend the [predominantly white] Franklin school because their families had always gone there." Was the segregation experienced by Mexican-American children the same as the segregation experienced by African-American children?

4. The *Westminster* case ultimately led to the repeal of California's segregation statutes. Then-governor Earl Warren signed the legislation repealing the segregation statutes. See the discussion of *Mendez* and its historical context at Chapter 4 § 1 F, *supra.*

5. The *Mendez* decision apparently was the first decision to explicitly reject the reasoning of *Plessy v. Ferguson.* For example, in *Mendez,* the court reasoned that a "paramount requisite in the American system of public education is social equality. It must be open to all children by unified school association regardless of lineage." The court also wrote that

> commingling of the entire student body instills and develops a common cultural attitude among the school children which is imperative for the perpetuation of American institutions and ideals. It is also established by the record that the methods of segregation prevalent in the defendant school districts foster antagonisms in the children and suggest inferiority among them where none exists.

Mendez, 64 F. Supp. at 549.

6. Consider the similarity in the reasoning of the *Mendez* decision and the Supreme Court's ultimate decision of the segregation issue in *Brown v. Board of Education, infra.* Should *Mendez* be considered one of the cases leading to the *Brown* decision? Consider Earl Warren's involvement with respect to both cases, as Governor of California signing the repeal of the segregation statutes, and as author of the *Brown* decision.

7. For additional sources on Latino/a desegregation efforts, see Guadalupe San Miguel, Jr. & Richard R. Valencia, *From the Treaty of Guadalupe Hidalgo to* Hopwood: *The Educational Plight and Struggle of Mexican Americans in the Southwest,* 68 Harv. Ed. Rev. 353 (1998); Juan F. Perea, *The Black/White Binary Paradigm of Race: The "Normal Science" of American Racial Thought,* 85 Calif. L. Rev. 1213 (1997); George A. Martinez, *Legal Indeterminacy, Judicial Discretion and the Mexican–American Litigation*

Experience, 1930–1980, 27 U.C. Davis L. Rev. 555, 574–602 (1994); Jorge C. Rangel & Carlos M. Alcala, *Project Report: De Jure Segregation of Chicanos in Texas Schools*, 7 Harv. C.R.-C.L. L. Rev. 307 (1972); see generally, Gilbert G. Gonzalez, *Chicano Education in the Era of Segregation* 136–56 (1990).

The Supreme Court decided a series of important educational segregation cases in graduate schools that preceded the Warren Court's repudiation of *Plessy v. Ferguson* in *Brown v. Board of Education.* Consider the following case:

SWEATT v. PAINTER

339 U.S. 629 (1950).

CHIEF JUSTICE VINSON delivered the opinion of the Court.

This case and *McLaurin v. Oklahoma State Regents*, 339 U.S. 637, present different aspects of this general question: To what extent does the Equal Protection Clause of the Fourteenth Amendment limit the power of a state to distinguish between students of different races in professional and graduate education in a state university? * * *

In the instant case, petitioner filed an application for admission to the University of Texas Law School for the February, 1946 term. His application was rejected solely because he is a Negro.[8] Petitioner thereupon brought this suit for *mandamus* against the appropriate school officials, respondents here, to compel his admission. At that time, there was no law school in Texas which admitted Negroes.

[The state court agreed that "the action of the State in denying petitioner the opportunity to gain a legal education while granting it to others deprived him of the equal protection of the laws guaranteed by the Fourteenth Amendment." The court denied relief when the university showed it planned to open "a law school for Negroes." The school opened, but Mr. Sweatt refused to register.] * * *

The University of Texas Law School, from which petitioner was excluded, was staffed by a faculty of sixteen full-time and three part-time professors, some of whom are nationally recognized authorities in their field. Its student body numbered 850. The library contained over 65,000 volumes. Among the other facilities available to the students were a law review, moot court facilities, scholarship funds, and Order of the Coif affiliation. The school's alumni occupy the most distinguished positions in the private practice of the law and in the public life of the State. It may properly be considered one of the nation's ranking law schools.

The law school for Negroes which was to have opened in February, 1947, would have had no independent faculty or library. The teaching was to be carried on by four members of the University of Texas Law School faculty, who were to maintain their offices at the University of Texas while teaching at both institutions. Few of the 10,000 volumes

---

8. It appears that the University has been restricted to white students, in accordance with the State law. See Tex.Const. Art. VII, §§ 7, 14; Tex.Rev.Civ.Stat. Arts. 2643b, 2719, 2900 (Vernon, 1925 and Supp.).

ordered for the library had arrived; nor was there any full-time librarian. The school lacked accreditation.

Since the trial of this case, respondents report the opening of a law school at the Texas State University for Negroes. It is apparently on the road to full accreditation. It has a faculty of five full-time professors; a student body of 23; a library of some 16,500 volumes serviced by a full-time staff; a practice court and legal aid association; and one alumnus who has become a member of the Texas Bar.

Whether the University of Texas Law School is compared with the original or the new law school for Negroes, we cannot find substantial equality in the educational opportunities offered white and Negro law students by the State. In terms of number of the faculty, variety of courses and opportunity for specialization, size of the student body, scope of the library, availability of law review and similar activities, the University of Texas Law School is superior. What is more important, the University of Texas Law School possesses to a far greater degree those qualities which are incapable of objective measurement but which make for greatness in a law school. Such qualities, to name but a few, include reputation of the faculty, experience of the administration, position and influence of the alumni, standing in the community, traditions and prestige. It is difficult to believe that one who had a free choice between these law schools would consider the question close.

Moreover, although the law is a highly learned profession, we are well aware that it is an intensely practical one. The law school, the proving ground for legal learning and practice, cannot be effective in isolation from the individuals and institutions with which the law interacts. Few students and no one who has practiced law would choose to study in an academic vacuum, removed from the interplay of ideas and the exchange of views with which the law is concerned. The law school to which Texas is willing to admit petitioner excludes from its student body members of the racial groups which number 85% of the population of the State and include most of the lawyers, witnesses, jurors, judges and other officials with whom petitioner will inevitably be dealing when he becomes a member of the Texas Bar. With such a substantial and significant segment of society excluded, we cannot conclude that the education offered petitioner is substantially equal to that which he would receive if admitted to the University of Texas Law School.

It may be argued that excluding petitioner from that school is no different from excluding white students from the new law school. This contention overlooks realities. It is unlikely that a member of a group so decisively in the majority, attending a school with rich traditions and prestige which only a history of consistently maintained excellence could command, would claim that the opportunities afforded him for legal education were unequal to those held open to petitioner. That such a claim, if made, would be dishonored by the State, is no answer. "Equal protection of the laws is not achieved through indiscriminate imposition of inequalities." *Shelley v. Kraemer*, 334 U.S. 1, 22 (1948).

It is fundamental that these cases concern rights which are personal and present. This Court has stated unanimously that "The State must provide (legal education) for (petitioner) in conformity with the Equal Protection Clause of the Fourteenth Amendment and provide it as soon as it does for applicants of any other group." *Sipuel v. Board of Regents*, 332 U.S. 631, 633 (1948). * * *

In accordance with these cases, petitioner may claim his full constitutional right: legal education equivalent to that offered by the State to students of other races. Such education is not available to him in a separate law school as offered by the State. We cannot, therefore, agree with respondents that the doctrine of *Plessy v. Ferguson*, 163 U.S. 537 (1896), requires affirmance of the judgment below. Nor need we reach petitioner's contention that *Plessy v. Ferguson* should be reexamined in the light of contemporary knowledge respecting the purposes of the Fourteenth Amendment and the effects of racial segregation.

We hold that the Equal Protection Clause of the Fourteenth Amendment requires that petitioner be admitted to the University of Texas Law School. The judgment is reversed and the cause is remanded for proceedings not inconsistent with this opinion.

Reversed.

Notes and Questions

1. In the companion case of *McLaurin v. Oklahoma*, 339 U.S. 637 (1950), appellant McLaurin was a "Negro citizen of Oklahoma," who applied for admission to the University of Oklahoma to earn a doctorate in education. The university denied his application because of his race. The Oklahoma legislature amended its segregation statute "to permit the admission of Negroes to institutions of higher learning attended by white students, in cases where such institutions offered courses not available in the Negro schools. The amendment provided, however, that in such cases the program of instruction 'shall be given at such colleges or institutions of higher education upon a segregated basis.'" Mr. McLaurin "was required to sit apart at a designated desk in an anteroom adjoining the classroom; to sit at a designated desk on the mezzanine floor of the library, but not to use the desks in the regular reading room; and to sit at a designated table and to eat at a different time from the other students in the school cafeteria."

The U.S. Supreme Court opinion explains:

> In the interval between the decision of the court below and the hearing in this Court, the treatment afforded appellant was altered. For some time, the section of the classroom in which appellant sat was surrounded by a rail on which there was a sign stating, "Reserved For Colored," but these have been removed. He is now assigned to a seat in the classroom in a row specified for colored students; he is assigned to a table in the library on the main floor; and he is permitted to eat at the same time in the cafeteria as other students, although here again he is assigned to a special table.

> It is said that the separations imposed by the State in this case are in form merely nominal. McLaurin uses the same classroom, library and cafeteria as students of other races; there is no indication that the seats to which he is assigned in these rooms have any disadvantage of

location. He may wait in line in the cafeteria and there stand and talk with his fellow students, but while he eats he must remain apart. * * *

Our society grows increasingly complex, and our need for trained leaders increases correspondingly. Appellant's case represents, perhaps, the epitome of that need, for he is attempting to obtain an advanced degree in education, to become, by definition, a leader and trainer of others. Those who will come under his guidance and influence must be directly affected by the education he receives. Their own education and development will necessarily suffer to the extent that his training is unequal to that of his classmates. State imposed restrictions which produce such inequalities cannot be sustained. * * *

We conclude that the conditions under which this appellant is required to receive his education deprive him of his personal and present right to the equal protection of the laws. See *Sweatt v. Painter*, 339 U.S. 629. We hold that under these circumstances the Fourteenth Amendment precludes differences in treatment by the state based upon race. 339 U.S. at 640–42.

2. If the Court believed that the facilities at the black law school in *Sweatt* did not equal that of the white law school, why did the Court not simply order more money to be spent on the black law school?

3. Mr. McLaurin's segregation from his white classmates hampered his "ability to study, to engage in discussion, and exchange views with other students." Does the Court's vision of education suggest an argument that supports diversity in education? Does this argument only apply to racial diversity?

4. In *Sweatt* the court said: "It may be argued that excluding petitioner from that school is no different from excluding white students from the new school. This contention overlooks realities." What realities does the argument overlook?

The mirror image argument, that all must be treated alike is a trap of liberal legalism. "Legal liberalism teaches us that all people should be treated equally, fairly, and the same. It is the solid underpinning of the notion of the color-blind Constitution * * *. It appeared when John F. Kennedy intoned, with great emotional force, 'Race shall play no part in American society.' This is our ideal, and it is attractive. The reality is that if we say race plays no part, then the invisible system of white privilege will inevitably continue." Stephanie M. Wildman with contributions by Margalynne Armstrong, Adrienne D. Davis & Trina Grillo, *Privilege Revealed: How Invisible Preference Undermines America* 170 (1996). How is the court able to avoid this trap in *Sweatt*, recognizing that exclusion from the majority institution is different from exclusion from the less privileged law school "for Negroes," yet unable to see the lack of parallelism in other cases of unequal privilege involving race or other identity categories?

BROWN v. BOARD OF EDUCATION
347 U.S. 483 (1954).

CHIEF JUSTICE WARREN delivered the opinion of the Court.

These cases come to us from the States of Kansas, South Carolina, Virginia, and Delaware. They are premised on different facts and different local conditions, but a common legal question justifies their consideration together in this consolidated opinion.

In each of the cases, minors of the Negro race, through their legal representatives, seek the aid of the courts in obtaining admission to the public schools of their community on a nonsegregated basis. In each instance, they have been denied admission to schools attended by white children under laws requiring or permitting segregation according to race. This segregation was alleged to deprive the plaintiffs of the equal protection of the laws under the Fourteenth Amendment. In each of the cases other than the Delaware case, a three-judge federal district court denied relief to the plaintiffs on the so-called "separate but equal" doctrine announced by this Court in *Plessy v. Ferguson*, 163 U.S. 537. Under that doctrine, equality of treatment is accorded when the races are provided substantially equal facilities, even though these facilities be separate. In the Delaware case, the Supreme Court of Delaware adhered to that doctrine, but ordered that the plaintiffs be admitted to the white schools because of their superiority to the Negro schools.

The plaintiffs contend that segregated public schools are not "equal" and cannot be made "equal," and that hence they are deprived of the equal protection of the laws. Because of the obvious importance of the question presented, the Court took jurisdiction. Argument was heard in the 1952 Term, and reargument was heard this Term on certain questions propounded by the Court.

Reargument was largely devoted to the circumstances surrounding the adoption of the Fourteenth Amendment in 1868. It covered exhaustively consideration of the Amendment in Congress, ratification by the states, then existing practices in racial segregation, and the views of proponents and opponents of the Amendment. This discussion and our own investigation convince us that, although these sources cast some light, it is not enough to resolve the problem with which we are faced. At best, they are inconclusive. The most avid proponents of the post-War Amendments undoubtedly intended them to remove all legal distinctions among "all persons born or naturalized in the United States." Their opponents, just as certainly, were antagonistic to both the letter and the spirit of the Amendments and wished them to have the most limited effect. What others in Congress and the state legislatures had in mind cannot be determined with any degree of certainty.

An additional reason for the inconclusive nature of the Amendment's history, with respect to segregated schools, is the status of public education at that time. In the South, the movement toward free common schools, supported by general taxation, had not yet taken hold. Education of white children was largely in the hands of private groups. Education of Negroes was almost nonexistent, and practically all of the race were illiterate. In fact, any education of Negroes was forbidden by law in some states. Today, in contrast, many Negroes have achieved outstanding success in the arts and sciences as well as in the business and professional world. It is true that public school education at the time of the Amendment had advanced further in the North, but the effect of the Amendment on Northern States was generally ignored in the congressional debates. Even in the North, the conditions of public education did not approximate those existing today. The curriculum was usually rudimentary; ungraded schools were common in rural areas; the school term was but three months a year in many states; and compulsory school attendance was virtually unknown. As a consequence, it is not surprising that there should be so little in the history of the Fourteenth Amendment relating to its intended effect on public education.

In the first cases in this Court construing the Fourteenth Amendment, decided shortly after its adoption, the Court interpreted it as proscribing all state-imposed discriminations against the Negro race. The doctrine of "separate but equal" did not make its appearance in this court until 1896 in the case of *Plessy v. Ferguson, supra*, involving not education but transportation. American courts have since labored with the doctrine for over half a century. In this Court, there have been six cases involving the "separate but equal" doctrine in the field of public education. In *Cumming v. Board of Education of Richmond County*, 175 U.S. 528, and *Gong Lum v. Rice*, 275 U.S. 78, the validity of the doctrine itself was not challenged. In more recent cases, all on the graduate school level, inequality was found in that specific benefits enjoyed by white students were denied to Negro students of the same educational qualifications. *State of Missouri ex rel. Gaines v. Canada*, 305 U.S. 337; *Sipuel v. Board of Regents of University of Oklahoma*, 332 U.S. 631; *Sweatt v. Painter*, 339 U.S. 629; *McLaurin v. Oklahoma State Regents*, 339 U.S. 637. In none of these cases was it necessary to re-examine the doctrine to grant relief to the Negro plaintiff. And in *Sweatt v. Painter, supra*, the Court expressly reserved decision on the question whether *Plessy v. Ferguson* should be held inapplicable to public education.

In the instant cases, that question is directly presented. Here, unlike *Sweatt v. Painter*, there are findings below that the Negro and white schools involved have been equalized, or are being equalized, with respect to buildings, curricula, qualifications and salaries of teachers, and other "tangible" factors. Our decision, therefore, cannot turn on merely a comparison of these tangible factors in the Negro and white schools involved in each of the cases. We must look instead to the effect of segregation itself on public education.

In approaching this problem, we cannot turn the clock back to 1868 when the Amendment was adopted, or even to 1896 when *Plessy v. Ferguson* was written. We must consider public education in the light of its full development and its present place in American life throughout the Nation. Only in this way can it be determined if segregation in public schools deprives these plaintiffs of the equal protection of the laws.

Today, education is perhaps the most important function of state and local governments. Compulsory school attendance laws and the great expenditures for education both demonstrate our recognition of the importance of education to our democratic society. It is required in the performance of our most basic public responsibilities, even service in the armed forces. It is the very foundation of good citizenship. Today it is a principal instrument in awakening the child to cultural values, in preparing him for later professional training, and in helping him to adjust normally to his environment. In these days, it is doubtful that any child may reasonably be expected to succeed in life if he is denied the opportunity of an education. Such an opportunity, where the state has undertaken to provide it, is a right which must be made available to all on equal terms.

We come then to the question presented: Does segregation of children in public schools solely on the basis of race, even though the physical facilities and other "tangible" factors may be equal, deprive the children of the minority group of equal educational opportunities? We believe that it does.

In *Sweatt v. Painter*, in finding that a segregated law school for Negroes could not provide them equal educational opportunities, this Court relied in large part on "those qualities which are incapable of objective measurement but which make for greatness in a law school." In *McLaurin v. Oklahoma State Regents*, the Court, in requiring that a Negro admitted to a white graduate school be treated like all other students, again resorted to intangible considerations: " * * * his ability to study, to engage in discussions and exchange views with other students, and, in general, to learn his profession." Such considerations apply with added force to children in grade and high schools. To separate them from others of similar age and qualifications solely because of their race generates a feeling of inferiority as to their status in the community that may affect their hearts and minds in a way unlikely ever to be undone. The effect of this separation on their educational opportunities was well stated by a finding in the Kansas case by a court which nevertheless felt compelled to rule against the Negro plaintiffs:

> "Segregation of white and colored children in public schools has a detrimental effect upon the colored children. The impact is greater when it has the sanction of the law; for the policy of separating the races is usually interpreted as denoting the inferiority of the negro group. A sense of inferiority affects the motivation of a child to learn. Segregation with the sanction of law, therefore, has a tendency to (retard) the educational and mental development of Negro children and to deprive them of some of the benefits they would receive in a racial(ly) integrated school system."

Whatever may have been the extent of psychological knowledge at the time of *Plessy v. Ferguson*, this finding is amply supported by modern authority. Any language in *Plessy v. Ferguson* contrary to this finding is rejected.

We conclude that in the field of public education the doctrine of "separate but equal" has no place. Separate educational facilities are inherently unequal. Therefore, we hold that the plaintiffs and others similarly situated for whom the actions have been brought are, by reason of the segregation complained of, deprived of the equal protection of the laws guaranteed by the Fourteenth Amendment. This disposition makes unnecessary any discussion whether such segregation also violates the Due Process Clause of the Fourteenth Amendment.

Because these are class actions, because of the wide applicability of this decision, and because of the great variety of local conditions, the formulation of decrees in these cases presents problems of considerable complexity. On reargument, the consideration of appropriate relief was necessarily subordinated to the primary question—the constitutionality of segregation in public education. We have now announced that such segregation is a denial of the equal protection of the laws.

* * *

Cases ordered restored to docket for further argument on question of appropriate decrees.

Notes and Questions

1. *Brown v. Board of Education*, 349 U.S. 294 (1955) (*Brown II*) affirmed "the fundamental principle that racial discrimination in public education is unconstitutional," 349 U.S. at 298, and acknowledged broad equity power in the judiciary to "take such proceedings and enter such orders and decrees consistent with this opinion as are necessary and proper to admit to public schools on a racially nondiscriminatory basis with all deliberate speed the parties to these cases." 349 U.S. at 301. Why was a second *Brown* decision, urging "all deliberate speed," necessary? For an excellent examination of the litigation strategy culminating in *Brown,* see Richard Kluger, *Simple Justice* (1976).

2. The reach of the *Brown* decision extended beyond education. In the years following *Brown*, the Court affirmed decisions finding segregation unconstitutional in a number of other public facilities. See, *e.g., Gayle v. Browder*, 352 U.S. 903 (1956) (buses in the city of Montgomery); *Holmes v. City of Atlanta*, 350 U.S. 879 (1955) (golf courses); *Mayor of Baltimore v. Dawson*, 350 U.S. 877 (beaches, bathhouses, and swimming pools).

3. Critics of *Brown* suggest that integration has meant admitting black students to white schools with the expectation that black students assimilate into the white environment. See Alex M. Johnson, Jr., *Bid Whist, Tonk, and United States v. Fordice: Why Integrationism Fails African–Americans Again*, 81 Calif. L. Rev. 1401 (1993). Does integration have to be synonymous with assimilation? Sharon Rush adamantly answers, "No," urging "an integrated environment is one in which people of all races share equal power and have equal voices in shaping policies and making decisions about how the environment will be structured." Sharon Rush, *The Heart of Equal Protection: Education and Race*, 23 N.Y.U. Rev. of L. & Social Change 1, 4 (1997). What policies or mechanism could make such a vision of integration possible? How can real tensions be resolved in an integrated environment?

4. *Brown* supporters often cite the case as a landmark making racial segregation in education illegal. Yet segregation persists. Consider this excerpt from Richard Thompson Ford, *The Boundaries of Race: Political Geography in Legal Analysis*, 107 Harv. L. Rev. 1841, 1844–45, 1848–49, 1875–76 (1994):*

> It is now passé to speak of racial segregation. In an America that is facing the identity crisis of multiculturalism, where racial diversity seems to challenge the norms and values of the nation's most fundamental institutions, to speak of segregation seems almost quaint. The

---

* Copyright © 1994 by Richard Thompson Ford and the Harvard Law Review. Used by permission.

physical segregation of the races would seem to be a relatively simple matter to address; indeed many believe it has already been addressed. Discrimination in housing, in the workplace, and in schools is illegal. Thus it is perhaps understandable that we have turned our attention to other problems, on the assumption that any segregation that remains is either vestigial or freely chosen. But even as racial segregation has fallen from the national agenda, it has persisted. Even as racial segregation is described as a natural expression of racial and cultural solidarity, a chosen and desirable condition for which government is not responsible and that government should not oppose, segregation continues to play the same role it always has in American race relations: to isolate, disempower, and oppress.

Segregation is oppressive and disempowering rather than desirable or inconsequential because it involves more than simply the relationship of individuals to other individuals; it also involves the relationship of groups of individuals to political influence and economic resources. Residence is more than a personal choice; it is also a primary source of political identity and economic security. Likewise, residential segregation is more than a matter of social distance; it is a matter of political fragmentation and economic stratification along racial lines, enforced by public policy and the rule of law.

Segregated minority communities have been historically impoverished and politically powerless. Today's laws and institutions need not be explicitly racist to ensure that this state of affairs continues—they need only to perpetuate historical conditions. * * * Race-neutral policies, set against an historical backdrop of state action in the service of racial segregation and thus against a contemporary backdrop of racially identified space—physical space primarily associated with and occupied by a particular racial group—predictably reproduce and entrench racial segregation and the racial-caste system that accompanies it. Thus, the persistence of racial segregation, even in the face of civil rights reform, is not mysterious. * * *

Both public and private actors laid the groundwork for the construction of racially identified spaces and, therefore, for racial segregation as well. Explicit governmental policy at the local, state, and federal levels has encouraged and facilitated racial segregation. * * * Although the federal government ended these discriminatory practices after 1950, it did nothing to remedy the damage it had done or to prevent private actors from perpetuating segregation until much later.

Racial segregation was also maintained by private associations of white homeowners who "lobbied city councils for zoning restrictions and for the closing of hotels and rooming houses . . . [,] threatened boycotts of real estate agents who sold homes to blacks . . . [, and] withdrew their patronage from white businesses that catered to black clients." These associations shaped the racial and economic landscape, and implemented what might well be described as public policies, by private fiat. Thus, private associations as well as governments defined political space. * * *

Racially identified spaces, demarcated by local boundaries, have distributive as well as political consequences. Our economic model demonstrates that, because localities administer many taxing and spending functions, boundaries that segregate on the basis of wealth or race ensure that taxes are higher and quality of services lower in some jurisdictions than in others. And because local boundaries are regarded as sacrosanct in the implementation of desegregation remedies, if inter-local rather than intra-local segregation is more prevalent, the remedies will be of little consequence.

In *Milliken v. Bradley* [418 U.S. 717 (1974)], the Supreme Court held that court-ordered school busing designed to remedy *de jure* racial segregation in the Detroit schools could not include predominantly white suburban school districts. The Court found that, because no evidence existed that the suburban districts that would be included under the court-ordered plan had themselves engaged in *de jure* discrimination, they could not be forced to participate in the busing remedy. This rationale is puzzling unless one views cities not as mere agents of state power, but as autonomous entities. If cities were mere agents of state power, the state as a whole would be ultimately responsible for their discriminatory actions. The state as a whole would therefore bear responsibility for remedying the discriminatory practices: An apportion-ment of blame and responsibility within the state would be arbitrary and any such apportionment that hindered effective desegregation would be unacceptable.

One may object that, because Michigan had allocated power and authority to cities, the Court correctly allocated blame and responsibility in the same manner. But the Court failed to examine the motivation for the position of local jurisdictional boundaries. Moreover, by conceiving of local political space as opaque—as defining a singular entity—the Court failed to consider the fact that Detroit's racial composition had changed and that responsibility for historical segregation could no more be confined within Detroit's city limits than could its white former resi-dents.

By accepting the municipal boundaries as given, the *Milliken* Court ironically segregated the scope of the remedy to racial segregation, and thereby may have allowed the historical segregation to become en-trenched rather than remedied. "The plaintiffs were to be trapped within the city's boundaries, without even an opportunity to demand that those boundary lines be justified as either rational or innocently nonrational."

Richard Ford describes the combination of private association and government action that results in political space being segregated. Given this connected role of public and private actors, can constitutional doctrine alone address segregation? Should it? Do the available statutory remedies provide sufficient redress?

5. Was *Brown* really a case about helping black school children or was it instead aimed mainly at advancing white self-interest? See Derrick Bell, Brown v. Board of Education *and the Interest–Convergence Dilemma,* 93 Harv. L. Rev. 518 (1980) (*Brown* decision helped U.S. cold war strategy). See also Mary L. Dudziak, *Desegregation as a Cold War Imperative,* 41 Stan. L. Rev. 61 (1988).

B. QUALITY OF EDUCATION

Once the U.S. Supreme Court viewed segregation as legally unaccep-table, issues relating to race and education did not disappear; rather they were reframed. The meaning of education, particularly high-quality education, remained contested in cases involving school financing and decisions exploring the boundaries of desegregation.

Classroom Exercise: *Huckleberry Finn* and the Eighth-Grade Classroom

In an integrated school, the eighth grade curriculum includes Mark Twain's *The Adventures of Huckleberry Finn*. A group of predominantly African–American parents want the book removed from the class reading list. They believe it is not age appropriate because children are at an impressionable age, particularly regarding race relations. They point out that the book uses the word "n____r" 213 times. While the use of that word is offensive in and of itself, they believe that if another classic about a young blond girl, such as *Heidi*, had used the word "b__ch" 213 times, it would be seen as offensive and removed from the curriculum.

Another parent group, composed primarily of white parents, but also including some people of color, want the book kept. They say that it is an important American classic, and the parents want their children reading the books that are part of the canon of education in the United States.

Divide into groups of six. Two students represent the parents who want the book removed, two represent the parents who want to keep the text, one represents the mediator selected to try to resolve the issue. The sixth person must listen and vote as a school board member. Then have school board members from each of the groups vote. What is the racial, ethnic, gender, and sexual orientation of the "school board" in your classroom? Do these identity categories have any bearing on the decision of the board?

See Robin D. Barnes, *Black America and School Choice: Charting a New Course*, 106 Yale L.J. 2375, 2393–2398 (1997) (describing a conflict about *Huckleberry Finn*). See also Stanley Fish, *Not of an Age, But for All Time: Canons and Postmodernism*, 43 J. Legal Educ. 11, 12 (1993), commenting:

> [W]e see two features possessed by canonical materials: (1) They carry their authority with them, seeming to have acquired it by natural right, and (2) they function not to encourage thought, but to stop it. Canonical materials, when they are exerting their full force, draw a line in the sand, but with an air suggesting that the sand is a monument of steel. When a piece of the canon is invoked in this way, it is assumed that there is nothing more to say. In fact there is always more that could be said; it is just that the structure of canonical authority is such that one is discouraged from saying it, or even thinking it.

Should *The Adventures of Huckleberry Finn* be part of the canon? What are the arguments for its inclusion and exclusion? What other book might you choose to assign instead and why would you choose it?

See also *Monteiro v. Tempe Union High Sch. Dist.*, 158 F.3d 1022 (9th Cir.1998), concerning *Huckleberry Finn* and concluding that "allegations that a school required that a book be read, and then refused to remove it from the curriculum" failed to state a discrimination claim under either the Equal Protection Clause or Title VI, but also finding that the complaint sufficiently alleged facts describing a hostile racial educational environment where plaintiff was the target of racial slurs and graffiti.

SAN ANTONIO INDEPENDENT SCHOOL DISTRICT v. RODRIGUEZ

411 U.S. 1 (1973).

JUSTICE POWELL delivered the opinion of the Court.

This suit attacking the Texas system of financing public education was initiated by Mexican–American parents whose children attend the elementary and secondary schools in the Edgewood Independent School District, an urban school district in San Antonio, Texas. They brought a class action on behalf of schoolchildren throughout the State who are members of minority groups or who are poor and reside in school districts having a low property tax base. * * * The school district in which appellees reside, the Edgewood Independent School District, has been compared throughout this litigation with the Alamo Heights Independent School District. This comparison between the least and most affluent districts in the San Antonio area serves to illustrate the manner in which the dual system of finance operates and to indicate the extent to which substantial disparities exist despite the State's impressive progress in recent years. Edgewood is one of seven public school districts in the metropolitan area. Approximately 22,000 students are enrolled in its 25 elementary and secondary schools. The district is situated in the core-city sector of San Antonio in a residential neighborhood that has little commercial or industrial property. The residents are predominantly of Mexican–American descent: Approximately 90% of the student population is Mexican–American and over 6% is Negro. The average assessed property value per pupil is $5,960—the lowest in the metropolitan area— and the median family income ($4,686) is also the lowest. At an equalized tax rate of $1.05 per $100 of assessed property—the highest in the metropolitan area—the district contributed $26 to the education of each child for the 1967–1968 school year above its Local Fund Assignment for the Minimum Foundation Program. The Foundation Program contributed $222 per pupil for a state-local total of $248. Federal funds added another $108 for a total of $356 per pupil.

Alamo Heights is the most affluent school district in San Antonio. Its six schools, housing approximately 5,000 students, are situated in a residential community quite unlike the Edgewood District. The school population is predominantly "Anglo," having only 18% Mexican–Americans and less than 1% Negroes. The assessed property value per pupil exceeds $49,000, and the median family income is $8,001. In 1967–1968 the local tax rate of $.85 per $100 of valuation yielded $333 per pupil over and above its contribution to the Foundation Program. Coupled with the $225 provided from that Program, the district was able to supply $558 per student. Supplemented by a $36 per-pupil grant from federal sources, Alamo Heights spent $594 per pupil. * * *

[S]ubstantial interdistrict disparities in school expenditures found by the District Court to prevail in San Antonio and in varying degrees throughout the State still exist. And it was these disparities, largely attributable to differences in the amounts of money collected through local property taxation, that led the District Court to conclude that Texas' dual system of public school financing violated the Equal Protection Clause. The District Court held that the Texas system discriminates on the basis of wealth in the manner in which education is provided for its people. Finding that wealth is a "suspect" classification and that education is a "fundamental" interest, the District Court held that the Texas system could be sustained only if the State could show that it was premised upon some compelling state interest. On this issue the court concluded that "[n]ot only are defendants unable to demonstrate compelling state interests ... they fail even to establish a reasonable basis for these classifications." * * *

The wealth discrimination discovered by the District Court in this case, and by several other courts that have recently struck down school-financing laws in other States, is quite unlike any of the forms of wealth discrimination heretofore reviewed by this Court. Rather than focusing on the unique features of the alleged discrimination, the courts in these cases have virtually assumed their findings of a suspect classification through a simplistic process of analysis: Since, under the traditional systems of financing public schools, some poorer people receive less expensive educations than other more affluent people, these systems discriminate on the basis of wealth. This approach largely ignores the hard threshold questions, including whether it makes a difference for purposes of consideration under the Constitution that the class of disadvantaged "poor" cannot be identified or defined in customary equal protection terms, and whether the relative—rather than absolute—nature of the asserted deprivation is of significant consequence. Before a State's laws and the justifications for the classifications they create are subjected to strict judicial scrutiny, we think these threshold considerations must be analyzed more closely than they were in the court below.

The case comes to us with no definitive description of the classifying facts or delineation of the disfavored class. Examination of the District Court's opinion and of appellees' complaint, briefs, and contentions at oral argument suggests, however, at least three ways in which the discrimination claimed here might be described. The Texas system of school financing might be regarded as discriminating (1) against "poor" persons whose incomes fall below some identifiable level of poverty or who might be characterized as functionally "indigent," or (2) against those who are relatively poorer than others, or (3) against all those who, irrespective of their personal incomes, happen to reside in relatively poorer school districts. Our task must be to ascertain whether, in fact, the Texas system has been shown to discriminate on any of these possible bases and, if so, whether the resulting classification may be regarded as suspect. * * *

Only appellees' first possible basis for describing the class disadvantaged by the Texas school-financing system—discrimination against a class of definably "poor" persons—might arguably meet the criteria established in these prior cases. Even a cursory examination, however, demonstrates that neither of the two distinguishing characteristics of wealth classifications can be found here. First, in support of their charge that the system discriminates against the "poor," appellees have made no effort to demonstrate that it operates to the peculiar disadvantage of any class fairly definable as indigent, or as composed of persons whose incomes are beneath any designated poverty level. Indeed, there is reason to believe that the poorest families are not necessarily clustered in the poorest property districts. A recent and exhaustive study of school districts in Connecticut concluded that * * * the poor were clustered around commercial and industrial areas—those same areas that provide the most attractive sources of property tax income for school districts. Whether a similar pattern would be discovered in Texas is not known, but there is no basis on the record in this case for assuming that the poorest people—defined by reference to any level of absolute impecunity—are concentrated in the poorest districts.

Second, neither appellees nor the District Court addressed the fact that, unlike each of the foregoing cases, lack of personal resources has not occasioned an absolute deprivation of the desired benefit. The argument here is not that the children in districts having relatively low assessable property values are receiving no public education; rather, it is that they are receiving a poorer quality education than that available to children in districts having more assessable wealth. Apart from the unsettled and disputed question whether the quality of education may be determined by the amount of money expended for it, a sufficient answer to appellees' argument is that, at least where wealth is involved, the Equal Protection Clause does not require absolute equality or precisely equal advantages. Nor indeed, in view of the infinite variables affecting the educational process, can any system assure equal quality of education except in the most relative sense. * * *

However described, it is clear that appellees' suit asks this Court to extend its most exacting scrutiny to review a system that allegedly discriminates against a large, diverse, and amorphous class, unified only by the common factor of residence in districts that happen to have less taxable wealth than other districts. The system of alleged discrimination and the class it defines have none of the traditional indicia of suspectness: The class is not saddled with such disabilities, or subjected to such a history of purposeful unequal treatment, or relegated to such a position of political powerlessness as to command extraordinary protection from the majoritarian political process.

We thus conclude that the Texas system does not operate to the peculiar disadvantage of any suspect class. But in recognition of the fact that this Court has never heretofore held that wealth discrimination alone provides an adequate basis for invoking strict scrutiny, appellees have not relied solely on this contention. They also assert that the State's system impermissibly interferes with the exercise of a "fundamental" right and that accordingly the prior decisions of this Court require the application of the strict standard of judicial review. It is this question—whether education is a fundamental right, in the sense that it is among the rights and liberties protected by the Constitution—which has so consumed the attention of courts and commentators in recent years.

In *Brown v. Board of Education*, 347 U.S. 483 (1954), a unanimous Court recognized that "education is perhaps the most important function of state and local governments." What was said there in the context of racial discrimination has lost none of its vitality with the passage of time:

> "Compulsory school attendance laws and the great expenditures for education both demonstrate our recognition of the importance of education to our democratic society. It is required in the performance of our most basic public responsibilities, even service in the armed forces. It is the very foundation of good citizenship. Today it is a principal instrument in awakening the child to cultural values, in preparing him for later professional training, and in helping him to adjust normally to his environment. In these days, it is doubtful that any child may reasonably be expected to succeed in life if he is denied the opportunity of an education. Such an opportunity, where the state has undertaken to provide it, is a right which must be made available to all on equal terms."

This theme, expressing an abiding respect for the vital role of education in a free society, may be found in numerous opinions of Justices of this Court writing both before and after *Brown* was decided.

Nothing this Court holds today in any way detracts from our historic dedication to public education. We are in complete agreement with the conclusion of the three-judge panel below that "the grave significance of education both to the individual and to our society" cannot be doubted. But the importance of a service performed by the State does not determine whether it must be regarded as fundamental for purposes of examination under the Equal Protection Clause. * * *

Education, of course, is not among the rights afforded explicit protection under our Federal Constitution. Nor do we find any basis for saying it is implicitly so protected. As we have said, the undisputed importance of education will not alone cause this Court to depart from the usual standard for reviewing a State's social and economic legislation. It is appellees' contention, however, that education is distinguishable from other services and benefits provided by the State because it bears a peculiarly close relationship to other rights and liberties accorded protection under the Constitution. Specifically, they insist that education is itself a fundamental personal right because it is essential to the effective exercise of First Amendment freedoms and to intelligent utilization of the right to vote. In asserting a nexus between speech and education, appellees urge that the right to speak is meaningless unless the speaker is capable of articulating his thoughts intelligently and persuasively. The "marketplace of ideas" is an empty forum for those lacking basic communicative tools. Likewise, they argue that the corollary right to receive information becomes little more than a hollow privilege when the recipient has not been taught to read, assimilate, and utilize available knowledge.

A similar line of reasoning is pursued with respect to the right to vote. Exercise of the franchise, it is contended, cannot be divorced from the educational foundation of the voter. The electoral process, if reality is to conform to the democratic ideal, depends on an informed electorate: A voter cannot cast his ballot intelligently unless his reading skills and thought processes have been adequately developed.

We need not dispute any of these propositions. The Court has long afforded zealous protection against unjustifiable governmental interference with the individual's rights to speak and to vote. Yet we have never presumed to possess either the ability or the authority to guarantee to the citizenry the most effective speech or the most informed electoral choice. That these may be desirable goals of a system of freedom of expression and of a representative form of government is not to be doubted. These are indeed goals to be pursued by a people whose thoughts and beliefs are freed from governmental interference. But they are not values to be implemented by judicial intrusion into otherwise legitimate state activities. * * *

Furthermore, the logical limitations on appellees' nexus theory are difficult to perceive. How, for instance, is education to be distinguished from the significant personal interests in the basics of decent food and shelter? Empirical examination might well buttress an assumption that the ill-fed, ill-clothed, and ill-housed are among the most ineffective participants in the political process, and that they derive the least enjoyment from the benefits of the First Amendment. * * *

* * * Every step leading to the establishment of the system Texas utilizes today—including the decisions permitting localities to tax and expend locally, and creating and continuously expanding the state aid— was implemented in an effort to extend public education and to improve its quality. Of course, every reform that benefits some more than others may be criticized for what it fails to accomplish. But we think it plain that, in substance, the thrust of the Texas system is affirmative and reformatory and, therefore, should be scrutinized under judicial principles sensitive to the nature of the State's efforts and to the rights reserved to the States under the Constitution.

It should be clear, for the reasons stated above and in accord with the prior decisions of this Court, that this is not a case in which the challenged state action must be subjected to the searching judicial scrutiny reserved for laws that create suspect classifications or impinge upon constitutionally protected rights.

We need not rest our decision, however, solely on the inappropriateness of the strict-scrutiny test. A century of Supreme Court adjudication under the Equal Protection Clause affirmatively supports the application of the traditional standard of review, which requires only that the State's system be shown to bear some rational relationship to legitimate state purposes. * * *

Thus, we stand on familiar grounds when we continue to acknowledge that the Justices of this Court lack both the expertise and the familiarity with local problems so necessary to the making of wise

decisions with respect to the raising and disposition of public revenues.
* * *

In addition to matters of fiscal policy, this case also involves the most persistent and difficult questions of educational policy, another area in which this Court's lack of specialized knowledge and experience counsels against premature interference with the informed judgments made at the state and local levels. Education, perhaps even more than welfare assistance, presents a myriad of "intractable economic, social, and even philosophical problems." The very complexity of the problems of financing and managing a statewide public school system suggests that "there will be more than one constitutionally permissible method of solving them," and that, within the limits of rationality, "the legislature's efforts to tackle the problems" should be entitled to respect. On even the most basic questions in this area the scholars and educational experts are divided. Indeed, one of the major sources of controversy concerns the extent to which there is a demonstrable correlation between educational expenditures and the quality of education—an assumed correlation underlying virtually every legal conclusion drawn by the District Court in this case. Related to the questioned relationship between cost and quality is the equally unsettled controversy as to the proper goals of a system of public education. And the question regarding the most effective relationship between state boards of education and local school boards, in terms of their respective responsibilities and degrees of control, is now undergoing searching re-examination. The ultimate wisdom as to these and related problems of education is not likely to be divined for all time even by the scholars who now so earnestly debate the issues. In such circumstances, the judiciary is well advised to refrain from imposing on the States inflexible constitutional restraints that could circumscribe or handicap the continued research and experimentation so vital to finding even partial solutions to educational problems and to keeping abreast of ever-changing conditions.
* * *

JUSTICE WHITE, with whom JUSTICE DOUGLAS and JUSTICE BRENNAN join, dissenting. * * *

I cannot disagree with the proposition that local control and local decisionmaking play an important part in our democratic system of government. Much may be left to local option, and this case would be quite different if it were true that the Texas system, while insuring minimum educational expenditures in every district through state funding, extended a meaningful option to all local districts to increase their per-pupil expenditures and so to improve their children's education to the extent that increased funding would achieve that goal. The system would then arguably provide a rational and sensible method of achieving the stated aim of preserving an area for local initiative and decision.

The difficulty with the Texas system, however, is that it provides a meaningful option to Alamo Heights and like school districts but almost none to Edgewood and those other districts with a low per-pupil real estate tax base. In these latter districts, no matter how desirous parents are of supporting their schools with greater revenues, it is impossible to do so through the use of the real estate property tax. In these districts, the Texas system utterly fails to extend a realistic choice to parents because the property tax, which is the only revenue-raising mechanism extended to school districts, is practically and legally unavailable. * * *

* * * If the State aims at maximizing local initiative and local choice, by permitting school districts to resort to the real property tax if they choose to do so, it utterly fails in achieving its purpose in districts with property tax bases so low that there is little if any opportunity for interested parents, rich or poor, to augment school district revenues. Requiring the State to establish only that unequal treatment is in furtherance of a permissible goal, without also requiring the State to show that the means chosen to effectuate that goal are rationally related to its achievement, makes equal protection analysis no more than an empty gesture. In my view, the parents and children in Edgewood, and in like districts, suffer from an invidious discrimination violative of the Equal Protection Clause. * * *

JUSTICE MARSHALL, with whom JUSTICE DOUGLAS concurs, dissenting. * * *

In my judgment, the right of every American to an equal start in life, so far as the provision of a state service as important as education is concerned, is far too vital to permit state discrimination on grounds as tenuous as those presented by this record. Nor can I accept the notion that it is sufficient to remit these appellees to the vagaries of the political process which, contrary to the majority's suggestion, has proved singularly unsuited to the task of providing a remedy for this discrimination. I, for one, am unsatisfied with the hope of an ultimate "political" solution sometime in the indefinite future while, in the meantime, countless children unjustifiably receive inferior educations "that may affect their hearts and minds in a way unlikely ever to be undone." * * *

The appellants do not deny the disparities in educational funding caused by variations in taxable district property wealth. They do contend, however, that whatever the differences in per-pupil spending among Texas districts, there are no discriminatory consequences for the children of the disadvantaged districts. They recognize that what is at stake in this case is the quality of the public education provided Texas children in the districts in which they live. But appellants reject the suggestion that the quality of education in any particular district is determined by money—beyond some minimal level of funding which they believe to be assured every Texas district by the Minimum Foundation School Program. In their view, there is simply no denial of equal educational opportunity to any Texas school children as a result of the widely varying per-pupil spending power provided districts under the current financing scheme.

In my view, though, even an unadorned restatement of this contention is sufficient to reveal its absurdity. Authorities concerned with educational quality no doubt disagree as to the significance of variations in per-pupil spending. Indeed, conflicting expert testimony was presented to the District Court in this case concerning the effect of spending variations on educational achievement. We sit, however, not to resolve disputes over educational theory but to enforce our Constitution. It is an inescapable fact that if one district has more funds available per pupil than another district, the former will have greater choice in educational planning than will the latter. In this regard, I believe the question of discrimination in educational quality must be deemed to be an objective one that looks to what the State provides its children, not to what the children are able to do with what they receive. That a child forced to attend an underfunded school with poorer physical facilities, less experienced teachers, larger classes, and a narrower range of courses than a school with substantially more funds—and thus with greater choice in educational planning—may nevertheless excel is to the credit of the child, not the State. Indeed, who can ever measure for such a child the opportunities lost and the talents wasted for want of a broader, more enriched education? Discrimination in the opportunity to learn that is afforded a child must be our standard. * * *

Despite the evident discriminatory effect of the Texas financing scheme, both the appellants and the majority raise substantial questions concerning the precise character of the disadvantaged class in this case. * * *

I believe it is sufficient that the overarching form of discrimination in this case is between the schoolchildren of Texas on the basis of the taxable property wealth of the districts in which they happen to live. * * * [T]he children of a district are excessively advantaged if that district has more taxable property per pupil than the average amount of taxable property per pupil considering the State as a whole. By contrast, the children of a district are disadvantaged if that district has less taxable property per pupil than the state average. * * *

* * * I must once more voice my disagreement with the Court's rigidified approach to equal protection analysis. The Court apparently seeks to establish today that equal protection cases fall into one of two neat categories which dictate the appropriate standard of review—strict scrutiny or mere rationality. But this Court's decisions in the field of equal protection defy such easy categorization. A principled reading of what this Court has done reveals that it has applied a spectrum of standards in reviewing discrimination allegedly violative of the Equal Protection Clause. This spectrum clearly comprehends variations in the degree of care with which the Court will scrutinize particular classifications, depending, I believe, on the constitutional and societal importance of the interest adversely affected and the recognized invidiousness of the basis upon which the particular classification is drawn. * * *

Nevertheless, the majority today attempts to force this case into the same category for purposes of equal protection analysis as decisions involving discrimination affecting commercial interests. By so doing, the majority singles this case out for analytic treatment at odds with what seems to me to be the clear trend of recent decisions in this Court, and thereby ignores the constitutional importance of the interest at stake and the invidiousness of the particular classification, factors that call for far more than the lenient scrutiny of the Texas financing scheme which the majority pursues. Yet if the discrimination inherent in the Texas scheme is scrutinized with the care demanded by the interest and classification present in this case, the unconstitutionality of that scheme is unmistakable. * * *

* * * [T]he fundamental importance of education is amply indicated by the prior decisions of this Court, by the unique status accorded public education by our society, and by the close relationship between education and some of our most basic constitutional values.

The special concern of this Court with the educational process of our country is a matter of common knowledge. Undoubtedly, this Court's most famous statement on the subject is that contained in *Brown v. Board of Education*:

> "Today, education is perhaps the most important function of state and local governments. Compulsory school attendance laws and the great expenditures for education both demonstrate our recognition of the importance of education to our democratic society. It is required in the performance of our most basic public responsibilities, even service in the armed forces. It is the very foundation of good citizenship. Today it is a principal instrument in awakening the child to cultural values, in preparing him for later professional training, and in helping him to adjust normally to his environment...."

* * *

Education directly affects the ability of a child to exercise his First Amendment rights, both as a source and as a receiver of information and ideas, whatever interests he may pursue in life. * * *

Of particular importance is the relationship between education and the political process. Education serves the essential function of instilling in our young an understanding of and appreciation for the principles and operation of our governmental processes. Education may instill the interest and provide the tools necessary for political discourse and debate. Indeed, it has frequently been suggested that education is the dominant factor affecting political consciousness and participation. * * * But of most immediate and direct concern must be the demonstrated effect of education on the exercise of the franchise by the electorate. * * *

* * * Our prior cases have dealt essentially with discrimination on the basis of personal wealth. Here, by contrast, the children of the disadvantaged Texas school districts are being discriminated against not necessarily because of their personal wealth or the wealth of their families, but because of the taxable property wealth of the residents of the district in which they happen to live. The appropriate question, then, is whether the same degree of judicial solicitude and scrutiny that has previously been afforded wealth classifications is warranted here.

As the Court points out, no previous decision has deemed the presence of just a wealth classification to be sufficient basis to call forth rigorous judicial scrutiny of allegedly discriminatory state action. That wealth classifications alone have not necessarily been considered to bear the same high degree of suspectness as have classifications based on, for instance, race or alienage may be explainable on a number of grounds. The "poor" may not be seen as politically powerless as certain discrete and insular minority groups. Personal poverty may entail much the same social stigma as historically attached to certain racial or ethnic groups. But personal poverty is not a permanent disability; its shackles may be escaped. Perhaps most importantly, though, personal wealth may not necessarily share the general irrelevance as a basis for legislative action that race or nationality is recognized to have. While the "poor" have frequently been a legally disadvantaged group, it cannot be ignored that social legislation must frequently take cognizance of the economic status of our citizens. Thus, we have generally gauged the invidiousness of wealth classifications with an awareness of the importance of the interests being affected and the relevance of personal wealth to those interests.

When evaluated with these considerations in mind, it seems to me that discrimination on the basis of group wealth in this case likewise calls for careful judicial scrutiny. First, it must be recognized that while local district wealth may serve other interests, it bears no relationship whatsoever to the interest of Texas schoolchildren in the educational opportunity afforded them by the State of Texas. Given the importance of that interest, we must be particularly sensitive to the invidious characteristics of any form of discrimination that is not clearly intended to serve it, as opposed to some other distinct state interest. Discrimination on the basis of group wealth may not, to be sure, reflect the social stigma frequently attached to personal poverty. Nevertheless, insofar as group wealth discrimination involves wealth over which the disadvantaged individual has no significant control, it represents in fact a more serious basis of discrimination than does personal wealth. For such discrimination is no reflection of the individual's characteristics or his abilities. * * *

The disability of the disadvantaged class in this case extends as well into the political processes upon which we ordinarily rely as adequate for the protection and promotion of all interests. Here legislative reallocation of the State's property wealth must be sought in the face of inevitable opposition from significantly advantaged districts that have a strong vested interest in the preservation of the status quo * * *.

Nor can we ignore the extent to which, in contrast to our prior decisions, the State is responsible for the wealth discrimination in this instance. * * * [W]e have no such simple *de facto* wealth discrimination here. The means for financing public education in Texas are selected and specified by the State. It is the State that has created local school districts, and tied educational funding to the local property tax and thereby to local district wealth. * * *

In the final analysis, then, the invidious characteristics of the group wealth classification present in this case merely serve to emphasize the need for careful judicial scrutiny of the State's justifications for the resulting interdistrict discrimination in the educational opportunity afforded to the schoolchildren of Texas. * * *

Notes and Questions

1. Jonathan Kozol, *Savage Inequalities* 213–14 (1991) reports:

It is 23 years now since Demetrio Rodriguez went to court. Things have not changed very much in the poor neighborhoods of Texas. After 23 years of court disputes and numerous state formula revisions, per-pupil spending ranges from $2,000 in the poorest districts to some $19,000 in the richest.

2. Why does the majority opinion find it of no apparent significance that in the poor Edgewood district "90% of the student population is Mexican–American and over 6% is Negro?" Is the Court engaging in quintessential "not noticing race" to the detriment of the children of color?

3. The majority mentions the correlation between education and an informed electorate, requisite for full democratic participation. Why does the Court dismiss the importance of this connection? Race and voting are treated in Chapter 8.

What is the significance of public schools for democracy as a form of government? "[L]egal education (indeed all education) shares a responsibility to consciously educate students for participation in democracy and with appreciation of democratic norms such as equity, civil rights, and mutual respect for the ideas of others." Stephanie M. Wildman, *Democratic Community and Privilege: The Mandate for Inclusive Education*, 81 Minn. L. Rev. 1429, 1431 (1997). "Youngsters learn their place in the social order and develop a system of responses to their placement that are hard to dislodge. They form 'an attitude' toward work, adults, the large public setting and what counts and what doesn't on the basis of schools." Deborah Meier, *The Power of Their Ideas: Lessons for America From a Small School in Harlem* 10 (1995). Meier muses "some children recognize the power of their ideas while others become alienated from their own genius." *Id*. at 3. She adds, "Democracy is based on our power to influence by our public statements and actions what we want the future to look like." *Id*. at 7.

4. Sharon Rush has observed: "[T]he *Brown* Court was only willing to abolish segregation in public schools because a quality education is important to every child. In addition to protecting and promoting racial equality by its holding, the *Brown* Court was also making a profound statement about the importance of a quality education to a child's welfare." Sharon Rush, *The Heart of Equal Protection: Education and Race*, 23 N.Y.U. Rev. of L. & Social Change 1, 5 (1997). If education is so important and that principle was central to the *Brown* decision, why did the *Rodriguez* Court decline to hold that education is a fundamental right?

5. The Court has consistently reiterated its *Rodriguez* holding that education is not a fundamental right. See *Plyler v. Doe*, 457 U.S. 202 (1982); *Martinez v. Bynum*, 461 U.S. 321 (1983); *Kadrmas v. Dickinson Pub. Sch.* 487 U.S. 450 (1988).

6. Consider this critique of *Rodriguez* by Richard Ford:

A similar pattern and misconception of space prevailed in *San Antonio Independent School District v. Rodriguez*, in which the Court held that a school-financing system that was based on local property taxes and produced large disparities in tax-burden/expenditure ratios among districts did not violate the Equal Protection Clause. The Court reasoned that a commitment to local control obliged it to uphold the

Texas school-financing scheme. The Court also rejected the argument that the Texas system of local funding was unconstitutionally arbitrary and asserted that "any scheme of local taxation—indeed the very existence of identifiable local governmental units—requires the establishment of jurisdictional boundaries that are inevitably arbitrary." The Court's argument here is essentially circular. The appellees began by challenging as arbitrary the use of local boundaries as a means of determining the distribution of educational funds. The Court's response asserted that arbitrariness is inevitable if local boundaries are to be respected. But this is precisely what was at issue: Are local boundaries to be used to determine school finance levels or not?

The Court's circular reasoning reflects another level of incongruence in its logic. While the Court based its refusal to overturn the Texas system on respect for local autonomy and local boundaries, at the same time it justified the arbitrariness of Texas's local boundaries on the grounds that local boundaries are irrelevant. If respect for local government were as important as the Court claimed, it would seem strange that the Court should so casually dismiss the fact that the boundaries that define these governments are arbitrary. But, if arbitrariness is inevitable, it seems illogical to accord arbitrarily defined subdivisions such respect.

The Court's decision rests on two conflicting conceptions of local government and the political space it occupies. On the one hand, the Court conceived of local space as transparent and thus viewed localities as mere subdivisions, the inconsequential and administratively necessary agents of centralized power. On the other hand, it conceived of local space as opaque and thus viewed localities as deserving of respect as autonomous political entities.

Richard Thompson Ford, *The Boundaries of Race: Political Geography in Legal Analysis*, 107 Harv. L. Rev. 1841, 1876–77 (1994).*

Should local boundaries be used to allocate funds for education? See *Serrano v. Priest*, 487 P.2d 1241 (1971) (*Serrano I*) and 557 P.2d 929 (1976) (*Serrano II*), *cert.* denied 432 U.S. 907 (1977) (reaching a result contrary to *Rodriguez*). See also Peter Enrich, *Leaving Equality Behind: New Directions in School Finance Reform*, 48 Vand. L. Rev. 101 (1995) (suggesting using adequacy arguments instead of relying on equality in education finance litigation).

7. Equal opportunity to education is a basic tenet of international human rights law. See Connie de la Vega, *The Right to Equal Education: Merely a Guiding Principle or Customary International Legal Right?*, 11 Harv. BlackLetter L.J. 37 (1994) (urging that international standards be used to convince state courts that a right to equal educational opportunity exists under state constitutions).

MISSOURI v. JENKINS

515 U.S. 70 (1995).

CHIEF JUSTICE REHNQUIST delivered the opinion of the Court.

As this school desegregation litigation enters its 18th year, we are called upon again to review the decisions of the lower courts. In this case, the State of Missouri has challenged the District Court's order of salary increases for virtually all instructional and noninstructional staff within the Kansas City, Missouri, School District (KCMSD) and the District Court's order requiring the State to continue to fund remedial "quality education" programs because student achievement levels were still "at or below national norms at many grade levels."

[The Court described the lengthy prior procedural history of the case. The District Court had ordered the school district to spend large amounts of money on capital improvements and to restructure its schools to eliminate all vestiges of prior segregation.] * * *

As part of its desegregation plan, the District Court has ordered salary assistance to the KCMSD. In 1987, the District Court initially ordered salary assistance only for teachers within the KCMSD. Since that time, however, the District Court has ordered salary assistance to all but three of the approximately 5,000 KCMSD employees. The total cost of this component of the desegregation remedy since 1987 is over $200 million.

The District Court's desegregation plan has been described as the most ambitious and expensive remedial program in the history of school desegregation. The annual cost per pupil at the KCMSD far exceeds that of the neighboring SSD's [suburban school districts] or of any school district in Missouri. Nevertheless, the KCMSD, which has pursued a "friendly adversary" relationship with the plaintiffs, has continued to propose ever more expensive programs. As a result, the desegregation costs have escalated and now are approaching an annual cost of $200 million. These massive expenditures have financed

> "high schools in which every classroom will have air conditioning, an alarm system, and 15 microcomputers; a 2,000–square-foot planetarium; green houses and vivariums; a 25–acre farm with an air-conditioned meeting room for 104 people; a Model United Nations wired for language translation; broadcast capable radio and television studios with an editing and animation lab; a temperature controlled art gallery; movie editing and screening rooms; a 3,500–square-foot dust-free diesel mechanics room; 1,875–square-foot elementary school animal rooms for use in a zoo project; swimming pools; and numerous other facilities."

Not surprisingly, the cost of this remedial plan has "far exceeded KCMSD's budget, or for that matter, its authority to tax." The State, through the operation of joint-and-several liability, has borne the brunt of these costs. The District Court candidly has acknowledged that it has "allowed the District planners to dream" and "provided the mechanism for th[ose] dreams to be realized." In short, the District Court "has gone to great lengths to provide KCMSD with facilities and opportunities not available anywhere else in the country."

With this background, we turn to the present controversy. First, the State has challenged the District Court's requirement that it fund salary increases for KCMSD instructional and noninstructional staff. The State claimed that funding for salaries was beyond the scope of the District Court's remedial authority. Second, the State has challenged the District Court's order requiring it to continue to fund the remedial quality education programs for the 1992–1993 school year. The State contended that under *Freeman v. Pitts*, 503 U.S. 467 (1992), it had achieved partial unitary status with respect to the quality education programs already in place. As a result, the State argued that the District Court should have relieved it of responsibility for funding those programs. * * *

Because of the importance of the issues, we granted *certiorari* to consider the following: (1) whether the District Court exceeded its constitutional authority when it granted salary increases to virtually all instructional and noninstructional employees of the KCMSD, and (2) whether the District Court properly relied upon the fact that student achievement test scores had failed to rise to some unspecified level when it declined to find that the State had achieved partial unitary status as to the quality education programs.

* * * We turn to the questions presented.

Almost 25 years ago, in *Swann v. Charlotte–Mecklenburg Bd. of Ed.*, 402 U.S. 1 (1971), we dealt with the authority of a district court to fashion remedies for a school district that had been segregated in law in violation of the Equal Protection Clause of the Fourteenth Amendment. Although recognizing the discretion that must necessarily adhere in a district court in fashioning a remedy, we also recognized the limits on such remedial power:

> "[E]limination of racial discrimination in public schools is a large task and one that should not be retarded by efforts to achieve broader purposes lying beyond the jurisdiction of the school authorities. One vehicle can carry only a limited amount of baggage. It would not serve the important objective of *Brown I* to seek to use school desegregation cases for purposes beyond their scope, although desegregation of schools ultimately will have impact on other forms of discrimination."

Three years later, in *Milliken I*, we held that a District Court had exceeded its authority in fashioning interdistrict relief where the surrounding school districts had not themselves been guilty of any constitutional violation. We said that a desegregation remedy "is necessarily designed, as all remedies are, to restore the victims of discriminatory conduct to the position they would have occupied in the absence of such conduct." "[W]ithout an interdistrict violation and interdistrict effect, there is no constitutional wrong calling for an interdistrict remedy." We also rejected "[t]he suggestion . . . that schools which have a majority of Negro students are not 'desegregated,' whatever the makeup of the school district's population and however neutrally the district lines have been drawn and administered." See also *Freeman*, 503 U.S. at 474 ("[A] critical beginning point is the degree of racial imbalance in the school district, that is to say a comparison of the proportion of majority to minority students in individual schools with the proportions of the races in the district as a whole").

Three years later, in *Milliken v. Bradley*, 433 U.S. 267 (1977) (*Milliken II*), we articulated a three-part framework derived from our prior cases to guide district courts in the exercise of their remedial authority.

> "In the first place, like other equitable remedies, the nature of the desegregation remedy is to be determined by the nature and scope of the constitutional violation. *Swann v. Charlotte–Mecklenburg Board of Education*, 402 U.S. at 16. The remedy must therefore be related to 'the condition alleged to offend the Constitution. . . .' *Milliken I*, 418 U.S. at 738. Second, the decree must indeed be remedial in nature, that is, it must be designed as nearly as possible 'to restore the victims of discriminatory conduct to the position they would have occupied in the absence of such conduct.' *Id.* at 746. Third, the federal courts in devising a remedy must take into account the interests of state and local authorities in managing their own affairs, consistent with the Constitution."

We added that the "principle that the nature and scope of the remedy are to be determined by the violation means simply that federal-court decrees must directly address and relate to the constitutional violation itself." In applying these principles, we have identified "student assignments, . . . 'faculty, staff, transportation, extracurricular activities and facilities,'" as the most important indicia of a racially segregated school system.

Because "federal supervision of local school systems was intended as a temporary measure to remedy past discrimination," we also have considered the showing that must be made by a school district operating under a desegregation order for complete or partial relief from that order. In *Freeman*, we stated that

> "[a]mong the factors which must inform the sound discretion of the court in ordering partial withdrawal are the following: [1] whether there has been full and satisfactory compliance with the decree in those aspects of the system where supervision is to be withdrawn; [2] whether retention of judicial control is necessary or practicable to achieve compliance with the decree in other facets of the school system; and [3] whether the school district has demonstrated, to the public and to the parents and students of the once disfavored race, its good-faith commitment to the whole of the courts' decree and to those provisions of the law and the Constitution that were the predicate for judicial intervention in the first instance."

The ultimate inquiry is "'whether the [constitutional violator] ha[s] complied in good faith with the desegregation decree since it was entered, and whether the vestiges of past discrimination ha[ve] been eliminated to the extent practicable.'"

Proper analysis of the District Court's orders challenged here, then, must rest upon their serving as proper means to the end of restoring the victims of discriminatory conduct to the position they would have occupied in the absence of that conduct and their eventual restoration of "state and local authorities to the control of a school system that is operating in compliance with the Constitution." We turn to that analysis.

The State argues that the order approving salary increases is beyond the District Court's authority because it was crafted to serve an "interdistrict goal," in spite of the fact that the constitutional violation in this case is "intradistrict" in nature. "[T]he nature of the desegregation remedy is to be determined by the nature and scope of the constitutional violation." The proper response to an intradistrict violation is an intradistrict remedy, that serves to eliminate the racial identity of the schools within the effected school district by eliminating, as far as practicable, the vestiges of *de jure* segregation in all facets of their operations.

Here, the District Court has found, and the Court of Appeals has affirmed, that this case involved no interdistrict constitutional violation that would support interdistrict relief. Thus, the proper response by the District Court should have been to eliminate to the extent practicable the vestiges of prior *de jure* segregation within the KCMSD: a system-wide reduction in student achievement and the existence of 25 racially identifiable schools with a population of over 90% black students.

The District Court and Court of Appeals, however, have felt that because the KCMSD's enrollment remained 68.3% black, a purely intradistrict remedy would be insufficient. But, as noted in *Milliken I*, we have rejected the suggestion "that schools which have a majority of Negro students are not 'desegregated' whatever the racial makeup of the school district's population and however neutrally the district lines have been drawn and administered." See *Milliken II*, 433 U.S. at 280 n.14, ("[T]he Court has consistently held that the Constitution is not violated by racial imbalance in the schools, without more").

Instead of seeking to remove the racial identity of the various schools within the KCMSD, the District Court has set out on a program to create a school district that was equal to or superior to the surrounding SSD's. Its remedy has focused on "desegregative attractiveness," coupled with "suburban comparability." Examination of the District Court's reliance on "desegregative attractiveness" and "suburban comparability" is instructive for our ultimate resolution of the salary-order issue.

The purpose of desegregative attractiveness has been not only to remedy the system-wide reduction in student achievement, but also to attract nonminority students not presently enrolled in the KCMSD. This remedy has included an elaborate program of capital improvements, course enrichment, and extracurricular enhancement not simply in the formerly identifiable black schools, but in schools throughout the district. The District Court's remedial orders have converted every senior high school, every middle school, and one-half of the elementary schools in the KCMSD into "magnet" schools. The District Court's remedial order has all but made the KCMSD itself into a magnet district.

We previously have approved of intradistrict desegregation remedies involving magnet schools. Magnet schools have the advantage of encouraging voluntary movement of students within a school district in a pattern that aids desegregation on a voluntary basis, without requiring extensive busing and redrawing of district boundary lines. As a component in an intradistrict remedy, magnet schools also are attractive because they promote desegregation while limiting the withdrawal of white student enrollment that may result from mandatory student reassignment.

The District Court's remedial plan in this case, however, is not designed solely to redistribute the students within the KCMSD in order to eliminate racially identifiable schools within the KCMSD. Instead, its purpose is to attract nonminority students from outside the KCMSD schools. But this interdistrict goal is beyond the scope of the intradistrict violation identified by the District Court. In effect, the District Court has devised a remedy to accomplish indirectly what it admittedly lacks the remedial authority to mandate directly: the interdistrict transfer of students. * * *

The District Court's pursuit of "desegregative attractiveness" cannot be reconciled with our cases placing limitations on a district court's remedial authority. It is certainly theoretically possible that the greater the expenditure per pupil within the KCMSD, the more likely it is that some unknowable number of nonminority students not presently attending schools in the KCMSD will choose to enroll in those schools. Under this reasoning, however, every increased expenditure, whether it be for teachers, noninstructional employees, books, or buildings, will make the KCMSD in some way more attractive, and thereby perhaps induce nonminority students to enroll in its schools. But this rationale is not susceptible to any objective limitation. This case provides numerous examples demonstrating the limitless authority of the District Court operating under this rationale. In short, desegregative attractiveness has been used "as the hook on which to hang numerous policy choices about improving the quality of education in general within the KCMSD." * * *

The District Court's pursuit of the goal of "desegregative attractiveness" results in so many imponderables and is so far removed from the task of eliminating the racial identifiability of the schools within the KCMSD that we believe it is beyond the admittedly broad discretion of the District Court. In this posture, we conclude that the District Court's order of salary increases, which was "grounded in remedying the vestiges of segregation by improving the desegregative attractiveness of the KCMSD," is simply too far removed from an acceptable implementation of a permissible means to remedy previous legally mandated segregation. * * *

* * * The basic task of the District Court is to decide whether the reduction in achievement by minority students attributable to prior *de jure* segregation has been remedied to the extent practicable. Under our precedents, the State and the KCMSD are "entitled to a rather precise statement of [their] obligations under a desegregation decree." Although the District Court has determined that "[s]egregation has caused a system wide reduction in achievement in the schools of the KCMSD," it never has identified the incremental effect that segregation has had on

minority student achievement or the specific goals of the quality education programs.

* * * Just as demographic changes independent of *de jure* segregation will affect the racial composition of student assignments, so too will numerous external factors beyond the control of the KCMSD and the State affect minority student achievement. So long as these external factors are not the result of segregation, they do not figure in the remedial calculus. Insistence upon academic goals unrelated to the effects of legal segregation unwarrantably postpones the day when the KCMSD will be able to operate on its own.

The District Court also should consider that many goals of its quality education plan already have been attained: The KCMSD now is equipped with "facilities and opportunities not available anywhere else in the country." KCMSD schools received an AAA rating eight years ago, and the present remedial programs have been in place for seven years. It may be that in education, just as it may be in economics, a "rising tide lifts all boats," but the remedial quality education program should be tailored to remedy the injuries suffered by the victims of prior *de jure* segregation. Minority students in kindergarten through grade 7 in the KCMSD always have attended AAA-rated schools; minority students in the KCMSD that previously attended schools rated below AAA have since received remedial education programs for a period of up to seven years.

On remand, the District Court must bear in mind that its end purpose is not only "to remedy the violation" to the extent practicable, but also "to restore state and local authorities to the control of a school system that is operating in compliance with the Constitution."

The judgment of the Court of Appeals is reversed. * * *

JUSTICE THOMAS, concurring.

It never ceases to amaze me that the courts are so willing to assume that anything that is predominantly black must be inferior. Instead of focusing on remedying the harm done to those black schoolchildren injured by segregation, the District Court here sought to convert the Kansas City, Missouri, School District (KCMSD) into a "magnet district" that would reverse the "white flight" caused by desegregation. In this respect, I join the Court's decision concerning the two remedial issues presented for review. * * *

Two threads in our jurisprudence have produced this unfortunate situation, in which a District Court has taken it upon itself to experiment with the education of the KCMSD's black youth. First, the court has read our cases to support the theory that black students suffer an unspecified psychological harm from segregation that retards their mental and educational development. This approach not only relies upon questionable social science research rather than constitutional principle, but it also rests on an assumption of black inferiority. Second, we have permitted the federal courts to exercise virtually unlimited equitable powers to remedy this alleged constitutional violation. The exercise of this authority has trampled upon principles of federalism and the separation of powers and has freed courts to pursue other agendas unrelated to the narrow purpose of precisely remedying a constitutional harm.

The mere fact that a school is black does not mean that it is the product of a constitutional violation. A "racial imbalance does not itself establish a violation of the Constitution." *United States v. Fordice*, 505 U.S. 717, 745 (1992) (Thomas, J., concurring). Instead, in order to find unconstitutional segregation, we require that plaintiffs "prove all of the essential elements of *de jure* segregation—that is, stated simply, a current condition of segregation resulting from intentional state action directed specifically to the [allegedly segregated] schools." *Keyes v. School Dist. No. 1, Denver*, 413 U.S. 189, 205–206 (1973). "[T]he differentiating factor between *de jure* segregation and so-called *de facto* segregation . . . is purpose or intent to segregate." *Id.* at 208.

In the present case, the District Court inferred a continuing constitutional violation from two primary facts: the existence of *de jure* segregation in the KCMSD prior to 1954, and the existence of *de facto* segregation today. The District Court found that in 1954, the KCMSD operated 16 segregated schools for black students and that, in 1974, 39 schools in the district were more than 90% black. Desegregation efforts reduced this figure somewhat, but the District Court stressed that 24 schools remained "racially isolated," that is, more than 90% black, in 1983–1984. For the District Court, it followed that the KCMSD had not dismantled the dual system entirely. The District Court also concluded that because of the KCMSD's failure to "become integrated on a system-wide basis," the dual system still exerted "lingering effects" upon KCMSD black students, whose "general attitude of inferiority" produced "low achievement . . . which ultimately limits employment opportunities and causes poverty." * * *

When a district court holds the State liable for discrimination almost 30 years after the last official state action, it must do more than show that there are schools with high black populations or low test scores. Here, the district judge did not make clear how the high black enrollments in certain schools were fairly traceable to the State of Missouri's actions. I do not doubt that Missouri maintained the despicable system of segregation until 1954. But I question the District Court's conclusion that because the State had enforced segregation until 1954, its actions, or lack thereof, proximately caused the "racial isolation" of the predominantly black schools in 1984. In fact, where, as here, the finding of liability comes so late in the day, I would think it incumbent upon the District Court to explain how more recent social or demographic phenomena did not cause the "vestiges." This the District Court did not do.

Without a basis in any real finding of intentional government action, the District Court's imposition of liability upon the State of Missouri improperly rests upon a theory that racial imbalances are unconstitutional. That is, the court has "indulged the presumption, often irrebuttable in practice, that a presently observed [racial] imbalance has been proximately caused by intentional state action during the prior *de jure* era." *United States v. Fordice*, 505 U.S. at 745 (Thomas, J., concurring). In effect, the court found that racial imbalances constituted an ongoing constitutional violation that continued to inflict harm on black students. This position appears to rest upon the idea that any school that is black is inferior, and that blacks cannot succeed without the benefit of the company of whites.

The District Court's willingness to adopt such stereotypes stemmed from a misreading of our earliest school desegregation case. In *Brown v. Board of Education*, 347 U.S. 483 (1954) [*Brown I*], the Court noted several psychological and sociological studies purporting to show that *de jure* segregation harmed black students by generating "a feeling of inferiority" in them. Seizing upon this passage in *Brown I*, the District Court asserted that "forced segregation ruins attitudes and is inherently unequal." The District Court suggested that this inequality continues in full force even after the end of *de jure* segregation:

> "The general attitude of inferiority among blacks produces low achievement which ultimately limits employment opportunities and causes poverty. While it may be true that poverty results in low achievement regardless of race, it is undeniable that most poverty-level families are black. The District stipulated that as of 1977 they had not eliminated all the vestiges of the prior dual system. The Court finds the inferior education indigenous of the state-compelled dual school system has lingering effects in the [KCMSD]."

Thus, the District Court seemed to believe that black students in the KCMSD would continue to receive an "inferior education" despite the end of *de jure* segregation, as long as *de facto* segregation persisted. As the District Court later concluded, compensatory educational programs were necessary "as a means of remedying many of the educational problems which go hand in hand with racially isolated minority student populations." Such assumptions and any social science research upon which they rely certainly cannot form the basis upon which we decide matters of constitutional principle.

It is clear that the District Court misunderstood the meaning of *Brown I*. *Brown I* did not say that "racially isolated" schools were inherently inferior; the harm that it identified was tied purely to *de jure* segregation, not *de facto* segregation. Indeed, *Brown I* itself did not need to rely upon any psychological or social-science research in order to announce the simple, yet fundamental truth that the Government cannot discriminate among its citizens on the basis of race. As the Court's unanimous opinion indicated: "[I]n the field of public education the doctrine of 'separate but equal' has no place. Separate educational facilities are inherently unequal." *Brown I*, 347 U.S. at 495. At the heart of this interpretation of the Equal Protection Clause lies the principle that the Government must treat citizens as individuals, and not as members of racial, ethnic or religious groups. It is for this reason that we must subject all racial classifications to the strictest of scrutiny, which (aside from two decisions rendered in the midst of wartime) has proven automatically fatal.

Segregation was not unconstitutional because it might have caused psychological feelings of inferiority. Public school systems that separated blacks and provided them with superior educational resources—making blacks "feel" superior to whites sent to lesser schools—would violate the Fourteenth Amendment, whether or not the white students felt stigmatized, just as do school systems in which the positions of the races are reversed. Psychological injury or benefit is irrelevant to the question whether state actors have engaged in intentional discrimination—the critical inquiry for ascertaining violations of the Equal Protection Clause. The judiciary is fully competent to make independent determinations concerning the existence of state action without the unnecessary and misleading assistance of the social sciences.

Regardless of the relative quality of the schools, segregation violated the Constitution because the State classified students based on their race. Of course, segregation additionally harmed black students by relegating them to schools with substandard facilities and resources. But neutral policies, such as local school assignments, do not offend the Constitution when individual private choices concerning work or residence produce schools with high black populations. The Constitution does not prevent individuals from choosing to live together, to work together, or to send their children to school together, so long as the State does not interfere with their choices on the basis of race.

Given that desegregation has not produced the predicted leaps forward in black educational achievement, there is no reason to think that black students cannot learn as well when surrounded by members of their own race as when they are in an integrated environment. Indeed, it may very well be that what has been true for historically black colleges is true for black middle and high schools. Despite their origins in "the shameful history of state-enforced segregation," these institutions can be " 'both a source of pride to blacks who have attended them and a source of hope to black families who want the benefits of . . . learning for their children.' " Because of their "distinctive histories and traditions," black schools can function as the center and symbol of black communities, and provide examples of independent black leadership, success, and achievement.

Thus, even if the District Court had been on firmer ground in identifying a link between the KCMSD's pre–1954 *de jure* segregation and the present "racial isolation" of some of the district's schools, mere *de facto* segregation (unaccompanied by discriminatory inequalities in educational resources) does not constitute a continuing harm after the end of *de jure* segregation. "Racial isolation" itself is not a harm; only state-enforced segregation is. After all, if separation itself is a harm, and if integration therefore is the only way that blacks can receive a proper education, then there must be something inferior about blacks. Under this theory, segregation injures blacks because blacks, when left on their own, cannot achieve. To my way of thinking, that conclusion is the result of a jurisprudence based upon a theory of black inferiority.

This misconception has drawn the courts away from the important goal in desegregation. The point of the Equal Protection Clause is not to enforce strict race-mixing, but to ensure that blacks and whites are treated equally by the State without regard to their skin color. The lower courts should not be swayed by the easy answers of social science, nor should they accept the findings, and the assumptions, of sociology and psychology at the price of constitutional principle. * * *

This Court should never approve a State's efforts to deny students, because of their race, an equal opportunity for an education. But the federal courts also should avoid using racial equality as a pretext for solving social problems that do not violate the Constitution. It seems apparent to me that the District Court undertook the worthy task of providing a quality education to the children of KCMSD. As far as I can tell, however, the District Court sought to bring new funds and facilities into the KCMSD by finding a constitutional violation on the part of the State where there was none. Federal courts should not lightly assume that States have caused "racial isolation" in 1984 by maintaining a segregated school system in 1954. We must forever put aside the notion that simply because a school district today is black, it must be educationally inferior.

Even if segregation were present, we must remember that a deserving end does not justify all possible means. The desire to reform a school district, or any other institution, cannot so captivate the Judiciary that it forgets its constitutionally mandated role. Usurpation of the traditionally local control over education not only takes the judiciary beyond its proper sphere, it also deprives the States and their elected officials of their constitutional powers. At some point, we must recognize that the judiciary is not omniscient, and that all problems do not require a remedy of constitutional proportions.

JUSTICE SOUTER, with whom JUSTICE STEVENS, JUSTICE GINSBURG, and JUSTICE BREYER join, dissenting.

[In the first part of his dissent Justice Souter objects to the "Court's failure to provide adequate notice of the issue to be decided (or to limit the decision to issues on which certiorari was clearly granted)." Justice Souter then described the Court's opinion in *Hills v. Gautreaux*, 425 U.S. 284 (1976), in which the Court found that the Chicago Housing Authority (CHA) and the federal Department of Housing and Urban Development (HUD) had maintained a racially segregated system of public housing. In *Gautreaux*, the Court approved a remedial order extending beyond the Chicago city limit to the metropolitan housing market.] * * *

On its face, the District Court's magnet school concept falls entirely within the scope of equitable authority recognized in *Gautreaux*. In *Gautreaux*, the fact that the CHA and HUD had the authority to operate outside the limits of the City of Chicago meant that an order to fund or build housing beyond those limits would "not necessarily entail coercion of uninvolved governmental units...." Here, by the same token, the District Court has not sought to "consolidate or in any way restructure" the SSDs, or, indeed, to subject them to any remedial obligation at all. The District Court's remedial measures go only to the operation and quality of schools within the KCMSD, and the burden of those measures accordingly falls only on the two proven constitutional wrongdoers in this case, the KCMSD and the State. And insofar as the District Court has ordered those violators to undertake measures to increase the

KCMSD's attractiveness to students from other districts and thereby to reverse the flight attributable to their prior segregative acts, its orders do not represent an abuse of discretion, but instead appear "wholly commensurate with the 'nature and extent of the constitutional violation.' " * * *

JUSTICE GINSBURG, dissenting.

I join Justice Souter's illuminating dissent and emphasize a consideration key to this controversy.

The Court stresses that the present remedial programs have been in place for seven years. But compared to more than two centuries of firmly entrenched official discrimination, the experience with the desegregation remedies ordered by the District Court has been evanescent.

In 1724, Louis XV of France issued the Code Noir, the first slave code for the Colony of Louisiana, an area that included Missouri. * * *

Before the Civil War, Missouri law prohibited the creation or maintenance of schools for educating blacks: "No person shall keep or teach any school for the instruction of negroes or mulattoes, in reading or writing, in this State." Act of February 16, 1847, § 1, 1847 Mo.Laws 103.

Beginning in 1865, Missouri passed a series of laws requiring separate public schools for blacks. See, *e.g.*, Act of March 29, 1866, § 20, 1865 Mo.Laws 177. The Missouri Constitution first permitted, then required, separate schools. See Mo. Const. 1865, Art. IX, § 2; Mo. Const. 1875, Art. XI, § 3.

After this Court announced its decision in *Brown v. Board of Education*, 347 U.S. 483 (1954), Missouri's Attorney General declared these provisions mandating segregated schools unenforceable. See *Jenkins v. Missouri*, 593 F. Supp. 1485, 1490 (W.D.Mo.1984). The statutes were repealed in 1957 and the constitutional provision was rescinded in 1976. Nonetheless, thirty years after *Brown I*, the District Court found that "the inferior education indigenous of the state-compelled dual school system has lingering effects in the Kansas City, Missouri School District." The District Court concluded that "the State ... cannot defend its failure to affirmatively act to eliminate the structure and effects of its past dual system on the basis of restrictive state law." Just ten years ago, in June 1985, the District Court issued its first remedial order. *Jenkins v. Missouri*, 639 F. Supp. 19 (W.D.Mo.1985).

Today, the Court declares illegitimate the goal of attracting nonminority students to the Kansas City, Missouri, School District and thus stops the District Court's efforts to integrate a school district that was, in the 1984/1985 school year, sorely in need and 68.3% black. See also *Jenkins v. Missouri*, 672 F. Supp. 400, 411 (W.D.Mo.1987) (reporting that physical facilities in the School District had "literally rotted"). Given the deep, inglorious history of segregation in Missouri, to curtail desegregation at this time and in this manner is an action at once too swift and too soon.

Notes and Questions

. 1.   The U.S. Supreme Court decided *Adarand v. Pena*, (see Chapter 7, § 3 *supra*), *Miller v. Johnson*, (see Chapter 8, § 3 *supra*), and *Jenkins* all in the same year—1995. What vision of race emerges from reading these three opinions, concerning affirmative action, voting, and education, together?

2.   Does the Court's distinction between interdistrict and intradistrict violations make sense in the world of residential segregation described by Armstrong, Mahoney, and Ford, *supra*?

3.   If the remedy of making an inner city school district attractive to outlying (predominantly white) areas is disallowed and residential housing patterns are well-established as segregated, can segregation by race in education ever be changed? Is it desirable that it should be? See Meredith Lee Bryant, *Combating School Resegregation Through Housing: A Need for a Reconceptualization of American Democracy and the Rights it Protects*, 13 Harv. BlackLetter L. J. 127 (1997) (urging the Court to address segregation in housing).

Consider also john powell, *Segregation and Educational Inadequacy in Twin Cities Public Schools*, 17 Hamline J. Pub. L. & Pol'y 337 (1996)* describing the Minneapolis terrain as representative of national trends. "American metropolitan areas have become increasingly characterized by a poor, minority urban core, with a white, middle-class suburban ring; and urban school populations have become majority-minority even in cities where whites constitute a majority." *Id.* at 338. Explaining that economic and racial isolation create inadequate schools, powell suggests the benefits of integration transcend test scores. "Segregation substantively denies minority students a basic education, and denies all students the integrated education to prepare them for citizenship in a multicultural society." *Id.* at 362.

According to powell, "As federal law has increasingly failed to address educational disparities substantively, litigators have turned to their state constitutions." *Id.* at 361. He explains that early state court litigation used equity theory to demand equal revenues among school districts, but that more recently the state cases address education substantively: "The adequacy theory insists that states have a constitutional duty to provide students an adequate educational opportunity. Courts, in turn, have responded to the shift from equity to adequacy theories, finding their state constitutions guarantee students adequate educational opportunities. * * * [T]he basis of the adequacy theory is quite simple." *Id.* at 361.

Virtually all states, by their constitution or statutes, guarantee some form of adequate education to their students. Where such provisions are found to be legally binding, the state has an obligation to provide, and students have an entitlement to receive, an adequate education. When the state can take reasonable measures to meet this obligation, and fails to do so, it has breached its constitutional duty. Courts are reluctant to impose definitions of adequacy, but education experts, state promulgated standards, and the opportunities provided by successful schools, can guide the court in defining adequacy. Thus, insufficient funding to support a basic education would violate the adequacy standard. Similarly, if it can be shown that segregation by race and socioeconomic status undermines students' ability to achieve an adequate education, the state violates its duty to provide an adequate education, where it allows such segregation.

Id. at 362.

4. Patricia Williams described a television report "about a particularly poignant phenomenon labeled 'theft of education.' It bristled with middle-class anxiety that poor blacks were escaping from the inner city and invading schools where they did not belong. Domestic servants had apparently been using their employers' addresses to enroll their children in schools in suburbs like Winnetka. They were lying! was the gist of this report. They were stealing tax dollars! They were raiding the Chicken Coop of Knowledge! It was sad, the images of those children at the train station, their books scattered, their way blocked as guards demanding proof of residence pressed them back onto the trains." Patricia J. Williams, *The Theft of Education,* The Nation, May 19, 1997 at 10.*

5. Is Justice Thomas correct that the District Court, in ordering remedies, assumed that a black school is inferior? Is his reading of *Brown I* correct? Is this then the legacy of *Brown I*, that it be used to argue against black inferiority and uphold a segregated school system? Why was segregation held unconstitutional under *Brown I*?

6. How does Justice Thomas' analysis that intent be required compare to Reva Siegel's in Chapter 7, § 1? What outcome might you expect from a requirement of proof of intentional discrimination on the part of school officials?

C. THE DESIRABILITY OF INTEGRATION

Given the intractability of segregation and inequality in education, scholars and educators have questioned the ideal of integration, wondering who has really benefited from the *Brown I* legacy.

DREW S. DAYS, III

Brown *Blues: Rethinking the Integrative Ideal*
34 Wm. & Mary L. Rev. 53, 53–74 (1992).*

* * * *Brown* was the culmination of a long campaign by the NAACP to overturn the "separate but equal" doctrine. It also ushered in, without doubt, more than a generation of court decisions and legislation that eradicated all vestiges of formal segregation in America. Blacks seemed to agree with the Supreme Court's pronouncement in *Brown* that children are unlikely to function effectively in America's pluralistic society unless they live and learn with people of different races from an early age.

Several developments in recent years suggest, however, that growing numbers of blacks may be turning away from this integrative ideal. Four examples of this shift are worth noting: First, black parents now express support for school board efforts to end desegregation plans that involve busing, favoring instead a return to neighborhood schools, even though this would result in increases in the number of virtually all-black schools in the inner city; second, at the urging of black parents, school boards in a number of major cities have attempted to create all-black male academies; third, black administrators, faculty, students, and alumni of historically black colleges in the South have joined state officials in opposition to court-ordered higher education desegregation plans; and fourth, black students on predominantly white college campuses have urged administrators to provide special facilities for the black students' social and cultural events. Some critics have dismissed these developments as perverse efforts by blacks to return to a "separate but equal" regime. In fact, these developments raise serious and complex questions about the future of race relations in America that deserve careful analysis, not simplistic characterization. This article is an attempt to contribute constructively to that process.

BLACKS AND NEIGHBORHOOD SCHOOLS

The school desegregation process has not been unproblematic, to say the least. Almost forty years after *Brown I*, there is still active litigation alleging constitutional violations. There is no gainsaying, however, that as a result of *Brown I* and its progeny, thousands of black, white, and Hispanic children have been able to receive integrated educations and develop both educational and social skills that will stand them in good stead in later life. At the very least, the mandatory presence of white children has saved some black and other minority children from the physically inferior facilities—and inferior resources—to which they had been assigned under segregation.

Acknowledging the important gains of desegregation, however, should not blind us to the continuing legacy of segregation within desegregated systems. In many schools, racially segregated classes make it unlikely that children of different races will have meaningful interaction during the school day. Moreover, the black community has paid, in some instances, a high price for desegregation. For example, schools that served not only as educational institutions but as community centers in predominantly black neighborhoods have been closed; the burden of busing has fallen disproportionately upon black children; black teachers and administrators have been dismissed and demoted disproportionately; and black students have encountered increased disciplinary action in recently desegregated schools.

Most important, perhaps, given the initial hope that desegregation would increase the quality of educational opportunity for black students, is the fact that the desegregation process has not necessarily brought about improvements. Indeed, in some cases, desegregation has limited opportunity. For example, where magnet schools offering innovative educational programs have replaced formerly all-black facilities, black student enrollment in the special programs has been limited by the need to maintain racial balance. This record establishes, contrary to common assumptions, that desegregation has not been an unmitigated benefit to previously segregated black students, teachers, and administrators.

One need not conclude that these negative consequences are the inevitable result of desegregation, however, and that the black community might have been better off seeking to improve educational opportunities within a segregated system. The more plausible explanation is that the same racist tendencies in America that created and maintained segregated schools did not disappear overnight once desegregation was mandated. Rather, they merely found new opportunities in this new arrangement to disadvantage the black community.

Whatever the pros and cons of desegregation, however, the reality is that demographic changes in the United States since 1954 have produced a pattern of residential segregation. This makes further progress in school desegregation in certain areas difficult to envision. Urban centers across the nation are predominantly black and Hispanic; the suburbs and rural areas are predominantly white. Even in those cities where the white population exceeds the minority, the public school populations are predominantly black and Hispanic. This latter phenomenon can be explained by the presence of childless white couples, older white couples, and white families with children enrolled in private and parochial, rather than public, schools.

Although some litigation efforts to achieve metropolitan-wide desegregation have been successful, the Supreme Court's 1974 decision in a Detroit school desegregation case [*Milliken v. Bradley*, 418 U.S. 717 (1974)] effectively limited the availability of that remedy in most urban areas. A few large cities have adopted voluntary desegregation plans involving urban and suburban communities, but their impact upon intercity segregation has been modest, largely because those participating in such programs have been disproportionately black. The result has been, therefore, a one-way rather than a two-way process, with urban blacks heading out to suburban schools but relatively few suburban whites coming into the city.

It is true that some predominantly black and Hispanic school districts have been able to obtain significant resources from their states based upon a second Supreme Court ruling involving Detroit schools. Still, the educational experiences of many black and Hispanic students in America will occur in one-race schools in poorly funded urban communities that have been abandoned by large numbers of white—as well as middle-class black—families. Even in those districts where it is still possible for blacks and whites to attend school together, some members of the black community have begun to question whether the result achieved is worth the time and expense that desegregation entails.

There is also a sense among some blacks that although some desegregation plans no longer produce meaningful numbers of whites and blacks studying together, the plans are maintained because of the mistaken belief that blacks cannot learn unless whites are sitting next to them in class. The blacks who challenge the continuation of such plans argue that a return to neighborhood school assignment makes more sense because parental and community involvement in the schools would be more likely to increase. Moreover, government resources expended on busing could be redirected to increasing the quality of materials and instruction available at those schools.

Blacks and whites who oppose efforts to roll back desegregation plans do so for a variety of reasons. First, they fear that such proposals are yet another attempt by school boards guilty of past intentional segregation to escape any further role in avoiding resegregation. Second, they suspect blacks who support such rollbacks of acting more in their own political and economic interests than in the interests of black children. What roll-back proponents seek, in fact, are more and better jobs for black administrators and teachers in exchange for reduced pressure for increasing or maintaining desegregation levels. Third, roll-back opponents fear that a return to all-black schools will result in "benign neglect" of those schools in terms of resources allocated for facilities, materials, and personnel.

This debate, although perhaps the subject of greater media focus in recent years, is not a new one. Blacks, having seen the bad, along with the good, of desegregation, have for some time questioned whether the process should be extended to the limits that the Supreme Court precedents allowed. This attitude has been particularly prevalent with respect to desegregation plans that require extensive busing. These voices of restraint often had no effective forum, however, because they were often white school boards correctly viewed as inherently untrustworthy spokespersons for this point of view. The major civil rights organizations representing the plaintiffs in desegregation cases, on the other hand, strongly reject any thought of stopping short of what the Constitution would permit.

The debate has taken on a new dimension, however, because black mayors, city council members, and school superintendents have begun to express similar concerns about the wisdom of what they see as "desegregation at any cost." Courts are justifiably perplexed over how to evaluate the views of this group, because their authority, as elected and appointed blacks, to speak for the black community certainly is equal to, if not greater than, that of plaintiffs and their lawyers in school desegregation cases. Although some might dismiss their views as perversely malevolent toward black students, the positions of black elected and appointed officials deserve an evaluation as expressions of concern about the most effective approach to educating black children under daunting circumstances.

For these and other reasons, blacks increasingly support efforts by school districts under court desegregation orders to return to neighborhood school arrangements, even though such modifications inevitably will return certain facilities in the black community to largely one-race status. Of course, one must not lose sight of the fact that constitutional rights are individual. Whether a school district has satisfied its responsibility under *Brown* and its progeny to dismantle a dual system is not subject to resolution by referendum. The difficult legal question, one with which the Supreme Court continues to grapple, is how one determines whether the dual system is still in place. Meanwhile, debates over modifications of desegregation plans continue.

Proponents of modification argue that once the school board has done all it can to eradicate the vestiges of its previously dual system, it has satisfied constitutional requirements. Continued segregation, they contend, is not the school board's fault, but rather, the consequence of residential segregation caused by private choice and market forces. Opponents of rolling back desegregation plans argue that the school board has a duty to continue making adjustments until the results of the pattern of segregation it created have been eradicated. They take the position that demographics cited by the board as an explanation of continued segregation are not adventitious, but rather, the consequence of past school board practices. Under current Supreme Court doctrines, the proponents of modification are likely to prevail because the Court consistently has refused to consider the extent to which segregative actions by governmental agencies other than school boards might justify maintenance of desegregation plans where modification would result in resegregation. Consequently, school desegregation plaintiffs are left with a wrong in search of a remedy. As they witness schools that were all-black before desegregation return to that status once the board's modifications go into effect, it must seem to them that years of effort have been in vain.

SCHOOLS FOR BLACK MALES

Media attention and public debate over the past few years have also focused on proposals to establish public schools or programs exclusively for black male students. In Milwaukee, for example, the school board planned to designate two schools as all-black or virtually all-black facilities where special attention would be given to the educational and developmental needs of black males. These "immersion schools" would offer features unavailable in other Milwaukee facilities: school days one hour longer and less rigidly structured than normal; a multicultural curriculum; and mandatory Saturday classes held in cooperation with the local branch of the Urban League. Weekend sessions would focus on nonacademic subjects such as "what it means to be a responsible male," "how to save and invest money," and "the practicalities of cooking and cleaning." The students would also be required to wear uniforms.

As a result of actual or threatened litigation, Milwaukee's proposal and similar ones in other urban school districts were modified to include female and white students who wished to participate. The legal and political debate continues, however. At the core of the controversy is the question of whether a school that admits only blacks is any more constitutional than the ones that *Brown* outlawed because they admitted only whites.

At one level, they clearly are not comparable. The system of state-imposed racial segregation in public education that *Brown* declared unconstitutional was designed to ensure that blacks remained a second-class, subjugated race in American society. Schools established for black males, in contrast, are not designed to subjugate whites or deny them first-class citizenship. Rather, they address what most would acknowledge is the critical plight of young black males in urban America. The premise of the theory is that "one of the most obvious psychosocial deficits in the environment of inner city black boys is the lack of consistent, positive, literate, black male role models."

At another level, however, our history counsels us to be wary of any racial classifications. For that reason, the Supreme Court has mandated that any use of racial criteria by government must be for the purpose of achieving a compelling interest and must be necessary to achieve that purpose. Dual school systems under segregation failed that test because maintaining segregation of the races did not constitute a compelling government interest. All-black academies, in contrast, concededly are designed to meet a compelling interest—saving black males from educational and social disaster. However, the case has not been made persuasively that this is an interest that necessarily requires the exclusion of whites.

The fact that the school district might be able to achieve its goals more efficiently employing a racially exclusive approach is no justification for such a system. Expedience cannot legitimize racial segregation. Even taking the proponents of all-black academies at their word, there is little evidence to support the view that mentoring, counseling, extended school days, small classes, and a curriculum that gives proper recognition to the contributions of blacks to American society, will improve black male educational and social functioning only in a racially segregated setting. Such an enriched educational environment is likely to produce positive effects irrespective of the racial setting.

Proponents may contend that only experimentation will determine the effectiveness of such programs. Racial classifications, however, are not proper subjects for experimentation. Of course, in many urban settings, the likelihood that whites will be enrolled in center city schools and thereby be displaced to accommodate the all-black academies, is slim. Similarly, whites likely will not apply to attend such schools. Under these circumstances, as a practical matter, school districts can set up programs for all-black student bodies without imposing any bar to whites.

Proposals to create all-black male academies have attracted adherents largely in those districts where a number of schools in the center city, as in Milwaukee, cannot feasibly be desegregated. Under these circumstances, it is hard to fault black parents and sympathetic school officials who do not believe that black male students can await the integration millennium. Consequently, they have joined forces to develop a structure that they hope will save their sons. Such approaches clearly reflect disenchantment with the *Brown* integrative ideal and may be educationally misguided. However, to the extent that whites and females may participate, the programs would not appear to violate constitutional limits.

HISTORICALLY BLACK COLLEGES AND UNIVERSITIES

NAACP lawyers prepared for their ultimate assault on the "separate but equal" doctrine in *Brown* by challenging successfully the exclusion of blacks from all-white graduate and professional schools. Indeed, it was in one of those earlier cases that the Supreme Court acknowledged the "intangible" inequality caused by segregation that would figure so prominently in its 1954 decision. The Court made clear shortly after *Brown II*, the desegregation implementation decision in 1955, that the concept of "all deliberate speed" had no application to higher education desegregation. Consequently, efforts by blacks to enroll in previously all-white colleges and universities during the late 1950s and early 1960s found support in the courts, as well as in the executive branch. In a few instances, the government even called out troops to ensure the admission of blacks.

Meanwhile, almost no attention was being given to the fact that southern and border states were continuing to operate dual systems of higher education. This arrangement was dictated, in large part, by the federal government's promotion in 1862, under the First Morrill Act, of state land grant colleges for whites and then, in 1890, under the Second Morrill Act, parallel institutions for blacks. Thereafter states systematically discriminated against black institutions in the allocation of funds for a period that extended well beyond 1954.

The historically black institutions, as a group, nevertheless, achieved remarkable success educating students from segregated and inferior secondary schools. They developed programs that provided their students with instruction and nurturing sufficient to prepare them to function effectively in society after graduation. In many cases, their graduates have pursued graduate and professional training at prestigious universities in the North and West.

Early attempts to challenge dual systems of higher education produced court orders that seemed to embrace a "freedom of choice" approach. State officials successfully argued that college students were not assigned to institutions, but rather, were free to select a college or university based upon considerations of curriculum, location, cost, and admissions requirements. Consequently, as long as states did not preclude students from attending an institution because of their race, the courts determined that dual systems did not offend the Constitution.

In the early 1970s, however, black plaintiffs initiated litigation in *Adams v. Richardson*, charging federal officials with illegally providing funds to states that maintained dual systems of higher education. As a result of this suit, the court ordered the Department of Health, Education and Welfare (HEW)—and later the Department of Education—to launch an enforcement campaign to dismantle those systems. Central to that campaign was the premise that the states in question had a constitutional duty to act affirmatively to remedy the conditions that created and perpetuated separate black and white institutions at the post-secondary level.

Unlike earlier court decisions, federal administrative directives rejected the notion that "freedom of choice" was the proper remedial model. They recognized that students' choices were shaped powerfully by the effects of longstanding mandated segregation and discriminatory resource allocations between black and white institutions. One example of this was the placement of new institutions with parallel curriculums in communities where previously only historically black public institutions existed. These parallel institutions effectively provided white students with segregated alternatives.

Black higher education groups were at odds with federal agencies and the NAACP Legal Defense Fund, which brought the *Adams* suit, regarding the wisdom of pressing desegregation of public colleges and universities. Black college presidents, faculty, and alumni were undoubtedly mindful of the burdens the black community had been forced to bear during desegregation of public, primary, and secondary systems. They feared that desegregation of higher education would result, at best, in whites displacing black teachers and administrators, as well as black students. At worst, given the relative inferiority of their institutions, desegregation might result in the closing of schools, or the absorption of traditionally black institutions into historically white schools. In either event, institutions important to the black community would lose their identity, and opportunities in higher education for black administrators, faculty, and students would be significantly diminished.

Despite similar concerns, however, proponents of desegregation in higher education believed that both litigation and administrative enforcement could increase resources available to historically black institutions. Reducing program duplication and forcing the states to locate especially attractive academic programs at traditionally black schools would also enhance the schools' long-term viability.

It is fair to say that this desegregation effort has not been very successful. Significant segregation between historically black and white institutions is still apparent. Since 1973, state officials have effectively utilized the administrative process to delay meaningful change. Ultimately, the Court of Appeals for the District of Columbia Circuit dismissed the *Adams* litigation on technical grounds. As a result, the federal government is able to decide upon the nature, scope, and timing of enforcement largely free of court oversight.

Two higher education desegregation efforts, one involving Louisiana and the other Mississippi, were severed from the *Adams* administrative process and referred by HEW to the Justice Department for judicial enforcement. Little systemic desegregation has occurred in either case over the many years they have been in court. The Supreme Court recently ruled on Mississippi's higher education desegregation case.

The case presented the Court with an opportunity to define a state's constitutional duty to dismantle formerly dual systems of higher education, a question which had produced conflicting answers in the lower federal courts. Some courts had taken the position that higher education authorities had an affirmative responsibility, similar to that imposed upon school boards in the case of primary and secondary school desegregation, to eradicate the vestiges of their dual systems. Like HEW in the *Adams* proceedings, these courts believed that this responsibility must be discharged by addressing a variety of practices that affect students' decisions about which institutions they attend, such as admissions standards, program duplication, institutional resources, and governance. Other courts rejected the notion that primary and secondary school desegregation doctrines had any applicability to higher education, principally because college and university attendance is not mandated by the state but depends upon individual student choice. Consequently, these courts—including both the trial and appellate courts in the Mississippi case—concluded that a state's constitutional responsibility ends once it has removed all racial bars to students' attending the college or university of their choice.

In *United States v. Fordice*, the Supreme Court essentially embraced the former "affirmative duty" doctrine and reversed the lower courts' determination that Mississippi had met its constitutional responsibility. The Court found that in at least four areas—admission standards, program duplication, institutional mission assignments, and continued operation of all eight public universities—the state had failed to show that the "policies and practices traceable to its prior system that continue to have segregative effects" had "sound educational justification" and could not "be practicably eliminated." The case was then returned to the lower courts for evaluation of the Mississippi system against the Court's newly articulated standard.

The Court's decision leaves in limbo, however, the future of Mississippi's three historically black institutions. Although the Court acknowledged that "closure of one or more institutions would decrease the discriminatory effects of the present system," it declined to find such action constitutionally required. However, it flatly rejected the notion that Mississippi had a constitutional duty to upgrade the historically black institutions, as such. Rather, it left to the lower courts the question of whether "an increase in funding is necessary to achieve a full dismantlement." Given this ambiguity, the possibility exists that Mississippi will be able to achieve a unitary higher education system by closing those institutions.

It is this fear that black institutions will be the inevitable casualties of higher education desegregation that has complicated the dismantling of dual systems. Take for example, the ostensibly odd alignment of parties in the Louisiana case. After concluding that Louisiana's desegregation plans were inadequate, the federal court commissioned its own strategy. That plan envisioned, among other things, merging the traditionally black Southern University Law Center into the law school of Louisiana State University (LSU), the state's traditionally white flagship institution. The two law schools are located in Baton Rouge, only a few miles apart.

That the state opposed the merger plan was not surprising. However, it was joined by the Southern University Board of Supervisors, which viewed the court's order as a step backward, rather than forward, for black education in Louisiana. The board claimed that blacks, the victims of the state's history of segregation and discrimination in higher education, were being required to bear a disproportionate burden in rectifying that situation. Specifically, they contended that the merger of Southern University's law school into LSU's would undoubtedly displace black faculty and staff and curtail opportunities for blacks seeking legal education. The court's plan did not envision LSU's absorbing Southern's faculty and staff, nor did it require LSU to expand to ensure against a net loss of law school seats for black students after the merger.

In defense of its plan, the court took the position that the merger was required by the Constitution and was in the long-term interests of the citizens of Louisiana, black and white. But for the state's creation and maintenance of segregated higher education, the court pointed out, there would not still be two public law schools in the same city, one white and the other black. The court concluded that desegregation could occur only if one of the institutions closed. Moreover, the court observed that in a fiscally strapped state, maintaining two law schools in Baton Rouge made no economic sense.

Because Southern University's law school had been denied adequate state support due to its status as a black institution, the condition of its physical plant and the quality of its educational program were inferior to those of LSU. Consequently, the court concluded that Southern's law school should be the one to close. In response to the Southern University Board of Supervisors' concerns about the desegregation process, the court suggested that the board was interested in protecting the jobs of Southern faculty and administrators, rather than in improving educational opportunities for blacks.

This controversy delineates starkly the dilemma confronting proponents of higher education desegregation. The court clearly was correct that the maintenance of dual, segregated law schools in one city makes no legal or fiscal sense and that merging the institutions would require blacks and whites to study law together rather than apart. But the black opponents of the merger also have compelling arguments. Absent the state's history of discriminatory treatment of Southern University Law Center, the school's facilities and program probably would not be so inferior to those of LSU. Had there been "tangible" equality over the years between the two institutions, white students might have opted to attend Southern rather than LSU based upon "intangible" considerations, such as the presence of particular faculty members or curricular emphases. Moreover, there is no reason why Southern's board should apologize for seeking to protect the jobs of faculty and administrators. They too are victims of the state's segregative practices.

Finally, Southern University Law Center and LSU Law School have different admissions criteria. As a consequence, Southern has been able to admit some black students who, based upon objective indicators such as GPA and LSAT scores, would not be competitive candidates at LSU. Southern nevertheless has been able to train and graduate generations of black lawyers who provide competent legal services to poor and minority communities in the state. Unless LSU ensured that black students whom Southern would have admitted would find seats at LSU, the merger would represent a net loss of educational opportunities for black students in Louisiana.

The Louisiana case eventually was dismissed in light of the Fifth Circuit's ruling in the Mississippi case. Solving the dilemma in Louisiana and in other states where higher education desegregation is underway will not be easy now that the Supreme Court has vacated that decision.

The solution cannot be achieved overnight, however. It must operate within the twin constraints of constitutional requirements and economic reality. At the same time, it must address responsibly the displacement effects of the desegregation process and the ironic price that the black community must pay for desegregation.

BLACKS ON WHITE CAMPUSES

The proposed merger of Southern University Law Center into LSU undoubtedly raised concerns in the minds of black students about the reception they were likely to receive upon enrolling at LSU. Would the administration be supportive? Would faculty members nurture their intellectual development? Would white students accept them as colleagues and peers? These are questions that many black applicants likely ask when considering a predominantly white college or university anywhere in the country. The alternative for these students is to attend one of a group of public and private historically black institutions with proven track records of providing students with excellent preparation for postgraduate employment or education.

These are not idle concerns. Blacks have always encountered difficulties in predominantly white institutions, as accounts of the "best and brightest" of pioneer black students at prestigious northern institutions attest. They had to overcome both social isolation and a lack of even-handed administrative and faculty support in order to excel. Even though black enrollment in these institutions has increased over the years, the schools generally have not succeeded in retaining and graduating blacks in proportions equal to those for white students.

Explanations for this disparity range from the failure of such institutions to provide adequate financial support to the academic deficiencies of the students. One of the major variables, however, appears to be black students' perception of the degree to which the institutions will offer supportive environments within which they can grow academically and socially. This concern is not unique to blacks, of course. Students from other racial or ethnic minorities, public school graduates, southerners going north, and northerners going south, want to know whether they are going to feel at home in the institutions they are considering. The stakes just seem to be higher for blacks.

The number of black students attending traditionally white institutions surpassed token levels in the late 1960s, largely through a combination of more aggressive recruiting of candidates clearly meeting normal admissions criteria, as well as the establishment of affirmative action programs for qualified but less competitive students. This development was not an unalloyed advance, however, in efforts to increase educational opportunities for black students and reduce racial segregation in higher education. Black students on predominantly white campuses began to express concern about the difficulties of their adjustment, unlike their predecessors, who usually opted to suffer in silence. With varying degrees of insistence, black students asked that college administrators provide facilities specifically to allow them opportunities for greater social interaction than the institutions were affording them.

These requests prompted a range of reactions from blacks and whites, many quite hostile to the idea of black "Afro–Am houses" on campus. Some blacks and whites who had fought to end segregation viewed such developments as striking at the very heart of what *Brown* symbolized. Some administrators wondered why blacks had sought admission to their predominantly white institutions in order to segregate themselves from their white classmates. Whites who would have preferred not to see any black students on campus pointed cynically to the demands for special "houses" to justify their support for social groups, such as Greek societies or eating clubs, that excluded blacks.

These considerations, even the cynical claims of racists, highlight the difficulty of defending university support for racially exclusive social clubs and living arrangements that bar nonblacks irrespective of their backgrounds or interests. Blacks-only clubs or dormitories are bad social policy in that they reinforce racial stereotypes and most likely are unconstitutional. Ensuring that a hostile campus environment does not force black students to terminate their studies prior to graduation may well qualify as a compelling interest that justifies the establishment of such clubs and dormitories. As in the case of all-black academies, however, it is not clear that racially exclusive facilities within the university are necessary to achieving that goal.

In contrast, administrative support for non-exclusive facilities to benefit black students is sound social policy. They may provide black students with a "safe harbor" from stormy weather, particularly for those who are encountering a predominantly white environment for the first time. When special facilities for blacks first appeared on campuses, some sympathetic observers thought, perhaps naively, that blacks would have decreasing need for such refuges as time passed. However, the ongoing debate over affirmative action issues—from the legality of minority scholarships to whether blacks are stigmatized by such efforts—and the growth of hate speech on college campuses have surely caused black students on predominantly white campuses to feel more embattled than ever before. Black students should not have to subject themselves to undue psychological and emotional stress in order to enjoy the prestige, rich resources, outstanding academic programs, and influential alumni networks that top predominantly white institutions provide their students. "Afro–Am houses," properly handled, need not be the source of racial divisiveness. Rather, they can serve to promote the healthy integration of black students and black culture into the life of predominantly white institutions. Such integration does not demand black assimilation but instead reflects respect for cultural diversity.

CONCLUSION

The *Brown* decision and the integrative ideal that it embraced have opened opportunities for black advancement that were previously unthinkable. *Brown* also transformed our entire society in other ways too numerous to recite under these circumstances. As the four developments discussed above suggest, however, the increasing racial polarization and residential segregation in America have put the integrative ideal to the test. Concerns about the burdens blacks have had to carry in the desegregation process, the degree to which integration requires assimilation and rejection of black values and institutions, and the seemingly intractable problems presented for largely black school systems in educational *extremis*, are causing growing numbers of blacks to rethink *Brown*'s integrative ideal. These are admittedly difficult questions. Nevertheless, they deserve to be asked—indeed, they cannot be avoided. They must also be answered, although the answers may be uncomfortable and disappointing, at least in the short run, for those of us who hoped that we would see a different America almost forty years after *Brown*.

Notes and Questions

1.   The views of the well-known debaters Derrick Bell and Nathaniel Jones, concerning whether integration really benefits the black community, appear in Derrick A. Bell, *Serving Two Masters: Integration Ideals and Client Interests in School Desegregation Litigation*, 85 Yale L.J. 470 (1976) (questioning desegregation as the best solution for increasing educational excellence) and Nathaniel R. Jones, *Letter*, 86 Yale L.J. 378 (1976) (defending the NAACP's focus on desegregation).

2.   On the viability of black male schools, Robin Barnes comments:

> * * * Conditions of extreme racial inequity in public schools were documented in a study of Negro education as early as 1916. Separate and horridly unequal conditions characterized public education earlier this century, when black children were taught in one room shacks in conditions that were "miserable beyond all description." Despite the work of civil rights lawyers, the quality of educational opportunities for black students relative to whites has improved only moderately. Black children have less access than white students to the limited number of quality public education programs, and they are significantly overrepresented in the worst.

> Urban schools generally face incredible, if not intractable, problems, as "dropout rates hover well above 50 percent, truancy is the norm rather than the exception, violence is common, students struggle for basic literacy . . . and the physical condition of the schools is a disgrace." Black males appear to be faring most poorly under current conditions.

> To address this problem, several states have introduced schools specifically for black males. One such program in Michigan was immediately challenged as unconstitutional in a lawsuit sponsored by the American Civil Liberties Union (ACLU) and the National Organization for Women (NOW). In Detroit, a proposal to convert three elementary schools into all-black male academies received widespread parental support to wage a " 'united front against a problem that many believe threatens the black family, black culture and black male-female relationships.' " The schools were to focus exclusively on black males at risk to help address complex inner-city problems. One writer discussed the crisis in Detroit as follows:

>> In one particular elementary school located in Detroit's inner-city, a majority of the students are born to unwed mothers, walk by crack houses on their way to school, and are habitually recruited by neighborhood gangs. The school's janitor was killed in a "drive-by"

shooting, a preschool child was shot in the head, and a third grade boy had his mother pull him out of school because he owed a drug dealer $300 and he felt that he needed the "cover." To say that this environment has created unique and vexing problems for the Detroit Board of Education would be a gross understatement.

After examining the crisis situation facing urban males in Detroit, a task force proposed the creation of a school to serve up to 250 boys. The academic program included a curriculum "superior to those in the coeducational public schools 'in areas such as linguistics, social sciences, math and technology. Other planned programs would focus on career development, test-taking skills, and social responsibility.' " The school's ultimate purpose was called into question when opponents pointed out that some of the males admitted were not "at risk" as defined in the mission statement. Another legitimate objection centered on the fact that there were no programs to address the fate of girls who were at risk in the Detroit school system. Ultimately, the school board's plan was struck down because of its gender exclusivity. A settlement eventually allowed the schools to open on a coeducational basis. However, as one mother of three boys argued, " '[W]e have zillions of schools that are mixed, so what's wrong with one that is not?' " Perhaps a more effective response to the claim that at-risk females were entitled to comparable services would have been to reorganize the plan to allow simultaneous operation of all-female academies. Because no student would have been involuntarily placed in the schools, for which "applications overwhelmingly outpaced available admission slots," the final result deprived the public schools of the opportunity to operate in the tradition of some of America's most highly regarded private schools.

One writer suggests that the legal standard applied to all-female schools demonstrates that sex-based regulations might withstand heightened scrutiny when "there exists a strong correlation to remedial aspects of past discrimination and if the effect of the classification would not be likely to further outdated stereotypes and generalizations regarding women and men." However, even though U.S. District Court Judge George Woods acknowledged the "status of urban [black] males as an 'endangered species,' " he found it insufficient to justify a gender-based school. The ultimate effect of the equal protection challenge was to force at-risk black males and their educators to reconcile themselves to an attenuated version of the original plan. This case forcefully presents the issue that lies at the heart of the school choice movement:

> Who shall be empowered to make decisions affecting the education of Detroit's children? Will it be the leadership of the ACLU and NOW, most of whom reside outside the city of Detroit? Or will Detroit's parents and voters retain the right to expend their tax money as they see fit on behalf of their children's education? Hence the role of constitutional adjudication will continue to be of particular interest to those who seek to improve the quality of educational opportunities for African–American children.

Black Americans acknowledge that court-ordered integration and other desegregation policies have failed to integrate most urban schools or significantly increase access to quality educational programs. The public school integration that was the promise of *Brown v. Board of*

Education has been, in other words, "sparingly delivered." Where integration has occurred, it has often resulted in heightened racial tension. The cogent lesson of the failed effort to integrate the nation's schools is that racial desegregation must be completely voluntary in order to realize long-term success. This lesson may explain why school choice advocates have not identified racial integration as a primary objective of their initiatives. One writer notes that "America's long and divisive experiment with school integration may be quietly coming to an end." Instead, advocates of choice favor race-neutral policies that focus on the quality of education; choice and quality are thought to be linked.

Efforts to create and sustain high levels of academic achievement by African–American children require new strategies. Educational alternatives that foster advanced social development, academic excellence, and collaborative governance that is free of bias and racially disparate outcomes are arguably the key to effective education for black America's children. Policymakers historically have been unwilling or unable to establish programs that effectively lead to racial integration and educational equality. The school choice movement is a response to this problem. It is aimed at offering parents the widest range of educational choices and lessens the mounting frustration of legislators who must answer to diverse constituencies. Advocates embrace school choice as a means of increasing competition among schools and providing needed alternatives to deteriorating, badly managed, and obsolete educational programs.

Among the newer school choice initiatives, charter schools represent a unique opportunity for reforming public education. Charter schools are publicly funded, secular institutions that operate under a license granted to applicants who present a proposal that becomes the basis for the contract with state authorities. They operate outside the local school board, free from many of the policies and regulations that govern other public schools. The higher degree of autonomy in running the school is given in exchange for a greater degree of accountability.

Robin D. Barnes, *Black America and School Choice: Charting a New Course*, 106 Yale L.J. 2375, 2375–80 (1997).* Will the charter school alternative, publicly funded but operating outside of school boards, increase democratic practice? Will it improve black schools? Hurt them?

3. For an argument that immersion schools for African–American youth are necessary, see Kevin Brown, *Do African–Americans Need Immersion Schools?: The Paradoxes Created by Legal Conceptualization of Race and Public Education*, 78 Iowa L. Rev. 813 (1993).

D. THE PERMISSIBILITY OF USING RACE IN AN EDUCATIONAL SETTING: REVISITING AFFIRMATIVE ACTION AND RACIAL CLASSIFICATION

Recollection of the pre-*Brown* detrimental categorization and segregation of students has fueled a desire to move away from racial classification in educational settings. So it is not surprising that the affirmative action debate first reached the Supreme Court in cases regarding admis-

* Reprinted by permission of The Yale Law Journal Company and Fred B. Rothman & Company.

sion to education, first with *DeFunis v. Odegaard*, 416 U.S. 312 (1974), a challenge to the law school admissions at the University of Washington. The U.S. Supreme Court declined to hear the issue until Allan Bakke's case challenged the admission process at the University of California at Davis Medical School. The *Bakke* case is described within the next case concerning Cheryl Hopwood's challenge to the use of race in admissions at the University of Texas Law School, the same institution that had contested the admission of Heman Marion Sweatt.

The District Court described Cheryl Hopwood's application as indicating that

> [s]he received an associate's degree in accounting from Montgomery County Community College in May 1984 and a bachelor's degree in accounting from California State University in Sacramento in 1988. The application further indicates she is a certified public accountant in California, she worked twenty to thirty hours a week while obtaining her undergraduate degree, and she was active in Big Brothers and Big Sisters in California. Hopwood submitted an additional letter to the law school dated January 22, 1992, requesting permission to attend law school on a limited basis the first year, if accepted, because of the needs of her child, who had been born with cerebral palsy. Hopwood's application file contains no letters of recommendation. Additionally, her responses to the questions are brief and do not elaborate on her background and skill. She provided no personal statement with the application.

Hopwood v. Texas, 861 F. Supp. 551, 564 (W.D. Texas 1994)

As you read this passage describing Ms. Hopwood's application, do you find yourself wondering about her grades and Law School Admission Test scores? Should such numbers be determinative of admission? Can they provide help in the admission process? What other criteria might be useful in reviewing applicant files? The circuit court decision explains the University of Texas admission procedure in effect at the time of Ms. Hopwood's application.

HOPWOOD v. STATE OF TEXAS

78 F.3d 932 (5th Cir.1996), *cert. denied*, 518 U.S. 1033 (1996).

JERRY E. SMITH, CIRCUIT JUDGE:

With the best of intentions, in order to increase the enrollment of certain favored classes of minority students, the University of Texas School of Law (the law school) discriminates in favor of those applicants by giving substantial racial preferences in its admissions program. The beneficiaries of this system are blacks and Mexican Americans, to the detriment of whites and non-preferred minorities. The question we decide today * * * is whether the Fourteenth Amendment permits the school to discriminate in this way.

We hold that it does not. The law school has presented no compelling justification, under the Fourteenth Amendment or Supreme Court precedent, that allows it to continue to elevate some races over others, even for the wholesome purpose of correcting perceived racial imbalance in the student body. "Racial preferences appear to 'even the score' . . . only if one embraces the proposition that our society is appropriately viewed as divided into races, making it right that an injustice rendered in the past to a black man should be compensated for by discriminating against a white." *City of Richmond v. J.A. Croson Co.*, 488 U.S. 469, 528 (1989) (Scalia, J., concurring in the judgment).

* * * [W]e reverse and remand, concluding that the law school may not use race as a factor in law school admissions. * * *

I.

A.

The University of Texas School of Law is one of the nation's leading law schools, consistently ranking in the top twenty. Accordingly, admission to the law school is fiercely competitive, with over 4,000 applicants a year competing to be among the approximately 900 offered admission to achieve an entering class of about 500 students. Many of these applicants have some of the highest grades and test scores in the country.

Numbers are therefore paramount for admission. In the early 1990s, the law school largely based its initial admissions decisions upon an applicant's so-called Texas Index (TI) number, a composite of undergraduate grade point average (GPA) and Law School [Admissions] Test (LSAT) score. The law school used this number as a matter of administrative convenience in order to rank candidates and to predict, roughly, one's probability of success in law school. Moreover, the law school relied heavily upon such numbers to estimate the number of offers of admission it needed to make in order to fill its first-year class.

Of course, the law school did not rely upon numbers alone. The admissions office necessarily exercised judgment in interpreting the individual scores of applicants, taking into consideration factors such as the strength of a student's undergraduate education, the difficulty of his major, and significant trends in his own grades and the undergraduate grades at his respective college (such as grade inflation). Admissions personnel also considered what qualities each applicant might bring to his law school class. Thus, the law school could consider an applicant's background, life experiences, and outlook. Not surprisingly, these hard-to-quantify factors were especially significant for marginal candidates.

Because of the large number of applicants and potential admissions factors, the TI's administrative usefulness was its ability to sort candidates. For the class entering in 1992—the admissions group at issue in this case—the law school placed the typical applicant in one of three categories according to his TI scores: "presumptive admit," "presumptive deny," or a middle "discretionary zone." An applicant's TI category determined how extensive a review his application would receive. * * *

Applications in the middle range were subjected to the most extensive scrutiny. For all applicants other than blacks and Mexican Americans, the files were bundled into stacks of thirty, which were given to admissions subcommittees consisting of three members of the full admissions committee. Each subcommittee member, in reviewing the thirty files, could cast a number of votes—typically from nine to eleven—among the thirty files. Subject to the chairman's veto, if a candidate received two or three votes, he received an offer; if he garnered one vote, he was put on the waiting list; those with no votes were denied admission.

Blacks and Mexican Americans were treated differently from other candidates, however. First, compared to whites and non-preferred minorities[4], the TI ranges that were used to place them into the three admissions categories were lowered to allow the law school to consider and admit more of them. In March 1992, for example, the presumptive TI admission score for resident whites and non-preferred minorities was 199. Mexican Americans and blacks needed a TI of only 189 to be presumptively admitted. The difference in the presumptive-deny ranges is even more striking. The presumptive denial score for "nonminorities" was 192; the same score for blacks and Mexican Americans was 179.

While these cold numbers may speak little to those unfamiliar with the pool of applicants, the results demonstrate that the difference in the two ranges was dramatic. According to the law school, 1992 resident white applicants had a mean GPA of 3.53 and an LSAT of 164. Mexican Americans scored 3.27 and 158; blacks scored 3.25 and 157. The category of "other minority" achieved a 3.56 and 160.

These disparate standards greatly affected a candidate's chance of admission. For example, by March 1992, because the presumptive denial score for whites was a TI of 192 or lower, and the presumptive admit TI for minorities was 189 or higher, a minority candidate with a TI of 189 or above almost certainly would be admitted, even though his score was considerably below[8] the level at which a white candidate almost certainly would be rejected. Out of the pool of resident applicants who fell within

---

4. As blacks and Mexican Americans were the only two minority categories granted preferential treatment in admissions, it is inaccurate to say that the law school conducted separate admissions programs for "minorities" and "non-minorities." While the law school application form segregated racial and ethnic classification into seven categories—"Black/African American," "Native American," "Asian American," "Mexican American," "Other Hispanic" (meaning non-Mexican descent), "White," and "Other (describe)"—only American blacks and Mexican Americans received the benefit of the separate admissions track.

Thus, for example, the law school decided that a black citizen of Nigeria would not get preferential treatment, but a resident alien from Mexico, who resided in Texas, would. Likewise, Asians, American Indians, Americans from El Salvador and Cuba, and many others did not receive a preference.

It is important to keep the composition of these categories in mind. For the sake of simplicity and readability, however, we

sometimes will refer to two broad categories: "whites" (meaning Texas residents who were whites and non-preferred minorities) and "minorities" (meaning Mexican Americans and black Americans).

8. To illustrate this difference, we consider the four plaintiffs in this case—Cheryl Hopwood, Douglas Carvell, Kenneth Elliott, and David Rogers. For a student similarly situated to Hopwood, with a GPA of 3.8, to avoid presumptive denial as a white, *i.e.*, to obtain a TI of 193 or above, her LSAT had to be at least a 155, a score in approximately the top 32% of test-takers. If she were black (thus, needing a 180 TI), she would have had to score a 142 on the LSAT, ranking her only in the top 80%. Likewise, a student similar to Carvell, who had a 3.28 GPA, would have needed a "white" LSAT of 160 (top 17%) and a "black" 147 (top 63%). A student like Rodgers with a 3.13 would have needed either a 162 (top 12%) as a white or 149 as a black (top 56%). Finally, a student like Elliott with a 2.98 GPA would have needed a 163 (top 10%) or 150 (top 53%), respectively.

this range (189–192 inclusive), 100% of blacks and 90% of Mexican Americans, but only 6% of whites, were offered admission.

The stated purpose of this lowering of standards was to meet an "aspiration" of admitting a class consisting of 10% Mexican Americans and 5% blacks, proportions roughly comparable to the percentages of those races graduating from Texas colleges. The law school found meeting these "goals" difficult, however, because of uncertain acceptance rates and the variable quality of the applicant pool. In 1992, for example, the entering class contained 41 blacks and 55 Mexican Americans, respectively 8% and 10.7% of the class.

In addition to maintaining separate presumptive TI levels for minorities and whites, the law school ran a segregated application evaluation process. Upon receiving an application form, the school color-coded it according to race. If a candidate failed to designate his race, he was presumed to be in a nonpreferential category. Thus, race was always an overt part of the review of any applicant's file.

The law school reviewed minority candidates within the applicable discretionary range differently from whites. Instead of being evaluated and compared by one of the various discretionary zone subcommittees, black and Mexican American applicants' files were reviewed by a minority subcommittee of three, which would meet and discuss every minority candidate. Thus, each of these candidates' files could get extensive review and discussion. And while the minority subcommittee reported summaries of files to the admissions committee as a whole, the minority subcommittee's decisions were "virtually final."

Finally, the law school maintained segregated waiting lists, dividing applicants by race and residence. Thus, even many of those minority applicants who were not admitted could be set aside in "minority-only" waiting lists. Such separate lists apparently helped the law school maintain a pool of potentially acceptable, but marginal, minority candidates.

B.

Cheryl Hopwood, Douglas Carvell, Kenneth Elliott, and David Rogers (the "plaintiffs") applied for admission to the 1992 entering law school class. All four were white residents of Texas and were rejected.

The plaintiffs were considered as discretionary zone candidates. Hopwood, with a GPA of 3.8 and an LSAT of 39 (equivalent to a three-digit LSAT of 160), had a TI of 199, a score barely within the presumptive-admit category for resident whites, which was 199 and up. She was dropped into the discretionary zone for resident whites (193 to 198), however, because Johanson [Professor Johanson, chair of the law school admissions committee] decided her educational background overstated the strength of her GPA. Carvell, Elliott, and Rogers had TI's of 197, at the top end of that discretionary zone. Their applications were reviewed by admissions subcommittees, and each received one or no vote.

II.

The plaintiffs sued primarily under the Equal Protection Clause of the Fourteenth Amendment; they also claimed derivative statutory violations of 42 U.S.C.A. §§ 1981 and 1983 and of Title VI of the Civil Rights Act of 1964, 42 U.S.C.A. § 2000d (Title VI). The plaintiffs' central claim is that they were subjected to unconstitutional racial discrimination by the law school's evaluation of their admissions applications. * * *

III.

The central purpose of the Equal Protection Clause "is to prevent the States from purposefully discriminating between individuals on the basis of race." *Shaw v. Reno*, 509 U.S. 630 (1993) (citing *Washington v. Davis*, 426 U.S. 229, 239). It seeks ultimately to render the issue of race irrelevant in governmental decisionmaking. See *Palmore v. Sidoti*, 466 U.S. 429, 432 (1984) ("A core purpose of the Fourteenth Amendment was to do away with all governmentally imposed discrimination.").

Accordingly, discrimination based upon race is highly suspect. "Distinctions between citizens solely because of their ancestry are by their very nature odious to a free people whose institutions are founded upon the doctrine of equality," and "racial discriminations are in most circumstances irrelevant and therefore prohibited...." *Hirabayashi v. United States*, 320 U.S. 81, 100 (1943). Hence, "[p]referring members of any one group for no reason other than race or ethnic origin is discrimination for its own sake. This the Constitution forbids." *Regents of Univ. of Cal. v. Bakke*, 438 U.S. 265, 307 (1978) (opinion of Powell, J.); see also *Loving v. Virginia*, 388 U.S. 1, 11 (1967); *Brown v. Board of Educ.*, 347 U.S. 483, 493–94 (1954). These equal protection maxims apply to all races. *Adarand Constructors v. Pena*, 515 U.S. 200 (1995).

In order to preserve these principles, the Supreme Court recently has required that any governmental action that expressly distinguishes between persons on the basis of race be held to the most exacting scrutiny. See, *e.g.*, *Adarand; Loving*, 388 U.S. at 11. Furthermore, there is now absolutely no doubt that courts are to employ strict scrutiny when evaluating all racial classifications, including those characterized by their proponents as "benign" or "remedial."

Strict scrutiny is necessary because the mere labeling of a classification by the government as "benign" or "remedial" is meaningless. * * *

Under the strict scrutiny analysis, we ask two questions: (1) Does the racial classification serve a compelling government interest, and (2) Is it narrowly tailored to the achievement of that goal? As the *Adarand* Court emphasized, strict scrutiny ensures that "courts will consistently give racial classifications ... detailed examination both as to ends and as to means."

Finally, when evaluating the proffered governmental interest for the specific racial classification, to decide whether the program in question narrowly achieves that interest, we must recognize that "the rights created by ... the Fourteenth Amendment are, by its terms, guaranteed to the individual. The rights established are personal rights." *Shelley v. Kraemer*, 334 U.S. 1, 22 (1948). Thus, the Court consistently has rejected arguments conferring benefits on a person based solely upon his membership in a specific class of persons.

With these general principles of equal protection in mind, we turn to the specific issue of whether the law school's consideration of race as a factor in admissions violates the Equal Protection Clause. The district court found both a compelling remedial and a non-remedial justification for the practice.

First, the court approved of the non-remedial goal of having a diverse student body, reasoning that "obtaining the educational benefits that flow from a racially and ethnically diverse student body remains a sufficiently compelling interest to support the use of racial classifications." Second, the court determined that the use of racial classifications could be justified as a remedy for the "present effects at the law school of past discrimination in both the University of Texas system and the Texas educational system as a whole."

A.

1.

Justice Powell's separate opinion in *Bakke* provided the original impetus for recognizing diversity as a compelling state interest in higher education. In that case, Allan Bakke, a white male, was denied admission to the Medical School of the University of California at Davis, a state-run institution. Claiming that the State had discriminated against him impermissibly because it operated two separate admissions programs for the medical school, he brought suit under the state constitution, Title VI, and the Equal Protection Clause.

Under the medical school's admissions system, the white applicants, who comprised the majority of the prospective students, applied through the general admissions program. A special admissions program was reserved for members of "minority groups" or groups designated as "economically and/or educationally disadvantaged." The university set aside sixteen of the one hundred positions in the entering class for candidates from the special program.

The California Supreme Court struck down the program on equal protection grounds, enjoined any consideration of race in the admissions process, and ordered that Bakke be admitted. The United States Supreme Court affirmed in part and reversed in part in an opinion announced by Justice Powell. 438 U.S. at 271–72 (opinion of Powell, J.). The Court reached no consensus on a justification for its result, however. Six Justices filed opinions, none of which garnered more than four votes (including the writer's). The two major opinions—one four-Justice opinion by Justices Brennan, White, Marshall, and Blackmun and one by Justice Stevens in which Chief Justice Burger and Justices Stewart and Rehnquist joined—reflected completely contrary views of the law.

While Justice Powell found the program unconstitutional under the Equal Protection Clause and affirmed Bakke's admission, Justice Stevens declined to reach the constitutional issue and upheld Bakke's admission under Title VI. Justice Powell also concluded that the California Supreme Court's proscription of the consideration of race in admissions could not be sustained. This became the judgment of the Court, as the four-Justice opinion by Justice Brennan opined that racial classifications designed to serve remedial purposes should receive only intermediate scrutiny. These Justices would have upheld the admissions program under this intermediate scrutiny, as it served the substantial and benign purpose of remedying past societal discrimination.

Hence, Justice Powell's opinion has appeared to represent the "swing vote," and though, in significant part, it was joined by no other Justice, it has played a prominent role in subsequent debates concerning the impact of *Bakke*. In the present case, the significance of Justice Powell's opinion is its discussion of compelling state interests under the Equal Protection Clause. Specifically, after Justice Powell recognized that the proper level of review for racial classifications is strict scrutiny, he rejected and accepted respective justifications for the school's program as "substantial enough to support the use of a suspect classification."

Notably, because the first step in reviewing an affirmative action program is a determination of the state's interests at stake, it often is the determinative step. Justice Powell outlined the four state interests proffered by the *Bakke* defendants:

> The special admissions program purports to serve the purposes of: (i) "reducing the historic deficit of traditionally disfavored minorities in medical schools and in the medical profession,"; (ii) countering the effects of societal discrimination; (iii) increasing the number of physicians who will practice in communities currently underserved; and (iv) obtaining the educational benefits that flow from an ethnically diverse student body.

Justice Powell reasoned that the second and third justifications—remedying societal discrimination and providing role models—were never appropriate. He determined that any remedial justification was limited to eliminating "identified discrimination" with "disabling effects." He specifically emphasized that a particularized finding of a constitutional or statutory violation must be present before a remedy is justified. He determined not only that such findings were not present in *Bakke*, but that the medical school was not even in a position to make such findings.

Justice Powell further reasoned that diversity is a sufficient justification for limited racial classification. "[The attainment of a diverse student body] clearly is a constitutionally permissible goal for an institution of higher education." He argued that diversity of minorities' viewpoints furthered "academic freedom," an interest under the Constitution. While acknowledging that "academic freedom" does not appear as a constitutional right, he argued that it had "long ... been viewed as a special concern of the First Amendment."

Justice Powell presented this "special concern" as in tension with the Fourteenth Amendment. "Thus, in arguing that its universities must be accorded the right to select those students who will contribute the most to the 'robust exchange of ideas,' petitioner invokes a countervailing constitutional interest, that of the First Amendment." The Justice then concluded that

[a]n otherwise qualified medical student with a particular background—whether it be ethnic, geographic, culturally advantaged or disadvantaged—may bring to a professional school of medicine experiences, outlooks, and ideas that enrich the training of its student body and better equip its graduates to render with understanding their vital service to humanity.

Justice Powell therefore approved of a consideration of ethnicity as "one element in a range of factors a university properly may consider in attaining the goal of a heterogeneous student body." The next step for Justice Powell was to decide whether the medical school's program was necessary to further the goal of diversity. He said it was not. As the program made race the only determining factor for a certain number of the open spots that had been set aside, it did not further full diversity but only a conception of that term limited to race.

Justice Powell speculated that a program in which "race or ethnic background may be deemed a 'plus' in a particular applicant's file, yet does not insulate the individual from comparison with all the other candidates for the available seats," might pass muster. The Justice did not define what he meant by a "plus," but he did write that a "plus" program would be one in which an

applicant who loses out to another candidate receiving a "plus" on the basis of ethnic background will not have been foreclosed from all consideration for that seat simply because he was not the right color or had the wrong surname. It would only mean that his combined qualifications, which may have included similar nonobjective factors, did not outweigh those of another applicant. His qualifications would have been weighted fairly and competitively, and he would have no basis to complain of unequal treatment under the Fourteenth Amendment.

Under this conception of the Fourteenth Amendment, a program that considered a host of factors that include race would be constitutional, even if an applicant's race "tipped the scales" among qualified applicants. What a school could not do is to refuse to compare applicants of different races or establish a strict quota on the basis of race. In sum, Justice Powell found the school's program to be an unconstitutional "quota" system, but he intimated that the Constitution would allow schools to continue to use race in a wide-ranging manner.

2.

Here, the plaintiffs argue that diversity is not a compelling governmental interest under superseding Supreme Court precedent. Instead, they believe that the Court finally has recognized that only the remedial use of race is compelling. In the alternative, the plaintiffs assert that the district court misapplied Justice Powell's *Bakke* standard, as the law school program here uses race as a strong determinant rather than a mere "plus" factor and, in any case, the preference is not narrowly applied. The law school maintains, on the other hand, that Justice Powell's formulation in *Bakke* is law and must be followed—at least in the context of higher education.

We agree with the plaintiffs that any consideration of race or ethnicity by the law school for the purpose of achieving a diverse student body is not a compelling interest under the Fourteenth Amendment. Justice Powell's argument in *Bakke* garnered only his own vote and has never represented the view of a majority of the Court in *Bakke* or any other case. Moreover, subsequent Supreme Court decisions regarding education state that non-remedial state interests will never justify racial classifications. Finally, the classification of persons on the basis of race for the purpose of diversity frustrates, rather than facilitates, the goals of equal protection.

Justice Powell's view in *Bakke* is not binding precedent on this issue. While he announced the judgment, no other Justice joined in that part of the opinion discussing the diversity rationale. In *Bakke*, the word "diversity" is mentioned nowhere except in Justice Powell's single-Justice opinion. In fact, the four-Justice opinion, which would have upheld the special admissions program under intermediate scrutiny, implicitly rejected Justice Powell's position. [See 438 U.S. at 326 n.1 (Brennan, White, Marshall, and Blackmun JJ., concurring in the judgment in part and dissenting) ("We also agree with Mr. Justice Powell that a plan like the 'Harvard' plan . . . is constitutional under our approach, at least so long as the use of race to achieve an integrated student body is necessitated by the lingering effects of past discrimination.").] Justice Stevens declined to discuss the constitutional issue.
* * *

Indeed, recent Supreme Court precedent shows that the diversity interest will not satisfy strict scrutiny. Foremost, the Court appears to have decided that there is essentially only one compelling state interest to justify racial classifications: remedying past wrongs. In *Croson*, 488 U.S. at 493 (plurality opinion), the Court flatly stated that "[u]nless [racial classifications] are strictly reserved for remedial settings, they may in fact promote notions of racial inferiority and lead to a politics of racial hostility." * * *

In short, there has been no indication from the Supreme Court, other than Justice Powell's lonely opinion in *Bakke*, that the state's interest in diversity constitutes a compelling justification for governmental race-based discrimination. Subsequent Supreme Court caselaw strongly suggests, in fact, that it is not.

Within the general principles of the Fourteenth Amendment, the use of race in admissions for diversity in higher education contradicts, rather than furthers, the aims of equal protection. Diversity fosters, rather than minimizes, the use of race. It treats minorities as a group, rather than as individuals. It may further remedial purposes but, just as likely, may promote improper racial stereotypes, thus fueling racial hostility.

The use of race, in and of itself, to choose students simply achieves a student body that looks different. Such a criterion is no more rational on its own terms than would be choices based upon the physical size or blood type of applicants. Thus, the Supreme Court has long held that governmental actors cannot justify their decisions solely because of race.

See, *e.g.*, *Croson*, 488 U.S. at 496 (plurality opinion); *Bakke*, 438 U.S. at 307 (opinion of Powell, J.).

Accordingly, we see the caselaw as sufficiently established that the use of ethnic diversity simply to achieve racial heterogeneity, even as part of the consideration of a number of factors, is unconstitutional. Were we to decide otherwise, we would contravene precedent that we are not authorized to challenge.

While the use of race *per se* is proscribed, state-supported schools may reasonably consider a host of factors—some of which may have some correlation with race—in making admissions decisions. The federal courts have no warrant to intrude on those executive and legislative judgments unless the distinctions intrude on specific provisions of federal law or the Constitution.

A university may properly favor one applicant over another because of his ability to play the cello, make a downfield tackle, or understand chaos theory. An admissions process may also consider an applicant's home state or relationship to school alumni. Law schools specifically may look at things such as unusual or substantial extracurricular activities in college, which may be atypical factors affecting undergraduate grades. Schools may even consider factors such as whether an applicant's parents attended college or the applicant's economic and social background.[28]

For this reason, race often is said to be justified in the diversity context, not on its own terms, but as a proxy for other characteristics that institutions of higher education value but that do not raise similar constitutional concerns.[29] Unfortunately, this approach simply replicates the very harm that the Fourteenth Amendment was designed to eliminate.

The assumption is that a certain individual possesses characteristics by virtue of being a member of a certain racial group. This assumption, however, does not withstand scrutiny. "[T]he use of a racial characteristic to establish a presumption that the individual also possesses other, and socially relevant, characteristics, exemplifies, encourages, and legitimizes the mode of thought and behavior that underlies most prejudice and bigotry in modern America." Richard A. Posner, *The DeFunis Case and the Constitutionality of Preferential Treatment of Racial Minorities*, 1974 Sup. Ct. Rev. 12 (1974).

To believe that a person's race controls his point of view is to stereotype him. The Supreme Court, however, "has remarked a number of times, in slightly different contexts, that it is incorrect and legally inappropriate to impute to women and minorities 'a different attitude about such issues as the federal budget, school prayer, voting, and foreign relations.' " Michael S. Paulsen, *Reverse Discrimination and Law*

---

28. The law school's admissions program makes no distinction among black and Mexican American applicants in an effort to determine which of them, for example, may have been culturally or educationally disadvantaged.

29. For example, Justice Powell apparently felt that persons with different ethnic backgrounds would bring diverse "experiences, outlooks, and ideas" to the medical school. *Bakke*, 438 U.S. at 314.

School Faculty Hiring: The Undiscovered Opinion, 71 Tex. L. Rev. 993, 1000 (1993) (quoting *Roberts v. United States Jaycees*, 468 U.S. 609, 627–28 (1984)).* "Social scientists may debate how peoples' thoughts and behavior reflect their background, but the Constitution provides that the government may not allocate benefits or burdens among individuals based on the assumption that race or ethnicity determines how they act or think." *Metro Broadcasting*, 497 U.S. at 602 (O'Connor, J., dissenting).

Instead, individuals, with their own conceptions of life, further diversity of viewpoint. Plaintiff Hopwood is a fair example of an applicant with a unique background. She is the now-thirty-two-year-old wife of a member of the Armed Forces stationed in San Antonio and, more significantly, is raising a severely handicapped child. Her circumstance would bring a different perspective to the law school. The school might consider this an advantage to her in the application process, or it could decide that her family situation would be too much of a burden on her academic performance.

We do not opine on which way the law school should weigh Hopwood's qualifications; we only observe that "diversity" can take many forms. To foster such diversity, state universities and law schools and other governmental entities must scrutinize applicants individually, rather than resorting to the dangerous proxy of race.

The Court also has recognized that government's use of racial classifications serves to stigmatize. See, *e.g.*, *Brown v. Board of Educ.* (observing that classification on the basis of race "generates a feeling of inferiority"). While one might argue that the stigmatization resulting from so-called "benign" racial classifications is not as harmful as that arising from invidious ones, the current Court has now retreated from the idea that so-called benign and invidious classifications may be distinguished. As the plurality in *Croson* warned, "[c]lassifications based on race carry the danger of stigmatic harm. Unless they are reserved for remedial settings, they may in fact promote notions of racial inferiority and lead to the politics of racial hostility."

Finally, the use of race to achieve diversity undercuts the ultimate goal of the Fourteenth Amendment: the end of racially-motivated state action. Justice Powell's conception of race as a "plus" factor would allow race always to be a potential factor in admissions decisionmaking. While Justice Blackmun recognized the tension inherent in using race-conscious remedies to achieve a race-neutral society, he nevertheless accepted it as necessary. Several Justices who, unlike Justices Powell and Blackmun, are still on the Court, have now renounced toleration of this tension, however.

In sum, the use of race to achieve a diverse student body, whether as a proxy for permissible characteristics, simply cannot be a state interest compelling enough to meet the steep standard of strict scrutiny. These latter factors may, in fact, turn out to be substantially correlated with race, but the key is that race itself not be taken into account. Thus, that

---

* [Eds. But see Richard Delgado, *Five Months Later (The Trial Court Opinion)*, 71 Tex. L. Rev. 1011 (1993) (replying to Paulsen).]

portion of the district court's opinion upholding the diversity rationale is reversibly flawed.

B.

We now turn to the district court's determination that "the remedial purpose of the law school's affirmative action program is a compelling government objective." The plaintiffs argue that the court erred by finding that the law school could employ racial criteria to remedy the present effects of past discrimination in Texas's primary and secondary schools. The plaintiffs contend that the proper unit for analysis is the law school, and the state has shown no recognizable present effects of the law school's past discrimination. The law school, in response, notes Texas's well-documented history of discrimination in education and argues that its effects continue today at the law school, both in the level of educational attainment of the average minority applicant and in the school's reputation.

In contrast to its approach to the diversity rationale, a majority of the Supreme Court has held that a state actor may racially classify where it has a "strong basis in the evidence for its conclusion that remedial action was necessary." *Croson*, 488 U.S. at 500 (quoting *Wygant*, 476 U.S. at 277 (plurality opinion)). Generally, "[i]n order to justify an affirmative action program, the State must show there are 'present effects of past discrimination.' "

Because a state does not have a compelling state interest in remedying the present effects of past societal discrimination, however, we must examine the district court's legal determination that the relevant governmental entity is the system of education within the state as a whole. Moreover, we also must review the court's identification of what types of present effects of past discrimination, if proven, would be sufficient under strict scrutiny review. Finally, where the state actor puts forth a remedial justification for its racial classifications, the district court must make a "factual determination" as to whether remedial action is necessary. *Wygant*, 476 U.S. at 277–78. We review such factual rulings for clear error.

1.

The Supreme Court has "insisted upon some showing of prior discrimination by the governmental unit involved before allowing limited use of racial classifications in order to remedy such discrimination." *Wygant*, 476 U.S. at 274 (plurality opinion of Powell, J.). In *Wygant*, the Court analyzed a collective bargaining agreement between a school board and a teacher's union that allowed the board to give minorities preferential treatment in the event of layoffs. A plurality rejected the theory that such a program was justified because it provided minority role models. Such a claim was based upon remedying "societal discrimination," a rationale the Court consistently has rejected as a basis for affirmative action. Accordingly, the state's use of remedial racial classifications is limited to the harm caused by a specific state actor. * * *

The *Croson* Court further discussed how to identify the relevant past discriminator. Writing for the Court, Justice O'Connor struck down a minority business set-aside program implemented by the City of Richmond and justified on remedial grounds. While the district court opined that sufficient evidence had been found by the city to believe that such a program was necessary to remedy the present effects of past discrimination in the construction industry, the Court held:

> Like the "role model" theory employed in *Wygant*, a generalized assertion that there had been past discrimination in an entire industry provides no guidance for a legislative body to determine the precise scope of the injury it seeks to remedy. It "has no logical stopping point." "Relief" for such an ill-defined wrong could extend until the percentage of public contracts awarded to [minority businesses] in Richmond mirrored the percentage of minorities in the population as a whole.

The Court refused to accept indicia of past discrimination in anything but "the Richmond construction industry."

In addition, in a passage of particular significance to the instant case, the Court analogized the employment contractor situation to that of higher education and noted that "[l]ike claims that discrimination in primary and secondary schooling justifies a rigid racial preference in medical school admissions, an amorphous claim that there has been past discrimination in a particular industry cannot justify the use of an unyielding racial quota." Such claims were based upon "sheer speculation" about how many minorities would be in the contracting business absent past discrimination.

Applying the teachings of *Croson* and *Wygant*, we conclude that the district court erred in expanding the remedial justification to reach all public education within the State of Texas. The Supreme Court repeatedly has warned that the use of racial remedies must be carefully limited, and a remedy reaching all education within a state addresses a putative injury that is vague and amorphous. It has "no logical stopping point."

The district court's holding employs no viable limiting principle. If a state can "remedy" the present effects of past discrimination in its primary and secondary schools, it also would be allowed to award broad-based preferences in hiring, government contracts, licensing, and any other state activity that in some way is affected by the educational attainment of the applicants. This very argument was made in *Croson* and rejected:

> The "evidence" relied upon by the dissent, history of school desegregation in Richmond and numerous congressional reports, does little to define the scope of any injury to minority contractors in Richmond or the necessary remedy. The factors relied upon by the dissent could justify a preference of any size or duration.

The defendants' argument here is equally expansive.

Strict scrutiny is meant to ensure that the purpose of a racial preference is remedial. Yet when one state actor begins to justify racial preferences based upon the actions of other state agencies, the remedial actor's competence to determine the existence and scope of the harm—

and the appropriate reach of the remedy—is called into question. The school desegregation cases, for example, concentrate on school districts—singular government units—and the use of interdistrict remedies is strictly limited. See *Missouri v. Jenkins*; *Milliken v. Bradley*, 418 U.S. 717, 745 (1974) ("[W]ithout an interdistrict violation and interdistrict effect, there is no constitutional wrong calling for an interdistrict remedy."). Thus, one justification for limiting the remedial powers of a state actor is that the specific agency involved is best able to measure the harm of its past discrimination.

Here, however, the law school has no comparative advantage in measuring the present effects of discrimination in primary and secondary schools in Texas. Such a task becomes even more improbable where, as here, benefits are conferred on students who attended out-of-state or private schools for such education. Such boundless "remedies" raise a constitutional concern beyond mere competence. In this situation, an inference is raised that the program was the result of racial social engineering rather a desire to implement a remedy.

No one disputes that in the past, Texas state actors have discriminated against some minorities in public schools. In this sense, some lingering effects of such discrimination is not "societal," if that term is meant to exclude all state action. But the very program at issue here shows how remedying such past wrongs may be expanded beyond any reasonable limits.

Even if, *arguendo*, the state is the proper government unit to scrutinize, the law school's admissions program would not withstand our review. For the admissions scheme to pass constitutional muster, the State of Texas, through its legislature, would have to find that past segregation has present effects; it would have to determine the magnitude of those present effects; and it would need to limit carefully the "plus" given to applicants to remedy that harm. A broad program that sweeps in all minorities with a remedy that is in no way related to past harms cannot survive constitutional scrutiny. Obviously, none of those predicates has been satisfied here.

We further reject the proposition that the University of Texas System, rather than the law school, is the appropriate governmental unit for measuring a constitutional remedy. The law school operates as a functionally separate unit within the system. As with all law schools, it maintains its own separate admissions program. The law school hires faculty members that meet the unique requirements of a law school and has its own deans for administrative purposes. Thus, for much the same reason that we rejected the educational system as the proper measure—generally ensuring that the legally-imposed racially discriminatory program is remedial—we conclude that the University of Texas System is itself too expansive an entity to scrutinize for past discrimination.

In sum, for purposes of determining whether the law school's admissions system properly can act as a remedy for the present effects of past discrimination, we must identify the law school as the relevant alleged past discriminator. The fact that the law school ultimately may be subject to the directives of others, such as the board of regents, the university president, or the legislature, does not change the fact that the relevant putative discriminator in this case is still the law school. In order for any of these entities to direct a racial preference program at the law school, it must be because of past wrongs at that school.

2.

Next, the relevant governmental discriminator must prove that there are present effects of past discrimination of the type that justify the racial classifications at issue:

> To have a present effect of past discrimination sufficient to justify the program, the party seeking to implement the program must, at a minimum, prove that the effect it proffers is caused by the past discrimination and that the effect is of sufficient magnitude to justify the program.

Podberesky v. Kirwan, 38 F.3d 147, 153 (4th Cir.1994), *cert.* denied, 514 U.S. 1128 (1995). Moreover, as part of showing that the alleged present effects of past discrimination in fact justify the racial preference program at issue, the law school must show that it adopted the program specifically to remedy the identified present effects of the past discrimination.

Here, according to the district court: "The evidence presented at trial indicates those effects include the law school's lingering reputation in the minority community, particularly with prospective students, as a 'white' school; an underrepresentation of minorities in the student body; and some perception that the law school is a hostile environment for minorities." Plaintiffs now argue that these three alleged effects are at most examples of societal discrimination, which the Supreme Court has found not to be a valid remedial basis. "The effects must themselves be examined to see whether they were caused by the past discrimination and whether they are of a type that justifies the program."

As a legal matter, the district court erred in concluding that the first and third effects it identified—bad reputation and hostile environment—were sufficient to sustain the use of race in the admissions process. The Fourth Circuit examined similar arguments in *Podberesky*, a recent case that struck down the use of race-based scholarships. The university in that case sought, in part, to justify a separate scholarship program based solely upon race because of the university's "poor reputation within the African–American community" and because "the atmosphere on campus [was] perceived as being hostile to African–American students."

The *Podberesky* court rejected the notion that either of these rationales could support the single-race scholarship program. The court reasoned that any poor reputation by the school "is tied solely to knowledge of the University's discrimination before it admitted African–American students." The court found that "mere knowledge of historical fact is not the kind of present effect that can justify a race-exclusive remedy. If it were otherwise, as long as there are people who have access to history books, there will be programs such as this."

We concur in the Fourth Circuit's observation that knowledge of historical fact simply cannot justify current racial classifications. Even if, as the defendants argue, the law school may have a bad reputation in the minority community, "[t]he case against race-based preferences does not rest on the sterile assumption that American society is untouched or unaffected by the tragic oppression of its past." "Rather, it is the very enormity of that tragedy that lends resolve to the desire to never repeat it, and find a legal order in which distinctions based on race shall have no place." Moreover, we note that the law school's argument is even weaker than that of the university in *Podberesky*, as there is no dispute that the law school has never had an admissions policy that excluded Mexican Americans on the basis of race.

The *Podberesky* court rejected the hostile-environment claims by observing that the "effects"—that is, racial tensions—were the result of present societal discrimination. There was simply no showing of action by the university that contributed to any racial tension. Similarly, one cannot conclude that the law school's past discrimination has created any current hostile environment for minorities. While the school once did practice *de jure* discrimination in denying admission to blacks, the Court in *Sweatt v. Painter* struck down the law school's program. Any other discrimination by the law school ended in the 1960s.

By the late 1960s, the school had implemented its first program designed to recruit minorities, and it now engages in an extensive minority recruiting program that includes a significant amount of scholarship money. The vast majority of the faculty, staff, and students at the law school had absolutely nothing to do with any discrimination that the law school practiced in the past.

In such a case, one cannot conclude that a hostile environment is the present effect of past discrimination. Any racial tension at the law school is most certainly the result of present societal discrimination and, if anything, is contributed to, rather than alleviated by, the overt and prevalent consideration of race in admissions.

Even if the law school's alleged current lingering reputation in the minority community—and the perception that the school is a hostile environment for minorities—were considered to be the present effects of past discrimination, rather than the result of societal discrimination, they could not constitute compelling state interests justifying the use of racial classifications in admissions. A bad reputation within the minority community is alleviated not by the consideration of race in admissions, but by school action designed directly to enhance its reputation in that community.

Minority students who are aided by the law school's racial preferences have already made the decision to apply, despite the reputation. And, while prior knowledge that they will get a "plus" might make potential minorities more likely to apply, such an inducement does nothing, *per se*, to change any hostile environment. As we have noted, racial preferences, if anything, can compound the problem of a hostile environment.

The law school wisely concentrates only on the second effect the district court identified: underrepresentation of minorities because of past discrimination. The law school argues that we should consider the prior discrimination by the State of Texas and its educational system rather than of the law school. The school contends that this prior discrimination by the state had a direct effect on the educational attainment of the pool of minority applicants and that the discriminatory admissions program was implemented partially to discharge the school's duty of eliminating the vestiges of past segregation.

As we have noted, the district court accepted the law school's argument that past discrimination on the part of the Texas school system (including primary and secondary schools), reaching back perhaps as far as the education of the parents of today's students, justifies the current use of racial classifications. No one disputes that Texas has a history of racial discrimination in education. We have already discussed, however, that the *Croson* Court unequivocally restricted the proper scope of the remedial interest to the state actor that had previously discriminated. The district court squarely found that "[i]n recent history, there is no evidence of overt officially sanctioned discrimination at the University of Texas." As a result, past discrimination in education, other than at the law school, cannot justify the present consideration of race in law school admissions.

The law school now attempts to circumvent this result by claiming that its racial preference program is really a "State of Texas" plan rather than a law school program. Under the law school's reading of the facts, its program was the direct result of the state's negotiations with what was then the United States Department of Health, Education and Welfare's Office for Civil Rights (OCR). To bring the Texas public higher education system into compliance with Title VI, the state adopted the so-called "Texas Plan."

In light of our preceding discussion on the relevant governmental unit, this argument is inapposite. Even if the law school were specifically ordered to adopt a racial preference program, its implementation at the law school would have to meet the requirements of strict scrutiny.

Moreover, these alleged actions in the 1980s are largely irrelevant for purposes of this appeal. There is no indication that the Texas Plan imposed a direct obligation upon the law school. To the contrary, the law school's admissions program was self-initiated. Moreover, the current admissions program was formulated primarily in the 1990s, and the district court did not hold otherwise. * * *

The district court also sought to find a remedial justification for the use of race and, at the same time, attempted to distinguish *Croson* using *United States v. Fordice*, 505 U.S. 717 (1992). The court held that the law school had a compelling interest to "desegregate" the school through affirmative action.

The reliance upon *Fordice* is misplaced, however. The district court held that *Fordice*'s mandate to schools "to eliminate every vestige of racial segregation and discrimination" made *Croson* inapplicable, and reasoned that this mandate includes the effects of such prior practices or policies.

Fordice does not overrule *Croson*. The central holding of *Fordice* is that a state or one of its subdivisions must act to repudiate the continuing "policies or practices" of discrimination. In other words, a state has an affirmative duty to remove policies, tied to the past, by which it continues to discriminate. The *Fordice* Court did not address, in any way, a state actor's duty to counter the present effects of past discrimination that it did not cause.

In sum, the law school has failed to show a compelling state interest in remedying the present effects of past discrimination sufficient to maintain the use of race in its admissions system. Accordingly, it is unnecessary for us to examine the district court's determination that the law school's admissions program was not narrowly tailored to meet the compelling interests that the district court erroneously perceived. * * *

VI.

In summary, we hold that the University of Texas School of Law may not use race as a factor in deciding which applicants to admit in order to achieve a diverse student body, to combat the perceived effects of a hostile environment at the law school, to alleviate the law school's poor reputation in the minority community, or to eliminate any present effects of past discrimination by actors other than the law school. Because the law school has proffered these justifications for its use of race in admissions, the plaintiffs have satisfied their burden of showing that they were scrutinized under an unconstitutional admissions system. The plaintiffs are entitled to reapply under an admissions system that invokes none of these serious constitutional infirmities. We also direct the district court to reconsider the question of damages, and we conclude that the proposed intervenors properly were denied intervention.

Notes and Questions

1. What "qualifies" someone to attend law school? Do grades and test scores tell the most important information about you? Is *Hopwood* persuasive or perverse in reasoning that the University of Texas Law School discriminates in favor of minority students?

The Circuit Court decision asserts that after *Sweatt v. Painter*, any "discrimination by the law school ended in the 1960s." Yet the district court

> held that the State of Texas's "institutions of higher education are inextricably linked to the primary and secondary schools in the system." Accordingly, the court found that Texas's long history of racially discriminatory practices in its primary and secondary schools in its not-too-distant past had the following present effects at UT law: "the law school's lingering reputation in the minority community, particularly with prospective students, as a 'white' school; an underrepresentation of minorities in the student body; and some perception that the law school is a hostile environment for minorities."

78 F.3d at 938–939.

Why didn't this "long history of racially discriminatory practices" play a greater role in the Court's decision?

Responding to *Bakke* at the state court level, the lone dissenter, Justice Mathew O. Tobriner, wrote, "There is, indeed, a very sad irony to the fact that the first admission program aimed at promoting diversity ever to be struck down under the Fourteenth Amendment is the program most consonant with the underlying purposes of the Fourteenth Amendment." *Bakke v. Regents of Univ. of Cal.*, 18 Cal.3d 34, 66, 132 Cal.Rptr. 680, 702, 553 P.2d 1152, 1174 (1976). To what purposes was Justice Tobriner referring? Can a remedy for societal racial discrimination be constructed without taking note of race? Would it be desirable to do so, if it were possible? See Michael A. Olivas, *The Education of Latino Lawyers: An Essay on Crop Cultivation*, 14 Chicano–Latino L. Rev. 117 (1994) (urging an increase in Latino/a law professors as "the single most important key to any hope for increasing Latino educational access" and noting the significant role of "Anglo racism" in preventing that access.).

2. The use of "standardized" testing remains for many the touchstone of merit in measuring intelligence. But the relationship of this merit to race is rarely discussed:

> In 1923 Carl Campbell Brigham, in *A Study of American Intelligence*, declared that Nordic white intelligence in the United States was being diluted because of the introduction of inferior Negro stock. A few years later, Brigham designed an intelligence test that professed to measure native ability but incorporated a bias that would award high scores for knowledge of facts associated with Anglo culture. Shortly thereafter, Brigham became director of testing for the College Board; his test became known as the Scholastic Aptitude Test and is still given to millions of high school students today. The organization has not repudiated his teaching; as Stanley Fish points out, the library at the College Board's Educational Testing Service still bears Brigham's name.

Jean Stefancic & Richard Delgado, *No Mercy: How Conservative Think Tanks and Foundations Changed America's Social Agenda* 35 (1996).

See Dorothy A. Brown, *The LSAT Sweepstakes*, 2 J. Gender Race & Just. 59 (1998) (providing a fictionalized account of a world in which Blacks outscored Whites on the LSAT); Daria Roithmayr, *Deconstructing the Distinction Between Bias and Merit*, 85 Calif. L. Rev. 1449 (1997) (reviewing history of law school admissions standards and the manipulation of standards to exclude immigrants and people of color); Leslie G. Espinoza, *The LSAT: Narratives and Bias*, 1 Am. U. J. Gender & L. 121 (1993) (exploring how the narrative content of standardized tests contributes to bias).

3. Classroom Exercise: The acrobat, boxer, and pole vaulter

Consider this typical Scholastic Aptitude Test analogy question:

> acrobat is to trapeze AS ...

(You have five choices, but you eliminate some and narrow it down to two possible answers):

> acrobat: trapeze as (1) boxer: ring or (2) vaulter: pole. Which do you choose?

How many think the answer is boxer? How many would answer vaulter? (Note the sample may be skewed because most law students have taken the review courses that teach how to answer these questions.) Shouldn't a good lawyer be able to construct an argument justifying either answer?

The Educational Testing Service considers vaulter to be the correct answer. Conversation with James Bell, Director of College Counseling, Lick–Wilmerding High School, San Francisco, March, 1999. It is a narrow response, lacking imagination, which does not see past the hands. Boxer is the gestalt answer which looks at the big picture. The trapeze is the domain of the acrobat, as the ring is the domain of the boxer. Don't we want legal thinkers to both see the forest and the trees? The legal profession needs both kinds of minds, yet the test is eliminating one kind from this opportunity.

See also Robert Hayman, *The Smart Culture: Society, Intelligence, and Law* (1998).

4.   In the *Bakke* case, Justice Powell reasoned that students from different racial and ethnic backgrounds would bring diverse "experiences, outlooks, and ideas" to the medical school? Is he correct? Is this argument for noticing race persuasive?

5.   Abram Chayes, *The Role of the Judge in Public Law Litigation*, 89 Harv. L. Rev. 1281 (1976) argued that the traditional adversarial model of private disputes between a plaintiff and defendant inadequately addressed the public impact of disputes that in reality involved multiple parties. In *Hopwood*, the Thurgood Marshall Legal Society and the Black Pre–Law Society sought to intervene in the litigation. The district court denial was affirmed on appeal. *Hopwood v. Texas*, 21 F.3d 603, 605 (5th Cir.1994). In *Bakke,* the NAACP petitioned the California Supreme Court to remand the case for a new trial that included the real parties in interest. That petition was denied. Emma Coleman Jones, *Litigation Without Representation: The Need for Intervention to Affirm Affirmative Action*, 14 Harv. C.R.-C.L. L. Rev. 31, 33 n.9 (1979).

Are the interests of the intervenors, who represented minority groups, the same as those of the parties? Can white plaintiffs claiming discrimination in admissions and the schools seeking to defend its admissions policies adequately address the policy issues of concern to people of color? What conclusion can be reached about a legal system in which the interests of these racial groups were not represented in these decisions?

6.   The *Hopwood* decision begins with a quote from Justice Scalia which casts racial disputes in terms of black and white. Ironically many University of Texas law school applicants might come from the San Antonio school district that was primarily Mexican American and received inferior funding in the *Rodriguez* case. Why are these Mexican Americans rendered invisible in the construction of race with which the court begins?

The thrust of the quote is about not noticing race. What does this failure to notice race mean for these Mexican Americans?

7.   The trial court held "that the State of Texas's 'institutions of higher education are inextricably linked to the primary and secondary schools in the system.' " Accordingly, the court found that Texas's long history of racially discriminatory practices in its primary and secondary schools in its not-too-distant past had the following present effects at the law school: "the law school's lingering reputation in the minority community, particularly with prospective students, as a 'white' school; an underrepresentation of minorities in the student body; and some perception that the law school is a hostile environment for minorities." Why does the Fifth Circuit opinion discount these lower court findings?

In response to the *Hopwood* decision the Texas legislature passed a bill mandating universities to admit applicants who graduated in the top 10 percent of their high school class. Eric Garcia, *New Law Could Boost Minority Enrollment*, Dallas Morning News, May 25, 1997, at 1A. Why would tying admissions to top performance in high school boost minority admissions? Is this plan a good solution to ensure diverse collegiate student bodies?

8. Notice the Fifth Circuit's construction of the categories as white and minority, even though "white includes non-favored minority." What does this use of race mean?

9. San Francisco public schools have operated under a court ordered desegregation plan for fifteen years, which required schools to admit no more than 40 percent from any racial group. The plan also required that each school enroll representation from four out of nine designated racial groups. In *Ho v. S. F. Unified Sch. Dist.*, 147 F.3d 854 (9th Cir.1998), Chinese American plaintiffs challenged this desegregation plan as preventing their admission to prestigious Lowell High School. See Selena Dong, *"Too Many Asians": The Challenge of Fighting Discrimination Against Asian–Americans and Preserving Affirmative Action*, 47 Stan. L. Rev. 1027 (1995) (exploring how Asian Americans can "simultaneously argue in favor of preferential treatment for some minority groups over whites and against the sort of discrimination that is occurring at Lowell").

Awaiting trial in the *Ho* case, a federal judge ordered attorneys for the school district to file a proposed race-neutral enrollment plan. "Hundreds of school districts nationwide" have moved away from desegregation programs. Research has shown that "such districts 'resegregate' and return to racially identifiable schools, often with high concentrations of poverty and low levels of achievement at those where most of the students are black." Nanette Asimov, *S.F. Schools Give Court 'Race–Neutral' Enrollment Proposal*, S. F. Chron., Feb. 2, 1999 at A13 & A18.

In February 1999, the *Ho* case settled with the parties agreeing to end the court ordered desegregation plan by December 31, 2002. They further agreed that San Francisco schools may no longer use race or ethnicity as the "primary or predominant consideration" in enrollment decisions, but that race could be considered with other factors. School admission decisions may take neighborhood into account, giving preference to low income zip codes. In 2000 and 2001 the school district will evaluate the ethnic composition of every school. The parties will discuss what to do if they find an "identifiable racial or ethnic concentration" at that time. Nancy Asimov, *Parents Ponder New World of S.F. School Enrollment: Settlement Ends Registration by Racial Quota*, S.F. Chron., Feb. 18, 1999, at A15 & A20.

Is this move toward a race-neutral admission procedure a positive step? Is considering race as one of several factors for admission a workable compromise? How can the district evaluate the racial/ethnic composition of schools without asking about race? Is it desirable for schools (and employers) to keep racial records?

For further analyses of affirmative action, see Eric K. Yamamoto, *Critical Race Praxis: Race Theory and Political Lawyering Practice in Post–Civil Rights America*, 95 Mich. L. Rev. 821 (1997) (describing the political divisions in the Asian–American community related to the *Ho* case and the absence of critical theorists); Haeryung Shin, *Safety in Numbers? Equal Protection, Desegregation, and Discrimination: School Desegregation in a Multi–Cultural Society*, 82 Cornell L. Rev. 182 (1996) (describing the *Ho* litigation as "ironic and inevitable"); Frank H. Wu, *Changing America: Three Arguments About Asian Americans and the Law*, 45 Am. U. L. Rev.

811 (1996) (examining the model minority myth, colorblindness, and the problem of representation in *Ho*); Frank H. Wu, *Neither Black nor White: Asian Americans and Affirmative Action*, 15 B.C. Third World L.J. 225 (1995); and Deborah Ramirez, *Multicultural Empowerment: It's Not Just Black and White Anymore*, 47 Stan. L. Rev. 957, 971–72 (1995) (discussing the *Ho* case).

10.   The use of race in admissions remains an important site of political disagreement. William G. Bowen and Derek Bok, *The Shape of the River: Long–Term Consequences of Considering Race in College and University Admissions* (1998) concludes that race conscious admissions policies at elite institutions proved successful for both admitted students of color and white students who benefited from the diverse educational environment. They also argued that eliminating affirmative action would have only a slight statistical effect on a white student's chance at admission. Like parking spaces reserved for handicapped drivers, which might frustrate those looking to park, the elimination of the reserved space would probably not cause parking (or admissions) to be available.

The political struggle over affirmative action is well-documented in Charles R. Lawrence III & Mari J. Matsuda, *We Won't Go Back: Making the Case for Affirmative Action* (1997). See also Charles R. Lawrence III, *Each Other's Harvest: Diversity's Deeper Meaning*, 31 U.S.F. L. Rev. 757 (1997) (explaining the connection between affirmative action and ending subordination and segregation); Sheila Foster, *Difference and Equality: A Critical Assessment of the Concept of "Diversity,"* 1993 Wis. L. Rev. 105 (critiquing the notion of diversity as empty and treating all differences the same) and John Martinez, *Trivializing Diversity: The Problem of Overinclusion in Affirmative Action Programs*, 12 Harv. BlackLetter L.J. 49 (1995).

11.   Too often debates about affirmative action focus on race, gendering race male. When the topic turns to gender, women are often raced as white. Why might women of color be rendered invisible in the discussion of affirmative action? See Laura M. Padilla, *Intersectionality and Positionality: Situating Women of Color in the Affirmative Action Dialogue*, 66 Fordham L. Rev. 843 (1997) (explaining that women of color constitute a category of identity uniquely implicated in the affirmative action debate).

12.   For a comprehensive look at affirmative action litigation and colleges see Michael A. Olivas, *The Law and Higher Education: Cases and Materials on Colleges in Court* 981–1125 (2d ed. 1997).

GODBY v. MONTGOMERY COUNTY BOARD OF EDUCATION

996 F. Supp. 1390 (M.D.Ala.1998).

ALBRITTON, CHIEF JUDGE.

This cause is before the court on the Motion for Summary Judgment filed on July 25, 1997, by the Defendants, Montgomery County Board of Education (MCBOE) * * * [and the school superintendent, principal, and teachers]. The case was filed by Bethany Godby because of events which occurred while she was a student at Cloverdale Junior High School. Her complaint is that the Defendants racially discriminated against her and violated other of her federal rights in violation of 42

U.S.C.A. §§ 1981, 1983, 1985, 1986, and Title VI; and violated Alabama state law by negligently supervising their employees and invading her privacy. * * *

The primary Plaintiff in this case, Bethany Godby, is a mixed-race child. Her father is white and her mother is black. Bethany thinks of herself as being "both" races; and when she has been asked for her race on forms, such as those at school, she has routinely checked both categories.

Homecoming queen elections at her school, Cloverdale Junior High in Montgomery, elect (or at least elected) the queens and their courts according to their race. Students are asked to nominate "white" students and "black" students, separately. The seventh and eighth grades each have two representatives on the homecoming court—a student of each race from each grade. Ninth grade has a queen, who is the top vote getter, and two attendants, a white one and a black one.

THE ELECTION.

Bethany Godby was in the ninth grade at Cloverdale Junior High School in 1996–97, when this dispute began. On September 10 of that school year, her homeroom held a vote to nominate students for the school-wide homecoming queen election. Godby's homeroom teacher. Defendant Bradford, was not present, so the vote was conducted by a substitute teacher (who is not a defendant). Students were asked to separately nominate students as either white or black. The winner from each category in the homeroom would be that homeroom's nominee for the school-wide ballot. The school-wide ballot was also divided into two racial categories: white and black.

Godby was not in her homeroom when the vote started. She learned upon returning, however, that she had been suggested by one of her classmates as a candidate for the homeroom's black nominee. Matters became complicated when one of her classmates said that she should run as the homeroom's white nominee. Other students complained that it would be unfair for Godby to run for both slots, and a discussion about race ensued among the students. The substitute teacher left to consult with Ms. Lovrich, the school's homecoming director.

Lovrich went to the room and talked to Godby about the situation. Lovrich took Godby into the hall and told her that she had to choose one or the other slot in which to run; Godby could not run for both. In effect, the biracial child had to choose: Was she white or black? Godby returned to the room and asked her classmates which slot she should choose. The majority of the classmates told her that she should run as the white nominee. Godby ran for the white slot and was selected as her homeroom's nominee.

Godby's nomination during the first vote never made it to the general student body for a vote, however. The school officials have maintained from early on that the first election was invalidated because the girl who received the black nomination from Godby's homeroom had helped count the votes. This was thought improper. Plaintiffs have not contested that the black nominee helped count the votes. Plaintiffs have noted facts, however, which at least make it appear that other reasons may have led to the invalidation of the first election. Ms. Lovrich has admitted that she used the school computer in the guidance counselor's office to look up Godby's race after the first ballot was taken. Ms. Lovrich testified in deposition that the registry on the school computer listed Godby as black. Lovrich did this search because she thought that it was her "duty to make sure what [Godby] was telling me was true."

In any event, however, the first set of nominations was invalidated. Lovrich asked Bradford to redo the elections for both the white and black nominees from his homeroom. On the next day, a second round of votes was taken to get nominations. The school officials have maintained that Godby simply did not win the white nomination of her homeroom during this second vote. Godby has presented evidence, however, that she did win the white nomination of her homeroom during the second vote. This evidence includes her own testimony, affidavits from other students, and the results of a questionnaire given to the students by school officials. Godby herself says that there were no other white nominees from her classroom, so she was selected by default. She was the only nominee, even though students in the homeroom were allowed to nominate anyone from throughout the school.

Taking the facts in the light most favorable to Godby, therefore, it appears that she was nominated by her homeroom as a white nominee for the school-wide election. Godby's name was not on the school-wide ballot when it appeared, however. That fact is uncontested. School officials have maintained that Godby was not removed from the school-wide ballot, but was simply not nominated by her homeroom on the second try. Godby suggests improper action, however, and presents the evidence of her election, and Ms. Lovrich's admitted actions.

Godby did not learn that her name was not on the ballot until it was distributed to everyone. She asked Mr. Bradford why her name was not on the ballot, but he said that he did not know. He admits that he at first said that he did not know. He would not allow her to leave the room to ask someone at that time. Later in the day, Godby asked Lovrich why her name had not been on the ballot. Lovrich at first told her that she had not been nominated, but then, according to Godby, told Godby that it was because Lovrich had looked up her school records and discovered that Godby was black.

THE POLICY OF THE SCHOOL.

After the election, Godby's parents met with the principal of Cloverdale, Jethro Wilson, on two occasions: once with just Mrs. Godby present, a second time with both parents in attendance. Wilson claimed to not know anything about the incident, but told them that he would look into it. Wilson says that he talked to Mrs. Godby about the perceptions of society that mixed children are thought of as black. As stated by Mrs. Godby, Wilson and she talked about how the biracial election system was set up in the '60s, "mulattos," "quadroons," the effects of "one or two drops of black blood," and how it had been back in New Orleans. Wilson also showed Mrs. Godby that Bethany's registration on the computer showed her to be black.

Wilson testified that Cloverdale had a dual election system at the time that he became principal and that he continued that policy. A student had to declare one race or the other to participate. ("Q. Now, if a person is neither black nor white, what category would they fall into under this 1996 procedure for homecoming at Cloverdale? A. That's no procedure that they would fall under. They have to be one or the other.") Wilson says that the "racial quota" in homecoming elections was done "in order to give equal opportunity to both races." Wilson did not think that there was a compelling reason to have the dual election system. In fact, other activities at Cloverdale do not have a dual election system.

Lovrich testified that Cloverdale did not use a racially-divided election system in 1994–95, but returned to that system after complaints from white children and one white parent. Eberhart, the school system superintendent, has affirmed that the Cloverdale employees were "vested with th[e] authority to conduct th[e] election as they saw fit." He made this statement in the context of discussing Principal Wilson, and teachers Bradford and Lovrich. Eberhart also testified that he had no knowledge of the system that individual schools used to select their homecoming queens. He did not know of a compelling reason to have a dual racial classification.

Mr. Charles Everett, the executive assistant to the superintendent, testified in deposition. He does not know that anyone on the superintendent's executive committee has a specific role to advise the superintendent regarding "racial classifications in the selection of students in extracurricular activities;" and states that he is not aware of any discussion regarding racial selection in extracurricular activities among the executive officers. Everett believes that the schools should operate a dual race selection system for extracurricular activities because such a system allows students to "feel a part of the school" as if they have an "ownership" in the school.

Mr. Clinton Carter is a part-time consultant to the superintendent. Carter was instructed to search the policies of the MCBOE to find if there was a policy relating to racial composition of homecoming courts; he stated that there was no such policy. The Board at one time had a policy which enforced a racial selection of cheerleaders. Carter knows of no policy which would have kept a principal from designing his own homecoming election system, even one which used race as a factor. He thinks that other schools may have had such policies. He does not know if there was a compelling reason for having such a system. Cloverdale has become progressively more minority over the past twenty years.

Defendants have presented evidence that the defendants have adjusted the school policy regarding selection and election of students for positions in response to the incident at Cloverdale. Wilson has testified that, because of a resolution of the MCBOE, during future student elections, the schools "won't have a classification." Eberhart appears uncertain of the exact effect of the new policy, however. The new policy is not legally relevant at this time, however, as the Defendants have raised no issues of standing or mootness in their present motion, and the scope of relief is not before the court. Therefore, the court is not required to make any determinations regarding the evidence presented on this issue. * * *

After the incident was brought to the attention of the media by the Godby family, the school decided that a response was necessary. The school held a press conference where Principal Wilson spoke. The Principal initially represented that the first election was nullified because of a counting problem; the young lady who won the position of black attendant had assisted in counting the ballots. He represented that when the second election was held, Godby simply did not receive the requisite number of votes in her homeroom to be put on the school-wide ballot. Godby was not removed from the ballot. Rather, she never made it on the ballot.

INVESTIGATION BY THE SCHOOL.

Mr. Everett distributed a questionnaire to the students in Godby's homeroom class asking them about the incident. He recalls that the answers to the questionnaires were inconclusive as to the results of the first and second ballots in the homeroom. * * * They are in fact inconclusive. Ten students stated that Godby was the winner of the second nomination by her homeroom; eleven were not sure; and four thought that another student had won. Although the court is apt to be suspicious of the results of a survey of ninth-graders taken by school officials with whom the students are not familiar, neither side has raised an objection to the admissibility of this evidence. In any event, there is also an affidavit from a fellow student of Godby, stating that Godby won the second election.

III. DISCUSSION

Plaintiffs have brought a number of claims in this suit, and have presented even more theories of liability. Plaintiffs appear to be a bit unsure, as are some of the school officials, of what the particular wrong is. Is the wrong the election that was "stolen" from Godby? Or is the wrong that there was not a separate "biracial" category? Or is the wrong that the school was operating a "separate-but-equal" system for homecoming elections?

At least some of the school officials even appear to believe that an election based on separate racial categories is in the best interest of students. Far be it from this court to second-guess school professionals on how best to educate children; nevertheless, even school officials must follow the law. Racial categorization by the government is unacceptable, even if it is done for supposedly "good" reasons. The court sustains the central claim of Godby's suit. Plaintiff has presented a case of racial discrimination that should be heard by a jury. * * *

Although the Supreme Court has been somewhat divided, and slow, in developing the law of racial preferences, this court believes that the law now bars the racial distinctions made by the MCBOE in its homecoming nominations. The Fourteenth Amendment states that "[n]o State shall ... deny to any person within its jurisdiction the equal protection of the laws." Although the language of the Amendment is somewhat vague—after all, for almost 100 years, the Supreme Court read it to allow government-mandated segregation—the principles that it stands for have ultimately been put into focus. As stated by Justice Kennedy, it is the "moral imperative of race neutrality [that] is the driving force of the Equal Protection Clause." *City of Richmond v. J.A. Croson Co.*, 488 U.S. 469, 518 (Kennedy concurring). Government racial categorization, for little or no reason, cannot stand. * * *

Finally, the court also notes that it would not know what to term this particular voting system: discrimination or reverse discrimination? From the assertions of counsel, it was apparently instituted to smooth the transition into integrated schools during the 1960s. School authorities cannot rely on its institution at a time when it arguably may have been needed, however, to justify its existence today. Further, the schools would apparently not know what justification to offer. Official after official testified that he knew of no compelling justification for its existence. Indeed, the attorneys for the defendants have not offered one, either.

The only reasons given for the existence of the voting system are troubling at best. For one thing, the evidence is anecdotal, which can "suffice" on its own to justify governmental discrimination "only in the rare case." The problems with the evidence are not limited to its form, however. There are also serious difficulties with the substance. The evidence offered by the MCBOE is itself evidence of racial discrimination by the school. One school official testified that the voting system was reinstituted at the insistence of white students, and their parents, who now constitute a small minority at the school. That would make it something like reverse-reverse-discrimination, whatever that may be. In any event, it is not legal. Another explanation offered justifies the voting system as a benefit to all students, to help the students find a role model, or leader, of their own race. This role model theory was discussed, and dismissed, by a plurality of the Supreme Court in *Wygant*. Since then, the Court has made it clear that reverse discrimination cannot be practiced by the government for generalized reasons, or for the purpose of combating societal discrimination. *Croson*, 488 U.S. at 498 ("Like the 'role model' theory employed in *Wygant*, a generalized assertion that there has been past discrimination ... provides no guidance for a legislative body to determine the precise scope of the injury it seeks to remedy.")

In any event, however, there is only one standard by which to judge this action of the MCBOE. Government in the United States—be it "federal, state, or local governmental actor"—"may treat people differently because of their race only for the most compelling reasons." *Adarand*, 515 U.S. at 227. Racial "classifications are constitutional only if they are narrowly tailored measures that further compelling governmental interests." *Id.* Defendants in this case have tried little, if anything, to defend the racial quotas, and the racial voting system, at issue. All they have offered does not even come close to being the "strong basis in evidence" that is necessary in order for the court to sustain racial classification by a government entity. Simply put, when a government body "chooses to employ a suspect classification, it cannot rest upon a generalized assertion" of necessity or the benign nature of the classification. A good defense—indeed, a compelling, narrowly tailored defense—must be raised. It simply has not been here. * * *

IV. CONCLUSION

* * * The court is denying summary judgment to the MCBOE because of the actions of officials who appear, at least on the face of the evidence, to have been motivated by a desire to improve the lives of school children and to improve the Montgomery County School System. This court is not oblivious to the problems of the Montgomery County School System, nor is it oblivious to the desires of educators to mollify racial issues, so that the more important task of education can be undertaken. Nevertheless, the MCBOE may not, at least after the Supreme Court's announcements in recent years, divide their students, or classify their students, on the basis of race without a compelling, narrowly drawn, reason. Such a reason is not present here.

Notes and Questions

1. In an omitted part of the opinion the court considered plaintiff's claim based on Title VI, observing:

Title VI is an exercise of Congress' Spending Clause power. The statute reads:

> No person in the United States shall, on the ground of race, color, or national origin, be excluded from participation in, be denied the benefits of, or be subjected to discrimination under any program or activity receiving federal financial assistance.

42 U.S.C.A. § 2000d. Basically, Title VI establishes that those who receive federal funds may not discriminate.

Godby, 996 F. Supp. at 1413. For a discussion of the use of Title VI to combat racial discrimination in education see Preston C. Green, *Can Title VI Prevent Law Schools from Adopting Admissions Practices That Discriminate Against African Americans?*, 24 S. U. L. Rev 237 (1997). See also Stuart Biegel, *School Choice Policy and Title VI: Maximizing Equal Access for K–12 Students in a Substantially Deregulated Educational Environment*, 47 Hastings L.J. 1533, 1550–1555 (1995) (describing recent Title VI education cases).

2. Why, in 1996, would the Cloverdale Junior High School elect homecoming queens on black and white separate ballots? Why aren't there homecoming kings? Suppose you are a Latina or female Asian–American student at Cloverdale Junior High. Could you run for election as homecoming queen? What race would you pick if you had to choose either "Black" or "White?" Why?

3. What role should schools play in discussing race? What conversation do you imagine occurred in Ms. Godby's homeroom when "a discussion about race" ensued?

4. The courts in both *Hopwood* and *Godby* object to noticing race. Are the situations comparable, justifying the same rule?

5.   On the topic of multiraciality consider Trina Grillo, *Anti-Essentialism and Intersectionality: Tools to Dismantle the Master's House*, 10 Berkeley Women's L.J. 16, 25 (1995):*

The move for a "multiracial" category, both on census and other forms, and in terms of how we talk in daily life, is in part an attempt to recognize what is in fact the case—that some people have parents of two races, that even people who have parents of the same race may have other ancestors of a different race. A multiracial category would permit children to claim a racial relationship to both, or all, their parents, rather than being forced to choose. Moreover, even though over the years many black leaders have been biracial, today some multiracial people, especially those with very light skin or who have been raised only by a white parent, may not feel completely comfortable or accepted in black groups.

But the move to define people as multiracial has serious risks. How would we distinguish between those who are multiracial because they have one white parent, such as myself, and the general black population of the United States, many of whom in one way or another have a similar amount of white ancestry? Why would we *want* to make such a distinction? * * * There is a fear that multiracial people want to "get out of" being Black, that it is a new form of passing.

Chapter 10

RACISM AND FREEDOM OF EXPRESSION

The following materials all converge on the way freedom of expression, protected by the First Amendment of the United States Constitution, sometimes clashes with values emanating from the equality-protecting amendments, especially the Thirteenth and Fourteenth. As the reader will see, reformist speech—the speech dear to minorities—is sometimes given scant protection, while that which insults and degrades them is afforded wide latitude. Why should this be, and is this asymmetry inherent in our constitutional system? If not, what can be done about it?

ED SPARER

Fundamental Human Rights, Legal Entitlements, and the Social Struggle:
A Friendly Critique of the Critical Legal Studies Movement
36 Stan. L. Rev. 509, 512–13, 530, 540–46 (1984).*

I believe that certain fundamental human rights are inalienable. They exist regardless of whether or not they have been legally recognized. These rights—the "individual" right to free speech and dissent and to develop and express an independent conscience, including the right to free religious expression; the "solidarity" right to associate with one's fellow humans for common endeavor, including the right of working people to organize in unions of their own choice—are part of ourselves as human beings, each one and all of us.

What is the source of these rights? Is it the Declaration of Independence? The text of the Constitution? The Declaration of the Rights of Man? Statements of positive law? Judicial recognition of moral consensus? Utilitarian theory? Socialist theory? A "natural law" proclaimed by God? In my view, such sources are merely guides to an understanding of whether there has been legal or intellectual recognition of these inalienable rights and what the range of argument has been. But certain fundamental human rights are inalienable, regardless of the arguments for legal recognition and regardless of whether there exists a "higher" natural law which human beings are obliged by God to obey. These rights are part of our potential, what we might be as living persons, even if they do not express what we are or do at any given moment in our lives. The recognition that they are part of each one of us underlies the concept of the "equality" of human beings, whether national, racial, or sexual. * * *

While it is easy to understand how one person's right to separately possess property limits another person's separate possession of property, I fail to see how one person's exercise of, for example, free speech and dissent necessarily limits another person's. Quite the contrary; the exercise of these latter rights can increase the next person's ability to exercise them. It is not the social legitimization which flows from the formal recognition of rights that inhibits transformative, humanizing social struggle. Many factors impede such struggle. But rights such as free speech and dissent protect the ability of groups of people—including working people—to change their society, better their group situation, and expand their human freedom. * * *

Like so many others, as a youth just into college, I became concerned with the condition of the less fortunate. Too many people were too poor. Too much racial and ethnic discrimination existed, * * * all of which are still with us.

Dissatisfied with both the Democratic and Republican parties of the day, I joined Henry Wallace's third-party revolt and went to the South in 1947 as a would-be organizer of textile workers for Wallace. I returned some months later, shaken to my core, radicalized, as were many others a generation later in the civil rights and antipoverty movements. What so shook me were my encounters with textile workers who were paralyzed with fear; with gaunt twenty-five-year-old mothers in the textile communities who looked as if they were forty years old; with one-time militant labor organizers who—literally—had had their life essence beaten out of them by thugs; with black poverty which surpassed my imagination (but whose victims somehow maintained themselves within communities of warm life and mutual support to which I would flee occasionally for respite). I also encountered young white men who followed me from place to place, calmly assuring me that they were going to kill me; decent moderate political leaders who warned me that violence was planned against me but who would not openly speak against it; and raging mobs that would not let Henry Wallace speak but drove him out of town after town in danger of his life. These experiences changed my life. Poverty, discrimination, fear and violence, and the absence of the freedom of speech I had assumed existed in our country became the issues to which I wanted to devote my life's energies. A socialist America began to make sense to me.

I returned to my college, the City College of New York, which was alive with liberal and left-wing student activities. The Communist Party section on campus, with some 200 members at the time, vigorously recruited students, but I and others resisted. Dissent, I argued, was not permitted by the Party, and I believed in free speech and dissent; my experience in the South had convinced me not that free speech was a specious value because it was so readily violated but that it was important and vital.

At the same time, City College itself was torn by well-documented charges of anti-Jewish and anti-black discriminatory practices committed by particular faculty and administrators. Soon, working with a coalition of liberals, socialists, Communists, many otherwise "apolitical" students, and some faculty, a well-supported sit-down strike was held, followed by a college-wide vote to have a general student strike—the first such strike on a major American campus since the nineteen-thirties. My life, in those months, became the work of the "movement" that had developed on campus.

We lost. We had sung "we shall not be moved," but it was the college administration that would not move. The thousands of striking students became discouraged and went back to classes. The two main perpetrators of discriminatory activity were retained (one was promoted), the two chief faculty supporters of the strike were "let go" (neither having tenure), and I, in a move whose swiftness was surprising even to me, joined the Communist Party. Why?

At the time I joined, I had not changed my mind about the importance of free speech and dissent. Instead, I said to myself, I would suspend thought on the question until I could study it further. Bitterness towards and disillusionment with a college administration that I once believed embodied the best of liberal values was an element in my decision to join. Observing how the Communist students had worked for our mutual cause while others gave up in despair was another. But I believe something more profound had taken hold of me.

My life before had been that of an individual with a keen awareness of his individual weakness and a sense of terror at his fragile existence. In the year I spent working closely with the Communist students, I shared their lives, and they shared mine. I shared their passions and felt my own spirit to be alive. Yet, my spirit seemed to transcend myself. I had become part of a larger whole. I had found "community" and "solidarity." * * *

I was a good and dedicated Communist for seven years. The Party was my community, and it determined where I lived and what I did. One of my jobs was to study and learn the theory which justified what I did. It was then that I studied Lenin and the critique of the "bourgeois" rights to free speech and dissent. And, of course, given my changed position and the task of rationalizing what I had already committed myself to—Lenin's attack on Kautsky, Lenin's building upon the phraseology of Marx and his use of Engels—all made sense.

Meanwhile, I was witnessing again the lack of respect for free speech in the United States. Joe McCarthy was in his heyday, and Communists, among many others, were hounded. Few of us in those days spoke freely, even inside our own homes, without covering our telephones with blankets and checking for other signs of electronic invasion. I had become a factory worker. It was not unknown for Communist factory workers, when their affiliation was discovered, to be thrown bodily out of the factory window. Life for a Communist in the United States was hard.

But with our shared community (even though we were "underground" and rarely saw each other) and our steady work for a new society, it was worthwhile.

Free speech in the United States seemed to be a liberal myth, and even the liberals were beginning to concede this. The new lesson to me was that there were no "universals"; history and social relations determined political substance. In a socialist state, the workers would be free and the opponents of socialism suppressed. Later, after class differences had disappeared, state force would no longer be necessary.

Then, one day in the winter of 1956, I picked up a copy of the *New York Times*. There was the text of Nikita Khrushchev's "secret" speech to the 20th Congress of the Communist Party of the Soviet Union.[94] I experienced the shock that thousands of Communists the world over were experiencing then and had experienced in earlier periods of history as a result of analogous events. At first, I believed it to be a fabrication of the newspaper, but later confirmation from "our" sources revealed what the anti-Soviet "fabricators" had charged all along: a history of bloodshed, murder, terror, and suppression unparalleled in modern times except by Hitler. The charge was not "simply" the murder of "capitalists" and "enemies of socialism"; it was murder of leading Communist cadres, Bolsheviks who made the 1917 revolution, and Communist poets and artists. Exposed also were the deportations of whole peoples in the Soviet Union and other atrocities. Murder and suppression, suppression and murder, of whites and reds, yellows and blacks. It made no difference.

In shock, I began to think again about the inalienable rights to free speech and dissent. The legally protected right to dissent is not opposed to socialism and community; it is instead necessary for their realization. The individualistic and liberal rights of speech and dissent do not have only a "privatistic" and "egoistic" content; they are necessary for social struggle and advancement in socialist as well as capitalist society. * * *

The rights to free speech and dissent must be understood as essential to the human condition that seems most explicitly valued in Critical legal writing: the state of "community," the experience of solidarity with one's fellow humans in common life and endeavor. On this point, Duncan Kennedy's formulation is one with which I completely agree:

> Embedded in the rights notion is a liberating accomplishment of our culture: the affirmation of free human subjectivity against the constraints of group life, along with the paradoxical countervision of a group life that creates and nurtures individuals capable of freedom.[99]

The "liberating accomplishment" and the "paradoxical countervision" fit together as parts of a whole. One task of scholarship, in my

94. The text has since been published in N. Khrushchev, *The Anatomy of Terror: Khrushchev's Revelations About Stalin's Regime* (1956). The text reprinted there was released by the U.S. Department of State on June 4, 1956. It follows a text released earlier by the *Times* and discussed in the *Daily Worker* and other left publications.

99. D. Kennedy, *Critical Labor Law Theory: A Comment*, 4 Indus. Rel. L.J. 503, 506 (1981).

view, should be to deepen our understanding of the kinds of group life and conditions for group life and community which nourish individual freedom and broaden its public base. It is a tragic mistake to ignore historical experience and undermine the notion of "the inalienable rights of mankind" which are part of the essence of that individual freedom.

Of course, when I say "historical experience," I do not mean historical experience devoid of values. Historical experience teaches no lessons by itself. The values I sought in my early life—the values I still seek to advance today—concern both individual self-expression and communal support and solidarity. Over the last half-century, the experience of diverse societies, many thousands of Communists, socialists, and just plain democrats counsels that the protection and enhancement of those values require many things, especially the legal right to free speech and dissent.

Notes and Questions

1. If, as Sparer writes, free speech is a necessary condition for community, solidarity, and self-fulfillment, can that same speech sometimes fracture community, shunting some to the side and excluding them from participation?

2. What about the many "exceptions" to free speech doctrine—libel, defamation, copyright, words of threat or conspiracy, plagiarism, fighting words, shouting fire in a crowded theater, official secrets, perjury, disrespectful words uttered to a judge, etc.? In allowing these exceptions, have we given away something inalienable, as Sparer puts it? Why *have* we allowed these exceptions?

SECTION 1. FREEDOM OF EXPRESSION USED BY MINORITIES FOR ADVANCEMENT: POLITICAL SPEECH AND PROTEST

The following cases, dealing with the relationship between the civil rights ideal and free speech, sound a number of themes. The reader should ask himself or herself, when is civil rights speech protected, and when not? When it is not, note the catalog of reasons courts give for holding as they do—too loud, too muscular, wrong time, wrong place, the speaker didn't ask politely enough first, etc. Notice, as well, the historical progression they evidence. Early courts tended to side with civil rights protestors, marchers, speakers, and sit-in participants—especially if their speech was prayerful, mannerly, and decorous. Later, when Black Power entered the picture, rulings began to go the other way. See Derrick Bell, *Race, Racism, and American Law*, (3d ed. 1992) (chapter 6: Parameters of Protest).

COX v. LOUISIANA
379 U.S. 536 (1965).

On December 14, 1961, 23 students from Southern University, a Negro college, were arrested in downtown Baton Rouge, Louisiana, for picketing stores that maintained segregated lunch counters. This picketing, urging a boycott of those stores, was part of a general protest movement against racial segregation, directed by the local chapter of the Congress of Racial Equality, a civil rights organization. The appellant, an ordained Congregational minister, the Reverend Mr. B. Elton Cox, a Field Secretary of CORE, was an advisor to this movement. On the evening of December 14, appellant and Ronnie Moore, student president of the local CORE chapter, spoke at a mass meeting at the college. The students resolved to demonstrate the next day in front of the courthouse in protest of segregation and the arrest and imprisonment of the picketers who were being held in the parish jail located on the upper floor of the courthouse building. * * *

Captain Font of the City Police Department and Chief Kling of the Sheriff's office approached the group and spoke to Cox at the northeast corner of the capitol grounds. Cox identified himself as the group's leader, and, according to Font and Kling, he explained that the students were demonstrating to protest "the illegal arrest of some of their people who were being held in jail." The version of Cox and his witnesses throughout was that they came not "to protest just the arrest but . . . [also] to protest the evil of discrimination." Kling asked Cox to disband the group and "take them back from whence they came." Cox did not acquiesce in this request but told the officers that they would march by the courthouse, say prayers, sing hymns, and conduct a peaceful program of protest. The officer repeated his request to disband, and Cox again refused. Kling and Font then returned to their car in order to report by radio to the Sheriff and Chief of Police who were in the immediate vicinity; while this was going on, the students, led by Cox, began their walk toward the courthouse.

They walked in an orderly and peaceful file, two or three abreast, one block east, stopping on the way for a red traffic light. In the center of this block they were joined by another group of students. The augmented group now totaling about 2,000 turned the corner and proceeded south, coming to a halt in the next block opposite the courthouse.

As Cox, still at the head of the group, approached the vicinity of the courthouse, he was stopped by Captain Font and Inspector Trigg and brought to Police Chief Wingate White, who was standing in the middle of St. Louis Street. The Chief then inquired as to the purpose of the demonstration. Cox, reading from a prepared paper, outlined his program to White, stating that it would include a singing of the Star Spangled Banner and a "freedom song," recitation of the Lord's Prayer and the Pledge of Allegiance, and a short speech. White testified that he told Cox that "he must confine" the demonstration "to the west side of the street." White added, "This, of course, was not—I didn't mean it in the import that I was giving him any permission to do it, but I was presented with a situation that was accomplished, and I had to make a decision." Cox testified that the officials agreed to permit the meeting. * * *

The students were then directed by Cox to the west sidewalk, across the street from the courthouse, 101 feet from its steps. They were lined up on this sidewalk about five deep and spread almost the entire length of the block. The group did not obstruct the street. * * *

The Sheriff, deeming Cox's appeal to the students to sit in at the lunch counters to be "inflammatory," then took a power microphone and said, "Now, you have been allowed to demonstrate. Up until now your demonstration has been more or less peaceful, but what you are doing now is a direct violation of the law, a disturbance of the peace, and it has got to be broken up immediately." The testimony as to what then happened is disputed. Some of the State's witnesses testified that Cox said, "don't move"; others stated that he made a "gesture of defiance." It is clear from the record, however, that Cox and the demonstrators did not then and there break up the demonstration. Two of the Sheriff's deputies immediately started across the street and told the group, "You have heard what the Sheriff said, now, do what he said." A state witness testified that they put their hands on the shoulders of some of the students "as though to shove them away."

Almost immediately thereafter—within a time estimated variously at two to five minutes—one of the policemen exploded a tear gas shell at the crowd. This was followed by several other shells. The demonstrators quickly dispersed, running back towards the State Capitol and the downtown area; Cox tried to calm them as they ran and was himself one of the last to leave.

No Negroes participating in the demonstration were arrested on that day. The only person then arrested was a young white man, not a part of the demonstration, who was arrested "because he was causing a disturbance." The next day appellant was arrested and charged with four offenses. * * *

II.

The Breach of the Peace Conviction

Appellant was convicted of violating a Louisiana "disturbing the peace" statute. * * *

It is clear to us that on the facts of this case, * * * Louisiana infringed appellant's rights of free speech and free assembly by convicting him under this statute. * * * We hold that Louisiana may not constitutionally punish appellant under this statute for engaging in the type of conduct which this record reveals, and also that the statute as authoritatively interpreted by the Louisiana Supreme Court is unconstitutionally broad in scope. * * *

[O]ur independent examination of the record, which we are required to make, shows no conduct which the State had a right to prohibit as a breach of the peace.

Appellant led a group of young college students who wished "to protest segregation" and discrimination against Negroes and the arrest of 23 fellow students. They assembled peaceably at the State Capitol building and marched to the courthouse where they sang, prayed and listened to a speech. A reading of the record reveals agreement on the part of the State's witnesses that Cox had the demonstration "very well controlled," and until the end of Cox's speech, the group was perfectly "orderly." * * * The Sheriff testified that the sole aspect of the program to which he objected was "[t]he inflammatory manner in which he [Cox] addressed that crowd and told them to go on up town, go to four places on the protest list, sit down and if they don't feed you, sit there for one hour." Yet this part of Cox's speech obviously did not deprive the demonstration of its protected character under the Constitution as free speech and assembly. See *Edwards v. South Carolina, supra; Cantwell v. State of Connecticut*, 310 U.S. 296; *Thornhill v. State of Alabama*, 310 U.S. 88; *Garner v. State of Louisiana*, 368 U.S. 157, 185 (concurring opinion of Mr. Justice Harlan). * * *

Our conclusion that the record does not support the contention that the students' cheering, clapping and singing constituted a breach of the peace is confirmed by the fact that these were not relied on as a basis for conviction by the trial judge, who, rather, stated as his reason for convicting Cox of disturbing the peace that "[i]t must be recognized to be inherently dangerous and a breach of the peace to bring 1,500 people, colored people, down in the predominantly white business district in the City of Baton Rouge and congregate across the street from the courthouse and sing songs as described to me by the defendant as the CORE national anthem carrying lines such as 'black and white together' and to urge those 1,500 people to descend upon our lunch counters and sit there until they are served. That has to be an inherent breach of the peace, and our statute 14:103.1 has made it so."

Finally, the State contends that the conviction should be sustained because of fear expressed by some of the state witnesses that "violence was about to erupt" because of the demonstration. It is virtually undisputed, however, that the students themselves were not violent and threatened no violence. The fear of violence seems to have been based upon the reaction of the group of white citizens looking on from across the street. One state witness testified that "he felt the situation was getting out of hand" as on the courthouse side of St. Louis Street "were small knots or groups of white citizens who were muttering words, who seemed a little bit agitated." A police officer stated that the reaction of the white crowd was not violent, but "was rumblings." Others felt the atmosphere became "tense" because of "mutterings," "grumbling," and "jeering" from the white group. There is no indication, however, that any member of the white group threatened violence. And this small crowd estimated at between 100 and 300 was separated from the students by "seventy-five to eighty" armed policemen, including "every available shift of the City Police," the "Sheriff's Office in full complement," and "additional help from the State Police," along with a "fire truck and the Fire Department." As Inspector Trigg testified, they could have handled the crowd. * * *

There is an additional reason why this conviction cannot be sustained. The statute at issue in this case, as authoritatively interpreted by the Louisiana Supreme Court, is unconstitutionally vague in its overly broad scope. The statutory crime consists of two elements: (1) congregating with others "with intent to provoke a breach of the peace, or under circumstances such that a breach of the peace may be occasioned," and (2) a refusal to move on after having been ordered to do so by a law enforcement officer. While the second part of this offense is narrow and specific, the first element is not. The Louisiana Supreme Court in this case defined the term "breach of the peace" as "to agitate, to arouse from a state of repose, to molest, to interrupt, to hinder, to disquiet." 244 La., at 1105, 156 So.2d, at 455. In *Edwards*, defendants had been convicted of a common-law crime similarly defined by the South Carolina Supreme Court. Both definitions would allow persons to be punished merely for peacefully expressing unpopular views. Yet, a "function of free speech under our system of government is to invite dispute. It may indeed best serve its high purpose when it induces a condition of unrest, creates dissatisfaction with conditions as they are, or even stirs people to anger. Speech is often provocative and challenging. It may strike at prejudices and preconceptions and have profound unsettling effects as it presses for acceptance of an idea. That is why freedom of speech . . . is . . . protected against censorship or punishment. . . . There is no room under our Constitution for a more restrictive view. For the alternative would lead to standardization of ideas either by legislatures, courts, or dominant political or community groups." *Terminiello v. City of Chicago*, 337 U.S. 1, 4–5. * * * The Louisiana statute, as interpreted by the Louisiana court, is likely to allow conviction for innocent speech. Therefore, the conviction under this statute must be reversed as the statute is unconstitutional in that it sweeps within its broad scope activities that are constitutionally protected free speech and assembly. Maintenance of the opportunity for free political discussion is a basic tenet of our constitutional democracy. * * *

III.

THE OBSTRUCTING PUBLIC PASSAGES CONVICTION

We now turn to the issue of the validity of appellant's conviction for violating the Louisiana statute, LSA–Rev.Stat. § 14:100.1 (Cum.Supp. 1962), which provides:

"Obstructing Public Passages

No person shall wilfully obstruct the free, convenient and normal use of any public sidewalk, street, highway, bridge, alley, road, or other passageway, or the entrance, corridor or passage of any public building, structure, watercraft or ferry, by impeding, hindering, stifling, retarding or restraining traffic or passage thereon or therein.

Providing however nothing herein contained shall apply to a bona fide legitimate labor organization or to any of its legal activities such as picketing, lawful assembly or concerted activity in the interest of its members for the purpose of accomplishing or securing more favorable wage standards, hours of employment and working conditions."

Appellant was convicted under this statute, not for leading the march to the vicinity of the courthouse, which the Louisiana Supreme Court stated to have been "orderly," 244 La., at 1096, 156 So.2d, at 451, but for leading the meeting on the sidewalk across the street from the courthouse. *Id.*, at 1094, 1106–1107, 156 So.2d, at 451, 455. In upholding appellant's conviction under this statute, the Louisiana Supreme Court thus construed the statute so as to apply to public assemblies which do not have as their specific purpose the obstruction of traffic. There is no doubt from the record in this case that this far sidewalk was obstructed, and thus, as so construed, appellant violated the statute.

Appellant, however, contends that as so construed and applied in this case, the statute is an unconstitutional infringement on freedom of speech and assembly. This contention on the facts here presented raises an issue with which this Court has dealt in many decisions, that is, the right of a State or municipality to regulate the use of city streets and other facilities to assure the safety and convenience of the people in their use and the concomitant right of the people of free speech and assembly. * * *

The rights of free speech and assembly, while fundamental in our democratic society, still do not mean that everyone with opinions or beliefs to express may address a group at any public place and at any time. The constitutional guarantee of liberty implies the existence of an organized society maintaining public order, without which liberty itself would be lost in the excesses of anarchy. * * * Governmental authorities have the duty and responsibility to keep their streets open and available for movement. * * *

We have no occasion in this case to consider the constitutionality of the uniform, consistent, and nondiscriminatory application of a statute forbidding all access to streets and other public facilities for parades and meetings. Although the statute here involved on its face precludes all street assemblies and parades, it has not been so applied and enforced by the Baton Rouge authorities. City officials who testified for the State clearly indicated that certain meetings and parades are permitted in Baton Rouge, even though they have the effect of obstructing traffic, provided prior approval is obtained. This was confirmed in oral argument before this Court by counsel for the State. He stated that parades and meetings are permitted, based on "arrangements ... made with officials." The statute itself provides no standards for the determination of local officials as to which assemblies to permit or which to prohibit. Nor are there any administrative regulations on this subject which have been called to our attention. From all the evidence before us it appears that the authorities in Baton Rouge permit or prohibit parades or street meetings in their completely uncontrolled discretion.

The situation is thus the same as if the statute itself expressly provided that there could only be peaceful parades or demonstrations in the unbridled discretion of the local officials. The pervasive restraint on freedom of discussion by the practice of the authorities under the statute is not any less effective than a statute expressly permitting such selective enforcement. A long line of cases in this Court makes it clear that a State or municipality cannot "require all who wish to disseminate ideas to present them first to police authorities for their consideration and approval, with a discretion in the police to say some ideas may, while others may not, be ... disseminate[d] * * *." Schneider v. State of New Jersey, 308 U.S. 147, 164.

This Court has recognized that the lodging of such broad discretion in a public official allows him to determine which expressions of view will be permitted and which will not. This thus sanctions a device for the suppression of the communication of ideas and permits the official to act as a censor. Also inherent in such a system allowing parades or meetings only with the prior permission of an official is the obvious danger to the right of a person or group not to be denied equal protection of the laws. It is clearly unconstitutional to enable a public official to determine which expressions of view will be permitted and which will not or to engage in invidious discrimination among persons or groups either by use of a statute providing a system of broad discretionary licensing power or, as in this case, the equivalent of such a system by selective enforcement of an extremely broad prohibitory statute. * * * It follows, therefore, that appellant's conviction for violating the statute as so applied and enforced must be reversed.

Notes and Questions

1. Do you think Cox's instruction to the students to "sit-in" at lunch counters that do not serve Blacks was a breach of peace?

2. Could clapping and singing ever be a breach of peace, or was the perception by the white bystanders distorted by their fear of black people?

ADDERLEY v. FLORIDA

385 U.S. 39 (1966).

JUSTICE BLACK delivered the opinion of the Court.

Petitioners, Harriett Louise Adderley and 31 other persons, were convicted by a jury in a joint trial in the County Judge's Court of Leon County, Florida, on a charge of "trespass with a malicious and mischievous intent" upon the premises of the county jail contrary to § 821.18 of the Florida statutes. Petitioners, apparently all students of the Florida A. & M. University in Tallahassee, had gone from the school to the jail about a mile away, along with many other students, to "demonstrate" at the jail their protests of arrests of other protesting students the day before, and perhaps to protest more generally against state and local policies and practices of racial segregation, including segregation of the jail. The county sheriff, legal custodian of the jail and jail grounds, tried to persuade the students to leave the jail grounds. When this did not work, he notified them that they must leave, that if they did not leave he would arrest them for trespassing, and that if they resisted he would charge them with that as well. Some of the students left but others, including petitioners, remained and they were arrested. On appeal the convictions were affirmed by the Florida Circuit Court and then by the Florida District Court of Appeal, 175 So.2d 249. That being the highest state court to which they could appeal, petitioners applied to us for *certiorari* contending that, in view of petitioners' purpose to protest against jail and other segregation policies, their conviction denied them "rights of free speech, assembly, petition, due process of law and equal protection of the laws as guaranteed by the Fourteenth Amendment to the Constitution of the United States." On this "Question Presented" we granted *certiorari*. * * *

I.

Petitioners have insisted from the beginning of this case that it is controlled by and must be reversed because of our prior cases of *Edwards v. South Carolina*, 372 U.S. 229, and *Cox v. State of Louisiana*, 379 U.S. 536. We cannot agree.

The *Edwards* case, like this one, did come up when a number of persons demonstrated on public property against their State's segregation policies. They also sang hymns and danced, as did the demonstrators in this case. But here the analogies to this case end. In *Edwards*, the demonstrators went to the South Carolina State Capital grounds to protest. In this case they went to the jail. Traditionally, state capitol grounds are open to the public. Jails, built for security purposes, are not. The demonstrators at the South Carolina Capital went in through a public driveway and as they entered they were told by state officials there that they had a right as citizens to go through the State House grounds as long as they were peaceful. Here the demonstrators entered the jail grounds through a driveway used only for jail purposes and without warning to or permission from the sheriff. More importantly, South Carolina sought to prosecute its State Capital demonstrators by charging them with the common-law crime of breach of the peace. This Court in *Edwards* took pains to point out at length the indefinite, loose, and broad nature of this charge; indeed, this Court pointed out * * * that the South Carolina Supreme Court had itself declared that the "breach of the peace" charge is "not susceptible of exact definition." South Carolina's power to prosecute, it was emphasized, * * * would have been different had the State proceeded under a "precise and narrowly drawn regulatory statute evincing a legislative judgment that certain specific conduct be limited or proscribed" such as, for example, "limiting the periods during which the State House grounds were open to the public...." The South Carolina breach-of-the-peace statute was thus struck down as being so broad and all-embracing as to jeopardize speech, press, assembly and petition, under the constitutional doctrine enunciated in *Cantwell v. State of Connecticut*, 310 U.S. 296, 307–308, and followed in many subsequent cases. And it was on this same ground of vagueness that in *Cox v. State of Louisiana*, * * * the Louisiana Breach-of-the-peace law used to prosecute Cox was invalidated.

The Florida trespass statute under which these petitioners were charged cannot be challenged on this ground. It is aimed at conduct of one limited kind, that is, for one person or persons to trespass upon the property of another with a malicious and mischievous intent. There is no lack of notice in this law, nothing to entrap or fool the unwary.

Petitioners seem to argue that the Florida trespass law is void for vagueness because it requires a trespass to be "with a malicious and mischievous intent...." But these words do not broaden the scope of trespass so as to make it cover a multitude of types of conduct as does the common-law breach-of-the-peace charge. On the contrary, these words narrow the scope of the offense. The trial court charged the jury as to their meaning and petitioners have not argued that this definition, set out below, is not a reasonable and clear definition of the terms. The use of these terms in the statute, instead of contributing to uncertainty and misunderstanding, actually makes its meaning more understandable and clear. * * *

These judgments are affirmed.

Affirmed.

JUSTICE DOUGLAS, with whom THE CHIEF JUSTICE [WARREN], JUSTICE BRENNAN, and JUSTICE FORTAS concur, dissenting.

The First Amendment, applicable to the States by reason of the Fourteenth (*Edwards v. South Carolina*), 372 U.S. 229, provides that "Congress shall make no law ... abridging ... the right of the people peaceably to assemble, and to petition the Government for a redress of grievances." These rights, along with religion, speech, and press, are preferred rights of the Constitution, made so by reason of that explicit guarantee. * * * With all respect, therefore, the Court errs in treating the case as if it were an ordinary trespass case or an ordinary picketing case.

The jailhouse, like an executive mansion, a legislative chamber, a courthouse, or the statehouse itself (*Edwards v. South Carolina, supra*) is one of the seats of governments whether it be the Tower of London, the Bastille, or a small county jail. And when it houses political prisoners or those who many think are unjustly held, it is an obvious center for protest. The right to petition for the redress of grievances has an ancient history and is not limited to writing a letter or sending a telegram to a congressman; it is not confined to appearing before the local city council, or writing letters to the President or Governor or Mayor. See *NAACP v. Button*, 371 U.S. 415, 429–431. Conventional methods of petitioning may be, and often have been, shut off to large groups of our citizens. Legislators may turn deaf ears; formal complaints may be routed endlessly through a bureaucratic maze; courts may let the wheels of justice grind very slowly. Those who do not control television and radio, those who cannot afford to advertise in newspapers or circulate elaborate pamphlets may have only a more limited type of access to public officials. Their methods should not be condemned as tactics of obstruction and harassment as long as the assembly and petition are peaceable, as these were.

There is no question that petitioners had as their purpose a protest against the arrest of Florida A. & M. students for trying to integrate public theatres. The sheriff's testimony indicates that he well understood the purpose of the rally. The petitioners who testified unequivocally stated that the group was protesting the arrests, and state and local policies of segregation, including segregation of the jail. This testimony was not contradicted or even questioned. The fact that no one gave a formal speech, that no elaborate handbills were distributed, and that the group was not laden with signs would seem to be immaterial. Such methods are not the *sine qua non* of petitioning for the redress of grievances. The group did sing "freedom" songs. And history shows that a song can be a powerful tool of protest. See *Cox v. State of Louisiana*,

379 U.S. 536. There was no violence; no threat of violence; no attempted jail break; no storming of a prison; no plan or plot to do anything but protest. The evidence is uncontradicted that the petitioners' conduct did not upset the jailhouse routine; things went on as they normally would. None of the group entered the jail. Indeed, they moved back from the entrance as they were instructed. There was no shoving, no pushing, no disorder or threat of riot. It is said that some of the group blocked part of the driveway leading to the jail entrance. * * * [Yet] the entrance to the jail was not blocked. And whenever the students were requested to move they did so. If there was congestion, the solution was a further request to move to lawns or parking areas, not complete ejection and arrest. * * *

We do violence to the First Amendment when we permit this "petition for redress of grievances" to be turned into a trespass action. It does not help to analogize this problem to the problem of picketing. Picketing is a form of protest usually directed against private interests. I do not see how rules governing picketing in general are relevant to this express constitutional right to assemble and to petition for redress of grievances. In the first place the jailhouse grounds were not marked with "NO TRESPASSING!" signs, nor does respondent claim that the public was generally excluded from the grounds. Only the sheriff's fiat transformed lawful conduct into an unlawful trespass. * * * The Court forgets that prior to this day our decisions have drastically limited the application of state statutes inhibiting the right to go peacefully on public property to exercise First Amendment rights. * * * Such was the case of *Edwards v. South Carolina*, where aggrieved people "peaceably assembled at the site of the State Government" to express their grievances to the citizens of the State as well as to the legislature. 372 U.S., at 235. *Edwards* was in the tradition of *Cox v. State of New Hampshire*, 312 U.S. 569, where the public streets were said to be "immemorially associated" with "the right of assembly and the opportunities for the communication of thought and the discussion of public questions." *Id.*, at 574, 61. When we allow Florida to construe her "malicious trespass" statute to bar a person from going on property knowing it is not his own and to apply that prohibition to public property, we discard *Cox* and *Edwards*. Would the case be any different if, as is common, the demonstration took place outside a building which housed both the jail and the legislative body? I think not. * * *

Today a trespass law is used to penalize people for exercising a constitutional right. Tomorrow a disorderly conduct statute, a breach-of-the-peace statute, a vagrancy statute will be put to the same end. It is said that the sheriff did not make the arrests because of the views which petitioners espoused. That excuse is usually given, as we know from the many cases involving arrests of minority groups for breaches of the peace, unlawful assemblies, and parading without a permit. * * * Yet by allowing these orderly and civilized protests against injustice to be suppressed, we only increase the forces of frustration which the conditions of second-class citizenship are generating amongst us.

Notes and Questions

1. Can you reconcile *Cox v. Louisiana* and *Adderley v. Florida*? Is their difference merely that one was a statehouse, the other a jailhouse case?

2. Does one have the right to protest under the First Amendment only in public places? Do you agree that the protesters should not be allowed to demonstrate in the actual jail section of the building? Should the relative reasonableness of their behavior mean they should be allowed to stay in the jail because it is a government building and they are protesting what goes on there?

3. The Court faced the public/private distinction in *Shelley v. Kraemer* 334 U.S. 1 (1948). In that case a state court was asked to enforce a restrictive covenant prohibiting occupation of residential houses by anyone other than Whites. Since the covenant was between private homeowners the issue was whether it violated the Fourteenth Amendment which requires state action. The Court found state action in the state courts' enforcement of the covenant. The covenant was therefore unconstitutional because it violated the Equal Protection Clause.

WALKER v. CITY OF BIRMINGHAM

388 U.S. 307 (1967).

JUSTICE STEWART delivered the opinion of the Court.

On Wednesday, April 10, 1963, officials of Birmingham, Alabama, filed a bill of complaint in a state circuit court asking for injunctive relief against 139 individuals and two organizations. The bill and accompanying affidavits stated that during the preceding seven days:

"(R)espondents (had) sponsored and/or participated in and/or conspired to commit and/or to encourage and/or to participate in certain movements, plans or projects commonly called 'sit-in' demonstrations, 'kneel-in' demonstrations, mass street parades, trespasses on private property after being warned to leave the premises by the owners of said property, congregating in mobs upon the public streets and other public places, unlawfully picketing private places of business in the City of Birmingham, Alabama; violation of numerous ordinances and statutes of the City of Birmingham and State of Alabama...."

It was alleged that this conduct was "calculated to provoke breaches of the peace," "threaten(ed) the safety, peace and tranquility of the City," and placed "an undue burden and strain upon the manpower of the Police Department."

The bill stated that these infractions of the law were expected to continue and would "lead to further imminent danger to the lives, safety, peace, tranquility and general welfare of the people of the City of Birmingham," and that the "remedy by law (was) inadequate." The circuit judge granted a temporary injunction as prayed in the bill, enjoining the petitioners from, among other things, participating in or encouraging mass street parades or mass processions without a permit as required by a Birmingham ordinance.

Five of the eight petitioners were served with copies of the writ early the next morning. Several hours later four of them held a press conference. There a statement was distributed, declaring their intention to disobey the injunction because it was "raw tyranny under the guise of maintaining law and order." At this press conference one of the petitioners stated: "That they had respect for the Federal Courts, or Federal Injunctions, but in the past the State Courts had favored local law enforcement, and if the police couldn't handle it, the mob would."

That night a meeting took place at which one of the petitioners announced that "(i)njunction or no injunction we are going to march tomorrow." The next afternoon, Good Friday, a large crowd gathered in the vicinity of Sixteenth Street and Sixth Avenue North in Birmingham. A group of about 50 or 60 proceeded to parade along the sidewalk while a crowd of 1,000 to 1,500 onlookers stood by, "clapping, and hollering, and (w)hooping." Some of the crowd followed the marchers and spilled out into the street. At least three of the petitioners participated in this march.

Meetings sponsored by some of the petitioners were held that night and the following night, where calls for volunteers to "walk" and go to jail were made. On Easter Sunday, April 14, a crowd of between 1,500 and 2,000 people congregated in the midafternoon in the vicinity of Seventh Avenue and Eleventh Street North in Birmingham. One of the petitioners was seen organizing members of the crowd in formation. A group of about 50, headed by three other petitioners, started down the sidewalk two abreast. At least one other petitioner was among the marchers. Some 300 or 400 people from among the onlookers followed in a crowd that occupied the entire width of the street and overflowed onto the sidewalks. Violence occurred. Members of the crowd threw rocks that injured a newspaperman and damaged a police motorcycle.

The next day the city officials who had requested the injunction applied to the state circuit court for an order to show cause why the petitioners should not be held in contempt for violating it. At the ensuing hearing the petitioners sought to attack the constitutionality of the injunction on the ground that it was vague and overbroad, and restrained free speech. They also sought to attack the Birmingham parade ordinance upon similar grounds, and upon the further ground that the ordinance had previously been administered in an arbitrary and discriminatory manner.

The circuit judge refused to consider any of these contentions, pointing out that there had been neither a motion to dissolve the injunction, nor an effort to comply with it by applying for a permit from the city commission before engaging in the Good Friday and Easter Sunday parades. Consequently, the court held that the only issues before it were whether it had jurisdiction to issue the temporary injunction, and whether thereafter the petitioners had knowingly violated it. Upon these issues the court found against the petitioners, and imposed upon each of them a sentence of five days in jail and a $50 fine, in accord with an Alabama statute.

The Supreme Court of Alabama affirmed. That court, too, declined to consider the petitioners' constitutional attacks upon the injunction and the underlying Birmingham parade ordinance. * * *

Howat v. State of Kansas, 258 U.S. 181, was decided by this Court almost 50 years ago. That was a case in which people had been punished by a Kansas trial court for refusing to obey an antistrike injunction issued under the state industrial relations act. They had claimed a right to disobey the court's order upon the ground that the state statute and the injunction based upon it were invalid under the Federal Constitution. The Supreme Court of Kansas had affirmed the judgment, holding that the trial court "had general power to issue injunctions in equity, and that even if its exercise of the power was erroneous, the injunction was not void, and the defendants were precluded from attacking it in this collateral proceeding ... that, if the injunction was erroneous, jurisdiction was not thereby forfeited, that the error was subject to correction only by the ordinary method of appeal, and disobedience to the order constituted contempt." 258 U.S., at 189. * * *

In the present case, however, we are asked to hold that this rule of law, upon which the Alabama courts relied, was constitutionally impermissible. We are asked to say that the Constitution compelled Alabama to allow the petitioners to violate this injunction, to organize and engage in these mass street parades and demonstrations, without any previous effort on their part to have the injunction dissolved or modified, or any attempt to secure a parade permit in accordance with its terms. Whatever the limits of *Howat v. State of Kansas*, we cannot accept the petitioners' contentions in the circumstances of this case.

Without question the state court that issued the injunction had, as a court of equity, jurisdiction over the petitioners and over the subject matter of the controversy. And this is not a case where the injunction was transparently invalid or had only a frivolous pretense to validity. We have consistently recognized the strong interest of state and local governments in regulating the use of their streets and other public places. * * * When protest takes the form of mass demonstrations, parades, or picketing on public streets and sidewalks, the free passage of traffic and the prevention of public disorder and violence become important objects of legitimate state concern. As the Court stated, in *Cox v. State of Louisiana*, "We emphatically reject the notion ... that the First and Fourteenth Amendments afford the same kind of freedom to those who would communicate ideas by conduct such as patrolling, marching, and picketing on streets and highways, as these amendments afford to those who communicate ideas by pure speech." 379 U.S. 536, 555. * * *

The generality of the language contained in the Birmingham parade ordinance upon which the injunction was based would unquestionably raise substantial constitutional issues concerning some of its provisions. * * * The petitioners, however, did not even attempt to apply to the Alabama courts for an authoritative construction of the ordinance. Had they done so, those courts might have given the licensing authority granted in the ordinance a narrow and precise scope. * * *

The breadth and vagueness of the injunction itself would also unquestionably be subject to substantial constitutional question. But the way to raise that question was to apply to the Alabama courts to have the injunction modified or dissolved. The injunction in all events clearly prohibited mass parading without a permit, and the evidence shows that the petitioners fully understood that prohibition when they violated it.

The petitioners also claim that they were free to disobey the injunction because the parade ordinance on which it was based had been administered in the past in an arbitrary and discriminatory fashion. In support of this claim they sought to introduce evidence that, a few days before the injunction issued, requests for permits to picket had been made to a member of the city commission. One request had been rudely rebuffed, and this same official had later made clear that he was without power to grant the permit alone, since the issuance of such permits was the responsibility of the entire city commission. Assuming the truth of this proffered evidence, it does not follow that the parade ordinance was void on its face. The petitioners, moreover, did not apply for a permit either to the commission itself or to any commissioner after the injunction issued. Had they done so, and had the permit been refused, it is clear that their claim of arbitrary or discriminatory administration of the ordinance would have been considered by the state circuit court upon a motion to dissolve the injunction.

This case would arise in quite a different constitutional posture if the petitioners, before disobeying the injunction, had challenged it in the Alabama courts, and had been met with delay or frustration of their constitutional claims. But there is no showing that such would have been the fate of a timely motion to modify or dissolve the injunction. There was an interim of two days between the issuance of the injunction and the Good Friday march. The petitioners give absolutely no explanation of why they did not make some application to the state court during that period. * * *

The rule of law that Alabama followed in this case reflects a belief that in the fair administration of justice no man can be judge in his own case, however exalted his station, however righteous his motives, and irrespective of his race, color, politics, or religion. This Court cannot hold that the petitioners were constitutionally free to ignore all the procedures of the law and carry their battle to the streets. One may sympathize with the petitioners' impatient commitment to their cause. But respect for judicial process is a small price to pay for the civilizing hand of law, which alone can give abiding meaning to constitutional freedom.

Affirmed.

* * *

CHIEF JUSTICE WARREN, whom JUSTICE BRENNAN and JUSTICE FORTAS join, dissenting.

* * * The Court concedes that "(t)he generality of the language contained in the Birmingham parade ordinance upon which the injunction was based would unquestionably raise substantial constitutional issues concerning some of its provisions." *Ante*, p. 1830. That concession

is well-founded but minimal. I believe it is patently unconstitutional on its face. Our decisions have consistently held that picketing and parading are means of expression protected by the First Amendment, and that the right to picket or parade may not be subjected to the unfettered discretion of local officials. *Cox v. State of Louisiana*, 379 U.S. 536 (1965); *Edwards v. South Carolina*, 372 U.S. 229 (1963); *Thornhill v. State of Alabama*, 310 U.S. 88 (1940). Although a city may regulate the manner of use of its streets and sidewalks in the interest of keeping them open for the movement of traffic, it may not allow local officials unbridled discretion to decide who shall be allowed to parade or picket and who shall not. "Wherever the title of streets and parks may rest, they have immemorially been held in trust for the use of the public and, time out of mind, have been used for purposes of assembly, communicating thoughts between citizens, and discussing public questions. Such use of the streets and public places has, from ancient times, been a part of the privileges, immunities, rights, and liberties of citizens. The privilege of a citizen of the United States to use the street and parks for communication of views on national questions may be regulated in the interest of all; it is not absolute, but relative, and must be exercised in subordination to the general comfort and convenience, and in consonance with peace and good order; but it must not, in the guise of regulation, be abridged or denied." *Hague v. C.I.O.*, 307 U.S. 496, 515–516 (1939) (opinion of Justice Roberts). When local officials are given totally unfettered discretion to decide whether a proposed demonstration is consistent with "public welfare, peace, safety, health, decency, good order, morals or convenience," as they were in this case, they are invited to act as censors over the views that may be presented to the public. The unconstitutionality of the ordinance is compounded, of course, when there is convincing evidence that the officials have in fact used their power to deny permits to organizations whose views they dislike. The record in this case hardly suggests that Commissioner Connor and the other city officials were motivated in prohibiting civil rights picketing only by their overwhelming concern for particular traffic problems. Petitioners were given to understand that under no circumstances would they be permitted to demonstrate in Birmingham, not that a demonstration would be approved if a time and place were selected that would minimize the traffic difficulties. The only circumstance that the court can find to justify anything other than a *per curiam* reversal is that Commissioner Connor had the foresight to have the unconstitutional ordinance included in an *ex parte* injunction issued without notice or hearing or any showing that it was impossible to have notice or a hearing, forbidding the world at large (insofar as it knew of the order) to conduct demonstrations in Birmingham without the consent of the city officials. This injunction was such potent magic that it transformed the command of an unconstitutional statute into an impregnable barrier, challengeable only in what likely would have been protracted legal proceedings and entirely superior in the meantime even to the United States Constitution. * * *

JUSTICE DOUGLAS, with whom THE CHIEF JUSTICE [WARREN], JUSTICE BRENNAN, and JUSTICE FORTAS concur, dissenting.

* * * The right to defy an unconstitutional statute is basic in our scheme. Even when an ordinance requires a permit to make a speech, to deliver a sermon, to picket, to parade, or to assemble, it need not be honored when it is invalid on its face. *Lovell v. City of Griffin*, 303 U.S. 444, 452–453; *Thornhill v. State of Alabama*, 310 U.S. 88, 97; *Jones v. City of Opelika*, 316 U.S. 584, 602, adopted *per curiam* on rehearing, 319 U.S. 103, 104; *Cantwell v. State of Connecticut*, 310 U.S. 296, 305–306.

By like reason, where a permit has been arbitrarily denied one need not pursue the long and expensive route to this Court to obtain a remedy. The reason is the same in both cases. For if a person must pursue his judicial remedy before he may speak, parade, or assemble, the occasion when protest is desired or needed will have become history and any later speech, parade, or assembly will be futile or pointless.

Howat v. State of Kansas, 258 U.S. 181, states the general rule that court injunctions are to be obeyed until error is found by normal and orderly review procedures. See *United States v. United Mine Workers*, 330 U.S. 258, 293–294. But there is an exception where "the question of jurisdiction" is "frivolous and not substantial." *Id.*, at 293. Moreover, a state court injunction is not *per se* sacred where federal constitutional questions are involved. In re *Green*, 369 U.S. 689, held that contempt could not be imposed without a hearing where the state decree bordered the federal domain in labor relations and only a hearing could determine whether there was federal pre-emption. In the present case the collision between this state court decree and the First Amendment is so obvious that no hearing is needed to determine the issue. * * *

JUSTICE BRENNAN, with whom THE CHIEF JUSTICE [WARREN], JUSTICE DOUGLAS, and JUSTICE FORTAS join, dissenting.

* * * Attempts by petitioners at the contempt hearing to show that they tried to obtain a permit but were rudely rebuffed by city officials were aborted when the trial court sustained objections to the testimony. It did appear, however, that on April 3, a member of the Alabama Christian Movement for Human Rights (ACMHR) was sent by one of the petitioners, the Reverend Mr. Shuttlesworth, to Birmingham city hall to inquire about permits for future demonstrations. The member stated at trial:

"I asked (Police) Commissioner Connor for the permit, and asked if he could issue the permit, or other persons who would refer me to, persons who would issue a permit. He said, 'No, you will not get a permit in Birmingham, Alabama to picket. I will picket you over to the City Jail,' and he repeated that twice."

Two days later the Reverend Mr. Shuttlesworth sent a telegram to Police Commissioner Connor requesting a permit on behalf of ACMHR to picket on given dates "against the injustices of segregation and discrimination." Connor replied that the permit could be granted only by the full Commission and stated, "I insist that you and your people do not start any picketing on the streets in Birmingham, Alabama." Petitioners were also frustrated in their attempts at the contempt hearing to show that permits were granted, not by the Commission, but by the city clerk at the request of the traffic department, and that they were issued in a discriminatory manner. * * *

II.

The holding of the Alabama Supreme Court, and the affirmance of its decision by this Court, rest on the assumption that petitioners may be criminally punished although the parade ordinance and the injunction be unconstitutional on their faces as in violation of the First Amendment, and even if the parade ordinance was discriminatorily applied. It must therefore be assumed, for purposes of review of the Alabama Supreme Court's decision, and in assessing the Court's affirmance, that petitioners could successfully sustain the contentions (into which the Alabama courts refused to inquire) that the ordinance and injunction are in fact facially unconstitutional as excessively vague prior restraints on First Amendment rights and that the ordinance had been discriminatorily applied. * * *

In the present case we are confronted with a collision between Alabama's interest in requiring adherence to orders of its courts and the constitutional prohibition against abridgment of freedom of speech, more particularly "the right of the people peaceably to assemble," and the right "to petition the Government for a redress of grievances." See, e.g., *Stromberg v. People of State of California*, 283 U.S. 359; *De Jonge v. State of Oregon*, 299 U.S. 353; *Thornhill v. State of Alabama*, 310 U.S. 88; *Edwards v. State of South Carolina*, 372 U.S. 229; *Cox v. State of Louisiana*, 379 U.S. 536. Special considerations have time and again been deemed by us to attend protection of these freedoms in the face of state interests the vindication of which results in prior restraints upon their exercise, or their regulation in a vague or overbroad manner, or in a way which gives unbridled discretion to limit their exercise to an individual or group of individuals. To give these freedoms the necessary "breathing space to survive," *NAACP v. Button*, 371 U.S. 415, 433, the Court has modified traditional rules of standing and prematurity. See *Dombrowski v. Pfister*, 380 U.S. 479. We have molded both substantive rights and procedural remedies in the face of varied conflicting interests to conform to our overriding duty to insulate all individuals from the "chilling effect" upon exercise of First Amendment freedoms generated by vagueness, overbreadth and unbridled discretion to limit their exercise. * * *

It is said that petitioners should have sought to dissolve the injunction before conducting their processions. That argument is plainly repugnant to the principle that First Amendment freedoms may be exercised in the face of legislative prior restraints, and *a fortiori* of *ex parte* restraints broader than such legislative restraints, which may be challenged in any subsequent proceeding for their violation. But at all events, prior resort to a motion to dissolve this injunction could not be required because of the complete absence of any time limits on the duration of the *ex parte* order. See *Freedman v. State of Maryland*, 380 U.S. 51. Even the Alabama Supreme Court's Rule 47 leaves the timing of full judicial consideration of the validity of the restraint to that court's untrammeled discretion. * * *

The Court today lets loose a devastatingly destructive weapon for infringement of freedoms jealously safeguarded not so much for the benefit of any given group of any given persuasion as for the benefit of all of us. We cannot permit fears of "riots" and "civil disobedience" generated by slogans like "Black Power" to divert our attention from what is here at stake—not violence or the right of the State to control its streets and sidewalks, but the insulation from attack of *ex parte* orders and legislation upon which they are based even when patently impermissible prior restraints on the exercise of First Amendment rights, thus arming the state courts with the power to punish as a "contempt" what they otherwise could not punish at all. Constitutional restrictions against abridgments of First Amendment freedoms limit judicial equally with legislative and executive power. Convictions for contempt of court orders which invalidly abridge First Amendment freedoms must be condemned equally with convictions for violation of statutes which do the same thing. I respectfully dissent.

Notes and Questions

1. Do you agree that the protesters should have gone to court and dissolved the injunction prior to marching? Suppose they knew this effort would be fruitless even though the injunction was transparently unconstitutional? Is the Court's ruling merely about respect for the courts and their injunctive powers? If so, is it a petulant and needless act of self-assertion, like a parent telling a teenager, "No you can't go. You should have asked me first, before planning that party with Jennifer?" See David Oppenheimer, *Kennedy, King, Shuttlesworth and Walker*, 29 USF L. Rev. 645 (1995).

2. The Court, in *Shuttlesworth v. City of Birmingham*, 394 U.S. 147 (1969), held that a city ordinance which gave officials absolute power to prohibit any procession/demonstration by requiring prior application for a permit and no standards to guide the licensing authority was unconstitutional. It abridged free speech and assembly rights. Why must a person go to court to dissolve an injunction which infringes their free speech and assembly rights, but may ignore a city ordinance that does the same thing? Should unconstitutional court rulings be treated differently from unconstitutional statutes?

3. In *Green v. Samuelson*, 168 Md. 421, 178 A. 109 (1935), Blacks picketed stores that refused to hire Blacks, asking customers not to shop there. The court held that their actions were not governed by labor law because the right to picket is a social question. Therefore, even though the protestors' actions may injure the business of the stores their conduct could not be enjoined.

4. In *NAACP v. Button*, 371 U.S. 415 (1963), a Virginia statute barring solicitation of legal business was found unconstitutional because it infringed on the NAACP's rights of expression and association. The statute prohibited any arrangement by which prospective litigants are advised to seek the assistance of a particular attorney and prohibited advising a person of his legal rights. Since Virginia failed to show a substantial regulatory interest in prohibiting such communications, the prohibition was unconstitutional.

5. In *Green* and *Button*, southern states attempted, unsuccessfully, to invoke non-speech doctrines to bridle speech. Why was this illegitimate? How far can one go in communicating a civil rights message?

6. In *NAACP v. Overstreet*, 384 U.S. 118 (1966), the Supreme Court upheld a jury award of $80,000 for loss of business and for punitive damages against the national NAACP for a boycott organized by a local chapter. Fifteen years later, in *NAACP v. Claiborne Hardware*, 458 U.S. 886 (1982), the Court held that boycotters could not be held liable for damages unless they acted violently, and then only for the damages resulting from the violence. Further, the court held that violent participation by some members of the NAACP alone does not mean the group itself is liable. The group must be shown to have unlawful goals to be liable.

7. Does *Claiborne Hardware* effectively reverse *Overstreet*? What is the current liability of the NAACP or similar organization, if it organizes a boycott? What activity or motives must be shown for liability to attach?

8. The issue in *Hughes v. Superior Court*, 339 U.S. 460 (1950), was whether the Fourteenth Amendment bars a state from using an injunction to prohibit picketing of a business to increase the proportion of African–American employees. The Court held that the state could use an injunction because the picketing subverted the state policy against forcing businesses to hire by race. Later, in *United States v. O'Brien*, 391 U.S. 367 (1968), the Court held that the government had a sufficient interest to justify criminally punishing O'Brien for burning his draft card. The Court said that since the punishment furthered the governmental interest of raising an army and since the incidental restrictions to his First Amendment rights were no greater than essential to further that interest, the punishment was constitutional.

9. When protesting or boycotting, does one have more protection as an individual or as an organization? Do you think the current Court would continue to uphold the line set in *Hughes* and *O'Brien*? Does this mean that states can subvert protests by declaring a state policy and issuing an injunction?

10. For discussion of an NAACP boycott of the TV show "Amos 'n' Andy," see Chapter 12.

CHARLES R. LAWRENCE III

If He Hollers Let Him Go: Regulating Racist Speech on Campus
1990 Duke L.J. 431, 438–49.*

The landmark case of *Brown v. Board of Education* is not one we normally think of as a case about speech. As read most narrowly, the case is about the rights of black children to equal educational opportunity. But *Brown* can also be read more broadly to articulate a principle central to any substantive understanding of the Equal Protection Clause, the foundation on which all antidiscrimination law rests. This is the principle of equal citizenship. Under that principle "every individual is presumptively entitled to be treated by the organized society as a respected, responsible, and participating member.''[36] Furthermore, it requires the affirmative disestablishment of societal practices that treat people as members of an inferior or dependent caste, as unworthy to participate in the larger community. The holding in *Brown*—that racially segregated schools violate the Equal Protection Clause—reflects the fact that segregation amounts to a demeaning, caste-creating practice.

The key to this understanding of *Brown* is that the practice of segregation, the practice the Court held inherently unconstitutional, was speech. *Brown* held that segregation is unconstitutional not simply because the physical separation of black and white children is bad or because resources were distributed unequally among black and white schools. *Brown* held that segregated schools were unconstitutional primarily because of the message segregation conveys—the message that black children are an untouchable caste, unfit to be educated with white children. Segregation serves its purpose by conveying an idea. It stamps a badge of inferiority upon blacks, and this badge communicates a message to others in the community, as well as to blacks wearing the badge, that is injurious to blacks. Therefore, *Brown* may be read as regulating the content of racist speech. As a regulation of racist speech, the decision is an exception to the usual rule that regulation of speech content is presumed unconstitutional.

THE CONDUCT/SPEECH DISTINCTION

Some civil libertarians argue that my analysis of *Brown* conflates speech and conduct. They maintain that the segregation outlawed in *Brown* was discriminatory conduct, not speech, and the defamatory message conveyed by segregation simply was an incidental by-product of that conduct. This position is often stated as follows: "Of course segregation conveys a message but this could be said of almost all conduct. To take an extreme example, a murderer conveys a message of hatred for his victim. [But], we would not argue that we can't punish the murder— the primary conduct—merely because of this message which is its secondary byproduct."[42] This objection to my reading of *Brown* misperceives the central point of the argument. I have not ignored the distinction between the speech and conduct elements of segregation by mistake. Rather, my analysis turns on that distinction. It asks the question whether there is a purpose for outlawing segregation that is unrelated to its message, and it concludes the answer is "no."

If, for example, John W. Davis, counsel for the Board of Education of Topeka, Kansas, had been asked during oral argument in *Brown* to state the Board's purpose in educating black and white children in separate schools, he would have been hard pressed to answer in a way unrelated to the purpose of designating black children as inferior. If segregation's primary goal is to convey the message of white supremacy, then *Brown*'s declaration that segregation is unconstitutional amounts to a regulation of the message of white supremacy. Properly understood, *Brown* and its

36. K. Karst, *Citizenship, Race and Marginality*, 30 Wm. & Mary L. Rev. 1, 1 (1988).

42. Remarks by Nadine Strossen, ACLU General Counsel, responding to Professor Charles Lawrence at the 1989 ACLU Biennial Conference plenary session "Racism on the Rise," June 15, 1989.

progeny require that the systematic group defamation of segregation be disestablished. Although the exclusion of black children from white schools and the denial of educational resources and association that accompany exclusion can be characterized as conduct, these particular instances of conduct are concerned primarily with communicating the idea of white supremacy. The nonspeech elements are by-products of the main message rather than the message simply a by-product of unlawful conduct.

The public accommodations provisions of the Civil Rights Act of 1964 provide another example illuminating why laws against discrimination are also regulation of racist speech. The legislative history and the Supreme Court's opinions upholding the Act establish that Congress was concerned that blacks have access to public accommodations to eliminate impediments to the free flow of interstate commerce, but this purpose could have been achieved through a regime of separate-but-equal accommodations. Title II goes further; it incorporates the principal of the inherent inequality of segregation, and prohibits restaurant owners from providing separate places at the lunch counter for "whites" and "coloreds." Even if the same food and the same service are provided, separate-but-equal facilities are unlawful. If the signs indicating separate facilities remain in place, then the statute is violated despite proof that restaurant patrons are free to disregard the signs. Outlawing these signs graphically illustrates my point that antidiscrimination laws are primarily regulations of the content of racist speech.

Another way to understand the inseparability of racist speech and discriminatory conduct is to view individual racist acts as part of a totality. When viewed in this manner, white supremacists' conduct or speech is forbidden by the Equal Protection Clause. The goal of white supremacy is not achieved by individual acts or even by the cumulative acts of a group, but rather by the institutionalization of the ideas of white supremacy. The institutionalization of white supremacy within our culture has created conduct on the societal level that is greater than the sum of individual racist acts. The racist acts of millions of individuals are mutually reinforcing and cumulative because the status quo of institutionalized white supremacy remains long after deliberate racist actions subside.

It is difficult to recognize the institutional significance of white supremacy or how it acts to harm, partially because of its ubiquity. We simply do not see most racist conduct because we experience a world in which whites are supreme as simply "the world." Much racist conduct is considered unrelated to race or regarded as neutral because racist conduct maintains the status quo, the status quo of the world as we have known it. Catharine MacKinnon has observed that "to the extent that pornography succeeds in constructing social reality, it becomes invisible as harm."[53] Thus, pornography "is more act-like than thought-like."[54] This truth about gender discrimination is equally true of racism.

53. Catharine MacKinnon, *Toward A Feminist Theory of The State* 204 (1989).

54. *Id.*

Just because one can express the idea or message embodied by a practice such as white supremacy does not necessarily equate that practice with the idea. Slavery was an idea as well as a practice, but the Court recognized the inseparability of idea and practice in the institution of slavery when it held the enabling clause of the Thirteenth Amendment clothed Congress with the power to pass "all laws necessary and proper for abolishing all badges and incidents of slavery in the United States."[56] This understanding also informs the regulation of speech/conduct in the public accommodations provisions of the Civil Rights Act of 1964 discussed above. When the racist restaurant or hotel owner puts a "whites only" sign in his window, his sign is more than speech. Putting up the sign is more than an act excluding black patrons who see the sign. The sign is part of the larger practice of segregation and white supremacy that constructs and maintains a culture in which nonwhites are excluded from full citizenship. The inseparability of the idea and practice of racism is central to *Brown*'s holding that segregation is inherently unconstitutional.

Racism is both 100 percent speech and 100 percent conduct. Discriminatory conduct is not racist unless it also conveys the message of white supremacy—unless it is interpreted within the culture to advance the structure and ideology of white supremacy. Likewise, all racist speech constructs the social reality that constrains the liberty of nonwhites because of their race. By limiting the life opportunities of others, this act of constructing meaning also makes racist speech conduct.

THE PUBLIC/PRIVATE DISTINCTION

There are critics who would contend that *Brown* is inapposite because the Equal Protection Clause only restricts government behavior, whereas the First Amendment protects the speech of private persons. They say, "Of course we want to prevent the state from defaming blacks, but we must continue to be vigilant about protecting the speech rights, even of racist individuals, from the government. In both cases our concern must be protecting the individual from the unjust power of the state."

At first blush, this position seems persuasive, but its persuasiveness relies upon the mystifying properties of constitutional ideology. In particular, I refer to the state action doctrine. By restricting the application of the Fourteenth Amendment to discrimination implicating the government, the state action rule immunizes private discriminators from constitutional scrutiny. In so doing, it leaves untouched the largest part of the vast system of segregation in the United States. *The Civil Rights Cases*, in which this doctrine was firmly established, stand as a monument preserving American racial discrimination. Although the origin of state action is textual, countervailing values of privacy, freedom of

---

56. *The Civil Rights Cases*, 109 U.S. 3, 20 (1883) (striking down the Civil Rights Act of 1875 on the ground that the Fourteenth Amendment did not empower Congress to prohibit racial discrimination by innkeepers, railroads, and places of public amusement); *Jones v. Alfred H. Mayer Co.*, 392 U.S. 409, 439 (1968) (upholding Congress' use of the "badge of servitude" idea to justify federal legislation prohibiting racially discriminatory practices by private persons).

association, and free speech all have been used to justify the rule's exculpation of private racism.

In the abstract, the right to make decisions about how we will educate our children or with whom we will associate is an important value in American society. But when we decontextualize by viewing this privacy value in the abstract, we ignore the way it operates in the real world. We do not ask ourselves, for example, whether it is a value to which all persons have equal access. And we do not inquire about who has the resources to send their children to private school or move to an exclusive suburb. The privacy value, when presented as an ideal, seems an appropriate limitation on racial justice because we naively believe that everyone has an equal stake in this value.

The argument that distinguishes private racist speech from the government speech outlawed by *Brown* suffers from the same decontextualizing ideology. If the government is involved in a joint venture with private contractors to engage in the business of defaming blacks, should it be able to escape the constitutional mandate that makes that business illegal simply by handing over the copyright and the printing presses to its partners in crime? I think not. And yet this is the essence of the position that espouses First Amendment protection for those partners. * * *.

When a person responds to the argument that *Brown* mandates the abolition of racist speech by reciting the state action doctrine, she fails to consider that the alternative to regulating racist speech is infringement of the claims of blacks to liberty and equal protection. The best way to constitutionally protect these competing interests is to balance them directly. To invoke the state action doctrine is to circumvent our value judgment as to how these competing interests should be balanced.

The deference usually given to the First Amendment values in this balance is justified using the argument that racist speech is unpopular speech, that, like the speech of civil rights activists, pacifists, and religious and political dissenters, it is in need of special protection from majoritarian censorship. But for over three hundred years, racist speech has been the liturgy of America's leading established religion, the religion of racism. Racist speech remains a vital and regrettably popular characteristic of the American vernacular. It must be noted that there has not yet been satisfactory retraction of the government-sponsored defamation in the slavery clauses, the *Dred Scott* decision, the black codes, the segregation statutes, and countless other group libels. The injury to blacks is hardly redressed by deciding the government must no longer injure our reputation if one then invokes the First Amendment to ensure that racist speech continues to thrive in an unregulated private market. * * *

It is a very sad irony that the first instinct of many civil libertarians has been to express concern for possible infringement of the assailants' liberties while barely noticing the constitutional rights of the assailed. Shortly after *Brown*, many southern communities tried to escape the mandate of desegregation by closing public schools and opening private (white) academies. These attempts to avoid the Fourteenth Amendment through the privatization of discrimination consistently were invalidated by the courts. In essence, the Supreme Court held that the defamatory message of segregation would not be insulated from constitutional proscription simply because the speaker was a non-government entity.

The Supreme Court also has indicated that Congress may enact legislation regulating private racist speech. In upholding the public accommodations provisions of Title II of the Civil Rights Act of 1964 in *Heart of Atlanta Motel v. United States*, the Court implicitly rejected the argument that the absence of state action meant that private discriminators were protected by First Amendment free speech and associational rights. Likewise in *Bob Jones University v. United States*, the Court sustained the Internal Revenue Service's decision to discontinue tax exempt status for a college with a policy against interracial dating and marriage. The college framed its objection in terms of the free exercise of religion, since their policy was religiously motivated, but the Supreme Court found that the government had "a fundamental, overriding interest in eradicating racial discrimination in education" that "substantially outweighs whatever burden denial of tax benefits" placed on the college's exercise of its religious beliefs. It is difficult to believe that the University would have fared any better under free speech analysis or if the policy had been merely a statement of principle rather than an enforceable disciplinary regulation. Regulation of private racist speech also has been held constitutional in the context of prohibition of race-designated advertisements for employees, home sales, and rentals.

Thus *Brown* and the antidiscrimination law it spawned provide precedent for my position that the content regulation of racist speech is not only permissible but may be required by the Constitution in certain circumstances. This precedent may not mean that we should advocate the government regulation of all racist speech, but it should give us pause in assuming absolutist positions about regulations aimed at the message or idea such speech conveys. If we understand *Brown*—the cornerstone of the civil rights movement and equal protection doctrine—correctly, and if we understand the necessity of disestablishing the system of signs and symbols that signal blacks' inferiority, then we should not proclaim that all racist speech that stops short of physical violence must be defended.

Notes and Questions

1. Is Lawrence right that *Brown v. Board of Education* was a hate-speech case, and not one about official action, *viz.*, segregated pupil assignment? Just how damaging are messages from one person to another saying that the first regards the second as inferior, lazy, stupid, unworthy, etc.? Can one not simply shrug them off? Of course, if the hateful words are libelous, fighting words, or inflict intentional emotional distress, they are covered by one of these other doctrines. If so, why do we need hate-speech regulations or codes? Does the state have an independent interest in discouraging that kind of speech? Consider *Beauharnais, infra*, an early Supreme Court decision that ruled that it does.

2. Imagine that the students of law school X (public, U.S.A.) are upset over the school's refusal to hire faculty of color. Months of polite lobbying,

leafletting, teach-ins, and a press conference aimed at shaming the faculty have brought no results. The students are considering three plans; they seek your advice about each in terms of (1) likely efficacy, and (2) legal jeopardy (they don't want to get arrested, or, if so, have the conviction stand up). The three proposals are:

- A noon rally, with amplified sound, held directly outside the law school and aimed at disrupting ordinary activity inside.

- A secret agreement that the group and its sympathizers will show up at class one day wearing "brownface" to symbolize the absence of brown professors, and black armbands to symbolize mourning.

- A week-long "starve-in" by otherwise peaceable protesters in the main law school corridor. The protesters will remain lying off to both sides of the corridor and not blocking passage to other users. If asked to leave when the building closes for the night, they are prepared to refuse and court arrest.

What do you advise?

3.   Although cases of black protest are the best-known and the ones that have reached the Supreme Court, other groups have resorted to picketing, boycotts, marches, and other forms of expressive activity and direct action.

For a sample of writing on the American Indian Movement, see: Ward Churchill & Jim Vander Wall, *Agents of Repression: The FBI's Secret War Against the Black Panther Party and the American Indian Movement* (1988); John W. Sayer, *Ghost Dancing the Law: The Wounded Knee Trials* (1997); Peter Matthiessen, *In the Spirit of Crazy Horse* (1983); Kenneth S. Stern, *Loud Hawk: The United States Versus the American Indian Movement* (1994); Russell Means, *Where White Men Fear to Tread: The Autobiography of Russell Means* (1995); Mary Brave Bird, *Ohitika Woman* (1993); Johanna Brand, *The Life and Death of Anna Mae Aquash* (1978); Rex Wyler, *Blood of the Land: The Government and Corporate War Against First Nations* (1992); Joseph C. Hogan III, *Note, Guilty Until Proven Innocent: Leonard Peltier and the Sublegal System*, 34 B.C. L. Rev. 901 (1993).

For information on César Chávez and the farmworkers' movement, see Jacques E. Levy, *César Chávez: Autobiography of La Causa* (1975); Richard Griswold del Castillo & Richard A. Garcia, *César Chávez: A Triumph of Spirit* (1995); Winthrop Yinger, *César Chávez: The Rhetoric of Nonviolence* (1975); Ronald B. Taylor, *Chávez and the Farm Workers* (1975); Fred Ross, *Conquering Goliath: César Chávez at the Beginning* (1989); John G. Dunne, *Delano: The Story of the California Grape Strike* (1967); Susan Ferriss & Ricardo Sandoval, *The Fight in the Fields: César Chávez and the Farmworkers Movement* (1997); Mark Day *Forty Acres: César Chávez and the Farm Workers* (1971); James P. Terzian & Kathryn Cramer, *Mighty Hard Road: The Story of César Chávez* (1970); Peter Matthiessen, *Sal Si Puedes: César Chávez and the New American Revolution* (1969); Joan London & Henry Anderson, *So Shall Ye Reap* (1970); Emilio Huerta, *How the Legacy of César Chávez Continues to Impact the Lives of Farm Workers Through the National Farm Workers Service Center*, 9 La Raza L.J. 183 (1996); Beatriz J. Hernandez, *Cesar's Ghost,* 13 Cal. Law. July 1993, at 48.

SECTION 2.   LANGUAGE USED AGAINST MINORITIES: THE CASE OF HATE SPEECH

CHARLES R. LAWRENCE III

If He Hollers Let Him Go: Regulating Racist Speech on Campus
1990 Duke L.J. 431, 459–62, 466–75, 482–83.*

To engage in a debate about the First Amendment and racist speech without a full understanding of the nature and extent of the harm of racist speech risks making the First Amendment an instrument of domination rather than a vehicle of liberation. Not everyone has known the experience of being victimized by racist, misogynist, and homophobic speech, and we do not share equally the burden of the societal harm it inflicts. Often we are too quick to say we have heard the victims' cries when we have not; we are too eager to assure ourselves we have experienced the same injury, and therefore we can strike a constitutional balance without danger of mismeasurement. For many of us who have fought for the rights of oppressed minorities, it is difficult to accept that—by underestimating the injury from racist speech—we too might be implicated in the vicious words we would never utter. Until we have eradicated racism and sexism and no longer share in the fruits of those forms of domination, we cannot justly strike the balance over the protest of those who are dominated. My plea is simply that we listen to the victims.

Members of my own family were involved in a recent incident at Wilmington Friends, a private school in Wilmington, Delaware, that taught me much about both the nature of the injury racist speech inflicts and the lack of understanding many whites have of that injury. * * * In recent years, the school strove to meet its commitment to human equality by enrolling a small (but significant) group of minority students and hiring an even smaller number of black faculty and staff. My sister Paula, a gifted, passionate, and dedicated teacher was the principal of the lower school. Her sons attend the high school. * * *

In May of their second year in Wilmington, an incident occurred that shook the entire school community but was particularly painful to my sister's family and others who found themselves the objects of hateful speech. In a letter to the school community explaining a decision to expel four students, the school's headmaster described the incident as follows:

On Sunday evening, May 1, four students in the senior class met by prearrangement to paint the soccer kickboard, a flat rectangular structure, approximately 8 ft. by 25 ft., standing in the midst of the Wilmington Friends School playing fields. They worked for approximately one hour under bright moonlight and then went home.

What confronted students and staff the following morning, depicted on the kickboard, were racist and anti-Semitic slogans and, most disturbing of all, threats of violent assault against one clearly identified member of the senior class. The slogans included "Save the land, join the Klan," and "Down with Jews"; among the drawings were at least twelve hooded Ku Klux Klansmen, Nazi swastikas, and a burning cross. The most disturbing depictions, however, were those that threatened violence against one of the senior black students. He was drawn, in cartoon figure, identified by his name, and his initials, and by the name of his mother. Directly to the right of his head was a bullet, and farther to the right was a gun with its barrel directed toward the head. Under the drawing, three Ku Klux Klansmen were depicted, one of whom was saying that the student "dies." Next to the gun was a drawing of a burning cross under which was written "Kill the Tarbaby."[110]

When I visited my sister's family a few days after this incident, the injury they had suffered was evident. The wounds were fresh. Their faces betrayed the aftershock of a recently inflicted blow and a newly discovered vulnerability. I knew the pain and scars were no less enduring because the injury had not been physical. And when I talked to my sister, I realized the greatest part of her pain came not from the incident itself but rather from the reaction of white parents who had come to the school in unprecedented numbers to protest the offending students' expulsion. "It was only a prank." "No one was physically attacked." "How can you punish these kids for mere words, mere drawings." Paula's pain was compounded by the failure of these people, with whom she had lived and worked, to recognize that she had been hurt, to understand in even the most limited way the reality of her pain and that of her family.

Many people called the incident "isolated." But black folks know that no racial incident is "isolated" in America. That is what makes the incidents so horrible, so scary. It is the knowledge that they are not the isolated unpopular speech of a dissident few that makes them so frightening. These incidents are manifestations of an ubiquitous and deeply ingrained cultural belief system, an American way of life. Too often in recent months, as I have debated this issue with friends and colleagues, I have heard people speak of the need to protect "offensive" speech. The word offensive is used as if we were speaking of a difference in taste, as if I should learn to be less sensitive to words that offend me. I cannot help but believe that those people who speak of offense—those who argue that this speech must go unchecked—do not understand the great difference between offense and injury: They have not known the injury my sister experienced, have not known the fear, vulnerability, and shame experienced by [other victims]. There is a great difference between the offensiveness of words that you would rather not hear—because they are labeled dirty, impolite, or personally demeaning—and the injury inflicted by words that remind the world that you are fair game for physical attack, evoke in you all of the millions of cultural lessons regarding your inferiority that you have so painstakingly repressed, and imprint upon you a badge of servitude and subservience for

110. Letter from Dulany O. Bennett to parents, alumni, and friends of the Wil-   mington Friends School (May 17, 1988).

all the world to see. It is instructive that the chief proponents for sanctioning people who inflict these injuries are women and people of color, and there are few among these groups who take the absolutist position that any regulation of this speech is too much. * * *

Psychic injury is no less an injury than being struck in the face, and it often is far more severe. *Brown v. Board of Education*[114] speaks directly to the psychic injury inflicted by racist speech in noting that the symbolic message of segregation affected "the hearts and minds" of Negro children "in a way unlikely ever to be undone." Racial epithets and harassment often cause deep emotional scarring, and feelings of anxiety and fear that pervade every aspect of a victim's life. Many victims of hate propaganda have experienced physiological and emotional symptoms ranging from rapid pulse rate and difficulty in breathing, to nightmares, post-traumatic stress disorder, psychosis and suicide.[116] * * *

THE OTHER SIDE OF THE BALANCE: DOES THE SUPPRESSION OF RACIAL EPITHETS WEIGH FOR OR AGAINST SPEECH?

In striking a balance, we also must think about what we are weighing on the side of speech. Most blacks—unlike many white civil libertarians—do not have faith in free speech as the most important vehicle for liberation. The First Amendment coexisted with slavery, and we still are not sure it will protect us to the same extent that it protects whites. It often is argued that minorities have benefited greatly from First Amendment protection and therefore should guard it jealously. We are aware that the struggle for racial equality has relied heavily on the persuasion of peaceful protest protected by the First Amendment, but experience also teaches us that our petitions often go unanswered until they disrupt business as usual and require the self-interested attention of those persons in power. * * *

Blacks and other people of color are equally skeptical about the absolutist argument that even the most injurious speech must remain unregulated because in an unregulated marketplace of ideas the best ideas will rise to the top and gain acceptance. Our experience tells us the opposite. We have seen too many demagogues elected by appealing to America's racism. We have seen too many good, liberal politicians shy away from the issues that might brand them as too closely allied with us. The American marketplace of ideas was founded with the idea of the

114. *Brown v. Board of Education*, 347 U.S. 483, 494 (1954).

116. See M. Matsuda, *Public Response to Racist Speech: Considering the Victim's Story*, 87 Mich. L. Rev. 2320, 2335–41 (1989) (physical and psychological harm of racist hate speech is significant). The effects of racial prejudice include displaced aggression, avoidance, retreat, and withdrawal, alcoholism and suicide. H. Kitano, *Race Relations* 69–85 (2d ed. 1974). See also R. Delgado, *Words That Wound: A Tort Action for Racial Insults, Epithets, and Name-Calling*, 17 Harv. C.R.-C.L. L. Rev. 133, 137–39 (1982) (noting, *inter alia*, high blood pressure, loss of self-worth, and special harm to children); G. Allport, *The Nature of Prejudice* 142–60 (1954). *Cf.* Hafner, *Psychological Disturbances Following Prolonged Persecution*, 3 Soc. Psychiatry 79 (1968) (discussing psychological symptoms including headaches, dizziness, social withdrawal, chronic depression and anxiety neurosis in survivors of extreme persecution); M. Denis, *Race Harassment Discrimination: A Problem That Won't Go Away?*, 10 Employment Rel. L.J. 415, 432–35 (1984) (discussing damages for psychic injury in race harassment cases).

racial inferiority of nonwhites as one of its chief commodities, and ever since the market opened, racism has remained its most active item in trade.[133]

But it is not just the prevalence and strength of the idea of racism that makes the unregulated marketplace of ideas an untenable paradigm for those individuals who seek full and equal personhood for all. The real problem is that the idea of the racial inferiority of nonwhites infects, skews, and disables the operation of the market (like a computer virus, sick cattle, or diseased wheat). Racism is irrational and often unconscious. Our belief in the inferiority of nonwhites trumps good ideas that contend with it in the market, often without our even knowing it. In addition, racism makes the words and ideas of blacks and other despised minorities less saleable, regardless of their intrinsic value, in the marketplace of ideas. It also decreases the total amount of speech that enters the market by coercively silencing members of those groups who are its targets. * * *

The disruptive and disabling effect on the market of an idea like racism that is ubiquitous and irrational, but seldom seen or acknowledged, should be apparent. If the community is considering competing ideas about providing food for children, shelter for the homeless, or abortions for pregnant women, and the choices made among the proposed solutions are influenced by the idea that some children, families, or women are less deserving of our sympathy because they are not white, then the market is not functioning as either John Stuart Mill or Oliver Wendell Holmes envisioned it. In John Ely's terms, it suffers a "process defect."[141] * * *

Prejudice that is unconscious or unacknowledged causes even more distortions in the market. When racism operates at a conscious level, opposing ideas may prevail in open competition for the rational or moral sensibilities of the market participant. But when an individual is unaware of his prejudice, neither reason nor moral persuasion will likely succeed.

Racist speech also distorts the marketplace of ideas by muting or devaluing the speech of blacks and other nonwhites. An idea that would be embraced by large numbers of individuals if it were offered by a white individual will be rejected or given less credence because its author belongs to a group demeaned and stigmatized by racist beliefs. [Consider, for example,] the black political candidate whose ideas go unheard or are rejected by white voters, although voters would embrace the same ideas if they were championed by a white candidate. Racial minorities have the same experiences on a daily basis when they endure the microaggression of having their words doubted, or misinterpreted, or assumed to be without evidentiary support, or when their insights are ignored and then

133. See C. Lawrence, *The Id, the Ego and Equal Protection: Reckoning with Unconscious Racism*, 39 Stan. L. Rev. 317, 330 (1987) ("[Racism] is a part of our common historical experience and, therefore, a part of our culture. . . . We attach significance to race even when we are not aware that we are doing so. . . . Racism's universality renders it normal.").

141. See John Hart Ely, *Democracy and Distrust: A Theory of Judicial Review* 103–04, 135–79 (1980).

appropriated by whites who are assumed to have been the original authority.

Finally, racist speech decreases the total amount of speech that reaches the market. Racist speech is inextricably linked with racist conduct. The primary purpose and effect of the speech/conduct that constitutes white supremacy is the exclusion of nonwhites from full participation in the body politic. Sometimes the speech/conduct of racism is direct and obvious. When the Klan burns a cross on the lawn of a black person who joined the NAACP or exercised his right to move to a formerly all-white neighborhood, the effect of this speech does not result from the persuasive power of an idea operating freely in the market. It is a threat, a threat made in the context of a history of lynchings, beatings, and economic reprisals that made good on earlier threats, a threat that silences a potential speaker. The black student who is subjected to racial epithets is likewise threatened and silenced. Certainly she, like the victim of a cross-burning, may be uncommonly brave or foolhardy and ignore the system of violence in which this abusive speech is only a bit player. But it is more likely that we, as a community, will be denied the benefit of many of her thoughts and ideas. * * *

ASKING VICTIM GROUPS TO PAY THE PRICE

Whenever we decide that racist hate speech must be tolerated because of the importance of tolerating unpopular speech we ask blacks and other subordinated groups to bear a burden for the good of society— to pay the price for the societal benefit of creating more room for speech. And we assign this burden to them without seeking their advice, or consent. This amounts to white domination, pure and simple. It is taxation without representation. We must be careful that the ease with which we strike the balance against the regulation of racist speech is in no way influenced by the fact the cost will be borne by others. We must be certain that the individuals who pay the price are fairly represented in our deliberation, and that they are heard. * * *

My good friend and former colleague john powell * * * told the following story:

> My family was having Thanksgiving dinner at the home of friends. We are vegetarians and my two kids were trying to figure out which of the two dressings on the table was the vegetarian dressing and which was the meat dressing. One of our hosts pointed to one of the dressings and said, "This is the regular dressing and the other is the vegetarian dressing." I corrected him saying, "There is no such thing as 'regular' dressing. There is meat dressing and there is vegetarian dressing, but neither one of them is regular dressing."

This incident reminded john of the discussions he has had with his colleagues on the subject of regulating racist speech. "Somehow," he said,

> I always come away from these discussions feeling that my white colleagues think about the First amendment the way my friend thought about "regular" [meat] dressing, as an amendment for

regular people or all people, and that they think of the Equal Protection Clause of the Fourteenth Amendment the way my friend thought about vegetarian dressing, as a special amendment for a minority of different people.

Inevitably, in these conversations, those of us who are nonwhite bear the burden of justification, of justifying our concern for protection under our "special" amendment. It is not enough that we have demonstrated tangible and continuing injury committed against the victims of racist speech. There can be no public remedy for our special Fourteenth Amendment injury until we have satisfied our interlocutors that there is no possible risk of encroachment on their First Amendment—the "regular" amendment.

If one asks why we always begin by asking whether we can afford to fight racism rather than asking whether we can afford not to, or if one asks why my colleagues who oppose all regulation of racist speech do not feel that the burden is theirs (to justify a reading of the First Amendment that requires sacrificing rights guaranteed under the Equal Protection Clause), then one sees an example of how unconscious racism operates in the marketplace of ideas.

Well-meaning individuals who are committed to equality without regard to race, and who have demonstrated that commitment in many arenas, do not recognize where the burden of persuasion has been placed in this discussion. When they do, they do not understand why. Even as I experienced the frustration of always bearing the burden of persuasion, I did not see the source of my frustration or understand its significance until john told his story about the Thanksgiving dressing. Unfortunately, our unconscious racism causes us (even those of us who are the direct victims of racism), to view the First Amendment as the "regular" amendment—an amendment that works for all people—and the Equal Protection Clause and racial equality as a special-interest amendment important to groups that are less valued. * * *

EPILOGUE

"Enie, menie, minie, mo."

It is recess time at the South Main Street School. It is 1952, and I am nine. Eddie Becker, Muck Makowski, John Thomas, Terry Flynn, Howie Martin, and I are standing in a circle. Right feet thrust forward, the toes of our black, high-top Keds sneakers touching, forming a tight hub of white rubber at the center, our skinny blue-jeaned legs extend like spokes from the hub. Heads bowed, we are intently watching Muck, who is hunkered down on one knee so that he can touch our toes as he calls out the rhyme. We are enthralled and entranced by the drama of this boyhood ritual, this customary pre-game incantation. It is no less important than the game itself.

But my mind is not on the ritual. I have lost track of the count that will determine whose foot must be removed from the hub, who will no longer have a chance to be a captain in this game. I hardly feel Muck's index finger as it presses through the rubber to my toes. My mind is on the rhyme. I am the only black boy in this circle of towheaded prepubescent males. Time stands still for me. My palms are sweaty and I feel a prickly heat at the back of my neck. I know that Muck will not say the word.

"Catch a tiger by the toe."

The heads stay down. No one looks at me. But I know that none of them is picturing the capture of a large striped animal. They are thinking of me, imagining my toe beneath the white rubber of my Keds sneaker—my toe attached to a large, dark, thick lipped, burr-headed American fantasy/nightmare.

"If he hollers let him go." * * *

I was good at games, not just a good athlete, but a strategist, a leader. I knew how to make my teammates feel good about themselves so that they played better. It just came naturally to me. I could choose up a team and make them feel like family. When other folks felt good, I felt good too. Being good at games was the main tool I used to knock down the wall I'd found when I came to this white school in this white town. I looked forward to recess because that was when I could do the most damage to the wall. But now this rhyme, this word, had undone all my labors.

"Enie menie minie mo." * * *

Notes and Questions

1. Were the author's friends really thinking of him as a dark, thick-lipped nightmare? Consciously or unconsciously?

2. Is it possible instead that they thought of him as Jackie Robinson, and hoped very much to be picked for his team? Is this equally demeaning?

3. Is the main effect of hate speech to stir up animosity between skinheads and uneducated or working-class whites, and minorities, and thus to prevent their uniting against factory owners who oppress them both?

BEAUHARNAIS v. STATE OF ILLINOIS
343 U.S. 250 (1952).

JUSTICE FRANKFURTER delivered the opinion of the Court. (JUSTICES JACKSON, DOUGLAS, REED, and BLACK dissented.)

The petitioner was convicted upon information in the Municipal Court of Chicago of violating § 224a of Division 1 of the Illinois Criminal Code, Ill. Rev. Stat. 1949, c. 38, § 471. He was fined $200. The section provides:

> It shall be unlawful for any person, firm or corporation to manufacture, sell, or offer for sale, advertise or publish, present or exhibit in any public place in this state any lithograph, moving picture, play, drama or sketch, which publication or exhibition portrays depravity, criminality, unchastity, or lack of virtue of a class of citizens, of any race, color, creed or religion which said publication or exhibition exposes the citizens of any race, color, creed or religion to contempt, derision, or obloquy or which is productive of breach of the peace or riots....

Beauharnais challenged the statute as violating the liberty of speech and of the press guaranteed as against the States by the Due Process Clause of the Fourteenth Amendment, and as too vague, under the restrictions implicit in the same Clause, to support conviction for crime. The Illinois courts rejected these contentions and sustained defendant's conviction. 408 Ill. 512, 97 N.E.2d 343. We granted *certiorari* in view of the serious questions raised concerning the limitations imposed by the Fourteenth Amendment on the power of a State to punish utterances promoting friction among racial and religious groups. 342 U.S. 809.

The [prosecutor] charged that Beauharnais "did unlawfully ... exhibit in public places lithographs, which publications portray depravity, criminality, unchastity or lack of virtue of citizens of Negro race and color and which exposes citizens of Illinois of the Negro race and color to contempt, derision, or obloquy. ..." The lithograph complained of was a leaflet setting forth a petition calling on the Mayor and City Council of Chicago "to halt the further encroachment, harassment and invasion of white people, their property, neighborhoods and persons, by the Negro. ..." Below was a call for "One million self respecting white people in Chicago to unite ..." with the statement added that "If persuasion and the need to prevent the white race from becoming mongrelized by the negro will not unite us, then the aggressions ... rapes, robberies, knives, guns and marijuana of the negro, surely will." This, with more language, similar if not so violent, concluded with an attached application for membership in the White Circle League of America, Inc.

The testimony at the trial was substantially undisputed. From it the jury could find that Beauharnais was president of the White Circle League; that, at a meeting on January 6, 1950, he passed out bundles of the lithographs in question, together with other literature, to volunteers for distribution on downtown Chicago street corners the following day; that he carefully organized that distribution, giving detailed instructions for it; and that the leaflets were in fact distributed on January 7 in accordance with his plan and instructions. The court, together with other charges on burden of proof and the like, told the jury "if you find ... that the defendant, Joseph Beauharnais, did ... manufacture, sell, or offer for sale, advertise or publish, present or exhibit in any public place the lithograph ... then you are to find the defendant guilty. ..." He refused to charge the jury, as requested by the defendant, that in order to convict they must find "that the article complained of was likely to produce a clear and present danger of a serious substantive evil that rises far above public inconvenience, annoyance or unrest." Upon this evidence and these instructions, the jury brought in the conviction here for review.

The statute before us is not a catchall enactment left at large by the State court which applied it. *Cf. Thornhill v. State of Alabama*, 310 U.S. 88; *Cantwell v. State of Connecticut*, 310 U.S. 296, 307. It is a law specifically directed at a defined evil, its language drawing from history and practice in Illinois and in more than a score of other jurisdictions a meaning confirmed by the Supreme Court of that State in upholding this conviction. We do not, therefore, parse the statute as grammarians or treat it as an abstract exercise in lexicography. We read it in the animating context of well-defined usage, and State court construction which determines its meaning for us. *Cox v. State of New Hampshire*, 312 U.S. 569; *Chaplinsky v. State of New Hampshire*, 315 U.S. 568.

The Illinois Supreme Court tells us that § 224a "is a form of criminal libel law," 408 Ill. 512, 517, 97 N.E.2d 343, 346. The defendant, the trial court and the Supreme Court consistently treated it as such. The defendant offered evidence tending to prove the truth of parts of the utterance, and the courts below considered and disposed of this offer in terms of ordinary criminal libel precedents. Section 224a does not deal with the defense of truth, but by the Illinois Constitution, Art. II, § 4, S.H.A., "in all trials for libel, both civil and criminal, the truth, when published with good motives and for justifiable ends, shall be a sufficient defense." See also Ill. Rev. Stat., 1949, c. 38, § 404. Similarly, the action of the trial court in deciding as a matter of law the libelous character of the utterance, leaving to the jury only the question of publication, follows the settled rule in prosecutions for libel in Illinois and other States. Moreover, the Supreme Court's characterization of the words prohibited by the statute as those "liable to cause violence and disorder" paraphrases the traditional justification for punishing libels criminally, namely their "tendency to cause breach of the peace."

Libel of an individual was a common-law crime, and thus criminal in the colonies. Indeed, at common law, truth or good motives was no defense. In the first decades after the adoption of the Constitution, this was changed by judicial decision, statute or constitution in most States, but nowhere was there any suggestion that the crime of libel be abolished. Today, every American jurisdiction—the forty-eight States, the District of Columbia, Alaska, Hawaii and Puerto Rico—punishes libels directed at individuals. "There are certain well-defined and narrowly limited classes of speech, the prevention and punishment of which has never been thought to raise any Constitutional problem. These include the lewd and obscene, the profane, the libelous, and the insulting or 'fighting' words—those which by their very utterance inflict injury or tend to incite an immediate breach of the peace. It has been well observed that such utterances are no essential part of any exposition of ideas, and are of such slight social value as a step to truth that any benefit that may be derived from them is clearly outweighed by the social interest in order and morality. 'Resort to epithets or personal abuse is not in any proper sense communication of information or opinion safeguarded by the Constitution, and its punishment as a criminal act would raise no question under that instrument.' " *Cantwell v. State of Connecticut*, 310 U.S. 296, 309, 310. Such were the views of a unanimous Court in *Chaplinsky v. State of New Hampshire, supra*, 315 U.S. at pages 571–572.

No one will gainsay that it is libelous falsely to charge another with being a rapist, robber, carrier of knives and guns, and user of marijuana. The precise question before us, then, is whether the protection of "liberty" in the Due Process Clause of the Fourteenth Amendment prevents a State from punishing such libels—as criminal libel has been defined, limited and constitutionally recognized time out of mind—directed at designated collectivities and flagrantly disseminated. There is even authority, however dubious, that such utterances were also crimes at common law. It is certainly clear that some American jurisdictions have sanctioned their punishment under ordinary criminal libel statutes. We cannot say, however, that the question is concluded by history and practice. But if an utterance directed at an individual may be the object of criminal sanctions, we cannot deny to a State power to punish the same utterance directed at a defined group, unless we can say that this a wilful and purposeless restriction unrelated to the peace and well-being of the State.

Illinois did not have to look beyond her own borders or await the tragic experience of the last three decades to conclude that wilful purveyors of falsehood concerning racial and religious groups promote strife and tend powerfully to obstruct the manifold adjustments required for free, ordered life in a metropolitan, polyglot community. From the murder of the abolitionist Lovejoy in 1837 to the Cicero riots of 1951, Illinois has been the scene of exacerbated tension between races, often flaring into violence and destruction. In many of these outbreaks, utterances of the character here in question, so the Illinois legislature could conclude, played a significant part. The law was passed on June 29, 1917, at a time when the State was struggling to assimilate vast numbers of new inhabitants, as yet concentrated in discrete racial or national or religious groups—foreign-born brought to it by the crest of the great wave of immigration, and Negroes attracted by jobs in war plants and the allurements of northern claims. Nine years earlier, in the very city where the legislature sat, what is said to be the first northern race riot had cost the lives of six people, left hundreds of Negroes homeless and shocked citizens into action far beyond the borders of the State. Less than a month before the bill was enacted, East St. Louis had seen a day's rioting, prelude to an out-break, only four days after the bill became law, so bloody that it led to Congressional investigation. A series of bombings had begun which was to culminate two years later in the awful race riot which held Chicago in its grip for seven days in the summer of 1919. Nor has tension and violence between the groups defined in the statute been limited in Illinois to clashes between whites and Negroes.

In the face of this history and its frequent obligato of extreme racial and religious propaganda, we would deny experience to say that the Illinois legislature was without reason in seeking ways to curb false or malicious defamation of racial and religious groups, made in public places and by means calculated to have a powerful emotional impact on those to whom it was presented. "There are limits to the exercise of these liberties (of speech and of the press). The danger in these times from the coercive activities of those who in the delusion of racial or religious conceit would incite violence and breaches of the peace in order to deprive others of their equal right to the exercise of their liberties, is emphasized by events familiar to all. These and other transgressions of those limits the states appropriately may punish." This was the conclusion, again of a unanimous Court, in 1940. *Cantwell v. State of Connecticut, supra*, 310 U.S. at 310.

It may be argued, and weightily, that this legislation will not help matters; that tension and on occasion violence between racial and religious groups must be traced to causes more deeply embedded in our society than the rantings of modern Know–Nothings. Only those lacking responsible humility will have a confident solution for problems as intractable as the frictions attributable to differences of race, color or religion. This being so, it would be out of bounds for the judiciary to deny the legislature a choice of policy, provided it is not unrelated to the problem and not forbidden by some explicit limitation on the State's power. That the legislative remedy might not in practice mitigate the evil, or might itself raise new problems, would only manifest once more the paradox of reform. It is the price to be paid for the trial-and-error inherent in legislative efforts to deal with obstinate social issues. "The science of government ... has but few fixed principles, and practically consists in little more than the exercise of a sound discretion, applied to the exigencies of the state as they arise. It is the science of experiment." *Anderson v. Dunn*, 6 Wheat. 204, 226, 5 L.Ed. 242. Certainly the Due Process Clause does not require the legislature to be in the vanguard of science—especially sciences as young as human ecology and cultural anthropology. See *Tigner v. State of Texas*, 310 U.S. 141, 148.

Long ago this Court recognized that the economic rights of an individual may depend for the effectiveness of their enforcement on rights in the group, even though not formally corporate, to which he belongs. *American Steel Foundries v. Tri–City Central Trades Council*, 257 U.S. 184, 189. Such group-protection on behalf of the individual may, for all we know, be a need not confined to the part that a trade union plays in effectuating rights abstractly recognized as belonging to its members. It is not within our competence to confirm or deny claims of social scientists as to the dependence of the individual on the position of his racial or religious group in the community. It would, however, be arrant dogmatism, quite outside the scope of our authority in passing on the powers of a State, for us to deny that the Illinois Legislature may warrantably believe that a man's job and his educational opportunities and the dignity accorded him may depend as much on the reputation of the racial and religious group to which he willy-nilly belongs, as on his own merits. This being so, we are precluded from saying that speech concededly punishable when immediately directed at individuals cannot be outlawed if directed at groups with whose position and esteem in society the affiliated individual may be inextricably involved. * * *

Every power may be abused, but the possibility of abuse is a poor reason for denying Illinois the power to adopt measures against criminal libels sanctioned by centuries of Anglo–American law. "While this Court sits" it retains and exercises authority to nullify action which encroaches on freedom of utterance under the guise of punishing libel. Of course discussion cannot be denied and the right, as well as the duty, of criticism must not be stifled. * * *

As to the defense of truth, Illinois in common with many States requires a showing not only that the utterance state the facts, but also that the publication be made "with good motives and for justifiable ends." Ill. Const. Art. II, § 4. Both elements are necessary if the defense is to prevail. What has been called "the common sense of American criminal law," as formulated, with regard to necessary safeguards in criminal libel prosecutions, in the New York Constitution of 1821, Art. VII, § 8, has been adopted in terms by Illinois. The teaching of a century and a half of criminal libel prosecutions in this country would go by the board if we were to hold that Illinois was not within her rights in making this combined requirement. Assuming that defendant's offer of proof directed to a part of the defense was adequate, it did not satisfy the entire requirement which Illinois could exact.

Libelous utterances not being within the area of constitutionally protected speech, it is unnecessary, either for us or for the State courts, to consider the issues behind the phrase "clear and present danger." Certainly no one would contend that obscene speech, for example, may be punished only upon a showing of such circumstances. Libel, as we have seen, is in the same class.

We find no warrant in the Constitution for denying to Illinois the power to pass the law here under attack. But it bears repeating—although it should not—that our finding that the law is not constitutionally objectionable carries no implication of approval of the wisdom of the legislation or of its efficacy. These questions may raise doubts in our minds as well as in others. It is not for us, however, to make the legislative judgment. We are not at liberty to erect those doubts into fundamental law.

Affirmed.

Notes and Questions

1. Is *Beauharnais* still good law? Reconsider this question after reading *New York Times v. Sullivan, infra.* Canada and several European countries control hate speech, sometimes imposing criminal penalties on the speaker. See *Striking a Balance: Hate Speech, Freedom of Expression and Non-discrimination* (S. Coliver ed. 1992).

2. As our society becomes more multiracial, the population denser, and opportunities for interaction—rough or smooth—greater, will hate speech law have to evolve, much as the law of personal jurisdiction did when faced with many of the same social and economic changes?

NEW YORK TIMES v. SULLIVAN

376 U.S. 254 (1964).

JUSTICE BRENNAN delivered the opinion of the Court.

* * *

We are required in this case to determine for the first time the extent to which the constitutional protections for speech and press limit a State's power to award damages in a libel action brought by a public official against critics of his official conduct. * * * Respondent's complaint alleged that he had been libeled by statements in a full-page advertisement that was carried in the *New York Times* on March 29, 1960. * * *

Of the 10 paragraphs of text in the advertisement, the third and a portion of the sixth were the basis of respondent's claim of libel. They read as follows:

Third paragraph:

"In Montgomery, Alabama, after students sang 'My Country, 'Tis of Thee' on the State Capitol steps, their leaders were expelled from school, and truckloads of police armed with shotguns and tear-gas ringed the Alabama State College Campus. When the entire student body protested to state authorities by refusing to re-register, their dining hall was padlocked in an attempt to starve them into submission."

Sixth paragraph:

"Again and again the Southern violators have answered Dr. King's peaceful protests with intimidation and violence. They have bombed his home almost killing his wife and child. They have assaulted his person. They have arrested him seven times—for 'speeding,' 'loitering' and similar 'offenses.' And now they have charged him with 'perjury'—a felony under which they could imprison him for ten years. . . ."

Although neither of these statements mentions respondent by name, he contended that the word "police" in the third paragraph referred to him as the Montgomery Commissioner who supervised the Police Department, so that he was being accused of "ringing" the campus with police. He further claimed that the paragraph would be read as imputing to the police, and hence to him, the padlocking of the dining hall in order to starve the students into submission. As to the sixth paragraph, he contended that since arrests are ordinarily made by the police, the statement "They have arrested (Dr. King) seven times" would be read as referring to him; he further contended that the "They" who did the arresting would be equated with the "They" who committed the other described acts and with the "Southern violators." Thus, he argued, the paragraph would be read as accusing the Montgomery police, and hence him, of answering Dr. King's protests with "intimidation and violence," bombing his home, assaulting his person, and charging him with perjury. Respondent and six other Montgomery residents testified that they read some or all of the statements as referring to him in his capacity as Commissioner. * * *

Because of the importance of the constitutional issues involved, we granted the separate petitions for *certiorari* of the individual petitioners and of the *Times*. 371 U.S. 946. We reverse the judgment. We hold that the rule of law applied by the Alabama courts is constitutionally deficient for failure to provide the safeguards for freedom of speech and of the press that are required by the First and Fourteenth Amendments in a libel action brought by a public official against critics of his official conduct. We further hold that under the proper safeguards the evidence presented in this case is constitutionally insufficient to support the judgment for respondent. * * *

To avoid placing a handicap upon the freedoms of expression, we hold that if the allegedly libelous statements would otherwise be constitutionally protected from the present judgment, they do not forfeit that protection because they were published in the form of a paid advertisement.

II.

Under Alabama law, a publication is "libelous per se" if the words "tend to injure a person ... in his reputation" or to "bring (him) into public contempt"; the trial court stated that the standard was met if the words are such as to "injure him in his public office, or impute misconduct to him in his office, or want of official integrity, or want of fidelity to a public trust...." The jury must find that the words were published "of and concerning" the plaintiff, but where the plaintiff is a public official his place in the governmental hierarchy is sufficient evidence to support a finding that his reputation has been affected by statements that reflect upon the agency of which he is in charge. Once "libel per se" has been established, the defendant has no defense as to stated facts unless he can persuade the jury that they were true in all their particulars. *Alabama Ride Co. v. Vance*, 235 Ala. 263, 178 So. 438 (1938); *Johnson Publishing Co. v. Davis*, 271 Ala. 474, 494–495, 124 So.2d 441, 457–458 (1960). His privilege of "fair comment" for expressions of opinion depends on the truth of the facts upon which the comment is based. *Parsons v. Age–Herald Publishing Co.*, 181 Ala. 439, 450, 61 So. 345, 350 (1913). Unless he can discharge the burden of proving truth, general damages are presumed, and may be awarded without proof of pecuniary injury. A showing of actual malice is apparently a prerequisite to recovery of punitive damages, and the defendant may in any event forestall a punitive award by a retraction meeting the statutory requirements. Good motives and belief in truth do not negate an inference of malice, but are relevant only in mitigation of punitive damages if the jury chooses to accord them weight. *Johnson Publishing Co. v. Davis, supra*, 271 Ala., at 495, 124 So.2d, at 458.

The question before us is whether this rule of liability, as applied to an action brought by a public official against critics of his official conduct, abridges the freedom of speech and of the press that is guaranteed by the First and Fourteenth Amendments.

Respondent relies heavily, as did the Alabama courts, on statements of this Court to the effect that the Constitution does not protect libelous publications. Those statements do not foreclose our inquiry here. None of the cases sustained the use of libel laws to impose sanctions upon expression critical of the official conduct of public officials. * * * In deciding the question now, we are compelled by neither precedent nor policy to give any more weight to the epithet "libel" than we have to other "mere labels" of state law. *N.A.A.C.P. v. Button*, 371 U.S. 415, 429. * * * [L]ibel can claim no talismanic immunity from constitutional limitations. It must be measured by standards that satisfy the First Amendment.

The general proposition that freedom of expression upon public questions is secured by the First Amendment has long been settled by our decisions. The constitutional safeguard, we have said, "was fashioned to assure unfettered interchange of ideas for the bringing about of political and social changes desired by the people." *Roth v. United States*, 354 U.S. 476, 484. "The maintenance of the opportunity for free political discussion to the end that government may be responsive to the will of the people and that changes may be obtained by lawful means, an opportunity essential to the security of the Republic, is a fundamental principle of our constitutional system." *Stromberg v. California*, 283 U.S. 359. "[I]t is a prized American privilege to speak one's mind, although not always with perfect good taste, on all public institutions," *Bridges v. California*, 314 U.S. 252, 270, and this opportunity is to be afforded for "vigorous advocacy" no less than "abstract discussion." *N.A.A.C.P. v. Button*, 371 U.S. 415, 429. The First Amendment, said Judge Learned Hand, "presupposes that right conclusions are more likely to be gathered out of a multitude of tongues, than through any kind of authoritative selection. To many this is, and always will be, folly; but we have staked upon it our all." *United States v. Associated Press*, 52 F. Supp. 362, 372 (D.C.S.D.N.Y.1943). * * *

Thus we consider this case against the background of a profound national commitment to the principle that debate on public issues should be uninhibited, robust, and wide-open, and that it may well include vehement, caustic, and sometimes unpleasantly sharp attacks on government and public officials. See *Terminiello v. Chicago*, 337 U.S. 1, 4; *De Jonge v. Oregon*, 299 U.S. 353, 365. The present advertisement, as an expression of grievance and protest on one of the major public issues of our time, would seem clearly to qualify for the constitutional protection. The question is whether it forfeits that protection by the falsity of some of its factual statements and by its alleged defamation of respondent.

Authoritative interpretations of the First Amendment guarantees have consistently refused to recognize an exception for any test of truth—whether administered by judges, juries, or administrative officials—and especially one that puts the burden of proving truth on the speaker. *Cf. Speiser v. Randall*, 357 U.S. 513, 525–526. The constitutional protection does not turn upon "the truth, popularity, or social utility of the ideas and beliefs which are offered." *N.A.A.C.P. v. Button*, 371 U.S. 415, 445. As Madison said, "Some degree of abuse is inseparable from the proper use of every thing; and in no instance is this more true than in that of the press." 4 *Elliot's Debates on the Federal Constitution* (1876), p. 571. * * *

That erroneous statement is inevitable in free debate, and that it must be protected if the freedoms of expression are to have the "breathing space" that they "need ... to survive," *N.A.A.C.P. v. Button*, 371 U.S. 415, 433, was also recognized by the Court of Appeals for the District of Columbia Circuit in *Sweeney v. Patterson*, 76 U.S. App. D.C. 23, 24, 128 F.2d 457, 458 (1942), *cert.* denied, 317 U.S. 678. Judge Edgerton spoke for a unanimous court which affirmed the dismissal of a Congressman's libel suit based upon a newspaper article charging him with anti-Semitism in opposing a judicial appointment. He said:

"Cases which impose liability for erroneous reports of the political conduct of officials reflect the obsolete doctrine that the governed must not criticize their governors.... The interest of the public here outweighs the interest of appellant or any other individual. The protection of the public requires not merely discussion, but information. Political conduct and views which some respectable people approve, and others condemn, are constantly imputed to Congressmen. Errors of fact, particularly in regard to a man's mental states and processes, are inevitable.... Whatever is added to the field of libel is taken from the field of free debate."

Injury to official reputation affords no more warrant for repressing speech that would otherwise be free than does factual error. Where judicial officers are involved, this Court has held that concern for the dignity and reputation of the courts does not justify the punishment as criminal contempt of criticism of the judge or his decision. *Bridges v. California*, 314 U.S. 252. This is true even though the utterance contains "half-truths" and "misinformation." *Pennekamp v. Florida*, 328 U.S. 331, 342, 343, n.5, 345. Such repression can be justified, if at all, only by a clear and present danger of the obstruction of justice. If judges are to be treated as "men of fortitude, able to thrive in a hardy climate," *Craig v. Harney*, 331 U.S. 367 at 376, surely the same must be true of other government officials, such as elected city commissioners. Criticism of their official conduct does not lose its constitutional protection merely because it is effective criticism and hence diminishes their official reputations.

If neither factual error nor defamatory content suffices to remove the constitutional shield from criticism of official conduct, the combination of the two elements is no less inadequate. * * *

There is no force in respondent's argument that the constitutional limitations ... apply only to Congress and not to the States. It is true that the First Amendment was originally addressed only to action by the Federal Government, and that Jefferson, for one, while denying the power of Congress "to controul the freedom of the press," recognized such a power in the States. See the 1804 *Letter to Abigail Adams* quoted in *Dennis v. United States*, 341 U.S. 494, 522, n.4 (concurring opinion). But this distinction was eliminated with the adoption of the Fourteenth Amendment and the application to the States of the First Amendment's restrictions. See, *e.g., Gitlow v. New York*, 268 U.S. 652, 666; *Schneider v. State*, 308 U.S. 147, 160; *Bridges v. California*, 314 U.S. 252; *Edwards v. South Carolina*, 372 U.S. 229, 235.

What a State may not constitutionally bring about by means of a criminal statute is likewise beyond the reach of its civil law of libel. The fear of damage awards under a rule such as that invoked by the Alabama courts here may be markedly more inhibiting than the fear of prosecution under a criminal statute. * * * And since there is no double-jeopardy limitation applicable to civil lawsuits, this is not the only judgment that may be awarded against petitioners for the same publication. Whether or not a newspaper can survive a succession of such judgments, the pall of fear and timidity imposed upon those who would give voice to public criticism is an atmosphere in which the First Amendment freedoms cannot survive. Plainly the Alabama law of civil libel is "a form of regulation that creates hazards to protected freedoms markedly greater than those that attend reliance upon the criminal law." *Bantam Books, Inc. v. Sullivan*, 372 U.S. 58, 70. * * *

The state rule of law is not saved by its allowance of the defense of truth. * * * A rule compelling the critic of official conduct to guarantee the truth of all his factual assertions—and to do so on pain of libel judgments virtually unlimited in amount—leads to a comparable "self-censorship." Allowance of the defense of truth, with the burden of proving it on the defendant, does not mean that only false speech will be deterred.[19] Even courts accepting this defense as an adequate safeguard have recognized the difficulties of adducing legal proofs that the alleged libel was true in all its factual particulars. See, *e.g., Post Publishing Co. v. Hallam*, 59 F. 530, 540 (C.A.6th Cir. 1893); see also Noel, *Defamation of Public Officers and Candidates*, 49 Col. L. Rev. 875, 892 (1949). Under such a rule, would-be critics of official conduct may be deterred from voicing their criticism, even though it is believed to be true and even though it is in fact true, because of doubt whether it can be proved in court or fear of the expense of having to do so. They tend to make only statements which "steer far wider of the unlawful zone." *Speiser v. Randall, supra*, 357 U.S., at 526. The rule thus dampens the vigor and limits the variety of public debate. It is inconsistent with the First and Fourteenth Amendments.

The constitutional guarantees require, we think, a federal rule that prohibits a public official from recovering damages for a defamatory falsehood relating to his official conduct unless he proves that the statement was made with "actual malice"—that is, with knowledge that it was false or with reckless disregard of whether it was false or not. * * *

Such a privilege for criticism of official conduct[21] is appropriately analogous to the protection accorded a public official when he is sued for libel by a private citizen. In *Barr v. Matteo*, 360 U.S. 564, 575, this Court held the utterance of a federal official to be absolutely privileged if made "within the outer perimeter" of his duties. The States accord the same immunity to statements of their highest officers, although some differentiate their lesser officials and qualify the privilege they enjoy. But all hold that all officials are protected unless actual malice can be proved. The reason for the official privilege is said to be that the threat of damage suits would otherwise "inhibit the fearless, vigorous, and effective administration of policies of government" and "dampen the ardor of all but the most resolute, or the most irresponsible, in the unflinching discharge of their duties." *Barr v. Matteo, supra*, 360 U.S., at 571.

---

19. Even a false statement may be deemed to make a valuable contribution to public debate, since it brings about "the clearer perception and livelier impression of truth, produced by its collision with error." Mill, *On Liberty* (Blackwell, 1947), at 15; see also Milton, *Areopagitica*, in *Prose Works* (Yale, 1959), Vol. II, at 561.

21. The privilege immunizing honest misstatements of fact is often referred to as a "conditional" privilege to distinguish it from the "absolute" privilege recognized in judicial, legislative, administrative and executive proceedings. See, *e.g.*, Prosser, *Torts* (2d ed. 1955), § 95.

Analogous considerations support the privilege for the citizen-critic of government. It is as much his duty to criticize as it is the official's duty to administer. See *Whitney v. California*, 274 U.S. 357, 375 (concurring opinion of Justice Brandeis). As Madison said, "the censorial power is in the people over the Government, and not in the Government over the people." It would give public servants an unjustified preference over the public they serve, if critics of official conduct did not have a fair equivalent of the immunity granted to the officials themselves.

We conclude that such a privilege is required by the First and Fourteenth Amendments.

III.

We hold today that the Constitution delimits a State's power to award damages for libel in actions brought by public officials against critics of their official conduct. Since this is such an action,[23] the rule requiring proof of actual malice is applicable. While Alabama law apparently requires proof of actual malice for an award of punitive damages, where general damages are concerned malice is "presumed." Such a presumption is inconsistent with the federal rule. "The power to create presumptions is not a means of escape from constitutional restrictions," *Bailey v. Alabama*, 219 U.S. 219, 239; "[t]he showing of malice required for the forfeiture of the privilege is not presumed but is a matter for proof by the plaintiff...." *Lawrence v. Fox*, 357 Mich. 134, 146, 97 N.W.2d 719, 725 (1959). Since the trial judge did not instruct the jury to differentiate between general and punitive damages, it may be that the verdict was wholly an award of one or the other. But it is impossible to know, in view of the general verdict returned. Because of this uncertainty, the judgment must be reversed and the case remanded. * * *

As to the *Times*, we conclude that the facts do not support a finding of actual malice. The statement by the *Times'* Secretary that, apart from the padlocking allegation, he thought the advertisement was "substantially correct," affords no constitutional warrant for the Alabama Supreme Court's conclusion that it was a "cavalier ignoring of the falsity of the advertisement (from which), the jury could not have but been impressed with the bad faith of the *Times,* and its maliciousness inferable therefrom." The statement does not indicate malice at the time of the publication; even if the advertisement was not "substantially correct"—although respondent's own proofs tend to show that it was—that opinion was at least a reasonable one, and there was no evidence to impeach the witness' good faith in holding it. * * *

We also think the evidence was constitutionally defective in another respect: It was incapable of supporting the jury's finding that the allegedly libelous statements were made "of and concerning" respon-

---

23. We have no occasion here to determine how far down into the lower ranks of government employees the "public official" designation would extend for purposes of this rule, or otherwise to specify categories of persons who would or would not be included. *Cf. Barr v. Matteo*, 360 U.S. 564, 573–575. Nor need we here determine the boundaries of the "official conduct" concept. It is enough for the present case that respondent's position as an elected city commissioner clearly made him a public official, and that the allegations in the advertisement concerned what was allegedly his official conduct as Commissioner in charge of the Police Department. * * *

dent. Respondent relies on the words of the advertisement and the testimony of six witnesses to establish a connection between it and himself. Thus, in his brief to this Court, he states:

> "The reference to respondent as police commissioner is clear from the ad. In addition, the jury heard the testimony of a newspaper editor ...; a real estate and insurance man ...; the sales manager of a men's clothing store ...; a food equipment man ...; a service station operator ...; and the operator of a truck line for whom respondent had formerly worked.... Each of these witnesses stated that he associated the statements with respondent...." (Citations to record omitted.)

There was no reference to respondent in the advertisement, either by name or official position. * * * Although the statements may be taken as referring to the police, they did not on their face make even an oblique reference to respondent as an individual. Support for the asserted reference must, therefore, be sought in the testimony of respondent's witnesses. But none of them suggested any basis for the belief that respondent himself was attacked in the advertisement beyond the bare fact that he was in overall charge of the Police Department and thus bore official responsibility for police conduct; to the extent that some of the witnesses thought respondent to have been charged with ordering or approving the conduct or otherwise being personally involved in it, they based this notion not on any statements in the advertisement, and not on any evidence that he had in fact been so involved, but solely on the unsupported assumption that, because of his official position, he must have been. * * *

For good reason, "no court of last resort in this country has ever held, or even suggested, that prosecutions for libel on government have any place in the American system of jurisprudence." *City of Chicago v. Tribune Co.*, 307 Ill. 595, 601, 139 N.E. 86, 88, 28 A.L.R. 1368 (1923). The present proposition would sidestep this obstacle by transmuting criticism of government, however impersonal it may seem on its face, into personal criticism, and hence potential libel, of the officials of whom the government is composed. There is no legal alchemy by which a State may thus create the cause of action that would otherwise be denied for a publication which, as respondent himself said of the advertisement, "reflects not only on me but on the other Commissioners and the community." Raising as it does the possibility that a good-faith critic of government will be penalized for his criticism, the proposition relied on by the Alabama courts strikes at the very center of the constitutionally protected area of free expression. We hold that such a proposition may not constitutionally be utilized to establish that an otherwise impersonal attack on governmental operations was a libel of an official responsible for those operations. Since it was relied on exclusively here, and there was no other evidence to connect the statements with respondent, the evidence was constitutionally insufficient to support a finding that the statements referred to respondent.

The judgment of the Supreme Court of Alabama is reversed and the case is remanded to that court for further proceedings not inconsistent with this opinion.

Reversed and remanded.

DOE v. UNIVERSITY OF MICHIGAN

721 F. Supp. 852 (E.D.Mich.1989).

OPINION

COHN, DISTRICT JUDGE.

It is an unfortunate fact of our constitutional system that the ideals of freedom and equality are often in conflict. The difficult and sometimes painful task of our political and legal institutions is to mediate the appropriate balance between these two competing values. Recently, the University of Michigan at Ann Arbor (the University), a state-chartered university, see Mich. Const. Art. VIII, adopted a Policy on Discrimination and Discriminatory Harassment of Students in the University Environment (the Policy) in an attempt to curb what the University's governing Board of Regents (Regents) viewed as a rising tide of racial intolerance and harassment on campus. The Policy prohibited individuals, under the penalty of sanctions, from "stigmatizing or victimizing" individuals or groups on the basis of race, ethnicity, religion, sex, sexual orientation, creed, national origin, ancestry, age, marital status, handicap or Vietnam-era veteran status. However laudable or appropriate an effort this may have been, the Court found that the Policy swept within its scope a significant amount of "verbal conduct" or "verbal behavior" which is unquestionably protected speech under the First Amendment. Accordingly, the Court granted plaintiff John Doe's (Doe) prayer for a permanent injunction as to those parts of the Policy restricting speech activity, but denied the injunction as to the Policy's regulation of physical conduct. The reasons follow. * * *

The Policy established a three-tiered system whereby the degree of regulation was dependent on the location of the conduct at issue. The broadest range of speech and dialogue was "tolerated" in variously described public parts of the campus. Only an act of physical violence or destruction of property was considered sanctionable in these settings. Publications sponsored by the University such as the *Michigan Daily* and the *Michigan Review* were not subject to regulation. The conduct of students living in University housing is primarily governed by the standard provisions of individual leases, however the Policy appeared to apply in this setting as well. The Policy by its terms applied specifically to "[e]ducational and academic centers, such as classroom buildings, libraries, research laboratories, recreation and study centers[.]" In these areas, persons were subject to discipline for:

1. Any behavior, verbal or physical, that stigmatizes or victimizes an individual on the basis of race, ethnicity, religion, sex, sexual orientation, creed, national origin, ancestry, age, marital status, handicap or Vietnam-era veteran status, and that

a. involves an express or implied threat to an individual's academic efforts, employment, participation in University sponsored extra-curricular activities or personal safety; or

b. has the purpose or reasonably foreseeable effect of interfering with an individual's academic efforts, employment, participation in University sponsored extra-curricular activities or personal safety; or

c. creates an intimidating, hostile, or demeaning environment for educational pursuits, employment or participation in University sponsored extra-curricular activities.

2. Sexual advances, requests for sexual favors, and verbal or physical conduct that stigmatizes or victimizes an individual on the basis of sex or sexual orientation where such behavior:

a. involves an express or implied threat to an individual's academic efforts, employment, participation in University sponsored extra-curricular activities or personal safety; or

b. has the purpose or reasonably foreseeable effect of interfering with an individual's academic efforts, employment, participation in University sponsored extra-curricular activities or personal safety; or

c. creates an intimidating, hostile, or demeaning environment for educational pursuits, employment or participation in University sponsored extra-curricular activities. * * *

The Policy by its terms recognizes that certain speech which might be considered in violation may not be sanctionable, stating: "The Office of the General Counsel will rule on any claim that conduct which is the subject of a formal hearing is constitutionally protected by the First Amendment." * * *

The Policy provided for progressive discipline based on the severity of the violation. It stated that the University encouraged hearing panels to impose sanctions that include an educational element in order to sensitize the perpetrator to the harmfulness of his or her conduct. The Policy provided, however, that compulsory class attendance should not be imposed "in an attempt to change deeply held religious or moral convictions." Depending on the intent of the accused student, the effect of the conduct, and whether the accused student is a repeat offender, one or more of the following sanctions may be imposed: (1) formal reprimand; (2) community service; (3) class attendance; (4) restitution; (5) removal from University housing; (6) suspension from specific courses and activities; (7) suspension; (8) expulsion. The sanctions of suspension and expulsion could only be imposed for violent or dangerous acts, repeated offenses, or a willful failure to comply with a lesser sanction. The University President could set aside or lessen any sanction. * * *

VAGUENESS AND OVERBREADTH

Doe initially moved for a preliminary injunction against the Policy on the grounds that it was unconstitutionally vague and overbroad and that it chilled speech and conduct protected by the First Amendment.

The University in response said that the Policy has never been applied to reach protected speech and a preliminary injunction should therefore be denied. * * *

Doe claimed that the Policy was invalid because it was facially overbroad. It is fundamental that statutes regulating First Amendment activities must be narrowly drawn to address only the specific evil at hand. *Broadrick v. Oklahoma*, 413 U.S. 601, 611. "Because First Amendment freedoms need breathing space to survive, government may regulate in the area only with narrow specificity." *NAACP v. Button, supra* 371 U.S. at 433. A law regulating speech will be deemed overbroad if it sweeps within its ambit a substantial amount of protected speech along with that which it may legitimately regulate. *Id.* 413 U.S. at 612; *Gooding v. Wilson*, 405 U.S. 518, 521–22 (1972).

The Supreme Court has consistently held that statutes punishing speech or conduct solely on the grounds that they are unseemly or offensive are unconstitutionally overbroad. In *Houston v. Hill, supra,* the Supreme Court struck down a City of Houston ordinance which provided that "[i]t shall be unlawful for any person to assault or strike or in any manner oppose, molest, and abuse or interrupt any policeman in the execution of his duty." The Supreme Court also found that the ordinance was overbroad because it forbade citizens from criticizing and insulting police officers, although such conduct was constitutionally protected. *Id.* 482 U.S. at 460–65. The fact that the statute also had a legitimate scope of application in prohibiting conduct which was clearly unprotected by the First Amendment was not enough to save it. In *Gooding v. Wilson, supra,* the Supreme Court struck down a Georgia statute which made it a misdemeanor for "[a]ny person [to], without provocation, use to or of another, and in his presence ... opprobrious words or abusive language, tending to cause a breach of the peace." The Supreme Court found that this statute was overbroad as well, because it punished speech which did not rise to the level of "fighting words," as defined in *Chaplinsky v. New Hampshire, supra.* * * * These cases stand generally for the proposition that the state may not prohibit broad classes of speech, some of which may indeed be legitimately regulable, if in so doing a substantial amount of constitutionally protected conduct is also prohibited. This was the fundamental infirmity of the Policy.

The University repeatedly argued that the Policy did not apply to speech that is protected by the First Amendment. It urged the Court to disregard the [accompanying] Guide as "inaccurate" and look instead to "the manner in which the Policy has been interpreted and applied by those charged with its enforcement." However, as applied by the University over the past year, the Policy was consistently applied to reach protected speech.

On December 7, 1988, a complaint was filed against a graduate student in the School of Social Work alleging that he harassed students based on sexual orientation and sex. The basis for the sexual orientation charge was apparently that in a research class, the student openly stated his belief that homosexuality was a disease and that he intended to develop a counseling plan for changing gay clients to straight. See

Discipline File 88–12–21, described *supra*. He also related to other students that he had been counseling several of his gay patients accordingly. The student apparently had several heated discussions with his classmates over the validity and morality of his theory and program. On January 11, 1989, the Interim Policy Administrator wrote to the student informing him that following an investigation of the complaints, there was sufficient evidence to warrant a formal hearing on the charges of sex and sexual orientation harassment. A formal hearing on the charges was held on January 28, 1989. The hearing panel unanimously found that the student was guilty of sexual harassment but refused to convict him of harassment on the basis of sexual orientation. The panel stated:

> In a divided decision the hearing panel finds that the evidence available to the panel indicates that _____ did not harass students on the basis of sexual orientation under the strict definition of "The University of Michigan Policy on Discrimination and Discriminatory Harassment by Students in the University Environment." In accordance with First Amendment rights to free speech and the University's policy of academic freedom, _____ did not violate the policy by discussing either the origins or "curability" of homosexuality in the School of Social Work.

Although the student was not sanctioned over the allegations of sexual orientation harassment, the fact remains that the Policy Administrator—the authoritative voice of the University on these matters—saw no First Amendment problem in forcing the student to a hearing to answer for allegedly harassing statements made in the course of academic discussion and research. Moreover, there is no indication that had the hearing panel convicted rather than acquitted the student, the University would have interceded to protect the interests of academic freedom and freedom of speech. * * *[14]

The manner in which [this and other] complaints were handled demonstrated that the University considered serious comments made in the context of classroom discussion to be sanctionable under the Policy. The innocent intent of the speaker was apparently immaterial to whether a complaint would be pursued. Moreover, the Administrator generally failed to consider whether a comment was protected by the First Amendment before informing the accused student that a complaint had been filed. The Administrator instead attempted to persuade the accused student to accept "voluntary" sanctions. Behind this persuasion was, of course, the subtle threat that failure to accept such sanctions might result in a formal hearing. There is no evidence in the record that the Administrator ever declined to pursue a complaint through attempted mediation because the alleged harassing conduct was protected by the

14. Only a single complaint involving allegedly harassing remarks made in the context of a classroom discussion was dismissed because of First Amendment concerns. A complaint of anti-Semitic harassment was filed on March 27, 1989, by a Jewish student in a class on the Holocaust who was offended by another student's suggestion that Jews cynically used the Holocaust to justify Israel's policies toward the Palestinians. Complaint No. 89–3–2. According to the Administrator's notes, the perpetrator refused to apologize for the comment. The Administrator phoned the complainant and informed her that the comment was protected speech, not covered by the policy.

First Amendment. Nor is there evidence that the Administrator ever informed an accused harasser during mediation negotiations that the complained of conduct might be protected. The Administrator's manner of enforcing the Policy was constitutionally indistinguishable from a full blown prosecution. The University could not seriously argue that the policy was never interpreted to reach protected conduct. It is clear that the policy was overbroad both on its face and as applied.

Doe also urges that the policy be struck down on the grounds that it is impermissibly vague. A statute is unconstitutionally vague when "men of common intelligence must necessarily guess at its meaning." *Broadrick, supra* 413 U.S. at 607. A statute must give adequate warning of the conduct which is to be prohibited and must set out explicit standards for those who apply it. *Id.* "No one may be required at the peril of life, liberty or property to speculate as to the meaning of penal statutes. All are entitled to be informed as to what the State commands or forbids." *Lanzetta v. New Jersey*, 306 U.S. 451, 453 (1939). These considerations apply with particular force where the challenged statute acts to inhibit freedoms affirmatively protected by the constitution. *Smith v. Goguen*, 415 U.S. 566, 573 (1974). However, the chilling effect caused by an overly vague statute must be both real and substantial, *Young v. American Mini Theatres*, 427 U.S. 50 (1976), and a narrowing construction must be unavailable before a court will set it aside, *Screws v. United States*, 325 U.S. 91, 98 (1945).

Looking at the plain language of the Policy, it was simply impossible to discern any limitation on its scope or any conceptual distinction between protected and unprotected conduct. The structure of the Policy was in two parts; one relates to cause and the other to effect. Both cause and effect must be present to state a *prima facie* violation of the Policy. The operative words in the cause section required that language must "stigmatize" or "victimize" an individual. However, both of these terms are general and elude precise definition. Moreover, it is clear that the fact that a statement may victimize or stigmatize an individual does not, in and of itself, strip it of protection under the accepted First Amendment tests. * * *

During the oral argument, the Court asked the University's counsel how he would distinguish between speech which was merely offensive, which he conceded was protected, and speech which "stigmatizes or victimizes" on the basis of an invidious factor. Counsel replied "very carefully." The response, while refreshingly candid, illustrated the plain fact that the University never articulated any principled way to distinguish sanctionable from protected speech. Students of common understanding were necessarily forced to guess at whether a comment about a controversial issue would later be found to be sanctionable under the Policy. The terms of the Policy were so vague that its enforcement would violate the Due Process Clause. See *Cramp v. Board of Public Instruction,* 368 U.S. 278, 285–88 (1961).

CONCLUSION

* * * While the Court is sympathetic to the University's obligation to ensure equal educational opportunities for all of its students, such

efforts must not be at the expense of free speech. Unfortunately, this was precisely what the University did. From the Acting President's December 14 memorandum forward to the adoption of the Policy and continuing through the August 25 hearing, there is no evidence in the record that any officials at the University ever seriously attempted to reconcile their efforts to combat discrimination with the requirements of the First Amendment. The apparent willingness to dilute the values of free speech is ironic in light of the University's previous statements of policy on this matter. In 1977, the Regents adopted the "Statement on Freedom of Speech and Artistic Expression: The Rights and Obligations of Speakers, Performers, Audience Members, and Protesters at the University of Michigan" (Statement) which "reaffirm[ed] formally [the University's] deep and lasting commitment to freedom of speech and artistic expression." The Statement provides in part that

> freedom of speech must not ordinarily be restricted, governed or curtailed in any way by content except where the law, as interpreted by the Supreme Court of Michigan or the Supreme Court of the United States, holds that such an expression does not fall within constitutionally protected free speech. In all instances, the University authorities should act with maximum constraint, even in the face of obvious bad taste or provocation. The belief that some opinion is pernicious, false, or in any other way detestable cannot be grounds for its suppression.

Needless to say, the philosophy expressed in the Statement is diametrically opposed to that reflected in the Acting President's December 14 Memorandum. Apparently, no one involved in the drafting process noted the apparent inconsistency with the Regents' views as expressed in the Statement.

Throughout the case, the University's counsel strenuously urged that First Amendment concerns held a top priority in the development and administration of the Policy. Counsel repeatedly argued that the University interpreted the Policy to reach conduct such as racial slurs and epithets in the classroom directed at an individual victim. However, as the Court observed in its August 25, 1989 bench opinion,

> what we have heard here this morning ... from University counsel is a revisionist view of the Policy on Discrimination and Discriminatory Harassment by Students in the University Environment, and it is a view and interpretation of the Policy that was not in the minds of the legislators when it was adopted. And there is nothing in the record that has been presented to the Court which suggests that this was an appropriate interpretation of the policy.

Not only has the administrative enforcement of the Policy been wholly inconsistent with counsel's interpretation, but withdrawal of the Guide, see *supra* at 13, and the eleventh hour suspension of section 1(c), see *supra* at 8, suggests that the University had no idea what the limits of the Policy were and it was essentially making up the rules as it went along. * * *

Notes and Questions

1.   As *Doe* suggests, university policies prohibiting hate speech on campus have not been very successful in court. See also *UWM Post v. Board of Regents*, 774 F. Supp. 1163 (E.D.Wis.1991), in which the University of Wisconsin's hate speech rule was found unconstitutional because it did not meet the requirements for "fighting words," since it did not require that the speech tend to incite a violent reaction and was overbroad and unduly vague. Is there a way to regulate hate speech without regulating protected speech? Can you imagine campus hate speech so extreme that the University's interest would justify regulation?

2.   Do you agree with the Court's decision in *Sullivan*? Should the courts allow regulation of criticisms of private individuals if we cannot regulate criticism of public officials? Is there a difference between criticizing the way a public official does his job and that aimed at a person for his or her race? Can you define that difference sufficiently so that a court could distinguish the two forms of speech under your test? Is "you dumb _____, go back to (Africa, Mexico, Japan, the reservation), you don't belong at this campus" criticism—or something else? If so, what?

R.A.V. v. CITY OF ST. PAUL

505 U.S. 377 (1992).

JUSTICE SCALIA delivered the opinion of the Court.

* * * Petitioner and several other teenagers * * * allegedly burned a cross inside the fenced yard of a black family that lived across the street from the house where petitioner was staying. * * * [R]espondent city of St. Paul chose to charge petitioner (then a juvenile) [under] the St. Paul Bias–Motivated Crime Ordinance, St. Paul, Minn., Legis.Code § 292.02 (1990), which provides:

> "Whoever places on public or private property a symbol, object, appellation, characterization or graffiti, including, but not limited to, a burning cross or Nazi swastika, which one knows or has reasonable grounds to know arouses anger, alarm or resentment in others on the basis of race, color, creed, religion or gender commits disorderly conduct and shall be guilty of a misdemeanor."

Petitioner moved to dismiss this count on the ground that the St. Paul ordinance was substantially overbroad and impermissibly content based and therefore facially invalid under the First Amendment. * * *

I

In construing the St. Paul ordinance, we are bound by the construction given to it by the Minnesota court. Accordingly, we accept the Minnesota Supreme Court's authoritative statement that the ordinance reaches only those expressions that constitute "fighting words" within the meaning of *Chaplinsky*, 464 N.W.2d, at 510–511. Petitioner and his *amici* urge us to modify the scope of the *Chaplinsky* formulation, thereby invalidating the ordinance as "substantially overbroad," *Broadrick v. Oklahoma*, 413 U.S. 601, 610 (1973). We find it unnecessary to consider this issue. Assuming, *arguendo*, that all of the expression reached by the ordinance is proscribable under the "fighting words" doctrine, we nonetheless conclude that the ordinance is facially unconstitutional in that it prohibits otherwise permitted speech solely on the basis of the subjects the speech addresses. * * *

The proposition that a particular instance of speech can be proscribable on the basis of one feature (*e.g.*, obscenity) but not on the basis of another (*e.g.*, opposition to the city government) is commonplace and has found application in many contexts. We have long held, for example, that nonverbal expressive activity can be banned because of the action it entails, but not because of the ideas it expresses—so that burning a flag in violation of an ordinance against outdoor fires could be punishable, whereas burning a flag in violation of an ordinance against dishonoring the flag is not. Similarly, we have upheld reasonable "time, place, or manner" restrictions, but only if they are "justified without reference to the content of the regulated speech." *Ward v. Rock Against Racism*, 491 U.S. 781, 791 (1989) (internal quotation marks omitted); see also *Clark v. Community for Creative Non–Violence*, 468 U.S. 288, 298 (1984) (noting that the *O'Brien* test differs little from the standard applied to time, place, or manner restrictions). And just as the power to proscribe particular speech on the basis of a noncontent element (*e.g.*, noise) does not entail the power to proscribe the same speech on the basis of a content element; so also, the power to proscribe it on the basis of one content element (*e.g.*, obscenity) does not entail the power to proscribe it on the basis of other content elements.

In other words, the exclusion of "fighting words" from the scope of the First Amendment simply means that, for purposes of that Amendment, the unprotected features of the words are, despite their verbal character, essentially a "nonspeech" element of communication. Fighting words are thus analogous to a noisy sound truck: Each is, as Justice Frankfurter recognized, a "mode of speech," *Niemotko v. Maryland*, 340 U.S. 268, 282 (1951) (opinion concurring in result); both can be used to convey an idea; but neither has, in and of itself, a claim upon the First Amendment. As with the sound truck, however, so also with fighting words: The government may not regulate use based on hostility—or favoritism—towards the underlying message expressed. Compare *Frisby v. Schultz*, 487 U.S. 474 (1988) (upholding, against facial challenge, a content-neutral ban on targeted residential picketing), with *Carey v. Brown*, 447 U.S. 455 (1980) (invalidating a ban on residential picketing that exempted labor picketing). * * *

* * * In our view, the First Amendment imposes not an "underinclusiveness" limitation but a "content discrimination" limitation upon a State's prohibition of proscribable speech. There is no problem whatever, for example, with a State's prohibiting obscenity (and other forms of proscribable expression) only in certain media or markets, for although that prohibition would be "underinclusive," it would not discriminate on the basis of content. See, *e.g.*, *Sable Communications*, 492 U.S., at 124–126 (upholding 47 U.S.C.A. § 223(b)(1), which prohibits obscene telephone communications).

Even the prohibition against content discrimination that we assert the First Amendment requires is not absolute. It applies differently in the context of proscribable speech than in the area of fully protected speech. The rationale of the general prohibition, after all, is that content discrimination "raises the specter that the Government may effectively drive certain ideas or viewpoints from the marketplace," *Simon & Schuster*, 502 U.S., at 116; *Leathers v. Medlock*, 499 U.S. 439, 448 (1991); *FCC v. League of Women Voters of Cal.*, 468 U.S. 364, 383–384 (1984); *Consolidated Edison Co.*, 447 U.S., at 536; *Police Dept. of Chicago v. Mosley*, 408 U.S., at 95–98. But content discrimination among various instances of a class of proscribable speech often does not pose this threat.

When the basis for the content discrimination consists entirely of the very reason the entire class of speech at issue is proscribable, no significant danger of idea or viewpoint discrimination exists. Such a reason, having been adjudged neutral enough to support exclusion of the entire class of speech from First Amendment protection, is also neutral enough to form the basis of distinction within the class. To illustrate: A State might choose to prohibit only that obscenity which is the most patently offensive in its prurience—*i.e.*, that which involves the most lascivious displays of sexual activity. But it may not prohibit, for example, only that obscenity which includes offensive political messages. See *Kucharek v. Hanaway*, 902 F.2d 513, 517 (C.A.7 1990), *cert.* denied, 498 U.S. 1041 (1991). And the Federal Government can criminalize only those threats of violence that are directed against the President, see 18 U.S.C.A. § 871—since the reasons why threats of violence are outside the First Amendment (protecting individuals from the fear of violence, from the disruption that fear engenders, and from the possibility that the threatened violence will occur) have special force when applied to the person of the President. See *Watts v. United States*, 394 U.S. 705, 707 (1969) (upholding the facial validity of § 871 because of the "overwhelmin[g] interest in protecting the safety of [the] Chief Executive and in allowing him to perform his duties without interference from threats of physical violence"). But the Federal Government may not criminalize only those threats against the President that mention his policy on aid to inner cities. * * *

Another valid basis for according differential treatment to even a content-defined subclass of proscribable speech is that the subclass happens to be associated with particular "secondary effects" of the speech, so that the regulation is "justified without reference to the content of the ... speech," *Renton v. Playtime Theatres, Inc.*, 475 U.S. 41, 48 (1986) (quoting *Virginia State Bd. of Pharmacy, supra*) 425 U.S., at 771; see also *Young v. American Mini Theatres*, Inc., 427 U.S. 50, 71, n.34 (1976) (plurality opinion); *id.*, at 80–82 (Powell, J., concurring); *Barnes*, 501 U.S., at 586 (Souter, J., concurring in judgment). A State could, for example, permit all obscene live performances except those involving minors. Moreover, since words can in some circumstances violate laws directed not against speech but against conduct (a law against treason, for example, is violated by telling the enemy the Nation's defense secrets), a particular content-based subcategory of a proscribable class of speech can be swept up incidentally within the reach of a statute directed at conduct rather than speech. See *id.*, at 571 (plurality opinion); id., at 577 (Scalia, J., concurring in judgment); id., at 582 (Souter, J., concurring in judgment); *FTC v. Superior Court Trial Lawyers Assn.*, 493 U.S. 411, 425–432 (1990); *O'Brien*, 391 U.S., at 376–377. * * *

These bases for distinction refute the proposition that the selectivity of the restriction is "even arguably 'conditioned upon the sovereign's agreement with what a speaker may intend to say.'" *Metromedia, Inc. v. San Diego*, 453 U.S. 490, 555 (1981) (Stevens, J., dissenting in part) (citation omitted). There may be other such bases as well. Indeed, to validate such selectivity (where totally proscribable speech is at issue) it may not even be necessary to identify any particular "neutral" basis, so long as the nature of the content discrimination is such that there is no realistic possibility that official suppression of ideas is afoot. (We cannot think of any First Amendment interest that would stand in the way of a State's prohibiting only those obscene motion pictures with blue-eyed actresses.) Save for that limitation, the regulation of "fighting words," like the regulation of noisy speech, may address some offensive instances and leave other, equally offensive, instances alone. See *Posadas de Puerto Rico*, 478 U.S., at 342–343.

II

Applying these principles to the St. Paul ordinance, we conclude that, even as narrowly construed by the Minnesota Supreme Court, the ordinance is facially unconstitutional. Although the phrase in the ordinance, "arouses anger, alarm or resentment in others," has been limited by the Minnesota Supreme Court's construction to reach only those symbols or displays that amount to "fighting words," the remaining, unmodified terms make clear that the ordinance applies only to "fighting words" that insult, or provoke violence, "on the basis of race, color, creed, religion or gender." Displays containing abusive invective, no matter how vicious or severe, are permissible unless they are addressed to one of the specified disfavored topics. Those who wish to use "fighting words" in connection with other ideas—to express hostility, for example, on the basis of political affiliation, union membership, or homosexuality—are not covered. The First Amendment does not permit St. Paul to impose special prohibitions on those speakers who express views on disfavored subjects. See *Simon & Schuster*, 502 U.S., at 116; *Arkansas Writers' Project, Inc. v. Ragland*, 481 U.S. 221, 229–230 (1987).

In its practical operation, moreover, the ordinance goes even beyond mere content discrimination, to actual viewpoint discrimination. Displays containing some words—odious racial epithets, for example—would be prohibited to proponents of all views. But "fighting words" that do not themselves invoke race, color, creed, religion, or gender—aspersions upon a person's mother, for example—would seemingly be usable *ad libitum* in the placards of those arguing in favor of racial, color, etc., tolerance and equality, but could not be used by those speakers' opponents. One could hold up a sign saying, for example, that all "anti-Catholic bigots" are misbegotten; but not that all "papists" are, for that would insult and provoke violence "on the basis of religion." St. Paul has no such authority to license one side of a debate to fight freestyle, while requiring the other to follow Marquis of Queensberry rules.

What we have here, it must be emphasized, is not a prohibition of fighting words that are directed at certain persons or groups (which would be facially valid if it met the requirements of the Equal Protection Clause); but rather, a prohibition of fighting words that contain (as the Minnesota Supreme Court repeatedly emphasized) messages of "bias-motivated" hatred and in particular, as applied to this case, messages "based on virulent notions of racial supremacy." 464 N.W.2d, at 508, 511. One must wholeheartedly agree with the Minnesota Supreme Court that "[i]t is the responsibility, even the obligation, of diverse communities to confront such notions in whatever form they appear," *id.*, at 508, but the manner of that confrontation cannot consist of selective limitations upon speech. St. Paul's brief asserts that a general "fighting words" law would not meet the city's needs because only a content-specific measure can communicate to minority groups that the "group hatred" aspect of such speech "is not condoned by the majority." Brief for Respondent 25. The point of the First Amendment is that majority preferences must be expressed in some fashion other than silencing speech on the basis of its content. * * *

[T]he Minnesota Supreme Court and St. Paul acknowledge that the ordinance is directed at expression of group hatred * * * What makes the anger, fear, sense of dishonor, etc., produced by violation of this ordinance distinct from the anger, fear, sense of dishonor, etc., produced by other fighting words is nothing other than the fact that it is caused by a distinctive idea, conveyed by a distinctive message. The First Amendment cannot be evaded that easily. It is obvious that the symbols which will arouse "anger, alarm or resentment in others on the basis of race, color, creed, religion or gender" are those symbols that communicate a message of hostility based on one of these characteristics. St. Paul concedes in its brief that the ordinance applies only to "racial, religious, or gender-specific symbols" such as "a burning cross, Nazi swastika or other instrumentality of like import." Brief for Respondent 8. Indeed, St. Paul argued in the Juvenile Court that "[t]he burning of a cross does express a message and it is, in fact, the content of that message which the St. Paul Ordinance attempts to legislate." Memorandum from the Ramsey County Attorney to the Honorable Charles A. Flinn, Jr., dated July 13, 1990, in In re *Welfare of R.A.V.*, No. 89–D–1231 (Ramsey Cty. Juvenile Ct.), p. 1, reprinted in App. to Brief for Petitioner C–1.

The content-based discrimination reflected in the St. Paul ordinance comes within neither any of the specific exceptions to the First Amendment prohibition we discussed earlier nor a more general exception for content discrimination that does not threaten censorship of ideas. It assuredly does not fall within the exception for content discrimination based on the very reasons why the particular class of speech at issue (here, fighting words) is proscribable. As explained earlier, see *supra*, at 2545, the reason why fighting words are categorically excluded from the protection of the First Amendment is not that their content communicates any particular idea, but that their content embodies a particularly intolerable (and socially unnecessary) mode of expressing whatever idea the speaker wishes to convey. St. Paul has not singled out an especially offensive mode of expression—it has not, for example, selected for prohibition only those fighting words that communicate ideas in a threatening (as opposed to a merely obnoxious) manner. Rather, it has proscribed fighting words of whatever manner that communicate messages of racial, gender, or religious intolerance. Selectivity of this sort creates the possibility that the city is seeking to handicap the expression of particular ideas. That possibility would alone be enough to render the ordinance presumptively invalid, but St. Paul's comments and concessions in this case elevate the possibility to a certainty.

St. Paul argues that the ordinance comes within another of the specific exceptions we mentioned, the one that allows content discrimination aimed only at the "secondary effects" of the speech, see *Renton v. Playtime Theatres, Inc.*, 475 U.S. 41 (1986). According to St. Paul, the ordinance is intended, "not to impact on [*sic*] the right of free expression of the accused," but rather to "protect against the victimization of a person or persons who are particularly vulnerable because of their membership in a group that historically has been discriminated against." Brief for Respondent 28. Even assuming that an ordinance that completely proscribes, rather than merely regulates, a specified category of speech can ever be considered to be directed only to the secondary effects of such speech, it is clear that the St. Paul ordinance is not directed to secondary effects within the meaning of *Renton*. As we said in *Boos v. Barry*, 485 U.S. 312 (1988), "Listeners' reactions to speech are not the type of 'secondary effects' we referred to in *Renton*." *Id.*, at 321. "The emotive impact of speech on its audience is not a 'secondary effect." *Ibid.* See also *id.*, at 334 (opinion of Brennan, J.).

It hardly needs discussion that the ordinance does not fall within some more general exception permitting all selectivity that for any reason is beyond the suspicion of official suppression of ideas. The statements of St. Paul in this very case afford ample basis for, if not full confirmation of, that suspicion.

Finally, St. Paul and its *amici* defend the conclusion of the Minnesota Supreme Court that, even if the ordinance regulates expression based on hostility towards its protected ideological content, this discrimination is nonetheless justified because it is narrowly tailored to serve compelling state interests. Specifically, they assert that the ordinance helps to ensure the basic human rights of members of groups that have historically been subjected to discrimination, including the right of such group members to live in peace where they wish. We do not doubt that these interests are compelling, and that the ordinance can be said to promote them. But the "danger of censorship" presented by a facially content-based statute, *Leathers v. Medlock*, 499 U.S., at 448, requires that that weapon be employed only where it is "necessary to serve the asserted [compelling] interest," *Burson v. Freeman*, 504 U.S. 191, 199 (1992) (plurality opinion); *Perry Ed. Assn. v. Perry Local Educators' Assn.*, 460 U.S. 37, 45 (1983). The existence of adequate content-neutral alternatives thus "undercut[s] significantly" any defense of such a statute, *Boos v. Barry, supra*, 485 U.S., at 329, casting considerable doubt on the government's protestations that "the asserted justification is in fact an accurate description of the purpose and effect of the law," *Burson, supra*, 504 U.S., at 213 (Kennedy, J., concurring). The dispositive question in this case, therefore, is whether content discrimination is reasonably necessary to achieve St. Paul's compelling interests; it plainly is not. An ordinance not limited to the favored topics, for example, would have precisely the same beneficial effect. In fact the only interest distinctively served by the content limitation is that of displaying the city council's special hostility towards the particular biases thus singled out. That is precisely what the First Amendment forbids. The politicians of St. Paul are entitled to express that hostility—but not through the means of imposing unique limitations upon speakers who (however benightedly) disagree. * * *

WISCONSIN v. MITCHELL

508 U.S. 476 (1993).

CHIEF JUSTICE REHNQUIST delivered the opinion of the Court.

Respondent Todd Mitchell's sentence for aggravated battery was enhanced because he intentionally selected his victim on account of the victim's race. The question presented in this case is whether this penalty enhancement is prohibited by the First and Fourteenth Amendments. We hold that it is not.

On the evening of October 7, 1989, a group of young black men and boys, including Mitchell, gathered at an apartment complex in Kenosha, Wisconsin. Several members of the group discussed a scene from the motion picture *Mississippi Burning,* in which a white man beat a young black boy who was praying. The group moved outside and Mitchell asked them: "Do you all feel hyped up to move on some white people?" Brief for Petitioner 4. Shortly thereafter, a young white boy approached the group on the opposite side of the street where they were standing. As the boy walked by, Mitchell said: "You all want to fuck somebody up? There goes a white boy; go get him." *Id.,* at 4–5. Mitchell counted to three and pointed in the boy's direction. The group ran toward the boy, beat him severely, and stole his tennis shoes. The boy was rendered unconscious and remained in a coma for four days.

After a jury trial in the Circuit Court for Kenosha County, Mitchell was convicted of aggravated battery. Wis. Stat. §§ 939.05 and 940.19(1m) (1989–1990). That offense ordinarily carries a maximum sentence of two years' imprisonment. §§ 940.19(1m) and 939.50(3)(e). But because the jury found that Mitchell had intentionally selected his victim because of the boy's race, the maximum sentence for Mitchell's offense was increased to seven years under § 939.645. That provision enhances the maximum penalty for an offense whenever the defendant "[i]ntentionally selects the person against whom the crime ... is committed ... because of the race, religion, color, disability, sexual orientation, national origin or ancestry of that person...." § 939.645(1)(b). The Circuit Court sentenced Mitchell to four years' imprisonment for the aggravated battery.

Mitchell unsuccessfully sought postconviction relief in the Circuit Court. Then he appealed his conviction and sentence, challenging the constitutionality of Wisconsin's penalty-enhancement provision on First Amendment grounds. * * *

We granted *certiorari* because of the importance of the question presented and the existence of a conflict of authority among state high courts on the constitutionality of statutes similar to Wisconsin's penalty-enhancement provision, 506 U.S. 1033 (1992). We reverse. * * *

The State argues that the statute does not punish bigoted thought, as the Supreme Court of Wisconsin said, but instead punishes only conduct. While this argument is literally correct, it does not dispose of Mitchell's First Amendment challenge. To be sure, our cases reject the "view that an apparently limitless variety of conduct can be labeled 'speech' whenever the person engaging in the conduct intends thereby to express an idea." *United States v. O'Brien*, 391 U.S. 367, 376 (1968); accord, *R.A.V.*, 505 U.S., at 385–386; *Spence v. Washington*, 418 U.S. 405, 409 (1974) (*per curiam*); *Cox v. Louisiana*, 379 U.S. 536, 555 (1965). Thus, a physical assault is not by any stretch of the imagination expressive conduct protected by the First Amendment. See *Roberts v. United States Jaycees*, 468 U.S. 609, 628 (1984) ("[V]iolence or other types of potentially expressive activities that produce special harms distinct from their communicative impact . . . are entitled to no constitutional protection"); *NAACP v. Claiborne Hardware Co.*, 458 U.S. 886, 916 (1982) ("The First Amendment does not protect violence").

But the fact remains that under the Wisconsin statute the same criminal conduct may be more heavily punished if the victim is selected because of his race or other protected status than if no such motive obtained. Thus, although the statute punishes criminal conduct, it enhances the maximum penalty for conduct motivated by a discriminatory point of view more severely than the same conduct engaged in for some other reason or for no reason at all. Because the only reason for the enhancement is the defendant's discriminatory motive for selecting his victim, Mitchell argues (and the Wisconsin Supreme Court held) that the statute violates the First Amendment by punishing offenders' bigoted beliefs.

Traditionally, sentencing judges have considered a wide variety of factors in addition to evidence bearing on guilt in determining what sentence to impose on a convicted defendant. * * * Thus, in many States the commission of a murder, or other capital offense, for pecuniary gain is a separate aggravating circumstance under the capital sentencing statute. See, *e.g.*, Ariz. Rev. Stat. Ann. § 13–703(F)(5) (1989); Fla. Stat. § 921.141(5)(f) (Supp.1992); Miss. Code Ann. § 99–19–101(5)(f) (Supp. 1992); N.C. Gen. Stat. § 15A–2000(e)(6) (1992); Wyo. Stat. § 6–2–102(h)(vi) (Supp.1992).

But it is equally true that a defendant's abstract beliefs, however obnoxious to most people, may not be taken into consideration by a sentencing judge. *Dawson v. Delaware*, 503 U.S. 159 (1992). In *Dawson*, the State introduced evidence at a capital sentencing hearing that the defendant was a member of a white supremacist prison gang. Because "the evidence proved nothing more than [the defendant's] abstract beliefs," we held that its admission violated the defendant's First Amendment rights. *Id.*, at 167. In so holding, however, we emphasized that "the Constitution does not erect a *per se* barrier to the admission of evidence concerning one's beliefs and associations at sentencing simply because those beliefs and associations are protected by the First Amendment." *Id.*, at 165. Thus, in *Barclay v. Florida*, 463 U.S. 939 (1983) (plurality opinion), we allowed the sentencing judge to take into account the defendant's racial animus towards his victim. The evidence in that case showed that the defendant's membership in the Black Liberation Army and desire to provoke a "race war" were related to the murder of a white man for which he was convicted. See *id.*, at 942–944. Because "the elements of racial hatred in [the] murder" were relevant to several aggravating factors, we held that the trial judge permissibly took this evidence into account in sentencing the defendant to death. *Id.*, at 949, and n.7.

Mitchell suggests that *Dawson* and *Barclay* are inapposite because they did not involve application of a penalty-enhancement provision. But in *Barclay* we held that it was permissible for the sentencing court to consider the defendant's racial animus in determining whether he should be sentenced to death, surely the most severe "enhancement" of all. And the fact that the Wisconsin Legislature has decided, as a general matter, that bias-motivated offenses warrant greater maximum penalties across the board does not alter the result here. For the primary responsibility for fixing criminal penalties lies with the legislature.

Mitchell argues that the Wisconsin penalty-enhancement statute is invalid because it punishes the defendant's discriminatory motive, or reason, for acting. But motive plays the same role under the Wisconsin statute as it does under federal and state antidiscrimination laws, which we have previously upheld against constitutional challenge. * * * Title VII of the Civil Rights Act of 1964, for example, makes it unlawful for an employer to discriminate against an employee "because of such individual's race, color, religion, sex, or national origin." 42 U.S.C.A. § 2000e–2(a)(1). In *Hishon*, we rejected the argument that Title VII infringed employers' First Amendment rights. And more recently, in *R.A.V. v. St. Paul*, 505 U.S., at 389–390, we cited Title VII (as well as 18 U.S.C.A. § 242 and 42 U.S.C.A. §§ 1981 and 1982) as an example of a permissible content-neutral regulation of conduct. * * * Whereas the ordinance struck down in *R.A.V.* was explicitly directed at expression (*i.e.*, "speech" or "messages"), *id.*, at 392, the statute in this case is aimed at conduct unprotected by the First Amendment.

Moreover, the Wisconsin statute singles out for enhancement bias-inspired conduct because this conduct is thought to inflict greater individual and societal harm. For example, according to the State and its *amici*, bias-motivated crimes are more likely to provoke retaliatory crimes, inflict distinct emotional harms on their victims, and incite community unrest. See, *e.g.*, Brief for Petitioner 24–27; Brief for United States as Amicus Curiae 13–15; Brief for Lawyers' Committee for Civil Rights Under Law as Amicus Curiae 18–22; Brief for the American Civil Liberties Union as Amicus Curiae 17–19; Brief for the Anti–Defamation

League et al. as Amici Curiae 9–10; Brief for Congressman Charles E. Schumer et al. as Amici Curiae 8–9. The State's desire to redress these perceived harms provides an adequate explanation for its penalty-enhancement provision over and above mere disagreement with offenders' beliefs or biases. As Blackstone said long ago, "it is but reasonable that among crimes of different natures those should be most severely punished, which are the most destructive of the public safety and happiness." 4 W. Blackstone, Commentaries *16.

Finally, there remains to be considered Mitchell's argument that the Wisconsin statute is unconstitutionally overbroad because of its "chilling effect" on free speech. Mitchell argues (and the Wisconsin Supreme Court agreed) that the statute is "overbroad" because evidence of the defendant's prior speech or associations may be used to prove that the defendant intentionally selected his victim on account of the victim's protected status. Consequently, the argument goes, the statute impermissibly chills free expression with respect to such matters by those concerned about the possibility of enhanced sentences if they should in the future commit a criminal offense covered by the statute. We find no merit in this contention.

The sort of chill envisioned here is far more attenuated and unlikely than that contemplated in traditional "overbreadth" cases. We must conjure up a vision of a Wisconsin citizen suppressing his unpopular bigoted opinions for fear that if he later commits an offense covered by the statute, these opinions will be offered at trial to establish that he selected his victim on account of the victim's protected status, thus qualifying him for penalty enhancement. To stay within the realm of rationality, we must surely put to one side minor misdemeanor offenses covered by the statute, such as negligent operation of a motor vehicle (Wis.Stat. § 941.01 (1989–1990)); for it is difficult, if not impossible, to conceive of a situation where such offenses would be racially motivated. We are left, then, with the prospect of a citizen suppressing his bigoted beliefs for fear that evidence of such beliefs will be introduced against him at trial if he commits a more serious offense against person or property. This is simply too speculative a hypothesis to support Mitchell's overbreadth claim.

The First Amendment, moreover, does not prohibit the evidentiary use of speech to establish the elements of a crime or to prove motive or intent. Evidence of a defendant's previous declarations or statements is commonly admitted in criminal trials subject to evidentiary rules dealing with relevancy, reliability, and the like. Nearly half a century ago, in *Haupt v. United States*, 330 U.S. 631 (1947), we rejected a contention similar to that advanced by Mitchell here. Haupt was tried for the offense of treason, which, as defined by the Constitution (Art. III, § 3), may depend very much on proof of motive. To prove that the acts in question were committed out of "adherence to the enemy" rather than "parental solicitude," *id.*, at 641, the Government introduced evidence of conversations that had taken place long prior to the indictment, some of which consisted of statements showing Haupt's sympathy with Germany and Hitler and hostility towards the United States. We rejected Haupt's argument that this evidence was improperly admitted. While "[s]uch testimony is to be scrutinized with care to be certain the statements are not expressions of mere lawful and permissible difference of opinion with our own government or quite proper appreciation of the land of birth," we held that "these statements ... clearly were admissible on the question of intent and adherence to the enemy." *Id.*, at 642. * * *

For the foregoing reasons, we hold that Mitchell's First Amendment rights were not violated by the application of the Wisconsin penalty-enhancement provision in sentencing him. The judgment of the Supreme Court of Wisconsin is therefore reversed, and the case is remanded for further proceedings not inconsistent with this opinion.

Notes and Questions

1. *R.A.V.* again shows how limiting racially motivated expression has been unsuccessful. However, *Mitchell* shows that increasing punishment due to racial motivation is acceptable to the courts. Is this a way to limit hate speech—namely through increased punishment when the language used meets some race-neutral standard (such as fighting words, intentional infliction of emotional distress, etc.)?

2. Does the requirement that racial motivation accompany violence or a similar harm mean that the courts have made us wait too long (until another crime has been committed) to take action? Why not take action earlier, before violence is committed?

3. In *Mitchell* the defendants against whom enhanced penalties were sought were Black; in *R.A.V.* they were white skinheads. One lost, the other won. What part might race have played, if only subliminally?

RICHARD DELGADO

Words That Wound: A Tort Action for Racial Insults, Epithets, and Name–Calling
17 Harv. C.R.-C.L. L. Rev. 133, 133–49, 179–81 (1982).*

In *Contreras v. Crown Zellerbach Corp.*[1] the Washington Supreme Court held that a Mexican American's allegations that fellow employees had subjected him to a campaign of racial abuse stated a claim against his employer for the tort of outrage. The plaintiff alleged that he had suffered "humiliation and embarrassment by reason of racial jokes, slurs and comments"[3] and that the defendant's agents and employees had wrongfully accused him of stealing the employer's property, thereby preventing him from gaining employment and holding him up to public ridicule. Focusing upon the alleged racial abuse, the court declared that "racial epithets which were once part of common usage may not now be looked upon as 'mere insulting language.' "[4]

Eleven months later, the United States Court of Appeals for the

---

* Copyright © 1982 by The President and Fellows of Harvard College; Richard Delgado. Used by permission.

1. 88 Wash. 2d 735, 565 P.2d 1173 (1977) (*en banc*).

3. 88 Wash. 2d at 736, 565 P.2d at 1174.

4. *Id.* at 741, 565 P.2d at 1177.

Seventh Circuit in *Collin v. Smith*[5] affirmed a federal district court's decision declaring unconstitutional certain ordinances of the Village of Skokie, Illinois, which had been drafted to block a demonstration by members of the National Socialist Party of America. The village argued that the demonstration, together with the intended display of Nazi uniforms and swastikas, would inflict psychological trauma on its many Jewish citizens, some of whom had lived through the Holocaust. The court of appeals acknowledged that "many people would find [the] demonstration extremely mentally and emotionally disturbing."[7] Mentioning *Contreras*, the court also noted that Illinois recognizes the "new tort" of intentional infliction of severe emotional distress, which might well include the uttering of racial slurs. Nevertheless, the threat of criminal penalties imposed by the ordinance was held impermissibly to abridge the plaintiffs' First Amendment rights.

The concatenation of these two cases and the unsettled condition in which *Collin* leaves tort actions for racial speech suggest that reappraisal of these tort actions is in order. * * *

American society remains deeply afflicted by racism. Long before slavery became the mainstay of the plantation society of the antebellum South, Anglo–Saxon attitudes of racial superiority left their stamp on the developing culture of colonial America. Today, over a century after the abolition of slavery, many citizens suffer from discriminatory attitudes and practices, infecting our economic system, our cultural and political institutions, and the daily interactions of individuals. The idea that color is a badge of inferiority and a justification for the denial of opportunity and equal treatment is deeply ingrained.

The racial insult remains one of the most pervasive channels through which discriminatory attitudes are imparted. Such language injures the dignity and self-regard of the person to whom it is addressed, communicating the message that distinctions of race are distinctions of merit, dignity, status, and personhood. Not only does the listener learn and internalize the messages contained in racial insults, these messages color our society's institutions and are transmitted to succeeding generations.

The psychological harms caused by racial stigmatization are often much more severe than those created by other stereotyping actions. Unlike many characteristics upon which stigmatization may be based, membership in a racial minority can be considered neither self-induced, like alcoholism or prostitution, nor alterable. Race-based stigmatization is, therefore, "one of the most fruitful causes of human misery. Poverty can be eliminated—but skin color cannot."[16] The plight of members of racial minorities may be compared with that of persons with physical disfigurements; the point has been made that

> [a] rebuff due to one's color puts [the victim] in very much the situation of the very ugly person or one suffering from a loathsome disease. The suffering . . . may be aggravated by a consciousness of

5.   578 F.2d 1197 (7th Cir.), *cert.* denied,   **16.**   P. Mason, *Race Relations* 2 (1970).
439 U.S. 916 (1978).
7.   *Id.* at 1200.

incurability and even blameworthiness, a self-reproaching which tends to leave the individual still more aware of his loneliness and unwantedness.[17]

The psychological impact of this type of verbal abuse has been described in various ways. Kenneth Clark has observed, "Human beings ... whose daily experience tells them that almost nowhere in society are they respected and granted the ordinary dignity and courtesy accorded to others will, as a matter of course, begin to doubt their own worth."[18] Minorities may come to believe the frequent accusations that they are lazy, ignorant, dirty, and superstitious. "The accumulation of negative images ... present[s] them with one massive and destructive choice: either to hate one's self, as culture so systematically demand[s], or to have no self at all, to be nothing."[20]

The psychological responses to such stigmatization consist of feelings of humiliation, isolation, and self-hatred. Consequently, it is neither unusual nor abnormal for stigmatized individuals to feel ambivalent about their self-worth and identity. This ambivalence arises from the stigmatized individual's awareness that others perceive him or her as falling short of societal standards, standards which the individual has adopted. Stigmatized individuals thus often are hypersensitive and anticipate pain at the prospect of contact with "normals." It is no surprise, then, that racial stigmatization injures its victims' relationships with others. Racial tags deny minority individuals the possibility of neutral behavior in cross-racial contacts, thereby impairing the victims' capacity to form close interracial relationships. Moreover, the psychological responses of self-hatred and self-doubt unquestionably affect even the victims' relationships with members of their own group.

The psychological effects of racism may also result in mental illness and psychosomatic disease. The affected person may react by seeking escape through alcohol, drugs, or other kinds of anti-social behavior. * * * The achievement of high socioeconomic status does not diminish the psychological harms caused by prejudice. The effort to achieve success in business and managerial careers exacts a psychological toll even among exceptionally ambitious and upwardly mobile members of minority groups. Furthermore, those who succeed "do not enjoy the full benefits of their professional status within their organizations, because of inconsistent treatment by others resulting in continual psychological stress, strain, and frustration."[27] As a result, the incidence of severe psychological impairment caused by the environmental stress of prejudice and discrimination is not lower among minority group members of high socioeconomic status.

One of the most troubling effects of racial stigmatization is that it may affect parenting practices among minority group members, thereby perpetuating a tradition of failure. A recent study of minority mothers found that many denied the real significance of color in their lives, yet

17. O. Cox, *Caste, Class And Race* 383 (1948).

18. K. Clark, *Dark Ghetto* 63–64 (1965).

20. J. Kovel, *White Racism: A Psychohistory* 195 (1970).

27. J. Martin & C. Franklin, *Minority Group Relations* 3 (1979).

were morbidly sensitive to matters of race. Some, as a defense against aggression, identified excessively with whites, accepting whiteness as superior. Most had negative expectations concerning life's chances. Such self-conscious, hypersensitive parents, preoccupied with the ambiguity of their own social position, are unlikely to raise confident, achievement-oriented, and emotionally stable children.

In addition to these long-term psychological harms of racial labeling, the stresses of racial abuse may have physical consequences. Evidence suggests that high blood pressure is associated with inhibited, constrained, or restricted anger, and that insults produce elevation in blood pressure. American blacks have higher blood pressure levels and higher morbidity and mortality rates from hypertension, hypertensive disease, and stroke than do white counterparts. Further, there exists a strong correlation between degree of darkness of skin for blacks and level of stress felt, a correlation that may be caused by the greater discrimination experienced by dark-skinned blacks.

In addition to such emotional and physical consequences, racial stigmatization may damage a victim's pecuniary interests. The psychological injuries severely handicap the victim's pursuit of a career. The person who is timid, withdrawn, bitter, hypertense, or psychotic will almost certainly fare poorly in employment settings. An experiment in which blacks and whites of similar aptitudes and capacities were put into a competitive situation found that the blacks exhibited defeatism, half-hearted competitiveness, and "high expectancies of failure."[34] For many minority group members, the equalization of such quantifiable variables as salary and entry level would be an insufficient antidote to defeatist attitudes because the psychological price of attempting to compete is unaffordable; they are "programmed for failure."[35] Additionally, career options for the victims of racism are closed off by institutional racism—the subtle and unconscious racism in schools, hiring decisions, and the other practices which determine the distribution of social benefits and responsibilities.

Unlike most of the actions for which tort law provides redress to the victim, racial labeling and racial insults directly harm the perpetrator. Bigotry harms the individuals who harbor it by reinforcing rigid thinking, thereby dulling their moral and social senses and possibly leading to a "mildly . . . paranoid" mentality.[38] There is little evidence that racial slurs serve as a "safety valve" for anxiety which would otherwise be expressed in violence. * * *

THE HARMS OF RACIAL INSULTS

Immediate mental or emotional distress is the most obvious direct harm caused by a racial insult. Without question, mere words, whether racial or otherwise, can cause mental, emotional, or even physical harm to their target, especially if delivered in front of others or by a person in a position of authority. Racial insults, relying as they do on the unaltera-

---

34. *Id.* at 43.

35. *Id.* at 4.

38. G. Allport, *The Bigot in Our Midst*, 40 Commonweal 582 (1944), reprinted in

Anatomy of Racial Prejudice 161, 164 (G. deHuszar ed. 1946).

ble fact of the victim's race and on the history of slavery and race discrimination in this country, have an even greater potential for harm than other insults.

Although the emotional damage caused is variable and depends on many factors, only one of which is its outrageousness, a racial insult is always a dignitary affront, a direct violation of the victim's right to be treated respectfully. Our moral and legal systems recognize the principle that individuals are entitled to treatment that does not denigrate their humanity through disrespect for their privacy or moral worth. This ideal occupies a high place in our traditions, finding expression in such principles as universal suffrage, the prohibition against cruel and unusual punishment, the protection of the Fourth Amendment against unreasonable searches, and the abolition of slavery. A racial insult is a serious transgression of this principle because it derogates by race, a characteristic central to one's self-image.

The wrong of this dignitary affront consists of the expression of a judgment that the victim of the racial slur is entitled to less than that to which all other citizens are entitled. Verbal tags provide a convenient means of categorization so that individuals may be treated as members of a class and assumed to share all the negative attitudes imputed to the class. They thus make it easier for their users to justify their own superior position with respect to others. Racial insults also serve to keep the victim compliant. Such dignitary affronts are certainly no less harmful than others recognized by the law. Clearly, a society whose public law recognizes harm in the stigma of separate but equal schooling and the potential offensiveness of the required display of a state motto on automobile license plates, and whose private law sees actionable conduct in an unwanted kiss or the forcible removal of a person's hat, should also recognize the dignitary harm inflicted by a racial insult.

The need for legal redress for victims also is underscored by the intentionality of racial insults. This intentionality is obvious: What other purpose could the insult serve? There can be little doubt that the dignitary affront of racial insults, except perhaps those that are overheard, is intentional and therefore most reprehensible. Most people today know that certain words are offensive and only calculated to wound. No other use remains for such words as "nigger," "wop," "spick," or "kike."

In addition to the harms of immediate emotional distress and infringement of dignity, racial insults inflict psychological harm upon the victim. Racial slurs may cause long-term emotional pain because they draw upon and intensify the effects of the stigmatization, labeling, and disrespectful treatment that the victim has previously undergone. Social scientists who have studied the effects of racism have found that speech that communicates low regard for an individual because of race "tends to create in the victim those very traits of 'inferiority' that it ascribes to him."[72] Moreover, "even in the absence of more objective forms of

72. M. Deutsch, I. Katz & A. Jensen,   *opment* 175 (1968).
Social Class, Race And Psychological Devel-

discrimination—poor schools, menial jobs, and substandard housing—traditional stereotypes about the low ability and apathy of Negroes and other minorities can operate as 'self-fulfilling prophecies.' "[73] These stereotypes, portraying members of a minority group as stupid, lazy, dirty, or untrustworthy, are often communicated either explicitly or implicitly through racial insults. * * *

It is, of course, impossible to predict the degree of deterrence a cause of action in tort would create. But "for most people living in racist societies racial prejudice is merely a special kind of convenient rationalization for rewarding behavior."[83] In other words, in racist societies "most members of the dominant group will exhibit both prejudice and discrimination,"[84] but only in conforming to social norms. Thus, "when social pressures and rewards for racism are absent, racial bigotry is more likely to be restricted to people for whom prejudice fulfills a psychological 'need.' In such a tolerant milieu prejudiced persons may even refrain from discriminating behavior to escape social disapproval."[86] Increasing the cost of racial insults thus would certainly decrease their frequency. Laws will never prevent violations altogether, but they will deter "whoever is deterrable."[87]

Because most citizens comply with legal rules, and this compliance in turn "reinforce[s] their own sentiments toward conformity,"[88] a tort action for racial insults would discourage such harmful activity through the teaching function of the law. The establishment of a legal norm "creates a public conscience and a standard for expected behavior that check overt signs of prejudice."[90] Legislation aims first at controlling only the acts that express undesired attitudes. But "when expression changes, thoughts too in the long run are likely to fall into line."[91] "Laws ... restrain the middle range of mortals who need them as a mentor in molding their habits."[92] Thus, "If we create institutional arrangements in which exploitative behaviors are no longer reinforced, we will then succeed in changing attitudes [that underlie these behaviors]."[93] Because racial attitudes of white Americans "typically follow rather than precede actual institutional [or legal] alteration,"[94] a tort for racial slurs is a promising vehicle for the eradication of racism.

* * *

ELEMENTS OF THE CAUSE OF ACTION

In order to prevail in an action for a racial insult, the plaintiff should be required to prove that

73. *Id.*

83. P. van den Berghe, *Race and Racism* 21 (2d ed. 1978).

84. *Id.* at 20.

86. *Id.*

87. G. Allport, *The Nature of Prejudice* 472 (1954).

88. R. Williams, *The Reduction of Intergroup Tensions* 73 (1947).

90. G. Allport, *supra* note 87, at 470.

91. *Id.*

92. *Id.* at 439. See also G. Allport, *Prejudice: A Problem in Psychological and Social Causation* 4, Supp. Ser. No. 4, J. Soc. Issues (1950) (examination of prejudice as a mode of mental functioning).

93. H. Triandis, *The Impact of Social Change on Attitudes,* in *Attitudes, Conflict and Social Changes* 132 (1972) (quoted in Katz, *Preface, Toward the Elimination of Racism* 8 (P. Katz ed. 1976)).

94. G. Myrdal, *An American Dilemma* 20 (1944) (fallacy of theory that law cannot change custom).

language was addressed to him or her by the defendant that was intended to demean through reference to race; that the plaintiff understood as intended to demean through reference to race; and that a reasonable person would recognize as a racial insult.

Thus, it would be expected that an epithet such as "You damn nigger" would almost always be found actionable, as it is highly insulting and highly racial. However, an insult such as "You incompetent fool," directed at a black person by a white, even in a context which made it highly insulting, would not be actionable because it lacks a racial component. "Boy," directed at a young black male, might be actionable, depending on the speaker's intent, the hearer's understanding, and whether a reasonable person would consider it a racial insult in the particular context. "Hey, nigger," spoken affectionately between black persons and used as a greeting, would not be actionable. An insult such as "You dumb honkey," directed at a white person, could be actionable under this formulation of the cause of action, but only in the unusual situations where the plaintiff would suffer harm from such an insult.

The plaintiff may be able to show aggravating circumstances, such as abuse of a position of power or authority or knowledge of the victim's susceptibility to racial insults, which may render punitive damages appropriate. The common law defenses of privilege and mistake may be applicable, and retraction of the insult may mitigate damages.

Notes and Questions

1. Is an independent (*i.e.*, freestanding) tort the best way to deal with racist hate speech? What disadvantages and advantages do you see with this solution? Note that tort actions impose penalties after the fact—that is, no governmental actor intervenes or threatens action beforehand—while redress is left to individual, not group or societal, initiative. Are these features good or bad in light of our historic concerns over free speech?

2. In *Public Response to Racist Speech: Considering the Victim's Story,* 87 Mich. L. Rev. 2320 (1989), Mari J. Matsuda argues for a *public,* as opposed to a private, tort-law response to racist speech. After enumerating many of the same harms as Delgado, *supra,* she posits that the behavior eliciting them deserves the full sanction of the state in the form of criminal penalties.

INTERNATIONAL AND EMERGING RESPONSES TO HATE SPEECH

The United States lags behind Canada and many European societies in its toleration of racist, homophobic and anti-Semitic speech and hate crimes, even though it has signed a number of international treaties and conventions requiring it to take action against them. See *Striking a Balance* (S. Coliver ed. 1992) for a review of the positions of countries such as Italy, England, Sweden, and South Africa on hate.

HER MAJESTY THE QUEEN v. JAMES KEEGSTRA

1989: December 5, 6; 1990: December 13.

Present: DICKSON C.J.* and WILSON, LA FOREST, L'HEUREUX-DUBE, SOPINKA, GONTHIER and McLACHLIN JJ.

ON APPEAL FROM THE COURT OF APPEAL FOR ALBERTA

The accused, an Alberta high school teacher, was charged under s. 319(2) of the Criminal Code with wilfully promoting hatred against an identifiable group by communicating anti-Semitic statements to his students. Prior to his trial, the accused applied to the Court of Queen's Bench for an order quashing the charge. The court dismissed the application on the ground that s. 319(2) of the Code did not violate freedom of expression as guaranteed by s. 2(b) of the Canadian Charter of Rights and Freedoms. The court, for want of proper notice to the Crown, did not entertain the accused's argument that s. 319(3)(a) of the Code violated the presumption of innocence protected by s. 11(d) of the Charter. Section 319(3)(a) affords a defence of "truth" to the wilful promotion of hatred but only where the accused proves the truth of the communicated statements on a balance of probabilities. The accused was thereafter tried and convicted. On appeal the accused's Charter arguments were accepted, the Court of Appeal holding that ss. 319(2) and 319(3)(a) infringed ss. 2(b) and 11(d) of the Charter respectively, and that the infringements were not justifiable under s. 1 of the Charter.
* * *

THE USE OF AMERICAN CONSTITUTIONAL JURISPRUDENCE

* * * I think it appropriate to address * * * the relationship between Canadian and American approaches to the constitutional protection of free expression, most notably in the realm of hate propaganda. Those who attack the constitutionality of s. 319(2) draw heavily on the tenor of First Amendment jurisprudence in weighing the competing freedoms and interests in this appeal, a reliance which is understandable given the prevalent opinion that the criminalization of hate propaganda violates the Bill of Rights (see, *e.g.,* L. H. Tribe, *American Constitutional Law* (2nd ed. 1988), at p. 861, n.2; K. Greenawalt, *Insults and Epithets: Are They Protected Speech?* (1990), 42 Rutgers L. Rev. 287, at p. 304). In response to the emphasis placed upon this jurisprudence, I find it helpful to summarize the American position and to determine the extent to which it should influence the s. 1 analysis in the circumstances of this appeal.

A myriad of sources—both judicial and academic—offer reviews of First Amendment jurisprudence as it pertains to hate propaganda. Central to most discussions is the 1952 case of *Beauharnais v. Illinois*, 343 U.S. 250, where the Supreme Court of the United States upheld as constitutional a criminal statute forbidding certain types of group defamation. Though never overruled, *Beauharnais* appears to have been weakened by later pronouncements of the Supreme Court (see, *e.g.,*

---

* Chief Justice at the time of hearing.

Garrison v. Louisiana, 379 U.S. 64 (1964); *Ashton v. Kentucky*, 384 U.S. 195 (1966); *New York Times Co. v. Sullivan*, 376 U.S. 254 (1964); *Brandenburg v. Ohio*, 395 U.S. 444 (1969); and *Cohen v. California*, 403 U.S. 15 (1971)). The trend reflected in many of these pronouncements is to protect offensive, public invective as long as the speaker has not knowingly lied and there exists no clear and present danger of violence or insurrection.

In the wake of subsequent developments in the Supreme Court, on several occasions *Beauharnais* has been distinguished and doubted by lower courts (see, *e.g., Anti–Defamation League of B'Nai B'rith v. Federal Communications Commission*, 403 F.2d 169 (D.C.Cir. 1968), at p. 174, n.5; *Tollett v. United States*, 485 F.2d 1087 (8th Cir. 1973), at p. 1094, n.14; *American Booksellers Ass'n, Inc. v. Hudnut*, 771 F.2d 323 (7th Cir. 1985), at pp. 331–32; and *Doe v. University of Michigan*, 721 F. Supp. 852 (E.D.Mich. 1989), at p. 863). Of the judgments expressing a shaken faith in *Beauharnais, Collin v. Smith*, 578 F.2d 1197 (7th Cir. 1978), *certiorari* denied, 439 U.S. 916 (1978), is of greatest relevance to this appeal. In *Collin*, the Court of Appeal for the Seventh Circuit invalidated a municipal ordinance prohibiting public demonstrations inciting "violence, hatred, abuse or hostility toward a person or group of persons by reason of reference to religious, racial, ethnic, national or regional affiliation" (p. 1199), and thereby allowed members of the American Nazi Party to march through Skokie, Illinois, home to a large number of Jewish Holocaust survivors (despite the ruling, however, no march was held in Skokie; I. Horowitz, *First Amendment Blues: On Downs, Nazis in Skokie*, [1986] Am. B. Found. Res. J. 535, at p. 540).

The question that concerns us in this appeal is not, of course, what the law is or should be in the United States. But it is important to be explicit as to the reasons why or why not American experience may be useful in the s. 1 analysis of s. 319(2) of the Criminal Code. In the United States, a collection of fundamental rights has been constitutionally protected for over two hundred years. The resulting practical and theoretical experience is immense, and should not be overlooked by Canadian courts. On the other hand, we must examine American constitutional law with a critical eye, and in this respect La Forest J. has noted in *R. v. Rahey*, [1987] 1 S.C.R. 588, at p. 639:

> While it is natural and even desirable for Canadian courts to refer to American constitutional jurisprudence in seeking to elucidate the meaning of Charter guarantees that have counterparts in the United States Constitution, they should be wary of drawing too ready a parallel between constitutions born to different countries in different ages and in very different circumstances. . . .

Canada and the United States are not alike in every way, nor have the documents entrenching human rights in our two countries arisen in the same context. It is only common sense to recognize that, just as similarities will justify borrowing from the American experience, differences may require that Canada's constitutional vision depart from that endorsed in the United States.

Having examined the American cases relevant to First Amendment jurisprudence and legislation criminalizing hate propaganda, I would be adverse to following too closely the line of argument that would overrule *Beauharnais* on the ground that incursions placed upon free expression are only justified where there is a clear and present danger of imminent breach of peace. Equally, I am unwilling to embrace various categorizations and guiding rules generated by American law without careful consideration of their appropriateness to Canadian constitutional theory. Though I have found the American experience tremendously helpful in coming to my own conclusions regarding this appeal, and by no means reject the whole of the First Amendment doctrine, in a number of respects I am thus dubious as to the applicability of this doctrine in the context of a challenge to hate propaganda legislation.

First, it is not entirely clear that *Beauharnais* must conflict with existing First Amendment doctrine. Credible arguments have been made that later Supreme Court cases do not necessarily erode its legitimacy (see, *e.g.*, K. Lasson, *Racial Defamation As Free Speech: Abusing the First Amendment* (1985). 17 Colum. Hum. Rts. L. Rev. 11). Indeed, there exists a growing body of academic writing in the United States which evinces a stronger focus upon the way in which hate propaganda can undermine the very values which free speech is said to protect. This body of writing is receptive to the idea that, were the issue addressed from this new perspective, First Amendment doctrine might be able to accommodate statutes prohibiting hate propaganda (see, *e.g.*, R. Delgado, *Words That Wound: A Tort Action for Racial Insults, Epithets, and Name–Calling* (1982), 17 Harv. C.R.-C.L. L. Rev. 133; I. Horowitz and V. Bramson, *Skokie, the ACLU and the Endurance of Democratic Theory* (1979), 43 Law & Contemp. Probs. 328; Lasson, *op. cit.*, at pp. 20–30; M. Matsuda, *Public Response to Racist Speech: Considering the Victim's Story* (1989), 87 Mich. L. Rev. 2320, at p. 2348; Comment, *Doe v. University of Michigan: First Amendment—Racist and Sexist Expression on Campus—Court Strikes Down University Limits on Hate Speech* (1990), 103 Harv. L. Rev. 1397).

Second, the aspect of First Amendment doctrine most incompatible with s. 319(2), at least as that doctrine is described by those who would strike down the legislation, is its strong aversion to content-based regulation of expression. I am somewhat skeptical, however, as to whether this view of free speech in the United States is entirely accurate. Rather, in rejecting the extreme position that would provide an absolute guarantee of free speech in the Bill of Rights, the Supreme Court has developed a number of tests and theories by which protected speech can be identified and the legitimacy of government regulation assessed. Often required is a content-based categorization of the expression under examination. As an example, obscenity is not protected because of its content (see, *e.g.*, *Roth v. United States*, 354 U.S. 476 (1957)) and laws proscribing child pornography have been scrutinized under a less than strict First Amendment standard even where they extend to expression beyond the realm of the obscene (see *New York v. Ferber*, 458 U.S. 747 (1982)). Similarly, the vigourous protection of free speech relaxes when commercial expression is scrutinized (see, *e.g.*,

Posadas de Puerto Rico Associates v. Tourism Co. of Puerto Rico, 478 U.S. 328 (1986)), and it is permissible to restrict government employees in their exercise of the right to engage in political activity (*Cornelius v. NAACP Legal Defense and Educational Fund, Inc.*, 473 U.S. 788 (1985)).

In short, a decision to place expressive activity in a category which either merits reduced protection or falls entirely outside of the First Amendment's ambit at least impliedly involves assessing the content of the activity in light of free speech values. As Professor F. Schauer has said, it is always necessary to examine the First Amendment value of the expression limited by state regulation (*The Aim and the Target in Free Speech Methodology* (1989), 83 Nw. U.L. Rev. 562, at p. 568). To recognize that content is often examined under the First Amendment is not to deny that content neutrality plays a real and important role in the American jurisprudence. Nonetheless, that the proscription against looking at the content of expression is not absolute, and that balancing is occasionally employed in First Amendment cases (see Professor T. A. Aleinikoff, *Constitutional Law in the Age of Balancing* (1987), 96 Yale L.J. 943, at pp. 966–68), reveals that even in the United States it is sometimes thought justifiable to restrict a particular message because of its meaning.

Third, applying the Charter to the legislation challenged in this appeal reveals important differences between Canadian and American constitutional perspectives. . . . Section I has no equivalent in the United States, a fact previously alluded to by this Court in selectively utilizing American constitutional jurisprudence (see, *e.g., Re B.C. Motor Vehicle Act*, [1985] 2 S.C.R. 486, *per* Lamer J., at p. 498). Of course, American experience should never be rejected simply because the Charter contains a balancing provision, for it is well known that American courts have fashioned compromises between conflicting interests despite what appears to be the absolute guarantee of constitutional rights. Where s. 1 operates to accentuate a uniquely Canadian vision of a free and democratic society, however, we must not hesitate to depart from the path taken in the United States. Far from requiring a less solicitous protection of Charter rights and freedoms, such independence of vision protects these rights and freedoms in a different way. As will be seen below, in my view the international commitment to eradicate hate propaganda and, most importantly, the special role given equality and multiculturalism in the Canadian Constitution necessitate a departure from the view, reasonably prevalent in America at present, that the suppression of hate propaganda is incompatible with the guarantee of free expression. (In support of this view, see the comments of Professors K. Mahoney and J. Cameron in *Language as Violence v. Freedom of Expression: Canadian and American Perspectives on Group Defamation* (1988–89), 37 Buffalo L. Rev. 337, beginning at pp. 344 and 353 respectively).

In sum, there is much to be learned from First Amendment jurisprudence with regard to freedom of expression and hate propaganda. It would be rash, however, to see First Amendment doctrine as demanding the striking down of s. 319(2). Not only are the precedents somewhat mixed, but the relaxation of the prohibition against content-based regulation of expression in certain areas indicates that American courts are not loath to permit the suppression of ideas in some circumstances. Most importantly, the nature of the s. 1 test as applied in the context of a challenge to s. 319(2) may well demand a perspective particular to Canadian constitutional jurisprudence when weighing competing interests. If values fundamental to the Canadian conception of a free and democratic society suggest an approach that denies hate propaganda the highest degree of constitutional protection, it is this approach which must be employed. * * *

FREEDOM OF EXPRESSION

* * * Communications which wilfully promote hatred against an identifiable group are protected by s. 2(b) of the Charter. When an activity conveys or attempts to convey a meaning, through a non-violent form of expression, it has expressive content and thus falls within the scope of the word "expression" as found in the guarantee. The type of meaning conveyed is irrelevant. Section 2(b) protects all content of expression. In enacting s. 319(2) of the Code, Parliament sought to prohibit communications which convey meaning. Section 319(2), therefore, represents an infringement of s. 2(b).

Communications which are intended to promote hatred against identifiable groups do not fall within the ambit of a possible s. 2(b) exception concerning expression manifested in a violent form. This exception refers only to expression communicated directly through physical harm. Hate propaganda is not analogous to violence. It conveys a meaning that is repugnant, but the repugnance stems from the content of the message and not from its form. As for threats of violence, they are not excluded from the definition of expression envisioned by s. 2(b).

Sections 15 and 27 of the Charter, which deal with equality and multiculturalism, and the international agreements signed by Canada on the prohibition of racist statements, should not be used to interpret the scope of s. 2(b). It is inappropriate to attenuate the s. 2(b) freedom on the grounds that a particular context so requires. The large and liberal interpretation given to freedom of expression indicates that the preferable course is to weigh the various contextual values and factors in s. 1 of the Charter. This section both guarantees and limits Charter rights and freedoms by reference to principles fundamental in a free and democratic society.

Section 319(2) of the Code constitutes a reasonable limit upon freedom of expression. Parliament's objective of preventing the harm caused by hate propaganda is of sufficient importance to warrant overriding a constitutional freedom. Parliament has recognized the substantial harm that can flow from hate propaganda and, in trying to prevent the pain suffered by target group members and to reduce racial, ethnic and religious tension and perhaps even violence in Canada, has decided to suppress the wilful promotion of hatred against identifiable groups. Parliament's objective is supported not only by the work of numerous study groups, but also by our collective historical knowledge of the potentially catastrophic effects of the promotion of hatred. Additionally, the international commitment to eradicate hate propaganda and Canada's commitment to the values of equality and multiculturalism in ss. 15 and 27 of the Charter strongly buttress the importance of this objective.

Section 319(2) of the Code is an acceptably proportional response to Parliament's valid objective. There is obviously a rational connection between the criminal prohibition of hate propaganda and the objective of protecting target group members and of fostering harmonious social relations in a community dedicated to equality and multiculturalism. Section 319(2) serves to illustrate to the public the severe reprobation with which society holds messages of hate directed towards racial and religious groups. It makes that kind of expression less attractive and hence decreases acceptance of its content. Section 319(2) is also a means by which the values beneficial to a free and democratic society in particular, the value of equality and the worth and dignity of each human person can be publicized.

Section 319(2) of the Code does not unduly impair freedom of expression. This section does not suffer from overbreadth or vagueness; rather, the terms of the offence indicate that s. 319(2) possesses definitional limits which act as safeguards to ensure that it will capture only expressive activity which is openly hostile to Parliament's objective, and will thus attack only the harm at which the prohibition is targeted. The word "wilfully" imports into the offence a stringent standard of *mens rea* which significantly restricts the reach of s. 319(2) by necessitating the proof of either an intent to promote hatred or knowledge of the substantial certainty of such a consequence. The word "hatred" further reduces the scope of the prohibition. This word, in the context of s. 319(2), must be construed as encompassing only the most severe and deeply felt form of opprobrium. Further, the exclusion of private communications from the scope of s. 319(2), the need for the promotion of hatred to focus upon an identifiable group and the presence of the s. 319(3) defences, which clarify the scope of s. 319(2), all support the view that the impugned section creates a narrowly confined offence. Section 319(2) is not an excessive impairment of freedom of expression merely because the defence of truth in s. 319(3)(a) does not cover negligent or innocent error as to the truthfulness of a statement. Whether or not a statement is susceptible to classification as true or false, such error should not excuse an accused who has wilfully used a statement in order to promote hatred against an identifiable group. Finally, while other noncriminal modes of combatting hate propaganda exist, it is eminently reasonable to utilize more than one type of legislative tool in working to prevent the spread of racist expression and its resultant harm. To send out a strong message of condemnation, both reinforcing the values underlying s. 319(2) and deterring the few individuals who would harm target group members and the larger community by communicating hate propaganda, will occasionally require use of the criminal law.

The effects of s. 319(2) are not of such a deleterious nature as to outweigh any advantage gleaned from the limitation of s. 2(b). The expressive activity at which s. 319(2) is aimed constitutes a special category, a category only tenuously connected with the values underlying the guarantee of freedom of expression. Hate propaganda contributes little to the aspirations of Canadians or Canada in either the quest for truth, the promotion of individual self-development or the protection and fostering of a vibrant democracy where the participation of all individuals is accepted and encouraged. Moreover, the narrowly drawn terms of s. 319(2) and its defences prevent the prohibition of expression lying outside of this narrow category. Consequently, the suppression of hate propaganda represents an impairment of the individual's freedom of expression which is not of a most serious nature. * * *

RICHARD DELGADO

Campus Antiracism Rules: Constitutional Narratives In Collision
85 Nw. U. L. Rev. 343, 345–48, 383–86 (1991).*

Persons tend to react to the problem of racial insults in one of two ways. On hearing that a university has enacted rules forbidding certain forms of speech, some will frame the issue as a First Amendment problem: The rules limit speech, something that the Constitution forbids without a very good reason. If one takes that starting point, several consequences follow. First, the burden shifts to the other side to show that the interest in protecting members of the campus community from insults and name-calling is compelling enough to overcome the presumption in favor of free speech. Further, there must be no less onerous way of accomplishing that objective. Other concerns rise to the fore: Will the enforcer of the regulation become a censor, imposing narrow-minded restraints on campus discussion? Finally, what about slippery slopes and line-drawing problems: If a campus restricts this type of expression, might the temptation arise to do the same with classroom speech or political satire in the campus newspaper?

Others, however, will frame the problem in radically different terms—as one of protection of equality. They will ask whether an educational institution does not have the power, to protect core values emanating from the Thirteenth and Fourteenth Amendments, to enact reasonable regulations aimed at assuring equal personhood on campus. If one characterizes the issue this way, other consequences follow. Now, the defenders of racially scathing speech are required to show that the interest in its protection is compelling enough to overcome the preference for equal personhood; and we will want to be sure that this interest is advanced in the way least damaging to equality. They, too, will raise concerns about the decisionmaker who will enforce the rules, but from the opposite standpoint: The enforcer of the regulation must be attuned to the nuances of insult and racial supremacy at issue, for example by incorporating multi-ethnic representation into the hearing process. Finally, a different set of slopes will look slippery. If we do not intervene to protect equality here, what will the next outrage be?

The legal analysis, therefore, leads to opposite conclusions depending on the starting point. But an even deeper indeterminacy looms: Both sides invoke different narratives to rally support. Protectors of the First Amendment see campus antiracism rules as parts of a much longer story: the centuries-old struggle of Western society to free itself from superstition and enforced ignorance. The tellers of this story invoke martyrs like Socrates, Galileo, and Peter Zenger, and heroes like Locke, Hobbes, Voltaire, and Hume who fought for the right of free expression. They conjure up struggles against official censorship, book burning, witch trials, and communist blacklists. Compared to that richly textured, deeply stirring account, the minority-protector's interest in freeing a few (supersensitive?) individuals from momentary discomfort looks thin. A textured, historical account is pitted against a particularized, slice-of-life, dignitary one.

Those on the minority-protection side invoke a different, and no less powerful, narrative. They see a nation's centuries-long struggle to free itself from racial and other forms of tyranny, including slavery, lynching, Jim Crow laws, and "separate-but-equal" schools. They conjure up different milestones—Lincoln's Emancipation Proclamation, *Brown v. Board of Education*; they look to different heroes—Martin Luther King, the early Abolitionists, Rosa Parks, and César Chávez, civil rights protesters who put their lives on the line for racial justice. Arrayed against that richly textured historical account, the racist's interest in insulting a person of color face-to-face looks thin.

One often hears that the problem of campus antiracism rules is that of balancing free speech and equality. But more is at stake than that. Each side wants not merely to have the balance struck in its favor; each wants to impose its own understanding of what is at stake. Minority protectors see the injury of one who has been subject to a racial assault as not a mere isolated event, but as part of an interrelated series of acts by which persons of color are subordinated, and which will follow the victim wherever she goes. First Amendment defenders see the wrong of silencing the racist as much more than a momentary inconvenience: Protection of his right to speak is part of the never-ending vigilance necessary to preserve freedom of expression in a society that is too prone to balance it away.

My view is that both stories are equally valid. Judges and university administrators have no easy, *a priori* way of choosing between them, of privileging one over the other. They could coin an exception to free speech, thus giving primacy to the equal protection values at stake. Or, they could carve an exception to equality, saying in effect that universities may protect minority populations except where this abridges speech. Nothing in constitutional or moral theory requires one answer rather than the other. Social science, case law, and the experience of other nations provide some illumination. But ultimately, judges and university administrators must *choose*. And in making this choice, we are in uncharted terrain: We lack a pole star. * * *

Neither the constitutional narrative of the First, nor of the Thirteenth and Fourteenth, Amendments clearly prevails in connection with campus antiracism rules. Judges must choose. The dilemma is embedded in the nature of our system of law and politics: We want and fear both equality and liberty. * * *

Might a postmodern insight offer a possible solution to the problem of campus antiracism rules? Perhaps the speech by which society "constructs" a stigma picture of minorities may be regulated consistently with the First Amendment because it is different from most other forms of speech in function and effect. Indeed, regulation may prove necessary for full effectuation of the values of equal personhood we hold equally dear.

The first step is recognizing that racism is, in almost all its aspects, a class harm—the essence of which is subordination of one people by another. The mechanism of this subordination is a complex, interlocking series of acts, some physical, some symbolic. Although the physical acts (like lynchings and cross burnings) are often the most striking, the symbolic acts are the most insidious. By communicating and constructing a shared cultural image of the victim group as inferior, we enable ourselves to feel comfortable about the disparity in power and resources between ourselves and the stigmatized group. Even civil rights law contributes to this stigmatization: The group is so vulnerable that it requires social help. The shared picture also demobilizes the victims of discrimination, particularly the young. Indeed, social scientists have seen evidence of self-hatred and rejection of their own identity in children of color as early as age three.

The ubiquity and incessancy of harmful racial depiction are thus the source of its virulence. Like water dripping on sandstone, it is a pervasive harm which only the most hardy can resist. Yet the prevailing First Amendment paradigm predisposes us to treat racist speech as an individual harm, as though we only had to evaluate the effect of a single drop of water. This approach—corresponding to liberal, individualistic theories of self and society—systematically misperceives the experience of racism for both victim and perpetrator. This mistake is natural, and corresponds to one aspect of our natures—our individualistic selves. In this capacity, we want and need liberty. But we also exist in a social capacity; we need others to fulfill ourselves as beings. In this group aspect, we require inclusion, equality, and equal respect. Constitutional narratives of equal protection and prohibition of slavery—narratives that encourage us to form and embrace collectivity and equal citizenship for all—reflect this second aspect of our existence.

When the tacit consent of a group begins to coordinate the exercise of individual rights so as seriously to jeopardize participation by a smaller group, the "rights" nature of the first group's actions acquires a different character and dimension. The exercise of an individual right now poses a group harm and must be weighed against this qualitatively different type of threat. * * *

Thus, a wealthy and well-regarded citizen who is victimized by a vicious defamation is able to recover in tort. His social "picture," in which he has a property interest, has been damaged, and will require laborious reconstruction. It would require only slight extension of this observation to provide protection from racial slurs and hate-speech. Indeed, the rich man has the dominant "story" on his side; repairing the defamation's damage will be relatively easy.

Racist speech, by contrast, is not so readily repaired—it separates the victim from the storytellers who alone have credibility. Not only does racist speech, by placing all the credibility with the dominant group, strengthen the dominant story, it also works to disempower minority groups by crippling the effectiveness of *their* speech in rebuttal. This situation makes free speech a powerful asset to the dominant group, but a much less helpful one to subordinate groups—a result at odds, certainly, with marketplace theories of the First Amendment. Unless society is able to deal with this incongruity, the Thirteenth and Fourteenth Amendments and our complex system of civil rights statutes will be of little avail. At best, they will be able to obtain redress for episodic, blatant acts of individual prejudice and bigotry. But they will do little to address the source of the problem: the speech that creates the stigma-picture that makes the acts hurtful in the first place, and that renders almost any other form of aid—social or legal—useless.

Could judges and legislators effectuate the suggestion that speech which constructs a stigma-picture of a subordinate group stands on a different footing from sporadic speech aimed at persons who are not disempowered? It might be argued that *all* speech constructs the world to some extent, and that every speech act could prove offensive to someone. Traditionalists find modern art troublesome, Republicans detest left-wing speech, and some men hate speech that constructs a sex-neutral world. Yet race—like gender and a few other characteristics—is different; our entire history and culture bespeak this difference. Thus, judges easily could differentiate speech which subordinates blacks or Latinos, for example, from that which disparages factory owners. Will they choose to do so? There is cause for doubt: Low-grade racism benefits the status quo. Moreover, our system's winners have a stake in liberal, marketplace interpretations of law and politics—the seeming neutrality and meritocratic nature of such interpretations reassure the decisionmakers that their social position is deserved.

Still, resurgent racism on our nation's campuses is rapidly becoming a national embarrassment. Almost daily, we are faced with headlines featuring some of the ugliest forms of ethnic conflict and the spectre of virtually all-white universities. The need to avoid these consequences may have the beneficial effect of causing courts to reflect on, and tailor, constitutional doctrine. As Harry Kalven pointed out twenty five years ago, it would not be the first time that insights born of the cauldron of racial justice yielded reforms that ultimately redounded to the benefit of all society.[353]

Notes and Questions

1. Should college campuses be "bastions of free speech"—or is the case for bridling it there just as strong as elsewhere, say, in a workplace?

2. Are private colleges free to enact hate-speech rules? If so, would these rules just drive racism underground?

3. Is characterizing hate speech as a controversy about speech the wrong way to look at the problem?

353. See Harry Kalven, *The Negro and the First Amendment* (1965) (pointing out that reforms born of the cauldron of civil rights often end up benefiting all society, not just Blacks).

4.   On an emerging "legal realist" view of the First Amendment that eschews mechanistic, archaic "tests" and special doctrines in favor of a more skeptical, nuanced view of that Amendment and what it can accomplish, see the concluding selection of Chapter 12, *infra.*

5.   Recently, commentators and a small number of courts have begun exploring a new "hostile environment" approach to controlling campus racism, drawing an analogy to the hostile-workplace doctrine that has sprung up in the Title VII (job discrimination) arena. *E.g.*, Catharine MacKinnon, *Only Words* (1993). What advantages and disadvantages do you see with this new approach?

6.   Classroom Exercise: Blue Eyes, Brown Eyes

As an exercise in role playing, divide the class into "blue eyes" and "brown eyes" groups. Groups appoint speakers and supply them with "research" (*e.g.*, books like *The Bell Curve*) based on which the speakers lecture the class for several days in a row on the inferiority—physical, moral, social, and intellectual—of the other group. Afterward, each student will write about his or her reaction to the experience. See, *e.g.*, William Peters, *A Class Divided: Then and Now* (1971).

7.   For further reading on hate speech, see Richard Delgado & Jean Stefancic, *Must We Defend Nazis? Hate Speech, Pornography, and the New First Amendment* (1997); *The Price We Pay: The Case Against Racist Speech, Hate Propaganda, and Pornography* (L. Lederer & R. Delgado eds. 1996); Stephen G. Gey, *The Case Against Postmodern Censorship Theory*, 145 U. Pa. L. Rev. 193 (1996); Samuel Walker, *Hate Speech: The History of an American Controversy* (1994).

8.   A good deal of hate speech is beginning to be delivered by means of the Internet. These messages may be general—sent to many users or posted on a website—or sent to single users *e.g.*, an African–American undergraduate. For an example of the former, see Chapter 6 § 5 (Racial Paranoia On–Line). Does dissemination of hate messages electronically pose any special issues? See Rachel Weintraub–Reiter, Note: *Hate Speech over the Internet: A Traditional Constitutional Analysis or a New Cyber Constitution?* 8 B.U. Pub. Int. L.J. 145 (1998). Does it matter if the sender is using a computer system owned and maintained by a workplace or university?

SECTION 3. LANGUAGE, CULTURAL IDENTITY, AND THE "OFFICIAL ENGLISH" MOVEMENT

JUAN F. PEREA

Demography and Distrust: An Essay on American Languages,
Cultural Pluralism, and Official English
77 Minn. L. Rev. 269, 328–33, 335–49 (1992).*

American nativism and racism have targeted many groups throughout our history. Native Americans, African Americans, Mexican Americans, and Asian Americans, among other groups, have been subjected to unequal treatment and oppression because of their differences from the majority culture. * * *

America during 1910–1914 experienced growing nativism, as the nation groped for a sense of national unity. World War I focused this nativism: "The struggle with Germany . . . called forth the most strenuous nationalism and the most pervasive nativism that the United States had ever known."[332] Nativism takes aim at the ethnicity of "enemy people." Germans were deemed disloyal merely for being, acting, speaking, and reading like Germans. At the time, Germans were the largest national-origin group of immigrants in America, numbering more than 2.3 million persons. Germans had also been the largest non-English-speaking group of American colonists.

Loyalty was equated with conformity to the core English-speaking culture. Difference from that culture and difference of opinion were equated with foreign influence and subversion of American identity. The wartime hysteria yielded unprecedented demands for conformity, embodied in the movement for "100 per cent Americanism."[335] One hundred percent Americans, mostly members of the core culture, "felt sure that the nation would never be safe until every vestige of German culture had been stamped out."[336] One writer on Americanization, echoing the words of John Jay in *The Federalist*, wrote that "[t]he war has taught us the need of a more united people, speaking one language, thinking one tradition, and holding allegiance to one patriotism—America."[337] The wartime nativism led to the imprisonment, public flogging and lynching of Germans.

To Kill or Use Our German Press? asked the Literary Digest of May 11, 1918. Killing the German press would eliminate "enemy publications" assumed to be under German influence. Others argued that "[t]he best use to which German-language papers can be put in these days is communicating American sentiments to people who can not read English."[339] Eliminating the German press went beyond rhetoric and into the law. A 1920 Oregon law prohibited publication of any foreign language newspaper unless it carried a full, conspicuous, and literal translation of all its contents. Such translation being prohibitively expensive, the law was intended to put the foreign-language press out of business. Advocates of such measures had forgotten "the service done by the foreign language press to the government during the war by aiding the loans and explaining the draft."[341] They would silence not only the press, but also the German voice. The governor of Iowa banned the use of any language other than English "in all schools, church services, conversations in public places or over the telephone."[342]

Killing the German culture in American society also meant killing it in the schools. Many states attempted to ban the teaching of German and other foreign languages in their schools. By 1919, fifteen states had banned the teaching of foreign languages, and required English to be the

---

332. See John Higham, *Strangers in the Land* 195 (2d ed. 1988).

335. *Id*. at 204.

336. *Id*. at 208.

337. Harry Rider, *Americanization*, 14 Am. Pol. Sci. Rev. 110, 110 (1920).

339. *To Kill or Use Our German Press?*, Literary Dig., May 11, 1918, at 12, 12.

341. *American by Decree*, The New Republic, Apr. 28, 1920, at 262, 262–63.

342. Higham, *supra* note 332, at 248.

sole language of instruction in primary schools, both public and private. Illinois made English its exclusive language of instruction

> [b]ecause the English language is the common as well as official language of our country, and because it is essential to good citizenship that each citizen shall have or speedily acquire, as his natural tongue, the language in which the laws of the land, the decrees of the courts, and the announcements and pronouncements of its officials are made.[344]

Although English was the dominant language of the country, apparently only Illinois, rather peremptorily, declared it the official language of the land.

A Nebraska statute prohibited teaching any language other than English to students who had not passed the eighth grade. In 1922 the Supreme Court of Nebraska affirmed the conviction of Robert Meyer, who had violated the statute by teaching biblical stories in German to a ten-year-old. In its opinion, the Nebraska court expressed fears of languages other than English, their inherent danger, and their perceived lack of relation to American identity:

> The legislature had seen the baneful effects of permitting foreigners, who had taken residence in this country, to rear and educate their children in the language of their native land. The result of that condition was found to be inimical to our own safety. To allow the children of foreigners, who had emigrated here, to be taught from early childhood the language of the country of their parents was to rear them with that language as their mother tongue. It was to educate them so that they must always think in that language, and, as a consequence, naturally inculcate in them the ideas and sentiments foreign to the best interest of this country. The statute, therefore, was intended not only to require that the education of all children be conducted in the English language, but that, until they had grown into that language and until it had become part of them, they should not be taught any other language.[347]

For the Nebraska court, as for many Americans past and present, a foreign mother tongue was "foreign to the best interests of this country." The pattern repeats itself often. The United States Supreme Court, more detached from the nativism of the time, reversed Meyer's conviction and found that the statute violated substantive due process rights under the Fourteenth Amendment. The Court wrote that "[t]he protection of the Constitution extends to all, to those who speak other languages as well as to those born with English on the tongue."[349]

The war against Germany produced an unprecedented fear of German–American ethnicity, resulting in intensified demands for conformity with the core culture and the concomitant dismemberment of the German culture and language in America. A wartime crisis spawned intense

---

344. Act of June 28, 1919, § 1, 1919 Ill. Laws 917, 917–18, quoted in Rider, *supra* note 337, at 111.

347. *Meyer v. State*, 187 N.W. 100, 102 (Neb.1922), rev'd, 262 U.S. 390 (1923).

349. 262 U.S. at 401.

social and legal suppression of ethnic traits associated with the enemy. America attempted to define her true identity as that of her core culture. The perception of foreignness, *i.e.*, difference from that core culture, was once again equated with disloyalty and subversion. At roughly this same time, nativists sought to reinforce the core American culture through the immigration and naturalization laws.

OFFICIAL LANGUAGE POLICY ENACTED THROUGH THE IMMIGRATION AND NATURALIZATION LAWS

Despite the absence of federal laws declaring English to be the official language of our country, some federal laws do, in effect, produce this result. Our current federal immigration and naturalization laws require English literacy for naturalized citizenship, and literacy in any language for admission to the United States. In addition, the Immigration Reform and Control Act of 1986 required aliens newly legalized under its amnesty provision to demonstrate "minimal understanding of ordinary English" in order to become permanent resident aliens.

The English-literacy requirement for citizenship is of tremendous symbolic importance. It is an important expression of federal policy in favor of English. It is through our naturalization laws that, in clearest form, the nation spells out the criteria that must be met by those who would join the American nation.

English literacy has not, however, always been a requirement for citizenship. Nor has literacy of any kind always been a requirement for initial admission to the nation. The evolution of the English-language literacy requirement further demonstrates that nativism finds expression through language restrictions.

A strong popular movement favoring coerced assimilation occurred for the first time near the beginning of the twentieth century. Before this time, until around 1880, immigration to the United States had been open and unrestricted. Most assumed that American society would assimilate new immigrants. Indeed, because most of the immigrants until this time were from northwestern Europe, and especially from Great Britain, Germany, and Scandinavia, traditional sources of the American population, their racial and cultural characteristics matched those of the existing population relatively well and they were able to assimilate with relatively little cultural friction.

By 1890, immigrants from these countries began to be outnumbered by immigrants from the countries of southern and eastern Europe: Italy, Poland, and the Austro–Hungarian empire. These new immigrants brought with them their distinctive cultural traits. In response to these new, culturally different immigrants, a strong popular movement, fueled by American nativism, developed in favor of restrictions on immigration to the United States.

The first goal of proponents of restricted immigration was a literacy test for immigrants that, in theory, would exclude a large proportion of those seeking admission to the United States. The literacy test, "though ostensibly selective in theory, would prove restrictive in operation."[358]

---

358. Robert Divine, *American Immigration Policy* 1924–1952, at 4 (1957).

The purpose of the literacy test was clear: to exclude people whose ethnicity differed from that of the majority. Advocates of the test hoped that it would reduce immigration by twenty-five percent.

Opponents of the new European immigration tried three times, without success, to enact restrictive legislation that included a literacy requirement in some language for admission to the United States. Such legislation passed the Congress on three occasions. It was consistently vetoed by successive presidents because it was such a departure from prior, liberal immigration policy. * * *

Later, more effective restrictive legislation passed establishing numerical quotas for immigrants. The prevailing idea among advocates of quota restrictions was that national unity depended on racial "homogeneity," which appeared to mean preservation of the existing racial character of the country. Thus, one congressman argued that "[t]he trouble grows out of a country composed of intermingled and mongrelized people. The stability of a country depends upon the homogeneity of population."[373] Another congressman coined the slogan, "one race, one country, one destiny."[374] As the advocates of restriction saw it, the survival of constitutional democracy depended on the Nordic race: "If, therefore, the principle of individual liberty, guarded by a constitutional government created on this continent nearly a century and a half ago, is to endure, the basic strain of our population must be maintained."[375]

These comments illustrate the theme, repeated throughout our history, that our national identity, unity, and loyalty to our government depend on uniformity—sometimes racial, sometimes linguistic. "Foreign influences," persons whose ethnicity differs from that of the majority, are perceived as a threat to the nation. America's supposedly uniform ethnicity had to be created and preserved through the law. In the case of the immigration laws, the idea was that national unity depended on racial purity and uniformity, with existing American races superior to any others seeking entry. An identical theme underlies the official English movement's claim that national unity depends on linguistic uniformity or purity. * * *

THE DEVELOPMENT OF LANGUAGE REQUIREMENTS FOR CITIZENSHIP

The first statutory requirement of English ability for naturalized citizenship appeared in 1906. The rationale for the statute was that a requirement of ability to speak English would improve the "quality" of naturalized citizens. The Commission on Naturalization of 1905 expressed the prevailing view: "[T]he proposition is incontrovertible that no man is a desirable citizen of the United States who does not know the English language."[379] * * * The Nationality Act of 1940 also contained the requirement that an applicant for citizenship speak English. Section

---

373. 65 Cong. Rec. 5673 (1924) (statement of Rep. Wilson), quoted in Divine, *supra* note 358 at 14.

374. *Id*. at 5868 (statement of Rep. Hershey), quoted in Divine, *supra* note 358, at 15.

375. H.R. Rep. No. 350, 68th Cong., 1st Sess. 13 (1924), quoted in Divine, *supra* note 358, at 15.

379. Commission on Naturalization, *Report to the President* (Nov. 8, 1905), reprinted in H.R. Doc. No. 46, 59th Cong., 1st. Sess. 11 (1905).

304 of the Act stated: "No person ... shall hereafter be naturalized as a citizen of the United States upon his own petition who cannot speak the English language."[383]

In 1950, at the height of the national hysteria over the threat of communism, Congress stiffened the language requirements for naturalization. The Subversive Activities Control Act of 1950 amended section 304 to demand full literacy in English:

No person ... shall hereafter be naturalized as a citizen of the United States upon his own petition who cannot demonstrate

(1) an understanding of the English language, including an ability to read, write and speak words in ordinary usage in the English language ..., [and]

(2) a knowledge and understanding of the fundamentals of the history, and of the principles and form of government, of the United States.[385]

These provisions of the naturalization statute remain essentially the same today.

The symbolic importance of an English literacy requirement for naturalization should not be underestimated. It is in the naturalization laws that the criteria for belonging to America, for participating in its government, are most clearly stated. As one leading commentator aptly stated it, "[a]n English literacy requirement ... establishes the fact that the United States is an English culture and that its citizens will have to learn English in order to participate fully in it. The very existence of a literacy test establishes the 'official' character of the language."[387] To date, this represents the maximum degree to which English is officially and legally recognized as the language of the United States.

It is revealing that increased requirements for citizenship were enacted as part of the Subversive Activities Control legislation. Once again, "foreign" characteristics, this time lack of English literacy, were associated with disloyalty and "subversive activities." * * * The legislation, just like the Alien and Sedition Acts, and with just as broad a legislative brush, aimed to exclude aliens from citizenship to keep the "foreign influence" out of America. Supreme fear and distrust of "foreign" traits and the "foreign language" press led to legal restrictions designed to reinforce the identity of the core American culture. Nativism demands that only English-speaking Americans and the English-language press can be trusted. The English literacy requirement for citizenship remains the same today.

THE OFFICIAL ENGLISH MOVEMENT: THE POLITICS OF CONFORMITY OR EXCLUSION

From the panorama of the legal treatment of ethnicity and language several distinctive features of nativist movements stand out. Nativism tends to grow and flourish at times of national stress, often in response

---

383. Nationality Act of 1940, ch. 876, § 304, 54 Stat. 1140 (repealed 1952).

385. *Id.* at § 30.

387. Arnold H. Leibowitz, *English Literacy: Legal Sanction for Discrimination*, 45 Notre Dame L. Rev. 7, 14 (1969).

to unwelcome immigration or wartime. Nativism triggers restrictive laws aimed at persons whose ethnicity differs from that of the core culture, ostensibly to serve the goals of national unity or national security. Nativist movements seek to reinforce their narrow view of American cultural identity through the law by restricting cultural traits deemed "foreign." Another feature common to these nativist movements is the desire to disenfranchise certain Americans, or to impede the naturalization of aspiring Americans, because of their difference from the core culture.

The official English movement of the 1980s is part of this tradition. Former Senator S.I. Hayakawa, acting through U.S. English, an organization he founded with Dr. John Tanton, sought an amendment to the Constitution making English the official language of the United States. Subcommittees of the Senate Judiciary Committee, in 1984, and the House Judiciary Committee, in 1988, conducted hearings on proposed official English amendments. Despite persistent efforts and publicity, proponents of official English have not yet succeeded in achieving a federal constitutional amendment. The official English movement now appears to have a two-fold strategy: first, to obtain official English laws or constitutional amendments in the states, and, second, to have enacted a federal statute making English the official language of the federal government. Since the movement's ultimate goal is still a federal constitutional amendment, it appears that official English proponents will attempt to strengthen their position by arguing that the presence of many state laws and a possible federal statute increases or proves the necessity for a federal constitutional amendment.

The movement has been quite successful at the state level. Seventeen states now have laws declaring English to be their official language. The movement has recently sought official English amendments to the state constitutions of Maryland, West Virginia, and Missouri. * * * Through a federal constitutional amendment or statute, the movement seeks the elimination of bilingual ballots in state and federal elections. To accomplish this result, they must, in effect, persuade Congress to repeal certain provisions of the Voting Rights Act that require bilingual ballots under some circumstances. * * *

The official English movement belongs squarely within the matrix of modern American nativism. The cause of the official English movement is the immigration of people unpopular in the eyes of the majority. Its manifestations are those of earlier nativist movements: a desire, now abandoned, to restrict immigration; an appeal to national unity or, conversely, raising the familiar spectre of national disunity and the disintegration of American culture caused by new immigration; and, most important, the desire to disenfranchise certain Americans.

Many commentators agree that the cause of the official English movement is the large, and largely unwelcome, immigration of many Hispanics and Southeast Asians during recent decades. Since the repeal of national origin quotas in 1965, increasing numbers of immigrants have come from non-European countries, thus changing the racial and cultural balance carefully preserved by the prior quota system. In addition to legal immigration, a large influx of aliens took place from Latin America, many of whom subsequently were legalized during the amnesty offered in 1987 and 1988. According to one estimate, 300,000 Hispanic immigrants a year flow into the southern and western regions of the United States.

Like all other immigrant groups, these immigrants have brought with them their native languages. The influx of Spanish-speaking Hispanic immigrants has antagonized many Americans. Immigrants from Southeast Asia have also encountered hostility, violence, and language restriction. The racial and cultural differences of recent immigrants from the core culture have not gone unnoticed.

Part of U.S. English's original program was to "control immigration so that it does not reinforce trends toward language segregation."[423] The organization intended to lobby for legislation to restrict immigration that would reinforce the maintenance of certain languages, particularly Spanish, which, after English, is the second most-used language in this country. This means limiting the immigration of Hispanics, who are depicted as advocates of "language segregation." * * *

The official English movement renews the claim that national unity depends on ethnic purity—really conformity with the Anglo core culture—this time in the form of language. According to Hayakawa, multilingual election ballots present an "open threat . . . to our cherished idea of 'one nation, indivisible'."[428] Senator Huddleston, sponsor of the proposed constitutional amendment in 1984, made explicit his view of the connection between the English language and our national identity: "This amendment addresses something so fundamental to our sense of identity as Americans."[429] According to Senator Denton, official English laws will "help to preserve the basic internal unity" of our country.[430]

This perceived threat to the English language, however, is not supported by fact. English is ubiquitous. Between 94 and 96 percent of the American population is already English-speaking. Fully 85 percent of the population claims English as its mother tongue. Furthermore, English enjoys virtual hegemony as an international language of business, commerce, and interaction between nations. Given the national and international status of English, concerns about its deterioration (and ours), echoed throughout our history, are greatly overstated. Since fact does not support claims of deterioration of the English language, nor of national disunity, something else must be going on.

Since its inception, one of the official English movement's principal goals has been to eliminate bilingual, or more correctly, multilingual voting ballots. This can be accomplished only through the Congress's repeal, or refusal to extend, provisions in the 1975 amendments to the

423. Wright, *U.S. English*, S.F. Chron., Mar. 20, 1983, at B9, quoted in The English Language Amendment: Hearing on S.J. Res. 167 Before the Subcomm. on the Constitution of the Senate Comm. on the Judiciary, 98th Cong., 2d Sess., at 64 (1984) [hereinafter Senate Hearing].

428. Senate Hearing, at 53.

429. *Id.* at 15.

430. *Id.* at 11. Senator Denton asserted that the "language barrier that plagues millions of Americans each year" is a major source of "discrimination [against] and exploitation" of those who do not speak English. *Id.*

Voting Rights Act. * * * Proponents argue that English-only ballots create incentives for citizens to learn English and to realize that they cannot enjoy full participation in American life without doing so. Furthermore, the argument runs, multilingual ballots impair the political process because they make some voters dependent on "interpreters or go-betweens," because they preserve "minority voting blocs," and because voters whose primary language is not English will not be "as fully informed as possible" when they go to the polls.[436] Proponents of official English thus claim that multilingual ballots reduce political participation, a claim glaringly at odds with the obvious access to political participation that multilingual ballots provide to non-English speakers.

These arguments deserve brief response. First, English-only ballots create no meaningful incentive to learn English, particularly given the overwhelming existing social and economic incentives to do so. English-only ballots disenfranchise citizens who, for various reasons, have retained a language other than English. According to a 1982 study by the Mexican American Legal Defense and Educational Fund, seventy-two percent of monolingual Spanish-speaking citizens would be less likely to vote without the language assistance the Voting Rights Act requires. Similarly, monolingual citizens speaking other non-English languages also would be disenfranchised.

Second, voters who rely on American newspapers printed in languages other than English, such as the *Miami Herald*, which is published daily in both Spanish and English editions, can be fully informed about the issues in an election. The Supreme Court recognized as much when, in 1966, it upheld the Voting Rights Act in *Katzenbach v. Morgan*.[441] The Court stated that ability to read or understand Spanish-language newspapers, radio, and television is as effective a means of obtaining political information as ability to read English.

The movement's concern about "minority voting blocs" defined by language both expresses fear of the political power of Hispanics and the offensive assumption that minority group members think alike and vote alike. If proponents of official English are truly concerned about ethnic voting blocs, they should also be equally concerned about English-speaking ethnic voting blocs. Their concern, however, is only about ethnicity, Hispanic or Asian, different from that of the core culture.

Furthermore, the movement vastly overstates the competence and political participation of members of the majority core culture. Only about half of all eligible voters usually vote. Are all voters "as fully informed as possible?" Why deny access to multilingual ballots to citizens who do care enough to vote? And why hold only minority voters to a standard of "being as fully informed as possible" for voting? The movement's arguments amount to saying that people who do not know English are too ignorant to make informed voting decisions, an offensive presumption common throughout our history.

436. *Id.* at 20 (testimony of Sen. Huddleston).

441. 384 U.S. 641 (1966).

S.I. HAYAKAWA

English Is Key to Opportunities of American Life
Reading Eagle (Reading, Pa) (Mar. 20, 1990).*

Should English be designated the official language of the United States?

Are you surprised that I'm even asking that question?

Most people think that English already is our official language, but they're wrong. It isn't. Not yet anyway.

Let me tell you how I came to believe that English must be designated our official language.

I was born and brought up in Canada. Canada, as I am sure you know, has two official languages, English and French—a fact which most probably doubles the cost of government in time consumed and money spent.

My father, who studied English in a Japanese high school, settled in Canada after traveling and living for a period in the United States.

He was a serious student of Edgar Allan Poe. In our home, we had sets of books by Dickens, Thackeray, and O. Henry. So majoring in English seemed a natural thing for me to do for my bachelor's, master's and doctor degrees.

On my first visit to the United States in 1927, I was refused entry because of my Japanese ancestry. However, in 1929, I was awarded a graduate fellowship in English at the University of Wisconsin.

After I got my doctorate, the university hired me as a full-time professor of English. In 1954, I finally ceased to be the one foreigner in my family of an American wife and three children, when I was sworn in as an American citizen during naturalization ceremonies in Chicago.

As a professor of English, I continued to teach, write, and give lectures. Then suddenly, in the midst of wild student turmoil in the mid '60s, I found myself president of San Francisco State University. My handling of the crisis made me a hero—the tough guy who "faced down the radicals at State."

A few years after that, the good people of California elected me their U.S. senator. While many had been surprised that someone of Japanese ancestry had become a senator, I am the most surprised.

When I took office and began dealing with our national problems, one thing stood out above all... And that is, that there are many barriers to effective communication which are entrenched in our society—prejudice, generation gaps, and social and economic inequality, to name a few.

I realized that the last thing we need to do in our country is to add a language barrier to all of these.

In fact, one effective way to help solve the problems we already have is to establish a common ground on which we can all come together. That common ground is our English language.

And so in 1981, I introduced a Constitutional Amendment in Congress to make English the official language of the U.S. government.

Thousands of citizens all across the country offered support. Since no organization existed at that time to represent the interests of these people and bind them together into a powerful force, great potential for citizen action was lost.

That's why, after I retired from the Senate in 1983, I founded U.S. English. This letter is your invitation to join with us in the preservation of our common language—English.

U.S. English was founded on the principles that English must be made the official language of government and that the opportunity to learn English must be guaranteed to all the people of the United States.

U.S. English members understand the natural instincts and rights of people from all cultures to preserve their own customs and traditions.

However, we believe that this is the responsibility of families, churches, and private organizations, not the responsibility of government or public schools.

U.S. English has maintained from its inception that we must preserve our common bond through the enactment of a Federal English Language Amendment. And in order to mobilize our citizens in support of this drive, U.S. English has begun by pressing for State English Language Amendments.

In 1986, after being rebuffed by the California Legislature in our attempts to designate English the official state language, we went directly to the voters.

U.S. English members collected hundreds of thousands of signatures on petitions to put the official English issue on the ballot. It passed with 74 percent of the vote.

In 1988, we passed similar initiatives in Arizona, Colorado, and Florida—bringing the total number of states with laws protecting English to 17.

Unfortunately, certain groups who do not, or will not, understand U.S. English's motives for a common unifying language are challenging our victories with costly legal actions. So you see, even after we've won, we have to keep fighting to defend the role of English in our society.

Our long-range goal is to establish English as the official language of the United States.

However, U.S. English is not only concerned that we preserve and protect our common language, we are also committed to ensuring that all citizens have the opportunity to learn English.

To this end, we promote effective and cost-efficient methods of teaching English to limited English proficient students.

Our objective is to ensure that bilingual programs be designed to make teaching English the standard by which they are measured.

And what do all these people that enter into the American mainstream have in common? English—our shared common language!

English is the key to individual participation in the opportunities of American life.

It is the linchpin of a productive and efficient economy for us all. I hope you agree that we must preserve the precious bond that unites all Americans into one nation.

Please join with us in this important endeavor by becoming a member of U.S. English. If we are to succeed in protecting our hard won state victories, move ahead with improved methods of teaching English, and ultimately secure passage of a Federal English Language Amendment, we need your support.

Former U.S. Sen. S. I. Hayakawa is honorary chairman of U.S. English.

BILL MARTINI

Preserve Unity: Make English the Official Language
Star–Ledger, Oct. 16, 1996.*

In a recent article, Representative Bill Martini campaigns for passage of a congressional official English bill. He warns that without this bill, America will be divided—as Canada was almost divided by French-speaking Quebec's failed secession attempt. Rep. Martini goes on to state that:

> When you consider that Americans can vote, pay taxes, take their driver's license exams and go to school entirely in languages other than English, you begin to realize how important it is that we establish English as our nation's official language. Our government policies should reinforce our common language rather than erode it.

> * * * The bill is a modest proposal that would simply declare English the official language of the U.S. government and require the federal government to conduct its official business in English. The bill does not affect the use of foreign languages in any nonofficial capacity (*i.e.* homes, churches, neighborhood, and private businesses). In addition, the bill does not prohibit any official of the federal government from communicating orally with other persons in a foreign language.

> Why has the subject of language suddenly become an issue of national importance? For most of our nation's history, the English language was the key to integrating new immigrants. When my Italian grandparents came to this country, mastering English was the key to success and opportunity. But sadly, our nation's approach has changed. We, a nation, are at risk of losing our common bond.

Our country is unique for many reasons, not the least of which is our cultural diversity. As a nation that continually receives immigrants from many different countries, it is imperative that we unite under our most important common denominator, the English language. America needs a common-sense, common-language policy to help us preserve our unity.

As simple and straightforward as this concept may seem, there are those attacking these efforts as mean and unfair to immigrants. Those emotional arguments may seem prudent in the campaign season, but as a matter of policy, we need not look further than our neighbors to the north to see the damage that occurs when a bilingual, bicultural society is allowed to thrive.

* * *

Bilingualism issues in the United States are not new. Seven years after the adoption of the Constitution, a proposal to print federal laws in German as well as English was narrowly defeated in the House of Representatives.

In recent years, the push for bilingualism has arisen again. The presumed purpose is to aid new immigrants in their transition into American society. However, bilingualism has not worked out as planned, rather the contrary.

Rep. Martini goes on to quote Arthur Schlesinger, an adviser to President Kennedy, who in *The Disuniting of America,* finds bilingual education holds new immigrants back rather than eases their integration into American society. Martini concludes by warning that:

A bilingual society is neither separate nor equal. Those using languages other than English are condemned to an existence in a perpetual underclass in American society. The foreign-speaking poor have the most to lose in a bilingual America. This is the land of opportunity, but the promise of economic prosperity is nothing but a carrot on a stick to those suffering from the language barrier.

For these reasons, we should encourage new immigrants to master English as quickly as possible when assimilating into American society.

* * *

Our future as one nation depends on the foundation of one common language. And establishing English as the language will help us go forward together.

Notes and Questions

1. Nearly one-half of the states have enacted English-only laws that require that English be spoken, or printed, in certain state transactions or documents. See, *e.g.,* Jean Stefancic & Richard Delgado, *No Mercy: How Conservative Think Tanks and Foundations Changed America's Social Agenda* (1996).

2. How can these regulations survive First Amendment challenges? If the hate speech of a neo-Nazi is protected, why should not the language of a

Spanish-speaking patient seeking medical attention in a state facility or other form of official assistance be so as well?

————

Arizona's English-only law was the first to receive close legal scrutiny. In the "Yniguez" litigation, a Spanish-surnamed plaintiff mounted a sustained challenge, which was ultimately successful in the Ninth Circuit—but not for long. The Supreme Court vacated the case as moot. Shortly thereafter, the Arizona State Supreme Court revisited the issue. The two opinions are reproduced below.

ARIZONANS FOR OFFICIAL ENGLISH v. ARIZONA

520 U.S. 43 (1997).

JUSTICE GINSBURG delivered the opinion of the Court.

* * * Federal courts lack competence to rule definitively on the meaning of state legislation, see, *e.g., Reetz v. Bozanich*, 397 U.S. 82, 86–87 (1970), nor may they adjudicate challenges to state measures absent a showing of actual impact on the challenger, see, *e.g., Golden v. Zwickler*, 394 U.S. 103, 110 (1969). The Ninth Circuit, in the case at hand, lost sight of these limitations. The initiating plaintiff, Maria–Kelly F. Yniguez, sought federal-court resolution of a novel question: the compatibility with the Federal Constitution of a 1988 amendment to Arizona's Constitution declaring English "the official language of the State of Arizona"—"the language of . . . all government functions and actions." Ariz. Const., Art. XXVIII, §§ 1(1), 1(2). Participants in the federal litigation, proceeding without benefit of the views of the Arizona Supreme Court, expressed diverse opinions on the meaning of the amendment.

Yniguez commenced and maintained her suit as an individual, not as a class representative. A state employee at the time she filed her complaint, Yniguez voluntarily left the State's employ in 1990 and did not allege she would seek to return to a public post. Her departure for a position in the private sector made her claim for prospective relief moot. Nevertheless, the Ninth Circuit held that a plea for nominal damages could be read into Yniguez's complaint to save the case, and therefore pressed on to an ultimate decision. A three-judge panel of the Court of Appeals declared Article XXVIII unconstitutional in 1994, and a divided *en banc* court, in 1995, adhered to the panel's position.

The Ninth Circuit had no warrant to proceed as it did. The case had lost the essential elements of a justiciable controversy and should not have been retained for adjudication on the merits by the Court of Appeals. We therefore vacate the Ninth Circuit's judgment, and remand the case to that court with directions that the action be dismissed by the District Court. We express no view on the correct interpretation of Article XXVIII or on the measure's constitutionality. * * *

RUIZ v. HULL

191 Ariz. 441, 957 P.2d 984 (1998).

OPINION

MOELLER, JUSTICE.

In October 1987, Arizonans for Official English (AOE) initiated a petition drive to amend Arizona's constitution to designate English as the state's official language and to require state and local governments in Arizona to conduct business only in English. As a result of the general election in November 1988, the Amendment was added to the Arizona Constitution, receiving affirmative votes from 50.5% of Arizona citizens casting ballots. See *Yniguez v. Arizonans for Official English (AOE)*, 69 F.3d 920, 924 (9th Cir.1995) (*en banc*). The Amendment, entitled "English as the Official Language," provides that "[t]he State and all political subdivisions of [the] State shall act in English and in no other language." The Amendment binds all government officials and employees in Arizona during the performance of all government business, and provides that any "person who resides in or does business in this State shall have standing to bring suit to enforce this article in a court of record of the State."

* * *

In November 1992, the ten plaintiffs in this case brought an action in superior court against then-Governor J. Fife Symington, III and the Attorney General. On September 5, 1997, Governor Symington resigned and was succeeded by Jane Dee Hull, who has been substituted pursuant to Rule 27(c)(1) of the Arizona Rules of Civil Appellate Procedure. The plaintiffs sought a declaratory judgment that the Amendment violates the First, Ninth, and Fourteenth Amendments of the United States Constitution. The plaintiffs are four elected officials, five state employees, and one public school teacher. They are all bilingual and regularly communicate in both Spanish and English as private citizens and during the performance of government business. Plaintiffs allege that they speak Spanish during the performance of their government jobs and that they "fear communicating in Spanish 'during the performance of government business' in violation of Article XXVIII of the Arizona Constitution."

* * *

DISCUSSION

Plaintiffs contend that the Amendment is a blanket prohibition against all publicly elected officials and government employees using any language other than English in the performance of any government business. Therefore, they reason that the Amendment is a content-based regulation of speech contrary to the First Amendment. Plaintiffs also argue that the Amendment constitutes discrimination against non-English-speaking minorities, thereby violating the Equal Protection Clause of the Fourteenth Amendment. AOE and the state defendants respond that the Amendment should be narrowly read and * * * construed as requiring the use of English only with regard to "official, binding government acts." They argue that this narrow construction renders the Amendment constitutional.

At the outset, we note that this case concerns the tension between the constitutional status of language rights and the state's power to restrict such rights. On the one hand, in our diverse society, the importance of establishing common bonds and a common language between citizens is clear. *Yniguez v. AOE*, 69 F.3d at 923, citing *Guadalupe Organization, Inc. v. Tempe Elementary Sch. Dist.*, 587 F.2d 1022, 1027 (9th Cir.1978). We recognize that the acquisition of English language skills is important in our society. * * *

However, the American tradition of tolerance "recognizes a critical difference between encouraging the use of English and repressing the use of other languages." *Yniguez v. AOE*, 69 F.3d at 923. We agree with the Ninth Circuit's statement that Arizona's rejection of that tradition by enacting the Amendment has severe consequences not only for Arizona's public officials and employees, but also for the many thousands of persons who would be precluded from receiving essential information from government employees and elected officials in Arizona's governments. *Id.* If the wide-ranging language of the prohibitions contained in the Amendment were to be implemented as written, the First Amendment rights of all those persons would be violated, *id.*, a fact now conceded by the proponents of the Amendment, who, instead, urge a restrictive interpretation in accordance with the Attorney General's narrow construction discussed below.

By this opinion, we do not imply that the intent of those urging passage of the Amendment or of those who voted for it stemmed from linguistic chauvinism or from any other repressive or discriminatory intent. Rather we assume, without deciding, that the drafters of the initiative urged passage of the Amendment to further social harmony in our state by having English as a common language among its citizens.

* * *

Plain Meaning Rule

The Attorney General maintains that although the Amendment declares English to be Arizona's "official" language, its proscriptions against the use of non-English languages should be interpreted to apply only to "official acts of government." Ariz. Att'y Gen. Op. 189–009, at 5–6. The Attorney General defines "official act" as "a decision or determination of a sovereign, a legislative council, or a court of justice." *Id.* at 7. Although he does not further explain what acts would be official, the Attorney General concludes that the Amendment should not be read to prohibit public employees from using non-English languages while performing their public functions that could not be characterized as official. The Attorney General opines that the provision "does not mean that languages other than English cannot be used when reasonable to facilitate the day-to-day operation of government." *Id.* at 10.

* * *

To arrive at his interpretation, the Attorney General takes the word "act" from § 3(1)(a) of the Amendment, which provides that, with limited exceptions, the "State and all political subdivisions of this State shall act in English and in no other language." The Attorney General proposes that the word "act" from § 3(1)(a) should be ascribed to the word "official," found in the Amendment's proclamation that English is the official language of Arizona. Therefore, the Attorney General interprets the Amendment to apply only to the official acts of the state and limits the definition of the noun "act" to a "decision or determination of a sovereign, a legislative council, or a court of justice." We agree with the Ninth Circuit in *Yniguez v. AOE* that the former Attorney General's opinion ignores the fact that "act," when used as a verb as in the Amendment, does not include among its meanings the limited definition he proposed. 69 F.3d at 929. Similarly, section 1(2) of the Amendment also describes English as the language of "all government functions and actions." The Amendment does not limit the terms "functions" and "actions" to official acts as urged by the Attorney General, and the ordinary meanings of those terms do not impose such a limitation. *Id.* at 929 n.13. We agree with the district court that originally evaluated the challenges to the Amendment in *Yniguez*: "The Attorney General's restrictive interpretation of the Amendment is in effect a 'remarkable job of plastic surgery upon the face of the [Amendment].'" *Yniguez v. Mofford*, 730 F. Supp. at 316, citing *Shuttlesworth v. City of Birmingham,* 394 U.S. 147, 153 (1969).

We hold that by ignoring the express language of the Amendment, the Attorney General's proposed construction violates the plain meaning rule that requires the words of the Amendment to be given their natural, obvious, and ordinary meaning. By its express terms, the Amendment is not limited to official governmental acts or to the "formal, policy making, enacting and binding activities of government." Rather, it is plainly written in the broadest possible terms, declaring that the "English language is the language of . . . all government functions and actions" and prohibiting all "government officials and employees" at every level of state and local government from using non-English languages "during the performance of government business." Amendment, §§ 1(2), 1(3)(a)(iv). * * *

LEGISLATIVE INTENT

We also believe the Attorney General's proposed construction is at odds with the intent of the drafters of the Amendment. The drafters perceived and obviously intended that the application of the Amendment would be widespread. They therefore inserted some limited exceptions to it. Those exceptions permit the use of non-English languages to protect the rights of criminal defendants and victims, to protect the public health and safety, to teach a foreign language, and to comply with federal laws. Amendment, § 3.2. Regardless of the precise limits of these general exceptions, their existence demonstrates that the drafters of the Amendment understood that it would apply to far more than just official acts.

For example, one exception allows public school teachers to instruct in a non-English language when teaching foreign languages or when teaching students with limited English proficiency. Such instruction by teachers is obviously not a "formal, policy making, enacting or binding activity by the government," the narrow construction urged by the Attorney General. The exceptions would have been largely, if not entirely, unnecessary under the Attorney General's proposed construction of the Amendment. When construing statutes, we must read the statute as a whole and give meaningful operation to each of its provisions. *Kaku v. Arizona Board of Regents*, 172 Ariz. 296, 297, 836 P.2d 1006, 1007 (App.1992).

In construing an initiative, we may consider ballot materials and publicity pamphlets circulated in support of the initiative. The ballot materials and publicity pamphlets pertaining to the Amendment do not support the Attorney General's limiting construction. In AOE's argument for the Amendment, Chairman Robert D. Park stated that the Amendment was intended to "require the government to function in English, except in certain circumstances," and then listed those exceptions set forth in section 4 of the Amendment. * * * Chairman Park's argument then went on to state that "[o]fficially sanctioned multilingualism causes tension and division within a state. Proposition 106 [enacting the Amendment] will avoid that fate in Arizona." * * * The Legislative Council's argument in support of the Amendment stated that the existence of a multilingual society would lead to "the fears and tensions of language rivalries and ethnic distrust." Arizona Publicity Pamphlet in Support of the Amendment, at 26. Therefore, the Amendment's legislative history supports a broad, comprehensive construction of the Amendment, not the narrow construction urged by the Attorney General.

AMBIGUITY

The Attorney General's interpretation would unnecessarily inject elements of vagueness into the Amendment. We feel confident that an average reader of the Amendment would never divine that he or she was free to use a language other than English unless one was performing an official act defined as "a decision or determination of a sovereign, a legislative council, or a court of justice."

Because we conclude that the narrow construction advocated by the Attorney General is untenable, we analyze the constitutionality of the Amendment based on the language of the Amendment itself.

ENGLISH-ONLY PROVISIONS IN OTHER JURISDICTIONS

Although English-only provisions have recently become quite common, Arizona's is unique. Thus, we receive little guidance from other state courts. Twenty-one states and forty municipalities have official English statutes. However, most of those provisions are substantially less encompassing and certainly less proscriptive than the Amendment. The official English provisions in most states appear to be primarily symbolic. See, *e.g., Puerto Rican Org. for Political Action v. Kusper*, 490

F.2d 575, 577 (7th Cir.1973) (noting that official English law appears with laws naming the state bird and state song, and does not restrict the use to non-English languages by state and city agencies). Indeed, the Amendment has been identified as "by far the most restrictively worded official-English law to date." M. Arrington, Note, *English Only Laws and Direct Legislation: The Battle in the States Over Language Minority Rights*, 7 J.L. & Pol. 325, 327 (1991). This observation is shared by other commentators—who note that the Amendment "is the most restrictive of the current wave of official-language laws," and "is so far the most restrictive Official English measure." See D. Baron, *The English–Only Question* 21 (1990), and J. Crawford, *Hold Your Tongue* 176 (1992). * * *

* * *

LANGUAGE IS SPEECH PROTECTED BY THE FIRST AMENDMENT

* * *

The First Amendment to the United States Constitution provides:

Congress shall make no law respecting an establishment of religion, or prohibiting the free exercise thereof; or abridging the freedom of speech, or of the press; or the right of the people peaceably to assemble, and to petition the government for a redress of grievances.

The First Amendment applies to the states as well as to the federal government. *Gitlow v. New York*, 268 U.S. 652, 665 (1925). The expression of one's opinion is absolutely protected by the First and Fourteenth Amendments. *AMCOR Inv. Corp. v. Cox Ariz. Publications, Inc.*, 158 Ariz. 566, 568, 764 P.2d 327, 329 (App.1988) (citation omitted); see also *Meyer v. Nebraska*, 262 U.S. 390, 401 (1923) (stating that the United States Constitution protects speakers of all languages). The trial court held that the Amendment is content-neutral, and, therefore, does not violate the First Amendment. *City of Renton v. Playtime Theatres, Inc.*, 475 U.S. 41, 47–48 (1986). That ruling is flawed.

"Whatever differences may exist about interpretations of the First Amendment, there is practically universal agreement that a major purpose of that Amendment was to protect the free discussion of governmental affairs." *Landmark Communications, Inc. v. Virginia*, 435 U.S. 829, 838 (1978) (footnote omitted) (quoting *Mills v. Alabama*, 384 U.S. 214, 218 (1966)). * * *

Notwithstanding [some] limited exceptions, we find that the Amendment unconstitutionally inhibits "the free discussion of governmental affairs" in two ways. First, it deprives limited- and non-English-speaking persons of access to information about the government when multilingual access may be available and may be necessary to ensure fair and effective delivery of governmental services to non-English-speaking persons. It is not our prerogative to impinge upon the Legislature's ability to require, under appropriate circumstances, the provision of services in languages other than English. See, *e.g.*, A.R.S. § 23–906(D) (providing that every employer engaged in occupations subject to Arizona's Workers' Compensation statutes shall post in a conspicuous place upon his premises, in English and Spanish, a notice informing employees that unless they specifically reject coverage under Arizona's compulsory compensation law, they are deemed to have accepted the provisions of that law). The United States Supreme Court has held that First Amendment protection is afforded to the communication, its source, and its recipient. *Virginia State Board of Pharmacy v. Virginia Citizens Consumer Council, Inc.*, 425 U.S. 748, 756–57 (1976).

In his concurring opinion in *Barnes,* Justice Scalia stated, "[W]hen any law restricts speech, even for a purpose that has nothing to do with the suppression of communication ..., we insist that it meet the high First–Amendment standard of justification." 501 U.S. at 576. The Amendment contravenes core principles and values undergirding the First Amendment—the right of the people to seek redress from their government—by directly banning pure speech on its face. By denying persons who are limited in English proficiency, or entirely lacking in it, the right to participate equally in the political process, the Amendment violates the constitutional right to participate in and have access to government, a right which is one of the "fundamental principle[s] of representative government in this country." See *Reynolds v. Sims*, 377 U.S. 533, 560 (1964). The First Amendment right to petition for redress of grievances lies at the core of America's democracy. *McDonald v. Smith*, 472 U.S. 479, 482–83, 485 (1985); *United Mine Workers of America v. Illinois State Bar Assn.*, 389 U.S. 217, 222 (1967) (right to petition is "among the most precious liberties safeguarded by the Bill of Rights"). In *Board of Education v. Pico*, 457 U.S. 853, 867 (1982), the Court recognized that "the right to receive ideas is a necessary predicate to the recipient's meaningful exercise of his own rights of speech, press and political freedom."

The Amendment violates the First Amendment by depriving elected officials and public employees of the ability to communicate with their constituents and with the public. With only a few exceptions, the Amendment prohibits all public officials and employees in Arizona from acting in a language other than English while performing governmental functions and policies. We do not prohibit government offices from adopting language rules for appropriate reasons. We hold that the Amendment goes too far because it effectively cuts off governmental communication with thousands of limited-English-proficient and non-English-speaking persons in Arizona, even when the officials and employees have the ability and desire to communicate in a language understandable to them. Meaningful communication in those cases is barred. Under such circumstances, prohibiting an elected or appointed governmental official or an employee from communicating with the public violates the employee's and the official's rights. * * * As the Ninth Circuit noted, the Amendment could "hardly be more inclusive"; it "prohibit[s] the use in all oral and written communications by persons connected with the government of all words and phrases in any language other than English." *Yniguez v. AOE*, 69 F.3d at 933.

* * *

AOE argues that the "First Amendment addresses [the] content not [the] mode of communication." The trial court adopted this argument, concluding that the Amendment was a permissible content-neutral prohibition of speech. Essentially, *AOE* argues that strict scrutiny should be reduced in this case because the decision to speak a non-English language does not implicate pure speech rights, but rather only affects the "mode of communication." By requiring that government officials communicate only in a language which is incomprehensible to non-English speaking persons, the Amendment effectively bars communication itself. Therefore, its effect cannot be characterized as merely a time, place, or manner restriction because such restrictions, by definition, assume and require the availability of alternative means of communication.

AOE also argues that the Amendment can be characterized as a regulation that serves purposes unrelated to the content of expression and therefore should be deemed neutral, even if it has an incidental effect on some speakers or messages but not others. See *Ward*, 491 U.S. at 791 (citing *City of Renton*, 475 U.S. at 47–48). We agree with the Ninth Circuit's emphatic rejection in *Yniguez v. AOE* of the suggestion that the decision to speak in a language other than English does not implicate free speech concerns, but is instead akin to expressive conduct. There, the court said that "[s]peech in any language is still speech and the decision to speak in another language is a decision involving speech alone." 69 F.3d at 936. See generally Cecilia Wong, *Language is Speech: The Illegitimacy of Official English After* Yniguez v. Arizonans for Official English, 30 U.C. Davis L. Rev. 277, 278 (1996).

The United States Supreme Court has observed that "[c]omplete speech bans, unlike content-neutral restrictions on time, place or manner of expression, are particularly dangerous because they all but foreclose alternative means of disseminating certain information." *44 Liquormart, Inc. v. Rhode Island*, 517 U.S. 484, 506 (1996); see also *City of Ladue v. Gilleo*, 512 U.S. 43, 55 (1994) ("Our prior decisions have voiced particular concern with laws that foreclose an entire medium of expression.").

The Amendment poses a more immediate threat to First Amendment values than does legislation that regulates conduct and only incidentally impinges upon speech. *Cf. United States v. O'Brien*, 391 U.S. 367, 375–76, 382 (1968) (statute prohibiting knowing destruction or mutilation of selective service certificate did not abridge free speech on its face); *Clark v. Community for Creative Non–Violence*, 468 U.S. 288, 293–94 (1984) (National Park Service regulation forbidding sleeping in certain areas was defensible as a regulation of symbolic conduct or a time, place, or manner restriction). Laws "directed at speech" and communication are subject to exacting scrutiny and must be "justified by the substantial showing of need that the First Amendment requires." *Texas v. Johnson*, 491 U.S. 397, 406 (1989); accord *First National Bank of Boston v. Bellotti*, 435 U.S. 765, 786 (1978); *Buckley v. Valeo*, 424 U.S. 1, 16–17 (1976). Here, the drafters of the Amendment articulated the need for its enactment as promoting English as a common language. The Legislative Council's official argument in favor of the Amendment stated: "The State of Arizona is at a crossroads. It can move toward the fears and tensions of language rivalries and ethnic distrust, or it can reverse this trend and strengthen our common bond, the English language."

Even if the Amendment were characterized as a content- and viewpoint-neutral ban, and we hold such a characterization does not apply, the Amendment violates the First Amendment because it broadly infringes on protected speech. See *National Treasury Employees Union*, 513 U.S. at 470 (striking down content-neutral provisions of Ethics Reform Act due to significant burdens on public employee speech and on the "public's right to read and hear what Government employees would otherwise have written and said"). In *National Treasury Employees Union*, the Court recognized that a ban on speech *ex ante* (such as that imposed by the Amendment) constitutes a "wholesale deterrent to a broad category of expression by a massive number of potential speakers" and thus "chills potential speech before it happens." *Id.* at 467–68 (footnote omitted) (citation omitted); see also *City of Ladue*, 512 U.S. at 55 (holding that even content- and viewpoint-neutral laws can "suppress too much speech"); *Board of Airport Comm'rs v. Jews for Jesus, Inc.*, 482 U.S. 569, 574 (1987) (viewpoint neutral regulation held unconstitutional because it "prohibited all protected expression").

The chilling effect of the Amendment's broad applications is reinforced by Section 4 which provides that elected officials and state employees can be sued for violating the Amendment's prohibitions. See Appendix. We conclude that the Amendment violates the First Amendment.

Equal Protection

Section One of the Fourteenth Amendment provides, in pertinent part, that "[n]o state shall ... deny to any person within its jurisdiction the equal protection of the laws." The right to petition for redress of grievances is one of the fundamental rights guaranteed by the First Amendment. *United Mine Workers*, 389 U.S. at 222 (right to petition for redress of grievances is among the most precious of the liberties safeguarded by the Bill of Rights). A corollary to the right to petition for redress of grievances is the right to participate equally in the political process. See *Reynolds*, 377 U.S. at 560, 556–68 (concept of equal protection has been traditionally viewed as requiring the uniform treatment of persons standing in the same relation to the governmental action questioned or challenged); accord *Evans v. Romer*, 854 P.2d 1270, 1276 (Colo.1993) ("the Equal Protection Clause guarantees the fundamental right to participate equally in the political process and ... any attempt to infringe on an independently identifiable group's ability to exercise that right is subject to strict judicial scrutiny"); see also *Dunn v. Blumstein*, 405 U.S. 330, 335 (1972) (recognizing fundamental right to participate in state elections on an equal basis with other citizens in the jurisdiction).

The Amendment is subject to strict scrutiny because it impinges upon the fundamental First Amendment right to petition the government for redress of grievances. *United Mine Workers*, 389 U.S. at 222. The right to petition bars state action interfering with access to the legislature, the executive branch and its various agencies, and the judicial branch. *Eastern R.R. Presidents Conference v. Noerr Motor Freight, Inc.*, 365 U.S. 127, 137–39 (1961) (legislature); *United Mine Workers v. Pennington*, 381 U.S. 657 (1965) (executive); *California Motor Transport Co. v. Trucking Unlimited*, 404 U.S. 508 (1972) (administrative agencies and courts); *United Mine Workers*, 389 U.S. at 221–22 (courts).

The trial court rejected plaintiffs' equal protection argument on the grounds that plaintiffs had not shown that the Amendment was driven by discriminatory intent. See *Hunter v. Underwood*, 471 U.S. 222, 229 (1985). Because the Amendment curtails First Amendment rights, however, it is presumed unconstitutional and must survive this court's strict scrutiny. See generally *Rosen*, 641 F.2d at 1246. *AOE* and the state defendants bear the burden of establishing the Amendment's constitutionality by demonstrating that it is drawn with narrow specificity to meet a compelling state interest. *Id.*

* * *

As discussed previously, the compelling state interest test applies to the Amendment because it affects fundamental First Amendment rights. Even assuming *arguendo* that *AOE* and the state defendants could establish a compelling state interest for the Amendment (and they have not met that burden), they cannot satisfy the narrow specificity requirement. Under certain very restricted circumstances, states may regulate speech. See, *e.g.*, *Kovacs v. Cooper*, 336 U.S. 77, 80 (1949) (the First Amendment permits regulation of the time, place, and manner of the use of sound trucks). However, the Amendment is not a "regulation." Rather, it is a general prohibition of the use of non-English languages by all state personnel during the performance of government business and by all persons seeking to interact with all levels of government in Arizona. The Amendment's goal to promote English as a common language does not require a general prohibition on non-English usage. English can be promoted without prohibiting the use of other languages by state and local governments. Therefore, the Amendment does not meet the compelling state interest test and thus does not survive First Amendment strict scrutiny analysis.

Finally, we note that any interference with First Amendment rights need not be an absolute bar to render it unconstitutional as violating equal protection; a substantial burden upon that right is sufficient to warrant constitutional protections. By permanently implementing a linguistic barrier between persons and the government they have a right to petition, the Amendment substantially burdens First Amendment rights. See *Eastern R.R. Presidents Conference*, 365 U.S. at 137 ("The whole concept of representation depends upon the ability of the people to make their wishes known to their representatives"). Therefore, the Amendment violates the Fourteenth Amendment's guarantees of equal protection because it impinges upon both the fundamental right to participate equally in the political process and the right to petition the government for redress.

Notes and Questions

1.   Was the Supreme Court's decision not to review *Yniguez* spineless?

2.   After *Ruiz*, what sort of official English law would pass constitutional muster?

3.   Are *any* official language laws—any regime of English orthodoxy—wise?

4.   Should everyone be encouraged to learn and speak as many languages as possible? Would this introduce pandemonium? Civilization? Impede or advance communication or useful economic activity?

JUAN F. PEREA

Los Olvidados: On The Making of Invisible People
70 N.Y.U. L. Rev. 965, 965–71 (1995).*

In his recent book, Latinos, Earl Shorris poignantly describes Bienvenida Petión, a Jewish Latina immigrant, who clings to her language and culture "as if they were life itself."[1] When Bienvenida dies, it is "not of illness, but of English."[2] Bienvenida dies of English when she is confined to a nursing home where no one speaks Spanish, an environment in which she cannot communicate and in which no one cares about her language and culture.

"Death by English" is a death of the spirit, the slow death that occurs when one's own identity is replaced, reconfigured, overwhelmed, or rejected by a more powerful, dominant identity not one's own. For Latinos, illness by English of varying degree, even death by English, is a common affliction, without known cure. It may be identified, however, by some of its symptoms.

The mere sound of Spanish offends and frightens many English-only speakers, who sense in the language a loss of control over what they regard as "their" country. Spanish also frightens many Latinos, for it proclaims their identity as Latinos, for all to hear. The Latino's fear is rational. Spanish may subject Latinos to the harsh price of difference in the United States: the loss of a job, instant scapegoating, and identification as an outsider. Giving in to this fear and denying one's own identity as a Latino is, perhaps, to begin to die of English.

Latino invisibility is, I believe, the principal cause of illness by English. When I write of Latino invisibility, I mean a relative lack of positive public identity and legitimacy. I believe invisibility in this sense is created in several ways. Sometimes we are rendered invisible through the absence of public recognition and portrayal. Sometimes we are silenced through prohibitions on the use of Spanish. Sometimes we are rendered politically invisible, or nearly invisible, through the attribution of foreignness, what I shall call "symbolic deportation." * * *

The media presentation of the Los Angeles riots in the spring of 1992 illustrates the creation of Latino invisibility by omission. * * * [See

1.   Earl Shorris, *Latinos: A Biography of the People* 3 (1992).

2.   *Id.*

Chapter 13 § 1 for the author's description of Latino invisibility in news coverage of the L.A. riots.]

SEARCHING FOR LATINOS IN THE BOOKSTORES

When I travel, I spend a lot of time in bookstores searching for books on Latino life and history. It is hard to find such books. Not that they do not exist, as I own many books about Latinos. Yet I have never found a bookstore with a section on Latinos. There must be at least one, somewhere, but I have not found it yet. Since bookstores never have a section of books on Latinos, I have to search through many corridors, many categories, to find what I want. * * * The absence of a Latino or Hispanic studies section in most bookstores demonstrates a point about racial and ethnic categories in popular and scholarly culture. The need to roam across various corridors and subjects to find books on Latinos is caused by the absence of recognition that Latinos constitute an important subject about which many books have been written. The absence of a section on Latino studies and the fairly random sprinkling of books on Latinos throughout sections of varying relevance to Latinos is a metaphor for our denied identity, our absence from the popular imagination. To place books on United States Latinos in the Latin American studies section [as many bookstores do] is to place us outside the borders of the United States. It is symbolic deportation to the nations of Latin America together with symbolic exclusion from identity within the United States.

The difficulty of finding books on Latinos contrasts sharply with the relative ease of finding books on African Americans and their history. Most bookstores have an African–American or Black Studies section, the result of African–American demands for books on their history and literature. That African–American history and writing are so much easier to locate than Latino history demonstrates a much greater degree of public acknowledgement and legitimacy for black identity and the lack thereof with respect to Latino identity.

Latinos must voice similar demands for the books on our history and culture, so we are not such a well-kept secret. To be scattered widely among disparate disciplines is to dissipate Latino identity without category. It is a metaphor for the popular and scholarly denial of our identity. It is another form of Latino invisibility.

RICHARD RODRIGUEZ

Hunger Of Memory
32–37 (1982).*

This boy became a man. In private now, alone, I brood over language and intimacy—the great themes of my past. In public I expect most of the faces I meet to be the faces of strangers. (How do you do?) If meetings are quick and impersonal, they have been efficiently managed. I rush past the sounds of voices attending only to the words addressed to me. Voices seem planed to an even surface of sound, soundless. A business associate speaks in a deep baritone, but I pass through the timbre to attend to his words. The crazy man who sells me a newspaper every night mumbles something crazy, but I have time only to pretend that I have heard him say hello. Accented versions of English make little impression on me. In the rush-hour crowd a Japanese tourist asks me a question, and I inch past his accent to concentrate on what he is saying. The Eastern European immigrant in a neighborhood delicatessen speaks to me through a marinade of sounds, but I respond to his words. I note for only a second the Texas accent of the telephone operator or the Mississippi accent of the man who lives in the apartment below me.

My city seems silent until some ghetto black teenagers board the bus I am on. Because I do not take their presence for granted, I listen to the sounds of their voices. Of all the accented versions of English I hear in a day, I hear theirs most intently. They are *the* sounds of the outsider. They annoy me for being loud—so self-sufficient and unconcerned by my presence. Yet for the same reason they seem to me glamorous. (A romantic gesture against public acceptance.) Listening to their shouted laughter, I realize my own quiet. Their voices enclose my isolation. I feel envious, envious of their brazen intimacy.

I warn myself away from such envy, however. I remember the black political activists who have argued in favor of using black English in schools. (Their argument varies only slightly from that made by foreign-language bilingualists.) I have heard "radical" linguists make the point that black English is a complex and intricate version of English. And I do not doubt it. But neither do I think that black English should be a language of public instruction. What makes black English inappropriate in classrooms is not something in the language. It is rather what lower-class speakers make of it. Just as Spanish would have been a dangerous language for me to have used at the start of my education, so black English would be a dangerous language to use in the schooling of teenagers for whom it reenforces feelings of public separateness.

This seems to me an obvious point. But one that needs to be made. In recent years there have been attempts to make the language of the alien public language. "Bilingual education, two ways to understand ...," television and radio commercials glibly announce. Proponents of bilingual education are careful to say that they want students to acquire good schooling. Their argument goes something like this: Children permitted to use their family language in school will not be so alienated and will be better able to match the progress of English-speaking children in the crucial first months of instruction. (Increasingly confident of their abilities, such children will be more inclined to apply themselves to their studies in the future.) But then the bilingualists claim another, very different goal. They say that children who use their family language in school will retain a sense of their individuality—their ethnic heritage and cultural ties. Supporters of bilingual education thus want it both ways. They propose bilingual schooling as a way of helping students acquire the skills of the classroom crucial for public success.

But they likewise insist that bilingual instruction will give students a sense of their identity apart from the public.

Behind this screen there gleams an astonishing promise: One can become a public person while still remaining a private person. At the very same time one can be both! There need be no tension between the self in the crowd and the self apart from the crowd! Who would not want to believe such an idea? Who can be surprised that the scheme has won the support of many middle-class Americans? If the barrio or ghetto child can retain his separateness even while being publicly educated, then it is almost possible to believe that there is no private cost to be paid for public success. Such is the consolation offered by any of the current bilingual schemes. Consider, for example, the bilingual voters' ballot. In some American cities one can cast a ballot printed in several languages. Such a document implies that a person can exercise that most public of rights—the right to vote—while still keeping apart, unassimilated from public life.

It is not enough to say that these schemes are foolish and certainly doomed. Middle-class supporters of public bilingualism toy with the confusion of those Americans who cannot speak standard English as well as they can. Bilingual enthusiasts, moreover, sin against intimacy. An Hispanic–American writer tells me, "I will never give up my family language; I would as soon give up my soul." Thus he holds to his chest a skein of words, as though it were the source of his family ties. He credits to language what he should credit to family members. A convenient mistake. For as long as he holds on to words, he can ignore how much else has changed in his life.

It has happened before. In earlier decades, persons newly successful and ambitious for social mobility similarly seized upon certain "family words." Working-class men attempting political power took to calling one another "brother." By so doing they escaped oppressive public isolation and were able to unite with many others like themselves. But they paid a price for this union. It was a public union they forged. The word they coined to address one another could never be the sound (brother) exchanged by two in intimate greeting. In the union hall the word "brother" became a vague metaphor; with repetition a weak echo of the intimate sound. Context forced the change. Context could not be overruled. Context will always guard the realm of the intimate from public misuse.

Today nonwhite Americans call "brother" to strangers. And white feminists refer to their mass union of "sisters." And white middle-class teenagers continue to prove the importance of context as they try to ignore it. They seize upon the idioms of the black ghetto. But their attempt to appropriate such expressions invariably changes the words. As it becomes a public expression, the ghetto idiom loses its sound—its message of public separateness and strident intimacy. It becomes with public repetition a series of words, increasingly lifeless.

WILCOMB E. WASHBURN

Red Man's Land, White Man's Law
218 (1971).*

"*Tradition* is the enemy of progress." This was the motto of an Indian school in the Southwest that I passed in 1952. The school was a boarding school, the form of schooling most favored by white administrators in the nineteenth and early twentieth century specifically because it tore the Indian child from his cultural matrix and dragged him into an alien world. It was a world marked by punctuality, discipline, competition, study and punishment; a cold and friendless passage to the culture that counted. I have often thought about the lone Indian who succeeded in graduating from Harvard in the seventeenth century. Many others entered, but despaired. Imagine the cultural shock of leaving the bosom of an Indian village for the sterile intricacies of Puritan theology at Harvard College in the seventeenth century! The shock would probably be fatal for most twentieth-century whites. The problem, it should be unnecessary to point out, is not intelligence, but culture. Similarly, the Indian boy of the Western United States, confronted with an equally confusing American culture of the twentieth century, must have been torn to the depths of his soul as he weighed the unfortunate choices open to him either by acceptance or rejection.

Notes and Questions

1. In Chapter 12 § 4, the reader learns about racial stereotypes of minority groups of color. One such stereotype that fiction and the movies attach to Native Americans is speaking in broken English—chiefs saying, "ugh," braves shrieking war whoops, Tonto and other sidekick types muttering "me gettum." See, *e.g.*, Robert F. Berkhofer, Jr., *The White Man's Indian* (1978); Ward Churchill, *Film Stereotyping of Native Americans*, 5 Book Forum 370 (1981); Philip J. Deloria, Jr., *Playing Indian* (1997).

Yet, Indian languages are fully complete and Indian speakers easily up to most ordinary challenges. Thomas Jefferson wished that Congress could speak half as well as the orators of the Indian nations, while William Penn praised the Lenni Lanape language of the Delaware for its subtlety. See *William Penn's Own Account of the Lenni Lenape or Delaware Indians* (A. Myers ed. 1970). The Cherokee, in a futile effort to blend in, adopted English as their official language and published an English-language newspaper, *The Cherokee Phoenix*.

2. For further discussion of Indians and stereotyping, see Chapter 12.

RONALD TAKAKI

Strangers from a Different Shore
127–28, 257–58 (1989).*

A uniquely *Chinese–American* social institution, the store was a center of life in the Chinese community, the "resort of all the Chinese in the colony" and "a place of call." There they were able to purchase

Chinese foods, books in Chinese, firecrackers, incense, ceremonial paper, Chinese herbs, and other Chinese sundries. There they escaped from the "strangeness and fierceness of their everyday world" and recalled "happier days at home when they crowded the village inns ... to drink tea and exchange gossip, or to listen to vagrant minstrels chant ballads." In the back rooms of stores, men spent many pleasant hours telling Chinese folktales and especially ghost stories, like the one about the sound of the slippers:

In China many years ago the father of a certain woman died ... the daughter had cared a great deal for him and when he died she grieved deeply. Not long after his death she was awakened one night by a familiar sound, the sound of her father's slippers walking across the floor. She was not afraid of ghosts or of darkness, so she got up to look, but she could not discover anything unusual. Many nights after that she heard the sound, always at the same time, and always she would wake up and investigate, but never did she discover what it meant.

Shortly afterwards the daughter was married and her husband took her over here, to America. She arrived in America and had forgotten all about the sound of the slippers. But one day she heard it again, here in her new home in America. She was very much surprised at this. She did not think it strange when she heard it in China. But here in America! The sound was exactly the same as that she had heard when she lived in her little house in the village. And, even today, ever so often always at the same hour, she hears it and she knows, that it is the sound of her dead father's slippers scratching across the floor.

In the back rooms of stores, as the Chinese gathered around the stove for warmth, they challenged each other at chess and checkers, played musical instruments, listened to the phonograph, and read newspapers. Some of them also taught each other English, struggling through *An English–Chinese Phrase Book*, compiled by Wong Sam and Assistants in San Francisco in 1875. The phrases reflected their everyday lives—the broad range of experiences, anxieties, and hopes of the Chinese in America. * * *

In the back rooms, the men found out what was happening in town and also in the homeland. "Letters for the colony were directed home," said a mother. "She is my country now because she is the mother country of my children." Through their children they had connected themselves to the land here, and many parents sacrificed for their children to make it possible for them to have what had been denied to the immigrant generation. They urged their children to study hard so that they would not be victimized by racism as the first generation had been, suffering indignities and "eating bitterness," *hec fu*. "I've worked my fingers to the bones for you boys to get yourself an education," an immigrant father told his son. "If you cannot be better than they [whites] are, try to be their equal anyway, because that way, one of these days, you can be up there too."

SEARCHING FOR BRIDGES: SECOND-GENERATION CHINESE AMERICANS

For the second-generation Chinese, education was viewed as the way to get "up there." In the old country, peasants were too poor to send their children to school; here the immigrants could enroll their children in public school. "Think of all the marvelous things you can learn here," Alice Yu's parents told her. "You can get one of the best educations here. This is a wonderful country. You can learn a lot here." The children went to the public schools, where they said the pledge of allegiance to the flag of the United States and learned about American culture. In American schools, they came under the influence of their teachers. * * * "In the English school they didn't believe in Chinese customs," recounted Victor Wong. The teachers tried to "dissuade us from speaking Cantonese; they tried to dissuade us from everything Chinese. Their view of the Chinese ways was that they were evil, heathen, non-Christian." One of his teachers scolded him: "If you're gonna be an American, ya might as well learn to speak English."

But to their parents, they were also Chinese and had to learn the Chinese language and the culture of the old country. Consequently, after attending American school all day, the children went to Chinese school. "My Chinese school career began when I was 5 years old," said Edward L. C. of San Francisco. "The school was on Grant Ave. We went to Chinese school immediately after American school which was about 4 or 5 p.m. and stayed there till about 7 or 8 p.m." They also had classes at Chinese school on Saturday from 9 a.m. to 1 p.m. There they learned Chinese language, history, literature, and philosophy. Many of the children thought Chinese school was burdensome. "In the American schools they are anxious to get ahead of their classmates, while their attitude toward the Chinese learning is indifferent," observed Julia I. Hsuan Chen, herself a second-generation Chinese. "Consequently, the only language which the majority of the Chinese Americans can read and write is English." Growing up in San Francisco's Chinatown in the 1920s, Thomas W. Chinn was sent to Chinese school. "Somehow," recounted Chinn, who founded the *Chinese Digest in 1935*, "we never became proficient in reading or writing Chinese—probably because we never thought of ourselves as needing Chinese. After all, weren't we Americans?"

Like the Nisei [second-generation Japanese Americans], the second-generation Chinese shuttled between the American school and their home. In the home, wrote Kit King Louis in an essay, "Problems of Second Generation Chinese" published in 1932, the two cultures met. There they also clashed. As they grew up, many second-generation Chinese saw America as their "permanent home" and China as "remote and foreign." Many changed their given names—from Soo Fei to Fay, Wei Lim to William, Teong to Ted, Mei Guen to Mae Gwen, Yim Jun to Jean, Yim Sunn to Shelley, and Yoon to June. They viewed themselves as Americans and wanted their first names to identify them as such. They also wanted to look American. Mrs. E. M. Findlay, who worked for the Congregational Mission in San Francisco's Chinatown for twenty-seven years, described the Chinese youth in 1924: "The Chinese girls bob their hair, wear sleeveless dresses, and look just like the little

American flappers." In their "extravagance," Chinese teenagers did not think too much about their daily mixing of the two cultures: "On weekends we'd go eat wonton and drink orange freeze at the soda fountain." Many youngsters saw themselves as modern. "My parents wanted me to grow up a good Chinese girl, but I am an American and I can't accept all the old Chinese ways and ideas," explained Flora Belle Jan of Fresno in 1924. "A few years ago when my Mother took me to worship at the shrine of my ancestor and offer a plate of food, I decided it was time to stop this foolish custom. So I got up and slammed down the rice in front of the idol and said, 'So long Old Top, I don't believe in you anyway.'" Sometimes the break from their parents and Chinese culture also involved self-rejection: "When I was young, before thirteen," admitted Grace Wen, "I used to wish I had light hair and blue eyes."

[Eds. See the excerpt from *The Bluest Eye* by Toni Morrison, Chapter 6 § 4.]

Notes and Questions

1. Is the English-only movement, as Perea suggests, an aspect of latter-day nativism? Note that many of the same organizations and individuals backing the English-only movement also have been active in the effort to limit immigration and militarize the border with Mexico. So, is the effort to require English-speaking evidence of hatred toward that which is foreign—or, specifically, brown or Asian? (And not, *e.g.*, Swedish or Norwegian.) Or can an argument be made that speaking a single language is necessary to preserve national unity and avoid fragmentation?

2. The percentage of Americans who speak English is in the high nineties. How much more national unity could we expect from a determined effort to enforce Official English?

Classroom Exercises

1. A public school district has offered bonuses to teachers who become proficient in "Ebonics," a dialect of English spoken by inner-city children and families. Sallie Mae Patterson III, an African–American teacher who is a member of the Republican Party, challenges the bonus as demeaning to students and unfair to teachers who prefer to teach standard English to young black children.

How would you argue on behalf of Patterson? On behalf of the school board?

2. It is the year 2060, and a representative of the Florida state legislature has just proposed a bill that would make Spanish the official language of that state. In support, Rep. Carrillo has produced a report showing that 51 percent of the state's populace now speaks Spanish as their first, or main, language. The bill also provides remedial assistance for non-Spanish speakers, and contains a grandfather clause so that none will lose jobs due to a Spanish-speaking deficiency for the first five years after the bill's passage. The bill's preamble recites that having a single, official language is important for the state's unity.

Would such a measure be constitutional? If you lived in Florida, would you vote for it? Learn Spanish as quickly as possible? Gladly, or grudgingly?

Chapter 11

RACE, SEXUALITY, AND
THE FAMILY

One of the most popular public attitudes toward race in the late twentieth century is the attitude of "color-blindness." For example, many people argue that with respect to the practices and institutions of public life, we should not "notice race," or at least not let race matter.

Yet this widespread commitment to color-blindness breaks down when it comes to "private" matters. As Rachel Moran has noted, although to take race into account in making decisions would be considered immoral and possibly illegal when it comes to education, employment, and public accommodations, Americans routinely take race into account when making decisions about whom to date, whom to marry, and whom to adopt. See Rachel Moran, *Interracial Intimacy* (forthcoming 2000). A quick scan of the personals ads in any newspaper reveals open race consciousness: For example, "SWM seeks S, W or AF for walks on the beach." Men and women make racial rules for themselves about their romantic possibilities: for example, an African–American woman may declare that she would never date "outside the race." Adoption markets and adoption decisions are color-coded: for example, the "market" values white babies over black and "mixed" babies, and many people argue that race-matching between families and adopted children is not only acceptable but appropriate.

Why this dramatic difference between "public" and "private" life? Feminists have long questioned the distinction drawn between these two spheres, arguing that it helps keep women's oppression in place. See, *e.g.*, Nadine Taub & Elizabeth M. Schneider, *Women's Subordination and the Role of Law*, in *The Politics of Law: A Progressive Critique* 151–57 (David Kairys ed., rev. ed. 1990). How does the distinction between public and private relate to matters of race? To what extent does race-consciousness in the "private" world affect the "public" world, and vice versa? How do gender, sexuality, and the legal and social institution known as "the family" interact with race and racism? These are some of the questions addressed in this chapter.

SECTION 1. SEXUALITY

CHRISTIAN F. FEEST

Pride and Prejudice: The Pocahontas Myth and the Pamunkey in *The
Invented Indian: Cultural Actions and Government Policies*
49–52, 54–56, 58–60 (James A. Clifton ed. 1990).*

Late in 1607, when the Jamestown colony was plagued by a dangerous relationship between scanty food supplies and excessive factional
strife, Captain John Smith ventured into Chickahominy Indian country
to trade for corn. When exploring the country beyond their lands at the
end of his foraging trip, he was apprehended by a sizable detachment of
warriors of the Powhatan chiefdom as a suspect in the murder case of a
Rappahannock Indian, who had been killed a few years earlier by an
unidentified Englishman. Although Smith was cleared of this charge, he
was taken before Powhatan at Pamunkey, tried, and (as far as he could
make out) sentenced to death on more general grounds. Just as the
tawny executioners readied themselves to knock out the Captain's
brains, Pocahontas—Powhatan's favorite daughter (and cherished subject of later romantic biographers)—threw herself over the Captain's
stocky body and thereby presumably saved his life.

Later * * * [she] intervened repeatedly to extend economic aid and
political advice to Smith and the fledgling colony. After Smith returned
to England, Pocahontas disappeared from the colonists' view, and a
moderately cold war ensued between the natives and these alien squatters. When, in 1613, Captain Samuel Argall had to go all the way to the
Potomacs' territory to trade for corn, he encountered Pocahontas again.
Seizing her as a hostage, Argall carried the young woman to Jamestown
to extort peace from Powhatan. Pocahontas was soon moved to the
settlement at Henrico where she was instructed in the doctrines of
Christianity, to which she readily converted. The following year she
eventually proved instrumental in mediating peace between her father's
people and those of her newly acquired fiancé—John Rolfe, the pioneer
of English tobacco cultivation in Virginia. This was a second marriage
for both, Pocahontas (now Mrs. Rebecca Rolfe) gave birth to Thomas
Rolfe in 1615, and a year later went to England with husband and son,
where she was introduced to Queen Anne and unexpectedly met John
Smith again. As she was preparing to return to Virginia in early 1617,
Mrs. Rolfe—or Pocahontas—fell ill and died at Gravesend. The lasting
power of images of this young woman and her associations with America's pioneer founders is evident in the title and jacket blurb of Leon
Phillips' 1973 *First Lady of America: A Romanticized Biography of
Pocahontas*, where she is touted for as being as "relevant today as she
was in 1612 * * * a woman of enormous power and intellect." * * *

The Pocahontas–Smith–Rolfe story has all the distinctive features of
an American origin myth. Of much significance is the era when what
had been a colorful local story achieved nationwide popularity. Before
the 1800s Pocahontas and her role were little known outside Virginia.

Thereafter the developing nation began to build and to catalog its own mythology, accounts of hero figures and basic values of America's beginning cast in epic form. Among these nationally favored tales was that of Pocahontas who, by repeatedly safeguarding the very existence of the first English colony on American soil, was drawn in an early image of Manifest Destiny. At the same time, likely of greater importance, Pocahontas was made to symbolize a virginal native America, for her representation was merged with the older Indian Queen and Indian Princess images. In mythic form, by saving Smith she legitimizes the Anglo–American presence in North America. By marrying Rolfe she conveys the aboriginals' title to the land to the English colonists and accepts a dependent status for native Americans. By her early death she makes room for Euroamerican expansion as all good Indians should do. For Virginians there were additional dimensions: Her alleged contribution to her husband's experiments with tobacco cultivation helped to establish the basis for Virginia's economic prosperity, while through her son, Thomas, she infused the blood of native American "royalty" into the veins of the colonial elite.

During the eighteenth century, some thoughtful Virginians lamented that so few colonists had followed John Rolfe's example in marrying an Indian woman, because such unions would have established a better claim to the land. Extolling the benefits of native American-immigrant American conjugal ties, William Byrd II concluded: "Besides, the poor Indians would have had less reason to complain that the English took their lands, if they had received it by way of a marriage portion with their daughters." A few decades later, Peter Fontaine agreed that "if * * * we had taken Indian wives in the first place, it would have been some compensation for their lands * * * We should [have] become the rightful heirs to their lands." Interestingly, these eighteenth-century sentiments conflicted with the existing laws of Virginia, which since 1691 had outlawed interracial marriage. The nineteenth-century Pocahontas story, however, was obviously not concerned with the quantities of Indian woman-American male marriages: A single richly symbolic case served the explanatory purposes of myth-making much better. * * *

After 1646 the Algonquian peoples of Virginia were quickly becoming an insignificant factor both politically and militarily. As tribal populations rapidly decreased, reservation land was allotted to the tribes on a per capita basis, but even these small patches became increasingly subject to the encroachment of the rapidly growing populations of colonial neighbors. Military and political conquest had proved to be a much more effective means for obtaining possession of the country than either interracial marriage or the proposed Christianity-for-land deal which had figured so prominently in early promotional literature. * * *

In the absence of clearly visible cultural symbols of their Indian status and with pressures mounting to distinguish themselves from the Colored category after Reconstruction, Virginia Algonquians had to find ways to establish their separate identity. Certificates of Indian descent had been issued by local authorities during the eighteenth and early nineteenth centuries, but these were simply not enough. * * *

In the 1880s the Pamunkey began to use the Pocahontas story to validate their Indian identity in the eyes and minds of their contemporaries: White, Black, and Red. This development should be seen as a profound emotional plea for a redefinition of their status in Virginia's race-class hierarchy. The Pocahontas story was of special value because it established a base for common ground between the Pamunkey and their neighbors, for the myth was long dear to other Virginians. But the Pamunkey drew different conclusions from the same mythic premises. Essentially, this process conformed to earlier Pamunkey practice—the adoption of broadly American criteria and symbols for defining their Indian identity. This tactic, the Pamunkey had learned, aided them in communicating their point of view.

The major vehicle used to transport the message to the public was a play reenacting Pocahontas's role in the salvation of Captain John Smith's life. This dramatic scene was more or less regularly performed between at least 1881 and 1915. It was probably intended as reminder of the debt owed by Virginians to the Indians, of the old alliance between these peoples, and the fact that Powhatan's children were still alive—if not well—in Virginia. Our information on this pageant comes from a variety of sources. The earliest known photograph of Virginia Algonquians, for example, shows a Pamunkey troupe staging what is labeled as the "John Smith Play" at the Yorktown Centennial in 1881. * * *

There is other evidence, however, relating to the importance of the Pocahontas myth to the Virginia Algonquians. A missionary visiting Pamunkey in 1915 (almost three centuries too late) offered the following observation gathered in the Indians' houses. There he saw: "On the walls, a copy of the original picture of Mrs. John Rolfe number two, better known as the Princess Pocahontas, and perhaps an old time print of Capt. John Smith, a character even at this day revered by these Indians." We may have doubts regarding the reasons for the alleged Indian sympathies for Smith, whose record as a friend of the Indians is—to say the least—equivocal. As part of the Pocahontas myth, however, his role was notably important to the Pamunkey. In contrast, if readers have not already noticed, conspicuously absent between 1881 and 1920 from all Pamunkey celebrations of the 1607 meeting and engagement was the figure of John Rolfe. This is especially noteworthy, for he had become their relative by marriage to Pocahontas. This relationship the Pamunkey certified later in the seventeenth century with the gift of a tract of land to Thomas Rolfe, which shows that this affinal tie was acknowledged by them as binding for some decades. Why the late nineteenth-century Pamunkey dropped his role in organizing and casting their pageant presents a puzzle. A useful interpretation is that the Pamunkey sense of their own history shifted with changes in their place in Virginia society. Their overriding concern in the late nineteenth century was to redefine their position—as Indians. Denying John Rolfe's role, and symbolically that of the numerous other later Englishmen who had married Pamunkey women, further reinforced their "racial purity" and the culturally redefined boundary between themselves and other Virginians. * * *

Though the Pocahontas–Smith pageant is no longer performed by the Pamunkey, the story continues to be important as a key symbol of their distinctive identity and their special relationship to American society. The myth lives on in a new art form. Pottery making was revived in 1932 when a pottery school was opened on the reservation with financial aid from the state of Virginia. Brightly painted and glazed wares in this newly invented traditional style continue to be made by a few Pamunkey ladies of the older generation for sale to tourists. Some of these pots and plates are decorated with a kind of picture writing also of twentieth-century origin and itself an attempt to produce something that could be recognized as "Indian" by other Virginians.

The story most often told in these pictographs is that of Pocahontas and Captain John Smith. The Pamunkey translation (which once again stresses the aspects of friendship between Indians and Whites) reads as follows: "1. Indians 2. While hunting 3. Discover 4. White man 5. Standing 6. In shallow water 7. Indians 8. Agree 9. To kill white man 10. at chief's seat 11. Indian maiden 12. Disagrees with 13. Indian men 14. (And) makes no harm for 15. White man 16. But good wishes." In this manner, an event of no great world-historical significance lives on symbolically, perpetuated by the few surviving Pamunkey, used by them to fix their identity and to win the hearts and minds of Captain John Smith's children.

Notes and Questions

1. Compare the Mexican legend of *"La Malinche"* with the myth of Pocahontas. As the story goes, La Malinche, also known as Malintzin

> was an Aztec noble woman who was presented to Cortes upon landing in Veracruz in 1519. She subsequently served Cortes as lover, translator and tactical advisor. * * * Malintzin's history, her legend and subsequent mythic dimensions as evil goddess and creator of a new race—the mestizo race, embroils her in a family quarrel, where many male members often prefer to see her as the mother-whore, bearer of illegitimate children, responsible for the foreign Spanish invasion; and where female members attempt to restore balance in ways that are sometimes painfully ambivalent. * * *

Norma Alarcón, *Chicana's Feminist Literature: A Re–Vision Through Malintzin/or Malintzin: Putting Flesh Back on the Object*, in *This Bridge Called My Back: Writings by Radical Women of Color* 182 (Cherríe Moraga and Gloria Anzaldúa eds. 1983). See also Sandra Messinger Cypess, *La Malinche in Mexican Literature: From History to Myth* (1991).

La Malinche is considered the mother of a "new race:" Mexicans commonly consider themselves a "mestizo" or mixed race, acknowledging their Indian, European, and (sometimes) their African heritage. In contrast, in the United States Whites have clung to the belief that their racial heritage is "pure." See F. James Davis, *Who Is Black? One Nation's Definition* (1991).

At the same time, however, La Malinche is considered something of a traitor who passed on secrets of her people to the marauding Spanish. Thus, attitudes toward her in Mexico are ambivalent. Could Pocahontas be viewed in the same way? Why is the dominant attitude toward her admiring rather than critical?

Feest notes that the liaison between Pocahontas and Captain John Smith was the exception, not the rule. In fact, in 1691 the Virginia Assembly passed an act "for prevention of that abominable mixture and spurious issue which hereafter may encrease in this dominion, as well as by negroes, mulattoes, and Indians intermarrying with English, or other white woman, as by their unlawfull accompanying with one another." See Edmund S. Morgan, *American Slavery, American Freedom: The Ordeal of Colonial Virginia* 335 (1975). Under the act, a white man or woman who married a Negro, mulatto, or Indian was to be banished from the colony. *Id.* In contrast, in the American West Anglo men frequently married "Spanish" or Mexican women of means. See Chapter 4, *supra* and this chapter, § 2 *infra*.

2. In 1924, the Virginia legislature passed a statute defining a white person as a person having "no trace whatsoever of any blood other than Caucasian." An exception was made, however, for a person with up to "one-sixteenth Indian ancestry." This exception was known as the "Pocahontas exception," for people who claimed descent from Captain John Smith and Pocahontas. See An Act to Preserve Racial Integrity, Ch. 371, § 5, 1927 Va. Sess. Laws 534, 535.

STEPHANIE L. PHILLIPS

Claiming Our Foremothers: The Legend of Sally Hemings
and the Tasks of Black Feminist Theory
8 Hastings Women's L.J. 401, 403–04, 406–17 (1997).*

Who was Sally Hemings? She was a slave owned by Thomas Jefferson who, according to legend, bore him several children. Both the historicity of the story and the meanings ascribed to it are hotly contested. Generally speaking, some historians and most African Americans, including those who believe themselves descendants of Hemings and Jefferson, think of Hemings as Jefferson's "slave wife" or long-time paramour. Arrayed against them are other historians who deny—some of them vehemently—that Jefferson had any sexual relationship with Hemings. It is unlikely that either of these contending versions will be vanquished any time soon, because the story is too important for the contestants to simply abandon it and because the factual record will remain incomplete. The story concerns, after all, events from almost two hundred years ago that would, of necessity, be shrouded in secrecy. It would not have been possible for Thomas Jefferson, leading revolutionary intellectual, slave-holding Virginia aristocrat, and two-term president of the United States, to openly acknowledge either his liaison with his slave or his paternity of their children. Sally Hemings was not Jefferson's lawfully wedded wife, nor could she be: The blood of her African grandmother was a taint that made Sally Hemings legally and socially less than a human being.

I have become convinced that the story of Sally Hemings, both factual and mythological, is an important one. * * * Of the innumerable stories that have been told by African–American women about sexual relationships between slave women and white men, only those that illustrate a paradigm of sexual oppression are usually treated as relevant to black feminist theory. This is problematic because other stories, wherein slave women have loving or ambivalent relationships with their masters, have present-day implications for black feminist theory and politics. Specifically, stories about love between master and slave present the question whether racial hierarchy can sometimes be transcended in the context of intimate relationships. Other stories, such as those about slave women who have ambivalent, perverse relationships with their masters, present the question whether black women form corrupt attachments to white men, to the detriment of "the race," in general, and black men, in particular.

I initially reacted with extreme distaste to the idea that Sally Hemings and Thomas Jefferson had a long-term, amorous relationship. I thought that their story, if told at all, should be told as a story of oppression. My feelings about the Hemings story began to shift, however, as I read the work of some of the historians who denied that Hemings and Jefferson had a romantic or sexual attachment. When these historians asserted that Jefferson could not possibly have loved Sally because she was a slave, I recognized their attack as a slur, directed not only against Sally Hemings, but also against all slave women and, possibly, African Americans in general. Thus, I came to a new understanding of the importance of the Sally Hemings story as a bone of contention between racist and antiracist forces.

ACT I: IN WHICH I DISCOVER DESCENDANTS OF THOMAS JEFFERSON IN MY FAMILY.

One day my then-spouse and I were touring the District of Columbia, tending to choose sites to visit and to slant our conversation with particular interest in African–American history. Jeffrey said to me, "You know, your cousin David is a descendant of Thomas Jefferson and his slave wife." My reaction? None. I neither believed nor disbelieved the story. More accurately, I suspended disbelief, affected enough by dominant cultural assumptions to be inclined to reject the story, aware enough of the counter-story as told and lived by African Americans to recognize the likely "truth" of the story, and tilted back toward disbelief by my feeling that claims to white ancestors, particularly famous ones, are undignified.

Next episode. I was raiding a friend's bookshelves, looking for something good to read. After inspecting the pile of books I had selected, Mary said, "I think you've missed one. Have you already read *Sally Hemings* (1979), by Barbara Chase–Riboud?" "Who's Sally Hemings?" I asked. "What!" exclaimed Mary. "How could you not know that she was the slave wife of Thomas Jefferson?" Suitably chastened, I added Sally Hemings to my gleanings and trotted on home.

Later that night, I pulled out Chase–Riboud's book. The painting on the book jacket is of (what I suppose you would call) a woman's chest: the part of her anatomy that begins at the base of the neck and runs to top-of-bosom. Delicate shading indicates where the gentle swell of breasts begins. Hanging over the nascent cleavage, which is oh-sotastefully rendered, lies an oval locket, suspended from a chain and opened upon its hinge to reveal a portrait. With astonishment verging on alarm, I reared back in my chair and loudly exclaimed, "Why, he looks just like David!" My former disbelief evaporated on the spot, and I "knew" that Thomas Jefferson and Sally Hemings had produced descendants, of whom my cousin was one. My "knowledge" was in the form of an intuitive flash, a subjective state of certainty which I thought beyond challenge.

ACT II: IN WHICH BARBARA CHASE-RIBOUD GIVES LIFE TO THE MYTH.

As I read Chase–Riboud's novel, *Sally Hemings*, I became more and more impressed by its cover which, as I have already mentioned, is adorned by a painting of a woman's chest, whereon reposes a portrait-in-locket of Thomas Jefferson. Seldom, if ever, have I come upon a book jacket with so apt a design. Barbara Chase–Riboud constructs the story of Thomas Jefferson and Sally Hemings as a great romance, as is clearly implied by the cover painting. For Sally to wear Jefferson's portrait, so near to both her bosom and her heart, means that she loves him. It also means that she possesses him.

With significant distaste, I endured Chase–Riboud's description of Sally Hemings as compellingly beautiful, to all appearances white and possessed of the supreme feminine virtues of submissiveness and devotion, along with a deep sensuality which, no doubt, was a manifestation of her otherwise-latent African blood. Chase–Riboud gives us a woman who is an affront to any feminist notion of what a woman should be. Furthermore, this Sally exemplifies a model of femininity unattainable by most black women, a feminine ideal that has been a painful component of black women's oppression. As for the idea that Sally loved Jefferson and he loved her, is that not obscene?

Among those who cry "obscenity," there is the most fundamental disagreement. For some, the obscenity in the alleged love between Jefferson and Sally is slavery. Not only did the hypocrite Jefferson hold Sally in bondage, but, perhaps as bad or worse, she accepted her status. She could have remained in France as a free woman, but chose to return to Virginia with Jefferson, as his slave. To others, the obscenity is Sally. She was technically black as well as a slave. What could Thomas Jefferson, Founding Father, widely-read scion of the Enlightenment, and shining white star, have possibly seen in her?

The two obscenity camps agree that, whatever there was between Thomas Jefferson and Sally Hemings, it was not love. The First Obscenity Group would say that the proper word for any sexual intercourse between these two is "rape." Members of the Second Obscenity Group reject even the idea of sexual congress with a black woman as a filthy slander upon a man whom they greatly admire.

There is a third group, of course, which includes Chase–Riboud, that sees no obscenity in the idea of love between Jefferson and Sally, but willingly accepts this version of the story as the only one that can square with respect for each of them, as well as respect for their descendants. And what, after all, is so implausible about the story? As told by Chase–Riboud, the key elements of the love between Jefferson and Sally turn out to be not uncommon: He was attracted to her sensuality, submission, and beauty; she was attracted to his sensuality and power. The hierarchical nature of their relationship was itself erotic. Moreover, Jefferson's dominance as male and master was not completely determinative: Sally's sexuality gave her power.

Chase–Riboud's characters and plot development are so compelling that I began to consider her construction of the Hemings/Jefferson story seriously, despite my aversion to her portrait of Sally and my political discomfort with her decision to treat this as a story of love, rather than oppression.

ACT III: IN WHICH I RUN ACROSS A FOOTNOTE
DENYING THE EXISTENCE OF MY COUSIN.

This story might have ended for me after I finished reading Barbara Chase–Riboud's deeply troubling, strangely seductive novel. I went on, I thought, to other things. Then, in pursuit of my study of the history of religion in American public life, in which Jefferson figures prominently, I ran across a footnote which informed me that the emerging consensus was that Thomas Jefferson did not have any children with Sally Hemings. I was dumbfounded. How could these historians have let the real story elude them? Wouldn't genealogical research include interviews with family members? The truth of the Thomas Jefferson/Sally Hemings story is stamped upon the face of my cousin, among others. Perhaps, I thought, I should try to unravel this mystery.

ACT IV: IN WHICH I ENDURE VIRGINIUS DABNEY'S OPINION THAT SALLY
HEMINGS AND, BY EXTENSION, HER DESCENDANTS AND [I] ARE SCUM.

Upon the advice of a helpful colleague, I decided to read a book by Virginius Dabney, *The Jefferson Scandals: A Rebuttal*. I approached the slim volume with curiosity and anticipatory outrage: Just how was this gentleman going to go about the task of whitewashing the alleged stain upon his hero's character? What perverted and prejudiced method did he deploy that enabled him to deny the plain truth that Sally Hemings bore children to Thomas Jefferson?

Dabney describes the genesis of the "Jefferson Scandals" thus:

> The debunking of Jefferson began when a vicious, unscrupulous disappointed office-seeker named James T. Callender disseminated to the nation in 1802 the allegation that Jefferson had the slave Sally Hemings as his concubine.

While the story of Jefferson and Sally Hemings has been the subject of speculation for nearly two hundred years, Dabney blames its late twentieth-century revival on Fawn Brodie, author of *Thomas Jefferson: An Intimate History*. Brodie's book, a much discussed best-seller, included material on Sally Hemings that became the foundation for Chase–Riboud's later, fictionalized account.

Dabney devotes the longest chapter of his book to a carefully constructed attempt to make Fawn Brodie look ridiculous. He certainly succeeds. Unfortunately, Fawn Brodie had done a sort of psychoanalysis of Jefferson's words, reading meanings into Jefferson's letters that seem strained and far-fetched. Given this material, Dabney rather easily manages to arouse contempt for Brodie and makes her look like an idiot.

Dabney also devotes substantial space in his monograph to descriptions of Jefferson and his accomplishments. This material, meant strongly to imply that the liaison between Jefferson and Hemings did not happen, is a tad overblown. For example:

> The lack of a Bill of Rights in the United States Constitution when it was adopted in 1788 was immediately noted by Jefferson, and he wrote at once from France, pressing for such an expansion of the new nation's organic law. All our civil liberties today are based on those amendments to the Constitution. In addition to his incomparable contributions in these areas, Jefferson's prodigious versatility made it possible for him to provide others of far-reaching significance in such fields as architecture, education, science, agriculture, and law. On top of all else, he was an accomplished musician, bibliophile, and philologist. No serious historian claims that Thomas Jefferson was without faults, but this philosopher-statesman is universally acknowledged to have been one of the most brilliant ornaments of the Enlightenment, an age that produced in America a group of men whose political genius astounded the world.

In addition to all that, Jefferson was an exemplary family man, devoted to his wife and devastated by her death, whereafter he lavished attention upon their daughters. Was Jefferson celibate from age thirty-nine, when his wife died, until his own death forty-four years later? No one knows for sure, but Dabney, at any rate, finds credible evidence of only one romantic entanglement: a brief fling with Maria Cosway. Dabney tells us:

> Maria and Jefferson met in Paris in the autumn of 1786, and the forty-three-year-old widower, whose wife had died four years before, was attracted at once to the lovely twenty-seven-year-old woman with the golden hair and violet eyes. She was not only easy to look upon but greatly gifted both as an artist and a musician. * * * Maria played well on the harp and pianoforte, was also a composer, and had a fine singing voice. In addition she was an accomplished linguist. All of which could not fail to appeal to Jefferson, whose interests were quite similar.

Why does Dabney devote several pages to reporting on the Jefferson/Cosway affair, topped off by her full-page portrait? It seems that Dabney wants to give us a complete picture of a woman who, in Dabney's opinion, was plausibly Jefferson's love interest. By contrast, we are led to conclude by negative inference that Sally Hemings emphatically was not.

Woven throughout Dabney's thin book are insinuations against Hemings, most notably his repeated references to her "brood" of "illegitimate" children. These snide references aside, Dabney's principal strategy with respect to an image of Sally is to insist that no one now living has any proof of what she was like, except for the fact that she was "a handsome light-skinned slave." Such a strategy serves multiple purposes.

First, Dabney means to emphasize that Brodie and Chase–Riboud lack specific evidence upon which to base their portrayals of Sally Hemings's character and personality. Thus, they, who believe that Jefferson and Sally had a long-term, amorous relationship, have had to use their imaginations to construct a Sally that Jefferson could plausibly have loved. Dabney, on the other hand, restrains himself from sketching in the details of the Sally he imagines, the one who, to his mind, could never have attracted, much less held, the attention of Jefferson. By failing to describe the Sally he so despises, Dabney, no doubt, strives to make himself relatively impregnable to charges of racist animus. More importantly, he forces his readers to supply from their own imaginations the degraded Sally that would be unworthy of anything but derision and scorn. Thus, Dabney enlists his readers in the task of constructing Sally as she must have been in order for Dabney's abhorrence to have arisen.

Confronting Dabney's treatment of Sally was a dreadful experience for me. I felt a boiling rage at Dabney as liar, slanderer, and racist. But my anger was overlaid with an even more powerful humiliation. I experienced all of Dabney's scorn of Sally as scorn of me. Not only did I feel that he was deriding my character, I could feel the sting on my cheeks as though I had been slapped by some hated-white-person-with-power, a slavemaster, perhaps. However, despite my overwrought feelings, I did not lose sight of what I viewed to be the bottom-line fact: There are a lot of people alive today who are partially of African descent and who look remarkably like Thomas Jefferson. So, Dabney, what do you say to that!

"It was the nephew." Well, I'll be damned. Dabney did not, after all, fail to admit that there are a number of Jefferson-looking African Americans abroad in the world. Rather, he offers the only possible explanation for his version of history: Sally Hemings's children were not fathered by Thomas Jefferson, but by one of Jefferson's nephews, either Samuel or Peter Carr. Thus, African Americans who bear a marked family resemblance to Thomas Jefferson are explained as his lateral, rather than direct, descendants, and Jefferson's virtue and honor are left intact.

While I must concede that Dabney's story line is not wholly implausible, the historical evidence remains inconclusive. The "Nephew Story," for example, was far from definitively established in Dabney's book. Dabney himself quotes Jefferson's grandson as saying that Sally's children "resembled Mr. Jefferson so closely that it was plain that they had his blood in their veins," and that "in one case the resemblance was so close, that at some distance or in the dusk, the slave dressed in the same way, might have been mistaken for Mr. Jefferson." However, this grandson, as well as Jefferson's granddaughter, and, more ambiguously, the former overseer of Monticello, were all of the opinion that one of Jefferson's nephews, Samuel or Peter Carr, had fathered Sally Hemings's children.

In flat contradiction to the "Nephew Story," as told by Jefferson's grandchildren and overseer, a detailed, published statement by Madison Hemings states that his parents were Thomas Jefferson and Sally

Hemings. Dabney, however, attempts to dispose of Madison's statement as a fabrication by some scalawag (on the supposition that Madison was surely too ignorant and backward to have produced so articulate an account). In the alternative, Dabney hypothesizes that Madison's story is based on lies told to him by his mother, Sally Hemings, who exhibited the oft-observed, deplorable, female trait of seeking vicarious glamour by telling everyone that her bastards were fathered by some great and famous man. Such a speculative attack on the credibility of Jefferson's putative son does not, of course, constitute evidence of what actually happened. In fact, Dabney has his own credibility problem: There surely are African Americans, members of the Jefferson family and others, who will never be impressed by the "evidence" turned up by bad-intentioned white people.

WHAT SEQUEL SHALL I WRITE?

Evidentiary and credibility issues aside, mainstream media include so many casual references to Sally Hemings as Jefferson's paramour that even an army of professional historians would be inadequate to rout the story. Thus, there is little doubt that the tale is fated for periodic retelling and reevaluation. As my contribution to evaluating this story, I could pursue one of several strategies. I could, for instance, delve further into the historical evidence in order to come closer to a firm opinion about what "really" happened. As another alternative, I could frame the issue as a dispute between those who affirm and those who seemingly question the full humanity of Sally Hemings, her descendants, and African Americans generally. This would be an historiographical inquiry into what is at stake for those who see the story largely in terms of its racial meanings and would include further analysis of Dabney and his book.

These projects, which emphasize different aspects of the historical debate about Sally Hemings, would be motivated largely by the desire to defend her, her descendants, and other African Americans (including myself) from racist slurs. After encountering Dabney, I am convinced that this is important work. If I chose one or both of these paths, however, I would leave unexplored my initial reactions to the Sally Hemings story, particularly as presented by Barbara Chase–Riboud. When I first encountered the story, I intensely disliked the idea that Sally Hemings and Thomas Jefferson loved each other, and I had strong political objections to an imaginative portrayal of their relationship as a romance, rather than a story of oppression. I do not want to lose sight of the possibility that, from the point of view of African–American culture and politics, Sally is somehow inauthentic and largely irrelevant, even though I want to move to her defense when she is attacked by apparent racists.

Notes and Questions

1. Phillips asks: "Are there divergent interpretations of the Sally Hemings story within the African–American community, particularly among women? Have other African–American women, besides myself, been offended when the story of Sally Hemings is told as a love story, rather than a story of oppression? As opponents of American race and gender hierarchies, have we

unduly privileged stories about slave-era sexual oppression so that the issues raised by other important stories are suppressed?" *Id*. at 416–17. What do you think?

2.   Phillips' article notes "that sexual interactions between white men and slave women were very common, despite the fact that such contact was illegal. Blaming slave women for the fact of this illicit sex, white supremacists have created the 'Jezebel' stereotype of a black women whose personality and character were entirely dominated by her quest for sexual indulgence. In opposition to the Jezebel stereotype, the antiracist movement has made a priority of teaching that most sexual intercourse between slave women and white men resulted from rape or other forms of coercion. This story of sexual oppression is not, however, the only one extant within the African–American community. There are, in fact, three stories that African Americans tell about slave-era sex between black women and white men."

Phillips continues:

I call the three stories "Primeval Stories" because of the foundational role they play with regard to American race and gender issues. The first, the "Hate Story," concerns situations where slave women hate their masters, who take sex by brutality, rape, or other acts of coercion. The key players in this story are an evil white man and a blameless slave woman. On the sidelines, there is a black man who is the preferred mate of the slave woman, but who is powerless to protect her from her master's predations. The "Hate Story" is paradigmatic, because it represents the most prevalent pattern of sexual interactions between slave women and white men, because it is the most relevant to the present-day circumstances of African Americans, and because the other two Primeval Stories cannot be fully understood without examining how they deviate from the Hate Story.

The second set of narratives illustrates the "Love Story," in which the slave and master love each other. The story of Sally Hemings and Thomas Jefferson reappears here as one example. In these narratives, the slave and master share, in addition to a sexual bond, some level of affection and commitment. This is a hierarchical relationship, but the slave woman is not merely an object of domination. Rather, her beauty, sensuality, and intuitive intelligence make her powerful. In addition to the other key character, a virile white man who is capable of love and devotion across lines of caste, there is a subsidiary character in some versions of the Love Story: the child of the union, who looks white, and suffers enormous identity confusion and various catastrophes because she is socially and legally categorized as "black." This is the "tragic mulatta."

* * * [In] the "Third Primeval Story," * * * the slave woman both loves and hates her master. These relationships are perverse, both psychologically and sexually. The subsidiary character, here, is a black man, who is in sexual competition with the white man for the slave woman's attention. The slave woman makes herself sexually indispensable to both male characters, but then chooses to align herself with the white man. This fact pattern is the origin of the age-old accusation that black women are traitors to the race and forms the basis for the idea that black women suffer less than black men, as victims of white supremacy.

Id. at 404–05.

3. Recent scientific evidence suggests that, in fact, Thomas Jefferson and Sally Hemings did indeed have children together. See Dinitia Smith & Nicholas Wade, *DNA Test Finds Evidence of Jefferson Child by Slave*, N.Y. Times, November 1, 1998, at 1–1, col. 5.

4. Compare the stories of Pocahontas, La Malinche, and Sally Hemings. Did these women "consent" to the relationships they found themselves in? What does "consent" mean in this context? To what extent are all these stories about what anthropologist Gayle Rubin famously called "the traffic in women"? What stories might these women tell if they could speak for themselves? Would they say they had consented? Were in love? Hated the powerful men in their lives?

HARRIET A. JACOBS

Incidents in the Life of a Slave Girl 27–36 (Jean Fagan Yellin ed. 1987).*

[Harriet Ann Jacobs, a freed slave and activist in the abolition movement, wrote *Incidents in the Life of a Slave Girl* in 1857. Using fictionalized names for the characters, Jacobs' narrator, Linda Brent, tells a story based on Jacobs' own life as a slave. When Linda Brent was eleven her mistress died and "bequeathed" Brent to Emily Flint, a family relative who was a young child. Emily Flint's father, Dr. Flint, sexually harassed Brent constantly, and continued to pursue her even after she ran away. Brent's grandmother was emancipated and worked as a baker.]

During the first years of my service in Dr. Flint's family, I was accustomed to share some indulgences with the children of my mistress. Though this seemed to me no more than right, I was grateful for it, and tried to merit the kindness by the faithful discharge of my duties. But I now entered on my fifteenth year—a sad epoch in the life of a slave girl. My master began to whisper foul words in my ear. Young as I was, I could not remain ignorant of their import. I tried to treat them with indifference or contempt. The master's age, my extreme youth, and the fear that his conduct would be reported to my grandmother, made him bear this treatment for many months. He was a crafty man, and resorted to many means to accomplish his purposes. Sometimes he had stormy, terrific ways, that made his victims tremble; sometimes he assumed a gentleness that he thought must surely subdue. Of the two, I preferred his stormy moods, although they left me trembling. He tried his utmost to corrupt the pure principles my grandmother had instilled. He peopled my young mind with unclean images, such as only a vile monster could think of. I turned from him with disgust and hatred. But he was my master. I was compelled to live under the same roof with him—where I saw a man forty years my senior daily violating the most sacred commandments of nature. He told me I was his property; that I must be subject to his will in all things. My soul revolted against the mean tyranny. But where could I turn for protection? No matter whether the slave girl be black as ebony or as fair as her mistress. In either case, there is no shadow of law to protect her from insult, from violence, or even from death; all these are inflicted by fiends who bear the shape of men. The mistress, who ought to protect the helpless victim, has no other feelings towards her but those of jealousy and rage. The degradation, the wrongs, the vices, that grow out of slavery, are more than I can describe. They are greater than you would willingly believe. Surely, if you credited one half the truths that are told you concerning the helpless millions suffering in this cruel bondage, you at the north would not help to tighten the yoke. You surely would refuse to do for the master, on your own soil, the mean and cruel work which trained bloodhounds and the lowest class of whites do for him at the south.

Everywhere the years bring to all enough of sin and sorrow; but in slavery the very dawn of life is darkened by these shadows. Even the little child, who is accustomed to wait on her mistress and her children, will learn, before she is twelve years old, why it is that her mistress hates such and such a one among the slaves. Perhaps the child's own mother is among those hated ones. She listens to violent outbreaks of jealous passion, and cannot help understanding what is the cause. She will become prematurely knowing in evil things. Soon she will learn to tremble when she hears her master's footfall. She will be compelled to realize that she is no longer a child. If God has bestowed beauty upon her, it will prove her greatest curse. That which commands admiration in the white woman only hastens the degradation of the female slave. I know that some are too much brutalized by slavery to feel the humiliation of their position; but many slaves feel it most acutely, and shrink from the memory of it. I cannot tell how much I suffered in the presence of these wrongs, nor how I am still pained by the retrospect. My master met me at every turn, reminding me that I belonged to him, and swearing by heaven and earth that he would compel me to submit to him. If I went out for a breath of fresh air, after a day of unwearied toil, his footsteps dogged me. If I knelt by my mother's grave, his dark shadow fell on me even there. The light heart which nature had given me became heavy with sad forebodings. The other slaves in my master's house noticed the change. Many of them pitied me; but none dared to ask the cause. They had no need to inquire. They knew too well the guilty practices under that roof; and they were aware that to speak of them was an offence that never went unpunished.

I longed for someone to confide in. I would have given the world to have laid my head on my grandmother's faithful bosom, and told her all my troubles. But Dr. Flint swore he would kill me, if I was not as silent as the grave. Then, although my grandmother was all in all to me, I feared her as well as loved her. I had been accustomed to look up to her with a respect bordering upon awe. I was very young, and felt shamefaced about telling her such impure things, especially as I knew her to be very strict on such subjects. Moreover, she was a woman of a high spirit. She was usually very quiet in her demeanor; but if her indignation was once roused, it was not very easily quelled. I had been told that she once chased a white gentleman with a loaded pistol, because he insulted one of her daughters. I dreaded the consequences of a violent outbreak; and both pride and fear kept me silent. But though I did not confide in my grandmother, and even evaded her vigilant watchfulness and inquiry, her presence in the neighborhood was some protection to me. Though she had been a slave, Dr. Flint was afraid of her. He dreaded her scorching rebukes. Moreover, she was known and patronized by many people; and he did not wish to have his villainy made public. It was lucky for me that I did not live on a distant plantation, but in a town not so large that the inhabitants were ignorant of each other's affairs. Bad as are the laws and customs in a slaveholding community, the doctor, as a professional man, deemed it prudent to keep up some outward show of decency.

Oh, what days and nights of fear and sorrow that man caused me! Reader, it is not to awaken sympathy for myself that I am telling you truthfully what I suffered in slavery. I do it to kindle a flame of compassion in your hearts for my sisters who are still in bondage, suffering as I once suffered.

I once saw two beautiful children playing together. One was a fair white child; the other was her slave, and also her sister. When I saw them embracing each other, and heard their joyous laughter, I turned sadly away from the lovely sight. I foresaw the inevitable blight that would fall on the little slave's heart. I knew how soon her laughter would be changed to sighs. The fair child grew up to be a still fairer women. From childhood to womanhood her pathway was blooming with flowers, and overarched by a sunny sky. Scarcely one day of her life had been clouded when the sun rose on her happy bridal morning.

How had those years dealt with her slave sister, the little playmate of her childhood? She, also, was very beautiful; but the flowers and sunshine of love were not for her. She drank the cup of sin, and shame, and misery, whereof her persecuted race are compelled to drink.

In view of these things, why are ye silent, ye free men and women of the north? Why do your tongues falter in maintenance of the right? Would that I had more ability! But my heart is so full, and my pen is so weak! There are noble men and women who plead for us, striving to help those who cannot help themselves. God bless them! God give them strength and courage to go on! God bless those, everywhere, who are laboring to advance the cause of humanity!

I would ten thousand times rather that my children should be the half-starved paupers of Ireland than to be the most pampered among the slaves of America. I would rather drudge out my life on a cotton plantation, till the grave opened to give me rest, than to live with an unprincipled master and a jealous mistress. The felon's home in a penitentiary is preferable. He may repent, and turn from the error of his ways, and so find peace; but it is not so with a favorite slave. She is not allowed to have any pride of character. It is deemed a crime in her to wish to be virtuous.

Mrs. Flint possessed the key to her husband's character before I was born. She might have used this knowledge to counsel and to screen the young and the innocent among her slaves; but for them she had no sympathy. They were the objects of her constant suspicion and malevolence. She watched her husband with unceasing vigilance; but he was well practiced in means to evade it. What he could not find opportunity to say in words he manifested in signs. He invented more than were ever thought of in a deaf and dumb asylum. I let them pass, as if I did not understand what he meant; and many were the curses and threats bestowed on me for my stupidity. One day he caught me teaching myself to write. He frowned, as if he was not well pleased; but I suppose he came to the conclusion that such an accomplishment might help to advance his favorite scheme. Before long, notes were often slipped into my hand. I would return them, saying, "I can't read them, sir." "Can't you?" he replied; "then I must read them to you." He always finished the reading by asking, "Do you understand?" Sometimes he would complain of the heat of the tea room, and order his supper to be placed on a small table in the piazza. He would seat himself there with a well-satisfied smile, and tell me to stand by and brush away the flies. He would eat very slowly, pausing between the mouthfuls. These intervals were employed in describing the happiness I was so foolishly throwing away, and in threatening me with the penalty that finally awaited my stubborn disobedience. He boasted much of the forbearance he had exercised towards me, and reminded me that there was a limit to his patience. When I succeeded in avoiding opportunities for him to talk to me at home, I was ordered to come to his office, to do some errand. When there, I was obliged to stand and listen to such language as he saw fit to address to me. Sometimes I so openly expressed my contempt for him that he would become violently enraged, and I wondered why he did not strike me. Circumstanced as he was, he probably thought it was better policy to be forbearing. But the state of things grew worse and worse daily. In desperation I told him that I must and would apply to my grandmother for protection. He threatened me with death, and worse than death, if I made any complaint to her. Strange to say, I did not despair. I was naturally of a buoyant disposition, and always I had a hope of somehow getting out of his clutches. Like many a poor, simple slave before me, I trusted that some threads of joy would yet be woven into my dark destiny.

I had entered my sixteenth year, and every day it became more apparent that my presence was intolerable to Mrs. Flint. Angry words frequently passed between her and her husband. He had never punished me himself, and he would not allow anybody else to punish me. In that respect, she was never satisfied; but, in her angry moods, no terms were too vile for her to bestow upon me. Yet, I, whom she detested so bitterly, had far more pity for her than he had, whose duty it was to make her life happy. I never wronged her, or wished to wrong her; and one word of kindness from her would have brought me to her feet.

After repeated quarrels between the doctor and his wife, he announced his intention to take his youngest daughter, then four years old, to sleep in his apartment. It was necessary that a servant should sleep in the same room, to be on hand if the child stirred. I was selected for that office, and informed for what purpose that arrangement had been made. By managing to keep within sight of people, as much as possible, during the day time, I had hitherto succeeded in eluding my master, though a razor was often held to my throat to force me to change this line of policy. At night I slept by the side of my great aunt, where I felt safe. He was too prudent to come into her room. She was an old woman, and had been in the family many years. Moreover, as a married man, and a professional man, he deemed it necessary to save appearances in some degree. But he resolved to remove the obstacle in the way of his scheme; and he thought he had planned it so that he should evade suspicion. He was well aware how much I prized my refuge by the side of my old aunt, and he determined to dispossess me of it. The first night the doctor had the little child in his room alone. The next morning, I was ordered to take my station as nurse the following night. A kind Providence interposed in my favor. During the day Mrs. Flint heard of this new arrangement, and a storm followed. I rejoiced to hear it rage.

After a while my mistress sent for me to come to her room. Her first question was, "Did you know you were to sleep in the doctor's room?"

"Yes, ma'am."

"Who told you?"

"My master."

"Will you answer truly all the questions I ask?"

"Yes, ma'am."

"Tell me, then, as you hope to be forgiven, are you innocent of what I have accused you?"

"I am."

She handed me a Bible, and said, "Lay your hand on your heart, kiss this holy book, and swear before God that you tell me the truth."

I took the oath she required, and I did it with a clear conscience.

"You have taken God's holy word to testify your innocence," said she. "If you have deceived me, beware! Now take this stool, sit down, look me directly in the face, and tell me all that has passed between your master and you."

I did as she ordered. As I went on with my account her color changed frequently, she wept, and sometimes groaned. She spoke in tones so sad, that I was touched by her grief. The tears came to my eyes; but I was soon convinced that her emotions arose from anger and wounded pride. She felt that her marriage vows were desecrated, her dignity insulted; but she had no compassion for the poor victim of her husband's perfidy. She pitied herself as a martyr; but she was incapable of feeling for the condition of shame and misery in which her unfortunate, helpless slave was placed.

Yet perhaps she had some touch of feeling for me; for when the conference was ended, she spoke kindly, and promised to protect me. I should have been much comforted by this assurance if I could have had confidence in it; but my experiences in slavery had filled me with distrust. She was not a very refined woman, and had not much control over her passions. I was an object of her jealousy, and, consequently, of her hatred; and I knew I could not expect kindness or confidence from her under the circumstances in which I was placed. I could not blame her. Slaveholders' wives feel as other women would under similar circumstances. The fire of her temper kindled from small sparks, and now the flame became so intense that the doctor was obliged to give up his intended arrangement.

I knew I had ignited the torch, and I expected to suffer for it afterwards; but I felt too thankful to my mistress for the timely aid she rendered me to care much about that. She now took me to sleep in a room adjoining her own. There I was an object of her especial care, though not of her especial comfort, for she spent many a sleepless night to watch over me. Sometimes I woke up, and found her bending over me. At other times she whispered in my ear, as though it was her husband who was speaking to me, and listened to hear what I would answer. If she startled me, on such occasions, she would glide stealthily away; and the next morning she would tell me I had been talking in my sleep, and ask who I was talking to. At last, I began to be fearful for my life. It had been often threatened; and you can imagine, better than I can describe, what an unpleasant sensation it must produce to wake up in the dead of night and find a jealous woman bending over you. Terrible as this experience was, I had fears that it would give place to one more terrible.

My mistress grew weary of her vigils; they did not prove satisfactory. She changed her tactics. She now tried the trick of accusing my master of crime, in my presence, and gave my name as the author of the accusation. To my utter astonishment, he replied, "I don't believe it: but if she did acknowledge it, you tortured her into exposing me." Tortured into exposing him! Truly, Satan had no difficulty in distinguishing the color of his soul! I understood his object in making this false representation. It was to show me that I gained nothing by seeking the protection of my mistress; that the power was still all in his own hands. I pitied Mrs. Flint. She was a second wife, many years the junior of her husband; and the hoary-headed miscreant was enough to try the patience of a wiser and better woman. She was completely foiled, and knew not how to proceed. She would gladly have had me flogged for my supposed false oath; but, as I have already stated, the doctor never allowed anyone to whip me. The old sinner was politic. The application of the lash might have led to remarks that would have exposed him in the eyes of his children and grandchildren. How often did I rejoice that I lived in a town where all the inhabitants knew each other! If I had been on a remote plantation, or lost among the multitude of a crowded city, I should not be a living woman at this day.

The secrets of slavery are concealed like those of the Inquisition. My master was, to my knowledge, the father of eleven slaves. But did the mothers dare to tell who was the father of their children? Did the other slaves dare to allude to it, except in whispers among themselves? No, indeed! They knew too well the terrible consequences.

My grandmother could not avoid seeing things which excited her suspicions. She was uneasy about me, and tried various ways to buy me; but the never changing answer was always repeated: "Linda does not belong to *me*. She is my daughter's property, and I have no legal right to sell her." The conscientious man! He was too scrupulous to *sell* me; but he had no scruples whatever about committing a much greater wrong against the helpless young girl placed under his guardianship, as his daughter's property. Sometimes my persecutor would ask me whether I would like to be sold. I told him I would rather be sold to any body than to lead such a life as I did. On such occasions he would assume the air of a very injured individual, and reproach me for my ingratitude. "Did I not take you into the house, and make you the companion of my own children?" he would say. "Have I ever treated you like a negro? I have never allowed you to be punished, not even to please your mistress. And this is the recompense I get, you ungrateful girl!" I answered that he had reasons of his own for screening me from punishment, and that the course he pursued made my mistress hate me and persecute me. If I wept, he would say, "Poor child! Don't cry! don't cry! I will make peace for you with your mistress. Only let me arrange matters in my own way. Poor, foolish girl! You don't know what is for your own good. I would cherish you. I would make a lady of you. Now go, and think of all I have promised you."

I did think of it.

Reader, I draw no imaginary pictures of southern homes. I am telling you the plain truth. Yet when victims make their escape from this wild beast of Slavery, northerners consent to act the part of blood-hounds, and hunt the poor fugitive back into his den, "full of dead men's bones, and all uncleanness." Nay, more, they are not only willing, but proud, to give their daughters in marriage to slaveholders. The poor girls have romantic notions of a sunny clime, and of the flowering vines that all the year round shade a happy home. To what disappointments are they destined! The young wife soon learns that the husband in whose hands she has placed her happiness pays no regard to his marriage vows. Children of every shade of complexion play with her own fair babies, and too well she knows that they are born unto him of his own household. Jealousy and hatred enter the flowery home, and it is ravaged of its loveliness.

Southern women often marry a man knowing that he is the father of many little slaves. They do not trouble themselves about it. They regard such children as property, as marketable as the pigs on the plantation; and it is seldom that they do not make them aware of this by passing them into the slavetrader's hands as soon as possible, and thus getting them out of their sight. I am glad to say there are some honorable exceptions.

I have myself known two southern wives who exhorted their husbands to free those slaves towards whom they stood in a "parental relation;" and their request was granted. These husbands blushed before the superior nobleness of their wives' natures. Though they had only counselled them to do that which it was their duty to do, it commanded their respect, and rendered their conduct more exemplary. Concealment was at an end, and confidence took the place of distrust.

Though this bad institution deadens the moral sense, even in white women, to a fearful extent, it is not altogether extinct. I have heard southern ladies say of Mr. Such a one, "He not only thinks it no disgrace to be the father of those little niggers, but he is not ashamed to call himself their master. I declare, such things ought not to be tolerated in any decent society!"

Notes and Questions

1. For a description of private law doctrine and the connection between sexual relationships, transfers of wealth, and legal personality under the regime of slavery, see Adrienne D. Davis, *The Private Law of Race and Sex: An Antebellum Perspective*, 51 Stan. L. Rev. 221 (1999). Elsewhere, Davis comments:

> The story of the planter who boasted of creating his entire plantation workforce of 50 to 60 from the issue of one enslaved woman "in the course of the lifetime of the original producers" leads one, inevitably, to speculate about how slave women must have felt to see themselves used as a return on capital, a means of reproduction, to see their children born into slavery, children they may well not have wanted, often fathered by rape or legitimized coercion. Under such circumstances, what does one do? To love, or not to love? To abort, to suicide, to poison, to murder? What would any of us do? And, for the final horror, the cycle would then repeat itself; imagine living to see your own enslaved grandchildren begin to repeat the whole evil process once more. I do not make this point to claim a winning ticket in the [oppression sweepstakes]; black men, too, suffered under such a system—both as parents and as children. There was brutality and oppression enough for all. Still, the mutable identity of enslaved women under the antebellum sexual economy—producers of both labor and capital, female breeding stock when convenient, "male" laborers when not—offers its own particular set of twists on slavery, twists that seem vital to an understanding of the whole.

Adrienne D. Davis, *The "Sexual Economy" of American Slavery*.

2. For a description of the implications of past and present property interests in women's bodies and fetuses, see Patricia J. Williams, *Fetal Fictions: An Exploration of Property Archetypes in Racial and Gendered Contexts*, 42 Fla. L. Rev. 81 (1990).

STORY v. STATE

59 So. 480, 178 Ala. 98 (1912).

McCLELLAN, J.

The indictment contained two counts; the first charging rape of Beatrice McClure, and the second charging the violation of the following penal statute (Code, § 7698): "Carnal knowledge of women by administering drug, etc.—Any person who has carnal knowledge of any woman above fourteen years of age, without her consent, by administering to her any drug or other substance which produces such stupor, imbecility of mind, or weakness of body, as to prevent effectual resistance, must, on conviction, be punished at the discretion of the jury, by death or by imprisonment in the penitentiary for not less than ten years." The conviction was under the second count only. * * *

In prosecutions for rape, and in kindred proceedings, where nonconsent is an element of the offense, in which the chastity of a woman may be brought into question, the character of the woman for chastity may be impeached; but this is usually done by evidence of her reputation in that respect, and not by proof of particular acts of unchastity. In other jurisdictions the rule is different; the courts holding that the substantive fact of unchastity may be shown, not only by general reputation therefor, but by evidence of particular acts. The view to which this court long ago gave its approval, as stated, found its chief support in 3 Green. on Evi. § 214, where that learned author said: "The character of the prosecutrix for chastity may also be impeached; but this must be done by general evidence of her reputation in that respect, and not by evidence of particular instances of unchastity. Nor can she be interrogated as to a criminal connection with any other person, except as to her previous intercourse with the prisoner himself; nor is such evidence of other instances admissible."

We are not disposed to enter, at this late day, upon a reinvestigation of the soundness of the general rule thus accepted by this court. The theory of the rule is that the essential (to the offense) fact of nonconsent of the woman to intercourse with the defendant may be negatived by evidence of general reputation for unchastity—a condition that argues the consent of the woman to meretricious intercourse with the defendant.

The woman here confessed that she had, for some time, pursued the vocation of a prostitute. She is a woman of the Caucasian race. The defendant is a negro. The defendant sought to show that the woman bore the reputation of having practiced her lewdness with negroes; and, also, that on one occasion in a neighboring state she was caught in bed with a negro other than the defendant. The court disallowed both characters of this evidence; evidently, in consequence of the application of the rule which we have stated as long prevailing in this state. * * * With respect to the stated effort to show particular conduct of the woman in a neighboring state, there can be, under the prevailing rule, no doubt of the correctness of the court's action. With respect to the matter of her reputation for prostitution among negroes, we have, after full consideration, reached a different conclusion. We think the proffered testimony to that effect should have been received.

As affecting the credibility of a witness, evidence in chief may be taken of the general character of the witness; but, while the notorious want of chastity in a female would of course blight her reputation and destroy confidence in her virtue in any respect, yet her general reputation for unchastity cannot be inquired into in order to reflect upon her credibility as a witness; for that would result in the original investigation of the cause of her repute, which is not permissible. So, the admissibility of the testimony now under consideration is to be referred to its office tending to negative the nonconsent of the woman to meretricious intercourse with the defendant (if such there was), and not to an effect reflecting upon her credibility as a witness.

The social status, as respects the white race and the negro race, in this state is universally known. The general relation of the races, each toward the other, is kind and cordial to a most marked and gratifying degree; and the impulse the dominant race manifests toward the inferior race is that of a commendable guardianship and abundant generosity, inspired by motives not only of fundamental justice but of sentiment engendered by the earlier legal dependence and subjection of the slave to the master. While this honorable condition is obvious and prevails, yet the social relation and practices of the races have, in the interest of our civilization as well as in expression of the natural pride of the dominant Anglo–Saxon race and of its preservation from the degeneration social equality, between the races, would inevitably bring, imperatively necessitated and created immutable rules of social conduct and social restraint, that the just ends indicated might be attained and permanently maintained. Since the fundamental, initial suggestion of the social separation of the races is conceived in nature and is nurtured by a social pride and self-respect that only ignorance or unholy purpose can question or assail, it was and is the natural result that laws should be enacted promotive of the social purpose of the dominant race. Among these are: The inhibition against the authorization or legalization of marriage between any white person and a negro, or the descendant of a negro (Const. §§ 102, 182); the penal prohibition of marriage between these races (Code, §§ 7421, 7422); and the statute-imposed separation of the races in public schools and in the cars of carriers of passengers in this state (Code, §§ 1757, 5487). The civilization adhering to and fostering such purposes visits upon those who practice immoral conduct, across the barrier, between these races, a severer condemnation than is visited upon those who, of the same race, practice a like moral violation. Whether such a distinction, in the two cases, is morally tenable, is not a question of presently important concern in the matter under consideration. It is the fact of the severer condemnation in the one case than in the other of which in the administration of justice we feel constrained to take account, and not of its justification, morally or otherwise. From this status of social relation between the races—the civilization in which we live—we know, as all do, that a universal public opinion, prevalent in both races, recognizes at least two grades of depravity among those women of the white race who make commerce of their virtue. Deeply depraved as are those white women who practice prostitution among members of their own race, those few white women (if such there be) who may practice their lewdness among negroes are yet lower in the scale of depravity—are yet beneath those who entirely forfeit respect by the barter of their very characters. Reclamation may be made of one; but, for the other, there is little, if any, hope. It is inevitable from this fact that, though a white woman be a prostitute, the presumption is strong, nearly conclusive, among both the races, that she will not yield—has not yielded—even in her confirmed depravity, to commerce with a negro charged with an offense against her person. The consensus of public opinion, unrestricted to either race, is that a white woman prostitute is yet, though lost of virtue, above the even greater sacrifice of the voluntary submission of her person to the embraces of the other race.

This leads us to the conclusion that the reputation of a white woman for unchastity, in cases where her nonconsent to the meretricious intercourse is essential to the inquiry of guilt laid against one of the negro race, does not comprehend a reputation for the practice of her lewdness with members of the negro race. That practice, if sufficient to invite a reputation therefor, affords the basis of a reputation for a character of unchastity distinct from that afforded by prostitution among members of the prostitute's own race. And if such a reputation, for that character and degree of prostitution, is found to exist, the natural and legitimate effect is to negative the prevalent notion that the white woman has not voluntarily yielded to the embraces of the accused negro.

There was therefore prejudicial error in declining to allow the defendant to submit to the jury, for their consideration on the issue of nonconsent, imported in the charge stated in the second count, the proffered testimony of witnesses called to show (if qualified to that end) that Beatrice McClure, a white woman, had the reputation of having practiced her prostitution among members of the negro race.

* * *

For the error indicated, the judgment is reversed, and the cause is remanded.

Notes and Questions

1. *Story v. State* illustrates how a white woman's nonconsent to intercourse may be proven by the blackness of the defendant. But when the rape victim is a black woman, consent to intercourse has been implied from the blackness of the victim. Jennifer Wriggins explains the historic background for this treatment:

The legal system [during slavery] rendered the rape of Black women by any man, white or Black, invisible. The rape of a Black woman was not a crime. In 1859 the Mississippi Supreme Court dismissed the indictment of a male slave for the rape of a female slave less than 10 years old, saying:

[T]his indictment can not be sustained, either at common law or under our statutes. It charges no offense known to either system. [Slavery] was unknown to the common law * * * and hence its provisions are inapplicable. * * * There is no act (of our legislature on this subject) which embraces either the attempted or actual commission of a rape by a slave on a female slave. * * * Masters and slaves can not be governed by the same system or laws; so different are their positions, rights and duties.

This decision is illuminating in several respects. First, Black men are held to lesser standards of sexual restraint with Black women than are white men with white women. Second, white men are held to lesser standards of restraint with Black women than are Black men with white women. Neither white nor Black men were expected to show sexual restraint with Black women. * * *

The legal system's denial that Black women experienced sexual abuse by both white and Black men also persisted [after the Civil War], although statutes had been made race-neutral. Even if a Black victim's case went to trial—in itself highly unlikely—procedural barriers and prejudice against Black women protected any man accused of rape or attempted rape. The racist rule which facilitated prosecutions of Black offender/white victim attempted rapes by allowing the jury to consider the defendant's race as evidence of his intent, for instance, was not applied where both persons were "of color and there was no evidence of their social standing." That is the fact that a defendant was Black was considered relevant only to prove intent to rape a white woman; it was not relevant to prove intent to rape a Black woman. By using disparate procedures, the court implicitly makes two assertions. First, Black men do not want to rape Black women with the same intensity or regularity that Black men want to rape white women. Second, Black women do not experience coerced sex in the sense that white women experience it. * * *

The criminal justice system continues to take the rape of Black women less seriously than the rape of white women. Studies show that judges generally impose harsher sentences for rape when the victim is white than when the victim is Black. * * *

Evidence concerning police behavior also documents the fact that the claims of Black rape victims are taken less seriously than those of whites. A 1968 study of Philadelphia police processing decisions concluded that the differential in police decisions to charge for rape "resulted primarily from a lack of confidence in the veracity of Black complainants and a belief in the myth of Black promiscuity."

The thorough denial of Black women's experiences of rape by the legal system is especially shocking in light of the fact that Black women are much more likely to be victims of rape than are white women. Based on data from national surveys of rape victims, "the profile of the most frequent rape victim is a young woman, divorced or separated, Black and poverty stricken."

Jennifer Wriggins, *Rape, Racism, and the Law*, 6 Harv. Women's L.J. 103, 118–122 (1983).*

DARREN LENARD HUTCHINSON
Out Yet Unseen: A Racial Critique of Gay and Lesbian Legal Theory and Political Discourse
29 Conn. L. Rev. 561, 562, 575–83 (1997).**

In the poem *Tongues Untied,* Marlon T. Riggs, a black gay filmmaker and writer, recounts childhood confrontations with racism and homophobia. Riggs remembers being labelled a "nigger" and excluded by white students at Hepzibah Junior High in Augusta, Georgia, where he was "bused" at age twelve, and being called a "homo" by the older brother of a childhood friend. Through these "coming-of-age" experiences, a young Riggs learns to "[dis]claim" his marginalized racial and sexual statuses: He hides "deep inside [him]self where it is still. Silent, safe. * * * "

While living in the largely white gay and lesbian community of San Francisco, an adult Riggs begins to acknowledge his gay identity. Riggs, however, tries to ignore the "absence of black images" in the "Castro" or the fact that the "few" existing images—"joke, fetish, cartoon, caricature or disco diva adored from a distance"—affirm racial hierarchy. Nevertheless, Riggs eventually learns that in the Castro, he is "an alien, unseen, and seen, unwanted."

The turning point in the poem—and in Riggs' life—occurs when, after persistent introspection and reclaiming of suppressed racial identity, Riggs escapes "delusion, pain, alienation, [and] silence"—and integrates (instead of treating as separate) his black and gay identities. Thus, at the poem's conclusion, the knots of silence and invisibility caused by interlocking racism and homophobia are "untied."

The symbolic meaning of the phrase "tongues untied" has grown to identify a small, yet expanding, cultural, intellectual, and artistic "movement" aimed at revealing—or ending the silence around—the interactions of race, class, gender, and sexuality. * * *

[Eds. The author seeks "to demonstrate the ready interplay between race, class, and sexual subordination—or the multidimensionality of oppression."]

One final illustration of the multidimensional nature of oppression is provided by the case of Jeffrey Dahmer. In July 1991 Dahmer, a young white male, confessed to police that he had killed and dismembered seventeen males in his Milwaukee apartment.[62] Most of Dahmer's victims were black gay men. Dahmer lived in an economically depressed neighborhood. Like [Julio] Rivera and Venus Xtravaganza, many of Dahmer's victims were lured to their deaths by promises of money for sexual favors, namely, posing nude for photographs.

Dahmer's confession stunned the nation. Perhaps more surprising than the murders, however, was the revelation that three white police officers had once (prior to Dahmer's confession) responded to emergency calls by Dahmer's neighbors—two black women—and found fourteen year-old Konerak Sinthasomphone, a Laotian youth, drugged, naked, bleeding, and fleeing Dahmer's apartment. Despite the imperiled condition in which they found Konerak, two of the officers returned him to the apartment after Dahmer convinced them that he and Konerak were "lovers involved in a spat." When the officers returned to the police station, they described the case as a "boy-boy" incident and joked that they needed "de-lousing." The officers also failed to enter Dahmer's name into police computers or file an official report of the incident. Dahmer killed Konerak after the police left. Subsequent to Dahmer's confession, it was revealed that he had previously been convicted of molesting an older brother of Konerak in 1988. Had the police officers conducted a computer search of Dahmer's name, they would have discovered his prior molestation conviction. The police inaction impli-

62. See *Sinthasomphone v. Milwaukee*, 838 F. Supp. 1320, 1321–22 (E.D.Wis.1993). On November 28, 1994, while serving fifteen consecutive life sentences for the murders, Dahmer was beaten to death by a fellow inmate. See Don Terry, *Jeffrey Dahmer, Multiple Killer, Is Bludgeoned to Death in Prison*, N.Y. Times, Nov. 29, 1994, at A1.

cates a combination of racial, class, gender, and sexual subordination issues.

The police officers dismissed the concerns of the two poor black women who reported their fear that a "child [was] being raped and molested by [Dahmer]." Instead, one officer tried to assure the women that "it wasn't a child, it was an adult * * * I can't do anything about somebody's sexual preferences in life." An officer also threatened to arrest one of the black women if she persisted in seeking help for Konerak. Finally, the officers turned away an ambulance crew that arrived on the scene—although one of the paramedics concluded that Konerak needed medical treatment.

Thus, the police ignored Konerak's obvious injuries, denied him necessary medical care, portrayed the incident pejoratively, dismissed the black women, and accepted Dahmer's characterization of the horrible scene they discovered as a lovers' quarrel. Furthermore, the officers apparently believed that violence, drugs, and dramatic differences in age are common features of "boy-boy" relationships—a patently homophobic conclusion. The officers may have also acted on racist stereotypes of Asian men as effeminate—thus "homosexual"—when they "read" the scene as a domestic dispute.

In response to the officers' egregious conduct, Konerak's estate and several of his family members have filed a lawsuit against the officers and the City of Milwaukee under Title 42 U.S.C.A. § 1983 (Section 1983). The complaint alleges that the officers' failure to provide protection for Konerak resulted from discrimination on the basis of race and sexual orientation in violation of the Equal Protection Clause of the Fourteenth Amendment of the United States Constitution. The complaint also alleges that the City of Milwaukee maintained a policy or custom of discrimination against people of color and sexual minorities, pursuant to which the officers acted. Thus, this litigation is one of the few reported discrimination cases brought by actual or perceived as gay or lesbian people of color, in which the racially and sexually subordinate statuses of the plaintiff is mentioned in the opinion. It is also the only reported case in which the court found as "factually viable" a multidimensional claim of sexual and racial discrimination. Therefore, although the case overall lacks controversy and any particularly groundbreaking judicial analysis, it nevertheless merits some attention in this article.

After conducting discovery, the officers and the City of Milwaukee moved for summary judgment, but the court denied both of these motions. In the affidavits accompanying their motion, the officers disputed that they acted with discriminatory intent. The court, however, held that the undisputed facts would permit a jury to infer that they acted with discriminatory intent. Discriminatory intent may be shown with direct or indirect evidence. In this case, the officers' intent, as in most discrimination cases, is subject to proof by circumstantial evidence. Because plaintiffs' discrimination claim requires proof of the officers' intent or motive through inferences from the surrounding—and compelling—evidence of bias, the claim does not lend itself to summary judgment. Thus, the court appropriately denied the officers' motion.

The City of Milwaukee moved for summary judgment on the grounds that in 1991—the same year Konerak was murdered—it allegedly implemented official measures to correct any problems of bias within its police department. The City of Milwaukee thus argued that the only relevant evidence for determining whether it has a policy of discrimination was its conduct subsequent to 1991 and that this evidence demonstrated that no such policy existed. The court rejected this argument and held that the police department's pre–1991 history of discrimination was relevant for determining whether the City of Milwaukee had an unwritten "policy" of discrimination against people of color and gays and lesbians at the time of Konerak's death. The court's ruling is consistent with legal precedent. As the Supreme Court has held, a custom or policy of discrimination may arise in the Section 1983 context when "practices of state officials could well be so permanent and well settled as to constitute a 'custom or usage' with the force of law." Thus, evidence of the department's pre–1991 history is necessary for the trier of fact to determine whether the police department had been engaging in a pattern of discriminatory practices at the time the officers returned Konerak to Dahmer's apartment and whether these practices were "so permanent and well settled" so as to carry "the force of law."

The court's rulings regarding the factual viability of plaintiffs' discrimination claims are consistent with my argument that both racial and sexual subordination informed the police's improper response to Konerak's subjugation. This case also demonstrates that multidimensionality need not remain exclusively a creature of legal scholarship, but that it may (and should) influence civil rights cases brought to remedy acts of discrimination.

One final aspect of the Dahmer tragedy merits attention. The officers' racial and sexual bias not only subordinated Konerak but also privileged Dahmer. Affirming racial privilege, the officers accorded Dahmer deference and credibility—allowing him to settle his "spat" alone. Thus, the police subjected Konerak to further "domestic abuse." Dahmer, meanwhile, negotiated a favorable resolution, from his perspective, of the encounter. He maintained dominion over his home and Konerak, who in this context becomes his sexual property (read "it"). The efforts of Konerak and the black women, on the other hand, proved unavailing. Their attempts to secure protection were met with threats, disregard, slurs, jokes, and inaction.

[The Dahmer tragedy illustrates] racial, class, and sexual subordination are interrelated. Several of these forces may contribute to a single act of discrimination, as * * * the police behavior in the * * * [Dahmer tragedy reveals]. These sources of disempowerment may also combine to limit an individual's life choices, as the short lives of * * * the Dahmer victims demonstrate. Moreover, because race and class also create privilege, these statuses may offer some insulation from forces of oppression. For instance, the police deferred to Dahmer, who was white (and male), although they believed he was gay.

Notes and Questions

1.   Hutchinson's article contains the following footnote:

During the completion of this article, the City of Milwaukee settled the suit with Konerak's estate and family, agreeing to pay them $850,000. See *Milwaukee to Pay $850,000 to Family of Dahmer Victim*, Wash. Post, Apr. 26, 1995, at A6. In a final show of "diplomacy" toward the Sinthasomphone family, the County of Milwaukee, upon discovering the terms of the settlement, asked Konerak's family to repay $65,000 (of a total of $106,368) in welfare benefits the family received during the past ten years. See *Give Back Welfare, County Tells Family*, Wis. St. J., Apr. 27, 1995, at 3B. A "county spokesman" stated that such demands are routinely made when families receive "windfalls" from other sources. See *id.*

Hutchinson, *supra* at n. 95.

2.   Hutchinson's notion of "multidimensionality" is echoed in the work of many scholars who identify themselves with critical race theory or critical race feminism. For example, Kimberlé Williams Crenshaw notes that "many of the experiences black women face are not subsumed within the traditional boundaries of race or gender discrimination as these boundaries are currently understood, and * * * the intersection of racism and sexism factors into black women's lives in ways that cannot be captured wholly by looking separately at the race or gender dimensions of those experiences." Kimberlé Williams Crenshaw, *Mapping the Margins: Intersectionality, Identity Politics, and Violence Against Women of Color,* in *Critical Race Theory: The Key Writings That Formed The Movement* 358 (Kimberlé Crenshaw, Neil Gotanda, Gary Peller & Kendall Thomas eds. 1995). Similarly, Mari Matsuda asks political activists and theorists to "ask the other question": "When I see something that looks racist, I ask, 'Where is the patriarchy in this?' When I see something that looks sexist, I ask, 'Where is the heterosexism in this?' When I see something that looks homophobic, I ask, 'Where are the class interests in this?' Working in coalition forces us to look for both the obvious and non-obvious relationships of domination, helping us to realize that no form of subordination ever stands alone." Mari J. Matsuda, *Beside My Sister, Facing the Enemy: Legal Theory Out of Coalition,* 43 Stan. L. Rev. 1183, 1189 (1991). See also Peter Kwan, *Jeffrey Dahmer and the Cosynthesis of Categories,* 48 Hastings L.J. 1257 (1997). See generally *Critical Race Feminism: A Reader* (Adrien K. Wing ed. 1997).

Where is the racism, sexism, and homophobia in the story Hutchinson tells about Dahmer? What can we learn about the relation among race, gender, and sexual orientation from the treatment of each of the participants in this tragedy?

3.   For the argument that "one of the most urgent tasks of gay and lesbian African Americans is to demand the inclusion of black sexual freedom on the antiracist agenda," see Kendall Thomas, *"Ain't Nothin' Like the Real Thing": Black Masculinity, Gay Sexuality, and the Jargon of Authenticity,* in *Representing Black Men* 55 (Marcellus Blount & George P. Cunningham eds. 1996).

4.   For a critique of traditional discrimination analysis and feminist theory for its failure to take adequate account of discrimination against gays

and lesbians, see Elvia R. Arriola, *Gendered Inequality: Lesbians, Gays and Feminist Legal Theory*, 9 Berkeley Women's L.J. 103 (1994).

CATHARINE A. MACKINNON

Crimes of War, Crimes of Peace
in *On Human Rights: The Oxford Amnesty Lectures 1993*
83–109 (S. Shute and S. Hurley eds. 1993).*

Women are violated in many ways that men are not, or rarely are; many of these violations are sexual and reproductive. Ranging from objectification to killing, from dehumanization and defilement to mutilation and torture to sexual murder, this abuse occurs in forms and settings and legal postures that overlap every recognized human rights convention but is addressed, effectively and as such, by none. What most often happens to women escapes the human rights net. Something—jurisdictional, evidentiary, substantive, customary, or habitual—is always wrong with it. Abuses of women as women rarely seem to fit what these laws and their enforcing bodies have in mind; the more abuses there are, the more they do not fit. Whether in war or in what is called peacetime, at home or abroad, in private or in public, by our side or the other side, man's inhumanity to woman is ignored.

Women's absence shapes human rights in substance and in form, effectively defining what a human and a right are. What does it mean to recognize a principle called human rights that does not really apply to the systemic and systematic violations of the dignity and integrity and security and life of over half the human race? It means that what violates the dignity of others is dignity for them; what violates the integrity of others is integrity for them; what violates the security of others is as much security as they are going to get. Even death to a full human being is less serious for them. Half of humanity is thus effectively defined as nonhuman, sub-human, properly rightsless creatures, beings whose reality of violation, to the extent it is somehow female, floats beneath international legal space.

For a compressed illustration of some current realities that are at once a hair's breadth and a gendered light-year away from the atrocities that ground human rights principles and fill the factual reports of Amnesty International, consider this communication from a researcher of Croatian descent gathering information in Croatia and Bosnia–Herzegovina:

> Serbian forces have exterminated over 200,000 Croatians and Muslims thus far in an operation they've coined "ethnic cleansing." In this genocide, in Bosnia–Herzegovina alone over 30,000 Muslim and Croatian girls and women are pregnant from mass rape. Of the 100 Serbian-run concentration camps, about 20 are solely rape/death camps for Muslim and Croatian women and children. * * * [There are] news reports and pictures here of Serbian tanks plastered with pornography * * * [and reports that those who] catch the eye of the

men looking at the pornography are killed. * * * Some massacres in villages as well as rapes and/or executions in camps are being videotaped as they're happening. One Croatian woman described being tortured by electroshocks and gang-raped in a camp by Serbian men dressed in Croatian uniforms who filmed the rapes and forced her to "confess" on film that Croatians raped her. In the streets of Zagreb, UN troops often ask local women how much they cost. * * * There are reports of refugee women being forced to sexually service them to receive aid. * * * Tomorrow I talk to two survivors of mass rape, thirty men per day for over three months * * *. The UN passed a resolution to collect evidence, a first step for a war crimes trial, but it is said there is no precedent for trying sexual atrocities. * * *

The war against Croatia and Bosnia–Herzegovina exemplifies how existing approaches to human rights can work to cover up and confuse who is doing what to whom and effectively condone atrocities. All state parties are apparently covered by most of the relevant international human rights guarantees and laws of war, certainly by customary international law. But nothing has yet been invoked to stop the abuses or to hold the perpetrators accountable. What is the problem? The fact of Serbian aggression is beyond question, just as the fact of male aggression against women is beyond question, here and everywhere. "Ethnic cleansing" is a Serbian policy of extermination of non-Serbs with the goal of "all Serbs in one nation," a "Greater Serbia" encompassing what was called Yugoslavia. Yet this genocidal war of aggression has repeatedly been construed as bilateral, a civil war or an ethnic conflict, to the accompaniment of much international wonderment that people cannot get along and pious clucking at the behavior of "all sides" reminiscent of blaming women for getting themselves raped by men they know. * * *

One result of this equalization of aggressor with aggressed-against is that these rapes are not grasped either as a strategy in genocide or as a practice of misogyny, far less as both at once, continuous at once with this ethnic war of aggression and with the gendered war of aggression of everyday life. This war is to everyday rape what the Holocaust was to everyday anti-Semitism. Muslim and Croatian women and girls are raped, then murdered, by Serbian military men, regulars and irregulars, in their homes, in rape/death camps, on hillsides, everywhere. Their corpses are raped as well. When this is noticed, it is either as genocide or as rape, or as femicide but not genocide, but not as rape as a form of genocide directed specifically at women. It is seen either as part of a campaign of Serbia against non-Serbia or an onslaught by combatants against civilians, but not an attack by men against women. Or, in the feminist whitewash, it becomes just another instance of aggression by all men against all women all the time, rather than what it is, which is rape by some men against certain women. The point seems to be to obscure, by any means available, exactly who is doing what to whom and why.

When the women survive, the rapes tend to be regarded as an inevitability of armed conflict, part of the war of all against all, or as a continuation of the hostilities of civil life, of all men against all women. Rape does occur in war among and between all sides; rape is a daily act by men against women and is always an act of domination by men over women. But the fact that these rapes are part of an ethnic war of extermination, being misrepresented as a civil war among equal aggressors, means that Muslim and Croatian women are facing twice as many rapists with twice as many excuses, two layers of men on top of them rather than one, and two layers of impunity serving to justify the rapes: just war and just life.

Notes and Questions

1. In *Kadic v. Karadzic*, 70 F.3d 232 (2d Cir.1995), *cert.* denied, 518 U.S. 1005 (1996), the Second Circuit permitted evidence of rapes arising out of the Bosnia conflict to serve as the basis for a genocide claim under international law.

2. Many feminists have argued that rape is a crime of violence against women. See Susan Brownmiller, *Against Our Will: Men, Women, and Rape* (1975). The previous excerpt shows how rape can be a genocidal crime as well. For an analysis of the distinction between rape as an example of everyday male dominance and sexual assault as "national security policy," see Margaret A. Baldwin, *Public Women and the Feminist State*, 20 Harv. Women's L.J. 47 (1997).

In her other writings, MacKinnon has argued that sexuality itself in Western culture is defined by the wants and needs of men, and that pornography plays a key role in constructing this domination-centered sexuality: "Along with the rape and prostitution in which it participates, pornography institutionalizes the sexuality of male supremacy, which fuses the erotization of dominance and submission with the social construction of male and female." See Catharine MacKinnon, *Not a Moral Issue*, in *Feminism Unmodified: Discourses on Life and Law* 148 (1987); see generally Catharine A. MacKinnon, *Only Words* (1993). To what extent might "the wants and needs of men" also be racialized? Are "the wants and needs" of *all* men incorporated into dominant Western sexual images, or only the wants and needs of some men? If the latter, which men?

3. Several human rights documents provide broad protection to individuals against discrimination. However, as MacKinnon suggests, it is questionable to what extent these documents protect against sex discrimination. Berta Hernández-Truyol notes:

> [H]uman rights instruments, including the UN charter, mandate non-discrimination on the basis of sex in their general nondiscrimination clauses. However, if one looks beyond those clauses to some of the substantive provisions granting specific rights, one finds, disturbingly, that some of the provisions exclude sex as the basis of protection. For example, while Article 2(1) of the International Covenant on Civil and Political Rights (ICCPR) mandates sex equality, Article 20 of the ICCPR provides that "any advocacy of national, racial or religious hatred that constitutes incitement to discrimination, hostility or violence shall be prohibited by law." On its face, Article 20 does not proscribe sex-based advocacy of hatred. Canons of construction—both domestic from contract law and international from the Vienna Convention on the Law of Treaties—provide that the general cedes to the specific. Therefore, the omission of sex from Article 20 signifies that the advocacy of sex-based "hatred that constitutes incitement to discrimination, hostility, or vio-

lence" is not proscribed. This interpretation suggests that sex-based violence—a global problem of such proportions that it succeeded in uniting women from the North and South, East and West, at the 1993 Human Rights Conference in Vienna in order to bring the subject to the forefront of the Human Rights meeting (a meeting that at the outset did not even include women on the agenda)—if bad at all, is not as bad as ethnic, race, or religion-based hatred. * * *

The hegemonic foundations of international human rights norms are further evident in the Race Convention's construction of sex, race, and racial power. This treaty contains a general nondiscrimination provision that includes sex. In its preambular message, moreover, it refers to a provision of the Universal Declaration [of Human Rights] that includes sex. Yet, somehow, the Race Convention manages to delete sex from the reference.

Berta Esperanza Hernández-Truyol, *Breaking Cycles of Inequality: Critical Theory, Human Rights, and the Family In/Justice.**

4. For the argument that minority female scholars must articulate their own "distinctive minority feminist jurisprudential stances," see Regina Austin, *Sapphire Bound!*, 1989 Wis. L. Rev. 539. For the argument that feminist legal theory must expand from a monocausal emphasis on gender and incorporate variables of race, ethnicity, and class, see Celina Romany, *Ain't I a Feminist?*, 4 Yale J.L. & Feminism 23 (1991).

ERIC T. BERKMAN

Note: *Responses to the International Child Sex Tourism Trade*
19 B.C. Int'l & Comp. L. Rev. 397, 401–03, 404–05 (1996).**

Each year, thousands of men from Western European consumer countries, as well as from consumer countries like the United States, New Zealand, and Australia, flock to Southeast Asia seeking young boys and girls to patronize what has become a lucrative child prostitution and pornography industry. In certain countries, the problem involves mature-looking teenaged girls who happen to be below the age of consent. Elsewhere, however, Western sex tourists specifically seek children younger than twelve, or even ten years of age. They do so for a variety of reasons. Among them are the beliefs that sex with children will give them longevity, and that sex with children will bring a lower risk of AIDS. Many others are simply attracted to children.

* * * Most of the countries where the child sex tourism trade occurs have laws prohibiting child prostitution and child pornography. Nonetheless, enforcement of these laws is generally very lax. * * *

In some instances, children take to the streets in an effort to support themselves, and perhaps their families, as street vendors, shoeshine boys, or in other "legitimate" jobs, and then turn to prostitution when they find they cannot survive on the income these jobs bring. These children range in age from under ten to their late teens.

* Reprinted by permission of the author.   ** Copyright © 1996 by the Boston College International & Comparative Law Review. Reprinted by permission.

Other children are essentially sold into prostitution by their parents. In these cases, children are generally turned over by their parents to recruiters in return for a cash advance, to be paid off by the child's labor. Frequently, parents do not know what kind of work their child is being "indentured" into. Parents often give up their child under the mistaken assumption that the child will be working in a legitimate capacity. Other parents, however, knowingly sell their children into prostitution, often in return for money to buy drugs.

Finally, some children leave their homes to escape violence and neglect, and find themselves unable to support themselves by any means other than prostitution. These children wind up at the mercy of their pimp or "madam" out of fear of exposure to the authorities, which would result either in their being sent back to their homes or being placed in state care.

Although the majority of children sold, indentured, or lured into prostitution remain in their home country, movement of children across international borders has become quite common. For example, children from Nepal, Bangladesh, and India have been discovered in Pakistan and the Gulf States; Thai children have been found in Japan. In Thailand, which has the world's largest child sex industry, the supply of young girls is diminishing. Thus, Thai traffickers have made inroads into Burma and China in search of young girls.

These children are essentially slaves to their procurers. Those who were sent to "work" off a "loan" to their parents face usurious interest rates, charges for room and board, and various other fraudulent expenses, making the prospect of ever actually working off the loan appear quite illusory. In Thailand, child prostitutes serve "an average of three customers a day, six or seven days a week, every week of the year." The effects of such a lifestyle are devastating, both psychologically and physically.

Psychologically, victims of child sexual exploitation live in constant fear. They live in fear of violence and sadistic acts by their clients, fear of being beaten by the gangsters and pimps who control the sex trade, and fear of being apprehended by the police. Additionally, they often suffer from feelings of depression and low self-esteem as a result of being constantly degraded, and from feelings of hopelessness as a result of their inability to change their circumstance. Among these children, "despair is the norm," and "suicide is common."

The physical damage among sexually exploited children in Asia, particularly among child prostitutes, is also very serious. Venereal diseases are endemic among these children, and infection of the AIDS virus is sweeping through at startling rates. Children rarely receive treatment and are generally taken for medical care only when they are seriously or terminally ill.

Child prostitutes are also poorly fed and sheltered and commonly suffer from malnutrition and tuberculosis. Despite these conditions, if they do not earn enough money, they are severely punished, often through beatings and starvation. These living conditions frequently lead to hard drug use among the children. The psychological, emotional, and physical repercussions of this lifestyle, in addition to the deprivation of education that the situation creates, prevents most of these children from ever making positive contributions as members of their communities. These children are deprived of their childhood and society is deprived of these children.

Many Asian nations have tourist areas that cater to foreigners seeking sex. Foreigners come primarily from Western Europe, the United States, and Australia seeking boys and girls for sex or pornography. Child welfare activists assert that these travelers, who are able to act with virtually no fear of punishment except deportation, enable the child sex trade to flourish. These excursions are facilitated, in many cases, by actual sex tours visibly marketed in the countries of the consumers, or by advertisements in travel magazines, highlighting the underage sex available in Asia and elsewhere. * * *

Despite * * * official attempts to curb the child sex trade, the problem remains prevalent. This is due largely to lack of enforcement * * * on the part of police and government officials. The lack of enforcement is attributable in part to corruption within the police forces. Additionally, countries affected by the sex tourism trade are, for the most part, very poor, and socio-economic realities lead the governments to concern themselves more with the money that such tourism brings in than with the effect it might have on the children. This might explain why Bradley Pendragon, a thirty-three year old Australian sex tourist recently convicted in Thailand for child pornography, was only the first foreign national ever tried in a Thai court for engaging in the child sex trade.

Notes and Questions

1. The preceding excerpt does not discuss what role race and ethnicity might play in the international child sex trade. However, pornography, including child pornography, often makes use of racial and cultural stereotypes. Indeed, some writers argue that attraction to the "exotic" plays an important role in cross-cultural, cross-ethnic, and interracial sexuality. See Laurie Shrage, *Moral Dilemmas of Feminism: Prostitution, Adultery, and Abortion* 148 (1994) (speculating that "culturally produced racial fantasies concerning the sexuality of these women" play a role in causing white American and European men to seek out women from other races and countries); Robert J.C. Young, *Colonial Desire: Hybridity in Theory, Culture and Race* (1995) (discussing nineteenth-century English desires for colored "others" in the colonial context); bell hooks, *Eating the Other: Desire and Resistance*, in *Black Looks: Race and Representation* 21 (1992) (discussing contemporary, consumerist versions of interracial desire); see also Vednita Nelson, *Prostitution: Where Racism and Sexism Intersect*, 1 Mich. J. Gender & L. 81 (1993).

2. The excerpts in this chapter so far have focused on situations where interracial sex is illegal, or where consent to sexuality is an issue. Does race also play a role in consensual sexual interactions? Consider the following excerpts.

FRANCES WINDDANCE TWINE

Heterosexual Alliances: The Romantic Management of Racial Identity, in
The Multiracial Experience: Racial Borders as the New Frontier
291, 294–96, 299–302, 303 (Maria P.P. Root ed. 1996).*

In both the academic and the popular press, we can find evidence of how romantic choices are "read" as indications of racial identity and racial allegiances. * * * The experiences of the Berkeley students whom I interviewed demonstrate how the selection of romantic partners enables some young adults of multiracial heritage to adjust themselves to the current racial order. The consequences of their need to make themselves "fit" the current system are reflected in the conscious decisions that young adults of multiracial heritage often make regarding who constitutes an appropriate and desirable romantic partner.

One of the questions I posed to my interviewees was whether there had been any changes in their friendship networks or romantic partners during the past several years. Most identified changes in the types of people they found desirable. * * * Shifts in racial self-identification were often partially expressed and grounded in romantic choices. This can be illustrated by the experiences of Alex, the 21–year-old son of an African–American mother and a white Jewish American father. Alex reported experiencing a dramatic shift in his identity during his first 3 years on the Berkeley campus. Prior to his attendance at UC [the University of California], he described a pattern of rejecting black women in dating and social life. He self-identified as "biracial" before coming to Berkeley and had attempted to assert a biracial identity as "black and Jewish." He said that he had been unsuccessful in this endeavor and had "given up" his white Jewish identity in favor of a monoracial African–American identity. * * *

Alex drew a clear link between his dating relationships and his racial identity. He was very conscious of the politics of desire and how his racial identity affected his desire for certain types of girls in junior high school. Alex went on to describe how he rejected his African–American mother's attempts to encourage him to date black girls. Dating a black girl was in conflict with his attempt to assert a biracial identity as a (white) Jewish American and African–American male. Alex recognized that demographics were not the single most important factor in his selection of white girls at his predominantly white high school. He argued against a demographic justification by clearly stating that he made a conscious decision to reject *all* of the black girls who expressed romantic interest in him:

> But I think that it's not just a coincidence that I never dated any black girls in high school. Looking back I definitely avoided it. I remember a [black] girl in my high school who had her mother ask my mother if I would be her escort for a cotillion. * * * I do realize that I was running away just because it would have been dating a *black* girl. And she was pretty too, nice, stylish, popular. Irrelevant. Totally irrelevant.

As someone who currently self-identifies as black and had embraced a monoracial identity, Alex interpreted his behavior during this period as his attempt to flee from a monoracial black identity because he wanted to assert a biracial identity at that time. His dating behavior, like that of other individuals who are biracial cannot be easily coded by race and whose appearance is racially ambiguous in some contexts, reveals that he was conscious of the importance of his romantic partner in coding him racially. Alex's partner provided the ground upon which he publicly asserted a black racial identity. His partner provided cues to others as to his racial identity and allegiances in cases where his physical appearance did not provide sufficient cues. * * *

Jessica, the 24–year-old daughter of an Anglo American woman and an African–American father, grew up in an exclusively white suburban community. She described her pre-Berkeley racial identity as neutral. She had shifted from a neutral racial identity in high school to a biracial identity in college. When asked how she was categorized by others, Jessica reported that when, as a child, she visited her relatives in a Spanish-speaking area of Los Angeles, she was often taken for a Mexican American, so the social context was crucial in how she was racially identified. To offset her ambiguous physical appearance, Jessica described how she consciously selects the social events that she will attend in her efforts to clarify her biracial identity as an African-descent woman.

> People always think I'm Hispanic. They think I'm Mexican or sometimes they think I'm Polynesian. Black people know I'm black though * * * when I'm in a black environment, people know [that I have a black parent]. Especially if I'm at a black conference or I'm in a black organization or at a black meeting.

Jessica went to these black conferences and meetings with men who were recognized as members of the black community. Heterosexual romance provided an arena in which she learned the expectations that the middle-class black community had of women recognized as *culturally black*. Romance provided an avenue to a publicly recognized black social identity. Her shift from a racially neutral or off-white identity to a biracial identity precipitated a shift in the types of men she found desirable. After returning from a year abroad in Africa, she began to see herself as biracial, which precipitated a shift in her romantic partners of choice.

> And when I came back [from Africa], I started dating predominantly black men. Actually since I've been back, I haven't dated any white men. And so there's been a big shift in the men I've seen. And the boyfriend I have currently is black.

Like other students of African descent who had been raised by European American or Asian American parents, Jessica described having had to "work hard" at establishing and maintaining ties to the African–American community in order to assert a biracial identity. * * * Thus, for Jessica, her membership in the black community was communicated to the public by her dating men who were recognized as black men exclusively and by participating in black events. * * *

Mimi, the 26–year-old, brown-skinned daughter of a Chinese father and an African-descent mother now identifies herself as "black and Asian." Mimi, who was born in Jamaica, grew up in Canada and Texas. Her Chinese father prohibited her mother from ever discussing her multiracial heritage and kept her African ancestry hidden. Her shift from a monoracial Chinese identity to a biracial identity occurred during her first year at Berkeley, but the ground was laid for this shift when she became integrated into a black friendship network on her job the year before attending Berkeley.

He controlled our family situation. I didn't know anything about my mother's family until very recently. He didn't want us to know anything about our black blood. So the whole time I was growing up I was led to believe that I was only Chinese. * * * But now and for the past 5 years when people ask me I tell them first that I'm Jamaican by birth but in terms of race I always say I'm Asian and black. * * * . I guess at one time [becoming a biracial black Asian] was a conscious effort to seek out the company of black people but now it's just a way of life. * * *

As a woman whose physical appearance and cultural training do not declare her African–American heritage, Mimi has learned to "work" at asserting a biracial identity by actively cultivating friendships and romances with black men. When asked how she asserts a biracial identity, she revealed her constant anxiety about not having the same cultural knowledge as individuals who had been socialized as black and grown up in African–American family networks.

I'm 24 years old. I feel like I ought to know more [about African–American history and culture] than I do now * * * even in social situations when we're having discussions, I'm afraid [a monoracial Black] will find out that I don't know about black history and say that I'm not really black. I feel all the time that I'm scrambling to catch up—to get to speed with everybody else, in terms of what I should know [about being Black].

The anxiety of not having the cultural information to claim a biracial identity was echoed by several women who were attempting to assert newly acquired multiracial identities. * * * Their black romantic partners were crucial in both providing them with cultural information and giving them access to these communities. * * *

Some informants experienced conflicts with their parents when they began to exclusively date men of African descent who self-identified as black, as they shifted from a biracial identity to a monoracial black identity. Tehmina, the 23–year-old daughter of a second-generation Russian–Jewish American mother and black American father, described how her mother responded to her preference for black men.

And my mom is wondering "[When] are you going to date a white person?" * * * She feels hurt because she sees me identifying with my African–American cultural heritage * * * especially when we have a conversation about who I'm dating and almost everybody I bring home is black. Almost everybody. And all the pictures on my wall. Almost everybody is black.

Prior to her attendance at UC Berkeley, Tehmina had self-identified as "Caucasian," which was an expression of her cultural connection and allegiance to her Russian Jewish American mother (biological) and her Anglo American stepfather. She had had no contact with the relatives of her black American father, and he did not participate in her upbringing. Her identity began to shift at Berkeley, and at the time of this interview she self-identified as a black Jewish American and restricted her dating to men who were publicly recognized as black. * * * She felt that because she was now a member of the black campus community and not the white Jewish campus community, she must demonstrate her allegiance to the community by not dating nonblacks. When she discussed her current boyfriend, she emphasized the disapproval that she might receive from the black campus community if she did not place emphasis upon the African heritage of her Puerto Rican boyfriend, who is of multiracial heritage. Tehmina reflects upon the response of the black community to her dating:

> Something that I noticed when I told [black students] that [my boyfriend] is Puerto Rican is that I had to back it up with "He's Afro–Puerto–Rican." He "acts black" and "looks black," too.

JOAN WALSH

Asian Women, Caucasian Men: The New Demographics of Love, San Francisco Examiner Image Magazine
December 2, 1990, at 11.*

There's no better place to take the dating temperature of the Bay Area than the personal ads section of the *San Francisco Bay Guardian*. In these teeming pages, being a woman of Asian descent is a marketing plus, the female version of being a straight man who wants kids. Unfortunately, as a 35–year-old romantic shopper named Ana Reyes learned, it also attracts men who might enjoy a Bangkok sex tour or import an Asian mail-order bride—men who, in other words, have some offensive notions about Asian women. "You should see some of the letters," groans Reyes, a saleswoman of Philippine descent who ventured into the personals market after a long-term relationship ended. "Some of them made me want to write back just to tell them off."

There was the Marine who reminisced about his tour of duty in the Philippines, where his Filipina girlfriend did his laundry. "He said he liked Filipinas best, because they really know how to treat their men," Ana recalls. Others were hot for the "exotic Asian look," she says.

This is 1990, in an increasingly Asian city, where Asian–American women are visible as newscasters, judges, political powerbrokers, university professors. But judging from the letters she received, Ana concludes, a lot of white guys still think "we're all nice girls who cater to men." (In fact, the notion that Asian women are "nice" may be the 1990s update on the stereotype that they're "submissive," the term is heard so often in discussions of Asian-white dating.) Of the 60–plus respondents to

Ana's ad, all but three were white. * * * Some were professional Asian-daters. Ana wasn't pleased.

"When a man tells me he usually dates Asian women, I tell him I'm very concerned about what that means," she says. "I know some are looking for 'Cherry Blossom' girls," inspired by the company that imports Asian women for marriage with traditional-minded American men. "Then there are the ones who are just into the 'exotic' look. I want to blow their stereotypes."

Ana shatters at least two stereotypes—that of Asian women as submissive, and personals advertisers as rejects. Analytical and articulate, the college-educated Reyes is also beautiful, with looks at the intersection of Hispanic and Asian. It's a look that she knows is in vogue now, and she's ambivalent about her current popularity. "Some of these guys who write, all they want to know is what I look like, and it really bothers me. But I guess I'm sort of asking for it by advertising that I'm Asian." Why did she put her race in the ad, I ask. "Everybody else does," she says. "To leave it out would seem dishonest." It would also be a marketing mistake. In the competitive world of the personals ads, hyping your assets is key, and being Asian gets results.

* * *

Ana's old boyfriend, and the boyfriend before that, are white. Despite discomfort with stereotyping, Ana and other Asian women are dating white men in increasing numbers, leaving some Asian men and white women watching with growing frustration from the sidelines.

High-profile women of Asian descent reflect the trend: writers Amy Tan and Maxine Hong Kingston, newscasters Connie Chung, Wendy Tokuda and Jan Yanehiro—all have Caucasian husbands. The phenomenon is spawning its own jargon. White men who prefer Asian women are said to "like rice"; they have "Asian-women syndrome"; they're "Asian-women-aholics" or "rice queens" (a term borrowed from the gay world, where white-Asian romance is also hot).

The high number of Asians in the Bay Area, along with their high education and income levels, makes some of the cross-cultural romance inevitable. In California, American-born Asians are more likely to marry outside their own group (or "outmarry," to use the sociological term) than any other race—in some Asian ethnic groups, the outmarriage rate is as high as 80 percent. And when they do outmarry, their partners are most likely to be white. But there's more to Asian-white romance than demography. If numbers told the whole story, Asian men would just as likely be involved with white women as the reverse. They're not, by a long shot. A recent sampling of marriage records for San Francisco County showed that four times as many Asian women as Asian men married whites, says Sonoma State University professor Larry Shinagawa; in Sacramento the ratio was 8 to 1. * * *

There's no proof that most white men who date and marry Asians are fleeing white women; many * * * may just happen to fall in love with someone who happens to be of Asian descent. * * * But among those who only date Asian women, or who voice strong preferences for Asians, there's frequently an undercurrent of frustration with feminism.

Mike Arnold describes himself as "maladroit" with women. He blames it on his father, a child abuser he likens to Hitler. Thanks to subtle sexual belittling—"I should write a WASP *Portnoy's Complaint*," he says—Mike didn't date until college, and then only fitfully. Now, at 42, he dates only Asians, with chilling self-awareness about his motivations.

"I get some breaks from Asian women. Their standards are lower," he says matter-of-factly. "It's a Darwinistic world, dating-wise, and I have an inferiority complex with white women. Most of them have a big chip on their shoulders, and I don't care how liberated they say they are, they're not interested in someone who doesn't make much money. I eventually realized that being white, I could make it with an Asian woman who's more physically attractive than I am, just because she's got a cultural inferiority complex." * * *

Tom Knight has had more luck in love than Mike has, with white women as well as Asians, but he too finds it difficult being emotional with some white women. "Men were raised to be tough, and though I'd like to be more emotional, there's a fear there with women I feel too much equality with." That's part of why he prefers dating Asian women.

"I see something of a feminist backlash in it," admits the fortysomething art professional. "I don't really understand it, but I know I feel less threatened by Asian women. I grew up in a culture where men acted a certain way and women acted a certain way, and I'm more comfortable with Asian culture, where interpersonal relations are more ritualized, and women are graceful, polite and considerate." Traveling in China cemented his preference for Asian looks. He started thinking of white women as "big, overweight Amazonians, with no bra, frizzy hair and lots of freckles. It made me feel kind of ugly myself."

When he met his first Japanese–American girlfriend, Tom recalls, "I liked looking at her. She didn't look threatening, mean or sad. She was pretty, but not beautiful—beautiful is threatening too. I thought, I could live with this person." He did, for six years. "She did a lot for me: She had tea ready when I came home, she scrubbed me in the bathtub. I liked it—you probably would too. My friends thought it was sick, but it made me happy. I think the Western world is too into individuality, and with her I had a mutual striving for harmony."

Eventually, though, the relationship ended. "There's such a thing as too much 'otherness.' We couldn't communicate. We weren't mental equals. Her whole world was her relationship with me." * * *

Their new popularity is a shock to a lot of Asian women. * * *

For white women, the surprise is similar and not entirely pleasant. * * *

Of course white women *are* disadvantaged by the defection of white men for Asian women—unless they're willing to date Asian men in comparable numbers. And generally, they're not.

"It's Asian men who really get the short end of the stick," admits Elizabeth Crandall, 20, a member of Berkeley's Alpha Phi sorority. "Asian women are with white men, but white women don't date Asians." That's not exactly news to Asian men at Berkeley. Doug Nishida, president of the predominantly Asian fraternity Lambda Phi Epsilon, pulled together a group of his friends to talk about the Asian women-white men phenomenon. Our conversation flashed back and forth between sociological theories and personal angst. Of the four, only Doug has a girlfriend right now, a trend they attribute at least partly to the preference of Asian women for white men. * * *

All four have discussed the trend with friends, with family, in Asian–American Studies classes. They believe American culture—white culture—has sought to emasculate men of color, and see the same impulse that insulted black men with the term "boy" neutering Asian men. "Look at the *Rambo* movies, or *The Karate Kid*," says Bryan Nobida, whose heritage is half-Chinese, half-Filipino. "Look at all movies and TV. Asian men are either celibate, sexless or else we're rapists, someone that a white man should save a woman from. The Asian never ends up with the woman." * * *

"As an Asian–American, I can't complain," [Dave] says, because he thinks all races should be free to date whomever they want. "But as a man, I get very upset. It wouldn't be as bad if white women were dating Asian men, but they aren't." Of the four—all good looking, funny, articulate—only Doug has ever dated a white woman, which shocked me, even though I know the statistics.

"So it's pretty upsetting," Dave continues. "It's a sexual thing, it's very primal—it's like your turf is being invaded, and it makes you angry."

The others laugh at his bluntness, but they mostly agree. "It wouldn't bother me as much if Asian women were also dating black men or Latino men," Bryan says. "But it's white guys. I've heard Asian women say they only date white guys. And it's because we live in a white culture. They do it for status. It's self-contempt." * * *

Shinagawa and colleague Gin Yong Pang, a doctoral candidate in Ethnic Studies at UC–Berkeley, have coined their own term, "hiergamy," to explain intermarriage patterns, including the tendency of Asian–American women to marry white men. Hiergamy, says Shinagawa, holds that in marriage, people "try to maximize their status opportunities, and their sense of wholeness, in the context of a society that's stratified by race, class and gender."

That's a mouthful, but it works like this: Given a choice between Asian men—who have some economic clout but less social status—and educated white men—who have economic clout and social status, as well as the more liberal attitudes social acceptance can bring—many Asian women would choose the latter. The concept also explains why many white men marry Asian women, Shinagawa says: "They are bright, educated and articulate women, but in the racial fantasies of white men they have always been portrayed as submissive, domestic and sexy— qualities they think white women have abandoned for feminism." White men, in other words, are trading a little public status for some private happiness, a reasonable compromise under hiergamy.

Notes and Questions

1. Should people take race into account in deciding whom to pursue romantically? Or is romantic choice a "private" matter that should have no political motivations or consequences? If race properly may or should make a difference, how should it play a role? Should people pursue romantic partners who are racially "different" or "the same" as themselves? Should it be considered appropriate to seek an "exotic" partner? A partner who will bring you and your family social status? Is it appropriate to encourage others not to date "outside the race"? Why or why not?

Why do you suppose personal ads are race-conscious? Would you support requiring them to be race-blind?

2. The Twine excerpt suggests that the racial choice of one's partner may be the cause or effect of one's racial self-identification. Do you approve or disapprove of the conscious choices "Alex," "Jessica," "Mimi," and "Tehmina" made to adopt certain racial identities? Why?

3. For an analysis of the racialization of Asian–American women, see Sumi K. Cho, *Converging Stereotypes in Racialized Sexual Harassment: Where the Model Minority Meets Suzie Wong*, 1 J. Gender Race & Just. 177 (1997).

4. Consider what it would be like to date someone of a different race (even if you do or have already). What are the implications for you of dating an African American, a Latino/a, a white American, or an Asian American? What are the costs and benefits of each choice, for you? What do these implications tell us about the social construction and valuation of different races?

5. The Walsh excerpt suggests that people of different races are ranked along hierarchies of "masculinity" and "femininity." Would you agree? Is there a social consensus about such a hierarchy, if it exists, or is it a purely individual, idiosyncratic matter?

Several writers have argued that in the contemporary United States, Asian–American men are treated as less masculine than white or black men. See, *e.g.*, David Mura, *How America Unsexes the Asian Male*, N.Y. Times, Aug. 22, 1996, at C9 (discussing sexual stereotyping of Asian men).

SECTION 2. MARRIAGE

In contemporary times, marriage is usually thought of as the highest expression of adult heterosexual love and romance. Yet in other times and places, the economic aspects of marriage have played a more important role in its legal and social expression than its romantic aspects. See Rachel Moran, *Interracial Intimacy* (forthcoming 2000). As Moran notes, the Western European tradition of chivalry, from which contemporary Americans get much of their mythology about romance, was explicitly focused on extra-marital affairs. Because the elite knights, lords and ladies who developed the concept of chivalric love married for money and power, the only "pure" love was love outside marriage.

More recently, critics of marriage have argued that it institutionalizes the domination of women and the marginalization of gay and lesbian people. In a famous article, anthropologist Gayle Rubin calls for a "political economy of sex" in order to address such questions. Gayle Rubin, *The Traffic in Women: Notes on the "Political Economy" of Sex*, in *Toward an Anthropology of Women* 157 (Rayna Reiter ed. 1975). Does marriage also institutionalize racial divisions?

Rubin notes that anthropologist Claude Levi–Strauss argued that the essence of kinship systems was an exchange of women between men, in which marriage and children embodied a cultural alliance between individual men and groups of men. Rubin goes further: "[T]here are other questions to ask of a marriage system than whether or not it exchanges women. Is the woman traded for a woman, or is there an equivalent? Is this equivalent only for women, or can it be turned into something else? If it can be turned into something else, is it turned into political power or wealth? On the other hand, can bridewealth be obtained only in marital exchange, or can it be obtained from elsewhere? Can women be accumulated through amassing wealth? Can wealth be accumulated by disposing of women? Is a marriage system part of a system of stratification?" Rubin at 207. She concludes:

> [S]exual systems cannot, in the final analysis, be understood in complete isolation. A full-bodied analysis of women in a single society, or throughout history, must take *everything* into account: the evolution of commodity forms in women, systems of land tenure, political arrangements, subsistence technology, etc. Equally important, economic and political analyses are incomplete if they do not consider women, marriage, and sexuality.

Rubin at 209–210.

As you read the excerpts that follow, see if you can trace some of the connections among marriage, race, wealth, and power.

ROLDAN v. LOS ANGELES COUNTY ET AL.

129 Cal.App. 267, 18 P.2d 706 (1933).

ARCHBALD, Justice pro tem.

Solvador Roldan applied to the county clerk of Los Angeles county for a license to wed a woman of Caucasian descent and was refused such license. On a hearing of his application before the superior court for a writ to compel the issuance thereof, he was found to be a "Filipino", *viz.*, "an Illocano, born in the Philippine Islands of Filipino progenitors in whose blood was co-mingled a strain of Spanish," and not a Mongolian. From a judgment making the alternative writ of mandate permanent, the defendants have appealed.

Section 69 of the Civil Code, relating to marriage licenses, was amended in 1880 (Code Amendments, 1880, p. 3) to prohibit the issuance of a license authorizing the marriage of a white person "with a * * * Mongolian." Section 60 of the Civil Code was amended in 1905 (Stats. 1905, p. 554, § 2) by adding "Mongolians" to the classes whose marriage with a "white" was made "illegal and void." The sole question involved in this appeal is whether or not the Legislature in 1880 and 1905 meant to include Filipinos in its use of the word "Mongolian."

We find no dissent to the statement that the Filipino is included among the Malays, although since the time of Huxley, at least, there has been some question among ethnologists as to whether the five grand subdivisions of the races of mankind, as classified by Blumenbach, is the proper classification, or whether the Malays are to be included among the "Mongoloid" group and as a branch of the Mongolian family. We are not, however, interested in what the best scientific thought of the day was, but in what was the common use of the word "Mongolian" in California at the time of the enactment of the legislation above mentioned.

* * *

[The court refers to various scientific racial classifications quoted in dictionary and encyclopedic sources.]

We think we have quoted enough to show that, regardless of the fine points of the argument from the ethnologist's standpoint, the early classification of Blumenbach left its impression on the writers from his day to 1905, at least, so that his classification is spoken of as the one "commonly" used; and we venture to think that in the recollection of those whose early schooling was anywhere in the period from 1850 to 1905 his classification of the races into the five divisions, the white, black, yellow, red, and brown, still persists.

From 1862 to 1885 the history of California is replete with legislation to curb the so-called "Chinese invasion," and as we read we are impressed with the fact that the terms "Asiatics," "Coolies," and "Mongolians" meant "Chinese" to the people who discussed and legislated on the problem, or at most that they only extended in their thought to natives of China and the inhabitants of adjacent countries having the same characteristics. * * *

* * * That the Malay race was not in the thoughts of any in the convention as being included in the designations used is clearly shown from the speech of Mr. James M. Shafter against the proposed amendment prohibiting the employment of Chinese by public officers and making a candidate for office ineligible who employed or had employed them within three months previously. After stating that such provision was the equivalent to debarring Chinese from employment (vol. 2, p. 676), he declared: "I have had in my employment natives of most European countries, of the isles of the sea, including the Cannibal Islands of the south Pacific. Why do you not exclude the Kanakas, the Fiji, the Malay or the criminal from Australia? No reason against the Chinaman but presses with greater force against these people." Apparently no one challenged this statement, which implied that the Malay, at least, was not included in the designation "Mongolian"; and we can draw but one conclusion from the debates, and that is that such an idea was not present in the minds of the members of the Convention.

Much more could be shown, but we think we have set down sufficient to indicate that in 1880, in a group that would compare very favorably with the average Legislature, there was no thought of applying the name Mongolian to a Malay; that the word was used to designate the class of residents whose presence caused the problem at which all the legislation was directed, *viz.*, the Chinese, and possibly contiguous peoples of like characteristics; that the common classification of the races was Blumenbach's, which made the "Malay" one of the five grand subdivisions, *i.e.*, the "brown race," and that such classification persisted until after section 60 of the Civil Code was amended in 1905 to make it consistent with section 69 of the same Code. As counsel for appellants have well pointed out, this is not a social question before us, as that was decided by the Legislature at the time the Code was amended; and if the common thought of today is different from what it was at such time, the matter is one that addresses itself to the Legislature and not to the courts.

Judgment affirmed.

Notes and Questions

1. From the founding of the nation until the Supreme Court's decision in *Loving v. Virginia*, 388 U.S. 1 (1967), antimiscegenation statutes in many states prevented Whites and nonwhites from marrying. California's antimiscegenation statute, Civil Code § 60, was enacted in 1872 and mandated that "[a]ll marriages of white persons with Negroes or mulattoes are illegal and void." Cal. Civ. Code § 60 (Deering 1872). It succeeded a statute that not only prohibited such marriages, but authorized criminal penalties as well. Cal. Civ. Code § 60, 68 (Deering 1871). In 1905, section 60 was amended to include "Mongolians." That version of the statute is the subject of the *Roldan* case. In 1933, presumably in response to *Roldan*, the legislature amended section 60 to include "members of the Malay race."

2. What was the purpose of antimiscegenation statutes? In 1948, the California Supreme Court overturned that state's antimiscegenation statute by a 4–3 decision in *Perez v. Lippold*, 32 Cal.2d 711, 198 P.2d 17 (1948). The court held both that the statute was a violation of the federal Equal Protection Clause and that it was void for vagueness. On the equal protection issue, Justice Traynor, for the majority, noted that because the statute discriminated against persons on the basis of race or color, only "exceptional circumstances" could justify it. The state offered several justifications for the statute.

First, the state relied on the following language from a nineteenth century Missouri case: " 'It is stated as a well authenticated fact that if the issue of a black man and a white woman, and a white man and a black woman intermarry, they cannot possibly have any progeny, and such a fact sufficiently justifies these laws which forbid the intermarriage of blacks and whites, laying out of view other sufficient grounds for such enactments.' " *Perez*, 32 Cal.2d. at 720, n.2 (quoting *State v. Jackson*, 80 Mo. 175, 179, 50 Am.Rep. 499).

Second, the state argued that "the prohibition of intermarriage between Caucasians and members of the specified races prevents the Caucasian race from being contaminated by races whose members are by nature physically and mentally inferior to Caucasians." *Id.* at 722.

Third, the state argued that "persons wishing to marry in contravention of race barriers come from the 'dregs of society' and that their progeny will therefore be a burden on the community." *Id.* at 724.

Fourth, the state argued that "race discrimination diminishes the contacts and therefore the tensions between races." *Id.* at 726.

Fifth, the state argued that interracial marriage has an adverse effect upon the children of such marriages, relying on *Buck v. Bell*, 274 U.S. 200, in which the Supreme Court upheld the sterilization of a woman deemed "feeble-minded" in the interests of the greater public. *Id.*

The court rejected each of these arguments as insufficiently supported by the evidence and the statutory scheme. It would be another two decades, however, before the U.S. Supreme Court would decide *Loving v. Virginia*, declaring similar statutes unconstitutional. Indeed, in *Pace v. Alabama*, 106 U.S. 583 (1883), the Court had upheld an Alabama statute imposing more severe punishment for adultery or fornication between a white person and a Negro than for such acts between individuals belonging to the same race. In a short opinion, the Court found no equal protection problem, since the statute treated white and Negro people the same.

3. As the widespread passage of antimiscegenation statutes suggests, marriages between White and nonwhite people were often punished in the United States. In the nineteenth-century West, however, it was common for Anglo men to marry Mexican women. As one sociologist describes the situation in nineteenth-century California:

> For their part, European Americans also were not oblivious to the advantages of marrying into wealthy ranchero families. With eligible white women being scarce in the territory, fair-complexioned, upper-class Mexican women were among the most valued marriage partners available. While white men derived a degree of status from marrying the Californio's daughters, more important were the tangible political and economic opportunities that such unions afforded. These marriages provided strategic access to land held by the old elite. Thousands of acres passed into the hands of Anglo men as part of the inheritances some Californio women brought to marriage. Moreover, Anglo sons-in-law were often the first ones given access to land sold by rancheros desperately needing cash.

Tomás Almaguer, *Racial Fault Lines: The Historical Origins of White Supremacy in California* 58–59 (1994). Almaguer also notes, however, that Mexicans, unlike other California minority groups at the time, had a claim to "whiteness" through their connection with Spain. The strength of this claim depended on the class status and ancestry of the person claiming it.

> White immigrants generally made racial distinctions among the Mexican population * * *. Those [Mexicans] whose class position and ostensible European ancestry placed them at the top of the hierarchy during the Mexican period, the "gente de razon," were reluctantly viewed as "white" by Anglo Americans. The dark complexioned, mestizo population (the "greasers" or *gente sin razon*—literally, "people without rea-

son"), on the other hand, were viewed as "nonwhite" and not significantly different from pure-blood, Indian "savages" in the state.

Id. at 55.

4. In *State v. Pass*, 59 Ariz. 16, 121 P.2d 882 (1942), the defendant was tried for second degree murder. The principal witness against him was his wife. At trial, the defendant objected to her testimony on the ground that a state statute disqualified wives from testifying against husbands except by the husband's consent. The court overruled the defendant's objection, holding that defendant and Ruby Contreras were not husband and wife "upon the ground * * * that a descendant of an Indian may not marry a member of the Caucasian race." On appeal, the court noted:

> The evidence is undisputed that defendant's mother was the child of an English father and a Piute Indian woman and that his father was a Mexican, so he was a descendant of three races, to wit, Caucasian, Indian and Mexican.
>
> Ruby Contreras Pass testified that her father was a Spaniard and her mother half French and half Mexican. And to the question "Do you have any Indian blood in you?" she answered, "Not that I know of." Thus she is a descendant of two races, to wit, Spanish and French.

Pass, 121 P.2d at 882.

The statute at issue prohibited the marriage of "persons of Caucasian blood, or their descendants, with Negroes, Hindus, Mongolians, members of the Malay race, or Indians, and their descendants." On appeal, the court held that the statute did apply to make the Passes' marriage void, and thus upheld the defendant's conviction.

What result under this statute if a person of mixed-white and African–American descent tried to marry? Can a "mixed-race" person marry anyone under the Arizona statutory language? Why does the court think this issue raises no constitutional problem? The court in *Pass* did have a comment on the wisdom of the statute:

> We think the language used by the lawmakers went far beyond what was intended. In trying to prevent the white race from interbreeding with Indians, Negroes, Mongolians, etc., it has made it unlawful for a person with 99% Indian blood and 1% Caucasian blood to marry an Indian, or a person with 99% Caucasian blood and 1% Indian blood to marry a Caucasian. We mention this and the absurd situations it creates believing and hoping that the legislature will correct it by naming the percentage of Indian and other tabooed blood that will invalidate a marriage. The miscegenation statutes of the different states do fix the degree or percentage of blood in a Negro, an Indian, etc., preventing marriage alliances with Caucasians.

121 P.2d at 883.

Why did the court assert "the language used by the lawmakers went far beyond what was intended," yet believe it was powerless to remedy the problem?

If Ruby Contreras' father was "a Spaniard" and her mother was "a Mexican of Spanish and French descent," she might well identify as a Latina today. Would she also be White? Should her classification matter for purposes of marriage? Should it matter for any purpose?

5.   The Virginia Supreme Court faced a challenge to their state antimiscegenation statute when Richard Loving, who was White, and Mildred Loving, who was African American, challenged their criminal conviction under the statute. Replying to the Lovings' arguments, which relied on decisions finding discrimination unconstitutional in other areas of life, the court observed:

> We have given consideration to these decisions, but it must be pointed out that none of them deals with miscegenation statutes or curtails a legal truth which has always been recognized—that there is an overriding state interest in the institution of marriage. None of these decisions takes away from what was said by the United States Supreme Court in *Maynard v. Hill*, 125 U.S. 190:
>
> > "Marriage, as creating the most important relation in life, as having more to do with the morals and civilization of a people than any other institution, has always been subject to the control of the Legislature."

Loving v. Virginia, 206 Va. 924, 929–30, 147 S.E.2d 78, 82 (1966).

Why should the "morals and civilization of a people" be legally regulated?

LOVING v. VIRGINIA
388 U.S. 1 (1967).

CHIEF JUSTICE WARREN delivered the opinion of the Court.

This case presents a constitutional question never addressed by this Court: whether a statutory scheme adopted by the State of Virginia to prevent marriages between persons solely on the basis of racial classifications violates the Equal Protection and Due Process Clauses of the Fourteenth Amendment. For reasons which seem to us to reflect the central meaning of those constitutional commands, we conclude that these statutes cannot stand consistently with the Fourteenth Amendment.

In June 1958, two residents of Virginia, Mildred Jeter, a Negro woman, and Richard Loving, a white man, were married in the District of Columbia pursuant to its laws. Shortly after their marriage, the Lovings returned to Virginia and established their marital abode in Caroline County. At the October Term, 1958, of the Circuit Court of Caroline County, a grand jury issued an indictment charging the Lovings with violating Virginia's ban on interracial marriages. On January 6, 1959, the Lovings pleaded guilty to the charge and were sentenced to one year in jail; however, the trial judge suspended the sentence for a period of 25 years on the condition that the Lovings leave the State and not return to Virginia together for 25 years. He stated in an opinion that:

> "Almighty God created the races white, black, yellow, malay and red, and he placed them on separate continents. And but for the interference with his arrangement there would be no cause for such marriages. The fact that he separated the races shows that he did not intend for the races to mix."

After their convictions, the Lovings took up residence in the District of Columbia. On November 6, 1963, they filed a motion in the state trial court to vacate the judgment and set aside the sentence on the ground that the statutes which they had violated were repugnant to the Fourteenth Amendment. * * *

The two statutes under which appellants were convicted and sentenced are part of a comprehensive statutory scheme aimed at prohibiting and punishing interracial marriages. The Lovings were convicted of violating § 20–58 of the Virginia Code:

> "Leaving State to evade law.—If any white person and colored person shall go out of this State, for the purpose of being married, and with the intention of returning, and be married out of it, and afterwards return to and reside in it, cohabiting as man and wife, they shall be punished as provided in § 20–59, and the marriage shall be governed by the same law as if it had been solemnized in this State. The fact of their cohabitation here as man and wife shall be evidence of their marriage."

Section 20–59, which defines the penalty for miscegenation, provides:

> "Punishment for marriage.—If any white person intermarry with a colored person, or any colored person intermarry with a white person, he shall be guilty of a felony and shall be punished by confinement in the penitentiary for not less than one nor more than five years."

Other central provisions in the Virginia statutory scheme are § 20–57, which automatically voids all marriages between "a white person and a colored person" without any judicial proceeding, and § 20–54 and 1–14 which, respectively, define "white persons" and "colored persons and Indians" for purposes of the statutory prohibitions.[4] The Lovings have never disputed in the course of this litigation that Mrs. Loving is a "colored person" or that Mr. Loving is a "white person" within the meanings given those terms by the Virginia statutes.

Virginia is now one of 16 States which prohibit and punish marriages on the basis of racial classifications. Penalties for miscegenation arose as an incident to slavery and have been common in Virginia since

---

4. Section 20–54 of the Virginia Code provides:

"Intermarriage prohibited; meaning of term 'white persons.'—It shall hereafter be unlawful for any white person in this State to marry any save a white person, or a person with no other admixture of blood than white and American Indian. For the purpose of this chapter, the term 'white person' shall apply only to such person as has no trace whatever of any blood other than Caucasian; but persons who have one-sixteenth or less of the blood of the American Indian and have no other non-Caucasic blood shall be deemed to be white persons. All laws heretofore passed and now in effect regarding the intermarriage of white and colored persons shall apply to marriages prohibited by this chapter." Va.Code Ann. § 20—54 (1960 Repl.Vol.). * * *

Section 1–14 of the Virginia Code provides:

Colored persons and Indians defined.— "Every person in whom there is ascertainable any Negro blood shall be deemed and taken to be a colored person, and every person not a colored person having one fourth or more of American Indian blood shall be deemed an American Indian; except that members of Indian tribes existing in this Commonwealth having one fourth or more of Indian blood and less than one sixteenth of Negro blood shall be deemed tribal Indians." Va.Code Ann. § 1–14 (1960 Repl.Vol.).

the colonial period. The present statutory scheme dates from the adoption of the Racial Integrity Act of 1924, passed during the period of extreme nativism which followed the end of the First World War. The central features of this Act, and current Virginia law, are the absolute prohibition of a "white person" marrying other than another "white person," a prohibition against issuing marriage licenses until the issuing official is satisfied that the applicants' statements as to their race are correct, certificates of "racial composition" to be kept by both local and state registrars, and the carrying forward of earlier prohibitions against racial intermarriage.

I.

In upholding the constitutionality of these provisions in the decision below, the Supreme Court of Appeals of Virginia referred to its 1955 decision in *Naim v. Naim*, 197 Va. 80, 87 S.E.2d 749, as stating the reasons supporting the validity of these laws. In *Naim*, the state court concluded that the State's legitimate purposes were "to preserve the racial integrity of its citizens," and to prevent "the corruption of blood," "a mongrel breed of citizens," and "the obliteration of racial pride," obviously an endorsement of the doctrine of White Supremacy. The court also reasoned that marriage has traditionally been subject to state regulation without federal intervention, and, consequently, the regulation of marriage should be left to exclusive state control by the Tenth Amendment.

While the state court is no doubt correct in asserting that marriage is a social relation subject to the State's police power, the State does not contend in its argument before this Court that its powers to regulate marriage are unlimited notwithstanding the commands of the Fourteenth Amendment. * * * Instead, the State argues that the meaning of the Equal Protection Clause, as illuminated by the statements of the Framers, is only that state penal laws containing an interracial element as part of the definition of the offense must apply equally to whites and Negroes in the sense that members of each race are punished to the same degree. Thus, the State contends that, because its miscegenation statutes punish equally both the white and the Negro participants in an interracial marriage, these statutes, despite their reliance on racial classifications do not constitute an invidious discrimination based upon race. The second argument advanced by the State assumes the validity of its equal application theory. The argument is that, if the Equal Protection Clause does not outlaw miscegenation statutes because of their reliance on racial classifications, the question of constitutionality would thus become whether there was any rational basis for a State to treat interracial marriages differently from other marriages. On this question, the State argues, the scientific evidence is substantially in doubt and, consequently, this Court should defer to the wisdom of the state legislature in adopting its policy of discouraging interracial marriages.

Because we reject the notion that the mere "equal application" of a statute containing racial classifications is enough to remove the classifications from the Fourteenth Amendment's proscription of all invidious racial discriminations, we do not accept the State's contention that these statutes should be upheld if there is any possible basis for concluding that they serve a rational purpose. * * * In the case at bar, * * * we deal with statutes containing racial classifications, and the fact of equal application does not immunize the statute from the very heavy burden of justification which the Fourteenth Amendment has traditionally required of state statutes drawn according to race.

The State argues that statements in the Thirty-ninth Congress about the time of the passage of the Fourteenth Amendment indicate that the Framers did not intend the Amendment to make unconstitutional state miscegenation laws. Many of the statements alluded to by the State concern the debates over the Freedmen's Bureau Bill, which President Johnson vetoed, and the Civil Rights Act of 1866, 14 Stat. 27, enacted over his veto. While these statements have some relevance to the intention of Congress in submitting the Fourteenth Amendment, it must be understood that they pertained to the passage of specific statutes and not to the broader, organic purpose of a constitutional amendment. As for the various statements directly concerning the Fourteenth Amendment, we have said in connection with a related problem, that although these historical sources "cast some light" they are not sufficient to resolve the problem; "[a]t best, they are inconclusive. The most avid proponents of the post-War Amendments undoubtedly intended them to remove all legal distinctions among 'all persons born or naturalized in the United States.' Their opponents, just as certainly, were antagonistic to both the letter and the spirit of the Amendments and wished them to have the most limited effect." * * *

The State finds support for its "equal application" theory in the decision of the Court in *Pace v. State of Alabama*, 106 U.S. 583 (1883). In that case, the Court upheld a conviction under an Alabama statute forbidding adultery or fornication between a white person and a Negro which imposed a greater penalty than that of a statute proscribing similar conduct by members of the same race. The Court reasoned that the statute could not be said to discriminate against Negroes because the punishment for each participant in the offense was the same. However, as recently as the 1964 Term, in rejecting the reasoning of that case, we stated *"Pace* represents a limited view of the Equal Protection Clause which has not withstood analysis in the subsequent decisions of this Court." *McLaughlin v. Florida*, 379 U.S. at 188. As we there demonstrated, the Equal Protection Clause requires the consideration of whether the classifications drawn by any statute constitute an arbitrary and invidious discrimination. The clear and central purpose of the Fourteenth Amendment was to eliminate all official state sources of invidious racial discrimination in the States.

There can be no question but that Virginia's miscegenation statutes rest solely upon distinctions drawn according to race. The statutes proscribe generally accepted conduct if engaged in by members of different races. Over the years, this Court has consistently repudiated "[d]istinctions between citizens solely because of their ancestry" as being "odious to a free people whose institutions are founded upon the doctrine of equality." *Hirabayashi v. United States*, 320 U.S. 81, 100 (1943). At the very least, the Equal Protection Clause demands that racial classifications, especially suspect in criminal statutes, be subjected to the "most rigid scrutiny," *Korematsu v. United States*, 323 U.S. 214, 216 (1944), and, if they are ever to be upheld, they must be shown to be necessary to the accomplishment of some permissible state objective, independent of the racial discrimination which it was the object of the Fourteenth Amendment to eliminate. Indeed, two members of this Court have already stated that they "cannot conceive of a valid legislative purpose * * * which makes the color of a person's skin the test of whether his conduct is a criminal offense." *McLaughlin v. Florida*, 379 U.S. at 198 (Stewart, J., joined by Douglas, J., concurring).

There is patently no legitimate overriding purpose independent of invidious racial discrimination which justifies this classification. The fact that Virginia prohibits only interracial marriages involving white persons demonstrates that the racial classifications must stand on their own justification, as measures designed to maintain White Supremacy. We have consistently denied the constitutionality of measures which restrict the rights of citizens on account of race. There can be no doubt that restricting the freedom to marry solely because of racial classifications violates the central meaning of the Equal Protection Clause.

II.

These statutes also deprive the Lovings of liberty without due process of law in violation of the Due Process Clause of the Fourteenth Amendment. The freedom to marry has long been recognized as one of the vital personal rights essential to the orderly pursuit of happiness by free men.

Marriage is one of the "basic civil rights of man," fundamental to our very existence and survival. To deny this fundamental freedom on so unsupportable a basis as the racial classifications embodied in these statutes, classifications so directly subversive of the principle of equality at the heart of the Fourteenth Amendment, is surely to deprive all the State's citizens of liberty without due process of law. The Fourteenth Amendment requires that the freedom of choice to marry not be restricted by invidious racial discriminations. Under our Constitution, the freedom to marry or not marry, a person of another race resides with the individual and cannot be infringed by the State.

These convictions must be reversed. It is so ordered.

Reversed.

JUSTICE STEWART, concurring.

I have previously expressed the belief that "it is simply not possible for a state law to be valid under our Constitution which makes the criminality of an act depend upon the race of the actor." *McLaughlin v. State of Florida*, 379 U.S. 184, 198 (concurring opinion). Because I adhere to that belief, I concur in the judgment of the Court.

Notes and Questions

1. Is *Loving v. Virginia* rightly decided? Why? Isn't it true that as a matter of equal protection, the statute treated white and nonwhite people

the same? If this is the case, shouldn't the statute be upheld as long as the state can articulate a rational reason for it?

Can you think of other groups, similarly situated, that are treated differently under the statute?

2. Note that *Loving* was decided relatively recently. Does it surprise you that states could and did prohibit interracial marriages as recently as 1967? Why has racial equality in marriage (in principle) been such a recent phenomenon?

3. Twenty–five years after *Loving* was decided, a reporter for the *New York Times* found Mrs. Loving still living a mile and a half from where Sheriff R. Garnett Brooks broke into the Lovings' bedroom to arrest husband and wife. Sheriff Brooks and Mrs. Loving, according to the reporter, have not spoken to one another for 34 years, although they see one another occasionally. When interviewed, Sheriff Brooks had no regrets about his actions.

"I was acting according to the law at the time, and I still think it should be on the books," said Sheriff Brooks, sitting with his wife on the porch of his home in Bowling Green. "I don't think a white person should marry a black person. I'm from the old school. The Lord made sparrows and robins, not to mix with one another."

Mr. Brooks said he had rarely pondered the case in the last 35 years. "If they'd been outstanding people, I would have thought something about it," he said. "But with this caliber of people, it didn't matter. They were both low class."

David Margolick, *A Mixed Marriage's 25th Anniversary of Legality*, N.Y. Times, June 12, 1992, at B20.

BETHANY RUTH BERGER
After Pocahontas: Indian Women and the Law, 1830 to 1934
21 Am. Indian L. Rev. 1, 28–39 (1997).*

The unique legal status of Indians as members of "dependent sovereign nations" attached a peculiar mix of privileges and liabilities to Indian status. Indians throughout the nineteenth century found their rights to independence on their own land repeatedly abrogated, and were persecuted when they refused to remain on the ever smaller pieces of land they were allotted. With the resulting constant upheaval and diminution of hunting lands, the Indian people were not only legally and militarily beset but economically impoverished. On the other hand, they were also immune from criminal prosecution for crimes against Indians committed on Indian land. In addition, as various treaties and then the Dawes Allotment Act divided and parcelled out tribal lands in efforts to "civilize" the Indians through ownership of private property, Indian status also equalled entitlement to often valuable property. In the century before the Indian New Deal, the federal courts considered a series of cases regarding which of the legal attributes of "Indianness" the white husbands of Indian women would hold.

[Eds. In *United States v. Rogers*, 45 U.S. (4 How.) 567 (1845), the Court held that a white man who had intermarried and been adopted into the Cherokee Nation was nevertheless not an "Indian" for purposes of federal criminal jurisdiction.] [W]hile this decision has obvious implications for Indian sovereignty, it affected the wives of intermarried white men as well. Their husbands could no longer fully assimilate themselves with their people, but remained subject to the authority of the white government, unable to regard an Indian nation as sovereign in the way that their wives could. Following *Rogers*, legal shifts in allegiance would occur only from the Indian, and almost always female, side.

After *Rogers* effectively determined that Indian women would not be vectors for increasing the size of the tribes, the federal government soon came to encourage the opposite process: intermarriage as a method to decrease adherence to tribal custom. This process probably began with local federal agents allocating land to white husbands as the heads of families and state court approval of these allocations. * * * By the Assimilationist Period [the 1880s through the 1920s], however, this process was codified in federal statutes. The year after the Dawes Act was passed [1887], Congress passed a statute declaring that Indian women who married white men would thereby become American citizens.

The law was ostensibly designed to protect Indian women from unscrupulous white men who would marry them only to gain rights to Indian land. Although the statute responded to a real problem, it equally addressed the fear raised by *Rogers* that white men would assimilate with their wives' tribes. The amendment was intended to ensure that the effect of the Dawes Act would be to "mak[e] citizens of the United States instead of making Indians of our citizens." The legislative history presents an unwitting contrast between the two paths for intermarriage, the approved path in which the Indian woman left her tribe for an allegiance with the United States, and that in which her husband joined her people:

> Mr. Ezra B. Taylor: Is not the object of this bill to prevent the marriage or miscegenation of these degenerate whites with the Indian squaws?
>
> * * *
>
> Mr. Weaver: The effect of the bill is to encourage Indians to marry white men and become citizens of the United States.

In gaining United States citizenship, intermarried Indian women were to lose their bonds with their tribes. * * *

As the federal courts were effectively declaring that white husbands of Indian women could gain their wives' rights to tribal property, but not their national identity, state courts were creating a body of jurisprudence under which men, Indian or white, had almost no legal obligation to their Indian wives. The dominant view of judicial treatment of Indian marriage and divorce is that stated by Felix Cohen, that "Indian tribes have been accorded the widest possible latitude in regulating the domestic relations of their members." This established doctrine, and the extension of the general rule that marriages would be upheld if valid where contracted, disguised the extent to which assumptions regarding the dissolute nature of sexual relations with Indian women often led courts to assume Indian marriages invalid without question. In 1832, for example, Circuit Judge James Duane Doty ended an era in the established Indian-white community of Green Bay, Wisconsin, by indicting thirty-six of its principal male inhabitants for fornication with their Indian and mixed-blood wives. In 1917, moreover, only one year after the Supreme Court announced that Indians cohabiting without the benefit of marriage according to state law could not be prosecuted for adultery, the Minnesota Supreme Court confidently declared that a majority of mixed blood Indians were not the issue of lawful wedlock. * * *

[Two important cases concerned "the validity of promissory notes made by Delilah Wall, a Choctaw woman, in light of the common law rule against a married woman's ability to contract."] Delilah and David Wall had been married by a justice of the peace in 1831, and had lived together until 1839 when David left for the Choctaw country west of the Mississippi. Although Delilah executed the note at issue in *Wall II* after David left her, and executed that in *Wall I* before, the court treated both as valid on the ground the husband took no part of the wife's property under Choctaw law. As a consequence of this "peculiarity," the court held, the wife must have the capacity to contract to protect her property.

The *gravamen* of these opinions, however, is whether abandonment of an Indian woman would dissolve a marriage. After stating that "[a]ll the testimony in relation to rights of husband and wife, under Choctaw law, may have been of a disputable or doubtful nature," Justice Goldthwaite proceeded to make law on that same doubtful testimony. The court immediately cast the custom of relatively easy dissolution of marriage as one designed for the convenience of the husband: "By [Choctaw] law, it appears that the husband may at pleasure dissolve the relation. His abandonment is evidence that he has done so." The court hearkens to various classical sources to justify the decision, stating that "[h]owever strange it may appear, at this day, that a marriage may thus easily be dissolved, the Choctaws are scarcely worse than the Romans, who permitted a husband to dismiss his wife for the most frivolous causes," and that "[m]arriages among the Indian tribes must be regarded as taking place in a state of nature. * * *" The court's recognition of the custom, however, seems to stem from a disdain for the perceived barbarism of the Indians, and it is grouped together with various other privileges of state law also denied to them:

> Do our laws allow Indians to participate equally with us in our civil and political privileges? Do they vote at our elections, or are they represented in our legislature, or have they any concern as jurors or magistrates, in the administration of justice? Are they subject to our laws of marriage and divorce, and would we sustain a criminal prosecution for bigamy, if they should change their wives and husbands at pleasure, and according to their own customs, and contract new matrimonial alliances? I apprehend that every one of these questions must be answered in the negative * * *.

There is evidence that the Alabama court and the later courts that held abandonment to equal divorce under tribal law were misinterpreting that law. Several sources note that separation was relatively rare and usually occurred among childless couples, and evidence from various tribes suggests that while informal divorce was allowed, stable marriages were encouraged and rewarded. * * *

Indeed, many of the marital customs decried by white reformers as degrading to Indian women may have been created instead to benefit women. The practice of having more than one or two wives, for example, may frequently have been more a matter of sharing work than an accommodation of male sexual desire. As one elderly Omaha man said in response to white prohibition of polygamy, "I must take another wife * * * my old wife is not strong enough now to do all her work alone." * * * In their study of domestic violence under Navajo common law, James and Elsie Zion suggest that the tradition of marrying sisters was also a way to ensure protection against domestic abuse where the couple would not live with her family. * * *

Moreover, while courts framed their recognition of abandonment of an Indian woman as a divorce as an acknowledgement of tribal sovereignty over domestic relations, they also tended to imply that because informal dissolution was available, the prior "connexion" was not a marriage at all. Regarding the ten year cohabitation and parenting of three children by Colonel Johnson, a government agent in Indian country, with Tapissee, the daughter of a chief, a Missouri court declared:

> [I]t is clear that all such connexions, which have taken place among the various tribes of North American Indians, either between persons of pure Indian blood, or between half breeds, or between the white and Indian races, must be regarded as a mere illicit intercourse, and the offspring be considered as illegitimate. * * *

In addition, because a majority of these cases involved white men leaving Indian women when the possibility of return to civilization came along, judges often framed divorce by abandonment as a male privilege. * * *

The women, moreover, were presented as degraded by their acquiescence to this practice: they were concubines or "article[s] of trade," they were "bought" and "abandoned." * * *

Perhaps more important, husbands retained no legal obligations to their Indian wives if they decided to move on: "It is plain that among the savage tribes on this continent, marriage is merely a natural contract, and that neither law, custom or religion has affixed to it any conditions or limitations or forms other than what nature has itself proscribed." Or, in the words of the North Carolina Supreme Court, "it can never be held that mere cohabitation, with an understanding that it may cease at pleasure, can constitute a marriage, or carry with it the rights and disabilities of that relation."

MARTINEZ v. SANTA CLARA PUEBLO

402 F. Supp. 5 (D.N.M.1975), rev'd and remanded, 540 F.2d
1039 (10th Cir.1976), rev'd, 436 U.S. 49 (1978).

MECHEM, District Judge.

Julia Martinez and her daughter Audrey Martinez bring this suit, each individually and as the representative of a class, against the Santa Clara Pueblo and Governor Lucario Padilla, individually and in his capacity as governor of the Pueblo. Plaintiffs claim that a portion of a tribal ordinance which denies Pueblo membership to the children of female but not male members of the Pueblo who marry non-members of the Pueblo, violates 25 U.S.C.A. § 1302(8). This statute prohibits a tribal government in the exercise of its power of self-government from denying "to any person within its jurisdiction the equal protection of its laws or (depriving) any person of liberty or property without due process of law." Plaintiffs seek an injunction against the further enforcement of the ordinance.

[Eds. 25 U.S.C.A. § 1302, the Indian Civil Rights Act (ICRA), was enacted by Congress in 1968. The purpose of the Act was to "single out the more important civil rights contained in the Constitution and to render those applicable to tribal members who reside on the reservation," *Martinez v. Santa Clara Pueblo*, 540 F.2d 1039, 1042 (1976). Congress did make some effort to square constitutional protections with existing tribal law and custom; for example, the nonestablishment clause of the First Amendment and the Fifteenth Amendment were omitted from the Act. Nevertheless, many Indian nations, including the Pueblo, were opposed to the ICRA, seeing it as an attempt to undermine tribal law. *Martinez v. Santa Clara Pueblo*, 540 F.2d at 1045.]

The ordinance, passed in 1939, reads as follows:

Be it ordained by the Council of the Pueblo of Santa Clara, New Mexico, in regular meeting duly assembled, that hereafter the following rules shall govern the admission to membership to the Santa Clara Pueblo:

1. All children born of marriages between members of the Santa Clara Pueblo shall be members of the Santa Clara Pueblo.

2. All children born of marriages between male members of the Santa Clara Pueblo and non-members shall be members of the Santa Clara Pueblo.

3. Children born of marriages between female members of the Santa Clara Pueblo and non-members shall not be members of the Santa Clara Pueblo.

4. Persons shall not be naturalized as members of the Santa Clara Pueblo under any circumstances.

Plaintiffs attack subparts two and three of the ordinance.

Julia Martinez is a female member of the Santa Clara Pueblo. She is and at all times pertinent to this action was married to Myles Martinez, a Navajo Indian who is not a member of the Pueblo. Plaintiff Audrey Martinez is one of the eight surviving children born to their marriage. Under the 1939 Ordinance, Audrey and the other Martinez children are not recognized as members of the Pueblo. By order previously entered, it has been determined that Audrey Martinez may properly bring this action as the representative of a class consisting of all children born to marriages between Santa Clara women and men who are not members of the Pueblo and that Julia Martinez may properly bring this action as the representative of a class consisting of all women who are members of the Santa Clara Pueblo, and who have married men who are not members of the Santa Clara Pueblo.

The social and political organization of the Pueblo must be discussed first. Santa Clara Pueblo was founded around 1300 A.D. The Pueblo now covers roughly 48,000 acres, held by the United States in trust for the Pueblo. Approximately 1,200 recognized members and between 150 and 200 non-members currently live on the Pueblo. Approximately 150 recognized members live elsewhere, one-third of them in other locations in New Mexico, and the rest scattered across twenty-two different states.

In its early days, Santa Clara culture made no distinction between what Anglo–Americans would term "political" and "religious" matters. However, with the Spanish invasion in the early seventeenth century, the Pueblo instituted a "secular" government to distract Spanish attention from the *caciques* (religious leaders) who were the real authorities in the Pueblo. The distinction between religious and secular spheres is now well established in the Santa Clara culture.

The membership of the Pueblo is and has been organized into what the anthropologists refer to as '*moieties*', specifically the Winter people and the Summer people. Each moiety is led by a cacique, and each is further divided into factions. The precise function and significance of moiety membership is not clear on the record; it is, however, clear that it is primarily a religious grouping. The caciques are still the dominant authorities in the Pueblo, nominating the candidates for secular office and exercising an effective veto by influence over the actions of the secular government.

The division of the moieties into factions is a relatively recent development. During the early part of the twentieth century sharp conflicts developed in the Pueblo over the importance of traditional customs and values in the life of the Pueblo. For example, a major source of controversy was whether the Governor should be an older, highly respected man who was well versed in the traditional ways, or a younger man, educated in Anglo–American schools, who could speak English and would be able to deal more effectively with non-Pueblo society. The disagreement literally split the Pueblo, and during the late 1920s and early 1930s the Pueblo had two governors, neither of whom recognized the authority of the other, and two separate Winter and Summer moieties. The Bureau of Indian Affairs (BIA) staff in Washington offered to arbitrate the dispute. The entire Pueblo agreed that the BIA officials from Washington were irrelevant.

They did agree to have the resident BIA agent, Elizabeth Sargent, help settle the difference. At her suggestion, and after much discussion, the Pueblo organized pursuant to the authority of the Wheeler–Howard Act, 25 U.S.C.A. § 476, and adopted a Constitution and By–Laws in 1935. As reorganized the secular government retained many of its traditional institutions, such as the unity of the legislative and "appellate" judicial functions in the Council, while at the same time incorporating and instituting certain Anglo–American institutions, principally voting for secular officials. Thus, the present Pueblo government is neither wholly traditional nor wholly anglicized.

Under the Constitution and By–Laws there is a single governing body, the Council, as noted, which possesses both legislative and "appellate" judicial powers. Santa Clara Constitution, Article IV, Sections 1 and 2. The Council consists of the secular officers of the Pueblo—the Governor, the Lieutenant Governor, the Secretary, the Treasurer, the Interpreter, and the Sheriff—and eight representatives. As a matter of custom and practice, the representatives represent the factions, which still exist.

The Governor is the chief executive of the Pueblo charged with enforcing the law "civil and criminal, written and unwritten." In addition he appears to have the initial responsibility for settling controversies among and concerning the members of the Pueblo. A person aggrieved by a ruling of the Governor may appeal to the Council, at which time the Governor may vote only to break a tie.

All other secular governmental power and responsibility is vested in the Council, including the power to enact ordinances governing Pueblo life. Most important for the present case, the Constitution specifically grants the Council the power to determine which children of mixed marriages shall be recognized as members of the Pueblo, and to determine who is a member for purposes of dealings in land and land use rights. The 1939 Ordinance was enacted by the Council pursuant to these powers, and is agreed by all parties to be in force at this time.

The factual development of the equal protection claims of the parties is best begun by identifying the interests of plaintiffs and defendants affected or served by the Ordinance.

As previously noted, Audrey Martinez is the daughter of the marriage of plaintiff Julia Martinez, a recognized member of the Pueblo and Myles Martinez, a non-member of the Pueblo. It is undisputed that the 1939 Ordinance bars recognition of Audrey as a member of the Pueblo. If Myles were a member of the Pueblo and Julia Martinez were not—or if Julia were not married, and Audrey had been born out of wedlock, the Ordinance would not bar her recognition as a member and the Council would in fact so recognize her.

Julia Martinez has lived at the Pueblo all her life, with the exception of a relatively brief absence to further her education. Myles Martinez has lived at the Pueblo ever since his marriage to Julia, with the exception of a relatively brief absence while serving in the armed forces. Audrey Martinez grew up on the Pueblo, although she does leave to pursue her education. Aside from the fact that she is not recognized as a member of the Pueblo and is therefore denied certain rights, she has been raised in the culture of Santa Clara, speaks Tewa, the traditional language, and clearly considers herself to be a Santa Claran.

As a factual matter, recognition as a member of the Pueblo would give Audrey Martinez three distinct types of rights which she is presently denied. First, she would gain political rights, primarily the right to vote, to take matters before the Pueblo Council, and the qualification to hold office as a secular official.

Secondly, she would be entitled to share in the material benefits of Pueblo membership. The most important of the material benefits is that referred to as land use rights. As noted above, title to the Pueblo land is held by the United States in trust for the Pueblo, rather than for the individual members of the Pueblo. The Council may designate specific areas of the land to be set aside for the use of particular individuals, and members of the Pueblo are equally entitled to use land not specifically assigned to an individual. As a matter of custom and practice, these use rights are passed down through families. However, only members of the Pueblo are entitled to use rights; thus in families such as the Martinez family, where the children are not members of the Pueblo, the land use rights cannot be passed on to succeeding generations. In the same manner, Article VII, Section 2 of the Santa Clara Constitution, provides that members may rent or sell their use rights, but again, only to other members. As noted above, the Council has the power under the Constitution to determine who is a member for purposes of land use rights. It is undisputed that since 1939 this determination has been governed by the 1939 Ordinance, although from the Constitution it would appear that the Council could, if it so decided, apply different criteria. Other material benefits and privileges include the right to hunt and fish on the land, the use of irrigation water, and an equal share in any distribution of pecuniary benefits made by the Pueblo, or any other programs, present or future, undertaken by the Pueblo for the benefit of its members.

Third, as members, Audrey and other children similarly situated would as of right be able to continue living at the Pueblo. While it is true that the Martinez family and a number of other families in their position live at the Pueblo, this is not as a matter of right. If and when Mrs. Martinez dies, the rest of the family, as non-members, would not have the right to continue living on the Pueblo, though it is not now known whether they would be forced to leave. Furthermore, under the Santa Clara Constitution, non-members and only non-members may be expelled from the Pueblo for violating a Pueblo Ordinance.

Lack of membership does not now affect entitlement to federal benefits accorded Indians generally, or participation in the religious life of the Pueblo. In 1968, Mr. and Mrs. Martinez obtained BIA census numbers for their children, and since then the children have received all federal benefits generally available to Indians, including educational and medical benefits. As to religion, Audrey Martinez is already allowed to participate in Pueblo religious ceremonies to the same extent that she would be if she were a recognized member of the Pueblo. Thus, the question presented is one of membership in the Pueblo for purposes of purely internal, secular, rights and privileges.

Julia Martinez claims that the operation of the Ordinance rendering her children non-members denies her the equal protection of the laws and deprives her of property without due process of law. More specifically, she claims that the Ordinance necessarily restricts her land use rights and other material benefits and rights which she could give to her children if they were recognized as members.

In addition to these relatively precise and legally protectible interests, Julia and Audrey Martinez and many of those similarly situated share a strong emotional involvement with the Pueblo. Regardless of official definitions of membership, Julia Martinez feels that her children, having grown up in Santa Clara, should be recognized as Santa Clarans. Audrey Martinez, despite official definitions, clearly considers herself to be a Santa Clara Indian. While the law may not recognize or protect these interests, it would be foolish to pretend that they do not exist.

While the factual context of the legal claims made by Audrey and Julia Martinez differs, it is clear that both ultimately present the same legal question—whether the 1939 Ordinance violates their rights to equal protection of tribal laws, as secured to them by the Indian Civil Rights Act, 25 U.S.C.A. § 1302(8).

The specific interests of the Pueblo in membership policies generally and in the particular policy of the 1939 Ordinance are of concern as well. Since 1680 the Pueblo has existed as a conquered people, identifiable as a group but surrounded by an alien culture, first Spanish and later American. From a practical political standpoint, the result has been a tension in the life of the Pueblo between traditional Pueblo customs and values and the "modern" customs and values of Anglo–American society. As noted above, this tension was once so acute that the Pueblo became divided against itself. The differences were eventually resolved by the adoption of the Constitution, which drew upon both traditional Pueblo and modern Anglo–American institutions, synthesizing them into a unique structure neither wholly traditional nor wholly modern.

The function of membership policies must be examined within this context. In *Dodge v. Nakai*, 298 F. Supp. 26 (D.Ariz.1969), the Court dealt with the interest of the Navajo tribe in geographically defining itself, and controlling who could and could not enter the reservation. Membership policies present the same interests on a different level. They are no more or less than a mechanism of social, and to an extent psychological and cultural, self-definition. The importance of this to Santa Clara or to any other Indian tribe cannot be overstressed. In deciding who is and who is not a member, the Pueblo decides what it is that makes its members unique, what distinguishes a Santa Clara Indian from everyone else in the United States. If its ability to do this is limited or restricted by an external authority, then a new definition of what it is to be a Santa Claran is imposed, and the culture of Santa Clara is inevitably changed.

The second major interest served by membership policies, and by the particular policy of the 1939 Ordinance, is that of economic survival of the tribal unit. As plaintiffs have demonstrated, the adoption of the 1939 Ordinance was in response to a sudden increase in mixed marriages, which had resulted in a proportionate strain on the economic resources of the Pueblo. Plaintiffs argue that economic integrity of the Pueblo is less important than cultural autonomy. The difficulty with this position is that the two are not easily separable. The ability of the Pueblo to control the use and distribution of its resources enhances its ability to maintain its cultural autonomy.

Plaintiffs do not challenge the power of the Pueblo, as delegated to and exercised by the Council, to make and enforce rules concerning membership. Their attack on the Ordinance is solely aimed at the criteria employed as to children of mixed marriages.

At trial the defendants sought to prove that the Ordinance was merely the written embodiment of ancient custom, or alternatively, that the Ordinance regulated membership for religious as well as secular purposes. The Ordinance does not regulate religious as well as political membership. As noted above, Audrey Martinez, although not a recognized member of the Pueblo, is allowed to participate in religious ceremonies to the same extent she would be if she were a member. While there is a relationship between religious life and secular, political life at Santa Clara, the distinction has been clear for nearly four hundred years. The Ordinance neither pertains to religious membership, nor necessarily affects it.

Whether or not the Ordinance is an embodiment of pre-existing ancient Pueblo custom is less clear. Before 1939 mixed marriages were relatively rare in the Pueblo, and consequently there was no need for a hard and fast rule concerning membership; rather, the Council considered each case separately. In that sense, the establishment of any one rule must be seen as a break with tradition.

On the other hand, the criteria employed in classifying children of mixed marriages as members or non-members are rooted in certain traditional values. It appears that Santa Clara was traditionally patrilineal and patrilocal—in other words, that kinship, name and location of residence generally were expected to follow the male rather than the female line. These cultural expectations have lost much of their force, but they are not entirely vitiated. The absentee voter lists of the Pueblo show that in 1971, 148 members of the Pueblo lived elsewhere. Of these, 59 were men and 89 were women. In 1973, 143 members lived elsewhere, of whom 59 were men and 84 were women. Furthermore, it is apparent that membership of the parents and marriage, either within or out of the Pueblo, has always been considered a highly significant factor in membership determinations as opposed to other possible criteria such as degree of Santa Clara ancestry. When a member of the Pueblo married a non-member, the status of children of the marriage was questionable. Consonant with this, children born to an unmarried Santa Clara woman traditionally have been and still are recognized as members, regardless of who the father is or might be.

It is clear that the interests of plaintiffs and defendants in the 1939 Ordinance are vitally important. Indeed, they are fundamentally the same. Both sides have political and property rights which are affected by the Ordinance. Both sides also have a deep psychological and cultural interest in the membership Ordinance which, if not legally quantifiable, cannot be ignored.

Courts faced with the necessity of construing 25 U.S.C.A. § 1302(8) have consistently held that the equal protection guarantee of the Indian Civil Rights Act is not identical to the constitutional guarantee of equal protection. Instead, the Act and its equal protection guarantee must be read against the background of tribal sovereignty and interpreted within the context of tribal law and custom. *Crowe v. Eastern Band of Cherokee Indians, Inc.*, 506 F.2d 1231 (4th Cir.1974); *Means v. Wilson*, 383 F. Supp. 378 (D.S.D.1974). Unfortunately this principle does not answer questions so much as teach the terms in which they must be asked. * * *

Plaintiffs do not suggest that the Indian Civil Rights Act should be interpreted in a manner which would impose an Anglo–American equal protection standard on tribes in derogation of their traditional values. To the contrary, they have consistently argued, as have the defendants, that the Act should be interpreted in such a manner as to preserve the cultural identity of Indian tribes in general and of Santa Clara in particular. Plaintiffs instead point out that the sex of the parent who is a member of the Pueblo bears little or no relationship to the strength of the parent's identification with traditional Santa Clara culture or the likelihood that the parent will attempt to pass the traditional cultural values on to the child. They point out, quite correctly, that Audrey Martinez and many other children similarly situated have been brought up on the Pueblo, speak the Tewa language, participate in its life, and are, culturally, for all practical purposes, Santa Clara Indians. On the other hand, there are certainly instances of children whose fathers are members of Santa Clara, but who have been raised far from the Pueblo, who cannot speak the language, who have not participated in the life of the Pueblo, and who know nothing of its values, customs and traditions, yet who are, under the 1939 Ordinance, recognized as members. Plaintiffs contend that this is not only irrational but actively destructive of the cultural identity of the Pueblo.

Even assuming plaintiffs are correct, the equal protection guarantee of the Indian Civil Rights Act should not be construed in a manner which would require or authorize this Court to determine which traditional values will promote cultural survival and therefore should be preserved and which of them are inimical to cultural survival and should therefore be abrogated. Such a determination should be made by the people of Santa Clara; not only because they can best decide what values are important, but also because they must live with the decision every day. Obviously they can and should be the judges of whether a particular rule is beneficial or inimical to their survival as a distinct cultural group.

Much has been written about tribal sovereignty. If those words have any meaning at all, they must mean that a tribe can make and enforce its decisions without regard to whether an external authority considers those decisions wise. To abrogate tribal decisions, particularly in the delicate area of membership, for whatever "good" reasons, is to destroy cultural identity under the guise of saving it. Congress has not indicated that they intended the Indian Civil Rights Act to be interpreted in such a manner.

Judgment will be entered in accordance with this opinion.

Notes and Questions

1. How does the Santa Clara Pueblo ordinance compare to the rules discussed in the Berger excerpt? Is the ordinance, even if legally valid, a good idea? What interests does it seek to protect? Is the ordinance due extra deference because it reflects "cultural difference"? Or is it not culturally "different" at all—that is, does the ordinance, reflecting American law in many other areas, disadvantage women's rights and the right to marriage in order to serve larger social policies?

2. On appeal, the Tenth Circuit held that because the classification included in the ordinance was based on sex, it was presumptively invidious and could be upheld only if justified by a compelling tribal interest. The court concluded that the tribe's interest was not substantial enough to justify its discriminatory effect. *Martinez v. Santa Clara Pueblo*, 540 F.2d 1039 (10th Cir.1976). The Supreme Court reversed, holding that the Indian Civil Rights Act does not authorize actions for equitable relief against a tribe or its officers. See *Santa Clara Pueblo v. Martinez*, 436 U.S. 49, 71 (1978) ("[E]fforts by the federal judiciary to apply the statutory prohibitions of section 1302 in a civil context may substantially interfere with a tribe's ability to maintain itself as a culturally and politically distinct entity.").

SECTION 3. CHILDREN AND FAMILIES

JANA LESLIE–MILLER

From Bell *to* Bell: Responsible Reproduction in the Twentieth Century
8 Md. J. Contemp. Legal Issues 123–25, 129–36 (1997).*

In 1927, the Supreme Court decided the case of *Buck v. Bell*. Carrie Buck, a Virginia resident who the state labeled feeble minded, gave birth to an illegitimate daughter. Consequently, the state committed Carrie to the State Colony for Epileptics and the Feeble Minded, a state hospital in Lynchburg, where she learned that she was to be sterilized pursuant to a state statute allowing for involuntary sterilization of mentally retarded persons contained in state institutions. Carrie, through her counsel, contested the procedure and argued that the statute was unconstitutional and violated both her substantive due process and equal protection rights under the Fourteenth Amendment.

Justice Holmes writing for the majority upheld the Virginia statute. In his opinion, Holmes declared that Carrie, her mother, and Carrie's illegitimate child were all feeble minded. Carrie's daughter was seven months old at the time this determination was made. Holmes went on to say that: "Three generations of imbeciles are enough." This seventy-year old case, although its precedential value questionable, has never been overruled.

In the early part of this century, Virginia and many other states maintained selective eugenic sterilization policies. The idea that the state should concern itself with the responsible reproduction of its citizens took root in this country largely as a result of the propaganda of Francis Galton, a cousin to Charles Darwin, and Charles B. Davenport, a eugenicist who committed his career to "the science of the improvement of the human race by better breeding." Undeniably, this science justified discrimination on the basis of race, class, and sex:

> There were [thought to be] definite grades of people within each race and these grades determined by fixed hereditary realities. [It was also thought] that there were unalterable grades of the races themselves, some being much more highly evolved than others. The best classes of people within the Caucasian race were not producing enough children whereas the inferior classes were producing too many offspring. A clear implication was that the upper classes must be encouraged to have more children and that the lower classes must somehow be compelled to have fewer.

Sterilization of these undesirable individuals was thereby justified and even encouraged by science. Eugenicists sold the American government and public on the idea that "the breeding habits of [inferior] populations" were an important matter of public policy.

A review of state statutes, case law, and the scientific literature on eugenic sterilization reveals the prevailing twentieth-century belief that the transfer of bad genes from generation to generation had to be contained, that responsible reproduction demanded it, and that it was none other than the government's job to do so. As a result, the government sponsored the eugenic sterilization of individuals of childbearing age who, like Carrie Buck, were considered "feeble minded." Harry H. Laughlin of the Eugenics Record Office, a leading eugenicist in the United States in the early part of this century, recommended sterilization for all who were "socially inadequate" and who failed "chronically as a useful member of the organized social life of the state." Many individuals were deemed "socially inadequate," the statistics suggest, as between the years 1907 and 1963, there were approximately 64,000 involuntary sterilizations performed throughout the United States.

The holding in *Buck* opened the flood gates. The Supreme Court placed its stamp of approval on localized management of reproduction of the fittest among state populations. With the Supreme Court's endorsement on such a broad and obscurely defined category as "feeble minded," states were free to institute eugenic sterilization policies to reach all of their inferior populations. As such, the movement to ensure responsible reproduction was in motion.

In Alabama, for example, the Partlow State School for Mental Deficients implemented a strong eugenic sterilization policy. In fact, this particular institution's policy was to sterilize all patients before they were approved for release from the institution. The president of the Medical Association of the State of Alabama (MASA) affirmed this policy in the late 1920s by arguing that, "it is not humane to allow the insane to propagate his species to the injury of himself and the public." This same president made the startling proclamation in 1928 that, "science can improve the human race by making the production of the mentally unfit impossible." Alabama's eugenic sterilization laws, in spite of the state's zealous leaders, were surprisingly more conservative in their reach than the law in many other states, leading several doctors and scientists in the state to criticize the law as inadequate. One leading eugenist presented his discontent before the Alabama legislature and praised, in comparison, the "bold experiment in mass sterilization" in Germany.

In California, the state code allowed for involuntary sterilization of various classes of "mental defectives" and "criminals." Unfortunately, as these classes of individuals extended to inmates in insane asylums, it also extended to "recovering alcoholics, people with mild cases of epilepsy, and others who today would not be considered 'insane,'" as these individuals were often placed in insane asylums along with the mentally ill. In 1910, the Attorney General for California, U.S. Webb, clarified how extensive the sterilization program in the state should be:

> Most of the insane, epileptic, imbecile, idiotic, sexual perverts; many of the confirmed inebriates, prostitutes, tramps and criminals, as well as the habitual paupers found in our country poor-asylums; also many of the children in our orphan homes, belong to the class known as degenerates. For this condition to go on unchecked eventually means a weakening of our nation.

In short, Webb justified involuntary sterilization from a public welfare perspective: The welfare of the nation naturally demanded the elimination of reproductive freedom for the socially unfit.

Throughout the mid-part of the twentieth-century, beliefs in the legitimacy of involuntary sterilization prevailed and states continued to sterilize the feeble minded, convicted criminals, and others thought to be unfit for the role of parenting. It was not until 1941 that the Supreme Court finally articulated opposition to involuntary sterilization, concluding that unequal application of sterilization, at least in the criminal context, is unconstitutional. In *Skinner v. Oklahoma*, the Court found that it is a violation of the Equal Protection Clause to sterilize one offender and not the other when the offenses are, for the most part, morally indistinguishable. In writing for the court, Justice Douglas made the following observations:

> We are dealing here with legislation which involves one of the basic civil rights of man. Marriage and procreation are fundamental to the very existence and survival of the race. The power to sterilize, if exercised, may have subtle, far-reaching and devastating effects . * * * There is no redemption for the individual whom the law touches. Any experiment which the State conducts is to his irreparable injury. He is forever deprived of a basic liberty. We mention these matters not to reexamine the scope of the police power of the States. We advert to them merely in emphasis of our view that strict

scrutiny of the classification which a State makes in a sterilization law is essential. * * *

The Court determined that for a state to subject a convicted criminal to involuntary sterilization, the state's regulation must survive the traditional strict scrutiny test. In other words, for a sterilization law to pass constitutional muster, there must be a compelling state interest. This is a much more stringent test than the Court used in *Buck v. Bell*. In *Buck*, the Court merely balanced the interests of the individual with that of the state and looked to see that the state's interests, as well as the means used, were rational. By requiring the state's interest to be compelling, the *Skinner* Court acknowledged that the reproductive autonomy of prison inmates outweighed the state's interest in controlling reproductive matters. The *Skinner* Court, however, when asked to distinguish *Buck v. Bell*, declined.

When the Court found, with *Skinner*, that procreation is a fundamental right, involuntary sterilization arguably should have come to an end. Unfortunately, this was not the result. Most states interpreted the Court's holding in *Skinner* to apply solely in the criminal context and were thereby able to maintain eugenic sterilization policies as applied against institutionalized individuals. Moreover, in future cases, it became clear that the compelling interest of the state did not extend so far as to protect those whom the state considered "deficient" from involuntarily being sterilized, and "deficiency" could be defined very broadly. "Of the states with eugenic sterilization laws as of 1968, the feeble-minded or mentally deficient were subject to sterilization in all 27, the mentally ill in 25, epileptics in 14, habitual criminals in 7, and 'moral degenerates and sexual perverts' in 7." As a result, regulations concerning state-sponsored sterilization programs which touched these individuals survived the Supreme Court's test of strict scrutiny.

We see an example of a state's sterilization statute surviving the strict scrutiny test in *Cook v. Oregon*. Oregon passed legislation which required that certain institutionalized individuals undergo mandatory sterilization. A majority of the Court found that:

> The state's concern for the welfare of its citizenry extends to future generations and when there is overwhelming evidence, as there is here, that a potential parent will not be able to provide a proper environment for a child because of his own mental illness or mental retardation, the State has sufficient interest to order sterilization.

When dealing with persons who are mentally ill or mentally retarded, this case demonstrates that the state's interest in prohibiting defective genes from being passed to subsequent generations can be construed as compelling. Even though the facts in the case suggested that the state of Oregon relied on insufficient data concerning the genetic origins of mental retardation, the Oregon Supreme Court found the state's interest sufficiently compelling to satisfy the strict scrutiny test. The Court seemed to believe that the state's interest in preventing "a line of law-breakers, such as murderers, sexual perverts, pyromaniacs and thieves" from being "brought into the world to become a burden and a menace to the state," outweighed the fundamental rights of the mentally retarded to procreate.

Another example of a state testing the Court's compelling interest standard occurred in California where some criminally convicted defendants were given the option of "voluntary" sterilization in lieu of serving prison time. The voluntariness of this option is debatable. One notable case involved a twenty-year old Chicano woman who was presented with this option. The woman who had been convicted for using marijuana, a relatively minor charge, was at the bottom of the socio-economic ladder and the mother of an illegitimate child. She was, therefore, a good candidate for the voluntary sterilization program. The presiding judge offered her the sterilization option, which she accepted, but before the operation took place, she changed her mind; thus she had to serve her prison time. The woman appealed and the case was heard by the California Supreme Court which rendered an interesting holding. The majority found that the trial judge "was in excess of his judicial power" and "only the Superior Court is given power to order sterilization of a human being and then in very limited special cases." Through this decision, the state's highest court avoided this controversial issue by acknowledging the existence of legitimate reasons for compulsory sterilization, but finding that the power to order them simply lay outside the domain of the state's trial courts.

South Carolina also tested the Supreme Court's limits by allowing physicians in one county to agree that medical services would only be provided to women with three or more illegitimate children if they consented to "postpartum sterilization." The impact of this early 1970s policy was that "more than one-third of all the welfare mothers in the county were said to have been rendered incapable of additional pregnancies by the end of the year." * * *

* * * In 1973, Ralph Nader, a public interest lobbyist, along with the Health Research Group which he pioneered, released a report accusing doctors of "cavalierly subjecting women to surgical sterilization without either explaining the hazards or describing alternative methods of birth control." His report highlighted a Baltimore City Hospital where doctors targeted women in their most vulnerable moments, in the heat of labor, with sterilization forms for them to sign. "Of twelve cases cited from Baltimore," the report claimed, "seven of the women were under age twenty and none had more than two children."

The practice of gaining sterilization consent from women while in the midst of labor was not unique to Baltimore. In Los Angeles, ten Mexican–American women who had agreed to sterilization either while they were experiencing labor or while they were under anesthesia sued the hospital and lost. Even though four out of the ten women did not actually realize that they had been sterilized until several years later the judge held that there was merely a "breakdown in communication between the patients and the doctors." Although the court recognized that the women had suffered severe emotional distress, it somehow determined that "one can hardly blame the doctors."

In recent years, sterilization has also been utilized to control reproduction rates within ethnic populations such as American Indians. At the Indian Health Service Hospital in Claremore, Oklahoma, for example, "194 sterilizations were performed in one year—one out of every four women admitted to the hospital." Reportedly, neither the irreversibility of sterilization procedures, nor other methods of birth control, were explained to these women, four of whom were under the age of twenty.

These examples are significant evidence of the racist and classist overtones in eugenic sterilization policies. The words of Alyce Gullattee, a black psychiatrist, resound with truth: "Sterilization will save society from poor parents rather than poor heredity. * * *" One need not look very far for confirmation of this charge. Study after study indicate that "there are significant differences in incidence of sterilization along income and welfare lines * * * the poor are sterilized at disproportionately higher rates." Even without research data, one finds evidence of a societal belief that some people are simply undeserving of procreation rights. For instance, columnist George Will wrote that "sterilization programs * * * weed the population." Who, one wonders, are the weeds? Welfare recipients? The mentally retarded? Unwed mothers?

Notes and Questions

1. For other cases on forced sterilization, see *Relf v. Weinberger*, 372 F. Supp. 1196, 1199 (D.D.C.1974) ("Although Congress has been insistent that all family planning programs function on a purely voluntary basis, there is uncontroverted evidence in the record that minors and other incompetents have been sterilized with federal funds and that an indefinite number of poor people have been improperly coerced into accepting a sterilization operation under the threat that various federally supported welfare benefits would be withdrawn unless they submitted to irreversible sterilization."), on remand *sub nom. Relf v. Mathews*, 403 F. Supp. 1235 (D.D.C.1975), vacated *sub nom. Relf v. Weinberger*, 565 F.2d 722 (D.C.Cir. 1977); *Walker v. Pierce*, 560 F.2d 609 (4th Cir. 1977), *cert.* denied, 434 U.S. 1075 (1978) (civil rights action against obstetrician who refused to treat Medicaid patients who already had two children if they failed to consent to a tubal ligation; dismissed on grounds that he was not acting under color of state law); *Avery v. County of Burke*, 660 F.2d 111, 115 (4th Cir. 1981) (county agency induced teenage girl to undergo unwanted sterilization on the basis of misrepresentation that she had sickle cell trait); Joelle S. Weiss, *Controlling HIV–Positive Women's Procreative Destiny: A Critical Equal Protection Analysis*, 2 Seton Hall Const. L.J. 643 (1992); Dick Grosboll, *Sterilization Abuse: Current State of the Law and Remedies for Abuse*, 10 Golden Gate U. L. Rev. 1147 (1980).

2. Efforts to control the reproductive behavior of low-status women, including women of color, by using the power of the state have taken many forms over the years. As the preceding excerpt suggests, one place where low-income women, including many women of color, have been vulnerable to such control is through the health care system. Women at public hospitals have been subjected to involuntary sterilization and sterilization with inadequate "consent." More recently, they have been targeted by prosecutors seeking to punish them criminally for smoking, drinking, and using controlled substances while pregnant. Dorothy Roberts argues that this targeting presents a constitutional issue:

A Black mother arrested in Pinellas County, Florida could make out a *prima facie* case of unconstitutional racial discrimination by showing that a disproportionate number of those chosen for prosecution for exposing newborns to drugs are Black. In particular, she could point out the disparity between the percentage of defendants who are Black and the percentage of pregnant substance abusers who are Black. *The New England Journal of Medicine* study of pregnant women in Pinellas County referred to earlier found that only about twenty-six percent of those who used drugs were Black. Yet over ninety percent of Florida prosecutions for drug abuse during pregnancy have been brought against Black women. The defendant could buttress her case with the study's finding that, despite similar rates of substance abuse, Black women were ten times more likely than white women to be reported to public health authorities for substance abuse during pregnancy. In addition, the defendant could show that both health care professionals and prosecutors wield a great deal of discretion in selecting women to be subjected to the criminal justice system. The burden would then shift to the state "to dispel the inference of intentional discrimination" by justifying the racial discrepancy in its prosecutions.

Dorothy E. Roberts, *Punishing Drug Addicts Who Have Babies: Women of Color, Equality, and the Right of Privacy*, 104 Harv. L. Rev. 1419 (1991); see also Dorothy E. Roberts, *Killing the Black Body: Race, Reproduction, and the Meaning of Liberty* (1997); Lisa C. Ikemoto, *The Code of Perfect Pregnancy: At the Intersection of the Ideology of Motherhood, the Practice of Defaulting to Science, and the Interventionist Mindset of Law*, 53 Ohio St. L.J. 1205 (1992).

Another important method of reproductive control of women of color has been through the welfare state. In the 1980s and 1990s, images of the black "welfare queen," lacking a man and having too many babies, fueled efforts to require women on welfare to use birth control techniques such as Norplant, as well as, in some states, caps on aid after a certain number of children. See, *e.g.*, Beverly Horsburgh, *Schrödinger's Cat, Eugenics, and the Compulsory Sterilization of Welfare Mothers: Deconstructing an Old/New Rhetoric and Constructing the Reproductive Right to Natality for Low-income Women of Color*, 17 Cardozo L. Rev. 531 (1996); Dorothy E. Roberts, *Crime, Race, and Reproduction*, 67 Tul. L. Rev. 1945 (1993).

Finally, women who are under the control of the criminal justice system are also vulnerable to state-coerced reproductive control. See, *e.g.*, Note (Kristyn M. Walker), *Judicial Control of Reproductive Freedom: The Use of Norplant as a Condition of Probation*, 78 Iowa L. Rev. 779 (1993).

3. The reproduction of undocumented persons has been targeted by legislation and by proposed constitutional amendments that would deny birthright citizenship to the children of illegal immigrants. See Dorothy Roberts, *Who May Give Birth to Citizens? Reproduction, Eugenics, and Immigration,* in *Immigrants Out! The New Nativism and the Anti–Immigrant Impulse in the United States* 205 (Juan F. Perea ed. 1997).

4. Although the popularity of the American eugenics project of the 1920s and 1930s waned when it became widely recognized that Hitler's genocidal policies were based on similar theories concerning the supposed genetic superiority of the "Aryan" race, the notion that certain racial-ethnic groups are biologically inferior to others periodically reappears within scientific and popular discourse. For example, a recent best-selling book by

Richard J. Herrnstein and Charles A. Murray, *The Bell Curve: Intelligence and Class Structure in American Life* (1994), suggests that African Americans are "naturally" less intelligent than Whites (based on the authors' examination of IQ scores for various groups). For responses to this argument from the social science community, see *The Bell Curve Wars: Race, Intelligence, and the Future of America* (Steve Fraser ed. 1995).

5.   In addition to the ideology of biological inferiority highlighted by the previous excerpt, ideologies of cultural inferiority have played an important role in justifying attempts to regulate or destroy women of color's reproductive capacities. Sometimes these theories target the family itself as inferior, and as the cause of greater social ills. For example, in 1965 Daniel Patrick Moynihan issued a report called *The Negro Family: The Case for National Action*. According to Moynihan:

> At the heart of the deterioration of the fabric of the Negro society is the deterioration of the Negro family. It is the fundamental cause of the weakness of the Negro community. * * * In essence, the Negro community has been forced into a matriarchal structure which, because it is so out of line with the rest of the American society, seriously retards the progress of the group as a whole.

U.S. Dep't of Labor, Office of Planning & Policy Research, *The Negro Family: the Case for National Action* 5 (1965).

In other cases, theories about cultural inferiority have led policymakers to target children and families as a means to disrupt or destroy the wider ethnic culture. Consider the materials on Indian families that follow.

K. TSIANINA LOMAWAIMA

*Domesticity in the Federal Indian Schools: The Power of Authority
Over Mind and Body*, in *Deviant Bodies: Critical Perspectives
on Difference in Science and Popular Culture*
197 (Jennifer Terry & Jacqueline Urla eds. 1995).*

In the early 1900s, federal boarding schools forbade native language use and religious practice, and they separated families. Policy makers calculated these practices to achieve far-reaching social goals, to civilize and Christianize young Indian people and so draw them away from tribal identification and communal living. The government's ambitious goals of individual transformation mobilized, in the boarding schools, a rigid and detailed military discipline that scheduled every waking moment, organized classrooms and work details, and even mandated a "correct" physical posture, "correct" ways of moving and exercising, and "correct" details of dress. * * *

In the 1870s, Congress authorized army officer Richard H. Pratt to convert military barracks at Carlisle, Pennsylvania, into the Carlisle Indian School, the first federal off-reservation boarding school for Indian youth. Carlisle had been preceded by, and was for many years contemporaneous with, the Indian School at Hampton Institute, a normal and industrial training school for black Americans in Hampton, Virginia. Pratt ran Carlisle in a military fashion, with issued uniforms, close order

* Essay adapted from K. Tsianina Lomawaima, *They Called It Prairie Light* (1994).   Copyright © 1994 by University of Nebraska Press. Reprinted with permission.

drill, and students organized by company and by rank. The educational experiment at Carlisle met with federal approval, and within five years schools had been established in Genoa, Nebraska; Lawrence, Kansas; and Chilocco, Oklahoma. Using a curriculum that emphasized piety, obedience, and manual labor, these schools aimed to transform the Indian child. The essential transformation would be internal, a matter of Christian belief, nontribal identification, mental discipline, and moral elevation. For female students, that meant training for domesticity; for male students, it meant instruction in semi-skilled trades and agriculture. The regimentation of the external body was the essential sign of a new life, of a successful transformation. The famous "before and after" pictures of Carlisle students are as much a part of American iconography as the images of Custer's Last Stand. "Savages" shed buckskin, feathers, robes, and moccasins; long black hair was shorn or bobbed or twisted into identical, "manageable" styles; pinafores, stiff starched collars, stockings, and black oxfords signified the "new woman." * * *

The struggle to reform the Indian home targeted the education of young women. They would serve as the matrons of allotment households, promoting a Christian, civilized lifestyle and supporting their husbands in the difficult climb up the evolutionary staircase (from hunter or pastoralist to farmer). The Victorian vision of Woman as Mother affirmed mother's capacity to bear this burden, to influence society and shape the future by nurturing their children. An epigraph by Helen Hunt prefaced a description of "Home Economics Class Instruction" at Chilocco: "A woman who creates and sustains a home, and under whose hand children grow up to be strong and pure men and women, is a Creator, second only to God." To create this godly creature, Indian schools had to convince or force Indian girls to renounce the teachings of their own mothers. Estelle Reel, superintendent of Indian schools from 1898 to 1910, encouraged the matrons to assure Indian girls who were being trained in housekeeping that "because our grandmothers did things in a certain way is no reason why we should do the same."

MISSISSIPPI BAND OF CHOCTAW INDIANS v. HOLYFIELD

490 U.S. 30 (1989).

JUSTICE BRENNAN delivered the opinion of the Court, in which JUSTICES WHITE, MARSHALL, BLACKMUN, O'CONNOR, and SCALIA joined. JUSTICE STEVENS filed a dissenting opinion, in which THE CHIEF JUSTICE REHNQUIST and KENNEDY joined.

This appeal requires us to construe the provisions of the Indian Child Welfare Act that establish exclusive tribal jurisdiction over child custody proceedings involving Indian children domiciled on the tribe's reservation.

A

The Indian Child Welfare Act of 1978 (ICWA), 92 Stat. 3069, 25 U.S.C.A. §§ 1901–1963, was the product of rising concern in the mid–1970s over the consequences to Indian children, Indian families, and

Indian tribes of abusive child welfare practices that resulted in the separation of large numbers of Indian children from their families and tribes through adoption or foster care placement, usually in non-Indian homes. Senate oversight hearings in 1974 yielded numerous examples, statistical data, and expert testimony documenting what one witness called "[t]he wholesale removal of Indian children from their homes, * * * the most tragic aspect of Indian life today." Indian Child Welfare Program, Hearings before the Subcommittee on Indian Affairs of the Senate Committee on Interior and Insular Affairs, 93d Cong., 2d Sess., 3 (statement of William Byler) (hereinafter 1974 Hearings). Studies undertaken by the Association on American Indian Affairs in 1969 and 1974, and presented in the Senate hearings, showed that 25 to 35% of all Indian children had been separated from their families and placed in adoptive families, foster care, or institutions. Adoptive placements counted significantly in this total: In the State of Minnesota, for example, one in eight Indian children under the age of 18 was in an adoptive home, and during the year 1971–1972 nearly one in every four infants under one year of age was placed for adoption. The adoption rate of Indian children was eight times that of non-Indian children. Approximately 90% of the Indian placements were in non-Indian homes. 1974 Hearings, at 75–83. A number of witnesses also testified to the serious adjustment problems encountered by such children during adolescence,[1] as well as the impact of the adoptions on Indian parents and the tribes themselves.

Further hearings, covering much the same ground, were held during 1977 and 1978 on the bill that became the ICWA. While much of the testimony again focused on the harm to Indian parents and their children who were involuntarily separated by decisions of local welfare authorities, there was also considerable emphasis on the impact on the tribes themselves of the massive removal of their children. For example, Mr. Calvin Isaac, Tribal Chief of the Mississippi Band of Choctaw Indians and representative of the National Tribal Chairmen's Association, testified as follows:

> "Culturally, the chances of Indian survival are significantly reduced if our children, the only real means for the transmission of the tribal

---

1. For example, Dr. Joseph Westermeyer, a University of Minnesota social psychiatrist, testified about his research with Indian adolescents who experienced difficulty coping in white society, despite the fact that they had been raised in a purely white environment:

"[T]hey were raised with a white cultural and social identity. They are raised in a white home. They attended, predominantly white schools, and in almost all cases, attended a church that was predominantly white, and really came to understand very little about Indian culture, Indian behavior, and had virtually no viable Indian identity. They can recall such things as seeing cowboys and Indians on TV and feeling that Indians were [] historical figure[s] but were not a viable contemporary social group.

"Then during adolescence, they found that society was not to grant them the white identity that they had. They began to find this out in a number of ways. For example, a universal experience was that when they began to date white children, the parents of the white youngsters were against this, and there were pressures among white children from the parents not to date these Indian children. * * *

"The other experience was derogatory name calling in relation to their racial identity. * * *

"[T]hey were finding that society was putting on them an identity which they didn't possess and taking from them an identity that they did possess."

heritage, are to be raised in non-Indian homes and denied exposure to the ways of their People. Furthermore, these practices seriously undercut the tribes' ability to continue as self-governing communities. Probably in no area is it more important that tribal sovereignty be respected than in an area as socially and culturally determinative as family relationships."

Chief Isaac also summarized succinctly what numerous witnesses saw as the principal reason for the high rates of removal of Indian children:

"One of the most serious failings of the present system is that Indian children are removed from the custody of their natural parents by nontribal government authorities who have no basis for intelligently evaluating the cultural and social premises underlying Indian home life and childrearing. Many of the individuals who decide the fate of our children are at best ignorant of our cultural values, and at worst contemptful of the Indian way and convinced that removal, usually to a non-Indian household or institution, can only benefit an Indian child."[4]

The congressional findings that were incorporated into the ICWA reflect these sentiments. * * *

At the heart of the ICWA are its provisions concerning jurisdiction over Indian child custody proceedings. Section 1911 lays out a dual jurisdictional scheme. Section 1911(a) establishes exclusive jurisdiction in the tribal courts for proceedings concerning an Indian child "who resides or is domiciled within the reservation of such tribe," as well as for wards of tribal courts regardless of domicile. Section 1911(b), on the other hand, creates concurrent but presumptively tribal jurisdiction in the case of children not domiciled on the reservation: On petition of either parent or the tribe, state-court proceedings for foster care placement or termination of parental rights are to be transferred to the tribal court, except in cases of "good cause," objection by either parent, or declination of jurisdiction by the tribal court.

* * *

The most important substantive requirement imposed on state courts is that of § 1915(a), which, absent "good cause" to the contrary, mandates that adoptive placements be made preferentially with (1) members of the child's extended family, (2) other members of the same tribe, or (3) other Indian families.

The ICWA thus, in the words of the House Report accompanying it, "seeks to protect the rights of the Indian child as an Indian and the rights of the Indian community and tribe in retaining its children in its society." It does so by establishing "a Federal policy that, where possible, an Indian child should remain in the Indian community," and by

---

4. One of the particular points of concern was the failure of non-Indian child welfare workers to understand the role of the extended family in Indian society. The House Report on the ICWA noted: "An Indian child may have scores of, perhaps more than a hundred, relatives who are counted as close, responsible members of the family. Many social workers, untutored in the ways of Indian family life or assuming them to be socially irresponsible, consider leaving the child with persons outside the nuclear family as neglect and thus as grounds for terminating parental rights."

making sure that Indian child welfare determinations are not based on "a white, middle-class standard which, in many cases, forecloses placement with [an] Indian family."

B

This case involves the status of twin babies, known for our purposes as B.B. and G.B., who were born out of wedlock on December 29, 1985. Their mother, J.B., and father, W.J., were both enrolled members of appellant Mississippi Band of Choctaw Indians (Tribe), and were residents and domiciliaries of the Choctaw Reservation in Neshoba County, Mississippi. J.B. gave birth to the twins in Gulfport, Harrison County, Mississippi, some 200 miles from the reservation. On January 10, 1986, J.B. executed a consent-to-adoption form before the Chancery Court of Harrison County. W.J. signed a similar form. On January 16, appellees Orrey and Vivian Holyfield filed a petition for adoption in the same court, and the chancellor issued a Final Decree of Adoption on January 28. Despite the court's apparent awareness of the ICWA, the adoption decree contained no reference to it, nor to the infants' Indian background.

Two months later the Tribe moved in the Chancery Court to vacate the adoption decree on the ground that under the ICWA exclusive jurisdiction was vested in the tribal court. On July 14, 1986, the court overruled the motion, holding that the Tribe "never obtained exclusive jurisdiction over the children involved herein. * * * " The court's one-page opinion relied on two facts in reaching that conclusion. The court noted first that the twins' mother "went to some efforts to see that they were born outside the confines of the Choctaw Indian Reservation" and that the parents had promptly arranged for the adoption by the Holyfields. Second, the court stated: "At no time from the birth of these children to the present date have either of them resided on or physically been on the Choctaw Indian Reservation."

The Supreme Court of Mississippi affirmed. It rejected the Tribe's arguments that the state court lacked jurisdiction and that it, in any event, had not applied the standards laid out in the ICWA. The court recognized that the jurisdictional question turned on whether the twins were domiciled on the Choctaw Reservation. * * *

The sole issue in this case is, as the Supreme Court of Mississippi recognized, whether the twins were "domiciled" on the reservation.

The meaning of "domicile" in the ICWA is, of course, a matter of Congress' intent. The ICWA itself does not define it. The initial question we must confront is whether there is any reason to believe that Congress intended the ICWA definition of "domicile" to be a matter of state law. * * *

It is clear from the very text of the ICWA, not to mention its legislative history and the hearings that led to its enactment, that Congress was concerned with the rights of Indian families and Indian communities *vis-a-vis* state authorities. More specifically, its purpose was, in part, to make clear that in certain situations the state courts did not have jurisdiction over child custody proceedings. Indeed, the congressional findings that are a part of the statute demonstrate that Congress perceived the States and their courts as partly responsible for the problem it intended to correct. See 25 U.S.C.A. § 1901(5) (state "judicial bodies * * * have often failed to recognize the essential tribal relations of Indian people and the cultural and social standards prevailing in Indian communities and families"). Under these circumstances it is most improbable that Congress would have intended to leave the scope of the statute's key jurisdictional provision subject to definition by state courts as a matter of state law.

Second, Congress could hardly have intended the lack of nationwide uniformity that would result from state-law definitions of domicile. * * *

We therefore think it beyond dispute that Congress intended a uniform federal law of domicile for the ICWA.

It remains to give content to the term "domicile" in the circumstances of the present case. The holding of the Supreme Court of Mississippi that the twin babies were not domiciled on the Choctaw Reservation appears to have rested on two findings of fact by the trial court: (1) that they had never been physically present there, and (2) that they were "voluntarily surrendered" by their parents. The question before us, therefore, is whether under the ICWA definition of "domicile" such facts suffice to render the twins nondomiciliaries of the Reservation. * * *

It is undisputed in this case that the domicile of the mother (as well as the father) has been, at all relevant times, on the Choctaw Reservation. Thus, it is clear that at their birth the twin babies were also domiciled on the reservation, even though they themselves had never been there. The statement of the Supreme Court of Mississippi that "[a]t no point in time can it be said the twins * * * were domiciled within the territory set aside for the reservation," may be a correct statement of that State's law of domicile, but it is inconsistent with generally accepted doctrine in this country and cannot be what Congress had in mind when it used the term in the ICWA.

Nor can the result be any different simply because the twins were "voluntarily surrendered" by their mother. Tribal jurisdiction under § 1911(a) was not meant to be defeated by the actions of individual members of the tribe, for Congress was concerned not solely about the interests of Indian children and families, but also about the impact on the tribes themselves of the large numbers of Indian children adopted by non-Indians. The numerous prerogatives accorded the tribes through the ICWA's substantive provisions, e.g., § 1911(a) (exclusive jurisdiction over reservation domiciliaries), 1911(b) (presumptive jurisdiction over nondomiciliaries), 1911(c) (right of intervention), 1912(a) (notice), 1914 (right to petition for invalidation of state-court action), 1915(c) (right to alter presumptive placement priorities applicable to state-court actions), 1915(e) (right to obtain records), 1919 (authority to conclude agreements with States), must, accordingly, be seen as a means of protecting not only the interests of individual Indian children and families, but also of the tribes themselves.

In addition, it is clear that Congress' concern over the placement of Indian children in non-Indian homes was based in part on evidence of the detrimental impact on the children themselves of such placements outside their culture. Congress determined to subject such placements to the ICWA's jurisdictional and other provisions, even in cases where the parents consented to an adoption, because of concerns going beyond the wishes of individual parents. As the 1977 Final Report of the congressionally established American Indian Policy Review Commission stated, in summarizing these two concerns, "[r]emoval of Indian children from their cultural setting seriously impacts a long-term tribal survival and has damaging social and psychological impact on many individual Indian children."

These congressional objectives make clear that a rule of domicile that would permit individual Indian parents to defeat the ICWA's jurisdictional scheme is inconsistent with what Congress intended. The appellees in this case argue strenuously that the twins' mother went to great lengths to give birth off the reservation so that her children could be adopted by the Holyfields. But that was precisely part of Congress' concern. Permitting individual members of the tribe to avoid tribal exclusive jurisdiction by the simple expedient of giving birth off the reservation would, to a large extent, nullify the purpose the ICWA was intended to accomplish. The Supreme Court of Utah expressed this well in its scholarly and sensitive opinion in what has become a leading case on the ICWA:

"To the extent that [state] abandonment law operates to permit [the child's] mother to change [the child's] domicile as part of a scheme to facilitate his adoption by non-Indians while she remains a domiciliary of the reservation, it conflicts with and undermines the operative scheme established by subsections [1911(a)] and [1913(a)] to deal with children of domiciliaries of the reservation and weakens considerably the tribe's ability to assert its interest in its children. The protection of this tribal interest is at the core of the ICWA, which recognizes that the tribe has an interest in the child which is distinct from but on a parity with the interest of the parents. This relationship between Indian tribes and Indian children domiciled on the reservation finds no parallel in other ethnic cultures found in the United States. It is a relationship that many non-Indians find difficult to understand and that non-Indian courts are slow to recognize. It is precisely in recognition of this relationship, however, that the ICWA designates the tribal court as the exclusive forum for the determination of custody and adoption matters for reservation-domiciled Indian children, and the preferred forum for nondomiciliary Indian children. [State] abandonment law cannot be used to frustrate the federal legislative judgment expressed in the ICWA that the interests of the tribe in custodial decisions made with respect to Indian children are as entitled to respect as the interests of the parents." In re *Adoption of Halloway*, 732 P.2d 962, 969–970 (1986).

We agree with the Supreme Court of Utah that the law of domicile Congress used in the ICWA cannot be one that permits individual reservation-domiciled tribal members to defeat the tribe's exclusive jurisdiction by the simple expedient of giving birth and placing the child for adoption off the reservation. Since, for purposes of the ICWA, the twin babies in this case were domiciled on the reservation when adoption proceedings were begun, the Choctaw tribal court possessed exclusive jurisdiction pursuant to 25 U.S.C.A. § 1911(a). The Chancery Court of Harrison County was, accordingly, without jurisdiction to enter a decree of adoption; under ICWA § 104, 25 U.S.C.A. § 1914, its decree of January 28, 1986, must be vacated. We are not unaware that over three years have passed since the twin babies were born and placed in the Holyfield home, and that a court deciding their fate today is not writing on a blank slate in the same way it would have in January 1986. Three years' development of family ties cannot be undone, and a separation at this point would doubtless cause considerable pain.

Whatever feelings we might have as to where the twins should live, however, it is not for us to decide that question. We have been asked to decide the legal question of who should make the custody determination concerning these children—not what the outcome of that determination should be. The law places that decision in the hands of the Choctaw tribal court. Had the mandate of the ICWA been followed in 1986, of course, much potential anguish might have been avoided. * * *

The judgment of the Supreme Court of Mississippi is reversed, and the case is remanded for further proceedings not inconsistent with this opinion.

JUSTICE STEVENS, with whom THE CHIEF JUSTICE and JUSTICE KENNEDY join, dissenting.

* * *

If J.B. and W.J. had established a domicile off the reservation, the state courts would have been required to give effect to their choice of jurisdiction; there should not be a different result when the parents have not changed their own domicile, but have expressed an unequivocal intent to establish a domicile for their children off the reservation. * * *

When an Indian child is temporarily off the reservation, but has not been abandoned to a person off the reservation, the tribe has an interest in exclusive jurisdiction. The ICWA expresses the intent that exclusive tribal jurisdiction is not so frail that it should be defeated as soon as the Indian child steps off the reservation. Similarly, when the child is abandoned by one parent to a person off the reservation, the tribe and the other parent domiciled on the reservation may still have an interest in the exercise of exclusive jurisdiction. That interest is protected by the rule that a child abandoned by one parent takes on the domicile of the other. But when an Indian child is deliberately abandoned by both parents to a person off the reservation, no purpose of the ICWA is served by closing the state courthouse door to them. * * *

The interpretation of domicile adopted by the Court * * * forces parents of Indian children who desire to invoke state-court jurisdiction to establish a domicile off the reservation. Only if the custodial parent has the wealth and ability to establish a domicile off the reservation will the parent be able to use the processes of state court. I fail to see how such a requirement serves the paramount congressional purpose of "promot[ing] the stability and security of Indian tribes and families."

The Court concludes its opinion with the observation that whatever anguish is suffered by the Indian children, their natural parents, and their adoptive parents because of its decision today is a result of their failure to initially follow the provisions of the ICWA. By holding that parents who are domiciled on the reservation cannot voluntarily avail themselves of the adoption procedures of state court and that all such proceedings will be void for lack of jurisdiction, however, the Court establishes a rule of law that is virtually certain to ensure that similar anguish will be suffered by other families in the future. Because that result is not mandated by the language of the ICWA and is contrary to its purposes, I respectfully dissent.

Notes and Questions

1. Why might a mother or father of any race seek an adoptive placement for an out-of-wedlock child? Should federal law be permitted to frustrate that maternal or paternal choice? Should choice reside exclusively in the mother? Do the issues surrounding Indian sovereignty or the special history of white interference in Indian families make the case of Indian children unique?

2. Louis La Rose, chairman of the Winnebago Tribe, testified:

I think the cruelest trick that the white man has ever done to Indian children is to take them into adoption courts, erase all of their records and send them off to some nebulous family that has a value system that is A–1 in the State of Nebraska and that child reaches 16 or 17, he is a little brown child residing in a white community and he goes back to the reservation and he has absolutely no idea who his relatives are, and they effectively make him a non-person and I think * * * they destroy him.

490 U.S. at 50, n.24.

3. In the cited *Halloway* case, the child's aunt testified that

she concealed her intention to remove Jeremiah from the reservation from the Navajo Division of Social Welfare despite her knowledge that the Division was attempting to handle Jeremiah's situation at the time. She explained that if the Division had learned of her concerns about Jeremiah's being raised by his maternal grandparents, it might have placed him in another Indian home on the reservation. She testified that she did not want him placed in an Indian home because she thought that other Indian homes would have drinking problems similar to those plaguing Jeremiah's family and that Jeremiah could learn about his Indian heritage later. The tribe learned of Jeremiah's proposed adoption only after the Utah court had found that the child's domicile had shifted to Utah, thus providing the state court with jurisdiction over him pursuant to the ICWA. The tribe was informed of both the proposed adoption and Jeremiah's new domicile by the notice sent at the direction of the Utah court. The tribe received this notice approximately five months after Jeremiah's mother executed the consent to adoption and seven months after Jeremiah had been removed from the reservation.

In re *Adoption of Halloway*, 732 P.2d 962, 968 (Utah 1986).

If a family member of a child, who is a member of a native tribe, makes a decision she/he believes is in the child's best interest, why should federal law nullify that decision? Doesn't federal or state legal intervention nullify the notion of extended family responsibility? What if a decision is made by the child's father or mother? How often have federal determinations dictated decisions in your family?

4.   Barbara Kingsolver, a novelist, has one of her characters remark:

> For this whole century, right up until 1978 when we got the Indian Child Welfare Act, social workers would come in here with no understanding of how our families worked. They would see a child who'd been left with someone outside the nuclear family, and they would call that neglect. To us, that is an insane rationale. We don't distinguish between father, uncle, mother, grandmother. We don't think of ourselves as having extended families. We look at you guys and think you have contracted families. We couldn't understand why they were taking us apart. My brother Gabe, going to a man and woman in Texas when we had a whole family here. I've seen babies carried off with no more thought than you'd give a bag of brown sugar you picked up at the market.

Jennifer Nutt Carleton, *The Indian Child Welfare Act: A Study in the Codification of the Ethnic Best Interests of the Child*, 81 Marq. L. Rev. 21 (1997) (quoting Barbara Kingsolver, *Pigs in Heaven* 284 (1993)); see also Alissa M. Wilson, *Best Interests of Children in the Cultural Context of the Indian Child Welfare Act*, 28 Loy. U. Chi. L.J. 839 (1997).

TWILA L. PERRY

The Transracial Adoption Controversy: An Analysis
of Discourse and Subordination
21 N.Y.U. Rev. of L. & Social Change 33, 42, 54–56 (1993–94).*

In a well-known 1972 position paper, the National Association of Black Social Workers (NABSW) took a strong position against transracial adoption. [Eds. The NABSW was concerned only with black-white transracial adoption.] This group argued that Black children belong physically, psychologically, and culturally in Black families and that transracial adoption constitutes a form of cultural genocide. Many writers have stated that, as a result of the position taken by the NABSW, transracial adoptions declined precipitously, falling from 2 percent of all adoptions in 1975 to 1 percent of all adoptions in 1987. The NABSW has not wavered from its position.

There is little agreement about the significance and impact of transracial adoption. Some contend that such adoptions are a necessary means of providing homes to Black children and that Black children raised in white families can grow up to be happy, healthy members of society. Others have argued that Black children will inevitably suffer if white parents raise them. These opponents of transracial adoption contend that there is no shortage of Black homes—only a shortage of resources and commitment by whites to recruit and support adoptive Black families and to encourage the placement of Black children in their own extended families. * * *

Some authors who write about transracial adoption from the colorblind individualist perspective contextualize transracial adoption within the broader governmental control over individual choices regarding family structure. Under this analysis, the acceptance of an individual's choice to transracially adopt is a logical extension of the 1967 Supreme Court decision in *Loving v. Virginia*, in which the Court struck down a state statute prohibiting interracial marriage. Before the *Loving* decision, a number of states had outlawed such marriages. *Loving* has served as a springboard for arguments supporting the right of personal choice in creating families in other contexts, such as artificial insemination, surrogate motherhood, nonnuclear family living arrangements, and gay and lesbian families. Thus, in attacking policy preferences for placing Black children with Black adoptive parents, Professor [Elizabeth] Bartholet cites *Loving* as the Supreme Court's endorsement of the idea that "the state is not permitted to insist that race count as a factor in the ordering of people's most private lives." Under this logic, the choice to create a multiracial family through adoption is an issue of individual rights as much as the choice to create a multiracial family through marriage.

From a perspective of color and community consciousness, a critical part of the analysis of autonomy and choice in the creation of families derives from both the history and the current conditions that affect the ability of Black people in this country to create and sustain families. Although *Loving* is important, the history of family and autonomy begins before that decision. The history dates back to the time of slavery, when white slaveowners had virtually complete control over the fate of Black families. Society accorded no respect to Black people's choices to become husbands and wives or to raise children. White slavemasters had complete control over Black children; slave mothers had no claim to their children under the law. The slaveowner could sell Black children, beat them, kill them, or remove them from their parents to be raised in his home as house servants. The slave had no right to engage in individual, autonomous decision making about family life.

The question for some Blacks may be whether the system of white control over the fate of Black children has really changed. The number of transracial adoptions in this country started to increase only after white babies became a scarce commodity. Social service agencies, largely dominated by whites, began to place Black children in white homes. To some Blacks, this may suggest that the disempowerment of enslaved Blacks has continued in modern-day America. Whites still hold power over the lives of Black children, determining where and with whom Black children will live. Black children are still commodities to be purchased and sold in a white-controlled marketplace.

In contrast, white ethnic and religious groups have placed an emphasis on intragroup adoptive placements for their own children. For example, historically Jewish and Catholic social services agencies have exercised great influence, if not complete control, over decisions regarding the adoptive placements of children from their ethnic or religious groups. The agenda of these groups has clearly been to place children intraethnically and intrareligiously. It is troubling that the NABSW is criticized for having the same goal—placing children within their group of origin.

In addition, many Blacks recognize that the oppressive conditions under which Black families live render Black families more vulnerable to state intervention by government agencies and thus cause disproportionate numbers of Blacks to lose custody of their children. For these families, surviving each day as an intact unit may be a constant struggle; they simply do not have the autonomy to make decisions about everyday family life that the more affluent take for granted. For many Blacks, then, transracial adoption is inextricably linked to the fragility of the Black family, which fragility is a result of racism and oppression. From this perspective, the issue is not autonomy—choosing an orange, green, or blue family—but the survival of Black families in a hostile environment.

Notes and Questions

1. In the 1990s, large numbers of Chinese girl babies have been adopted by families in the United States. Most of these families have been white. Does this practice pose a threat to Asian-American culture? To the individual children? Is the black-white transracial adoption controversy a good parallel to this situation?

2. Amerasian children of war often find themselves ostracized in their home countries, for complex reasons. See Chapter 6 § 1, *supra*.

SHIRLEE TAYLOR HAIZLIP

The Sweeter the Juice: A Family Memoir in Black and White
13–15 (1994).*

Sometimes I look at people and wonder if they are related to me. I do this in public places and private spaces. There I am, in airport terminals, and train stations, on ballroom floors and sandy beaches, studying people who might be my relatives. At parties and dances I have become momentarily distracted by familiar yet unknown faces. I scrutinize the shape of the nose, the cast of the eyes, the curve of the lips and the jut of the chin. Whenever I see a tall white man with the slightly kinky golden brown hair, subtly flared nostrils and large ears of my brother, I say, "There's a Morris."

I often wonder what those I observe would think if they knew what I was doing. Would they be amused, insulted, nervous? I have indulged in this curious pastime since I was eight years old, when I first understood that all but one of my mother's family had become white.

I am a black woman, but many of you would never know it. On the other hand, I do subscribe to the racial mythology that black people know their own. My skin is as light as that of an average white person. The skin of my sisters and brother is as light as, if not lighter than, mine. But we have lived as, worked as, and mostly married black people. Our psyches, souls, and sensibilities are black. Sociologists would say we have been "socialized" as black people. Yet our lives have been deeply colored by our absence of deep color.

The mirror would say that my mother's skin is the fairest of them all. She has always been a beautiful woman with dark hair, large and expressively sad, dark eyes, a heart-shaped face and a gracefully defined mouth. Her nose is prominent and long. All of her life, like many other people whose light color does not immediately define their race, she has been called "exotic-looking." I too have inherited that label and unwillingly passed it along to my daughters.

Most of us are curious as to who we are and why we look the way we do. Many of us know the answers to those questions. Some of us have no idea. This primeval need to know informs my search for my relatives. I liken my curiosity to that of adopted children looking for their kin. I am not entirely sure, if and when the time comes, that I will be comforted to know the sculpture of their cheeks or the architecture of their noses.

Mysteries of color have encased my family for five generations. Putting together the bits and pieces of my past creates a quilt of melanin patches shading from dark to light, red to brown, tan to pink. There are ragged edges and missing segments. I dream I will find some of myself in those holes and gaps. I need to finish the quilt, wearing it smooth until its edges feel soft to my touch, blending its clashing colors to my own notion of harmony. Only then can I store it away in a safe place, taking it out every once in a while to look at.

Make no mistake. I do not lust after my whiteness. More often than not, I feel ambivalent about the white part of me and those circumstances, both known and imagined, that resulted in the mix. I am not really sure what the white portion of me means, if anything. Is it a separate self? Does it think differently from my black self? Does it have a subconscious racial memory? How can I love it when it may not love me?

Finding the missing souls of my family has supplied some of the answers. I will keep looking for those who can provide the vanished biographies; those who can restore the limbs amputated from the family tree. In searching for my family, I yearn to close the circle of my existence.

What is it I will get from confronting these living ghosts? A knowledge of life on the other side? The opportunity to feel superior? The revenge of exposure and embarrassment? Recognition, contrition, forgiveness or what might have been their sin of abandonment? A gathering unto their bosoms? Sometimes I believe I want all of these things. Often I think I want none of them. More than anything, it is the attempt to understand and consolidate identity that drives my exploration.

In a broader sense, my family's story reflects white and black America's historical attitude toward skin color. Our experience suggests that America is not what it presents itself to be. Some geneticists have said that 95 percent of "white" Americans have widely varying degrees of black heritage. According to *The Source: A Guidebook to American Genealogy,* 75 percent of all African–Americans have at least one white ancestor and 15 percent have predominantly white blood lines. All statistics, of course, are subject to interpretation and reinterpretation, but the fact that anthropologists and biologists continue to glean these truths from their study of genetic data gives weight to the claim that there are no "real white Americans." As Adrian Piper wrote, "[t]he longer a person's family has lived in this country, the higher the probable percentage of African ancestry—bad news for the DAR, I'm afraid."

In other words, many Americans are not who they think they are; hundreds of thousands of white people in America are not "white." Some know it; others don't. Ten thousand people each year cross the visible and invisible color line and become "white." If a new sociological method of determining race were devised, equal numbers of black people might no longer be black. What happened in my family and many others like it calls into question the concept of color as a means of self-definition.

Genes and chromosomes from Africa, Europe and a pristine America commingled and created me. I have been called Egyptian, Italian, Jewish, French, Iranian, Armenian, Syrian, Spanish, Portuguese and Greek. I have also been called black and Peola and nigger and high yellow and bright. I am an American anomaly. I am an American ideal. I am the American nightmare. I am the Martin Luther King dream. I am the new America.

Notes and Questions

1.   The division of many American families into separate "black" and "white" tributaries has had an effect not only on the individual psyches of those who have lost relatives or never had a chance to know them. It has also affected patterns of wealth. For instance, Melvin L. Oliver and Thomas M. Shapiro found that, despite the gradually converging incomes of middle-class African Americans and middle-class Whites following the Second Reconstruction, middle-class Whites continue to enjoy the lion's share of wealth, meaning assets like houses, businesses, jewelry, antiques, and financial instruments that can be passed from generation to generation. See Melvin L. Oliver & Thomas M. Shapiro, *Black Wealth/White Wealth* (1995).

Part of this imbalance is due to the fact that over the centuries, white testators directed their property toward their "white" heirs and left little or nothing to their "black" heirs. Even when white fathers, for example, desired to leave property to their African–American mistresses or "mixed" children, the law often made it difficult to do this. See Virginia R. Dominguez, *White by Definition: Social Classification in Creole Louisiana* (1986) (detailing how the Louisiana Civil Code made it difficult both for white fathers to acknowledge their "illegitimate" children of color and for those fathers to bequeath property to them). Miscegenation laws and strong social sanctions against interracial relationships also played a part in creating this imbalance in wealth. Compare this imbalance to the transfers of wealth from

Latino/a and Indian people to white people through intermarriage discussed earlier in this chapter.

LISA JONES

Bulletproof Diva: Tales of Race, Sex, and Hair
53–66 (1994).*

Who are you, what are you, where are you from, no, where are you really from, where are your parents from, are your grandparents Americans? Are you from here, what's your background, what's your nationality, where do you live? Are you black, are you white, do you speak Spanish? Are you really white, are you really black? Are you Puerto Rican, are you half and half, are you biracial, multiracial, interracial, transracial, racially unknown, race neutral, colorless, colorblind, down with the rat race or the human race? Who are you? Where are you coming from? Who are your people?

THE IDENTITY FAIRY: Excuse me, before you get all up in my business, don't you want to know my name?

Should we keep it simple or run the extended-play version? I hail from the Afro-rainbow tribe. Papa's black by way of Newark and South Carolina, Mom's Jewish by way of Brooklyn and Eastern Europe. Ethnically I'm African American. Politically I'm a person of color. My résumé: Womanist-theater producing circa the eighties; day jobbing at an alternative newspaper, looking to define the role of race woman in the multiculti nineties. My faith is strictly rhythm and blues. Still hung up on soul music, poetry and jazz, sixties girl groups. Air guitar to the Isley Brothers and Living Colour. Marley heals my soul. Al Green and Sting wake me up in the morning. I go to Aretha and Joni Mitchell when I need to cry.

I know a Panamanian–American computer technician who is deep brown as a Senegalese and ethnically Latino. He speaks Spanish and Brooklyn–Italian blue-collar English. Ask him what he is, he'll tell you black Hispanic. I know a Caribbean–American architect who has lived on three continents, calls soccer football, and has a white great-grandfather and a Chinese great-grandfather, though he himself is gingerbread brown. This guy is from Grenada originally, though he identifies politically as African American. I also know a music promoter, black, who was raised by his mother, Jewish, in the suburbs of San Francisco. But from the way this guy swaggers and curses you'd think he was gangsta straight out of Compton. Trust me, all three guys are cute.

Say I marry one of these guys, will our children be multiracial, multiethnic, African American, black, people of color? Will they be called "niggers," "cocos," or "spics"? Will they live in an America where race, as Cornel West reports, still matters? Will they live in a war zone like Bosnia, where ethnicity, culture, and religion still matter? Or will AIDS and toxic waste cut their lives short before they can begin their pontificating, philosophizing, awfulizing, agonizing, rejoicing, preachifying, and signifying over just who they are in this shaky home we call the Americas?

Last night I had dinner with a group of friends who are Asian, Latino, and African American, and combinations of the above mixed with European. I love us dearly. We take David Dinkins's gorgeous mosaic quite literally and we aren't alone. We value the ethnic histories, rituals, stories passed down to us from our families of origin, from our families of choice, and from our book learning. We swap these traditions, make up new ones. At home, we identify each other by turf: Peter is Miss Mott Street, I'm Miss Bowery, Miss Dorado Beach is Maria. Yet we'd probably be more comfortable with the public monikers black, Latino, or Asian, than with "biracial" or "multiracial."

Most of us just hit the big three-oh. We saw the sixties as grade-school kids. We memorized TV pictures of dogs sicced on black folks in Mississippi and stories our grandparents told of Japanese internment camps out West. We can tell you about the years before English-as-a-second-language programs, when little girls like María, Margie, and Gladys were thrown into English-only class-rooms and left to sink or tread water. We got to Ivy League colleges thanks to affirmative action programs. Corporate America hired us under diversity initiatives.

The idea of a "multiracial" category on the census fills us with ambivalence. Is this just one more polite, largely academic game of identity hopscotch folks are playing while Los Angeles burns? Still, we're keeping our ears open.

What do you know about the groups that are behind this census movement? Are they a multiracial, interracial Mafia? Biracial Rambos and contras? Are they white parents of mixed-race bambinos bartering for a safety zone for their café-au-lait kids? Or are they regular folks searching for a new way to identify their families?

THE IDENTITY FAIRY: This is what I know so far. There's the Association of MultiEthnic Americans (AMEA), a nationwide confederation of the inter-racial/multiethnic support groups based in San Francisco. And there's Project RACE (short for Reclassify All Children Equally), a lobbying organization out of Atlanta that campaigns on the local level. As of May 1993, due to the labors of Project RACE, three states have passed and two are reviewing legislation that adds the category "multiracial" to school forms.

AMEA and project RACE are at the forefront of the census movement. [These groups and several others converged] on Washington at hearings before a subcommittee on the census. If their efforts pay off, "multiracial" will replace "other race" on census forms in the year 2000. What this will mean, no one's sure. Could there be a massive flight from the categories Hispanic and black? Will the 9.8 million Americans who checked "other race" in 1990 switch over without a hitch to "multira-cial"? By the turn of the new century, will the numbers in the "other race," now "multiracial" category, have multiplied dramatically? Will America have become the brown stew pot that *Time* and *Newsweek* have been warning us about since the mid-eighties? And call them black, multiracial, or Hispanic (another ethnic appellation concocted by politics), will the majority of these brown ones still be poor folks? Or might all Americans check "multiracial," finally recognizing their heritage for what it is?

Give us your off-the-cuff take on this census movement.

THE IDENTITY FAIRY: I haven't been to any meetings, but I did speak at length with several organizers and foot soldiers, including, among others, Carlos Fernandez, president of AMEA, Susan Graham, executive director of Project RACE, Kendra Wallace, Project's vice president in California, and Michelle Erickson of Chicago. Erickson pulled her five-year-old son out of the public school system rather than choose between existing racial categories. (She identifies Andrew, her son, as biracial.) Instigated by Erickson's letter-writing campaign and the lobbying of Project RACE, the state of Illinois is now considering the "multiracial" category.

Many in the census movement see the bottom line of their crusade as a fight for the self-esteem of their children. Graham of Project RACE, who is a white mother of two, as she calls them, "multiracial kids," says children are psychologically healthiest when they have accurate racial labels at their disposal. But what on earth constitutes an accurate racial label? And if the census movement is ultimately out to do away with such sacrosanct labels, will creating new ones accomplish this?

Beyond the children's self-esteem issue, the movement's larger agenda and philosophical goals registered blurry. Race is configured as choice, as a category on a school form. Race is not seen as a political/economic construct, a battleground where Americans vie for power and turf, but a question of color, a stick-on, peel-off label. If there *is* an end goal to the census movement's efforts, it appears to be assimilation. I don't mean this is in the didactic sense of chiding others for wanting their piece of American pie; I mean it as finding a place to fit in, creating a space of comfort for self, away from the choke hold of race. The business as usual of discrimination, against the have-nots, who are usually shades of brown, and in favor of the have-sos, who are usually shades of pink, is left undisturbed.

When I heard that all state legislation for school forms would remain symbolic until the Congress and the Office of Management and Budget vote to add multiracial to the list of official categories, I scratched my head. And when I heard that the activists couldn't agree on whether those who checked the "multiracial" box would be considered a disadvantaged minority deserving of federal protections under the Voting Rights Act, I scratched some more. Why was this movement—potentially a vital movement for the acknowledgment of hybrid cultures/lives—being tied to a kite that no one could steer?

Do you have other concerns about the census movement?

THE IDENTITY FAIRY: Let's look at a few:

Is race (and racism) left intact? Instead of fighting for a new racial category, if the end goal is, as census activists say, to do away with the biological pseudoscience of race, why aren't they in the trenches casting stones at institutional racism? Anna Deavere Smith's *Fires in the Mirror* quotes an interview the playwright did with Angela Davis. Davis says she feels tentative about the meaning of race these days, but not tentative at all about racism. People of color, whether they call themselves biracial, Swirls (as they do in Fostorio, Ohio), or zebra Americans, are disproportionately members of America's underclass. Here's a meaningful contrast: Ohio became the first state last year to adopt the multiracial category on school forms. This year [Eds. 1993], Ohio saw a bloody uprising at the Lucasville state prison. Almost 60 percent of prisoners there are black men, though African Americans make up barely one quarter of the state's population. Will the symbolic recognition of multiracial identity reverse numbers like these?

I was struck that the census movement had no alliances with progressive organizations representing other people of color. None of these organizations had staged a teach-in or protested over the miscarriage of justice in the Rodney King case. Was biraciality being constructed as a less progressive stance than identifying as a "person of color," that catchphrase invented in the eighteenth century, then popularized in the seventies, as an expression of solidarity with other p.o.c.s. worldwide?

Cape Town, U.S.A.? It's been asked before, and until I hear a good comeback, the question stands: Would "multiracial" be akin to South Africa's "colored" caste created under apartheid? Carlos Fernandez of AMEA believes that an "in-between" racial category isn't racist in itself, it is how such a category is used. Yet why wouldn't multiracial/colored be mythologized or positioned politically any differently in America?

Are we special? The census movement and its "interracial/biracial nationalists," as I refer to them playfully, claim biraciality as a mark of "racial" singularity, one that in America (where most racial groups are multiethnic and multicultural) has little grounding. Their insistence on biraciality's unique status borders on elitism. They marvel at the perks of biraciality: that biracials have several cultures at their disposal. (Though don't we all as Americans?) They say things like "biracial people are free of bias because they embody both black and white." Can you fight essentialism with essentialism? Are we to believe that all biracials are chosen people, free of prejudice, self-interest, and Republican Christian fundamentalism?

By proclaiming specialness[,] aren't biracials still clinging to the niche of exotic other? "How could we not love them, they're so cute," boasted one white mother active in the census movement of her biracial children. Minus butter-pecan skin and Shirley Temple curls would they be less an attractive proposition? * * *

What's history got to do with it? As black/white biracials, when we distance ourselves from the African–American freedom struggle, from aging, though historically critical, ideas like "black power" and "black community," do we fail to honor a history that brought us to where we are today? Is biraciality political sedition? And if it feels that way, and it shouldn't, how can we make it feel less so? Are there ways to be responsible to a history that we are indebted to without being imprisoned by it?

I found the generalizations the census movers made about African Americans disturbing. Resistance from some blacks to the multiracial category was translated into resistance from the entire African–American population. Aren't some of the parents involved in the census movement African Americans? The bills to add the "multiracial" category on the state level have all been introduced by African–American legislators. The census initiative has garnered support from local chapters of the NAACP. *Essence* magazine and other black publications spread the word about AMEA and fellow interracial groups long before their white counterparts.

To say that biracials have been cold-shouldered by African Americans throughout history, as some activists suggested, is selective ignorance. Black communities have always been shelter to multiethnic people, perhaps not an unproblematic shelter, yet a shelter nonetheless. Black folks, I'd venture, have welcomed difference in their communities more than most Americans. * * *

Are we family? Shouldn't we ask what makes biracial people a community? What holds us together other than a perceived sense of our own difference from the ethnic mainstream? Consider if the Mexican–Samoan kid in San Diego has the same needs as the black-Jewish kid from New York's Upper West Side? Maybe politically as people of color, but do they share a definitive mixed-race culture? And if they do, should we call it "biraciality" or should we call it "American culture"?

Does blackness remain a stigma? As my telephone travels made clear, the census camp is not minus attitudes of: "If you had a choice you'd be anything but black." Biraciality was posited by some as an escape from the "blemish of blackness." Chicago mother Michelle Erickson asked me quite innocently if I knew how degrading it was "to be attached to categories like black or Hispanic." Kendra Wallace, a biracial woman in her early twenties, pronounced rules of membership in the black community to be too stiff–based, she feels, on such criteria as "hair texture and whether one speaks proper English or not." (Is African–American diversity still that invisible to the world? One could have come away with a picture far more complex by watching a week's worth of sitcoms.)

A moment of cruel and unusual irony took place in a conversation with Project RACE's Susan Graham. During Black History Month, Graham's son returned home with some materials on Langston Hughes. Graham was disappointed that the school had failed to focus on "Langston Hughes's biraciality." I reminded Graham that African Americans as a whole were a multiethnic and multiracial folk, and that Hughes never hid the fact that he had white family, yet he "cast his lot," as the expression went back then, with his darker kin. Hughes's writing, one can safely say, celebrates, if not romanticizes African–American culture. Graham seemed irritated. The one-drop rule was the only thing that kept him in the black community, she insisted. If Hughes were alive today, he would choose to be multiracial, he would identify first with mixed-race people and the work of her lobbying group.

People of all races and cultures should feel free to claim Hughes as an idol, but wasn't Graham aware of a rather painful history? One where black people have had their every gift confiscated and attributed to others? Would this now happen in the name of multiracialism?

Seems like you've exhausted the critical tip. Did you happen upon anything constructive in your telephone encounters with the biracial movement?

THE IDENTITY FAIRY: Carlos Fernandez said something that made sense. Official recognition of multiracial identity may not end racism; it is, however, a necessary step. If we refuse to recognize that any material reality exists between black and white, we do nothing except enshrine these social boundaries—and enshrine the political divide that upholds them.

Certainly the daguerreotype of mixed-race people as freaks of nature could use a long overdue slashing. If the biracial lobby can help in this regard, bless them. Says Kendra Wallace: "We're invisible or our identities are always problematized and sexualized." Our "bloods" are at war inside of us. If mixed race were made normal, we could look forward to the comic mulatto, the introspective, the slovenly. We might one day come to miss ye olde tragic mulatto, the world's pet mule.

As much as I found myself resisting the biracial nationalists, to deny a group the right to identify as they wish to seems equally reactionary. In October last year the San Diego Unified School District, known for its conservatism, balked at admitting a little boy to grammar school until his mother, Patricia Whitebread, who is black, assigned him an "appropriate race." (Unlike many school forms nationally, San Diego's has no "other" designation.) White-bread refused. The school district admitted the child anyway. Later the district classified her son as black without Whitebread's permission.

The activists I spoke to framed their cause as a civil rights movement. Perhaps one not as transparently vital as a movement for equal opportunity in employment or fair access to housing, but certainly one consummate with religious freedom of expression. In *Interrace*, psychologist Francis Wardle, director of the Center for the Study of Biracial Children, a clearinghouse in Colorado, makes a passionate appeal for interracial family networks not to be seen as a threat to African Americans:

"We are so aware of the need to improve conditions for so many blacks in this country that we are very puzzled some high profile blacks spend time and energy fighting us.

"We are not the enemy. . . . Don't insist we must raise our children to belong to a distinctive (and arbitrary) racial or ethnic category. Don't say that history and society must define who we are and what we want our children to become."

Perhaps the arrival of the biracialists might finally drive home to traditional ethnic communities the need for more proactive coalition politics. Kendra Wallace thought biracial organizing would allow people to leave racial enclaves, build bridges, and in time, return. In the lore of the passing novels, those who "passed for white" (or in this case "stood for colored") always found their way back to the black hearth. Of course the black hearth, as we approach the twenty-first century is more fragmented and scattered than ever. * * *

What's your idea of art and scholarship that politicizes multiracialism?

THE IDENTITY FAIRY: Certainly the visual art and writings of Adrian Piper provide keen example. Piper works genius at demystifying the political economy of what she tags "racial classification." Her call to American whites to face up to their black heritage (and to blacks to do the reverse) takes multiracialism/multiculturalism beyond politically correct arts programming and into the realm of configuring a new American identity.

The work of writers and media artists Guillermo Gómez-Peña and Coco Fusco also stands out. In her contribution to the anthology *Black Popular Culture* Fusco tells us that in Cuba, where black people in her family come from, there's an expression that goes *"Chivo que rompe tambor con su pellejo paga,"* which translates literally, "The goat who breaks the drum will have to pay with his skin." The phrase has another meaning as well: "The troublemaker turns him- or herself into the instrument to continue the music." Fusco argues that "black popular cultures, especially musical cultures, have generated an abundance of archetypes that embrace dissonance and contend with internal difference; these [are] semantic residues of histories of contradiction and conflict. Maybe one of these days our intellectual debate will catch up with our popular cultural ability to engage dissent, without the defensiveness that continuously rears its head."

Gómez-Peña's work takes on America in the "intercultural crisis." Writes critic Richard Schechner: "Interculturalists [such as Gómez-Peña] refuse utopian schemes, refuse to cloak power arrangements and struggles. Instead, interculturalists probe the confrontations, ambivalences, disruptions, fears, disturbances, and difficulties when and where cultures collide, overlap or pull away from each other. Interculturalists explore misunderstandings, broken messages, and failed translations—what is not pure and what cannot successfully fuse. These are seen not as disasters, but as fertile rifts of creative possibilities."

Any last words of advice to those swimming in the identity pool?

THE IDENTITY FAIRY: As you get older, chances are you will define yourself by your alliances with a multitude of communities. No one community will speak for you completely and no one community should be so static as to not let you share in others.

As for the biracial nationalists and their movement: Check them out, debate them, start your own. Don't accept any position—be it biracial/multiracial/interracial/African/Asian/or Latin American—as a political catchall.

Challenge all your communities to live up to you. The late poet Audre Lorde, African American, Caribbean American, feminist, gay, and supporter of the global causes of people of color, always spoke as a member of all her many homes.

In coming to self, balance individual identity with a responsibility to and critical eye on history. I'll never forget visiting the Afro–American

Cultural Center at Yale as a prefreshman. I wandered around the building looking at the posters and murals, remnants of the late sixties, of the days when black students were admitted to mainstream universities in sizable numbers, of student protest for admission and retention initiatives, of sit-ins for ethnic studies departments. Alone, I walked the rooms of the House, as we call it, and felt the spirits of those students. A priceless moral and intellectual inheritance was being passed to me. On the train back home, I wept all kinds of tears: angry tears, tears of pride, gratitude tears. Later I would move away from the House and find other homes, but I always took the House and that inheritance with me.

Welcome to America. It ain't as airbrushed as a Benetton ad, but it's a happening place. Hope you brought your Rollerblades *and* your Air Jordans.

Notes and Questions

1. For the 2000 Census, the Office of Management and Budget declined to create a new category called "multiracial." However, respondents will be permitted to select more than one racial-ethnic category. OMB also made several other changes to its racial-ethnic definitions and categories:

• The Asian or Pacific Islander category was broken into two categories: one called "Asian" and the other called "Native Hawaiian or Other Pacific Islander." The Native Hawaiian or Other Pacific Islander category will be defined as "a person having origins in any of the original peoples of Hawaii, Guam, Samoa, or other Pacific Islands." The "Asian" category will be defined as "a person having origins in any of the original peoples of the Far East, Southeast Asia, or the Indian subcontinent including, for example, Cambodia, China, India, Japan, Korea, Malaysia, Pakistan, the Philippine Islands, Thailand, and Vietnam."

• The "Hispanic" category will be renamed "Hispanic or Latino."

• The definition of the "American Indian or Alaska Native" category will be modified to include "the original peoples from Central and South America."

• The "Black" category will be renamed "Black or African American."

OMB also noted two areas where in its view further research was needed: (1) how to deal with people of part "Hispanic or Latino" origin, who at present are asked either to identify themselves as either of Hispanic or Latino origin or not; (2) whether there should be an ethnic category for Arabs/Middle Easterners.

Office of Management and Budget, *Revisions to the Standards for the Classification of Federal Data on Race and Ethnicity*, February 12, 1998, http://www.whitehouse.gov/WH/EOP/OMB/html/fedreg/Ombdir15.html

2. What is at stake in the redefinition of census categories? Tanya Hernández argues that both symbolic and material politics are involved, and that the two are sometimes in conflict. For her critical assessment of the Multiracial Category Movement, see Tanya Hernández, *"Multiracial" Discourse: Racial Classifications in an Era of Color–Blind Jurisprudence*, 57 Md. L. Rev. 97 (1998) (excerpted in Chapter 1). For an analysis of the literature about multiracialism, see Jean Stefancic, *Multiracialism: A Bibliographic Essay and Critique in Memory of Trina Grillo*, 81 Minn. L. Rev. 1521 (1997).

Chapter 12

RACISM AND POPULAR CULTURE: HISTORICAL IMAGES AND CURRENT SUCCESSES

Perhaps abetted by the climate of free expression discussed in Chapter 10, *supra*, much of American popular culture is deeply and carelessly racist. Why is this so, and what can be done about it?

SECTION 1. CULTURAL IMAGERY

RICHARD DELGADO & JEAN STEFANCIC

Images of the Outsider in American Law and Culture: Can Free Expression Remedy Systemic Social Ills?
77 Cornell L. Rev. 1258, 1260–81 (1992).*

Examining the history of ethnic depiction for each of the four main minority subgroups of color—Mexicans, African American, Asians, and Native Americans—in the United States, in each case we found the same sad story: Each group is depicted, in virtually every epoch, in terms that can only be described as demeaning or worse. In addition, we found striking parallels among the stigma-pictures that society disseminated of the four groups. The stock characters may have different names and appear at different times, but they bear remarkable likenesses and seem to serve similar purposes for the majority culture. * * *

The belief that we can somehow control our consciousness despite limitations of time and positionality we call the *empathic fallacy*. In literature, the pathetic fallacy holds that nature is like us, that it is endowed with feelings, moods, and goals we can understand. It is raining. The poet, feeling sad, writes that the world weeps with him or her. A correlate, which we term the empathic fallacy, consists of believing that we can enlarge our sympathies through linguistic means alone. By exposing ourselves to ennobling narratives, we broaden our experience, deepen our empathy, and achieve new levels of sensitivity and fellow-feeling. We can, in short, think, talk, read, and write our way out of bigotry and narrow-mindedness, out of our limitations of experience and perspective. As we illustrate, however, we can do this only to a very limited extent. * * *

IMAGES OF THE OUTSIDER

African Americans

Early in our history, as everyone knows, slave traders rounded up African villagers and transported them to the New World in chains. En route, many died; those who survived were sold and forced to work in the fields and houses of a colonial nation bent on economic development and expansion. By the eve of the Civil War, over 4,000,000 African Americans were condemned to exist in some form of this American Nightmare.

Slave codes regulated behavior, deterring rebellion and forbidding intermarriage. They also prohibited Southern blacks from learning to read and write, thereby denying them access to the world of print then replete with arguments about "the rights of man." The dominant image of blacks in the popular theater and literature of the late eighteenth century was that of the docile and contented slave—child-like, lazy, illiterate, and dependent on the protection and care of a white master. The first appearance of Sambo, a "comic Negro" stereotype, occurred in 1781 in a play called *The Divorce*.[20] This black male character, portrayed by a white in blackface, danced, sang, spoke nonsense, and acted the buffoon. The black man's potential as a sexual and economic competitor was minimized by portraying him as an object of laughter.

Blackface minstrelsy found a new popularity in the 1830s when Thomas D. Rice created Jim Crow, modeled on an elderly crippled black slave who shuffle-danced and sang.[22] Rice even borrowed the old man's shabby clothes for a more authentic stage performance. Rice's performance of Jump Jim Crow won him immediate success in the United States and England. By the 1840s minstrel shows were standard fare in American music halls. In these shows, whites in blackface created and disseminated stereotypes of African Americans as inept urban dandies or happy child-like slaves. Probably more whites—at least in the North— received their understanding of African–American culture from minstrel shows than from first hand acquaintance with blacks.

Because laws forbade slaves to learn to read or write, slave culture was primarily oral. Thus, it is highly significant that former slaves such as Frederick Douglass and William Wells Brown published accounts of captivity, life on plantations, and escapes to freedom. These early slave narratives, published in the North and circulated among abolitionist societies, presented counterimages to the prevailing myths of the dominant culture. The abolitionist movement reached its apogee with the publication of Harriet Beecher Stowe's *Uncle Tom's Cabin*. Though Stowe was successful in presenting the slave master as villain, her portrayal of Uncle Tom changed the stereotype of the black slave only a little: Previously he had been docile, content, or comic, while in her

20. *Split Image: African Americans In The Mass Media* 5–6 (Jannette L. Dates & William Barlow eds. 1990) [hereinafter *Split Image*].

22. See *Split Image, supra* note 20, at 7.

depiction he became gentle, long-suffering, and imbued with Christian piety.

After the Civil War, the black image bifurcated. The "good slave" image continued, but was soon joined by an ominous "shadow" figure. The Uncle Tom character became romanticized, a black mouthpiece espousing an apologia for the beliefs of the old genteel white Confederacy. Though never overtly sexual, his masculine form re-emerged as the avuncular storyteller Uncle Remus, as well as various other "uncles." His feminine form evolved into a "mammy" figure—cook, washerwoman, nanny, and all-round domestic servant—responsible for the comfort of the Southern white household. With no life of her own, imbued with practical wisdom, she took an intense interest in the welfare and well-being of the white family she cared for.

During the tumultuous Reconstruction period, the sexuality denied to uncles and mammies found a crude outlet in a new stereotype of the recently freed male Negro as brutish and bestial. The Ku Klux Klan and other illegal raiding parties justified their reign of terror as necessary to control newly freed blacks whom they believed ready to force sex on any white woman they might encounter. This stereotype, appearing in novels with titles like *The Negro a Beast*,[32] was offered to justify the widespread lynching that took 2,500 black lives between 1885 and 1900.

The myth of the out-of-control ambitious black was fueled by currents prevalent in the marketplace of Western thought during the late nineteenth century: (1) the growth of American imperialism; (2) the absorption of "inferior races;" (3) the white man's burden mentality—the white South bearing the burden in the U.S.; (4) the manifest destiny belief of the Anglo Saxons; and (5) the new social science theory concerning genetic inferiority.[34]

Many of these ideas found expression in the powerful, crass, and influential writings of Thomas Dixon. His work represented an effort to satisfy his two goals in life: Making money and converting people to racism. He believed that whites, both Northern and Southern, were duty bound to protect the Anglo–Saxon heritage, particularly white women, who were destined to produce a superior race.[35] In 1905, Dixon wrote *The Clansman*, a tale of two families, one Northern and one Southern, united through marriage.[36] It proved a sensation, particularly in the South. Ten years later, filmmaker D.W. Griffith used the plots of this and another of Dixon's novels[37] for his epic three-hour film, *The Birth of a Nation*.[38]

The film transformed Dixon's novels into vivid visual images, featuring uncles, mammies, buffoons, an interfering mulatto mistress, and a

32. Charles Carroll, *The Negro a Beast, or In the Image of God* (1900); see also H. Faulkner, *Homespun Justice: The Lynching in American Fiction*, 22 S.D. Rev. 104 (1984).

34. Catherine Silk & John Silk, *Racism and Anti–Racism in American Popular Culture* 49 (1990).

35. *Id.* at 50; see Russell Merritt, *D.W. Griffith's The Birth of a Nation: Going After Little Sister*, in *Close Viewings: An Anthology of New Film Criticism* 215 (1990).

36. Silk & Silk, *supra* note 34, at 50.

37. *The Leopard's Spots* (1902).

38. Silk & Silk, *supra* note 34, at 125.

chase scene in which an animalistic black man pursues a young white woman until she leaps to her death from a pedestal-like perch at the edge of a cliff. The film played to audiences throughout the country. New white immigrants from eastern and southern Europe saw the film in innumerable movie houses in poor neighborhoods, where it played for almost a year. In the South it played for fifteen years. A special screening was held at the White House for Dixon's former classmate, President Woodrow Wilson, his guests, and the entire Supreme Court. Wilson later described the film as "like writing history with lightning."[41]

Blacks could do little to confront the film's overwhelming popularity. The NAACP, by then established with its own newspaper, mobilized opposition. But the film's momentum was unstoppable. Film critics, many of them liberal, though decrying its racism, praised the film for its technical and artistic merits.

In contrast, efforts to present the story of Reconstruction from a black point of view were unsuccessful. Novelist Albion Tourgee, a white superior court judge and activist, used black characters who spoke in their own voices to show the freed man as a person who worked hard and attempted to succeed, but was victimized by the Ku Klux Klan. Tourgee believed the answer to racism lay in portraying blacks as normal—like everyone else. His novel, *Bricks Without Straw*, attracted a devoted but small audience; the South's treatment of blacks no longer interested many Northerners, and few Southerners were willing to listen. Black writers suffered a similar fate. While Charles Chesnutt, author of *The Conjure Woman*, was included in a list of "the foremost storytellers of the time," his publisher refused to release his next novel because the previous two about racial themes had been commercially unsuccessful.[45] As Silk and Silk point out, "[M]essages only reach those people who are willing to listen. Only when a later audience became receptive . . . could [their] tales be . . . appreciated."[46]

Although blacks had gained formal legal equality, the Supreme Court, in 1896, upheld segregation in *Plessy v. Ferguson*.[47] Lynchings continued; racist stereotypes prevailed. Blacks had little access to the press or the film industry and could do little to change the racism that both industries reinforced. Nevertheless, blacks joined the army in droves during World War I. Segregation in the ranks was rigidly enforced, however, and many blacks returned angry and disheartened. After the war, unrest in the country led to at least twenty-five urban race riots, many in the previously peaceful North. Repressive images immediately increased and prevailed for a little over a decade. Then, as the disruption abated, a few writers, such as Eugene O'Neill and Sinclair Lewis, portrayed blacks and their plight sympathetically. Black writers and artists in New York created the Harlem Renaissance. Blacks' image metamorphosed yet again. Whites, excited and enthusiastic over this new

41. *Id*. at 127. Wilson's comment probably was intended as praise, for he added: "[O]ne of my regrets is that it is so horribly true." *Id*.

45. *Id*. at 45; *Split Image, supra* note 20, at 11–12. On the status of the Negro at that time, see Raymond W. Logan, *The Negro in American Life and Thought: The Nadir, 1877–1901* (1954).

46. Silk & Silk, *supra* note 34, at 46.

47. 163 U.S. 537 (1896).

artistic rapprochement with blacks, quickly praised them and their work for elements of the exoticism and primitivism popularized by Gauguin. Echoing early images of good-natured, happy-go-lucky blacks, white society began to regard African Americans as musically talented, rhythmical, passionate, and entertaining. Although these developments heralded a somewhat more positive image, nevertheless the new images retained elements of condescension and previous stereotypes. The majority-race critics, intellectuals, and artists who were entranced by the Renaissance may have intended no harm, yet they perpetuated views of African Americans as the exotic other.

With World War II, black soldiers and workers were needed for the war effort; the more virulent forms of racism were held in abeyance. However, when the war ended and the soldiers returned, racial hostilities again sharpened. Having experienced a relatively racism-free environment during the war, black workers and soldiers were not prepared to return to lives of menial work and subservience to whites. For many, expectations of improvement were fed by war propaganda depicting the U.S. as fighting for freedom. Activism sprang up; the Civil Rights movement began, and once again the dominant image of blacks took on new forms: the cocky, street-smart black who knows his rights; the unreasonable, opportunistic community leader and militant; the safe, comforting, cardigan-wearing ("nice") black of TV sitcoms; and the Black Bomber of superstud films, all mutations of, and permutations of, old familiar forms.

Native Americans

The experience of other groups parallels that of blacks. For example, when the colonists arrived in Virginia and Massachusetts in the seventeenth century, they brought with them images of the Indian created in England and Europe. Early explorers described native peoples of the "new world" as innocent, ingenuous, friendly, and naked. At first, relations between the two groups were cordial. Later, however, more settlers arrived, bringing with them English concepts of property—land transfer, titles, deeds—that were foreign to Indian thought. Indians who did not cooperate with the settlers' plans were forced off their lands; eventually hostilities broke out, resulting in a conflict that lasted over two centuries.

Early writings about Native Americans reflected two romanticized images—"the Indian princess," incarnated most notably in Pocahontas, and "the man Friday," found in Robinson Crusoe, earlier as the troublesome servant Caliban, later as the faithful loyal Chingachgook, and in the twentieth century the buffoon and sidekick Tonto. The first instance of the "captivity narrative" appeared in Massachusetts in 1682 with Mary Rowlandson's *Captivity and Restoration*.[65] Early fiction portrayed Indians as looters, burners, and killers—but not rapists, because New Englanders knew that Indians rarely committed rape. But the erotic

65. Raymond W. Stedman, *Shadows of the Indian: Stereotypes in American Culture* 75 (1982); see M. Rowlandson, *The Sovereignty & Goodness of God, Together with the Faithfulness of His Promises Displayed: Being a Narrative of the Captivity and Restoration of Mrs. Mary Rowlandson* (1682).

elements of Rowlandson's story, although mild and subordinated to her religious message, made it the prototype for later captivity tales that emphasized sexual aggression directed toward Simon-pure captives.

Other writers followed suit without Rowlandson's delicacy, portraying Indians as animal-like and sub-human, a characterization whose roots go back to Paracelsus (1493–1541), who proposed that Indians were not among "the sons of Adam."[71] Shakespeare explored this theme when he wrote *The Tempest* and created a servant for Prospero—Caliban— whose name was an anagram of the newly coined word "cannibal." Cotton Mather and other Puritan writers called Indians wolves, lions, sorcerers, and demons possessed by Satan. By the nineteenth century, Indians had become savage, barbarous, and half-civilized. In early movies, restless natives and jungle beasts were practically interchangeable elements. No wonder, then, that Indians were removed, with little protest from the dominant society, to reservations, just as wild and rare beasts were confined to animal reserves.

Later movies of the "cowboys and Indians" genre built on these images when they featured war dances, exotic dress, drunkenness, surprise attacks, scalping, raiding, raping, tomahawks, tomtoms, and torture. D.W. Griffith, creator of *The Birth of a Nation*, incorporated these elements and more in *The Battle of Elderbush Gulch* (1913). In that movie, a white woman, trapped in a cabin surrounded by Indians, awaits her fate, not knowing whether the Indian attackers will kill her or whether one of her white defenders will shoot her before letting the Indians take her alive. By 1911, portrayal of Indians in film had become so demeaning that representatives of four western tribes protested to President William Howard Taft and to Congress. But little change occurred until World War II, when Hollywood transferred the enemy role to the Japanese and Germans. Many of these early Indian movies are still shown on television, feeding the psyches of new generations of Americans with the familiar stereotypes.

Shortly after the end of the war, Hollywood released *Broken Arrow* (1950), the first movie ever to feature an Indian as hero—Cochise of the Apaches. Though artistically and historically flawed, it was widely praised. Other "noble savage" films reversed the stereotype in the opposite direction, portraying Native Americans with exaggerated nobleness—a striking parallel to the treatment adulating whites gave black writers during the Harlem Renaissance.

In 1969, N. Scott Momaday, a Kiowa–Cherokee writer, won the Pulitzer Prize for his novel *House Made of Dawn*. In 1972, PBS ran a BBC production of *The Last of the Mohicans*. In each of these cases, the audience was struck by the intelligence of the Native American voice—a far cry from the earlier steady diet (still heard today) of chiefs saying "ugh," braves shrieking war whoops, and Tonto saying "me gettum." It was not always so. Thomas Jefferson wished Congress could speak half as well as orators of Indian nations. William Penn praised the Lenni Lanape language of the Delaware for its subtlety. Yet, speech of the Indians—as well as that of African Americans, Mexicans, and Asians—

---

71. Stedman, *supra* note 65, at 121.

has been mangled, blunted, and rendered inarticulate by whites who then became entitled to speak for them. Like the other groups of color, Native Americans have been disempowered by the very element which, they are told, will save them.

Asian Americans

With Asian Americans, we find the same pattern we found elsewhere: The dominant depiction in popular culture is negative—although rarely seen as such at the time—with the stereotype shifting to accommodate society's changing needs.

In the middle years of the nineteenth century, Chinese were welcomed into the land for their labor: They were needed to operate the mines, build railroads, and carry out other physical tasks necessary to the country's development. The industrious immigrants soon, however, began to surpass white American workers. They opened small businesses, succeeded in making profitable mines that others had abandoned. Not surprisingly, Chinese became the scapegoats for the 1870s Depression. Unionists and writers exaggerated negative traits thought associated with them—opium smoking, gambling—and succeeded in having anti-Chinese legislation enacted. By 1882 public sentiment had been mobilized sufficiently so that Congress was able to pass an Exclusion Act, which reduced the number of Chinese in the U.S. from 105,000 in 1880 to 65,000 in 1908.

During this period, Japan's international position was on the rise, yet U.S. writers and politicians depicted all Asians as inferior, unassimilable, willing to work inhuman hours at low wages, and loyal to foreign despots. When Japan defeated first China and then Russia, it began to replace China as the "yellow peril." By 1924, all Asians were barred, an exclusion the Supreme Court had upheld for the Chinese in 1889. During a period of increasing tensions between the two countries, the film industry portrayed Japanese and other Asians—during this period few distinctions were made—in unremittingly negative terms. As with African Americans and Native Americans, Asian men were depicted as cunning, savage, and as potential rapists interested in defiling white women. (In sharp contrast, white male actors were seen as having legitimate access to Asian women.)

As U.S. militancy grew, films began to devalue Asian—principally Japanese—life. Not even they valued life, the narratives of the day said. Why should we value theirs? During earlier periods, when racism against Asians was relatively quiescent, writers and film-makers employed the stock character of the Charlie Chan, the hapless, pidgin-talking Asian, in many respects the functional equivalent of the Sambo or uncle. But as anti-Japanese sentiment increased, we began depicting even domestic Asians as foul and tricky. Anti–Asian films were easy to produce and profitable; Hollywood would often assign a Japanese actor to play a Chinese villain and vice versa.

W.R. Hearst sponsored *Patria*, an anti-Asian film serial that began in 1919 and continued for several years, depicting Asians as a Yellow Menace. At one point, Woodrow Wilson became disturbed by the virulence of Hearst's production and wrote asking him to soften it. Hearst responded by changing the series so that it became dominantly anti-Mexican. In the period immediately preceding and following World War II, anti-Japanese images continued to proliferate. A stock character was the master Oriental criminal, often played by Anglo actors in make-up. By this time, films and novels were distinguishing between Chinese (who were good), and Japanese (who were bad). After Pearl Harbor, intense anti-Japanese propaganda resulted in federal action to intern 110,000 Japanese Americans, many of whom had lived in the United States all their lives. Many lost farms, houses, and other property. It later came to light that much of the evidence of likely sabotage and fifth column activities had been fabricated.

Following World War II, depictions of blacks and Indians were upgraded to some extent, but those of Asians only a little. Many of James Bond's villains, for example, have been Asian. In recent days, Japan has once again become a serious economic rival of the United States, producing automobiles, computers, and other products at a price and quality American industry has proven unable to match. Predictably, a further wave of anti-Asian sentiment and stereotyping is re-emerging.

Mexican Americans

Images of Mexican Americans ("Chicanos") fall into three or four well-delineated stereotypes—the greaser, the conniving, treacherous bandito, the happy-go-lucky shiftless lover of song, food, and dance, and the tragic, silent "Spanish" tall, dark, and handsome type of romantic fiction—which change according to society's needs. As with blacks, Asians, and Indians, most Americans have relatively few interpersonal contacts with Mexican Americans; therefore, these images become the individual's only reality. When such a person meets an actual Mexican American, he or she tends to place the other in one of the ready-made categories. Stereotyping thus denies members of both groups the opportunity to interact with each other on anything like a complex, nuanced human level.

During and just after the Conquest, when the U.S. was seizing and then settling large tracts of Mexican territory in the Southwest, "Western" or "conquest" fiction depicted Anglos bravely displacing shifty, brutal, and treacherous Mexicans. After the war ended and control of the Southwest passed to American hands, a subtle shift occurred. Anglos living and settling in the new regions were portrayed as Protestant, independent, thrifty, industrious, mechanically resourceful, and interested in progress; Mexicans, as traditional, sedate, lacking in mechanical resourcefulness and ambition. Writers both on and off the scene created the same images of indolent, pious Mexicans—ignoring the two centuries of enterprising farmers and ranchers who withstood or negotiated with Apaches and Comanches and built a sturdy society with irrigation, land tenure, and mining codes.

In the late Conquest period, depiction of this group bifurcated. As happened at a different period with African Americans, majority-race writers created two images of the Mexican: the "good" (loyal) Mexican peon or sidekick, and the "bad" fighter/greaser Mexican who did not know his place. The first was faithful and domestic; the second, treacherous and evil. As with other groups, the second ("bad") image had sexual overtones: The greaser coveted Anglo women and would seduce or rape them if given the opportunity. Children's books of this time, like the best-selling Buffalo Bill series, were full of Mexican stereotypes used to reinforce moral messages to the young: They are like this, we like that. The series ended in 1912.

The first thirty years of this century saw heavy Mexican immigration of mainly poor workers. The first Bracero programs—official, temporary importation of field hands—appeared. With increasing numbers, whites-only signs, segregated housing and schools appeared, aimed now at Mexicans in addition to blacks. With increased risk of interaction and intermarriage, novels and newspaper writing reinforced the notion of these immigrants' baseness, simplicity, and inability to assimilate.

The movies of this period depicted Latins as buffoons, sluts, or connivers; even some of the titles were disparaging: for example, *The Greaser's Gauntlet*. Films featured brown-skinned desperadoes stealing horses or gold, lusting after pure Anglo women, shooting noble Saxon heroes in the back, or acting the part of hapless buffoons. Animated cartoons and short subjects, still shown on television, featured tequila-drinking Mexicans, bullfighters, Speedy Gonzalez and Slowpoke Rodriguez, and clowns—as well as Castilian caballeras, light-skinned, upper class, and prone to wearing elaborate dresses and carrying castanets.

World War II brought the need for factory and agricultural workers and a new flood of immigrants. Images softened to include "normal," or even noble, Mexicans, like the general of Marlon Brando's *Viva Zapata*. Perhaps realizing it had overstepped, America diminished the virulence of its anti-Mexican imagery. Yet the Western genre, with Mexican villains and bandits, continues; and the immigrant speaking gibberish still makes an appearance. Even the most favorable novel and film of the post-war period, *The Milagro Beanfield War*, ends in stereotypes.

A few writers found their own culture alienating or sick and sought relief in a more serene Southwest culture. As with the Harlem Renaissance, these creative artists tended to be more generous to Mexicans, but nevertheless retained the Anglo hero as the central figure or Samaritan who uplifts the Mexican from his or her traditional ignorance.

How Could They?

Lessons from the History of Racial Depiction

As we saw, the depiction of ethnic groups of color is littered with negative images, although the content of those images changes over time. In some periods, society needed to suppress a group, as with blacks during Reconstruction. Society then coined an image to suit that purpose—that of primitive, powerful larger than life blacks, terrifying and barely under control. At other times, for example during slavery, society needed reassurance that blacks were docile, cheerful, and content with their lot. Images of sullen, rebellious blacks dissatisfied with their condition would have made white society uneasy. Accordingly, images of simple, happy blacks, content to do the master's work, were disseminated.

In every era, then, ethnic imagery comes bearing an enormous amount of social weight. Nevertheless, we sense that we are in control, that things need not be that way. We believe we can use speech, jiujitsu fashion, on behalf of oppressed peoples. We believe speech can serve as a tool of destabilization; indeed, it is virtually a prime tenet of liberal jurisprudence that by talk, dialog, exhortation, and so on, we present each other with passionate, appealing messages that will counter the evil ones of racism and sexism, and thereby advance society to greater levels of fairness and humanity. * * *

But both history and modernist and postmodern insights about language and the social construction of reality show that reliance on countervailing speech that will, in theory, wrestle with bad or vicious speech is often misplaced. This is so for two interrelated reasons: First, the account rests on simplistic and erroneous notions of narrativity and change, and second, on a misunderstanding of the relation between the subject, or self, and new narratives.

Our review showed that we simply do not see many forms of discrimination, bias, and prejudice as wrong at the time. The racism of other times and places does stand out, does strike us as glaringly and appallingly wrong. But this happens only decades or centuries later; we acquiesce in today's version with little realization that it is wrong, that a later generation will ask "How could they?" about us. We only condemn the racism of another place (South Africa) or time. But that of our own place and time strikes us, if at all, as unexceptionable, trivial, or well within literary license. Every form of creative work (we tell ourselves) relies on stock characters. What's so wrong with a novel that employs a black who ..., or a Mexican who.... ? Besides, the argument goes, those groups are disproportionately employed as domestics, are responsible for a high proportion of our crime, are they not? And some actually talk this way; why, just last week, I overheard....

This time-warp aspect of racism makes speech an ineffective tool to counter it. Racism is woven into the warp and woof of the way we see and organize the world. One of the many preconceptions we bring to experience and use to construct and make sense of our social world, it forms part of the dominant narrative, the group of received understandings and basic principles that form the baseline from which we reason. How could these be in question? Recent scholarship shows that the dominant narrative changes very slowly and resists alteration. We interpret new stories in light of the old. Ones that deviate too markedly from our pre-existing stock are dismissed as extreme, coercive, political, and wrong. The only stories about race we are prepared to condemn, then, are the old ones giving voice to the racism of an earlier age, ones that society has already begun to reject. We can condemn Justice Brown for writing as he did in *Plessy v. Ferguson*, but not university administrators who refuse remedies for campus racism, failing to notice the remarkable parallels between the two.

THE SECOND REASON: OUR NARRATIVES, OUR SELVES

Racial change is slow, then, because the story of race is part of the dominant narrative we use to interpret experience. The narrative teaches that race matters, that people are different, with the differences lying always in a predictable direction. It holds that certain cultures, unfortunately, have less ambition than others, that the majority group is largely innocent of racial wrongdoing, that the current distribution of comfort and well-being is roughly what merit and fairness dictate. Within that general framework, only certain matters are open for discussion: How different? In what ways? With how many exceptions? And what measures are due to deal with this unfortunate situation and at what cost to whites? This is so because the narrative leaves only certain things intelligible; other arguments and texts would seem alien.

A second and related insight from modern scholarship focuses not on the role of narratives in confining change to manageable proportions, but on the relationship between our selves and those narratives. The reigning First Amendment metaphor—the marketplace of ideas—implies a separation between subjects who do the choosing and the ideas or messages that vie for their attention. Subjects are "in here," the messages "out there." The pre-existing subjects choose the idea that seems most valid and true—somewhat in the manner of a diner deciding what to eat at a buffet.

But scholars are beginning to realize that this mechanistic view of an autonomous subject choosing among separate, external ideas is simplistic. In an important sense, we are our current stock of narratives, and they us. We subscribe to a stock of explanatory scripts, plots, narratives, and understandings that enable us to make sense of—to construct—our social world. Because we then live in that world, it begins to shape and determine us, who we are, what we see, how we select, reject, interpret and order subsequent reality.

These observations imply that our ability to escape the confines of our own preconceptions is quite limited. The contrary belief—that through speech and remonstrance alone we can endlessly reform ourselves and each other—we call the *empathic fallacy*. It and its companion, the pathetic fallacy, are both based on *hubris*, the belief that we can be more than we are. The empathic fallacy holds that through speech and remonstrance we can surmount our limitations of time, place and culture, can transcend our own situatedness. But our examination of the cultural record, as well as postmodern understandings of language and personhood, both point to the same conclusion: The notion of ideas competing with each other, with truth and goodness emerging victorious from the competition, has proven seriously deficient when applied to evils, like racism, that are deeply inscribed in the culture. We have constructed the social world so that racism seems normal, part of the status quo, in need of little correction. It is not until much later that what we believed begins to seem incredibly, monstrously wrong. How could we have believed *that*?

True, every few decades an occasional genius will rise up and offer a work that recognizes and denounces the racism of the day. Unfortunately, they are ignored—they have no audience. Witness, for example, the recent "discovery" of long-forgotten black writers such as Charles Chesnutt, Zora Neale Hurston, or the slave narratives. Consider that Nadine

Gordimer won the Nobel Prize after nearly 40 years of writing about the evils of apartheid; Harriet Beecher Stowe's book sold well only after years of abolitionist sentiment and agitation had sensitized her public to the possibility that slavery was wrong. One should, of course, speak out against social evils. But we should not accord speech greater efficacy than it has.

Notes and Questions

1.   In 1951, the National Association for the Advancement of Colored People (NAACP) protested against the television version of the Amos 'n' Andy show.[1] The protests were based on the opinion held by many (but not all) Blacks that the show's depiction of those of the black race was demeaning to the black audience and misleading to the white audience.[2] Others felt that the show was valuable as the only all-black series on television at that time, showing that black actors were as talented as white actors.[3] The methods of the protest included talking to newspapers and CBS, on which the show was broadcast, talking to product sponsors and threatening boycotts of such products. However, with divided support in the black community and next to none in the white community, the protests resulted in few changes to the show.[4] With whom do you agree?

2.   If Blacks laugh at Amos 'n' Andy humor depicting African Americans in derogatory fashion, should that end any argument?

MARGARET M. RUSSELL

Race and the Dominant Gaze: Narratives of Law and Inequality in Popular Film
15 Legal Stud. F. 243, 246–51, 253 (1991).*

Black filmmaker Robert Townsend in the 1987 comedy *Hollywood Shuffle* lambastes the Hollywood film and television community as manipulative buffoons who use black actors only for roles as pimps, drug addicts, and prostitutes; accordingly, the film's black characters realize that their livelihood depends upon conforming to these debilitating images—that is, doing the "Hollywood Shuffle." * * * How has the dominant gaze operated to perpetuate the subordination of blacks in mainstream Hollywood films? Consider three distinct ways: (1) in the proliferation of degrading stereotypes which serve to dehumanize blacks' history, lives and experiences; (2) in the marginalization or complete absence of indigenous perspectives on blacks' history, lives and experiences; and (3) in the co-optation—or "Hollywood-ization"—of trendy, ostensibly "racial," themes. In marginalizing blacks and other minorities from popular discourse, the three trends frequently overlap in particular films. * * *

It is important to understand the history of exploitation of blacks in American films, for it is from this ideological cinema-scape that contemporary movies emerge. Over time, such distortion and erasure create

1. Melvin Patrick Ely, *The Adventures of Amos 'n' Andy: A Social History of an American Phenomenon* (1991).

2. *Id.* at 215–16.

3. *Id.* at 216–17.

4. *Id.* at 237.

* Originally published in Legal Studies Forum. Used by permission.

damage both subtle and severe. The unchallenged transmission of racial stereotypes in films not only weakens resistance to their falsity, but also strengthens the legitimacy of their narrative source. With these concerns in mind, I must concede that I approach movies not only with an avid fan's enthusiasm and curiosity, but with a skeptic's critical eye as well. It was in this frame of mind that I first saw *Soul Man*—a fairytale romance of a white student who pretends to be black so that he can go to Harvard Law School.

"This is the Eighties! It's the Cosby decade—America LOVES black people!" With these cheery words, the white protagonist of *Soul Man* attempts to reassure a doubting friend of the wisdom of his decision to "turn black" in order to win a minority scholarship to Harvard Law School. As the flippancy of this dialogue might suggest, *Soul Man* aims both stylistically and substantively to be very much a modern flick. It sparkles with several (by now de rigueur) attributes bound to please the youthful, upwardly mobile movie-goer: a hip title; a musical soundtrack studded with soul, rock and blues standards; and a plot featuring attractive, well-educated, and basically conventional young people. The slickly packaged story provides carefully measured doses of comedy, romance, sex, conflict, and moralizing before reaching a happy and uncomplicated denouement.

Not coincidentally, *Soul Man*'s narrative premise is also characteristic of its era—a post-*Bakke* fantasy about the dangerous possibilities of affirmative action, minority scholarships, and other race-conscious remedies. Mark Watson, an upper middle-class, white male college graduate, fears that he will be prevented from attending the law school of his dreams. To obtain his "rightful" place at Harvard, he decides to fake being black so that he can win a minority scholarship. With the help of a friend, Mark obtains chemicals to darken his skin, interviews successfully for the scholarship, and—viola!—embarks on his new life as a black man at Harvard. * * * What renders this movie an especially revealing artifact of its era is its willingness (indeed eagerness) to use race explicitly as a gimmick to advance its old-fashioned story line. *Soul Man*'s comic effectiveness depends upon the viewer's willingness to accept racial stereotypes as comedy and racial identity as a gag. Significantly, the movie transmits its putative wisdom about black experience not through the eyes of its black characters, but through the gaze of a white person aiming to carry out a self-serving schoolboy scheme. In using such a dominant gaze, the film undermines its own "enlightened" pretensions in commenting on law, race, and the reality of racial discrimination. To understand how this diminution is accomplished, it is helpful to clarify the perspective of race that permeates the film. * * *

Once introductory scenes have established the film's narrative framework, the rest of *Soul Man* focuses on Mark's blackface experience at Harvard Law. Notice that *Soul Man*'s central plot gimmick—a white protagonist in blackface—is hardly a new phenomenon; films such as *The Birth of a Nation* and *Uncle Tom's Cabin* featured white actors playing black roles, and vaudevillian blackface constituted a major entertainment form in the early part of the century. The effect of blackface in *Soul Man*—as in these earlier representations—is to create a disquieting narrative undercurrent, a dysfunction between surface and substance. The viewer is expected not to question this dissonance, but to accept it as a gag for the purposes of being entertained.

In this respect, *Soul Man*'s use of blackface more closely resembles these earlier regressive films than it does two more recent movies using blackface themes to advance serious points. *Watermelon Man* (1971) focuses on the tragicomic dilemma of a white character who wakes up one day and discovers that he has turned black overnight; however, a critical distinction between this film and *Soul Man* rests upon the viewer's knowledge that the white character is in fact played by a black actor, Godfrey Cambridge. *Black Like Me* (1965), based on the well-known autobiography of John Howard Griffin, dramatizes the prejudice and hatred confronted by a white journalist who deliberately darkens his skin to learn first-hand the treatment of blacks in the South in the early 1960s. Unlike *Soul Man, Black Like Me is* a serious tale of degradation and cruelty; the protagonist cannot find lodging, work, transportation, or even a place to go to the bathroom. He suffers the indignities of racial slurs, ignorant comments, and outright threats of violence; his experience of life in the South is almost unremittingly somber and bleak.

Unlike *Watermelon Man* or *Black Like Me, Soul Man* uses blackface to portray the issue of crossing the color line as a farcical, frat-boy romp. Mark Watson's indignities seem to be limited to suffering the occasional bigoted apartment manager or tasteless racist joke from fellow students—hardly an inconvenience when compared to the "benefits" that he derives from being black. Moreover, *Soul Man* presents these incidents as comic fodder, intended to amuse rather than to provoke or disturb. As a result, the depiction of racist incidents in this film is stripped of affective power and validity and subsumed within Mark's dominant gaze.

In scene after scene, the plot trots out hoary old stereotypes and invites the viewer to find them amusing. In a pivotal scene, we watch Mark's tense visit to the home of the white Radcliffe student's wealthy and bigoted family, and are asked to observe the event through Mark's eyes. Through his gaze, we see racist stereotypes which Mark imagines are being projected upon him by the family: that he is vicious drug addict and pimp who will abuse their pure daughter; or a lascivious island native who wants to seduce the mother; or a Prince-style, pelvis-thrusting rocker who will corrupt the young son. By filtering its parody of ignorance and bias through the eyes of Mark—hardly a true "victim" of prejudice—the scene lacks both the irony and the empathic power necessary to convey its ostensibly well-intended message. * * * Instead, since Mark is clearly not black and not in a subordinate role to anyone, I was left with the sense that his dilettantish exposure to racism in this scene was somehow equated with blacks' everyday experiences with racism, and that the hyperbolically bigoted whites were being equated with blacks' everyday experiences with racists. Such a message is not enlightened but distressingly discourages viewers from recognizing that often bigotry wears a mask not burlesque-style and latent, but subtle and insidious. * * *

In defending his film, *Do the Right Thing* (1989) against the criticism that it might make mainstream white audiences feel uncomfortable, Spike Lee asserted, "[T]hat's the way it is all the time for black people."[20] Lee's point was that the dominant gaze still prevails; "uncomfortable" perspectives are marginalized, criticized, or worst of all, simply ignored. A film such as *Soul Man,* which capitalizes on an ostensibly alternative perspective to tell a tale about contemporary race relations, is ultimately fatally flawed by the dominance of its vision. By exploiting racial stereotypes without reminding the viewers of their continuing destructive force, *Soul Man* misses the opportunity to make—either seriously or comically—a truly instructive comment about the nature of racism in our society.

Notes and Questions

1.   Does every movie have a point of view? Does every movie have a racial point of view—*viz.*, White, Jewish, Black, etc.? Do we just not notice the ones that are made from the white standpoint because we are so used to seeing them?

2.   Do even white-made movies sometimes contain derogatory stories of Whites? For example—the father as a sap, the teenager as hedonistic airhead, the college professor as dithering nerd, the young woman as sex object and siren.

3.   Consider the movie *A Family Thing*, starring Robert Duvall and James Earl Jones, in which Duvall discovers that he is Black. A Southerner, with the ingrained prejudices of that region, he has to come to terms with the realization that James Earl Jones is his brother. Are movies like this one healthy and antiracist? Or do they, too, reinforce stereotypes such as black otherness? See James Gordon, *Did the First Justice Harlan Have a Black Brother?* 15 W. New Eng. L. Rev. 159 (1993), suggesting that close family contact among races is healthy and may ameliorate prejudice.

4.   Consider, as well, Gregory Williams, *Life on the Color Line* (1996), describing how the author, now a law school dean, was first raised as a White, then as a young teenager was sent to live with the black relatives in his family. Williams, who looks white but has a black father, describes how he and his brother were deposited in a poor, run-down home, where they encountered loving relatives and came to terms with their own blackness. The book reveals in painful detail how the brothers adjusted to their new lives. See the excerpt in Chapter 6 § 2 *supra*.

5.   Early television featured unredeemably racist cartoons, such as Amos 'n' Andy, shuffling Sambos, pickaninnies, whooping Indians, and tequila-drinking, sombrero-wearing Mexican banditos. Some of these devastating images still appear as reruns on Saturday morning TV, where they are watched by children. What should concerned parents do about this?

6.   Leading African–American filmmaker Spike Lee was recently interviewed by *Ebony* magazine.[1] Asked about his film, *Crooklyn*, which has no violence, profanity, crack or explicit sex, Lee replied:

---

20. bell hooks, *Yearning: Race, Gender, and Cultural Politics* 173 (1990).

1. Lynn Norment, *A Revealing Look at Spike Lee's Changing Life*, Ebony, May 1994, at 28.

"When is the last time you saw a film about a black family with a father, a family that was not dysfunctional, where nobody's on crack and the kids aren't in gangs?" [He went on to observe that] "we have to understand [that] * * * [all] Black people do not like just one type of movie or one type of music or one type of TV program. We are diverse. * * * We should branch out. The audience is ready. People are getting tired of repetition. . . . I'm not trying to tell Black filmmakers what they should make. I just hope we can make more films about different things." * * *

Lee has helped * * * other Black filmmakers, writers, and actors [get their start in film, and takes satisfaction in] that "never before in the history of cinema have we had the access to film that we have now."

* * * [Yet] some of his colleagues are not taking advantage of the opportunities to create quality television shows and films about Blacks. "There are no Black dramas," he points out. "Everything is just shucking and jiving, rolling your eyes, that kind of stuff." * * *

"There was a time when we said as a people, once we get the opportunity to get in front of the camera and in back of the camera directing, producing and writing these shows, things would be different. But that's not precisely the case because we're writing a lot of this stuff we're doing." * * *

MARLON RIGGS

Ethnic Notions.*

NARR: The mammy, the pickaninny, the coon, the Sambo, the uncle: Well into the middle of the twentieth century, these were some of the most popular depictions of black Americana. By 1941 * * * images like these permeated American culture. These were the images that decorated our homes, that served and amused and made us laugh. Taken for granted, they worked their way into the mainstream of American life. Of ethnic caricatures in America, these have been the most enduring. Today there's little doubt that they shaped the most gut-level feelings about race.

LARRY LEVINE: When you see hundreds of them, in all parts of the country persisting over a very long period of time, they have to have meaning. They obviously appeal to people. They appeal to the creator, but they appeal also to the consumers, those who look at the cartoons, or read the novels, or buy the artifacts.

BARBARA CHRISTIAN: It is not just that it's in the figurines, and the coffee pots and so on, it is that we are seen that way, perceived that way, even in terms of public policy. And that our lives are lived under that shadow, and sometimes we then even become to believe it ourselves.

LARRY LEVINE: Blacks don't really look like that. So why is it so appealing to people to think they look like that, and pretend they look like that, and to like to look at icons that look like that. You look at them often enough and black people begin to look like that, even

* California Newsreel, 1987. Used by permission of Signifyin' Works.

though they don't. So that they've had a great impact in our society. They therefore tell us both about the inner desires of the people who create and consume them, and also they tell us about some of the forces that shape reality, for large portions of our population.

VIDEO/SYNC: *Uncle Tom's Cabana* (Film, 1947)

Well now, chil'ren, ol' Oncle Tom's gon' tell you the real true story about Uncle Tom's Cabin.

NARR: Contained in these cultural images is the history of our national conscience: a conscience striving to reconcile the paradox of racism in a nation founded on human equality—a conscience coping with this profound contradiction through caricature. What were the consequences of these caricatures? How did they mold and mirror the reality of racial tensions in America for more than 100 years?

VOICE-OVER: Laughing Ben: "I got a hat on my head, shoes on my feet, so what need I care, cuz I'm the luckiest coon in this town (laughter)"

NARR: In the early 1900s, images and songs portrayed a simple, docile, laughing black man: the Sambo. This image became one of the classic portrayals of black men in film. Carefree and irresponsible, the Sambo was quick to avoid work while revelling in the easy pleasures of food, dance, and song. His life was one of child-like contentment.

VIDEO/SYNC: *Rhapsody in Black and Blue* (Film, 1932)

Man: Dog gonnit, can't this boy go to town! Listen here. Ha, ha, ha!

Woman: Come away from that old box.

Man: Well, can I help it 'cause I got an ear for music?

Woman: Yeah, that's all you got, is an ear for music, and a mouth for po'k chop. You better get a desire for work.

NARR: The happy Sambo began his stage life in the late 1820s when a man named T.D. Rice brought a new sensation to American theater. Rice was known as an Ethiopian delineator, a white comedian who performed in blackface. The name of his routine would later become *the* symbol of segregation in the South.

LENI SLOAN: The Jim Crow was a dance that started on the plantation as a result of dancing being outlawed in 1690. Dancing was said by the church to be crossing your feet. And so the slaves created a way of shuffling and sliding to safely glide around the laws without crossing their feet.

NARR: The slaves had a saying for their cunning in skirting the law.

LENI SLOAN: "Wheel about, and turn about, and jump just so, every time I wheel about, I jump Jim Crow."

NARR: According to legend, T.D. Rice saw a crippled black man dancing an exaggerated Jim Crow dance. Rice took the man's tattered clothes and that night imitated him on stage.

LENI SLOAN: It was an instant success. And America loved it. And a bevy of imitators came about, literally hundreds of men tore up their clothes, discarded their perfect dialects of the black man, and began to do this exaggerated character dance which became known as the Jim Crow character. And so here we have Jim Crow, T.D. Rice, taking a dance which was altered by a law, from a man who was crippled, and exaggerating it again. And he had no intention of presenting truth. But what was bought by the majority of the people in Ohio, and the Louisiana Territory, and along the Erie Canal, was that this was a true image. And it was a devastating image. People in small towns who had never seen blacks, you know, and suddenly saw Rice, bought that as a black image.

NARR: In 1843, a group of blackface performers joined together to form a single troupe. Instead of delineators, they called themselves minstrels. The minstrel show captivated broad audiences, mostly in the North, and emerged as America's first form of national popular entertainment. Like movies today, successful minstrels played to the tastes and values of their audiences. Jim Crow, reflecting popular demand, evolved into the singing dancing Sambo. This light-hearted figure became one of the most potent forces in the politics of slavery.

PAT TURNER: The minstrelsy era really took off at the same time as the abolitionist movement took off. And you could almost sort of chart the two. As there were people working to end slavery, people working to eradicate slavery, there were also people increasing the exaggerated portrayals that we find in the minstrel material.

NARR: Minstrel caricatures mirrored the prevailing belief that slavery was good for the slave since it drew upon his "natural" inferiority and willingness to serve. Slaves were content. The proof was offered in the image of the happy Sambo.

Notes and Questions

1. Do you agree with the *functional* view of media imagery, set out by Delgado and Stefancic, according to which cultural images of minorities are either soothing or alarming, according to the shifting demands of society and the labor pool?

2. Is this a conspiracy theory?

3. Can minorities flip things and create their own counter-imagery? Compare Spike Lee's words with the following selection on Mexican street theatre.

YOLANDA BROYLES–GONZÁLEZ

El Teatro Campesino: Theater in the Chicano Movement
xi, xii, 10, 19–20 (1994).*

The numerous social and political struggles of the 1960s and the 1970s—such as the civil rights movement, the United Farm Workers movement, the antiwar movement, and the women's liberation movement—were intimately bound to a multifaceted cultural renaissance. Perhaps the single most inspirational struggle for Chicanas/os was the

David and Goliath standoff between the United Farm Workers Union and the agribusiness giants in California and other states. * * *

One manifestation of that spirit of activism was the Chicana/o theater movement, which spread across the Southwest, the Northwest, and the Midwest in the 1960s and the 1970s. In virtually all centers of Chicana/o population as well as on campuses everywhere, theater groups sprang up dedicated to portraying the life, heritage, and problems of Chicanas/os in this country.

Under the wing of the United Farm Workers Union based in Delano, California, El Teatro Campesino (The Farm Workers' Theater) emerged in 1965, conceived as a union tool for organizing, fund-raising, and politicizing. In its beginnings El Teatro Campesino performed numerous highly improvisational skits (called *actos),* which expressed the exploitive living and working conditions of farmworkers in boldly satirical words and actions. All of the early skits also underscored the need to unionize against the abuses of agribusiness. In addition to regular performances— often on the backs of flatbed trucks before farmworkers—the group also played college campuses and toured Europe repeatedly. A group viewed and appreciated by farmworkers simply as an effective organizational tool, became, curiously, idolized in intellectual circles and was converted into a Chicano icon for the academy. Euro–American scholarship and the press followed suit. Today the name Teatro Campesino enjoys almost mythical status, even though the ensemble that established that reputation no longer exists. (El Teatro Campesino, Inc., exists only as a production company.) * * *

The *carpa* [Eds. tent show, often ribald, and forerunner of today's Teatro Campesino] played with full force into the 1950s and the early 1960s, a resilience probably attributable to its native and working-class roots, as well as its ability to speak to the daily reality of Mexican workers in an entertaining manner. This is the world of working-class performance inherited by El Teatro Campesino.

On numerous occasions Luis Valdez and other members of the Teatro Campesino ensemble have affirmed and reaffirmed their strong roots in the carpa tradition and the carpa aesthetic, usually referred to as the Rasquachi Aesthetic within the Teatro Campesino. ("Rasquachi" is rich in connotations and can be used to express affection or disaffection while referring to something earthy, unpretentious, gaudy, resourceful, etc.) Valdez indicates: "We evolved—in our own earthiness— characters that emerged from Cantinflas and the whole comic Mexican tradition of the carpa, the tent" (Broyles 1983:38). It was particularly the performing family of El Circo Escalante that made a great impression on the young Valdez. The Escalantes were itinerant artists who at times lived from performance income and at other times from farm labor income. That was to become a model for the early Teatro Campesino.

Linguistic markers pointing to a relationship between El Teatro Campesino and the Mexican popular tradition also abound: The term "carpa" appears in the titles of Teatro Campesino performance pieces such as the classic La gran carpa de los Rasquachis; another piece, for example, was entitled Carpa Cantinflesca. Like most Teatro Campesino pieces the latter is based in the Mexican performance style embodied by the great carpa comedian Cantinflas, particularly popular from the 1930s through the 1950s and now legendary. Charlie Chaplin, in fact, referred to Cantinflas as "the world's greatest comedian" (Tobar 1993). * * *

It is interesting that much of the transmission of the Mexican popular performance tradition happened not from the top down, as is often assumed by critics, but from the bottom up. This is evident not only in the collective work mode, which relied on the collective talents of a group, but also in the fact that farmworker audiences often gave the Teatro performance guidance or feedback. It was the farmworker audience, for example, that demanded of the Teatro Campesino a performance aesthetic foregrounding action. Valdez ("The Talk of the Town," 1967) recalls how the Teatro grew in response to farmworker input: "When we started the Teatro, workers came up to us after performances and said, 'There's not enough action,' so we introduced more slapstick. We use even more slapstick when we perform for Mexican–American farmworkers than when we perform for a middle-class audience in New York." * * *

The human body, memory, and community are intertwined phenomena that came to bear on the carpa and Teatro Campesino oral culture of performance in yet other very significant ways. For one thing, memory extends far beyond the momentary absorption and retention of dramatic dialogue. In other words, memory here is associated not only with short-term memorization but with long-term historical memory and physical knowledge of life in the urban barrios and rural enclaves, of social relations of oppression and resistance. Within an orally based culture, memory and the body are the sites of a community's self-knowledge. Memory in this context signifies a remembrance of lived experience within a community, usually one's directly lived experience combined with the greater communal historical experience transmitted to youth by elders in oral historical discourse. * * *

Within the oral performance mode of the Teatro Campesino, historical memory provided the very raw materials from which all production was generated. Performers relied directly on the memory of the Mexican working-class community's experience within the dominant society. The dynamism of memory provided the foundation for an understanding and critique of the present. A critical exploration of that social experience lay at the heart of all Teatro Campesino performance work. Teatro Campesino ensemble member Olivia Chumacero (interview, 1/19/1983) commented on the intimate and direct relationship of continuity between the individual's performance work and life experience: "You had to draw from yourself, from where you were coming from. Things came out from you, from what you thought, from where you were coming from, from what you had experienced in life. It was wonderful. It was not a mechanical learning of lines, word for word. Words that someone had put in your mouth. It was your life."

The creation of pieces within the Teatro was a collective process of discussion and improvisation, with the human memory as repository and foundation. The key within this collective process of creation is the body, or physical memory. Within the collective creation process creational faith is vested in the social wisdom of the body, a wisdom that emerges in the process of improvisation. Improvisation in the Mexican oral performance mode entails thinking something through with the body. * * * The generation of ideas and plays within El Teatro Campesino was achieved through the active work of the entire body. Improvisation is the bodily process of thinking. As an exploratory process, improvisation involved a trial-and-error system of rehearsal. Meaning was rehearsed through the body until a play took on a general form. In 1967 Luis Valdez described the process: "We take a real situation—often something that happens on the picket line and we improvise around it. When we get an improvisation that we like, we're ready. An acto is never written down" ("The Talk of the Town," 1967).

All Teatro Campesino performance pieces went through various transformations and discussions before being committed to memory (not to written form).Yet that form was always subject to new improvisation, not least of all during performance. This approach to theatrical creation and performance was also championed by Enrique Buenaventura, who worked intensely with Chicana/o theater groups in addition to elaborating his own system of collective creation in Colombia. Buenaventura affirms (personal communication, 10/18/1990): *"El cuerpo sabe mas que la cabeza. Las ideas vienen del cuerpo a la cabeza. Es importante que el cuerpo guie la cabeza y no al reves. La idea debe de nacer del trabajo corporal"* (The body knows more than the head. Ideas come from the body to the head. It is important that the body guide the mind and not the other way around. Ideas should be generated by bodily work).

Born of and for the working-class farmworker community, the Teatro Campesino's actos directly enacted the physical sociocultural memory of that community's experience. Memory indeed was the prime conduit for all performance work within El Teatro Campesino. And the power and instrumentality of memory, rooted in the community and in the body, made possible the immediacy, authenticity, and vitality characteristic of the ensemble's work.

CYNTHIA KWEI YUNG LEE

Race and Self–Defense: Toward a Normative Conception of Reasonableness
81 Minn. L. Rev. 367, 423–24, 426–32, 438–41 (1996).*

* * *

Most discussions on the subject of race and the American criminal justice system have focused on the Black–White paradigm. Such focus may be justified because of the history of slavery and the current discrimination practiced against Blacks in this country. Nonetheless, because of this focus, issues concerning other non-Whites tend to be overlooked. This is unfortunate because other non-Whites are also subject to socially constructed notions about race.

The ways in which Asian Americans have been socially constructed in American society are contradictory. While racial representations of

* Used by permission of the Minnesota Law Review.

Blacks are largely negative, Asian Americans have been racially represented in conflicting ways. For example, Asian Americans appear to benefit from the model minority stereotype that seems to have become the predominant image in the 1990s. Under this stereotype, Asian Americans are perceived as smart, hard-working, law-abiding, and respectful of authority. * * *

* * * [T]he model minority stereotype can benefit some Asian Americans. What is often overlooked, however, is that the positive attributes of the stereotype (*e.g.*, intelligent, hard-working, law-abiding) are linked with corresponding negative attributes (*e.g.*, lacking personality, unfairly competitive, clannish, unwilling to assimilate, rigidly rulebound): * * * To be intelligent is to lack personality. To be hard-working is to be unfairly competitive. To be family-oriented is to be clannish, "too ethnic," and unwilling to assimilate. To be law-abiding is to be rigidly rule-bound, tied to traditions in the homeland, unappreciative of democracy and free expression.

In times of economic uncertainty, resentment against Asian Americans seems to increase, perhaps because of the perception that "model" Asian Americans take away valuable job opportunities from other Americans. Reactions to the Los Angeles riots of 1992 following the Simi Valley jury's acquittal of the four White police officers who brutally beat African–American Rodney King reflected conflicting sentiments of sympathy for and resentment against the Korean Americans caught up in the destruction. On the one hand, Korean American store owners were constructed oppositionally to African–American and Latino looters as unfortunate victims of the riots and looting. On the other hand, Korean Americans were portrayed as property-loving, gun-toting store owners who valued material possessions over human life.

The Asian-as-Foreigner

Fear of the foreign is sometimes a black streak that runs through America's political culture. We see instances of [this] when it involves hate crimes, not necessarily directed at black Americans, but at foreign Americans.

—Mike McCurry White House Press Secretary[222]

It is almost oxymoronic to speak of foreign Americans, yet the term conveys meaning—Asian Americans and Latinos. Many Americans associate Asian Americans with foreignness. The person who asks an Asian American "Where are you from?" usually expects a response like "Japan" (or China or Korea)—not "Texas" (or Ohio or Northern California). This focus on the Asian in Asian American is deep-rooted. During World War II, when the United States was at war with Japan, hostility toward Japan extended to all persons of Japanese ancestry. From 1942 to 1945, Japanese Americans were incarcerated in internment camps because of their heritage. The internment took place even though there

222. John Marelius, *Clinton Issues Call for Healing*, S.D. Union Trib., June 11, 1996, at A1.

was no evidence that Americans of Japanese descent were disloyal to the United States. Even though the United States was at war with Germany and Italy, as well as with Japan, persons of German and Italian ancestry were not similarly incarcerated.

The Asian-as-foreigner stereotype is evident today, though it has taken on more subtle forms. During the O.J. Simpson trial, much of the racial joking in the case was directed at two Asian Americans associated with the case. The Honorable Lance Ito, the judge who presided over the trial, and criminalist Dennis Fung, two Asian Americans who speak articulately and without a noticeable accent, were portrayed as bumbling, heavily-accented Asians who could barely speak English by radio station disc jockeys, publishing houses, and even a United States senator.[229] During the Simpson trial, the historical impulse to mock others on the basis of racial difference was fulfilled by poking fun at the Asian Americans associated with the trial, constructing them as Asians with heavy accents characteristic of the Asian-as-foreigner stereotype.

Sometimes the Asian-as-foreigner stereotype takes on more ominous manifestations. In 1982, Vincent Chin, a Chinese American, was beaten to death with a baseball bat by Ronald Ebens and Michael Nitz, two White Detroit autoworkers. Before killing Chin, Ebens and Nitz, illustrating the all-too-common confusion between Chinese Americans and Japanese Americans and between Asian Americans and Asian nationals, called Chin a "Nip." They also accused Chin of contributing to the loss of jobs in the automobile industry, yelling "It's because of you little mother fuckers that we're out of work."[232] They pled guilty to manslaughter and were each sentenced to three years of probation and fined $3,780. When discussing the no jail time sentence that he imposed on the two men, the judge explained, "Had it been a brutal murder, those fellows would be in jail now."[234] It is unclear what led the judge to think the baseball bat beating was not a brutal murder, yet the judge was not alone in his sentiments. Friends of Ebens and Nitz claimed the beating was just an accident, despite witnesses' reports that Ebens swung the baseball bat at Chin's head as if he were hitting a home run, Chin's skull was fractured in several places, and police officers who arrived on the scene said pieces of Chin's brain were splattered all over the sidewalk.

* * *

THE ASIAN-AS-MARTIAL ARTIST

Another common belief about Asians and Asian Americans is the Asian-as-martial artist stereotype. Many people assume that young Asian men know martial arts. In *State v. Simon*,[284] the Asian-as-martial artist stereotype helped secure an acquittal for a man who shot his Chinese

229. Cynthia Kwei Yung Lee, *Beyond Black and White: Racializing Asian Americans in a Society Obsessed with O.J.*, 6 Hastings Women's L.J. 165, 175, 181–83, 187, 191–92, 193–94, 199 (1995).

232. Dana Sachs, *The Murderer Next Door*, Mother Jones, July/August 1989, at 54; *Who Killed Vincent Chin?* (a film by Renee Tajima & Christine Choy).

234. *Id.*, at 54.

284. 646 P.2d 1119 (Kan.1982).

neighbor and then claimed self-defense. Anthony Simon, an elderly homeowner, shot his neighbor, Steffen Wong, a Chinese man, as Wong was entering his own duplex. Simon was charged with two counts of aggravated assault.

At trial, Simon testified that he assumed, by virtue of Wong's racial heritage, that Wong was an expert in the martial arts. Simon claimed he was afraid of Wong and that heated words had been exchanged between the two neighbors. Simon also said he was fearful because more Orientals were moving into the neighborhood and one had even expressed interest in purchasing Simon's home. In addition to Simon's testimony, the defense called a clinical psychologist who testified Simon was a psychological invalid who suffered from anxiety neurosis. Defense counsel argued to the jury that the evidence showed Simon reasonably believed Wong was an imminent threat to him.

The jury acquitted Simon on all counts. Although the judge's jury instruction on self-defense utilized a subjective standard of reasonableness, that the jury could find Simon's fear to be reasonable when it was quite clear that his fear of Wong was based almost solely on a racial stereotype is quite astounding. The Asian-as-martial artist stereotype may have influenced jurors to sympathize with Simon's misplaced belief that because of his Asian heritage, Wong must have been a dangerous martial arts expert.

Racial representations of Asian Americans can have a subtle, but far-reaching impact. The judge who sentenced the men who killed Vincent Chin by beating him with a baseball bat felt that what happened to Chin was not a brutal murder even though Chin's brains were splattered all over the sidewalk and his skull fractured in several places. Likewise, the jury that acquitted Anthony Simon believed the defendant's claim of self-defense even though it is difficult to understand how the jurors could find these defendants' beliefs and actions objectively reasonable. Racial stereotypes about Asians as foreigners, economic rivals, "gooks" we fought in Vietnam, "Japs" responsible for Pearl Harbor, "chinks" who take our jobs, not only deindividualize, they also dehumanize Asian Americans. Racial representations can also influence legal decisionmakers to accept more readily claims of self-defense by defendants who kill Asian Americans, not necessarily because Asian Americans are thought to be more violent or more dangerous than others (although this may occur under the Asian-as-martial artist stereotype), but because Asian and Asian American lives, seen as foreign or outside the American community, are not valued to the same extent as other lives.

* * *

[Eds. See also Chapter 13 § 3 *infra* for further discussion of Lee's thesis and its implications for the trial process.]

JOHN M. KANG
Deconstructing the Ideology of White Aesthetics
2 Mich. J. Race & L. 283, 345, 347–51 (1997).*

ASIAN AND ASIAN-AMERICAN MEN: "WITHOUT SINFUL MANHOOD"

While African–American men tend to be embraced for their super masculinity, Asian–American men tend to be rejected for lacking the masculinity associated with bodily aesthetics. Early White American rhetoric surrounding Black men focused on their masculine appearance, but the rhetoric surrounding Asian men emphasized either their asexuality or their perceived femininity. This is not to say, of course, that Asian men were not stereotyped as sexual threats to White women. However, the prevalent caricature of Asian men in the nineteenth century as well as today has been unmistakably imbued with those stereotypically patronizing qualities we generally associate with women. * * *

The stereotypic view of effeminate Asian–American men continued throughout the twentieth century and up to today. In cinema, American viewers were introduced to the very popular Charlie Chan, "the detective who outsmarted others with his cleverness [and who unlike] white American males acting in leading roles ... was depicted as sexless or effeminate."[238] We see this same theme in John Hughes' 1984 comedy, *Sixteen Candles*. There, a sixteen-year-old Molly Ringwald encounters a foreign exchange student from China. Portrayed as infantile, feeble and weak, he is also juxtaposed against a strong, physically large White man, Molly's love interest. The Asian male is reduced to the role of a boy, while the White male, by virtue of his race, stands out as a man. If masculinity requires disassociating one's self from boyhood and trying to reach manhood, this infantilization of Asian men would seem to mean that they have failed to develop, sexually. Through Asian male characters, White men can see themselves as men and point to their Asian counterparts as impotent, helpless boys. Whereas the racial exoticism of Black American men was used to demonize a threatening masculinity that allowed White men to see themselves as rational and intelligent, the racial exoticism of Asian–American men allows White men to reaffirm their physical superiority and manhood.

The media's emasculation of Asian men has provoked some Asian–American male artists to respond. Perhaps the most colorful spokesman is Chinese–American writer Frank Chin. Chin argues that acceptance of Asian Americans as Americans is especially important for Asian men because this would help confer onto them a masculine identity that is otherwise denied them by their racial stereotype. For Chin, racial aesthetic acceptance is more than acquiring an identity as an American; it also means acquiring an identity as a man. This is an obstacle that White male immigrants have never encountered in America. * * *

ASIAN-AMERICAN WOMEN: ALL THE BUTTERFLIES—MADAME, MISS, AND M

While Asian men tend to be devalued because their bodily aesthetics contradict popular White notions of masculinity, the bodily aesthetics of

---

* Used by permission of the author and the Michigan Journal of Race & Law.

238. Pat K. Chew, *Asian Americans: The "Reticent" Minority And Their Paradoxes*, 36 Wm. & Mary L. Rev. 1, 39 (1994).

Asian women are lauded because they complement, and perhaps even symbolize, the ideal of femininity. As Asian men are perceived as physically small and weak, so too are Asian women. However, a small physical build has been traditionally associated with submissiveness, passivity, and vulnerability—qualities associated with feminine beauty. Therefore, it is not unusual to find White men being fascinated with the racial exoticism of Asian women, often to such an extent that it eclipses the femininity of White women. In numerous films, plays, books, and stories, Asian women are presented as the ideal woman by virtue of their feminine physique. Femininity, however, is a racially relative concept that exists only in contrast to something else. And in all of these films and stories, the femininity of Asian women is realized largely because it is contrasted with the physical masculinity of White characters.

Perhaps the most well-known example of this relationship is Puccini's *Madame Butterfly*. Canonized as one of the great operas, Puccini's opera is based on an 1898 short story by American John Luther Long. Puccini's work begins soon after what is euphemistically referred to as the American "opening" of Japan. Pinkerton, a naval officer stationed in Nagasaki, represents Western culture as a decidedly masculine figure existing in the public sphere of combat. He is physically taller and bigger than the Japanese girl, Cho–Cho–San, our little Butterfly. Pinkerton's juxtaposed masculinity is highlighted by other trappings of manhood. He rides a battleship. He wears an officer's uniform. He is a captain. And he is a member of an occupying military force. Cho–Cho–San, our little Butterfly, has no such public identity. She is the feminine private sphere of emotion, bias, irrationality, and delicacy. She cannot hide behind a battleship, a uniform, and the title of captain; she has nowhere to hide at all. Instead, her Japanese family oppresses her into feminine submission. Thus, she hopes that Captain Pinkerton will save her from this suffocating Asian culture. They marry, but Pinkerton only desires a night of passion without any commitments. He leaves her, but she remains in Japan and faithfully awaits her savior's return to rescue her from Asian culture. Pinkerton returns, but not for Butterfly. He only returns for their child.

Cho–Cho–San kills herself knowing that "death with honor is better than life with dishonor." By having killed herself, she confirms both her racial and sexual stereotype. As Catherine Clement states, this honorable death reunites Butterfly with her Oriental culture. For Western viewers, Asians become authentic through suicide. Death also confirms her femininity. To transcend Pinkerton's refusal and seek to find her own life would not be feminine. Instead, through suicide, she engages in the ultimate act of femininity, a complete relinquishment of resolve and the greatest abnegation of self-worth; through death, she is redeemed as the purest embodiment of femininity, and Cho–Cho–San dies beautifully as both a Japanese and as the feminine Butterfly. * * *

Upon closer analysis, the fascination with Butterfly reflects not just a fascination with a particular submissive Asian female body, but with a submissive Asian body in general. An illuminating work by playwright

David Henry Hwang[251] suggests this to be the case. In his *M. Butterfly*, Hwang resurrects Puccini's opera. As in *Madame Butterfly*, the Asian woman character is noticeably shorter and slighter than her White male co-star. But unlike Madame Butterfly, in *M. Butterfly*, an Asian American subverts the traditional Western characterizations of Cho–Cho–San. Hwang's play takes place primarily during the Chinese Cultural Revolution in the 1960s. Based on a true story, a French diplomat named Gallimard becomes obsessed with Song Liling, a Chinese opera star. After seeing Liling perform Puccini's opera, Gallimard tells her, "You were utterly convincing. It's the first time ... I've seen the beauty of the story."[253] Liling responds,

> It's one of your favorite fantasies, isn't it? The submissive Oriental woman and the cruel white man.... Consider it this way: What would you say if a blonde homecoming queen fell in love with a short Japanese businessman? He treats her cruelly, then goes home for three years, during which time she prays to his picture and turns down marriage from a young Kennedy. Then, when she learns he has remarried, she kills herself. Now, I believe you would consider this girl to be a deranged idiot, correct? But because it's an Oriental who kills herself for a Westerner—ah!—you find it beautiful.[254]

Gallimard is nonetheless obsessed with Liling. * * *

LINDA L. AMMONS

Mules, Madonnas, Babies, Bath Water, Racial Imagery and Stereotypes:
The African–American Woman and the Battered Woman Syndrome
1995 Wis. L. Rev. 1003, 1045–48, 1056–61, 1065, 1067–68.*

The subtlest and most pervasive of all influences are those which create and maintain the repertory of stereotypes. We are told about the world before we see it. We imagine most things before we experience them. And those preconceptions, unless education has made us acutely aware, govern deeply the whole process of perception.

> Next comes a warmer race, from sable sprung,
> To love each thought, to lust each nerve is strung;
> The Samboe dark, and Mulatto brown,
> The Mestize fair, the well-limb'd Quaderoon,
> And jetty Afric, from no spurious sire,
> Warm as her soil, and as her sun-on fire.
> These sooty dames, well vers'd in Venus' school,
> Make love an art, and boast they kiss by rule.[155]

> White girls are pretty funny,
> sometimes they drive me mad,

251. David H. Hwang, *M. Butterfly* (1988).

253. *Id.* at 17.

254. *Id.*

* Copyright © 1995 by The Board of Regents of the University of Wisconsin System. Reprinted by permission of the Wisconsin Law Review.

155. *Jamaica, A Poem in Three Parts,* quoted in Winthrop D. Jordan, *White Over Black: American Attitudes Toward the Negro* 150 (1968).

black girls just want to get fucked all night
I just don't have that much jam.[156]

A stereotype is a fixed impression that "conforms very little to the facts ... and results from our defining first and observing second."[157] Sociologists and psychologists have researched the phenomenon of stereotyping. In his classic work, *The Nature of Prejudice*, Gordon Allport defines a stereotype as "an exaggerated belief associated with a category. Its function is to justify (rationalize) our conduct in relation to that category."[158] Stereotypes are "the language of prejudice."[159] Attitudes about ethnic groups are a part of the social heritage of a society. They appear in a range of materials from academic sources to rock-and-roll lyrics. For example, although the above quotation cited by Jordan and the lyrics by The Rolling Stones were written more that 200 years apart, the statements promote the same stereotype about black women: They are sexually available. * * *

By the time a child is four or five, he or she has learned the significance of skin color and racial membership. Whites have been taught either expressly or implicitly that they are better than blacks. Even when adults conform their public behavior to what is socially acceptable because of the changing laws and/or mores, the indoctrination of childhood can create psychological conflicts. Psychologist Thomas Pettigrew provides an example: "Many Southerners have confessed to me, for instance, that even though in their minds they no longer feel prejudice against blacks, they still feel squeamish when they shake hands with a black."[166]

Stereotypes about African Americans have been a frequent topic of research. Scientists repeatedly find that blacks consistently receive the most unfavorable attributions. Among the historical stereotypes that were created to keep black women marginalized were Mammy, Aunt Jemima, and Jezebel. Modern caricatures include Sapphire, the matriarch and the welfare queen. These representations are so powerful that the sight of a woman of African descent can trigger responses of violence, disdain, fear, or invisibility. * * *

Extra-legal factors are ones that affect the outcome of a trial, but are not directly related to the evidence before the jury. For example, social and demographic characteristics, jury composition, and group dynamics may influence a verdict. When African Americans are brought to trial, extra-legal factors like these may easily alter their ability to get

156. The Rolling Stones, *Some Girls*, on *Some Girls* (Warner Communications 1978).

157. John C. Brigham, *Ethnic Stereotypes*, 76 Psychol. Bull. 15, 17 (1971) (quoting Katz & Braly, *Racial Prejudice and Racial Stereotypes*, 30 J. Abnormal & Soc. Psychol. 175, 181 (1935)).

158. Gordon Allport, *The Nature of Prejudice* 191, 192 (1979). ("The stereotype acts both as a justificatory device for categorical acceptance or rejection of a group, and as a screening or selective device to maintain simplicity in perception and in thinking.") bell hooks defines stereotypes as "a fantasy, a projection onto the Other that makes them less threatening." bell hooks, *Representations of Whiteness in the Black Imagination,* in *Black Looks, Race And Representation* 165, 170 (1992).

159. Howard J. Ehrlich, *The Social Psychology of Prejudice* 21 (1973).

166. Daniel Goleman, *Useful Modes of Thought Contribute to the Power of Prejudice*, N.Y. Times, May 12, 1987, at C1.

a fair trial. Justice Blackmun's dissent in *Callins v. Collins*[191] raised this issue in connection with capital cases and the death penalty. Racial bias in the courtroom is *de jure* illegal, but *de facto* bias is widespread.

The objective of the *voir dire* process is impartiality. *Voir dire* should reveal and remove those persons from the jury whose biases, as a matter of law (*e.g.*, juror having some previous history with defendant), might prevent them from fairly deliberating about the guilt or innocence of the defendant. In such a situation the juror is to be struck for cause. However, actual bias, based on subjective factors (*e.g.*, race or religion), may be harder to discern and counter. Peremptory challenges can be used to remove potential jurors for reasons other than race or sex. Although peremptory removals are not "(c)onstitutionally protected fundamental rights,"[202] the Supreme Court considers the process, "one of the most important of the rights secured to the accused."[203] Justice Marshall expressed concern that the court take a hard look at racially motivated challenges that might be disguised as facially neutral. Marshall explained that pretext anchored in racial stereotyping could be very subtle:

> A prosecutor's own conscious or unconscious racism may lead him easily to the conclusion that a prospective black juror is "sullen," or "distant," a characterization that would not have come to his mind if a white juror had acted identically. A judge's own conscious or unconscious racism may lead him to accept such an explanation as well supported.[205]

The reality of the jury selection process does not always conform to the normative theory, however. Prosecutors and/or defense attorneys want jurors with certain predispositions in order to get a conviction or acquittal. Justice may be blind, but jurors are not. Jurors do not come to the courtroom with a blank slate. The most fair-minded person has opinions about how the world operates. A juror's experiential base is a function of many factors, including sex, race, age, personality, class, and religion. Justice O'Connor acknowledged this reality in *J.E.B. v. Alabama ex rel T.B.*[208] when she stated, "(w)e know that people do not ignore as jurors what they know as men or women."[209] What we do not know empirically is the extent to which extra-legal factors influence verdicts. However, our judicial system requires that jurors render verdicts that are based on the facts of the trial and not on pre-existing attitudes about issues or persons. * * *

Whether plaintiff or defendant, the black woman in the courtroom faces obstacles to being considered a believable, reasonable person. Because she is so far removed from the mythical norm, her very existence is deviant. The treatment of Anita Hill and Lani Guinier, two accomplished black female attorneys, by presidents, Congress, the media,

---

191. 114 S. Ct. 1127 (1994).

202. *Georgia v. McCollum*, 112 S. Ct. 2348, 2358 (1992).

203. *Swain v. Alabama*, 380 U.S. 202, 219 (1965) (quoting *Pointer v. United States*, 151 U.S. 396, 408 (1894)).

205. *Batson v. Kentucky*, 476 U.S. 79, 106 (1986) (Marshall, J., concurring).

208. 114 S. Ct. 1419 (1994).

209. *Id*. at 1432.

and the public, demonstrates how the credibility of a black woman in a public forum can be called into question and how the stereotypes are used. Although not a trial, the Anita Hill/Clarence Thomas hearings illustrate how a well-respected, established black woman is vulnerable to attack when she challenges the veracity of a soon-to-be-appointed Justice of the United States Supreme Court. Justice Thomas used racial imagery to deflect attention from the disputed facts of his alleged misconduct (sexual harassment of Anita Hill) while director of the Equal Employment Opportunities Commission. Hill received the verbal lashing of senators, and was portrayed not just as unworthy of belief, but as mad (a Jezebel–Sapphire combination). * * *

African–American women's courtroom credibility issues have not gone unnoticed. Documented juror and judicial attitudes concerning the veracity of black women's claims of rape reveal stereotypes that inhibit the black female victim at trial. Researcher Gary LaFree conducted a study of jurors in Indianapolis which revealed that jurors are less likely to render a guilty verdict in rape trials when the complainant is a black woman. LaFree stated, "[p]erhaps jurors were influenced by stereotypes of black women as more likely to consent to sex, as more sexually experienced and hence less harmed by an assault. Or they may have simply accorded less priority to black victims' claims for justice."[230] LaFree then cites a response of a juror who argued for an acquittal of an accused rapist. The juror said, "a girl of her age from that kind of neighborhood probably wasn't a virgin anyway." LaFree gives other examples of how alleged rapes of black women are discounted because of their race. He quotes one juror who said, "Negroes have a way of not telling the truth. They've a knack for coloring the story. So you know you can't believe everything they say."[232]

RAYMOND STEDMAN

Shadows of the Indian
3–5, 69–73 (1982).*

Brownies they were, at least a dozen of them, clustered beneath a warm Georgia sun that spring day to poke into Indian life and lore. With their Scout leader and a few harried mothers the exuberant nine-year-olds had come to the outskirts of bustling Macon to tramp the ceremonial mounds and peek into the carefully reconstructed buildings of a thousand-year-old village designated Ocmulgee National Monument. Their thirsts thoroughly slaked by innumerable dashes to a well-tested water fountain, the young ladies stood ready to meet the patient park assistant who would be their guide.

Enriched by a thousand such moments, the "ranger" knew exactly how to begin: "Tell me, what do you know about Indians?"

Nine hands went into the air. The assistant selected the girl who seemed to have the largest twinkle in her eye. "I know a lot about

---

230. See Gary D. Lafree et al., *Jurors' Responses, Victim's Behavior and Legal Issues in Sexual Assault Trials*, 32 Soc. Probs. 389, 402 (1995).

232. Gary D. LaFree, *Rape and Criminal Justice: The Social Construction of Sexual Assault* 220 (1989).

Indians," she asserted. "They wear feathers and put paint on their faces and yell in real high voices when they attack white people and kill them with tomahawks!" Her friends nodded in agreement, one of them grunting, "Ugh, ugh."

"How did you learn those things?" the guide asked.

"Oh, from movies on television. I watch them all the time. And sometimes we talk about Indians in school."

"Have you ever seen a real Indian?"

"No, . . . I don't think so."

The guide pointed to a young member of the park staff coming out of the information area. "That fellow's an Indian," he said. "Sometimes we fish or hunt together. And he's as good a person as you'd ever want to meet. Does he look dangerous?"

Silence. Then a few quick "no's."

"Of course not. Now let me tell you about Indians. . . . "

Before the hour had passed, one more set of budding citizens had for the first time passed beyond the stereotypes and cliches of the Indian image and learned something concrete about the American continent's first inhabitants. But what if they had not come to Ocmulgee? What about those children (or adults) who have no Indian parks to visit, no Indians to see? What about tens of millions of residents of the United States who leave the whole matter to the popular media?

Their viewpoint might not differ much from that of the Brownie at Ocmulgee, or those of the students of Mrs. Lillian Rosen at New York City's Public School 183. Killing, once again, seemed to be an Indian's main function, to judge by her pupils' replies to her questions one day. "If an Indian moved to the city," said one boy, "he'd kill people. He's not smart and he would think people were cowboys and would kill dogs because he would think they were water buffalo or fish." Other comments from Mrs. Rosen's class followed the same line: Slaughter and stupidity in imaginary situations. Said the dismayed teacher, "The kids don't have the faintest idea that Indians are real people."

Yet is it surprising that children, and children now grown, have at best a mixed conception of those mysterious peoples they meet through history books or mass media? The Indian portrait of the moment may be bellicose or ludicrous or romantic, but almost never is the portrait we see that of a real person. At one instant a phantom Indian passes before us as a statuelike denizen of forest or prairie, sharing food with the Pilgrims, bowing his head before Manitou, shielding the body of John Smith from death clubs, speaking in periodic sentences of the Happy Hunting Ground or the Great White Father or the encroachment of the Long Knives. * * *

They are everywhere before us, the shadow Indians. They wear many fictional hats, but few are flattering. They sing and dance, but rarely as they really did * * * or do. They fight desperately on screen in defense of their asserted rights, but die trying to kill the white hero. They pledge their love to handsome army scouts, but soon their white doeskin dresses are stained with their own blood. They inspire thousands of athletic spectators, but usually disguised as court fools. They strike it rich in middle western oil fields and roar around, overdressed in long roadsters. They drink too much white man's whiskey and stagger about shouting, "Hallelujah!" Yes, they are fascinating figures, the American Indians. But have we ever seen them?

INDIAN TALK

Hist, Chingachgook's bride-to-be in *The Deerslayer*, 1841, written after *Nick of the Woods* talks to Hetty Hutter in almost comic-Indian fashion:

> "No t'ink more of him—no say more of scalp . . . you pale-face, I redskin; we bring up different fashion. . . . Better not talk of any but fader and Hurry; Mingo understand *dat*; he no understand *t'udder*. Promise you no talk about what you no understand."

The talking Indian of fiction has been if not drowned then at least engulfed by a sea of confusions. His first words to white men, in whatever area or dialect, were recorded by untrained ears—sometimes by ears listening for special clues to lands of riches like "Cathay." Often those words traveled circuitous routes even through several European tongues to the English dictionary (or frontier equivalent). Some of an Indian's sounds did not exist in the language of his hearers and were lost entirely or were turned in to grunted approximations (in books beyond count Indian speech is described as "guttural"). Then came the generalizations, based upon the misconception that all the nations spoke something called "Indian." Thus "How!" (an approximation of Sioux or Osage words of greeting) was put into the mouth of every Indian from Canada to Mexico, and beyond; "squaw" was applied to all Indian women, though the term was an approximation of regional Algonquin; and so on. Respected writers, for example Francis Parkman, did not help the generalization problem by calling "How!" "a monosyllable by which an Indian contrives to express half the emotions of which he is susceptible." Ernest Thompson Seton assumed universal affirmatives and negatives and in his well-intentioned *Rolf of the Woods* (1911) misled young readers by stating that "ugh (yes) and wah (no) are Indianisms that continue no matter how well the English has been acquired."

Compounding generalization was imitation. One "heap big" (whatever its slight foundation in forest grammar) was followed by thousands of "heap bigs." One ancient contraction of the English "him"—as in "Make'm drunk"—was in some lost decade mindlessly converted into a verbal ending sans pronoun "See-um clouds" and generations of lazy authors followed suit. Abundant imitation came also on the heels of supposedly direct translations of imagery: "Great White Father," "Happy Hunting Grounds," "squawman." These phrases, along with "heap big chief," suggested H. L. Mencken in *The American Language,* "owed more to the imagination of the pioneers than to the actual usage of the Indians." Yet how many novelists or screenplay writers would get through an Indian story without them?

The time has passed for fully reconstructing the actual manner in which Indians handled English conversation in the days before the mass-media era colored all language. We have only recollections and rough transcriptions of spoken exchanges in colonial and frontier days by persons whose own English phrasing and pronunciation would be far from the standard American of radio and television. Still, if we do not know precisely how to treat Indian dialogue, we know, most assuredly, how not to. The oldtime Indian talk is wrong, dead wrong. Someday even writers for the popular media will realize that fact. Someday.

Notes and Questions

1. If jurors bring ideas, acquired as children, of Indians and other people of color to the courtroom, can they set them aside by an act of will?

2. If an attorney asks them to do so, is that playing the race card and inviting special consideration for a black or brown defendant?

3. What is wrong with Brownies, Girl Scouts, and burned-out Anglos who resettle in New Mexico "playing Indian"? If done in humility and a desire to learn?

4. Compare the selections in this chapter and section with those appearing in Chapter 10 on languages. Do you think that the same mechanism underlying prohibitions on non-English languages also underlies stereotypes in popular culture?

5. Would increasing the number of Indian, black, Chicano/a, etc., authors, movie producers and directors mitigate some of the harmful images described above? Or do commercial forces and audience demand prove too powerful, so that black directors will continue to make movies about antisocial black characters, violent detectives, etc.?

MAGDA LEWIS

"Are Indians Nicer Now?": What Children Learn
From Books About Native North Americans
135–52 (1988).*

My son Geoffrey has just turned five years old. On the evening that I brought home my bundle of books, his eyes grew large and interested. He immediately appropriated the books, retired to a quiet corner and began looking through them. After some time, having leafed through all of the books, he emerged from his quiet place and asked soberly, "Are Indians nicer now?" The message so clearly given through the visual representations in these books was obvious to him and did not fail to make its impact.

What is typical of the style of most of the books I found is that the pictures tended to be presented as snapshots. The text tended mostly to refer to the picture descriptively but made no attempt at connecting one picture to the next or indeed to locate the picture in a larger context. Hence the overall effect was one of disjointedness as the images were decontextualized and made to appear unconnected to a wider, reasonable, and sufficient cultural base. Generally, the books did not sufficient-

* From *How Much Truth Do We Tell the Children?* (Betty Bacon ed. 1988). Used by permission.

ly explain the Native peoples' culturally based behavior, behavior which, therefore, tended to seem arbitrary, irrational, and "quaint." This approach impedes the reader's ability to penetrate the culture with a reasonable amount of understanding.

The images presented in these books work successfully on two levels. For very young readers, the disjointed and decontextualized visual impact is immediate and implies a way of seeing the world. In the absence of counter images, the young child begins to assimilate this point of view and assumes it to be a direct representation of reality, much the same as she assumes family photographs to be a direct representation of reality. For older readers who have already had experience with this kind of imagery and who, therefore, bring a stock of preconceived notions to the text, these images work to reinforce those very notions. The individual, in projecting her knowledge onto the image, has its "truth" reaffirmed through the dialectic process: The image feeds the common understanding, which in turn, in part, defines the image. Hence, it is clear that, in order for the images to make any sense at all, they depend to a large extent on what the reader already brings to the content. A good example of this process is provided by the title page of a book called *The North American Indians* by Ernest Berke. We are provided here with a picture of a lone Native man. He is typically naked on his upper torso. He is wearing elaborate ornamentation. Three feathers protrude from his hair at variously skewed angles. On his lower torso he is wearing buckskin, fringed leggings and a small blanket drapes loosely around his waist. On his belt a large knife rests in an ornamented case. He is wearing moccasins and in his hand he is holding a pipe. He is sitting "Indian style" (note how the stereotypical images have invaded the very language used to describe them) on a buffalo skin blanket on which rests an ornamental item—rather prominently placed. His head is at a 45 degree angle turned toward the sky. A small fire burns in front of him from which the smoke is rising straight up in the air in a thin, wispy shaft. His horse, also adorned with feathers and what appears to be a shield, grazes nearby. The man and his horse are alone on top of what appears to be a small hill, the terrain of which is very rough and rocky and looks hard and inhospitable. There are a few scrub bushes about. The man has a sullen look on his face, his mouth is downturned and his eyes are half closed. That this picture appears on the title page is particularly interesting because no explanatory text accompanies it. However, the picture is so heavily laden with stereotypical images that although we have no idea of what this man is doing or why, we almost seem to "know."

What has been presented here is a myth, specifically in that the images of the Native peoples are overlaid by a socially determined understanding of the meaning of these images. Hence, for example, when we see the Native man, with his horse and pipe on the barren hill, his head turned toward the sky, we also see the "loner," the "mysterious," the "sinister," the "religious": Someone who is doing strange, yet strangely familiar, things. These are often repeated images of the Native peoples—images that reinforce our particular understanding of them. The images we see in these books are laden with predetermined meaning and hence present themselves as statements of fact. Indeed, the hegemonic process has worked to its full potential here as the particular point of view of the dominant group; their ideological penetration into the warp and weft of the social fabric has so infused our common understanding and everyday knowledge that its validity and source are never questioned. In the process, Native reality is reified as their activities are abstracted from any sensible context.

What is totally lost in these books as a result of this approach is that first, they make it practically impossible for the child to become aware that a culture, foreign though it may be to the reader, has a reasonable and sufficient base which dictates certain acceptable behavior (acceptable within the parameters of that culture). And second, they conceal from the child that it is necessary to have an understanding of different cultures from this perspective so that her knowledge of these differences does not feed bias but rather enables her to understand life situations from different perspectives. Inasmuch as there is on the one hand a proliferation of this type of children's material and on the other hand a suppression of the culture of the oppressed, it therefore appears that the agenda of the dominant culture is precisely the denial of such an understanding in order that their superiority, through cultural and therefore economic and political means, may be maintained. In other words, in order that the invader's treatment of the Native people, both through physical and cultural abuse and extermination, may be justified, in their own minds and historically in the minds of their children, these books serve as a vehicle for Dehumanization of the Native in the eyes of non-Native children and for Mystification of the Native in the eyes of Native children. That, until only very recently, few publications offered perspectives that could effectively counter the standard images of Native peoples attests to the success of these processes: Both the dominator and the dominated have internalized the desired effects of dehumanization and mystification respectively. * * *

Significantly the vast majority of the images in these books are premised on a notion of Native people as individuals from a distant past rather than as a current reality. That they are written in the past tense and the fact that the images are almost always contextualized in a typical noncurrent setting implies a distant past which has no relationship to the present. Typical of this is the book *Plains Indians*. The last page of this book shows a group of Native people being removed on horseback and in wagons to the Indian reservations. The text reads, "The Indians were finally defeated in 1890 at Wounded Knee. They were herded onto reservations on land that white people did not want. With no buffalo to hunt, their lives became dependent on the government. They lost their freedom, and their whole way of life on the plains they loved" (*id.* at 28). And so it ended. * * *

That these images of the vanished "Indian" permeate the cultural fabric of the child's social context is emphasized by their ubiquity. *Everywhere:* Children's nursery rhymes; advertising; and common language (*e.g.*, acting like a bunch of wild Indians). The logo for Mutual of Omaha personifies this use of the Native image. It consists of a head wearing a feathered headdress covering the eyes. Below it is a bulbous nose and below that a down-turned mouth. What makes this logo particularly interesting is that the image is not only rigidly stereotypical and immediately recognizable as that of an "Indian" but it is difficult to imagine what religious/cultural artifact of any other group in North America could be used so blatantly, be so immediately recognized by the wide majority of the population and go so routinely unchallenged. * * * Children's nursery rhymes are particularly relevant in that they are littered with Native images. The one that addresses itself specifically to the vanishing Indian, however, is the familiar "one little, two little, three little Indians." As the rhyme proceeds up to ten little Indians, the countdown starts in the other direction until it stops at "one little Indian boy." They are all gone but one. One can almost see the "little Indian boys" jumping out from behind trees, where they had been "lurking" and being "popped off" by the ever ready, vigilant white man. This is no mere fanciful extrapolation, overdone analytic zeal, or stretching an analogy. As Hartmut Lutz points out, economic, political, and ideological reasons supported mythologizing the white man as superhero and the Native people as the evil that lurks behind every tree and which, therefore, had to be eliminated. * * *

The cliches, in fact, are legion. These images of Native people are not confined to one book but rather this version of Native history and culture has a consistency in children's picture books which the child cannot escape. Given the social, political, and economic context within which the publishing industry functions, it is perhaps not surprising that the books, both from the school library and from the public library, were so blatant in their biases and represented often and with noticeable impact the view of the dominant culture. In general, as can be seen, the culturally biased view of the Native peoples is the familiar one often represented through other popular media such as television, consumer items and service industries catering to the tourist trade. These various and wide-ranging vehicles for the dissemination of the popular culture work in remarkable concert to bring forth the accepted version of Native reality.

GARRETT EPPS

What's Loving *Got To Do With It?*
81 Iowa L. Rev. 1489, 1498–1500 (1996).*

Pocahontas, the daughter of Chief Powhatan, must stand as the quintessential assimilationist. At the age of 18, she was abducted from her family and taken as a hostage by the English settlers at Jamestown. The colonists originally hoped to use Pocahontas as a lever with which to blackmail Powhatan into giving them back captured English prisoners and weapons, and granting them favorable peace terms and "also a great quantitie of Corne."[53] But Pocahontas found that her father was unwilling to bargain for her freedom. Powhatan left her in the care of her

---

* Used by permission of the Iowa Law Review.

53. Grace Steele Woodward, *Pocahontas* 156 (1969) (quoting Edward D. Neill, *History of the Virginia Company of London, with Letters to and from the First Colony Never Before Printed* 86 (1869)).

captors, Sir Thomas Gates and Sir Thomas Dale, "the two highest-ranking colonists in Virginia."[55]

Gates and Dale soon realized that if Pocahontas was to be used as pawn in their political chess game with the Indians, the abduction in itself was not going to produce checkmate. Several other moves would have to be made.... Thus, while they waited hopefully for some positive response from Chief Powhatan, they attended more or less deliberately to the transformation of Pocahontas into a "model Indian princess." Pocahontas was placed in the care of the Reverend Alexander Whitaker, who took her to his farm near Henrico. His women parishioners taught her to wear English dress, and he undertook the Pygmalion-like role of molding the young savage into an English lady. No longer was she permitted to offer sacrifices to Ahone at mealtime or repeat traditional Powhatan chants to the god.... Finally, in the spring of 1614, Whitaker reviewed her in the catechism, received her renunciation of paganism, heard her confession of faith in Jesus Christ, and through the sacrament of baptism renamed her Rebecca and welcomed her into the fellowship of the Church of England.

The Englishman John Rolfe married the new Christian, even though, he admitted, her "education hath bin rude, her manners barbarous, her generation accursed, and her nutriture so discrepant in all things from myself."[57] Further, Rolfe was aware of the Biblical and civil prohibitions against marrying "strange wives."[58] However, Pocahontas's captors gave permission because the marriage would be "justification for attempting once again to press Chief Powhatan for a peaceful settlement of hostilities."[59] Pocahontas herself agreed to marry Rolfe because of her pain at her father's indifference to her captivity. King James of England sought to prosecute Rolfe for high treason for the marriage, but his wrath subsided when the Privy Council assured him that Rebecca's issue would not be heirs to England's holdings in Virginia. Rolfe and his Rebecca were married on April 5, 1614. The next year, Rebecca Rolfe bore John Rolfe a son, Thomas Rolfe. In 1616 the Virginia Company prevailed upon her to come to England to help raise money for the colony. But once in England, her health quickly deteriorated, and in 1617 she died and was buried at Gravesend as "Rebecca Rolfe."

The life and death of this model princess is a painful story—of dual disinheritance and misunderstanding, of apostasy, exploitation, alienation, exile and lonely, premature death; its legacy is the odd phenomenon of aristocratic Virginia segregationists who proudly (and often falsely) claimed her as an ancestor—who claimed proudly to be "white," in other words, only by an act of legislative grace.

What does the Pocahontas proviso prove? Nothing definitively. But to me it suggests that to hope that mere intermarriage can dismantle an oppressive scheme of domination is, at best, naive. The wishful thought behind it is that if my children, or their children, can simply look

55. *Id*. at 156.

57. *Id*. at 158–59 (quoting Raphe Hanor, *A True Discourse of the Present Estate of Virginia* 64 (1615)).

58. Woodward, *supra* note 53, at 162.

59. *Id*. at 163.

different from me, then those who hate me because of how I look will be transformed from enemies into brothers and friends.

But social reality is rarely so forgiving. It did not happen so for poor Rebecca Rolfe; after she died, the heirs of her half-white son displaced and exterminated the heirs of her Native father, creating in the process a system of racial domination previously unparalleled in history. Their motive was not the simple joy of hurting those who did not look like them—it was profit from the unjust labor system needed to grow tobacco. For those who ally themselves with American racism, which grows historically from the system those colonists created, the enemy is not truly those who look a certain way, but those who question an economic and social structure that rewards some with unmerited benefit and others with undeserved suffering. Those committed to privilege can always find compelling reasons why those beneath them are not worthy of equal dignity and voice; if it is not their race, it will be their "culture," or their educational level, or their language, or any excuse at all to keep the structure of domination intact.

Notes and Questions

1.   Can one make a movie or tell a story without using *any* stock characters or stereotypes, such as the bumbling Asian tourist, the crafty spy or desperado from some evil empire, or the handsome Latino romantic idol? Or, are stock characters necessary for any narrative?

2.   Can some of these stock figures—*e.g.*, the martial arts expert Asian man—be neutral, or even positive? What about Pocahontas?

3.   On the way sex and race interact in the creation of Asian imagery, see the selection by John Kang, *supra* this chapter.

4.   In *The Bluest Eye*, Toni Morrison describes how a young black female character longs to have white features. See Chapter 6, § 4, *supra*. Where would a young black woman get these insidious ideas of her own ugliness and inferiority?

5.   If media representations, songs like White Christmas, and children's books depicting princesses as beautiful and invariably Nordic-looking are in part responsible, should society destroy those books? Refuse to buy them? Tell black, brown, and Asian children to toughen up?

6.   For a discussion of *Snow White*, see Chapter 6, § 4.

7.   Class Exercise

This class has just received a notice that the law school film society plans to show D.W. Griffith's *The Birth of a Nation*, a critically acclaimed but virulently racist movie. A section of the minority students' association is protesting the showing because of its glorification of white supremacy. These students invoke an obscure campus rule, laid down sixty years ago when the school had an affiliation with a religious denomination, that requires advance notice of disturbing content for any presentation, speech, or classroom lecture, if the content is apt to cause psychological or cultural pain in the audience. The law school chapter of the ACLU threatens to file suit if the students' objections prevail.

Half the class: Please be prepared to argue the ACLU position. Other half: The minority association's.

8.   For further reading and viewing, see Patricia Williams, *The Alchemy of Race and Rights* (1991); Patricia Williams, *The Rooster's Egg* (1995); Lisa Ikemoto, *Traces of the Master Narrative in the Story of African American/Korean American Conflict: How We Constructed "Los Angeles,"* 66 S. Cal. L. Rev. 1581 (1993); Marlon Riggs, Ethnic Notions (California Newsreel, 1987); Marlon Riggs, Color Adjustment (California Newsreel, 1991); *"I" Is Not for Indian: The Portrayal of Native Americans* in *Books for Young People* (Naomi Caldwell–Wood & Lisa A. Mitten comps. 1991); *From Different Shores: Perspectives on Race and Ethnicity in America* (Ronald Takaki ed. 1987); Richard Griffith & Arthur Mayer, *The Movies* (Rev. ed. 1970)

SECTION 2.   MINIMIZING CULTURAL PREJUDICE

Certain areas of American culture are less racist than others. What makes them different? The following materials explore this question.

RICHARD DELGADO, et al.

*Fairness and Formality: Minimizing the Risk of
Prejudice in Alternative Dispute Resolution*
1985 Wis. L. Rev. 1359, 1387–91, 1400–04.*

The selection of one mode or another of dispute resolution can do little, at least in the short run, to counter prejudice that stems from authoritarian personalities or historical currents. Prejudice that results from social-psychological factors is, however, relatively controllable. Much prejudice is environmental—people express it because the setting encourages or tolerates it. In some settings people feel free to vent hostile or denigrating attitudes toward members of minority groups; in others they do not. * * *

Prejudiced persons are least likely to act on their beliefs if the immediate environment confronts them with the discrepancy between their professed ideals and their personal hostilities against out-groups. According to social psychologists, once most persons realize that their attitudes and behavior deviate from what is expected, they will change or suppress them.

Given this human tendency to conform, American institutions have structured and defined situations to encourage appropriate behavior. Our judicial system, in particular, has incorporated societal norms of fairness and even-handedness into institutional expectations and rules of procedure at many points. These norms create a "public conscience and a standard for expected behavior that check overt signs of prejudice."[222] * * * They do this in a variety of ways. First, the formalities of a court trial—the flag, the black robes, the ritual—remind those present that the occasion calls for the higher, "public" values, rather than the lesser values embraced during moments of informality and intimacy. In a courtroom trial the American Creed, with its emphasis on fairness, equality, and respect for personhood, governs. Equality of status, or

222.   G. Allport, *The Nature of Prejudice* 470 (25th Anniv. Ed. 1979).

something approaching it, is preserved—each party is represented by an attorney and has a prescribed time and manner for speaking, putting on evidence, and questioning the other side. Equally important, formal adjudication avoids the unstructured, intimate interactions that, according to social scientists, foster prejudice. The rules of procedure maintain distance between the parties. Counsel for the parties do not address one another, but present the issue to the trier of fact. The rules preserve the formality of the setting by dictating in detail how this confrontation is to be conducted.

That the formality of adversarial adjudication deters prejudice is borne out by the few empirical studies that have investigated the question. An experiment conducted by Walker and his colleagues showed that subjects viewed adversarial procedures as "the most preferable and the fairest mode of dispute resolution,"[223] a preference that may even extend to persons in countries that do not use an adversarial system of justice. Another experiment placed subjects in a laboratory setting behind a "veil of ignorance"[225] and asked them to choose among a variety of procedural alternatives. Almost all the subjects chose the adversarial system. The authors concluded that the adversary system introduces a systematic evidentiary bias in favor of the weaker party.

Another experiment showed that the "competitive presentation of evidence counteracts decisionmaker bias ..."[227] In one experiment, subjects were presented with a test case; they were given a list of both "lawful" and "unlawful" factors, but were told to consider only the "lawful" ones in making a decision. The results showed that in a simulated adversarial framework, even those subjects predetermined to be biased gave less weight to unlawful factors in their decisionmaking. The authors hypothesized that adversarial procedure counteracts decisionmaker bias because it combats the natural human tendency to "judge too swiftly in terms of the familiar that which is not yet fully known."[230] The human propensity to prejudge and make irrational categorizations is thus checked by procedural safeguards found in an adversarial system.

Formality and adversarial procedures thus counteract bias among legal decisionmakers and disputants. But it seems likely that those factors increase fairness in yet a further way—by strengthening the resolve of minority disputants to pursue their legal rights.

Early in life, minority children become aware of themselves as different, an awareness that is often not merely neutral, but associated with feelings of inferiority. Separate studies by psychologists Kenneth Clark and Mary Goodman in which minority children were presented with dolls of various colors illustrate this graphically. For example, when asked to make a choice between a white and black doll, "the doll that

223. Thibaut, Walker, LaTour & Houlden, *Procedural Justice as Fairness*, 26 Stan L. Rev. 1271, 1288 (1974).

225. *Id.* at 1272. The term "veil of ignorance" was coined by John Rawls. J. Rawls, *A Theory of Justice* (1971); the purpose of the device is to cancel out self-interest in the analysis of hypothetical social arrangements.

227. Thibaut, Walker & Lind, *Adversary Presentation and Bias in Legal Decisionmaking*, 86 Harv. L. Rev. 386, 401 (1972).

230. *Id.* at 390, 401.

looks like you," most black children chose the white one. A black child justified his choice of the white over the black doll as a friend because "his feet, hands, ears, elbows, knees, and hair are clean."[235] In another experiment, a black child hated her skin color so much that she "vigorously lathered her arms and face with soap in an effort to wash away the dirt."[236] As minority children grow, they are "likely to experience a long series of events, from exclusion from play groups and cliques to violence and threats of violence, that are far less likely to be experienced by the average member of the majority group."[237] Against a background of "slights, rebuffs, forbidden opportunities, restraints, and often violence . . . the minority group member shapes that fundamental aspect of personality—a sense of oneself and one's place in the total scheme of things."[238]

Discriminatory treatment can trigger a variety of responses, of which three are most common: Avoidance, aggression, and acceptance. A minority group member may display one or more of these responses, depending on the setting. In some situations, victims of discrimination are likely to respond with apathy or defeatism; in others, the same individuals may forthrightly and effectively assert their interests. In general, when a person feels "he is the master of his fate, that he can control to some extent his own destiny, that if he works hard things will go better for him, he is then likely to achieve more. . . ."[242] That is, minority group members are more apt to participate in processes which they believe will respond to reasonable efforts. They are understandably less likely to participate in proceedings where the results are random and unpredictable.

Thus, a favored forum for redress of race-based wrongs has been the traditional adjudicatory setting. Minorities recognize that public institutions, with their defined rules and formal structure, are more subject to rational control than private or informal structures. Informal settings allow wider scope for the participants' emotional and behavioral idiosyncrasies; in these settings majority group members are most likely to exhibit prejudicial behavior. Thus, a formal adjudicative forum increases the minority group member's sense of control and, therefore, may be seen as the fairer forum. This perception becomes self-fulfilling: Minority persons are encouraged to pursue their legal rights as though prejudice were unlikely and thus the possibility of prejudice is in fact lessened.
* * *

PREJUDICE IN ALTERNATIVE DISPUTE RESOLUTION (ADR)—
ASSESSING AND BALANCING THE RISKS

ADR increases the risk of prejudice toward vulnerable disputants. The rules and structures of formal justice tend to suppress bias, whereas

235. Clark & Clark, *Racial Identification and Preference in Negro Children*, in *Readings in Social Psychology* 602, 611 (E. Maccoby, T. Newcomb & E. Hartley eds. 1958).

236. M. Goodman, *Race Awareness in Young Children* 56 (rev. ed. 1964).

237. See G. Simpson & J. Yinger, *Racial and Cultural Minorities: An Analysis of*

Prejudice and Discrimination 168 (4th ed. 1972).

238. *Id.* at 192.

242. Grambs, *Negro Self–Concept Reappraised*, in *Black Self–Concept: Implications for Education and Social Science* 184 (J. Banks & J. Grambs eds. 1972).

informality tends to increase it. ADR's leftwing critics see ADR as increasing the power of authoritarian social institutions over individuals, extending state coercive power into new areas of citizens' lives, and discouraging collective action. * * *

If ADR increases the risk of prejudice or bias in adjudication, it does not follow immediately that ADR should be curtailed. Equity concerns are only one value among many; conceivably, the gains in flexibility, speed, and economy that ADR's proponents cite could override moderate losses in fairness. A survey of the role of the ideal of fairness in American procedural law suggests, however, that the balance should be struck on the side of fairness.

American procedural law's history evidences a strong and steady evolution toward fairness, an evolution that has at times overshadowed the impulse toward economy and efficiency. Over a century ago, the Field code simplified pleading rules, largely to eliminate traps for the unwary and to render legal paper work intelligible to ordinary persons. The great procedural reforms of this century, civil discovery and long-arm jurisdiction, were likewise intended to equalize power and opportunity among litigants. Discovery enables litigants of modest means to learn facts about the dispute that might otherwise remain in the exclusive possession of the more powerful party. Long-arm jurisdiction enables citizens injured by corporations and other powerful entities to bring them to account where the injury occurred, instead of being forced to sue where the defendant is found.

Civil and criminal reforms have made access to court cheaper and more readily available to all. Public defenders and legal aid attorneys represent individuals who cannot afford the costs of a private lawyer. Transcripts on appeal in some cases have been held a defendant's constitutional right. A panoply of rules and procedures have developed to assure fairness, despite the added costs they impose. Many of these are minor, such as the rule permitting modification of time rules for good cause. Others are broader, cutting across areas and stages of litigation, such as the requirement of trial by jury. Although efficiency and fairness are often in tension, our jurisprudence regards fairness in litigation as an important ideal not to be discarded lightly—and certainly not in broadbased, systemic fashion. How can we preserve that value in informal proceedings without sacrificing the benefits of informality?

ADR offers a number of clear-cut benefits. It can shape a decree flexibly so as to protect a continuing relationship between the parties. It is low-cost, speedy, and, for some at least, nonintimidating. Yet there is little benefit for a minority disputant in a quick, painless hearing that renders an adverse decision tainted by prejudice.

The risk of prejudice is greatest when a member of an in-group confronts a member of an out-group; when that confrontation is direct, rather than through intermediaries; when few rules constrain conduct; when the setting is closed and does not make clear that "public" values are to preponderate; and when the controversy concerns an intimate, personal matter rather than some impersonal question. Many minority participants will press their claims most vigorously when they believe that what they do and say will make a difference, that the structure will respond, and that the outcome is predictable and related to effort and merit.

It follows that ADR is most apt to incorporate prejudice when a person of low status and power confronts a person or institution of high status and power. In such situations, the party of high status is more likely than in other situations to attempt to call up prejudiced responses; at the same time, the individual of low status is less likely to press his or her claim energetically. The dangers increase when the mediator or other third party is a member of the superior group or class. Examples of ADR settings that may contain these characteristics are prison and other institutional review boards, consumer complaint panels, and certain types of cases referred to an ombudsman. In these situations, minorities and members of other out-groups should opt for formal in-court adjudication, and the justice system ought to avoid pressuring them to accept an alternate procedure. ADR should be reserved for cases in which parties of comparable power and status confront each other.

ADR also poses heightened risks of prejudice when the issue to be adjudicated touches a sensitive or intimate area of life, for example, housing or culture-based conduct. Thus, many landlord-tenant, inter-neighbor, and intrafamilial disputes are poor candidates for ADR. When the parties are of unequal status and the question litigated concerns a sensitive, intimate area, the risks of an outcome colored by prejudice are especially great. If, for reasons of economy or efficiency ADR must be resorted to in these situations, the likelihood of bias can be reduced by providing rules that clearly specify the scope of the proceedings and forbid irrelevant or intrusive inquiries, by requiring open proceedings, and by providing some form of higher review. The third-party facilitator or decisionmaker should be a professional and be acceptable to both parties. Any party desiring one should be provided with an advocate, ideally an attorney, experienced with representation before the forum in question. To avoid atomization and lost opportunities to aggregate claims and inject public values into dispute resolution, ADR mechanisms should not be used in cases that have a broad societal dimension, but forward them to court for appropriate treatment.

Would measures like these destroy the very advantages of economy, simplicity, speed, and flexibility that make ADR attractive? They do increase the costs, but, on balance, those costs seem worth incurring. The ideal of equality before the law is too insistent a value to be compromised in the name of more mundane advantages. Continued growth of ADR consistent with goals of basic fairness will require two essential adjustments: (1) It will be necessary to identify those areas and types of ADR in which the dangers of prejudice are greatest and to direct those grievances to formal court adjudication; (2) In those areas in which the risk of prejudice exists, but is not so great as to require an absolute ban, checks and formalities must be built into ADR to ameliorate these risks as much as possible. * * *

Notes and Questions

1. Do you agree that formality and clearcut rules offer an environment more conducive than their opposites to minorities' success? People of color have always gravitated to government service, sports, and the military—settings governed by formal, well-understood rules. (See the selection by Richard Estrada *infra*). Is this the reason?

2. Is formal adjudication, despite its superficial promise of fairness, an even deeper trap for minority reformers? See Derrick Bell, *And We Are Not Saved: The Elusive Quest for Racial Justice* (1987).

3. If the mere existence of rules (and without consideration of their enforcement) minimizes the racist impulse, is this an argument for campus hate-speech regulations? See Chapter 10.

PAUL BUTLER

Jackie Robinson: Breaking the Barrier
Dallas Morning News, Sunday, April 6, 1997, at 1J.*

Fifty years ago this month, many white Americans first demonstrated their willingness to be entertained by, and profit from, a black athlete. * * * This white "progress" has been, for black people, a mixed blessing. If, however, America's pastime is a metaphor for life in the U.S.A., then Jackie Robinson failed. Or rather, white people have. * * *

Some people have compared, favorably, desegregation in baseball to desegregation in public education. The myth is that the former was accomplished by a few good white men * * * and one fine African-American role model, Jackie Robinson. And look at their fruit today: Black players dominate professional basketball and football and constitute a significant percentage of major league baseball players as well. Integrating the public schools, on the other hand, took an order of the Supreme Court, and it has proved a colossal failure: More African-American students attend virtually all-black schools in 1997 than when *Brown v. Board of Education* was decided. * * * Integration happened in major league baseball in large part because World War II depleted the supply of excellent white players, and, accordingly, the games were not as profitable or entertaining as they might have been.

In 1946, the Dodgers, especially, were hurting, athletically and fiscally. They were the least popular team in a city that had three professional baseball organizations. Rickey [the general manager] believed the Dodgers could profit by raiding the best players, and much of the audience, of the Negro Leagues. * * * Jackie Robinson was not the best player in the Negro Leagues, but he was the most marketable one. He was college-educated and married, which would keep him away from white girls. He had a temper, but he was willing to check it if that were the price of his ticket to the big time. * * *

[T]he reason that integration worked in baseball is that white people were persuaded that black participation was in whites' interest. Jackie Robinson was the 1947 Rookie of the Year, and the Brooklyn Dodgers won the National League pennant. Other teams realized that if they

* Reprinted with permission of the Dallas Morning News.

wanted to win, they had to hire African–American players. * * * The white body politic still has not been persuaded that integration in the non-entertainment aspects of American life is in its best interests. That is why integration has failed outside of popular culture.

Jackie Robinson should be our role model because he understood that baseball is not important. He also understood that racial justice remains an elusive goal in the United States, even with success stories like him and me. Shortly before he died, Robinson wrote that "virtually every time the black stands up like a man to make a protest or to tell the truth as he sees it, white folks and some white-minded black folks try to hush or shame him by singing out that 'you've come a long way' routine. They fail to see that we've still got a long way to go. * * *"

Notes and Questions

1.   Jackie Robinson wrote in his autobiography that "[t]here was a time when I deeply believed in America. I have become bitterly disillusioned." Is this indicative of the feelings of most integrationists or people in the civil rights movement?

2.   Have you ever felt that way about race relations in the United States?

3.   Do you consider Jackie Robinson a hero? Does his disillusionment affect your feelings?

4.   If the United States contains (tolerates?) a few dozen black, Latino, and Asian millionaires in sports or entertainment, but rarely in any other field, is this a good or a bad sign?

RICHARD ESTRADA

Military Success for Hispanics is Tied to Education
Chicago Tribune, February 25, 1997, Commentary at 19.*

When my late father dropped out of high school to join the military in the 1940s, he did so out of patriotism and economic necessity. The son of a non-English-speaking widow from Mexico, his occupational alternatives at the time included the filling stations and copper mines of southwestern New Mexico.

Yet, based on that initial two-year stint in the Army, he made something of himself. He returned home, finished high school and proceeded to become the first in his family to earn a college diploma and a commission in the U.S. Army. He was forever grateful, respectively, to the GI Bill and the Reserve Officers' Training Corps program at New Mexico State University in Las Cruces. But the story of one gutsy Mexican–American kid from the Southwest was hardly unique. As General Colin Powell has written in his memoir, *My American Journey*, the military has served as a steppingstone for minorities since the days of the Buffalo Soldiers, black enlisted men who helped pacify the West after the Civil War. General Powell, the former chairman of the Joint Chiefs of Staff, was himself an ROTC product.

* Used by permission of the author.

Still, the participation and status of minorities in the military may be changing, and not for the better. Last year, for example, it was reported that, for the first time in this century, the interest of African Americans in enlisting in the military was experiencing more than a brief dip.

Military recruiters note that heightened standards for enlistment dating from the late 1970s represent a hurdle for minority youth that has been increasingly hard to overcome. Hispanics may be facing an especially difficult challenge. As reporter George Wilson pointed out in the February 17 issue of the *Navy Times*, while 11.5 percent of Americans between 18 and 44 are Hispanic, Hispanics represent only about 6.3 percent of those personnel on active duty in the armed forces. Among Hispanics who are serving, success has been most notable at the top of the enlisted ranks. The grades E–7 through E–9 have witnessed a growth in the proportion of Hispanics every year and in every branch of the service between 1987 and 1996. During that period, the percentage of Hispanics in those ranks in the Navy went from 1.9 percent to 3.2 percent; Marines, 5.1 percent to 8.2 percent; Army, 4.3 percent to 6.8 percent; while the Air Force went from 3.4 to 4.1 percent.

Hispanics are less represented in the officer ranks, where their advancement is not as fast, either. Wilson notes that in the leadership grades O–1 through O–3, Hispanics were barely 2 percent in all the services in 1987. In the following decade, that representation has increased to just 3.3 percent. Hispanic naval officers have gone from 2.3 percent to 4.4 percent; Marine Corps, 2.1 percent to 4.7 percent; Army, 1.5 percent to 3.8 percent. Only the Air Force has shown a decline, going from 2.4 percent to just under 2 percent.

Already about 24 million, the Hispanic population is exploding. The group is projected to overtake blacks as the nation's largest minority as early as 2010. In that context, *Navy Times* reporter Wilson says the real hurdle to an expanded and more influential Hispanic presence in the military is low educational attainment rates.

"Hispanics nationwide are statistically less likely to finish high school," he writes, "and that makes it harder for them to get into the military." He emphasizes a 1994 survey by the American Council on Education that found 82.6 percent of whites and 77 percent of blacks to be high school graduates. But among Hispanics, the figure was a dismal 56.6 percent.

Is difficulty with English the root of the problem? That explanation is overblown, according to Hispanic observers quoted by the *Navy Times*. Yet, the article doesn't address whether young immigrants who do speak English are dropping out to work because they are expected to contribute to the household. In any event, low levels of educational attainment comprise the real barrier to greater Hispanic participation in the military. The *Navy Times* has put its finger on a key point. Education is the road map by which a greater number of Hispanics may be able to use the military as a jumping-off point to upward mobility. It was a lesson well-learned by Hispanics after World War II that should not be forgotten today.

MICHAEL ORIARD

College Athletics as a Vehicle for Social Reform
22 J.C. & U.L. 77, 77–78, 80–81 (1995).*

Does college athletics help or hinder the quest for higher education for underprivileged students? * * *

Although we tend to see the problems in intercollegiate athletics, and universities' seeming inability to solve these problems, as recent things, in reality the problems date from the early 1890s when university administrators first confronted that they had lost considerable control of college football to the popular press and its huge public. What in 1880 was an extracurricular activity of interest to no one outside a few elite university communities and their alumni in the Northeast, became by the early 1890s a great popular spectacle attracting up to 50,000 for the Thanksgiving Day college football game in New York and generating interest throughout the country. Ever since, even the most high-minded university administrators have struggled, with limited success, to put their intercollegiate athletic programs in the service of their institutions' educational missions, against the demands of an increasingly enormous public that, more simply, wants to be entertained.

* * * Intercollegiate athletics emerged as part of the expansion and transformation of higher education in the late nineteenth century: Colleges now recruiting the sons and daughters of the great emerging middle class (instead of just the sons of the elite and future clergymen); a college education now understood to be a necessary preparation for, not a hindrance to, achieving success in business and the professions. The football team in particular became a center of student life and alumni loyalty. Big-time college athletics are not about participation, but about university relations. * * *

The answer to the question whether intercollegiate athletics help or hinder underprivileged students cannot lie simply in interpreting the most recent NCAA data on graduation rates. * * * The ladder of athletic success goes up a very steep pyramid, hugely wide at the bottom, extremely narrow at the top. The argument is by now familiar: that the "hoop dreams" of inner-city kids to become the next Michael Jordan misdirect the ambitions and commitment of the most disadvantaged children in the United States into a futile pursuit for athletic wealth and glory. And universities are found particularly culpable in this massive delusion, serving, as they do, as the gateway to the NFL and NBA. This argument indeed can be grounded in hard data. For the millions on the playground and the hundreds of thousands who play in high school, there are only 13,000 or so spots for incoming freshmen athletes at the college level, and for those 13,000, only a few hundred will move on to play at the professional level. To be more specific about one sport, football: If each of the 106 NCAA Division I–A schools offers twenty-five football scholarships each year, that means opportunities, at most, for only 2,650 high school graduates each year. Considering only black

* Used by permission of the author and the Journal of College and University Law.

freshman football players—but expanding the pool to include all 301 NCAA Division I institutions in a given year (1987–88)—the number of opportunities is only 1,513. Of those 2,650 or 1,513—whichever number seems more meaningful—something like 150 to 200 will make it to the NFL, assuming that teams average five to seven rookies each season. For those who make it, the average career in the NFL is a little over three years.

Faced with such figures, one still can ask whether eliminating the NFL would guarantee that inner-city kids would redirect their energies into reading and math, and whether eliminating intercollegiate athletics would guarantee that they would aspire to higher education rather than higher sport. We should also remind ourselves to avoid the tendency to find simple cultural explanations for complicated political and economic problems. Murphy Brown, rather than poverty, is blamed for the disintegration of the American family among the poor. Arnold Schwarzenegger movies, rather than poverty, are blamed for urban violence. In a similar way, are the false hopes inspired by sport perhaps too easily blamed for the ultimate hopelessness of the inner city?

One also can confront data with other data, a different set of figures that would seem to challenge the suggestion that sport is a dead end: Of the 156,918 total freshmen who enrolled in Division I schools in 1987, just 7,772 (5%) were African American; of those 7,772, 1,184 (15%) were athletes (compared to 2.3% of white students who were athletes). The disproportionate number of black athletes in relation to black non-athletes at many universities today might lead to a conclusion that, without sport, minority access to higher education would be considerably more dismal than it currently is.

* * *

Notes and Questions

1. Harry Edwards, in *Sociology of Sport* (1973), argues that athletics' value for communities, and especially those of color, is overrated. Statistics show that college athletes, particularly ones of color, fail to complete their degree, take easy courses, and are cast out injured, limping, and underprepared. Few of them make it in the pros. The movie *Hoop Dreams* (1994) depicts the trap of athletic success for youth of color, a theme Jesse Jackson and the Rainbow Coalition have repeated.

2. You are a black or brown parent. Your child is tall for his age, exceptionally well-coordinated, quick, and powerful. He loves sports, but is also good at his classes. Mega State University (public, U.S.A.) is offering him a huge scholarship to play big-time football. Princeton is offering a much smaller academic scholarship and the chance to play intramural sports. Would you put your foot down, and if so, in which direction?

3. Is sports a trap and a perpetuation of stereotypes? For all, or for just minority youths?

4. Can white men jump? What do you make of the rash of recent news stories about the plight of the white athlete who simply cannot compete with the superior black sprinter, middle-distance runner, or basketball star? Is this self-righteous whining on the part of athletes who want to win without

training hard? Recall how various national road races have been passing rules designed to minimize the number of foreign, especially Kenyan, competitors. Would this have happened had Sweden or Ireland been the countries sending dozens of superbly qualified runners to scoop up all the prizes? Recall how Adolf Hitler showed shock and displeasure over Jesse Owens' successes at the 1936 Olympics. (Owens was a top sprinter, long jumper, and an African American.) Is the reaction one sees today in the U.S. any different from Hitler's?

See Special Report, *What Ever Happened to the White Athlete? Newsweek*, Dec. 9, 1997.

5. In sports, the military, and other relatively formal settings, racism seems to hold less sway than it does in other arenas. (For example, professional baseball and football are about 70 percent minority—although the percentage of coaches, managers, and quarterbacks is much lower, just as it is in the officer ranks in the military.) Is this so because the rules discourage outward expression of prejudice? Because persons of different races and backgrounds work and interact together and thus get to know each other as individuals? If so, radical immersion in another culture might dispel prejudice even without stern, omnipresent rules.

6. Could the wrong sort of immersion *increase* prejudice?

7. Consider how Blacks and other minorities seem to obtain success most readily only in powerless roles that serve utilitarian purposes for the white majority: In national defense, minorities and poor Whites die; in sports, disproportionate numbers of minorities serve to entertain and amuse Whites. These roles, while bringing respectability (in the case of the military) or high salaries (in the case of the entertainment/sports world) only reinforce the view that people of color are good as cannon fodder or sources of entertainment. See Iris Marion Young, *Justice and the Politics of Difference* (1990), discussing the concept of marginalization—the idea that we come to expect people of color to act only in certain roles *and* then make that expectation reality by hiring people of color only for those roles (*e.g.*, as athlete, custodian, bellhop, entertainer, etc.).

Is General Colin Powell a counter-example to what is written in the previous paragraph?

JOHN HOWARD GRIFFIN

Black Like Me
13–14, 42–48, 99 (1996).*

NOVEMBER 6

For the past four days, I had spent my time at the doctor's or closed up in my room with cotton pads over my eyes and the sun lamp turned on me. They had made blood tests twice and found no indication of damage to the liver. But the medication produced lassitude and I felt constantly on the verge of nausea.

The doctor, well-disposed, gave me many warnings about the dangers of this project in so far as my contact with Negroes was concerned.

Now that he had had time to think, he was beginning to doubt the wisdom of this course, or perhaps he felt strongly his responsibility. In any event, he warned me that I must have some contact in each major city so my family could check on my safety from time to time.

"I believe in the brotherhood of man," he said. "I respect the race. But I can never forget when I was an intern and had to go down on South Rampart Street to patch them up. Three or four would be sitting in a bar or at a friend's house. They were apparently friends one minute and then something would come up and one would get slashed up with a knife. We're willing enough to go all the way for them, but we've got this problem—how can you render the duties of justice to men when you're afraid they'll be so unaware of justice they may destroy you?—especially since their attitude toward their own race is a destructive one." He said this with real sadness. I told him my contacts indicated that Negroes themselves were aware of this dilemma and they were making strong efforts to unify the race, to condemn among themselves any tactic or any violence or injustice that would reflect against the race as a whole.

"I'm glad to hear that," he said, obviously unconvinced.

He also told me things that Negroes had told him that the lighter the skin the more trustworthy the Negro. I was astonished to see an intelligent man fall for this cliche, and equally astonished that Negroes would advance it, for in effect it placed the dark Negro in an inferior position and fed the racist idea of judging a man by his color.

When not lying under the lamp, I walked the streets of New Orleans to orient myself. Each day I stopped at a sidewalk shoeshine stand near the French Market. The shine boy was an elderly man, large, keenly intelligent and a good talker. He had lost a leg during World War I. He showed none of the obsequiousness of the Southern Negro, but was polite and easy to know. (Not that I had any illusions that I knew him, for he was too astute to allow any white man that privilege.) I told him I was a writer, touring the Deep South to study living conditions, civil rights, etc., but I did not tell him I would do this as a Negro. Finally, we exchanged names. He was called Sterling Williams. I decided he might be the contact for my entry into the Negro community.

* * *

NOVEMBER 10–12

Two days of incessant walking, mostly looking for jobs. I wanted to discover what sort of work an educated Negro, nicely dressed, could find. I met no rebuffs, only gentleness when they informed me they could not use my services as typist, bookkeeper, etc.

The patterns became the same. Each day at the shine stand we had the same kind of customers; each day we cooked food and ate on the sidewalk; each day we fed the beggar and the pigeons. * * *

The next morning I went to the Y cafe next door for breakfast of grits and eggs. The elderly gentleman who ran the cafe soon had me talking—or rather listening. He foresaw a new day for the race. Great strides had been made, but greater ones were to be made still. I told him of my unsuccessful job-hunting. He said it was all part of the pattern of economics—economic injustice.

"You take a young white boy. He can go through school and college with a real incentive. He knows he can make good money in any profession when he gets out. But can a Negro—in the South? No, I've seen many make brilliant grades in college. And yet when they come home in the summers to earn a little money, they have to do the most menial work. And even when they graduate it's a long hard pull. Most take postal jobs, or preaching or teaching jobs. This is the cream. What about the others, Mr. Griffin? A man knows no matter how hard he works, he's never going to quite manage * * * taxes and prices eat up more than he can earn. He can't see how he'll ever have a wife and children. The economic structure just doesn't permit it unless he's prepared to live down in poverty and have his wife work too. That's part of it. Our people aren't educated because they either can't afford it or else they know education won't earn them the jobs it would a white man. Any kind of family life, any decent standard of living seems impossible from the outset. So a lot of them, without even understanding the cause, just give up. They take what they can—mostly in pleasure, and they make the grand gesture, the wild gesture, because what have they got to lose if they do die in a car wreck or a knife fight or something else equally stupid."

"Yes, and then it's these things that cause the whites to say we're not worthy of first-class citizenship."

"Ah ..." he dropped his hands to his sides hard in frustration. "Isn't it so? They make it impossible for us to earn, to pay much in taxes because we haven't much in income, and then they say that because they pay most of the taxes, they have the right to have things like they want. It's a vicious circle, Mr. Griffin, and I don't know how we'll get out of it. They put us low, and then blame us for being down there and say that since we are low, we can't deserve our rights."

Others entered, ordered breakfast and joined the conversation.

"Equal job opportunities," Mr. Gayle said. "That's the answer to much of the tragedy of our young people."

"What's needed?" I asked. "What kind of wisdom can overcome the immense propaganda of the racists and the hate groups? People read this poison and it's often presented in a benevolent tone, even a kind tone. Many sincerely think the Negro, because of his very Negro-ness, could not possibly measure up to white standards in work performance. I read recently where one of them said that equality of education and job opportunity would be an even greater tragedy for us. He said it would quickly prove to us that we can't measure up—disillusion us by showing us that we are, in fact, inferior."

"I wish those kind souls wouldn't be so protective. I know plenty who'd be willing to take the chance of being 'disillusioned,'" the proprietor laughed.

"They're about fifty years behind the times," an elderly man said. "The social scientists have shown this is wrong. Our own people have proven themselves in every field not just a few, but thousands. How can the racists deny these proofs?"

"They don't bother to find out about them," Mr. Gayle said flatly.

"We need a conversion of morals," the elderly man said. "Not just superficially, but profoundly. And in both races. We need a great saint— some enlightened common sense. Otherwise, we'll never have the right answers when these pressure groups—those racists, superpatriots, whatever you want to call them—tag every move toward racial justice as communist-inspired, Zionist-inspired, Illuminati-inspired, Satan-inspired, * * * part of some secret conspiracy to overthrow the Christian civilization."

"So, if you want to be a good Christian, you mustn't act like one. That makes sense," Mr. Gayle said.

"That's what they claim. The minute you give me my rights to vote when I pay taxes, to have a decent job, a decent home, a decent education then you're taking that first step toward 'race-mixing' and that's part of the great secret conspiracy to ruin civilization, to ruin America."

"So, if you want to be a good American, you've got to practice bad Americanism. That makes sense, too," Mr. Gayle sighed. "Maybe it'd take a saint after all to straighten such a mess out."

"We've reached a poor state when people are afraid that doing the decent and right thing is going to help the communist conspiracy," the proprietor said. "I'm sure a lot of people are held back just on that point."

"Any way you look at it, we're in the middle. It's hard for me to understand how letting me have a decent job, so I can raise my children in a better home and give them a better education is going to help the enemies of my country. * * * "

Walking along Dryades, through the ghetto, I realized that every informed man with whom I had spoken, in the intimate freedom of the colored bond, had acknowledged a double problem for the Negro. First, the discrimination against him. Second, and almost more grievous, his discrimination against himself; his contempt for the blackness that he associates with his suffering; his willingness to sabotage his fellow Negroes because they are part of the blackness he has found so painful. * * *

On Chartres Street in the French Quarter I walked toward Brennan's, one of New Orleans' famed restaurants. Forgetting myself for a moment, I stopped to study the menu that was elegantly exposed in a show window. I read, realizing that a few days earlier I could have gone in and ordered anything on the menu. But now, though I was the same person with the same appetite, the same appreciation and even the same wallet, no power on earth could get me inside this place for a meal. I recalled hearing some Negro say, "You can live here all your life, but you'll never get inside one of the great restaurants except as kitchen boy." The Negro often dreams of things separated from him only by a door, knowing that he is forever cut off from experiencing them.

I read the menu carefully, forgetting that Negroes do not do such things. It is too poignant, like the little boy peering in the candy store window. It might affect the tourist.

I looked up to see the frowns of disapproval that can speak so plainly and so loudly without words. The Negro learns this silent language fluently. He knows by the white man's look of disapproval and petulance that he is being told to get on his way, that he is "stepping out of line."

It was a day of giving the gracious smile and receiving the gracious rebuff as I asked again and again about jobs.

Finally, I gave up and went to the shine stand. From there I set out to return at dusk to Dryades. But I had walked too far. My legs gave out. At Jackson Square, a public park, I found a long, curving bench and sat down to rest for a moment. The park appeared deserted. A movement through the bushes attracted my attention. I looked to see a middle-aged white man across the park slowly fold the newspaper he was reading, get to his feet and amble toward me. The fragrance of his pipe tobacco preceded him, reassuring me. Racists are not the pipe-smoking type, I thought to myself.

With perfect courtesy he said, "You'd better find yourself someplace else to rest."

I took it as a favor. He was warning me so I could get out before someone insulted me. "Thank you," I said. "I didn't know we weren't allowed in here."

Later, I told the story at the Y, and discovered that Negroes have the right to sit in Jackson Square. This individual simply did not want me there.

But at the time I did not know it. I left, sick with exhaustion, wondering where a Negro could sit to rest. It was walk constantly until you could catch a bus, but keep on the move unless you have business somewhere. If you stop to sit on the curb, a police car will pass and probably ask you what you're doing. I have heard none of the Negroes speak of police harassment, but they have warned me that any time the police see a Negro idling, especially one they do not recognize, they will surely question him. This is worrisome, certainly an experience any Negro wants to avoid.

I walked over to Claiborne and caught the first bus that passed. It took me out to Dillard University, a beautiful campus. I was too tired to explore it, however, and sat on the bench waiting to catch another bus into town. Buses were inexpensive to ride and it was a good way to rest.

Night was near when I finally caught the bus going toward town. Two blocks before Canal, the bus makes a left turn off Claiborne. I rang the bell to get off at this stop. The driver pulled to a halt and opened the door. He left it open until I reached it. I was ready to step off when the door banged shut in my face. Since he had to remain there waiting for a clear passage through traffic, I asked him to let me off.

"I can't leave the door open all night," he said impatiently.

He waited another full minute, but refused to open the door.

"Will you please let me off on the next corner, then?" I asked, controlling my temper, careful not to do or say anything that would jeopardize the Negroes' position in the area.

He did not answer. I returned to my seat. A woman watched me with sympathetic anger, as though she in no way approved of this kind of treatment. However, she did not speak.

At each stop, I sounded the buzzer, but the driver continued through the next two stops. He drove me eight full blocks past my original stop and pulled up then only because some white passengers wanted to get off. I followed them to the front. He watched me, his hand on the lever that would spring the doors shut.

"May I get off now?" I asked quietly when the others had stepped down.

"Yeah, go ahead," he said finally, as though he had tired of the cat-and-mouse game. I got off, sick, wondering how I could ever walk those eight blocks back to my original stop.

In all fairness, I must add that this is the only example of deliberate cruelty I encountered on any of the city buses of New Orleans. Even though I was outraged, I knew he did not commit this indignity against me, but against my black flesh, my color. This was an individual act by an individual, and certainly not typical.

November 14

After a week of wearying rejection, the newness had worn off. My first vague, favorable impression that it was not as bad as I had thought it would be came from courtesies of the whites toward the Negro in New Orleans. But this was superficial. All the courtesies in the world do not cover up the one vital and massive discourtesy—that the Negro is treated not even as a second-class citizen, but as a tenth-class one. His day-to-day living is a reminder of his inferior status. He does not become calloused to these things—the polite rebuffs when he seeks better employment; hearing himself referred to as nigger, coon, jigaboo; having to bypass available rest-room facilities or eating facilities to find one specified for him. Each new reminder strikes at the raw spot, deepens the wound. I do not speak here only from my personal reaction. * * *

November 21

Three days in Mobile. I spent them walking through the town, searching jobs, and then every night I met my host on the corner opposite the bus station and we went to his house to sleep.

Again, an important part of my daily life was spent searching for the basic things that all whites take for granted: a place to eat, or somewhere to find a drink of water, a rest room, somewhere to wash my hands. More than once I walked into drugstores where a Negro can buy cigarettes or anything else except soda fountain service. I asked politely where I might find a glass of water. Though they had water not three yards away, they carefully directed me to the nearest Negro cafe. Had I asked outright for a drink, they would perhaps have given it. But I never asked. The Negro dreads rejection, and I waited for them to offer the drink. Not one ever did. No matter where you are, the nearest Negro cafe is always far away, it seems. I learned to eat a great deal when it was available and convenient, because it might not be available or convenient when the belly next indicated its hunger. I have been told that many distinguished Negroes whose careers have brought them South encounter similar difficulties. All the honors in the world cannot buy them a cup of coffee in the lowest greasy-spoon joint. It is not that they crave service in the white man's cafe over their own—it is simply that in many sparsely settled areas Negro cafes do not exist; and even in densely settled areas, one must sometimes cross town for a glass of water. It is rankling, too, to be encouraged to buy all of one's goods in white stores and then be refused soda-fountain or rest-room service.

CLASS EXERCISE: "DON'T TRY THIS AT HOME"

Compare the preceding selection by author John Howard Griffin and the selection in Chapter 6, § 3, *supra*, by Joshua Solomon, who attempted to replicate Griffin's example in turning himself into a Black and travelling the country in search of experiences.

Joshua Solomon lasted three days. He discontinued the experiment because he could not face the loneliness and isolation brought on by his new, black identity. What experiences have equipped you with the ability to understand being in a demonized group (other than a member of your own)? How would you feel if you woke up one morning to find yourself changed into a _____ (place here your own favorite demonized group)? Would you spend a week in the gay community (if you are straight), made up as a Black, or confined totally to a wheelchair if you wanted to become more empathic? Or do other ways lend themselves to deepening cross-group identification and sympathy? What are they?

Finally, reconsider the issue of the First Amendment discussed in Chapter 10, *supra*, in connection with hate-speech controls. Any type of direct regulation of media stereotypes will, of course, run up against this amendment. Is it possible that the extreme deference for racially disparaging cultural messages we now exhibit because of that amendment—or the way we interpret it—may change? Consider the following selection, which suggests that it may:

RICHARD DELGADO

First Amendment Formalism is Giving Way to First Amendment Legal Realism
29 Harv. C.R.-C.L. L. Rev. 169, 171–76 (1994).*

* * * The [constitutional] ground itself is shifting. The prevailing First Amendment paradigm is undergoing a slow, inexorable transformation. We are witnessing the arrival, nearly seventy years after its appearance in other areas of law, of *First Amendment legal realism*. The

old, formalist view of speech as a near-perfect instrument for testing ideas and promoting social progress is passing into history. Replacing it is a much more nuanced, skeptical, and realistic view of what speech can do, one that looks to self and class interest, linguistic science, politics, and other tools of the realist approach to understand how expression functions in our political system. We are losing our innocence about the First Amendment, but we will all be wiser, not to mention more humane, when that process is complete.

Early in American history, we thought the First Amendment was the crowning jewel of our jurisprudence. As recently as 1970, prominent scholars described our system of free expression in sweeping, exalted terms. But shortly thereafter some writers began expressing doubts about whether First Amendment doctrine was capable of delivering on its promises. In the last few years, under the impetus of challenges from Critical Race Theory, feminist and other writers, the trickle of doubts has turned into a flood.

The transition to the new paradigm is, however, far from complete. Those who write in the new tradition still expend much energy defending it from charges that they are Satanic, forgetful of history, deluded, in league with fascism, etc. It is impossible to predict what the new understanding of the First Amendment will look like when it is fully mature, just as the early Realists, seventy years ago, could scarcely have predicted how their movement would lead the way to clinical legal education, perspectivalism, critical legal studies, and elite law reviews. With these cautions, here are what I see as the themes and outlines of the new conception of the First Amendment.

First, the paradigm includes an awareness of the First Amendment's limitations. Early in our history, we made grandiose claims for what the system of free expression could do. But recently, scholars have shown that our much-vaunted marketplace of ideas works best in connection with questions that are narrowly limited in scope. Is this parking space safer to leave the car in than another? Does a heavy object fall faster than a light one in a vacuum? Would a voucher school-finance scheme adversely affect the poor? With such clearly bounded disputes, First Amendment free speech can often help us avoid error and arrive at a consensus. But with systemic social ills like racism and sexism, the marketplace of ideas is much less effective. These broadscale ills are embedded in the reigning paradigm, the set of meanings and conventions by which we construct and interpret reality. Someone who speaks out against the racism of his or her day is seen as extreme, political, or incoherent. Speech is least effective where we need it most.

A second theme of First Amendment legal realism is the understanding of the free expression paradigm as a tool for legitimating the status quo. If, as a starting point, we posit a perfect marketplace of ideas, then, according to the old paradigm, the current distribution of social power and resources must be roughly what fairness and justice would dictate. Our more energetic, European ideas, for example, competed with others and won in a fair fight. But, of course, it was not fair: Communication is expensive, so the poor are often excluded; the dominant paradigm renders certain ideas unsayable or incomprehensible; and our system of ideas and images constructs certain people so that they have little credibility in the eyes of listeners.

This leads to a third component of the new approach, namely the idea that language and expression can sometimes serve as instruments of positive harm. Incessant depiction of a group as lazy, stupid, and hypersexual—or ornamental for that matter—constructs social reality so that members of that group are always one-down. Thereafter, even the most scrupulously neutral laws and rules will not save them from falling further and further behind as private actions compound their disadvantage. Affirmative action becomes necessary, which in turn reinforces the view that members of these groups are naturally inferior (because they need special help). Pornography and hate speech are the two most visible fronts on which the fight to make the legal order recognize and prevent these harms is waged, often against great resistance from critics who preach tolerance of offending speech. But when powerful groups find a particular type of speech offensive and likely to render *them* one-down, they pass a law to curtail it. We rarely notice these "exceptions" and special doctrines, however, because they are time-honored and second nature. *Of course* there would be an exception for state secrets, plagiarism, false advertising, and dozens of other types of speech, we say. But one to protect seventeen-year-old black undergraduates at dominantly white institutions? Oh no, we say, the First Amendment must be a seamless web.

First Amendment realism leads us to notice how even labeling something a First Amendment problem channels and predetermines analysis. Why, feminists and civil rights activists ask, should I be a mere compelling state interest in your jurisprudence, and not you one in my equality-based analysis? We are belatedly realizing that treating hate speech as a First Amendment problem may make as little sense as treating murder under the Commerce Clause.

We are beginning to scrutinize such sweeping generalizations as: Speech is minorities' best friend; suppressing racism only causes it to explode in more virulent forms later; talking back is the best solution to bigotry and sexism; and tolerating face-to-face insults is necessary to a university's role as a bastion of free speech and inquiry. We are beginning to ask the "who-benefits?" question about free speech and to raise the possibility that scoundrels and bigots can easily hide under its mantle. We are questioning whether the continuum of high-value (*viz.*, normal) and low-value speech may not be all there is. Could there be no-value speech, or negative-value speech, which not only could, but should be restricted?

We are beginning to flip stock arguments. Until now, the following argument has been determinative: The First Amendment condemns that; therefore it is wrong. We are raising the possibility that the correct argument may sometimes be: The First Amendment condemns that, therefore the First Amendment (or the way we understand it) is wrong. Although it is often said that free speech is the best protector of equality, perhaps equality is a precondition of effective speech, at least in the grand, dialogic sense. We can now take statements such as "The campus ought to be a bastion of free speech," and render them as, "The campus ought to be a bastion of equal, respectful treatment." Or, finally, from the old saw "The cure is more speech," why not, "The cure is more equality?"

We are beginning to realize that even judges who set out to be scrupulously fair may not be able to *balance* values in cases, such as those concerning hate speech, when free speech and another value (say community) come into conflict. Speech-community is in reality a dyad, not two separate things that a judge can balance, like Jones' right to build a fence and Smith's right to have more sun in his living room.

On the level of ideas, then, the ground is inexorably shifting. The ACLU's own internal struggles reveal the anxiety and ferment that presage a paradigm shift. It is all there—the *ad hominem* arguments, the effort to have it both ways, accusations of straying from holy truth, a sense of beleaguerment, an increase of the decibel level, a resort to paternalistic arguments ("if those minorities knew their own best interest, they would not be clamoring for.... "), and the strategic retreat ("how about the narrowest possible speech code?").

What will the new paradigm mean for civil rights and civil liberties activism and scholarship? Will we not lose a valuable tool for convincing judges to be equitable and to protect human values if we discard the old paradigm? The answer today is the same as it would have been if we put the question to Felix Cohen, Jerome Frank, or any of the early legal realist scholars seventy years ago. They might have replied that misplaced faith in law as a science could not possibly benefit minorities and the oppressed. They might have replied that understanding how law really works is a first step to marshaling that discipline in the service of causes one holds dear. They might have replied that safety does not lie in pleasant fictions. For these reasons, those championing equality and human values have nothing to fear from the new paradigm.

In any event, it is too late to turn back. First Amendment realism has arrived. The last outpost of formalist thought and faith has fallen. Unless the ACLU adjusts its thinking to take account of the more nuanced, skeptical view now emerging, its program, counsels, and pronouncements will seem more and more the futile products of a backwater of legal thought.

Notes and Questions

1. Do we need to "get real" about the First Amendment?

2. Does classic free-speech absolutism stand in the way of cultural change by assuring that outgroups remain where they are?

3. If so, this would be at odds with a classic First Amendment rationale—allowing orderly social change—and would constitute a major paradox for First Amendment defenders.

4. Putting aside the issue of official regulation, would self-regulation and conscience work? That is (to put it bluntly), could an antiracist novel or movie make money in a society such as ours? If a major movie studio decided to stop making films that traded on sexual and racial stereotypes, would they go out of business?

5. If so, is reform "unrealistic"?

Chapter 13

RACE AND CRIME

SECTION 1. STUDYING RACE AND CRIME: BEYOND THE BLACK/WHITE PARADIGM?

Juan F. Perea

Los Olvidados: *On the Making of Invisible People*
70 N.Y.U. L. Rev. 965, 967–69 (1995).*

* * * The [1992] Los Angeles riots, precipitated by the acquittal of four white police officers who had severely beaten Rodney King, have been characterized as the worst urban riots of this century. Over fifty persons died, and over 2400 persons were injured, during the riots. Estimates of the value of property destroyed or damaged during the riots run in the billions of dollars.

I identify three images that emerged from the riots as perhaps the most compelling. First is the horrifying image of organized police brutality and violence inflicted upon Rodney King, fortuitously videotaped and then widely broadcast nationally. The videotaped images resonate with centuries of similar violence suffered by African Americans at the hands of armed Whites intent on brutalizing them. Without the coincidental videotape as witness and testimony to King's beating, I am confident that he would have been an invisible victim of police violence.

The second image is the horrible violence inflicted upon Reginald Denny, also captured and widely broadcast on videotape. Many commentators and journalists presented this image as a kind of symbolic counterpoint to the violence against Rodney King, as though both events were comparable. Reginald Denny's beating created possibilities for certain artificial and misleading symmetries: Even if the Los Angeles police were out of control, so were the black rioters; a black victim is matched by a paired white victim.

A third image from the Los Angeles riots is that of armed Korean or Korean American merchants protecting their stores with firearms. The media covered the riots as if they were the outcome of simmering conflict between Korean Americans and African Americans. The conflict was cast as an ethnic and racial conflict between two minority groups—one labeled good, one labeled bad. Koreans were the good ethnics, "model minority members"—hardworking, quiet, law-abiding property owners striving to climb the ladder of the American dream. Blacks were the bad—violent, criminal, and out of control. The good minority versus bad minority oppositional pairing disguises our traditional racial hierarchy and racism by displacing it onto two oppressed minority groups.

Now a fourth image: groups of Latino-looking people rushing from a storefront, arms laden with stolen merchandise. While images like this were broadcast frequently, they were treated as incidental in public discussion of the Los Angeles riots. Yet this image contains a remarkably important part of the story of the riots. According to statistics reported by David Hayes–Bautista, Werner Schink, and Maria Hayes–Bautista, most of the early victims of crowd violence were Latinos; one-third of the dead were Latino; between twenty and forty percent of the businesses damaged were Latino owned; and one-half of those arrested were Latino. Particularly by the beginning of the second day, the Los Angeles riots were heavily Latino riots, not black-white riots.

The story of the Los Angeles riots is, therefore, a largely Latino story too. This makes perfect sense because half of the population of South Central Los Angeles was Latino, mostly Mexican American with more recent Mexican and other Central American immigrants. Yet neither the stories of Latino victimization nor Latino criminality entered public debate about the riots at all. Despite widespread Latino anger at conditions in South Central Los Angeles similar to those faced by African Americans, the needs of the Latino community in South Central were neither seen nor discussed publicly at all. It is a story that continues to be difficult to find and tell.

[Eds. For further discussion of this article, see Chapter 7 § 2 and Chapter 10 § 3.]

Notes and Questions

1. When searching for information about the relationship between race and crime in the United States, one fact becomes clear. Nearly all of the articles, essays, surveys, and statistics available that discuss racial minorities and crime focus on one group: African Americans. As a consequence, while the literature on African Americans and crime is enormous, and the literature on white Americans and crime is substantial, very little is even known about other racialized groups when it comes to crime.

Thus, for example, although the Bureau of Justice Statistics, which compiles data on the criminal justice system for the federal government, estimates that "Hispanics" were the fastest-growing minority group in prison from 1980 to 1993, accurate statistical data on this group are difficult to find. See Report of the National Criminal Justice Commission, *The Real War on Crime* 104 (Steven R. Donziger ed. 1996). Some organizations do not report criminal justice statistics concerning persons of "Hispanic" origin at all, instead classifying them as either Black or White. *Id.* at 103. Other organizations use a category called "Hispanic," but treat it as an "ethnic" rather than "racial" category, making it difficult to compare data on "Hispanics" with data for African Americans and other racialized groups.

See Ronald Barri Flowers, *Minorities and Criminality* 33 (1988) (describing the National Crime Survey). Moreover, Asian Americans and Native Americans are frequently lumped together as "Other" in criminal justice data sets, making it impossible to discover rates of victimization or perpetration for these groups.

What is the reason for this focus on Black and White, to the exclusion of other racialized groups? One reason might be that African Americans are heavily overrepresented both as perpetrators and as victims of crime, and white Americans make up the majority in this country. Another reason might be that, as D. Marvin Jones suggests, in the American popular imagination "criminals are stereotyped as black and * * * innocent victims are stereotyped as white." See D. Marvin Jones, *Darkness Made Visible: Law, Metaphor, and the Racial Self*, 82 Geo. L.J. 437, 499 (1993). As you read the materials that follow, consider the extent to which cultural images of crime and criminals are racialized. Consider, in this context, the significance of the issues and groups researchers and policymakers study, and the issues and groups they fail to study.

SECTION 2.   RACE, ETHNICITY, AND VICTIMS

A. HATE CRIMES

NOTE, RACIAL VIOLENCE AGAINST ASIAN AMERICANS

106 Harv. L. Rev. 1926, 1928–30, 1933–37, 1938–39 (1993).*

In 1982, Vincent Chin, a Chinese American, was murdered by two white men, a father-and-son team of laid-off auto workers, in Detroit, Michigan. Ronald Ebens, the father, provoked a barroom scuffle by yelling at Chin, "It's because of you little mother fuckers, that we're out of work." Afterward, Ebens and his stepson, Michael Nitz, chased down Vincent Chin at a nearby McDonald's and bludgeoned him comatose with a baseball bat. A few days later, Chin was disconnected from life support. This attack stands out as a perverse symbol of racist violence. Even if one presumes that their unemployment was caused by unjust trade practices of the Japanese government, when Ebens and Nitz brained Vincent Chin, they transferred blame not only from the Japanese people to United States citizens of Japanese descent, but finally from Japanese Americans to anyone unlucky enough to bear Asian features.

Nothing is especially noteworthy about a crime whose victim by chance is of Asian descent. But unique, pernicious harms arise from being consciously targeted as a victim either by rational calculus or by racial animus because of race. Physically, hate crimes are usually more brutal than other crimes. Psychologically, they invoke a feeling of helplessness, because race—the only characteristic that could be changed to avoid future attacks—is immutable.

Because rationally targeted and racially animated violence endangers everyone with Asian features, these acts not only terrorize individuals, but also ripple fear throughout the entire Asian–American community. Consider, for example, the trepidation in the Asian Indian community in Jersey City, wrought by a public letter from a gang called the "Dotbusters" that stated: "We will go to any extreme to get Indians to move out. * * * If I'm walking down the street and I see a Hindu and the setting is right, I will just hit him or her. We plan some of our more extreme attacks. * * * We use the phone book and look up the name Patel." By discouraging an entire community from participating in social and political life, such ethnic intimidation denies Asian Americans an equal opportunity to exercise the rights and privileges that constitute and signify membership in the greater community. These two interconnected impacts particularly to racial violence—individual psychological debilitation and community subordination—make such violence warrant special concern.

Unfortunately, common generalizations about Asian Americans have prompted criminals to target them as choice victims of street crime. Asian Americans appear to promise a larger than average benefit because they are seen as members of a merchant-entrepreneurial class or as rich tourists, who tend to carry and use cash instead of less convertible forms of money. At the same time, criminals view Asian Americans as less costly targets. Regarded as physically weak and culturally averse to defending themselves, Asian Americans are considered low direct risks in any physical confrontation. Asian Americans also pose lower indirect risks because they report crimes to the police less often. This reluctance to complain, particularly among recent immigrants, may stem from language barriers, cultural norms, ignorance of the American legal system, mistrust of the police from adverse experiences in the United States or in their country of origin, or general skepticism about the efficacy of legal recourse. Whatever the causes, the proclivity not to report crimes makes Asian Americans even more attractive victims. * * *

Although acts of racist violence against Asian Americans do not all fit into any single theory, a simple psychological model of racist violence may provide a useful heuristic to probe how stereotypes spark and sustain the causal chain of violence. This model posits three structural elements in the chain of violence, which need not occur as distinct moments in a linear mode of rational deliberation: First, the actor becomes hostile toward Asian Americans as a group; second, he decides to commit violence; third, he chooses a particular victim.

I. Becoming Hostile.—(a) Turf Wars: Battle Against the Foreigners.—Violently attacking another human being, although normally condemnable to all, can become justified in the eyes of the attacker if its immoral quality is muted or transfigured. Protecting the racial purity of one's territory or neighborhood provides one such justification for hostility towards Asian Americans who "invade" the "turf" of another racial community. Turf invasion can occur when an Asian American travels into an unwelcoming neighborhood, or more seriously, when an Asian–American family moves into an intolerant community. The pattern of move-in violence is unexceptional: Asian–American families moving into all-white neighborhoods have been greeted with burning crosses, rocks, and mob attacks. On a larger social scale, when entire Asian–American neighborhoods encroach on previously non-Asian areas, hostility may erupt along the intercommunal interface, sometimes abating only when Asian Americans abandon the area.

The stereotype of foreignness animates this territorial response. Because Asian Americans are different, and because this difference is conceived as foreign—not in a cosmopolitan sense, but in the aberrant, un-American sense—they are denied the respect granted to fellow members of our national community.

(b) Scapegoating: Blaming the Unfair Competitors and the Model Minority.—Besides turf invasion, another principal reason for hostility towards Asian Americans is the sentiment that they are responsible for various social problems. Although Asian Americans are not likely to be the true causes of the multifarious economic and social problems plaguing America, they have nevertheless become convenient targets of displaced frustration. This scapegoating response is mediated by stereotypes of Asian Americans as unfair competitors and model minorities.

Asian Americans are seen as unfair competitors by people on every rung of the socio-economic ladder. Because scapegoating others allows us to skirt self-criticism, politicians, business managers, and workers alike blame the present national economic doldrums on unfair trade practices of Japan and other Asian countries. The scapegoating rationale asserts that if Asian nations would not exploit the rules of global capitalism, then America would be in fine economic shape. This backlash, felt by all Americans of Asian descent, can sometimes kill, as it did Vincent Chin.

On the domestic front, Asian Americans are viewed as unfair competitors for jobs. Although much evidence suggests that recent immigrants do not significantly affect the employment rates of other groups, the misperception that Asian Americans steal valuable employment opportunities remains. This response typifies the general pattern of increased racial hostility in periods of economic frustration. Just as in the nineteenth-century Chinese immigrant laborers were terrorized and killed for taking white jobs in the economically depressed Western states, Asian Americans are again being victimized for economic reasons.

In addition, Asian Americans are deemed unfair competitors because they consume resources that would otherwise go to "real" Americans. Despite the popular belief that Asian Americans are economically prosperous, certain Asian–American groups, such as recently resettled refugees from Southeast Asia, occupy the lowest rungs of our nation's economic ladder. It is, again, widely but erroneously supposed that these refugees receive substantial special treatment from the government in the form of low-interest loans, cash grants, and more generous welfare benefits. Many balk at even meager grants of aid, because Asian immigrants are seen as incorrigibly foreign.

Finally, Asian Americans are stereotyped as unfair competitors by other racial minorities. Recent Asian immigrants, unable to find employment elsewhere, often start small businesses such as groceries or liquor stores in urban, economically depressed, and predominantly non-Asian minority areas. In addition to the sundry burdens common to all small business owners, these Asian Americans experience a unique difficulty because they are accused of exploiting the local community. Worse, it is often assumed that federal and state governments and private banks grant Asian Americans preferential treatment to initiate entrepreneurial ventures, privileges denied to other racial groups. In such situations, the turf protection and scapegoating responses combine to create an especially volatile environment, prone to sharp intercommunal tensions and racist violence.

Complementing the unfair competitor image, the stereotype of Asian Americans as the model minority stokes other, separate, scapegoating mechanisms. By waving the supposed successes of Asian Americans in the faces of other minority groups, the majority obliquely implies that, but for their incompetence or indolence, they too would be succeeding in America. This tactic, at once obfuscating and provocative, amounts to interracial baiting that heightens resentment against Asian Americans.

The model minority myth, in conjunction with the unfair competitor stereotype, also creates resentment of Asian Americans among whites. Particularly in educational settings, the performance of Asian Americans has come to challenge and threaten the status of white students. Graffiti strewn on campus walls captures the situation poignantly: "Chink, chink, cheating chink!" "Stop the Yellow Hordes." "Stop the Chinese before they flunk you out."

2. *Deciding to Commit Violence.*—Neither territorial encroachment by nor scapegoating of Asian Americans will in itself cause physical violence without the aid of other stereotypes that tip the decision-making process towards committing violence. As discussed above, the stereotype of submissiveness encourages crimes against Asian Americans by making violence appear less risky. Physical violence is also easier to perform on a dehumanized victim, because the social and psychological inhibitions against committing violence on a fellow human being become disengaged. For Asian–American victims, the psychological process of dehumanization is achieved via the stereotype of foreignness, which denies them "in-group" status, and that of fungibility, which strips them of individual dignity. * * *

3. *Choosing a Victim: Broadening the Victim Class.*—Stereotypes enlarge the scope of the Asian–American victim class in two ways. First, the foreigner stereotype bridges national boundaries and holds Asian Americans culpable for the deeds of Asian governments. As foreigners, Japanese Americans, born and raised in the United States, were exiled to internment camps for the carnage of Pearl Harbor. Second, as the 1992 riots in Los Angeles made clear, the stereotype of Asian Americans as fungible licenses the targeting of all Asian Americans instead of one particular individual of Asian descent or one particular Asian ethnicity. This phenomenon, repeated throughout history, ensures that individuals are attacked because they are assumed to be members of an ethnicity to which they do not belong or, more fundamentally, because they simply happen to be of Asian descent. Fungibility explains what happened to

two Cambodian residents assaulted by Vietnam veterans "who were angry that Vietnamese were coming to this country and buying new cars." When told that their victims were Cambodians, not Vietnamese, the assailants retorted, "it's the same thing." * * *

Decreasing violence against Asian Americans can be pursued along two mutually reinforcing paths. The standard approach employs traditional law enforcement techniques to make such crimes less attractive to the actor. By contrast, the sociocultural approach attacks the problem at a broader, cultural level by disenabling the stereotypes that catalyze the causal chain of racist violence. Because bias crimes signal a more general malady in our culture, a systemic cultural reconstitution of how Asian Americans are regarded is necessary to decrease substantially the problem of racist violence. This sociocultural approach demands a broad coalition of media, government, community organizations, and schools to work together to terminate those deleterious stereotypes, subtly perpetuated, that impel violence.

Notes and Questions

1. In *R.A.V. v. City of St. Paul*, 505 U.S. 377 (1992), the U.S. Supreme Court considered an ordinance enacted by the city of St. Paul, Minnesota, which made it a misdemeanor to place on public or private property a symbol, object, appellation, characterization, or graffiti—including a burning cross—which one knows or has reasonable grounds to know arouses anger, alarm, or resentment in others on the basis of race, color, creed, religion, or gender. A teenager who allegedly burned a cross inside the fenced yard of a black family was charged with violating this ordinance, and challenged it as a violation of the First Amendment right to freedom of speech. The Court struck down the ordinance as "viewpoint discrimination," reasoning that those who used "fighting words" in the service of tolerance could do so under the ordinance but those who used such language or symbols in the service of hatred could not. See Chapter 10 *supra*.

In *Wisconsin v. Mitchell*, 508 U.S. 476 (1993), however, the Supreme Court sustained a state statute that provided a longer maximum sentence for a criminal offense whenever an accused intentionally selected a victim because of the victim's race, religion, color, disability, sexual orientation, national origin, or ancestry. Such "enhancement" statutes thus remain constitutional.

According to the U.S. Department of Justice:

Forty-seven jurisdictions across the United States have enacted some form of legislation designed to combat hate crimes. Thirty-nine States have enacted laws against bias-motivated violence and intimidation. Nineteen States have statutes that specifically mandate the collection of hate crime data. Meanwhile, dozens of law enforcement agencies have promulgated new policies and procedures to address hate crimes.

U.S. Department of Justice, Bureau of Justice Assistance, *A Policymaker's Guide to Hate Crimes* xiii (March 1997). The *R.A.V.* and *Mitchell* cases are excerpted in Chapter 6, *supra*.

2. The Hate Crime Statistics Act of 1990, Pub. L. No. 101–275, Apr. 23, 1990, 104 Stat. 140 (codified at 28 U.S.C.A. § 534) defines hate crimes as "crimes that manifest evidence of prejudice based on race, religion, sexual

orientation, or ethnicity, including where appropriate the crimes of murder, non-negligent manslaughter, forcible rape, aggravated assault, simple assault, intimidation, arson, and destruction, damage or vandalism of property." As of 1993, fewer than half the States had adopted the federal definition of a hate crime. Some states have added more victim categories. As the Department of Justice reports, "Connecticut, for example, adds people with physical disabilities to the list of possible victims; Illinois' definition includes 'color, creed, ancestry, and physical and mental disability'; and Rhode Island's definition includes disability and gender. On the other hand, Pennsylvania does not recognize sexual orientation as a victim classification." *Id.* at 2–3.

What is the relationship between hate crimes and hate speech? See Chapter 10, § 2.

3.   There is a long history of white violence against communities of color. The history begins, of course, with the genocide and attempted genocide of Indian nations by Whites from the period of "discovery" through the nineteenth century. After the Civil War, lynchings of African Americans reached a peak; it was also common for Whites to riot in black communities, destroying homes, stores, and public facilities. On the West Coast, Whites regularly participated in anti-Chinese riots in the nineteenth century, as well as campaigns of terror against local indigenous populations. Mexican Americans living in the Southwest also regularly faced violence or the threat of violence, particularly when Mexican Americans appeared to pose an economic threat to Whites. Are there other examples you can think of, historical or contemporary?

4.   In February, 1999, the U.S. Department of Justice Bureau of Justice Statistics released a study finding that American Indians are the victims of violent crimes at more than twice the national average. The study found that the rate of violent crime experienced by Indian women was nearly 50 percent higher than that by black men. In addition, according to the study, 60 percent of those committing violent crimes against Indians were Whites; 29 percent were other Indians and 10 percent were Black. This is in sharp contrast to crimes against white and black people, in which the perpetrator is usually of the same race as the victim. See Lawrence Greenfield & Steven K. Smith, *American Indians and Crime* (1999).

A commentator was quoted as saying that "much of the violence against Indians by other racial groups was attributable to racism and alcohol, 'with Indians being victimized by poor, drunken whites, people on the margins hurting each other.' There are still high levels of prejudice against Indians in the West, where most Indians live, he said, and a culture that lives on the edges of Indian reservations 'that tolerates this violence,' even among law enforcement officials." *Crimes Against Indians On Rise,* S.F. Chron., Feb. 15, 1999, at p. A3, col. 5 (quoting Sidney Harring, professor of law at the City University of New York School of Law).

Should this violence be conceptualized as "hate crime?" If not, is it related to hate crimes in any way?

5.   According to the U.S. Department of Justice, at present African Americans are more likely to be targets of hate crimes than members of any other group. "Of the nearly 8,000 hate crimes reported in 1995, almost 3,000 of them were motivated by bias against African Americans. Other typical victims are Jews, homosexuals, Muslims, and, increasingly, Asian Ameri-

cans." See U.S. Department of Justice, Bureau of Justice Assistance, *A Policymaker's Guide to Hate Crimes* x (March 1997). The report provides a snapshot of hate crimes committed in 1996:

- In North Carolina three soldiers from Fort Bragg were charged in the racially motivated killing of an African–American couple in Fayetteville in December 1995. The incident led to an Army investigation in March 1996 into the involvement of U.S. soldiers in extremist and hate groups.

- Three predominantly African–American churches were burned in Louisiana in February 1996, and four churches had been burned in Alabama since December 22, 1995.

- Also in February 1996, Virginia State police were asked to help local police investigate attacks on area houses of worship. The vandalizing of two Jewish synagogues brought the number of religious facilities that had been attacked in the State in recent months to four.

- Police in St. Alban, Vermont, arrested two teens in a racially motivated beating in February 1996 that left a 19–year-old Hispanic man blind in one eye. A pipe, a tree limb, and a broken hockey stick apparently were used in the attack, police said.

- In Mamaroneck, New York, a $15,000 reward was offered for the arrest of vandals who spray painted hate messages on seven houses in February 1996; six of the homes belonged to Jewish families.

Id. at 1–2. The report continues:

Most hate crimes are committed not by members of an organized hate group but by individual citizens. * * * Some perpetrators resent the growing economic power of a particular racial or ethnic group and engage in "scapegoating"; others react to a perceived threat to the safety and property value of their neighborhood. * * * Other offenders include the "thrill seekers"—those who randomly target interchangeable representatives of minority groups for harassment and violence—and the "mission offenders," those who believe they are on a mission to rid the world of some perceived evil. The last group, the "mission offenders," comprises less than 2 percent of bias-motivated offenders. The majority of offenders—and passive observers—are merely individuals who believe racial and ethnic stereotypes and act on spur-of-the-moment impulses. Frequently, alcohol or drug use is a factor.

Id. at 20–21.

The Hate Crime Statistics Act of 1990 (HCSA) directs the U.S. Attorney General to collect data from State and local law enforcement agencies about crimes that "manifest evidence of prejudice based upon race, religion, sexual orientation, or ethnicity." Submission of such data is voluntary. The Federal Bureau of Investigation's (FBI) Uniform Crime Report (UCR) Program is the Nation's central repository of hate crime statistics.

When the UCR issued its first report on hate crimes in January 1993, fewer than one in five of the Nation's law enforcement agencies were providing data on these crimes. As of October 1996, nearly 60 percent of the 16,000 law enforcement agencies that participated in the UCR were contributing hate crime data, and 19 States had enacted statutes that mandated hate crime data collection. More agencies are expected to provide data on hate crimes as States convert to the National Incident Based Reporting System (NIBRS), a new, more comprehensive crime reporting system that collects a variety of crime information, including whether a crime was motivated by bias and the demographic characteristics of both the victim and offender.

Id. at xi.

Because not all law enforcement agencies track hate crimes, because the definition of a hate crime varies among jurisdictions, and because hate crimes are consistently underreported, it is difficult to know whether hate crimes are increasing or decreasing.

B. DOMESTIC VIOLENCE

KIMBERLÉ CRENSHAW

Mapping the Margins: Intersectionality, Identity Politics,
and Violence Against Women of Color
in *Critical Race Theory: The Key Writings That Formed the Movement* (Kimberlé
Crenshaw, Neil Gotanda, Gary Peller, & Kendall Thomas eds. 1995).*

Where systems of race, gender, and class domination converge, as they do in the experiences of battered women of color, intervention strategies based solely on the experiences of women who do not share the same class or race backgrounds will be of limited help to women who because of race and class face different obstacles. Such was the case in 1990 when Congress amended the marriage fraud provisions of the Immigration and Nationality Act to protect immigrant women who were battered or exposed to extreme cruelty by the United States citizens or permanent residents these women immigrated to the United States to marry. Under the marriage fraud provisions of the Act, a person who immigrated to the United States to marry a United States citizen or permanent resident had to remain "properly" married for two years before even applying for permanent resident status, at which time applications for the immigrant's permanent status were required of both spouses. Predictably, under these circumstances, many immigrant women were reluctant to leave even the most abusive of partners for fear of being deported. When faced with the choice between protection from their batterers and protection against deportation, many immigrant women chose the latter. Reports of the tragic consequences of this double subordination put pressure on Congress to include in the Immigration Act of 1990 a provision amending the marriage fraud rules to allow for an explicit waiver for hardship caused by domestic violence. Yet many immigrant women, particularly immigrant women of color, have remained vulnerable to battering because they are unable to meet the conditions established for a waiver. The evidence required to support a waiver "can include, but is not limited to, reports and affidavits from police, medical personnel, psychologists, school officials, and social service agencies." For many immigrant women, limited access to these resources can make it difficult for them to obtain the evidence needed for a waiver. And cultural barriers often further discourage immigrant women from reporting or escaping battering situations. Tina Shum, a family counselor at a social service agency, points out that "[t]his law sounds so easy to apply, but there are cultural complications in the Asian community that make even these requirements difficult. * * * Just to find the opportunity and courage to call us is an accomplishment for many." The typical immigrant spouse, she suggests, may live "[i]n an extended family where several generations live together, there may be no privacy on the telephone, no opportunity to leave the house and no understanding of public phones." As a consequence, many immigrant women are wholly dependent on their husbands as their link to the world outside their homes.

Immigrant women are also vulnerable to spousal violence because so many of them depend on their husbands for information regarding their legal status. Many women who are now permanent residents continue to suffer abuse under threats of deportation by their husbands. Even if the threats are unfounded, women who have no independent access to information will still be intimidated by such threats. And even though the domestic violence waiver focuses on immigrant women whose husbands are United States citizens or permanent residents, there are countless women married to undocumented workers (or who are themselves undocumented) who suffer in silence for fear that the security of their entire families will be jeopardized should they seek help or otherwise call attention to themselves.[27]

Language barriers present another structural problem that often limits opportunities of non-English-speaking women to take advantage of existing support services. Such barriers not only limit access to information about shelters, but also limit access to the security shelters provide. Some shelters turn non-English-speaking women away for lack of bilingual personnel and resources. * * *

Women of color are differently situated in the economic, social, and political worlds. When reform efforts undertaken on behalf of women neglect this fact, women of color are less likely to have their needs met than women who are racially privileged. For example, counselors who provide rape crisis services to women of color report that a significant proportion of the resources allocated to them must be spent handling problems other than rape itself. Meeting these needs often places these

---

27.   Incidents of sexual abuse of undocumented women abound. Marta Rivera, director of the Hostos College Center for Women's and Immigrant's Rights, tells of how a 19–year-old Dominican woman had "arrived shaken ... after her boss raped her in the women's restroom at work." The woman told Rivera that "70 to 80 percent of the workers [in a Brooklyn garment factory] were undocumented, and they all accepted sex as part of the job.... She said a 13–year-old girl had been raped there a short while before her, and the family sent her back to the Dominican Republic." * * *

In another example, a "Latin American woman, whose husband's latest attack left her with two broken fingers, a swollen face and bruises on her neck and chest, refused to report the beating to police." She returned to her home after a short stay in a shelter. She did not leave the abusive situation because she was "an undocumented, illiterate laborer whose children, passport and money are tightly controlled by her husband." Although she was informed of her rights, she was not able to hurdle the structural obstacles in her path. * * *

counselors at odds with their funding agencies, which allocate funds according to standards of need that are largely white and middle-class. These uniform standards of need ignore the fact that different needs often demand different priorities in terms of resource allocation, and consequently, these standards hinder the ability of counselors to address the needs of nonwhite and poor women. A case in point: Women of color occupy positions both physically and culturally marginalized within dominant society, and so information must be targeted directly to them in order to reach them. Accordingly, rape crisis centers must earmark more resources for basic information dissemination in communities of color than in white ones.

Notes and Questions

1. Crenshaw argues that the solutions for women who suffer from domestic violence may vary according to the woman's position in racial, ethnic, and class hierarchies. At the same time, domestic violence is a serious problem for all women. For example, the National Crime Victimization Survey (NCVS) found that nearly 30 percent of all female homicide victims were known to have been killed by "intimates" (defined as current or former husbands or boyfriends). In contrast, just over 3 percent of male homicide victims were known to have been killed by their current or former wives or girlfriends. Twenty-six percent of rapes and sexual assaults against women were committed by intimates. Moreover, female victims of violence were more likely to be injured when attacked by someone they knew than female victims of violence who were attacked by strangers. The NCVS found that the rate of victimization did not vary according to race. See Ronet Bachman & Linda E. Saltzman, *Violence Against Women: Estimates from the Redesigned Survey, Special Report,* U.S. Department of Justice, Bureau of Justice Statistics (NCJ 154348), August 1995. For an analysis of domestic violence in the Latino/a community, see Jenny Rivera, *Domestic Violence Against Latinas by Latino Males: An Analysis of Race, National Origin, and Gender Differentials,* 14 B.C. Third World L.J. 231 (1994).

These figures by definition do not include victimization by intimates who are women, or male victimization by male intimate partners. Gay and lesbian domestic violence has seldom been studied, but researchers know that it exists. See generally Carla M. da Luz, *A Legal and Social Comparison of Heterosexual and Same–Sex Domestic Violence: Similar Inadequacies in Legal Recognition and Response,* 4 S. Cal. Rev. L. & Women's Stud. 251 (1994); Ruthann Robson, *Lavender Bruises: Intra–Lesbian Violence, Law and Lesbian Legal Theory,* 20 Golden Gate U. L. Rev. 567, 568 (1990).

C. POLICE BRUTALITY

GREGORY HOWARD WILLIAMS

Controlling the Use of Non-deadly Force: Policy and Practice
10 Harv. BlackLetter J. 79, 80, 82–90, 100–01, 103–04 (1993).*

* * * [P]olice not only use a broad range of force, but their determination of when to use force is often racially based. One recent study that

reviewed complaints of police brutality in New York City found that "there exists a perpetual pattern of police violence in New York City led primarily by white officers, and directed at African–American males particularly, and people of color generally." Regarding police brutality in Los Angeles, the Christopher Report was even more blunt. "The problem of excessive force is aggravated by racism and bias within the LAPD [Los Angeles Police Department]." A survey of 960 officers found that approximately one-quarter agreed that prejudice against minority citizens exists within the LAPD and may lead to the use of excessive force. * * *

While evidence shows that police brutality actually has declined in recent years in New York, Chicago, New Orleans and even Los Angeles, the costs of unbridled discretion are huge. In the 1980s, riots resulting from police-citizen conflicts in Miami caused more than $100 million in damage. The riots set off by the acquittal of the officers accused of beating Rodney King in the spring of 1992 resulted in more than fifty deaths and approximately $800 million in damage. These events have created a "crisis of confidence in law enforcement." Since the ability of the police to carry out their duties largely depends on the degree to which the public is willing to assist and support them, a public not only skeptical of the police but antagonistic to them has tremendous repercussions on how well the police can accomplish the myriad of tasks they are assigned. While the public expects the police to exercise discretion in the performance of their duties, that discretion is expected to be reasonable and kept within appropriate boundaries. As evidenced by the public reaction following the Rodney King beating, there is little that can have a more negative impact on the public view of the police than examples of polices officers' flagrant abuse of physical power and authority. This has special significance in minority communities across America, as the skepticism about even-handed treatment by the police has always been higher in those communities than in predominantly white communities. Vivid public events like the Rodney King beating intensify and reinforce pervasive feelings of mistreatment by the police in minority communities. This mistrust of the police spills over into all areas of interaction between the police and the public. * * *

Although there are many police departments that can be singled out for criticism, the LAPD has been in the news most recently. It serves as a striking example of a police department that fails to specify and carefully monitor the use of force. In the early 1980s, a series of federal cases, emanating from Los Angeles citizens, challenged the police department's excessive use of "chokeholds." Compared to the use of force in other departments nationwide, the Los Angeles police appeared to use the chokeholds indiscriminately, even on offenders arrested for minor traffic violations. Despite the fact that the litigation revealed that between 1975 and 1982 sixteen persons were killed by the use of the "chokehold," primarily African Americans, Los Angeles police officials virtually ignored the need to address the problem of controlling the use of non-deadly force. (Not) surprisingly, former Los Angeles Police chief Daryl Gates blamed the disproportionate deaths of African–American males from the use of chokeholds on his presumption of physiological differences between whites and Blacks. This type of leadership undoubtedly had a substantial impact on how use-of-force issues were viewed by officers on the street. In fact, in a remarkably counter-intuitive justification, Sergeant Stacey Koon, the supervising sergeant in the Rodney King beating, blamed the ban of the use of the chokehold for the beating. In what may have been a case of pigeons coming home to roost, Koon expressed shock and surprise when he and his fellow officers were reprimanded by Chief Gates for the Rodney King beating.

Contrary to the sentiments articulated by Sergeant Koon and others, civil rights committees in several states have noted the lack of guidance for officers on the escalating use of non-deadly force. These committees have called for more explicit instructions and limitations on the use of force and for increased training in the areas of persuasion and other non-physical coercive tactics. An Ohio committee, for example, warned that police officers "must learn to control their fears and anxiety, they must learn to examine people for signs of resistance, flight and threat. * * * They must learn how to establish and express authority by cajoling, requesting and negotiating to avoid using force." A Kansas committee urged for additional training on the use of force at police academies and during in-service programs, "so as to thoroughly indoctrinate the officers." A Minnesota committee has also sought formal education of officers in non-physical techniques such as negotiation and arbitration, noting that the lack of training impedes professional maturity, so that "civilians continue to bear the brunt of unnecessarily heavy-handed police conduct." * * *

A number of recent events around the country demonstrate the need for direction and supervision in law enforcement. In some instances, officers have shown not only resentment toward control and supervision, but in fact have broken and flouted the law in public protest and demonstrations organized to express their resistance to law enforcement policies established by civilian officials. For example, the lawless actions of New York police officers in blocking bridges and hurling racial epithets at Mayor Dinkins during mass demonstrations will remain an infamous part of police history in America. These incidents reveal an institution in which there is widespread resistance to the types of control effectively applied to other politically created organizations. Thus it is not surprising that these officers abuse their power and exercise an unreasonable use of force. Fortunately, not all police officers in America subscribe to the ethos expressed by some of New York's "finest." * * *

Perhaps a more effective means than controlling the use of non-deadly force through punitive sanctions is that of fostering an internal "respect for justice" that prevents a police officer from using excessive force in the first place. Police officers often see themselves as isolated and separated from the communities in which they serve. The Christopher Commission, established to review the LAPD following the Rodney King beating, detailed vivid examples of feelings of separateness and an attitude of disdain on the part of Los Angeles officers serving Los Angeles' ethnic minority communities. Racial epithets and disparaging comments about minority citizens in the recorded radio transmission are clear evidence that minority citizens are considered less than human by many police officers. Similar remarks repeatedly documented in the records of the LAPD further demonstrate the violent and antagonistic mentality that has developed toward minority communities. If police officials continue to refuse to bring officers under control, citizens will have to demand political accountability through their government officials.

In some respects, one could argue that the problems we are facing as a result of police abusing their power speaks to the failure of previous and ongoing efforts to develop "politically independent" police agencies. Around the turn of the century, efforts were made to insulate the police from "politics." For example, in Los Angeles the position of Police Chief was established as a life tenure appointment. However, rather than establishing a position through which an appointee could rise above the vicissitudes of local politics, the police chief became a major political figure, with no constituency other than the officers whom he commanded. Consequently, departmental positions on such issues as the use of force have been largely shaped and formed internally and not subjected to external review and criticism. * * *

Unfortunately, the courts have also failed to adequately review and monitor the actions of police departments, and have not held them accountable for their conduct. No doubt the courts, like the rest of American society, have embraced the view that politics has no place in law enforcement decisions. That approach has evolved into a mindset that has not only removed police from politics but from political accountability as well.

Only in rare cases have state courts addressed the issue of the use of police discretion. In general, federal courts have taken a similarly minimalist role in the review of police practices. *Rizzo v. Goode* is a prime example of the federal "hands-off" policy toward local police departments. In *Rizzo*, the Philadelphia police department, Mayor Rizzo and other city officials were defendants in two separate civil-rights class actions charging misconduct in the treatment of citizens at the hands of police officers in twenty-eight separate incidents. Complaints detailed several instances of beatings by police officers utilizing bare hands, blackjacks and nightsticks during arrests. Although the U.S. district court found violations of complainants' civil rights in some of the incidents, the court did not find existence of a police policy that violated the constitutional rights of the plaintiff classes. The district court did order that the City follow court guidelines in drafting a detailed program for dealing adequately with civilian complaints and in making revisions in police manuals and procedures. However, the U.S. Supreme Court reversed the Third Circuit, holding essentially that the incidents complained of were not sufficiently representative of Philadelphia police officers' conduct to warrant judicial intervention, which the Court believed would sharply limit the police department's necessary "latitude in the 'dispatch of its own internal affairs.' " Despite countless examples of Philadelphia police officers misusing their authority and brutalizing citizens, especially African Americans, the Supreme Court relied on the doctrine of federalism in refusing to intercede to protect the citizenry of

Philadelphia. The *Rizzo* Court reinforced its "hands-off" approach in *Los Angeles v. Lyons*, which challenged the use of the chokehold by Los Angeles police officers.

The use of deadly force is one of the few areas in which the Supreme Court has recently become willing to intervene. Although for years the Supreme Court allowed state and local governments virtually free rein to determine the appropriate use of deadly force, the Court in *Tennessee v. Garner* established baseline requirements concerning the use of deadly force. In this unprecedented decision, the Court abolished the "fleeing felon" rule that had been virtually etched in stone in state codes and local police department practices. For over a hundred years, the common law "fleeing felon" rule allowed officers to shoot on sight any "fleeing felon." That rule governed the application of the use of deadly force in many states. In *Garner* the Court held under the Fourth Amendment that "force may not be used unless it is necessary to prevent * * * escape and the officer has probable cause to believe that the suspect poses a significant threat of death or serious physical injury to the officers or others." In deciding to use deadly force, the officer's determination of whether a seizure is constitutional, "must balance the nature and quality of the intrusion on the individual's Fourth Amendment interest against the importance of the governmental interests."

The major limitation with the *Garner* "reasonableness" standard is that while it provides some vague parameters for the use of force, police departments are still left with the responsibility of turning it into practical guidelines suitable for daily use by officers. Without additional guidance, the reasonableness test is simply a sham. In reality, citizens' interest in limiting police power is rarely able to carry the day against the government and general public interest in fighting crime. The only way for the reasonableness test to be regarded as credible is for it to be applied fairly in the form of more explicit guidance. With respect to the use of deadly force, some state statutes explicitly detail the circumstances under which the use of deadly force is appropriate. These statutes typically list the crimes or activities that must occur. Unfortunately, "reasonableness" of the use of force has not received analogous clarifying definitions in the area of non-deadly force. * * *

While federal statutes provide a potential plaintiff with a claim of violation of civil rights under 42 U.S.C.A. § 1983 and also provide for criminal prosecution of police misconduct under 42 U.S.C.A. § 842, such cases are difficult to win. Thus in the past few years, there has been a great deal of discussion about the need for additional action at the federal level.

At present, the Justice Department lacks authority to address systemic patterns or practices of police misconduct. Also, the Justice Department does not have authority to sue offending departments to change underlying policies. Under the Civil Rights of Institutionalized Persons Act, the Justice Department can sue to change the policy of jails or prisons that tolerate guards beating inmates. However, the Department cannot sue to change the policy of police departments that tolerate or encourage officers beating and killing citizens on the streets of America.

In 1991, the Police Accountability Act was introduced into Congress. The Act would give standing to the U.S. Attorney General, and in some cases, to private parties, to seek injunctive relief against police departments that engage in patterns or practices of unconstitutional or unlawful conduct. The legislation was introduced in the aftermath of the Rodney King beating by LAPD officers. It was designed to move the federal government from its normal "backstop" role in monitoring police brutality cases to the front line in the effort to control the use of force by police nationwide.

Hearings were held in the Spring of 1991 on the Police Accountability Act. Those testifying at the hearings recounted how the "war on drugs" focus of most police departments has minimized concerns about the use of force by police officers. The hearings highlighted another especially important dimension of situations involving excessive use of force. Such force is primarily directed against Black and Latino citizens.

The Justice Department was not strongly supportive of the Police Accountability Act. The Assistant Attorney General in charge of the Civil Rights Division felt that it was important for the Justice Department to continue to play a secondary role in monitoring police abuse cases. According to Assistant Attorney General W. Lee Rawls, police agencies themselves and state and local prosecutors should take primary responsibility for monitoring the conduct of individual police officers. However, there are problems with this approach. The public, especially persons of color, have very little confidence in the ability or desire of police agencies or state and local prosecutors to undertake the task of ferreting out and prosecuting cases where police officers abuse their authority. The representatives of the NAACP made this point in their testimony for the legislation. They stressed the need for communities to coalesce and become actively involved in monitoring local problems of police abuse. However, there is a corresponding need for the federal government to be able to play a strong role and there must be statutory provisions that permit such a role to be played. * * *

Remedial measures are the responsibility not only of the police, but also of prosecutors, legislators and other actors. For various reasons, these actors have not taken the necessary steps. Courts disapprove of unfettered discretion but want to leave police agencies free to conduct their business. Legislators have the authority to make policy but are reluctant to do so because they do not want to appear to be handicapping police in their fight against crime. Prosecutors desire not to call attention to their own discretionary powers and often will not challenge arrests, especially for low-visibility crimes. Local government action has been precluded by partisan politics and basic neglect in following the usual methods of supervision, even though continuing cases alleging municipal liability for violations of civil rights may be an impetus for change. * * *

As some states have done, lawmakers should require local police agencies to develop rules on the use of force, based upon guidelines from the state. In addition, state agencies should review local lawmaking on the issue of non-deadly force. Input from local officials, the public and patrol officers should be taken into account in formulating new policy. New rules should target the laws that allow the greatest discretion, and the rules should be enforced by local police agencies and used as the basis for discipline. One noted problem is that local agencies have not been vigilant in punishing officers who have repeatedly used excessive force:

> [D]iscipline rates on the whole are virtually nil. In the Miami area, Metro–Dade officials have sustained 10 of 172 excessive force complaints since 1988, resulting in only one cop's leaving the 2,457 officer force. * * * One disquieting analysis by the Detroit Free Press found that the department reserves its lightest discipline for officers who assault citizens.

* * * There are a number of emerging programs and ideas designed to deal with the serious crime issues facing America. It is important to remember that as we design efforts to combat crime, we must make sure that such efforts continue to respect the rights of citizens and not allow the police to ride roughshod over the citizens' rights in their efforts to ferret out crime and criminals.

Notes and Questions

1. A recent report by Human Rights Watch which studied 14 American cities concluded:

> Race continues to play a central role in police brutality in the United States. Indeed, despite gains in many areas since the civil rights movement of the 1950s and 1960s, one area that has been stubbornly resistant to change has been the treatment afforded racial minorities by police. In the cities we have examined where such data are available, minorities have alleged human rights violations by police more frequently than white residents and far out of proportion to their representation in those cities. Police have subjected minorities to apparently discriminatory treatment and have physically abused minorities while using racial epithets. Each new incident involving police mistreatment of an African American, Hispanic American or other minority—and particularly those that receive media attention—reinforces a belief that some residents are subjected to particularly harsh treatment and racial bias.

Human Rights Watch, *Shielded from Justice: Police Brutality and Accountability in the United States* 2 (1998).

2. Think about your experience with the police as you were growing up. Were the police a presence in your neighborhood? Were you taught to trust or distrust the police? Why?

3. Suppose you are a police chief in charge of a police department known for its poor race relations with the community. What steps would you take to improve the relationship between the police and the community?

SECTION 3. RACE, ETHNICITY, AND PERPETRATORS
FLOYD D. WEATHERSPOON

The Devastating Impact of the Justice System on the Status
of African–American Males: An Overview Perspective
23 Cap. U. L. Rev. 23, 25–26 (1994).*

The most frequently cited data on African–American males include:

One in four black men in the United States in the age group 20–29 is under the control of the criminal justice system—in prison or jail, on probation or parole.

African–American males presently represent 48% of all individuals arrested for drug violations.

African–American males represent almost 40% of individuals on death row.

More African–American males are incarcerated than enrolled in college.

On any given day, African–American males are at least 8 times more likely to be in prison than white males.

The devastating impact of the justice system on the status of African–American males also directly or indirectly affects other institutional systems and processes. African–American males typically rank at the bottom of every study or statistical report regarding education, health, and employment. For example:

> The death rate from homicide . . . for black males ages 25–34 is almost 5 times as high as for black females (108 vs. 21.9), 7.4 times as high as for white males (108 vs. 13.6), and 24 times as high as . . . for white females (108 vs. 4.4).

African–American males have a lower life expectancy than all other groups.

Notes and Questions

1. As the Weatherspoon excerpt suggests, the data concerning the entanglement of African–American men with the criminal justice system are startling. Other data concerning this group include the following:

> The United States imprisons African–American men at a rate six times that of white men. African Americans are incarcerated at a rate of 1,947 per 100,000 African–American citizens compared to a rate of 306 per 100,000 for white citizens. African–American males make up less than 7 percent of the U.S. population, yet they comprise almost half of the prison and jail population. In 1992, 56 percent of all African–American men aged 18 to 35 in Baltimore were under some form of criminal justice supervision on any given day. In the District of Columbia, the figure was 42 percent. One out of every three African–American men between the ages of 20 and 29 in the entire country—including subur-

ban and rural areas—was under some form of criminal justice supervision in 1994.

The Report of the National Criminal Justice Commission, *The Real War on Crime* 102 (Steven R. Donziger ed. 1996). See generally Jerome G. Miller, *Search and Destroy: African–American Males in the Criminal Justice System* (1996).

2. One measure of the involvement of groups with the criminal justice system is the arrest rate. One researcher, using 1986 data, studied arrest rates both across racial-ethnic groups and within racial-ethnic groups:

[E]xcept for Asian Americans, minority groups are overrepresented in UCR* arrests compared to their respective proportions in the U.S. population. * * *

[I]n 1986 blacks were arrested for 46.5 percent of violent crimes and 30.2 percent of property crimes * * * [T]he total percentage of blacks arrested in that year was more than twice (27 percent) the percentage of blacks in the U.S. population (12 percent). Further, the proportion of blacks arrested for violent crime (46.5 percent) is almost four times the black population percentage, while property crime (30.2 percent) and the total Crime Index (33.7 percent) percentages are more than twice that proportion. * * *

* * * Another way of examining these UCR statistics is within the subgroup instead of between subgroups. * * * Looked at from this internal perspective, we find that only 7.7 percent of black arrests are for violent crimes, and 18.4 are for property crimes, yielding a total within-group Crime Index of 26.1 percent. * * *

* * * [A]lthough there is obvious disproportionate involvement of African Americans in official arrest statistics compared with Euro–Americans and other minorities, with the exception of larceny-theft, the types of crime in which blacks are involved for the most part tend to reflect vague offenses peculiar to each jurisdiction ("all other offenses"), offenses against the public order (drugs, disorderly conduct, driving under the influence), or violent offenses most commonly committed against other blacks (other assaults, aggravated assault.) * * *

* * * Hispanic Americans are an estimated 6.5 percent of the U.S. population, but compared to non-Hispanics they were 12.7 percent of all persons arrested in 1986, a proportion almost twice that of their population. * * * Within the Hispanic American subgroup, Index crimes account for 21.3 percent of their total arrests, a percentage that ranks them second to blacks and Asian Americans (both at 26.1 percent). The majority of their arrests are for non-Index offenses (78.7 percent). * * *

* * * [T]he Index crimes for which Hispanics are arrested most frequently are the same, and in the same order, as those for whites, Native Americans, and Asian Americans: larceny-theft (10.6 percent), burglary (4.1 percent), and aggravated assault (3.3 percent). * * *

As with whites, in 1986 the percentage of Asian American UCR arrests was lower than their representation in the U.S. population.

---

* [Eds. The FBI annually publishes *Uniform Crime Reports* tracking a number of offenses. The UCR keeps statistics on eight "Crime Index" offenses (murder/nonnegligent manslaughter, forcible rape, robbery, and aggravated assault) and four "Property Index crimes" (burglary, larceny/theft, motor vehicle theft, and arson).]

Asian Americans are 1.4 percent of the nation's population, while their arrests make up less than 1 percent (0.7 percent) of total arrests, with Index crimes at .8 percent of all arrests, and violent and property crimes at .6 percent and .9 percent, respectively. * * *

* * * Asian Americans and African Americans have identical percentages of Index crimes (26.1 percent) as a proportion of all crimes for which they are arrested. Second, among all their arrests, violent crime arrests of Asian Americans (3.8 percent) slightly exceed those of whites (3.3 percent). A third, and unexpected, finding is that arrests for Index property crimes are higher among Asian Americans (22.3 percent) than in any other within-group examination. * * * Larceny-theft, at 17.2 percent of Asian American index crimes, is substantially higher than the within-group proportion of whites or any of the other minorities. * * *

The within-group analysis suggests that Asian Americans, at least in terms of arrests, are more similar to African Americans with regard to crime statistics than to any other minority subgroup, or to Euro–Americans. * * *

* * * Native Americans are estimated at less than 1 percent of the population (0.6 percent) but constituted 1 percent of those persons arrested in 1986 for total Index crimes and Index property crimes, and 0.7 percent of those arrested for violent Index crimes. * * *

With the exception of larceny-theft (12.3 percent), Native Americans have the lowest within-group proportions of Index crime arrests of any of the minority groups examined. They are lowest in violent Index crime (3.2 percent), with only whites slightly lower in both Index property crime (15.6 compared to 16.2 percent for Native Americans) and the overall Crime Index (18.9 percent vs. 19.4 percent). * * *

* * * Whereas "all other offenses" (17.4 percent) is the lowest arrest category compared to the other four groups, the next three most frequent Native American arrest offenses—drunkenness (16.8 percent), driving under the influence (14.2 percent), and liquor law violations (9.1 percent)—clearly distinguish this group from all other subgroups and demonstrate the influence of alcohol use on the arrests of Native Americans.

Coramae Richey Mann, *Unequal Justice: A Question of Color* 37, 39–44 (1993).*

Another researcher, using 1985 data, also notes that Native Americans "show [a higher] arrest rate than any other race/ethnic group for liquor law and drunkenness violations," while Asian Americans have "an extremely low arrest rate relative to their population size and well below that of any other minority." Ronald Barri Flowers, *Minorities and Criminality* 46 (1988). "[B]lacks are arrested 5 times as often as Asians and 2.6 times as often as whites for all crimes. Among Crime Index offenses, the black arrest rate is 11 times greater than the Asian arrest rate for murder and 6.4 times that of whites for forcible rape. Other comparisons are just as noteworthy, such as the Native–American rate of arrest for drunkenness being 28.9 times the

Asian arrest rate and the Hispanic arrestees for drug abuse violations outnumbering whites by more than 3 to 1." *Id.*

Another measure of group involvement with the criminal justice system is the imprisonment rate. The National Criminal Justice Commission reports the following:

> The difference between the numbers of minorities and whites in prison has widened as sentences for crimes have gotten longer. In 1930, 75 percent of all prison admissions were white and 22 percent were African–American. That ratio has roughly reversed. In 1992, 29 percent of prison admissions were white, while 51 percent were African–American and 20 percent were Hispanic. Almost three out of four prison admissions today are either African–American or Hispanic. Ninety percent of the prison admissions for drug offenses are African–American or Hispanic. * * *

>   * * * [T]he Bureau of Justice Statistics (which compiles data on the criminal justice system for the federal government) estimates that Hispanics constituted the fastest-growing minority group in prison from 1980 to 1993. During that period, the proportion of inmates of Hispanic origin increased from 7.7 percent to 14.3 percent and the rate of imprisonment for Hispanics more than tripled, from 163 to 529 prison inmates per 100,000 Hispanic residents.

The Report of the National Criminal Justice Commission, *The Real War on Crime* 102, 103–104, 115 (Steven R. Donziger ed. 1996).* The Commission also notes that because crimes committed on Indian reservations fall under federal jurisdiction, Indians who commit ordinary crimes are subject to higher penalties that were designed under the federal system for serious or interstate offenders. *Id.*

As previously noted, however, all of these statistics are flawed due to poor record keeping by race. As the National Criminal Justice Commission notes, "Some states simply do not report data on persons of Hispanic origin, preferring instead to classify them as either black or white. * * * Similarly, Asians and Pacific Islanders are rarely tracked as a separate statistical category. Los Angeles, which has a significant Asian and Pacific Islander population, did not keep statistics on this minority group until 1991." *Id.* at 103–04. Coramae Richey Mann reports: "Until 1983, UCR statistics for Asian Americans were categorized as Chinese or Japanese, a classification that often revealed different arrest profiles for the two groups. * * * The new UCR category, 'Asian or Pacific Islander,' * * * leaves much to be desired, since any differences between cultural groups are masked." *Unequal Justice* at 42.

For a probing analysis of race and crime, see Katheryn K. Russell, *The Color of Crime* (1998).

3. Although the disproportionate involvement of minority groups with the criminal justice system is obvious and shocking, it is not clear how these data should be interpreted. For example, to what extent do these figures reflect a higher crime rate among certain racialized groups, and to what extent do they measure racial discrimination throughout the criminal justice system? Answering this question is problematic. For example, because Afri-

can Americans are arrested for all crimes at a much higher rate than other racialized groups, one might hypothesize that they commit crimes at a higher rate than the other groups. However, it might be that African Americans are disproportionately arrested for crimes because police officers are consciously or unconsciously influenced by racial stereotypes about the criminality of African Americans. Similarly, the high rate of African American and "Hispanic" incarceration might be because those groups commit more crime, or it might be that legislators see crimes committed by African Americans and Latinos as being the most serious and therefore tailor penal regulations to target these groups. In any case, because stereotypes often become self-fulfilling prophecies when treated as truth, it is difficult to separate the two when it comes to racialized groups and crime.

Although researchers dispute to what extent it accounts for the disproportionate representation of African Americans and Latinos in the criminal justice system, racial bias has been located at each step of the process, from reporting to policing to recording and measurement of crime. Both white and black rape victims, for example, tend to report black offenders to the police more often than white offenders; and Latino offenders are often reported as black. Coramae Richey Mann, *Unequal Justice: A Question of Color* 32 (1993). A Florida study of 1,017 homicide defendants found that crimes involving white victims and African–American offenders were much more likely to be upgraded in severity by the prosecutor, while crimes involving African–American victims and white offenders were more likely to be downgraded. National Criminal Justice Commission, *The Real War on Crime*, at 110. Scattered empirical studies also suggest that people of color pay higher bail than Whites, are more likely to be incarcerated before trial, and are less successful than Whites at getting charges dropped, getting cases dismissed, avoiding harsher punishment, avoiding extra charges, and having their criminal records wiped clean. *Id.* at 111–12. Finally, research suggests that people of color are subject to longer and harsher sentences than Whites. *Id.* at 113.

4.   One reason for the dramatically large number of African Americans and Latinos in U.S. jails and prisons is the "war on drugs" launched in the mid–1980s by President Ronald Reagan. Although available research suggests that illegal drug use is fairly evenly spread across racialized groups, African Americans are far more likely to be arrested, prosecuted, convicted, and imprisoned for drug crimes. For example:

African–American arrest rates for drugs during the height of the "drug war" in 1989 were five times higher than arrest rates for whites *even though whites and African–Americans were using drugs at the same rate*. African–Americans make up 12 percent of the U.S. population and constitute 13 percent of all monthly drug users, but represent 35 percent of those arrested for drug possession, 55 percent of those convicted of drug possession, and 74 percent of those sentenced to prison for drug possession. * * *

Surveys conducted by the National Institute for Drug Abuse have consistently found that arrest rates bear no relation to drug use. African–Americans and whites use cocaine and marijuana at roughly the same rate, yet African–Americans suffer five times the number of arrests of whites for these drugs. Between 1985 and 1989, the number of African–American arrests for drug offenses nationwide more than doubled from 210,000 to 452,000, while the number of white arrests grew by only 27 percent.

National Criminal Justice Commission, *The Real War on Crime*, at 115. The overwhelming majority of new prison admissions for drug offenses since the inauguration of the War on Drugs have been African–American and Latino men.

5.   The Sentencing Reform Act of 1984, Pub. L. No. 98–473, 98 Stat. 1987 (1984) radically changed criminal sentencing in the federal system. The Act created the U.S. Sentencing Commission to promulgate sentencing guidelines, abolished parole, and sharply limited the "good time" prisoners can earn to reduce their sentences. In the 1980s, Congress also enacted a series of "mandatory minimum" sentencing statutes for drug offenders. The combination of guidelines and mandatory minimum sentences dramatically reduced the power of judges and prison officials over an individual offender's sentence.

Under the guidelines, neither race nor gender may be a sentencing factor. See U.S. Sentencing Commission, *Federal Sentencing Guidelines Manual*, § 5H1.10 (policy statement) (1992). Yet, under the seemingly "color-blind" sentencing guidelines and minimums, researchers have found that white offenders continue to receive lower sentences than nonwhite offenders. Indeed, one researcher remarks that "[r]ace, or factors related to race but not controlled for by this analysis, is a more important factor in sentencing now than it was before." Barbara S. Meierhoefer, *The Role of Offense and Offender Characteristics in Federal Sentencing*, 66 S. Cal. L. Rev. 367, 388 (1992); see also Barbara S. Meierhoefer, Federal Judicial Center, *The General Effect of Mandatory Minimum Prison Terms: a Longitudinal Study* (1992).

At least one scholar argues that race should be considered as a mitigating factor in sentencing when "race" is a proxy for relevant cultural differences; when it is likely that racial discrimination has occurred at previous stages of the criminal process; and "when racial bias has made it likely that the defendant's criminal history improperly magnifies the seriousness of his crime or the likelihood that he will commit future ones." Placido G. Gómez, *The Dilemma of Difference: Race as a Sentencing Factor,* 24 Golden Gate U. L. Rev 357, 360–61 (1994). Do you agree that race should sometimes be a mitigating factor? Does it follow that race should sometimes be an aggravating factor?

6.   Another gap in our information regarding race and the criminal justice system has to do with the impact of the system on women, particularly women of color. As Paula Johnson notes in an article on black women and the criminal justice system:

Angela Davis observed over twenty years ago that "sufficient attention has not been devoted to women in prison." This need remains urgent and largely unfulfilled, particularly with regard to African–American women. Although the American Correctional Association's (ACA) national survey of imprisoned women in the United States found the majority to be young, women of color, and single mothers, recent studies have produced important research about women in crime and punishment, but have virtually ignored the experiences of African–American women. Similarly, research in African–American criminality has focused almost exclusively on males. This is a stark omission considering that African–American women have been disproportionately incarcerated relative to their numbers in the overall population. African–American women represent over forty percent of the women in United States federal prisons. This statistic is alarming given that the *total* African–American population comprises but a mere twelve percent of the entire U.S. population. * * *

In the twentieth century, as in the past, poverty is the major correlative in African-American women's involvement in criminality. Two-thirds of offenders sent to prison are convicted of property, drug and public disorder crimes. The median net worth for African Americans in 1988 was $4,606, less than a tenth of the median net worth for white Americans. Female-headed households are at substantially greater risk of poverty. In the United States, 44% of African–American families are headed by single mothers, compared with 13% of white families. The median income for an African–American household headed by a single woman is 38% of that for an African–American married couple.

Another major reason for the increased incarceration of black women is the nation's "war on drugs." Mandatory and guideline sentencing laws, particularly those assessing higher penalties for all levels of drug involvement are having a devastating impact on African–American women who are receiving the severe punishments. Women are particularly affected by the Rockefeller Drug Laws. While male drug commitments increased from 32% in 1987 to 43.7% in 1989, the proportion of the female population imprisoned for drug offenses rose from 42.4% to 66.4% in the same period. * * *

According to the New York State Department of Correctional Services, most female "inmates report that their offenses involved cocaine, crack or opiates.... In 1988, 43.3% of women reported that the drug leading to their conviction was cocaine, and another 30.6%, specified crack. This self-reported pattern of commitment was reversed in 1989, with 44.8% of females citing crack, and 33.9% [citing] cocaine." The Department also reports that in 1988, those incarcerated for either selling or possessing crack in 1988, 49.4% were black, 43.3% Hispanic and 7.3% white. The percentage of Hispanic [women's] crack admissions in 1989 was nearly identical to that of 1988, while black [women's] crack admissions were up and white, down. The proportion of women incarcerated from New York City in 1989 for crack offenses was nearly double the proportion incarcerated for cocaine offenses (40.7% versus 20.7%).

Many women find themselves incarcerated because they have been forced or tricked into carrying drugs for dealers. Often the dealers are boyfriends, spouses or other relatives that use the threat of retaliation if the women do not agree to carry large amounts of drugs, frequently across state or national borders. These women are victimized again by the criminal justice system by serving long sentences for drug possession.

Paula C. Johnson, *At the Intersection of Injustice: Experiences of African American Women in Crime and Sentencing,* 4 Am. U. J. Gender & Law 1, 5–6, 42–43, 44–45 (1995).*

7. Researchers agree that most crime, particularly violent personal crimes such as homicide, rape, and robbery, is intra-racial rather than interracial. In addition, most victims of violent crimes are victimized by someone they know, rather than a stranger. Nevertheless, fear of crime in the United States is often focused on stranger crime, and particularly on interracial stranger crime. What role might stereotypes play in this divergence of fear from reality?

8. Although people of color, particularly African Americans and Latinos, are vastly overrepresented among those under the control of the criminal justice system, they are also overrepresented among those who are victimized by crime. Coramae Richey Mann reports:

> Homicide is the primary cause of death for African–American males age fifteen to twenty-four years * * * A black male has 1 chance in 21 to be murdered, whereas a white male's lifetime chances of being murdered are 1 in 131. The odds of being a homicide victim are far greater for a black female (1 in 124) than for a white female (1 in 606), which ranks black females second to black males as high-risk homicide victims. * * *
>
> The data are limited, but a few studies reveal that other minorities are also overrepresented as homicide offenders and victims. * * * A report on high-risk homicide among racial and ethnic groups from 1970 to 1983 revealed that Native Americans are only 12 percent among the nonblack U.S. minority population, yet in 1980 their homicide rate was 70 percent higher than that for whites; in 1982 they accounted for 43 percent of all the homicides in the nonblack minority group. * * *
>
> A study * * * of Hispanic (Mexican) and Anglo (white) homicide in Arizona, California, Colorado, New Mexico, and Texas from 1976 through 1980 found that the Hispanic victim rate to be more than three times the national white rate, and almost three times (21.6 per 100,000) the five-state Anglo rate (7.7 per 100,000).

Unequal Justice at 46–47.

The fact that members of racialized minority groups are likely to be the victims of, as well as arrested for, serious crime has led to controversy about the best way to protect minority communities. Consider the readings that follow.

A. RACE AND CRIMINALIZATION

RANDALL KENNEDY
The State, Criminal Law, and Racial Discrimination: A Comment
107 Harv. L. Rev. 1255, 1255–61, 1267–68 (1994).*

Crime is widely perceived as a major blight that decreases happiness, productivity, and security in the United States. Defining crimes and protecting people from criminality are central tasks that we assign to the state. Like many social ills, crime afflicts African Americans with a special vengeance. African Americans are considerably more likely than whites to be raped, robbed, assaulted, and murdered. Many of those who seek to champion the interests of African Americans, however, wrongly retard efforts to control criminality. They charge that the state, at least in its role as administrator of criminal justice, is now (as it has been historically) an instrument of racist oppression. In all too many instances, these allegations are overblown and counterproductive; they exaggerate the extent of racial prejudice in the criminal justice system and detract attention from other problems of law enforcement that warrant more consideration. What such critiques ignore or minimize is that the main problem confronting black communities in the United States is not excessive policing and invidious punishment but rather a failure of the state to provide black communities with the equal protection of the laws. Although this failure often stems from a pervasive and racist devaluation of black victims of crime, ironically, a substantial contributing cause is a misguided antagonism toward efforts to preserve public safety. * * *

Conventional racial critiques of the state maintain that the criminal justice system is infected with a pervasive, systemic racial bias. This bias, the argument goes, subjects African Americans (particularly men) to unfair targeting at every level of contact that individuals have with officials charged with protecting the public safety: surveillance, stops, arrests, prosecutions, and sentencing. These critics (depending on age) allude to bitter memories of the Scottsboro Boys or Rodney King, and portray the police as colonial forces of occupation and prisons as centers of racist oppression. * * *

Fueled by the conviction that invidious racial discrimination pervades definitions of criminality and the administration of law enforcement, these beliefs give rise to a distinctive stance characterized by hostility toward the agencies of crime control, sympathetic identification with defendants and convicts, and a commitment to policies aimed at narrowly constraining the powers of law enforcement authorities. Those who adopt this stance frequently proceed as if there existed no dramatic discontinuities in American history, as if there existed little difference between the practices and sentiments that characterized the eras of slavery and *de jure* segregation and those prevalent today, as if African Americans had completely failed in their efforts to reform and participate in the creation and implementation of government policy, and as if black mayors, chiefs of police, and legislators did not exist. But, of course, there has been substantial change in the terrain of race relations, and today, some of the policies most heatedly criticized by certain sectors of black communities are supported and enforced by other African Americans within these same communities. These facts call for a reconsideration of old paradigmatic images that guide intuitions about the meaning of racial disparities in arrests, prosecutions, and sentencing. Although the administration of criminal justice has, at times, been used as an instrument of racial oppression, the principal problem facing African Americans in the context of criminal justice today is not over-enforcement but under-enforcement of the laws. The most lethal danger facing African Americans in their day-to-day lives is not white, racist officials of the state, but private, violent criminals (typically black) who attack those most vulnerable to them without regard to racial identity.

Acknowledgment of these realities gives rise to attitudes that differ greatly from the attitudes of those who view the criminal justice system with fear and loathing. These attitudes include a perception of criminal law enforcement as a public good, a sympathetic identification with the actual and potential victims of crime, and a commitment to policies that offer greater physical security to minority communities, even if that means ceding greater powers to law enforcement agencies and thus concomitantly narrowing the formal liberties that individuals currently enjoy. * * *[20]

Unfortunately, efforts to address the danger crime poses to minority communities are confused and hobbled by a reflexive, self-defeating resort to charges of racism when a policy, racially neutral on its face, gives rise to racial disparities when applied. Such overheated allegations of racism obscure analysis of a wide range of problems in the criminal justice system. Consider, for instance, the stifling of intelligent debate over drug policy by the rhetoric of paranoia. On the one hand, some condemn as "genocide" the punitive "war on drugs" because a disproportionate number of those subjected to arrest, prosecution, and incarceration for drug use are black. At the same time, others, including Representative Charles Rangel [D–NY] and Director of the Office of National Drug Control Policy Lee Brown, condemn proposals for decriminalizing drug use on the grounds that such policies would amount to genocide because racial minorities would constitute a disproportionate number of those allowed to pursue their drug habits without deterrent intervention by the state. No one in either of these camps has come forward with credible evidence to suggest that American drug policy is truly genocidal—that is, deliberately designed to eradicate a people. Yet the rhetoric of racial genocide clearly influences the public debate about this aspect of criminal law enforcement policy. * * *

When discussing racial issues and the administration of criminal justice, some commentators think immediately and, all too often, *solely* about invidious criminal prosecution of people of color. There is reason for that. Throughout American history, officials have wielded the criminal law as a weapon with which to intimidate blacks and other people of color. But the flip side of racially invidious over-enforcement of the criminal law is often minimized. Racially invidious under-enforcement purposefully denies African–American victims of violence the things that all persons legitimately expect from the state: civil order and, in the

---

20. The position I adopt closely resembles a strand of thought within African–American communities that Professor Regina Austin terms the "politics of distinction." This school of thought stresses "the difference that exists between the 'better' elements of [the African–American community] and the stereotypical 'lowlifes' who richly merit the bad reputations the dominant society accords them." Regina Austin, *"The Black Community," Its Lawbreakers, and a Politics of Identification*, 65 S. Cal. L. Rev. 1769, 1772 (1992). Although Professor Austin is ambivalent toward this strand of thought, she describes it aptly:

According to the politics of distinction, little enough attention is being paid to the law-abiding people who are the lawbreakers' victims. Drive-by shootings and random street crime have replaced lynchings as a source of intimidation, and the "culture of terror" practiced by armed crack dealers and warring adolescents has turned them into the urban equivalents of the Ku Klux Klan. Cutting the lawbreakers loose, so to speak, by dismissing them as aberrations and excluding them from the orbit of our concern to concentrate on the innocent is a wise use of political resources.

event that crimes are committed, best efforts to apprehend and punish offenders. For most of the nation's history, blacks were denied this public good. The history of antiblack lynching and the failure of the states and the federal government to combat it effectively offers only the most notorious example. In many contexts, in comparison to the treatment accorded to whites, blacks have been denied quite literally the equal *protection* of the law.

PAUL BUTLER

Racially Based Jury Nullification: Black Power in the Criminal Justice System
105 Yale L.J. 677, 679, 680, 698, 714–15, 723 (1995).*

* * * This essay examines the question of what role race should play in black jurors' decisions to acquit defendants in criminal cases. Specifically, I consider trials that include both African–American defendants and African–American jurors. I argue that the race of a black defendant is sometimes a legally and morally appropriate factor for jurors to consider in reaching a verdict of not guilty or for an individual juror to consider in refusing to vote for conviction.

My thesis is that, for pragmatic and political reasons, the black community is better off when some nonviolent lawbreakers remain in the community rather than go to prison. The decision as to what kind of conduct by African Americans ought to be punished is better made by African Americans themselves, based on the costs and benefits to their community, than by the traditional criminal justice process, which is controlled by white lawmakers and white law enforcers. Legally, the doctrine of jury nullification gives the power to make this decision to African–American jurors who sit in judgment of African–American defendants. Considering the costs of law enforcement to the black community and the failure of white lawmakers to devise significant nonincarcerative responses to black antisocial conduct, it is the moral responsibility of black jurors to emancipate some guilty black outlaws. * * *

My goal is the subversion of American criminal justice, at least as it now exists. Through jury nullification, I want to dismantle the master's house with the master's tools. My intent, however, is not purely destructive; this project is also constructive, because I hope that the destruction of the status quo will not lead to anarchy, but rather to the implementation of certain noncriminal ways of addressing antisocial conduct. Criminal conduct among African Americans is often a predictable reaction to oppression. Sometimes black crime is a symptom of internalized white supremacy; other times it is a reasonable response to the racial and economic subordination every African American faces every day. Punishing black people for the fruits of racism is wrong if that punishment is premised on the idea that it is the black criminal's "just deserts." * * *

I agree that criminal law enforcement constitutes a public good for African Americans when it serves the social protection goals that Professor Kennedy highlights. In other words, when locking up black men means that "violent criminals ... who attack those most vulnerable" are off the streets, most people—including most law enforcement critics—would endorse the incarceration. But what about when locking up a black man has no or little net effect on public safety, when, for example, the crime with which he was charged is victimless? Putting aside for a moment the legal implications, couldn't an analysis of the costs and benefits to the African–American community present an argument against incarceration? I argue "yes," in light of the substantial costs to the community of law enforcement. I accept that other reasonable people may disagree. But the law enforcement enthusiasts seldom acknowledge that racial critics even weigh the costs and benefits; their assumption seems to be that the racial critics are foolish or blinded by history or motivated by their own ethnocentrism.

[Eds. Professor Butler reviews the statistics on African Americans and the criminal justice system, and argues that a plausible interpretation of them is that criminal law is an instrument of white supremacy. He then argues that jury nullification, for a juror who holds this view, is morally proper for two reasons: because the myth of the "rule of law" is simply a myth for African Americans, and because African Americans do not have a fair say in the laws that govern them, because of systematic anti-black bias in the American democratic system.]

* * * Let us assume that there is a black defendant who, the evidence suggests, is guilty of the crime with which he has been charged, and a black juror who thinks that there are too many black men in prison. The black juror has two choices: She can vote for conviction, thus sending another black man to prison and implicitly allowing her presence to support public confidence in the system that puts him there, or she can vote "not guilty," thereby acquitting the defendant, or at least causing a mistrial. In choosing the latter, the juror makes a decision not to be a passive symbol of support for a system for which she has no respect. Rather than signaling her displeasure with the system by breaching "community peace," the black juror invokes the political nature of her role in the criminal justice system and votes "no." In a sense, the black juror engages in an act of civil disobedience, except that her choice is better than civil disobedience because it is lawful. Is the black juror's race-conscious act moral? Absolutely. It would be farcical for her to be the sole colorblind actor in the criminal process, especially when it is her blackness that advertises the system's fairness.

At this point, every African American should ask herself whether the operation of the criminal law in the United States advances the interests of black people. If it does not, the doctrine of jury nullification affords African–American jurors the opportunity to control the authority of the law over some African–American criminal defendants. In essence, black people can "opt out" of American criminal law. * * *

To allow African–American jurors to exercise their responsibility in a principled way, I make the following proposal: African–American jurors should approach their work cognizant of its political nature and their prerogative to exercise their power in the best interests of the black community. In every case, the juror should be guided by her view of what is "just." For the reasons stated in the preceding parts of this essay, I have more faith in the average black juror's idea of justice than I do in the idea that is embodied in the "rule of law." * * *

In cases involving violent *malum in se* crimes like murder, rape, and assault, jurors should consider the case strictly on the evidence presented, and, if they have no reasonable doubt that the defendant is guilty, they should convict. For nonviolent *malum in se* crimes such as theft or perjury, nullification is an option that the juror should consider, although there should be no presumption in favor of it. A juror might vote for acquittal, for example, when a poor woman steals from Tiffany's, but not when the same woman steals from her next-door neighbor. Finally, in cases involving nonviolent, *malum prohibitum* offenses, including "victimless" crimes like narcotics offenses, there should be a presumption in favor of nullification. * * *

Why would a juror who is willing to ignore a law created through the democratic process be inclined to follow my proposal? There is no guarantee that she would. But when we consider that black jurors are already nullifying on the basis of race because they do not want to send another black man to prison, we recognize that these jurors are willing to use their power in a politically conscious manner. Many black people have concerns about their participation in the criminal justice system as jurors and might be willing to engage in some organized political conduct, not unlike the civil disobedience that African Americans practiced in the South in the 1950s and 1960s. It appears that some black jurors now excuse some conduct—like murder—that they should not excuse. My proposal, however, provides a principled structure for the exercise of the black juror's vote. I am not encouraging anarchy. Instead, I am reminding black jurors of their privilege to serve a higher calling than law: justice. I am suggesting a framework for what justice means in the African–American community.

TRACEY L. MEARES

Social Organization and Drug Law Enforcement
35 Am. Crim. L. Rev. 191, 192–94, 196–98, 203, 205–211, 219–20 (1998).*

One undisputed consequence of the War on Drugs is that disproportionate numbers of African Americans (poor African Americans in particular) have been convicted and imprisoned for drug offending. President Bush's Attorney General, William Barr, touted this piece of data, claiming that "the benefits of increased incarceration would be enjoyed disproportionately by black Americans." Assessing the extent to which African Americans enjoyed the claimed benefits of the policy, however, is difficult. Unfortunately, drug selling and drug use are prevalent in modern urban ghettoes where many poor African Americans reside, suggesting that many African Americans could benefit from federal and state crackdowns on drug offenders. At the same time, it is impossible to ignore that "the young men wreaking havoc in the ghetto are still [considered] 'our youngsters' in the eyes of the many decent poor and working-class black people who are sometimes their victims." In light of such beliefs, it is difficult to be confident that the members of the black community who are supposedly helped by prevalent and lengthy sentences for drug offenders wholeheartedly support them. In short, while African Americans disproportionately suffer the problems associated with drug use and marketing, they also suffer the negative consequences associated with the current drug-law enforcement regime. Therefore, a theory that holistically and systematically assesses the costs and benefits of the current regime is necessary in order to determine whether today's "get tough" approach really benefits those who have the most to gain—and to lose—from it. * * *

* * * [P]roblems related to drugs and violence in many inner city communities are unlikely to be remedied unless a community-level approach is adopted. * * *

Unlike other poor Americans, African Americans who are poor often live in poor communities. * * * William Julius Wilson has pinpointed structural economic changes as a major contributing factor to the poverty of inner-city urban neighborhoods. In the 1970s, the socioeconomic structure of many inner-city ghettoes changed for the worse as industrial jobs vanished. African Americans who were dependent on these jobs for living wages lost income, and existing racially segregated urban communities became pockets of extreme poverty because residential racial segregation ensured the spatial concentration of poverty.

Economic dislocations and residential segregation do not tell the whole story behind many very poor urban communities, however. Another important part of the story involves the bleeding of non-poor families from urban ghettoes. While many African Americans were losing industrial jobs, the strongest barriers to residential integration were withering away. Middle class African Americans who were able to leave the poorest inner city communities did so, amplifying the effects of concentrated poverty in African–American neighborhoods.

The overwhelmingly poor communities in which many poor African Americans live are marked by unemployment, family disruption, and residential instability. Non–African Americans who are poor are unlikely to live in such desolate conditions. Importantly, then, the "same" poor individuals from different communities face different challenges. Problems associated with drug use, drug marketing, and drug-law enforcement interact with the unique ecological context of very poor neighborhoods, producing a distinct set of experiences for the many disadvantaged African Americans who live in them. Analysis of the experiences produced by the ecological context of urban inner city life through the lens of social organization theory suggests that law enforcement policies that are beneficial to highly organized (and often non-poor) communities may not work as well in communities that are less well organized and poor.

While the relationship between the structural determinants of weakened social processes and crime is incredibly important, there is also an important cultural aspect of social organization that cannot be ignored. Socially organized or cohesive communities are better able to engage in informal social control that can lead to lower levels of crime than communities that are not cohesive. But cohesive communities are able to do so because such communities are able to realize common values, which can be continually reinforced in daily community life through conduct and discourse that center on law-abidingness. Such a community can be considered culturally organized. A community's inability to settle on common values is an indicator of less organization. So one way to assess cultural disorganization in a community is by looking to the diversity or fragmentation of community values and norms that is likely to flow from weak community organizational structures. Recent urban ethnography helps to make this point. In his book *Streetwise*, Elijah Anderson compellingly recounts how the weakened structural fabric of an urban community attended the transmission of diffuse norms in the community of "Northton." Anderson describes in great detail the clash between "decent" values (norms associated with hard work, family life, the church and law-abiding behavior) held by some families in Northton and "streetwise" values (norms associated with drug culture, unemployment, little family responsibility, and crime) held by others. Anderson's finding that streetwise values did not completely overtake decent values in Northton is critical to thinking about cultural disorganization in a community. While many in Northton continued to adhere to decent values, the streetwise code of conduct presented a significant and rival set of values that Northton residents were forced to negotiate in their daily lives. It should be obvious that it is more difficult for a community in which there are competing value systems to achieve and reinforce a common set of values.

Attention to both the structural and cultural components of community social organization holds great potential for crime-fighting goals. Policies that enhance community social processes and reduce the fragmentation of values in impoverished neighborhoods can assist residents in reducing crime. * * *

In the face of the high levels of victimization caused by drug use and marketing in poor communities, some argue that law enforcement efforts should be ratcheted up. Note that this argument may be particularly salient to those who, unlike the large numbers of middle class African Americans in the 1970s and 1980s who were able to leave the very poor inner city communities for safer communities elsewhere, are unable to distance themselves from the very poor neighborhoods in which they used to live. * * *

While law-abiders might understandably hope that making distinctions between themselves and drug offenders through harsh sentences will improve social organization, there is another side of the story. High levels of drug-law enforcement, as currently implemented anyway, are likely to produce negative consequences for community social organization in poor, minority neighborhoods that mimic the consequences that prevalent illegal drug use is likely to generate in the same places—family disruption, unemployment, and low economic status. When these negative consequences are visited on a class of offenders that are not geographically dispersed but that are instead spatially concentrated, as are lowlevel drug retailers, it is possible that the policy that leads to these consequences will *confound* its own crime-fighting ends.

* * *

First, imprisonment contributes to the already high percentage of families headed by single African–American women. Because the mortality rate for African–American men is somewhat higher than that for African–American women, the female to male ratio is already quite high in some African–American communities. High levels of incarceration of African–American men add to this ratio. Increases in the ratio of African–American women to African–American men are likely to lead to a lower probability of marriage and formation of two-parent families.

Second, the removal of young adults from the community means fewer adults to monitor and supervise children. Inadequate supervision leads to increased opportunities for children to become involved in delinquency and crime. The increasing rate of African–American women sentenced to prison presents an additional hazard to poor African–American communities and especially to the children growing up in them, although the absolute numbers are small compared to the numbers of African–American men imprisoned. According to my analysis of Bureau of Justice Statistics data, between 1986 and 1991 the number of non-Hispanic, African–American women incarcerated in state prisons for drug offenses mushroomed from 667 to 6,193—an 828% increase. Because African–American women often are the primary caretakers of children in poor communities, there is a growing risk that children are in danger of losing both parents to the criminal justice system. As a result, these children face a very high risk of future criminal involvement. Moreover, communities will suffer a loss because each additional incarcerated adult erodes the important community adult/child ratio that is a predictor of greater neighborhood supervision.

In addition to the negative consequences that high rates of imprisonment undoubtedly have on the amount of emotional support and caregiving available to the families of incarcerated individuals, high imprisonment rates are also likely to have a detrimental effect on the economic well-being of families in impoverished neighborhoods. The prevalence of low economic status and unemployment among families predicts low levels of community social organization. Given the well-established association between poverty and families headed by single women, there can be little doubt that high rates of incarceration of African–American men will contribute to the deepening poverty in the African–American community. Recent Census estimates indicate that an astonishing 31.3% of African–American families have incomes below the poverty level, compared to 9.4% for whites. Families of the incarcerated necessarily lose whatever financial support the offenders could have given them. Although the majority of those incarcerated are ill-educated and although many have shallow work histories, many still manage to contribute financially to their families prior to being imprisoned. Some participate in the "informal economy," running unlicensed cab businesses, car repair businesses, and unlicensed street vending businesses, to name a few, in order to assist their families, and some of them engage in illegal activity in order to contribute to their families. A recent RAND study documents the importance of drug selling as an economic activity for young black males in the District of Columbia. This study found that over half of the men sampled provided monthly support to a child, spouse, girlfriend, family member, or friend. Another study of Chicago Public Housing found that many public housing residents rely on gang members for financial support to supplement public assistance benefits.

Most drug offenders will not remain in prison forever, and we should expect some of the negative financial consequences that families suffer when a contributor is sent away to prison to be alleviated, if only in part, when the offender is released. However, the negative consequences to the community are not likely to be remedied simply by the release of drug offenders. In fact, release of convicted drug offenders back into their communities may worsen the social organization of poor communities, even while the convict's return may improve the financial situation of his family.

The vast majority of formerly incarcerated men return to their homes in the inner city, where job prospects for everyone already are glum, even if they are aware of better job prospects elsewhere. In 1993 the Bureau of Labor Statistics estimated the unemployment rate in central cities to be 8.2%, compared to 6.2% in suburbs of central cities and 6.5% in the balance of the country; however, researchers have documented unemployment rates as high as 60% in some hyper-poverty areas in central cities. Of course, legitimate job prospects for ex-convicts are likely to be worse than the already weak prospects for inner city residents generally. Few people with the typical convict's credentials would be competitive in today's service-oriented economy, which emphasizes educational attainment and training. Thus, a released convict likely will have even fewer employment opportunities than he had before he was imprisoned, so he will inevitably contribute to the already high rates of unemployment in the central cities when he returns home—unemployment that erodes community social organization.

One might think that the argument I have just made is undercut by the fact that many drug offenders did not participate in the formal labor force prior to incarceration. Under those conditions, it is hard to see how a convict's return to his neighborhood would substantially worsen the neighborhood's social organization. In fact, one might even predict that many families would be better off once an offender is released because the newly-released offender is able to contribute to his family financially, or in other ways, as he was not able to do in prison. Notwithstanding the fact that the unemployed released convict may be able to enhance his family's welfare when he returns home, it is important to see that the release of convicted drug offenders back into poor communities has the potential to erode a community's social organization even if the proportion of unemployed individuals in the community is essentially unchanged.

Widespread human capital in a community facilitates the formation of networks and relationships among individuals that form the backbone of the structural components of social organization; however, the status of "convict" severely compromises the released felon's ability to make investments in human capital. A released convict may perceive further investment in human capital to be useless because he may understandably reason that sinking money and time into education and training will not overcome the stigma of a felony conviction on a job application. When he makes the decision to refrain from further investment, he weakens existing relationships he has with people who will be less likely to depend on him, because his ability to provide them with benefits through interaction is compromised. Additionally, the individual who decides not to make further investments in education, skills and training cuts himself off from potential useful relationships with others who have no incentive to form relationships with him. It is true that many law abiders in the neighborhoods I am concerned with here possess low levels of human capital, as poverty often is correlated with low levels of education. By distinguishing convicted drug offenders from law abiders, I do not mean to imply that it is a fairly simple proposition for residents of poor urban communities to invest in human capital by acquiring better educations and vocational skills. However, I do mean to argue that to the extent that it is difficult for anyone in poor communities to do so, it is that much harder for a released convict, and the marginal effect of this additional hurdle may make a large difference in the potential of the convict to form important networks with his neighbors. The basic point is this: All unemployed populations are not equal, and any incremental increase in the proportion of convicts among the unemployed population of the ghetto portends incrementally worse consequences for the vitality of the community.

* * * Voting is another indicator of participation in the life of a community. In at least fifteen states, convicts are unable to vote. Voting is connected to other forms of political participation such as membership in formal organizations, an important structural component of social organization. * * *

Finally, release of incarcerated drug offenders is unlikely to remedy the first precursor to social organization disruption referred to earlier—family disruption. Even though a released convict may contribute to his family in small and helpful ways, it is unlikely that release will lead to strengthening of family ties and aversion of family disruption. With dismal employment prospects, the released convict may not be viewed as a favorable "marriage prospect." If the released convict was married prior to incarceration, his now impaired economic circumstances likely will place strains on his relationship. Higher numbers of families headed by single women seem inevitable even after incarcerated men are released. And to the extent that a single woman has managed to create a stable home life while the father of her children was incarcerated, his release may lead to disruptive domestic violence.

The previous analysis illustrates that a drug-law enforcement strategy that depends on the high prevalence of long sentences to generate benefits may ultimately backfire. The strategy leads to disruption of family life, unemployment, and lower levels of civic participation. Thus, to the extent that the strategy produces crime reduction benefits, it does so only by exacerbating the preconditions of social organization disruption. * * *

The analysis in this article suggests a few directions for drug-law enforcement. First, it suggests that high incarceration strategies should not be favored to eradicate the serious problems associated with drugs in poor neighborhoods in central cities. Second, it suggests that community-based policies with local control, and community control in particular, should be favored. Thus, my analysis argues against national uniform strategies. And third, it suggests that law enforcement is a critical part of a program to rebuild the social organization of communities.

This third point may be the most contentious. Scholars who discuss social organization theory often focus on the potential for attention to "root causes" to repair damaged communities. Moreover, [Clifford] Shaw and [Henry] McKay * * * suggested that individualized treatment, which often is consistent with traditional law enforcement strategies, is unlikely to effectively reduce crime and delinquency in communities with low social organization. Nevertheless, these important points should not be used to undermine the great potential for public law enforcement to improve social organization. Greater resources for housing and even employment may not be enough to repair seriously damaged communities without an organizational "spur." Governmental entities, including law enforcement agencies, are uniquely situated to provide resources and direction for affirmative organizational efforts. In fact, participation by residents in formal community policing programs is an example of precisely the type of activity that predicts social organization improvement, as participation in formal organization is an aspect of local community solidarity. Moreover, participation in a neighborhood-based group in support of community policing is likely to lead to law-abiding behavior directly. When citizens participate in these programs they are engaged directly in the business of constructing and transmitting law-abiding norms. Finally, as a practical matter, the political impetus for such inputs may be lacking where crime problems are serious. Thus, a carefully considered law enforcement strategy can make other resources politically viable. We cannot overlook the fact that minority residents of crime-plagued neighborhoods are themselves demanding higher levels of law enforcement as a way to repair their communities.

Notes and Questions

1.   Who is right—Kennedy or Butler? Could they both be right? Does Meares' approach offer a viable middle ground? For a fuller account of Kennedy's argument, see Randall Kennedy, *Race, Crime, and the Law* (1997).

For an analysis of the "politics of distinction" within the black community, see Regina Austin, *"The Black Community," Its Lawbreakers, and a Politics of Identification*, 65 S. Cal. L. Rev. 1769 (1992).

2.   Is Butler's proposal for jury nullification strategically problematic, even if morally persuasive? What if African–American potential jurors are systematically removed from petit juries on the grounds that they will not promise to follow the law? What if white jurors also begin to nullify?

3. Why is Butler's proposal addressed only to African Americans? Should not all Americans nullify verdicts against African–American defendants in the circumstances Butler describes? Do other racialized groups have a stake in the concerns Butler outlines?

4. Under the federal sentencing guidelines and congressional mandatory minimum penalties, drug offenses involving "crack" cocaine are punished more harshly than the same offenses involving "powder" cocaine. Because crack and powder cocaine are pharmacologically identical, in *United States v. Clary*, 846 F. Supp. 768 (E.D.Mo.1994), a district judge held the 100–1 punishment ratio between crack and powder cocaine to violate the equal protection element of the Fifth Amendment. Reviewing the history of drug crimes, the court found that Congress was motivated by unconscious racism, specifically against African Americans, when it enacted this punishment structure. (The court cited, among other sources, Charles R. Lawrence's article, *The Id, the Ego, and Equal Protection*, excerpted in Chapter 1.) As the court described this process:

> Crack cocaine eased into the mainstream of the drug culture about 1985 and immediately absorbed the media's attention. Between 1985 and 1986, over 400 reports had been broadcast by the networks. Media accounts of crack-user horror stories appeared daily on every major channel and in every major newspaper. Many of the stories were racist. Despite the statistical data that whites were prevalent among crack users, rare was the interview with a young black person who had avoided drugs and the drug culture, and even rarer was any media association with whites and crack. Images of young black men daily saturated the screens of our televisions. These distorted images branded onto the public mind and the minds of legislators that young black men were solely responsible for the drug crisis in America. The media created a stereotype of a crack dealer as a young black male, unemployed, gang affiliated, gun toting, and a menace to society. These stereotypical descriptions of drug dealers may be accurate, but not all young black men are drug dealers. The broad brush of uninformed public opinion paints them all as the same.

> Legislators used these media accounts as informational support for the enactment of the crack statute. The *Congressional Record*, prior to enactment of the statute, is replete with news articles submitted by members for their colleagues' consideration which labeled crack dealers as black youths and gangs. Members of Congress also introduced into the record media reports containing language that was either overtly or subtly racist, and which exacerbated white fears that the "crack problem" would spill out of the ghettos.

> These stereotypical images undoubtedly served as the touchstone that influenced racial perceptions held by legislators and the public as related to the "crack epidemic." The fear of increased crime as a result of crack cocaine fed white society's fear of the black male as a crack user and as a source of social disruption. The prospect of black crack migrating to the white suburbs led the legislators to reflexively punish crack violators more harshly than their white, suburban, powder cocaine dealing counterparts. The ultimate outcome resulted in the legislators drafting the crack statute with its Draconian punishment.

Clary, 846 F. Supp. at 783–84.

The court's decision was reversed on appeal. Relying on standard equal protection jurisprudence, the Eighth Circuit held that before "strict scrutiny" could be applied to a statute, there must first be a showing that the government action was taken pursuant to a conscious, deliberate intent to harm a racial group. Therefore, the district court's theory of "unconscious racism" was invalid. *United States v. Clary*, 34 F.3d 709 (8th Cir.1994). For more on intent and theories of equality, see Chapter 7.

All of the other federal circuit courts to consider the equal protection claim made in *Clary* have similarly upheld the 500–1 ratio.

5.   Distinctions between powder and crack cocaine frequently appear in state statutes as well as in the federal system. For a useful overview of the pertinent state statutes, see Knoll D. Lowney, *Smoked Not Snorted: Is Racism Inherent in Our Crack Cocaine Laws?*, 45 Wash. U. J. Urb. & Contemp. L. 121 (1994).

6.   In *State v. Russell*, 477 N.W.2d 886 (Minn.1991), the Minnesota Supreme Court held that a 10–1 disparity in punishment between powder and crack cocaine imposed by Minnesota law violated the state equal protection clause. The court applied what it described as the "rational basis test," but interpreted the state rational basis test as requiring more scrutiny than the federal rational basis test. The court in *Russell* held that there was inadequate evidence that the distinction between powder and crack cocaine facilitated prosecution of street level drug dealers or more violent criminals; the court also found that the state's evidence failed to adequately support the proposition that crack cocaine was a substance more addictive and dangerous than powder cocaine.

Professor Randall Kennedy has written that "*Russell* was wrongly decided. * * * As a constitutional matter, the state [of Minnesota] was justified in penalizing possession of crack cocaine more harshly than possession of powdered cocaine notwithstanding the racial demographics that emerged from the operation of this sentencing scheme." Kennedy, *supra*, at 1256. Do you agree? What role should the history of racist administration of the criminal law play in the decision?

The Minnesota legislature responded to the *Russell* decision by increasing the penalties for powder cocaine to match those for crack cocaine. See Minn. Stat. 152.023–.025 (Supp. 1993). Was this a win for communities of color?

7.   As Professor Paula C. Johnson notes, another constitutional challenge to the crack and powder cocaine disparity in punishment has been the Eighth Amendment doctrine of cruel and unusual punishment.

In *Harmelin v. Michigan* [501 U.S. 957 (1991)], the defendant was sentenced to life imprisonment without possibility of parole pursuant to a Michigan statute requiring such punishment for the possession of more than 650 grams of any mixture containing cocaine. The majority of the Court reaffirmed the principle that gross disproportionality of a sentence of imprisonment violates the Eighth Amendment's Cruel and Unusual Punishments Clause. However, the Court simultaneously distanced itself from the standards announced in [*Solem v. Helm*, 463 U.S. 277 (1983)]. The Court was sharply divided on the issue of whether Harmelin's life sentence constituted cruel and unusual punishment. In writing for the plurality, Justice Scalia's opinion affirmed the Michigan

Court of Appeals' decision upholding the sentence. Two members of the Court, however, voted to affirm because they found no Eighth Amendment proportionality requirement applicable to noncapital sentences. Three members voted to affirm because, based on the severity of the crime of cocaine distribution, the sentence was constitutional under the narrow proportionality test that they concluded was applicable to noncapital sentences. The four dissenters believed that the sentence was unconstitutionally disproportionate to the offense.

Paula C. Johnson, *At the Intersection of Injustice, supra* at 51.

8. In 1995, the President refused the recommendations of the United States Sentencing Commission to equalize the penalties for possession of crack and powder cocaine. See President's Statement on Signing S. 1254 (Oct. 30, 1995), available in 1995 WL 634347, at 1.

9. As the previous notes suggest, critics of the racial effects of the criminal justice system have questioned statutes that target crimes committed by nonwhites for particularly harsh punishment. Is the focus on "street crime" proper? Or is "white" crime more of a problem? See Richard Delgado, *Rodrigo's Eighth Chronicle: Black Crime, White Fears—On the Social Construction of Threat*, 80 Va. L. Rev. 503 (1994). Delgado notes that the United States Census and the FBI annual crime reports "show that the figure for white-collar crime exceeds the dollar losses from all the crimes associated with African Americans put together." 80 Va. L. Rev. at 518.

10. Another concern is the use of police discretion to focus on minority individuals and groups within minority communities. For example, the police practice of "racial profiling" has been widely criticized in the scholarly literature, but widely deferred to by the courts. As Mark Kadish explains:

> Police officers rely on drug courier profiles to justify stopping and questioning citizens about whether they are carrying illegal drugs. A nationally recognized profile does not exist; federal, state, local, and even individual law enforcement officials may have their own "profile." Citizens easily may match one of these profiles, because the profiles list general and often contradictory characteristics: traveling by plane, train, automobile, or bus; traveling alone, with friends, or with your children; being young, middle-aged, or "older"; having short or long hair; traveling to or from Fort Lauderdale, Miami, New York, Los Angeles, San Diego, Atlanta, Chicago, Detroit, Austin, Birmingham, Chattanooga, Charlotte, Dayton, Indianapolis, Kansas City, Newark, Tulsa, Dallas–Fort Worth, or any foreign country; traveling in a business suit, casual clothes, or disheveled clothing; paying cash for your ticket; traveling without checking your luggage, carrying only a garment bag, or checking several large suitcases; traveling and returning home in twenty-four to forty-eight hours; being nervous or anxious when traveling; glancing around the airport, bus, or train terminal; looking over your shoulder; making telephone calls immediately after arriving at your destination; and taking public transportation to your destination. If any of these characteristics match you and your travel habits, you may well fit a version of the drug courier profile.

Mark J. Kadish, *The Drug Courier Profile: In Planes, Trains, and Automobiles; and Now in the Jury Box*, 46 Am. U. L. Rev. 747, 748–749 (1997).*

Studies indicate that race is often used as a primary factor in drug courier profiles. For example:

* * * In Volusia County, Florida, videotapes and other documents relating to stops on Interstate 95, made by the Sheriff's drug squad, disclosed that highway stops were based in large measure on the race of the driver. Seventy percent of the motorists stopped were black or Hispanic; 80 percent of the cars that were searched were driven by blacks or Hispanics; only 1 percent of those stopped received a traffic citation; and over five hundred motorists were subjected to searches and frisks without any cause or suspicion. By comparison, only 5 percent of the drivers on this stretch of Interstate 95 were black or Hispanic, and only 15 percent of all persons convicted in Florida for traffic violations during this period were of a minority race.

David Rudovsky, *The Impact of the War on Drugs on Procedural Fairness and Racial Equality,* 1994 U. Chi. Legal F. 237, 250–251.

Yet the use of drug courier profiles has been upheld by the courts, with very little interest in the possible equal protection and selective enforcement problems raised by their existence. See, e.g., *Florida v. Bostick*, 501 U.S. 429 (1991) (upholding a search of passengers on a bus); *United States v. Taylor*, 956 F.2d 572 (6th Cir.1992) (no need to decide whether defendant, the only black person exiting from a plane from Memphis to Miami, was stopped because of his race, or whether the incorporation of a racial component into the Drug Enforcement Administration's drug courier profile would violate equal protection and due process guarantees, since the search was "consensual"); see also *United States v. Beck*, 602 F.2d 726, 729 (5th Cir.1979); *United States v. Carrizoza–Gaxiola*, 523 F.2d 239, 241 (9th Cir.1975); Sheri L. Johnson, *Race and the Decision to Detain a Suspect*, 93 Yale L.J. 214 (1983). For a race-conscious theoretical critique of *Bostick*, see Dwight L. Greene, *Justice Scalia and Tonto, Judicial Pluralistic Ignorance, and the Myth of Colorless Individualism in* Bostick v. Florida, 67 Tul. L. Rev. 1979 (1993); Robin K. Magee, *The Myth of the Good Cop and the Inadequacy of Fourth Amendment Remedies for Black Men: Contrasting Presumptions of Innocence and Guilt*, 23 Cap. U. L. Rev. 151 (1994). See also Erika L. Johnson, *"A Menace To Society:" The Use of Criminal Profiles and Its Effects on Black Males*, 38 How. L.J. 629 (1995).

For the argument that pretextual traffic stops targeting mostly Blacks and Latinos/as should violate the Fourth Amendment, see Tracey Maclin, *Race and the Fourth Amendment*, 51 Vand. L. Rev. 333 (1998).

11.　The issue of gang-related crime, like the issue of the "war on drugs," provides a vivid forum for the debate between Randall Kennedy and Paul Butler. Consider the case that follows.

PEOPLE EX REL. JOAN R. GALLO v. ACUNA

14 Cal.4th 1090, 60 Cal.Rptr.2d 277, 929 P.2d 596 (1997).

Brown, J.

At the request of the City Attorney of the City of San Jose (hereafter the City), we granted review to resolve an array of challenges to two provisions of a preliminary injunction entered by the superior court against individual members of an alleged "criminal street gang." * * *

The 48 declarations submitted by the City in support of its plea for injunctive relief paint a graphic portrait of life in the community of Rocksprings. Rocksprings is an urban war zone. The four-square-block neighborhood, claimed as the turf of a gang variously known as Varrio Sureo Town, Varrio Sureo Treces (VST), or Varrio Sureo Locos (VSL), is an occupied territory. Gang members, all of whom live elsewhere, congregate on lawns, on sidewalks, and in front of apartment complexes at all hours of the day and night. They display a casual contempt for notions of law, order, and decency—openly drinking, smoking dope, sniffing toluene, and even snorting cocaine laid out in neat lines on the hoods of residents' cars. The people who live in Rocksprings are subjected to loud talk, loud music, vulgarity, profanity, brutality, fistfights and the sound of gunfire echoing in the streets. Gang members take over sidewalks, driveways, carports, apartment parking areas, and impede traffic on the public thoroughfares to conduct their drive-up drug bazaar. Murder, attempted murder, drive-by shootings, assault and battery, vandalism, arson, and theft are commonplace. The community has become a staging area for gang-related violence and a dumping ground for the weapons and instrumentalities of crime once the deed is done. Area residents have had their garages used as urinals; their homes commandeered as escape routes; their walls, fences, garage doors, sidewalks, and even their vehicles turned into a sullen canvas of gang graffiti.

The people of this community are prisoners in their own homes. Violence and the threat of violence are constant. Residents remain indoors, especially at night. They do not allow their children to play outside. Strangers wearing the wrong color clothing are at risk. Relatives and friends refuse to visit. The laundry rooms, the trash dumpsters, the residents' vehicles, and their parking spaces are used to deal and stash drugs. Verbal harassment, physical intimidation, threats of retaliation, and retaliation are the likely fate of anyone who complains of the gang's illegal activities or tells police where drugs may be hidden.

Among other allegations, the City's complaint asserted that the named defendants and others "[f]or more than 12 months precedent to the date of [the] complaint, continuing up to the present time . . . [have] occupied [and] used the area commonly known as 'Rocksprings' . . . in such a manner so as to constitute a public nuisance . . . injurious to the health, indecent or offensive to the senses, [and] an obstruction to the free use of property so as to interfere with the comfortable enjoyment of life or property by those persons living in the . . . neighborhood."

After alleging the usual requisites for equitable relief—the prospect of "great and irreparable injury" and the absence of "a plain, adequate and speedy remedy at law"—the complaint prayed for a broad and comprehensive injunction against defendants' alleged activities in Rocksprings. The superior court granted an *ex parte* temporary restraining order enjoining all 38 defendants named in the complaint and issued an order to show cause (OSC) why a preliminary injunction should not be entered. * * *

* * * After the matter was briefed and argued, the superior court entered a preliminary injunction. * * *

The Court of Appeal disagreed with the superior court, upholding only provisions of the preliminary injunction enjoining acts or conduct defined as crimes under specific provisions of the Penal Code. Although its premise is never clearly articulated, that ruling effectively limits the scope of permissible injunctive relief under California's public nuisance statutes to independently criminal conduct. The Court of Appeal also concluded many of the provisions of the preliminary injunction were void and unenforceable under either the First and Fifth Amendments to the federal Constitution as unconstitutionally vague or overbroad. Altogether, 15 of the 24 provisions of the trial court's preliminary injunction were partially or entirely invalidated. However, the City's petition only sought review of two provisions—paragraphs (a) and (k). We granted the City's petition and now reverse.

* * * The state has not only a right to "maintain a decent society," but an obligation to do so. In the public nuisance context, the community's right to security and protection must be reconciled with the individual's right to expressive and associative freedom. Reconciliation begins with the acknowledgment that the interests of the community are not invariably less important than the freedom of individuals. Indeed, the security and protection of the community is the bedrock on which the superstructure of individual liberty rests. From Montesquieu to Locke to Madison, the description of the pivotal compact remains unchanged: By entering society, individuals give up the unrestrained right to act as they think fit; in return, each has a positive right to society's protection. * * * As we explain, a principal office of the centuries-old doctrine of the "public nuisance" has been the maintenance of public order—tranquillity, security and protection—when the criminal law proves inadequate. * * *

The Court of Appeal held that paragraph (a) of the preliminary injunction, enjoining defendants from "Standing, sitting, walking, driving, gathering or appearing anywhere in public view with any other defendant . . . or with any other known 'VST' (Varrio Sureno Town or Varrio Sureno Treces) or 'VSL' (Varrio Sureno Locos) member" was invalid on associational grounds; that is, the provision infringed defendants' right to associate with fellow gang members, a right protected by the First Amendment. We disagree.

In a series of opinions, the United States Supreme Court has made it clear that, although the Constitution recognizes and shields from government intrusion a limited right of association, it does not recognize "a generalized right of 'social association.' " As we explain, neither does the First Amendment protect the collective public activities of the gang members within the four-block precinct of Rocksprings, activities directed in the main at trafficking in illegal drugs and securing control of the community through systematic acts of intimidation and violence. * * *

The Court of Appeal found paragraph (k), enjoining defendants from "confronting, intimidating, annoying, harassing, threatening, challenging, provoking, assaulting and/or battering any residents or patrons, or visitors to 'Rocksprings' ... known to have complained about gang activities," impermissibly vague in two respects. First, like paragraph (a), it speaks of persons "known to have complained about gang activities," without indicating how or even whether a defendant is to be charged with this knowledge. * * *

Second, according to the Court of Appeal, provision (k) fails to define sufficiently the words "confront," "annoy," "provoke," "challenge," or "harass"; it thus fails to provide a standard of conduct for those whose activities are proscribed. Yet similar words were upheld against claims of vagueness by the Supreme Court in [*Madsen*, 512 U.S. 753, a case involving harassment in front of an abortion clinic]. * * *

Here again, "[t]he particular context is all important." The words of provision (k) which the Court of Appeal considered irretrievably vague are simply not, at least in the constitutional sense, when the objectives of the injunction are considered and the words of the provision are read in context. Finally, the declarations filed by the City in support of preliminary relief leave little doubt as to what kind of conduct the decree seeks to enjoin. One Rocksprings resident recounted an incident in which gang members had threatened to cut out the tongue of her nine-year-old daughter if she talked to the police; she stated that other residents had been threatened as well. Another resident reported her neighbor's property had been vandalized and the resident threatened after complaining to police that gang members had urinated in her garage. A police officer declared Rocksprings residents had told him gang members confront and threaten them with physical violence when asked to leave residential property. Others refused to furnish declarations, fearing for their lives if any gang member should discover their identities. We conclude neither of the two provisions should have been invalidated by the Court of Appeal on vagueness grounds.

Do provisions (a) and (k) of the superior court's preliminary injunction meet the constitutional test formulated by the Supreme Court in *Madsen*, by "burden[ing] no more speech than necessary to serve" an important governmental interest? We conclude both provisions satisfy the constitutional test. As noted, provision (a) effectively forbids gang members from engaging in any form of social intercourse with anyone known to them to be a gang member "anywhere in public view" within the four-block area of Rocksprings. The provision's ban on all forms of association—"standing, sitting, walking, driving, gathering or appearing anywhere in public view"—does not violate the *Madsen* standard merely because of its breadth. The provision seeks to ensure that, within the circumscribed area of Rocksprings, gang members have no opportunity to combine.

It is the threat of collective conduct by gang members loitering in a specific and narrowly described neighborhood that the provision is sensibly intended to forestall. Given that overriding purpose, the prohibitions enumerated in provision (a) are not easily divisible. Permitting two or more gang members to drive together but not sit, or to stand together but not walk, would obviously defeat the core purpose behind the proscription. Moreover, given the factual showing made by the City in support of preliminary relief—the carnival-like atmosphere of collective mayhem described above—we cannot say that the ban on any association between gang members within the neighborhood goes beyond what is required to abate the nuisance.

The effect of provision (a)'s ban on defendants' protected speech is minimal. To judge from the evidence placed before the superior court, the gangs appear to have had no constitutionally protected or even lawful goals within the limited territory of Rocksprings. So far as the record before the trial court shows, the gangs and their members engaged in no expressive or speech-related activities which were not either criminally or civilly unlawful or inextricably intertwined with unlawful conduct. According to the declaration of Officer Mikael Niehoff, an eight-year veteran of the San Jose Police Department: "Illegal drug dealing by Sureno gang members, including VSL/VST, is a common practice, and the gang entity provides protection to the individual members, allowing them to establish areas where they can conduct their illegal activities. The protective shield of the gang has allowed individual members to commit crimes such as narcotic trafficking that result in personal gain. These crimes are committed in association with the gang because of the protection offered to the members by virtue of their gang affiliation. In the Rocksprings area, the fact that numerous narcotics transactions occurred is a direct result of the protective shield provided by VSL/VST. Individuals who claimed membership in VSL or VST were at liberty to deal drugs in a veritable 'safe' zone."

Does provision (a)'s prohibition on a gang member associating with even a single fellow gang member within Rocksprings transgress the test of *Madsen*? Could not the restriction be limited to barring associations between, say, three other gang members? Two gang members? On such a highly particular question, we are compelled to defer to the superior knowledge of the trial judge, who is in a better position than we to determine what conditions "on the ground" in Rocksprings will reasonably permit. Outside the perimeter of Rocksprings, the superior court's writ does not run; gang members are subject to no special restrictions that do not affect the general population. Given the limited area within which the superior court's injunction operates, the absence of any showing of constitutionally protected activity by gang members within that area, the aggravated nature of gang misconduct, the fact that even within Rocksprings gang members may associate freely out of public view, and the kind of narrow yet irreducible arbitrariness that inheres in such line-drawing, we conclude that this aspect of provision (a) passes muster as well under the standard of *Madsen*.

We reach a similar resolution with respect to provision (k). That provision forbids those subject to the injunction from confronting, intimidating or similarly challenging—including assaulting and battering—residents of Rocksprings, "or any other persons" who gang members know have complained about their conduct within the neighborhood. It has long been the rule, of course, that physical violence and the threat of violence are not constitutionally protected: "The First Amendment does not protect violence." Because the conduct proscribed by provision (k) consists of threats of violence and violent acts themselves, it "fall[s] outside the protection of the First Amendment because [such acts] coerce by unlawful conduct, rather than persuade by expression, and thus play no part in the 'marketplace of ideas.' As such, they are punishable because of the state's interest in protecting individuals from the fear of violence, the disruption fear engenders and the possibility the threatened violence will occur." "[A] physical assault is not by any stretch of the imagination expressive conduct protected by the First Amendment." By the same token, "utterance in a context of violence can lose its significance as an appeal to reason and become part of an instrument of force. Such utterance was not meant to be sheltered by the Constitution." * * *

* * * [T]here was sufficient evidence before the superior court to support the conclusions that the gang and its members present in Rocksprings were responsible for the public nuisance, that each of the individual defendants either admitted gang membership or was identified as a gang member, and that each was observed by police officials in the Rocksprings neighborhood. Although all but three of the eleven defendants who chose to contest entry of the preliminary injunction—Miguel Moreno, Rafael Ruiz, and Blanca Gonzalez—were shown to have committed acts, primarily drug related, comprising specific elements of the public nuisance, such individualized proof is not a condition to the entry of preliminary relief based on a showing that it is the gang, acting through its individual members, that is responsible for the conditions prevailing in Rocksprings. Additional proceedings will be required to enforce the specific terms of the preliminary injunction. Should contempt proceedings ensue, each individual defendant will have an opportunity to contest any claim by the City that he or she has violated specific terms of the preliminary injunction. * * *

MOSK, J., dissenting.

No doubt Montesquieu, Locke, and Madison will turn over in their graves when they learn they are cited in an opinion that does not enhance liberty but deprives a number of simple rights to a group of Latino youths who have not been convicted of a crime. Mindful of the admonition of another great 18th century political philosopher, Benjamin Franklin, that "[t]hey that can give up essential liberty to obtain a little temporary safety deserve neither liberty nor safety," I would, unlike the majority, in large part affirm the judgment of the Court of Appeal.[1] * * *[4]

* * *

1. [Eds. relocated footnote] The City "validates" as a criminal street gang an association of three or more persons with a common name or symbol whose members collectively or individually engage in a pattern of criminal conduct, as defined by [the] * * * Penal Code * * *. It does not, however, adhere to the statutory definition of a gang member. * * * Instead, to "validate" specific gang members, the City merely reviews police records to identify individuals who admit membership in a gang to a peace officer, probation officer, juvenile hall or youth ranch employee, or who meet two or more of the following conditions: wear clothing or tattoos indicating gang affiliation or use gang hand signs; are named by

4. See note 4 on page 1063.

Paragraph (a) enjoins "[s]tanding, sitting, walking, driving, gathering or appearing anywhere in public with any other defendant herein, or with any other known 'VST' ... or 'VSL' ... member." It applies without any requirement or condition that a defendant or his associate be engaged in any illegal activity or misconduct related to the alleged public nuisance.

The provision is impermissibly vague. Who is a "known" VST or VSL member? And by whom is such membership "known"? In the absence of any specific definition of gang membership, neither police officers nor courts are provided with a consistent standard for determining when a violation of the injunction occurred.

Thus, even if we were to accept the City's argument that the only reasonable construction of the prohibition is that it requires a defendant to know that the person he or she is standing, sitting, driving, walking, driving, gathering, or appearing with is a gang member, it remains susceptible to arbitrary enforcement. Without a definition of gang membership, how would a defendant know when he or she was violating the injunction? It is also unclear how a police officer would know whether or not a defendant knows that he or she is engaging in these activities with a gang member. Under the City's construction, a defendant could be arrested and prosecuted for walking down the street or simply appearing in public with another person, based on a police officer's mere supposition that such defendant "knew" he or she was in the company of a "known" gang member. As the Court of Appeal recognized: "it is apparent a defendant could be engaged in one of the activities prohibited in paragraph (a) with a person not known to him or to her but known to police as a gang member, and suffer penalties for refusing to obey the injunction as a result. This is a classic case of vagueness."

Apart from these fundamental vagueness problems, the prohibitions under paragraph (a) go "further than is absolutely necessary to protect the lawful rights of the parties seeking such injunction" by penalizing much ordinary and lawful activity that does not fall within the statutory definition of a public nuisance. The prohibitions are not only sweeping, but absolute: They apply without regard to the defendant's intent or to the circumstances. * * *

two or more members of a gang as a member; actively participate in a gang crime; are identified by a reliable informant as a gang member; or are observed associating with gang members two or more times. Using similar broad criteria, the Los Angeles Sheriff's Department has estimated that 47 percent of all African–American males between the ages of 21 and 24 are actual or suspected gang members.

4. * * * [A]s it indicated in written and oral argument, the City did not challenge the Court of Appeal's determination that the following conduct, *inter alia*, was improperly enjoined: possession or use in Rocksprings of such everyday items as beepers, pens, spray paint cans, nails, screwdrivers, or any "sharp objects capable of defacing private or public property"; "encouraging" or "participating" in the use or possession of narcotics; "engaging in conversation, or otherwise communicating with the occupants of any vehicle"; using communicative hand signs or signals describing or referring to the gangs; wearing clothing bearing the name or letters associated with the gangs; climbing trees or walls or "passing through" fences. The City impliedly concedes that the Court of Appeal correctly struck these provisions of the injunction as enjoining more conduct than was necessary to abate the nuisance and on constitutional grounds.

The City asserts, and the majority apparently agree, that the associational rights of the members of the loosely formed VSL and VST gangs are not "worthy" of constitutional protection; they argue that only "intimate" and "expressive" associations are entitled to such protection. Although I, too, deplore gang violence, I am unwilling, despite the apparent nature of the Sureo gangs, to conclude that their members do not also engage in innocent intimate or expressive conduct. * * *

Although the terms "harassing" and "intimidating" are not specifically defined in the preliminary injunction, I disagree with the Court of Appeal's conclusion that they are too vague. * * *

The remainder of the provision, however, is too vague to withstand due process challenge. Activity in Rocksprings that consists of "[i]n any manner confronting, ... annoying, ... challenging, [or] provoking" others may include so much ordinary social behavior—and so much that depends on the individual sensibilities of those who might feel annoyed, challenged, or provoked—that it impermissibly invites arbitrary enforcement. * * *

As the City concedes, an individual may be "validated" as a VSL/VST gang member simply because he or she wears gang colors (including "neutral" colors like khaki, black, white, and blue) and is seen in the company of other "validated" gang members. I would agree with the Court of Appeal that, absent any showing that an individual "validated" as a gang member is likely to commit acts constituting a public nuisance in Rocksprings, he or she may not properly be subjected to the injunction, at least to the extent that it enjoins ordinary and innocent conduct within the Rocksprings neighborhood. * * * *[11]

As to one of the named defendants, Blanca Gonzalez, the evidence consisted solely of a police officer's statement to the effect that she was the driver of a car that was circling up and down the street in a purportedly Norteo-dominated neighborhood—apparently not Rocksprings. On that occasion, she was dressed in a black top and black jeans, consistent with members of Sureo gangs; she told the police officer that she belonged to the VST and VCT (also known as "Varrio Colonio Treces") gangs. On another occasion, a police officer on patrol in Rocksprings entered into a conversation with Gonzalez and another young Hispanic woman, after they drove up to an address in the Rocksprings neighborhood. Gonzalez told him that she did not live in Rocksprings and that she was a member of the VSL gang. * * *

The record also fails to support enjoining Miguel Moreno or Rafael Ruiz. Although both at one time "admitted" gang membership, neither

---

11. Use of the word "gang" has a tendency to strike fear in the hearts of countless persons. The trial court and now a majority of this court have succumbed to that somewhat irrational fear. The Court of Appeal is to be commended for looking at the issue dispassionately and objectively. Some of these defendants have not been convicted of, or even charged with, any crime. Yet they are, under the injunction, deprived of a number of personal rights generally reserved to all free citizens—including the right to walk or drive through the Rocksprings neighborhood with a "known" gang member even for an innocent purpose.

was adequately shown to have engaged in conduct amounting to a public nuisance in or around Rocksprings. Moreno was merely "identified" by an unknown party as having been involved in a drug offense in Rocksprings. Ruiz was identified by a police officer responding to a citizen call concerning a drug transaction as loosely matching a description of one of the participants. * * *

The majority would permit our cities to close off entire neighborhoods to Latino youths who have done nothing more than dress in blue or black clothing or associate with others who do so; they would authorize criminal penalties for ordinary, nondisruptive acts of walking or driving through a residential neighborhood with a relative or friend. In my view, such a blunderbuss approach amounts to both bad law and bad policy. Justice Black warned in *Jay v. Boyd* (1956) 351 U.S. 345, 367: "Unfortunately there are some who think that the way to save freedom in this country is to adopt the techniques of tyranny." The majority here appear to embrace that misguided belief. Accordingly, I dissent.

Notes and Questions

1.   Did the injunction granted in *Acuna* go too far? How might you feel about it if you lived in the Rocksprings neighborhood?

2.   Is race an important issue in the *Acuna* case? The majority opinion never mentions race, while Justice Mosk, in his dissent, several times pointedly refers to the defendants as "Latinos." Does it matter that the defendants *and*, most likely, the victims of the behavior enjoined as a public nuisance were Latinos/as? If so, in what way?

3.   For more on gang profiling, see Margaret A. Russell, *Entering Great America: Reflections on Race and the Convergence of Progressive Legal Theory and Practice,* 43 Hastings L.J. 749 (1992).

4.   In Chicago v. Morales, 119 S.Ct. 1849 (1999), the Supreme Court, in a highly divided opinion, found that Chicago's Gang Congregation Ordinance violated the Due Process Clause of the Fourteenth Amendment because it was unconstitutionally vague. The ordinance stated that

> whenever a police officer observes a person whom he reasonably believes to be a criminal street gang member loitering in any public place with one or more other persons, he shall order all such persons to disperse and remove themselves from the area. Any person who does not promptly obey such an order is in violation of this section.

Id. at n.2.

Justice Stevens, in a section of the opinion joined only by Justices Souter and Ginsburg, concluded that "in this instance the city has enacted an ordinance that affords too much discretion to the police and too little notice to citizens who wish to use the public streets." Justice Scalia, and Justice Thomas, joined by Justices Scalia and Chief Justice Rehnquist, filed dissenting opinions.

B. RACE AND THE TRIAL PROCESS

CYNTHIA KWEI YUNG LEE

Race and Self–Defense: Toward a Normative Conception of Reasonableness
81 Minn. L. Rev. 367, 429–30, 432–34, 437–40, 444–52 (1996).*

It is almost oxymoronic to speak of foreign Americans, yet the term "foreign American" conveys meaning—Asian Americans and Latinos. Many Americans associate Asian Americans with foreignness. The person who asks an Asian American "Where are you from?" usually expects a response like "Japan" (or China or Korea)—not "Texas" (or Ohio or Northern California). This focus on the Asian in Asian American is deep-rooted. During World War II, when the United States was at war with Japan, hostility toward Japan was extended to all persons of Japanese ancestry. From 1942 to 1945, Japanese Americans were incarcerated in internment camps because of their Japanese heritage. The internment took place even though there was no evidence that Americans of Japanese descent were disloyal to the United States. Even though the United States was at war with Germany and Italy, as well as with Japan, persons of German and Italian ancestry were not similarly incarcerated.

The Asian-as-foreigner stereotype is evident today, though it has taken on more subtle forms. During the O.J. Simpson trial, much of the racial joking in the case was directed at two Asian Americans associated with the case. The Honorable Lance Ito, the judge who presided over the trial, and criminalist Dennis Fung, two Asian Americans who speak articulately and without a noticeable accent, were portrayed as bumbling, heavily-accented Asians who could barely speak English by radio station disc jockeys, publishing houses, and even a United States senator. During the Simpson trial, the historical impulse to mock others on the basis of racial difference was fulfilled by poking fun at the Asian Americans associated with the trial, constructing them as Asians with heavy accents characteristic of the Asian-as-foreigner stereotype. * * *

Because of the confusion between Asian Americans and Asian nationals, symptomatic of the Asian-as-foreigner stereotype, the killing of Yoshihiro Hattori, a Japanese foreign exchange student, by Rodney Peairs, a Louisiana homeowner who claimed he acted in self-defense and was acquitted, has special significance for both Asian nationals and Asian Americans. On October 17, 1992, two sixteen-year-old high school students, Yoshihiro Hattori and Webb Haymaker were looking for a Halloween party in the suburbs of Baton Rouge, Louisiana when they came to the home of Rodney and Bonnie Peairs and rang the doorbell. The Peairs's home was decorated for Halloween and was only a few doors away from the correct house. Hattori was dressed as the character played by John Travolta in "Saturday Night Fever," wearing a white tuxedo jacket and carrying a small camera. No one answered the front door, but the boys heard the clinking of window blinds coming from the rear of the carport area. The boys walked around the house in that direction. A moment later, Bonnie Peairs opened the door. Webb Haymaker started to say, "We're here for the party." When Yoshi came around the corner to join Webb, Mrs. Peairs slammed the door and screamed for her husband to get the gun. Without asking any questions, Rodney Peairs went to the bedroom and grabbed a laser-scoped .44 magnum Smith and Wesson, one of a number of guns Peairs owned.

The two boys had walked away from the house and were on the sidewalk about ten yards from the house when Peairs rushed out of the house and into the carport area. The carport light was on and a street light was located in front of the house, illuminating the carport and sidewalk area. Hattori, the Japanese exchange student, turned and approached Peairs, smiling apologetically and explaining, "We're here for the party," in heavily accented English. Rather than explaining to Hattori that he had the wrong house, Peairs pointed his gun at Hattori and shouted the word "freeze." Hattori, who did not understand the English word "freeze," continued to approach Peairs. Peairs fired one shot at Hattori's chest. Hattori collapsed and died on the spot. The entire incident—from the time Peairs opened the door to the time he fired his gun at Hattori—took place in approximately three seconds.

Peairs was charged with manslaughter. At trial, Peairs's attorney argued that Peairs shot Hattori because he honestly and reasonably believed the unarmed Hattori was about to kill or seriously harm him. The judge instructed the jury that in order to acquit Peairs on the ground of self-defense, the jury needed to find that Peairs reasonably believed he was in imminent danger of losing his life or receiving great bodily harm and that the killing was necessary to save himself from that danger. After little more than three hours of deliberating, the jury returned a verdict of not guilty. Spectators in the courtroom responded to the verdict with applause. In contrast to the public's outrage at the perceived shortness of the deliberation process in the O.J. Simpson case when jurors in that case reached a verdict in less than four hours, there was little if any public outrage at the three hours of deliberation and resulting acquittal in the Peairs case. * * *

Just as the attorney representing Bernhard Goetz covertly and effectively played the race card, Peairs's attorney subtly and effectively appealed to prejudice against the Japanese "enemy." Playing on the Asian-as-foreigner stereotype, which was all the more readily believed in this case involving a true Asian foreigner, Peairs's attorney told the jury that Hattori was acting in a menacing, aggressive fashion, "like a stranger invading someone's home turf." The use of language suggesting an invasion of home turf is striking in light of the way Japanese people have been viewed in this country. Historically, Japanese nationals and Japanese Americans have been viewed as the enemy. In more recent times, the Japanese have also been viewed as the enemy—the economic yellow peril responsible for the loss of American jobs. Indicative of this tendency to view Japan as the enemy, one writer, commenting on Japanese outrage at the not guilty verdict in the Peairs case, wrote: "America excels at overreaction to a singular occurrence; *it's gratifying to witness our economic arch rival suffer the same weakness. They've bloodied our nose enough in the business markets of the world.* * * * At least Americans can see hysteria is no less common in 'perfect Japan.' " The notion of foreignness embedded in this "invasion of home turf" language was so subtle that this indirect reference to national origin went unnoticed by the prosecution.

Bonnie Peairs's trial testimony is also significant. When asked to describe Hattori, Mrs. Peairs responded, *"I guess he appeared Oriental. He could have been Mexican or whatever."* Mrs. Peairs was unable to tell whether Hattori was "Oriental" or "Mexican" or neither. All she knew was that Hattori looked different, foreign. Her comment highlights the way minorities are often lumped together as a homogenous group outside the American community.

If Webb Haymaker had been the victim, it is unlikely that the spectators in the courtroom would have responded with applause to the not guilty verdict. If Haymaker, the boy from the neighborhood, rather than Hattori, a foreigner from Japan, had been the victim in this case, the defense would have had a more difficult time portraying the victim as "a crazy man," "frightening," or "scary," terms used to describe Hattori. If Haymaker had been the victim, the presence of Haymaker's parents in the courtroom and in the community would have made it much more difficult for the defense to paint a credible picture of the victim as the bad guy. But Haymaker was not the victim; Hattori, a Japanese foreigner, was the one shot and killed. * * *

Another common belief about Asians and Asian Americans is encompassed in the Asian-as-martial artist stereotype. Many people assume that young Asian men know martial arts. In *State v. Simon*, the Asian-as-martial artist stereotype helped secure an acquittal for a man who shot his Chinese neighbor and then claimed self-defense. Anthony Simon, an elderly homeowner, shot his neighbor, Steffen Wong, a Chinese man, as Wong was entering his own duplex. Simon was charged with two counts of aggravated assault.

At trial, Simon argued that he assumed, by virtue of Wong's racial heritage, that Wong was an expert in the martial arts. Simon claimed he was afraid of Wong and that heated words had been exchanged between the two neighbors. Simon also said he was fearful because more Orientals were moving into the neighborhood and one had even expressed interest in purchasing Simon's home. In addition to Simon's testimony, the defense called a clinical psychologist who testified Simon was a psychological invalid who suffered from anxiety neurosis. Defense counsel argued to the jury that the evidence showed Simon reasonably believed Wong was an imminent threat to him.

The jury acquitted Simon on all counts. Although the instruction on self-defense given to the jury utilized a subjective standard of reasonableness, the fact that the jury could find Simon's fear to be reasonable when it was quite clear that his fear of Wong was based almost solely on a racial stereotype is quite astounding. The Asian-as-martial artist stereotype may have influenced jurors to sympathize with Simon's misplaced belief that because of Wong's Asian heritage, Wong must have been a dangerous martial arts expert. * * *

The perception that young Latinos who dress a certain way are dangerous criminal gang members who pose a threat of serious bodily injury to those who confront them, coupled with the notion that Latinos tend to be hot-blooded and prone to violence, may contribute to the frequency with which homicide and assault cases involving Latino victims are not prosecuted. In numerous instances, Latinos have been shot, beaten, and/or killed by citizens or police officers claiming justifiable use of deadly force under circumstances calling into question whether the use of deadly force was truly warranted. In many of these cases, despite the fact that the Latino victim was unarmed or shot in the back, criminal charges were not brought against the person claiming justifiable homicide. In recent history, the most widely publicized incident of this type occurred in January 1995.

On January 31, 1995, eighteen-year-old Cesar Rene Arce and twenty-year-old David Hillo, two young Mexican Americans, were spray-painting columns supporting the Hollywood Freeway in Los Angeles at about 1:00 a.m. William Masters II, a white man carrying a loaded gun without a permit in his fanny pack, was out for a late-night walk and saw the two boys spray-painting the columns. Masters picked up a piece of paper from the ground and wrote down the license plate number of the young men's car. Masters claims that when Arce saw him writing, Arce blocked the sidewalk and demanded that he hand over the paper. A scuffle ensued in which Arce tried to rip the paper from Masters's hand and Masters tried to jam the rest of the paper into his pocket. According to Masters, when Hillo held up a screwdriver in a threatening manner, Masters handed over the piece of paper and began walking away. Masters claims he thought the boys were behind him, so he swung around, and fired at Arce. Masters then shot Hillo in the buttocks. Arce died from the shot which entered him from his back.

Masters told the first police officers at the scene, "I shot him because he was spray-painting." Later, Masters claimed he shot the boys in self-defense. In yet another explanation, Masters claimed that he shot the boys because they tried to rob him. Masters was arrested and jailed on suspicion of murder. When he was released from custody, Masters called the two youths he shot "skinhead Mexicans," blamed Arce's mother for his death because she failed to raise Arce well, and said that as a former Marine, he was trained to take down as many of the enemy as he could.

The Los Angeles County District Attorney's Office declined to prosecute Masters on the ground that Masters acted in self-defense when he shot Arce. The determination that Masters reasonably believed he was about to be attacked by Arce is surprising given the fact that the shot that killed Arce entered him from his back. In contrast, the Los Angeles County District Attorney's Office filed murder and manslaughter charges against two Black men (one of whom was the rap singer known as Snoop Doggy Dogg) who claimed they shot another Black man in self-defense, disbelieving their self-defense claim largely because the victim was shot in the back and buttocks.

The decision not to file criminal homicide charges against Masters was also based on the prediction that the government would have had a difficult time convincing a jury to return a conviction against Masters. The government's case would have rested primarily on testimony by Hillo, the young man who survived the shooting. Hillo would have been a problematic witness since he gave conflicting versions of the facts in interviews with the police. Moreover, judging from public reaction to the event, the community was extremely supportive of Masters. Telephone calls reportedly flooded into the police station where Masters was held, offering money and legal assistance. Sandi Webb, a Simi Valley Council-woman, declared her support for Masters by stating, "Kudos to William Masters for his vigilant anti-graffiti efforts and for his foresight in carrying a gun for self protection. If [Los Angeles] refuses to honor Masters as a crime-fighting hero, then I invite him to relocate to our town."

While the Masters case is about the exercise of prosecutorial, not jury, discretion, it is nevertheless relevant to the discussion of the effect of racial stereotypes on legal decisionmaking. Racial stereotypes affect all people, including prosecutors, judges, and jurors. The Masters case is difficult because fear of crime and increasing gang violence are legitimate fears held by many people, particularly in Southern California. Graffiti on freeway overpasses, public buildings, and private property is a reminder that the threat of violent crime is not far off. Supporters of Masters were likely reacting to this fear of crime and gang violence. As one supporter explained, "Whatever he did doesn't bother me. I'm not saying shooting people is the way to do it.... But [the graffiti] is just disgusting. It doesn't seem like anyone's doing anything about it." * * *

The support William Masters generated for shooting two young Mexican American males engaged in spray-painting is striking when contrasted with the Michael Fay incident, involving a non-Latino white American teenager who was caught engaging in graffiti in Singapore, which occurred less than one year earlier. In 1994, Michael Fay pled guilty to two counts of vandalism and two counts of mischief, admitting that he was one of a group of youths who spray-painted eighteen cars, threw eggs at other cars, and switched license plates on still other cars. When a Singaporean judge sentenced Fay to four months in prison, a $2,230 fine, and *six lashes with a rattan cane*, many Americans rallied to Fay's defense. Fay's mother appealed to U.S. government officials, asking them to assist in gaining clemency for her son. When explaining why her son should not be subjected to caning, the punishment typically imposed in Singapore for vandalism, Fay's mother stated, "Caning is not something the *American* public would want an *American* to go through. It's barbaric." Fay's mother further described her son as "a *typical* teen-ager" who played on the American football team. U.S. Embassy officials and members of the American Chamber of Commerce responded to Fay's mother's request, condemning the severity of the sentence. Ralph Boyce, Charge d'Affaires of the American Embassy, stated "We see a large discrepancy between the offence and the punishment. The cars were not permanently damaged. The paint was removed with paint thinner. Caning leaves permanent scars." Even U.S. President Bill Clinton made a strong protest to the Singapore government, asking for reconsideration of the sentence.

In the Masters case, a white American shot two Mexican Americans after catching them in the act of spray-painting columns supporting a public freeway, and was called a crime-fighting hero even though he killed one of the youths. In the Michael Fay case, the Singaporean government prosecuted a white American teenager for spray-painting eighteen cars and engaging in other acts of vandalism. Many Americans were outraged at the caning punishment the Singaporean government imposed on Fay. If a Singaporean citizen had shot and killed Fay after catching him in the act of spray-painting the Singaporean citizen's car, it is unlikely that Americans would view the Singaporean as a hero, even if the Singaporean claimed, as Masters did, that he thought Fay was going to hurt him and shot Fay in self-defense. Stereotypes of Mexican American youths as criminal gang members likely influenced the general public's reaction to the Masters case.

Stereotypes play a more important role in our thinking and interactions with other people than we may be willing to admit. We all make assumptions about people. Often our assumptions are linked to perceived racial identities. Stereotyping, in and of itself, is not necessarily evil but can become evil when it results in harmful consequences. Because one of the purposes of the law is to ensure fair and equal treatment, the law should discourage reliance on stereotypes, especially when such reliance results in harmful action such as the use of deadly force.

Notes and Questions

1.   Angela Davis, a former defense attorney, notes that among her colleagues it was a joke that if one could not successfully defend a white client, one would lose one's license to practice. Less facetiously, Professor Davis argues that the decision to charge and to plea bargain is extensively influenced by race, yet prosecutorial discretion is largely unreviewed and unreviewable. See Angela J. Davis, *Prosecution and Race: The Power and Privilege of Discretion,* 67 Fordham L. Rev. 13 (1998).

2.   Professor Lee's article concerns the ways in which racial stereotypes can play a role in the perception that an assailant poses a threat of imminent death or great bodily harm for the purpose of self-defense doctrine. Race also enters the courtroom in other ways. As Sheri Lynn Johnson notes:

> Racial imagery can be conveyed in pictures, stories, examples, and generalizations. These visual and auditory experiences may themselves generate a racial image, or they may recall for the observer racial imagery to which she was exposed at an earlier time. Because race is such a salient characteristic in our society, a juror will notice the race of the defendant, the witnesses, the attorneys, the judge, and other jurors. What each juror will "see" when she observes an African–American judge, a white defendant, a Latino witness, or an Asian–American prosecutor will be affected by what happens in the courtroom, but what she "sees" happening in the courtroom will be affected by her prior exposure to racial imagery.

Sheri Lynn Johnson, *Racial Imagery in Criminal Cases*, 67 Tul. L. Rev. 1739, 1743 (1993). For more on how stereotyping operates as a matter of cognitive psychology, see Chapter 1, § 1B and Chapter 12 § 1 *supra*.

Professor Johnson notes that there are no "race shield laws" that prevent attorneys from playing upon racial stereotypes in the courtroom, and she proposes that such statutes be passed. In a similar vein, Anthony Alfieri argues that attorneys have an ethical duty to avoid playing upon such stereotypes, even when representing criminal defendants. See Anthony V. Alfieri, *Defending Racial Violence,* 95 Colum. L. Rev. 1301 (1995); see also Anthony V. Alfieri, *Race Trials*, 76 Tex. L. Rev. 1293 (1998).

3. Are there ever times when race and ethnicity *should* enter the courtroom? Consider the problem of "culture" in the excerpt that follows.

LETI VOLPP

(Mis)Identifying Culture: Asian Women and the "Cultural Defense"
17 Harv. Women's L.J. 57, 57–58, 84–89 (1994).*

The "cultural defense" is a legal strategy that defendants use in attempts to excuse criminal behavior or to mitigate culpability based on a lack of requisite *mens rea*. Defendants may also use "cultural defenses" to present evidence relating to state of mind when arguing self defense or mistake of fact. The theory underlying the defense is that the defendant, usually a recent immigrant to the United States, acted according to the dictates of his or her "culture," and therefore deserves leniency. There is, however, no formal "cultural defense"; individual defense attorneys and judges use their discretion to present or consider cultural factors affecting the mental state or culpability of a defendant. In my discussion of this strategy, I focus on the significance of its use for Asian women. * * *

After strangling her son, Sidney Wu, with the cord from a window blind, Helen Wu was convicted of second degree murder and was sentenced to a term of fifteen years to life by a California Superior Court. She appealed, claiming in part that the trial court committed reversible error by refusing to give a jury instruction about the effect her cultural background might have had on her state of mind when she killed her son. * * *

Helen Wu was born in 1943 in Saigon, Indochina. In 1963 she met Gary Wu, who emigrated to the United States that same year and married another woman. In 1978 or 1979 Gary Wu contacted Helen and said that he heard she had been married, was divorced and had a daughter. He told her that his marriage was unsatisfactory because his wife was infertile and that he planned to divorce her. They discussed the possibility of Helen emigrating to the United States and bearing a child for him. Helen, who was in love with him, believed that Gary would marry her after he divorced his wife.

Gary Wu sent Helen money so that she could apply for a visa and in November 1979 she came to the United States. At his request, Helen brought most of the money he had sent her. Upon her arrival he told her his divorce proceedings would be completed soon and that he would marry her. Gary then obtained a divorce but did not tell Helen.

Helen Wu conceived a child with Gary in early 1980. After Sidney was born, Gary still made no overtures regarding marriage. Helen was depressed, could not speak English, could not drive, and had no support system in the United States. She told Gary that she intended to return to Macau, thinking that he would persuade her to stay. After he failed to do so, she returned to Macau without Sidney because she did not wish people in Macau to know she had had a baby out of wedlock.

For the next eight years Helen repeatedly asked Gary to bring Sidney to visit her in Macau. In 1987 he said that he needed money and agreed to bring Sidney in return. During his visit, Helen showed him a certificate of deposit for a million Hong Kong dollars, which belonged to a friend. He proposed marriage, but she declined, depressed because the proposal seemed to be because of "her" money and because she did not know if he was still married. She was so distraught she tried to kill herself.

Helen came to the United States again in 1989 and visited Gary's ill mother, who said that Helen should take Sidney when she died because Gary would not take good care of him. That September Gary and Helen were married in Las Vegas. On the drive back, she asked him if he married her for her money, and he responded that until she produced the money, she had no right to speak.

Eight days later Helen saw Gary beat Sidney. Sidney then told her that the house they were staying in belonged to another woman, Rosemary, who was Gary's girlfriend. Sidney also told her that Gary called Helen "psychotic" and "very troublesome," and that Gary beat him.

After hearing this, Helen began to experience heart palpitations and have trouble breathing. She told Sidney that she wanted to die and asked him if he would go too. He clung to her neck and cried. Helen cut the cord off a window blind and strangled her son. She stopped breathing, and when she started again, she was surprised how quickly he had died.

Helen wrote Gary a note saying that he had bullied her too much and that "now this air is vented. I can die with no regret." After failing in an attempt to strangle herself, she then slashed her left wrist with a knife in the kitchen. Helen returned to the bedroom and lay down next to Sidney on the bed, after first placing a waste-paper basket under her wrist so the floor would not be dirtied with her blood. Gary returned several hours later to find Sidney dead and Helen in a decreased state of consciousness. She was taken to an emergency room and revived.

Based on these facts and the evidence at trial, the appellate court reversed and remanded the case. The court found that the trial judge should have instructed the jurors that they could choose to consider Helen Wu's cultural background in determining the presence or absence of the various mental states that were elements of murder. The trial court had refused to give the instruction, commenting that it did not want to put the "stamp of approval on [defendant's] actions in the

United States, which would have been acceptable in China." The appellate court held that evidence of Helen's cultural background was relevant to the elements of premeditation and deliberation, and found that cultural information was also relevant to the issues of malice aforethought and the existence of heat of passion because it could potentially reduce an intentional killing to voluntary manslaughter.

At the initial trial, the prosecution and defense attempted to paint very divergent views of Helen Wu. They both focused on whether she had "motherly" feelings towards Sidney, and whether she was a "traditional Chinese woman."

> Initially, we note that the facts presented at trial, while not in conflict as to certain specific events, did vary considerably as to whether defendant had "motherly" feelings toward the victim, her son, whether she was a "traditional" Chinese woman, and, based on the above noted factors, whether the motive for his death was a desire for revenge against Sidney's father or guilt over having not taken good care of the child and fear that he would be ill-treated in the future.

On appeal, the prosecution argued that the court did not give the instruction because the evidence that Helen Wu had the values and motives of a traditional Chinese mother was contradicted by other evidence, and because their expert noted that nothing in Chinese culture or religion encouraged filicide. The appellate court responded that a conflict in evidence did not mean the jury should not have been given an instruction.

The appellate court held that there was ample evidence of both Helen Wu's cultural background and the impact that her background might have had on her mental state. Unlike in the Chen case, the defense offered some of this information through experts on "transcultural psychology." These experts testified that Helen Wu's emotional state was intertwined with and explained by her cultural background. They described Helen's actions in killing her son as stemming not from an evil motive, but from her love for Sidney, her feeling of failure as a mother and her desire to be with her son in another life. One expert, Dr. Chien, testified about the cultural context within which Helen acted:

> She thought the only way to find out a way out is to bring this Sidney to go together so the mother and son can finally live together in the other heaven, other world if that cannot be done in this realistic earth.... [S]he was under the heat of passion when she realized that her son was unwanted son, uncared by Gary, passed around from one woman to the other woman, and now the grandmother is dying and she was planning to leave, 'What will happen to Sidney?' And all this information came up to her mind to stimulate all her guilt feeling which was probably more than ordinary guilt feeling that some depressive person would feel.... [I]n my expertise as a transcultural psychiatr[ist] ... with my familiarity with the Chinese culture ... and from the information interview I obtain from Helen, she thought she was doing that out from the mother's love, mother's responsibility....

It's a mother's altruism. This may be very difficult for the Western-
er to understand.... But in the Asian culture when the mother
commits suicide and leaves the children alone, usually they'll be
considered to be a totally irresponsible behavior, and the mother will
usually worry what would happen if she died....

In addition to Dr. Chien, the defense called another expert to
explain the influence of Helen's cultural context on her behavior. Psychologist Terry Gock stated:

[S]he in many ways is a product of her past experiences, including
her culture.... [I]n some sense the kind of alternatives that she ...
saw how to get out of that situation was quite culturally determined
... perhaps in this country, even with a traditional woman may,
may see other options. But in her culture, in her own mind, there
are no other options but to, for her at that time, but to kill herself
and take the son along with her so that they could sort of step over
to the next world where she could devote herself, all of herself to the
caring of the son, caring of Sidney.... Her purpose ... in many
ways ... is a benevolent one.

Notes and Questions

1.   To what extent did the testimony in the *Wu* case just described rely
on stated or unstated stereotypes about culture, ethnicity, and gender?
Professor Volpp notes that such cultural evidence suggests that the defendant's behavior is "determined" by her identity. Does that mean it should be
excluded? What is the relationship between this kind of evidence and the
kind of racial defense decried by Professor Lee?

2.   Is the use of "cultural" evidence in the courtroom determined by its
acceptability in the dominant culture? Daina Chiu argues that cultural
evidence about Asians is only taken seriously in the courtroom when it
confirms existing stereotypes (for example, the testimony in *Wu* arguably
confirms white American stereotypes about the passive, self-sacrificing Asian
woman). See Daina C. Chiu, *The Cultural Defense: Beyond Exclusion,
Assimilation, and Guilty Liberalism*, 82 Calif. L. Rev. 1053 (1994); see also
Sherene Razack, *Looking White People in the Eye: Gender, Race and Culture
in Courtrooms and Classrooms* (1998) (discussing the use of cultural stereotypes about foreign "others" in Canadian refugee cases). If this is true, can
the problem be avoided?

3.   Professor Volpp concludes:

While a formalized "cultural defense" is problematic because it will
force defendants' actions to be defined through a group-based identity
and reify cultural stereotypes, in some circumstances a defense that
presents cultural background will be appropriate. In formulating a legal
recourse to the predicament of a particular individual whose behavior
was influenced by forces such as racism, sexism and subordination in
the form of violence, admission of cultural factors should not function as
a reductive "explanation" of that individual's actions as fitting into
group behavior or "culture." Rather, the choice to provide an individual
defendant with cultural information should be made for the purpose of
explaining that individual's state of mind, in much the same way that
the criminal law allows other information about a defendant's life

history to mitigate sentences or charges in a criminal trial. Even when we attempt to use cultural information to explain an individual's oppressions or her state of mind, we are forced to label and define, in other words, to essentialize, certain behavior as "cultural." This can be done in the spirit of what might be called "strategic essentialism"—consciously choosing to essentialize a particular community for the purpose of a specific political goal. Strategic essentialism ideally should be undertaken by the affected community, which is best situated to undertake the process of selecting the appropriate circumstances in which to offer cultural information.

Volpp at 95–96.

Do you agree? How should "the affected community" undertake the project of "strategic essentialism?"

C. RACE AND SENTENCING

McCLESKEY v. KEMP
481 U.S. 279 (1987).

JUSTICE POWELL delivered the opinion of the Court, in which CHIEF JUSTICE REHNQUIST and JUSTICES WHITE, O'CONNOR, and SCALIA joined.

This case presents the question whether a complex statistical study that indicates a risk that racial considerations enter into capital sentencing determinations proves that petitioner McCleskey's capital sentence is unconstitutional under the Eighth or Fourteenth Amendments.

[Warren McCleskey, an African–American man, was convicted of the murder of a white police officer during the course of a robbery. In the post-conviction sentencing hearing, the jury recommended the death penalty based on the existence of two statutory aggravating circumstances—that the killing occurred during the commission of a robbery, and that the victim was a peace officer engaged in the performance of his duties—and no mitigating circumstances. The judge followed the recommendation and sentenced McCleskey to death. On appeal, the state supreme court affirmed the conviction and sentence.]

McCleskey next filed a petition for a writ of *habeas corpus* in the Federal District Court for the Northern District of Georgia. His petition raised 18 claims, one of which was that the Georgia capital sentencing process is administered in a racially discriminatory manner in violation of the Eighth and Fourteenth Amendments to the United States Constitution. In support of his claim, McCleskey proffered a statistical study performed by Professors David C. Baldus, Charles Pulaski, and George Woodworth (the Baldus study) that purports to show a disparity in the imposition of the death sentence in Georgia based on the race of the murder victim and, to a lesser extent, the race of the defendant. The Baldus study is actually two sophisticated statistical studies that examine over 2,000 murder cases that occurred in Georgia during the 1970s. The raw numbers collected by Professor Baldus indicate that defendants charged with killing white persons received the death penalty in 11% of the cases, but defendants charged with killing blacks received the death penalty in only 1% of the cases. The raw numbers also indicate a reverse racial disparity according to the race of the defendant: 4% of the black defendants received the death penalty, as opposed to 7% of the white defendants.

Baldus also divided the cases according to the combination of the race of the defendant and the race of the victim. He found that the death penalty was assessed in 22% of the cases involving black defendants and white victims; 8% of the cases involving white defendants and white victims; 1% of the cases involving black defendants and black victims; and 3% of the cases involving white defendants and black victims. Similarly, Baldus found that prosecutors sought the death penalty in 70% of the cases involving black defendants and white victims; 32% of the cases involving white defendants and white victims; 15% of the cases involving black defendants and black victims; and 19% of the cases involving white defendants and black victims.

Baldus subjected his data to an extensive analysis, taking account of 230 variables that could have explained the disparities on nonracial grounds. One of his models concludes that, even after taking account of 39 nonracial variables, defendants charged with killing white victims were 4.3 times as likely to receive a death sentence as defendants charged with killing blacks. According to this model, black defendants were 1.1 times as likely to receive a death sentence as other defendants. Thus, the Baldus study indicates that black defendants, such as McCleskey, who kill white victims have the greatest likelihood of receiving the death penalty.[1] * * *

McCleskey's first claim is that the Georgia capital punishment statute violates the Equal Protection Clause of the Fourteenth Amendment.[7] He argues that race has infected the administration of Georgia's statute in two ways: Persons who murder whites are more likely to be sentenced to death than persons who murder blacks, and black murderers are more likely to be sentenced to death than white murderers. As a black defendant who killed a white victim, McCleskey claims that the Baldus study demonstrates that he was discriminated against because of

---

1. Baldus' 230–variable model divided cases into eight different ranges, according to the estimated aggravation level of the offense. Baldus argued in his testimony to the District Court that the effects of racial bias were most striking in the midrange cases. "When the cases become tremendously aggravated so that everybody would agree that if we're going to have a death sentence, these are the cases that should get it, the race effects go away. It's only in the mid-range of cases where the decisionmakers have a real choice as to what to do. If there's room for the exercise of discretion, then the [racial] factors begin to play a role." Under this model, Baldus found that 14.4% of the black-victim midrange cases received the death penalty, and 34.4% of the white-victim cases received the death penalty. According to Baldus, the facts of McCleskey's case placed it within the midrange.

7. Although the District Court rejected the findings of the Baldus study as flawed, the Court of Appeals assumed that the study is valid and reached the constitutional issues. Accordingly, those issues are before us. As did the Court of Appeals, we assume the study is valid statistically without reviewing the factual findings of the District Court. Our assumption that the Baldus study is statistically valid does not include the assumption that the study shows that racial considerations actually enter into any sentencing decisions in Georgia. Even a sophisticated multiple-regression analysis such as the Baldus study can only demonstrate a risk that the factor of race entered into some capital sentencing decisions and a necessarily lesser risk that race entered into any particular sentencing decision.

his race and because of the race of his victim. In its broadest form, McCleskey's claim of discrimination extends to every actor in the Georgia capital sentencing process, from the prosecutor who sought the death penalty and the jury that imposed the sentence, to the State itself that enacted the capital punishment statute and allows it to remain in effect despite its allegedly discriminatory application. We agree with the Court of Appeals, and every other court that has considered such a challenge, that this claim must fail.

Our analysis begins with the basic principle that a defendant who alleges an equal protection violation has the burden of proving "the existence of purposeful discrimination." A corollary to this principle is that a criminal defendant must prove that the purposeful discrimination "had a discriminatory effect" on him. Thus, to prevail under the Equal Protection Clause, McCleskey must prove that the decisionmakers in his case acted with discriminatory purpose. He offers no evidence specific to his own case that would support an inference that racial considerations played a part in his sentence. Instead, he relies solely on the Baldus study. McCleskey argues that the Baldus study compels an inference that his sentence rests on purposeful discrimination. McCleskey's claim that these statistics are sufficient proof of discrimination, without regard to the facts of a particular case, would extend to all capital cases in Georgia, at least where the victim was white and the defendant is black.

The Court has accepted statistics as proof of intent to discriminate in certain limited contexts. First, this Court has accepted statistical disparities as proof of an equal protection violation in the selection of the jury venire in a particular district. Although statistical proof normally must present a "stark" pattern to be accepted as the sole proof of discriminatory intent under the Constitution, "because of the nature of the jury-selection task, ... we have permitted a finding of constitutional violation even when the statistical pattern does not approach [such] extremes." Second, this Court has accepted statistics in the form of multiple-regression analysis to prove statutory violations under Title VII of the Civil Rights Act of 1964. * * *

But the nature of the capital sentencing decision, and the relationship of the statistics to that decision, are fundamentally different from the corresponding elements in the venire-selection or Title VII cases. Most importantly, each particular decision to impose the death penalty is made by a petit jury selected from a properly constituted venire. Each jury is unique in its composition, and the Constitution requires that its decision rest on consideration of innumerable factors that vary according to the characteristics of the individual defendant and the facts of the particular capital offense.

Thus, the application of an inference drawn from the general statistics to a specific decision in a trial and sentencing simply is not comparable to the application of an inference drawn from general statistics to a specific venire-selection or Title VII case. In those cases, the statistics relate to fewer entities, and fewer variables are relevant to the challenged decisions.

Another important difference between the cases in which we have accepted statistics as proof of discriminatory intent and this case is that, in the venire-selection and Title VII contexts, the decisionmaker has an opportunity to explain the statistical disparity. Here, the State has no practical opportunity to rebut the Baldus study. "Controlling considerations of * * * public policy," dictate that jurors "cannot be called * * * to testify to the motives and influences that led to their verdict." Similarly, the policy considerations behind a prosecutor's traditionally "wide discretion" suggest the impropriety of our requiring prosecutors to defend their decisions to seek death penalties, "often years after they were made." Moreover, absent far stronger proof, it is unnecessary to seek such a rebuttal, because a legitimate and unchallenged explanation for the decision is apparent from the record: McCleskey committed an act for which the United States Constitution and Georgia laws permit imposition of the death penalty.

Finally, McCleskey's statistical proffer must be viewed in the context of his challenge. McCleskey challenges decisions at the heart of the State's criminal justice system. "One of society's most basic tasks is that of protecting the lives of its citizens and one of the most basic ways in which it achieves the task is through criminal laws against murder." Implementation of these laws necessarily requires discretionary judgments. Because discretion is essential to the criminal justice process, we would demand exceptionally clear proof before we would infer that the discretion has been abused. The unique nature of the decisions at issue in this case also counsels against adopting such an inference from the disparities indicated by the Baldus study. Accordingly, we hold that the Baldus study is clearly insufficient to support an inference that any of the decisionmakers in McCleskey's case acted with discriminatory purpose.

McCleskey also suggests that the Baldus study proves that the State as a whole has acted with a discriminatory purpose. He appears to argue that the State has violated the Equal Protection Clause by adopting the capital punishment statute and allowing it to remain in force despite its allegedly discriminatory application. But " 'discriminatory purpose' * * * implies more than intent as volition or intent as awareness of consequences. It implies that the decisionmaker, in this case a state legislature, selected or reaffirmed a particular course of action at least in part 'because of,' not merely 'in spite of,' its adverse effects upon an identifiable group." For this claim to prevail, McCleskey would have to prove that the Georgia Legislature enacted or maintained the death penalty statute because of an anticipated racially discriminatory effect. In *Gregg v. Georgia, supra,* this Court found that the Georgia capital sentencing system could operate in a fair and neutral manner. There was no evidence then, and there is none now, that the Georgia Legislature enacted the capital punishment statute to further a racially discriminatory purpose.[20] * * *

---

20. McCleskey relies on "historical evidence" to support his claim of purposeful discrimination by the State. This evidence focuses on Georgia laws in force during and just after the Civil War. Of course, the "historical background of the decision is one evidentiary source" for proof of intentional discrimination. *Arlington Heights v.*

Accordingly, we reject McCleskey's equal protection claims.

McCleskey also argues that the Baldus study demonstrates that the Georgia capital sentencing system violates the Eighth Amendment. * * *

* * * Because McCleskey's sentence was imposed under Georgia sentencing procedures that focus discretion "on the particularized nature of the crime and the particularized characteristics of the individual defendant," *id.* at 206, we lawfully may presume that McCleskey's death sentence was not "wantonly and freakishly" imposed, *id.* at 207, and thus that the sentence is not disproportionate within any recognized meaning under the Eighth Amendment.

Although our decision in [*Gregg v. Georgia*, upholding the constitutionality of capital punishment imposed with certain procedural safeguards] appears to foreclose McCleskey's disproportionality argument, he further contends that the Georgia capital punishment system is arbitrary and capricious in application, and therefore his sentence is excessive, because racial considerations may influence capital sentencing decisions in Georgia. We now address this claim.

To evaluate McCleskey's challenge, we must examine exactly what the Baldus study may show. Even Professor Baldus does not contend that his statistics prove that race enters into any capital sentencing decisions or that race was a factor in McCleskey's particular case. Statistics at most may show only a likelihood that a particular factor entered into some decisions. There is, of course, some risk of racial prejudice influencing a jury's decision in a criminal case. There are similar risks that other kinds of prejudice will influence other criminal trials. The question "is at what point that risk becomes constitutionally unacceptable," McCleskey asks us to accept the likelihood allegedly shown by the Baldus study as the constitutional measure of an unacceptable risk of racial prejudice influencing capital sentencing decisions. This we decline to do.

Because of the risk that the factor of race may enter the criminal justice process, we have engaged in "unceasing efforts" to eradicate racial prejudice from our criminal justice system. Our efforts have been guided by our recognition that "the inestimable privilege of trial by jury * * * is a vital principle, underlying the whole administration of criminal justice." Thus, it is the jury that is a criminal defendant's fundamental "protection of life and liberty against race or color prejudice." Specifically, a capital sentencing jury representative of a criminal defendant's community assures a " 'diffused impartiality,' " in the jury's task of "express[ing] the conscience of the community on the ultimate question of life or death."

Individual jurors bring to their deliberations "qualities of human nature and varieties of human experience, the range of which is un-

---

Metropolitan Housing Dev. Corp., 429 U.S., at 267. But unless historical evidence is reasonably contemporaneous with the challenged decision, it has little probative value. Cf. *Hunter v. Underwood*, 471 U.S. 222, 228–233 (1985) (relying on legislative histo- ry to demonstrate discriminatory motivation behind state statute). Although the history of racial discrimination in this country is undeniable, we cannot accept official actions taken long ago as evidence of current intent.

known and perhaps unknowable." The capital sentencing decision requires the individual jurors to focus their collective judgment on the unique characteristics of a particular criminal defendant. It is not surprising that such collective judgments often are difficult to explain. But the inherent lack of predictability of jury decisions does not justify their condemnation. On the contrary, it is the jury's function to make the difficult and uniquely human judgments that defy codification and that "buil[d] discretion, equity, and flexibility into a legal system."

McCleskey's argument that the Constitution condemns the discretion allowed decisionmakers in the Georgia capital sentencing system is antithetical to the fundamental role of discretion in our criminal justice system. Discretion in the criminal justice system offers substantial benefits to the criminal defendant. Not only can a jury decline to impose the death sentence, it can decline to convict or choose to convict of a lesser offense. Whereas decisions against a defendant's interest may be reversed by the trial judge or on appeal, these discretionary exercises of leniency are final and unreviewable. Similarly, the capacity of prosecutorial discretion to provide individualized justice is "firmly entrenched in American law." As we have noted, a prosecutor can decline to charge, offer a plea bargain, or decline to seek a death sentence in any particular case. Of course, "the power to be lenient [also] is the power to discriminate," but a capital punishment system that did not allow for discretionary acts of leniency "would be totally alien to our notions of criminal justice."

At most, the Baldus study indicates a discrepancy that appears to correlate with race. Apparent disparities in sentencing are an inevitable part of our criminal justice system. The discrepancy indicated by the Baldus study is "a far cry from the major systemic defects identified in *Furman*." As this Court has recognized, any mode for determining guilt or punishment "has its weaknesses and the potential for misuse." Specifically, "there can be 'no perfect procedure for deciding in which cases governmental authority should be used to impose death.' " Despite these imperfections, our consistent rule has been that constitutional guarantees are met when "the mode [for determining guilt or punishment] itself has been surrounded with safeguards to make it as fair as possible." Where the discretion that is fundamental to our criminal process is involved, we decline to assume that what is unexplained is invidious. In light of the safeguards designed to minimize racial bias in the process, the fundamental value of jury trial in our criminal justice system, and the benefits that discretion provides to criminal defendants, we hold that the Baldus study does not demonstrate a constitutionally significant risk of racial bias affecting the Georgia capital sentencing process. * * *

Two additional concerns inform our decision in this case. First, McCleskey's claim, taken to its logical conclusion, throws into serious question the principles that underlie our entire criminal justice system. The Eighth Amendment is not limited in application to capital punishment, but applies to all penalties .. Thus, if we accepted McCleskey's claim that racial bias has impermissibly tainted the capital sentencing decision, we could soon be faced with similar claims as to other types of penalty. Moreover, the claim that his sentence rests on the irrelevant factor of race easily could be extended to apply to claims based on unexplained discrepancies that correlate to membership in other minority groups,[39] and even to gender. Similarly, since McCleskey's claim relates to the race of his victim, other claims could apply with equally logical force to statistical disparities that correlate with the race or sex of other actors in the criminal justice system, such as defense attorneys or judges. Also, there is no logical reason that such a claim need be limited to racial or sexual bias. If arbitrary and capricious punishment is the touchstone under the Eighth Amendment, such a claim could—at least in theory—be based upon any arbitrary variable, such as the defendant's facial characteristics, or the physical attractiveness of the defendant or the victim, that some statistical study indicates may be influential in jury decisionmaking. As these examples illustrate, there is no limiting principle to the type of challenge brought by McCleskey. The Constitution does not require that a State eliminate any demonstrable disparity that correlates with a potentially irrelevant factor in order to operate a criminal justice system that includes capital punishment. As we have stated specifically in the context of capital punishment, the Constitution does not "plac[e] totally unrealistic conditions on its use." *Gregg v. Georgia*, 428 U.S. at 199, n.50.

39. In *Regents of the University of California v. Bakke*, 438 U.S. 265, 295 (1978) (opinion of Powell, J.), we recognized that the national "majority" "is composed of various minority groups, most of which can lay claim to a history of prior discrimination at the hands of the State and private individuals." See *id.*, at 292 (citing *Strauder v. West Virginia*, 100 U.S., at 308 (Celtic Irishmen) (dictum); *Yick Wo v. Hopkins*, 118 U.S. 356 (1886) (Chinese); *Truax v. Raich*, 239 U.S. 33, 36, 41–42 (1915) (Austrian resident aliens); *Korematsu v. United States*, 323 U.S. 214, 216 (1944) (Japanese); *Hernandez v. Texas*, 347 U.S. 475 (1954) (Mexican–Americans)). See also *Uniform Guidelines on Employee Selection Procedures* (1978), 29 CFR § 1607.4(B) (1986) (employer must keep records as to the "following races and ethnic groups: Blacks, American Indians (including Alaskan Natives), Asians (including Pacific Islanders), Hispanics (including persons of Mexican, Puerto Rican, Cuban, Central or South American, or other Spanish origin or culture regardless of race), and whites (Caucasians) other than Hispanics"); U.S. Bureau of the Census, 1980 *Census of the Population*, Vol. 1, ch. B (PC80–1–B), reprinted in 1986 *Statistical Abstract of the United States* 29 (dividing United States population by "race and Spanish origin" into the following groups: White, Black, American Indian, Chinese, Filipino, Japanese, Korean, Vietnamese, Spanish origin, and all other races); U.S. Bureau of the Census, 1980 *Census of the Population, Supplementary Report*, series PC80–S1–10, reprinted in 1986 *Statistical Abstract of the United States* 34 (listing 44 ancestry groups and noting that many individuals reported themselves to belong to multiple ancestry groups).

We also have recognized that the ethnic composition of the Nation is ever shifting. *Crawford v. Board of Ed. of Los Angeles*, 458 U.S. 527 (1982), illustrates demographic facts that we increasingly find in our country, namely, that populations change in composition, and may do so in relatively short timespans. We noted: "In 1968 when the case went to trial, the [Los Angeles] District was 53.6% white, 22.6% black, 20% Hispanic, and 3.8% Asian and other. By October 1980, the demographic composition had altered radically: 23.7% white, 23.3% black, 45.3% Hispanic, and 7.7% Asian and other." *Id.*, at 530, n.1. Increasingly whites are becoming a minority in many of the larger American cities. There appears to be no reason why a white defendant in such a city could not make a claim similar to McCleskey's if racial disparities in sentencing arguably are shown by a statistical study.

Finally, in our heterogeneous society the lower courts have found the boundaries of race and ethnicity increasingly difficult to determine. [Eds. The Court cited lower court decisions in *Shaare Tefila Congregation v. Cobb*, 481 U.S. 615 (1987) and *St. Francis College v. Al-Khazraji*, 481 U.S. 604 (1987) (concluding that Jews and Arabs, respectively, were among the "races" intended to be protected under 42 U.S.C.A. §§ 1981 and 1982).]

Second, McCleskey's arguments are best presented to the legislative bodies. It is not the responsibility—or indeed even the right—of this Court to determine the appropriate punishment for particular crimes. It is the legislatures, the elected representatives of the people, that are "constituted to respond to the will and consequently the moral values of the people." Legislatures also are better qualified to weigh and "evaluate the results of statistical studies in terms of their own local conditions and with a flexibility of approach that is not available to the courts." Capital punishment is now the law in more than two-thirds of our States. It is the ultimate duty of courts to determine on a case-by-case basis whether these laws are applied consistently with the Constitution. Despite McCleskey's wide-ranging arguments that basically challenge the validity of capital punishment in our multiracial society, the only question before us is whether in his case, the law of Georgia was properly applied. We agree with the District Court and the Court of Appeals for the Eleventh Circuit that this was carefully and correctly done in this case. * * *

Accordingly, we affirm the judgment of the Court of Appeals for the Eleventh Circuit.

JUSTICE BRENNAN, with whom JUSTICE MARSHALL joins, and with whom JUSTICE BLACKMUN and JUSTICE STEVENS join in all but Part I, dissenting.

At some point in this case, Warren McCleskey doubtless asked his lawyer whether a jury was likely to sentence him to die. A candid reply to this question would have been disturbing. First, counsel would have to tell McCleskey that few of the details of the crime or of McCleskey's past criminal conduct were more important than the fact that his victim was white. Furthermore, counsel would feel bound to tell McCleskey that defendants charged with killing white victims in Georgia are 4.3 times as likely to be sentenced to death as defendants charged with killing blacks. In addition, frankness would compel the disclosure that it was more likely than not that the race of McCleskey's victim would determine whether he received a death sentence: 6 of every 11 defendants convicted of killing a white person would not have received the death penalty if their victims had been black, while, among defendants with aggravating and mitigating factors comparable to McCleskey's, 20 of every 34 would not have been sentenced to die if their victims had been black. Finally, the assessment would not be complete without the information that cases involving black defendants and white victims are more likely to result in a death sentence than cases featuring any other racial combination of defendant and victim. The story could be told in a variety of ways, but McCleskey could not fail to grasp its essential narrative line: There was a significant chance that race would play a prominent role in determining if he lived or died.

The Court today holds that Warren McCleskey's sentence was constitutionally imposed. It finds no fault in a system in which lawyers must tell their clients that race casts a large shadow on the capital sentencing process. * * *

These adjusted figures are only the most conservative indication of the risk that race will influence the death sentences of defendants in

Georgia. Data unadjusted for the mitigating or aggravating effect of other factors show an even more pronounced disparity by race. The capital sentencing rate for all white-victim cases was almost 11 times greater than the rate for black-victim cases. Furthermore, blacks who kill whites are sentenced to death at nearly 22 times the rate of blacks who kill blacks, and more than 7 times the rate of whites who kill blacks. In addition, prosecutors seek the death penalty for 70% of black defendants with white victims, but for only 15% of black defendants with black victims, and only 19% of white defendants with black victims. Since our decision upholding the Georgia capital sentencing system in *Gregg*, the State has executed seven persons. All of the seven were convicted of killing whites, and six of the seven executed were black. Such execution figures are especially striking in light of the fact that, during the period encompassed by the Baldus study, only 9.2% of Georgia homicides involved black defendants and white victims, while 60.7% involved black victims. * * *

Evaluation of McCleskey's evidence cannot rest solely on the numbers themselves. We must also ask whether the conclusion suggested by those numbers is consonant with our understanding of history and human experience. Georgia's legacy of a race-conscious criminal justice system, as well as this Court's own recognition of the persistent danger that racial attitudes may affect criminal proceedings, indicates that McCleskey's claim is not a fanciful product of mere statistical artifice.

For many years, Georgia operated openly and formally precisely the type of dual system the evidence shows is still effectively in place. The criminal law expressly differentiated between crimes committed by and against blacks and whites, distinctions whose lineage traced back to the time of slavery. During the colonial period, black slaves who killed whites in Georgia, regardless of whether in self-defense or in defense of another, were automatically executed. * * *

This Court has invalidated portions of the Georgia capital sentencing system three times over the past 15 years. The specter of race discrimination was acknowledged by the Court in striking down the Georgia death penalty statute in *Furman*. Justice Douglas cited studies suggesting imposition of the death penalty in racially discriminatory fashion, and found the standardless statutes before the Court "pregnant with discrimination." Justice Marshall pointed to statistics indicating that "Negroes [have been] executed far more often than whites in proportion to their percentage of the population. Studies indicate that while the higher rate of execution among Negroes is partially due to a higher rate of crime, there is evidence of racial discrimination." Although Justice Stewart declined to conclude that racial discrimination had been plainly proved, he stated that "my concurring Brothers have demonstrated that, if any basis can be discerned for the selection of these few to be sentenced to die, it is the constitutionally impermissible basis of race." In dissent, Chief Justice Burger acknowledged that statistics "suggest, at least as a historical matter, that Negroes have been sentenced to death with greater frequency than whites in several States, particularly for the crime of interracial rape." Finally, also in dissent, Justice Powell intimated that an Equal Protection Clause argument would be available for a black "who could demonstrate that members of his race were being singled out for more severe punishment than others charged with the same offense." * * * It is clear that the Court regarded the opportunity for the operation of racial prejudice a particularly troublesome aspect of the unbounded discretion afforded by the Georgia sentencing scheme.

Five years later, the Court struck down the imposition of the death penalty in Georgia for the crime of rape. *Coker v. Georgia*, 433 U.S. 584 (1977). Although the Court did not explicitly mention race, the decision had to have been informed by the specific observations on rape by both the Chief Justice and Justice Powell in *Furman*. Furthermore, evidence submitted to the Court indicated that black men who committed rape, particularly of white women, were considerably more likely to be sentenced to death than white rapists. For instance, by 1977 Georgia had executed 62 men for rape since the Federal Government began compiling statistics in 1930. Of these men, 58 were black and 4 were white.

Three years later, the Court in *Godfrey* found one of the State's statutory aggravating factors unconstitutionally vague, since it resulted in "standardless and unchanneled imposition of death sentences in the uncontrolled discretion of a basically uninstructed jury. * * * Justice Marshall, concurring in the judgment, noted that 'the disgraceful distorting effects of racial discrimination and poverty continue to be painfully visible in the imposition of death sentences.' "

This historical review of Georgia criminal law is not intended as a bill of indictment calling the State to account for past transgressions. Citation of past practices does not justify the automatic condemnation of current ones. But it would be unrealistic to ignore the influence of history in assessing the plausible implications of McCleskey's evidence. "Americans share a historical experience that has resulted in individuals within the culture ubiquitously attaching a significance to race that is irrational and often outside their awareness." Lawrence, *The Id, the Ego, and Equal Protection: Reckoning With Unconscious Racism*, 39 Stan. L. Rev. 327 (1987). As we said in *Rose v. Mitchell*, 443 U.S. 545, 558–559 (1979):

> "We * * * cannot deny that, 114 years after the close of the War Between the States and nearly 100 years after *Strauder*, racial and other forms of discrimination still remain a fact of life, in the administration of justice as in our society as a whole. Perhaps today that discrimination takes a form more subtle than before. But it is not less real or pernicious."

The ongoing influence of history is acknowledged, as the majority observes, by our " 'unceasing efforts' to eradicate racial prejudice from our criminal justice system." These efforts, however, signify not the elimination of the problem but its persistence. Our cases reflect a realization of the myriad of opportunities for racial considerations to influence criminal proceedings: in the exercise of peremptory challenges; in the selection of the grand jury; in the selection of the petit jury; in the exercise of prosecutorial discretion; in the conduct of argument; and in the conscious or unconscious bias of jurors.

The discretion afforded prosecutors and jurors in the Georgia capital sentencing system creates such opportunities. No guidelines govern prosecutorial decisions to seek the death penalty, and Georgia provides juries with no list of aggravating and mitigating factors, nor any standard for balancing them against one another. Once a jury identifies one aggravating factor, it has complete discretion in choosing life or death, and need not articulate its basis for selecting life imprisonment. The Georgia sentencing system therefore provides considerable opportunity for racial considerations, however subtle and unconscious, to influence charging and sentencing decisions. * * *

Considering the race of a defendant or victim in deciding if the death penalty should be imposed is completely at odds with this concern that an individual be evaluated as a unique human being. Decisions influenced by race rest in part on a categorical assessment of the worth of human beings according to color, insensitive to whatever qualities the individuals in question may possess. Enhanced willingness to impose the death sentence on black defendants, or diminished willingness to render such a sentence when blacks are victims, reflects a devaluation of the lives of black persons. When confronted with evidence that race more likely than not plays such a role in a capital sentencing system, it is plainly insufficient to say that the importance of discretion demands that the risk be higher before we will act—for in such a case the very end that discretion is designed to serve is being undermined. * * *

The Court next states that its unwillingness to regard petitioner's evidence as sufficient is based in part on the fear that recognition of McCleskey's claim would open the door to widespread challenges to all aspects of criminal sentencing. Taken on its face, such a statement seems to suggest a fear of too much justice. Yet surely the majority would acknowledge that if striking evidence indicated that other minority groups, or women, or even persons with blond hair, were disproportionately sentenced to death, such a state of affairs would be repugnant to deeply rooted conceptions of fairness. The prospect that there may be more widespread abuse than McCleskey documents may be dismaying, but it does not justify complete abdication of our judicial role. The Constitution was framed fundamentally as a bulwark against governmental power, and preventing the arbitrary administration of punishment is a basic ideal of any society that purports to be governed by the rule of law. * * *

Those whom we would banish from society or from the human community itself often speak in too faint a voice to be heard above society's demand for punishment. It is the particular role of courts to hear these voices, for the Constitution declares that the majoritarian chorus may not alone dictate the conditions of social life. The Court thus fulfills, rather than disrupts, the scheme of separation of powers by closely scrutinizing the imposition of the death penalty, for no decision of a society is more deserving of "sober second thought." * * *

It is tempting to pretend that minorities on death row share a fate in no way connected to our own, that our treatment of them sounds no echoes beyond the chambers in which they die. Such an illusion is ultimately corrosive, for the reverberations of injustice are not so easily confined. "The destinies of the two races in this country are indissolubly linked together," and the way in which we choose those who will die reveals the depth of moral commitment among the living.

The Court's decision today will not change what attorneys in Georgia tell other Warren McCleskeys about their chances of execution. Nothing will soften the harsh message they must convey, nor alter the prospect that race undoubtedly will continue to be a topic of discussion. McCleskey's evidence will not have obtained judicial acceptance, but that will not affect what is said on death row. However many criticisms of today's decision may be rendered, these painful conversations will serve as the most eloquent dissents of all.

Notes and Questions

1. Consider the uses of history in the dissent in *McCleskey*. Consider also the majority's dismissal of history in *McCleskey*. How important is historical context in deciding contemporary issues of constitutional law?

2. Consider the majority's suggestion in *McCleskey* that the multicultural character of the United States, and the dynamic quality of "race," make claims of group racial discrimination difficult, if not impossible, to recognize. Do you agree? For an analysis of other opinions in which the Court seems to suggest that claims of racial discrimination are nonjusticiable because "we are all minorities," see Alexandra Natapoff, *Trouble in Paradise: Equal Protection and the Dilemma of Interminority Group Conflict*, 47 Stan. L. Rev. 1059 (1995).

3. As the majority opinion indicates, statistical evidence is admissible to prove discrimination in Title VII employment cases. Why does the Court reject such evidence in more consequential capital cases?

4. In 1994, the House of Representatives approved the Racial Justice Act, but it was later dropped from the crime bill in conference with the Senate. A 1990 version had met with the same fate. The Act would have permitted defendants to present data raising an inference that the death sentence was imposed with a racial motivation. The Act also specified the process by which the government could rebut the inference. If it was unable to do so, the Act prohibited the imposition of the death penalty. See *Symposium: Violent Crime Control and Law Enforcement Act of 1994*, 20 U. Dayton L. Rev. 557, 653 (1995). See generally Don Edwards & John Conyers, Jr., *The Racial Justice Act—A Simple Matter of Justice*, 20 U. Dayton L. Rev. 699 (1995); Daniel E. Lungren & Mark L. Krotoski, *The Racial Justice Act of 1994—Undermining Enforcement of the Death Penalty Without Promoting Racial Justice*, 20 U. Dayton L. Rev. 655 (1995).

D.   CONCLUSION: JUSTICE OR "JUST US"?

PAUL BUTLER

Affirmative Action and the Criminal Law
68 U. Colo. L. Rev. 841, 843–44, 861–62 (1997).*

[I]n addressing the problems of African Americans, affirmative action largely has been limited to the contexts of education, employment, and voting. Affirmative action has ignored one of the most troubling disparities between the white majority and the black minority in the United States. The purpose of this article is to make the case for affirmative action in criminal law. * * *

I recommend six proposals for affirmative action in criminal law, which I discuss at the end of this article. I suggest that retribution shall not justify punishment of African–American criminals, and that rehabilitation must be the primary justification for their punishment. I recommend that black criminal defendants have majority black juries that are authorized to sentence them. I propose that black people not be sentenced to death for interracial homicide. I recommend that African Americans be arrested, tried, and sentenced for drug crimes only in proportion to their actual commission of those crimes. Finally, I urge, as a goal for the year 2000, a prison population that more accurately reflects the racial diversity of America.

Affirmative action in criminal law is not as radical a proposition as it may initially seem. Within the criminal justice system, some criminal procedures are race conscious; some criminal procedures, moreover, reflect non-racial fairness preferences even when such preferences defeat formal notions of equality. Using affirmative action to correct race-based injuries suffered by African Americans would be consistent with the policies that underlie these procedures. * * *

[D]isproportionate black criminality results from something other than a disproportionate evil in black people. African–American criminality is a predictable response to the United States' historical policy of official hatred of the black race. This hatred is evidenced by slavery and by the subsequent widespread discrimination, whether *de jure* (mainly in the South) or *de facto* (in every part of the country), against black people in every sector of American life, including criminal justice, education, housing, employment, voting rights, health care, and family law.

Affirmative action acknowledges that this grotesque history is responsible for the environment of African Americans, and for their substandard performance under almost every "objective" measure of achievement. When we understand that the explanation for the disproportionate frequency of black crime is environmental, we discern the connection between past discrimination and black criminality. Black criminality—like low standardized test scores, poor grades, depressed wages, and poorly capitalized businesses—is another symptom of the disease of white supremacy. It is a disease that no reasonable person would choose, if she had a choice. Under the affirmative action paradigm, reparations are warranted in criminal law.

MARGARET E. MONTOYA

Of "Subtle Prejudices," White Supremacy, and Affirmative
Action: A Reply to Paul Butler
68 U. Colo. L. Rev. 891, 919–26 (1997).*

I am frankly of two minds about Professor Butler's proposals. I agree with much of his underlying analysis of the inequities of the criminal justice system: People of color are more involved in criminal activity because of the squalor of their living conditions and lack of training or job possibilities. Thus, they are arrested, imprisoned, and sentenced to death in numbers that are greatly disproportional to their representation in the total population, and communities of color are seriously weakened because of this cycling of people in and out of prisons. I also agree that race (and racism) play a significant role in the operation and implementation of the criminal law, including the use of the death penalty. I agree that race-conscious measures are necessary to correct many of these abuses. However, I do not agree that affirmative action can be the legal architecture with which to rebuild the criminal justice system. Thus, Professor Butler and I differ in the means we would employ to accomplish our agreed-upon objective of radically changing the criminal justice system. * * *

Professor Butler explains that he focuses "on African Americans because of their extreme participation in the criminal justice system compared with other groups." I believe his statement reveals a weakness in his understanding of the power of white supremacy.

Professor Butler's claim that African–American criminality is rooted in "the disease of white supremacy" oddly disregards the comparable reality of Latino/a economic deprivation and disproportionate incarceration rates. On January 30, 1997, the *New York Times* carried a front page, top of the fold, article with the following headline: "Hispanic Households Struggle Amid Broad Decline in Income." This article included a graph showing that while the family income of whites increased by 2.2%, and that of African Americans by 9.9% in the period from 1992–1996, the family income of Hispanics, whether American-born or newly arrived, fell by 6.9%. These economic statistics have their unfortunate corollaries in Latino imprisonment rates: The states with the four largest prison populations, California, Texas, New York, and Florida, all have substantial Latino/a populations. Approximately one-third of the prison populations of California and New York are Latino/a, although the percentages of Latinos/as in the general population are 27 percent and 13 percent, respectively.

I am not trying to make a dash for the bottom on behalf of Latinos/as, nor am I taking issue with the fact that African Americans are unconscionably overrepresented in prisons. Instead, I am making a somewhat different point: Race relations in this country are extremely complex. White supremacy is experienced by non-white groups in different ways in different geographic regions under different historical conditions. Professor [Tomás] Almaguer provides a particularly cogent analysis of this complexity. Because the scholarly understanding of "race" has developed in the shadow of the black/white encounter, academics have typically focused on national racial demographics and have overlooked racial dynamics in the American Southwest. He identifies three consequences of this academic oversimplification:

(1) We tend to see "race relations" as a binary and bipolar relationship, a perspective that offers little understanding of what happens when more than two racialized groups are competing; (2) we often view race and class hierarchies as neatly corresponding or symmetrical, as in the prototypical slaveowner/slave relationship; and (3) we generally assume that racializing discourses and practices are derived from or mask other, more fundamental underlying structures such as the class relationship between capital and labor.

Thus, I posit that a multiracial and cross-gendered analysis would reveal structures of subordination within the context of the criminal justice system more accurately than Professor Butler's binary racial construct. Moreover, such an analysis is more consistent with the historicity of "race" and provides a vocabulary that moves us beyond the black/white model that characterizes much of what is written about racial groups.

Notes and Questions

1. Do you agree with Professor Butler? With Professor Montoya? What should be done about the problem of race and crime?

Chapter 14

RESPONSES TO RACISM

The story of how people of all races have resisted oppression is long, complex, and inspiring. That resistance has taken many forms, including outright rebellion and warfare, voting registration drives, nonviolent campaigns, storytelling and counterstorytelling, and filing the lawsuits that became the court decisions in this text. Boycott, protest, demonstration, coalition work, and education have all played roles as well. This variety of methods should not be surprising: Recall how varied and complex are the forms that racialization and racism take (see preceding chapters in this text), and how they change over time. One strategy that might work for one group in one era might fail miserably for another at a different period. No formula allows an easy answer to the question, "How can we combat racism?" except perhaps, "Keep trying."

SECTION 1. THE ROLE OF LAW

Threaded through these methods of resistance and strategies for future action remains an underlying question about the role of law and the legal system. As E.P. Thompson observed:

[P]eople are not as stupid as some structuralist philosophers suppose them to be. They will not be mystified by the first man who puts on a wig. It is inherent in the especial character of law, as a body of rules and procedures, that it shall apply logical criteria with reference to standards of universality and equity. It is true that certain categories of person may be excluded from this logic (as children or slaves), that other categories may be debarred from access to parts of the logic (as women or, for many forms of eighteenth-century law, those without certain kinds of property), and that the poor may often be excluded, through penury, from the law's costly procedures. All this, and more, is true. But if too much of this is true, then the consequences are plainly counterproductive. Most men have a strong sense of justice, at least with regard to their own interests. If the law is evidently partial and unjust, then it will mask nothing, legitimize nothing, contribute nothing to any class's hegemony. The essential precondition for the effectiveness of law, in its function as ideology, is that it shall display an independence from gross manipulation and shall seem to be just. It cannot seem to be so without upholding its own logic and criteria of equity; indeed, on occasion, by actually *being* just.

E.P. Thompson, *Whigs and Hunters: The Origin of the Black Act* 262–263 (1975).*

Do the cases in this casebook suggest that Thompson is correct that on occasion the law must in fact be or appear to be just? Progressive lawyering and organizing seek to push law to live up to its promises. But can they alter the "logic" of law? Can law play a positive role in the struggle against racism?

See Derrick Bell, *Racial Realism*, 24 Conn. L. Rev. 363 (1992), suggesting that the struggle for racial justice will never be won, and that racism, once embedded fully in a society like ours, can never be cast off. One must, nevertheless, struggle against racism; meaning derives from the act of struggle. Do you agree? If so, what is the role of the reform-minded lawyer?

RENNARD STRICKLAND

To Do the Right Thing: Reaffirming Indian Traditions of Justice Under Law
in Rennard Strickland, *Tonto's Revenge* 77–84 (1997).**

No people on the North American continent are more closely identified with law than the Cherokee. Even today, whenever issues of Indian law are joined in the courts, the early nineteenth-century Cherokee removal cases—*Cherokee Nation v. Georgia* and *Worcester v. Georgia*—are cited [see Chapter 3 *supra*]. When the story of the birth of tribal constitutionalism is documented, the Cherokees are listed as the first Indian tribe to adopt a written law and establish a formal constitution. The United States, on the occasion of the two-hundredth anniversary of the U.S. Constitution, acknowledged the contribution of the Iroquoian peoples, of whom the Cherokees are the southernmost tribe. The legal heritage of the wampums entrusted to the Keetoowah begins at the very beginning of life on this continent. It can be said, without equivocation, that the Cherokee are truly a people of law. * * *

From 1808 until 1898 the Cherokee tribe operated tribal courts based upon their own written laws, codes, and constitutions. Throughout the nineteenth century, outside observers who came into the nation chronicled the honesty and efficiency of the system. They also noted that support for Cherokee law was nearly universal among all tribal groups, from fullblood traditionalists to mixed-blood acculturationists. * * * [A]t the beginning of the nineteenth century, the Cherokees cast their fate into the mainstream of the American legal process. Few have done the process greater honor than the Cherokee.

In the struggle to retain their ancestral homes in Georgia in the 1830s, the Cherokee awaited the decision of Chief Justice John Marshall and the Supreme Court. The Marshall Court, in the famous *Worcester v. Georgia*, supported the Cherokee cause and reaffirmed the Cherokee belief in the legal process. Then [President Andrew] Jackson is purported to have issued his famous challenge to the judiciary—"Marshall has made his law, let him enforce it." Marshall and the Cherokees had the law. Jackson had the troops.

With a Supreme Court decision in their favor, fifteen thousand Cherokees were driven by General Winfield Scott and his troops out of their beloved southern mountain homelands. Only eleven thousand finished the journey; four thousand died along the trek, which we know as the "Trail of Tears." This incident * * * vividly illustrates the Indians' historic dilemma. As soon as a tribe adapted to new ways in an effort to survive, the United States, through force of arms or legislation, destroyed what the tribe had done. The pattern was repeated again and again.

At the close of the nineteenth century, the Cherokee and their brother and sister tribes, the Creeks, Chickasaws, Choctaws, and Seminoles, had developed legal systems more just and efficient than most states. They stood ready to accept the dream that their negotiations had held-out—admission to the Union as an Indian state. The Cherokees had moved to a truly well-run, almost a model, court process and now waited for the long-promised Indian state that would culminate their historic compromise. Instead, the United States Congress and the instrument of their creation, the Dawes Commission, divided tribal lands, abolished Indian courts, and attempted to end forever the governing powers of the Indian nations. The Cherokees and the other Civilized Tribes were forced to abandon their Indian State of Sequoyah and were involuntarily merged into the state of Oklahoma.

It is during this dark period that Redbird Smith, the visionary leader of the Keetoowah traditionalists, said:

> My greatest ambition has always been to think right and do right. It is my belief that this is the fulfilling of the law of the Great Creator.... I have always believed the Great Creator had a great design for my people, the Cherokees. I have been taught that from my childhood up and now in my mature manhood I recognize it as a great truth. Our forces have been dissipated by external forces, perhaps it has been just a training, but we must now get together ... and render our contribution to mankind. We are endowed with intelligence, we are industrious, we are loyal, and we are spiritual but we are overlooking the particular Cherokee mission on earth— for no man nor race is endowed with these qualifications without a designed purpose.... Our pride in our ancestral heritage is our great incentive for handing something worthwhile to our posterity. It is this pride in ancestry that makes men strong and loyal for their principle in life.

Surely, it is so. * * *

Nearly a century ago, it did not appear that law, much less the Cherokee Nation and its ancestral heritage, would endure for tribal posterity. In 1898, the clerk of the Cherokee Supreme Court * * * wrote the last entry on the ledger pages of the official record book: The end of the court session and the absence of the Cherokee tribal justices were duly noted. The Supreme Court record book for that final year opens with the federal orders closing Cherokee courts; then the pages are blank. Thus, in 1898, Cherokee courts closed and their formal use of the Cherokee written law summarily ended. Under federal law, Cherokee judges were no longer allowed to enforce their own tribal regulation; indeed, to have held court would have made the judges criminals.

We are here this morning to formally mark the end of that federal interdict and acknowledge the tribal rebirth of the Cherokee court system. * * * In preparation for this speech, I went to the archives of the Oklahoma Historical Society and once again examined the leather-bound volumes which are the official record of the seven Cherokee district courts and the Supreme Court of the Cherokee Nation. I reviewed the court volumes—district by district. It is an impressive judicial lineage, a great ancestral heritage.

As I looked at the faded pages with the flourish of elaborate, handwritten nineteenth-century records of hearings and trials and appeals, I saw, in my mind's eye, that group of Cherokee deputies, in Washington, in January of 1809. And I heard * * * Thomas Jefferson speaking to them about the introduction of what the president called "the regular administration of laws." Jefferson, author of the Declaration of Independence, spoke the following words to the assembled Cherokee delegation: "I sincerely wish you may succeed in your laudable endeavors to save ... your nation, by adopting industrious occupations and government of regular laws."

Less than ninety years later a new president and his federal marshals did not wish the Cherokee Nation well, indeed, they did not wish the Cherokees to continue what Jefferson had urged them to begin. And so, in 1898, the federal government forcibly closed—they believed forever—the ongoing legal system of the Cherokee Nation. We are here, today, celebrating the fact that they were wrong, so very wrong. The Jeffersonian view has prevailed, and the Cherokee Nation is officially following "industrious occupations and government of regular laws."

Today, we are witnessing the opening of another chapter in a heroic story. Students of Indian history are familiar with the triumphant tale of how bands of Cherokees forged themselves into a political state, created their own native alphabet, adopted a written constitution, and ultimately provided political, social, and economic leadership not only for the tribe, but in a new state and for the entire nation. What is not as well understood is that the Cherokees were not an anemic people given only to simple domestic pursuits, but were a tribe of fierce warriors and intrepid hunters whose conquest had given them military dominion over the great heartland of the southern mountain ranges.

That the Cherokees were eventually to be known as one of the "Five Civilized Tribes" is testimony to their ingenuity. The Cherokees believed, paradoxically, that in change was the best hope of survival as an Indian people. Historical proof of the significance of this attitude is found in the testimony of Charles Hicks, a Cherokee chief and one of the earliest advocates of this policy. At the beginning of the nineteenth century, Hicks wrote to the missionary Daniel Sabin Buttrick that abandonment of old ways and adoption of new ones represented "the [tribe's] conviction that their very existence as a people depends upon it."

There is a widely held belief that between 1808 and 1809, under the tutelage of Jefferson and other leaders, the Cherokees dramatically broke with their ancient law ways and passed from a state of "savage" lawlessness to a highly sophisticated, efficiently operating "civilized" system of tribal laws and courts. To anyone familiar with law and the development of legal institutions, this is obviously rhetoric of mythical proportions. The Cherokees did not, as is commonly believed, break all threads of cultural continuity. They built upon their own ancient traditions. In 1808 the tribe drafted the first written law, prohibiting the execution of clan revenge, but this act should not be taken as evidence that all native aspects of tribal law were purged. In fact, Cherokee records affirm that traditional tribal values played, and hopefully will continue to play, a vital role in the development of the Cherokee legal system.

The Cherokee legal experience illustrates that it is possible to retain a tribal worldview within the context of evolving Anglo–Saxon institutions. The result of the creation of a Cherokee constitution and court system, however, was not what Jefferson and the "civilizers" had expected. Instead of a weak carbon copy, an anemic shadow people, the Cherokees emerged as worthy adversaries who demanded that their own Cherokee institutions be respected. The tribe had been schooled in the ways of the white man, but retained their own sense of Indian values, which demanded that they too be extended the rights to which they were entitled by the U.S. Constitution and laws. * * *

The Cherokee experience demonstrates that law is more—much more—than powdered wigs, black robes, leather-bound statutes, silver stars, and blinded ladies with balanced scales. Law is also a Cherokee religious leader listening to the spirit world while holding the sacred wampums in hand, just as it is the Cheyenne Soldier—Society warrior draped in the skin of a wolf. In fact, a command from the spirit world can have greater force as law than the most elaborate of codes devised by the most learned of men. For law is organic. Law is part of a time and a place, the product of a specific time and an actual place. Thus law was to the traditional Cherokee a part of a larger worldview, a command from the spirit world. And it is as such that we must view the law of the Cherokees. * * *

* * * Today, for all Americans, there is a pragmatic as well as a philosophical reason for seeking to find this Cherokee spirit. For that spirit may help redefine the American image, help America rediscover traditional values in this world of change.

How can the nation learn what the Cherokee has to offer? We can begin by teaching the philosophy, religion, art, literature, music, and dance of the Native American. The tribe is already beginning the task of creating such a curriculum. The story of the Indian is the literature of America. It is not trite to say that the Indian sings the song of our forests, of our birds, of our souls. His world is our world. He is of

America. And he is America. Why, indeed, are the tales of the Brothers Grimm, Hans Christian Andersen, and the politically minded Mother Goose a better fare for American children than the friendship of Thunder and the origin of corn?

Notes and Questions

1. Consider Indians' status today. In light of the brutal treatment of Native peoples, are you as optimistic about the role of law and the legal system in society as Strickland is? See Robert A. Williams, *The American Indian in Western Legal Thought: The Discourses of Conquest* (1990); *Linking Arms Together: American Indian Treaty Visions of Law and Peace, 1600–1800* (1997) (pointing out that the U.S. government's treatment of Indians is a nearly continuous chain of broken promises).

2. Does assuming a lawyer's role present special dangers for an Indian? John Rollin Ridge, also known as Yellow Bird, became the first Native American to practice law in California. Rennard Strickland observes:

> Yellow Bird illustrates that being a lawyer makes one no more or less an Indian. It is what one does with the law that matters. Going to law school—indeed, excelling in the law—gives us a tool, nothing more. * * * The message for Indian law and Indian lawyers is that Native peoples must remain true to their own spirit, their own traditions, and their own values. * * * [T]he man will be back, asking you to re-create yourself in yet another image. There is never a last treaty or a last demand. If you change too much, there is little worthy of saving.

Yellow Bird's Song in Rennard Strickland, *Tonto's Revenge* 10–11 (1997).

3. Wilma P. Mankiller served as deputy principal chief of the Cherokee Nation from 1983 to 1985 and principal chief from 1985 to 1995. In Wilma P. Mankiller, *Entering the Twenty–First Century—On Our Own Terms*, she writes:

> In the old days, the Cherokee people believed that the world existed in a precarious balance, and only right or correct actions kept it from tumbling. Wrong actions were believed to disturb the balance. An important part of the balance was harmony and equality between men and women. Cherokee government once was described as "petticoat government" because of the strong influence of women.
>
> Cherokee assimilation into the culture and values of the larger society eventually forced Cherokee women into a secondary role. * * * Unfortunately, by the time I ran in my first election for deputy chief in 1983, our history of balance between men and women seemed to be long forgotten.

In *A Voice of Our Own* 213 (Nancy M. Neuman ed. 1996).*

4. For an appraisal of the "blurred legacy" of twentieth century civil rights statutes, see Linda S. Greene, *Twenty Years of Civil Rights: How Firm A Foundation?*, 37 Rutgers L. Rev. 707 (1985).

5. For a critique of Supreme Court decisionmaking as "veiled majoritarianism" with respect to race, see Girardeau A. Spann, *Pure Politics*, 88 Mich. L. Rev. 1971 (1990).

SECTION 2.   RESISTING WHITE SUPREMACY

BY BOYCOTT AND NON–VIOLENT ACTION

Eight prominent, moderate Alabama clergymen had published an open letter in January calling on Dr. Martin Luther King to allow the battle for integration to continue in the local and federal courts. They warned that nonviolent resistance as supported by Dr. King would incite civil disturbances. King wrote the following classic statement on resisting unjust laws on April 16, 1963, while he was serving a sentence for participating in civil rights demonstrations in Birmingham, Alabama.

MARTIN LUTHER KING, JR.

Letter from a Birmingham Jail
(1963).*

My Dear Fellow Clergymen,

While confined here in the Birmingham city jail, I came across your recent statement calling our present activities "unwise and untimely." * * *

You deplore the demonstrations that are presently taking place in Birmingham. But I am sorry that your statement did not express a similar concern for the conditions that brought the demonstrations into being. I am sure that each of you would want to go beyond the superficial social analyst who looks merely at effects, and does not grapple with underlying causes. I would not hesitate to say that it is unfortunate that so-called demonstrations are taking place in Birmingham at this time, but I would say in more emphatic terms that it is even more unfortunate that the white power structure of this city left the Negro community with no other alternative.

In any nonviolent campaign there are four basic steps: (1) collection of the facts to determine whether injustices are alive, (2) negotiation, (3) self-purification, and (4) direct action. We have gone through all of these steps in Birmingham. There can be no gainsaying of the fact that racial injustice engulfs this community.

Birmingham is probably the most thoroughly segregated city in the United States. Its ugly record of police brutality is known in every section of this country. Its unjust treatment of Negroes in the courts is a notorious reality. There have been more unsolved bombings of Negro homes and churches in Birmingham than any city in this nation. These are the hard, brutal and unbelievable facts. On the basis of these conditions Negro leaders sought to negotiate with the city fathers. But the political leaders consistently refused to engage in good faith negotiation. * * *

* * *So we had no alternative except that of preparing for direct action, whereby we would present our very bodies as a means of laying

our case before the conscience of the local and national community. We were not unmindful of the difficulties involved. So we decided to go through a process of self-purification. We started having workshops on nonviolence and repeatedly asked ourselves the questions, "Are you able to accept blows without retaliating?" "Are you able to endure the ordeals of jail?" We decided to set our direct-action program around the Easter season, realizing that with the exception of Christmas, this was the largest shopping period of the year. Knowing that a strong economic withdrawal program would be the by-product of direct action, we felt that this was the best time to bring pressure on the merchants for the needed changes. * * *

You may well ask, "Why direct action? Why sit-ins, marches, etc.? Isn't negotiation a better path?" You are exactly right in your call for negotiation. Indeed, this is the purpose of direct action. Nonviolent direct action seeks to create such a crisis and establish such creative tension that a community that has constantly refused to negotiate is forced to confront the issue. It seeks so to dramatize the issue that it can no longer be ignored. I just referred to the creation of tension as a part of the work of the nonviolent resister. This may sound rather shocking. But I must confess that I am not afraid of the word *tension*. I have earnestly worked and preached against violent tension, but there is a type of constructive nonviolent tension that is necessary for growth. Just as Socrates felt that it was necessary to create a tension in the mind so that individuals could rise from the bondage of myths and half-truths to the unfettered realm of creative analysis and objective appraisal, we must see the need of having nonviolent gadflies to create the kind of tension in society that will help men to rise from the dark depths of prejudice and racism to the majestic heights of understanding and brotherhood. So the purpose of the direct action is to create a situation so crisis-packed that it will inevitably open the door to negotiation. We, therefore, concur with you in your call for negotiation. Too long has our beloved Southland been bogged down in the tragic attempt to live in monologue rather than dialogue. * * *

We know through painful experience that freedom is never voluntarily given by the oppressor; it must be demanded by the oppressed. Frankly, I have never yet engaged in a direct action movement that was "well-timed," according to the timetable of those who have not suffered unduly from the disease of segregation. For years now I have heard the word "Wait!" It rings in the ear of every Negro with a piercing familiarity. This "Wait" has almost always meant "Never." It has been a tranquilizing thalidomide, relieving the emotional stress for a moment, only to give birth to an ill-formed infant of frustration. We must come to see with the distinguished jurist of yesterday that "justice too long delayed is justice denied." We have waited for more than 340 years for our constitutional and God-given rights. The nations of Asia and Africa are moving with jet-like speed toward the goal of political independence, and we still creep at horse and buggy pace toward the gaining of a cup of coffee at a lunch counter. I guess it is easy for those who have never felt the stinging darts of segregation to say, "Wait." But when you have seen vicious mobs lynch your mothers and fathers at will and drown your sisters and brothers at whim; when you have seen hate-filled policemen curse, kick, brutalize and even kill your black brothers and sisters with impunity; when you see the vast majority of your twenty million Negro brothers smothering in an airtight cage of poverty in the midst of an affluent society; when you suddenly find your tongue twisted and your speech stammering as you seek to explain to your six-year-old daughter why she can't go to the public amusement park that has just been advertised on television, and see the depressing clouds of inferiority begin to form in her little mental sky, and see her begin to distort her little personality by unconsciously developing a bitterness toward white people; when you have to concoct an answer for a five-year-old son asking in agonizing pathos: "Daddy, why do white people treat colored people so mean?"; when you take a cross-country drive and find it necessary to sleep night after night in the uncomfortable corners of your automobile because no motel will accept you; when you are humiliated day in and day out by nagging signs reading "white" and "colored " when your first name becomes "nigger" and your middle name becomes "boy" (however old you are) and your last name becomes "John," and when your wife and mother are never given the respected title "Mrs."; when you are harried by day and haunted by night by the fact that you are a Negro, living constantly at tiptoe stance never quite knowing what to expect next, and plagued with inner fears and outer resentments; when you are forever fighting a degenerating sense of "nobodiness"; then you will understand why we find it difficult to wait. There comes a time when the cup of endurance runs over, and men are no longer willing to be plunged into an abyss of injustice where they experience the blackness of corroding despair. I hope, sirs, you can understand our legitimate and unavoidable impatience.

You express a great deal of anxiety over our willingness to break laws. This is certainly a legitimate concern. Since we so diligently urge people to obey the Supreme Court's decision of 1954 outlawing segregation in the public schools, it is rather strange and paradoxical to find us consciously breaking laws. One may well ask, "How can you advocate breaking some laws and obeying others?" The answer is found in the fact that there are two types of laws: There are *just* and there are *unjust* laws. I would agree with Saint Augustine that "An unjust law is no law at all."

Now what is the difference between the two? How does one determine when a law is just or unjust? A just law is a man-made code that squares with the moral law or the law of God. An unjust law is a code that is out of harmony with the moral law. To put it in the terms of Saint Thomas Aquinas, an unjust law is a human law that is not rooted in eternal and natural law. Any law that uplifts human personality is just. Any law that degrades human personality is unjust. All segregation statutes are unjust because segregation distorts the soul and damages the personality. It gives the segregator a false sense of superiority, and the segregated a false sense of inferiority. To use the words of Martin Buber, the great Jewish philosopher, segregation substitutes an "I-it" relationship for the "I-thou" relationship, and ends up relegating persons to the status of things. So segregation is not only politically, economically and sociologically unsound, but it is morally wrong and sinful. Paul Tillich has said that sin is separation. Isn't segregation an existential expression of man's tragic separation, an expression of his awful estrangement, his terrible sinfulness? So I can urge men to disobey segregation ordinances because they are morally wrong.

Let us turn to a more concrete example of just and unjust laws. An unjust law is a code that a majority inflicts on a minority that is not binding on itself. This is difference made legal. On the other hand a just law is a code that a majority compels a minority to follow that it is willing to follow itself. This is sameness made legal.

Let me give another explanation. An unjust law is a code inflicted upon a minority which that minority had no part in enacting or creating because they did not have the unhampered right to vote. Who can say that the legislature of Alabama which set up the segregation laws was democratically elected? Throughout the state of Alabama all types of conniving methods are used to prevent Negroes from becoming registered voters and there are some counties without a single Negro registered to vote despite the fact that the Negro constitutes a majority of the population. Can any law set up in such a state be considered democratically structured?

There are just a few examples of unjust and just laws. There are some instances when a law is just on its face and unjust in its application. For instance, I was arrested Friday on a charge of parading without a permit. Now there is nothing wrong with an ordinance which requires a permit for a parade, but when the ordinance is used to preserve segregation and to deny citizens the First Amendment privilege of peaceful assembly and peaceful protest, then it becomes unjust.

I hope you can see the distinction I am trying to point out. In no sense do I advocate evading or defying the law as the rabid segregationist would do. This would lead to anarchy. One who breaks an unjust law must do it *openly, lovingly* (not hatefully as the white mothers did in New Orleans when they were seen on television screaming, "nigger, nigger, nigger"), and with a willingness to accept the penalty. I submit that an individual who breaks a law that conscience tells him is unjust, and willingly accepts the penalty by staying in jail to arouse the conscience of the community over its injustice, is in reality expressing the very highest respect for law. * * *

We can never forget that everything Hitler did in Germany was "legal" and everything the Hungarian freedom fighters did in Hungary was "illegal." It was "illegal" to aid and comfort a Jew in Hitler's Germany. But I am sure that if I had lived in Germany during that time I would have aided and comforted my Jewish brothers even though it was illegal. If I lived in a Communist country today where certain principles dear to the Christian faith are suppressed, I believe I would openly advocate disobeying these anti-religious laws. I must make two honest confessions to you, my Christian and Jewish brothers. First, I must confess that over the last few years I have been gravely disappointed with the white moderate. I have almost reached the regrettable conclusion that the Negro's great stumbling block in the stride toward freedom is not the White Citizens Counciler or the Ku Klux Klanner, but the white moderate who is more devoted to "order" than to justice; who prefers a negative peace which is the absence of tension to a positive peace which is the presence of justice; who constantly says, "I agree with you in the goal you seek, but I can't agree with your methods of direct action" who paternalistically feels that he can set the timetable for another man's freedom; who lives by the myth of time and who constantly advised the Negro to wait until a "more convenient season." Shallow understanding from people of good will is more frustrating than absolute misunderstanding from people of ill will. Lukewarm acceptance is much more bewildering than outright rejection.

I had hoped that the white moderate would understand that law and order exist for the purpose of establishing justice, and that when they fail to do this they become dangerously structured dams that block the flow of social progress. I had hoped that the white moderate would understand that the present tension of the South is merely a necessary phase of the transition from an obnoxious negative peace, where the Negro passively accepted his unjust plight, to a substance-filled positive peace, where all men will respect the dignity and worth of human personality. Actually, we who engage in nonviolent direct action are not the creators of tension. We merely bring to the surface the hidden tension that is already alive. We bring it out in the open where it can be seen and dealt with. Like a boil that can never be cured as long as it is covered up but must be opened with all its pus-flowing ugliness to the natural medicines of air and light, injustice must likewise be exposed, with all of the tension its exposing creates, to the light of human conscience and the air of national opinion before it can be cured. * * *

You spoke of our activity in Birmingham as extreme. At first I was rather disappointed that fellow clergymen would see my nonviolent efforts as those of the extremist. I started thinking about the fact that I stand in the middle of two opposing forces in the Negro community. One is a force of complacency made up of Negroes who, as a result of long years of oppression, have been so completely drained of self-respect and a sense of "somebodiness" that they have adjusted to segregation, and, of a few Negroes in the middle class who, because of a degree of academic and economic security, and because at points they profit by segregation, have unconsciously become insensitive to the problems of the masses. The other force is one of bitterness and hatred, and comes perilously close to advocating violence. It is expressed in the various black nationalist groups that are springing up over the nation, the largest and best known being Elijah Muhammad's Muslim movement. This movement is nourished by the contemporary frustration over the continued existence of racial discrimination. It is made up of people who have lost faith in America, who have absolutely repudiated Christianity, and who have concluded that the white man is an incurable "devil." I have tried to stand between these two forces, saying that we need not follow the "do-nothingism" of the complacent or the hatred and despair of the black nationalist. There is the more excellent way of love and nonviolent protest. I'm grateful to God that, through the Negro church, the dimension of nonviolence entered our struggle. If this philosophy had not emerged, I am convinced that by now many streets of the South would be flowing with floods of blood. And I am further convinced that if our white brothers dismiss as "rabble-rousers" and "outside agitators" those of us who are working through the channels of nonviolent direct action and refuse to support our nonviolent efforts, millions of Negroes, out of frustration and despair, will seek solace and security in black nationalist ideologies, a development that will lead inevitably to a frightening racial nightmare.

Oppressed people cannot remain oppressed forever. The urge for freedom will eventually come. This is what happened to the American Negro. Something within has reminded him of his birthright of freedom; something without has reminded him that he can gain it. Consciously and unconsciously, he has been swept in by what the Germans call *Zeitgeist*, and with his black brothers of Africa, and his brown and yellow brothers of Asia, South America and the Caribbean, he is moving with a sense of cosmic urgency toward the promised land of racial justice. Recognizing this vital urge that has engulfed the Negro community, one should readily understand public demonstrations. The Negro has many pent-up resentments and latent frustrations. He has to get them out. So let him march sometime; let him have his prayer pilgrimages to the city hall; understand why he must have sit-ins and freedom rides. If his repressed emotions do not come out in these nonviolent ways, they will come out in ominous expressions of violence. This is not a threat; it is a fact of history. So I have not said to my people "get rid of your discontent." But I have tried to say that this normal and healthy discontent can be channelized through the creative outlet of nonviolent direct action. Now this approach is being dismissed as extremist. I must admit that I was initially disappointed in being so categorized.

But as I continued to think about the matter I gradually gained a bit of satisfaction from being considered an extremist. Was not Jesus an extremist in love—"Love your enemies, bless them that curse you, pray for them that despitefully use you." Was not Amos an extremist for justice—"Let justice roll down like waters and righteousness like a mighty stream." Was not Paul an extremist for the gospel of Jesus Christ—"I bear in my body the marks of the Lord Jesus." Was not Martin Luther an extremist—"Here I stand; I can do none other so help me God." Was not John Bunyan an extremist—"I will stay in jail to the end of my days before I make a butchery of my conscience." Was not Abraham Lincoln an extremist—"This nation cannot survive half slave and half free." Was not Thomas Jefferson an extremist—"We hold these truths to be self-evident, that all men are created equal." So the question is not whether we will be extremist but what kind of extremist will we be. Will we be extremists for hate or will we be extremists for love? Will we be extremists for the preservation of injustice—or will we be extremists for the cause of justice? In that dramatic scene on Calvary's hill, three men were crucified. We must not forget that all three were crucified for the same crime—the crime of extremism. Two were extremists for immorality, and thusly fell below their environment. The other, Jesus Christ, was an extremist for love, truth and goodness, and thereby rose above his environment. So, after all, maybe the South, the nation and the world are in dire need of creative extremists. * * *

I hope the church as a whole will meet the challenge of this decisive hour. But even if the church does not come to the aid of justice, I have no despair about the future. I have no fear about the outcome of our struggle in Birmingham, even if our motives are presently misunderstood. We will reach the goal of freedom in Birmingham and all over the nation, because the goal of America is freedom. Abused and scorned though we may be, our destiny is tied up with the destiny of America. Before the Pilgrims landed at Plymouth we were here. Before the pen of Jefferson etched across the pages of history the majestic words of the Declaration of Independence, we were here. For more than two centuries our foreparents labored in this country without wages; they made cotton king; and they built the homes of their masters in the midst of brutal injustice and shameful humiliation—and yet out of a bottomless vitality they continued to thrive and develop. If the inexpressible cruelties of slavery could not stop us, the opposition we now face will surely fail. We will win our freedom because the sacred heritage of our nation and the eternal will of God are embodied in our echoing demands.

I must close now. But before closing I am impelled to mention one other point in your statement that troubled me profoundly. You warmly commended the Birmingham police force for keeping "order" and "preventing violence." I don't believe you would have so warmly commended the police force if you had seen its angry violent dogs literally biting six unarmed, nonviolent Negroes. I don't believe you would so quickly commend the policemen if you would observe their ugly and inhuman treatment of Negroes here in the city jail; if you would watch them push and curse old Negro women and young Negro girls; if you would see them slap and kick old Negro men and young boys; if you will observe them, as they did on two occasions, refuse to give us food because we wanted to sing our grace together. I'm sorry that I can't join you in your praise for the police department.

It is true that they have been rather disciplined in their public handling of the demonstrators. In this sense they have been rather publicly "nonviolent." But for what purpose? To preserve the evil system of segregation. Over the last few years I have consistently preached that nonviolence demands that the means we use must be as pure as the ends we seek. So I have tried to make it clear that it is wrong to use immoral means to attain moral ends. But now I must affirm that it is just as wrong, or even more so, to use moral means to preserve immoral ends. Maybe Mr. Connor and his policemen have been rather publicly nonviolent, as Chief Pritchett was in Albany, Georgia, but they have used the moral means of nonviolence to maintain the immoral end of flagrant racial injustice. T.S. Eliot has said that there is no greater treason than to do the right deed for the wrong reason.

I wish you had commended the Negro sit-inners and demonstrators of Birmingham for their sublime courage, their willingness to suffer and their amazing discipline in the midst of the most inhuman provocation. One day the South will recognize its real heroes. They will be the James

Merediths, courageously and with a majestic sense of purpose facing jeering and hostile mobs and the agonizing loneliness that characterizes the life of the pioneer. They will be old, oppressed, battered Negro women, symbolized in a seventy-two-year-old woman of Montgomery, Alabama, who rose up with a sense of dignity and with her people decided not to ride the segregated buses, and responded to one who inquired about her tiredness with ungrammatical profundity: "My feet is tired, but my soul is rested." They will be the young high school and college students, young ministers of the gospel and a host of their elders courageously and non-violently sitting-in at lunch counters and willingly going to jail for conscience's sake. One day the South will know that when these disinherited children of God sat down at lunch counters they were in reality standing up for the best in the American dream and the most sacred values in our Judeo–Christian heritage, and thusly, carrying our whole nation back to those great wells of democracy which were dug deep by the Founding Fathers in the formulation of the Constitution and the Declaration of Independence. * * *

Yours for the cause of Peace and Brotherhood,

Martin Luther King, Jr.

Notes and Questions

1. Dr. King states that an unjust law is "out of harmony with the moral law." Is this definition workable in a culturally diverse society? Is his explanation that an unjust law is one inflicted without the consent of the governed a more useful definition?

2. Notice how close Dr. King's definition of an unjust law comes to one of the Supreme Court's rationales for heightened scrutiny of certain laws. See *e.g.*, *Carolene Products v. United States*, 323 U.S. 18, n.4 (1944).

3. Dr. King describes the tension necessary for social change and learning. Have you experienced such tension in the classroom? Was the outcome positive? What, precisely, did you do? See Jerome McCristal Culp, Jr., *Autobiography and Legal Scholarship and Teaching: Finding the Me in the Legal Academy*, 77 Va. L. Rev. 539 (1991) (urging the importance of telling one's own truths in the classroom).

4. How do you, personally, feel about breaking an unjust law? Have you done so? Would you be willing to defend someone like Dr. King, who has? Would you prosecute him?

SECTION 3. COALITION
BERNICE JOHNSON REAGON

Coalition Politics: Turning the Century in Home
Girls: A Black Feminist Anthology
356–368 (Barbara Smith ed. 1983).*

* * * I'm Bernice Reagon. I was born in Georgia, and I'd like to talk about the fact that * * * we'll [soon] turn up another century. I believe that we are positioned to have the opportunity to have something to do

with what makes it into the next century. And the principles of coalition are directly related to that. You don't go into coalition because you just *like* it. The only reason you would consider trying to team up with somebody who could possibly kill you, is because that's the only way you can figure you can stay alive. * * *

We've pretty much come to the end of a time when you can have a space that is "yours only"—just for the people you want to be there. Even when we have our "women-only" festivals, there is no such thing. The fault is not necessarily with the organizers of the gathering. To a large extent it's because we have just finished with that kind of isolating. There is no hiding place. There is nowhere you can go and only be with people who are like you. It's over. Give it up.

Now every once in awhile there is a need for people to try to clean out corners and bar the doors and check everybody who comes in the door, and check what they carry in and say, "Humph, inside this place the only thing we are going to deal with is X or Y or Z." And so only the X's or Y's or Z's get to come in. That place can then become a nurturing place or a very destructive place. Most of the time when people do that, they do it because of the heat of trying to live in this society where being an X or Y or Z is very difficult, to say the least. The people running the society call the shots as if they're still living in one of those little villages, where they kill the ones they don't like or put them in the forest to die. * * * When somebody else is running a society like that, and you are the one who would be put out to die, it gets too hard to stay out in that society all the time. And that's when you find a place, and you try to bar the door and check all the people who come in. You come together to see what you can do about shouldering up all of your energies so that you and your kind can survive.

There is no chance that you can survive by staying *inside* the barred room. That will not be tolerated. The door of the room will just be painted red and then when those who call the shots get ready to clean house, they have easy access to you.

But that space while it lasts should be a nurturing space where you sift out what people are saying about you and decide who you really are. And you take the time to try to construct within yourself and within your community who you would be if you were running society. In fact, in that little barred room where you check everybody at the door, you act out community. * * *

Of course the problem with the experiment is that there ain't nobody in there but folk like you, which by implication means you wouldn't know what to do if you were running it with all of the other people who are out there in the world. Now that's nationalism. I mean it's nurturing, but it is also nationalism. At a certain stage nationalism is crucial to a people if you are going to ever impact as a group in your own interest. Nationalism at another point becomes reactionary because it is totally inadequate for surviving in the world with many peoples.

Sometimes you get comfortable in your little barred room, and you decide you in fact are going to live there and carry out all of your stuff in there. And you gonna take care of everything that needs to be taken care of in the barred room. If you're white and in the barred room and if everybody's white, one of the first things you try to take care of is making sure that people don't think that the barred room is a racist barred room. So you begin to talk about racism and the first thing you do is say, "Well, maybe we better open the door and let some Black folks in the barred room." Then you think, "Well, how we gonna figure out whether they're X's or not?" Because there's nothing in the room but X's. You go down the checklist. You been working a while to sort out who you are, right? So you go down the checklist and say, "If we can find Black folk like that we'll let them in the room." You don't really want Black folks, you are just looking for yourself with a little color to it.

And there are those of us Black folk who are like that. So if you're lucky you can open the door and get one or two. Right? And everything's wonderful. But no matter what, there will be one or two of us who have not bothered to be like you and you know it. We come knocking on your door and say, "Well, you let them in, you let me in too." And we will break your door down trying to get in. As far as we can see we are also X's. Cause you didn't say, "THIS BARRED ROOM IS FOR WHITE X'S ONLY." You just said it was for X's. So everybody who thinks they're an X comes running to get into the room. And because you trying to take care of everything in this room, and you know you're not racist, you get pressed to let us all in.

The first thing that happens is that the room don't feel like the room anymore. And it ain't home no more. It is not a womb no more. And you can't feel comfortable no more. And what happens at that point has to do with trying to do too much in it. You don't do no coalition building in a womb. It's just like trying to get a baby used to taking a drink when they're in your womb. It just don't work too well. Inside the womb you generally are very soft and unshelled. You have no covering. And you have no ability to handle what happens if you start to let folks in who are not like you.

Coalition work is not work done in your home. Coalition work has to be done in the streets. And it is some of the most dangerous work you can do. And you shouldn't look for comfort. Some people will come to a coalition and they rate the success of the coalition on whether or not they feel good when they get there. They're not looking for a coalition; they're looking for a home! They're looking for a bottle with some milk in it and a nipple, which does not happen in a coalition. You don't get a lot of food in a coalition. You don't get fed a lot in a coalition. In a coalition you have to give, and it is different from your home. You can't stay there all the time. You go to the coalition for a few hours and then you go back and take your bottle wherever it is, and then you go back and coalesce some more.

It is very important not to confuse them—home and coalition. * * *

* * * At this festival [Yosemite] they said: Whatever you drink, bring it with you—tea, honey, you know, whatever it is—and we will provide hot water. Now I understand that you got here and there was no hot water. Can't get nothing! That is the nature of coalition. You have to give it all. It is not to feed you; you have to feed it. And it's a monster. It

never gets enough. It always wants more. So you better be sure you got your home someplace for you to go to so that you will not become a martyr to the coalition. Coalition *can* kill people; however, it is not by nature fatal. You do not have to die because you are committed to coalition. I'm not so old, and I don't know nothing else. But you do have to know how to pull back, and you do have to have an old-age perspective. * * *

What would you be like if you had white hair and had not given up your principles? It might be wise as you deal with coalition efforts to think about the possibilities of going for fifty years. It calls for some care. I'm not gonna be suicidal, if I can help it. Sometimes you don't even know you just took a step that could take your head off cause you can't know everything when you start to coalesce with these people who sorta look like you in just one aspect but really they belong to another group. That is really the nature of women. It does not matter at all that biologically we have being women in common. We have been organized to have our primary cultural signals come from some other factors than that we are women. We are not from our base acculturated to be women people, capable of crossing our first people boundaries—Black, White, Indian, etc.

Now if we are the same women from the same people in this barred room, we never notice it. That stuff stays wherever it is. It does not show up until somebody walks into the room who happens to be a woman but really is also somebody else. And then out comes who we really are. And at that point you are not a woman. You are Black or you are Chicana or you are Disabled or you are Racist or you are White. The fact that you are a woman is not important at all and it is not the governing factor to your existence at that moment. I am now talking about bigotry and everybody's got it. I am talking about turning the century with some principles intact. Today wherever women gather together it is not necessarily nurturing. It is coalition building. And if you feel the strain, you may be doing some good work. * * * If coalition is so bad, and so terrible, and so uncomfortable, why is it necessary? That's what you're asking. Because the barred rooms will not be allowed to exist. They will all be wiped out. * * *

Now these little rooms were created by some of the most powerful movements we have seen in this country. I'm going to start with the Civil Rights movement because of course I think that that was the first one in the era we're in. Black folks started it, Black folks did it, so everything you've done politically rests on the efforts of my people— that's my arrogance! Yes, and it's the truth; it's my truth. You can take it or leave it, but that's the way I see it. So once we did what we did, then you've got women, you've got Chicanos, you've got the Native Americans, and you've got homosexuals, and you got all of these people who also got sick of somebody being on their neck. And maybe if they come together, they can do something about it. And I claim all of you as coming from something that made me who I am. You can't tell me that you ain't in the Civil Rights movement. You are in the Civil Rights movement that we created that just rolled up to your door. But it could not stay the same, because if it was gonna stay the same it wouldn't have done you no good. Some of you would not have caught yourself dead near no Black folks walking around talking about freeing themselves from racism and lynching. So by the time our movement got to you it had to sound like something you knew about. * * *

* * * At some point, you cannot be fighting oppression and be oppressed yourself and not feel it. * * * And as you became aware of that you tried to talk to these movement people about how you felt. And they say, "Well let's take that up next week. Because the most important thing now is that Black people are being oppressed and we must work with that." Watch these mono-issue people. They ain't gonna do you no good. I don't care who they are. And there are people who prioritize the cutting line of the struggle. And they say the cutting line is this issue, and more than anything we must move on this issue and that's automatically saying that whatever's bothering you will be put down if you bring it up. You have to watch these folks. Watch these groups that can only deal with one thing at a time. On the other hand, learn about space within coalition. You can't have everybody sitting up there talking about everything that concerns you at the same time or you won't get no place.

There is not going to be the space to continue as we are or as we were. There was a time when folks saw the major movement force coming out of the Black community. Then, the hottest thing became the Native Americans and the next, students' rights and the next, the anti-war movement or whatever. The movement force just rolled around hitting various issues. Now, there were a few people who kept up with many of those issues. *They are very rare.* Anytime you find a person showing up at all of those struggles, and they have some sense of sanity by your definition, not theirs (cause almost everybody thinks they're sane), one, study with them, and two, protect them. They're gonna be in trouble shortly because they are the most visible ones. They hold the key to turning the century with our principles and ideals intact. They can teach you how to cross cultures and not kill yourself. * * *

There is an offensive movement that started in this country in the 60s that is continuing. The reason we are stumbling is that we are at the point where in order to take the next step we've got to do it with some folk we don't care too much about. * * * We must just keep going. The media says that nothing happened in the 70s, and most of us get up on stage and we talk as if that in fact is the case, and it's a lie. The only way it will be true is if you believe them and do not take the next step. Everybody who is in this space at this time belongs here. And it's a good thing if you came. I don't care what you went through or what somebody did to you. Go for yourself. *You* give this weekend everything you can. Because no matter how much of a coalition space this is, it ain't nothing like the coalescing you've got to do tomorrow, and Tuesday and Wednesday, when you really get out there, back into the world: That is ours too.

These festival weekends are places of crisis and you can do wonderful things in a crisis. * * * You go beyond yourself anyway, and you talk about it for years. In fact, that's all you pay attention to: when that great day happen. You go wishing everyday was like that. Everyday ain't like that, and what really counts is not what you do this weekend, but take what this weekend has meant—try to digest it. And first thing, Monday, Tuesday morning at work, before twenty-four hours go around, apply it. And then do it everyday you get up and find yourself alive. Thank you.

Notes and Questions

1. How does the discomfort Bernice Johnson Reagon describes as inherent in coalition work relate to the creative tension described by Dr. Martin Luther King?

2. Consider the next excerpt in which Francisco Valdes considers coalition between critical outsider groups.

FRANCISCO VALDES
*Theorizing "OutCrit" Theories: Comparative Antisubordination Experience and Postsubordination Vision as Jurisprudential Method.**

* * * Postsubordination vision expands this focus [on "different" forms of subordination] beyond experience or struggle to include hope and aspiration as another way of assessing the possibility and design of critical coalitions. This expanded focus asks: Regardless of where we have been, where do we want to go[, and] have we arrived at similar conclusions and aspirations even though we may have traveled different routes to these conclusions and aspirations? Though our hopes and aims partially may be shaped by past and present circumstances, this expanded focus provides a different entry point toward critical coalitions because it asks OutCrits [Eds. OutCrits includes critical outsider groups such as LatCrit, RaceCrit, FemCrit, and Queer theorists.] a different question: Whether we can join forces now due to the hopes or aspirations that we harbor and perhaps share. As such, this focus asks not whether we can travel together based first and foremost on present or past positions, but whether outgroups can work together to arrive at a common destination; rather than prompting outsiders to determine whether our past and present are sufficiently alike to create a common path toward social justice, postsubordination vision prompts us to determine first and foremost whether our destination coordinates are compatible—whether our critical conceptions of substantive social justice match, or can be made to. By shifting the focus to this forward-looking question, postsubordination vision may help coalition-building where backward-looking assessments of sameness and difference may not. Postsubordination vision therefore is best viewed as a complement to, not a substitute for, constructive sameness/difference dialog.

Postsubordination vision also may be useful as OutCrit method because it sometimes is helpful to begin a project by first envisioning as concretely as possible where one wants to be at its end, and then to work back from that vision to plan the journey. And it sometimes is useful to imagine and spell out for one's self (and others) not only what the project is "against" but what it is "for". This utility is magnified when the project or journey is long, controversial, complex or arduous. Because coalitional antisubordination projects and journeys are each of these, and more, critical legal scholars from varied subject positions constructively can begin coalitional OutCrit theorizing by imagining the end goal of our antisubordination activities.

The move to progressive postsubordination vision occasions another possibility for theoretical and political advancement: Postsubordination vision pushes for the linkage of identities to ideas and supports the move from reactive to proactive antisubordination theory and praxis. Plainly, the attainment of a postsubordination society requires RaceCrits, Queer-Crits, LatCrits and other "crits" to expose and dismantle entrenched rules, structures and conditions that breed injustice and inequality. But the composition of postsubordination vision goes beyond critique, beyond unpacking and deconstructing; postsubordination discourse entails artic-ulation of substantive visions about reconstructed social relations and legal fields. By focusing attention on the specific socio-legal character of a postsubordination era, this move encourages identity critiques to go beyond oppositional criticism and to set forth the alternative(s) to the status quo that motivate our work.

Postsubordination vision as jurisprudential method therefore calls for some hard thinking and honest talking about the type of postsubordi-nation society that "we" are struggling toward. This concreteness might reveal difference and produce conflict, as the ongoing LatCrit experiment annually illustrates. But, as the LatCrit experiment also illustrates, this engagement is precisely the crucible that forges progress. To transcend as well as test the limits of past injustices and present practices, CRT's second decade must in part be organized around the need to join LatCrit (and Queer legal) theory in imaginative and productive ways to success-fully articulate, and materially produce, a postsubordination order that actually delivers social justice across the many troubled categories of life and hope that law and policy daily affect.

To that end, the vision I pursue here and elsewhere is a society where "difference" is not only tolerated and accepted but cultivated and celebrated, a society where legal principles and cultural practices accom-modate and affirm, rather than burden or disdain, the public perfor-mance of difference across multiple axes of social and legal personhood. Rather than utopian, this vision seeks to reclaim and apply the demand for human agency and dignity proclaimed stirringly at the founding of this nation, but betrayed since then by the many acts of *de jure* or *de facto* domination and exploitation that have wracked the nation's soul, and that still do. Thus, for legal scholars of whatever affiliation or affinity willing to share and toil for this progressive postsubordination vision, the pressing question is: How do we help to theorize, and thereby help to produce in material terms, this vision?

The means are several, if not numerous, as suggested both by the gains and limits of CRT's first decade: CRT, Queer discourse and LatCrit theory uniformly teach that outsider legal scholars must move beyond single-axis projects, we must rise above essentialist thinking, we must blend theory with practice, we must come together periodically for intellectual and human sustenance, we must engage in careful but caring self-critique, we must remain dedicated to pushing beyond hard-fought gains and despite daunting limits. But a crucial and often-missing link in this array of insights is: To get there from here every one of us must own the struggle against white supremacy, as well as against male supremacy, as well as straight and other supremacies. To realize a progressive vision of social justice for all, I personally must resist oppression in all its permutations and on multiple fronts and levels at once, I personally must resist a single-axis conflation of identity and substance. And so must you. Our common and everyday project must be "fighting for a world where we *all* have seats at the table." Progressive postsubordination vision thus helps to place a premium on a widescale recognition that all of us must own the struggles against all forms of hegemony.

This method and vision thereby can help outsider scholars join forces and build OutCrit solidarity around outgroup struggles that otherwise we might not appreciate as personal—or, at minimum, as linked to our own. Progressive vision can bring into sharp relief the relational and interdependent operation of "different" supremacies, highlighting the importance of *practicing* intersectionality, multiplicity and multidimensionality in consistent and expansive ways to produce social justice. Progressive postsubordination vision can help remove lingering doubts about the importance of critical coalitions by underscoring how "different" forms of hegemony may combine to produce mutually-reinforcing vectors of oppression that mutate in myriad ways time and again to oppose or coopt any effort toward transformation on any front. If OutCrit scholars practice critical legal theory in this way, and if we do so responsibly, insistently, collectively and mutually, our respective and shared visions of a progressive postsubordination order just may help bring us together to decide to build a common table of justice, dignity and prosperity for all.

Notes and Questions

1.　The work of building coalition may be eased by assuring recognition time. As Trina Grillo and Stephanie M. Wildman explain:

> Recognition time is time devoted exclusively to examining one oppression. It may mitigate one problem created when we make analogies to race—the marginalizing and obscuring of racism/white supremacy. Recognition time acknowledges both the need to honor the pain of those oppressed by other *isms*, each in their turn, and the need to allow the oppression being focused on to remain center stage.

> Creating recognition time may not be easy, and it raises problems of its own. An African–American woman law professor who teaches a seminar on women of color and the law has said that she finds it difficult to focus the students on gender issues; they want to stay with race. Why might this happen? If the first filter through which one looks at the world is not acknowledged, one cannot move on to other, perhaps even equally important, filters. When we combine several socially subordinated groups into one discussion (as analogies implicitly do) and do not set aside a distinct time to recognize one specific oppression or another, other than to use them as reference points for an analogy, we create an inability to focus on any one of them. This does not mean that the oppressions are unrelated, but rather, that they must be studied

separately as well as together. To allow these separate and focused recognition times might relax people.

Stephanie M. Wildman with contributions by Margalynne Armstrong, Adrienne D. Davis, and Trina Grillo, *Privilege Revealed: How Invisible Preference Undermines America* 99–100 (1996).*

2. Bernice Johnson Reagon and Francisco Valdes underscore the difficulty of coalition work. Even the best efforts may lead to inter-group conflict between groups seeking to combat white supremacy.

Eric Yamamoto examines a particular case of intergroup dispute, originating at Lowell High School in San Francisco. The NAACP sued the school for race discrimination resulting in a court ordered consent-decree mandating that the school could not admit more than 40 percent of students from any racial group. Chinese–American plaintiffs sued a decade later, challenging the original court order, seeking to compel the school to admit more than 40 percent Chinese Americans, who qualified for admission based on grades and test scores.

Yamamoto observes that the *Ho* case, brought by the Chinese–American plaintiffs, demonstrates

> an intensifying dissociation of law (as it conceives of justice) from racial justice (as it is experienced by racialized groups). *Ho* illuminates three dimensions of this dissociation through its awkward embrace of a constricted civil rights law paradigm: First, the Chinese–American plaintiffs appear to ignore the historical linkage of law and cultural representations to legalized racial oppression. They support their civil rights claims to equality under the law by disparaging other "less deserving" racial groups. Second, they uncritically employ rhetoric and assert claims shaped initially by African–American civil rights struggles and recast later by neoconservative politicians and jurists to undermine minority claims of institutional racism and to sanction white claims of "reverse discrimination." In doing so, the plaintiffs generate confusion and anger among African Americans, Latinos, and other Asian Americans about the purpose of antidiscrimination laws and about *Ho*'s social meaning and impact. Third, and related, the plaintiffs invoke a civil rights paradigm that understands racial conflict narrowly in white-on-black, perpetrator-and-victim terms and fails to account for the unique dimensions of interracial group grievances and to facilitate possibilities for intergroup healing.

Eric K. Yamamoto, *Critical Race Praxis: Race Theory and Political Lawyering Practice in Post-Civil Rights America*, 95 Mich. L. Rev. 821, 828 (1997).**

What might be done about the dissociation Yamamoto describes? Can coalition work provide a solution? What problems might occur in seeking to form coalitions to surmount such differences? Would an analysis that keeps the presence of white privilege foremost help overcome some obstacles?

Yamamoto proposes a "critical race praxis." He describes three implications of such a praxis:

The first is the grounding of justice in concrete racial realities. It requires exploring the experiences of racial communities and locating theory development and application within their antisubordination struggles. The second is the reframing of racial justice claims and court process as cultural performances. This requires rethinking the cultural and communicative dimensions of justice claims, starting with law and emphasizing pragmatic conceptions of justice for racial groups. The third implication is the development of an interracial praxis. This praxis acknowledges continuing white dominance in many spheres of socio-economic life and expands justice inquiry beyond white on black and even white on color to encompass color on color. As part of that inquiry, an interracial praxis explores prospects of intergroup healing and assesses racial group agency and responsibility both enlivened and constrained by multiple contexts.

Id. at 830.

For an extended discussion of interracial conflict management, see Eric K. Yamamoto, *Interracial Justice: Conflict and Reconciliation in Post–Civil Rights America* (1999).

3. An important method to contribute to coalition building is offered by Mari Matsuda who urges those resisting racism and all forms of oppression to look for the links between systems of oppression and to "Ask the other question." Matsuda explains:

When I see something that looks racist, I ask, "Where is the patriarchy in this?" When I see something that looks sexist, I ask, "Where is the heterosexism in this?" When I see something that looks homophobic, I ask, "Where are the class interests in this?" Working in coalition forces us to look for both the obvious and non-obvious relationships of domination, helping us to realize that no form of subordination ever stands alone.

* * * In trying to explain this to my own community, I sometimes try to shake people up by suggesting that patriarchy killed Vincent Chin. Most people think racism killed Vincent Chin. When white men with baseball bats, hurling racist hate speech, beat a man to death, it is obvious that racism is a cause. It is only slightly less obvious, however, when you walk down the aisles of Toys R Us, that little boys grow up in this culture with toys that teach dominance and aggression, while little girls grow up with toys that teach about being pretty, baking, and changing a diaper. And the little boy who is interested in learning how to nurture and play house is called a "sissy." When he is a little older he is called a "f_g." He learns that acceptance for men in this society is premised on rejecting the girl culture and taking on the boy culture, and I believe that this, as much as racism, killed Vincent Chin. I have come to see that homophobia is the disciplinary system that teaches men that they had better talk like 2 Live Crew or someone will think they "aren't real men," and I believe that this homophobia is a cause of rape and violence against women. I have come to see how that same homophobia makes women afraid to choose women, sending them instead into the arms of men who beat them. I have come to see how class oppression creates the same effect, cutting off the chance of economic independence that could free women from dependency upon abusive men.

Mari J. Matsuda, *Beside My Sister, Facing the Enemy: Legal Theory out of Coalition*, 43 Stan. L. Rev. 1183, 1189–90 (1991).*

4. Are all coalitions inherently unstable? If so, what politics follows from that assumption?

5. For an analysis of the sometimes violent discourse between African Americans and Korean Americans, see Reginald Leamon Robinson, *"The Other Against Itself": Deconstructing the Violent Discourse between Korean and African Americans*, 67 S. Cal. L. Rev. 15 (1993).

6. For an analysis of the intergroup conflict between Blacks and Latinos/as, see Bill Piatt, *Black and Brown in America: The Case for Cooperation* (1997).

CHARLES R. LAWRENCE, III

Who Are We? And Why Are We Here?: Doing
*Critical Race Theory in Hard Times***

* * *How do we talk to one another about the hard stuff—sexism, heterosexism, nationalism, class privilege, internalized racism—moving beyond the black/white paradigm and still understanding its special place in the construction of American racism? "Who are we? And why are we here?"

* * *I offer this short and tentative list not as an answer to my question but as a place to begin our conversations. Here is my list:

1. Speaking simple truths to power

2. Making our own communities our first audience

3. Creating homeplace for refuge and hard conversations

4. Defining boundaries (knowing who is us and who is them)

5. Starting small (knowing that small is important and good)

6. Remembering that we are beautiful and that we are bad (or "the bomb")

7. Nurturing the new generation (mentoring and parenting)

* * *

When a member of the audience asked [Roger] Wilkins why the children of middle-class Black folk like him should benefit from affirmative action, he answered, "Because fighting racism in white institutions is hand to hand combat. And if my daughter is among the best trained and most committed freedom fighters, we must have her here with us. We need every warrior we can muster."

These are simple truths, simply said. The dismantling of affirmative action is segregation. Its purpose and meaning are the same as the Jim Crow. We need to call Pete Wilson and Orrin Hatch what they are—old-fashioned segregationists. When our liberal colleagues stand by and

---

wring their hands saying "Now that these measures are law nothing can be done," we need to ask, "Which side are you on?" and tell them we will judge them by the results of their actions. Law faculties determine the standards by which we judge who is qualified to attend our schools, and, if we are unwilling to reexamine measures of merit that replicate white privilege, we must explain our collaboration with segregationists. Just as respectable white folks in Birmingham, Alabama and Jackson, Mississippi were responsible for the bombings and lynchings of the Klan, because they had the power to put a stop to them, we and our colleagues are responsible for the crime that is done by the resegregation of our law schools and that simple truth must be told.

These are truths that have been lost and forgotten amidst the revisionist rhetoric of "color blindness" and "racial preferences." When our colleagues accuse us of "being polemical and lacking balance" or engaging in "identity politics" and "vulgar racial essentialism" or being "radical nihilist" when today's political climate calls for pragmatism and compromise, or when they attack our scholarship as "unanalytic," "unsophisticated," "untruthful," "beyond all reason," and even "anti Semitic," we must know that these are words designed not just to discredit and defame but to intimidate and pressure us to self-censor. I am worried that our enemies have achieved some success in this project, that too often we seek the safety of abstract theory, and avoid the narratives that implicate our colleagues. * * *

Critical Race Theory was born as part of the resistance to retrenchment and it is not surprising that we and our work have been subject to relentless attack throughout the past ten years. We know the colleagues who have established careers and gained name recognition by critical race bashing. More importantly, impugning our ideas and silencing our message is central to the ideological war that is being waged by the right. Most of us live and work in a largely white world, and our work is paid for and judged by a white audience. Powerful white folks have the power to make and enforce law, and it is natural that, as lawyers and law professors, we so often find ourselves speaking to them first and foremost: responding to attacks, seeking to influence legislation, writing articles for white tenure committees, lecturing and writing in venues where few in our audience are colored or poor. This is often important work. Much of it is the hand-to-hand combat that Roger Wilkins spoke of. But I want to suggest that in these times of backlash and retrenchment it is especially important that we find ways to speak to and with the folks from our own communities. * * *

[Lawrence explains that the lack of access to mainstream media has forced us into a reactive posture in conversations about race and racial issues. He urges spending "less time talking to white folks and more to our folks" to foster continuing education. He explains that the best theory evolves from these conversations and within the context of activism with those communities.]

There is much teaching to be done in communities of color, both the teaching of the skills that are denied our children in the public schools (each of us should find a young person to tutor) and the teaching of politics—helping young black people put the lie of their inferiority outside of them, helping men of color understand how patriarchy harms them as well as their sisters, teaching colored professionals the importance of coming out of the closet as beneficiaries of affirmative action.

We would not be here but for the ideologically informed struggles of the communities from which we come, and we will not be here for long if the folks in those communities do not know that they belong here and that they must fight for our inclusion and theirs. * * *

bell hooks * * * has said,

Home, however fragile and tenuous, (the slave hut, the wooden shack), had a radical dimension. Despite the brutal reality of racial apartheid, of domination, one's homeplace was the site where one could freely confront the issue of humanization, where one could resist.

In hard times it is especially important to create homeplaces, safe places among trusted friends to seek refuge and dress the wounds of battle, and also places for hard conversations, where differences can be aired and strategy mapped, where we can struggle with and affirm one another. As we have increased our numbers, it has become more difficult for Critical Race Theory meetings to be a homeplace for us all. From the beginning we have also been about coalition building, and that wondrous musical/political voice Bernice Johnson Reagon has said of coalition: "Coalition work is not done in your home. Coalition work is done in the streets. It is some of the most dangerous work you can do. And you shouldn't look for comfort."

Critical Race Theory has always lived with this tension. Folks have come seeking refuge from hostile workplaces, and often they have encountered the unsafety of coalition building. We have struggled to teach each other about the intersections that gender and race and heterosexism make and to confront our own internalization and participation in those subordinations. Some of us have said, "I am marginalized or made invisible or even dehumanized by this discussion." and we have not always heard them. Inevitably, I will hear gossip about some falling-out or a faction forming, but I take this news of Critical Race conflict as evidence of growing pain. I am reassured that we are alive and not unlike other families. I also believe it is not necessarily a bad thing that, as we grow in number, we form smaller more intimate groups of younger and older, Lat–Crits and queer-race-Crits and mid-Atlantic-women-of-color-crits, homeplaces within a collective too large now to be a homeplace itself. I think this is good because there is some wonderful work that is produced in these smaller groups and because I do not experience them as excluding or divisive. Many of us move freely among them and identify with more than one.

There is another tension that has been with us always. This is the tension between our desire to create a community of kinship and safe harbor for all people of color who self-identify as progressive and our need to define our politics with sufficient clarity to make that politics meaningful and functional. In hard times I think it more important than ever to clearly define who we are and what we stand for. I am not talking about the silly debate over whether certain individuals have been, or should be, barred from attending Critical Race Theory workshops. I am not advocating the adoption of a party platform or the recitation of an apostle's creed. I believe that our work suffers when we are not prepared to engage in serious criticism of ourselves and of one another. But, in a time when we are misrepresented and caricatured by our enemies, when there are people of color who are misogynist, or homophobic or anti-other but still call themselves progressive race-men, we must be clear about what we stand for. We must know who is us and who is them.

What do we do when there is no mass movement, when the river of liberation is not pulling us along in a rushing torrent but only moving in its deep streams? I have been thinking about those who have gone before us, earlier generations of radical teachers who kept the flames of freedom alive in hard times. There is a poster on my office wall at home with a picture of the brothers of the Niagara movement, all in hats. When I look at that picture, I am always struck by what a small group they were. I think of Ida Wells mounting an anti-lynching campaign, almost single-handed at first. In Spike Lee's movie *Four Little Girls,* a retrospective documentary about the infamous Easter Sunday bombing of the Sixteenth Street Church in Birmingham, Alabama, Andy Young, reflecting on the massive civil rights movement that grew in that city so long known for the brutality of its racism, says, "Everybody always thinks of the movement as hundreds and thousands of people marching and going to jail, but when we first came to Birmingham we'd have ten or twelve people show up for a march." In hard times we must continue to be activists. In hard times it is important and necessary and good to start small. * * *

One morning not too long ago Mari Matsuda walked into her office. Scrolling across the screen of her computer in three inch high letters were the words. "Professor Matsuda is the Bomb." Was this a threat or a not so funny practical joke? Had some member of a hate group found a way to write this message on her computer. Thinking it was better to be safe than sorry, Mari called the associate dean and the dean called security. It was the security guard, a young brother, who said, "Professor Matsuda, I think someone is trying to pay you a compliment."

* * *For me this story is not just an artifact of the generation gap. It is a reminder that in hard times it is important to remember that we are "the bomb," or "bad," as we first generation critical race theorists used to say when we were young. Each of you is "the bomb" and collectively we are a nuclear explosion of beauty. * * *

Derrick Bell says that racism is permanent. One thing is for certain, none of us will live long enough to know if he is right. So we're in this fight for the long haul, and Derrick is certainly right when he says we struggle because that is what gives life meaning, that is what gives us joy. I for one am glad I'm in this struggle with all of you.

Notes and Questions

1. Can Lawrence's list provide workable guidelines for engaging in the "long haul" fight against racism? If racism is permanent, how should that

reality influence political decisions about coalition building or about anti-racist work?

2. For further discussion on the difficulty of talking about race and racial issues and the importance of coalition work see Leslie Espinoza & Angela P. Harris, *Afterword: Embracing the Tar–Baby—LatCrit Theory and the Sticky Mess Of Race*, 85 Calif. L. Rev. 1585, 1612 (1997); 10 La Raza L.J. 499, 526 (1998), observing:

> Tension and conflict within and between oppressed racial groups keep us from forming coalitions. Yet, united action is the only hope for effectively changing the vast disparities in wealth between social strata in this country. * * * Race definitions operate to define the "have-nots" and to mask the correlation between race and the "haves."

Id. at 526.

See also Gerald López, *Rebellious Lawyering: One Chicano's Vision of Progressive Law Practice* (1992)(explaining how lawyers can work to empower their clients).

3. Assume that two groups, Blacks and Latinos both want University X to create an ethnic studies department. What, if anything, might be gained by seeking coalition as opposed to working independently to achieve this goal? What stands to be lost?

SECTION 4.   WHITES RESISTING RACISM
RICHARD DELGADO

Rodrigo's Eleventh Chronicle: Empathy and False Empathy
84 Calif. L. Rev. 61, 95–100 (1996).*

"The first role for white folks who would like to be helpful is what Noel Ignatiev and John Garvey call the race traitor. Have you heard of the idea?"

I strained to remember. "I think I have. * * * Tell me how you see the race traitor idea applying to our empathy dilemma."

"White people who want to help can become traitors to the white race. As Ignatiev and Garvey put it, 'Treason to whiteness is loyalty to humanity.' For example, if a white person is in a group of whites and one of them tells a racist joke or story, the white can look up in surprise and say: 'Oh, you must have told that story in front of me because you assumed I am white. I'm not. I'm black. I may look white, but my ancestry is black. And let me tell you why I found that story offensive.' "

"In other words," I said, "they identify with blacks radically and completely, not by imagining how they would feel if they were black, but by identifying themselves with blacks when other whites ask for their help in reinforcing white supremacy."

"Yes," Rodrigo continued. "And that includes rejecting white privilege, so far as a white-looking person is capable of doing that. In dozens of encounters in life, one takes on the role of being, acting, and speaking out as though one were a black—that is, one of us."

"I'm not sure how that is possible," I said. "Could you give me an example?"

"Ignatiev and Garvey themselves give many. Whiteness is a social construct, basically a readiness to accept many privileges that come to you if you look and act a certain way. If you refuse to be white you begin the process of destabilizing this construction that society relies on to preserve the current system of racial subordination. So, suppose a neatly dressed white person, who happens to be a race traitor, is pulled over by a police officer and then let go with a warning. The person ought to question the officer, 'Would you have done this if I had been black?' "

"So whites ought to reject racial privilege and challenge manifestations of racism that they observe."

"Yes. And if enough people do this, the system will collapse, because whites will never be sure which other whites are confederates—are loyal to the white race in the sense of accepting unearned privilege and conspiring tacitly to keep blacks down. The race traitor not only opposes racism but seeks to disrupt its normal functioning, and does so from within. Therein lies the concept's power. The color line is not the work of a few racist individuals but of a system of institutions and practices. Race traitors challenge each of these at every turn: tracking in public schools; location of public housing on the other side of the tracks; so-called meritocratic criteria that firms and institutions rely on unthinkingly, even though they exclude blacks and women. They put their lives on the line." * * *

"A radical proposal, Rodrigo," I said. "I'm not sure many of our white friends would adopt it."

"It does entail a radical commitment," Rodrigo conceded. "But, as I mentioned, if only a small proportion of whites did, it would seriously jeopardize the system of white-over-black hegemony that has reigned in this country for over four hundred years. And the form of identification it would generate would be real. * * *"

"Could a progressive lawyer * * * be a race traitor? Is this a solution to law's confining role?" I asked.

"I'd like to think so," Rodrigo replied. "But I'm skeptical, for all the reasons we just mentioned. Law is structurally biased against empathy. Of course nothing prevents a lawyer from being a race traitor outside his or her work in a law office, nor from using law strategically, from time to time, to advocate the race traitor objective."

"Very interesting, Rodrigo, and it just might work, even if not for lawyers. But I think you said you had a second plan."

"My second plan sounds almost like the opposite of the first, but as you'll see it's not. * * * [It] would envision whites working with whites to lift the yokes of oppression that burden both them and us. [I'm sure you recall] the closing speech by the famous white radical at the recent Critical Legal Studies conference. * * * He described his own upbringing as a member of the ruling class, as he put it—prep school, Harvard, antiwar rebellions, SDS [Eds. Students for a Democratic Society, a radical student group]. He was a creature of the sixties, and when he grew up turned to CLS for inspiration and support."

"He not only turned to Critical Legal Studies, he helped develop it," I interjected. "He was a founding father, helping the new movement carve out such notions as indeterminacy and the theory that law is essentially politics."

"And do you remember what he said, Professor, about his own engagement with racial identity groups?"

"I do. He said he had sided with Black Power and the Panthers, although as a more or less distant cheerleader and fellow traveler. He said quite candidly that he thought he had little role beyond that, and that as a member of the white privileged class he could not do much more, that there is a sort of built-in limitation. Consequently he turned to institutional politics, the politics of daily life, teaching elite law students how to survive in the corporate world and subvert their own offices and institutions. That and deconstructing legal doctrine. * * *"

"But you feel there is more he could have done?"

"Yes. I keep thinking that someone with his charisma and prodigious talent could have done more. All it would have taken would have been a slight shift—a few degrees this way, rather than that."

"And that shift is . . . ," I cajoled.

"I think our famous friend should have devoted himself, at least in part, to working with his own race, that is, with disaffected working-class whites. He could have supplied them with the analyses and leadership that they needed, and at a crucial time. Working-class, blue-collar whites, ethnic whites, and poor Southern whites today are arrayed against minorities. They have turned against us with a vengeance. They are the 'angry white men' who helped bring about the Republican revolution that is setting back the cause of social and racial justice, challenging affirmative action, and demanding the end of welfare to the poor and desperate."

"You are saying that if the famous white radical, and people like him, had stopped flirting with radical chic social movements like the Panthers back in the sixties and gone to preach to their own blue-collar brothers and sisters, we would not be in the fix we are in today?"

"Yes. They might have listened to him. Lower-class whites are not our natural enemies. Quite the contrary. But they think they are. Elite whites neatly use them to deflect attention from their own crass materialism, manipulation, and profits—from the way they maintain unsafe workplaces for the workers; pay bare subsistence wages; phase out factories at the drop of a hat, creating real destitution; and send jobs overseas if it suits their interest, all at the expense of workers."

"So you are saying fancy Crits in elite positions at the top schools aided the Republican revolution and the terrible turn things have taken for our people and for the poor?"

"I am," Rodrigo replied with conviction. "They took the easy way out. Instead of taking their campaign to the factories and lower-class tenement districts, they listened to the Panthers, shivered a little, and went and wrote elegant law review articles about the structure of Western legal thought, mostly for each other's benefit. They abandoned their own people. Empathy—the shallow, chic kind—is always more attractive than responsibility, which is hard work."

"Is it too late?" I asked.

"It's never too late. Look at what Ralph Nader is doing. He's writing for workers in dangerous factories, consumers who buy unsafe products. He communicates effectively. He has a fancy law degree, yet he addresses his message to those who unfortunately have been led to think we are the cause of their economic pain. He's trying to redirect their attention upward, to the corporate elite that is oppressing us all, much as Martin Luther King was preparing to do toward the end of his life, just before he was assassinated. Robert Kennedy, too. Workers and middle-class whites listen to Nader—some of them, at least. There's no reason he should be working at this alone."

Notes and Questions

1. Is it realistic to expect Whites to have a stake in responding to racism? Derrick Bell has suggested that racial progress only occurs when it is in white self-interest. Derrick Bell, Brown v. Board of Education *and the Interest–Convergence Dilemma,* 93 Harv. L. Rev. 518, 524 (1980).

2. Should Whites, seeking to form multi-racial coalitions, follow any rules to guide their conduct?

> Whites do not look at the world through a filter of racial awareness, even though whites, of course, have a race. The power to ignore race, when white is the race, is a privilege, a societal advantage. All whites are the beneficiaries of racism in this use of the term because we gain from systemic white privilege. Generally whites think of racism as voluntary, intentional conduct, done by someone else.

> Whites spend a lot of time trying to persuade ourselves and each other that racism has nothing to do with us. A big step would be for whites to admit that we do benefit from racism and then to consider what to do about it.

Stephanie M. Wildman, Looking Squarely at *"White Bashing,"* S. F. Chron., Feb. 26, 1998 at A21, col.2.*

3. What other methods could Whites use to resist racism? Stephanie M. Wildman gives the advice "Make a friend." Wildman explains:

> The importance of friendship in talking about power systems should not be underestimated. In a class I once taught, an African–American student observed, "white people always ask me what they can do to fight racism. My answer to them is: Make a friend of color as the first step in this long process."

> This advice is important, but I worry about it being misunderstood. For many white people, making a friend of color means they are able to

convince themselves that they must not be racist because they have this trophy friend. Another woman of color I know commented that she has many white friends, but avoids discussing race with them. She is afraid of being hurt by her white friends' small stake in issues of race, when her stake is so large. It is easier for her just to avoid the whole conversation.

Given these difficulties, let me say why I am so taken by this simple, yet serious, advice—"Make a friend." Most of us who are white lead lives that are segregated by race. Race is imprinted on most neighborhood patterns, which means it is replicated in schools. Our lives as straight people are generally segregated by sexual orientation also. * * * The lives we lead affect what we can see and hear in the world around us; but we can perceive more of the world through the experiences of those close to us. So if you make a friend across categories of difference, realize that this means working on listening to what is important to your friend.

Stephanie M. Wildman, with contributions by Margalynne Armstrong, Adrienne D. Davis & Trina Grillo, *Privilege Revealed: How Invisible Preference Undermines America* 3–4 (1996).*

How should a person of color respond to a White who says, "I want to be your friend?"

4. Can friendship be overdone or cloying? Consider the following passage:

When Western Apaches stage joking imitations of Anglo Americans, they portray them as gross incompetents in the conduct of social relations. Judged according to Apache standards for what is normal and "right," the joker's actions are intended to seem extremely peculiar and altogether "wrong." In other words, the image the joker presents of "the Whiteman" is an image of ineffectively guided behavior, of social action gone haywire, of an individual stunningly ignorant of how to comport himself appropriately in public situations. * * *

[In a joke performance by J, who begins with "Hello, my friend!" and continues to use the phrase, "my friend" is] an expression that Apaches think Anglo Americans bandy about in a thoroughly irresponsible way. There is no word in Western Apache that corresponds precisely to the English lexeme *friend*. The nearest equivalent is *schich inzhoni* ("toward me, he is good"), an expression used only by individuals who have known each other for many years and, on the basis of this experience, have developed strong feelings of mutual confidence and respect. In contrast, Apaches note, Anglo Americans refer to and address as "friends" persons they have scarcely met, persisting in this practice even when it is evident from other things they say and do that they hold these individuals in low esteem. More specifically, Whitemen are said to make liberal use of the term when they want something from someone, apparently believing that by professing affection and concern they can improve their chances of getting it. In short, Anglo Americans pretend to what cannot and should not be pretended to—hasty friendship—and it strikes Apaches as the height of folly and presumptuousness that they do. One of my consultants put it succinctly: "Whitemen say you're their friend like it was nothing, like it was air."

Keith H. Basso, *Portraits of "The Whiteman:" Linguistic Play and Cultural Symbols among the Western Apache* 48 (1979).*

SECTION 5. RACIAL HEALING
ERIC K. YAMAMOTO

Race Apologies
1 J. Gender Race & Just. 47, 47–55, 64–67 (1997).**

"S[outh] Africa opens wounds to heal wrongs of [the] past."

* * * [H]ow can racial groups redress historical wrongs inflicted by one group upon the other in order to overcome present-day obstacles to peaceable and productive group interactions? In particular I focus on race apologies—or more encompassingly, apologies and reparations.

Since the United States' 1988 apology to and monetary reparations for Japanese Americans wrongfully interned during World War II, America has experienced a spate of race-related apologies. The apologies range from Congress' apology to indigenous Hawaiians in 1993 for the illegal United States-aided overthrow of the sovereign Hawaiian nation, to the Southern Baptists' apology to African–American church members for the denomination's endorsement of slavery, to the Florida legislature's $2 million reparations to black survivors of government-backed murder and mayhem in the black town of Rosewood, to Ice Cube's apology to Korean–American merchants for his rap "Black Korea" that threatened the burning of Korean stores, to Rutgers University President's apology for indicating that blacks lacked the "genetic background" to perform well on standardized tests, to Senator D'Amato's pseudo-apology for his linguistic mocking of Judge Lance Ito's Japanese ancestry. Several racial justice grievances with pending claims for apologies and reparations include African–American claims for reparations for the harms of slavery, a suit for reparations by Peruvian Japanese abducted from Peru by the United States during World War II and interned in America's concentration camps, and Native Hawaiian claims for reparations from the United States.

These recent past and potential future race apologies in the United States are part of a worldwide phenomenon that includes Queen Elizabeth's apology to and reparations for New Zealand's Maoris for British-initiated nineteenth-century bloody race wars, French President Chirac's recognition of French complicity in the deportation of 76,000 Jews to Nazi concentration camps, the Catholic Church's apology for its assimilationist policy in Australia that contributed to Aborigines' spiritual and cultural destruction, and the Evangelical Lutheran Church of America's apology for founder Martin Luther's damaging anti-Semitism. * * *

While I employ the term race apologies to emphasize race concerns, many of the apologies are also in important respects gendered and class-related. The call for the Japanese government to apologize to and provide reparations for the poor Korean women enslaved and forced into prostitution during the Second World War is an example.

What potential does the wave of race apologies hold for the redress of justice grievances among racial groups in the United States? For, where appropriate, interracial reconciliation? When do apologies lead to meaningful restructuring of intergroup relations? When are they simply masks for continuing status quo oppression? As a beginning response to these questions, I examine in this essay the reparatory efforts of South Africa's Truth and Reconciliation Commission. As the epigraph suggests, the Commission is endeavoring to foster racial reconciliation by healing the wounds of human rights abuses. The Commission's work * * * is relevant to racial groups in the United States who harbor justice grievances against one another while endeavoring to "live together peaceably but also work together politically." * * *

Following the fall of apartheid, Nelson Mandela joined hands with F.W. de Klerk and declared, "Let's forget the past! What's done is done!" Mandela, head of South Africa's new government and former prisoner of de Klerk's white National Party regime, sent a clear message: Reconciliation between whites and blacks is a fundamental first step toward healing historic wounds and rebuilding the nation. Since this optimistic proclamation, the process of interracial healing has lurched forward.

Among his first presidential acts, Mandela signed the Promotion of National Unity and Reconciliation Bill and established the Truth and Reconciliation Commission. Headed by Nobel Peace Laureate Archbishop Desmond Tutu, the seventeen-member Commission includes psychologists, lawyers, and scholars selected by experts and appointed by Mandela. Its staff numbers 150 and its two-year budget is $40 million. The Commission is composed of three committees with distinct but related functions: The first function is to investigate gross violations of human rights; the second, to consider amnesty for those who confess to political crimes; and the third, to recommend nonmonetary reparations for victims.

According to Justice Minister Dullah Omar, an author of the Reconciliation Bill, the Commission's larger task is to initiate a healing process that fosters genuine reconciliation between the races. "There is a need for understanding, but not for vengeance, a need for reparation, but not for retaliation." Commission proponents believe that healing is achievable and that South African society can move beyond apartheid if those who inflicted racial wounds acknowledge the suffering they wrought and accept appropriate responsibility. The Commission's work is deemed especially important by many in light of the perceived failure of the current South African courts and criminal laws to bring apartheid abusers to justice—as evidenced by the recent acquittal of former apartheid Defense Minister Magnus Malan and others on charges of ordering a massacre in a black township.

A first step in the Commission's process is storytelling by those physically and emotionally scarred. For Archbishop Tutu, the catharsis of personal storytelling is as necessary to South Africa's healing as the broader legal and governmental changes: "The consequences of apartheid cannot be wiped away simply by democratic decisionmaking structures or even by large sums of money for housing, education, health, and job creation." Saths Cooper, director of the Family Institute in Johannesburg, agrees, maintaining that "a broad commission allowing the victims to articulate their suffering is essential for reconciliation. 'The degree of hurt, bitterness, and anger is still palpable. . . . No amount of legislation will remove that.'"

A second step in the Commission's process is acknowledgment of harm by wrongdoers. The Commission "hopes to encourage political criminals on all sides to confess in detail to their acts." Criminal confessions are fostered by assurances of amnesty, offering "perpetrators of human-rights abuses a kind of giant national plea bargain." Their stories and apologies, Commission proponents hope, will lead to a sense of closure for those who suffered. Commission supporters believe that perpetrator storytelling and amnesty will also prevent protracted litigation and adversarialness in reconstructing the nation.

In light of storytelling by both perpetrators and those suffering, Archbishop Tutu echoes Justice Minister Omar's view of the Commission and emphasizes that the Commission's goal is reconciliation, not retribution. Telling stories is a beginning step toward forgiveness, and therefore, nation-building: "It's realpolitik, this forgiveness thing. It's not just something in the realm of religion or the spiritual. If [retributive] justice is your last word, you've had it. You've got to go beyond it." According to Tutu, retributive justice is "largely Western. . . . The justice we hope for is restorative of the dignity of the people." This kind of restorative justice is reflective of the African notion of *ubuntu*, or interconnectedness. Ubuntu is the idea that no one can be healthy when the community is sick: "Ubuntu says I am human only because you are human. If I undermine your humanity, I dehumanise myself." It characterizes justice as community restoration—the rebuilding of the community to include those harmed or formerly excluded.

Contrary to critics' initial fears, the Commission's work has not opened the floodgates to demands for revenge or exorbitant compensation. Some participants appear satisfied in having their suffering acknowledged. * * * [H]owever, others worry about "empty apologies"— that storytelling about personal trauma and words of apology alone are unlikely to be enough to engender meaningful reconciliation. Those who suffered need to perceive an apology as complete and sincere, with the former aggressors recognizing the historical roots of present hurts and accepting responsibility for the harm inflicted. For many, the acknowledgment and the apology must also be accompanied by meaningful social, structural and attitudinal changes. These dimensions of reconciliation are part of what I have elsewhere termed interracial justice.

The approach to interracial justice I am developing does not present a universal theory of justice so much as offer a way to inquire into, ruminate on and act upon real-life intergroup tensions marked both by conflict and underlying hostility and by a desire for peaceable and productive relations. My specific focus is on justice grievances among communities of color, although I believe the approach has broader implications. It reflects a praxis approach to intergroup conflict where participants, at some deep level, desire to move toward the establishment of "right relationships" or the restoration of "broken relationships."

Interracial justice thus embraces antisubordination principles and draws upon concepts of healing from several different disciplines, including law, theology, social psychology, political theory, and indigenous practices. In appropriate situations, interracial justice may assist groups seeking to rethink alliances by bridging the chasm between presently-felt racial wounds and the establishment or restoration of workable intergroup relations. As a praxis approach, interracial justice suggests inquiry and action in four related areas—acknowledgment, affirmative efforts, material change and reframing.

Briefly stated, acknowledgment is comprised of three facets. First, it asks racial groups to recognize and, if needed, jointly reconstruct the historic basis for current disabling racial constraints and resultant human suffering. Second, it asks the groups to recognize their respective agency in and responsibility for the imposition of those constraints. Sometimes the line between perpetrators and victims is clearly marked, in which event, group responsibility for racial harms is easily attributable. At other times the line blurs according to changing circumstances— some groups simultaneously are oppressed in certain situations and oppressive in others—in which event, thoughtful critical socio-legal analysis of group agency and responsibility is in order. Finally, acknowledgment asks both groups to accept responsibility for healing so that the groups can begin to address historical antipathies undermining contemporary relations. Acknowledgment is akin to the first step in healing a festering wound; the wound must be carefully and realistically assessed for the infection to be properly treated.

In some circumstances, acknowledgment of responsibility for a racial group's historical wounds may itself be enough to foster healing. In other instances, something more may be needed because "repentance without restitution is empty." That something more is addressed by the second area of interracial justice inquiry: affirmative efforts. This area is performative. It entails cleansing the wound and treating the infection. It means acting upon acknowledgments about disabling group constraints and constrained, yet extant, group agency and responsibility. It means mutual performance, often in the form of an apology and reparations and corresponding forgiveness. Affirmative efforts mean moving beyond acknowledgments and reaching out to heal the hurt with purposeful actions.

The third area of inquiry is material change in intergroup relations. It reflects the consequences of acknowledgments and affirmative efforts. It signals a change both in group attitudes and relational structure. Change occurs after, or sometimes during, the assessment of historical injuries and the undertaking of affirmative efforts, when groups begin to rearticulate identities and restructure intergroup interactions. Material change reflects, on one level, acceptance and forgiveness and, on another level, institutional restructuring and the redistribution of group power.

The fourth area of interracial justice inquiry is reframing. At this stage of healing, the groups together begin to weave a new narrative about their relationship. This new narrative speaks not only to a joint reconstruction of history. It also speaks to a transformation of the relationship in terms of both the ways the groups characterize one another and their mutual commitment to antisubordination in future interactions. * * *

* * * [T]he interracial justice approach reveals that while an apology is seemingly a necessary step toward reconciliation, it is only one step in an inexact, difficult process. If those with power intend to retain power over the "other" and exercise attendant privileges, then no apology will lead to reconciliation. Repairing the damaged relationship between the racial groups "requires that the victimizers accept responsibility for their acts or those of their predecessor governments and people, recognize [and act upon] the injustice done, and in some way ask forgiveness of the victims."

Interracial reconciliation is a messy, complex process. The interracial justice areas of inquiry—acknowledgment, affirmative efforts, material change and reframing—are rarely ascertainable in an orderly or predictable way. What is clear, however, is that all four dimensions of interracial justice are significant to the process of interracial reconciliation. Without careful attention to each dimension, even where all groups share the same ultimate goal of interracial healing, old enmities will continue to smolder until some external force causes them to re-ignite.

Theologian Donald Shriver notes the "pertinence of all sides of a forgiving-forgiven transaction in present and future South African politics." South Africans, he says, believe:

> the white government and the white citizens of their country . . . must make public apology for the sins of racism; there must soon be some tangible restitution for its deep damage to millions of human lives; the country must begin to fashion for itself a pluralistic political culture that sustains both difference and connection between diverse groups of its population; and it must do so with due haste—it does not have forever to recover from its collective misdeeds if it is to save its collective humanity.

How will the Commission's work play out over time? What will be the long-term effect of the apologies elicited by the Commission? What lessons lie for contemplated race apology strategies in the United States? How can we assess and evaluate? As mentioned, the answers to these questions are wide open. Despite the Commission's success in fostering public acknowledgment of survivor suffering, and perhaps in light of its difficulty in procuring consistently meaningful confessions, the Commission's work still meets with strong criticism from both ends of the philosophical spectrum.

Some argue that the public airing of old hurts serves only to stir resentment and impede reconciliation. David Walsh, professor of political studies at the University of Cape Town, shares this view: "If anything, it's had the reverse effect. I see no signs of the truth, followed by catharsis, followed by healing. I think that is the sheerest mythology."

Instead, he and others believe that the storytelling forces open old wounds and interrupts their healing. Apartheid hurt South Africans of all colors, they argue. In the interest of peace, all citizens of the new society should simply forget the past and focus on immediate, concrete concerns about employment, education, and the like. Some take the "forget and forgive" argument a step further. They assert that every white South African who benefitted from white privilege under apartheid shares some responsibility for the suffering it caused. Given such universal white culpability, it is practically impossible to bring every individual "responsible" for apartheid to justice. And since justice is an impossibility, they argue, the goal should simply be peace. At the other end of the spectrum, some argue that peace is impossible without justice, and justice is impossible without reparations and a change in attitude and behavior on the part of former oppressors. Churchill Mxenge, the brother of Griffith Mxenge, a prominent ANC lawyer who was murdered during the apartheid era, argues that "people who are hurt and bleeding [cannot] simply . . . forget about their wounds and forget about justice. . . . [T]hat is not normal. That doesn't happen. Unless justice [in the courts] is done it's difficult for any person to think of forgiving." A South African reporter similarly observed, "precisely because reconciliation has not been earned, it functions as nothing more than a bandage that splits as soon as there is any pressure applied to it."

Meager white involvement in the Commission's work has heightened this "split bandage" view. While black spectators pack each hearing, white attendance reportedly is sparse. Many whites apparently perceive the Commission and its work as a "black thing" that does not affect them. Alex Boraine, Deputy Chairman of the Commission, warned that white South Africans' "disappointingly poor" participation could impede national healing.

What is evident at this stage of the Commission's work is that no collective reframing of "what happened," "who is responsible," and "how we are to get on with a new South Africa" has emerged. No new societal narrative has been fashioned yet acknowledging the past and transforming it into a foundation for the future. As Donald Shriver observes about the Commission's work, and as the interracial justice approach offered here suggests, reconciliation through framing of a new societal narrative requires more than survivor storytelling and incomplete apologies. When those suffering see material change in societal attitudes and institutional structure, when some form of meaningful reparations is forthcoming, then in new South Africa those long disenfranchised may sense a kind of justice that contributes to intergroup healing, to restoring the community—ubuntu.

Notes and Questions

1. Could a truth commission approach work in the United States? Is an apology, unaccompanied by concrete reparations, such as monetary payment, hollow? Would meaningful dialogue about race be a prerequisite to its success?

2.   The *San Francisco Chronicle* ran a special Sunday section on race, in order to foster such dialogue. Consider this follow-up column by Joan Ryan, *A Few Home Truths About Race*, S. F. Chron., Oct 4, 1998 at Zone 1.*

Two weeks ago, in our special Sunday issue on race, I invited readers to share their views on how "to instill in our children the ideal that color doesn't matter."

The response has made me feel frighteningly stupid (an emotion always close to the surface anyway)—but also uplifted. Reading the letters and e-mails was like sitting in on the kind of frank and unvarnished discussion you hear at family dinner tables, where the real-life issues of the world are hashed out.

Of course color matters, readers said. "I get angry with all this talk about our having achieved a color-blind society," wrote one Chinese–American man with two children. "I feel that is a lie that really just sets up people of color to work harder at an unachievable goal.... Color-blind means we all have to pretend that we can be white ..."

An African–American woman with a 12–year-old son wrote: "You posed the wrong question. I've often thought that this premise ... is at the core of the problem of race relations. Color matters, because it's who we are."

Another African American, a 32–year-old man in Berkeley, wrote: "Being told (by my parents) that 'People are people' was not helpful when I was consistently receiving the message from others that I was, in fact, different."

A Japanese–American woman pointed out that kids "have enough brains to look around and see that we live in a white-dominated society. It's important," she says, to "give children the vocabulary for naming what they see, so that racial hurts are not locked away inside them in silence."

Many also felt I gave my son a bad answer when, as we read a book about Abraham Lincoln, he wanted to know why people were slaves. I told him that white Americans used their power and prejudice to enslave blacks for free labor.

"You taught him it's better to be white than to be black. I would have been ashamed to do that to my kids," wrote one.

Others said I should have explained that slavery is not a uniquely American horror. "Tell your son that other people of different skin colors have also been held in slavery over history," one man said.

Another wrote: "Slavery, you might have said, is a bad thing no matter who does it. In this way, you would have put the focus where it belongs: on slavery (rather than race)."

One father in Sonoma said I could have broadened the discussion from slavery to oppression. "Kids understand that the powerful take advantage of the less powerful—they see it in the schoolyard and in the playing fields. It was more important for us that our kids understand they should never allow themselves to be oppressors.... The virtue we hoped to instill was compassion."

Several parents said they tried to teach their children racial tolerance by moving into racially diverse neighborhoods and sending their children to diverse schools. "Then we raised them with the Golden Rule, simply to treat all people as they would like to be treated," wrote a mother in Berkeley.

A white Oakland mother of two who is married to an African–Caribbean man says the key is to talk. When her daughters asked why flesh-colored Band-aids didn't come in their "cafe au lait" skin color and why the good people on TV were white and the bad people weren't, "we discussed it so that it wouldn't become some kind of shameful secret." "When our daughters were very young," the mother wrote, "we told them that people are like the flowers in the garden. They all come in different colors, and no color is better than any other."

Thanks for the lessons.

What race do you think the "father in Sonoma" is? Why isn't his race made explicit, when other races in the article are expressly mentioned? Should noticing race be part of a strategy of seeking meaningful discourse? Can we keep ourselves from noticing?

HARLON L. DALTON

Racial Healing
206–210, 222–234 (1995).*

It is high time we began a frank and open dialogue with the folks with whom we share the bottom of the hill. For too long we have viewed other people of color primarily as rivals for "the crumbs that fall from the master's table." Occasionally, we have sought to unite with them around common interests as we define them, but it doesn't take much for us to lapse back into a thinly disguised free-for-all. At best, we tend to ignore the rest of the rainbow, despite the efforts of Jesse Jackson and a few others to build bridges. It is remarkable how little we know about other people of color. We, and they, have been so fixated on our relationships with White America that we have failed to engage each other.

But there is more to the story than just externally forged rivalry and massive disengagement. Many Black folk are sincerely of the view that we *deserve* more from society than do other people of color. First off, we are entitled to special treatment because we are America's largest racial minority. Needless to say, this claim is a bit inconvenient in places like Miami and Los Angeles, and will be untrue across the board in forty years or so. More fundamentally, the logic of the claim is far from self-evident. In fact, a pretty decent argument can be made that the larger a group is, the less protection it needs from majority tyranny. Then there is the view that we are entitled to special consideration because we have been standing in line longer than anyone else. If you don't count Native Americans. On the other hand, we may have gained certain advantages by being here first, not least of which is that we have had plenty of time to figure out how to work the system.

One of our favorite trumps is that, unlike other people of color, we were brought to America's shores involuntarily. The implication is that the horrors of the middle passage and the unseemliness of our having been kidnaped or purchased entitle us to a special measure of solicitude and respect. (Once again, we conveniently leave out Native Americans, who hopelessly complicate the picture.) However, the difficulty with relying on our forced importation is that no African American living today came by slave ship, and neither did any of our parents. Nor is it exactly the case that most Latinos and Asian Americans arrived on the *QE 2*. To take just one contemporary example, several times in recent years vessels teeming with Chinese asylum seekers have made it to our shores. The circumstances of their passage have proved horrific, and we have learned to our dismay that these would-be Americans often were indentured to the people who arranged for their escape. True, the United States government was not implicated in their exploitation (by, for example, facilitating trafficking in human beings), but that fact did not make the new arrival's voyage any more pleasant.

We also invoke the experience of slavery and its grim aftermath as a basis for favoring us over other people of color. We have suffered the greatest deprivation, historically, and therefore deserve the most in reparations. That may well be a legitimate argument, assuming there are reparations to be had. But the truth is that most of us are not in any position to draw meaningful comparisons. We are largely ignorant of the history of other people of color. Most Black people know very little, for example, about coolie labor laws, about the slavery-like conditions of many migrant labor camps, or about the Trail of Tears, the forced relocation of the Cherokee Nation during which a fourth of the population died.

Nor do we fare much better when we glibly assert that in contemporary America, Blacks are worse off than other people of color. Most of us know very little about Laotian, Bangladeshi, or other Asian–American communities that are visibly struggling to survive. And even though we do know that many Latinos and Native Americans are having a hard time of it, we conveniently forget that fact when we are trying to stay at the front of the parade of color. Finally, we aren't above playing the nativist card. We deserve to be elevated above Asian Americans and Latinos because we are more truly American than they. After all, English is our native tongue. We go back several generations. Although our distant African heritage is important to us, we owe no allegiance to any other country. Of course, in trading on the fact that many Whites view Asian Americans and Latinos as foreign even if they are American-born, we implicitly recognize that at least in that respect they are worse off than we are.

Quite apart from our sense that we are more deserving than other people of color, Black people tend to resent what we often perceive as the unfair advantages possessed by other people of color. In particular, many Blacks believe that Latinos are more "acceptable" to White society by virtue of their lighter color (on average). I am reminded of a ditty I often heard as a child. "If you are white, you're all right. If you're brown, stick around. If you're black, stay back." Although this bit of wisdom was usually offered as a commentary on color consciousness *within* the Black community, it captures our sense of external color consciousness as well. Many of us also begrudge Asian Americans their relative success in commerce and in the classroom. We discount their effort and determination and cast about for less attractive explanation. Even if we do not resent them directly, we take justifiable umbrage at the fact that the accomplishments of Asian Americans are constantly flung in our faces by White folk bent on mischief. More generally, we are not happy at the prospect of being leapfrogged by groups we thought were beneath us or at best beside us in the pecking order. And we truly get perturbed when we sense that the new kids on the block disdain or disrespect us.

Our resentment frequently expresses itself in a lack of charity. Too often we speak of Korean–American and Asian–Indian merchants in the same unflattering terms we employed to describe Jewish shopkeepers thirty years ago. Many of our stand-up comics seem to think that burlesquing an Asian accent is a clever thing to do, and too often their audiences reward them with laughter. We take perverse pleasure in the fact that many Latinos have to struggle at least as much as we do. We give Native Americans a break, partly because we are more aware of their oppression, but in large part because we do not ordinarily consider them a threat to us.

It is critically important for Black folk to own up to these sentiments and to question our assumptions and beliefs about other communities of color. It is also important for Latinos, Asian Americans, and Native Americans to engage us around these issues and to put their own stuff on the table as well. If we do not explore the real differences that exist among us, we will never discover what we truly have in common. We cannot in good conscience insist that White folk take up the cause of racial justice if we are not equally willing to struggle with the issues of pecking order and bias among ourselves. And as we head into a century in which we collectively will become the majority, we need to make sure that we develop new patterns of relating so that we do [not] become enmeshed in an even more complex version of king of the hill. * * *

In my version of the Promised Land, I would not eliminate race, but I would eliminate the pecking order to which it is so closely tied. I have no idea what meaning, if any, race would acquire once it was detached from issues of privilege and power. That is rather like asking whether men would still be from Mars and women from Venus if gender hierarchy were eliminated. But for now at least, I would be happy to just let it evolve. I would also take steps to undo at least some of the continuing effects of historical racial privileging, in part to level the playing field and in part to reduce the likelihood that the pecking order would simply reassert itself. In the absence of a racial hierarchy, I would not be bothered by the existence of predominantly White, partially Asian–American symphony orchestras. I'd be perfectly happy to have the NBA remain predominantly black (though if there are any more John Stocktons or Dan Majerles out there, bring 'em on) and the NHL close to lily white. And I certainly wouldn't want every neighborhood, schoolroom, and workplace in America to resemble a racial and ethnic Noah's Ark. On the other hand, the composition of the Senate would have to change dramatically. If it did not do so through the normal electoral process, I would question seriously whether we had succeeded in uncoupling race and power.

Which bring us to the heart of the matter: How *do* we uncouple race and power? How do we dismantle the pecking order? Let me begin by saying that I share Derrick Bell's conviction that racial progress for Blacks (and, I would add, for other people of color) is achieved only when Whites view it as serving their own interests as well. So it all boils down to whether it is in White people's perceived interest to dismantle the pecking order.

Putting the question of perception to the side for a moment, I do believe that racial justice *is* in White people's self-interest. People of color are not alone in suffering psychically from the racial status quo. White folk expend enormous amounts of energy justifying the awkward persistence of racial disparities in America, hiding from the reality of White skin privilege, and masking even from themselves the ways in which it operates. For over two hundred years we have struggled with the contradiction between our nation's commitment to true equality and the reality of racial stratification. It would be a great relief for all concerned to resolve that contradiction in favor of our national ideals.

Less loftily, it is fast becoming evident that attitudes and practices that inhibit a large chunk of the population from fulfilling its potential are a luxury this country can no longer afford. If America is to maintain its exalted position in a highly competitive world economy, she will need to unshackle all of her citizens. Even less loftily given the fact that in little more than a generation Whites will likely become a racial minority in America, they would be well advised to firmly establish, in practice as well as theory, the principle that systematically disadvantaging people on the basis of race is illegitimate.

It is one thing for me to believe this. It is quite another for White Americans across the board to embrace the notion that dismantling racial hierarchy is in their best interest. Perhaps it is the Pollyanna in me, or simply the part that needs a shore in sight, but I genuinely believe that this too is possible. White folk *can* see the light. But first they must work through their fears about what a brave new world would actually feel like and be like. When they are consumed by fear or paralyzed by uncertainty, people often do not do what is good for them. Ask anyone who is stuck in a relationship that she knows isn't working for her. So even granting that there are rewards aplenty to be gained from transforming race relations, a huge question remains: If we go that way, what will our lives be like? * * *

The key to taming fear and reducing uncertainty is for all of us to find ways to actually experience racial equality firsthand. Today, before we reach the Promised Land. That has always been possible to accomplish on a micro level, even in the midst of broadscale *in*equality. After all, oppression is rarely monolithic or total. And now, more than ever, opportunities exist for White people to deal with Blacks (and other people of color) as true peers; to, in effect, try equality on for size.

Indeed the very process of racial engagement puts us all on the same plane. When we are open and honest with each other; when we abandon our hiding places, take risks, and own up to our own self-interest, when we place on the table our assumptions, fears, trepidations, and secret desires, *by that very act* we are connecting with one another as equals. For we do not, as a rule, make ourselves truly vulnerable to people we think are beneath us or beyond us. Of course, verbal engagement is just the start. For White folk to truly come to appreciate the stake they have in racial equality, they must actually experience it in their lives.

I mean more than just working, living, or even worshipping in an integrated setting. For being together in the same place and time does not necessarily mean that people are interacting on terms of true equality. More often than not, integration occurs exclusively on White people's terms. It consists of people of color being allowed to participate in a culture, or undertaking, or an environment from which they previously were, or felt, excluded. At best they are the new kids on the block, dependent on Whites for guidance, support, and even approval. Too often, there is a missionary quality to the relationship, as Whites "groom" people of color (there's an interesting word) to take over more responsible positions in time. Someday. Even when Whites and people of color are peers, there is often a significant difference in their comfort level, sense of security, and sense of belonging. Frequently the new kids feel out of their element, especially if they are having to perform on unfamiliar terrain or in a language in which they feel less than comfortable. And constrained. They feel forever on probation, and under enormous pressure to mimic the behavior and attitudes of their White colleagues.

So even in environments that look inviting on the surface, it is important to look past appearances and determine whether an invisible hierarchy is in place. The most promising settings for genuinely egalitarian interaction are ones where White folk are out of their element, where the pecking order is reversed, or where the natives get to bring religion to the missionaries instead of the other way around. Unfortunately, such settings are altogether too rare. Not surprisingly, Whites who find themselves in such settings often have difficulty adjusting to not being on top. But that, of course, is part of the lesson to be learned, for in a world in which race and power are unhinged, power will have to be shared. * * *

[Dalton offers the Salt and Pepper Gospel Singers as "a rare example of integration, African–American style." Dalton describes how the Singers worked through a difficult period during which they adopted a race-conscious policy of encouraging more black singers to join and not accepting more white singers until the group had reached its original balance of fifty-fifty, Black and White.] * * *

Is Salt and Pepper the Promised Land? In many ways yes, but it is an awfully tiny land indeed. The choir is, of course, a work-in-progress, as is every human endeavor. Yet certain features seem fixed. We have not run away from race or tried to make it go away. In fact, we have placed it front and center. And in that very act we have created the

possibility of altering its meaning. * * * Integration has not meant homogenization.

The same is true on a personal level. Although it is fair to say that each and every member of Salt and Pepper has been transformed by the experience of performing with the choir, in important respects we also remain the same people we were when we joined. No one has changed color. No one has changed race. No one's culture has been lost or sacrificed. We have managed to blend and be respectful of difference at the same time. The only thing we have given up is the right to dominate one another. No one's history has been altered. But together we have the power to transform the future.

That is my vision of the Promised Land. It is not grand, but it is real. And it is attainable. All it takes is genuine commitment to the process of racial healing.

Notes and Questions

1. Why does Dalton draw a distinction between a predominantly white U.S. Senate, asserting it would have to "change dramatically," and a predominantly black NBA and white NHL? Is this a distinction based on a traditional view of power? Does it ring true, when athletes garner million dollar endorsement contracts?

2. Is Dalton's vision of racial transformation premised on the commitment of all people to social equality and healing? Is it viable for other social institutions beyond the choir?

3. Lerone Bennett, Jr. in *The Challenge of Blackness* 39 (1972) wrote:

George Washington and George Washington's slaves lived different realities. And if we extend that insight to all the dimensions of white American history, we will realize that blacks lived a different time and a different reality in this country. And the terrifying implications of all this ... is that there is another time, another reality, another America ....

Angela Harris cites this quote and describes the other Americas inhabited by science fiction heroes Scully and Mulder and the protagonist of Thomas Pynchon's *The Crying of Lot 49*—Oedipa Maas. These heroes are "trying to expose the truth to the world ... hoping ... America will rise up in righteous indignation and sweep away injustice. Like Oedipa Maas, and like people of color generally when suspecting the effects of racism, they are forced to wonder whether they are seeing an inner truth or are merely paranoid." Angela Harris, *Afterword: Other Americas*, 95 Mich. L. Rev. 1150, 1155 (1997). Harris' essay explores the other Americas, the divergent realities, created by different experiences of race.

Harris observes: "The liberal dream of a beloved American community has traditionally been of an America without race. More specifically, it has been Justice Scalia's dream of a melting-pot America in which 'we are all just one race'—the 'American' race." [See *Adarand*, Chapter 7 *supra*]. Harris suggests another possibility: "a community that begins to take shape here and now, a justice that acknowledges race rather than making it magically disappear, a language that tries to bridge 'reality' and 'counterreality,' a world that includes 'nonwhite others' rather than only black and white." *Id*.

4.   In an earlier essay describing the evolution of Critical Race Theory and its intellectual challenges, Angela Harris described the significance of antiracist struggle in the face of racism:

> [Derrick] Bell urges contemporary anti-racists to struggle against racism in order to make their lives meaningful rather than in the hope of someday magically sweeping racism away. The logic Bell uses in this argument is not the familiar "either/or" logic, but a "both and" logic:

> It is not a matter of choosing between the pragmatic recognition that racism is permanent no matter what we do, or an idealism based on the long-held dream of attaining a society free of racism. Rather, it is a question of both, and. Both the recognition of the futility of action—where action is more civil rights strategies destined to fail—and the unalterable conviction that something must be done, that action must be taken.[quoting Derrick A. Bell, *Faces at the Bottom of the Well: The Permanence of Racism* 199 (1992).]

> Bell's urgings fit with the religious orientation of Anthony Cook and Cornel West. They also fit with the reconstruction jurisprudence I have been imagining in this Foreword. Reconstructing modernism requires both sophistication and disenchantment—both a commitment to building intellectual structures that are strong, complex, capacious, and sound, and a knowledge that reason and logic alone will never end racism, that words alone can never break down the barrier between ourselves and those we set out to persuade. The jurisprudence of reconstruction, like the world the slaves made, is only one of meaning—neither magic nor the abyss.

See Angela P. Harris, *Foreword: The Jurisprudence of Reconstruction*, 82 Calif. L. Rev. 741, 784–85 (1994). See also Anthony E. Cook, *Reflections on Postmodernism*, 26 New Eng. L. Rev. 751 (1992); Cornel West, *Keeping Faith: Philosophy and Race in America* (1993).

5.   john powell states: "Race remains important despite the fact that it is to a great degree a social construction. * * * Racial classifications shape how we talk about race. While racial classifications in the law may constrain the ability of the law to effectively address the needs of certain communities, racial classifications at the same time work to give credence to certain historical narratives." john a. powell, *An Agenda for the Post–Civil Rights Era*, 29 U.S.F. L. Rev. 889, 899 (1995).

JOHN O. CALMORE

Dismantling the Master's House: Essay in Memory of Trina Grillo—Random Notes of an Integration Warrior
81 Minn. L. Rev. 1441, 1443–57, 1459, 1475–77 (1997).*

Although it has been over forty years since the Supreme Court ruled that state-sanctioned separate-but-equal educational polices were unconstitutional, and almost thirty years since Congress declared that "fair housing" was to be a national policy, integration remains a problematic feature in African–American life. Some days I think that integration represents eminently good common sense. Some days I think that it is a necessary evil to be dealt with in order to overcome racial separation,

stratification, and inequality. Other days, particularly when I find myself in poor black neighborhoods or public schools, I think integration is simply irrelevant. * * * Today, integration in public schools, in suburban neighborhoods, and in employment settings remains a difficult proposition. * * *

Nonetheless, some of us * * * have integrated and benefitted. I think that integration works very well, but only for a very small group of black people. We who are in the best position to benefit are HFS blacks; we represent the "Huxtable Family Syndrome." [Because the Cosby family is an ordinary family, a lot of white viewers who might otherwise think, "Gee, we don't want blacks in our neighborhood," might decide, "Hey, the members of the Cosby family would be dynamite neighbors!"] We are affluent, and we have options and choices not available to most Americans (white or black). To a degree, we represent the old saw that "money whitens." We translate human capital into socioeconomic status, which, in turn, translates into social mobility. Still, blacks have been far less successful in this translation than Asians and Latinos. Indeed, in their study of residential segregation, Douglas Massey and Nancy Denton found that black people who have $50,000 in family income are as segregated as blacks who have less than $5,000 in income.

In light of the requirements of HFS, to integrate fully into American society the paradigm integration warrior will be a college graduate, hold a professional or managerial job, and have family income in excess of $50,000. As of 1992, few blacks could fit this profile. Only twelve percent had a college degree. Seventeen percent held professional or managerial jobs, but many of these were in the diminishing public sector rather than in the growing private sector. Only eleven percent had family income between $50,000 and $75,000. In 1992, only three percent of blacks had incomes between $75,000 and $100,000. Arguably, the physician-attorney combined incomes of the Huxtables exceeded $100,000. Families "living this large" constituted just two percent of the black population of the United States. These Huxtable-like blacks are the primary integration warriors.

I am willing to relax the HFS standards and presume that all blacks whose income exceeds $50,000 are potential integration warriors. While thirty-six percent of whites have this level of income, only sixteen percent of blacks do. Although this group of blacks is a small percentage of the total black population, it is a large number of people: approximately 4.8 million blacks out of a total black population of 30 million. Many of us in this group have integrated and, in varying degrees, met with white acceptance. Yet many of us seem to feel short-changed. For example, in reporting on the laments of "integration warriors," Charisse Jones states, "Among blacks who have worked, learned and lived in predominantly white settings, one theme occurs over and over again: This interaction has not made many whites accept blacks as equals, and perhaps never will." In a similar vein, Ellis Cose's study of this privileged class found many of its members enraged at the treatment they have received within the mainstream opportunity structure:

Despite its very evident prosperity, much of America's black middle class is in excruciating pain. And that distress—although most of the country does not see it—illuminates a serious American problem: the problem of the broken covenant, of the pact that if you work hard, get a good education, and play by the rules, you will be allowed to advance and to achieve to the limits of your ability.

* * * [Calmore discusses the notion of biological passing explaining: "To 'pass' meant to cross the color line—to pass over it—and gain acceptance as White in the white world. Some Blacks passed completely, while others passed only part-time or inadvertently (as when they were mistaken as white and did not correct the impression)."]

Integration, the keystone of the civil rights movement and now its keepsake, represents a sociological and cultural passing by people of color. To appreciate the hard balance between costs and benefits, even for some of the affluent class, I recall the story of Cheryl Harris's beloved grandmother. I think her story makes my analogy clearer. Sometime in the 1930s, Harris's Mississippi-born grandmother moved to Chicago and faced the harshness of economic survival for herself and her two daughters. She sought employment with a major retailer that was located in the city's central business district. This story would have been unremarkable for a white woman similarly situated, but for her grandmother this job search was "an act of great daring and self-denial, for in so doing she was presenting herself as a white woman." In the parlance of racist America, she was, then, passing. As Harris puts it:

[I]n the burgeoning landscape of urban America, anonymity was possible for a Black person with "white" features. She was transgressing boundaries, crossing borders, spinning on margins, traveling between dualities of Manichean space, rigidly bifurcated into light/dark; good/bad, white/black. No longer immediately identified as "Lula's daughter," she could thus enter the white world, albeit on a false passport, not merely passing, but trespassing.

This success through use of a "false passport," such as credentials discounted because gained through affirmative action, and "trespassing" on heretofore white property interests, are also implicated in sociological and cultural passing as blacks "integrate." As we come to view the socially constructed features of race, we recognize that phenotypically identifiable Asians and Pacific Islanders can pass ethnically as "model minorities." Even dark-skinned, nappy-headed African Americans like me can pass sociologically and culturally if we have the right history of socialization, the right credentials, a respectable job, an affluent income, and a proper street address or zip code.

Even with this individual package, though, integration for the group is problematic for four primary reasons: (1) its anchor is individualistic assimilation, (2) its progress is gradual, (3) its acceptable extent is tokenistic, and (4) worst of all, its unintended consequence is to support and reinforce white dominance and hegemony. In sociological and cultural passing, the intersectional issues of race and class loom large. As Harris has explained, passing in the biological sense is related to "the historical and continuing pattern of white racial domination and economic exploitation that has given passing a certain economic logic." So, too, with integration's sociological passing, there is "a certain economic logic" in living with white suburbanites. Except in minimal terms, though, this logic is entirely theoretical for the blacks among the concentrated and isolated ghetto poor. For Harris's grandmother, by becoming white, "it was automatically assured that she would receive higher economic returns in the short term, as well as greater economic, political, and social security in the long run." Many would make the same claim about the fruits of sociological passing in order to integrate. Moreover, passing allowed Harris's grandmother to access "a whole set of public and private privileges that materially and permanently guaranteed basic subsistence needs and, therefore, survival. Becoming white increased the possibility of controlling critical aspects of one's life rather than being the object of others' domination." Again, sociological passing has similar goals and motivations.

Passing has a price, and the associated costs are often hidden from public expression and view. Sociologist F. James Davis notes that those who pass biologically sacrifice loyalty to the black community in order to secure economic opportunities and societal status. White on the outside, but black on the inside, those who pass biologically experience difficult adjustments and ambiguous identities. Sociological passing has the same costs.

While I realize that the concept of status passing is not perfectly analogous to the biological phenomenon, the family resemblance is sufficient to point to some of the relational and operational difficulties associated with integration. In actuality, I have experienced and observed that status passing more resembles the marginalized, distressing, and contradictory experiences of the light-skinned mulatto, part black and part white. Here, passing often is imperfect, resulting in a placement between two worlds. It may provoke a number of reactions. Davis summarizes the various ways of trying to cope with the problems of mulatto marginality, and these observations also describe status passing quite well:

(1) They may become preoccupied with expressing strong hatred of all whites, an aggressive pattern that often seems to suggest ambivalent feelings about oneself and the black community. (2) They may accept the black identity but worry about color discrimination and conflict within the black community and hope that color difference can be minimized. . . . (3) They may make a conscious commitment to the black identity, to embrace the symbols of blackness, and to work hard to prove their pride in being black. (4) They may become strongly committed to reducing discrimination by the white community against all blacks. . . . (5) They may accept and make use of the marginal status position, adopting a marginal identity rather than a black identity, perceiving and dealing objectively with the black and white communities both while not being fully a part of either, and often being a liaison person between the two. (6) They may suppress the dilemma and reject any kind of racial identity, focusing instead on a professional identity or some absorbing role. . . . (7) They may decide to pass as white, experiencing all the stress and risks involved

in assuming a white identity. Sometimes a person will switch from one mode of adjustment to another, and sometimes adopt more than one style at a time.

I have quoted the Davis summary completely because it provides significant insight into the problems integration warriors experience. It helps as well to explain why a significant number of blacks, regardless of class position, are profoundly alienated from the very mainstream of society upon which they rely in order to access opportunity, material gain, and status. It also helps to explain why so many blacks remain ambivalent and conflicted about both the normative weight and instrumental prospects of an integrated future. There is, in short, a fundamental problem with the black costs of admission to the white world.

I learned of these costs when, at eighteen, I left my black northwest Pasadena neighborhood to return to Stanford. I first went to Stanford as a two-year-old to live with my Aunt Loretta and Uncle Jack shortly after my mother died in 1947. I lived with them for five years, until I returned to Pasadena to live with my father and grandparents. My aunt was a domestic and my uncle was a cook; both worked for a Stanford fraternity. We lived in a very humble "guest house" on campus behind the fraternity. I went to kindergarten and first grade with the professors' and graduate students' children at the University Elementary School. I was the only black. Upon returning to Pasadena, I went to Grover Cleveland Elementary School and George Washington Junior High School. Both were mixed with whites, Asians, Latinos, and other blacks. My high school, John Muir, was mixed, but the student body was about two-thirds white, most of whom came from affluent Altadena and La Canada.

Although no one in my extended family had gone to college, everybody worked hard. My father worked at Lockheed Aircraft for more than twenty years, mostly as a parts expediter. My grandmother taught adult education, teaching the art of hooked-rug making at Pasadena City College. From my earliest memory, my grandfather was retired, having been first a barber and later a chauffeur. We all prized education and I was driven to be a good student. My Aunt Loretta so "loved" Stanford that my family chose the university as my higher-education goal. It was the only school to which I applied.

I went to college one month after Martin Luther King, Jr.'s inspirational speech on August 28, 1963, when he voiced his dream that his four children would one day be judged by the content of their character rather than by their black skin; that freedom would ring not only from the mountains of New York, Colorado, and California, but also from Stone Mountain in Georgia, Lookout Mountain in Tennessee, and "from every hill and molehill of Mississippi." Watching the live telecast of King's speech with my father, John Harold, and my grandmother, Rhoda, three generations of African Americans tearfully bought into his color-blind dream. I was to test it. My future was to be our pay-off as we ran an intergenerational relay race to high achievement and success. Each generation was highly intelligent and had worked hard, but only I had an opportunity to win out. From that day on, I have never run just for myself. At Stanford, it was my heavy obligation to make not only my extended family proud, but also, as my grandmother instructed, "to do the race proud." I remember her telling me, "John Otis, there will not be very many Negro boys up there and what you do will be magnified— the bad more than the good. You must demonstrate that we belong." I was to keep my hair cut short, to be clean-cut, and to remember my manners. My admission to Stanford was similar to a draft notice, and like many of the blacks and Latinos sent to fight in Vietnam, I was drafted to be a point man.

I thus began college not only before affirmative action and multicultural understandings, but also before the 1964 civil rights legislation governing freedom from discrimination in public accommodations and in employment, before the 1965 voting rights provisions, and before the 1968 Fair Housing Act. I was an integration warrior with very little back-up, under the auspices of an inchoate national commitment to equality of opportunity. My freshman class included eleven blacks, joining the four sophomores, two juniors, and two seniors already there. With graduate and professional students, I believe the total black student body was about twenty-five out of over ten thousand. Combining college and law school, I had one black professor and one female professor. When I look back at those days and I think about my commitment to integration, I am reminded of the story about the pig and the chicken in the afterlife discussing their contribution to the meal of breakfast. The chicken bragged about contributing the eggs that made the scones and pancakes, not to mention those that were scrambled. Unimpressed, the pig referred to the bacon, sausage, and ham. He informed the chicken, that while she had, indeed, made a contribution, the pig had made a commitment.

While at Stanford, people of African descent changed radically from Negro to black. Nappy hair was in as Afros grew wild. Expressions of cultural nationalism were manifested from the wearing of dashikis to the motto of the organization US—"wherever we are, US is." Along with these developments, black power, Black Student Unions, Black Panthers, black nationalism, and black-as-beautiful seemed to challenge not only King's dream, but everything else we seemed to know. In many ways I was living in, as Dickens said, the best of times and the worst of times.

Riding these waves of change, I, along with twenty-four other blacks, entered Harvard Law School in a class of around 525 students. Before 1965, no more than four blacks had been admitted in a given year. My class was bigger than earlier classes because black students from elite white schools were, for the first time in significant numbers (twelve), admitted along with those from the historically black colleges. The world beyond Langdell Hall was crazy, as cities burned; as Robert Kennedy and Dr. King were assassinated; as more cities burned; as the Vietnam War made less and less sense, morally and otherwise; as student protests intensified here and there; as local police were called to Harvard Yard in 1969, bringing "police brutality" home to elite sons and daughters; as they took Muhammed Ali's title; and as the Kerner Commission declared the nation to be "racist" (new word, then) and comprised of "two societies, one black and one white, separate and unequal."

Quite frankly, during the whole time I was at Harvard, I never quite figured out why I was there, what I was to do with the education I was receiving, how it was constructively relevant to anything I cared about. Except in a paper-chase kind of way—getting valued credentials—I had a lot of trouble focusing on the relevance of the formal education I was receiving. At law school, the institutional channeling of aspiration and the peer orientations of white male students were too narrow. If you were not aspiring for a partnership shot at a major Wall Street law firm, a thin blonde wife, and a Greenwich address, it was not clear what the Harvard Law man was to do (Harvard Law women were as few and as marginal as were most blacks). Only the force of habit from being a good student since age five cranked me through. It was this way for many of the blacks at that time. I spent a lot of time working for the Boston Legal Assistance office in Roxbury, and, there, I found myself and my future. There, I decided I would never practice law simply as an amoral technician, equally adept at arguing both sides.

After I graduated, I went into Legal Services, where I stayed for the next fourteen years: as a Reginald Heber Smith Fellow in Roxbury; as a staff attorney at the Watts office of the Legal Aid Foundation of Los Angeles; at the Western Center on Law and Poverty in Los Angeles; at the National Housing Law Project in Berkeley; and as the Director of Litigation at the Legal Aid Foundation. I later taught at the law school at North Carolina Central in Durham, the state's separate-but-equal counterpart to the University of North Carolina at Chapel Hill. I have also taught at Loyola Law School and spent a couple of years as a program officer in the Ford Foundation's Rights and Social Justice Program. I describe myself as working toward achieving a more just society.

From all of these experiences, I have learned how to have difficult conversations about race; how to maintain a high level of civility and respect for others in my dealings with them, even when it is not returned; and how to never, never give up. From my college days on, I have learned that most blacks achieve not only against the odds, but with a kind of blind faith that our good efforts will be rewarded commensurably. I have found hope more often stemming from serendipitous good luck than from reasonable expectation. As I remember the blacks who were with me at Stanford and Harvard Law, I am impressed less with their bottom-line achievements, which are varied and outstanding, but, instead with the difficulty of their journey and conversion. Most of us came from so far back, over so many hurdles, with so little privileged background. As graduates, we often represented what Bart Landry calls "the new middle class," because eighty percent of the African American middle class in the 1970s was first-generation middle class. * * *

To disregard black achievement and the racial circumstances under which it is attained is to render a terrible disservice to the achiever, to discount too much. So often, my peers dug success out of a bedrock of racist resistance. Before the race for success had begun, we had already run far to get to the starting line of equal opportunity, to compete on "the level playing field" with whites. Once there, we often realized that we had to form a league of our own and chart a very different course than our white peers. The future they saw so self-assuredly, we viewed skeptically. Their guarantees were our gambles. Beyond my elite peers, black achievement too often gets decontextualized and reduced to bottom-line comparisons that do not tell half the story. It distorts our achievement syndrome and discounts our worth. * * *

In the 1970s, a significant number of people of color sought to articulate and endorse cultural pluralism even as the assimilationist mainstream opportunity structure began to invite our participation. The proposition was not just empirically difficult, but conceptually as well, because core assimilationism also, paradoxically, paid lip service to pluralism. As Newfield and Gordon point out:

> Assimilationist pluralists continually insist on conformity to [the] core, even as they profess their belief in plurality. This assimilationist-pluralist position is contradictory, and yet it forms a pillar of the American Creed, standing next to its fellow pillars "democracy" and "free enterprise" and transforming these into elements of the core political culture.

The pressures of assimilationism to adapt are unrelenting. Moreover, its explanations for and justifications of status-quo America are compelling to most members of the national community. It pretends to value diversity and promote equal opportunity, but it also seeks to impose a "single explanatory system or view of reality [that purports to] account for all the phenomena of life." Thus, its primary objective is to subsume diverse groups into a single whole at the center, with pluralism lightly tolerated at the margins.

In opposing assimilationism, even while assimilating, those of us who press for enhanced equality and social justice cannot be deterred by others who characterize us as threats to social harmony. We cannot let our individual upward mobility dissuade us from challenging "unjust ground rules" merely because that mobility may be contingent on obeying those rules. We cannot buy into standards that our social group—colored people—had no share in formulating and little stake in implementing. We must disrupt the operation of these standards and destroy their masquerade as inclusive, neutral, and unifying when they are, in truth, themselves racial and divisive. As Newfield and Gordon conclude, "Assimilationism is the general operating system for everybody's software of cultural interaction. And it is an immensely powerful opponent of all kinds of equity movements in American life." As an integration warrior, I am fighting more against assimilationism than I am fighting for integration. It is just difficult, however, because I am fighting from within integrated settings, having necessarily assimilated to a degree. But I have been doing it for the last thirty years and I am committed to do so for another thirty if I am able.

Progressives who act from a critical feminist, "queer," or race-critical standpoint, must be insurgent, critical multiculturalists. Our position demands it, because the assimilationist ideology seeks to suppress our claims for a more inclusionary and just society. Moreover, monoculturalism sets the stage for sexism, heterosexism, and racism. For those of us who occupy cultural borderlands, our values, interests, and life experiences are reduced to "annoying exceptions rather than central areas for inquiry." We must react to monoculturalism and its handmaiden, assimilationism, by reclaiming our status on the borderlands and positioning it center stage. As Peter McLaren states, "We must create new narratives—new 'border narratives'—in order to reauthor the discourses of oppression in politically subversive ways as well as create sites of possibility and enablement."

Notes and Questions

1. Several of the excerpts in this section imply that black people should not give up on white people nor on themselves. If you are Black, do you agree? What role should other groups play in the effort to be integration warriors, seeking to establish a multicultural, more just society? If you are White, how can you colorize yourself? Would you want to be a "race traitor?" See Chapter 6 § 4 *supra*. Are you prepared to make the sacrifices that role entails?

2. Is integration useful in responding to racism or is it more useful as a visionary image in discussing responses? Would you want to be an integration warrior?

3. Does America have a "common ground, shared values, and rules of the game?" If not, what implications might that absence have for intergroup dealing and coalition?

4. Does our very language encode white supremacy, so that even talking with each other makes the matter worse?

5. Is violent resistance to an unjust social order ever justified? If your answer is no, do you believe the American Revolution was a mistake?

Recall that only a short time after Dr. Martin Luther King issued his famous letter (Section 2, *supra*), the Black Power movement exploded onto the national scene. In dozens of cities, Black Panthers and similar groups abandoned the ideal of prayerful, respectful protest and petition, stopped talking with mainstream white people, purchased arms, and, in a turn toward nationalism, began offering programs such as free breakfasts for young black schoolchildren.

Around the same time, Corky Gonzalez's Denver-based Crusade for Justice began confronting racist police and indifferent school officials, leading to a shootout in which one police officer and several members of the Crusade were shot.

6. Would you defend a black, Indian, or Chicano nationalist who has little respect for law and believes our court system is corrupt and serves the interests of the white elite? See, *e.g.*, Eldridge Cleaver, *Soul on Ice* (1969); Oscar "Zeta" Acosta, *Uncollected Essays* (Ilan Stavans ed. 1995); Michael A. Olivas, *"Breaking the Law on Principle:" An Essay on Lawyers' Dilemmas, Unpopular Cases, and Legal Regimes*, 52 U. Pitt. L. Rev. 815 (1991). See also Paul Harris, *Black Rage Confronts the Law* (1997).

7. If corporate/government power will grant Blacks and other people of color concessions only when the change also advances white elite interest, as Derrick Bell argues, is the threat of destabilization (rioting, unrest, law-breaking), unfortunately, one of the few ways outsiders have at their disposal for getting the power structure's attention? Is this principle true at some times, but not others? Today, the gap between Blacks, Latinos, and Indians on the one hand, and Whites on the other, stands wider than it has at any recent point in income, school completion, infant mortality, and longevity. Do these disparities increase the likelihood of social unrest in the foreseeable future? If so, what part will you play? See Richard Delgado, *The Coming Race War? And Other Apocalyptic Tales of America After Affirmative Action and Welfare* (1996).

SECTION 6. RESPONDING TO RACISM IN THE CLASSROOM AND THE LEGAL PROFESSION

While no single formula will serve to counter every form of racism, one must somehow begin and continue. Since many of our lives are lived in classrooms, this text closes with an examination of the classroom community in which these issues may arise.

MARGARET E. MONTOYA

Máscaras, Trenzas, y Greñas:*
Un/masking the Self While Un/braiding Latina Stories and Legal Discourse
15 Chicano–Latino L. Rev. 1, 2–26; 17 Harv. Women's L.J. 185, 186–209 (1994).**

One of the earliest memories from my school years is of my mother braiding my hair, making my *trenzas*. In 1955, I was seven years old. I was in second grade at the Immaculate Conception School in Las Vegas, New Mexico. Our family home with its outdoor toilet was on an unpaved street, one house from the railroad track. I remember falling asleep to the subterranean rumble of the trains.

Nineteen-fifty-five was an extremely important year in my development, in my understanding of myself in relation to Anglo Society. I remember 1955 as the year I began to think about myself in relation to my classmates and their families. I began to feel different and to adjust my behavior accordingly.

We dressed in front of the space heater in the bedroom we shared with my older brother. Catholic school girls wore uniforms. We wore blue jumpers and white blouses. I remember my mother braiding my hair and my sister's. I can still feel the part she would draw with the point of the comb. She would begin at the top of my head pressing down as she drew the comb down to the nape of my neck. "Don't move," she'd say as she held the two hanks of hair, checking to make sure that the part was straight. Only then would she begin, braiding as tightly as our squirming would allow, so the braids could withstand our running, jumping, and hanging from the monkey bars at recess. "I don't want you to look *greñudas*," my mother would say. ["I don't want you to look uncombed."]

Hearing my mother use both English and Spanish gave emphasis to what she was saying. She used Spanish to talk about what was really important: her feelings, her doubts, her worries. She also talked to us in Spanish about *gringos*, Mexicanos, and the relations between them. Her stories were sometimes about being treated outrageously by *gringos*, her anger controlled and her bitterness implicit. She also told stories about Anglos she admired—those who were egalitarian, smart, well-spoken and well-mannered.

Sometimes Spanish was spoken so as not to be understood by Them. Usually, though, Spanish and English were woven together. *Greñuda* was one of many words encoded with familial and cultural meaning. My mother used the word to admonish us, but she wasn't warning us about name-calling: *Greñuda* was not an epithet that our schoolmates were likely to use. Instead, I heard my mother saying something that went beyond well-groomed hair and being judged by our appearance—she could offer strategies for passing *that* scrutiny. She used the Spanish word, partly because there is no precise English equivalent, but also because she was interpreting the world for us.

The real message of *greñudas* was conveyed through the use of the Spanish word—it was unspoken and subtextual. She was teaching us that our world was divided, that They–Who–Don't-Speak–Spanish would see us as different, would judge us, would find us lacking. Her lessons about combing, washing and doing homework frequently relayed a deeper message: Be prepared, because you will be judged by your skin color, your names, your accents. They will see you as ugly, lazy, dumb and dirty.

As I put on my uniform and as my mother braided my hair, I changed; I became my public self. My *trenzas* announced that I was clean and well-cared-for at home. My *trenzas* and school uniform blurred the differences between my family's economic and cultural circumstances and those of the more economically comfortable Anglo students. I welcomed the braids and uniform as a disguise which concealed my minimal wardrobe and the relative poverty in which my family lived.
* * *

When I arrived as a student at Harvard Law School, I dressed so as to proclaim my politics. During my first day of orientation, I wore a Mexican peasant blouse and cutoff jeans on which I had embroidered the Chicano symbol of the *águila* (a stylized eagle) on one seat pocket and the woman symbol on the other. The *águila* reminded me of the red and black flags of the United Farm Worker rallies; it reminded me that I had links to a particular community. I was never to finish the fill-in stitches in the woman symbol. My symbols, like my struggles, were ambiguous.

The separation of the two symbols reminds me today that my participation in the Chicano movement had been limited by my gender, while in the women's movement it had been limited by my ethnicity. I drew power from both movements—I identified with both—but I knew that I was at the margin of each one.

As time went on, my clothes lost their political distinctiveness. My clothes signified my ambivalence: Perhaps if I dressed like a lawyer, eventually I would acquire more conventional ideas and ideals and fit in with my peers. Or perhaps if I dressed like a lawyer, I could harbor for some future use the disruptive and, at times, unwelcome thoughts that entered my head. My clothing would become protective coloration. Chameleon-like, I would dress to fade into the ideological, political and cultural background rather than proclaim my differences. * * *

For stigmatized groups, such as people of color, the poor, women, gays and lesbians, assuming a mask is comparable to being "on stage." Being "on stage" is frequently experienced as being acutely aware of one's words, affect, tone of voice, movements and gestures because they seem out of sync with what one is feeling and thinking. At unexpected moments, we fear that we will be discovered to be someone or something other than who or what we pretend to be. Lurking just behind our carefully constructed disguises and lodged within us is the child whom no one would have mistaken for being anything other than what she was. Her masking was yet imperfect, still in rehearsal, and at times unnecessary.

For Outsiders, being masked in the legal profession has psychological as well as ideological consequences. Not only do we perceive ourselves as being "on stage," but the experience of class-jumping—being born poor but later living on the privileged side of the economic divide as an adult—can also induce schizoid feelings. As first-year law students don their three-piece suits, they make manifest the class ascendancy implicit in legal education. Most Latinas/os in the legal profession now occupy an economic niche considerably higher than that of our parents, our relatives and frequently that of our students. Our speech, clothes, cars, homes and lifestyle emphasize this difference.

The masks we choose can impede our legal representation and advocacy by driving a wedge between self, our *familias*, and our communities. As our economic security increases, we escape the choicelessness and lack of control over vital decisions that oppress communities of color. To remain connected to the community requires one to be Janus-faced, able to present one face to the larger society and another among ourselves. Janus-faced not in the conventional meaning of being deceitful, but in the sense of having two faces simultaneously. One face is the adult face that allows us to make our way through the labyrinth of the dominant culture. The other, the face of the child, is one of difference, free of artifice. This image with its dichotomized character fails to capture the multiplicity, fluidity and interchangeability of faces, masks and identities upon which we rely. * * *

The legal profession provides ample opportunity for role-playing, drama, story-telling and posturing. Researchers have studied the use of masks and other theatrical devices among practicing lawyers and in the law school environment. Mask imagery has been used repeatedly to describe different aspects of legal education, lawyering and law making. * * *

Some law students are undoubtedly attracted to the profession by the opportunity to disguise themselves and have no desire or need to look for their hidden selves. Some law students, however, may resent the role-playing they know to be necessary to succeed in their studies and in their relations with professors and peers. Understanding how and why we mask ourselves can help provide opportunities for students to explore their public and private personalities and to give expression to their feelings. * * *

My memories from law school begin with the first case I ever read in Criminal Law. I was assigned to seat number one in a room that held some 175 students.

The case was entitled *People of the State of California v. Josephine Chavez.* [176 P.2d 92 (Cal.App.1947)] It was the only case in which I remember encountering a Latina, and she was the defendant in a manslaughter prosecution. The facts, as I think back and before I have searched out the casebook, involved a young woman giving birth one night over the toilet in her mother's home without waking her child, brothers, sisters or mother. The baby dropped into the toilet. Josefina cut the umbilical cord with a razor blade. She recovered the body of the baby, wrapped it in newspaper and hid it under the bathtub. She ran away, but later she turned herself in to her probation officer.

The legal issue was whether the baby had been born alive for purposes of the California manslaughter statute: whether the baby had been born alive and was therefore subject to being killed. The class wrestled with what it meant to be alive in legal terms. Had the lungs filled with air? Had the heart pumped blood?

For two days I sat mute, transfixed while the professor and the students debated the issue. Finally, on the third day, I timidly raised my hand. I heard myself blurt out: What about the other facts? What about her youth, her poverty, her fear over the pregnancy, her delivery in silence? I spoke for perhaps two minutes, and when I finished, my voice was high-pitched and anxious.

An African–American student in the back of the room punctuated my comments with "Hear! Hear!" Later other students thanked me for speaking up and in other ways showed their support.

I sat there after class had ended, in seat number one on day number three, wondering why it had been so hard to speak. Only later would I begin to wonder whether I would ever develop the mental acuity, the logical clarity to be able to sort out the legally relevant facts from what others deemed sociological factoids. Why did the facts relating to the girl-woman's reality go unvoiced? Why were her life, her anguish, her fears rendered irrelevant? Engaging in analyses about The Law, her behavior and her guilt demanded that I disembody Josefina, that I silence her reality which screamed in my head. * * *

A discussion raising questions about the gender-, class-, and ethnicity-based interpretations in the opinion, however, would have run counter to traditional legal discourse. Interjecting information about the material realities and cultural context of a poor Latina woman's life introduces taboo information into the classroom. Such information would transgress the prevalent ideological discourse. The puritanical and elitist protocol governing the classroom, especially during the 1970s, supported the notion that one's right to a seat in the law school classroom could be brought into question if one were to admit knowing about the details of pregnancies and self abortions, or the hidden motivations of a *pachuca* (or a *chola*, a "homegirl" in today's Latino gang parlance). By overtly linking oneself to the life experiences of poor women, especially *pachucas*, one would emphasize one's differences from those who seemed to have been admitted to law school by right.

Information about the cultural context of Josephine Chavez's life would also transgress the linguistic discourse within the classroom. One would find it useful, and perhaps necessary, to use Spanish words and concepts to describe accurately and to contextualize Josephine Chavez's experience. In the 1970s, however, Spanish was still the language of Speedy Gonzales, José Jimenez and other racist parodies.

To this day, I have dozens of questions about this episode in Josephine Chavez's life. I yearn to read an appellate opinion which reflects a sensitivity to her story, told in her own words. What did it take to conceal her pregnancy from her familia? With whom did she share her secret? How could she have given birth with "the doors open and no lights ... turned on?" How did she do so without waking the others who were asleep? How did she brace herself as she delivered the baby into the toilet? Did she shake as she cut the umbilical cord?

I long to hear Josephine Chavez's story told in what I will call Mothertalk and Latina–Daughtertalk. Mothertalk is about the blood and mess of menstruation, about the every month-ness of periods or about the fear in the pit of the stomach and the ache in the heart when there is no period. Mothertalk is about the blood and mess of pregnancy, about placentas, umbilical cords and stitches. Mothertalk is about sex and its effects. Mothertalk helps make sense of our questions: How does one give birth in darkness and in silence? How does one clean oneself after giving birth? How does one heal oneself? Where does one hide from oneself after seeing one's dead baby in a toilet?

Latina–Daughtertalk is about feelings reflecting the deeply ingrained cultural values of Latino families: in this context, feelings of *vergüenza de sexualidad* ("sexual shame"). Sexual experience comes enshrouded in sexual shame; have sex and you risk being known as *sinvergüenza*, shameless. Another Latina–Daughtertalk value is *respeto á la máma y respeto á la familia*. Familias are not nuclear nor limited by blood ties; they are extended, often including foster siblings and *comadres y compadres, madrinas y padrinos* (godmothers, godfathers and other religion-linked relatives).

Josephine Chavez's need to hide her pregnancy (with her head-to-toe mask) can be explained by a concern about the legal consequences as well as by the *vergüenza* within and of her *familia* that would accompany the discovery of the pregnancy, a pregnancy that was at once proof and reproof of her sexuality. Josephine's unwanted pregnancy would likely have been interpreted within her community, her *familia*, and by her mother as a lack of *respeto*.

I sense that students still feel vulnerable when they reveal explicitly gendered or class-based knowledge, such as information about illicit sexuality and its effects, or personal knowledge about the lives of the poor and the subordinated. Even today there is little opportunity to use Spanish words or concepts within the legal academy. Students respond to their feelings of vulnerability by remaining silent about these tabooed areas of knowledge.

The silence had profound consequences for me and presumably for others who identified with Josephine Chavez because she was Latina, or because she was female, or because she was poor. For me, the silence invalidated my experience. I reexperienced the longing I felt that day in Criminal Law many times. At the bottom of that longing was a desire to be recognized, a need to feel some reciprocity. As I engaged in His/Their reality, I needed to feel Him/Them engage in mine.

Embedded in Josephine Chavez's unfortunate experience are various lessons about criminal law specifically and about the law and its effects more generally. The opinion's characteristic avoidance of context and obfuscation of important class- and gender-based assumptions is equally important to the ideological socialization and doctrinal development of law students. Maintaining a silence about Chavez's ethnic and socio-economic context lends credence to the prevailing perception that there is only one relevant reality. * * *

Over time, I figured out that my interpretations of the facts in legal opinions were at odds with the prevailing discourse in the classroom, regardless of the subject matter. Much of the discussion assumed that we all shared common life experiences. I remember sitting in the last row and being called on in Tax, questioned about a case involving the liability of a father for a gift of detached and negotiable bond coupons to his son. It was clear that I was befuddled by the facts of the case. Looking at his notes on the table, the professor asked with annoyance whether I had ever seen a bond. My voice quivering, I answered that I had not. His head shot up in surprise. He focused on who I was; I waited, unmasked. He became visibly flustered as he carefully described the bond with its tear-off coupons to me. Finally, he tossed me an easy question, and I choked out the answer.

This was one instance of feeling publicly unmasked. In this case, it was class-based ignorance which caused my mask(s) to slip. Other students also may have lacked knowledge about bonds. Maybe other students, especially those from families with little money and certainly no trust funds, stocks or bonds, also would have felt unmasked by the questioning. But I felt isolated and different because I could be exposed in so many ways—through class, ethnicity, race, gender, and the subtleties of language, dress, make-up, voice and accent.

For multiple and overlapping reasons I felt excluded from the experiences of others, experiences that provided them with knowledge that better equipped them, indeed privileged them, in the study of The

Law, especially within the upper class domain that is Harvard. Not knowing about bonds linked the complexities of class-jumping with the fearful certainty that, in the eyes of some, and most painfully in my own/my mother's eyes, I would be seen as *greñuda*: dirty, ugly, dumb and uncombed.

It was not possible for me to guard against the unexpected visibility—or, paradoxically, the invisibility—caused by class, gender or ethnic differences that lurked in the materials we studied. Such issues were, after all, pervasive, and I was very sensitive to them.

Sitting in the cavernous classrooms at Harvard under the stern gaze of patrician jurists was an emotionally wrenching experience. I remember the day one of the students was called on to explain *Erie v. Tompkins*. His identification of the salient facts, his articulation of the major and minor issues and his synopsis of the Court's reasoning was so precise and concise that it left a hush in the room. He had already achieved and was able to model for the rest of us the objectivity, clarity, and mental acuity that we/I aspired to.

The respect shown for this type of analysis was qualitatively different than that shown for contextual or cultural analysis. Such occurrences in the classroom were memorable because they were defining: Rational objectivity trumped emotional subjectivity. What They had to say trumped what I wanted to say but didn't.

I have no memory of ever speaking out again to explain facts from my perspective as I had done that one day in Criminal Law. There was to be only one Latina in any of my cases, only one Josephine. While I was at Harvard, my voice was not heard again in the classroom examining, exploring or explaining the life situations of either defendants or victims. Silence accommodated the ideological uniformity, but also revealed the inauthenticity implicit in discursive assimilation.

As time went on, I felt diminished and irrelevant. It wasn't any one discussion, any one class or any one professor. The pervasiveness of the ideology marginalized me, and others; its efficacy depended upon its subtextual nature, and this masked quality made it difficult to pinpoint.

I had arrived at Harvard feeling different. I understood difference to be ineluctably linked with, and limited to, race, class and gender. The kernel of that feeling I first associated with Josephine Chavez, that scrim of silence, remains within me. It is still my experience that issues of race, ethnicity, gender or class are invisible to most of my white and/or male colleagues. Issues of sexual orientation, able-bodiedness, and sometimes class privilege can be invisible to me. I still make conscious choices about when to connect such issues to the topic at hand and when to remain silent. I'm still unclear about strategies and tactics, about being frontal or oblique.

Issues of race or gender are never trivial or banal from my perspective. Knowing how or when to assert them effectively as others react with hostility, boredom or weariness can be a "crazy-making" endeavor. Sometimes it seems that every interaction requires that I overlook the terms of the discourse or that I affirmatively redefine them. My truths require that I say unconventional things in unconventional ways.

Speaking out assumes prerogative. Speaking out is an exercise of privilege. Speaking out takes practice.

Silence ensures invisibility. Silence provides protection. Silence masks.

Notes and Questions

1. Does Montoya describe reactions you have had in the classroom? Did you speak out as she did? Why or why not? Reflect for a moment on how it is to be an outsider surrounded by a culture that does not acknowledge your values or your sense of reality. What would you do?

2. Addressing the difficulties faced by students of color, Kimberlé Williams Crenshaw observes:

> In many instances, minority students' values, beliefs, and experiences clash not only with those of their classmates but also with those of their professors. Yet because of the dominant view in academe that legal analysis can be taught without directly addressing conflicts of individual values, experiences, and world views, these conflicts seldom, if ever, reach the surface of the classroom discussion. Dominant beliefs in the objectivity of legal discourse serve to suppress the conflict by discounting the relevance of any particular perspective in legal analysis and by positing an analytical stance that has no specific cultural, political, or class characteristics. I call this dominant mode "perspectivelessness."

> This norm of perspectivelessness is problematic in general, and particularly burdensome on minority students. While it seems relatively straightforward that objects, issues, and other phenomena are interpreted from the vantage point of the observer, many law classes are conducted as though it is possible to create, weigh, and evaluate rules and arguments in ways that neither reflect nor privilege any particular perspective or world view. Thus, law school discourse proceeds with the expectation that students will learn to perform the standard mode of legal reasoning and embrace its presumption of perspectivelessness. When this expectation is combined with the fact that what is understood as objective or neutral is often the embodiment of a white middle-class world view, minority students are placed in a difficult situation. To assume the air of perspectivelessness that is expected in the classroom, minority students must participate in the discussion as though they were not African American or Latino, but colorless legal analysts. The consequence of adopting this colorless mode is that when the discussion involves racial minorities, minority students are expected to stand apart from their history, their identity, and sometimes their own immediate circumstances and discuss issues without making reference to the reality that the "they" or "them" being discussed is from their perspective "we" or "us." Conversely, on the few occasions when minority students are invited to incorporate their racial identity and experiences into their comments, they often feel as though they have been put on the spot. Moreover, their comments are frequently disregarded by other students who believe that since race figures prominently in such comments, the minority students—unlike themselves—are expressing biased, self-interested, or subjective opinions. The result is that minority students can

seldom ground their analysis in their own racial experiences without risking some kind of formal or informal sanction. Minority students escape the twin problems of objectification and subjectification in discussions when minority experiences are deemed to be completely irrelevant, or are obscured by the centering of the discussion elsewhere. The price of this sometimes welcomed invisibility, however, can be intense alienation.

Kimberlé Williams Crenshaw, *Foreword: Toward a Race–Conscious Pedagogy in Legal Education*, 4 S. Cal. Rev. L. & Women's Stud. 33, 34–36 (1994).*

3.   Progressive legal work can provide relief from the law school experience, but introduce other tensions. Julie Su describes her legal work, representing Thai and Latina garment workers:

> I experience tensions as a community lawyer, or lawyer activist. As an Asian-American woman, I embody traits traditionally excluded from the environments, the profession, and the system to which I have sought access. I engage in my own struggle to be heard, to find words that describe my life and vision and make my experiences resonate within the narrow language of the law, and to change a legal system and a society that does not recognize my experience of injustice or exclusion. Other lawyers treat and view the lawyer activist as an outsider. Here, I am not just talking about the times I have been ignored, when a white male attorney representing a garment manufacturer reached directly past me to shake the hands of my white male co-counsel, for example. I am not talking about those many instances.

> I am talking about the attorneys on our side who say, "If you want to do all that political and educational stuff, organize meetings with the workers and visit them in their homes at night, go ahead and do that. But leave the 'real' lawyering—the hard-core strategizing, brief writing and arguing—to the real lawyers." But to me, the traditional, so-called "real" lawyers, who are not engaged in the workers' lives, cannot represent them in the lawsuit in a way that is true to the workers. The lawyer activist has to be an active participant in the litigation to ensure that the workers' lives guide the litigation. Lawyer activists have to be active participants in litigation to transform the practice of law.

> Lawyer activists are often marginalized by non-lawyers as well. Many progressive activists with whom I have worked refer to lawyers as "necessary evils." They feel that lawyers distort and destroy a struggle, wanting to speak for the workers and take over the cause, insisting on leading rather than joining. Non-lawyer activists often seek to limit the role of the lawyer activist to that more suited to a traditional lawyer—at the margins of the struggle.

> So what is our role as lawyers? How can we make transformative work—both in our profession and our communities—real? I do not know the answers to these difficult questions. I do not even know if finding answers is the ultimate goal. But I believe that anyone who tells you these tensions are not worth struggling over misses the essence of what it means to be an advocate for people and an advocate for justice. Law school does a good job of telling you that all of these tensions are really nonsense, or at best, that they make for interesting discussions in those

"soft, fuzzy" courses but have no place in the real practice of law. I want to tell you that is absolutely wrong.

I have learned more, gained more, cared more, smiled and cried more by sharing my life, work, and passion with the Thai and Latina garment workers, who live with the violence of poverty and suffer the brutality of sweatshops, than I thought I could by choosing to become a lawyer. The workers have inspired me, personally and professionally, to be more than I ever imagined. My work with them has been more gratifying than anything I thought possible during law school. Working not for them, but with them, it is not only their lives, but mine that has been changed.

Julie A. Su, *Making the Invisible Visible: The Garment Industry's Dirty Laundry*, 1 J. Gender Race & Just. 405, 416–417 (1998).*

4. Classroom Exercise: See Frank McClellan, *The Dark Side of Tort Reform: Searching for Racial Justice*, 48 Rutgers L. Rev. 761 (1996).

Your law firm represents the plaintiff in a medical malpractice case, involving an improper dose of anaesthesia that was administered before surgery. Your firm is suing the doctor. A senior partner in the firm comes to tell you about the case.

STOP. Did you picture the plaintiff and the doctor? Picture them. Do they have a race? A gender? Do you ask the senior partner about the race of the parties? [Many white people assume the parties are White; that is part of white privilege as the default race.]

Now picture a black plaintiff suing a white doctor. Do you want to ask questions about race on *voir dire*? Why or why not? Does it change your answer if you picture a white plaintiff suing a black doctor?

As an attorney, you are not representing your client adequately if you do not consider race. Attorneys have an obligation to learn about race and strategize about how it could affect each case. See Anthony V. Alfieri, *Race Trials*, 76 Tex. L. Rev. 1293 (1998). See also Phoebe A. Haddon, *Education for a Public Calling in the 21st Century*, 69 Wash. L. Rev. 573 (1994) (urging that good lawyering "emphasizes a professional obligation to promote equality in the legal system.")

5. Who do you know who needs to learn some of the insights you have gained from this book? How will you teach them? What will you do today to address these issues and respond to racism?

Index

A

F

G

H

I

J

K

L

R

S

T

U